Department of Defense FAR Supplement

as of January 1, 2020

Compiled from GOVERNMENT CONTRACTS REPORTER

(As of January 1, 2020)

2700 Lake Cook Road
Riverwoods, IL, 60015
866 529 6600
www.WoltersKluwerLR.com

Printed in the United States of America
ISBN 978-1-5438-1941-0
Media Issue 10031717-0011

About the Defense Federal Acquisition Regulation Supplement

This volume contains the full text of the Department of Defense Federal Acquisition Regulation Supplement and the Department of Defense Procedures, Guidance, and Information as of January 1, 2020.

The DFARS and PGI are issued under authority of the Secretary of Defense to implement and supplement the requirements of the Federal Acquisition Regulation. The DFARS contains requirements of law, DoD-wide policies, delegations of FAR authorities, deviations from FAR requirements, and policies and procedures that have a significant effect beyond the internal operating procedures of DoD or a significant cost or administrative impact on contractors or offerors. Relevant procedures, guidance and information which do not meet these criteria are contained in the PGI.

Amendments to the DFARS were previously issued as Defense Acquisition Circulars, and are now issued in the form of interim and final rules. Amendments to the PGI are issued as Publication Notices. The source for any text changes to the DFARS or PGI since their origination appears in brackets following the amended text.

This book is intended for use as a convenient reference when it is not essential to have a text that reflects the latest amendments. Thus, no updating service will be provided. Future amendments will be reported as issued and incorporated in the DFARS and PGI as they appear in the GOVERNMENT CONTRACTS REPORTER, FEDERAL PROCUREMENT REGULATIONS and future editions of this book.

January 1, 2020

WoltersKluwer

Editorial

George M. Gullo, Esq.
Marilyn Helt, Esq.
David L. Stephanides, Esq.
William A. Van Huis, Esq.

Editorial Support

Theresa J. Jensen
Corann Kelly

Table of Contents

Defense Federal Acquisition Regulation Supplement

Procedures, Guidance, and Information

Page

Sources 13

DEFENSE FEDERAL ACQUISITION REGULATION SUPPLEMENT

SUBCHAPTER A—GENERAL

Part 201—Federal Acquisition Regulations System 43
Part 202—Definitions of Words and Terms 53
Part 203—Improper Business Practices and Personal Conflicts of Interest 61
Part 204—Administrative and Information Matters 71

SUBCHAPTER B—ACQUISITION PLANNING

Part 205—Publicizing Contract Actions 97
Part 206—Competition Requirements 103
Part 207—Acquisition Planning 109
Part 208—Required Sources of Supplies and Services 119
Part 209—Contractor Qualifications 129
Part 210—Market Research 145
Part 211—Describing Agency Needs 149
Part 212—Acquisition of Commercial Items 159

SUBCHAPTER C—CONTRACTING METHODS AND CONTRACT TYPES

Part 213—Simplified Acquisition Procedures 179

Page
Part 214—Sealed Bidding 187
Part 215—Contracting by Negotiation 191
Part 216—Types of Contracts 227
Part 217—Special Contracting Methods 239
Part 218—Emergency Acquisitions 263

SUBCHAPTER D—SOCIOECONOMIC PROGRAMS
Part 219—Small Business Programs 269
Part 220—[NO FAR SUPPLEMENT]
Part 221—[NO FAR SUPPLEMENT]
Part 222—Application of Labor Laws to Government Acquisitions 285
Part 223—Environment, Energy and Water Efficiency, Renewable Energy Technologies, Occupational Safety, and Drug-Free Workplace 301
Part 224—Protection of Privacy and Freedom of Information 309
Part 225—Foreign Acquisition 313
Part 226—Other Socioeconomic Programs 393

SUBCHAPTER E—GENERAL CONTRACTING REQUIREMENTS
Part 227—Patents, Data, and Copyrights 401
Part 228—Bonds and Insurance 449
Part 229—Taxes 455
Part 230—Cost Accounting Standards Administration 461
Part 231—Contract Cost Principles and Procedures 465
Part 232—Contract Financing 473
Part 233—Protests, Disputes, and Appeals 493

SUBCHAPTER F—SPECIAL CATEGORIES OF CONTRACTING
Part 234—Major System Acquisition 497
Part 235—Research and Development Contracting 507
Part 236—Construction and Architect-Engineer Contracts 515
Part 237—Service Contracting 523

Page

Part 238—[NO FAR SUPPLEMENT]

Part 239—Acquisition of Information Technology 545

Part 240—[NO FAR SUPPLEMENT]

Part 241—Acquisition of Utility Services 559

SUBCHAPTER G—CONTRACT MANAGEMENT

Part 242—Contract Administration and Audit Services 567

Part 243—Contract Modifications 585

Part 244—Subcontracting Policies and Procedures 591

Part 245—Government Property 597

Part 246—Quality Assurance 609

Part 247—Transportation 623

Part 248—[NO FAR SUPPLEMENT]

Part 249—Termination of Contracts 633

Part 250—Extraordinary Contractual Actions and the Safety Act 639

Part 251—Use of Government Sources by Contractors 643

SUBCHAPTER H—CLAUSES AND FORMS

Part 252—Solicitation Provisions and Contract Clauses 649

Part 253—Forms 1029

APPENDICES

A—Armed Services Board of Contract Appeals 1119

B—[Removed] 1139

D—[Removed] 1143

E—[Removed] 1147

F—Material Inspection and Receiving Report 1151

G—[Removed] 1177

H—Debarment and Suspension Procedures 1181

I—Policy and Procedures for the DoD Pilot Mentor-Protege Program 1185

Page

PROCEDURES, GUIDANCE, AND INFORMATION

SUBCHAPTER A—GENERAL

Part 201—Federal Acquisition Regulations System 1205
Part 202—Definitions of Words and Terms 1219
Part 203—Improper Business Practices and Personal Conflicts of Interest 1223
Part 204—Administrative Matters 1227

SUBCHAPTER B—COMPETITION AND ACQUISITION PLANNING

Part 205—Publicizing Contract Actions 1281
Part 206—Competition Requirements 1285
Part 207—Acquisition Planning 1291
Part 208—Required Sources of Supplies and Services 1301
Part 209—Contractor Qualifcations 1333
Part 210—Market Research 1341
Part 211—Describing Agency Needs 1345
Part 212—Acquisition of Commercial Items 1351

SUBCHAPTER C—CONTRACTING METHODS AND CONTRACT TYPES

Part 213—Simplified Acquisition Procedures 1355
Part 215—Contracting by Negotiation 1361
Part 216—Types of Contracts 1379
Part 217—Special Contracting Methods 1393
Part 218—Emergency Acquisitions 1427

SUBCHAPTER D—SOCIOECONOMIC PROGRAMS

Part 219—Small Business Programs 1431
Part 222—Application of Labor Laws to Government Acquisitions 1437
Part 223—Environment, Energy and Water Efficiency, Renewable Energy Technologies, Occupational Safety and Drug-Free Workplace 1447
Part 225—Foreign Acquisition 1451
Part 226—Other Socioeconomic Programs 1489

Page

SUBCHAPTER E—GENERAL CONTRACTING REQUIREMENTS

Part 228—Bonds and Insurance 1493
Part 229—Taxes 1499
Part 230—Cost Accounting Standards Administration 1505
Part 231—Contract Cost Principles and Procedures 1509
Part 232—Contract Financing 1513
Part 233—Protests, Disputes, and Appeals 1521

SUBCHAPTER F—SPECIAL CATEGORIES OF CONTRACTING

Part 234—Major System Acquisition 1525
Part 235—Research and Development Contracting 1529
Part 236—Construction and Architect-Engineer Contracts 1533
Part 237—Service Contracting 1539
Part 239—Acquisition of Information Technology . . . 1547
Part 241—Acquisition of Utility Services 1553

SUBCHAPTER G—CONTRACT MANAGEMENT

Part 242—Contract Administration and Audit Services 1557
Part 243—Contract Modifications 1571
Part 244—Subcontracting Policies and Procedures 1575
Part 245—Government Property 1579
Part 246—Quality Assurance 1591
Part 247—Transportation 1597
Part 249—Termination of Contracts 1605
Part 250—Extraordinary Contractual Actions and the Safety Act 1615
Part 251—Use of Government Sources by Contractors 1621

SUBCHAPTER H—CLAUSES AND FORMS

Part 252—Solicitation Provisions and Contract Clauses 1625
Part 253—Forms 1629

Page

APPENDICES

F—Material Inspection and Receiving Report....... 1641

TOPICAL INDEX

Topical Index.................................. 1651

Department of Defense FAR Supplement

SOURCES

Final rule, 84 FR 72563, 12-31-2019, effective 12-31-2019; see ¶ 70,017.30.
Final rule, 84 FR 72561, 12-31-2019, effective 12-31-2019; see ¶ 70,017.29.
Final rule, 84 FR 72554, 12-31-2019, effective 12-31-2019; see ¶ 70,017.28.
Final rule, 84 FR 72247, 12-31-2019, effective 12-31-2019; see ¶ 70,017.27.
Final rule, 84 FR 72245, 12-31-2019, effective 1-1-2020; see ¶ 70,017.26.
Final rule, 84 FR 72239, 12-31-2019, effective 12-31-2019; see ¶ 70,017.25.
Interim rule, 84 FR 72231, 12-31-2019, effective 12-31-2019; see ¶ 70,017.24.
Final rule, 84 FR 65311, 11-27-2019, effective 11-27-2019; see ¶ 70,017.23.
Final rule, 84 FR 65310, 11-27-2019, effective 11-27-2019; see ¶ 70,017.22.
Final rule, 84 FR 65308, 11-27-2019, effective 11-27-2019; see ¶ 70,017.21.
Final rule, 84 FR 65304, 11-27-2019, effective 11-27-2019; see ¶ 70,017.20.
Final rule, 84 FR 58337, 10-31-2019, effective 10-31-2019; see ¶ 70,017.19.
Final rule, 84 FR 58336, 10-31-2019, effective 10-31-2019; see ¶ 70,017.18.
Final rule, 84 FR 58334, 10-31-2019, effective 10-31-2019; see ¶ 70,017.17.
Final rule, 84 FR 58332, 10-31-2019, effective 10-31-2019; see ¶ 70,017.16.
Final rule, 84 FR 58331, 10-31-2019, effective 10-31-2019; see ¶ 70,017.15.
Final rule, 84 FR 50785, 9-26-2019, effective 10-1-2019; see ¶ 70,017.14.
Final rule, 84 FR 48510, 9-13-2019, effective 9-13-2019; see ¶ 70,017.13.
Final rule, 84 FR 48508, 9-13-2019, effective 9-13-2019; see ¶ 70,017.12.
Final rule, 84 FR 48507, 9-13-2019, effective 9-13-2019; see ¶ 70,017.11.
Final rule, 84 FR 48506, 9-13-2019, effective 9-13-2019; see ¶ 70,017.10.
Final rule, 84 FR 48504, 9-13-2019, effective 9-13-2019; see ¶ 70,017.09.
Final rule, 84 FR 48503, 9-13-2019, effective 9-13-2019; see ¶ 70,017.08.
Final rule, 84 FR 48501, 9-13-2019, effective 9-13-2019; see ¶ 70,017.07.
Final rule, 84 FR 48500, 9-13-2019, effective 9-13-2019; see ¶ 70,017.06.
Final rule, 84 FR 48499, 9-13-2019, effective 9-13-2019; see ¶ 70,017.05.
Final rule, 84 FR 48498, 9-13-2019, effective 9-13-2019; see ¶ 70,017.04.
Final rule, 84 FR 48496, 9-13-2019, effective 9-13-2019; see ¶ 70,017.03.
Final rule, 84 FR 39207, 8-9-2019, effective 8-9-2019; see ¶ 70,017.02.
Final rule, 84 FR 39204, 8-9-2019, effective 8-9-2019; see ¶ 70,017.01.
Final rule, 84 FR 39203, 8-9-2019, effective 8-9-2019; see ¶ 70,017.
Final rule, 84 FR 39201, 8-9-2019, effective 8-9-2019; see ¶ 70,016.999.
Final rule, 84 FR 33858, 7-16-2019, effective 7-31-2019; see ¶ 70,016.998.
Final rule, 84 FR 30953, 6-28-2019, effective 6-28-2019; see ¶ 70,016.997.
Final rule, 84 FR 30952, 6-28-2019, effective 6-28-2019; see ¶ 70,016.996.
Final rule, 84 FR 30950, 6-28-2019, effective 6-28-2019; see ¶ 70,016.995.
Final rule, 84 FR 30947, 6-28-2019, effective 7-31-2019; see ¶ 70,016.994.
Final rule, 84 FR 30946, 6-28-2019, effective 6-28-2019; see ¶ 70,016.993.
Final rule, 84 FR 25194, 5-31-2019, effective 5-31-2019; see ¶ 70,016.992.
Final rule, 84 FR 25194, 5-31-2019, effective 5-31-2019; see ¶ 70,016.991.
Final rule, 84 FR 25192, 5-31-2019, effective 5-31-2019; see ¶ 70,016.990.
Final rule, 84 FR 25190, 5-31-2019, effective 5-31-2019; see ¶ 70,016.989.
Final rule, 84 FR 25188, 5-31-2019, effective 5-31-2019; see ¶ 70,016.988.
Final rule, 84 FR 25187, 5-31-2019, effective 5-31-2019; see ¶ 70,016.987.
Final rule, 84 FR 18161, 4-30-2019, effective 4-30-2019; see ¶ 70,016.986.

Final rule, 84 FR 18160, 4-30-2019, effective 4-30-2019; see ¶ 70,016.985.
Final rule, 84 FR 18156, 4-30-2019, effective 4-30-2019; see ¶ 70,016.984.
Final rule, 84 FR 18155, 4-30-2019, effective 4-30-2019; see ¶ 70,016.983.
Final rule, 84 FR 18153, 4-30-2019, effective 4-30-2019; see ¶ 70,016.982.
Final rule, 84 FR 12141, 4-1-2019, effective 4-1-2019; see ¶ 70,016.981.
Final rule, 84 FR 12140, 4-1-2019, effective 4-1-2019; see ¶ 70,016.980.
Final rule, 84 FR 12140, 4-1-2019, effective 4-1-2019; see ¶ 70,016.979.
Final rule, 84 FR 12139, 4-1-2019, effective 4-1-2019; see ¶ 70,016.978.
Final rule, 84 FR 12138, 4-1-2019, effective 4-1-2019; see ¶ 70,016.977.
Final rule, 84 FR 12137, 4-1-2019, effective 4-1-2019; see ¶ 70,016.976.
Final rule, 84 FR 4371, 2-15-2019, effective 2-15-2019; see ¶ 70,016.975.
Final rule, 84 FR 4370, 2-15-2019, effective 2-15-2019; see ¶ 70,016.974.
Final rule, 84 FR 4368, 2-15-2019, effective 2-15-2019; see ¶ 70,016.973.
Final rule, 84 FR 4366, 2-15-2019, effective 2-15-2019; see ¶ 70,016.972.
Final rule, 84 FR 4364, 2-15-2019, effective 2-15-2019; see ¶ 70,016.971.
Final rule, 84 FR 4362, 2-15-2019, effective 2-15-2019; see ¶ 70,016.970.
Final rule, 84 FR 4360, 2-15-2019, effective 2-15-2019; see ¶ 70,016.969.
Interim rule, 83 FR 66066, 12-21-2018, effective 12-21-2018; see ¶ 70,016.968.
Final rule, 83 FR 66062, 12-21-2018, effective 12-21-2018; see ¶ 70,016.967.
Final rule, 83 FR 65562, 12-21-2018, effective 12-21-2018; see ¶ 70,016.966.
Final rule, 83 FR 65560, 12-21-2018, effective 12-21-2018; see ¶ 70,016.965.
Final rule, 83 FR 65559, 12-21-2018, effective 12-21-2018; see 70,016.964.
Final rule, 83 FR 62502, 12-4-2018, effective 12-4-2018; see ¶ 70,016.963.
Final rule, 83 FR 62501, 12-4-2018, effective 12-4-2018; see ¶ 70,016.962.
Final rule, 83 FR 62498, 12-4-2018, effective 12-5-2018; see ¶ 70,016.961.
Final rule, 83 FR 54681, 10-31-2018, effective 10-31-2018; see ¶ 70,016.960.
Final rule, 83 FR 54680, 10-31-2018, effective 10-31-2018; see ¶ 70,016.959.
Final rule, 83 FR 54679, 10-31-2018, effective 10-31-2018; see ¶ 70,016.958.
Final rule, 83 FR 54677, 10-31-2018, effective 10-31-2018; see ¶ 70,016.957.
Final rule, 83 FR 54676, 10-31-2018, effective 10-31-2018; see ¶ 70,016.956.
Final rule, 83 FR 49181, 9-28-2018, effective 9-28-2018; see ¶ 70,016.955.
Final rule, 83 FR 49180, 9-28-2018, effective 9-28-2018; see ¶ 70,016.954.
Final rule, 83 FR 49179, 9-28-2018, effective 9-28-2018; see ¶ 70,016.953.
Final rule, 83 FR 49178, 9-28-2018, effective 9-28-2018; see ¶ 70,016.952.
Final rule, 83 FR 42788, 8-24-2018, effective 8-24-2018; see ¶ 70,016.951.
Final rule, 83 FR 42787, 8-24-2018, effective 8-24-2018; see ¶ 70,016.950.
Final rule, 83 FR 30825, 6-29-2018, effective 6-29-2018; see ¶ 70,016.949.
Final rule, 83 FR 30824, 6-29-2018, effective 6-29-2018; see ¶ 70,016.948.
Final rule, 83 FR 30587, 6-29-2018, effective 6-29-2018; see ¶ 70,016.947.
Final rule, 83 FR 30584, 6-29-2018, effective 6-29-2018; see ¶ 70,016.946.
Final rule, 83 FR 24895, 5-30-2018, effective 5-30-2018; see ¶ 70,016.945.
Final rule, 83 FR 24894, 5-30-2018, effective 5-30-2018; see ¶ 70,016.944.
Final rule, 83 FR 24892, 5-30-2018, effective 5-30-2018; see ¶ 70,016.943.
Final rule, 83 FR 24891, 5-30-2018, effective 5-30-2018; see ¶ 70,016.942.
Final rule, 83 FR 24890, 5-30-2018, effective 10-1-2018; see ¶ 70,016.941.
Final rule, 83 FR 24888, 5-30-2018, effective 5-30-2018; see ¶ 70,016.940.
Final rule, 83 FR 24887, 5-30-2018, effective 5-30-2018; see ¶ 70,016.939.

Final rule, 83 FR 24886 , 5-30-2018, effective 5-30-2018; see ¶ 70,016.938.
Final rule, 83 FR 19645, 5-4-2018, effective 5-4-2018; see ¶ 70,016.937.
Final rule, 83 FR 19641, 5-4-2018, effective 5-4-2018; see ¶ 70,016.936.
Final rule, 83 FR 19641, 5-4-2018, effective 5-4-2018; see ¶ 70,016.935.
Final rule, 83 FR 16004, 4-13-2018, effective 4-13-2018; see ¶ 70,016.934.
Final rule, 83 FR 16003, 4-13-2018, effective 4-13-2018; see ¶ 70,016.933.
Final rule, 83 FR 16001, 4-13-2018, effective 4-13-2018; see ¶ 70,016.932.
Final rule, 83 FR 15996, 4-13-2018, effective 4-13-2018; see ¶ 70,016.931.
Final rule, 83 FR 15995, 4-13-2018, effective 4-13-2018; see ¶ 70,016.930.
Final rule, 83 FR 15994, 4-13-2018, effective 4-13-2018; see ¶ 70,016.929.
Final rule, 83 FR 12681, 3-23-2018, effective 3-23-2018; see ¶ 70,016.928.
Final rule, 83 FR 12682, 3-23-2018, effective 3-23-2018; see ¶ 70,016.927.
Final rule, 83 FR 4447, 1-31-2018, effective 1-31-2018; see ¶ 70,016.926.
Final rule, 83 FR 4431, 1-31-2018, effective 1-31-2018; see ¶ 70,016.925.
Final rule, 81 FR 93841, 12-22-2016, effective 12-22-2016; see ¶ 70,016.921.
Final rule, 81 FR 93840, 12-22-2016, effective 12-22-2016; see ¶ 70,016.920.
Final rule, 81 FR 78012, 11-4-2016, effective 11-4-2016; see ¶ 70,016.919.
Final rule, 81 FR 78011, 11-4-2016, effective 11-4-2016; see ¶ 70,016.918.
Final rule, 81 FR 78008, 11-4-2016, effective 11-4-2016; see ¶ 70,016.917.
Final rule, 81 FR 73005, 10-21-2016, effective 10-21-2016; see ¶ 70,016.916.
Final rule, 81 FR 72986, 10-21-2016, effective 10-21-2016; see ¶ 70,016.915.
Final rule, 81 FR 72738, 10-21-2016, effective 10-21-2016; see 70,016.914.
Final rule, 81 FR 65567, 9-23-2016, effective 9-23-2016; see ¶ 70,016.913.
Final rule, 81 FR 65565, 9-23-2016, effective 9-23-2016; see ¶ 70,016.912.
Final rule, 81 FR 65563, 9-23-2016, effective 9-23-2016; see ¶ 70,016.911.
Final rule, 81 FR 65563, 9-23-2016, effective 9-23-2016; see ¶ 70,016.910.
Final rule, 81 FR 59515, 8-30-2016, effective 9-29-2016; see ¶ 70,016.909.
Final rule, 81 FR 59510, 8-30-2016, effective 8-30-2016; see ¶ 70,016.908.
Final rule, 81 FR 59510, 8-30-2016, effective 8-30-2016; see ¶ 70,016.907.
Final rule, 81 FR 53045, 8-11-2016, effective 8-11-2016; see ¶ 70,016.906.
Final rule, 81 FR 50652, 8-2-2016, effective 8-2-2016; see ¶ 70,016.905.
Final rule, 81 FR 50650, 8-2-2016, effective 8-2-2016; see ¶ 70,016.904.
Final rule, 81 FR 50635, 8-2-2016, effective 8-2-2016; see ¶ 70,016.903.
Final rule, 81 FR 42563, 6-30-2016, effective 6-30-2016; see ¶ 70,016.902.
Final rule, 81 FR 42562, 6-30-2016, effective 6-30-2016; see ¶ 70,016.901.
Final rule, 81 FR 42559, 6-30-2016, effective 6-30-2016; see ¶ 70,016.900.
Interim rule, 81 FR 42557, 6-30-2016, effective 6-30-2016; see ¶ 70,016.899.
Final rule, 81 FR 42556, 6-30-2016, effective 6-30-2016; see ¶ 70,016.898.
Final rule, 81 FR 36473, 6-7-2016, effective 6-7-2016; see ¶ 70,016.897.
Final rule, 81 FR 28733, 5-10-2016, effective 5-10-2016; see ¶ 70,016.896.
Final rule, 81 FR 28732, 5-10-2016, effective 5-10-2016; see ¶ 70,016.895.
Final rule, 81 FR 28732, 5-10-2016, effective 5-10-2016; see ¶ 70,016.894.
Final rule, 81 FR 28730, 5-10-2016, effective 5-10-2016; see ¶ 70,016.893.
Final rule, 81 FR 28729, 5-10-2016, effective 5-10-2016; see ¶ 70,016.892.
Final rule, 81 FR 28724, 5-10-2016, effective 5-10-2016; see ¶ 70,016.891.
Final rule, 81 FR 17048, 3-25-2016, effective 3-25-2016; see ¶ 70,016.890.
Final rule, 81 FR 17047, 3-25-2016, effective 3-25-2016; see ¶ 70,016.889.

Final rule, 81 FR 17045, 3-25-2016, effective 3-25-2016; see ¶ 70,016.888.
Final rule, 81 FR 17044, 3-25-2016, effective 3-25-2016; see ¶ 70,016.887.
Final rule, 81 FR 17041, 3-25-2016, effective 3-25-2016; see ¶ 70,016.886.
Final rule, 81 FR 9783, 2-26-2016, effective 2-26-2016; see ¶ 70,016.885.
Interim rule, 80 FR 81472, 12-30-2015, effective 12-30-2015; see ¶ 70,016.884.
Final rule, 80 FR 81470, 12-30-2015, effective 12-30-2015; see ¶ 70,016.883.
Final rule, 80 FR 81467, 12-30-2015, effective 12-30-2015; see ¶ 70,016.882.
Final rule, 80 FR 74694, 11-30-2015, effective 11-30-2015; see ¶ 70,016.881.
Final rule, 80 FR 72607, 11-20-2015, effective 11-20-2015; see ¶ 70,016.880.
Final rule, 80 FR 72606, 11-20-2015, effective 11-20-2015; see ¶ 70,016.879.
Final rule, 80 FR 72599, 11-20-2015, effective 11-20-2015; see ¶ 70,016.878.
Final rule, 80 FR 72357, 11-19-2015, effective 11-19-2015; see ¶ 70,016.877.
Final rule, 80 FR 67254, 10-30-2015, effective 10-30-2015; see ¶ 70,016.876.
Final rule, 80 FR 67253, 10-30-2015, effective 10-30-2015; see ¶ 70,016.875.
Final rule, 80 FR 67252, 10-30-2015, effective 10-30-2015; see ¶ 70,016.874.
Final rule, 80 FR 67243, 10-30-2015, effective 10-30-2015; see ¶ 70,016.873.
Interim rule, 80 FR 63928, 10-22-2015, effective 11-20-2015; see ¶ 70,016.872.
Final rule, 80 FR 58632, 9-30-2015, effective 9-30-2015; see ¶ 70,016.871.
Final rule, 80 FR 58630, 9-30-2015, effective 9-30-2015; see ¶ 70,016.870.
Final rule, 80 FR 56929, 9-21-2015, effective 9-21-2015; see ¶ 70,016.869.
CFR correction, 80 FR 56398, 9-18-2015; see ¶ 70,016.868.
Final rule, 80 FR 51752, 8-26-2015, effective 8-26-2015; see ¶ 70,016.867.
Interim rule, 80 FR 51751, 8-26-2015, effective 8-26-2015; see ¶ 70,016.866.
Final rule, 80 FR 51750, 8-26-2015, effective 8-26-2015; see ¶ 70,016.865.
Final rule, 80 FR 51750, 8-26-2015, effective 8-26-2015; see ¶ 70,016.864.
Final rule, 80 FR 51748, 8-26-2015, effective 8-26-2015; see ¶ 70,016.863.
Interim rule, 80 FR 51739, 8-26-2015, effective 8-26-2015; see ¶ 70,016.862.
Final rule, 80 FR 45899, 8-3-2015, effective 10-1-2015; see ¶ 70,016.861.
Final rule, 80 FR 36903, 6-26-2015, effective 10-1-2015; see ¶ 70,016.860.
Final rule, 80 FR 36900, 6-26-2015, effective 6-26-2015; see ¶ 70,016.859.
Final rule, 80 FR 36897, 6-26-2015, effective 6-26-2015; see ¶ 70,016.858.
Final rule, 80 FR 36719, 6-26-2015, effective 6-26-2015; see ¶ 70,016.857.
Final rule, 80 FR 36718, 6-26-2015, effective 6-26-2015; see ¶ 70,016.856.
Final rule, 80 FR 31309, 6-2-2015, effective 6-2-2015; see ¶ 70,016.855.
Final rule, 80 FR 30117, 5-26-2015, effective 5-26-2015; see ¶ 70,016.854.
Final rule, 80 FR 30115, 5-26-2015, effective 5-26-2015; see ¶ 70,016.853.
Final rule, 80 FR 29983, 5-26-2015, effective 5-26-2015; see ¶ 70,016.852.
Final rule, 80 FR 29981, 5-26-2015, effective 5-26-2015; see ¶ 70,016.851.
Final rule, 80 FR 29980, 5-26-2015, effective 5-26-2015; see ¶ 70,016.850.
Final rule, 80 FR 21656, 4-20-2015, effective 4-20-2015; see ¶ 70,016.849.
Final rule, 80 FR 15912, 3-26-2015, effective 3-26-2015; see ¶ 70,016.847.
Final rule, 80 FR 15912, 3-26-2015, effective 3-26-2015; see ¶ 70,016.846.
Interim rule, 80 FR 15909, 3-26-2015, effective 3-26-2015; see ¶ 70,016.845.
Final rule, 80 FR 10391, 2-26-2015, effective 2-26-2015; see ¶ 70,016.844.
Final rule, 80 FR 10390, 2-26-2015, effective 2-26-2015; see ¶ 70,016.843.
Final rule, 80 FR 10389, 2-26-2015, effective 2-26-2015; see ¶ 70,016.842.
Final rule, 80 FR 4999, 1-29-2014, effective 1-29-2015; see ¶ 70,016.841.

Final rule, 80 FR 4997, 1-29-2014, effective 1-29-2015; see ¶ 70,016.840.
Final rule, 80 FR 4806 1-29-2014, effective 1-29-2015; see ¶ 70,016.839.
Final rule, 80 FR 4805, 1-29-2014, effective 1-29-2015; see ¶ 70,016.838.
Final rule, 80 FR 2018, 1-15-2014, effective 1-15-2015; see ¶ 70,016.837.
Correcting amendments, 79 FR 75757, 12-19-2014, effective 12-19-2014; see ¶ 70,016.836.
Final rule, 79 FR 73652, 12-16-2014, effective 12-16-2014; see ¶ 70,016.835.
Final rule, 79 FR 73500, 12-11-2014, effective 12-11-2014; see ¶ 70,016.834.
Final rule, 79 FR 73499, 12-11-2014, effective 12-11-2014; see ¶ 70,016.833.
Final rule, 79 FR 73498, 12-11-2014, effective 12-11-2014; see ¶ 70,016.832.
Final rule, 79 FR 73493, 12-11-2014, effective 12-11-2014; see ¶ 70,016.831.
Final rule, 79 FR 73492, 12-11-2014, effective 12-11-2014; see ¶ 70,016.830.
Final rule, 79 FR 73490, 12-11-2014, effective 12-11-2014; see ¶ 70,016.829.
Final rule, 79 FR 73488, 12-11-2014, effective 12-11-2014; see ¶ 70,016.828.
Final rule, 79 FR 73487, 12-11-2014, effective 12-11-2014; see ¶ 70,016.827.
Final rule, 79 FR 68635, 11-18-2014, effective 11-18-2014; see ¶ 70,016.826.
Final rule, 79 FR 67356, 11-13-2014, effective 11-13-2014; see ¶ 70,016.825.
Final rule, 79 FR 65815, 11-5-2014, effective 11-5-2014; see ¶ 70,016.824.
Final rule, 79 FR 65592, 11-5-2014, effective 11-5-2014; see ¶ 70,016.823.
Final rule, 79 FR 61584, 10-14-2014, effective 10-14-2014; see ¶ 70,016.822.
Final rule, 79 FR 61583, 10-14-2014, effective 10-14-2014; see ¶ 70,016.821.
Interim rule, 79 FR 61579, 10-14-2014, effective 10-14-2014; see ¶ 70,016.820.
Final rule, 79 FR 58699, 9-30-2014, effective 9-30-2014; see ¶ 70,016.819.
Final rule, 79 FR 58697, 9-30-2014, effective 9-30-2014; see ¶ 70,016.818.
Final rule, 79 FR 58696, 9-30-2014, effective 9-30-2014; see ¶ 70,016.817.
Final rule, 79 FR 58694, 9-30-2014, effective 9-30-2014; see ¶ 70,016.816.
Final rule, 79 FR 58693, 9-30-2014, effective 9-30-2014; see ¶ 70,016.815.
Final rule, 79 FR 56278, 9-19-2014, effective 9-19-2014; see ¶ 70,016.814.
Final rule, 79 FR 51501, 8-29-2014, effective 8-29-2014; see ¶ 70,016.813.
Interim rule, 79 FR 45661, 8-5-2014, effective 8-5-2014; see ¶ 70,016.812.
Interim rule, 79 FR 44314, 7-31-2014, effective 7-31-2014; see ¶ 70,016.811.
Final rule, 79 FR 44314, 7-31-2014, effective 7-31-2014; see ¶ 70,016.810.
Final rule, 79 FR 44313, 7-31-2014, effective 7-31-2014; see ¶ 70,016.809.
Final rule, 79 FR 42214, 7-21-2014, effective 7-21-2014; see ¶ 70,016.808.
Final rule, 79 FR 35700, 6-24-2014, effective 6-24-2014; see ¶ 70,016.807.
Final rule, 79 FR 35699, 6-24-2014, effective 6-24-2014; see ¶ 70,016.806.
Final rule, 79 FR 30474, 5-28-2014, effective 5-28-2014; see ¶ 70,016.805.
Final rule, 79 FR 30469, 5-28-2014, effective 5-28-2014; see ¶ 70,016.804.
Final rule, 79 FR 23278, 4-28-2014, effective 4-28-2014; see ¶ 70,016.802.
Final rule, 79 FR 22042, 4-21-2014, effective 4-21-2014; see ¶ 70,016.801.
Final rule, 79 FR 22041, 4-21-2014, effective 4-21-2014; see ¶ 70,016.800.
Final rule, 79 FR 22036, 4-21-2014, effective 4-21-2014; see ¶ 70,016.799.
Final rule, 79 FR 22036, 4-21-2014, effective 4-21-2014; see ¶ 70,016.798.
Final rule, 79 FR 18654, 4-3-2014, effective 4-3-2014; see ¶ 70,016.797.
Final rule, 79 FR 17931, 3-31-2014, effective 3-31-2014; see ¶ 70,016.796.
Final rule, 79 FR 17448, 3-28-2014, effective 3-28-2014; see ¶ 70,016.795.
Final rule, 79 FR 17447, 3-28-2014, effective 3-28-2014; see ¶ 70,016.794.

Final rule, 79 FR 17446, 3-28-2014, effective 3-28-2014; see ¶ 70,016.793.
Final rule, 79 FR 17445, 3-28-2014, effective 3-28-2014; see ¶ 70,016.792.
Final rule, 79 FR 13568, 3-11-2014, effective 3-11-2014; see ¶ 70,016.791.
Final rule, 79 FR 11342, 2-28-2014, effective 2-28-2014; see ¶ 70,016.790.
Final rule, 79 FR 11341, 2-28-2014, effective 2-28-2014; see ¶ 70,016.789.
Interim rule, 79 FR 11337, 2-28-2014, effective 2-28-2014; see ¶ 70,016.788.
Final rule, 79 FR 11336, 2-28-2014, effective 2-28-2014; see ¶ 70,016.787.
Final rule, 79 FR 4633, 1-29-2014, effective 1-29-2014; see ¶ 70,016.786.
Final rule, 79 FR 4631, 1-29-2014, effective 1-29-2014; see ¶ 70,016.785.
Final rule, 79 FR 3519, 1-22-2014, effective 1-22-2014; see ¶ 70,016.784.
Final rule, 78 FR 79620, 12-31-2013, effective 1-1-2014; see ¶ 70,016.783.
Final rule, 78 FR 76993, 12-20-2013, effective 12-20-2013; see ¶ 70,016.782.
Final rule, 78 FR 76067, 12-16-2013, effective 12-16-2013; see ¶ 70,016.781.
Final rule, 78 FR 73451, 12-6-2013, effective 12-6-2013; see ¶ 70,016.780.
Final rule, 78 FR 73450, 12-6-2013, effective 12-6-2013; see ¶ 70,016.779.
Final rule, 78 FR 73450, 12-6-2013, effective 12-6-2013; see ¶ 70,016.778.
Final rule, 78 FR 69282, 11-18-2013, effective 11-18-2013; see ¶ 70,016.777.
Final rule, 78 FR 69273, 11-18-2013, effective 11-18-2013; see ¶ 70,016.776.
Interim rule, 78 FR 69267, 11-18-2013, effective 11-18-2013; see ¶ 70,016.775.
Final rule, 78 FR 65221, 10-31-2013, effective 10-31-2013; see ¶ 70,016.774.
Final rule, 78 FR 65220, 10-31-2013, effective 10-31-2013; see ¶ 70,016.773.
Final rule, 78 FR 65219, 10-31-2013, effective 10-31-2013; see ¶ 70,016.772.
Interim rule, 78 FR 65218, 10-31-2013, effective 10-31-2013; see ¶ 70,016.771.
Final rule, 78 FR 65214, 10-31-2013, effective 10-31-2013; see ¶ 70,016.770.
Interim rule, 78 FR 59859, 9-30-2013, effective 9-30-2013; see ¶ 70,016.769.
Interim rule, 78 FR 59854, 9-30-2013, effective 9-30-2013; see ¶ 70,016.768.
Interim rule, 78 FR 59851, 9-30-2013, effective 9-30-2013; see ¶ 70,016.767.
Final rule, 78 FR 54968, 9-9-2013, effective 9-9-2013; see ¶ 70,016.766.
Final rule, 78 FR 48333, 8-8-2013, effective 8-8-2013; see ¶ 70,016.765.
Final rule, 78 FR 48331, 8-8-2013, effective 8-8-2013; see ¶ 70,016.764.
Final rule, 78 FR 41331, 7-10-2013, effective 7-10-2013; see ¶ 70,016.763.
Final rule, 78 FR 40043, 7-3-2013, effective 7-3-2013; see ¶ 70,016.762.
Final rule, 78 FR 38325, 6-26-2013, effective 6-26-2013; see ¶ 70,016.761.
Final rule, 78 FR 38324, 6-26-2013, effective 6-26-2013; see ¶ 70,016.760.
Final rule, 78 FR 37980, 6-25-2013, effective 6-25-2013; see ¶ 70,016.759.
Final rule, 78 FR 36113, 6-17-2013, effective 6-17-2013; see ¶ 70,016.758.
Final rule, 78 FR 36108, 6-17-2013, effective 6-17-2013; see ¶ 70,016.757.
Final rule, 78 FR 33994, 6-16-2013, effective 6-16-2013; see ¶ 70,016.756.
Final rule, 78 FR 33993, 6-6-2013, effective 6-6-2013; see ¶ 70,016.755.
Final rule, 78 FR 30233, 5-22-2013, effective 5-22-2013; see ¶ 70,016.754.
Final rule, 78 FR 30232, 5-22-2013, effective 5-22-2013; see ¶ 70,016.753.
Final rule, 78 FR 30231, 5-22-2013, effective 5-22-2013; see ¶ 70,016.752.
Final rule, 78 FR 28756, 5-16-2013, effective 5-16-2013; see ¶ 70,016.751.
Final rule, 78 FR 21850, 4-12-2013, effective 4-12-2013; see ¶ 70,016.750.
Final rule, 78 FR 18877, 3-28-2013, effective 3-28-2013; see ¶ 70,016.749.
Final rule, 78 FR 18877, 3-28-2013, effective 3-28-2013; see ¶ 70,016.748.
Final rule, 78 FR 18876, 3-28-2013, effective 3-28-2013; see ¶ 70,016.747.

Final rule, 78 FR 18865, 3-28-2013, effective 3-28-2013; see ¶ 70,016.746.
Final rule, 78 FR 13547, 2-28-2013, effective 2-28-2013; see ¶ 70,016.745.
Final rule, 78 FR 13546, 2-28-2013, effective 2-28-2013; see ¶ 70,016.744.
Final rule, 78 FR 13544, 2-28-2013, effective 2-28-2013; see ¶ 70,016.743.
Final rule, 78 FR 13543, 2-28-2013, effective 2-28-2013; see ¶ 70,016.742.
Final rule, 77 FR 76941, 12-31-2012, effective 12-31-2012; see ¶ 70,016.741.
Final rule, 77 FR 76939, 12-31-2012, effective 12-31-2012; see ¶ 70,016.740.
Final rule, 77 FR 76938, 12-31-2012, effective 1-30-2013; see ¶ 70,016.739.
Final rule, 77 FR 76936, 12-31-2012, effective 12-31-2012; see ¶ 70,016.738.
Interim rule, 77 FR 68699, 11-16-2012, effective 11-16-2012; see ¶ 70,016.737.
CFR Correction, 77 FR 59343, 9-27-2012; see ¶ 70,016.736.
CFR Correction, 77 FR 59339, 9-27-2012; see ¶ 70,016.735.
CFR Correction, 77 FR 59339, 9-27-2012; see ¶ 70,016.734.
CFR Correction, 77 FR 59339, 9-27-2012; see ¶ 70,016.733.
CFR Correction, 77 FR 59339, 9-27-2012; see ¶ 70,016.732.
Final rule, 77 FR 52258, 8-29-2012, effective 8-29-2012; see ¶ 70,016.731.
Final rule, 77 FR 52254, 8-29-2012, effective 8-29-2012; see ¶ 70,016.730.
Final rule, 77 FR 52253, 8-29-2012, effective 8-29-2012; see ¶ 70,016.729.
Final rule, 77 FR 52252, 8-29-2012, effective 8-29-2012; see ¶ 70,016.728.
Final rule, 77 FR 43470, 7-24-2012, effective 7-24-2012; see ¶ 70,016.727.
Final rule, 77 FR 43470, 7-24-2012, effective 7-24-2012; see ¶ 70,016.726.
Final rule, 77 FR 39141, 6-29-2012, effective 6-29-2012; see ¶ 70,016.725.
Final rule, 77 FR 39140, 6-29-2012, effective 6-29-2012; see ¶ 70,016.724.
Final rule, 77 FR 39125, 6-29-2012, effective 6-29-2012; see ¶ 70,016.723.
Final rule, 77 FR 38736, 6-29-2012, effective 6-29-2012; see ¶ 70,016.722.
Interim rule, 77 FR 38734, 6-29-2012, effective 6-29-2012; see ¶ 70,016.721.
Final rule, 77 FR 38731, 6-29-2012, effective 6-29-2012; see ¶ 70,016.720.
Final rule, 77 FR 35883, 6-15-2012, effective 6-15-2012; see ¶ 70,016.719.
Final rule, 77 FR 35879, 6-15-2012, effective 6-15-2012; see ¶ 70,016.718.
Final rule, 77 FR 31536, 5-29-2012, effective 5-29-2012; see ¶ 70,016.717.
Final rule, 77 FR 30368, 5-22-2012, effective 5-22-2012; see ¶ 70,016.716.
Final rule, 77 FR 30367, 5-22-2012, effective 5-22-2012; see ¶ 70,016.715.
Final rule, 77 FR 30366, 5-22-2012, effective 5-22-2012; see ¶ 70,016.714.
Final rule, 77 FR 30365, 5-22-2012, effective 5-22-2012; see ¶ 70,016.713.
Interim rule, 77 FR 30361, 5-22-2012, effective 5-22-2012; see ¶ 70,016.712.
Interim rule, 77 FR 30359, 5-22-2012, effective 5-22-2012; see ¶ 70,016.711.
Interim rule, 77 FR 30356, 5-22-2012, effective 5-22-2012; see ¶ 70,016.710.
Final rule, 77 FR 23631, 4-30-2012, effective 4-30-2012; see ¶ 70,016.709.
Final rule, 77 FR 19132, 3-30-2012, effective 3-30-2012; see ¶ 70,016.708.
Final rule, 77 FR 19128, 3-30-2012, effective 3-30-2012; see ¶ 70,016.707.
Final rule, 77 FR 19128, 3-30-2012, effective 3-30-2012; see ¶ 70,016.706.
Interim rule, 77 FR 19127, 3-30-2012, effective 3-30-2012; see ¶ 70,016.705.
Final rule, 77 FR 19126, 3-30-2012, effective 4-30-2012; see ¶ 70,016.704.
Final rule, 77 FR 14480, 3-12-2012, effective 3-12-2012; see ¶ 70,016.703.
Final rule, 77 FR 13013, 3-5-2012, effective 3-5-2012; see ¶ 70,016.702.
Final rule, 77 FR 11775, 2-28-2012, effective 2-28-2012; see ¶ 70,016.701.
Final rule, 77 FR 11367, 2-24-2012, effective 2-24-2012; see ¶ 70,016.700.

Final rule, 77 FR 11367, 2-24-2012, effective 2-24-2012; see ¶ 70,016.699.
Final rule, 77 FR 11355, 2-24-2012, effective 2-24-2012; see ¶ 70,016.698.
Final rule, 77 FR 11354, 2-24-2012, effective 2-24-2012; see ¶ 70,016.697.
Final rule, 77 FR 10976, 2-24-2012, effective 2-24-2012; see ¶ 70,016.696.
Final rule, 77 FR 4632, 1-30-2012, effective 1-30-2012; see ¶ 70,016.695.
Final rule, 77 FR 4631, 1-30-2012, effective 1-30-2012; see ¶ 70,016.694.
Final rule, 77 FR 4630, 1-30-2012, effective 1-30-2012; see ¶ 70,016.693.
Final rule, 77 FR 2653, 1-19-2012, effective 1-19-2012; see ¶ 70,016.692.
Interim rule, 76 FR 78858, 12-20-2011, effective 12-20-2011; see ¶ 70,016.691.
Final rule, 76 FR 76318, 12-7-2011, effective 12-7-2011; see ¶ 70,016.690.
Final rule, 76 FR 71833, 11-18-2011, effective 11-18-2011; see ¶ 70,016.689.
Final rule, 76 FR 71831, 11-18-2011, effective 11-18-2011; see ¶ 70,016.688.
Final rule, 76 FR 71830, 11-18-2011, effective 11-18-2011; see ¶ 70,016.687.
Final rule, 76 FR 71826, 11-18-2011, effective 11-18-2011; see ¶ 70,016.686.
Final rule, 76 FR 71824, 11-18-2011, effective 11-18-2011; see ¶ 70,016.685.
Final rule, 76 FR 71468, 11-18-2011, effective 11-18-2011; see ¶ 70,016.684.
Final rule, 76 FR 71467, 11-18-2011, effective 11-18-2011; see ¶ 70,016.683.
Final rule, 76 FR 71465, 11-18-2011, effective 11-18-2011; see ¶ 70,016.682.
Final rule, 76 FR 71465, 11-18-2011, effective 11-18-2011; see ¶ 70,016.681.
Final rule, 76 FR 71464, 11-18-2011, effective 11-18-2011; see ¶ 70,016.680.
Final rule, 76 FR 61282, 10-4-2011, effective 10-4-2011; see ¶ 70,016.679.
Final rule, 76 FR 61279, 10-4-2011, effective 10-40-2011; see ¶ 70,016.678.
Final rule, 76 FR 58155, 9-20-2011, effective 9-20-2011; see ¶ 70,016.677.
Final rule, 76 FR 58152, 9-20-2011, effective 9-20-2011; see ¶ 70,016.676.
Final rule, 76 FR 58150, 9-20-2011, effective 9-20-2011; see ¶ 70,016.675.
Final rule, 76 FR 58149, 9-20-2011, effective 9-20-2011; see ¶ 70,016.674.
Final rule, 76 FR 58144, 9-20-2011, effective 9-20-2011; see ¶ 70,016.673.
Final rule, 76 FR 58142, 9-20-2011, effective 9-20-2011; see ¶ 70,016.672.
Final rule, 76 FR 58140, 9-20-2011, effective 9-20-2011; see ¶ 70,016.671.
Final rule, 76 FR 58138, 9-20-2011, effective 9-20-2011; see ¶ 70,016.670.
Final rule, 76 FR 58137, 9-20-2011, effective 9-20-2011; see ¶ 70,016.669.
Final rule, 76 FR 58136, 9-20-2011, effective 9-20-2011; see ¶ 70,016.668.
Final rule, 76 FR 58122, 9-20-2011, effective 9-20-2011; see ¶ 70,016.667.
Final rule, 76 FR 57677, 9-16-2011, effective 9-16-2011; see ¶ 70,016.666.
Interim rule, 76 FR 57674, 9-16-2011, effective 9-16-2011; see ¶ 70,016.665.
Final rule, 76 FR 57671, 9-16-2011, effective 9-16-2011; see ¶ 70,016.664.
Final rule, 76 FR 52139, 8-19-2011, effective 8-19-2011; see ¶ 70,016.663.
Final rule, 76 FR 52138, 8-19-2011, effective 8-19-2011; see ¶ 70,016.662.
Interim rule, 76 FR 52133, 8-19-2011, effective 8-19-2011; see ¶ 70,016.661.
Final rule, 76 FR 52132, 8-19-2011, effective 8-19-2011; see ¶ 70,016.660.
Final rule, 76 FR 44282, 7-25-2011, effective 7-25-2011; see ¶ 70,016.659.
Interim rule, 76 FR 44280, 7-25-2011, effective 7-25-2011; see ¶ 70,016.658.
Final rule, 76 FR 38053, 6-29-2011, effective 6-29-2011; see ¶ 70,016.657.
Final rule, 76 FR 38051, 6-29-2011, effective 6-29-2011; see ¶ 70,016.656.
Interim rule, 76 FR 38050, 6-29-2011, effective 6-29-2011; see ¶ 70,016.655.
Interim rule, 76 FR 38048, 6-29-2011, effective 6-29-2011; see ¶ 70,016.654.
Final rule, 76 FR 38047, 6-29-2011, effective 6-29-2011; see ¶ 70,016.653.

Final rule, 76 FR 38046, 6-29-2011, effective 6-29-2011; see ¶ 70,016.652.
Final rule, 76 FR 36883, 6-23-2011, effective 6-23-2011; see ¶ 70,016.651.
Final rule, 76 FR 33170, 6-8-2011, effective 6-8-2011; see ¶ 70,016.650.
Final rule, 76 FR 33166, 6-8-2011, effective 6-8-2011; see ¶ 70,016.649.
Interim rule, 76 FR 32843, 6-6-2011, effective 6-6-2011; see ¶ 70,016.648.
Final rule, 76 FR 32841, 6-6-2011, effective 6-6-2011; see ¶ 70,016.647.
Final rule, 76 FR 32840, 6-6-2011, effective 6-6-2011; see ¶ 70,016.646.
Interim rule, 76 FR 28856, 5-18-2011, effective 5-18-2011; see ¶ 70,016.645.
Final rule, 76 FR 27274, 5-11-2011, effective 5-11-2011; see ¶ 70,016.644.
Final rule, 76 FR 27274, 5-11-2011, effective 5-11-2011; see ¶ 70,016.643.
Final rule, 76 FR 27274, 5-11-2011, effective 5-11-2011; see ¶ 70,016.642.
Final rule, 76 FR 25569, 5-5-2011, effective 5-5-2011; see ¶ 70,016.641.
Final rule, 76 FR 25566, 5-5-2011, effective 5-5-2011; see ¶ 70,016.640.
Final rule, 76 FR 25565, 5-5-2011, effective 5-5-2011; see ¶ 70,016.639.
Final rule, 76 FR 23505, 4-27-2011, effective 4-27-2011; see ¶ 70,016.638.
Final rule, 76 FR 23504, 4-27-2011, effective 4-27-2011; see ¶ 70,016.637.
Final rule, 76 FR 21809, 4-19-2011, effective 4-19-2011; see ¶ 70,016.636.
Final rule, 76 FR 21812, 4-19-2011, effective 4-19-2011; see ¶ 70,016.635.
Final rule, 76 FR 21810, 4-19-2011, effective 4-19-2011; see ¶ 70,016.634.
Final rule, 76 FR 14590, 3-17-2011, effective 3-17-2011; see ¶ 70,016.633.
Final rule, 76 FR 14589, 3-17-2011, effective 3-17-2011; see ¶ 70,016.632.
Interim rule, 76 FR 14588, 3-17-2011, effective 3-17-2011; see ¶ 70,016.631.
Final rule, 76 FR 14587, 3-17-2011, effective 3-17-2011; see ¶ 70,016.630.
Final rule, 76 FR 13297, 3-11-2011, effective 3-11-2011; see ¶ 70,016.629.
CFR Correction, 76 FR 11969, 3-4-2011, effective 3-4-2011; see ¶ 70,016.628.
Final rule, 76 FR 11371, 3-2-2011, effective 3-2-2011; see ¶ 70,016.627.
Interim rule, 76 FR 11363, 3-2-2011, effective 3-2-2011; see ¶ 70,016.626.
Final rule, 76 FR 11361, 3-2-2011, effective 3-2-2011; see ¶ 70,016.625.
Final rule, 76 FR 9680, 2-22-2011, effective 23-22-2011; see ¶ 70,016.624.
Final rule, 76 FR 9680, 2-22-2011, effective 2-22-2011; see ¶ 70,016.623.
Final rule, 76 FR 9679, 2-22-2011, effective 2-22-2011; see ¶ 70,016.622.
Final rule, 76 FR 8303, 2-14-2011, effective 2-14-2011; see ¶ 70,016.621.
Final rule, 76 FR 6006, 2-2-2011, effective 2-2-2011; see ¶ 70,016.620.
Final rule, 76 FR 6004, 2-2-2011, effective 2-2-2011; see ¶ 70,016.619.
Final rule, 76 FR 3536, 1-20-2011, effective 1-20-2011; see ¶ 70,016.618.
Final rule, 76 FR 25, 1-3-2011, effective 1-3-2011; see ¶ 70,016.617.
Final rule, 75 FR 81915, 12-29-2010, effective 12-29-2010; see ¶ 70,016.616.
Final rule, 75 FR 81908, 12-29-2010, effective 12-29-2010; see ¶ 70,016.615.
Final rule, 75 FR 78619, 12-16-2010, effective 12-16-2010; see ¶ 70,016.614.
Final rule, 75 FR 76297, 12-8-2010, effective 12-8-2010; see ¶ 70,016.613.
Final rule, 75 FR 76295, 12-8-2010, effective 12-8-2010; see ¶ 70,016.612.
Final rule, 75 FR 71564, 11-24-2010, effective 11-24-2010; see ¶ 70,016.611.
Final rule, 75 FR 71563, 11-24-2010, effective 11-24-2010; see ¶ 70,016.610.
Final rule, 75 FR 71562, 11-24-2010, effective 11-24-2010; see ¶ 70,016.609.
Final rule, 75 FR 71560, 11-24-2010, effective 11-24-2010; see ¶ 70,016.608.
Interim rule, 75 FR 69360, 11-12-2010, effective 11-12-2010; see ¶ 70,016.607.
Interim rule, 75 FR 67632, 11-3-2010, effective 11-3-2010; see ¶ 70,016.606.

Final rule, 75 FR 66686, 10-29-2010, effective 10-29-2010; see ¶ 70,016.605.
Interim rule, 75 FR 66683, 10-29-2010, effective 10-29-2010; see ¶ 70,016.604.
Final rule, 75 FR 66680, 10-29-2010, effective 10-29-2010; see ¶ 70,016.603.
Final rule, 75 FR 66680, 10-29-2010, effective 10-29-2010; see ¶ 70,016.602.
Final rule, 75 FR 66679, 10-29-2010, effective 10-29-2010; see ¶ 70,016.601.
Interim rule, 75 FR 65439, 10-25-2010, effective 10-25-2010; see ¶ 70,016.600.
Interim rule, 75 FR 65437, 10-25-2010, effective 10-25-2010; see ¶ 70,016.599.
Final rule, 75 FR 59103, 9-27-2010, effective 9-27-2010; see ¶ 70,016.598.
Final rule, 75 FR 59102, 9-27-2010, effective 9-27-2010; see ¶ 70,016.597.
Final rule, 75 FR 59102, 9-27-2010, effective 9-27-2010; see ¶ 70,016.596.
Final rule, 75 FR 59101, 9-27-2010, effective 9-27-2010; see ¶ 70,016.595.
Final rule, 75 FR 54527, 9-8-2010, effective 9-8-2010; see ¶ 70,016.594.
Final rule, 75 FR 54526, 9-8-2010, effective 9-8-2010; see ¶ 70,016.593.
Final rule, 75 FR 54526, 9-8-2010, effective 9-8-2010; see ¶ 70,016.592.
Interim rule, 75 FR 54524, 9-8-2010, effective 9-8-2010; see ¶ 70,016.591.
Final rule, 75 FR 54524, 9-8-2010, effective 9-8-2010; see ¶ 70,016.590.
Interim rule, 75 FR 52650, 8-27-2010, effective 8-27-2010; see ¶ 70,016.589.
Final rule, 75 FR 51416, 8-20-2010, effective 8-20-2010; see ¶ 70,016.588.
Final rule, 75 FR 51416, 8-20-2010, effective 8-20-2010; see ¶ 70,016.587.
Final rule, 75 FR 49849, 8-16-2010, effective 8-16-2010; see ¶ 70,016.586.
Final rule, 75 FR 48279, 8-10-2010, effective 8-10-2010; see ¶ 70,016.585.
Final rule, 75 FR 48276, 8-10-2010, effective 8-10-2010; see ¶ 70,016.584.
Final rule, 75 FR 48278, 8-10-2010, effective 8-10-2010; see ¶ 70,016.583.
Final rule, 75 FR 45072, 8-2-2010, effective 10-1-2010; see ¶ 70,016.582.
Final rule, 75 FR 40717, 7-13-2010, effective 7-13-2010; see ¶ 70,016.581.
Interim rule, 75 FR 40716, 7-13-2010, effective 7-13-2010; see ¶ 70,016.580.
Interim rule, 75 FR 40714, 7-13-2010, effective 7-13-2010; see ¶ 70,016.579.
Interim rule, 75 FR 40711, 7-13-2010, effective 7-13-2010; see ¶ 70,016.578.
Interim rule, 75 FR 35684, 6-23-2010, effective 6-23-2010; see ¶ 70,016.577.
Final rule, 75 FR 34946, 6-21-2010, effective 6-21-2010; see ¶ 70,016.576.
Final rule, 75 FR 34943, 6-21-2010, effective 6-21-2010; see ¶ 70,016.575.
Interim rule, 75 FR 34942, 6-21-2010, effective 6-21-2010; see ¶ 70,016.574.
Final rule, 75 FR 33195, 6-11-2010, effective 6-11-2010; see ¶ 70,016.573.
Final rule, 75 FR 32642, 6-8-2010, effective 6-8-2010; see ¶ 70,016.572.
Final rule, 75 FR 32641, 6-8-2010, effective 6-8-2010; see ¶ 70,016.571.
Final rule, 75 FR 32640, 6-8-2010, effective 6-8-2010; see ¶ 70,016.570.
Interim rule, 75 FR 32639, 6-8-2010, effective 6-8-2010; see ¶ 70,016.569.
Interim rule, 75 FR 32638, 6-8-2010, effective 6-8-2010; see ¶ 70,016.568.
Interim rule, 75 FR 32637, 6-8-2010, effective 6-8-2010; see ¶ 70,016.567.
Interim rule, 75 FR 27946, 5-19-2010, effective 5-19-2010; see ¶ 70,016.566.
Final rule, 75 FR 25119, 5-7-2010, effective 5-7-2010; see ¶ 70,016.565.
Final rule, 75 FR 22706, 4-30-2010, effective 4-30-2010; see ¶ 70,016.564.
Final rule, 75 FR 18035, 4-8-2010, effective 4-8-2010; see ¶ 70,016.563.
Final rule, 75 FR 18034, 4-8-2010, effective 4-8-2010; see ¶ 70,016.562.
Final rule, 75 FR 18029, 4-8-2010, effective 4-8-2010; see ¶ 70,016.561.
Final rule, 75 FR 14095, 3-24-2010, effective 3-24-2010; see ¶ 70,016.560.
Interim rule, 75 FR 10191, 3-5-2010, effective 3-5-2010; see ¶ 70,016.559.

Interim rule, 75 FR 10190, 3-5-2010, effective 3-5-2010; see ¶ 70,016.558.
Interim rule, 75 FR 9114, 3-1-2010, effective 3-1-2010; see ¶ 70,016.557.
Interim rule, 75 FR 8272, 2-24-2010, effective 2-24-2010; see ¶ 70,016.556.
Final rule, 75 FR 6819, 2-11-2010, effective 3-15-2010; see ¶ 70,016.555.
Final rule, 75 FR 3179, 1-20-2010, effective 1-20-2010; see ¶ 70,016.554.
Final rule, 75 FR 3178, 1-20-2010, effective 1-20-2010; see ¶ 70,016.553.
Final rule, 74 FR 68699, 12-29-2009, effective 12-29-2009; see ¶ 70,016.552.
Final rule, 74 FR 68384, 12-24-2009, effective 12-24-2009; see ¶ 70,016.551.
Final rule, 74 FR 68383, 12-24-2009, effective 12-24-2009; see ¶ 70,016.550.
Final rule, 74 FR 68382, 12-24-2009, effective 12-24-2009; see ¶ 70,016.549.
Interim rule, 74 FR 61045, 11-23-2009, effective 11-23-2009; see ¶ 70,016.548.
Interim rule, 74 FR 61043, 11-23-2009, effective 11-23-2009; see ¶ 70,016.547.
Final rule, 74 FR 59914, 11-19-2009, effective 11-19-2009; see ¶ 70,016.546.
Final rule, 74 FR 59914, 11-19-2009, effective 11-19-2009; see ¶ 70,016.545.
Final rule, 74 FR 59916, 11-19-2009, effective 11-19-2009; see ¶ 70,016.544.
Final rule, 74 FR 59913, 11-19-2009, effective 11-19-2009; see ¶ 70,016.543.
Final rule, 74 FR 59916, 11-19-2009, effective 11-19-2009; see ¶ 70,016.542.
Final rule, 74 FR 59914, 11-19-2009, effective 11-19-2009; see ¶ 70,016.541.
Final rule, 74 FR 53413, 10-19-2009, effective 10-19-2009; see ¶ 70,016.540.
Final rule, 74 FR 53412, 10-19-2009, effective 10-19-2009; see ¶ 70,016.539.
Final rule, 74 FR 52895, 10-15-2009, effective 10-15-2009; see ¶ 70,016.538.
Correction, 74 FR 44769, 8-31-2009, effective 8-31-2009; see ¶ 70,016.534.
Final rule, 74 FR 42779, 8-25-2009, effective 8-25-2009; see ¶ 70,016.533.
Interim rule, 74 FR 37652, 7-29-2009, effective 7-29-2009; see ¶ 70,016.532.
Interim rule, 74 FR 37650, 7-29-2009, effective 7-29-2009; see ¶ 70,016.531.
Final rule, 74 FR 37649, 7-29-2009, effective 7-29-2009; see ¶ 70,016.530.
Final rule, 74 FR 37648, 7-29-2009, effective 7-29-2009; see ¶ 70,016.529.
Final rule, 74 FR 37645, 7-29-2009, effective 7-29-2009; see ¶ 70,016.528.
Final rule, 74 FR 37644, 7-29-2009, effective 7-29-2009; see ¶ 70,016.527.
Final rule, 74 FR 37642, 7-29-2009, effective 7-29-2009; see ¶ 70,016.526.
Final rule, 74 FR 37642, 7-29-2009, effective 7-29-2009; see ¶ 70,016.525.
Final rule, 74 FR 37626, 7-29-2009, effective 7-29-2009; see ¶ 70,016.524.
Final rule, 74 FR 37625, 7-29-2009, effective 7-29-2009; see ¶ 70,016.523.
Correction, 74 FR 35825, 7-21-2009, effective 7-21-2009; see ¶ 70,016.522.
Interim rule, 74 FR 34270, 7-15-2009, effective 7-15-2009; see ¶ 70,016.521.
Final rule, 74 FR 34269, 7-15-2009, effective 7-15-2009; see ¶ 70,016.520.
Interim rule, 74 FR 34266, 7-15-2009, effective 7-15-2009; see ¶ 70,016.519.
Final rule, 74 FR 34265, 7-15-2009, effective 7-15-2009; see ¶ 70,016.518.
Final rule, 74 FR 34264, 7-15-2009, effective 7-15-2009; see ¶ 70,016.517.
Final rule, 74 FR 34264, 7-15-2009, effective 7-15-2009; see ¶ 70,016.517.
Interim rule, 74 FR 34263, 7-15-2009, effective 7-15-2009; see ¶ 70,016.516.
Interim rule, 74 FR 2422, 1-15-2009, effective 1-15-2009; see ¶ 70,016.515.
Final rule, 74 FR 2421, 1-15-2009, effective 1-15-2009; see ¶ 70,016.514.
Final rule, 74 FR 2421, 1-15-2009, effective 1-15-2009; see ¶ 70,016.513.
Final rule, 74 FR 2418, 1-15-2009, effective 1-15-2009; see ¶ 70,016.512.
Interim rule, 74 FR 2417, 1-15-2009, effective 1-15-2009; see ¶ 70,016.511.
Final rule, 74 FR 2416, 1-15-2009, effective 1-15-2009; see ¶ 70,016.510.

Interim rule, 74 FR 2415, 1-15-2009, effective 1-15-2009; see ¶ 70,016.509.
Final rule, 74 FR 2414, 1-15-2009, effective 1-15-2009; see ¶ 70,016.508.
Final rule, 74 FR 2414, 1-15-2009, effective 1-15-2009; see ¶ 70,016.507.
Final rule, 74 FR 2413, 1-15-2009, effective 1-15-2009; see ¶ 70,016.506.
Final rule, 74 FR 2411, 1-15-2009, effective 1-15-2009; see ¶ 70,016.505.
Interim rule, 74 FR 2410, 1-15-2009, effective 1-15-2009; see ¶ 70,016.504.
Interim rule, 74 FR 2408, 1-15-2009, effective 1-15-2009; see ¶ 70,016.503.
Final rule, 74 FR 2407, 1-15-2009, effective 1-15-2009; see ¶ 70,016.502.
Final rule, 74 FR 2407, 1-15-2009, effective 1-15-2009; see ¶ 70,016.501.
Final rule, 73 FR 76971, 12-18-2008, effective 12-18-2008; see ¶ 70,016.500.
Interim rule, 73 FR 76970, 12-18-2008, effective 12-18-2008; see ¶ 70,016.499.
Final rule, 73 FR 76969, 12-18-2008, effective 12-18-2008; see ¶ 70,016.498.
Final rule, 73 FR 70913, 11-24-2008, effective 11-24-2008; see ¶ 70,016.497.
Final rule, 73 FR 70912, 11-24-2008, effective 11-24-2008; see ¶ 70,016.496.
Final rule, 73 FR 70909, 11-24-2008, effective 11-24-2008; see ¶ 70,016.495.
Final rule, 73 FR 70906, 11-24-2008, effective 11-24-2008; see ¶ 70,016.494.
Final rule, 73 FR 70905, 11-24-2008, effective 11-24-2008; see ¶ 70,016.493.
Interim rule, 73 FR 53156, 9-15-2008, effective 9-15-2008; see ¶ 70,016.489.
Final rule, 73 FR 53156, 9-15-2008, effective 9-15-2008; see ¶ 70,016.490.
Interim rule, 73 FR 53151, 9-15-2008, effective 9-15-2008; see ¶ 70,016.489.
Final rule, 73 FR 53151, 9-15-2008, effective 9-15-2008; see ¶ 70,016.488.
Final rule, 73 FR 46819, 8-12-2008, effective 8-12-2008; see ¶ 70,016.487.
Final rule, 73 FR 46818, 8-12-2008, effective 8-12-2008; see ¶ 70,016.486.
Final rule, 73 FR 46817, 8-12-2008, effective 8-12-2008; see ¶ 70,016.485.
Final rule, 73 FR 46817, 8-12-2008, effective 8-12-2008; see ¶ 70,016.484.
Interim rule, 73 FR 46816, 8-12-2008, effective 8-12-2008; see ¶ 70,016.483.
Final rule, 73 FR 46814, 8-12-2008, effective 8-12-2008; see ¶ 70,016.482.
Final rule, 73 FR 46813, 8-12-2008, effective 8-12-2008; see ¶ 70,016.481.
Interim rule, 73 FR 42274, 7-21-2008, effective 7-21-2008; see ¶ 70,016.480.
Interim rule, 73 FR 27464, 5-13-2008, effective 5-13-2008; see ¶ 70,016.479.
Final rule, 73 FR 27464, 5-13-2008, effective 5-13-2008; see ¶ 70,016.478.
Final rule, 73 FR 21846, 4-23-2008, effective 4-23-2008; see ¶ 70,016.477.
Final rule, 73 FR 21845, 4-23-2008, effective 4-23-2008; see ¶ 70,016.476.
Final rule, 73 FR 21845, 4-23-2008, effective 4-23-2008; see ¶ 70,016.475.
Final rule, 73 FR 21844, 4-23-2008, effective 4-23-2008; see ¶ 70,016.474.
Final rule, 73 FR 16764, 3-31-2008, effective 3-31-2008; see ¶ 70,016.473.
Final rule, 73 FR 11356, 3-3-2008, effective 3-3-2008; see ¶ 70,016.472.
Final rule, 73 FR 11354, 3-3-2008, effective 3-3-2008; see ¶ 70,016.471.
Interim rule, 73 FR 4117, 1-24-2008, effective 1-24-2008; see ¶ 70,016.470.
Final rule, 73 FR 4116, 1-24-2008, effective 1-24-2008; see ¶ 70,016.469.
Interim rule, 73 FR 4115, 1-24-2008, effective 1-24-2008; see ¶ 70,016.468.
Final rule, 73 FR 4115, 1-24-2008, effective 1-24-2008; see ¶ 70,016.467.
Final rule, 73 FR 4114, 1-24-2008, effective 1-24-2008; see ¶ 70,016.466.
Final rule, 73 FR 4113, 1-24-2008, effective 1-24-2008; see ¶ 70,016.465.
Final rule, 73 FR 4113, 1-24-2008, effective 1-24-2008; see ¶ 70,016.464.
Final rule, 73 FR 1830, 1-10-2008, effective 1-10-2008; see ¶ 70,016.463.
Final rule, 73 FR 1830, 1-10-2008, effective 1-10-2008; see ¶ 70,016.462.

Final rule, 73 FR 1828, 1-10-2008, effective 1-10-2008; see ¶ 70,016.461.
Interim rule, 73 FR 1826, 1-10-2008, effective 1-10-2008; see ¶ 70,016.460.
Final rule, 73 FR 1826, 1-10-2008, effective 1-10-2008; see ¶ 70,016.459.
Interim rule, 73 FR 1823, 1-10-2008, effective 1-10-2008; see ¶ 70,016.458.
Final rule, 73 FR 1822, 1-10-2008, effective 1-10-2008; see ¶ 70,016.457.
Final rule, 72 FR 69159, 12-7-2007, effective 12-7-2007; see ¶ 70,016.456.
Final rule, 72 FR 69158, 12-7-2007, effective 12-7-2007; see ¶ 70,016.455.
Final rule, 72 FR 63113, 11-8-2007, effective 11-8-2007; see ¶ 70,016.454.
Interim rule, 72 FR 52293, 9-13-2007, effective 9-13-2007; see ¶ 70,016.453.
Final rule, 72 FR 51194, 9-6-2007, effective 9-6-2007; see ¶ 70,016.452.
Final rule, 72 FR 51193, 9-6-2007, effective 9-6-2007; see ¶ 70,016.451.
Interim rule, 72 FR 51192, 9-6-2007, effective 9-6-2007; see ¶ 70,016.450.
Final rule, 72 FR 51189, 9-6-2007, effective 9-6-2007; see ¶ 70,016.449.
Final rule, 72 FR 51189, 9-6-2007, effective 9-6-2007; see ¶ 70,016.448.
Final rule, 72 FR 51189, 9-6-2007, effective 9-6-2007; see ¶ 70,016.447.
Interim rule, 72 FR 51188, 9-6-2007, effective 9-6-2007; see ¶ 70,016.446.
Final rule, 72 FR 51187, 9-6-2007, effective 9-6-2007; see ¶ 70,016.445.
Final rule, 72 FR 51187, 9-6-2007, effective 9-6-2007; see ¶ 70,016.444.
Interim rule, 72 FR 49204, 8-28-2007, effective 8-28-2007; see ¶ 70,016.443.
Correction, 72 FR 46534, 8-20-2007, effective 8-20-2007; see ¶ 70,016.442.
Final rule, 72 FR 30278, 5-31-2007, effective 5-31-2007; see ¶ 70,016.437.
Final rule, 72 FR 20765, 4-26-2007, effective 4-26-2007; see ¶ 70,016.436.
Final rule, 72 FR 20764, 4-26-2007, effective 4-26-2007; see ¶ 70,016.435.
Final rule, 72 FR 20763, 4-26-2007, effective 4-26-2007; see ¶ 70,016.434.
Final rule, 72 FR 20761, 4-26-2007, effective 4-26-2007; see ¶ 70,016.433.
Interim rule, 72 FR 20758, 4-26-2007, effective 4-26-2007; see ¶ 70,016.432.
Final rule, 72 FR 20758, 4-26-2007, effective 4-26-2007; see ¶ 70,016.431.
Final rule, 72 FR 20757, 4-26-2007, effective 4-26-2007; see ¶ 70,016.430.
Interim rule, 72 FR 14242, 3-27-2007, effective 3-27-2007; see ¶ 70,016.429.
Final rule, 72 FR 14241, 3-27-2007, effective 3-27-2007; see ¶ 70,016.428.
Final rule, 72 FR 14240, 3-27-2007, effective 3-27-2007; see ¶ 70,016.427.
Final rule, 72 FR 14239, 3-27-2007, effective 3-27-2007; see ¶ 70,016.426.
Final rule, 72 FR 14239, 3-27-2007, effective 3-27-2007; see ¶ 70,016.425.
Final rule, 72 FR 6486, 2-12-2007, effective 2-12-2007; see ¶ 70,016.424.
Final rule, 72 FR 6485, 2-12-2007, effective 2-12-2007; see ¶ 70,016.423.
Final rule, 72 FR 6485, 2-12-2007, effective 2-12-2007; see ¶ 70,016.422.
Final rule, 72 FR 6484, 2-12-2007, effective 2-12-2007; see ¶ 70,016.421.
Final rule, 72 FR 6484, 2-12-2007, effective 2-12-2007; see ¶ 70,016.420.
Final rule, 72 FR 6480, 2-12-2007, effective 2-12-2007; see ¶ 70,016.419.
Interim rule, 72 FR 2637, 1-22-2007, effective 1-22-2007; see ¶ 70,016.418.
Final rule, 72 FR 2633, 1-22-2007, effective 1-22-2007; see ¶ 70,016.417.
Interim rule, 72 FR 2631, 1-22-2007, effective 1-22-2007; see ¶ 70,016.416.
Final rule, 71 FR 75893, 12-19-2006, effective 12-19-2006; see ¶ 70,016.415.
Final rule, 71 FR 75891, 12-19-2006, effective 12-19-2006; see ¶ 70,016.414.
Final rule, 71 FR 75890, 12-19-2006, effective 12-19-2006; see ¶ 70,016.413.
Interim rule, 71 FR 74469, 12-12-2006, effective 2-12-2007; see ¶ 70,016.412.
Final rule, 71 FR 69492, 12-1-2006, effective 12-1-2006; see ¶ 70,016.411.

Final rule, 71 FR 69489, 12-1-2006, effective 12-1-2006; see ¶ 70,016.410.
Final rule, 71 FR 69489, 12-1-2006, effective 12-1-2006; see ¶ 70,016.409.
Final rule, 71 FR 69488, 12-1-2006, effective 12-1-2006; see ¶ 70,016.408.
Final rule, 71 FR 65752, 11-9-2006, effective 11-9-2006; see ¶ 70,016.407.
Final rule, 71 FR 62566, 10-26-2006, effective 10-26-2006; see ¶ 70,016.406.
Final rule, 71 FR 62566, 10-26-2006, effective 10-26-2006; see ¶ 70,016.405.
Final rule, 71 FR 62565, 10-26-2006, effective 10-26-2006; see ¶ 70,016.404.
Interim rule, 71 FR 62560, 10-26-2006, effective 10-26-2006; see ¶ 70,016.403.
Final rule, 71 FR 62559, 10-26-2006, effective 10-26-2006; see ¶ 70,016.402.
Interim rule, 71 FR 58541, 10-4-2006, effective 10-4-2006; see ¶ 70,016.401.
Interiml rule, 71 FR 58540, 10-4-2006, effective 10-4-2006; see ¶ 70,016.400.
Final rule, 71 FR 58539, 10-4-2006, effective 10-4-2006; see ¶ 70,016.399.
Interim rule, 71 FR 58537, 10-4-2006, effective 10-4-2006; see ¶ 70,016.398.
Final rule, 71 FR 58537, 10-4-2006, effective 10-4-2006; see ¶ 70,016.397.
Interim rule, 71 FR 58536, 10-4-2006, effective 10-4-2006; see ¶ 70,016.396.
Final rule, 71 FR 53047, 9-8-2006, effective 9-8-2006; see ¶ 70,016.395.
Interim rule, 71 FR 53045, 9-8-2006, effective 9-8-2006; see ¶ 70,016.394.
Final rule, 71 FR 53044, 9-8-2006, effective 9-8-2006; see ¶ 70,016.393.
Final rule, 71 FR 53044, 9-8-2006, effective 9-8-2006; see ¶ 70,016.392.
Interim rule, 71 FR 53042, 9-8-2006, effective 9-8-2006; see ¶ 70,016.391.
Final rule, 71 FR 44928, 8-8-2006, effective 8-8-2006; see ¶ 70,016.389.
Final rule, 71 FR 44926, 8-8-2006, effective 8-8-2006; see ¶ 70,016.388.
Final rule, 71 FR 44926, 8-8-2006, effective 8-8-2006; see ¶ 70,016.387.
Final rule, 71 FR 39010, 7-11-2006, effective 7-11-2006; see ¶ 70,016.386.
Final rule, 71 FR 39009, 7-11-2006, effective 7-11-2006; see ¶ 70,016.385.
Final rule, 71 FR 39008, 7-11-2006, effective 7-11-2006; see ¶ 70,016.384.
Final rule, 71 FR 39008, 7-11-2006, effective 7-11-2006; see ¶ 70,016.383.
Final rule, 71 FR 39006, 7-11-2006, effective 7-11-2006; see ¶ 70,016.382.
Final rule, 71 FR 39005, 7-11-2006, effective 7-11-2006; see ¶ 70,016.381.
Final rule, 71 FR 39004, 7-11-2006, effective 7-11-2006; see ¶ 70,016.380.
Interim rule, 71 FR 29084, 5-19-2006, effective 5-19-2006; see ¶ 70,016.374.
Final rule, 71 FR 27646, 5-12-2006, effective 5-12-2006; see ¶ 70,016.373.
Final rule, 71 FR 27645, 5-12-2006, effective 5-12-2006; see ¶ 70,016.372.
Final rule, 71 FR 27644, 5-12-2006, effective 5-12-2006; see ¶ 70,016.371.
Final rule, 71 FR 27643, 5-12-2006, effective 5-12-2006; see ¶ 70,016.370.
Final rule, 71 FR 27642, 5-12-2006, effective 5-12-2006; see ¶ 70,016.369.
Final rule, 71 FR 27641, 5-12-2006, effective 5-12-2006; see ¶ 70,016.368.
Final rule, 71 FR 27640, 5-12-2006, effective 5-12-2006; see ¶ 70,016.367.
Final rule, 71 FR 18671, 4-12-2006, effective 4-12-2006; see ¶ 70,016.366.
Final rule, 71 FR 18671, 4-12-2006, effective 4-12-2006; see ¶ 70,016.365.
Final rule, 71 FR 18669, 4-12-2006, effective 4-12-2006; see ¶ 70,016.364.
Final rule, 71 FR 18667, 4-12-2006, effective 4-12-2006; see ¶ 70,016.363.
Final rule, 71 FR 14110, 3-21-2006, effective 3-21-2006; see ¶ 70,016.362.
Final rule, 71 FR 14108, 3-21-2006, effective 3-21-2006; see ¶ 70,016.361.
Final rule, 71 FR 14106, 3-21-2006, effective 3-21-2006; see ¶ 70,016.360.
Final rule, 71 FR 14104, 3-21-2006, effective 3-21-2006; see ¶ 70,016.359.
Final rule, 71 FR 14102, 3-21-2006, effective 3-21-2006; see ¶ 70,016.358.

Final rule, 71 FR 14101, 3-21-2006, effective 3-21-2006; see ¶ 70,016.357.
Final rule, 71 FR 14100, 3-21-2006, effective 3-21-2006; see ¶ 70,016.356.
Final rule, 71 FR 14099, 3-21-2006, effective 3-21-2006; see ¶ 70,016.355.
Final rule, 71 FR 9273, 2-23-2006, effective 2-23-2006; see ¶ 70,016.354.
Final rule, 71 FR 9272, 2-23-2006, effective 2-23-2006; see ¶ 70,016.353.
Final rule, 71 FR 9271, 2-23-2006, effective 2-23-2006; see ¶ 70,016.352.
Interim rule, 71 FR 9269, 2-23-2006, effective 2-23-2006; see ¶ 70,016.351.
Final rule, 71 FR 9269, 2-23-2006, effective 2-23-2006; see ¶ 70,016.350.
Final rule, 71 FR 9268, 2-23-2006, effective 2-23-2006; see ¶ 70,016.349.
Final rule, 71 FR 9267, 2-23-2006, effective 2-23-2006; see ¶ 70,016.348.
Final rule, 71 FR 3418, 1-23-2006, effective 1-23-2006; see ¶ 70,016.347.
Final rule, 71 FR 3416, 1-23-2006, effective 1-23-2006; see ¶ 70,016.346.
Final rule, 71 FR 3415, 1-23-2006, effective 1-23-2006; see ¶ 70,016.345.
Final rule, 71 FR 3414, 1-23-2006, effective 1-23-2006; see ¶ 70,016.344.
Final rule, 71 FR 3413, 1-23-2006, effective 1-23-2006; see ¶ 70,016.343.
Final rule, 71 FR 3412, 1-23-2006, effective 1-23-2006; see ¶ 70,016.342.
Final rule, 70 FR 75412, 12-20-2005, effective 12-20-2005; see ¶ 70,016.341.
Final rule, 70 FR 75411, 12-20-2005, effective 12-20-2005; see ¶ 70,016.340.
Final rule, 70 FR 75411, 12-20-2005, effective 12-30-2005; see ¶ 70,016.339.
Final rule, 70 FR 73153, 12-9-2005, effective 12-9-2005; see ¶ 70,016.338.
Final rule, 70 FR 73152, 12-9-2005, effective 12-9-2005; see ¶ 70,016.337.
Final rule, 70 FR 73151, 12-9-2005, effective 12-9-2005; see ¶ 70,016.336.
Final rule, 70 FR 73150, 12-9-2005, effective 12-9-2005; see ¶ 70,016.335.
Final rule, 70 FR 73148, 12-9-2005, effective 12-9-2005; see ¶ 70,016.334..
Final rule, 70 FR 67924, 11-9-2005, effective 11-9-2005; see ¶ 70,016.333.
Final rule, 70 FR 67923, 11-9-2005, effective 11-9-2005; see ¶ 70,016.332.
Final rule, 70 FR 67922, 11-9-2005, effective 11-9-2005; see ¶ 70,016.331.
Final rule, 70 FR 67921, 11-9-2005, effective 11-9-2005; see ¶ 70,016.330.
Final rule, 70 FR 67919, 11-9-2005, effective 11-9-2005; see ¶ 70,016.329.
Final rule, 70 FR 67919, 11-9-2005, effective 11-9-2005; see ¶ 70,016.328.
Final rule, 70 FR 67918, 11-9-2005, effective 11-9-2005; see ¶ 70,016.327.
Final rule, 70 FR 67917, 11-9-2005, effective 11-9-2005; see ¶ 70,016.326.
Final rule, 70 FR 58980, 10-11-2005, effective 10-11-2005; see ¶ 70,016.325.
Final rule, 70 FR 57193, 9-30-2005, effective 9-30-2005; see ¶ 70,016.324.
Interim rule, 70 FR 57191, 9-30-2005, effective 9-30-2005; see ¶ 70,016.323.
Final rule, 70 FR 57191, 9-30-2005, effective 9-30-2005; see ¶ 70,016.322.
Final rule, 70 FR 57190, 9-30-2005, effective 9-30-2005; see ¶ 70,016.321.
Final rule, 70 FR 57188, 9-30-2005, effective 9-30-2005; see ¶ 70,016.320.
Final rule, 70 FR 57188, 9-30-2005, effective 9-30-2005; see ¶ 70,016.319.
Final rule, 70 FR 54651, 9-16-2005, effective 9-16-2005; see ¶ 70,016.318.
Final rule, 70 FR 54651, 9-16-2005, effective 9-16-2005; see ¶ 70,016.317.
Final rule, 70 FR 53955, 9-13-2005, effective 11-14-2005; see ¶ 70,016.316.
Correction, 70 FR 53716, 9-9-2005, effective 9-1-2005; see ¶ 70,016.315.
Final rule, 70 FR 52034, 9-1-2005, effective 9-1-2005; see ¶ 70,016.314.
Interim rule, 70 FR 52032, 9-1-2005, effective 9-1-2005; see ¶ 70,016.313.
Interim rule, 70 FR 52031, 9-1-2005, effective 9-1-2005; see ¶ 70,016.312.
Final rule, 70 FR 52030, 9-1-2005, effective 9-1-2005; see ¶ 70,016.311.

Final rule, 70 FR 43073, 7-26-2005, effective 7-26-2005; see ¶ 70,016.310.
Interim rule, 70 FR 43074, 7-26-2005, effective 7-26-2005; see ¶ 70,016.309.
Interim rule, 70 FR 43072, 7-26-2005, effective 7-26-2005; see ¶ 70,016.308.
Final rule, 70 FR 35543, 6-21-2005, effective 6-21-2005; see ¶ 70,016.307.
Final rule, 70 FR 35549, 6-21-2005, effective 6-21-2005; see ¶ 70,016.306.
Interim rule, 70 FR 29640, 5-24-2005, effective 5-24-2005; see ¶ 70,016.305.
Interim rule, 70 FR 29643, 5-24-2005, effective 5-24-2005; see ¶ 70,016.304.
Interim rule, 70 FR 29644, 5-24-2005, effective 5-24-2005; see ¶ 70,016.303.
Interim rule, 70 FR 24323, 5-9-2005, effective 5-9-2005; see ¶ 70,016.302.
Final rule, 70 FR 23790, 5-5-2005, effective 6-6-2005; see ¶ 70,016.301.
Final rule, 70 FR 23804, 5-5-2005, effective 5-5-2005; see ¶ 70,016.300.
Final rule, 70 FR 20831, 4-22-2005, effective 4-22-2005; see ¶ 70,016.299.
Final rule, 70 FR 20838, 4-22-2005, effective 4-22-2005; see¶ 70,016.298.
Final rule, 70 FR 19003, 4-12-2005, effective 4-12-2005; see ¶ 70,016.297.
Final rule, 70 FR 14576, 3-23-2005, effective 3-23-2005; see ¶ 70,016.296.
Final rule, 70 FR 14574, 3-23-2005, effective 3-23-2005; see ¶ 70,016.295.
Final rule, 70 FR 14574, 3-23-2005, effective 3-23-2005; see ¶ 70,016.294.
Final rule, 70 FR 14573, 3-23-2005, effective 3-23-2005; see ¶ 70,016.293.
Interim rule, 70 FR 14572, 3-23-2005, effective 3-23-2005; see ¶ 70,016.292.
Final rule, 70 FR 8538, 2-22-2005, effective 2-22-2005; see ¶ 70,016.291.
Interim rule, 70 FR 8536, 2-22-2005, effective 2-22-2005; see ¶ 70,016.290.
Correction , 70 FR 8537, 2-22-2005, effective 2-7-2005; see ¶ 70,016.289.
Final rule, 70 FR 8539, 2-22-2005, effective 2-22-2005; see ¶ 70,016.288.
Final rule, 70 FR 8537, 2-22-2005, effective 2-22-2005; see ¶ 70,016.287.
Final rule, 70 FR 6375, 2-7-2005, effective 2-7-2005; see ¶ 70,016.286.
Final rule, 70 FR 6374, 2-7-2005, effective 2-7-2005; see ¶ 70,016.285.
Final rule, 70 FR 6373, 2-7-2005, effective 2-7-2005; see ¶ 70,016.284.
Final rule, 70 FR 2361, 1-13-2005, effective 12-15-2004; see ¶ 70,016.283.
Interim rule, 70 FR 2361, 1-13-2005, effective 1-13-2005; see ¶ 70,016.282.
Final rule, 69 FR 75000, 12-15-2004, effective 12-15-2004; see ¶ 70,016.281.
Final rule, 69 FR 74991, 12-15-2004, effective 12-15-2004; see ¶ 70,016.280.
Interim rule, 69 FR 74992, 12-15-2004, effective 12-15-2004; see ¶ 70,016.279.
Final rule, 69 FR 74995, 12-15-2004, effective 12-15-2004; see ¶ 70,016.278.
Final rule, 69 FR 74989, 12-15-2004, effective 12-15-2004; see ¶ 70,016.277.
Final rule, 69 FR 75000, 12-15-2004, effective 12-15-2004; see ¶ 70,016.276.
Final rule, 69 FR 74990, 12-15-2004, effective 12-15-2004; see ¶ 70,016.275.
Final rule, 69 FR 67856, 11-22-2004, effective 11-22-2004; see ¶ 70,016.274.
Final rule, 69 FR 67854, 11-22-2004, effective 11-22-2004; see ¶ 70,016.273.
Final rule, 69 FR 67855, 11-22-2004, effective 11-22-2004; see ¶ 70,016.272.
Final rule, 69 FR 67857, 11-22-2004, effective 11-22-2004; see ¶ 70,016.271.
Final rule, 69 FR 67858, 11-22-2004, effective 11-22-2004; see ¶ 70,016.270.
Final rule, 69 FR 67856, 11-22-2004, effective 11-22-2004; see ¶ 70,016.269.
Final rule, 69 FR 67855, 11-22-2004, effective 11-22-2004; see ¶ 70,016.268.
Final rule, 69 FR 65089, 11-10-2004, effective 11-10-2004; see ¶ 70,016.267.
Final rule, 69 FR 65091, 11-10-2004, effective 11-10-2004; see ¶ 70,016.266.
Final rule, 69 FR 65090, 11-10-2004, effective 11-10-2004; see ¶ 70,016.265.
Final rule, 69 FR 65088, 11-10-2004, effective 11-10-2004; see ¶ 70,016.264.

Final rule, 69 FR 65089, 11-10-2004, effective 11-10-2004; see ¶ 70,016.263.
Final rule, 69 FR 63331, 11-1-2004, effective 11-1-2004; see ¶ 70,016.262.
Final rule, 69 FR 63330, 11-1-2004, effective 11-1-2004; see ¶ 70,016.261.
Interim rule, 69 FR 63329, 11-1-2004, effective 11-1-2004; see ¶ 70,016.260.
Final rule, 69 FR 63328, 11-1-2004, effective 11-1-2004; see ¶ 70,016.259.
Final rule, 69 FR 63327, 11-1-2004, effective 11-1-2004; see ¶ 70,016.258.
Final rule, 69 FR 63327, 11-1-2004, effective 11-1-2004; see ¶ 70,016.257.
Final rule, 69 FR 63326, 11-1-2004, effective 11-1-2004; see ¶ 70,016.256.
Correction, 69 FR 59648, 10-5-2004; see ¶ 70,016.255.
Final rule, 69 FR 58353, 9-30-2004, effective 9-30-2004; see ¶ 70,016.254.
Final rule, 69 FR 58353, 9-30-2004, effective 9-30-2004; see ¶ 70,016.253.
Interim rule, 68 FR 56563, 10-1-2003, effective 10-1-2003; see ¶ 70,016.252.
Interim rule, 68 FR 56561, 10-1-2003, effective 10-1-2003; see ¶ 70,016.251.
Final rule, 68 FR 56560, 10-1-2003, effective 10-1-2003; see ¶ 70,016.250.
Interim rule, 69FR 55987, 9-17-2004, effective 9-17-2004; see ¶ 70,016.249.
Final rule, 69 FR 55989, 9-17-2004, effective 9-17-2004; see ¶ 70,016.248.
Interim rule, 69 FR 55986, 9-17-2004, effective 9-17-2004; see ¶ 70,016.247.
Final rule, 69 FR 55986, 9-17-2004, effective 9-17-2004; see ¶ 70,016.246.
Final rule, 69 FR 55989, 9-17-2004, effective 9-17-2004; see ¶ 70,016.245.
Interim rule, 69 FR 55991, 9-17-2004, effective 9-17-2004; see ¶ 70,016.244.
Final rule, 69 FR 55992, 9-17-2004, effective 9-17-2004; see ¶ 70,016.243.
Final rule, 69 FR 35532, 6-25-2004, effective 6-25-2004; see ¶ 70,016.242.
Final rule, 69 FR 35535, 6-25-2004, effective 6-25-2004; see ¶ 70,016.241.
Final rule, 69 FR 35533, 6-25-2004, effective 6-25-2004; see ¶ 70,016.240.
Interim rule, 69 FR 35532, 6-25-2004, effective 6-25-2004; see ¶ 70,016.239.
Interim rule, 69 FR 31911, 6-8-2004, effective 6-8-2004; see ¶ 70,016.238.
Final rule, 69 FR 31912, 6-8-2004, effective 6-8-2004; see ¶ 70,016.237.
Final rule, 69 31907, 6-8-2004, effective 6-8-2004; see ¶ 70,016.236.
Final rule, 69 FR 31910, 6-8-2004, effective 6-8-2004; see ¶ 70,016.235.
Interim rule, 69 FR 31909, 6-8-2004, effective 6-8-2004; see ¶ 70,016.234.
Final rule, 69 FR 26509, 5-13-2004, effective 5-13-2004; see ¶ 70,016.233.
Final rule, 69 FR 26507, 5-13-2004, effective 5-13-2004; see ¶ 70,016.232.
Interim rule, 69 FR 26508, 5-13-2004, efective 5-13-2004; see ¶ 70,016.231.
Interim rule, 69 FR 13478, 3-23-2004, effective 3-23-2004; see ¶ 70,016.230.
Interim rule, 69 FR 13478, 3-23-2004, effective 3-23-2004; see ¶ 70,016.229.
Interim rule, 69 FR 13477, 3-23-2004, effective 3-23-2004; see ¶ 70,016.228.
Final rule, 69 FR 8115, 2-23-2004, effective 2-23-2004; see ¶ 70,016,227.
Interim rule, 69 FR 1926, 1-13-2004, effective 1-13-2004; see ¶ 70,016.226.
Final rule, 69 FR 1926, 1-13-2004, effective 1-13-2004; see ¶ 70,016.225.
Interim rule, 68 FR 75196, 12-30-2003, effective 1-1-2004; see ¶ 70,016.224.
Final rule, 68 FR 69631, 12-15-2003, effective 12-15-2003; see ¶ 70,016.223.
Final rule, 68 FR 69628, 12-15-2003, effective 12-15-2003; see ¶ 70,016.222.
Final rule, 68 FR 64559, 11-14-2003, effective 12-15-2003; see ¶ 70,016.221.
Final rule, 68 FR 64561, 11-14-2003, effective 1-13-2004; see ¶ 70,016.220.
Interim rule, 68 FR 64557, 11-14-2003, effective 11-14-2003; see ¶ 70,016.219.
Final rule, 68 FR 64555, 11-14-2003, effective 11-14-2003; see ¶ 70,016.218.
Interim rule, 68 FR 58631, 10-10-2003, effective 1-1-2004; see ¶ 70,016.217.

Final rule, 68 FR 50477, 8-21-2003, effective 8-21-2003; see ¶ 70,016.216.
Final rule, 68 FR 50476, 8-21-2003, effective 8-21-2003; see ¶ 70,016.215.
Interim rule, 68 FR 50474, 8-21-2003, effective 8-21-2003; see ¶ 70,016.214.
Final rule, 68 FR 50476, 8-21-2003, effective 8-21-2003; see ¶ 70,016.213.
Final rule, 68 FR 50477, 8-21-2003, effective 8-21-2003; see ¶ 70,016.212.
Interim rule, 68 FR 43332, 7-22-2003, effective 7-22-2003; see ¶ 70,016.211.
Interim rule, 68 FR 43331, 7-22-2003, effecitve 7-22-2003; see ¶ 70,016.210.
Final rule, 68 FR 36944, 6-20-2003, effective 6-20-2003; see ¶ 70,016.209.
Final rule, 68 FR 36944, 6-20-2003, effective 6-20-2003; see ¶ 70,016.208.
Final rule, 68 FR 36945, 6-20-2003, effective 10-1-2003; see ¶ 70,016.207.
Final rule, 68 FR 33026, 6-3-2003, effective 6-3-2003; see ¶ 70,016.206.
Final rule, 68 FR 23088, 4-30-2003, effective 4-30-2003; see ¶ 70,016.205.
Final rule, 68 FR 15381, 3-31-2003, effective 3-31-2003; see ¶ 70,016.204.
Final rule, 68 FR 15380, 3-31-2003, effective 3-31-2003; see ¶ 70,016.203.
Final rule, 68 FR 15615, 3-31-2003, effective 4-30-2003; see ¶ 70,016.202.
Interim rule, 68 FR 8450, 2-21-2003, effective 3-1-2003; see ¶ 70,016.201.
Final rule, 68 FR 7438, 2-14-2003, effective 2-14-2003; see ¶ 70,016.200.
Interim rule, 68 FR 7441, 2-14-2003, effective 4-15-2003; see ¶ 70,016.199.
Interim rule, 68 FR 7443, 2-14-2003, effective 4-15-2003; see ¶ 70,016.198.
Interim rule, 68 FR 7441, 2-14-2003, effective 4-15-2003; see ¶ 70,016.197.
Final rule, 67 FR 77937, 12-20-2002, effective 12-20-2002; see ¶ 70,016.196.
Final rule, 67 FR 77936, 12-20-2002, effective 12-20-2002; see ¶ 70,016.195.
Final rule, 67 FR 77936, 12-20-2002, effective 12-20-2002; see ¶ 70,016.194.
Final rule, 67 FR 70325, 11-22-2002, effective 11-22-2002; see ¶ 70,016.193.
Final rule, 67 FR 70323, 11-22-2002, effective 11-22-2002; see ¶ 70,016.192.
Final rule, 67 FR 65514, 10-25-2002, effective 10-25-2002; see ¶ 70,016.191.
Final rule, 67 FR 65509, 10-25-2002, effective 10-25-2002; see ¶ 70,016.190.
Final rule, 67 FR 65509, 10-25-2002, effective 10-25-2002; see ¶ 70,016.189.
Final rule, 67 FR 65505, 10-25-2002, effective 10-25-2002; see ¶ 70,016.188.
Final rule, 67 FR 65512, 10-25-2002, effective 10-25-2002; see ¶ 70,016.187.
Final rule, 67 FR 61516, 10-1-2002, effective 10-1-2002; see ¶ 70,016.186.
Final rule, 67 FR 61516, 10-1-2002, effective 10-1-2002; see ¶ 70,016.186.
Final rule, 67 FR 55730, 8-30-2002, effective 8-30-2002; see ¶ 70,016.185.
Final rule, 67 FR 49253, 7-30-2002, effective 7-30-2002; see ¶ 70,016.184.
Final rule, 67 FR 49254, 7-30-2002, effective 7-30-2002; see ¶ 70,016.183.
Final rule, 67 FR 49251, 7-30-2002, effective 7-30-2002; see ¶ 70,016.182.
Final rule, 67 FR 49255, 7-30-2002, effective 7-30-2002; see ¶ 70,016.181.
Final rule, 67 FR 49256, 7-30-2002, effective 7-30-2002; see ¶ 70,016.180.
Final rule, 67 FR 46112, 7-12-2002, effective 10-1-2002; see ¶ 70,016.179.
Final rule, 67 FR 38022, 5-31-2002, effective 5-31-2002; see ¶ 70,016.178.
Final rule, 67 FR 38023, 5-31-2002, effective 5-31-2002; see ¶ 70,016.177.
Final rule, 67 FR 38020, 5-31-2002, effective 5-31-2002; see ¶ 70,016.176.
Final rule, 67 FR 20699, 4-26-2002, effective 4-26-2002; see ¶ 70,016.175.
Interim rule, 67 FR 20687, 4-26-2002, effective 4-26-2002; see ¶ 70,016.174.
Final rule, 67 FR 20688, 4-26-2002, effective 4-26-2002; see ¶ 70,016.173.
Final rule, 67 FR 20692, 4-26-2002, effective 4-26-2002; see ¶ 70,016.172.
Interim rule, 67 FR 20697, 4-26-2002, effective 4-26-2002; see ¶ 70,016.171.

Final rule, 67 FR 20693, 4-26-2002, effective 4-26-2002; see ¶ 70,016.170.

Final rule, 67 FR 11435, 3-14-2002, effective 3-14-2002; see ¶ 70,016.169.

Interim rule, 67 FR 11438, 3-14-2002, effective 3-14-2002; see ¶ 70,016.168.

Interim rule, 67 FR 11435, 3-14-2002, effective 3-14-2002; see ¶ 70,016.167.

Final rule, 67 FR 11438, 3-14-2002, effective 3-14-2002; see ¶ 70,016.166.

Final rule, 67 FR 1137, 3-14-2002, effective 3-14-2002; see ¶ 70,016.165.

Final rule, 67 FR 4209, 1-29-2002, effective 1-29-2002; see ¶ 70,016.164.

Final rule, 67 FR 4208, 1-29-2002, effective 1-29-2002; see ¶ 70,016.163.

Final rule, 67 FR 4210, 1-29-2002, effective 1-29-2002; see ¶ 70,016.162.

Final rule, 67 FR 4209, 1-29-2002, effective 1-29-2002; see ¶ 70,016.161.

Final rule, 67 FR 4207, 1-29-2002, effective 1-29-2002; see ¶ 70,016.160.

Final rule, 66 FR 63334, 12-6-2001, effective 12-6-2001; see ¶ 70,016.159.

Final rule, 66 FR 63335, 12-6-2001, effective 12-6-2001; see ¶ 70,016.158.

Final rule, 66 FR 63336, 12-6-2001, effective 12-6-2001; see ¶ 70,016.157.

Final rule, 66 FR 55123, 11-1-2001, effective 11-1-2001; see ¶ 70,016.156.

Final rule, 66 FR 55121, 11-1-2001, effective 11-1-2001; see ¶ 70,016.155.

Final rule, 66 FR 55121, 11-1-2001, effective 11-1-2001; see ¶ 70,016.154.

Final rule, 66 FR 49860, 10-1-2001, effective 10-1-2001; see ¶ 70,016.153.

Final rule, 66 FR 49865, 10-1-2001, effective 10-1-2001, corrected 66 FR 51515, 10-9-2001; see ¶ 70,016.152.

Final rule, 66 FR 49862, 10-1-2001, effective 10-1-2001; see ¶ 70,016.151.

Final rule, 66 FR 49862, 10-1-2001, effective 10-1-2001; see ¶ 70,016.150.

Final rule, 66 FR 49864, 10-1-2001, effective 10-1-2001; see ¶ 70,016.149.

Final rule, 66 FR 49864, 10-1-2001, effective 10-1-2001; see ¶ 70,016.148.

Final rule, 66 FR 49863, 10-1-2001, effective 10-1-2001; see ¶ 70,016.147.

Interim rule, 66 FR 47108, 9-11-2001, effective 9-11-2001; see ¶ 70,016.146.

Interim rule, 66 FR 47110, 9-11-2001, effective 9-11-2001; see ¶ 70,016.145.

Final rule, 66 FR 47107, 9-11-2001, effective 9-11-2001; see ¶ 70,016.144.

Final rule, 66 FR 47096, 9-11-2001, effective 10-1-2001, corrected 66 FR 48621, 9-21-2001, effective 10-1-2001; see ¶ 70,016.143.

Interim rule, 66 FR 47113, 9-11-2001, effective 9-11-2001; see ¶ 70,016.142.

Final rule, 66 FR 47112, 9-11-2001, effective 9-11-2001; see ¶ 70,016.141.

Final rule, 65 FR 77835, 12-13-2000, effective 12-13-2000; see ¶ 70,016.140.

Final rule, 65 FR 77832, 12-13-2000, effective 12-13-2000; see ¶ 70,016.139.

Final rule, 65 FR 77832, 12-13-2000, effective 12-13-2000; see ¶ 70,016.138.

Final rule, 65 FR 77831, 12-13-2000, effective 12-13-2000; see ¶ 70,016.137.

Final rule, 65 FR 77829, 12-13-2000, effective 12-13-2000; see ¶ 70,016.136.

Interim rule, 65 FR 77827, 12-13-2000, effective 12-13-2000; see ¶ 70,016.135.

Final rule, 65 FR 63804, 10-25-2000, effective 10-25-2000; see ¶ 70,016.134.

Final rule, 65 FR 63806, 10-25-2000, effective 10-25-2000; see ¶ 70,016.133.

Final rule, 65 FR 63802, 10-25-2000, effective 10-25-2000; see ¶ 70,016.132.

Final rule, 65 FR 52951, 8-31-2000, effective 8-31-2000; see ¶ 70,016.131; corrected, 65 FR 58607, 9-29-2000.

Final rule, 65 FR 52954, 8-31-2000, effective 8-31-2000; see ¶ 70,016.130.

Final rule, 65 FR 50152, 8-17-2000, effective 8-17-2000; see ¶ 70,016.128.

Final rule, 65 FR 50151, 8-17-2000, effective 8-17-2000; see ¶ 70,016.127.

Final rule, 65 FR 50150, 8-17-2000, effective 8-17-2000; see ¶ 70,016.126.

Final rule, 65 FR 50149, 8-17-2000, effective 8-17-2000; see ¶ 70,016.129.

Final rule, 65 FR 50143, 8-17-2000, effective 8-17-2000; see ¶ 70,016.125.

Interim rule, 65 FR 50148, 8-17-2000, effective 10-1-2000; see ¶ 70,016.124; finalized without change, 65 FR 77831, 12-13-2000, effective 12-13-2000, see ¶ 70,016.137.

Final rule, 65 FR 46626, 7-31-2000, effective 7-31-2000; see ¶ 70,016.123.

Final rule, 65 FR 46625, 7-31-2000, effective 7-31-2000; see ¶ 70,016.122.

Final rule, 65 FR 39722, 6-27-2000, effective 6-27-2000; see ¶ 70,016.121.

Final rule, 65 FR 39722, 6-27-2000, effective 6-27-2000; see ¶ 70,016.120.

Final rule, 65 FR 39721, 6-27-2000, effective 6-27-2000; see ¶ 70,016.119.

Final rule, 65 FR 39707, 6-27-2000, effective 10-1-2000; see ¶ 70,016.118.

Final rule, 65 FR 39703, 6-27-2000, effective 6-27-2000; see ¶ 70,016.117.

Final rule, 65 FR 36034, 6-6-2000, effective 6-6-2000; see ¶ 70,016.116.

Final rule, 65 FR 36033, 6-6-2000, effective 6-6-2000; see ¶ 70,016.115.

Final rule, 65 FR 32041, 5-22-2000, effective 5-22-2000; see ¶ 70,016.114.

Final rule, 65 FR 32040, 5-22-2000, effective 5-22-2000; see ¶ 70,016.113.

Final rule, 65 FR 32040, 5-22-2000, effective 5-22-2000; see ¶ 70,016.112.

Final rule, 65 FR 19859, 4-13-2000, effective 4-13-2000; see ¶ 70,016.111.

Final rule, 65 FR 19859, 4-13-2000, effective 4-13-2000; see ¶ 70,016.110.

Final rule, 65 FR 19858, 4-13-2000, effective 4-13-2000; see ¶ 70,016.109.

Final rule, 65 FR 19849, 4-13-2000, effective 4-13-2000; see ¶ 70,016.108.

Final rule, 65 FR 14397, 3-16-2000, effective 3-16-2000; see ¶ 70,016.107.

Final rule, 65 FR 14400, 3-16-2000, effective 3-16-2000; see ¶ 70,016.106.

Interim rule, 65 FR 14402, 3-16-2000, effective 3-16-2000; see ¶ 70,016.105.

Final rule, 65 FR 14400, 3-16-2000, effective 3-16-2000; see ¶ 70,016.104.

Final rule, 65 FR 14380, 3-16-2000, effective 3-16-2000; see ¶ 70,016.103.

Interim rule, 65 FR 6554, 2-10-2000, effective 2-10-2000; see ¶ 70,016.102; corrected, 65 FR 30191, 5-10-2000.

Final rule, 65 FR 6553, 2-10-2000, effective 2-10-2000; see ¶ 70,016.101.

Final rule, 65 FR 6553, 2-10-2000, effective 2-10-2000; see ¶ 70,016.100.

Final rule, 65 FR 6551, 2-10-2000, effective 2-10-2000; see ¶ 70,016.99.

Interim rule, 65 FR 2058, 1-13-2000, effective 1-13-2000; see ¶ 70,016.98, corrected 65 FR 19818, 4-12-2000.

Interim rule, 65 FR 2057, 1-13-2000, effective 1-13-2000; see ¶ 70,016.97; finalized without change, 65 FR 19859, 4-13-2000, effective 4-13-2000, see ¶ 70,016.110.

Interim rule, 65 FR 2056, 1-13-2000, effective 1-13-2000; see ¶ 70,016.96.

Final rule, 65 FR 2055, 1-13-2000, effective 1-13-2000; see ¶ 70,016.95.

Final rule, 64 FR 62986, 11-18-99, effective 11-18-99; see ¶ 70,016.94.

Final rule, 64 FR 62984, 11-18-99, effective 11-18-99, corrected 65 FR 4864, 2-1-2000; see ¶ 70,016.93.

Final rule, 64 FR 62987, 11-18-99, effective 11-18-99; see ¶ 70,016.92.

Final rule, 64 FR 62986, 11-18-99, effective 11-18-99; see ¶ 70,016.91.

Final rule, 64 FR 61031, 11-9-99, effective 11-9-99; see ¶ 70,016.90.

Final rule, 64 FR 61030, 11-9-99, effective 11-9-99; see ¶ 70,016.89.

Final rule, 64 FR 61028, 11-9-99, effective 11-9-99; see ¶ 70,016.88.

Final rule, 64 FR 56704, 10-21-99, effective 10-21-99; see ¶ 70,016.87; corrected, 64 FR 63380, 11-19-99.

Final rule, 64 FR 55632, 10-14-99, effective 10-14-99; see ¶ 70,016.86.

Final rule, 64 FR 55632, 10-14-99, effective 10-14-99; see ¶ 70,016.85.

Final rule, 64 FR 52672, 9-21-99, effective 10-1-99; see ¶ 70,016.84.

Final rule, 64 FR 52670, 9-30-99, effective 9-30-99; see ¶ 70,016.83.

Final rule, 64 FR 51077, 9-21-99, effective 9-21-99; see ¶ 70,016.82.

Final rule, 64 FR 51074, 9-21-99, effective 9-21-99; see ¶ 70,016.81.

Final rule, 64 FR 49684, 9-14-99, effective 9-14-99; see ¶ 70,016.80.

Final rule, 64 FR 49683, 9-14-99, effective 9-14-99; see ¶ 70,016.79.

Final rule, 64 FR 45197, 8-19-99, effective 10-1-99; see ¶ 70,016.78.

Final rule, 64 FR 45196, 8-19-99, effective 8-19-99; see ¶ 70,016.77.

Final rule, 64 FR 43098, 8-9-99, effective 8-9-99; see ¶ 70,016.76; corrected 64 FR 46474, 8-25-99.

Final rule, 64 FR 43096, 8-9-99, effective 8-9-99; see ¶ 70,016.75.

Final rule, 64 FR 39431, 7-22-99, effective 7-22-99; see ¶ 70,016.74.

Final rule, 64 FR 39430, 7-22-99, effective 7-22-99; see ¶ 70,016.73.

Final rule, 64 FR 39429, 7-22-99, effective 7-22-99; see ¶ 70,016.72.

Interim rule, 64 FR 31732, 6-14-99, effective 6-14-99; see ¶ 70,016.71.

Final rule, 64 FR 31732, 6-14-99, effective 6-14-99; see ¶ 70,016.70; finalized without change, 64 FR 55632, 10-14-99.

Final rule, 64 FR 28109, 5-25-99, effective 5-25-99; see ¶ 70,016.69.

Final rule, 64 FR 28109, 5-25-99, effective 5-25-99; see ¶ 70,016.68.

Final rule, 64 FR 8726, 2-23-99, effective 2-23-99; see ¶ 70,016.67-1.

Final rule, 64 FR 8727, 2-23-99, effective 2-23-99; see ¶ 70,016.67.

Final rule, 64 FR 8730, 2-23-99, effective 2-23-99; see ¶ 70,016.66.

Interim rule, 64 FR 8727, 2-23-99, effective 2-23-99; see ¶ 70,016.65; finalized with changes, 65 FR 6553, 2-10-2000, see ¶ 70,016.101.

Final rule, 64 FR 24528, 5-7-99, effective 5-7-99; see ¶ 70,016.64.

Final rule, 64 FR 24528, 5-7-99, effective 5-7-99; see ¶ 70,016.63.

Final rule, 64 FR 24529, 5-7-99, effective 5-7-99; see ¶ 70,016.62.

Interim rule, 64 FR 18829, 4-16-99, effective 4-16-99; see ¶ 70,016.61; corrected, 64 FR 48459, 9-3-99; finalized without change, 64 FR 51077, 9-21-99, effective 9-21-99, see ¶ 70,016.82.

Final rule, 64 FR 18828, 4-16-99, effective 5-3-99; see ¶ 70,016.60.

Final rule, 64 FR 18827, 4-16-99, effective 4-16-99; see ¶ 70,016.59.

Final rule, 64 FR 14399, 3-25-99, effective 3-25-99; see ¶ 70,016.58.

Final rule, 64 FR 14398, 3-25-99, effective 3-25-99, corrected, 64 FR 28875, 5-27-99; see ¶ 70,016.57.

Final rule, 64 FR 14397, 3-25-99, effective 3-25-99; see ¶ 70,016.56.

Final rule, 64 FR 8731, 2-23-99, effective 2-23-99; see ¶ 70,016.55.

Final rule, 64 FR 8726, 2-23-99, effective 2-23-99; see ¶ 70,016.54.

Final rule, 64 FR 8729, 2-23-99, effective 2-23-99; see ¶ 70,016.53.

Interim rule, 64 FR 2599, 1-15-99, effective 1-15-99; see ¶ 70,016.52.

Final rule, 64 FR 2600, 1-15-99, effective 1-15-99; see ¶ 70,016.51.

Final rule, 64 FR 2595, 1-15-99, effective 1-15-99; see ¶ 70,016.50.

Final rule, 63 FR 71230, 12-24-98, effective 12-24-98; see ¶ 70,016.49.

Final rule, 63 FR 69007, 12-15-98, effective 12-15-98; see ¶ 70,016.48.

Final rule, 63 FR 69006, 12-15-98, effective 12-15-98; see ¶ 70,016.47.

Final rule, 63 FR 69007, 12-15-98, effective 12-15-98; see ¶ 70,016.46.

Final rule, 63 FR 69006, 12-15-98, effective 12-15-98; see ¶ 70,016.45.

Final rule, 63 FR 69005, 12-15-98, effective 12-15-98; see ¶ 70,016.44.

Final rule, 63 FR 67804, 12-9-98, effective 12-9-98; see ¶ 70,016.43.

Final rule, 63 FR 67804, 12-9-98, effective 12-9-98; see ¶ 70,016.42

Final rule, 63 FR 67803, 12-9-98, effective 12-9-98; see ¶ 70,016.41.

Final rule, 63 FR 67803, 12-9-98, effective 12-9-98; see ¶ 70,016.40.

Interim rule, 63 FR 64427, 11-20-98, effective 1-1-99; see ¶ 70,016.39.

Final rule, 63 FR 64426, 11-20-98, effective 11-20-98; see ¶ 70,016.38.

Final rule, 63 FR 63799, 11-17-98, effective 11-17-98; see ¶ 70,016.37.

Final rule, 63 FR 60217, 11-9-98, effective 11-9-98; see ¶ 70,016.36.

Final rule, 63 FR 60216, 11-9-98, effective 11-9-98; see ¶ 70,016.35.

Final rule, 63 FR 55040, 10-14-98, effective 10-14-98; see ¶ 70,016.34, corrected 63 FR 56290, 10-21-98.

Final rule, 63 FR 43889, 8-17-98, effective 8-17-98; see ¶ 70,016.33.

Final rule, 63 FR 43890, 8-17-98, effective 8-17-98; see ¶ 70,016.32.

Interim rule, 63 FR 43887, 8-17-98, effective 8-17-98; see ¶ 70,016.31.

Final rule, 63 FR 41972, 8-6-98, effective 10-1-98; see ¶ 70,016.30.

Final rule, 63 FR 40374, 7-29-98, effective 7-29-98; see ¶ 70,016.29.

Interim rule, 63 FR 34605, 6-25-98, effective 6-25-98; see ¶ 70,016.28.

Interim rule, 63 FR 33586, 6-19-98, effective 6-19-98; see ¶ 70,016.26.

Final rule, 63 FR 31937, 6-11-98, effective 6-11-98, see ¶ 70,016.25.

Interim rule, 63 FR 31935, 6-11-98, effective 6-11-98, see ¶ 70,016.24; finalized with changes, 64 FR 52670, 9-30-99, see ¶ 70,016.83.

Final rule, 63 FR 31934, 6-11-98, effective 6-11-98, see ¶ 70,016.23.

Interim rule, 63 FR 31936, 6-11-98, effective 6-11-98, see ¶ 70,016.22.

Final rule, 63 FR 28284, 5-22-98, effective 5-22-98, see ¶ 70,016.21.

Interim rule, 63 FR 27682, 5-20-98, effective 6-1-98, see ¶ 70,016.20.

Final rule, 63 FR 15316, 3-31-98, effective 3-31-98, see ¶ 70,016.18, corrected 63 FR 20447, 4-24-98.

Interim rule, 63 FR 14836, 3-27-98, effective 3-27-98, see ¶ 70,017.17.

Final rule, 63 FR 14640, 3-26-98, effective 3-26-98, see ¶ 70,016.16.

Interim rule, 63 FR 14640, 3-26-98, effective 3-26-98 see ¶ 70,016.15.

Interim rule, 63 FR 11850, 3-11-98, effective 3-11-98, see ¶ 70,016.14.

DAC 91-13, 63 FR 11522, 3-9-98, effective 3-9-98; see ¶ 70,010.48; corrected 63 FR 17124, 4-8-98, corrected 63 FR 29061, 5-27-98.

Interim rule, 63 FR 7308, 2-13-98, effective 2-13-98; see ¶ 70,016.13, corrected 63 FR 12862, 3-16-98.

Final rule, 63 FR 6109, 2-6-98, effective 2-6-98; see ¶ 70,016.12.

Interim rule, 63 FR 5744, 2-4-98, effective 2-4-98; see ¶ 70,016.11.

Final rule, 62 FR 63035, 11-26-97, effective 11-26-97; see ¶ 70,016.10.

Final rule, 62 FR 48181, 9-15-97, effective 10-1-97; see ¶ 70,016.09.

Final rule, 62 FR 47154, 9-8-97, effective 9-8-97; see ¶ 70,016.08.

Final rule, 62 FR 47153, 9-8-97, effective 9-8-97; see ¶ 70,016.07.

Final rule, 62 FR 44223, 8-20-97, effective 8-20-97; see ¶ 70,016.06.

Final rule, 62 FR 44221, 8-20-97, effective 10-1-97; see ¶ 70,016.05.

Final rule, 62 FR 40471, 7-29-97, effective 7-29-97; see ¶ 70,016.04.

Final rule, 62 FR 37147, 7-11-97, effective 7-11-97; see ¶ 70,016.03.

Interim rule, 62 FR 37146, 7-11-97, effective 7-11-97; see ¶ 70,016.02.

DAC 91-12, 62 FR 34114, 6-24-97, effective 6-24-97; see ¶ 70,010.47; corrected 62 FR 49304, 9-19-97.

Final rule, 62 FR 16099, 4-4-97, effective 4-4-97; see ¶ 70,016.

Interim rule, 62 FR 9990, 3-5-97, effective 3-5-97; see ¶ 70,015.99; corrected 62 FR 11953, 3-13-97; corrected 62 FR 49304, 9-19-97.

Interim rule, 62 FR 9375, 3-3-97, effective 3-3-97; see ¶ 70,015.98.

Interim rule, 62 FR 5779, 2-7-97, effective 2-7-97; see ¶ 70,015.97; corrected 62 FR 49304, 9-19-97.

Final rule, 62 FR 2611, 1-17-97, effective 1-17-97; see ¶ 70,015.96.

Interim rule, 62 FR 2856, 1-17-97, effective 1-17-97; see ¶ 70,015.95.

Interim rule, 62 FR 2857, 1-17-97, effective 1-17-97; see ¶ 70,015.94.

Final rule, 62 FR 2615, 1-17-97, effective 1-17-97; see ¶ 70,015.93.

Interim rule, 62 FR 2615, 1-17-97, effective 1-17-97; see ¶ 70,015.92.

Interim rule, 62 FR 2616, 1-17-97, effective 1-17-97; see ¶ 70,015.91.

Final rule, 62 FR 2612, 1-17-97, effective 1-17-97; see ¶ 70,015.90.

Interim rule, 62 FR 1058, 1-8-97, effective 1-8-97; see ¶ 70,015.88; corrected 62 FR 49305, 9-19-97.

Final rule, 62 FR 1058, 1-8-97, effective 1-8-97; see ¶ 70,015.89; corrected 62 FR 1817, 1-13-97; corrected 62 FR 49305, 9-19-97.

Final rule, 61 FR 67952, 12-26-96, effective 12-26-96; see ¶ 70,015.87.

Final rule, 61 FR 65478, 12-13-96, effective 12-13-96; see ¶ 70,015.86.

Interim rule, 61 FR 64636, 12-6-96, effective 12-6-96; see ¶ 70,015.85; corrected 62 FR 49304, 9-19-97.

Interim rule, 61 FR 64635, 12-6-96, effective 12-6-96; see ¶ 70,015.84.

Final rule, 61 FR 58490, 11-15-96, effective 11-15-96; see ¶ 70,015.83.

Final rule, 61 FR 58488, 11-15-96, effective 11-15-96; see ¶ 70,015.82.

Final rule, 61 FR 58489, 11-15-96, effective 11-15-96; see ¶ 70,015.81.

Final rule, 61 FR 54346, 10-18-96, effective 10-18-96; see ¶ 70,015.18.

Final rule, 61 FR 51030, 9-30-96, effective 10-1-96; see ¶ 70,015.79; corrected 62 FR 49304, 9-19-97.

DAC 91-11, 61 FR 50446, 9-26-96, effective 9-26-96; see ¶ 70,010.46.

Interim rule, 61 FR 39900, 7-31-96, effective 7-31-96; corrected, 61 FR 49008, 9-17-96; see ¶ 70,015.78.

Interim rule, 61 FR 37841, 7-22-96, effective 7-22-96; see ¶ 70,015.77.

Final rule, 61 FR 36305, 7-10-96, effective 7-10-96; see ¶ 70,015.76.

Interim rule, 61 FR 25408, 5-21-96, effective 5-21-96; see ¶ 70,015.75.

Final rule, 61 FR 25409, 5-21-96, effective 5-21-96; see ¶ 70,015.74.

Interim rule, 61 FR 21973, 5-13-96, effective 5-13-96; see ¶ 70,015.73.

Interim rule, 61 FR 18987, 4-30-96, effective 4-30-96; corrected, 61 FR 49531, 9-20-96; see ¶ 70,015.72.

Final rule, 61 FR 18686, 4-29-96, effective 4-29-96; corrected, 61 FR 49531, 9-20-96; see ¶ 70,015.71.

Final rule, 61 FR 16880, 4-18-96, effective 4-18-96; see ¶ 70,015.70.

Final rule, 61 FR 16881, 4-18-96, effective 4-18-96; corrected, 61 FR 49531, 9-20-96; see ¶ 70,015.69.

Interim rule, 61 FR 16879, 4-18-96, effective 4-18-96; see ¶ 70,015.68.

Interim rule, 61 FR 13106, 3-26-96, effective 4-1-96; see ¶ 70,015.67.

Interim rule, 61 FR 10899, 3-18-96, effective 3-18-96; see ¶ 70,015.66.

Final rule, 61 FR 10285, 3-13-96, effective 4-12-96; see ¶ 70,015.65.

DAC 91-10, 61 FR 7739, 2-29-96, effective 2-29-96; see ¶ 70,010.45.

Interim rule, 61 FR 7077, 2-26-96, effective 2-26-96; see ¶ 70,015.64.

Interim rule, 61 FR 3600, 2-1-96, effective 2-1-96; see ¶ 70,015.63.

Final rule, 61 FR 130, 1-3-96, effective 1-1-96; see ¶ 70,015.62.

DAC 91-9, 60 FR 61586, 11-30-95, effective 11-30-95; corrected, 61 FR 43119, 8-20-96; see ¶ 70,010.44.

Suspended, 60 FR 54954, 10-27-95, effective 10-23-95; see ¶ 70,015.61.

Final rule, 60 FR 43563, 8-22-95, effective 8-22-95.

Interim rule, 60 FR 40106, 8-7-95, effective 8-7-95; see ¶ 70,015.57.

Final rule, 60 FR 35668, 7-10-95, effective 7-10-95.

Interim rule, 60 FR 34471, 7-3-95, effective 7-3-95.

Final rule, 60 FR 34467, 7-3-95, effective 7-3-95, corrected, 60 FR 43191, 8-18-95.

Interim rule, 60 FR 34471, 7-3-95, effective 7-3-95.

DAC 91-8, 60 FR 33464, 6-28-95, effective 6-30-95; see ¶ 70,010.43.

DAC 91-7, 60 FR 29491, 6-5-95, effective 5-17-95; see ¶ 70,010.42.

Interim rule, 60 FR 19531, 4-19-95, effective 4-10-95.

Interim rule, 60 FR 13076, 3-10-95, effective 3-3-95.

Interim rule, 60 FR 13075, 3-10-95, effective 3-6-95.

Interim rule, 60 FR 13074, 3-10-95, effective 2-27-95.

Interim rule, 60 FR 13073, 3-10-95, effective 3-6-95.

Interim rule, 60 FR 4569, 1-24-95, effective 1-17-95.

Interim rule, 60 FR 2888, 1-12-95, effective 1-5-95.

Interim rule, 60 FR 2330, 1-9-95, effective 12-14-94.

Interim rule, 60 FR 1747, 1-5-95, effective 12-29-94.

Final rule, 59 FR 53116, 10-21-94, effective 10-18-94; see ¶ 70,015.38.

Final rule, 59 FR 52442, 10-18-94, effective 10-1-94; revised 60 FR 15689, 3-27-95, effective 3-21-95; see ¶ 70,015.49.

Final rule, 59 FR 51132, 10-7-94, effective 9-29-94; see ¶ 70,015.37.

Interim rule, 59 FR 50851, 10-6-94, effective 9-29-94; see ¶ 70,015.34.

Final rule, 59 FR 50851, 10-6-94, effective 9-29-94.

Final rule, 59 FR 50511, 10-4-94, effective 9-28-94; see ¶ 70,015.33.

Interim rule, 59 FR 36088, 7-15-94, effective 7-8-94.

DAC 91-6, 59 FR 27662, 5-27-94, effective 5-27-94; see ¶ 70,010.41.

Interim rule, 59 FR 26143, 5-19-94, effective 5-5-94.

Interim rule, 59 FR 24958, 5-13-94, effective 5-3-94.

Final rule, 59 FR 23169, 5-5-94; effective 4-26-94; see ¶ 70,015.28.

Final rule, 59 FR 22759, 5-3-94, effective 4-25-94; see ¶ 70,015.27.

Interim rule, 59 FR 22130, 4-29-94, effective 4-21-94.

Interim rule, 59 FR 19145, 4-22-94, effective 4-13-94.

Interim rule, 59 FR 12191, 3-16-94, effective 3-8-94.

Final rule, 59 FR 10579, 3-7-94, effective 2-25-94; see ¶ 70,015.22.

Final rule, 59 FR 10579, 3-7-94, effective 2-14-94; see ¶ 70,015.21.

Official correction, 59 FR 8041, 2-17-94.

Interim rule, 59 FR 1288, 1-10-94, effective 1-1-94; corrected, 59 FR 8041, 2-17-94.

Interim rule, 58 FR 62045, 11-24-93, effective 11-11-93.

Interim rule, 58 FR 46091, 9-1-93, effective 8-23-93; see ¶ 70,015.13.

Final rule, 58 FR 32062, 6-8-93; ¶ 70,015.12.

Interim rule, 58 FR 43285, 8-16-93, effective 8-9-93.

DAC 91-5, 58 FR 28458, 5-13-93, effective 4-30-93; 58 FR 32416, 6-9-93; see ¶ 70,010.40.

Final rule, 58 FR 16782, 3-31-93, effective 3-24-93; see ¶ 70,015.11.

DAC 91-4, 57 FR 53596, 11-12-92, effective 10-30-92; corrected, 57 FR 55472, 11-25-92; see ¶ 70,010.39.

Interim rule, 57 FR 52593, 11-4-92, effective 10-26-92.

Interim rule, 57 FR 47270, 10-15-92, effective 10-5-92.

Final rule, 57 FR 42707, 9-16-92, effective 9-8-92.

DAC 91-3, 57 FR 42626, 9-15-92; see ¶ 70,010.38.

Interim rule, 57 FR 41422, 9-10-92, effective 9-1-92.

Interim rule, 57 FR 38286, 8-24-92, effective 8-14-92.

Interim rule, 57 FR 32736, 7-23-92, effective 7-16-92.

Interim rule, 57 FR 29041, 6-30-92, effective 6-23-92.

DAC 91-2, 57 FR 14988, 4-23-92; see ¶ 70,010.37.

Interim rule, 57 FR 4741, 2-7-92, effective 12-31-91.

DAC 91-1, 56 FR 67208, 12-30-91; see ¶ 70,010.36.

Final rule, 59 FR 10579, 3-7-94, effective 2-14-94; see ¶ 70,015.21.

Official correction, 59 FR 8041, 2-17-94.

Interim rule, 59 FR 1288, 1-10-94, effective 1-1-94; corrected, 59 FR 8041, 2-17-94.

Interim rule, 58 FR 62045, 11-24-93, effective 11-11-93.

Interim rule, 58 FR 46091, 9-1-93, effective 8-23-93; see ¶ 70,015.13.

Final rule, 58 FR 32062, 6-8-93; see ¶ 70,015.12.

Interim rule, 58 FR 43285, 8-16-93, effective 8-9-93.

DAC 91-5, 58 FR 28458, 5-13-93, effective 4-30-93; corrected, 58 FR 32416, 6-9-93; see ¶ 70,010.40.

Final rule, 58 FR 16782, 3-31-93, effective 3-24-93; see ¶ 70,015.11.

DAC 91-4, 57 FR 53596, 11-12-92, effective 10-30-92; corrected, 57 FR 55472, 11-25-92; see ¶ 70,010.39.

Interim rule, 57 FR 52593, 11-4-92, effective 10-26-92.

Interim rule, 57 FR 47270, 10-15-92, effective 10-5-92.

Final rule, 57 FR 42707, 9-16-92, effective 9-8-92.

DAC 91-3, 57 FR 42626, 9-15-92; see ¶ 70,010.38.

Interim rule, 57 FR 41422, 9-10-92, effective 9-1-92.

Interim rule, 57 FR 38286, 8-24-92, effective 8-14-92.

Interim rule, 57 FR 32736, 7-23-92, effective 7-16-92.

Interim rule, 57 FR 29041, 6-30-92, effective 6-23-92.

DAC 91-2, 57 FR 14988, 4-23-92; see ¶ 70,010.37.

Interim rule, 57 FR 4741, 2-7-92, effective 12-31-91.

DAC 91-1, 56 FR 67208, 12-30-91; see ¶ 70,010.36.

Note: The ¶ 70, __._ citations in the Sources list refer to the location of the source documents in **Government Contracts Reporter**, which is also available from **Wolters Kluwer Law and Business**.

Codification and Numbering

The official source for the Defense Federal Acquisition Regulation Supplement is Title 48, Chapter 2 of the United States Code of Federal Regulations. The numbering of the DFARS parallels the FAR. For example, DFARS section 204.105 consists of material that applies only to the Department of Defense but relates to FAR section 4.105; DFARS section 245.505-14(a)(3) consists of DoD material that supplements FAR section 45.505-14(a)(3).

DFARS materials that cannot be integrated intellegibly with a FAR counterpart are assigned numbers ending in 70 and up. This applies to the part, subpart, section, and subsection levels. Thus, Part 270 is the first part that can be used by DoD to add coverage that has no direct parallel anywhere in the FAR. Subpart 215.70 contains material supplementing FAR Part 15. Section 215.470 supplements FAR 15.4; subsection 215.402-70 supplements FAR 15.402. Below the subsection level, supplementary material is designated in the DFARS by units designated as (S-70) through (S-89).

Defense Federal Acquisition Regulation Supplement Parts 201—212

GENERAL
ACQUISITION PLANNING

Table of Contents

Page

SUBCHAPTER A—GENERAL

Part 201—Federal Acquisition Regulations System 43
Part 202—Definitions of Words and Terms 53
Part 203—Improper Business Practices and Personal Conflicts of Interest 61
Part 204—Administrative and Information Matters 71

SUBCHAPTER B—ACQUISITION PLANNING

Part 205—Publicizing Contract Actions 97
Part 206—Competition Requirements 103
Part 207—Acquisition Planning 109
Part 208—Required Sources of Supplies and Services 119
Part 209—Contractor Qualifications 129
Part 210—Market Research 145
Part 211—Describing Agency Needs 149
Part 212—Acquisition of Commercial Items 159

See page 39 for an explanation of the numbering of the DFARS.

PART 201—FEDERAL ACQUISITION REGULATIONS SYSTEM

Table of Contents

Subpart 201.1—Purpose, Authority, Issuance

Purpose 201.101
Applicability 201.104
Issuance 201.105
Copies 201.105-3
OMB approval under the Paperwork Reduction Act 201.106
Certifications 201.107
Statutory acquisition-related dollar thresholds–adjustment for inflation . 201.109
Peer Reviews 201.170

Subpart 201.2—Administration

Maintenance of the FAR 201.201
The two councils 201.201-1
Maintenance of Procedures, Guidance, and Information 201.201-70

Subpart 201.3—Agency Acquisition Regulations

Policy 201.301
Publication and codification 201.303
Agency control and compliance procedures 201.304

Subpart 201.4—Deviations from the FAR

Policy 201.402
Individual deviations 201.403
Class deviations 201.404

Subpart 201.6—Career Development, Contracting Authority, and Responsibilities

Contracting officers 201.602
Responsibilities 201.602-2
Contract clause 201.602-70
Selection, appointment, and termination of appointment for contracting officers 201.603
Selection 201.603-2
Appointment 201.603-3
Appointment of property administrators and plant clearance officers . . . 201.670

SUBCHAPTER A—GENERAL (Parts 201-204)

PART 201—FEDERAL ACQUISITION REGULATIONS SYSTEM

SUBPART 201.1—PURPOSE, AUTHORITY, ISSUANCE

201.101 Purpose.

(1) The defense acquisition system, as defined in 10 U.S.C. 2545, exists to manage the investments of the United States in technologies, programs, and product support necessary to achieve the national security strategy prescribed by the President pursuant to section 108 of the National Security Act of 1947 (50 U.S.C. 3043) and to support the United States Armed Forces.

(2) The investment strategy of DoD shall be postured to support not only the current United States armed forces, but also future armed forces of the United States.

(3) The primary objective of DoD acquisition is to acquire quality supplies and services that satisfy user needs with measurable improvements to mission capability and operational support at a fair and reasonable price.

[Final rule, 83 FR 19641, 5/4/2018, effective 5/4/2018]

201.104 Applicability.

The FAR and the Defense Federal Acquisition Regulation Supplement (DFARS) also apply to purchases and contracts by DoD contracting activities made in support of foreign military sales or North Atlantic Treaty Organization cooperative projects without regard to the nature or sources of funds obligated, unless otherwise specified in this regulation.

[Redesignated from 201.103, Final rule, 64 FR 39429, 7/22/99, effective 7/22/99]

201.105 Issuance. (No Text)

[Redesignated from 201.104, Final rule, 64 FR 39429, 7/22/99, effective 7/22/99]

201.105-3 Copies.

The DFARS and the DFARS Procedures, Guidance, and Information (PGI) are available electronically via the World Wide Web at *http://www.acq.osd.mil/dpap/dars/index.htm*.

[Final rule, 64 FR 39429, 7/22/99, effective 7/22/99; Final rule, 69 FR 63326, 11/1/2004, effective 11/1/2004]

201.106 OMB approval under the Paperwork Reduction Act.

See PGI 201.106 for a list of the information collection and recordkeeping requirements contained in this regulation that have been approved by the Office of Management and Budget.

[Final rule, 80 FR 67254, 10/30/2015, effective 10/30/2015]

201.107 Certifications.

In accordance with 41 U.S.C. 1304, a new requirement for a certification by a contractor or offeror may not be included in the DFARS unless—

(1) The certification requirement is specifically imposed by statute; or

(2) Written justification for such certification is provided to the Secretary of Defense by the Under Secretary of Defense (Acquisition, Technology, and Logistics), and the Secretary of Defense approves in writing the inclusion of such certification requirement.

[DAC 91-13, 63 FR 11522, 3/9/98, effective 3/9/98; Final rule, 65 FR 39703, 6/27/2000, effective 6/27/2000; Final rule, 76 FR 58137, 9/20/2011, effective 9/20/2011; Final rule, 77 FR 35879, 6/15/2012, effective 6/15/2012]

201.109 Statutory acquisition-related dollar thresholds–adjustment for inflation.

(a) (i) 41 U.S.C. 1908(d) requires the adjustment for inflation of all statutory acquisition-related dollar thresholds in the DFARS be applied to contracts and subcontracts without regard to the date of award of the contract or subcontract, except thresholds based on the Wage Rate Requirements statute, the Service Contract Labor Standards statute, or established by the United States Trade Representative pursuant to the Trade Agreement Act, which are not escalated by the statute.

(ii) Section 814(b) of the National Defense Authorization Act for Fiscal Year 2012 (Pub. L. 112-81) requires that the threshold established in 10 U.S.C. 2253(a)(2) for the acquisition of right-hand drive passenger sedans be included in the list of dollar thresholds that are subject to adjustment for inflation in accordance with the requirements of 41 U.S.C. 1908, and is adjusted pursuant to such provisions, as appropriate.

(d) A matrix showing the most recent escalation adjustments of statutory acquisition-related dollar thresholds is available PGI 201.109.

[Final rule, 71 FR 75891, 12/19/2006, effective 12/19/2006; Interim rule, 77 FR 19127, 3/30/2012, effective 3/30/2012; Final rule, 77 FR 52252, 8/29/2012, effective 8/29/2012; Final rule, 84 FR 25186, 5/31/2019, effective 5/31/2019]

201.170 Peer Reviews.

(a) *DoD peer reviews.* (1) The Office of the Director, Defense Procurement and Acquisition Policy, will organize teams of reviewers and facilitate peer reviews for solicitations and contracts, as follows using the procedures at PGI 201.170—

(i) Preaward peer reviews for competitive procurements will be conducted in three phases for all solicitations valued at $1 billion or more (including options).

(ii) Preaward peer reviews for noncompetitive procurements will be conducted in three phases for new contract actions valued at $5 million or more; and

(iii) Postaward peer reviews will be conducted for all contracts for services valued at $1 billion or more.

(2) To facilitate planning for peer reviews, the military departments and defense agencies shall provide a rolling annual forecast of acquisitions at the end of each quarter (*i.e.*, March 31; June 30; September 30; December 31), to the Deputy Director, Defense Procurement and Acquisition Policy (Contract Policy and International Contracting) via email to *osd.pentagon.ousd-atl.mbx.peer-reviews@mail.mil.*

(b) *Component peer reviews.* The military departments and defense agencies shall establish procedures for—

(1) Preaward peer reviews of solicitations for competitive procurements valued at less than $1 billion;

(2) Preaward peer reviews for noncompetitive procurements valued at less than $500 million; and

(3) Postaward peer reviews of all contracts for services valued at less than $1 billion.

[Final rule, 74 FR 37625, 7/29/2009, effective 7/29/2009; Final rule, 77 FR 19126, 3/30/2012, effective 4/30/2012; Final rule, 78 FR 54968, 9/9/2013, effective 9/9/2013; Final rule, 79 FR 51264, 8/28/2014, effective 8/28/2014]

SUBPART 201.2—ADMINISTRATION

201.201 Maintenance of the FAR. (No Text)

201.201-1 The two councils.

(c) The composition and operation of the DAR Council is prescribed in DoD Instruction 5000.35, Defense Acquisition Regulations (DAR) System.

(d)(i) Departments and agencies process proposed revisions of FAR or DFARS through channels to the Director of the DAR Council. Process the proposed revision as a memorandum in the following format, addressed to the Director, DAR Council, OUSD(AT&L), 3060 Defense Pentagon, Washington, DC 20301-3060; datafax (571) 372-6094:

I. PROBLEM: Succinctly state the problem created by current FAR and/or DFARS coverage and describe the factual and/or legal reasons necessitating the change to the regulation.

II. RECOMMENDATION: Identify the FAR and/or DFARS citations to be revised. Attach as TAB A, a copy of the text of the existing coverage, conformed to include the proposed additions and deletions. Indicate deleted coverage with dashed lines through the current words being deleted and insert proposed language in brackets at the appropriate locations within the existing coverage. If the proposed deleted portion is extensive, it may be outlined by lines forming a box with diagonal lines drawn connecting the corners.

III. DISCUSSION: Include a complete, convincing explanation of why the change is necessary and how the recommended revision will solve the problem. Address advantages and disadvantages of the proposed revision, as well as any cost or administrative impact on Government activities and contractors. Identify any potential impact of the change on automated systems, e.g., automated financial and procurement systems. Provide any other background information that would be helpful in explaining the issue.

IV. COLLATERALS: Address the need for public comment (FAR 1.301(b) and subpart 1.5), the Paperwork Reduction Act, and the Regulatory Flexibility Act (FAR 1.301(c)).

V. DEVIATIONS: If a recommended revision of DFARS is a FAR deviation, identify the deviation and include under separate TAB a justification for the deviation that addresses the requirements of 201.402(2). The justification should be in the form of a memorandum for the Director of Defense Procurement and Acquisition Policy, Office of the Under Secretary of Defense (Acquisition, Technology, and Logistics).

(ii) The public may offer proposed revisions of FAR or DFARS by submission of a memorandum, in the format (including all of the information) prescribed in paragraph (d)(i) of this subsection, to the Director of the DAR Council.

[DAC 91-9, 60 FR 61586, 11/30/95, effective 11/30/95; DAC 91-11, 61 FR 50446, 9/26/96, effective 9/26/96; DAC 91-13, 63 FR 11522, 3/9/98, effective 3/9/98; Final rule, 65 FR 6551, 2/10/2000, effective 2/10/2000, Final rule, 68 FR 7438, 2/14/2003, effective 2/14/2003; Final rule, 73 FR 70905, 11/24/2008, effective 11/24/2008; Final rule, 77 FR 76936, 12/31/2012, effective 12/31/2012; Final rule, 78 FR 13543, 2/28/2013, effective 2/28/2013]

201.201-70 Maintenance of Procedures, Guidance, and Information.

The DAR Council is also responsible for maintenance of the DFARS Procedures, Guidance, and Information (PGI).

[Final rule, 69 FR 63326, 11/1/2004, effective 11/1/2004]

SUBPART 201.3—AGENCY ACQUISITION REGULATIONS

201.301 Policy.

(a)(1) DoD implementation and supplementation of the FAR is issued in the Defense Federal Acquisition Regulation Supplement (DFARS) under authorization and subject to the authority, direction, and control of the Secretary of Defense. The DFARS contains—

(i) Requirements of law;

(ii) DoD-wide policies;

(iii) Delegations of FAR authorities;

(iv) Deviations from FAR requirements; and

(v) Policies/procedures that have a significant effect beyond the internal operating procedures of DoD or a significant cost or administrative impact on contractors or offerors.

(2) Relevant procedures, guidance, and information that do not meet the criteria in paragraph (a)(1) of this section are issued in the DFARS Procedures, Guidance, and Information (PGI).

(b) When **Federal Register** publication is required for any policy, procedure, clause, or form, the department or agency requesting Under Secretary of Defense (Acquisition, Technology, and Logistics) (USD(AT&L)) approval for use of the policy, procedure, clause, or form (see 201.304(1)) must include an analysis of the public comments in the request for approval. Information on determining when a clause requires publication in the **Federal Register** and approval in accordance with 201.304(1) is provided at PGI 201.301(b).

[DAC 91-9, 60 FR 61586, 11/30/95, effective 11/30/95; Final rule, 65 FR 6551, 2/10/2000, effective 2/10/2000; Final rule,

69 FR 63326, 11/1/2004, effective 11/1/2004; Final rule, 80 FR 36718, 6/26/2015, effective 6/26/2015]

201.303 Publication and codification.

(a) (i) The DFARS is codified under chapter 2 in title 48, Code of Federal Regulations.

(ii) To the extent possible, all DFARS text (whether implemental or supplemental) is numbered as if it were implemental. Supplemental numbering is used only when the text cannot be integrated intelligibly with its FAR counterpart.

(A) Implemental numbering is the same as its FAR counterpart, except when the text exceeds one paragraph, the subdivisions are numbered by skipping a unit in the FAR 1.105-2(b)(2) prescribed numbering sequence. For example, three paragraphs implementing FAR 19.501 would be numbered 219.501 (1), (2), and (3) rather than (a), (b), and (c). Three paragraphs implementing FAR 19.501(a) would be numbered 219.501(a) (i), (ii), and (iii) rather than (a) (1), (2), and (3). Further subdivision of the paragraphs follows the prescribed numbering sequence, e.g., 219.501(1)(i)(A)(*1*)(*i*).

(B) Supplemental numbering is the same as its FAR counterpart, with the addition of a number of 70 and up or (S-70) and up. Parts, subparts, sections, or subsections are supplemented by the addition of a number of 70 and up. Lower divisions are supplemented by the addition of a number of (S-70) and up. When text exceeds one paragraph, the subdivisions are numbered using the FAR 1.105-2(b)(2) prescribed sequence, without skipping a unit. For example, DFARS text supplementing FAR 19.501 would be numbered 219.501-70. Its subdivisions would be numbered 219.501-70(a), (b), and (c).

(C) Subdivision numbering below the 4th level does not repeat the numbering sequence. It uses italicized Arabic numbers and then italicized lower case Roman numerals.

(D) An example of DFARS numbering is in Table 1-1, DFARS Numbering.

(iii) Department/agency and component supplements must parallel the FAR and DFARS numbering, except department/agency supplemental numbering uses subsection numbering of 90 and up, instead of 70 and up.

TABLE 1-1—DFARS NUMBERING

FAR	Is implemented as	Is supplemented as
19	219	219.70
19.5	219.5	219.570
19.501	219.501	219.501-70
19.501-1	219.501-1	219.501-1-70
19.501-1(a)	219.501-1(a)	219.501-1(a)(S-70)
19.501-1(a)(1)	219.501-1(a)(1)	219.501-1(a)(1)(S-70)

[Final rule, 64 FR 51074, 9/21/99, effective 9/21/99]

201.304 Agency control and compliance procedures.

Departments and agencies and their component organizations may issue acquisition regulations as necessary to implement or supplement the FAR or DFARS.

(1) (i) Approval of the USD(AT&L) is required before including in a department/agency or component supplement, or any other contracting regulation document such as a policy letter or clause book, any policy, procedure, clause, or form that—

(A) Has a significant effect beyond the internal operating procedures of the agency; or

(B) Has a significant cost or administrative impact on contractors or offerors.

(ii) Except as provided in paragraph (2) of this section, the USD(AT&L) has delegated authority to the Director of Defense Procurement and Acquisition Policy (OUSD(AT&L)DPAP) to approve or disapprove the policies, procedures, clauses, and forms subject to paragraph (1)(i) of this section.

(2) In accordance with 41 U.S.C. 1304, a new requirement for a certification by a contractor or offeror may not be included in a department/agency or component procurement regulation unless—

(i) The certification requirement is specifically imposed by statute; or

(ii) Written justification for such certification is provided to the Secretary of Defense by USD(AT&L), and the Secretary of Defense approves in writing the inclusion of such certification requirement.

(3) Contracting activities must obtain the appropriate approval (see 201.404) for any class deviation (as defined in FAR Subpart 1.4) from the FAR or DFARS, before its inclusion in a department/agency or component supplement or any other contracting regulation document such as a policy letter or clause book.

(4) Each department and agency must develop and, upon approval by OUSD(AT&L)DPAP, implement, maintain, and comply with a plan for controlling the use of clauses other than those prescribed by FAR or DFARS. Additional information on department and agency clause control plan requirements is available at PGI 201.304(4).

(5) Departments and agencies must submit requests for the Secretary of Defense, USD(AT&L), and OUSD(AT&L)DPAP approvals required by this section through the Director of the DAR Council. Procedures for requesting approval of department and agency clauses are provided at PGI 201.304(5).

(6) The Director of Defense Procurement publishes changes to the DFARS in the Federal Register and electronically via the World Wide Web. Each change includes an effective date. Unless guidance accompanying a change states otherwise, contracting officers must include any new or revised clauses, provisions, or forms in solicitations issued on or after the effective date of the change.

[DAC 91-9, 60 FR 61586, 11/30/95, effective 11/30/95; DAC 91-13, 63 FR 11522, 3/9/98, effective 3/9/98; Final rule, 64 FR 39429, 7/22/99, effective 7/22/99; Final rule, 65 FR 6551, 2/10/2000, effective 2/10/2000; Final rule, 68 FR 7438, 2/14/2003, effective 2/14/2003; CFR Correction, 74 FR 49826, 9/29/2009; Final rule, 76 FR 58137, 9/20/2011, effective 9/20/2011; Final rule, 77 FR 35879, 6/15/2012, effective 6/15/2012; Final rule, 80 FR 36718, 6/26/2015, effective 6/26/2015]

SUBPART 201.4—DEVIATIONS FROM THE FAR

201.402 Policy.

(1) The Director of Defense Procurement and Acquisition Policy, Office of the Under Secretary of Defense (Acquisition, Technology and Logistics), (OUSD(AT&L)DPAP), is the approval authority within DoD for any individual or class deviation from—

(i) FAR 3.104, Procurement Integrity, or DFARS 203.104, Procurement Integrity;

(ii) FAR Subpart 27.4, Rights in Data and Copyrights, or DFARS Subpart 227.4, Rights in Data and Copyrights;

(iii) FAR Part 30, Cost Accounting Standards Administration, or DFARS Part 230, Cost Accounting Standards Administration;

(iv) FAR Subpart 31.1, Applicability, or DFARS Subpart 231.1, Applicability (contract cost principles);

(v) FAR Subpart 31.2, Contracts with Commercial Organizations; or

(vi) FAR Part 32, Contract Financing (except Subparts 32.7and FAR 32.8 and the payment clauses prescribed by Subpart 31.1), or DFARS Part 232, Contract Financing (except Subparts 232.7 and 232.8).

(2) Submit requests for deviation approval through department/agency channels to the approval authority in paragraph (1) of this section, 201.403, or 201.404, as appropriate. Submit deviations that require OUSD(AT&L)DPAP approval through the Director of the DAR Council. At a minimum, each request must—

(i) Identify the department/agency, and component if applicable, requesting the deviation;

(ii) Identify the FAR or DFARS citation from which a deviation is needed, state what is required by that citation, and indicate whether an individual or class deviation is requested;

(iii) Describe the deviation and indicate which of paragraphs (a) through (f) of FAR 1.401 best categorizes the deviation;

(iv) State whether the deviation will have a significant effect beyond the internal operating procedures of the agency and/or a significant cost of administrative impact on contractors or offerors, and give reasons to support the statement;

(v) State the period of time for which the deviation is required;

(vi) State whether approval for the same deviation has been received previously, and if so, when;

(vii) State whether the proposed deviation was published (see FAR subpart 1.5 for publication requirements) in the Federal Register and provide analysis of comments;

(viii) State whether the request for deviation has been reviewed by legal counsel, and if so, state results; and

(ix) Give detailed rationale for the request. State what problem or situation will be avoided, corrected, or improved if request is approved.

[DAC 91-9, 60 FR 61586, 11/30/95, effective 11/30/95; DAC 91-11, 61 FR 50446, 9/26/96, effective 9/26/96; Final rule, 64 FR 8726, 2/23/99, effective 2/23/99; Final rule 65 FR 6551 2/10/2000, effective 2/10/2000; Final rule, 68 FR 7438, 2/14/2003, effective 2/14/2003]

201.403 Individual deviations.

(1) Individual deviations, except those described in 201.402(1) and paragraph (2) of this section, must be approved in accordance with the department/agency plan prescribed by 201.304(4).

(2) Contracting officers outside the United States may deviate from prescribed nonstatutory FAR and DFARS clauses when—

(i) Contracting for support services, supplies, or construction, with the governments of North Atlantic Treaty Organization (NATO) countries or other allies (as described in 10 U.S.C. 2341(2)), or with United Nations or NATO organizations; and

(ii) Such governments or organizations will not agree to the standard clauses.

[Final rule, 65 FR 6551, 2/10/2000, effective 2/10/2000]

201.404 Class deviations.

(b)(i) Except as provided in paragraph (b)(ii) of this section, OUSD(AT&L)DPAP is the approval authority within DoD for any class deviation.

(ii) The senior procurement executives for the Army, Navy, and Air Force, and the Directors of the Defense Commissary Agency, the Defense Contract Management Agency, and the Defense Logistics Agency, may approve any class deviation, other than those described in 201.402(1), that does not—

(A) Have a significant effect beyond the internal operating procedures of the department or agency;

(B) Have a significant cost or administrative impact on contractors or offerors;

(C) Diminish any preference given small business concerns by the FAR or DFARS; or

(D) Extend to requirements imposed by statute or by regulations of other agencies such as the Small Business Administration and Department of Labor.

[Final rule, 65 FR 6551, 2/10/2000, effective 2/10/2000; Final rule, 65 FR 52951, 8/31/2000, effective 8/31/2000; Final rule, 68 FR 7438, 2/14/2003, effective 2/14/2003]

SUBPART 201.6—CAREER DEVELOPMENT, CONTRACTING AUTHORITY, AND RESPONSIBILITIES

201.602 Contracting officers. (No Text)

201.602-2 Responsibilities.

(d) Follow the procedures at PGI 201.602-2 regarding designation, assignment, and responsibilities of a contracting officer's representative (COR).

(1) A COR shall be an employees, military or civilian, of the U.S. Government, a foreign government, or a North Atlantic Treaty Organization/coalition partner. In no case shall contractor personnel serve as CORs.

[Final rule, 70 FR 75411, 12/20/2005, effective 12/20/2005; Final rule, 71 FR 69488, 12/1/2006, effective 12/1/2006; Final rule, 75 FR 22706, 4/30/2010, effective 4/30/2010; Final rule, 76 FR 58136, 9/20/2011, effective 9/20/2011; Final rule, 79 FR 22036, 4/21/2014, effective 4/21/2014]

201.602-70 Contract clause.

Use the clause at 252.201-7000, Contracting Officer's Representative, in solicitations and contracts when appointment of a contracting officer's representative is anticipated.

201.603 Selection, appointment, and termination of appointment for contracting officers. (No Text)

[Final rule, 78 FR 73450, 12/6/2013, effective 12/6/2013]

201.603-2 Selection.

(1) In accordance with 10 U.S.C. 1724, in order to qualify to serve as a contracting officer with authority to award or administer contracts for amounts above the simplified acquisition threshold, a person must

(i) Have completed all contracting courses required for a contracting officer to serve in the grade in which the employee or member of the armed forces will serve;

(ii) Have at least 2 years experience in a contracting position;

(iii) Have—

(A) Received a baccalaureate degree from an accredited educational institution; and

(B) Completed at least 24 semester credit hours, or equivalent, of study from an accredited institution of higher education in any of the following disciplines: accounting, business finance, law, contracts, purchasing, economics, industrial management, marketing, quantitative methods, and organization and management; and

(iv) Meet such additional requirements, based on the dollar value and complexity of the contracts awarded or administered in the position, as may be established by the Secretary of Defense.

(2) The qualification requirements in paragraph (1)(iii) of this subsection do not apply to a DoD employee or member of the armed forces who

(i) On or before September 30, 2000, occupied

(A) A contracting officer position with authority to award or administer contracts above the simplified acquisition threshold; or

(B) A position either as an employee in the GS-1102 occupational series or a member of the armed forces in an occupational specialty similar to the GS-1102 series;

(ii) Is in a contingency contracting force; or

(iii) Is an individual appointed to a 3-year developmental position. Information on developmental opportunities is contained in DoD Instruction 5000.66, Operation of the Defense Acquisition, Technology, and Logistics Workforce Education, Training, and Career Development Program.

(3) Waivers to the requirements in paragraph (1) of this subsection may be authorized. Information on waivers is contained in DoD Instruction 5000.66.

[DAC 91-5, 58 FR 28458, 5/13/93, effective 4/30/93; DAC 91-12, 62 FR 34114, 6/24/97, effective 6/24/97; Final rule, 67 FR 65509, 10/25/2002, effective 10/25/2002; Final rule, 73 FR 21844, 4/23/2008, effective 4/23/2008]

201.603-3 Appointment.

(a) Certificates of Appointment executed under the Armed Services Procurement Regulation or the Defense Acquisition Regulation have the same effect as if they had been issued under FAR.

(b) Agency heads may delegate the purchase authority in 213.301 to DoD civilian employees and members of the U.S. Armed Forces.

[Final rule, 64 FR 56704, 10/21/99, effective 10/21/99]

201.670 Appointment of property administrators and plant clearance officers.

(a) The appropriate agency authority shall appoint or terminate (in writing) property administrators and plant clearance officers.

(b) In appointing qualified property administrators and plant clearance officers, the appointing authority shall consider experience, training, education, business acumen, judgment, character, and ethics.

[Final rule, 76 FR 52139, 8/19/2011, effective 8/19/2011]

PART 202—DEFINITIONS OF WORDS AND TERMS

Table of Contents

Subpart 202.1—Definitions

Definitions 202.101

PART 202—DEFINITIONS OF WORDS AND TERMS

SUBPART 202.1—DEFINITIONS

202.101 Definitions.

Authorized aftermarket manufacturer means an organization that fabricates an electronic part under a contract with, or with the express written authority of, the original component manufacturer based on the original component manufacturer's designs, formulas, and/or specifications.

Compromise means disclosure of information to unauthorized persons, or a violation of the security policy of a system, in which unauthorized intentional or unintentional disclosure, modification, destruction, or loss of an object, or the copying of information to unauthorized media may have occurred.

Congressional defense committees means—

(1) In accordance with 10 U.S.C. 101(a)(16), except as otherwise specified in paragraph (2) of this definition or as otherwise specified by statute for particular applications—

(i) The Committee on Armed Services of the Senate;

(ii) The Committee on Appropriations of the Senate;

(iii) The Committee on Armed Services of the House of Representatives; and

(iv) The Committee on Appropriations of the House of Representatives.

(2) For use in subpart 217.1, see the definition at 217.103.

Contract administration office also means a contract management office of the Defense Contract Management Agency.

Contracting activity for DoD also means elements designated by the director of a defense agency which has been delegated contracting authority through its agency charter. DoD contracting activities are listed at PGI 202.101.

Contract manufacturer means a company that produces goods under contract for another company under the label or brand name of that company.

Contracting officer's representative means an individual designated and authorized in writing by the contracting officer to perform specific technical or administrative functions.

Contractor-approved supplier means a supplier that does not have a contractual agreement with the original component manufacturer for a transaction, but has been identified as trustworthy by a contractor or subcontractor.

Counterfeit electronic part means an unlawful or unauthorized reproduction, substitution, or alteration that has been knowingly mismarked, misidentified, or otherwise misrepresented to be an authentic, unmodified electronic part from the original manufacturer, or a source with the express written authority of the original manufacturer or current design activity, including an authorized aftermarket manufacturer. Unlawful or unauthorized substitution includes used electronic parts represented as new, or the false identification of grade, serial number, lot number, date code, or performance characteristics.

Cyber incident means actions taken through the use of computer networks that result in a compromise or an actual or potentially adverse effect on an information system and/or the information residing therein.

Departments and agencies, as used in DFARS, means the military departments and the defense agencies. The military departments are the Departments of the Army, Navy, and Air Force (the Marine Corps is a part of the Department of the Navy). The defense agencies are the Defense Advanced Research Projects Agency, the Defense Business Transformation Agency, the Defense Commissary Agency, the Defense Contract Management Agency, the Defense Finance and Accounting Service, the Defense Information Systems Agency, the Defense Intelligence Agency, the Defense Logistics Agency, the Defense Security Cooperation Agency, the Defense Security Service, the Defense Threat Reduction Agency, the Missile Defense Agency, the National Geospatial-Intelligence Agency, and the National Security Agency, the United States Special

Operations Command, and the United States Transportation Command.

Department of Defense (DoD), as used in DFARS, means the Department of Defense, the military departments, and the defense agencies.

Electronic part means an integrated circuit, a discrete electronic component (including, but not limited to, a transistor, capacitor, resistor, or diode), or a circuit assembly (section 818(f)(2) of Pub. L. 112–81).

Executive agency means for DoD, the Department of Defense, the Department of the Army, the Department of the Navy, and the Department of the Air Force.

Head of the agency means, for DoD, the Secretary of Defense, the Secretary of the Army, the Secretary of the Navy, and the Secretary of the Air Force. Subject to the direction of the Secretary of Defense, the Under Secretary of Defense (Acquisition, Technology, and Logistics), and the Director of Defense Procurement and Acquisition Policy, the directors of the defense agencies have been delegated authority to act as head of the agency for their respective agencies (i.e., to perform functions under the FAR or DFARS reserved to a head of agency or agency head), except for such actions that by terms of statute, or any delegation, must be exercised within the Office of the Secretary of Defense. For emergency acquisition flexibilities, see DFARS 218.270.

Major defense acquisition program is defined in 10. U.S.C. 2430(a).

Micro-purchase threshold, for DoD acquisition of supplies or services funded by DoD appropriations, in lieu of the definition at FAR 2.101, means $5,000 (10 U.S.C. 2338), except—

(1) For DoD acquisition of supplies or services for basic research programs and for activities of the DoD science and technology reinvention laboratories (*https://www.acq.osd.mil/rd/laboratories/labs/liststrl.html*), it means $10,000 (10 U.S.C. 2339);

(2) For acquisitions of construction subject to 40 U.S.C. chapter 31, subchapter IV, Wage Rate Requirements (Construction), $2,000;

(3) For acquisitions of services subject to 41 U.S.C. chapter 67, Service Contract Labor Standards, $2,500; and

(4) For acquisitions of supplies or services that, as determined by the head of the contracting activity, are to be used to support a contingency operation; or to facilitate defense against or recovery from cyber, nuclear, biological, chemical or radiological attack; to support a request from the Secretary of State or the Administrator of the United States Agency for International Development to facilitate provision of international disaster assistance pursuant to 22 U.S.C. 2292 *et seq.;* or to support response to an emergency, or major disaster (42 U.S.C. 5122), as described in 13.201(g)(1), except for construction subject to 40 U.S.C. chapter 31, subchapter IV, Wage Rate Requirements (Construction) (41 U.S.C. 1903)—

(i) $20,000 in the case of any contract to be awarded and performed, or purchase to be made, inside the United States; and

(ii) $30,000 in the case of any contract to be awarded and performed, or purchase to be made, outside the United States.

Milestone decision authority, with respect to a major defense acquisition program, major automated information system, or major system, means the official within the Department of Defense designated with the overall responsibility and authority for acquisition decisions for the program or system, including authority to approve entry of the program or system into the next phase of the acquisition process (10 U.S.C. 2431a).

Non-Government sales means sales of the supplies or services to non-Governmental entities for purposes other than governmental purposes.

Obsolete electronic part means an electronic part that is no longer available from the original manufacturer or an authorized aftermarket manufacturer.

Offset means a benefit or obligation agreed to by a contractor and a foreign government or international organization as an inducement or condition to purchase supplies or services pursuant to a foreign military sale (FMS). There are two types of offsets: direct offsets and indirect offsets.

(1) A direct offset involves benefits or obligations, including supplies or services that are directly related to the item(s) being purchased and are integral to the deliverable of the FMS contract. For example, as a condition of a foreign military sale, the contractor may require or agree to permit the customer to produce in its country certain components or subsystems of the item being sold. Generally, direct offsets must be performed within a specified period, because they are integral to the deliverable of the FMS contract.

(2) An indirect offset involves benefits or obligations, including supplies or services that are not directly related to the specific item(s) being purchased and are not integral to the deliverable of the FMS contract. For example, as a condition of a foreign military sale, the contractor may agree to purchase certain manufactured products, agricultural commodities, raw materials, or services, or make an equity investment or grant of equipment required by the FMS customer, or may agree to build a school, road or other facility. Indirect offsets would also include projects that are related to the FMS contract but not purchased under said contract (e.g., a project to develop or advance a capability, technology transfer, or know-how in a foreign company). Indirect offsets may be accomplished without a clearly defined period of performance.

Offset costs means the costs to the contractor of providing any direct or indirect offsets required (explicitly or implicitly) as a condition of a foreign military sale.

Original component manufacturer means an organization that designs and/or engineers a part and is entitled to any intellectual property rights to that part.

Original equipment manufacturer means a company that manufactures products that it has designed from purchased components and sells those products under the company's brand name.

Original manufacturer means the original component manufacturer, the original equipment manufacturer, or the contract manufacturer.

Procedures, Guidance, and Information (PGI) means a companion resource to the DFARS that—

(1) Contains mandatory internal DoD procedures. The DFARS will direct compliance with mandatory procedures using imperative language such as "Follow the procedures at . . ." or similar directive language;

(2) Contains non-mandatory internal DoD procedures and guidance and supplemental information to be used at the discretion of the contracting officer. The DFARS will point to non-mandatory procedures, guidance, and information using permissive language such as "The contracting officer may use . . . " or "Additional information is available at . . . " or other similar language;

(3) Is numbered similarly to the DFARS, except that each PGI numerical designation is preceded by the letters "PGI"; and

(4) Is available electronically at *http://www.acq.osd.mil/dpap/dars/index.htm*.

Senior procurement executive means, for DoD—

Department of Defense (including the defense agencies)—Under Secretary of Defense (Acquisition, Technology, and Logistics);

Department of the Army—Assistant Secretary of the Army (Acquisition, Logistics, and Technology);

Department of the Navy—Assistant Secretary of the Navy (Research, Development and Acquisition);

Department of the Air Force—Assistant Secretary of the Air Force (Acquisition).

The directors of the defense agencies have been delegated authority to act as senior procurement executive for their respective agencies, except for such actions that by terms of statute, or any delegation, must be exercised by the Under Secretary of Defense (Acquisition, Technology, and Logistics).

Sufficient non-Government sales means relevant sales data that reflects market pricing and contains enough information to make adjustments covered by FAR 15.404-1(b)(2)(ii)(B).

Suspect counterfeit electronic part means an electronic part for which credible evidence (including, but not limited to, visual inspection or testing) provides reasonable doubt that the electronic part is authentic.

Tiered evaluation of offers, also known as cascading evaluation of offers, means a procedure used in negotiated acquisitions, when market research is inconclusive for justifying limiting competition to small business concerns, whereby the contracting officer—

(1) Solicits and receives offers from both small and other than small business concerns;

(2) Establishes a tiered or cascading order of precedence for evaluating offers that is specified in the solicitation; and

(3) If no award can be made at the first tier, evaluates offers at the next lower tier, until award can be made.

Uncertified cost data means the subset of "data other than certified cost or pricing data" (see FAR 2.101) that relates to cost.

[DAC 91-1, 56 FR 67212, 12/30/91, effective 12/31/91; DAC 91-3, 57 FR 42629, 9/15/92, effective 8/31/92; DAC 91-6, 59 FR 27662, 5/27/94, effective 5/27/94; DAC 91-7, 60 FR 29491, 6/5/95, effective 5/17/95; DAC 91-9, 60 FR 61586, 11/30/95, effective 11/30/95; DAC 91-10, 61 FR 7739, 2/29/96, effective 2/29/96; DAC 91-11, 61 FR 50446, 9/26/96, effective 9/26/96; DAC 91-12, 62 FR 34114, 6/24/97, effective 6/24/97; DAC 91-13, 63 FR 11522, 3/9/98, effective 3/9/98; Final rule, 64 FR 43096, 8/9/99, effective 8/9/99; Final rule, 64 FR 51074, 9/21/99, effective 9/21/99; Final rule, 65 FR 14397, 3/16/2000, effective 3/16/2000; Final rule, 65 FR 39703, 6/27/2000, effective 6/27/2000; Final rule, 65 FR 52951, 8/31/2000, effective 8/31/2000, corrected, 65 FR 58607 9/29/2000; Final rule, 66 FR 49860, 10/1/2001, effective 10/1/2001; Final rule, 66 FR 63334, 12/6/2001, effective 12/6/2001; Final rule, 67 FR 4207,1/29/2002, effective 1/29/2002; Final rule, 68 FR 7438, 2/14/2003, effective 2/14/2003; Final rule, 68 FR 15380, 3/31/2003, effective 3/31/2003; Final rule, 68 FR 23088, 4/30/2003, effective 4/30/2003; Final rule, 68 FR 56560, 10/1/2003, effective 10/1/2003; Interim rule, 68 FR 58631, 10/10/2003, effective 1/1/2004; Interim rule, 68 FR 75196, 12/30/2003, effective 1/1/2004; Final rule, 69 FR 1926, 1/13/2004, effective 1/13/2004; Final rule, 69 FR 58353, 9/30/2004, effective 9/30/2004; Final rule, 69 FR 63326, 11/1/2004, effective 11/1/2004, finalized without change, 70 FR 20831, 4/22/2005, effective 4/22/2005; Interim rule, 71 FR 53042, 9/8/2006, effective 9/8/2006; Final rule, 72 FR 42313, 8/2/2007, effective 8/2/2007; Correction, 72 FR 46534, 8/20/2007, effective 8/20/2007; Final rule, 72 FR 51187, 9/6/2007, effective 9/6/2007; Final rule, 72 FR 61113, 11/8/2007, effective 11/8/2007; Final rule, 73 FR 53151, 9/15/2008, effective 9/15/2008; Final rule, 73 FR 70905, 11/24/2008, effective 11/24/2008; Final rule, 74 FR 2407, 1/15/2009, effective 1/15/2009; Interim rule, 74 FR 34263, 7/15/2009, effective 7/15/2009; Final rule, 74 FR 37626, 7/29/2009, effective 7/29/2009; Final rule, 74 FR 37642, 7/29/2009, effective 7/29/2009; Final rule, 74 FR 42779, 8/25/2009, effective 8/25/2009; Correction, 74 FR 44769, 8/31/2009, effective 8/31/2009; Final rule, 75 FR 51416, 8/20/2010, effective 8/20/2010; Interim rule; delay in confirmation as final, 75 FR 52650, 8/27/2010; Final rule, 76 FR 21810, 4/19/2011, effective 4/19/2011; Final rule, 76 FR 21809, 4/19/2011, effective 4/19/2011; Interim rule, 76 FR 44280, 7/25/2011, effective 7/25/2011; Final rule, 76 FR 71833, 11/18/2011, effective 11/18/2011; Final rule, 76 FR 76318, 12/7/2011, effective 12/7/2011; Final rule, 77 FR 23631, 4/20/2012, effective 4/20/2012, Final rule, 77 FR 76938, 12/31/2012, effective 1/30/2013; Interim rule, 79 FR 4631, 1/29/2014, effective 1/29/2014; Final rule, 79 FR 26091, 5/6/2014, effective 5/6/2014; Final rule, 79 FR 35699, 6/24/2014, effective 6/24/2014; Final rule, 79 FR 58693, 9/30/2014, effective 9/30/2014; Final rule, 80 FR 36903, 6/26/2015, effective 10/1/2015; Interim rule, 80 FR 51739, 8/26/2015, effective 8/26/2015; Final rule, 80 FR 67243, 10/30/2015, effective 10/30/2015; Final rule, 81 FR 42556, 6/30/2016, effective 6/30/2016; Final rule, 81 FR 50635,

8/2/2016, effective 8/2/2016; Publication notice, 20160923; Final rule, 81 FR 72986, 10/21/2016, effective 10/21/2016; Final rule, 83 FR 4431, 1/31/2018, effective 1/31/2018; Final rule, 83 FR 15994, 4/13/2018, effective 4/13/2018; Final rule, 83 FR 24895, 5/30/2018, effective 5/30/2018; Final rule, 83 FR 30825, 6/29/2018, effective 6/29/2018; Final rule, 84 FR 12137, 4/1/2019, effective 4/1/2019; Final rule, 84 FR 65304, 11/27/2019, effective 11/27/2019]

PART 203—IMPROPER BUSINESS PRACTICES AND PERSONAL CONFLICTS OF INTEREST

Table of Contents

Reporting of violations and suspected violations 203.070

Subpart 203.1—Safeguards

[Removed] 203.103
[Removed] 203.103-2
Procurement integrity 203.104
Disclosure, protection, and marking of contractor bid or proposal information and source selection information 203.104-4
[Removed] 203.104-5
[Removed] 203.104-10
Business practices 203.170
Senior DoD officials seeking employment with defense contractors 203.171
Scope 203.171-1
Definition 203.171-2
Policy 203.171-3
Contract clause 203.171-4

Subpart 203.2—[Removed]

[Removed] 203.203

Subpart 203.3—[Removed]

[Removed] 203.301

Subpart 203.4—[Removed]

[Removed] 203.405

Subpart 203.5—Other Improper Business Practices

[Removed] 203.502
Subcontractor kickbacks 203.502-2
Prohibition on persons convicted of fraud or other defense-contract-related felonies 203.570
Scope 203.570-1
Prohibition period 203.570-2
Contract clause 203.570-3
[Removed] 203.570-4
[Redesignated] 203.570-5

Subpart 203.7—Voiding and Rescinding Contracts

Authority 203.703

Subpart 203.8—Limitations on the Payment of Funds To Influence Federal Transactions

Processing suspected violations 203.806

Subpart 203.9—Whistleblower Protections for Contractor Employees

Scope of subpart 203.900
Definitions 203.901

Policy 203.903
Procedures for filing complaints 203.904
Procedures for investigating complaints 203.905
Remedies 203.906
[Removed] 203.907
Contract clause 203.970

Subpart 203.10—Contractor Code of Business Ethics and Conduct

Requirements 203.1003
Contract clauses 203.1004

Subpart 203.70—[Removed]

PART 203—IMPROPER BUSINESS PRACTICES AND PERSONAL CONFLICTS OF INTEREST

203.070 Reporting of violations and suspected violations.

Report violations and suspected violations of the following requirements in accordance with 209.406-3 or 209.407-3 and DoD 7050.5, Coordination of Remedies for Fraud and Corruption Related to Procurement Activities:

(a) Certificate of Independent Price Determination (FAR 3.103).

(b) Procurement integrity (FAR 3.104).

(c) Gratuities clause (FAR 3.203).

(d) Antitrust laws (FAR 3.303).

(e) Covenant Against Contingent Fees (FAR 3.405).

(f) Kickbacks (FAR 3.502).

(g) Prohibitions on persons convicted of defense-related contract felonies (203.570).

[Final rule, 69 FR 74989, 12/15/2004, effective 12/15/2004; Final rule, 77 FR 35879, 6/15/2012, effective 6/15/2012]

SUBPART 203.1—SAFEGUARDS

203.103 [Removed]

[Final rule, 69 FR 74989, 12/15/2004, effective 12/15/2004]

203.103-2 [Removed]

[Final rule, 64 FR 62984, 11/18/99, effective 11/18/99; Final rule, 69 FR 74989, 12/15/2004, effective 12/15/2004]

203.104 Procurement integrity. (No Text)

203.104-4 Disclosure, protection, and marking of contractor bid or proposal information and source selection information.

(d) (3) For purposes of FAR 3.104-4(d) (3) only, DoD follows the notification procedures in FAR 27.404-5(a). However, FAR 27.404-5(a) (1) does not apply to DoD.

[Interim rule, 74 FR 2408, 1/15/2009, effective 1/15/2009; Final rule, 74 FR 59913, 11/19/2009, effective 11/19/2009]

203.104-5 [Removed]

[Final rule, 62 FR 2611, 1/17/97, effective 1/17/97; Interim rule, 74 FR 2408, 1/15/2009, effective 1/15/2009; Final rule, 74 FR 59913, 11/19/2009, effective 11/19/2009]

203.104-10 [Removed]

[Final rule, 64 FR 62984, 11/18/99, effective 11/18/99; corrected 65 FR 4864, 2/1/2000; Final rule, 69 FR 74989, 12/15/2004, effective 12/15/2004]

203.170 Business practices.

To ensure the separation of functions for oversight, source selection for a major weapon system or major service acquisition.

(a) Senior leaders shall not perform multiple roles in source selection for a major weapon system or major service acquisition.

(b) Vacant acquisition positions shall be filled on an "acting" basis from below until a permanent appointment is made. To provide promising professionals an opportunity to gain experience by temporarily filling higher positions, these oversight duties shall not be accrued at the top.

(c) Acquisition process reviews of the military departments shall be conducted to assess and improve acquisition and management processes, roles, and structures. The scope of the reviews should include—

(1) Distribution of acquisition roles and responsibilities among personnel;

(2) Processes for reporting concerns about unusual or inappropriate actions; and

(3) Application of DoD Instruction 5000.2, Operation of the Defense Acquisition System, and the disciplines in the Defense Acquisition Guidebook.

(d) Source selection processes shall be—

(1) Reviewed and approved by cognizant organizations responsible for oversight;

(2) Documented by the head of the contracting activity or at the agency level; and

(3) Periodically reviewed by outside officials independent of that office or agency.

(e) Legal review of documentation of major acquisition system source selection shall be conducted prior to contract award, including the supporting documentation of the source selection evaluation board, source selection advisory council, and source selection authority.

(f) Procurement management reviews shall determine whether clearance threshold authorities are clear and that independent review is provided for acquisitions exceeding the simplified acquisition threshold.

[Final rule, 72 FR 20757, 4/26/2007, effective 4/26/2007; Final rule, 74 FR 2407, 1/15/2009, effective 1/15/2009; Final rule, 79 FR 73487, 12/11/2014, effective 12/11/2014]

203.171 Senior DoD officials seeking employment with defense contractors. (No Text)

[Interim rule, 74 FR 2408, 1/15/2009, effective 1/15/2009; Final rule, 74 FR 59913, 11/19/2009, effective 11/19/2009]

203.171-1 Scope.

This section implements Section 847 of the National Defense Authorization Act for Fiscal Year 2008 (Public Law 110-181).

[Interim rule, 74 FR 2408, 1/15/2009, effective 1/15/2009; Final rule, 74 FR 59913, 11/19/2009, effective 11/19/2009]

203.171-2 Definition.

Covered DoD official as used in this section, is defined in the clause at 252.203-7000, Requirements Relating to Compensation of Former DoD Officials.

[Interim rule, 74 FR 2408, 1/15/2009, effective 1/15/2009; Final rule, 74 FR 59913, 11/19/2009, effective 11/19/2009]

203.171-3 Policy.

(a) A DoD official covered by the requirements of Section 847 of Public Law 110-181 (a "covered DoD official") who, within 2 years after leaving DoD service, expects to receive compensation from a DoD contractor, shall, prior to accepting such compensation, request a written opinion from the appropriate DoD ethics counselor regarding the applicability of post-employment restrictions to activities that the official may undertake on behalf of a contractor.

(b) A DoD contractor may not knowingly provide compensation to a covered DoD official within 2 years after the official leaves DoD service unless the contractor first determines that the official has received, or has requested at least 30 days prior to receiving compensation from the contractor, the post-employment ethics opinion described in paragraph (a) of this section.

(c) If a DoD contractor knowingly fails to comply with the requirements of the clause at DFARS 252.203-7000, administrative and contractual actions may be taken, including cancellation of a procurement, rescission of a contract, or initiation of suspension or debarment proceedings.

[Interim rule, 74 FR 2408, 1/15/2009, effective 1/15/2009; Final rule, 74 FR 59913, 11/19/2009, effective 11/19/2009]

203.171-4 Contract clause.

(a) Use the clause at 252.203-7000, Requirements Relating to Compensation of Former DoD Officials, in all solicitations and contracts, including solicitations and contracts using FAR part 12 procedures for the acquisition of commercial items.

(b) Use the provision at 252.203-7005, Representation Relating to Compensation of Former DoD Officials, in all solicitations, including solicitations using FAR part 12 procedures for the acquisition of commercial items and solicitations for task and delivery orders.

[Interim rule, 74 FR 2408, 1/15/2009, effective 1/15/2009; Final rule, 74 FR 59913, 11/19/2009, effective 11/19/2009; Final rule, 76 FR 71826, 11/18/2011, effective 11/18/2011; Final rule, 78 FR 37980, 6/25/2013, effective 6/25/2013]

SUBPART 203.2—[REMOVED]

203.203 [Removed]

[Final rule, 64 FR 62984, 11/18/99, effective 11/18/99; Final rule, 69 FR 74989, 12/15/2004, effective 12/15/2004]

SUBPART 203.3—[REMOVED]

203.301 [Removed]

[Final rule, 64 FR 62984, 11/18/99, effective 11/18/99; Final rule, 69 FR 74989, 12/15/2004, effective 12/15/2004]

SUBPART 203.4—[REMOVED]

203.405 [Removed]

[Redesignated from 203.409, DAC 91-12, 62 FR 34114, 6/24/97, effective 6/24/97; Final rule, 64 FR 62984, 11/18/99, effective 11/18/99; Final rule, 69 FR 74989, 12/15/2004, effective 12/15/2004]

SUBPART 203.5—OTHER IMPROPER BUSINESS PRACTICES

203.502 [Removed]

[Final rule, 64 FR 62984, 11/18/99, effective 11/18/99; Final rule, 69 FR 74989, 12/15/2004, effective 12/15/2004]

203.502-2 Subcontractor kickbacks.

(h) The DoD Inspector General has designated Special Agents of the following investigative organizations as representatives for conducting inspections and audits under 41 U.S.C. chapter 87, Kickbacks:

(i) U.S. Army Criminal Investigation Command.

(ii) Naval Criminal Investigative Service.

(iii) Air Force Office of Special Investigations.

(iv) Defense Criminal Investigative Service.

[DAC 91-7, 60 FR 29491, 6/5/95, effective 5/17/95; Final rule, 69 FR 74989, 12/15/2004, effective 12/15/2004; Final rule, 77 FR 35879, 6/15/2012, effective 6/15/2012]

203.570 Prohibition on persons convicted of fraud or other defense-contract-related felonies. (No Text)

[Final rule, 69 FR 74989, 12/15/2004, effective 12/15/2004; Final rule, 71 FR 14099, 3/21/2006, effective 3/21/2006]

203.570-1 Scope.

This subpart implements 10 U.S.C. 2408. For information on 10 U.S.C. 2408, see PGI 203.570-1.

203.570-2 Prohibition period.

DoD has sole responsibility for determining the period of the prohibition described in a paragraph (b) of the clause at 252.203-7001, Prohibition on Persons Convicted of Fraud or Other Defense-Contract-Related Felonies. The prohibition period—

(a) Shall not be less than 5 years from the date of conviction unless the agency head or a designee grants a waiver in the interest of national security. Follow the waiver procedures at PGI 203.570-2(a); and

(b) May be more than 5 years from the date of conviction if the agency head or designee makes a written determination of the need for the longer period. The agency shall provide a copy of the determination to the address at PGI 203.570-2(b).

[Final rule, 64 FR 14397, 3/25/99, effective 3/25/99; Final rule, 69 FR 74989, 12/15/2004, effective 12/15/2004]

203.570-3 Contract clause.

Use the clause at 252.203-7001, Prohibition on Persons Convicted of Fraud or Other Defense-Contract-Related Felonies, in all solicitations and contracts exceeding the simplified acquisition threshold, except solicitations and contracts for commercial items.

[Final rule, 64 FR 14397, 3/25/99, effective 3/25/99; redesignated from 203.570-5, Final rule, 69 FR 74989, 12/15/2004, effective 12/15/2004]

203.570-4 [Removed]

[Final rule, 64 FR 62984, 11/18/99, effective 11/18/99; Final rule, 69 FR 74989, 12/15/2004, effective 12/15/2004]

203.570-5 [Redesignated]

[Final rule, 64 FR 14397, 3/25/99, effective 3/25/99; redesignated to 203.507-3, Final rule, 69 FR 74989, 12/15/2004, effective 12/15/2004]

SUBPART 203.7—VOIDING AND RESCINDING CONTRACTS

203.703 Authority.

The authority to act for the agency head under this subpart is limited to a level no lower than an official who is appointed by and with the advice of the Senate, without power of redelegation. For the defense agencies, for purposes of this subpart, the agency head designee is the Under Secretary of Defense (Acquisition, Technology, and Logistics).

[DAC 91-9, 60 FR 61586, 11/30/95, effective 11/30/95; Final rule, 65 FR 39703, 6/27/2000, effective 6/27/2000]

SUBPART 203.8—LIMITATIONS ON THE PAYMENT OF FUNDS TO INFLUENCE FEDERAL TRANSACTIONS

203.806 Processing suspected violations.

Report suspected violations to the address at PGI 203.8(a).

[Final rule, 77 FR 19128, 3/30/2012, effective 3/30/2012]

SUBPART 203.9—WHISTLEBLOWER PROTECTIONS FOR CONTRACTOR EMPLOYEES

203.900 Scope of subpart.

This subpart applies to DoD instead of FAR subpart 3.9.

(1) This subpart implements 10 U.S.C. 2409 as amended by section 846 of the National Defense Authorization Act for Fiscal Year 2008 (Pub. L. 110–181), section 842 of the National Defense Authorization Act for Fiscal Year 2009 (Pub. L. 110–417), and section 827 of the National Defense Authorization Act for Fiscal Year 2013 (Pub. L. 112–239).

(2) This subpart does not apply to any element of the intelligence community, as defined in 50 U.S.C. 3003(4). This subpart does not apply to any disclosure made by an employee of a contractor or subcontractor of an element of the intelligence community if such disclosure—

(i) Relates to an activity or an element of the intelligence community; or

(ii) Was discovered during contract or subcontract services provided to an element of the intelligence community.

[Interim rule, 74 FR 2410, 1/15/2009, effective 1/15/2009; Final rule, 74 FR 59914, 11/19/2009, effective 11/19/2009; Interim rule, 78 FR 59851, 9/30/2013, effective 9/30/2013; Final rule, 79 FR 11336, 2/28/2014, effective 2/28/2014]

203.901 Definition.

Abuse of authority, as used in this subpart, means an arbitrary and capricious exercise of authority that is inconsistent with the mission of DoD or the successful performance of a DoD contract.

[Interim rule, 78 FR 59851, 9/30/2013, effective 9/30/2013; Final rule, 79 FR 11336, 2/28/2014, effective 2/28/2014]

203.903 Policy.

(1) *Prohibition.* 10 U.S.C. 2409 prohibits contractors and subcontractors from discharging, demoting, or otherwise discriminating against an employee as a reprisal for disclosing, to any of the entities listed at paragraph (3) of this section, information that the employee reasonably believes is evidence of gross mismanagement of a DoD contract, a gross waste of DoD funds, an abuse of authority relating to a DoD contract, a violation of law, rule, or regulation related to a DoD contract (including the competition for or negotiation of a contract), or a substantial and specific danger to public health or safety. Such reprisal is prohibited even if it is undertaken at the request of an executive branch official, unless the request takes the form of a non-discretionary directive and is within the authority of the executive branch official making the request.

(2) *Classified information.* As provided in section 827(h) of the National Defense Authorization Act for Fiscal Year 2013, nothing in this subpart provides any rights to disclose classified information not otherwise provided by law.

(3) Entities to whom disclosure may be made:

(i) A Member of Congress or a representative of a committee of Congress.

(ii) An Inspector General that receives funding from or has oversight over contracts awarded for or on behalf of DoD.

(iii) The Government Accountability Office.

(iv) A DoD employee responsible for contract oversight or management.

(v) An authorized official of the Department of Justice or other law enforcement agency.

(vi) A court or grand jury.

(vii) A management official or other employee of the contractor or subcontractor who has the responsibility to investigate, discover, or address misconduct.

(4) *Disclosure clarified.* An employee who initiates or provides evidence of contractor or subcontractor misconduct in any judicial or administrative proceeding relating to waste, fraud, or abuse on a DoD contract shall be deemed to have made a disclosure.

(5) *Contracting officer actions.* A contracting officer who receives a complaint of reprisal of the type described in paragraph (1) of this section shall forward it to legal counsel or to the appropriate party in accordance with agency procedures.

[Interim rule, 74 FR 2410, 1/15/2009, effective 1/15/2009; Final rule, 74 FR 59914, 11/19/2009, effective 11/19/2009; Interim rule, 78 FR 59851, 9/30/2013, effective 9/30/2013; Final rule, 79 FR 11336, 2/28/2014, effective 2/28/2014; Final rule, 79 FR 23278, 4/28/2014, effective 4/28/2014]

203.904 Procedures for filing complaints.

(1) Any employee of a contractor or subcontractor who believes that he or she has been discharged, demoted, or otherwise discriminated against contrary to the policy in 203.903 may file a complaint with the Inspector General of the Department of Defense.

(2) A complaint may not be brought under this section more than three years after the date on which the alleged reprisal took place.

(3) The complaint shall be signed and shall contain—

(i) The name of the contractor;

(ii) The contract number, if known; if not, a description reasonably sufficient to identify the contract(s) involved;

(iii) The violation of law, rule, or regulation giving rise to the disclosure;

(iv) The nature of the disclosure giving rise to the discriminatory act, including the party to whom the information was disclosed; and

(v) The specific nature and date of the reprisal.

[Interim rule, 74 FR 2410, 1/15/2009, effective 1/15/2009; Final rule, 74 FR 59914, 11/19/2009, effective 11/19/2009; Interim rule, 78 FR 59851, 9/30/2013, effective 9/30/2013; Final rule, 79 FR 11336, 2/28/2014, effective 2/28/2014]

203.905 Procedures for investigating complaints.

(1) Unless the DoD Inspector General makes a determination that the complaint is frivolous, fails to allege a violation of the prohibition in 203.903, or has been previously addressed in another Federal or State judicial or administrative proceeding initiated by the complainant, the DoD Inspector General will investigate the complaint.

(2) If the DoD Inspector General investigates the complaint, the DoD Inspector General will—

(i) Notify the complainant, the contractor alleged to have committed the violation, and the head of the agency; and

(ii) Provide a written report of findings to the complainant, the contractor alleged to have committed the violation, and the head of the agency.

(3) Upon completion of the investigation, the DoD Inspector General—

(i) Either will determine that the complaint is frivolous, fails to allege a violation of the prohibition in 203.903, or has been previously addressed in another Federal or State judicial or administrative proceeding initiated by the complainant, or will submit the report addressed in paragraph (2) of this section within 180 days after receiving the complaint; and

(ii) If unable to submit a report within 180 days, will submit the report within the additional time period, up to 180 days, as agreed to by the person submitting the complaint.

(4) The DoD Inspector General may not respond to any inquiry or disclose any information from or about any person alleging the reprisal, except to the extent that such response or disclosure is—

(i) Made with the consent of the person alleging reprisal;

(ii) Made in accordance with 5 U.S.C. 552a (the Freedom of Information Act) or as required by any other applicable Federal law; or

(iii) Necessary to conduct an investigation of the alleged reprisal.

(5) The legal burden of proof specified at paragraph (e) of 5 U.S.C. 1221 (Individual Right of Action in Certain Reprisal Cases) shall be controlling for the purposes of an investigation conducted by the DoD Inspector General, decision by the head of an agency, or judicial or administrative proceeding to determine whether prohibited discrimination has occurred.

[Interim rule, 74 FR 2410, 1/15/2009, effective 1/15/2009; Final rule, 74 FR 59914, 11/19/2009, effective 11/19/2009; Interim rule, 78 FR 59851, 9/30/2013, effective 9/30/2013; Final rule, 79 FR 11336, 2/28/2014, effective 2/28/2014]

203.906 Remedies.

(1) Not later than 30 days after receiving a DoD Inspector General report in accordance with 203.905, the head of the agency shall determine whether sufficient basis exists to conclude that the contractor has subjected the complainant to a reprisal as prohibited by 203.903 and shall either issue an order denying relief or shall take one or more of the following actions:

(i) Order the contractor to take affirmative action to abate the reprisal.

(ii) Order the contractor to reinstate the person to the position that the person held before the reprisal, together with compensatory damages (including back pay), employment benefits, and other terms and conditions of employment that would apply to the person in that position if the reprisal had not been taken.

(iii) Order the contractor to pay the complainant an amount equal to the aggregate amount of all costs and expenses (including attorneys' fees and expert witnesses' fees) that were reasonably incurred by the complainant for, or in connection with, bringing the complaint regarding the reprisal, as determined by the head of the agency.

(2) If the head of the agency issues an order denying relief or has not issued an order within 210 days after the submission of the complaint or within 30 days after the expiration of an extension of time granted in accordance with 203.905(3)(ii), and there is no showing that such delay is due to the bad faith of the complainant—

(i) The complainant shall be deemed to have exhausted all administrative remedies with respect to the complaint; and

(ii) The complainant may bring a de novo action at law or equity against the contractor to seek compensatory damages and other relief available under 10 U.S.C. 2409 in the appropriate district court of the United States, which shall have jurisdiction over such an action without regard to the amount in controversy. Such an action shall, at the request of either party to the action, be tried by the court with a jury. An action under this authority may not be brought more than two years after the date on which remedies are deemed to have been exhausted.

(3) An Inspector General determination and an agency head order denying relief under paragraph (2) of this section shall be admissible in evidence in any de novo action at law or equity brought pursuant to 10 U.S.C. 2409(c).

(4) Whenever a contractor fails to comply with an order issued by the head of agency in accordance with 10 U.S.C. 2409, the head of the agency or designee shall request the Department of Justice to file an action for enforcement of such order in the United States district court for a district in which the reprisal was found to have occurred. In any action brought under this paragraph, the

court may grant appropriate relief, including injunctive relief, compensatory and exemplary damages, and reasonable attorney fees and costs. The person upon whose behalf an order was issued may also file such an action or join in an action filed by the head of the agency.

(5) Any person adversely affected or aggrieved by an order issued by the head of the agency in accordance with 10 U.S.C. 2409 may obtain judicial review of the order's conformance with the law, and the implementing regulation, in the United States Court of Appeals for a circuit in which the reprisal is alleged in the order to have occurred. No petition seeking such review may be filed more than 60 days after issuance of the order by the head of the agency or designee. Review shall conform to Chapter 7 of Title 5, Unites States Code. Filing such an appeal shall not act to stay the enforcement of the order by the head of an agency, unless a stay is specifically entered by the court.

(6) The rights and remedies provided for in this subpart may not be waived by any agreement, policy, form, or condition of employment.

[Interim rule, 74 FR 2410, 1/15/2009, effective 1/15/2009; Final rule, 74 FR 59914, 11/19/2009, effective 11/19/2009; Interim rule, 78 FR 59851, 9/30/2013, effective 9/30/2013; Final rule, 78 FR 73450, 12/6/2013, effective 12/6/2013; Final rule, 79 FR 11336, 2/28/2014, effective 2/28/2014]

203.907 [Removed]

[Interim rule, 78 FR 59851, 9/30/2013, effective 9/30/2013; Final rule, 78 FR 73450, 12/6/2013, effective 12/6/2013; Final rule, 79 FR 11336, 2/28/2014, effective 2/28/2014]

203.970 Contract clause.

Use the clause at 252.203-7002, Requirement to Inform Employees of Whistleblower Rights, in all solicitations and contracts.

[Interim rule, 74 FR 2410, 1/15/2009, effective 1/15/2009; Final rule, 74 FR 59914, 11/19/2009, effective 11/19/2009]

SUBPART 203.10—CONTRACTOR CODE OF BUSINESS ETHICS AND CONDUCT

203.1003 Requirements.

(b) *Notification of possible contractor violation.* Upon notification of a possible contractor violation of the type described in FAR 3.1003(b), coordinate the matter with the following office:

Department of Defense Office of Inspector General, Administrative Investigations Contractor Disclosure Program, 4800 Mark Center Drive, Suite 14L25, Arlington, VA 22350-1500; Toll-Free Telephone: 866-429-8011. Website: *https://www.dodig.mil/Programs/Contractor-Disclosure-Program/*.

(c) *Fraud hotline poster.* For contracts performed outside the United States, when security concerns can be appropriately demonstrated, the contracting officer may provide the contractor the option to publicize the program to contractor personnel in a manner other than public display of the poster required by 203.1004(b)(2)(ii), such as private employee written instructions and briefings.

[Final rule, 74 FR 53412, 10/19/2009, effective 10/19/2009; Final rule, 77 FR 76936, 12/31/2012, effective 12/31/2012; Final rule, 81 FR 73005, 10/21/2016, effective 10/21/2016; Final rule, 84 FR 39201, 8/9/2019, effective 8/9/2019]

203.1004 Contract clauses.

(a) Use the clause at 252.203-7003, Agency Office of the Inspector General, in solicitations and contracts, including solicitations and contracts using FAR part 12 procedures for the acquisition of commercial items, that include the FAR clause 52.203-13, Contractor Code of Business Ethics and Conduct.

(b)(2)(ii) Unless the contract is for the acquisition of a commercial item, use the clause at 252.203-7004, Display of Hotline Posters, in lieu of the clause at FAR 52.203-14, Display of Hotline Poster(s), in solicitations and contracts, if the contract value exceeds $5.5 million. If the Department of Homeland Security (DHS) provides disaster relief funds for the contract, DHS will provide information on how to obtain and display the DHS fraud hotline poster (see FAR 3.1003).

[Final rule, 73 FR 46814, 8/12/2008, effective 8/12/2008; Final rule, 74 FR 53412, 10/19/2009, effective 10/19/2009; Final rule, 75 FR 59101, 9/27/2010, effective 9/27/2010; Final rule, 76 FR 32840, 6/6/2011, effective 6/6/2011; Final rule, 76 FR 57671, 9/16/2011, effective 9/16/2011; Final rule, 78 FR 37980, 6/25/2013, effective 6/25/2013; Final rule, 80 FR 4999, 1/29/2015, effective 1/29/2015; Final rule, 80 FR 36903, 6/26/2015, effective 10/1/2015]

SUBPART 203.70—[REMOVED]

203.7000 [Removed]

[Final rule, 73 FR 46814, 8/12/2008, effective 8/12/2008]

203.7001 [Removed]

[Final rule, 73 FR 46814, 8/12/2008, effective 8/12/2008]

203.7002 [Removed]

[Final rule, 73 FR 46814, 8/12/2008, effective 8/12/2008]

PART 204—ADMINISTRATIVE AND INFORMATION MATTERS

Table of Contents

Subpart 204.1—Contract Execution

Contracting officer's signature . . . 204.101

Subpart 204.2—Contract Distribution

Procedures . . . 204.201
[Removed] . . . 204.202
Taxpayer identification information . . . 204.203
Electronic Document Access . . . 204.270
Policy . . . 204.270-1
Procedures . . . 204.270-2

Subpart 204.4—Safeguarding Classified Information Within Industry

General . . . 204.402
Responsibilities of contracting officers . . . 204.403
Contract clause . . . 204.404
Additional contract clauses . . . 204.404-70
U.S.-International Atomic Energy Agency Additional Protocol . . . 204.470
General . . . 204.470-1
National security exclusion . . . 204.470-2
Contract clause . . . 204.470-3

Subpart 204.6—Contract Reporting

General . . . 204.602
Responsibilities . . . 204.604
Reporting data . . . 204.606
[Removed] . . . 204.670

Subpart 204.8—Contract Files

Contract files . . . 204.802
Closeout of contract files . . . 204.804
[Removed] . . . 204.804-1
[Removed] . . . 204.804-2
Disposal of contract files . . . 204.805

Subpart 204.9—Taxpayer Identification Number Information

General . . . 204.902
[Removed] . . . 204.904
[Removed] . . . 204.905

Subpart 204.11—System for Award Management

Procedures . . . 204.1103
[Removed] . . . 204.1105

Subpart 204.12—Annual Representations and Certifications

Solicitation provision . . . 204.1202

Subpart 204.16—Uniform Procurement Instrument Identifiers

Policy . . . 204.1601

Procedures . . . 204.1603
Cross reference to Federal Procurement Data System . . . 204.1670
Order of application for modifications . . . 204.1671

Subpart 204.18—Commercial Government Entity Code

Procedures . . . 204.1870

Subpart 204.21—Prohibition on Contracting for Certain Telecommunications and Video Surveillance Services or Equipment

Scope of subpart . . . 204.2100
Definitions . . . 204.2101
Prohibition . . . 204.2102
Procedures . . . 204.2103
Waivers . . . 204.2104
Solicitation provisions and contract clause . . . 204.2105

Subpart 204.70—Procurement Acquisition Lead Time

Procedures . . . 204.7001

Subpart 204.71—Uniform Contract Line Item Numbering System

Scope . . . 204.7100
Definitions . . . 204.7101
Policy . . . 204.7102
Contract line items . . . 204.7103
Criteria for establishing . . . 204.7103-1
Numbering procedures . . . 204.7103-2
Contract subline items . . . 204.7104
Criteria for establishing . . . 204.7104-1
Numbering procedures . . . 204.7104-2
Contract exhibits and attachments . . . 204.7105
Contract modifications . . . 204.7106
Contract accounting classification reference number (ACRN) and agency accounting identifier (AAI) . . . 204.7107
Payment instructions . . . 204.7108
Contract clause . . . 204.7109

Subpart 204.72—Antiterrorism Awareness Training

Scope of subpart . . . 204.7200
Definition . . . 204.7201
Policy . . . 204.7202
Contract clause . . . 204.7203

Subpart 204.73—Safeguarding Covered Defense Information and Cyber Incident Reporting

Scope . . . 204.7300
Definitions . . . 204.7301
Policy . . . 204.7302
Procedures . . . 204.7303
Solicitation provision and contract clauses . . . 204.7304

Subpart 204.74—Disclosure of Information to Litigation Support Contractors

Scope of subpart 204.7400
Definitions 204.7401
Policy 204.7402
Contract clauses 204.7403

PART 204—ADMINISTRATIVE AND INFORMATION MATTERS

SUBPART 204.1—CONTRACT EXECUTION

204.101 Contracting officer's signature.

Follow the procedures at PGI 204.101 for signature of contract documents.

[Final rule, 63 FR 69005, 12/15/98, effective 12/15/98; Final rule, 71 FR 9267, 2/23/2006, effective 2/23/2006]

SUBPART 204.2—CONTRACT DISTRIBUTION

204.201 Procedures.

Follow the procedures at PGI 204.201 for the distribution of contracts and modifications.

(a) In lieu of the requirement at FAR 4.201 (a), contracting officers shall distribute one signed copy or reproduction of the signed contract to the contractor.

[DAC 91-6, 59 FR 27662, 5/27/94, effective 5/27/94; Final rule, 63 FR 31934, 6/11/98, effective 6/11/98; Final rule, 64 FR 51074, 9/21/99, effective 9/21/99; Final rule, 70 FR 58980, 10/11/2005, effective 10/11/2005; Final rule, 80 FR 58630, 9/30/2015, effective 9/30/2015]

204.202 [Removed]

[DAC 91-10, 61 FR 7739, 2/29/96, effective 2/29/96; Final rule, 63 FR 31934, 6/11/98, effective 6/11/98; Final rule, 64 FR 51074, 9/21/99, effective 9/21/99; Final rule, 64 FR 61028, 11/9/99, effective 11/9/99; Final rule, 70 FR 58980, 10/11/2005, effective 10/11/2005]

204.203 Taxpayer identification information.

(b) The procedure at FAR 4.203(b) does not apply to contracts that include the provision at FAR 52.204-7, System for Award Management. The payment office obtains the taxpayer identification number and the type of organization from the System for Award Management database.

[Final rule, 64 FR 43098, 8/9/99, effective 8/9/99; Interim rule, 68 FR 64557, 11/14/2003, effective 11/14/2003; Final rule, 70 FR 57188, 9/30/2005, effective 9/30/2005; Final rule, 78 FR 13543, 2/28/2013, effective 2/28/2013; Final rule, 78 FR 28756, 5/16/2013, effective 5/16/2013]

204.270 Electronic Document Access. (No Text)

[Final rule, 75 FR 59102, 9/27/2010, effective 9/27/2010; Final rule, 80 FR 58630, 9/30/2015, effective 9/30/2015]

204.270-1 Policy.

(a) The Electronic Data Access (EDA) system, an online repository for contractual instruments and supporting documents, is DoD's primary tool for electronic distribution of contract documents and contract data. Contract attachments shall be uploaded to EDA, except for contract attachments that are classified, are too sensitive for widespread distribution (*e.g.*, personally identifiable information and Privacy Act and Health Insurance Portability and Accountability Act, or cannot be practicably converted to electronic format (*e.g.*, samples, drawings, and models). Section J (or similar location when the Uniform Contract Format is not used) shall include the annotation "provided under separate cover" for any attachment not uploaded to EDA.

(b) Agencies are responsible for ensuring the following when posting documents, including contractual instruments, to EDA—

(1) The timely distribution of documents; and

(2) That internal controls are in place to ensure that—

(i) The electronic version of a contract document in EDA is an accurate representation of the contract; and

(ii) The contract data in EDA is an accurate representation of the underlying contract.

[Final rule, 80 FR 58630, 9/30/2015, effective 9/30/2015; Final rule, 84 FR 48510, 9/13/2019, effective 9/13/2019]

204.270-2 Procedures.

(b) The procedures at PGI 204.270-2 provide details on how to record the results of data verification in EDA. When these procedures are followed, contract documents and data in EDA are an accurate representation of the contract and therefore may be used for audit purposes.

(c) The procedures at PGI 204.270-2(c) provide details on the creation and processing of contract deficiency reports, which are used to correct problems with contracts distributed in EDA.

[Final rule, 80 FR 58630, 9/30/2015, effective 9/30/2015; Final rule, 81 FR 72738, 10/21/2016, effective 10/21/2016]

SUBPART 204.4—SAFEGUARDING CLASSIFIED INFORMATION WITHIN INDUSTRY

204.402 General.

DoD employees or members of the Armed Forces who are assigned to or visiting a contractor facility and are engaged in oversight of an acquisition program will retain control of their work products, both classified and unclassified (See PGI 204.402).

[DAC 91-2, 57 FR 14992, 4/23/92, effective 4/16/92; Final rule, 64 FR 51074, 9/21/99, effective 9/21/99; Final rule, 71 FR 9267, 2/23/2006, effective 2/23/2006; Final rule, 76 FR 76318, 12/7/2011, effective 12/7/2011]

204.403 Responsibilities of contracting officers.

(1) Contracting officers shall ensure that solicitations comply with PGI 204.403(1).

(2) For additional guidance on determining a project to be fundamental research in accordance with 252.204-7000(a)(3), see PGI 204.403(2).

[Final rule, 76 FR 76318, 12/7/2011, effective 12/7/2011; Final rule, 79 FR 56278, 9/19/2014, effective 9/19/2014]

204.404 Contract clause. (No Text)

204.404-70 Additional contract clauses.

(a) Use the clause at 252.204-7000, Disclosure of Information, in solicitations and contracts when the contractor will have access to or generate unclassified information that may be sensitive and inappropriate for release to the public.

(b) Use the clause at 252.204-7003, Control of Government Personnel Work Product, in all solicitations and contracts.

[DAC 91-2, 57 FR 14992, 4/23/92, effective 4/16/92; Final rule, 64 FR 45196, 8/19/99, effective 8/19/99; Final rule, 84 FR 12138, 4/1/2019, effective 4/1/2019]

204.470 U.S.-International Atomic Energy Agency Additional Protocol. (No Text)

[Final rule, 74 FR 2411, 1/15/2009, effective 1/15/2009]

204.470-1 General.

Under the U.S.-International Atomic Energy Agency Additional Protocol (U.S.-IAEA AP), the United States is required to declare a wide range of public and private nuclear-related activities to the IAEA and potentially provide access to IAEA inspectors for verification purposes.

[Final rule, 74 FR 2411, 1/15/2009, effective 1/15/2009]

204.470-2 National security exclusion.

(a) The U.S.-IAEA AP permits the United States unilaterally to declare exclusions from inspection requirements for activities, or locations or information associated with such activities, with direct national security significance.

(b) In order to ensure that all relevant activities are reviewed for direct national security significance, both current and former activities, and associated locations or information, are to be considered for applicability for a national security exclusion.

(c) If a DoD program manager receives notification from a contractor that the contractor is required to report any of its activities in accordance with the U.S.-IAEA AP, the program manager will—

(1) Conduct a security assessment to determine if, and by what means, access may be granted to the IAEA; or

(2) Provide written justification to the component or agency treaty office for application of the national security exclusion at that location to exclude access by the IAEA, in accordance with DoD Instruction 2060.03, Application of the National Security Exclusion to the Agreements Between the United States of America and the International Atomic Energy Agency for the Application of Safeguards in the United States of America.

[Final rule, 74 FR 2411, 1/15/2009, effective 1/15/2009]

204.470-3 Contract clause.

Use the clause at 252.204-7010, Requirement for Contractor to Notify DoD if the Contractor's Activities are Subject to Reporting Under the U.S.-International Atomic Energy Agency Additional Protocol, in solicitations and contracts for research and development or major defense acquisition programs involving—

(a) Any fissionable materials (e.g., uranium, plutonium, neptunium, thorium, americium);

(b) Other radiological source materials; or

(c) Technologies directly related to nuclear power production, including nuclear or radiological waste materials.

[Final rule, 74 FR 2411, 1/15/2009, effective 1/15/2009]

SUBPART 204.6—CONTRACT REPORTING

204.602 General.

See PGI 204.602 for additional information on the Federal Procurement Data System (FPDS) and procedures for resolving technical or policy issues relating to FPDS.

[Final rule, 74 FR 37644, 7/29/2009, effective 7/29/2009]

204.604 Responsibilities.

(1) The process for reporting contract actions to FPDS should, where possible, be automated by incorporating it into contract writing systems.

(2) Data in FPDS is stored indefinitely and is electronically retrievable. Therefore, the contracting officer may reference the contract action report (CAR) approval date in the associated Government contract file instead of including a paper copy of the electronically submitted CAR in the file. Such reference satisfies contract file documentation requirements of FAR 4.803(a).

(3) By December 15th of each year, the chief acquisition officer of each DoD component required to report its contract actions shall submit to the Director, Defense Procurement and Acquisition Policy, its annual certification and data validation results for the preceding fiscal year in accordance with the DoD Data Improvement Plan requirements at *http://www.acq.osd.mil/dpap/pdi/eb*. The Director, Defense Procurement and Acquisition Policy, will submit a consolidated DoD annual certification to the Office of Management and Budget by January 5th of each year.

[Final rule, 74 FR 37644, 7/29/2009, effective 7/29/2009]

204.606 Reporting data.

In addition to FAR 4.606, follow the procedures at PGI 204.606 for reporting data to FPDS.

[Final rule, 74 FR 37644, 7/29/2009, effective 7/29/2009]

204.670 [Removed]

[Final rule, 71 FR 44926, 8/8/2006, effective 8/8/2006; Final rule, 74 FR 37644, 7/29/2009, effective 7/29/2009]

SUBPART 204.8—CONTRACT FILES

204.802 Contract files.

(a) Any document posted to the Electronic Data Access (EDA) system is part of the contract file and is accessible by multiple parties, including the contractor. Do not include in EDA contract documents that are classified, too sensitive for widespread distribution (*e.g.*, personally identifiable information and Privacy Act and Health Insurance Portability and Accountability Act), or attachments that cannot be practicably converted to electronic format (*e.g.*, samples, drawings, and models). Inclusion of any document in EDA other than contracts, modifications, and orders is optional.

(f) A photocopy, facsimile, electronic, mechanically-applied and printed signature, seal, and date are considered to be an original signature, seal, and date.

[Final rule, 80 FR 58630, 9/30/2015, effective 9/30/2015; Final rule, 84 FR 48510, 9/13/2019, effective 9/13/2019]

204.804 Closeout of contract files.

(1) Except as provided in paragraph (3) of this section, contracting officers shall close out contracts in accordance with the procedures at PGI 204.804. The closeout date for file purposes shall be determined and documented by the procuring contracting officer.

(2) The head of the contracting activity shall assign the highest priority to closeout of contracts awarded for performance in a contingency area. Heads of contracting activities shall monitor and assess on a regular basis the progress of contingency contract closeout activities and take appropriate steps if a backlog occurs. For guidance on the planning and execution of closing out such contracts, see PGI 207.105(b)(20)(C)(8) and PGI 225.373(e).

(3)(i) In accordance with section 836 of the National Defense Authorization Act for Fiscal Year 2017 (Pub. L. 114-328) and section 824 of the National Defense Authorization Act for Fiscal Year 2018 (Pub. L. 115-91), contracting officers may close out contracts or groups of contracts through issuance of one or more modifications to such contracts without completing a reconciliation audit or other corrective action in accordance with FAR 4.804-5(a)(3) through (15), as appropriate, if each contract—

(A) Was entered into on a date that is at least 17 fiscal years before the current fiscal year;

(B) Has no further supplies or services due under the terms of the contract; and

(C) Has been determined by a contracting official, at least one level above the contracting officer, to be not otherwise reconcilable, because—

(*1*) The contract or related payment records have been destroyed or lost; or

(*2*) Although contract or related payment records are available, the time or effort required to establish the exact amount owed to the U.S. Government or amount owed to the contractor is disproportionate to the amount at issue.

(ii) Any contract or group of contracts meeting the requirements of paragraph (3)(i) of this section may be closed out through a negotiated settlement with the contractor. Except as provided in paragraph (3)(ii)(B) of this section, the contract closeout process shall include a bilateral modification of the affected contract, including those contracts that are closed out in accordance with a negotiated settlement.

(A) For a contract or groups of contracts, the contracting officer shall prepare a negotiation settlement memorandum that describes how the requirements of paragraph (3)(i) of this section have been met.

(B) For a group of contracts, a bilateral modification of at least one contract shall be made to reflect the negotiated settlement for a group of contracts, and unilateral modifications may be made, as appropriate, to other contracts in the group to reflect the negotiated settlement.

(iii) For contract closeout actions under paragraph (3) of this section, remaining contract balances—

(A) May be offset with balances in other contract line items within the same contract, regardless of the year or type of appropriation obligated to fund each contract line item and regardless of whether the appropriation obligated to fund such contract line item has closed; and

(B) May be offset with balances on other contracts, regardless of the year or type of appropriations obligated to fund each contract and regardless of whether such appropriations have closed.

(iv) USD(A&S) is authorized to waive any provision of acquisition law or regulation in order to carry out the closeout procedures authorized in paragraph (3)(i) of this section (see procedures at PGI 204.804(3)(iv)).

[Final rule, 73 FR 4113, 1/24/2008, effective 1/24/2008; Final rule, 77 FR 30366, 5/22/2012, effective 5/22/2012; Final rule, 80 FR 36900, 6/26/2015, effective 6/26/2015; Final rule, 84 FR 18153, 4/30/2019, effective 4/30/2019]

204.804-1 [Removed]

[Final rule, 64 FR 2595, 1/15/99, effective 1/15/99; Final rule, 73 FR 4113, 1/24/2008, effective 1/24/2008]

204.804-2 [Removed]

[Final rule, 73 FR 4113, 1/24/2008, effective 1/24/2008]

204.805 Disposal of contract files.

(1) The sources of the period for which contract files must be retained are General Records Schedule 3 (Procurement, Supply, and Grant Records) and General Records Schedule 6 (Accountable Officers' Accounts Records). Copies of the General Records Schedule may be obtained from the National Archives and Records Administration, Washington, DC 20408.

(2) Deviations from the periods cannot be granted by the Defense Acquisition Regulatory Council. Forward requests for deviations to both the Government Accountability and the National Archives and Records Administration.

(3) Hold completed contract files in the office responsible for maintaining them for a period of 12 months after completion. After the initial 12 month period, send the records to the local records holding or staging area until they are eligible for destruction. If no space is available locally, transfer the files to the General Services Administration Federal Records Center that services the area.

(4) Duplicate or working contract files should contain no originals of materials that properly belong in the official files. Destroy working files as soon as practicable once they are no longer needed.

(5) Retain pricing review files, containing documents related to reviews of the contractor's price proposals, subject to certified cost or pricing data (see FAR 15.403-4), for six years. If it is impossible to determine the final payment date in order to measure the six year period, retain the files for nine years.

[Final rule, 62 FR 40471, 7/29/97, effective 7/29/97; DAC 91-13, 63 FR 11522, 3/9/98, effective 3/9/98; Final rule, 71 FR 53044, 9/8/2006, effective 9/8/2006; Final rule, 77 FR 76939, 12/31/2012, effective 12/31/2012; Final rule, 80 FR 58630, 9/30/2015, effective 9/30/2015]

SUBPART 204.9—TAXPAYER IDENTIFICATION NUMBER INFORMATION

204.902 General.

(b) DoD uses the Federal Procurement Data System (FPDS) to meet these reporting requirements.

[Final rule, 64 FR 43098, 8/9/99, effective 8/9/99; Final rule, 71 FR 9267, 2/23/2006, effective 2/23/2006; Final rule, 74 FR 37644, 7/29/2009, effective 7/29/2009]

204.904 [Removed]

[Final rule, 64 FR 43098, 8/9/99, effective 8/9/99; Interim rule, 68 FR 64557, 11/14/2003, effective 11/14/2003; Final rule, 70 FR 35543, 6/21/2005, effective 6/21/2005; Final rule, 70 FR 57188, 9/30/2005, effective 9/30/2005; Final rule, 71 FR 9267, 2/23/2006, effective 2/23/2006]

204.905 [Removed]

[Final rule, 64 FR 43098, 8/9/99, effective 8/9/99; Removed by interim rule, 68 FR 64557, 11/14/2003, effective 11/14/2003; Final rule, 70 FR 57188, 9/30/2005, effective 9/30/2005]

SUBPART 204.11—SYSTEM FOR AWARD MANAGEMENT

204.1103 Procedures.

See PGI 204.1103 for helpful information on navigation and data entry in the System for Award Management (SAM) database.

(1) On contract award documents, use the contractor's legal or "doing business as" name and physical address information as recorded in the SAM database at the time of award.

(2) When making a determination to exercise an option, or at any other time before

issuing a modification other than a unilateral modification making an administrative change, ensure that—

(i) The contractor's record is active in the SAM database; and

(ii) The contractor's Data Universal Numbering System (DUNS) number, Commercial and Government Entity (CAGE) code, name, and physical address are accurately reflected in the contract document.

(3) At any time, if the DUNS number, CAGE code, contractor name, or physical address on a contract no longer matches the information on the contractor's record in the SAM database, the contracting officer shall process a novation or change-of-name agreement, or an address change, as appropriate.

(4) See PGI 204.1103 for additional requirements relating to use of information in the SAM database.

(5) On contractual documents transmitted to the payment office, provide the CAGE code, instead of the DUNS number or DUNS+4 number, in accordance with agency procedures.

[Added, interim rule, 68 FR 64557, 11/14/2003, effective 11/14/2003; Final rule, 70 FR 57188, 9/30/2005, effective 9/30/2005; Final rule, 74 FR 37642, 7/29/2009, effective 7/29/2009; Final rule, 78 FR 28756, 5/16/2013, effective 5/16/2013]

204.1105 [Removed]

[Added, interim rule, 68 FR 64557, 11/14/2003, effective 11/14/2003; Final rule, 70 FR 57188, 9/30/2005, effective 9/30/2005; Final rule, 77 FR 76936, 12/31/2012, effective 12/31/2012; Final rule, 78 FR 28756, 5/16/2013, effective 5/16/2013; Final rule, 78 FR 30232, 5/22/2013, effective 5/22/2013; Final rule, 79 FR 11341, 2/28/2014, effective 2/28/2014; Publication notice, 20151230; Final rule, 83 FR 24894, 5/30/2018, effective 5/30/2018]

SUBPART 204.12—ANNUAL REPRESENTATIONS AND CERTIFICATIONS

204.1202 Solicitation provision.

When using the provision at FAR 52.204–8, Annual Representations and Certifications—

(1) Use the provision with 252.204–7007, Alternate A, Annual Representations and Certifications; and

(2) When the provision at 52.204-7, System for Award Management, is included in the solicitation, do not include separately in the solicitation the following provisions, which are included in DFARS 252.204-7007:

(i) 252.204–7016, Covered Defense Telecommunications Equipment or Services—Representation.

(ii) 252.209-7002, Disclosure of Ownership or Control by a Foreign Government.

(iii) 252.209-7003, Reserve Officer Training Corps and Military Recruiting on Campus—Representation.

(iv) 252.216-7008, Economic Price Adjustment—Wage Rates or Material Prices Controlled by a Foreign Government—Representation.

(v) 252.225-7000, Buy American—Balance of Payments Program Certificate.

(vi) 252.225-7020, Trade Agreements Certificate.

(vii) 252.225-7031, Secondary Arab Boycott of Israel.

(viii) 252.225-7035, Buy American—Free Trade Agreements—Balance of Payments Program Certificate.

(ix) 252.225-7042, Authorization to Perform.

(x) 252.225-7049, Prohibition on Acquisition of Certain Foreign Commercial Satellite Services—Representations.

(xi) 252.225-7050, Disclosure of Ownership or Control by the Government of a Country that is a State Sponsor of Terrorism.

(xii) 252.226-7002, Representation for Demonstration Project for Contractors Employing Persons with Disabilities.

(xiii) 252.229-7012, Tax Exemptions (Italy)—Representation.

(xiv) 252.229-7013, Tax Exemptions (Spain)—Representation.

(xv) 252.247-7022, Representation of Extent of Transportation by Sea.

[Final rule, 73 FR 1822, 1/10/2008, effective 1/10/2008; Final rule, 76 FR 58140, 9/20/2011, effective 9/20/201; Final rule, 77 FR 19128, 3/30/2012, effective 3/30/2012; Final rule, 77 FR 35879, 6/15/2012, effective 6/15/2012; Final rule, 78 FR 37980, 6/25/2013, effective 6/25/2013; Final rule, 78 FR 40043, 7/3/2013, effective 7/3/2013; Interim rule, 79 FR 45661, 8/5/2014, effective 8/5/2014; Final rule, 79 FR 51264, 8/28/2014, effective 8/28/2014; Final rule, 79 FR 73488 12/11/2014, effective 12/11/2014; Final rule, 79 FR 73490 12/11/2014, effective 12/11/2014; Final rule, 80 FR 4999, 1/29/2015, effective 1/29/2015; Final rule, 83 FR 24887, 5/30/2018, effective 5/30/2018; Interim rule, 83 FR 66066, 12/21/2018, effective 12/21/2018; Final rule, 84 FR 30946, 6/28/2019, effective 6/28/2019; Interim rule, 84 FR 72231, 12/31/2019, effective 12/31/2019; Final rule, 84 FR 72554, 12/31/2019, effective 12/31/2019]

SUBPART 204.16—UNIFORM PROCUREMENT INSTRUMENT IDENTIFIERS

204.1601 Policy.

(a) *Establishment of a Procurement Instrument Identifier (PIID).* Do not reuse a PIID once it has been assigned. Do not assign the same PIID to more than one task or delivery order, even if they are issued under different base contracts or agreements.

(b) *Transition of PIID numbering.* Effective October 1, 2016, all DoD components shall comply with the PIID numbering requirements of FAR subpart 4.16 and this subpart for all new solicitations, contracts, orders, and agreements issued, and any amendments and modifications to those new actions. See also PGI 204.1601(b).

(c) *Change in the PIID after its assignment.* When a PIID is changed after contract award, the new PIID is known as a continued contract.

(i) A continued contract—

(A) Does not constitute a new procurement;

(B) Incorporates all prices, terms, and conditions of the predecessor contract effective at the time of issuance of the continued contract;

(C) Operates as a separate contract independent of the predecessor contract once issued; and

(D) Shall not be used to evade competition requirements, expand the scope of work, or extend the period of performance beyond that of the predecessor contract.

(ii) When issuing a continued contract, the contracting officer shall—

(A) Issue an administrative modification to the predecessor contract to clearly state that—

(*1*) Any future awards provided for under the terms of the predecessor contract (*e.g.*, issuance of orders or exercise of options) will be accomplished under the continued contract; and

(*2*) Supplies and services already acquired under the predecessor contract shall remain solely under that contract for purposes of Government inspection, acceptance, payment, and closeout; and

(B) Follow the procedures at PGI 204.1601(c).

[Final rule 81 FR 9783, 2/26/2016, effective 2/26/2016]

204.1603 Procedures.

(a) *Elements of a PIID.* DoD-issued PIIDs are thirteen characters in length. Use only alpha-numeric characters, as prescribed in FAR 4.1603 and this subpart. Do not use the letter I or O in any part of the PIID.

(3) *Position 9.*

(A) DoD will use three of the letters reserved for departmental or agency use in FAR 4.1603(a)(3) in this position as follows:

(*1*) Use M to identify purchase orders and task or delivery orders issued by the enterprise FedMall system.

(*2*) Use S to identify broad agency announcements.

(*3*) Use T to identify automated requests for quotations by authorized legacy contract writing systems. See PGI 204.1603(a)(3)(A)(*3*) for the list of authorized systems.

(B) Do not use other letters identified in FAR 4.1603(a)(3) as "Reserved for future Federal Governmentwide use" or "Reserved for departmental or agency use" in position 9 of the PIID.

(C) Do not use the letter C or H for contracts or agreements with provisions for orders or calls.

(4) *Positions 10 through 17.* In accordance with FAR 4.1603(a)(4), DoD-issued PIIDs shall only use positions 10 through 13 to complete the PIID. Enter the serial number of the instrument in these positions. A separate series of serial numbers may be used for any type of instrument listed in FAR 4.1603(a)(3). DoD components assign such series of PIID numbers sequentially. A DoD component may reserve blocks of numbers or alpha-numeric numbers for use by its various activities.

(b) *Elements of a supplementary PIID.* In addition to the supplementary PIID numbering procedures in FAR 4.1603(b), follow the procedures contained in paragraphs (b)(2)(ii)(*1*) and (*2*) of this section. See PGI 204.1603(b) for examples of proper supplementary PIID numbering.

(2)(ii) *Positions 2 through 6.* In accordance with FAR 4.1603(b)(2)(ii), DoD-issued supplementary PIIDs shall, for positions 2 through 6 of modifications to contracts and agreements, comply with the following:

(*1*) *Positions 2 and 3.* These two digits may be either alpha or numeric characters, except—

(*i*) Use K, L, M, N, P, and Q only in position 2, and only if the modification is issued by the Air Force and is a provisioned item order;

(*ii*) Use S only in position 2, and only to identify modifications issued to provide initial or amended shipping instructions when—

(*a*) The contract has either FOB origin or destination delivery terms; and

(*b*) The price changes;

(*iii*) Use T, U, V, W, X, or Y only in position 2, and only to identify modifications issued to provide initial or amended shipping instructions when—

(*a*) The contract has FOB origin delivery terms; and

(*b*) The price does not change; and

(*iv*) Use Z only in position 2, and only to identify a modification which definitizes a letter contract or a previously issued undefinitized modification.

(*2*) *Positions 4 through 6.* These positions are always numeric. Use a separate series of serial numbers for each type of modification listed in paragraph (b)(2)(ii) of this section.

[Final rule 81 FR 9783, 2/26/2016, effective 2/26/2016]

204.1670 Cross reference to Federal Procurement Data System.

Detailed guidance on mapping PIID and supplementary PIID numbers stored in the Electronic Data Access system to data elements reported in the Federal Procurement Data System can be found in PGI 204.1670.

[Final rule 81 FR 9783, 2/26/2016, effective 2/26/2016; Final rule, 84 FR 48510, 9/13/2019, effective 9/13/2019]

204.1671 Order of application for modifications.

(a) Circumstances may exist in which the numeric order of the modifications to a contract is not the order in which the changes to the contract actually take effect.

(b) In order to determine the sequence of modifications to a contract or order, the modifications will be applied in the following order—

(1) Modifications will be applied in order of the effective date on the modification;

(2) In the event of two or more modifications with the same effective date, modifications will be applied in signature date order; and

(3) In the event of two or more modifications with the same effective date and the

same signature date, procuring contracting office modifications will be applied in numeric order, followed by contract administration office modifications in numeric order.

[Final rule 81 FR 9783, 2/26/2016, effective 2/26/2016]

SUBPART 204.18—COMMERCIAL GOVERNMENT ENTITY CODE

204.1870 Procedures.

Follow the procedures and guidance at PGI 204-1870 concerning Commercial and Government Entity (CAGE) codes and CAGE file maintenance.

[Final rule 79 FR 73492, 12/11/2014, effective 12/11/2014]

SUBPART 204.21—PROHIBITION ON CONTRACTING FOR CERTAIN TELECOMMUNICATIONS AND VIDEO SURVEILLANCE SERVICES OR EQUIPMENT

204.2100 Scope of subpart.

This subpart implements section 1656 of the National Defense Authorization Act for Fiscal Year 2018 (Pub. L. 115–91) and section 889(a)(1)(A) of the National Defense Authorization Act for Fiscal Year 2019 (Pub. L. 115–232).

[Interim rule, 84 FR 72231, 12/31/2019, effective 12/31/2019]

204.2101 Definitions.

As used in this subpart—

Covered defense telecommunications equipment or services means—

(1) Telecommunications equipment produced by Huawei Technologies Company or ZTE Corporation, or any subsidiary or affiliate of such entities;

(2) Telecommunications services provided by such entities or using such equipment; or

(3) Telecommunications equipment or services produced or provided by an entity that the Secretary of Defense reasonably believes to be an entity owned or controlled by, or otherwise connected to, the government of a covered foreign country.

Covered foreign country means—

(1) The People's Republic of China; or

(2) The Russian Federation.

Covered missions means—

(1) The nuclear deterrence mission of DoD, including with respect to nuclear command, control, and communications, integrated tactical warning and attack assessment, and continuity of Government; or

(2) The homeland defense mission of DoD, including with respect to ballistic missile defense.

[Interim rule, 84 FR 72231, 12/31/2019, effective 12/31/2019]

204.2102 Prohibition.

(a) *Prohibited equipment, systems, or services.* In addition to the prohibition at FAR 4.2102(a), unless the covered defense telecommunications equipment or services are subject to a waiver described in 204.2104, the contracting officer shall not procure or obtain, or extend or renew a contract (e.g., exercise an option) to procure or obtain, any equipment, system, or service to carry out covered missions that uses covered defense telecommunications equipment or services as a substantial or essential component of any system, or as critical technology as part of any system.

[Interim rule, 84 FR 72231, 12/31/2019, effective 12/31/2019]

204.2103 Procedures.

(a) *Representations.*

(1)(i) If the offeror selects "does not" in response to the provision at DFARS 252.204–7016, the contracting officer may rely on the representation, unless the contracting officer has an independent reason to question the representation. If the contracting officer has a reason to question the "does not" representation in FAR 52.204–26, FAR 52.212–3(v), or 252.204–7016, then the contracting officer shall consult with the requiring activity and legal counsel.

(ii) If the offeror selects "does" in paragraph (c) of the provision at DFARS 252.204–7016, the offeror must complete the representation at DFARS 252.204–7017.

(2)(i) If the offeror selects "will not" in paragraph (d) of the provision at DFARS

252.204–7017, the contracting officer may rely on the representation, unless the contracting officer has an independent reason to question the representation. If the contracting officer has a reason to question the "will not" representation in FAR 52.204–24 or DFARS 252.204–7017, then the contracting officer shall consult with the requiring activity and legal counsel.

(ii) If an offeror selects "will" in paragraph (d) of the provision at DFARS 252.204–7017, the offeror must provide the information required by paragraph

(e) of the provision. When an offeror completes paragraph (e) of either of the provisions at FAR 52.204–24 or DFARS 252.204–7017, the contracting officer shall—

(A) Forward the offeror's representation and disclosure information to the requiring activity; and

(B) Not award to the offeror unless the requiring activity advises—

(1) For equipment, systems, or services that use covered telecommunications equipment or services as a substantial or essential component of any system, or as critical technology as part of any system, that a waiver as described at FAR 4.2104 has been granted; or

(2) For equipment, systems, or services to be used to carry out covered missions that use covered defense telecommunications equipment or services as a substantial or essential component of any system, or as critical technology as part of any system, that a waiver as described at DFARS 204.2104 has been granted.

(b) *Reporting.* If a contractor reports information to ***https://dibnet.dod.mil*** in accordance with the clause at FAR 52.204–25 or DFARS 252.204–7018, the Defense Cyber Crime Center will notify the contracting officer, who will consult with the requiring activity on how to proceed with the contract.

[Interim rule, 84 FR 72231, 12/31/2019, effective 12/31/2019]

204.2104 Waivers.

The Secretary of Defense may waive the prohibition in 204.2102(a) on a caseby-case basis for a single, one-year period, if the Secretary—

(a) Determines such waiver to be in the national security interests of the United States; and

(b) Certifies to the Congressional defense committees that—

(1) There are sufficient mitigations in place to guarantee the ability of the Secretary to carry out the covered missions; and

(2) The Secretary is removing the use of covered defense telecommunications equipment or services in carrying out such missions.

[Interim rule, 84 FR 72231, 12/31/2019, effective 12/31/2019]

204.2105 Solicitation provisions and contract clause.

(a) Use the provision at 252.204–7016, Covered Defense Telecommunications Equipment or Services—Representation, in all solicitations, including solicitations using FAR part 12 procedures for the acquisition of commercial items and, solicitations for task and delivery orders, basic ordering agreements (BOAs), orders against BOAs, blanket purchase agreements (BPAs), and calls against BPAs.

(b) Use the provision at 252.204–7017, Prohibition on the Acquisition of Covered Defense Telecommunications Equipment or Services—Representation, in all solicitations, including solicitations using FAR part 12 procedures for the acquisition of commercial items, and solicitations for task and delivery orders, BOAs, orders against BOAs, BPAs, and calls against BPAs.

(c) Use the clause at 252.204–7018, Prohibition on the Acquisition of Covered Defense Telecommunications Equipment or Services, in all solicitations and resultant awards, including solicitations and contracts using FAR part 12 procedures for the acquisition of commercial items, and solicitations and awards for task and delivery orders, BOAs, orders against BOAs, BPAs, and calls against BPAs.

[Interim rule, 84 FR 72231, 12/31/2019, effective 12/31/2019]

SUBPART 204.70—PROCUREMENT ACQUISITION LEAD TIME

204.7000 [Removed and Reserved]

[DAC 91-1, 56 FR 67212, 12/30/91, effective 12/31/91; Final rule, 68 FR 64555, 11/14/2003, effective 11/14/2003; Final rule 81 FR 9783, 2/26/2016, effective 2/26/2016]

204.7001 Procedures.

Follow the procedures at PGI 204.7001 for reporting procurement acquisition lead time milestones in the Procurement Integrated Enterprise Environment module.

[Final rule, 71 FR 27640, 5/12/2006, effective 5/12/2006; Final rule 81 FR 9783, 2/26/2016, effective 2/26/2016; Final rule, 84 FR 72563, 12/31/2019, effective 12/31/2019]

204.7002 [Removed and Reserved]

[Final rule, 65 FR 14397, 3/16/2000, effective 3/16/2000; Final rule, 68 FR 64555, 11/14/2003, effective 11/14/2003; Final rule 81 FR 9783, 2/26/2016, effective 2/26/2016]

204.7003 [Removed and Reserved]

[DAC 91-1, 56 FR 67212, 12/30/91, effective 12/31/91; DAC 91-6, 59 FR 27662, 5/27/94, effective 5/27/94; DAC 91-9, 60 FR 61586, 11/30/95, effective 11/30/95; DAC 91-11, 61 FR 50446, 9/26/96, effective 9/26/96; DAC 91-12, 62 FR 34114, 6/24/97, effective 6/24/97; Final rule, 64 FR 51074, 9/21/99, effective 9/21/99; Final rule, 65 FR 14397, 3/16/2000, effective 3/16/2000; Final rule, 65 FR 39703, 6/27/2000, effective 6/27/2000; Final rule, 68 FR 7438, 2/14/2003, effective 2/14/2003; Final rule, 68 FR 64555, 11/14/2003, effective 11/14/2003; Final rule 69 FR 63327, 11/1/2004, effective 11/1/2004; Final rule, 74 FR 37644, 7/29/2009, effective 7/29/2009; Final rule, 77 FR 35879, 6/15/2012, effective 6/15/2012; Final rule, 78 FR 30231, 5/22/2013, effective 5/22/2013; Correction, 78 FR 33993, 6/6/2013, effective 6/6/2013; Final rule, 79 FR 13568, 3/11/2014, effective 3/11/2014; Final rule 81 FR 9783, 2/26/2016, effective 2/26/2016]

204.7004 [Removed and Reserved]

[Final rule, 68 FR 64555, 11/14/2003, effective 11/14/2003; Final rule, 78 FR 30231, 5/22/2013, effective 5/22/2013; Final rule 81 FR 9783, 2/26/2016, effective 2/26/2016]

204.7005 [Removed and Reserved]

[Final rule, 68 FR 64555, 11/14/2003, effective 11/14/2003; Final rule, 69 FR 63327, 11/1/2004, effective 11/1/2004; Final rule, 72 FR 42313, 8/2/2007, effective 8/2/2007; Final rule, 73 4113, 1/24/2008, effective 1/24/2008; Final rule, 73 FR 27464, 5/13/2008, effective 5/13/2008; Final rule, 76 FR 38046, 6/29/2011, effective 6/29/2011; Final rule 81 FR 9783, 2/26/2016, effective 2/26/2016]

204.7006 [Removed and Reserved]

[Final rule, 75 FR 59102, 9/27/2010, effective 9/27/2010; Final rule 81 FR 9783, 2/26/2016, effective 2/26/2016]

204.7007 [Removed and Reserved]

[Final rule, 77 FR 30367, 5/22/2012, effective 5/22/2012; Final rule 81 FR 9783, 2/26/2016, effective 2/26/2016]

SUBPART 204.71—UNIFORM CONTRACT LINE ITEM NUMBERING SYSTEM

204.7100 Scope.

This subpart prescribes policies and procedures for assigning contract line item numbers.

204.7101 Definitions.

Accounting classification reference number (ACRN) means any combination of a two position alpha/numeric code used as a method of relating the accounting classification citation to detailed line item information contained in the schedule.

Attachment means any documentation, appended to a contract or incorporated by reference, which does not establish a requirement for deliverables.

Definitized item, as used in this subpart, means an item for which a firm price has been established in the basic contract or by modification.

Exhibit means a document, referred to in a contract, which is attached and establishes requirements for deliverables. The term shall not be used to refer to any other kind of attachment to a contract. The DD Form 1423, Contract Data Requirements List, is always an exhibit, rather than an attachment.

Nonseverable deliverable, as used in this subpart, means a deliverable item that is a single end product or undertaking, entire in nature, that cannot be feasibly subdivided into discrete elements or phases without losing its identity.

Undefinitized item, as used in this subpart, means an item for which a price has not been established in the basic contract or by modification.

[Final rule, 60 FR 34467, 7/3/95, effective 7/3/95; Final rule, 70 FR 58980, 10/11/2005, effective 10/11/2005]

204.7102 Policy.

(a) The numbering procedures of this subpart shall apply to all—

(1) Solicitations;

(2) Solicitation line and subline item numbers;

(3) Contracts as defined in FAR Subpart 2.1;

(4) Contract line and subline item numbers;

(5) Exhibits;

(6) Exhibit line items; and

(7) Any other document expected to become part of the contract.

(b) The numbering procedures are mandatory for all contracts where separate contract line item numbers are assigned, unless—

(1) The contract is an indefinite-delivery type for petroleum products against which posts, camps, and stations issue delivery orders for products to be consumed by them; or

(2) The contract is a communications service authorization issued by the Defense Information Systems Agency's Defense Information Technology Contracting Organization.

[DAC 91-1, 56 FR 67212, 12/30/91, effective 12/31/91; Final rule, 60 FR 34467, 7/3/95, effective 7/3/95; Final rule, 64 FR 61028, 11/9/99, effective 11/9/99; Final rule, 71 FR 9268, 2/23/2006, effective 2/23/2006; Final rule 77 FR 76936, 12/31/2012, effective 12/31/2012]

204.7103 Contract line items.

Follow the procedures at PGI 204.7103 for establishing contract line times.

[Final rule, 79 FR 51264, 8/28/2014, effective 8/28/2014]

204.7103-1 Criteria for establishing.

Contracts shall identify the items or services to be acquired as separate contract line items unless it is not feasible to do so.

(a) Contract line items shall have all four of the following characteristics; however, there are exceptions within the characteristics, which may make establishing a separate contract line item appropriate even though one of the characteristics appears to be missing—

(1) *Single unit price.* The item shall have a single unit price or a single total price, except—

(i) If the item is not separately priced (NSP) but the price is included in the unit price of another contract line item, enter NSP instead of the unit price;

(ii) When there are associated subline items, established for other than informational reasons, and those subline items are priced in accordance with 204.7104;

(iii) When the items or services are being acquired on a cost-reimbursement contract;

(iv) When the contract is for maintenance and repair services (e.g., a labor hour contract) and firm prices have been established for elements of the total price of an item but the actual number and quantity of the elements are not known until performance. The contracting officer may structure these contracts to reflect a firm or estimated total amount for each line item;

(v) When the contract line item is established to refer to an exhibit or an attachment (if management needs dictate that a unit price be entered, the price shall be set forth in the item description block and enclosed in parentheses); or

(vi) When the contract is an indefinite delivery type contract and provides that the price of an item shall be determined at the time a delivery order is placed and the price is influenced by such factors as the quantity ordered (*e.g.*, 10-99 $1.00, 100-249 $.98, 250+ @$.95), the destination, the FOB point, or the type of packaging required.

(2) *Separately identifiable.* A contract line item must be identified separately from any other items or services on the contract.

(i) Supplies are separately identifiable if they have no more than one—

(A) National stock number (NSN);

(B) Item description; or

(C) Manufacturer's part number.

(ii) Services are separately identifiable if they have no more than one—

(A) Scope of work; or

(B) Description of services.

(iii) This requirement does not apply if there are associated subline items, established for other than informational reasons, and those subline items include the actual detailed identification in accordance with 204.7104. Where this exception applies, use a general narrative description instead of the contract item description.

(3) *Separate delivery schedule.* Each contract line item or service shall have its own delivery schedule, period of performance, or completion date expressly stated ("as required" constitutes an expressly stated delivery term).

(i) The fact that there is more than one delivery date, destination, performance date, or performance point may be a determining factor in the decision as to whether to establish more than one contract line item.

(ii) If a contract line item has more than one destination or delivery date, the contracting officer may create individual contract line items for the different destinations or delivery dates, or may specify the different delivery dates for the units by destination in the delivery schedule.

(4) *Single accounting classification citation.*

(i) Each contract line item shall reference a single accounting classification citation except as provided in paragraph (a)(4)(ii) of this subsection.

(ii) The use of multiple accounting classification citations for a contract line item is authorized in the following situations:

(A) A single, nonseverable deliverable to be paid for with R&D or other funds properly incrementally obligated over several fiscal years in accordance with DoD policy;

(B) A single, nonseverable deliverable to be paid for with different authorizations or appropriations, such as in the acquisition of a satellite or the modification of production tooling used to produce items being acquired by several activities; or

(C) A modification to an existing contract line item for a nonseverable deliverable that results in the delivery of a modified item(s) where the item(s) and modification are to be paid for with different accounting classification citations.

(iii) When the use of multiple accounting classification citations is authorized for a single contract line item, establish informational subline items for each accounting classification citation in accordance with 204.7104-1(a).

(b) All subline items and exhibit line items under one contract line item shall be the same contract type as the contract line item.

(c) For a contract that contains a combination of fixed-price line items, time-and-materials/labor-hour line items, and/or cost-reimbursement line items, identify the contract type for each contract line item in Section B, Supplies or Services and Prices/Costs, to facilitate appropriate payment.

(d) Exhibits may be used as an alternative to putting a long list of contract line items in the schedule. If exhibits are used, create a contract line item citing the exhibit's identifier. See 204.7105.

(e) If the contract involves a test model or a first article which must be approved, establish a separate contract line item or subline item for each item of supply or service which must be approved. If the test model or first article consists of a lot composed of a mixture of items, a single line item or subline item may be used for the lot.

(f) If a supply or service involves ancillary functions, like packaging and handling, transportation, payment of state or local taxes, or use of reusable containers, and these functions are normally performed by the contractor and the contractor is normally entitled to reimbursement for performing these functions, do not establish a separate contract line item solely to account for these functions. However, do identify the functions in the contract schedule. If the offeror separately prices these functions, contracting officers may establish separate contract line items for the functions; however, the separate line items must conform to the requirements of paragraph (a) of this subsection.

(g) Certain commercial items and initial provisioning spares for weapons systems are requested and subsequently solicited using units of measure such as kit, set, or lot. However, there are times when individual items within that kit, set, or lot are not grouped and delivered in a single shipment. This creates potential contract administration issues with inspection, acceptance, and payment. In such cases, solicitations should be structured to allow offerors to provide information about products that may not have been known to the Government prior to solicitation and propose an alternate line item structure as long as the alternate is consistent with the requirements of 204.71, which provides explicit guidance on the use of contract line items and subline items, and with PGI 204.71.

[Final rule, 60 FR 34467, 7/3/95, effective 7/3/95, corrected 60 FR 43191, 8/18/95; Final rule, 70 FR 58980, 10/11/2005, effective 10/11/2005; Final rule, 76 FR 58138, 9/20/2011, effective 9/20/2011; Final rule, 79 FR 11341, 2/28/2014, effective 2/28/2014]

204.7103-2 Numbering procedures.

Follow the procedures at PGI 204.7103-2 for numbering contract line items.

[Final rule, 70 FR 58980, 10/11/2005, effective 10/11/2005]

204.7104 Contract subline items. (No Text)

204.7104-1 Criteria for establishing.

Contract subline items provide flexibility to further identify elements within a contract line item for tracking performance or simplifying administration. There are only two kinds of subline items: those which are informational in nature and those which consist of more than one item that requires separate identification.

(a) *Informational subline items.* (1) This type of subline item identifies information that relates directly to the contract line item and is an integral part of it (e.g., parts of an assembly or parts of a kit). These subline items shall not be scheduled separately for delivery, identified separately for shipment or performance, or priced separately for payment purposes.

(2) The informational subline item may include quantities, prices, or amounts, if necessary to satisfy management requirements. However, these elements shall be included within the item description in the supplies/services column and enclosed in parentheses to prevent confusing them with quantities, prices, or amounts that have contractual significance. Do not enter these elements in the quantity and price columns.

(3) Informational subline items shall be used to identify each accounting classification citation assigned to a single contract line item number when use of multiple citations is authorized (see 204.7103-1(a)(4)(ii)).

(b) *Separately identified subline items.* (1) Subline items will be used instead of contract line items to facilitate payment, delivery tracking, contract funds accounting, or other management purposes. Such subline items shall be used when items bought under one contract line item number—

(i) Are to be paid for from more than one accounting classification. A subline item shall be established for the quantity associated with the single accounting classification citation. Establish a line item rather than a subline item if it is likely that a subline item may be assigned additional accounting classification citations at a later date. Identify the funding as described in 204.7104-1(a)(3);

(ii) Are to be packaged in different sizes, each represented by its own NSN;

(iii) Have collateral costs, such as packaging costs, but those costs are not a part of the unit price of the contract line item;

(iv) Have different delivery dates or destinations or requisitions, or a combination of the three; or

(v) Identify parts of an assembly or kit which—

(A) Have to be separately identified at the time of shipment or performance; and

(B) Are separately priced.

(2) Each separately identified contract subline item shall have its own—

(i) Delivery schedule, period of performance, or completion date;

(ii) Unit price or single total price or amount (not separately priced (NSP) is acceptable as an entry for price or amount if the price is included in another subline item or a different contract line item). This requirement does not apply—

(A) If the subline item was created to refer to an exhibit or an attachment. If management needs dictate that a unit price be entered, the price shall be set forth in the item description block of the schedule and enclosed in parentheses; or

(B) In the case of indefinite delivery contracts described at 204.7103-1(a)(1)(vi).

(iii) Identification (e.g., NSN, item description, manufacturer's part number, scope of work, description of services).

(3) Unit prices and extended amounts.

(i) The unit price and total amount for all subline items may be entered at the contract line item number level if the unit price for the subline items is identical. If there is any variation, the subline item unit prices shall be entered at the subline item level only.

(ii) The unit price and extended amounts may be entered at the subline items level.

(iii) The two methods in paragraphs (b)(3)(i) and (ii) of this subsection shall not be combined in a contract line item.

(iv) When the price for items not separately priced is included in the price of another subline item or contract line item, it may be necessary to withhold payment on the priced subline item until all the related subline items that are not separately priced have been delivered. In those cases, use the clause at 252.204-7002, Payment for Subline Items Not Separately Priced.

[Final rule, 60 FR 34467, 7/3/95, effective 7/3/95; Interim rule, 68 FR 58631, 10/10/2003, effective 1/1/2004; Interim rule, 68 FR 75196, 12/30/2003, effective 1/1/2004, finalized without change, 70 FR 20831, 4/22/2005, effective 4/22/2005]

204.7104-2 Numbering procedures.

Follow the procedures at PGI 240.7104-2 for numbering contract line items.

[Final rule, 60 FR 34467, 7/3/95, effective 7/3/95; Interim rule, 68 FR 58631, 10/10/2003, effective 1/1/2004; Interim rule, 68 FR 75196, 12/30/2003, effective 1/1/2004, finalized without change, 70 FR 20831, 4/22/2005, effective 4/22/2005; Final rule, 70 FR 58980, 10/11/2005, effective 10/11/2005]

204.7105 Contract exhibits and attachments.

Follow the procedures at PGI 204.7105 for use and numbering of contract exhibits and attachments.

[Final rule, 71 FR 9268, 2/23/2006, effective 2/23/2006]

204.7106 Contract modifications.

(a) If new items are added, assign new contract line or subline item numbers or exhibit line item numbers, in accordance with the procedures established at 204.7103, 204.7104, and 204.7105.

(b) *Modifications to existing contract line items or exhibit line items.* (1) If the modification relates to existing contract line items or exhibit line items, the modification shall refer to those item numbers.

(2) If the contracting officer decides to assign new identifications to existing contract or exhibit line items, the following rules apply—

(i) *Definitized and undefinitized items.* (A) The original line item or subline item number may be used if the modification applies to the total quantity of the original line item or subline.

(B) The original line item or subline item number may be used if the modification makes only minor changes in the specifications of some of the items ordered on the original line item or subline item and the resulting changes in unit price can be averaged to provide a new single unit price for the total quantity. If the changes in the specifications make the item significantly distinguishable from the original item or the resulting changes in unit price cannot be averaged, create a new line item.

(C) If the modification affects only a partial quantity of an existing contract line item or subline item or exhibit line item and the change does not involve either the delivery date or the ship-to/mark-for data, the original contract line item or subline item or exhibit line item number shall remain with the unchanged quantity. Assign the changed quantity the next available number.

(ii) *Undefinitized items.* In addition to the rules in paragraph (b)(2)(1), the following additional rules apply to undefinitized items—

(A) If the modification is undefinitized and increases the quantity of an existing definitized item, assign the undefinitized quantity the next available number.

(B) If the modification increases the quantity of an existing undefinitized item, the original contract line item or subline item or exhibit line item may be used if the unit price for the new quantity is expected to be the same as the price for the original quantity. If the unit prices of the two quantities will be different, assign the new quantity the next available number.

(C) If the modification both affects only a partial quantity of the existing contract line item or subline item or exhibit line item and definitizes the price for the affected portion, the definitized portion shall retain the original item number. However, if the modification definitizes the price for the whole quantity of the line item, and price impact of the changed work can be apportioned equally over the whole to arrive at a new unit price, the quantity with the changes can be added into the quantity of the existing item.

(D) If the modification affects only a partial quantity of an existing contract line item or subline item or exhibit line item but does not change the delivery schedule or definitize price, the unchanged portion shall retain the original contract line item or subline item or exhibit item number. Assign the changed portion the next available number.

(3) If the modification will decrease the amount obligated—

(i) There shall be coordination between the administrative and procuring contracting offices before issuance of the modification; and

(ii) The contracting officer shall not issue the modification unless sufficient unliquidated obligation exists or the purpose is to recover monies owed to the Government.

[Final rule, 70 FR 58980, 10/11/2005, effective 10/11/2005; Final rule, 77 FR 76936, 12/31/2012, effective 12/31/2012; Final rule, 78 FR 13543, 2/28/2013, effective 2/28/2013]

204.7107 Contract accounting classification reference number (ACRN) and agency accounting identifier (AAI).

Traceability of funds from accounting systems to contract actions is accomplished using ACRNs and AAIs. Follow the procedures at PGI 204.7107 for use of ACRNs and AAIs.

[Final rule, 60 FR 34467, 7/3/95, effective 7/3/95, corrected 60 FR 43191, 8/18/95; Final rule, 70 FR 58980, 10/11/2005, effective 10/11/2005; Final rule, 74 FR 52895, 10/15/2009, effective 10/15/2009]

204.7108 Payment instructions.

Follow the procedures at PGI 204.7108 for inclusion of payment instructions in contracts.

[Final rule, 70 FR 58980, 10/11/2005, effective 10/11/2005]

204.7109 Contract clause.

Use the clause at 252.204-7006, Billing Instructions, in solicitations and contracts if Section G includes—

(a) Any of the standard payment instructions at PGI 204.7108) (d) (1) through (6); or

(b) Other payment instructions, in accordance with PGI 204.7108(d) (12), that require contractor identification of the contract line item(s) on the payment request.

[Final rule, 70 FR 58980, 10/11/2005, effective 10/11/2005; Final rule, 76 FR 58138, 9/20/2011, effective 9/20/2011; Final rule, 78 FR 37980, 6/25/2013, effective 6/25/2013; Final rule, 83 FR 24886, 5/30/2018, effective 5/30/2018]

SUBPART 204.72—ANTITERRORISM AWARENESS TRAINING

204.7200 Scope of subpart.

This subpart provides policy and guidance related to antiterrorism awareness training for contractor personnel who require routine physical access to a Federally-controlled facility or military installation.

[Final rule, 84 FR 4362, 2/15/2019, effective 2/15/2019]

204.7201 Definition.

As used in this subpart—

Military installation means a base, camp, post, station, yard, center, or other activity under the jurisdiction of the Secretary of a military department or, in the case of an activity in a foreign country, under the operational control of the Secretary of a military department or the Secretary of Defense (see 10 U.S.C. 2801(c) (4)).

[Final rule, 84 FR 4362, 2/15/2019, effective 2/15/2019]

204.7202 Policy.

It is DoD policy that—

(a) Contractor personnel who, as a condition of contract performance, require routine physical access to a Federally-controlled facility or military installation are required to complete Level I antiterrorism awareness training within 30 days of requiring access and annually thereafter; and

(b) In accordance with Department of Defense Instruction O-2000.16, Volume 1, DoD Antiterrorism (AT) Program Implementation: DoD AT Standards, Level I antiterrorism awareness training may be completed—

(1) Through a DoD-sponsored and certified computer or web-based distance learning instruction for Level I antiterrorism awareness; or

(2) Under the instruction of a qualified Level I antiterrorism awareness instructor.

[Final rule, 84 FR 4362, 2/15/2019, effective 2/15/2019]

204.7203 Contract clause.

Include the clause at 252.204-7004, DoD Antiterrorism Awareness Training for Contractors, in solicitations and contracts, including solicitations and contracts using FAR part 12 procedures for the acquisition of commercial items, when contractor personnel require routine physical access to a Federally-controlled facility or military installation.

[Final rule, 84 FR 4362, 2/15/2019, effective 2/15/2019]

SUBPART 204.73—SAFEGUARDING COVERED DEFENSE INFORMATION AND CYBER INCIDENT REPORTING

204.7300 Scope.

(a) This subpart applies to contracts and subcontracts requiring contractors and subcontractors to safeguard covered defense information that resides in or transits through covered contractor information systems by applying specified network security requirements. It also requires reporting of cyber incidents.

(b) This subpart does not abrogate any other requirements regarding contractor physical, personnel, information, technical, or general administrative security operations governing the protection of unclassified information, nor does it affect requirements of the National Industrial Security Program.

[Interim rule, 73 FR 42274, 7/21/2008, effective 7/21/2008; Final rule, 75 FR 18029, 4/8/2010, effective 4/8/2010; Final rule, 78 FR 36108, 6/17/2013, effective 6/21/2013; Final rule, 78 FR 69273, 11/18/2013, effective 11/18/2013; Interim rule, 80 FR 51739, 8/26/2015, effective 8/26/2015; Final rule, 81 FR 72986, 10/21/2016, effective 10/21/2016]

204.7301 Definitions.

As used in this subpart—

Adequate security means protective measures that are commensurate with the consequences and probability of loss, misuse, or unauthorized access to, or modification of information.

Contractor attributional/proprietary information means information that identifies the contractor(s), whether directly or indirectly, by the grouping of information that can be traced back to the contractor(s) (e.g., program description, facility locations), personally identifiable information, as well as trade secrets, commercial or financial information, or other commercially sensitive information that is not customarily shared outside of the company.

Controlled technical information means technical information with military or space application that is subject to controls on the access, use, reproduction, modification, performance, display, release, disclosure, or dissemination. Controlled technical information would meet the criteria, if disseminated, for distribution statements B through F using the criteria set forth in DoD Instruction 5230.24, Distribution Statements on Technical Documents. The term does not include information that is lawfully publicly available without restrictions.

Covered contractor information system means an unclassified information system that is owned, or operated by or for, a contractor and that processes, stores, or transmits covered defense information

Covered defense information means unclassified controlled technical information or other information (as described in the Controlled Unclassified Information (CUI) Registry at *http://www.archives.gov/cui/registry/category-list.html*) that requires safeguarding or dissemination controls pursuant to and consistent with law, regulations, and Governmentwide policies, and is—

(1) Marked or otherwise identified in the contract, task order, or delivery order and provided to the contractor by or on behalf of DoD in support of the performance of the contract; or

(2) Collected, developed, received, transmitted, used, or stored by or on behalf of the contractor in support of the performance of the contract.

Information system means a discrete set of information resources organized for the collection, processing, maintenance, use, sharing, dissemination, or disposition of information.

Media means physical devices or writing surfaces including, but not limited to, magnetic tapes, optical disks, magnetic disks, large scale integration memory chips, and printouts onto which covered defense information is recorded, stored, or printed within a covered contractor information system.

Rapidly report means within 72 hours of discovery of any cyber incident.

Technical information means technical data or computer software, as those terms are defined in the clause at DFARS 252.227-7013, Rights in Technical Data-Non Commercial Items, regardless of whether or not the clause is incorporated in this solicitation or contract. Examples of technical information include research and engineering data, engineering drawings, and associated lists, specifications, standards, process sheets, manuals, technical reports, technical orders, catalog-item identifications, data sets, studies and analyses and related information, and computer software executable code and source code.

[Interim rule, 73 FR 42274, 7/21/2008, effective 7/21/2008; Final rule, 75 FR 18029, 4/8/2010, effective 4/8/2010; Final rule, 78 FR 36108, 6/17/2013, effective 6/21/2013; Final rule, 78 FR 69273, 11/18/2013, effective 11/18/2013; Interim rule, 80 FR 51739, 8/26/2015, effective 8/26/2015; Final rule, 81 FR 72986, 10/21/2016, effective 10/21/2016]

204.7302 Policy.

(a) Contractors and subcontractors are required to provide adequate security on all covered contractor information systems.

(b) Contractors and subcontractors are required to rapidly report cyber incidents directly to DoD at *http://dibnet.dod.mil*. Subcontractors provide the incident report number automatically assigned by DoD to the prime contractor. Lower-tier subcontractors likewise report the incident report number automatically assigned by DoD to their higher-tier subcontractor, until the prime contractor is reached.

(1) If a cyber incident occurs, contractors and subcontractors submit to DoD—

(i) A cyber incident report;

(ii) Malicious software, if detected and isolated; and

(iii) Media (or access to covered contractor information systems and equipment) upon request.

(2) Contracting officers shall refer to PGI 204.7303-4(c) for instructions on contractor submissions of media and malicious software.

(c) Information shared by the contractor may include contractor attributional/proprietary information that is not customarily shared outside of the company, and that the unauthorized use or disclosure of such information could cause substantial competitive harm to the contractor that reported the information. The Government shall protect against the unauthorized use or release of information that includes contractor attributional/proprietary information.

(d) A cyber incident that is reported by a contractor or subcontractor shall not, by itself, be interpreted as evidence that the contractor or subcontractor has failed to provide adequate security on their covered contractor information systems, or has otherwise failed to meet the requirements of the clause at 252.204-7012, Safeguarding Covered Defense Information and Cyber Incident Reporting. When a cyber incident is reported, the contracting officer shall consult with the DoD component Chief Information Officer/cyber security office prior to assessing contractor compliance (see PGI 204.7303-3(a)(3)). The contracting officer shall consider such cyber incidents in the context of an overall assessment of a contractor's compliance with the requirements of the clause at 252.204-7012.

(e) Support services contractors directly supporting Government activities related to safeguarding covered defense information and cyber incident reporting (e.g., forensic analysis, damage assessment, or other services that require access to data from another contractor) are subject to restrictions on use and disclosure of reported information.

[Interim rule, 73 FR 42274, 7/21/2008, effective 7/21/2008; Final rule, 75 FR 18029, 4/8/2010, effective 4/8/2010; Final rule, 78 FR 36108, 6/17/2013, effective 6/21/2013; Final rule, 78 FR 69273, 11/18/2013, effective 11/18/2013; Final rule, 79 FR 74652, 12/16/2014, effective 12/16/2014; Interim rule, 80 FR 51739, 8/26/2015, effective 8/26/2015; Final rule, 81 FR 72986, 10/21/2016, effective 10/21/2016]

204.7303 Procedures.

Follow the procedures relating to safeguarding covered defense information at PGI 204.7303.

[Interim rule, 73 FR 42274, 7/21/2008, effective 7/21/2008; Final rule, 75 FR 18029, 4/8/2010, effective 4/8/2010; Final rule, 78 FR 36108, 6/17/2013, effective 6/21/2013; Final rule, 78 FR 69273, 11/18/2013, effective 11/18/2013; Interim rule, 79 FR 74652, 12/16/2014, effective 12/16/2014; Interim rule, 80 FR 51739, 8/26/2015, effective 8/26/2015]

204.7304 Solicitation provision and contract clauses.

(a) Use the provision at 252.204-7008, Compliance with Safeguarding Covered Defense Information Controls, in all solicitations, including solicitations using FAR part 12 procedures for the acquisition of commercial items, except for solicitations solely for the acquisition of commercially available off-the-shelf (COTS) items.

(b) Use the clause at 252.204-7009, Limitations on the Use or Disclosure of Third-Party

Contractor Reported Cyber Incident Information, in all solicitations and contracts, including solicitations and contracts using FAR part 12 procedures for the acquisition of commercial items, for services that include support for the Government's activities related to safeguarding covered defense information and cyber incident reporting.

(c) Use the clause at 252.204-7012, Safeguarding Covered Defense Information and Cyber Incident Reporting, in all solicitations and contracts, including solicitations and contracts using FAR part 12 procedures for the acquisition of commercial items, except for solicitations and contracts solely for the acquisition of COTS items.

[Interim rule, 73 FR 42274, 7/21/2008, effective 7/21/2008; Final rule, 75 FR 18029, 4/8/2010, effective 4/8/2010; Final rule, 78 FR 36108, 6/17/2013, effective 6/21/2013; Final rule, 79 FR 74652, 12/16/2014, effective 12/16/2014; Interim rule, 80 FR 51739, 8/26/2015, effective 8/26/2015; Final rule, 80 FR 56929 , 9/21/2015, effective 9/21/2015; Final rule, 81 FR 72986, 10/21/2016, effective 10/21/2016; Final rule, 82 FR 61479, 12/28/2017, effective 12/28/2017]

SUBPART 204.74—DISCLOSURE OF INFORMATION TO LITIGATION SUPPORT CONTRACTORS

204.7400 Scope of subpart.

This subpart prescribes policies and procedures for the release and safeguarding of information to litigation support contractors. It implements the requirements at 10 U.S.C. 129d.

[Interim rule, 79 FR 11337, 2/28/2014, effective 2/28/2014; Final rule, 81 FR 28724, 5/10/2016, effective 5/10/2016]

204.7401 Definitions.

As used in this subpart—

Computer software means computer programs, source code, source code listings, object code listings, design details, algorithms, processes, flow charts, formulae, and related material that would enable the software to be reproduced, recreated, or recompiled. Computer software does not include computer data bases or computer software documentation.

Litigation information means any information, including sensitive information, that is furnished to the contractor by or on behalf of the Government, or that is generated or obtained by the contractor in the performance of litigation support under a contract. The term does not include information that is lawfully, publicly available without restriction, including information contained in a publicly available solicitation.

Litigation support means administrative, technical, or professional services provided in support of the Government during or in anticipation of litigation.

Litigation support contractor means a contractor (including its experts, technical consultants, subcontractors, and suppliers) providing litigation support under a contract that contains the clause at 252.204-7014, Limitations on the Use or Disclosure of Information by Litigation Support Contractors.

Sensitive information means controlled unclassified information of a commercial, financial, proprietary, or privileged nature. The term includes technical data and computer software, but does not include information that is lawfully, publicly available without restriction.

Technical data means recorded information, regardless of the form or method of the recording, of a scientific or technical nature (including computer software documentation). The term does not include computer software or data incidental to contract administration, such as financial and/or management information.

[Interim rule, 79 FR 11337, 2/28/2014, effective 2/28/2014; Final rule, 81 FR 28724, 5/10/2016, effective 5/10/2016; Final rule, 81 FR 28724, 5/10/2016, effective 5/10/2016]

204.7402 Policy.

(a) Any release or disclosure of litigation information that includes sensitive information to a litigation support contractor, and the litigation support contractor's use and handling of such information, shall comply with the requirements of 10 U.S.C. 129d.

(b) To the maximum extent practicable, DoD will provide notice to an offeror or contractor submitting, delivering, or otherwise providing information to DoD in connection with an offer or performance of a contract that such information may be released or disclosed to litigation support contractors.

(c) Information that is publicly available without restriction, including publicly available solicitations for litigation support services, will not be protected from disclosure as litigation information.

(d) When sharing sensitive information with a litigation support contractor, contracting officers shall ensure that all other applicable requirements for handling and safeguarding the relevant types of sensitive information are included in the contract (*e.g.*, FAR subparts 4.4 and 24.1; DFARS subparts 204.4 and 224.1).

[Interim rule, 79 FR 11337, 2/28/2014, effective 2/28/2014; Final rule, 81 FR 28724, 5/10/2016, effective 5/10/2016; Final rule, 81 FR 28724, 5/10/2016, effective 5/10/2016]

204.7403 Contract clauses.

(a) Use the clause at 252.204-7014, Limitations on the Use or Disclosure of Information by Litigation Support Contractors, in all solicitations and contracts that involve litigation support services, including solicitations and contracts using FAR part 12 procedures for the acquisition of commercial items.

(b) Use the clause at 252.204-7015, Notice of Authorized Disclosure of Information for Litigation Support, in all solicitations and contracts, including solicitations and contracts using FAR part 12 procedures for the acquisition of commercial items.

[Interim rule, 79 FR 11337, 2/28/2014, effective 2/28/2014; Final rule, 79 FR 13568, 3/11/2014, effective 3/11/2014; Final rule, 81 FR 28724, 5/10/2016, effective 5/10/2016; Final rule, 84 FR 58331, 10/31/2019, effective 10/31/2019]

PART 205—PUBLICIZING CONTRACT ACTIONS

Table of Contents

Subpart 205.2—Synopses of Proposed Contract Actions

Publicizing and response time 205.203
Special situations 205.205
Notification of bundling of DoD contracts 205.205-70
Only one responsible source 205.205-71
Preparation and transmittal of synopses 205.207

Subpart 205.3—Synopses of Contract Awards

General 205.301
Announcement of contract awards 205.303

Subpart 205.4—Release of Information

Contract clause 205.470
[Removed] 205.470-1
[Removed] 205.470-2

Subpart 205.5—Paid Advertisements

Authority 205.502

SUBCHAPTER B—ACQUISITION PLANNING (Parts 205-212)

PART 205—PUBLICIZING CONTRACT ACTIONS

SUBPART 205.2—SYNOPSES OF PROPOSED CONTRACT ACTIONS

205.203 Publicizing and response time.

(b) Allow at least 45 days response time when requested by a qualifying or designated country source (as these terms are used in part 225) and the request is consistent with the Government's requirement.

(S–70) When using competitive procedures, if a solicitation allowed fewer than 30 days for receipt of offers and resulted in only one offer, the contracting officer shall resolicit, allowing an additional period of at least 30 days for receipt of offers, except as provided in 215.371-4 and 215.371-5.

[Final rule, 77 FR 39125, 6/29/2012, effective 6/29/2012]

205.205 Special situations. (No Text)

[Interim rule, 75 FR 40714, 7/13/2010, effective 7/13/2010; Final rule, 76 FR 9679, 2/22/2011, effective 2/22/2011]

205.205-70 Notification of bundling of DoD contracts.

(a) When a proposed acquisition is funded entirely using DoD funds and potentially involves bundling, the contracting officer shall, at least 30 days prior to the release of a solicitation or 30 days prior to placing an order without a solicitation, publish in FedBizOpps.gov (or any successor site) a notification of the intent to bundle the requirement. In addition, if the agency has determined that measurably substantial benefits are expected to be derived as a result of bundling, the notification shall include a brief description of those benefits (see FAR 7.107).

(b) This requirement is in addition to the notification requirements at FAR 10.001(c)(2)(i) and (ii)

[Interim rule, 75 FR 40714, 7/13/2010, effective 7/13/2010; Final rule, 76 FR 9679, 2/22/2011, effective 2/22/2011]

205.205-71 Only one responsible source.

Follow the procedures at PGI 206.302-1(d) prior to soliciting a proposal without providing for full and open competition under the authority at FAR 6.302-1.

[Final rule, 80 FR 21656, 4/20/2015, effective 4/20/2015]

205.207 Preparation and transmittal of synopses.

(a)(i) For numbering synopsis notices, follow the procedures at PGI 205.207(a)(i).

(d) For special notices for small business events, follow the procedures at PGI 205.207(d).

[Interim rule, 63 FR 41972, 8/6/98, effective 10/1/98, finalized without change, 64 FR 52670 9/30/99; Final rule, 69 FR 63327, 11/1/2004, effective 11/1/2004; Final rule, 70 FR 73148, 12/9/2005, effective 12/9/2005; Final rule, 76 FR 76318, 12/7/2011, effective 12/7/2011; Interim rule, 79 FR 61579, 10/14/2014, effective 10/14/2014; Final rule, 80 FR 15912, 3/26/2015, effective 3/26/2015]

SUBPART 205.3—SYNOPSES OF CONTRACT AWARDS

205.301 General.

(a)(S-70) Synopsis of exceptions to domestic source requirements.

(i) In accordance with 10 U.S.C. 2533a(k), contracting officers also must synopsize through the GPE, awards exceeding the simplified acquisition threshold that are for the acquisition of any clothing, fiber, yarn, or fabric items described in 225.7002-1(a)(1)(ii) through (x), if—

(A) The Secretary concerned has determined that domestic items are not available, in accordance with 225.7002-2(b); or

(B) The acquisition is for chemical warfare protective clothing, and the contracting officer has determined that an exception to domestic source requirements applies because the acquisition furthers an agreement with a qualifying country, in accordance with 225.7002-2(n).

(ii) The synopsis must be submitted in sufficient time to permit its publication not later than 7 days after contract award.

(iii) In addition to the information otherwise required in a synopsis of contract award, the synopsis must include one of the following statements as applicable:

(A) "The exception at DFARS 225.7002-2(b) applies to this acquisition, because the Secretary concerned has determined that items grown, reprocessed, reused, or produced in the United States cannot be acquired as and when needed in satisfactory quality and sufficient quantity at U.S. market prices."

(B) "The exception at DFARS 225.7002-2(n) applies to this acquisition, because the contracting officer has determined that this acquisition of chemical warfare protective clothing furthers an agreement with a qualifying country identified in DFARS 225.003(10)."

[Interim rule, 71 FR 58536, 10/4/2006, effective 10/4/2006; Final rule, 72 FR 42315, 8/2/2007, effective 8/2/2007; Final rule, 74 FR 52895, 10/15/2009, effective 10/15/2009; Final rule, 74 FR 59914, 11/19/2009, effective 11/19/2009; Interim rule, 80 FR 51739, 8/26/2015, effective 8/26/2015]

205.303 Announcement of contract awards.

(a) *Public Announcement.*

(i) The threshold for DoD awards is $7 million. Report all contractual actions, including modifications, that have a face value, excluding unexercised options, of more than $7 million.

(A) For undefinitized contractual actions, report the not-to-exceed (NTE) amount. Later, if the definitized amount exceeds the NTE amount by more than $7 million, report only the amount exceeding the NTE.

(B) For indefinite delivery, time and material, labor hour, and similar contracts, report the initial award if the estimated face value, excluding unexercised options, is more than $7 million. Do not report orders up to the estimated value, but after the estimated value is reached, report subsequent modifications and orders that have a face value of more than $7 million.

(C) Do not report the same work twice.

(ii) Departments and agencies submit the information—

(A) To the Office of the Assistant Secretary of Defense (Public Affairs);

(B) By the close of business the day before the date of the proposed award;

(C) Using report control symbol DD-LA-(AR) 1279;

(D) Including, as a minimum, the following—

(*1*) *Contract data.* Contract number, modification number, or delivery order number, face value of this action, total cumulative face value of the contract, description of what is being bought, contract type, whether any of the buy was for foreign military sales (FMS) and identification of the FMS customer;

(*2*) *Competition information.* Number of solicitations mailed and number of offers received;

(*3*) *Contractor data.* Name, address, and place of performance (if significant work is performed at a different location);

(*4*) *Funding data.* Type of appropriation and fiscal year of the funds, and whether the contract is multiyear (see FAR Subpart 17.1); and

(*5*) *Miscellaneous data.* Identification of the contracting office, the contracting office point of contact, known congressional interest, and the information release date.

(iii) Departments and agencies, in accordance with department/agency procedures and concurrent with the public announcement, shall provide information similar to that required by paragraph (a)(ii) of this section to members of Congress in whose state or district the contractor is located and the work is to be performed.

[DAC 91-1, 56 FR 67212, 12/30/91, effective 12/31/91; Final rule, 71 FR 75891, 12/19/2006, effective 12/19/2006; Final rule, 75 FR 45072, 8/2/2010, effective 10/1/2010;

Final rule, 80 FR 36903, 6/26/2015, effective 10/1/2015]

SUBPART 205.4—RELEASE OF INFORMATION

205.470 Contract clause.

Use the clause at 252.205-7000, Provision of Information to Cooperative Agreement Holders, in solicitations and contracts, including solicitations and contracts using FAR part 12 procedures for the acquisition of commercial items, that are expected to exceed $1,000,000. This clause implements 10 U.S.C. 2416.

[Final rule, 69 FR 63327, 11/1/2004, effective 11/1/2004; Interim rule, 70 FR 8536, 2/22/2005, effective 2/22/2005; Final rule without change, 70 FR 54651, 9/16/2005, effective 9/16/2005; CFR Correction, 74 FR 48170, 9/22/2009; CFR Correction, 77 FR 59339, 9/27/2012; Final rule, 78 FR 37980, 6/25/2013, effective 6/25/2013]

205.470-1 [Removed]

[Final rule, 69 FR 63327, 11/1/2004, effective 11/1/2004]

205.470-2 [Removed]

[Final rule, 69 FR 63327, 11/1/2004, effective 11/1/2004]

SUBPART 205.5—PAID ADVERTISEMENTS

205.502 Authority.

(a) *Newspapers.* Heads of contracting activities are delegated authority to approve the publication of paid advertisements in newspapers.

[Final rule, 65 FR 2056, 1/13/2000, effective 1/13/2000; Final rule, 69 FR 63327, 11/1/2004, effective 11/1/2004]

PART 206—COMPETITION REQUIREMENTS

Table of Contents

Scope of part 206.000
Applicability 206.001

Subpart 206.1—Full and Open Competition

Use of competitive procedures 206.102

Subpart 206.2—Full and Open Competition After Exclusion of Sources

Establishing or maintaining alternative sources 206.202
[Removed] 206.203

Subpart 206.3—Other Than Full and Open Competition

Circumstances permitting other than full and open competition 206.302
Only one responsible source and no other supplies or services will satisfy agency requirements 206.302-1
Unusual and compelling urgency 206.302-2
Industrial mobilization, engineering, developmental, or research capability, or expert services 206.302-3
Solicitation provision 206.302-3-70
International agreement 206.302-4
Authorized or required by statute 206.302-5
Public interest 206.302-7
Justifications 206.303
[Removed] 206.303-1
Content 206.303-2
Acquisitions in support of operations in Afghanistan 206.303-70
Approval of the justification 206.304
Availability of the justification 206.305

PART 206—COMPETITION REQUIREMENTS

206.000 Scope of part.

For information on the various approaches that may be used to competitively fulfill DoD requirements, see PGI 206.000.

[Final rule, 80 FR 21656, 4/20/2015, effective 4/20/2015]

206.001 Applicability.

(b) As authorized by 10 U.S.C. 1091, contracts awarded to individuals using the procedures at 237.104(b)(ii) are exempt from the competition requirements of FAR Part 6.

(S-70) Also excepted from this part are follow-on production contracts for products developed pursuant to the "other transactions" authority of 10 U.S.C. 2371 for prototype projects when—

(1) The other transaction agreement includes provisions for a follow-on production contract;

(2) The contracting officer receives sufficient information from the agreements officer and the project manager for the prototype other transaction agreement, which documents that the conditions set forth in 10 U.S.C. 2371 note, subsections (f)(2) (A) and (B) (see 32 CFR 3.9(d)), have been met; and

(3) The contracting officer establishes quantities and prices for the follow-on production contract that do not exceed the quantities and target prices established in the other transaction agreement.

[DAC 91-9, 60 FR 61586, 11/30/95, effective 11/30/95; Final rule, 69 FR 31907, 6/8/2004, effective 6/8/2004; Final rule, 69 FR 74990, 12/15/2004, effective 12/15/2004; Final rule, 70 FR 2361, 1/13/2005, effective 12/15/2004]

SUBPART 206.1—FULL AND OPEN COMPETITION

206.102 Use of competitive procedures.

(d) *Other competitive procedures.*

(2) In lieu of FAR 6.102(d)(2), competitive selection of science and technology proposals resulting from a broad agency announcement with peer or scientific review, as described in 235.016(a) (10 U.S.C. 2302(2)(B)).

[Final rule, 84 FR 4364, 2/15/2019, effective 2/15/2019]

SUBPART 206.2—FULL AND OPEN COMPETITION AFTER EXCLUSION OF SOURCES

206.202 Establishing or maintaining alternative sources.

(a) Agencies may use this authority to totally or partially exclude a particular source from a contract action.

(b) The determination and findings (D&F) and the documentation supporting the D&F must identify the source to be excluded from the contract action. Include the following information at PGI 206.202(b), as applicable, and any other information that may be pertinent, in the supporting documentation.

[Final rule, 69 FR 74990, 12/15/2004, effective 12/15/2004]

206.203 [Removed]

[Interim rule, 63 FR 41972, 8/6/98, effective 10/1/98, finalized without change, 64 FR 52670 9/30/99; Final rule, 76 FR 76318, 12/7/2011, effective 12/7/2011; Interim rule, 79 FR 61579, 10/14/2014, effective 10/14/2014; Final rule, 80 FR 15912, 3/26/2015, effective 3/26/2015]

SUBPART 206.3—OTHER THAN FULL AND OPEN COMPETITION

206.302 Circumstances permitting other than full and open competition. (No Text)

206.302-1 Only one responsible source and no other supplies or services will satisfy agency requirements.

(a) *Authority.*

(2)(i) Section 8059 of Pub. L. 101-511 and similar sections in subsequent defense appropriations acts, prohibit departments and agencies from entering into contracts for studies, analyses, or consulting services (see

FAR Subpart 37.2) on the basis of an unsolicited proposal without providing for full and open competition, unless—

(*1*) The head of the contracting activity, or a designee no lower than chief of the contracting office, determines that—

(*i*) Following thorough technical evaluation, only one source is fully qualified to perform the proposed work;

(*ii*) The unsolicited proposal offers significant scientific or technological promise, represents the product of original thinking, and was submitted in confidence; or

(*iii*) The contract benefits the national defense by taking advantage of a unique and significant industrial accomplishment or by ensuring financial support to a new product or idea;

(*2*) A civilian official of the DoD, whose appointment has been confirmed by the Senate, determines the award to be in the interest of national defense; or

(*3*) The contract is related to improvement of equipment that is in development or production.

(b) *Application.* This authority may be used for acquisitions of test articles and associated support services from a designated foreign source under the DoD Foreign Comparative Testing Program.

(c) *Application for brand-name descriptions.*

(2) Notwithstanding FAR 6.302-1(c)(2), in accordance with section 888(a) of the National Defense Authorization Act for Fiscal Year 2017 (Pub. L. 114-328), the justification and approval addressed in FAR 6.303 is required in order to use brand name or equal descriptions.

(d) *Limitations.* Follow the procedures at PGI 206.302-1(d) prior to soliciting a proposal without providing for full and open competition under this authority.

(S-70) *Application for proprietary specifications or standards.* In accordance with section 888(a) of the National Defense Authorization Act for Fiscal Year 2017 (Pub. L. 114-328), the justification and approval addressed in FAR 6.303 is required in order to use proprietary specifications and standards.

[DAC 91-2, 57 FR 14992, 4/23/92, effective 4/16/92; DAC 91-5, 58 FR 28458, 5/13/93, effective 4/30/93; Final rule, 69 FR 74990, 12/15/2004, effective 12/15/2004; Final rule, 80 FR 21656, 4/20/2015, effective 4/20/2015; Final rule, 84 FR 25190, 5/31/2019, effective 5/31/2019]

206.302-2 Unusual and compelling urgency.

(b) *Application.* For guidance on circumstances under which use of this authority may be appropriate, see PGI 206.302-2(b).

[Final rule, 67 FR 61516, 10/1/2002, effective 10/1/2002; Final rule, 69 FR 74990, 12/15/2004, effective 12/15/2004]

206.302-3 Industrial mobilization, engineering, developmental, or research capability, or expert services. (No Text)

206.302-3-70 Solicitation provision.

Use the provision at 252.206-7000, Domestic Source Restriction, in all solicitations that are restricted to domestic sources under the authority of FAR 6.302-3.

206.302-4 International agreement.

(c) *Limitations.* Pursuant to 10 U.S.C. 2304(f)(2)(E), the justifications and approvals described in FAR 6.303 and 6.304 are not required if the head of the contracting activity prepares a document that describes the terms of an agreement or treaty or the written directions, such as a Letter of Offer and Acceptance, that have the effect of requiring the use of other than competitive procedures for the acquisition.

[Final rule, 63 FR 67803, 12/9/98, effective 12/9/98]

206.302-5 Authorized or required by statute.

(b) *Application.*

Agencies may use this authority to—

(i) Acquire supplies and services from military exchange stores outside the United States for use by the armed forces outside the United States in accordance with 10 U.S.C. 2424(a) and subject to the limitations of 10 U.S.C. 2424(b). The limitations of 10 U.S.C. 2424(b) (1) and (2) do not apply to the purchase of soft drinks that are manufactured in the United States. For the purposes of 10 U.S.C. 2424, soft drinks manufactured in the United States are brand name carbonated sodas, manufactured in the United States, as evidenced by product markings.

(ii) Acquire police, fire protection, airfield operation, or other community services from local governments at military installations to be closed under the circumstances in 237.7401 (Section 2907 of Fiscal Year 1994 Defense Authorization Act (Pub. L. 103-160)).

(c) *Limitations.* (i) 10 U.S.C. 2361 precludes use of this exception for awards to colleges or universities for the performance of research and development, or for the construction of any research or other facility, unless—

(A) The statute authorizing or requiring award specifically—

(1) States that the statute modifies or supersedes the provisions of 10 U.S.C. 2361,

(2) Identifies the particular college or university involved, and

(3) States that award is being made in contravention of 10 U.S.C. 2361(a); and

(B) The Secretary of Defense provides Congress written notice of intent to award. The contract cannot be awarded until 180 days have elapsed since the date Congress received the notice of intent to award. Contracting activities must submit a draft notice of intent with supporting documentation through channels to the Director of Defense Procurement and Acquisition Policy, Office of the Under Secretary of Defense (Acquisition, Technology, and Logistics).

(ii) The limitation in paragraph (c)(i) of this subsection applies only if the statute authorizing or requiring award was enacted after September 30, 1989.

(iii) Subsequent statutes may provide different or additional constraints on the award of contracts to specified colleges and universities. Contracting officers should consult legal counsel on a case-by-case basis.

[DAC 91-2, 57 FR 14992, 4/23/92, effective 4/16/92; DAC 91-4, 57 FR 53598, 11/12/92, effective 10/30/92; DAC 91-5, 58 FR 28458, 5/13/93, effective 4/30/93; Interim rule, 59 FR 36088, 7/15/94, effective 7/8/94; DAC 91-7, 60 FR 29491, 6/5/95, effective 5/17/95; Interim rule, 60 FR 40106, 8/7/95, effective 8/7/95, finalized without change, DAC 91-9, 60 FR 61586, 11/30/95, effective 11/30/95; Final rule, 65 FR 39703, 6/27/2000, effective 6/27/2000; Final rule, 68 FR 7438, 2/14/2003, effective 2/14/2003]

206.302-7 Public interest.

(c) *Limitations.* For the defense agencies, the written determination to use this authority must be made by the Secretary of Defense.

206.303 Justifications. (No Text)

[Final rule, 72 FR 20758, 4/26/2007, effective 4/26/2007; Interim rule, 73 FR 53151, 9/15/2008, effective 9/15/2008; Final rule, 75 FR 18035, 4/8/2010, effective 4/8/2010]

206.303-1 [Removed]

[DAC 91-9, 60 FR 61586, 11/30/95, effective 11/30/95; Final rule, 68 FR 15615, 3/31/2003, effective 4/30/2003; Final rule, 69 FR 74990, 12/15/2004, effective 12/15/2004; Final rule, 72 FR 20758, 4/26/2007, effective 4/26/2007]

206.303-2 Content.

(b) (i) Include the information required by PGI 206.303-2(b)(i) in justifications citing the authority at FAR 6.302-1.

[Final rule, 69 FR 74990, 12/15/2004, effective 12/15/2004; Final rule, 80 FR 21656, 4/20/2015, effective 4/20/2015]

206.303-70 Acquisitions in support of operations in Afghanistan.

The justification and approval addressed in FAR 6.303 is not required for acquisitions conducted using a procedure specified in 225.7703-1(a).

[Final rule, 69 FR 74990, 12/15/2004, effective 12/15/2004; Interim rule, 73 FR 53151, 9/15/2008, effective 9/15/2008; Final rule, 75 FR 18035, 4/8/2010, effective 4/8/2010; Interim rule, 78 FR 59854, 9/30/2013, effective 9/30/2013; Final rule, 79 FR 11342, 2/28/2014, effective 2/28/2014]

206.304 Approval of the justification.

(a)(4) The Under Secretary of Defense (Acquisition, Technology, and Logistics) may delegate this authority to—

(S-70) For a noncompetitive follow-on acquisition to a previous award for the same supply or service supported by a justification for other than full and open competition citing the authority at FAR 6.302-1, follow the procedures at PGI 206.304(a)(S-70).

(A) An Assistant Secretary of Defense; or

(B) For a defense agency, an officer or employee serving in, assigned, or detailed to that agency who—

(1) If a member of the armed forces, is serving in a rank above brigadier general or rear admiral (lower half); or

(2) If a civilian, is serving in a position with a grade under the General Schedule (or any other schedule for civilian officers or employees) that is comparable to or higher than the grade of major general or rear admiral.

[Final rule, 61 FR 10285, 3/13/96, effective 4/12/96; DAC 91-11, 61 FR 50446, 9/26/96, effective 9/26/96; Final rule, 65 FR 39703, 6/27/2000, effective 6/27/2000; Final rule, 80 FR 21656, 4/20/2015, effective 4/20/2015]

206.305 Availability of the justification.

See PGI 206.305 for further guidance on the requirements for preparing, obtaining approval, and posting justification and approval documents for contracts awarded using the authority of FAR 6.302-2.

[Final rule, 80 FR 67254, 10/30/2015, effective 10/30/2015]

PART 207—ACQUISITION PLANNING

Table of Contents

Subpart 207.1—Acquisition Plans

Policy 207.102
Agency-head responsibilities 207.103
General procedures 207.104
Contents of written acquisition plans 207.105
Additional requirements for major systems 207.106
[Removed and Reserved] 207.170
[Removed] 207.170-1
[Removed] 207.170-2
[Removed] 207.170-3
Component breakout 207.171
Scope 207.171-1
Definition 207.171-2
Policy 207.171-3
Procedures 207.171-4
Human research 207.172

Subpart 207.3—Contractor Versus Government Performance

Policy 207.302

Subpart 207.4—Equipment Lease or Purchase

Acquisition considerations 207.401
Statutory requirement 207.470
Funding requirements 207.471

Subpart 207.5—Inherently Governmental Functions

Scope of subpart 207.500
Policy 207.503

Subpart 207.70—Buy-to-Budget—Additional Quantities of End Items

Definition 207.7001
Authority to acquire additional quantities of end items 207.7002
Limitation 207.7003

PART 207—ACQUISITION PLANNING

SUBPART 207.1—ACQUISITION PLANS

207.102 Policy.

(a)(1) See 212.102 regarding requirements for a written determination that the commercial item definition has been met when using FAR Part 12 procedures.

[DAC 91-9, 60 FR 61586, 11/30/95, effective 11/30/95; Final rule, 71 FR 53044, 9/8/2006, effective 9/8/2006; Final rule, 73 FR 4114, 1/24/2008, effective 1/24/2008]

207.103 Agency-head responsibilities.

(d)(i) Prepare written acquisition plans for—

(A) Acquisitions for development, as defined in FAR 35.001, when the total cost of all contracts for the acquisition program is estimated at $10 million or more;

(B) Acquisitions for production or services when the total cost of all contracts for the acquisition program is estimated at $50 million or more for all years or $25 million or more for any fiscal year; and

(C) Any other acquisition considered appropriate by the department or agency.

(ii) Written plans are not required in acquisitions for a final buy out or one-time buy. The terms "final buy out" and "one-time buy" refer to a single contract that covers all known present and future requirements. This exception does not apply to a multiyear contract or a contract with options or phases.

(e) Prepare written acquisition plans for acquisition programs meeting the thresholds of paragraphs (d)(i)(A) and (B) of this section on a program basis. Other acquisition plans may be written on either a program or an individual contract basis.

(g) The program manager, or other official responsible for the program, has overall responsibility for acquisition planning.

(h) For procurement of conventional ammunition, as defined in DoDD 5160.65, Single Manager for Conventional Ammunition (SMCA), the SMCA will review the acquisition plan to determine if it is consistent with retaining national technology and industrial base capabilities in accordance with 10 U.S.C. 2304(c)(3) and Section 806 of Public Law 105-261. The department or agency—

(i) Shall submit the acquisition plan to the address in PGI 207.103(h); and

(ii) Shall not proceed with the procurement until the SMCA provides written concurrence with the acquisition plan. In the case of a non-concurrence, the SMCA will resolve issues with the Army Office of the Executive Director for Conventional Ammunition.

[DAC 91-11, 61 FR 50446, 9/26/96, effective 9/26/96; Final rule, 66 FR 47107, 9/11/2001, effective 9/11/2001; Final rule, 67 FR 61516, 10/1/2002, effective 10/1/2002; Final rule, 68 FR 15380, 3/31/2003, effective 3/31/2003; Final rule, 71 FR 53044, 9/8/2006, effective 9/8/2006; Final rule, 71 FR 58537, 10/4/2006, effective 10/4/2006]

207.104 General procedures.

In developing an acquisition plan, agency officials shall take into account the requirement for scheduling and conducting a Peer Review in accordance with 201.170.

[DAC 91-11, 61 FR 50446, 9/26/96, effective 9/26/96; Final rule, 71 FR 53044, 9/8/2006, effective 9/8/2006; Final rule, 74 FR 37625, 7/29/2009, effective 7/29/2009]

207.105 Contents of written acquisition plans.

In addition to the requirements of FAR 7.105, planners shall follow the procedures at PGI 207.105.

[DAC 91-5, 58 FR 28458, 5/13/93, effective 4/30/93; Interim rule, 58 FR 32061, 6/8/93, effective 5/21/93; DAC 91-7, 60 FR 29491, 6/5/95, effective 5/17/95; DAC 91-9, 60 FR 61586, 11/30/95, effective 11/30/95; DAC 91-11, 61 FR 50446, 9/26/96, effective 9/26/96; Final rule, 64 FR 51074, 9/21/99, effective 9/21/99; Final rule, 65 FR 14397, 3/16/2000, effective 3/16/2000; Final rule, 65 FR 63804, 10/25/2000, effective 10/25/2000; Final rule, 67 FR 61516,

10/1/2002, effective 10/1/2002; Final rule, 69 FR 55986, 9/17/2004, effective 9/17/2004; Final rule, 70 FR 23790, 5/5/2005, effective 6/6/2005; Interim rule, 70 FR 29640, 5/24/2005, effective 5/24/2005; Final rule, 71 FR 14099, 3/21/2006, effective 3/21/2006; Final rule, 71 FR 14102, 3/21/2006, effective 3/21/2006; Final rule, 71 FR 53044, 9/8/2006, effective 9/8/2006]

207.106 Additional requirements for major systems.

(b) (1) (A) The contracting officer is prohibited by 10 U.S.C. 2305(d) (4) (A) from requiring offers for development or production of major systems that would enable the Government to use technical data to competitively reprocure identical items or components of the system if the item or component were developed exclusively at private expense, unless the contracting officer determines that—

(1) The original supplier of the item or component will be unable to satisfy program schedule or delivery requirements;

(2) Proposals by the original supplier of the item or component to meet mobilization requirements are insufficient to meet the agency's mobilization needs; or

(3) The Government is otherwise entitled to unlimited rights in technical data.

(B) If the contracting officer makes a determination, under paragraphs (b) (1) (A) *(1)* and *(2)* of this section, for a competitive solicitation, 10 U.S.C. 2305(d) (4) (B) requires that the evaluation of items developed at private expense be based on an analysis of the total value, in terms of innovative design, life-cycle costs, and other pertinent factors, of incorporating such items in the system.

(S-70) (1) In accordance with section 802(a) of the National Defense Authorization Act for Fiscal Year 2007 (Pub. L. 109-364) and DoD policy requirements, acquisition plans for major weapon systems and subsystems of major weapon systems shall—

(i) Assess the long-term technical data and computer software needs of those systems and subsystems; and

(ii) Establish acquisition strategies that provide for the technical data and computer software deliverables and associated license rights needed to sustain those systems and subsystems over their life cycle. The strategy may include—

(A) The development of maintenance capabilities within DoD; or

(B) Competition for contracts for sustainment of the systems or subsystems.

(2) Assessments and corresponding acquisition strategies developed under this section shall—

(i) Be developed before issuance of a solicitation for the weapon system or subsystem;

(ii) In accordance with 10 U.S.C. 2443, to emphasize reliability and maintainability in weapon system design, ensure that reliability and maintainability are included in the performance attributes of the key performance parameters on sustainment during the development of capabilities requirements. For additional guidance see PGI 207.105(b) (14) (ii) *(2)*;

(iii) Address the merits of including a priced contract option for the future delivery of technical data and computer software, and associated license rights, that were not acquired upon initial contract award;

(iv) Address the potential for changes in the sustainment plan over the life cycle of the weapon system or subsystem; and

(v) Apply to weapon systems and subsystems that are to be supported by performance-based logistics arrangements as well as to weapon systems and subsystems that are to be supported by other sustainment approaches.

(S-71) See 209.570 for policy applicable to acquisition strategies that consider the use of lead system integrators.

(S-72) (1) In accordance with section 202 of the Weapon Systems Acquisition Reform Act of 2009 (Pub. L. 111-23), acquisition plans for major defense acquisition programs as defined in 10 U.S.C. 2430, shall include measures that—

(i) Ensure competition, or the option of competition, at both the prime contract level and subcontract level (at such tier or tiers as are appropriate) throughout the program life cycle as a means to improve contractor performance; and

(ii) Document the rationale for the selection of the appropriate subcontract tier or tiers under paragraph (S-72)(1)(i) of this section, and the measures which will be employed to ensure competition, or the option of competition.

(2) Measures to ensure competition, or the option of competition, may include, but are not limited to, cost-effective measures intended to achieve the following:

(i) Competitive prototyping.

(ii) Dual-sourcing.

(iii) Unbundling of contracts.

(iv) Funding of next-generation prototype systems or subsystems.

(v) Use of modular, open architectures to enable competition for upgrades.

(vi) Use of build-to-print approaches to enable production through multiple sources.

(vii) Acquisition of complete technical data packages.

(viii) Periodic competitions for subsystem upgrades.

(ix) Licensing of additional suppliers.

(x) Periodic system or program reviews to address long-term competitive effects of program decisions.

(3) In order to ensure fair and objective "make-or-buy" decisions by prime contractors, acquisition strategies and resultant solicitations and contracts shall—

(i) Require prime contractors to give full and fair consideration to qualified sources other than the prime contractor for the development or construction of major subsystems and components of major weapon systems;

(ii) Provide for Government surveillance of the process by which prime contractors consider such sources and determine whether to conduct such development or construction in-house or through a subcontract; and

(iii) Provide for the assessment of the extent to which the prime contractor has given full and fair consideration to qualified sources in sourcing decisions as a part of past performance evaluations.

(4) Whenever a source-of-repair decision results in a plan to award a contract for the performance of maintenance and sustainment services on a major weapon system, to the maximum extent practicable and consistent with statutory requirements, the acquisition plan shall prescribe that award will be made on a competitive basis after giving full consideration to all sources (including sources that partner or subcontract with public or private sector repair activities).

(5) In accordance with 10 U.S.C. 2443, acquisition plans for engineering manufacturing and development and production of major systems as defined in 10 U.S.C. 2302 and 2302d and for major defense acquisition programs as defined in 202.101, shall include performance measures that are developed using best practices for responding to the positive or negative performance of a contractor for the engineering and manufacturing development or production of a weapon system, including embedded software. At a minimum the contracting officer shall—

(i) Encourage the use of incentive fees and penalties as appropriate; and

(ii) Allow the program manager or comparable requiring activity official exercising program management responsibilities, to base determinations of a contractor's performance on reliability and maintainability data collected during the program. Such data collection and associated evaluation metrics shall be described in detail in the contract; and to the maximum extent practicable, the data shall be shared with appropriate contractor and Government organizations.

(S-73) In accordance with section 815 of the National Defense Authorization Act for Fiscal Year 2009 (Pub. L. 110-417) and DoD policy requirements, acquisition plans for major weapons systems shall include a plan for the preservation and storage of special tooling associated with the production of hardware for major defense acquisition programs through the end of the service life of the related weapons system. The plan shall include the identification of any contract clauses, facilities, and funding required for the preservation and storage of such tooling. The Undersecretary of Defense for Acquisition, Technology, and Logistics (USD (AT&L)) may waive this requirement if USD (AT&L) determines that it is in the best interest of DoD.

(S-74) When selecting contract type, see 234.004 (section 811 of the National Defense Authorization Act for Fiscal Year 2013 (Pub. L. 112-239)).

[Interim rule, 72 FR 51188, 9/6/2007, effective 9/6/2007; Interim rule, 73 FR 1823, 1/10/2008, effective 1/10/2008; Final rule, 74 FR 68699, 12/29/2009, effective 12/29/2009; Interim rule, 75 FR 8272, 2/24/2010, effective 2/24/2010; Final rule, 75 FR 54524, 9/8/2010, effective 9/8/2010; Final rule, 76 FR 11361, 3/2/2011, effective 3/2/2011; Interim rule, 79 FR 4631, 1/20/2014, effective 1/29/2014; Final rule, 79 FR 58693, 9/30/2014, effective 9/30/2014; Final rule, 84 FR 58332, 10/31/2019, effective 10/31/2019]

207.170 [Removed and Reserved]

[Interim rule, 69 FR 55986, 9/17/2004, effective 9/17/2004; Final rule, 71 FR 14104, 3/21/2006, effective 3/21/2006; Final rule, 83 FR 15995, 4/13/2018, effective 4/13/2018]

207.170-1 [Removed]

[Interim rule, 69 FR 55986, 9/17/2004, effective 9/17/2004; Final rule, 71 FR 14104, 3/21/2006, effective 3/21/2006; Final rule, 83 FR 15995, 4/13/2018, effective 4/13/2018]

207.170-2 [Removed]

[Interim rule, 69 FR 55986, 9/17/2004, effective 9/17/2004; Final rule, 71 FR 14104, 3/21/2006, effective 3/21/2006; Final rule, 76 FR 23504, 4/27/2011, effective 4/27/2011; Final rule, 83 FR 15995, 4/13/2018, effective 4/13/2018]

207.170-3 [Removed]

[Interim rule, 69 FR 55986, 9/17/2004, effective 9/17/2004; Final rule, 71 FR 14104, 3/21/2006, effective 3/21/2006; Final rule, 71 FR 75891, 12/19/2006, effective 12/19/2006; Final rule, 75 FR 45072, 8/2/2010, effective 10/1/2010; Final rule, 80 FR 36903, 6/26/2015, effective 10/1/2015; Final rule, 80 FR 45899, 8/3/2015, effective 10/1/2015; Final rule, 83 FR 15995, 4/13/2018, effective 4/13/2018]

207.171 Component breakout. (No Text)

[Final rule, 71 FR 14101, 3/21/2006, effective 3/21/2006]

207.171-1 Scope.

(a) This section provides policy for breaking out components of end items for future acquisitions so that the Government can purchase the components directly from the manufacturer or supplier and furnish them to the end item manufacturer as Government-furnished material.

(b) This section does not apply to—

(1) The initial decisions on Government-furnished equipment or contractor-furnished equipment that are made at the inception of an acquisition program; or

(2) Breakout of parts for replenishment (see Appendix E).

[Final rule, 71 FR 14101, 3/21/2006, effective 3/21/2006]

207.171-2 Definition.

Component, as used in this section, includes subsystems, assemblies, subassemblies, and other major elements of an end item; it does not include elements of relatively small annual acquisition value.

[Final rule, 71 FR 14101, 3/21/2006, effective 3/21/2006]

207.171-3 Policy.

DoD policy is to break out components of weapons systems or other major end items under certain circumstances.

(a) When it is anticipated that a prime contract will be awarded without adequate price competition, and the prime contractor is expected to acquire any component without adequate price competition, the agency shall break out that component if—

(1) Substantial net cost savings probably will be achieved; and

(2) Breakout action will not jeopardize the quality, reliability, performance, or timely delivery of the end item.

(b) Even when either or both the prime contract and the component will be acquired with adequate price competition, the agency shall consider breakout of the component if substantial net cost savings will result from—

(1) Greater quantity acquisitions; or

(2) Such factors as improved logistics support (through reduction in varieties of spare parts) and economies in operations and training (through standardization of design).

(c) Breakout normally is not justified for a component that is not expected to exceed $1 million for the current year's requirement.

[Final rule, 71 FR 14101, 3/21/2006, effective 3/21/2006]

207.171-4 Procedures.

Agencies shall follow the procedures at PGI 207.171-4 for component breakout.

[Final rule, 71 FR 14101, 3/21/2006, effective 3/21/2006]

207.172 Human research.

Any DoD component sponsoring research involving human subjects—

(a) Is responsible for oversight of compliance with 32 CFR Part 219, Protection of Human Subjects; and

(b) Must have a Human Research Protection Official, as defined in the clause at 252.235-7004, Protection of Human Subjects, and identified in the DoD component's Human Research Protection Management Plan. This official is responsible for the oversight and execution of the requirements of the clause at 252.235-7004 and shall be identified in acquisition planning.

[Final rule, 74 FR 37648, 7/29/2009, effective 7/29/2009]

SUBPART 207.3—CONTRACTOR VERSUS GOVERNMENT PERFORMANCE

207.302 Policy.

See PGI 207.302 for information on the Governmentwide moratorium and restrictions on public-private competitions conducted pursuant to Office of Management and Budget (OMB) Circular A-76.

[Final rule, 81 FR 36473, 6/7/2016, effective 6/7/2016]

SUBPART 207.4—EQUIPMENT LEASE OR PURCHASE

207.401 Acquisition considerations.

If the equipment will be leased for more than 60 days, the requiring activity must prepare and provide the contracting officer with the justification supporting the decision to lease or purchase.

207.470 Statutory requirements.

(a) *Requirement for authorization of certain contracts relating to vessels, aircraft, and combat vehicles.* The contracting officer shall not enter into any contract for the lease or charter of any vessel, aircraft, or combat vehicle, or any contract for services that would require the use of the contractor's vessel, aircraft, or combat vehicle, unless the Secretary of the military department concerned has satisfied the requirements of 10 U.S.C. 2401, when—

(1) The contract will be a long-term lease or charter as defined in 10 U.S.C. 2401(d)(1); or

(2) The terms of the contract provide for a substantial termination liability as defined in 10 U.S.C. 2401(d)(2). Also see PGI 207.470.

(b) *Limitation on contracts with terms of 18 months or more.* As required by 10 U.S.C. 2401a, the contracting officer shall not enter into any contract for any vessel, aircraft, or vehicle, through a lease, charter, or similar agreement with a term of 18 months or more, or extend or renew any such contract for a term of 18 months or more, unless the head of the contracting activity has—

(1) Considered all costs of such a contract (including estimated termination liability); and

(2) Determined in writing that the contract is in the best interest of the Government.

(c) *Leasing of commercial vehicles and associated equipment.* Except as provided in paragraphs (a) and (b) of this section, the contracting officer may use leasing in the acquisition of commercial vehicles and associated equipment whenever the contracting officer determines that leasing of such vehicles is practicable and efficient (10 US.C. 2401a).

[Interim rule, 61 FR 16879, 4/18/96, effective 4/18/96; DAC 91-11, 61 FR 50446, 9/26/96, effective 9/26/96; Final rule, 74 FR 34265, 7/15/2009, effective 7/15/2009]

207.471 Funding requirements.

(a) Fund leases in accordance with DoD Financial Management Regulation (FMR) 7000.14-R, Volume 2A, Chapter 1.

(b) DoD leases are either capital leases or operating leases. See FMR 7000.14-R, Volume 4, Chapter 6, Section 060206.

(c) Use procurement funds for capital leases, as these are essentially installment purchases of property.

[Final rule, 64 FR 31732, 6/14/99, effective 6/14/99; Final rule, 66 FR 55121, 11/1/2001, effective 11/1/2001; Final rule, 71 FR 53044, 9/8/2006, effective 9/8/2006; Final rule, 76 FR 76318, 12/7/2011, effective 12/7/2011]

SUBPART 207.5—INHERENTLY GOVERNMENTAL FUNCTIONS

207.500 Scope of subpart.

This subpart also implements 10 U.S.C. 2383.

[Interim rule, 70 FR 14572, 3/23/2005, effective 3/23/2005; Final rule, 71 FR 14100, 3/21/2006, effective 3/21/2006]

207.503 Policy.

(e) The written determination required by FAR 7.503(e), that none of the functions to be performed by contract are inherently governmental—

(i) Shall be prepared using DoD Instruction 1100.22, Guidance for Determining Workforce Mix; and

(ii) Shall include a determination that none of the functions to be performed are exempt from private sector performance, as addressed in DoD Instruction 1100.22.

(S-70) Contracts for acquisition functions.

(1) In accordance with 10 U.S.C. 2383, the head of an agency may enter into a contract for performance of the acquisition functions closely associated with inherently governmental functions that are listed at FAR 7.503(d) only if—

(i) The contracting officer determines that appropriate military or civilian DoD personnel—

(A) Cannot reasonably be made available to perform the functions;

(B) Will oversee contractor performance of the contract; and

(C) Will perform all inherently governmental functions associated with the functions to be performed under the contract; and

(ii) The contracting officer ensures that the agency addresses any potential organizational conflict of interest of the contractor in the performance of the functions under the contract (see FAR Subpart 9.5).

(2) See related information at PGI 207.503(S-70).

[Interim rule, 70 FR 14572, 3/23/2005, effective 3/23/2005; Final rule, 71 FR 14100, 3/21/2006, effective 3/21/2006; Interim rule, 73 FR 1826, 1/10/2008, effective 1/10/2008]

SUBPART 207.70—BUY-TO-BUDGET - ADDITIONAL QUANTITIES OF END ITEMS

207.7001 Definition.

End item, as used in this subpart, means a production product assembled, completed, and ready for issue or deployment.

[Final rule, 69 FR 13477, 3/23/2004, effective 3/23/2004]

207.7002 Authority to acquire additional quantities of end items.

10 U.S.C. 2308 authorizes DoD to use funds available for the acquisition of an end item to acquire a higher quantity of the end item than the quantity specified in a law providing for the funding of that acquisition, if the head of an agency determines that—

(a) The agency has an established requirement for the end item that is expected to remain substantially unchanged throughout the period of the acquisition;

(b) It is possible to acquire the higher quantity of the end item without additional funding because of production efficiencies or other cost reductions;

(c) The amount of funds used for the acquisition of the higher quantity of the end item will not exceed the amount provided under that law for the acquisition of the end item; and

(d) The amount provided under that law for the acquisition of the end item is sufficient to ensure that each unit of the end item acquired within the higher quantity is fully funded as a complete end item.

[Final rule, 69 FR 13477, 3/23/2004, effective 3/23/2004]

207.7003 Limitation.

For noncompetitive acquisitions, the acquisition of additional quantities is limited to not more than 10 percent of the quantity approved in the justification and approval prepared in accordance with FAR Part 6 for the acquisition of the end item.

[Interim rule, 68 FR 43331, 7/22/2003, effective 7/22/2003; Final rule, 69 FR 13477, 3/23/2004, effective 3/23/2004]

PART 208—REQUIRED SOURCES OF SUPPLIES OR SERVICES

Table of Contents

Priorities for use of Government supply sources 208.002
[Removed] 208.003

Subpart 208.4—Federal Supply Schedules

Use of Federal Supply Schedules 208.404
[Removed] 208.404-1
[Removed] 208.404-2
[Removed] 208.404-70
Ordering procedures for Federal Supply Schedules 208.405
[Removed] 208.405-2
Limiting sources 208.405-6
[Removed] 208.405-70
Ordering activity responsibilities 208.406
Order placement 208.406-1

Subpart 208.6—Acquisition from Federal Prison Industries, Inc.

Acquisition of items for which FPI has a significant market share 208.602-70

Subpart 208.7—Acquisition from Nonprofit Agencies Employing People Who Are Blind or Severely Disabled

Procedures 208.705

Subpart 208.70—Coordinated Acquisition

Scope of subpart 208.7000
Definitions 208.7001
Assignment authority 208.7002
Acquiring department responsibilities 208.7002-1
Requiring department responsibilities 208.7002-2
Applicability 208.7003
Assignments under integrated materiel management (IMM) 208.7003-1
Assignments under coordinated acquisition 208.7003-2
Procedures 208.7004
[Removed] 208.7004-1
[Removed] 208.7004-2
[Removed] 208.7004-3
[Removed] 208.7004-4
[Removed] 208.7004-5
[Removed] 208.7004-6
[Removed] 208.7004-7
[Removed] 208.7004-8
[Removed] 208.7004-9
[Removed] 208.7004-10
Military interdepartmental purchase requests 208.7005
Coordinated acquisition assignments 208.7006

Subpart 208.71—Acquisition for National Aeronautics and Space Administration (NASA)

Authorization 208.7100
Policy 208.7101
Procedures 208.7102
[Removed] 208.7103
Changes in estimated total prices 208.7104
[Removed] 208.7105

Subpart 208.72—[Removed and Reserved]

Subpart 208.73—Use of Government-Owned Precious Metals

Definitions 208.7301
Policy 208.7302
Procedures 208.7303
Refined precious metals 208.7304
Contract clause 208.7305

Subpart 208.74—Enterprise Software Agreements

Scope of Subpart 208.7400
Definitions 208.7401
General 208.7402
Acquisition Procedures 208.7403

PART 208—REQUIRED SOURCES OF SUPPLIES OR SERVICES

208.002 Priorities for use of Government supply sources.

(a) (1) (v) See Subpart 208.70, Coordinated Acquisition, and Subpart 208.74, Enterprise Software Agreements.

[Final rule, 67 FR 65509, 10/25/2002, effective 10/25/2002; Final rule, 67 FR 77936, 12/20/2002, effective 12/20/2002; Final rule, 71 FR 39004, 7/11/2006, effective 7/11/2006]

208.003 [Removed]

[DAC 91-12, 62 FR 34114, 6/24/97, effective 6/24/97; Final rule, 67 FR 77936, 12/20/2002, effective 12/20/2002; Final rule, 71 FR 39004, 7/11/2006, effective 7/11/2006]

SUBPART 208.4—FEDERAL SUPPLY SCHEDULES

208.404 Use of Federal Supply Schedules.

(a) (i) If only one offer is received in response to an order exceeding the simplified acquisition threshold that is placed on a competitive basis, the procedures at 215.371 apply.

(ii) Departments and agencies shall comply with the review, approval, and reporting requirements established in accordance with subpart 217.7 when placing orders for supplies or services in amounts exceeding the simplified acquisition threshold.

(iii) When a schedule lists both foreign and domestic items that will meet the needs of the requiring activity, the ordering office must apply the procedures of part 225 and FAR part 25, Foreign Acquisition. When purchase of an item of foreign origin is specifically required, the requiring activity must furnish the ordering office sufficient information to permit the determinations required by part 225 and FAR part 25 to be made.

(iv) Use the provisions at 252.215-7007, Notice of Intent to Resolicit, and 252.215-7008, Only One Offer, as prescribed at 215.371-6 and 215.408(3), respectively.

[Final rule, 67 FR 65505, 10/25/2002, effective 10/25/2002; Final rule, 69 FR 63327, 11/1/2004, effective 11/1/2004; Interim rule, 70 FR 29640, 5/24/2005, effective 5/24/2005; Final rule, 71 FR 14102, 3/21/2006, effective 3/21/2006; Final rule, 71 FR 14106, 3/21/2006, effective 3/21/2006; Final rule, 77 FR 39125, 6/29/2012, effective 6/29/2012; Final rule, 78 FR 38234, 6/26/2013, effective 6/26/2013; Final rule, 80 FR 67254, 10/30/2015, effective 10/30/2015; Final rule, 83 FR 30824, 6/29/2018, effective 6/29/2018]

208.404-1 [Removed]

[Final rule, 71 FR 14106, 3/21/2006, effective 3/21/2006]

208.404-2 [Removed]

[Final rule, 71 FR 14106, 3/21/2006, effective 3/21/2006]

208.404-70 [Removed]

[Final rule, 67 FR 65505, 10/25/2002, effective 10/25/2002; Final rule, 71 FR 14106, 3/21/2006, effective 3/21/2006]

208.405 Ordering procedures for Federal Supply Schedules.

(1) Include an evaluation factor regarding supply chain risk (see subpart 239.73) when acquiring information technology, whether as a service or as a supply, that is a covered system, is a part of a covered system, or is in support of a covered system, as defined in 239.7301.

(2) See 215.101-2-70 for the limitations and prohibitions on the use of the lowest price technically acceptable source selection process, which are applicable to orders placed under Federal Supply Schedules.

(3) See 217.7801 for the prohibition on the use of reverse auctions for personal protective equipment and aviation critical safety items.

[Final rule, 71 FR 14106, 3/21/2006, effective 3/21/2006; Interim rule, 78 FR 69267, 11/18/2013, effective 11/18/2013; Final rule, 80 FR 67243, 10/30/2015, effective 10/30/2015; Final rule, 84 FR 50785, 9/26/2019, effective 10/1/2019]

208.405-2 [Removed]

[Final rule, 64 FR 2595, 1/15/99, effective 1/15/99; Final rule, 65 FR 46625, 7/31/2000, effective 7/31/2000; Final rule, 71 FR 14106, 3/21/2006, effective 3/21/2006]

208.405-6 Limiting sources.

For an order or blanket purchase agreement (BPA) exceeding the simplified acquisition threshold that is a follow-on to an order or BPA for the same supply or service previously issued based on a limiting sources justification citing the authority at FAR 8.405-6(a)(1)(i)(B) or (C), follow the procedures at PGI 208.405-6.

[Final rule, 80 FR 21656, 4/20/2015, effective 4/20/2015]

208.405-70 [Removed]

[Final rule, 71 FR 14106, 3/21/2006, effective 3/21/2006; Final rule, 75 FR 45072, 8/2/2010, effective 10/1/2010; Final rule, 77 FR 39125, 6/29/2012, effective 6/29/2012; Final rule, 78 FR 38234, 6/26/2013, effective 6/26/2013]

208.406 Ordering activity responsibilities. (No Text)

[Final rule, 71 FR 14106, 3/21/2006, effective 3/21/2006]

208.406-1 Order placement.

Follow the procedures at PGI 208.406-1 when ordering from schedules.

[Final rule, 71 FR 14106, 3/21/2006, effective 3/21/2006]

SUBPART 208.6—ACQUISITION FROM FEDERAL PRISON INDUSTRIES, INC.

208.602-70 Acquisition of items for which FPI has a significant market share.

(a) *Scope.* This subsection implements Section 827 of the National Defense Authorization Act for Fiscal Year 2008 (Pub. L. 110-181).

(b) *Definition. Item for which FPI has a significant market share,* as used in this subsection, means an item for which FPI's share of the DoD market for the federal supply class including that item is greater than 5 percent, as determined by DoD in consultation with the Office of Federal Procurement Policy. A list of the federal supply classes of items for which FPI has a significant market share is maintained at *http://www.acq.osd.mil/dpap/cpic/cp/specific_policy_areas.html#federal_prison.*

(c) *Policy.*

(1) When acquiring an item for which FPI has a significant market share—

(i) Acquire the item using—

(A) Competitive procedures (e.g., the procedures in FAR 6.102, the set-aside procedures in FAR Subpart 19.5, or competition conducted in accordance with FAR Part 13); or

(B) The fair opportunity procedures in FAR 16.505, if placing an order under a multiple award delivery-order contract; and

(ii) Include FPI in the solicitation process, consider a timely offer from FPI, and make an award in accordance with the policy at FAR 8.602(a)(4)(ii) through (v).

(2) When acquiring an item for which FPI does not have a significant market share, acquire the item in accordance with the policy at FAR 8.602.

[Interim rule, 73 FR 46816, 8/12/2008, effective 8/12/2008; Final rule, 74 FR 59914, 11/19/2009, effective 11/19/2009]

SUBPART 208.7—ACQUISITION FROM NONPROFIT AGENCIES EMPLOYING PEOPLE WHO ARE BLIND OR SEVERELY DISABLED

208.705 Procedures.

Follow the procedures at PGI 208.705 when placing orders with central nonprofit agencies.

[Final rule, 71 FR 39004, 7/11/2006, effective 7/11/2006]

SUBPART 208.70—COORDINATED ACQUISITION

208.7000 Scope of subpart.

This subpart prescribes policy and procedures for acquisition of items for which contracting responsibility is assigned to one or more of the departments/agencies or the

General Services Administration. Contracting responsibility is assigned through—

(a) The Coordinated Acquisition Program (commodity assignments are listed in PGI 208.7006); or

(b) The Integrated Materiel Management Program (assignments are in DoD 4140.26-M, Defense Integrated Materiel Management Manual for Consumable Items).

[Final rule, 67 FR 77936, 12/20/2002, effective 12/20/2002; Final rule, 71 FR 39004, 7/11/2006, effective 7/11/2006]

208.7001 Definitions.

For purposes of this subpart—

Acquiring department means the department, agency, or General Services Administration which has contracting responsibility under the Coordinated Acquisition Program.

Integrated materiel management means assignment of acquisition management responsibility to one department, agency, or the General Service Administration for all of DoD's requirements for the assigned item. Acquisition management normally includes computing requirements, funding, budgeting, storing, issuing, cataloging, standardizing, and contracting functions.

Requiring department means the department or agency which has the requirement for an item.

208.7002 Assignment authority.

(a) Under the DoD Coordinated Acquisition Program, contracting responsibility for certain commodities is assigned to a single department, agency, or the General Services Administration (GSA). Commodity assignments are made—

(1) To the departments and agencies, by the Deputy Under Secretary of Defense (Logistics);

(2) To GSA, through agreement with GSA, by the Deputy Under Secretary of Defense (Logistics);

(3) Outside the contiguous United States, by the Unified Commanders; and

(4) For acquisitions to be made in the contiguous United States for commodities not assigned under paragraphs (a) (1), (2), or (3) of this section, by agreement of agency heads (10 U.S.C. 2311).

(i) Agreement may be on either a one-time or a continuing basis. The submission of a military interdepartmental purchase request (MIPR) by a requiring activity and its acceptance by the contracting activity of another department, even though based on an oral communication, constitutes a one-time agreement.

(ii) Consider repetitive delegated acquisition responsibilities for coordinated acquisition assignment. If not considered suitable for coordinated acquisition assignment, formalize continuing agreements and distribute them to all activities concerned.

(b) Under the Integrated Materiel Management Program, assignments are made by the Deputy Under Secretary of Defense (Logistics)—

(1) To the departments and agencies; and

(2) To GSA, through agreement with GSA.

[Final rule, 64 FR 51074, 9/21/99, effective 9/21/99; Final rule, 70 FR 35543, 6/21/2005, effective 6/21/2005]

208.7002-1 Acquiring department responsibilities.

See PGI 208.7002-1 for the acquiring department's responsibilities.

[Final rule, 71 FR 39004, 7/11/2006, effective 7/11/2006]

208.7002-2 Requiring department responsibilities.

See PGI 208.7002-2 for the requiring department's responsibilities.

[Final rule, 65 FR 52951, 8/31/2000, effective 8/31/2000; Final rule, 71 FR 39004, 7/11/2006, effective 7/11/2006]

208.7003 Applicability. (No Text)

208.7003-1 Assignments under integrated materiel management (IMM).

(a) Acquire all items assigned for IMM from the IMM manager except—

(1) Items purchased under circumstances of unusual and compelling urgency as de-

fined in FAR 6.302-2. After such a purchase is made, the requiring activity must send one copy of the contract and a statement of the emergency to the IMM manager;

(2) Items for which the IMM manager assigns a supply system code for local purchase or otherwise grants authority to purchase locally; or

(3) When purchase by the requiring activity is in the best interest of the Government in terms of the combination of quality, timeliness, and cost that best meets the requirement. This exception does not apply to items—

(i) Critical to the safe operation of a weapon system;

(ii) With special security characteristics; or

(iii) Which are dangerous (e.g., explosives, munitions).

(b) Follow the procedures at PGI 208.7003-1(b) when an item assigned for IMM is to be acquired by the requiring department in accordance with paragraph (a)(3) of this subsection.

[DAC 91-9, 60 FR 61586, 11/30/95, effective 11/30/95; Final rule, 64 FR 51074, 9/21/99, effective 9/21/99; Final rule, 64 FR 61030, 11/9/99, effective 11/9/99; Final rule, 71 FR 39004, 7/11/2006, effective 7/11/2006]

208.7003-2 Assignments under coordinated acquisition.

Requiring departments must submit to the acquiring department all contracting requirements for items assigned for coordinated acquisition, except—

(a) Items obtained through the sources in FAR 8.002(a)(1)(i) through (vii);

(b) Items obtained under 208.7003-1(a);

(c) Requirements not in excess of the simplified acquisition threshold in FAR part 2, when contracting by the requiring department is in the best interest of the Government;

(d) In an emergency. When an emergency purchase is made, the requiring department must send one copy of the contract and a statement of the emergency to the contracting activity of the acquiring department;

(e) Requirements for which the acquiring department's contracting activity delegates contracting authority to the requiring department;

(f) Items in a research and development stage (as described in FAR part 35). Under this exception, the military departments may contract for research and development requirements, including quantities for testing purposes and items undergoing in-service evaluation (not yet in actual production, but beyond prototype). Generally, this exception applies only when research and development funds are used.

(g) Items peculiar to nuclear ordnance material where design characteristics or test-inspection requirements are controlled by the Department of Energy (DoE) or by DoD to ensure reliability of nuclear weapons.

(1) This exception applies to all items designed for and peculiar to nuclear ordnance regardless of agency control, or to any item which requires test or inspection conducted or controlled by DoE or DoD.

(2) This exception does not cover items used for both nuclear ordnance and other purposes if the items are not subject to the special testing procedures.

(h) Items to be acquired under FAR 6.302-6 (national security requires limitation of sources);

(i) Items to be acquired under FAR 6.302-1 (supplies available only from the original source for follow-on contract);

(j) Items directly related to a major system and which are design controlled by and acquired from either the system manufacturer or a manufacturer of a major subsystem;

(k) Items subject to rapid design changes, or to continuous redesign or modification during the production and/or operational use phases, which require continual contact between industry and the requiring department to ensure that the item meets the requirements:

(1) This exception permits the requiring department to contract for items of highly unstable design. For use of this exception, it

must be clearly impractical, both technically and contractually, to refer the acquisition to the acquiring department. Anticipation that contracting by negotiation will be appropriate, or that a number of design changes may occur during contract performance is not in itself sufficient reason for using this exception.

(2) This exception also applies to items requiring compatibility testing, provided such testing requires continual contact between industry and the requiring department;

(l) Containers acquired only with items for which they are designed;

(m) One-time buy of a noncataloged item.

(1) This exception permits the requiring departments to contract for a nonrecurring requirement for a noncataloged item. This exception could cover a part or component for a prototype which may be stock numbered at a later date.

(2) This exception does not permit acquisitions of recurring requirements for an item, based solely on the fact that the item is not stock numbered, nor may it be used to acquire items which have only slightly different characteristics than previously cataloged items.

[DAC 91-9, 60 FR 61586, 11/30/95, effective 11/30/95; Final rule, 64 FR 51074, 9/21/99, effective 9/21/99; Final rule, 71 FR 69489, 12/1/2006, effective 12/1/2006]

208.7004 Procedures.

Follow the procedures at PGI 208.7004 for processing coordinated acquisition requirements.

[Final rule, 71 FR 39004, 7/11/2006, effective 7/11/2006]

208.7004-1 [Removed]

[Final rule, 71 FR 39004, 7/11/2006, effective 7/11/2006]

208.7004-2 [Removed]

[Final rule, 71 FR 39004, 7/11/2006, effective 7/11/2006]

208.7004-3 [Removed]

[Final rule, 71 FR 39004, 7/11/2006, effective 7/11/2006]

208.7004-4 [Removed]

[Final rule, 71 FR 39004, 7/11/2006, effective 7/11/2006]

208.7004-5 [Removed]

[Final rule, 71 FR 39004, 7/11/2006, effective 7/11/2006]

208.7004-6 [Removed]

[Final rule, 71 FR 39004, 7/11/2006, effective 7/11/2006]

208.7004-7 [Removed]

[Final rule, 71 FR 39004, 7/11/2006, effective 7/11/2006]

208.7004-8 [Removed]

[Final rule, 71 FR 39004, 7/11/2006, effective 7/11/2006]

208.7004-9 [Removed]

[Final rule, 71 FR 39004, 7/11/2006, effective 7/11/2006]

208.7004-10 [Removed]

[Final rule, 71 FR 39004, 7/11/2006, effective 7/11/2006]

208.7005 Military interdepartmental purchase requests.

Follow the procedures at—

(a) PGI 253.208-1 when using DD Form 448, Military Interdepartmental Purchase Request; and

(b) PGI 253.208-2 when using DD Form 448-2, Acceptance of MIPR.

[Final rule, 71 FR 39004, 7/11/2006, effective 7/11/2006]

208.7006 Coordinated acquisition assignments.

See PGI 208.7006 for coordinated acquisition assignments.

[Final rule, 71 FR 39004, 7/11/2006, effective 7/11/2006]

SUBPART 208.71—ACQUISITION FOR NATIONAL AERONAUTICS AND SPACE ADMINISTRATION (NASA)

208.7100 Authorization.

NASA is authorized by Public Law 85-568 to use the acquisition services, personnel, equipment, and facilities of DoD departments and agencies with their consent, with or without reimbursement, and on a similar basis to cooperate with the departments/agencies in the use of acquisition services, equipment, and facilities.

208.7101 Policy.

Departments and agencies shall cooperate fully with NASA in making acquisition services, equipment, personnel, and facilities available on the basis of mutual agreement.

[Final rule, 71 FR 39004, 7/11/2006, effective 7/11/2006]

208.7102 Procedures.

Follow the procedures at PGI 208.7102 when contracting or performing services for NASA.

[Final rule, 71 FR 39004, 7/11/2006, effective 7/11/2006]

208.7103 [Removed]

[Final rule, 71 FR 39004, 7/11/2006, effective 7/11/2006]

208.7104 [Removed]

[Final rule, 71 FR 39004, 7/11/2006, effective 7/11/2006]

208.7105 [Removed]

[Final rule, 71 FR 39004, 7/11/2006, effective 7/11/2006]

SUBPART 208.72—[REMOVED AND RESERVED]

208.7201 [Removed]

[Final rule, 71 FR 39004, 7/11/2006, effective 7/11/2006]

208.7202 [Removed]

[Final rule, 71 FR 39004, 7/11/2006, effective 7/11/2006]

208.7203 [Removed]

[DAC 91-3, 57 FR 42629, 9/15/92, effective 8/31/92; DAC 91-12, 62 FR 34114, 6/24/97, effective 6/24/97; Final rule, 68 FR 15615, 3/31/2003, effective 4/30/2003; Final rule, 71 FR 39004, 7/11/2006, effective 7/11/2006]

208.7204 [Removed]

[Final rule, 64 FR 2595, 1/15/99, effective 1/15/99; Final rule, 71 FR 39004, 7/11/2006, effective 7/11/2006]

SUBPART 208.73—USE OF GOVERNMENT-OWNED PRECIOUS METALS

208.7301 Definitions.

As used in this subpart—

Defense Supply Center, Philadelphia (DSCP) means the Defense Logistics Agency field activity located at 700 Robbins Avenue, Philadelphia, PA 19111-5096, which is the assigned commodity integrated material manager for refined precious metals and is responsible for the storage and issue of such material.

Refined precious metal means recovered silver, gold, platinum, palladium, iridium, rhodium, or ruthenium, in bullion, granulation or sponge form, which has been purified to at least .999 percentage of fineness.

[Final rule, 65 FR 14397, 3/16/2000, effective 3/16/2000; Final rule, 65 FR 52951, 8/31/2000, effective 8/31/2000, corrected, 65 FR 58607, 9/29/2000; Final rule, 71 FR 39004, 7/11/2006, effective 7/11/2006]

208.7302 Policy.

DoD policy is for maximum participation in the Precious Metals Recovery Program. DoD components shall furnish recovered precious metals contained in the DSCP inventory to production contractors rather than use contractor-furnished precious metals whenever the contracting officer determines it to be in the Government's best interest.

[Final rule, 65 FR 52951, 8/31/2000, effective 8/31/2000; Final rule, 71 FR 39004, 7/11/2006, effective 7/11/2006]

208.7303 Procedures.

Follow the procedures at PGI 208.7303 for use of the Precious Metals Recovery Program.

[Final rule, 65 FR 52951, 8/31/2000, effective 8/31/2000, corrected, 65 FR 58607, 9/29/2000; Final rule, 71 FR 39004, 7/11/2006, effective 7/11/2006]

208.7304 Refined precious metals.

See PGI 208.7304 for a list of refined precious metals managed by DSCP.

[Final rule, 65 FR 52951, 8/31/2000, effective 8/31/2000; Final rule, 71 FR 39004, 7/11/2006, effective 7/11/2006]

208.7305 Contract clause.

(a) Use the clause at 252.208-7000, Intent to Furnish Precious Metals as Government-Furnished Material, in all solicitations and contracts except—

(1) When the contracting officer has determined that the required precious metals are not available from DSCP;

(2) When the contracting officer knows that the items being acquired do not require precious metals in their manufacture; or

(3) For acquisitions at or below the simplified acquisition threshold.

(b) To make the determination in paragraph (a)(1) of this section, the contracting officer shall consult with the end item inventory manager and comply with the procedures in Chapter 11, DoD 4160.21-M, Materiel Disposition Manual.

[Final rule, 64 FR 2595, 1/15/99, effective 1/15/99; Final rule, 65 FR 14397, 3/26/2000, effective 3/26/2000; Final rule, 65 FR 52951, 8/31/2000, effective 8/31/2000]

SUBPART 208.74—ENTERPRISE SOFTWARE AGREEMENTS

208.7400 Scope of subpart.

This subpart prescribes policy and procedures for acquisition of commercial software and software maintenance, including software and software maintenance that is acquired—

(a) As part of a system or system upgrade, where practicable;

(b) Under a service contract;

(c) Under a contract or agreement administered by another agency (e.g., under an interagency agreement);

(d) Under a Federal Supply Schedule contract or blanket purchase agreement established in accordance with FAR 8.405; or

(e) By a contractor that is authorized to order From a Government supply source pursuant to FAR 51.101.

[Final rule, 67 FR 65509, 10/25/2002, effective 10/25/2002; Final rule, 71 FR 62559, 10/26/2006, effective 10/26/2006; Final rule, 78 FR 38234, 6/26/2013, effective 6/26/2013]

208.7401 Definitions.

As used in this subpart—

Enterprise software agreement means an agreement or a contract that is used to acquire designated commercial software or related services such as software maintenance.

Enterprise Software Initiative means an initiative led by the DoD Chief Information Officer to develop processes for DoD-wide software asset management.

Software maintenance means services normally provided by a software company as standard services at established catalog or market prices, e.g., the right to receive and use upgraded versions of software, updates, and revisions.

[Final rule, 67 FR 65509, 10/25/2002, effective 10/25/2002; Final rule, 71 FR 39004, 7/11/2006, effective 7/11/2006]

208.7402 General.

(1) Departments and agencies shall fulfill requirements for commercial software and related services, such as software maintenance, in accordance with the DoD Enterprise Software Initiative (ESI) (see Web site at *http://www.don-imit.navy.mil/esi*). ESI promotes the use of enterprise software agreements (ESAs) with contractors that allow DoD to obtain favorable terms and pricing for commercial software and related services. ESI does not dictate the products or services to be acquired.

(2) Include an evaluation factor regarding supply chain risk (see subpart 239.73) when

acquiring information technology, whether as a service or as a supply, that is a covered system, is a part of a covered system, or is in support of a covered system, as defined in 239.7301.

[Final rule, 67 FR 65509, 10/25/2002, effective 10/25/2002; Interim rule, 78 FR 69267, 11/18/2013, effective 11/18/2013; Final rule, 80 FR 67243, 10/30/2015, effective 10/30/2015]

208.7403 Acquisition procedures.

Follow the procedures at PGI 208.7403 when acquiring commercial software and related services.

[Final rule, 67 FR 65509, 10/25/2002, effective 10/25/2002; Final rule, 71 FR 39004, 7/11/2006, effective 7/11/2006]

PART 209—CONTRACTOR QUALIFICATIONS

Table of Contents

Subpart 209.1—Responsible Prospective Contractors

Definitions 209.101
[Removed] 209.103
[Removed] 209.103-70
Standards 209.104
General standards 209.104-1
Subcontractor responsibility 209.104-4
Solicitation provision 209.104-70
Procedures 209.105
Obtaining information 209.105-1
Determinations and documentation 209.105-2
Inclusion of determination of contractor fault in Federal Awardee Performance and Integrity Information System (FAPIIS) 209.105-2-70
Preaward surveys 209.106
[Removed] 209.106-1
[Removed] 209.106-2

Subpart 209.2—Qualifications Requirements

Policy 209.202
Aviation and ship critical safety items 209.270
Scope 209.270-1
Definitions 209.270-2
Policy 209.270-3
Procedures 209.270-4
Contract clause 209.270-5

Subpart 209.3—[Removed]

Subpart 209.4—Debarment, Suspension, and Ineligibility

Policy 209.402
Definitions 209.403
Effect of listing 209.405
[Removed] 209.405-1
Restrictions on subcontracting 209.405-2
Debarment 209.406
General 209.406-1
Causes for debarment 209.406-2
Procedures 209.406-3
Suspension 209.407
Procedures 209.407-3
Solicitation provision and contract clause 209.409
Reserve Officer Training Corps and military recruiting on campus 209.470
Definition 209.470-1
Policy 209.470-2
Procedures 209.470-3

Solicitation provision and contract clause 209.470-4
Congressional Medal of Honor 209.471

Subpart 209.5—Organizational and Consultant Conflicts of Interest

General rules 209.505
Obtaining access to proprietary information 209.505-4
Limitations on contractors acting as lead system integrators 209.570
Definitions 209.570-1
Policy 209.570-2
Procedures 209.570-3
Solicitation provision and contract clause 209.570-4
Organizational conflicts of interest in major defense acquisition programs 209.571
Scope of subpart. 209.571-0
Definitions. 209.571-1
Applicability. 209.571-2
Policy. 209.571-3
Mitigation. 209.571-4
Lead system integrators. 209.571-5
Identification of organizational conflicts of interest. 209.571-6
Systems engineering and technical assistance contracts. 209.571-7
Solicitation provision and contract clause. 209.571-8

PART 209—CONTRACTOR QUALIFICATIONS

SUBPART 209.1—RESPONSIBLE PROSPECTIVE CONTRACTORS

209.101 Definition

Entity controlled by a foreign government, foreign government, and *proscribed information*, are defined in the provision at 252.209-7002, Disclosure of Ownership or Control by a Foreign Government.

[Final rule, 59 FR 51132, 10/7/94, effective 9/29/94]

209.103 [Removed]

[DAC 91-7, 60 FR 29491, 6/5/95, effective 5/17/95; DAC 91-11, 61 FR 50446, 9/26/96, effective 9/26/96; Final rule, 65 FR 39703, 6/27/2000, effective 6/27/2000; Final rule, 69 FR 65088, 11/10/2004, effective 11/10/2004]

209.103-70 [Removed]

[DAC 91-9, 60 FR 61586, 11/30/95, effective 11/30/95; DAC 91-11, 61 FR 50446, 9/26/96, effective 9/26/96; Final rule, 69 FR 65088, 11/10/2004, effective 11/10/2004]

209.104 Standards. (No Text)

209.104-1 General standards.

(e) For cost-reimbursement or incentive type contracts, or contracts which provide for progress payments based on costs or on a percentage or stage of completion, the prospective contractor's accounting system and related internal controls must provide reasonable assurance that—

(i) Applicable laws and regulations are complied with;

(ii) The accounting system and cost data are reliable;

(iii) Risk of misallocations and mischarges are minimized; and

(iv) Contract allocations and charges are consistent with invoice procedures.

(g) (i) *Ownership or control by the government of a terrorist country.* (See 225.771.)

(A) Under 10 U.S.C. 2327(b), a contracting officer shall not award a contract of $150,000 or more to a firm or to a subsidiary of a firm when a foreign government—

(1) Either directly or indirectly, has a significant interest—

(i) In the firm; or

(ii) In the subsidiary or the firm that owns the subsidiary; and

(2) Has been determined by the Secretary of State under 50 U.S.C. App. 2405(j)(1)(A) to be a government of a country that has repeatedly provided support for acts of international terrorism.

(B) Whenever the contracting officer has a question about application of the provision at 252.209-7002, the contracting officer may seek advice from the Security Directorate, Office of the Deputy Under Secretary of Defense, Human Intelligence, Counterintelligence, and Security.

(C) Forward any information indicating that a firm or a subsidiary of a firm may be owned or controlled by the government of a terrorist country, through agency channels, to: Deputy Director, Defense Procurement (Contract Policy and International Contracting, OUSD(AT&L)DPAP(CPIC)), 3060 Defense Pentagon, Washington, DC 20301-3060.

(ii) *Ownership or control by a foreign government when access to proscribed information is required to perform the contract.*

(A) Under 10 U.S.C. 2536(a), no DoD contract under a national security program may be awarded to an entity controlled by a foreign government if that entity requires access to proscribed information to perform the contract.

(B) Whenever the contracting officer has a question about application of the provision at 252.209-7002, the contracting officer may seek advice from the Director, Defense Security Programs, Office of the Assistant Secretary of Defense for Command, Control, Communications and Intelligence.

(C) In accordance with 10 U.S.C. 2536(b)(1)(A), the Secretary of Defense may waive the prohibition in paragraph (g)(ii)(A) of this subsection upon determining that the waiver is essential to the national security interests of the United States. The Secretary has delegated authority to grant this waiver to the Undersecretary of Defense for Intelligence. Waiver requests, prepared by the requiring activity in coordination with the contracting officer, shall be processed through the Director of Defense Procurement and Acquisition Policy, Office of the Under Secretary of Defense (Acquisition, Technology, and Logistics), and shall include a proposed national interest determination. The proposed national interest determination, prepared by the requiring activity in coordination with the contracting officer, shall include:

(1) Identification of the proposed awardee, with a synopsis of its foreign ownership (include solicitation and other reference numbers to identify the action);

(2) General description of the acquisition and performance requirements;

(3) Identification of the national security interests involved and the ways award of the contract helps advance those interests;

(4) The availability of another entity with the capacity, capability and technical expertise to satisfy defense acquisition, technology base, or industrial base requirements; and

(5) A description of any alternate means available to satisfy the requirement, e.g., use of substitute products or technology or alternate approaches to accomplish the program objectives.

(D) In accordance with 10 U.S.C. 2536(b)(1)(B), the Secretary of Defense may, in the case of a contract awarded for environmental restoration, remediation, or waste management at a DoD facility, waive the prohibition in paragraph (g)(ii)(A) of this subsection upon—

(1) Determining that—

(i) The waiver will advance the environmental restoration, remediation, or waste management objectives of DoD and will not harm the national security interests of the United States; and

(ii) The entity to which the contract is awarded is controlled by a foreign government with which the Secretary is authorized to exchange Restricted Data under section 144c. of the Atomic Energy Act of 1954 (42 U.S.C. 2164(c)); and

(2) Notifying Congress of the decision to grant the waiver. The contract may be awarded only after the end of the 45-day period beginning on the date the notification is received by the appropriate Congressional committees.

[DAC 91-5, 58 FR 28458, 5/13/93, effective 4/30/93; Interim rule, 59 FR 51130, 10/7/94, effective 9/29/94; Final rule, 59 FR 51132, 10/7/94, effective 9/29/94; DAC 91-7, 60 FR 29491, 6/5/95, effective 5/17/95; DAC 91-12, 62 FR 34114, 6/24/97, effective 6/24/97; Interim rule, 63 FR 11850, 3/11/98, effective 3/11/98; Interim rule, 63 FR 14836, 3/27/98, effective 3/27/98, finalized without change, 63 FR 64426, 11/20/98; Final rule, 65 FR 39703, 6/27/2000, effective 6/27/2000; Final rule, 67 FR 4208, 1/29/2002, effective 1/29/2002; Final rule, 68 FR 7438, 2/14/2003, effective 2/14/2003; Final rule, 74 FR 2413, 1/15/2009, effective 1/15/2009; Interim rule, 75 FR 35684, 6/23/2010, effective 6/23/2010; Final rule, 75 FR 45072, 8/2/2010, effective 10/1/2010; Final rule, 76 FR 21812, 4/19/2011, effective 4/19/2011; Final rule, 79 FR 73488, 12/11/2014, effective 12/11/2014]

209.104-4 Subcontractor responsibility.

Generally, the Canadian Commercial Corporation's (CCC) proposal of a firm as its subcontractor is sufficient basis for an affirmative determination of responsibility. However, when the CCC determination of responsibility is not consistent with other information available to the contracting officer, the contracting officer shall request from CCC and any other sources whatever additional information is necessary to make the responsibility determination.

209.104-70 Solicitation provision.

Use the provision at 252.209-7002, Disclosure of Ownership or Control by a Foreign Government, in all solicitations, including those subject to the procedures in FAR part 13, when access to proscribed information is necessary for contract performance. If the solicitation includes the provision at FAR

52.204-7, do not separately list the provision 252.209-7002 in the solicitation.

[DAC 91-5, 58 FR 28458, 5/13/93, effective 4/30/93; Interim rule, 59 FR 51130, 10/7/94, effective 9/29/94; DAC 91-12, 62 FR 34114, 6/24/97, effective 6/24/97; Interim rule, 63 FR 11850, 3/11/98, effective 3/11/98; Interim rule, 63 FR 14836, 3/27/98, effective 3/27/98, finalized without change, 63 FR 64426, 11/20/98; Final rule, 65 FR 39703, 6/27/2000, effective 6/27/2000; Final rule, 67 FR 4208, 1/29/2002, effective 1/29/2002; Final rule, 68 FR 7438, 2/14/2003, effective 2/14/2003; Final rule, 72 FR 30278, 5/31/2007, effective 5/31/2007; Final rule, 74 FR 2413, 1/15/2009, effective 1/15/2009; Final rule, 75 FR 45072, 8/2/2010, effective 10/1/2010; CFR Correction, 77 FR 59339, 9/27/2012; Final rule, 78 FR 37980, 6/25/2013, effective 6/25/2013; Final rule, 78 FR 40043, 7/3/2013, effective 7/3/2013; Final rule, 79 FR 73488, 12/11/2014, effective 12/11/2014]

209.105 Procedures. (No Text)

209.105-1 Obtaining information.

(1) For guidance on using the Exclusions section of the System for Award Management, see PGI 209.105-1.

(2) A satisfactory performance record is a factor in determining contractor responsibility (see FAR 9.104–1(c)). One source of information relating to contractor performance is the Contractor Performance Assessment Reporting System (CPARS) available at *https://www.cpars.gov/*. Information relating to contract terminations for cause and for default is also available through the Federal Awardee Performance and Integrity Information System (FAPIIS) module of CPARS, available at *https://www.fapiis.gov* (see subpart 42.15). This termination information is just one consideration in determining contractor responsibility.

[Final rule, 71 FR 14099, 3/21/2006, effective 3/21/2006; Final rule, 74 FR 2414, 1/15/2009, effective 1/15/2009; Final rule, 76 FR 76318, 12/7/2011, effective 12/7/2011; Final rule, 78 FR 28756, 5/16/2013, effective 5/16/2013; Final rule, 79 FR 17445, 3/28/2014, effective 3/28/2014; Final rule, 84 FR 48507, 9/13/2019, effective 9/13/2019]

209.105-2 Determinations and documentation.

(a) The contracting officer shall submit a copy of a determination of nonresponsibility to the appropriate debarring and suspending official listed in 209.403.

[Final rule, 64 FR 62984, 11/18/99, effective 11/18/99; Final rule, 69 FR 74989, 12/15/2004, effective 12/15/2004; Final rule, 71 FR 14099, 3/21/2006, effective 3/21/2006; Final rule, 71 FR 62559, 10/26/2006, effective 10/26/2006]

209.105-2-70 Inclusion of determination of contractor fault in Federal Awardee Performance and Integrity Information System (FAPIIS).

If the contractor or a subcontractor at any tier is not subject to the jurisdiction of the U.S. courts and the DoD appointing official that requested a DoD investigation makes a final determination that a contractor's or subcontractor's gross negligence or reckless disregard for the safety of civilian or military personnel of the Government caused serious bodily injury or death of such personnel, the contracting officer shall enter in FAPIIS the appropriate information regarding such determination within three days of receiving notice of the determination, pursuant to section 834 of the National Defense Authorization Act for Fiscal Year 2011 (Pub. L. 111-383). Information posted in FAPIIS regarding such determinations will be publicly available.

[Interim rule, 76 FR 57674, 9/16/2011, effective 9/16/2011; Final rule, 77 FR 11354, 2/24/2012, effective 2/24/2012]

209.106 Preaward surveys.

When requesting a preaward survey, follow the procedures at PGI 209.106.

[Final rule, 69 FR 65088, 11/10/2004, effective 11/10/2004]

209.106-1 [Removed]

[DAC 91-9, 60 FR 61586, 11/30/95, effective 11/30/95; Final rule, 69 FR 65088, 11/10/2004, effective 11/10/2004]

209.106-2 [Removed]

[DAC 91-5, 58 FR 28458, 5/13/93, effective 4/30/93; Final rule, 64 FR 61028, 11/9/99, effective 11/9/99; Final rule, 69 FR 65088, 11/10/2004, effective 11/10/2004]

SUBPART 209.2—QUALIFICATIONS REQUIREMENTS

209.202 Policy.

(a) (1) Except for aviation or ship critical safety items, obtain approval in accordance with PGI 209.202(a) (1) when establishing qualification requirements. See 209.270 for approval of qualification requirements for aviation or ship critical safety items.

[DAC 91-9, 60 FR 61586, 11/30/95, effective 11/30/95; Final rule, 65 FR 63804, 10/25/2000, effective 10/25/2000; Final rule, 69 FR 65088, 11/10/2004, effective 11/10/2004; Interim rule, 73 FR 1826, 1/10/2008, effective 1/10/2008; Final rule, 73 FR 46817, 8/12/2008, effective 8/12/2008]

209.270 Aviation and ship critical safety items. (No Text)

[Interim rule, 69 FR 55987, 9/17/2004, effective 9/17/2004; Final rule, 70 FR 57188, 9/30/2005, effective 9/30/2005; Interim rule, 73 FR 1826, 1/10/2008, effective 1/10/2008; Final rule, 73 FR 46817, 8/12/2008, effective 8/12/2008]

209.270-1 Scope.

This section—

(a) Implements—

(1) Section 802 of the National Defense Authorization Act for Fiscal Year 2004 (Pub. L. 108-136); and

(2) Section 130 of the National Defense Authorization Act for Fiscal Year 2007 (Pub. L. 109-364); and

(b) Prescribes policy and procedures for qualification requirements in the procurement of aviation and ship critical safety items and the modification, repair, and overhaul of those items.

[Interim rule, 69 FR 55987, 9/17/2004, effective 9/17/2004; Final rule, 70 FR 57188, 9/30/2005, effective 9/30/2005; Interim rule, 73 FR 1826, 1/10/2008, effective 1/10/2008; Final rule, 73 FR 46817, 8/12/2008, effective 8/12/2008]

209.270-2 Definitions.

As used in this section—

Aviation critical safety item means a part, an assembly, installation equipment, launch equipment, recovery equipment, or support equipment for an aircraft or aviation weapon system if the part, assembly, or equipment contains a characteristic any failure, malfunction, or absence of which could cause—

(1) A catastrophic or critical failure resulting in the loss of or serious damage to the aircraft or weapon system;

(2) An unacceptable risk of personal injury or loss of life; or

(3) An uncommanded engine shutdown that jeopardizes safety.

Design control activity—

(1) With respect to an aviation critical safety item, means the systems command of a military department that is specifically responsible for ensuring the air worthiness of an aviation system or equipment in which an aviation critical safety item is to be used; and

(2) With respect to a ship critical safety item, means the systems command of a military department that is specifically responsible for ensuring the seaworthiness of a ship or ship equipment in which a ship critical safety item is to be used.

Ship critical safety item means any ship part, assembly, or support equipment containing a characteristic the failure, malfunction, or absence of which could cause—

(1) A catastrophic or critical failure resulting in loss of or serious damage to the ship; or

(2) An unacceptable risk of personal injury or loss of life.

[Interim rule, 69 FR 55987, 9/17/2004, effective 9/17/2004; Final rule, 70 FR 57188, 9/30/2005, effective 9/30/2005; Interim rule, 73 FR 1826, 1/10/2008, effective 1/10/2008; Final rule, 73 FR 46817, 8/12/2008, effective 8/12/2008]

209.270-3 Policy.

(a) The head of the contracting activity responsible for procuring an aviation or ship critical safety item may enter into a contract for the procurement, modification, repair, or overhaul of such an item only with a source approved by the head of the design control activity.

(b) The approval authorities specified in this section apply instead of those otherwise specified in FAR 9.202(a)(1), 9.202(c), or 9.206-1(c), for the procurement, modification, repair, and overhaul of aviation or ship critical safety items.

[Interim rule, 69 FR 55987, 9/17/2004, effective 9/17/2004; Final rule, 70 FR 57188, 9/30/2005, effective 9/30/2005; Interim rule, 73 FR 1826, 1/10/2008, effective 1/10/2008; Final rule, 73 FR 46817, 8/12/2008, effective 8/12/2008]

209.270-4 Procedures.

(a) The head of the design control activity shall—

(1) Identify items that meet the criteria for designation as aviation or ship critical safety items. See additional information at PGI 209.270-4;

(2) Approve qualification requirements in accordance with procedures established by the design control activity; and

(3) Qualify and identify aviation and ship critical safety item suppliers and products.

(b) The contracting officer shall—

(1) Ensure that the head of the design control activity has determined that a prospective contractor or its product meets or can meet the established qualification standards before the date specified for award of the contract;

(2) Refer any offers received from an unapproved source to the head of the design control activity for approval. The head of the design control activity will determine whether the offeror or its product meets or can meet the established qualification standards before the date specified for award of the contract; and

(3) Refer any requests for qualification to the design control activity.

(c) See 246.407(S-70) and 246.504 for quality assurance requirements.

[Interim rule, 69 FR 55987, 9/17/2004, effective 9/17/2004; Final rule, 70 FR 57188, 9/30/2005, effective 9/30/2005; Interim rule, 73 FR 1826, 1/10/2008, effective 1/10/2008; Final rule, 73 FR 46817, 8/12/2008, effective 8/12/2008]

209.270-5 Contract clause.

The contracting officer shall insert the clause at 252.209-7010, Critical Safety Items, in solicitations and contracts when the acquisition includes one or more items designated by the design control activity as critical safety items.

[Final rule, 76 FR 52138, 8/19/2011, effective 8/19/2011]

SUBPART 209.3—[REMOVED]

209.303 [Removed]

[Final rule, 69 FR 65088, 11/10/2004, effective 11/10/2004]

209.305 [Removed]

[Final rule, 69 FR 65088, 11/10/2004, effective 11/10/2004]

209.306 [Removed]

[Final rule, 69 FR 65088, 11/10/2004, effective 11/10/2004]

209.308 [Removed]

[Final rule, 69 FR 65088, 11/10/2004, effective 11/10/2004]

SUBPART 209.4—DEBARMENT, SUSPENSION, AND INELIGIBILITY

209.402 Policy.

(d) The suspension and debarment procedures in appendix H are to be followed by all debarring and suspending officials.

(e) The department or agency shall provide a copy of Appendix H, Debarment and Suspension Procedures, to contractors at the time of their suspension or when they are proposed for debarment, and upon request to other interested parties.

[DAC 91-6, 59 FR 27662, 5/27/94, effective 5/27/94]

209.403 Definitions.

Debarring and suspending official.

(1) For DoD, the designees are—

Army—Director, Soldier & Family Legal Services

Navy/Marine Corps—The Assistant General Counsel (Acquisition Integrity)

Air Force—Deputy General Counsel (Contractor Responsibility)

Defense Advanced Research Projects Agency—The Director

Defense Information Systems Agency—The General Counsel

Defense Intelligence Agency—The Senior Procurement Executive

Defense Logistics Agency—The Special Assistant for Contracting Integrity

National Geospatial—Intelligence Agency—The General Counsel

Defense Threat Reduction Agency—The Director

National Security Agency—The Senior Acquisition Executive

Missile Defense Agency—The General Counsel

United States Cyber Command—The Staff Judge Advocate

Defense Health Agency—The General Counsel

Overseas installations—as designated by the agency head

(2) Overseas debarring and suspending officials—

(i) Are authorized to debar or suspend contractors located within the official's geographic area of responsibility under any delegation of authority they receive from their agency head.

(ii) Debar or suspend in accordance with the procedures in FAR Subpart 9.4 or under modified procedures approved by the agency head based on consideration of the laws or customs of the foreign countries concerned.

(iii) In addition to the bases for debarment in FAR 9.406-2, may consider the following additional bases—

(A) The foreign country concerned determines that a contractor has engaged in bid-rigging, price-fixing, or other anti-competitive behavior; or

(B) The foreign country concerned declares the contractor to be formally debarred, suspended, or otherwise ineligible to contract with that foreign government or its instrumentalities.

(3) The Defense Logistics Agency Special Assistant for Contracting Integrity is the exclusive representative of the Secretary of Defense to suspend and debar contractors from the purchase of Federal personal property under the Federal Property Management Regulations (41 CFR 101-45.6) and the Defense Materiel Disposition Manual (DoD 4160.21-M).

[DAC 91-1, 56 FR 67212, 12/30/91, effective 12/31/91; DAC 91-6, 59 FR 27662, 5/27/94, effective 5/27/94; DAC 91-9, 60 FR 61586, 11/30/95, effective 11/30/95; DAC 91-11, 61 FR 50446, 9/26/96, effective 9/26/96; DAC 91-13, 63 FR 11522, 3/9/98, effective 3/9/98; Final rule, 64 FR 51074, 9/21/99, effective 9/21/99; Final rule, 64 FR 62984, 11/18/99, effective 11/18/99; Final rule, 68 FR 7438, 2/14/2003, effective 2/14/2003; Final rule, 70 FR 14573, 3/23/2005, effective 3/23/2005; Final rule, 74 FR 42779, 8/25/2009, effective 8/25/2009; Final rule, 74 FR 52895, 10/15/2009, effective 10/15/2009; Interim rule, 76 FR 11363, 3/2/2011, effective 3/2/2011; Final rule, 76 FR 76318, 12/7/2011, effective 12/7/2011; Final rule, 77 FR 23631, 4/20/2012, effective 4/20/2012; Final rule, 77 FR 52253, 8/29/2012, effective 8/29/2012; Final rule, 78 FR 30233, 5/22/2013, effective 5/22/2013; Final rule, 84 FR 18155, 4/30/2019, effective 4/30/2019]

209.405 Effect of listing.

(a) Under 10 U.S.C. 2393(b), when a department or agency determines that a compelling reason exists for it to conduct business with a contractor that is debarred or suspended from procurement programs, it must provide written notice of the determination to the General Services Administration (GSA), GSA Suspension and Debarment

Official, Office of Acquisition Policy, 1275 First Street, NE., Washington, DC 20417. Examples of compelling reasons are—

(i) Only a debarred or suspended contractor can provide the supplies or services;

(ii) Urgency requires contracting with a debarred or suspended contractor;

(iii) The contractor and a department or agency have an agreement covering the same events that resulted in the debarment or suspension and the agreement includes the department or agency decision not to debar or suspend the contractor; or

(iv) The national defense requires continued business dealings with the debarred or suspended contractor.

(b) (i) The Procurement Cause and Treatment Code "H" annotation in the Exclusions section of the System for Award Management (SAM Exclusions) identifies contractor facilities where no part of a contract or subcontract may be performed because of a violation of the Clean Air Act (42 U.S.C. 7606) or the Clean Water Act (33 U.S.C. 1368).

(ii) Under the authority of Section 8 of Executive Order 11738, the agency head may grant an exemption permitting award to a contractor using a Code "H" ineligible facility if the agency head determines that such an exemption is in the paramount interest of the United States.

(A) The agency head may delegate this exemption authority to a level no lower than a general or flag officer or a member of the Senior Executive Service.

(B) The official granting the exemption—

(1) Shall promptly notify the Environmental Protection Agency suspending and debarring official of the exemption and the corresponding justification; and

(2) May grant a class exemption only after consulting with the Environmental Protection Agency suspending and debarring official.

(C) Exemptions shall be for a period not to exceed one year. The continuing necessity for each exemption shall be reviewed annually and, upon the making of a new determination, may be extended for periods not to exceed one year.

(D) All exemptions must be reported annually to the Environmental Protection Agency suspending and debarring official.

(E) See PGI 209.405 for additional procedures and information.

[Final rule, 65 FR 52954, 8/31/2000, effective 8/31/2000; Final rule, 74 FR 2414, 1/15/2009, effective 1/15/2009; Final rule, 76 FR 27274, 5/11/2011, effective 5/11/2011; Final rule, 79 FR 73488, 12/11/2014, effective 12/11/2014]

209.405-1 [Removed]

[DAC 91-7, 60 FR 29491, 6/5/95, effective 5/17/95; DAC 91-9, 60 FR 61586, 11/30/95, effective 11/30/95; Final rule, 75 FR 66679, 10/29/2010, effective 10/29/2010]

209.405-2 Restrictions on subcontracting.

(a) The contracting officer shall not consent to any subcontract with a firm, or a subsidiary of a firm, that is identified by the Secretary of Defense in SAM Exclusions as being owned or controlled by the government of a country that is a state sponsor of terrorism unless the agency head states in writing the compelling reasons for the subcontract. (See also 225.771.)

[Interim rule, 63 FR 14836, 3/27/98, effective 3/27/98, finalized without change, 63 FR 64426, 11/20/98; Final rule, 79 FR 73488, 12/11/2014, effective 12/11/2014]

209.406 Debarment. (No Text)

209.406-1 General.

(a) (i) When the debarring official decides that debarment is not necessary, the official may require the contractor to enter into a written agreement which includes—

(A) A requirement for the contractor to establish, if not already established, and to maintain the standards of conduct and internal control systems prescribed by FAR subpart 3.10; and

(B) Other requirements the debarring official considers appropriate.

(ii) Before the debarring official decides not to suspend or debar in the case of an indictment or conviction for a felony, the debarring official must determine that the contractor has addressed adequately the circumstances that gave rise to the misconduct, and that appropriate standards of ethics and integrity are in place and are working.

[DAC 91-2, 57 FR 14992, 4/23/92, effective 4/16/92; Final rule, 76 FR 76318, 12/7/2011, effective 12/7/2011]

209.406-2 Causes for debarment.

(1) Any person shall be considered for debarment if criminally convicted of intentionally affixing a label bearing a "Made in America" inscription to any product sold in or shipped to the United States or its outlying areas that was not made in the United Staters or its outlying areas (10 U.S.C. 2410f).

(i) The debarring official will make a determination concerning debarment not later than 90 days after determining that a person has been so convicted.

(ii) In cases where the debarring official decides not to debar, the debarring official will report that decision to the Director of Defense Procurement and Acquisition Policy who will notify Congress within 30 days after the decision is made.

(2) Any contractor that knowingly provides compensation to a former DoD official in violation of section 847 of the National Defense Authorization Act for Fiscal Year 2008 may face suspension and debarment proceedings in accordance with 41 U.S.C. 2105 (c)(1)(C).

[DAC 91-5, 58 FR 28458, 5/13/93, effective 4/30/93; Final rule, 68 FR 7438, 2/14/2003, effective 2/14/2003; Final rule, 70 FR 35543, 6/21/2005, effective 6/21/2005; Interim rule, 74 FR 2408, 1/15/2009, effective 1/15/2009; Final rule, 74 FR 59913, 11/19/2009, effective 11/19/2009; Final rule, 76 FR 58137, 9/20/2011, effective 9/20/2011]

209.406-3 Procedures.

Refer all matters appropriate for consideration by an agency debarring and suspending official as soon as practicable to the appropriate debarring and suspending official identified in 209.403. Any person may refer a matter to the debarring and suspending official. Follow the procedures at PGI 209.406-3.

[Final rule, 64 FR 62984, 11/18/99, effective 11/18/99, corrected by 65 FR 4864, 2/1/2000; Final rule, 69 FR 74989, 12/15/2004, effective 12/15/2004]

209.407 Suspension. (No Text)

209.407-3 Procedures.

Refer all matters appropriate for consideration by an agency debarring and suspending official as soon as practicable to the appropriate debarring and suspending official identified in 209.403. Any person may refer a matter to the debarring and suspending official. Follow the procedures at PGI 209.407-3.

[Final rule, 64 FR 62984, 11/18/99, effective 11/18/99, corrected by 65 FR 4864, 2/1/2001; Final rule, 69 FR 74989, 12/15/2004, effective 12/15/2004]

209.409 Solicitation provision and contract clause.

Use the clause at 252.209-7004, Subcontracting with Firms that are Owned or Controlled by the Government of a Country that is a State Sponsor of Terrorism, in solicitations and contracts with a value of $150,000 or more.

[Interim rule, 63 FR 14836, 3/27/98, effective 3/27/98, finalized without change, 63 FR 64426, 11/20/98; Final rule, 75 FR 45072, 8/2/2010, effective 10/1/2010; Final rule, 79 FR 73488, 12/11/2014, effective 12/11/2014]

209.470 Reserve Officer Training Corps and military recruiting on campus. (No Text)

209.470-1 Definition.

Institution of higher education, as used in this section, means an institution that meets the requirements of 20 U.S.C. 1001 and includes all subelements of such an institution.

[Interim rule, 65 FR 2056, 1/13/2000, effective 1/13/2000; Final rule, 67 FR 49253, 7/30/2002, effective 7/30/2002]

209.470-2 Policy.

(a) Except as provided in paragraph (b) of this subsection, 10 U.S.C. 983 prohibits DoD from providing funds by contract or grant to an institution of higher education if the Secretary of Defense determines that the institution has a policy or practice that prohibits or in effect prevents—

(1) The Secretary of a military department from maintaining, establishing, or operating a unit of the Senior Reserve Officer Training Corps (ROTC) at that institution;

(2) A student at that institution from enrolling in a unit of the senior ROTC at another institution of higher education;

(3) The Secretary of a military department or the Secretary of Transportation from gaining entry to campuses, or access to students on campuses, for purposes of military recruiting; or

(4) Military recruiters from accessing certain information pertaining to students enrolled at that institution.

(b) The prohibition in paragraph (a) of this subsection does not apply to an institution of higher education if the Secretary of Defense determines that—

(1) The institution has ceased the policy or practice described in paragraph (a) of this subsection; or

(2) The institution has a long-standing policy of pacifism based on historical religious affiliation.

[Interim rule, 65 FR 2056, 1/13/2000, effective 1/13/2000; Final rule, FR 49253, 7/30/2002, effective 7/30/2002]

209.470-3 Procedures.

If the Secretary of Defense determines that an institution of higher education is ineligible to receive DoD funds because of a policy or practice described in 209.470-2(a)—

(a) The Secretary of Defense will list the institution on the List of Parties Excluded from Federal Procurement and Nonprocurement Programs published by General Services Administration (also see FAR 9.404 and 32 CFR part 216); and

(b) DoD components—

(1) Shall not solicit offers from, award contracts to, or consent to subcontracts with the institution;

(2) Shall make no further payments under existing contracts with the institution; and

(3) Shall terminate existing contracts with the institution.

[Interim rule, 65 FR 2056, 1/13/2000, effective 1/13/2000; Final rule, 67 FR 49253, 7/30/2002, effective 7/30/2002]

209.470-4 Solicitation provision and contract clause.

(a) Use the provision at 252.209-7003, Reserve Officer Training Corps and Military Recruiting on Campus—Representation, in all solicitations with institutions of higher education. If the solicitation includes the provision at FAR 52.204-7, do not separately list the provision 2252.209-7003 in the solicitation.

(b) Use the clause at 252.209-7005, Reserve Officer Training Corps and Military Recruiting on Campus, in all solicitations and contracts with institutions of higher education.

[Interim rule, 65 FR 2056, 1/13/2000, effective 1/13/2000; Final rule, 67 FR 49253, 7/30/2002, effective 7/30/2002; Final rule, 77 FR 19128, 3/30/2012, effective 3/30/2012; Final rule, 78 FR 37980, 6/25/2013, effective 6/25/2013; Final rule, 78 FR 40043, 7/3/2013, effective 7/3/2013]

209.471 Congressional Medal of Honor.

In accordance with Section 8118 of Pub. L. 105-262, do not award a contract to, extend a contract with, or approve the award of a subcontract to any entity that, within the preceding 15 years, has been convicted under 18 U.S.C. 704 of the unlawful manufacture or sale of the Congressional Medal of Honor. Any entity so convicted will be listed as ineligible on the List of Parties Excluded from Federal Procurement and Nonprocurement Programs published by the General Services Administration.

[Interim rule, 64 FR 31732, 6/14/99, effective 6/14/99, finalized without change, 64 FR 55632, 10/14/99]

SUBPART 209.5—ORGANIZATIONAL AND CONSULTANT CONFLICTS OF INTEREST

209.505 General rules. (No Text)

[Interim rule, 76 FR 11363, 3/2/2011, effective 3/2/2011; Final rule, 78 FR 30233, 5/22/2013, effective 5/22/2013]

209.505-4 Obtaining access to proprietary information.

(b) (i) For contractors, other than litigation support contractors, accessing third party proprietary technical data or computer software, non-disclosure requirements are addressed at 227.7103-7(b), through use of the clause at 252.227-7025 as prescribed at 227.7103-6(c) and 227.7203-6(d). Pursuant to that clause, covered Government support contractors may be required to enter into non-disclosure agreements directly with the third party asserting restrictions on limited rights technical data, commercial technical data, or restricted rights computer software. The contracting officer is not required to obtain copies of these agreements or to ensure that they are properly executed.

(ii) For litigation support contractors accessing litigation information, including that originating from third parties, use and non-disclosure requirements are addressed through the use of the clause at 252.204-7014, as prescribed at 204.7403(a). Pursuant to the clause, litigation support contractors are not required to enter into non-disclosure agreements directly with any third party asserting restrictions on any litigation information.

[Interim rule, 76 FR 11363, 3/2/2011, effective 3/2/2011; Final rule, 78 FR 30233, 5/22/2013, effective 5/22/2013; Final rule, 81 FR 28724, 5/10/2016, effective 5/10/2016; Final rule, 81 FR 36473, 6/7/2016, effective 6/7/2016; Final rule, 84 FR 58331, 10/31/2019, effective 10/31/2019]

209.570 Limitations on contractors acting as lead system integrators. (No Text)

[Interim rule, 73 FR 1823, 1/10/2008, effective 1/10/2008]

209.570-1 Definition.

Lead system integrator, as used in this section, is defined in the clause at 252.209-7007, Prohibited Financial Interests for Lead System Integrators. See PGI 209.570-1 for additional information.

[Interim rule, 73 FR 1823, 1/10/2008, effective 1/10/2008]

209.570-2 Policy.

(a) Except as provided in paragraph (b) of this subsection, 10 U.S.C. 2410p prohibits any entity performing lead system integrator functions in the acquisition of a major system by DoD from having any direct financial interest in the development or construction of any individual system or element of any system of systems.

(b) The prohibition in paragraph (a) of this subsection does not apply if—

(1) The Secretary of Defense certifies to the Committees on Armed Services of the Senate and the House of Representatives that—

(i) The entity was selected by DoD as a contractor to develop or construct the system or element concerned through the use of competitive procedures; and

(ii) DoD took appropriate steps to prevent any organizational conflict of interest in the selection process; or

(2) The entity was selected by a subcontractor to serve as a lower-tier subcontractor, through a process over which the entity exercised no control.

(c) In accordance with Section 802 of the National Defense Authorization Act for Fiscal Year 2008 (Pub. L. 110-181), DoD may award a new contract for lead system integrator functions in the acquisition of a major system only if—

(1) The major system has not yet proceeded beyond low-rate initial production; or

(2) The Secretary of Defense determines in writing that it would not be practicable to carry out the acquisition without continuing to use a contractor to perform lead system integrator functions and that doing so is in the best interest of DoD. The authority to make this determination may not be dele-

gated below the level of the Under Secretary of Defense for Acquisition, Technology, and Logistics. (*Also see* 209.570-3(b).)

(d) Effective October 1, 2010, DoD is prohibited from awarding a new contract for lead system integrator functions in the acquisition of a major system to any entity that was not performing lead system integrator functions in the acquisition of the major system prior to January 28, 2008.

[Interim rule, 73 FR 1823, 1/10/2008, effective 1/10/2008; Interim rule, 74 FR 34266, 7/15/2009, effective 7/15/2009; Final rule, 75 FR 3178, 1/20/2010, effective 1/20/2010]

209.570-3 Procedures.

(a) In making a responsibility determination before awarding a contract for the acquisition of a major system, the contracting officer shall—

(1) Determine whether the prospective contractor meets the definition of "lead system integrator";

(2) Consider all information regarding the prospective contractor's direct financial interests in view of the prohibition at 209.570-2(a); and

(3) Follow the procedures at PGI 209.570-3.

(b) A determination to use a contractor to perform lead system integrator functions in accordance with 209.570-2(c)(2)—

(1) Shall specify the reasons why it would not be practicable to carry out the acquisition without continuing to use a contractor to perform lead system integrator functions, including a discussion of alternatives, such as use of the DoD workforce or a system engineering and technical assistance contractor;

(2) Shall include a plan for phasing out the use of contracted lead system integrator functions over the shortest period of time consistent with the interest of the national defense; and

(3) Shall be provided to the Committees on Armed Services of the Senate and the House of Representatives at least 45 days before the award of a contract pursuant to the determination.

[Interim rule, 73 FR 1823, 1/10/2008, effective 1/10/2008; Interim rule, 74 FR 34266, 7/15/2009, effective 7/15/2009; Final rule, 75 FR 3178, 1/20/2010, effective 1/20/2010]

209.570-4 Solicitation provision and contract clause.

(a) Use the provision at 252.209-7006, Limitations on Contractors Acting as Lead System Integrators, in solicitations for the acquisition of a major system when the acquisition strategy envisions the use of a lead system integrator.

(b) Use the clause at 252.209-7007, Prohibited Financial Interests for Lead System Integrators—

(1) In solicitations that include the provision at 252.209-7006; and

(2) In contracts when the contractor will fill the role of a lead system integrator for the acquisition of a major system.

[Interim rule, 73 FR 1823, 1/10/2008, effective 1/10/2008]

209.571 Organizational conflicts of interest in major defense acquisition programs. (No Text)

[Final rule, 75 FR 81908, 12/29/2010, effective 12/29/2010]

209.571-0 Scope of subpart.

This subpart implements section 207 of the Weapons System Acquisition Reform Act of 2009 (Pub. L. 111–23).

[Final rule, 75 FR 81908, 12/29/2010, effective 12/29/2010]

209.571-1 Definitions.

As used in this section—

Lead system integrator includes *lead system integrator with system responsibility* and *lead system integrator without system responsibility.*

(i) *Lead system integrator with system responsibility* means a prime contractor for the development or production of a major system, if the prime contractor is not expected at the time of award to perform a substantial portion of the work on the system and the major subsystems.

(ii) *Lead system integrator without system responsibility* means a prime contractor under a contract for the procurement of services, the primary purpose of which is to perform acquisition functions closely associated with inherently governmental functions (see section 7.503(d) of the Federal Acquisition Regulation) with respect to the development or production of a major system.

Major subcontractor means a subcontractor that is awarded a subcontract that equals or exceeds—

(i) Both the certified cost or pricing data threshold and 10 percent of the value of the contract under which the subcontract is awarded; or

(ii) $55 million.

Pre-Major Defense Acquisition Program means a program that is in the Materiel Solution Analysis or Technology Development Phases preceding Milestone B of the Defense Acquisition System and has been identified to have the potential to become a major defense acquisition program.

Systems engineering and technical assistance.

(1) *Systems engineering* means an interdisciplinary technical effort to evolve and verify an integrated and total life cycle balanced set of system, people, and process solutions that satisfy customer needs.

(2) *Technical assistance* means the acquisition support, program management support, analyses, and other activities involved in the management and execution of an acquisition program.

(3) *Systems engineering and technical assistance*—

(i) Means a combination of activities related to the development of technical information to support various acquisition processes. Examples of systems engineering and technical assistance activities include, but are not limited to, supporting acquisition efforts such as—

(A) Deriving requirements;

(B) Performing technology assessments;

(C) Developing acquisition strategies;

(D) Conducting risk assessments;

(E) Developing cost estimates;

(F) Determining specifications;

(G) Evaluating contractor performance and conducting independent verification and validation;

(H) Directing other contractors' (other than subcontractors) operations;

(I) Developing test requirements and evaluating test data;

(J) Developing work statements (but see paragraph (ii)(B) of this definition).

(ii) Does not include—

(A) Design and development work of design and development contractors, in accordance with FAR 9.505–2(a)(3) or FAR 9.505–2(b)(3), and the guidance at PGI 209.571–7; or

(B) Preparation of work statements by contractors, acting as industry representatives, under the supervision and control of Government representatives, in accordance with FAR 9.505–2(b)(1)(ii).

[Final rule, 75 FR 81908, 12/29/2010, effective 12/29/2010; Interim rule, 79 FR 4631, 1/29/2014, effective 1/29/2014; Final rule, 79 FR 58693, 9/30/2014, effective 9/30/2014; Final rule, 84 FR 25186, 5/31/2019, effective 5/31/2019]

209.571-2 Applicability.

(a) This subsection applies to major defense acquisition programs.

(b) To the extent that this section is inconsistent with FAR subpart 9.5, this section takes precedence.

[Final rule, 75 FR 81908, 12/29/2010, effective 12/29/2010]

209.571-3 Policy.

It is DoD policy that—

(a) Agencies shall obtain advice on major defense acquisition programs and pre-major defense acquisition programs from sources that are objective and unbiased; and

(b) Contracting officers generally should seek to resolve organizational conflicts of interest in a manner that will promote competition and preserve DoD access to the expertise and experience of qualified contractors. Accordingly, contracting officers should, to the extent feasible, employ organizational conflict of interest resolution strategies that do not unnecessarily restrict the pool of potential offerors in current or future acquisitions. Further, contracting activities shall not impose across-the-board restrictions or limitations on the use of particular resolution methods, except as may be required under 209.571–7 or as may be appropriate in particular acquisitions.

[Final rule, 75 FR 81908, 12/29/2010, effective 12/29/2010]

209.571-4 Mitigation.

(a) Mitigation is any action taken to minimize an organizational conflict of interest. Mitigation may require Government action, contractor action, or a combination of both.

(b) If the contracting officer and the contractor have agreed to mitigation of an organizational conflict of interest, a Government-approved Organizational Conflict of Interest Mitigation Plan, reflecting the actions a contractor has agreed to take to mitigate a conflict, shall be incorporated into the contract.

(c) If the contracting officer determines, after consultation with agency legal counsel, that the otherwise successful offeror is unable to effectively mitigate an organizational conflict of interest, then the contracting officer, taking into account both the instant contract and longer term Government needs, shall use another approach to resolve the organizational conflict of interest, select another offeror, or request a waiver in accordance with FAR 9.503 (but see statutory prohibition in 209.571–7, which cannot be waived).

(d) For any acquisition that exceeds $1 billion, the contracting officer shall brief the senior procurement executive before determining that an offeror's mitigation plan is unacceptable.

[Final rule, 75 FR 81908, 12/29/2010, effective 12/29/2010]

209.571-5 Lead system integrators.

For limitations on contractors acting as lead systems integrators, see 209.570.

[Final rule, 75 FR 81908, 12/29/2010, effective 12/29/2010]

209.571-6 Identification of organizational conflicts of interest.

When evaluating organizational conflicts of interest for major defense acquisition programs or pre-major defense acquisition programs, contracting officers shall consider—

(a) The ownership of business units performing systems engineering and technical assistance, professional services, or management support services to a major defense acquisition program or a pre-major defense acquisition program by a contractor who simultaneously owns a business unit competing (or potentially competing) to perform as—

(1) The prime contractor for the same major defense acquisition program; or

(2) The supplier of a major subsystem or component for the same major defense acquisition program.

(b) The proposed award of a major subsystem by a prime contractor to business units or other affiliates of the same parent corporate entity, particularly the award of a subcontract for software integration or the development of a proprietary software system architecture; and

(c) The performance by, or assistance of, contractors in technical evaluation.

[Final rule, 75 FR 81908, 12/29/2010, effective 12/29/2010]

209.571-7 Systems engineering and technical assistance contracts.

(a) Agencies shall obtain advice on systems architecture and systems engineering matters with respect to major defense acquisition programs or pre-major defense acquisition programs from Federally Funded Research and Development Centers or other sources independent of the major defense acquisition program contractor.

(b) *Limitation on Future Contracting.* (1) Except as provided in paragraph (c) of this subsection, a contract for the performance of systems engineering and technical assistance for a major defense acquisition program or a pre-major defense acquisition program shall prohibit the contractor or any affiliate of the contractor from participating as a contractor or major subcontractor in the development or production of a weapon system under such program.

(2) The requirement in paragraph (b)(1) of this subsection cannot be waived.

(c) *Exception*. (1) The requirement in paragraph (b)(1) of this subsection does not apply if the head of the contracting activity determines that—

(i) An exception is necessary because DoD needs the domain experience and expertise of the highly qualified, apparently successful offeror; and

(ii) Based on the agreed-to resolution strategy, the apparently successful offeror will be able to provide objective and unbiased advice, as required by 209.571-3(a), without a limitation on future participation in development and production.

(2) The authority to make this determination cannot be delegated.

[Final rule, 75 FR 81908, 12/29/2010, effective 12/29/2010]

209.571-8 Solicitation provision and contract clause.

(a) Use the provision at 252.209-7008, Notice of Prohibition Relating to Organizational Conflict of Interest—Major Defense Acquisition Program, if the solicitation includes the clause at 252.209-7009, Organizational Conflict of Interest—Major Defense Acquisition Program; and

(b) Use the clause at 252.209-7009, Organizational Conflict of Interest—Major Defense Acquisition Program, in solicitations and contracts for systems engineering and technical assistance for major defense acquisition programs or pre-major defense acquisition programs.

[Final rule, 75 FR 81908, 12/29/2010, effective 12/29/2010]

PART 210—MARKET RESEARCH

Table of Contents

Policy 210.001
Procedures 210.002

PART 210—MARKET RESEARCH

210.001 Policy.

(a) In addition to the requirements of FAR 10.001(a), agencies shall—

(i) Conduct market research appropriate to the circumstances before issuing a solicitation with tiered evaluation of offers (section 816 of Pub. L. 109-163); and

(ii) Use the results of market research to determine whether the criteria in FAR part 19 are met for setting aside the acquisition for small business or, for a task or delivery order, whether there are a sufficient number of qualified small business concerns available to justify limiting competition under the terms of the contract. If the contracting officer cannot determine whether the criteria are met, the contracting officer shall include a written explanation in the contract file as to why such a determination could not be made (section 816 of Pub. L. 109-163).

(c)(2) In addition to the notification requirements at FAR 10.001(c)(2)(i) and (ii), see 205.205-70 for the bundling notification publication requirement.

[Interim rule, 67 FR 20687 4/26/2002, effective 4/26/2002; Final rule, 69 FR 63328, 11/1/2004, effective 11/1/2004; Final rule, 71 FR 14104, 3/21/2006, effective 3/21/2006; Interim rule, 71 FR 53042, 9/8/2006, effective 9/8/2006; Final rule, 72 FR 42313, 8/2/2007, effective 8/2/2007; Interim rule, 75 FR 40714, 7/13/2010, effective 7/13/2010; Final rule, 76 FR 9679, 2/22/2011, effective 2/22/2011; Final rule, 83 FR 15995, 4/13/2018, effective 4/13/2018]

210.002 Procedures.

(e)(i) When contracting for services, see PGI 210.070 for the "Market Research Report Guide for Improving the Tradecraft in Services Acquisition."

(ii) See PGI 210.002(e)(ii) regarding potential offerors that express an interest in an acquisition.

(iii) Follow the procedures at PGI 210.002(e)(iii) regarding contract file documentation.

[Final rule, 77 FR 52253, 8/29/2012, effective 8/29/2012; Final rule, 80 FR 21656, 4/20/2015, effective 4/20/2015; Final rule, 81 FR 65563, 9/23/2016, effective 9/23/2016]

PART 211—DESCRIBING AGENCY NEEDS

Table of Contents

Policy 211.002
[Removed] 211.002-70

Subpart 211.1—Selecting and Developing Requirements Documents

Use of brand name or equal purchase descriptions 211.104
Items peculiar to one manufacturer 211.105
Purchase descriptions for service contracts 211.106
Solicitation provision 211.107
Use of proprietary specifications or standards 211.170

Subpart 211.2—Using and Maintaining Requirements Documents

Identification and availability of specifications 211.201
Solicitation provisions and contract clauses 211.204
[Reserved] 211.270
Elimination of use of class I ozone-depleting substances 211.271
Alternate preservation, packaging, and packing 211.272
Substitutions for military or Federal specifications and standards 211.273
Definition 211.273-1
Policy 211.273-2
Procedures 211.273-3
Contract clauses 211.273-4
Item identification and valuation requirements 211.274
General 211.274-1
Policy for item unique identification 211.274-2
Policy for valuation 211.274-3
Policy for reporting of Government-furnished property 211.274-4
Policy for assignment of Government-assigned serial numbers 211.274-5
Contract clauses 211.274-6
Passive radio frequency identification. 211.275
Definitions 211.275-1
Policy 211.275-2
Contract clause 211.275-3

Subpart 211.5—Liquidated Damages

Scope 211.500
Contract clauses 211.503

Subpart 211.6—Priorities and Allocations

General 211.602

Subpart 211.70—Purchase Requests

Procedures 211.7001

PART 211—DESCRIBING AGENCY NEEDS

211.002 Policy.

All defense technology and acquisition programs in DoD are subject to the policies and procedures in DoDD 5000.01, The Defense Acquisition System, and DoDI 5000.02, Operation of the Defense Acquisition System.

[DAC 91-9, 60 FR 61586, 11/30/95, effective 11/30/95; Final rule, 71 FR 27641, 5/12/2006, effective 5/12/2006; Final rule, 76 FR 76318, 12/7/2011, effective 12/7/2011]

211.002-70 [Removed]

[DAC 91-9, 60 FR 61586, 11/30/95, effective 11/30/95; Final rule, 83 FR 54676, 10/31/2018, effective 10/31/2018]

SUBPART 211.1—SELECTING AND DEVELOPING REQUIREMENTS DOCUMENTS

211.104 Use of brand name or equal purchase descriptions.

A justification and approval is required to use brand name or equal purchase descriptions—

(1) When using sealed bidding or negotiated acquisition procedures (see 206.302-1(c)(2) for justification requirements); or

(2) When using the simplified procedures for certain commercial items at FAR 13.5 (see 213.501(a)(ii) for justification requirement).

[Final rule, 84 FR 25190, 5/31/2019, effective 5/31/2019]

211.105 Items peculiar to one manufacturer.

Follow the publication requirements at PGI 211.105.

[Final rule, 70 FR 23804, 5/5/2005, effective 5/5/2005]

211.106 Purchase descriptions for service contracts.

Agencies shall require that purchase descriptions for service contracts and resulting requirements documents, such as statements of work or performance work statements, include language to provide a clear distinction between Government employees and contractor employees. Agencies shall be guided by the characteristics and descriptive elements of personal-services contracts at FAR 37.104. Service contracts shall require contractor employees to identify themselves as contractor personnel by introducing themselves or being introduced as contractor personnel and displaying distinguishing badges or other visible identification for meetings with Government personnel. In addition, contracts shall require contractor personnel to appropriately identify themselves as contractor employees in telephone conversations and in formal and informal written correspondence.

[Interim rule, 75 FR 54524, 9/8/2010, effective 9/8/2010; Final rule, 76 FR 25565, 5/5/2011, effective 5/5/2011]

211.107 Solicitation provision.

(b) To comply with section 875(c) of the National Defense Authorization Act for Fiscal Year 2017 (Pub. L. 114-328), use the provision at FAR 52.211-7, Alternatives to Government-Unique Standards, in DoD solicitations that include military or Government-unique specifications and standards.

[Final rule, 65 FR 6553, 2/10/2000, effective 2/10/2000; Final rule, 84 FR 4366, 2/15/2019, effective 2/15/2019]

211.170 Use of proprietary specifications or standards.

A justification and approval is required to use proprietary specifications and standards—

(1) When using sealed bidding or negotiated acquisition procedures (see 206.302-1(S-70) for justification requirements); or,

(2) When using the simplified procedures for certain commercial items at FAR 13.5 (see 213.501(a)(ii) for justification requirements).

[Final rule, 84 FR 25190, 5/31/2019, effective 5/31/2019]

SUBPART 211.2—USING AND MAINTAINING REQUIREMENTS DOCUMENTS

211.201 Identification and availability of specifications.

Follow the procedures at PGI 211.201 for obtaining specifications, standards, and data item descriptions from the ASSIST database, including DoD adoption notices on voluntary consensus standards.

[DAC 91-9, 60 FR 61586, 11/30/95, effective 11/30/95; Final rule, 64 FR 8727, 2/23/99, effective 2/23/99; Final rule, 64 FR 51074, 9/21/99, effective 9/21/99; Final rule, 69 FR 67854, 11/22/2004, effective 11/22/2004; Final rule, 71 FR 27641, 5/12/2006, effective 5/12/2006; Final rule, 84 FR 4366, 2/15/2019, effective 2/15/2019]

211.204 Solicitation provisions and contract clauses.

(c) When contract performance requires use of specifications, standards, and data item descriptions that are not listed in the Acquisition Streamlining and Standardization Information System database, use a provision, as appropriate, substantially the same as 252.211-7002, Availability for Examination of Specifications, Standards, Plans, Drawings, Data Item Descriptions, and Other Pertinent Documents.

[DAC 91-9, 60 FR 61586, 11/30/95, effective 11/30/95; Final rule, 71 FR 27641, 5/12/2006, effective 5/12/2006; Final rule, 84 FR 25192, 5/31/2019, effective 5/31/2019]

211.270 [Reserved]

[Removed and reserved, 64 FR 55632, 10/14/99, effective 10/14/99]

211.271 Elimination of use of class I ozone-depleting substances.

See subpart 223.8 for restrictions on contracting for ozone-depleting substances.

[DAC 91-9, 60 FR 61586, 11/30/95, effective 11/30/95; Final rule, 70 FR 73150, 12/9/2005, effective 12/9/2005]

211.272 Alternate preservation, packaging, and packing.

Use the provision at 252.211-7004, Alternate Preservation, Packaging, and Packing, in solicitations which include military preservation, packaging, or packing specifications when it is feasible to evaluate and award using commercial or industrial preservation, packaging, or packing.

[DAC 91-9, 60 FR 61586, 11/30/95, effective 11/30/95]

211.273 Substitutions for military or Federal specifications and standards. (No Text)

211.273-1 Definition.

SPI process, as used in this section, is defined in the clause at 252.211-7005, Substitutions for Military or Federal Specifications and Standards.

[Final rule, 62 FR 44223, 8/20/97, effective 8/20/97]

211.273-2 Policy.

(a) Under the Single Process Initiative (SPI), DoD accepts SPI processes in lieu of specific military or Federal specifications or standards that specify a management or manufacturing process.

(b) DoD acceptance of an SPI process follows the decision of a Management Council, which includes representatives of the contractor, the Defense Contract Management Agency, the Defense Contract Audit Agency, and the military departments.

(c) In procurements of previously developed items, SPI processes that previously were accepted by the Management Council shall be considered valid replacements for military or Federal specifications or standards, absent a specific determination to the contrary.

[Final rule, 62 FR 44223, 8/20/97, effective 8/20/97; Final rule, 64 FR 14398, 3/25/99, effective 3/25/99; Final rule, 65 FR 52951, 8/31/2000, effective 8/31/2000; Final rule, 71 FR 27641, 5/12/2006, effective 5/12/2006]

211.273-3 Procedures.

Follow the procedures at PGI 211.273-3 for encouraging the use of SPI processes instead of military or Federal specifications and standards.

[Final rule, 64 FR 14398, 3/25/99, effective 3/25/99; Final rule, 71 FR 27641, 5/12/2006, effective 5/12/2006]

211.273-4 Contract clause.

Use the clause at 252.211-7005, Substitutions for Military or Federal Specifications and Standards, in solicitations and contracts exceeding the micro-purchase threshold, when procuring previously developed items.

[Final rule, 62 FR 44223, 8/20/97, effective 8/20/97]

211.274 Item Identification and valuation requirements. (No Text)

[Interim rule, 72 FR 52293, 9/13/2007, effective 9/13/2007; Final rule, 73 FR 70906, 11/24/2008, effective 11/24/2008]

211.274-1 General.

Unique item identification and valuation is a system of marking and valuing items delivered to DoD that will enhance logistics, contracting, and financial business transactions supporting the United States and coalition troops. Through unique item identification policy, which capitalizes on leading practices and embraces open standards, DoD can—

(a) Achieves lower life-cycle cost of item management and improves lifecycle property management;

(b) Improves operational readiness;

(c) Provides reliable accountability of property and asset visibility throughout the life cycle;

(d) Reduces the burden on the workforce through increased productivity and efficiency; and

(e) Ensures item level traceability throughout lifecycle to strengthen supply chain integrity, enhance cyber security, and combat counterfeiting.

[Final rule, 70 FR 20831, 4/22/2005, effective 4/22/2005; Final rule, 78 FR 76067, 12/16/2013, effective 12/16/2013]

211.274-2 Policy for item unique identification.

(a) It is DoD policy that DoD item unique identification, or a DoD recognized unique identification equivalent, is required for all delivered items, including items of contractor-acquired property delivered on contract line items (see PGI 245.402–71 for guidance when delivery of contractor acquired property is required)—

(1) For which the Government's unit acquisition cost is $5,000 or more;

(2) For which the Government's unit acquisition cost is less than $5,000 when the requiring activity determines that item unique identification is required for mission essential or controlled inventory items; or

(3) Regardless of value for any—

(i) DoD serially managed item (reparable or nonreparable) or subassembly, component, or part embedded within a subassembly, component, or part;

(ii) Parent item (as defined in 252.211–7003(a)) that contains the embedded subassembly, component, or part;

(iii) Warranted serialized item;

(iv) Item of special tooling or special test equipment, as defined at FAR 2.101, for a major defense acquisition program that is designated for preservation and storage in accordance with the requirements of section 815 of the National Defense Authorization Act for Fiscal Year 2009 (Pub. L. 110–417); and

(v) High risk item identified by the requiring activity as vulnerable to supply chain threat, a target of cyber threats, or counterfeiting.

(b) *Exceptions*. The contractor will not be required to provide DoD item unique identification if—

(1) The items, as determined by the head of the contracting activity, are to be used to support a contingency or humanitarian or peacekeeping operation; to facilitate defense against or recovery from nuclear, biological, chemical, or radiological attack; to facilitate the provision of international disaster assistance; or to support response to an emergency or major disaster; or

(2) A determination and findings has been executed concluding that it is more cost effective for the Government requiring activity to assign, mark, and register the unique item identifier after delivery, and the item is either acquired from a small business concern, or is a commercial item acquired under FAR part 12 or part 8.

(i) The determination and findings shall be executed by—

(A) The Component Acquisition Executive for an acquisition category (ACAT) I program; or

(B) The head of the contracting activity for all other programs.

(ii) The DoD Unique Identification Policy Office must receive a copy of the determination and findings required by paragraph (b)(2)(i) of this subsection. Follow the procedures at PGI 211.274-2.

[Interim rule, 68 FR 58631, 10/10/2003, effective 1/1/2004; Interim rule, 68 FR 75196, 12/30/2003, effective 1/1/2004; Final rule, 70 FR 20831, 4/22/2005, effective 4/22/2005; Final rule, 76 FR 33166, 6/8/2011, effective 6/8/2011; Final rule, 77 FR 52254, 8/29/2012, effective 8/29/2012; Final rule, 78 FR 76067, 12/16/2013, effective 12/16/2013; Final rule, 83 FR 24888, 5/30/2018, effective 5/30/2018]

211.274-3 Policy for valuation.

(a) It is DoD policy that contractors shall be required to identify the Government's unit acquisition cost for all deliverable end items to which item unique identification applies.

(b) The Government's unit acquisition cost is—

(1) For fixed-price type line, subline, or exhibit line items, the unit price identified in the contract at the time of delivery;

(2) For cost-type or undefinitized line, subline, or exhibit line items, the contractor's estimated fully burdened unit cost to the Government at the time of delivery; and

(3) For items delivered under a time-and-materials contract, the contractor's estimated fully burdened unit cost to the Government at the time of delivery.

(c) The Government's unit acquisition cost of subassemblies, components, and parts embedded in delivered items shall not be separately identified.

[Interim rule, 68 FR 58631, 10/10/2003, effective 1/1/2004; Interim rule, 68 FR 75196, 12/30/2003, effective 1/1/2004; Final rule, 70 FR 20831, 4/22/2005, effective 4/22/2005; Final rule, 78 FR 76067, 12/16/2013, effective 12/16/2013]

211.274-4 Policy for reporting of Government-furnished property.

(a) It is DoD policy that all Government-furnished property be recorded in the DoD Item Unique Identification (IUID) Registry, as defined in the clause at 252.211-7007, Reporting of Government-Furnished Property.

(b) The following items are not required to be reported:

(1) Contractor-acquired property, as defined in FAR part 45.

(2) Property under any statutory leasing authority.

(3) Property to which the Government has acquired a lien or title solely because of partial, advance, progress, or performance-based payments.

(4) Intellectual property or software.

(5) Real property.

(6) Property released as work in process.

(7) Non-serial managed items (reporting is limited to receipt transactions only).

[Interim rule, 68 FR 58631, 10/10/2003, effective 1/1/2004; Interim rule, 68 FR 75196, 12/30/2003, effective 1/1/2004; Final rule, 70 FR 20831, 4/22/2005, effective 4/22/2005; Interim rule, 72 FR 52293, 9/13/2007, effective 9/13/2007; Final rule, 73 FR 70906, 11/24/2008, effective 11/24/2008; Final rule, 77 FR 52254, 8/29/2012, effective 8/29/2012]

211.274-5 Policy for assignment of Government-assigned serial numbers.

It is DoD policy that contractors apply Government-assigned serial numbers, such as tail numbers/hull numbers and equipment registration numbers, in human-readable format on major end items when required by law, regulation, or military operational necessity. The latest version of MIL-STD-130, Marking of U.S. Military Property, shall be used for the marking of human-readable information.

[Final rule, 75 FR 59102, 9/27/2010, effective 9/27/2010]

211.274-6 Contract clauses.

(a)(1) Use the clause at 252.211-7003, Item Unique Identification and Valuation, in solicitations and contracts, including solicitations and contracts using FAR part 12 procedures for the acquisition of commercial items, for supplies, and for services involving the furnishing of supplies, unless the conditions in 211.274-2(b) apply.

(2) Identify in paragraph (c)(1)(ii) of the clause the contract line, subline, or exhibit line item number and description of any item(s) below $5,000 in unit acquisition cost for which DoD item unique identification or a DoD recognized unique identification equivalent is required in accordance with 211.274-2(a)(2).

(3) Identify in paragraph (c)(1)(iii) of the clause the applicable attachment number, when DoD item unique identification or a DoD recognized unique identification equivalent is required in accordance with 211.274-2(a)(3)(i) through (v).

(b) Use the clause at 252.211-7007, Reporting of Government-Furnished Property, in solicitations and contracts that contain the clause at FAR 52.245- 1, Government Property.

(c) Use the clause at 252.211-7008, Use of Government-Assigned Serial Numbers, in solicitations and contracts, including solicitations and contracts using FAR part 12 procedures for the acquisition of commercial items, that—

(1) Contain the clause at 252.211-7003, Item Unique Identification and Valuation.

(2) Require the contractor to mark major end items under the terms and conditions of the contract.

[Interim rule, 72 FR 52293, 9/13/2007, effective 9/13/2007; Final rule, 73 FR 70906, 11/24/2008, effective 11/24/2008; Redesignated from 211.274-5, Final rule, 75 FR 59102, 9/27/2010, effective 9/27/2010; Final rule, 77 FR 52254, 8/29/2012, effective 8/29/2012; Final rule, 78 FR 37980, 6/25/2013, effective 6/25/2013; Final rule, 78 FR 76067, 12/16/2013, effective 12/16/2013; Final rule, 79 FR 44313, 7/31/2014, effective 7/31/2014; Final rule, 79 FR 44313, 7/31/2014, effective 7/31/2014; Final rule, 80 FR 51750, 8/26/2015, effective 8/26/2015]

211.275 Passive radio frequency identification. (No Text)

211.275-1 Definitions.

Bulk commodities, case, palletized unit load, passive RFID tag, and *radio frequency identification* are defined in the clause at 252.211-7006, Passive Radio Frequency Identification.

[Final rule, 70 FR 53955, 9/13/2005, effective 11/14/2005; Final rule, 76 FR 58142, 9/20/2011, effective 9/20/2011]

211.275-2 Policy.

(a) Except as provided in paragraph (b) of this section, radio frequency identification (RFID), in the form of a passive RFID tag, is required for cases and palletized unit loads packaging levels and any additional consolidation level(s) deemed necessary by the requiring activity for shipments of items that—

(1) Contain items in any of the following classes of supply, as defined in DoD Manual 4140.01, Volume 6, DoD Supply Chain Materiel Management Procedures: Materiel Returns, Retention, and Disposition:

(i) Subclass of Class I—Packaged operational rations.

(ii) Class II—Clothing, individual equipment, tentage, organizational tool kits, hand tools, and administrative and housekeeping supplies and equipment.

(iii) Class IIIP—Packaged petroleum, lubricants, oils, preservatives, chemicals, and additives.

(iv) Class IV—Construction and barrier materials.

(v) Class VI—Personal demand items (non-military sales items).

(vi) Subclass of Class VIII—Medical materials (excluding pharmaceuticals, biologicals, and reagents—suppliers should limit the mixing of excluded and non-excluded materials).

(vii) Class IX—Repair parts and components including kits, assemblies and subassemblies, reparable and consumable items required for maintenance support of all equipment, excluding medical-peculiar repair parts; and

(2) Will be shipped to one of the locations listed at *https://www.acq.osd.mil/log/sci/RFID_ship-to-locations.html* or to—

(i) A location outside the contiguous United States when the shipment has been assigned Transportation Priority 1; or

(ii) Any additional location(s) deemed necessary by the requiring activity.

(iii) Defense Distribution Depot, Albany, GA: DoDAAC SW3121.

(iv) Defense Distribution Depot, Anniston, AL: DoDAAC W31G1Z or SW3120.

(v) Defense Distribution Depot, Barstow, CA: DoDAAC SW3215.

(vi) Defense Distribution Depot, Cherry Point, NC: DoDAAC SW3113.

(vii) Defense Distribution Depot, Columbus, OH: DoDAAC SW0700.

(viii) Defense Distribution Depot, Corpus Christi, TX: DoDAAC W45H08 or SW3222.

(ix) Defense Distribution Depot, Hill, UT: DoDAAC SW3210.

(x) Defense Distribution Depot, Jacksonville, FL: DoDAAC SW3122.

(xi) Defense Distribution Depot, Oklahoma City, OK: DoDAAC SW3211.

(xii) Defense Distribution Depot, Norfolk, VA: DoDAAC SW3117.

(xiii) Defense Distribution Depot, Puget Sound, WA: DoDAAC SW3216.

(xiv) Defense Distribution Depot, Red River, TX: DoDAAC W45G19 or SW3227.

(xv) Defense Distribution Depot, Richmond, VA: DoDAAC SW0400.

(xvi) Defense Distribution Depot, San Diego, CA: DoDAAC SW3218.

(xvii) Defense Distribution Depot, Tobyhanna, PA: DoDAAC W25G1W or SW3114.

(xviii) Defense Distribution Depot, Warner Robins, GA: DoDAAC SW3119.

(xix) Air Mobility Command Terminal, Charleston Air Force Base, Charleston, SC: Air Terminal Identifier Code CHS.

(xx) Air Mobility Command Terminal, Naval Air Station, Norfolk, VA: Air Terminal Identifier Code NGU.

(xxi) Air Mobility Command Terminal, Travis Air Force Base, Fairfield, CA: Air Terminal Identifier Code SUU.

(xxii) A location outside the contiguous United States when the shipment has been assigned Transportation Priority 1.

(b) The following are excluded from the requirements of paragraph (a) of this subsection:

(1) Shipments of bulk commodities.

(2) Shipments to locations other than Defense Distribution Depots when the contract includes the clause at FAR 52.213-1, Fast Payment Procedures.

[Final rule, 70 FR 53955, 9/13/2005, effective 11/14/2005; Interim rule, 71 FR 29084, 5/19/2006, effective 5/19/2006; Final rule, 72 FR 6480, 2/12/2007, effective 2/12/2007; Final rule, 76 FR 58142, 9/20/2011, effective 9/20/2011; Final rule, 81 FR 36473, 6/7/2016, effective 6/7/2016; Final rule, 82 FR 61479, 12/28/2017, effective 12/28/2017; Final rule, 83 FR 12681, 3/23/2018, effective 3/23/2018]

211.275-3 Contract clause.

Use the clause at 252.211-7006, Passive Radio Frequency Identification, in solicitations and contracts, including solicitations and contracts using FAR part 12 procedures for the acquisition of commercial items, that will require shipment of items meeting the criteria at 211.275-2, and complete paragraph (b)(1)(ii) of the clause at 252.211-7006 as appropriate.

[Final rule, 70 FR 53955, 9/13/2005, effective 11/14/2005; Final rule, 76 FR 58142, 9/20/2011, effective 9/20/2011; Final rule,

78 FR 37980, 6/25/2013, effective 6/25/2013]

SUBPART 211.5—LIQUIDATED DAMAGES

211.500 Scope.

This subpart and FAR subpart 11.5 do not apply to liquidated damages for comprehensive subcontracting plans under the Test Program for Negotiation of Comprehensive Small Business Subcontracting Plans. See 219.702-70 for coverage of liquidated damages for comprehensive subcontracting plans.

[Final rule, 83 FR 15996, 4/13/2018, effective 4/13/2018]

211.503 Contract clauses.

(b) Use the clause at FAR 52.211-12, Liquidated Damages Construction, in all construction contracts exceeding $700,000, except cost-plus-fixed-fee contracts or contracts where the contractor cannot control the pace of the work. Use of the clause in contracts of $700,000 or less is optional.

[DAC 91-9, 60 FR 61586, 11/30/95, effective 11/30/95; Redesignated at 66 FR 49860, 10/1/2001, effective 10/1/2001; Final rule, 71 FR 75891, 12/19/2006, effective 12/19/2006; Final rule, 75 FR 45072, 8/2/2010, effective 10/1/2010; Final rule, 80 FR 36903, 6/26/2015, effective 10/1/2015]

SUBPART 211.6—PRIORITIES AND ALLOCATIONS

211.602 General.

DoD implementation of the Defense Priorities and Allocations Systems is in DoDD 4400.1, Defense Production Act Programs.

[Final rule, 64 FR 51074, 9/21/99, effective 9/21/99]

SUBPART 211.70—PURCHASE REQUESTS

211.7001 Procedures.

Follow the procedures at PGI 211.7001 for developing and distributing purchase requests, except for the requirements for Military Interdepartmental Purchase Requests (DD Form 448) addressed in 253.208-1.

[Final rule, 79 FR 51264, 8/28/2014, effective 8/28/2014]

PART 212—ACQUISITION OF COMMERCIAL ITEMS

Table of Contents

Definitions 212.001

Subpart 212.1—Acquisition of Commercial Items—General

Applicability 212.102

Subpart 212.2—Special Requirements for the Acquisition of Commercial Items

Procedures for solicitation, evaluation, and award 212.203
Offers 212.205
Contract type 212.207
Determination of price reasonableness 212.209
Technical data 212.211
Computer software 212.212
Major weapon systems as commercial items 212.270
Limitation on acquisition of right-hand drive passenger sedans 212.271
Preference for certain commercial products and services 212.272

Subpart 212.3—Solicitation Provisions and Contract Clauses for the Acquisition of Commercial Items

Solicitation provisions and contract clauses for the acquisition of commercial items 212.301
Tailoring of provisions and clauses for the acquisition of commercial items 212.302
[Removed] 212.303

Subpart 212.5—Applicability of Certain Laws to the Acquisition of Commercial Items

Applicability of certain laws to executive agency contracts for the acquisition of commercial items 212.503
Applicability of certain laws to subcontracts for the acquisition of commercial items 212.504
Applicability of certain laws to contracts and subcontracts for the acquisition of commercially available off-the-shelf items 212.570

Subpart 212.6—Streamlined Procedures for Evaluation and Solicitation for Commercial Items

Streamlined evaluation of offers 212.602

Subpart 212.70—Limitation on Conversion of Procurement from Commercial Acquisition Procedures

Scope 212.7000
Procedures 212.7001

Subpart 212.71—Pilot Program for Acquisition of Military-Purpose Nondevelopmental Items

Scope 212.7000
Procedures 212.7001

Scope 212.7100
Definitions 212.7101
Pilot program 212.7102
Contracts under the program 212.7102-1
Reporting requirements 212.7102-2
Sunset of the pilot authority 212.7102-3
Solicitation provision 212.7103

PART 212—ACQUISITION OF COMMERCIAL ITEMS

212.001 Definitions.

As used in this part—

Market research means a review of existing systems, subsystems, capabilities, and technologies that are available or could be made available to meet the needs of DoD in whole or in part. The review shall include, at a minimum, contacting knowledgeable individuals in Government and industry regarding existing market capabilities and pricing information, and may include any of the techniques for conducting market research provided in FAR 10.002(b)(2) (section 855 of the National Defense Authorization Act for Fiscal Year 2016 (Pub. L. 114-92)).

Nontraditional defense contractor means an entity that is not currently performing and has not performed any contract or subcontract for DoD that is subject to full coverage under the cost accounting standards prescribed pursuant to 41 U.S.C. 1502 and the regulations implementing such section, for at least the 1-year period preceding the solicitation of sources by DoD for the procurement (10 U.S.C. 2302(9)).

[Final rule, 83 FR 4431, 1/31/2018, effective 1/31/2018]

SUBPART 212.1—ACQUISITION OF COMMERCIAL ITEMS—GENERAL

212.102 Applicability.

(a)(i) *Commercial item determination*. When using FAR part 12 procedures for acquisitions exceeding $1 million in value, except for acquisitions made pursuant to FAR 12.102(f)(1), the contracting officer shall—

(A) Determine in writing that the acquisition meets the commercial item definition in FAR 2.101;

(B) Include the written determination in the contract file; and

(C) Obtain approval at one level above the contracting officer when a commercial item determination relies on subsections (1)(ii), (3), (4), or (6) of the *commercial item* definition at FAR 2.101.

(D) Follow the procedures and guidance at PGI 212.102(a)(i) regarding file documentation and commercial item determinations.

(ii) *Prior commercial item determination*. This section implements 10 U.S.C. 2306a(b)(4) and 10 U.S.C. 2380(b).

(A) The contracting officer may presume that a prior commercial item determination made by a military department, a defense agency, or another component of DoD shall serve as a determination for subsequent procurements of such item. See PGI 212.102(a)(ii) for information about items that the Department has historically acquired as military unique, noncommercial items.

(B) If the contracting officer does not make the presumption that a prior commercial item determination is valid, and instead chooses to proceed with a procurement of an item previously determined to be a commercial item using procedures other than the procedures authorized for the procurement of a commercial item, the contracting officer shall request a review of the commercial item determination by the head of the contracting activity that will conduct the procurement. Not later than 30 days after receiving a request for review of a commercial item determination, the head of a contracting activity shall—

(*1*) Confirm that the prior determination was appropriate and still applicable; or

(*2*) Issue a determination that the prior use of FAR part 12 procedures was improper or that it is no longer appropriate to acquire the item using FAR part 12 procedures, with a written explanation of the basis for the determination (see 212.70).

(iii) *Nontraditional defense contractors*. In accordance with 10 U.S.C. 2380a, contracting officers may treat supplies and services provided by nontraditional defense contractors as commercial items. This permissive authority is intended to enhance defense innovation and investment, enable DoD to acquire items that otherwise might not have been available, and create incentives for nontraditional defense contractors to do business with DoD. It is not intended to recategorize current noncommercial items, however, when appropriate, contracting officers may consider applying commercial item procedures to the procurement of supplies and services from business segments that meet the definition of "nontraditional defense contractor" even though they have been established under traditional defense contractors. The decision to apply commercial item procedures to the procurement of supplies and services from nontraditional defense contractors does not require a commercial item determination and does not mean the item is commercial.

[Removed by final rule, 69 FR 35532, 6/25/2004, effective 6/25/2004; Final rule, 73 FR 4114, 1/24/2008, effective 1/24/2008; Final rule, 77 FR 14480, 3/12/2012, effective 3/12/2012; Final rule 80 FR 10389, 2/26/2015, effective 2/26/2015; Final rule, 81 FR 65563, 9/23/2016, effective 9/23/2016; Final rule, 83 FR 4431, 1/31/2018, effective 1/31/2018]

SUBPART 212.2—SPECIAL REQUIREMENTS FOR THE ACQUISITION OF COMMERCIAL ITEMS

212.203 Procedures for solicitation, evaluation, and award.

(1) See 215.101-2-70 for the limitations and prohibitions on the use of the lowest price technically acceptable source selection process, which are applicable to the acquisition of commercial items.

(2) See 217.7801 for the prohibition on the use of reverse auctions for personal protective equipment and aviation critical safety items.

[Final rule, 84 FR 50785, 9/26/2019, effective 10/1/2019]

212.205 Offers.

(c) When using competitive procedures, if only one offer is received, the contracting officer shall follow the procedures at 215.371.

[Final rule, 77 FR 39125, 6/29/2012, effective 6/29/2012]

212.207 Contract type.

(b) In accordance with section 805 of the National Defense Authorization Act for Fiscal Year 2008 (Pub. L. 110-181), use of time-and-materials and labor-hour contracts for the acquisition of commercial items is authorized only for the following:

(i) Services acquired for support of a commercial item, as described in paragraph (5) of the definition of *commercial item* at FAR 2.101 (41 U.S.C. 103).

(ii) Emergency repair services.

(iii) Any other commercial services only to the extent that the head of the agency concerned approves a written determination by the contracting officer that—

(A) The services to be acquired are commercial services as defined in paragraph (6) of the definition of *commercial item* at FAR 2.101 (41 U.S.C. 103);

(B) If the services to be acquired are subject to FAR 15.403-1(c)(3)(ii), the offeror of the services has submitted sufficient information in accordance with that subsection;

(C) Such services are commonly sold to the general public through use of time-and-materials or labor-hour contracts; and

(D) The use of a time-and-materials or labor-hour contract type is in the best interest of the Government.

[Interim rule, 74 FR 34263, 7/15/2009, effective 7/15/2009; Correction, 74 FR 35825, 7/21/2009, effective 7/21/2009; Final rule, 75 FR 51416, 8/20/2010, effective 8/20/2010; Interim rule; delay in confirmation as final, 75 FR 52650, 8/27/2010; Final rule, 76 FR 21810, 4/19/2011, effective 4/19/2011; Final rule, 76 FR 58137, 9/20/2011, effective 9/20/2011]

212.209 Determination of price reasonableness.

(a) Market research shall be used, where appropriate, to inform price reasonableness determinations.

(b) If the contracting officer determines that the information obtained through market research pursuant to paragraph (a) of this section, is insufficient to determine the reasonableness of price, the contracting officer shall consider information submitted by the offeror of recent purchase prices paid by the Government and commercial customers for the same or similar commercial items under comparable terms and conditions in establishing price reasonableness on a subsequent purchase if the contracting officer is satisfied that the prices previously paid remain a valid reference for comparison. In assessing whether the prices previously paid remain a valid reference for comparison, the contracting officer shall consider the totality of other relevant factors such as the time elapsed since the prior purchase and any differences in the quantities purchased (10 U.S.C. 2306a(b)).

(c) If the contracting officer determines that the offeror cannot provide sufficient information as described in paragraph (b) of this section to determine the reasonableness of price, the contracting officer should request the offeror to submit information on—

(1) Prices paid for the same or similar items sold under different terms and conditions;

(2) Prices paid for similar levels of work or effort on related products or services;

(3) Prices paid for alternative solutions or approaches; and

(4) Other relevant information that can serve as the basis for determining the reasonableness of price.

(d) Nothing in this section shall be construed to preclude the contracting officer from requiring the contractor to supply information that is sufficient to determine the reasonableness of price, regardless of whether or not the contractor was required to provide such information in connection with any earlier procurement. If the contracting officer determines that the pricing information submitted is not sufficient to determine the reasonableness of price, the contracting officer may request other relevant information regarding the basis for price or cost, including uncertified cost data such as labor costs, material costs, and other direct and indirect costs.

[Final rule, 83 FR 4431, 1/31/2018, effective 1/31/2018]

212.211 Technical data.

The DoD policy for acquiring technical data for commercial items is at 227.7102.

[DAC 91-9, 60 FR 61586, 11/30/95, effective 11/30/95]

212.212 Computer software.

(1) Departments and agencies shall identify and evaluate, at all stages of the acquisition process (including concept refinement, concept decision, and technology development), opportunities for the use of commercial computer software and other non-developmental software in accordance with Section 803 of the National Defense Authorization Act for Fiscal Year 2009 (Pub. L. 110-417).

(2) See Subpart 208.74 when acquiring commercial software or software maintenance. See 227.7202 for policy on the acquisition of commercial computer software and commercial computer software documentation.

[Interim rule, 69 FR 63329, 11/1/2004, effective 11/1/2004; Final rule, 71 FR 18667, 4/12/2006, effective 4/12/2006; Final rule, 74 FR 34269, 7/15/2009, effective 7/15/2009]

212.270 Major weapon systems as commercial items.

The DoD policy for acquiring major weapon systems as commercial items is in Subpart 234.70.

[Interim rule, 69 FR 63329, 11/1/2004, effective 11/1/2004; Final rule, 71 FR 18667, 4/12/2006, effective 4/12/2006; Interim rule, 71 FR 58537, 10/4/2006, effective 10/4/2006; Final rule, 72 FR 51189, 9/6/2007, effective 9/6/2007]

212.271 Limitation on acquisition of right-hand drive passenger sedans.

10 U.S.C. 2253 (a)(2) limits the authority to purchase right-hand drive passenger sedans to a cost of not more than $40,000 per vehicle.

[Interim rule, 77 FR 19127, 3/30/2012, effective 3/30/2012; Final rule, 77 FR 52252, 8/29/2012, effective 8/29/2012]

212.272 Preference for certain commercial products and services.

(a) As required by section 855 of the National Defense Authorization Act for Fiscal Year 2016 (Pub. L. 114-92), for requirements relating to the acquisition of commercial information technology products and services, see 239.101.

(b)(1) As required by section 876 of the National Defense Authorization Act of Fiscal Year 2017 (Pub. L. 114-328), a contracting officer may not enter into a contract above the simplified acquisition threshold for facilities-related services, knowledge-based services (except engineering services), medical services, or transportation services that are not commercial services, unless the appropriate official specified in paragraph (b)(2) of this section determines in writing that no commercial services are suitable to meet the agency's needs as provided in section 10 U.S.C. 2377(c)(2).

(2) The following officials are authorized to make the determination specified in paragraph (b)(1) of this section:

(i) For contracts above $10 million, the head of the contracting activity, the combatant commander of the combatant command concerned, or the Under Secretary of Defense for Acquisition and Sustainment (as applicable).

(ii) For contracts in an amount above the simplified acquisition threshold and at or below $10 million, the contracting officer.

[Final rule, 84 FR 39203, 8/9/2019, effective 8/9/2019]

SUBPART 212.3—SOLICITATION PROVISIONS AND CONTRACT CLAUSES FOR THE ACQUISITION OF COMMERCIAL ITEMS

212.301 Solicitation provisions and contract clauses for the acquisition of commercial items.

(c) Include an evaluation factor regarding supply chain risk (see subpart 239.73) when acquiring information technology, whether as a service or as a supply, that is a covered system, is a part of a covered system, or is in support of a covered system, as defined in 239.7301.

(f) The following additional provisions and clauses apply to DoD solicitations and contracts using FAR part 12 procedures for the acquisition of commercial items. If the offeror has completed any of the following provisions listed in this paragraph electronically as part of its annual representations and certifications at *https://www.acquisition.gov*, the contracting officer shall consider this information instead of requiring the offeror to complete these provisions for a particular solicitation.

(i) *Part 203—Improper Business Practices and Personal Conflicts of Interest.* (A) Use the FAR clause at 52.203-3, Gratuities, as prescribed in FAR 3.202, to comply with 10 U.S.C. 2207.

(B) Use the clause at 252.203-7000, Requirements Relating to Compensation of Former DoD Officials, as prescribed in 203.171-4(a), to comply with section 847 of Pub. L. 110-181.

(C) Use the clause at 252.203-7003, Agency Office of the Inspector General, as prescribed in 203.1004(a), to comply with section 6101 of Pub. L. 110-252 and 41 U.S.C. 3509.

(D) Use the provision at 252.203-7005, Representation Relating to Compensation of Former DoD Officials, as prescribed in 203.171-4(b).

(ii) *Part 204—Administrative and Information Matters.*

(A) Use the clause at 252.204-7004, Antiterrorism Awareness Training for Contractors, as prescribed in 204.7203.

(B) Use the provision at 252.204-7008, Compliance with Safeguarding Covered Defense Information Controls, as prescribed in 204.7304(a).

(C) Use the clause at 252.204-7009, Limitations on the Use or Disclosure of Third-Party Contractor Reported Cyber Incident Information, as prescribed in 204.7304(b).

(D) Use the clause at 252.204-7012, Safeguarding of Covered Defense Information and Cyber Incident Reporting, as prescribed in 204.7304(c).

(E) Use the clause at 252.204-7014, Limitations on the Use or Disclosure of Information by Litigation Support Contractors, as prescribed in 204.7403(a), to comply with 10 U.S.C. 129d.

(F) Use the clause at 252.204-7015, Notice of Authorized Disclosure of Information for

Litigation Support, as prescribed in 204.7403(b), to comply with 10 U.S.C. 129d.

(H) Use the provision at 252.204–7016, Covered Defense Telecommunications Equipment or Services—Representation, as prescribed in 204.2105(a), to comply with section 1656 of the National Defense Authorization Act for Fiscal Year 2018 (Pub. L. 115–91).

(I) Use the provision at 252.204–7017, Prohibition on the Acquisition of Covered Defense Telecommunications Equipment or Services—Representation, as prescribed in 204.2105(b), to comply with section 1656 of the National Defense Authorization Act for Fiscal Year 2018 (Pub. L. 115–91).

(J) Use the clause at 252.204–7018, Prohibition on the Acquisition of Covered Defense Telecommunications Equipment or Services, as prescribed in 204.2105(c), to comply with section 1656 of the National Defense Authorization Act for Fiscal Year 2018 (Pub. L. 115–91).

(iii) *Part 205—Publicizing Contract Actions.* Use the clause at 252.205-7000, Provision of Information to Cooperative Agreement Holders, as prescribed in 205.470, to comply with 10 U.S.C. 2416.

(iv) *Part 211—Describing Agency Needs.* (A) Use the clause at 252.211-7003, Item Unique Identification and Valuation, as prescribed in 211.274-6(a)(1).

(B) Use the provision at 252.211-7006, Passive Radio Frequency Identification, as prescribed in 211.275-3.

(C) Use the clause at 252.211-7007, Reporting of Government-Furnished Property, as prescribed in 211.274-6.

(D) Use the clause at 252.211-7008, Use of Government-Assigned Serial Numbers, as prescribed in 211.274-6(c).

(v) Part 213—*Simplified Acquisition Procedures.* Use the provision at 252.213–7000, Notice to Prospective Suppliers on Use of Supplier Performance Risk System in Past Performance Evaluations, as prescribed in 213.106–2–70.

(vi) *Part 215—Contracting by Negotiation.* (A) Use the provision at 252.215-7003, Requirements for Submission of Data Other Than Certified Cost or Pricing Data—Canadian Commercial Corporation, as prescribed at 215.408(2)(i).

(B) Use the clause at 252.215-7004, Requirement for Submission of Data other Than Certified Cost or Pricing Data—Modifications—Canadian Commercial Corporation, as prescribed at 215.408(2)(ii).

(C) Use the provision at 252.215-7007, Notice of Intent to Resolicit, as prescribed in 215.371-6.

(D) Use the provision 252.215-7008, Only One Offer, as prescribed at 215.408(3).

(E) Use the provision 252.215-7010, Requirements for Certified Cost or Pricing Data and Data Other Than Certified Cost or Pricing Data, as prescribed at 215.408(5)(i) to comply with section 831 of the National Defense Authorization Act for Fiscal Year 2013 (Pub. L. 112-239) and sections 851 and 853 of the National Defense Authorization Act for Fiscal Year 2016 (Pub. L. 114-92).

(*1*) Use the basic provision as prescribed at 215.408(5)(i)(A).

(*2*) Use the alternate I provision as prescribed at 215.408(5)(i)(B).

(vii) *Part 219—Small Business Programs.* (A) Use the clause at 252.219-7003, Small Business Subcontracting Plan (DoD Contracts), to comply with 15 U.S.C. 637.

(1) Use the basic clause as prescribed in 219.708(b)(1)(A)(*1*).

(2) Use the alternate I clause as prescribed in 219.708(b)(1)(A)(*2*)

(3) Use the alternate II clause as prescribed in 219.708(b)(1)(A)(3).

(B) Use the clause at 252.219-7004, Small Business Subcontracting Plan (Test Program), as prescribed in 219.708(b)(1)(B), to comply with 15 U.S.C. 637 note.

(C) Use the provision at 252.219-7000, Advancing Small Business Growth, as prescribed in 219.309(1), to comply with 10 U.S.C. 2419.

(D) Use the provision at 252.219-7012, Competition for Religious-Related Services, as prescribed in 219.270-3.

(viii) *Part 223—Environment, Energy and Water Efficiency, Renewable Energy Technolo-*

gies, Occupational Safety, and Drug-Free Workplace. Use the clause at 252.223-7008, Prohibition of Hexavalent Chromium, as prescribed in 223.7306.

(ix) *Part 225—Foreign Acquisition*. (A) Use the provision at 252.225-7000, Buy American—Balance of Payments Program Certificate, to comply with 41 U.S.C. chapter 83 and Executive Order 10582 of December 17, 1954, Prescribing Uniform Procedures for Certain Determinations Under the Buy-American Act.

(*1*) Use the basic provision as prescribed in 225.1101(1)(i).

(*2*) Use the alternate I provision as prescribed in 225.1101(1)(ii).

(B) Use the clause at 252.225-7001, Buy American and Balance of Payments Program, to comply with 41 U.S.C. chapter 83 and Executive Order 10582 of December 17, 1954, Prescribing Uniform Procedures for Certain Determinations Under the Buy-American Act.

(*1*) Use the basic clause as prescribed in 225.1101(2)(ii).

(*2*) Use the alternate I clause as prescribed in 225.1101(2)(iii).

(C) Use the clause at 252.225-7006, Acquisition of the American Flag, as prescribed in 225.7002-3(c), to comply with section 8123 of the DoD Appropriations Act, 2014 (Pub. L. 113-76, division C, title VIII), and the same provision in subsequent DoD appropriations acts.

(D) Use the clause at 252.225-7007, Prohibition on Acquisition of Certain Items from Communist Chinese Military Companies, as prescribed in 225.1103(4), to comply with section 1211 of the National Defense Authorization Act (NDAA) for Fiscal Year (FY) 2006 (Pub. L. 109-163) as amended by the NDAAs for FY 2012 and FY 2017.

(E) Use the clause at 252.225-7008, Restriction on Acquisition of Specialty Metals, as prescribed in 225.7003-5(a)(1), to comply with 10 U.S.C. 2533b.

(F) Use the clause at 252.225-7009, Restriction on Acquisition of Certain Articles Containing Specialty Metals, as prescribed in 225.7003-5(a)(2), to comply with 10 U.S.C. 2533b.

(G) Use the provision at 252.225-7010, Commercial Derivative Military Article—Specialty Metals Compliance Certificate, as prescribed in 225.7003-5(b), to comply with 10 U.S.C. 2533b.

(H) Use the clause at 252.225-7012, Preference for Certain Domestic Commodities, as prescribed in 225.7002-3(a), to comply with 10 U.S.C. 2533a.

(I) Use the clause at 252.225-7015, Restriction on Acquisition of Hand or Measuring Tools, as prescribed in 225.7002-3(b), to comply with 10 U.S.C. 2533a.

(J) Use the clause at 252.225-7016, Restriction on Acquisition of Ball and Roller Bearings, as prescribed in 225.7009-5, to comply with section 8065 of Pub. L. 107-117 and the same restriction in subsequent DoD appropriations acts.

(K) Use the clause at 252.225-7017, Photovoltaic Devices, as prescribed in 225.7017-4(a), to comply with section 846 of Public Law 111-383.

(L) Use the provision at 252.225-7018, Photovoltaic Devices—Certificate, as prescribed in 225.7017-4(b), to comply with section 846 of Public Law 111-383.

(M) Use the provision at 252.225-7020, Trade Agreements Certificate, to comply with 19 U.S.C. 2501-2518 and 19 U.S.C. 3301 note. Alternate I also implements section 886 of the National Defense Authorization Act for Fiscal Year 2008 (Pub. L. 110-181).

(*1*) Use the basic provision as prescribed in 225.1101(5)(i).

(*2*) Use the alternate I provision as prescribed in 225.1101(5)(ii).

(N) Use the clause at 252.225-7021, Trade Agreements to comply with 19 U.S.C. 2501-2518 and 19 U.S.C. 3301 note.

(*1*) Use the basic clause as prescribed in 225.1101(6)(i).

(*2*) Use the alternate II clause as prescribed in 225.1101(6)(iii).

(O) Use the provision at 252.225-7023, Preference for Products or Services from Afghanistan, as prescribed in 225.7703-4(a), to comply with section 886 of the National Defense Authorization Act for Fiscal Year 2008 (Pub. L. 110-181).

(P) Use the clause at 252.225-7024, Requirement for Products or Services from Afghanistan, as prescribed in225.7703-4(b), to comply with section 886 of the National Defense Authorization Act for Fiscal Year 2008 (Pub. L. 110-181).

(Q) Use the clause at 252.225-7026, Acquisition Restricted to Products or Services from Afghanistan, as prescribed in 225.7703-4(c), to comply with section 886 of the National Defense Authorization Act for Fiscal Year 2008 (Pub. L. 110-181).

(R) Use the clause at 252.225-7027, Restriction on Contingent Fees for Foreign Military Sales, as prescribed in 225.7307(a), to comply with 22 U.S.C. 2779.

(S) Use the clause at 252.225-7028, Exclusionary Policies and Practices of Foreign Governments, as prescribed in 225.7307(b), to comply with 22 U.S.C. 2755.

(T) Use the clause at 252.225-7029, Acquisition of Uniform Components for Afghan Military or Afghan National Police, as prescribed in 225.7703-4(d).

(U) Use the provision at 252.225-7031, Secondary Arab Boycott of Israel, as prescribed in 225.7605, to comply with 10 U.S.C. 2410i.

(V) Use the provision at 252.225-7035, Buy American—Free Trade Agreements—Balance of Payments Program Certificate, to comply with 41 U.S.C. chapter 83 and 19 U.S.C. 3301 note. Alternates II, III, and V also implement section 886 of the National Defense Authorization Act for Fiscal Year 2008 (Pub. L. 110-181).

(*1*) Use the basic provision as prescribed in 225.1101(9)(i).

(*2*) Use the alternate I provision as prescribed in 225.1101(9)(ii).

(*3*) Use the alternate II provision as prescribed in 225.1101(9)(iii).

(*4*) Use the alternate III provision as prescribed in 225.1101(9)(iv).

(*5*) Use the alternate IV provision as prescribed in 225.1101(9)(v).

(*6*) Use the alternate V provision as prescribed in 225.1101(9)(vi).

(W) Use the clause at 252.225-7036, Buy American—Free Trade Agreements—Balance of Payments Program to comply with 41 U.S.C. chapter 83 and 19 U.S.C. 3301 note. Alternates II, III, and V also implement section 886 of the National Defense Authorization Act for Fiscal Year 2008 (Pub. L. 110-181).

(*1*) Use the basic clause as prescribed in 225.1101(10)(i)(A).

(*2*) Use the alternate I clause as prescribed in 225.1101(10)(i)(B).

(*3*) Use the alternate II clause as prescribed in 225.1101(10)(i)(C).

(*4*) Use the alternate III clause as prescribed in 225.1101(10)(i)(D).

(*5*) Use the alternate IV clause as prescribed in 225.1101(10)(i)(E).

(*6*) Use the alternate V clause as prescribed in 225.1101(10)(i)(F).

(X) Use the provision at 252.225-7037, Evaluation of Offers for Air Circuit Breakers, as prescribed in 225.7006-4(a), to comply with 10 U.S.C. 2534(a)(3).

(Y) Use the clause at 252.225-7038, Restriction on Acquisition of Air Circuit Breakers, as prescribed in 225.7006-4(b), to comply with 10 U.S.C. 2534(a)(3).

(Z) Use the clause at 252.225-7039, Defense Contractors Performing Private Security Functions Outside the United States, as prescribed in 225.302-6, to comply with section 2 of Pub. L. 110–181, as amended.

(AA) Use the clause at 252.225-7040, Contractor Personnel Supporting U.S. Armed Forces Deployed Outside the United States, as prescribed in 225.371-5(a).

(BB) Use the clause at 252.225-7043, Antiterrorism/Force Protection Policy for Defense Contractors Outside the United States, as prescribed in 225.372-2.

(CC) Use the provision at 252.225-7049, Prohibition on Acquisition of Certain Foreign Commercial Satellite Services—Representations, as prescribed at 225.772-5(a), to comply with 10 U.S.C. 2279.

(DD) Use the provision at 252.225-7050, Disclosure of Ownership or Control by the Government of a Country that is a State Sponsor of Terrorism, as prescribed in 225.771-5, to comply with 10 U.S.C. 2327(b).

(EE) Use the clause at 252.225-7051, Prohibition on Acquisition for Certain Foreign Commercial Satellite Services, as prescribed in 225.772-5(b), to comply with 10 U.S.C. 2279.

(FF) Use the clause at 252.225-7052, Restriction on the Acquisition of Certain Magnets and Tungsten, as prescribed in 225.7018-5.

(x) *Part 226—Other Socioeconomic Programs.* (A) Use the clause at 252.226-7001, Utilization of Indian Organizations, Indian-Owned Economic Enterprises, and Native Hawaiian Small Business Concerns, as prescribed in 226.104, to comply with section 8021 of Pub. L. 107-248 and similar sections in subsequent DoD appropriations acts.

(B) Use the provision at 252.226–7002, Representation for Demonstration Project for Contractors Employing Persons with Disabilities, as prescribed in 226.7203.

(xi) *Part 227—Patents, Data, and Copyrights.* (A) Use the clause at 252.227-7013, Rights in Technical Data-Noncommercial Items, as prescribed in 227.7103-6(a). Use the clause with its Alternate I as prescribed in 227.7103-6(b)(1). Use the clause with its Alternate II as prescribed in 227.7103-6(b)(2), to comply with 10 U.S.C. 7317 and 17 U.S.C. 1301, *et seq.*

(B) Use the clause at 252.227-7015, Technical Data-Commercial Items, as prescribed in 227.7102-4(a)(1), to comply with 10 U.S.C. 2320. Use the clause with its Alternate I as prescribed in 227.7102-4(a)(2), to comply with 10 U.S.C. 7317 and 17 U.S.C. 1301, *et seq.*

(C) Use the clause at 252.227-7037, Validation of Restrictive Markings on Technical Data, as prescribed in 227.7102-4(c).

(xii) *Part 229—Taxes.* (A) Use the clause at 252.229-7014, Taxes—Foreign Contracts in Afghanistan, as prescribed at 229.402-70(k).

(B) Use the clause at 252.229-7015,Taxes—Foreign Contracts in Afghanistan (North Atlantic Treaty Organization Status of Forces Agreement), as prescribed at 229.402-70(l).

(xiii) *Part 232—Contract Financing.* (A) Use the clause at 252.232-7003, Electronic Submission of Payment Requests and Receiving Reports, as prescribed in 232.7004, to comply with 10 U.S.C. 2227.

(B) Use the clause at 252.232-7006,, Wide Area WorkFlow Payment Instructions, as prescribed in 232.7006(b).

(C) Use the clause at 252.232-7009, Mandatory Payment by Governmentwide Commercial Purchase Card, as prescribed in 232.1110.

(D) Use the clause at 252.232-7010, Levies on Contract Payments, as prescribed in 232.7102.

(E) Use the clause at 252.232-7011, Payments in Support of Emergencies and Contingency Operations, as prescribed in 232.908.

(F) Use the provision at 252.232-7014, Notification of Payment in Local Currency (Afghanistan), as prescribed in 232.7202.

(xiv) *Part 237—Service Contracting.* (A) Use the clause at 252.237-7010, Prohibition on Interrogation of Detainees by Contractor Personnel, as prescribed in 237.173-5, to comply with section 1038 of Pub. L. 111-84.

(B) Use the clause at 252.237-7019, Training for Contractor Personnel Interacting with Detainees, as prescribed in 237.171-4, to comply with section 1092 of Pub. L. 108-375.

(xv) *Part 239—Acquisition of Information Technology.*

(A) Use the provision 252.239-7009, Representation of Use of Cloud Computing, as prescribed in 239.7604(a).

(B) Use the clause 252.239-7010, Cloud Computing Services, as prescribed in 239.7604(b).

(C) Use the provision at 252.239-7017, Notice of Supply Chain Risk, as prescribed in 239.7306(a), to comply with 10 U.S.C. 2339a.

(D) Use the clause at 252.239-7018, Supply Chain Risk, as prescribed in 239.7306(b), to comply with 10 U.S.C. 2339a.

(xvi) *Part 243—Contract Modifications.* Use the clause at 252.243-7002, Requests for Equitable Adjustment, as prescribed in 243.205-71, to comply with 10 U.S.C. 2410.

(xvii) *Part 244—Subcontracting Policies and Procedures.* Use the clause at 252.244-7000, Subcontracts for Commercial Items, as prescribed in 244.403.

(xviii) *Part 246—Quality Assurance.* (A) Use the clause at 252.246-7003, Notification of Potential Safety Issues, as prescribed in 246.370(a).

(B) Use the clause at 252.246-7004, Safety of Facilities, Infrastructure, and Equipment for Military Operations, as prescribed in 246.270-4, to comply with section 807 of Pub. L. 111-84.

(C) Use the clause at 252.246-7008, Sources of Electronic Parts, as prescribed in 246.870-3(b), to comply with section 818(c)(3) of Pub. L. 112-81, as amended by section 817 of the National Defense Authorization Act for Fiscal Year 2015 (Pub. L. 113-291 and section 885 of the National Defense Authorization Act for Fiscal Year 2016 (Pub. L. 114-92)).

(xix) *Part 247—Transportation.* (A) Use the clause at 252.247-7003, Pass-Through of Motor Carrier Fuel Surcharge Adjustment to the Cost Bearer, as prescribed in 247.207, to comply with section 884 of Pub. L. 110-417.

(B) Use the provision at 252.247-7022, Representation of Extent of Transportation by Sea, as prescribed in 247.574(a).

(C) Use the basic or one of the alternates of the clause at 252.247-7023, Transportation of Supplies by Sea, as prescribed in 247.574(b), to comply with the Cargo Preference Act of 1904 (10 U.S.C. 2631(a)).

(*1*) Use the basic clause as prescribed in 247.574(b)(1).

(*2*) Use the alternate I clause as prescribed in 247.5744(b)(2).

(*3*) Use the alternate II clause as prescribed in 2247.574(b)(3).

(D) Use the clause 252.247-7025, Reflagging or Repair Work, as prescribed in 247.574(c), to comply with 10 U.S.C. 2631(b).

(E) Use the provision at 252.247-7026, Evaluation Preference for Use of Domestic Shipyards—Applicable to Acquisition of Carriage by Vessel for DoD Cargo in the Coastwise or Noncontiguous Trade, as prescribed in 247.574(d), to comply with section 1017 of Pub. L. 109-364.

(F) Use the clause at 252.247-7027, Riding Gang Member Requirements, as prescribed in 247.574(e), to comply with section 3504 of the National Defense Authorization Act for Fiscal Year 2009 (Pub. L. 110-417).

(G) Use the clause at 252.247-7028, Application for U.S. Government Shipping Documentation/Instructions, as prescribed in 247.207.

[DAC 91-9, 60 FR 61586, 11/30/95, effective 11/30/95; DAC 91-11, 61 FR 50446, 9/26/96, effective 9/26/96; DAC 91-12, 62 FR 34114, 6/24/97, effective 6/24/97; DAC 91-13, 63 FR 11522, 3/9/98, effective 3/9/98; Final rule, 63 FR 15316, 3/31/98, effective 3/31/98; Interim rule, 64 FR 8727, 2/23/99, effective 2/23/99; Final rule, 64 FR 43098, 8/9/99, effective 8/9/99; Final rule, 65 FR 46625, 7/31/2000, effective 7/31/2000; Final rule, 66 FR 49860, 10/1/2001, effective 10/1/2001; Final rule, 66 FR 55121, 11/1/2001, effective 11/1/2001; Final rule, 68 FR 7438, 2/14/2003, effective 2/14/2003; Final rule, 68 FR 15615, 3/31/2003, effective 4/30/2003; Interim rule, 68 FR 58631, 10/10/2003, effective 1/1/2004; Interim rule, 68 FR 58633, 10/10/2003, effective 1/1/2004; Interim rule, 68 FR 64557, 11/14/2003, effective 11/14/2003; Interim rule, 68 FR 75196, 12/30/2003, effective 1/1/2004; Interim rule, 69 FR 1926, 1/13/2004, effective 1/13/2004; Final rule, 70 FR 20831, 4/22/2005, effective 4/22/2005; Final rule, 70 FR 23790, 5/5/2005, effective 6/6/2005; Final rule, 70 FR 53955, 9/13/2005, effective 11/14/2005; Final rule, 70 FR 57188, 9/30/2005, effective 9/30/2005; Final rule, 71 FR 9269, 2/23/2006, effective 2/23/2006; Interim rule, 71 FR 34826, 6/16/2006, effective 6/16/2006; Final rule, 71 FR 39005, 7/11/2006, effective 7/11/2006; Interim rule, 71 FR 62560, 10/26/2006, effective

10/26/2006; Final rule, 71 FR 69489, 12/1/2006, effective 12/1/2006; Final rule, 72 FR 2633, 1/22/2007, effective 1/22/2007; Interim rule, 72 FR 49204, 8/28/2007, effective 8/28/2007; Final rule, 73 FR 1822, 1/10/2008, effective 1/10/2008; Final rule, 73 FR 4115, 1/24/2008, effective 1/24/2008; Final rule, 73 FR 16764, 3/31/2008, effective 3/31/2008; Final rule, 73 FR 70909, 11/24/2008, effective 11/24/2008; Final rule, 74 FR 37626, 7/29/2009, effective 7/29/2009; Interim rule, 75 FR 40711, 7/13/2010, effective 7/13/2010; Interim rule, 75 FR 65437, 10/25/2010, effective 10/25/2010; Final rule, 76 FR 11371, 3/2/2011, effective 3/2/2011; Final rule, 76 FR 58138, 9/20/2011, effective 9/20/2011; Final rule, 76 FR 61279, 10/4/2011, effective 10/4/2011; Final rule, 76 FR 71464, 11/18/2011, effective 11/18/2011; Interim rule, 76 FR 78858, 12/20/2011, effective 12/20/2011; Final rule, 77 FR 23631, 4/20/2012, effective 4/20/2012; Final rule, 77 FR 30368, 5/22/2012, effective 5/22/2012; Final rule, 77 FR 35879, 6/15/2012, effective 6/15/2012; Final rule, 77 FR 39125, 6/29/2012, effective 6/29/2012; Final rule, 77 FR 39140, 6/29/2012, effective 6/29/2012; Final rule, 77 FR 39141, 6/29/2012, effective 6/29/2012; Final rule, 77 FR 52254, 8/29/2012, effective 8/29/2012; Final rule, 78 FR 37980, 6/25/2013, effective 6/25/2013; Interim rule, 78 FR 59854, 9/30/2012, effective 9/30/2013; Final rule, 78 FR 65214, 10/31/2013, effective 10/31/2013; Interim rule, 78 FR 69267, 11/18/2013, effective 11/18/2013; Final rule 78 FR 69273, 11/18/2013, effective 11/18/2013; Final rule, 78 FR 73450, 12/6/2013, effective 12/6/2013; Final rule, 78 FR 76067, 12/16/2013, effective 12/13/2013; Interim rule, 79 FR 11337, 2/282014, effective 2/28/2014; Final rule, 79 FR 22036, 4/21/2014, effective 4/21/2014; Final rule, 79 FR 30469, 5/28/2014, effective 5/28/2014; Final rule, 79 FR 44313, 7/31/2014, effective 7/31/2014; Interim rule, 79 FR 45661, 8/5/2014, effective 8/5/2014; Final rule, 79 FR 58694, 9/30/2014, effective 9/30/2014; Final rule, 79 FR 65815, 11/5/2014, effective 11/5/2014; Final rule, 79 FR 73488, 12/11/2014, effective 12/11/2014; Final rule, 79 FR 73490, 12/11/2014, effective 12/11/2014; Final rule, 80 FR 2018, 1/15/2015, effective 1/15/2015; Final rule, 80 FR 4997, 1/29/2015, effective 1/29/2015; Final rule, 80 FR 4999, 1/29/2015, effective 1/29/2015; Final rule, 80 FR 30115, 5/26/2015, effective 5/26/2015; Final rule, 80 FR 30117, 5/26/2015, effective 5/26/2015; Final rule, 80 FR 36900, 6/26/2015, effective 6/26/2015; Interim rule, 80 FR 51739, 8/26/2015, effective 8/26/2015; Final rule, 80 FR 56929, 9/21/2015, effective 9/21/2015; Final rule, 80 FR 67243, 10/30/2015, effective 10/30/2015; Final rule, 80 FR 72599, 11/20/2015, effective 11/20/2015; Final rule, 80 FR 81467, 12/30/2015, effective 12/30/2015; Final rule, 81 FR 17045, 3/25/2016, effective 3/25/2016; Final rule, 81 FR 28724, 5/10/2016, effective 5/10/2016; Final rule, 81 FR 28729, 5/10/2016, effective 5/10/2016; Final rule, 81 FR 28730, 5/10/2016, effective 5/10/2016; Final rule, 81 FR 50635, 8/2/2016, effective 8/2/2016; Final rule, 81 FR 72986, 10/21/2016, effective 10/21/2016; Final rule, 82 FR 61479, 12/28/2017, effective 12/28/2017; Final rule, 83 FR 4431, 1/31/2018, effective 1/31/2018; Final rule, 83 FR 16001, 4/13/2018, effective 4/13/2018; Final rule, 83 FR 19641, 5/4/2018, effective 5/4/2018; Final rule, 83 FR 24886, 5/30/2018, effective 5/30/2018; Final rule, 83 FR 24887, 5/30/2018, effective 5/30/2018; Final rule, 83 FR 30824, 6/29/2018, effective 6/29/2018; Final rule, 83 FR 62498, 12/4/2018, effective 12/5/2018; Final rule, 83 FR 66062, 12/21/2018, effective 12/21/2018; Interim rule, 83 FR 66066, 12/21/2018, effective 12/21/2018; Final rule, 84 FR 4362, 2/15/2019, effective 2/15/2019; Final rule, 84 FR 4368, 2/15/2019, effective 2/15/2019; Final rule, 84 FR 4370, 2/15/2019, effective 2/15/2019; Interim rule, 84 FR 18156, 4/30/2019, effective 4/30/2019; Final rule, 84 FR 25188, 5/31/2019, effective 5/31/2019; Final rule, 84 FR 48507, 9/13/2019, effective 9/13/2019; Final rule, 84 FR 48510, 9/13/2019, effective 9/13/2019; Final rule, 84 FR 58331, 10/31/2019, effective 10/31/2019; Interim rule, 84 FR 72231, 12/31/2019, effective 12/31/2019; Final rule, 84 FR 72554, 12/31/2019, effective 12/31/2019]

212.302 Tailoring of provisions and clauses for the acquisition of commercial items.

(c) *Tailoring inconsistent with customary commercial practice*. The head of the contracting activity is the approval authority within the DoD for waivers under FAR 12.302(c).

[DAC 91-9, 60 FR 61586, 11/30/95, effective 11/30/95]

212.303 [Removed]

[Final rule, 65 FR 46625, 7/31/2000, effective 7/31/2000; Final rule, 69 FR 65089, 11/10/2004, effective 11/10/2004]

SUBPART 212.5—APPLICABILITY OF CERTAIN LAWS TO THE ACQUISITION OF COMMERCIAL ITEMS

212.503 Applicability of certain laws to executive agency contracts for the acquisition of commercial items.

(a) The following laws are not applicable to contracts for the acquisition of commercial items:

(i) 10 U.S.C. 2306(b), Prohibition on Contingent Fees.

(ii) 10 U.S.C. 2324, Allowable Costs Under Defense Contracts.

(iii) 10 U.S.C. 2384(b), Requirement to Identify Suppliers.

(iv) 10 U.S.C. 2397(a)(1), Reports by Employees or Former Employees of Defense Contractors.

(v) 10 U.S.C. 2397b(f), Limits on Employment for Former DoD Officials.

(vi) 10 U.S.C. 2397c, Defense Contractor Requirements Concerning Former DoD Officials.

(vii) 10 U.S.C. 2408(a), Prohibition on Persons Convicted of Defense Related Felonies.

(viii) 10 U.S.C. 2410b, Contractor Inventory Accounting System Standards (see 252.242-7004).

(ix) 107 Stat 1720 (Section 843(a), Public Law 103-160), Reporting Requirement Regarding Dealings with Terrorist Countries.

(x) Domestic Content Restrictions in the National Defense Appropriations Acts for Fiscal Years 1996 and Subsequent Years, unless the restriction specifically applies to commercial items. For the restriction that specifically applies to commercial ball or roller bearings as end items, see 225.7009-3 (Section 8065 of Public Law 107-117).

(xi) Section 8116 of the Defense Appropriations Act for Fiscal Year 2010 (Pub. L. 111-118) and similar sections in subsequent DoD appropriations acts.

(c) The applicability of the following laws has been modified in regard to contracts for the acquisition of commercial items:

(i) 10 U.S.C. 2402, Prohibition on Limiting Subcontractor Direct Sales to the United States (see FAR 3.503 and 52.203-6).

(ii) 10 U.S.C. 2306a, Truth in Negotiations Act (see FAR 15.403-1(b)(3)).

[DAC 91-9, 60 FR 61586, 11/30/95, effective 11/30/95; Interim rule, 63 FR 11850, 3/11/98, effective 3/11/98; Final rule, 63 FR 55040, 10/14/98, effective 10/14/98; Final rule, 64 FR 51074, 9/21/99, effective 9/21/99; Interim rule, 65 FR 77827, 12/13/2000, effective 12/13/2000, finalized without change, 66 FR 49862, 10/1/2001, effective 10/1/2001; Final rule, 67 4208, 1/29/2002, effective 1/29/2002; Final rule, 69 FR 65089, 11/10/2004, effective 11/10/2004; Final rule, 73 FR 76969, 12/18/2008, effective 12/18/2008; Interim rule, 75 FR 27946, 5/19/2010, effective 5/19/2010; Final rule, 75 FR 76295, 12/8/2010, effective 12/8/2010; Final rule, 76 FR 38047, 6/29/2011, effective 6/29/2011; Final rule, 76 FR 76318, 12/7/2011, effective 12/7/2011]

212.504 Applicability of certain laws to subcontracts for the acquisition of commercial items.

(a) The following laws are not applicable to subcontracts at any tier for the acquisition of commercial items or commercial components:

(i) 10 U.S.C. 2306(b) Prohibition on Contingent Fees.

(ii) 10 U.S.C. 2313(c), Examination of Records of a Contractor.

(iii) 10 U.S.C. 2324, Allowable Costs Under Defense Contracts.

(iv) 10 U.S.C. 2327, Reporting Requirement Regarding Dealings with Terrorist Countries.

(v) 10 U.S.C. 2384(b), Requirement to Identify Suppliers.

(vi) 10 U.S.C. 2391 note, Notification of Substantial Impact on Employment.

(vii) 10 U.S.C. 2393, Prohibition Against Doing Business with Certain Offerors or Contractors.

(viii) 10 U.S.C. 2397(a)(1), Reports by Employees or Former Employees of Defense Contractors.

(ix) 10 U.S.C. 2397b(f), Limits on Employment for Former DoD Officials.

(x) 10 U.S.C. 2397c, Defense Contractor Requirements Concerning Former DoD Officials.

(xi) 10 U.S.C. 2408(a) Prohibition on Persons Convicted of Defense Related Felonies.

(xii) 10 U.S.C. 2410b, Contractor Inventory Accounting System Standards.

(xiii) 10 U.S.C. 2501 note, Notification of Proposed Program Termination.

(xiv) 10 U.S.C. 2534, Miscellaneous Limitations on the Procurement of Goods Other Than United States Goods.

(xv) Effective May 1, 1996: 10 U.S.C. 2631, Transportation of Supplies by Sea.

(xvi) Domestic Content Restrictions in the National Defense Appropriations Acts for Fiscal Years 1996 and Subsequent Years, unless the restriction specifically applies to commercial items. For the restriction that specifically applies to commercial ball or roller bearings as end items, see 225.7009-3 (Section 8065 of Public Law 107-117).

(b) Certain requirements of the following laws have been eliminated for subcontracts at any tier for the acquisition of commercial items or commercial components:

(i) 10 U.S.C. 2393(d), Subcontractor Reports Under Prohibition Against Doing Business with Certain Offerors (see FAR 52.209-6).

(ii) 10 U.S.C. 2402, Prohibition on Limiting Subcontractor Direct Sales to the United States (see FAR 3.503 and 52.203-6).

[DAC 91-9, 60 FR 61586, 11/30/95, effective 11/30/95; Final rule, 61 FR 58488, 11/15/96; effective 11/15/96; Interim rule, 62 FR 5779, 2/7/97, effective 2/7/97; Final rule, 65 FR 14400, 3/16/2000, effective 3/16/2000; Final rule, 65 FR 39703, 6/27/2000, effective 6/27/2000; Interim rule, 12/13/2000, effective 12/13/2000, finalized without change, 66 FR 49862, 10/1/2001, effective 10/1/2001; Final rule, 69 FR 63330, 11/1/2004, effective 11/1/2004; Final rule, 73 FR 76969, 12/18/2008, effective 12/18/2008; Interim rule, 75 FR 27946, 5/19/2010, effective 5/19/2010; Final rule, 75 FR 76295, 12/8/2010, effective 12/8/2010; Final rule, 76 FR 38047, 6/29/2011, effective 6/29/2011; Final rule, 76 FR 58144, 9/20/2011, effective 9/20/2011; Final rule, 76 FR 76318, 12/7/2011, effective 12/7/2011; CFR Correction, 77 FR 59339, 9/27/2012]

212.570 Applicability of certain laws to contracts and subcontracts for the acquisition of commercially available off-the-shelf items.

Paragraph (a)(1) of 10 U.S.C. 2533b, Requirement to buy strategic materials critical to national security from American sources, is not applicable to contracts and subcontracts for the acquisition of commercially available off-the-shelf items, except as provided at 225.7003-3(b)(2)(i).

[Final rule, 72 FR 63113, 11/8/2007, effective 11/8/2007; Final rule, 74 FR 37626, 7/29/2009, effective 7/29/2009]

SUBPART 212.6—STREAMLINED PROCEDURES FOR EVALUATION AND

SOLICITATION FOR COMMERCIAL ITEMS

212.602 Streamlined evaluation of offers.

(b) (i) For the acquisition of transportation and transportation-related services, also consider evaluating offers in accordance with the criteria at 247.206(1).

(ii) For the acquisition of transportation in supply contracts that will include a significant requirement for transportation of items outside the contiguous United States, also evaluate offers in accordance with the criterion at 247.301-71.

(iii) For the direct purchase of ocean transportation services, also evaluate offers in accordance with the criteria at 247.573-2(c).

[Final rule, 65 FR 50143, 8/17/2000, effective 8/17/2000; Final rule, 70 FR 35543, 6/21/2005, effective 6/21/2005; Interim rule, 72 FR 49204, 8/28/2007, effective 8/28/2007; Final rule, 73 FR 70909, 11/24/2008, effective 11/24/2008]

SUBPART 212.70—LIMITATION ON CONVERSION OF PROCUREMENT FROM COMMERCIAL ACQUISITION PROCEDURES

212.7000 Scope.

This subpart implements section 856 of the National Defense Authorization Act for Fiscal Year 2016 (Pub. L. 114-92).

[Interim rule, 69 FR 63329, 11/1/2004, effective 11/1/2004; Final rule, 71 FR 18667, 4/12/2006, effective 4/12/2006; Interim rule, 72 FR 49204, 8/28/2007, effective 8/28/2007; Final rule, Removed and reserved, 80 FR 10389, 2/26/2015, effective 2/26/2015; Final rule, 83 FR 4431, 1/31/2018, effective 1/31/2018]

212.7001 Procedures.

(a) *Limitation.* (1) For a procurement valued at more than $1 million, but less than $100 million, previously procured under a prime contract using FAR part 12 procedures based on a commercial item determination made by a military department, a defense agency, or another DoD component, prior to converting the procurement from commercial acquisition procedures to noncommercial acquisition procedures under FAR part 15, the head of the contracting activity shall determine in writing, upon recommendation from the contracting officer for the procurement that—

(i) The earlier use of commercial acquisition procedures under FAR part 12 was in error or based on inadequate information; and

(ii) DoD will realize a cost savings compared to the cost of procuring a similar quantity or level of such item or service using commercial acquisition procedures.

(2) In the case of a procurement valued at $100 million or more, a contract may not be awarded pursuant to a conversion of the procurement described in paragraph (a)(1) of this section until a copy of the head of contracting activity determination is provided to the Office of the Under Secretary of Defense for Acquisition, Technology, and Logistics.

(b) In making a determination under paragraph (a) of this section, the determining official shall, at a minimum, consider the following factors:

(1) The estimated cost of research and development to be performed by the existing contractor to improve future products or services.

(2) The costs for DoD and the contractor in assessing and responding to data requests to support a conversion to noncommercial acquisition procedures.

(3) Changes in purchase quantities.

(4) Costs associated with potential procurement delays resulting from the conversion.

(c) The requirements of this subpart terminate November 25, 2020.

[Interim rule, 69 FR 63329, 11/1/2004, effective 11/1/2004; Final rule, 71 FR 18667, 4/12/2006, effective 4/12/2006; Final rule, Removed and reserved, 80 FR 10389, 2/26/2015, effective 2/26/2015; Final rule, 83 FR 4431, 1/31/2018, effective 1/31/2018]

212.7002 [Removed and Reserved]

[Interim rule, 69 FR 63329, 11/1/2004, effective 11/1/2004; Final rule, 71 FR 18667,

4/12/2006, effective 4/12/2006; Final rule, 80 FR 10389, 2/26/2015, effective 2/26/2015]

212.7002-1 [Removed and Reserved]

[Interim rule, 69 FR 63329, 11/1/2004, effective 11/1/2004; Final rule, 71 FR 18667, 4/12/2006, effective 4/12/2006; Final rule, 73 FR 21845, 4/23/2008, effective 4/23/2008; Interim rule, 74 FR 2415, 1/15/2009, effective 1/15/2009; Final rule, 74 FR 59916, 11/19/2009, effective 11/19/2009; Final rule, 80 FR 10389, 2/26/2015, effective 2/26/2015]

212.7002-2 [Removed and Reserved]

(b) See 212.7003 for special procedures pertaining to technical data and computer software.

[Interim rule, 69 FR 63329, 11/1/2004, effective 11/1/2004; Final rule, 71 FR 18667, 4/12/2006, effective 4/12/2006; Final rule, 73 FR 21845, 4/23/2008, effective 4/23/2008; Interim rule, 74 FR 2415, 1/15/2009, effective 1/15/2009; Final rule, 74 FR 59916, 11/19/2009, effective 11/19/2009; Final rule, 80 FR 10389, 2/26/2015, effective 2/26/2015]

212.7002-3 [Removed and Reserved]

[Final rule, 76 FR 33170, 6/8/2011, effective 6/8/2011; Final rule, 80 FR 10389, 2/26/2015, effective 2/26/2015]

212.7003 [Removed and Reserved]

[Interim rule, 69 FR 63329, 11/1/2004, effective 11/1/2004; Final rule, 71 FR 18667, 4/12/2006, effective 4/12/2006; Final rule, 80 FR 10389, 2/26/2015, effective 2/26/2015]

SUBPART 212.71—PILOT PROGRAM FOR ACQUISITION OF MILITARY-PURPOSE NONDEVELOPMENTAL ITEMS

212.7100 Scope.

This subpart establishes the pilot program authorized by section 866 of the National Defense Authorization Act for Fiscal Year 2011 (Pub. L. 111-383), as modified by section 892 of the National Defense Authorization Act for Fiscal Year 2016 (Pub. L. 114-92).

[Interim rule, 76 FR 38048, 6/29/2011, effective 6/29/2011; Final rule, 77 FR 2653, 1/19/2012, effective 1/19/2012; Interim rule, 81 FR 42557, 6/30/2016, effective 6/30/2016; Final rule, 81 FR 78012, 11/4/2016, effective 11/4/2016]

212.7101 Definitions.

As used in this subpart—

Military–purpose nondevelopmental item means a nondevelopmental item that meets a validated military requirement, as determined in writing by the responsible program manager, and has been developed exclusively at private expense. An item shall not be considered to be developed at private expense if development of the item was paid for in whole or in part through—

(1) Independent research and development costs or bid and proposal costs, per the definition in FAR 31.205-18, that have been reimbursed directly or indirectly by a Federal agency or have been submitted to a Federal agency for reimbursement; or

(2) Foreign government funding.

Nondevelopmental item is defined in FAR 2.101 and also includes previously developed items of supply that require modifications other than those customarily available in the commercial marketplace if such modifications are consistent with the requirement at 212.7102-1(c)(1).

[Interim rule, 76 FR 38048, 6/29/2011, effective 6/29/2011; Final rule, 77 FR 2653, 1/19/2012, effective 1/19/2012; Interim rule, 81 FR 42557, 6/30/2016, effective 6/30/2016]

212.7102 Pilot program. (No Text)

[Interim rule, 76 FR 38048, 6/29/2011, effective 6/29/2011; Final rule, 77 FR 2653, 1/19/2012, effective 1/19/2012]

212.7102-1 Contracts under the program.

The contracting officer may utilize this pilot program to enter into contracts for the acquisition of military-purpose nondevelopmental items. See PGI 212.7102 for file documentation requirements. Each contract entered into under the pilot program shall—

(a) Be a firm-fixed-price contract, or a fixed-price contract with an economic price adjustment clause;

(b) Be in an amount not in excess of $100 million;

(c) Provide—

(1) For the delivery of an initial lot of production quantities of completed items not later than nine months after the date of the award of such contract; and

(2) That failure to make delivery as provided for under paragraph (c)(1) may result in termination for cause; and

(d) Be—

(1) Exempt from the requirement to submit certified cost or pricing data;

(2) Exempt from the cost accounting standards under 41 U.S.C. 1502; and

(3) Subject to the requirement to provide data other than certified cost or pricing data for the purpose of price reasonableness determinations.

[Interim rule, 76 FR 38048, 6/29/2011, effective 6/29/2011; Final rule, 77 FR 2653, 1/19/2012, effective 1/19/2012; Final rule, 77 FR 35879, 6/15/2012, effective 6/15/2012; Final rule, 80 FR 36903, 6/26/2015, effective 10/1/2015; Interim rule, 81 FR 42557, 6/30/2016, effective 6/30/2016; Final rule, 81 FR 78012, 11/4/2016, effective 11/4/2016]

212.7102-2 Reporting requirements.

Departments and agencies shall prepare a consolidated annual report to provide information about contracts awarded under this pilot authority. The report shall be submitted to the Office of the Deputy Director, Defense Procurement and Acquisition Policy (Contract Policy and International Contracting), by October 31 each year in accordance with the procedures at PGI 212.7102. See PGI 212.7102 for annual reporting format.

[Interim rule, 76 FR 38048, 6/29/2011, effective 6/29/2011; Final rule, 77 FR 2653, 1/19/2012, effective 1/19/2012]

212.7102-3 Sunset of the pilot authority.

(a) The authority to carry out the pilot program described in this subpart expires on December 31, 2019.

(b) The expiration under paragraph (a) of this section of the authority to carry out the pilot program will not affect the validity of any contract awarded under the pilot program before the expiration of the pilot program under that paragraph.

[Interim rule, 76 FR 38048, 6/29/2011, effective 6/29/2011; Final rule, 77 FR 2653, 1/19/2012, effective 1/19/2012; Final rule, 79 FR 17446, 3/28/2014, effective 3/28/2014]

212.7103 Solicitation provision.

Use the provision at 252.212-7002, Pilot Program for Acquisition of Military-Purpose Non developmental Items, in solicitations when use of the pilot program is planned and the applicability criteria of 212.7102-1 are met.

[Interim rule, 76 FR 38048, 6/29/2011, effective 6/29/2011; Final rule, 77 FR 2653, 1/19/2012, effective 1/19/2012; Interim rule, 81 FR 42557, 6/30/2016, effective 6/30/2016; Final rule, 81 FR 78012, 11/4/2016, effective 11/4/2016]

Defense Federal Acquisition Regulation Supplement Parts 213—226

CONTRACTING METHODS AND CONTRACT TYPES SOCIOECONOMIC PROGRAMS

Table of Contents

Page

SUBCHAPTER C—CONTRACTING METHODS AND CONTRACT TYPES

Part 213—Simplified Acquisition Procedures 179
Part 214—Sealed Bidding 187
Part 215—Contracting by Negotiation 191
Part 216—Types of Contracts 227
Part 217—Special Contracting Methods 239
Part 218—Emergency Acquisitions 263

SUBCHAPTER D—SOCIOECONOMIC PROGRAMS

Part 219—Small Business Programs 269
Part 220—[NO FAR SUPPLEMENT]
Part 221—[NO FAR SUPPLEMENT]
Part 222—Application of Labor Laws to Government Acquisitions 285
Part 223—Environment, Energy and Water Efficiency, Renewable Energy Technologies, Occupational Safety, and Drug-Free Workplace 301
Part 224—Protection of Privacy and Freedom of Information 309
Part 225—Foreign Acquisition 313
Part 226—Other Socioeconomic Programs 393

See page 39 for an explanation of the numbering of the DFARS.

PART 213—SIMPLIFIED ACQUISITION PROCEDURES

Table of Contents

Subpart 213.1—Procedures

General 213.101
Promoting competition 213.104
Soliciting competition 213.106-1
Soliciting competition—tiered evaluation of offers 213.106-1-70
Evaluation of quotations or offers 213.106-2
Solicitation provision. 213.106-2-70
[Removed] 213.106-3

Subpart 213.2—Actions At or Below the Micro-Purchase Threshold

General 213.201
Use of the Governmentwide commercial purchase card 213.270

Subpart 213.3—Simplified Acquisition Methods

Government wide commercial purchase card 213.301
Purchase orders 213.302
Obtaining contractor acceptance and modifying purchase orders 213.302-3
Clauses 213.302-5
Blanket Purchase Agreements (BPAs) 213.303
Purchases under BPAs 213.303-5
Imprest funds and third party drafts 213.305
[Removed] 213.305-1
Conditions for use 213.305-3
SF 44, Purchase Order-Invoice-Voucher 213.306
Forms 213.307

Subpart 213.4—Fast Payment Procedure

Conditions for use 213.402

Subpart 213.5—Simplified Procedures for Certain Commercial Items

Only one offer 213.500-70
Special documentation requirements 213.501

Subpart 213.70—Simplified Acquisition Procedures Under the 8(a) Program

Procedures 213.7001
Purchase orders 213.7002
[Removed] 213.7003-1
[Removed] 213.7003-2

SUBCHAPTER C—CONTRACTING METHODS AND CONTRACT TYPES (Parts 213-218)

PART 213—SIMPLIFIED ACQUISITION PROCEDURES

213.005 [Removed]

[Removed by 67 FR 4208, 1/29/2002, effective 1/29/2002]

SUBPART 213.1—PROCEDURES

213.101 General.

Structure awards valued above the micro-purchase threshold (e.g., contract line items, delivery schedule, and invoice instructions) in a manner that will minimize the generation of invoices valued at or below the micro-purchase threshold.

[Final rule, 65 FR 46625, 7/31/2000, effective 7/31/2000]

213.104 Promoting competition.

For information on the various approaches that may be used to competitively fulfill DoD requirements, see PGI 213.104.

[Final rule, 80 FR 21656, 4/20/2015, effective 4/20/2015]

213.106-1 Soliciting competition.

(a) *Considerations.*

(2) (i) Include an evaluation factor regarding supply chain risk (see subpart 239.73) when acquiring information technology, whether as a service or as a supply, that is a covered system, is a part of a covered system, or is in support of a covered system, as defined in 239.7301.

(ii) See 215.101-2-70 for limitations and prohibitions on the use of the lowest price technically acceptable source selection process, which are applicable to simplified acquisitions.

(iii) See 217.7801 for the prohibition on the use of reverse auctions for personal protective equipment and aviation critical safety items.

[Final rule, 80 FR 67243, 10/30/2015, effective 10/30/2015; Final rule, 84 FR 50785, 9/26/2019, effective 10/1/2019]

213.106-1-70 Soliciting competition—tiered evaluation of offers.

See limitations on the use of tiered evaluation of offers at 215.203-70.

[Interim rule, 71 FR 53042, 9/8/2006, effective 9/8/2006; Final rule, 72 FR 42313, 8/2/2007, effective 8/2/2007]

213.106-2 Evaluation of quotations or offers.

(b) (i) For competitive solicitations for supplies using FAR part 13 simplified acquisition procedures, including acquisitions valued at less than or equal to $1 million under the authority at FAR subpart 13.5, the contracting officer shall—

(A) Consider data available in the statistical reporting module of the Supplier Performance Risk System (SPRS) regarding the supplier's past performance history for the Federal supply class (FSC) and product or service code (PSC) of the supplies being purchased. Procedures for the use of SPRS in the evaluation of quotations or offers are provided in the SPRS User's Manual available under the references section of the SPRS website at *https://www.sprs.csd.disa.mil/reference.htm.*

(B) Ensure the basis for award includes an evaluation of each supplier's past performance history in SPRS for the FSC and PSC of the supplies being purchased; and

(C) In the case of a supplier without a record of relevant past performance history in SPRS for the FSC or PSC of the supplies being purchased, the supplier may not be evaluated favorably or unfavorably for its past performance history.

[Final rule, 80 FR 30117, 5/26/2015, effective 5/26/2015; Final rule, 80 FR 30117, 5/26/2015, effective 5/26/2015; Publication notice, 20171208; Final rule, 83 FR 12681, 3/23/2018, effective 3/23/2018; Final rule, 84 FR 48507, 9/13/2019, effective 9/13/2019]

213.106-2-70 Solicitation provision.

Use the provision at 252.213-7000, Notice to Prospective Suppliers on Use of Supplier Performance Risk System in Past Performance Evaluations, in competitive solicitations for supplies when using FAR part 13 simplified acquisition procedures, including competitive solicitations using FAR part 12 procedures for the acquisition of commercial items and acquisitions valued at less than or equal to $1 million under the authority at FAR subpart 13.5.

[Final rule, 80 FR 30117, 5/26/2015, effective 5/26/2015; Final rule, 80 FR 30117, 5/26/2015, effective 5/26/2015; Final rule, 84 FR 48507, 9/13/2019, effective 9/13/2019]

213.106-3 [Removed]

[Final rule, 64 FR 43098, 8/9/99, effective 8/9/99, corrected, 64 FR 51587, 10/7/99; Removed by interim rule, 68 FR 64557, 11/14/2003, effective 11/14/2003; Final rule, 70 FR 57188, 9/30/2005, effective 9/30/2005]

SUBPART 213.2—ACTIONS AT OR BELOW THE MICRO-PURCHASE THRESHOLD

213.201 General.

(g) See PGI 213.201(g) for guidance on use of the higher micro-purchase thresholds prescribed in FAR 13.201(g) to support a declared contingency operation or to facilitate defense against or recovery from nuclear, biological, chemical, or radiological attack.

(j) Do not procure or obtain, or extend or renew a contract to procure or obtain, any equipment, system, or service to carry out covered missions that use covered defense telecommunications equipment or services as a substantial or essential component of any system, or as critical technology as part of any system, unless a waiver is granted. (See subpart 204.21.)

[Final rule, 81 FR 53045, 8/11/2016, effective 8/11/2016; Interim rule, 84 FR 72231, 12/31/2019, effective 12/31/2019]

213.270 Use of the Governmentwide commercial purchase card.

Use the Governmentwide commercial purchase card as the method of purchase and/or method of payment for purchases valued at or below the micro-purchase threshold. This policy applies to all types of contract actions authorized by the FAR unless—

(a) The Deputy Secretary of Defense has approved an exception for an electronic commerce/electronic data interchange system or operational requirement that results in a more cost-effective payment process;

(b) (1) A general or flag officer or a member of the Senior Executive Service (SES) makes a written determination that—

(i) The source or sources available for the supply or service do not accept the purchase card; and

(ii) The contracting office is seeking a source that accepts the purchase card.

(2) To prevent mission delays, if an activity does not have a resident general or flag officer of SES member, delegation of this authority to the level of the senior local commander or director is permitted; or

(c) The purchase or payment meets one or more of the following criteria:

(1) The place of performance is entirely outside the United States and its outlying areas.

(2) The purchase is a Standard Form 44 purchase for aviation fuel or oil.

(3) The purchase is an overseas transaction by a contracting officer in support of a contingency operation as defined in 10 U.S.C. 101(a)(13) or a humanitarian or peacekeeping operation as defined in 10 U.S.C. 2302(8).

(4) The purchase is a transaction in support of intelligence or other specialized activities addressed by Part 2.7 of Executive Order 12333.

(5) The purchase is for training exercises in preparation for overseas contingency, humanitarian, or peacekeeping operations.

(6) The payment is made with an accommodation check.

(7) The payment is for a transportation bill.

(8) The purchase is under a Federal Supply Schedule contract that does not permit use of the Governmentwide commercial purchase card.

(9) The purchase is for medical services and—

(i) It involves a controlled substance or narcotic;

(ii) It requires the submission of a Health Care Summary Record to document the nature of the care purchased;

(iii) The ultimate price of the medical care is subject to an independent determination that changes the price paid based on application of a mandatory CHAMPUS Maximum Allowable Charge determination that reduces the Government liability below billed charges;

(iv) The Government already has entered into a contract to pay for the services without the use of a purchase card;

(v) The purchaser is a beneficiary seeking medical care; or

(vi) The senior local commander or director of a hospital or laboratory determines that use of the purchase card is not appropriate or cost-effective. The Medical Prime Vendor Program and the DoD Medical Electronic Catalog Program are two examples where use of the purchase card may not be cost-effective.

[Final rule, 65 FR 46625, 7/31/2000, effective 7/31/2000; Final rule, 70 FR 35543, 6/21/2005, effective 6/21/2005]

SUBPART 213.3—SIMPLIFIED ACQUISITION METHODS

213.301 Governmentwide commercial purchase card.

Follow the procedures at PGI 213.301 for authorizing, establishing, and operating a Governmentwide commercial purchase card program.

(1) *United States,* as used in this section, means the 50 States and the District of Columbia, the Commonwealth of Puerto Rico, the Virgin Islands, the Commonwealth of the Northern Mariana Islands, Guam, American Samoa, Wake Island, Johnston Island, Canton Island, the outer Continental Shelf, and any other place subject to the jurisdiction of the United States (but not including leased bases).

(2) An individual appointed in accordance with 201.603-3(a) also may use the Governmentwide commercial purchase card to make a purchase that exceeds the micro-purchase threshold but does not exceed $25,000, if—

(i) The purchase—

(A) Is made outside the United States for use outside the United States; and

(B) Is for a commercial item; but

(C) Is not for work to be performed by employees recruited within the United States;

(D) Is not for supplies or services originating from, or transported from or through, sources identified in FAR Subpart 25.7;

(E) Is not for ball or roller bearings as end items;

(F) Does not require access to classified or Privacy Act information; and

(G) Does not require transportation of supplies by sea; and

(ii) The individual making the purchase—

(A) Is authorized and trained in accordance with agency procedures;

(B) Complies with the requirements of FAR 8.002 in making the purchase; and–

(C) Seeks maximum practicable competition for the purchase in accordance with FAR 13.104(b).

(3) A contracting officer supporting a contingency operation as defined in 10 U.S.C. 101(a)(13) or a humanitarian or peacekeeping operation as defined in 10 U.S.C. 2302(8) also may use the Governmentwide commercial purchase card to make a purchase that exceeds the micro-purchase threshold but does not exceed the simplified acquisition threshold, if—

(i) The supplies or services being purchased are immediately available;

(ii) One delivery and one payment will be made; and

(iii) The requirements of paragraphs (2)(i) and (ii) of this section are met.

(4) Guidance on DoD purchase, travel, and fuel card programs is available in the "Department of Defense Government Charge Card Guidebook for Establishing and Managing Purchase, Travel, and Fuel Card Programs" at *http://www.acq.osd.mil/dpap/pdi/pc/policy/_documents.html*. Additional guidance on the fuel card programs is available at *http://www.energy.dla.mil*.

[Final rule, 64 FR 56704, 10/21/99, effective 10/21/99, corrected, 64 FR 63380, 11/19/99; Final rule, 66 FR 55123, 11/1/2001, effective 11/1/2001, correction 66 FR 56902, 11/13/2001; Final rule, 67 FR 38020, 5/31/2002, effective 5/31/2002; Final rule, 68 FR 56560, 10/1/2003, effective 10/1/2003; Final rule, 70 FR 75411, 12/20/2005, effective 12/20/2005; Final rule, 72 FR 6484, 2/12/2007, effective 2/12/2007; Final rule, 73 FR 70905, 11/24/2008, effective 11/24/2008; Final rule, 76 FR 76318, 12/7/2011, effective 12/7/2011; Final rule, 77 FR 23631, 4/20/2012, effective 4/20/2012; Final rule, 77 FR 35879, 6/15/2012, effective 6/15/2012; Final rule, 79 FR 56278, 9/19/2014, effective 9/19/2014]

213.302 Purchase orders. (No Text)

213.302-3 Obtaining contractor acceptance and modifying purchase orders.

(1) Require written acceptance of purchase orders for classified acquisitions.

(2) See PGI 213.302-3 for guidance on the use of unilateral modifications.

(3) A supplemental agreement converts a unilateral purchase order to a bilateral agreement. If not previously included in the purchase order, incorporate the clause at 252.243-7001, Pricing of Contract Modifications, in the Standard Form 30, and obtain the contractor's acceptance by signature on the Standard Form 30.

[Final rule, 64 FR 2595, 1/15/99, effective 1/15/99; Final rule, 71 FR 3412, 1/23/2006, effective 1/23/2006]

213.302-5 Clauses.

(a) Use the clause at 252.243-7001, Pricing of Contract Modifications, in all bilateral purchase orders.

(d) When using the clause at FAR 52.213-4, delete the reference to the clause at FAR 52.225-1, Buy American—Supplies. Instead, if the Buy American statute applies to the acquisition, use the clause at—

(i) 252.225-7001, Buy American and Balance of Payments Program, as prescribed at 225.1101(2); or

(ii) 252.225-7036, Buy American—Free Trade Agreements—Balance of Payments Program, as prescribed at 225.1101(10).

[Final rule, 64 FR 24528, 5/7/99, effective 5/7/99; Final rule, 65 FR 19849, 4/13/2000, effective 4/13/2000; Final rule, 65 FR 39703, 6/27/2000, effective 6/27/2000; Final rule, 68 FR 56560, 10/1/2003, effective 10/1/2003; Interim rule, 69 FR 1926, 1/13/2004, effective 1/13/2004; Final rule, 77 FR 35879, 6/15/2012, effective 6/15/2012]

213.303 Blanket purchase agreements (BPAs). (No Text)

213.303-5 Purchases under BPAs.

(b) Individual purchases for subsistence may be made at any dollar value; however, the contracting officer must satisfy the competition requirements of FAR Part 6 for any action not using simplified acquisition procedures.

[Final rule, 64 FR 2595, 1/15/99, effective 1/15/99]

213.305 Imprest funds and third party drafts. (No Text)

213.305-1 [Removed]

[Final rule, 64 FR 2595, 1/15/99, effective 1/15/99; Final rule, 71 FR 3412, 1/23/2006, effective 1/23/2006]

213.305-3 Conditions for use.

(d)(i) On a very limited basis, installation commanders and commanders of other activities with contracting authority may be granted authority to establish imprest funds and third party draft (accommodation check) accounts. Use of imprest funds and third party drafts must comply with—

(A) DoD 7000.14-R, DoD Financial Management Regulation, Volume 5, Disbursing Policy and Procedures; and

(B) The Treasury Financial Manual, Volume I, Part 4, Chapter 3000.

(ii) Use of imprest funds requires approval by the Director for Financial Commerce, Office of the Deputy Chief Financial Officer, Office of the Under Secretary of Defense (Comptroller), except as provided in paragraph (d) (iii) of this subsection.

(iii) Imprest funds are authorized for use without further approval for—

(A) Overseas transactions at or below the micro-purchase threshold in support of a contingency operation as defined in 10 U.S.C. 101(a) (13) or a humanitarian or peacekeeping operation as defined in 10 U.S.C. 2302(8); and

(B) Classified transactions.

[Final rule, 64 FR 2595, 1/15/99, effective 1/15/99; Final rule, 71 FR 3412, 1/23/2006, effective 1/23/2006]

213.306 SF 44, Purchase Order-Invoice-Voucher.

(a) (1) The micro-purchase limitation applies to all purchases, except that purchases not exceeding the simplified acquisition threshold may be made for—

(A) Fuel and oil. U.S. Government fuel cards may be used in lieu of an SF 44 for fuel, oil, and authorized refueling-related items (see PGI 213.306 for procedures on use of fuel cards);

(B) Overseas transactions by contracting officers in support of a contingency operation as defined in 10 U.S.C. 101(a) (13) or a humanitarian or peacekeeping operation as defined in 10 U.S.C. 2302(8); and

(C) Transactions in support of intelligence and other specialized activities addressed by Part 2.7 of Executive Order 12333.

[Final rule, 64 FR 2595, 1/15/99, effective 1/15/99; Final rule, 71 FR 3412, 1/23/2006, effective 1/23/2006; Final rule, 72 FR 6484, 2/12/2007, effective 2/12/2007; Final rule, 76 FR 58149, 9/20/2011, effective 9/20/2011]

213.307 Forms.

See PGI 213.307 for procedures on use of forms for purchases made using simplified acquisition procedures.

[Final rule, 64 FR 2595, 1/15/99, effective 1/15/99; Final rule, 70 FR 35543, 6/21/2005, effective 6/21/2005; Final rule, 71 FR 3412, 1/23/2006, effective 1/23/2006]

SUBPART 213.4—FAST PAYMENT PROCEDURE

213.402 Conditions for use.

(a) Individual orders may exceed the simplified acquisition threshold for—

(i) Brand-name commissary resale subsistence; and

(ii) Medical supplies for direct shipment overseas.

[Final rule, 64 FR 2595, 1/15/99, effective 1/15/99]

SUBPART 213.5—SIMPLIFIED PROCEDURES FOR CERTAIN COMMERCIAL ITEMS

213.500-70 Only one offer.

If only one offer is received in response to a competitive solicitation issued using simplified acquisition procedures authorized under FAR subpart 13.5, follow the procedures at 215.371-2.

[Final rule, 80 FR 21656, 4/20/2015, effective 4/20/2015; Final rule, 80 FR 36718, 6/26/2015, effective 6/26/2015; Final rule, 80 FR 56929, 9/21/2015, effective 9/21/2015]

213.501 Special documentation requirements.

(a) (i) *Sole source (including brand name) acquisitions.* For noncompetitive follow-on acquisitions of supplies or services previously awarded on a noncompetitive basis, include the additional documentation required by PGI 206.303-2(b) (i) and follow the procedures at PGI 206.304(a) (S-70).

(ii) In accordance with section 888(a) of the National Defense Authorization Act for Fiscal Year 2017 (Pub. L. 114-328), the justification and approval addressed in FAR 13.501(a) is required in order to use brand name or equal descriptions or proprietary specifications and standards.

[Final rule, 80 FR 21656, 4/20/2015, effective 4/20/2015; Final rule, 80 FR 56929, 9/21/2015, effective 9/21/2015; Final rule, 84 FR 25190, 5/31/2019, effective 5/31/2019]

SUBPART 213.70—SIMPLIFIED ACQUISITION PROCEDURES UNDER THE 8(a) PROGRAM

213.7001 Procedures.

For acquisitions that are otherwise appropriate to be conducted using procedures set forth in this part, and also eligible for the 8(a) Program, contracting officers may use—

(a) (i) For sole source purchase orders not exceeding the simplified acquisition threshold, the procedures in PGI 219.804-2(2); or

(ii) For other types of acquisitions, the procedures in PGI 219.8, excluding the procedures in PGI 219.804-2(2); or

(a) (2) The procedures for award to the Small Business Administration in FAR subpart 19.8.

(b) To comply with section 898 of the National Defense Authorization Act for Fiscal Year 2016 (Pub. L. 114-92), contracting officers shall not use the sole source authority at FAR 6.302-5(b)(4) to purchase religious-related services to be performed on a U.S. military installation. For competitive purchases under the 8(a) program, contracting officers shall not exclude a nonprofit organization from the competition. See 219.270 for additional procedures.

[Final rule, 64 FR 2595, 1/15/99, effective 1/15/99; Redesignated from 213.7002, Final rule, 71 FR 3412, 1/23/2006, effective 1/23/2006; Final rule, 81 FR 65563, 9/23/2016, effective 9/23/2016; Final rule, 83 FR 16001, 4/13/2018, effective 4/13/2018]

213.7002 Purchase orders.

The contracting officer need not obtain a contractor's written acceptance of a purchase order or modification of a purchase order for an acquisition under the 8(a) Program pursuant to 219.804-2(2).

[Redesignated from 213.7003, Final rule, 71 FR 3412, 1/23/2006, effective 1/23/2006]

213.7003-1 [Removed]

[Final rule, 64 FR 2595, 1/15/99, effective 1/15/99; Final rule, 71 FR 3412, 1/23/2006, effective 1/23/2006]

213.7003-2 [Removed]

[Final rule, 64 FR 2595, 1/15/99, effective 1/15/99; Final rule, 71 FR 3412, 1/23/2006, effective 1/23/2006]

PART 214—SEALED BIDDING

Table of Contents

Subpart 214.2—Solicitation of Bids

[Removed] 214.201-1
Part IV—Representations and instructions 214.201-5
Solicitation provisions 214.201-6
General rules for solicitation of bids 214.202
Descriptive literature 214.202-5
Cancellation of invitations before opening 214.209

Subpart 214.4—Opening of Bids and Award of Contract

Rejection of bids 214.404
Cancellation of invitations after opening 214.404-1
Mistakes in bids 214.407
Other mistakes disclosed before award 214.407-3
Award 214.408
General 214.408-1

Subpart 214.5—Two-Step Sealed Bidding

Procedures 214.503
Step one 214.503-1

PART 214—SEALED BIDDING

SUBPART 214.2—SOLICITATION OF BIDS

214.201-1 [Removed]

[Final rule, 65 FR 46625, 7/31/2000, effective 7/31/2000; Final rule, 69 FR 65089, 11/10/2004, effective 11/10/2004]

214.201-5 Part IV—Representations and instructions

(c) Include an evaluation factor regarding supply chain risk (see subpart 239.73) when acquiring information technology, whether as a service or as a supply, that is a covered system, is a part of a covered system, or is in support of a covered system, as defined in 239.7301.

[Final rule, 80 FR 67243, 10/30/2015, effective 10/30/2015]

214.201-6 Solicitation provisions.

(2) Use the provisions at 252.215-7007, Notice of Intent to Resolicit, and 252.215-7008, Only One Offer, as prescribed at 215.371-6 and 215.408(3), respectively.

[Final rule, 77 FR 39125, 6/29/2012, effective 6/29/2012; Final rule, 83 FR 30824, 6/29/2018, effective 6/29/2018]

214.202 General rules for solicitation of bids. (No Text)

214.202-5 Descriptive literature.

(c) *Requirements of invitation for bids.* When brand name or equal purchase descriptions are used, use of the provision at FAR 52.211-6, Brand Name or Equal, satisfies this requirement.

[DAC 91-13, 63 FR 11522, 3/9/98, effective 3/9/98; Final rule, 64 FR 55632, 10/14/99, effective 10/14/99; Final rule, 69 FR 65089, 11/10/2004, effective 11/10/2004]

214.209 Cancellation of invitations before opening.

If an invitation for bids allowed fewer than 30 days for receipt of offers, and resulted in only one offer, the contracting officer shall cancel and resolicit, allowing an additional period of at least 30 days for receipt of offers, as provided in 215.371.

[Final rule, 77 FR 39125, 6/29/2012, effective 6/29/2012]

SUBPART 214.4—OPENING OF BIDS AND AWARD OF CONTRACT

214.404 Rejection of bids. (No Text)

214.404-1 Cancellation of invitations after opening.

(1) The contracting officer shall make the written determinations required by FAR 14.404-1(c) and (e)(1).

(2) If only one offer is received, follow the procedures at 215.371 in lieu of the procedures at FAR 14.404-1(f).

[Final rule, 76 FR 76318, 12/7/2011, effective 12/7/2011; Final rule, 77 FR 39125, 6/29/2012, effective 6/29/2012]

214.407 Mistakes in bids. (No Text)

214.407-3 Other mistakes disclosed before award.

(e) Authority for making a determination under FAR 14.407-3(a), (b), and (d) is delegated for the defense agencies, without power of redelegation, as follows:

(i) Defense Advanced Research Projects Agency: General Counsel, DARPA.

(ii) Defense Information Systems Agency:

General Counsel, DISA.

(iii) Defense Intelligence Agency:

Principal Assistant for Acquisition.

(iv) Defense Logistics Agency:

(A) General Counsel, DLA; and

(B) Associate General Counsel, DLA.

(v) National Geospatial-Intelligence Agency: General Counsel, NGA.

(vi) Defense Threat Reduction Agency: General Counsel, DTRA.

(vii) National Security Agency: Director of Procurement, NSA.

(viii) Missile Defense Agency: General Counsel, MDA

(ix) Defense Contract Management Agency: General Counsel, DCMA.

[DAC 91-3, 57 FR 42629, 9/15/92, effective 8/31/92; DAC 91-6, 59 FR 27662, 5/27/94, effective 5/27/94; DAC 91-9, 60 FR 61586, 11/30/95, effective 11/30/95; DAC 91-11, 61 FR 50446, 9/26/96, effective 9/26/96; Redesignated from 214.406-3, DAC 91-12, 62 FR 34114, 6/24/97, effective 6/24/97; Final rule, 64 FR 51074, 9/21/99, effective 9/21/99; Final rule, 68 FR 7438, 2/14/2003, effective 2/14/2003; Correction, 68 FR 9580, 2/28/2003, effective 2/28/2003; Final rule, 69 FR 65089, 11/10/2004, effective 11/10/2004; Final rule, 74 FR 42779, 8/25/2009, effective 8/25/2009]

214.408 Award.

[Final rule, 77 FR 39125, 6/29/2012, effective 6/29/2012]

214.408-1 General.

(b) For acquisitions that exceed the simplified acquisition threshold, if only one offer is received, follow the procedures at 215.371.

[Final rule, 77 FR 39125, 6/29/2012, effective 6/29/2012]

SUBPART 214.5—TWO-STEP SEALED BIDDING SEC.

214.503 Procedures (No Text).

[Final rule, 69 FR 65089, 11/10/2004, effective 11/10/2004; Final rule, 80 FR 67243, 10/30/2015, effective 10/30/2015]

214.503-1 Step one.

(a) (4) Include an evaluation factor regarding supply chain risk (see subpart 239.73) when acquiring information technology, whether as a service or as a supply, that is a covered system, is a part of a covered system, or is in support of a covered system, as defined in 239.7301.

[DAC 91-4, 57 FR 53599, 11/12/92, effective 10/30/92; Final rule, 69 FR 65089, 11/10/2004, effective 11/10/2004; Final rule, 80 FR 67243, 10/30/2015, effective 10/30/2015]

PART 215—CONTRACTING BY NEGOTIATION

Table of Contents

[Removed] . . . 215.000

Subpart 215.1—Source Selection Processes and Techniques

Lowest price technically acceptable source selection process . . . 215.101-2
Limitations and prohibitions . . . 215.101-2-70
Best value continuum . . . 215.101
Best value when acquiring tents or other temporary structures . . . 215.101-70

Subpart 215.2—Solicitation and Receipt of Proposals and Information

Requests for proposals—tiered evaluation of offers . . . 215.203-70
Solicitation provisions and contract clauses . . . 215.209
Peer Reviews . . . 215.270

Subpart 215.3—Source Selection

Scope of subpart . . . 215.300
Responsibilities . . . 215.303
Evaluation factors and significant subfactors . . . 215.304
Proposal evaluation . . . 215.305
Exchanges with offerors after receipt of proposals . . . 215.306
Evaluation factor for employing or subcontracting with members of the Selected Reserve . . . 215.370
Definition . . . 215.370-1
Evaluation factor . . . 215.370-2
Solicitation provision and contract clause . . . 215.370-3
Only one offer . . . 215.371
Policy . . . 215.371-1
Promote competition . . . 215.371-2
Fair and reasonable price and the requirement for additional cost or pricing data . . . 215.371-3
Exceptions . . . 215.371-4
Waiver . . . 215.371-5
Solicitation provision . . . 215.371-6

Subpart 215.4—Contract Pricing

Definitions . . . 215.401
Pricing policy . . . 215.402
Obtaining certified cost or pricing data. . . . 215.403
Prohibition on obtaining certified cost or pricing data (10 U.S.C. 2306a and 41 U.S.C. chapter 35) . . . 215.403-1
Requiring data other than certified cost or pricing data . . . 215.403-3
Instructions for submission of certified cost or pricing data and data other than certified cost or pricing data. . . . 215.403-5
Proposal analysis. . . . 215.404
Proposal analysis techniques. . . . 215.404-1
Data to support proposal analysis. . . . 215.404-2
Subcontract pricing considerations. . . . 215.404-3

Profit. 215.404-4
DD Form 1547, Record of Weighted Guidelines Method Application 215.404-70
Weighted guidelines method. 215.404-71
General. 215.404-71-1
Performance risk. 215.404-71-2
Contract type risk and working capital adjustment. 215.404-71-3
Facilities capital employed. 215.404-71-4
Cost efficiency factor. 215.404-71-5
Modified weighted guidelines method for nonprofit organizations other than FFRDCs. 215.404-72
Alternate structured approaches. 215.404-73
Fee requirements for cost-plus-award-fee contracts. 215.404-74
Fee requirements for FFRDCs. 215.404-75
[Removed] 215.404-76
Prenegotiation objectives. 215.406-1
Certificate of Current Cost or Pricing Data. 215.406-2
Documenting the negotiation. 215.406-3
Special cost or pricing areas. 215.407
Defective certified cost or pricing data. 215.407-1
Make-or-buy programs. 215.407-2
Forward pricing rate agreements. 215.407-3
Should-cost review. 215.407-4
Estimating systems 215.407-5
Disclosure, maintenance, and review requirements. 215.407-5-70
Solicitation provisions and contract clauses. 215.408
Estimated data prices. 215.470

Subpart 215.5—Preaward, Award, and Postaward Notifications, Protests, and Mistakes

Notifications to unsuccessful offerors 215.503
Postaward debriefing of offerors 215.506

PART 215—CONTRACTING BY NEGOTIATION

215.000 [Removed]

[Final rule, 63 FR 55040, 10/14/98, effective 10/14/98; Final rule, 71 FR 3413, 1/23/2006, effective 1/23/2006]

SUBPART 215.1—SOURCE SELECTION PROCESSES AND TECHNIQUES

215.101-2 Lowest price technically acceptable source selection process. (No Text)

[Final rule, 84 FR 50785, 9/26/2019, effective 10/1/2019]

215.101-2-70 Limitations and prohibitions.

The following limitations and prohibitions apply when considering the use of the lowest price technically acceptable source selection procedures.

(a) *Limitations.*

(1) In accordance with section 813 of the National Defense Authorization Act for Fiscal Year 2017 (Pub. L. 114-328) as amended by section 822 of the National Defense Authorization Act for Fiscal Year 2018 (Pub. L. 115-91) (see 10 U.S.C. 2305 note), the lowest price technically acceptable source selection process shall only be used when—

(i) Minimum requirements can be described clearly and comprehensively and expressed in terms of performance objectives, measures, and standards that will be used to determine the acceptability of offers;

(ii) No, or minimal, value will be realized from a proposal that exceeds the minimum technical or performance requirements;

(iii) The proposed technical approaches will require no, or minimal, subjective judgment by the source selection authority as to the desirability of one offeror's proposal versus a competing proposal;

(iv) The source selection authority has a high degree of confidence that reviewing the technical proposals of all offerors would not result in the identification of characteristics that could provide value or benefit;

(v) No, or minimal, additional innovation or future technological advantage will be realized by using a different source selection process;

(vi) Goods to be procured are predominantly expendable in nature, are nontechnical, or have a short life expectancy or short shelf life (See PGI 215.101-2-70(a)(1)(vi) for assistance with evaluating whether a requirement satisfies this limitation);

(vii) The contract file contains a determination that the lowest price reflects full life-cycle costs (as defined at FAR 7.101) of the product(s) or service(s) being acquired (see PGI 215.101-2-70(a)(1)(vii) for information on obtaining this determination); and

(viii) The contracting officer documents the contract file describing the circumstances justifying the use of the lowest price technically acceptable source selection process.

(2) In accordance with section 813 of the National Defense Authorization Act for Fiscal Year 2017, as amended by section 822 of the National Defense Authorization Act for Fiscal Year 2018 (Pub. L. 115-91) (see 10 U.S.C. 2305 note), contracting officers shall avoid, to the maximum extent practicable, using the lowest price technically acceptable source selection process in the case of a procurement that is predominately for the acquisition of—

(i) Information technology services, cybersecurity services, systems engineering and technical assistance services, advanced electronic testing, or other knowledge-based professional services;

(ii) Items designated by the requiring activity as personal protective equipment (except see paragraph (b)(1) of this section); or

(iii) Services designated by the requiring activity as knowledge-based training or logistics services in contingency operations or other operations outside the United States, including in Afghanistan or Iraq.

(b) *Prohibitions.*

(1) In accordance with section 814 of the National Defense Authorization Act for Fiscal Year 2017 as amended by section 882 of the National Defense Authorization Act for Fiscal Year 2018 (see 10 U.S.C. 2302 note),

contracting officers shall not use the lowest price technically acceptable source selection process to procure items designated by the requiring activity as personal protective equipment or an aviation critical safety item, when the requiring activity advises the contracting officer that the level of quality or failure of the equipment or item could result in combat casualties. See 252.209-7010 for the definition and identification of critical safety items.

(2) In accordance with section 832 of the National Defense Authorization Act for Fiscal Year 2018 (see 10 U.S.C. 2442 note), contracting officers shall not use the lowest price technically acceptable source selection process to acquire engineering and manufacturing development for a major defense acquisition program for which budgetary authority is requested beginning in fiscal year 2019.

(3) Contracting officers shall make award decisions based on best value factors and criteria, as determined by the resource sponsor (in accordance with agency procedures), for an auditing contract. The use of the lowest price technically acceptable source selection process is prohibited (10 U.S.C. 254b).

[Final rule, 84 FR 50785, 9/26/2019, effective 10/1/2019]

215.101 Best value continuum. (No Text)

215.101-70 Best value when acquiring tents or other temporary structures.

(a) In accordance with section 368 of the National Defense Authorization Act for Fiscal Year 2012 (Pub. L. 112-81), when acquiring tents or other temporary structures for use by the Armed Forces, the contracting officer shall award contracts that provide the best value. Temporary structures covered by this paragraph are nonpermanent buildings, including tactical shelters, nonpermanent modular or pre-fabricated buildings, or portable or relocatable buildings, such as trailers or equipment configured for occupancy (see also 246.270-2). Determination of best value includes consideration of the total life-cycle costs of such tents or structures, including the costs associated with any equipment, fuel, or electricity needed to heat, cool, or light such tents or structures (see FAR 7.105(a)(3)(i) and PGI 207.105(a)(3)(i)).

(b) The requirements of this section apply to any agency or department that acquires tents or other temporary structures on behalf of DoD (see FAR 17.503(d)(2)).

[Final rule, 78 FR 13544, 2/28/2013, effective 2/28/2013]

SUBPART 215.2—SOLICITATION AND RECEIPT OF PROPOSALS AND INFORMATION

215.203-70 Requests for proposals—tiered evaluation of offers.

(a) The tiered or cascading order of precedence used for tiered evaluation of offers shall be consistent with FAR part 19.

(b) Consideration shall be given to the tiers of small businesses (e.g., 8(a), HUBZone small business, service-disabled veteran-owned small business, small business) before evaluating offers from other than small business concerns.

(c) The contracting officer is prohibited from issuing a solicitation with a tiered evaluation of offers unless—

(1) The contracting officer conducts market research, in accordance with FAR part 10 and part 210, to determine—

(i) Whether the criteria in FAR part 19 are met for setting aside the acquisition for small business; or

(ii) For a task or delivery order, whether there are a sufficient number of qualified small business concerns available to justify limiting competition under the terms of the contract; and

(2) If the contracting officer cannot determine whether the criteria in paragraph (c)(1) of this section are met, the contracting officer includes a written explanation in the contract file as to why such a determination could not be made (Section 816 of Public Law 109-163).

[Interim rule, 71 FR 53042, 9/8/2006, effective 9/8/2006; Final rule 72 FR 42313, 8/2/2007, effective 8/2/2007]

215.204-1 [Removed]

[Final rule, 65 FR 46625, 7/31/2000, effective 7/31/2000; Final rule, 71 FR 3413, 1/23/2006, effective 1/23/2006]

215.204-2 [Removed]

[Final rule, 63 FR 55040, 10/14/98, effective 10/14/98; Final rule, 70 FR 58980, 10/11/2005, effective 10/11/2005; Final rule, 71 FR 3413, 1/23/2006, effective 1/23/2006]

215.209 Solicitation provisions and contract clauses.

(a) For source selections when the procurement is $100 million or more, contracting officers should use the provision at FAR 52.215-1, Instructions to Offerors—Competitive Acquisition, with its Alternate I.

[Final rule, 76 FR 58150, 9/20/2011, effective 9/20/2011]

215.270 Peer Reviews.

Agency officials shall conduct Peer Reviews in accordance with 201.170.

[Final rule, 74 FR 37625, 7/29/2009, effective 7/29/2009]

SUBPART 215.3—SOURCE SELECTION

215.300 Scope of subpart.

Contracting officers shall follow the principles and procedures in Director, Defense Procurement and Acquisition Policy memorandum dated April 1, 2016, entitled "Department of Defense Source Selection Procedures," when conducting negotiated, competitive acquisitions utilizing FAR part 15 procedures. See PGI 215.300.

[Final rule, 76 FR 13297, 3/11/2011, effective 3/11/2011; Final rule, 81 FR 28729, 5/10/2016, effective 5/10/2016; Final rule, 81 FR 28729, 5/10/2016, effective 5/10/2016]

215.303 Responsibilities.

(b) (2) For high-dollar value and other acquisitions, as prescribed by agency procedures, the source selection authority shall approve a source selection plan before the solicitation is issued. Follow the procedures at PGI 215.303 (b) (2) for preparation of the source selection plan.

[Final rule, 63 FR 55040, 10/14/98, effective 10/14/98; Final rule, 71 FR 3413, 1/23/2006, effective 1/23/2006]

215.304 Evaluation factors and significant subfactors.

(c) (i) In acquisitions that require use of the clause at FAR 52.219-9, Small Business Subcontracting Plan, other than those based on the lowest price technically acceptable source selection process (see FAR 15.101-2), the extent of participation of small businesses (to include service-disabled veteran-owned small business concerns, HUBZone small business concerns, small disadvantaged business concerns, and women-owned small business concerns) in performance of the contract shall be addressed in source selection. The contracting officer shall evaluate the extent to which offerors identify and commit to small business performance of the contract, whether as a joint venture, teaming arrangement, or subcontractor.

(A) See PGI 215.304 (c) (i) (A) for examples of evaluation factors.

(B) Proposals addressing the extent of small business performance shall be separate from subcontracting plans submitted pursuant to the clause at FAR 52.219-9 and shall be structured to allow for consideration of offers from small businesses.

(C) When an evaluation assesses the extent that small businesses are specifically identified in proposals, the small businesses considered in the evaluation shall be listed in any subcontracting plan submitted pursuant to FAR 52.219-9 to facilitate compliance with 252.219-7003 (e).

(ii) In accordance with 10 U.S.C. 2436, consider the purchase of capital assets (including machine tools) manufactured in the United States, in source selections for all major defense acquisition programs as defined in 10 U.S.C. 2430.

(iii) See 247.573-2 (c) for additional evaluation factors required in solicitations for the direct purchase of ocean transportation services.

(iv) In accordance with section 812 of the National Defense Authorization Act for Fiscal Year 2011, consider the manufacturing readiness and manufacturing-readiness processes of potential contractors and subcontractors as a part of the source selection process for major defense acquisition programs.

(v) Include an evaluation factor regarding supply chain risk (see subpart 239.73) when acquiring information technology, whether as a service or as a supply, that is a covered system, is a part of a covered system, or is in support of a covered system, as defined in 239.7301. For additional guidance see PGI 215.304(c) (v).

(vi) Ensure source selections emphasize sustainment factors and objective reliability and maintainability evaluation criteria in competitive contracts for the—

(A) Technical maturation and risk reduction phase of weapon system design (see guidance at PGI 207.105(b) (14) (ii) (*2*));

(B) Engineering and manufacturing development phase of a weapon system, including embedded software (10 U.S.C. 2443); or

(C) Production and deployment phase of a weapon system, including embedded software (10 U.S.C. 2443).

(vii) See 226.7202 for an additional evaluation factor required in solicitations when using the Demonstration Project for Contractors Employing Persons with Disabilities.

[Interim rule, 63 FR 64427, 11/20/98, effective 1/1/99, finalized without change, 64 FR 52670, 9/30/99; Final rule, 64 FR 51074, 9/21/99, effective 9/21/99; Interim rule, 70 FR 29643, 5/24/2005, effective 5/24/2005; Final rule, 71 FR 3413, 1/23/2006, effective 1/23/2006; Final rule, 71 FR 14108, 3/21/2006, effective 3/21/2006; Interim rule, 72 FR 49204, 8/28/2007, effective 8/28/2007; Final rule, 73 FR 70909, 11/24/2008, effective 11/24/2008; Interim rule, 76 FR 38050, 6/29/2011, effective 6/29/2011; Final rule, 76 FR 71465, 11/18/2011, effective 11/18/2011; Interim rule, 78 FR 69267, 11/18/2013, effective 11/18/2013; Interim rule, 79 FR 61579, 10/14/2014, effective 10/14/2014; Final rule, 80 FR 15912, 3/26/2015, effective 3/26/2015; Final rule, 80 FR 67243, 10/30/2015, effective 10/30/2015; Final rule, 80 FR 67254, 10/30/2015, effective 10/30/2015; Final rule, 84 FR 58332, 10/31/2019, effective 10/31/2019; Final rule, 84 FR 72554, 12/31/2019, effective 12/31/2019]

215.305 Proposal evaluation.

(a) (2) (A) Past performance evaluation. When a past performance evaluation is required by FAR 15.304, and the solicitation includes the clause at FAR 52.219-8, Utilization of Small Business Concerns, the evaluation factors shall include the past performance of offerors in complying with requirements of that clause. When a past performance evaluation is required by FAR 15.304, and the solicitation includes the clause at FAR 52.219-9, Small Business Subcontracting Plan, the evaluation factors shall include the past performance of offerors in complying with requirements of that clause.

(B) Contracting officers shall consider an offeror's failure to make a good faith effort to comply with its comprehensive subcontracting plan under the Test Program described at 219.702-70 as part of the evaluation of the past performance.

[Final rule, 63 FR 55040, 10/14/98, effective 10/14/98; Final rule, 65 FR 39721, 6/27/2000, effective 6/27/2000; Final rule, 71 FR 3413, 1/23/2006, effective 1/23/2006; Final rule, 83 FR 15996, 4/13/2018, effective 4/13/2018]

215.306 Exchanges with offerors after receipt of proposals.

(c) *Competitive range.*

(1) For acquisitions with an estimated value of $100 million or more, contracting officers should conduct discussions. Follow the procedures at FAR 15.306(c) and (d).

[Final rule, 76 FR 58150, 9/20/2011, effective 9/20/2011]

215.370 Evaluation factor for employing or subcontracting with members of the Selected Reserve. (No Text)

[Final rule, 73 FR 62211, 10/20/2008, effective 10/20/2008]

215.370-1 Definition.

Selected Reserve, as used in this section, is defined in the provision at 252.215-7005, Evaluation Factor for Employing or Subcontracting with Members of the Selected Reserve.

[Final rule, 73 FR 62211, 10/20/2008, effective 10/20/2008]

215.370-2 Evaluation factor.

In accordance with Section 819 of the National Defense Authorization Act for Fiscal Year 2006 (Pub. L. 109-163), the contracting officer may use an evaluation factor that considers whether an offeror intends to perform the contract using employees or individual subcontractors who are members of the Selected Reserve. See PGI 215.370-2 for guidance on use of this evaluation factor.

[Final rule, 73 FR 62211, 10/20/2008, effective 10/20/2008]

215.370-3 Solicitation provision and contract clause.

(a) Use the provision at 252.215-7005, Evaluation Factor for Employing or Subcontracting with Members of the Selected Reserve, in solicitations that include an evaluation factor considering whether an offeror intends to perform the contract using employees or individual subcontractors who are members of the Selected Reserve.

(b) Use the clause at 252.215-7006, Use of Employees or Individual Subcontractors Who are Members of the Selected Reserve, in solicitations that include the provision at 252.215-7005. Include the clause in the resultant contract only if the contractor stated in its proposal that it intends to perform the contract using employees or individual subcontractors who are members of the Selected Reserve, and that statement was used as an evaluation factor in the award decision.

[Final rule, 73 FR 62211, 10/20/2008, effective 10/20/2008]

215.371 Only one offer. (No Text)

[Final rule, 77 FR 39125, 6/29/2012, effective 6/29/2012]

215.371-1 Policy.

It is DoD policy, if only one offer is received in response to a competitive solicitation—

(a) To take the required actions to promote competition (see 215.371-2); and

(b) To ensure that the price is fair and reasonable (see 215.371-3) and to comply with the statutory requirement for certified cost or pricing data (see FAR 15.403-4).

[Final rule, 77 FR 39125, 6/29/2012, effective 6/29/2012]

215.371-2 Promote competition.

Except as provided in sections 215.371-4 and 215.371-5—

(a) If only one offer is received when competitive procedures were used and the solicitation allowed fewer than 30 days for receipt of proposals, the contracting officer shall—

(1) Consult with the requiring activity as to whether the requirements document should be revised in order to promote more competition (see FAR 6.502(b) and 11.002); and

(2) Resolicit, allowing an additional period of at least 30 days for receipt of proposals; and

(b) For competitive solicitations in which more than one potential offeror expressed an interest in an acquisition, but only one offer was ultimately received, follow the procedures at PGI 215.371-2.

[Final rule, 77 FR 39125, 6/29/2012, effective 6/29/2012; Final rule, 80 FR 21656, 4/20/2015, effective 4/20/2015]

215.371-3 Fair and reasonable price and the requirement for additional cost or pricing data.

For acquisitions that exceed the simplified acquisition threshold, if only one offer is received when competitive procedures were used and it is not necessary to resolicit in accordance with 215.371-2(a), then then the contracting officer shall comply with the following:

(a) If no additional cost or pricing data are required to determine through cost or price analysis that the offered price is fair and reasonable, the contracting officer shall require that any cost or pricing data provided in the proposal be certified if the acquisition exceeds the certified cost or pricing data threshold and an exception to the requirement for certified cost or pricing data at FAR 15.403-1(b)(2) through (5) does not apply.

(b) Otherwise, the contracting officer shall obtain additional cost or pricing data to determine a fair and reasonable price. If the acquisition exceeds the certified cost or pricing data threshold and an exception to the requirement for certified cost or pricing data at FAR 15.403-1(b)(2) through (5) does not apply, the cost or pricing data shall be certified.

(c) If the contracting officer is still unable to determine that the offered price is fair and reasonable, the contracting officer shall enter into negotiations with the offeror to establish a fair and reasonable price. The negotiated price should not exceed the offered price.

(d) If the contracting officer is unable to negotiate a fair and reasonable price, see FAR 15.405(d).

[Final rule, 77 FR 39125, 6/29/2012, effective 6/29/2012; Final rule, 78 FR 65214, 10/31/2013, effective 10/31/2013; Final rule, 84 FR 30947, 6/28/2019, effective 7/31/2019]

215.371-4 Exceptions.

(a) The requirements at sections 215.371-2 do not apply to—

(1) Acquisitions at or below the simplified acquisition threshold;

(2) Acquisitions, as determined by the head of the contracting activity, in support of contingency or humanitarian or peacekeeping operations; to facilitate defense against or recovery from cyber, nuclear, biological, chemical, or radiological attack; to facilitate the provision of international disaster assistance; or to support response to an emergency or major disaster;

(3) Small business set-asides under FAR subpart 19.5, set asides offered and accepted into the 8(a) Program under FAR subpart 19.8, or set-asides under the HUBZone Program (see FAR 19.1305(c)), the Service-Disabled Veteran-Owned Small Business Procurement Program (see FAR 19.1405(c)), or the Women-Owned Small Business Program (see FAR 19.1505(d));

(4) Acquisitions of science and technology, as specified in 235.016(a); or

(5) Acquisitions of architect-engineer services (see FAR 36.601-2).

(b) The applicability of an exception in paragraph (a) of this section does not eliminate the need for the contracting officer to seek maximum practicable competition and to ensure that the price is fair and reasonable.

[Final rule, 77 FR 39125, 6/29/2012, effective 6/29/2012; Final rule, 78 FR 65214, 10/31/2013, effective 10/31/2013; Final rule, 83 FR 24888, 5/30/2018, effective 5/30/2018; Final rule, 84 FR 4364, 2/15/2019, effective 2/15/2019]

215.371-5 Waiver.

(a) The head of the contracting activity is authorized to waive the requirement at 215.371-2 to resolicit for an additional period of at least 30 days.

(b) This waiver authority cannot be delegated below one level above the contracting officer.

[Final rule, 77 FR 39125, 6/29/2012, effective 6/29/2012]

215.371-6 Solicitation provision.

Use the provision at 252.215-7007, Notice of Intent to Resolicit, in competitive solicitations, including solicitations using FAR part 12 procedures for the acquisition of commercial items, that will be solicited for fewer than 30 days, unless an exception at 215.371-4 applies or the requirement is waived in accordance with 215.371-5.

[Final rule, 78 FR 65214, 10/31/2013, effective 10/31/2013]

SUBPART 215.4—CONTRACT PRICING

215.401 Definitions.

As used in this subpart—

Market prices means current prices that are established in the course of ordinary trade between buyers and sellers free to bargain and that can be substantiated through competition or from sources independent of the offerors.

Relevant sales data means information provided by an offeror of sales of the same or similar items that can be used to establish price reasonableness taking into consideration the age, volume, and nature of the transactions (including any related discounts, refunds, rebates, offsets, or other adjustments).

[Final rule, 83 FR 4431, 1/31/2018, effective 1/31/2018]

215.402 Pricing policy.

(a) (i) Pursuant to section 831 of the National Defense Authorization Act for Fiscal Year 2013 (Pub. L. 112-239)—

(A) The contracting officer is responsible for determining if the information provided by the offeror is sufficient to determine price reasonableness. This responsibility includes determining whether information on the prices at which the same or similar items have previously been sold is adequate for evaluating the reasonableness of price, and determining the extent of uncertified cost data that should be required in cases in which price information is not adequate;

(B) The contracting officer shall not limit the Government's ability to obtain any data that may be necessary to support a determination of fair and reasonable pricing by agreeing to contract terms that preclude obtaining necessary supporting information; and

(C) When obtaining uncertified cost data, the contracting officer shall require the offeror to provide the information in the form in which it is regularly maintained in the offeror's business operations.

(ii) Follow the procedures at PGI 215.402 when conducting cost or price analysis, particularly with regard to acquisitions for sole source commercial items.

[Final rule, 72 FR 30278, 5/31/2007, effective 5/31/2007; Final rule, 83 FR 4431, 1/31/2018, effective 1/31/2018]

215.403 Obtaining certified cost or pricing data. (No Text)

[Final rule, 77 FR 39125, 6/29/2012, effective 6/29/2012; Final rule, 77 FR 76939, 12/31/2012, effective 12/31/2012]

215.403-1 Prohibition on obtaining certified cost or pricing data (10 U.S.C. 2306a and 41 U.S.C. chapter 35).

(b) *Exceptions to certified cost or pricing data requirements.* (i) Follow the procedures at PGI 215.403-1(b).

(ii) Submission of certified cost or pricing data shall not be required in the case of a contract, subcontract, or modification of a contract or subcontract to the extent such data relates to an indirect offset.

(c) *Standards for exceptions from certified cost or pricing data requirements*—(1) *Adequate price competition.*

(A) For acquisitions under dual or multiple source programs—

(*1*) The determination of adequate price competition must be made on a case-by-case basis. Even when adequate price competition exists, in certain cases it may be appropriate to obtain additional data to assist in price analysis; and

(*2*) Adequate price competition normally exists when—

(*i*) Prices are solicited across a full range of step quantities, normally including a 0–100 percent split, from at least two offerors that are individually capable of producing the full quantity; and

(*ii*) The reasonableness of all prices awarded is clearly established on the basis of price analysis (see FAR 15.404–1(b)).

(B) If only one offer is received in response to a competitive solicitation, see 215.371–3.

(3) *Commercial items.*

(A) Follow the procedures at PGI 215.403-1(c)(3)(A) for pricing commercial items.

(B) By November 30th of each year, departments and agencies shall provide a report to the Director, Defense Procurement and Acquisition Policy (DPAP), ATTN:

DPAP/CPIC, of all contracting officer determinations that commercial item exceptions apply under FAR 15.403-1(b)(3), during the previous fiscal year, for any contract, subcontract, or modification expected to have a value of $19.5 million or more. See PGI 215.403-1(c)(3)(B) for the format and guidance for the report. The Director, DPAP, will submit a consolidated report to the congressional defense committees exceptions apply under FAR 15.403-1(b)(3), during the previous fiscal year, for any contract, subcontract, or modification expected to have a value of $19.5 million or more. See PGI 215.403-1(c)(3) for the format and guidance for the report. The Director, DPAP, will submit a consolidated report to the congressional defense committees.

(C) When applying the commercial item exception under FAR 15.403-1(b)(3), see 212.102(a)(ii) regarding prior commercial item determinations.

(4) *Waivers.*

(A) The head of the contracting activity may, without power of delegation, apply the exceptional circumstances authority when a determination is made that—

(*1*) The property or services cannot reasonably be obtained under the contract, subcontract, or modification, without the granting of the waiver;

(*2*) The price can be determined to be fair and reasonable without the submission of certified cost or pricing data; and

(*3*) There are demonstrated benefits to granting the waiver. Follow the procedures at PGI 215.403-1(c)(4)(A) for determining when an exceptional case waiver is appropriate, for approval of such waivers, for partial waivers, and for waivers applicable to unpriced supplies or services.

(B) By November 30th of each year, departments and agencies shall provide a report to the Director, DPAP, ATTN: DPAP/CPIC, of all waivers granted under FAR 15.403-1(b)(4), during the previous fiscal year, for any contract, subcontract, or modification expected to have a value of $19.5 million or more. See PGI 215.403-1(c)(4)(B) for the format and guidance for the report. The Director, DPAP, will submit a consolidated report to the congressional defense committees.

(C) DoD has waived the requirement for submission of certified cost or pricing data for the Canadian Commercial Corporation and its subcontractors (but see 215.408(3) and 225.870-4(c)).

(D) DoD has waived certified cost or pricing data requirements for nonprofit organizations (including educational institutions) on cost-reimbursement-no-fee contracts. The contracting officer shall require—

(*1*) Submission of data other than certified cost or pricing data to the extent necessary to determine price reasonableness and cost realism; and

(*2*) Certified cost or pricing data from subcontractors that are not nonprofit organizations when the subcontractor's proposal exceeds the certified cost or pricing data threshold at FAR 15.403-4(a)(1).

[Final rule, 63 FR 55040, 10/14/98, effective 10/14/98; Final rule, 71 FR 69492, 12/1/2006, effective 12/1/2006; Final rule, 72 FR 30278, 5/31/2007, effective 5/31/2007; Final rule, 76 FR 58137, 9/20/2011, effective 9/20/2011; Final rule, 77 FR 39125, 6/29/2012, effective 6/29/2012; Final rule, 77 FR 43470, 7/24/2012, effective 7/24/2012; Final rule, 77 FR 52253, 8/29/2012, effective 8/29/2012; Final rule, 77 FR 76936, 12/31/2012, effective 12/31/2012; Final rule 77 FR 76939, 12/31/2012, effective 12/31/2012; Final rule, 78 FR 13543, 2/28/2013, effective 2/28/2013; Final rule, 78 FR 65214, 10/31/2013, effective 10/31/2013; Final rule, 80 FR 36903, 6/26/2015, effective 10/1/2015; Final rule, 83 FR 4431, 1/31/2018, effective 1/31/2018; Final rule, 83 FR 30825, 6/29/2018, effective 6/29/2018]

215.403-3 Requiring data other than certified cost or pricing data.

Follow the procedures at PGI 215.403-3.

[Final rule, 72 FR 30278, 5/31/2007, effective 5/31/2007; Final rule 77 FR 76939, 12/31/2012, effective 12/31/2012]

215.403-5 Instructions for submission of certified cost or pricing

data and data other than certified cost or pricing data.

(b) (3) For contractors following the contract cost principles in FAR subpart 31.2, Contracts With Commercial Organizations, pursuant to the procedures in FAR 42.1701 (b), the administrative contracting officer shall require contractors to comply with the submission items in Table 215.403–1 in order to ensure that their forward pricing rate proposal is submitted in an acceptable form in accordance with FAR 15.403–5(b) (3). The contracting officer should request that the proposal be submitted to the Government at least 90 days prior to the proposed effective date of the rates. To ensure the proposal is complete, the contracting officer shall request that the contractor complete the Contractor Forward Pricing Rate Proposal Adequacy Checklist at Table 215.403–1, and submit it with the forward pricing rate proposal.

Table 215.403–1—Contractor Forward Pricing Rate Proposal Adequacy Checklist

Complete the following checklist, providing the location of requested information, or an explanation of why the requested information is not provided, and submit it with the forward pricing rate proposal.

CONTRACTOR FORWARD PRICING RATE PROPOSAL ADEQUACY CHECKLIST

Submission item	Proposal page No. (if applicable)	If not provided, explain (may use continuation pages)
General Instructions		
1. Is there a properly completed first page of the proposal as specified by the contracting officer? Initial proposal elements include: a. Name and address of contractor; b. Name and telephone number of point of contact; c. Period covered; d. The page of the proposal that addresses— 1. Whether your organization is subject to cost accounting standards (CAS); 2. Whether your organization has submitted a CAS Disclosure Statement, and whether it has been determined adequate; 3. Whether you have been notified that you are or may be in noncompliance with your Disclosure Statement or CAS (other than a noncompliance that the cognizant Federal agency official had determined to have an immaterial cost impact), and if yes, an explanation;	Proposal Cover Page.	

Submission item	Proposal page No. (if applicable)	If not provided, explain (may use continuation pages)
4. Whether any aspect of this proposal is inconsistent with your disclosed practices or applicable CAS, and, if so, an explanation; and whether the proposal is consistent with established estimating and accounting principles and procedures and FAR part 31, Cost Principles, and, if not, an explanation;		
e. The following statement: "This forward pricing rate proposal reflects our estimates, as of the date of submission entered in (f) below and conforms with Table 215.4031. By submitting this proposal, we grant the Contracting Officer and authorized representative(s) the right to examine those records, which include books, documents, accounting procedures and practices, and other data, regardless of type and form or whether such supporting information is specifically referenced or included in the proposal as the basis for each estimate, that will permit an adequate evaluation of the proposed rates and factors.";		
f. Date of submission; and		
g. Name, title, and signature of authorized representative.		
2. Summary of proposed direct and indirect rates and factors, including the proposed pool and base costs for each proposed indirect rate and factor.	Immediately following the proposal cover page.	
3. Table of Contents or index.		
a. Does the proposal include a table of contents or index identifying and referencing all supporting data accompanying or identified in the proposal?		
b. For supporting documentation not provided with the proposal, does the basis of each estimate in the proposal include the location of the documentation and the point of contact (custodian) name, phone number, and email address? Does the proposal disclose known or anticipated changes in business activities or processes that could materially impact the proposed rates (if not previously provided)? For example—		

Submission item	Proposal page No. (if applicable)	If not provided, explain (may use continuation pages)
4. a. Management initiatives to reduce costs; b. Changes in management objectives as a result of economic conditions and increased competitiveness; c. Changes in accounting policies, procedures, and practices including (i) reclassification of expenses from direct to indirect or vice versa; (ii) new methods of accumulating and allocating indirect costs and the related impact; and (iii) advance agreements; d. Company reorganizations (including acquisitions or divestitures); e. Shutdown of facilities; or f. Changes in business volume and/or contract mix/type.		
5. Do proposed costs based on judgmental factors include an explanation of the estimating processes and methods used, including those used in projecting from known data?		
6. Does the proposal show trends and budgetary data? Does the proposal provide an explanation of how the data, as well as any adjustments to the data, were used?		
7. The proposal should reconcile to the supporting data referenced. If the proposal does not reconcile to the supporting data referenced, identify applicable page(s) and explain.		
8. The proposal should be internally consistent. If the proposal is not internally consistent, identify applicable page(s) and explain.		
Direct Labor		
Direct Labor Rates Methodology and Basis of Each Estimate		
9. a. Does the proposal include an explanation of the methodology used to develop the direct labor rates and identify the basis of each estimate?		

Submission item	Proposal page No. (if applicable)	If not provided, explain (may use continuation pages)
b. Does the proposal include or identify the location of the supporting documents for the base-period labor rates (e.g., payroll records)?		
10. Does the proposal identify escalation factors for the out-year labor rates, the costs to which escalation is applicable, and the basis of each factor used?		
11. Does the proposal identify planned or anticipated changes in the composition of labor rates, labor categories, union agreements, headcounts, or other factors that could significantly impact the direct labor rates?		
Indirect Rates (Fringe, Overhead, G&A, etc.)		
12. Indirect Rates Methodology and Basis of Each Estimate.		
a. Does the proposal identify the basis of each estimate and provide an explanation of the methodology used to develop the indirect rates?		
b. Does the proposal include or identify the location of the supporting documents for the proposed rates?		
13. Does the proposal identify indirect expenses by burden center, by cost element, by year (including any voluntary deletions, if applicable) in a format that is consistent with the accounting system used to accumulate actual expenses?		
14. Does the proposal identify any contingencies?		
15. Does the proposal identify planned or anticipated changes in the nature, type, or level of indirect costs, including fringe benefits?		
16. Does the proposal identify corporate, home office, shared services, or other incoming allocated costs and the source for those costs, including location and point of contact (custodian) name, phone number, and email address?		

Submission item	Proposal page No. (if applicable)	If not provided, explain (may use continuation pages)
17. Does the proposal separately identify all intermediate cost pools and provide a reconciliation to show where the costs will be allocated?		
18. Does the proposal identify the escalation factors used to escalate indirect costs for the out-years, the costs to which escalation is applicable, and the basis of each factor used?		
19. Does the proposal provide details of the development of the allocation base?		
20. Does the proposal include or reference the supporting data for the allocation base such as program budgets, negotiation memoranda, proposals, contract values, etc.?		
21. Does the proposal identify how the proposed allocation bases reconcile with its long range plans, strategic plan, operating budgets, sales forecasts, program budgets, etc.?		
Cost of Money (COM)		
22. Cost of Money. a. Are Cost of Money rates submitted on Form CASB-CMF, with the Treasury Rate used to compute COM identified and a summary of the net book value of assets, identified as distributed and non-distributed? b. Does the proposal identify the support for the Form CASB-CMF, for example, the underlying reports and records supporting the net book value of assets contained in the form?		
Other		
23. Does the proposal include a comparison of prior forecasted costs to actual results in the same format as the proposal and an explanation/analysis of any differences?		

Submission item	Proposal page No. (if applicable)	If not provided, explain (may use continuation pages)
24. If this is a revision to a previous rate proposal or a forward pricing rate agreement, does the new proposal provide a summary of the changes in the circumstances or the facts that the contractor asserts require the change to the rates?		

[Final rule, 63 FR 55040, 10/14/98, effective 10/14/98; Final rule, 71 FR 69492, 12/1/2006, effective 12/1/2006; Final rule, 75 FR 71560, 11/24/2010, effective 11/24/2010; Final rule 79 FR 73493, 12/11/202014, effective 12/11/2014]

215.404 Proposal analysis. (No Text)

215.404-1 Proposal analysis techniques.

(a) (i) *General.* Follow the procedures at PGI 215.404-1 for proposal analysis.

(ii) For spare parts or support equipment, perform an analysis of—

(ii) (A) Those line items where the proposed price exceeds by 25 percent or more the lowest price the Government has paid within the most recent 12-month period based on reasonably available data;

(ii) (B) Those line items where a comparison of the item description and the proposal price indicates a potential for overpricing;

(ii) (C) Significant high-dollar-value items. If there are no obvious high-dollar-value items, include an analysis of a random sample of items; and

(ii) (D) A random sample of the remaining low-dollar value items. Sample size may be determined by subjective judgment, e.g., experience with the offeror and the reliability of its estimating and accounting systems.

(b) *Price analysis for commercial and non-commercial items.* (i) In the absence of adequate price competition in response to the solicitation, pricing based on market prices is the preferred method to establish a fair and reasonable price (see PGI 215.404-1(b) (i)).

(ii) If the contracting officer determines that the information obtained through market research is insufficient to determine the reasonableness of price, the contracting officer shall consider information submitted by the offeror of recent purchase prices paid by the Government and commercial customers for the same or similar commercial items under comparable terms and conditions in establishing price reasonableness on a subsequent purchase if the contracting officer is satisfied that the prices previously paid remain a valid reference for comparison. The contracting officer shall consider the totality of other relevant factors such as the time elapsed since the prior purchase and any differences in the quantities purchased (section 853 of the National Defense Authorization Act for Fiscal Year 2016 (Pub. L. 114-92)).

(iii) If the contracting officer determines that the offeror cannot provide sufficient information as described in paragraph (b)(ii) of this section to determine the reasonableness of price, the contracting officer should request the offeror to submit information on—

(A) Prices paid for the same or similar items sold under different terms and conditions;

(B) Prices paid for similar levels of work or effort on related products or services;

(C) Prices paid for alternative solutions or approaches; and

(D) Other relevant information that can serve as the basis for determining the reasonableness of price.

(iv) If the contracting officer determines that the pricing information submitted is not sufficient to determine the reasonableness of price, the contracting officer shall request other relevant information, to include cost data. However, no cost data may be required in any case in which there are sufficient non-Government sales of the same item to establish reasonableness of price (section 831 of the National Defense Authorization Act for Fiscal Year 2013 (Pub. L. 112-239)).

(v) When evaluating pricing data, the contracting officer shall consider materially differing terms and conditions, quantities, and market and economic factors. For similar items, the contracting officer shall also consider material differences between the similar item and the item being procured (see FAR 15.404-1(b)(2)(ii)(B) and PGI 215.404-1(b)(v)). Material differences are those that could reasonably be expected to influence the contracting officer's determination of price reasonableness. The contracting officer shall consider the following factors when evaluating the relevance of the information available:

(A) *Market prices.*

(B) *Age of data.*

(*1*) Whether data is too old to be relevant depends on the industry (e.g., rapidly evolving technologies), product maturity (e.g., stable), economic factors (e.g., new sellers in the marketplace), and various other considerations.

(*2*) A pending sale may be relevant if, in the judgement of the contracting officer, it is probable at the anticipated price, and the sale could reasonably be expected to materially influence the contracting officer's determination of price reasonableness. The contracting officer may consult with the cognizant administrative contracting officers (ACOs) as they may have information about pending sales.

(C) *Volume and completeness of transaction data.* Data must include a sufficient number of transactions to represent the range of relevant sales to all types of customers. The data must also include key information, such as date, quantity sold, part number, part nomenclature, sales price, and customer. If the number of transactions is insufficient or the data is incomplete, the contracting officer shall request additional sales data to evaluate price reasonableness. If the contractor cannot provide sufficient sales data, the contracting officer shall request other relevant information.

(D) *Nature of transactions.* The nature of a sales transaction includes the information necessary to understand the transaction, such as terms and conditions, date, quantity sold, sale price, unique requirements, the type of customer (government, distributor, retail end-user, etc.), and related agreements. It also includes warranties, key product technical specifications, maintenance agreements, and preferred customer rewards.

(vi) The contracting officer shall consider catalog prices to be reliable when they are regularly maintained and supported by relevant sales data (including any related discounts, refunds, rebates, offsets, or other adjustments). The contracting officer may request that the offeror support differences between the proposed price(s), catalog price(s), and relevant sales data.

(vii) The contracting officer may consult with the DoD cadre of experts who are available to provide expert advice to the acquisition workforce in assisting with commercial item and price reasonableness determinations. The DoD cadre of experts is identified at PGI 215.404-1(b)(vii).

(h) *Review and justification of passthrough contracts.* Follow the procedures at PGI 215.404–1(h)(2) when considering alternative approaches or making the determination that the contracting approach selected is in the best interest of the Government, as required by FAR 15.404–1(h)(2).

[Final rule, 63 FR 55040, 10/14/98, effective 10/14/98; Final rule, 71 FR 69492, 12/1/2006, effective 12/1/2006; Final rule, 72 FR 30278, 5/31/2007, effective 5/31/2007; Final rule, 77 FR 76939, 12/31/2012, effective 12/31/2012; Final rule, 83 FR 4431, 1/31/2018, effective 1/31/2018; Final rule, 84 FR 72563, 12/31/2019, effective 12/31/2019]

215.404-2 Data to support proposal analysis.

See PGI 215.404-2 for guidance on obtaining field pricing or audit assistance.

[Final rule, 63 FR 55040, 10/14/98, effective 10/14/98; Final rule, 71 FR 69492, 12/1/2006, effective 12/1/2006; Final rule, 77 FR 76939, 12/31/2012, effective 12/31/2012]

215.404-3 Subcontract pricing considerations.

Follow the procedures at PGI 215.404-3 when reviewing a subcontractor's proposal.

[Final rule, 63 FR 55040, 10/14/98, effective 10/14/98; Final rule, 71 FR 69492, 12/1/2006, effective 12/1/2006]

215.404-4 Profit.

(b) *Policy.*

(1) Contracting officers shall use a structured approach for developing a prenegotiation profit or fee objective on any negotiated contract action when certified cost or pricing data is obtained, except for cost-plus-award-fee contracts (see 215.404-74, 216.405-2, and FAR 16.405-2) or contracts with Federally Funded Research and Development Centers (FFRDCs) (see 215.404-75). There are three structured approaches—

(A) The weighted guidelines method;

(B) The modified weighted guidelines method; and

(C) An alternate structured approach.

(c) *Contracting officer responsibilities.*

(1) Also, do not perform a profit analysis when assessing cost realism in competitive acquisitions.

(2) When using a structured approach, the contracting officer—

(A) Shall use the weighted guidelines method (see 215.404-71), except as provided in paragraphs (c) (2) (B) and (c) (2) (C) of this subsection.

(B) Shall use the modified weighted guidelines method (see 215.404-72) on contract actions with nonprofit organizations other than FFRDCs.

(C) May use an alternate structured approach (see 215.404-73) when—

(*1*) The contract action is—

(*i*) At or below the certified cost or pricing data threshold (see FAR 15.403-4(a)(1));

(*ii*) For architect-engineer or construction work;

(*iii*) Primarily for delivery of material from subcontractors; or

(*iv*) A termination settlement; or

(*2*) The weighted guidelines method does not produce a reasonable overall profit objective and the head of the contracting activity approves use of the alternate approach in writing.

(D) Shall use the weighted guidelines method to establish a basic profit rate under a formula-type pricing agreement, and may then use the basic rate on all actions under the agreement, provided that conditions affecting profit do not change.

(E) Shall document the profit analysis in the contract file.

(5) Although specific agreement on the applied weights or values for individual profit factors shall not be attempted, the contracting officer may encourage the contractor to—

(A) Present the details of its proposed profit amounts in the weighted guidelines format or similar structured approach; and

(B) Use the weighted guidelines method in developing profit objectives for negotiated subcontracts.

(6) The contracting officer must also verify that relevant variables have not materially changed (e.g., performance risk, interest rates, progress payment rates, distribution of facilities capital).

(d) *Profit-analysis factors.*—

(1) *Common factors.* The common factors are embodied in the DoD structured approaches and need not be further considered by the contracting officer.

[Final rule, 63 FR 55040, 10/14/98, effective 10/14/98; Final rule, 63 FR 63799, 11/17/98, effective 11/17/98; Final rule, 65 FR 77829, 12/13/2000, effective 12/13/2000; Final rule, 66 FR 49862, 10/1/2001, effective 10/1/2001; Final rule, 71 FR 69492, 12/1/2006, effective 12/1/2006; Final rule,

77 FR 76939, 12/31/2012, effective 12/31/2012]

215.404-70 DD Form 1547, Record of Weighted Guidelines Method Application.

Follow the procedures at PGI 215.404-70 for use of DD Form 1547 whenever a structured approach to profit analysis is required.

[Final rule, 63 FR 55040, 10/14/98, effective 10/14/98; Final rule, 71 FR 69492, 12/1/2006, effective 12/1/2006]

215.404-71 Weighted guidelines method. (No Text)

215.404-71-1 General.

(a) The weighted guidelines method focuses on three profit factors—

(1) Performance risk;

(2) Contract type risk; and

(3) Facilities capital employed.

(4) Cost efficiency.

(b) The contracting officer assigns values to each profit factor; the value multiplied by the base results in the profit objective for that factor. Each profit factor has a normal value and a designated range of values. The normal value is representative of average conditions on the prospective contract when compared to all goods and services acquired by DoD. The designated range provides values based on above normal or below normal conditions. In the negotiation documentation, the contracting officer need not explain assignment of the normal value, but should address conditions that justify assignment of other than the normal value. The cost efficiency special factor has no normal value. The contracting officer shall exercise sound business judgment in selecting a value when this special factor is used (see 215.404-71-5).

[Final rule, 63 FR 55040, 10/14/98, effective 10/14/98, Final rule, 67 FR 20688, 4/26/2002, effective 4/26/2002; Final rule, 67 FR 49254, 7/30/2002, effective 7/30/2002]

215.404-71-2 Performance risk.

(a) *Description*. This profit factor addresses the contractor's degree of risk in fulfilling the contract requirements. The factor consists of two parts:

(1) Technical—the technical uncertainties of performance.

(2) Management/cost control—the degree of management effort necessary—

(i) To ensure that contract requirements are met; and

(ii) To reduce and control costs.

(b) *Determination*. The following extract from the DD Form 1547 is annotated to describe the process.

Item	*Contractor risk factors*	*Assigned weighting*	*Assigned value*	*Base (item 20)*	*Profit objective*
21	Technical	(1)	(2)	N/A	N/A
22	Management/Cost Control	(1)	(2)	N/A	N/A
23	Performance Risk (Composite) . . .	N/A	(3)	(4)	(5)

(1) Assign a weight (percentage) to each element according to its input to the total performance risk. The total of the two weights equals 100 percent.

(2) Select a value for each element from the list in paragraph (c) of this subsection using the evaluation criteria in paragraphs (d) and (e) of this subsection.

(3) Compute the composite as shown in the following example:

[In Percentage]

	Assigned weighting	Assigned value	Weighted value
Technical	60	5.0	3.0
Management/Cost Control	40	4.0	1.6
Composite Value	100	. . . .	4.6

(4) Insert the amount from Block 20 of the DD Form 1547. Block 20 is total contract costs, excluding facilities capital cost of money.

(5) Multiply (3) by (4).

(c) *Values: Normal and designated ranges.*

[In Percentage]

	Normal value	Designated range
Standard	5	3% to 7%.
Technology Incentive	9	7% to 11%.

(1) *Standard.* The standard designated range should apply to most contracts.

(2) *Technology incentive.* For the technical factor only, contracting officers may use the technology incentive range for acquisitions that include development, production, or application of innovative new technologies. The technology incentive range does not apply to efforts restricted to studies, analyses, or demonstrations that have a technical report as their primary deliverable.

(d) *Evaluation criteria for technical.*

(1) *Review the contract requirements and focus on the critical performance elements in the statement of work or specifications.* Factors to consider include—

(i) Technology being applied or developed by the contractor;

(ii) Technical complexity;

(iii) Program maturity;

(iv) Performance specifications and tolerances;

(v) Delivery schedule; and

(vi) Extent of a warranty or guarantee.

(2) *Above normal conditions.*

(i) The contracting officer may assign a higher than normal value in those cases where there is a substantial technical risk. Indicators are—

(A) Items are being manufactured using specifications with stringent tolerance limits;

(B) The efforts require highly skilled personnel or require the use of state-of-the-art machinery;

(C) The services and analytical efforts are extremely important to the Government and must be performed to exacting standards;

(D) The contractor's independent development and investment has reduced the Government's risk or cost;

(E) The contractor has accepted an accelerated delivery schedule to meet DoD requirements; or

(F) The contractor has assumed additional risk through warranty provisions.

(ii) Extremely complex, vital efforts to overcome difficult technical obstacles that require personnel with exceptional abilities, experience, and professional credentials may justify a value significantly above normal.

(iii) The following may justify a maximum value—

(A) Development or initial production of a new item, particularly if performance or quality specifications are tight; or

(B) A high degree of development or production concurrency.

(3) *Below normal conditions.*

(i) The contracting officer may assign a lower than normal value in those cases where the technical risk is low. Indicators are—

(A) Requirements are relatively simple;

(B) Technology is not complex;

(C) Efforts do not require highly skilled personnel;

(D) Efforts are routine;

(E) Programs are mature; or

(F) Acquisition is a follow-on effort or a repetitive type acquisition.

(ii) The contracting officer may assign a value significantly below normal for—

(A) Routine services;

(B) Production of simple items;

(C) Rote entry or routine integration of Government-furnished information; or

(D) Simple operations with Government-furnished property.

(4) *Technology incentive range.*

(i) The contracting officer may assign values within the technology incentive range when contract performance includes the introduction of new, significant technological innovation. Use the technology incentive range only for the most innovative contract efforts. Innovation may be in the form of—

(A) Development or application of new technology that fundamentally changes the characteristics of an existing product or system and that results in increased technical performance, improved reliability, or reduced costs; or

(B) New products or systems that contain significant technological advances over the products or systems they are replacing.

(ii) When selecting a value within the technology incentive range, the contracting officer should consider the relative value of the proposed innovation to the acquisition as a whole. When the innovation represents a minor benefit, the contracting officer should consider using values less than the norm. For innovative efforts that will have a major positive impact on the product or program, the contracting officer may use values above the norm.

(e) *Evaluation criteria for management/cost control.*

(1) *The contracting officer should evaluate—*

(i) The contractor's management and internal control systems using contracting office data, information and reviews made by field contract administration offices or other DoD field offices;

(ii) The management involvement expected on the prospective contract action;

(iii) The degree of cost mix as an indication of the types of resources applied and value added by the contractor;

(iv) The contractor's support of Federal socioeconomic programs;

(v) The expected reliability of the contractor's cost estimates (including the contractor's cost estimating system);

(vi) The adequacy of the contractor's management approach to controlling cost and schedule; and

(vii) Any other factors that affect the contractor's ability to meet the cost targets (e.g., foreign currency exchange rates and inflation rates).

(2) *Above normal conditions.*

(i) The contracting officer may assign a higher than normal value when the management effort is intense. Indicators of this are—

(A) The contractor's value added is both considerable and reasonably difficult;

(B) The effort involves a high degree of integration or coordination;

(C) The contractor has a good record of past performance;

(D) The contractor has a substantial record of active participation in Federal socioeconomic programs;

(E) The contractor provides fully documented and reliable cost estimates;

(F) The contractor makes appropriate make-or-buy decisions; or

(G) The contractor has a proven record of cost tracking and control.

(ii) The contracting officer may justify a maximum value when the effort—

(A) Requires large scale integration of the most complex nature;

(B) Involves major international activities with significant management coordination (e.g., offsets with foreign vendors); or

(C) Has critically important milestones.

(iii) If the contractor demonstrates efficient management and cost control through the submittal of a timely, qualifying proposal (as defined in 217.7401) in furtherance of definitization of an undefinitized contract action, and the proposal demonstrates effective cost control from the time of award to the present, the contracting officer may add 1 percentage point to the value determined for management/cost control up to the maximum of 7 percent.

(3) *Below normal conditions.*

(i) The contracting officer may assign a lower than normal value when the management effort is minimal. Indicators of this are—

(A) The program is mature and many end item deliveries have been made;

(B) the contractor adds minimal value to an item;

(C) The efforts are routine and require minimal supervision;

(D) The contractor provides poor quality, untimely proposals;

(E) The contractor fails to provide an adequate analysis of subcontractor costs;

(F) The contractor does not cooperate in the evaluation and negotiation of the proposal;

(G) The contractor's cost estimating system is marginal;

(H) The contractor has made minimal effort to initiate cost reduction programs;

(I) The contractor's cost proposal is inadequate; or

(J) The contractor has a record of cost overruns or another indication of unreliable cost estimates and lack of cost control; or

(K) The contractor has a poor record of past performance.

(ii) The following may justify a value significantly below normal—

(A) Reviews performed by the field contract administration offices disclose unsatisfactory management and internal control systems (e.g., quality assurance, property control, safety, security); or

(B) The effort requires an unusually low degree of management involvement.

[Final rule, 65 FR 77829, 12/13/2000, effective 12/13/2000, Final rule, 67 FR 20688, 4/26/2002, effective 4/26/2002; Final rule, 67 FR 49254, 7/30/2002, effective 7/30/2002; Final rule, 78 FR 13543, 2/28/2013, effective 2/28/2013; Final rule, 83 FR 30584, 6/29/2018, effective 6/29/2018; Final rule, 84 FR 39204, 8/9/2019, effective 8/9/2019]

215.404-71-3 Contract type risk and working capital adjustment.

(a) *Description.* The contract type risk factor focuses on the degree of cost risk accepted by the contractor under varying contract types. The working capital adjustment is an adjustment added to the profit objective for contract type risk. It only applies to fixed-price contracts that provide for progress payments. Though it uses a formula approach, it is not intended to be an exact calculation of the cost of working capital. Its purpose is to give general recognition to the contractor's cost of working capital under varying contract circumstances, financing policies, and the economic environment.

(b) *Determination.* The following extract from the DD 1547 is annotated to explain the process.

Item	*Contractor risk factors*	*Assigned value*	*Base*	*Profit objective*
24a	Contract Type Risk (based on incurred costs at the time of qualifying proposal submission).	(1)	(2) (i)	(3)
24b	Contract Type Risk (based on Government estimated cost to complete)	(1)	(2) (ii)	(3)
24b	Totals		(3)	(3)

Item	Contractor risk factors	Costs financed	Length factor	Interest rate	Profit objective
25	Working Capital (4)	(5)	(6)	(7)	(8)

(1) Select a value from the list of contract types in paragraph (c) of this section using the evaluation criteria in paragraph (d) of this section. See paragraph (d)(2) of this section.

(2)(i) Insert the amount of costs incurred as of the date the contractor submits a qualifying proposal, such as under an undefinitized contract action, (excluding facilities capital cost of money) into the Block 24a column titled Base.

(ii) Insert the amount of Government estimated cost to complete (excluding facilities capital cost of money) into the Block 24b column titled Base.

(3) Multiply (1) by (2)(i) and (2)(ii), respectively for Blocks 24a and 24b. Add Blocks 24a and 24b and insert the totals in Block 24c.

(4) Only complete this block when the prospective contract is a fixed-price contract containing provisions for progress payments.

(5) Insert the amount computed per paragraph (e) of this subsection.

(6) Insert the appropriate figure from paragraph (f) of this subsection.

(7) Use the interest rate established by the Secretary of the Treasury (see *https://www.fiscal.treasury.gov/fsservices/gov/pmt/promptPayment/rates.htm*). Do not use any other interest rate.

(8) Multiply (5) by (6) by (7). This is the working capital adjustment. It shall not exceed 4 percent of the contract costs in Block 20.

(c) *Values: Normal and designated ranges.*

Contract type	Notes	Normal value (percent)	Designated range (percent)
Firm-fixed-price, no financing	(1)	5.0	4 to 6.
Firm-fixed-price, with performance-based payments	(6)	4.0	2.5 to 5.5
Firm-fixed-price, with progress payments . .	(2)	3.0	2 to 4.
Fixed-price incentive, no financing	(1)	3.0	2 to 4.
Fixed-price incentive, with performance-based payments.	(6)	2.0	0.5 to 3.5.
Fixed-price with redetermination provision .	(3)		
Fixed-price incentive, with progress payments	(2)	1.0	0 to 2.
Cost-plus-incentive-fee	(4)	1.0	0 to 2.
Cost-plus-fixed-fee	(4)	0.5	0 to 1.
Time-and-materials (including overhaul contracts priced on time-and- materials basis).	(5)	0.5	0 to 1.
Labor-hour	(5)	0.5	0 to 1.
Firm-fixed-price, level-of-effort	(5)	0.5	0 to 1.

(1) *No financing* means either that the contract does not provide progress payments or performance-based payments, or that the contract provides them only on a limited basis, such as financing of first articles. Do not compute a working capital adjustment.

(2) When the contract contains provisions for progress payments, compute a working capital adjustment (Block 25).

(3) For the purposes of assigning profit values, treat a fixed-price contract with redetermination provisions as if it were a fixed-price incentive contract with below normal conditions.

(4) Cost-plus contracts shall not receive the working capital adjustment.

(5) These types of contracts are considered cost-plus-fixed-fee contracts for the purposes of assigning profit values. They shall not receive the working capital adjustment in Block 25. However, they may receive higher than normal values within the designated range to the extent that portions of cost are fixed.

(6) When the contract contains provisions for performance-based payments, do not compute a working capital adjustment.

(d) *Evaluation criteria.*

(1) *General.* The contracting officer should consider elements that affect contract type risk such as—

(i) Length of contract;

(ii) Adequacy of cost data for projections;

(iii) Economic environment;

(iv) Nature and extent of subcontracted activity;

(v) Protection provided to the contractor under contract provisions (e.g., economic price adjustment clauses);

(vi) The ceilings and share lines contained in incentive provisions;

(vii) Risks associated with contracts for foreign military sales (FMS) that are not funded by U.S. appropriations; and

(viii) When the contract contains provisions for performance-based payments—

(A) The frequency of payments;

(B) The total amount of payments compared to the maximum allowable amount specified at FAR 32.1004 (b) (2); and

(C) The risk of the payment schedule to the contractor.

(2) *Mandatory.* (i) The contracting officer shall assess the extent to which costs have been incurred prior to definitization of the contract action (also see 217.7404-6(a) and 243.204-70-6). When costs have been incurred prior to definitization, generally regard the contract type risk to be in the low end of the designated range. If a substantial portion of the costs have been incurred prior to definitization, the contracting officer may assign a value as low as zero percent, regardless of contract type. However, if a contractor submits a qualifying proposal to definitize an undefinitized contract action and the contracting officer for such action definitizes the contract after the end of the 180-day period beginning on the date on which the contractor submitted the qualifying proposal (as defined in 217.7401), the profit allowed on the contract shall accurately reflect the cost risk of the contractor as such risk existed on the date the contractor submitted the qualifying proposal.

(ii) Contracting officers shall document in the price negotiation memorandum the reason for assigning a specific contract type risk value, to include the extent to which any reduced cost risk during the undefinitized period of performance was considered, in determining the negotiation objective.

(3) *Above normal conditions.* The contracting officer may assign a higher than normal value when there is substantial contract type risk. Indicators of this are—

(i) Efforts where there is minimal cost history;

(ii) Long-term contracts without provisions protecting the contractor, particularly when there is considerable economic uncertainty;

(iii) Incentive provisions (e.g., cost and performance incentives) that place a high degree of risk on the contractor;

(iv) FMS sales (other than those under DoD cooperative logistics support arrangements or those made from U.S. Government inventories or stocks) where the contractor can demonstrate that there are substantial risks above those normally present in DoD contracts for similar items; or

(v) An aggressive performance-based payment schedule that increases risk.

(4) *Below normal conditions.* The contracting officer may assign a lower than normal value when the contract type risk is low. Indicators of this are—

(i) Very mature product line with extensive cost history;

(ii) Relatively short-term contracts;

(iii) Contractual provisions that substantially reduce the contractor's risk;

(iv) Incentive provisions that place a low degree of risk on the contractor;

(v) Performance-based payments totaling the maximum allowable amount(s) specified at FAR 32.1004 (b)(2); or

(vi) A performance-based payment schedule that is routine with minimal risk.

(e) *Costs financed.*

(1) Costs financed equal total costs multiplied by the portion (percent) of costs financed by the contractor.

(2) Total costs equal Block 20 (i.e., all allowable costs excluding facilities capital cost of money), reduced as appropriate when—

(i) The contractor has little cash investment (e.g., subcontractor progress payments liquidated late in period of performance);

(ii) Some costs are covered by special financing provisions, such as advance payments; or

(iii) The contract is multiyear and there are special funding arrangements.

(3) The portion that the contractor finances is generally the portion not covered by progress payments, i.e., 100 percent minus the customary progress payment rate (see FAR 32.501). For example, if a contractor receives progress payments at 80 percent, the portion that the contractor finances is 20 percent. On contracts that provide progress payments to small businesses, use the customary progress payment rate for large businesses.

(f) *Contract length factor.*

(1) This is the period of time that the contractor has a working capital investment in the contract. It—

(i) Is based on the time necessary for the contractor to complete the substantive portion of the work;

(ii) Is not necessarily the period of time between contract award and final delivery (or final payment), as periods of minimal effort should be excluded;

(iii) Should not include periods of performance contained in option provisions; and

(iv) Should not, for multiyear contracts, include periods of performance beyond that required to complete the initial program year's requirements.

(2) The contracting officer—

(i) Should use the following table to select the contract length factor;

(ii) Should develop a weighted average contract length when the contract has multiple deliveries; and

(iii) May use sampling techniques provided they produce a representative result.

Period to perform substantive portion (in months)	*Contract length factor*
21 or less	.40
22 to 27	.65
28 to 33	.90
34 to 39	1.15
40 to 45	1.40
46 to 51	1.65
52 to 57	1.90
58 to 63	2.15
64 to 69	2.40
70 to 75	2.65
76 or more	2.90

(3) Example: A prospective contract has a performance period of 40 months with end items being delivered in the 34th, 36th, 38th, and 40th months of the contract. The average period is 37 months and the contract length factor is 1.15.

[Final rule, 63 FR 55040, 10/14/98, effective 10/14/98; Final rule, 64 FR 61031, 11/9/99 effective 11/9/99; Final rule, 66 FR 63334, 12/6/2001, effective 12/6/2001, Final rule, 67 FR 20688, 4/26/2002, effective 4/26/2002; Final rule, 67 FR 49254, 7/30/2002, effective 7/30/2002; Final rule, 72 FR 14239, 3/27/2007, effective

3/27/2007; Final rule, 75 FR 48276, 8/10/2010, effective 8/10/2010; Final rule, 80 FR 56929, 9/21/2015, effective 9/21/2015; Final rule, 83 FR 30584, 6/29/2018, effective 6/29/2018; Final rule, 84 FR 39204, 8/9/2019, effective 8/9/2019]

215.404-71-4 Facilities capital employed.

(a) *Description.* This factor focuses on encouraging and rewarding capital investment in facilities that benefit DoD. It recognizes both the facilities capital that the contractor will employ in contract performance and the contractor's commitment to improving productivity.

(b) *Contract facilities capital estimates.* The contracting officer shall estimate the facilities capital cost of money and capital employed using—

(1) An analysis of the appropriate Forms CASB-CMF and cost of money factors (48 CFR 9904.414 and FAR 31.205-10); and

(2) DD Form 1861, Contract Facilities Capital Cost of Money.

(c) *Use of DD Form 1861.* See PGI 215.404-71-4(c) for obtaining field pricing support for preparing DD Form 1861.

(1) *Purpose.* The DD Form 1861 provides a means of linking the Form CASB-CMF and DD Form 1547, Record of Weighted Guidelines Application. It—

(i) Enables the contracting officer to differentiate profit objectives for various types of assets (land, buildings, equipment). The procedure is similar to applying overhead rates to appropriate overhead allocation bases to determine contract overhead costs.

(ii) Is designed to record and compute the contract facilities capital cost of money and capital employed which is carried forward to DD Form 1547.

(2) *Completion instructions.* Complete a DD Form 1861 only after evaluating the contractor's cost proposal, establishing cost of money factors, and establishing a prenegotiation objective on cost. Complete the form as follows:

(i) List overhead pools and direct-charging service centers (if used) in the same structure as they appear on the contractor's cost proposal and Form CASB-CMF. The structure and allocation base units-of-measure must be compatible on all three displays.

(ii) Extract appropriate contract overhead allocation base data, by year, from the evaluated cost breakdown or prenegotiation cost objective and list against each overhead pool and direct-charging service center.

(iii) Multiply each allocation base by its corresponding cost of money factor to get the facilities capital cost of money estimated to be incurred each year. The sum of these products represents the estimated contract facilities capital cost of money for the year's effort.

(iv) Total contract facilities cost of money is the sum of the yearly amounts.

(v) Since the facilities capital cost of money factors reflect the applicable cost of money rate in Column 1 of Form CASB-CMF, divide the contract cost of money by that same rate to determine the contract facilities capital employed.

(d) *Preaward facilities capital applications.* To establish cost and price objectives, apply the facilities capital cost of money and capital employed as follows:

(1) *Cost of Money.* (i) *Cost Objective.* Use the imputed facilities capital cost of money, with normal, booked costs, to establish a cost objective or the target cost when structuring an incentive type contract. Do not adjust target costs established at the outset even though actual cost of money rates become available during the period of contract performance.

(ii) *Profit Objective.* When measuring the contractor's effort for the purpose of establishing a prenegotiation profit objective, restrict the cost base to normal, booked costs. Do not include cost of money as part of the cost base.

(2) *Facilities Capital Employed.* Assess and weight the profit objective for risk associated with facilities capital employed in accordance with the profit guidelines at 215.404-71-4.

(e) *Determination.* The following extract from the DD Form 1547 has been annotated to explain the process.

Item	Contractor risk factors	Assigned value	Amount employed	Profit objective
26.	Land	N/A	(2)	N/A
27.	Buildings	N/A	(2)	N/A
28.	Equipment	(1)	(2)	(3)

(1) Select a value from the list in paragraph (f) of this subsection using the evaluation criteria in paragraph (g) of this subsection.

(2) Use the allocated facilities capital attributable to land, buildings, and equipment, as derived in DD Form 1861, Contract Facilities Capital Cost of Money.

(i) In addition to the net book value of facilities capital employed, consider facilities capital that is part of a formal investment plan if the contractor submits reasonable evidence that—

(A) Achievable benefits to DoD will result from the investment; and

(B) The benefits of the investment are included in the forward pricing structure.

(ii) If the value of intracompany transfers has been included in Block 20 at cost (i.e., excluding general and administrative (G&A) expenses and profit), add to the contractor's allocated facilities capital, the allocated facilities capital attributable to the buildings and equipment of those corporate divisions supplying the intracompany transfers. Do not make this addition if the value of intracompany transfers has been included in Block 20 at price (i.e., including G&A expenses and profit).

(3) Multiply (1) by (2).

(f) *Values: Normal and designated ranges.*

Notes	Asset type	Normal value (percent)	Designated range (percent)
(1)	Land	0	N/A
(1)	Buildings	0	N/A
(1)	Equipment	17.5	10 to 25

(g) *Evaluation criteria.*

(1) *In evaluating facilities capital employed, the contracting officer—*

(i) Should relate the usefulness of the facilities capital to the goods or services being acquired under the prospective contract;

(ii) Should analyze the productivity improvements and other anticipated industrial base enhancing benefits resulting from the facilities capital investment, including—

(A) The economic value of the facilities capital, such as physical age, undepreciated value, idleness, and expected contribution to future defense needs; and

(B) The contractor's level of investment in defense related facilities as compared with the portion of the contractor's total business that is derived from DoD; and

(iii) Should consider any contractual provisions that reduce the contractor's risk of investment recovery, such as termination protection clauses and capital investment indemnification.

(2) *Above normal conditions.*

(i) The contracting officer may assign a higher than normal value if the facilities capital investment has direct, identifiable, and exceptional benefits. Indicators are—

(A) New investments in state-of-the-art technology that reduce acquisition cost of yield other tangible benefits such as improved product quality or accelerated deliveries;

(B) Investments in new equipment for research and development applications.

(ii) The contracting officer may assign a value significantly above normal when there are direct and measurable benefits in efficiency and significantly reduced acquisition costs on the effort being priced. Maximum values apply only to those cases where the benefits of the facilities capital investment are substantially above normal.

(3) *Below normal conditions.*

(i) The contracting officer may assign a lower than normal value if the facilities capital investment has little benefit to DoD. Indicators are—

(A) Allocations of capital apply predominantly to commercial item lines;

(B) Investments are for such things as furniture and fixtures, home or group level administrative offices, corporate aircraft and hangars, gymnasiums; or

(C) Facilities are old or extensively idle.

(ii) The contracting officer may assign a value significantly below normal when a significant portion of defense manufacturing is done in an environment characterized by outdated, inefficient, and labor-intensive capital equipment.

[Final rule, 63 FR 55040, 10/14/98, effective 10/14/98, Final rule, 67 FR 20688, 4/26/2002, effective 4/26/2002; Final rule, 67 FR 49254, 7/30/2002, effective 7/30/2002; Final rule 71 FR 69492, 12/1/2006, effective 12/1/2006; Final rule, 72 FR 14239, 3/27/2007, effective 3/27/2007; Final rule, 73 FR 70905, 11/24/2008, effective 11/24/2008]

215.404-71-5 Cost efficiency factor.

(a) This special factor provides an incentive for contractors to reduce costs. To the extent that the contractor can demonstrate cost reduction efforts that benefit the pending contract, the contracting officer may increase the prenegotiation profit objective by an amount not to exceed 4 percent of total objective cost (Block 20 of the DD Form 1547) to recognize these efforts (Block 29).

(b) To determine if using this factor is appropriate, the contracting officer shall consider criteria, such as the following, to evaluate the benefit the contractor's cost reduction efforts will have on the pending contract:

(1) The contractor's participation in Single Process Initiative improvements;

(2) Actual cost reductions achieved on prior contracts;

(3) Reduction or elimination of excess or idle facilities;

(4) The contractor's cost reduction initiatives (e.g., competition advocacy programs, technical insertion programs, obsolete parts control programs, spare parts pricing reform, value engineering, outsourcing of functions such as information technology). Metrics developed by the contractor such as fully loaded labor hours (i.e., cost per labor hour, including all direct and indirect costs) or other productivity measures may provide the basis for assessing the effectiveness of the contractor's cost reduction initiatives over time;

(5) The contractor's adoption of process improvements to reduce costs;

(6) Subcontractor cost reduction efforts;

(7) The contractor's effective incorporation of commercial items and processes; or

(8) The contractor's investment in new facilities when such investments contribute to better asset utilization or improved productivity.

(c) When selecting the percentage to use for this special factor, the contracting officer has maximum flexibility in determining the best way to evaluate the benefit the contractor's cost reduction efforts will have on the pending contract. However, the contracting officer shall consider the impact that quantity differences, learning, changes in scope, and economic factors such as inflation and deflation will have on cost reduction.

[Final rule, 67 FR 20688, 4/26/2002, effective 4/26/2002; Final rule, 67 FR 49254, 7/30/2002, effective 7/30/2002]

215.404-72 Modified weighted guidelines method for nonprofit organizations other than FFRDCs.

(a) *Definition.* As used in this subpart, a *nonprofit organization* is a business entity—

(1) That operates exclusively for charitable, scientific, or educational purposes;

(2) Whose earnings do not benefit any private shareholder or individual;

(3) Whose activities do not involve influencing legislation or political campaigning for any candidate for public office; and

(4) That is exempted from Federal income taxation under section 501 of the Internal Revenue Code.

(b) For nonprofit organizations that are entities that have been identified by the Secretary of Defense or a Secretary of a Department as receiving sustaining support on a cost-plus-fixed-fee basis from a particular DoD department or agency, compute a fee objective for covered actions using the weighted guidelines method in 215.404-71, with the following modifications:

(1) *Modifications to performance risk (Blocks 21-23 of the DD Form 1547).*

(i) If the contracting officer assigns a value from the standard designated range (see 215.404-71-2 (c)), reduce the fee objective by an amount equal to 1 percent of the costs in Block 20 of the DD Form 1547. Show the net (reduced) amount on the DD Form 1547.

(ii) Do not assign a value from the technology incentive designated range.

(2) *Modifications to contract type risk (Block 24 of the DD Form 1547).* Use a designated range of 1 percent to 0 percent instead of the values in 215.404-71-3. There is no normal value.

(c) For all other nonprofit organizations except FFRDCs, compute a fee objective for covered actions using the weighted guidelines method in 215.404-71, modified as described in paragraph (b)(1) of this subsection.

[Final rule, 63 FR 63799, 11/17/98, effective 11/17/98; Final rule, 65 FR 77829, 12/13/2000, effective 12/13/2000; Final rule, 67 FR 49254, 7/30/2002, effective 7/30/2002]

215.404-73 Alternate structured approaches.

(a) The contracting officer may use an alternate structured approach under 215.404-4 (c).

(b) The contracting officer may design the structure of the alternate, but it shall include—

(1) Consideration of the three basic components of profit—performance risk, contract type risk (including working capital), and facilities capital employed. However, the contracting officer is not required to complete Blocks 21 through 30 of the DD Form 1547.

(2) Offset for facilities capital cost of money.

(i) The contracting officer shall reduce the overall prenegotiation profit objective by the amount of facilities capital cost of money under Cost Accounting Standard (CAS) 414, Cost of Money as an Element of the Cost of Facilities Capital (48 CFR 9904.414). Cost of money under CAS 417, Cost of Money as an Element of the Cost of Capital Assets Under Construction (48 CFR 9904.417), should not be used to reduce the overall prenegotiation profit objective. The profit amount in the negotiation summary of the DD Form 1547 must be net of the offset.

(ii) This adjustment is needed for the following reason: The values of the profit factors used in the weighted guidelines method were adjusted to recognize the shift in facilities capital cost of money from an element of profit to an element of contract cost (see FAR 31.205-10) and reductions were made directly to the profit factors for performance risk. In order to ensure that this policy is applied to all DoD contracts that allow facilities capital cost of money, similar adjustments shall be made to contracts that use alternate structured approaches.

[Final rule, 63 FR 55040, 10/14/98, effective 10/14/98, Final rule, 67 FR 20688, 4/26/2002, effective 4/26/2002; Final rule, 71 FR 69492, 12/1/2006, effective 12/1/2006]

215.404-74 Fee requirements for cost-plus-award-fee contracts.

In developing a fee objective for cost-plus-award-fee contracts, the contracting officer shall—

(a) Follow the guidance in FAR 16.405-2 and 216.405-2;

(b) Not use the weighted guidelines method or alternate structured approach;

(c) Apply the offset policy in 215.404-73 (b) (2) for facilities capital cost of money, i.e., reduce the base fee by the amount of facilities capital cost of money; and

(d) Not complete a DD Form 1547

[Final rule, 63 FR 55040, 10/14/98, effective 10/14/98, Final rule, 67 FR 20688, 4/26/2002, effective 4/26/2002]

215.404-75 Fee requirements for FFRDCs.

For nonprofit organizations that are FFRDCs, the contracting officer—

(a) Should consider whether any fee is appropriate. Considerations shall include the FFRDC's—

(1) Proportion of retained earnings (as established under generally accepted accounting methods) that relates to DoD contracted effort;

(2) Facilities capital acquisition plans;

(3) Working capital funding as assessed on operating cycle cash needs; and

(4) Provision for funding unreimbursed costs deemed ordinary and necessary to the FFRDC.

(b) Shall, when a fee is considered appropriate, establish the fee objective in accordance with FFRDC fee policies in the DoD FFRDC Management Plan.

(c) Shall not use the weighted guidelines method or an alternate structured approach.

[Final rule, 63 FR 63799, 11/17/98, effective 11/17/98]

215.404-76 [Removed]

[Final rule, 63 FR 55040, 10/14/98, effective 10/14/98; Redesignated from 215.404-75, Final rule, 63 FR 63799, 11/17/98, effective 11/17/98; Final rule, 65 FR 52951, 8/31/2000, effective 8/31/2000, corrected, 65 FR 58607, 9/29/2000; Final rule, 66 FR 49862, 10/1/2001, effective 10/1/2001; Final rule, 66 FR 63334, 12/6/2001, effective 12/6/2001; Final rule, 67 FR 4207, 1/29/2002, effective 1/29/2002; Final rule, 70 FR 35543, 6/21/2005, effective 6/21/2005; Final rule, 71 FR 69492, 12/1/2006, effective 12/1/2006; Final rule, 80 FR 67254, 10/30/2015, effective 10/30/2015]

215.406-1 Prenegotiation objectives.

Follow the procedures at PGI 215.406-1 for establishing prenegotiation objectives.

[Final rule, 63 FR 55040, 10/14/98, effective 10/14/98; Final rule, 71 FR 69492, 12/1/2006, effective 12/1/2006]

215.406-2 Certificate of Current Cost or Pricing Data.

See PGI 215.406-2 for additional information and guidance on Certificates of Current Cost or Pricing Data.

[Final rule, 84 FR 25194, 5/31/2019, effective 5/31/2019]

215.406-3 Documenting the negotiation.

Follow the procedures at PGI 215.406-3 for documenting the negotiation and uploading sole source business clearance documentation into the Contract Business Analysis Repository.

[Final rule, 63 FR 55040, 10/14/98, effective 10/14/98; Final rule, 71 FR 69492, 12/1/2006, effective 12/1/2006; Final rule, 78 FR 21850, 4/12/2013, effective 4/12/2013]

215.407 Special cost or pricing areas. (No Text)

[Final rule, 83 FR 19645, 5/4/2018, effective 5/4/2018]

215.407-1 Defective certified cost or pricing data.

(c) (i) When a contractor voluntarily discloses defective pricing after contract award, the contracting officer shall discuss the disclosure with the Defense Contract Audit Agency (DCAA). This discussion will assist in the contracting officer determining the involvement of DCAA, which could be a limited-scope audit (*e.g.*, limited to the affected cost elements of the defective pricing disclosure), a full-scope audit, or technical assistance as appropriate for the circumstances (*e.g.*, nature or dollar amount of the defective pricing disclosure). At a minimum, the contracting officer shall discuss with DCAA the following:

(A) Completeness of the contractor's voluntary disclosure on the affected contract.

(B) Accuracy of the contractor's cost impact calculation for the affected contract.

(C) Potential impact on existing contracts, task or deliver orders, or other proposals the contractor has submitted to the Government.

(ii) Voluntary disclosure of defective pricing is not a voluntary refund as defined in 242.7100 and does not waive the Government entitlement to the recovery of any overpayment plus interest on the overpayments in accordance with FAR 15.407-1(b)(7).

(iii) Voluntary disclosure of defective pricing does not waive the Government's rights to pursue defective pricing claims on the affected contract or any other Government contract.

[Final rule, 83 FR 19645, 5/4/2018, effective 5/4/2018]

215.407-2 Make-or-buy programs.

(a) *General.* See PGI 215.407-2 for guidance on factors to consider when deciding whether to request a make-or-buy plan and for factors to consider when evaluating make-or-buy plan submissions.

(e) *Program requirements.*

(1) *Items and work included.* The minimum dollar amount is $1.5 million.

[Final rule, 63 FR 55040, 10/14/98, effective 10/14/98; Final rule, 75 FR 45072, 8/2/2010, effective 10/1/2010; Final rule, 76 FR 76318, 12/7/2011, effective 12/7/2011]

215.407-3 Forward pricing rate agreements.

(b) (i) Use forward pricing rate agreement (FPRA) rates when such rates are available, unless waived on a case-by-case basis by the head of the contracting activity.

(ii) Advise the ACO of each case waived.

(iii) Contact the ACO for questions on FPRAs or recommended rates.

[Final rule, 63 FR 55040, 10/14/98, effective 10/14/98]

215.407-4 Should-cost review.

(a) *General.* See PGI 215.407-4 for guidance on determining whether to perform a program or overhead should-cost review.

(b) *Program should-cost review.* Major weapon system should-cost program reviews shall be conducted in a manner that is transparent, objective, and provides for the efficiency of the DoD systems acquisition process (section 837 of the National Defense Authorization Act for Fiscal Year 2018 (Pub. L. 115-91)).

(i) Major weapon system should-cost reviews may include the following features:

(A) A thorough review of each contributing element of the program cost and the justification for each cost.

(B) An analysis of non-value added overhead and unnecessary reporting requirements.

(C) Benchmarking against similar DoD programs, similar commercial programs (where appropriate), and other programs by the same contractor at the same facility.

(D) An analysis of supply chain management to encourage competition and incentive cost performance at lower tiers.

(E) A review of how to restructure the program (Government and contractor) team in a streamlined manner, if necessary.

(F) Identification of opportunities to break out Government-furnished equipment versus prime contractor-furnished materials.

(G) Identification of items or services contracted through third parties that result in unnecessary pass-through costs.

(H) Evaluation of ability to use integrated developmental and operational testing and modeling and simulation to reduce overall costs.

(I) Identification of alternative technology and materials to reduce developmental or lifecycle costs for a program.

(J) Identification and prioritization of cost savings opportunities.

(K) Establishment of measurable targets and ongoing tracking systems.

(ii) The should-cost review shall provide for sufficient analysis while minimizing the impact on program schedule by engaging stakeholders early, relying on information already available before requesting additional data, and establishing a team with the relevant expertise early.

(iii) The should-cost review team shall be comprised of members, including third-party experts if necessary, with the training, skills, and experience in analysis of cost elements, production or sustainment processes, and technologies relevant to the program under review. The review team may include members from the Defense Contract Management Agency, the department or agency's cost analysis center, and appropriate functional organizations, as necessary.

(iv) The should-cost review team shall establish a process for communicating and collaborating with the contractor throughout the should-cost review, including notification to the contractor regarding which elements of the contractor's operations will be reviewed and what information will be necessary to perform the review, as soon as practicable, both prior to and during the review.

(v) The should-cost review team report shall ensure, to the maximum extent practicable, review of current, accurate, and complete data, and shall identify cost savings opportunities associated with specific engineering or business changes that can be quantified and tracked.

[Final rule, 63 FR 55040, 10/14/98, effective 10/14/98; Final rule, 65 FR 52951, 8/31/2000, effective 8/31/2000, corrected, 65 FR 58607, 9/29/2000; Final rule, 67 FR 49251, 7/30/2002, effective 7/30/2002; Final rule, 67 FR 49254, 7/30/2002, effective 7/30/200; Final rule, 71 FR 69492, 12/1/2006, effective 12/1/2006; Final rule, 84 FR 65308, 11/27/2019, effective 11/27/2019]

215.407-5 Estimating systems. (No text)

215.407-5-70 Disclosure, maintenance, and review requirements.

(a) *Definitions.*

(1) *Acceptable estimating system* is defined in the clause at 252.215-7002, Cost Estimating System Requirements.

(i) Is established, maintained, reliable, and consistently applied; and

(ii) Produces verifiable, supportable, and documented cost estimates.

(2) *Contractor* means a business unit as defined in FAR 2.101.

(3) *Estimating system* is as defined in the clause at 252.215-7002, Cost Estimating System Requirements.

(4) *Significant deficiency* is defined in the clause at 252.215-7002, Cost Estimating System Requirements.

(b) *Applicability.*

(1) DoD policy is that all contractors have acceptable estimating systems that consistently produce well-supported proposals that are acceptable as a basis for negotiation of fair and reasonable prices.

(i) Are acceptable;

(ii) Consistently produce well-supported proposals that are acceptable as a basis for negotiation of fair and reasonable prices;

(iii) Are consistent with and integrated with the contractor's related management systems; and

(iv) Are subject to applicable financial control systems.

(2) A large business contractor is subject to estimating system disclosure, maintenance, and review requirements if—

(i) In its preceding fiscal year, the contractor received DoD prime contracts or subcontracts totaling $50 million or more for which certified cost or pricing data were required; or

(ii) In its preceding fiscal year, the contractor received DoD prime contracts or subcontracts totaling $10 million or more (but less than $50 million) for which certified cost or pricing data were required and the contracting officer, with concurrence or at the request of the ACO, determines it to be in the best interest of the Government (e.g., significant estimating problems are believed to exist or the contractor's sales are predominantly Government).

(c) *Policy.* (1) The contracting officer shall—

(i) Through use of the clause at 252.215-7002, Cost Estimating System Requirements, apply the disclosure, maintenance, and review requirements to large business contractors meeting the criteria in paragraph (b)(2)(i) of this section;

(ii) Consider whether to apply the disclosure, maintenance, and review requirements to large business contractors under paragraph (b)(2)(ii) of this section; and

(iii) Not apply the disclosure, maintenance, and review requirements to other than large business contractors.

(2) The cognizant contracting officer, in consultation with the auditor, for contractors subject to paragraph (b)(2) of this section, shall—

(i) Determine the acceptability of the disclosure and approve or disapprove the system: and

(ii) Pursue correction of any deficiencies.

(3) The auditor conducts estimating system reviews.

(4) An acceptable system shall provide for the use of appropriate source data, utilize sound estimating techniques and good judgment, maintain a consistent approach, and adhere to established policies and procedures.

(5) In evaluating the acceptability of a contractor's estimating system, the contracting officer, in consultation with the auditor, shall determine whether the contractor's estimating system complies with the system criteria for an acceptable estimating system as prescribed in the clause at 252.215-7002, Cost Estimating System Requirements.

(d) *Disposition of findings*—(1) *Reporting of findings.* The auditor shall document findings and recommendations in a report to the contracting officer. If the auditor identifies any significant estimating system deficiencies, the report shall describe the deficiencies in sufficient detail to allow the contracting officer to understand the deficiencies.

(2) *Initial determination.* (i) The contracting officer shall review all findings and recommendations and, if there are no significant deficiencies, shall promptly notify the contractor, in writing, that the contractor's estimating system is acceptable and approved; or

(ii) If the contracting officer finds that there are one or more significant deficiencies (as defined in the clause at 252.215-7002, Cost Estimating System Requirements) due to the contractor's failure to meet one or more of the estimating system criteria in the clause at 252.215-7002, the contracting officer shall—

(A) Promptly make an initial written determination on any significant deficiencies and notify the contractor, in writing, providing a description of each significant deficiency in sufficient detail to allow the contractor to understand the deficiency;

(B) Request the contractor to respond in writing to the initial determination within 30 days; and

(C) Promptly evaluate the contractor's responses to the initial determination, in consultation with the auditor or functional specialist, and make a final determination.

(3) *Final determination.* (i) The contracting officer shall make a final determination and notify the contractor in writing that—

(A) The contractor's estimating system is acceptable and approved, and no significant deficiencies remain, or

(B) Significant deficiencies remain. The notice shall identify any remaining significant deficiencies, and indicate the adequacy of any proposed or completed corrective action. The contracting officer shall—

(*1*) Request that the contractor, within 45 days of receipt of the final determination, either correct the deficiencies or submit an acceptable corrective action plan showing milestones and actions to eliminate the deficiencies;

(*2*) Disapprove the system in accordance with the clause at 252.215-7002, Cost Estimating System Requirements; and

(*3*) Withhold payments in accordance with the clause at 252.242-7005, Contractor Business Systems, if the clause is included in the contract.

(ii) Follow the procedures relating to monitoring a contractor's corrective action and the correction of significant deficiencies in PGI 215.407-5-70(e).

(e) *System approval.* The contracting officer shall promptly approve a previously disapproved estimating system and notify the contractor when the contracting officer determines that there are no remaining significant deficiencies.

(f) *Contracting officer notifications.* The cognizant contracting officer shall promptly distribute copies of a determination to approve a system, disapprove a system and withhold payments, or approve a previously disapproved system and release withheld payments, to the auditor; payment office; affected contracting officers at the buying activities; and cognizant contracting officers in contract administration activities.

[Final rule, 63 FR 55040, 10/14/98, effective 10/14/98; Final rule, 67 FR 49251, 7/30/2002, effective 7/30/2002; Final rule, 71 FR 69492, 12/1/2006, effective 12/1/2006; Interim rule, 76 FR 28856, 5/18/2011, effective 5/18/2011; Final rule, 77 FR 11355, 2/24/2012, effective 2/24/2012; Final rule, 77 FR 76939, 12/31/2012, effective 12/31/2012]

215.408 Solicitation provisions and contract clauses.

(1) Use the clause at 252.215-7002, Cost Estimating System requirements, in all solicitations and contracts to be awarded on the basis of certified cost or pricing data.

(2) When contracting with the Canadian Commercial Corporation—

(i) (A) Use the provision at 252.215-7003, Requirement for Submission of Data Other Than Certified Cost or Pricing Data—Canadian Commercial Corporation—

(*1*) In lieu of DFARS 252.215-7010, Requirements for Certified Cost or Pricing Data and Data Other Than Certified Cost or Pricing Data, in a solicitation, including solicitations using FAR part 12 procedures for the acquisition of commercial items, for a sole source acquisition from the Canadian Commercial Corporation that is—

(*i*) Cost-reimbursement, if the contract value is expected to exceed $700,000; or

(*ii*) Fixed-price, if the contract value is expected to exceed $500 million; or

(*2*) In lieu of DFARS 252.215-7010, in a solicitation, including solicitations using FAR part 12 procedures for the acquisition of commercial items, for a sole source acquisition from the Canadian Commercial Corporation that does not meet the thresholds specified in paragraph (2) (i) (A) (*1*), if approval is obtained as required at 225.870-4(c) (2) (ii); and

(B) Do not use 252.225-7003 in lieu of DFARS 252.215–7010 in competitive acquisitions; and

(ii) (A) Use the clause at 252.215-7004, Requirement for Submission of Data Other Than Certified Cost or Pricing Data—Modifications—Canadian Commercial Corporation—

(*1*) In a solicitation, including solicitations using FAR part 12 procedures for the acquisition of commercial items, for a sole source acquisition, from the Canadian Commercial Corporation and resultant contract that is—

(*i*) Cost-reimbursement, if the contract value is expected to exceed $700,000; or

(*ii*) Fixed-price, if the contract value is expected to exceed $500 million;

(*2*) In a solicitation, including solicitations using FAR part 12 procedures for the acquisition of commercial items, for a sole source acquisition from the Canadian Commercial Corporation and resultant contract that does not meet the thresholds specified in paragraph (2) (ii) (A) (*1*), if approval is obtained as required at 225.870-4(c) (2) (ii); or

(3) (i) In a solicitation, including solicitations using FAR part 12 procedures for the acquisition of commercial items, for a competitive acquisition that includes FAR 52.215-21, Requirement for Data Other Than Certified Cost or Pricing Data—Modifications, or that meets the thresholds specified in paragraph (2) (ii) (A) *(1)*.

(ii) The contracting officer shall then select the appropriate clause to include in the contract (52.215-21 only if award is not to the Canadian Commercial Corporation; or 252.215- 7004 if award is to the Canadian Commercial Corporation and necessary approval is obtained in accordance with 225.870-4(c) (2) (ii)); and

(B) Do not use 252.225-7003 in lieu of DFARS 252.215-7010 in competitive acquisitions; and

(3) Use the provision at 252.215-7008, Only One Offer, in competitive solicitations that exceed the simplified acquisition threshold, including solicitations using FAR part 12 procedures for the acquisition of commercial items.

(4) When the solicitation requires the submission of certified cost or pricing data, the contracting officer should include 252.215-7009, Proposal Adequacy Checklist, in the solicitation to facilitate submission of a thorough, accurate, and complete proposal.

(5) When reasonably certain that the submission of certified cost or pricing data or data other than certified cost or pricing data will be required or when using the provision at 252.215-7008—

(i) Use the basic or alternate of the provision at 252.215-7010, Requirements for Certified Cost or Pricing Data and Data Other Than Certified Cost or Pricing Data, in lieu of the provision at FAR 52.215-20, Requirements for Certified Cost or Pricing Data and Data Other Than Certified Cost or Pricing Data, in solicitations, including solicitations using FAR part 12 procedures for the acquisition of commercial items.

(A) Use the basic provision when submission of certified cost or pricing data is required to be in the FAR Table 15-2 format, or if it is anticipated, at the time of solicitation, that the submission of certified cost or pricing data may not be required.

(B) Use the alternate I provision to specify a format for certified cost or pricing data other than the format required by FAR Table 15-2;

(ii) Use the provision at 252.215-7011, Requirements for Submission of Proposals to the Administrative Contracting Officer and Contract Auditor, when using the basic or alternate of the provision at 252.215-7010 and copies of the proposal are to be sent to the ACO and contract auditor; and

(iii) Use the provision at 252.215-7012, Requirements for Submission of Proposals via Electronic Media, when using the basic or alternate of the provision at 252.215-7010 and submission via electronic media is required.

(6) Use the provision at 252.215-7013, Supplies and Services Provided by Nontraditional Defense Contractors, in all solicitations.

(7) Use the clause at 252.215-7014, Exception from Certified Cost or Pricing Data Requirements for Foreign Military Sales Indirect Offsets, in solicitations and contracts that contain the provision at 252.215-7010, Requirements for Certified Cost or Pricing Data and Data Other Than Certified Cost or Pricing Data, when it is reasonably certain that—

(i) The contract is expected to include costs associated with an indirect offset; and

(ii) The submission of certified cost or pricing data or data other than certified cost or pricing data will be required.

(8) Use the clause at 252.215-7015, Program Should-Cost Review, in all solicitations and contracts for the development or production of a major weapon system, as defined in 234.7001.

[Final rule, 63 FR 55040, 10/14/98, effective 10/14/98; Interim rule, 72 FR 20758, 4/26/2007, effective 4/26/2007; Interim rule, 73 FR 27464, 5/13/2008, effective 5/13/2008; Final rule, 75 FR 48278, 8/10/2010, effective 8/10/2010; Final rule, 77 FR 39125, 6/29/2012, effective 6/29/2012; Final rule, 77 FR 43470, 7/24/2012, effective 7/24/2012; Final rule,

77 FR 76939, 12/31/2012, effective 12/31/2012; Final rule, 78 FR 13543, 2/28/2013, effective 2/28/2013; Final rule, 78 FR 18865, 3/28/2013, effective 3/28/2013; Final rule, 78 FR 37980, 6/25/2013, effective 6/25/2013; Final rule, 78 FR 65214, 10/31/2013, effective 10/31/2013; Final rule, 81 FR 28729, 5/10/2016, effective 5/10/2016; Final rule, 81 FR 36473, 6/7/2016, effective 6/7/2016; Final rule, 83 FR 4431, 1/31/2018, effective 1/31/2018; Final rule, 83 FR 30824, 6/29/2018, effective 6/29/2018; Final rule, 83 FR 30825, 6/29/2018, effective 6/29/2018; Final rule, 84 FR 30947, 6/28/2019, effective 7/31/2019; Final rule, 84 FR 65308, 11/27/2019, effective 11/27/2019]

215.470 Estimated data prices.

(a) DoD requires estimates of the prices of data in order to evaluate the cost to the Government of data items in terms of their management, product, or engineering value.

(b) When data are required to be delivered under a contract, include DD Form 1423, Contract Data Requirements List, in the solicitation. See PGI 215.470(b) for guidance on the use of DD Form 1423.

(c) The contracting officer shall ensure that the contract does not include a requirement for data that the contractor has delivered or is obligated to deliver to the government under another contract or subcontract, and that the successful offeror identifies any such data required by the solicitation. However, where duplicate data are desired, the contract price shall include the costs of duplication, but not of preparation, of such data.

[Final rule, 63 FR 55040, 10/14/98, effective 10/14/98; Final rule, 71 FR 69492, 12/1/2006, effective 12/1/2006]

SUBPART 215.5—PREAWARD, AWARD, AND POSTAWARD NOTIFICATIONS, PROTESTS, AND MISTAKES

215.503 Notifications to unsuccessful offerors.

If the Government exercises the authority provided in 239.7305(d), the notifications to unsuccessful offerors, either preaward or postaward, shall not reveal any information that is determined to be withheld from disclosure in accordance with 10 U.S.C. 2339a (see subpart 239.73).

[Interim rule, 78 FR 69267, 11/18/2013, effective 11/18/2013; Final rule, 80 FR 67243, 10/30/2015, effective 10/30/2015; Final rule, 84 FR 4368, 2/15/2019, effective 2/15/2019]

215.506 Postaward debriefing of offerors.

(e) If the Government exercises the authority provided in 239.7305(d), the debriefing shall not reveal any information that is determined to be withheld from disclosure in accordance with 10 U.S.C. 2339a (see subpart 239.73).

[Interim rule, 78 FR 69267, 11/18/2013, effective 11/18/2013; Final rule, 80 FR 67243, 10/30/2015, effective 10/30/2015; Final rule, 84 FR 4368, 2/15/2019, effective 2/15/2019]

PART 216—TYPES OF CONTRACTS

Table of Contents

Subpart 216.1—Selecting Contract Types

Policies 216.102
Factors in selecting contract type 216.104
Research and development 216.104-70

Subpart 216.2—Fixed-Price Contracts

Fixed-price contracts with economic price adjustment 216.203
Contract clauses 216.203-4
Additional provisions and clauses 216.203-4-70

Subpart 216.3—Cost-Reimbursement Contracts

Limitations 216.301-3
Cost-plus-fixed-fee contracts 216.306
Contract clauses 216.307

Subpart 216.4—Incentive Contracts

General 216.401
[Removed] 216.401-70
Objective criteria 216.401-71
Application of predetermined, formula-type incentives 216.402
Technical performance incentives 216.402-2
Fixed-price incentive contracts 216.403
Fixed-price incentive (firm target) contracts 216.403-1
Fixed-price incentive (successive targets) contracts 216.403-2
[Removed] 216.404
Cost-reimbursement incentive contracts 216.405
Cost-plus-incentive-fee contracts 216.405-1
Cost-plus-award-fee contracts 216.405-2
Award fee reduction or denial for jeopardizing the health or safety of Government personnel 216.405-2-70
Award fee reduction or denial for failure to comply with requirements relating to performance of private security functions 216.405-2-71
Contract clauses 216.406
Other applications of award fees 216.470

Subpart 216.5—Indefinite-Delivery Contracts

[Removed] 216.501-1
[Removed] 216.501-2
General 216.501-2-70
Indefinite-quantity contracts 216.504
Ordering 216.505
Orders under multiple-award contracts 216.505-70
Solicitation provisions and contract clauses 216.506

Subpart 216.6—Time-and-Materials, Labor-Hour, and Letter Contracts

Time-and-materials contracts 216.601

Letter contracts 216.603
Application 216.603-2
Limitations 216.603-3
Contract clauses 216.603-4

Subpart 216.7—Agreements

Basic ordering agreements 216.703

PART 216—TYPES OF CONTRACTS

SUBPART 216.1—SELECTING CONTRACT TYPES

216.102 Policies.

(1) In accordance with section 829 of the National Defense Authorization Act for Fiscal Year 2017 (Pub. L. 114-328), the contracting officer shall first consider the use of fixed-price contracts, including fixed-price incentive contracts, in the determination of contract type. See 216.301-3(2) for approval requirements for certain cost-reimbursement contracts.

(2) In accordance with section 811 of the National Defense Authorization Act for Fiscal Year 2013 (Pub. L. 112-239), use of any cost-reimbursement line item for the acquisition of production of major defense acquisition programs is prohibited unless the exception at 234.004(2)(ii) applies.

(3) See 225.7301-1 for the requirement to use fixed-price contracts for acquisitions for foreign military sales.

[Interim rule, 79 FR 4631, 1/29/2014, effective 1/29/2014; Final rule, 79 FR 58693, 9/30/2014, effective 9/30/2014; Final rule, 84 FR 65304, 11/27/2019, effective 11/27/2019]

216.104 Factors in selecting contract type.

Contracting officers shall follow the principles and procedures in Director, Defense Procurement and Acquisition Policy memorandum dated April 1, 2016, entitled "Guidance on Using Incentive and Other Contract Types," when selecting and negotiating the most appropriate contract type for a given procurement. See PGI 216.104.

[Final rule, 71 FR 39006, 7/11/2006, effective 7/11/2006; Final rule, 81 FR 28729, 5/10/2016, effective 5/10/2016]

216.104-70 Research and development.

Follow the procedures at PGI 216.104-70 for selecting the appropriate research and development contract type, and see 235.006(b) for additional approval requirements.

[Final rule, 71 FR 39006, 7/11/2006, effective 7/11/2006; Final rule, 84 FR 65304, 11/27/2019, effective 11/27/2019]

SUBPART 216.2—FIXED-PRICE CONTRACTS

216.203 Fixed-price contracts with economic price adjustment. (No Text)

216.203-4 Contract clauses.

(1) Generally, use the clauses at FAR 52.216-2, Economic Price Adjustment—Standard Supplies, FAR 52.216-3, Economic Price Adjustment—Semistandard Supplies, and FAR 52.216-4, Economic Price Adjustment—Labor and Material, only when—

(i) The total contract price exceeds the simplified acquisition threshold; and

(ii) Delivery or performance will not be completed within 6 months after contract award.

(2) Follow the procedures at PGI 216.203-4 when using an economic price adjustment clause based on cost indexes of labor or material.

[Final rule, 62 FR 40471, 7/29/97, effective 7/29/97; DAC 91-13, 63 FR 11522, 3/9/98, effective 3/9/98; Final rule, 64 FR 2595, 1/15/99, effective 1/15/99; Final rule, 71 FR 39006, 7/11/2006, effective 7/11/2006]

216.203-4-70 Additional provisions and clauses.

(a) *Price adjustment for basic steel, aluminum, brass, bronze, or copper mill products.* (1)(i) The price adjustment clause at 252.216-7000, Economic Price Adjustment—Basic Steel, Aluminum, Brass, Bronze, or Copper Mill Products, may be used in fixed-price supply solicitations and contracts for basic steel, aluminum, brass, bronze, or copper mill products, such as sheets, plates, and bars, when an established catalog or market price exists for the particular product being acquired.

(ii) The 10 percent figure in paragraph (d)(1) of the clause shall not be exceeded unless approval is obtained at a level above the contracting officer.

(2) Use the price adjustment provision at 252.216-7007, Economic Price Adjustment—Basic Steel, Aluminum, Brass, Bronze, or Copper Mill Products—Representation, in solicitations that include the clause at 252.216-7000, Economic Price Adjustment—Basic Steel, Aluminum, Brass, Bronze, or Copper Mill Products.

(b) *Price adjustment for nonstandard steel items.*

(1) The price adjustment clause at 252.216-7001, Economic Price Adjustment—Nonstandard Steel Items, may be used in fixed-price supply contracts when—

(i) The contractor is a steel producer and actually manufacture the standard steel mill item referred to in the "base steel index" definition of the clause; and

(ii) The items being acquired are nonstandard steel items made wholly or in part of standard steel mill items.

(2) When this clause is included in invitations for bids, omit Note 6 of the clause and all references to Note 6.

(3) Solicitations shall instruct offerors to complete all blanks in accordance with the applicable notes.

(4) When the clause is to provide for adjustment on a basis other than "established price" (see Note 6 of the clause), that price must be verified.

(5) The 10 percent figure in paragraph (e)(4) of the clause shall not be exceeded unless approval is obtained at a level above the contracting officer.

(c) *Price adjustment for wage rates or material prices controlled by a foreign government.* (1)(i) The price adjustment clause at 252.216-7003, Economic Price Adjustment—Wage Rates or Material Prices Controlled by a Foreign Government, may be used in fixed-price supply and service solicitations and contracts when—

(A) The contract is to be performed wholly or in part in a foreign country; and

(B) A foreign government controls wage rates or material prices and may, during contract performance, impose a mandatory change in wages or prices of material.

(ii) Verify the base wage rates and material prices prior to contract award and prior to making any adjustment in the contract price.

(2) Use the provision at 252.216-7008, Economic Price Adjustment–Wage Rates or Material Prices Controlled by a Foreign Government—Representation, in solicitations that include the clause at 252.216-7003, Economic Price Adjustment–Wage Rates or Material Prices Controlled by a Foreign Government. If the solicitation includes the provision at FAR 52.204-7, do not separately list the provision 252.216-7008 in the solicitation.

[DAC 91-12, 62 FR 34114, 6/24/97, effective 6/24/97; Final rule, 62 FR 40471, 7/29/97, effective 7/29/97; Final rule, 77 FR 19128, 3/30/2012, effective 3/30/2012; Final rule, 78 FR 37980, 6/25/2013, effective 6/25/2013; Final rule, 78 FR 40043, 7/3/2013, effective 7/3/2013]

SUBPART 216.3—COST-REIMBURSEMENT CONTRACTS

216.301-3 Limitations.

(1) For contracts in connection with a military construction project or a military family housing project, contracting officers shall not use cost-plus-fixed-fee, cost-plus-award-fee, or cost-plus-incentive-fee contract types (10 U.S.C. 2306(c)). This applies notwithstanding a declaration of war or the declaration by the President of a national emergency under section 201 of the National Emergencies Act (50 U.S.C. 1621) that includes the use of the Armed Forces.

(2) Except as provided in 235.006(b), in accordance with section 829 of the National Defense Authorization Act for Fiscal Year 2017 (Pub. L. 114-328), approval of the head of the contracting activity is required prior to awarding cost-reimbursement contracts in excess of $25 million.

[Final rule, 81 FR 65563, 9/23/2016, effective 9/23/2016; Final rule, 84 FR 65304, 11/27/2019, effective 11/27/2019]

216.306 Cost-plus-fixed-fee contracts.

(c) *Limitations.* For contracts in connection with a military construction project or military family housing project, see the prohibition at 216.301–3.

(i) Except as provided in paragraph (c)(ii) of this section, annual military construction appropriations acts prohibit the use of cost-plus-fixed-fee contracts that—

(A) Are funded by a military construction appropriations act;

(B) Are estimated to exceed $25,000; and

(C) Will be performed within the United States, except Alaska.

(ii) The prohibition in paragraph (c)(i) of this section does not apply to contracts specifically approved in writing, setting forth the reasons therefor, in accordance with the following:

(A) The Secretaries of the military departments are authorized to approve such contracts that are for environmental work only, provided the environmental work is not classified as construction, as defined by 10 U.S.C. 2801.

(B) The Secretary of Defense or designee must approve such contracts that are not for environmental work only or are for environmental work classified as construction.

[Final rule, 62 FR 1058, 1/8/97, effective 1/8/97, corrected 62 FR 49305, 9/19/97; Final rule, 71 FR 39006, 7/11/2006, effective 7/11/2006; Final rule, 81 FR 65563, 9/23/2016, effective 9/23/2016]

216.307 Contract clauses.

(a) As required by section 827 of the National Defense Authorization Act for Fiscal Year 2013 (Pub. L. 112-239), use the clause at 252.216-7009, Allowability of Costs Incurred in Connection With a Whistleblower Proceeding—

(1) In task orders entered pursuant to contracts awarded before September 30, 2013, that include the clause at FAR 52.216-7, Allowable Cost and Payment; and

(2) In contracts awarded before September 30, 2013, that—

(i) Include the clause at FAR 52.216-7, Allowable Cost and Payment; and

(ii) Are modified to include the clause at DFARS 252.203-7002, Requirement to Inform Employees of Whistleblower Rights, dated September 2013 or later.

[Interim rule, 78 FR 59859, 9/30/2013, effective 9/30/2012; Final rule, 80 FR 36719, 6/26/2015, effective 6/26/2015]

SUBPART 216.4—INCENTIVE CONTRACTS

216.401 General.

(c) See PGI 216.401(c) for information on the Defense Acquisition University Award and Incentive Fees Community of Practice.

(d)(i) Except as provided in paragraph (d)(ii), the determination and findings justifying that the use of an incentive- or award-fee contract is in the best interest of the Government, may be signed by the head of contracting activity or a designee—

(A) No lower than one level below the head of the contracting activity for award fee contracts; or

(B) One level above the contracting officer for incentive fee contracts.

(ii) For cost-reimbursement incentive- or award fee contracts valued in excess of $25 million, the determination and findings justifying that the use of this type of contract is in the best interest of the Government shall be signed by the head of the contracting activity. See DFARS 216.301-3(2).

(e) Award-fee plans required in FAR 16.401(e) shall be incorporated into all award-fee type contracts. Follow the procedures at PGI 216.401(e) when planning to award an award-fee contract.

[Final rule, 75 FR 78619, 12/16/2010, effective 12/16/2010; Final rule, 76 FR 8303, 2/14/2011, effective 2/14/2011; Final rule, 84 FR 65304, 11/27/2019, effective 11/27/2019]

216.401-70 [Removed]

[Final rule, 75 FR 78619, 12/16/2010, effective 12/16/2010; Final rule, 80 FR 18323, 4/6/2015, effective 4/6/2015; Final rule, 80 FR 72606, 11/20/2015, effective 11/20/2015]

216.401-71 Objective criteria.

(1) Contracting officers shall use objective criteria to the maximum extent possible to

measure contract performance. Objective criteria are associated with cost-plus-incentive-fee and fixed-price-incentive contracts.

(2) When objective criteria exist but the contracting officer determines that it is in the best interest of the Government also to incentivize subjective elements of performance, the most appropriate contract type is a multiple-incentive contract containing both objective incentives and subjective award-fee criteria (i.e., cost-plus-incentive-fee/award-fee or fixed-price-incentive/award-fee).

(3) See PGI 216.401(e) for guidance on the use of award-fee contracts.

[Final rule, 75 FR 78619, 12/16/2010, effective 12/16/2010; Final rule, 76 FR 8303, 2/14/2011, effective 2/14/2011]

216.402 Application of predetermined, formula-type incentives. (No Text)

216.402-2 Technical performance incentives.

(1) See PGI 216.402-2 for guidance on establishing performance incentives.

(2) Contracting officers shall ensure requirements about the payment of incentive fees or the imposition of penalties are included in the solicitation for a contract for the engineering and manufacturing development or production of a weapon system, including embedded software, if the program manager or comparable requiring activity official exercising program manager responsibilities includes—

(i) Provisions for the payment of incentive fees to the contractor, based on achievement of design specification requirements for reliability and maintainability of weapons systems under the contract; or

(ii) The imposition of penalties to be paid by the contractor to the Government for failure to achieve such design specification requirements (10 U.S.C. 2443).

[Final rule, 71 FR 39006, 7/11/2006, effective 7/11/2006; Final rule, 84 FR 58332, 10/31/2019, effective 10/31/2019]

216.403 Fixed-price incentive contracts. (No Text)

[Final rule, 71 FR 39006, 7/11/2006, effective 7/11/2006]

216.403-1 Fixed-price incentive (firm target) contracts.

(b) *Application.*

(1) The contracting officer shall give particular consideration to the use of fixed-price incentive (firm target) contracts, especially for acquisitions moving from development to production.

(2) The contracting officer shall pay particular attention to share lines and ceiling prices for fixed-price incentive (firm target) contracts, with a 120 percent ceiling and a 50/50 share ratio as the point of departure for establishing the incentive arrangement.

(3) See PGI 216.403-1 for guidance on the use of fixed-price incentive (firm target) contracts.

[Final rule, 76 FR 57677, 9/16/2011, effective 9/16/2011]

216.403-2 Fixed-price incentive (successive targets) contracts.

See PGI 216.403-2 for guidance on the use of fixed-price incentive (successive targets) contracts.

[Final rule, 71 FR 39006, 7/11/2006, effective 7/11/2006]

216.404 [Removed]

[DAC 91-13, 63 FR 11522, 3/9/98, effective 3/9/98; Final rule, 71 FR 39006, 7/11/2006, effective 7/11/2006]

216.405 Cost-reimbursement incentive contracts. (No Text)

[DAC 91-13, 63 FR 11522, 3/9/98, effective 3/9/98]

216.405-1 Cost-plus-incentive-fee contracts.

See PGI 216.405-1 for guidance on the use of cost-plus-incentive-fee contracts.

[Redesignated from 216.404-1, DAC 91-13, 63 FR 11522, 3/9/98, effective 3/9/98; Final rule, 71 FR 39006, 7/11/2006, effective 7/11/2006]

216.405-2 Cost-plus-award-fee contracts.

(1) *Award-fee pool.* The award-fee pool is the total available award fee for each evaluation period for the life of the contract. The contracting officer shall perform an analysis of appropriate fee distribution to ensure at least 40 percent of the award fee is available for the final evaluation so that the award fee is appropriately distributed over all evaluation periods to incentivize the contractor throughout performance of the contract. The percentage of award fee available for the final evaluation may be set below 40 percent if the contracting officer determines that a lower percentage is appropriate, and this determination is approved by the head of the contracting activity (HCA). The HCA may not delegate this approval authority.

(2) *Award-fee evaluation and payments.* Award-fee payments other than payments resulting from the evaluation at the end of an award-fee period are prohibited. (This prohibition does not apply to base-fee payments.) The fee-determining official's rating for award-fee evaluations will be provided to the contractor within 45 calendar days of the end of the period being evaluated. The final award-fee payment will be consistent with the fee-determining official's final evaluation of the contractor's overall performance against the cost, schedule, and performance outcomes specified in the award-fee plan.

(3) *Limitations.*

(i) The cost-plus-award-fee contract shall not be used—

(A) To avoid—

(*1*) Establishing cost-plus-fixed-fee contracts when the criteria for cost-plus-fixed-fee contracts apply; or

(*2*) Developing objective targets so a cost-plus-incentive-fee contract can be used; or

(B) For either engineering development or operational system development acquisitions that have specifications suitable for simultaneous research and development and production, except a cost-plus-award-fee contract may be used for individual engineering development or operational system development acquisitions ancillary to the development of a major weapon system or equipment, where—

(*1*) It is more advantageous; and

(*2*) The purpose of the acquisition is clearly to determine or solve specific problems associated with the major weapon system or equipment.

(ii) Do not apply the weighted guidelines method to cost-plus-award-fee contracts for either the base (fixed) fee or the award fee.

(iii) The base fee shall not exceed three percent of the estimated cost of the contract exclusive of the fee.

(4) See PGI 216.405-2 for guidance on the use of cost-plus-award-fee contracts.

[Redesignated from 216.404-2, DAC 91-13, 63 FR 11522, 3/9/98, effective 3/9/98; Final rule, 68 FR 64561, 11/14/2003, effective date 1/13/2004; Final rule, 71 FR 39006, 7/11/2006, effective 7/11/2006; Final rule, 76 FR 8303, 2/14/2011, effective 2/14/2011]

216.405-2-70 Award fee reduction or denial for jeopardizing the health or safety of Government personnel.

(a) *Definitions.*

Covered incident and *serious bodily injury,* as used in this section, are defined in the clause at 252.216-7004, Award Fee Reduction or Denial for Jeopardizing the Health or Safety of Government Personnel.

(b) The contracting officer shall include in the evaluation criteria of any award-fee plan, a review of contractor and subcontractor actions that jeopardized the health or safety of Government personnel, through gross negligence or reckless disregard for the safety of such personnel, as determined through—

(1) Conviction in a criminal proceeding, or finding of fault and liability in a civil or administrative proceeding (in accordance with section 823 of the National Defense Authorization Act for Fiscal Year 2010 (Pub. L. 111-84)); or

(2) If a contractor or a subcontractor at any tier is not subject to the jurisdiction of the U.S. courts, a final determination of contractor or subcontractor fault resulting from a DoD investigation (in accordance with section 834 of the National Defense Authoriza-

tion Act for Fiscal Year 2011 (Pub. L. 111-383)).

(c) In evaluating the contractor's performance under a contract that includes the clause at 252.216-7004, Award Fee Reduction or Denial for Jeopardizing the Health or Safety of Government Personnel, the contracting officer shall consider reducing or denying award fees for a period if contractor or subcontractor actions cause serious bodily injury or death of civilian or military Government personnel during such period. The contracting officer's evaluation also shall consider recovering all or part of award fees previously paid for such period.

[Interim rule, 75 FR 69360, 11/12/2010, effective 11/12/2010; Redesignated, Interim rule, 76 FR 52133, 8/19/2011, effective 8/19/2011; Interim rule, 76 FR 57674, 9/16/2011, effective 9/16/2011; Final rule, 77 FR 11354, 2/24/2012, effective 2/24/2012; Final rule, 77 FR 35883, 6/15/2012, effective 6/15/2012]

216.405-2-71 Award fee reduction or denial for failure to comply with requirements relating to performance of private security functions.

(a) In accordance with section 862 of the National Defense Authorization Act for Fiscal Year 2008, as amended, the contracting officer shall include in any award-fee plan a requirement to review contractor compliance with, or violation of, applicable requirements of the contract with regard to the performance of private security functions in an area of contingency operations, complex contingency operations, or other military operations or exercises that are designated by the combatant commander (see 225.370).

(b) In evaluating the contractor's performance under a contract that includes the clause at 252.225-7039, Defense Contractors Performing Private Security Functions Outside the United States, the contracting officer shall consider reducing or denying award fees for a period if the contractor fails to comply with the requirements of the clause during such period. The contracting officer's evaluation also shall consider recovering all or part of award fees previously paid for such period.

[Interim rule, 76 FR 52133, 8/19/2011, effective 8/19/2011; Final rule, 77 FR 35883, 6/15/2012, effective 6/15/2012; Final rule, 78 FR 73450, 12/6/2013, effective 12/6/2013; Final rule, 81 FR 42559, 6/30/2016, effective 6/30/2016]

216.406 Contract clauses.

(e) Use the clause at 252.216-7004, Award Fee Reduction or Denial for Jeopardizing the Health or Safety of Government Personnel, in all solicitations and contracts containing award-fee provisions.

[Interim rule, 75 FR 69360, 11/12/2010, effective 11/12/2010; Publication notice 20110112; Final rule, 76 FR 8303, 2/14/2011, effective 2/14/2011; Final rule, 77 FR 11354, 2/24/2012, effective 2/24/2012; Final rule, 83 FR 49180, 9/28/2018, effective 9/28/2018]

216.470 Other applications of award fees.

See PGI 216.470 for guidance on other applications of award fees.

[Interim rule, 70 FR 29643, 5/24/2005, effective 5/24/2005; Final rule, 71 FR 14108, 3/21/2006, effective 3/21/2006; Final rule, 71 FR 39006, 7/11/2006, effective 7/11/2006]

SUBPART 216.5—INDEFINITE-DELIVERY CONTRACTS

216.501-1 [Removed]

[Final rule, 67 FR 65505, 10/25/2002, effective 10/25/2002; Final rule, 78 FR 38234, 6/26/2013, effective 6/26/2013]

216.501-2 [Removed]

[Interim rule, 69 FR 13478, 3/23/2004, effective 3/23/2004; Final rule, 70 FR 73151, 12/9/2005, effective 12/9/2005; Final rule, 78 FR 38234, 6/26/2013, effective 6/26/2013]

216.501-2-70 General.

(a)(i) For items with a shelf-life of less than 6 months, consider the use of indefinite-delivery type contracts with orders to be placed either—

(A) Directly by the users; or

(B) By central purchasing offices with deliveries direct to users.

(ii) Whenever an indefinite-delivery contract is issued, the issuing office must furnish all ordering offices sufficient information for the ordering office to complete its contract reporting responsibilities under 204.670-2. This data must be furnished to the ordering activity in sufficient time for the activity to prepare its report for the action within 3 working days of the order.

(b) See 217.204(e)(i) for limitations on the period for task order or delivery order contracts awarded by DoD pursuant to 10 U.S.C. 2304a.

[DAC 91-3, 57 FR 42630, 9/15/92, effective 8/31/92; DAC 91-13, 63 FR 11522, 3/9/98, effective 3/9/98; Redesignated Final rule, 78 FR 38234, 6/26/2013, effective 6/26/2013]

216.504 Indefinite-quantity contracts.

(c) *Multiple award preference*—(1) *Planning the acquisition.* (ii)(D)(1) The senior procurement executive has the authority to make the determination authorized in FAR 16.504(c)(1)(ii)(D)(1)

(*i*) In accordance with section 816 of the National Defense Authorization Act for Fiscal Year 2019 (Pub. L. 115-232), when making the determination at FAR 16.504(c)(1)(ii)(D)(1)(*i*),the senior procurement executive shall determine that the task or delivery orders expected under the contract are so integrally related that only a single source can "efficiently perform the work," instead of "reasonably perform the work" as required by the FAR.

(2) The congressional notification requirement at FAR 16.504(c)(1)(ii)(D)(2) does not apply to DoD.

[Final rule, 74 FR 2416, 1/15/2009, effective 1/15/2009; Interim rule, 75 FR 40716, 7/13/2010, effective 7/13/2010; Publication notice, 20100917; Publication notice, 20101007; Final rule, 76 FR 3536, 1/20/2011, effective 1/20/2011; Final rule, 76 FR 71465, 11/18/2011, effective 11/18/2011; Final rule, 77 FR 19132, 3/30/2012, effective 3/30/2012; Final rule, 77 FR 23631, 4/20/2012, effective 4/20/2012; Final rule, 80 FR 56929, 9/21/2015, effective 9/21/2015; Final rule, 83 FR 65559, 12/21/2018, effective 12/21/2018; Final rule, 84 FR 12139, 4/1/2019, effective 4/1/2019]

216.505 Ordering.

(a) *General.*

(6) Orders placed under indefinite-delivery contracts may be issued on DD Form 1155, Order for Supplies or Services.

(S-70) Departments and agencies shall comply with the review, approval, and reporting requirements established in accordance with subpart 217.7 when placing orders under non-DoD contracts in amounts exceeding the simplified acquisition threshold.

(b) *Orders under multiple-award contracts.*

(1) *Fair opportunity.*

(A) See 215.101-2-70 for the limitations and prohibitions on the use of the lowest price technically acceptable source selection process, which are applicable to orders placed against multiple award indefinite delivery contracts.

(B) See 217.7801 for the prohibition on the use of reverse auctions for personal protective equipment and aviation critical safety items.

(2) *Exceptions to the fair opportunity process.* For an order exceeding the simplified acquisition threshold, that is a follow-on to an order previously issued for the same supply or service based on a justification for an exception to fair opportunity citing the authority at FAR 16.505(b)(2)(i)(B) or (C), follow the procedures at PGI 216.505(b)(2).

[DAC 91-13, 63 FR 11522, 3/9/98, effective 3/9/98; Interim rule, 70 FR 29640, 5/24/2005, effective 5/24/2005; Final rule, 71 FR 14102, 3/21/2006, effective 3/21/2006; Final rule, 80 FR 21656, 4/20/2015, effective 4/20/2015; Final rule, 80 FR 67254, 10/30/2015, effective 10/30/2015; Final rule, 84 FR 50785, 9/26/2019, effective 10/1/2019]

216.505-70 Orders under multiple-award contracts.

(a) If only one offer is received in response to an order exceeding the simplified acquisition threshold that is placed on a competitive basis, the contracting officer shall follow the procedures at 215.371.

(b) See PGI 216.505-70 for guidance regarding minimum labor category qualifications for orders issued under multiple-award services contracts.

[Final rule, 67 FR 65505, 10/25/2002, effective 10/25/2002; Final rule, 71 FR 14106, 3/21/2006, effective 3/21/2006; Final rule, 75 FR 45072, 8/2/2010, effective 10/1/2010; Final rule, 77 FR 39125, 6/29/2012, effective 6/29/2012; Final rule, 78 FR 38234, 6/26/2013, effective 6/26/2013; Final rule, 84 FR 48510, 9/13/2019, effective 9/13/2019]

216.506 Solicitation provisions and contract clauses.

(a) Insert the clause at 252.216-7006, Ordering, in lieu of the clause at 52.216-18, Ordering, in solicitations and contracts when a definite-quantity contract, a requirements contract, or an indefinite-quantity contract is contemplated.

(S-70) Use the provisions at 252.215-7007, Notice of Intent to Resolicit, and 252.215-7008, Only One Offer, as prescribed at 215.371-6 and 215.408(3), respectively.

[DAC 91-13, 63 FR 11522, 3/9/98, effective 3/9/98; Final rule, 76 FR 25566, 5/5/2011, effective 5/5/2011; Final rule, 77 FR 23631, 4/20/2012, effective 4/20/2012; Final rule, 79 FR 22036, 4/21/2014, effective 4/21/2014; Final rule, 83 FR 30587, 6/29/2018, effective 6/29/2018; Final rule, 83 FR 30824, 6/29/2018, effective 6/29/2018]

SUBPART 216.6—TIME-AND-MATERIALS, LABOR-HOUR, AND LETTER CONTRACTS

216.601 Time-and-materials contracts.

(d) *Limitations.*

(i) (A) *Approval of determination and findings for time-and-materials or labor-hour contracts.*

(*1*) *Base period plus any option periods is three years or less.*

(*i*) For contracts (including indefinite-delivery contracts) and orders in which the portion of the requirement performed on a time-and-materials or labor-hour basis exceeds $1 million, the approval authority for the determination and findings shall be the senior contracting official within the contracting activity. This authority may not be delegated.

(*ii*) For contracts (including indefinite-delivery contracts) and orders in which the portion of the requirement performed on a time-and-materials or labor-hour basis is less than or equal to $1 million, the determination and findings shall be approved one level above the contracting officer.

(*2*) *Base period plus any option periods exceeds three years.* The authority of the head of the contracting activity to approve the determination and findings may not be delegated.

(*3*) *Exception.* The approval requirements in paragraphs (d)(i)(A)(*1*) and (*2*) of this section do not apply to contracts that, as determined by the head of the contracting activity—

(*i*) Support contingency or humanitarian or peacekeeping operations;

(*ii*) Facilitate defense against or recovery from conventional, cyber, nuclear, biological, chemical or radiological attack;

(*iii*) Facilitate the provision of international disaster assistance; or

(*iv*) Support response to an emergency or major disaster.

(B) *Content of determination and findings.* The determination and findings shall contain sufficient facts and rationale to justify that no other contract type is suitable. At a minimum, the determination and findings shall—

(*1*) Include a description of the market research conducted;

(*2*) Establish that it is not possible at the time of placing the contract or order to accurately estimate the extent or duration of the work or to anticipate costs with any reasonable degree of certainty;

(*3*) Address why a cost-plus-fixed-fee term or other cost-reimbursement, incentive, or fixed-price contract or order is not appropriate; for contracts (including indefinite-delivery contracts) and orders for noncommercial items awarded to contractors with adequate accounting systems, a cost-plus-fixed-fee term contract type shall be preferred over a time-and-materials or labor-hour contract type;

(*4*) Establish that the requirement has been structured to minimize the use of time-and-materials and labor-hour requirements (*e.g.*, limiting the value or length of the time-and-materials or labor-hour portion of the contract or order; establishing fixed prices for portions of the requirement); and

(*5*) Describe the actions planned to minimize the use of time-and-materials and labor-hour contracts on future acquisitions for the same requirements.

(C) *Indefinite-delivery contracts.* For indefinite-delivery contracts, the contracting officer shall structure contracts that authorize time-and-materials orders or labor-hour orders to also authorize orders on a cost-reimbursement, incentive, or fixed-price basis, to the maximum extent practicable.

(e) *Solicitation provisions.* Use the provision at 52.216-29, Time-and-Materials/Labor-Hour Proposal Requirements—Non-Commercial Item Acquisition with Adequate Price Competition, with 252.216-7002, Alternate A, in solicitations contemplating the use of a time-and-materials or labor-hour contract type for non-commercial items if the price is expected to be based on adequate competition.

[Interim rule, 71 FR 74469, 12/12/2006, effective 2/12/2007; Final rule, 72 FR 51189, 9/6/2007, effective 9/6/2007; Final rule, 73 FR 70912, 11/24/2008, effective 11/24/2008; Final rule, 80 FR 29980, 5/26/2015, effective 5/26/2015; Final rule, 83 FR 24888, 5/30/2018, effective 5/30/2018]

216.603 Letter contracts. (No Text)

216.603-2 Application.

(c) (3) In accordance with 10 U.S.C. 2326, establish definitization schedules for letter contracts following the requirements at 217.7404-3(a) instead of the requirements at FAR 16.603-2(c)(3).

[Final rule, 75 FR 32641, 6/8/2010, effective 6/8/2010]

216.603-3 Limitations.

See subpart 217.74 for additional limitations on the use of letter contracts.

216.603-4 Contract clauses.

(b)(2) See 217.7406(a) for additional guidance regarding use of the clause at FAR 52.216-24, Limitation of Government Liability.

(3) Use the clause at 252.217-7027, Contract Definitization, in accordance with its prescription at 217.7406(b), instead of the clause at FAR 52.216-25, Contract Definitization.

[DAC 91-10, 61 FR 7739, 2/29/96, effective 2/29/96; Final rule, 71 FR 58537, 10/4/2006, effective 10/4/2006; Final rule, 72 FR 69158, 12/7/2007, effective 12/7/2007; Final rule, 76 FR 76318, 12/7/2011, effective 12/7/2011]

SUBPART 216.7—AGREEMENTS

216.703 Basic ordering agreements.

(c) *Limitations.* The period during which orders may be placed against a basic ordering agreement may not exceed 5 years.

(d) *Orders.* Follow the procedures at PGI 216.703(d) for issuing orders under basic ordering agreements.

[DAC 91-10, 61 FR 7739, 2/29/96, effective 2/29/96, corrected, 61 FR 18195, 4/24/96; Final rule, 71 FR 39006, 7/11/2006, effective 7/11/2006]

PART 217—SPECIAL CONTRACTING METHODS

Table of Contents

Subpart 217.1—Multiyear Contracting

Definitions 217.103
General 217.170
Multiyear contracts for services 217.171
Multiyear contracts for supplies 217.172
Multiyear contracts for military family housing 217.173
Multiyear contracts for electricity from renewable energy sources 217.174

Subpart 217.2—Options

Use of options 217.202
Contracts 217.204
Exercise of options 217.207
Solicitation provisions and contract clauses 217.208
Additional clauses 217.208-70

Subpart 217.4—[Removed]

Subpart 217.5—Interagency Acquisitions

Scope of subpart 217.500
Procedures 217.502
General 217.502-1
Ordering procedures 217.503

Subpart 217.6—Management and Operating Contracts

Scope of subpart 217.600

Subpart 217.7—Interagency Acquisitions: Acquisitions by Nondefense Agencies on Behalf of the Department of Defense

Scope of subpart 217.700
Definitions 217.701
Procedures 217.770

Subpart 217.70—Exchange of Personal Property

Scope of subpart 217.7000
Definitions 217.7001
Policy 217.7002
Purchase request 217.7003
Solicitation and award 217.7004
Solicitation provision 217.7005

Subpart 217.71—Master Agreement for Repair and Alteration of Vessels

Scope of subpart 217.7100
Definitions 217.7101
General 217.7102
Master agreements and job orders 217.7103
Content and format of master agreements 217.7103-1
Period of agreement 217.7103-2

Solicitations for job orders 217.7103-3
Emergency work 217.7103-4
Repair costs not readily ascertainable 217.7103-5
Modification of master agreements 217.7103-6
Contract clauses 217.7104

Subpart 217.72—[Removed and Reserved]

Subpart 217.73—Identification of Sources of Supply

Scope 217.7300
Policy 217.7301
Procedures 217.7302
Solicitation provision 217.7303

Subpart 217.74—Undefinitized Contract Actions

Scope 217.7400
Definitions 217.7401
Exceptions 217.7402
Policy 217.7403
Limitations 217.7404
Authorization 217.7404-1
Price ceiling 217.7404-2
Definitization schedule 217.7404-3
Limitations on obligations 217.7404-4
Exceptions 217.7404-5
Allowable profit 217.7404-6
Plans and reports 217.7405
Contract clauses 217.7406

Subpart 217.75—Acquisition of Replenishment Parts

Scope of subpart 217.7500
Definition 217.7501
General 217.7502
Spares acquisition integrated with production 217.7503
Acquisition of parts when data is not available 217.7504
Limitations on price increases 217.7505
Spare parts breakout program 217.7506

Subpart 217.76—Contracts with Provisioning Requirements

[Removed] 217.7600
Provisioning 217.7601
[Removed] 217.7602
[Removed] 217.7602-1
[Removed] 217.7602-2
[Removed] 217.7603
[Removed] 217.7603-1
[Removed] 217.7603-2
[Removed] 217.7603-3

Subpart 217.77—Over and Above Work

[Removed] 217.7700
Procedures 217.7701
Contract clause 217.7702

Subpart 217.78—Reverse Auctions

Prohibition 217.7801

PART 217—SPECIAL CONTRACTING METHODS

SUBPART 217.1—MULTIYEAR CONTRACTING

217.103 Definitions.

As used in this subpart—

Advance procurement means an exception to the full funding policy that allows acquisition of long lead time items (advance long lead acquisition) or economic order quantities (EOQ) of items (advance EOQ acquisition) in a fiscal year in advance of that in which the related end item is to be acquired. Advance procurements may include materials, parts, components, and effort that must be funded in advance to maintain a planned production schedule.

Congressional defense committees means—

(1) The Committee on Armed Services of the Senate;

(2) The Committee on Appropriations of the Senate;

(3) The Subcommittee on Defense of the Committee on Appropriations of the Senate;

(4) The Committee on Armed Services of the House of Representatives;

(5) The Committee on Appropriations of the House of Representatives; and

(6) The Subcommittee on Defense of the Committee on Appropriations of the House of Representatives.

Military installation means a base, camp, post, station, yard, center, or other activity under the jurisdiction of the Secretary of a military department or, in the case of an activity in a foreign country, under the operational control of the Secretary of a military department or the Secretary of Defense (10 U.S.C. 2801(c)(4)).

[DAC 91-13, 63 FR 11522, 3/9/98, effective 3/9/98; Interim rule, 68 FR 43332, 7/22/2003, effective 7/22/2003; Final rule, 69 FR 26507, 5/13/2004, effective 5/13/2004; Final rule, 79 FR 35699, 6/24/2014, effective 6/24/2014; Final rule, 80 FR 29981, 5/26/2015, effective 5/26/2015]

217.170 General.

(a) Before awarding a multiyear contract, the head of the agency must compare the cost of that contract to the cost of an annual procurement approach, using a present value analysis. Do not award the multiyear contract unless the analysis shows that the multiyear contract will result in the lower cost (10 U.S.C. 2306b(l)(7); section 8008(a) of Pub. L. 105-56, and similar sections in subsequent DoD appropriations acts).

(b) The head of the agency must provide written notice to the congressional defense committees at least 30 days before termination of any multiyear contract (section 8010 of Division C, Title VIII, of the Consolidated and Further Continuing Appropriations Act, 2015 (Pub. L. 113–235) and similar sections in subsequent DoD appropriations acts).

(c) Every multiyear contract must comply with FAR 17.104(c), unless an exception is approved through the budget process in coordination with the cognizant comptroller.

(d)(1) DoD must provide notification to the congressional defense committees at least 30 days before entering into a multiyear contract for certain procurements, including those expected to—

(i) Employ an unfunded contingent liability in excess of $20 million (see 10 U.S.C. 2306b(l)(1)(B)(i)(II), 10 U.S.C. 2306c(d)(1), and section 8008(a) of Pub. L. 105-56 and similar sections in subsequent DoD appropriations acts);

(ii) Employ economic order quantity procurement in excess of $20 million in any one year of the contract (see 10 U.S.C. 2306b(l)(1)(B)(i)(I) and section 8008(a) of Pub. L. 105-56 and similar sections in subsequent DoD appropriations acts);

(iii) Involve a contract for advance procurement leading to a multiyear contract that employs economic order quantity procurement in excess of $20 million in any one year (see 10 U.S.C. 2306b(l)(1)(B)(ii) and section 8008(a) of Pub. L. 105-56 and similar sections in subsequent DoD appropriations acts); or

(iv) Include a cancellation ceiling in excess of $135.5 million (see 10 U.S.C. 2306c(d)(4) and 10 U.S.C. 2306b(g)(1)).

(2) A DoD component must submit a request for authority to enter into a multiyear contract described in paragraphs (d)(1)(i) through (iv) of this section as part of the component's budget submission for the fiscal year in which the multiyear contract will be initiated. DoD will include the request, for each candidate it supports, as part of the President's budget for that year and in the Appendix to that budget as part of proposed legislative language for the appropriations bill for that year (section 8008(b) of Pub. L. 105-56).

(3) If the advisability of using a multiyear contract becomes apparent too late to satisfy the requirements in paragraph (d)(2) of this section, the request for authority to enter into a multiyear contract must be—

(i) Formally submitted by the President as a budget amendment; or

(ii) Made by the Secretary of Defense, in writing, to the congressional defense committees (see section 8008(b) of Pub. L. 105-56).

(4) Agencies must establish reporting procedures to meet the congressional notification requirements of paragraph (d)(1) of this section. The head of the agency must submit a copy of each notice to the Director of Defense Procurement and Acquisition Policy, Office of the Under Secretary of Defense (Acquisition, Technology, and Logistics) (OUSD(AT&L)DPAP), and to the Deputy Under Secretary of Defense (Comptroller) (Program/Budget) (OUSD(C)(P/B)).

(5) If the budget for a contract that contains a cancellation ceiling in excess of $135.5 million does not include proposed funding for the costs of contract cancellation up to the cancellation ceiling established in the contract—

(i) The notification required by paragraph (d)(1) of this section shall include—

(A) The cancellation ceiling amounts planned for each program year in the proposed multiyear contract, together with the reasons for the amounts planned;

(B) The extent to which costs of contract cancellation are not included in the budget for the contract; and

(C) A financial risk assessment of not including budgeting for costs of contract cancellation (10 U.S.C. 2306b(g) and 10 U.S.C. 2306c(d)); and

(ii) The head of the agency shall provide copies of the notification to the Office of Management and Budget at least 14 days before contract award.

[Final rule, 66 FR 63336, 12/6/2001, effective 12/6/2001; Final rule, 68 FR 7438, 2/14/2003, effective 2/14/2003; Interim rule, 70 FR 24323, 5/9/2005, effective 5/9/2005; Final rule without change, 70 FR 54651, 9/16/2005, effective 9/16/2005; Final rule, 71 FR 75891, 12/19/2006, effective 12/19/2006; Interim rule, 75 FR 9114, 3/1/2010, effective 3/1/2010; Final rule, 75 FR 45072, 8/2/2010, effective 10/1/2010; Final rule, 75 FR 54526, 9/8/2010, effective 9/8/2010; Final rule, 76 FR 58152, 9/20/2011, effective 9/20/2011; Final rule, 80 FR 29981, 5/26/2015, effective 5/26/2015; Final rule, 80 FR 36903, 6/26/2015, effective 10/1/2015; Final rule, 81 FR 28730, 5/10/2016, effective 5/10/2016]

217.171 Multiyear contracts for services.

(a) The head of the agency may enter into a multiyear contract for a period of not more than 5 years for the following types of services (and items of supply relating to such services), even though funds are limited by statute to obligation only during the fiscal year for which they were appropriated (10 U.S.C. 2306c(a)). Covered services are—

(1) Operation, maintenance, and support of facilities and installations;

(2) Maintenance or modification of aircraft, ships, vehicles, and other highly complex military equipment;

(3) Specialized training requiring high-quality instructor skills (*e.g.,* training for pilots and aircrew members or foreign language training);

(4) Base services (*e.g.,* ground maintenance, in-plane refueling, bus transportation, and refuse collection and disposal); and

(5) Environmental remediation services for—

(i) An active military installation;

(ii) A military installation being closed or realigned under a base closure law as defined in 10 U.S.C. 2667(h)(2); or

(iii) A site formerly used by DoD (10 U.S.C. 2306c(b)).

(b) The head of the agency must be guided by the following principles when entering into a multiyear contract for services:

(1) The portion of the cost of any plant or equipment amortized as a cost of contract performance should not exceed the ratio between the period of contract performance and the anticipated useful commercial life of the plant or equipment. As used in this section, *useful commercial life* means the commercial utility of the facilities rather than the physical life, with due consideration given to such factors as the location, specialized nature, and obsolescence of the facilities.

(2) Consider the desirability of obtaining an option to extend the term of the contract for a reasonable period not to exceed 3 years at prices that do not include charges for plant, equipment, or other nonrecurring costs already amortized.

(3) Consider the desirability of reserving the right to take title, under the appropriate circumstances, to the plant or equipment upon payment of the unamortized portion of the cost (10 U.S.C. 2306c(c)).

(c) Before entering into a multiyear contract for services, the head of the agency must make a written determination that—

(1) There will be a continuing requirement for the services consistent with current plans for the proposed contract period;

(2) Furnishing the services will require—

(i) A substantial initial investment in plant or equipment; or

(ii) The incurrence of substantial contingent liabilities for the assembly, training, or transportation of a specialized work force; and

(3) Using a multiyear contract will promote the best interests of the United States by encouraging effective competition and promoting economies in operations (10 U.S.C. 2306c(a)).

(d) The head of an agency may not initiate a multiyear contract for services if the value of the multiyear contract exceeds $678.5 million unless a law specifically provides authority for the contract (10 U.S.C. 2306c(d)(2)).

[Final rule, 66 FR 63336, 12/6/2001, effective 12/6/2001; Interim rule, 68 FR 43332, 7/22/2003, effective 7/22/2003; Final rule, 69 FR 26507, 5/13/2004, effective 5/134/2004; Interim rule, 70 FR 24323, 5/9/2005, effective 5/9/2005; Final rule without change, 70 FR 54651, 9/16/2005, effective 9/16/2005; Final rule, 71 FR 75891, 12/19/2006, effective 12/19/2006; Final rule, 75 FR 45072, 8/2/2010, effective 10/1/2010; Final rule, 76 FR 58152, 9/20/2011, effective 9/20/2011; Final rule, 76 FR 76318, 12/7/2011, effective 12/7/2011; Final rule, 80 FR 29981, 5/26/2015, effective 5/26/2015; Final rule, 80 FR 36903, 6/26/2015, effective 10/1/2015]

217.172 Multiyear contracts for supplies.

(a) This section applies to all multiyear contracts for supplies, including weapon systems and other multiyear acquisitions specifically authorized by law (10 U.S.C. 2306b).

(b) The head of the agency may enter into a multiyear contract for supplies if, in addition to the conditions listed in FAR 17.105-1(b), the use of such a contract will promote the national security of the United States (10 U.S.C. 2306b(a)(6)).

(c) Multiyear contracts in amounts exceeding $678.5 million must be specifically authorized by law in an act other than an appropriations act (10 U.S.C. 2306b(i)(1)).

(d) The head of the agency may not initiate a multiyear procurement contract for any system (or component thereof) if the value of the multiyear contract would exceed $678.5 million unless authority for the contract is specifically provided in an appropriations act (10 U.S.C. 2306b(l)(3)).

(e) The head of the agency shall not enter into a multiyear contract unless—

(1) The Secretary of Defense has submitted to Congress a budget request for full funding of units to be procured through the contract;

(2) In the case of a contract for procurement of aircraft, the budget request includes full funding of procurement funds for production beyond advance procurement activities of aircraft units to be produced in the fiscal year covered by the budget;

(3) Cancellation provisions in the contract do not include consideration of recurring manufacturing costs of the contractor associated with the production of unfunded units to be delivered under the contract;

(4) The contract provides that payments to the contractor under the contract shall not be made in advance of incurred costs on funded units; and

(5) The contract does not provide for a price adjustment based on a failure to award a follow-on contract (section 8010 of Division C, Title VIII, of the Consolidated and Further Continuing Appropriations Act, 2015 (Pub. L. 113–235) and similar sections in subsequent DoD appropriations acts).

(f)(1) The head of the agency must not enter into or extend a multiyear contract that exceeds $678.5 million (when entered into or extended) until the Secretary of Defense identifies the contract and any extension in a report submitted to the congressional defense committees (10 U.S.C. 2306b(l)(5)).

(2) In addition, for contracts equal to or greater than $678.5 million, the head of the contracting activity must determine that the conditions required by paragraph (h)(2)(i) through (vii) of this section will be met by such contract, in accordance with the Secretary's certification and determination required by paragraph (h)(2) of this section.

(g) The head of the agency may enter into a multiyear contract for—

(1) A weapon system and associated items, services, and logistics support for a weapon system (10 U.S.C. 2306b(h)(1)); and

(2) Advance procurement of components, parts, and materials necessary to manufacture a weapon system, including advance procurement to achieve economic lot purchases or more efficient production rates (see paragraphs (h)(3) and (4) of this section regarding economic order quantity procurements) (10 U.S.C. 2306b(h)(2)). Before initiating an advance procurement, the contracting officer must verify that it is consistent with DoD policy (*e.g.,* the full funding policy in Volume 2A, chapter 1, of DoD 7000.14-R, Financial Management Regulation).

(h) The head of the agency shall ensure that the following conditions are satisfied before awarding a multiyear contract for a defense acquisition program that has been specifically authorized by law to be carried out using multiyear contract authority:

(1) The multiyear exhibits required by DoD 7000.14-R, Financial Management Regulation, are included in the agency's budget estimate submission and the President's budget request.

(2) The Secretary of Defense certifies to Congress in writing, by no later than 30 days before entry into such contracts, that each of the conditions in paragraphs (h)(2)(i) through (vii) of this section is satisfied (10 U.S.C. 2306b(i)(1)(A) through (G)) (10 U.S.C. 2306b(i)(3)).

(i) The Secretary has determined that each of the requirements in FAR 17.105–1, paragraphs (b)(1) through (5), will be met by such contract and has provided the basis for such determination to the congressional defense committees (10 U.S.C. 2306b(i)(3)(A)).

(ii) The Secretary's determination under paragraph (h)(2)(i) of this section was made after the completion of a cost analysis performed by the Defense Cost and Resource Center of the Department of Defense and such analysis supports the findings (10 U.S.C. 2306b(i)(3)(B)).

(iii) The system being acquired pursuant to such contract has not been determined to have experienced cost growth in excess of the critical cost growth threshold pursuant to 10 USC 2433(d) within 5 years prior to the date the Secretary anticipates such contract (or a contract for advance procurement entered into consistent with the authorization for such contract) will be awarded (10 U.S.C. 2306b (i) (3) (C)).

(iv) A sufficient number of end items of the system being acquired under such contract have been delivered at or within the most current estimates of the program acquisition unit cost or procurement unit cost for such system to determine that current estimates of such unit costs are realistic (10 U.S.C. 2306b (i) (3) (D)).

(v) Sufficient funds will be available in the fiscal year in which the contract is to be awarded to perform the contract, and the future-years defense program for such fiscal year will include the funding required to execute the program without cancellation (10 U.S.C. 2306b (i) (3) (E)).

(vi) The contract is a fixed price type contract (10 U.S.C. 2306b (i) (3) (F)).

(vii) The proposed multiyear contract provides for production at not less than minimum economic rates, given the existing tooling and facilities (10 U.S.C. 2306b (i) (3) (G)). The head of the agency shall submit to OUSD (C) (P/B) information supporting the agency's determination that this requirement has been met.

(viii) The head of the agency shall submit information supporting this certification to OUSD (C) (P/B) for transmission to Congress through the Secretary of Defense.

(A) The head of the agency shall, as part of this certification, give written notification to the congressional defense committees of—

(1) The cancellation ceiling amounts planned for each program year in the proposed multiyear contract, together with the reasons for the amounts planned;

(2) The extent to which costs of contract cancellation are not included in the budget for the contract; and

(3) A financial risk assessment of not including the budgeting for costs of contract cancellation (10 U.S.C. 2306b (g)); and

(B) The head of the agency shall provide copies of the notification to the Office of Management and Budget at least 14 days before contract award.

(3) The contract is for the procurement of a complete and usable end item (10 U.S.C. 2306b (i) (5) (A)).

(4) Funds appropriated for any fiscal year for advance procurement are obligated only for the procurement of those long-lead items that are necessary in order to meet a planned delivery schedule for complete major end items that are programmed under the contract to be acquired with funds appropriated for a subsequent fiscal year (including an economic order quantity of such long-lead items when authorized by law (10 U.S.C. 2306b (i) (5) (B)).

(5) The Secretary may make the certification under paragraph (h) (2) of this section notwithstanding the fact that one or more of the conditions of such certification are not met if the Secretary determines that, due to exceptional circumstances, proceeding with a multiyear contract under this section is in the best interest of the Department of Defense and the Secretary provides the basis for such determination with the certification (10 U.S.C. 2306b (i) (6)).

(6) The Secretary of Defense may not delegate this authority to make the certification under paragraph (h) (2) of this section or the determination under paragraph (h) (5) of this section to an official below the level of the Under Secretary of Defense for Acquisition, Technology, and Logistics (10 U.S.C. 2306b (i) (7)).

(7) All other requirements of law are met and there are no other statutory restrictions on using a multiyear contract for the specific system or component. One such restriction may be the achievement of specified cost savings. If the agency finds, after negotiations with the contractor(s), that the specified savings cannot be achieved, the head of the agency shall assess the savings that, nevertheless, could be achieved by using a multiyear contract. If the savings are substantial, the head of the agency may request relief from the law's specific savings requirement (10 U.S.C. 2306b (i) (4)). The request shall—

(i) Quantify the savings that can be achieved;

(ii) Explain any other benefits to the Government of using the multiyear contract;

(iii) Include details regarding the negotiated contract terms and conditions; and

(iv) Be submitted to OUSD(AT&L)DPAP for transmission to Congress via the Secretary of Defense and the President.

(i) The Secretary of Defense may instruct the head of the agency proposing a multiyear contract to include in that contract negotiated priced options for varying the quantities of end items to be procured over the life of the contract (10 U.S.C. 2306b(j)).

(j) Any requests for increased funding or reprogramming for procurement of a major system under a multiyear contract shall be accompanied by an explanation of how the request for increased funding affects the determinations made by the Secretary of Defense under 217.172(h)(2) (10 U.S.C. 2306b(m)).

[Final rule, 66 FR 63336, 12/6/2001, effective 12/6/2001; Interim rule, 68 FR 50474, 8/21/2003, effective 8/21/2003; Final rule, 69 FR 13478, 3/23/2004, effective 3/23/2004; Interim rule, 70 FR 24323, 5/9/2005, effective 5/9/2005; Final rule without change, 70 FR 54651, 9/16/2005, effective 9/16/2005; Interim rule, 75 FR 9114, 3/1/2010, effective 3/1/2010; Final rule, 75 FR 54526, 9/8/2010, effective 9/8/2010; Final rule, 76 FR 58152, 9/20/2011, effective 9/20/2011; Final rule, 80 FR 29981, 5/26/2015, effective 5/26/2015; Final rule, 80 FR 36903, 6/26/2015, effective 10/1/2015; Final rule, 81 FR 28730, 5/10/2016, effective 5/10/2016]

217.173 Multiyear contracts for military family housing.

The head of the agency may enter into multiyear contracts for periods up to 4 years for supplies and services required for management, maintenance, and operation of military family housing and may pay the costs of such contracts for each year from annual appropriations for that year (10 U.S.C. 2829).

[Final rule, 64 FR 43096, 8/9/99, effective 8/9/99; Final rule, 65 FR 39703, 6/27/2000, effective 6/27/2000; Final rule ,68 FR 7438, 2/14/2003, effective 2/14/2003; Interim rule, 68 FR 50474, 8/21/2003, effective 8/21/2003; Final rule, 69 FR 13478, 3/23/2004, effective 3/24/2004; Interim rule, 70 FR 24323, 5/9/2005, effective 5/9/2005; Final rule without change, 70 FR 54651, 9/16/2005, effective 9/16/2005; Final rule, 76 FR 58152, 9/20/2011, effective 9/20/2011; Final rule, 80 FR 29981, 5/26/2015, effective 5/26/2015]

217.174 Multiyear contracts for electricity from renewable energy sources.

(a) The head of the contracting activity may enter into a contract for a period not to exceed 10 years for the purchase of electricity from sources of renewable energy, as that term is defined in section 203(b)(2) of the Energy Policy Act of 2005 (42 U.S.C. 15852(b)(2)).

(b) *Limitations.* The head of the contracting activity may exercise the authority in paragraph (a) of this section to enter into a contract for a period in excess of 5 years only if the head of the contracting activity determines, on the basis of a business case analysis (see PGI 217.174 for a business case analysis template and guidance*) prepared by the requiring activity, that—

(1) The proposed purchase of electricity under such contract is cost effective; and

(2) It would not be possible to purchase electricity from the source in an economical manner without the use of a contract for a period in excess of 5 years.

(c) Nothing in this section shall be construed to preclude the DoD from using other multiyear contracting authority of DoD to purchase renewable energy.

* [*http://www.acq.osd.mil/dpap/dars/dfars/changenotice/2010/20100621/2008-D006%20PGI%20Template.doc*]

[Interim rule, 75 FR 34942, 6/21/2010, effective 6/21/2010; Final rule, 76 FR 14587, 3/17/2011, effective 3/17/2011; Redesignated from 217.175, Final rule, 76 FR 58152, 9/20/2011, effective 9/20/2011]

SUBPART 217.2—OPTIONS

217.202 Use of options.

(1) See PGI 217.202 for guidance on the use of options.

(i) See PGI 217.202(1) for guidance on the use of options with foreign military sales (FMS).

(ii) See PGI 217.202(2) for the use options with sole source major systems for U.S. and U.S./FMS combined procurements.

(2) See 234.005-1 for limitations on the use of contract options for the provision of advanced component development, prototype, or initial production of technology developed under the contract or the delivery of initial or additional items.

[DAC 91-10, 61 FR 7739, 2/29/96, effective 2/29/96; Final rule, 71 FR 27642, 5/12/2006, effective 5/12/2006; Interim rule, 75 FR 32638, 6/8/2010, effective 6/8/2010; Confirmation of interim final rule, 75 FR 71562, 11/24/2010, effective 11/24/2010; Final rule, 81 FR 17044, 3/25/2016, effective 3/25/2016; Final rule, 84 FR 65304, 11/27/2019, effective 11/27/2019]

217.204 Contracts.

(e) (i) Notwithstanding FAR 17.204(e), the ordering period of a task order or delivery order contract (including a contract for information technology) awarded by DoD pursuant to 10 U.S.C. 2304a—

(A) May be for any period up to 5 years;

(B) May be subsequently extended for one or more successive periods in accordance with an option provided in the contract or a modification of the contract; and

(C) Shall not exceed 10 years unless the head of the agency determines in writing that exceptional circumstances require a longer ordering period.

(ii) Paragraph (e)(i) of this section does not apply to the following:

(A) Contracts, including task or delivery order contracts, awarded under other statutory authority.

(B) Advisory and assistance service task order contracts (authorized by 10 U.S.C. 2304B that are limited by statute to 5 years, with the authority to extend an additional 6 months (see FAR 16.505(c)).

(C) Definite-quantity contracts.

(D) GSA schedule contracts.

(E) Multi-agency contracts awarded by agencies other than NASA, DoD, or the Coast Guard.

(iii) Obtain approval from the senior procurement executive before issuing an order against a task or delivery order contract subject to paragraph (e)(i) of this section, if performance under the order is expected to extend more than 1 year beyond the 10-year limit or extended limit described in paragraph (e)(i)(C) of this section (see FAR 37.106 for funding and term of service contracts).

[Interim rule, 69 FR 13478, 3/23/2004, effective 3/23/2004; Interim rule, 69 FR 74992, 12/15/2004, effective 12/15/2004; Final rule, 70 FR 73151, 12/9/2005, effective 12/9/2005; Final rule, 79 FR 58696, 9/30/2014, effective 9/30/2014]

217.207 Exercise of options.

(c) In addition to the requirements at FAR 17.207(c), exercise an option only after determining that the contractor's record in the System for Award Management database is active and the contractor's Data Universal Numbering System (DUNS) number, Commercial and Government Entity (CAGE) code, name, and physical address are accurately reflected in the contract document. See PGI 217.207 for the requirement to perform cost or price analysis of spare parts prior to exercising any option for firm-fixed-price contracts containing spare parts.

[Removed by 67 FR 4208, 1/29/2002, effective 1/29/2002; Final rule, 74 FR 37642, 7/29/2009, effective 7/29/2009; Final rule, 78 FR 28756, 5/16/2013, effective 5/16/2013; Final rule, 79 FR 67356, 11/13/2014, effective 11/13/2014]

217.208 Solicitation provisions and contract clauses.

Sealed bid solicitations shall not include provisions for evaluations of options unless the contracting officer determines that there is a reasonable likelihood that the options will be exercised (10 U.S.C. 2305(a)(5)). This limitation also applies to sealed bid solicitations for the contracts excluded by FAR 17.200.

[Final rule, 71 FR 27642, 5/12/2006, effective 5/12/2006]

217.208-70 Additional clauses.

(a) Use the basic or alternate of the clause at 252.217-7000, Exercise of Option to Fulfill Foreign Military Sales Commitments, in solicitations and contracts when an option may be used for foreign military sale requirements. Do not use the basic or the alternate of this clause in contracts for establishment or replenishment of DoD inventories or stocks, or acquisitions made under DoD cooperative logistics support arrangements.

(1) Use the basic clause when the foreign military sales country is known at the time of solicitation or award.

(2) Use the alternate I clause when the foreign military sale country is not known at the time of solicitation or award.

(b) When a surge option is needed in support of industrial capability production planning, use the clause at 252.217-7001, Surge Option, in solicitations and contracts.

(1) Insert the percentage or quantity of increase the option represents in paragraph (a) of the clause to ensure adequate quantities are available to meet item requirements.

(2) Change 30 days in paragraphs (b)(2) and (d)(1) to longer periods, if appropriate.

(3) Change the 24-month period in paragraph (c)(3), if appropriate.

[Final rule, 71 FR 27642, 5/12/2006, effective 5/12/2006; Final rule, 79 FR 65592, 11/5/2014, effective 11/5/2014; Final rule, 83 FR 62502, 12/4/2018, effective 12/4/2018]

SUBPART 217.4—[REMOVED]

217.401 [Removed]

[Interim rule, 63 FR 64427, 11/20/98, effective 1/1/99, finalized without change, 64 FR 52670, 9/30/99; Interim rule, 65 FR 50148, 8/17/2000, effective 10/1/2000, finalized without change, 65 FR 77831, 12/13/2000; Final rule, 69 FR 67855, 11/22/2004, effective 11/22/2004]

SUBPART 217.5—INTERAGENCY ACQUISITIONS

217.500 Scope of subpart.

(a) Unless more specific statutory authority exists, the procedures in FAR subpart 17.5 and this subpart apply to all purchases, except micro-purchases, made for DoD by another agency. This includes orders under a task or delivery order contract entered into by the other agency. (Pub. L. 105-261, Section 814.)

(b) A contracting activity from one DoD Component may provide acquisition assistance to deployed DoD units or personnel from another DoD Component. See PGI 217.502-1 for guidance and procedures.

[Final rule, 64 FR 14399, 3/25/99, effective 3/25/99; Final rule, 76 FR 76318, 12/7/2011, effective 12/7/2011; Final rule, 80 FR 36718, 6/26/2015, effective 6/26/2015; Final rule, 80 FR 74694, 11/30/2015, effective 11/30/2015]

217.502 Procedures. (No Text).

[Final rule, 80 FR 74694, 11/30/2015, effective 11/30/2015]

217.502-1 General.

(a) *Written agreement on responsibility for management and administration*—

(1) *Assisted acquisitions.* Follow the procedures at PGI 217.502-1(a)(1), when a contracting activity from a DoD Component provides acquisition assistance to deployed DoD units or personnel from another DoD Component.

[Final rule, 80 FR 74694, 11/30/2015, effective 11/30/2015; Final rule, 83 FR 62501, 12/4/2018, effective 12/4/2018]

217.503 Ordering procedures.

(a) When the requesting agency is within DoD, a copy of the executed determination and findings required by FAR 17.502-2 shall be furnished to the servicing agency as an attachment to the order. When a DoD contracting office is acting as the servicing agency, a copy of the executed determination and findings shall be obtained from the requesting agency and placed in the contract file for the Economy Act order.

[DAC 91-13, 63 FR 11522, 3/9/98, effective 3/9/98; Final rule, 76 FR 76318, 12/7/2011, effective 12/7/2011]

SUBPART 217.6—MANAGEMENT AND OPERATING CONTRACTS

217.600 Scope of subpart.

FAR Subpart 17.6 does not apply to DoD.

SUBPART 217.7—INTERAGENCY ACQUISITIONS: ACQUISITIONS BY NONDEFENSE AGENCIES ON BEHALF OF THE DEPARTMENT OF DEFENSE

217.700 Scope of subpart.

This subpart—

(a) Implements section 854 of the National Defense Authorization Act for Fiscal Year 2005 (Pub. L. 108-375), section 801 of the National Defense Authorization Act for Fiscal Year 2008 (Pub. L. 110-181), and section 806 of the National Defense Authorization Act for Fiscal Year 2010 (Pub. L. 111-84); and

(b) Prescribes policy for the acquisition of supplies and services through the use of contracts or orders issued by non-DoD agencies.

[Final rule, 80 FR 51750, 8/26/2015, effective 8/26/2015]

217.701 Definitions.

As used in this subpart—

Assisted acquisition means the type of interagency contracting through which acquisition officials of a non-DoD agency award a contract or a task or delivery order for the acquisition of supplies or services on behalf of DoD.

Direct acquisition means the type of interagency contracting through which DoD orders a supply or service from a Governmentwide acquisition contract maintained by a non-DoD agency.

Governmentwide acquisition contract means a task or delivery order contract that—

(1) Is entered into by a non-defense agency; and

(2) May be used as the contract under which property or services are procured for one or more other departments or agencies of the Federal Government.

[Final rule, 80 FR 51750, 8/26/2015, effective 8/26/2015]

217.770 Procedures.

Departments and agencies shall establish and maintain procedures for reviewing and approving orders placed for supplies and services under non-DoD contracts, whether through direct acquisition or assisted acquisition, when the amount of the order exceeds the simplified acquisition threshold. These procedures shall include—

(a) Evaluating whether using a non-DoD contract for the acquisition is in the best interest of DoD. Factors to be considered include—

(1) Satisfying customer requirements;

(2) Schedule;

(3) Cost effectiveness (taking into account discounts and fees). In order to ensure awareness of the total cost of fees associated with use of a non-DoD contract, follow the procedures at PGI 217.770(a)(3); and

(4) Contract administration (including oversight);

(b) Determining that the tasks to be accomplished or supplies to be provided are within the scope of the contract to be used;

(c) Reviewing funding to ensure that it is used in accordance with appropriation limitations; and

(d) Collecting and reporting data on the use of assisted acquisition for analysis. Follow the reporting requirements in subpart 204.6.

[Final rule, 80 FR 51750, 8/26/2015, effective 8/26/2015; Final rule, 80 FR 56929, 9/21/2015, effective 9/21/2015]

SUBPART 217.70—EXCHANGE OF PERSONAL PROPERTY

217.7000 Scope of subpart.

This subpart prescribes policy and procedures for exchange of nonexcess personal property concurrent with an acquisition. 40 U.S.C. 503 permits exchange of personal property and application of the exchange allowance to the acquisition of similar property. This subpart does not authorize the sale of nonexcess personal property.

[Final rule, 77 FR 35879, 6/15/2012, effective 6/15/2012]

217.7001 Definitions.

As used in this subpart—

(a) *Exchange (trade-in) property* means property which—

(1) Is not excess but is eligible for replacement (because of obsolescence, unserviceability, or other reason); and

(2) Is applied as whole or partial payment toward the acquisition of similar items (*i.e.*, items designed and constructed for the same purpose).

(b) *Property* means items that fall within one of the generic categories listed in DoD Manual 4140.01, Volume 9, DoD Supply Chain Materiel Management Procedures: Materiel Programs.

[Final rule, 65 FR 39703, 6/27/2000, effective 6/27/2000; Final rule, 77 FR 23631, 4/20/2012, effective 4/20/2012; Final rule, 82 FR 61479, 12/28/2017, effective 12/28/2017]

217.7002 Policy.

DoD policy is to exchange, rather than replace, eligible nonexcess property whenever exchange promotes economical and efficient program accomplishment. Exchange policy, authority, and applicability are governed by—

(a) The Federal Property Management Regulations issued by the Administrator of the General Services Administration; and

(b) DoD Manual 4140.01, Volume 9, DoD Supply Chain Materiel Management Procedures: Materiel Programs.

[Final rule, 65 FR 39703, 6/27/2000, effective 6/27/2000; Final rule, 77 FR 23631, 4/20/2012, effective 4/20/2012; Final rule, 82 FR 61479, 12/28/2017, effective 12/28/2017]

217.7003 Purchase request.

Ensure that the requiring activity provides all of the following in support of the purchase request—

(a) A certification that the property is eligible for exchange and complies with all conditions and limitations of DoD Manual 4140.01, Volume 9, DoD Supply Chain Materiel Management Procedures: Materiel Programs;

(b) A written determination of economic advantage indicating—

(1) The anticipated economic advantage to the Government from use of the exchange authority;

(2) That exchange allowances shall be applied toward, or in partial payment of, the items to be acquired; and

(3) That, if required, the exchange property has been rendered safe or innocuous or has been demilitarized;

(c) All applicable approvals for the exchange; and

(d) A description of the property available for exchange (e.g., nomenclature, location, serial number, estimated travel value).

[Final rule, 65 FR 39703, 6/27/2000, effective 6/27/2000; Final rule, 77 FR 23631, 4/20/2012, effective 4/20/2012; Final rule, 82 FR 61479, 12/28/2017, effective 12/28/2017]

217.7004 Solicitation and award.

(a) Solicitations shall include a request for offerors to state prices—

(1) For the new items being acquired without any exchange; and

(2) For the new items with the exchange (trade-in allowance) for the exchange property listed.

(b) The contracting officer is not obligated to award on an exchange basis. If the lowest evaluated offer is an offer for the new items without any exchange, the contracting officer may award on that basis and forgo the exchange.

(c) Exchanges may be made only with the successful offeror. When the successful offer includes an exchange, award one contract for both the acquisition of the new property and the trade-in of the exchange property. The only exception is when the items must be acquired against a mandatory Federal supply schedule contract, in which case, award a separate contract for the exchange.

217.7005 Solicitation provision.

Use the provision at 252.217-7002, Offering Property for Exchange, when offering nonexcess personal property for exchange. Allow a minimum of 14 calendar days for the inspection period in paragraph (b) of the clause if the exchange property is in the contiguous United States. Allow at least 21 calendar days outside the contiguous United States.

[Final rule, 70 FR 35543, 6/21/2005, effective 6/21/2005]

SUBPART 217.71—MASTER AGREEMENT FOR REPAIR AND ALTERATION OF VESSELS

217.7100 Scope of subpart.

This subpart contains acquisition policies and procedures for master agreements for repair and alteration of vessels.

217.7101 Definitions.

(a) *Master agreement for repair and alteration of vessels—*

(1) Is a written instrument of understanding, negotiated between a contracting activity and a contractor that—

(A) Contains contract clauses, terms, and conditions applying to future contracts for repairs, alterations, and/or additions to vessels; and

(B) Contemplates separate future contracts that will incorporate by reference or attachment the required and applicable clauses agreed upon in the master agreement.

(2) Is not a contract.

(b) *Job order—*

(1) Is a fixed price contract incorporating, by reference or attachment, a master agreement for repair and alteration of vessels;

(2) May include clauses pertaining to subjects not covered by the master agreement; but applicable to the job order being awarded; and

(3) Applies to a specific acquisition and sets forth the scope of work, price, delivery date, and other appropriate terms that apply to the particular job order.

217.7102 General.

(a) Activities shall enter into master agreements for repair and alteration of vessels with all prospective contractors located within the United States or its outlying areas, which—

(1) Request ship repair work; and

(2) Possess the organization and facilities to perform the work satisfactorily. (Issuance of a master agreement does not indicate approval of the contractor's facility for any particular acquisition and is not an affirmative determination of responsibility under FAR subpart 9.1 for any particular acquisition.)

(b) Activities may use master agreements in work with prospective contractors located outside the United States and its outlying areas.

(c) Activities may issue job orders under master agreements to effect repairs, alterations, and/or additions to vessels belonging to foreign governments.

(1) Contractors shall treat vessels of a foreign government as if they were vessels of the U.S. Government whenever requested to do so by the contracting officer.

(2) Identify the vessel and the foreign government in the solicitation and job order.

[Final rule, 70 FR 35543, 6/21/2005, effective 6/21/2005]

217.7103 Master agreements and job orders. (No Text)

[Final rule, 71 FR 27642, 5/12/2006, effective 5/12/2006]

217.7103-1 Content and format of master agreements.

Follow the procedures at PGI 217.7103-1 for preparation of master agreements.

[Final rule, 71 FR 27642, 5/12/2006, effective 5/12/2006]

217.7103-2 Period of agreement.

(a) Master agreements remain in effect until canceled by either the contractor or the contracting officer.

(b) Master agreements can be canceled by either the contractor or the contracting officer by giving 30 days written notice to the other.

(c) Cancellation of a master agreement does not affect the rights and liabilities under any job order existing at the time of cancellation. The contractor must continue to perform all work covered by any job order issued before the effective date of cancellation of the master agreement.

217.7103-3 Solicitations for job orders.

(a) When a requirement arises within the United States or its outlying areas for the type of work covered by the master agreement, solicit offers from prospective contractors that—

(1) Previously executed a master agreement; or

(2) Have not previously executed a master agreement, but possess the necessary qualifications to perform the work and agree to execute a master agreement before award of a job order.

(b) Follow the procedures at PGI 217.7103-3 when preparing solicitations for job orders.

[Final rule, 63 FR 55040, 10/14/98, effective 10/14/98, corrected, 63 FR 56290, 10/21/98; Final rule, 70 FR 35543, 6/21/2005, effective 6/21/2005; Final rule, 71 FR 27642, 5/12/2006, effective 5/12/2006]

217.7103-4 Emergency work.

(a) The contracting officer, without soliciting offers, may issue a written job order to a contractor that has previously executed a master agreement when—

(i) Delay in the performance of necessary repair work would endanger a vessel, its cargo or stores; or

(ii) Military necessity requires immediate work on a vessel.

(b) Follow the procedures at PGI 217.7103-4 when processing this type of undefinitized contract action.

[Redesignated from 217.7103-5, Final rule, 71 FR 27642, 5/12/2006, effective 5/12/2006]

217.7103-5 Repair costs not readily ascertainable.

Follow the procedures at PGI 217.7103-5 if the nature of any repairs is such that their extent and probable cost cannot be ascertained readily.

[Redesignated from 217.7103-6, Final rule, 71 FR 27642, 5/12/2006, effective 5/12/2006]

217.7103-6 Modification of master agreements.

(a) Review each master agreement at least annually before the anniversary of its effective date and revise it as necessary to conform to the requirements of the FAR and DFARS. Statutory or other mandatory changes may require review and revision earlier than one year.

(b) A master agreement shall be changed only by modifying the master agreement itself. It shall not be changed through a job order.

(c) A modification to a master agreement shall not affect job orders issued before the effective date of the modification.

[Redesignated from 217.7103-7, Final rule, 71 FR 27642, 5/12/2006, effective 5/12/2006]

217.7104 Contract clauses.

(a) Use the following clauses in solicitations for, and in, master agreements for repair and alteration of vessels:

(1) 252.217-7003, Changes.

(2) 252.217-7004, Job Orders and Compensation.

(3) 252.217-7005, Inspection and Manner of Doing Work.

(4) 252.217-7006, Title.

(5) 252.217-7007, Payments.

(6) 252.217-7008, Bonds.

(7) 252.217-7009, Default.

(8) 252.217-7010, Performance.

(9) 252.217-7011, Access to Vessel.

(10) 252.217-7012, Liability and Insurance.

(11) 252.217-7013, Guarantees.

(12) 252.217-7014, Discharge of Liens.

(13) 252.217-7015, Safety and Health.

(14) 252.217-7016, Plant Protection, as applicable.

(b) (1) Incorporate in solicitations for, and in, job orders, the clauses in the master agreement, and any other clauses on subjects not covered by the master agreement, but applicable to the job order to be awarded.

(2) Use the clause at 252.217-7016, Plant Protection, in job orders where performance is to occur at the contractor's facility.

SUBPART 217.72—[REMOVED AND RESERVED]

217.7200 [Removed and Reserved]

[Final rule, 71 FR 27642, 5/12/2006, effective 5/12/2006]

217.7201 [Removed and Reserved]

[Final rule, 71 FR 27642, 5/12/2006, effective 5/12/2006]

217.7202 [Removed and Reserved]

[Final rule, 71 FR 27642, 5/12/2006, effective 5/12/2006]

217.7203 [Removed and Reserved]

[Final rule, 71 FR 27642, 5/12/2006, effective 5/12/2006]

SUBPART 217.73—IDENTIFICATION OF SOURCES OF SUPPLY

217.7300 Scope.

This subpart implements 10 U,S.C. 2384. It contains policy and procedures for requiring contractors to identify the actual manufacturer of supplies furnished to DoD.

217.7301 Policy.

Contractors shall identify their sources of supply in contracts for supplies. Contractor identification of sources of supply enables solicitation, in subsequent acquisitions, of actual manufacturers or other suppliers of items. This enhances competition and potentially avoids payment of additional costs for no significant added value.

217.7302 Procedures.

(a) Whenever practicable, include a requirement for contractor identification of sources of supply in all contracts for the delivery of supplies. The identification shall include—

(1) The item's actual manufacturer or producer, or all the contractor's sources for the item;

(2) The item's national stock number (if there is one);

(3) The item identification number used by—

(i) The actual manufacturer or producer of the item; or

(ii) Each of the contractor's sources for the item; and

(4) The source of any technical data delivered under the contract.

(b) The requirement in paragraph (a) of this section does not apply to contracts that are—

(1) For commercial items; or

(2) Valued at or below the simplified acquisition threshold.

[DAC 91-9, 60 FR 61586, 11/30/95, effective 11/30/95; Final rule, 64 FR 2595, 1/15/99, effective 1/15/99]

217.7303 Solicitation provision.

(a) Use the provision at 252.217-7026, Identification of Sources of Supply, or one substantially the same, in all solicitations for supplies when the acquisition is being conducted under other than full and open competition, except when—

(1) Using FAR 6.302-5;

(2) The contracting officer already has the information required by the provision (e.g., the information was obtained under other acquisitions);

(3) The contract is for subsistence, clothing or textiles, fuels, or supplies purchased and used outside the United States;

(4) The contracting officer determines that it would not be practicable to require offerors/contractors to provide the information, e.g., nonrepetitive local purchases; or

(5) The contracting officer determines that the exception at 217.7302(b) applies to all items under the solicitation.

(b) If appropriate, use the provision at 252.217-7026, Identification of Sources of Supply, or one substantially the same, in service contracts requiring the delivery of supplies.

SUBPART 217.74—UNDEFINITIZED CONTRACT ACTIONS

217.7400 Scope.

This subpart prescribes policies and procedures implementing 10 U.S.C. 2326.

217.7401 Definitions.

As used in this subpart—

Contract action means an action which results in a contract.

(1) It includes contract modifications for additional supplies or services.

(2) It includes task orders and delivery orders.

(3) It does not include change orders, administrative changes, funding modifications, or any other contract modifications that are within the scope and under the terms of the contract, *e.g.,* engineering change proposals, value engineering change proposals, and over and above work requests as described in subpart 217.77. For policy relating to definitization of change orders, see 243.204-70.

Definitization means the agreement on, or determination of, contract terms, specifications, and price, which converts the undefinitized contract action to a definitive contract.

Qualifying proposal means a proposal that contains sufficient information to enable DoD to conduct meaningful analyses and audits of the information contained in the proposal.

Undefinitized contract action means any contract action for which the contract terms, specifications, or price are not agreed upon before performance is begun under the action. Examples are letter contracts, orders under basic ordering agreements, and provisioned item orders, for which the price has not been agreed upon before performance has begun. For policy relating to definitization of change orders, see 243.204-70.

[Interim rule, 75 FR 10190, 3/5/2010, effective 3/5/2010; Final rule, 75 FR 48276, 8/10/2010, effective 8/10/2010; Final rule, 75 FR 54526, 9/8/2010, effective 9/8/2010; Final rule, 77 FR 76939, 12/31/2012, effective 12/31/2012; Final rule, 84 FR 39204, 8/9/2019, effective 8/9/2019]

217.7402 Exceptions.

(a) The following undefinitized contract actions (UCAs) are not subject to this subpart. However, the contracting officer shall apply the policy and procedures to them to the maximum extent practicable (also see paragraph (b) of this section):

(1) Purchases at or below the simplified acquisition threshold.

(2) Special access programs.

(3) Congressionally mandated long-lead procurement contracts.

(b) If the contracting officer determines that it is impracticable to adhere to the procedures of this subpart for a particular contract action that falls within one of the categories in paragraph (a) of this section, the contracting officer shall provide prior notice, through agency channels, electronically via email to the Principal Director, Defense Pricing and Contracting (Contract Policy), at *osd.pentagon.ousd-a-s.mbx.dpc-cp@mail.mil.*

[DAC 91-10, 61 FR 7739, 2/29/96, effective 2/29/96; Final rule, 75 FR 48276, 8/10/2010, effective 8/10/2010; Final rule, 80 FR 72607, 11/20/2015, effective 11/20/2015; Final rule, 84 FR 39204, 8/9/2019, effective 8/9/2019; Final rule, 84 FR 48510, 9/13/2019, effective 9/13/2019]

217.7403 Policy.

DoD policy is that undefinitized contract actions shall—

(a) Be used only when—

(1) The negotiation of a definitive contract action is not possible in sufficient time to meet the Government's requirements; and

(2) The Government's interest demands that the contractor be given a binding commitment so that contract performance can begin immediately.

(b) Be as complete and definite as practicable under the particular circumstances.

217.7404 Limitations.

See PGI 217.7404 for additional guidance on obtaining approval to authorize use of an undefinitized contact action, documentation requirements, and other limitations on their use.

(a) *Foreign military sales contracts*.

(1) A contracting officer may not enter into a UCA for a foreign military sale unless—

(i) The UCA provides for agreement upon contractual terms, specifications, and price by the end of the 180-day period beginning on the date on which the contractor submits a qualifying proposal; and

(ii) The contracting officer obtains approval from the head of the contracting activity to enter into a UCA in accordance with 217.7404-1.

(2) The head of the contracting activity may waive the requirements of paragraph (a)(1) of this section, if a waiver is necessary in order to support any of the following operations:

(i) A contingency operation.

(ii) A humanitarian or peacekeeping operation.

(b) *Unilateral definitization by a contracting officer*. Any UCA with a value greater than $50 million may not be unilaterally definitized until—

(1) The earlier of—

(i) The end of the 180-day period, beginning on the date on which the contractor submits a qualifying proposal to definitize the contractual terms, specifications, and price; or

(ii) The date on which the amount of funds expended under the contractual action is equal to more than 50 percent of the negotiated overall not-to-exceed price for the contractual action;

(2) The head of the contracting activity, without power of redelegation, approves the definitization in writing;

(3) The contracting officer provides a copy of the written approval to the contractor; and

(4) A period of 30 calendar days has elapsed after the written approval is provided to the contractor.

[Final rule, 77 FR 52253, 8/29/2012, effective 8/29/2012; Final rule, 84 FR 39204, 8/9/2019, effective 8/9/2019]

217.7404-1 Authorization.

The contracting officer shall obtain approval from the head of the contracting activity before—

(a) Entering into a UCA. The request for approval must fully explain the need to begin performance before definitization, including the adverse impact on agency requirements resulting from delays in beginning performance.

(b) Including requirements for non-urgent spare parts and support equipment in a UCA. The request should show that inclusion of the non-urgent items is consistent with good business practices and in the best interest of the United States.

(c) Modifying the scope of a UCA when performance has already begun. The request should show that the modification is consistent with good business practices and in the best interests of the United States.

217.7404-2 Price ceiling.

UCAs shall include a not-to-exceed price.

217.7404-3 Definitization schedule.

(a) UCAs shall contain definitization schedules that provide for definitization by the earlier of—

(1) The date that is 180 days after the contractor submits a qualifying proposal. This date may not be extended beyond an additional 90 days without a written determination by the head of the contracting activity without power of redelegation, the commander of the combatant command con-

cerned, or the Under Secretary of Defense for Acquisition and Sustainment that it is in the best interests of the military department or the defense agency, the combatant command, or the Department of Defense, respectively, to continue the action; or

(2) The date on which the amount of funds obligated under the contract action is equal to more than 50 percent of the not-to-exceed price.

(b) Submission of a qualifying proposal in accordance with the definitization schedule is a material element of the contract. If the contractor does not submit a timely qualifying proposal, the contracting officer may suspend or reduce progress payments under FAR 32.503-6, or take other appropriate action.

[DAC 91-7, 60 FR 29491, 6/5/95, effective 5/17/95; DAC 91-10, 61 FR 7739, 2/29/96, effective 2/29/96; Final rule, 63 FR 67803, 12/9/98, effective 12/9/98; Publication notice, 20171208; Final rule, 84 FR 39204, 8/9/2019, effective 8/9/2019]

217.7404-4 Limitations on obligations.

(a) The Government shall not obligate more than 50 percent of the not-to-exceed price before definitization. However, if a contractor submits a qualifying proposal before 50 percent of the not-to-exceed price has been obligated by the Government, then the limitation on obligations before definitization may be increased to no more than 75 percent (see 232.102-70 for coverage on provisional delivery payments).

(b) In determining the appropriate amount to obligate, the contracting officer shall assess the contractor's proposal for the undefinitized period and shall obligate funds only in an amount consistent with the contractor's requirements for the undefinitized period.

[DAC 91-7, 60 FR 29491, 6/5/95, effective 5/17/95; Final rule, 74 FR 37649, 7/29/2009, effective 7/29/2009]

217.7404-5 Exceptions.

(a) The limitations in 217.7404-2, 217.7404-3, and 217.7404-4 do not apply to UCAs for the purchase of initial spares.

(b) The head of an agency may waive the limitations in 217.7404(a), 217.7404-2, 217.7404-3, and 217.7404-4 for UCAs if the head of the agency determines that the waiver is necessary to support—

(1) A contingency operation; or

(2) A humanitarian or peacekeeping operation.

[DAC 91-7, 60 FR 29491, 6/5/95, effective 5/17/95; Final rule, 63 FR 67803, 12/9/98, effective 12/9/98; Final rule, 71 FR 27642, 5/12/2006, effective 5/12/2006; Final rule, 84 FR 39204, 8/9/2019, effective 8/9/2019]

217.7404-6 Allowable profit.

When the final price of a UCA is negotiated after a substantial portion of the required performance has been completed, the head of the contracting activity shall ensure the profit allowed reflects—

(a) Any reduced cost risk to the contractor for costs incurred during contract performance before negotiation of the final price. However, if a contractor submits a qualifying proposal to definitize a UCA, and the contracting officer for such action definitizes the contract after the end of the 180-day period beginning on the date on which the contractor submitted the qualifying proposal, the profit allowed on the contract shall accurately reflect the cost risk of the contractor as such risk existed on the date the contractor submitted the qualifying proposal;

(b) Any reduced cost risk to the contractor for costs expected to be incurred during performance of the remainder of the contract after negotiation of the final price; and

(c) The requirements at 215.404-71-3(d)(2). The risk assessment shall be documented in the price negotiation memorandum.

[Final rule, 71 FR 27642, 5/12/2006, effective 5/12/2006; Final rule, 74 FR 37649, 7/29/2009, effective 7/29/2009; Final rule, 83 FR 30584, 6/29/2018, effective 6/29/2018; Final rule, 84 FR 39204, 8/9/2019, effective 8/9/2019]

217.7405 Plans and reports.

(a) To provide for enhanced management and oversight of UCAs, departments and agencies shall—

(1) Prepare and maintain a Consolidated UCA Management Plan; and

(2) Prepare semi-annual Consolidated UCA Management Reports addressing each UCA with an estimated value exceeding $5 million.

(b) Consolidated UCA Management Reports and Consolidated UCA Management Plan updates shall be submitted to the Office of the Director, Defense Procurement and Acquisition Policy, by October 31 and April 30 of each year in accordance with the procedures at PGI 217.7405.

(c) Consolidated UCA Management Reports shall include information about all change orders that are not forward priced (i.e., unpriced) and have an estimated value exceeding $5 million.

[Final rule, 74 FR 37649, 7/29/2009, effective 7/29/2009; Final rule, 75 FR 48276, 8/10/2010, effective 8/10/2010]

217.7406 Contract clauses.

(a) Use the clause at FAR 52.216-24, Limitation of Government Liability, in—

(1) All UCAs;

(2) Solicitations associated with UCAs;

(3) Basic ordering agreements;

(4) Indefinite-delivery contracts;

(5) Any other type of contract providing for the use of UCAs; and

(6) Unpriced change orders with an estimated value exceeding $5 million.

(b)(1) Use the clause at 252.217-7027, Contract Definitization, in—

(i) All UCAs;

(ii) Solicitations associated with UCAs;

(iii) Basic ordering agreements;

(iv) Indefinite-delivery contracts;

(v) Any other type of contract providing for the use of UCAs; and

(vi) Unpriced change orders with an estimated value exceeding $5 million.

(2) Insert the applicable information in paragraphs (a), (b), and (d) of the clause.

(3) If, at the time of entering into the UCA or unpriced change order, the contracting officer knows that the definitive contract action will meet the criteria of FAR 15.403-1, 15.403-2, or 15.403-3 for not requiring submission of certified cost or pricing data, the words "and certified cost or pricing data" may be deleted from paragraph (a) of the clause.

[DAC 91-10, 61 FR 7739, 2/29/96, effective 2/29/96; Final rule, 63 FR 55040, 10/14/98, effective 10/14/98; Redesignated from 217.7406, Final rule, 71 FR 27642, 5/12/2006, effective 5/12/2006; Redesignated from 217.7405, Final rule, 74 FR 37649, 7/29/2009, effective 7/29/2009; Final rule, 75 FR 48276, 8/10/2010, effective 8/10/2010; Final rule, 77 FR 76939, 12/31/2012, effective 12/31/2012]

SUBPART 217.75—ACQUISITION OF REPLENISHMENT PARTS

217.7500 Scope of subpart.

This subpart provides guidance on additional requirements related to acquisition of replenishment parts.

[Final rule, 71 FR 27642, 5/12/2006, effective 5/12/2006]

217.7501 Definition.

Replenishment parts, as used in this subpart, means repairable or consumable parts acquired after the initial provisioning process.

[Final rule, 71 FR 27642, 5/12/2006, effective 5/12/2006]

217.7502 General.

Departments and agencies—

(a) May acquire replenishment parts concurrently with production of the end item.

(b) Shall provide for full and open competition when fully adequate drawings and any other needed data are available with the right to use for acquisition purposes (see part 227). However—

(1) When data is not available for a competitive acquisition, use one of the procedures in PGI 217.7504.

(2) Replenishment parts must be acquired so as to ensure the safe, dependable, and effective operation of the equipment. Where this assurance is not possible with new sources, competition may be limited to the original manufacturer of the equipment or other sources that have previously manufactured or furnished the parts as long as the action is justified. See 209.270 for requirements applicable to replenishment parts for aviation or ship critical safety items.

(c) Shall follow the limitations on price increases in 217.7505.

[Interim rule, 69 FR 55987, 9/17/2004, effective 9/17/2004; Final rule, 70 FR 57188, 9/30/2005, effective 9/30/2005; Redesignated from 217.7501, Final rule, 71 FR 27642, 5/12/2006, effective 5/12/2006; Interim rule, 73 FR 1826, 1/10/2008, effective 1/10/2008; Final rule, 73 FR 46817, 8/12/2008, effective 8/12/2008]

217.7503 Spares acquisition integrated with production.

Follow the procedures at PGI 217.7503 for acquiring spare parts concurrently with the end item.

[Final rule, 65 FR 39703, 6/27/2000, effective 6/27/2000; Redesignated from 217.7501, Final rule, 71 FR 27642, 5/12/2006, effective 5/12/2006]

217.7504 Acquisition of parts when data is not available.

Follow the procedures at PGI 217.7504 when acquiring parts for which the Government does not have the necessary data.

[Redesignated from 217.7501, Final rule, 71 FR 27642, 5/12/2006, effective 5/12/2006]

217.7505 Limitations on price increases.

This section provides implementing guidance for section 1215 of Public Law 98-94 (10 U.S.C. 2452 note).

(a) The contracting officer shall not award, on a sole source basis, a contract for any centrally managed replenishment part when the price of the part has increased by 25 percent or more over the most recent 12-month period.

(1) Before computing the percentage difference between the current price and the prior price, adjust for quantity, escalation, and other factors necessary to achieve comparability.

(2) Departments and agencies may specify an alternate percentage or percentages for contracts at or below the simplified acquisition threshold.

(b) The contracting officer may award a contract for a part, the price of which exceeds the limitation in paragraph (a) of this section, if the contracting officer certifies in writing to the head of the contracting activity before award that—

(1) The contracting officer has evaluated the price of the part and concluded that the price increase is fair and reasonable; or

(2) The national security interests of the United States require purchase of the part despite the price increase.

(c) The fact that a particular price has not exceeded the limitation in paragraph (a) of this section does not relieve the contracting officer of the responsibility for obtaining a fair and reasonable price.

(d) Contracting officers may include a provision in sole source solicitations requiring that the offeror supply with its proposal, price and quantity data on any government orders for the replenishment part issued within the most recent 12 months.

[Final rule, 64 FR 2595, 1/15/99, effective 1/15/99; Redesignated from 217.7501, Final rule, 71 FR 27642, 5/12/2006, effective 5/12/2006]

217.7506 Spare parts breakout program.

See PGI 217.7506 and DoD Manual 4140.01, Volume 9, DoD Supply Chain Materiel Management Procedures: Materiel Programs, for spare parts breakout requirements.

[Final rule, 71 FR 27642, 5/12/2006, effective 5/12/2006; Final rule, 82 FR 61479, 12/28/2017, effective 12/28/2017]

SUBPART 217.76—CONTRACTS WITH PROVISIONING REQUIREMENTS

217.7600 [Removed]

[Final rule, 67 FR 61516, 10/1/2002, effective 10/1/2002; Final rule, 71 FR 27642, 5/12/2006, effective 5/12/2006]

217.7601 Provisioning.

(a) Follow the procedures at PGI 217.7601 for contracts with provisioning requirements.

(b) For technical requirements of provisioning, see DoD Manual 4140.01, Volume 2, DoD Supply Chain Materiel Management Procedures: Demand and Supply Planning.

[Final rule, 71 FR 27642, 5/12/2006, effective 5/12/2006; Final rule, 82 FR 61479, 12/28/2017, effective 12/28/2017]

217.7602 [Removed]

[Final rule, 71 FR 27642, 5/12/2006, effective 5/12/2006]

217.7602-1 [Removed]

[Final rule, 71 FR 27642, 5/12/2006, effective 5/12/2006]

217.7602-2 [Removed]

[Final rule, 71 FR 27642, 5/12/2006, effective 5/12/2006]

217.7603 [Removed]

[Final rule, 71 FR 27642, 5/12/2006, effective 5/12/2006]

217.7603-1 [Removed]

[Final rule, 71 FR 27642, 5/12/2006, effective 5/12/2006]

217.7603-2 [Removed]

[Final rule, 71 FR 27642, 5/12/2006, effective 5/12/2006]

217.7603-3 [Removed]

[Final rule, 71 FR 27642, 5/12/2006, effective 5/12/2006]

SUBPART 217.77—OVER AND ABOVE WORK

217.7700 [Removed]

[Final rule, 71 FR 27642, 5/12/2006, effective 5/12/2006]

217.7701 Procedures.

Follow the procedures at PGI 217.7701 when acquiring over and above work.

[Final rule, 71 FR 27642, 5/12/2006, effective 5/12/2006]

217.7702 Contract clause.

Use the clause at 252.217-7028, Over and Above Work, in solicitations and contracts containing requirements for over and above work, except as provided for in subpart 217.71.

SUBPART 217.78—REVERSE AUCTIONS

217.7801 Prohibition.

In accordance with section 814 of the National Defense Authorization Act for Fiscal Year 2017 (Pub. L. 114-328) as amended by section 882 of the National Defense Authorization Act for Fiscal Year 2018 (Pub. L. 115-91) (see 10 U.S.C. 2302 note), contracting officers shall not use reverse auctions when procuring items designated by the requiring activity as personal protective equipment or an aviation critical safety item, when the requiring activity advises the contracting officer that the level of quality or failure of the equipment or item could result in combat casualties. See 252.209-7010 for the definition and identification of critical safety items.

[Interim rule, 70 FR 29640, 5/24/2005, effective 5/24/2005; Final rule, 71 FR 14102, 3/21/2006, effective 3/21/2006; Interim rule, 74 FR 34270, 7/15/2009, effective 7/15/2009; Final rule, 75 FR 6819, 2/11/2010, effective 3/15/2010; Interim rule, 75 FR 32639, 6/8/2010, effective 6/8/2010; Final rule, 76 FR 9680, 2/22/2011, effective 2/22/2011; Final rule, 80 FR 51750, 8/26/2015, effective 8/26/2015; Final rule, 84 FR 50785, 9/26/2019, effective 10/1/2019]

PART 218—EMERGENCY ACQUISITIONS

Table of Contents

Subpart 218.1—Available Acquisition Flexibilities

Additional acquisition flexibilities 218.170

Subpart 218.2—Emergency Acquisition Flexibilities

Contingency operation 218.201
Defense or recovery from certain events 218.202
Incidents of national significance, emergency declaration, or major disaster declaration 218.203
Humanitarian or peacekeeping operation 218.204
Head of contracting activity determinations 218.270
Use of electronic business tools 218.271

PART 218—EMERGENCY ACQUISITIONS

SUBPART 218.1—AVAILABLE ACQUISITION FLEXIBILITIES

218.170 Additional acquisition flexibilities.

Additional acquisition flexibilities available to DoD are as follows:

(a) *Circumstances permitting other than full and open competition.* Use of the authority at FAR 6.302-2, Unusual and compelling urgency, may be appropriate under certain circumstances. See PGI 206.302-2.

(b) *Use of advance Military Interdepartmental Purchase Request (MIPR).* For urgent requirements, the advance MIPR may be transmitted electronically. See PGI 208.7004-3.

(c) *Use of the Governmentwide commercial purchase card.* Governmentwide commercial purchase cards do not have to be used for purchases valued at or below the micro-purchase threshold if the place of performance is entirely outside the United States. See 213.270(c)(1).

(d) *Master agreement for repair and alteration of vessels.* The contracting officer, without soliciting offers, may issue a written job order for emergency work to a contractor that has previously executed a master agreement, when delay would endanger a vessel, its cargo or stores, or when military necessity requires immediate work on a vessel. See 217.7103-4, 252.217-7010, and PGI 217.7103-4.

(e) *Spare parts breakout program.* An urgent immediate buy need not be delayed if an evaluation of the additional information cannot be completed in time to meet the required delivery date. See PGI 217.7506, paragraph 1-105(e).

(f) *Storage and disposal of toxic and hazardous materials.* Under certain emergency situations, exceptions apply with regard to the prohibition on storage or disposal of non-DoD-owned toxic or hazardous materials on DoD installations. See 223.7102(a)(3) and (7).

(g) *Authorization Acts, Appropriations Acts, and other statutory restrictions on foreign acquisition.* Acquisitions in the following categories are not subject to the restrictions of 225.7002, Restrictions on food, clothing, fabrics, specialty metals, and hand or measuring tools: (1) Acquisitions at or below the simplified acquisition threshold; (2) Acquisitions outside the United States in support of combat operations; (3) Acquisitions of perishable foods by or for activities located outside the United States for personnel of those activities; (4) Acquisitions of food, specialty metals, or hand or measuring tools in support of contingency operations, or for which the use of other than competitive procedures has been approved on the basis of unusual and compelling urgency in accordance with FAR 6.302-2; (5) Emergency acquisitions by activities located outside the United States for personnel of those activities; and (6) Acquisitions by vessels in foreign waters. See 225.7002-2.

(h) *Rights in technical data.* The agency head may notify a person asserting a restriction that urgent or compelling circumstances (e.g., emergency repair or overhaul) do not permit the Government to continue to respect the asserted restriction. See 227.7102-2; 227.7103-5; 227.7103-13; 227.7104; 227.7103-13; 252.227-7013; 252.227-7014; 252.227-7015; 252.227-7018; and 252.227-7037.

(i) *Tax exemption in Spain.* If copies of a contract are not available and duty-free import of equipment or materials is urgent, the contracting officer may send the Joint United States Military Group copies of the Letter of Intent or a similar document indicating the pending award. See PGI 229.7001.

(j) *Electronic submission and processing of payment requests.* Exceptions to the use of Wide Area Workflow are at 232.7002(a).

(k) *Mortuary services.* In an epidemic or other emergency, the contracting activity may obtain services beyond the capacity of the contractor's facilities from other sources. See 237.7003(a) and 252.237-7003.

[Interim rule, 72 FR 2631, 1/22/2007, effective 1/22/2007; Final rule, 72 FR 51187, 9/6/2007, effective 9/6/2007; Final rule, 77 FR 38731, 6/29/2012, effective 6/29/2012;

Final rule, 84 FR 48504, 9/13/2019, effective 9/13/2019]

SUBPART 218.2—EMERGENCY ACQUISITION FLEXIBILITIES

218.201 Contingency operation.

(1) *Selection, appointment, and termination of appointment.* Contracting officer qualification requirements pertaining to a baccalaureate degree and 24 semester credit hours of business related courses do not apply to DoD employees or members of the armed forces who are in a contingency contracting force. See 201.603-2(2).

(2) *Policy for item unique identification.* Contractors will not be required to provide DoD item unique identification if the items, as determined by the head of the contracting activity, are to be used to support a contingency operation. See 211.274–2(b).

(3) *Use of the Governmentwide commercial purchase card.* Governmentwide commercial purchase cards do not have to be used for purchases valued at or below the micro-purchase threshold if the purchase or payment is for an overseas transaction by a contracting officer in support of a contingency operation, or for training exercises in preparation for overseas contingency, humanitarian, or peacekeeping operations. See 213.201(g) and 213.270(c)(3) and (5).

(4) *Governmentwide commercial purchase card.* A contracting office supporting a contingency operation or a humanitarian or peacekeeping operation may use the Governmentwide commercial purchase card to make a purchase that exceeds the micro-purchase threshold but does not exceed the simplified acquisition threshold if certain conditions are met. See 213.301(3).

(5) *Imprest funds and third party drafts.* Imprest funds are authorized for use without further approval for overseas transactions at or below the micro-purchase threshold in support of a contingency operation or a humanitarian or peacekeeping operation. See 213.305- 3(d)(iii)(A).

(6) *Standard Form (SF) 44, Purchase Order-Invoice-Voucher.* SF 44s may be used for purchases not exceeding the simplified acquisition threshold for overseas transactions by contracting officers in support of a contingency operation or a humanitarian or peacekeeping operation. See 213.306(a)(1)(B).

(7) *Only one offer.* The requirements at sections 215.371-2 do not apply to acquisitions, as determined by the head of the contracting activity, in support of a contingency operation. See 215.371-4(a)(2).

(8) *Approval of determination and findings for time-and-materials or labor-hour contracts.* The approval requirements in paragraphs (d)(i)(A)(*1*) and (*2*) of this section do not apply to contracts that, as determined by the head of the contracting activity, support contingency. See 216.601(d)(3).

(9) *Undefinitized contract actions.* The head of the agency may waive certain limitations for undefinitized contract actions if the head of the agency determines that the waiver is necessary to support a contingency operation or a humanitarian or peacekeeping operation. See 217.7404-5(b).

(10) *Prohibited sources.* DoD personnel are authorized to make emergency acquisitions in direct support of U.S. or allied forces deployed in military contingency, humanitarian, or peacekeeping operations in a country or region subject to economic sanctions administered by the Department of the Treasury, Office of Foreign Assets Control. See 225.701-70.

(11) *Authorization Acts, Appropriations Acts, and other statutory restrictions on foreign acquisition.* Acquisitions in the following categories are not subject to the restrictions of 225.7002, Restrictions on food, clothing, fabrics, specialty metals, and hand or measuring tools: (1) Acquisitions at or below the simplified acquisition threshold; (2) Acquisitions outside the United States in support of combat operations; (3) Acquisitions of perishable foods by or for activities located outside the United States for personnel of those activities; (4) Acquisitions of food, specialty metals, or hand or measuring tools in support of contingency operations, or for which the use of other than competitive procedures has been approved on the basis of unusual and compelling urgency in accordance with FAR 6.302-2; (5) Emergency acquisitions by activities located outside the

United States for personnel of those activities; and (6) Acquisitions by vessels in foreign waters. See 225.7002-2.

(12) *Electronic submission and processing of payment requests.* Contractors do not have to submit payment requests in electronic form for contracts awarded by deployed contracting officers in the course of military operations, including contingency operations or humanitarian or peacekeeping operations. See 232.7002(a)(4).

[Interim rule, 72 FR 2631, 1/22/2007, effective 1/22/2007; Final rule, 72 FR 51187, 9/6/2007, effective 9/6/2007; Final rule, 78 FR 76067, 12/16/2013, effective 12/16/2013; Final rule, 81 FR 53045, 8/11/2016, effective 8/11/2016; Final rule, 83 FR 24888, 5/30/2018, effective 5/30/2018]

218.202 Defense or recovery from certain events.

For acquisitions that, as determined by the head of the contracting activity, are to facilitate defense against or recovery from cyber, nuclear, biological, chemical, or radiological attack; to facilitate provision of international disaster assistance; or to support response to an emergency or major disaster, the following requirements do not apply:

(1) *Policy for unique item identification at 211.274-2(a).* Contractors are not required to provide DoD unique item identification if the items are to be used to facilitate defense against or recovery from nuclear, biological, chemical, or radiological attack. However, contractors are not exempt from this requirement if the items are to be used to facilitate defense against or recovery from cyber attack. See 211.274-2(b).

(2) *Only one offer requirements at section 215.371-2.* See 215.371-4(a)(2).

(3) *Approval of determination and findings for time-and-materials or labor-hour contracts at 216.601(d)(i)(A)(1) and (2).* See 216.601(d)(3).

[Interim rule, 72 FR 2631, 1/22/2007, effective 1/22/2007; Final rule, 72 FR 51187, 9/6/2007, effective 9/6/2007; Final rule, 83 FR 24888, 5/30/2018, effective 5/30/2018]

218.203 Incidents of national significance, emergency declaration, or major disaster declaration.

(1) *Establishing or maintaining alternative sources.* PGI contains a sample format for Determination and Findings citing the authority of FAR 6.202(a), regarding exclusion of a particular source in order to establish or maintain an alternative source or sources. Alternate 2 of the sample format addresses having a supplier available for furnishing supplies or services in case of a national emergency. See PGI 206.202.

(2) *Electronic submission and processing of payment requests.* Contractors do not have to submit payment requests in electronic form for contracts awarded by contracting officers in the conduct of emergency operations, such as responses to natural disasters or national or civil emergencies. See 232.7002(a)(4).

[Interim rule, 72 FR 2631, 1/22/2007, effective 1/22/2007; Final rule, 72 FR 51187, 9/6/2007, effective 9/6/2007]

218.204 Humanitarian or peacekeeping operation.

The following requirements do not apply to acquisitions that, as determined by the head of the contracting activity, are in support of humanitarian or peacekeeping operations:

(1) *Policy for item unique identification at 211.274-2(a).* See 211.274-2(b).

(2) *Only one offer requirements at sections* 215.371-2. See 215.371-4(a)(2).

(3) *Approval of determination and findings for time-and-materials or labor-hour contracts at 216.601(d)(i)(A)(1) and (2).* See 216.601(d)(3).

[Final rule, 83 FR 24888, 5/30/2018, effective 5/30/2018]

218.270 Head of contracting activity determinations.

For contract actions supporting contingency operations or facilitating defense against or recovery from nuclear, biological, chemical, or radiological attack, the term *head of the contracting activity,* is replaced with *head of the contracting activity*, as defined in FAR 2.101, in the following locations:

(a) FAR 2.101: definition of “simplified acquisition threshold.”

(1) Definition of *Micro-purchase threshold*, paragraph (3).

(2) Definition of *Simplified acquisition threshold.*

(b) FAR 12.102(f).

(c) FAR 13.201(g).

(d) FAR 13.500(c)(1).

(e) FAR 18.2.

[Interim rule, 72 FR 2631, 1/22/2007, effective 1/22/2007; Final rule, 72 FR 51187, 9/6/2007, effective 9/6/2007; Final rule, 74 FR 2407, 1/15/2009, effective 1/15/2009; Redesignated, Interim rule, 76 FR 44280, 7/25/2011, effective 7/25/2011; Redesignated, Final rule, 76 FR 71833, 11/18/2011, effective 11/18/2011; Final rule, 82 FR 61479, 12/28/2017, effective 12/28/2017; Redesignated from 218.271, Final rule, 83 FR 24888, 5/30/2018, effective 5/30/2018]

218.271 Use of electronic business tools.

When supporting a contingency operation or humanitarian or peacekeeping operation, follow the procedures at PGI 218.271 concerning the use of electronic business tools,

[Final rule, 80 FR 10390, 2/26/2015, effective 2/26/2015; Redesignated from 218.272, Final rule, 83 FR 24888, 5/30/2018, effective 5/30/2018]

PART 219—SMALL BUSINESS PROGRAMS

Table of Contents

[Removed] . . . 219.000
[Removed] . . . 219.001

Subpart 219.2—Policies

General policy . . . 219.201
Specific policies . . . 219.202
Encouraging small business participation in acquisitions . . . 219.202-1
[Removed] . . . 219.202-5
Religious-related services—inclusion of nonprofit organizations . . . 219.270
Definition . . . 219.270-1
Procedures . . . 219.270-2
Solicitation provision . . . 219.270-3

Subpart 219.3—Determination of Small Business Status for Small Business Programs

Rerepresentation by a contractor that represented itself as a small business concern . . . 219.301-2
Rerepresentation by a contractor that represented itself as other than a small business concern . . . 219.301-3
Determining North American Industry Classification System codes and size standards . . . 219.303
Solicitation provisions and contract clauses . . . 219.309

Subpart 219.4—Cooperation with the Small Business Administration

General . . . 219.401
Small Business Administration procurement center representatives . . . 219.402

Subpart 219.5—Set-Asides for Small Business

Setting aside acquisitions . . . 219.502
Requirements for setting aside acquisitions . . . 219.502-1
Total set-asides . . . 219.502-2
[Removed] . . . 219.502-3
[Removed] . . . 219.502-70
Rejecting Small Business Administration recommendations . . . 219.505
[Removed] . . . 219.508

Subpart 219.6—Certificates of Competency and Determinations of Responsibility

Procedures . . . 219.602
[Removed] . . . 219.602-1
[Removed] . . . 219.602-3

Subpart 219.7—The Small Business Subcontracting Program

Statutory requirements for the Test Program for Negotiation of Comprehensive Small Business Subcontracting Plans . . . 219.702-70
Eligibility requirements for participating in the program . . . 219.703
Subcontracting plan requirements . . . 219.704

Responsibilities of the contracting officer under the subcontracting assistance program 219.705
[Removed] 219.705-2
Reviewing the subcontracting plan 219.705-4
Postaward responsibilities of the contracting officer 219.705-6
Responsibilities of the cognizant administrative contracting officer 219.706
Contract clauses 219.708

Subpart 219.8—Contracting with the Small Business Administration (The 8(a) Program)

General 219.800
Selecting acquisitions for the 8(a) Program 219.803
Evaluation, offering, and acceptance 219.804
Agency evaluation 219.804-1
[Removed] 219.804-2
[Removed] 219.804-3
Competitive 8(a) 219.805
General 219.805-1
Procedures 219.805-2
Pricing the 8(a) contract 219.806
Contract negotiations 219.808
Sole source 219.808-1
Preparing the contracts 219.811
[Removed] 219.811-1
[Removed] 219.811-2
Contract clauses 219.811-3
[Removed] 219.812

Subpart 219.10—[Removed]

Subpart 219.11—[Removed]

Subpart 219.12—[Removed]

Subpart 219.13—Historically Underutilized Business Zone (HUBZone) Program

Price evaluation preference for HUBZone small business concerns 219.1307

Subpart 219.70—[Reserved]

Subpart 219.71—Pilot Mentor-Protege Program

Scope 219.7100
Policy 219.7101
General 219.7102
Procedures 219.7103
General 219.7103-1
Contracting officer responsibilities 219.7103-2
Developmental assistance costs eligible for reimbursement or credit 219.7104
Reporting 219.7105
Performance reviews 219.7106

SUBCHAPTER D—SOCIOECONOMIC PROGRAMS (Parts 219-226)

PART 219—SMALL BUSINESS PROGRAMS

219.000 [Removed]

[DAC 91-6, 59 FR 27662, 5/27/94, effective 5/27/94; Final rule, 64 FR 62987, 11/18/99, effective 11/18/99; Final rule, 68 FR 15381, 3/31/2003, effective 3/31/2003; Final rule, 71 FR 39008, 7/11/2006, effective 7/11/2006; Final rule, 72 FR 20761, 4/26/2007, effective 4/26/2007; Interim rule, 79 FR 61579, 10/14/2014, effective 10/14/2014; Final rule, 80 FR 15912, 3/26/2015, effective 3/26/2015]

219.001 [Removed]

[Interim rule, 63 FR 64427, 11/20/98, effective 1/1/99, finalized without change, 64 FR 52670, 9/30/99; Final rule, 74 FR 37644, 7/29/2009, effective 7/29/2009; Interim rule, 79 FR 61579, 10/14/2014, effective 10/14/2014; Final rule, 80 FR 15912, 3/26/2015, effective 3/26/2015]

SUBPART 219.2—POLICIES

219.201 General policy.

(c) For the defense agencies, the director of the Office of Small Business Programs must be appointed by, be responsible to, and report directly to the director or deputy director of the defense agency.

(8) The responsibility for assigning small business technical advisors is delegated to the head of the contracting activity.

(10) Contracting activity small business specialists perform this function by—

(A) Reviewing and making recommendations for all acquisitions (including orders placed against Federal Supply Schedule contracts) over $10,000, except those under the simplified acquisition threshold that are totally set aside for small business concerns in accordance with FAR 19.502-2. Follow the procedures at PGI 219.201 (c) (10) regarding such reviews.

(B) Making the review before issuance of the solicitation or contract modification and documenting it on DD Form 2579, Small Business Coordination Record (see PGI 253.219-70 for instructions on completing the form); and

(C) Referring recommendations that have been rejected by the contracting officer to the Small Business Administration (SBA) procurement center representative. If an SBA procurement center representative is not assigned, see FAR 19.402(a).

(11) Also conduct annual reviews to assess—

(A) The extent of consolidation of contract requirements that has occurred (see FAR 7.107); and

(B) The impact of those consolidations on the availability of small business concerns to participate in procurements as both contractors and subcontractors.

(d) For information on the appointment and functions of small business specialists, see PGI 219.201(d).

[Interim rule, 63 FR 41972, 8/6/98, effective 10/1/98, finalized without change, 64 FR 52670 9/30/99; Final rule, 64 FR 2595, 1/15/99, effective 1/15/99; Final rule, 65 FR 39703, 6/27/2000, effective 6/27/2000; Interim rule, 65 FR 50148, 8/17/2000, effective 10/1/2000, finalized without change, 65 FR 77831, 12/13/2000; Final rule, 65 FR 63806, 10/25/2000, effective 10/25/2000; Interim rule, 69 FR 55986, 9/17/2004, effective 9/17/2004; Final rule, 71 FR 14104, 3/21/2006, effective 3/21/2006; Final rule, 71 FR 44926, 8/8/2006, effective 8/8/2006; Final rule, 73 FR 46813, 8/12/2008, effective 8/12/2008; Final rule, 75 FR 45072, 8/2/2010, effective 10/1/2010; Interim rule, 79 FR 61579, 10/14/2014, effective 10/14/2014; Final rule, 79 FR 67356, 11/13/2014, effective 11/13/2014; Final rule, 79 FR 68635, 11/18/2014, effective 11/18/2014; Final rule, 80 FR 15912, 3/26/2015, effective 3/26/2015; Final rule, 80 FR 56929 , 9/21/2015, effective 9/21/2015; Final rule, 83 FR 15995, 4/13/2018, effective 4/13/2018]

219.202 Specific policies. (No Text)

219.202-1 Encouraging small business participation in acquisitions.

See PGI 205.207(d) for information on how to advertise a small business event on the Government point of entry.

[Final rule, 72 FR 20761, 4/26/2007, effective 4/26/2007; Final rule, 76 FR 76318, 12/7/2011, effective 12/7/2011; Final rule, 77 FR 76936, 12/31/2012, effective 12/31/2012; Interim rule, 79 FR 61579, 10/14/2014, effective 10/14/2014; Final rule, 80 FR 15912, 3/26/2015, effective 3/26/2015]

219.202-5 [Removed]

[Interim rule, 63 FR 41972, 8/6/98, effective 10/1/98, finalized without change, 64 FR 52670 9/30/99; Final rule, 65 FR 63804, 10/25/2000, effective 10/25/2000; Final rule, 74 FR 37644, 7/29/2009, effective 7/29/2009; Interim rule, 79 FR 61579, 10/14/2014, effective 10/14/2014; Final rule, 80 FR 15912, 3/26/2015, effective 3/26/2015]

219.270 Religious-related services–inclusion of nonprofit organizations.(No Text)

[Final rule, 83 FR 16001, 4/13/2018, effective 4/13/2018]

219.270-1 Definition.

As used in this section—

Nonprofit organization means any organization that is—

(1) Described in section 501(c) of the Internal Revenue Code of 1986; and

(2) Exempt from tax under section 501(a) of that Code.

[Final rule, 83 FR 16001, 4/13/2018, effective 4/13/2018]

219.270-2 Procedures.

(a) To comply with section 898 of the National Defense Authorization Act for Fiscal Year 2016 (Pub. L. 114-92), when acquiring religious-related services to be performed on a U.S. military installation—

(1) Do not preclude a nonprofit organization from competing, even when the acquisition is set aside for small businesses as identified in FAR 19.000(a)(3); and

(2) Do not use any of the sole source exceptions at FAR 6.302-5(b)(4) through (7) for such acquisitions.

(b) If the apparently successful offeror has not represented in its quotation or offer that it is one of the small business concerns identified in FAR 19.000(a)(3), the contracting officer shall verify that the offeror is registered in the System for Award Management database as a nonprofit organization.

[Final rule, 83 FR 16001, 4/13/2018, effective 4/13/2018]

219.270-3 Solicitation provision.

Use the provision DFARS 252.219-7012, Competition for Religious-Related Services, in solicitations, including solicitations using FAR part 12 procedures for the acquisition of commercial items, for the acquisition of religious-related services to be performed on U.S. military installations, when the acquisition is set aside for any of the small business concerns identified in FAR 19.000(a)(3).

[Final rule, 83 FR 16001, 4/13/2018, effective 4/13/2018]

SUBPART 219.3—DETERMINATION OF SMALL BUSINESS STATUS FOR SMALL BUSINESS PROGRAMS

219.301-2 Rerepresentation by a contractor that represented itself as a small business concern.

Follow the procedures at PGI 204.606(4)(vii) for reporting modifications for rerepresentation actions.

[Final rule, 76 FR 76318, 12/7/2011, effective 12/7/2011]

219.301-3 Rerepresentation by a contractor that represented itself as other than a small business concern.

Follow the procedures at PGI 204.606(4)(vii) for reporting modifications for rerepresentation actions.

[Final rule, 76 FR 76318, 12/7/2011, effective 12/7/2011]

219.303 Determining North American Industry Classification System codes and size standards.

Contracting officers shall follow the procedures for "Correctly Identifying Size Status of Contractors" in the OUSD (AT&L) DPAP memorandum dated July 21, 2010.

[Final rule, 76 FR 3536, 1/20/2011, effective 1/20/2011; Final rule, 80 FR 30115 , 5/26/2015, effective 5/26/2015; Final rule, 80 FR 30116, 5/26/2015, effective 5/26/2015]

219.309 Solicitation provisions and contract clauses.

(1) Use the provision at 252.219-7000, Advancing Small Business Growth, in solicitations, including solicitations using FAR part 12 procedures for acquisition of commercial items, when the estimated annual value of the contract is expected to exceed—

(i) The small business size standard, if expressed in dollars, for the North American Industry Classification System (NAICS) code assigned by the contracting officer; or

(ii) $70 million, if the small business size standard is expressed as number of employees for the NAICS code assigned by the contracting officer.

[Final rule, 80 FR 30115, 5/26/2015, effective 5/26/2015; Final rule, 80 FR 30116, 5/26/2015, effective 5/26/2015]

SUBPART 219.4—COOPERATION WITH THE SMALL BUSINESS ADMINISTRATION

219.401 General.

(b) The contracting activity small business specialist is the primary activity focal point for interface with the SBA.

219.402 Small Business Administration procurement center representatives.

(c)(i) *Authority.* This section implements section 1811 of the National Defense Authorization Act for Fiscal Year 2017 (Pub. L. 114–328).

(ii) *Definition.* As used in this section—

Humanitarian and civic assistance means any of the following activities carried out in conjunction with authorized military operations in a foreign country:

(A) Medical, surgical, dental, and veterinary care provided in areas of a country that are rural or underserved by professionals in those fields, including education, training, and technical assistance related to the care provided.

(B) Construction of rudimentary surface transportation systems.

(C) Well drilling and construction of basic sanitation facilities.

(D) Rudimentary construction and repair of public facilities. (10 U.S.C. 401(e))

(iii) *Exclusions.* Unless the contracting activity requests a review, SBA procurement center representatives will not review acquisitions conducted by or for DoD if the acquisition is—

(A) For foreign military sales (see 225.7300);

(B) In support of humanitarian and civic assistance;

(C) In support of a contingency operation;

(D) Awarded pursuant to a Status of Forces Agreement or other agreement with the government of a foreign country in which U.S. Armed Forces are deployed; or

(E) Both awarded and performed outside the United States and its outlying areas.

[Final rule, 84 FR 72561, 12/31/2019, effective 12/31/2019]

SUBPART 219.5—SET-ASIDES FOR SMALL BUSINESS

219.502 Setting aside acquisitions. (No Text)

219.502-1 Requirements for setting aside acquisitions.

Do not set aside acquisitions—

(1) For supplies that were developed and financed, in whole or in part, by Canadian sources under the U.S.-Canadian Defense Development Sharing Program; or

(2) Excluded from procurement center representative review (see 219.402(c)(iii)).

[DAC 91-5, 58 FR 28458, 5/13/93, effective 4/30/93; Interim rule, 69 FR 31909,

6/8/2004, effective 6/8/2004; Final rule, 69 FR 67855, 11/22/2004, effective 11/22/2004; Final rule, 75 FR 45072, 8/2/2010, effective 10/1/2010; Final rule, 80 FR 36903, 6/26/2015, effective 10/1/2015; Final rule, 84 FR 18160, 4/30/2019, effective 4/30/2019; Final rule, 84 FR 72561, 12/31/2019, effective 12/31/2019]

219.502-2 Total set-asides.

(a) Unless the contracting officer determines that the criteria for set-aside cannot be met, set aside for small business concerns acquisitions for—

(i) Construction, including maintenance and repairs, under $2.5 million;

(ii) Dredging under $1.5 million; and

(iii) Architect-engineer services for military construction or family housing projects under $1 million (10 U.S.C. 2855).

[DAC 91-5, 58 FR 28458, 5/13/93, effective 4/30/93; Interim rule, 69 FR 31909, 6/8/2004, effective 6/8/2004; Final rule, 69 FR 67855, 11/22/2004, effective 11/22/2004; Final rule, 71 FR 75891, 12/19/2006, effective 12/19/2006; Final rule, 75 FR 45072, 8/2/2010, effective 10/1/2010; Publication notice, 20101007; Publication notice, 20101025; Final rule, 80 FR 36903, 6/26/2015, effective 10/1/2015; Final rule, 84 FR 18160, 4/30/2019, effective 4/30/2019]

219.502-3 [Removed]

[Interim rule, 65 FR 50148, 8/17/2000, effective 10/1/2000, finalized without change, 65 FR 77831, 12/13/2000; Interim rule, 79 FR 61579, 10/14/2014, effective 10/14/2014]

219.502-70 [Removed]

[Final rule, 68 FR 64559, 11/14/2003, effective date 12/15/2003; Final rule, 69 FR 63328, 11/1/2004, effective 11/1/2004; Final rule, 80 FR 15912, 3/26/2015, effective 3/26/2015]

219.505 Rejecting Small Business Administration recommendations.

(b) The designee shall be at a level no lower than chief of the contracting office.

219.508 [Removed]

[Final rule, 68 FR 64559, 11/14/2002, effective date 12/15/2003; Final rule, 69 FR 63328, 11/1/2004, effective 11/1/2004]

SUBPART 219.6—CERTIFICATES OF COMPETENCY AND DETERMINATIONS OF RESPONSIBILITY

219.602 Procedures.

When making a nonresponsibility determination for a small business concern, follow the procedures at PGI 219.602.

[Final rule, 72 FR 20761, 4/26/2007, effective 4/26/2007]

219.602-1 [Removed]

[Interim rule, 60 FR 40106, 8/7/95, effective 8/7/95, finalized without change, DAC 91-9, 60 FR 61586, 11/30/95, effective 11/30/95; Final rule, 72 FR 20761, 4/26/2007, effective 4/26/2007]

219.602-3 [Removed]

[DAC 91-12, 62 FR 34114, 6/24/97, effective 6/24/97; Final rule, 72 FR 20761, 4/26/2007, effective 4/26/2007]

SUBPART 219.7—THE SMALL BUSINESS SUBCONTRACTING PROGRAM

219.702-70 Statutory requirements for the Test Program for Negotiation of Comprehensive Small Business Subcontracting Plans.

(a) *Test Program*. In accordance with 15 U.S.C. 637 note, DoD has established a test program to determine whether comprehensive subcontracting plans on a corporate, division, or plant-wide basis will reduce administrative burdens while enhancing subcontracting opportunities for small and small disadvantaged business concerns. This program is referred to as the Test Program for Negotiation of Comprehensive Small Business Subcontracting Plans (Test Program).

(b) *Eligibility requirements*. To become and remain eligible to participate in the Test Program, a business concern is required to have furnished supplies or services (including construction) under at least three DoD contracts during the preceding fiscal year, having an aggregate value of at least $100 million.

(c) *Comprehensive subcontracting plans.* (1) The Defense Contract Management Agency will designate the contracting officer who shall negotiate and approve comprehensive subcontracting plans with eligible participants on an annual basis.

(2) Test Program participants use their comprehensive subcontracting plans, in lieu of individual subcontracting plans, when performing any DoD contract or subcontract that requires a subcontracting plan.

(d) *Assessment.* The contracting officer designated to manage the comprehensive subcontracting plan shall conduct a compliance review during the fiscal year after the close of the fiscal year for which the plan is applicable. The contracting officer shall compare the approved percentage or dollar goals to the total, actual subcontracting dollars covered by the comprehensive subcontracting plan.

(1) If the contractor has failed to meet its approved subcontracting goal(s), the contracting officer shall give the contractor written notice specifying the failure, advising of the potential for assessment of liquidated damages, permitting the contractor to demonstrate what good faith efforts have been made, and providing a period of 15 working days (or longer period at the contracting officer's discretion) within which to respond. The contracting officer may take the contractor's failure to respond to the notice as an admission that no valid explanation exists.

(2) The contracting officer shall review all available information to determine whether the contractor has failed to make a good faith effort to comply with the plan.

(3) If, after consideration of all relevant information, the contracting officer determines that the contractor failed to make a good faith effort to comply with the comprehensive subcontracting plan, the contracting officer shall issue a final decision. The contracting officer's final decision shall include the right of the contractor to appeal under the Disputes clause. The contracting officer shall distribute a copy of the final decision to all cognizant contracting officers for the contracts covered under the plan.

(e) *Liquidated damages.* The amount of liquidated damages shall be the amount of anticipated damages sustained by the Government, including but not limited to additional expenses of administration, reporting, and contract monitoring, and shall be identified in the comprehensive subcontracting plan. Liquidated damages shall be in addition to any other remedies the Government may have.

(f) *Expiration date.* The Test Program expires on December 31, 2017.

[DAC 91-5, 58 FR 28458, 5/13/93, effective 4/30/93, Corrected, 58 FR 32416, 6/9/93; Final rule, 60 FR 35668, 7/10/95, effective 7/10/95; Interim rule, 61 FR 39900, 7/31/96, effective 7/31/96, corrected, 61 FR 49008, 9/17/96, finalized without change, DAC 91-12, 62 FR 34114, 6/24/97, effective 6/24/97; Interim rule, 63 FR 14640, 3/26/98, effective 3/26/98, finalized without change, 63 FR 64426, 11/20/98; Final rule, 64 FR 62986, 11/18/99, effective 11/18/99; Final rule, 70 FR 14574, 3/23/2005, effective 3/23/2005; Final rule, 72 FR 20761, 4/26/2007, effective 4/26/2007; Final rule, 77 FR 11367, 2/24/2012, effective 2/24/2012; Final rule, 83 FR 15996, 4/13/2018, effective 4/13/2018]

219.703 Eligibility requirements for participating in the program.

(a) Qualified nonprofit agencies for the blind and other severely disabled, that have been approved by the Committee for Purchase from People Who Are Blind or Severely Disabled under 41 U.S.C. chapter 85, are eligible to participate in the program as a result of 10 U.S.C. 2410d and section 9077 of Pub. L. 102-396 and similar sections in subsequent Defense appropriations acts. Under this authority, subcontracts awarded to such entities may be counted toward the prime contractor's small business subcontracting goal.

(b) A contractor may also rely on the written representation as to status of—

(i) A historically black college or university or minority institution; or

(ii) A qualified nonprofit agency for the blind or other severely disabled approved by the Committee for Purchase from People Who Are Blind or Severely Disabled.

[DAC 91-3, 57 FR 42630, 9/15/92, effective 8/31/92; DAC 91-5, 58 FR 28458, 5/13/93, effective 4/30/93; Interim rule, 60 FR 13074, 3/10/95, effective 2/27/95, corrected, 60 FR 41157, 8/11/95; DAC 91-9, 60 FR 61586, 11/30/95, effective 11/30/95; DAC 91-13, 63 FR 11522, 3/9/98, effective 3/9/98; Interim rule, 63 FR 41972, 8/6/98, effective 10/1/98, finalized without change, 64 FR 52670 9/30/99; Final rule, 64 FR 51074, 9/21/99, effective 9/21/99; Final rule, 64 FR 62986, 11/18/99, effective 11/18/99; Final rule, 72 FR 20761, 4/26/2007, effective 4/26/2007; Final rule 76 FR 58137, 9/20/2011, effective 9/20/2011; Final rule, 77 FR 35879, 6/15/2012, effective 6/15/2012; Interim rule, 79 FR 61579, 10/14/2014, effective 10/14/2014; Final rule, 80 FR 15912, 3/26/2015, effective 3/26/2015]

219.704 Subcontracting plan requirements.

(1) In those subcontracting plans which specifically identify small businesses, prime contractors shall notify the administrative contracting officer of any substitutions of firms that are not small business firms, for the small business firms specifically identified in the subcontracting plan. Notifications shall be in writing and shall occur within a reasonable period of time after award of the subcontract. Contractor-specified formats shall be acceptable.

(2) See 215.304 for evaluation of offers in acquisitions that require a subcontracting plan.

[DAC 91-9, 60 FR 61586, 11/30/95, effective 11/30/95; Final rule, 61 FR 18686, 4/29/96, effective 4/29/96; Final rule, 72 FR 20761, 4/26/2007, effective 4/26/2007; Interim rule, 79 FR 61579, 10/14/2014, effective 10/14/2014; Final rule, 80 FR 15912, 3/26/2015, effective 3/26/2015]

219.705 Responsibilities of the contracting officer under the subcontracting assistance program. (No Text)

219.705-2 [Removed]

[DAC 91-6, 59 FR 27662, 5/27/94, effective 5/27/94; Final rule, 64 FR 51074, 9/21/99, effective 9/21/99; Final rule, 72 FR 20761, 4/26/2007, effective 4/26/2007]

219.705-4 Reviewing the subcontracting plan.

(d) (i) Challenge any subcontracting plan that does not contain positive goals. A small disadvantaged business goal of less than five percent must be approved one level above the contracting officer.

(ii) The contracting officer may use the checklist at PGI 219.705-4 when reviewing subcontracting plans in accordance with FAR 19.705-4.

[Interim rule, 63 FR 41972, 8/6/98, effective 10/1/98, finalized without change, 64 FR 52670 9/30/99; Final rule, 69 FR 67855, 11/22/2004, effective 11/22/2004; Interim rule, 79 FR 61579, 10/14/2014, effective 10/14/2014; Final rule, 80 FR 15912, 3/26/2015, effective 3/26/2015; Final rule, 82 FR 61479, 12/28/2017, effective 12/28/2017]

219.705-6 Postaward responsibilities of the contracting officer.

(f) See PGI 219.705-6(f) for guidance on reviewing subcontracting reports.

[Final rule, 82 FR 61479, 12/28/2017, effective 12/28/2017]

219.706 Responsibilities of the cognizant administrative contracting officer.

(a) (i) The contract administration office also is responsible for reviewing, evaluating, and approving master subcontracting plans.

(ii) The small business specialist supports the administrative contracting officer in evaluating a contractor's performance and compliance with its subcontracting plan.

219.708 Contract clauses.

(b) (1) (A) Use the basic, alternate I, or alternate II clause at 252.219-7003, Small

Business Subcontracting Plan (DoD Contracts), in solicitations and contracts, including solicitations and contracts using FAR part 12 procedures for the acquisition of commercial items, that contain the clause at FAR 52.219-9 Small Business Subcontracting Plan.

(*1*) Use the basic clause at 252.219–7003, when using the basic, alternate I, or alternate II of FAR 52.219-9.

(*2*) Use the alternate I clause at 252.219–7003, when using Alternate III ofFAR 52.219–9.

(B) In contracts with contractors that have comprehensive subcontracting plans approved under the Test Program described in 219.702-70, including contracts using FAR part 12 procedures for the acquisition of commercial items, use the clause at 252.219-7004, Small Business Subcontracting Plan (Test Program), instead of the clauses at 252.219-7003, Small Business Subcontracting Plan (DoD Contracts), FAR 52.219-9, Small Business Subcontracting Plan, and FAR 52.219-16, Liquidated Damages—Subcontracting Plan.

(*2*) However, also include in the prime contract, solely for the purpose of flowing the clauses down to subcontractors—

(*i*)FAR 52.219-9, Small Business Subcontracting Plan, and DFARS 252.219-7003; or

(*ii*) When the contract will not be reported in FPDS (see FAR 4.606(c)(5)), FAR clause FAR 52.219-9, Small Business Subcontracting Plan with its Alternate III and DFARS 252.219-7003, Small Business Subcontracting Plan (DoD Contracts), with its Alternate I.

(2) In contracts with contractors that have comprehensive subcontracting plans approved under the Test Program described in 219.702-70, do not use the clause at FAR 52.219-16, Liquidated Damages—Subcontracting Plan.

(3) Use the alternate II clause at 252.219–7003 when using the Demonstration Project described at 226.72.

(c)(1) Do not use the clause at FAR 52.219-10, Incentive Subcontracting Program, in contracts with contractors that have comprehensive subcontracting plans approved under the Test Program described in 219.702-70.

[DAC 91-1, 56 FR 67213, 12/30/91, effective 12/31/91; Interim rule, 61 FR 39900, 7/31/96, effective 7/31/96, finalized without change, DAC 91-12, 62 FR 34114, 6/24/97, effective 6/24/97; Interim rule, 63 FR 64427, 11/20/98, effective 1/1/99, finalized without change, 64 FR 52670, 9/30/99; Final rule, 65 FR 52951, 8/31/2000, effective 8/31/2000, corrected, 65 FR 58607, 9/29/2000; Final rule, 67 FR 49251, 7/30/2002, effective 7/30/2002; Final rule, 72 FR 20761, 4/26/2007, effective 4/26/2007; Final rule, 74 FR 34264, 7/15/2009, effective 7/15/2009; Interim rule, 75 FR 65439, 10/25/2010, effective 10/25/2010; Final rule, 78 FR 13546, 2/28/2013, effective 2/28/2013; Final rule, 78 FR 37980, 6/25/2013, effective 6/25/2013; Final rule, 81 FR 17045, 3/25/2016, effective 3/25/2016; Final rule, 83 FR 15996, 4/13/2018, effective 4/13/2018; Final rule, 84 FR 72554, 12/31/2019, effective 12/31/2019]

SUBPART 219.8—CONTRACTING WITH THE SMALL BUSINESS ADMINISTRATION (THE 8(A) PROGRAM)

219.800 General.

(a) By Partnership Agreement (PA) between the Small Business Administration (SBA) and the Department of Defense (DoD), the SBA has delegated to the Under Secretary of Defense (Acquisition, Technology, and Logistics) its authority under paragraph 8(a)(1)(A) of the Small Business Act (15 U.S.C. 637(a)) to enter into 8(a) prime contracts, and its authority under 8(a)(1)(B) of the Small Business Act to award the performance of those contracts to eligible 8(a) Program participants. However, the SBA remains the prime contractor on all 8(a) contracts, continues to determine eligibility of concerns for contract award, and retains appeal rights under FAR 19.810. The SBA delegates only the authority to sign contracts on its behalf. Consistent with the provisions of the PA, this authority is hereby redelegated to DoD contracting officers. A copy of the

PA, which includes the PA's expiration date, is available at PGI 219.800.

(b) Contracts awarded under the PA may be awarded directly to the 8(a) participant on either a sole source or competitive basis. An SBA signature on the contract is not required.

(c) Notwithstanding the PA, the contracting officer may elect to award a contract pursuant to the provisions of FAR Subpart 19.8.

[Interim rule, 67 FR 11435, 3/14/2002, effective 3/14/2002; Final rule, 67 FR 49255, 7/30/2002, effective 7/30/2002; Final rule, 69 FR 58353, 9/30/2004, effective 9/30/2004; Correction, 69 FR 59648, 10/5/2004; Final rule, 70 FR 35543, 6/21/2005, effective 6/21/2005; Final rule, 70 FR 57190, 9/30/2005, effective 9/30/2005; Final rule, 72 FR 20761, 4/26/2007, effective 4/26/2007]

219.803 Selecting acquisitions for the 8(a) Program.

When selecting acquisitions for the 8(a) Program, follow the procedures at PGI 219.803.

[Interim rule, 63 FR 41972, 8/6/98, effective 10/1/98, finalized without change, 64 FR 52670, 9/30/99; Final rule, 72 FR 20761, 4/26/2007, effective 4/26/2007]

219.804 Evaluation, offering, and acceptance.

When processing requirements under the PA, follow the procedures at PGI 219.804.

[Final rule, 72 FR 20761, 4/26/2007, effective 4/26/2007]

219.804-1 Agency evaluation.

(f) The 8(a) firms should be offered the opportunity to give a technical presentation.

[Interim rule, 63 FR 41972, 8/6/98, effective 10/1/98, finalized without change, 64 FR 52670, 9/30/99]

219.804-2 [Removed]

[Interim rule, 67 FR 11435, 3/14/2002, effective 3/14/2002; Final rule, 67 FR 49255, 7/30/2002, effective 7/30/2002; Final rule, 72 FR 20761, 4/26/2007, effective 4/26/2007]

219.804-3 [Removed]

[Interim rule, 63 FR 33586, 6/19/98, effective 6/19/98, finalized without change, 63 FR 64426, 11/20/98; Interim rule, 67 FR 11435, 3/14/2002, effective 3/14/2002; Final Rule, 67 FR 49255, 7/30/2002, effective 7/30/2002; Final rule, 72 FR 20761, 4/26/2007, effective 4/26/2007]

219.805 Competitive 8(a). (No Text)

219.805-1 General.

(b) (2) (A) For acquisitions that exceed the competitive threshold, the SBA also may accept the requirement for a sole source 8(a) award on behalf of a small business concern owned by a Native Hawaiian Organization (Section 8020 of Pub. L. 109-148).

(B) *Native Hawaiian Organization*, as used in this subsection and as defined by 15 U.S.C. 637(a)(15) and 13 CFR 124.3, means any community service organization serving Native Hawaiians in the State of Hawaii—

(1) That is a not-for-profit organization chartered by the State of Hawaii;

(2) That is controlled by Native Hawaiians; and

(3) Whose business activities will principally benefit such Native Hawaiians.

[Interim rule, 70 FR 43072, 7/26/2005, effective 7/26/2005; Final rule, 71 FR 34831, 6/16/2006, effective 6/16/2006]

219.805-2 Procedures.

When processing requirements under the PA, follow the procedures at PGI 219.805-2 for requesting eligibility determinations.

[Interim rule, 63 FR 33586, 6/19/98, effective 6/19/98, finalized without change, 63 FR 64426, 11/20/98; Interim rule, 67 FR 11435, 3/14/2002, effective 3/14/2002; Final rule, 67 FR 49255, 7/30/2002, effective 7/30/2002; Final rule, 72 FR 20761, 4/26/2007, effective 4/26/2007]

219.806 Pricing the 8(a) contract.

For requirements processed under the PA cited in 219.800—

(1) The contracting officer shall obtain certified cost or pricing data from the 8(a)

contractor, if required by FAR subpart 15.4; and

(2) SBA concurrence in the negotiated price is not required. However, except for purchase orders not exceeding the simplified acquisition threshold, the contracting officer shall notify the SBA prior to withdrawing a requirement from the 8(a) Program due to failure to agree on price or other terms and conditions.

[Interim rule, 63 FR 33586, 6/19/98, effective 6/19/98, finalized without change, 63 FR 64426, 11/20/98; Interim rule, 67 FR 11435, 3/14/2002, effective 3/14/2002; Final rule, 67 FR 49255, 7/30/2002, effective 7/30/2002; Final rule, 77 FR 76939, 12/31/2012, effective, 12/31/2012]

219.808 Contract negotiations. (No Text)

219.808-1 Sole source.

For sole source requirements processed under the PA, follow the procedures at PGI 219.808-1.

[Interim rule, 63 FR 33586, 6/19/98, effective 6/19/98, finalized without change, 63 FR 64426, 11/20/98; Interim rule, 67 FR 11435, 3/14/2002, effective 3/14/2002; Final Rule, 67 FR 49255, 7/30/2002, effective 7/30/2002; Final rule, 72 FR 20761, 4/26/2007, effective 4/26/2007]

219.811 Preparing the contracts.

When preparing awards under the PA, follow the procedures at PGI 219.811.

[Final rule, 72 FR 20761, 4/26/2007, effective 4/26/2007]

219.811-1 [Removed]

[Interim rule, 63 FR 33586, 6/19/98, effective 6/19/98, finalized without change, 63 FR 64426, 11/20/98; Interim rule, 67 FR 11435, 3/14/2002, effective 3/14/2002; Final rule, 67 FR 49255, 7/30/2002, effective 7/30/2002; Final rule, 72 FR 20761, 4/26/2007, effective 4/26/2007]

219.811-2 [Removed]

[Interim rule, 63 FR 33586, 6/19/98, effective 6/19/98, finalized without change, 63 FR 64426, 11/20/98; Interim rule, 67 FR 11435, 3/14/2002, effective 3/14/2002; Final rule, 67 FR 49255, 7/30/2002, effective 7/30/2002; Final rule, 72 FR 20761, 4/26/2007, effective 4/26/2007]

219.811-3 Contract clauses.

(1) Use the clause at 252.219-7009, Section 8(a) Direct Award, instead of the clauses at FAR 52.219-11, Special 8(a) Contract Conditions, FAR 52.219-12, Special 8(a) Subcontract Conditions, and FAR 52.219-17, Section 8(a) Award, in solicitations and contracts processed in accordance with the PA cited in 219.800.

(2) Use the clause at 252.219-7010, Notification of Competition Limited to Eligible 8(a) Participants—Partnership Agreement, in lieu of the clause at FAR 52.219-18, Notification of Competition Limited to Eligible 8(a) Participants, in competitive solicitations and contracts when the acquisition is accomplished using the procedures ofFAR 19.805 and processed in accordance with the PA cited in 219.800.

(3) Use the clause at 252.219-7011, Notification to Delay Performance, in solicitations and purchase orders issued under the PA cited in 219.800.

[Interim rule, 63 FR 33586, 6/19/98, effective 6/19/98, finalized without change, 63 FR 64426, 11/20/98; Interim rule, 67 FR 11435, 3/14/2002, effective 3/14/2002; Final Rule, 67 FR 49255, 7/30/2002, effective 7/30/2002; Final rule, 72 FR 20761, 4/26/2007, effective 4/26/2007; Final rule, 81 FR 17045, 3/25/2016, effective 3/25/2016; Final rule, 84 FR 58334, 10/31/2019, effective 10/31/2019]

219.812 [Removed]

[Interim rule, 63 FR 33586, 6/19/98, effective 6/19/98, finalized without change, 63 FR 64426, 11/20/98; Interim rule, 67 FR 11435, 3/14/2002, effective 3/14/2002; Final Rule, 67 FR 49255, 7/30/2002, effective 7/30/2002; Final rule, 72 FR 20761, 4/26/2007, effective 4/26/2007]

SUBPART 219.10—[REMOVED]

219.1005 [Removed]

[DAC 91-5, 58 FR 28458, 5/13/93, effective 4/30/93; DAC 91-6, 59 FR 27662,

5/27/94, effective 5/27/94; DAC 91-12, 62 FR 34114, 6/24/97, effective 6/24/97; Interim rule, 63 FR 41972, 8/6/98, effective 10/1/98, finalized without change, 64 FR 52670 9/30/99; Interim rule, 65 FR 50148, 8/17/2000, effective 10/1/2000, finalized without change, 65 FR 77831, 12/13/2000; Final rule, 66 FR 49860, 10/1/2001, effective 10/1/2001; Final rule, 68 FR 50476, 8/21/2003, effective 8/21/2003; Interim rule, 69 FR 31909, 6/8/2004, effective 6/8/2004; Final rule, 69 FR 67855, 11/22/2004, effective 11/22/2004; Final rule, 75 FR 45072, 8/2/2010, effective 10/1/2010; Final rule, 76 FR 9680 , 2/22/2011, effective 2/22/2011]

219.1007 [Removed]

[Final rule, 65 FR 39703, 6/27/2000, effective 6/27/2000; Final rule, 68 FR 7438, 2/14/2003, effective 2/14/2003; Final rule, 70 FR 6373, 2/7/2005, effective 2/7/2005; Final rule, 73 FR 46813, 8/12/2008, effective 8/12/2008; Final rule, 76 FR 9680 , 2/22/2011, effective 2/22/2011]

SUBPART 219.11—[REMOVED]

219.1101 [Removed]

[Final rule, 72 FR 20761, 4/26/2007, effective 4/26/2007; Interim rule, 79 FR 61579, 10/14/2014, effective 10/14/2014; Final rule, 80 FR 15912, 3/26/2015, effective 3/26/2015]

219.1102 [Removed]

[Interim rule, 63 FR 41972, 8/6/98, effective 10/1/98, finalized without change, 64 FR 52670 9/30/99; Interim rule, 71 FR 53042, 9/8/2006, effective 9/8/2006; Final rule, 72 FR 42313, 8/2/2007, effective 8/2/2007; Interim rule, 79 FR 61579, 10/14/2014, effective 10/14/2014; Final rule, 80 FR 15912, 3/26/2015, effective 3/26/2015]

SUBPART 219.12—[REMOVED]

219.1203 [Removed]

[Interim rule, 63 FR 64427, 11/20/98, effective 1/1/99, finalized without change, 64 FR 52670, 9/30/99; Interim rule, 65 FR 50148, 8/17/2000, effective 10/1/2000, finalized without change, 65 FR 77831, 12/13/2000; Interim rule, 79 FR 61579, 10/14/2014, effective 10/14/2014; Final rule, 80 FR 15912, 3/26/2015, effective 3/26/2015]

219.1204 [Removed]

[Interim rule, 63 FR 64427, 11/20/98, effective 1/1/99, finalized without change, 64 FR 55632, 10/14/99; Final rule, 74 FR 34264, 7/15/2009, effective 7/15/2009; Interim rule, 79 FR 61579, 10/14/2014, effective 10/14/2014; Final rule, 80 FR 15912, 3/26/2015, effective 3/26/2015]

SUBPART 219.13—HISTORICALLY UNDERUTILIZED BUSINESS ZONE (HUBZONE) PROGRAM

219.1307 Price evaluation preference for HUBZone small business concerns.

(a) Also, do not use the price evaluation preference in acquisitions that use tiered evaluation of offers, until a tier is reached that considers offers from other than small business concerns.

[Interim rule, 71 FR 53042, 9/8/2006, effective 9/8/2006; Final rule, 72 FR 42313, 8/2/2007, effective 8/2/2007]

SUBPART 219.70—[RESERVED]

[Removed and reserved, Interim rule, 63 FR 41972, 8/6/98, effective 10/1/98, finalized without change, 64 FR 52670, 9/30/99]

SUBPART 219.71—PILOT MENTOR-PROTEGE PROGRAM

219.7100 Scope.

This subpart implements the Pilot Mentor-Protege Program (hereafter referred to as the "Program") established under section 831 of the National Defense Authorization Act for Fiscal Year 1991 (Public Law 101-510; 10 U.S.C. 2302 note), as amended through December 23, 2016. The purpose of the Program is to provide incentives for DoD contractors to assist protege firms in enhancing their capabilities and to increase participation of such firms in Government and commercial contracts.

[Interim rule, 66 FR 47108, 9/11/2001, effective 9/11/2001, finalized without change, 67 FR 11435, 3/14/2002, effective

3/14/2002; Final rule, 69 FR 74995, 12/15/2004, effective 12/15/2004; Final rule, 83 FR 12682, 3/23/2018, effective 3/23/2018; Final rule, 83 FR 54677, 10/31/2018, effective 10/31/2018]

219.7101 Policy.

DoD policy and procedures for implementation of the Program are contained in Appendix I, Policy and Procedures for the DoD Pilot Mentor-Protege Program.

[Interim rule, 65 FR 6554, 2/10/2000, effective 2/10/2000, finalized without change, 65 FR 50149, 8/17/2000]

219.7102 General.

The Program includes—

(a) Mentor firms and protégé firms that meet the criteria in Appendix I, section I-102.

(b) Mentor-protege agreements that establish a developmental assistance program for a protege firm.

(c) Incentives that DoD may provide to mentor firms, including—

(1) Reimbursement for developmental assistance costs through—

(i) A separately priced contract line item on a DoD contract; or

(ii) A separate contract, upon written determination by the cognizant Component Director, Small Business Programs (SBP), that unusual circumstances justify reimbursement using a separate contract; or

(2) Credit toward applicable subcontracting goals, established under a subcontracting plan negotiated under FAR subpart 19.7 or under the DoD Comprehensive Subcontracting Test Program, for developmental assistance costs that are not reimbursed.

[Interim rule, 65 FR 6554, 2/10/2000, effective 2/10/2000, corrected 65 FR 30191, 5/10/2000, finalized without change, 65 FR 50149, 8/17/2000; Interim rule, 66 FR 47108, 9/11/2001, effective 9/11/2001, finalized without change, 67 FR 11435, 3/14/2002, effective 3/14/2002; Final rule, 69 FR 74995, 12/15/2004, effective 12/15/2004; Interim rule, 70 FR 29644, 5/24/2005, effective 5/24/2005; Final rule, 71 FR 3414, 1/23/2006, effective 1/23/2006; Final rule, 73 FR 46813, 8/12/2008, effective 8/12/2008; Final rule, 83 FR 12682, 3/23/2018, effective 3/23/2018]

219.7103 Procedures. (No Text)

219.7103-1 General.

The procedures for application, acceptance, and participation in the Program are in Appendix I, Policy and Procedures for the DoD Pilot Mentor-Protege Program. The Director, SBP, of each military department or defense agency has the authority to approve contractors as mentor firms, approve mentor-protege agreements, and forward approved mentor-protege agreements to the contracting officer when funding is available.

[Interim rule, 65 FR 6554, 2/10/2000, effective 2/10/2000, finalized without change, 65 FR 50149, 8/17/2000; Final rule, 69 FR 74995, 12/15/2004, effective 12/15/2004; Final rule, 73 FR 46813, 8/12/2008, effective 8/12/2008]

219.7103-2 Contracting officer responsibilities.

Contracting officers must—

(a) Negotiate an advance agreement on the treatment of developmental assistance costs for either credit or reimbursement if the mentor firm proposes such an agreement, or delegate authority to negotiate to the administrative contracting officer (see FAR 31.109).

(b) Modify (without consideration) applicable contract(s) to incorporate the clause at 252.232-7005, Reimbursement of Subcontractor Advance Payments—DoD Pilot Mentor-Protege Program, when a mentor firm provides advance payments to a protege firm under the Program and the mentor firm requests reimbursement of advance payments.

(c) Modify (without consideration) applicable contract(s) to incorporate other than customary progress payments for protege firms in accordance with FAR 32.504(c) if a mentor firm provides such payments to a protege firm and the mentor firm requests reimbursement.

(d) Modify applicable contract(s) to establish a contract line item for reimbursement of developmental assistance costs if—

(1) A DoD program manager or the cognizant Component Director, SBP, has made funds available for that purpose; and

(2) The contractor has an approved mentor-protege agreement.

(e) Negotiate and award a separate contract for reimbursement of developmental assistance costs only if—

(1) Funds are available for that purpose;

(2) The contractor has an approved mentor-protege agreement; and

(3) The cognizant Component Director, SBP, has made a determination in accordance with 219.7102(c)(1)(ii).

(f) Not authorize reimbursement for costs of assistance furnished to a protege firm in excess of $1,000,000 in a fiscal year unless a written determination from the cognizant Component Director, SBP, is obtained.

(g) Advise contractors of reporting requirements in Appendix I.

(h) Provide a copy of the approved Mentor-Protege agreement to the Defense Contract Management Agency administrative contracting officer responsible for conducting the annual performance review (see Appendix I, Section I-113).

[Interim rule, 65 FR 6554, 2/10/2000, effective 2/10/2000, corrected 65 FR 30191, 5/10/2000; Final rule, 65 FR 50149, 8/17/2000, effective 8/17/2000; Interim rule, 66 FR 47108, 9/11/2001, effective 9/11/2001, finalized without change, 67 FR 11435, 3/14/2002, effective 3/14/2002; Final rule, 69 FR 74995, 12/15/2004, effective 12/15/2004; Final rule, 73 FR 46813, 8/12/2008, effective 8/12/2008; Final rule, 83 FR 12682, 3/23/2018, effective 3/23/2018]

219.7104 Developmental assistance costs eligible for reimbursement or credit.

(a) Developmental assistance provided under an approved mentor-protege agreement is distinct from, and must not duplicate, any effort that is the normal and expected product of the award and administration of the mentor firm's subcontracts. The mentor firm must accumulate and charge costs associated with the latter in accordance with its approved accounting practices. Mentor firm costs that are eligible for reimbursement are set forth in Appendix I.

(b) Before incurring any costs under the Program, mentor firms must establish the accounting treatment of developmental assistance costs eligible for reimbursement or credit. To be eligible for reimbursement under the Program, the mentor firm must incur the costs not later than September 30, 2021.

(c) If the mentor firm is suspended or debarred while performing under an approved mentor-protege agreement, the mentor firm may not be reimbursed or credited for developmental assistance costs incurred more than 30 days after the imposition of the suspension or debarment.

(d) Developmental assistance costs incurred by a mentor firm not later than September 30, 2021, that are eligible for crediting under the Program, may be credited toward subcontracting plan goals as set forth in Appendix I.

[Interim rule, 65 FR 6554, 2/10/2000, effective 2/10/2000, corrected 65 FR 30191, 5/10/2000, finalized without change, 65 FR 50149, 8/17/2000; Final rule, 67 FR 77936, 12/20/2002, effective 12/20/2002; Interim rule, 70 FR 29644, 5/24/2005, effective 5/24/2005; Final rule, 71 FR 3414, 1/23/2006, effective 1/23/2006; Final rule, 76 FR 71467, 11/18/2011, effective 11/18/2011; Final rule, 77 FR 11367, 2/24/2012, effective 2/24/2012; Final rule, 83 FR 12682, 3/23/2018, effective 3/23/2018]

219.7105 Reporting.

Mentor and protege firms must report on the progress made under mentor-protege agreements as indicated in Appendix I, Section I-112.

[Interim rule, 65 FR 6554, 2/10/2000, effective 2/10/2000, finalized without change, 65 FR 50149, 8/17/2000; Final rule, 69 FR 74995, 12/15/2004, effective 12/15/2004]

219.7106 Performance reviews.

The Defense Contract Management Agency will conduct annual performance reviews of all mentor-protege agreements as indicated in Appendix I, Section I-113. The determinations made in these reviews should be a major factor in determinations of amounts of reimbursement, if any, that the mentor firm is eligible to receive in the remaining years of the Program participation term under the agreement.

[Final rule 65 FR 50149, 8/17/2000, effective 8/17/2000; Final rule, 69 FR 74995, 12/15/2004, effective 12/15/2004]

PART 220—[NO FAR SUPPLEMENT]

PART 221—[NO FAR SUPPLEMENT]

PART 222—APPLICATION OF LABOR LAWS TO GOVERNMENT ACQUISITIONS

Table of Contents

Definitions 222.001

Subpart 222.1—Basic Labor Policies

Labor relations 222.101
General 222.101-1
Reporting labor disputes 222.101-3
Impact of labor disputes on defense programs 222.101-3-70
Removal of items from contractors' facilities affected by work stoppages 222.101-4
Acquisition of stevedoring services during labor disputes 222.101-70
Federal and State labor requirements 222.102
Policy 222.102-1
Overtime 222.103
Approvals 222.103-4

Subpart 222.3—Contract Work Hours and Safety Standards

Liquidated damages and overtime pay 222.302

Subpart 222.4—Labor Standards for Contracts Involving Construction

Applicability 222.402
Installation support contracts 222.402-70
Statutory and regulatory requirements 222.403
Department of Labor regulations 222.403-4
Construction Wage Rate Requirements statute wage determinations 222.404
General requirements 222.404-2
Administration and enforcement 222.406
Policy 222.406-1
Payrolls and statements 222.406-6
Investigations 222.406-8
Withholding from or suspension of contract payments 222.406-9
Disposition of disputes concerning construction contract labor standards enforcement 222.406-10
Semiannual enforcement reports 222.406-13

Subpart 222.6—Contracts for Materials, Supplies, Articles, and Equipment Exceeding $15,000

Exemptions 222.604
Regulatory exemptions 222.604-2

Subpart 222.8—Equal Employment Opportunity

Inquiries 222.806
Exemptions 222.807

Subpart 222.10—Service Contract Labor Standards

Applicability 222.1003
General 222.1003-1

Procedures for obtaining wage determinations 222.1008
Obtaining wage determinations 222.1008-1
[Removed] 222.1008-2
[Removed] 222.1008-7
[Removed] 222.1014

Subpart 222.13—Equal Opportunity for Veterans

Waivers 222.1305
Complaint procedures 222.1308
Solicitation provision and contract clauses 222.1310

Subpart 222.14—Employment of Workers with Disabilities

Waivers 222.1403
Complaint procedures 222.1406

Subpart 222.17—Combating Trafficking in Persons

[Removed] 222.1700
[Removed] 222.1701
[Removed] 222.1702
Policy 222.1703
Violations and remedies 222.1704
[Removed] 222.1704-70
[Removed] 222.1705
Procedures 222.1770
[Removed] 222.1771

Subpart 222.70—Restrictions on the Employment of Personnel for Work on Construction and Service Contracts in Noncontiguous States

Scope of subpart 222.7000
Definition 222.7001
General 222.7002
Waivers 222.7003
Contract clause 222.7004

Subpart 222.71—[Removed and Reserved]

Subpart 222.72—Compliance with Labor Laws of Foreign Governments

Contract clauses 222.7201

Subpart 222.73—Limitations Applicable to Contracts Performed on Guam

Scope of subpart 222.7300
Prohibition on use of nonimmigrant aliens 222.7301
Contract clause 222.7302
[Removed] 222.7303

Subpart 222.74—Restrictions on the Use of Mandatory Arbitration Agreements

Scope of subpart 222.7400
Definition 222.7401
Policy 222.7402
Applicability 222.7403

Waiver 222.7404
Contract clause 222.7405

PART 222—APPLICATION OF LABOR LAWS TO GOVERNMENT ACQUISITIONS

222.001 Definition.

Labor advisor, as used in this part, means the departmental or agency headquarters labor advisor.

[Final rule, 72 FR 20763, 4/26/2007, effective 4/26/2007]

SUBPART 222.1—BASIC LABOR POLICIES

222.101 Labor Relations. (No Text)

222.101-1 General.

Follow the procedures at PGI 222.101-1 for referral of labor relations matters to the appropriate authorities.

[Final rule, 71 FR 18669, 4/12/2006, effective 4/12/2006]

222.101-3 Reporting labor disputes.

Follow the procedures at PGI 222.101-3 for reporting labor disputes.

[Final rule, 64 FR 28109, 5/25/99, effective 5/25/99; Final rule, 71 FR 18669, 4/12/2006, effective 4/12/2006; Final rule, 71 FR 27643, 5/12/2006, effective 5/12/2006]

222.101-3-70 Impact of labor disputes on defense programs.

(a) Each department and agency shall determine the degree of impact of potential or actual labor disputes on its own programs and requirements. For guidance on determining the degree of impact, see PGI 222.101-3-70 (a).

(b) Each contracting activity shall obtain and develop data reflecting the impact of a labor dispute on its requirements and programs. Upon determining that the impact of the labor dispute is significant, the head of the contracting activity shall submit a report of findings and recommendations to the labor advisor in accordance with departmental procedures.

[Final rule, 64 FR 28109, 5/25/99, effective 5/25/99; Final rule, 65 FR 52951, 8/31/2000, effective 8/31/2000, Final rule, 71 FR 18669, 4/12/2006, effective 4/12/2006; Final rule, 80 FR 67254, 10/30/2015, effective 10/30/2015]

222.101-4 Removal of items from contractors' facilities affected by work stoppages.

(a) When a contractor is unable to deliver urgent and critical items because of a work stoppage at its facility, the contracting officer, before removing any items from the facility, shall—

(i) Before initiating any action, contact the labor advisor to obtain the opinion of the national office of the Federal Mediation and Conciliation Service or other mediation agency regarding the effect movement of the items would have on labor negotiations. Normally removals will not be made if they will adversely affect labor negotiations.

(ii) Upon the recommendation of the labor advisor, provide a written request for removal of the material to the cognizant contract administration office. Include in the request the information specified at PGI 222.101-4 (a) (ii).

(iii) With the assistance of the labor advisor or the commander of the contract administration office, attempt to have both the management and the labor representatives involved agree to shipment of the material by normal means.

(iv) If agreement for removal of the needed items cannot be reached following the procedures in paragraphs (a) (i) through (iii) of this subsection, the commander of the contract administration office, after obtaining approval from the labor advisor, may seek the concurrence of the parties to the dispute to permit movement of the material by military vehicles with military personnel. On receipt of such concurrences, the commander may proceed to make necessary arrangements to move the material.

(v) If agreement for removal of the needed items cannot be reached following any of the procedures in paragraphs (a) (i) through (iv) of this subsection, refer the matter to the labor advisor with the information required by 222.101-3-70(b). If the labor advisor is unsuccessful in obtaining concurrence of the parties for the movement of the material and further action to obtain the material is deemed necessary, refer the matter to the agency head. Upon review and verification that the items are urgently or critically needed and cannot be moved with the consent of the parties, the agency head, on a nondelegable basis, may order removal of the items from the facility.

[Final rule, 71 FR 18669, 4/12/2006, effective 4/12/2006]

222.101-70 Acquisition of stevedoring services during labor disputes.

(a) Use the following procedures only in the order listed when a labor dispute delays performance of a contract for stevedoring services which are urgently needed.

(1) Attempt to have management and labor voluntarily agree to exempt military supplies from the labor dispute by continuing the movement of such material.

(2) Divert vessels to alternate ports able to provide necessary stevedoring services.

(3) Consider contracting with reliable alternative sources of supply within the stevedoring industry.

(4) Utilize civil service stevedores to perform the work performed by contract stevedores.

(5) Utilize military personnel to handle the cargo which was being handled by contract stevedores prior to the labor dispute.

(b) Notify the labor advisor when a deviation from the procedures in paragraph (a) of this subsection is required.

222.102 Federal and State labor requirements. (No Text)

222.102-1 Policy.

(1) Direct all inquiries from contractors or contractor employees regarding the applicability or interpretation of Occupational Safety and Health Act (OSHA) regulations to the Department of Labor.

(2) Upon request, provide the address of the appropriate field office of the Occupational Safety and Health Administration of the Department of Labor.

(3) Do not initiate any application for the suspension or relaxation of labor requirements without prior coordination with the labor advisor. Any requests for variances or alternative means of compliance with OSHA requirements must be approved by the Occupational Safety and Health Administration of the Department of Labor.

[Final rule, 71 FR 18669, 4/12/2006, effective 4/12/2006]

222.103 Overtime. (No Text)

222.103-4 Approvals.

(a) The department/agency approving official shall—

(i) Obtain the concurrence of other appropriate approving officials; and

(ii) Seek agreement as to the contracts under which overtime premiums will be approved when—

(A) Two or more contracting offices have current contracts at the same contractor facility; and

(B) The approval of overtime by one contracting office will affect the performance or cost of contracts of another office. In the absence of evidence to the contrary, a contracting officer may rely on a contractor's statement that approval of overtime premium pay for one contract will not affect performance or payments under any other contract.

SUBPART 222.3—CONTRACT WORK HOURS AND SAFETY STANDARDS

222.302 Liquidated damages and overtime pay.

Upon receipt of notification of Contract Work Hours and Safety Standards violations, the contracting officer shall—

(1) Immediately withhold such funds as are available;

(2) Give the contractor written notification of the withholding and a statement of the basis for the liquidated damages assessment. The written notification shall also inform the contractor of its 60 days right to appeal the assessment, through the contracting officer, to the agency official responsible for acting on such appeals; and

(3) If funds available for withholding are insufficient to cover liquidated damages, ask the contractor to pay voluntarily such funds

as are necessary to cover the total liquidated damage assessment.

(d) (i) The assessment shall become the final administrative determination of contractor liability for liquidated damages when—

(A) The contractor fails to appeal to the contracting agency within 60 days from the date of the withholding of funds;

(B) The department agency, following the contractor's appeals, issues a final order which affirms the assessment of liquidated damages or waives damages of $500 or less; or

(C) The Secretary of Labor takes final action on a recommendation of the agency head to waive or adjust liquidated damages in excess of $500.

(ii) Upon final administrative determination of the contractor's liability for liquidated damages, the contracting officer shall transmit withheld or collected funds determined to be owed the Government as liquidated damages to the servicing finance and accounting officer for crediting to the appropriate Government Treasury account. The contracting officer shall return any excess withheld funds to the contractor.

[Final rule, 77 FR 35879, 6/15/2012, effective 6/15/2012]

SUBPART 222.4—LABOR STANDARDS FOR CONTRACTS INVOLVING CONSTRUCTION

222.402 Applicability. (No Text)

222.402-70 Installation support contracts.

(a) Apply both the Service Contract Labor Standards statute and the Construction Wage Rate Requirements statute to installation support contracts if—

(1) The contract is principally for services but also requires a substantial and segregable amount of construction, alteration, renovation, painting, or repair work; and

(2) The aggregate dollar value of such construction work exceeds or is expected to exceed $2,000.

(b) *Service Contract Labor Standards statute coverage under the contract.* Contract installation support requirements, such as plant operation and installation services (i.e., custodial, snow removal, etc.) are subject to the Service Contract Labor Standards. Apply Service Contract Labor Standards clauses and minimum wage and fringe benefit requirements to all contract service calls or orders for such maintenance and support work.

(c) *Construction Wage Rate Requirements statute coverage under the contract.* Contract construction, alteration, renovation, painting, and repair requirements (i.e., roof shingling, building structural repair, paving repairs, etc.) are subject to the Construction Wage Rate Requirements statute. Apply Construction Wage Rate Requirements clauses and minimum wage requirements to all contract service calls or orders for construction, alteration, renovation, painting, or repairs to buildings or other works.

(d) *Repairs versus maintenance.* Some contract work may be characterized as either Construction Wage Rate Requirements painting/repairs or Service Contract Labor Standards maintenance. For example, replacing broken windows, spot painting, or minor patching of a wall could be covered by either the Construction Wage Rate Requirements or the Service Contract Labor Standards. In those instances where a contract service call or order requires construction trade skills (i.e., carpenter, plumber, painter, etc.), but it is unclear whether the work required is Service Contract Labor Standards maintenance or Construction Wage Rate Requirements painting/repairs, apply the following rules:

(1) Individual service calls or orders which will require a total of 32 or more work hours to perform shall be considered to be repair work subject to the Construction Wage Rate Requirements.

(2) Individual service calls or orders which will require less than 32 work hours to perform shall be considered to be maintenance subject to the Service Contract Labor Standards.

(3) Painting work of 200 square feet or more to be performed under an individual service call or order shall be considered to be subject to the Construction Wage Rate

Requirements statute regardless of the total work hours required.

(e) The determination of labor standards application shall be made at the time the solicitation is prepared in those cases where requirements can be identified. Otherwise, the determination shall be made at the time the service call or order is placed against the contract. The service call or order shall identify the labor standards law and contract wage determination which will apply to the work required.

(f) Contracting officers may not avoid application of the Construction Wage Rate Requirements statute by splitting individual tasks between orders or contracts.

[Final rule, 77 FR 35879, 6/15/2012, effective 6/15/2012]

222.403 Statutory and regulatory requirements. (No Text)

222.403-4 Department of Labor regulations.

Direct all questions regarding Department of Labor regulations to the labor advisor.

222.404 Construction Wage Rate Requirements statute wage determinations.

Not later than April 1 of each year, each department and agency shall furnish the Administrator, Wage and Hour Division, with a general outline of its proposed construction program for the coming fiscal year. The Department of Labor uses this information to determine where general wage determination surveys will be conducted.

(1) Indicate by individual project of $500,000 or more—

(i) The anticipated type of construction;

(ii) The estimated dollar value; and

(iii) The location in which the work is to be performed (city, town, village, county, or other civil subdivision of the state).

(2) The report format is contained in Department of Labor All Agency Memo 144, December 27, 1985.

(3) The report control number is 1671-DOL-AN.

[Final rule, 77 FR 35879, 6/15/2012, effective 6/15/2012]

222.404-2 General requirements.

(c)(5) Follow the procedures at PGI 222.404-2(c)(5) when seeking clarification of the proper application of construction wage rate schedules.

[Final rule, 71 FR 18669, 4/12/2006, effective 4/12/2006; Final rule, 72 FR 20763, 4/26/2007, effective 4/26/2007]

222.404-3 [Removed]

[Final rule, 71 FR 18669, 4/12/2006, effective 4/12/2006]

222.404-11 [Removed]

[Final rule, 71 FR 18669, 4/12/2006, effective 4/12/2006]

222.406 Administration and enforcement. (No Text)

222.406-1 Policy.

(a) *General.* The program shall also include—

(i) Training appropriate contract administration, labor relations, inspection, and other labor standards enforcement personnel in their responsibilities; and

(ii) Periodic review of field enforcement activities to ensure compliance with applicable regulations and instructions.

(b) *Preconstruction letters and conferences.*

(1) Promptly after award of the contract, the contracting officer shall provide a preconstruction letter to the prime contractor. This letter should accomplish the following, as appropriate—

(A) Indicate that the labor standards requirements contained in the contract are based on the following statutes and regulations—

(1) Construction Wage Rate Requirements statute;

(2) Contract Work Hours and Safety Standards statute;

(3) Copeland (Anti-Kickback) Act;

(4) Parts 3 and 5 of the Secretary of Labor's Regulations (parts 3 and 5, subtitle A, title 29, CFR); and

(5) Executive Order 11246 (Equal Employment Opportunity);

(B) Call attention to the labor standards requirements in the contract which relate to—

(1) Employment of foremen, laborers, mechanics, and others;

(2) Wages and fringe benefits payments, payrolls, and statements;

(3) Differentiation between subcontractors and suppliers;

(4) Additional classifications;

(5) Benefits to be realized by contractors and subcontractors in keeping complete work records;

(6) Penalties and sanctions for violations of the labor standards provisions; and

(7) The applicable provisions of FAR 22.403; and

(C) Ensure that the contractor sends a copy of the preconstruction letter to each subcontractor.

(2) Before construction begins, the contracting officer shall confer with the prime contractor and any subcontractor designated by the prime to emphasize their labor standards obligations under the contract when—

(A) The prime contractor has not performed previous Government contracts;

(B) The prime contractor experienced difficulty in complying with labor standards requirements on previous contracts; or

(C) It is necessary to determine whether the contractor and its subcontractors intend to pay any required fringe benefits in the manner specified in the wage determination or to elect a different method of payment. If the latter, inform the contractor of the requirements of FAR 22.406-2.

[Final rule, 77 FR 35879, 6/15/2012, effective 6/15/2012]

222.406-6 Payrolls and statements.

(a) *Submission.* Contractors who do not use Department of Labor Form WH 347 or its equivalent must submit a DD Form 879, Statement of Compliance, with each payroll report.

222.406-8 Investigations.

(a) Before beginning an investigation, the investigator shall inform the contractor of the general scope of the investigation, and that the investigation will include examining pertinent records and interviewing employees. In conducting the investigation, follow the procedures at PGI 222.406-8 (a).

(c) *Contractor notification.*

(4) (A) Notify the contractor by certified mail of any finding that it is liable for liquidated damages under the Contract Work Hours and Safety Standards (CWHSS) statute. The notification shall inform the contractor that—

(*1*) It has 60 days after receipt of the notice to appeal the assessment of liquidated damages; and

(*2*) The appeal must demonstrate either that the alleged violations did not occur at all, occurred inadvertently notwithstanding the exercise of due care, or the assessment was computed improperly.

(B) If an appeal is received, the contracting officer shall process the appeal in accordance with department or agency regulations.

(d) *Contracting officer's report.*

Forward a detailed enforcement report or summary report to the agency head in accordance with agency procedures. Include in the report, as a minimum, the information specified at PGI 222.406-8(d).

[Final rule, 71 FR 18669, 4/12/2006, effective 4/12/2006; Final rule, 77 FR 35879, 6/15/2012, effective 6/15/2012]

222.406-9 Withholding from or suspension of contract payments.

(a) *Withholding from contract payments.* The contracting officer shall contact the labor advisor for assistance when payments due a contractor are not available to satisfy that contractor's liability for Construction Wage Rate Requirements or CWHSS statute wage underpayments or liquidated damages.

(c) *Disposition of contract payments withheld or suspended.*

(3) *Limitation on forwarding or returning funds.* When disposition of withheld funds

remains the final action necessary to close out a contract, the Department of Labor will retain withheld funds pending completion of an investigation or other administrative proceedings.

(4) *Liquidated damages.*

(A) The agency head may adjust liquidated damages of $500 or less when the amount assessed is incorrect or waive the assessment when the violations—

(*1*) Were nonwillful or inadvertent; and

(*2*) Occurred notwithstanding the exercise of due care by the contractor, its subcontractor, or their agents.

(B) The agency head may recommend to the Administrator, Wage and Hour Division, that the liquidated damages over $500 be adjusted because the amount assessed is incorrect. The agency head may also recommend the assessment be waived when the violations—

(*1*) Were nonwillful or inadvertent; and

(*2*) Occurred notwithstanding the exercise of due care by the contractor, the subcontractor, or their agents.

[Final rule, 77 FR 35879, 6/15/2012, effective 6/15/2012; Final rule, 82 FR 61479, 12/28/2017, effective 12/28/2017]

222.406-10 Disposition of disputes concerning construction contract labor standards enforcement.

(d) Forward the contracting officer's findings and the contractor's statement through the labor advisor.

222.406-13 Semiannual enforcement reports.

Forward these reports through the head of the contracting activity to the labor advisor within 15 days following the end of the reporting period. These reports shall not include information from investigations conducted by the Department of Labor. These reports shall contain the following information, as applicable, for construction work subject to the Construction Wage Rate Requirements statute and the CWSS statute—

(1) Period covered;

(2) Number of prime contracts awarded;

(3) Total dollar amount of prime contracts awarded;

(4) Number of contractors/subcontractors against whom complaints were received;

(5) Number of investigations conducted;

(6) Number of contractors/subcontractors found in violation;

(7) Amount of wage restitution found due under—

(i) Construction Wage Rate Requirements statute; and

(ii) CWSS statute;

(8) Number of employees due wage restitution under—

(i) Construction Wage Rate Requirements statute; and

(ii) CWHSS statute;

(9) Amount of liquidated damages assessed under the CWSS—

(i) Total amount;

(ii) Number of contracts involved;

(10) Number of employees and amount paid/withheld under—

(i) Construction Wage Rate Requirements statute;

(ii) CWSS statute;

(iii) Copeland Act; and

(11) Preconstruction activities—

(i) Number of compliance checks performed

(ii) Preconstruction letters sent.

[Final rule, 77 FR 35879, 6/15/2012, effective 6/15/2012]

222.407 [Removed]

[Final rule, 71 FR 18669, 4/12/2006, effective 4/12/2006]

SUBPART 222.6—CONTRACTS FOR MATERIALS, SUPPLIES, ARTICLES,

AND EQUIPMENT EXCEEDING $15,000

222.604 Exemptions. (No Text)

222.604-2 Regulatory exemptions.

(b) Submit all applications for such exemptions through contracting channels to the labor advisor.

[Final rule, 65 FR 14397, 3/16/2000, effective 3/16/2000]

SUBPART 222.8—EQUAL EMPLOYMENT OPPORTUNITY

222.804 [Removed]

[Final rule, 71 FR 18669, 4/12/2006, effective 4/12/2006]

222.804-2 [Removed]

[Final rule, 71 FR 18669, 4/12/2006, effective 4/12/2006]

222.805 [Removed]

[Final rule, 71 FR 18669, 4/12/2006, effective 4/12/2006]

222.806 Inquiries.

(b) Refer inquiries through the labor advisor.

222.807 Exemptions.

(c) Follow the procedures at PGI 222.807 (c) when submitting a request for an exemption.

[Final rule, 71 FR 18669, 4/12/2006, effective 4/12/2006]

SUBPART 222.10—SERVICE CONTRACT LABOR STANDARDS

222.1003 Applicability. (No Text)

222.1003-1 General.

For contracts having a substantial amount of construction, alteration, renovation, painting, or repair work, see 222.402-70.

222.1003-7 [Removed]

[Final rule, 71 FR 18669, 4/12/2006, effective 4/12/2006]

222.1008 Procedures for obtaining wage determinations. (No Text)

[Final rule, 72 FR 20763, 4/26/2007, effective 4/26/2007]

222.1008-1 Obtaining wage determinations.

Follow the procedures at PGI 222.1008-1 regarding use of the Service Contract Act Directory of Occupations when preparing the e98.

[Final rule, 72 FR 20763, 4/26/2007, effective 4/26/2007]

222.1008-2 [Removed]

[Final rule, 71 FR 18669, 4/12/2006, effective 4/12/2006; Final rule, 72 FR 20763, 4/26/2007, effective 4/26/2007]

222.1008-7 [Removed]

[Final rule, 72 FR 20763, 4/26/2007, effective 4/26/2007]

222.1014 [Removed]

[Final rule, 71 FR 18669, 4/12/2006, effective 4/12/2006; Final rule, 72 FR 20763, 4/26/2007, effective 4/26/2007]

SUBPART 222.13—EQUAL OPPORTUNITY FOR VETERANS

222.1303 [Removed]

[Final rule, 71 FR 18669, 4/12/2006, effective 4/12/2006]

222.1304 [Removed]

[Removed by 67 FR 4208, 1/29/2002, effective 1/29/2002]

222.1305 Waivers.

(c) Follow the procedures at PGI 222.1305(c) for submission of waiver requests.

[Final rule, 71 FR 18669, 4/12/2006, effective 4/12/2006]

222.1306 [Removed]

[Final rule, 71 FR 18669, 4/12/2006, effective 4/12/2006]

222.1308 Complaint procedures.

The contracting officer shall—

(1) Forward each complaint received as indicated in FAR 22.1308; and

(2) Notify the complainant of the referral. The contractor in question shall not be advised in any manner or for any reason of the complainant's name, the nature of the complaint, or the fact that the complaint was received.

[DAC 91-5, 58 FR 28458, 5/13/93, effective 4/30/93; Final rule, 71 FR 18669, 4/12/2006, effective 4/12/2006]

222.1310 Solicitation provision and contract clauses.

(a) (1) Use of the clause at FAR 52.222-35, Equal Opportunity for Veterans, with its paragraph (c), Listing Openings, also satisfies the requirement of 10 U.S.C. 2410k.

[Final rule, 71 FR 18669, 4/12/2006, effective 4/12/2006; Final rule, 80 FR 67254, 10/30/2015, effective 10/30/2015]

SUBPART 222.14—EMPLOYMENT OF WORKERS WITH DISABILITIES

222.1403 Waivers.

(c) The contracting officer shall submit a waiver request through contracting channels to the labor advisor. If the request is justified, the labor advisor will endorse the request and forward it for action to—

(i) The agency head for waivers under FAR 22.1403(a). For the defense agencies, waivers must be approved by the Under Secretary of Defense for Acquisition.

(ii) The Secretary of Defense, without the power of redelegation, for waivers under FAR 22.1403(b).

222.1406 Complaint procedures.

The contracting officer shall notify the complainant of such referral. The contractor in question shall not be advised in any manner or for any reason of the complainant's name, the nature of the complaint, or the fact that the complaint was received.

[Final rule, 71 FR 18669, 4/12/2006, effective 4/12/2006]

SUBPART 222.17—COMBATING TRAFFICKING IN PERSONS

222.1700 [Removed]

[Interim rule, 71 FR 62560, 10/26/2006, effective 10/26/2006; Final rule, 73 FR 4115, 1/24/2008, effective 1/24/2008]

222.1701 [Removed]

[Interim rule, 71 FR 62560, 10/26/2006, effective 10/26/2006; Final rule, 73 FR 4115, 1/24/2008, effective 1/24/2008]

222.1702 [Removed]

[Interim rule, 71 FR 62560, 10/26/2006, effective 10/26/2006; Final rule, 73 FR 4115, 1/24/2008, effective 1/24/2008]

222.1703 Policy.

See PGI 222.1703 for additional information regarding DoD policy for combating trafficking in persons outside the United States.

[Interim rule, 71 FR 62560, 10/26/2006, effective 10/26/2006; Final rule, 73 FR 4115, 1/24/2008, effective 1/24/2008]

222.1704 Violations and remedies.

Follow the procedures at PGI 222.1704 for notifying the Combatant Commander if a violation occurs.

[Interim rule, 71 FR 62560, 10/26/2006, effective 10/26/2006; Final rule, 73 FR 4115, 1/24/2008, effective 1/24/2008]

222.1704-70 [Removed]

[Interim rule, 71 FR 62560, 10/26/2006, effective 10/26/2006; Final rule, 73 FR 4115, 1/24/2008, effective 1/24/2008]

222.1705 [Removed]

[Interim rule, 71 FR 62560, 10/26/2006, effective 10/26/2006; Final rule, 73 FR 4115, 1/24/2008, effective 1/24/2008]

222.1770 Procedures.

For a sample checklist for auditing compliance with Combating Trafficking in Persons policy, see the Defense Contract Management Agency checklist, Afghanistan Universal Examination Record Combating Trafficking in Persons, available at DFARS Procedures Guidance and Information 222.17.

[Final rule, 80 FR 4999, 1/29/2015, effective 1/29/2015]

222.1771 [Removed]

[Final rule, 80 FR 4999, 1/29/2015, effective 1/29/2015; Final rule, 83 FR 24887, 5/30/2018, effective 5/30/2018]

SUBPART 222.70—RESTRICTIONS ON THE EMPLOYMENT OF PERSONNEL FOR WORK ON CONSTRUCTION AND SERVICE CONTRACTS IN NONCONTIGUOUS STATES

222.7000 Scope of subpart.

(a) This subpart implements Section 8071 of the Fiscal Year 2000 Defense Appropriations Act, Public Law 106-79, and similar sections in subsequent Defense Appropriations Acts.

(b) This subpart applies only—

(1) To construction and service contracts to be performed in whole or in part within a noncontiguous State; and

(2) When the unemployment rate in the noncontiguous State is in excess of the national average rate of unemployment as determined by the Secretary of Labor.

[Interim rule, 65 FR 14402, 3/16/2000, effective 3/16/2000, finalized without change, 65 FR 50150, 8/17/2000]

222.7001 Definition.

Noncontiguous State, as used in this subpart, means Alaska, Hawaii, Puerto Rico, the Northern Mariana Islands, American Samoa, Guam, the U.S. Virgin Islands, Baker Island, Howland Island, Jarvis Island, Johnston Atoll, Kingman Reef, Midway Islands, Navassa Island, Palmyra Atoll, and Wake Island.

[Final rule, 65 FR 50150, 8/17/2000, effective 8/17/2000]

222.7002 General.

A contractor awarded a contract subject to this subpart must employ, for the purpose of performing that portion of the contract work within the noncontiguous State, individuals who are residents of that noncontiguous State and who, in the case of any craft or trade, possess or would be able to acquire promptly the necessary skills to perform the contract.

[Interim rule, 65 FR 14402, 3/16/2000, effective 3/16/2000, finalized without change, 65 FR 50150, 8/17/2000]

222.7003 Waivers.

The head of the agency may waive the requirements of 222.7002 on a case-by-case basis in the interest of national security.

[Final rule, 65 FR 50150, 8/17/2000, effective 8/17/2000]

222.7004 Contract clause.

Use the clause at 252.222-7000, Restrictions on Employment of Personnel, in all solicitations and contracts subject to this subpart. Insert the name of the appropriate noncontiguous State in paragraph (a) of the clause.

[Interim rule, 65 FR 14402, 3/16/2000, effective 3/16/2000, finalized without change, 65 FR 50150, 8/17/2000]

SUBPART 222.71—[REMOVED AND RESERVED]

222.7100 [Removed]

[Interim rule, 57 FR 52593, 11/4/92, effective 10/26/92; Final rule, 71 FR 18669, 4/12/2006, effective 4/12/2006]

222.7101 [Removed and Reserved]

[Interim rule, 57 FR 52593, 11/4/92, effective 10/26/92; Final rule, 83 FR 24887, 5/30/2018, effective 5/30/2018]

222.7102 [Removed and Reserved]

[Interim rule, 57 FR 52593, 11/4/92, effective 10/26/92; Final rule, 83 FR 24887, 5/30/2018, effective 5/30/2018]

SUBPART 222.72—COMPLIANCE WITH LABOR LAWS OF FOREIGN GOVERNMENTS

222.7200 [Removed]

[DAC 91-12, 62 FR 34114, 6/24/97, effective 6/24/97; Final rule, 71 FR 18669, 4/12/2006, effective 4/12/2006]

222.7201 Contract clauses.

(a) Use the clause at 252.222-7002, Compliance with Local Labor Laws (Overseas), in solicitations and contracts for services or construction to be performed outside the United States and its outlying areas.

(b) Use the clause at 252.222-7003, Permit from Italian Inspectorate of Labor, in solicitations and contracts for porter, janitorial, or ordinary facility and equipment maintenance services to be performed in Italy.

(c) Use the clause at 252.222-7004, Compliance with Spanish Social Security Laws and Regulations, in solicitations and contracts for services or construction to be performed in Spain.

[DAC 91-12, 62 FR 34114, 6/24/97, effective 6/24/97; Final rule, 70 FR 35543, 6/21/2005, effective 6/21/2005]

SUBPART 222.73—LIMITATIONS APPLICABLE TO CONTRACTS PERFORMED ON GUAM

222.7300 Scope of subpart.

This subpart—

(a) Implements Section 390 of the National Defense Authorization Act for Fiscal Year 1998 (Pub. L. 105-85); and

(b) Applies to contracts for base operations support on Guam that—

(1) Are awarded as a result of a competition conducted under OMB Circular A-76; and

(2) Are entered into or modified on or after November 18, 1997.

[Final rule, 64 FR 52672, 9/30/99, effective 9/30/99; Final rule, 72 FR 20764, 4/26/2007, effective 4/26/2007]

222.7301 Prohibition on use of nonimmigrant aliens.

(a) Any alien who is issued a visa or otherwise provided nonimmigrant status under Section 101(a)(15)(H)(ii) of the Immigration and Nationality Act (8 U.S.C. 1101(a)(15)(H)(ii)) is prohibited from performing work under a contract for base operations support on Guam.

(b) Lawfully admitted citizens of the freely associated states of the Republic of the Marshall Islands, the Federated States of Micronesia, or the Republic of Palau are not subject to the prohibition in paragraph (a) of this section.

[Final rule, 64 FR 52672, 9/30/99, effective 9/30/99; Final rule, 72 FR 20764, 4/26/2007, effective 4/26/2007]

222.7302 Contract clause.

Use the clause at 252.222-7005, Prohibition on Use of Nonimmigrant Aliens—Guam, in solicitations and contracts subject to this subpart.

[Final rule, 64 FR 52672, 9/30/99, effective 9/30/99; Final rule, 72 FR 20764, 4/26/2007, effective 4/26/2007]

222.7303 [Removed]

[Final rule, 64 FR 52672, 9/30/99, effective 9/30/99; Final rule, 72 FR 20764, 4/26/2007, effective 4/26/2007]

SUBPART 222.74—RESTRICTIONS ON THE USE OF MANDATORY ARBITRATION AGREEMENTS

222.7400 Scope of subpart.

This subpart implements section 8116 of the Defense Appropriations Act for Fiscal Year 2010 (Pub. L. 111-118).

[Interim rule, 75 FR 29746, 5/19/2010, effective 5/19/2010; Final rule, 75 FR 76295, 12/8/2010, effective 12/8/2010; Final rule, 76 FR 38047, 6/29/2011, effective 6/29/2011]

222.7401 Definition.

Covered subcontractor, as used in this subpart, is defined in the clause at 252.222-7006 , Restrictions on the Use of Mandatory Arbitration Agreements.

[Interim rule, 75 FR 29746, 5/19/2010, effective 5/19/2010; Final rule, 75 FR 76295, 12/8/2010, effective 12/8/2010]

222.7402 Policy.

(a) Departments and agencies are prohibited from using funds appropriated or otherwise made available by the Fiscal Year 2010 Defense Appropriations Act (Pub. L. 111-118) or subsequent DoD appropriations acts for any contract (including task or delivery orders and bilateral modifications adding new work) in excess of $1 million, unless the contractor agrees not to—

(1) Enter into any agreement with any of its employees or independent contractors

that requires, as a condition of employment, that the employee or independent contractor agree to resolve through arbitration—

(i) Any claim under title VII of the Civil Rights Act of 1964; or

(ii) Any tort related to or arising out of sexual assault or harassment, including assault and battery, intentional infliction of emotional distress, false imprisonment, or negligent hiring, supervision, or retention; or

(2) Take any action to enforce any provision of an existing agreement with an employee or independent contractor that mandates that the employee or independent contractor resolve through arbitration—

(i) Any claim under title VII of the Civil Rights Act of 1964; or

(ii) Any tort related to or arising out of sexual assault or harassment, including assault and battery, intentional infliction of emotional distress, false imprisonment, or negligent hiring, supervision, or retention.

(b) No funds appropriated or otherwise made available by the Fiscal Year 2010 Defense Appropriations Act (Pub. L. 111-118) or subsequent DoD appropriations acts may be expended unless the contractor certifies that it requires each covered subcontractor to agree not to enter into, and not to take any action to enforce, any provision of any agreement, as described in paragraph (a) of this section, with respect to any employee or independent contractor performing work related to such subcontract.

[Interim rule, 75 FR 29746, 5/19/2010, effective 5/19/2010; Final rule, 75 FR 76295, 12/8/2010, effective 12/8/2010; Final rule, 76 FR 38047, 6/29/2011, effective 6/29/2011]

222.7403 Applicability.

This requirement does not apply to the acquisition of commercial items (including commercially available off-the-shelf items).

[Interim rule, 75 FR 29746, 5/19/2010, effective 5/19/2010; Final rule, 75 FR 76295, 12/8/2010, effective 12/8/2010]

222.7404 Waiver.

(a) The Secretary of Defense may waive, in accordance with paragraphs (b) through (d) of this section, the applicability of paragraphs (a) or (b) of 222.7402 to a particular contract or subcontract, if the Secretary or the Deputy Secretary personally determines that the waiver is necessary to avoid harm to national security interests of the United States, and that the term of the contract or subcontract is not longer than necessary to avoid such harm.

(b) The waiver determination shall set forth the grounds for the waiver with specificity, stating any alternatives considered, and explain why each of the alternatives would not avoid harm to national security interests.

(c) The contracting officer shall submit requests for waivers in accordance with agency procedures and PGI 222.7404(c).

(d) The Secretary of Defense will transmit the determination to Congress and simultaneously publish it in the **Federal Register**, not less than 15 business days before the contract or subcontract addressed in the determination may be awarded.

[Interim rule, 75 FR 29746, 5/19/2010, effective 5/19/2010; Final rule, 75 FR 76295, 12/8/2010, effective 12/8/2010; Final rule, 78 FR 36113, 6/17/2013, effective 6/17/2013]

222.7405 Contract clause.

Use the clause at 252.222-7006, Restrictions on the Use of Mandatory Arbitration Agreements, in all solicitations and contracts (including task or delivery orders and bilateral modifications adding new work) valued in excess of $1 million utilizing funds appropriated or otherwise made available by the Defense Appropriations Act for Fiscal Year 2010 (Pub. L. 111-118), or subsequent DoD appropriations acts, except in contracts for the acquisition of commercial items, including commercially available off-the-shelf items.

[Interim rule, 75 FR 29746, 5/19/2010, effective 5/19/2010; Final rule, 75 FR 76295, 12/8/2010, effective 12/8/2010; Final rule,

76 FR 38047, 6/29/2011, effective 6/29/2011]

PART 223—ENVIRONMENT, ENERGY AND WATER EFFICIENCY, RENEWABLE ENERGY TECHNOLOGIES, OCCUPATIONAL SAFETY, AND DRUG-FREE WORKPLACE

Table of Contents

Subpart 223.3—Hazardous Material Identification and Material Safety Data

[Removed] 223.300
Policy 223.302
Contract clause 223.303
Safety precautions for ammunition and explosives 223.370
Scope 223.370-1
Definition 223.370-2
Policy 223.370-3
Procedures 223.370-4
Contract clauses 223.370-5

Subpart 223.4—Use of Recovered Materials

[Removed] 223.404
Procedures 223.405

Subpart 223.5—Drug-Free Workplace

Drug-free work force 223.570
Policy 223.570-1
Contract clause 223.570-2
[Removed] 223.570-3

Subpart 223.8—Ozone-Depleting Substances

Policy 223.803

Subpart 223.70—[Reserved]

Subpart 223.71—Storage, Treatment, and Disposal of Toxic or Hazardous Materials

Definitions 223.7101
Policy 223.7102
Procedures 223.7103
Exceptions 223.7104
Reimbursement 223.7105
Contract clause 223.7106

Subpart 223.72—Safeguarding Sensitive Conventional Arms, Ammunition, and Explosives

Definition 223.7200
Policy 223.7201
Preaward responsibilities 223.7202
Contract clause 223.7203

Subpart 223.73—Minimizing the Use of Materials Containing Hexavalent Chromium

Definition 223.7300

Policy 223.7301
Authorities 223.7302
Prohibition 223.7303
Exceptions 223.7304
Authorization and approval 223.7305
Contract clause 223.7306

PART 223—ENVIRONMENT, ENERGY AND WATER EFFICIENCY, RENEWABLE ENERGY TECHNOLOGIES, OCCUPATIONAL SAFETY, AND DRUG-FREE WORKPLACE

SUBPART 223.3—HAZARDOUS MATERIAL IDENTIFICATION AND MATERIAL SAFETY DATA

223.300 [Removed]

[Final rule, 70 FR 73150, 12/9/2005, effective 12/9/2005]

223.302 Policy.

(e) The contracting officer shall also provide hazard warning labels, that are received from apparent successful offerors, to the cognizant safety officer.

[DAC 91-1, 56 FR 67215, 12/30/91, effective 12/31/91; Final rule, 70 FR 73150, 12/9/2005, effective 12/9/2005]

223.303 Contract clause.

Use the clause at 252.223-7001, Hazard Warning Labels, in solicitations and contracts which require submission of hazardous material data sheets (see FAR 23.302(c)).

[DAC 91-1, 56 FR 67215, 12/30/91, effective 12/31/91]

223.370 Safety precautions for ammunition and explosives. (No Text)

223.370-1 Scope.

(a) This section applies to all acquisitions involving the use of ammunition and explosives, including acquisitions for—

(1) Development;

(2) Testing;

(3) Research;

(4) Manufacturing;

(5) Handling or loading;

(6) Assembling;

(7) Packaging;

(8) Storage;

(9) Transportation;

(10) Renovation;

(11) Demilitarization;

(12) Modification;

(13) Repair;

(14) Disposal;

(15) Inspection; or

(16) Any other use, including acquisitions requiring the use or the incorporation of materials listed in paragraph (b) of this subsection for initiation, propulsion, or detonation as an integral or component part of an explosive, an ammunition, or explosive end item or weapon system.

(b) This section does not apply to acquisitions solely for—

(1) Inert components containing no explosives, propellants, or pyrotechnics;

(2) Flammable liquids;

(3) Acids;

(4) Oxidizers;

(5) Powdered metals; or

(6) Other materials having fire or explosive characteristics.

223.370-2 Definition.

Ammunition and explosives, as used in this section, is defined in the clause at 252.223-7002, Safety Precautions for Ammunition and Explosives.

223.370-3 Policy.

(a) DoD policy is to ensure that its contractors take reasonable precautions in handling ammunition and explosives so as to minimize the potential for mishaps.

(b) This policy is implemented by DoD Manual 4145.26-M, DoD Contractors' Safety Manual for Ammunition and Explosives, which is incorporated into contracts under which ammunition and explosives are handled. The manual contains mandatory safety requirements for contractors. When work is to be performed on a Government-owned installation, the contracting officer may use the ammunition and explosives regulation of the DoD component or installation as a substitute for, or supplement to, DoD Manual 4145.26-M, as long as the contract cites these regulations.

[Final rule, 70 FR 73150, 12/9/2005, effective 12/9/2005]

223.370-4 Procedures.

Follow the procedures at PGI 223.370-4.

[DAC 91-6, 59 FR 27662, 5/27/94, effective 5/27/94; Final rule, 64 FR 51074, 9/21/99, effective 9/21/99; Final rule, 70 FR 73150, 12/9/2005, effective 12/9/2005]

223.370-5 Contract clauses.

Use the clauses at 252.223-7002, Safety Precautions for Ammunition and Explosives, and 252.223-7003, Change in Place of Performance—Ammunition and Explosives, in all solicitations and contracts for acquisition to which this section applies.

SUBPART 223.4—USE OF RECOVERED MATERIALS

223.404 [Removed]

[Removed by final rule, 66 FR 49864, 10/1/2001, effective 10/1/2001]

223.405 Procedures.

Follow the procedures at PGI 223.405.

[Final rule, 66 FR 49864, 10/1/2001, effective 10/1/2001; Final rule, 70 FR 73150, 12/9/2005, effective 12/9/2005]

SUBPART 223.5—DRUG-FREE WORKPLACE

223.570 Drug-free work force. (No Text)

223.570-1 Policy.

DoD policy is to ensure that its contractors maintain a program for achieving a drug-free work force.

[Interim final rule, 57 FR 32737, 7/23/92, effective 7/16/92, finalized without change, DAC 91-11, 61 FR 50446, 9/26/96; Redesignated 223.570-2, Final rule, 70 FR 73150, 12/9/2005, effective 12/9/2005]

223.570-2 Contract clause.

(a) Use the clause at 252.223-7004, Drug-Free Work Force, in all solicitations and contracts—

(1) That involve access to classified information; or

(2) When the contracting officer determines that the clause is necessary for reasons of national security or for the purpose of protecting the health or safety of those using or affected by the product of, or performance of, the contract.

(b) Do not use the clause in solicitations and contracts—

(1) For commercial items;

(2) When performance or partial performance will be outside the United States and its outlying areas, unless the contracting officer determines such inclusion to be in the best interest of the Government; or

(3) When the value of the acquisition is at or below the simplified acquisition threshold.

[Interim final rule, 57 FR 32737, 7/23/92, effective 7/16/92; DAC 91-9, 60 FR 61586, 11/30/95, effective 11/30/95, finalized without change, DAC 91-11, 61 FR 50446, 9/26/96; Final rule, 64 FR 2595, 1/15/99, effective 1/15/99; Final rule, 70 FR 35543, 6/21/2005, effective 6/21/2005; Redesignated 223.570-4, Final rule, 70 FR 73150, 12/9/2005, effective 12/9/2005]

223.570-3 [Removed]

[Final rule, 70 FR 73150, 12/9/2005, effective 12/9/2005]

SUBPART 223.8—OZONE-DEPLETING SUBSTANCES

223.803 Policy.

No DoD contract may include a specification or standard that requires the use of a class I ozone-depleting substance or that can be met only through the use of such a substance unless the inclusion of the specification or standard is specifically authorized at a level no lower than a general or flag officer or a member of the Senior Executive Service of the requiring activity in accordance with Section 326, Public Law 102-484 (10 U.S.C. 2301 (repealed) note). This restriction is in addition to any imposed by the Clean Air Act and applies after June 1, 1993, to all DoD contracts, regardless of place of performance.

[DAC 91-11, 61 FR 50446, 9/26/96, effective 9/26/96; Final rule, 70 FR 73150,

12/9/2005, effective 12/9/2005; Final rule, 71 FR 75891, 12/19/2006, effective 12/19/2006]

SUBPART 223.70—[RESERVED]

[Removed and reserved, final rule, 63 FR 67804, 12/9/98, effective 12/9/98]

SUBPART 223.71—STORAGE, TREATMENT, AND DISPOSAL OF TOXIC OR HAZARDOUS MATERIALS

223.7101 Definitions.

As used in this subpart, the terms *storage* and *toxic* or *hazardous materials* are defined in the clause at 252.223–7006, Prohibition on Storage, Treatment, and Disposal of Toxic or Hazardous Materials.

[Final rule, 79 FR 58697, 9/30/2014, effective 9/30/2014]

223.7102 Policy.

(a) 10 U.S.C. 2692 prohibits storage, treatment, or disposal on DoD installations of toxic or hazardous materials that are not owned either by DoD or by a member of the armed forces (or a dependent of the member) assigned to or provided military housing on the installation, unless an exception in 223.7104 applies.

(b) When storage of toxic or hazardous materials is authorized based on an imminent danger, the storage provided shall be temporary and shall cease once the imminent danger no longer exists. In all other cases of storage or disposal, the storage or disposal shall be terminated as determined by the Secretary of Defense.

[Final rule, 79 FR 58697, 9/30/2014, effective 9/30/2014]

223.7103 Procedures.

(a) (1) Storage, treatment, or disposal of toxic or hazardous materials not owned by DoD on a DoD installation is prohibited unless—

(i) One or more of the exceptions set forth in 223.7104(a) is met including requisite approvals; or

(ii) Secretary of Defense authorization is obtained under the conditions set forth in 223.7104(b).

(2) When storage, treatment, or disposal of toxic or hazardous materials not owned by DoD is authorized in accordance with this subpart, the contract shall specify the types and quantities of toxic or hazardous materials that may be temporarily stored, treated, or disposed of in connection with the contract or as a result of the authorized use of a DoD facility or space launch facility. All solicitations and contracts shall specify the conditions under which storage, treatment, or disposal is authorized.

(b) If the contracting officer is uncertain as to whether particular activities are prohibited or fall under one of the exceptions in 223.7104, the contracting officer should seek advice from the cognizant office of counsel.

[Final rule, 79 FR 58697, 9/30/2014, effective 9/30/2014]

223.7104 Exceptions.

(a) The prohibition of 10 U.S.C. 2692 does not apply to any of the following:

(1) The storage, treatment, or disposal of materials that will be or have been used in connection with an activity of DoD or in connection with a service to be performed on a DoD installation for the benefit of DoD.

(2) The storage of strategic and critical materials in the National Defense Stockpile under an agreement for such storage with the Administrator of General Services Administration.

(3) The temporary storage or disposal of explosives in order to protect the public or to assist agencies responsible for Federal, State, or local law enforcement in storing or disposing of explosives when no alternative solution is available, if such storage or disposal is made in accordance with an agreement between the Secretary of Defense and the head of the Federal, State, or local agency concerned.

(4) The temporary storage or disposal of explosives in order to provide emergency lifesaving assistance to civil authorities.

(5) The disposal of excess explosives produced under a DoD contract, if the head of the military department concerned determines, in each case, that an alternative feasible means of disposal is not available to the

contractor, taking into consideration public safety, available resources of the contractor, and national defense production requirements.

(6) The temporary storage of nuclear materials or nonnuclear classified materials in accordance with an agreement with the Secretary of Energy.

(7) The storage of materials that constitute military resources intended to be used during peacetime civil emergencies in accordance with applicable DoD regulations.

(8) The temporary storage of materials of other Federal agencies in order to provide assistance and refuge for commercial carriers of such material during a transportation emergency.

(9) The storage of any material that is not owned by DoD, if the Secretary of the military department concerned determines that the material is required or generated in connection with the authorized and compatible use of a facility of DoD, including the use of such a facility for testing material or training personnel.

(10) The treatment and disposal of any toxic or hazardous materials not owned by DoD, if the Secretary of the military department concerned determines that the material is required or generated in connection with the authorized and compatible use of a facility of that military department and the Secretary enters into a contract or agreement with the prospective user that—

(i) Is consistent with the best interest of national defense and environmental security; and

(ii) Provides for the prospective user's continued financial and environmental responsibility and liability with regard to the material.

(11) The storage of any material that is not owned by DoD if the Secretary of the military department concerned determines that the material is required or generated in connection with the use of a space launch facility located on a DoD installation or on other land controlled by the United States.

(b) The Secretary of Defense may grant an exception to the prohibition in 10 U.S.C. 2692 when essential to protect the health and safety of the public from imminent danger if the Secretary otherwise determines the exception is essential and if the storage or disposal authorized does not compete with private enterprise.

[Final rule, 79 FR 58697, 9/30/2014, effective 9/30/2014]

223.7105 Reimbursement.

The Secretary of Defense may assess a charge for any storage or disposal provided under this subpart. If a charge is to be assessed, then such assessment shall be identified in the contract with payment to the Government on a reimbursable cost basis.

[Final rule, 79 FR 58697, 9/30/2014, effective 9/30/2014]

223.7106 Contract clause.

Use the basic or the alternate of the clause at 252.223-7006, Prohibition on Storage, Treatment, and Disposal of Toxic or Hazardous Materials, in all solicitations and contracts which require, may require, or permit contractor access to a DoD installation.

(a) Use the basic clause, unless a determination is made under 223.7104(a)(10).

(b) Use the alternate I clause when the Secretary of the military department issues a determination under the exception at 223.7104(a)(10).

[Final rule, 79 FR 58697, 9/30/2014, effective 9/30/2014]

SUBPART 223.72—SAFEGUARDING SENSITIVE CONVENTIONAL ARMS, AMMUNITION, AND EXPLOSIVES

223.7200 Definition.

Arms, ammunition, and explosives (AA&E), as used in this subpart, means those items within the scope (chapter 1, paragraph B) of DoD 5100.76-M, Physical Security of Sensitive Conventional Arms, Ammunition, and Explosives.

[DAC 91-10, 61 FR 7739, 2/29/96, effective 2/29/96]

223.7201 Policy.

(a) The requirements of DoD 5100.76-M, Physical Security of Sensitive Conventional

Arms, Ammunition, and Explosives, shall be applied to contracts when—

(1) AA&E will be provided to the contractor or subcontractor as Government-furnished property; or

(2) The principal development, production, manufacture, or purchase of AA&E is for DoD use.

(b) The requirements of DoD 5100.76-M need not be applied to contracts when—

(1) The AA&E to be acquired under the contract is a commercial item within the meaning of FAR 2.101; or

(2) The contract will be performed in a Government-owned contractor-operated ammunition production facility. However, if subcontracts issued under such a contract will meet the criteria of paragraph (a) of this section, the requirements of DoD 5100.76-M shall apply.

[DAC 91-10, 61 FR 7739, 2/29/96, effective 2/29/96]

223.7202 Preaward responsibilities.

When an acquisition involves AA&E, technical or requirements personnel shall specify in the purchase request—

(a) That AA&E is involved; and

(b) Which physical security requirements of DoD 5100.76-M apply.

[DAC 91-10, 61 FR 7739, 2/29/96, effective 2/29/96]

223.7203 Contract clause.

Use the clause at 252.223-7007, Safeguarding Sensitive Conventional Arms, Ammunition, and Explosives, in all solicitations and contracts to which DoD 5100.76-M applies, in accordance with the policy at 223.7201. Complete paragraph (b) of the clause based on information provided by cognizant technical or requirements personnel.

[DAC 91-10, 61 FR 7739, 2/29/96, effective 2/29/96, corrected, 61 FR 18195, 4/24/96]

SUBPART 223.73—MINIMIZING THE USE OF MATERIALS CONTAINING HEXAVALENT CHROMIUM

223.7300 Definition.

Legacy system, as used in this subpart, means any program that has passed Milestone A in the defense acquisition management system, as defined in DoD Instruction 5000.02.

[Final rule, 76 FR 25569, 5/5/2011, effective 5/5/2011]

223.7301 Policy.

It is DoD policy to minimize hexavalent chromium (an anti-corrosive) in items acquired by DoD (deliverables and construction material), due to the serious human health and environmental risks related to its use. Executive Order 13423, section 3, paragraph (a) requires that the heads of agencies reduce or eliminate the acquisition and use of toxic or hazardous chemicals. Executive Order 13514 requires that the heads of agencies are responsible for "reducing and minimizing the quantity of toxic and hazardous chemicals and materials acquired, used, or disposed of."

[Final rule, 76 FR 25569, 5/5/2011, effective 5/5/2011]

223.7302 Authorities.

(a) Executive Order 13423 of January 24, 2007, Strengthening Federal Environmental, Energy, and Transportation Management.

(b) Executive Order 13514 of October 5, 2009, Federal Leadership in Environmental, Energy, and Economic Performance.

[Final rule, 76 FR 25569, 5/5/2011, effective 5/5/2011]

223.7303 Prohibition.

(a) Except as provided in 223.7304 and 223.7305, no contract may include a specification or standard that results in a deliverable or construction material containing more than 0.1 percent hexavalent chromium by weight in any homogeneous material in the deliverable or construction material where proven substitutes are available that provide acceptable performance for the application.

(b) This prohibition is in addition to any imposed by the Clean Air Act regardless of the place of performance.

[Final rule, 76 FR 25569, 5/5/2011, effective 5/5/2011]

223.7304 Exceptions.

The prohibition in 223.7303 does not apply to—

(a) Legacy systems and their related parts, subsystems, and components that already contain hexavalent chromium. However, alternatives to hexavalent chromium shall be considered by the appropriate official during system modifications, follow-on procurements of legacy systems, or maintenance procedure updates; and

(b) Additional sustainment related contracts (*e.g.*, parts, services) for a system in which use of hexavalent chromium was previously approved.

[Final rule, 76 FR 25569, 5/5/2011, effective 5/5/2011]

223.7305 Authorization and approval.

(a) The prohibition in 223.7303 does not apply to critical defense applications if no substitute can meet performance requirements. The DoD policy of April 8, 2009, "Minimizing the Use of Hexavalent Chromium," contains requirements for weighing hexavalent chromium versus substitutes. DoD Program Managers must consider the following factors—

(1) Cost effectiveness of alternative materials or processes;

(2) Technical feasibility of alternative materials or processes;

(3) Environment, safety, and occupational health risks associated with the use of the hexavalent chromium or substitute materials in each specific application;

(4) Achieving a DoD Manufacturing Readiness Level of at least eight for any qualified alternative;

(5) Materiel availability of hexavalent chromium and the proposed alternatives over the projected life span of the system; and

(6) Corrosion performance difference of alternative materials or processes as determined by agency corrosion subject matter experts.

(b) However, unless an exception in 223.7304 applies, the incorporation of hexavalent chromium in items acquired by DoD shall be specifically authorized at a level no lower than a general or flag officer or a member of the Senior Executive Service from the Program Executive Office or equivalent level, in coordination with the component Corrosion Control and Prevention Executive. Follow the procedures in PGI 223.7305.

[Final rule, 76 FR 25569, 5/5/2011, effective 5/5/2011]

223.7306 Contract clause.

Unless an exception in 223.7304 applies, or use has been authorized in accordance with PGI 223.7305, use the clause at 252.223-7008, Prohibition of Hexavalent Chromium, in solicitations and contracts, including solicitations and contracts using FAR part 12 procedures for the acquisition of commercial items, that are for supplies, maintenance and repair services, or construction.

[Final rule, 76 FR 25569, 5/5/2011, effective 5/5/2011; Final rule, 78 FR 37980, 6/25/2013, effective 6/25/2013]

PART 224—PROTECTION OF PRIVACY AND FREEDOM OF INFORMATION

Table of Contents

Subpart 224.1—Protection of Individual Privacy

[Removed] 224.102
Procedures 224.103

Subpart 224.2—Freedom of Information Act

Policy 224.203

PART 224—PROTECTION OF PRIVACY AND FREEDOM OF INFORMATION

SUBPART 224.1—PROTECTION OF INDIVIDUAL PRIVACY

224.102 [Removed]

[Final rule, 69 FR 67856, 11/22/2004, effective 11/22/2004]

224.103 Procedures.

(b) (2) DoD rules and regulations are contained in DoDD 5400.11, Department of Defense Privacy Program, and DoD 5400.11-R, Department of Defense Privacy Program.

SUBPART 224.2—FREEDOM OF INFORMATION ACT

224.203 Policy.

(a) DoD implementation is in DoDD 5400.7, DoD Freedom of Information Act Program, and DoD 5400.7-R, DoD Freedom of Information Act Program.

[Redesignated from 224.202, DAC 91-12, 62 FR 34114, 6/24/97, effective 6/24/97]

PART 225—FOREIGN ACQUISITION

Table of Contents

[Removed] 225.000
General 225.001
Definitions 225.003
Reporting of acquisition of end products manufactured outside the United States 225.070

Subpart 225.1—Buy American—Supplies

General 225.101
Exceptions 225.103
Determining reasonableness of cost 225.105
Acquisition from or through other Government agencies 225.170
[Removed] 225.171

Subpart 225.2—Buy American—Construction Materials

Exceptions 225.202
Noncompliance 225.206

Subpart 225.3—Contracts Performed Outside the United States

Contractor personnel in a designated operational area or supporting a diplomatic or consular mission outside the United States. 225.301
Scope 225.301-1
Contract clause 225.301-4
Contractors performing private security functions outside the United States 225.302
Contract clause. 225.302-6
Contracts requiring performance or delivery in a foreign country 225.370
[Removed] 225.370-1
[Removed] 225.370-2
[Removed] 225.370-3
[Removed] 225.370-4
[Removed] 225.370-5
[Removed] 225.370-6
Contractor personnel supporting U.S. Armed Forces deployed outside the United States 225.371
Scope 225.371-1
Definition 225.371-2
Government support 225.371-3
Law of war training 225.371-4
Contract clauses 225.371-5
Antiterrorism/force protection 225.372
General 225.372-1
Contract clause 225.372-2
Contract administration in support of contingency operations 225.373
Use of electronic business tools 225.374

Subpart 225.4—Trade Agreements

Exceptions 225.401
End products subject to trade agreements 225.401-70
Products or services in support of operations in Afghanistan 225.401-71
General 225.402
World Trade Organization Government Procurement Agreement and Free Trade Agreements 225.403
Procedures 225.408

Subpart 225.5—Evaluating Foreign Offers—Supply Contracts

Application 225.502
Group Offers 225.503
Evaluation examples 225.504

Subpart 225.6—[Removed]

Subpart 225.7—Prohibited Sources

Restrictions 225.701
Exception 225.701-70
Prohibition on acquisition of certain items from Communist Chinese military companies 225.770
Definitions 225.770-1
Prohibition 225.770-2
Exceptions 225.770-3
Identifying items covered by the USML or the 600 series of the CCL . . . 225.770-4
Waiver of prohibition 225.770-5
Prohibition on contracting or subcontracting with a firm that is owned or controlled by the government of a country that is a state sponsor of terrorism. 225.771
Scope 225.771-0
Definition 225.771-1
Prohibition 225.771-2
Notification 225.771-3
Waiver of prohibition 225.771-4
Solicitation provision 225.771-5
Prohibition on acquisition of certain foreign commercial satellite services 225.772
Scope 225.772-0
Definitions 225.772-1
Prohibitions 225.772-2
Procedures 225.772-3
Exception 225.772-4
Solicitation provision and contract clauses 225.772-5

Subpart 225.8—Other International Agreements and Coordination

Procedures 225.802
Contracts for performance outside the United States and Canada 225.802-70
End use certificates 225.802-71
Contracting with Canadian contractors 225.870

General 225.870-1
Solicitation of Canadian contractors 225.870-2
Submission of offers 225.870-3
Contracting procedures 225.870-4
Contract administration 225.870-5
Termination procedures 225.870-6
Acceptance of Canadian supplies 225.870-7
Industrial security 225.870-8
North Atlantic Treaty Organization (NATO) cooperative projects 225.871
Scope 225.871-1
Definitions 225.871-2
General 225.871-3
Statutory waivers 225.871-4
Directed subcontracting 225.871-5
Disposal of property 225.871-6
Congressional notification 225.871-7
Contracting with qualifying country sources 225.872
General 225.872-1
Applicability 225.872-2
Solicitation procedures 225.872-3
Individual determinations 225.872-4
Contract administration 225.872-5
Request for audit services 225.872-6
Industrial security for qualifying countries 225.872-7
Subcontracting with qualifying country sources 225.872-8
Waiver of United Kingdom commercial exploitation levies 225.873
Policy 225.873-1
Procedures 225.873-2

Subpart 225.9—Customs and Duties

Definition 225.900-70
Policy 225.901
Procedures 225.902
Exempted supplies 225.903

Subpart 225.10—Additional Foreign Acquisition Regulations

Clause deviations in overseas contracts 225.1070

Subpart 225.11—Solicitation Provisions and Contract Clauses

Scope of subpart 225.1100
Acquisition of supplies 225.1101
Other provisions and clauses 225.1103

Subpart 225.70—Authorization Acts, Appropriations Acts, and Other Statutory Restrictions on Foreign Acquisition

Scope of subpart 225.7000
Definitions 225.7001
Restrictions on food, clothing, fabrics, hand or measuring tools, and flags. 225.7002

Restrictions 225.7002-1
Exceptions 225.7002-2
Contract clauses 225.7002-3
Restrictions on acquisition of specialty metals 225.7003
Definitions 225.7003-1
Restrictions 225.7003-2
Exceptions 225.7003-3
[Removed and Reserved] 225.7003-4
Solicitation provision and contract clauses 225.7003-5
Restriction on acquisition of foreign buses 225.7004
Restriction 225.7004-1
Applicability 225.7004-2
Exceptions 225.7004-3
Waiver 225.7004-4
[Removed and Reserved] 225.7005
[Removed] 225.7005-1
[Removed] 225.7005-2
[Removed] 225.7005-3
Restriction on air circuit breakers for naval vessels 225.7006
Restriction 225.7006-1
Exceptions 225.7006-2
Waiver 225.7006-3
Solicitation provision and contract clause 225.7006-4
Restriction on anchor and mooring chain 225.7007
Restrictions 225.7007-1
Waiver 225.7007-2
Contract clause 225.7007-3
Waiver of restrictions of 10 U.S.C. 2534 .... 225.7008
[Removed] 225.7008-1
[Removed] 225.7008-2
[Removed] 225.7008-3
[Removed] 225.7008-4
Restrictions on ball and roller bearings 225.7009
Scope 225.7009-1
Restriction 225.7009-2
Exception 225.7009-3
Waiver 225.7009-4
Contract clause 225.7009-5
Restriction on certain naval vessel components. 225.7010
Restriction. 225.7010-1
Exceptions. 225.7010-2
Waiver. 225.7010-3
Implementation. 225.7010-4
Restriction on carbon, alloy, and armor steel plate 225.7011
Restriction 225.7011-1
Waiver 225.7011-2
Contract clause 225.7011-3

Restriction on supercomputers 225.7012
Restriction 225.7012-1
Waiver 225.7012-2
Contract clause 225.7012-3
Restrictions on construction or repair of vessels in foreign shipyards . . . 225.7013
Restriction on military construction 225.7014
Restriction on overseas architect-engineer services 225.7015
[Removed] 225.7016
[Removed] 225.7016-1
[Removed] 225.7016-2
[Removed] 225.7016-3
[Removed] 225.7016-4
Utilization of domestic photovoltaic devices 225.7017
Definitions 225.7017-1
Restriction 225.7017-2
Exceptions 225.7017-3
Solicitation provision and contract clause 225.7017-4
Restriction on acquisition of certain magnets and tungsten 225.7018
Definitions 225.7018-1
Restriction 225.7018-2
Exceptions 225.7018-3
Nonavailability determination 225.7018-4
Contract clause 225.7018-5

Subpart 225.71—Other Restrictions on Foreign Acquisition

Scope of subpart 225.7100
Definitions 225.7101
Forgings 225.7102
Policy 225.7102-1
Exceptions 225.7102-2
Waiver 225.7102-3
Contract clause 225.7102-4
[Removed] 225.7103
[Removed] 225.7103-1
[Removed] 225.7103-2
[Removed] 225.7103-3

Subpart 225.72—Reporting Contract Performance Outside the United States

Policy 225.7201
Exception 225.7202
Contracting officer distribution of reports 225.7203
Solicitation provision and contract clauses 225.7204

Subpart 225.73—Acquisitions for Foreign Military Sales

Scope of subpart 225.7300
General 225.7301
Requirement to use firm-fixed-price contracts 225.7301-1

Solicitation approval for sole source contracts . . . 225.7301-2
Preparation of letter of offer and acceptance . . . 225.7302
Pricing acquisitions for FMS . . . 225.7303
Contractor sales to other foreign customers . . . 225.7303-1
Cost of doing business with a foreign government or an international organization . . . 225.7303-2
Government-to-government agreements . . . 225.7303-3
Contingent fees . . . 225.7303-4
Acquisitions wholly paid for from nonrepayable funds . . . 225.7303-5
FMS customer involvement . . . 225.7304
Limitation of liability . . . 225.7305
Offset arrangements . . . 225.7306
Contract clauses . . . 225.7307

Subpart 225.74—[Removed and Reserved]

Subpart 225.75—Balance of Payments Program

Scope of subpart . . . 225.7500
Policy . . . 225.7501
Procedures . . . 225.7502
Contract clauses . . . 225.7503

Subpart 225.76—Secondary Arab Boycott of Israel

Restriction . . . 225.7601
Procedures . . . 225.7602
Exceptions . . . 225.7603
Waivers . . . 225.7604
Solicitation provision . . . 225.7605

Subpart 225.77—Acquisitions in Support of Operations in Afghanistan

Scope . . . 225.7700
Definitions . . . 225.7701
Acquisitions not subject to the enhanced authority to acquire products or services from Afghanistan . . . 225.7702
Acquisition of small arms . . . 225.7702-1
Acquisition of uniform components for the Afghan military or the Afghan police . . . 225.7702-2
Enhanced authority to acquire products or services from Afghanistan . . . 225.7703
Acquisition procedures . . . 225.7703-1
Determination requirements . . . 225.7703-2
Evaluating offers . . . 225.7703-3
Solicitation provisions and contract clauses . . . 225.7703-4
Acquisitions of products and services from South Caucasus/Central and South Asian (SC/CASA) state in support of operations in Afghanistan . . . 225.7704
Applicability of trade agreements . . . 225.7704-1
Applicability of Balance of Payments Program . . . 225.7704-2
Solicitation provisions and contract clauses . . . 225.7704-3

Prohibition on use of funds for contracts of certain programs and projects in Afghanistan that cannot be safely accessed 225.7705
Prohibition 225.7705-1
Waiver of prohibition 225.7705-2
Procedures 225.7705-3

Subpart 225.78—Acquisitions in Support of Geographic Combatant Command's Theater Security Cooperation Efforts

Policy 225.7801

Subpart 225.79—Export Control

Scope of subpart 225.7900
Export-controlled items 225.7901
Definitions 225.7901-1
General 225.7901-2
Policy 225.7901-3
Contract clause 225.7901-4
Defense Trade Cooperation Treaties 225.7902
Definitions 225.7902-1
Purpose 225.7902-2
Policy 225.7902-3
Procedures 225.7902-4
Solicitation provision and contract clause 225.7902-5

PART 225—FOREIGN ACQUISITION

225.000 [Removed]

[Final rule, 68 FR 15615, 3/31/2003, effective 4/30/2003; Final rule, 70 FR 73153, 12/9/2005, effective 12/9/2005]

225.001 General.

For guidance on evaluating offers or foreign end products, see PGI 225.001.

[Final rule, 65 FR 19849, 4/13/2000, effective 4/13/2000; Final rule, 67 FR 77937, 12/20/2002, effective 12/20/2002; Final rule, 68 FR 15615, 3/31/2003, effective 4/30/2003; Final rule, 70 FR 73153, 12/9/2005, effective 12/9/2005]

225.003 Definitions.

As used in this part—

600 series of the Commerce Control List means the series of 5-character export control classification numbers (ECCNs) of the Commerce Control List of the Export Administration Regulations in 15 CFR part 774, supplement no. 1, that have a "6" as the third character. The 600 series constitutes the munitions and munitions-related ECCNs within the larger Commerce Control List. (See definition of "600 series" in 15 CFR 772.)

Caribbean Basin country end product includes petroleum or any product derived from petroleum.

Communist Chinese military company means any entity, regardless of geographic location, that is—

(1) A part of the commercial or defense industrial base of the People's Republic of China (including a subsidiary or affiliate of such entity); or

(2) Owned or controlled by, or affiliated with, an element of the Government or armed forces of the People's Republic of China.

Defense equipment means any equipment, item of supply, component, or end product purchased by DoD.

Domestic concern means—

(1) A concern incorporated in the United States (including a subsidiary that is incorporated in the United States, even if the parent corporation is a foreign concern); or

(2) An unincorporated concern having its principal place of business in the United States.

Domestic end product has the meaning given in the clauses at 252.225-7001, Buy American and Balance of Payments Program; and 252.225-7036, Buy American—Free Trade Agreements—Balance of Payments Program, instead of the meaning in FAR 25.003.

Eligible product means, instead of the definition in FAR 25.003—

(1) A foreign end product that—

(1) (i) Is in a category listed in 225.401-70; and

(1) (ii) Is not subject to discriminatory treatment, due to the applicability of a trade agreement to a particular acquisition;

(2) A foreign construction material that is not subject to discriminatory treatment, due to the applicability of a trade agreement to a particular acquisition; or

(3) A foreign service that is not subject to discriminatory treatment, due to the applicability of a trade agreement to a particular acquisition.

Foreign concern means any concern other than a domestic concern.

Free Trade Agreement country does not include Oman.

Nonqualifying country means a country other than the United States or a qualifying country.

Nonqualifying country component means a component mined, produced, or manufactured in a nonqualifying country.

Qualifying country means a country with a reciprocal defense procurement memorandum of understanding or international agreement with the United States in which both countries agree to remove barriers to purchases of supplies produced in the other country or services performed by sources of the other country, and the memorandum or agreement complies, where applicable, with the requirements of section 36 of the Arms

Export Control Act (22 U.S.C. 2776) and with 10 U.S.C. 2457. Accordingly, the following are qualifying countries:

Australia

Austria

Belgium

Canada

Czech Republic

Denmark

Egypt

Estonia

Finland

France

Germany

Greece

Israel

Italy

Japan

Latvia

Luxembourg

Netherlands

Norway

Poland

Portugal

Slovenia

Spain

Sweden

Switzerland

Turkey

United Kingdom of Great Britain and Northern Ireland

(11) *Qualifying country component* and *qualifying country end product* are defined in the clauses at 252.225-7001, Buy American and Balance of Payments Program; and 252.225-7036, Buy American—Free Trade Agreements—Balance of Payments Program. Qualifying country end product is also defined in the clause at 252.225-7021, Trade Agreements.

Qualifying country offer means an offer of a qualifying country end product, including the price of transportation to destination.

Source, when restricted by words such as foreign, domestic, or qualifying country, means the actual manufacturer or producer of the end product or component.

South Caucasus/Central and South Asian (SC/CASA) state means Armenia, Azerbaijan, Georgia, Kazakhstan, Kyrgyzstan, Pakistan, Tajikistan, Turkmenistan, or Uzbekistan.

South Caucasus/Central and South Asian (SC/CASA) state construction material means construction material that—

(1) Is wholly the growth, product, or manufacture of an SC/CASA state; or

(2) In the case of a construction material that consists in whole or in part of materials from another country, has been substantially transformed in an SC/CASA state into a new and different construction material distinct from the material from which it was transformed.

South Caucasus/Central and South Asian (SC/CASA) state end product means an article that—

(1) Is wholly the growth, product, or manufacture of an SC/CASA state; or

(2) In the case of an article that consists in whole or in part of materials from another country, has been substantially transformed in an SC/CASA state into a new and different article of commerce with a name, character, or use distinct from that of the article or articles from which it was transformed. The term refers to a product offered for purchase under a supply contract, but for purposes of calculating the value of the end product, includes services (except transportation services) incidental to its supply, provided that the value of those incidental services does not exceed the value of the product itself.

United States Munitions List means the munitions list of the International Traffic in Arms Regulation in 22 CFR part 121.

[Final rule, 65 FR 19849, 4/13/2000, effective 4/13/2000; Final rule, 67 FR 77937, 12/20/2002, effective 12/20/2002; Final rule, 68 FR 15615, 3/31/2003, effective 4/30/2003; Interim rule, 69 FR 1926, 1/13/2004, effective 1/13/2004; Final rule, 70 FR 73152, 12/9/2005, effective

12/9/2005; Final rule, 73 FR 76970, 12/18/2008, effective 12/18/2008; Interim rule, 74 FR 37650, 7/29/2009, effective 7/29/2009; Final rule, 75 FR 3179, 1/20/2010, effective 1/20/2010; Final rule, 75 FR 34943, 6/21/2010, effective 6/21/2010; Final rule, 75 FR 81915, 12/29/2010, effective 12/29/2010; Final rule, 77 FR 35879, 6/15/2012, effective 6/15/2012; Final rule, 77 FR 38736, 6/29/2012, effective 6/29/2012; Final rule, 77 FR 76941, 12/31/2012, effective 12/31/2012; Final rule, 81 FR 50650, 8/2/2016, effective 8/2/2016; Final rule, 81 FR 93840, 12/22/2016, effective 12/22/2016; Final rule, 82 FR 61483, 12/28/2017, effective 12/28/2017; Interim rule, 83 FR 66066, 12/21/2018, effective 12/21/2018; Final rule, 84 FR 25188, 5/31/2019, effective 5/31/2019]

225.070 Reporting of acquisition of end products manufactured outside the United States.

Follow the procedures at PGI 225.070 for entering the data on the acquisition of end products manufactured outside the United States.

[Final rule, 71 FR 62559, 10/26/2006, effective 10/26/2006; Redesignated, Final rule, 79 FR 11341, 2/28/2014, effective 2/28/2014]

SUBPART 225.1—BUY AMERICAN—SUPPLIES

225.101 General.

(a) For DoD, the following two-part test determines whether a manufactured end product is a domestic end product:

(i) The end product is manufactured in the United States; and

(ii) The cost of its U.S. and qualifying country components exceeds 50 percent of the cost of all its components. This test is applied to end products only and not to individual components.

(c) Additional exceptions that allow the purchase of foreign end products are listed at 225.103.

[Final rule, 68 FR 15615, 3/31/2003, effective 4/30/2003]

225.103 Exceptions.

(a) (i) (A) Public interest exceptions for certain countries are in 225.872.

(B) For procurements covered by the World Trade Organization Procurement Agreement, the Under Secretary of Defense (Acquisition, Technology, and Logistics) has determined that it is inconsistent with the public interest to apply the Buy American statute to end products that are substantially transformed in the United States.

(ii) (A) Normally, use the evaluation procedures in subpart 225.5, but consider recommending a public interest exception if the purposes of the Buy American statute are not served, or in order to meet a need set forth in 10 U.S.C. 2533. For example, a public interest exception may be appropriate—

(1) If accepting the low domestic offer will involve substantial foreign expenditures, or accepting the low foreign offer will involve substantial domestic expenditures;

(2) To ensure access to advanced state-of-the-art commercial technology; or

(3) To maintain the same source of supply for spare and replacement parts (also see paragraph (b) (iii) (B) of this section)—

(i) For an end item that qualifies as a domestic end product; or

(ii) In order not to impair integration of the military and commercial industrial base.

(B) Except as provided in PGI 225.872-4, process a determination for a public interest exception after consideration of the factors in 10 U.S.C. 2533—

(1) At a level above the contracting officer for acquisitions valued at or below the simplified acquisition threshold;

(2) By the head of the contracting activity for acquisitions with a value greater than the simplified acquisition threshold but less than $1.5 million; or

(3) By the agency head for acquisitions valued at $1.5 million or more.

(b) (i) A determination that an article, material, or supply is not reasonably available is required when domestic offers are insufficient to meet the requirement and award is to be made on other than a qualifying country or eligible end product.

(ii) Except as provided in FAR 25.103(b)(3), the determination shall be approved—

(A) At a level above the contracting officer for acquisitions valued at or below the simplified acquisition threshold;

(B) By the chief of the contracting office for acquisitions with a value greater than the simplified acquisition threshold but less than $1.5 million; or

(C) By the head of the contracting activity or immediate deputy for acquisitions valued at $1.5 million or more.

(iii) A separate determination as to whether an article is reasonably available is not required for the following articles. DoD has already determined that these articles are not reasonably available from domestic sources:

(A) Spare or replacement parts that must be acquired from the original foreign manufacturer or supplier.

(B) Foreign drugs acquired by the Defense Supply Center, Philadelphia, when the Director, Pharmaceuticals Group, Directorate of Medical Materiel, determines that only the requested foreign drug will fulfill the requirements.

(iv) Under coordinated acquisition (see Subpart 208.70), the determination is the responsibility of the requiring department when the requiring department specifies acquisition of a foreign end product.

(c) The cost of a domestic end product is unreasonable if it is not the low evaluated offer when evaluated under Subpart 225.5.

[Final rule, 65 FR 19849, 4/13/2000, effective 4/13/2000; Final rule, 65 FR 39703, 6/27/2000, effective 6/27/2000; Final rule, 67 FR 49251, 7/30/2002, effective 7/30/2002; Final rule, 67 FR 77937, 12/20/2002, effective 12/20/2002; Final rule, 68 FR 15615, 3/31/2003, effective 4/30/2003; Interim rule, 70 FR 2361, 1/13/2005, effective 1/13/2005; Final rule, 70 FR 73152, 12/9/2005, effective 12/9/2005; Final rule, 73 FR 4113, 1/24/2008, effective 1/24/2008; Final rule, 75 FR 45072, 8/2/2010, effective 10/1/2010; Final rule, 77 FR 35879, 6/15/2012, effective 6/15/2012; Final rule, 80 FR 15912, 3/26/2015, effective 3/26/2015]

225.104 [Removed]

[Final rule, 68 FR 15615, 3/31/2003, effective 4/30/2003; Final rule, 79 FR 44314, 7/31/2014, effective 7/31/2014]

225.105 Determining reasonableness of cost.

(b) Use an evaluation factor of 50 percent instead of the factors specified in FAR 25.105(b).

[Final rule, 65 FR 19849, 4/13/2000, effective 4/13/2000; Final rule, 68 FR 15615, 3/31/2003, effective 4/30/2003]

225.170 Acquisition from or through other Government agencies.

Contracting activities must apply the evaluation procedures in Subpart 225.5 when using Federal supply schedules.

[Final rule, 65 FR 19849, 4/13/2000, effective 4/13/2000; Final rule, 68 FR 15615, 3/31/2003, effective 4/30/2003]

225.171 [Removed]

[Final rule, 65 FR 19849, 4/13/2000, effective 4/13/2000; Final rule, 68 FR 15615, 3/31/2003, effective 4/30/2003; Final rule, 70 FR 73153, 12/9/2005, effective 12/9/2005]

SUBPART 225.2—BUY AMERICAN—CONSTRUCTION MATERIALS

225.202 Exceptions.

(a)(2) A nonavailability determination is not required for construction materials listed in FAR 25.104(a). For other materials, a nonavailability determination shall be approved at the levels specified in 225.103(b)(ii). Use the estimated value of the construction materials to determine the approval level.

[Final rule, 65 FR 19849, 4/13/2000, effective 4/13/2000; Final rule, 68 FR 15615, 3/31/2003, effective 4/30/2003; Final rule, 80 FR 15912, 3/26/2015, effective 3/26/2015]

225.206 Noncompliance.

(c) (4) Prepare any report of noncompliance in accordance with the procedures at 209.406-3 or 209.407-3.

[Final rule, 64 FR 62984, 11/18/99, effective 11/18/99]

SUBPART 225.3—CONTRACTS PERFORMED OUTSIDE THE UNITED STATES

225.301 Contractor personnel in a designated operational area or supporting a diplomatic or consular mission outside the United States. (No Text)

[Final rule, 73 FR 16764, 3/31/2008, effective 3/31/2008]

225.301-1 Scope.

(a) *Performance in a designated operational area,* as used in this section, means performance of a service or construction, as required by the contract. For supply contracts, the term includes services associated with the acquisition of supplies (e.g., installation or maintenance), but does not include production of the supplies or associated overhead functions.

(c) For DoD, this section also applies to all personal services contracts.

[Final rule, 73 FR 16764, 3/31/2008, effective 3/31/2008]

225.301-4 Contract clause.

(1) Use the clause at FAR 52.225-19, Contractor Personnel in a Designated Operational Area or Supporting a Diplomatic or Consular Mission Outside the United States, in accordance with the prescription at FAR 25.301-4, except that—

(i) The clause shall also be used in personal services contracts with individuals; and

(ii) The clause shall not be used when all contractor personnel performing outside the United States will be covered by the clause at 252.225-7040.

(2) When using the clause at FAR 52.225-19, the contracting officer shall inform the contractor that the Synchronized Predeployment and Operational Tracker (SPOT) is the appropriate automated system to use for the list of contractor personnel required by paragraph (g) of the clause. Information on the SPOT system is available at *https://spot.dmdc.mil* and *http://www.acq.osd.mil/log/PS/ctr mgt accountability.html.*

[Final rule, 73 FR 16764, 3/31/2008, effective 3/31/2008; Final rule, 74 FR 34264, 7/15/2009, effective 7/15/2009; Final rule, 80 FR 67254, 10/30/2015, effective 10/30/2015]

225.302 Contractors performing private security functions outside the United States. (No Text)

[Final rule, 80 FR 4997, 1/29/2015, effective 1/29/2015]

225.302-6 Contract clause.

Use the clause at 252.225-7039, Defense Contractors Performing Private Security Functions Outside the United States, instead of FAR clause 52.225-26, Contractors Performing Private Security Functions Outside the United States, in solicitations and contracts, including solicitations and contracts using FAR part 12 procedures for the acquisition of commercial items, when private security functions are to be performed outside the United States in—

(1) Contingency operations;

(2) Combat operations, as designated by the Secretary of Defense;

(3) Other significant military operations (as defined in 32 CFR part 159), designated by the Secretary of Defense, and only upon agreement of the Secretary of Defense and the Secretary of State;

(4) Peace operations, consistent with Joint Publication 3–07.3; or

(5) Other military operations or military exercises, when designated by the Combatant Commander.

[Final rule, 80 FR 4997, 1/29/2015, effective 1/29/2015; Final rule, 81 FR 42559, 6/30/2016, effective 6/30/2016]

225.370 Contracts requiring performance or delivery in a foreign country.

(a) If the acquisition requires the performance of services or delivery of supplies in an area outside the United States, follow the procedures at PGI 225.370(a).

(b) For work performed in Germany, eligibility for logistics support or base privileges of contractor employees is governed by U.S.-German bilateral agreements. Follow the procedures at Army in Europe Regulation 715-9, available at *http://www.eur.army.mil/g1/content/CPD/docper/docper_germany-Links.html* under "AE Regs & Resources."

(c) For work performed in Japan or Korea, see PGI 225.370(b) for information on bilateral agreements and policy relating to contractor employees in Japan or Korea.

(d) For work performed in the U.S. Central Command area of responsibility, follow the procedures for theater business clearance/contract administration delegation instructions at PGI 225.370(d).

[Interim rule, 76 FR 52133, 8/19/2011, effective 8/19/2011; Final rule, 77 FR 35883, 6/15/2012, effective 6/15/2012; Final rule, 78 FR 69282, 11/18/2013, effective 11/18/2013; Final rule, 80 FR 36900, 6/26/2015, effective 6/26/2015; Final rule, 80 FR 56929, 9/21/2015, effective 9/21/2015]

225.370-1 [Removed]

[Interim rule, 76 FR 52133, 8/19/2011, effective 8/19/2011; Final rule, 77 FR 35883, 6/15/2012, effective 6/15/2012; Final rule, 78 FR 69282, 11/18/2013, effective 11/18/2013; Final rule, 78 FR 73450, 12/6/2013, effective 12/6/2013]

225.370-2 [Removed]

[Interim rule, 76 FR 52133, 8/19/2011, effective 8/19/2011; Final rule, 77 FR 35883, 6/15/2012, effective 6/15/2012; Final rule, 78 FR 69282, 11/18/2013, effective 11/18/2013; Final rule, 78 FR 73450, 12/6/2013, effective 12/6/2013]

225.370-3 [Removed]

[Interim rule, 76 FR 52133, 8/19/2011, effective 8/19/2011; Final rule, 77 FR 35883, 6/15/2012, effective 6/15/2012; Final rule, 78 FR 69282, 11/18/2013, effective 11/18/2013; Final rule, 78 FR 73450, 12/6/2013, effective 12/6/2013]

225.370-4 [Removed]

[Interim rule, 76 FR 52133, 8/19/2011, effective 8/19/2011; Final rule, 77 FR 35883, 6/15/2012, effective 6/15/2012; Final rule, 78 FR 69282, 11/18/2013, effective 11/18/2013; Final rule, 78 FR 73450, 12/6/2013, effective 12/6/2013]

225.370-5 [Removed]

[Interim rule, 76 FR 52133, 8/19/2011, effective 8/19/2011; Final rule, 77 FR 35883, 6/15/2012, effective 6/15/2012; Final rule, 78 FR 69282, 11/18/2013, effective 11/18/2013; Final rule, 78 FR 73450, 12/6/2013, effective 12/6/2013]

225.370-6 [Removed]

[Interim rule, 76 FR 52133, 8/19/2011, effective 8/19/2011; Final rule, 77 FR 35883, 6/15/2012, effective 6/15/2012; Final rule, 78 FR 37980, 6/25/2013, effective 6/25/2013; Final rule, 78 FR 69282, 11/18/2013, effective 11/18/2013; Final rule, 78 FR 73450, 12/6/2013, effective 12/6/2013]

225.371 Contractor personnel supporting U.S. Armed Forces deployed outside the United States.

For additional information on contractor personnel supporting U.S. Armed Forces, see PGI 225.371.

[Final rule, 80 FR 36900, 6/26/2015, effective 6/26/2015]

225.371-1 Scope.

(a) This section applies to contracts that involve contractor personnel supporting U.S. Armed Forces deployed outside the United States in—

(1) Contingency operations;

(2) Humanitarian or peacekeeping operations; or

(3) Other military operations or military exercises, when designated by the combatant commander.

(b) Any of the types of operations listed in paragraph (a) of this section may include stability operations such as—

(1) Establishment or maintenance of a safe and secure environment; or

(2) Provision of emergency infrastructure reconstruction, humanitarian relief, or essential governmental services (until feasible to transition to local government).

[Final rule, 80 FR 36900, 6/26/2015, effective 6/26/2015]

225.371-2 Definition.

Designated operational area is defined in the clause at 252.225-7040. See PGI 225.371-2 for additional information on designated operational areas.

[Final rule, 80 FR 36900, 6/26/2015, effective 6/26/2015]

225.371-3 Government support.

(a) Government support that may be authorized or required for contractor personnel performing in a designated operational area may include, but is not limited to, the types of support listed in PGI 225.371-3(a).

(b) The agency shall provide logistical or security support only when the appropriate agency official, in accordance with agency guidance, determines in coordination with the combatant commander that—

(1) Such Government support is available and is needed to ensure continuation of essential contractor services; and

(2) The contractor cannot obtain adequate support from other sources at a reasonable cost.

(c) The contracting officer shall specify in the solicitation and contract—

(1) Valid terms, approved by the combatant commander, that specify the responsible party, if a party other than the combatant commander is responsible for providing protection to the contractor personnel performing in the designated operational area; and

(2) Any other Government support to be provided, and whether this support will be provided on a reimbursable basis, citing the authority for the reimbursement.

(d) *Medical support of contractor personnel.* The contracting officer shall provide direction to the contractor when the contractor is required to reimburse the Government for medical treatment or transportation of contractor personnel to a selected civilian facility in accordance with paragraph (c)(2)(ii) of the clause at 252.225-7040. For additional information, see PGI 225.371-3(d).

(e) *Letter of authorization.* Contractor personnel must have a Synchronized Predeployment and Operational Tracker (SPOT)-generated letter of authorization (LOA) signed by the contracting officer in order to process through a deployment center or to travel to, from, or within the designated operational area. The LOA also will identify any additional authorizations, privileges, or Government support that the contractor personnel are entitled to under the contract. For additional information on LOAs, see PGI 225.371-3(e).

[Final rule, 80 FR 36900, 6/26/2015, effective 6/26/2015]

225.371-4 Law of war training.

(a) *Basic training.* Basic law of war training is required for all contractor personnel supporting U.S. Armed Forces deployed outside the United States. The basic training normally will be provided through a military-run training center. The contracting officer may authorize the use of an alternate basic training source, provided the servicing DoD legal advisor concurs with the course content. An example of an alternate source of basic training is the web-based training provided by the Defense Acquisition University at *https://acc.dau.mil/CommunityBrowser.aspx?id=18014&lang=en-US.*

(b) *Advanced law of war training.* (1) The types of personnel that must obtain advanced law of war training include the following:

(i) Private security contractors.

(ii) Security guards in or near areas of military operations.

(iii) Interrogators, linguists, interpreters, guards, report writers, information technology technicians, or others who will come into contact with enemy prisoners of war, civilian internees, retained persons, other detainees, terrorists, or criminals who are captured, transferred, confined, or detained during or in the aftermath of hostilities.

(iv) Other personnel when deemed necessary by the contracting officer.

(2) If contractor personnel will be required to obtain advanced law of war training, the solicitation and contract shall specify—

(i) The types of personnel subject to advanced law of war training requirements;

(ii) Whether the training will be provided by the Government or the contractor;

(iii) If the training will be provided by the Government, the source of the training; and

(iv) If the training will be provided by the contractor, a requirement for coordination of the content with the servicing DoD legal advisor to ensure that training content is commensurate with the duties and responsibilities of the personnel to be trained.

[Final rule, 80 FR 36900, 6/26/2015, effective 6/26/2015]

225.371-5 Contract clauses.

(a) Use the clause at 252.225-7040, Contractor Personnel Supporting U.S. Armed Forces Deployed Outside the United States, instead of the clause at FAR 52.225-19, Contractor Personnel in a Designated Operational Area or Supporting a Diplomatic or Consular Mission Outside the United States, in solicitations and contracts, including solicitations and contracts using FAR part 12 procedures for the acquisition of commercial items, for performance in a designated operational area that authorize contractor personnel (including both contractors authorized to accompany the Force (CAAF) and non-CAAF) to support U.S. Armed Forces deployed outside the United States in—

(1) Contingency operations;

(2) Peace operations consistent with Joint Publication 3-07.3; or

(3) Other military operations or military exercises, when designated by the combatant commander or as directed by the Secretary of Defense.

(b) For additional guidance on clauses to consider when using the clause at 252.225-7040, see PGI 225.371-5(b).

[Interim rule, 76 FR 52133, 8/19/2011, effective 8/19/2011; Final rule, 77 FR 35883, 6/15/2012, effective 6/15/2012; Final rule, 78 FR 37980, 6/25/2013, effective 6/25/2013; Final rule, 78 FR 69282, 11/18/2013, effective 11/18/2013; Final rule, 78 FR 73450, 12/6/2013, effective 12/6/2013; Final rule, 80 FR 36900, 6/26/2015, effective 6/26/2015; Interim rule, 80 FR 51739, 8/26/2015, effective 8/26/2015; Final rule, 80 FR 51752, 8/26/2015, effective 8/26/2015]

225.372 Antiterrorism/force protection. (No Text)

[Final rule, 80 FR 36900, 6/26/2015, effective 6/26/2015]

225.372-1 General.

Information and guidance pertaining to DoD antiterrorism/force protection policy for contracts that require performance or travel outside the United States can be obtained from the offices listed in PGI 225.372-1.

[Final rule, 80 FR 36900, 6/26/2015, effective 6/26/2015]

225.372-2 Contract clause.

Use the clause at 252.225-7043, Antiterrorism/Force Protection Policy for Defense Contractors Outside the United States, in solicitations and contracts, including solicitations and contracts using FAR part 12 procedures for the acquisition of commercial items, that require performance or travel outside the United States, except for contracts with—

(a) Foreign governments;

(b) Representatives of foreign governments; or

(c) Foreign corporations wholly owned by foreign governments.

[Final rule, 80 FR 36900, 6/26/2015, effective 6/26/2015]

225.373 Contract administration in support of contingency operations.

For additional guidance on contract administration considerations when supporting contingency operations, see PGI 225.373.

[Final rule, 80 FR 36900, 6/26/2015, effective 6/26/2015]

225.374 Use of electronic business tools.

See 218.271 concerning the use of electronic business tools in support of a contingency operation or humanitarian or peacekeeping operation.

[Final rule, 80 FR 36900, 6/26/2015, effective 6/26/2015; Final rule, 83 FR 24888, 5/30/2018, effective 5/30/2018]

SUBPART 225.4—TRADE AGREEMENTS

225.401 Exceptions.

(a) (2) (A) If a department or agency considers an individual acquisition of a product to be indispensable for national security or national defense purposes and appropriate for exclusion from the provisions of FAR subpart 25.4, it may submit a request with supporting rationale to the Director of Defense Procurement and Acquisition Policy (OUSD (AT&L) DPAP). Approval by OUSD (AT&L) DPAP is not required if—

(*1*) Purchase from foreign sources is restricted by statute (see subpart 225.70);

(*2*) Another exception in FAR 25.401 applies to the acquisition; or

(*3*) Competition from foreign sources is restricted under subpart 225.71.

(B) Public interest exceptions for certain countries when acquiring products or services in support of operations in Afghanistan are in 225.7704–1.

[Final rule, 65 FR 19849, 4/13/2000, effective 4/13/2000; Final rule, 68 FR 15615, 3/31/2003, effective 4/30/2003; Final rule, 75 FR 81915, 12/29/2010, effective 12/29/2010]

225.401-70 End products subject to trade agreements.

Acquisitions of end products in the following product service groups (PSGs) are covered by trade agreements if the value of the acquisition is at or above the applicable trade agreement threshold and no exception applies. If an end product is not in one of the listed groups, the trade agreements do not apply. The definition of Caribbean Basin country end products in FAR 25.003 excludes those end products that are not eligible for duty-free treatment under 19 U.S.C. 2703 (b). Therefore certain watches, watch parts, and luggage from certain Caribbean Basin countries are not eligible products. However, 225.003 expands the definition of Caribbean Basin country end products to include petroleum and any product derived from petroleum, in accordance with Section 8094 of Pub. L. 103-139.

PSG	*Category/description*
22	Railway equipment
23	Motor vehicles, trailers, and cycles (except 2305, 2350 and buses under 2310)
24	Tractors
25	Vehicular equipment components
26	Tires and tubes
29	Engine accessories
30	Mechanical power transmission equipment
32	Woodworking machinery and equipment
34	Metalworking machinery
35	Service and trade equipment
36	Special industry machinery (except 3690)
37	Agricultural machinery and equipment
38	Construction, mining, excavating, and highway maintenance equipment
39	Materials handling equipment
40	Rope, cable, chain, and fittings
41	Refrigeration, air conditioning, and air circulating equipment
42	Fire fighting, rescue and safety equipment; and environmental protection equipment and materials
43	Pumps and compressors
44	Furnace, steam plant, and drying equipment (except 4470)
45	Plumbing, heating, and waste disposal equipment
46	Water purification and sewage treatment equipment
47	Pipe, tubing, hose, and fittings
48	Valves
49	Maintenance and repair shop equipment (except 4920-4927, 4931-4935, 4960, 4970)
53	Hardware and abrasives
54	Prefabricated structures and scaffolding
55	Lumber, millwork, plywood, and veneer
56	Construction and building materials
61	Electric wire, and power and distribution equipment
62	Lighting fixtures and lamps
63	Alarm, signal, and security detection systems
65	Medical, dental, and veterinary equipment and supplies
66	Instruments and laboratory equipment (except aircraft clocks under 6645)—See FAR 25.003 exclusion of certain watches and watch parts for certain Caribbean Basin countries
67	Photographic equipment
68	Chemicals and chemical products

PSG	Category/description
69	Training aids and devices
70	Automatic data processing equipment (including firmware), software, supplies, and support equipment
71	Furniture
72	Household and commercial furnishings and appliances
73	Food preparation and serving equipment
74	Office machines, text processing systems and visible record equipment
75	Office supplies and devices
76	Books, maps, and other publications
77	Musical instruments, phonographs, and home-type radios
78	Recreational and athletic equipment
79	Cleaning equipment and supplies
80	Brushes, paints, sealers, and adhesives
81	Containers, packaging, and packing supplies (except 8140)
83	Pins, needles, and sewing kits (only part of 8315) and flagstaffs, flagpoles, and flagstaff trucks (only part of 8345)
84	Luggage (only 8460)—See FAR 25.003 for exclusion of luggage for Caribbean Basin countries
85	Toiletries
87	Agricultural supplies
88	Live animals
89	Tobacco products (only 8975)
91	Fuels, lubricants, oils, and waxes
93	Nonmetallic fabricated materials
94	Nonmetallic crude materials
96	Ores, minerals, and their primary products
99	Miscellaneous

[Final rule, 65 FR 19849, 4/13/2000, effective 4/13/2000; Final rule, 68 FR 15615, 3/31/2003, effective 4/30/2003; Interim rule, 69 FR 1926, 1/13/2004, effective 1/13/2004; Interim rule, 70 FR 2361, 1/13/2005, effective 1/13/2005; Final rule, 70 FR 73153, 12/9/2005, effective 12/9/2005; Interim rule, 71 FR 9269, 2/23/2006, effective 2/23/2006; Final rule, 71 FR 65752, 11/9/2006, effective 11/9/2006; Final rule, 80 FR 4805, 1/29/2015, effective 1/29/2015]

225.401-71 Products or services in support of operations in Afghanistan.

When acquiring products or services, other than small arms, in support of operations in Afghanistan, if using a procedure specified in 225.7703-1(a)(2) or (3), the procedures of subpart 25.4 are not applicable.

[Interim rule, 73 FR 53151, 9/15/2008, effective 9/15/2008; Final rule, 75 FR 18035, 4/8/2010, effective 4/8/2010; Interim rule, 78 FR 59854, 9/30/2013, effective 9/30/2013; Final rule, 79 FR 11342, 2/28/2014, effective 2/28/2014; Publication notice, 20151230]

225.402 General.

To estimate the value of the acquisition, use the total estimated value of end products covered by trade agreements (see 225.401-70).

[Final rule, 65 FR 19849, 4/13/2000, effective 4/13/2000; Final rule, 67 FR 77937, 12/20/2002, effective 12/20/2002; Interim rule, 70 FR 2361, 1/13/2005, effective 1/13/2005; Final rule, 70 FR 73152, 12/9/2005, effective 12/9/2005]

225.403 World Trade Organization Government Procurement Agreement and Free Trade Agreements.

(c) For acquisitions or supplies covered by the World Trade Organization Government Procurement Agreement, acquire only U.S.-made, qualifying country, or designated country end products unless—

(i) The contracting officer determines that offers of U.S.-made, qualifying country, or designated country end products from responsive, responsible offerors are either—

(A) Not received; or

(B) Insufficient to fill the Government's requirements. In this case, accept all responsive, responsible offers of U.S.-made, qualifying country, and eligible products before accepting any other offers;

(ii) A national interest waiver under 19 U.S.C. 2512(b)(2) is granted on a case-by-case basis. Except as delegated in paragraphs (c)(i)(A) and (B) of this section, submit any request for a national interest waiver to the Director of Defense Procurement and Acquisition Policy in accordance with department or agency procedures. Include supporting rationale with the request.

(A) The head of the contracting activity may approve a national interest waiver for a purchase by an overseas purchasing activity, if the waiver is supported by a written statement from the requiring activity that the products being acquired are critical for the support of U.S. forces stationed abroad.

(B) The Commander or Director, Defense Energy Support Center, may approve national interest waivers for purchases of fuel for use by U.S. forces overseas; or

(iii) The acquisition is in support of operations in Afghanistan (see 225.7704-1).

[Final rule, 65 FR 19849, 4/13/2000, effective 4/13/2000; Final rule, 68 FR 15615, 3/31/2003, effective 4/30/2003; Interim rule, 70 FR 2361, 1/13/2005, effective 1/13/2005; Final rule, 70 FR 73152, 12/9/2005, effective 12/9/2005; Final rule, 75 FR 81915, 12/29/2010, effective 12/29/2010; Final rule, 76 FR 76318, 12/7/2011, effective 12/7/2011]

225.408 Procedures.

(a) (4) The requirements of FAR 25.408(a) (4), on submission of offers in U.S. dollars, do not apply to overseas acquisitions or to Defense Energy Support Center post, camp, or station overseas requirements.

[Final rule, 65 FR 19849, 4/13/2000, effective 4/13/2000; Final rule, 70 FR 73153, 12/9/2005, effective 12/9/2005]

SUBPART 225.5—EVALUATING FOREIGN OFFERS—SUPPLY CONTRACTS

225.502 Application.

(a) Whenever the acquisition is in support of operations in Afghanistan, treat the offers of end products from South Caucasus or Central and South Asian states listed in 225.401-70 the same as qualifying country offers.

(b) Use the following procedures instead of the procedures in FAR 25.502(b) for acquisitions subject to the World Trade Organization Government Procurement Agreement:

(i) Consider only offers of U.S.-made, qualifying country, or designated country end products, except as permitted by 225.403 or 225.7703-1.

(ii) If price is the determining factor, award on the low offer.

(c) Use the following procedures instead of those in FAR 25.502(c) for acquisitions subject to the Buy American statute or the Balance of Payments Program:

(i) (A) If the acquisition is subject only to the Buy American statute or the Balance of Payments Program, then only qualifying country end products are exempt from application of the Buy American or Balance of Payments Program evaluation factor.

(B) If the acquisition is also subject to a Free Trade Agreement, then eligible products of the applicable Free Trade Agreement country are also exempt from application of the Buy American or Balance of Payments Program evaluation factor.

(ii) If price is the determining factor, use the following procedures:

(A) If the low offer is a domestic offer, award on that offer.

(B) If there are no domestic offers, award on the low offer (see example in 225.504(1)).

(C) If the low offer is foreign offer that is exempt from application of the Buy American or Balance of Payments Program evaluation factor, award on that offer. (If the low offer is a qualifying country offer from a country listed at 225.872-1(b), execute a determination in accordance with 225.872-4.)

(D) If the low offer is a foreign offer that is not exempt from application of the Buy American or Balance of Payments Program evaluation factor, and there is another foreign offer that is exempt and is lower than the lowest domestic offer, award on the low foreign offer (see example in 225.504(2)).

(E) Otherwise, apply the 50 percent evaluation factor to the low foreign offer.

(1) If the price of the low domestic offer is less than the evaluated price of the low foreign offer, award on the low domestic offer (see example in 225.504(3)).

(2) If the evaluated price of the low foreign offer remains less than the low domestic offer, award on the low foreign offer (see example in 225.504(4)).

(iii) If price is not the determining factor, use the following procedures:

(A) If there are domestic offers, apply the 50 percent Buy American or Balance of Payments Program evaluation factor to all foreign offers unless an exemption applies.

(B) Evaluate in accordance with the criteria of the solicitation.

(C) If these procedures will not result in award on a domestic offer, reevaluate offers without the 50 percent factor. If this will result in award on an offer to which the Buy American statute or Balance of Payments Program applies, but evaluation in accordance with paragraph (c)(ii) of this section would result in award on a domestic offer, proceed with award only after execution of a determination in accordance with 225.103(a)(ii)(B), that domestic preference would be inconsistent with the public interest.

(iv) If the solicitation includes the provision at 252.225-7023, Preference for Products or Services from Afghanistan, use the evaluation procedures at 225.7703-3.

[Final rule, 65 FR 19849, 4/13/2000, effective 4/13/2000; Final rule, 67 FR 77937, 12/20/2002, effective 12/20/2002; Final rule, 68 FR 15615, 3/31/2003, effective 4/30/2003; Interim rule, 69 FR 1926, 1/13/2004, effective 1/13/2004; Final rule, 69 FR 74991, 12/15/2004, effective 12/15/2004; Interim rule, 70 FR 2361, 1/13/2005, effective 1/13/2005; Final rule, 70 FR 73152, 12/9/2005, effective 12/9/2005; Interim rule, 73 FR 53151, 9/15/2008, effective 9/15/2008; Final rule, 75 FR 18035, 4/8/2010, effective 4/8/2010; Final rule, 75 FR 81915, 12/29/2010, effective 12/29/2010; Final rule, 77 FR 35879, 6/15/2012, effective 6/15/2012; Interim rule, 78 FR 59854, 9/30/2013, effective 9/30/2013; Final rule, 79 FR 11342, 2/28/2014, effective 2/28/2014]

225.503 Group offers.

Evaluate group offers in accordance with FAR 25.503, but apply the evaluation procedures of 225.502.

[Final rule, 68 FR 15615, 3/31/2003, effective 4/30/2003]

225.504 Evaluation examples.

For examples that illustrate the evaluation procedures in 225.502(c)(ii), see PGI 225.504.

[Final rule, 65 FR 19849, 4/13/2000, effective 4/13/2000; Final rule, 67 FR 77939, 12/20/2002, effective 12/20/2002; Final rule, 68 FR 15615, 3/31/2003, effective 4/30/2003; Final rule, 70 FR 73153, 12/9/2005, effective 12/9/2005]

SUBPART 225.6—[REMOVED]

225.670 [Removed]

225.670-1 [Removed]

[Final rule, 68 FR 15615, 3/31/2003, effective 4/30/2003; Final rule, 71 FR 39005, 7/11/2006, effective 7/11/2006]

225.670-2 [Removed]

[Final rule, 68 FR 15615, 3/31/2003, effective 4/30/2003; Final rule, 71 FR 39005, 7/11/2006, effective 7/11/2006]

225.670-3 [Removed]

[Final rule, 68 FR 15615, 3/31/2003, effective 4/30/2003; Final rule, 71 FR 39005, 7/11/2006, effective 7/11/2006]

225.670-4 [Removed]

[Final rule, 68 FR 15615, 3/31/2003, effective 4/30/2003; Final rule, 71 FR 39005, 7/11/2006, effective 7/11/2006]

SUBPART 225.7—PROHIBITED SOURCES

225.701 Restrictions. (No Text)

[Final rule, 59 FR 51132, 10/7/94, effective 9/29/94; redesignated from 225.702, Final rule, 65 FR 19849, 4/13/2000, effective 4/13/2000; Final rule, 68 FR 15615, 3/31/2003, effective 4/30/2003; Final rule, 70 FR 73153, 12/9/2005, effective 12/9/2005; Final rule, 79 FR 73488, 12/11/2014, effective 12/11/2014]

225.701-70 Exception.

DoD personnel are authorized to make emergency acquisitions in direct support of U.S. or allied forces deployed in military contingency, humanitarian, or peacekeeping operations in a country or region subject to economic sanctions administered by the Department of the Treasury, Office of Foreign Assets Control.

[Interim rule, 68 FR 7441, 2/14/2003, effective 2/14/2003]

225.770 Prohibition on acquisition of certain items from Communist Chinese military companies.

This section implements section 1211 of the National Defense Authorization Act for Fiscal Year 2006 (Pub. L. 109-163), section 1243 of the National Defense Authorization Act for Fiscal Year 2012 (Pub. L. 112-81), and section 1296 of the National Defense Authorization Act for Fiscal Year 2017 (Pub. L. 114-328). See PGI 225.770 for additional information relating to this statute, the terms used in this section, the United States Munitions List (USML), and the 600 series of the Commerce Control List (CCL).

[Final rule, 68 FR 15615, 3/31/2003, effective 4/30/2003; Interim rule, 71 FR 53045, 9/8/2006, effective 9/8/2006; Final rule, 72 FR 14239, 3/27/2007, effective 3/27/2007; Final rule, 77 FR 30365, 5/22/2012, effective 5/22/2012; Interim rule, 83 FR 66066, 12/21/2018, effective 12/21/2018; Final rule, 84 FR 25188, 5/31/2019, effective 5/31/2019]

225.770-1 Definitions.

As used in this section—

Component means an item that is useful only when used in conjunction with an end item (15 CFR 772.1 and 22 CFR 120.45(b)).

Item means—

(1) A USML defense article, as defined at 22 CFR 120.6;

(2) A USML defense service, as defined at 22 CFR 120.9; or

(3) A 600 series item, as defined at 15 CFR 772.1.

Part means any single unassembled element of a major or minor component, accessory, or attachment, that is not normally subject to disassembly without the destruction or impairment of designed use (15 CFR 772.1 and 22 CFR 120.45(d)).

[DAC 91-4, 57 FR 53599, 11/12/92, effective 10/30/92; Final rule, 68 FR 15615, 3/31/2003, effective 4/30/2003; Interim rule, 71 FR 53045, 9/8/2006, effective 9/8/2006; Final rule, 72 FR 14239, 3/27/2007, effective 3/27/2007; Interim rule, 83 FR 66066, 12/21/2018, effective 12/21/2018; Final rule, 84 FR 25188, 5/31/2019, effective 5/31/2019]

225.770-2 Prohibition.

Do not acquire items covered by the USML or the 600 series of the CCL, through a contract or subcontract at any tier, from any Communist Chinese military company. This prohibition does not apply to components and parts of covered items unless the components and parts are themselves covered by the USML or the 600 series of the CCL.

[Interim rule, 71 FR 53045, 9/8/2006, effective 9/8/2006; Final rule, 72 FR 14239, 3/27/2007, effective 3/27/2007; Interim rule, 83 FR 66066, 12/21/2018, effective 12/21/2018; Final rule, 84 FR 25188, 5/31/2019, effective 5/31/2019]

225.770-3 Exceptions.

The prohibition in DFARS 225.770-2 does not apply to items acquired—

(a) In connection with a visit to the People's Republic of China by a vessel or an aircraft of the U.S. armed forces;

(b) For testing purposes; or

(c) For the purpose of gathering intelligence.

[DAC 91-4, 57 FR 53599, 11/12/92, effective 10/30/92; Final rule, 64 FR 2595, 1/15/99, effective 1/15/99; Final rule, 68 FR 15615, 3/31/2003, effective 4/30/2003; Interim rule, 71 FR 53045, 9/8/2006, effective 9/8/2006; Final rule, 72 FR 14239, 3/27/2007, effective 3/27/2007; Interim rule, 83 FR 66066, 12/21/2018, effective 12/21/2018; Final rule, 84 FR 25188, 5/31/2019, effective 5/31/2019]

225.770-4 Identifying items covered by the USML or the 600 series of the CCL.

(a) Before issuance of a solicitation, the requiring activity will notify the contracting officer in writing whether the items to be acquired are covered by the USML or the 600 series of the CCL. The notification will identify any covered item(s) and will provide the pertinent USML reference(s) from 22 CFR part 121 or the 600 series of the CCL references from 15 CFR part 774, supplement no. 1.

(b) The USML includes defense articles and defense services that fall into 21 categories. The CCL includes ten categories and five product groups in each category, many of which contain 600 series items. Since not all items covered by the USML or 600 series of the CCL are themselves munitions (*e.g.*, protective personnel equipment, military training equipment), the requiring activity should consult the USML and the 600 series of the CCL before concluding that an item is or is not covered. See PGI 225.770-4.

[DAC 91-4, 57 FR 53599, 11/12/92, effective 10/30/92; DAC 91-9, 60 FR 61586, 11/30/95, effective 11/30/95; Final rule, 65 FR 39703, 6/27/2000, effective 6/27/2000; Final rule, 68 FR 15615, 3/31/2003, effective 4/30/2003; Interim rule, 71 FR 53045, 9/8/2006, effective 9/8/2006; Final rule, 72 FR 14239, 3/27/2007, effective 3/27/2007; Interim rule, 83 FR 66066, 12/21/2018, effective 12/21/2018; Final rule, 84 FR 25188, 5/31/2019, effective 5/31/2019]

225.770-5 Waiver of prohibition.

(a) The prohibition in 225.770-2 may be waived, on a case-by-case basis, if an official identified in paragraph (b) of this subsection determines that a waiver is necessary for national security purposes.

(b) The following officials are authorized, without power of delegation, to make the determination specified in paragraph (a) of this subsection:

(1) The Under Secretary of Defense (Acquisition and Sustainment).

(2) The Secretaries of the military departments.

(3) The Component Acquisition Executive of the Defense Logistics Agency.

(c) (1) The official granting a waiver shall submit a report to the congressional defense committees, with a copy to the Director of Defense Procurement and Acquisition Policy (see PGI 225.770-5), not less than 15 days before issuing the waiver.

(2) In the report, the official shall—

(i) Identify the specific reasons for the waiver; and

(ii) Include recommendations as to what actions may be taken to develop alternative sourcing capabilities in the future.

[DAC 91-4, 57 FR 53599, 11/12/92, effective 10/30/92; Final rule, 68 FR 15615, 3/31/2003, effective 4/30/2003; Interim rule, 71 FR 53045, 9/8/2006, effective 9/8/2006; Final rule, 72 FR 14239, 3/27/2007, effective 3/27/2007; Final rule, 77 FR 30365, 5/22/2012, effective 5/22/2012; Interim rule, 83 FR 66066, 12/21/2018, effective 12/21/2018; Final rule, 84 FR 25188, 5/31/2019, effective 5/31/2019]

225.771 Prohibition on contracting or subcontracting with a firm that is owned or controlled by the government of a country that is a state sponsor of terrorism. (No Text)

[Final rule, 68 FR 15615, 3/31/2003, effective 4/30/2003; Interim rule, 79 FR 45661, 8/5/2014, effective 8/5/2014; Final rule, 79 FR 73488, 12/11/2014, effective 12/11/2014; Final rule, 79 FR 73490, 12/11/2014, effective 12/11/2014]

225.771-0 Scope.

This section implements 10 U.S.C. 2327(b).

[Final rule, 79 FR 73488, 12/11/2014, effective 12/11/2014]

225.771-1 Definition.

State sponsor of terrorism, as used in this section, is defined in the provision at 252.225-7050, Disclosure of Ownership or Control by the Government of a Country that is a State Sponsor of Terrorism.

Interim rule, 64 FR 8727, 2/23/99, effective 2/23/99; Final rule, 68 FR 15615, 3/31/2003, effective 4/30/2003; Interim rule, 79 FR 45661, 8/5/2014, effective 8/5/2014; Final rule, 79 FR 73488, 12/11/2014, effective 12/11/2014]

225.771-2 Prohibition.

(a) The contracting officer shall not award a contract of $150,000 or more to a firm when a foreign government that is a state sponsor of terrorism owns or controls, either directly or indirectly, a significant interest in—

(i) The firm;

(ii) A subsidiary of the firm; or

(iii) Any other firm that owns or controls the firm.

(b) For restrictions on subcontracting with a firm, or a subsidiary of a firm, that is identified by the Secretary of Defense as being owned or controlled by the government of a country that is a state sponsor of terrorism, see 209.405-2.

[Interim rule, 64 FR 8727, 2/23/99, effective 2/23/99; Final rule, 65 FR 6553, 2/10/2000, effective 2/10/2000; Interim rule, 79 FR 45661, 8/5/2014, effective 8/5/2014; Final rule, 79 FR 73488, 12/11/2014, effective 12/11/2014]

225.771-3 Notification.

Any disclosure that the government of a country that is a state sponsor of terrorism has a significant interest in an offeror, a subsidiary of an offeror, or any other firm that owns or controls an offeror shall be forwarded through agency channels to the address at PGI 225.771-3.

[Final rule, 65 FR 6553, 2/10/2000, effective 2/10/2000; Final rule, 68 FR 15615, 3/31/2003, effective 4/30/2003; Interim rule, 79 FR 45661, 8/5/2014, effective 8/5/2014; Final rule, 79 FR 73488, 12/11/2014, effective 12/11/2014]

225.771-4 Waiver of prohibition.

The prohibition in 225.771-2 may be waived if the Secretary of Defense determines that a waiver is not inconsistent with the national security objectives of the United States in accordance with 10 U.S.C. 2327(c).

[Final rule, 65 FR 6553, 2/10/2000, effective 2/10/20002000; Final rule, 68 FR 15615, 3/31/2003, effective 4/30/2003; Interim rule, 79 FR 45661, 8/5/2014, effective 8/5/2014; Final rule, 79 FR 73488, 12/11/2014, effective 12/11/2014]

225.771-5 Solicitation provision.

Use the provision at 252.225-7050, Disclosure of Ownership or Control by the Government of a Country that is a State Sponsor of Terrorism, in solicitations, including solicitations using FAR part 12 procedures for the acquisition of commercial items (other than commercial satellite services), that are expected to result in contracts of $150,000 or more. If the solicitation includes the provision at FAR 52.204-7, do not separately list the provision 252.225-7050 in the solicitation.

[Final rule, 65 FR 6553, 2/10/2000, effective 2/10/2000; Final rule, 68 FR 15615, 3/31/2003, effective 4/30/2003; Interim rule, 79 FR 45661, 8/5/2014, effective 8/5/2014; Final rule, 79 FR 73488, 12/11/2014, effective 12/11/2014]

225.772 Prohibition on acquisition of certain foreign commercial satellite services. (No Text)

[Interim rule, 79 FR 45661, 8/5/2014, effective 8/5/2014; Final rule, 79 FR 73490, 12/11/2014, effective 12/11/2014; Interim rule, 83 FR 66066, 12/21/2018, effective 12/21/2018; Final rule, 84 FR 25188, 5/31/2019, effective 5/31/2019]

225.772-0 Scope.

This section implements 10 U.S.C. 2279.

[Interim rule, 79 FR 45661, 8/5/2014, effective 8/5/2014; Final rule, 79 FR 73490, 12/11/2014, effective 12/11/2014]

225.772-1 Definitions.

As used in this section—

Covered foreign country means—

(1) The People's Republic of China;

(2) North Korea;

(3) The Russian Federation; or

(4) Any country that is a state sponsor of terrorism. (10 U.S.C. 2279)

Cybersecurity risk means threats to and vulnerabilities of information or information systems and any related consequences caused by or resulting from unauthorized access, use, disclosure, degradation, disruption, modification, or destruction of such information or information systems, including such related consequences caused by an act of terrorism. (10 U.S.C. 2279)

Foreign entity means—

(1) Any branch, partnership, group or subgroup, association, estate, trust, corporation or division of a corporation, or organization organized under the laws of a foreign state if either its principal place of business is

outside the United States or its equity securities are primarily traded on one or more foreign exchanges.

(2) Notwithstanding paragraph (1) of this definition, any branch, partnership, group or sub-group, association, estate, trust, corporation or division of a corporation, or organization that demonstrates that a majority of the equity interest in such entity is ultimately owned by U.S. nationals is not a foreign entity. (31 CFR 800.212)

Government of a covered foreign country includes the state and the government of a covered foreign country, as well as any political subdivision, agency, or instrumentality thereof.

Launch vehicle means a fully integrated space launch vehicle. (10 U.S.C. 2279)

Satellite services means communications capabilities that utilize an on-orbit satellite for transmitting the signal from one location to another.

State sponsor of terrorism means a country determined by the Secretary of State, under section 1754(c)(1)(A)(i) of the Export Control Reform Act of 2018 (Title XVII, Subtitle B, of the National Defense Authorization Act for Fiscal Year 2019, Pub. L. 115-232), to be a country the government of which has repeatedly provided support for acts of international terrorism. As of December 21, 2018, state sponsors of terrorism include: Iran, North Korea, Sudan, and Syria. (10 U.S.C. 2327)

[Interim rule, 79 FR 45661, 8/5/2014, effective 8/5/2014; Final rule, 79 FR 73490, 12/11/2014, effective 12/11/2014; Interim rule, 83 FR 66066, 12/21/2018, effective 12/21/2018; Final rule, 84 FR 25188, 5/31/2019, effective 5/31/2019]

225.772-2 Prohibitions.

Except as provided in 225.772-4, the contracting officer shall not award a contract for commercial satellite services to—

(a)(1) A foreign entity if the Under Secretary of Defense for Acquisition and Sustainment or the Under Secretary of Defense for Policy reasonably believes that—

(i) The foreign entity is an entity in which the government of a covered foreign country has an ownership interest that enables the government to affect satellite operations;

(ii) The foreign entity plans to or is expected to provide satellite services under the contract from a covered foreign country; or

(iii) Entering into such contract would create an unacceptable cybersecurity risk for DoD, as determined by the Under Secretary of Defense for Acquisition and Sustainment or the Under Secretary of Defense for Policy; or

(2) An offeror that is offering commercial satellite services provided by a foreign entity as described in paragraph (a) of this section; or

(b)(1) Any entity, except as provided in paragraph (b)(2) of this section, for a launch that occurs on or after December 31, 2022, if the Under Secretary of Defense for Acquisition and Sustainment or the Under Secretary of Defense for Policy reasonably believes that such satellite services will be provided using satellites that will be—

(i) Designed or manufactured—

(A) In a covered foreign country; or

(B) By an entity controlled in whole or in part by, or acting on behalf of, the government of a covered foreign country; or

(ii) Launched outside the United States using a launch vehicle that is—

(A) Designed or manufactured in a covered foreign country; or

(B) Provided by—

(*1*) The government of a covered foreign country; or

(*2*) An entity controlled in whole or in part by, or acting on behalf of, the government of a covered foreign country.

(2) The prohibition in paragraph (b)(1) of this section does not apply with respect to launch services for which a satellite service provider has a contract or other agreement that, prior to June 10, 2018, was either fully paid for by the satellite service provider or covered by a legally binding commitment of the satellite service provider to pay for such services.

[Interim rule, 79 FR 45661, 8/5/2014, effective 8/5/2014; Final rule, 79 FR 73490,

12/11/2014, effective 12/11/2014; Interim rule, 83 FR 66066, 12/21/2018, effective 12/21/2018; Final rule, 84 FR 25188, 5/31/2019, effective 5/31/2019]

225.772-3 Procedures.

(a)(1) The contracting officer shall not award to any source that is a foreign satellite service provider or is offering satellite services provided by a foreign entity if such award presents an unacceptable cybersecurity risk, as determined by the Under Secretary of Defense for Acquisition and Sustainment or the Under Secretary of Defense for Policy.

(2) When procuring commercial satellite services from a foreign entity, the contracting officer shall review the exclusion records in the System for Award Management (SAM) database as required at FAR 9.405, to ensure that an entity identified in, or otherwise known to be involved in, the otherwise successful offer is not listed as ineligible in the SAM database (see FAR 9.405).

(b) If an offeror discloses information in accordance with paragraph (c) of the provision 252.225-7049, Prohibition on Acquisition of Certain Foreign Commercial Satellite Services—Representations, the contracting officer—

(1) Shall forward the information regarding the offeror through agency channels to the address at PGI 225.772-3; and

(2) Shall not award to that offeror, unless an exception is determined to apply in accordance with 225.772-4.

(c)(1) If the otherwise successful offeror provides negative responses to all representations in the provision at 252.225-7049, the contracting officer may rely on the representations, unless the contracting officer has an independent reason to question the representations.

(2) If the contracting officer has an independent reason to question a negative representation of the otherwise successful offeror, the contracting officer shall consult with the office specified in PGI 225.772-3, prior to deciding whether to award to that offeror.

[Interim rule, 79 FR 45661, 8/5/2014, effective 8/5/2014; Final rule, 79 FR 73490, 12/11/2014, effective 12/11/2014; Interim rule, 83 FR 66066, 12/21/2018, effective 12/21/2018; Final rule, 84 FR 25188, 5/31/2019, effective 5/31/2019]

225.772-4 Exception.

(a) The prohibitions in 225.772-2(a) and (b) do not apply if—

(1) The Under Secretary of Defense for Acquisition and Sustainment, or the Under Secretary of Defense for Policy, without power of redelegation, determines that it is in the national security interest of the United States to enter into such contract; and

(2) Not later than seven days before entering into such contract, the Under Secretary of Defense making the determination in paragraph (a)(1) of this section, in consultation with the Director of National Intelligence, submits to the congressional defense committees a national security assessment, in accordance with 10 U.S.C. 2279.

(b) If requesting an exception pursuant to paragraph (a) of this section, the contracting officer shall forward the request through agency channels to the address at PGI 225.772-3, providing any available information necessary for the Under Secretary of Defense making the determination in paragraph (a)(1) of this section to evaluate the request and perform a national security assessment, in accordance with 10 U.S.C. 2279.

[Interim rule, 79 FR 45661, 8/5/2014, effective 8/5/2014; Final rule, 79 FR 73490, 12/11/2014, effective 12/11/2014; Interim rule, 83 FR 66066, 12/21/2018, effective 12/21/2018; Final rule, 84 FR 25188, 5/31/2019, effective 5/31/2019]

225.772-5 Solicitation provision and contract clauses.

(a) Use the provision at 252.225-7049, Prohibition on Acquisition of Certain Foreign Commercial Satellite Services—Representations, in solicitations that include the clause at 252.225-7051, Prohibition on Acquisition of Certain Foreign Commercial Satellite Services. If the solicitation includes the provision at FAR 52.204-7, do not separately list the provision 252.225-7049 in the solicitation.

(b) Use the clause at 252.225-7051, Prohibition on Acquisition of Certain Foreign Commercial Satellite Services, in solicitations and contracts for the acquisition of commercial satellite services, including solicitation and contracts using FAR part 12 procedures for the acquisition of commercial items.

(c) Use the clause at 252.239-7018, Supply Chain Risk, as prescribed at 239.7306(b), when applicable.

[Interim rule, 79 FR 45661, 8/5/2014, effective 8/5/2014; Final rule, 79 FR 73490, 12/11/2014, effective 12/11/2014; Interim rule, 83 FR 66066, 12/21/2018, effective 12/21/2018; Final rule, 84 FR 25188, 5/31/2019, effective 5/31/2019]

SUBPART 225.8—OTHER INTERNATIONAL AGREEMENTS AND COORDINATION

225.802 Procedures.

(b) Information on memoranda of understanding and other international agreements is available at PGI 225.802(b).

[Final rule, 68 FR 15615, 3/31/2003, effective 4/30/2003; Final rule, 70 FR 73153, 12/9/2005, effective 12/9/2005]

225.802-70 Contracts for performance outside the United States and Canada.

Follow the procedures at PGI 802-70 when placing a contract requiring performance outside the United States and Canada. Also see subpart 225.3, Contracts Performed Outside the United States.

[Final rule, 65 FR 52951, 8/31/2000, effective 8/31/2000; Final rule, 68 FR 15615, 3/31/2003, effective 4/30/2003; Final rule, 70 FR 23790, 5/5/2005, effective 6/6/2005; Final rule, 77 FR 43470, 7/24/2012, effective 7/24/2012; Final rule, 80 FR 36900, 6/26/2015, effective 6/26/2015]

225.802-71 End use certificates.

Contracting officers considering the purchase of an item from a foreign source may encounter a request for the signing of a certificate to indicate that the Armed Forces of the United States is the end user of the item, and that the U.S. Government will not transfer the item to third parties without authorization from the Government of the country selling the item. When encountering this situation, refer to DoD Directive 2040.3, End Use Certificates, for guidance.

[DAC 91-3, 57 FR 42630, 9/15/92, effective 8/31/92; Final rule, 68 FR 15615, 3/31/2003, effective 4/30/2003]

225.870 Contracting with Canadian contractors. (No Text)

225.870-1 General.

(a) The Canadian government guarantees to the U.S. Government all commitments, obligations, and covenants of the Canadian Commercial Corporation under any contract or order issued to the Corporation by any contracting office of the U.S. Government. The Canadian government has waived notice of any change or modification that may be made, from time to time, in these commitments, obligations, or covenants.

(b) For production planning purposes, Canada is part of the defense industrial base (see 225.870-2(b)).

(c) The Canadian Commercial Corporation will award and administer contracts with contractors located in Canada, except for—

(1) Negotiated acquisitions for experimental, developmental, or research work under projects other than the Defense Development Sharing Program;

(2) Acquisitions of unusual or compelling urgency;

(3) Acquisitions at or below the simplified acquisition threshold; or

(4) Acquisitions made by DoD activities located in Canada.

(d) For additional information on production rights, data, and information; services provided by Canadian Commercial Corporation; audit; and inspection, see PGI 225.870-1(d).

[Final rule, 65 FR 52951, 8/31/2000, effective 8/31/2000; Final rule, 68 FR 15615, 3/31/2003, effective 4/30/2003; Final rule, 70 FR 73153, 12/9/2005, effective

12/9/2005; Final rule, 77 FR 43470, 7/24/2012, effective 7/24/2012]

225.870-2 Solicitation of Canadian contractors.

(a) If requested, furnish a solicitation to the Canadian Commercial Corporation even if no Canadian firm is solicited.

(b) Handle acquisitions at or below the simplified acquisition threshold directly with Canadian firms and not through the Canadian Commercial Corporation.

[DAC 91-3, 57 FR 42630, 9/15/92, effective 8/31/92; Final rule, 68 FR 15615, 3/31/2003, effective 4/30/2003; Final rule, 72 FR 20758, 4/26/2007, effective 4/26/2007]

225.870-3 Submission of offers.

(a) As indicated in 225.870-4, the Canadian Commercial Corporation is the prime contractor. To indicate acceptance of offers by individual Canadian companies, the Canadian Commercial Corporation issues a letter supporting the Canadian offer and containing the following information:

(1) Name of the Canadian offeror.

(2) Confirmation and endorsement of the offer in the name of the Canadian Commercial Corporation.

(3) A statement that the Corporation shall subcontract 100 percent with the offeror.

(b) When a Canadian offer cannot be processed through the Canadian Commercial Corporation in time to meet the date for receipt of offers, the Corporation may permit Canadian firms to submit offers directly. However, the contracting officer shall receive the Canadian Commercial Corporation's endorsement before contract award.

(c) The Canadian Commercial Corporation will submit all sealed bids in terms of U.S. currency. Do not adjust contracts awarded under sealed bidding for losses or gains from fluctuation in exchange rates.

(d) Except for sealed bids, the Canadian Commercial Corporation normally will submit offers and quotations in terms of Canadian currency. The Corporation may, at the time of submitting an offer, elect to quote and receive payment in terms of U.S. currency, in which case the contract—

(1) Shall provide for payment in U.S. currency; and

(2) Shall not be adjusted for losses or gains from fluctuation in exchange rates.

[Final rule, 68 FR 15615, 3/31/2003, effective 4/30/2003]

225.870-4 Contracting procedures.

(a) Except for contracts described in225.870-1(c)(1) through (4), award individual contracts covering purchases from suppliers located in Canada to the Canadian Commercial Corporation, 350 Albert Street, Suite 700, Ottawa, ON K1R 1A4.

(b) Direct communication with the Canadian supplier is authorized and encouraged in connection with all technical aspects of the contract, provided the Corporation's approval is obtained on any matters involving changes to the contract.

(c) *Requirement for data other than certified cost or pricing data.* (1) DoD has waived the requirement for submission of certified cost or pricing data for the Canadian Commercial Corporation and its subcontractors (see 215.403-1(c)(4)(C)).

(2) The Canadian Commercial Corporation is not exempt from the requirement to submit data other than certified cost or pricing data, as defined in FAR 2.101. In accordance with FAR 15.403-3(a)(1)(ii), the contracting officer shall require submission of data other than certified cost or pricing data from the offeror, to the extent necessary to determine a fair and reasonable price.

(i) No further approval is required to request data other than certified cost or pricing data from the Canadian Commercial Corporation in the following circumstances:

(A) In a solicitation for a sole source acquisition that is—

(1) Cost-reimbursement, if the contract value is expected to exceed $700,000; or

(2) Fixed-price, if the contract value is expected to exceed $500 million.

(B) If the Canadian Commercial Corporation submits the only offer in response to a competitive solicitation that meets the thresholds specified in paragraph (c)(2)(i)(A) of this section.

(C) For modifications that exceed $150,000 in contracts that meet the criteria in paragraph (c)(2)(i)(A) or (B) of this section.

(D) In competitive solicitations in which data other than certified cost or pricing data are required from all offerors.

(ii) In any circumstances other than those specified in paragraph (c)(2)(i) of this section, the contracting officer shall only require data other than certified cost or pricing data from the Canadian Commercial Corporation if the head of the contracting activity, or designee no lower than two levels above the contracting officer, determines that data other than certified cost or pricing data are needed (or in the case of modifications that it is reasonably certain that data other than certified cost or pricing data will be needed) in order to determine that the price is fair and reasonable) (see FAR 15.403-3(a).

(3) The contracting officer shall use the provision at 252.215-7003, Requirement for Submission of Data Other Than Certified Cost or Pricing Data—Canadian Commercial Corporation, and the clause at 252.215-7004, Requirement for Submission of Data Other Than Certified Cost or Pricing Data—Modifications—Canadian Commercial Corporation, as prescribed at 215.408(2)(i) and (ii), respectively.

(4) Except for contracts described in 225.870-1(c)(1) through (4), Canadian suppliers will provide required data other than certified cost or pricing data exclusively through the Canadian Commercial Corporation.

(5) As specified in FAR 15.403-3(a)(4), an offeror who does not comply with a requirement to submit data that the contracting officer has deemed necessary to determine price reasonableness or cost realism is ineligible for award, unless the head of the contracting activity determines that it is in the best interest of the Government to make the award to that offeror, based on consideration of the following:

(i) The effort made to obtain the data.

(ii) The need for the item or service.

(iii) Increased cost or significant harm to the Government if award is not made.

(d) Identify in the contract, the type of currency, i.e., U.S. or Canadian. Contracts that provide for payment in Canadian currency shall—

(1) Quote the contract price in terms of Canadian dollars and identify the amount by the initials "CN", e.g., $1,647.23CN; and

(2) Clearly indicate on the face of the contract the U.S./Canadian conversion rate at the time of award and the U.S. dollar equivalent of the Canadian dollar contract amount.

[DAC 91-3, 57 FR 42630, 9/15/92, effective 8/31/92; Final rule, 68 FR 15615, 3/31/2003, effective 4/30/2003; Final rule, 77 FR 43470, 7/24/2012, effective 7/24/2012; Final rule, 78 FR 65214, 10/31/2013, effective 10/31/2013; Final rule, 80 FR 36718, 6/26/2015, effective 6/26/2015; Final rule, 82 FR 61479, 12/28/2017, effective 12/28/2017; Final rule, 83 FR 30824, 6/29/2018, effective 6/29/2018]

225.870-5 Contract administration.

Follow the contract administration procedures at PGI 225.870-5.

[Final rule, 65 FR 52951, 8/31/2000, effective 8/31/2000; Final rule, 68 FR 15615, 3/31/2003, effective 4/30/2003; Final rule, 69 FR 58353, 9/30/2004, effective 9/30/2004; Final rule, 70 FR 73153, 12/9/2005, effective 12/9/2005]

225.870-6 Termination procedures.

When contract termination is necessary, follow the procedures at 249.7000.

[Final rule, 68 FR 15615, 3/31/2003, effective 4/30/2003; Final rule, 71 FR 27644, 5/12/2006, effective 5/12/2006]

225.870-7 Acceptance of Canadian supplies.

For information on the acceptance of Canadian supplies, see PGI 225.870-7.

[Final rule, 68 FR 15615, 3/31/2003, effective 4/30/2003; Final rule, 70 FR 73153, 12/9/2005, effective 12/9/2005]

225.870-8 Industrial security.

Industrial security for Canada shall be in accordance with the U.S.-Canada Industrial Security Agreement of March 31, 1952, as amended.

[Final rule, 68 FR 15615, 3/31/2003, effective 4/30/2003]

225.871 North Atlantic Treaty Organization (NATO) cooperative projects. (No Text)

[Final rule, 70 FR 73153, 12/9/2005, effective 12/9/2005]

225.871-1 Scope.

This section implements 22 U.S.C. 2767 and 10 U.S.C. 2350b.

[Final rule, 68 FR 15615, 3/31/2003, effective 4/30/2003; Final rule, 70 FR 73153, 12/9/2005, effective 12/9/2005]

225.871-2 Definitions.

As used in this section—

(a) *Cooperative project* means a jointly managed arrangement—

(1) Described in a written agreement between the parties;

(2) Undertaken to further the objectives of standardization, rationalization, and interoperability of the armed forces of NATO member countries; and

(3) Providing for—

(i) One or more of the other participants to share with the United States the cost of research and development, testing, evaluation, or joint production (including follow-on support) of certain defense articles;

(ii) Concurrent production in the United States and in another member country of a defense article jointly developed; or

(iii) Acquisition by the United States of a defense article or defense service from another member country.

(b) *Other participant* means a cooperative project participant other than the United States.

[Final rule, 68 FR 15615, 3/31/2003, effective 4/30/2003]

225.871-3 General.

(a) *Cooperative project authority.*

(1) Departments and agencies, that have authority to do so, may enter into cooperative project agreements with NATO or with one or more member countries of NATO under DoDD 5530.3, International Agreements.

(2) Under laws and regulations governing the negotiation and implementation of cooperative project agreements, departments and agencies may enter into contracts, or incur other obligations, on behalf of other participants without charge to any appropriation or contract authorization.

(3) Agency heads are authorized to solicit and award contracts to implement cooperative projects.

(b) *Contracts implementing cooperative projects shall comply with all applicable laws relating to Government acquisition, unless a waiver is granted under 225.871-4.* A waiver of certain laws and regulations may be obtained if the waiver—

(1) Is required by the terms of a written cooperative project agreement;

(2) Will significantly further NATO standardization, rationalization, and interoperability; and

(3) Is approved by the appropriate DoD official.

[Final rule, 68 FR 15615, 3/31/2003, effective 4/30/2003]

225.871-4 Statutory waivers.

(a) For contracts or subcontracts placed outside the United States, the Deputy Secretary of Defense may waive any provision of law that specifically prescribes—

(1) Procedures for the formation of contracts;

(2) Terms and conditions for inclusion in contracts;

(3) Requirements or preferences for—

(i) Goods grown, produced, or manufactured in the United States or in U.S. Government-owned facilities; or

(ii) Services to be performed in the United States; or

(4) Requirements regulating the performance of contracts.

(b) There is no authority for waiver of—

(1) Any provision of the Arms Export Control Act (22 U.S.C. 2751);

(2) Any provision of 10 U.S.C. 2304;

(3) The cargo preference laws of the United States, including the Military Cargo Preference Act of 1904 (10 U.S.C. 2631) and the Cargo Preference Act of 1954 (46 U.S.C. 1241(b)); or

(4) Any of the financial management responsibilities administered by the Secretary of the Treasury.

(c) To request a waiver under a cooperative project, follow the procedures at PGI 225.871-4.

(d) Obtain the approval of the Deputy Secretary of Defense before committing to make a waiver in an agreement or a contract.

[Final rule, 68 FR 15615, 3/31/2003, effective 4/30/2003; Final rule, 71 FR 62565, 10/26/2006, effective 10/26/2006]

225.871-5 Directed subcontracting.

(a) The Director of Defense Procurement and Acquisition Policy may authorize the direct placement of subcontracts with particular subcontractors. Directed subcontracting is not authorized unless specifically addressed in the cooperative project agreement.

(b) In some instances, it may not be feasible to name specific subcontractors at the time the agreement is concluded. However, the agreement shall clearly state the general provisions for work sharing at the prime and subcontract level. For additional information on cooperative project agreements, see PGI 225.871-5.

[Final rule, 68 FR 15615, 3/31/2003, effective 4/30/2003; Final rule, 70 FR 73153, 12/9/2005, effective 12/9/2005]

225.871-6 Disposal of property.

Dispose of property that is jointly acquired by the members of a cooperative project under the procedures established in the agreement or in a manner consistent with the terms of the agreement, without regard to any laws of the United States applicable to the disposal of property owned by the United States.

[Final rule, 68 FR 15615, 3/31/2003, effective 4/30/2003; Final rule, 70 FR 73153, 12/9/2005, effective 12/9/2005]

225.871-7 Congressional notification.

(a) Congressional notification is required when DoD makes a determination to award a contract or subcontract to a particular entity, if the determination was not part of the certification made under 22 U.S.C. 2767(f) before finalizing the cooperative agreement.

(1) Departments and agencies shall provide a proposed Congressional notice to the Director of Defense Procurement and Acquisition Policy in sufficient time to forward to Congress before the time of contract award.

(2) The proposed notice shall include the reason it is necessary to use the authority to designate a particular contractor or subcontractor.

(b) Congressional notification is also required each time a statutory waiver under 225.871-4 is incorporated in a contract or a contract modification, if such information was not provided in the certification to Congress before finalizing the cooperative agreement.

[DAC 91-9, 60 FR 61586, 11/30/95, effective 11/30/95; Final rule, 65 FR 39703, 6/27/2000, effective 6/27/2000; Final rule, 68 FR 15615, 3/31/2003, effective 4/30/2003]

225.872 Contracting with qualifying country sources. (No Text)

225.872-1 General.

(a) As a result of memoranda of understanding and other international agreements, DoD has determined it inconsistent with the public interest to apply restrictions of the Buy American statute or the Balance of Payments Program to the acquisition of qualifying country end products from the following qualifying countries:

Australia

Belgium

Canada

Czech Republic

Denmark

Egypt

Estonia

Federal Republic of Germany

Finland

France

Greece

Israel

Italy

Japan

Latvia

Luxembourg

Netherlands

Norway

Poland

Portugal

Slovenia

Spain

Sweden

Switzerland

Turkey

United Kingdom of Great Britain and Northern Ireland

(b) Individual acquisitions of qualifying country end products from the following qualifying country may, on a purchase-by-purchase basis (see 225.872-4), be exempted from application of the Buy American statute and the Balance of Payments Program as inconsistent with the public interest:

Austria

(c) The determination in paragraph (a) of this subsection does not limit the authority of the Secretary concerned to restrict acquisitions to domestic sources or reject an otherwise acceptable offer from a qualifying country source when considered necessary for national defense reasons.

[DAC 91-4, 57 FR 53599, 11/12/92, effective 10/30/92; DAC 91-9, 60 FR 61586, 11/30/95, effective 11/30/95; DAC 91-12, 62 FR 34114, 6/24/97, effective 6/24/97; Interim rule, 63 FR 5744, 2/4/98, effective 2/4/98; Final rule, 68 FR 15615, 3/31/2003, effective 4/30/2003; Final rule, 69 FR 8115, 2/23/2004, effective 2/23/2004; Final rule, 75 FR 32640, 6/8/2010, effective 6/8/2010; Final rule, 77 FR 35879, 6/15/2012, effective 6/15/2012; Final rule, 77 FR 38736, 6/29/2012, effective 6/29/2012; Final rule, 77 FR 76941, 12/31/2012, effective 12/31/2012; Final rule, 81 FR 50650, 8/2/2016, effective 8/2/2016; Final rule, 81 FR 93840, 12/22/2016, effective 12/22/2016; Final rule, 82 FR 61483, 12/28/2017, effective 12/28/2017]

225.872-2 Applicability.

(a) This section applies to all acquisitions of supplies except those restricted by—

(1) U.S. National Disclosure Policy, DoDD 5230.11, Disclosure of Classified Military Information to Foreign Governments and International Organizations;

(2) U.S. defense mobilization base requirements purchased under the authority of FAR 6.302-3(a)(2)(i), except for quantities in excess of that required to maintain the defense mobilization base. This restriction does not apply to Canadian planned producers.

(i) Review individual solicitations to determine whether this restriction applies.

(ii) Information concerning restricted items may be obtained from the Deputy Under Secretary of Defense (Industrial Affairs);

(3) Other U.S. laws or regulations (*e.g.*, the annual DoD appropriations act); and

(4) U.S. industrial security requirements.

(b) This section does not apply to construction contracts.

[DAC 91-9, 60 FR 61586, 11/30/95, effective 11/30/95; DAC 91-12, 62 FR 34114, 6/24/97, effective 6/24/97; Final rule, 65 FR 39703, 6/27/2000, effective 6/27/2000; Final rule, 68 FR 15615, 3/31/2003, effective 4/30/2003]

225.872-3 Solicitation procedures.

(a) Except for items developed under the U.S./Canadian Development Sharing Program, use the criteria for soliciting and awarding contracts to small business concerns under FAR Part 19 without regard to whether there are potential qualifying country sources for the end product. Do not consider an offer of a qualifying country end product if the solicitation is identified for the exclusive participation of small business concerns.

(b) Send solicitations directly to qualifying country sources. Solicit Canadian sources through the Canadian Commercial Corporation in accordance with DFARS 225.870.

(c) Use international air mail if solicitation destinations are outside the United States and security classification permits such use.

(d) If unusual technical or security requirements preclude the acquisition of otherwise acceptable defense equipment from qualifying country sources, review the need for such requirements. Do not impose unusual technical or security requirements solely for the purpose of precluding the acquisition of defense equipment from qualifying countries.

(e) Do not automatically exclude qualifying country sources from submitting offers because their supplies have not been tested and evaluated by the department or agency.

(1) Consider the adequacy of qualifying country service testing on a case-by-case basis. Departments or agencies that must limit solicitations to sources whose items have been tested and evaluated by the department or agency shall consider supplies from qualifying country sources that have been tested and accepted by the qualifying country for service use.

(2) The department or agency may perform a confirmatory test, if necessary.

(3) Apply U.S. test and evaluation standards, policies, and procedures when the department or agency decides that confirmatory tests of qualifying country end products are necessary.

(4) If it appears that these provisions might adversely delay service programs, obtain the concurrence of the Under Secretary of Defense (Acquisition, Technology, and Logistics), before excluding the qualifying country source from consideration.

(f) Permit industry representatives from a qualifying country to attend symposia, program briefings, prebid conferences (see FAR 14.207 and 15.201(c)), and similar meetings that address U.S. defense equipment needs and requirements. When practical, structure these meetings to allow attendance by representatives of qualifying country concerns.

[DAC 91-9, 60 FR 61586, 11/30/95, effective 11/30/95; Final rule, 63 FR 55040, 10/14/98, effective 10/14/98; Final rule, 65 FR 39703, 6/27/2000, effective 6/27/2000; Final rule, 68 FR 15615, 3/31/2003, effective 4/30/2003; Final rule, 72 FR 20758, 4/26/2007, effective 4/26/2007]

225.872-4 Individual determinations.

If the offer of an end product from a qualifying country source listed in 225.872-1(b), as evaluated, is low or otherwise eligible for award, prepare a determination and findings exempting the acquisition from the Buy American statute and the Balance of Payments Program as inconsistent with the public interest, unless another exception such as the Trade Agreements Act applies. Follow the procedures at PGI 225.872-4.

[DAC 91-3, 57 FR 42630, 9/15/92, effective 8/31/92; DAC 91-13, 63 FR 11522, 3/9/98, effective 3/9/98; Final rule, 65 FR 39703, 6/27/2000, effective 6/27/2000; Final rule, 68 FR 15615, 3/31/2003, effective 4/30/2003; Final rule, 70 FR 73153, 12/9/2005, effective 12/9/2005; Final rule, 77 FR 35879, 6/15/2012, effective 6/15/2012]

225.872-5 Contract administration.

(a) Arrangements exist with some qualifying countries to provide reciprocal contract administration services. Some arrangements are at no cost to either government. To determine whether such an arrangement has been negotiated and what contract administration functions are covered, contact the Deputy Director of Defense Procurement and Acquisition Policy (Contract Policy and International Contracting), ((703) 697-9351, DSN 227-9351).

(b) Follow the contract administration procedures at PGI 225.872-5(b).

(c) Information on quality assurance delegations to foreign governments is in Subpart

246.4, Government Contract Quality Assurance.

[DAC 91-7, 60 FR 29491, 6/5/95, effective 5/17/95; Final rule, 68 FR 15615, 3/31/2003, effective 4/30/2003; Final rule, 70 FR 73153, 12/9/2005, effective 12/9/2005; Final rule, 72 FR 30278, 5/31/2007, effective 5/31/2007]

225.872-6 Request for audit services.

Handle requests for audit services in France, Germany, the Netherlands, or the United Kingdom in accordance with PGI 215.404-2(c), but follow the additional procedures at PGI 225.872-6.

[DAC 91-7, 60 FR 29491, 6/5/95, effective 5/17/95; Final rule, 63 FR 55040, 10/14/98, effective 10/14/98, Final rule, 64 FR 61028, 11/9/99, effective 11/9/99; Final rule, 68 FR 15615, 3/31/2003, effective 4/30/2003; Final rule, 70 FR 73153, 12/9/2005, effective 12/9/2005; Final rule, 72 FR 30278, 5/31/2007, effective 5/31/2007; Final rule, 81 FR 59510, 8/30/2016, effective 8/30/2016]

225.872-7 Industrial security for qualifying countries.

The required procedures for safeguarding classified defense information necessary for the performance of contracts awarded to qualifying country sources are in the DoD Industrial Security Regulation DoD 5220.22-R (implemented for the Army by AR 380-49; for the Navy by SECNAV Instruction 5510.1H; for the Air Force by AFI 31-601; for the Defense Information Systems Agency by DCA Instruction 240-110-8; and for the National Imagery and Mapping Agency by NIMA Instruction 5220.22).

[DAC 91-1, 56 FR 67215, 12/30/91, effective 12/31/91; Final rule, 64 FR 51074, 9/21/99, effective 9/21/99, Final rule, 64 FR 61028, 11/9/99, effective 11/9/99; Final rule, 68 FR 15615, 3/31/2003, effective 4/30/2003]

225.872-8 Subcontracting with qualifying country sources.

In reviewing contractor subcontracting procedures, the contracting officer shall ensure that the contract does not preclude qualifying country sources from competing for subcontracts, except when restricted by national security interest reasons, mobilization base considerations, or applicable U.S. laws or regulations (see the clause at 252.225-7002, Qualifying Country Sources as Subcontractors).

[Final rule, 68 FR 15615, 3/31/2003, effective 4/30/2003]

225.873 Waiver of United Kingdom commercial exploitation levies. (No Text)

225.873-1 Policy.

DoD and the Government of the United Kingdom (U.K.) have agreed to waive U.K. commercial exploitation levies and U.S. nonrecurring cost recoupment charges on a reciprocal basis. For U.K. levies to be waived, the offeror or contractor shall identify the levies and the contracting officer shall request a waiver before award of the contract or subcontract under which the levies are charged.

[DAC 91-4, 57 FR 53599, 11/12/92, effective 10/30/92; Final rule, 68 FR 15615, 3/31/2003, effective 4/30/2003]

225.873-2 Procedures.

When an offeror or a contractor identifies a levy included in an offered or contract price, follow the procedures at PGI 225.873-2.

[DAC 91-4, 57 FR 53599, 11/12/92, effective 10/30/92; Final rule, 64 FR 51074, 9/21/99, effective 9/21/99; Final rule, 68 FR 15615, 3/31/2003, effective 4/30/2003; Final rule, 70 FR 73153, 12/9/2005, effective 12/9/2005]

SUBPART 225.9—CUSTOMS AND DUTIES

225.900-70 Definitions.

Component as used in this subpart, means any item supplied to the Government as part of an end product or of another component.

[Final rule, 74 FR 68383, 12/24/2009, effective 12/24/2009]

225.901 Policy.

Unless the supplies are entitled to duty-free treatment under a special category in the Harmonized Tariff Schedule of the United States (*e.g.*, the Caribbean Basin Economic Recovery Act or a Free Trade Agreement), or unless the supplies already have entered into the customs territory of the United States and the contractor already has paid the duty, DoD will issue duty-free entry certificates for—

(1) Qualifying country supplies (end products and components);

(2) Eligible products (end products but not components) under contracts covered by the World Trade Organization Government Procurement Agreement or a Free Trade Agreement; and

(3) Other foreign supplies for which the contractor estimates that duty will exceed $300 per shipment into the customs territory of the United States.

[Final rule, 65 FR 19849, 4/13/2000, effective 4/13/2000; Final rule, 68 FR 15615, 3/31/2003, effective 4/30/2003; Interim rule, 69 FR 1926, 1/13/2004, effective 1/13/2004; Interim rule, 70 FR 2361, 1/13/2005, effective 1/13/2005; Final rule, 70 FR 73152, 12/9/2005, effective 12/9/2005; Final rule, 81 FR 28732, 5/10/2016, effective 5/10/2016; Final rule, 81 FR 28732, 5/10/2016, effective 5/10/2016]

225.902 Procedures.

Follow the entry and release procedures at PGI 225.902.

[Final rule, 65 FR 19849, 4/13/2000, effective 4/13/2000; Final rule, 65 FR 52951, 8/31/2000, effective 8/31/2000; Final rule, 68 FR 15615, 3/27/2003, effective 4/30/2003; Final rule, 70 FR 73153, 12/9/2005, effective 12/9/2005]

225.903 Exempted supplies.

(b) (i) For an explanation of the term *supplies*, see PGI 225.903(b) (i).

(ii) The duty-free certificate shall be printed, stamped, or typed on the face of, or attached to, Customs Form 7501. A duly designated officer or civilian official of the appropriate department or agency shall execute the certificate in the format provided at PGI 225.903(b) (ii).

[Final rule, 65 FR 19849, 4/13/2000, effective 4/13/2000; Final rule, 68 FR 15615, 3/27/2003, effective 4/30/2003; Final rule, 70 FR 73153, 12/9/2005, effective 12/9/2005]

SUBPART 225.10—ADDITIONAL FOREIGN ACQUISITION REGULATIONS

225.1070 Clause deviations in overseas contracts.

See 201.403(2) for approval authority for clause deviations in overseas contracts with governments of North Atlantic Treaty Organization (NATO) countries or other allies or with United Nations or NATO organizations.

[Final rule, 65 FR 19849, 4/13/2000, effective 4/13/2000]

SUBPART 225.11—SOLICITATION PROVISIONS AND CONTRACT CLAUSES

225.1100 Scope of subpart.

This subpart prescribes the clauses that implement subparts 225.1 through 225.10. The clauses that implement subparts 225.70 through 225.75 are prescribed within those subparts.

[Final rule, 68 FR 15615, 3/27/2003, effective 4/30/2003; Final rule, 81 FR 17047, 3/25/2016, effective 3/25/2016]

225.1101 Acquisition of supplies.

(1) Use the basic or the alternate of the provision at 252.225–7000, Buy American—Balance of Payments Program Certificate, instead of the provision at FAR 52.225–2, Buy American Certificate, in any solicitation, including solicitations using FAR part 12 procedures for the acquisition of commercial items, that includes the basic or the alternate of the clause at 252.225–7001, Buy American and Balance of Payments Program. If the solicitation includes the provision at FAR 52.204–7, do not separately list the provision 252.225–7000 in the solicitation.

(i) Use the basic provision when the solicitation includes the basic clause at 252.225–7001.

(ii) Use the alternate I provision when the solicitation includes alternate I of the clause at 252.225–7001.

(2)(i) Use the basic or alternate of the clause at 252.225–7001, Buy American and Balance of Payments Program, instead of the clause at FAR 52.225-1, Buy American—Supplies, in solicitations and contracts, including solicitations and contracts using FAR part 12 procedures for the acquisition of commercial items, unless—

(A) All line items will be acquired from a particular source or sources under the authority of FAR 6.3023;

(B) All line items require domestic or qualifying country end products in accordance with subpart 225.70, but note that this exception does not apply if subpart 225.70 only requires manufacture of the end product in the United States or in the United States or Canada, without a corresponding requirement for use of domestic components;

(C) The acquisition is for supplies for use within the United States and an exception to the Buy American statute applies, e.g., nonavailability or public interest (see FAR 25.103, 25.103, and 225.103);

(D) The acquisition is for supplies for use outside the United States and an exception to the Balance of Payments Program applies (see DFARS 225.7501);

(E) One or more of the basic or the alternates of the following clauses will apply to all line items in the contract:

(*1*) 252.225-7021, Trade Agreements.

(*2*) 252.225-7036, Buy American—Free Trade Agreements—Balance of Payments Program; or

(F) All line items will be acquired using a procedure specified in 225.7703-1(a).

(ii) Use the basic clause if the acquisition is not of end products listed in 225.401–70 in support of operations in Afghanistan.

(iii) Use the alternate I clause when the acquisition is of end products listed in 225.401–70 in support of operations in Afghanistan.

(3) Use the clause at 252.225-7002, Qualifying Country Sources as Subcontractors, in solicitations and contracts that include the basic or one of the alternates of the following clauses:

(i) 252.225-7001, Buy American and Balance of Payments Program.

(ii) 252.225-7021, Trade Agreements.

(iii) 252.225–7036, Buy American—Free Trade Agreements—Balance of Payments Program.

(4) Use the clause at 252.225-7013, Duty-Free Entry, instead of the clause at FAR 52.225-8. Do not use the clause for acquisitions of supplies that will not enter the customs territory of the United States.

(5) Use the basic or the alternate of the provision at 252.225–7020, Trade Agreements Certificate, instead of the provision at FAR 52.225–6, Trade Agreements Certificate, in solicitations, including solicitations using FAR part 12 procedures for the acquisition of commercial items, that include the basic or alternate II of the clause at 252.225–7021, Trade Agreements. If the solicitation includes the provision at FAR 52.204–7, do not separately list the provision 252.225–7020 in the solicitation.

(i) Use the basic provision if the solicitation includes the basic clause at 252.225–7021.

(ii) Use the alternate I provision if the solicitation includes alternate II of the clause at 252.225–7021.

(6) Except as provided in paragraph (6)(iv) of this section, use the basic or an alternate of the clause at 252.225–7021, Trade Agreements, instead of the clause at FAR 52.225–5, Trade Agreements, in solicitations and contracts, including solicitations and contracts using FAR part 12 procedures for the acquisition of commercial items, if the World Trade Organization Government Procurement Agreement applies, i.e., the acquisition is of end products listed at 225.401–70, the value of the acquisition equals or exceeds $182,000, and none of the exceptions at 25.401(a) applies.

(i) Use the basic clause in solicitations and contracts that are not of end products in support of operations in Afghanistan, or that include the clause at 252.225–7024, Requirement for Products or Services from Afghanistan.

(ii) Use the alternate II clause in solicitations and contracts that do not include the clause at 252.225–7024, Requirement for Products or Services from Afghanistan, when the acquisition is of end products in support of operations in Afghanistan.

(iii) Do not use the basic or an alternate of the clause if—

(A) Purchase from foreign sources is restricted, unless the contracting officer anticipates a waiver of the restriction; or

(B) The clause at 252.225-7026, Acquisition Restricted to Products or Services from Afghanistan, is included in the solicitation and contract.

(iv) The acquisition of eligible and noneligible products under the same contract may result in the application of trade agreements to only some of the items acquired. In such case, indicate in the Schedule those items covered by the Trade Agreements clause.

(7) Use the provision at DFARS 252.225-7032, Waiver of United Kingdom Levies—Evaluation of Offers, in solicitations if a U.K. firm is expected to—

(i) Submit an offer; or

(ii) Receive a subcontract exceeding $1 million.

(8) Use the clause at 252.225-7033, Waiver of United Kingdom Levies, in solicitations and contracts if a U.K. firm is expected to—

(i) Submit an offer; or

(ii) Receive a subcontract exceeding $1 million.

(9) Use the basic or an alternate of the provision at 252.225–7035, Buy American—Free Trade Agreements—Balance of Payments Program Certificate, instead of the provision at FAR 52.225–4, Buy American—Free Trade Agreements—Israeli Trade Act Certificate, in solicitations, including solicitations using FAR part 12 procedures for the acquisition of commercial items, that include the basic or an alternate of the clause at 252.225–7036, Buy American—Free Trade Agreements—Balance of Payments Program. If the solicitation includes the provision at FAR 52.204–7, do not separately list the provision 252.225–7035 in the solicitation.

(i) Use the basic provision in solicitations when the basic of the clause at 252.225–7036 is used.

(ii) Use the alternate I provision when the solicitation includes alternate I of the clause at 252.225–7036.

(iii) Use the alternate II provision when the solicitation includes alternate II of the clause at 252.225–7036.

(iv) Use the alternate III provision when the solicitation includes alternate III of the clause at 252.225–7036.

(v) Use the alternate IV provision when the solicitation includes alternate IV of the clause at 252.225–7036.

(vi) Use the alternate V provision when the solicitation includes alternate V of the clause at 252.225–7036.

(10)(i) Except as provided in paragraph (10)(ii) of this section, use the basic or an alternate of the clause at 252.225–7036, Buy American—Free Trade Agreements—Balance of Payments Program, instead of the clause at FAR 52.225–3, Buy American—Free Trade Agreements—Israeli Trade Act, in solicitations and contracts, including solicitations and contracts using FAR part 12 procedures for the acquisition of commercial items, for the items listed at 225.401–70, when the estimated value equals or exceeds $25,000, but is less than $182,000, unless an exception at FAR 25.401 or 225.401 applies.

(A) Use the basic clause in solicitations and contracts when the estimated value equals or exceeds $100,000 but is less than $182,000, except if the acquisition is of end products in support of operations in Afghanistan.

(B) Use the alternate I clause in solicitations and contracts when the estimated value equals or exceeds $25,000, but less than $83,099, except if the acquisition is of end products in support of operations in Afghanistan.

(C) Use the alternate II clause in solicitations and contracts when the estimated value equals or exceeds $100,000, but is less than $182,000, and the acquisition is of end products in support of operations in Afghanistan.

(D) Use the alternate III clause in solicitations and contracts when the estimated value equals or exceeds $25,000, but is less than $83,099, and the acquisition is of end products in support of operations in Afghanistan.

(E) Use the alternate IV clause in solicitations and contracts when the estimated value equals or exceeds $83,099 but is less than $100,000, except if the acquisition is of end products in support of operations in Afghanistan.

(F) Use the alternate V clause in solicitations and contracts when the estimated value equals or exceeds $83,099 but is less than $100,000 and the acquisition is of end products in support of operations in Afghanistan.

(ii) Do not use the basic or an alternate of the clause in paragraph (10)(i) of this section if—

(A) Purchase from foreign sources is restricted (see 225.401(a)(2)), unless the contracting officer anticipates a waiver of the restriction;

(B) Acquiring information technology that is a commercial item, using fiscal year 2004 or subsequent funds (Section 535 of Division F of the Consolidated Appropriations Act, 2004 (Pub. L. 108–199), and the same provision in subsequent appropriations acts); or

(C) Using a procedure specified in 225.7703-1(a).

(iii) The acquisition of eligible and noneligible products under the same contract may result in the application of a Free Trade Agreement to only some of the items acquired. In such case, indicate in the Schedule those items covered by the Buy American—Free Trade Agreements—Balance of Payments Program clause.

[Final rule, 65 FR 19849, 4/13/2000, effective 4/13/2000; Final rule, 65 FR 36033, 6/6/2000, effective 6/6/2000; Final rule, 67 FR 20693, 4/26/2002, effective 4/26/2002; Final rule, 67 FR 77937, effective 12/20/2002, effective 12/20/2002; Final rule, 68 FR 15615, 3/31/2003, effective 4/30/2003; Interim rule, 69 FR 1926, 1/13/2004, effective 1/13/2004; Interim rule, 71 FR 9269, 2/23/2006, effective 2/23/2006; Final rule, 71 FR 58539, 10/4/2006, effective 10/4/2006; Final rule, 71 FR 65752, 11/9/2006, effective 11/9/2006; Interim rule, 73 FR 4115, 1/24/2008, effective 1/24/2008; Final rule, 73 FR 46818, 8/12/2008, effective 8/12/2008; Interim rule, 73 FR 53151, 9/15/2008, effective 9/15/2008; Final rule, 74 FR 34264, 7/15/2009, effective 7/15/2009; Final rule, 75 FR 18035, 4/8/2010, effective 4/8/2010; Interim rule, 75 FR 32637, 6/8/2010, effective 6/8/2010; Final rule, 75 FR 66680, 10/29/2010, effective 10/29/2010; Final rule, 75 FR 81915, 12/29/2010, effective 12/29/2010; Final rule, 77 FR 4630, 1/30/2012, effective 1/30/2012; Interim rule, 77 FR 30356, 5/22/2012, effective 5/22/2012; Final rule, 77 FR 35879, 6/15/2012, effective 6/15/2012; Final rule, 78 FR 18876, 3/28/2013, effective 3/28/2013; Final rule, 78 FR 37980, 6/25/2013, effective 6/25/2013; Final rule, 78 FR 40043, 7/3/2013, effective 7/3/2013; Interim rule, 78 FR 59854, 9/30/2013, effective 9/30/2013; Final rule, 78 FR 79620, 12/31/2013, effective 1/1/2014; Final rule, 79 FR 3519, 1/22/2014, effective 1/22/2014; Final rule, 79 FR 11342, 2/28/2014, effective 2/28/2014; Final rule, 79 FR 65815, 11/5/2014, effective 11/5/2014; Final rule, 80 FR 2018, 1/15/2015, effective 1/15/2015; Final rule, 80 FR 36897, 6/26/2015, effective 6/26/2015; Final rule, 80 FR 81470, 12/30/2015, effective 1/1/2016; Final rule, 81 FR 17047, 3/25/2016, effective 3/25/2016; Final rule, 82 FR 61481, 12/28/2017, effective 1/1/2018; Final rule, 84 FR 72245, 12/31/2019, effective 1/1/2020]

225.1103 Other provisions and clauses.

(1) Unless the contracting officer knows that the prospective contractor is not a domestic concern, use the clause at 252.225-7005, Identification of Expenditures

in the United States, in solicitations and contracts that—

(i) Exceed the simplified acquisition threshold; and

(ii) Are for the acquisition of—

(A) Supplies for use outside the United States;

(B) Construction to be performed outside the United States; or

(C) Services to be performed primarily outside the United States.

(2) Use the clause at DFARS 252.225-7041, Correspondence in English, in solicitations and contracts when contract performance will be wholly or in part in a foreign country.

(3) Use the provision at 252.225-7042, Authorization to Perform, in solicitations when contract performance will be wholly or in part in a foreign country. If the solicitation includes the provision at FAR 52.204-7, do not separately list the provision 252.225-7042 in the solicitation.

(4) Unless an exception in 225.770-3 applies, use the clause at 252.225-7007, Prohibition on Acquisition of Certain Items from Communist Chinese Military Companies, in solicitations and contracts involving the delivery of items covered by the United States Munitions List or the 600 series of the Commerce Control List.

[Final rule, 65 FR 19849, 4/13/2000, effective 4/13/2000; Final rule, 67 FR 20693, 4/26/2002, effective 4/26/2002; Final rule, 67 FR 77937, 12/20/2002, effective 12/20/2002; Final rule, 68 FR 15615, 3/31/2003, effective 4/30/2003; Final rule, 71 FR 39005, 7/11/2006, effective 7/11/2006; Interim rule, 71 FR 53045, 9/8/2006, effective 9/8/2006; Final rule, 72 FR 14239, 3/27/2007, effective 3/27/2007; Final rule, 78 FR 37980, 6/25/2013, effective 6/25/2013; Final rule, 78 FR 40043, 7/3/2013, effective 7/3/2013; Interim rule, 83 FR 66066, 12/21/2018, effective 12/21/2018; Final rule, 84 FR 25188, 5/31/2019, effective 5/31/2019]

SUBPART 225.70—AUTHORIZATION ACTS, APPROPRIATIONS ACTS, AND OTHER STATUTORY RESTRICTIONS ON FOREIGN ACQUISITION

225.7000 Scope of subpart.

(a) This subpart contains restrictions on the acquisition of foreign products and services, imposed by DoD appropriations and authorization acts and other statutes. Refer to the acts to verify current applicability of the restrictions.

(b) Nothing in this subpart affects the applicability of the Buy American statute or the Balance of Payments Program.

[Interim rule, 62 FR 2856, 1/17/97, effective 1/17/97, finalized without change, DAC 91-12, 62 FR 34114, 6/24/97, effective 6/24/97; Final rule, 68 FR 15615, 3/31/2003, effective 4/30/2003; Final rule, 77 FR 35879, 6/15/2012, effective 6/15/2012]

225.7001 Definitions.

As used in this subpart—

Assembly means an item forming a portion of a system or subsystem that—

(1) Can be provisioned and replaced as an entity; and

(2) Incorporates multiple, replaceable parts.

Bearing components means the bearing element, retainer, inner race, or outer race.

Component means any item supplied to the Government as part of an end item or of another component except that for use in 225.7007, the term means an article, material, or supply incorporated directly into an end product.

End item, as used in sections 225.7003 and 225.7018, means the final production product when assembled or completed and ready for delivery under a line item of the contract (10 U.S.C. 2533b(m)).

End product means supplies delivered under a line item of the contract.

Hand or measuring tools means those tools listed in Federal supply classifications 51 and 52, respectively.

Structural component of a tent—

(1) Means a component that contributes to the form and stability of the tent (e.g.,

poles, frames, flooring, guy ropes, pegs); and

(2) Does not include equipment such as heating, cooling, or lighting.

Subsystem means a functional grouping of items that combine to perform a major function within an end item, such as electrical power, altitude control, and propulsion.

[Interim rule, 61 FR 10899, 3/18/96, effective 3/18/96; DAC 91-11, 61 FR 50446, 9/26/96, effective 9/26/96; Interim rule, 67 FR 20697, 4/26/2002, effective 4/26/2002; Final rule, 71 FR 14110, 3/21/2006, effective 3/21/2006; Final rule, 73 11354, 3/3/2008, effective 3/3/2008; Final rule, 74 FR 37626, 7/29/2009, effective 7/29/2009; Final rule, 74 FR 68383, 12/24/2009, effective 12/24/2009; Interim rule, 77 FR 38734, 6/29/2012, effective 6/29/2012; Final rule 78 FR 13544, 2/28/2013, effective 2/28/2013; Final rule, 84 FR 72239, 12/31/2019, effective 12/31/2019]

225.7002 Restrictions on food, clothing, fabrics, hand or measuring tools, and flags.

[Final rule, 74 FR 37626, 7/29/2009, effective 7/29/2009; Final rule, 80 FR 51748, 8/26/2015, effective 8/26/2015]

225.7002-1 Restrictions.

(a) The following restrictions implement 10 U.S.C. 2533a (the "Berry Amendment").

(1) Any of the following items, either as end products or components, unless the items have been grown, reprocessed, reused, or produced in the United States:

(i) Food.

(ii) Clothing and the materials and components thereof, other than sensors, electronics, or other items added to, and not normally associated with, clothing and the materials and components thereof. Clothing includes items such as outerwear, headwear, underwear, nightwear, footwear, hosiery, handwear, belts, badges, and insignia. For additional guidance and examples, see PGI 225.7002-1(a)(1)(ii).

(iii) *Tents and the structural components of tents, tarpaulins, or covers.* In addition, in accordance with section 368 of the National Defense Authorization Act for Fiscal Year 2012 (Pub. L. 112–81)—

(A) Tents and the structural components of tents;

(B) Tarpaulins; or

(C) Covers.

(iv) Cotton and other natural fiber products.

(v) Woven silk or woven silk blends.

(vi) Spun silk yarn for cartridge cloth.

(vii) Synthetic fabric or coated synthetic fabric, including all textile fibers and yarns that are for use in such fabrics.

(viii) Canvas products.

(ix) Wool (whether in the form of fiber or yarn or contained in fabrics, materials, or manufactured articles).

(x) Any item of individual equipment (Product or Service Code (PSC) 8465) manufactured from or containing any of the fibers, yarns, fabrics, or materials listed in this paragraph (a)(1).

(2) Hand or measuring tools, unless the tools were produced in the United States. For additional guidance, see see PGI 225.7002-1(a)(2).

(b) In accordance with section 8123 of the Department of Defense Appropriations Act, 2014 (Pub. L. 113-76, division C, title VIII), and the same provision in subsequent Defense appropriations acts, except as provided in 225.7002-2, do not acquire a flag of the United States (PSC 8345), unless such flag, including the materials and components thereof, is manufactured in the United States, consistent with the requirements at 10 U.S.C. 2533a. This restriction does not apply to the acquisition of any end-items or components related to flying or displaying the flag (e.g., flag poles and accessories).

[DAC 91-2, 57 FR 14993, 4/23/92, effective 4/16/92; DAC 91-6, 59 FR 27662, 5/27/94, effective 5/27/94; Interim rule, 62 FR 5779, 2/7/97, effective 2/7/97; Final rule, 62 FR 47153, 9/8/97, effective 9/8/97; Interim rule, 67 FR 20697, 4/26/2002, effective 4/26/2002; Final rule, 71 FR 39008, 7/11/2006, effective 7/11/2006; Interim rule, 71 FR 58536, 10/4/2006, effective

10/4/2006; Interim rule, 72 FR 2637, 1/22/2007, effective 1/22/2007; Final rule, 72 FR 42315, 8/2/2007, effective 8/2/2007; Final rule, 73 FR 11354, 3/3/2008, effective 3/3/2008; Final rule, 74 FR 37626, 7/29/2009, effective 7/29/2009; Final rule, 76 FR 52132, 8/19/2011, effective 8/19/2011; Interim rule, 77 FR 38734, 6/29/2012, effective 6/29/2012; Final rule 78 FR 13544, 2/28/2013, effective 2/28/2013; Final rule, 80 FR 51748, 8/26/2015, effective 8/26/2015]

225.7002-2 Exceptions.

Acquisitions in the following categories are not subject to the restrictions in 225.7002-1:

(a) Acquisitions at or below the simplified acquisition threshold, except for athletic footwear purchased by DoD for use by members of the Army, Navy, Air Force, or Marine Corps upon their initial entry into the Armed Forces (section 817 of the National Defense Authorization Act for Fiscal Year 2017 (Pub. L. 114-328)).

(b) Acquisitions of any of the items in 225.7002-1, if the Secretary concerned determines that items grown, reprocessed, reused, or produced in the United States cannot be acquired as and when needed in a satisfactory quality and sufficient quantity at U.S. market prices. (See the requirement in 205.301 for synopsis within 7 days after contract award when using this exception.)

(1) The following officials are authorized, without power of redelegation, to make such a domestic nonavailability determination:

(i) The Under Secretary of Defense (Acquisition, Technology, and Logistics).

(ii) The Secretary of the Army.

(iii) The Secretary of the Navy.

(iv) The Secretary of the Air Force.

(v) The Director of the Defense Logistics Agency.

(2) The supporting documentation for the determination shall include—

(i) An analysis of alternatives that would not require a domestic nonavailability determination; and

(ii) A written certification by the requiring activity, with specificity, why such alternatives are unacceptable.

(3) Defense agencies other than the Defense Logistics Agency shall follow the procedures at PGI 225.7002-2(b)(3) when submitting a request for a domestic nonavailability determination.

(c) Acquisitions of items listed in FAR 25.104(a).

(d) Acquisitions outside the United States in support of combat operations.

(e) Acquisitions of perishable foods by or for activities located outside the United States for personnel of those activities.

(f) Acquisitions of food, or hand or measuring tools—

(1) In support of contingency operations; or

(2) For which the use of other than competitive procedures has been approved on the basis of unusual and compelling urgency in accordance with FAR 6.302-2.

(g) Emergency acquisitions by activities located outside the United States for personnel of those activities.

(h) Acquisitions by vessels in foreign waters.

(i) Acquisitions of items specifically for commissary resale.

(j) Acquisitions of incidental amounts of cotton, other natural fibers, or wool incorporated in an end product, for which the estimated value of the cotton, other natural fibers, or wool—

(1) Is not more than 10 percent of the total price of the end product; and

(2) Does not exceed the simplified acquisition threshold.

(k) Acquisitions of waste and byproducts of cotton or wood fiber for use in the production or propellants and explosives.

(l) Acquisitions of foods manufactured or processed in the United States, regardless of where the foods (and any component if applicable) were grown or produced. However, in accordance with section 8118 of the DoD Appropriations Act for Fiscal Year 2005 (Pub. L. 108-287), this exception does not apply to fish, shellfish, or seafood manufactured or processed in the United States or fish, shellfish, or seafood contained in foods manufactured or processed in the United States.

(m) Acquisitions of fibers and yarns that are for use in synthetic fabric or coated synthetic fabric (but not the purchase of the synthetic or coated synthetic fabric itself), if—

(1) The fabric is to be used as a component of an end product that is not a textile product. Examples of textile products, made in whole or in part of fabric, include—

(i) Draperies, floor coverings, furnishings, and bedding (Product or Service Group (PSG) 72, Household and Commercial Furnishings and Appliances);

(ii) Items made in whole or in part of fabric in PSG 83, Textile/leather/furs/apparel/findings/tents/flags, or PSG 84, Clothing, Individual Equipment and Insignia;

(iii) Upholstered seats (whether for household, office, or other use); and

(iv) Parachutes (PSC 1670); or

(2) The fibers and yarns are para-aramid fibers and continuous filament para-aramid yarns manufactured in a qualifying country.

(n) Acquisitions of chemical warfare protective clothing when the acquisition furthers an agreement with a qualifying country. (See 225.003(10) and the requirement in 205.301 for synopsis within 7 days after contract award when using this exception.)

(o) Acquisitions that are interagency, State, or local purchases that are executed by DoD as a result of the transfer of contracts from the General Services Administration or for which DoD serves as an item manager for products on behalf of the General Services Administration. According to section 897 of the National Defense Authorization Act for Fiscal Year 2016 (Pub. L. 114–92), such contracts shall not be subject to requirements under chapter 148 of title 10, United States Code (including 10 U.S.C. 2533a), to the extent such contracts are for purchases of products by other Federal agencies or State or local governments.

[DAC 91-5, 58 FR 28458, 5/13/93, effective 4/30/93; DAC 91-6, 59 FR 27662, 5/27/94, effective 5/27/94; DAC 91-9, 60 FR 61586, 11/30/95, effective 11/30/95; DAC 91-11, 61 FR 50446, 9/26/96, effective 9/26/96; Interim rule, 62 FR 5779, 2/7/97, effective 2/7/97; Final rule, 62 FR 47153, 9/8/97, effective 9/8/97; Interim rule, 64 FR 2599, 1/15/99, effective 1/15/99; Final rule, 64 FR 24528, 5/7/99, effective 5/7/99; Final rule, 65 FR 39703, 6/27/2000, effective 6/27/2000; Final rule, 65 FR 52951, 8/31/2000, effective 8/31/2000; Interim rule, 67 FR 20697, 4/26/2002, effective 4/26/2002; Interim rule, 68 FR 7441, 2/14/2003, effective 2/14/2003; Interim rule, 69 FR 26508, 5/13/2004, effective 5/13/2004; Final rule, 69 FR 31910, 6/8/2004, effective 6/8/2004; Final rule, 69 FR 55989, 9/17/2004, effective 9/17/2004; Final rule, 70 FR 43073, 7/26/2005, effective 7/26/2005; Interim rule, 71 FR 34832, 6/16/2006, effective 6/16/2006; Interim rule, 71 FR 58536, 10/4/2006, effective 10/4/2006; Final rule, 72 FR 6484, 2/12/2007, effective 2/12/2007; Final rule, 72 FR 20765, 4/26/2007, effective 4/26/2007; Final rule 72 FR 42315, 8/2/2007, effective 8/2/2007; Final rule, 72 FR 63113, 11/8/2007, effective 11/8/2007; Final rule, 73 FR 11354, 3/3/2008, effective 3/3/2008; Final rule, 73 FR 76970, 12/18/2008, effective 12/18/2008; Final rule, 74 FR 37626, 7/29/2009, effective 7/29/2009; Final rule, 74 FR 52895, 10/15/2009, effective 10/15/2009; Final rule, 75 FR 34943, 6/21/2010, effective 6/21/2010; Interim rule, 76 FR 14588, 3/17/2011, effective 3/17/2011; Final rule, 76 FR 52132, 8/19/2011, effective 8/19/2011; Final rule, 80 FR 36718, 6/26/2015, effective 6/26/2015; Final rule, 80 FR 51748, 8/26/2015, effective 8/26/2015; Final rule, 81 FR 42562, 6/30/2016, effective 6/30/2016; Final rule, 83 FR 65560, 12/21/2018, effective 12/21/2018]

225.7002-3 Contract clauses.

Unless an exception at 225.7002-2 applies—

(a) Use the clause at 252.225-7012, Preference for Certain Domestic Commodities, in solicitations and contracts, including solicitations and contracts using FAR part 12 procedures for the acquisition of commercial items.

(b) Use the clause at 252.225-7015, Restriction on Acquisition of Hand or Measuring Tools, in solicitations and contracts, including solicitations and contracts using FAR part 12 procedures for the acquisition of commercial items, that exceed the simplified acquisition threshold that require delivery of hand or measuring tools.

(c) Use the clause at 252.225-7006, Acquisition of the American Flag, in solicitations and contracts, including solicitations and contracts using FAR part 12 procedures for the acquisition of commercial items, that are for the acquisition of the American flag, with an estimated value that exceeds the simplified acquisition threshold.

[DAC 91-11, 61 FR 50446, 9/26/96, effective 9/26/96; Interim rule, 67 FR 20697, 4/26/2002, effective 4/26/2002; Final rule, 68 FR 15615, 3/31/2003, effective 4/30/2003; Final rule, 73 FR 11354, 3/3/2008, effective 3/3/2008; Final rule, 74 FR 37626, 7/29/2009, effective 7/29/2009; Final rule, 78 FR 37980, 6/25/2013, effective 6/25/2013; Final rule, 80 FR 51748, 8/26/2015, effective 8/26/2015; Final rule, 80 FR 67254, 10/30/2015, effective 10/30/2015; Final rule, 83 FR 65560, 12/21/2018, effective 12/21/2018]

225.7003 Restrictions on acquisition of specialty metals. (No Text)

[Interim rule, 62 FR 2856, 1/17/97, effective 1/17/97, finalized without change, DAC 91-12, 62 FR 34114, 6/24/97, effective 6/24/97; Final rule, 68 FR 15615, 3/31/2003, effective 4/30/2003; Final rule, 70 FR 73153, 12/9/2005, effective 12/9/2005; Final rule, 71 FR 14110, 3/21/2006, effective 3/21/2006; Final rule, 74 FR 37626, 7/29/2009, effective 7/29/2009]

225.7003-1 Definitions.

As used in this section—

Alloy means a metal consisting of a mixture of a basic metallic element and one or more metallic, or non-metallic, alloying elements.

(1) For alloys named by a single metallic element (e.g., titanium alloy), it means that the alloy contains 50 percent or more of the named metal (by mass).

(2) If two metals are specified in the name (e.g., nickel-iron alloy), those metals are the two predominant elements in the alloy, and together they constitute 50 percent or more of the alloy (by mass).

Automotive item—

(1) Means a self-propelled military transport tactical vehicle, primarily intended for use by military personnel or for carrying cargo, such as—

(i) A high-mobility multipurpose wheeled vehicle;

(ii) An armored personnel carrier; or

(iii) A troop/cargo-carrying truckcar, truck, or van; and

(2) Does not include—

(i) A commercially available off-the-shelf vehicle; or

(ii) Construction equipment (such as bulldozers, excavators, lifts, or loaders) or other self-propelled equipment (such as cranes or aircraft ground support equipment).

Commercial derivative military article means an item acquired by the Department of Defense that is or will be produced using the same production facilities, a common supply chain, and the same or similar production processes that are used for the production of articles predominantly used by the general public or by nongovernmental entities for purposes other than governmental purposes.

Electronic component means an item that operates by controlling the flow of electrons or other electrically charged particles in circuits, using interconnections of electrical devices such as resistors, inductors, capacitors, diodes, switches, transistors, or integrated circuits. The term does not include structural or mechanical parts of an assembly containing an electronic component and does not include any high performance magnets that may be used in the electronic component.

High performance magnet means a permanent magnet that obtains a majority of its magnetic properties from rare earth metals (such as samarium).

Produce means—

(1) Atomization;

(2) Sputtering; or

(3) Final consolidation of non-melt derived metal powders.

Specialty metal means—

(1) Steel—

(i) With a maximum alloy content exceeding one or more of the following limits: manganese, 1.65 percent; silicon, 0.60 percent; or copper, 0.60 percent; or

(ii) Containing more than 0.25 percent of any of the following elements: aluminum, chromium, cobalt, molybdenum, nickel, niobium (columbium), titanium, tungsten, or vanadium;

(2) Metal alloys consisting of—

(i) Nickel or iron-nickel alloys that contain a total of alloying metals other than nickel and iron in excess of 10 percent; or

(ii) Cobalt alloys that contain a total of alloying metals other than cobalt and iron in excess of 10 percent;

(3) Titanium and titanium alloys; or

(4) Zirconium and zirconium alloys.

Steel means an iron alloy that includes between .02 and 2 percent carbon and may include other elements.

[Final rule, 74 FR 37626, 7/29/2009, effective 7/29/2009; Final rule, 84 FR 72239, 12/31/2019, effective 12/31/2019]

225.7003-2 Restrictions.

(a) The following restrictions implement 10 U.S.C. 2533b. Except as provided in 225.7003-3—

(1) Do not acquire the following items, or any components of the following items, unless any specialty metals contained in the items or components are melted or produced in the United States (also see guidance at PGI 225.7003-2(a)):

(i) Aircraft.

(ii) Missile or space systems.

(iii) Ships.

(iv) Tank or automotive items.

(v) Weapon systems.

(vi) Ammunition.

(2) Do not acquire a specialty metal (*e.g.*, raw stock, including bar, billet, slab, wire, plate, and sheet; castings; and forgings) as an end item, unless the specialty metal is melted or produced in the United States. This restriction applies to specialty metal acquired by a contractor for delivery to DoD as an end item, in addition to specialty metal acquired by DoD directly from the entity that melted or produced the specialty metal.

(b) For more information on specialty metals restrictions and reporting of noncompliances, see *http://www.acq.osd.mil/dpap/cpic/ic/restrictions_on_specialty_metals_10_usc_2533b.html.*

[Final rule, 74 FR 37626, 7/29/2009, effective 7/29/2009; Final rule, 81 FR 28729, 5/10/2016, effective 5/10/2016; Final rule, 81 FR 28730, 5/10/2016, effective 5/10/2016]

225.7003-3 Exceptions.

(a) *Acquisitions in the following categories are not subject to the restrictions in 225.7003-2*:

(1) Acquisitions at or below the simplified acquisition threshold.

(2) Acquisitions outside the United States in support of combat operations.

(3) Acquisitions in support of contingency operations.

(4) Acquisitions for which the use of other than competitive procedures has been approved on the basis of unusual and compelling urgency in accordance with FAR 6.302-2.

(5) Acquisitions of items specifically for commissary resale.

(6) Acquisitions of items for test and evaluation under the foreign comparative testing program (10 U.S.C. 2350a(g)). However, this exception does not apply to any acquisitions under follow-on production contracts.

(b) *One or more of the following exceptions may apply to an end item or component that includes any of the following, under a prime contract or subcontract at any tier*. The restrictions in 225.7003-2do not apply to the following:

(1) Electronic components, unless the Secretary of Defense, upon the recommendation of the Strategic Materials Protection Board pursuant to 10 U.S.C. 187, determines that the domestic availability of a particular electronic component is critical to national security.

(2) (i) Commercially available off-the-shelf (COTS) items containing specialty metals, except the restrictions do apply to contracts or subcontracts for the acquisition of—

(A) Specialty metal mill products, such as bar, billet, slab, wire, plate, and sheet, that have not been incorporated into end items, subsystems, assemblies, or components. Specialty metal supply contracts issued by COTS producers are not subcontracts for the purposes of this exception;

(B) Forgings or castings of specialty metals, unless the forgings or castings are incorporated into COTS end items, subsystems, or assemblies;

(C) Commercially available high performance magnets that contain specialty metal, unless such high performance magnets are incorporated into COTS end items or subsystems (see PGI 225.7003-3(b)(6) for a table of applicability of specialty metals restrictions to magnets); and

(D) COTS fasteners, unless—

(1) The fasteners are incorporated into COTS end items, subsystems, or assemblies; or

(2) The fasteners qualify for the commercial item exception in paragraph (b)(3) of this subsection.

(ii) If this exception is used for an acquisition of COTS end items valued at $5 million or more per item, the acquiring department or agency shall submit an annual report to the Director, Defense Procurement and Acquisition Policy, in accordance with the procedures at PGI 225.7003-3(b)(2).

(3) Fasteners that are commercial items and are acquired under a contract or subcontract with a manufacturer of such fasteners, if the manufacturer has certified that it will purchase, during the relevant calendar year, an amount of domestically melted or produced specialty metal, in the required form, for use in the production of fasteners for sale to DoD and other customers, that is not less than 50 percent of the total amount of the specialty metal that the manufacturer will purchase to carry out the production of such fasteners for all customers.

(4) Items listed in 225.7003-2(a), manufactured in a qualifying country or containing specialty metals melted or produced in a qualifying country.

(5) Specialty metal in any of the items listed in 225.7003–2 if the USD(A&S), or an official authorized in accordance with paragraph (b)(5)(i) of this section, determines that specialty metal melted or produced in the United States cannot be acquired as and when needed at a fair and reasonable price in a satisfactory quality, a sufficient quantity, and the required form (i.e., a domestic nonavailability determination). In accordance with 10 U.S.C. 2533b(m)(4), the term "required form" in this section refers to the form of the mill product, such as bar, billet, wire, slab, plate, or sheet, in the grade appropriate for the production of a finished end item to be delivered to the Government under this contract; or a finished component assembled into an end item to be delivered to the Government under the contract. See guidance in PGI 225.7003–3(b)(5).

(i) The Secretary of the military department concerned is authorized, without power of redelegation, to make a domestic nonavailability determination that applies to only one contract.

The supporting documentation for the determination shall include—

(A) An analysis of alternatives that would not require a domestic nonavailability determination; and

(B) Written documentation by the requiring activity, with specificity, why such alternatives are unacceptable.

(ii) A domestic nonavailability determination that applies to more than one contract (*i.e.*, a class domestic nonavailability determination), requires the approval of the USD(A&S).

(A) At least 30 days before making a domestic nonavailability determination that would apply to more than one contract, the USD(A&S) will, to the maximum extent practicable, and in a manner consistent with the protection of national security and confidential business information—

(1) Publish a notice on the Federal Business Opportunities Web site (*http://www.FedBizOpps.gov* or any successor site) of the intent to make the domestic nonavailability determination; and

(2) Solicit information relevant to such notice from interested parties, including producers of specialty metal mill products.

(B) The USD(A&S)—

(1) Will take into consideration all information submitted in response to the notice in making a class domestic nonavailability determination;

(2) May consider other relevant information that cannot be made part of the public record consistent with the protection of national security information and confidential business information; and

(3) Will ensure that any such domestic nonavailability determination and the rationale for the determination are made publicly available to the maximum extent consistent with the protection of national security and confidential business information.

(6) End items containing a minimal amount of otherwise noncompliant specialty metals (*i.e.*, specialty metals not melted or produced in the United States that are not covered by another exception listed in this paragraph (b)), if the total weight of noncompliant specialty metal does not exceed 2 percent of the total weight of all specialty metal in the end item. This exception does not apply to high performance magnets containing specialty metals. See PGI 225.7003-3(b)(6) for a table of applicability of specialty metals restrictions to magnets.

(c) *Compliance for commercial derivative military articles*. The restrictions at 225.7003-2(a) do not apply to an item acquired under a prime contract if—

(1) The offeror has certified, and subsequently demonstrates, that the offeror and its subcontractor(s) will individually or collectively enter into a contractual agreement or agreements to purchase a sufficient quantity of domestically melted or produced specialty metal in accordance with the provision at 252.225-7010; and

(2) The USD(A&S), or the Secretary of the military department concerned, determines that the item is a commercial derivative military article (defense agencies see procedures at PGI 225.7003-3(c)). The contracting officer shall submit the offeror's certification and a request for a determination to the appropriate official, through agency channels, and shall notify the offeror when a decision has been made.

(d) *National security waiver*. The USD(A&S) may waive the restrictions at 225.7003-2 if the USD(A&S) determines in writing that acceptance of the item is necessary to the national security interests of the United States (*see* procedures at PGI 225.7003-3(d)). This authority may not be delegated.

(1) The written determination of the USD(A&S)—

(i) Shall specify the quantity of end items to which the national security waiver applies;

(ii) Shall specify the time period over which the national security waiver applies; and

(iii) Shall be provided to the congressional defense committees before the determination is executed, except that in the case of an urgent national security requirement, the determination may be provided to the congressional defense committees up to 7 days after it is executed.

(2) After making such a determination, the USD(A&S) will—

(i) Ensure that the contractor or subcontractor responsible for the noncompliant specialty metal develops and implements an effective plan to ensure future compliance; and

(ii) Determine whether or not the noncompliance was knowing and willful. If the USD(A&S) determines that the noncompliance was knowing and willful, the appropriate debarring and suspending official shall consider suspending or debarring the contractor or subcontractor until such time as the contractor or subcontractor has effectively addressed the issues that led to the noncompliance.

(3) Because national security waivers will only be granted when the acquisition in question is necessary to the national security interests of the United States, the requirement for a plan will be applied as a condition subsequent, and not a condition precedent, to the granting of a waiver.

[Final rule, 74 FR 37626, 7/29/2009, effective 7/29/2009; Final rule, 75 FR 48279, 8/10/2010, effective 8/10/2010; Final rule, 79 FR 17445, 3/28/2014, effective 3/28/2014; Final rule, 84 FR 72239, 12/31/2019, effective 12/31/2019]

225.7003-4 [Removed and Reserved]

[Final rule, 74 FR 37626, 7/29/2009, effective 7/29/2009; Final rule, 84 FR 65310, 11/27/2019, effective 11/27/2019]

225.7003-5 Solicitation provision and contract clauses.

(a) Unless the acquisition is wholly exempt from the specialty metals restrictions at 225.7003-2 because the acquisition is covered by an exception in 225.7003-3(a) or (d) (but see paragraph (d) of this subsection)—

(1) Use the clause at 252.225-7008, Restriction on Acquisition of Specialty Metals, in solicitations and contracts, including solicitations and contracts using FAR part 12 procedures for the acquisition of commercial items, that—

(i) Exceed the simplified acquisition threshold; and

(ii) Require the delivery of specialty metals as end items.

(2) Use the clause at 252.225-7009, Restriction on Acquisition of Certain Articles Containing Specialty Metals, in solicitations and contracts, including solicitations and contracts using FAR part 12 procedures for the acquisition of commercial items, that—

(i) Exceed the simplified acquisition threshold; and

(ii) Require delivery of any of the following items, or components of the following items, if such items or components contain specialty metal:

(A) Aircraft.

(B) Missile or space systems.

(C) Ships.

(D) Tank or automotive items.

(E) Weapon systems.

(F) Ammunition.

(b) Use the provision at 252.225-7010, Commercial Derivative Military Article—Specialty Metals Compliance Certificate, in solicitations, including solicitations using FAR part 12 procedures for the acquisition of commercial items,—

(1) That contain the clause at 252.225-7009; and

(2) For which the contracting officer anticipates that one or more offers of commercial derivative military articles may be received.

(c) If an agency cannot reasonably determine at time of acquisition whether some or all of the items will be used in support of combat operations or in support of contingency operations, the contracting officer should not rely on the exception at 225.7003-3(a)(2) or (3), but should include the appropriate specialty metals clause or provision in the solicitation and contract.

(d) If the solicitation and contract require delivery of a variety of contract line items containing specialty metals, but only some of the items are subject to domestic specialty metals restrictions, identify in the Schedule those items that are subject to the restrictions.

[Final rule, 74 FR 37626, 7/29/2009, effective 7/29/2009; Final rule, 75 FR 48279, 8/10/2010, effective 8/10/2010; Final rule, 78 FR 37980, 6/25/2013, effective 6/25/2013]

225.7004 Restriction on acquisition of foreign buses. (No Text)

[Interim rule, 62 FR 2857, 1/17/97, effective 1/17/97, finalized without change, DAC

91-12, 62 FR 34114, 6/24/97, effective 6/24/97; Final rule, 68 FR 15615, 3/31/2003, effective 4/30/2003]

225.7004-1 Restriction.

In accordance with 10 U.S.C. 2534, do not acquire a multipassenger motor vehicle (bus) unless it is manufactured in the United States, Australia, Canada, or the United Kingdom.

[Final rule, 68 FR 15615, 3/31/2003, effective 4/30/2003; Final rule, 83 FR 65560, 12/21/2018, effective 12/21/2018]

225.7004-2 Applicability.

Apply this restriction if the buses are purchased, leased, rented, or made available under contracts for transportation services.

[Final rule, 68 FR 15615, 3/31/2003, effective 4/30/2003]

225.7004-3 Exceptions.

This restriction does not apply in any of the following circumstances:

(a) Buses manufactured outside the United States, Australia, Canada, or the United Kingdom are needed for temporary use because buses manufactured in the United States, Australia, Canada, or the United Kingdom are not available to satisfy requirements that cannot be postponed. Such use may not, however, exceed the lead time required for acquisition and delivery of buses manufactured in the United States, Australia, Canada, or the United Kingdom.

(b) The requirement for buses is temporary in nature. For example, to meet a special, nonrecurring requirement or a sporadic and infrequent recurring requirement, buses manufactured outside the United States, Australia, Canada, or the United Kingdom may be used for temporary periods of time. Such use may not, however, exceed the period of time needed to meet the special requirement.

(c) Buses manufactured outside the United States, Australia, Canada, or the United Kingdom are available at no cost to the U.S. Government.

(d) The acquisition is for an amount at or below the simplified acquisition threshold.

[Final rule, 68 FR 15615, 3/31/2003, effective 4/30/2003; Final rule, 83 FR 65560, 12/21/2018, effective 12/21/2018]

225.7004-4 Waiver.

The waiver criteria at 225.7008(a) apply to this restriction.

[Final rule, 68 FR 15615, 3/31/2003, effective 4/30/2003; Final rule, 74 FR 37626, 7/29/2009, effective 7/29/2009]

225.7005 [Removed and Reserved]

[Interim rule, 63 FR 5744, 2/4/98, effective 2/4/98; Final rule, 63 FR 28284, 5/22/98, effective 5/22/98; Interim rule, 63 FR 43887, 8/17/98, effective 8/17/98, finalized without change, 63 FR 64426, 11/20/98; Final rule, 65 FR 39703, 6/27/2000, effective 6/27/2000; Final rule, 68 FR 15615, 3/31/2003, effective 4/30/2003; Final rule, 83 FR 24890, 5/30/2018, effective 10/1/2018]

225.7005-1 [Removed]

[Final rule, 68 FR 15615, 3/31/2003, effective 4/30/2003; Final rule, 71 FR 39004, 7/11/2006, effective 7/11/2006; Final rule, 74 FR 63883, 12/24/2009, effective 12/24/2009; Final rule, 83 FR 24890, 5/30/2018, effective 10/1/2018]

225.7005-2 [Removed]

[Final rule, 68 FR 15615, 3/31/2003, effective 4/30/2003; Final rule, 83 FR 24890, 5/30/2018, effective 10/1/2018]

225.7005-3 [Removed]

[Final rule, 68 FR 15615, 3/31/2003, effective 4/30/2003; Final rule, 74 FR 37626, 7/29/2009, effective 7/29/2009; Final rule, 83 FR 24890, 5/30/2018, effective 10/1/2018]

225.7006 Restriction on air circuit breakers for naval vessels.

[Final rule, 68 FR 15615, 3/31/2003, effective 4/30/2003]

225.7006-1 Restriction.

In accordance with 10 U.S.C. 2534, do not acquire air circuit breakers for naval vessels unless they are manufactured in the United States, Australia, Canada, or the United Kingdom.

[Final rule, 68 FR 15615, 3/31/2003, effective 4/30/2003; Final rule, 83 FR 65560, 12/21/2018, effective 12/21/2018]

225.7006-2 Exceptions.

This restriction does not apply if the acquisition is—

(a) For an amount at or below the simplified acquisition threshold; or

(b) For spare or repair parts needed to support air circuit breakers manufactured outside the United States. Support includes the purchase of spare air circuit breakers when those from alternate sources are not interchangeable.

[Final rule, 68 FR 15615, 3/31/2003, effective 4/30/2003]

225.7006-3 Waiver.

The waiver criteria at 225.7008(a) apply to this restriction.

[Final rule, 68 FR 15615, 3/31/2003, effective 4/30/2003; Final rule, 74 FR 37626, 7/29/2009, effective 7/29/2009; Final rule, 78 FR 13543, 2/28/2013, effective 2/28/2013; Final rule, 83 FR 65560, 12/21/2018, effective 12/21/2018]

225.7006-4 Solicitation provision and contract clause.

(a) Use the provision at 252.225-7037, Evaluation of Offers for Air Circuit Breakers, in solicitations, including solicitations using FAR part 12 procedures for the acquisition of commercial items, that require air circuit breakers for naval vessels unless—

(1) An exception applies; or

(2) A waiver has been granted.

(b) Use the clause at 252.225-7038, Restriction on Acquisition of Air Circuit Breakers, in solicitations and contracts, including solicitations and contracts using FAR part 12 procedures for the acquisition of commercial items, that require air circuit breakers for naval vessels unless—

(1) An exception at 225.7006-2 applies; or

(2) A waiver has been granted.

[Final rule, 68 FR 15615, 3/31/2003, effective 4/30/2003; Final rule, 78 FR 37980, 6/25/2013, effective 6/25/2013; Final rule, 83 FR 65560, 12/21/2018, effective 12/21/2018]

225.7007 Restrictions on anchor and mooring chain. (No Text)

[Final rule, 68 FR 15615, 3/31/2003, effective 4/30/2003]

225.7007-1 Restrictions.

(a) In accordance with Section 8041 of the Fiscal Year 1991 DoD Appropriations Act (Public Law 101-511) and similar sections in subsequent DoD appropriations acts, do not acquire welded shipboard anchor and mooring chain, four inches or less in diameter, unless—

(1) It is manufactured in the United States, including cutting, heat treating, quality control, testing, and welding (both forging and shot blasting process); and

(2) The cost of the components manufactured in the United States exceeds 50 percent of the total cost of components.

(b) 10 U.S.C. 2534 also restricts acquisition of welded shipboard anchor and mooring chain, four inches or less in diameter, when used as a component of a naval vessel. However, the Appropriations Act restriction described in paragraph (a) of this subsection takes precedence over the restriction of 10 U.S.C. 2534.

[Interim rule, 63 FR 5744, 2/4/98, effective 2/4/98; Final rule, 68 FR 15615, 3/31/2003, effective 4/30/2003]

225.7007-2 Waiver.

(a) The Secretary of the department responsible for acquisition may waive the restriction in 225.7007-1(a), on a case-by-case basis, if—

(1) Sufficient domestic suppliers are not available to meet DoD requirements on a timely basis; and

(2) The acquisition is necessary to acquire capability for national security purposes.

(b) Document the waiver in a written determination and findings containing—

(1) The factors supporting the waiver; and

(2) A certification that the acquisition must be made in order to acquire capability for national security purposes.

(c) Provide a copy of the determination and findings to the House and Senate Committees on Appropriations.

[Interim rule, 60 FR 19531, 4/19/95, effective 4/10/95, finalized without change, DAC 91-9, 60 FR 61586, 11/30/95, effective 11/30/95; Final rule, 68 FR 15615, 3/31/2003, effective 4/30/2003]

225.7007-3 Contract clause.

Unless a waiver has been granted, use the clause at 252.225-7019, Restriction on Acquisition of Anchor and Mooring Chain, in solicitations and contracts requiring welded shipboard anchor or mooring chain four inches or less in diameter.

[Interim rule, 63 FR 5744, 2/4/98, effective 2/4/98; Final rule, 68 FR 15615, 3/31/2003, effective 4/30/2003]

225.7007-4 [Removed]

[Interim rule, 63 FR 5744, 2/4/98, effective 2/4/98; Interim rule, 63 FR 43887, 8/17/98, effective 8/17/98, finalized without change, 63 FR 64426, 11/20/98; Final rule, 68 FR 15615, 3/31/2003, effective 4/30/2003]

225.7008 Waiver of restrictions of 10 U.S.C. 2534.

(a) When specifically authorized by reference elsewhere in this subpart, the restrictions on certain foreign purchases under 10 U.S.C. 2534(a) may be waived as follows:

(1)(i) The Under Secretary of Defense (Acquisition, Technology, and Logistics) (USD(AT&L)), without power of delegation, may waive a restriction for a particular item for a particular foreign country upon determination that—

(A) United States producers of the item would not be jeopardized by competition from a foreign country, and that country does not discriminate against defense items produced in the United States to a greater degree than the United States discriminates against defense items produced in that country; or

(B) Application of the restriction would impede cooperative programs entered into between DoD and a foreign country, or would impede the reciprocal procurement of defense items under a memorandum of understanding providing for reciprocal procurement of defense items under 225.872, and that country does not discriminate against defense items produced in the United States to a greater degree than the United States discriminates against defense items produced in that country.

(ii) A notice of the determination to exercise the waiver authority shall be published in the **Federal Register** and submitted to the congressional defense committees at least 15 days before the effective date of the waiver.

(iii) The effective period of the waiver shall not exceed 1 year.

(iv) For contracts entered into prior to the effective date of a waiver, provided adequate consideration is received to modify the contract, the waiver shall be applied as directed or authorized in the waiver to—

(A) Subcontracts entered into on or after the effective date of the waiver; and

(B) Options for the procurement of items that are exercised after the effective date of the waiver, if the option prices are adjusted for any reason other than the application of the waiver.

(2) The head of the contracting activity may waive a restriction on a case-by-case basis upon execution of a determination and findings that any of the following applies:

(i) The restriction would cause unreasonable delays.

(ii) Satisfactory quality items manufactured in the United States or Canada are not available.

(iii) Application of the restriction would result in the existence of only one source for the item in the United States or Canada.

(iv) Application of the restriction is not in the national security interests of the United States.

(v) Application of the restriction would adversely affect a U.S. company.

(3) A restriction is waived when it would cause unreasonable costs. The cost of an item of U.S. or Canadian origin is unreasonable if it exceeds 150 percent of the offered

price, inclusive of duty, of items that are not of U.S. or Canadian origin.

(b) In accordance with the provisions of paragraphs (a)(1)(i) through (iii) of this section, the USD(AT&L) has waived the restrictions of 10 U.S.C. 2534(a) for certain items manufactured in the United Kingdom, including air circuit breakers for naval vessels (see 225.7006) and the naval vessel components listed at 225.7010-1.

[Final rule, 68 FR 15615, 3/31/2003, effective 4/30/2003; Final rule, 70 FR 52030, 9/1/2005, effective 9/1/2005; Final rule, 74 FR 37626, 7/29/2009, effective 7/29/2009; Final rule, 78 FR 13543, 2/28/2013, effective 2/28/2013; Final rule, 80 FR 10391, 2/26/2015, effective 2/26/2015]

225.7008-1 [Removed]

[Final rule, 68 FR 15615, 3/31/2003, effective 4/30/2003; Final rule, 70 FR 52030, 9/1/2005, effective 9/1/2005]

225.7008-2 [Removed]

[Final rule, 68 FR 15615, 3/31/2003, effective 4/30/2003; Final rule, 70 FR 52030, 9/1/2005, effective 9/1/2005]

225.7008-3 [Removed]

[Final rule, 68 FR 15615, 3/31/2003, effective 4/30/2003; Final rule, 70 FR 52030, 9/1/2005, effective 9/1/2005]

225.7008-4 [Removed]

[Final rule, 68 FR 15615, 3/31/2003, effective 4/30/2003; Final rule, 70 FR 52030, 9/1/2005, effective 9/1/2005]

225.7009 Restriction on ball and roller bearings. (No Text)

[Removed and reserved, DAC 91-12, 62 FR 34114, 6/24/97, effective 6/24/97; Final rule, 68 FR 15615, 3/31/2003, effective 4/30/2003; Final rule, 71 FR 14110, 3/21/2006, effective 3/21/2006]

225.7009-1 Scope.

This section implements Section 8065 of the Fiscal Year 2002 DoD Appropriations Act (Pub. L. 107-117) and the same restriction in subsequent DoD appropriations acts.

[Final rule, 68 FR 15615, 3/31/2003, effective 4/30/2003; Final rule, 71 FR 14110, 3/21/2006, effective 3/21/2006]

225.7009-2 Restriction.

(a) Do not acquire ball and roller bearings unless—

(1) The bearings are manufactured in the United States or Canada; and

(2) For each ball or roller bearing, the cost of the bearing components manufactured in the United States or Canada exceeds 50 percent of the total cost of the bearing components of that ball or roller bearing.

(b) The restriction at 225.7003-2 may also apply to bearings that are made from specialty metals, such as high carbon chrome steel (bearing steel).

[Final rule, 68 FR 15615, 3/31/2003, effective 4/30/2003; Final rule, 71 FR 14110, 3/21/2006, effective 3/21/2006; Final rule, 75 FR 76297, 12/8/2010, effective 12/8/2010; Final rule, 76 FR 32841, 6/6/2011, effective 6/6/2011]

225.7009-3 Exception.

The restriction in 225.7009-2 does not apply to contracts or subcontracts for the acquisition of commercial items, except for commercial ball and roller bearings acquired as end items.

[Final rule, 68 FR 15615, 3/31/2003, effective 4/30/2003; Final rule, 70 FR 57191, 9/30/2005, effective 9/30/2005; Final rule, 71 FR 14110, 3/21/2006, effective 3/21/2006]

225.7009-4 Waiver.

The Secretary of the department responsible for acquisition or, for the Defense Logistics Agency, the Component Acquisition Executive, may waive the restriction in 225.7009-2, on a case-by-case basis, by certifying to the House and Senate Committees on Appropriations that—

(a) Adequate domestic supplies are not available to meet DoD requirements on a timely basis; and

(b) The acquisition must be made in order to acquire capability for national security purposes.

[Final rule, 68 FR 15615, 3/31/2003, effective 4/30/2003; Final rule, 71 FR 14110, 3/21/2006, effective 3/21/2006]

225.7009-5 Contract clause.

Use the clause at 252.225-7016, Restriction on Acquisition of Ball and Roller Bearings, in solicitations and contracts, including solicitations and contracts using FAR part 12 procedures for the acquisition of commercial items, unless—

(a) The items being acquired are commercial items other than ball or roller bearings acquired as end items;

(b) The items being acquired do not contain ball and roller bearings; or

(c) A waiver has been granted in accordance with 225.7009-4.

[Final rule, 71 FR 14110, 3/21/2006, effective 3/21/2006; Final rule, 78 FR 37980, 6/25/2013, effective 6/25/2013]

225.7010 Restriction on certain naval vessel components. (No Text)

[Final rule, 68 FR 15615, 3/31/2003, effective 4/30/2003; Final rule, 73 FR 21845, 4/23/2008, effective 4/23/2008; Final rule, 78 FR 37980, 6/25/2013, effective 6/25/2013; Final rule, 80 FR 10391, 2/26/2015, effective 2/26/2015]

225.7010-1 Restriction.

In accordance with 10 U.S.C. 2534, do not acquire the following components of naval vessels, to the extent they are unique to marine applications, unless manufactured in the United States or Canada:

(a) Gyrocompasses.

(b) Electronic navigation chart systems.

(c) Steering controls.

(d) Pumps.

(e) Propulsion and machinery control systems.

(f) Totally enclosed lifeboats.

[Interim rule, 60 FR 19531, 4/19/95, effective 4/10/95, finalized without change, DAC 91-9, 60 FR 61586, 11/30/95, effective 11/30/95; DAC 91-12, 62 FR 34114, 6/24/97, effective 6/24/97; Interim rule, 63 FR 5744, 2/4/98, effective 2/4/98; Final rule, 68 FR 15615, 3/31/2003, effective 4/30/2003; Final rule, 73 FR 21845, 4/23/2008, effective 4/23/2008; Final rule, 80 FR 10391, 2/26/2015, effective 2/26/2015]

225.7010-2 Exceptions.

This restriction does not apply to—

(a) Contracts or subcontracts that do not exceed the simplified acquisition threshold; or

(b) Acquisition of spare or repair parts needed to support components for naval vessels manufactured outside the United States. Support includes the purchase of spare gyrocompasses, electronic navigation chart systems, steering controls, pumps, propulsion and machinery control systems, or totally enclosed lifeboats, when those from alternate sources are not interchangeable.

[Interim rule, 63 FR 5744, 2/4/98, effective 2/4/98; Final rule, 68 FR 15615, 3/31/2003, effective 4/30/2003; Final rule, 73 FR 21845, 4/23/2008, effective 4/23/2008; Final rule, 80 FR 10391, 2/26/2015, effective 2/26/2015]

225.7010-3 Waiver.

(a) The waiver criteria at 225.7008(a) apply to this restriction.

(b) The Under Secretary of Defense (Acquisition, Technology, and Logistics) has waived the restriction of 10 U.S.C. 2534 for certain items manufactured in the United Kingdom, including the items listed in section 225.7010-1. See 225.7008.

[Interim rule, 63 FR 5744, 2/4/98, effective 2/4/98; Interim rule, 63 FR 43887, 8/17/98, effective 8/17/98, finalized without change, 63 FR 64426, 11/20/98; Final rule, 68 FR 15615, 3/31/2003, effective 4/30/2003; Final rule, 73 FR 21845, 4/23/2008, effective 4/23/2008; Final rule, 80 FR 10391, 2/26/2015, effective 2/26/2015]

225.7010-4 Implementation.

(a) 10 U.S.C. 2534(h) prohibits the use of contract clauses or certifications to implement this restriction.

(b) Agencies shall accomplish implementation of this restriction through use of management and oversight techniques that achieve the objectives of this section without imposing a significant management burden on the Government or the contractor involved.

[Final rule, 68 FR 15615, 3/31/2003, effective 4/30/2003; Final rule, 73 FR 21845, 4/23/2008, effective 4/23/2008; Final rule, 80 FR 10391, 2/26/2015, effective 2/26/2015]

225.7011 Restriction on carbon, alloy, and armor steel plate. (No Text)

[Final rule, 68 FR 15615, 3/31/2003, effective 4/30/2003]

225.7011-1 Restriction.

(a) In accordance with Section 8111 of the Fiscal Year 1992 DoD Appropriations Act (Pub. L. 102-172) and similar sections in subsequent DoD appropriations acts, do not acquire any of the following types of carbon, alloy, or armor steel plate for use in a Government-owned facility or a facility under the control of (e.g., leased by) DoD, unless it is melted and rolled in the United States or Canada:

(1) Carbon, alloy, or armor steel plate in Federal Supply Class 9515.

(2) Carbon, alloy, or armor steel plate described by specifications of the American Society for Testing Materials or the American Iron and Steel Institute.

(b) This restriction—

(1) Applies to the acquisition of carbon, alloy, or armor steel plate as a finished steel mill product that may be used "as is" or may be used as an intermediate material for the fabrication of an end product; and

(2) Does not apply to the acquisition of an end product (e.g., a machine tool), to be used in the facility, that contains carbon, alloy, or armor steel plate as a component.

[DAC 91-6, 59 FR 27662, 5/27/94, effective 5/27/94; Final rule, 68 FR 15615, 3/31/2003, effective 4/30/2003; Final rule, 71 FR 75893, 12/19/2006, effective 12/19/2006]

225.7011-2 Waiver.

The Secretary of the department responsible for acquisition may waive this restriction, on a case-by-case basis, by certifying to the House and Senate Committees on Appropriations that—

(a) Adequate U.S. or Canadian supplies are not available to meet DoD requirements on a timely basis; and

(b) The acquisition must be made in order to acquire capability for national security purposes.

[DAC 91-6, 59 FR 27662, 5/27/94, effective 5/27/94; Final rule, 68 FR 15615, 3/31/2003, effective 4/30/2003]

225.7011-3 Contract clause.

Unless a waiver has been granted, use the clause at 252.225-7030, Restriction on Acquisition of Carbon, Alloy, and Armor Steel Plate, in solicitations and contracts that–

(a) Require the delivery to the Government of carbon, alloy, or armor steel plate that will be used in a Government-owned facility or a facility under the control of DoD; or

(b) Require contractors operating in a Government-owned facility or a facility under the control of DoD to purchase carbon, alloy, or armor steel plate.

[Final rule, 68 FR 15615, 3/31/2003, effective 4/30/2003; Final rule, 71 FR 75893, 12/19/2006, effective 12/19/2006]

225.7011-4 [Removed]

[DAC 91-6, 59 FR 27662, 5/27/94, effective 5/27/94; DAC 91-11, 61 FR 50446, 9/26/96, effective 9/26/96; DAC 91-13,63 FR 11522, 3/9/98, effective 3/9/98; Final rule, 68 FR 15615, 3/31/2003, effective 4/30/2003]

225.7011-5 [Removed]

[DAC 91-6, 59 FR 27662, 5/27/94, effective 5/27/94; Final rule, 68 FR 15615, 3/31/2003, effective 4/30/2003]

225.7012 Restriction on supercomputers. (No Text)

[Final rule, 68 FR 15615, 3/31/2003, effective 4/30/2003]

225.7012-1 Restriction.

In accordance with Section 8112 of Public Law 100-202, and similar sections in subsequent DoD appropriations acts, do not purchase a supercomputer unless it is manufactured in the United States.

[Interim rule, 61 FR 13106, 3/26/96, effective 4/1/96, finalized without change, DAC 91-11, 61 FR 50446, 9/26/96; Final rule, 68 FR 15615, 3/31/2003, effective 4/30/2003]

225.7012-2 Waiver.

The Secretary of Defense may waive this restriction, on a case-by-case basis, after certifying to the Armed Services and Appropriations Committees of Congress that—

(a) Adequate U.S. supplies are not available to meet requirements on a timely basis; and

(b) The acquisition must be made in order to acquire capability for national security purposes.

[Interim rule, 61 FR 13106, 3/26/96, effective 4/1/96, finalized without change, DAC 91-11, 61 FR 50446, 9/26/96; Final rule, 68 FR 15615, 3/31/2003, effective 4/30/2003]

225.7012-3 Contract clause.

Unless a waiver has been granted, use the clause at DFARS 252.225-7011, Restriction on Acquisition of Supercomputers, in solicitations and contracts for the acquisition of supercomputers.

[Interim rule, 61 FR 13106, 3/26/96, effective 4/1/96; DAC 91-11, 61 FR 50446, 9/26/96, effective 9/26/96; Final rule, 68 FR 15615, 3/31/2003, effective 4/30/2003]

225.7013 Restrictions on construction or repair of vessels in foreign shipyards.

In accordance with 10 U.S.C. 7309 and 7310—

(a) Do not award a contract to construct in a foreign shipyard—

(1) A vessel for any of the armed forces; or

(2) A major component of the hull or superstructure of a vessel for any of the armed forces; and

(b) Do not overhaul, repair, or maintain in a foreign shipyard, a naval vessel (or any other vessel under the jurisdiction of the Secretary of the Navy) homeported in the United States. This restriction does not apply to voyage repairs.

[Removed and reserved, DAC 91-12, 62 FR 34114, 6/24/97, effective 6/24/97; Final rule, 68 FR 15615, 3/31/2003, effective 4/30/2003; Final rule, 71 FR 58537, 10/4/2006, effective 10/4/2006]

225.7014 Restrictions on military construction.

(a) For restriction on award of military construction contracts to be performed in the United States outlying areas in the Pacific and on Kwajalein Atoll, or in countries bordering the Arabian Gulf, see 236.273(a).

(b) For restriction on acquisition of steel for use in military construction projects, see 236.274.

[DAC 91-6, 59 FR 27662, 5/27/94, effective 5/27/94; Final rule, 68 FR 15615, 3/31/2003, effective 4/30/2003; Final rule, 70 FR 35543, 6/21/2005, effective 6/21/2005; Final rule, 72 FR 14239, 3/27/2007, effective 3/27/2007; Interim rule, 74 FR 2417, 1/15/2009, effective 1/15/2009; Final rule, 74 FR 59916, 11/19/2009, effective 11/19/2009; Interim rule, 79 FR 44314, 7/31/2014, effective 7/31/2014; Final rule 79 FR 73498, 12/11/2014, effective 12/11/2014; Interim rule, 80 FR 15909, 3/26/2015, effective 3/26/2015; Interim rule, 80 FR 51751, 8/26/2015, effective 8/26/2015]

225.7015 Restriction on overseas architect-engineer services.

For restriction on award of architect-engineer contracts to be performed in Japan, in any North Atlantic Treaty Organization member country, or in countries bordering the Arabian Gulf, see 236.602-70.

[Final rule, 68 FR 15615, 3/31/2003, effective 4/30/2003; Interim rule, 79 FR 44314, 7/31/2014, effective 7/31/2014; Final rule 79 FR 73498, 12/11/2014, effective 12/11/2014; Interim rule, 80 FR 15909, 3/26/2015, effective 3/26/2015; Interim rule, 80 FR 51751, 8/26/2015, effective 8/26/2015]

225.7015-1 [Removed]

[DAC 91-5, 58 FR 28458, 5/13/93, effective 4/30/93; Final rule, 68 FR 15615, 3/31/2003, effective 4/30/2003]

225.7015-2 [Removed]

[Final rule, 68 FR 15615, 3/31/2003, effective 4/30/2003]

225.7015-3 [Removed]

[DAC 91-5, 58 FR 28458, 5/13/93, effective 4/30/93; Final rule, 68 FR 15615, 3/31/2003, effective 4/30/2003]

225.7016 [Removed]

[Final rule, 68 FR 15615, 3/31/2003, effective 4/30/2003; Redesignated, Final rule, 74 FR 53413, 10/19/2009, effective 10/19/2009; Final rule, 76 FR 14589, 3/17/2011, effective 3/17/2011; Interim rule, 76 FR 32843, 6/6/2011, effective 6/6/2011; Final rule, 76 FR 71831, 11/18/2011, effective 11/18/2011; Final rule, 81 FR 17048, 3/25/2016, effective 3/25/2016]

225.7016-1 [Removed]

[DAC 91-5, 58 FR 28458, 5/13/93, effective 4/30/93; Final rule, 68 FR 15615, 3/31/2003, effective 4/30/2003; Redesignated, Final rule, 74 FR 53413, 10/19/2009, effective 10/19/2009; Final rule, 76 FR 14589, 3/17/2011, effective 3/17/2011]

225.7016-2 [Removed]

[DAC 91-5, 58 FR 28458, 5/13/93, effective 4/30/93; Final rule, 68 FR 15615, 3/31/2003, effective 4/30/2003; Redesignated, Final rule, 74 FR 53413, 10/19/2009, effective 10/19/2009; Final rule, 76 FR 14589, 3/17/2011, effective 3/17/2011]

225.7016-3 [Removed]

[DAC 91-2, 57 FR 14994, 4/23/92, effective 4/16/92; Final rule, 68 FR 15615, 3/31/2003, effective 4/30/2003; Redesignated, Final rule, 71 FR 62565, 10/26/2006, effective 10/26/2006; Redesignated, Final rule, 74 FR 53413, 10/19/2009, effective 10/19/2009; Final rule, 76 FR 14589, 3/17/2011, effective 3/17/2011]

225.7016-4 [Removed]

[DAC 91-2, 57 FR 14994, 4/23/92, effective 4/16/92; DAC 91-4, 57 FR 53600, 11/12/92, effective 10/30/92; Final rule, 68 FR 15615, 3/31/2003, effective 4/30/2003; Redesignated, Final rule, 74 FR 53413, 10/19/2009, effective 10/19/2009; Final rule, 76 FR 14589, 3/17/2011, effective 3/17/2011]

225.7017 Utilization of domestic photovoltaic devices. (No Text)

225.7017-1 Definitions.

As used in this section—

Caribbean Basin country photovoltaic device means a photovoltaic device that—

(1) Is wholly manufactured in a Caribbean Basin country; or

(2) In the case of a photovoltaic device that consists in whole or in part of materials from another country, has been substantially transformed in a Caribbean Basin country into a new and different article of commerce with a name, character, or use distinct from that of the article or articles from which it was transformed, provided that the photovoltaic device is not subsequently substantially transformed outside of a Caribbean Basin country.

Covered contract means an energy savings performance contract, a utility services contract, or a private housing contract awarded by DoD, to be performed in the United States, if such contract results in DoD ownership of photovoltaic devices, by means other than DoD purchase as end products. DoD is deemed to own a photovoltaic device if the device is—

(1) Installed in the United States on DoD property or in a facility owned by DoD; and

(2) Reserved for the exclusive use of DoD in the United States for the full economic life of the device.

Designated country photovoltaic device means a World Trade Organization Government Procurement Agreement (WTO GPA) country photovoltaic device, a Free Trade Agreement country photovoltaic device, a least developed country photovoltaic device, or a Caribbean Basin country photovoltaic device.

Domestic photovoltaic device means a photovoltaic device that is manufactured in the United States.

Foreign photovoltaic device means a photovoltaic device other than a domestic photovoltaic device.

Free Trade Agreement country photovoltaic device means a photovoltaic device that—

(1) Is wholly manufactured in a Free Trade Agreement country; or

(2) In the case of a photovoltaic device that consists in whole or in part of materials from another country, has been substantially transformed in a Free Trade Agreement country into a new and different article of commerce with a name, character, or use distinct from that of the article or articles from which it was transformed, provided that the photovoltaic device is not subsequently substantially transformed outside of a Free Trade Agreement country.

Least developed country photovoltaic device means a photovoltaic device that—

(1) Is wholly manufactured in a least developed country; or

(2) In the case of a photovoltaic device that consists in whole or in part of materials from another country, has been substantially transformed in a least developed country into a new and different article of commerce with a name, character, or use distinct from that of the article or articles from which it was transformed, provided that the photovoltaic device is not subsequently substantially transformed outside of a least developed country.

Photovoltaic device means a device that converts light directly into electricity through a solid-state, semiconductor process.

Qualifying country photovoltaic device means a photovoltaic device manufactured in a qualifying country.

U.S.-made photovoltaic device means a photovoltaic device that—

(1) Is manufactured in the United States; or

(2) Is substantially transformed in the United States into a new and different article of commerce with a name, character, or use distinct from that of the article or articles from which it was transformed, provided that the photovoltaic device is not subsequently substantially transformed outside of the United States.

WTO GPA country photovoltaic device means a photovoltaic device that—

(1) Is wholly manufactured in a WTO GPA country; or

(2) In the case of a photovoltaic device that consists in whole or in part of materials from another country, has been substantially transformed in a WTO GPA country into a new and different article of commerce with a name, character, or use distinct from that of the article or articles from which it was transformed, provided that the photovoltaic device is not subsequently substantially transformed outside of a WTO GPA country.

[Interim rule, 76 FR 78858, 12/20/2011, effective 12/20/2011; Final rule, 77 FR 30368, 5/22/2012, effective 5/22/2012; Final rule, 80 FR 72599, 11/20/2015, effective 11/20/2015; Publication notice 20151118; Final rule, 83 FR 62498, 12/4/2018, effective 12/5/2018]

225.7017-2 Restriction.

In accordance with section 846 of the National Defense Authorization Act for Fiscal Year 2011 (Pub. L. 111-383), photovoltaic devices provided under any covered contract shall comply with 41 U.S.C. chapter 83, Buy American, subject to the exceptions to that statute provided in the Trade Agreements Act of 1979 (19 U.S.C. 2501 *et seq.*).

[Interim rule, 76 FR 78858, 12/20/2011, effective 12/20/2011; Final rule, 77 FR 30368, 5/22/2012, effective 5/22/2012; Final rule, 80 FR 72599, 11/20/2015, effective 11/20/2015; Final rule, 83 FR 62498, 12/4/2018, effective 12/5/2018]

225.7017-3 Exceptions.

DoD requires the contractor to utilize domestic photovoltaic devices in covered contracts that exceed the simplified acquisition threshold, with the following exceptions:

(a) *Qualifying country.* Qualifying country photovoltaic devices may be utilized in any covered contract, because 225.103(a)(i)(A) provides an exception to the Buy American statute for products of qualifying countries, as defined in 225.003.

(b) *Buy American—unreasonable cost.* For a covered contract that utilizes photovoltaic devices valued at less than $182,000, the exception for unreasonable cost may apply (see FAR 25.103(c). If the cost of a foreign photovoltaic device plus 50 percent is less than the cost of a domestic photovoltaic device, then the foreign photovoltaic device may be utilized.

(c) *Trade agreements*—(1) *Free Trade Agreements.* For a covered contract that utilizes photovoltaic devices valued at $25,000 or more, photovoltaic devices may be utilized from a country covered under the acquisition by a Free Trade Agreement, depending upon dollar threshold (see FAR subpart 25.4).

(2) *World Trade Organization—Government Procurement Agreement.* For covered contracts that utilize photovoltaic devices that are valued at $180,000 or more, only U.S.-made photovoltaic devices, designated country photovoltaic devices, or qualifying country photovoltaic devices may be utilized.

[Interim rule, 76 FR 78858, 12/20/2011, effective 12/20/2011; Final rule, 77 FR 13013, 3/5/2012, effective 3/5/2012; Final rule, 77 FR 30368, 5/22/2012, effective 5/22/2012; Final rule, 77 FR 35879, 6/15/2012, effective 6/15/2012; Final rule, 78 FR 79620, 12/31/2013, effective 1/1/2014; Final rule, 80 FR 72599, 11/20/2015, effective 11/20/2015; Final rule, 80 FR 81470, 12/30/2015, effective 1/1/2016; Final rule, 82 FR 61481, 12/28/2017, effective 1/1/2018; Final rule, 83 FR 62498, 12/4/2018, effective 12/5/2018; Final rule, 84 FR 72245, 12/31/2019, effective 1/1/2020]

225.7017-4 Solicitation provision and contract clause.

(a)(1) Use the clause at 252.225-7017, Photovoltaic Devices, in solicitations, including solicitations using FAR part 12 procedures for the acquisition of commercial items, for a contract expected to exceed the simplified acquisition threshold that may be a covered contract, *i.e.*, an energy savings performance contract, a utility service contract, or a private housing contract awarded by DoD, if such contract will result in DoD ownership of photovoltaic devices, by means other than DoD purchase as end products.

(i) Is expected to exceed the simplified acquisition threshold; and

(ii) May be a covered contract, *i.e.*, a contract that provides for a photovoltaic device to be—

(A) Installed in the United States on DoD property or in a facility owned by DoD; or

(B) Reserved for the exclusive use of DoD in the United States for the full economic life of the device.

(2) Use the clause in the resultant contract, including contracts using FAR part 12 procedures for the acquisition of commercial items, if it is a covered contract.

(b) Use the provision at 252.225-7018, Photovoltaic Devices—Certificate, in solicitations, including solicitations using FAR part 12 procedures for the acquisition of commercial items, that contain the clause at 252.225-7017.

[Interim rule, 76 FR 78858, 12/20/2011, effective 12/20/2011; Final rule, 77 FR 30368, 5/22/2012, effective 5/22/2012; Final rule, 78 FR 37980, 6/25/2013, effective 6/25/2013; Final rule, 80 FR 72599, 11/20/2015, effective 11/20/2015; Final rule, 83 FR 62498, 12/4/2018, effective 12/5/2018]

225.7018 Restriction on acquisition of certain magnets and tungsten. (No Text)

[Final rule, 68 FR 15615, 3/31/2003, effective 4/30/2003; Interim rule, 84 FR 18156, 4/30/2019, effective 4/30/2019]

225.7018-1 Definitions.

As used in this section—

Covered country means—

(1) The Democratic People's Republic of North Korea;

(2) The People's Republic of China;

(3) The Russian Federation; and

(4) The Islamic Republic of Iran.

Covered material means—

(1) Samarium-cobalt magnets;

(2) Neodymium-iron-boron magnets;

(3) Tungsten metal powder; and

(4) Tungsten heavy alloy or any finished or semi-finished component containing tungsten heavy alloy.

Electronic device means an item that operates by controlling the flow of electrons or other electrically charged particles in circuits, using interconnections such as resistors, inductors, capacitors, diodes, switches, transistors, or integrated circuits.

Tungsten heavy alloy means a tungsten base pseudo alloy that—

(1) Meets the specifications of ASTM B777 or SAE–AMS–T–21014 for a particular class of tungsten heavy alloy; or

(2) Contains at least 90 percent tungsten in a matrix of other metals (such as nickel-iron or nickel-copper) and has density of at least 16.5 g/cm3).

[DAC 91-6, 59 FR 27662, 5/27/94, effective 5/27/94; Final rule, 68 FR 15615, 3/31/2003, effective 4/30/2003; Interim rule, 84 FR 18156, 4/30/2019, effective 4/30/2019; Final rule, 84 FR 72239, 12/31/2019, effective 12/31/2019]

225.7018-2 Restriction.

(a) Except as provided in 225.7018-3 and 225.7018-4, do not acquire any covered material melted or produced in any covered country, or any end item, manufactured in any covered country, that contains a covered material (10 U.S.C. 2533c).

(b) (1) For samarium-cobalt magnets and neodymium iron-boron magnets, this restriction includes—

(i) Melting samarium with cobalt to produce the samarium-cobalt alloy or melting neodymium with iron and boron to produce the neodymium-iron-boron alloy; and

(ii) All subsequent phases of production of the magnets, such as powder formation, pressing, sintering or bonding, and magnetization.

(2) The restriction on melting and producing of samarium-cobalt magnets is in addition to any applicable restrictions on melting of specialty metals at 225.7003 and the clause at 252.225-7009, Restriction on Acquisition of Certain Articles Containing Specialty Metals.

(c) For production of tungsten metal powder and tungsten heavy alloy, this restriction includes—

(1) Atomization;

(2) Calcination and reduction into powder;

(3) Final consolidation of non-melt derived metal powders; and

(4) All subsequent phases of production of tungsten metal powder, tungsten heavy alloy, or any finished or semi-finished component containing tungsten heavy alloy.

[DAC 91-5, 58 FR 28458, 5/13/93, effective 4/30/93; DAC 91-9, 60 FR 61586, 11/30/95, effective 11/30/95; Final rule, 65 FR 39703, 6/27/2000, effective 6/27/2000; Final rule, 68 FR 15615, 3/31/2003, effective 4/30/2003; Interim rule, 84 FR 18156, 4/30/2019, effective 4/30/2019; Final rule, 84 FR 72239, 12/31/2019, effective 12/31/2019]

225.7018-3 Exceptions.

The restriction in section 225.7018-2 does not apply to an acquisition—

(a) At or below the simplified acquisition threshold;

(b) Outside the United States of an item for use outside the United States; or

(c) Of an end item that is—

(1) A commercially available off-theshelf item (but see PGI 225.7018–3(c)(1)(i) with regard to commercially available samarium-cobalt magnets), other than—

(i) A commercially available off-the-shelf item that is 50 percent or more tungsten by weight; or

(ii) A tungsten heavy alloy mill product, such as bar, billet, slab, wire, cube, sphere, block, blank, plate, or sheet, that has not been incorporated into an end item, subsystem, assembly, or component;

(2) An electronic device, unless the Secretary of Defense, upon the recommendation of the Strategic Materials Protection Board pursuant to 10 U.S.C. 187 determines that the domestic availability of a particular electronic device is critical to national security (but see PGI 225.7018–3(c)(1)(ii) with regard to samariumcobalt magnets used in electronic components); or

(3) A neodymium-iron-boron magnet manufactured from recycled material if the milling of the recycled material and sintering of the final magnet takes place in the United States.

(d) If the authorized agency official concerned determines that compliant covered materials of satisfactory quality and quantity, in the required form, cannot be procured as and when needed at a reasonable price.

(1) For tungsten heavy alloy, the term "required form" refers to the form of the mill product, such as bar, billet, wire, slab, plate, or sheet, in the grade appropriate for the production of a finished end item to be delivered to the Government under this contract; or a finished component assembled into an end item to be delivered to the Government under the contract.

(2) For samarium-cobalt magnets or neodymium-iron-boron magnets, the term "required form" refers to the form and properties of the magnets.

[DAC 91-6, 59 FR 27662, 5/27/94, effective 5/27/94; Final rule, 68 FR 15615, 3/31/2003, effective 4/30/2003; Interim rule, 84 FR 18156, 4/30/2019, effective 4/30/2019; Final rule, 84 FR 72239, 12/31/2019, effective 12/31/2019]

225.7018-4 Nonavailability determination.

(a) *Individual nonavailability determinations.*

(1) The head of the contracting activity is authorized to make a nonavailability determination described in 225.7018–3(d) on an individual basis (i.e., applies to only one contract).

(i) The Under Secretary of Defense (Acquisition and Sustainment).

(ii) The Secretary of the Army.

(iii) The Secretary of the Navy.

(iv) The Secretary of the Air Force.

(v) The Director of the Defense Logistics Agency.

(2) The supporting documentation for the determination shall include—

(i) An analysis of alternatives that would not require a nonavailability determination; and

(ii) A written certification by the requiring activity that describes, with specificity, why such alternatives are unacceptable.

(3) Provide to USD(A&S) DASD (Industrial Policy), in accordance with the procedures at PGI 225.7018–4(a)(3)—

(i) A copy of individual nonavailability determinations with supporting documentation; and

(ii) Notification when individual waivers are requested, but denied.

(b) *Class nonavailability determinations.* A class nonavailability determination (*i.e.*, a nonavailability determinations that applies to more than one contract) requires the approval of the USD(A&S). Follow the procedures at PGI 225.7018-4(b) when submitting a request for a class nonavailability determination.

(1) At least 30 days before making a nonavailability determination that would apply to more than one contract, the USD(A&S) will, to the maximum extent practicable, and in a manner consistent with the protection of national security and confidential business information—

(i) Publish a notice on the Federal Business Opportunities website (*www.FedBizOpps.gov*) of the intent to make the nonavailability determination; and

(ii) Solicit information relevant to such notice from interested parties, including producers of mill products from covered materials.

(2) The USD(A&S)—

(i) Will take into consideration all information submitted in response to the notice in making a class nonavailability determination;

(ii) May consider other relevant information that cannot be made part of the public record consistent with the protection of national security information and confidential business information; and

(iii) Will ensure that any such nonavailability determination and the rationale for the determination are made publicly available to the maximum extent consistent with the protection of national security and confidential business information.

[Interim rule, 84 FR 18156, 4/30/2019, effective 4/30/2019; Final rule, 84 FR 72239, 12/31/2019, effective 12/31/2019]

225.7018-5 Contract clause.

Unless acquiring items outside the United States for use outside the United States or a nonavailability determination has been made in accordance with 225.7018-4, use the clause at 252.225-7052, Restriction on Acquisition of Certain Magnets and Tungsten, in solicitations and contracts, including solicitations and contracts using FAR part 12 procedures for the acquisition of commercial items, that exceed the simplified acquisition threshold.

[Interim rule, 84 FR 18156, 4/30/2019, effective 4/30/2019]

225.7019 [Removed]

[Final rule, 68 FR 15615, 3/31/2003, effective 4/30/2003]

225.7019-1 [Removed]

[Interim rule, 61 FR 10899, 3/18/96, effective 3/18/96, finalized without change, DAC 91-11, 61 FR 50446, 9/26/96; Final rule, 61 FR 58488, 11/15/96, effective 11/15/96; DAC 91-12, 62 FR 34114, 6/24/97, effective 6/24/97; Interim rule, 63 FR 5744, 2/4/98, effective 2/4/98; Interim rule, 63 FR 43887, 8/17/98, effective 8/17/98, finalized without change, 63 FR 64426, 11/20/98; Interim rule, 65 FR 77827, 12/13/2000, effective 12/13/2000, finalized without change, 66 FR 49862, 10/1/2001, effective 10/1/2001; Final rule, 68 FR 15615, 3/31/2003, effective 4/30/2003]

225.7019-2 [Removed]

[DAC 91-11, 61 FR 50446, 9/26/96, effective 9/26/96; Final rule, 65 FR 52951, 8/31/2000, effective 8/31/2000, corrected, 65 FR 58607, 9/29/2000; Interim rule, 65 FR 77827, 12/13/2000, effective 12/13/2000, finalized without change, 66 FR 49862, 10/1/2001, effective 10/1/2001; Final rule, 68 FR 15615, 3/31/2003, effective 4/30/2003]

225.7019-3 [Removed]

[Interim rule, 61 FR 10899, 3/18/96, effective 3/18/96; DAC 91-11, 61 FR 50446, 9/26/96, effective 9/26/96; Interim rule, 62 FR 2615, 1/17/97, effective 1/17/97; DAC 91-12, 62 FR 34114, 6/24/97, effective 6/24/97; Interim rule, 63 FR 5744, 2/4/98, effective 2/4/98; Final rule, 63 FR 28284, 5/22/98, effective 5/22/98; Interim rule, 63 FR 43887, 8/17/98, effective 8/17/98, finalized without change, 63 FR 64426, 11/20/98; Final rule, 65 FR 39703, 6/27/2000, effective 6/27/2000; Final rule, 68 FR 15615, 3/31/2003, effective 4/30/2003]

225.7019-4 [Removed]

[Interim rule, 65 FR 77827, 12/13/2000, effective 12/13/2000, finalized without change, 66 FR 49862, 10/1/2001, effective 10/1/2001; Final rule, 68 FR 15615, 3/31/2003, effective 4/30/2003]

225.7020 [Removed]

[Final rule, 68 FR 15615, 3/31/2003, effective 4/30/2003]

225.7020-1 [Removed]

[Interim rule, 65 FR 77827, 12/13/2000, effective 12/13/2000, finalized without change, 66 FR 49862, 10/1/2001, effective 10/1/2001; Final rule, 68 FR 15615, 3/31/2003, effective 4/30/2003]

225.7020-2 [Removed]

[Interim rule, 65 FR 77827, 12/13/2000, effective 12/13/2000, finalized without change, 66 FR 49862, 10/1/2001, effective 10/1/2001; Final rule, 68 FR 15615, 3/31/2003, effective 4/30/2003]

225.7020-3 [Removed]

[Interim rule, 65 FR 77827, 12/13/2000, effective 12/13/2000, finalized without change, 66 FR 49862, 10/1/2001, effective 10/1/2001; Final rule, 68 FR 15615, 3/31/2003, effective 4/30/2003]

225.7020-4 [Removed]

[Interim rule, 65 FR 77827, 12/13/2000, effective 12/13/2000, finalized without change, 66 FR 49862, 10/1/2001, effective 10/1/2001; Final rule, 67 FR 11437, 3/14/2002, effective 3/14/2002; Final rule, 68 FR 15615, 3/31/2003, effective 4/30/2003]

225.7021 [Removed]

[Final rule, 68 FR 15615, 3/31/2003, effective 4/30/2003]

225.7021-1 [Removed]

[DAC 91-7, 60 FR 29491, 6/5/95, effective 5/17/95; Final rule, 68 FR 15615, 3/31/2003, effective 4/30/2003]

225.7021-2 [Removed]

[Interim rule, 59 FR 11729, 3/14/94, effective 3/7/94; Final rule, 68 FR 15615, 3/31/2003, effective 4/30/2003]

225.7021-3 [Removed]

[DAC 91-7, 60 FR 29491, 6/5/95, effective 5/17/95; Final rule, 68 FR 15615, 3/31/2003, effective 4/30/2003]

225.7022 [Removed]

[Final rule, 68 FR 15615, 3/31/2003, effective 4/30/2003]

225.7022-1 [Removed]

[Interim rule, 61 FR 13106, 3/26/96, effective 4/1/96, finalized without change, DAC 91-11, 61 FR 50446, 9/26/96; DAC 91-12, 62 FR 34114, 6/24/97, effective 6/24/97; Interim rule, 63 FR 5744, 2/4/98, effective 2/4/98; Interim rule, 63 FR 43887, 8/17/98, effective 8/17/98, finalized without change, 63 FR 64426, 11/20/98; Final rule, 68 FR 15615, 3/31/2003, effective 4/30/2003]

225.7022-2 [Removed]

[DAC 91-12, 62 FR 34114, 6/24/97, effective 6/24/97; Interim rule, 63 FR 5744, 2/4/98, effective 2/4/98; Interim rule, 63 FR 43887, 8/17/98, effective 8/17/98, finalized without change, 63 FR 64426, 11/20/98; Final rule, 68 FR 15615, 3/31/2003, effective 4/30/2003]

225.7022-3 [Removed]

[Interim rule, 63 FR 5744, 2/4/98, effective 2/4/98; Interim rule, 63 FR 43887, 8/17/98, effective 8/17/98, finalized without change, 63 FR 64426, 11/20/98; Final rule, 68 FR 15615, 3/31/2003, effective 4/30/2003]

225.7022-4 [Removed]

[Interim rule, 61 FR 13106, 3/26/96, effective 4/1/96, finalized without change, DAC 91-11, 61 FR 50446, 9/26/96; Final rule, 68 FR 15615, 3/31/2003, effective 4/30/2003]

225.7023 [Removed]

[Final rule, 68 FR 15615, 3/31/2003, effective 4/30/2003

225.7023-1 [Removed]

[Interim rule, 60 FR 34471, 7/3/95, effective 7/3/95; DAC 91-9, 60 FR 61586, 11/30/95, effective 11/30/95; Final rule, 68 FR 15615, 3/31/2003, effective 4/30/2003]

225.7023-2 [Removed]

[Interim rule, 60 FR 34471, 7/3/95, effective 7/3/95, finalized without change, DAC 91-9, 60 FR 61586, 11/30/95, effective 11/30/95; Final rule, 68 FR 15615, 3/31/2003, effective 4/30/2003]

225.7023-3 [Removed]

[Interim rule, 60 FR 34471, 7/3/95, effective 7/3/95; DAC 91-9, 60 FR 61586, 11/30/95, effective 11/30/95; Final rule, 68 FR 15615, 3/31/2003, effective 4/30/2003]

SUBPART 225.71—OTHER RESTRICTIONS ON FOREIGN ACQUISITION

225.7100 Scope of subpart.

This subpart contains foreign product restrictions that are based on policies designed to protect the defense industrial base.

[DAC 91-12, 62 FR 34114, 6/24/97, effective 6/24/97; Final rule, 68 FR 15615, 3/31/2003, effective 4/30/2003]

225.7101 Definition.

Component and *domestic manufacture*, as used in this subpart, are defined in the clause at 252.225-7025, Restriction on Acquisition of Forgings.

[DAC 91-12, 62 FR 34114, 6/24/97, effective 6/24/97; Final rule, 68 FR 15615, 3/31/2003, effective 4/30/2003; Final rule, 74 FR 68383, 12/24/2009, effective 12/24/2009]

225.7102 Forgings. (No Text)

[Final rule, 68 FR 15615, 3/31/2003, effective 4/30/2003]

225.7102-1 Policy.

When acquiring the following forging items, whether as end items or components, acquire items that are of domestic manufacture to the maximum extent practicable:

Items	*Categories*
Ship propulsion shafts	Excludes service and landing craft shafts.
Periscope tubes	All.
Ring forgings for bull gears	All greater than 120 inches in diameter.

[DAC 91-12, 62 FR 34114, 6/24/97, effective 6/24/97; Final rule, 68 FR 15615, 3/31/2003, effective 4/30/2003]

225.7102-2 Exceptions.

The policy in 225.7102-1 does not apply to acquisitions—

(a) Using simplified acquisition procedures, unless the restricted item is the end item being purchased;

(b) Overseas for overseas use; or

(c) When the quantity acquired exceeds the amount needed to maintain the U.S. defense mobilization base (provided the excess quantity is an economical purchase quantity). The requirement for domestic manufacture does not apply to the quantity above that required to maintain the base, in which case, qualifying country sources may compete.

[DAC 91-12, 62 FR 34114, 6/24/97, effective 6/24/97; Final rule, 68 FR 15615, 3/31/2003, effective 4/30/2003]

225.7102-3 Waiver.

Upon request from a contractor, the contracting officer may waive the requirement for domestic manufacture of the items listed in 225.7102-1.

[DAC 91-12, 62 FR 34114, 6/24/97, effective 6/24/97; Final rule, 68 FR 15615, 3/31/2003, effective 4/30/2003]

225.7102-4 Contract clause.

Use the clause at 252.225-7025, Restriction on Acquisition of Forgings, in solicitations and contracts, unless—

(a) The supplies being acquired do not contain any of the items listed in 225.7102-1; or

(b) An exception in 225.7102-2 applies. If an exception applies to only a portion of the acquisition, specify the excepted portion in the solicitation and contract.

[DAC 91-12, 62 FR 34114, 6/24/97, effective 6/24/97; Final rule, 68 FR 15615, 3/31/2003, effective 4/30/2003]

225.7103 [Removed]

[Final rule, 68 FR 15615, 3/31/2003, effective 4/30/2003; Final rule, 71 FR 62566, 10/26/2006, effective 10/26/2006]

225.7103-1 [Removed]

[Final rule, 65 FR 77832, 12/13/2000, effective 12/13/2000; Final rule, 68 FR 15615, 3/31/2003, effective 4/30/2003; Final rule, 70 FR 6374, 2/7/2005, effective 2/7/2005; Final rule, 71 FR 62566, 10/26/2006, effective 10/26/2006]

225.7103-2 [Removed]

[DAC 91-12, 62 FR 34114, 6/24/97, effective 6/24/97; Final rule, 68 FR 15615, 3/31/2003, effective 4/30/2003; Final rule, 71 FR 62566, 10/26/2006, effective 10/26/2006]

225.7103-3 [Removed]

[Final rule, 65 FR 77832, 12/13/2000, effective 12/13/2000; Final rule, 68 FR 15615, 3/31/2003, effective 4/30/2003; Final rule, 70 FR 6374, 2/7/2005, effective 2/7/2005; correction, 70 FR 8537, 2/22/2005, effective 2/7/2005; Final rule, 71 FR 62566, 10/26/2006, effective 10/26/2006]

SUBPART 225.72—REPORTING CONTRACT PERFORMANCE OUTSIDE THE UNITED STATES

225.7201 Policy

10 U.S.C. 2410g requires offerors and contractors to notify DoD of any intention to perform a DoD contract outside the United States and Canada when the contract could be performed inside the United States or Canada.

[Final rule, 70 FR 20838, 4/22/2005, effective 4/22/2005; Final rule, 79 FR 73499, 12/11/2014. effective 12/11/2014.]

225.7202 Exception.

This subpart does not apply to contracts for commercial items, construction, ores, natural gas, utilities, petroleum products and crudes, timber (logs), or subsistence.

[DAC 91-9, 60 FR 61586, 11/30/95, effective 11/30/95; Final rule, 70 FR 20838, 4/22/2005, effective 4/22/2005]

225.7203 Contracting officer distribution of reports.

Follow the procedures at PGI 225.7203 for distribution of reports submitted with offers in accordance with the provision at 252.225-7003, Report of Intended Performance Outside the United States and Canada—Submission with Offer.

[DAC 91-5, 58 FR 28458, 5/13/93, effective 4/30/93; DAC 91-7, 60 FR 29491, 6/5/95, effective 5/17/95; Final rule, 65 FR 39703, 6/27/2000, effective 6/27/2000; Final rule, 68 FR 15615, 3/31/2003, effective 4/30/2003; Final rule, 70 FR 20838, 4/22/2005, effective 4/22/2005]

225.7204 Solicitation provision and contract clauses.

Except for acquisitions described in 225.7202—

(a) Use the provision at 252.225-7003, Report of Intended Performance Outside the United States and Canada—Submission with Offer, in solicitations with a value exceeding $13.5 million; and

(b) Use the clause at 252.225-7004, Report of Intended Performance Outside the United States and Canada—Submission after Award, in solicitations and contracts with a value exceeding $13.5 million.

[DAC 91-5, 58 FR 28458, 5/13/93, effective 4/30/93; Final rule, 68 FR 15615, 3/31/2003, effective 4/30/2003; Final rule, 70 FR 20838, 4/22/2005, effective 4/22/2005; Final rule, 71 FR 75891, 12/19/2006, effective 12/19/2006; Final rule, 75 FR 45072, 8/2/2010, effective 10/1/2010; Final rule, 79 FR 73499, 12/11/2014, effective 12/11/2014; Final rule, 80 FR 36903, 6/26/2015, effective 10/1/2015]

SUBPART 225.73—ACQUISITIONS FOR FOREIGN MILITARY SALES

225.7300 Scope of subpart.

(a) This subpart contains policies and procedures for acquisitions for foreign military sales (FMS) under the Arms Export Control Act (22 U.S.C. Chapter 39). Section 22 of the Arms Export Control Act (22 U.S.C. 2762) authorizes DoD to enter into contracts for resale to foreign countries or international organizations.

(b) This subpart does not apply to—

(1) FMS made from inventories or stocks;

(2) Acquisitions for replenishment of inventories or stocks; or

(3) Acquisitions made under DoD cooperative logistic supply support arrangements.

[Final rule, 63 FR 43889, 8/17/98, effective 8/17/98]

225.7301 General.

(a) The U.S. Government sells defense articles and services to foreign governments or international organizations through FMS agreements. The agreement is documented in a Letter of Offer and Acceptance (LOA) (see the Defense Security Cooperation Agency (DSCA) Security Assistance Management Manual (DSCA 5105.38-M)).

(b) Conduct FMS acquisitions under the same acquisition and contract management procedures used for other defense acquisitions.

(c) Follow the additional procedures at PGI 225.7301 (c) for preparation of solicitations and contracts that include FMS requirements.

(d) See 229.170 for policy on contracts financed under U.S. assistance programs that involve payment of foreign country value added taxes or customs duties.

[Final rule, 63 FR 43889, 8/17/98, effective 8/17/98; Final rule, 68 FR 15615, 3/31/2003, effective 4/30/2003; Final rule, 70 FR 57191, 9/30/2005, effective 9/30/2005; Final rule, 70 FR 73153, 12/9/2005, effective 12/9/2005; Final rule, 71 FR 18671, 4/12/2006, effective 4/12/2006; Interim rule, 80 FR 31309, 6/2/2015, effective 6/2/2015]

225.7301-1 Requirement to use firm-fixed-price contracts.

(a) *Requirement.* In accordance with section 830 of the National Defense Authorization Act for Fiscal Year 2017 (Pub. L. 114-328), a firm-fixed-price contract shall be used for FMS, unless the foreign country that is the counterparty to FMS—

(1) Has established in writing a preference for a different contract type; or

(2) Requests in writing that a different contract type be used for a specific FMS. See PGI 217.202(2) on the use of priced options for FMS requirements.

(b) *Waiver.* The requirement in paragraph (a) of this section may be waived, if the chief of the contracting office determines, on a case-by-case basis, that a different contract type is in the best interest of the United States and American taxpayers.

[Final rule, 84 FR 65304, 11/27/2019, effective 11/27/2019]

225.7301-2 Solicitation approval for sole source contracts.

The contracting officer shall coordinate through agency channels with the Principal Director, Defense Pricing and Contracting, prior to issuing a solicitation for a sole source contract for U.S./FMS combined requirements for a major system that has an estimated contract value that exceeds $500 million. See also 201.170 and PGI 216.403-1(1)(ii)(B) and (C).

[Final rule, 84 FR 65304, 11/27/2019, effective 11/27/2019]

225.7302 Preparation of letter of offer and acceptance.

For FMS programs that will require an acquisition, the contracting officer shall assist the DoD implementing agency responsible for preparing the Letter of Offer and Acceptance (LOA) by—

(1) Working with prospective contractors to—

(i) Identify, in advance of the LOA, any unusual provisions or deviations (such as those requirements for Pseudo LOAs identified at PGI 225.7301);

(ii) Advise the contractor if the DoD implementing agency expands, modifies, or does not accept any key elements of the prospective contractor's proposal;

(iii) Identify any logistics support necessary to perform the contract (such as those requirements identified at PGI 225.7301); and

(iv) For noncompetitive acquisitions over $10,000, ask the prospective contractor for information on price, delivery, and other relevant factors. The request for information shall identify the fact that the information is for a potential foreign military sale and shall identify the foreign customer; and

(2) Working with the DoD implementing agency responsible for preparing the LOA, as specified in PGI 225.7302.

[Interim rule, 62 FR 2616, 1/17/97, effective 1/17/97; Final rule, 63 FR 43889, 8/17/98, effective 8/17/98; Final rule, 68 FR 15615, 3/31/2003, effective 4/30/2003; Final rule, 70 FR 73153, 12/9/2005, effective 12/9/2005; Final rule, 78 FR 73450, 12/6/2013, effective 12/6/2013]

225.7303 Pricing acquisitions for FMS.

(a) Price FMS contracts using the same principles used in pricing other defense contracts. However, application of the pricing principles in FAR parts 15 and 31 to an FMS contract may result in prices that differ from other defense contract prices for the same item due to the considerations in this section.

(b) If the foreign government has conducted a competition resulting in adequate price competition (see FAR 15.403-1(b)(1)), the contracting officer shall not require the submission of certified cost or pricing data. The contracting officer should consult with the foreign government through security assistance personnel to determine if adequate price competition has occurred.

[Final rule, 64 FR 49683, 9/14/99, effective 9/14/99; Final rule, 68 FR 15615, 3/31/2003, effective 4/30/2003; Final rule, 77 FR 76939, 12/31/2012, effective 12/31/2012]

225.7303-1 Contractor sales to other foreign customers.

If the contractor has made sales of the item required for the foreign military sale to foreign customers under comparable conditions, including quantity and delivery, price the FMS contract in accordance with FAR part 15.

225.7303-2 Cost of doing business with a foreign government or an international organization.

(a) In pricing FMS contracts where non-U.S. Government prices as described in 225.7303-1 do not exist, except as provided in 225.7303-5, recognize the reasonable and allocable costs of doing business with a foreign government or international organization, even though such costs might not be recognized in the same amounts in pricing other defense contracts. Examples of such costs include, but are not limited to, the following:

(1) Selling expenses (not otherwise limited by FAR Part 31), such as—

(i) Maintaining international sales and service organizations;

(ii) Sales commissions and fees in accordance with FAR Subpart 3.4;

(iii) Sales promotions, demonstrations, and related travel for sales to foreign governments. Section 126.8 of the International Traffic in Arms Regulations (22 CFR 126.8) may require Government approval for these costs to be allowable, in which case the appropriate Government approval shall be obtained; and

(iv) Configuration studies and related technical services undertaken as a direct selling effort to a foreign country.

(2) Product support and post-delivery service expenses, such as—

(i) Operations or maintenance training, training or tactics films, manuals, or other related data; and

(ii) Technical field services provided in a foreign country related to accident investigations, weapon system problems, or operations/tactics enhancement, and related travel to foreign countries.

(3) *Offsets.* For additional information see 225.7306.

(i) An offset agreement is the contractual arrangement between the FMS customer and the U.S. defense contractor that identifies the offset obligation imposed by the FMS customer that has been accepted by the U.S. defense contractor as a condition of the FMS customer's purchase. These agreements are distinct and independent of the LOA and the FMS contract. Further information about offsets and LOAs may be found in the Defense Security Cooperation Agency (DSCA) Security Assistance Management Manual (DSCA 5105.38-M), chapter 6, paragraph 6.3.9. (*http://samm.dsca.mil/chapter/chapter-6*).

(ii) A U.S. defense contractor may recover all costs incurred for offset agreements with a foreign government or international organization if the LOA is financed wholly with foreign government or international organization customer cash or repayable foreign military finance credits.

(iii) The U.S. Government assumes no obligation to satisfy or administer the offset agreement or to bear any of the associated costs.

(iv) Indirect offset costs are deemed reasonable for purposes of FAR parts 15 and 31 with no further analysis necessary on the part of the contracting officer, provided that the U.S. defense contractor submits to the contracting officer a signed offset agreement or other documentation showing that the FMS customer has made the provision of an indirect offset a condition of the FMS acquisition. FMS customers are placed on notice through the LOA that indirect offset costs are deemed reasonable without any further analysis by the contracting officer.

(4) Costs that are the subject of advance agreement under the appropriate provisions of FAR part 31; or where the advance understanding places a limit on the amounts of cost that will be recognized as allowable in defense contract pricing, and the agreement contemplated that it will apply only to DoD contracts for the U.S. Government's own requirement (as distinguished from contracts for FMS).

(b) Costs not allowable under FAR part 31 are not allowable in pricing FMS contracts, except as noted in paragraphs (c) and (e) of this subsection.

(c) The limitations for major contractors on independent research and development and bid and proposal (IR&D/B&P) costs for projects that are of potential interest to DoD, in231.205-18(c)(iii), do not apply to FMS contracts, except as provided in 225.7303-5. The allowability of IR&D/B&P costs on contracts for FMS not wholly paid for from funds made available on a nonrepayable basis is limited to the contract's allocable share of the contractor's total IR&D/B&P expenditures. In pricing contracts for such FMS—

(1) Use the best estimate of reasonable costs in forward pricing.

(2) Use actual expenditures, to the extent that they are reasonable, in determining final cost.

(d) Under paragraph (e)(1)(A) of Section 21 of the Arms Export Control Act (22 U.S.C. 2761), the United States must charge for administrative services to recover the estimated cost of administration of sales made under the Army Export Control Act.

(e) The limitations in 231.205-1 on allowability of costs associated with leasing Government equipment do not apply to FMS contracts.

[DAC 91-1, 56 FR 67216, 12/30/91, effective 12/31/91; DAC 91-3, 57 FR 42631, 9/15/92, effective 8/31/92; DAC 91-4, 57 FR 53600, 11/12/92, effective 10/30/92; Final rule, 59 FR 50511, 10/4/94, effective 9/28/94; DAC 91-10, 61 FR 7739, 2/29/96, effective 2/29/96; Interim rule, 61 FR 18987, 4/30/96, effective 4/30/96, finalized without change, DAC 91-11, 61 FR 50446, 9/26/96; Final rule, 63 FR 43889, 8/17/98, effective 8/17/98; Final rule, 64 FR 8729, 2/23/99, effective 2/23/99; Final rule, 64 FR 49683, 9/14/99, effective 9/14/99; Final rule, 68 FR 15615, 3/31/2003, effective 4/30/2003; Final rule, 70 FR 73153, 12/9/2005, effective 12/9/2005; Final rule, 74 FR 68382, 12/24/2009, effective 12/24/2009; Interim rule, 80 FR 31309, 6/2/2015, effective 6/2/2015; Final rule, 83 FR 30825, 6/29/2018, effective 6/29/2018]

225.7303-3 Government-to-government agreements.

If a government-to-government agreement between the United States and a foreign government for the sale, coproduction, or cooperative logistic support of a specifically defined weapon system, major end item, or support item, contains language in conflict with the provisions of this section, the language of the government-to-government agreement prevails.

225.7303-4 Contingent fees.

(a) Except as provided in paragraph (b) of this subsection, contingent fees are generally allowable under DoD contracts, provided—

(1) The fees are paid to a bona fide employee or a bona fide established commercial or selling agency maintained by the prospective contractor for the purpose of securing business (see FAR Part 31 and FAR Subpart 3.4); and

(2) The contracting officer determines that the fees are fair and reasonable.

(b)(1) Under DoD 5105.38-M, LOAs for requirements for the governments of Australia, Taiwan, Egypt, Greece, Israel, Japan, Jordan, Republic of Korea, Kuwait, Pakistan, Philippines, Saudi Arabia, Turkey, Thailand, or Venezuela (Air Force) shall provide that all U.S. Government contracts resulting from the LOAs prohibit the reimbursement of contingent fees as an allowable cost under the contract, unless the contractor identifies the payments and the foreign customer approves the payments in writing before contract award (see 225.7307(a)).

(2) For FMS to countries not listed in paragraph (b)(1) of this subsection, contingent fees exceeding $50,000 per FMS case are unallowable under DoD contracts, unless the contractor identifies the payment and the foreign customer approves the payment in writing before contract award.

[DAC 91-13, 63 FR 11522, 3/9/98, effective 3/9/98; Final rule, 63 FR 43889, 8/17/98, effective 8/17/98; Final rule, 68 FR 15615, 3/31/2003, effective 4/30/2003; Final rule, 70 FR 73153, 12/9/2005, effective 12/9/2005]

225.7303-5 Acquisitions wholly paid for from nonrepayable funds.

(a) In accordance with 22 U.S.C. 2762(d), price FMS wholly paid for from funds made available on a nonrepayable basis on the same costing basis with regard to profit, overhead, IR&D/B&P, and other costing elements as is applicable to acquisitions of like items purchased by DoD for its own use.

(b) Direct costs associated with meeting a foreign customer's additional or unique requirements are allowable under such contracts. Indirect burden rates applicable to such direct costs are permitted at the same rates applicable to acquisitions of like items purchased by DoD for its own use.

(c) A U.S. defense contractor may not recover costs incurred for offset agreements with a foreign government or international organization if the LOA is financed with funds made available on a nonrepayable basis.

[Interim rule, 61 FR 18987, 4/30/96, effective 4/30/96, corrected, 61 FR 49531, 9/20/96, finalized without change, DAC 91-11, 61 FR 50446, 9/26/96; Final rule, 63 FR 43889, 8/17/98, effective 8/17/98; Final rule, 64 FR 49683, 9/14/99, effective 9/14/99; Final rule, 68 FR 15615, 3/31/2003, effective 4/30/2003]

225.7304 FMS customer involvement.

(a) FMS customers may request that a defense article or defense service be obtained from a particular contractor. In such cases, FAR 6.302-4 provides authority to contract without full and open competition. The FMS customer may also request that a subcontract be placed with a particular firm. The contracting officer shall honor such requests from the FMS customer only if the LOA or other written direction sufficiently fulfills the requirements of FAR Subpart 6.3.

(b) FMS customers should be encouraged to participate with U.S. Government acquisition personnel in discussions with industry to—

(1) Develop technical specifications;

(2) Establish delivery schedules;

(3) Identify any special warranty provisions or other requirements unique to the FMS customer; and

(4) Review prices of varying alternatives, quantities, and options needed to make price-performance tradeoffs.

(c) Do not disclose to the FMS customer any data, including certified cost or pricing data, that is contractor proprietary unless the contractor authorizes its release.

(d) Except as provided in paragraph (e)(3) of this section, the degree of FMS customer participation in contract negotiations is left to the discretion of the contracting officer after consultation with the contractor. The contracting officer shall provide an explanation to the FMS customer if its participation in negotiations will be limited. Factors that may limit FMS customer participation include situations where—

(1) The contract includes requirements for more than one FMS customer;

(2) The contract includes unique U.S. requirements; or

(3) Contractor proprietary data is a subject of negotiations.

(e) Do not allow representatives of the FMS customer to—

(1) Direct the exclusion of certain firms from the solicitation process (they may suggest the inclusion of certain firms);

(2) Interfere with a contractor's placement of subcontracts; or

(3) Observe or participate in negotiations between the U.S. Government and the contractor involving certified cost or pricing

data, unless a deviation is granted in accordance with subpart 201.4.

(f) Do not accept directions from the FMS customer on source selection decisions or contract terms (except that, upon timely notice, the contracting officer may attempt to obtain any special contract provisions, warranties, or other unique requirements requested by the FMS customer).

(g) Do not honor any requests by the FMS customer to reject any bid or proposal.

(h) If an FMS customer requests additional data concerning FMS contract prices, the contracting officer shall, after consultation with the contractor, provide sufficient data to demonstrate the reasonableness of the price and reasonable responses to relevant questions concerning contract price. This data—

(1) May include tailored responses, top-level pricing summaries, historical prices, or an explanation of any significant differences between the actual contract price and the estimated contract price included in the initial LOA; and

(2) May be provided orally, in writing, or by any other method acceptable to the contracting officer.

[Final rule, 63 FR 43889, 8/17/98, effective 8/17/98; Final rule, 67 FR 70323, 11/22/2002, effective 11/22/2002; Final rule, 77 FR 76939, 12/31/2012, effective 12/31/2012]

225.7305 Limitation of liability.

Advise the contractor when the foreign customer will assume the risk for loss or damage under the appropriate limitation of liability clause(s) (see FAR Subpart 46.8). Consider the costs of necessary insurance, if any, obtained by the contractor to cover the risk of loss or damage in establishing the FMS contract price.

[Final rule, 68 FR 15615, 3/31/2003, effective 4/30/2003]

225.7306 Offset arrangements.

In accordance with the Presidential policy statement of April 16, 1990, DoD does not encourage, enter into, or commit U.S. firms to FMS offset arrangements. The decision whether to engage in offsets, and the responsibility for negotiating and implementing offset arrangements, resides with the companies involved. (Also see 225.7303-2(a)(3).)

[DAC 91-12, 62 FR 34114, 6/24/97, effective 6/24/97; Redesignated 225.7306, Final rule, 70 FR 73153, 12/9/2005, effective 12/9/2005]

225.7307 Contract clauses.

(a) Use the clause at 252.225-7027, Restriction on Contingent Fees for Foreign Military Sales, in solicitations and contracts, including solicitations and contracts using FAR part 12 procedures for the acquisition of commercial items, that are for FMS. Insert in paragraph (b)(1) of the clause the name(s) of any foreign country customer(s) listed in 225.7303-4(b).

(b) Use the clause at 252.225-7028, Exclusionary Policies and Practices of Foreign Governments, in solicitations and contracts, including solicitations and contracts using FAR part 12 procedures for the acquisition of commercial items, that are for the purchase of supplies and services for international military education training and FMS.

[Interim rule, 62 FR 2616, 1/17/97, effective 1/17/97; Final rule, 63 FR 43889, 8/17/98, effective 8/17/98; Final rule, 68 FR 15615, 3/31/2003, effective 4/30/2003; Redesignated 225.7307, Final rule, 70 FR 73153, 12/9/2005, effective 12/9/2005; Final rule, 78 FR 37980, 6/25/2013, effective 6/25/2013]

SUBPART 225.74—[REMOVED AND RESERVED]

225.7401 [Removed and Reserved]

[Interim rule, 63 FR 31936, 6/11/98, effective 6/11/98, finalized without change, 64 FR 24529, 5/7/99; Final rule, 68 FR 15615, 3/31/2003, effective 4/30/2003; Final rule, 70 FR 23790, 5/5/2005, effective 6/6/2005; Final rule, 71 FR 39008, 7/11/2006, effective 7/11/2006; Final rule, 72 FR 14239, 3/27/2007, effective 3/27/2007; Final rule, 78 FR 73450, 12/6/2013, effective 12/6/2013; Final rule, 80 FR 36900, 6/26/2015, effective 6/26/2015]

225.7402 [Removed and Reserved]

[Interim rule, 63 FR 31936, 6/11/98, effective 6/11/98, finalized without change, 64 FR 24529, 5/7/99; Final rule, 70 FR 23790, 5/5/2005, effective 6/6/2005; Interim rule, 71 FR 34826, 6/16/2006, effective 6/16/2006; Final rule, 73 FR 16764, 3/31/2008, effective 3/31/2008; Final rule, 79 FR 30469, 5/28/2014, effective 5/28/2014; Final rule, 80 FR 36900, 6/26/2015, effective 6/26/2015]

225.7402-1 [Removed and Reserved]

[Final rule, 70 FR 23790, 5/5/2005, effective 6/6/2005; Interim rule, 71 FR 34826, 6/16/2006, effective 6/16/2006; Final rule, 73 FR 16764, 3/31/2008, effective 3/31/2008; Final rule, 80 FR 36900, 6/26/2015, effective 6/26/2015]

225.7402-2 [Removed and Reserved]

[Final rule, 70 FR 23790, 5/5/2005, effective 6/6/2005; Interim rule, 71 FR 34826, 6/16/2006, effective 6/16/2006; Final rule, 73 FR 16764, 3/31/2008, effective 3/31/2008; Final rule, 79 FR 30469, 5/28/2014, effective 5/28/2014; Final rule, 80 FR 36900, 6/26/2015, effective 6/26/2015]

225.7402-3 [Removed and Reserved]

[Final rule, 70 FR 23790, 5/5/2005, effective 6/6/2005; Interim rule, 71 FR 34826, 6/16/2006, effective 6/16/2006; Final rule, 73 FR 16764, 3/31/2008, effective 3/31/2008; Final rule, 76 FR 36883, 6/23/2011, effective 6/23/2011; Final rule, 80 FR 36900, 6/26/2015, effective 6/26/2015]

225.7402-4 [Removed and Reserved]

[Final rule, 74 FR 2418, 1/15/2009, effective 1/15/2009; Final rule, 80 FR 36900, 6/26/2015, effective 6/26/2015]

225.7402-5 [Removed and Reserved]

[Final rule, 70 FR 23790, 5/5/2005, effective 6/6/2005; Interim rule, 71 FR 34826, 6/16/2006, effective 6/16/2006; Final rule, 73 FR 16764, 3/31/2008, effective 3/31/2008; Final rule, 74 FR 2418, 1/15/2009, effective 1/15/2009; Final rule, 76 FR 36883, 6/23/2011, effective 6/23/2011; Final rule, 78 FR 37980, 6/25/2013, effective 6/25/2013; Final rule, 79 FR 30469, 5/28/2014, effective 5/28/2014; Final rule, 80 FR 36900, 6/26/2015, effective 6/26/2015]

225.7403 [Removed and Reserved]

[Final rule, 70 FR 23790, 5/5/2005, effective 6/6/2005; Final rule, 80 FR 36900, 6/26/2015, effective 6/26/2015]

225.7403-1 [Removed and Reserved]

[Final rule, 70 FR 23790, 5/5/2005, effective 6/6/2005; Final rule, 80 FR 36900, 6/26/2015, effective 6/26/2015]

225.7403-2 [Removed and Reserved]

[Final rule, 70 FR 23790, 5/5/2005, effective 6/6/2005; Final rule, 78 FR 37980, 6/25/2013, effective 6/25/2013; Final rule, 80 FR 36900, 6/26/2015, effective 6/26/2015]

225.7404 [Removed and Reserved]

[Final rule, 76 FR 27274, 5/11/2011, effective 5/11/2011; Final rule, 80 FR 36900, 6/26/2015, effective 6/26/2015]

225.7405 [Removed and Reserved]

[Final rule, 80 FR 10390, 2/26/2015, effective 2/26/2015; Final rule, 80 FR 36900, 6/26/2015, effective 6/26/2015]

SUBPART 225.75—BALANCE OF PAYMENTS PROGRAM

225.7500 Scope of subpart.

This subpart provides policies and procedures implementing the Balance of Payments Program. It applies to contracts for the acquisition of—

(a) Supplies for use outside the United States; and

(b) Construction to be performed outside the United States.

225.7501 Policy.

Acquire only domestic end products for use outside the United States, and use only domestic construction material for construction to be performed outside the United States, including end products and construction material for foreign military sales, unless—

(a) Before issuing the solicitation—

(1) The estimated cost of the acquisition or the value of a particular construction material is at or below the simplified acquisition threshold;

(2) The end product or particular construction material is—

(i) Listed;

(ii) A petroleum product;

(iii) A spare part for foreign-manufactured vehicles, equipment, machinery, or systems, provided the acquisition is restricted to the original manufacturer or its supplier;

(iv) An industrial gas;

(v) A brand drug specified by the Defense Medical Materiel Board; or

(vi) Information technology that is a commercial item, using fiscal year 2004 or subsequent funds (Section 535 of Division F of the Consolidated Appropriations Act, 2004 (Pub. L. 108-199), and the same provision in subsequent appropriations acts);

(3) The acquisition is covered by the World Trade Organization Government Procurement Agreement;

(4) The acquisition of foreign end products or construction material is required by a treaty or executive agreement between governments;

(5) Use of a procedure specified in 225.7703-1(a) is authorized for an acquisition in support of operations in Afghanistan;

(6) The end product is acquired for commissary resale; or

(7) The contracting officer determines that a requirement can best be filled by a foreign end product or construction material, including determinations that—

(i) A subsistence product is perishable and delivery from the United States would significantly impair the quality at the point of consumption;

(ii) An end product or construction material, by its nature or as a practical matter, can best be acquired in the geographic area concerned, e.g., ice or books; or bulk material, such as sand, gravel, or other soil material, stone, concrete masonry units, or fired brick;

(iii) A particular domestic construction material is not available;

(iv) The cost of domestic construction material would exceed the cost of foreign construction material by more than 50 percent, calculated on the basis of—

(A) A particular construction material; or

(B) The comparative cost of application of the Balance of Payments Program to the total acquisition; or

(v) Use of a particular domestic construction material is impracticable;

(b) After receipt of offers—

(1) The evaluated low offer (see Subpart 225.5) is an offer of an end product that—

(i) Is a qualifying country end product;

(ii) Is an eligible product; or

(iii) If the acquisition is in support of operations in Afghanistan, a South Caucasus/Central and South Asian state end product listed in 225.401–70 (see 225.7704-2); or

(iv) Is a nonqualifying country end product, but application of the Balance of Payments Program evaluation factor would not result in award on a domestic offer; or

(2) The construction material is an eligible product or, if the acquisition is in support of operations in Afghanistan, the construction material is a South Caucasus/Central and South Asian state construction material (see 225.7704-2); or

(c) At any time during the acquisition process, the head of the agency determines that it is not in the public interest to apply the restrictions of the Balance of Payments Program to the end product or construction material.

[Final rule, 67 FR 77936, 12/20/2002, effective 12/20/2002; Interim rule, 69 FR 1926, 1/13/2004, effective 1/13/2004; Interim rule, 70 FR 2361, 1/13/2005, effective 1/13/2005; Final rule, 70 FR 73153, 12/9/2005, effective 12/9/2005; Final rule, 71 FR 58539, 10/4/2006, effective 10/4/2006; Interim rule, 73 FR 53151, 9/15/2008, effective 9/15/2008; Final rule, 75 FR 18035, 4/8/2010, effective 4/8/2010; Final rule, 75 FR 81915, 12/29/2010, effective 12/29/2010; Final rule, 76 FR 76318, 12/7/2011, effective 12/7/2011; Interim rule, 78 FR 59854, 9/30/2013, effective 9/30/2013; Final rule, 79 FR 11342, 2/28/2014, effective 2/28/2014; Final rule, 82 FR 61479, 12/28/2017, effective 12/28/2017]

225.7502 Procedures.

If the Balance of Payments Program applies to the acquisition, follow the procedures at PGI 225.7502.

[Final rule, 71 FR 62565, 10/26/2006, effective 10/26/2006]

225.7503 Contract clauses.

Unless the entire acquisition is exempt from the Balance of Payments Program—

(a) Use the basic or an alternate of the clause at DFARS 252.225–7044, Balance of Payments Program—Construction Material, in solicitations and contracts for construction to be performed outside the United States, including acquisitions of commercial items or components, with an estimated value greater than the simplified acquisition threshold but less than $7,008,000.

(1) Use the basic clause unless the acquisition is in support of operations in Afghanistan.

(2) Use the alternate I clause if the acquisition is in support of operations in Afghanistan.

(b) Use the basic or an alternate of the clause at 252.225–7045, Balance of Payments Program—Construction Material Under Trade Agreements, in solicitations and contracts for construction to be performed outside the United States with an estimated value of $7,008,000 or more, including acquisitions of commercial items or components.

(1) Use the basic clause in solicitations and contracts with an estimated value of $10,802,884 or more, unless the acquisition is in support of operations in Afghanistan.

(2) Use the alternate I clause in solicitations and contracts with an estimated value of $7,008,000 or more, but less than $10,802,884 unless the acquisition is in support of operations in Afghanistan.

(3) Use the alternate II clause in solicitations and contracts with an estimated value of $10,802,884 or more and is in support of operations in Afghanistan.

(4) Use the alternate III clause in solicitations and contracts with an estimated value of $7,008,000 or more, but less than $10,802,884, and is in support of operations in Afghanistan.

[Final rule, 67 FR 20693, 4/26/2002, effective 4/26/2002; Final rule, 67 FR 49256, 7/30/2002, effective 7/30/2002; Interim rule, 69 FR 1926, 1/13/2004, effective 1/13/2004; Interim rule, 71 FR 9269, 2/23/2006, effective 2/23/2006; Final rule, 71 FR 65752, 11/9/2006, effective 11/9/2006; Interim rule, 73 FR 4115, 1/24/2008, effective 1/24/2008; Final rule, 73 FR 46818, 8/12/2008, effective 8/12/2008; Interim rule, 75 FR 32637, 6/8/2010, effective 6/8/2010; Final rule, 75 FR 66680, 10/29/2010, effective 10/29/2010; Final rule, 75 FR 81915, 12/29/2010, effective 12/29/2010; Final rule, 76 FR 3536, 1/20/2011, effective 1/20/2011; Final rule, 77 FR 4630, 1/30/2012, effective 1/30/2012; Final rule, 78 FR 79620, 12/31/2013, effective 1/1/2014; Final rule, 79 FR 65815, 11/5/2014, effective 11/5/2014; Final rule, 80 FR 81470, 12/30/2015, effective 1/1/2016; Final rule, 82 FR 61481, 12/28/2017, effective 1/1/2018; Final rule, 84 FR 72245, 12/31/2019, effective 1/1/2020]

SUBPART 225.76—SECONDARY ARAB BOYCOTT OF ISRAEL

225.7601 Restriction.

In accordance with 10 U.S.C. 2410i, do not enter into a contract with a foreign entity unless it has certified that it does not comply with the secondary Arab boycott of Israel.

[Final rule, 71 FR 39005, 7/11/2006, effective 7/11/2006]

225.7602 Procedures.

For contracts awarded to the Canadian Commercial Corporation (CCC), the CCC will submit a certification from its proposed subcontractor with the other required precontractual information (see 225.870).

[Final rule, 71 FR 39005, 7/11/2006, effective 7/11/2006]

225.7603 Exceptions.

This restriction does not apply to—

(a) Purchases at or below the simplified acquisition threshold;

(b) Contracts for consumable supplies, provisions, or services for the support of United States forces or of allied forces in a foreign country; or

(c) Contracts pertaining to the use of any equipment, technology, data, or services for intelligence or classified purposes, or to the acquisition or lease thereof, in the interest of national security.

[Final rule, 71 FR 39005, 7/11/2006, effective 7/11/2006]

225.7604 Waivers.

The Secretary of Defense may waive this restriction on the basis of national security interests. To request a waiver, follow the procedures at PGI 225.7604.

[Final rule, 71 FR 39005, 7/11/2006, effective 7/11/2006; Final rule, 71 FR 62565, 10/26/2006, effective 10/26/2006]

225.7605 Solicitation provision.

Unless an exception at 225.7603 applies or a waiver has been granted in accordance with 225.7604, use the provision at 252.225-7031, Secondary Arab Boycott of Israel, in all solicitations, including solicitations using FAR part 12 procedures for the acquisition of commercial items. If the solicitation includes the provision at FAR 52.204-7, do not separately list 252.225-7031 in the solicitation.

[Final rule, 71 FR 39005, 7/11/2006, effective 7/11/2006; Final rule, 78 FR 37980, 6/25/2013, effective 6/25/2013; Final rule, 78 FR 40043, 7/3/2013, effective 7/3/2013]

SUBPART 225.77—ACQUISITIONS IN SUPPORT OF OPERATIONS IN AFGHANISTAN

225.7700 Scope.

This subpart implements—

(a) Section 892 of the National Defense Authorization Act for Fiscal Year 2008 (Pub. L. 110–181);

(b) Section 886 of the National Defense Authorization Act for Fiscal Year 2008 (Pub. L. 110–181), as amended by section 842 of the National Defense Authorization Act for Fiscal Year 2013 (Pub. L. 112–239);

(c) Section 826 of the National Defense Authorization Act for Fiscal Year 2013 (Pub. L. 112–239); and

(d) The determinations by the Deputy Secretary of Defense regarding participation of the countries of the South Caucasus or Central and South Asia in acquisitions in support of operations in Afghanistan.

(e) Section 216 of the National Defense Authorization Act for Fiscal Year 2017 (Pub. L. 114-328).

[Interim rule, 73 FR 53151, 9/15/2008, effective 9/15/2008; Final rule, 75 FR 18035, 4/8/2010, effective 4/8/2010; Final rule, 75 FR 81915, 12/29/2010, effective 12/29/2010; Interim rule, 78 FR 59854, 9/30/2013, effective 9/30/2013; Final rule, 79 FR 11342, 2/28/2014, effective 2/28/2014; Final rule, 83 FR 16003, 4/13/2018, effective 4/13/2018]

225.7701 Definitions.

As used in this subpart—

Product from Afghanistan means a product that is mined, produced, or manufactured in Afghanistan.

Service from Afghanistan means a service including construction that is performed in Afghanistan predominantly by citizens or permanent resident aliens of Afghanistan.

Small arms means pistols and other weapons less than 0.50 caliber.

Source from Afghanistan means a source that—

(1) Is located in Afghanistan; and

(2) Offers products or services from Afghanistan.

Textile component is defined in the clause at 252.225-7029, Acquisition of Uniform Components for Afghan Military or Afghan National Police.

[Interim rule, 73 FR 53151, 9/15/2008, effective 9/15/2008; Final rule, 75 FR 18035, 4/8/2010, effective 4/8/2010; Interim rule, 78 FR 59854, 9/30/2013, effective 9/30/2013; Final rule, 79 FR 11342, 2/28/2014, effective 2/28/2014]

225.7702 Acquisitions not subject to the enhanced authority to acquire products or services from Afghanistan. (No Text)

[Interim rule, 78 FR 59854, 9/30/2013, effective 9/30/2013; Final rule, 79 FR 11342, 2/28/2014, effective 2/28/2014]

225.7702-1 Acquisition of small arms.

(a) Except as provided in paragraph (b) of this section, when acquiring small arms for assistance to the Army of Afghanistan, the Afghani Police Forces, or other Afghani security organizations—

(1) Use full and open competition to the maximum extent practicable, consistent with the provisions of 10 U.S.C. 2304;

(2) If use of other than full and open competition is justified in accordance with FAR Subpart 6.3, ensure that—

(i) No responsible U.S. manufacturer is excluded from competing for the acquisition; and

(ii) Products manufactured in the United States are not excluded from the competition; and

(3) If the exception at FAR 6.302-2 (unusual and compelling urgency) applies, do not exclude responsible U.S. manufacturers or products manufactured in the United States from the competition for the purpose of administrative expediency. However, such an offer may be rejected if it does not meet delivery schedule requirements.

(b) Paragraph (a)(2) of this section does not apply when—

(1) The exception at FAR 6.302-1 (only one or a limited number of responsible sources) applies, and the only responsible source or sources are not U.S. manufacturers or are not offering products manufactured in the United States; or

(2) The exception at FAR 6.302-4 (international agreement) applies, and United States manufacturers or products manufactured in the United States are not the source(s) specified in the written directions of the foreign government reimbursing the agency for the cost of the acquisition of the property or services for such government.

[Interim rule, 73 FR 53151, 9/15/2008, effective 9/15/2008; Final rule, 75 FR 18035, 4/8/2010, effective 4/8/2010; Interim rule, 78 FR 59854, 9/30/2013, effective 9/30/2013; Final rule, 79 FR 11342, 2/28/2014, effective 2/28/2014]

225.7702-2 Acquisition of uniform components for the Afghan military or the Afghan police.

Any textile components supplied by DoD to the Afghan National Army or the Afghan National Police for purpose of production of uniforms shall be produced in the United States.

[Interim rule, 78 FR 59854, 9/30/2013, effective 9/30/2013; Final rule, 79 FR 11342, 2/28/2014, effective 2/28/2014]

225.7703 Enhanced authority to acquire products or services from Afghanistan. (No Text)

[Interim rule, 73 FR 53151, 9/15/2008, effective 9/15/2008; Final rule, 75 FR 18035, 4/8/2010, effective 4/8/2010; Interim rule, 78 FR 59854, 9/30/2013, effective 9/30/2013; Final rule, 79 FR 11342, 2/28/2014, effective 2/28/2014]

225.7703-1 Acquisition procedures.

(a) Subject to the requirements of 225.7703-2, except as provided in 225.7702, a product or service (including construction), in support of operations in Afghanistan may be acquired by—

(1) Providing a preference for products or services from Afghanistan in accordance with the evaluation procedures at 225.7703-3;

(2) Limiting competition to products or services from Afghanistan; or

(3) Using procedures other than competitive procedures to award a contract to a particular source or sources from Afghanistan. When other than competitive procedures are used, the contracting officer shall document the contract file with the rationale for selecting the particular source(s).

(b) For acquisitions conducted using a procedure specified in paragraph (a) of this subsection, the justification and approval addressed in FAR Subpart 6.3 is not required.

(c) When issuing solicitations and contracts for performance in Afghanistan, follow the procedures at PGI 225.7703-1(c).

[Interim rule, 73 FR 53151, 9/15/2008, effective 9/15/2008; Final rule, 75 FR 18035, 4/8/2010, effective 4/8/2010; Interim rule, 78 FR 59854, 9/30/2013, effective 9/30/2013; Final rule, 79 FR 11342, 2/28/2014, effective 2/28/2014; Final rule, 79 FR 58694, 9/30/2014, effective 9/30/2014]

225.7703-2 Determination requirements.

Before use of a procedure specified in 225.7703-1(a), a written determination must be prepared and executed as follows:

(a) For products or services to be used only by the military forces, police, or other security personnel of Afghanistan, the contracting officer shall—

(1) Determine in writing that the product or service is to be used only by the military forces, police, or other security personnel of Afghanistan; and

(2) Include the written determination in the contract file.

(b) For products or services not limited to use by the military forces, police, or other security personnel of Afghanistan, the following requirements apply:

(1) The appropriate official specified in paragraph (b)(2) of this subsection must determine in writing that it is in the national security interest of the United States to use a procedure specified in 225.7703-1(a), because—

(i) The procedure is necessary to provide a stable source of jobs in Afghanistan; and

(ii) Use of the procedure will not adversely affect—

(A) Operations in Afghanistan (including security, transition, reconstruction, and humanitarian relief activities); or

(B) The U.S. industrial base. The authorizing official generally may presume that there will not be an adverse effect on the U.S. industrial base. However, when in doubt, the authorizing official should coordinate with the applicable subject matter expert specified in PGI 225.7703-2(b).

(2) Determinations may be made for an individual acquisition or a class of acquisitions meeting the criteria in paragraph (b)(1) of this subsection as follows:

(i) The head of the contacting activity is authorized to make a determination that applies to an individual acquisition with a value of less than $93 million.

(ii) The Director, Defense Procurement and Acquisition Policy, and the following officials, without power of redelegation, are authorized to make a determination that applies to an individual acquisition with a value of $93 million or more or to a class of acquisitions:

(A) Defense Logistics Agency Component Acquisition Executive.

(B) Army Acquisition Executive.

(C) Navy Acquisition Executive.

(D) Air Force Acquisition Executive.

(E) Commander of the United States Central Command Joint Theater Support Contracting Command (C-JTSCC).

(3) The contracting officer—

(i) Shall include the applicable written determination in the contract file; and

(ii) Shall ensure that each contract action taken pursuant to the authority of a class determination is within the scope of the class determination, and shall document the contract file for each action accordingly.

(c) See PGI 225.7703-2(c) for formats for use in preparation of the determinations required by this subsection.

[Interim rule, 73 FR 53151, 9/15/2008, effective 9/15/2008; Final rule, 75 FR 18035, 4/8/2010, effective 4/8/2010; Final rule, 75 FR 45072, 8/2/2010, effective 10/1/2010; Interim rule, 78 FR 59854, 9/30/2013, effective 9/30/2013; Final rule, 79 FR 11342, 2/28/2014, effective 2/28/2014; Final rule, 80 FR 36903, 6/26/2015, effective 10/1/2015]

225.7703-3 Evaluating offers.

Evaluate offers submitted in response to solicitations that include the provision at 252.225-7023, Preference for Products or Services from Afghanistan, as follows:

(a) If the low offer is an offer of a product or service from Afghanistan, award on that offer.

(b) If there are no offers of a product or service from Afghanistan, award on the low offer.

(c) Otherwise, apply the evaluation factor specified in the solicitation to the low offer.

(1) If the price of the low offer of a product or service from Afghanistan is less than the evaluated price of the low offer, award on the low offer of a product or service from Afghanistan.

(2) If the evaluated price of the low offer remains less than the low offer of a product or service from Afghanistan, award on the low offer.

[Interim rule, 73 FR 53151, 9/15/2008, effective 9/15/2008; Final rule, 75 FR 18035, 4/8/2010, effective 4/8/2010; Final rule, 78 FR 41331, 7/10/2013, effective 7/10/2013; Interim rule, 78 FR 59854, 9/30/2013, effective 9/30/2013; Final rule, 79 FR 11342, 2/28/2014, effective 2/28/2014; Final rule, 79 FR 56278, 9/19/2014, effective 9/19/2014; Final rule, 80 FR 72607, 11/20/2015, effective 11/20/2015]

225.7703-4 Solicitation provisions and contract clauses.

(a) Use the provision at 252.225-7023, Preference for Products or Services from Afghanistan, in solicitations, including solicitations using FAR part 12 procedures for the acquisition of commercial items, that provide a preference for products or services from Afghanistan in accordance with 225.7703-1(a)(1). The contracting officer may modify the 50 percent evaluation factor in accordance with contracting office procedures.

(b) Use the clause at 252.225-7024, Requirement for Products or Services from Afghanistan, in solicitations, including solicitations using FAR part 12 procedures for the acquisition of commercial items, that include the provision at 252.225-7023, Preference for Products or Services from Afghanistan, and in the resulting contract.

(c) Use the clause at 252.225-7026, Acquisition Restricted to Products or Services from Afghanistan, in solicitations and contracts, including solicitations and contracts using FAR part 12 procedures for the acquisition of commercial items, that—

(1) Are restricted to the acquisition of products or services from Afghanistan in accordance with 225.7703-1(a)(2); or

(2) Will be directed to a particular source or sources from Afghanistan in accordance with 225.7703-1(a)(3).

(d) Use the clause at 252.225-7029, Acquisition of Uniform Components for Afghan Military or Afghan National Police, in solicitations and contracts, including solicitations and contracts using FAR part 12 procedures for the acquisition of commercial items, for the acquisition of any textile components that DoD intends to supply to the Afghan National Army or the Afghan National Police for purposes of production of uniforms.

(e) When the Trade Agreements Act applies to the acquisition, use the appropriate clause and provision as prescribed at 225.1101 (5) and (6).

(f) Do not use any of the following provisions or clauses in solicitations or contracts that include the provision at 252.225-7023, the clause at 252.225-7024, or the clause at 252.225-7026:

(1) 252.225-7000, Buy American—Balance of Payments Program Certificate.

(2) 252.225-7001, Buy American and Balance of Payments Program.

(3) 252.225-7002, Qualifying Country Sources as Subcontractors.

(4) 252.225-7035, Buy American—Free Trade Agreements—Balance of Payments Program Certificate.

(5) 252.225-7036, Buy American—Free Trade Agreements—Balance of Payments Program.

(6) 252.225-7044, Balance of Payments Program—Construction Material.

(7) 252.225-7045, Balance of Payments Program—Construction Material Under Trade Agreements.

(g) Do not use the following clause or provision in solicitations or contracts that include the clause at 252.225-7026:

(1)252.225-7020, Trade Agreements Certificate.

(2) 252.225-7021, Trade Agreements.

(3) 252.225-7022, Trade Agreements Certificate—Inclusion of Iraqi End Products.

[Interim rule, 73 FR 53151, 9/15/2008, effective 9/15/2008; Final rule, 75 FR 18035, 4/8/2010, effective 4/8/2010; Final rule, 78 FR 37980, 6/25/2013, effective 6/25/2013; Redesignated by Interim rule, 78 FR 59854,9/30/2013, effective 9/30/2013; Final rule, 79 FR 11342, 2/28/2014, effective 2/28/2014; Final rule, 84 FR 12140, 4/1/2019, effective 4/1/2019]

225.7704 Acquisitions of products and services from South Caucasus/ Central and South Asian (SC/CASA) state in support of operations in Afghanistan. (No Text)

[Final rule, 75 FR 81915, 12/29/2010, effective 12/29/2010]

225.7704-1 Applicability of trade agreements.

As authorized by the United States Trade Representative, the Secretary of Defense has waived the prohibition in section 302(a) of the Trade Agreements Act (see subpart 225.4) for acquisitions by DoD, and by GSA on behalf of DoD, of products and services from SC/CASA states in direct support of operations in Afghanistan.

[Final rule, 75 FR 81915, 12/29/2010, effective 12/29/2010]

225.7704-2 Applicability of Balance of Payments Program.

The Deputy Secretary of Defense has determined, because of importance to national security, that it would be inconsistent with the public interest to apply the provisions of the Balance of Payments Program (see subpart 225.75) to offers of end products other than arms, ammunition, and war materials (i.e., end products listed in 225.401-70) and construction materials from the SC/CASA states that are being acquired by or on behalf of DoD in direct support of operations in Afghanistan.

[Final rule, 75 FR 81915, 12/29/2010, effective 12/29/2010]

225.7704-3 Solicitation provisions and contract clauses.

Appropriate solicitation provisions and contract clauses are prescribed as alternates to the Buy American-Trade Agreements-Balance of Payments Program solicitation provisions and contract clauses prescribed at 225.1101 and 225.7503.

[Final rule, 75 FR 81915, 12/29/2010, effective 12/29/2010]

225.7705 Prohibition on use of funds for contracts of certain programs and projects in Afghanistan that cannot be safely accessed.

This section implements section 1216 of the National Defense Authorization Act for Fiscal Year 2017 (Pub. L. 114-328).

[Final rule, 83 FR 16003, 4/13/2018, effective 4/13/2018]

225.7705-1 Prohibition.

The contracting officer shall not obligate or expend funds for a construction or other infrastructure program or project of the Department in Afghanistan if military or civilian personnel of the United States Government or their representatives, with authority to conduct oversight of such program or project, cannot safely access such program or project. In limited circumstances, this prohibition may be waived in accordance with section 225.7705-2.

[Final rule, 83 FR 16003, 4/13/2018, effective 4/13/2018]

225.7705-2 Waiver of prohibition.

(a) The prohibition in 225.7705-1 may be waived upon issuance of a determination, approved in accordance with paragraph (b) of this section, that—

(1) The program or project clearly contributes to United States national interests or strategic objectives;

(2) The Government of Afghanistan has requested or expressed a need for the program or project;

(3) The program or project has been coordinated with the Government of Afghanistan, and with any other implementing agencies or international donors;

(4) Security conditions permit effective implementation and oversight of the program or project;

(5) Safeguards to detect, deter, and mitigate corruption and waste, fraud, and abuse of funds are in place;

(6) Adequate arrangements have been made for the sustainment of the program or project following its completion, including arrangements with respect to funding and technical capacity for sustainment; and

(7) Meaningful metrics have been established to measure the progress and effectiveness of the program or project in meeting its objectives.

(b) The following officials are authorized to approve the determination described in paragraph (a) of this section:

(1) In the case of a program or project with an estimated lifecycle cost of less than $1 million, by the contracting officer.

(2) In the case of a program or project with an estimated lifecycle cost of $1 million or more, but less than $20 million, by the senior U.S. officer in the Combined Security Transition Command-Afghanistan.

(3) In the case of a program or project with an estimated lifecycle cost of $20 million or more, but less than $40 million, by the Commander of United States Forces-Afghanistan.

(4) In the case of a program or project with an estimated lifecycle cost of $40 million or more, by the Secretary of Defense.

(c) Congressional notification is required within 15 days of issuance of a determination to waive the prohibition for programs or projects valued at $40 million or more in accordance with paragraph (b)(4) of this section.

[Final rule, 83 FR 16003, 4/13/2018, effective 4/13/2018]

225.7705-3 Procedures.

(a) The contracting officer shall not obligate or expend funds for contracts for a construction or other infrastructure program or project in Afghanistan, awarded after December 23, 2016, unless the requiring activity provides the following documentation:

(1) Written affirmation that military or civilian personnel of the United States Government or their representatives, with authority to conduct oversight of such program or project, can safely access such program or project; or

(2)(i) For programs or projects valued at less than $1 million, sufficient information upon which to base the determination described in 225.7705-2(a); or

(ii)(A) For programs or projects valued at $1 million or more, a copy of the approved determination described in 225.7705-2(a) and (b); and

(B) For programs or projects valued at $40 million or more, a copy of the Congressional notification described in 225.7705-2(c).

(b) After contract award, the contracting officer shall review the requiring activity's progress reports (*e.g.*, contracting officer's representative reports) that addresses whether access continues to be safe or security conditions continue to permit effective implementation and oversight of the contract. If the requiring activity does not affirm continued safe access or, if a determination to waive the prohibition has been approved, that security conditions continue to permit effective implementation and oversight of the contract, then the contracting officer shall consult with the requiring activity to take any appropriate actions.

[Final rule, 83 FR 16003, 4/13/2018, effective 4/13/2018]

SUBPART 225.78—ACQUISITIONS IN SUPPORT OF GEOGRAPHIC COMBATANT COMMAND'S THEATER SECURITY COOPERATION EFFORTS

225.7801 Policy.

For guidance on procurement support of the geographic combatant command's theater security cooperation efforts, see PGI 225.78.

[Final rule, 76 FR 27274, 5/11/2011, effective 5/11/2011]

SUBPART 225.79—EXPORT CONTROL

225.7900 Scope of subpart.

This subpart implements—

(a) Section 890(a) of the National Defense Authorization Act for Fiscal Year 2008 (Pub. L. 110-181); and

(b) The requirements regarding export control of Title I of the Security Cooperation Act of 2010 (Pub. L. 111-266); the Treaty Between the Government of the United States of America and the Government of Australia Concerning Defense Trade Cooperation (the U.S.-Australia DTC Treaty); and the Treaty Between the Government of the United States of America and the Government the United Kingdom of Great Britain and Northern Ireland Concerning Defense Trade Cooperation (the U.S.-U.K. DTC Treaty). See PGI 225.7902 for additional information.

[Interim rule, 77 FR 30361, 5/22/2012, effective 5/22/2012; Final rule, 78 FR 36108, 6/17/2013, effective 6/17/2013]

225.7901 Export-comtrolled items.

This section implements section 890(a) of the National Defense Authorization Act for Fiscal Year 2008 (Pub. L. 110-181).

[Interim rule, 77 FR 30361, 5/22/2012, effective 5/22/2012; Final rule, 78 FR 36108, 6/17/2013, effective 6/17/2013]

225.7901-1 Definitions.

Export-controlled items, as used in this section, is defined in the clause at 252.225-7048.

[Interim rule, 77 FR 30361, 5/22/2012, effective 5/22/2012; Final rule, 78 FR 36108, 6/17/2013, effective 6/17/2013]

225.7901-2 General.

Certain types of items are subject to export controls in accordance with the Arms Export Control Act (22 U.S.C. 2751, *et seq.*), the International Traffic in Arms Regulations (22 CFR parts 120-130), the Export Administration Act of 1979, as amended (50 U.S.C. App. 2401 *et seq.*), and the Export Administration Regulations (15 CFR parts 730-774). See PGI 225.7901-2 for additional information.

[Interim rule, 77 FR 30361, 5/22/2012, effective 5/22/2012; Final rule, 78 FR 36108, 6/17/2013, effective 6/17/2013]

225.7901-3 Policy.

(a) It is in the interest of both the Government and the contractor to be aware of export controls as they apply to the performance of DoD contracts.

(b) It is the contractor's responsibility to comply with all applicable laws and regulations regarding export-controlled items. This responsibility exists independent of, and is not established or limited by, this section.

[Interim rule, 77 FR 30361, 5/22/2012, effective 5/22/2012; Final rule, 78 FR 36108, 6/17/2013, effective 6/17/2013]

225.7901-4 Contract clause.

Use the clause at 252.225-7048, Export-Controlled Items, in all solicitations and contracts.

[Interim rule, 77 FR 30361, 5/22/2012, effective 5/22/2012; Final rule, 78 FR 36108, 6/17/2013, effective 6/17/2013]

225.7902 Defense Trade Cooperation Treaties.

This section implements the Defense Trade Cooperation (DTC) Treaties with Australia and the United Kingdom and the associated Implementing Arrangements for DoD solicitations and contracts that authorize prospective contractors and contractors to use the DTC Treaties to respond to DoD solicitations and in the performance of DoD contracts.

[Interim rule, 77 FR 30361, 5/22/2012, effective 5/22/2012; Final rule, 78 FR 36108, 6/17/2013, effective 6/17/2013]

225.7902-1 Definitions.

Approved community, defense articles, Defense Trade Cooperation (DTC) Treaty, export, Implementing Arrangement, qualifying defense articles, transfer, and *U.S. DoD Treaty-eligible requirements* are defined in contract clause DFARS 252.225-7047, Exports by Approved Community Members in Performance of the Contract.

[Interim rule, 77 FR 30361, 5/22/2012, effective 5/22/2012; Final rule, 78 FR 36108, 6/17/2013, effective 6/17/2013]

225.7902-2 Purpose.

The DTC Treaties permit the export of certain U.S. defense articles, technical data, and defense services, without U.S. export licenses or other written authorization under the International Traffic in Arms Regulation (ITAR) into and within the Approved Community, as long as the exports are in support of purposes specified in the DTC Treaties. All persons must continue to comply with statutory and regulatory requirements outside of DFARS and ITAR concerning the import of defense articles and defense services or the possession or transfer of defense articles, including, but not limited to, regulations issued by the Bureau of Alcohol, Tobacco, Firearms and Explosives found at 27 CFR parts 447, 478, and 479, which are unaffected by the DTC Treaties. The Approved Community consists of U.S. entities that are registered with the Department of State and are eligible exporters, the U.S. Government, and certain governmental and commercial facilities in Australia and the United Kingdom that are approved and listed by the U.S. Government. See PGI 225.7902-2 for additional information.

[Interim rule, 77 FR 30361, 5/22/2012, effective 5/22/2012; Final rule, 78 FR 36108, 6/17/2013, effective 6/17/2013]

225.7902-3 Policy.

DoD will facilitate maximum use of the DTC Treaties by prospective contractors responding to DoD solicitations and by contractors eligible to export qualifying defense articles under DoD contracts in accordance with 22 CFR 126.16(g) and 22 CFR 126.17(g).

[Interim rule, 77 FR 30361, 5/22/2012, effective 5/22/2012; Final rule, 78 FR 36108, 6/17/2013, effective 6/17/2013]

225.7902-4 Procedures.

(a) For all solicitations and contracts that may be eligible for DTC Treaty coverage (see PGI 225.7902-4(1)), the program manager shall identify in writing and submit to the contracting officer prior to issuance of a solicitation and prior to award of a contract—

(1) The qualifying DTC Treaty Scope paragraph (Article 3(1)(a), 3(1)(b), or 3(1)(d) of the U.S.-Australia DTC Treaty or Article (3)(1)(a), (3(1)(b), or 3(1)(d) of the U.S.-U.K. DTC Treaty); and

(2) The qualifying defense article(s) using the categories described in 22 CFR 126.16(g) and 22 CFR 126.17(g).

(b) If applicable, the program manager shall also identify in writing and submit to the contracting officer any specific Part C, DTC Treaty-exempted technology list items, terms and conditions for applicable contract line item numbers (See PGI 225.7902-4(2)).

[Interim rule, 77 FR 30361, 5/22/2012, effective 5/22/2012; Final rule, 78 FR 36108, 6/17/2013, effective 6/17/2013]

225.7902-5 Solicitation provision and contract clause.

(a) Use the provision at 252.225-7046, Exports by Approved Community Members in Response to the Solicitation, in solicitations containing the clause at 252.225-7047.

(b)(1) Use the clause at 252.225-7047, Exports by Approved Community Members in Performance of the Contract, in solicitations and contracts when—

(i) Export-controlled items are expected to be involved in the performance of the contract and the clause at 252.225-7048 is used; and

(ii) At least one contract line item is intended to satisfy a U.S. DoD Treaty-eligible requirement.

(2) The contracting officer shall complete paragraph (b) of the clause using information the program manager provided as required by PGI 225.7902-4(a).

[Interim rule, 77 FR 30361, 5/22/2012, effective 5/22/2012; Final rule, 78 FR 36108, 6/17/2013, effective 6/17/2013; Final rule, 78 FR 38235, 6/26/2013, effective 6/26/2013; Final rule, 78 FR 40043, 7/3/2013, effective 7/3/2013]

PART 226—OTHER SOCIOECONOMIC PROGRAMS

Table of Contents

Subpart 226.1—Indian Incentive Program

Procedures 226.103
Contract clause 226.104

Subpart 226.3—[Removed]

Subpart 226.70—[Removed and Reserved]

Subpart 226.71—Preference for Local and Small Businesses

Scope of subpart 226.7100
Definition 226.7101
Policy 226.7102
Procedure 226.7103
Other considerations 226.7104

Subpart 226.72—Demonstration Project for Contractors Employing Persons With Disabilities

Scope of subpart 226.7200
Definitions 226.7201
Policy and procedures 226.7202
Solicitation provision 226.7203

PART 226—OTHER SOCIOECONOMIC PROGRAMS

SUBPART 226.1—INDIAN INCENTIVE PROGRAM

226.103 Procedures.

Follow the procedures at PGI 226.103 when submitting a request for funding of an Indian incentive.

[Final rule, 65 FR 19858, 4/13/2000, effective 4/13/2000; Interim rule, 68 FR 56561, 10/1/2003, effective 10/1/2003; Final rule, 69 FR 55989, 9/17/2004, effective 9/17/2004; Final rule, 70 FR 73148, 12/9/2005, effective 12/9/2005]

226.104 Contract clause.

Use the clause at 252.226-7001, Utilization of Indian Organizations, Indian-Owned Economic Enterprises, and Native Hawaiian Small Business Concerns, in solicitations and contracts, including solicitations and contracts using FAR part 12 procedures for the acquisition of commercial items, that are for supplies or services exceeding $500,000 in value.

[Final rule, 65 FR 19858, 4/13/2000, effective 4/13/2000; Final rule, 65 FR 52951, 8/31/2000, effective 8/31/2000, corrected, 65 FR 58607, 9/29/2000; Interim rule, 66 FR 47110, 9/11/2001, effective 9/11/2001; Final rule, 67 FR 38022, 5/31/2002, effective 5/31/2002; Final rule, 67 FR 65512, 10/25/2002, effective 10/25/2002; Interim rule, 68 FR 56561, 10/1/2003, effective 10/1/2003; Final rule, 69 FR 55989, 9/17/2004, effective 9/17/2004; Final rule, 78 FR 37980, 6/25/2013, effective 6/25/2013]

SUBPART 226.3—[REMOVED]

226.370 [Removed]

[Final rule, 70 FR 73148, 12/9/2005, effective 12/9/2005; Interim rule, 79 FR 61579, 10/14/2014, effective 10/14/2014; Final rule, 80 FR 15912, 3/26/2015, effective 3/26/2015]

226.370-1 [Removed]

[Final rule, 70 FR 73148, 12/9/2005, effective 12/9/2005; Interim rule, 79 FR 61579, 10/14/2014, effective 10/14/2014; Final rule, 80 FR 15912, 3/26/2015, effective 3/26/2015]

226.370-2 [Removed]

[Final rule, 70 FR 73148, 12/9/2005, effective 12/9/2005; Interim rule, 79 FR 61579, 10/14/2014, effective 10/14/2014; Final rule, 80 FR 15912, 3/26/2015, effective 3/26/2015]

226.370-3 [Removed]

[Final rule, 70 FR 73148, 12/9/2005, effective 12/9/2005; Interim rule, 79 FR 61579, 10/14/2014, effective 10/14/2014; Final rule, 80 FR 15912, 3/26/2015, effective 3/26/2015]

226.370-4 [Removed]

[Final rule, 70 FR 73148, 12/9/2005, effective 12/9/2005; Interim rule, 79 FR 61579, 10/14/2014, effective 10/14/2014; Final rule, 80 FR 15912, 3/26/2015, effective 3/26/2015]

226.370-5 [Removed]

[Final rule, 70 FR 73148, 12/9/2005, effective 12/9/2005; Interim rule, 79 FR 61579, 10/14/2014, effective 10/14/2014; Final rule, 80 FR 15912, 3/26/2015, effective 3/26/2015]

226.370-6 [Removed]

[Final rule, 70 FR 73148, 12/9/2005, effective 12/9/2005; Interim rule, 79 FR 61579, 10/14/2014, effective 10/14/2014; Final rule, 80 FR 15912, 3/26/2015, effective 3/26/2015]

226.370-7 [Removed]

[Final rule, 70 FR 73148, 12/9/2005, effective 12/9/2005; Interim rule, 79 FR 61579, 10/14/2014, effective 10/14/2014; Final rule, 80 FR 15912, 3/26/2015, effective 3/26/2015]

226.370-8 [Removed]

[Final rule, 70 FR 73148, 12/9/2005, effective 12/9/2005; Interim rule, 79 FR 61579, 10/14/2014, effective 10/14/2014; Final rule,

80 FR 15912, 3/26/2015, effective 3/26/2015]

226.370-9 [Removed]

[Final rule, 70 FR 73148, 12/9/2005, effective 12/9/2005; Interim rule, 79 FR 61579, 10/14/2014, effective 10/14/2014; Final rule, 80 FR 15912, 3/26/2015, effective 3/26/2015]

SUBPART 226.70—[REMOVED AND RESERVED]

[Final rule, 70 FR 73148, 12/9/2005, effective 12/9/2005]

SUBPART 226.71—PREFERENCE FOR LOCAL AND SMALL BUSINESSES

226.7100 Scope of subpart.

This subpart implements Section 2912 of the Fiscal Year 1994 Defense Authorization Act (Pub. L. 103-160) and Section 817 of the Fiscal Year 1995 Defense Authorization Act (Pub. L. 103-337).

[Interim rule, 60 FR 5870, 1/31/95, effective 1/26/95, finalized without change, DAC 91-9, 60 FR 61586, 11/30/95, effective 11/30/95]

226.7101 Definition.

Vicinity, as used in this subpart, means the county or counties in which the military installation to be closed or realigned is located and all adjacent counties, unless otherwise defined by the agency head.

[DAC 91-7, 60 FR 29491, 6/5/95, effective 5/17/95]

226.7102 Policy.

Businesses located in the vicinity of a military installation that is being closed or realigned under a base closure law, including 10 U.S.C. 2687, and small and small disadvantaged businesses shall be provided maximum practicable opportunity to participate in acquisitions that support the closure or realignment, including acquisitions for environmental restoration and mitigation.

[Interim rule, 59 FR 12191, 3/16/94, effective 3/8/94]

226.7103 Procedure.

In considering acquisitions for award through the section 8(a) program (subpart 219.8 and FAR subpart 19.8) or in making set-aside decisions under subpart 219.5 and FAR subpart 19.5 for acquisitions in support of a base closure or realignment, the contracting officer shall—

(a) Determine whether there is a reasonable expectation that offers will be received from responsible business concerns located in the vicinity of the military installation that is being closed or realigned.

(b) If offers can not be expected from business concerns in the vicinity, proceed with section 8(a) or set-aside consideration as otherwise indicated in part 219 and FAR part 19.

(c) If offers can be expected from business concerns in the vicinity—

(1) Consider section 8(a) only if at least one eligible 8(a) contractor is located in the vicinity.

(2) Set aside the acquisition for small business only if at least one of the expected offers is from a small business located in the vicinity.

[DAC 91-7, 60 FR 29491, 6/5/95, effective 5/17/95; Interim rule, 63 FR 41972, 8/6/98, effective 10/1/98, finalized without change, 64 FR 52670 9/30/99; Final rule 67 FR 11438 3/14/2002, effective 3/14/2002]

226.7104 Other considerations.

When planning for contracts for services related to base closure activities at a military installation affected by a closure or realignment under a base closure law, contracting officers shall consider including, as a factor in source selection, the extent to which offerors specifically identify and commit, in their proposals, to a plan to hire residents of the vicinity of the military installation that is being closed or realigned.

[DAC 91-9, 60 FR 61586, 11/30/95, effective 11/30/95]

SUBPART 226.72—DEMONSTRATION PROJECT FOR CONTRACTORS

EMPLOYING PERSONS WITH DISABILITIES

226.7200 Scope of subpart.

This subpart implements section 853 of the National Defense Authorization Act for Fiscal Year 2004 (Pub. L. 108–136, 10 U.S.C. 2302 note). Nothing in this subpart supersedes the requirement to use the mandatory sources in FAR part 8 or the small business programs in FAR part 19.

[Final rule, 84 FR 72554, 12/31/2019, effective 12/31/2019]

226.7201 Definitions.

As used in this subpart—

Eligible contractor means a business entity operated on a for-profit or nonprofit basis that—

(1) Employs severely disabled individuals at a rate that averages not less than 33 percent of its total workforce over the 12-month period prior to issuance of the solicitation;

(2) Pays not less than the minimum wage prescribed pursuant to 29 U.S.C. 206 to the employees who are severely disabled individuals; and

(3) Provides, for its employees, health insurance and a retirement plan comparable to those provided for employees by business entities of similar size in its industrial sector or geographic region.

Severely disabled individual means an individual with a disability (as defined in 42 U.S.C. 12102) who has a severe physical or mental impairment that seriously limits one or more functional capacities.

[Final rule, 84 FR 72554, 12/31/2019, effective 12/31/2019]

226.7202 Policy and procedures.

(a) (1) Contracting officers may use this Demonstration Project to award one or more contracts to an eligible contractor for the purpose of providing defense contracting opportunities for entities that employ severely disabled individuals. To determine if there are eligible contractors capable of fulfilling the agency's requirement, conduct market research as described in 210.002 and FAR 10.002. For services, see also PGI 210.070.

(2) If the contracting officer elects to use this Demonstration Project, FAR 6.302–5 requires a written justification and approval to limit competition to eligible contractors. In the justification, identify the statutory authority for the Demonstration Project (10 U.S.C. 2302 note).

(b) When using this Demonstration Project, one of the evaluation factors shall be the percentage of the offeror's total workforce that consists of severely disabled individuals employed by the offeror. Contracting officers may use a rating method in which a higher percentage of the offeror's total workforce consisting of severely disabled individuals would result in a higher rating for this evaluation factor.

(c) (1) Contracts awarded to eligible contractors under this Demonstration Project shall be counted toward DoD's small disadvantaged business goal. The contractor must be an eligible contractor when options under the contract are exercised, in order for DoD to continue to receive credit for the contract toward its small disadvantaged business goal.

(2) Contracting officers shall verify the contractor's representation (e.g., by checking the System for Award Management) prior to exercising an option on a contract awarded under the Demonstration Project. Contracting officers may exercise the option if the contractor has represented that it is not an eligible contractor; however, the contract shall no longer be counted toward DoD's small disadvantaged business goal.

[Final rule, 84 FR 72554, 12/31/2019, effective 12/31/2019]

226.7203 Solicitation provision.

Use the provision at 252.226–7002, Representation for Demonstration Project for Contractors Employing Persons with Disabilities, in solicitations when using this Demonstration Project, including solicitations using FAR part 12 procedures for the acquisition of commercial items.

[Final rule, 84 FR 72554, 12/31/2019, effective 12/31/2019]

Defense Federal Acquisition Regulation Supplement Parts 227—241

GENERAL CONTRACTING REQUIREMENTS SPECIAL CATEGORIES OF CONTRACTING

Table of Contents

Page

SUBCHAPTER E—GENERAL CONTRACTING REQUIREMENTS

Part 227—Patents, Data, and Copyrights 401
Part 228—Bonds and Insurance 449
Part 229—Taxes 455
Part 230—Cost Accounting Standards Administration 461
Part 231—Contract Cost Principles and Procedures 465
Part 232—Contract Financing 473
Part 233—Protests, Disputes, and Appeals 493

SUBCHAPTER F—SPECIAL CATEGORIES OF CONTRACTING

Part 234—Major System Acquisition 497
Part 235—Research and Development Contracting 507
Part 236—Construction and Architect-Engineer Contracts 515
Part 237—Service Contracting 523
Part 238—[NO FAR SUPPLEMENT]
Part 239—Acquisition of Information Technology 545
Part 240—[NO FAR SUPPLEMENT]
Part 241—Acquisition of Utility Services 559

See page 39 for an explanation of the numbering of the DFARS.

PART 227—PATENTS, DATA, AND COPYRIGHTS

Table of Contents

Subpart 227.3—Patent Rights under Government Contracts

Contract clauses 227.303
Procedures 227.304
General 227.304-1
[Removed] 227.304-4

Subpart 227.4—Rights in Data and Copyrights

Scope of subpart 227.400

Subpart 227.6—Foreign License and Technical Assistance Agreements

Scope 227.670
General 227.671
Policy 227.672
Foreign license and technical assistance agreements between the Government and domestic concerns 227.673
Supply contracts between the Government and a foreign government or concern 227.674
Foreign license and technical assistance agreements between a domestic concern and a foreign government or concern 227.675
International Traffic in Arms Regulations 227.675-1
Review of agreements 227.675-2
Foreign patent interchange agreements 227.676

Subpart 227.70—Infringement Claims, Licenses, and Assignments

Scope 227.7000
Policy 227.7001
Statutes pertaining to administrative claims of infringement 227.7002
Claims for copyright infringement 227.7003
Requirements for filing an administrative claim for patent infringement . . 227.7004
Indirect notice of patent infringement claims 227.7005
Investigation and administrative disposition of claims 227.7006
Notification and disclosure of claimants 227.7007
Settlement of indemnified claims 227.7008
Patent releases, license agreements, and assignments 227.7009
Required clauses 227.7009-1
Clauses to be used when applicable 227.7009-2
Additional clauses—contracts except running royalty contracts 227.7009-3
Additional clauses—contracts providing for payment of a running royalty 227.7009-4
Assignments 227.7010
Procurement of rights in inventions, patents, and copyrights 227.7011
Contract format 227.7012
Recordation 227.7013

Subpart 227.71—Rights in Technical Data

Scope of subpart 227.7100

Definitions 227.7101
Commercial items, components, or processes 227.7102
Policy 227.7102-1
Rights in technical data 227.7102-2
Government right to review, verify, challenge and validate asserted restrictions 227.7102-3
Contract clauses 227.7102-4
Noncommercial items or processes 227.7103
Policy 227.7103-1
Acquisition of technical data 227.7103-2
Early identification of technical data to be furnished to the Government with restrictions on use, reproduction or disclosure 227.7103-3
License rights 227.7103-4
Government rights 227.7103-5
Contract clauses 227.7103-6
Use and non-disclosure agreement 227.7103-7
Deferred delivery and deferred ordering of technical data 227.7103-8
Copyright 227.7103-9
Contractor identification and marking of technical data to be furnished with restrictive markings 227.7103-10
Contractor procedures and records 227.7103-11
Government right to establish conformity of markings 227.7103-12
Government right to review, verify, challenge, and validate asserted restrictions 227.7103-13
Conformity, acceptance, and warranty of technical data 227.7103-14
Subcontractor rights in technical data 227.7103-15
Providing technical data to foreign governments, foreign contractors, or international organizations 227.7103-16
Overseas contracts with foreign sources 227.7103-17
Contracts under the Small Business Innovation Research (SBIR) Program 227.7104
Contracts for the acquisition of existing works 227.7105
General 227.7105-1
Acquisition of existing works without modification 227.7105-2
Acquisition of modified existing works 227.7105-3
Contracts for special works 227.7106
Contracts for architect-engineer services 227.7107
Architectural designs and data clauses for architect- engineer or construction contracts 227.7107-1
Contracts for construction supplies and research and development work 227.7107-2
Approval of restricted designs 227.7107-3
Contractor data repositories 227.7108

Subpart 227.72—Rights in Computer Software and Computer Software Documentation

Scope of subpart 227.7200
Definitions 227.7201

Commercial computer software and commercial computer software documentation 227.7202
Policy 227.7202-1
[Reserved] 227.7202-2
Rights in commercial computer software or commercial computer software documentation 227.7202-3
Contract clause 227.7202-4
Noncommercial computer software and noncommercial computer software documentation 227.7203
Policy 227.7203-1
Acquisition of noncommercial computer software and computer software documentation 227.7203-2
Early identification of computer software or computer software documentation to be furnished to the Government with restrictions on use, reproduction or disclosure 227.7203-3
License rights 227.7203-4
Government rights 227.7203-5
Contract clauses 227.7203-6
[Removed] 227.7203-7
Deferred delivery and deferred ordering of computer software and computer software documentation 227.7203-8
Copyright 227.7203-9
Contractor identification and marking of computer software or computer software documentation to be furnished with restrictive markings 227.7203-10
Contractor procedures and records 227.7203-11
Government right to establish conformity of markings 227.7203-12
Government right to review, verify, challenge, and validate asserted restrictions 227.7203-13
Conformity, acceptance, and warranty of computer software and computer software documentation 227.7203-14
Subcontractor rights in computer software or computer software documentation 227.7203-15
Providing computer software or computer software documentation to foreign governments, foreign contractors, or international organizations 227.7203-16
Overseas contracts with foreign sources 227.7203-17
Contracts under the Small Business Innovative Research Program 227.7204
Contracts for special works 227.7205
Contracts for architect-engineer services 227.7206
Contractor data repositories 227.7207

SUBCHAPTER E—GENERAL CONTRACTING REQUIREMENTS (Parts 227-233)

PART 227—PATENTS, DATA, AND COPYRIGHTS

SUBPART 227.3—PATENT RIGHTS UNDER GOVERNMENT CONTRACTS

227.303 Contract clauses.

(1) Use the clause at 252.227-7039, Patents—Reporting of Subject Inventions, in solicitations and contracts containing the clause at FAR 52.227-11, Patent Rights—Ownership by the Contractor.

(2) (i) Use the clause at 252.227-7038, Patent Rights—Ownership by the Contractor (Large Business), instead of the clause at FAR 52.227-11, in solicitations and contracts for experimental, developmental, or research work if—

(A) The contractor is other than a small business concern or nonprofit organization; and

(B) No alternative patent rights clause is used in accordance with FAR 27.303 (c) or (e).

(ii) Use the clause with its Alternate I if—

(A) The acquisition of patent rights for the benefit of a foreign government is required under a treaty or executive agreement;

(B) The agency head determines at the time of award that it would be in the national interest to acquire the right to sublicense foreign governments or international organizations pursuant to any existing or future treaty of agreement; or

(C) Other rights are necessary to effect a treaty or agreement, in which case Alternate I may be appropriately modified.

(iii) Use the clause with its Alternate II in long-term contracts if necessary to effect treaty or agreements to be entered into.

[Final rule, 72 FR 69159, 12/7/2007, effective 12/7/2007]

227.304 Procedures. (No Text)

227.304-1 General.

Interim and final invention reports and notification of all subcontracts for experimental, developmental, or research work may be submitted on DD Form 882, Report of Inventions and Subcontracts.

[DAC 91-4, 57 FR 53600, 11/12/92, effective 10/30/92; Final rule, 76 FR 76318, 12/7/2011, effective 12/7/2011]

227.304-4 [Removed]

[Final rule, 72 FR 69159, 12/7/2007, effective 12/7/2007]

SUBPART 227.4—RIGHTS IN DATA AND COPYRIGHTS

227.400 Scope of subpart.

DoD activities shall use the guidance in subparts 227.71 and 227.72 instead of the guidance in FAR subpart 27.4.

[DAC 91-8, 60 FR 33464, 6/28/95, effective 6/30/95]

SUBPART 227.6—FOREIGN LICENSE AND TECHNICAL ASSISTANCE AGREEMENTS

227.670 Scope.

This subpart prescribes policy with respect to foreign license and technical assistance agreements.

227.671 General.

In furtherance of the Military Assistance Program or for other national defense purposes, the Government may undertake to develop or encourage the development of foreign additional sources of supply. The development of such sources may be accomplished by an agreement, often called a foreign licensing agreement or technical assistance agreement, wherein a domestic concern, referred to in this subpart as a “primary source,” agrees to furnish to a foreign concern or government, herein referred to as a “second source;” foreign patent rights; technical assistance in the form of data, know-how, trained personnel of the primary source, instruction and guidance of the personnel of the second source, jigs, dies, fixtures, or other manufacturing aids, or such other assistance, information, rights, or licenses as are needed to enable the second source to produce particular supplies or perform particular services. Agreements calling for one or more of the foregoing may be entered into between the primary source and the Government, a foreign government, or a foreign concern. The consideration for providing such foreign license and technical assistance may be in the form of a lump sum payment, payments for each item manufactured by the second source, an agreement to exchange data and patent rights on improvements made to the article or service, capital stock transactions, or any combination of these. The primary source's bases for computing such consideration may include actual costs; charges for the use of patents, data, or know-how reflecting the primary source's investment in developing and engineering and production techniques; and the primary source's "price" for setting up a second source. Such agreements often refer to the compensation to be paid as a royalty or license fee whether or not patent rights are involved.

227.672 Policy.

It is Government policy not to pay in connection with its contracts, and not to allow to be paid in connection with contracts made with funds derived through the Military Assistance Program or otherwise through the United States Government, charges for use of patents in which it holds a royalty-free license or charges for data which it has a right to use and disclose to others, or which is in the public domain, or which the Government has acquired without restriction upon its use and disclosure to others. This policy shall be applied by the Departments in negotiating contract prices for foreign license technical assistance contracts (227.675) or supply contracts with second sources (227.674); and in commenting on such agreements when they are referred to the Department of Defense by the Department of State pursuant to section 414 of the Mutual Security Act of 1954 as amended (22 U.S.C. 1934) and the International Traffic in Arms Regulations (see 227.675).

227.673 Foreign license and technical assistance agreements between the Government and domestic concerns.

(a) Contracts between the Government and a primary source to provide technical assistance or patent rights to a second source for the manufacture of supplies or performance of services shall, to the extent practicable, specify the rights in patents and data and any other rights to be supplied to the second source. Each contract shall provide, in connection with any separate agreement between the primary source and the second source for patent rights or technical assistance relating to the articles or services involved in the contract, that—

(1) The primary source and his subcontractors shall not make, on account of any purchases by the Government or by others with funds derived through the Military Assistance Program or otherwise through the Government, any charge to the second source for royalties or amortization for patents or inventions in which the Government holds a royalty-free license; or data which the Government has the right to possess, use, and disclose to others; or any technical assistance provided to the second source for which the Government has paid under a contract between the Government and the primary source; and

(2) The separate agreement between the primary and second source shall include a statement referring to the contract between the Government and the primary source, and shall conform to the requirements of the International Traffic in Arms Regulations (see 227.675-1).

(b) The following factors, among others, shall be considered in negotiating the price to be paid the primary source under contracts within (a) of this section:

(1) The actual cost of providing data, personnel, manufacturing aids, samples, spare parts, and the like;

(2) The extent to which the Government has contributed to the development of the supplies or services, and to the methods of manufacture or performance, through past contracts for research and development or for manufacture of the supplies or performance of the services; and

(3) The Government's patent rights and rights in data relating to the supplies or services and to the methods of manufacture or of performance.

227.674 Supply contracts between the Government and a foreign government or concern.

In negotiating contract prices with a second source, including the redetermination of contract prices, or in determining the allowability of costs under a cost-reimbursement contract with a second source, the contracting officer:

(a) Shall obtain from the second source a detailed statement (see FAR 27.204-1(a)(2)) of royalties, license fees, and other compensation paid or to be paid to a primary source (or any of his subcontractors) for patent rights, rights in data, and other technical assistance provided to the second source, including identification and description of such patents, data, and technical assistance; and

(b) Shall not accept or allow charges which in effect are—

(1) For royalties or amortization for patents or inventions in which the Government holds a royalty-free license; or

(2) For data which the Government has a right to possess, use, and disclose to others; or

(3) For any technical assistance provided to the second source for which the Government has paid under a contract between the Government and a primary source.

227.675 Foreign license and technical assistance agreements between a domestic concern and a foreign government or concern. (No Text)

227.675-1 International Traffic in Arms Regulations.

Pursuant to section 414 of the Mutual Security Act of 1954, as amended (22 U.S.C. 1934), the Department of State controls the exportation of data relating to articles designated in the United States Munitions List as arms, ammunition, or munitions of war. (The Munitions List and pertinent procedures are set forth in the International Traffic in Arms Regulations, 22 CFR, *et seq.*) Before authorizing such exportation, the Department of State generally requests comments from the Department of Defense. On request of the Office of the Assistant Secretary of Defense (International Security Affairs), each Department shall submit comments thereon as the basis for a Department of Defense reply to the Department of State.

227.675-2 Review of agreements.

(a) In reviewing foreign license and technical assistance agreements between primary and second sources, the Department concerned shall, insofar as its interests are involved, indicate whether the agreement meets the requirements of sections 124.07-124.10 of the International Traffic in Arms Regulations or in what respects it is deficient. Paragraphs (b) through (g) of this subsection provide general guidance.

(b) When it is reasonably anticipated that the Government will purchase from the second source the supplies or services involved in the agreement, or that Military Assistance Program funds will be provided for the procurement of the supplies or services, the following guidance applies.

(1) If the agreement specifies a reduction in charges thereunder, with respect to purchases by or for the Government or by others with funds derived through the Military Assistance Program or otherwise through the Government, in recognition of the Government's rights in patents and data, the Department concerned shall evaluate the amount of the reduction to determine whether it is fair and reasonable in the circumstances, before indicating its approval.

(2) If the agreement does not specify any reduction in charges or otherwise fails to give recognition to the Government's rights in the patents or data involved, approval shall be conditioned upon amendment of the agreement to reflect a reduction, evaluated by the Department concerned as acceptable to the Government, in any charge thereunder with respect to purchases made by or for the Government or by others with funds derived through the Military Assistance Program or otherwise through the Government, in accordance with Section 124.10 of the International Traffic in Arms Regulations.

(3) If the agreement provides that no charge is to be made to the second source for data or patent rights to the extent of the

Government's rights, the Department concerned shall evaluate the acceptability of the provision before indicating its approval.

(4) If time or circumstances do not permit the evaluation called for in (b) (1), (2), or (3) of this subsection, the guidance in (c) of this subsection shall be followed.

(c) When it is not reasonably anticipated that the Government will purchase from the second source the supplies or services involved in the agreement nor that Military Assistance Program funds will be provided for the purchase of the supplies or services, then the following guidance applies.

(1) If the agreement provides for charges to the second source for data or patent rights, it may suffice to fulfill the requirements of Section 124.10 insofar as the Department of Defense is concerned if:

(i) The agreement requires the second source to advise the primary source when he has knowledge of any purchase made or to be made from him by or for the Government or by others with funds derived through the Military Assistance Program or otherwise through the Government;

(ii) The primary source separately agrees with the Government that upon such advice to him from the second source or from the Government or otherwise as to any such purchase or prospective purchase, he will negotiate with the Department concerned an appropriate reduction in his charges to the second source in recognition of any Government rights in patents or data; and

(iii) The agreement between the primary and second sources further provides that in the event of any such purchase and resulting reduction in charges, the second source shall pass on this reduction to the Government by giving the Government a corresponding reduction in the purchase price of the article or service.

(2) If the agreement provides that no charge is to be made to the second source for data or patent rights to the extent to which the Government has rights, the Department concerned shall:

(i) Evaluate the acceptability of the provision before indicating its approval; or

(ii) Explicitly condition its approval on the right to evaluate the acceptability of the provision at a later time.

(d) When there is a technical assistance agreement between the primary source and the Government related to the agreement between the primary and second sources that is under review, the latter agreement shall reflect the arrangements contemplated with respect thereto by the Government's technical assistance agreement with the primary source.

(e) Every agreement shall provide that any license rights transferred under the agreement are subject to existing rights of the Government.

(f) In connection with every agreement referred to in (b) of this section, a request shall be made to the primary source—

(1) To identify the patents, data, and other technical assistance to be provided to the second source by the primary source or any of his subcontractors,

(2) To identify any such patents and data in which, to the knowledge of the primary source, the Government may have rights, and

(3) To segregate the charges made to the second source for each such category or item of patents, data, and other technical assistance.

Reviewing personnel shall verify this information or, where the primary source does not furnish it, obtain such information from Governmental sources so far as practicable.

(g) The Department concerned shall make it clear that its approval of any agreement does not necessarily recognize the propriety of the charges or the amounts thereof, or constitute approval of any of the business arrangements in the agreement, unless the Department expressly intends by its approval to commit itself to the fairness and reasonableness of a particular charge or charges. In any event, a disclaimer should be made to charges or business terms not affecting any purchase made by or for the Government or by others with funds derived through the Military Assistance Program or otherwise through the Government.

227.676 Foreign patent interchange agreements.

(a) Patent interchange agreements between the United States and foreign governments provide for the use of patent rights, compensation, free licenses, and the establishment of committees to review and make recommendations on these matters. The agreements also may exempt the United States from royalty and other payments. The contracting officer shall ensure that royalty payments are consistent with patent interchange agreements.

(b) Assistance with patent rights and royalty payments in the United States European Command (USEUCOM) area of responsibility is available from HQ USEUCOM, ATTN: ECLA, Unit 30400, Box 1000, APO 09128; Telephone: DSN 430-8001/7263, Commercial 49-0711-680-8001/7263; Telefax: 49-0711-680-5732.

[DAC 91-12, 62 FR 34114, 6/24/97, effective 6/24/97; DAC 91-13, 63 FR 11522, 3/9/98, effective 3/9/98]

SUBPART 227.70—INFRINGEMENT CLAIMS, LICENSES, AND ASSIGNMENTS

227.7000 Scope.

This subpart prescribes policy, procedures, and instructions for use of clauses with respect to processing licenses, assignments, and infringement claims.

227.7001 Policy.

Whenever a claim of infringement of privately owned rights in patented inventions or copyrighted works is asserted against any Department or Agency of the Department of Defense, all necessary steps shall be taken to investigate, and to settle administratively, deny, or otherwise dispose of such claim prior to suit against the United States. This subpart 227.70 does not apply to licenses or assignments acquired by the Department of Defense under the Patent Rights clauses.

227.7002 Statutes pertaining to administrative claims of infringement.

Statutes pertaining to administrative claims of infringement in the Department of Defense include the following: the Foreign Assistance Act of 1961, 22 U.S.C. 2356 (formerly the Mutual Security Acts of 1951 and 1954); the Invention Secrecy Act, 35 U.S.C. 181-188; 10 U.S.C. 2386; 28 U.S.C. 1498; and 35 U.S.C. 286.

227.7003 Claims for copyright infringement.

The procedures set forth herein will be followed, where applicable, in copyright infringement claims.

227.7004 Requirements for filing an administrative claim for patent infringement.

(a) A patent infringement claim for compensation, asserted against the United States under any of the applicable statutes cited in 227.7002, must be actually communicated to and received by a Department, agency, organization, office, or field establishment within the Department of Defense. Claims must be in writing and should include the following:

(1) An allegation of infringement;

(2) A request for compensation, either expressed or implied;

(3) A citation of the patent or patents alleged to be infringed;

(4) A sufficient designation of the alleged infringing item or process to permit identification, giving the military or commercial designation, if known, to the claimant;

(5) A designation of at least one claim of each patent alleged to be infringed; or

(6) As an alternative to (a) (4) and (5) of this section, a declaration that the claimant has made a bona fide attempt to determine the item or process which is alleged to infringe, but was unable to do so, giving reasons, and stating a reasonable basis for his belief that his patent or patents are being infringed.

(b) In addition to the information listed in (a) of this section, the following material and information is generally necessary in the course of processing a claim of patent infringement. Claimants are encouraged to furnish this information at the time of filing a claim to permit the most expeditious processing and settlement of the claim.

(1) A copy of the asserted patent(s) and identification of all claims of the patent alleged to be infringed.

(2) Identification of all procurements known to claimant which involve the alleged infringing item or process, including the identity of the vendor or contractor and the Government procuring activity.

(3) A detailed identification of the accused article or process, particularly where the article or process relates to a component or subcomponent of the item procured, an element by element comparison of the representative claims with the accused article or process. If available, this identification should include documentation and drawings to illustrate the accused article or process in suitable detail to enable verification of the infringement comparison.

(4) Names and addresses of all past and present licenses under the patent(s), and copies of all license agreements and releases involving the patent(s).

(5) A brief description of all litigation in which the patent(s) has been or is now involved, and the present status thereof.

(6) A list of all persons to whom notices of infringement have been sent, including all departments and agencies of the Government, and a statement of the ultimate disposition of each.

(7) A description of Government employment or military service, if any, by the inventor and/or patent owner.

(8) A list of all Government contracts under which the inventor, patent owner, or anyone in privity with him performed work relating to the patented subject matter.

(9) Evidence of title to the patent(s) alleged to be infringed or other right to make the claim.

(10) A copy of the Patent Office file of each patent if available to claimant.

(11) Pertinent prior art known to claimant, not contained in the Patent Office file, particularly publications and foreign art.

In addition in the foregoing, if claimant can provide a statement that the investigation may be limited to the specifically identified accused articles or processes, or to a specific procurement, it may materially expedite determination of the claim.

(c) Any department receiving an allegation of patent infringement which meets the requirements of this paragraph shall acknowledge the same and supply the other departments that may have an interest therein with a copy of such communication and the acknowledgment thereof.

(1) For the Department of the Army—Chief, Patents, Copyrights, and Trademarks Division, U.S. Army Legal Services Agency;

(2) For the Department of the Navy—the Patent Counsel for Navy, Office of Naval Research;

(3) For the Department of the Air Force—Chief, Patents Division, Office of the Judge Advocate General;

(4) For the Defense Logistics Agency—the Office of Counsel;

(5) For the National Security Agency—the General Counsel;

(6) For the Defense Information Systems Agency—the Counsel;

(7) For the Defense Threat Reduction Agency—the General Counsel; and

(8) For the National Geospatial-Intelligence Agency—the Counsel.

(d) If a communication alleging patent infringement is received which does not meet the requirements set forth in paragraph (c) of this section, the sender shall be advised in writing—

(1) That his claim for infringement has not been satisfactorily presented, and

(2) Of the elements considered necessary to establish a claim.

(e) A communication making a proffer of a license in which no infringement is alleged shall not be considered as a claim for infringement.

[DAC 91-1, 56 FR 67216, 12/30/91, effective 12/31/91; DAC 91-11, 61 FR 50446, 9/26/96, effective 9/26/96; Final rule, 62 FR 2612, 1/17/97, effective 1/17/97; Final rule, 64 FR 51074, 9/21/99, effective 9/21/99; Final rule, 74 FR 42779, 8/25/2009, effective

8/25/2009; Final rule, 76 FR 3536, 1/20/2011, effective 1/20/2011]

227.7005 Indirect notice of patent infringement claims.

(a) A communication by a patent owner to a Department of Defense contractor alleging that the contractor has committed acts of infringement in performance of a Government contract shall not be considered a claim within the meaning of 227.7004 until it meets the requirements specified therein.

(b) Any Department receiving an allegation of patent infringement which meets the requirements of 227.7004 shall acknowledge the same and supply the other Departments (see 227.7004(c)) which may have an interest therein with a copy of such communication and the acknowledgment thereof.

(c) If a communication covering an infringement claim or notice which does not meet the requirements of 227.7004(a) is received from a contractor, the patent owner shall be advised in writing as covered by the instructions of 227.7004(d).

227.7006 Investigation and administrative disposition of claims.

An investigation and administrative determination (denial or settlement) of each claim shall be made in accordance with instructions and procedures established by each Department, subject to the following:

(a) When the procurement responsibility for the alleged infringing item or process is assigned to a single Department or only one Department is the purchaser of the alleged infringing item or process, and the funds of that Department only are to be charged in the settlement of the claim, that Department shall have the sole responsibility for the investigation and administrative determination of the claim and for the execution of any agreement in settlement of the claim. Where, however, funds of another Department are to be charged, in whole or in part, the approval of such Department shall be obtained as required by 208.7002. Any agreement in settlement of the claim, approved pursuant to 208.7002 shall be executed by each of the Departments concerned.

(b) When two or more Departments are the respective purchasers of alleged infringing items or processes and the funds of those Departments are to be charged in the settlement of the claim, the investigation and administrative determination shall be the responsibility of the Department having the predominant financial interest in the claim or of the Department or Departments as jointly agreed upon by the Departments concerned. The Department responsible for negotiation shall, throughout the negotiation, coordinate with the other Departments concerned and keep them advised of the status of the negotiation. Any agreement in the settlement of the claim shall be executed by each Department concerned.

227.7007 Notification and disclosure to claimants.

When a claim is denied, the Department responsible for the administrative determination of the claim shall so notify the claimant or his authorized representative and provide the claimant a reasonable rationale of the basis for denying the claim. Disclosure of information or the rationale referred to above shall be subject to applicable statutes, regulations, and directives pertaining to security, access to official records, and the rights of others.

227.7008 Settlement of indemnified claims.

Settlement of claims involving payment for past infringement shall not be made without the consent of, and equitable contribution by, each indemnifying contractor involved, unless such settlement is determined to be in the best interests of the Government and is coordinated with the Department of Justice with a view to preserving any rights of the Government against the contractors involved. If consent of and equitable contribution by the contractors are obtained, the settlement need not be coordinated with the Department of Justice.

227.7009 Patent releases, license agreements, and assignments.

This section contains clauses for use in patent release and settlement agreements, license agreements, and assignments, executed by the Government, under which the Government acquires rights. Minor modifications of language (*e.g.*, pluralization of “Secretary” or “Contracting Officer”) in multi-departmental agreements may be made if necessary.

227.7009-1 Required clauses.

(a) Covenant Against Contingent Fees. Insert the clause at FAR 52.203-5.

(b) Gratuities. Insert the clause at FAR 52.203-3.

(c) Assignment of Claims. Insert the clause at FAR 52.232-23.

(d) Disputes. Pursuant to FAR Subpart 33.2, insert the clause at FAR 52.233-1.

(e) Non-Estoppel. Insert the clause at 252.227-7000.

[DAC 91-11, 61 FR 50446, 9/26/96, effective 9/26/96]

227.7009-2 Clauses to be used when applicable.

(a) *Release of past infringement.* The clause at 252.227-7001, Release of Past Infringement, is an example which may be modified or omitted as appropriate for particular circumstances, but only upon the advice of cognizant patent or legal counsel. (See footnotes at end of clause.)

(b) *Readjustment of payments.* The clause at 252.227-7002, Readjustment of Payments, shall be inserted in contracts providing for payment of a running royalty.

(c) *Termination.* The clause at 252.227-7003, Termination, is an example for use in contracts providing for the payment of a running royalty. This clause may be modified or omitted as appropriate for particular circumstances, but only upon the advice of cognizant patent or legal counsel (see 227.7004(c)).

227.7009-3 Additional clauses—contracts except running royalty contracts.

The following clauses are examples for use in patent release and settlement agreements, and license agreements not providing for payment by the Government of a running royalty.

(a) *License Grant.* Insert the clause at 252.227-7004.

(b) *License Term.* Insert one of the clauses at 252.227-7005 Alternate I or Alternate II, as appropriate.

227.7009-4 Additional clauses—contracts providing for payment of a running royalty.

The clauses set forth below are examples which may be used in patent release and settlement agreements, and license agreements, when it is desired to cover the subject matter thereof and the contract provides for payment of a running royalty.

(a) *License grant—running royalty.* No Department shall be obligated to pay royalties unless the contract is signed on behalf of such Department. Accordingly, the License Grant clause at 252.227-7006 should be limited to the practice of the invention by or for the signatory Department or Departments.

(b) *License term—running royalty.* The clause at 252.227-7007 is a sample form for expressing the license term.

(c) *Computation of royalties.* The clause at 252.227-7008 providing for the computation of royalties, may be of varying scope depending upon the nature of the royalty bearing article, the volume of procurement, and the type of contract pursuant to which the procurement is to be accomplished.

(d) *Reporting and payment of royalties.* (1) The contract should contain a provision specifying the office designated within the specific Department involved to make any necessary reports to the contractor of the extent of use of the licensed subject matter by the entire Department, and such office shall be charged with the responsibility of obtaining from all procuring offices of that Department the information necessary to make the required reports and corresponding vouchers necessary to make the required payments. The clause at 252.227-7009 is a sample for expressing reporting and payment of royalties requirements.

(2) Where more than one Department or Government Agency is licensed and there is a ceiling on the royalties payable in any reporting period, the licensing Departments or

Agencies shall coordinate with respect to the pro rata share of royalties to be paid by each.

(e) *License to other government agencies.* When it is intended that a license on the same terms and conditions be available to other departments and agencies of the Government, the clause at 252.227-7010 is an example which may be used.

227.7010 Assignments.

(a) The clause at 252.227-7011 is an example which may be used in contracts of assignment of patent rights to the Government.

(b) To facilitate proof of contracts of assignments, the acknowledgment of the contractor should be executed before a notary public or other officer authorized to administer oaths (35 U.S.C. 261).

227.7011 Procurement of rights in inventions, patents, and copyrights.

Even though no infringement has occurred or been alleged, it is the policy of the Department of Defense to procure rights under patents, patent applications, and copyrights whenever it is in the Government's interest to do so and the desired rights can be obtained at a fair price. The required and suggested clauses at 252.227-7004 and 252.227-7010 shall be required and suggested clauses, respectively, for license agreements and assignments made under this paragraph. The instructions at 227.7009-3 and 227.7010 concerning the applicability and use of those clauses shall be followed insofar as they are pertinent.

227.7012 Contract format.

The format at 252.227-7012 appropriately modified where necessary, may be used for contracts of release, license, or assignment.

227.7013 Recordation.

Executive Order No. 9424 of 18 February 1944 requires all executive Departments and agencies of the Government to forward through appropriate channels to the Commissioner of Patents and Trademarks, for recording, all Government interests in patents or applications for patents.

SUBPART 227.71—RIGHTS IN TECHNICAL DATA

227.7100 Scope of subpart.

This subpart—

(a) Prescribes policies and procedures for the acquisition of technical data and the rights to use, modify, reproduce, release, perform, display, or disclose technical data. It implements requirements in the following laws and Executive Order:

(1) 10 U.S.C. 2302(4).

(2) 10 U.S.C. 2305 (subsection (d)(4)).

(3) 10 U.S.C. 2320.

(4) 10 U.S.C. 2321.

(5) 10 U.S.C. 2325.

(6) 10 U.S.C. 7317.

(7) 17 U.S.C. 1301, *et seq.*

(8) Pub. L. 103-355.

(9) Executive Order 12591 (Subsection 1(b)(6)).

(b) Does not apply to—

(1) Computer software or technical data that is computer software documentation (see subpart 227.72); or

(2) Releases of technical data to litigation support contractors (see subpart 204.74).

[DAC 91-8, 60 FR 33464, 6/28/95, effective 6/30/95; Interim rule, 74 FR 61043, 11/23/2009, effective 11/23/2009; Final rule, 75 FR 54527, 9/8/2010, effective 9/8/2010; Interim rule, 79 FR 11337, 2/28/2014, effective 2/28/2014; Interim rule, 81 FR 28724, 5/10/2016, effective 5/10/2016]

227.7101 Definitions.

(a) As used in this subpart, unless otherwise specifically indicated, the terms *offeror* and *contractor* include an offeror's or contractor's subcontractors, suppliers, or potential subcontractors or suppliers at any tier.

(b) Other terms used in this subpart are defined in the clause at 252.227-7013, Rights in Technical Data—Noncommercial Items.

[DAC 91-8, 60 FR 33464, 6/28/95, effective 6/30/95; DAC 91-9, 60 FR 61586, 11/30/95, effective 11/30/95]

227.7102 Commercial items, components, or processes. (No Text)

[DAC 91-8, 60 FR 33464, 6/28/95, effective 6/30/95; Final rule, 76 FR 58144, 9/20/2011, effective 9/20/2011]

227.7102-1 Policy.

(a) DoD shall acquire only the technical data customarily provided to the public with a commercial item or process, except technical data that—

(1) Are form, fit, or function data;

(2) Are required for repair or maintenance of commercial items or processes, or for the proper installation, operating, or handling of a commercial item, either as a stand alone unit or as a part of a military system, when such data are not customarily provided to commercial users or the data provided to commercial users is not sufficient for military purposes; or

(3) Describe the modifications made at Government expense to a commercial item or process in order to meet the requirements of a Government solicitation.

(b) To encourage offerors and contractors to offer or use commercial products to satisfy military requirements, offerors, and contractors shall not be required, except for the technical data described in paragraph (a) of this subsection, to—

(1) Furnish technical information related to commercial items or processes that is not customarily provided to the public; or

(2) Relinquish to, or otherwise provide, the Government rights to use, modify, reproduce, release, perform, display, or disclose technical data pertaining to commercial items or processes except for a transfer of rights mutually agreed upon.

(c) The Government's rights in a vessel design, and in any useful article embodying a vessel design, must be consistent with the Government's rights in technical data pertaining to the design (10 U.S.C. 7317; 17 U.S.C. 1301(a)(3)).

[DAC 91-8, 60 FR 33464, 6/28/95, effective 6/30/95; Interim rule, 74 FR 61043, 11/23/2009, effective 11/23/2009; Final rule, 75 FR 54527, 9/8/2010, effective 9/8/2010; CFR Correction, 77 FR 59339, 9/27/2012]

227.7102-2 Rights in technical data.

(a) The clause at 252.227-7015, Technical Data—Commercial Items, provides the Government specific license rights in technical data pertaining to commercial items or processes. DoD may use, modify, reproduce, release, perform, display, or disclose data only within the Government. The data may not be used to manufacture additional quantities of the commercial items and, except for emergency repair or overhaul and for covered Government support contractors, may not be released or disclosed to, or used by, third parties without the contractor's written permission. Those restrictions do not apply to the technical data described in 227.7102-1(a).

(2) Use the clause at 252.227-7015 with its Alternate I in contracts for the development or delivery of a vessel design or any useful article embodying a vessel design.

(b) If additional rights are needed, contracting activities must negotiate with the contractor to determine if there are acceptable terms for transferring such rights. The specific additional rights granted to the Government shall be enumerated in a license agreement made part of the contract.

[DAC 91-8, 60 FR 33464, 6/28/95, effective 6/30/95; Interim rule, 74 FR 61043, 11/23/2009, effective 11/23/2009; Interim rule, 76 FR 11363, 3/2/2011, effective 3/2/2011; Final rule, 78 FR 30233, 5/22/2013, effective 5/22/2013]

227.7102-3 Government right to review, verify, challenge and validate asserted restrictions.

Follow the procedures at 227.7103-13 and the clause at 252.227-7037, Validation of Restrictive Markings on Technical Data, regarding the validation of asserted restrictions on technical data related to commercial items.

[Final rule, 76 FR 58144, 9/20/2011, effective 9/20/2011]

227.7102-4 Contract clauses.

(a)(1) Except as provided in paragraph (b) of this subsection, use the clause at 252.227-7015, Technical Data-Commercial Items, in all solicitations and contracts, including solicitations and contracts using FAR part 12 procedures for the acquisition of commercial items, when the Contractor will be required to deliver technical data pertaining to commercial items, components, or processes.

(2) Use the clause at 252.227-7015 with its Alternate I in solicitations and contracts, including solicitations and contracts using FAR part 12 procedures for the acquisition of commercial items, for the development or delivery of a vessel design or any useful article embodying a vessel design.

(b) In accordance with the clause prescription at 227.7103-6(a), use the clause at 252.227-7013, Rights in Technical Data-Noncommercial Items, in addition to the clause at 252.227-7015, if the Government will have paid for any portion of the development costs of a commercial item. The clause at 252.227-7013 will govern the technical data pertaining to any portion of a commercial item that was developed in any part at Government expense, and the clause at 252.227-7015 will govern the technical data pertaining to any portion of a commercial item that was developed exclusively at private expense.

(c) Use the clause at 252.227-7037, Validation of Restrictive Markings on Technical Data, in solicitations and contracts using FAR part 12 procedures for the acquisition of commercial items that include the clause at 252.227-7015 or the clause at 252.227-7013.

[DAC 91-8, 60 FR 33464, 6/28/95, effective 6/30/95; DAC 91-9, 60 FR 61586, 11/30/95, effective 11/30/95; Interim rule, 74 FR 61043, 11/23/2009, effective 11/23/2009; Final rule, 75 FR 54527, 9/8/2010, effective 9/8/2010; Final rule, 76 FR 58144, 9/20/2011, effective 9/20/2011; Final rule 78 FR 37980, 6/25/2013, effective 6/25/2013]

227.7103 Noncommercial items or processes. (No Text)

227.7103-1 Policy.

(a) DoD policy is to acquire only the technical data, and the rights in that data, necessary to satisfy agency needs.

(b) Solicitations and contracts shall—

(1) Specify the technical data to be delivered under a contract and delivery schedules for the data;

(2) Establish or reference procedures for determining the acceptability of technical data;

(3) Establish separate contract line items, to the extent practicable, for the technical data to be delivered under a contract and require offerors and contractors to price separately each deliverable data item; and

(4) Require offerors to identify, to the extent practicable, technical data to be furnished with restrictions on the Government's rights and require contractors to identify technical data to be delivered with such restrictions prior to delivery.

(c) Offerors shall not be required, either as a condition of being responsive to a solicitation or as a condition for award, to sell or otherwise relinquish to the Government any rights in technical data related to items, components or processes developed at private expense except for the data identified at 227.7103-5(a)(2) and (a)(4) through (9).

(d) Offerors and contractors shall not be prohibited or discouraged from furnishing or offering to furnish items, components, or processes developed at private expense solely because the Government's rights to use, modify, release, reproduce, perform, display, or disclose technical data pertaining to those items may be restricted.

(e) As provided in 10 U.S.C. 2305, solicitations for major systems development contracts shall not require offerors to submit proposals that would permit the Government to acquire competitively items identical to items developed at private expense unless a determination is made at a level above the contracting officer that—

(1) The offeror will not be able to satisfy program schedule or delivery requirements; or

(2) The offeror's proposal to meet mobilization requirements does not satisfy mobilization needs.

(f) For acquisitions involving major weapon systems or subsystems of major weapon systems, the acquisition plan shall address acquisition strategies that provide for technical data and the associated license rights in accordance with 207.106(S-70).

(g) The Government's rights in a vessel design, and in any useful article embodying a vessel design, must be consistent with the Government's rights in technical data pertaining to the design (10 U.S.C. 7317; 17 U.S.C. 1301(a)(3)).

[DAC 91-8, 60 FR 33464, 6/28/95, effective 6/30/95; Interim rule, 72 FR 51188, 9/6/2007, effective 9/6/2007; Interim rule, 74 FR 61043, 11/23/2009, effective 11/23/2009; Final rule, 74 FR 68699, 12/29/2009, effective 12/29/2009; Final rule, 75 FR 54527, 9/8/2010, effective 9/8/2010]

227.7103-2 Acquisition of technical data.

(a) Contracting officers shall work closely with data managers and requirements personnel to assure that data requirements included in solicitations are consistent with the policy expressed in 227.7103-1.

(b)(1) Data managers or other requirements personnel are responsible for identifying the Government's minimum needs for technical data. Data needs must be established giving consideration to the contractor's economic interests in data pertaining to items, components, or processes that have been developed at private expense; the Government's costs to acquire, maintain, store, retrieve, and protect the data; reprocurement needs; repair, maintenance and overhaul philosophies; spare and repair part considerations; and whether procurement of the items, components, or processes can be accomplished on a form, fit, or function basis. When it is anticipated that the Government will obtain unlimited or government purpose rights in technical data that will be required for competitive spare or repair parts procurements, such data should be identified as deliverable data items. Reprocurement needs may not be a sufficient reason to acquire detailed manufacturing or process data when items or components can be acquired using performance specifications, form, fit and function data, or when there are a sufficient number of alternate sources which can reasonably be expected to provide such items on a performance specification or form, fit, or function basis.

(2) When reviewing offers received in response to a solicitation or other request for data, data managers must balance the original assessment of the Government's data needs with data prices contained in the offer.

(c) Contracting officers are responsible for ensuring that, wherever practicable, solicitations and contracts—

(1) Identify the type and quantity of the technical data to be delivered under the contract and the format and media in which the data will be delivered;

(2) Establish each deliverable data item as a separate contract line item (this requirement may be satisfied by listing each deliverable data item on an exhibit to the contract);

(3) Identify the prices established for each deliverable data item under a fixed-price type contract;

(4) Include delivery schedules and acceptance criteria for each deliverable data item; and

(5) Specifically identify the place of delivery for each deliverable item of technical data.

[DAC 91-8, 60 FR 33464, 6/28/95, effective 6/30/95]

227.7103-3 Early identification of technical data to be furnished to the Government with restrictions on use, reproduction or disclosure.

(a) 10 U.S.C. 2320 requires, to the maximum extent practicable, an identification prior to delivery of any technical data to be delivered to the Government with restrictions on use.

(b) Use the provision at 252.227-7017, Identification and Assertion of Use, Release, or Disclosure Restrictions, in all solicitations that include the clause at 252.227-7013, Rights in Technical Data—Noncommercial Items. The provision requires offerors to identify any technical data for which restrictions, other than copyright, on use, release, or disclosure are asserted and to attach the identification and assertions to the offer.

(c) Subsequent to contract award, the clause at 252.227-7013 permits a contractor, under certain conditions, to make additional assertions of use, release, or disclosure restrictions. The prescription for the use of that clause and its alternate is at 227.7103-6 (a) and (b).

[DAC 91-8, 60 FR 33464, 6/28/95, effective 6/30/95; Final rule 78 FR 13543, 2/28/2013, effective 2/28/2013]

227.7103-4 License rights.

(a) *Grant of license.* The Government obtains rights in technical data, including a copyright license, under an irrevocable license granted or obtained for the Government by the contractor. The contractor or licensor retains all rights in the data not granted to the Government. For technical data that pertain to items, components, or processes, the scope of the license is generally determined by the source of funds used to develop the item, component, or process. When the technical data do not pertain to items, components, or processes, the scope of the license is determined by the source of funds used to create the data.

(1) *Technical data pertaining to items, components, or processes.* Contractors or licensors may, with some exceptions (see 227.7103-5(a)(2) and (a)(4) through (9)), restrict the Government's rights to use, modify, release, reproduce, perform, display or disclose technical data pertaining to items, components, or processes developed exclusively at private expense (limited rights). They may not restrict the Government's rights in items, components, or processes developed exclusively at Government expense (unlimited rights) without the Government's approval. When an item, component, or process is developed with mixed funding, the Government may use, modify, release, reproduce, perform, display or disclose the data pertaining to such items, components, or processes within the Government without restriction but may release or disclose the data outside the Government only for government purposes (government purpose rights).

(2) *Technical data that do not pertain to items, components, or processes.* Technical data may be created during the performance of a contract for a conceptual design or similar effort that does not require the development, manufacture, construction, or production of items, components or processes. The Government generally obtains unlimited rights in such data when the data were created exclusively with Government funds, government purpose rights when the data were created with mixed funding, and limited rights when the data were created exclusively at private expense.

(b) *Source of funds determination.* The determination of the source of development funds for technical data pertaining to items, components, or processes should be made at any practical sub-item or subcomponent level or for any segregable portion of a process. Contractors may assert limited rights in a segregable sub-item, subcomponent, or portion of a process which otherwise qualifies for limited rights under the clause at 252.227-7013, Rights in Technical Data—Noncommercial Items.

[DAC 91-8, 60 FR 33464, 6/28/95, effective 6/30/95]

227.7103-5 Government rights.

The standard license rights that a licensor grants to the Government are unlimited rights, government purpose rights, or limited rights. Those rights are defined in the clause at 252.227-7013, Rights in Technical Data—Noncommercial Items. In unusual situations, the standards rights may not satisfy the Government's needs or the Government may be willing to accept lesser rights in data in return for other consideration. In those cases, a special license may be negotiated. However, the licensor is not obligated to provide the Government greater rights and the contracting officer is not required to accept lesser rights than the rights provided in the standard grant of license. The situations under which a particular grant of license applies are enumerated in paragraphs (a) through (d) of this subsection.

(a) *Unlimited rights.* The Government obtains unlimited rights in technical data that are—

(1) Data pertaining to an item, component, or process which has been or will be developed exclusively with Government funds;

(2) Studies, analyses, test data, or similar data produced in the performance of a contract when the study, analysis, test, or similar work was specified as an element of performance;

(3) Created exclusively with Government funds in the performance of a contract that does not require the development, manufacture, construction, or production of items, components, or processes;

(4) Form, fit, and function data;

(5) Necessary for installation, operation, maintenance, or training purposes (other than detailed manufacturing or process data);

(6) Corrections or changes to technical data furnished to the contractor by the Government;

(7) Publicly available or have been released or disclosed by the contractor or subcontractor without restrictions on further use, release or disclosure other than a release or disclosure resulting from the sale, transfer, or other assignment of interest in the software to another party or the sale or transfer of some or all of a business entity or its assets to another party;

(8) Data in which the Government has obtained unlimited rights under another Government contract or as a result of negotiations; or

(9) Data furnished to the Governme[...] under a Government contract or subcontra[...] thereunder, with—

(i) Government purpose license rights or limited rights and the restrictive condition(s) has/have expired; or

(ii) Government purpose rights and the contractor's exclusive right to use such data for commercial purposes has expired.

(b) *Government purpose rights.* (1) The Government obtains government purpose rights in technical data—

(i) That pertain to items, components, or processes developed with mixed funding except when the Government is entitled to unlimited rights as provided in paragraphs (a)(2) and (a)(4) through (9) of this subsection; or

(ii) Created with mixed funding in the performance of a contract that does not require the development, manufacture, construction, or production of items, components, or processes.

(2) The period during which government purpose rights are effective is negotiable. The clause at 252.227-7013 provides a nominal five-year period. Either party may request a different period. Changes to the government purpose rights period may be made at any time prior to delivery of the technical data without consideration from either party. Longer periods should be negotiated when a five-year period does not provide sufficient time to apply the data for commercial purposes or when necessary to recognize subcontractors' interests in the data.

(3) The government purpose rights period commences upon execution of the contract, subcontract, letter contract (or similar contractual instrument), contract modification, or option exercise that required the development. Upon expiration of the Government rights period, the Government has unlimited rights in the data including the right to authorize others to use the data for commercial purposes.

(4) Durin[...] purpose rights pe[...]ot use, or au-[...]chnical data [...]e rights leg-[...]he Govern-[...]se data in [...] rights to [...]o do so, [...] or disclosure, the in-[...]pient is subject to the use and n[...]disclosure agreement at 227.7103-7; or

N41756-11-C-3894
RAYTHEON BLACKBIRD TECHNOLOGIES, INC
PROJECT: "LIGHTHOUSE"

(ii) The intended recipient is a Government contractor receiving access to the data for performance of a Government contract that contains the clause at 252.227-7025, Limitations on the Use or Disclosure of Government-Furnished Information Marked with Restrictive Legends.

(5) When technical data marked with government purpose rights legends will be released or disclosed to a Government contractor performing a contract that does not include the clause at 252.227-7025, the contract may be modified, prior to release or disclosure, to include that clause in lieu of requiring the contractor to complete a use and non-disclosure agreement.

(6) Contracting activities shall establish procedures to assure that technical data marked with government purpose rights legends are released or disclosed, including a release or disclosure through a Government solicitation, only to persons subject to the use and nondisclosure restrictions. Public announcements in the Commerce Business Daily or other publications must provide notice of the use and nondisclosure requirements. Class use and non-disclosure agreements (*e.g.*, agreements covering all solicitations received by the XYZ company within a reasonable period) are authorized and may be obtained at any time prior to release or disclosure of the government purpose rights data. Documents transmitting government purpose rights data to persons under class agreements shall identify the technical data subject to government purpose rights and the class agreement under which such data are provided.

(c) *Limited rights*. (1) The Government obtains limited rights in technical data—

(i) That pertain to items, components, or processes developed exclusively at private expense except when the Government is entitled to unlimited rights as provided in paragraphs (a)(2) and (a)(4) through (9) of this subsection; or

(ii) Created exclusively at private expense in the performance of a contract that does not require the development, manufacture, construction, or production of items, components, or processes.

(2) Data in which the Government has limited rights may not be used, released, or disclosed outside the Government without the permission of the contractor asserting the restriction except for a use, release, or disclosure that is—

(i) Necessary for emergency repair and overhaul; or

(ii) To a covered Government support contractor; or

(iii) To a foreign government, other than detailed manufacturing or process data, when use, release, or disclosure is in the interest of the United States and is required for evaluational or informational purposes.

(3) The person asserting limited rights must be notified of the Government's intent to release, disclose, or authorize others to use such data prior to release or disclosure of the data except notification of an intended release, disclosure, or use for emergency repair or overhaul which shall be made as soon as practicable.

(4) When the person asserting limited rights permits the Government to release, disclose, or have others use the data subject to restrictions on further use, release, or disclosure, or for a release under paragraph (c)(2)(i), (ii), or (iii) of this subsection, the intended recipient must complete the use and non-disclosure agreement at 227.7103-7, or receive the data for performance of a Government contract that contains the clause at 252.227-7025, Limitations on the Use or Disclosure of Government-Furnished Information Marked with Restrictive Legends, prior to release or disclosure of the limited rights data.

(d) *Specifically negotiated license rights*. (1) Negotiate specific licenses when the parties agree to modify the standard license rights granted to the government or when the government wants to obtain rights in data in which it does not have rights. When negotiating to obtain, relinquish, or increase the Government's rights in technical data, consider the acquisition strategy for the item, component, or process, including logistics support and other factors which may have relevance for a particular procurement. The Government may accept lesser rights when it has unlimited or government purpose rights in data but may not accept less than limited rights in such data. The negotiated license rights must stipulate what rights the Government has to release or disclose the data to other persons or to authorize others to use the data. Identify all negotiated rights in a license agreement made part of the contract.

(2) When the Government needs additional rights in data acquired with government purpose or limited rights, the contracting officer must negotiate with the contractor to determine whether there are acceptable terms for transferring such rights. Generally, such negotiations should be conducted only when there is a need to disclose the data outside the Government or if the additional rights are required for competitive reprocurement and the anticipated savings expected to be obtained through competition are estimated to exceed the acquisition cost of the additional rights. Prior to negotiating for additional rights in limited rights data, consider alternatives such as—

(i) Using performance specifications and form, fit, and function data to acquire or develop functionally equivalent items, components, or processes;

(ii) Obtaining a contractor's contractual commitment to qualify additional sources and maintain adequate competition among the sources; or

(iii) Reverse engineering, or providing items from Government inventories to contractors who request the items to facilitate the development of equivalent items through reverse engineering.

[DAC 91-8, 60 FR 33464, 6/28/95, effective 6/30/95; Interim rule, 76 FR 11363, 3/2/2011, effective 3/2/2011; Final rule, 78 FR 30233, 5/22/2013, effective 5/22/2013]

227.7103-6 Contract clauses.

(a) Use the clause at 252.227-7013, Rights in Technical Data—Noncommercial Items, in solicitations and contracts, including solicitations and contracts using FAR part 12 procedures for the acquisition of commercial items, when the successful offeror(s) will be required to deliver to the Government technical data pertaining to noncommercial items, or pertaining to commercial items for which the Government will have paid for any portion of the development costs (in which case the clause at 252.227-7013 will govern the technical data pertaining to any portion of a commercial item that was developed in any part at Government expense, and the clause at 252.227-7015 will govern the technical data pertaining to any portion of a commercial item that was developed exclusively at private expense). Do not use the clause when the only deliverable items are computer software or computer software documentation (see 227.72), commercial items developed exclusively at private expense (see DFARS 227.7102-4), existing works (see 227.7105), special works (see 227.7106), or when contracting under the Small Business Innovation Research Program (see 227.7104). Except as provided in 227.7107-2, do not use the clause in architect-engineer and construction contracts.

(b) (1) Use the clause at 252.227-7013 with its Alternate I in research solicitations and contracts, including research solicitations and contracts using FAR part 12 procedures for the acquisition of commercial items, when the contracting officer determines, in consultation with counsel, that public dissemination by the contractor would be—

(i) In the interest of the government; and

(ii) Facilitated by the Government relinquishing its right to publish the work for sale, or to have others publish the work for sale on behalf of the Government.

(2) Use the clause at 252.227-7013 with its Alternate II in solicitations and contracts, including solicitations and contracts using FAR part 12 procedures for the acquisition of commercial items, that are for the development or delivery of a vessel design or any useful article embodying a vessel design.

(c) Use the clause at 252.227-7025, Limitations on the Use or Disclosure of Government Furnished Information Marked with Restrictive Legends, in solicitations and contracts when it is anticipated that the Government will provide the contractor (other than a litigation support contractor covered by 252.204-7014), for performance of its contract, technical data marked with another contractor's restrictive legend(s).

(d) Use the provision at 252.227-7028, Technical Data or Computer Software Previously Delivered to the Government, in solicitations when the resulting contract will require the contractor to deliver technical data. The provision requires offerors to identify any technical data specified in the solicitations as deliverable data items that are the same or substantially the same as data items the offeror has delivered or is obligated to deliver, either as a contractor or subcontractor, under any other federal agency contract.

(e) Use the following clauses in solicitations and contracts that include the clause at 252.227-7013:

(1) 252.227-7016, Rights in Bid or Proposal Information;

(2) 252.227-7030, Technical Data—Withholding of Payment; and

(3) 252.227-7037, Validation of Restrictive Markings on Technical Data (paragraph (e) of the clause contains information that must be included in a challenge).

[DAC 91-8, 60 FR 33464, 6/28/95, effective 6/30/95, corrected, 60 FR 41157, 8/11/95; DAC 91-9, 60 FR 61586, 11/30/95, effective 11/30/95; Final rule, 62 FR 2612, 1/17/97, effective 1/17/97; Interim rule, 69 FR 31911, 6/8/2004, effective 6/8/2004; Final rule, 69 FR 67856, 11/22/2004, effective 11/22/2004; Interim rule, 74 FR 61043, 11/23/2009, effective 11/23/2009; Final rule, 75 FR 54527, 9/8/2010, effective 9/8/2010; Final rule, 76 FR 58144, 9/20/2011, effective 9/20/2011; Final rule 78 FR 37980, 6/25/2013, effective 6/25/2013; Interim rule, 79 FR 11337, 2/28/2014, effective 2/28/2014; Interim rule, 81 FR 28724, 5/10/2016, effective 5/10/2016]

227.7103-7 Use and non-disclosure agreement.

(a) Except as provided in paragraph (b) of this subsection, technical data or computer software delivered to the Government with restrictions on use, modification, reproduction, release, performance, display, or disclosure may not be provided to third parties unless the intended recipient completes and signs the use and non-disclosure agreement at paragraph (c) of this subsection prior to release, or disclosure of the data.

(1) The specific conditions under which an intended recipient will be authorized to use, modify, reproduce, release, perform, display, or disclose technical data subject to limited rights or computer software subject to restricted rights must be stipulated in an attachment to the use and non-disclosure agreement.

(2) For an intended release, disclosure, or authorized use of technical data or computer software subject to special license rights, modify paragraph (1)(d) of the use and non-disclosure agreement to enter the conditions, consistent with the license requirements, governing the recipient's obligations regarding use, modification, reproduction, release, performance, display or disclosure of the data or software.

(b) The requirement for use and non-disclosure agreements does not apply to Government contractors which require access to a third party's data or software for the performance of a Government contract that contains the clause at 252.227-7025, Limitations on the Use or Disclosure of Government-Furnished Information Marked with Restrictive Legends.

(c) The prescribed use and non-disclosure agreement is:

Use and Non-Disclosure Agreement

The undersigned, ___ (Insert Name) ___, an authorized representative of the ___ (Insert Company Name) ___, (which is hereinafter referred to as the "Recipient") requests the Government to provide the Recipient with technical data or computer software (hereinafter referred to as "Data") in which the Government's use, modification, reproduction, release, performance, display or disclosure rights are restricted. Those Data are identified in an attachment to this Agreement. In consideration for receiving such Data, the Recipient agrees to use the Data strictly in accordance with this Agreement:

(1) The Recipient shall—

(a) Use, modify, reproduce, release, perform, display, or disclose Data marked with government purpose rights or SBIR data rights legends only for government purposes and shall not do so for any commercial purpose. The Recipient shall not release, perform, display, or disclose these Data, without the express written permission of the contractor whose name appears in the restrictive legend (the "Contractor"), to any person other than its subcontractors or suppliers, or prospective subcontractors or suppliers, who require these Data to submit offers for, or perform, contracts with the Recipient. The Recipient shall require its subcontractors or suppliers, or prospective subcontractors or suppliers, to sign a use and non-disclosure agreement prior to disclosing or releasing these Data to such persons. Such agreement must be consistent with the terms of this agreement.

(b) Use, modify, reproduce, release, perform, display, or disclose technical data marked with limited rights legends only as specified in the attachment to this Agreement. Release, performance, display, or disclosure to other persons is not authorized unless specified in the attachment to this Agreement or expressly permitted in writing by the Contractor. The Recipient shall promptly notify the Contractor of the execution of this Agreement and identify the Contractor's Data that has been or will be provided to the Recipient, the date and place the Data were or will be received, and the name and address of the Government office that has provided or will provide the Data.

(c) Use computer software marked with restricted rights legends only in performance of Contract Number ___ (insert contract number(s)) ___. The recipient shall not, for example, enhance, decompile, disassemble, or reverse engineer the software; time share, or use a computer program with more than one computer at a time. The recipient may not release, perform, display, or disclose such software to others unless expressly permitted in writing by the licensor whose name appears in the restrictive legend. The Recipient shall promptly notify the software licensor of the execution of this Agreement and identify the software that has been or will be provided to the Recipient, the date and place the software were or will be received, and the name and address of the Government office that has provided or will provide the software.

(d) Use, modify, reproduce, release, perform, display, or disclose Data marked with special license rights legends (To be completed by the contracting officer. See 227.7103-7(a)(2). Omit if none of the Data requested is marked with special license rights legends).

(2) The Recipient agrees to adopt or establish operating procedures and physical security measures designed to protect these Data from inadvertent release, or disclosure to unauthorized third parties.

(3) The Recipient agrees to accept these Data "as is" without any Government representation as to suitability for intended use or warranty whatsoever. This disclaimer does not affect any obligation the Government may have regarding Data specified in a contract for the performance of that contract.

(4) The Recipient may enter into any agreement directly with the Contractor with respect to the use, modification, reproduction, release, performance, display, or disclosure of these Data.

(5) The Recipient agrees to indemnify and hold harmless the Government, its agents, and employees from every claim or liability, including attorneys fees, court costs, and expenses arising out of, or in any way related to, the misuse or unauthorized modification, reproduction, release, performance, display, or disclosure of Data received from the Government with restrictive legends by the Recipient or any person to whom the Recipient has released or disclosed the Data.

(6) The Recipient is executing this Agreement for the benefit of the Contractor. The Contractor is a third party beneficiary of this Agreement who, in addition to any other rights it may have, is intended to have the rights of direct action against the Recipient or any other person to whom the Recipient has released or disclosed the Data, to seek damages from any breach of this Agreement or to otherwise enforce this Agreement.

(7) The Recipient agrees to destroy these Data, and all copies of the Data in its possession, no later than 30 days after the date shown in paragraph (8) of this Agreement, to have all persons to whom it released the Data do so by that date, and to notify the Contractor that the Data have been destroyed.

(8) This Agreement shall be effective for the period commencing with the Recipient's execution of this Agreement and ending

upon ___ (Insert Date) ___. The obligations imposed by this Agreement shall survive the expiration or termination of the Agreement.

Recipient's Business Name ___________

By ___________

Authorized Representative

____

Date

Representative's Typed Name ___________

and Title ___________

(End of use and non-disclosure agreement)

[DAC 91-8, 60 FR 33464, 6/28/95, effective 6/30/95]

227.7103-8 Deferred delivery and deferred ordering of technical data.

(a) *Deferred delivery.* Use the clause at 252.227-7026, Deferred Delivery of Technical Data or Computer Software, when it is in the Government's interests to defer the delivery of technical data. The clause permits the contracting officer to require the delivery of technical data identified as "deferred delivery" data at any time until two years after acceptance by the Government of all items (other than technical data or computer software) under the contract or contract termination, whichever is later. The obligation of subcontractors or suppliers to deliver such technical data expires two years after the date the prime contractor accepts the last item from the subcontractor or supplier for use in the performance of the contract. The contract must specify which technical data is subject to deferred delivery. The contracting officer shall notify the contractor sufficiently in advance of the desired delivery date for such data to permit timely delivery.

(b) *Deferred ordering.* Use the clause at 252.227-7027, Deferred Ordering of Technical Data or Computer Software, when a firm requirement for a particular data item(s) has not been established prior to contract award but there is a potential need for the data. Under this clause, the contracting officer may order any data that has been generated in the performance of the contract or any subcontract thereunder at any time until three years after acceptance of all items (other than technical data or computer software) under the contract or contract termination, whichever is later. The obligation of subcontractors to deliver such data expires three years after the date the contractor accepts the last item under the subcontract. When the data are ordered, the delivery dates shall be negotiated and the contractor compensated only for converting the data into the prescribed form, reproduction costs, and delivery costs.

[DAC 91-8, 60 FR 33464, 6/28/95, effective 6/30/95]

227.7103-9 Copyright.

(a) *Copyright license.* (1) The clause at 252.227-7013, Rights in Technical Data—Noncommercial Items, requires a contractor to grant or obtain for the Government license rights which permit the Government to reproduce data, distribute copies of the data, publicly perform or display the data or, through the right to modify data, prepare derivative works. The extent to which the Government, and others acting on its behalf, may exercise these rights varies for each of the standard data rights licenses obtained under the clause. When nonstandard license rights in technical data will be negotiated, negotiate the extent of the copyright license concurrent with negotiations for the data rights license. Do not negotiate a copyright license that provides less rights than the standard limited rights license in technical data.

(2) The clause at 252.227-7013 does not permit a contractor to incorporate a third party's copyrighted data into a deliverable data item unless the contractor has obtained an appropriate license for the Government and, when applicable, others acting on the Government's behalf, or has obtained the contracting officer's written approval to do so. Grant approval to use third party copyrighted data in which the Government will not receive a copyright license only when the Government's requirements cannot be satisfied without the third party material or when the use of the third party material will result in cost savings to the Government which outweigh the lack of a copyright license.

(b) *Copyright considerations—acquisition of existing and special works.* See 227.7105 or 227.7106 for copyright considerations when acquiring existing or special works.

[DAC 91-8, 60 FR 33464, 6/28/95, effective 6/30/95]

227.7103-10 Contractor identification and marking of technical data to be furnished with restrictive markings.

(a) *Identification requirements.* (1) The solicitation provision at 252.227-7017, Identification and Assertion of Use, Release, or Disclosure Restrictions, requires offerors to identify to the contracting officer, prior to contract award, any technical data that the offeror asserts should be provided to the Government with restrictions on use, modification, reproduction, release or disclosure. This requirement does not apply to restrictions based solely on copyright. The notification and identification must be submitted as an attachment to the offer. If an offeror fails to submit the attachment or fails to complete the attachment in accordance with the requirements of the solicitation provision, such failure shall constitute a minor informality. Provide offerors an opportunity to remedy a minor informality in accordance with the procedures at FAR 14.405 or 15.306. An offeror's failure to correct the informality within the time prescribed by the contracting officer shall render the offer ineligible for award.

(2) The procedures for correcting minor informalities shall not be used to obtain information regarding asserted restrictions or an offeror's suggested asserted rights category. Questions regarding the justification for an asserted restriction or asserted rights category must be pursued in accordance with the procedures at 227.7103-13.

(3) The restrictions asserted by a successful offeror shall be attached to its contract unless, in accordance with the procedures at 227.7103-13, the parties have agreed that an asserted restriction is not justified. The contract attachment shall provide the same information regarding identification of the technical data, the asserted rights category, the basis for the assertion, and the name of the person asserting the restrictions as required by paragraph (d) of the solicitation provision at 252.227-7017. Subsequent to contract award, the clause at 227.7103-13, Rights in Technical Data—Noncommercial Items, permits the contractor to make additional assertions under certain conditions. The additional assertions must be made in accordance with the procedures and in the format prescribed by that clause.

(4) Neither the pre- or post-award assertions made by the contractor, nor the fact that certain assertions are identified in the attachment to the contract, determine the respective rights of the parties. As provided at 227.7103-13, the Government has the right to review, verify, challenge and validate restrictive markings.

(5) Information provided by offerors in response to the solicitation provision may be used in the source selection process to evaluate the impact on evaluation factors that may be created by restrictions on the Government's ability to use or disclose technical data. However, offerors shall not be prohibited from offering products for which the offeror is entitled to provide the Government limited rights in the technical data pertaining to such products and offerors shall not be required, either as a condition of being responsive to a solicitation or as a condition for award, to sell or otherwise relinquish any greater rights in technical data when the offeror is entitled to provide the technical data with limited rights.

(b) *Contractor marking requirements.* The clause at 227.7103-13, Rights in Technical Data—Noncommercial Items—

(1) Requires a contractor that desires to restrict the Government's rights in technical data to place restrictive markings on the data, provides instructions for the placement of the restrictive markings, and authorizes the use of certain restrictive markings; and

(2) Requires a contractor to deliver, furnish, or otherwise provide to the Government any technical data in which the Government has previously obtained rights with the Government's pre-existing rights in that data unless the parties have agreed otherwise or restrictions on the Government's rights to use, modify, reproduce, release,

perform, display, or disclose the data have expired. When restrictions are still applicable, the contractor is permitted to mark the data with the appropriate restrictive legend for which the data qualified.

(c) *Unmarked technical data*. (1) Technical data delivered or otherwise provided under a contract without restrictive markings shall be presumed to have been delivered with unlimited rights and may be released or disclosed without restriction. To the extent practicable, if a contractor has requested permission (see paragraph (c)(2) of this subsection) to correct an inadvertent omission of markings, do not release or disclose the technical data pending evaluation of the request.

(2) A contractor may request permission to have appropriate legends placed on unmarked technical data at its expense. The request must be received by the contracting officer within six months following the furnishing or delivery of such data, or any extension of that time approved by the contracting officer. The person making the request must:

(i) Identify the technical data that should have been marked;

(ii) Demonstrate that the omission of the marking was inadvertent, the proposed marking is justified and conforms with the requirements for the marking of technical data contained in the clause at 252.227-7013; and

(iii) Acknowledge, in writing, that the Government has no liability with respect to any disclosure, reproduction, or use of the technical data made prior to the addition of the marking or resulting from the omission of the marking.

(3) Contracting officers should grant permission to mark only if the technical data were not distributed outside the Government or were distributed outside the Government with restrictions on further use or disclosure.

[DAC 91-8, 60 FR 33464, 6/28/95, effective 6/30/95; Final rule, 82 FR 61479, 12/28/2017, effective 12/28/2017]

227.7103-11 Contractor procedures and records.

(a) The clause at 227.7103-13, Rights in Technical Data—Noncommercial Items, requires a contractor, and its subcontractors or suppliers that will deliver technical data with other than unlimited rights, to establish and follow written procedures to assure that restrictive markings are used only when authorized and to maintain records to justify the validity of asserted restrictions on delivered data.

(b) The clause at 252.227-7037, Validation of Restrictive Markings on Technical Data requires contractors and their subcontractors at any tier to maintain records sufficient to justify the validity of restrictive markings on technical data delivered or to be delivered under a Government contract.

[DAC 91-8, 60 FR 33464, 6/28/95, effective 6/30/95]

227.7103-12 Government right to establish conformity of markings.

(a) *Nonconforming markings*. (1) Authorized markings are identified in the clause at 227.7103-13, Rights in Technical Data—Noncommercial Items. All other markings are nonconforming markings. An authorized marking that is not in the form, or differs in substance, from the marking requirements in the clause at 227.7103-13 is also a nonconforming marking.

(2) The correction of nonconforming markings on technical data is not subject to 252.227-7037, Validation of Restrictive Markings on Technical Data. To the extent practicable, the contracting officer should return technical data bearing nonconforming markings to the person who has placed the nonconforming markings on such data to provide that person an opportunity to correct or strike the nonconforming marking at that person's expense. If that person fails to correct the nonconformity and return the corrected data within 60 days following the person's receipt of the data, the contracting officer may correct or strike the nonconformity at that person's expense. When it is impracticable to return technical data for correction, contracting officers may unilaterally correct any nonconforming markings at

Government expense. Prior to correction, the data may be used in accordance with the proper restrictive marking.

(b) *Unjustified markings.* (1) An unjustified marking is an authorized marking that does not depict accurately restrictions applicable to the Government's use, modification, reproduction, release, performance, display, or disclosure of the marked technical data. For example, a limited rights legend placed on technical data pertaining to items, components, or processes that were developed under a Government contract either exclusively at Government expense or with mixed funding (situations under which the Government obtains unlimited or government purpose rights) is an unjustified marking.

(2) Contracting officers have the right to review and challenge the validity of unjustified markings. However, at any time during performance of a contract and notwithstanding existence of a challenge, the contracting officer and the person who has asserted a restrictive marking may agree that the restrictive marking is not justified. Upon such agreement, the contracting officer may, at his or her election, either—

(i) Strike or correct the unjustified marking at that person's expense; or

(ii) Return the technical data to the person asserting the restriction for correction at that person's expense. If the data are returned and that person fails to correct or strike the unjustified restriction and return the corrected data to the contracting officer within 60 days following receipt of the data, the unjustified marking shall be corrected or stricken at that person's expense.

[DAC 91-8, 60 FR 33464, 6/28/95, effective 6/30/95]

227.7103-13 Government right to review, verify, challenge, and validate asserted restrictions.

(a) *General.* An offeror's assertion(s) of restrictions on the Government's rights to use, modify, reproduce, release, or disclose technical data do not, by themselves, determine the extent of the Government's rights in the technical data. Under 10 U.S.C. 2321, the Government has the right to challenge asserted restrictions when there are reasonable grounds to question the validity of the assertion and continued adherence to the assertion would make it impractical to later procure competitively the item to which the data pertain.

(b) *Pre-award considerations.* The challenge procedures required by 10 U.S.C. 2321 could significantly delay awards under competitive procurements. Therefore, avoid challenging asserted restrictions prior to a competitive contract award unless resolution of the assertion is essential for successful completion of the procurement.

(c) *Challenge considerations and presumption.*

(1) *Requirements to initiate a challenge.* Contracting officers shall have reasonable grounds to challenge the validity of an asserted restriction. Before issuing a challenge to an asserted restriction, carefully consider all available information pertaining to the assertion. The contracting officer shall not challenge a contractor's assertion that a commercial item was developed exclusively at private expense unless the Government can demonstrate that it contributed to development of that item.

(2) *Presumption regarding development exclusively at private expense.* 10 U.S.C. 2320(b)(1) and 2321(f) establish a presumption and procedures regarding validation of asserted restrictions for technical data related to commercial items, and to major systems, on the basis of development exclusively at private expense.

(i) *Commercial items.* Except as provided in paragraph (c)(2)(ii) of this section, contracting officers shall presume that a commercial item was developed exclusively at private expense whether or not a contractor or subcontractor submits a justification in response to a challenge notice. When a challenge is warranted, a contractor's or subcontractor's failure to respond to the challenge notice cannot be the sole basis for issuing a final decision denying the validity of an asserted restriction.

(ii) *Major weapon systems.* When the contracting officer challenges an asserted restriction regarding technical data for a major weapon system or a subsystem or component thereof on the basis that the technology was not developed exclusively at private expense—

(A) The presumption in paragraph (c)(2)(i) of this section applies to—

(*1*) A commercial subsystem or component of a major weapon system, if the major weapon system was acquired as a commercial item in accordance with subpart 234.70 (10 U.S.C. 2379(a));

(*2*) A component of a subsystem, if the subsystem was acquired as a commercial item in accordance with subpart 234.70 (10 U.S.C. 2379(b)); and

(*3*) Any other component, if the component is a commercially available off-the-shelf item or a commercially available off-the-shelf item with modifications of a type customarily available in the commercial marketplace or minor modifications made to meet Federal Government requirements; and

(B) In all other cases, the contracting officer shall sustain the challenge unless information provided by the contractor or subcontractor demonstrates that the item was developed exclusively at private expense.

(d) *Challenge and validation.* All challenges shall be made in accordance with the provisions of the clause at 252.227-7037, Validation of Restrictive Markings on Technical Data.

(1) *Challenge period.* Asserted restrictions should be reviewed before acceptance of technical data deliverable under the contract. Assertions must be challenged within three years after final payment under the contract or three years after delivery of the data, whichever is later. However, restrictive markings may be challenged at any time if the technical data—

(i) Are publicly available without restrictions;

(ii) Have been provided to the United States without restriction; or

(iii) Have been otherwise made available without restriction other than a release or disclosure resulting from the sale, transfer, or other assignment of interest in the technical data to another party or the sale or transfer of some or all of a business entity or its assets to another party.

(2) *Pre-challenge requests for information.* (i) After consideration of the situations described in paragraph (d)(3) of this subsection, contracting officers may request the person asserting a restriction to furnish a written explanation of the facts and supporting documentation for the assertion in sufficient detail to enable the contracting officer to ascertain the basis of the restrictive markings. Additional supporting documentation may be requested when the explanation provided by the person making the assertion does not, in the contracting officer's opinion, establish the validity of the assertion.

(ii) If the person asserting the restriction fails to respond to the contracting officer's request for information or additional supporting documentation, or if the information submitted or any other available information pertaining to the validity of a restrictive marking does not justify the asserted restriction, a challenge should be considered.

(3) *Transacting matters directly with subcontracts.* The clause at 252.227-7037 obtains the contractor's agreement that the Government may transact matters under the clause directly with a subcontractor, at any tier, without creating or implying privity of contract. Contracting officers should permit a subcontractor or supplier to transact challenge and validation matters directly with the Government when—

(i) A subcontractor's or supplier's business interests in its technical data would be compromised if the data were disclosed to a higher tier contractor;

(ii) There is reason to believe that the contractor will not respond in a timely manner to a challenge and an untimely response would jeopardize a subcontractor's or suppliers right to assert restrictions; or

(iii) Requested to do so by a subcontractor or supplier.

(4) *Challenge notice.* The contracting officer shall not issue a challenge notice unless there are reasonable grounds to question the validity of an assertion. The contracting officer may challenge an assertion whether or not supporting documentation was re-

quested under paragraph (d)(2) of this subsection. Challenge notices shall be in writing and issued to the contractor or, after consideration of the situations described in paragraph (d)(3) of this subsection, the person asserting the restriction. The challenge notice shall include the information in paragraph (e) of the clause at 252.227-7037.

(5) *Extension of response time.* The contracting officer, at his or her discretion, may extend the time for response contained in a challenge notice, as appropriate, if the contractor submits a timely written request showing the need for additional time to prepare a response.

(6) *Contracting officer's final decision.* Contracting officers must issue a final decision for each challenged assertion, whether or not the assertion has been justified.

(i) A contracting officer's final decision that an assertion is not justified must be issued a soon as practicable following the failure of the person asserting the restriction to respond to the contracting officer's challenge within 60 days, or any extension to that time granted by the contracting officer.

(ii) A contracting officer who, following a challenge and response by the person asserting the restriction, determines that an asserted restriction is justified, shall issue a final decision sustaining the validity of the asserted restriction. If the asserted restriction was made subsequent to submission of the contractor's offer, add the asserted restriction to the contract attachment.

(iii) A contracting officer who determines that the validity of an asserted restriction has not been justified shall issue a contracting officer's final decision within the time frames prescribed in 252.227-7037. As provided in paragraph (g) of that clause, the Government is obligated to continue to respect the asserted restrictions through final disposition of any appeal unless the agency head notifies the person asserting the restriction that urgent or compelling circumstances do not permit the Government to continue to respect the asserted restriction.

(7) *Multiple challenges to an asserted restriction.* When more than one contracting officer challenges an asserted restriction, the contracting officer who made the earliest challenge is responsible for coordinating the Government challenges. That contracting officer shall consult with all other contracting officers making challenges, verify that all challenges apply to the same asserted restriction and, after consulting with the contractor, subcontractor, or supplier asserting the restriction, issue a schedule that provides that person a reasonable opportunity to respond to each challenge.

(8) *Validation.* Only a contracting officer's final decision, or actions of an agency board of contract appeals or a court of competent jurisdiction, that sustain the validity of an asserted restriction constitute validation of the asserted restriction.

[DAC 91-8, 60 FR 33464, 6/28/95, effective 6/30/95; Final rule, 76 FR 58144, 9/20/2011, effective 9/20/2011; Final rule, 81 FR 65565, 9/23/2016, effective 9/23/2016]

227.7103-14 Conformity, acceptance, and warranty of technical data.

(a) *Statutory requirements.* 10 U.S.C. 2320—

(1) Provides for the establishment of remedies applicable to technical data found to be incomplete, inadequate, or not to satisfy the requirements of the contract concerning such data; and

(2) Authorizes agency heads to withhold payments (or exercise such other remedies an agency head considers appropriate) during any period if the contractor does not meet the requirements of the contract pertaining to the delivery of technical data.

(b) *Conformity and acceptance.* (1) Solicitations and contracts requiring the delivery of technical data shall specify the requirements the data must satisfy to be acceptable. Contracting officers, or their authorized representatives, are responsible for determining whether technical data tendered for acceptance conform to the contractual requirements.

(2) The clause at 252.227-7030, Technical Data—Withholding of Payment, provides for withholding up to 10 percent of the contract

price pending correction or replacement of the nonconforming technical data or negotiation of an equitable reduction in contract price. The amount subject to withholding may be expressed as a fixed dollar amount or as a percentage of the contract price. In either case, the amount shall be determined giving consideration to the relative value and importance of the data. For example—

(i) When the sole purpose of a contract is to produce the data, the relative value of that data may be considerably higher than the value of data produced under a contract where the production of the data is a secondary objective; or

(ii) When the Government will maintain or repair items, repair and maintenance data may have a considerably higher relative value than data that merely describe the item or provide performance characteristics.

(3) Do not accept technical data that do not conform to the contractual requirements in all respects. Except for nonconforming restrictive markings (see paragraph (b)(4) of this subsection), correction or replacement of nonconforming data or an equitable reduction in contract price when correction or replacement of the nonconforming data is not practicable or is not in the Government's interests, shall be accomplished in accordance with—

(i) The provisions of a contract clause providing for inspection and acceptance of deliverables and remedies for nonconforming deliverables; or

(ii) The procedures at FAR 46.407(c) through (g), if the contract does not contain an inspection clause providing remedies for nonconforming deliverables.

(4) Follow the procedures at DFARS 227.7103-12(a)(2) if nonconforming markings are the sole reason technical data fail to conform to contractual requirements. The clause at DFARS 252.227-7030 may be used to withhold an amount for payment, consistent with the terms of the clause, pending correction of the nonconforming markings.

(c) *Warranty*. (1) The intended use of the technical data and the cost, if any, to obtain the warranty should be considered before deciding to obtain a data warranty (see FAR 46.703). The fact that a particular item, component, or process is or is not warranted is not a consideration in determining whether or not to obtain a warranty for the technical data that pertain to the item, component, or process. For example, a data warranty should be considered if the Government intends to repair or maintain an item and defective repair or maintenance data would impair the Government's effective use of the item or result in increased costs to the Government.

(2) As prescribed in 246.710, use the clause at 252.246-7001, Warranty of Data, and its alternates, or a substantially similar clause when the Government needs a specific warranty of technical data.

[DAC 91-8, 60 FR 33464, 6/28/95, effective 6/30/95; Interim rule, 69 FR 31911, 6/8/2004, effective 6/8/2004; Final rule, 69 FR 67856, 11/22/2004, effective 11/22/2004]

227.7103-15 Subcontractor rights in technical data.

(a) 10 U.S.C. 2320 provides subcontractors at all tiers the same protection for their rights in data as is provided to prime contractors. The clauses at 252.227-7013, Rights in Technical Data—Noncommercial Items, and 252.227-7037, Validation of Restrictive Markings on Technical Data, implement the statutory requirements.

(b) 10 U.S.C. 2321 permits a subcontractor to transact directly with the Government matters relating to the validation of its asserted restrictions on the Government's rights to use or disclose technical data. The clause at 252.227-7037obtains a contractor's agreement that the direct transaction of validation or challenge matters with subcontractors at any tier does not establish or imply privity of contract. When a subcontractor or supplier exercise its right to transact validation matters directly with the Government, contracting officers shall deal directly with such persons, as provided at 227.7103-13(c)(3).

(c) Require prime contractors whose contracts include the following clauses to include those clauses, without modification except for appropriate identification of the parties, in contracts with subcontractors or suppliers, at all tiers, who will be furnishing technical data for non-commercial items in response to a Government requirement:

(1) 252.227-7013, Rights in Technical Data—Noncommercial Items;

(2) 252.227-7025, Limitations on the Use or Disclosure of Government-Furnished Information Marked with Restrictive Legends;

(3) 252.227-7028, Technical Data or Computer Software Previously Delivered to the Government; and

(4) 252.227-7037, Validation of Restrictive Markings on Technical Data.

(d) Do not require contractors to have their subcontractors or suppliers at any tier relinquish rights in technical data to the contractor, a higher tier subcontractor, or to the Government, as a condition for award of any contract, subcontract, purchase order, or similar instrument except for the rights obtained by the Government under the Rights in Technical Data—Noncommercial Items clause contained in the contractor's contract with the Government.

[DAC 91-8, 60 FR 33464, 6/28/95, effective 6/30/95; DAC 91-9, 60 FR 61586, 11/30/95, effective 11/30/95]

227.7103-16 Providing technical data to foreign governments, foreign contractors, or international organizations.

Technical data may be released or disclosed to foreign governments, foreign contractors, or international organizations only if release or disclosure is otherwise permitted both by Federal export controls and other national security laws or regulations. Subject to such laws and regulations, the Department of Defense—

(a) May release or disclose technical data in which it has obtained unlimited rights to such foreign entities or authorize the use of such data by those entities; and

(b) Shall not release or disclose technical data for which restrictions on use, release, or disclosure have been asserted to foreign entities, or authorize the use of technical data by those entities, unless the intended recipient is subject to the same provisions as included in the use and non-disclosure agreement at 227.7103-7 and the requirements of the clause at 252.227-7013, Rights in Technical Data—Noncommercial Items, governing use, modification, reproduction, release, performance, display, or disclosure of such data have been satisfied.

[DAC 91-8, 60 FR 33464, 6/28/95, effective 6/30/95]

227.7103-17 Overseas contracts with foreign sources.

(a) The clause at 252.227-7032, Rights in Technical Data and Computer Software (Foreign), may be used in contracts with foreign contractors to be performed overseas, except Canadian purchases (see paragraph (c) of this subsection), in lieu of the clause at 252.227-7013, Rights in Technical Data—Noncommercial Items, when the Government requires the unrestricted right to use, modify, reproduce, perform, display, release or disclose all technical data to be delivered under the contract. Do not use the clause in contracts for existing or special works.

(b) When the Government does not require unlimited rights, the clause at 252.227-7032 may be modified to accommodate the needs of a specific overseas procurement situation. The Government should obtain rights in the technical data that are not less than the rights the Government would have obtained under the data rights clause(s) prescribed in this part for a comparable procurement performed within the United States or its outlying areas.

(c) Contracts for Canadian purchases shall include the appropriate data rights clause prescribed in this part for a comparable procurement performed within the United States or its outlying areas.

[DAC 91-8, 60 FR 33464, 6/28/95, effective 6/30/95; Final rule, 70 FR 35543, 6/21/2005, effective 6/21/2005]

227.7104 Contracts under the Small Business Innovation Research (SBIR) Program.

(a) Use the clause at 252.227-7018, Rights in Noncommercial Technical Data and Computer Software—Small Business Innovation Research (SBIR) Program, when technical data or computer software will be generated during performance of contracts under the SBIR program.

(b) Under the clause at 252.227-7018, the Government obtains SBIR data rights in technical data and computer software generated under the contract and marked with the SBIR data rights legend. SBIR data rights provide the Government limited rights in such technical data and restricted rights in such computer software during the SBIR data protection period commencing with contract award and ending five years after completion of the project under which the data were generated. Upon expiration of the five-year restrictive license, the Government has unlimited rights in the SBIR technical data and computer software.

(c) During the SBIR data protection period, the Government may not release or disclose SBIR technical data or computer software to any person except as authorized for limited rights technical data or restricted rights computer software, respectively.

(d) Use the clause at 252.227-7018 with its Alternate I in research contracts when the contracting officer determines, in consultation with counsel, that public dissemination by the contractor would be—

(1) In the interest of the Government; and

(2) Facilitated by the Government relinquishing its right to publish the work for sale, or to have others publish the work for sale on behalf of the Government.

(e) Use the following provision and clauses in SBIR solicitations and contracts that include the clause at 252.227-7018:

(1) 252.227-7016, Rights in Bid or Proposal Information;

(2) 252.227-7017, Identification and Assertion of Use, Release, or Disclosure Restrictions;

(3) 252.227-7019, Validation of Asserted Restrictions—Computer Software;

(4) 252.227-7030, Technical Data—Withholding of Payment; and

(5) 252.227-7037, Validation of Restrictive Markings on Technical Data (paragraph (e) of the clause contains information that must be included in a challenge).

(f) Use the following clauses and provision in SBIR solicitations and contracts in accordance with the guidance at 227.7103-6 (c) and (d):

(1) 252.227-7025, Limitations on the Use or Disclosure of Government-Furnished Information Marked with Restrictive Legends; and

(2) 252.227-7028, Technical Data or Computer Software Previously Delivered to the Government.

[DAC 91-8, 60 FR 33464, 6/28/95, effective 6/30/95; DAC 91-9, 60 FR 61586, 11/30/95, effective 11/30/95; Final rule, 62 FR 2612, 1/17/97, effective 1/17/97; Interim rule, 69 FR 31911, 6/8/2004, effective 6/8/2004; Final rule, 69 67856, 11/22/2004, effective 11/22/2004; Final rule, 78 FR 30233, 5/22/2013, effective 5/22/2013]

227.7105 Contracts for the acquisition of existing works. (No Text)

227.7105-1 General.

(a) Existing works include motion pictures, television recordings, video recordings, and other audiovisual works in any medium; sound recordings in any medium; musical, dramatic, and literary works; pantomimes and choreographic works; pictorial, graphic, and sculptural works; and works of a similar nature. Usually, these or similar works were not first created, developed, generated, originated, prepared, or produced under a Government contract. Therefore, the Government must obtain a license in the work if it intends to reproduce the work, distribute copies of the work, prepare derivative works, or perform or display the work publicly. When the Government is not responsible for the content of an existing work, it should require the copyright owner to indemnify the Government for liabilities that may arise out of the content, performance, use, or disclosure of such data.

(b) Follow the procedures at 227.7106 for works which will be first created, developed, generated, originated, prepared, or produced under a Government contract and the Government needs to control distribution of the work or has a specific need to obtain indemnity for liabilities that may arise out of the creation, content, performance, use, or disclosure of the work or from libelous or other unlawful material contained in the work. Follow the procedures at 227.7103 when the Government does not need to control distribution of such works or obtain such indemnities.

[DAC 91-8, 60 FR 33464, 6/28/95, effective 6/30/95]

227.7105-2 Acquisition of existing works without modification.

(a) Use the clause at 252.227-7021, Rights in Data—Existing Works, in lieu of the clause at 252.227-7013, Rights in Technical Data—Noncommercial Items, in solicitations and contracts exclusively for existing works when—

(1) The existing works will be acquired without modification; and

(2) The Government requires the right to reproduce, prepare derivative works, or publicly perform or display the existing works; or

(3) The Government has a specific need to obtain indemnity for liabilities that may arise out of the content, performance, use, or disclosure of such data.

(b) The clause at 252.227-7021 provides the Government, and others acting on its behalf, a paid-up, non-exclusive, irrevocable, world-wide license to reproduce, prepare derivative works and publicly perform or display the works called for by a contract and to authorize others to do so for government purposes.

(c) A contract clause is not required to acquire existing works such as books, magazines and periodicals, in any storage or retrieval medium, when the Government will not reproduce the books, magazines or periodicals, or prepare derivative works.

[DAC 91-8, 60 FR 33464, 6/28/95, effective 6/30/95]

227.7105-3 Acquisition of modified existing works.

Use the clause at 252.227-7020, Rights in Special Works, in solicitations and contracts for modified existing works in lieu of the clause at DFARS 252.227-7021, Rights in Data—Existing Works.

[DAC 91-8, 60 FR 33464, 6/28/95, effective 6/30/95]

227.7106 Contracts for special works.

(a) Use the clause at 252.227-7020, Rights in Special Works, in solicitations and contracts where the Government has a specific need to control the distribution of works first produced, created, or generated in the performance of a contract and required to be delivered under that contract, including controlling distribution by obtaining an assignment of copyright, or a specific need to obtain indemnity for liabilities that may arise out of the creation, delivery, use, modification, reproduction, release, performance, display, or disclosure of such works. Use the clause—

(1) In lieu of the clause at 252.227-7013, Rights in Technical Data—Noncommercial Items, when the Government must own or control copyright in all works first produced, created, or generated and required to be delivered under a contract; or

(2) In addition to the clause at 252.227-7013 when the Government must own or control copyright in a portion of a work first produced, created, or generated and required to be delivered under a contract. The specific portion in which the Government must own or control copyright must be identified in a special contract requirement.

(b) Although the Government obtains an assignment of copyright and unlimited rights in a special work under the clause at 252.227-7020, the contractor retains use and disclosure rights in that work. If the Government needs to restrict a contractor's rights to use or disclose a special work, it must also negotiate a special license which specifically restricts the contractor's use or disclosure rights.

(c) The clause at 252.227-7020 does not permit a contractor to incorporate into a special work any works copyrighted by others unless the contractor obtains the contracting officer's permission to do so and obtains for the Government a non-exclusive, paid up, world-wide license to make and distribute copies of that work, to prepare derivative works, to perform or display publicly any portion of the work, and to permit others to do so for government purposes. Grant permission only when the Government's requirements cannot be satisfied unless the third party work is included in the deliverable work.

(d) Examples of works which may be procured under the Rights in Special Works clause include, but are not limited, to audiovisual works, computer data bases, computer software documentation, scripts, soundtracks, musical compositions, and adaptations; histories of departments, agencies, services or units thereof; surveys of Government establishments; instructional works or guidance to Government officers and employees on the discharge of their official duties; reports, books, studies, surveys or similar documents; collections of data containing information pertaining to individuals that, if disclosed, would violate the right of privacy or publicity of the individuals to whom the information relates; or investigative reports.

[DAC 91-8, 60 FR 33464, 6/28/95, effective 6/30/95]

227.7107 Contracts for architect-engineer services.

This section sets forth policies and procedures, pertaining to data, copyrights, and restricted designs unique to the acquisition of construction and architect-engineer services.

[DAC 91-8, 60 FR 33464, 6/28/95, effective 6/30/95]

227.7107-1 Architectural designs and data clauses for architect-engineer or construction contracts.

(a) Except as provided in paragraph (b) of this subsection and in 227.7107-2, use the clause at 252.227-7022, Government Rights (Unlimited), in solicitations and contracts for architect-engineer services and for construction involving architect-engineer services.

(b) When the purpose of a contract for architect-engineer services, or for construction involving architect-engineer services, is to obtain a unique architectural design of a building, a monument, or construction of similar nature, which for artistic, aesthetic or other special reasons the Government does not want duplicated, the Government may acquire exclusive control of the data pertaining to the design by including the clause at 252.227-7023, Drawings and Other Data to Become Property of Government, in solicitations and contracts.

(c) The Government shall obtain unlimited rights in shop drawings for construction. In solicitations and contracts calling for delivery of shop drawings, include the clause at 252.227-7033, Rights in Shop Drawings.

[DAC 91-8, 60 FR 33464, 6/28/95, effective 6/30/95]

227.7107-2 Contracts for construction supplies and research and development work.

Use the provisions and clauses required by 227.7103-6 and 227.7203-6 when the acquisition is limited to—

(a) Construction supplies or materials;

(b) Experimental, developmental, or research work, or test and evaluation studies of structures, equipment, processes, or materials for use in construction; or

(c) Both.

[DAC 91-8, 60 FR 33464, 6/28/95, effective 6/30/95]

227.7107-3 Approval of restricted designs.

The clause at 252.227-7024, Notice and Approval of Restricted Designs, may be included in architect-engineer contracts to permit the Government to make informed decisions concerning noncompetitive aspects of the design.

[DAC 91-8, 60 FR 33464, 6/28/95, effective 6/30/95]

227.7108 Contractor data repositories.

(a) Contractor data repositories may be established when permitted by agency procedures. The contractual instrument establishing the data repository must require, as a minimum, the data repository management contractor to—

(1) Establish and maintain adequate procedures for protecting technical data delivered to or stored at the repository from unauthorized release or disclosure;

(2) Establish and maintain adequate procedures for controlling the release or disclosure of technical data from the repository to third parties consistent with the Government's rights in such data;

(3) When required by the contracting officer, deliver data to the Government on paper or in other specified media;

(4) Be responsible for maintaining the currency of data delivered directly by Government contractors or subcontractors to the repository;

(5) Obtain use and non-disclosure agreements (see 227.7103-7) from all persons to whom government purpose rights data is released or disclosed; and

(6) Indemnify the Government from any liability to data owners or licensors resulting from, or as a consequence of, a release or disclosure of technical data made by the data repository contractor or its officers, employees, agents, or representatives.

(b) If the contractor is or will be the data repository manager, the contractor's data management and distribution responsibilities must be identified in the contract or the contract must reference the agreement between the Government and the contractor that establishes those responsibilities.

(c) If the contractor is not and will not be the data repository manager, do not require a contractor or subcontractor to deliver technical data marked with limited rights legends to a data repository managed by another contractor unless the contractor or subcontractor who has asserted limited rights agrees to release the data to the repository or has authorized, in writing, the Government to do so.

(d) Repository procedures may provide for the acceptance, delivery, and subsequent distribution of technical data in storage media other than paper, including direct electronic exchange of data between two computers. The procedures must provide for the identification of any portions of the data provided with restrictive legends, when appropriate. The acceptance criteria must be consistent with the authorized delivery format.

[DAC 91-8, 60 FR 33464, 6/28/95, effective 6/30/95]

SUBPART 227.72—RIGHTS IN COMPUTER SOFTWARE AND COMPUTER SOFTWARE DOCUMENTATION

227.7200 Scope of subpart.

This subpart—

(a) Prescribes policies and procedures for the acquisition of computer software and computer software documentation, and the rights to use, modify, reproduce, release, perform, display, or disclose such software or documentation. It implements requirements in the following laws and Executive Order:

(1) 10 U.S.C. 2302(4).

(2) 10 U.S.C. 2305 (subsection (d)(4)).

(3) 10 U.S.C. 2320.

(4) 10 U.S.C. 2321.

(5) 10 U.S.C. 2325.

(6) Executive Order 12591 (subsection 1(b)(6)).

(b) Does not apply to—

(1) Computer software or computer software documentation acquired under GSA schedule contracts; or

(2) Releases of computer software or computer software documentation to litigation support contractors (see subpart 204.74).

[DAC 91-8, 60 FR 33464, 6/28/95, effective 6/30/95; Interim rule, 79 FR 11337, 2/28/2014, effective 2/28/2014; Interim rule, 81 FR 28724, 5/10/2016, effective 5/10/2016]

227.7201 Definitions.

(a) As used in this subpart, unless otherwise specifically indicated, the terms *offeror* and *contractor* include an offeror's or contractor's subcontractors, suppliers, or potential subcontractors or suppliers at any tier.

(b) Other terms used in this subpart are defined in the clause at 252.227-7014, Rights in Noncommercial Computer Software and Noncommercial Computer Software Documentation.

[DAC 91-8, 60 FR 33464, 6/28/95, effective 6/30/95]

227.7202 Commercial computer software and commercial computer software documentation. (No Text)

227.7202-1 Policy.

(a) Commercial computer software or commercial computer software documentation shall be acquired under the licenses customarily provided to the public unless such licenses are inconsistent with Federal procurement law or do not otherwise satisfy user needs.

(b) Commercial computer software and commercial computer software documentation shall be obtained competitively, to the maximum extent practicable, using firm-fixed-price contracts or firm-fixed-priced orders under available pricing schedules.

(c) Offerors and contractors shall not be required to—

(1) Furnish technical information related to commercial computer software or commercial computer software documentation that is not customarily provided to the public except for information documenting the specific modifications made at Government expense to such software or documentation to meet the requirements of a Government solicitation; or

(2) Relinquish to, or otherwise provide, the Government rights to use, modify, reproduce, release, perform, display, or disclose commercial computer software or commercial computer software documentation except for a transfer of rights mutually agreed upon.

[DAC 91-8, 60 FR 33464, 6/28/95, effective 6/30/95]

227.7202-2 [Reserved]

[Reserved, DAC 91-9, 60 FR 61586, 11/30/95, effective 11/30/95]

227.7202-3 Rights in commercial computer software or commercial computer software documentation.

(a) The Government shall have only the rights specified in the license under which the commercial computer software or commercial computer software documentation was obtained.

(b) If the Government has a need for rights not conveyed under the license customarily provided to the public, the Government must negotiate with the contractor to determine if there are acceptable terms for transferring such rights. The specific rights granted to the Government shall be enumerated in the contract license agreement or an addendum thereto.

[DAC 91-8, 60 FR 33464, 6/28/95, effective 6/30/95]

227.7202-4 Contract clause.

A specific contract clause governing the Government's rights in commercial computer software or commercial computer software documentation is not prescribed. As required by 227.7202-3, the Government's rights to use, modify, reproduce, release, perform, display, or disclose computer software or computer software documentation shall be identified in a license agreement.

[DAC 91-8, 60 FR 33464, 6/28/95, effective 6/30/95]

227.7203 Noncommercial computer software and noncommercial computer software documentation. (No Text)

227.7203-1 Policy.

(a) DoD policy is to acquire only the computer software and computer software documentation, and the rights in such software or documentation, necessary to satisfy agency needs.

(b) Solicitations and contracts shall—

(1) Specify the computer software or computer software documentation to be delivered under a contract and the delivery schedules for the software or documentation;

(2) Establish or reference procedures for determining the acceptability of computer software or computer software documentation;

(3) Establish separate contract line items, to the extent practicable, for the computer software or computer software documentation to be delivered under a contract and require offerors and contractors to price separately each deliverable data item; and

(4) Require offerors to identify, to the extent practicable, computer software or computer software documentation to be furnished with restrictions on the Government's rights and require contractors to identify computer software or computer software documentation to be delivered with such restrictions prior to delivery.

(c) Offerors shall not be required, either as a condition of being responsive to a solicitation or as a condition for award, to sell or otherwise relinquish to the Government any rights in computer software developed exclusively at private expense except for the software identified at 227.7203-5(a) (3) through (6).

(d) Offerors and contractors shall not be prohibited or discouraged from furnishing or offering to furnish computer software developed exclusively at private expense solely because the Government's rights to use, modify, release, reproduce, perform, display, or disclose the software may be restricted.

(e) For acquisitions involving major weapon systems or subsystems of major weapon systems, the acquisition plan shall address acquisition strategies that provide for computer software and computer software documentation, and the associated license rights, in accordance with 207.106(S-70).

[DAC 91-8, 60 FR 33464, 6/28/95, effective 6/30/95; Interim rule, 72 FR 51188, 9/6/2007, effective 9/6/2007; Final rule, 74 FR 68699, 12/29/2009, effective 12/29/2009]

227.7203-2 Acquisition of noncommercial computer software and computer software documentation.

(a) Contracting officers shall work closely with data managers and requirements personnel to assure that computer software and computer software documentation requirements included in solicitations are consistent with the policy expressed in 227.7203-1.

(b) (1) Data managers or other requirements personnel are responsible for identifying the Government's minimum needs. In addition to desired software performance, compatibility, or other technical considerations, needs determinations should consider such factors as multiple site or shared use requirements, whether the Government's software maintenance philosophy will require the right to modify or have third parties modify the software, and any special computer software documentation requirements.

(2) When reviewing offers received in response to a solicitation or other request for computer software or computer software documentation, data managers must balance the original assessment of the Government's needs with prices offered.

(c) Contracting officers are responsible for ensuring that, wherever practicable, solicitations and contracts—

(1) Identify the types of computer software and the quantity of computer programs and computer software documentation to be delivered, any requirements for multiple users at one site or multiple site licenses, and the format and media in which the software or documentation will be delivered;

(2) Establish each type of computer software or computer software documentation to be delivered as a separate contract line item (this requirement may be satisfied by an exhibit to the contract);

(3) Identify the prices established for each separately priced deliverable item of computer software or computer software documentation under a fixed-price type contract;

(4) Include delivery schedules and acceptance criteria for each deliverable item; and

(5) Specifically identify the place of delivery for each deliverable item.

[DAC 91-8, 60 FR 33464, 6/28/95, effective 6/30/95]

227.7203-3 Early identification of computer software or computer software documentation to be furnished to the Government with restrictions on use, reproduction or disclosure.

(a) Use the provision at 252.227-7017, Identification and Assertion of Use, Release, or Disclosure Restrictions, in all solicitation that include the clause at 252.227-7014, Rights in Noncommercial Computer Software and Noncommercial Computer Software Documentation. The provision requires offerors to identify any computer software or computer software documentation for which restrictions, other than copyright, on use, modification, reproduction, release, performance, display, or disclosure are asserted and to attach the identification and assertion to the offer.

(b) Subsequent to contract award, the clause at 252.227-7014 permits a contractor, under certain conditions, to make additional assertions of restrictions. The prescriptions for the use of that clause and its alternates are at 227.7203-6(a).

[DAC 91-8, 60 FR 33464, 6/28/95, effective 6/30/95]

227.7203-4 License rights.

(a) *Grant of license*. The Government obtains rights in computer software or computer software documentation, including a copyright license, under an irrevocable license granted or obtained by the contractor which developed the software or documentation or the licensor of the software or documentation if the development contractor is not the licensor. The contractor or licensor retains all rights in the software or documentation not granted to the Government. The scope of a computer software license is generally determined by the source of funds used to develop the software. Contractors or licensors may, with some exceptions, restrict the Government's rights to use, modify, reproduce, release, perform, display, or disclose computer software developed exclusively or partially at private expense (see 227.7203-5 (b) and (c)). They may not, without the Government's agreement (see 227.7203-5(d)), restrict the Government's rights in computer software developed exclusively with Government funds or in computer software documentation required to be delivered under a contract.

(b) *Source of funds determination*. The determination of the source of funds used to develop computer software should be made at the lowest practicable segregable portion of the software or documentation (e.g., a software sub-routine that performs a specific function). Contractors may assert restricted rights in a segregable portion of computer software which otherwise qualifies for restricted rights under the clause at 252.227-7014, Rights in Noncommercial Computer Software and Noncommercial Computer Software Documentation.

[DAC 91-8, 60 FR 33464, 6/28/95, effective 6/30/95]

227.7203-5 Government rights.

The standard license rights in computer software that a licensor grants to the Government are unlimited rights, government purpose rights, or restricted rights. The standard license in computer software documentation conveys unlimited rights. Those rights are defined in the clause at 252.227-7014, Rights in Noncommercial Computer Software and Noncommercial Computer Software Documentation. In unusual situations, the standard rights may not satisfy the Government's needs or the Government may be willing to accept lesser rights in return for other consideration. In those cases, a special license may be negotiated. However, the licensor is not obligated to provide the Government greater rights and the contracting officer is not required to accept lesser rights than the rights provided in the standard grant of license. The situations under which a particular grant of license applies are enumerated in paragraphs (a) through (d) of this subsection.

(a) *Unlimited rights*. The Government obtains an unlimited rights license in—

(1) Computer software developed exclusively with Government funds;

(2) Computer software documentation required to be delivered under a Government contract;

(3) Corrections or changes to computer software or computer software documentation furnished to the contractor by the Government;

(4) Computer software or computer software documentation that is otherwise publicly available or has been released or disclosed by the contractor or subcontractor without restrictions on further use, release or disclosure other than a release or disclosure resulting from the sale, transfer, or other assignment of interest in the software to another party or the sale or transfer of some or all of a business entity or it assets to another party;

(5) Computer software or computer software documentation obtained with unlimited rights under another Government contract or as a result of negotiations; or

(6) Computer software or computer software documentation furnished to the Government, under a Government contract or subcontract with—

(i) Restricted rights in computer software, limited rights in technical data, or government purpose license rights and the restrictive conditions have expired; or

(ii) Government purpose rights and the contractor's exclusive right to use such software or documentation for commercial purposes has expired.

(b) *Government purpose rights.* (1) Except as provided in paragraph (a) of this subsection, the Government obtains government purpose rights in computer software developed with mixed funding.

(2) The period during which government purpose rights are effective is negotiable. The clause at 252.227-7014 provides a nominal five-year period. Either party may request a different period. Changes to the government purpose rights period may be made at any time prior to delivery of the software without consideration from either party. Longer periods should be negotiated when a five-year period does not provide sufficient time to commercialize the software or, for software developed by subcontractors, when necessary to recognize the subcontractors' interests in the software.

(3) The government purpose rights period commences upon execution of the contract, subcontract, letter contract (or similar contractual instrument), contract modification, or option exercise that required development of the computer software. Upon expiration of the government purpose rights period, the Government has unlimited rights in the software including the right to authorize others to use data for commercial purposes.

(4) During the government purpose rights period, the Government may not use, or authorize other persons to use, computer software marked with government purpose rights legends for commercial purposes. The Government shall not release or disclose, or authorize others to release or disclose, computer software in which it has government purpose rights to any person unless—

(i) Prior to release or disclosure, the intended recipient is subject to the use and non-disclosure agreement at 227.7103-7; or

(ii) The intended recipient is a Government contractor receiving access to the software for performance of a Government contract that contains the clause at 252.227-7025, Limitations on the Use or Disclosure of Government-Furnished Information Marked with Restrictive Legends.

(5) When computer software marked with government purpose rights legends will be released or disclosed to a Government contractor performing a contract that does not include the clause at 2252.227-7025, the contract may be modified, prior to release or disclosure, to include such clause in lieu of requiring the contractor to complete a use and non-disclosure agreement.

(6) Contracting activities shall establish procedures to assure that computer software or computer software documentation marked with government purpose rights legends are released or disclosed, including a release or disclosure through a Government solicitation, only to persons subject to the

use and non-disclosure restrictions. Public announcements in the Commerce Business Daily or other publications must provide notice of the use and non-disclosure requirements. Class use and non-disclosure agreements (e.g., agreements covering all solicitations received by the XYZ company within a reasonable period) are authorized and may be obtained at any time prior to release or disclosure of the government purpose rights software or documentation. Documents transmitting government purpose rights software or documentation to persons under class agreements shall identify the specific software or documentation subject to government purpose rights and the class agreement under which such software or documentation are provided.

(c) *Restricted rights.*

(1) The Government obtains restricted rights in noncommercial computer software, required to be delivered or otherwise provided to the Government under a contract, that was developed exclusively at private expense.

(2) Contractors are not required to provide the Government additional rights in computer software delivered or otherwise provided to the Government with restricted rights. When the Government has a need for additional rights, the Government must negotiate with the contractor to determine if there are acceptable terms for transferring such rights. List or describe all software in which the contractor has granted the Government additional rights in a license agreement made part of the contract (see paragraph (d) of this subsection). The license shall enumerate the specific additional rights granted to the Government.

(d) *Specifically negotiated license rights.* Negotiate specific licenses when the parties agree to modify the standard license rights granted to the Government or when the Government wants to obtain rights in computer software in which it does not have rights. When negotiating to obtain, relinquish, or increase the Government's rights in computer software, consider the planned software maintenance philosophy, anticipated time or user sharing requirements, and other factors which may have relevance for a particular procurement. If negotiating to relinquish rights in computer software documentation, consider the administrative burden associated with protecting documentation subject to restrictions from unauthorized release or disclosure. The negotiated license rights must stipulate the rights granted the Government to use, modify, reproduce, release, perform, display, or disclose the software or documentation and the extent to which the Government may authorize others to do so. Identify all negotiated rights in a license agreement made part of the contract.

(e) *Rights in derivative computer software or computer software documentation.* The clause at 252.227-7014 protects the Government's rights in computer software, computer software documentation, or portions thereof that the contractor subsequently uses to prepare derivative software or subsequently embeds or includes in other software or documentation. The Government retains the rights it obtained under the development contract in the unmodified portions of the derivative software or documentation.

[DAC 91-8, 60 FR 33464, 6/28/95, effective 6/30/95; Final rule, 76 FR 3536, 1/20/2011, effective 1/20/2011]

227.7203-6 Contract clauses.

(a) (1) Use the clause at 252.227-7014, Rights in Noncommercial Computer Software and Noncommercial Computer Software Documentation, in solicitations and contracts when the successful offeror(s) will be required to deliver computer software or computer software documentation. Do not use the clause when the only deliverable items are technical data (other than computer software documentation), commercial computer software or commercial computer software documentation, commercial items (see 227.7102-3), special works (see 227.7205), or contracts under the Small Business Innovation Research Program (see 227.7104), Except as provided in 227.7107-2, do not use the clause in architect-engineer and construction contracts.

(2) Use the clause at 252.227-7014 with its Alternate I in research contracts when the

contracting officer determines, in consultation with counsel, that public dissemination by the contractor would be—

(i) In the interest of the Government; and

(ii) Facilitated by the Government relinquishing its right to publish the work for sale, or to have others publish the work for sale on behalf of the Government.

(b) Use the clause at 252.227-7016, Rights in Bid or Proposal Information, in solicitations and contracts that include the clause at 252.227-7014.

(c) Use the clause at 252.227-7019, Validation of Asserted Restrictions—Computer Software, in solicitations and contracts that include the clause at 252.227-7014. The clause provides procedures for the validation of asserted restrictions on the Government's rights to use, release, or disclose computer software.

(d) Use the provision at 252.227-7025, Limitations on the Use or Disclosure of Government-Furnished Information Marked with Restrictive Legends, in solicitations and contracts when it is anticipated that the Government will provide the contractor (other than a litigation support contractor covered by 252.204-7014), for performance of its contract, computer software or computer software documentation marked with another contractor's restrictive legend(s).

(e) Use the provision at 252.227-7028, Technical Data or Computer Software Previously Delivered to the Government, in solicitations when the resulting contract will require the contractor to deliver computer software or computer software documentation. The provision requires offerors to identify any software or documentation specified in the solicitation as deliverable items that are the same or substantially the same as software or documentation which the offeror has delivered or is obligated to deliver, either as a contractor or subcontractor, under any other federal agency contract.

(f) Use the clause at 252.227-7037, Validation of Restrictive Markings on Technical Data, in solicitations and contracts that include the clause at 252.227-7014 when the contractor will be required to deliver noncommercial computer software documentation (technical data). The clause implements statutory requirements under 10 U.S.C. 2321. Paragraph (e) of the clause contains information that must be included in a formal challenge.

[DAC 91-8, 60 FR 33464, 6/28/95, effective 6/30/95; Final rule, 76 FR 3536, 1/20/2011, effective 1/20/2011; Interim rule, 79 FR 11337, 2/28/2014, effective 2/28/2014; Final rule, 81 FR 28724, 5/10/2016, effective 5/10/2016]

227.7203-7 [Removed]

[Reserved, DAC 91-8, 60 FR 33464, 6/28/95, effective 6/30/95; Final rule, 78 FR 73450, 12/6/2013, effective 12/6/2013]

227.7203-8 Deferred delivery and deferred ordering of computer software and computer software documentation.

(a) *Deferred delivery.* Use the clause at 252.227-7026, Deferred Delivery of Technical Data or Computer Software, when it is in the Government's interests to defer the delivery of computer software or computer software documentation. The clause permits the contracting officer to require the delivery of data identified as "deferred delivery" data or computer software at any time until two years after acceptance by the Government of all items (other than technical data or computer software) under the contract or contract termination, whichever is later. The obligation of subcontractors or suppliers to deliver such data expires two years after the date the prime contractor accepts the last item from the subcontractor or supplier for use in the performance of the contract. The contract must specify the computer software or computer software documentation that is subject to deferred delivery. The contracting officer shall notify the contractor sufficiently in advance of the desired delivery date for such software or documentation to permit timely delivery.

(b) *Deferred ordering.* Use the clause at 252.227-7027, Deferred Ordering of Technical Data or Computer Software, when a firm requirement for software or documentation has not been established prior to contract award but there is a potential need for computer software or computer software documentation. Under this clause the contracting officer may order any computer software or computer software documentation generated in the performance of the contract or any subcontract thereunder at any time until three years after acceptance of all items (other than technical data or computer software) under the contract or contract termination, whichever is later. The obligation of subcontractors to deliver such technical data or computer software expires three years after the date the contractor accepts the last item under the subcontract. When the software or documentation are ordered, the delivery dates shall be negotiated and the contractor compensated only for converting the software or documentation into the prescribed form, reproduction costs, and delivery costs. [DAC 91-8, 60 FR 33464, 6/28/95, effective 6/30/95]

227.7203-9 Copyright.

(a) *Copyright license.* (1) The clause at 252.227-7014, Rights in Noncommercial Computer Software and Noncommercial Computer Software Documentation, requires a contractor to grant, or obtain for the Government license rights which permit the Government to reproduce the software or documentation, distribute copies, perform or display the software or documentation and, through the right to modify data, prepare derivative works. The extent to which the Government, and others acting on its behalf, may exercise these rights varies for each of the standard data rights licenses obtained under the clause. When non-standard license rights in computer software or computer software documentation will be negotiated, negotiate the extent of the copyright license concurrent with negotiations for the data rights license. Do not negotiate copyright licenses for computer software that provide less rights than the standard restricted rights in computer software license. For computer software documentation, do not negotiate a copyright license that provides less rights than the standard limited rights in technical data license.

(2) The clause at 252.227-7013, Rights in Technical Data—Noncommercial Items, does not permit a contractor to incorporate a third party's copyrighted software into a deliverable software item unless the contractor has obtained an appropriate license for the Government and, when applicable, others acting on the Government's behalf, or has obtained the contracting officer's written approval to do so. Grant approval to use third party copyrighted software in which the Government will not receive a copyright license only when the Government's requirements cannot be satisfied without the third party material or when the use of the third party material will result in cost savings to the Government which outweigh the lack of a copyright license.

(b) *Copyright considerations—special works.* See 227.7205 for copyright considerations when acquiring special works.

[DAC 91-8, 60 FR 33464, 6/28/95, effective 6/30/95]

227.7203-10 Contractor identification and marking of computer software or computer software documentation to be furnished with restrictive markings.

(a) *Identification requirements.* (1) The solicitation provision at 252.227-7017, Identification and Assertion of Use, Release, or Disclosure Restrictions, requires offerors to identify, prior to contract award, any computer software or computer software documentation that an offeror asserts should be provided to the Government with restrictions on use, modification, reproduction, release, or disclosure. This requirement does not apply to restrictions based solely on copyright. The notification and identification must be submitted as an attachment to the offer. If an offeror fails to submit the attachment or fails to complete the attachment in accordance with the requirements of the solicitation provision, such failure shall constitute a minor informality. Provide offerors an opportunity to remedy a minor informality in accordance with the procedures at FAR 14.405 or 15.306(a). An offeror's failure to correct an informality within the time prescribed by the contracting officer shall render the offer ineligible for award.

(2) The procedures for correcting minor informalities shall not be used to obtain information regarding asserted restrictions or

an offeror's suggested asserted rights category. Questions regarding the justification for an asserted restriction or asserted rights category must be pursued in accordance with the procedures at 227.7203-13.

(3) The restrictions asserted by a successful offeror shall be attached to its contract unless, in accordance with the procedures at 227.7203-13, the parties have agreed that an asserted restriction is not justified. The contract attachment shall provide the same information regarding identification of the computer software or computer software documentation, the asserted rights category, the basis for the assertion, and the name of the person asserting the restrictions as required by paragraph (d) of the solicitation provision at 252.227-7017. Subsequent to contract award, the clause at 252.227-7014, Rights in Noncommercial Computer Software and Noncommercial Computer Software Documentation, permits a contractor to make additional assertions under certain conditions. The additional assertions must be made in accordance with the procedures and in the format prescribed by that clause.

(4) Neither the pre- or post-award assertions made by the contractor nor the fact that certain assertions are identified in the attachment to the contract, determine the respective rights of the parties. As provided at 227.7203-13, the Government has the right to review, verify, challenge and validate restrictive markings.

(5) Information provided by offerors in response to the solicitation provision at 252.227-7017 may be used in the source selection process to evaluate the impact on evaluation factors that may be created by restrictions on the Government's ability to use or disclose computer software or computer software documentation.

(b) *Contractor marking requirements.* The clause at 252.227-7014, Rights in Noncommercial Computer Software and Noncommercial Computer Software Documentation—

(1) Requires a contractor who desires to restrict the Government's rights in computer software or computer software documentation to place restrictive markings on the software or documentation, provides instructions for the placement of the restrictive markings, and authorizes the use of certain restrictive markings. When it is anticipated that the software will or may be used in combat or situations which simulate combat conditions, do not permit contractors to insert instructions into computer programs that interfere with or delay operation of the software to display a restrictive rights legend or other license notice; and

(2) Requires a contractor to deliver, furnish, or otherwise provide to the Government any computer software or computer software documentation in which the Government has previously obtained rights with the Government's pre-existing rights in that software or documentation unless the parties have agreed otherwise or restrictions on the Government's rights to use, modify, produce, release, or disclose the software or documentation have expired. When restrictions are still applicable, the contractor is permitted to mark the software or documentation with the appropriate restrictive legend.

(c) *Unmarked computer software or computer software documentation.* (1) Computer software or computer software documentation delivered or otherwise provided under a contract without restrictive markings shall be presumed to have been delivered with unlimited rights and may be released or disclosed without restriction. To the extent practicable, if a contractor has requested permission (see paragraph (c)(2) of this subsection) to correct an inadvertent omission of markings, do not release or disclose the software or documentation pending evaluation of the request.

(2) A contractor may request permission to have appropriate legends placed on unmarked computer software or computer software documentation at its expense. The request must be received by the contracting officer within six months following the furnishing or delivery of such software or documentation, or any extension of that time approved by the contracting officer. The person making the request must—

(i) Identify the software or documentation that should have been marked;

(ii) Demonstrate that the omission of the marking was inadvertent, the proposed marking is justified and conforms with the requirements for the marking of computer software or computer software documentation contained in the clause at 252.227-7014; and

(iii) Acknowledge, in writing, that the Government has no liability with respect to any disclosure, reproduction, or use of the software or documentation made prior to the addition of the marking or resulting from the omission of the marking.

(3) Contracting officers should grant permission to mark only if the software or documentation were not distributed outside the Government or were distributed outside the Government with restrictions on further use or disclosure.

[DAC 91-8, 60 FR 33464, 6/28/95, effective 6/30/95; Final rule, 63 FR 55040, 10/14/98, effective 10/14/98]

227.7203-11 Contractor procedures and records.

(a) The clause at 252.227-7014, Rights in Noncommercial Computer Software and Noncommercial Computer Software Documentation, requires a contractor, and its subcontractors or suppliers that will deliver computer software or computer software documentation with other than unlimited rights, to establish and follow written procedures to assure that restrictive markings are used only when authorized and to maintain records to justify the validity of restrictive markings.

(b) The clause at 252.227-7019, Validation of Asserted Restrictions—Computer Software, requires contractors and their subcontractors or suppliers at any tier to maintain records sufficient to justify the validity of markings that assert restrictions on the use, modification, reproduction, release, performance, display, or disclosure of computer software.

[DAC 91-8, 60 FR 33464, 6/28/95, effective 6/30/95]

227.7203-12 Government right to establish conformity of markings.

(a) *Nonconforming markings.* (1) Authorized markings are identified in the clause at 252.227-7014, Rights in Noncommercial Computer Software and Noncommercial Computer Software Documentation. All other markings are nonconforming markings. An authorized marking that is not in the form, or differs in substance, from the marking requirements in the clause at 252.227-7014 is also a nonconforming marking.

(2) The correction of nonconforming markings on computer software is not subject to 252.227-7019, Validation of Asserted Restrictions—Computer Software, and the correction of nonconforming markings on computer software documentation (technical data) is not subject to 252.227-7037, Validation of Restrictive Markings on Technical Data. To the extent practicable, the contracting officer should return computer software or computer software documentation bearing nonconforming markings to the person who has placed the nonconforming markings on the software or documentation to provide that person an opportunity to correct or strike the nonconforming markings at that person's expense. If that person fails to correct the nonconformity and return the corrected software or documentation within 60 days following the person's receipt of the software or documentation, the contracting officer may correct or strike the nonconformity at the person's expense. When it is impracticable to return computer software or computer software documentation for correction, contracting officers may unilaterally correct any nonconforming markings at Government expense. Prior to correction, the software or documentation may be used in accordance with the proper restrictive marking.

(b) *Unjustified markings.* (1) An unjustified marking is an authorized marking that does not depict accurately restrictions applicable to the Government's use, modification, reproduction, release, or disclosure of the marked computer software or computer software documentation. For example, a restricted rights legend placed on computer software developed under a Government contract either exclusively at Government expense or with mixed funding (situations under which the Government obtains unlimited or government purpose rights) is an unjustified marking.

(2) Contracting officers have the right to review and challenge the validity of unjustified markings. However, at any time during performance of a contract and notwithstanding existence of a challenge, the contracting officer and the person who has asserted a restrictive marking may agree that the restrictive marking is not justified. Upon such agreement, the contracting officer may, at his or her election, either—

(i) Strike or correct the unjustified marking at that person's expense; or

(ii) Return the computer software or computer software documentation to the person asserting the restriction for correction at that person's expense. If the software or documentation are returned and that person fails to correct or strike the unjustified restriction and return the corrected software or documentation to the contracting officer within 60 days following receipt of the software or documentation, the unjustified marking shall be corrected or stricken at that person's expense.

[DAC 91-8, 60 FR 33464, 6/28/95, effective 6/30/95]

227.7203-13 Government right to review, verify, challenge, and validate asserted restrictions.

(a) *General*. An offeror's or contractor's assertion(s) of restrictions on the Government's rights to use, modify, reproduce, release, or disclose computer software or computer software documentation do not, by themselves, determine the extent of the Government's rights in such software or documentation. The Government may require an offeror or contractor to submit sufficient information to permit an evaluation of a particular asserted restriction and may challenge asserted restrictions when there are reasonable grounds to believe that an assertion is not valid.

(b) *Requests for information*. Contracting officers should have a reason to suspect that an asserted restriction might not be correct prior to requesting information. When requesting information, provide the offeror or contractor the reason(s) for suspecting that an asserted restriction might not be correct. A need for additional license rights is not, by itself, a sufficient basis for requesting information concerning an asserted restriction. Follow the procedures at 227.7203-5(d) when additional license rights are needed but there is no basis to suspect that an asserted restriction might not be valid.

(c) *Transacting matters directly with subcontractors*. The clause at 252.227-7019, Validation of Asserted Restrictions—Computer Software, obtains the contractor's agreement that the Government may transact matters under the clause directly with a subcontractor or supplier, at any tier, without creating or implying privity of contract. Contracting officers should permit a subcontractor or supplier to transact challenge and validation matters directly with the Government when—

(1) A subcontractor's or supplier's business interests in its technical data would be compromised if the data were disclosed to a higher tier contractor.

(2) There is reason to believe that the contractor will not respond in a timely manner to a challenge and an untimely response would jeopardize a subcontractor's or supplier's right to assert restrictions; or

(3) Requested to do so by a subcontractor or supplier.

(d) *Challenging asserted restrictions*. (1) *Pre-award considerations*. The challenge procedures in the clause at 252.227-7019 could significantly delay competitive procurements. Therefore, avoid challenging asserted restrictions prior to a competitive contract award unless resolution of the assertion is essential for successful completion of the procurement.

(2) *Computer software documentation*. Computer software documentation is technical data. Challenges to asserted restrictions on the Government's rights to use, modify, reproduce, release, perform, display, or disclose computer software documentation must be made in accordance with the clause

at 252.227-7037, Validation of Restrictive Markings on Technical Data, and the guidance at 227.7103-13. The procedures in the clause at 252.227-7037 implement requirements contained in 10 U.S.C. 2321. Resolution of questions regarding the validity of asserted restrictions using the process described at 227.7103-12(b)(2) is strongly encouraged.

(3) *Computer software.* (i) Asserted restrictions should be reviewed before acceptance of the computer software deliverable under a contract. The Government's right to challenge an assertion expires three years after final payment under the contract or three years after delivery of the software, whichever is later. Those limitations on the Government's challenge rights do not apply to software that is publicly available, has been furnished to the Government without restrictions, or has been otherwise made available without restrictions.

(ii) Contracting officers must have reasonable grounds to challenge the current validity of an asserted restriction. Before challenging an asserted restriction, carefully consider all available information pertaining to the asserted restrictions. Resolution of questions regarding the validity of asserted restrictions using the process described at 227.7203-12(b)(2) is strongly encouraged. After consideration of the situations described in paragraph (c) of this subsection, contracting officers may request the person asserting a restriction to furnish a written explanation of the facts and supporting documentation for the assertion in sufficient detail to enable the contracting officer to determine the validity of the assertion. Additional supporting documentation may be requested when the explanation provided by that person does not, in the contracting officer's opinion, establish the validity of the assertion.

(iii) Assertions may be challenged whether or not supporting documentation was requested. Challenges must be in writing and issued to the person asserting the restriction.

(4) *Extension of response time.* The contracting officer, at his or her discretion, may extend the time for response contained in a challenge, as appropriate, if the contractor submits a timely written request showing the need for additional time to prepare a response.

(e) *Validating or denying asserted restrictions.* (1) Contracting officers must promptly issue a final decision denying or sustaining the validity of each challenged assertion unless the parties have agreed on the disposition of the assertion. When a final decision denying the validity of an asserted restriction is made following a timely response to a challenge, the Government is obligated to continue to respect the asserted restrictions through final disposition of any appeal unless the agency head notifies the person asserting the restriction that urgent or compelling circumstances do not permit the Government to continue to respect the asserted restriction. See 252.227-7019(g) for restrictions applicable following a determination of urgent and compelling circumstances.

(2) Only a contracting officer's final decision, or actions of an agency Board of Contract Appeals or a court of competent jurisdiction, that sustain the validity of an asserted restriction constitute validation of the restriction.

(f) *Multiple challenges to an asserted restriction.* When more than one contracting officer challenges an asserted restriction, the contracting officer who made the earliest challenge is responsible for coordinating the Government challenges. That contracting officer shall consult with all other contracting officers making challenges, verify that all challenges apply to the same asserted restriction and, after consulting with the contractor, subcontractor, or supplier asserting the restriction, issue a schedule that provides that person a reasonable opportunity to respond to each challenge.

[DAC 91-8, 60 FR 33464, 6/28/95, effective 6/30/95; Final rule, 76 FR 58144, 9/20/2011, effective 9/20/2011; Final rule, 81 FR 65565, 9/23/2016, effective 9/23/2016]

227.7203-14 Conformity, acceptance, and warranty of

computer software and computer software documentation.

(a) *Computer software documentation.* Computer software documentation is technical data. See 227.7103-14 for appropriate guidance and statutory requirements.

(b) *Computer software. (1) Conformity and acceptance. Solicitations and contracts requiring the delivery of computer software shall specify the requirements the software must satisfy to be acceptable.* Contracting officers, or their authorized representatives, are responsible for determining whether computer software tendered for acceptance conforms to the contractual requirements. Except for nonconforming restrictive markings (follow the procedures at 227.7203-12(a) if nonconforming markings are the sole reason computer software tendered for acceptance fails to conform to contractual requirements), do not accept software that does not conform in all respects to applicable contractual requirements. Correction or replacement of nonconforming software, or an equitable reduction in contract price when correction or replacement of the nonconforming data is not practicable or is not in the Government's interests, shall be accomplished in accordance with—

(i) The provisions of a contract clause providing for inspection and acceptance of deliverables and remedies for nonconforming deliverables; or

(ii) The procedures at FAR 46.407(c) through (g), if the contract does not contain an inspection clause providing remedies for nonconforming deliverables.

(2) *Warranties. (i) Weapon systems.* Computer software that is a component of a weapon system or major subsystem should be warranted as part of the weapon system warranty. Follow the procedures at 246.7.

(ii) *Non-weapon systems.* Approval of the chief of the contracting office must be obtained to use a computer software warranty other than a weapon system warranty. Consider the factors at FAR 46.703 in deciding whether to obtain a computer software warranty. When approval for a warranty has been obtained, the clause at 252.246-7001, Warranty of Data, and its alternates, may be appropriately modified for use with computer software or a procurement specific clause may be developed.

[DAC 91-8, 60 FR 33464, 6/28/95, effective 6/30/95; Final rule, 76 FR 3536, 1/20/2011, effective 1/20/2011]

227.7203-15 Subcontractor rights in computer software or computer software documentation.

(a) Subcontractors and suppliers at all tiers should be provided the same protection for their rights in computer software or computer software documentation as are provided to prime contractors.

(b) The clauses at 252.227-7019, Validation of Asserted Restrictions—Computer Software, and 252.227-7037, Validation of Restrictive Markings on Technical Data, obtain a contractor's agreement that the Government's transaction of validation or challenge matters directly with subcontractors at any tier does not establish or imply privity of contract. When a subcontractor or supplier exercises its right to transact validation matters directly with the Government, contracting officers shall deal directly with such persons, as provided at 227.7203-13(c) for computer software and 227.7103-13(c)(3) for computer software documentation (technical data).

(c) Require prime contractors whose contracts include the following clauses to include those clauses, without modification except for appropriate identification of the parties, in contracts with subcontractors or suppliers who will be furnishing computer software in response to a Government requirement (see 227.7103-15(c) for clauses required when subcontractors or suppliers will be furnishing computer software documentation (technical data)):

(1) 252.227-7014, Rights in Noncommercial Computer Software and Noncommercial Computer Software Documentation;

(2) 252.227-7019, Validation of Asserted Restrictions—Computer Software;

(3) 252.227-7025, Limitations on the Use or Disclosure of Government Furnished Information Marked with Restrictive Legends; and

(4) 252.227-7028, Technical Data or Computer Software Previously Delivered to the Government.

(d) Do not require contractors to have their subcontractors or suppliers at any tier relinquish rights in technical data to the contractor, a higher tier subcontractor, or to the Government, as a condition for award of any contract, subcontract, purchase order, or similar instrument except for the rights obtained by the Government under the provisions of the Rights in Noncommercial Computer Software and Noncommercial Computer Software Documentation clause contained in the contractor's contract with the Government.

[DAC 91-8, 60 FR 33464, 6/28/95, effective 6/30/95; Final rule, 76 FR 76318, 12/7/2011, effective 12/7/2011]

227.7203-16 Providing computer software or computer software documentation to foreign governments, foreign contractors, or international organizations.

Computer software or computer software documentation may be released or disclosed to foreign governments, foreign contractors, or international organizations only if release or disclosure is otherwise permitted both by Federal export controls and other national security laws or regulations. Subject to such laws and regulations, the Department of Defense—

(a) May release or disclose computer software or computer software documentation in which it has obtained unlimited rights to such foreign entities or authorize the use of such data by those entities; and

(b) Shall not release or disclose computer software or computer software documentation for which restrictions on use, release, or disclosure have been asserted to such foreign entities or authorize the use of such data by those entities, unless the intended recipient is subject to the same provisions as included in the use and nondisclosure agreement at 227.7103-7 and the requirements of the clause at 252.227-7014, Rights in Noncommercial Computer Software and Noncommercial Computer Software Documentation, governing use, modification, reproduction, release, performance, display, or disclosure of such data have been satisfied.

[DAC 91-8, 60 FR 33464, 6/28/95, effective 6/30/95]

227.7203-17 Overseas contracts with foreign sources.

(a) The clause at 252.227-7032, Rights in Technical Data and Computer Software (Foreign), may be used in contracts with foreign contractors to be performed overseas, except Canadian purchases (see paragraph (c) of this subsection) in lieu of the clause at 252.227-7014, Rights in Noncommercial Computer Software and Noncommercial Computer Software Documentation, when the Government requires the unrestricted right to use, modify, reproduce, release, perform, display, or disclose all computer software or computer software documentation to be delivered under the contract. Do not use the clause in contracts for special works.

(b) When the Government does not require unlimited rights, the clause at 252.227-7032 may be modified to accommodate the needs of a specific overseas procurement situation. The Government should obtain rights to the computer software or computer software documentation that are not less than the rights the Government would have obtained under the software rights clause(s) prescribed in this part for a comparable procurement performed within the United States or its outlying areas.

(c) Contracts for Canadian purchases shall include the appropriate software rights clause prescribed in this part for a comparable procurement performed within the United States or its outlying areas.

[DAC 91-8, 60 FR 33464, 6/28/95, effective 6/30/95; Final rule, 70 FR 35543, 6/21/2005, effective 6/21/2005]

227.7204 Contracts under the Small Business Innovative Research Program.

When contracting under the Small Business Innovation Research Program, follow the procedures at 227.7104.

[DAC 91-8, 60 FR 33464, 6/28/95, effective 6/30/95; Final rule, 76 FR 3536, 1/20/2011, effective 1/20/2011]

227.7205 Contracts for special works.

(a) Use the clause at 252.227-7020, Rights in Special Works, in solicitations and contracts where the Government has a specific need to control the distribution of computer software or computer software documentation first produced, created, or generated in the performance of a contract and required to be delivered under that contract, including controlling distribution by obtaining an assignment of copyright, or a specific need to obtain indemnity for liabilities that may arise out of the creation, delivery, use, modification, reproduction, release, performance, display, or disclosure of such software or documentation. Use the clause—

(1) In lieu of the clause at 252.227-7014, Rights in Noncommercial Computer Software and Noncommercial Computer Software Documentation, when the Government must own or control copyright in all computer software or computer software documentation first produced, created, or generated and required to be delivered under a contract; or

(2) In addition to the clause at 252.227-7014 when the Government must own or control copyright in some of the computer software or computer software documentation first produced, created, or generated and required to be delivered under a contract. The specific software or documentation in which the Government must own or control copyright must be identified in a special contract requirement.

(b) Although the Government obtains an assignment of copyright and unlimited rights in the computer software or computer software documentation delivered as a special work under the clause at 252.227-7020, the contractor retains use and disclosure rights in that software or documentation. If the Government needs to restrict a contractor's rights to use or disclose a special work, it must also negotiate a special license which specifically restricts the contractor's use or disclosure rights.

(c) The clause at 252.227-7020 does not permit a contractor to incorporate into a special work any work copyrighted by others unless the contractor obtains the contracting officer's permission to do so and obtains for the Government a non-exclusive, paid up, world-wide license to make and distribute copies of that work, to prepare derivative works, to perform or display any portion of that work, and to permit others to do so for government purposes. Grant permission only when the Government's requirements cannot be satisfied unless the third party work is included in the deliverable work.

(d) Examples of other works which may be procured under the clause at 252.227-7020 include, but are not limited to, audiovisual works, scripts, soundtracks, musical compositions, and adaptations; histories of departments, agencies, services or units thereof; surveys of Government establishments; instructional works or guidance to Government officers and employees on the discharge of their official duties; reports, books, studies, surveys or similar documents; collections of data containing information pertaining to individuals that, if disclosed, would violate the right of privacy or publicity of the individuals to whom the information relates; or investigative reports.

[DAC 91-8, 60 FR 33464, 6/28/95, effective 6/30/95]

227.7206 Contracts for architect-engineer services.

Follow 227.7107 when contracting for architect-engineer services.

[DAC 91-8, 60 FR 33464, 6/28/95, effective 6/30/95]

227.7207 Contractor data repositories.

Follow 227.7108 when it is in the Government's interests to have a data repository include computer software or to have a separate computer software repository. Contractual instruments establishing the repository requirements must appropriately reflect the repository manager's software responsibilities.

[DAC 91-8, 60 FR 33464, 6/28/95, effective 6/30/95]

PART 228—BONDS AND INSURANCE

Table of Contents

Subpart 228.1—Bonds

Performance and payment bonds for construction contracts 228.102
General 228.102-1
Defense Environmental Restoration Program construction contracts ... 228.102-70
Other types of bonds 228.105
Administration 228.106
Withholding contract payments 228.106-7
[Removed] 228.170

Subpart 228.3—Insurance

Risk-pooling arrangements 228.304
Overseas workers' compensation and war-hazard insurance 228.305
Insurance under cost-reimbursement contracts 228.307
Group insurance plans 228.307-1
Solicitation provision and contract clause on liability insurance under cost-reimbursement contracts 228.311
Contract clause 228.311-1
Additional clauses 228.370

PART 228—BONDS AND INSURANCE

SUBPART 228.1—BONDS

228.102 Performance and payment bonds for construction contracts. (No Text)

228.102-1 General.

The requirement for performance and payment bonds is waived for cost-reimbursement contracts. However, for cost-type contracts with fixed-price construction subcontracts over $35,000, require the prime contractor to obtain from each of its construction subcontractors performance and payment protections in favor of the prime contractor as follows:

(1) For fixed-price construction subcontracts over $35,000, but not exceeding $150,000, payment protection sufficient to pay labor and material costs, using any of the alternatives listed at FAR 28.102-1(b)(1).

(2) For fixed-price construction subcontracts over $150,000—

(i) A payment bond sufficient to pay labor and material costs; and

(ii) A performance bond in an equal amount if available at no additional cost.

[DAC 91-3, 57 FR 42631, 9/15/92, effective 8/31/92; DAC 91-5, 58 FR 28458, 5/13/93, effective 4/30/93; DAC 91-7, 60 FR 29491, 6/5/95, effective 5/17/95; Final rule, 68 FR 36944, 6/20/2003, effective 6/20/2003; Final rule, 71 FR 75891, 12/19/2006, effective 12/19/2006; Final rule, 75 FR 45072, 8/2/2010, effective 10/1/2010; Final rule, 80 FR 36903, 6/26/2015, effective 10/1/2015]

228.102-70 Defense Environmental Restoration Program construction contracts.

For Defense Environmental Restoration Program construction contracts entered into pursuant to 10 U.S.C. 2701

(a) Any rights of action under the performance bond shall only accrue to, and be for the exclusive use of, the obligee named in the bond;

(b) In the event of default, the surety's liability on the performance bond is limited to the cost of completion of the contract work, less the balance of unexpended funds. Under no circumstances shall the liability exceed the penal sum of the bond;

(c) The surety shall not be liable for indemnification or compensation of the obligee for loss or liability arising from personal injury or property damage, even if the injury or damage was caused by a breach of the bonded contract; and

(d) Once it has taken action to meet its obligations under the bond, the surety is entitled to any indemnification and identical standard of liability to which the contractor was entitled under the contract or applicable laws and regulations.

[Final rule, 68 FR 36944, 6/20/2003, effective 6/20/2003]

228.105 Other types of bonds.

Fidelity and forgery bonds generally are not required but are authorized for use when—

(1) Necessary for the protection of the Government or the contractor; or

(2) The investigative and claims services of a surety company are desired.

[Final rule, 70 FR 8537, 2/22/2005, effective 2/22/2005]

228.106 Administration. (No Text)

228.106-7 Withholding contract payments.

(a) Withholding may be appropriate in other than construction contracts (see FAR 32.112-1(b)).

[Final rule, 57 FR 42707, 9/16/92, effective 9/8/92; Final rule, 70 FR 8537, 2/22/2005, effective 2/22/2005]

228.170 [Removed]

[Final rule, 83 FR 54679, 10/31/2018, effective 10/31/2018]

SUBPART 228.3—INSURANCE

228.304 Risk-pooling arrangements.

DoD has established the National Defense Projects Rating Plan, also known as the Special Casualty Insurance Rating Plan, as a risk-pooling arrangement to minimize the cost to the Government of purchasing the liability insurance listed in FAR 28.307-2. Use the plan in accordance with the procedures at PGI 228.304 when it provides the necessary coverage more advantageously than commercially available coverage.

[Final rule, 69 FR 65090, 11/10/2004, effective 11/10/2004]

228.305 Overseas workers' compensation and war-hazard insurance.

(d) When submitting requests for waiver, follow the procedures at PGI 228.305(d).

[Final rule, 69 FR 65090, 11/10/2004, effective 11/10/2004]

228.307 Insurance under cost-reimbursement contracts. (No Text)

228.307-1 Group insurance plans.

The Defense Department Group Term Insurance Plan is available for contractor use under cost-reimbursement type contracts when approved as provided in department or agency regulations. A contractor is eligible if—

(a) The number of covered employees is 500 or more; and

(b) The contractor has all cost-reimbursement contracts; or

(c) At least 90 percent of the payroll for contractor operations to be covered by the Plan is under cost-reimbursement contracts.

228.311 Solicitation provision and contract clause on liability insurance under cost-reimbursement contracts. (No Text)

228.311-1 Contract clause.

Use the clause at FAR 52.228-7, Insurance—Liability to Third Persons, in solicitations and contracts, other than those for construction and those for architect-engineer services, when a cost-reimbursement contract is contemplated, unless the head of the contracting activity waives the requirement for use of the clause.

[Redesignated from 228.311-2, DAC 91-11, 61 FR 50446, 9/26/96, effective 9/26/96]

228.370 Additional clauses.

(a) Use the clause at 252.228-7000, Reimbursement for War-Hazard Losses, when—

(1) The clause at FAR 52.228-4, Worker's Compensation and War-Hazard Insurance Overseas, is used; and

(2) The head of the contracting activity decides not to allow the contractor to buy insurance for war-hazard losses.

(b) (1) Use the clause at 252.228-7001, Ground and Flight Risk, in all solicitations and contracts for the acquisition, development, production, modification, maintenance, repair, flight, or overhaul of aircraft, except those solicitations and contracts—

(i) That are strictly for activities incidental to the normal operations of the aircraft (*e.g.*, refueling operations, minor non-structural actions not requiring towing such as replacing aircraft tires due to wear and tear);

(ii) That are awarded under FAR Part 12 procedures and are for the development, production, modification, maintenance, repair, flight, or overhaul of aircraft; or otherwise involving the furnishing of aircraft;

(iii) For which a non-DoD customer (including a foreign military sales customer) has not agreed to assume the risk for loss or destruction of, or damages to, the aircraft; or

(iv) For commercial derivative aircraft that are to be maintained to Federal Aviation Administration (FAA) airworthiness when the work will be performed at a licensed FAA repair station.

(2) The clause at 252.228-7001 may be modified only as follows:

(i) Include a modified definition of "aircraft" if the contract covers other than conventional types of winged aircraft, *i.e.*, helicopters, vertical take-off or landing aircraft, lighter-than-air airships, unmanned aerial vehicles, or other nonconventional aircraft. The modified definition should describe a stage of manufacture comparable to the standard definition.

(ii) Modify "in the open" to include "hush houses," test hangars and comparable structures, and other designated areas.

(iii) Expressly define the "contractor's premises" where the aircraft will be located during and for contract performance. These locations may include contract premises which are owned or leased by the contractor or subcontractor, or premises where the contractor or subcontractor is a permittee or licensee or has a right to use, including Government airfields.

(iv) Revise paragraph (e)(3) of the clause to provide Government assumption of risk for transportation by conveyance on streets or highways when transportation is—

(A) Limited to the vicinity of contractor premises; and

(B) Incidental to work performed under the contract.

(3) Follow the procedures at PGI 228.370(b) when using the clause at 252.228-7001.

(c) The clause at 252.228-7003, Capture and Detention, may be used when contractor employees are subject to capture and detention and may not be covered by the War Hazards Compensation Act (42 U.S.C. 1701 *et seq.*).

(d) Use the clause at 252.228-7005, Mishap Reporting and Investigation Involving Aircraft, Missiles, and Space Launch Vehicles, in solicitations and contracts that involve the manufacture, modification, overhaul, or repair of aircraft, missiles, and space launch vehicles.

(e) Use the clause at 252.228-7006, Compliance with Spanish Laws and Insurance, in solicitations and contracts for services or construction to be performed in Spain, unless the contractor is a Spanish concern.

[DAC 91-3, 57 FR 42631, 9/15/92, effective 8/31/92; DAC 91-11, 61 FR 50446, 9/26/96, effective 9/26/96; DAC 91-12, 62 FR 34114, 6/24/97, effective 6/24/97; Final rule, 63 FR 69006, 12/15/98, effective 12/15/98; Final rule, 75 FR 32642, 6/8/2010, effective 6/8/2010; Final rule, 84 FR 65311, 11/27/2019, effective 11/27/2019]

PART 229—TAXES

Table of Contents

Subpart 229.1—General

Resolving tax problems 229.101
Reporting of foreign taxation on U.S. assistance programs 229.170
Definition 229.170-1
Policy 229.170-2
Reports 229.170-3
Contract clause 229.170-4

Subpart 229.4—Contract Clauses

Foreign contracts 229.402
Foreign fixed-price contracts 229.402-1
Additional provisions and clauses 229.402-70

Subpart 229.70—Special Procedures for Overseas Contracts

PART 229—TAXES

SUBPART 229.1—GENERAL

229.101 Resolving tax problems.

(a) Within DoD, the agency-designated legal counsels are the defense agency General Counsels, the General Counsels of the Navy and Air Force, and for the Army, the Chief, Contract Law Division, Office of the Judge Advocate General. For additional information on the designated legal counsels, see PGI 229.101(a).

(b) For information on fuel excise taxes, see PGI 229.101(b).

(c) For guidance on directing a contractor to litigate the applicability of a particular tax, see PGI 229.101(c).

(d) For information on tax relief agreements between the United States and European foreign governments, see PGI 229.101(d).

[DAC 91-12, 62 FR 34114, 6/24/97, effective 6/24/97; DAC 91-13, 63 FR 11522, 3/9/98, effective 3/9/98; Final rule, 70 FR 8538, 2/22/2005, effective 2/22/2005; Final rule, 71 FR 14099, 3/21/2006, effective 3/21/2006]

229.170 Reporting of foreign taxation on U.S. assistance programs. (No Text)

[Interim rule, 70 FR 57191, 9/30/2005, effective 9/30/2005; Final rule, 71 FR 18671, 4/12/2006, effective 4/12/2006]

229.170-1 Definition.

Commodities, as used in this section, means any material, articles, supplies, goods, or equipment.

[Interim rule, 70 FR 57191, 9/30/2005, effective 9/30/2005; Final rule, 71 FR 18671, 4/12/2006, effective 4/12/2006]

229.170-2 Policy

(a) By law, bilateral agreements with foreign governments must include a provision that commodities acquired under contracts funded by U.S. assistance programs shall be exempt from taxation by the foreign government. If taxes or customs duties nevertheless are imposed, the foreign government must reimburse the amount of such taxes to the U.S. Government (Section 579 of Division E of the Consolidated Appropriations Act, 2003 (Pub. L. 108-7), as amended by Section 506 of Division D of the Consolidated Appropriations Act, 2004 (Pub. L. 108-199), and similar sections in subsequent acts).

(b) This foreign tax exemption—

(1) applies to a contract or subcontract for commodities when—

(i) The funds are appropriated by the annual foreign operations appropriations act; and

(ii) the value of the contract or subcontract is $500 or more;

(2) Does not apply to the acquisition of services;

(3) Generally is implemented through letters of offer and acceptance, other country-to-country agreements, or Federal interagency agreements; and

(4) Requires reporting of noncompliance for effective implementation.

[Interim rule, 70 FR 57191, 9/30/2005, effective 9/30/2005; Final rule 71 FR 18671, 4/12/2006, effective 4/12/2006]

229.170-3 Reports.

The contracting officer shall submit a report to the designated Security Assistance Office when a foreign government or entity imposes tax or customs duties on commodities acquired under contracts or subcontracts meeting the criteria of 229.170-2(b)(1). Follow the procedures at PGI 229-170-3 for submission of reports.

[Interim rule, 70 FR 57191, 9/30/2005, effective 9/30/2005; Final rule, 71 FR 18671, 4/12/2006, effective 4/12/2006]

229.170-4 Contract clause.

Use the clause at 252.229-7011, Reporting of Foreign Taxes—U.S. Assistance programs, in solicitations and contracts funded with U.S. assistance appropriations provided in the annual foreign operations appropriations act.

[Interim rule, 70 FR 57191, 9/30/2005, effective 9/30/2005; Final rule, 71 FR 18671, 4/12/2006, effective 4/12/2006]

SUBPART 229.4—CONTRACT CLAUSES

229.402 Foreign contracts. (No Text)

229.402-1 Foreign fixed-price contracts.

Use the clause at 252.229-7000, Invoices Exclusive of Taxes or Duties, in solicitations and contracts when a fixed-price contract will be awarded to a foreign concern.

[DAC 91-12, 62 FR 34114, 6/24/97, effective 6/24/97]

229.402-70 Additional provisions and clauses.

(a) Use the basic or the alternate of the clause at 252.229–7001, Tax Relief, in solicitations and contracts when a contract will be awarded to a foreign concern for performance in a foreign country.

(1) Use the basic clause in solicitations and contracts when the contract will be performed in a foreign country other than Germany.

(2) Use the alternate I clause in solicitations and contracts when the contract will be performed in Germany.

(b) Use the clause at 252.229-7002, Customs Exemptions (Germany), in solicitations and contracts requiring the import of U.S. manufactured products into Germany.

(c) (1) Use the clause at 252.229-7003, Tax Exemptions (Italy), in solicitations and contracts when contract performance will be in Italy.

(2) Use the provision at 252.229-7012, Tax Exemptions (Italy)—Representation, in solicitations that contain the clause at 252.229-7003, Tax Exemptions (Italy). If the solicitation includes the provision at FAR 52.204-7, do not separately list 252.229-7012 in the solicitation.

(d) Use the clause at 252.229-7004, Status of Contractor as a Direct Contractor (Spain), in solicitations and contracts requiring the import into Spain of supplies for construction, development, maintenance, or operation of Spanish-American installations and facilities.

(e) (1) Use the clause at 252.229-7005, Tax Exemptions (Spain), in solicitations and contracts when contract performance will be in Spain.

(2) Use the provision at 252.229-7013, Tax Exemptions (Spain)—Representation, in solicitations that contain the clause at 252.229-7005, Tax Exemptions (Spain). If the solicitation includes the provision at FAR 52.204-7, do not separately list 252.229-7013 in the solicitation.

(f) Use the clause at DFARS 252.229-7006, Value Added Tax Exclusion (United Kingdom), in solicitations and contracts when contract performance will be in the United Kingdom.

(g) Use the clause at 252.229-7007, Verification of United States Receipt of Goods, in solicitations and contracts when contract performance will be in the United Kingdom.

(h) Use the clause at 252.229-7008, Relief from Import Duty (United Kingdom), in solicitations issued and contracts awarded in the United Kingdom.

(i) Use the clause at 252.229-7009, Relief from Customs Duty and Value Added Tax on Fuel (Passenger Vehicles) (United Kingdom), in solicitations issued and contracts awarded in the United Kingdom for fuels (gasoline or diesel) and lubricants used in passenger vehicles (excluding taxis).

(j) Use the clause at 252.229-7010, Relief from Customs Duty on Fuel (United Kingdom), in solicitations issued and contracts awarded in the United Kingdom that require the use of fuels (gasoline or diesel) and lubricants in taxis or vehicles other than passenger vehicles.

(k) Use the clause at 252.229-7014, Taxes—Foreign Contracts in Afghanistan, in solicitations and contracts, including solicitations and contracts using FAR part 12 procedures for the acquisition of commercial items, with performance in Afghanistan, unless the clause at 252.229-7015 is used.

(l) Use the clause at 252.229-7015, Taxes—Foreign Contracts in Afghanistan (North Atlantic Treaty Organization Status of Forces Agreement), instead of the clause at 252.229-7014, Taxes—Foreign Contracts in Afghanistan, in solicitations and contracts, including solicitations and contracts using FAR part 12 procedures for the acquisition of commercial items, with performance in Afghanistan awarded on behalf of the North Atlantic Treaty Organization (NATO), which are governed by the NATO Status of Forces Agreement (SOFA), if approval from the Director, Defense Procurement and Acquisition Policy, Office of the Under Secretary of Defense for Acquisition, Technology, and Logistics, has been obtained prior to each use.

[DAC 91-12, 62 FR 34114, 6/24/97, effective 6/24/97; Final rule, 77 FR 19128, 3/30/2012, effective 3/30/2012; Final rule, 78 FR 37980, 6/25/2013, effective 6/25/2013; Final rule, 78 FR 40043, 7/3/2013, effective 7/3/2013; Final rule, 79 FR 58699, 9/30/2014, effective 9/30/2014; Final rule, 80 FR 81467, 12/30/2015, effective 12/30/2015]

SUBPART 229.70—SPECIAL PROCEDURES FOR OVERSEAS CONTRACTS

To obtain tax relief for overseas contracts, follow the procedures at PGI 229.70.

[Final rule, 70 FR 6375, 2/7/2005, effective 2/7/2005]

PART 230—COST ACCOUNTING STANDARDS ADMINISTRATION

Table of Contents

Subpart 230.2—CAS Program Requirements

Waiver 230.201-5

Subpart 230.70—[Removed]

Subpart 230.71—[Removed]

PART 230—COST ACCOUNTING STANDARDS ADMINISTRATION

SUBPART 230.2—CAS PROGRAM REQUIREMENTS

230.201-5 Waiver.

(a) (1) (A) The military departments and the Director, Defense Procurement and Acquisition Policy, Office of the Under Secretary of Defense (Acquisition, Technology, and Logistics)—

(1) May grant CAS waivers that meet the conditions in FAR 30.201- 5(b) (1); and

(2) May grant CAS waivers that meet the conditions in FAR 30.201- 5(b) (2), provided the cognizant Federal agency official granting the waiver determines that—

(i) The property or services cannot reasonably be obtained under the contract, subcontract, or modification, as applicable, without granting the waiver;

(ii) The price can be determined to be fair and reasonable without the application of the Cost Accounting Standards; and

(iii) There are demonstrated benefits to granting the waiver.

(B) Follow the procedures at PGI 230.201-5(a) (1) for submitting waiver requests to the Director, Defense Procurement and Acquisition Policy.

(2) The military departments shall not delegate CAS waiver authority below the individual responsible for issuing contracting policy for the department.

(e) By November 30th of each year, the military departments shall provide a report to the Director, Defense Procurement and Acquisition Policy, ATTN: DPAP/CPIC, of all waivers granted under FAR 30.201-5(a), during the previous fiscal year, for any contract, subcontract, or modification expected to have a value of $15,000,000 or more. See PGI 230.201-5(e) for format and guidance for the report. The Director, Defense Procurement and Acquisition Policy, will submit a consolidated report to the CAS Board and the congressional defense committees.

(ii) The Director of Defense Procurement and Acquisition Policy will submit a consolidated DoD report to the CAS Board.

[Final rule, 65 FR 36034, 6/6/2000, effective 6/6/2000; Final rule, 68 FR 7438, 2/14/2003, effective 2/14/2003; Final rule, 71 FR 69492, 12/1/2006, effective 12/1/2006; Final rule, 77 FR 52253, 8/29/2012, effective 8/29/2012]

SUBPART 230.70—[REMOVED]

230.7000 [Removed]

[Final rule, 71 FR 69492, 12/1/2006, effective 12/1/2006]

230.7001 [Removed]

[Final rule, 71 FR 69492, 12/1/2006, effective 12/1/2006]

230.7001-1 [Removed]

[Final rule, 71 FR 69492, 12/1/2006, effective 12/1/2006]

230.7001-2 [Removed]

[Final rule, 71 FR 69492, 12/1/2006, effective 12/1/2006]

230.7002 [Removed]

[Final rule, 63 FR 55040, 10/14/98, effective 10/14/98; Final rule, 71 FR 69492, 12/1/2006, effective 12/1/2006]

230.7003 [Removed]

[Final rule, 71 FR 69492, 12/1/2006, effective 12/1/2006]

230.7003-1 [Removed]

[Final rule, 71 FR 69492, 12/1/2006, effective 12/1/2006]

230.7003-2 [Removed]

[Final rule, 71 FR 69492, 12/1/2006, effective 12/1/2006]

230.7004 [Removed]

[Final rule, 71 FR 69492, 12/1/2006, effective 12/1/2006]

230.7004-1 [Removed]

[Final rule, 63 FR 55040, 10/14/98, effective 10/14/98; Final rule, 71 FR 69492, 12/1/2006, effective 12/1/2006]

230.7004-2 [Removed]

[Final rule, 71 FR 69492, 12/1/2006, effective 12/1/2006]

SUBPART 230.71—[REMOVED]

230.7100 [Removed]

[Final rule, 71 FR 69492, 12/1/2006, effective 12/1/2006]

230.7101 [Removed]

[Final rule, 71 FR 69492, 12/1/2006, effective 12/1/2006]

230.7101-1 [Removed]

[Final rule, 71 FR 69492, 12/1/2006, effective 12/1/2006]

230.7101-2 [Removed]

[Final rule, 71 FR 69492, 12/1/2006, effective 12/1/2006]

230.7102 [Removed]

[Final rule, 71 FR 69492, 12/1/2006, effective 12/1/2006]

230.7103 [Removed]

[Final rule, 63 FR 55040, 10/14/98, effective 10/14/98; Final rule, 71 FR 69492, 12/1/2006, effective 12/1/2006]

PART 231—CONTRACT COST PRINCIPLES AND PROCEDURES

Table of Contents

Subpart 231.1—Applicability

Scope of subpart 231.100
Contract clause 231.100-70

Subpart 231.2—Contracts with Commercial Organizations

[Removed] 231.201-2
[Removed] 231.203
Selected costs 231.205
Public relations and advertising costs 231.205-1
Compensation for personal services 231.205-6
[Removed] 231.205-10
Independent research and development and bid and proposal costs 231.205-18
Insurance and indemnification 231.205-19
Legislative lobbying costs 231.205-22
External restructuring costs 231.205-70
Costs related to counterfeit electronic parts and suspect counterfeit electronic parts 231.205-71

Subpart 231.3—Contracts with Educational Institutions

Requirements 231.303

Subpart 231.6—Contracts with State, Local, and Federally Recognized Indian Tribal Governments

Requirements 231.603

Subpart 231.7—Contracts with Nonprofit Organizations

Requirements 231.703

PART 231—CONTRACT COST PRINCIPLES AND PROCEDURES

SUBPART 231.1—APPLICABILITY

231.100 Scope of subpart. (No Text)

231.100-70 Contract clause.

Use the clause at 252.231-7000, Supplemental Cost Principles, in all solicitations and contracts which are subject to the principles and procedures described in FAR subparts 31.1, 31.2, 31.6, or 31.7.

[DAC 91-6, 59 FR 27662, 5/27/94, effective 5/27/94]

SUBPART 231.2—CONTRACTS WITH COMMERCIAL ORGANIZATIONS

231.201-2 [Removed]

[Interim rule, 72 FR 20758, 4/26/2007, effective 4/26/2007; Final rule, 75 FR 48178, 8/10/2010, effective 8/10/2010]

231.203 [Removed]

[Interim rule, 72 FR 20758, 4/26/2007, effective 4/26/2007; Interim rule, 73 FR 27464, 5/13/2008, effective 5/13/2008; Final rule, 75 FR 48178, 8/10/2010, effective 8/10/2010]

231.205 Selected costs. (No Text)

231.205-1 Public relations and advertising costs.

See 225.7303-2(e) for allowability provisions affecting foreign military sales contracts.

(f) Unallowable public relations and advertising costs also include monies paid to the Government associated with the leasing of Government equipment, including lease payments and reimbursement for support services, except for foreign military sales contracts as provided for at 225.7303-2.

[Final rule, 74 FR 68382, 12/24/2009, effective 12/24/2009]

231.205-6 Compensation for personal services.

(f) (1) In accordance with Section 8122 of Pub. L. 104-61, and similar sections in subsequent Defense appropriations acts, costs for bonuses or other payments in excess of the normal salary paid by the contractor to an employee, that are part of restructuring costs associated with a business combination, are unallowable under DoD contracts funded by fiscal year 1996 or subsequent appropriations. This limitation does not apply to severance payments or early retirement incentive payments. (See 231.205-70(b) for the definitions of *business combination* and *restructuring costs*.)

(m) (1) Fringe benefit costs that are contrary to law, employer-employee agreement, or an established policy of the contractor are unallowable.

[DAC 91-4, 57 FR 53600, 11/12/92, effective 10/30/92; DAC 91-5, 58 FR 28458, 5/13/93, effective 4/30/93; Interim rule, 60 FR 2330, 1/9/95, effective 12/14/94; DAC 91-9, 60 FR 61586, 11/30/95, effective 11/30/95; Interim rule, 61 FR 7077, 2/26/96, effective 2/26/96; Interim rule, 61 FR 36305, 7/10/96, effective 7/10/96, finalized without change, DAC 91-12, 62 FR 34114, 6/24/97, effective 6/24/97; DAC 91-11, 61 FR 50446, 9/26/96, effective 9/26/96; Interim rule, 61 FR 58490, 11/15/96, effective 11/15/96, finalized without change, DAC 91-12, 62 FR 34114, 6/24/97, effective 6/24/97; Interim rule, 61 FR 65478, 12/13/96, effective 12/13/96, finalized without change, DAC 91-12, 62 FR 34114, 6/24/97, effective 6/24/97; Interim rule, 62 FR 63035, 11/26/97, effective 11/26/97, finalized without change, 63 FR 64426, 11/20/98; Final rule, 63 FR 14640, 3/26/98, effective 3/26/98; Final rule, 78 FR 73451, 12/6/2013, effective 12/6/2013]

231.205-10 [Removed]

[Final rule, 69 FR 63331, 11/1/2004, effective 11/1/2004]

231.205-18 Independent research and development and bid and proposal costs.

(a) *Definitions.* As used in this subsection—

(i) *Covered contract* means a DoD prime contract for an amount exceeding the simplified acquisition threshold, except for a fixed-price contract without cost incentives. The term also includes a subcontract for an amount exceeding the simplified acquisition threshold, except for a fixed-price subcontract without cost incentives under such a prime contract.

(ii) *Covered segment* means a product division of the contractor that allocated more than $1,100,000 in independent research and development and bid and proposal (IR&D/B&P) costs to covered contracts during the preceding fiscal year. In the case of a contractor that has no product divisions, the term means that contractor as a whole. A product division of the contractor that allocated less than $1,100,000 in IR&D/B&P costs to covered contracts during the preceding fiscal year is not subject to the limitations in paragraph (c) of this subsection.

(iii) *Major contractor* means any contractor whose covered segments allocated a total of more than $11,000,000 in IR&D/B&P costs to covered contracts during the preceding fiscal year. For purposes of calculating the dollar threshold amounts to determine whether a contractor meets the definition of "major contractor," do not include contractor segments allocating less than $1,100,000 of IR&D/B&P costs to covered contracts during the preceding fiscal year.

(c) *Allowability.*

(i) Departments/agencies shall not supplement this regulation in any way that limits IR&D/B&P cost allowability.

(ii) See 225.7303-2(c) for allowability provisions affecting foreign military sale contracts.

(iii) For major contractors, the following limitations apply:

(A) The amount of IR&D/B&P costs allowable under DoD contracts shall not exceed the lesser of—

(1) Such contracts' allocable share of total incurred IR&D/B&O costs; or

(2) The amount of incurred IR&D/B&P costs for projects having potential interest to DoD.

(B) Allowable IR&D/B&P costs are limited to those for projects that are of potential interest to DoD, including activities intended to accomplish any of the following:

(1) Enable superior performance of future U.S. weapon systems and components.

(2) Reduce acquisition costs and life-cycle costs of military systems.

(3) Strengthen the defense industrial and technology base of the United States.

(4) Enhance the industrial competitiveness of the United States.

(5) Promote the development of technologies identified as critical under 10 U.S.C. 2522.

(6) Increase the development and promotion of efficient and effective applications of dual-use technologies.

(7) Provide efficient and effective technologies for achieving such environmental benefits as: Improved environmental data gathering, environmental cleanup and restoration, pollution reduction in manufacturing, environmental conservation, and environmentally safe management of facilities.

(C) For annual IR&D costs to be allowable—

(1) The IR&D projects generating the costs must be reported to the Defense Technical Information Center (DTIC) using the DTIC's online input form and instructions at *http://www.defenseinnovationmarketplace.mil*;

(2) The inputs must be updated at least annually and when the project is completed; and

(3) Copies of the input and updates must be made available for review by the cognizant administrative contracting officer (ACO) and the cognizant Defense Contract Audit Agency auditor to support the allowability of the costs.

[Final rule, 64 FR 8729, 2/23/99, effective 2/23/99; Final rule, 77 FR 4632, 1/30/2012, effective 1/30/2012; Final rule, 81 FR 78008, 11/4/2016, effective 11/4/2016; Publication notice, 20171208; Final rule, 83 FR 42787, 8/24/2018, effective 8/24/2018]

231.205-19 Insurance and indemnification.

(e) In addition to the cost limitations in FAR 31.205-19(e), self-insurance and purchased insurance costs are subject to the requirements of the clauses at 252.217-7012, Liability and Insurance, and 252.228-7001, Ground and Flight Risk.

[Final rule, 75 FR 32642, 6/8/2010, effective 6/8/2010]

231.205-22 Legislative lobbying costs.

(a) Costs associated with preparing any material, report, list, or analysis on the actual or projected economic or employment impact in a particular State or congressional district of an acquisition program for which all research, development, testing, and evaluation has not been completed also are unallowable (10 U.S.C. 2249).

[Final rule, 62 FR 47154, 9/8/97, effective 9/8/97; Final rule, 69 FR 63331, 11/1/2004, effective 11/1/2004]

231.205-70 External restructuring costs.

(a) *Scope.* This subsection—

(1) Prescribes policies and procedures for allowing contractor external restructuring costs when savings would result for DoD; and

(2) Implements 10 U.S.C. 2325.

(b) *Definitions.* As used in this subsection:

(1) *Business combination* means a transaction whereby assets or operations of two or more companies not previously under common ownership or control are combined, whether by merger, acquisition, or sale/purchase of assets.

(2) *External restructuring activities* means restructuring activities occurring after a business combination that affect the operations of companies not previously under common ownership or control. They do not include restructuring activities occurring after a business combination that affect the operations of only one of the companies not previously under common ownership or control, or, when there has been no business combination, restructuring activities undertaken within one company. External restructuring activities are a direct outgrowth of a business combination. They normally will be initiated within 3 years of the business combination.

(3) *Restructuring activities* means nonroutine, nonrecurring, or extraordinary activities to combine facilities, operations, or workforce, in order to eliminate redundant capabilities, improve future operations, and reduce overall costs. Restructuring activities do not include routine or ongoing repositionings and redeployments of a contractor's productive facilities or workforce (e.g., normal plant rearrangement or employee relocation), nor do they include other routine or ordinary activities charged as indirect costs that would otherwise have been incurred (e.g., planning and analysis, contract administration and oversight, or recurring financial and administrative support).

(4) *Restructuring costs* means the costs, including both direct and indirect, of restructuring activities. Restructuring costs that may be allowed include, but are not limited to, severance pay for employees, early retirement incentive payments for employees, employee retraining costs, relocation expense for retained employees, and relocation and rearrangement of plant and equipment. For purposes of this definition, if restructuring costs associated with external restructuring activities allocated to DoD contracts are less than $2.5 million, the costs shall not be subject to the audit, review, and determination requirements of paragraph (c) (4) of this subsection; instead, the normal rules for determining cost allowability in accordance with FAR part 31 shall apply.

(5) *Restructuring savings* means cost reductions, including both direct and indirect cost reductions, that result from restructuring activities. Reassignments of cost to future periods are not restructuring savings.

(c) *Limitations on cost allowability.*

Restructuring costs associated with external restructuring activities shall not be allowed unless—

(1) Such costs are allowable in accordance with FAR part 31 and DFARS part 231;

(2) An audit of projected restructuring costs and restructuring savings is performed;

(3) The cognizant administrative contracting officer (ACO) reviews the audit report and the projected costs and projected

savings, and negotiates an advance agreement in accordance with paragraph (d) of this subsection; and

(4) (i) The official designated in paragraph (c) (4) (ii) of this subsection determines in writing that the audited projected savings, on a present value basis, for DoD resulting from the restructuring will exceed either—

(A) The costs allowed by a factor of at least two to one; or

(B) The cost allowed, and the business combination will result in the preservation of a critical capability that might otherwise be lost to DoD.

(ii) (A) If the amount of restructuring costs is expected to exceed $25 million over a 5-year period, the designated official is the Under Secretary of Defense (Acquisition, Technology, and Logistics) or the Principal Deputy. This authority may not be delegated below the level of an Assistant Secretary of Defense.

(B) For all other cases, the designated official is the Director of the Defense Contract Management Agency. The Director may not delegate this authority.

(d) *Procedures and ACO responsibilities.*

As soon as it is known that the contractor will incur restructuring costs for external restructuring activities, the cognizant ACO shall follow the procedures at PGI 231.205-70(d).

(e) *Information needed to obtain a determination.*

(1) The novation agreement (if one is required).

(2) The contractor's restructuring proposal.

(3) The proposed advance agreement.

(4) The audit report.

(5) Any other pertinent information.

(6) The cognizant ACO's recommendation for a determination. This recommendation must clearly indicate one of the following, consistent with paragraph (c) (4) (i) of this subsection:

(i) The audited projected savings for DoD will exceed the costs allowed by a factor of at least two to one on a present value basis.

(ii) The business combination will result in the preservation of a critical capability that might otherwise be lost to DoD, and the audited projected savings for DoD will exceed the costs allowed on a present value basis.

(f) *Contracting officer responsibilities.*

(1) The contracting officer, in consultation with the cognizant ACO, should consider including a repricing clause in noncompetitive fixed-price contracts that are negotiated during the period between—

(i) The time a business combination is announced; and

(ii) The time the contractor's forward pricing rates are adjusted to reflect the impact of restructuring.

(2) The decision to use a repricing clause will depend upon the particular circumstances involved, including—

(i) When the restructuring will take place;

(ii) When restructuring savings will begin to be realized;

(iii) The contract performance period;

(iv) Whether the contracting parties are able to make a reasonable estimate of the impact of restructuring on the contract; and

(v) The size of the potential dollar impact of restructuring on the contract.

(3) If the contracting officer decides to use a repricing clause, the clause must provide for a downward-only price adjustment to ensure that DoD receives its appropriate share of restructuring net savings.

[Interim rule, 63 FR 7308, 2/13/98, effective 2/13/98; corrected 63 FR 12862, 3/16/98; finalized without change, 63 FR 64426, 11/20/98; Final rule, 64 FR 18827, 4/16/99, effective 4/16/99; Final rule, 65 FR 39703, 6/27/2000, effective 6/27/2000; Final rule, 68 FR 7438, 2/14/2003, effective 2/14/2003; Final rule, 69 FR 63331, 11/1/2004, effective 11/1/2004; Interim rule, 70 FR 43074, 7/26/2005, effective 7/26/2005; Final rule, 71 FR 9271, 2/23/2006, effective 2/23/2006]

231.205-71 Costs related to counterfeit electronic parts and suspect counterfeit electronic parts.

(a) *Scope*. This section implements the requirements of section 818(c)(2), National Defense Authorization Act for Fiscal Year 2012 (Pub. L. 112-81), as modified by section 833, National Defense Authorization Act for Fiscal Year 2013 (Pub. L. 112-239), and section 885 of the National Defense Authorization Act for Fiscal Year 2016 (Pub. L. 114-92).

(b) The costs of counterfeit electronic parts and suspect counterfeit electronic parts and the costs of rework or corrective action that may be required to remedy the use or inclusion of such parts are unallowable, unless—

(1) The contractor has an operational system to detect and avoid counterfeit electronic parts and suspect counterfeit electronic parts that has been reviewed and approved by DoD pursuant to 244.303(b);

(2) The counterfeit electronic parts or suspect counterfeit electronic parts are Government-furnished property as defined in FAR 45.101 or were obtained by the contractor in accordance with the clause at 252.246-7008, Sources of Electronic Parts; and

(3) The contractor—

(i) Becomes aware of the counterfeit electronic parts or suspect counterfeit electronic parts through inspection, testing, and authentication efforts of the contractor or its subcontractors; through a Government Industry Data Exchange Program (GIDEP) alert; or by other means; and

(ii) Provides timely (*i.e.*, within 60 days after the contractor becomes aware) written notice to—

(A) The cognizant contracting officer(s); and

(B) GIDEP (unless the contractor is a foreign corporation or partnership that does not have an office, place of business, or fiscal paying agent in the United States; or the counterfeit electronic part or suspect counterfeit electronic part is the subject of an on-going criminal investigation).

[Final rule, 79 FR 26091, 5/6/2014, effective 5/6/2014; Final rule, 81 FR 59510, 8/30/2016, effective 8/30/2016]

SUBPART 231.3—CONTRACTS WITH EDUCATIONAL INSTITUTIONS

231.303 Requirements.

(1) Pursuant to section 841 of the National Defense Authorization Act for Fiscal Year 1994 (Pub. L. 103-160), no limitation may be placed on the reimbursement of otherwise allowable indirect costs incurred by an institution of higher education under a DoD contract awarded on or after November 30, 1993, unless that same limitation is applied uniformly to all other organizations performing similar work under DoD contracts. The 26 percent limitation imposed on administrative indirect costs by OMB Circular No. A-21 shall not be applied to DoD contracts awarded on or after November 30, 1993, to institutions of higher education because the same limitation is not applied to other organizations performing similar work.

(2) The cognizant administrative contracting officer may waive the prohibition in 231.303(1) if the governing body of the institution of higher education requests the waiver to simplify the institution's overall management of DoD cost reimbursements under DoD contracts.

(3) Under 10 U.S.C. 2249, the costs cited in 231.205-22(a) are unallowable.

[Interim rule, 59 FR 26143, 5/19/94, effective 5/5/94; Interim rule, 60 FR 2330, 1/9/95, effective 12/14/94, finalized without change, DAC 91-9, 60 FR 61586, 11/30/95, effective 11/30/95; Interim rule, 61 FR 36305, 7/10/96, effective 7/10/96, finalized without change, DAC 91-12, 62 FR 34114, 6/24/97, effective 6/24/97; Final rule, 62 FR 47154, 9/8/97, effective 9/8/97; Final rule, 63 FR 14640, 3/26/98, effective 3/26/98]

SUBPART 231.6—CONTRACTS WITH STATE, LOCAL, AND FEDERALLY RECOGNIZED INDIAN TRIBAL GOVERNMENTS

231.603 Requirements.

Under 10 U.S.C. 2249, the costs cited in 231.205-22(a) are unallowable.

[Interim rule, 61 FR 36305, 7/10/96, effective 7/10/96, finalized without change, DAC 91-12, 62 FR 34114, 6/24/97, effective 6/24/97; Final rule, 62 FR 47154, 9/8/97, effective 9/8/97; Final rule, 63 FR 14640, 3/26/98, effective 3/26/98]

SUBPART 231.7—CONTRACTS WITH NONPROFIT ORGANIZATIONS

231.703 Requirements.

Under 10 U.S.C. 2249, the costs cited in 231.205-22(a) are unallowable.

[Interim rule, 61 FR 36305, 7/10/96, effective 7/10/96, finalized without change, DAC 91-12, 62 FR 34114, 6/24/97, effective 6/24/97; Final rule, 62 FR 47154, 9/8/97, effective 9/8/97; Final rule, 63 FR 14640, 3/26/98, effective 3/26/98]

PART 232—CONTRACT FINANCING

Table of Contents

Definitions . . . 232.001
Reduction or suspension of contract payments upon finding of fraud . . . 232.006
Reporting . . . 232.006-5
Contract financing payments . . . 232.007
Responsibilities . . . 232.070
[Removed and Reserved] . . . 232.071
Financial responsibility of contractors . . . 232.072
Required financial reviews . . . 232.072-1
Appropriate information . . . 232.072-2
Cash flow forecasts . . . 232.072-3

Subpart 232.1—Non-Commercial Item Purchase Financing

Description of contract financing methods . . . 232.102
Provisional delivery payments . . . 232.102-70
Providing contract financing . . . 232.104
[Removed] . . . 232.108
[Removed] . . . 232.111

Subpart 232.2—Commercial Item Purchase Financing

Security for Government financing . . . 232.202-4
Solicitation provisions and contract clauses . . . 232.206
[Removed] . . . 232.207

Subpart 232.3—Loan Guarantees for Defense Production

Authority . . . 232.302

Subpart 232.4—Advance Payments for Non-Commercial Items

Exclusions . . . 232.404
Contracting officer action . . . 232.409
Recommendation for approval . . . 232.409-1
Findings, determination, and authorization . . . 232.410
Contract clause . . . 232.412
Additional clauses . . . 232.412-70
Advance payment pool . . . 232.470

Subpart 232.5—Progress Payments Based on Costs

General . . . 232.501
Customary progress payment rates . . . 232.501-1
Unusual progress payments . . . 232.501-2
Contract price . . . 232.501-3
Preaward matters . . . 232.502
[Removed] . . . 232.502-1
Contract clauses . . . 232.502-4
Additional clauses . . . 232.502-4-70
Postaward matters . . . 232.503
Suspension or reduction of payments . . . 232.503-6

Application of Government title terms 232.503-15

Subpart 232.6—Contract Debts

Responsibilities 232.602
Debt determination 232.603
Demand for payment 232.604
Compromising debts 232.610
Contract clause 232.611
Transfer of responsibility for debt collection 232.670
Bankruptcy reporting 232.671

Subpart 232.7—Contract Funding

Policy 232.702
Contract funding requirements 232.703
General 232.703-1
Contracts crossing fiscal years 232.703-3
Military construction appropriations act restriction 232.703-70
Limitation of cost or funds 232.704
Incrementally funded fixed-price contracts 232.704-70
Contract clauses 232.705
Clause for limitation of government's obligation 232.705-70

Subpart 232.8—Assignment of Claims

Policies 232.803
Procedure 232.805
Contract clause 232.806

Subpart 232.9—Prompt Payment

Applicability 232.901
Responsibilities 232.903
Determining payment due dates 232.904
Payment documentation and process 232.905
Making payments 232.906
Contract clauses 232.908

Subpart 232.10—Performance-Based Payments

Policy 232.1001
Criteria for use 232.1003-70
Procedures 232.1004
Contract clauses 232.1005-70
[Removed] 232.1007

Subpart 232.11—Electronic Funds Transfer

[Removed] 232.1108
Solicitation provision and contract clauses 232.1110

Subpart 232.70—Electronic Submission and Processing of Payment Requests and Receiving Reports

Scope of subpart 232.7000
Definitions 232.7001

Policy 232.7002
Procedures 232.7003
Contract clauses 232.7004

Subpart 232.71—Levies on Contract Payments

Scope of subpart 232.7100
Policy and procedures 232.7101
Contract clause 232.7102

Subpart 232.72—Payment in Local Currency (Afghanistan)

Scope of subpart 232.7200
Policy and procedures 232.7201
Solicitation provision 232.7202

PART 232—CONTRACT FINANCING

232.001 Definitions.

Incremental funding means the partial funding of a contract or an exercised option, with additional funds anticipated to be provided at a later time.

[Final rule, 71 FR 18671, 4/12/2006, effective 4/12/2006]

232.006 Reduction or suspension of contract payments upon finding of fraud. (No Text)

[DAC 91-13, 63 FR 11522, 3/9/98, effective 3/9/98]

232.006-5 Reporting.

Departments and agencies in accordance with department/agency procedures, shall prepare and submit to the Under Secretary of Defense (Acquisition, Technology, and Logistics), through the Director of Defense Procurement and Acquisition Policy, annual reports (Report Control Symbol DD-AT&L (A) 1891) containing the information required by FAR 32.006-5.

[DAC 91-13, 63 FR 11522, 3/9/98, effective 3/9/98; Final rule, 65 FR 39703, 6/27/2000, effective 6/27/2000; Final rule, 68 FR 7438, 2/14/2003, effective 2/14/2003]

232.007 Contract financing payments.

(a) DoD policy is to make contract financing payments as quickly as possible. Generally, the contracting officer shall insert the standard due dates of 7 days for progress payments, and 14 days for performance-based payments and interim payments on cost-type contracts, in the appropriate paragraphs of the respective payment clauses. For interim payments on cost-reimbursement contracts for services, see 232.906(a)(i).

(b) The contracting officer should coordinate contract financing payment terms with offices that will be involved in the payment process to ensure that specified terms can be met. Where justified, the contracting officer may insert a due date greater than, but not less than, the standard. In determining payment terms, consider—

(i) Geographical separation;

(ii) Workload;

(iii) Contractor ability to submit a proper request; and

(iv) Other factors that could affect timing of payment.

[Final rule, 70 FR 75412, 12/20/2005, effective 12/20/2005]

232.070 Responsibilities.

(a) The Director of Defense Procurement and Acquisition Policy, Office of the Under Secretary of Defense (Acquisition, Technology, and Logistics) (OUSD(AT&L)DPAP) is responsible for ensuring uniform administration of DoD contract financing, including DoD contract financing policies and important related procedures. Agency discretion under FAR part 32 is at the DoD level and is not delegated to the departments and agencies. Proposals by the departments and agencies, to exercise agency discretion, shall be submitted to OUSD(AT&L)DPAP.

(b) Departments and agencies are responsible for their day-to-day contract financing operations. Refer specific cases involving financing policy or important procedural issues to OUSD (AT&L) DPAP for consideration through the department/agency Contract Finance Committee members (also see Subpart 201.4 for deviation request and approval procedures).

(c) See PGI 232.070(c) for information on department/agency contract financing offices.

[DAC 91-13, 63 FR 11522, 3/9/98, effective 3/9/98; Final rule, 65 FR 39703, 6/27/2000, effective 6/27/2001; Final rule, 68 FR 7438, 2/14/2003, effective 2/14/2003; Final rule, 70 FR 75412, 12/20/2005, effective 12/20/2005; Final rule, 72 FR 20765, 4/26/2007, effective 4/26/2007]

232.071 [Removed and Reserved]

[DAC 91-13, 63 FR 11522, 3/9/98, effective 3/9/98; Final rule, 65 FR 39703, 6/27/2000, effective 6/27/2000; Final rule, 68 FR 7438, 2/14/2003, effective 2/14/2003; Final rule, 70 FR 75412, 12/20/2005, effective 12/20/2005]

232.072 Financial responsibility of contractors.

Use the policies and procedures in this section in determining the financial capability of current or prospective contractors.

[DAC 91-13, 63 FR 11522, 3/9/98, effective 3/9/98]

232.072-1 Required financial reviews.

The contracting officer shall perform a financial review when the contracting officer does not otherwise have sufficient information to make a positive determination of financial responsibility. In addition, the contracting officer shall consider performing a financial review—

(a) Prior to award of a contract, when—

(1) The contractor is on a list requiring preaward clearance or other special clearance before award;

(2) The contractor is listed on the Consolidated List of Contractors Indebted to the Government (Hold-Up List), or is otherwise known to be indebted to the Government;

(3) The contractor may receive Government assets such as contract financing payments or Government property;

(4) The contractor is experiencing performance difficulties on other work; or

(5) The contractor is a new company or a new supplier of the item.

(b) At periodic intervals after award of a contract, when—

(1) Any of the conditions in paragraphs (a)(2) through (a)(5) of this subsection are applicable; or

(2) There is any other reason to question the contractor's ability to finance performance and completion of the contract.

[DAC 91-13, 63 FR 11522, 3/9/98, effective 3/9/98]

232.072-2 Appropriate information.

(a) The contracting officer shall obtain the type and depth of financial and other information that is required to establish a contractor's financial capability or disclose a contractor's financial condition. While the contracting officer should not request information that is not necessary for protection for the Government's interests, the contracting officer must insist upon obtaining the information that is necessary. The unwillingness or inability of a contractor to present reasonably requested information in a timely manner, especially information that a prudent business person would be expected to have and to use in the professional management of a business, may be a material fact in the determination of the contractor's responsibility and prospects for contract completion.

(b) The contracting officer shall obtain the following information to the extent required to protect the Government's interest. In addition, if the contracting officer concludes that information not listed in paragraphs (b)(1) through (b)(10) of this subsection is required to comply with 232.072-1, that information should be requested. The information must be for the person(s) who are legally liable for contract performance. If the contractor is not a corporation, the contracting officer shall obtain the required information for each individual/joint venturer/partner:

(1) Balance sheet and income statement—

(i) For the current fiscal year (interim);

(ii) For the most recent fiscal year and, preferably, for the 2 preceding fiscal years. These should be certified by an independent public accountant or by an appropriate officer of the firm; and

(iii) Forecasted for each fiscal year for the remainder of the period of contract performance.

(2) Summary history of the contractor and its principal managers, disclosing any previous insolvencies—corporate or personal, and describing its products or services.

(3) Statement of all affiliations disclosing—

(i) Material financial interests of the contractor;

(ii) Material financial interests in the contractor;

(iii) Material affiliations of owners, officers, directors, major stockholders; and

(iv) The major stockholders if the contractor is not a widely-traded, publicly-held corporation.

(4) Statement of all forms of compensation to each officer, manager, partner, joint venturer, or proprietor, as appropriate—

(i) Planned for the current year;

(ii) Paid during the past 2 years; and

(iii) Deferred to future periods.

(5) Business base and forecast that—

(i) Shows, by significant markets, existing contracts and outstanding offers, including those under negotiation; and

(ii) Is reconcilable to indirect cost rate projections.

(6) Cash forecast for the duration of the contract (see 232.072-3).

(7) Financing arrangement information that discloses—

(i) Availability of cash to finance contract performance;

(ii) Contractor's exposure to financial crisis from creditor's demands;

(iii) Degree to which credit security provisions could conflict with Government title terms under contract financing;

(iv) Clearly stated confirmations of credit with no unacceptable qualifications;

(v) Unambiguous written agreement by a creditor if credit arrangements include deferred trade payments or creditor subordinations/repayment suspensions.

(8) Statement of all state, local, and Federal tax accounts, including special mandatory contributions, *e.g.*, environmental superfund.

(9) Description and explanation of the financial effect of issues such as—

(i) Leases, deferred purchase arrangements, or patent or royalty arrangements;

(ii) Insurance, when relevant to the contract;

(iii) Contemplated capital expenditures, changes in equity, or contractor debt load;

(iv) Pending claims either by or against the contractor;

(v) Contingent liabilities such as guarantees, litigation, environmental, or product liabilities;

(vi) Validity of accounts receivable and actual value of inventory, as assets; and

(vii) Status and aging of accounts payable.

(10) Significant ratios such as—

(i) Inventory to annual sales;

(ii) Inventory to current assets;

(iii) Liquid assets to current assets;

(iv) Liquid assets to current liabilities;

(v) Current assets to current liabilities; and

(vi) Net worth to net debt.

[DAC 91-13, 63 FR 11522, 3/9/98, effective 3/9/98]

232.072-3 Cash flow forecasts.

(a) *A contractor must be able to sustain a sufficient cash flow to perform the contract.* When there is doubt regarding the sufficiency of a contractor's cash flow, the contracting officer should require the contractor to submit a cash flow forecast covering the duration of the contract.

(b) A contractor's inability of refusal to prepare and provide cash flow forecasts or to reconcile actual cash flow with previous forecasts is a strong indicator of serious managerial deficiencies or potential contract cost or performance problems.

(c) *Single or one-time cash flow forecasts are of limited forecasting power.* As such, they should be limited to preaward survey situations. Reliability of cash flow forecasts can be established only by comparing a series of previous actual cash flows with the corresponding forecasts and examining the causes of any differences.

(d) *Cash flow forecasts must*—

(1) Show the origin and use of all material amounts of cash within the entire business unit responsible for contract performance, period by period, for the length of the contract (or until the risk of a cash crisis ends); and

(2) Provide an audit trail to the data and assumptions used to prepare it.

(e) *Cash flow forecasts can be no more reliable than the assumptions on which they are based. Most important of these assumptions are—*

(1) Estimated amounts and timing of purchases and payments for materials, parts, components, subassemblies, and services;

(2) Estimated amounts and timing of payments of purchase or production of capital assets, test facilities, and tooling;

(3) Amounts and timing of fixed cash charges such as debt installments, interest, rentals, taxes, and indirect costs;

(4) Estimated amounts and timing of payments for projected labor, both direct and indirect;

(5) Reasonableness of projected manufacturing and production schedules;

(6) Estimated amounts and timing of billings to customers (including progress payments), and customer payments;

(7) Estimated amounts and timing of cash receipts from lenders or other credit sources, and liquidation of loans; and

(8) Estimated amount and timing of cash receipt from other sources.

(f) *The contracting officer should review the assumptions underlying the cash flow forecasts. In determining whether the assumptions are reasonable and realistic, the contracting officer should consult with—*

(1) The contractor;

(2) Government personnel in the areas of finance, engineering, production, cost, and price analysis; or

(3) Prospective supply, subcontract, and loan or credit sources.

[DAC 91-13, 63 FR 11522, 3/9/98, effective 3/9/98]

SUBPART 232.1—NON-COMMERCIAL ITEM PURCHASE FINANCING

232.102 Description of contract financing methods.

(e) (2) Progress payments based on percentage or stage of completion are authorized only for contracts for construction (as defined in FAR 36.102), shipbuilding, and ship conversion, alteration, or repair. However, percentage or state of completion methods of measuring contractor performance may be used for performance-based payments in accordance with FAR Subpart 32.10.

[DAC 91-13, 63 FR 11522, 3/9/98, effective 3/9/98]

232.102-70 Provisional delivery payments.

(a) The contracting officer may establish provisional delivery payments to pay contractors for the costs of supplies and services delivered to and accepted by the Government under the following contract actions if undefinitized:

(1) Letter contracts contemplating a fixed-price contract.

(2) Orders under basic ordering agreements.

(3) Spares provisioning documents annexed to contracts.

(4) Unpriced equitable adjustments on fixed-price contracts.

(5) Orders under indefinite-delivery contracts.

(b) Provisional delivery payments shall be—

(1) Used sparingly;

(2) Priced conservatively; and

(3) Reduced by liquidating previous progress payments in accordance with the Progress Payments clause.

(c) Provisional delivery payments shall not—

(1) Include profit;

(2) Exceed funds obligated for the undefinitized contract action; or

(3) Influence the definitized contract price.

[DAC 91-13, 63 FR 11522, 3/9/98, effective 3/9/98]

232.104 Providing contract financing.

For fixed-price contracts with a period of performance in excess of a year that meet the dollar thresholds established in FAR 32.104(d), and for solicitations expected to result in such contracts, in lieu of the requirement at FAR 32.104(d)(1)(ii) for the contractor to demonstrate actual financial need or the unavailability of private financing, DoD has determined that—

(1) The use of customary contract financing (see FAR 32.113), other than loan guarantees and advance payments, is in DoD's best interest; and

(2) Further justification of its use in individual acquisitions is unnecessary.

[Final rule, 81 FR 93841, 12/22/2016, effective 12/22/2016]

232.108 [Removed]

[DAC 91-13, 63 FR 11522, 3/9/98, effective 3/9/98; Final rule, 70 FR 75412, 12/20/2005, effective 12/20/2005]

232.111 [Removed]

[Final rule, 68 FR 69631, 12/15/2003, effective 12/15/2003; Final rule, 73 FR 4116, 1/24/2008, effective 1/24/2008]

SUBPART 232.2—COMMERCIAL ITEM PURCHASE FINANCING

232.202-4 Security for Government financing.

(a)(2) When determining whether an offeror's financial condition is adequate security, see 232.072-2 and 232.072-3 for guidance. It should be noted that an offeror's financial condition may be sufficient to make the contractor responsible for award purposes, but may not be adequate security for commercial contract financing.

[DAC 91-13, 63 FR 11522, 3/9/98, effective 3/9/98]

232.206 Solicitation provisions and contract clauses.

(f) *Prompt payment for commercial purchase payments.* The contracting officer shall incorporate the following standard prompt payment terms for commercial item contract financing:

(i) *Commercial advance payments*: The contractor entitlement date specified in the contract, or 30 days after receipt by the designated billing office of a proper request for payment, whichever is later.

(ii) *Commercial interim payments*: The contractor entitlement date specified in the contract, or 14 days after receipt by the designated billing office of a proper request for payment, whichever is later. The prompt payment standards for commercial delivery payments shall be the same as specified in FAR Subpart 32.9 for invoice payments for the item delivered.

(g) *Installment payment financing for commercial items.* Installment payment financing shall not be used for DoD contracts, unless market research has established that this form of contract financing is both appropriate and customary in the commercial marketplace. When installment payment financing is used, the contracting officer shall use the ceiling percentage of contract price that is customary in the particular marketplace (not to exceed the maximum rate established in FAR 52.232-30).

[DAC 91-13, 63 FR 11522, 3/9/98, effective 3/9/98; Final rule, 70 FR 75412, 12/20/2005, effective 12/20/2005]

232.207 [Removed]

[DAC 91-13, 63 FR 11522, 3/9/98, effective 3/9/98; Final rule, 70 FR 75412, 12/20/2005, effective 12/20/2005]

SUBPART 232.3—LOAN GUARANTEES FOR DEFENSE PRODUCTION

232.302 Authority.

(a) The use of guaranteed loans as a contract financing mechanism requires the availability of certain congressional authority. The DoD has not requested such authority in recent years, and none is now available.

SUBPART 232.4—ADVANCE PAYMENTS FOR NON-COMMERCIAL ITEMS

232.404 Exclusions.

(a)(9) The requirements of FAR Subpart 32.4 do not apply to advertisements in high school and college publications for military recruitment efforts under 10 U.S.C. 503 when the contract cost does not exceed the micro-purchase threshold.

[Final rule, 70 FR 75412, 12/20/2005, effective 12/20/2005; Final rule, 71 FR 75891, 12/19/2006, effective 12/19/2006; Final rule, 75 FR 45072, 8/2/2010, effective 10/1/2010]

232.409 Contracting officer action. (No Text)

232.409-1 Recommendation for approval.

Follow the procedures at PGI 232.409-1 for preparation of the documents required by FAR 32.409-1(e) and (f).

[Final rule, 70 FR 75412, 12/20/2005, effective 12/20/2005]

232.410 Findings, determination, and authorization.

If an advance payment procedure is used without a special bank account, follow the procedures at PGI 232.410.

[Final rule, 70 FR 75412, 12/20/2005, effective 12/20/2005]

232.412 Contract clause. (No Text)

232.412-70 Additional clauses.

(a) Use the clause at 252.232-7000, Advance Payment Pool, in any contract that will be subject to the terms of an advance payment pool agreement with a nonprofit organization or educational institution. Normally, use the clause in all cost reimbursement type contracts with the organization or institution.

(b) Use the clause at 252.232-7001, Disposition of Payments, in contracts when payments under the contract are to be made by a disbursing office not designated in the advance payment pool agreement.

(c) Use the clause at 252.232-7005, Reimbursement of Subcontractor Advance Payments-DoD Pilot Mentor-Protege Program, when advance payments will be provided by the contractor to a subcontractor pursuant to an approved mentor-protege agreement (See subpart 219.71).

[DAC 91-1, 56 FR 67217, 12/30/91, effective 12/31/91]

232.470 Advance payment pool.

(a) An advance payment pool agreement—

(1) Is a means of financing the performance of more than one contract held by a single contractor;

(2) Is especially convenient for the financing of cost-type contracts with nonprofit educational or research institutions for experimental or research and development work when several contracts require financing by advance payments. When appropriate, pooled advance payments may also be used to finance other types of contracts held by a single contractor; and

(3) May be established—

(i) Without regard to the number of appropriations involved;

(ii) To finance contracts for one or more department(s) or contracting activity(ies); or

(iii) In addition to any other advance payment pool agreement at a single contractor location when it is more convenient or otherwise preferable to have more than one agreement.

SUBPART 232.5—PROGRESS PAYMENTS BASED ON COSTS

232.501 General. (No Text)

232.501-1 Customary progress payment rates.

(a) The customary progress payment rates for DoD contracts, including contracts that contain foreign military sales (FMS) requirements, are 80 percent for large business concerns and 90 percent for small business concerns.

[Final rule, 66 FR 49864, 10/1/2001, effective 10/1/2001; Interim rule, 79 FR 61579, 10/14/2014, effective 10/14/2014; Final rule, 80 FR 15912, 3/26/2015, effective 3/26/2015]

232.501-2 Unusual progress payments.

Follow the procedures at PGI 232.501-2for approval of unusual progress payments.

[Final rule, 65 FR 39722, 6/27/2000, effective 6/27/2000; Final rule, 65 FR 39703,

6/27/2000, effective 6/27/2000; Final rule, 68 FR 7438, 2/14/2003, effective 2/14/2003; Final rule, 70 FR 75412, 12/20/2005, effective 12/20/2005]

232.501-3 Contract price.

(b) The contracting officer may approve progress payments when the contract price exceeds the funds obligated under the contract, provided the contract limits the Government's liability to the lesser of—

(i) The applicable rate (i.e., the lower of the progress payment rate, the liquidation rate, or the loss-ratio adjusted rate); or

(ii) 100 percent of the funds obligated.

[Final rule, 65 FR 39722, 6/27/2000, effective 6/27/2000; Final rule, 70 FR 75412, 12/20/2005, effective 12/20/2005]

232.502 Preaward matters. (No Text)

232.502-1 [Removed]

[Final rule, 71 FR 75891, 12/19/2006, effective 12/19/2006; Final rule 75 FR 45072, 8/2/2010, effective 10/1/2010; Interim rule, 79 FR 61579, 10/14/2014, effective 10/14/2014; Final rule, 80 FR 15912, 3/26/2015, effective 3/26/2015]

232.502-4 Contract clauses. (No text)

232.502-4-70 Additional clauses.

(a) Use the clause at 252.232-7002, Progress Payments for Foreign Military Sales Acquisitions, in solicitations and contracts that—

(i) Contain FMS requirements; and

(ii) Provide for progress payments.

(b) Use the clause at 252.232-7004, DoD Progress Payment Rates, instead of Alternate I of the clause at FAR 52.232-16, if the contractor is a small business concern.

[DAC 91-1, 56 FR 67217, 12/30/91, effective 12/31/91; Final rule, 64 FR 8731, 2/23/99, effective 2/23/99; Final rule, 65 FR 39722, 6/27/2000, effective 6/27/2000; Final rule, 66 FR 49864, 10/1/2001, effective 10/1/2001; Interim rule, 79 FR 61579, 10/14/2014, effective 10/14/2014; Final rule, 80 FR 15912, 3/26/2015, effective 3/26/2015]

232.503 Postaward matters. (No Text)

232.503-6 Suspension or reduction of payments.

(b) *Contractor noncompliance.* See also 242.7503.

(g) *Loss contracts.* Use the following loss ratio adjustment procedures for making adjustments required by FAR 32.503-6(f) and (g)—

(i) Except as provided in paragraph (g) (ii) of this subsection, the contracting officer must prepare a supplementary analysis of the contractor's request for progress payments and calculate the loss ratio adjustment using the procedures in FAR 32.503-6(g).

(ii) The contracting officer may request the contractor to prepare the supplementary analysis as an attachment to the progress payment request when the contracting officer determines that the contractor's methods of estimating the "Costs to Complete" are reliable, accurate, and not susceptible to improper influences.

(iii) To maintain an audit trail and permit verification of calculations, do not make the loss ratio adjustments by altering or replacing data on the contractor's original request for progress payment (SF 1443, Contractor's Request for Progress Payment, or computer generated equivalent).

[DAC 91-7, 60 FR 29491, 6/5/95, effective 5/17/95; Final rule, 65 FR 39722, 6/27/2000, effective 6/27/2000]

232.503-15 Application of Government title terms.

(d) An administrative contracting officer (ACO) determination that the contractor's material management and accounting system conforms to the system criteria at 252.242-7004(d) (7) constitutes the contracting officer approval requirement of FAR 32.503-15(d). Prior to granting blanket approval of cost transfers between contracts, the ACO should determine that—

(i) The contractor retains records of the transfer activity that took place in the prior month;

(ii) The contractor prepares, at least monthly, a summary of the transfer activity that took place in the prior month; and

(iii) The summary report includes as a minimum, the total number and dollar value of transfers.

[DAC 91-3, 57 FR 42632, 9/15/92, effective 8/31/92; Final rule, 70 FR 75412, 12/20/2005, effective 12/20/2005; Final rule, 77 FR 11355, 2/24/2012, effective 2/24/2012]

SUBPART 232.6—CONTRACT DEBTS

232.602 Responsibilities.

(b) Disbursing officers are those officials designated to make payments under a contract or to receive payments of amounts due under a contract. The disbursing officer is responsible for determining the amount and collecting contract debts whenever overpayments or erroneous payments have been made. The disbursing officer also has primary responsibility when the amounts due and dates for payment are contained in the contract, and a copy of the contract has been furnished to the disbursing officer with notice to collect as amounts become due.

[Final rule, 70 FR 75412, 12/20/2005, effective 12/20/2005; Final rule, 80 FR 58632, 9/30/2015, effective 9/30/2015]

232.603 Debt determination.

When transferring a case to the contract financing office, follow the procedures at PGI 232.603.

[Final rule, 70 FR 75412, 12/20/2005, effective 12/20/2005; Final rule, 80 FR 58632, 9/30/2015, effective 9/30/2015]

232.604 Demand for payment.

When issuing a demand for payment of a contract debt, follow the procedures at PGI 232.604.

[Final rule, 70 FR 75412, 12/20/2005, effective 12/20/2005; Final rule, 80 FR 58632, 9/30/2015, effective 9/30/2015]

232.610 Compromising debts.

Only the department/agency contract financing offices (see PGI 232.070(c)) are authorized to compromise debts covered by this subpart.

[Final rule, 70 FR 75412, 12/20/2005, effective 12/20/2005; Final rule, 80 FR 58632, 9/30/2015, effective 9/30/2015]

232.611 Contract clause.

(a) The Director of Defense Procurement and Acquisition Policy, Office of the Under Secretary of Defense (Acquisition, Technology, and Logistics), may exempt the contracts in FAR 32.611(a)(2)through (5) and other contracts, in exceptional circumstances, from the administrative interest charges required by this subpart.

(7) Other exceptions are—

(A) Contracts for instructions of military or ROTC personnel at civilian schools, colleges, and universities;

(B) Basic agreements with telephone companies for communications services and facilities, and purchases under such agreements; and

(C) Transportation contracts with common carriers for common carrier services.

[DAC 91-9, 60 FR 61586, 11/30/95, effective 11/30/95; Final rule, 65 FR 39703, 6/27/2000, effective 6/27/2000; Final rule, 68 FR 7438, 2/14/2003, effective 2/14/2003; Final rule, 70 FR 75412, 12/20/2005, effective 12/20/2005; Final rule, 80 FR 58632, 9/30/2015, effective 9/30/2015]

232.670 Transfer of responsibility for debt collection.

Follow the procedures at PGI 232.670 for transferring responsibility for debt collection.

[Final rule, 70 FR 75412, 12/20/2005, effective 12/20/2005]

232.671 Bankruptcy reporting.

Follow the procedures at PGI 232.671 for bankruptcy reporting.

[Final rule, 70 FR 75412, 12/20/2005, effective 12/20/2005]

SUBPART 232.7—CONTRACT FUNDING

232.702 Policy.

Fixed-price contracts shall be fully funded except as permitted by 232.703-1.

[Interim rule, 58 FR 46091, 9/1/93, effective 8/23/93; Final rule, 71 FR 18671, 4/12/2006, effective 4/12/2006]

232.703 Contract funding requirements. (No Text)

[Final rule, 71 FR 18671, 4/12/2006, effective 4/12/2006]

232.703-1 General.

(1) A fixed-price contract may be incrementally funded only if—

(i) The contract (excluding any options) or any exercised option—

(A) Is for severable services;

(B) Does not exceed one year in length; and

(C) Is incrementally funded using funds available (unexpired) as of the date the funds are obligated; or

(ii) The contract uses funds available from multiple (two or more) fiscal years and—

(A) The contract is funded with research and development appropriations; or

(B) Congress has otherwise authorized incremental funding.

(2) An incrementally funded fixed-price contract shall be fully funded as soon as funds are available.

[Interim rule, 58 FR 46091, 9/1/93, effective 8/23/93; Final rule, 71 FR 18671, 4/12/2006, effective 4/12/2006]

232.703-3 Contracts crossing fiscal years.

(b) The contracting officer may enter into a contract, exercise an option, or place an order under a contract for severable services for a period that begins in one fiscal year and ends in the next fiscal year if the period of the contract awarded, option exercised, or order placed does not exceed 1 year (10 U.S.C. 2410a).

[Final rule, 64 FR 28109, 5/25/99, effective 5/25/99]

232.703-70 Military construction appropriations act restriction.

Annual military construction appropriations acts restrict the use of funds appropriated by the acts for payments under cost-plus-fixed-fee contracts (see 216.306(c)).

[DAC 91-10, 61 FR 7739, 2/29/96, effective 2/29/96]

232.704 Limitation of cost or funds. (No Text)

[Interim rule, 58 FR 46091, 9/1/93, effective 8/23/93; Final rule, 71 FR 18671, 4/12/2006, effective 4/12/2006]

232.704-70 Incrementally funded fixed-price contracts.

(a) Upon receipt of the contractor's notice under paragraph (c) of the clause at 252.232-7007, Limitation of Government's Obligation, the contracting officer shall promptly provide written notice to the contractor that the Government is—

(1) Allotting additional funds for continued performance and increasing the Government's limitation of obligation in a specified amount;

(2) Terminating the contract; or

(3) Considering whether to allot additional funds; and

(i) The contractor is entitled by the contract terms to stop work when the Government's limitation of obligation is reached; and

(ii) Any costs expended beyond the Government's limitation of obligation are at the contractor's risk.

(b) Upon learning that the contract will receive no further funds, the contracting officer shall promptly give the contractor written notice of the Government's decision and terminate for the convenience of the Government.

(c) The contracting officer shall ensure that, in accordance with paragraph (b) of the clause at 252.232-7007, Limitation of Government's Obligation, sufficient funds are allotted to the contract to cover the total amount payable to the contractor in the event of termination for the convenience of the Government.

[Interim rule, 58 FR 46091, 9/1/93, effective 8/23/93; Final rule, 71 FR 18671, 4/12/2006, effective 4/12/2006]

232.705 Contract clauses. (No Text)

[Interim rule, 58 FR 46091, 9/1/93, effective 8/23/93; Final rule, 71 FR 18671, 4/12/2006, effective 4/12/2006]

232.705-70 Clause for limitation of government's obligation.

Use the clause at 252.232-7007, Limitation of Government's Obligation, in solicitations and resultant incrementally funded fixed-price contracts. The contracting officer may revise the contractor's notification period, in paragraph (c) of the clause, from "ninety" to "thirty" or "sixty" days, as appropriate.

[Interim rule, 58 FR 46091, 9/1/93, effective 8/23/93; Final rule, 71 FR 18671, 4/12/2006, effective 4/12/2006]

SUBPART 232.8—ASSIGNMENT OF CLAIMS

232.803 Policies.

(b) Only contracts for personal services may prohibit the assignment of claims.

(d) Pursuant to 41 U.S.C. 6305, and in accordance with Presidential delegation dated October 3, 1995, Secretary of Defense delegation dated February 5, 1996, and Under Secretary of Defense (Acquisition, Technology, and Logistics) delegation dated February 23, 1996, the Director of Defense Procurement determined on May 10, 1996, that a need exists for DoD to agree not to reduce or set off any money due or to become due under the contract when the proceeds under the contract have been assigned in accordance with the Assignment of Claims provision of the contract. This determination was published in the Federal Register on June 11, 1996, as required by law. Nevertheless, if departments/agencies decide it is in the Government's interests, or if the contracting officer makes a determination in accordance with FAR 32.803(d) concerning a significantly indebted offeror, they may exclude the no-setoff commitment.

[DAC 91-11, 61 FR 50446, 9/26/96, effective 9/26/96; Final rule, 65 FR 39703, 6/27/2000, effective 6/27/2000; Final rule, 76 FR 58137, 9/20/2011, effective 9/20/2011]

232.805 Procedure.

(b) The assignee shall forward—

(i) To the administrative contracting officer (ACO), a true copy of the instrument of assignment and an original and three copies of the notice of assignment. The ACO shall acknowledge receipt by signing and dating all copies of the notice of assignment and shall—

(A) File the true copy of the instrument of assignment and the original of the notice in the contract file;

(B) Forward two copies of the notice to the disbursing officer of the payment office cited in the contract;

(C) Return a copy of the notice to the assignee; and

(D) Advise the contracting officer of the assignment.

(ii) To the surety or sureties, if any, a true copy of the instrument of assignment and an original and three copies of the notice of assignment. The surety shall return three acknowledged copies of the notice to the assignee, who shall forward two copies to the disbursing officer designated in the contract.

(iii) To the disbursing officer of the payment office cited in the contract, a true copy of the instrument of assignment and an original and one copy of the notice of assignment. The disbursing officer shall acknowledge and return to the assignee the copy of the notice and shall file the true copy of the instrument and original notice.

232.806 Contract clause.

(a)(1) Use the clause at 252.232-7008, Assignment of Claims (Overseas), instead of the clause at FAR 52.232-23, Assignment of Claims, in solicitations and contracts when contract performance will be in a foreign country.

(2) Use Alternate I with the clause at FAR 52.232-23, Assignment of Claims, unless otherwise authorized under 232.803(d).

[DAC 91-12, 62 FR 34114, 6/24/97, effective 6/24/97]

SUBPART 232.9—PROMPT PAYMENT

232.901 Applicability.

(1) Except for FAR 32.908, FAR subpart 32.9, Prompt Payment, does not apply when—

(i) There is—

(A) An emergency, as defined in the Disaster Relief Act of 1974;

(B) A contingency operation (see FAR 2.101(b)); or

(C) The release or threatened release of hazardous substances (as defined in 4 U.S.C. 9606, section 106); and

(ii) The head of the contracting activity has made a determination, after consultation with the cognizant comptroller, that conditions exist that limit normal business operations; and

(iii) Payments will be made in the operational area or made contingent upon receiving supporting documentation (i.e., contract, invoice, and receiving report) from the operational area.

(2) Criteria limiting normal business operations during emergencies and contingency operations that restrict the use of FAR 32.9 may include such conditions as—

(i) Support infrastructure, hardware, communications capabilities, and bandwidth are not consistently available such that normal business operations can be carried out;

(ii) Support resources, facilities, and banking needs are not consistently available for use as necessary in carrying out normal business operations;

(iii) Military mission priorities override the availability of appropriately skilled personnel in support of back-office operations;

(iv) Mobility impairments and security concerns restrict free movement of personnel and documents necessary for timely processing;

(v) Foreign vendors are not familiar with or do not understand DoD contract requirements (i.e., proper invoice, receiving documentation, and contracting terms); or

(vi) Documents received in support of payment requests and shipments require language translations that cannot be performed and documented within normal business processing times.

(3) Subsequent Determinations. The head of the contracting activity shall make subsequent determinations, after consultation with the cognizant comptroller, as the operational area evolves into either a more stable or less stable environment.

(i) If the head of the contracting activity determines that the operational area has evolved into a more stable environment, the contracting officer shall notify, by issuance of a contract modification, each contractor performing in the operational area under review. The modification deactivates clause 252.232-7011 and activates the applicable FAR Prompt Payment clause in the contract.

(ii) If after deactivation of clause 252.232-7011, the head of the contracting activity subsequently determines that the operational area has evolved into a less stable environment, the head of the contracting activity will make a determination that conditions exist that limit normal business operations. The contracting officer will then reactivate clause 252.232-7011 by issuance of a contract modification.

[Interim rule, 75 FR 40711, 7/13/2010, effective 7/13/2010; Final rule, 76 FR 11371, 3/2/2011, effective 3/2/2011]

232.903 Responsibilities.

DoD policy is to assist small business concerns by paying them as quickly as possible after invoices and all proper documentation, including acceptance, are received and before normal payment due dates established in the contract (*see* 232.906(a)).

[Final rule, 70 FR 75412, 12/20/2005, effective 12/20/2005; Interim rule, 76 FR 23505, 4/27/2011, effective 4/27/2011; Final rule, 76 FR 71468, 11/18/2011, effective 11/18/2011]

232.904 Determining payment due dates.

(d) In most cases, Government acceptance or approval can occur within the 7-day constructive acceptance period specified in the FAR Prompt Payment clauses. Government payment of construction progress payments can, in most cases, be made within the 14-day period allowed by the Prompt Payment for Construction Contracts clause. While the contracting officer may specify a longer period because the period specified in the contract is not reasonable or practical, such change should be coordinated with the Government offices responsible for acceptance or approval and for payment. Reasons for specifying a longer period include but are not limited to: the nature of the work or supplies or services, inspection or testing requirements, shipping and acceptance terms, and resources available at the acceptance activity. A constructive acceptance period of less than the cited 7 or 14 days is not authorized.

[Final rule, 70 FR 75412, 12/20/2005, effective 12/20/2005]

232.905 Payment documentation and process.

(b) (1) (iii) For task and delivery orders numbered in accordance with FAR 4.1603 and 204.1603, the 13-character order number may serve as the contract number on invoices and receiving reports. The contract or agreement number under which the order was placed may be omitted from invoices and receiving reports. The contractor may choose to identify both the contract number and the 13-character order number on invoices and receiving reports. Task and delivery orders numbered with a four-position alphanumeric call or order serial number shall include both the 13-position basic contract Procurement Instrument Identifier and the four-position order number.

[Final rule, 63 FR 69006, 12/15/98, effective 12/15/98; Final rule, 70 FR 75412, 12/20/2005, effective 12/20/2005; Final rule 81 FR 9783, 2/26/2016, effective 2/26/2016]

232.906 Making payments.

(a) (i) Generally, the contracting officer shall insert the standard due date of 14 days for interim payments on cost-reimbursement contracts for services in the clause at FAR 52.232-25, Prompt Payment, when using the clause with its Alternate I.

(ii) The restrictions of FAR 32.906 prohibiting early payment do not apply to invoice payments made to small business concerns. However, contractors shall not be entitled to interest penalties if the Government fails to make early payment.

[Final rule, 64 FR 51074, 9/21/99, effective 9/21/99; Final rule, 70 FR 75412, 12/20/2005, effective 12/20/2005; Interim rule, 76 FR 23505, 4/27/2011, effective 4/27/2011; Final rule, 76 FR 71468, 11/18/2011, effective 11/18/2011]

232.908 Contract clauses.

Use the clause at 252.232-7011, Payments in Support of Emergencies and Contingency Operations, in solicitations and contracts, including solicitations and contracts using FAR part 12 procedures for the acquisition of commercial items, in acquisitions that meet the applicability criteria at 232.901(1). Use of this clause is in addition to use of either the approved Payment clause prescribed in FAR 32.908 or the clause at FAR 52.212-4, Contract Terms and Conditions—Commercial Items.

[Interim rule, 75 FR 40711, 7/13/2010, effective 7/13/2010; Final rule, 76 FR 11371, 3/2/2011, effective 3/2/2011; Final rule, 78 FR 37980, 6/25/2013, effective 6/25/2013]

SUBPART 232.10—PERFORMANCE-BASED PAYMENTS

232.1001 Policy.

(a) As with all contract financing, the purpose of performance-based payments is to assist the contractor in the payment of costs incurred during the performance of the contract. Therefore, performance-based payments should never exceed total cost incurred at any point during the contract. See PGI 232.1001(a) for additional information on use of performance-based payments.

(d) The contracting officer shall use the following standard payment terms for performance-based payments: The contractor entitlement date, if any, specified in the contract, or 14 days after receipt by the designated billing office of a proper request for payment, whichever is later.

[DAC 91-13, 63 FR 11522, 3/9/98, effective 3/9/98; Final rule, 79 FR 17931, 3/31/2014, effective 3/31/2014]

232.1003-70 Criteria for use.

The contracting officer will consider the adequacy of an offeror's or contractor's accounting system prior to agreeing to use performance-based payments.

[Final rule, 79 FR 17931, 3/31/2014, effective 3/31/2014]

232.1004 Procedures.

(b) Prior to using performance-based payments, the contracting officer shall—

(i) Agree with the offeror on price using customary progress payments before negotiation begins on the use of performance-based payments, except for modifications to contracts that already use performance-based payments;

(ii) Analyze the performance-based payment schedule using the performance-based payments (PBP) analysis tool. The PBP analysis tool is on the DPAP website in the Cost, Pricing & Finance section, Performance Based Payments—Guide Book & Analysis Tool tab, at *http://www.acq.osd.mil/dpap/cpic/cp/Performance_based_payments.html.*

(A) When considering performance-based payments, obtain from the offeror/contractor a proposed performance-based payments schedule that includes all performance-based payments events, completion criteria and event values along with the projected expenditure profile in order to negotiate the value of the performance events. If performance-based payments are deemed practical, the Government will evaluate and negotiate the details of the performance-based payments schedule.

(B) For modifications to contracts that already use performance-based payments financing, the basis for negotiation must include performance-based payments. The PBP analysis tool will be used in the same manner to help determine the price for the modification. The only difference is that the baseline assuming customary progress payments will reflect an objective profit rate instead of a negotiated profit rate;

(iii) Negotiate the consideration to be received by the Government if the performance-based payments payment schedule will be more favorable to the contractor than customary progress payments;

(iv) Obtain the approval of the business clearance approving official, or one level above the contracting officer, whichever is higher, for the negotiated consideration; and

(v) Document in the contract file that the performance-based payment schedule provides a mutually beneficial settlement position that reflects adequate consideration to the Government for the improved contractor cash flow.

(c) *Instructions for multiple appropriations.* If the contract contains foreign military sales requirements, the contracting officer shall provide instructions for distribution of the contract financing payments to each country's account.

[DAC 91-13, 63 FR 11522, 3/9/98, effective 3/9/98; Final rule, 79 FR 17931, 3/31/2014, effective 3/31/2014]

232.1005-70 Contract clauses.

The contracting officer shall include the following clauses with appropriate fill-ins in solicitations and contracts that include performance-based payments:

(a) For performance-based payments made on a whole-contract basis, use the clause at 252.232-7012, Performance-Based Payments—Whole–Contract Basis.

(b) For performance-based payments made on a deliverable-item basis, use the clause at 252.232-7013, Performance-Based Payments—Deliverable–Item Basis.

[Final rule, 79 FR 17931, 3/31/2014, effective 3/31/2014]

232.1007 [Removed]

[DAC 91-13, 63 FR 11522, 3/9/98, effective 3/9/98; Final rule, 70 FR 75412, 12/20/2005, effective 12/20/2005]

SUBPART 232.11—ELECTRONIC FUNDS TRANSFER

232.1108 [Removed]

[Final rule, 65 FR 46625, 7/31/2000, effective 7/31/2000; Final rule, 70 FR 75412, 12/20/2005, effective 12/20/2005]

232.1110 Solicitation provision and contract clauses.

Use the clause at 252.232-7009, Mandatory Payment by Governmentwide Commercial Purchase Card, in solicitations, contracts, and agreements, including solicitations, contracts, and agreements using FAR part 12 procedures for the acquisition of commercial items, when—

(1) Placement of orders or calls valued at or below the micro-purchase threshold is anticipated; and

(2) Payment by Governmentwide commercial purchase card is required for orders or calls valued at or below the micro-purchase threshold under the contract or agreement.

[Final rule, 65 FR 46625, 7/31/2000, effective 7/31/2000; Final rule, 78 FR 37980, 6/25/2013, effective 6/25/2013]

SUBPART 232.70—ELECTRONIC SUBMISSION AND PROCESSING OF PAYMENT REQUESTS AND RECEIVING REPORTS

232.7000 Scope of subpart.

This subpart prescribes policies and procedures for submitting and processing payment requests in electronic form to comply with 10 U.S.C. 2227.

[Interim rule, 68 FR 8450, 2/21/2003, effective 3/1/2003]

232.7001 Definitions.

As used in this subpart—

Electronic form means any automated system that transmits information electronically from the initiating system to affected systems.

Payment request means any request for contract financing payment or invoice payment submitted by the contractor under a contract or task or delivery order.

Receiving report means the data prepared in the manner and to the extent required by appendix F of this chapter, Material Inspection and Receiving Report.

[Interim rule, 68 FR 8450, 2/21/2003, effective 3/1/2003; Final rule, 83 FR 66062, 12/21/2018, effective 12/21/2018]

232.7002 Policy.

(a) Payment requests and receiving reports are required to be submitted in electronic form, except for—

(1) Classified contracts or purchases when electronic submission and processing of payment requests and receiving reports could compromise the safeguarding of classified information or national security;

(2) Cases in which contractor submission of electronic payment requests and receiving reports is not feasible (*e.g.*, when contract performance is in an environment where internet connectivity is not available);

(3) Cases in which DoD is unable to receive payment requests or provide acceptance in electronic form;

(4) Cases in which the contractor has requested permission in writing to submit payment requests and receiving reports by nonelectronic means, and the contracting officer has provided instructions for a temporary alternative method of submission of payment requests and receiving reports in the contract administration data section of the contract or task or delivery order (*e.g.*, section G, an addendum to FAR 52.212-4, or applicable clause); and

(5) When the Governmentwide commercial purchase card is used as the method of payment, in which case only submission of the receiving report in electronic form is required.

(b)(1) The only acceptable electronic form for submission of payment requests and receiving reports is Wide Area WorkFlow (WAWF) (*https://wawf.eb.mil/*), except as follows:

(i) For payment of commercial transportation services provided under a Government rate tender, contract, or task or delivery order for transportation services, the use of a DoD-approved electronic third party payment system or other exempted vendor payment/invoicing system (*e.g.*, PowerTrack, Transportation Financial Management System, and Cargo and Billing System) is permitted.

(ii) For submitting and processing payment requests and receiving reports for contracts or task or delivery orders for rendered health care services, the use of TRICARE Encounter Data System as the electronic form is permitted.

(2) Facsimile, email, and scanned documents are not acceptable electronic forms of payment requests or receiving reports.

[Interim rule, 68 FR 8450, 2/21/2003, effective 3/1/2003; Final rule, 68 FR 69628, 12/15/2003, effective 12/15/2003; Final rule, 72 FR 14240, 3/27/2007, effective 3/27/2007; Final rule, 73 FR 11356, 3/3/2008, effective 3/3/2008; Final rule, 77 FR 38731, 6/29/2012, effective 6/29/2012; Final rule, 83 FR 66062, 12/21/2018, effective 12/21/2018]

232.7003 Procedures.

(a) DoD officials receiving payment requests in electronic form shall process the payment requests in electronic form. The WAWF system provides the method to electronically process payment requests and receiving reports.

(1) Documents necessary for payment, such as receiving reports, invoice approvals, contracts, contract modifications, and required certifications, shall also be processed in electronic form.

(2) Scanned documents and other commonly used file formats are only acceptable for processing supporting documentation.

(b) If one of the exceptions to submission in electronic form at 232.7002(a) applies, the contracting officer shall—

(1) Consult the payment office and the contract administration office regarding the alternative method to be used for submission of payment requests or receiving reports (*e.g.*, facsimile or conventional mail); and

(2) Provide procedures for invoicing in the contract administration data section of the contract or task or delivery order (*e.g.*, section G, an addendum to FAR 52.212-4, or applicable clause) for submission of invoices by nonelectronic means. If submission of invoices by nonelectronic means is temporary, the procedures should specify the time period for which they apply.

[Interim rule, 68 FR 8450, 2/21/2003, effective 3/1/2003; Final rule, 69 FR 1926, 1/13/2004, effective 1/13/2004; Final rule, 71 FR 27643, 5/12/2006, effective 5/12/2006; Final rule, 72 FR 14240, 3/27/2007, effective 3/27/2007; Final rule, 73 FR 11356, 3/3/2008, effective 3/3/2008; Final rule, 77 FR 38731, 6/29/2012, effective 6/29/2012; Final rule, 83 FR 66062, 12/21/2018, effective 12/21/2018]

232.7004 Contract clauses.

(a) Unless an exception to submission in electronic form at 232.7002(a) applies and instructions for invoices are contained in the contract administration data section of the contract or task or delivery order, use the clause at 252.232-7003, Electronic Submission of Payment Requests and Receiving Reports, in solicitations and contracts, including solicitations and contracts using FAR part 12 procedures for the acquisition of commercial items.

(b) Use the clause at 252.232-7006, Wide Area WorkFlow Payment Instructions, in solicitations and contracts or task or delivery orders, including solicitations and contracts using FAR part 12 procedures for the acquisition of commercial items, when 252.232-7003 is used and none of the exceptions at 232.7002(b)(1) apply. See PGI 232.7004 for instructions on completing the clause.

[Interim rule, 68 FR 8450, 2/21/2003, effective 3/1/2003; Final rule, 73 FR 11356, 3/3/2008, effective 3/3/2008; Final rule, 77 FR 38731, 6/29/2012, effective 6/29/2012; Final rule, 78 FR 37980, 6/25/2013, effective 6/25/2013; Final rule, 79 FR 44313, 7/31/2014, effective 7/31/2014; Final rule, 83 FR 66062, 12/21/2018, effective 12/21/2018]

SUBPART 232.71—LEVIES ON CONTRACT PAYMENTS

232.7100 Scope of subpart.

This subpart prescribes policies and procedures concerning the effect of levies pursuant to 26 U.S.C. 6331(h) on contract payments. The Internal Revenue Service (IRS) is authorized to levy up to 100 percent of all payments made under a DoD contract, up to the amount of the tax debt.

[Interim rule, 70 FR 52031, 9/1/2005, effective 9/1/2005; Final rule, 71 FR 69489, 12/1/2006, effective 12/1/2006]

232.7101 Policy and procedures.

(a) The contracting officer shall require the contractor to—

(1) Promptly notify the contracting officer when a levy may result in an inability to perform the contract; and

(2) Advise the contracting officer whether the inability to perform may adversely affect national security.

(b) The contracting officer shall promptly notify the Director, Defense Procurement and Acquisition Policy (DPAP), when the contractor's inability to perform will adversely affect national security or will result in significant additional costs to the Government. Follow the procedures at PGI 232.7101(b) for reviewing the contractor's rationale and submitting the required notification.

(c) The Director, DPAP, will promptly evaluate the contractor's rationale and will notify the IRS, the contracting officer, and the payment office, as appropriate, in accordance with the procedures at PGI 232.7101(c).

(d) The contracting officer shall then notify the contractor in accordance with paragraph (c) of the clause at 252.232-7010 and in accordance with the procedures at PGI 232.7101(d).

[Interim rule, 70 FR 52031, 9/1/2005, effective 9/1/2005; Final rule, 71 FR 69489, 12/1/2006, effective 12/1/2006]

232.7102 Contract clause.

Use the clause at 252.232-7010, Levies on Contract Payments, in all solicitations and contracts, including solicitations and contracts using FAR part 12 procedures for the acquisition of commercial items.

[Interim rule, 70 FR 52031, 9/1/2005, effective 9/1/2005; Final rule, 71 FR 69489, 12/1/2006, effective 12/1/2006; Final rule, 78 FR 37980, 6/25/2013, effective 6/25/2013]

SUBPART 232.72—PAYMENT IN LOCAL CURRENCY (AFGHANISTAN)

232.7200 Scope of subpart.

This subpart prescribes policies and procedures concerning the payment of contracts for performance in Afghanistan.

[Final rule, 79 FR 58694, 9/30/2014, effective 9/30/2014]

232.7201 Policy and procedures.

Payment currency used for contracts performed in Afghanistan shall be dependent on the nationality of the vendor pursuant to the authority of USCENTCOM Fragmentary Orders (FRAGOs) 09–1567 and 10–143. If the contract is awarded to a host nation vendor (Afghan), the contractor will be paid in Afghani (local currency) via electronic funds transfer to a local (Afghan) banking institution. Contracts shall not be awarded to host nation vendors who do not bank locally. If awarded to other than a host nation vendor, the contract will be awarded in U.S. dollars.

[Final rule, 79 FR 58694, 9/30/2014, effective 9/30/2014]

232.7202 Solicitation provision.

Use the provision at 252.232–7014, Notification of Payment in Local Currency (Afghanistan), in all solicitations, including solicitations using FAR part 12 procedures for the acquisition of commercial items, for performance in Afghanistan.

[Final rule, 79 FR 58694, 9/30/2014, effective 9/30/2014]

PART 233—PROTESTS, DISPUTES, AND APPEALS

Table of Contents

Subpart 233.1—Protests

General 233.102
Briefing requirement for protested acquisitions valued at $1 billion or more 233.170
Reporting requirement for protests of solicitations or awards 233.171

Subpart 233.2—Disputes and Appeals

[Removed] 233.204
Limitations on payment 233.204-70
Contracting officer's authority 233.210
Contract clause 233.215
Additional contract clause 233.215-70

PART 233—PROTESTS, DISPUTES, AND APPEALS

SUBPART 233.1—PROTESTS

233.102 General

If the government exercises the authority provided in 239.7305(d) to limit disclosure of information, no action undertaken by the Government under such authority shall be subject to review in a bid protest before the Government Accountability Office or in any Federal court (see subpart 239.73).

[Interim rule, 78 FR 69267, 11/18/2013, effective 11/18/2013; Final rule, 80 FR 67243, 10/30/2015, effective 10/30/2015]

233.170 Briefing requirement for protested acquisitions valued at $1 billion or more.

Follow the procedures at PGI 233.170 for briefing protested acquisitions valued at $1 billion or more.

[Final rule, 76 FR 3536, 1/20/2011, effective 1/20/2011]

233.171 Reporting requirement for protests of solicitations or awards.

Follow the procedures at PGI 233.171 for reporting information on protests involving the same contract award or proposed award that have been filed at both the Government Accountability Office and the United States Court of Federal Claims.

[Final rule, 84 FR 25194, 5/31/2019, effective 5/31/2019]

SUBPART 233.2—DISPUTES AND APPEALS

233.204 [Removed]

[DAC 91-13, 63 FR 11522, 3/9/98, effective 3/9/98; Final rule, 72 FR 6485, 2/12/2007, effective 2/12/2007]

233.204-70 Limitations on payment.

See 10 U.S.C. 2410(b) for limitations on Congressionally directed payment of a claim under 41 U.S.C. chapter 71 (Contract Disputes), a request for equitable adjustment to contract terms, or a request for relied under Pub. L. 85-804.

[DAC 91-13, 63 FR 11522, 3/9/98, effective 3/9/98; Final rule, 72 FR 6485, 2/12/2007, effective 2/12/2007; Final rule, 77 FR 35879, 6/15/2012, effective 6/15/2012]

233.210 Contracting officer's authority.

See PGI 232.210 for guidance on reviewing a contractor's claim.

[Final rule, 72 FR 6485, 2/12/2007, effective 2/12/2007]

233.215 Contract clause.

Use Alternate I of the clause at FAR 52.233-1, Disputes, when—

(1) The acquisition is for—

(i) Aircraft

(ii) Spacecraft and launch vehicles

(iii) Naval vessels

(iv) Missile systems

(v) Tracked combat vehicles

(vi) Related electronic systems;

(2) The contracting officer determines that continued performance is—

(i) Vital to the national security, or

(ii) Vital to the public health and welfare; or

(3) The head of the contracting activity determines that continued performance is necessary pending resolution of any claim that might arise under or be related to the contract.

[Redesignated from 233.214, DAC 91-12, 62 FR 34114, 6/24/97, effective 6/24/97]

233.215-70 Additional contract clause.

Use the clause at 252.233-7001, Choice of Law (Overseas), in solicitations and contracts when contract performance will be outside of the United States and its outlying areas, unless otherwise provided for in a government-to-government agreement.

[DAC 91-12, 62 FR 34114, 6/24/97, effective 6/24/97; Final rule, 70 FR 35543, 6/21/2005, effective 6/21/2005]

PART 234—MAJOR SYSTEM ACQUISITION

Table of Contents

Definitions 234.001
Responsibilities 234.003
Acquisition strategy 234.004
General requirements 234.005
Competition 234.005-1
Mission-oriented solicitation 234.005-2
[Removed] 234.005-70
[Removed] 234.005-71

Subpart 234.2—Earned Value Management System

Policy 234.201
Solicitation provisions and contract clause 234.203

Subpart 234.70—Acquisition of Major Weapon Systems as Commercial Items

Scope of subpart 234.7000
Definition 234.7001
Policy 234.7002

Subpart 234.71—Cost and Software Data Reporting

Policy 234.7100
Solicitation provision and contract clause 234.7101

SUBCHAPTER F—SPECIAL CATEGORIES OF CONTRACTING (Parts 234-241)

PART 234—MAJOR SYSTEM ACQUISITION

234.001 Definitions.

As used in this subpart—

Acceptable earned value management system and *earned value management system* are defined in the clause at 252.234-7002, Earned Value Management System.

Production of major defense acquisition program means the production and deployment of a major system that is intended to achieve an operational capability that satisfies mission needs, or an activity otherwise defined as Milestone C under Department of Defense Instruction 5000.02 or related authorities.

Significant deficiency is defined in the clause at 252.234-70022, Earned Value Management System, and is synonymous with *noncompliance.*

[DAC 91-9, 60 FR 61586, 11/30/95, effective 11/30/95; Final rule, 70 FR 14574, 3/23/2005, effective 3/23/2005; Interim rule, 76 FR 28856, 5/18/2011, effective 5/18/2011; Final rule, 77 FR 11355, 2/24/2012, effective 2/24/2012; Interim rule, 79 FR 4631, 1/29/2014, effective 1/29/2014; Final rule, 79 FR 58693, 9/30/2014, effective 9/30/2014]

234.003 Responsibilities.

DoDD 5000.01, The Defense Acquisition System, and DoDI 5000.02, Operation of the Defense Acquisition System, contain the DoD implementation of OMB Circular A-109 and OMB Circular A-11.

[DAC 91-12, 62 FR 34114, 6/24/97, effective 6/24/97; Final rule, 70 FR 14574, 3/23/2005, effective 3/23/2005; Final rule, 76 FR 76318, 12/7/2011, effective 12/7/2011]

234.004 Acquisition strategy.

(1) See 209.570 for policy applicable to acquisition strategies that consider the use of lead system integrators.

(2) *Contract type.*

(i) In accordance with section 818 of the National Defense Authorization Act for Fiscal Year 2007 (Pub. L. 109-364), for major defense acquisition programs at Milestone B—

(A) The milestone decision authority shall select, with the advice of the contracting officer, the contract type for a development program at the time of Milestone B approval or, in the case of a space program, Key Decision Point B approval;

(B) The basis for the contract type selection shall be documented in the acquisition strategy. The documentation—

(1) Shall include an explanation of the level of program risk; and

(2) If program risk is determined to be high, shall outline the steps taken to reduce program risk and the reasons for proceeding with Milestone B approval despite the high level of program risk; and

(C) If a cost-reimbursement type contract is selected, the contract file shall include the milestone decision authority's written determination that—

(1) The program is so complex and technically challenging that it would not be practicable to reduce program risk to a level that would permit the use of a fixed-price type contract; and

(2) The complexity and technical challenge of the program is not the result of a failure to meet the requirements of 10 U.S.C. 2366a.

(ii) In accordance with section 811 of the National Defense Authorization Act for Fiscal Year 2013 (Pub. L. 112-239), the contracting officer shall—

(A) Not use cost-reimbursement line items for the acquisition of production of major defense acquisition programs, unless the Under Secretary of Defense for Acquisition and Sustainment (USD(A&S)), or the milestone decision authority when the milestone decision authority is the service acquisition executive of the military department that is managing the program, submits to the congressional defense committees—

(1) A written certification that the particular cost-reimbursement line items are

needed to provide a required capability in a timely and cost effective manner; and

(2) An explanation of the steps taken to ensure that cost-reimbursement line items are used only to achieve the purposes of the exception; and

(B) Include a copy of such congressional certification in the contract file.

(iii) See 216.301-3 for additional contract type approval requirements for cost-reimbursement contracts.

(iv) For fixed-price incentive (firm target) contracts, contracting officers shall comply with the guidance provided at PGI 216.403-1(1) (ii) (B) and (C).

(3) The contracting officer shall include in solicitations for contracts for the technical maturation and risk reduction phase, engineering and manufacturing development phase or production phase of a weapon system, including embedded software—

(i) Clearly defined measurable criteria for engineering activities and design specifications for reliability and maintainability provided by the program manager, or the comparable requiring activity official performing program management responsibilities; or

(ii) Ensure a copy of the justification, executed by the program manager or the comparable requiring activity official performing program management responsibilities for the decision that engineering activities and design specifications for reliability and maintainability should not be a requirement, is included in the contract file (10 U.S.C. 2443).

[DAC 91-12, 62 FR 34114, 6/24/97, effective 6/24/97; Final rule, 70 FR 14574, 3/23/2005, effective 3/23/2005; Interim rule, 73 FR 1823, 1/10/2008, effective 1/10/2008; Interim rule, 73 FR 4117, 1/24/2008, effective 1/24/2008; Final rule, 75 FR 18034, 4/8/2010, effective 4/8/2010; Interim rule, 79 FR 4631, 1/29/2014, effective 1/29/2014; Final rule, 79 FR 23278, 4/28/2014, effective 4/28/2014; Final rule, 79 FR 58693, 9/30/2014, effective 9/30/2014; Final rule, 84 FR 58332, 10/31/2019, effective 10/31/2019; Final rule, 84 FR 65304, 11/27/2019, effective 11/27/2019]

234.005 General requirements.

[Final rule, 70 FR 14574, 3/23/2005, effective 3/23/2005; Final rule, 73 FR 21846, 4/23/2008, effective 4/23/2008; Interim rule, 79 FR 4631, 1/29/2014, effective 1/29/2014; Final rule, 79 FR 58693, 9/30/2014, effective 9/30/2014]

234.005-1 Competition.

A contract that is initially awarded from the competitive selection of a proposal resulting from a broad agency announcement may contain a contract line item or contract option for the provision of advanced component development, prototype, or initial production of technology developed under the contract or the delivery of initial or additional items if the item or a prototype thereof is created as the result of work performed under the contract only when it adheres to the following limitations:

(1) The contract line item or contract option shall be limited to the minimal amount of initial or additional prototype items that will allow for timely competitive solicitation and award of a follow-on development or production contract for those items.

(2) The term of the contract line item or contract option shall be for not more than 2 years.

(3) The dollar value of the work to be performed pursuant to the contract line item or contract option shall not exceed $100 million in fiscal year 2017 constant dollars. (10 U.S.C. 2302e)

[Interim rule, 75 FR 32638, 6/8/2010, effective 6/8/2010; Confirmation of interim final rule, 75 FR 71562, 11/24/2010, effective 11/24/2010; Final rule, 81 FR 17044, 3/25/2016, effective 3/25/2016; Final rule, 84 FR 4364, 2/15/2019, effective 2/15/2019]

234.005-2 Mission-oriented solicitation.

See 215.101-2-70(b) (2) for the prohibition on the use of the lowest price technically acceptable source selection process for engineering and manufacturing development of a major defense acquisition program for which budgetary authority is requested beginning in fiscal year 2019.

[Final rule, 84 FR 50785, 9/26/2019, effective 10/1/2019]

234.005-70 [Removed]

[Interim rule, 62 FR 9990, 3/5/97, effective 3/5/97; DAC 91-13, 63 FR 11522, 3/9/98, effective 3/9/98; Final rule, 70 FR 14574, 3/23/2005, effective 3/23/2005]

234.005-71 [Removed]

[Interim rule, 62 FR 9990, 3/5/97, effective 3/5/97, corrected 62 FR 11953, 3/13/97, corrected, 62 FR 49305, 9/19/97, adopted as final, DAC 91-13, 63 FR 11522, 3/9/98; Final rule, 70 FR 14574, 3/23/2005, effective 3/23/2005]

SUBPART 234.2—EARNED VALUE MANAGEMENT SYSTEM

234.201 Policy.

(1) DoD applies the earned value management system requirement as follows:

(i) For cost or incentive contracts and subcontracts valued at $20,000,000 or more, the earned value management system shall comply with the guidelines in the American National Standards Institute/Electronic Industries Alliance Standard 748, Earned Value Management Systems (ANSI/EIA-748).

(ii) For cost or incentive contracts and subcontracts valued at $50,000,000 or more, the contractor shall have an earned value management system that has been determined by the cognizant Federal agency to be in compliance with the guidelines in ANSI/EIA-748.

(iii) For cost or incentive contracts and subcontracts valued at less than $20,000,000—

(A) The application of earned value management is optional and is a risk-based decision;

(B) A decision to apply earned value management shall be documented in the contract file; and

(C) Follow the procedures at PGI 234.201(1)(iii) for conducting a cost-benefit analysis.

(iv) For firm-fixed-price contracts and subcontracts of any dollar value—

(A) The application of earned value management is discouraged; and

(B) Follow the procedures at PGI 234.201(1)(iv) for obtaining a waiver before applying earned value management.

(2) When an offeror proposes a plan for compliance with the earned value management system guidelines in ANSI/EIA-748, follow the review procedures at PGI 234.201(2).

(3) The Defense Contract Management Agency is responsible for determining earned value management system compliance when DoD is the cognizant Federal agency.

(4) See PGI 234.201(3) for additional guidance on earned value management.

(5) The cognizant contracting officer, in consultation with the functional specialist and auditor, shall—

(i) Determine the acceptability of the contractor's earned value management system and approve or disapprove the system; and

(ii) Pursue correction of any deficiencies.

(6) In evaluating the acceptability of a contractor's earned value management system, the contracting officer, in consultation with the functional specialist and auditor, shall determine whether the contractor's earned value management system complies with the system criteria for an acceptable earned value management system as prescribed in the clause at 252.234-7002, Earned Value Management System.

(7) *Disposition of findings*—(i) *Reporting of findings.* The functional specialist or auditor shall document findings and recommendations in a report to the contracting officer. If the functional specialist or auditor identifies any significant deficiencies in the contractor's earned value management system, the report shall describe the deficiencies in sufficient detail to allow the contracting officer to understand the deficiencies.

(ii) *Initial determination.* (A) The contracting officer shall review all findings and recommendations and, if there are no significant deficiencies, shall promptly notify the contractor, in writing, that the contractor's earned value management system is acceptable and approved; or

(B) If the contracting officer finds that there are one or more significant deficiencies (as defined in the clause at 252.234-7002, Earned Value Management System) due to the contractor's failure to meet one or more of the earned value management system criteria in the clause at 252.234-7002, the contracting officer shall—

(*1*) Promptly make an initial written determination on any significant deficiencies and notify the contractor, in writing, providing a description of each significant deficiency in sufficient detail to allow the contractor to understand the deficiencies;

(*2*) Request the contractor to respond, in writing, to the initial determination within 30 days; and

(*3*) Evaluate the contractor's response to the initial determination, in consultation with the auditor or functional specialist, and make a final determination.

(iii) *Final determination.* (A) The contracting officer shall make a final determination and notify the contractor, in writing, that—

(*1*) The contractor's earned value management system is acceptable and approved, and no significant deficiencies remain, or

(*2*) Significant deficiencies remain. The notice shall identify any remaining significant deficiencies, and indicate the adequacy of any proposed or completed corrective action. The contracting officer shall—

(*i*) Request that the contractor, within 45 days of receipt of the final determination, either correct the deficiencies or submit an acceptable corrective action plan showing milestones and actions to eliminate the deficiencies;

(*ii*) Disapprove the system in accordance with the clause at 252.234-7002, Earned Value Management System, when initial validation is not successfully completed within the timeframe approved by the contracting officer, or the contracting officer determines that the existing earned value management system contains one or more significant deficiencies in high-risk guidelines in ANSI/EIA-748 standards (guidelines 1, 3, 6, 7, 8, 9, 10, 12, 16, 21, 23, 26, 27, 28, 30, or 32). When the contracting officer determines that the existing earned value management system contains one or more significant deficiencies in one or more of the remaining 16 guidelines in ANSI/EIA-748 standards, the contracting officer shall use discretion to disapprove the system based on input received from functional specialists and the auditor; and

(*iii*) Withhold payments in accordance with the clause at 252.242-7005, Contractor Business Systems, if the clause is included in the contract.

(B) Follow the procedures relating to monitoring a contractor's corrective action and the correction of significant deficiencies at PGI 234.201(7).

(8) *System approval.* The contracting officer shall promptly approve a previously disapproved earned value management system and notify the contractor when the contracting officer determines that there are no remaining significant deficiencies.

(9) *Contracting officer notifications.* The cognizant contracting officer shall promptly distribute copies of a determination to approve a system, disapprove a system and withhold payments, or approve a previously disapproved system and release withheld payments to the auditor; payment office; affected contracting officers at the buying activities; and cognizant contracting officers in contract administration activities.

[Final rule, 73 FR 21846, 4/23/2008, effective 4/23/2008; Interim rule, 76 FR 28856, 5/18/2011, effective 5/18/2011; Final rule, 76 FR 76318, 12/7/2011, effective 12/7/2011; Final rule, 77 FR 11355, 2/24/2012, effective 2/24/2012]

234.203 Solicitation provisions and contract clause.

For cost or incentive contracts valued at $20,000,000 or more, and for other contracts for which EVMS will be applied in accordance with 234.201(1)(iii) and (iv)—

(1) Use the provision at 252.234-7001, Notice of Earned Value Management System, instead of the provisions at FAR 52.234-2,

Notice of Earned Value Management System—Pre-Award IBR, and FAR 52.234-3, Notice of Earned Value Management System—Post-Award IBR, in the solicitation; and

(2) Use the clause at 252.234-7002, Earned Value Management System, instead of the clause at FAR 52.234-4, Earned Value Management System, in the solicitation and contract.

[Final rule, 73 FR 21846, 4/23/2008, effective 4/23/2008]

SUBPART 234.70—ACQUISITION OF MAJOR WEAPON SYSTEMS AS COMMERCIAL ITEMS

234.7000 Scope of subpart.

This subpart—

(a) Implements 10 U.S.C. 2379; and

(b) Requires a determination by the Secretary of Defense and a notification to Congress before acquiring a major weapon system as a commercial item.

[Interim rule, 71 FR 58537, 10/4/2006, effective 10/4/2006; Final rule, 72 FR 51189, 9/6/2007, effective 9/6/2007]

234.7001 Definition.

Major weapon system, as used in this subpart, means a weapon system acquired pursuant to a major defense acquisition program.

[Interim rule, 71 FR 58537, 10/4/2006, effective 10/4/2006; Final rule, 72 FR 51189, 9/6/2007, effective 9/6/2007; Final rule, 80 FR 36903, 6/26/2015, effective 10/1/2015]

234.7002 Policy.

(a) *Major weapon systems.* (1) A DoD major weapon system may be treated as a commercial item, or acquired under procedures established for the acquisition of commercial items, only if—

(i) The Secretary of Defense determines that—

(A) The major weapon system is a commercial item as defined in FAR 2.101; and

(B) Such treatment is necessary to meet national security objectives; and

(ii) The congressional defense committees are notified at least 30 days before such treatment or acquisition occurs. Follow the procedures at PGI 234.7002.

(2) The authority of the Secretary of Defense to make a determination under paragraph (a)(1) of this section may not be delegated below the level of the Deputy Secretary of Defense.

(b) *Subsystems.* A subsystem of a major weapon system (other than a commercially available off-the-shelf item) shall be treated as a commercial item and acquired under procedures established for the acquisition of commercial items if—

(1) The subsystem is intended for a major weapon system that is being acquired, or has been acquired, under procedures established for the acquisition of commercial items in accordance with paragraph (a) of this section; or

(2) The contracting officer determines in writing that the subsystem is a commercial item.

(i) The subsystem is a commercial item; and

(ii) The offeror has submitted sufficient information to evaluate, through price analysis, the reasonableness of the price for the subsystem.

(c) *Components and spare parts.* (1) A component or spare part for a major weapon system (other than a commercially available off-the-shelf item) may be treated as a commercial item if—

(i) The component or spare part is intended for—

(A) A major weapon system that is being acquired, or has been acquired, under procedures established for the acquisition of commercial items in accordance with paragraph (a) of this section; or

(B) A subsystem of a major weapon system that is being acquired, or has been acquired, under procedures established for the acquisition of commercial items in accordance with paragraph (b) of this section; or

(ii) The contracting officer determines in writing that the component or spare part is a commercial item.

(A) The component or spare part is a commercial item; and

(B) The offeror has submitted sufficient information to evaluate, through price analysis, the reasonableness of the price for the component or spare part.

(2) This paragraph (c) shall apply only to components and spare parts that are acquired by DoD through a prime contract or a modification to a prime contract, or through a subcontract under a prime contract or modification to a prime contract on which the prime contractor adds no, or negligible, value.

(d) *Relevant information.* This section implements 10 U.S.C. 2379.

(1) To the extent necessary to make a determination of price reasonableness, the contracting officer shall require the offeror to submit prices paid for the same or similar commercial items under comparable terms and conditions by both Government and commercial customers.

(2) If the contracting officer determines that the offeror cannot provide sufficient information described in paragraph (d)(1) of this section to determine the reasonableness of price, the contracting officer shall request the offeror to submit information on—

(i) Prices paid for the same or similar items under different terms and conditions;

(ii) Prices paid for similar levels of work or effort on related products or services;

(iii) Prices paid for alternative solutions or approaches; and

(iv) Other relevant information that can serve as the basis for a price reasonableness determination.

(3) If the contracting officer determines that the information submitted pursuant to paragraphs (d)(1) and (2) of this section is not sufficient to determine the reasonableness of price, the contracting officer shall request the offeror to submit other relevant information, including uncertified cost data. However, no uncertified cost data may be required in any case in which there are sufficient non-Government sales of the same item to establish reasonableness of price.

(4) An offeror shall not be required to submit information described in paragraph (d)(3) of this section with regard to a commercially available off-the-shelf item. An offeror may be required to submit such information with regard to any other item that was developed exclusively at private expense only after the head of the contracting activity determines in writing that the information submitted pursuant to paragraphs (d)(1) and (2) of this section is not sufficient to determine the reasonableness of price.

[Interim rule, 71 FR 58537, 10/4/2006, effective 10/4/2006; Final rule, 72 FR 51189, 9/6/2007, effective 9/6/2007; Interim rule, 74 FR 34263, 7/15/2009, effective 7/15/2009; Final rule, 75 FR 51416, 8/20/2010, effective 8/20/2010; Interim rule; delay in confirmation as final, 75 FR 52650, 8/27/2010; Final rule, 76 FR 21810, 4/19/2011, effective 4/19/2011; Final rule, 83 FR 4431, 1/31/2018, effective 1/31/2018]

SUBPART 234.71—COST AND SOFTWARE DATA REPORTING

234.7100 Policy.

(a) The cost and software data reporting (CSDR) requirement is mandatory for major defense acquisition programs (as defined in 10 U.S.C. 2430), and major automated information system programs (as defined in 10 U.S.C. 2445a) as specified in DoDI 5000.02, Operation of the Defense Acquisition System and the DoD 5000.04-M-1, CSDR Manual. The CSDR system is applied in accordance with the reporting requirements established in DoDI 5000.02. The two principal components of the CSDR system are contractor cost data reporting and software resources data reporting.

(b) Prior to contract award, contracting officers shall consult with the Defense Cost and Resource Center to determine that the offeror selected for award has proposed a standard CSDR system, as described in the offeror's proposal in response to the provision at 252.234-7003, that is in compliance with DoDI 5000.02, Operation of the Defense Acquisition System, and the DoD 5000.04-M-1, CSDR Manual.

(c) Contact information for the Defense Cost and Resource Center and the Deputy Director, Cost Assessment, is located at PGI 234.7100.

[Final rule, 75 FR 71560, 11/24/2010, effective 11/24/2010]

234.7101 Solicitation provision and contract clause.

(a) Use the basic or the alternate of the provision at 252.234–7003, Notice of Cost and Software Data Reporting System, in any solicitation that includes the basic or the alternate of the clause at 252.234–7004, Cost and Software Data Reporting.

(1) Use the basic provision when the solicitation includes the clause at 252.234–7004, Cost and Software Data Reporting—Basic.

(2) Use the alternate I provision when the solicitation includes the clause at 252.234–7004, Cost and Software Data Reporting—Alternate I.

(b) Use the basic or the alternate of the clause at 252.234–7004, Cost and Software Data Reporting System, in solicitations that include major defense acquisition programs or major automated information system programs as follows:

(1) Use the basic clause in solicitations and contracts for major defense acquisition programs or major automated information system programs that exceed $50 million.

(2) Use the alternate I clause in solicitations and contracts for major defense acquisition programs or major automated information system programs with a value equal to or greater than $20 million, but less than or equal to $50 million, when so directed by the program manager with the approval of the OSD Deputy Director, Cost Assessment.

[Final rule, 75 FR 71560, 11/24/2010, effective 11/24/2010; Final rule, 79 FR 65592, 11/5/2014, effective 11/5/2014]

PART 235—RESEARCH AND DEVELOPMENT CONTRACTING

Table of Contents

Definitions 235.001
Contracting methods and contract type 235.006
Manufacturing Technology Program 235.006-70
Competition 235.006-71
[Removed] 235.007
Evaluation for award 235.008
Scientific and technical reports 235.010
[Removed] 235.015
Special use allowances for research facilities acquired by educational institutions 235.015-70
Broad agency announcement 235.016
Federally Funded Research and Development Centers 235.017
Sponsoring agreements 235.017-1
Indemnification against unusually hazardous risks 235.070
Indemnification under research and development contracts 235.070-1
Indemnification under contracts involving both research and development and other work 235.070-2
Contract clauses 235.070-3
Export-controlled items 235.071
Additional contract clauses 235.072

Subpart 235.70—[Removed]

PART 235—RESEARCH AND DEVELOPMENT CONTRACTING

235.001 Definitions.

Research and development means those efforts described by the Research, Development, Test, and Evaluation (RDT&E) budget activity definitions found in the DoD Financial Management Regulation (DoD 7000.14-R), Volume 2B, Chapter 5.

[Final rule, 65 FR 32040, 5/22/2000, effective 5/22/2000]

235.006 Contracting methods and contract type.

(b) (i) Consistent with section 829 of the National Defense Authorization Act for Fiscal Year 2017 (Pub. L. 114-328), the Under Secretary of Defense for Acquisition and Sustainment (USD (A&S)) has determined that the use of cost-reimbursement contracts for research and development in excess of $25 million is approved, if the contracting officer executes a written determination and findings that—

(A) The level of program risk does not permit realistic pricing; and

(B) It is not possible to provide an equitable and sensible allocation of program risk between the Government and the contractor.

(ii) For major defense acquisition programs as defined in 10 U.S.C. 2430—

(A) Follow the procedures at 234.004; and

(B) Notify the milestone decision authority of an intent not to exercise a fixed-price production option on a development contract for a major weapon system reasonably in advance of the expiration of the option exercise period.

(iii) For other than major defense acquisition programs—

(A) Do not award a fixed-price type contract for a development program effort unless—

(1) The level of program risk permits realistic pricing;

(2) The use of a fixed-price type contract permits an equitable and sensible allocation of program risk between the Government and the contractor; and

(3) A written determination that the criteria of paragraphs (b) (iii) (A) (1) and (2) of this section have been met is executed—

(i) By the USD (A&S) if the contract is over $25 million and is for: research and development for a non-major system; the development of a major system (as defined in FAR 2.101); or the development of a subsystem of a major system; or

(ii) By the contracting officer for any development not covered by paragraph (b) (iii) (A) (3) (i) of this section.

(B) Obtain USD (A&S) approval of the Government's prenegotiation position before negotiations begin, and obtain USD (AT&L) approval of the negotiated agreement with the contractor before the agreement is executed, for any action that is—

(1) An increase of more than $250 million in the price or ceiling price of a fixed-price type development contract, or a fixed-price type contract for the lead ship of a class;

(2) A reduction in the amount of work under a fixed-price type development contract or a fixed-price type contract for the lead ship of a class, when the value of the work deleted is $100 million or more; or

(3) A repricing of fixed-price type production options to a development contract, or a contract for the lead ship of a class, that increases the price or ceiling price by more than $250 million for equivalent quantities.

[Interim rule, 64 FR 18829, 4/16/99, effective 4/16/99, corrected 64 FR 48459, 9/3/99, finalized without change, 64 FR 51077 9/21/99; Final rule, 65 FR 39703, 6/27/2000, effective 6/27/2000; Interim rule, 73 FR 4117, 1/24/2008, effective 1/24/2008; Final rule, 75 FR 18034, 4/8/2010, effective 4/8/2010; Final rule, 84 FR 65304, 11/27/2019, effective 11/27/2019]

235.006-70 Manufacturing Technology Program.

In accordance with 10 U.S.C. 2521(d), for acquisitions under the Manufacturing Technology Program—

(a) Award all contracts using competitive procedures; and

(b) Include in all solicitations an evaluation factor that addresses the extent to which offerors propose to share in the cost of the project (see FAR 15.304).

[Interim rule, 65 FR 2057, 1/13/2000, effective 1/13/2000, finalized without change, 65 FR 19859, 4/13/2000; Final rule, 69 FR 65091, 11/10/2004, effective 11/10/2004]

235.006-71 Competition.

(a) Use of a broad agency announcement with peer or scientific review for the award of science and technology proposals in accordance with 235.016(a) fulfills the requirement for full and open competition (see 206.102(d)(2)).

(b) See 234.005-1 for limitations on the use of contract line items or contract options for the provision of advanced component development or prototypes of technology developed under a competitively awarded proposal.

[Confirmation of interim final rule, 75 FR 71562, 11/24/2010, effective 11/24/2010; Final rule, 84 FR 4364, 2/15/2019, effective 2/15/2019]

235.007 [Removed]

[Final rule, 69 FR 65091, 11/10/2004, effective 11/10/2004]

235.008 Evaluation for award.

See 209.570 for limitations on the award of contracts to contractors acting as lead system integrators.

[Final rule, 69 FR 65091, 11/10/2004, effective 11/10/2004; Interim rule, 73 FR 1823, 1/10/2008, effective 1/10/2008]

235.010 Scientific and technical reports.

(b) For DoD, the Defense Technical Information Center is responsible for collecting all scientific and technical reports. For access to these reports, follow the procedures at PGI 235.010(b).

[DAC 91-7, 60 FR 29491, 6/5/95, effective 5/17/95; DAC 91-12, 62 FR 34114, 6/24/97, effective 6/24/97; Final rule, 69 FR 65091, 11/10/2004, effective 11/10/2004]

235.015 [Removed]

[DAC 91-6, 59 FR 27662, 5/27/94, effective 5/27/94; Final rule, 69 FR 65091, 11/10/2004, effective 11/10/2004]

235.015-70 Special use allowances for research facilities acquired by educational institutions.

(a) *Definitions.* As used in this subsection—

(1) *Research facility* means—

(i) Real property, other than land; and

(ii) Includes structures, alterations, and improvements, acquired for the purpose of conducting scientific research under contracts with departments and agencies of the DoD.

(2) *Special use allowance* means a negotiated direct or indirect allowance—

(i) For construction or acquisition of buildings, structures, and real property, other than land; and

(ii) Where the allowance is computed at an annual rate exceeding the rate which normally would be allowed under FAR subpart 31.3.

(b) *Policy.* (1) Educational institutions are to furnish the facilities necessary to perform Defense contracts. FAR 31.3 governs how much the Government will reimburse the institution for the research programs. However, in extraordinary situations, the Government may give special use allowances to an educational institution when the institution is unable to provide the capital for new laboratories or expanded facilities needed for Defense contracts.

(2) Decisions to provide a special use allowance must be made on a case-by-case basis, using the criteria in paragraph (c) of this subsection.

(c) *Authorization for special use allowance.* The head of a contracting activity may approve special use allowances only when all of the following conditions are met—

(1) The research facility is essential to the performance of DoD contracts;

(2) Existing facilities, either Government or nongovernment, cannot meet program requirements practically or effectively;

(3) The proposed agreement for special use allowances is a sound business arrangement;

(4) The Government's furnishing of Government-owned facilities is undesirable or impractical; and

(5) The proposed use of the research facility is to conduct essential Government research which requires the new or expanded facilities.

(d) *Application of the special use allowance.* (1) In negotiating a special use allowance—

(i) Compare the needs of DoD and of the institution for the research facility to determine the amount of the special use allowance;

(ii) Consider rental costs for similar space in the area where the research facility is or will be located to establish the annual special use allowance;

(iii) Do not include or allow—

(A) The costs of land; or

(B) Interest charges on capital;

(iv) Do not include maintenance, utilities, or other operational costs;

(v) The period of allowance generally will be—

(A) At least ten years; or

(B) A shorter period if the total amount to be allowed is less than the construction or acquisition cost for the research facility;

(vi) Generally, provide for allocation of the special use allowance equitably among the Government contracts using the research facility;

(vii) Special use allowances apply only in the years in which the Government has contracts in effect with the institution. However, if in any given year there is a reduced level of Government research effort which results in the special use allowance being excessive compared to the Government research funding, a separate special use allowance may be negotiated for that year;

(viii) Special use allowances may be adjusted for the period before construction is complete if the facility is partially occupied and used for Government research during that period.

(2) A special use allowance may be based on either total or partial cost of construction or acquisition of the research facility.

(i) When based on total cost neither the normal use allowance nor depreciation will apply—

(A) During the special use allowance period; and

(B) After the educational institution has recovered the total construction or acquisition cost from the Government or other users.

(ii) When based on partial cost, normal use allowance and depreciation—

(A) Apply to the balance of costs during the special use allowance period to the extent negotiated in the special use allowance agreement; and

(B) Do not apply after the special use allowance period, except for normal use allowance applied to the balance.

(3) During the special use allowance period, the research facility—

(i) Shall be available for Government research use on a priority basis over nongovernment use; and

(ii) Cannot be put to any significant use other than that which justified the special use allowance, unless the head of the contracting activity, who approved the special use allowance, consents.

(4) The Government will pay only an allocable share of the special use allowance when the institution makes any substantial use of the research facility for parties other than the Government during the period when the special use allowance is in effect.

(5) In no event shall the institution be paid more than the acquisition costs.

[DAC 91-7, 60 FR 29491, 6/5/95, effective 5/17/95]

235.016 Broad agency announcement.

(a) *General.* A broad agency announcement with peer or scientific review may be used for the award of science and technology proposals. Science and technology proposals include proposals for the following:

(i) Basic research (budget activity 6.1).

(ii) Applied research (budget activity 6.2).

(iii) Advanced technology development (budget activity 6.3).

(iv) Advanced component development and prototypes (budget activity 6.4).

[Final rule, 84 FR 4364, 2/15/2019, effective 2/15/2019]

235.017 Federally Funded Research and Development Centers.

(a) Policy.

(2) No DoD fiscal year 1992 or later funds may be obligated or expended to finance activities of a DoD Federally Funded Research and Development Center (FFRDC) if a member of its board of directors or trustees simultaneously serves on the board of directors or trustees of a profit-making company under contract to DoD, unless the FFRDC has a DoD-approved conflict of interest policy for its members (Section 8107 of Pub. L. 102-172 and similar sections in subsequent Defense appropriations acts).

[DAC 91-2, 57 FR 14994, 4/23/92, effective 4/16/92; DAC 91-4, 57 FR 53601, 11/12/92, effective 10/30/92; DAC 91-5, 58 FR 28458, 5/13/93, effective 4/30/93]

235.017-1 Sponsoring agreements.

(c) (4) DoD-sponsoring FFRDCs that function primarily as research laboratories (C3I Laboratory operated by the Institute for Defense Analysis, Lincoln Laboratory operated by Massachusetts Institute of Technology, and Software Engineering Institute operated by Carnegie Mellon) may respond to solicitations and announcements for programs which promote research, development, demonstration, or transfer of technology (Section 217, Public Law 103-337).

[DAC 91-9, 60 FR 61586, 11/30/95, effective 11/30/95; Final rule, 69 FR 65091, 11/10/2004, effective 11/10/2004]

235.070 Indemnification against unusually hazardous risks. (No Text)

235.070-1 Indemnification under research and development contracts.

(a) Under 10 U.S.C. 2354, and if authorized by the Secretary concerned, contracts for research and/or development may provide for indemnification of the contractor or subcontractors for—

(1) Claims by third persons (including employees) for death, bodily injury, or loss of or damage to property; and

(2) Loss of or damage to the contractor's property to the extent that the liability, loss, or damage—

(i) Results from a risk that the contract defines as "unusually hazardous;"

(ii) Arises from the direct performance of the contract; and

(iii) Is not compensated by insurance or other means.

(b) Clearly define the specific unusually hazardous risks to be indemnified. Submit this definition for approval with the request for authorization to grant indemnification. Include the approved definition in the contract.

[Final rule, 64 FR 51074, 9/21/99, effective 9/21/99]

235.070-2 Indemnification under contracts involving both research and development and other work.

These contracts may provide for indemnification under the authority of both 10 U.S.C. 2354 and Public Law 85-804. Public Law 85-804 will apply only to work to which 10 U.S.C. 2354 does not apply. Actions under Public Law 85-804 must also comply with FAR 50.104-3.

[Final rule, 78 FR 21850, 4/12/2013, effective 4/12/2013]

235.070-3 Contract clauses.

When the contractor is to be indemnified in accordance with 235.070-1, use either—

(a) The clause at 252.235-7000, Indemnification Under 10 U.S.C. 2354—Fixed Price; or

(b) The clause at 252.235-7001, Indemnification Under 10 U.S.C. 2354—Cost-Reimbursement, as appropriate.

235.071 Export-controlled items.

For requirements regarding access to export-controlled items, see 225.7901.

[Interim rule, 73 FR 42274, 7/21/2008, effective 7/21/2008; Final rule, 75 FR 18029, 4/8/2010, effective 4/8/2010; Final rule, 78 FR 36108, 6/17/2013, effective 6/17/2013]

235.072 Additional contract clauses.

(a) Use a clause substantially the same as the clause at 252.235-7002, Animal Welfare, in solicitations and contracts involving research, development, test, and evaluation or training that use live vertebrate animals.

(b) Use the basic or the alternate of the clause at 252.235-7003, Frequency Authorization, in solicitations and contracts for developing, producing, constructing, testing, or operating a device requiring a frequency authorization.

(1) Use the basic clause if agency procedures do not authorize the use of DD Form 1494, Application for Equipment Frequency Allocation, to obtain radio frequency authorization.

(2) Use the alternate I clause if agency procedures authorize the use of DD Form 1494, Application for Equipment Frequency Allocation, to obtain frequency authorization.

(c) Use the clause at 252.235-7010, Acknowledgment of Support and Disclaimer, in solicitations and contracts for research and development.

(d) Use the clause at 252.235-7011, Final Scientific or Technical Report, in solicitations and contracts for research and development.

(e) Use the clause at 252.235-7004, Protection of Human Subjects, in solicitations and contracts that include or may include research involving human subjects in accordance with 32 CFR Part 219, DoD Directive 3216.02, and 10 U.S.C. 980, including research that meets exemption criteria under 32 CFR 219.101(b). The clause—

(1) Applies to solicitations and contracts awarded by any DoD component, regardless of mission or funding Program Element Code; and

(2) Does not apply to use of cadaver materials alone, which are not directly regulated by 32 CFR Part 219 or DoD Directive 3216.02, and which are governed by other DoD policies and applicable State and local laws.

[DAC 91-7, 60 FR 29491, 6/5/95, effective 5/17/95; Final rule, 70 FR 35543, 6/21/2005, effective 6/21/2005; redesignated Interim rule, 73 FR 42274, 7/21/2008, effective 7/21/2008; Final rule, 74 FR 37648, 7/29/2009, effective 7/29/2009; Final rule, 75 FR 18029, 4/8/2010, effective 4/8/2010; Final rule, 79 FR 17447, 3/28/2014, effective 3/28/2014; Final rule, 79 FR 73500, 12/11/2014, effective 12/11/2014]

SUBPART 235.70—[REMOVED]

235.7000 [Removed]

[Interim rule, 63 FR 34605, 6/25/98, effective 6/25/98, finalized without change, 63 FR 64426, 11/20/98; Final rule, 69 FR 67857, 11/22/2004, effective 11/22/2004]

235.7001 [Removed]

[Interim rule, 63 FR 34605, 6/25/98, effective 6/25/98, finalized without change, 63 FR 64426, 11/20/98; Final rule, 69 FR 67857, 11/22/2004, effective 11/22/2004]

235.7002 [Removed]

[Interim rule, 63 FR 34605, 6/25/98, effective 6/25/98, finalized without change, 63 FR 64426, 11/20/98; Final rule, 69 FR 67857, 11/22/2004, effective 11/22/2004]

235.7003 [Removed]

[Final rule, 69 FR 67857, 11/22/2004, effective 11/22/2004]

235.7003-1 [Removed]

[Interim rule, 63 FR 34605, 6/25/98, effective 6/25/98, finalized without change, 63 FR 64426, 11/20/98; Final rule, 69 FR 67857, 11/22/2004, effective 11/22/2004]

235.7003-2 [Removed]

[Interim rule, 63 FR 34605, 6/25/98, effective 6/25/98, finalized without change, 63 FR 64426, 11/20/98; Final rule 67 FR 20699, 4/26/2002, effective 4/26/2002; Final rule, 69 FR 67857, 11/22/2004, effective 11/22/2004]

235.7003-3 [Removed]

[Interim rule, 63 FR 34605, 6/25/98, effective 6/25/98, finalized without change, 63 FR

64426, 11/20/98; Final rule, 69 FR 67857, 11/22/2004, effective 11/22/2004]

235.7003-4 [Removed]

[Interim rule, 63 FR 34605, 6/25/98, effective 6/25/98, finalized without change, 63 FR 64426, 11/20/98; Final rule, 69 FR 67857, 11/22/2004, effective 11/22/2004]

PART 236—CONSTRUCTION AND ARCHITECT-ENGINEER CONTRACTS

Table of Contents

Subpart 236.1—General

Definitions 236.102

Subpart 236.2—Special Aspects of Contracting for Construction

[Removed] 236.201
Government estimate of construction costs 236.203
Disclosure of the magnitude of construction projects 236.204
Liquidated damages 236.206
Special procedures for sealed bidding in construction contracting 236.213
Special procedures for cost-reimbursement contracts for construction . . 236.215
[Removed] 236.213-70
Expediting construction contracts 236.270
Cost-plus-fixed-fee contracts 236.271
Prequalification of sources 236.272
Construction in foreign countries 236.273
Restriction on acquisition of steel for use in military construction projects 236.274
Construction of industrial resources 236.275

Subpart 236.3—Two-Phase Design-Build Selection Procedures

Phase One 236.303-1

Subpart 236.5—Contract Clauses

Additional provisions and clauses 236.570

Subpart 236.6—Architect-Engineering Services

Policy 236.601
Selection of firms for architect-engineer contracts 236.602
Selection criteria 236.602-1
[Removed] 236.602-2
[Removed] 236.602-4
Restriction on award of overseas architect-engineer contracts to foreign firms 236.602-70
Performance evaluation 236.604
Negotiations 236.606
Statutory fee limitation 236.606-70
Contract clauses 236.609
Additional provision 236.609-70

Subpart 236.7—Standard and Optional Forms for Contracting for Construction, Architect-Engineer Services, and Dismantling, Demolition, or Removal of Improvements

Standard and optional forms for use in contracting for construction or dismantling, demolition, or removal of improvements 236.701

PART 236—CONSTRUCTION AND ARCHITECT-ENGINEER CONTRACTS

SUBPART 236.1—GENERAL

236.102 Definitions.

Construction activity means an activity at any organizational level of the DoD that—

(1) Is responsible for the architectural, engineering, and other related technical aspects of the planning, design, and construction of facilities; and

(2) Receives its technical guidance from the Army Office of the Chief of Engineers, Naval Facilities Engineering Command, or Air Force Directorate of Civil Engineering.

Marshallese firm is defined in the provision at 252.236-7012, Military Construction on Kwajalein Atoll—Evaluation Preference.

United States firm is defined in the provisions at 252.236-7010, Overseas Military Construction-Preference for United States Firms, and 252.236-7011, Overseas Architect-Engineer Services-Restriction to United States firms.

[Interim rule, 62 FR 2857, 1/17/97, effective 1/17/97, finalized without change, DAC 91-12, 62 FR 34114, 6/24/97, effective 6/24/97; DAC 91-13, 63 FR 11522, 3/9/98, effective 3/9/98, finalized without change, 63 FR 64426, 11/20/98; Final rule, 71 FR 9272, 2/23/2006, effective 2/23/2006; Final rule, 76 FR 58155, 9/20/2011, effective 9/20/2011]

SUBPART 236.2—SPECIAL ASPECTS OF CONTRACTING FOR CONSTRUCTION

236.201 [Removed]

[DAC 91-10, 61 FR 7739, 2/29/96, effective 2/29/96; Final rule, 66 FR 49860, 10/1/2001, effective 10/1/2001; Final rule, 71 FR 9272, 2/23/2006, effective 2/23/2006; Final rule, 76 FR 58155, 9/20/2011, effective 9/20/2011]

236.203 Government estimate of construction costs.

Follow the procedures at PGI 236.203 for handling the Government estimate of construction costs.

[Final rule, 71 FR 9272, 2/23/2006, effective 2/23/2006]

236.204 Disclosure of the magnitude of construction projects.

Additional price ranges are—

(i) Between $10,000,000 and $25,000,000;

(ii) Between $25,000,000 and $100,000,000;

(iii) Between $100,000,000 and $250,000,000;

(iv) Between $250,000,000 and $500,000,000; and

(v) Over $500,000,000.

[DAC 91-10, 61 FR 7739, 2/29/96, effective 2/29/96]

236.206 Liquidated damages.

See 211.503 for instructions on use of liquidated damages.

[Final rule, 66 FR 49860, 10/1/2001, effective 10/1/2001]

236.213 Special procedures for sealed bidding in construction contracting.

If it appears that sufficient funds may not be available for all the desired construction features, consider using a bid schedule with additive or deductive items in accordance with PGI 236.213.

[Final rule, 71 FR 9272, 2/23/2006, effective 2/23/2006]

236.215 Special procedures for cost-reimbursement contracts for construction.

For contracts in connection with a military construction project or military family housing project, see the prohibition at 216.301-3.

[Final rule, 81 FR 65563, 9/23/2016, effective 9/23/2016]

236.213-70 [Removed]

[Final rule, 65 FR 39703, 6/27/2000, effective 6/27/2000; Final rule, 71 FR 9272, 2/23/2006, effective 2/23/2006]

236.270 Expediting construction contracts.

(a) 10 U.S.C. 2858 requires agency head approval to expedite the completion date of a contract funded by a Military Construction Appropriations Act, if additional costs are involved. This approval authority may not be redelegated. The approval authority must—

(1) Certify that the additional expenditures are necessary to protect the National interest; and

(2) Establish a reasonable completion date for the project.

(b) The contracting officer may approve an expedited completion date if no additional costs are involved.

236.271 Cost-plus-fixed-fee contracts.

Annual military construction appropriations acts restrict the use of cost-plus-fixed-fee contracts (see 216.306(c)). See also 216.301-3 regarding the prohibition on the use of certain cost-reimbursement contracts in connection with a military construction project or military family housing project.

[DAC 91-10, 61 FR 7739, 2/29/96, effective 2/29/96; Final rule, 81 FR 65563, 9/23/2016, effective 9/23/2016]

236.272 Prequalification of sources.

(a) Prequalification procedures may be used when necessary to ensure timely and efficient performance of critical construction projects. Prequalification—

(1) Results in a list of sources determined to be qualified to perform a specific construction contract; and

(2) Limits offerors to those with proven competence to perform in the required manner.

(b) The head of the contracting activity must—

(1) Authorize the use of prequalification by determining, in writing, that a construction project is of an urgency or complexity that requires prequalification; and

(2) Approve the prequalification procedures.

(c) For small businesses, the prequalification procedures must require the qualifying authority to—

(1) Request a preliminary recommendation from the appropriate Small Business Administration regional office, if the qualifying authority believes a small business is not responsible;

(2) Permit the small business to submit a bid or proposal if the preliminary recommendation is that the small business is responsible; and

(3) Follow the procedures in FAR 19.6, if the small business is in line for award and is found nonresponsible.

236.273 Construction in foreign countries.

(a) In accordance with section 112 of the Military Construction and Veterans Affairs and Related Agencies Appropriations Act, 2015 (Division I of Pub. L. 113-235) and the same provision in subsequent military construction appropriations acts, military construction contracts funded with military construction appropriations, that are estimated to exceed $1,000,000 and are to be performed in the United States outlying areas in the Pacific and on Kwajalein Atoll, or in countries bordering the Arabian Gulf (*i.e.*, Iran, Oman, United Arab Emirates, Saudi Arabia, Qatar, Bahrain, Kuwait, and Iraq), shall be awarded only to United States firms, unless—

(1) The lowest responsive and responsible offer of a United States firm exceeds the lowest responsive and responsible offer of a foreign firm by more than 20 percent; or

(2) The contract is for military construction on Kwajalein Atoll and the lowest responsive and responsible offer is submitted by a Marshallese firm.

(b) See PGI 236.273(b) for guidance on technical working agreements with foreign governments.

[Interim rule, 62 FR 2856, 1/17/97, effective 1/17/97; DAC 91-12, 62 FR 34114, 6/24/97, effective 6/24/97; DAC 91-13, 63 FR 11522, 3/9/98, effective 3/9/98, finalized without change, 63 FR 64426, 11/20/98; Final rule, 66 FR 49860, 10/1/2001, effective 10/1/2001; Final rule, 70 FR 35543, 6/21/2005, effective 6/21/2005; Redesignated from 236.274, Final rule, 71 FR 9272, 2/23/2006, effective 2/23/2006; Interim rule, 79 FR 44314, 7/31/2014, effective

7/31/2014; Final rule 79 FR 73498, 12/11/2014, effective 12/11/2014; Interim rule, 80 FR 15909, 3/26/2015, effective 3/26/2015; Interim rule, 80 FR 51751, 8/26/2015, effective 8/26/2015]

236.274 Restriction on acquisition of steel for use in military construction projects.

In accordance with section 108 of the Military Construction and Veterans Affairs Appropriations Act, 2009 (Pub. L. 110-329, Division E) and the same provision in subsequent military construction appropriations acts, do not acquire, or allow a contractor to acquire, steel for any construction project or activity for which American steel producers, fabricators, or manufacturers have been denied the opportunity to compete for such acquisition of steel.

[Interim rule, 74 FR 2417, 1/15/2009, effective 1/15/2009; Final rule, 74 FR 59916, 11/19/2009, effective 11/19/2009; Interim rule, 80 FR 15909, 3/26/2015, effective 3/26/2015; Interim rule, 80 FR 51751, 8/26/2015, effective 8/26/2015]

236.275 Construction of industrial resources.

See Subpart 237.75 for policy relating to facilities projects.

[Final rule, 74 FR 37645, 7/29/2009, effective 7/29/2009]

SUBPART 236.3—TWO-PHASE DESIGN-BUILD SELECTION PROCEDURES

236.303-1 Phase One.

(a) (4) In lieu of the limitations on the maximum number of offerors that may be selected to submit phase-two proposals at FAR 36.303-1 (a) (4), for DoD—

(i) If the contract value exceeds $4 million, the maximum number of offerors specified in the solicitation that are to be selected to submit phase-two proposals shall not exceed five, unless—

(A) The solicitation is issued for an indefinite-delivery indefinite-quantity contract for design-build construction; or

(B) The head of the contracting activity, delegable to a level no lower than the senior contracting official within the contracting activity, approves the contracting officer's decision with respect to an individual solicitation, that a maximum number greater than five is in the best interest of the Government and is consistent with the purposes and objectives of the two-phase selection procedures. The decision shall be documented in the contract file (10 U.S.C 2305a(d)).

(ii) If the contract value is at or below $4 million, the maximum number of offerors specified in the solicitation that are to be selected to submit phase-two proposals is at the discretion of the contracting officer.

[Final rule, 84 FR 4371, 2/15/2019, effective 2/15/2019]

SUBPART 236.5—CONTRACT CLAUSES

236.570 Additional provisions and clauses.

(a) Use the following clauses in all fixed-price construction solicitations and contracts—

(1) 252.236-7000, Modification Proposals-Price Breakdown; and

(2) 252.236-7001, Contract Drawings and Specifications.

(b) Use the following provisions and clauses in fixed-price construction contracts and solicitations as applicable—

(1) 252.236-7002, Obstruction of Navigable Waterways, when the contract will involve work near or on navigable waterways.

(2) When the head of the contracting activity has approved use of a separate bid item for mobilization and preparatory work, use either—

(i) 252.236-7003, Payment for Mobilization and Preparatory Work. Use this clause for major construction contracts that require—

(A) Major or special items of plant and equipment; or

(B) Large stockpiles of material which are in excess of the type, kind, and quantity which would be normal for a contractor qualified to undertake the work; or

(ii) 252.236-7004, Payment for Mobilization and Demobilization. Use this clause for contracts involving major mobilization expense, or plant equipment and material (other than the situations covered in paragraph (b)(2)(i) of this section) made necessary by the location or nature of the work.

(A) Generally, allocate 60 percent of the lump sum price in paragraph (a) of the clause to the cost of mobilization.

(B) Vary this percentage to reflect the circumstances of the particular contract, but in no event should mobilization exceed 80 percent of the payment item.

(3) 252.236-7005, Airfield Safety Precautions, when construction will be performed on or near airfields.

(4) 252.236-7006, Cost Limitation, if the solicitation's bid schedule contains one or more items subject to statutory cost limitations, and if a waiver has not been granted (FAR 36.205).

(5) 252.236-7007, Additive or Deductive Items, if the procedures in 236.213 are being used.

(6) 252.236-7008, Contract Prices—Bidding Schedule, if the contract will contain only unit prices for some items.

(c) Use the following provisions in solicitations for military construction contracts that are funded with military construction appropriations and are estimated to exceed $1,000,000:

(1) 252.236-7010, Overseas Military Construction—Preference for United States Firms, when contract performance will be in a United States outlying area in the Pacific or in a country bordering the Arabian Gulf.

(2) 252.236-7012, Military Construction on Kwajalein Atoll—Evaluation Preference, when contract performance will be on Kwajalein Atoll.

(d) Use the clause at 252.236-7013, Requirement for Competition Opportunity for American Steel Producers, Fabricators, and Manufacturers, in solicitations and contracts that—

(1) Use funds appropriated for military construction; and

(2) May require the acquisition of steel as a construction material.

(e) Also see 246.710(4) for an additional clause applicable to construction contracts to be performed in Germany.

[DAC 91-3, 57 FR 42632, 9/15/92, effective 8/31/92; Interim rule, 62 FR 2856, 1/17/97, effective 1/17/97; DAC 91-12, 62 FR 34114, 6/24/97, effective 6/24/97; DAC 91-13, 63 FR 11522, 3/9/98, effective 3/9/98, finalized without change, 63 FR 64426, 11/20/98; Final rule, 65 FR 63804, 10/25/2000, effective 10/25/2000; Final rule, 68 FR 7438, 2/14/2003, effective 2/14/2003; Final rule, 70 FR 35543, 6/21/2005, effective 6/21/2005; Final rule, 73 FR 46817, 8/12/2008, effective 8/12/2008; Interim rule, 74 FR 2417, 1/15/2009, effective 1/15/2009; Final rule, 74 FR 59916, 11/19/2009, effective 11/19/2009; Interim rule, 79 FR 44314, 7/31/2014, effective 7/31/2014; Final rule 79 FR 73498, 12/11/2014, effective 12/11/2014; Interim rule, 80 FR 15909, 3/26/2015, effective 3/26/2015; Interim rule, 80 FR 51751, 8/26/2015, effective 8/26/2015]

SUBPART 236.6—ARCHITECT-ENGINEER SERVICES

236.601 Policy.

(1) Written notification to the congressional defense committees is required if the total estimated contract price for architect-engineer services or construction design, in connection with military construction, military family housing, or restoration or replacement of damaged or destroyed facilities, exceeds $1.5 million. In accordance with 10 U.S.C. 480, unclassified notifications must be provided by electronic medium.

(i) For military construction or military family housing (10 U.S.C. 2807(b)), the notification—

(A) Must include the scope of the project and the estimated contract price; and

(B)(1) If provided by electronic medium, must be provided at least 14 days before the initial obligation of funds; or

(2) If provided by other than electronic medium, must be received by the congres-

sional defense committees at least 21 days before the initial obligation of funds.

(ii) For restoration or replacement of damaged or destroyed facilities (10 U.S.C. 2854(b)), the notification—

(A) Must include the justification for the project, the estimated contract price, and the source of the funds for the project; and

(B) (1) If provided by electronic medium, must be provided at least 7 days before the initial obligation of funds; or

(2) If provided by other than electronic medium, must be received by the congressional defense committees at least 21 days before the initial obligation of funds.

(2) During the applicable notice period, synopsis of the proposed contract action and administrative actions leading to the award may be started.

[Final rule, 63 FR 69007, 12/15/98, effective 12/15/98; Interim rule, 71 FR 58540, 10/4/2006, effective 10/4/2006; Final rule, 72 FR 51191, 9/6/2007, effective 9/6/2007; Final rule, 80 FR 36903, 6/26/2015, effective 10/1/2015]

236.602 Selection of firms for architect-engineer contracts. (No Text)

236.602-1 Selection criteria.

(a) Establish the evaluation criteria before making the public announcement required by FAR 5.205(d) and include the criteria and their relative order of importance in the announcement. Follow the procedures at PGI 236.602-1(a).

[DAC 91-6, 59 FR 27662, 5/27/94, effective 5/27/94; Interim rule, 63 FR 41972, 8/6/98, effective 10/1/98, finalized without change, 64 FR 52670, 9/30/99; Interim rule, 63 FR 64427, 11/20/98, effective 1/1/99; Interim rule 65 FR 50148, 8/17/2000, effective 10/1/2000, finalized without change, 65 FR 77831, 12/13/2000; Final rule, 69 FR 75000, 12/15/2004, effective 12/15/2004; Final rule, 71 FR 53044, 9/8/2006, effective 9/8/2006]

236.602-2 [Removed]

[DAC 91-13, 63 FR 11522, 3/9/98, effective 3/9/98; Final rule, 69 FR 75000, 12/15/2004, effective 12/15/2004]

236.602-4 [Removed]

[DAC 91-13, 63 FR 11522, 3/9/98, effective 3/9/98; Final rule, 69 FR 75000, 12/15/2004, effective 12/15/2004]

236.602-70 Restriction on award of overseas architect-engineer contracts to foreign firms.

In accordance with section 111 of the Military Construction and Veterans Affairs and Related Agencies Appropriations Act, 2015 (Division I of Pub. L. 113-235) and the same provision in subsequent military construction appropriations acts, architect-engineer contracts funded by military construction appropriations that are estimated to exceed $500,000 and are to be performed in Japan, in any North Atlantic Treaty Organization member country, or in countries bordering the Arabian Gulf (*i.e.*, Iran, Oman, United Arab Emirates, Saudi Arabia, Qatar, Bahrain, Kuwait, and Iraq), shall be awarded only to United States firms or to joint ventures of United States and host nation firms.

[Interim rule, 62 FR 2857, 1/17/97, effective 1/17/97, finalized without change, DAC 91-12, 62 FR 34114, 6/24/97, effective 6/24/97; Final rule, 76 FR 58155, 9/20/2011, effective 9/20/2011; Interim rule, 79 FR 44314, 7/31/2014, effective 7/31/2014; Final rule 79 FR 73498, 12/11/2014, effective 12/11/2014; Interim rule, 80 FR 15909, 3/26/2015, effective 3/26/2015; Interim rule, 80 FR 51751, 8/26/2015, effective 8/26/2015]

236.604 Performance evaluation.

Prepare a separate performance evaluation after actual construction of the project. Ordinarily, the evaluating official should be the person most familiar with the architect-engineer contractor's performance.

[DAC 91-10, 61 FR 7739, 2/29/96, effective 2/29/96; Final rule, 64 FR 51074, 9/21/99, effective 9/21/99; Final rule, 69 FR 75000, 12/15/2004, effective 12/15/2004; Final rule, 76 FR 58155, 9/20/2011, effective 9/20/2011]

236.606 Negotiations. (No Text)

236.606-70 Statutory fee limitation.

(a) 10 U.S.C. 4540, 7212, and 9540 limit the contract price (or fee) for architect-engineer services for the preparation of designs, plans, drawings, and specifications to six percent of the project's estimated construction cost.

(b) The six percent limit also applies to contract modifications, including modifications involving—

(1) Work not initially included in the contract. Apply the six percent limit to the revised total estimated construction cost.

(2) Redesign. Apply the six percent limit as follows—

(i) Add the estimated construction cost of the redesign features to the original estimated construction cost;

(ii) Add the contract cost for the original design to the contract cost for redesign; and

(iii) Divide the total contract design cost by the total estimated construction cost. The resulting percentage may not exceed the six percent statutory limitation.

(c) The six percent limit applies only to that portion of the contract (or modification) price attributable to the preparation of designs, plans, drawings, and specifications. If a contract or modification also includes other services, the part of the price attributable to the other services is not subject to the six percent limit.

[Final rule, 76 FR 58155, 9/20/2011, effective 9/20/2011]

236.609 Contract clauses. (No Text)

236.609-70 Additional provision.

Use the provision at 252.236-7011, Overseas Architect-Engineer Services—Restriction to United States Firms, in solicitations for architect-engineer contracts that are—

(1) Funded with military construction appropriations;

(2) Estimated to exceed $500,000; and

(3) To be performed in Japan, in any North Atlantic Treaty Organization member country, or in countries bordering the Arabian Gulf.

[Interim rule, 62 FR 2857, 1/17/97, effective 1/17/97; DAC 91-12, 62 FR 34114, 6/24/97, effective 6/24/97; DAC 91-13, 63 FR 11522, 3/9/98, effective 3/9/98; Final rule, 76 FR 58155, 9/20/2011, effective 9/20/2011; Interim rule, 79 FR 44314, 7/31/2014, effective 7/31/2014; Final rule 79 FR 73498, 12/11/2014, effective 12/11/2014; Interim rule, 80 FR 15909, 3/26/2015, effective 3/26/2015; Interim rule, 80 FR 51751, 8/26/2015, effective 8/26/2015; Final rule, 83 FR 54680, 10/31/2018, effective 10/31/2018]

SUBPART 236.7—STANDARD AND OPTIONAL FORMS FOR CONTRACTING FOR CONSTRUCTION, ARCHITECT-ENGINEER SERVICES, AND DISMANTLING, DEMOLITION, OR REMOVAL OF IMPROVEMENTS

236.701 Standard and optional forms for use in contracting for construction or dismantling, demolition, or removal of improvements.

(c) Do not use Optional Form 347, Order for Supplies or Services (see 213.307).

[Final rule, 65 FR 63804, 10/25/2000, effective 10/25/2000]

PART 237—SERVICE CONTRACTING

Table of Contents

Subpart 237.1—Service Contracts—General

Definitions 237.101
Policy 237.102
Prohibition on contracting for firefighting or security- guard functions 237.102-70
Limitation on service contracts for military flight simulators 237.102-71
Contracts for management services 237.102-72
Prohibition on contracts for services of senior mentors 237.102-73
Taxonomy for the acquisition of services, and supplies and equipment . . . 237.102-74
Guidebook for the acquisition of services 237.102-75
Review criteria for the acquisition of services 237.102-76
Acquisition requirements roadmap tool 237.102-77
Market research report guide for improving the tradecraft in services acquisition 237.102-78
Private sector notification requirements in support of in-sourcing actions 237.102-79
Personal services contracts 237.104
Funding and term of service contracts 237.106
Services of quasi-military armed forces 237.109
Approval of contracts and task orders for services 237.170
Scope 237.170-1
Approval requirements 237.170-2
[Removed] 237.170-3
Training for contractor personnel interacting with detainees 237.171
Scope 237.171-1
Definition 237.171-2
Policy 237.171-3
Contract clause 237.171-4
Service Contracts Surveillance 237.172
Prohibition on interrogation of detainees by contractor personnel 237.173
Scope 237.173-1
Definitions 237.173-2
Policy 237.173-3
Waiver 237.173-4
Contract clause 237.173-5
Disclosure of information to litigation support contractors 237.174
Training that uses live vertebrate animals 237.175

Subpart 237.2—Advisory and Assistance Services

[Removed] 237.201
[Removed] 237.203
Acquisition of audit services 237.270
[Removed] 237.271
[Removed] 237.272

Subpart 237.5—Management Oversight of Service Contracts

Agency-head responsibilities 237.503

Subpart 237.6—[Removed]

Subpart 237.70—Mortuary Services

Scope 237.7000
Method of acquisition 237.7001
Area of performance and distribution of contracts 237.7002
Solicitation provisions and contract clauses 237.7003

Subpart 237.71—Laundry and Dry Cleaning Services

Scope 237.7100
Solicitation provisions and contract clauses 237.7101

Subpart 237.72—Educational Service Agreements

Scope 237.7200
Educational service agreement 237.7201
Limitations 237.7202
Duration 237.7203
Format and clauses for educational service agreements 237.7204

Subpart 237.73—Services of Students at Research and Development Laboratories

Scope 237.7300
Definitions 237.7301
General 237.7302
Contract clauses 237.7303

Subpart 237.74—Services at Installations Being Closed

Scope 237.7400
Policy 237.7401
Contract clause 237.7402

Subpart 237.75—Acquisition and Management of Industrial Resources

Definition 237.7501
Policy 237.7502

Subpart 237.76—Continuation of Essential Contractor Services

Scope 237.7600
Definitions 237.7601
Policy 237.7602
Solicitation provision and contract clause 237.7603

Subpart 237.77—Competition for Religious-Related Services

Scope of subpart 237.7700
Definition 237.7701
Policy 237.7702

PART 237—SERVICE CONTRACTING

SUBPART 237.1—SERVICE CONTRACTS—GENERAL

237.101 Definitions.

Increased performance of security-guard functions, as used in this subpart, means—

(1) In the case of an installation or facility where no security-guard functions were performed as of September 10, 2001, the entire scope or extent of the performance of security-guard functions at the installation or facility after such date; and

(2) In the case of an installation or facility where security-guard functions were performed within a lesser scope of requirements or to a lesser extent as of September 10, 2001, than after such date, the increment of the performance of security-guard functions at the installation or facility that exceeds such lesser scope of requirements or extent of performance.

Senior mentor means a retired flag, general, or other military officer or retired senior civilian official who provides expert experience-based mentoring, teaching, training, advice, and recommendations to senior military officers, staff, and students as they participate in war games, warfighting courses, operational planning, operational exercises, and decision-making exercises.

[Interim rule, 68 FR 7443, 2/14/2003, effective 2/14/2003; Final rule, 68 FR 50476, 8/21/2003, effective 8/21/2003; Final rule, 75 FR 71563, 11/24/2010, effective 11/24/2010]

237.102 Policy.

(b) (1) *Preference for certain commercial services.* See 212.272 for procedures for implementation of the preference for commercial facilities-related services, knowledge-based services (except engineering services), medical services, or transportation services, as required by section 876 of the National Defense Authorization Act for Fiscal Year 2017 (Pub. L. 114-328).

(2) *Public-private competitions.* See PGI 207.302 for information on the Governmentwide moratorium and restrictions on public-private competitions conducted pursuant to Office of Management and Budget (OMB) Circular A-76.

(c) In addition to the prohibition on award of contracts for the performance of inherently governmental functions, contracting officers shall not award contracts for functions that are exempt from private sector performance. See 207.503(e) for the associated documentation requirement.

(e) Program officials shall obtain assistance from contracting officials through the Peer Review process at 201.170.

[Final rule, 73 FR 1826, 1/10/2008, effective 1/10/2008; Final rule, 74 FR 37625, 7/29/2009, effective 7/29/2009; Final rule, 81 FR 36473, 6/7/2016, effective 6/7/2016; Final rule, 84 FR 39203, 8/9/2019, effective 8/9/2019]

237.102-70 Prohibition on contracting for firefighting or security-guard functions.

(a) Under 10 U.S.C. 2465, the DoD is prohibited for entering into contracts for the performance of firefighting or security-guard functions at any military installation or facility unless—

(1) The contract is to be carried out at a location outside the United States and its outlying areas at which members of the armed forces would have to be used for the performance of firefighting or security-guard functions at the expense of unit readiness;

(2) The contract will be carried out on a Government-owned but privately operated installation;

(3) The contract (or renewal of a contract) is for the performance of a function under contract on September 24, 1983; or

(4) The contract—

(i) Is for the performance of firefighting functions;

(ii) Is for a period of 1 year or less; and

(iii) Covers only the performance of firefighting functions that, in the absence of the contract, would have to be performed by members of the armed forces who are not readily available to perform such functions by reason of a deployment.

(b) Under Section 2907 of Public Law 103-160, this prohibition does not apply to services at installations being closed (see subpart 237.74).

(c)(1) Under section 332 of Public Law 107-314, as amended by section 333 of Public Law 109-364 and section 343 of Public Law 110-181, this prohibition does not apply to any contract that is entered into for any increased performance of security-guard functions at a military installation or facility undertaken in response to the terrorist attacks on the United States on September 11, 2001, if—

(i) Without the contract, members of the Armed Forces are or would be used to perform the increased security-guard functions;

(ii) The agency has determined that—

(A) Recruiting and training standards for the personnel who are to perform the security-guard functions are comparable to the recruiting and training standards for DoD personnel who perform the same security-guard functions;

(B) Contractor personnel performing such functions will be effectively supervised, reviewed, and evaluated; and

(C) Performance of such functions will not result in a reduction in the security of the installation or facility;

(iii) Contract performance will not extend beyond September 30, 2012; and

(iv) The total number of personnel employed to perform security-guard functions under all contracts entered into pursuant to this authority does not exceed the following limitations:

(A) For fiscal year 2007, the total number of such personnel employed under such contracts on October 1, 2006.

(B) For fiscal year 2008, the number equal to 90 percent of the total number of such personnel employed under such contracts on October 1, 2006.

(C) For fiscal year 2009, the number equal to 80 percent of the total number of such personnel employed under such contracts on October 1, 2006.

(D) For fiscal year 2010, the number equal to 70 percent of the total number of such personnel employed under such contracts on October 1, 2006.

(E) For fiscal year 2011, the number equal to 60 percent of the total number of such personnel employed under such contracts on October 1, 2006.

(F) For fiscal year 2012, the number equal to 50 percent of the total number of such personnel employed under such contracts on October 1, 2006.

(2) Follow the procedures at PGI 237.102-70(c) to ensure that the personnel limitations specified in paragraph (c)(1)(iv) of this section are not exceeded.

[DAC 91-9, 60 FR 61586, 11/30/95, effective 11/30/95; Interim rule, 67 FR 11438, 3/14/2002, effective 3/14/2002; Interim rule, 68 FR 7443, 2/14/2003, effective 2/14/2003; Final rule, 68 FR 50476, 8/21/2003, effective 8/21/2003; Interim rule, 69 FR 35532, 6/25/2004, effective 6/25/2004; Final rule, 69 FR 75000, 12/15/2004, effective 12/15/2004; Final rule, 70 FR 14576, 3/23/2005, effective 3/23/2005; Final rule, 70 FR 35543, 6/21/2005, effective 6/21/2005; Interim rule, 71 FR 34833, 6/16/2006, effective 6/16/2006; Final rule, 72 FR 6485, 2/12/2007, effective 2/12/2007; Interim rule, 72 FR 51192, 9/6/2007, effective 9/6/2007; Interim rule, 73 FR 53156, 9/15/2008, effective 9/15/2008; Final rule, 74 FR 2421, 1/15/2009, effective 1/15/2009; CFR correction, 80 FR 56398, 9/18/2015, effective 9/18/2015; Final rule, 84 FR 65310, 11/27/2019, effective 11/27/2019]

237.102-71 Limitation on service contracts for military flight simulators.

(a) *Definitions.* As used in this subsection—

(1) *Military flight simulator* means any system to simulate the form, fit, and function of a military aircraft that has no commonly available commercial variant.

(2) *Service contract* means any contract entered into by DoD, the principal purpose of which is to furnish services in the United States through the use of service employees as defined in 41 U.S.C. 6701.

(b) Under Section 832 of Public Law 109-364, as amended by Section 883(b) of Public Law 110-181, DoD is prohibited from entering into a service contract to acquire a military flight simulator. However, the Secretary of Defense may waive this prohibition with respect to a contract, if the Secretary—

(1) Determines that a waiver is in the national interest; and

(2) Provides an economic analysis to the congressional defense committees at least 30 days before the waiver takes effect. This economic analysis shall include, at a minimum—

(i) A clear explanation of the need for the contract; and

(ii) An examination of at least two alternatives for fulfilling the requirements that the contract is meant to fulfill, including the following with respect to each alternative:

(A) A rationale for including the alternative.

(B) A cost estimate of the alternative and an analysis of the quality of each cost estimate.

(C) A discussion of the benefits to be realized from the alternative.

(D) A best value determination of each alternative and a detailed explanation of the life-cycle cost calculations used in the determination.

(c) When reviewing requirements or participating in acquisition planning that would result in a military department or defense agency acquiring a military flight simulator, the contracting officer shall notify the program officials of the prohibition in paragraph (b) of this subsection. If the program officials decide to request a waiver from the Secretary of Defense under paragraph (b) of this subsection, the contracting officer shall follow the procedures at PGI 237.102-71.

[Final rule, 72 FR 51193, 9/6/2007, effective 9/6/2007; Final rule, 73 FR 53156, 9/15/2008, effective 9/15/2008; Final rule 76 FR 58137, 9/20/2011, effective 9/20/2011]

237.102-72 Contracts for management services.

In accordance with Section 802 of the National Defense Authorization Act for Fiscal Year 2008 (Pub. L. 110-181), DoD may award a contract for the acquisition of services the primary purpose of which is to perform acquisition support functions with respect to the development or production of a major system, only if—

(a) The contract prohibits the contractor from performing inherently governmental functions;

(b) The DoD organization responsible for the development or production of the major system ensures that Federal employees are responsible for determining—

(1) Courses of action to be taken in the best interest of the Government; and

(2) Best technical performance for the warfighter; and

(c) The contract requires that the prime contractor for the contract may not advise or recommend the award of a contract or subcontract for the development or production of the major system to an entity owned in whole or in part by the prime contractor.

[Interim rule, 74 FR 34266, 7/15/2009, effective 7/15/2009; Final rule, 75 FR 3178, 1/20/2010, effective 1/20/2010]

237.102-73 Prohibition on contracts for services of senior mentors.

DoD is prohibited from entering into contracts for the services of senior mentors. See PGI 237.102-73 for references to DoD policy and implementation guidance.

[Final rule, 75 FR 71563, 11/24/2010, effective 11/24/2010]

237.102-74 Taxonomy for the acquisition of services, and supplies and equipment.

See PGI 237.102-74 for further guidance on the taxonomy for the acquisition of services and the acquisition of supplies and equipment.

[Final rule, 75 FR 78619, 12/16/2010, effective 12/16/2010; Final rule, 79 FR 51264, 8/28/2014, effective 8/28/2014]

237.102-75 Guidebook for the acquisition of services.

See PGI 237.102-75 for information on the Defense Acquisition Guidebook, Chapter 10, Acquisition of Services.

[Final rule, 76 FR 76318, 12/7/2011, effective 12/7/2011; Final rule, 81 FR 36473, 6/7/2016, effective 6/7/2016; Final rule, 82 FR 61479, 12/28/2017, effective 12/28/2017]

237.102-76 Review criteria for the acquisition of services.

See PGI 237.102-76 for tenets and review criteria to be used when conducting preaward and postaward reviews for the acquisition of services.

[Final rule, 76 FR 76318, 12/7/2011, effective 12/7/2011]

237.102-77 Acquisition requirements roadmap tool.

See PGI 237.102-77 for guidance on using the Acquisition Requirements Roadmap Tool to develop and organize performance requirements into draft versions of the performance work statement, the quality assurance surveillance plan, and the performance requirements summary.

[Final rule, 77 FR 52253, 8/29/2012, effective 8/29/2012; Final rule, 81 FR 36473, 6/7/2016, effective 6/7/2016]

237.102-78 Market research report guide for improving the tradecraft in services acquisition.

See PGI 210.070 for guidance on use of the market research report guide to conduct and document market research for service acquisitions.

[Final rule, 77 FR 52253, 8/29/2012, effective 8/29/2012]

237.102-79 Private sector notification requirements in support of in-sourcing actions.

In accordance with 10 U.S.C. 2463, contracting officers shall provide written notification to affected incumbent contractors of Government in-sourcing determinations. Notification shall be provided within 20 business days of the contracting officer's receipt of a decision from the cognizant component in-sourcing program official. The notification will summarize the requiring official's final determination as to why the service is being in-sourced and shall be coordinated with the component's in-sourcing program official. No formal hiring or contract-related actions may be initiated prior to such notification, except for preliminary internal actions associated with hiring or contract modification. See the OASD (RFM) memorandum entitled "Private Sector Notification Requirements in Support of In-sourcing Actions," dated January 29, 2013, for further information, which is available at PGI 237.102-79.

[Final rule, 78 FR 21850, 4/12/2013, effective 4/12/2013; Interim rule, 78 FR 65218, 10/31/2013, effective 10/31/2013; Final rule, 79 FR 35700, 6/24/2014, effective 6/24/2014]

237.104 Personal services contracts.

(b) (i) Authorization to acquire the personal services of experts and consultants is included in 10 U.S.C. 129b. Personal service contracts for expert and consultant services must also be authorized by a determination and findings (D&F) in accordance with department/agency regulations.

(A) Generally, the D&F should authorize one contract at a time; however, an authorizing official may issue a blanket D&F for classes of contracts.

(B) Prepare each D&F in accordance with FAR 1.7 and include a determination that—

(*1*) The duties are of a temporary or intermittent nature;

(*2*) Acquisition of the services is advantageous to the national defense;

(*3*) DoD personnel with necessary skills are not available;

(*4*) Excepted appointment cannot be obtained;

(*5*) A nonpersonal services contract is not practicable;

(*6*) Statutory authority, 5 U.S.C. 3109 and other legislation, apply; and

(*7*) Any other determination required by statues has been made.

(ii) Personal services contracts for health care are authorized by 10 U.S.C. 1091.

(A) This authority may be used to acquire—

(*1*) Direct health care services provided in medical treatment facilities;

(*2*) Health care services at locations outside of medical treatment facilities (such as the provision of medical screening examinations at military entrance processing stations); and

(*3*) Services of clinical counselors, family advocacy program staff, and victim's services representatives to members of the Armed Forces and covered beneficiaries who require such services, provided in medical treatment facilities or elsewhere. Persons with whom a personal services contract may be entered into under this authority include clinical social workers, psychologists, psychiatrists, and other comparable professionals who have advanced degrees in counseling or related academic disciplines and who meet all requirements for State licensure and board certification requirements, if any, within their fields of specialization.

(B) Sources for personal services contracts with individuals under the authority of 10 U.S.C. 1091 shall be selected through the procedures in this section. These procedures do not apply to contracts awarded to business entities other than individuals. Selections made using the procedures in this section are exempt by statute from FAR part 6 competition requirements (see 206.001(b)).

(C) Approval requirements for—

(*1*) Direct health care personal services contracts (see paragraphs (b)(ii)(A)(1) and (2) of this section) and a pay cap are in DoDI 6025.5, Personal Services Contracts for Health Care Providers.

(i) A request to enter into a personal services contract for direct health care services must be approved by the commander of the medical/dental treatment facility where the services will be performed.

(ii) A request to enter into a personal services contract for a location outside of a medical treatment facility must be approved by the chief of the medical facility who is responsible for the area in which the services will be performed.

(*2*) Services of clinical counselors, family advocacy program staff, and victim's services representatives (see paragraph (b)(ii)(A)(3) of this section), shall be in accordance with agency procedures.

(D) The contracting officer must ensure that the requiring activity provides a copy of the approval with the purchase request.

(E) The contracting officer must provide adequate advance notice of contracting opportunities to individuals residing in the area of the facility. The notice must include the qualification criteria against which individuals responding will be evaluated. The contracting officer shall solicit applicants through at least one local publication which serves the area of the facility. Acquisitions under this section for personal service contracts are exempt from the posting and synopsis requirements of FAR Part 5.

(F) The contracting officer shall provide the qualifications of individuals responding to the notice to the commander of the facility for evaluation and ranking in accordance with agency procedures. Individuals must be considered solely on the basis of the professional qualifications established for the particular personal services being acquired and the Government's estimate of reasonable rates, fees, or other costs. The commander of the facility shall provide the contracting officer with rationale for the ranking of individuals, consistent with the required qualifications.

(G) Upon receipt from the facility of the ranked listing of applicants, the contracting officer shall either—

(*1*) Enter into negotiations with the highest ranked applicant. If a mutually satisfactory contract cannot be negotiated, the contracting officer shall terminate negotiations with the highest ranked applicant and enter into negotiations with the next highest.

(*2*) Enter into negotiations with all qualified applicants and select on the basis of qualifications and rates, fees, or other costs.

(H) In the event only one individual responds to an advertised requirement, the contracting officer is authorized to negotiate the contract award. In this case, the individual must still meet the minimum qualifications of the requirement and the contracting officer must be able to make a determination that the price is fair and reasonable.

(I) If a fair and reasonable price cannot be obtained from a qualified individual, the requirement should be canceled and acquired using procedures other than those set forth in this section.

(iii) (A) In accordance with 10 U.S.C. 129b(d), an agency may enter into a personal services contract if—

(*1*) The personal services—

(i) Are to be provided by individuals outside the United States, regardless of their nationality;

(ii) Directly support the mission of a defense intelligence component or counter-intelligence organization of DoD; or

(iii) Directly support the mission of the special operations command of DoD; and

(*2*) The head of the contracting activity provides written approval for the proposed contract. The approval shall include a determination that addresses the following:

(i) The services to be procured are urgent or unique;

(ii) It would not be practical to obtain such services by other means; and

(iii) For acquisition of services in accordance with paragraph (b) (iii) (A) (1) (i) of this section, the services to be acquired are necessary and appropriate for supporting DoD activities and programs outside the United States.

(B) The contracting officer shall ensure that the applicable requirements of paragraph (b) (iii) (A) (2) of this section have been satisfied and shall include the approval documentation in the contract file.

(iv) The requirements of 5 U.S.C. 3109, Employment of Experts and Consultants; Temporary or Intermittent, do not apply to contracts entered into in accordance with paragraph (b) (iii) of this section.

(d) See 237.503(c) for requirements for certification and approval of requirements for services to prevent contracts from being awarded or administered in a manner that constitutes an unauthorized personal services contract.

(f) (i) Payment to each expert or consultant for personal services under 5 U.S.C. 3109 shall not exceed the highest rate fixed by the Classification Act Schedules for grade GS-15 (see 5 CFR 304.105(a)).

(ii) The contract may provide for the same per diem and travel expenses authorized for a Government employee, including actual transportation and per diem in lieu of subsistence for travel between home or place of business and official duty station.

(iii) Coordinate with the civilian personnel office on benefits, taxes, personnel ceilings, and maintenance of records.

[Interim rule, 60 FR 2888, 1/12/95, effective 1/5/95; DAC 91-9, 60 FR 61586, 11/30/95, effective 11/30/95; DAC 91-13, 63 FR 11522, 3/9/98, effective 3/9/98; Final rule, 67 FR 61516, 10/1/2002, effective 10/1/2002; Interim rule, 69 FR 55991, 9/17/2004, effective 9/17/2004; Finalized without change; Final rule, 70 FR 19003, 4/12/2005, effective 4/12/2005; Final rule, 76 FR 25565, 5/5/2011, effective 5/5/2011]

237.106 Funding and term of service contracts.

(1) Personal service contracts for expert or consultant services shall not exceed 1 year. The nature of the duties must be—

(i) Temporary (not more than 1 year); or

(ii) Intermittent (not cumulatively more than 130 days in 1 year).

(2) The contracting officer may enter into a contract, exercise an option, or place an order under a contract for severable services for a period that begins in one fiscal year and ends in the next fiscal year if the period of the contract awarded, option exercised, or order placed does not exceed 1 year (10 U.S.C. 2410a).

[Final rule, 64 FR 28109, 5/25/99, effective 5/25/99]

237.109 Services of quasi-military armed forces.

See 237.102-70(b) for prohibition on contracting for firefighting or security-guard functions.

[DAC 91-9, 60 FR 61586, 11/30/95, effective 11/30/95]

237.170 Approval of contracts and task orders for services. (No Text)

[Interim rule, 68 FR 56563, 10/1/2003, effective 10/1/2003; Final rule, 71 FR 14102, 3/21/2006, effective 3/21/2006]

237.170-1 Scope.

This section—

(a) Implements 10 U.S.C. 2330; and

(b) Applies to services acquired for DoD, regardless of whether the services are acquired through—

(1) A DoD contract or task order; or

(2) A contract or task order awarded by an agency other than DoD.

[Interim rule, 68 FR 56563, 10/1/2003, effective 10/1/2003; Final rule, 71 FR 14102, 3/21/2006, effective 3/21/2006]

237.170-2 Approval requirements.

(a) *Acquisition of services through a contract or task order that is not performance based.*

(1) For acquisitions at or below $93 million obtain the approval of the official designated by the department or agency.

(2) For acquisitions exceeding $93 million obtain the approval of the senior procurement executive.

(b) *Acquisition of services through use of a contract or task order issued by a non-DoD agency.* Comply with the review, approval, and reporting requirements established in accordance with subpart 217.7 when acquiring services through use of a contract or task order issued by a non-DoD agency.

[Interim rule, 68 FR 56563, 10/1/2003, effective 10/1/2003; Interim rule, 70 FR 29640, 5/24/2005, effective 5/24/2005; Final rule, 71 FR 14102, 3/21/2006, effective 3/21/2006; Final rule, 71 FR 75891, 12/19/2006, effective 12/19/2006; Final rule, 75 FR 45072, 8/2/2010, effective 10/1/2010; Final rule, 80 FR 36903, 6/26/2015, effective 10/1/2015; Final rule, 80 FR 67254, 10/30/2015, effective 10/30/2015]

237.170-3 [Removed]

[Interim rule, 68 FR 56563, 10/1/2003, effective 10/1/2003; Interim rule, 70 FR 29640, 5/24/2005, effective 5/24/2005; Final rule, 71 FR 14102, 3/21/2006, effective 3/21/2006]

237.171 Training for contractor personnel interacting with detainees. (No Text)

[Interim rule, 70 FR 52032, 9/1/2005, effective 9/1/2005; Final rule, 71 FR 53047, 9/8/2006, effective 9/8/2006]

237.171-1 Scope.

This section prescribes policies to prevent the abuse of detainees, as required by Section 1092 of the National Defense Authorization Act for Fiscal Year 2005 (Pub. L. 108-375).

[Interim rule, 70 FR 52032, 9/1/2005, effective 9/1/2005; Final rule, 71 FR 53047, 9/8/2006, effective 9/8/2006]

237.171-2 Definition.

Combatant commander, detainee, and *personnel interacting with detainees*, as used in this section, are defined in the clause at 252.237-7019, Training for Contractor Personnel Interacting with Detainees.

[Interim rule, 70 FR 52032, 9/1/2005, effective 9/1/2005; Final rule, 71 FR 53047, 9/8/2006, effective 9/8/2006]

237.171-3 Policy.

(a) Each DoD contract in which contractor personnel, in the course of their duties, interact with detainees shall include a requirement that such contractor personnel—

(1) Receive Government-provided training regarding the international obligations and laws of the United States applicable to the detention of personnel, including the Geneva Conventions; and

(2) Provide a copy of the training receipt document to the contractor.

(b) The combatant commander responsible for the area where the detention or interrogation facility is located will arrange for the training and a training receipt document to be provided to contractor personnel. For information on combatant commander geographic areas of responsibility and point of contact information for each command, see PGI 237.171-3(b).

[Interim rule, 70 FR 52032, 9/1/2005, effective 9/1/2005; Final rule, 71 FR 53047, 9/8/2006, effective 9/8/2006]

237.171-4 Contract clause.

Use the clause at 252.237-7019, Training for Contractor Personnel Interacting with Detainees, in solicitations and contracts, including solicitations and contracts using FAR part 12 procedures for the acquisition of commercial items, that are for the acquisition of services if—

(a) The clause at 252.225-7040, Contractor Personnel Supporting U.S. Armed Forces Deployed Outside the United States, is included in the solicitation or contract; or

(b) The services will be performed at a facility holding detainees, and contractor personnel in the course of their duties may be expected to interact with the detainees.

[Interim rule, 70 FR 52032, 9/1/2005, effective 9/1/2005; Final rule, 71 FR 53047, 9/8/2006, effective 9/8/2006; Final rule, 78 FR 37980, 6/25/2013, effective 6/25/2013; Final rule, 79 FR 30469, 5/28/2014, effective 5/28/2014]

237.172 Service contracts surveillance.

(a) Ensure that quality assurance surveillance plans are prepared in conjunction with the preparation of the statement of work or statement of objectives for solicitations and contracts for services. These plans should be tailored to address the performance risks inherent in the specific contract type and the work effort addressed by the contract. (See FAR subpart 46.4.) Retain quality assurance surveillance plans in the contract file. See *http://sam.dau.mil*, Step Four—Requirements Definition, for examples of quality assurance surveillance plans.

(b) See PGI 216.505-70 for guidance regarding minimum labor category qualifications for orders issued under multiple award services contracts.

[Final rule, 75 FR 22706, 4/30/2010, effective 4/30/2010; Final rule, 80 FR 58630, 9/30/2015, effective 9/30/2015; Final rule, 84 FR 48510, 9/13/2019, effective 9/13/2019]

237.173 Prohibition on interrogation of detainees by contractor personnel. (No Text)

[Interim rule, 75 FR 67632, 11/3/2010, effective 11/3/2010; Final rule, 76 FR 44282, 7/25/2011, effective 7/25/2011]

237.173-1 Scope.

This section prescribes policies that prohibit interrogation of detainees by contractor personnel, as required by section 1038 of the Fiscal Year 2010 National Defense Authorization Act (Pub. L. 111-84).

[Interim rule, 75 FR 67632, 11/3/2010, effective 11/3/2010; Final rule, 76 FR 44282, 7/25/2011, effective 7/25/2011]

237.173-2 Definitions.

As used in this subpart—

Detainee means any person captured, detained, held, or otherwise under the effective control of DoD personnel (military or civilian) in connection with hostilities. This includes, but is not limited to, enemy prisoners of war, civilian internees, and retained personnel. This does not include DoD personnel or DoD contractor personnel being held for law enforcement purposes.

Interrogation of detainees means a systematic process of formally and officially questioning a detainee for the purpose of obtaining reliable information to satisfy foreign intelligence collection requirements.

[Interim rule, 75 FR 67632, 11/3/2010, effective 11/3/2010; Final rule, 76 FR 44282, 7/25/2011, effective 7/25/2011]

237.173-3 Policy.

(a) No detainee may be interrogated by contractor personnel.

(b) Contractor personnel with proper training and security clearances may be used as linguists, interpreters, report writers, information technology technicians, and other employees filling ancillary positions, including as trainers of and advisors to interrogators, in interrogations of detainees if—

(1) Such personnel are subject to the same laws, rules, procedures, and policies (including DoD Instruction 1100.22, Policy and Procedures for Determining Workforce Mix (*http://www.dtic.mil/whs/directives/corres/pdf/110022p.pdf*); DoD Directive 2310.01E, The Department of Defense Detainee Program (*http://www.dtic.mil/whs/directives/corres/pdf/231001p.pdf*); and DoD Directive 3115.09, DoD Intelligence Interrogations, Detainee Debriefings, and Tactical Questioning (*http://www.dtic.mil/whs/directives/corres/pdf/311509p.pdf*)); pertaining to detainee operations and interrogations as those that apply to Government personnel in such positions in such interrogations; and

(2) Appropriately qualified and trained DoD personnel (military or civilian) are available to oversee the contractor's performance and to ensure that contractor personnel do not perform activities that are prohibited under this section.

[Interim rule, 75 FR 67632, 11/3/2010, effective 11/3/2010; Final rule, 76 FR 44282, 7/25/2011, effective 7/25/2011]

237.173-4 Waiver.

The Secretary of Defense may waive the prohibition in 237.173-3(a) for a period of 60 days, if the Secretary determines such a waiver is vital to the national security interests of the United States. The Secretary may renew a waiver issued pursuant to this paragraph for an additional 30-day period, if the Secretary determines that such a renewal is vital to the national security interests of the United States. Not later than five days after issuance of the waiver, the Secretary shall submit written notification to Congress. See specific waiver procedures at DoDI 1100.22.

[Interim rule, 75 FR 67632, 11/3/2010, effective 11/3/2010; Final rule, 76 FR 44282, 7/25/2011, effective 7/25/2011]

237.173-5 Contract clause.

Insert the clause at 252.237-7010, Prohibition on Interrogation of Detainees by Contractor Personnel, in solicitations and contracts, including solicitations and contracts using FAR part 12 procedures for the acquisition of commercial items, that are for the provision of services.

[Interim rule, 75 FR 67632, 11/3/2010, effective 11/3/2010; Final rule, 76 FR 44282, 7/25/2011, effective 7/25/2011; Final rule, 78 FR 37980, 6/25/2013, effective 6/25/2013]

237.174 Disclosure of information to litigation support contractors.

See 204.74 for disclosure of information to litigation support contractors.

[Interim rule, 75 FR 67632, 11/3/2010, effective 11/3/2010; Final rule, 76 FR 44282, 7/25/2011, effective 7/25/2011; Final rule, 78 FR 37980, 6/25/2013, effective 6/25/2013; Interim rule, 79 FR 11337, 2/28/2014, effective 2/28/2014; Interim rule, 81 FR 28724, 5/10/2016, effective 5/10/2016]

237.175 Training that uses live vertebrate animals.

Use the clause at 252.235-7002, Animal Welfare, as prescribed in 235.072(a), when contracting for training that will use live vertebrate animals.

[Final rule, 79 FR 73500, 12/11/2014, effective 12/11/2014]

SUBPART 237.2—ADVISORY AND ASSISTANCE SERVICES

237.201 [Removed]

[Final rule, 64 FR 39430, 7/22/99, effective 7/22/99; Final rule, 66 FR 49860, 10/1/2001, effective 10/1/2001; Final rule, 70 FR 57193, 9/30/2005, effective 9/30/2005]

237.203 [Removed]

[DAC 91-13, 63 FR 11522, 3/9/98, effective 3/9/98; Final rule, 64 FR 39430, 7/22/99, effective 7/22/99; Final rule, 70 FR 57193, 9/30/2005, effective 9/30/2005]

237.270 Acquisition of audit services.

(a) *General policy.* (1) Do not contract for audit services unless—

(i) The cognizant DoD audit organization determines that expertise required to perform the audit is not available within the DoD audit organization; or

(ii) Temporary audit assistance is required to meet audit reporting requirements mandated by law or DoD regulation.

(2) See 215.101-2-70(b)(3) for the prohibition on the use of the lowest price technically acceptable source selection process when acquiring audit services.

(3) See PGI 237.270 for a list of DoDD publications that govern the conduct of audits.

(b) *Contract period*. Except in unusual circumstances, award contracts for recurring audit services for a 1-year period with at least 2 option years.

(c) *Approvals*. Do not issue a solicitation for audit services unless the requiring activity provides evidence that the cognizant DoD audit organization has approved the statement of work. The requiring agency shall obtain the same evidence of approval for subsequent material changes to the statement of work.

(d) *Solicitation provisions and contract clauses*. (1) Use the provision at 252.237-7000, Notice of Special Standards of Responsibility, in solicitations for audit services.

(2) Use the clause at 252.237-7001, Compliance with Audit Standards, in solicitations and contracts for audit services.

[DAC 91-3, 57 FR 42632, 9/15/92, effective 8/31/92; Redesignated from 237.203-70, DAC 91-13, 63 FR 11522, 3/9/98, effective 3/9/98; Final rule, 70 FR 57193, 9/30/2005, effective 9/30/2005; Final rule, 84 FR 50785, 9/26/2019, effective 10/1/2019]

237.271 [Removed]

[Final rule, 64 FR 39430, 7/22/99, effective 7/22/99; Final rule, 70 FR 57193, 9/30/2005, effective 9/30/2005]

237.272 [Removed]

[Redesignated from 237.206, DAC 91-13, 63 FR 11522, 3/9/98, effective 3/9/98; Final rule, 70 FR 57193, 9/30/2005, effective 9/30/2005]

SUBPART 237.5—MANAGEMENT OVERSIGHT OF SERVICE CONTRACTS

237.503 Agency-head responsibilities.

(c) The agency head or designee shall employ procedures to ensure that requirements for service contracts are vetted and approved as a safeguard to prevent contracts from being awarded or administered in a manner that constitutes an unauthorized personal services contract. Contracting officers shall follow the procedures at PGI 237.503, include substantially similar certifications in conjunction with service contract requirements, and place the certification in the contract file. The program manager or other official responsible for the requirement, at a level specified by the agency, should execute the certification. In addition, contracting officers and program managers should remain aware of the descriptive elements at FAR 37.104(d) to ensure that a service contract does not inadvertently become administered as a personal-services contract.

[Interim rule, 75 FR 54524, 9/8/2010, effective 9/8/2010; Final rule, 76 FR 25565, 5/5/2011, effective 5/5/2011]

SUBPART 237.6—[REMOVED]

237.601 [Removed]

[Final rule, 69 FR 35532, 6/25/2004, effective 6/25/2004]

SUBPART 237.70—MORTUARY SERVICES

237.7000 Scope.

This subpart—

(a) Applies to contracts for mortuary services (the care of remains) for military personnel within the United States; and

(b) May be used as guidance in areas outside the United States for mortuary services for deceased military and civilian personnel.

[Final rule, 71 FR 3415, 1/23/2006, effective 1/23/2006]

237.7001 Method of acquisition.

(a) *Requirements type contract.* By agreement among the military activities, one activity in each geographical area will contract for the estimated requirements for the care of remains for all military activities in the area. Use a requirements type contract (see FAR 16.503) when the estimated annual requirements for the activities in the area are ten or more.

(b) *Purchase order.* Where no contract exists, use DD Form 1155, Order for Supplies or Services, to obtain mortuary services.

[Final rule, 71 FR 3415, 1/23/2006, effective 1/23/2006]

237.7002 Area of performance and distribution of contracts.

Follow the procedures at PGI 237.7002 for—

(a) Defining the geographical area to be covered by the contract; and

(b) Distributing copies of the contract.

[Final rule, 71 FR 3415, 1/23/2006, effective 1/23/2006]

237.7003 Solicitation provisions and contract clauses.

(a) Use the following clauses in all mortuary service solicitations and contracts, except do not use the clauses at 252.237-7004, Area of Performance, in solicitations or contracts that include port of entry requirements:

(1) 252.237-7003, Requirements, (insert activities authorized to place orders in paragraph (e) of the clause).

(2) 252.237-7004, Area of Performance.

(3) 252.237-7005, Performance and Delivery.

(4) 252.237-7006, Subcontracting.

(5) 252.237-7007, Termination for Default.

(6) 252.237-7008, Group Interment.

(7) 252.237-7009, Permits.

(8) 252.237-7011, Preparation History.

(b) Use the clause at FAR 52.245-1, Government Property, with its Alternate I, in solicitations and contracts that include port of entry requirements.

[Final rule, 71 FR 3415, 1/23/2006, effective 1/23/2006; Final rule, 74 FR 37645, 7/29/2009, effective 7/29/2009; Final rule, 79 FR 65592, 11/5/2014, effective 11/5/2014; Final rule, 84 FR 48504, 9/13/2019, effective 9/13/2019]

SUBPART 237.71—LAUNDRY AND DRY CLEANING SERVICES

237.7100 Scope.

This subpart—

(a) Applies to contracts for laundry and dry cleaning services within the United States; and

(b) May be used as guidance in areas outside the United States.

[Final rule, 71 FR 3415, 1/23/2006, effective 1/23/2006]

237.7101 Solicitation provisions and contract clauses.

(a) Use the provision at 252.237-7012, Instruction to Offerors (Count-of-Articles), in solicitations for laundry and dry cleaning services to be provided on a count-of-articles basis.

(b) Use the provision at 252.237-7013, Instruction to Offerors (Bulk Weight), in solicitations for laundry services to be provided on a bulk weight basis.

(c) Use the clause at 252.237-7014, Loss or Damage (Count-of-Articles), in solicitations and contracts for laundry and dry cleaning services to be provided on a count-of-articles basis.

(d) Use the clause at 252.237-7015, Loss or Damage (Weight of Articles), in solicitations and contracts for laundry and dry cleaning services to be provided on a bulk weight basis.

(1) Insert a reasonable per pound price in paragraph (b) of the clause, based on the average per pound value. When the contract requires laundry services on a bag type basis, insert reasonable per pound prices by bag type.

(2) Insert an appropriate percentage in paragraph (e) of the clause, not to exceed eight percent.

(e) Use the basic or an alternate of the clause at 252.237–7016, Delivery Tickets, in all solicitations and contracts for laundry and dry cleaning services.

(1) Use the basic clause when services are not to be provided on a bulk weight basis.

(2) Use the alternate I clause when services are for bag type laundry to be provided on a bulk weight basis.

(3) Use the alternate II clause when services are unsorted laundry to be provided on a bulk weight basis.

(f) Use the clause at 252.237-7017, Individual Laundry, in solicitations and contracts for laundry and dry cleaning services to be provided to individual personnel.

(1) Insert the number of pieces of outer garments in paragraphs (d) (1) and (2) of the clause.

(2) The number of pieces and composition of a bundle in paragraphs (d) (1) and (2) of the clause may be modified to meet local conditions.

(g) Use the clause at 252.237-7018, Special Definitions of Government Property, in all solicitations and contracts for laundry and dry cleaning services.

[DAC 91-12, 62 FR 34114, 6/24/97, effective 6/24/97; Redesignated from 237.7102, Final rule, 71 FR 3415, 1/23/2006, effective 1/23/2006; Final rule, 79 FR 65592, 11/5/2014, effective 11/5/2014]

SUBPART 237.72—EDUCATIONAL SERVICE AGREEMENTS

237.7200 Scope.

(a) This subpart prescribes acquisition procedures for educational services from schools, colleges, universities, or other educational institutions. This subpart does not include tuition assistance agreements, i.e., payment by the Government of partial tuition under the off-duty educational program.

(b) As used in the subpart—

(1) *Facilities* do not include the institution's dining rooms or dormitories; and

(2) *Fees* does not include charges for meals or lodging.

237.7201 Educational service agreement.

(a) An educational service agreement is not a contract, but is an ordering agreement under which the Government may order educational services.

(b) Educational service agreements provide for ordering educational services when—

(1) The Government pays normal tuition and fees for educational services provided to a student by the institution under its normal schedule of tuition and fees applicable to all students generally; and

(2) Enrollment is at the institution under the institution's normal rules and in courses and curricula which the institution offers to all students meeting admission requirements.

237.7202 Limitations.

Educational service agreements are not used to provide special courses or special fees for Government students.

[Final rule, 83 FR 16004, 4/13/2018, effective 4/13/2018]

237.7203 Duration.

(a) Educational service agreements are for an indefinite duration and remain in effect until terminated.

(b) The issuing activity must establish procedures to review each educational service agreement at least once each year. Review dates should consider the institution's academic calendar and occur at least 30 days before the beginning of a term. The purpose of the review is to incorporate changes to reflect requirements of any statute, Executive Order, FAR, or DFARS.

(c) If the contracting officer and the institution do not agree on required changes, terminate the agreement.

237.7204 Format and clauses for educational service agreements.

Educational service agreements under this subpart shall be in the following format. Add to the schedule any other provisions necessary to describe the requirements, if they are consistent with the following provisions and the policy of acquiring educational services in the form of standard course offerings at the prevailing rates of the institution.

Educational Service Agreement

Agreement No. ______________

1. This agreement entered into on the ___ day of ______, is between the Government, represented by the Contracting Officer, and the Contractor, (name of institution), an educational institution located in ___ (city), ___ (state).

2. This agreement is for educational services to be provided by the Contractor to Government personnel at the Contractor's institution. The Contractor shall provide instruction with standard offerings of courses available to the public.

3. The Government shall pay for services under the Contractor's normal schedule of tuition and fees applicable to the public and in effect at the time the services are performed.

4. The Government will review this agreement annually before the anniversary of its effective date for the purpose of incorporating changes required by statutes, executive orders, the Federal Acquisition Regulation, or the Defense Federal Acquisition Regulation Supplement. Changes required to be made by modification to this agreement or by issuance of a superseding agreement. If mutual agreement on the changes cannot be reached, the Government will terminate this agreement.

5. The parties may amend this agreement only by mutual consent.

6. This agreement shall start on the date in paragraph 1 and shall continue until terminated.

7. The estimated annual cost of this agreement is $________. This estimate is for administrative purposes only and does not impose any obligation on the Government to request any services or make any payment.

8. Advance payments are authorized by 10 U.S.C. 2396(a)(3).

9. Submit invoices to: ___ (name and address of activity).

Schedule Provisions

1. *Ordering procedures and services to be provided.* (a) The Contractor shall promptly deliver to the Contracting Officer one copy of each catalog applicable to this agreement, and one copy of any subsequent revision.

(b) The Government will request educational services under this agreement by a (insert type of request, such as, delivery order, official Government order, or other written communication). The (insert type of request, such as, delivery order, official Government order, or other written communication) will contain the number of this agreement and will designate as students at the Contractor's institution one or more Government-selected persons who have already been accepted for admission under the Contractor's usual admission standards.

(c) All students under this agreement shall register in the same manner, be subject to the same academic regulations, and have the same privileges, including the use of all facilities and equipment as any other students enrolled in the institution.

(d) Upon enrolling each student under this agreement, the Contractor shall, where the resident or nonresident status involves a difference in tuition or fees—

(i) Determine the resident or nonresident status of the student;

(ii) Notify the student and the Contracting Officer of the determination. If there is an appeal of the determination;

(iii) If there is an appeal of the determination, process the appeal under the Contractor's standard procedures;

(iv) Notify the student and Contracting Officer of the result; and

(v) Make the determination a part of the student's permanent record.

(e) The Contractor shall not furnish any instruction or other services to any student under this agreement before the effective date of a request for services in the form specified in paragraph (b) of this schedule.

2. *Change in curriculum.* The Contracting Officer may vary the curriculum for any student enrolled under this agreement but shall

not require or make any change in any course without the Contractor's consent.

3. *Payment.* (a) The Government shall pay the Contractor the normal tuition and fees which the Contractor charges any students pursuing the same or similar curricula, except for any tuition and fees which this agreement excludes. The Contractor may change any tuition and fees, provided—

(1) The Contractor publishes the revisions in a catalog or otherwise publicly announces the revisions;

(2) Applies the revisions uniformly to all students studying the same or similar curricula;

(3) Provides the Contracting Officer notice of changes before their effective date.

(b) The Contractor shall not establish any tuition or fees which apply solely to students under this agreement.

(c) If the Contractor regularly charges higher tuition and fees for nonresident students, the Contractor may charge the Government the normal nonresident tuition and fees for students under this agreement who are nonresidents. The Government shall not claim resident tuition and fees for any student solely on the basis of the student residing in the State as a consequence of enrollment under this agreement.

(d) The Contractor shall charge the Government only the tuition and fees which relate directly to enrollment as a student. Tuition and fees may include—

(i) Penalty fees for late registration or change of course caused by the Government;

(ii) Mandatory health fees and health insurance charges; and

(iii) Any flat rate charge applicable to all students registered for research that appears in the Contractor's publicly announced fee schedule.

(e) The Contractor shall not charge the Government for—

(i) Permit charges, such as vehicle registration or parking fees, unless specifically authorized in the request for service; and

(ii) Any equipment, refundable deposits, or any items or services (such as computer time) related to student research.

(f) Normally, the Contractor shall not directly charge individual students for application fees or any other fee chargeable to this agreement. However, if the Contractor's standard procedures require payment of any fee before the student is enrolled under this agreement, the Contractor may charge the student. When the Contractor receives payment from the Government, the Contractor shall fully reimburse the student.

(g) For each term the Contractor enrolls students under this agreement, the Contractor shall submit ___ copies of an invoice listing charges for each student separately. The Contractor shall submit invoices within ___ days after the start of the term and shall include—

(i) Agreement number and inclusive dates of the term;

(ii) Name of each student;

(iii) A list showing each course for each student if the school charges by credit hour;

(iv) The resident or nonresident status of each student (if applicable to the Contractor's school); and

(v) A breakdown of charges for each student, including credit hours, tuition, application fee, and other fees. Provide a total for each student and a grand total for all students listed on the invoice.

(h) If unforeseen events require additional charges that are otherwise payable under the Contractor's normal tuition and fee schedule, the Contractor may submit a supplemental invoice or make the adjustment on the next regular invoice under this agreement. The Contractor shall clearly identify and explain the supplemental invoice or the adjustment.

(i) The Contractor shall apply any credits resulting from withdrawal of students, or from any other cause under its standard procedures, to subsequent invoices submitted under this agreement. Credits should appear on the first invoice submitted after the action resulting in the credits. If no subsequent invoice is submitted, the Contractor shall deliver to the Contracting Officer a check drawn to the order of the office designated for contract administration. The Contractor shall identify the reason for the credit and the applicable term dates in all cases.

4. *Withdrawal of students.* (a) The Government may, at its option and at any time, withdraw financial support for any student by issuing official orders. The Government will furnish — copies of the orders to the Contractor within a reasonable time after publication.

(b) The Contractor may request withdrawal by the Government of any student for academic or disciplinary reasons.

(c) If withdrawal occurs before the end of a term, the Government will pay any tuition and fees due for the current term. The Contractor shall credit the Government with any charges eligible for refund under the Contractor's standard procedures for any students in effect on the date of withdrawal.

(d) Withdrawal of students by the Government will not be the basis for any special charge or claim by the Contractor other than charges under the Contractor's standard procedures.

5. *Transcripts.* Within a reasonable time after withdrawal of a student for any reason, or after graduation, the Contractor shall send to the Contracting Officer (or to an address supplied by the Contracting Officer) one copy of an official transcript showing all work by the student at the institution until such withdrawal or graduation.

6. *Student teaching.* The Government does not anticipate the Contractor awarding fellowships and assistantships to students attending school under this agreement. However, for graduate students, should both the student and the Contractor decide it to be in the student's best interests to assist in the institution's teaching program, the Contractor may provide nominal compensation for part-time service. Base the compensation on the Contractor's practices and procedures for other students of similar accomplishment in that department or field. The Contractor shall apply the compensation as a credit against any invoices presented for payment for any period in which the student performed the part-time teaching service.

7. *Termination of agreement.* (a) Either party may terminate this agreement by giving 30 days advance written notice of the effective date of termination. In the event of termination, the Government shall have the right, at its option, to continue to receive educational services for those students already enrolled in the contractor's institution under this agreement until such time that the students complete their courses or curricula or the Government withdraws them from the Contractor's institution. The terms and conditions of this agreement in effect on the effective date of the termination shall continue to apply to such students remaining in the Contractor's institution.

(b) Withdrawal of students under Schedule provision 4 shall not be considered a termination within the meaning of this provision 7.

(c) Termination by either party shall not be the basis for any special charge or claim by the Contractor, other than as provided by the Contractor's standard procedures.

GENERAL PROVISIONS

Use the following clauses in educational service agreements:

1. FAR 52.202-1, Definitions, and add the following paragraphs (h) through (m).

(h) *Term* means the period of time into which the Contractor divides the academic year for purposes of instruction. This includes "semester," "trimester," "quarter," or any similar word the Contractor may use.

(i) *Course* means a series of lectures or instructions, and laboratory periods, relating to one specific representation of subject matter, such as Elementary College Algebra, German 401, or Surveying. Normally, a student completes a course in one term and receives a certain number of semester hours credit (or equivalent) upon successful completion.

(j) *Curriculum* means a series of courses having a unified purpose and belonging primarily to one major academic field. It will usually include certain required courses and elective courses within established criteria.

Examples include Business Administration, Civil Engineering, Fine and Applied Arts, and Physics. A curriculum normally covers more than one term and leads to a degree or diploma upon successful completion.

(k) *Catalog* means any medium by which the Contractor publicly announces terms and conditions for enrollment in the Contractor's institution, including tuition and fees to be charged. This includes "bulletin," "announcement," or any other similar word the Contractor may use.

(l) *Tuition* means the amount of money charged by an educational institution for instruction, not including fees.

(m) *Fees* means those applicable charges directly related to enrollment in the Contractor's institution. Unless specifically allowed in the request for services, fees shall not include—

(1) Any permit charge, such as parking and vehicle registration; or

(2) Charges for services of a personal nature, such as food, housing, and laundry.

2. FAR 52.203-3, Gratuities.

3. FAR 52.203-5, Covenant Against Contingent Fees.

4. FAR 52.204-1, Approval of Contract, if required by department/agency procedures.

5. FAR 52.215-2, Audit and Records—Negotiation.

6. FAR 52.215-8, Order of Precedence—Uniform Contract Format.

7. Conflicts Between Agreement and Catalog. Insert the following clause:

CONFLICTS BETWEEN AGREEMENT AND CATALOG

If there is any inconsistency between this agreement and any catalog or other document incorporated in this agreement by reference or any of the Contractor's rules and regulations, the provisions of this agreement shall govern.

8. FAR 52.222-3, Convict Labor.

9. Under FAR 22.802, FAR 22.807, and FAR 22.810, use the appropriate clause from FAR 52.222-26, Equal Opportunity.

10. FAR 52.233-1, Disputes.

11. Assignment of Claims. Insert the following clause:

ASSIGNMENT OF CLAIMS

No claim under this agreement shall be assigned.

12. FAR 52.252-4, Alterations in Contract, if required by department/agency procedures.

SIGNATURE PAGE

Agreement No. ____________

Date ____________

The United States of America

By: (Contracting Officer) ____________

Activity ____________

Location (Name of Contractor) ____________

By: ____________

(Title) ____________

[DAC 91-9, 60 FR 61586, 11/30/95, effective 11/30/95; Final rule, 63 FR 55040, 10/14/98, effective 10/14/98; Final rule, 64 FR 49684, 9/14/99, effective 9/14/99, corrected, 64 FR 53447, 10/1/99; Final rule, 74 FR 42779, 8/25/2009, effective 8/25/2009; Publication notice, 20171208]

SUBPART 237.73—SERVICES OF STUDENTS AT RESEARCH AND DEVELOPMENT LABORATORIES

237.7300 Scope.

This subpart prescribes procedures for acquisition of temporary or intermittent services of students at institutions of higher learning for the purpose of providing technical support at Defense research and development laboratories (10 U.S.C. 2360).

237.7301 Definitions.

As used in this subpart—

(a) *Institution of higher learning* means any public or private post-secondary school, junior college, college, university, or other degree granting educational institution that—

(1) Is located in the United States or its outlying areas;

(2) Has an accredited education program approved by an appropriate accrediting body; and

(3) Offers a program of study at any level beyond high school.

(b) *Nonprofit organization* means any organization described by section 501(c)(3) of title 26 of the U.S.C. which is exempt from taxation under section 501(a) of title 26.

(c) *Student* means an individual enrolled (or accepted for enrollment) at an institution of higher learning before the term of the student technical support contract. The individual shall remain in good standing in a curriculum designed to lead to the granting of a recognized degree, during the term of the contract.

(d) *Technical support* means any scientific or engineering work in support of the mission of the DoD laboratory involved. It does not include administrative or clerical services.

[Final rule, 70 FR 35543, 6/21/2005, effective 6/21/2005]

237.7302 General.

Generally, agencies will acquire services of students at institutions of higher learning by contract between a nonprofit organization employing the student and the Government. When it is in the best interest of the Government, contracts may be made directly with students. These services are not subject to the requirements of FAR part 19, FAR 13.003(b)(1), or DFARS part 219. Award authority for these contracts is 10 U.S.C. 2304(a)(1) and 10 U.S.C. 2360.

[DAC 91-7, 60 FR 29491, 6/5/95, effective 5/17/95; Final rule, 64 FR 2595, 1/15/99, effective 1/15/99]

237.7303 Contract clauses.

Contracts made directly with students are nonpersonal service contracts but shall include the clauses at FAR 52.232-3, Payments Under Personal Services Contracts, and FAR 52.249-12, Termination (Personal Services).

SUBPART 237.74—SERVICES AT INSTALLATIONS BEING CLOSED

237.7400 Scope.

This subpart prescribes procedures for contracting, through use of other than full and open competition, with local governments for police, fire protection, airfield operation, or other community services at military installations to be closed under the Defense Authorization Amendments and Base Closure and Realignment Act (Pub. L. 100-526), as amended, and the Defense Base Closure and Realignment Act of 1990 (Pub. L. 101-510), as amended.

[Interim rule, 59 FR 36088, 7/15/94, effective 7/8/94; DAC 91-7, 60 FR 29491, 6/5/95, effective 5/17/95]

237.7401 Policy.

The authority in 206.302-5(b)(ii) to contract with local governments—

(a) May be exercised without regard to the provisions of 10 U.S.C. Chapter 146, Contracting for Performance of Civilian Commercial or Industrial Type Functions;

(b) May not be exercised earlier than 180 days before the date the installation is scheduled to be closed;

(c) Requires a determination by the head of the contracting activity that the services being acquired under contract with the local government are in the best interests of the Department of Defense.

[Interim rule, 59 FR 36088, 7/15/94, effective 7/8/94; DAC 91-7, 60 FR 29491, 6/5/95, effective 5/17/95; Final rule, 83 FR 24892, 5/30/2018, effective 5/30/2018]

237.7402 Contract clause.

Use the clause at 252.237-7022, Services at Installations Being Closed, in solicitations and contracts based upon the authority of this subpart.

[Interim rule, 59 FR 36088, 7/15/94, effective 7/8/94; DAC 91-7, 60 FR 29491, 6/5/95, effective 5/17/95]

SUBPART 237.75—ACQUISITION AND MANAGEMENT OF INDUSTRIAL RESOURCES

237.7501 Definition.

Facilities project, as used in this subpart, means a Government project to provide, modernize, or replace real property for use by a contractor in performing a Government contract or subcontract.

[Final rule, 74 FR 37645, 7/29/2009, effective 7/29/2009]

237.7502 Policy.

(a) Comply with DoD Directive 4275.5, Acquisition and Management of Industrial Resources, in processing requests for facilities projects.

(b) Departments and agencies shall submit reports of facilities projects to the House and Senate Armed Services Committees—

(1) At least 30 days before starting facilities projects involving real property (10 U.S.C. 2662); and

(2) In advance of starting construction for a facilities project regardless of cost. Use DD Form 1391, FY__ Military Construction Project Data, to notify congressional committees of projects that are not included in the annual budget.

[Final rule, 74 FR 37645, 7/29/2009, effective 7/29/2009]

SUBPART 237.76—CONTINUATION OF ESSENTIAL CONTRACTOR SERVICES

237.7600 Scope.

This subpart prescribes procedures for the acquisition of essential contractor services which support mission-essential functions.

[Interim rule, 75 FR 10191, 3/5/2010, effective 3/5/2010; Final rule, 75 FR 66680, 10/29/2010, effective 10/29/2010]

237.7601 Definitions.

As used in this subpart, *essential contractor service* and *mission-essential functions* are defined in the clause at 252.237-7023, Continuation of Essential Contractor Services.

[Interim rule, 75 FR 10191, 3/5/2010, effective 3/5/2010; Final rule, 75 FR 66680, 10/29/2010, effective 10/29/2010]

237.7602 Policy.

(a) Contractors providing services designated as essential contractor services shall be prepared to continue providing such services, in accordance with the terms and conditions of their contracts, during periods of crisis. As a general rule, the designation of services as essential contractor services will not apply to an entire contract but will apply only to those service functions that have been specifically identified as essential contractor services by the functional commander or civilian equivalent.

(b) Contractors who provide Government-determined essential contractor services shall provide a written plan to be incorporated in the contract, to ensure the continuation of these services in crisis situations. Contracting officers shall consult with a functional manager to assess the sufficiency of the contractor-provided written plan. Contractors will activate such plans only during periods of crisis, as authorized by the contracting officer, who does so at the direction of the appropriate functional commander or civilian equivalent.

(c) The contracting officer shall follow the procedures at PGI 207.105U(b)(20)(C) in preparing an acquisition plan.

[Interim rule, 75 FR 10191, 3/5/2010, effective 3/5/2010; Final rule, 75 FR 66680, 10/29/2010, effective 10/29/2010]

237.7603 Solicitation provision and contract clause.

(a) Use the clause at 252.237-7023, Continuation of Essential Contractor Services in all solicitations and contracts for services that are in support of mission-essential functions.

(b) Use the provision at 252.237-7024, Notice of Continuation of Essential Contractor Services in all solicitations for services that include the clause 252.237-7023.

[Interim rule, 75 FR 10191, 3/5/2010, effective 3/5/2010; Final rule, 75 FR 66680, 10/29/2010, effective 10/29/2010]

SUBPART 237.77—COMPETITION FOR RELIGIOUS-RELATED SERVICES

237.7700 Scope of subpart.

This subpart provides policy and guidance for the acquisition of religious-related services to be performed on a U.S. military installation in accordance with section 898 of the National Defense Authorization Act for Fiscal Year 2016 (Pub. L. 114-92).

[Final rule, 83 FR 16001, 4/13/2018, effective 4/13/2018]

237.7701 Definition.

As used in this subpart—

Nonprofit organization means any organization that is—

(1) Described in section 501(c) of the Internal Revenue Code of 1986; and

(2) Exempt from tax under section 501(a) of that Code.

[Final rule, 83 FR 16001, 4/13/2018, effective 4/13/2018]

237.7702 Policy.

(a) A nonprofit organization shall not be precluded from competing for a contract for religious-related services to be performed on a U.S. military installation.

(b) See 219.270 when an acquisition for religious-related services to be performed on a U.S. military installation is set aside for any of the small business concerns identified in FAR 19.000(a)(3).

[Final rule, 83 FR 16001, 4/13/2018, effective 4/13/2018]

PART 238—[NO FAR SUPPLEMENT]

PART 239—ACQUISITION OF INFORMATION TECHNOLOGY

Table of Contents

Subpart 239.1—General

Applicability 239.001
Policy 239.101

Subpart 239.70—Exchange or Sale of Information Technology

[Removed] 239.7000
Policy 239.7001
[Removed] 239.7002
[Removed] 239.7003

Subpart 239.71—Security and Privacy for Computer Systems

Scope of subpart 239.7100
Definition 239.7101
Policy and responsibilities 239.7102
General 239.7102-1
Compromising emanations—TEMPEST or other standard 239.7102-2
Information assurance contractor training and certification 239.7102-3
Contract clauses 239.7103

Subpart 239.72—Standards

[Removed] 239.7200
Solicitation requirements 239.7201
[Removed] 239.7202

Subpart 239.73—Requirements for Information Relating to Supply Chain Risk

Scope of subpart 239.7300
Definitions 239.7301
Applicability 239.7302
Authorized individuals 239.7303
Determination and notification 239.7304
Exclusion and limitation on disclosure 239.7305
Solicitation provision and contract clause 239.7306

Subpart 239.74—Telecommunications Services

Scope 239.7400
Definitions 239.7401
Policy 239.7402
[Removed and Reserved] 239.7403
[Removed and Reserved] 239.7404
Delegated authority for telecommunications resources 239.7405
Certified cost or pricing data and data other than certified cost or pricing data 239.7406
Type of contract 239.7407
[Removed] 239.7407-1
[Removed] 239.7407-2

Special construction 239.7408
General 239.7408-1
Applicability of construction labor standards for special construction 239.7408-2
Special assembly 239.7409
Cancellation and termination 239.7410
Contract clauses 239.7411

Subpart 239.75—[Removed]

Subpart 239.76—Cloud Computing

Scope of subpart 239.7600
Definitions 239.7601
Policy and responsibilities 239.7602
General 239.7602-1
Required storage of data within the United States or outlying areas 239.7602-2
Procedures 239.7603
Solicitation provision and contract clause 239.7604

PART 239—ACQUISITION OF INFORMATION TECHNOLOGY

SUBPART 239.1—GENERAL

239.001 Applicability.

Notwithstanding FAR 39.001, this part applies to acquisitions of information technology, including national security systems.

[Final rule, 80 FR 67243, 10/30/2015, effective 10/30/2015]

239.101 Policy.

(1) A contracting officer may not enter into a contract in excess of the simplified acquisition threshold for information technology products or services that are not commercial items unless the head of the contracting activity determines in writing that no commercial items are suitable to meet the agency's needs, as determined through the use of market research appropriate to the circumstances (see FAR 10.001(a)(3)) (section 855 of the National Defense Authorization Act for Fiscal Year 2016 (Pub. L. 114-92)).

(2) See subpart 208.74 when acquiring commercial software or software maintenance.

(3) See 227.7202 for policy on the acquisition of commercial computer software and commercial computer software documentation.

[Final rule, 67 FR 65509, 10/25/2002, effective 10/25/2002; Final rule, 74 FR 34269, 7/15/2009, effective 7/15/2009; Final rule, 83 FR 4431, 1/31/2018, effective 1/31/2018]

SUBPART 239.70—EXCHANGE OR SALE OF INFORMATION TECHNOLOGY

239.7000 [Removed]

[Interim rule, 62 FR 1058, 1/8/97, effective 1/8/97, finalized without change, DAC 91-12, 62 FR 34114, 6/24/97, effective 6/24/97; Final rule, 71 FR 39009, 7/11/2006, effective 7/11/2006]

239.7001 Policy.

Agencies shall follow the procedures in DoD Manual 4140.01, Volume 9, DoD Supply Chain Materiel Management Procedures: Materiel Programs, when considering the exchange or sale of Government-owned information technology.

[Final rule, 62 FR 1058, 1/8/97, effective 1/8/97, finalized without change, DAC 91-12, 62 FR 34114, 6/24/97, effective 6/24/97; Final rule, 71 FR 39009, 7/11/2006, effective 7/11/2006; Final rule, 82 FR 61479, 12/28/2017, effective 12/28/2017]

239.7002 [Removed]

[Final rule, 62 FR 1058, 1/8/97, effective 1/8/97, finalized without change, DAC 91-12, 62 FR 34114, 6/24/97, effective 6/24/97; Final rule, 71 FR 39009, 7/11/2006, effective 7/11/2006]

239.7003 [Removed]

[Final rule, 62 FR 1058, 1/8/97, effective 1/8/97, corrected 62 FR 49305, 9/19/97; DAC 91-12, 62 FR 34114, 6/24/97, effective 6/24/97.; Final rule, 71 FR 39009, 7/11/2006, effective 7/11/2006]

SUBPART 239.71—SECURITY AND PRIVACY FOR COMPUTER SYSTEMS

239.7100 Scope of subpart.

This subpart includes information assurance and Privacy Act considerations. Information assurance requirements are in addition to provisions concerning protection of privacy of individuals (see FAR Subpart 24.1).

[Final rule, 69 FR 35533, 6/25/2004, effective 6/25/2004]

239.7101 Definition.

Information assurance, as used in this subpart, means measures that protect and defend information, that is entered, processed, transmitted, stored, retrieved, displayed, or destroyed, and information systems, by ensuring their availability, integrity, authentication, confidentiality, and non-repudiation. This includes providing for the restoration of information systems by incorporating protection, detection, and reaction capabilities.

[Final rule, 69 FR 35533, 6/25/2004, effective 6/25/2004]

239.7102 Policy and responsibilities (No Text)

[Final rule, 69 FR 35533, 6/25/2004, effective 6/25/2004]

239.7102-1 General.

(a) Agencies shall ensure that information assurance is provided for information technology in accordance with current policies, procedures, and statutes, to include—

(1) The National Security Act;

(2) The Clinger-Cohen Act;

(3) National Security Telecommunications and Information Systems Security Policy No. 11;

(4) Federal Information Processing Standards;

(5) DoD Directive 8500.1, Information Assurance;

(6) DoD Instruction 8500.2, Information Assurance Implementation;

(7) DoD Directive 8140.01, Cyberspace

Workforce Management; and

(8) DoD Manual 8570.01-M, Information Assurance Workforce Improvement Program.

(b) For all acquisitions, the requiring activity is responsible for providing to the contracting officer—

(1) Statements of work, specifications, or statements of objectives that meet information assurance requirements as specified in paragraph (a) of this subsection;

(2) Inspection and acceptance contract requirements; and

(3) A determination as to whether the information technology requires protection against compromising emanations.

[Final rule, 69 FR 35533, 6/25/2004, effective 6/25/2004; Final rule, 73 FR 1828, 1/10/2008, effective 1/10/2008; Final rule, 75 FR 34946, 6/21/2010, effective 6/21/2010; Final rule, 80 FR 56929, 9/21/2015, effective 9/21/2015]

239.7102-2 Compromising emanations—TEMPEST or other standard.

For acquisitions requiring information assurance against compromising emanations, the requiring activity is responsible for providing to the contracting officer—

(a) The required protections, *i.e.*, an established National TEMPEST standard (*e.g.*, NSTISSAM TEMPEST 1-92) or a standard used by other authority;

(b) The required identification markings to include markings for TEMPEST or other standard, certified equipment (especially if to be reused);

(c) Inspection and acceptance requirements addressing the validation of compliance with TEMPEST or other standards; and

(d) A date through which the accreditation is considered current for purposes of the proposed contract.

[Final rule, 69 FR 35533, 6/25/2004, effective 6/25/2004; Final rule, 84 FR 58336, 10/31/2019, effective 10/31/2019]

239.7102-3 Information assurance contractor training and certification.

(a) For acquisitions that include information assurance functional services for DoD information systems, or that require any appropriately cleared contractor personnel to access a DoD information system to perform contract duties, the requiring activity is responsible for providing to the contracting officer—(1) A list of information assurance functional responsibilities for DoD information systems by category (*e.g.*, technical or management) and level (*e.g.*, computing environment, network environment, or enclave); and

(2) The information assurance training, certification, certification maintenance, and continuing education or sustainment training required for the information assurance functional responsibilities.

(b) After contract award, the requiring activity is responsible for ensuring that the certifications and certification status of all contractor personnel performing information assurance functions as described in DoD 8570.01-M, Information Assurance

Workforce Improvement Program, are in compliance with the manual and are identified, documented, and tracked.

(c) The responsibilities specified in paragraphs (a) and (b) of this section apply to all DoD information assurance duties supported by a contractor, whether performed full-time or part-time as additional or embedded duties, and when using a DoD contract, or a contract or agreement administered by another agency (e.g., under an interagency agreement).

(d) See PGI 239.7102-3 for guidance on documenting and tracking certification status of contractor personnel, and for additional information regarding the requirements of DoD 8570.01-M.

[Final rule, 73 FR 1828, 1/10/2008, effective 1/10/2008]

239.7103 Contract clauses.

(a) Use the clause at 252.239-7000, Protection Against Compromising Emanations, in solicitations and contracts involving information technology that requires protection against compromising emanations.

(b) Use the clause at 252.239-7001, Information Assurance Contractor Training and Certification, in solicitations and contracts involving contractor performance of information assurance functions as described in DoD 8570.01-M.

[Final rule, 69 FR 35533, 6/25/2004, effective 6/25/2004; Final rule, 73 FR 1828, 1/10/2008, effective 1/10/2008]

SUBPART 239.72—STANDARDS

239.7200 [Removed]

[Final rule, 71 FR 39010, 7/11/2006, effective 7/11/2006]

239.7201 Solicitation requirements.

Contracting officers shall ensure that all applicable Federal Information Processing Standards are incorporated into solicitations.

[Removed and reserved, Final rule, 62 FR 1058, 1/8/97, effective 1/8/97; Final rule, 71 FR 39010, 7/11/2006, effective 7/11/2006]

239.7202 [Removed]

[Final rule, 62 FR 1058, 1/8/97, effective 1/8/97, finalized without change, DAC 91-12, 62 FR 34114, 6/24/97, effective 6/24/97; Final rule, 71 FR 39010, 7/11/2006, effective 7/11/2006]

SUBPART 239.73—REQUIREMENTS FOR INFORMATION RELATING TO SUPPLY CHAIN RISK

239.7300 Scope of subpart.

This subpart implements 10 U.S.C. 2339a and elements of DoD Instruction 5200.44, Protection of Mission Critical Functions to Achieve Trusted Systems and Networks (TSN), at *https://www.esd.whs.mil/Portals/54/Documents/DD/issuances/dodi/520044p.pdf?ver=2018-11-08-075800-903*.

[Final rule, 70 FR 67917, 11/9/2005, effective 11/9/2005; Interim rule, 78 FR 69267, 11/18/2013, effective 11/18/2013; Final rule, 80 FR 67243, 10/30/2015, effective 10/30/2015; Final rule, 84 FR 4368, 2/15/2019, effective 2/15/2019]

239.7301 Definitions.

As used in this subpart—

Covered item of supply means an item of information technology that is purchased for inclusion in a covered system, and the loss of integrity of which could result in a supply chain risk for a covered system (see 10 U.S.C. 2339a).

Covered system means a national security system, as that term is defined at 44 U.S.C. 3552(b) (see 10 U.S.C. 2339a). It is any information system, including any telecommunications system, used or operated by an agency or by a contractor of an agency, or other organization on behalf of an agency—

(1) The function, operation, or use of which—

(i) Involves intelligence activities;

(ii) Involves cryptologic activities related to national security;

(iii) Involves command and control of military forces;

(iv) Involves equipment that is an integral part of a weapon or weapons system; or

(v) Is critical to the direct fulfillment of military or intelligence missions but this does not include a system that is to be used for routine administrative and business applications, including payroll, finance, logistics, and personnel management applications; or

(2) Is protected at all times by procedures established for information that have been specifically authorized under criteria established by an Executive order or an Act of Congress to be kept classified in the interest of national defense or foreign policy.

Information technology (see 40 U.S.C 11101(6)) means, in lieu of the definition at FAR 2.1, any equipment, or interconnected system(s) or subsystem(s) of equipment, that is used in the automatic acquisition, storage, analysis, evaluation, manipulation, management, movement, control, display, switching, interchange, transmission, or reception of data or information by the agency.

(1) For purposes of this definition, equipment is used by an agency if the equipment is used by the agency directly or is used by a contractor under a contract with the agency that requires—

(i) Its use; or

(ii) To a significant extent, its use in the performance of a service or the furnishing of a product.

(2) The term "information technology" includes computers, ancillary equipment (including imaging peripherals, input, output, and storage devices necessary for security and surveillance), peripheral equipment designed to be controlled by the central processing unit of a computer, software, firmware and similar procedures, services (including support services), and related resources.

(3) The term "information technology" does not include any equipment acquired by a contractor incidental to a contract.

Supply chain risk means the risk that an adversary may sabotage, maliciously introduce unwanted function, or otherwise subvert the design, integrity, manufacturing, production, distribution, installation, operation, or maintenance of a covered system so as to surveil, deny, disrupt, or otherwise degrade the function, use, or operation of such system (see 10 U.S.C. 2339a).

[Interim rule, 78 FR 69267, 11/18/2013, effective 11/18/2013; Final rule, 80 FR 67243, 10/30/2015, effective 10/30/2015; Final rule, 83 FR 15994, 4/13/2018, effective 4/13/2018; Final rule, 84 FR 4368, 2/15/2019, effective 2/15/2019]

239.7302 Applicability.

Notwithstanding FAR 39.001, this subpart shall be applied to acquisition of information technology for covered systems (see 10 U.S.C. 2339a) for procurements involving—

(a) A source selection for a covered system or a covered item of supply involving either a performance specification (see 10 U.S.C. 2305(a)(1)(C)(ii)), or an evaluation factor (see 10 U.S.C. 2305(a)(2)(A)), relating to supply chain risk;

(b) The consideration of proposals for and issuance of a task or delivery order for a covered system or a covered item of supply where the task or delivery order contract concerned includes a requirement relating to supply chain risk (see 10 U.S.C. 2304c(d)(3) and FAR 16.505(b)(1)(iv)(D)); or (c) Any contract action involving a contract for a covered system or a covered item of supply where such contract includes a requirement relating to supply chain risk.

[Interim rule, 78 FR 69267, 11/18/2013, effective 11/18/2013; Final rule, 80 FR 67243, 10/30/2015, effective 10/30/2015; Final rule, 84 FR 4368, 2/15/2019, effective 2/15/2019]

239.7303 Authorized individuals.

(a) Subject to 239.7304, the following individuals are authorized to take the actions authorized by 239.7305:

(1) The Secretary of Defense.

(2) The Secretary of the Army.

(3) The Secretary of the Navy

(4) The Secretary of the Air Force.

(b) The individuals authorized at paragraph (a) may not delegate the authority to take the actions at 239.7305 or the responsibility for making the determination required by 239.7304 to an official below the level of—

(1) For the Department of Defense, the Under Secretary of Defense for Acquisition and Sustainment; and,

(2) For the military departments, the service acquisition executive for the department concerned.

[Interim rule, 78 FR 69267, 11/18/2013, effective 11/18/2013; Final rule, 84 FR 4368, 2/15/2019, effective 2/15/2019]

239.7304 Determination and notification.

The individuals authorized in 239.7303 may exercise the authority provided in 239.7305 only after—

(a) Obtaining a joint recommendation by the Under Secretary of Defense for Acquisition and Sustainment and the Chief Information Officer of the Department of Defense, on the basis of a risk assessment by the Under Secretary of Defense for Intelligence, that there is a significant supply chain risk to a covered system;

(b) Making a determination in writing, in unclassified or classified form, with the concurrence of the Under Secretary of Defense for Acquisition and Sustainment, that—(1) Use of the authority in 239.7305(a), (b), or (c) is necessary to protect national security by reducing supply chain risk;

(2) Less intrusive measures are not reasonably available to reduce such supply chain risk; and

(3) In a case where the individual authorized in 239.7303 plans to limit disclosure of information under 239.7305(d), the risk to national security due to the disclosure of such information outweighs the risk due to not disclosing such information; and

(c)(1) Providing a classified or unclassified notice of the determination made under paragraph (b) of this section—

(i) In the case of a covered system included in the National Intelligence Program or the Military Intelligence Program, to the Select Committee on Intelligence of the Senate, the Permanent Select Committee on Intelligence of the House of Representatives, and the congressional defense committees; and

(ii) In the case of a covered system not otherwise included in paragraph (a) of this section, to the congressional defense committees; and

(2) The notice shall include—

(i) The following information (see 10 U.S.C. 2304(f)(3)):

(A) A description of the agency's needs.

(B) An identification of the statutory exception from the requirement to use competitive procedures and a demonstration, based on the proposed contractor's qualifications or the nature of the procurement, of the reasons for using that exception.

(C) A determination that the anticipated cost will be fair and reasonable.

(D) A description of the market survey conducted or a statement of the reasons a market survey was not conducted.

(E) A listing of the sources, if any, that expressed in writing an interest in the procurement.

(F) A statement of the actions, if any, the agency may take to remove or overcome any barrier to competition before a subsequent procurement for such needs;

(ii) The joint recommendation by the Under Secretary of Defense for Acquisition and Sustainment and the Chief Information Officer of the Department of Defense as specified in paragraph (a) of this section;

(iii) A summary of the risk assessment by the Under Secretary of Defense for Intelligence that serves as the basis for the joint recommendation specified in paragraph (a) of this section; and

(iv) A summary of the basis for the determination, including a discussion of less intrusive measures that were considered and why they were not reasonably available to reduce supply chain risk.

[Interim rule, 78 FR 69267, 11/18/2013, effective 11/18/2013; Final rule, 80 FR 67243, 10/30/2015, effective 10/30/2015; Final rule, 84 FR 4368, 2/15/2019, effective 2/15/2019]

239.7305 Exclusion and limitation on disclosure.

Subject to 239.7304, the individuals authorized in 239.7303 may, in the course of procuring information technology, whether as a service or as a supply, that is a covered system, is a part of a covered system, or is in support of a covered system—

(a) Exclude a source that fails to meet qualification standards established in accordance with the requirements of 10 U.S.C. 2319, for the purpose of reducing supply chain risk in the acquisition of covered systems;

(b) Exclude a source that fails to achieve an acceptable rating with regard to an evaluation factor providing for the consideration of supply chain risk in the evaluation of proposals for the award of a contract or the issuance of a task or delivery order;

(c) Withhold consent for a contractor to subcontract with a particular source or direct a contractor for a covered system to exclude a particular source from consideration for a subcontract under the contract; and

(d) Limit, notwithstanding any other provision of law, in whole or in part, the disclosure of information relating to the basis for carrying out any of the actions authorized by paragraphs (a) through (c) of this section, and if such disclosures are so limited—

(1) No action undertaken by the individual authorized under such authority shall be subject to review in a bid protest before the Government Accountability Office or in any Federal court; and

(2) The authorized individual shall—

(i) Notify appropriate parties of action taken under paragraphs (a) through (d) of this section and the basis for such action only to the extent necessary to effectuate the action;

(ii) Notify other Department of Defense components or other Federal agencies responsible for procurements that may be subject to the same or similar supply chain risk, in a manner and to the extent consistent with the requirements of national security; and

(iii) Ensure the confidentiality of any such notifications.

[Interim rule, 78 FR 69267, 11/18/2013, effective 11/18/2013; Final rule, 80 FR 67243, 10/30/2015, effective 10/30/2015]

239.7306 Solicitation provision and contract clause.

(a) Insert the provision at 252.239-7017, Notice of Supply Chain Risk, in solicitations, including solicitations using FAR part 12 procedures for the acquisition of commercial items, for information technology, whether acquired as a service or as a supply, that is a covered system, is a part of a covered system, or is in support of a covered system, as defined at 239.7301.

(b) Insert the clause at 252.239-7018, Supply Chain Risk, in solicitations and contracts, including solicitations and contracts using FAR part 12 procedures for the acquisition of commercial items, for information technology, whether acquired as a service or as a supply, that is a covered system, is a part of a covered system, or is in support of a covered system, as defined at 239.7301.

[Interim rule, 78 FR 69267, 11/18/2013, effective 11/18/2013; Final rule, 80 FR 67243, 10/30/2015, effective 10/30/2015]

SUBPART 239.74—TELECOMMUNICATIONS SERVICES

239.7400 Scope.

This subpart prescribes policy and procedures for acquisition of telecommunications services and maintenance of telecommunications security. Telecommunications services meet the definition of information technology.

[Final rule, 62 FR 1058, 1/8/97, effective 1/8/97, finalized without change, DAC 91-12, 62 FR 34114, 6/24/97, effective 6/24/97; Final rule, 71 FR 39010, 7/11/2006, effective 7/11/2006]

239.7401 Definitions.

As used in this subpart—

Common carrier means any entity engaged in the business of providing telecommunications services which are regulated by the Federal Communications Commission or other governmental body.

Foreign carrier means any person, partnership, association, joint-stock company, trust, governmental body, or corporation not subject to regulation by a U.S. governmental regulatory body and not doing business as a citizen of the United States, providing telecommunications services outside the territorial limits of the United States.

Governmental regulatory body means the Federal Communications Commission, any statewide regulatory body, or any body with less than statewide jurisdiction when operating under the State authority. The following are not *governmental regulatory bodies*—

(1) Regulatory bodies whose decisions are not subject to judicial appeal; and

(2) Regulatory bodies which regulate a company owned by the same entity which creates the regulatory body.

Long-haul telecommunications means all general and special purpose long-distance telecommunications facilities and services (including commercial satellite services, terminal equipment and local circuitry supporting the long-haul service) to or from the post, camp, base, or station switch and/or main distribution frame (except for trunk lines to the first-serving commercial central office for local communications services).

Noncommon carrier means any entity other than a common carrier offering telecommunications facilities, services, or equipment for lease.

Securing, sensitive information, and *telecommunications systems* have the meaning given in the clause at 252.239-7016, Telecommunications Security Equipment, Devices, Techniques, and Services.

Telecommunications means the transmission, emission, or reception of signals, signs, writing, images, sounds, or intelligence of any nature, by wire, cable, satellite, fiber optics, laser, radio, or any other electronic, electric, electromagnetic, or acoustically coupled means.

Telecommunications services means the services acquired, whether by lease or contract, to meet the Government's telecommunications needs. The term includes the telecommunications facilities and equipment necessary to provide such services.

[Final rule, 70 FR 67918, 11/9/2005, effective 11/9/2005; Final rule, 81 FR 28732, 5/10/2016, effective 5/10/2016]

239.7402 Policy.

(a) *Acquisition.* DoD policy is to acquire telecommunications services from common and noncommon telecommunications carriers—

(1) On a competitive basis, except when acquisition using other than full and open competition is justified;

(2) Recognizing the regulations, practices, and decisions of the Federal Communications Commission (FCC) and other governmental regulatory bodies on rates, cost principles, and accounting practices; and

(3) Making provision in telecommunications services contracts for adoption of—

(i) FCC approved practices; or

(ii) The generally accepted practices of the industry on those issues concerning common carrier services where—

(A) The governmental regulatory body has not expressed itself;

(B) The governmental regulatory body has declined jurisdiction; or

(C) There is no governmental regulatory body to decide.

(b) *Security.* (1) The contracting officer shall ensure, in accordance with agency procedures, that purchase requests identify—

(i) The nature and extent of information requiring security during telecommunications;

(ii) The requirement for the contractor to secure telecommunications systems;

(iii) The telecommunications security equipment, devices, techniques, or services with which the contractor's telecommunications security equipment, devices, techniques, or services must be interoperable; and

(iv) The approved telecommunications security equipment, devices, techniques, or services, such as found in the National Security Agency's Information Systems Security Products and Services Catalogue.

(2) Contractors and subcontractors shall provide all telecommunications security techniques or services required for performance of Government contracts.

(3) Except as provided in paragraph (b)(4) of this section, contractors and subcontractors shall normally provide all required property, to include telecommunications security equipment or related devices, in accordance with FAR 45.102. In some cases, such as for communications security (COMSEC) equipment designated as controlled cryptographic item (CCI), contractors or subcontractors must also meet ownership eligibility conditions.

(4) The head of the agency may authorize provision of the necessary property as Government-furnished property or acquisition as contractor-acquired property, as long as conditions of FAR 45.102(b) are met.

(c) *Foreign carriers.* For information on contracting with foreign carriers, see PGI 239.7402(c).

(d) *Long-haul telecommunications services.* When there is a requirement for procurement of long-haul telecommunications services, follow PGI 239.7402(d).

[DAC 91-1, 56 FR 67220, 12/30/91, effective 12/31/91; Final rule, 62 FR 1058, 1/8/97, effective 1/8/97, finalized without change, DAC 91-12, 62 FR 34114, 6/24/97, effective 6/24/97; Final rule, 71 FR 39010, 7/11/2006, effective 7/11/2006; Final rule, 74 FR 37645, 7/29/2009, effective 7/29/2009; Final rule, 81 FR 28732, 5/10/2016, effective 5/10/2016]

239.7403 [Removed and Reserved]

[Final rule, 71 FR 39010, 7/11/2006, effective 7/11/2006]

239.7404 [Removed and Reserved]

[Final rule, 71 FR 39010, 7/11/2006, effective 7/11/2006]

239.7405 Delegated authority for telecommunications resources.

The contracting officer may enter into a telecommunications service contract on a month-to-month basis or for any longer period or series of periods, not to exceed a total of 10 years. See PGI 239.7405 for documents relating to this contracting authority, which the General Services Administration has delegated to DoD.

[DAC 91-13, 63 FR 11522, 3/9/98, effective 3/9/98; Final rule, 70 FR 67918, 11/9/2005, effective 11/9/2005]

239.7406 Certified cost or pricing data and data other than certified cost or pricing data.

(a) Common carriers are not required to submit certified cost or pricing data before award of contracts for tariffed services. Rates or preliminary estimates quoted by a common carrier for tariffed telecommunications services are considered to be prices set by regulation within the provisions of 10 U.S.C. 2306a. This is true even if the tariff is set after execution of the contract.

(b) Rates or preliminary estimates quoted by a common carrier for nontariffed telecommunications services or by a noncommon carrier for any telecommunications service are not considered prices set by law or regulation.

(c) Contracting officers shall obtain sufficient data to determine that the prices are reasonable in accordance with FAR 15.403-3 or FAR 15.403-4. See PGI 239.7406 for examples of instances where additional data may be necessary to determine price reasonableness.

[Final rule, 62 FR 40471, 7/29/97, effective 7/29/97; DAC 91-13, 63 FR 11522, 3/9/98, effective 3/9/98; Final rule, 70 FR 67919, 11/9/2005, effective 11/9/2005; Final rule, 71 FR 39010, 7/11/2006, effective 7/11/2006; Final rule, 77 FR 76939, 12/31/2012, effective 12/31/2012]

239.7407 Type of contract.

When acquiring telecommunications services, the contracting officer may use a basic agreement (see FAR 16.702) in conjunction with communication service authorizations. When using this method, follow the procedures at PGI 239.7407.

[Final rule, 71 FR 27645, 5/12/2006, effective 5/12/2006]

239.7407-1 [Removed]

[Final rule, 71 FR 27645, 5/12/2006, effective 5/12/2006]

239.7407-2 [Removed]

[Final rule, 71 FR 27645, 5/12/2006, effective 5/12/2006]

239.7408 Special construction. (No Text)

239.7408-1 General.

(a) Special construction normally involves a common carrier giving a special service or facility related to the performance of the basic telecommunications service requirements.

This may include—

(1) Moving or relocating equipment;

(2) Providing temporary facilities;

(3) Expediting provision of facilities; or

(4) Providing specially constructed channel facilities to meet Government requirements.

(b) Use this subpart instead of FAR part 36 for acquisition of "special construction."

(c) Special construction costs may be—

(1) A contingent liability for using telecommunications services for a shorter time than the minimum to reimburse the contractor for unamortized nonrecoverable costs. These costs are usually expressed in terms of a termination liability, as provided in the contract or by tariff;

(2) A onetime special construction charge;

(3) Recurring charges for constructed facilities;

(4) A minimum service charge;

(5) An expediting charge; or

(6) A move or relocation charge.

(d) When a common carrier submits a proposal or quotation which has special construction requirements, the contracting officer shall require a detailed special construction proposal. Analyze all special construction proposals to—

(1) Determine the adequacy of the proposed construction;

(2) Disclose excessive or duplicative construction; and

(3) When different forms of charge are possible, provide for the form of charge most advantageous to the Government.

(e) When possible, analyze and approve special construction charges before receiving the service. Impose a ceiling on the special construction costs before authorizing the contractor to proceed, if prior approval is not possible. The contracting officer must approve special construction charges before final payment.

[Final rule, 71 FR 39010, 7/11/2006, effective 7/11/2006]

239.7408-2 Applicability of construction labor standards for special construction.

(a) The construction labor standards in FAR Subpart 22.4 ordinarily do not apply to special construction. However, if the special construction includes construction, alteration, or repair (as defined in FAR 22.401) of a public building or public work, the construction labor standards may apply. Determine applicability under FAR 22.402.

(b) Each CSA or other type contract which is subject to construction labor standards under FAR 22.402 shall cite that fact.

[Final rule, 71 FR 39010, 7/11/2006, effective 7/11/2006]

239.7409 Special assembly.

(a) Special assembly is the designing, manufacturing, arranging, assembling, or wiring of equipment to provide telecommunications services that cannot be provided with general use equipment.

(b) Special assembly rates and charges shall be based on estimated costs. The contracting officer should negotiate special assembly rates and charges before starting service. When it is not possible to negotiate in advance, use provisional rates and charges subject to adjustment, until final rates and charges are negotiated. The CSAs authorizing the special assembly shall be modified to reflect negotiated final rates and charges.

[Final rule, 71 FR 39010, 7/11/2006, effective 7/11/2006]

239.7410 Cancellation and termination.

(a) (1) Cancellation is stopping a requirement after placing of an order but before service starts.

(2) Termination is stopping a requirement after placing an order and after service starts.

(b) Determine cancellation or termination charges under the provisions of the applicable tariff or agreement/contract.

239.7411 Contract clauses.

(a) In addition to other appropriate FAR and DFARS clauses, use the following clauses in solicitations, contracts, and basic agreements for telecommunications services. Modify the clauses only if necessary to meet the requirements of a governmental regulatory agency.

(1) 252.239-7002, Access.

(2) 252.239-7004, Orders for Facilities and Services.

(3) 252.239-7006, Tariff Information.

(4) 252.239-7007, Cancellation or Termination of Orders.

(b) Use the following clauses in solicitations, contracts, and basic agreements for telecommunications services when the acquisition includes or may include special construction. Modify the clauses only if necessary to meet the requirements of a governmental regulatory agency—

(1) 252.239-7011, Special Construction and Equipment Charges; and

(2) 252.239-7012, Title to Telecommunication Facilities and Equipment.

(c) Use the basic or alternate of the clause at 252.239-7013, Term of Agreement and Continuation of Services, in basic agreements for telecommunications services.

(1) Use the basic clause in basic agreements that do not supersede an existing basic agreement with the contractor.

(2) Use the alternate I clause in basic agreements that supersede an existing basic agreement with the contractor. Complete paragraph (c) (1) of the clause with the basic agreement number, date, and contacting office that issued the basic agreement being superseded.

(d) Use the clause at 252.239-7016, Telecommunications Security Equipment, Devices, Techniques, and Services, in solicitations and contracts when performance of a contract requires secure telecommunications.

[DAC 91-3, 57 FR 42632, 9/15/92, effective 8/31/92; Final rule, 62 FR 40471, 7/29/97, effective 7/29/97; Final rule, 70 FR 67919, 11/9/2005, effective 11/9/2005; Final rule, 71 FR 39010, 7/11/2006, effective 7/11/2006; Final rule, 84 FR 48496, 9/13/2019, effective 9/13/2019; Final rule, 84 FR 48498, 9/13/2019, effective 9/13/2019; Final rule, 84 FR 58337, 10/31/2019, effective 10/31/2019]

SUBPART 239.75—[REMOVED]

239.7500 [Removed]

[DAC 91-2, 57 FR 14995, 4/23/92, effective 4/16/92; DAC 91-12, 62 FR 34114, 6/24/97, effective 6/24/97; Final rule, 71 FR 39010, 7/11/2006, effective 7/11/2006]

239.7501 [Removed]

[Final rule, 62 FR 1058, 1/8/97, effective 1/8/97, finalized without change, DAC 91-12, 62 FR 34114, 6/24/97, effective 6/24/97; Final rule, 71 FR 39010, 7/11/2006, effective 7/11/2006]

SUBPART 239.76—CLOUD COMPUTING

239.7600 Scope of subpart.

This subpart prescribes policies and procedures for the acquisition of cloud computing services.

[Interim rule, 80 FR 51739, 8/26/2015, effective 8/26/2015]

239.7601 Definitions.

As used in this subpart—

Authorizing official, as described in DoD Instruction 8510.01, Risk Management Framework (RMF) for DoD Information Technology (IT), means the senior Federal official or executive with the authority to formally assume responsibility for operating an information system at an acceptable level of risk to organizational operations (including mission, functions, image, or reputation), organizational assets, individuals, other organizations, and the Nation.

Cloud computing means a model for enabling ubiquitous, convenient, on-demand network access to a shared pool of configurable computing resources (e.g., networks, servers, storage, applications, and services) that can be rapidly provisioned and released with minimal management effort or service provider interaction. This includes other commercial terms, such as on-demand self-service, broad network access, resource pooling, rapid elasticity, and measured service. It also includes commercial offerings for software-as-a-service, infrastructure-as-a-service, and platform-as-a-service.

Government data means any information, document, media, or machine readable material regardless of physical form or characteristics, that is created or obtained by the Government in the course of official Government business.

Government-related data means any information, document, media, or machine readable material regardless of physical form or characteristics that is created or obtained by a contractor through the storage, processing, or communication of Government data. This does not include a contractor's business records (e.g., financial records, legal records, etc.) or data such as operating procedures, software coding, or algorithms that are not uniquely applied to the Government data.

Information system means a discrete set of information resources organized for the collection, processing, maintenance, use, sharing, dissemination, or disposition of information.

Media means physical devices or writing surfaces including, but not limited to, magnetic tapes, optical disks, magnetic disks, large-scale integration memory chips, and printouts onto which information is recorded, stored, or printed within an information system.

[Interim rule, 80 FR 51739, 8/26/2015, effective 8/26/2015; Final rule, 81 FR 72986, 10/21/2016, effective 10/21/2016]

239.7602 Policy and responsibilities. (No Text)

[Interim rule, 80 FR 51739, 8/26/2015, effective 8/26/2015]

239.7602-1 General.

(a) Generally, DoD shall acquire cloud computing services using commercial terms and conditions that are consistent with Federal law, and an agency's needs, including those requirements specified in this subpart. Some examples of commercial terms and conditions are license agreements, End User License Agreements (EULAs), Terms of Service (TOS), or other similar legal instruments or agreements. Contracting officers shall incorporate any applicable service provider terms and conditions into the contract by attachment or other appropriate mechanism. Contracting officers shall carefully review commercial terms and conditions and consult counsel to ensure these are consistent with Federal law, regulation, and the agency's needs.

(b) (1) Except as provided in paragraph (b) (2) of this section, the contracting officer shall only award a contract to acquire cloud computing services from a cloud service provider (e.g., contractor or subcontractor, regardless of tier) that has been granted provisional authorization by Defense Information Systems Agency, at the level appropriate to the requirement, to provide the relevant cloud computing services in accordance with the Cloud Computing Security Requirements Guide (SRG) (version in effect at the time the solicitation is issued or as authorized by the contracting officer) found at *http://iase.disa.mil/cloud_security/Pages/index.aspx.*

(2) The contracting officer may award a contract to acquire cloud computing services from a cloud service provider that has not been granted provisional authorization when—

(i) The requirement for a provisional authorization is waived by the DoD Chief Information Officer; or

(ii) The cloud computing service requirement is for a private, on-premises version that will be provided from U.S. Government facilities. Under this circumstance, the cloud service provider must obtain a provisional authorization prior to operational use.

(c) When contracting for cloud computing services, the contracting officer shall ensure the following information is provided by the requiring activity:

(1) Government data and Government-related data descriptions.

(2) Data ownership, licensing, delivery and disposition instructions specific to the relevant types of Government data and Government-related data (e.g., DD Form 1423, Contract Data Requirements List; work statement task;, line item). Disposition instructions shall provide for the transition of data in commercially available, or open and non-proprietary format (and for permanent records, in accordance with disposition guidance issued by National Archives and Record Administration).

(3) Appropriate requirements to support applicable inspection, audit, investigation, or other similar authorized activities specific to the relevant types of Government data and Government-related data, or specific to the type of cloud computing services being acquired.

(4) Appropriate requirements to support and cooperate with applicable system-wide search and access capabilities for inspections, audits, investigations, and similar authorized activities.

[Interim rule, 80 FR 51739, 8/26/2015, effective 8/26/2015; Final rule, 81 FR 72986, 10/21/2016, effective 10/21/2016]

239.7602-2 Required storage of data within the United States or outlying areas.

(a) Cloud computing service providers are required to maintain within the 50 states, the District of Columbia, or outlying areas of the United States, all Government data that is not physically located on DoD premises, unless otherwise authorized by the authorizing official, as described in DoD Instruction 8510.01, in accordance with the SRG.

(b) The contracting officer shall provide written notification to the contractor when the contractor is permitted to maintain Government data at a location outside the 50 States, the District of Columbia, and outlying areas of the United States.

[Interim rule, 80 FR 51739, 8/26/2015, effective 8/26/2015; Final rule, 81 FR 72986, 10/21/2016, effective 10/21/2016]

239.7603 Procedures.

Follow the procedures relating to cloud computing at PGI 239.7603.

[Final rule, 80 FR 74694, 11/30/2015, effective 11/30/2015]

239.7604 Solicitation provision and contract clause.

(a) Use the provision at 252.239-7009, Representation of Use of Cloud Computing, in solicitations, including solicitations using FAR part 12 procedures for the acquisition of commercial item, for information technology services.

(b) Use the clause at 252.239-7010, Cloud Computing Services, in solicitations and contracts, including solicitations and contracts using FAR part 12 procedures for the acquisition of commercial item, for information technology services.

[Interim rule, 80 FR 51739, 8/26/2015, effective 8/26/2015; Final rule, 80 FR 74694, 11/30/2015, effective 11/30/2015]

PART 240—[NO FAR SUPPLEMENT]

PART 241—ACQUISITION OF UTILITY SERVICES

Table of Contents

Subpart 241.1—General

Definitions 241.101
Applicability 241.102
Statutory and delegated authority 241.103

Subpart 241.2—Acquiring Utility Services

Policy 241.201
Procedures 241.202
[Removed] 241.203
Separate contracts 241.205
[Removed] 241.270

Subpart 241.5—Solicitation Provision and Contract Clauses

Solicitation provision and contract clauses 241.501
Additional clauses 241.501-70

PART 241—ACQUISITION OF UTILITY SERVICES

SUBPART 241.1—GENERAL

241.101 Definitions.

As used in this part—

Independent regulatory body means the Federal Energy Regulatory Commission, a state-wide agency, or an agency with less than state-wide jurisdiction when operating pursuant to state authority. The body has the power to fix, establish, or control the rates and services of utility suppliers.

Nonindependent regulatory body means a body that regulates a utility supplier which is owned or operated by the same entity that created the regulatory body, *e.g.*, a municipal utility.

Regulated utility supplier means a utility supplier regulated by an independent regulatory body.

Service power procurement officer means for the—

(1) Army, the Chief of Engineers;

(2) Navy, the Commander, Naval Facilities Engineering Command;

(3) Air Force, the head of a contracting activity; and

(4) Defense Logistics Agency, the head of a contracting activity.

[DAC 91-13, 63 FR 11522, 3/9/98, effective 3/9/98; Final rule, 71 FR 3416, 1/23/2006, effective 1/23/2006]

241.102 Applicability.

(a) This part applies to purchase of utility services from nonregulated and regulated utility suppliers. It includes the acquisition of liquefied petroleum gas as a utility service when purchased from regulated utility suppliers.

(b) (7) This part does not apply to third party financed projects. However, it may be used for any purchased utility services directly resulting from such projects, including those authorized by—

(A) 10 U.S.C. 2394 for energy, fuels, and energy production facilities for periods not to exceed 30 years;

(B) 10 U.S.C. 2394a for renewable energy for periods not to exceed 25 years;

(C) 10 U.S.C. 2689 for geothermal resources that result in energy production facilities;

(D) 10 U.S.C. 2809 for potable and waste water treatment plants for periods not to exceed 32 years; and

(E) 10 U.S.C. 2812 for lease/purchase of energy production facilities for periods not to exceed 32 years.

[DAC 91-13, 63 FR 11522, 3/9/98, effective 3/9/98]

241.103 Statutory and delegated authority.

(1) The contracting officer may enter into a utility service contract related to the conveyance of a utility system for a period not to exceed 50 years (10 U.S.C. 2688(d) (2)).

(2) The contracting officer may enter into an energy savings contract under 10 U.S.C. 2913 for a period not to exceed 25 years.

(3) See 217.174 for authority to enter into multiyear contracts for electricity from renewable energy sources.

(4) See PGI 241.103 for statutory authorities and maximum contract periods for utility and energy contracts.

[Interim rule, 65 FR 2058, 1/13/2000, effective 1/13/2000, corrected 65 FR 19818, 4/12/2000, finalized without change, 65 FR 32040, 5/22/2000; Final rule, 71 FR 3416, 1/23/2006, effective 1/23/2006; Final rule, 74 FR 52895, 10/15/2009, effective 10/15/2009; Interim rule, 75 FR 34942, 6/21/2010, effective 6/21/2010; Final rule, 76 FR 14587, 3/17/2011, effective 3/17/2011; Final rule, 76 FR 58152, 9/20/2011, effective 9/20/2011; Final rule, 81 FR 28733, 5/10/2016, effective 5/10/2016]

SUBPART 241.2—ACQUIRING UTILITY SERVICES

241.201 Policy.

(1) DoD, as a matter of comity, generally complies with the current regulations, practices, and decisions of independent regula-

tory bodies. This policy does not extend to nonindependent regulatory bodies.

(2) Purchases of utility services outside the United States may use—

(i) Formats and technical provisions consistent with local practice; and

(ii) Dual language forms and contracts.

(3) Rates established by an independent regulatory body—

(i) Are considered "prices set by law or regulation";

(ii) Are sufficient to set prices without obtaining certified cost or pricing data (see FAR subpart 15.4); and

(iii) Are a valid basis on which prices can be determined fair and reasonable.

(4) Compliance with the regulations, practices, and decisions of independent regulatory bodies as a matter of comity is not a substitute for the procedures at FAR 41.202(a).

[DAC 91-13, 63 FR 11522, 3/9/98, effective 3/9/98; Final rule, 71 FR 3418, 1/23/2006, effective 1/23/2006; Final rule, 77 FR 76939, 12/31/2012, effective 12/31/2012]

241.202 Procedures.

(1) *Connection and service charges.* The Government may pay a connection charge when required to cover the cost of the necessary connecting facilities. A connection charge based on the estimated labor cost of installing and removing the facility shall not include salvage cost. A lump-sum connection charge shall be no more than the agreed cost of the connecting facilities less net salvage. The order of precedence for contractual treatment of connection and service charges is—

(i) *No connection charge.*

(ii) *Termination liability.* Use when an obligation is necessary to secure the required services. The obligation must be not more than the agreed connection charge, less any net salvage material costs. Use of a termination liability instead of a connection charge requires the approval of the service power procurement officer or designee.

(iii) *Connection charge, refundable.* Use a refundable connection charge when the supplier refuses to provide the facilities based on lack of capital or published rules which prohibit providing up-front funding. The contract should provide for refund of the connection charge within five years unless a longer period or omission of the refund requirement is authorized by the service power procurement officer or designee.

(iv) *Connection and service charges, nonrefundable.* The Government may pay certain nonrefundable, nonrecurring charges including service initiation charges, a contribution in aid of construction, membership fees, and charges required by the supplier's rules and regulations to be paid by the customer. If possible, consider sharing with other than Government users the use of (and costs for) facilities when large nonrefundable charges are required.

(2) *Construction and labor requirements.* Follow the procedures at PGI 241.202(2) for construction and labor requirements associated with connection and service charges.

[DAC 91-13, 63 FR 11522, 3/9/98, effective 3/9/98; Final rule, 71 FR 3416, 1/23/2006, effective 1/23/2006]

241.203 [Removed]

[DAC 91-13, 63 FR 11522, 3/9/98, effective 3/9/98; Final rule, 71 FR 3416, 1/23/2006, effective 1/23/2006]

241.205 Separate contracts.

Follow the procedures at PGI 241.205 when acquiring utility services by separate contract.

[DAC 91-13, 63 FR 11522, 3/9/98, effective 3/9/98; Final rule, 71 FR 3416, 1/23/2006, effective 1/23/2006]

241.270 [Removed]

[DAC 91-13, 63 FR 11522, 3/9/98, effective 3/9/98; Final rule, 71 FR 3416, 1/23/2006, effective 1/23/2006]

SUBPART 241.5—SOLICITATION PROVISION AND CONTRACT CLAUSES

241.501 Solicitation provision and contract clauses.

(d) (1) Use a clause substantially the same as the clause at FAR 52.241-7, Change in Rates or Terms and Conditions of Service for Regulated Services, when the utility services to be provided are subject to an independent regulatory body.

(2) Use a clause substantially the same as the clause at FAR 52.241-8, Change in Rates or Terms and Conditions of Service for Unregulated Services, when the utility services to be provided are not subject to a regulatory body or are subject to a nonindependent regulatory body.

[Final rule, 71 FR 3418, 1/23/2006, effective 1/23/2006]

241.501-70 Additional clauses.

(a) If the Government must execute a superseding contract and capital credits, connection charge credits, or termination liability exist, use the clause at 252.241-7000, Superseding Contract.

(b) Use the clause at 252.241-7001, Government Access, when the clause at FAR 52.241-5, Contractor's Facilities, is used.

[DAC 91-13, 63 FR 11522, 3/9/98, effective 3/9/98]

Defense Federal Acquisition Regulation Supplement Parts 242—251

CONTRACT MANAGEMENT

Table of Contents

Page

SUBCHAPTER G—CONTRACT MANAGEMENT

Part 242—Contract Administration and Audit Services 567
Part 243—Contract Modifications 585
Part 244—Subcontracting Policies and Procedures 591
Part 245—Government Property 597
Part 246—Quality Assurance 609
Part 247—Transportation 623
Part 248—[NO FAR SUPPLEMENT]
Part 249—Termination of Contracts 633
Part 250—Extraordinary Contractual Actions and the Safety Act 639
Part 251—Use of Government Sources by Contractors 643

See page 39 for an explanation of the numbering of the DFARS.

PART 242—CONTRACT ADMINISTRATION AND AUDIT SERVICES

Table of Contents

Interagency agreements 242.002

Subpart 242.2—Contract Administration Services

Scope of subpart 242.200-70
Assignment of contract administration 242.202

Subpart 242.3—Contract Administration Office Functions

General 242.301
Contract administration functions 242.302

Subpart 242.4—[Removed]

Subpart 242.5—Postaward Orientation

Postaward conferences 242.503
Postaward conference procedure 242.503-2
[Removed] 242.503-3
[Removed] 242.570

Subpart 242.6—Corporate Administrative Contracting Officer

Assignment and location 242.602

Subpart 242.7—Indirect Cost Rates

[Removed] 242.704
Final indirect cost rates 242.705
Contracting officer determination procedure 242.705-1
Auditor determination procedure 242.705-2
[Removed] 242.705-3
Independent research and development and bid and proposal costs 242.771
Scope 242.771-1
Policy 242.771-2
Responsibilities 242.771-3

Subpart 242.8—Disallowance of Costs

[Removed] 242.801
Disallowing costs after incurrence 242.803

Subpart 242.11—Production Surveillance and Reporting

Surveillance requirements 242.1104
Assignment of criticality designator 242.1105
Reporting requirements 242.1106
Contract clause 242.1107
[Removed] 242.1107-70

Subpart 242.12—Novation and Change-of-Name Agreements

[Removed] 242.1202
Processing agreements 242.1203
Agreement to recognize a successor in interest (novation agreement) 242.1204

Subpart 242.14—[Removed]

Subpart 242.15—Contractor Performance Information

Policy 242.1502

Subpart 242.70—Contractor Business Systems

Contractor business system deficiencies 242.7000
Contract clause 242.7001

Subpart 242.71—Voluntary Refunds

General 242.7100
[Removed] 242.7101
[Removed] 242.7102

Subpart 242.72—Contractor Material Management and Accounting System

Scope of subpart 242.7200
Definitions 242.7201
Policy 242.7202
Review procedures 242.7203
Contract clause 242.7204

Subpart 242.73—Contractor Insurance/Pension Review

[Removed] 242.7300
General 242.7301
Requirements 242.7302
Responsibilities 242.7303

Subpart 242.74—Technical Representation at Contractor Facilities

General 242.7400
Procedures 242.7401

Subpart 242.75—Contractor Accounting Systems and Related Controls

Definitions 242.7501
Policy 242.7502
Contract clause 242.7503

SUBCHAPTER G—CONTRACT MANAGEMENT (Parts 242-251)

PART 242—CONTRACT ADMINISTRATION AND AUDIT SERVICES

242.002 Interagency agreements.

(b) (i) DoD requires reimbursement, at a rate set by the Under Secretary of Defense (Comptroller/Chief Financial Officer), from non-DoD organizations, except for—

(A) Quality assurance, contract administration, and audit services provided under a no-charge reciprocal agreement;

(B) Services performed under subcontracts awarded by the Small Business Administration under FAR subpart 19.8; and

(C) Quality assurance requests performed for the Canadian Department of National Defence and pricing services performed for Public Works and Government Services Canada (PWGSC), operating as Public Services and Procurment Canada (PSPC).

(ii) Departments and agencies may request an exception from the reimbursement policy in paragraph (b) (i) of this section from the Under Secretary of Defense (Comptroller/Chief Financial Officer). A request must show that an exception is in the best interest of the Government.

(iii) Departments and agencies must pay for services performed by non-DoD activities, foreign governments, or international organizations, unless otherwise provided by reciprocal agreements.

(S-70) (i) Foreign governments and international organizations may request contract administration services on their direct purchases from U.S. producers. Direct purchase is the purchase of defense supplies in the United States through commercial channels for use by the foreign government or international organization.

(ii) PWGSC, operating as PSPC, is permitted to submit its requests for contract administration services directly to the cognizant contract administration office.

(iii) Other foreign governments (including Canadian government organizations other than PSPC) and international organizations send their requests for contract administration services to the DoD Central Control Point (CCP) at the Headquarters, Defense Contract Management Agency, International and Federal Business Team. Contract administration offices provide services only upon request from the CCP. The CCP shall follow the procedures at PGI 242.002(S-70) (iii).

[Final rule, 64 FR 61028, 11/9/99, effective 11/9/99; Final rule, 65 FR 52951, 8/31/2000, effective 8/31/2000; Final rule, 65 FR 63804, 10/25/2000, effective 10/25/2000; Final rule, 70 FR 67919, 11/9/2005, effective 11/9/2005; Final rule, 83 FR 12681, 3/23/2018, effective 3/23/2018]

SUBPART 242.2—CONTRACT ADMINISTRATION SERVICES

242.200-70 Scope of subpart.

This subpart does not address the contract administration role of a contracting officer's representative (see 201.602).

[Final rule, 64 FR 61028, 11/9/99, effective 11/9/99]

242.202 Assignment of contract administration.

(a) (i) DoD activities shall not retain any contract for administration that requires performance of any contract administration function at or near contractor facilities, except contracts for—

(A) The National Security Agency;

(B) Research and development with universities;

(C) Flight training;

(D) Management and professional support services;

(E) Mapping, charting, and geodesy services;

(F) Base, post, camp, and station purchases;

(G) Operation or maintenance of, or installation of equipment at, radar or communication network sites;

(H) Communications services;

(I) Installation, operation, and maintenance of space-track sensors and relays;

(J) Dependents Medicare program contracts;

(K) Stevedoring contracts;

(L) Construction and maintenance of military and civil public works, including harbors, docks, port facilities, military housing, development of recreational facilities, water resources, flood control, and public utilities;

(M) Architect-engineer services;

(N) Airlift and sealift services (Air Mobility Command and Military Sealift Command may perform contract administration services at contractor locations involved solely in performance of airlift or sealift contracts);

(O) Subsistence supplies;

(P) Ballistic missile sites (contract administration offices may perform supporting administration of these contracts at missile activation sites during the installation, test, and checkout of the missiles and associated equipment);

(Q) Operation and maintenance of, or installation of equipment at, military test ranges, facilities, and installations; and

(R) The Defense Energy Support Center, Defense Logistics Agency.

(ii) Contract administration functions for base, post, camp, and station contracts on a military installation are normally the responsibility of the installation or tenant commander. However, the Defense Contract Management Agency (DCMA) shall, upon request of the military department, and subject to prior agreement, perform contract administration services on a military installation.

(iii) DCMA shall provide preaward survey assistance for post, camp, and station work performed on a military installation. The contracting office and the DCMA preaward survey monitor should jointly determine the scope of the survey and individual responsibilities.

(iv) To avoid duplication, contracting offices shall not locate their personnel at contractor facilities, except—

(A) In support of contracts retained for administration in accordance with paragraph (a)(i) of this section; or

(B) As permitted under subpart 242.74.

(e)(1)(A) In special circumstances, a contract administration office may request support from a component not listed in the Federal Directory of Contract Administration Services Components (available via the Internet at *https:/pubapp.dcma.mil/CASD/main.jsp*). An example is a situation where the contractor's work site is on a military base and a base organization is asked to provide support. Before formally sending the request, coordinate with the office concerned to ensure that resources are available for, and capable of, providing the support.

(B) When requesting support on a subcontract that includes foreign contract military sale (FMS) requirements, the contract administration office shall—

(*1*) Mark "FMS Requirement" on the face of the documents; and

(*2*) For each FMS case involved, provide the FMS case identifier, associated item quantities, DoD prime contract number, and prime contract line/subline item number.

[Final rule, 64 FR 61028, 11/09/99; effective 11/09/99; Final rule, 65 FR 52951, 8/31/2000, effective 8/31/2000; Final rule, 66 FR 49860, 10/1/2001, effective 10/1/2001; Final rule, 66 FR 63334, 12/6/2001, effective 12/6/2001; Final rule, 70 FR 52034, 9/1/2005, effective 9/1/2005; Final rule, 70 FR 67919, 11/9/2005, effective 11/9/2005; Final rule, 77 FR 23631, 4/20/2012, effective 4/20/2012]

SUBPART 242.3—CONTRACT ADMINISTRATION OFFICE FUNCTIONS

242.301 General.

Contract administration services performed outside the U.S. should be performed in accordance with FAR 42.301 unless there are no policies and procedures covering a given situation. In this case, coordinate proposed actions with the appropriate U.S. country teams or commanders of unified and specified commands.

242.302 Contract administration functions.

(a) (7) See 242.7502 for ACO responsibilities with regard to receipt of an audit report identifying significant accounting system or related internal control deficiencies.

(9) For additional contract administration functions related to IR&D/B&P projects performed by major contractors, see 242.771-3(a).

(12) Also perform all payment administration in accordance with any applicable payment clauses.

(13) (A) Do not delegate the responsibility to make payments to the Defense Contract Management Agency (DCMA).

(B) Follow the procedures at PGI 242.302(a) (13) (B) for designation of payment offices.

(39) See 223.370 for contract administration responsibilities on contracts for ammunition and explosives.

(67) Also support program offices and buying activities in precontractual efforts leading to a solicitation or award.

(S-70) Serve as the single point of contact for all Single Process Initiative (SPI) Management Council activities. The ACO shall negotiate and execute facilitywide class modifications and agreements for SPI processes, when authorized by the affected components.

(S-71) DCMA has responsibility for reviewing earned value management system (EVMS) plans and for verifying initial and continuing contractor compliance with DoD EVMS criteria. The contracting officer shall not retain this function.

(S-72) Ensure implementation of the Synchronized Predeployment and Operational Tracker (SPOT) by the contractor and maintain surveillance over contractor compliance with SPOT business rules available at the Web site provided at PGI 207.105(b) (20) (C) (*9*) for contracts incorporating the clause at 252.225-7040, Contractor Personnel Supporting U.S. Armed Forces Deployed Outside the United States. See PGI 242.302(a) (S-72) for guidance on assessing contractor's implementation of SPOT.

(S-73) Maintain surveillance over contractor compliance with trafficking in persons requirements for all DoD contracts for services incorporating the clause at FAR 52.222-50, Combating Trafficking in Persons, and, when necessary, its Alternate I, as identified in the clause prescription at FAR 22.1705. (see PGI 222.1703.)

(S-74) Approve or disapprove contractor business systems, as identified in the clause at 252.242-7005, Contractor Business Systems.

(S-75) See PGI 242.302(a) (S-75) for guidelines for monitoring contractor costs.

(S-76) Review and audit contractor identification of contractor-approved suppliers for the acquisition of electronic parts, as identified in the clause at 252.246-7008, Sources of Electronic Parts.

(b) (S-70) Issue, negotiate, and execute orders under basic ordering agreements for overhaul, maintenance, and repair.

[DAC 91-4, 57 FR 53601, 11/12/92, effective 10/30/92; DAC 91-7, 60 FR 29491, 6/5/95, effective 5/17/95; DAC 91-11, 61 FR 50446, 9/26/96, effective 9/26/96; Interim rule, 62 FR 9990, 3/5/97, effective 3/5/97; Final rule, 62 FR 44223, 8/20/97, effective 8/20/97; DAC 91-13, 63 FR 11522, 3/9/98, effective 3/9/98; Final rule, 64 FR 61028, 11/9/99, effective 11/9/99; Final rule, 65 FR 19849, 4/13/2000, effective 4/13/2000; Final rule, 65 FR 52951, 8/31/2000, effective 8/31/2000, corrected, 65 FR 58607, 9/29/2000; Final rule, 66 FR 49860, 10/1/2001, effective 10/1/2001; Final rule, 66 FR 63334, 12/6/2001, effective 12/6/2001; Final rule, 68 FR 15615, 3/31/2003, effective 4/30/2003; Final rule, 71 FR 44928, 8/8/2006, effective 8/8/2006; Final rule, 76 FR 36883, 6/23/2011, effective 6/23/2011; Final rule, 76 FR 71830, 11/18/2011, effective 11/18/2011; Final rule, 77 FR 11355, 2/24/2012, effective 2/24/2012; Final rule, 77 FR 23631, 4/20/2012, effective 4/20/2012; Final rule, 78 FR 13544, 2/28/2013, effective 2/28/2013; Final rule, 79 FR 30469, 5/28/2014, effective 5/28/2014; Final rule, 80 FR 36900, 6/26/2015, effective 6/26/2015; Final rule, 81 FR 50635, 8/2/2016, effective 8/2/2016]

SUBPART 242.4—[REMOVED]

[Final rule, 70 FR 67919, 11/9/2005, effective 11/9/2005]

SUBPART 242.5—POSTAWARD ORIENTATION

242.503 Postaward conferences. (No Text)

242.503-2 Postaward conference procedure.

(a) DD Form 1484, Post-Award Conference Record, may be used in conducting the conference and in preparing the conference report.

(b) For contracts that include the clause at 252.234-7004, Cost and Software Data Reporting, postaward conferences shall include a discussion of the contractor's standard cost and software data reporting (CSDR) process that satisfies the guidelines contained in the DoD 5000.04-M-1, CSDR Manual, and the requirements in the Government-approved CSDR plan for the contract, DD Form 2794, and related Resource Distribution Table.

[Final rule, 70 FR 67919, 11/9/2005, effective 11/9/2005; Final rule, 75 FR 71560, 11/24/2010, effective 11/24/2010]

242.503-3 [Removed]

[Final rule, 70 FR 67919, 11/9/2005, effective 11/9/2005]

242.570 [Removed]

[Final rule, 70 FR 67919, 11/9/2005, effective 11/9/2005]

SUBPART 242.6—CORPORATE ADMINISTRATIVE CONTRACTING OFFICER

242.602 Assignment and location.

(c) (2) If the agencies cannot agree, refer the matter to the Director of Defense Procurement and Acquisition Policy.

[Final rule, 68 FR 7438, 2/14/2003, effective 2/14/2003]

SUBPART 242.7—INDIRECT COST RATES

242.704 [Removed]

[Final rule, 70 FR 67919, 11/9/2005, effective 11/9/2005]

242.705 Final indirect cost rates. (No Text)

242.705-1 Contracting officer determination procedure.

(a) *Applicability and responsibility.*

(1) The corporate administrative contracting officer and individual administrative contracting officers shall jointly decide how to conduct negotiations. Follow the procedures at PGI 242.705-1(a) (1) when negotiations are conducted on a coordinated basis.

[DAC 91-9, 60 FR 61586, 11/30/95, effective 11/30/95; Final rule, 64 FR 61028, 11/9/99, effective 11/9/99; Final rule, 70 FR 67919, 11/9/2005, effective 11/9/2005]

242.705-2 Auditor determination procedure.

(b) *Procedures.*

(2) (iii) When agreement cannot be reached with the contractor, the auditor will issue a DCAA Form 1, Notice of Contract Costs Suspended and/or Disapproved, in addition to the advisory report to the administrative contracting officer.

[DAC 91-9, 60 FR 61586, 11/30/95, effective 11/30/95, Final rule, 64 FR 61028, 11/9/99, effective 11/9/99; Final rule, 70 FR 67919, 11/9/2005, effective 11/9/2005]

242.705-3 [Removed]

[Final rule, 59 FR 53116, 10/21/94, effective 10/18/94; Final rule, 70 FR 67919, 11/9/2005, effective 11/9/2005]

242.771 Independent research and development and bid and proposal costs. (No Text)

242.771-1 Scope.

This section implements 10 U.S.C. 2372, Independent research and development and bid and proposal costs: Payments to contractors.

[Final rule, 64 FR 8729, 2/23/99, effective 2/23/99]

242.771-2 Policy.

Defense contractors are encouraged to engage in independent research and development and bid and proposal (IR&D/B&P) activities of potential interest to DoD, including activities cited in 231.205-18(c)(iii)(B).

[Final rule, 64 FR 8729, 2/23/99, effective 2/23/99]

242.771-3 Responsibilities.

(a) The cognizant administrative contracting officer (ACO) or corporate ACO shall—

(1) Determine cost allowability of IR&D/B&P costs as set forth in 231.205-18 and FAR 31.205-18.

(2) Determine whether IR&D/B&P projects performed by major contractors (see 231.205-18(a)) are of potential interest to DoD; and

(3) Notify the contractor promptly of any IR&D/B&P activities that are not of potential interest to DoD.

(b) The Defense Contract Management Agency or the military department responsible for performing contract administration functions is responsible for providing the Defense Contract Audit Agency (DCAA) with IR&D/B&P statistical information, as necessary, to assist DCAA in the annual report required by paragraph (c) of this subsection.

(c) DCAA is responsible for submitting an annual report to the Director of Defense Procurement and Acquisition Policy, Office of the Under Secretary of Defense (Acquisition, Technology, and Logistics) (OUSD (AT&L))), setting forth required statistical information relating to the DoD-wide IR&D/B&P program.

(d) The Office of the Assistant Secretary of Defense for Research and Engineering (OASD R&E), is responsible for establishing a regular method for communication—

(1) From DoD to contractors, of timely and comprehensive information regarding planned or expected DoD future needs; and

(2) From contractors to DoD, of brief technical descriptions of contractor IR&D projects.

[Final rule, 64 FR 8729, 2/23/99, effective 2/23/99; Final rule, 65 FR 39703, 6/27/2000, effective 6/27/2000; Final rule, 65 FR 52951, 8/31/2000, effective 8/31/2000; Final rule, 68 FR 7438, 2/14/2003, effective 2/14/2003; Final rule, 81 FR 78008, 11/4/2016, effective 11/4/2016]

SUBPART 242.8—DISALLOWANCE OF COSTS

242.801 [Removed]

[Final rule, 70 FR 67919, 11/9/2005, effective 11/9/2005]

242.803 Disallowing costs after incurrence.

(a) *Contracting officer receipt of vouchers.* Contracting officer receipt of vouchers is applicable only for cost-reimbursement contracts with the Canadian Commercial Corporation. See 225.870-5(b) for invoice procedures.

(b) *Auditor receipt of voucher.*

(i) The contract auditor is the authorized representative of the contracting officer for—

(A) Receiving vouchers from contractors electronically or by other delivery methods as directed by the terms of the contract;

(B) Approving interim vouchers that were selected using sampling methodologies for provisional payment and sending them to the disbursing office after a pre-payment review. Interim vouchers not selected for a pre-payment review will be considered to be provisionally approved and will be sent directly to the disbursing office. All provisionally approved interim vouchers are subject to a later audit of actual costs incurred;

(C) Reviewing completion/final vouchers and sending them to the administrative contracting officer; and

(D) Issuing DCAA Forms 1, Notice of Contract Costs Suspended and/or Disapproved, to deduct costs where allowability is questionable.

(ii) The administrative contracting officer—

(A) Approves all completion/final vouchers and sends them to the disbursing officer; and

(B) May issue or direct the issuance of DCAA Form 1 on any cost when there is reason to believe it should be suspended or disallowed.

[Final rule, 61 FR 25409, 5/21/96, effective 5/21/96; DAC 91-11, 61 FR 50446, 9/26/96, effective 9/26/96; Final rule, 77 FR 52258, 8/29/2012, effective 8/29/2012]

SUBPART 242.11—PRODUCTION SURVEILLANCE AND REPORTING

242.1104 Surveillance requirements.

(a) The cognizant contract administration office (CAO)—

(i) Shall perform production surveillance on all contractors that have Criticality Designator A or B contracts;

(ii) Shall not perform production surveillance on contractors that have only Criticality Designator C contracts, unless specifically requested by the contracting officer; and

(iii) When production surveillance is required, shall—

(A) Conduct a periodic risk assessment of the contractor to determine the degree of production surveillance needed for all contracts awarded to that contractor. The risk assessment shall consider information provided by the contractor and the contracting officer;

(B) Develop a production surveillance plan based on the risk level determined during a risk assessment;

(C) Modify the production surveillance plan to incorporate any special surveillance requirements for individual contracts, including any requirements identified by the contracting officer; and

(D) Monitor contract progress and identify potential contract delinquencies in accordance with the production surveillance plan. Contracts with Criticality Designator C are exempt from this requirement unless specifically requested by the contracting officer.

[Final rule, 65 FR 39722, 6/27/2000, effective 6/27/2000; Final rule, 69 FR 31912, 6/8/2004, effective 6/8/2004]

242.1105 Assignment of criticality designator.

(1) Contracting officers shall—

(i) Assign criticality designator A to items with a priority 01, 02, 03, or 06 (if emergency supply of clothing) under DoD Manual 4140.01, Volume 5, DoD Supply Chain Materiel Management Procedures: Delivery of Materiel; and

(ii) Ordinarily assign criticality designator C to unilateral purchase orders.

(2) Only the contracting officer shall change the assigned designator.

[Final rule, 67 FR 61516, 10/1/2002, effective 10/1/2002; Final rule, 82 FR 61479, 12/28/2017, effective 12/28/2017]

242.1106 Reporting requirements.

(a) See DoDI 5000.2, Operation of the Defense Acquisition System, for reporting requirements for defense technology projects and acquisition programs.

(b) (i) Within four working days after receipt of the contractor's report, the CAO must provide the report and any required comments to the contracting officer and, unless otherwise specified in the contract, the inventory control manager.

(ii) If the contractor's report indicates that the contract is on schedule and the CAO agrees, the CAO does not need to add further comments. In all other cases, the CAO must add comments and recommend a course of action.

[Final rule, 65 FR 39722, 6/27/2000, effective 6/27/2000; Final rule, 70 FR 14574, 3/23/2005, effective 3/23/2005; Final rule, 73 FR 21846, 4/23/2008, effective 4/23/2008]

242.1107 Contract clause.

(b) When using the clause at FAR 52.242-2, include the following instructions in the contract schedule—

(i) Frequency and timing of reporting (normally 5 working days after each reporting period);

(ii) Contract line items, exhibits, or exhibit line items requiring reports;

(iii) Offices (with addresses/codes) where reports should be sent (always include the contracting office and contract administration office); and

(iv) The following requirements for report content—

(A) The problem, actual or potential, and its cause;

(B) Items and quantities affected;

(C) When the delinquency started or will start;

(D) Actions taken to overcome the delinquency;

(E) Estimated recovery date; and/or

(F) Proposed schedule revision.

242.1107-70 [Removed]

[DAC 91-13, 63 FR 11522, 3/9/98, effective 3/9/98; Final rule, 70 FR 14574, 3/23/2005, effective 3/23/2005; Final rule, 73 FR 21846, 4/23/2008, effective 4/23/2008]

SUBPART 242.12—NOVATION AND CHANGE-OF-NAME AGREEMENTS

242.1202 [Removed]

[Interim rule, 60 FR 1747, 1/5/95, effective 12/29/94; Final rule, 70 FR 67919, 11/9/2005, effective 11/9/2005]

242.1203 Processing agreements.

The responsible contracting officer shall process and execute novation and change-of-name agreements in accordance with the procedures at PGI 242.1203.

[DAC 91-6, 59 FR 27662, 5/27/94, effective 5/27/94; Final rule, 64 FR 51074, 9/21/99, effective 9/21/99; Final rule, 65 FR 39703, 6/27/2000, effective 6/27/2000; Final rule, 65 FR 63804, 10/25/2000, effective 10/25/2000; Final rule, 67 FR 4207, 1/29/2002, effective 1/29/2002; Final rule, 68 FR 7438, 2/14/2003, effective 2/14/2003; Final rule, 70 FR 67919, 11/9/2005, effective 11/9/2005]

242.1204 Agreement to recognize a successor in interest (novation agreement).

(i) When a novation agreement is required and the transferee intends to incur restructuring costs as defined at 213.205-70, the cognizant contracting officer shall include the following provisions as paragraph (b)(7) of the novation agreement instead of the paragraph (b)(7) provided in the sample format at FAR 42.1204(i):

"(7)(i) Except as set forth in subparagraph (7)(ii) below, the Transferor and the Transferee agree that the Government is not obligated to pay or reimburse either of them, for, or otherwise give effect to, any costs, taxes, or other expenses, or any related increases, directly or indirectly arising out of or resulting from the transfer or this Agreement, other than those that the Government in the absence of this transfer or Agreement would have been obligated to pay or reimburse under the terms of the contracts.

(ii) The Government recognizes that restructuring by the Transferee incidental to the acquisition/merger may be in the best interests of the Government. Restructuring costs that are allowable under Part 31 of the Federal Acquisition Regulation (FAR) or Part 231 of the Defense Federal Acquisition Regulation Supplement (DFARS) may be reimbursed under flexibly-priced novated contracts, provided the Transferee demonstrates that the restructuring will reduce overall costs to the Department of Defense (DoD) (and to the National Aeronautics and Space Administration (NASA), where there is a mix of DoD and NASA contracts), and the requirements included in DFARS 231.205-70 are met. Restructuring costs shall not be allowed on novated contracts unless there is an audit of the restructuring proposal; a determination by the contracting officer of overall reduced costs to DoD/NASA; and an Advance Agreement setting forth a cumulative cost ceiling for restructuring projects and the period to which such costs shall be assigned."

[Final rule, 61 FR 16881, 4/18/96, effective 4/18/96; Final rule, 65 FR 63804, 10/25/2000, effective 10/25/2000]

SUBPART 242.14—[REMOVED]

242.1402 [Removed]

[Final rule, 65 FR 50143, 8/17/2000, effective 8/17/2000; Final rule, 70 FR 35543, 6/21/2005, effective 6/21/2005; Final rule, 77 FR 39140 77 FR 39140, 6/29/2012, effective 6/29/2012]

242.1403 [Removed]

[Final rule, 65 FR 50143, 8/17/2000, effective 8/17/2000; Final rule, 77 FR 39140 77 FR 39140, 6/29/2012, effective 6/29/2012]

242.1404 [Removed]

[Final rule, 77 FR 39140 77 FR 39140, 6/29/2012, effective 6/29/2012]

242.1404-1 [Removed]

[DAC 91-1, 56 FR 67220, 12/30/91, effective 12/31/91; Final rule, 77 FR 39140 77 FR 39140, 6/29/2012, effective 6/29/2012]

242.1404-2 [Removed]

[Final rule, 77 FR 39140 77 FR 39140, 6/29/2012, effective 6/29/2012]

242.1404-2-70 [Removed]

[DAC 91-12, 62 FR 34114, 6/24/97, effective 6/24/97; Final rule, 77 FR 39140 77 FR 39140, 6/29/2012, effective 6/29/2012]

242.1405 [Removed]

[Final rule, 65 FR 50143, 8/17/2000, effective 8/17/2000; Final rule, 77 FR 39140 77 FR 39140, 6/29/2012, effective 6/29/2012]

242.1470 [Removed]

[Final rule, 65 FR 50143, 8/17/2000, effective 8/17/2000; Final rule, 77 FR 39140 77 FR 39140, 6/29/2012, effective 6/29/2012]

SUBPART 242.15—CONTRACTOR PERFORMANCE INFORMATION

242.1502 Policy.

(g) Past performance evaluations in the Contractor Performance Assessment Reporting System shall include an assessment of the contractor's performance against, and efforts to achieve, the goals identified in its comprehensive small business subcontracting plan when the contract contains the clause at 252.219-7004, Small Business Subcontracting Plan (Test Program).

[Final rule, 83 FR 15996, 4/13/2018, effective 4/13/2018]

SUBPART 242.70—CONTRACTOR BUSINESS SYSTEMS

242.7000 Contractor business system deficiencies.

(a) *Definitions.* As used in this subpart—

Acceptable contractor business systems and *contractor business systems* are defined in the clause at 252.242-7005, Contractor Business Systems.

Covered contract means a contract that is subject to the Cost Accounting Standards under 41 U.S.C. chapter 15, as implemented in regulations found at 48 CFR 9903.201-1 (see the FAR Appendix) (10 U.S.C. 2302 note, as amended by section 816 of Pub. L. 112-81).

Significant deficiency is defined in the clause at 252.242-7005, Contractor Business Systems.

(b) *Determination to withhold payments.* If the contracting officer makes a final determination to disapprove a contractor's business system in accordance with the clause at 252.242-7005, Contractor Business Systems, the contracting officer shall—

(1) In accordance with agency procedures, identify one or more covered contracts containing the clause at 252.242-7005, Contractor Business Systems, from which payments will be withheld. When identifying the covered contracts from which to withhold payments, the contracting officer shall ensure that the total amount of payment withholding under 252.242-7005, does not exceed 10 percent of progress payments, performance-based payments, and interim payments under cost-reimbursement, labor-hour, and time-and-materials contracts billed under each of the identified covered contracts. Similarly, the contracting officer shall ensure that the total amount of payment withholding under the clause at 252.242-7005, Contractor Business Systems, for each business system does not exceed five percent of progress payments, performance-based payments, and interim payments

under cost, labor-hour, and time-and-materials contracts billed under each of the identified covered contracts. The contracting officer has the sole discretion to identify the covered contracts from which to withhold payments.

(2) Promptly notify the contractor, in writing, of the contracting officer's determination to implement payment withholding in accordance with the clause at 252.242-7005, Contractor Business Systems. The notice of payment withholding shall be included in the contracting officer's written final determination for the contractor business system and shall inform the contractor that—

(i) Payments shall be withheld from the contract or contracts identified in the written determination in accordance with the clause at 252.242-7005, Contractor Business Systems, until the contracting officer determines that there are no remaining significant deficiencies; and

(ii) The contracting officer reserves the right to take other actions within the terms and conditions of the contract.

(3) Provide all contracting officers administering the selected contracts from which payments will be withheld, a copy of the determination. The contracting officer shall also provide a copy of the determination to the auditor; payment office; affected contracting officers at the buying activities; and cognizant contracting officers in contract administration activities.

(c) *Monitoring contractor's corrective action*. The contracting officer, in consultation with the auditor or functional specialist, shall monitor the contractor's progress in correcting the deficiencies. The contracting officer shall notify the contractor of any decision to decrease or increase the amount of payment withholding in accordance with the clause at 252.242-7005, Contractor Business Systems.

(d) *Correction of significant deficiencies*. (1) If the contractor notifies the contracting officer that the contractor has corrected the significant deficiencies, the contracting officer shall request the auditor or functional specialist to review the correction to verify that the deficiencies have been corrected. If, after receipt of verification, the contracting officer determines that the contractor has corrected all significant deficiencies as directed by the contracting officer's final determination, the contracting officer shall discontinue the withholding of payments, release any payments previously withheld, and approve the system, unless other significant deficiencies remain.

(2) Prior to the receipt of verification, the contracting officer may discontinue withholding payments pending receipt of verification, and release any payments previously withheld, if the contractor submits evidence that the significant deficiencies have been corrected, and the contracting officer, in consultation with the auditor or functional specialist, determines that there is a reasonable expectation that the corrective actions have been implemented and are expected to correct the significant deficiencies.

(3) Within 90 days of receipt of the contractor notification that the contractor has corrected the significant deficiencies, the contracting officer shall—

(i) Make a determination that—

(A) The contractor has corrected all significant deficiencies as directed by the contracting officer's final determination in accordance with paragraph (d)(1) of this section;

(B) There is a reasonable expectation that the corrective actions have been implemented in accordance with paragraph (d)(2) of this section; or

(C) The contractor has not corrected all significant deficiencies as directed by the contracting officer's final determination in accordance with paragraph (d)(1) of this section, or there is not a reasonable expectation that the corrective actions have been implemented in accordance with paragraph (d)(2) of this section; or

(ii) Reduce withholding directly related to the significant deficiencies covered under the corrective action plan by at least 50 percent of the amount being withheld from progress payments and performance-based payments, and direct the contractor, in writing, to reduce the percentage withheld on interim cost vouchers by at least 50 percent, until the contracting officer makes a determination in accordance with paragraph (d) (3) (i) of this section.

(4) If, at any time, the contracting officer determines that the contractor has failed to correct the significant deficiencies identified in the contractor's notification, the contracting officer will continue, reinstate, or increase withholding from progress payments and performance-based payments, and direct the contractor, in writing, to continue, reinstate, or increase the percentage withheld on interim cost vouchers to the percentage initially withheld, until the contracting officer determines that the contractor has corrected all significant deficiencies as directed by the contracting officer's final determination.

(e) For sample formats for written notifications of contracting officer determinations to initiate payment withholding, reduce payment withholding, and discontinue payment withholding in accordance with the clause at DFARS 252.242-7005, Contractor Business Systems, see PGI 242.7000.

[Interim rule, 76 FR 28856, 5/18/2011, effective 5/18/2011; Final rule, 77 FR 11355, 2/24/2012, effective 2/24/2012]

242.7001 Contract clause.

Use the clause at 252.242-7005, Contractor Business Systems, in solicitations and contracts (other than in contracts with educational institutions, Federally Funded Research and Development Centers (FFRDCs), or University Associated Research Centers (UARCs) operated by educational institutions) when—

(a) The resulting contract will be a covered contract as defined in 242.7000(a); and

(b) The solicitation or contract includes any of the following clauses:

(1) 252.215-7002, Cost Estimating System Requirements.

(2) 252.234-7002, Earned Value Management System.

(3) 252.242-7004, Material Management and Accounting System.

(4) 252.242-7006, Accounting System Administration.

(5) 252.244-7001, Contractor Purchasing System Administration.

(6) 252.245-7003, Contractor Property Management System Administration.

[Interim rule, 76 FR 28856, 5/18/2011, effective 5/18/2011; Final rule, 77 FR 11355, 2/24/2012, effective 2/24/2012]

SUBPART 242.71—VOLUNTARY REFUNDS

242.7100 General.

A voluntary refund is a payment or credit (adjustment under one or more contracts or subcontracts) to the Government from a contractor or subcontractor that is not required by any contractual or other legal obligation. Follow the procedures at PGI 242.7100 for voluntary refunds.

[Final rule, 70 FR 67919, 11/9/2005, effective 11/9/2005]

242.7101 [Removed]

[Final rule, 70 FR 67919, 11/9/2005, effective 11/9/2005]

242.7102 [Removed]

[Final rule, 70 FR 67919, 11/9/2005, effective 11/9/2005]

SUBPART 242.72—CONTRACTOR MATERIAL MANAGEMENT AND ACCOUNTING SYSTEM

242.7200 Scope of subpart.

(a) This subpart provides policies, procedures, and standards for use in the evaluation of a contractor's material management and accounting system (MMAS).

(b) The policies, procedures, and standards in this subpart—

(1) Apply only when the contractor has contracts exceeding the simplified acquisition threshold that are not for the acquisition of commercial items and are either—

(i) Cost-reimbursement contracts; or

(ii) Fixed-price contracts with progress payments made on the basis of costs incurred by the contractor as work progresses under the contract; and

(2) Do not apply to small businesses, educational institutions, or nonprofit organizations.

[Final rule, 65 FR 77832, 12/13/2000, effective 12/13/2000]

242.7201 Definitions.

Acceptable material management and accounting system, material management and accounting system, and *valid time-phased requirements* are defined in the clause at 252.242-7004, Material Management and Accounting System.

Significant deficiency is defined in the clause at 252.242-7004, Material Management and Accounting System.

[Final rule, 65 FR 77832, 12/13/2000, effective 12/13/2000; Interim rule, 76 FR 28856 76 FR 28856, 5/18/2011, effective 5/18/2011; Final rule, 77 FR 11355, 2/24/2012, effective 2/24/2012]

242.7202 Policy.

(a) DoD policy is for its contractors to have an MMAS that conforms to the standards in paragraph (d) of the clause at 252.242-7004, Material Management and Accounting System, so that the system—

(1) Reasonably forecasts material requirements;

(2) Ensures the costs of purchased and fabricated material charged or allocated to a contract are based on valid time-phased requirements; and

(3) Maintains a consistent, equitable, and unbiased logic for costing of material transactions.

(b) The cognizant contracting officer, in consultation with the auditor and functional specialist, if appropriate, shall—

(1) Determine the acceptability of the contractor's MMAS and approve or disapprove the system; and

(2) Pursue correction of any deficiencies.

(c) In evaluating the acceptability of the contractor's MMAS, the contracting officer, in consultation with the auditor and functional specialist, if appropriate, shall determine whether the contractor's MMAS complies with the system criteria for an acceptable MMAS as prescribed in the clause at 252.242-7004, Material Management and Accounting System.

[Final rule, 65 FR 77832, 12/13/2000, effective 12/13/2000; Interim rule, 76 FR 28856 76 FR 28856, 5/18/2011, effective 5/18/; Final rule, 77 FR 11355, 2/24/2012, effective 2/24/2012; Final rule, 81 FR 36473, 6/7/2016, effective 6/7/2016]

242.7203 Review procedures.

(a) *Criteria for conducting reviews.* Conduct an MMAS review when—

(1) A contractor has $40 million of qualifying sales to the Government during the contractor's preceding fiscal year; and

(2) The administrative contracting officer (ACO), with advice from the auditor, determines an MMAS review is needed based on a risk assessment of the contractor's past experience and current vulnerability.

(b) *Qualifying sales.* Qualifying sales are sales for which certified cost or pricing data were required under 10 U.S.C. 2306a, as implemented in FAR 15.403, or that are contracts priced on other than a firm-fixed-price or fixed-price with economic price adjustment basis. Sales include prime contracts, subcontracts, and modifications to such contracts and subcontracts.

(c) *Disposition of findings*—(1) *Reporting of findings.* The auditor or functional specialist shall document findings and recommendations in a report to the contracting officer. If the auditor or functional specialist identifies any significant MMAS deficiencies, the report shall describe the deficiencies in sufficient detail to allow the contracting officer to understand the deficiencies.

(2) *Initial determination.* (i) The contracting officer shall review findings and recommendations and, if there are no significant deficiencies, shall promptly notify the contractor, in writing, that the contractor's MMAS is acceptable and approved; or

(ii) If the contracting officer finds that there are one or more significant deficiencies (as defined in the clause at 252.242-7004, Material Management and Accounting System) due to the contractor's failure to meet one or more of the MMAS system criteria in the clause at 252.242-7004, Material Management and Accounting System, the contracting officer shall—

(A) Promptly make an initial written determination on any significant deficiencies and notify the contractor, in writing, providing a description of each significant deficiency in sufficient detail to allow the contractor to understand the deficiency;

(B) Request the contractor to respond, in writing, to the initial determination within 30 days; and

(C) Promptly evaluate the contractor's response to the initial determination in consultation with the auditor or functional specialist, and make a final determination.

(3) *Final determination*. (i) The ACO shall make a final determination and notify the contractor that—

(A) The contractor's MMAS is acceptable and approved, and no deficiencies remain, or

(B) Significant deficiencies remain. The notice shall identify any remaining significant deficiencies, and indicate the adequacy of any proposed or completed corrective action. The contracting officer shall—

(*1*) Request that the contractor, within 45 days of receipt of the final determination, either correct the deficiencies or submit an acceptable corrective action plan showing milestones and actions to eliminate the deficiencies;

(*2*) Disapprove the system in accordance with the clause at 252.242-7004, Material Management and Accounting System; and

(*3*) Withhold payments in accordance with the clause at 252.242-7005, Contractor Business Systems, if the clause is included in the contract.

(ii) Follow the procedures relating to monitoring a contractor's corrective action and the correction of significant deficiencies in PGI 242.7203.

(d) *System approval*. The contracting officer shall promptly approve a previously disapproved MMAS and notify the contractor when the contracting officer determines that there are no remaining significant deficiencies.

(e) *Contracting officer notifications*. The cognizant contracting officer shall promptly distribute copies of a determination to approve a system, disapprove a system and withhold payments, or approve a previously disapproved system and release withheld payments to the auditor; payment office; affected contracting officers at the buying activities; and cognizant contracting officers in contract administration activities.

[Final rule, 65 FR 77832, 12/13/2000, effective 12/13/2000; Interim rule, 76 FR 28856 76 FR 28856, 5/18/2011, effective 5/18/2011; Final rule, 77 FR 11355, 2/24/2012, effective 2/24/2012; Final rule, 77 FR 76939, 12/31/2012, effective 12/31/2012]

242.7204 Contract clause.

Use the clause at 252.242-7004, Material Management and Accounting System, in all solicitations and contracts exceeding the simplified acquisition threshold that are not for the acquisition of commercial items and—

(a) Are not awarded to small businesses, educational institutions, or nonprofit organizations; and

(b) Are either—

(1) Cost-reimbursement contracts; or

(2) Fixed-price contracts with progress payments made on the basis of costs incurred by the contractor as work progresses under the contract.

[Final rule, 65 FR 77832, 12/13/2000, effective 12/13/2000]

SUBPART 242.73—CONTRACTOR INSURANCE/PENSION REVIEW

242.7300 [Removed]

[Final rule, 71 FR 9273, 2/23/2006, effective 2/23/2006]

242.7301 General.

(a) The administrative contracting officer (ACO) is responsible for determining the allowability of insurance/pension costs in Government contracts and for determining the need for a Contractor/Insurance Pension Review (CIPR). Defense Contract Management Agency (DCMA) insurance/

pension specialists and Defense Contract Audit Agency (DCAA) auditors assist ACOs in making these determinations, conduct CIPRs when needed, and perform other routine audits as authorized under FAR 42.705 and 52.215-2. A CIPR is a DCMA/DCAA joint review that—

(1) Provides an in-depth evaluation of a contractor's—

(i) Insurance programs;

(ii) Pension plans;

(iii) Other deferred compensation plans; and

(iv) Related policies, procedures, practices, and costs; or

(2) Concentrates on specific areas of the contractor's insurance programs, pension plans, or other deferred compensation plans.

(b) DCMA is the DoD Executive Agent for the performance of all CIPRs.

(c) DCAA is the DoD agency designated for the performance of contract audit responsibilities related to Cost Accounting Standards administration as described in FAR subparts 30.2 and 30.6 as they relate to a contractor's insurance programs, pension plans, and other deferred compensation plans.

[Final rule, 63 FR 40374, 7/29/98, effective 7/29/98; Final rule, 65 FR 52951, 8/31/2000, effective 8/31/2000; Final rule, 71 FR 9273, 2/23/2006, effective 2/23/2006; Final rule, 77 FR 76939, 12/31/2012, effective 12/31/2012; Final rule, 82 FR 61479, 12/28/2017, effective 12/28/2017]

242.7302 Requirements.

(a) (1) An in-depth CIPR as described at DFARS 242.7301 (a) (1) shall be conducted only when—

(i) A contractor has $50 million of qualifying sales to the Government during the contractor's preceding fiscal year; and

(ii) The ACO, with advice from DCMA insurance/pension specialists and DCAA auditors, determines a CIPR is needed based on a risk assessment of the contractor's past experience and current vulnerability.

(2) Qualifying sales are sales for which certified cost or pricing data were required under 10 U.S.C. 2306a, as implemented in FAR 15.403, or that are contracts priced on other than a firm-fixed-price or fixed-price with economic price adjustment basis. Sales include prime contracts, subcontracts, and modifications to such contracts and subcontracts.

(b) A special CIPR that concentrates on specific areas of a contractor's insurance programs, pension plans, or other deferred compensation plans shall be performed for a contractor (including, but not limited to, a contractor meeting the requirements in paragraph (a) of this section) when any of the following circumstances exists, but only if the circumstance(s) may result in a material impact on Government contract costs:

(1) Information or data reveals a deficiency in the contractor's insurance/pension program.

(2) The contractor proposes or implements changes in its insurance, pension, or deferred compensation plans.

(3) The contractor is involved in a merger, acquisition, or divestiture.

(4) The Government needs to follow up on contractor implementation of prior CIPR recommendations.

(c) The DCAA auditor shall use relevant findings and recommendations of previously performed CIPRs in determining the scope of any audits of insurance and pension costs.

(d) When a Government organization believes that a review of the contractor's insurance/pension program should be performed, that organization should provide a recommendation for a review to the ACO. If the ACO concurs, the review should be performed as part of an ACO-initiated special CIPR or as part of a CIPR already scheduled for the near future.

[Final rule, 63 FR 40374, 7/29/98, effective 7/29/98; Final rule, 65 FR 52951, 8/31/2000, effective 8/31/2000; Final rule, 71 FR 9273, 2/23/2006, effective 2/23/2006; Final rule, 75 FR 71564, 11/24/2010, effective 11/24/2010; Final rule, 77 FR 76939, 12/31/2012, effective 12/31/2012; Final rule, 78 FR 13543, 2/28/2013, effective 2/28/2013]

242.7303 Responsibilities.

Follow the procedures at PGI 242.7303 when conducting a CIPR.

[Final rule, 63 FR 40374, 7/29/98, effective 7/29/98; Final rule, 65 FR 52951, 8/31/2000, effective 8/31/2000; Final rule, 71 FR 9273, 2/23/2006]

SUBPART 242.74—TECHNICAL REPRESENTATION AT CONTRACTOR FACILITIES

242.7400 General.

(a) Program managers may conclude that they need technical representation in contractor facilities to perform non-contract administration service (CAS) technical duties and to provide liaison, guidance, and assistance on systems and programs. In these cases, the program manager may assign technical representatives under the procedures in 242.7401.

(b) A technical representative is a representative of a DoD program, project, or system office performing non-CAS technical duties at or near a contractor facility. A technical representative is not—

(1) A representative of a contract administration or contract audit component; or

(2) A contracting officer's representative (see 201.602).

[Final rule, 64 FR 61028, 11/9/99, effective 11/9/99; Final rule, 70 FR 67919, 11/9/2005, effective 11/9/2005]

242.7401 Procedures.

When the program, project, or system manager determines that a technical representative is required, follow the procedures at PGI 242.7401.

[Final rule, 70 FR 67919, 11/9/2005, effective 11/9/2005]

SUBPART 242.75—CONTRACTOR ACCOUNTING SYSTEMS AND RELATED CONTROLS

242.7501 Definitions.

As used in this subpart—

Acceptable accounting system, and *accounting system* are defined in the clause at 252.242-7006, Accounting System Administration.

Significant deficiency is defined in the clause at 252.242-7006, Accounting System Administration.

[DAC 91-7, 60 FR 29491, 6/5/95, effective 5/17/95; Final rule, 70 FR 67919, 11/9/2005, effective 11/9/2005; Interim rule, 76 FR 28856, 5/18/2011, effective 5/18/2011; Final rule, 77 FR 11355, 2/24/2012, effective 2/24/2012]

242.7502 Policy.

(a) Contractors receiving cost-reimbursement, incentive type, time-and-materials, or labor-hour contracts, or contracts which provide for progress payments based on costs or on a percentage or stage of completion, shall maintain an accounting system.

(b) The cognizant contracting officer, in consultation with the auditor or functional specialist, shall—

(1) Determine the acceptability of a contractor's accounting system and approve or disapprove the system; and

(2) Pursue correction of any deficiencies.

(c) In evaluating the acceptability of a contractor's accounting system, the contracting officer, in consultation with the auditor or functional specialist, shall determine whether the contractor's accounting system complies with the system criteria for an acceptable accounting system as prescribed in the clause at 252.242-7006, Accounting System Administration.

(d) *Disposition of findings*— (1) *Reporting of findings*. The auditor shall document findings and recommendations in a report to the contracting officer. If the auditor identifies any significant accounting system deficiencies, the report shall describe the deficiencies in sufficient detail to allow the contracting officer to understand the deficiencies. Follow the procedures at PGI 242.7502 for reporting of deficiencies.

(2) *Initial determination*. (i) The contracting officer shall review findings and recommendations and, if there are no significant deficiencies, shall promptly notify the contractor, in writing, that the contrac-

tor's accounting system is acceptable and approved; or

(ii) If the contracting officer finds that there are one or more significant deficiencies (as defined in the clause at 252.242-7006, Accounting System Administration) due to the contractor's failure to meet one or more of the accounting system criteria in the clause at 252.242-7006, the contracting officer shall—

(A) Promptly make an initial written determination on any significant deficiencies and notify the contractor, in writing, providing a description of each significant deficiency in sufficient detail to allow the contractor to understand the deficiency;

(B) Request the contractor to respond, in writing, to the initial determination within 30 days; and

(C) Promptly evaluate the contractor's response to the initial determination, in consultation with the auditor or functional specialist, and make a final determination.

(3) *Final determination*. (i) The contracting officer shall make a final determination and notify the contractor, in writing, that—

(A) The contractor's accounting system is acceptable and approved, and no significant deficiencies remain, or

(B) Significant deficiencies remain. The notice shall identify any remaining significant deficiencies, and indicate the adequacy of any proposed or completed corrective action. The contracting officer shall—

(*1*) Request that the contractor, within 45 days of receipt of the final determination, either correct the deficiencies or submit an acceptable corrective action plan showing milestones and actions to eliminate the deficiencies;

(*2*) Make a determination to disapprove the system in accordance with the clause at 252.242-7006, Accounting System Administration; and

(*3*) Withhold payments in accordance with the clause at 252.242-7005, Contractor Business Systems, if the clause is included in the contract.

(ii) Follow the procedures relating to monitoring a contractor's corrective action and the correction of significant deficiencies in PGI 242.7502.

(e) *System approval*. The contracting officer shall promptly approve a previously disapproved accounting system and notify the contractor when the contracting officer determines that there are no remaining significant deficiencies.

(f) *Contracting officer notifications*. The cognizant contracting officer shall promptly distribute copies of a determination to approve a system, disapprove a system and withhold payments, or approve a previously disapproved system and release withheld payments to the auditor; payment office; affected contracting officers at the buying activities; and cognizant contracting officers in contract administration activities.

(g) *Mitigating the risk of accounting system deficiencies on specific proposals*.

(1) Field pricing teams shall discuss identified accounting system deficiencies and their impact in all reports on contractor proposals until the deficiencies are resolved.

(2) The contracting officer responsible for negotiation of a proposal generated by an accounting system with an identified deficiency shall evaluate whether the deficiency impacts the negotiations. See also PGI 242.7502(g)(2). If it does not, the contracting officer should proceed with negotiations. If it does, the contracting officer should consider other alternatives, *e.g.*—

(i) Allowing the contractor additional time to correct the accounting system deficiency and submit a corrected proposal;

(ii) Considering another type of contract;

(iii) Using additional cost analysis techniques to determine the reasonableness of the cost elements affected by the accounting system's deficiency;

(iv) Reducing the negotiation objective for profit or fee; or

(v) Including a contract (reopener) clause that provides for adjustment of the contract amount after award.

(3) The contracting officer who incorporates a reopener clause into the contract is

responsible for negotiating price adjustments required by the clause. Any reopener clause necessitated by an accounting system deficiency should—

(i) Clearly identify the amounts and items that are in question at the time of negotiation;

(ii) Indicate a specific time or subsequent event by which the contractor will submit a supplemental proposal, including certified cost or pricing data, identifying cost impact adjustment necessitated by the deficient accounting system;

(iii) Provide for the contracting officer to adjust the contract price unilaterally if the contractor fails to submit the supplemental proposal; and

(iv) Provide that failure of the Government and the contractor to agree to the price adjustment shall be a dispute under the Disputes clause.

[Interim rule, 76 FR 28856, 5/18/2011, effective 5/18/2011; Final rule, 77 FR 11355, 2/24/2012, effective 2/24/2012; Final rule, 77 FR 76939, 12/31/2012, effective 12/31/2012; Final rule, 80 FR 10390, 2/26/2015, effective 2/26/2015]

242.7503 Contract clause.

Use the clause at 252.242-7006, Accounting System Administration, in solicitations and contracts when contemplating—

(a) A cost-reimbursement, incentive type, time-and-materials, or labor-hour contract; or

(b) A contract with progress payments made on the basis of costs incurred by the contractor or on a percentage or stage of completion.

[Interim rule, 76 FR 28856, 5/18/2011, effective 5/18/2011; Final rule, 77 FR 11355, 2/24/2012, effective 2/24/2012; Final rule, 82 FR 61479, 12/28/2017, effective 12/28/2017]

PART 243—CONTRACT MODIFICATIONS

Table of Contents

Subpart 243.1—General

[Removed] 243.102
[Removed] 243.105
[Removed] 243.107
Notification of substantial impact on employment 243.107-70
Identification of foreign military sale (FMS) requirements 243.170
Obligation or deobligation of funds 243.171
Application of modifications 243.172

Subpart 243.2—Change Orders

Administration 243.204
Definitization of change orders 243.204-70
Scope 243.204-70-1
Price ceiling 243.204-70-2
Definitization schedule 243.204-70-3
Limitations on obligations 243.204-70-4
Exceptions 243.204-70-5
Allowable profit 243.204-70-6
Plans and reports 243.204-70-7
Certification of requests for equitable adjustment 243.204-71
Contract clauses 243.205
Pricing of contract modifications 243.205-70
Requests for equitable adjustment 243.205-71
Unpriced change orders 243.205-72

PART 243—CONTRACT MODIFICATIONS

SUBPART 243.1—GENERAL

243.102 [Removed]

[Final rule, 70 FR 67921, 11/9/2005, effective 11/9/2005]

243.105 [Removed]

[Interim rule, 61 FR 25408, 5/21/96, effective 5/21/96, finalized without change, DAC 91-12, 62 FR 34114, 6/24/97, effective 6/24/97; Interim rule, 65 FR 2057, 1/13/2000; Final rule, 67 FR 49253, 7/30/2002, effective 7/30/2002; Final rule, 70 FR 67921, 11/9/2005, effective 11/9/2005]

243.107 [Removed]

[Final rule, 70 FR 67921, 11/9/2005, effective 11/9/2005]

243.107-70 Notification of substantial impact on employment.

The Secretary of Defense is required to notify the Secretary of Labor if a modification of a major defense contract or subcontract will have a substantial impact on employment. The clause prescribed at 249.7003(c) requires that the contractor notify its employees, its subcontractors, and State and local officials when a contract modification will have a substantial impact on employment.

[DAC 91-1, 56 FR 67220, 12/30/91, effective 12/31/91; Final rule, 70 FR 67921, 11/9/2005, effective 11/9/2005]

243.170 Identification of foreign military sale (FMS) requirements.

Follow the procedures at PGI 243.170 for identifying contract modifications that add FMS requirements.

[Redesignated from 243.107-70, DAC 91-1, 56 FR 67220, 12/30/91, effective 12/31/91; Final rule, 70 FR 67921, 11/9/2005, effective 11/9/2005]

243.171 Obligation or deobligation of funds.

Follow the procedures at PGI 243.171 when obligating or deobligating funds.

[Final rule, 60 FR 34467, 7/3/95, effective 7/3/95; Interim rule, 68 FR 58631, 10/10/2003, effective 1/1/2004; Interim rule, 68 FR 75196, 12/30/2003, effective 1/1/2004, finalized without change, 70 FR 20831, 4/22/2005, effective 4/22/2005; Final rule, 70 FR 67921, 11/9/2005, effective 11/9/2005]

243.172 Application of modifications.

Follow the procedures in 204.1671 for determining the sequence for application of modifications to a contract or order.

[Final rule, 77 FR 30367, 5/22/2012, effective 5/22/2012; Final rule 81 FR 9783, 2/26/2016, effective 2/26/2016]

SUBPART 243.2—CHANGE ORDERS

243.204 Administration.

Follow the procedures at PGI 243.204 for administration of change orders.

[Final rule, 70 FR 67921, 11/9/2005, effective 11/9/2005; Final rule, 75 FR 48276, 8/10/2010, effective 8/10/2010]

243.204-70 Definitization of change orders. (No Text)

[Final rule, 75 FR 48276, 8/10/2010, effective 8/10/2010]

243.204-70-1 Scope.

(a) This subsection applies to unpriced change orders with an estimated value exceeding $5 million.

(b) Unpriced change orders for foreign military sales and special access programs are not subject to this subsection, but the contracting officer shall apply the policy and procedures to them to the maximum extent practicable. If the contracting officer determines that it is impracticable to adhere to the policy and procedures of this subsection for an unpriced change order for a foreign military sale or a special access program, the contracting officer shall provide prior notice, through agency channels, to the Deputy Director, Defense Procurement and Acquisition Policy (Contract Policy and International Contracting), 3060 Defense Pentagon, Washington, DC 20301-3060.

[Final rule, 75 FR 48276, 8/10/2010, effective 8/10/2010]

243.204-70-2 Price ceiling.

Unpriced change orders shall include a not-to-exceed price.

[Final rule, 75 FR 48276, 8/10/2010, effective 8/10/2010]

243.204-70-3 Definitization schedule.

(a) Unpriced change orders shall contain definitization schedules that provide for definitization by the earlier of—

(1) The date that is 180 days after issuance of the change order (this date may be extended but may not exceed the date that is 180 days after the contractor submits a qualifying proposal); or

(2) The date on which the amount of funds obligated under the change order is equal to more than 50 percent of the not-to-exceed price.

(b) Submission of a qualifying proposal in accordance with the definitization schedule is a material element of the contract. If the contractor does not submit a timely qualifying proposal, the contracting officer may suspend or reduce progress payments under FAR 32.503-6, or take other appropriate action.

[Final rule, 75 FR 48276, 8/10/2010, effective 8/10/2010; Final rule, 82 FR 61479, 12/28/2017, effective 12/28/2017]

243.204-70-4 Limitations on obligations.

(a) The Government shall not obligate more than 50 percent of the not-to-exceed price before definitization. However, if a contractor submits a qualifying proposal before 50 percent of the not-to-exceed price has been obligated by the Government, the limitation on obligations before definitization may be increased to no more than 75 percent (see 232.102-70 for coverage on provisional delivery payments).

(b) Obligations should be consistent with the contractor's requirements for the undefinitized period.

[Final rule, 75 FR 48276, 8/10/2010, effective 8/10/2010]

243.204-70-5 Exceptions.

(a) The limitations in 243.204-70-2, 243.204-70-3, and 243.204-70-4 do not apply to unpriced change orders for the purchase of initial spares.

(b) The limitations in 43.204-70-4(a) do not apply to unpriced change orders for ship construction and ship repair.

(c) The head of the agency may waive the limitations in 243.204-70-2, 243.204-70-3, and 43.204-70-4 for unpriced change orders if the head of the agency determines that the waiver is necessary to support—

(1) A contingency operation; or

(2) A humanitarian or peacekeeping operation.

[Final rule, 75 FR 48276, 8/10/2010, effective 8/10/2010]

243.204-70-6 Allowable profit.

When the final price of an unpriced change order is negotiated after a substantial portion of the required performance has been completed, the head of the contracting activity shall ensure the profit allowed reflects—

(a) Any reduced cost risk to the contractor for costs incurred during contract performance before negotiation of the final price;

(b) Any reduced cost risk to the contractor for costs expected to be incurred during performance of the remainder of the contract; and

(c) The extent to which costs have been incurred prior to definitization of the unpriced change order (see 215.404-71-3(d)(2)). The risk assessment shall be documented in the price negotiation memorandum.

[Final rule, 75 FR 48276, 8/10/2010, effective 8/10/2010; Final rule, 83 FR 30584, 6/29/2018, effective 6/29/2018]

243.204-70-7 Plans and reports.

To provide for enhanced management and oversight of unpriced change orders, departments and agencies shall—

(a) Include in the Consolidated Undefinitized Contract Action (UCA) Management Plan required by 217.7405, the actions planned and taken to ensure that unpriced change orders are definitized in accordance with this subsection; and

(b) Include in the Consolidated UCA Management Report required by 217.7405, each unpriced change order with an estimated value exceeding $5 million.

[Final rule, 75 FR 48276, 8/10/2010, effective 8/10/2010]

243.204-71 Certification of requests for equitable adjustment.

(a) A request for equitable adjustment to contract terms that exceeds the simplified acquisition threshold may not be paid unless the contract certifies the request in accordance with the clause at 252.243-7002.

(b) To determine if the dollar threshold for requiring certification is met, add together the absolute value of each cost increase and each cost decrease. See PGI 243.204-71(b) for an example.

(c) The certification required by 10 U.S.C. 2410(a), as implemented in the clause at 252.243-7002, is different from the certification required by 41 U.S.C. 7103, Disputes. If the contractor has certified a request for equitable adjustment in accordance with 10 U.S.C. 2410(a), and desires to convert the request to a claim under the Contract Disputes statute, the contractor shall certify the claim in accordance with FAR subpart 33.2.

[Interim rule, 62 FR 37146, 7/11/97, effective 7/11/97; DAC 91-13, 63 FR 11522, 3/9/98, effective 3/9/98; Final rule, 66 FR 49865, 10/1/2001, effective 10/1/2001; Final rule, 70 FR 67921, 11/9/2005, effective 11/9/2005; Redesignated, Final rule, 75 FR 48276, 8/10/2010, effective 8/10/2010; Final rule 76 FR 58137, 9/20/2011, effective 9/20/2011; Final rule, 76 FR 76318, 12/7/2011, effective 12/7/2011; Final rule, 77 FR 35879, 6/15/2012, effective 6/15/2012]

243.205 Contract clauses. (No Text)

243.205-70 Pricing of contract modifications.

Use the clause at 252.243-7001, Pricing of Contract Modifications, in solicitations and contracts when anticipating and using a fixed price type contract.

[Redesignated by 66 FR 49865, 10/1/2001, effective 10/1/2001]

243.205-71 Requests for equitable adjustment.

Use the clause at 252.243-7002, Requests for Equitable Adjustment, in solicitations and contracts, including solicitations and contracts using FAR part 12 procedures for the acquisition of commercial items, that are estimated to exceed the simplified acquisition threshold.

[Interim rule, 62 FR 37146, 7/11/97, effective 7/11/97; Correction to DAC 91-13, 63 FR 17124, 4/8/98, effective 3/9/98; Redesignated by 66 FR 49865, 10/1/2001, effective 10/1/2001; Final rule, 78 FR 37980, 6/25/2013, effective 6/25/2013]

243.205-72 Unpriced change orders.

See the clause prescriptions at 217.7406 for all unpriced change orders with an estimated value exceeding $5 million.

[Final rule, 75 FR 48276, 8/10/2010, effective 8/10/2010]

PART 244—SUBCONTRACTING POLICIES AND PROCEDURES

Table of Contents

Subpart 244.1—General

Definitions 244.101

Subpart 244.2—Consent to Subcontracts

Consent and advance notification requirements 244.201
Consent requirements 244.201-1
Contracting officer's evaluation 244.202
Considerations 244.202-2

Subpart 244.3—Contractors' Purchasing Systems Reviews

Objective 244.301
Requirements 244.302
Extent of review 244.303
[Removed] 244.304
Granting, withholding, or withdrawing approval 244.305
Policy 244.305-70
Contract clause 244.305-71

Subpart 244.4—Subcontracts for Commercial Items and Commercial Components

Policy requirements 244.402
Contract clause 244.403

PART 244—SUBCONTRACTING POLICIES AND PROCEDURES

SUBPART 244.1—GENERAL

244.101 Definitions.

As used in this subpart—

Acceptable purchasing system and *purchasing system* are defined in the clause at 252.244-7001, Contractor Purchasing System Administration.

Significant deficiency is defined in the clause at 252.244-7001, Contractor Purchasing System Administration.

[Interim rule, 76 FR 28856, 5/18/2011, effective 5/18/2011; Final rule, 77 FR 11355, 2/24/ 2012, effective 2/24/2012]

SUBPART 244.2—CONSENT TO SUBCONTRACTS

244.201 Consent and advance notification requirements. (No Text)

244.201-1 Consent requirements.

(a) In accordance with section 824 of the National Defense Authorization Act for Fiscal Year 2019 (Pub. L. 115-232), notwithstanding the requirements in FAR 44.201-1(a), the contracting officer shall not withhold consent to subcontract without the written approval of the program manager, or comparable requiring activity official exercising program management responsibilities, if the contractor has an approved purchasing system, as defined in FAR 44.101.

(S–70) In solicitations and contracts for information technology, whether acquired as a service or as a supply, that is a covered system or covered item of supply as those terms are defined at 239.7301, consider the need for a consent to subcontract requirement regarding supply chain risk (see subpart 239.73). For additional guidance see PGI 244.201-1.

[Interim rule, 78 FR 69267, 11/18/2013, effective 11/18/2013; Final rule, 80 FR 67243, 10/30/2015, effective 10/30/2015; Final rule, 84 FR 12140, 4/1/2019, effective 4/1/2019]

244.202 Contracting officer's evaluation. (No Text)

244.202-2 Considerations.

(a) Where other than lowest price is the basis for subcontractor selection, has the contractor adequately substantiated the selection as offering the greatest value to the Government?

[DAC 91-7, 60 FR 29491, 6/5/95, effective 5/17/95]

SUBPART 244.3—CONTRACTORS' PURCHASING SYSTEMS REVIEWS

244.301 Objective.

The administrative contracting officer (ACO) is solely responsible for initiating reviews the contractor's purchasing systems, but other organizations may request that the ACO initiate such reviews.

[Final rule, 70 FR 67922, 11/9/2005, effective 11/9/2005]

244.302 Requirements.

(a) In lieu of the threshold at FAR 44.302(a), the ACO shall determine the need for a CPSR if a contractor's sales to the Government are expected to exceed $50 million during the next 12 months.

[Final rule, 84 FR 72247, 12/31/2019, effective 12/31/2019]

244.303 Extent of review.

(a) Also review the adequacy of rationale documenting commercial item determinations to ensure compliance with the definition of *commercial item* in FAR 2.101.

(b) Also review the adequacy of the contractor's counterfeit electronic part detection and avoidance system under clause 252.246-7007, Contractor Counterfeit Electronic Part Detection and Avoidance System.

[Final rule, 79 FR 26091, 5/6/2014, effective 5/6/2014]

244.304 [Removed]

[DAC 91-11, 61 FR 50446, 9/26/96, effective 9/26/96; Final rule, 67 FR 38023, 5/31/2002, effective 5/31/2002; Final rule, 70 FR 67922, 11/9/2005, effective

11/9/2005; Final rule, 73 FR 4113, 1/24/2008, effective 1/24/2008; Interim rule, 76 FR 28856, 5/18/2011, effective 5/18/2011]

244.305 Granting, withholding, or withdrawing approval. (No Text)

[Interim rule, 76 FR 28856, 5/18/2011, effective 5/18/2011]

244.305-70 Policy.

Use this subsection instead of FAR 44.305-2(c) and 44.305-3(b).

(a) The cognizant contracting officer, in consultation with the purchasing system analyst or auditor, shall—

(1) Determine the acceptability of the contractor's purchasing system and approve or disapprove the system; and

(2) Pursue correction of any deficiencies.

(b) In evaluating the acceptability of the contractor's purchasing system, the contracting officer, in consultation with the purchasing system analyst or auditor, shall determine whether the contractor's purchasing system complies with the system criteria for an acceptable purchasing system as prescribed in the clause at 252.244-7001, Contractor Purchasing System Administration.

(c) *Disposition of findings*—(1) *Reporting of findings.* The purchasing system analyst or auditor shall document findings and recommendations in a report to the contracting officer. If the auditor or purchasing system analyst identifies any significant purchasing system deficiencies, the report shall describe the deficiencies in sufficient detail to allow the contracting officer to understand the deficiencies.

(2) *Initial determination.* (i) The contracting officer shall review all findings and recommendations and, if there are no significant deficiencies, shall promptly notify the contractor that the contractor's purchasing system is acceptable and approved; or

(ii) If the contracting officer finds that there are one or more significant deficiencies (as defined in the clause at 252.244-7001, Contractor Purchasing System Administration) due to the contractor's failure to meet one or more of the purchasing system criteria in the clause at 252.244-7001, the contracting officer shall—

(A) Promptly make an initial written determination on any significant deficiencies and notify the contractor, in writing, providing a description of each significant deficiency in sufficient detail to allow the contractor to understand the deficiency;

(B) Request the contractor to respond, in writing, to the initial determination within 30 days; and

(C) Evaluate the contractor's response to the initial determination in consultation with the auditor or purchasing system analyst, and make a final determination.

(3) *Final determination.* (i) The contracting officer shall make a final determination and notify the contractor, in writing, that—

(A) The contractor's purchasing system is acceptable and approved, and no significant deficiencies remain, or

(B) Significant deficiencies remain. The notice shall identify any remaining significant deficiencies, and indicate the adequacy of any proposed or completed corrective action. The contracting officer shall—

(*1*) Request that the contractor, within 45 days of receipt of the final determination, either correct the deficiencies or submit an acceptable corrective action plan showing milestones and actions to eliminate the deficiencies;

(*2*) Disapprove the system in accordance with the clause at 252.244-7001, Contractor Purchasing System Administration; and

(*3*) Withhold payments in accordance with the clause at 252.244-7005, Contractor Business Systems, if the clause is included in the contract.

(ii) Follow the procedures relating to monitoring a contractor's corrective action and the correction of significant deficiencies in PGI 244.305-70.

(d) *System approval.* The contracting officer shall promptly approve a previously disapproved purchasing system and notify the contractor when the contracting officer determines that there are no remaining significant deficiencies.

(e) *Contracting officer notifications.* The cognizant contracting officer shall promptly distribute copies of a determination to approve a system, disapprove a system and withhold payments, or approve a previously disapproved system and release withheld payments to the auditor; payment office; affected contracting officers at the buying activities; and cognizant contracting officers in contract administration activities.

(f) *Mitigating the risk of purchasing system deficiencies on specific proposals.*

(1) Source selection evaluation teams shall discuss identified purchasing system deficiencies and their impact in all reports on contractor proposals until the deficiencies are resolved.

(2) The contracting officer responsible for negotiation of a proposal generated by a purchasing system with an identified deficiency shall evaluate whether the deficiency impacts the negotiations. If it does not, the contracting officer should proceed with negotiations. If it does, the contracting officer should consider other alternatives, *e.g.*—

(i) Allowing the contractor additional time to correct the purchasing system deficiency and submit a corrected proposal;

(ii) Considering another type of contract, *e.g.*, a fixed-price incentive (firm target) contract instead of firm-fixed-price;

(iii) Using additional cost analysis techniques to determine the reasonableness of the cost elements affected by the purchasing system's deficiency;

(iv) Segregating the questionable areas as a cost-reimbursable line item;

(v) Reducing the negotiation objective for profit or fee; or

(vi) Including a contract (reopener) clause that provides for adjustment of the contract amount after award.

(3) The contracting officer who incorporates a reopener clause into the contract is responsible for negotiating price adjustments required by the clause. Any reopener clause necessitated by a purchasing system deficiency should—

(i) Clearly identify the amounts and items that are in question at the time of negotiation;

(ii) Indicate a specific time or subsequent event by which the contractor will submit a supplemental proposal, including certified cost or pricing data, identifying the cost impact adjustment necessitated by the deficient purchasing system;

(iii) Provide for the contracting officer to adjust the contract price unilaterally if the contractor fails to submit the supplemental proposal; and

(iv) Provide that failure of the Government and the contractor to agree to the price adjustment shall be a dispute under the Disputes clause.

[Interim rule, 76 FR 28856, 5/18/2011, effective 5/18/2011; Final rule, 77 FR 11355, 2/24/2012, effective 2/24/2012]

244.305-71 Contract clause.

Use the Contractor Purchasing System Administration basic clause or its alternate as follows:

(a) Use the clause at 252.244-7001, Contractor Purchasing System Administration—Basic, in solicitations and contracts containing the clause at FAR 52.244-2, Subcontracts.

(b) Use the clause at 252.244-7001, Contractor Purchasing System Administration—Alternate I, in solicitations and contracts that contain the clause at 252.246-7007, Contractor Counterfeit Electronic Part Detection and Avoidance System, but do not contain FAR 52.244-2, Subcontracts.

[Interim rule, 76 FR 28856, 5/18/2011, effective 5/18/2011; Final rule, 77 FR 11355, 2/24/ 2012, effective 2/24/2012; Final rule, 79 FR 26091, 5/6/2014, effective 5/6/2014]

SUBPART 244.4—SUBCONTRACTS FOR COMMERCIAL ITEMS AND COMMERCIAL COMPONENTS

244.402 Policy requirements.

(a) Contractors shall determine whether a particular subcontract item meets the definition of a commercial item. This requirement does not affect the contracting officer's responsibilities or determinations made under FAR 15.403-1(c)(3). Contractors are expected to exercise reasonable business judgment in making such determinations, consistent with the guidelines for conducting market research in FAR part 10.

244.403 Contract clause.

Use the clause at 252.244-7000, Subcontracts for Commercial Items, in solicitations and contracts, including solicitations and contracts using FAR part 12 procedures for the acquisition of commercial items.

[Interim rule, 62 FR 5779, 2/7/97, effective 2/7/97, corrected, 62 FR 49305, 9/19/97; 65 FR 14401, 3/16/2000; Final rule, 67 FR 38023, 5/31/2002, effective 5/31/2002; Final rule, 72 FR 2633, 1/22/2007, effective 1/22/2007; Final rule, 74 FR 52895, 10/15/2009, effective 10/15/2009; Final rule, 77 FR 39141, 6/29/2012, effective 6/29/2012; Final rule, 78 FR 37980, 6/25/2013, effective 6/25/2013]

PART 245—GOVERNMENT PROPERTY

Table of Contents

Subpart 245.1—General

Definitions 245.101
Policy 245.102
Furnishing Government property to contractors 245.103-70
Transferring Government property accountability 245.103-71
Government-furnished property attachments to solicitations and awards 245.103-72
Government property under sustainment contracts 245.103-73
Contracting office responsibilities 245.103-74
Responsibility and liability for Government property 245.104
Contractor's property management system compliance 245.105
Contract clauses 245.107

Subpart 245.2—Solicitation and Evaluation Procedures

Solicitation 245.201
Definitions 245.201-70
Security classification 245.201-71
Removed 245.201-72

Subpart 245.3—Authorizing the Use and Rental of Government Property

Contracts with foreign governments or international organizations. 245.302

Subpart 245.4—Title to Government Property

Title to contractor-acquired property 245.402
Policy. 245.402-70
Delivery of contractor-acquired property 245.402-71

Subpart 245.5—Support Government Property Administration

Storage at the Government's expense 245.570

Subpart 245.6—Reporting, Reutilization, and Disposal

Reutilization of Government property 245.602
Inventory disposal schedules 245.602-1
Screening 245.602-3
Plant clearance procedures 245.602-70
Disposal of surplus property 245.604
Sale of surplus property 245.604-3

Subpart 245.70—Plant Clearance Forms

Forms 245.7001
Standard Form 97, Certificate of Release of a Motor Vehicle (Agency Record Copy) 245.7001-1
DD Form 1149, Requisition and Invoice Shipping Document 245.7001-2
DD Form 1348-1, DoD Single Line Item Release/Receipt Document 245.7001-3
DD Form 1640, Request for Plant Clearance 245.7001-4
DD Form 1641, Disposal Determination/Approval 245.7001-5
DLA Form 1822, End Use Certificate 245.7001-6

Subpart 245.72—[Removed]

Subpart 245.73—[Removed]

PART 245—GOVERNMENT PROPERTY

SUBPART 245.1—GENERAL

245.101 Definitions.

Mapping, charting, and geodesy property, as used in this subpart, is defined in the clause at 252.245-7000, Government-Furnished Mapping, Charting, and Geodesy Property.

[Final rule, 74 FR 37645, 7/29/2009, effective 7/29/2009]

245.102 Policy.

(See the policy guidance at PGI 245.102-70.)

(1) *Mapping, charting, and geodesy property*. All Government-furnished mapping, charting, and geodesy (MC&G) property is under the control of the Director, National Geospatial Intelligence Agency.

(i) MC&G property shall not be duplicated, copied, or otherwise reproduced for purposes other than those necessary for contract performance.

(ii) Upon completion of contract performance, the contracting officer shall—

(A) Contact the Director, National Geospatial-Intelligence Agency, 7500 Geoint Drive, Springfield, VA 22150, for disposition instructions;

(B) Direct the contractor to destroy or return all Government-furnished MC&G property not consumed during contract performance; and

(C) Specify the destination and means of shipment for property to be returned to the Government.

(2) *Government supply sources*. When a contractor will be responsible for preparing requisitioning documentation to acquire Government-furnished property from Government supply sources, include in the contract the requirement to prepare the documentation in accordance with DoD 4000.25-1-M, Military Standard Requisitioning and Issue Procedures (MILSTRIP). Copies are available from the address cited at PGI 251.102.

(3) *Acquisition and management of industrial resources*. See Subpart 237.75 for policy relating to facilities projects.

(4) *Government-furnished property identification*.

(i) It is DoD policy that Government-furnished property be tagged, labeled, or marked based on DoD marking standards (MIL Standard 130) or other standards, when the requiring activity determines that such items are subject to serialized item management (serially-managed items). The list of Government-furnished property subject to serialized item management will be identified in the contract in accordance with PGI 245.103-72, GFP attachments to solicitations and awards.

(ii) *Exceptions*. The Contractor will not be required to tag, label, or mark—

(A) Government-furnished property that was previously tagged, labeled, or marked;

(B) Items, as determined by the head of the agency, that are to be used to support a contingency operation; or to facilitate defense against or recovery from nuclear, biological, chemical, or radiological attack;

(C) Items for which a determination and findings has been executed concluding that it is more cost effective for the Government requiring activity to assign, mark, and register the unique item identification after delivery of an item acquired from a small business concern or a commercial item acquired under FAR part 12 or part 8.

(1) The determination and findings shall be executed by—

(i) The Component Acquisition Executive for an Acquisition Category (ACAT) I program; or

(ii) The head of the contracting activity for all other programs.

(2) A copy of the executed determination and findings shall be provided to the DoD Unique Item Identification Policy Office at this address: OUSD (AT&L) DPAP/Program Development and Implementation, Room 3B855, 3060 Defense Pentagon, Washington, DC 20301-3060; or by facsimile to 703-602-6047.

(D) Items that are contractor-acquired property;

(E) Property under any statutory leasing authority;

(F) Property to which the Government has acquired a lien or title solely because of partial, advance, progress, or performance-based payments;

(G) Intellectual property or software; or

(H) Real property.

(5) *Reporting loss of Government property.* The Defense Contract Management Agency (DCMA) eTools software application is the DoD data repository for reporting loss of Government property in the possession of contractors. The requirements and procedures for reporting loss of Government property to eTools are set forth in the clause at 252.245-7002, Reporting Loss of Government Property, prescribed at 245.107.

[Final rule, 74 FR 37645, 7/29/2009, effective 7/29/2009; Final rule, 76 FR 3536, 1/20/2011, effective 1/20/2011; Final rule, 76 FR 6004, 2/2/2011, effective 2/2/2011; Final rule, 76 FR 6006, 2/2/2011, effective 2/2/2011; Final rule, 80 FR 2018, 1/15/2015, effective 1/15/2015; Final rule, 81 FR 36473, 6/7/2016, effective 6/7/2016]

245.103 General.

(1) Follow the procedures at PGI 245.103-70 for furnishing Government property to contractors.

(2) Follow the procedures at PGI 245.103-71 for transferring Government property accountability.

[Final rule, 74 FR 37645, 7/29/2009, effective 7/29/2009; Final rule, 76 FR 3536, 1/20/2011, effective 1/20/2011]

245.103-70 Furnishing Government property to contractors. (No Text)

[Final rule, 77 FR 76936, 12/31/2012, effective 12/31/2012]

245.103-71 Transferring Government property accountability. (No Text)

[Final rule, 77 FR 76936, 12/31/2012, effective 12/31/2012]

245.103-72 Government-furnished property attachments to solicitations and awards.

When performance will require the use of Government-furnished property, contracting officers shall use the fillable electronic "Requisitioned Government Furnished Property" and/or "Scheduled Government Furnished Property" formats as attachments to solicitations and awards. See PGI 245.103-72 for links to the formats and procedures for preparing Government-furnished property attachments to solicitations and awards.

[Final rule, 77 FR 76936, 12/31/2012, effective 12/31/2012; Final rule, 78 FR 13543, 2/28/2013, effective 2/28/2013]

245.103-73 Government property under sustainment contracts.

See PGI 245.103-73 for information on the reporting requirements for Government inventory held by contractors under sustainment contracts in accordance with DoD Manual 4140.01, Volume 6, DoD Supply Chain Materiel Management Procedures: Materiel Returns, Retention, and Disposition.

[Final rule, 82 FR 61479, 12/28/2017, effective 12/28/2017]

245.103-74 Contracting office responsibilities.

See PGI 245.103-74 for contracting office responsibilities.

[Final rule, 77 FR 76936, 12/31/2012, effective 12/31/2012; Final rule, 82 FR 61479, 12/28/2017, effective 12/28/2017; Final rule, 83 FR 12681, 3/23/2018, effective 3/23/2018]

245.104 Responsibility and liability for Government property.

In addition to the contract types listed at FAR 45.104, contractors are not held liable for loss of Government property under negotiated fixed-price contracts awarded on a basis other than submission of certified cost or pricing data.

[Final rule, 76 FR 71824, 11/18/2011, effective 11/18/2011]

245.105 Contractor's property management system compliance.

(a) *Definitions*—

(1) *Acceptable property management system* and *property management system* are defined in the clause at 252.245-7003, Contractor Property Management System Administration.

(2) *Significant deficiency* is defined in the clause at 252.245-7003, Contractor Property Management System Administration.

(b) *Policy*. The cognizant contracting officer, in consultation with the property administrator, shall—

(1) Determine the acceptability of the system and approve or disapprove the system; and

(2) Pursue correction of any deficiencies.

(c) In evaluating the acceptability of a contractor's property management system, the contracting officer, in consultation with the property administrator, shall determine whether the contractor's property management system complies with the system criteria for an acceptable property management system as prescribed in the clause at 252.245-7003, Contractor Property Management System Administration.

(d) *Disposition of findings*—(1) *Reporting of findings*. The property administrator shall document findings and recommendations in a report to the contracting officer. If the property administrator identifies any significant property system deficiencies, the report shall describe the deficiencies in sufficient detail to allow the contracting officer to understand the deficiencies.

(2) *Initial determination*. (i) The contracting officer shall review findings and recommendations and, if there are no significant deficiencies, shall promptly notify the contractor, in writing, that the contractor's property management system is acceptable and approved; or

(ii) If the contracting officer finds that there are one or more significant deficiencies (as defined in the clause at 252.245-7003, Contractor Property Management System Administration) due to the contractor's failure to meet one or more of the property management system criteria in the clause at 252.245-7003, the contracting officer shall—

(A) Promptly make an initial written determination on any significant deficiencies and notify the contractor, in writing, providing a description of each significant deficiency in sufficient detail to allow the contractor to understand the deficiency;

(B) Request the contractor to respond, in writing, to the initial determination within 30 days and;

(C) Evaluate the contractor's response to the initial determination, in consultation with the property administrator, and make a final determination.

(3) *Final determination*. (i) The contracting officer shall make a final determination and notify the contractor, in writing, that—

(A) The contractor's property management system is acceptable and approved, and no significant deficiencies remain, or

(B) Significant deficiencies remain. The notice shall identify any remaining significant deficiencies, and indicate the adequacy of any proposed or completed corrective action. The contracting officer shall—

(*1*) Request that the contractor, within 45 days of receipt of the final determination, either correct the deficiencies or submit an acceptable corrective action plan showing milestones and actions to eliminate the deficiencies;

(*2*) Disapprove the system in accordance with the clause at 252.245-7003, Contractor Property Management System Administration; and

(*3*) Withhold payments in accordance with the clause at 252.242-7005, Contractor Business Systems, if the clause is included in the contract.

(ii) Follow the procedures relating to monitoring a contractor's corrective action and the correction of significant deficiencies in PGI 245.105.

(e) *System approval*. The contracting officer shall promptly approve a previously disapproved property management system and notify the contractor when the contracting officer determines, in consultation with the property administrator, that there are no remaining significant deficiencies.

(f) *Contracting officer notifications.* The cognizant contracting officer shall promptly distribute copies of a determination to approve a system, disapprove a system and withhold payments, or approve a previously disapproved system and release withheld payments to the auditor; payment office; affected contracting officers at the buying activities; and cognizant contracting officers in contract administration activities.

[Final rule, 74 FR 37645, 7/29/2009, effective 7/29/2009; Interim rule, 76 FR 28856, 5/18/2011, effective 5/18/2011; Final rule, 77 FR 11355, 2/24/2012, effective 2/24/2012]

245.107 Contract clauses.

(1) (i) In lieu of the prescription at FAR 45.107(d), use the clause at FAR 52.245-1, Government Property, in all purchase orders for repair, maintenance, overhaul, or modification of Government property regardless of the unit acquisition cost of the items to be repaired.

(ii) For negotiated fixed-price contracts awarded on a basis other than submission of certified cost or pricing data for which Government property is provided, use the clause at FAR 52.245-1, Government Property, without its Alternate I.

(2) Use the clause at 252.245-7000, Government-Furnished Mapping, Charting, and Geodesy Property, in solicitations and contracts when mapping, charting, and geodesy property is to be furnished.

(3) Use the clause at 252.245-7001, Tagging, Labeling, and Marking of Government-Furnished Property, in solicitations and contracts that contain the clause at FAR 52.245-1, Government Property.

(4) Use the clause at 252.245-7002, Reporting Loss of Government Property, in solicitations and contracts that contain the clause at FAR 52.245-1, Government Property.

(5) Use the clause at 252.245-7003, Contractor Property Management System Administration, in solicitations and contracts containing the clause at FAR 52.245-1, Government Property.

(6) Use the clause at 252.245-7004, Reporting, Reutilization, and Disposal, in solicitations and contracts that contain the clause at FAR 52.245-1, Government Property.

[Final rule, 74 FR 37645, 7/29/2009, effective 7/29/2009; Redesignated as 245.107-70; Final rule, 76 FR 6004, 2/2/2011, effective 2/2/2011; Final rule, 76 FR 6006, 2/2/2011, effective 2/2/2011; Interim rule, 76 FR 28856, 5/18/2011, effective 5/18/2011; Final rule, 76 FR 52139, 8/19/2011, effective 8/19/2011; Final rule, 76 FR 71824, 11/18/2011, effective 11/18/2011; Final rule, 77 FR 11355, 2/24/2012, effective 2/24/2012; Final rule, 84 FR 18161, 4/30/2019, effective 4/30/2019]

SUBPART 245.2—SOLICITATION AND EVALUATION PROCEDURES

245.201 Solicitation. (No Text)

[Final rule, 76 FR 3536, 1/20/2011, effective 1/20/2011]

245.201-70 Definitions.

See the definitions at PGI 245.201-70.

[Final rule, 76 FR 3536, 1/20/2011, effective 1/20/2011]

245.201-71 Security classification.

Follow the procedures at PGI 245.201-71 for security classification.

[Final rule, 76 FR 3536, 1/20/2011, effective 1/20/2011; Redesignated Final rule, 77 FR 76936, 12/31/2012, effective 12/31/2012]

245.201-72 [Removed]

[Final rule, 76 FR 3536, 1/20/2011, effective 1/20/2011; Final rule, 77 FR 76936, 12/31/2012, effective 12/31/2012]

SUBPART 245.3—AUTHORIZING THE USE AND RENTAL OF GOVERNMENT PROPERTY

245.302 Contracts with foreign governments or international organizations.

(1) *General.*

(i) *Approval.* A contractor may use Government property on work for foreign governments and international organizations only when approved in writing by the contracting officer having cognizance of the property. The contracting officer may grant approval, provided—

(A) The use will not interfere with foreseeable requirements of the United States;

(B) The work is undertaken as a DoD foreign military sale; or

(C) For a direct commercial sale, the foreign country or international organization would be authorized to contract with the department concerned under the Arms Export Control Act.

(ii) *Use charges.*

(A) The Use and Charges clause is applicable on direct commercial sales to foreign governments or international organizations.

(B) When a particular foreign government or international organization has funded the acquisition of property, do not assess the foreign government or international organization rental charges or nonrecurring recoupments for the use of such property.

(2) *Special tooling and special test equipment.*

(i) DoD normally recovers a fair share of nonrecurring costs of special tooling and special test equipment by including these costs in its calculation of the nonrecurring cost recoupment charge when major defense equipment is sold by foreign military sales or direct commercial sales to foreign governments or international organizations. "Major defense equipment" is defined in DoD Directive 2140.2, Recoupment of Nonrecurring Costs on Sales of U.S. Items, as any item of significant military equipment on the United States Munitions List having a nonrecurring research, development, test, and evaluation cost of more than $50 million or a total production cost of more than $200 million.

(ii) When the cost thresholds in paragraph (2)(i) of this section are not met, the contracting officer shall assess rental charges for use of special tooling and special test equipment pursuant to the Use and Charges clause if administratively practicable.

(3) *Waivers.*

(i) Rental charges for use of U.S. production and research property on commercial sales transactions to the Government of Canada are waived for all commercial contracts. This waiver is based on an understanding wherein the Government of Canada has agreed to waive its rental charges.

(ii) Requests for waiver or reduction of charges for the use of Government property on work for foreign governments or international organizations shall be submitted to the contracting officer, who is authorized to approve the requests in consultation with the appropriate functional specialist.

[Final rule, 74 FR 37645, 7/29/2009, effective 7/29/2009; Final rule, 78 FR 65219, 10/31/2013, effective 10/31/2013]

SUBPART 245.4—TITLE TO GOVERNMENT PROPERTY

245.402 Title to contractor-acquired property. (No Text)

[Final rule, 76 FR 3536, 1/20/2011, effective 1/20/2011]

245.402-70 Policy.

Review the guidance at PGI 245.402-70 with regard to oversight and surveillance of contractor-acquired property.

[Final rule, 76 FR 3536, 1/20/2011, effective 1/20/2011; Final rule, 81 FR 50652, 8/2/2016, effective 8/2/2016]

245.402-71 Delivery of contractor-acquired property.

Follow the procedures at PGI 245.402-71 for the delivery of contractor-acquired property.

[Final rule, 76 FR 3536, 1/20/2011, effective 1/20/2011]

SUBPART 245.5—SUPPORT GOVERNMENT PROPERTY ADMINISTRATION

245.505 [Removed]

[Final rule, 74 FR 37645, 7/29/2009, effective 7/29/2009]

245.505-3 [Removed]

[Final rule, 74 FR 37645, 7/29/2009, effective 7/29/2009]

245.505-5 [Removed]

[Final rule, 74 FR 37645, 7/29/2009, effective 7/29/2009]

245.505-6 [Removed]

[Final rule, 74 FR 37645, 7/29/2009, effective 7/29/2009]

245.505-14 [Removed]

[DAC 91-6, 59 FR 27662, 5/27/94, effective 5/27/94; Interim rule, 72 FR 52293, 9/13/2007, effective 9/13/2007; Final rule, 73 FR 70906, 11/24/2008, effective 11/24/2008; Final rule, 74 FR 37645, 7/29/2009, effective 7/29/2009]

245.570 Storage at the Government's expense.

All storage contracts or agreements shall be separately priced and shall include all costs associated with the storage.

[Final rule, 76 FR 52139, 8/19/2011, effective 8/19/2011]

SUBPART 245.6—REPORTING, REUTILIZATION, AND DISPOSAL

245.602 Reutilization of Government property. (No Text)

[Final rule, 76 FR 52139, 8/19/2011, effective 8/19/2011]

245.602-1 Inventory disposal schedules.

For termination inventory, plant clearance officers shall verify inventory schedules, either directly or through appropriate technical personnel, to determine the following:

(a) *Allocability.*

(1) Review contract requirements, delivery schedules, bills of material, and other pertinent documents to determine whether schedules include property that—

(i) Is appropriate for use on the contract; or

(ii) Exceeds the quantity required for completion of the contract, but could be diverted to other commercial work or Government use.

(2) Review the contractor's—

(i) Recent purchases of similar material;

(ii) Plans for current and scheduled production;

(iii) Stock record entries; and

(iv) Bills of material for similar items.

(b) *Quantity.* Take measures to provide assurance that available inventory is in accordance with quantities listed on the inventory schedules. Quantities may be verified by actual item count, acceptance of labeled quantities in unopened/sealed packages, scale counts, or other appropriate methods.

(c) *Condition.* Ensure that the physical condition of the property is reasonably consistent with the Federal Condition Code supplied by the contractor.

[Final rule, 76 FR 52139, 8/19/2011, effective 8/19/2011]

245.602-3 Screening.

Property will be screened DoD-wide, including the contracting agency, requiring agency, and, as appropriate, the General Services Administration. The requiring agency shall have priority for retention of listed items. All required screening must be completed before any sale of contractor inventory, including contractor inventory in overseas locations (foreign excess personal property) can take place. Upon request of the prospective reutilization, transfer, donation, or sales customer, the plant clearance officer shall arrange for inspection of property at the contractor's plant in such a manner as to avoid interruption of the contractor's operations, and consistent with any security requirements.

[Final rule, 76 FR 52139, 8/19/2011, effective 8/19/2011]

245.602-70 Plant clearance procedures.

Follow the procedures at PGI 245.602-70 for establishing and processing a plant clearance case.

[DAC 91-1, 56 FR 67220, 12/30/91, effective 12/31/91; Final rule, 76 FR 52139, 8/19/2011, effective 8/19/2011]

245.604 Disposal of surplus property. (No Text)

[Final rule, 76 FR 52139, 8/19/2011, effective 8/19/2011]

245.604-3 Sale of surplus property.

(a) Plant clearance officers shall determine a best value sales approach (formal or informal sales), to include due consideration for costs, risks, and benefits, e.g., potential sales proceeds.

(b) *Informal bid procedures*. The plant clearance officer may direct the contractor to issue informal invitations for bid (orally, telephonically, or by other informal media), provided—

(1) Maximum practical competition is obtained;

(2) Sources solicited are recorded; and

(3) Informal bids are confirmed in writing.

(c) *Sale approval and award*. Plant clearance officers shall—

(1) Evaluate bids to establish that the sale price is fair and reasonable, taking into consideration—

(i) Knowledge or tests of the market;

(ii) Current published prices for the property;

(iii) The nature, condition, quantity, and location of the property; and

(iv) Past sale history for like or similar items;

(2) Approve award to the responsible bidder whose bid is most advantageous to the Government. The plant clearance officer shall not approve award to any bidder who is an ineligible transferee, as defined in 252.245-7004, Reporting, Reutilization, and Disposal; and

(3) Notify the contractor of the bidder to whom an award will be made within five working days from receipt of bids.

(d) *Noncompetitive sales*.

(1) Noncompetitive sales include purchases or retention at less than cost by the contractor. Noncompetitive sales may be made when—

(i) The plant clearance officer determines that this method is essential to expeditious plant clearance; and

(ii) The Government's interests are adequately protected.

(2) Noncompetitive sales shall be at fair and reasonable prices, not less than those reasonably expected under competitive sales.

(3) Conditions justifying noncompetitive sales are—

(i) No acceptable bids are received under competitive sale;

(ii) Anticipated sales proceeds do not warrant competitive sale;

(iii) Specialized nature of the property would not create bidder interest;

(iv) Removal of the property would reduce its value or result in disproportionate handling expenses; or

(v) Such action is essential to the Government's interests.

(e) Plant clearance officers shall consider any special disposal requirements such as demilitarization or trade security control requirements in accordance with DoDM 4160.28-M, Defense Demilitarization Manual, and DoDI 2030.08, Implementation of Trade Security Controls, respectively (See PGI 245.6).

[Final rule, 76 FR 52139, 8/19/2011, effective 8/19/2011]

SUBPART 245.70—PLANT CLEARANCE FORMS

245.7001 Forms.

Use the forms listed below in performance of plant clearance actions.

[Final rule, 76 FR 52139, 8/19/2011, effective 8/19/2011]

245.7001-1 Standard Form 97, Certificate of Release of a Motor Vehicle (Agency Record Copy).

Use for transfers, donations, and sales of motor vehicles. The contracting officer shall execute the SF 97 and furnish it to the purchaser.

[Final rule, 76 FR 52139, 8/19/2011, effective 8/19/2011]

245.7001-2 DD Form 1149, Requisition and Invoice Shipping Document.

Use for transfer and donation of contractor inventory.

[Final rule, 76 FR 52139, 8/19/2011, effective 8/19/2011]

245.7001-3 DD Form 1348-1, DoD Single Line Item Release/Receipt Document.

Use when authorized by the plant clearance officer.

[Final rule, 76 FR 52139, 8/19/2011, effective 8/19/2011]

245.7001-4 DD Form 1640, Request for Plant Clearance.

Use to request plant clearance assistance or transfer plant clearance.

[Final rule, 76 FR 52139, 8/19/2011, effective 8/19/2011]

245.7001-5 DD Form 1641, Disposal Determination/Approval.

Use to record rationale for the following disposal determinations:

(a) Downgrade useable property to scrap.

(b) Abandonment or destruction.

(c) Noncompetitive sale of surplus property.

(d) Other disposal actions.

[Final rule, 76 FR 52139, 8/19/2011, effective 8/19/2011]

245.7001-6 DLA Form 1822, End Use Certificate.

Use when directed by the plant clearance officer.

[Final rule, 76 FR 52139, 8/19/2011, effective 8/19/2011; Final rule, 77 FR 52253, 8/29/2012, effective 8/29/2012]

SUBPART 245.72—[REMOVED]

245.7201 [Removed]

[Final rule, 76 FR 52139, 8/19/2011, effective 8/19/2011]

245.7202 [Removed]

[Final rule, 76 FR 52139, 8/19/2011, effective 8/19/2011]

245.7203 [Removed]

[Final rule, 64 FR 51074, 9/21/99, effective 9/21/99; Final rule, 63 FR 31937, 6/11/98, effective 6/11/98; Final rule, 76 FR 52139, 8/19/2011, effective 8/19/2011]

245.7204 [Removed]

[Final rule, 76 FR 52139, 8/19/2011, effective 8/19/2011]

245.7205 [Removed]

[Final rule, 76 FR 52139, 8/19/2011, effective 8/19/2011]

245.7206 [Removed]

[DAC 91-12, 62 FR 34114, 6/24/97, effective 6/24/97; Final rule, 63 FR 31937, 6/11/98, effective 6/11/98; Final rule, 76 FR 52139, 8/19/2011, effective 8/19/2011]

SUBPART 245.73—[REMOVED]

245.7301 [Removed]

[Final rule, 63 FR 31937, 6/11/98, effective 6/11/98; Final rule, 76 FR 52139, 8/19/2011, effective 8/19/2011]

245.7302 [Removed]

[Final rule, 76 FR 52139, 8/19/2011, effective 8/19/2011]

245.7302-1 [Removed]

[Final rule, 76 FR 52139, 8/19/2011, effective 8/19/2011]

245.7302-2 [Removed]

[Final rule, 76 FR 52139, 8/19/2011, effective 8/19/2011]

245.7302-3 [Removed]

[Final rule, 76 FR 52139, 8/19/2011, effective 8/19/2011]

245.7302-4 [Removed]

[Final rule, 76 FR 52139, 8/19/2011, effective 8/19/2011]

245.7302-5 [Removed]

[Final rule, 76 FR 52139, 8/19/2011, effective 8/19/2011]

245.7303 [Removed]

[Final rule, 76 FR 52139, 8/19/2011, effective 8/19/2011]

245.7304 [Removed]

[Final rule, 76 FR 52139, 8/19/2011, effective 8/19/2011]

245.7305 [Removed]

[Final rule, 76 FR 52139, 8/19/2011, effective 8/19/2011]

245.7306 [Removed]

[Final rule, 76 FR 52139, 8/19/2011, effective 8/19/2011]

245.7307 [Removed]

[Final rule, 76 FR 52139, 8/19/2011, effective 8/19/2011]

245.7307-1 [Removed]

[Final rule, 76 FR 52139, 8/19/2011, effective 8/19/2011]

245.7307-2 [Removed]

[Final rule, 76 FR 52139, 8/19/2011, effective 8/19/2011]

245.7308 [Removed]

[DAC 91-3, 57 FR 42633, 9/15/92, effective 8/31/92; DAC 91-4, 57 FR 53601, 11/12/92, effective 10/30/92; Final rule, 76 FR 52139, 8/19/2011, effective 8/19/2011]

245.7309 [Removed]

[Final rule, 76 FR 52139, 8/19/2011, effective 8/19/2011]

245.7309-1 [Removed]

[Final rule, 76 FR 52139, 8/19/2011, effective 8/19/2011]

245.7309-2 [Removed]

[Final rule, 76 FR 52139, 8/19/2011, effective 8/19/2011]

245.7309-3 [Removed]

[Final rule, 76 FR 52139, 8/19/2011, effective 8/19/2011]

245.7309-4 [Removed]

[Final rule, 76 FR 52139, 8/19/2011, effective 8/19/2011]

245.7309-5 [Removed]

[Final rule, 76 FR 52139, 8/19/2011, effective 8/19/2011]

245.7309-6 [Removed]

[Final rule, 76 FR 52139, 8/19/2011, effective 8/19/2011]

245.7309-7 [Removed]

[Final rule, 76 FR 52139, 8/19/2011, effective 8/19/2011]

245.7309-8 [Removed]

[Final rule, 76 FR 52139, 8/19/2011, effective 8/19/2011]

245.7309-9 [Removed]

[Final rule, 76 FR 52139, 8/19/2011, effective 8/19/2011]

245.7309-10 [Removed]

[Final rule, 76 FR 52139, 8/19/2011, effective 8/19/2011]

245.7309-11 [Removed]

[Final rule, 76 FR 52139, 8/19/2011, effective 8/19/2011]

245.7309-12 [Removed]

[Final rule, 76 FR 52139, 8/19/2011, effective 8/19/2011]

245.7309-13 [Removed]

[Final rule, 76 FR 52139, 8/19/2011, effective 8/19/2011]

245.7309-14 [Removed]

[Final rule, 76 FR 52139, 8/19/2011, effective 8/19/2011]

245.7310 [Removed]

[Final rule, 76 FR 52139, 8/19/2011, effective 8/19/2011]

245.7310-1 [Removed]

[Final rule, 76 FR 52139, 8/19/2011, effective 8/19/2011]

245.7310-2 [Removed]

[Final rule, 76 FR 52139, 8/19/2011, effective 8/19/2011]

245.7310-3 [Removed]

[Final rule, 76 FR 52139, 8/19/2011, effective 8/19/2011]

245.7310-4 [Removed]

[Final rule, 76 FR 52139, 8/19/2011, effective 8/19/2011]

245.7310-5 [Removed]

[Final rule, 76 FR 52139, 8/19/2011, effective 8/19/2011]

245.7310-6 [Removed]

[Final rule, 76 FR 52139, 8/19/2011, effective 8/19/2011]

245.7310-7 [Removed]

[Final rule, 76 FR 52139, 8/19/2011, effective 8/19/2011]

245.7310-8 [Removed]

[Final rule, 76 FR 52139, 8/19/2011, effective 8/19/2011]

245.7311 [Removed]

[Final rule, 76 FR 52139, 8/19/2011, effective 8/19/2011]

245.7311-1 [Removed]

[Final rule, 76 FR 52139, 8/19/2011, effective 8/19/2011]

245.7311-2 [Removed]

[Final rule, 76 FR 52139, 8/19/2011, effective 8/19/2011]

245.7311-3 [Removed]

[Final rule, 76 FR 52139, 8/19/2011, effective 8/19/2011]

245.7311-4 [Removed]

[Final rule, 76 FR 52139, 8/19/2011, effective 8/19/2011]

PART 246—QUALITY ASSURANCE

Table of Contents

Subpart 246.1—General

Definitions 246.101
Policy 246.102
Contracting office responsibilities 246.103
[Removed] 246.104

Subpart 246.2—Contract Quality Requirements

Types of contract quality requirements 246.202
Higher-level contract quality requirements 246.202-4
[Removed] 246.203
Safety of facilities, infrastructure, and equipment for military operations .. 246.270
Scope 246.270-1
Policy 246.270-2
Exceptions 246.270-3
Contract clause 246.270-4

Subpart 246.3—Contract Clauses

Notification of potential safety issues 246.370

Subpart 246.4—Government Contract Quality Assurance

General 246.401
Government contract quality assurance at source 246.402
Government contract quality assurance for acquisitions at or below the simplified acquisition threshold 246.404
Foreign governments 246.406
Nonconforming supplies or services 246.407
Single-agency assignments of Government contract quality assurance 246.408
Subsistence 246.408-70
Aircraft 246.408-71
[Removed] 246.408-72
Government contract quality assurance actions 246.470
Assessment of additional costs 246.470-1
Quality evaluation data 246.470-2
[Removed] 246.470-3
[Removed] 246.470-4
[Removed] 246.470-5
Authorizing shipment of supplies 246.471
Inspection stamping 246.472

Subpart 246.5—Acceptance

Certificate of conformance 246.504

Subpart 246.6—Material Inspection and Receiving Reports

General 246.601
[Removed] 246.670
[Removed] 246.671

Subpart 246.7—Warranties

Definitions 246.701
[Removed] 246.702
[Removed] 246.703
Authority for use of warranties 246.704
Limitations 246.705
Warranty terms and conditions 246.706
Warranties of data 246.708
Contract clauses 246.710
Warranty attachments 246.710-70

Subpart 246.8—Contractor Liability for Loss of or Damage to Property of the Government

Contractor counterfeit electronic part detection and avoidance 246.870
Scope 246.870-0
Definition 246.870-1
Policy 246.870-2
Contract clauses 246.870-3

PART 246—QUALITY ASSURANCE

SUBPART 246.1—GENERAL

246.101 Definitions.

Discipline Working Group, as used in this subpart, is defined in the clause at 252.246-7004, Safety of Facilities, Infrastructure, and Equipment for Military Operations.

[Interim rule, 60 FR 33144, 6/27/95, effective 6/13/95, finalized without change, DAC 91-9, 60 FR 61586, 11/30/95, effective 11/30/95; Final rule, 71 FR 27646, 5/12/2006, effective 5/12/2006; Interim rule, 75 FR 66683, 10/29/2010, effective 10/29/2010; Final rule, 76 FR 14590, 3/17/2011, effective 3/17/2011]

246.102 Policy.

Departments and agencies shall also—

(1) Develop and manage a systematic, cost-effective Government contract quality assurance program to ensure that contract performance conforms to specified requirements. Apply Government quality assurance to all contracts for services and products designed, developed, purchased, produced, stored, distributed, operated, maintained, or disposed of by contractors.

(2) Conduct quality audits to ensure the quality of products and services meet contractual requirements.

(3) Base the type and extent of Government contract quality assurance actions on the particular acquisition.

(4) Provide contractors the maximum flexibility in establishing efficient and effective quality programs to meet contractual requirements. Contractor quality programs may be modeled on military, commercial, national, or international quality standards.

[Interim rule, 60 FR 33144, 6/27/95, effective 6/13/95, finalized without change, DAC 91-9, 60 FR 61586, 11/30/95, effective 11/30/95; Final rule, 71 FR 27646, 5/12/2006, effective 5/12/2006]

246.103 Contracting office responsibilities.

(1) The contracting office must coordinate with the quality assurance activity before changing any quality requirement.

(2) The activity responsible for technical requirements may prepare instructions covering the type and extent of Government inspections for acquisitions that are complex, have critical applications, or have unusual requirements. Follow the procedures at PGI 246.103(2) for preparation of instructions.

[Final rule, 71 FR 27646, 5/12/2006, effective 5/12/2006]

246.104 [Removed]

[Final rule, 71 FR 27646, 5/12/2006, effective 5/12/2006]

SUBPART 246.2—CONTRACT QUALITY REQUIREMENTS

246.202 Types of contract quality requirements. (No Text)

246.202-4 Higher-level contract quality requirements.

(1) Higher-level contract quality requirements are used in addition to a standard inspection requirement.

(2) Higher-level contract quality requirements, including nongovernment quality system standards adopted to meet DoD needs, are listed in the DoD Index of Specifications and Standards.

[Interim rule, 60 FR 33144, 6/27/95, effective 6/13/95; Redesignated from 246.202-3, DAC 91-9, 60 FR 61586, 11/30/95, effective 11/30/95]

246.203 [Removed]

[Final rule, 71 FR 27646, 5/12/2006, effective 5/12/2006]

246.270 Safety of facilities, infrastructure, and equipment for military operations. (No Text)

[Interim rule, 75 FR 66683, 10/29/2010, effective 10/29/2010; Final rule, 76 FR 14590, 3/17/2011, effective 3/17/2011]

246.270-1 Scope.

This section implements section 807 of the National Defense Authorization Act for Fiscal Year 2010 (Pub. L. 111-84). It establishes policies and procedures intended to ensure the safety and habitability of facilities, infrastructure, and equipment acquired for use by DoD military or civilian personnel during military operations performed outside the United States, Guam, Puerto Rico, and the Virgin Islands.

[Interim rule, 75 FR 66683, 10/29/2010, effective 10/29/2010; Final rule, 76 FR 14590, 3/17/2011, effective 3/17/2011]

246.270-2 Policy.

(a) Contracts (including task and delivery orders) for the construction, installation, repair, maintenance, or operation of facilities, infrastructure, and equipment configured for occupancy, including but not limited to, existing host nation facilities, new construction, and relocatable buildings acquired for use by DoD military or civilian personnel, shall require a pre-occupancy safety and habitability inspection.

(b) To minimize safety and health risks, each contract covered by this policy shall require the contractor's compliance with the Unified Facilities Criteria (UFC) 1-200-01 and its referenced standards for—

(1) Fire protection;

(2) Structural integrity;

(3) Electrical systems;

(4) Plumbing;

(5) Water treatment;

(6) Waste disposal; and

(7) Telecommunications networks.

(c) Existing host nation facilities constructed to standards equivalent to or more stringent than UFC 1-200-01 are acceptable upon a written determination of the acceptability of the standards by the Discipline Working Group.

(d) Inspections to ensure compliance with UFC 1-200-01 standards shall be conducted in accordance with the inspection clause of the contract.

[Interim rule, 75 FR 66683, 10/29/2010, effective 10/29/2010; Final rule, 76 FR 14590, 3/17/2011, effective 3/17/2011]

246.270-3 Exceptions.

The combatant commander may waive compliance with the foregoing standards when it is impracticable to comply with such standards under prevailing operational conditions.

[Interim rule, 75 FR 66683, 10/29/2010, effective 10/29/2010; Final rule, 76 FR 14590, 3/17/2011, effective 3/17/2011]

246.270-4 Contract clause.

Use the clause at 252.246-7004, Safety of Facilities, Infrastructure, and Equipment for Military Operations, in solicitations and contracts, including solicitations and contracts using FAR part 12 procedures for the acquisition of commercial items, for the construction, installation, repair, maintenance, or operation of facilities, infrastructure, or for equipment configured for occupancy, planned for use by DoD military or civilian personnel during military operations.

[Interim rule, 75 FR 66683, 10/29/2010, effective 10/29/2010; Final rule, 76 FR 14590, 3/17/2011, effective 3/17/2011; Final rule, 78 FR 37980, 6/25/2013, effective 6/25/2013]

SUBPART 246.3—CONTRACT CLAUSES

246.370 Notification of potential safety issues.

(a) Use the clause at 252.246-7003, Notification of Potential Safety Issues, in solicitations and contracts, including solicitations and contracts using FAR part 12 procedures for the acquisition of commercial items, for the acquisition of—

(1) Repairable or consumable parts identified as critical safety items;

(2) Systems and subsystems, assemblies, and subassemblies integral to a system; or

(3) Repair, maintenance, logistics support, or overhaul services for systems and subsystems, assemblies, subassemblies, and parts integral to a system.

(b) Follow the procedures at PGI 246.370 for the handling of notifications received under the clause at 252.246-7003.

[Final rule, 72 FR 2633, 1/22/2007, effective 1/22/2007; Final rule, 78 FR 37980, 6/25/2013, effective 6/25/2013; Final rule, 83 FR 66062, 12/21/2018, effective 12/21/2018]

SUBPART 246.4—GOVERNMENT CONTRACT QUALITY ASSURANCE

246.401 General.

The requirement for a quality assurance surveillance plan shall be addressed and documented in the contract file for each contract except for those awarded using simplified acquisition procedures. For contracts for services, the contracting officer should prepare a quality assurance surveillance plan to facilitate assessment of contractor performance, see 237.172. For contracts for supplies, the contracting officer should address the need for a quality assurance surveillance plan.

[Final rule, 75 FR 22706, 4/30/2010, effective 4/30/2010]

246.402 Government contract quality assurance at source.

Do not require Government contract quality assurance at source for contracts or delivery orders valued below $300,000, unless—

(1) Mandated by DoD regulation;

(2) Required by a memorandum of agreement between the acquiring department or agency and the contract administration agency; or

(3) The contracting officer determines that—

(i) Contract technical requirements are significant (e.g., the technical requirements include drawings, test procedures, or performance requirements);

(ii) The product being acquired—

(A) Has critical characteristics;

(B) Has specific features identified that make Government contract quality assurance at source necessary; or

(C) Has specific acquisition concerns identified that make Government contract quality assurance at source necessary; and

(iii) The contract is being awarded to—

(A) A manufacturer or producer; or

(B) A non-manufacturer or non-producer and specific Government verifications have been identified as necessary and feasible to perform.

[Final rule, 70 FR 8539, 2/22/2005, effective 2/22/2005; Final rule, 75 FR 45072, 8/2/2010, effective 10/1/2010]

246.404 Government contract quality assurance for acquisitions at or below the simplified acquisition threshold.

Do not require Government contract quality assurance at source for contracts or delivery orders valued at or below the simplified acquisition threshold unless the criteria at 246.402 have been met.

[Final rule, 70 FR 8539, 2/22/2005, effective 2/22/2005]

246.406 Foreign governments.

(1) Quality assurance among North Atlantic Treaty Organization (NATO) countries.

(i) NATO Standardization Agreement (STANAG) 4107, Mutual Acceptance of Government Quality Assurance and Usage of the Allied Quality Assurance Publications—

(A) Contains the processes, procedures, terms, and conditions under which one NATO member nation will perform quality assurance for another NATO member nation or NATO organization;

(B) Standardizes the development, updating, and application of the Allied Quality Assurance Publications; and

(C) Has been ratified by the United States and other nations in NATO with certain reservations identified in STANAG 4107.

(ii) Departments and agencies shall follow STANAG 4107 when—

(A) Asking a NATO member nation to perform quality assurance; or

(B) Performing quality assurance when requested by a NATO member nation or NATO organization.

(2) *International military sales (non-NATO)*. Departments and agencies shall—

(i) Perform quality assurance services on international military sales contracts or in accordance with existing agreements;

(ii) Inform host or U.S. Government personnel and contractors on the use of quality assurance publications; and

(iii) Delegate quality assurance to the host government when satisfactory services are available.

(3) *Reciprocal quality assurance agreements*. A Memorandum of Understanding (MOU) with a foreign country may contain an annex that provides for the reciprocal performance of quality assurance services. MOUs should be checked to determine whether such an annex exists for the country where a defense contract will be performed. (See Subpart 225.8 for more information about MOUs.)

[Final rule, 63 FR 43890, 8/17/98, effective 8/17/98; Final rule, 71 FR 27646, 5/12/2006, effective 5/12/2006]

246.407 Nonconforming supplies or services.

(f) If nonconforming material or services are discovered after acceptance, the defect appears to be the fault of the contractor, any warranty has expired, and there are no other contractual remedies, the contracting officer—

(i) Shall notify the contractor in writing of the nonconforming material or service;

(ii) Shall request that the contractor repair or replace the material, or perform the service, at no cost to the Government; and

(iii) May accept consideration if offered. For guidance on solicitation of a refund, see subpart 242.71.

(S-70) The head of the design control activity is the approval authority for acceptance of any nonconforming aviation or ship critical safety items or nonconforming modification, repair, or overhaul of such items (see 209.270). Authority for acceptance of minor nonconformances in aviation or ship critical safety items may be delegated as determined appropriate by the design control activity. See additional information at PGI 246.407.

[Final rule, 67 FR 4207, 1/29/2002, effective 1/29/2002; Interim rule, 69 FR 55987, 9/17/2004, effective 9/17/2004; Final rule, 70 FR 57188, 9/30/2005, effective 9/30/2005; Interim rule, 73 FR 1826, 1/10/2008, effective 1/10/2008; Final rule, 73 FR 46817, 8/12/2008, effective 8/12/2008]

246.408 Single-agency assignments of Government contract quality assurance. (No Text)

246.408-70 Subsistence.

(a) The Surgeons General of the military departments are responsible for—

(1) Acceptance criteria;

(2) Technical requirements; and

(3) Inspection procedures needed to assure wholesomeness of foods.

(b) The contracting office may designate any Federal activity, capable of assuring wholesomeness and quality in food, to perform quality assurance for subsistence contract items. The designation may—

(1) Include medical service personnel of the military departments; and

(2) Be on a reimbursable basis.

246.408-71 Aircraft.

(a) The Federal Aviation Administration (FAA) has certain responsibilities and prerogatives in connection with some commercial aircraft and of aircraft equipment and accessories (Pub. L. 85-726 (72 Stat 776, 49 U.S.C. 1423)). This includes the issuance of various certificates applicable to design, manufacture, and airworthiness.

(b) FAA evaluations are not a substitute for normal DoD evaluations of the contractor's quality assurance measures. Actual records of FAA evaluations may be of use to the contract administration office (CAO) and should be used to their maximum advantage.

(c) The CAO shall ensure that the contractor possesses any required FAA certificates prior to acceptance.

[Final rule, 71 FR 27646, 5/12/2006, effective 5/12/2006]

246.408-72 [Removed]

[Final rule, 71 FR 27646, 5/12/2006, effective 5/12/2006]

246.470 Government contract quality assurance actions. (No Text)

246.470-1 Assessment of additional costs.

(a) Under the clause at FAR 52.246-2, Inspection of Supplies—Fixed-Price, after considering the factors in paragraph (c) of this subsection, the quality assurance representative (QAR) may believe that the assessment of additional costs is warranted. If so, the representative shall recommend that the contracting officer take the necessary action and provide a recommendation as to the amount of additional costs. Costs are based on the applicable Federal agency, foreign military sale, or public rate in effect at the time of the delay, reinspection, or retest.

(b) If the contracting officer agrees with the QAR, the contracting officer shall—

(1) Notify the contractor, in writing, of the determination to exercise the Government's right under the clause at FAR 52.246-2, Inspection of Supplies—Fixed-Price; and

(2) Demand payment of the costs in accordance with the collection procedures contained in FAR Subpart 32.6.

(c) In making a determination to assess additional costs, the contracting officer shall consider—

(1) The frequency of delays, reinspection, or retest under both current and prior contracts;

(2) The cause of such delay, reinspection, or retest; and

(3) The expense of recovering the additional costs.

[Final rule, 71 FR 27646, 5/12/2006, effective 5/12/2006]

246.470-2 Quality evaluation data.

The contract administration office shall establish a system for the collection, evaluation, and use of the types of quality evaluation data specified in PGI 246.470-2.

[Final rule, 71 FR 27646, 5/12/2006, effective 5/12/2006]

246.470-3 [Removed]

[Final rule, 71 FR 27646, 5/12/2006, effective 5/12/2006]

246.470-4 [Removed]

[Final rule, 71 FR 27646, 5/12/2006, effective 5/12/2006]

246.470-5 [Removed]

[Final rule, 71 FR 27646, 5/12/2006, effective 5/12/2006]

246.471 Authorizing shipment of supplies.

(a) *General.* (1) Ordinarily, a representative of the contract administration office signs or stamps the shipping papers that accompany Government source-inspected supplies to release them for shipment. This is done for both prime and subcontracts.

(2) An alternative procedure (see paragraph (b) of this section) permits the contractor to assume the responsibility for releasing the supplies for shipment.

(3) The alternative procedure may include prime contractor release of supplies inspected at a subcontractor's facility.

(4) The use of the alternative procedure releases DoD manpower to perform technical functions by eliminating routine signing or stamping of the papers accompanying each shipment.

(b) *Alternative Procedures—Contract Release for Shipment.*

(1) For foreign military sales contracts, do not use alternative procedures.

(2) The contract administration office may authorize, in writing, the contractor to release supplies for shipment when—

(i) The stamping or signing of the shipping papers by a representative of the contract administration office interferes with the operation of the Government contract quality assurance program or takes too much of the Government representative's time;

(ii) There is sufficient continuity of production to permit the Government to establish a systematic and continuing evaluation of the contractor's control of quality; and

(iii) The contractor has a record of satisfactory quality, including that pertaining to preparation for shipment.

(3) The contract administration office shall withdraw, in writing, the authorization

when there is an indication that the conditions in paragraph (b)(2) of this subsection no longer exist.

(4) When the alternative procedure is used, require the contractor to—

(i) Type or stamp, and sign, the following statement on the required copy or copies of the shipping paper(s), or on an attachment—

The supplies in this shipment—

1. Have been subjected to and have passed all examinations and tests required by the contract;

2. Were shipped in accordance with authorized shipping instructions;

3. Conform to the quality, identity, and condition called for by the contract; and

4. Are of the quantity shown on this document.

This shipment was—

1. Released in accordance with section 246.471 of the Defense FAR Supplement; and

2. Authorized by (name and title of the authorized representative of the contract administration office) in a letter dated (date of authorizing letter). (Signature and title of contractor's designated official.)

(ii) Release and process, in accordance with established instructions, the DD Form 250, Material Inspection and Receiving Report, or other authorized receiving report.

[Final rule, 83 FR 66062, 12/21/2018, effective 12/21/2018]

246.472 Inspection stamping.

(a) DoD quality inspection approval marking designs (stamps) may be used for both prime contracts and subcontracts. Follow the procedures at PGI 246.472(a) for use of DoD inspection stamps.

(b) Policies and procedures regarding the use of National Aeronautics and Space Administration (NASA) quality status stamps are contained in NASA publications. When requested by NASA centers, the DoD inspector shall use NASA quality status stamps in accordance with current NASA requirements.

[Final rule, 71 FR 27646, 5/12/2006, effective 5/12/2006]

SUBPART 246.5—ACCEPTANCE

246.504 Certificate of conformance.

Before authorizing a certificate of conformance for aviation or ship critical safety items, obtain the concurrence of the head of the design control activity (see 209.270).

[Interim rule, 69 FR 55987, 9/17/2004, effective 9/17/2004; Final rule, 70 FR 57188, 9/30/2005, effective 9/30/2005; Interim rule, 73 FR 1826, 1/10/2008, effective 1/10/2008; Final rule, 73 FR 46817, 8/12/2008, effective 8/12/2008]

SUBPART 246.6—MATERIAL INSPECTION AND RECEIVING REPORTS

246.601 General.

See Appendix F, Material Inspection and Receiving Report, for procedures and instructions for the use, preparation, and distribution of—

(1) The Material Inspection and Receiving Report (DD Form 250 series); and

(2) Supplier's commercial shipping/packing lists used to evidence Government contract quality assurance.

[Final rule, 71 FR 27646, 5/12/2006, effective 5/12/2006]

246.670 [Removed]

[Final rule, 71 FR 27646, 5/12/2006, effective 5/12/2006]

246.671 [Removed]

[Final rule, 71 FR 27646, 5/12/2006, effective 5/12/2006]

SUBPART 246.7—WARRANTIES

246.701 Definitions.

As used in this subpart—

Acceptance as used in this subpart and in the warranty clauses at FAR 52.246-17, Warranty of Supplies of a Noncomplex Nature; FAR 52.246-18, Warranty of Supplies of a Complex Nature; FAR 52.246-19, Warranty of Systems and Equipment Under Performance Specifications or Design Criteria; and FAR 52.246-20, Warranty of Services, includes the execution of an official document (*e.g.*, DD Form 250, Material Inspection and Receiving Report) by an authorized representative of the Government.

Defect means any condition or characteristic in any supply or service furnished by the contractor under the contract that is not in compliance with the requirements of the contract.

Enterprise means the entity (e.g., a manufacturer or vendor) responsible for granting the warranty and/or assigning unique item identifiers to serialized warranty items.

Enterprise identifier means a code that is uniquely assigned to an enterprise by an issuing agency.

Issuing agency means an organization responsible for assigning a globally unique identifier to an enterprise, as indicated in the Register of Issuing Agency Codes for International Standards Organization/International Electrotechnical Commission 15459, located at *http://www.aimglobal.org/ ?Reg_Authority15459*.

Serialized item means each item produced is assigned a serial number that is unique among all the collective tangible items produced by the enterprise, or each item of a particular part, lot, or batch number is assigned a unique serial number within that part, lot, or batch number assignment within the enterprise identifier. The enterprise is responsible for ensuring unique serialization within the enterprise identifier or within the part, lot, or batch numbers, and that serial numbers, once assigned, are never used again.

Unique item identifier means a set of data elements marked on an item that is globally unique and unambiguous.

Warranty tracking means the ability to trace a warranted item from delivery through completion of the effectivity of the warranty.

[Final rule, 76 FR 33166, 6/8/2011, effective 6/8/2011; Final rule, 81 FR 17041, 3/25/2016, effective 3/25/2016]

246.702 [Removed]

[Final rule, 71 FR 27646, 5/12/2006, effective 5/12/2006]

246.703 [Removed]

[Final rule, 63 FR 6109, 2/6/98, effective 2/6/98; Final rule, 71 FR 27646, 5/12/2006, effective 5/12/2006]

246.704 Authority for use of warranties.

(1) The chief of the contracting office must approve use of a warranty, except in acquisitions for—

(i) Commercial items (see FAR 46.709);

(ii) Technical data, unless the warranty provides for extended liability (see 246.708);

(iii) Supplies and services in fixed-price type contracts containing quality assurance provisions that reference higher-level contract quality requirements (see 246.202-4); or

(iv) Supplies and services in construction contracts when using the warranties that are contained in Federal, military, or construction guide specifications.

(2) The chief of the contracting office shall approve the use of a warranty only when the benefits are expected to outweigh the cost.

[Interim rule, 60 FR 33144, 6/27/95, effective 6/13/95; DAC 91-9, 60 FR 61586, 11/30/95, effective 11/30/95; Final rule, 63 FR 6109, 2/6/98, effective 2/6/98; Final rule, 71 FR 27646, 5/12/2006, effective 5/12/2006]

246.705 Limitations.

(a) In addition to the exceptions provided in FAR 46.705(a), warranties in the clause at 252.246-7001, Warranty of Data, may be used in cost-reimbursement contracts.

[Final rule, 71 FR 27646, 5/12/2006, effective 5/12/2006]

246.706 Warranty terms and conditions.

(b) (5) *Markings*. For non-commercial items, use MIL-STD-129, Marking for Shipments and Storage, and MIL-STD-130, Identification Marking of U.S. Military Property, when marking warranty items.

[Final rule, 71 FR 27646, 5/12/2006, effective 5/12/2006]

246.708 Warranties of data.

Obtain warranties on technical data when practicable and cost effective. Consider the factors in FAR 46.703 in deciding whether to obtain warranties of technical data. Consider the following in deciding whether to use extended liability provisions—

(1) The likelihood that correction or replacement of the nonconforming data, or a price adjustment, will not give adequate protection to the Government; and

(2) The effectiveness of the additional remedy as a deterrent against furnishing nonconforming data.

246.710 Contract clauses.

(1) Use a clause substantially the same as the basic or one of the alternates of the clause at 252.246-7001, Warranty of Data, in solicitations and contracts that include the clause at 252.227-7013, Rights in Technical Data and Computer Software, when there is a need for greater protection or period of liability than provided by the inspection and warranty clauses prescribed in FAR part 46.

(i) Use the basic clause in solicitations and contracts that are not firm-fixed price or fixed-price incentive.

(ii) Use alternate in fixed-price-incentive solicitations and contracts.

(iii) Use alternate II in firm-fixed-price solicitations and contracts.

(2) Use the clause at 252.246-7002, Warranty of Construction (Germany), instead of the clause at FAR 52.246-21, Warranty of Construction, in solicitations and contracts for construction when a fixed-price contract will be awarded and contract performance will be in Germany.

(3) When the solicitation includes the clause at 252.211-7003, Item Unique Identification and Valuation, which is prescribed in 211.274-6(a), and it is anticipated that the resulting contract will include a warranty for serialized items—

(i) Use the provision 252.246-7005, Notice of Warranty Tracking of Serialized Items, in the solicitation if the Government does not specify a warranty and offerors will be required to enter data with the offer;

(ii) Use the clause at 252.246-7006, Warranty Tracking of Serialized Items, in the solicitation and contract; and

(iii) Include the following warranty attachments, available at *https://www.pdrep.csd.disa.mil/pdrep_files/ other/wsr.htm*, in the solicitation and contract and see 246.710-70:

(A) Warranty Tracking Information.

(B) Source of Repair Instructions.

[DAC 91-12, 62 FR 34114, 6/24/97, effective 6/24/97; Final rule, 64 FR 51074, 9/21/99, effective 9/21/99; Final rule, 71 FR 27646, 5/12/2006, effective 5/12/2006; Final rule, 76 FR 33166, 6/8/2011, effective 6/8/2011; Final rule, 78 FR 76067, 12/16/2013, effective 12/16/2013; Final rule, 79 FR 17448, 3/28/2014, effective 3/28/2014; Final rule, 79 FR 18654, 4/3/2014, effective 4/3/2014; Final rule, 81 FR 17041, 3/25/2016, effective 3/25/2016]

246.710-70 Warranty attachments.

Follow the procedures at PGI 246.710–70 regarding warranty attachments.

[Final rule, 76 FR 33166, 6/8/2011, effective 6/8/2011; Final rule, 81 FR 17041, 3/25/2016, effective 3/25/2016]

SUBPART 246.8—CONTRACTOR LIABILITY FOR LOSS OF OR DAMAGE TO PROPERTY OF THE GOVERNMENT

246.870 Contractor counterfeit electronic part detection and avoidance. (No Text)

[Final rule, 79 FR 26091, 5/6/2014, effective 5/6/2014; Final rule, 81 FR 50635, 8/2/2016, effective 8/2/2016]

246.870-0 Scope.

This section—

(a) Partially implements section 818(c) and (e) of the National Defense Authorization Act for Fiscal Year 2012 (Pub. L. 112-81), as amended by section 817 of the National Defense Authorization Act for Fiscal Year 2015 (Pub. L. 113-291) and section 885 of the National Defense Authorization Act for Fiscal Year 2016 (Pub. L. 114-92); and

(b) Prescribes policy and procedures for preventing counterfeit electronic parts and suspect counterfeit electronic parts from entering the supply chain when procuring electronic parts or end items, components, parts, or assemblies that contain electronic parts.

[Final rule, 79 FR 26091, 5/6/2014, effective 5/6/2014; Final rule, 81 FR 50635, 8/2/2016, effective 8/2/2016; Final rule, 83 FR 19641, 5/4/2018, effective 5/4/2018]

246.870-1 Definition.

Authorized supplier, as used in this subpart, means a supplier, distributor, or an aftermarket manufacturer with a contractual arrangement with, or the express written authority of, the original manufacturer or current design activity to buy, stock, repackage, sell, or distribute the part.

[Final rule, 81 FR 50635, 8/2/2016, effective 8/2/2016]

246.870-2 Policy.

(a) *Sources of electronic parts*. (1) Except as provided in paragraph (a)(2) of this section, the Government requires contractors and subcontractors at all tiers, to—

(i) Obtain electronic parts that are in production by the original manufacturer or an authorized aftermarket manufacturer or currently available in stock from—

(A) The original manufacturers of the parts;

(B) Their authorized suppliers; or

(C) Suppliers that obtain such parts exclusively from the original manufacturers of the parts or their authorized suppliers; and

(ii) Obtain electronic parts that are not in production by the original manufacturer or an authorized aftermarket manufacturer, and that are not currently available in stock from a source listed in paragraph (a)(1)(i) of this section, from suppliers identified by the Contractor as contractor-approved suppliers, provided that—

(A) For identifying and approving such contractor-approved suppliers, the contractor uses established counterfeit prevention industry standards and processes (including inspection, testing, and authentication), such as the DoD-adopted standards at *https://assist.dla.mil*;

(B) The contractor assumes responsibility for the authenticity of parts provided by such contractor-approved suppliers (see 231.205-71); and

(C) The selection of such contractor-approved suppliers is subject to review, audit, and approval by the Government, generally in conjunction with a contractor purchasing system review or other surveillance of purchasing practices by the contract administration office, or if the Government obtains credible evidence that a contractor-approved supplier has provided counterfeit parts. The contractor may proceed with the acquisition of electronic parts from a contractor-approved supplier unless otherwise notified by DoD.

(2) The Government requires contractors and subcontractors to comply with the notification, inspection, testing, and authentication requirements of paragraph (b)(3)(ii) of the clause at 252.246-7008, Sources of Electronic Parts, if the contractor—

(i) Obtains an electronic part from—

(A) A source other than any of the sources identified in paragraph (a)(1) of this section, due to nonavailability from such sources; or

(B) A subcontractor (other than the original manufacturer) that refuses to accept flowdown of this clause; or

(ii) Cannot confirm that an electronic part is new or not previously used and that it has not been commingled in supplier new production or stock with used, refurbished, reclaimed, or returned parts.

(3) Contractors and subcontractors are still required to comply with the requirements of paragraphs (a)(1) or (2) of this section, as applicable, if—

(i) Authorized to purchase electronic parts from the Federal Supply Schedule;

(ii) Purchasing electronic parts from suppliers accredited by the Defense Microelectronics Activity; or

(iii) Requisitioning electronic parts from Government inventory/stock under the authority of the clause at 252.251- 7000, Ordering from Government Supply Sources.

(A) The cost of any required inspection, testing, and authentication of such parts may be charged as a direct cost.

(B) The Government is responsible for the authenticity of the requisitioned electronic parts. If any such part is subsequently found to be counterfeit or suspect counterfeit, the Government will—

(*1*) Promptly replace such part at no charge; and

(*2*) Consider an adjustment in the contract schedule to the extent that replacement of the counterfeit or suspect counterfeit electronic parts caused a delay in performance.

(b) *Contractor counterfeit electronic part detection and avoidance system.* (1) Contractors that are subject to the cost accounting standards and that supply electronic parts or products that include electronic parts, and their subcontractors that supply electronic parts or products that include electronic parts, are required to establish and maintain an acceptable counterfeit electronic part detection and avoidance system. Failure to do so may result in disapproval of the purchasing system by the contracting officer and/or withholding of payments (see 252.244-7001, Contractor Purchasing System Administration).

(2) *System criteria.* A counterfeit electronic part detection and avoidance system shall include risk-based policies and procedures that address, at a minimum, the following areas (see the clause at 252.246-7007, Contractor Counterfeit Electronic Part Detection and Avoidance System):

(i) The training of personnel.

(ii) The inspection and testing of electronic parts, including criteria for acceptance and rejection.

(iii) Processes to abolish counterfeit parts proliferation.

(iv) Processes for maintaining electronic part traceability.

(v) Use of suppliers in accordance with paragraph (a) of this section.

(vi) The reporting and quarantining of counterfeit electronic parts and suspect counterfeit electronic parts.

(vii) Methodologies to identify suspect counterfeit electronic parts and to rapidly determine if a suspect counterfeit electronic part is, in fact, counterfeit.

(viii) Design, operation, and maintenance of systems to detect and avoid counterfeit electronic parts and suspect counterfeit electronic parts.

(ix) Flow down of counterfeit detection and avoidance requirements.

(x) Process for keeping continually informed of current counterfeiting information and trends.

(xi) Process for screening the Government-Industry Data Exchange Program (GIDEP) reports and other credible sources of counterfeiting information.

(xii) Control of obsolete electronic parts.

[Final rule, 79 FR 26091, 5/6/2014, effective 5/6/2014; Final rule, 81 FR 50635, 8/2/2016, effective 8/2/2016; Final rule, 81 FR 72738, 10/21/2016, effective 10/21/2016; Final rule, 83 FR 19641, 5/4/2018, effective 5/4/2018]

246.870-3 Contract clauses.

(a) (1) Except as provided in paragraph (a) (2) of this section, use the clause at 252.246-7007, Contractor Counterfeit Electronic Part Detection and Avoidance System, in solicitations and contracts when procuring—

(i) Electronic parts;

(ii) End items, components, parts, or assemblies containing electronic parts; or

(iii) Services, if the contractor will supply electronic parts or components, parts, or assemblies containing electronic parts as part of the service.

(2) Do not use the clause in solicitations and contracts that are set aside for small business.

(b) Use the clause at 252.246-7008, Sources of Electronic Parts, in solicitations and contracts, including solicitations and contracts using FAR part 12 procedures for the acquisition of commercial items, when procuring—

(1) Electronic parts;

(2) End items, components, parts, or assemblies containing electronic parts; or

(3) Services, if the contractor will supply electronic parts or components, parts, or assemblies containing electronic parts as part of the service.

[Final rule, 79 FR 26091, 5/6/2014, effective 5/6/2014; Final rule, 81 FR 50635, 8/2/2016, effective 8/2/2016]

PART 247—TRANSPORTATION

Table of Contents

Definitions 247.001

Subpart 247.1—General

Policies 247.101
[Removed] 247.104-5
[Removed] 247.105

Subpart 247.2—Contracts for Transportation or for Transportation-Related Services

Scope of subpart 247.200
Preparation of solicitations and contracts 247.206
Solicitation provisions, contract clauses, and special requirements. 247.207
Stevedoring contracts 247.270
Definitions 247.270-1
Technical provisions 247.270-2
Evaluation of bids and proposals 247.270-3
Contract clauses 247.270-4
[Removed] 247.270-5
Contracts for the preparation of personal property for shipment or storage or for performance of intra-city or intra-area movement 247.271
Policy 247.271-1
Procedures 247.271-2
Solicitation provisions, schedule formats, and contract clauses 247.271-3

Subpart 247.3—Transportation in Supply Contracts

General 247.301
Definition 247.301-70
Evaluation factor or subfactor 247.301-71
Solicitation provisions, contract clauses, and transportation factors 247.305
Packing, marking, and consignment instructions 247.305-10
[Removed] 247.305-70
DD Form 1384, Transportation Control and Movement Document 247.370
DD Form 1653, Transportation Data for Solicitations 247.371
DD Form 1654, Evaluation of Transportation Cost Factors 247.372

Subpart 247.5—Ocean Transportation by U.S.-Flag Vessels

Scope 247.570
Definitions 247.571
Policy 247.572
General 247.573
[Removed] 247.573-1
[Removed] 247.573-2
[Removed] 247.573-3
Solicitation provision and contract clauses 247.574

PART 247—TRANSPORTATION

247.001 Definitions.

For definitions of *Civil Reserve Air Fleet* and *Voluntary Intermodal Sealift Agreement*, see Joint Pub 1-02, DoD Dictionary of Military and Associated Terms. See additional information at PGI 247.001 for the Voluntary Intermodal Sealift Agreement program.

[Final rule, 65 FR 50143, 8/17/2000, effective 8/17/2000; Final rule, 75 FR 51416, 8/20/2010, effective 8/20/2010]

SUBPART 247.1—GENERAL

247.101 Policies.

(h) Shipping documents covering f.o.b. origin shipments.

(i) Procedures for the contractor to obtain bills of lading are in the clause at 252.247-7028, Application for U.S. Government Shipping Documentation/Instructions.

(ii) The term *commercial bills of lading* includes the use of any commercial form or procedure.

[Final rule, 77 FR 39140, 6/29/2012, effective 6/29/2012]

247.104-5 [Removed]

[Final rule, 65 FR 50143, 8/17/2000, effective 8/17/2000; Final rule, 75 FR 51416, 8/20/2010, effective 8/20/2010]

247.105 [Removed]

[DAC 91-6, 59 FR 27662, 5/27/94, effective 5/27/94; Final rule, 65 FR 50143, 8/17/2000, effective 8/17/2000; CFR Correction, 74 FR 48170, 9/22/2009; Final rule, 75 FR 51416, 8/20/2010, effective 8/20/2010]

SUBPART 247.2—CONTRACTS FOR TRANSPORTATION OR FOR TRANSPORTATION-RELATED SERVICES

247.200 Scope of subpart.

This subpart does not apply to the operation of vessels owned by, or bareboat chartered by, the Government. See additional guidance at PGI 247.200 for procurement of transportation or related services.

[Final rule, 65 FR 50143, 8/17/2000, effective 8/17/2000; Final rule, 75 FR 51416, 8/20/2010, effective 8/20/2010]

247.206 Preparation of solicitations and contracts.

Consistent with FAR 15.304 and 215.304, consider using the following as evaluation factors or subfactors:

(1) Record of claims involving loss or damage; and

(2) Commitment of transportation assets to readiness support (*e.g.,* Civil Reserve Air Fleet and Voluntary Intermodal Sealift Agreement).

[Final rule, 65 FR 50143, 8/17/2000, effective 8/17/2000; Final rule, 75 FR 51416, 8/20/2010, effective 8/20/2010]

247.207 Solicitation provisions, contract clauses, and special requirements.

(1) Use the clause at 252.247-7003, Pass-Through of Motor Carrier Fuel Surcharge Adjustment to the Cost Bearer, in solicitations and contracts, including solicitations and contracts using FAR part 12 procedures for the acquisition of commercial items, that are for carriage in which a motor carrier, broker, or freight forwarder will provide or arrange truck transportation services that provide for a fuel-related adjustment.

(2) Use the clause at 252.247-7028, Application for U.S. Government Shipping Documentation/Instructions in solicitations and contracts, including solicitations and contracts using FAR part 12 procedures for the acquisition of commercial items, when shipping under Bills of Lading Domestic Route Order under FOB origin contracts, Export Traffic Release regardless of FOB terms, or foreign military sales shipments.

[Interim rule, 74 FR 37652, 7/29/2009, effective 7/29/2009; Final rule, 75 FR 59103, 9/27/2010, effective 9/27/2010; Final rule, 77 FR 39140, 6/29/2012, effective 6/29/2012; Final rule, 78 FR 37980, 6/25/2013, effective 6/25/2013]

247.270 Stevedoring contracts. (No Text)

247.270-1 Definitions.

Commodity rate is—

(1) The price quoted for handling a ton (weight or measurement) of a specified commodity; and

(2) Computed by dividing the hourly stevedoring gang cost by the estimated number of tons of the specified commodity that can be handled in 1 hour.

Gang cost is—

(1) The total hourly wages paid to the workers in the gang, in accordance with the collective bargaining agreement between the maritime industry and the unions at a specific port; and

(2) Payments for workmen's compensation, social security taxes, unemployment insurance, taxes, liability and property damage insurance, general and administrative expenses, and profit.

Stevedoring is the—

(1) Loading of cargo from an agreed point of rest on a pier or lighter and its storage aboard a vessel; or

(2) Breaking out and discharging of cargo from any space in the vessel to an agreed point of rest dockside or in a lighter.

[Final rule, 65 FR 50143, 8/17/2000, effective 8/17/2000; Redesignated 247.270-1, Final rule, 75 FR 51416, 8/20/2010, effective 8/20/2010]

247.270-2 Technical provisions.

(a) Because conditions vary at different ports, and sometimes within the same port, it is not practical to develop standard technical provisions covering all phases of stevedoring operations.

(b) When including rail car, truck, or intermodal equipment loading and unloading, or other dock and terminal work under a stevedoring contract, include these requirements as separate items of work.

[Final rule, 65 FR 50143, 8/17/2000, effective 8/17/2000; Redesignated 247.270-2, Final rule, 75 FR 51416, 8/20/2010, effective 8/20/2010]

247.270-3 Evaluation of bids and proposals.

As a minimum, require that offers include—

(a) Tonnage or commodity rates that apply to the bulk of the cargo worked under normal conditions;

(b) Labor-hour rates that apply to services not covered by commodity rates, or to work performed under hardship conditions; and

(c) Rates for equipment rental.

[Final rule, 65 FR 50143, 8/17/2000, effective 8/17/2000; Redesignated 247.270-3, Final rule, 75 FR 51416, 8/20/2010, effective 8/20/2010]

247.270-4 Contract clauses.

Use the following clauses in solicitations and contracts for stevedoring services as indicated:

(a) 252.247-7000, Hardship Conditions.

(b) 252.247-7002, Revision of Prices, when using negotiation.

(c) 252.247-7007, Liability and Insurance.

[Final rule, 65 FR 50143, 8/17/2000, effective 8/17/2000; Redesignated 247.270-4, Final rule, 75 FR 51416, 8/20/2010, effective 8/20/2010; Final rule, 83 FR 42788, 8/24/2018, effective 8/24/2018; Final rule, 83 FR 49179, 9/28/2018, effective 9/28/2018; Final rule, 83 FR 49181, 9/28/2018, effective 9/28/2018; Final rule, 84 FR 30952, 6/28/2019, effective 6/28/2019]

247.271 Contracts for the preparation of personal property for shipment or storage or for performance of intra-city or intra-area movement. (No Text)

[Final rule, 79 FR 22036, 4/21/2014, effective 4/21/2014]

247.271-1 Policy.

(a) *Annual contracts*. Normally—

(1) Use requirements contracts to acquire services for the—

(i) Preparation of personal property for shipment or storage; and

(ii) Performance of intra-area movement.

(2) Award contracts on a calendar year basis.

(3) Provide for option years.

(4) Award contracts, or exercise option years, before November 1 of each year, if possible.

(b) *Areas of performance.* Define clearly in the solicitation each area of performance.

(1) Establish one or more areas; however, hold the number to a minimum consistent with local conditions.

(2) Each schedule may provide for the same or different areas of performance. Determine the areas as follows—

(i) Use political boundaries, streets, or any other features as lines of demarcation. Consider such matters as—

(A) Total volume;

(B) Size of overall area; and

(C) The need to service isolated areas of high population density.

(ii) Specifically identify frequently used terminals, and consider them as being included in each area of performance described in the solicitation.

(c) *Maximum requirements-minimum capability.* The contracting officer must—

(1) Establish realistic quantities on the Estimated Quantities Report in DoD 4500.9-R, Defense Transportation Regulation, Part IV;

(2) Ensure that the Government's minimum acceptable daily capability—

(i) Will at least equal the maximum authorized individual weight allowance as prescribed by the Joint Federal Travel Regulations; and

(ii) Will encourage maximum participation of small business concerns as offerors.

[Final rule, 65 FR 50143, 8/17/2000, effective 8/17/2000; Redesignated 247.271-1, Final rule, 75 FR 51416, 8/20/2010, effective 8/20/2010]

247.271-2 Procedures.

Follow the procedures at PGI 247.271-2 for contracting for the preparation of personal property for shipment or storage.

[Final rule, 64 FR 2595, 1/15/99, effective 1/15/99; Final rule, 65 FR 50143, 8/17/2000, effective 8/17/2000; Redesignated 247.271-2, Final rule, 75 FR 51416, 8/20/2010, effective 8/20/2010]

247.271-3 Solicitation provisions, schedule formats, and contract clauses.

When acquiring services for the preparation of personal property for movement or storage, or for performance of intra-city or intra-area movement, use the following provisions, clauses, and schedules. Revise solicitation provisions and schedules, as appropriate, if using negotiation rather than sealed bidding. Overseas commands, except those in Alaska and Hawaii, may modify these clauses to conform to local practices, laws, and regulations.

(a) In solicitations and resulting contracts, the schedules provided by the installation personal property shipping office. Follow the procedures at PGI 247.271-3(c) for use of schedules.

(1) When there is no requirement for an item or subitem in a schedule, indicate that item or subitem number, in its proper numerical sequence, and add the statement "No Requirement."

(2) Within Schedules I (Outbound) and II (Inbound), item numbers are reserved to permit inclusion of additional items as required by local conditions.

(3) Overseas activities, except those in Alaska and Hawaii, may modify the schedules when necessary to conform with local trade practices, laws, and regulations.

(4) All generic terminology, schedule, and item numbers in proper sequence must follow those contained in the basic format.

(5) When it is in the Government's best interest to have both outbound and inbound services within a given area of performance furnished by the same contractor, modify the schedule format to combine both services in a single schedule. However, items must follow the same sequential order as in the basic format.

(6) Process any modification of schedule format, other than those authorized in

paragraphs (c)(1) through (5) of this subsection, as a request for deviation to the Commander, MTMC.

(b) In addition to designating each ordering activity, as required by the clause at FAR 52.216-18, Ordering, identify by name or position title the individuals authorized to place orders for each activity. When provisions are made for placing oral orders in accordance with FAR 16.505(a)(4)(vii), document the oral orders in accordance with department or agency instructions.

(c) The clause at 252.247-7013, Contract Areas of Performance.

(d) The clause at 252.247-7014, Demurrage. See additional information at PGI 247.271-3(c)(1) for demurrage and detention charges.

(e) The clause at 252.247-7019, Drayage.

[Final rule, 65 FR 50143, 8/17/2000, effective 8/17/2000; Redesignated 247.271-3, Final rule, 75 FR 51416, 8/20/2010, effective 8/20/2010; Final rule, 78 FR 38234, 6/26/2013, effective 6/26/2013; Final rule, 79 FR 22036, 4/21/2014, effective 4/21/2014; Final rule, 83 FR 30587, 6/29/2018, effective 6/29/2018; Final rule, 83 FR 49178, 9/28/2018, effective 9/28/2018; Final rule, 84 FR 25194, 5/31/2019, effective 5/31/2019; Final rule, 84 FR 30950, 6/28/2019, effective 6/28/2019]

SUBPART 247.3—TRANSPORTATION IN SUPPLY CONTRACTS

247.301 General.

See PGI 247.301 for transportation guidance relating to Government Purchase Card purchases.

[Final rule, 75 FR 51416, 8/20/2010, effective 8/20/2010; Final rule, 81 FR 78011, 11/4/2016, effective 11/4/2016]

247.301-70 Definition.

Integrated logistics managers or *third-party logistics providers* means providers of multiple logistics services. Some examples of logistics services are the management of transportation, demand forecasting, information management, inventory maintenance, warehousing, and distribution.

[Final rule, 65 FR 50143, 8/17/2000, effective 8/17/2000]

247.301-71 Evaluation factor or subfactor.

For contracts that will include a significant requirement for transportation of items outside the contiguous United States, include an evaluation factor or subfactor that favors suppliers, third-party logistics providers, and integrated logistics managers that commit to using carriers that participate in one of the readiness programs (e.g., Civil Reserve Air Force Fleet and Voluntary Intermodal Sealift Agreement).

[Final rule, 65 FR 50143, 8/17/2000, effective 8/17/2000; Final rule, 81 FR 78011, 11/4/2016, effective 11/4/2016]

247.305 Solicitation provisions, contract clauses, and transportation factors. (No Text)

247.305-10 Packing, marking, and consignment instructions.

Follow the procedures at PGI 247.305-10 for preparation of consignment instructions.

[Final rule, 65 FR 50143, 8/17/2000, effective 8/17/2000; Final rule, 67 FR 61516, 10/1/2002, effective 10/1/2002; Final rule, 75 FR 51416, 8/20/2010, effective 8/20/2010]

247.305-70 [Removed]

[DAC 91-7, 60 FR 29491, 6/5/95, effective 5/17/95; Final rule, 75 FR 51416, 8/20/2010, effective 8/20/2010; Final rule, 84 FR 48506, 9/13/2019, effective 9/13/2019]

247.370 DD Form 1384, Transportation Control and Movement Document.

The transportation office of the shipping activity prepares the DD Form 1384 to accompany all shipments made through a military air or water port, in accordance with DoD 4500.9-R, Defense Transportation Regulation, Part II, Chapter 203. A link to this document is available in PGI 247.370.

[Final rule, 67 FR 61516, 10/1/2002, effective 10/1/2002; Redesignated 247.370, Final rule, 75 FR 51416, 8/20/2010, effective 8/20/2010]

247.371 DD Form 1653, Transportation Data for Solicitations.

The transportation specialist prepares the DD Form 1653 to accompany requirements for the acquisition of supplies. The completed form should contain recommendations for suitable f.o.b. terms and other suggested transportation provisions for inclusion in the solicitation.

[Redesignated 247.371, Final rule, 75 FR 51416, 8/20/2010, effective 8/20/2010]

247.372 DD Form 1654, Evaluation of Transportation Cost Factors.

Contracting personnel may use the DD Form 1654 to furnish information to the transportation office for development of cost factors for use by the contracting officer in the evaluation of f.o.b. origin offers.

[Redesignated 247.372, Final rule, 75 FR 51416, 8/20/2010, effective 8/20/2010]

SUBPART 247.5—OCEAN TRANSPORTATION BY U.S.-FLAG VESSELS

247.570 Scope.

(a) Implements—

(1) The Cargo Preference Act of 1904 ("the 1904 Act"), 10 U.S.C. 2631, which applies to the ocean transportation of cargo owned by, or destined for use by, DoD;

(2) Section 1017 of the National Defense Authorization Act for Fiscal Year 2007 (Pub. L. 109-364), which requires consideration, in solicitations requiring a covered vessel, of the extent to which offerors have had overhaul, repair, and maintenance work performed in shipyards located in the United States or Guam; and

(3) Section 3504 of the National Defense Authorization Act for Fiscal Year 2009 (Pub. L. 110-417), which addresses requirements that apply to riding gang members and DoD-exempted individuals (see 252.247-7027(c)) who perform work on U.S.-flag vessels under DoD contracts for transportation services documented under chapter 121, title 46 U.S.C.

(b) Does not specifically implement the Cargo Preference Act of 1954 ("the 1954 Act"), 46 U.S.C. 1241(b). The 1954 Act is applicable to DoD, but DFARS coverage is not required because compliance with the 1904 Act historically has resulted in DoD exceeding the 1954 Act's requirements; and

(c) Does not apply to ocean transportation of the following products, in which case FAR subpart 47.5 applies:

(1) Products obtained for contributions to foreign assistance programs.

(2) Products owned by agencies other than DoD, unless the products are clearly identifiable for eventual use by DoD.

[Final rule, 65 FR 50143, 8/17/2000, effective 8/17/2000; Interim rule 72 FR 49204, 8/28/2007, effective 8/28/2007; Final rule, 73 FR 70909, 11/24/2008, effective 11/24/2008; Interim rule, 75 FR 65437, 10/25/2010, effective 10/25/2010; Final rule, 76 FR 61279, 10/4/2011, effective 10/4/2011]

247.571 Definitions.

As used in this subpart—

(a) *Components, foreign flag vessel, ocean transportation, supplies,* and *U.S.-flag vessel* have the meaning given in the clause at DFARS 252.247-7023, Transportation of Supplies by Sea.

(b) *Reflagging or repair work* has the meaning given in the clause at 252.247-7025, Reflagging or Repair Work.

(c) *Covered vessel, foreign shipyard, overhaul, repair, and maintenance work, shipyard,* and *U.S. shipyard* have the meaning given in the provision at 252.247-7026, Evaluation Preference for Use of Domestic Shipyards—Applicable to Acquisition of Carriage by Vessel for DoD Cargo in the Coastwise or Noncontiguous Trade.

[Interim rule 72 FR 49204, 8/28/2007, effective 8/28/2007; Final rule, 73 FR 70909, 11/24/2008, effective 11/24/2008; Final rule, 78 FR 37980, 6/25/2013, effective 6/25/2013]

247.572 Policy.

(a) In accordance with 10 U.S.C. 2631(a), DoD contractors shall transport supplies, as defined in the clause at 252.247-7023, Transportation of Supplies by Sea, exclusively on U.S.-flag vessels unless—

(1) Those vessels are not available;

(2) The proposed charges to the Government are higher than charges to private persons for the transportation of like goods; or

(3) The proposed freight charges are excessive or unreasonable.

(b) Contracts must provide for the use of Government-owned vessels when security classifications prohibit the use of other than Government-owned vessels.

(c) In accordance with 10 U.S.C. 2631(b)—

(1) Any vessel used under a time charter contract for the transportation of supplies under this section shall have any reflagging or repair work, as defined in the clause at 252.247-7025, Reflagging or Repair Work, performed in the United States or its outlying areas, if the reflagging or repair work is performed—

(i) On a vessel for which the contractor submitted an offer in response to the solicitation for the contract; and

(ii) Prior to the acceptance of the vessel by the Government.

(2) The Secretary of Defense may waive this requirement if the Secretary determines that such waiver is critical to the national security of the United States.

(d) In accordance with Section 1017 of the National Defense Authorization Act for Fiscal Year 2007 (Public Law 109-364)—

(1) When obtaining carriage requiring a covered vessel, the contracting officer must consider the extent to which offerors have had overhaul, repair, and maintenance work for covered vessels performed in shipyards located in the United States or Guam; and

(2) DoD must submit an annual report to the congressional defense committees, addressing the information provided by offerors with regard to overhaul, repair, and maintenance for covered vessels performed in the United States or Guam.

(e) In accordance with section 3504 of the National Defense Authorization Act for Fiscal Year 2009 (Pub. L. 110-417), DoD may not award, renew or extend, or exercise an option under a charter of, or contract for carriage of cargo by, a U.S.-flag vessel documented under chapter 121 of title 46 U.S.C., unless the contract contains the clause at 252.247-7027.

[Final rule, 65 FR 50143, 8/17/2000, effective 8/17/2000; Final rule, 70 FR 35543, 6/21/2005, effective 6/21/2005; Interim rule, 72 FR 49204, 8/28/2007, effective 8/28/2007; Final rule, 73 FR 70909, 11/24/2008, effective 11/24/2008; Interim rule, 75 FR 65437, 10/25/2010, effective 10/25/2010; Final rule, 76 FR 61279, 10/4/2011, effective 10/4/2011; Final rule, 78 FR 37980, 6/25/2013, effective 6/25/2013; Final rule, 79 FR 61583, 10/14/2014, effective 10/14/2014]

247.573 General.

(a) *Delegated authority.* Pursuant to 10 U.S.C. 2631(a) and Secretary of Defense Memorandum dated February 7, 2012, (see PGI 245.573) the authority to make determinations of excessive ocean liner rates and excessive charter rates is delegated to—

(1) The Commander, United States Transportation Command, for excessive ocean liner rate determinations; and

(2) The Secretary of the Navy for excessive charter rate determinations.

(b) *Procedures.* (1) Contracting officers shall follow the procedures at PGI 247.573(b)(1) when purchase of ocean transportation services is incidental to a contract for supplies, services, or construction.

(2) Contracting officers shall follow the procedures at PGI 247.573(b)(2) when direct purchase of ocean transportation services is the principal purpose of the contract.

(3) Agency and department procedures relating to annual reporting requirements of information received from offerors in response to solicitation provision 252.247-7026, Evaluation Preference for Use of Domestic Shipyards—Applicable to Acquisition of Carriage by Vessel for DoD Cargo in the Coastwise of Noncontiguous Trade, are found at PGI 247.573(b)(3).

(4) Procedures are provided at PGI 247.573(b)(4) to accomplish security background checks pursuant to clause 252.247-7027, Riding Gang Member Requirements.

[Interim rule, 72 FR 49204, 8/28/2007, effective 8/28/2007; Final rule, 73 FR 70909, 11/24/2008, effective 11/24/2008; Final rule, 79 FR 61583, 10/14/2014, effective 10/14/2014]

247.573-1 [Removed]

[Final rule, 65 FR 50143, 8/17/2000, effective 8/17/2000; Final rule, 67 FR 38020, 5/31/2002, effective 5/31/2002; Interim rule, 72 FR 49204, 8/28/2007, effective 8/28/2007; Final rule, 73 FR 70909, 11/24/2008, effective 11/24/2008; Final rule, 75 FR 51416, 8/20/2010, effective 8/20/2010; Final rule, 79 FR 61583, 10/14/2014, effective 10/14/2014]

247.573-2 [Removed]

[Final rule, 65 FR 50143, 8/17/2000, effective 8/17/2000; Interim rule, 72 FR 49204, 8/28/2007, effective 8/28/2007; Final rule, 73 FR 70909, 11/24/2008, effective 11/24/2008; Final rule, 75 FR 51416, 8/20/2010, effective 8/20/2010; Final rule, 79 FR 61583, 10/14/2014, effective 10/14/2014]

247.573-3 [Removed]

[Interim rule, 72 FR 49204, 8/28/2007, effective 8/28/2007; Final rule, 73 FR 70909, 11/24/2008, effective 11/24/2008; Final rule, 79 FR 61583, 10/14/2014, effective 10/14/2014]

247.574 Solicitation provisions and contract clauses.

(a)(1) Use the provision at 252.247-7022, Representation of Extent of Transportation by Sea, in all solicitations, including solicitations using FAR part 12 procedures for the acquisition of commercial items, except—

(i) Those for direct purchase of ocean transportation services; or

(ii) Those with an anticipated value at or below the simplified acquisition threshold.

(2) If the solicitation includes the provision at FAR 52.204-7, do not separately list 252.247-7022 in the solicitation.

(b) Use the basic or one of the alternates of the clause at 252.247-7023, Transportation of Supplies by Sea, in all solicitations and contracts, including solicitations and contracts using FAR part 12 procedures for the acquisition of commercial items, except those for direct purchase of ocean transportation services.

(1) Use the basic clause unless any of the supplies to be transported are commercial items that are—

(i) Shipped in direct support of U.S. military contingency operations, exercises, or forces deployed in humanitarian or peacekeeping operations when the contract is not a construction contract; or

(ii) Commissary or exchange cargoes transported outside of the Defense Transportation System when the contract is not a construction contract.

(2) Use the alternate I clause if any of the supplies to be transported are commercial items that are shipped in direct support of U.S. military contingency operations, exercises, or forces deployed in humanitarian or peacekeeping operations when the contract is not a construction contract.

(3) Use the alternate II clause if any of the supplies to be transported are commercial items that are commissary or exchange cargoes transported outside of the Defense Transportation System (10 U.S.C. 2643), when the contract is not a construction contract.

(c) Use the clause at 252.247-7025, Reflagging or Repair Work, in all time charter solicitations and contracts, including time charter solicitations and contracts using FAR part 12 procedures for the acquisition of commercial items, that are for the use of a vessel for the transportation of supplies, unless a waiver has been granted in accordance with 247.572(c)(2).

(d) Use the provision at 252.247-7026, Evaluation Preference for Use of Domestic Shipyards—Applicable to Acquisition of Carriage by Vessel for DoD Cargo in the Coastwise or Noncontiguous Trade, in solicitations, including solicitations using FAR part 12 procedures for the acquisition of commercial items, that require a covered vessel for carriage of cargo for DoD.

(e) Use the clause at 252.247-7027, Riding Gang Member Requirements, in solicitations and contracts, including solicitations and contracts using FAR part 12 procedures for the acquisition of commercial items, that are for the charter of, or contract for carriage of cargo by, a U.S.-flag vessel documented under chapter 121 of title 46 U.S.C.

[Interim rule, 59 FR 10579, 3/7/94, effective 2/25/94; DAC 91-7, 60 FR 29491, 6/5/95, effective 5/17/95; Final rule, 64 FR 2595, 1/15/99, effective 1/15/99; Final rule, 65 FR 14400, 3/16/2000, effective 3/16/2000; Final rule, 67 FR 38020, 5/31/2002, effective 5/31/2002; Interim rule, 72 FR 49204, 8/28/2007, effective 8/28/2007; Final rule, 73 FR 70909, 11/24/2008, effective 11/24/2008; Interim rule, 75 FR 65437, 10/25/2010, effective 10/25/2010; Final rule, 76 FR 61279, 10/4/2011, effective 10/4/2011; Final rule, 78 FR 37980, 6/25/2013, effective 6/25/2013; Final rule, 78 FR 40043, 7/3/2013, effective 7/3/2013; Final rule, 79 FR 22036, 4/21/2014, effective 4/21/2014; Final rule, 79 FR 61583, 10/14/2014, effective 10/14/2014; Final rule, 84 FR 4370, 2/15/2019, effective 2/15/2019]

PART 248—[NO FAR SUPPLEMENT]

PART 249—TERMINATION OF CONTRACTS

Table of Contents

Subpart 249.1—General Principles

Duties of termination contracting officer after issuance of notice of termination 249.105
Termination status report 249.105-1
Release of excess funds 249.105-2
[Removed] 249.106
[Removed] 249.108
[Removed] 249.108-4
Settlement agreements 249.109
Settlement by determination 249.109-7
Limitation on pricing of the terminated effort 249.109-70
Settlement negotiation memorandum 249.110

Subpart 249.5—Contract Termination Clauses

General 249.501
Special termination costs 249.501-70

Subpart 249.70—Special Termination Requirements

Terminated contracts with Canadian Commercial Corporation 249.7000
Congressional notification on significant contract terminations 249.7001
[Reserved] 249.7002
Notification of anticipated contract terminations or reductions 249.7003

PART 249—TERMINATION OF CONTRACTS

SUBPART 249.1—GENERAL PRINCIPLES

249.105 Duties of termination contracting officer after issuance of notice of termination. (No Text)

249.105-1 Termination status report.

Follow the procedures at PGI 249.105-1 for reporting status of termination actions.

[DAC 91-6, 59 FR 27662, 5/27/94, effective 5/27/94; Final rule, 64 FR 51074, 9/21/99, effective 9/21/99; Final rule, 65 FR 39703, 6/27/2000, effective 6/27/2000; Final rule, 71 FR 27644, 5/12/2006, effective 5/12/2006]

249.105-2 Release of excess funds.

See PGI 249.105-2 for guidance on recommending the release of excess funds.

[Final rule, 71 FR 27644, 5/12/2006, effective 5/12/2006]

249.106 [Removed]

[Final rule, 64 FR 62984, 11/18/99, effective 11/18/99; Final rule, 71 FR 27644, 5/12/2006, effective 5/12/2006]

249.108 [Removed]

[Final rule, 71 FR 27644, 5/12/2006, effective 5/12/2006]

249.108-4 [Removed]

[Final rule, 71 FR 27644, 5/12/2006, effective 5/12/2006]

249.109 Settlement agreements. (No Text)

249.109-7 Settlement by determination.

Follow the procedures at PGI 249.109-7 for settlement of a convenience termination by determination.

[Final rule, 71 FR 27644, 5/12/2006, effective 5/12/2006]

249.109-70 Limitation on pricing of the terminated effort.

When there is a termination for convenience (partial or whole) or a change that reduces scope, follow the procedures at PGI 249.109-70 for limitation on pricing of the terminated or reduced effort.

[Final rule, 84 FR 30953, 6/28/2019, effective 6/28/2019]

249.110 Settlement negotiation memorandum.

Follow the procedures at PGI 249.110 for preparation of a settlement negotiation memorandum.

[DAC 91-12, 62 FR 34114, 6/24/97, effective 6/24/97; Final rule, 71 FR 27644, 5/12/2006, effective 5/12/2006]

SUBPART 249.5—CONTRACT TERMINATION CLAUSES

249.501 General. (No Text)

249.501-70 Special termination costs.

(a) The clause at 252.249-7000, Special Termination Costs, may be used in an incrementally funded contract when its use is approved by the agency head.

(b) The clause is authorized when—

(1) The contract term is 2 years or more;

(2) The contract is estimated to require—

(i) Total RDT&E financing in excess of $25 million; or

(ii) Total production investment in excess of $100 million; and

(3) Adequate funds are available to cover the contingent reserve liability for special termination costs.

(c) The contractor and the contracting officer must agree upon an amount that represents their best estimate of the total special termination costs to which the contractor would be entitled in the event of termination of the contract. Insert this amount in paragraph (c) of the clause.

(d) (1) Consider substituting an alternate paragraph (c) for paragraph (c) of the basic clause when—

(i) The contract covers an unusually long performance period; or

(ii) The contractor's cost risk associated with contingent special termination costs is expected to fluctuate extensively over the period of the contract.

(2) The alternate paragraph (c) should provide for periodic negotiation and adjustment of the amount reserved for special termination costs. Occasions for periodic adjustment may include—

(i) The Government's incremental assignment of funds to the contract;

(ii) The time when certain performance milestones are accomplished by the contractor; or

(iii) Other specific time periods agreed upon by the contracting officer and the contractor.

SUBPART 249.70—SPECIAL TERMINATION REQUIREMENTS

249.7000 Terminated contracts with Canadian Commercial Corporation.

(a) Terminate contracts with the Canadian Commercial Corporation in accordance with—

(1) The Letter of Agreement (LOA) between the Department of Defence Production (Canada) and the U.S. DoD, "Canadian Agreement" (for a copy of the LOA or for questions on its currency, contact the Office of the Director of Defense Procurement and Acquisition Policy (Contract Policy and International Contracting), *osd.pentagon.ousd-atl.mbx.cpic@mail.mil*:

(2) Policies in the Canadian Agreement and part 249; and

(3) The Canadian Supply Manual, Chapter 8, Annex 8.3, available at *http://www.tpsgc-pwgsc.gc.ca/app-acq/ga-sm/index-eng.html*, "Termination for Convenience Process, Public Works and Government Services Canada."

(b) Contracting officers shall ensure that the Canadian Commercial Corporation submits termination settlement proposals in the format prescribed in FAR 49.602 and that they contain the amount of settlements with subcontractors. The termination contracting officer (TCO) shall prepare an appropriate settlement agreement. (See FAR 49.603.) The letter transmitting a settlement proposal must certify—

(1) That disposition of inventory has been completed; and

(2) That the Contract Claims Resolution Board of the Public Works and Government Services Canada has approved settlements with Canadian subcontractors when the Procedures Manual on Termination of Contracts requires such approval.

(c) (1) The Canadian Commercial Corporation will—

(i) Settle all Canadian subcontractor termination claims under the Canadian Agreement; and

(ii) Submit schedules listing serviceable and usable contractor inventory for screening to the TCO (see FAR 45.6).

(2) After screening, the TCO must provide guidance to the Canadian Commercial Corporation for disposition of the contractor inventory.

(3) Settlement of Canadian subcontractor claims are not subject to the approval and ratification of the TCO. However, when the proposed negotiated settlement exceeds the total contract price of the prime contract, the TCO shall obtain from the U.S. contracting officer prior to final settlement—

(i) Ratification of the proposed settlement; and

(ii) A contract modification increasing the contract price and obligating the additional funds.

(d) The Canadian Commercial Corporation should send all termination settlement proposals submitted by U.S. subcontractors and suppliers to the TCO of the cognizant contract administration office of the Defense Contract Management Agency for settlement. The TCO will inform the Canadian Commercial Corporation of the amount of the net settlement of U.S. subcontractors and suppliers so that this amount can be included in the Canadian Commercial Corporation termination proposal. subcontractors and suppliers so that this amount can be included in the CCC termination proposal. The Canadian Commercial Corporation is responsible for execution of the settlement agreement with these subcontractors.

(e) The Canadian Commercial Corporation will continue administering contracts that the U.S. contracting officer terminates.

(f) The Canadian Commercial Corporation will settle all Canadian subcontracts in accordance with the policies, practices, and procedures of the Canadian Government.

(g) The U.S. agency administering the contract with the Canadian Commercial Corporation shall provide any services required by the Canadian Commercial Corporation, including disposal of inventory, for settlement of any subcontracts placed in the United States. Settlement of such U.S. subcontracts will be in accordance with this regulation.

[Final rule, 65 FR 39703, 6/27/2000, effective 6/27/2000; Final rule, 68 FR 7438, 2/14/2003, effective 2/14/2003; Final rule, 71 FR 27644, 5/12/2006, effective 5/12/2006; Final rule, 72 FR 30278, 5/31/2007, effective 5/31/2007; Final rule, 76 FR 3536, 1/20/2011, effective 1/20/2011; Final rule, 79 FR 56268, 9/19/2014, effective 9/19/2014]

249.7001 Congressional notification on significant contract terminations.

Congressional notification is required for any termination involving a reduction in employment of 100 or more contractor employees. Proposed terminations must be cleared through department/agency liaison offices before release of the termination notice, or any information on the proposed termination, to the contractor. Follow the procedures at PGI 249.7001 for congressional notification and release of information.

[DAC 91-1, 56 FR 67220, 12/30/91, effective 12/31/91; DAC 91-6, 59 FR 27662, 5/27/94, effective 5/27/94; DAC 91-11, 61 FR 50446, 9/26/96, effective 9/26/96; Final rule, 64 FR 51074 9/21/99, effective 9/21/99; Final rule, 65 FR 39703, 6/27/2000, effective 6/27/2000; Final rule, 68 FR 7438, 2/14/2003, effective 2/14/2003; Final rule, 71 FR 27644, 5/12/2006, effective 5/12/2006]

249.7002 [Reserved]

[Reserved, Final rule, 61 FR 67952, 12/26/96, effective 12/26/96]

249.7003 Notification of anticipated contract terminations or reductions.

(a) Section 1372 of the National Defense Authorization Act for Fiscal Year 1994 (Pub. L. 103-160) and Section 824 of the National Defense Authorization Act for Fiscal Year 1997 (Pub. L. 104-201) are intended to help establish benefit eligibility under the Job Training Partnership Act (29 U.S.C. 1661 and 1662) for employees of DoD contractors and subcontractors adversely affected by termination or substantial reductions in major defense programs.

(b) Departments and agencies are responsible for establishing procedures to:

(1) Identify which contracts (if any) under major defense programs will be terminated or substantially reduced as a result of the funding levels provided in an appropriations act.

(2) Within 60 days of the enactment of such an act, provide notice of the anticipated termination of or substantial reduction in the funding of affected contracts—

(i) Directly to the Secretary of Labor; and

(ii) Through the contracting officer to each prime contractor.

(c) Use the clause at 252.249-7002, Notification of Anticipated Contract Termination or Reduction, in all contracts under a major defense program.

[Interim rule, 61 FR 64636, 12/6/96, effective 12/6/96, finalized without change, DAC 91-12, 62 FR 34114, 6/24/97, effective 6/24/97, corrected 62 FR 49304, 9/19/97]

PART 250—EXTRAORDINARY CONTRACTUAL ACTIONS AND THE SAFETY ACT

Table of Contents

Subpart 250.1—Extraordinary Contractual Actions

Definitions 250.100
General 250.101
Policy 250.101-2
Limitations on payment 250.101-2-70
Records 250.101-3
Delegation of and limitations on exercise of authority 250.102
Delegation of authority 250.102-1
Delegations 250.102-1-70
Contract adjustment boards 250.102-2
Contract adjustments 250.103
Contract adjustment 250.103-3
Processing cases 250.103-5
Disposition 250.103-6
Residual powers 250.104
Special procedures for unusually hazardous or nuclear risks 250.104-3
Indemnification under contracts involving both research and development and other work 250.104-3-70

PART 250—EXTRAORDINARY CONTRACTUAL ACTIONS AND THE SAFETY ACT

SUBPART 250.1—EXTRAORDINARY CONTRACTUAL ACTIONS

250.100 Definitions.

Secretarial level, as used in this subpart, means—

(1) An official at or above the level of an Assistant Secretary (or Deputy) of Defense or of the Army, Navy, or Air Force; and

(2) A contract adjustment board established by the Secretary concerned.

[Final rule, 73 FR 46814, 8/12/2008, effective 8/12/2008]

250.101 General. (No Text)

250.101-2 Policy. (No Text)

250.101-2-70 Limitations on payment.

See 10 U.S.C. 2410(b) for limitations on Congressionally directed payment of a request for equitable adjustment to contract terms or a request for relief under Public Law 85-804.

[Final rule, 73 FR 46814, 8/12/2008, effective 8/12/2008]

250.101-3 Records.

Follow the procedures at PGI 250.101-3 for preparation of records.

[Final rule, 73 FR 46814, 8/12/2008, effective 8/12/2008]

250.102 Delegation of and limitations on exercise of authority. (No Text)

[Final rule, 73 FR 46814, 8/12/2008, effective 8/12/2008]

250.102-1 Delegation of authority.

(b) Authority under FAR 50.104 to approve actions obligating $70,000 or less may not be delegated below the level of the head of the contracting activity.

(d) In accordance with the acquisition authority of the Under Secretary of Defense (Acquisition, Technology, and Logistics (USD (AT&L)) under 10 U.S.C. 133, in addition to the Secretary of Defense and the Secretaries of the military departments, the USD (AT&L) may exercise authority to indemnify against unusually hazardous or nuclear risks.

[Final rule, 73 FR 46814, 8/12/2008, effective 8/12/2008; Final rule, 75 FR 45072, 8/2/2010, effective 10/1/2010; Final rule, 80 FR 36903, 6/26/2015, effective 10/1/2015]

250.102-1-70 Delegations.

(a) *Military departments.* The Departments of the Army, Navy, and Air Force will specify delegations and levels of authority for actions under the Act and the Executive Order in departmental supplements or agency acquisition guidance.

(b) *Defense agencies.* Subject to the restrictions on delegations of authority in 250.102-1(b) and FAR 50.102-1, the directors of the defense agencies may exercise and redelegate the authority contained in the Act and the Executive Order. The agency supplements or agency acquisition guidance shall specify the delegations and levels of authority.

(1) Requests to obligate the Government in excess of $70,000 must be submitted to the USD (AT&L) for approval.

(2) Requests for indemnification against unusually hazardous or nuclear risks must be submitted to the USD(AT&L) for approval before using the indemnification clause at FAR 52.250-1, Indemnification Under Public Law 85-804.

(c) *Approvals.* The Secretary of the military department or the agency director must approve any delegations in writing.

[Final rule, 73 FR 46814, 8/12/2008, effective 8/12/2008; Final rule, 75 FR 45072, 8/2/2010, effective 10/1/2010; Final rule, 80 FR 36903, 6/26/2015, effective 10/1/2015]

250.102-2 Contract adjustment boards.

The Departments of the Army, Navy, and Air Force each have a contract adjustment board. The board consists of a Chair and not less than two nor more than six other members, one of whom may be designated the Vice-Chair. A majority constitutes a quorum for any purpose and the concurring vote of a majority of the total board membership constitutes an action of the board. Alternates may be appointed to act in the absence of any member.

[Final rule, 73 FR 46814, 8/12/2008, effective 8/12/2008]

250.103 Contract adjustments. (No Text)

[Final rule, 73 FR 46814, 8/12/2008, effective 8/12/2008]

250.103-3 Contract adjustment.

(a) Contractor requests should be filed with the procuring contracting officer (PCO). However, if filing with the PCO is impractical, requests may be filed with an authorized representative, an administrative contracting officer, or the Office of General Counsel of the applicable department or agency, for forwarding to the cognizant PCO.

[Final rule, 73 FR 46814, 8/12/2008, effective 8/12/2008]

250.103-5 Processing cases.

(1) At the time the request is filed, the activity shall prepare the record described at PGI 250.101-3(1)(i) and forward it to the appropriate official within 30 days after the close of the month in which the record is prepared.

(2) The officer or official responsible for the case shall forward to the contract adjustment board, through departmental channels, the documentation described at PGI 250.103-5.

(3) Contract adjustment boards will render decisions as expeditiously as practicable. The Chair shall sign a memorandum of decision disposing of the case. The decision shall be dated and shall contain the information required by FAR 50.103-6.The memorandum of decision shall not contain any information classified "Confidential" or higher. The board's decision will be sent to the appropriate official for implementation.

[Final rule, 73 FR 46814, 8/12/2008, effective 8/12/2008]

250.103-6 Disposition.

For requests denied or approved below the Secretarial level, follow the disposition procedures at PGI 250.103-6.

[Final rule, 73 FR 46814, 8/12/2008, effective 8/12/2008]

250.104 Residual powers. (No Text)

[Final rule, 73 FR 46814, 8/12/2008, effective 8/12/2008]

250.104-3 Special procedures for unusually hazardous or nuclear risks. (No Text)

[Final rule, 73 FR 46814, 8/12/2008, effective 8/12/2008]

250.104-3-70 Indemnification under contracts involving both research and development and other work.

When indemnification is to be provided on contracts requiring both research and development work and other work, the contracting officer shall insert an appropriate clause using the authority of both 10 U.S.C. 2354 and Public Law 85-804.

(a) The use of Public Law 85-804 is limited to work which cannot be indemnified under 10 U.S.C. 2354 and is subject to compliance with FAR 50.104.

(b) Indemnification under 10 U.S.C. 2354 is covered by 235.070.

[Final rule, 73 FR 46814, 8/12/2008, effective 8/12/2008]

PART 251—USE OF GOVERNMENT SOURCES BY CONTRACTORS

Table of Contents

Subpart 251.1—Contractor Use of Government Supply Sources

Authorization to use government supply sources 251.102
[Removed] 251.105
Contract clause 251.107

Subpart 251.2—Contractor Use of Interagency Fleet Management System (IFMS) Vehicles

Authorization 251.202
Contract clause 251.205

PART 251—USE OF GOVERNMENT SOURCES BY CONTRACTORS

SUBPART 251.1—CONTRACTOR USE OF GOVERNMENT SUPPLY SOURCES

251.102 Authorization to use government supply sources.

(e) When authorizing contractor use of Government supply sources, follow the procedures at PGI 251.102.

(3) (ii) The contracting officer may also authorize the contractor to use the DD Form 1155 when requisitioning from the Department of Veterans Affairs.

(f) The authorizing agency is also responsible for promptly considering requests of the DoD supply source for authority to refuse to honor requisitions from a contractor that is indebted to DoD and has failed to pay proper invoices in a timely manner.

[DAC 91-7, 60 FR 29491, 6/5/95, effective 5/17/95; Final rule, 64 FR 61030, 11/9/99, effective 11/9/99; Final rule, 67 FR 65509, 10/25/2002, effective 10/25/2002; Final rule, 67 FR 70325, 11/22/2002, effective 11/22/2002; Final rule, 69 FR 67858, 11/22/2004, effective 11/22/2004]

251.105 [Removed]

[DAC 91-7, 60 FR 29491, 6/5/95, effective 5/17/95; Final rule, 69 FR 67858, 11/22/2004, effective 11/22/2004]

251.107 Contract clause.

Use the clause at 252.251-7000, Ordering From Government Supply Sources, in solicitations and contracts which include the clause at FAR 52.251-1, Government Supply Sources.

SUBPART 251.2—CONTRACTOR USE OF INTERAGENCY FLEET MANAGEMENT SYSTEM (IFMS) VEHICLES

251.202 Authorization.

(a) (2) (A) See FAR 28.307-2(c) for policy on contractor insurance.

(B) See FAR 28.308 for policy on self-insurance.

(C) See FAR 31.205-19 for allowability of insurance costs.

(5) Paragraph (d) of the clause at 252.251-7001 satisfies the requirement of FAR 51.202 (a) (5) for a written statement.

251.205 Contract clause.

Use the clause at 252.251-7001, Use of Interagency Fleet Management System (IFMS) Vehicles and Related Services, in solicitations and contracts which include the clause at FAR 52.251-2, Interagency Fleet Management System (IFMS) Vehicles and Related Services.

Defense Federal Acquisition Regulation Supplement Part 252

SOLICITATION PROVISIONS AND CONTRACT CLAUSES

Table of Contents

Page

SUBCHAPTER H—CLAUSES AND FORMS

Part 252—Solicitation Provisions and Contract Clauses 649

See page 39 for an explanation of the numbering of the DFARS.

PART 252—SOLICITATION PROVISIONS AND CONTRACT CLAUSES

Table of Contents

Subpart 252.1—Instructions for Using Provisions and Clauses

Using Part 252 . . . . 252.101
Identification of provisions and clauses 252.103

Subpart 252.2—Text of Provisions and Clauses

Federal Acquisition Regulations system, provisions and clauses for DFARS Part 201 . . . . 252.201
Contracting officer's representative 252.201-7000
Improper Business Practices and Personal Conflicts of Interest, provisions and clauses for DFARS Part 203 . . . . 252.203
Requirements Relating to Compensation of Former DoD Officials 252.203-7000
Prohibition on persons convicted of fraud or other Defense Contract-Related felonies 252.203-7001
Requirement to Inform Employees of Whistleblower Rights 252.203-7002
Agency Office of the Inspector General 252.203-7003
Display of Hotline Posters 252.203-7004
Representation Relating to Compensation of Former DoD Officials 252.203-7005
Administrative Matters, provisions and clauses for DFARS Part 204 . . . . 252.204
Disclosure of information 252.204-7000
[Removed and Reserved] 252.204-7001
Payment for subline items not separately priced 252.204-7002
Control of government personnel work product 252.204-7003
Antiterrorism Awareness Training for Contractors 252.204-7004
[Removed and Reserved] 252.204-7005
Billing Instructions 252.204-7006
Alternate A, Annual Representations and Certifications 252.204-7007
Compliance with Safeguarding Covered Defense Information Controls . 252.204-7008
Limitations on the Use or Disclosure of Third-Party Contractor Reported Cyber Incident Information 252.204-7009
Requirement for Contractor to Notify DoD if the Contractor's Activities are Subject to Reporting Under the U.S.-International Atomic Energy Agency Additional Protocol. 252.204-7010
[Removed and Reserved] 252.204-7011
Safeguarding Covered Defense Information and Cyber Incident Reporting 252.204-7012
[Removed and Reserved] 252.204-7013
Limitations on the Use or Disclosure of Information by Litigation Support Contractors 252.204-7014
Notice of Authorized Disclosure of Information for Litigation Support . . 252.204-7015
Covered Defense Telecommunications Equipment or Services—Representation 252.204-7016
Prohibition on the Acquisition of Covered Defense Telecommunications Equipment or Services—Representation 252.204-7017
Prohibition on the Acquisition of Covered Defense Telecommunications Equipment or Services 252.204-7018

Publicizing contract actions, provisions and clauses for DFARS Part 205 252.205
Provision of information to cooperative agreement holders 252.205-7000
Competition requirements, provisions and clauses for DFARS Part 206 . 252.206
Domestic source restriction 252.206-7000
Required Source of supplies and services, provisions and clauses for DFARS Part 208 .... 252.208
Intent to furnish precious metals as Government-furnished material ... 252.208-7000
Contractor qualifications, provisions and clauses for DFARS Part 209 . . 252.209
[Removed and Reserved] 252.209-7000
[Removed and Reserved] 252.209-7001
Disclosure of ownership or control by a foreign government 252.209-7002
Reserve Officer Training Corps and Military Recruiting on Campus-Representation 252.209-7003
Subcontracting with Firms that are Owned or Controlled by the Government of a Country That is a State Sponsor of Terrorism 252.209-7004
Reserve Officer Training Corps and military recruiting on campus 252.209-7005
Limitations on Contractors Acting as Lead System Integrators 252.209-7006
Prohibited Financial Interests for Lead System Integrators 252.209-7007
Notice of Prohibition Relating to Organizational Conflict of Interest—Major Defense Acquisition Program. 252.209-7008
Organizational Conflict of Interest—Major Defense Acquisition Program. 252.209-7009
Critical Safety Items 252.209-7010
Acquisition and distribution of commercial products, provisions and clauses for DFARS Part 211 .... 252.211
[Removed and Reserved] 252.211-7000
[Removed and Reserved] 252.211-7001
Availability for examination of specifications, standards, plans, drawings, data item descriptions, and other pertinent documents 252.211-7002
Item unique identification and valuation 252.211-7003
Alternate preservation, packaging, and packing 252.211-7004
Substitutions for military or Federal specifications and standards 252.211-7005
Passive Radio Frequency Identification 252.211-7006
Reporting of Government-Furnished Property 252.211-7007
Use of Government-assigned serial numbers 252.211-7008
Acquisition of commercial items—general, provision and clauses for DFARS Part 212 .... 252.212
[Removed and Reserved] 252.212-7000
[Removed and Reserved] 252.212-7001
Pilot Program for Acquisition of Military-purpose Nondevelopmental Items 252.212-7002
Simplified acquisition procedures DFARS Part 213 252.213
Notice to Prospective Suppliers on Use of Supplier Performance Risk System in Past Performance Evaluations 252.213-7000
Contracting by negotiation, provisions and clauses for DFARS Part 215 .... 252.215
[Removed and Reserved] 252.215-7000

[Reserved] . . . 252.215-7001
Cost estimating system requirements . . . 252.215-7002
Requirement for Submission of Data Other Than Certified Cost or Pricing Data—Canadian Commercial Corporation . . . 252.215-7003
Requirement for Submission of Data Other Than Certified Cost or Pricing Data—Modifications—Canadian Commercial Corporation . . . 252.215-7004
Evaluation Factor for Employing or Subcontracting with Members of the Selected Reserve . . . 252.215-7005
Use of Employees or Individual Subcontractors Who Are Members of the Selected Reserve . . . 252.215-7006
Notice of Intent to Resolicit . . . 252.215-7007
Only One Offer . . . 252.215-7008
Proposal adequacy checklist . . . 252.215-7009
Requirements for Certified Cost or Pricing Data and Data Other Than Certified Cost or Pricing Data . . . 252.215-7010
Requirements for Submission of Proposals to the Administrative Contracting Officer and Contract Auditor . . . 252.215-7011
Requirements for Submission of Proposals via Electronic Media . . . 252.215-7012
Supplies and Services Provided by Nontraditional Defense Contractors . . . 252.215-7013
Exception from Certified Cost or Pricing Data Requirements for Foreign Military Sales Indirect Offsets Contractors . . . 252.215-7014
Program Should-Cost Review . . . 252.215-7015
Type of contracts, provisions and clauses for DFARS Part 216 . . . 252.216
Economic price adjustment—basic steel, aluminum, brass, bronze, or copper mill products . . . 252.216-7000
Economic price adjustment—Nonstandard steel items . . . 252.216-7001
Alternate A, Time-and-Materials/Labor-Hour Proposal Requirements—Non-Commercial Item Acquisition with Adequate Price Competition . 252.216-7002
Economic price adjustment—wage rates or material prices controlled by a foreign government . . . 252.216-7003
Award Fee Reduction or Denial for Jeopardizing the Health or Safety of Government Personnel. . . . 252.216-7004
[Removed and Reserved] . . . 252.216-7005
Ordering . . . 252.216-7006
Economic price adjustment—basic steel, aluminum, brass, bronze, or copper mill products—representation . . . 252.216-7007
Economic price adjustment—wage rates or material prices controlled by a foreign government—representation . . . 252.216-7008
Allowability of legal costs incurred in connection with a whistleblower proceeding . . . 252.216-7009
[Removed] . . . 252.216-7010
Special contracting methods, provisions and clauses for DFARS Part 217 252.217
Exercise of option to fulfill foreign military sales commitments . . . 252.217-7000
Surge option . . . 252.217-7001
Offering property for exchange . . . 252.217-7002
Changes . . . 252.217-7003
Job orders and compensation . . . 252.217-7004

Inspection and manner of doing work 252.217-7005
Title 252.217-7006
Payments 252.217-7007
Bonds 252.217-7008
Default 252.217-7009
Performance 252.217-7010
Access to vessel 252.217-7011
Liability and insurance 252.217-7012
Guarantees 252.217-7013
Discharge of liens 252.217-7014
Safety and health 252.217-7015
Plant protection 252.217-7016
[Removed and Reserved] 252.217-7017
[Removed and Reserved] 252.217-7018
[Removed and Reserved] 252.217-7019
[Removed and Reserved] 252.217-7020
[Removed and Reserved] 252.217-7021
[Removed and Reserved] 252.217-7022
[Removed and Reserved] 252.217-7023
[Removed and Reserved] 252.217-7024
[Removed and Reserved] 252.217-7025
Identification of sources of supply 252.217-7026
Contract definitization 252.217-7027
Over and above work 252.217-7028
Small business and small disadvantaged business concerns, provisions and clauses for DFARS Part 219 . . . . 252.219
Advancing Small Business Growth 252.219-7000
[Reserved] 252.219-7001
[Reserved] 252.219-7002
Small Business Subcontracting Plan (DoD Contracts) 252.219-7003
Small Business Subcontracting Plan (Test Program) 252.219-7004
[Removed and Reserved] 252.219-7005
[Removed and Reserved] 252.219-7006
[Reserved] 252.219-7007
[Reserved] 252.219-7008
Section 8(a) direct award 252.219-7009
Notification of Competition Limited to Eligible 8(a) Participants—Partnership Agreement 252.219-7010
Notification to delay performance 252.219-7011
Competition for Religious-Related Services 252.219-7012
Application of labor laws to government acquisitions, provisions and clauses for DFARS Part 222 . . . . 252.222
Restrictions on employment of personnel 252.222-7000
[Removed and Reserved] 252.222-7001
Compliance with local labor laws (overseas) 252.222-7002
Permit from Italian Inspectorate of Labor 252.222-7003
Compliance with Spanish social security laws and regulations 252.222-7004

Prohibition on use of nonimmigrant aliens—Guam 252.222-7005
Restrictions on the Use of Mandatory Arbitration Agreements 252.222-7006
[Removed] 252.222-7007
Environment, conservation, occupational safety, and drug-free workplace, provisions and clauses for DFARS Part 223 . . . . 252.223
[Reserved] 252.223-7000
Hazard warning labels 252.223-7001
Safety precautions for ammunition and explosives 252.223-7002
Change in place of performance—ammunition and explosives 252.223-7003
Drug-free work force 252.223-7004
[Reserved] 252.223-7005
Prohibition on Storage, Treatment, and Disposal of Toxic or Hazardous Materials 252.223-7006
Safeguarding sensitive conventional arms, ammunition, and explosives . 252.223-7007
Prohibition of Hexavalent Chromium 252.223-7008
Foreign acquisition, provisions and clauses for DFARS Part 225 . . . . 252.225
Buy American—Balance of Payments Program Certificate 252.225-7000
Buy American and Balance of Payments Program 252.225-7001
Qualifying country sources as subcontractors 252.225-7002
Report of intended performance outside the United States and Canada—Submission with offer 252.225-7003
Report of Intended Performance Outside the United States and Canada—Submission after Award 252.225-7004
[Removed and Reserved] 252.225-7005
Acquisition of the American Flag 252.225-7006
Prohibition on Acquisition of Certain Items from Communist Chinese Military Companies 252.225-7007
Restriction on Acquisition of Specialty Metals 252.225-7008
Restriction on Acquisition of Certain Articles Containing Specialty Metals 252.225-7009
Commercial Derivative Military Article—Specialty Metals Compliance Certificate 252.225-7010
Restriction on acquisition of supercomputers 252.225-7011
Preference for certain domestic commodities 252.225-7012
Duty-free entry 252.225-7013
[Removed and Reserved] 252.225-7014
Restriction on acquisition of hand or measuring tools 252.225-7015
Restriction on acquisition of ball and roller bearings 252.225-7016
Photovoltaic Devices 252.225-7017
Photovoltaic Devices—Certificate 252.225-7018
Restriction on acquisition of foreign anchor and mooring chain 252.225-7019
Trade Agreements Certificate 252.225-7020
Trade agreements 252.225-7021
[Removed and Reserved] 252.225-7022
Preference for products or services from Afghanistan 252.225-7023
Requirement for products or services from Afghanistan 252.225-7024
Restriction on acquisition of forgings 252.225-7025

Acquisition Restricted to Products or Services from Afghanistan 252.225-7026
Restriction on contingent fees for foreign military sales 252.225-7027
Exclusionary policies and practices of foreign governments 252.225-7028
Acquisition of Uniform Components for Afghan Military or Afghan National Police 252.225-7029
Restriction on Acquisition of Carbon, Alloy, and Armor Steel Plate 252.225-7030
Secondary Arab boycott of Israel 252.225-7031
Waiver of United Kingdom Levies—Evaluation of Offers 252.225-7032
Waiver of United Kingdom Levies 252.225-7033
[Reserved] 252.225-7034
Buy American—Free Trade Agreements—Balance of Payments Program Certificate 252.225-7035
Buy American—Free Trade Agreements—Balance of Payments Program 252.225-7036
Evaluation of Offers for Air Circuit Breakers 252.225-7037
Restriction on Acquisition of Air Circuit Breakers 252.225-7038
Defense Contractors Performing Private Security Functions Outside the United States 252.225-7039
Contractor Personnel Supporting U.S. Armed Forces Deployed Outside the United States 252.225-7040
Correspondence in English 252.225-7041
Authorization to perform 252.225-7042
Antiterrorism/force protection policy for defense contractors outside the United States 252.225-7043
Balance of Payments Program—Construction Material 252.225-7044
Balance of Payments Program—Construction Material Under Trade Agreements. 252.225-7045
Exports by Approved Community Members in Response to the Solicitation 252.225-7046
Exports by Approved Community Members in Performance of the Contract 252.225-7047
Export-Controlled Items 252.225-7048
Prohibition on Acquisition of Certain Foreign Commercial Satellite Services—Representations 252.225-7049
Disclosure of Ownership or Control by the Government of a Country that is a State Sponsor of Terrorism 252.225-7050
Prohibition on Acquisition of Certain Foreign Commercial Satellite Services 252.225-7051
Restriction on the Acquisition of Certain Magnets and Tungsten 252.225-7052
Other socioeconomic programs, provisions and clauses for DFARS Part 226 . . . . 252.226
[Removed] 252.226-7000
Utilization of Indian organizations and Indian-owned economic enterprises, and native Hawaiian small business concerns 252.226-7001
Representation for Demonstration Project for Contractors Employing Persons with Disabilities 252.226-7002
Patents, data and copyrights, provisions and clauses for DFARS Part 227 252.227
Non-estoppel 252.227-7000

Release of past infringement 252.227-7001
Readjustment of payments 252.227-7002
Termination 252.227-7003
License grant 252.227-7004
License term 252.227-7005
License grant—running royalty 252.227-7006
License term—running royalty 252.227-7007
Computation of royalties 252.227-7008
Reporting and payment of royalties 252.227-7009
License to other Government agencies 252.227-7010
Assignments 252.227-7011
Patent license and release contract 252.227-7012
Rights in technical data—Noncommercial items 252.227-7013
Rights in noncommercial computer software and noncommercial computer software documentation 252.227-7014
Technical data—Commercial items 252.227-7015
Rights in bid or proposal information 252.227-7016
Identification and assertion of use, release, or disclosure restrictions . . . 252.227-7017
Rights in noncommercial technical data and computer software—Small Business Innovation Research (SBIR) Program 252.227-7018
Validation of asserted restrictions—Computer software 252.227-7019
Rights in special works 252.227-7020
Rights in data—existing works 252.227-7021
Government rights (unlimited) 252.227-7022
Drawings and other data to become property of Government 252.227-7023
Notice and approval of restricted designs 252.227-7024
Limitations on the Use or Disclosure of Government-Furnished Information Marked with Restrictive Legends 252.227-7025
Deferred delivery of technical data or computer software 252.227-7026
Deferred ordering of technical data or computer software 252.227-7027
Technical data or computer software previously delivered to the government 252.227-7028
[Reserved] 252.227-7029
Technical data—withholding of payment 252.227-7030
[Reserved] 252.227-7031
Rights in technical data and computer software (foreign) 252.227-7032
Rights in shop drawings 252.227-7033
[Reserved] 252.227-7034
[Reserved] 252.227-7035
[Reserved] 252.227-7036
Validation of restrictive markings on technical data 252.227-7037
Patent Rights—Ownership by the Contractor (Large Business) 252.227-7038
Patents—reporting of subject inventions 252.227-7039
Bonds and insurance, provisions and clauses for DFARS Part 228 . . . . 252.228
Reimbursement for war-hazard losses 252.228-7000
Ground and flight risk 252.228-7001
[Removed and Reserved] 252.228-7002

Capture and detention 252.228-7003
[Removed and Reserved] 252.228-7004
Mishap reporting and investigation involving aircraft, missiles, and space launch vehicles 252.228-7005
Compliance with Spanish laws and insurance 252.228-7006
Taxes, provisions and clauses for DFARS Part 229 . . . . 252.229
Invoices exclusive of taxes or duties 252.229-7000
Tax relief 252.229-7001
Customs exemptions (Germany) 252.229-7002
Tax Exemptions (Italy) 252.229-7003
Status of contractors as a direct contractor (Spain) 252.229-7004
Tax exemptions (Spain) 252.229-7005
Value Added Tax Exclusion (United Kingdom) 252.229-7006
Verification of United States receipt of goods 252.229-7007
Relief from Import Duty (United Kingdom) 252.229-7008
Relief from customs duty and value added tax on fuel (passenger vehicles) (United Kingdom) 252.229-7009
Relief from customs duty on fuel (United Kingdom) 252.229-7010
Reporting of Foreign Taxes—U.S. Assistance Programs 252.229-7011
Tax exemptions (Italy)—representation 252.229-7012
Tax exemptions (Spain)—representation 252.229-7013
Taxes—Foreign Contracts in Afghanistan 252.229-7014
Taxes—Foreign Contracts in Afghanistan (North Atlantic Treaty Organization Status of Forces Agreement) 252.229-7015
Contract cost principles and procedures, provisions and clauses for DFARS Part 231 . . . . 252.231
Supplemental cost principles 252.231-7000
Contract financing provisions and clauses for DFARS Part 232 . . . . 252.232
Advance payment pool 252.232-7000
Disposition of payments 252.232-7001
Progress payments for foreign military sales acquisitions 252.232-7002
Electronic submission of payment requests and receiving reports 252.232-7003
DoD progress payment rates 252.232-7004
Reimbursement of subcontractor advance payments—DoD pilot-mentor protégé program 252.232-7005
Wide Area WorkFlow Payment Instructions 252.232-7006
Limitation of Government's obligation 252.232-7007
Assignment of claims (overseas) 252.232-7008
Mandatory payment by Governmentwide commercial purchase card 252.232-7009
Levies on Contract Payments 252.232-7010
Payments in Support of Emergencies and Contingency Operations 252.232-7011
Performance-Based Payments—Whole-Contract Basis 252.232-7012
Performance-Based Payments—Deliverable-Item Basis 252.232-7013
Notification of Payment in Local Currency (Afghanistan) 252.232-7014
Protests, disputes, and appeals, provisions, and clauses for DFARS Part 233 . . . . 252.233
[Reserved] 252.233-7000

Choice of law (overseas) 252.233-7001
Major system acquisition, provisions and clauses for DFARS Part 234 . . 252.234
[Removed] 252.234-7000
Notice of Earned Value Management System 252.234-7001
Earned Value Management System 252.234-7002
Notice of Cost and Software Data Reporting System 252.234-7003
Cost and Software Data Reporting System 252.234-7004
Research and development contracting, provisions and clauses for DFARS Part 235 . . . . . 252.235
Indemnification under 10 U.S.C. 2354—fixed price 252.235-7000
Indemnification under 10 U.S.C. 2354—cost reimbursement 252.235-7001
Animal welfare 252.235-7002
Frequency authorization 252.235-7003
Protection of Human Subjects 252.235-7004
[Reserved] 252.235-7005
[Reserved] 252.235-7006
[Reserved] 252.235-7007
[Reserved] 252.235-7008
[Reserved] 252.235-7009
Acknowledgment of support and disclaimer 252.235-7010
Final scientific or technical report 252.235-7011
Construction and architect-engineer contracts, provisions and clauses for DFARS Part 236 . . . . . 252.236
Modification proposals—price breakdown 252.236-7000
Contract drawings and specifications 252.236-7001
Obstruction of navigable waterways 252.236-7002
Payment for mobilization and preparatory work 252.236-7003
Payment for mobilization and demobilization 252.236-7004
Airfield safety precautions 252.236-7005
Cost limitation 252.236-7006
Additive or deductive items 252.236-7007
Contract prices—bidding schedules 252.236-7008
[Removed and Reserved] 252.236-7009
Overseas military construction—Preference for United States firms 252.236-7010
Overseas architect-engineer services—Restriction to United States firms 252.236-7011
Military construction on Kwajalein Atoll—evaluation preference 252.236-7012
Requirement for competition opportunity for American steel producers, fabricators, and manufacturers 252.236-7013
Service contracting, provisions and clauses for DFARS Part 237 . . . . . 252.237
Notice of special standards of responsibility 252.237-7000
Compliance with audit standards 252.237-7001
[Removed and Reserved] 252.237-7002
Requirements 252.237-7003
Area of performance 252.237-7004
Performance and delivery 252.237-7005
Subcontracting 252.237-7006
Termination for default 252.237-7007

Group interment 252.237-7008
Permits 252.237-7009
Prohibition on interrogation of detainees by contractor personnel 252.237-7010
Preparation history 252.237-7011
Instruction to offerors (count-of-articles) 252.237-7012
Instruction to offerors (bulk weight) 252.237-7013
Loss or damage (count-of-articles) 252.237-7014
Loss or damage (weight of articles) 252.237-7015
Delivery tickets 252.237-7016
Individual laundry 252.237-7017
Special definitions of Government property 252.237-7018
Training for Contractor Personnel Interacting with Detainees 252.237-7019
[Reserved] 252.237-7020
[Reserved] 252.237-7021
Services at installations being closed 252.237-7022
Continuation of Essential Contractor Services 252.237-7023
Notice of Continuation of Essential Contractor Services 252.237-7024
Acquisition of information resources, provisions and clauses for DFARS Part 239 . . . . 252.239
Protection against compromising emanations 252.239-7000
Information Assurance Contractor Training and Certification 252.239-7001
Access 252.239-7002
[Removed and Reserved] 252.239-7003
Orders for facilities and services 252.239-7004
[Removed and Reserved] 252.239-7005
Tariff information 252.239-7006
Cancellation or termination of orders 252.239-7007
[Removed and Reserved] 252.239-7008
Representation of Use of Cloud Computing 252.239-7009
Cloud Computing Services 252.239-7010
Special construction and equipment charges 252.239-7011
Title to telecommunication facilities and equipment 252.239-7012
Term of Agreement and Continuation of Services 252.239-7013
[Removed and Reserved] 252.239-7014
[Removed and Reserved] 252.239-7015
Telecommunications security equipment, devices, techniques, and services 252.239-7016
Notice of supply chain risk 252.239-7017
Supply chain risk 252.239-7018
Acquisition of utility services, provisions and clauses for DFARS Part 241 . . . . 252.241
Superseding contract 252.241-7000
Government access 252.241-7001
Contract administration, provisions and clauses for DFARS Part 242 . . . 252.242
[Removed and Reserved] 252.242-7000
[Removed and Reserved] 252.242-7001
[Removed and Reserved] 252.242-7002

[Removed and Reserved] 252.242-7003
Material Management and Accounting System 252.242-7004
Contractor business systems 252.242-7005
Accounting system administration 252.242-7006
Contract modification, provisions and clauses for DFARS Part 243 . . . . . 252.243
[Reserved] 252.243-7000
Pricing of contract modifications 252.243-7001
Requests for equitable adjustment 252.243-7002
Subcontracting policies and procedures, provisions and clauses for DFARS Part 244 . . . . 252.244
Subcontracts for Commercial Items 252.244-7000
Contractor purchasing system administration 252.244-7001
Government property, provisions and clauses for DFARS Part 245 . . . . 252.245
Government-furnished mapping, charting, and geodesy property 252.245-7000
Tagging, labeling, and marking of government-furnished property 252.245-7001
Reporting Loss of Government Property 252.245-7002
Contractor Property Management System Administration 252.245-7003
Reporting, Reutilization, and Disposal 252.245-7004
Quality assurance, provisions and clauses for DFARS Part 246 . . . . 252.246
[Removed and Reserved] 252.246-7000
Warranty of data 252.246-7001
Warranty of construction (Germany) 252.246-7002
Notification of Potential Safety Issues 252.246-7003
Safety of Facilities, Infrastructure, and Equipment of Military Operations 252.246-7004
Notice of Warranty Tracking of Serialized Items 252.246-7005
Warranty Tracking of Serialized Items 252.246-7006
Contractor counterfeit electronic part detection and avoidance system . . 252.246-7007
Sources of Electronic Parts 252.246-7008
Transportation, provisions and clauses for DFARS Part 247 . . . . 252.247
Hardship conditions 252.247-7000
[Removed and Reserved] 252.247-7001
Revision of prices 252.247-7002
Pass-Through of Motor Carrier Fuel Surcharge Adjustment to the Cost Bearer 252.247-7003
[Removed and Reserved] 252.247-7004
[Removed and Reserved] 252.247-7005
[Removed and Reserved] 252.247-7006
Liability and insurance 252.247-7007
[Removed and Reserved] 252.247-7008
[Removed and Reserved] 252.247-7009
[Removed and Reserved] 252.247-7010
[Removed and Reserved] 252.247-7011
[Removed and Reserved] 252.247-7012
[Removed and Reserved] 252.247-7013
Demurrage 252.247-7014
[Removed and Reserved] 252.247-7015

Contractor liability for loss or damage 252.247-7016
[Removed and Reserved] 252.247-7017
[Removed and Reserved] 252.247-7018
[Removed and Reserved] 252.247-7019
[Removed and Reserved] 252.247-7020
[Removed and Reserved] 252.247-7021
Representation of extent of transportation by sea 252.247-7022
Transportation of supplies by sea 252.247-7023
[Removed and Reserved] 252.247-7024
Reflagging or repair work 252.247-7025
Evaluation Preference for Use of Domestic Shipyards—Applicable to Acquisition of Carriage by Vessel for DoD Cargo in the Coastwise or Noncontiguous Trade 252.247-7026
Riding gang member requirements 252.247-7027
Application for U.S. Government Shipping Documentation/Instructions . 252.247-7028
Value engineering, provisions and clauses for DFARS Part 248 . . . . 252.248
[Removed] 252.248-7000
Termination of contracts, provisions and clauses for DFARS Part 249 . . . 252.249
Special termination costs 252.249-7000
[Reserved] 252.249-7001
Notification of Anticipated Contract Termination or Reduction 252.249-7002
Use of government sources by contractors, provisions and clauses for DFARS Part 251 . . . . 252.251
Ordering from Government supply sources 252.251-7000
Use of Interagency Fleet Management System (IFMS) vehicles and related services 252.251-7001

SUBCHAPTER H—CLAUSES AND FORMS (Parts 252-253)

PART 252—SOLICITATION PROVISIONS AND CONTRACT CLAUSES

SUBPART 252.1—INSTRUCTIONS FOR USING PROVISIONS AND CLAUSES

252.101 Using Part 252.

(b) *Numbering.*

(2) *Provisions or clauses that supplement the FAR.*

(ii) (B) DFARS provisions or clauses use a four digit sequential number in the 7000 series, e.g., -7000, -7001, -7002. Department or agency supplemental provisions or clauses use four digit sequential numbers in the 9000 series.

252.103 Identification of provisions and clauses.

For guidance on numbering department or agency provisions and clauses, see PGI 252.103.

[Final rule, 80 FR 36718, 6/26/2015, effective 6/26/2015]

SUBPART 252.2—TEXT OF PROVISIONS AND CLAUSES

252.201 Federal Acquisition Regulations System, provisions and clauses for DFARS Part 201

252.201-7000 Contracting officer's representative.

As prescribed in 201.602-70, use the following clause:

CONTRACTING OFFICER'S REPRESENTATIVE (DEC 1991)

(a) *Definition. Contracting officer's representative* means an individual designated in accordance with subsection 201.602-2 of the Defense Federal Acquisition Regulation Supplement and authorized in writing by the contracting officer to perform specific technical or administrative functions.

(b) If the Contracting Officer designates a contracting officer's representative (COR), the Contractor will receive a copy of the written designation. It will specify the extent of the COR's authority to act on behalf of the contracting officer. The COR is not authorized to make any commitments or changes that will affect price, quality, quantity, delivery, or any other term or condition of the contract.

(End of clause)

[DAC 91-3, 57 FR 42633, 9/15/92, effective 8/31/92]

252.203 Improper Business Practices and Personal Conflicts of Interest, provisions and clauses for DFARS Part 203

252.203-7000 Requirements Relating to Compensation of Former DoD Officials.

As prescribed in 203.171-4(a), use the following clause:

REQUIREMENTS RELATING TO COMPENSATION OF FORMER DoD OFFICIALS (SEP 2011)

(a) *Definition. Covered DoD official,* as used in this clause, means an individual that—

(1) Leaves or left DoD service on or after January 28, 2008; and

(2) (i) Participated personally and substantially in an acquisition as defined in 41 U.S.C. 131 with a value in excess of $10 million, and serves or served—

(A) In an Executive Schedule position under subchapter II of chapter 53 of Title 5, United States Code;

(B) In a position in the Senior Executive Service under subchapter VIII of chapter 53 of Title 5, United States Code; or

(C) In a general or flag officer position compensated at a rate of pay for grade O-7 or above under section 201 of Title 37, United States Code; or

(ii) Serves or served in DoD in one of the following positions: Program manager, deputy program manager, procuring contracting officer, administrative contracting officer, source selection authority, member of the source selection evaluation board, or chief of a financial or technical evaluation team for a contract in an amount in excess of $10 million.

(b) The Contractor shall not knowingly provide compensation to a covered DoD official within 2 years after the official leaves DoD service, without first determining that the official has sought and received, or has not received after 30 days of seeking, a written opinion from the appropriate DoD ethics counselor regarding the applicability of post-employment restrictions to the activities that the official is expected to undertake on behalf of the Contractor.

(c) Failure by the Contractor to comply with paragraph (b) of this clause may subject the Contractor to rescission of this contract, suspension, or debarment in accordance with 41 U.S.C. 2105(c).

(End of clause)

[Removed and reserved, final rule, 62 FR 2611, 1/17/97, effective 1/17/97; Interim rule, 74 FR 2408, 1/15/2009, effective 1/15/2009; Final rule, 74 FR 59913, 11/19/2009, effective 11/19/2009; Final rule, 76 FR 58137, 9/20/2011, effective 9/20/2011; Final rule, 78 FR 37980, 6/25/2013, effective 6/25/2013]

252.203-7001 Prohibition on persons convicted of fraud or other defense-contract-related felonies.

As prescribed in 203.570-5, use the following clause:

PROHIBITION ON PERSONS CONVICTED OF FRAUD OR OTHER DEFENSE-CONTRACT-RELATED FELONIES (DEC 2008)

(a) *Definitions.*

As used in this clause—

(1) *Arising out of a contract with the DoD* means any act in connection with—

(i) Attempting to obtain;

(ii) Obtaining; or

(iii) Performing a contract or first-tier subcontract of any agency, department, or component of the Department of Defense (DoD).

(2) *Conviction of fraud or any other felony* means any conviction for fraud or a felony in violation of state or Federal criminal statutes, whether entered on a verdict or plea, including a plea of *nolo contendere*, for which sentence has been imposed.

(3) *Date of conviction* means the date judgment was entered against the individual.

(b) Any individual who is convicted after September 29, 1988, of fraud or any other felony arising out of a contract with the DoD is prohibited from serving—

(1) In a management or supervisory capacity on this contract;

(2) On the board of directors of the Contractor;

(3) As a consultant, agent, or representative for the Contractor; or

(4) In any other capacity with the authority to influence, advise, or control the decisions of the Contractor with regard to this contract.

(c) Unless waived, the prohibition in paragraph (b) of this clause applies for not less than 5 years from the date of conviction.

(d) 10 U.S.C. 2408 provides that the Contractor shall be subject to a criminal penalty of not more than $500,000 if convicted of knowingly—

(1) Employing a person under a prohibition specified in paragraph (b) of this clause; or

(2) Allowing such a person to serve on the board of directors of the contractor or first-tier subcontractor.

(e) In addition to the criminal penalties contained in 10 U.S.C. 2408, the Government may consider other available remedies, such as—

(1) Suspension or debarment;

(2) Cancellation of the contract at no cost to the Government; or

(3) Termination of the contract for default.

(f) The Contractor may submit written requests for waiver of the prohibition in paragraph (b) of this clause to the Contracting Officer. Requests shall clearly identify—

(1) The person involved;

(2) The nature of the conviction and resultant sentence or punishment imposed;

(3) The reasons for the requested waiver; and

(4) An explanation of why a waiver is in the interest of national security.

(g) The Contractor agrees to include the substance of this clause, appropriately modified to reflect the identity and relationship of the parties, in all first-tier subcontracts exceeding the simplified acquisition threshold in part 2 of the Federal Acquisition Regulation, except those for commercial items or components.

(h) Pursuant to 10 U.S.C. 2408(c), defense contractors and subcontractors may obtain information as to whether a particular person has been convicted of fraud or any other felony arising out of a contract with the DoD by contacting The Office of Justice Programs, The Denial of Federal Benefits Office, U.S. Department of Justice, telephone 301-937-1542; *www.ojp.usdoj.gov/BJA/grant/DFFC.html.*

(End of clause)

[DAC 91-5, 58 FR 28458, 5/13/93, effective 4/30/93; DAC 91-6, 59 FR 27662, 5/27/94, effective 5/27/94; DAC 91-9, 60 FR 61586, 11/30/95, effective 11/30/95; DAC 91-12, 62 FR 34114, 6/24/97, effective 6/24/97; Final rule, 64 FR 14397, 3/25/99, effective 3/25/99; Final rule, 69 FR 74989, 12/15/2004, effective 12/15/2004; Final rule, 73 FR 76971, 12/18/2008, effective 12/18/2008]

252.203-7002 Requirement to Inform Employees of Whistleblower Rights.

As prescribed in 203.970, use the following clause:

REQUIREMENT TO INFORM EMPLOYEES OF WHISTLEBLOWER RIGHTS (SEP 2013)

(a) The Contractor shall inform its employees in writing, in the predominant native language of the workforce, of contractor employee whistleblower rights and protections under 10 U.S.C. 2409, as described in subpart 203.9 of the Defense Federal Acquisition Regulation Supplement.

(b) The Contractor shall include the substance of this clause, including this paragraph (b), in all subcontracts.

(End of clause)

[Interim rule, 74 FR 2410, 1/15/2009, effective 1/15/2009; Final rule, 74 FR 59914, 11/19/2009, effective 11/19/2009; Interim rule, 78 FR 59851, 9/30/2013, effective 9/30/2013; Final rule, 79 FR 11336, 2/28/2014, effective 2/28/2014; Final rule, 80 FR 36719, 6/26/2015, effective 6/26/2015]

252.203-7003 Agency Office of the Inspector General.

As prescribed in 203.1004(a), use the following clause:

AGENCY OFFICE OF THE INSPECTOR GENERAL (AUG 2019)

The agency office of the Inspector General referenced in paragraphs (c) and (d) of FAR clause 52.203-13, Contractor Code of Business Ethics and Conduct, is the DoD Office of Inspector General at the following address:

Department of Defense Office of Inspector General, Administrative Investigations, Contractor Disclosure Program, 4800 Mark Center Drive, Suite 14L25, Alexandria, VA 22350-1500, Toll Free Telephone: 866-429-8011. Website: *https://www.dodig.mil/Programs/Contractor-Disclosure-Program/.*

(End of clause)

[Final rule, 75 FR 59101, 9/27/2010, effective 9/27/2010; Final rule, 76 FR 76318, 12/7/2011, effective 12/7/2011; Final rule, 77 FR 23631, 4/20/2012, effective 4/20/2012; Final rule, 77 FR 76936, 12/31/2012, effective 12/31/2012; Final rule, 84 FR 39201, 8/9/2019, effective 8/9/2019]

252.203-7004 Display of Hotline Posters.

As prescribed in 203.1004(b)(2)(ii), use the following clause:

DISPLAY OF HOTLINE POSTERS (AUG 2019)

(a) *Definition.* As used in this clause—

United States means the 50 States, the District of Columbia, and outlying areas.

(b) *Display of hotline poster(s)*.

(1) (i) The Contractor shall display prominently the DoD fraud, waste, and abuse hotline poster prepared by the DoD Office of the Inspector General, in effect at time of contract award, in common work areas within business segments performing work under Department of Defense (DoD) contracts.

(ii) For contracts performed outside the United States, when security concerns can be appropriately demonstrated, the contracting officer may provide the contractor the option to publicize the program to contractor personnel in a manner other than public display of the poster, such as private employee written instructions and briefings.

(2) If the contract is funded, in whole or in part, by Department of Homeland Security (DHS) disaster relief funds and the work is to be performed in the United States, the DHS fraud hotline poster shall be displayed in addition to the DoD hotline poster. If a display of a DHS fraud hotline poster is required, the Contractor may obtain such poster from—

(i) DHS Office of Inspector General/MAIL STOP 0305, Attn: Office of Investigations – Hotline, 245 Murray Lane SW, Washington, DC 20528-0305; or

(ii) Via the internet at *https://www.oig.dhs.gov/assets/Hotline/DHS_OIG_Hotlineoptimized.jpg*.

(c) (1) The DoD hotline poster may be obtained from: Defense Hotline, The Pentagon, Washington, D.C. 20301-1900, or is also available via the internet at *https://www.dodig.mil/Resources/Posters-and-Brochures/*.

(2) If a significant portion of the employee workforce does not speak English, then the poster is to be displayed in the foreign languages that a significant portion of the employees speak.

(3) Additionally, if the Contractor maintains a company website as a method of providing information to employees, the Contractor shall display an electronic version of the required poster at the website.

(d) *Subcontracts*. The Contractor shall include the substance of this clause, including this paragraph (d), in all subcontracts that exceed the threshold specified in Defense Federal Acquisition Regulation Supplement 203.1004(b) (2) (ii) on the date of subcontract award, except when the subcontract is for the acquisition of a commercial item.

(End of clause)

[Interim rule, 76 FR 57674, 9/16/2011, effective 9/16/2011; Final rule, 77 FR 76936, 12/31/2012, effective 12/31/2012; Final rule, 80 FR 4999, 1/29/2015, effective 1/29/2015; Final rule, 80 FR 36903, 6/26/2015, effective 10/1/2015; Final rule, 81 FR 73005, 10/21/2016, effective 10/21/2016; Final rule, 84 FR 25186, 5/31/2019, effective 5/31/2019; Final rule, 84 FR 39201, 8/9/2019, effective 8/9/2019]

252.203-7005 Representation Relating to Compensation of Former DoD Officials.

As prescribed in 203.171-4(b), insert the following provision:

REPRESENTATION RELATING TO COMPENSATION OF FORMER DoD OFFICIALS (NOV 2011)

(a) *Definition. Covered DoD official* is defined in the clause at 252.203-7000, Requirements Relating to Compensation of Former DoD Officials.

(b) By submission of this offer, the offeror represents, to the best of its knowledge and belief, that all covered DoD officials employed by or otherwise receiving compensation from the offeror, and who are expected to undertake activities on behalf of the offeror for any resulting contract, are presently in compliance with all post-employment restrictions covered by 18 U.S.C. 207, 41 U.S.C. 2101-2107, and 5 CFR parts 2637 and 2641, including Federal Acquisition Regulation 3.104-2.

(End of provision)

[Final rule, 76 FR 71826, 11/18/2011, effective 11/18/2011]

252.204 Administrative Matters, provisions and clauses for DFARS Part 204

252.204-7000 Disclosure of information.

As prescribed in 204.404-70(a), use the following clause:

DISCLOSURE OF INFORMATION (OCT 2016)

(a) The Contractor shall not release to anyone outside the Contractor's organization any unclassified information, regardless of medium (e.g., film, tape, document), pertaining to any part of this contract or any program related to this contract, unless—

(1) The Contracting Officer has given prior written approval;

(2) The information is otherwise in the public domain before the date of release; or

(3) The information results from or arises during the performance of a project that involves no covered defense information (as defined in the clause at DFARS 252.204-7012, Safeguarding Covered Defense Information and Cyber Incident Reporting) and has been scoped and negotiated by the contracting activity with the contractor and research performer and determined in writing by the contracting officer to be fundamental research (which by definition cannot involve any covered defense information), in accordance with National Security Decision Directive 189, National Policy on the Transfer of Scientific, Technical and Engineering Information, in effect on the date of contract award and the Under Secretary of Defense (Acquisition, Technology, and Logistics) memoranda on Fundamental Research, dated May 24, 2010, and on Contracted Fundamental Research, dated June 26, 2008 (available at DFARS PGI 204.4).

(b) Requests for approval under paragraph (a)(1) shall identify the specific information to be released, the medium to be used, and the purpose for the release. The Contractor shall submit its request to the Contracting Officer at least 10 business days before the proposed date for release.

(c) The Contractor agrees to include a similar requirement, including this paragraph (c), in each subcontract under this contract. Subcontractors shall submit requests for authorization to release through the prime contractor to the Contracting Officer.

(End of clause)

[DAC 91-2, 57 FR 14996, 4/23/92, effective 4/16/92; Final rule, 78 FR 48331, 8/8/2013, effective 8/8/2013; Final rule, 81 FR 72986, 10/21/2016, effective 10/21/2016]

252.204-7001 [Removed and Reserved]

[Final rule, 64 FR 43098, 8/9/99, effective 8/9/99; Final rule, 66 FR 47096, 9/11/2001, effective 10/1/2001; Final rule, 79 FR 73492, 12/11/2014, effective 12/11/2014]

252.204-7002 Payment for subline items not separately priced.

As prescribed in 204.7104-1(b)(3)(iv), use the following clause:

PAYMENT FOR SUBLINE ITEMS NOT SEPARATELY PRICED (DEC 1991)

(a) If the schedule in this contract contains any contract subline items or exhibit subline items identified as not separately priced (NSP), it means that the unit price for that subline item is included in the unit price of another, related line or subline item.

(b) The Contractor shall not invoice the Government for any portion of a contract line item or exhibit line item which contains an NSP until—

(1) The Contractor has delivered the total quantity of all related contract subline items or exhibit subline items; and

(2) The Government has accepted them.

(c) This clause does not apply to technical data.

(End of clause)

252.204-7003 Control of government personnel work product.

As prescribed in 204.404-70(b), use the following clause:

CONTROL OF GOVERNMENT PERSONNEL WORK PRODUCT (APR 1992)

The Contractor's procedures for protecting against unauthorized disclosure of information shall not require Department of Defense employees or members of the Armed Forces to relinquish control of their work products, whether classified or not, to the contractor.

(End of clause)

[DAC 91-2, 57 FR 14996, 4/23/92, effective 4/16/92]

252.204-7004 Antiterrorism Awareness Training for Contractors.

As prescribed in 204.7203, use the following clause:

LEVEL I ANTITERRORISM AWARENESS TRAINING FOR CONTRACTORS (FEB 2019)

(a) *Definition*. As used in this clause—

Military installation means a base, camp, post, station, yard, center, or other activity under the jurisdiction of the Secretary of a military department or, in the case of an activity in a foreign country, under the operational control of the Secretary of a military department or the Secretary of Defense (see 10 U.S.C. 2801(c)(4)).

(b) *Training*. Contractor personnel who require routine physical access to a Federally-controlled facility or military installation shall complete Level I antiterrorism awareness training within 30 days of requiring access and annually thereafter. In accordance with Department of Defense Instruction O-2000.16 Volume 1, DoD Antiterrorism (AT) Program Implementation: DoD AT Standards, Level I antiterrorism awareness training shall be completed—

(1) Through a DoD-sponsored and certified computer or web-based distance learning instruction for Level I antiterrorism awareness; or

(2) Under the instruction of a Level I antiterrorism awareness instructor.

(c) *Additional information*. Information and guidance pertaining to DoD antiterrorism awareness training is available at *https://jko.jten.mil/* or as otherwise identified in the performance work statement.

(d) *Subcontracts*. The Contractor shall include the substance of this clause, including this paragraph (d), in subcontracts, including subcontracts for commercial items, when subcontractor performance requires routine physical access to a Federally-controlled facility or military installation.

(End of clause)

[Final rule, 84 FR 4362, 2/15/2019, effective 2/15/2019]

252.204-7005 [Removed and Reserved]

[Final rule, 64 FR 45196, 8/19/99, effective 8/19/99; Final rule, 66 FR 55121, 11/1/2001, effective 11/1/2001; Final rule, 84 FR 12138, 4/1/2019, effective 4/1/2019]

252.204-7006 Billing instructions.

As prescribed in 204.7109, use the following clause:

BILLING INSTRUCTIONS (OCT 2005)

When submitting a request for payment, the Contractor shall—

(a) Identify the contract line item(s) on the payment request that reasonably reflect contract work performance; and

(b) Separately identify a payment amount for each contract line item included in the payment request.

(End of clause)

[Final rule, 70 FR 58980, 10/11/2005, effective 10/11/2005]

252.204-7007 Alternate A, Annual Representations and Certifications.

As prescribed in 204.1202, use the following provision:

ALTERNATE A, ANNUAL REPRESENTATIONS AND CERTIFICATIONS (DEC 2019)

Substitute the following paragraphs (b), (d), and (e) for paragraphs (b) and (d) of the provision at FAR 52.204–8:

(b)(1) If the provision at FAR 52.204–7, System for Award Management, is included in this solicitation, paragraph (e) of this provision applies.

(2) If the provision at FAR 52.204–7, System for Award Management, is not included in this solicitation, and the Offeror has an active registration in the System for Award Management (SAM), the Offeror may choose to use paragraph (e) of this provision instead of completing the corresponding individual representations and certifications in the solicitation. The Offeror shall indicate which option applies by checking one of the following boxes:

(i) __Paragraph (e) applies.

(ii) __Paragraph (e) does not apply and the Offeror has completed the individual representations and certifications in the solicitation.

(d) (1) The following representations or certifications in the SAM database are applicable to this solicitation as indicated:

(i) 252.204–7016, Covered Defense Telecommunications Equipment or Services—Representation. Applies to all solicitations.

(ii) 252.209-7003, Reserve Officer Training Corps and Military Recruiting on Campus—Representation. Applies to all solicitations with institutions of higher education.

(iii) 252.216-7008, Economic Price Adjustment—Wage Rates or Material Prices Controlled by a Foreign Government. Applies to solicitations for fixed-price supply and service contracts when the contract is to be performed wholly or in part in a foreign country, and a foreign government controls wage rates or material prices and may during contract performance impose a mandatory change in wages or prices of materials.

(iv) 252.225-7042, Authorization to Perform. Applies to all solicitations when performance will be wholly or in part in a foreign country.

(v) 252.225-7049, Prohibition on Acquisition of Certain Foreign Commercial Satellite Services—Representations. Applies to solicitations for the acquisition of commercial satellite services.

(vi) 252.225-7050, Disclosure of Ownership or Control by the Government of a Country that is a State Sponsor or Terrorism. Applies to all solicitations expected to result in contracts of $150,000 or more.

(vii) 252.229-7012, Tax Exemptions (Italy)—Representation. Applies to solicitations when contract performance will be in Italy.

(viii) 252.229-7013, Tax Exemptions (Spain)—Representation. Applies to solicitations when contract performance will be in Spain.

(ix) 252.247-7022, Representation of Extent of Transportation by Sea. Applies to all solicitations except those for direct purchase of ocean transportation services or those with an anticipated value at or below the simplified acquisition threshold.

(2) The following representations or certifications in SAM are applicable to this solicitation as indicated by the Contracting Officer: [*Contracting Officer check as appropriate.*]

__ (i) 252.209-7002, Disclosure of Ownership or Control by a Foreign Government.

__ (ii) 252.225-7000, Buy American Act—Balance of Payments Program Certificate.

__ (iii) 252.225-7020, Trade Agreements Certificate.

__ Use with Alternate I.

__ (iv) 252.225-7031, Secondary Arab Boycott of Israel.

__ (v) 252.225-7035, Buy American Act—Free Trade Agreements—Balance of Payments Program Certificate.

__ (vi) 252.226-7002, Representation for Demonstration Project for Contractors Employing Persons with Disabilities.

__ Use with Alternate I.

__ Use with Alternate II.

__ Use with Alternate III.

__ Use with Alternate IV.

__ Use with Alternate V.

(e) The offeror has completed the annual representations and certifications electronically via the SAM Web site at *https://*

www.acquisition.gov/. After reviewing the SAM database information, the offeror verifies by submission of the offer that the representations and certifications currently posted electronically that apply to this solicitation as indicated in FAR 52.204-8(c) and paragraph (d) of this provision have been entered or updated within the last 12 months, are current, accurate, complete, and applicable to this solicitation (including the business size standard applicable to the NAICS code referenced for this solicitation), as of the date of this offer, and are incorporated in this offer by reference (see FAR 4.1201); except for the changes identified below [*offeror to insert changes, identifying change by provision number, title, date*]. These amended representation(s) and/or certification(s) are also incorporated in this offer and are current, accurate, and complete as of the date of this offer.

FAR/DFARS provision No.	Title	Date	Change

Any changes provided by the offeror are applicable to this solicitation only, and do not result in an update to the representations and certifications located in the SAM database.

(End of provision)

[Final rule, 73 FR 1822, 1/10/2008, effective 1/10/2008; Final rule, 75 FR 25119, 5/7/2010, effective 5/7/2010; Final rule 76 FR 58140, 9/20/2011, effective 9/20/2011; Final rule, 76 FR 71464, 11/18/2011, effective 11/18/2011; Final rule, 77 FR 19128, 3/30/2012, effective 3/30/2012; Interim rule, 77 FR 30356, 5/22/2012, effective 5/22/2012; Final rule, 77 FR 43470, 7/24/2012, effective 7/24/2012; Final rule, 78 FR 18876, 3/28/2013, effective 3/28/2013; Final rule, 78 FR 28756, 5/16/2013, effective 5/16/2013; Final rule, 78 FR 30232, 5/22/2013, effective 5/22/2013; Final rule, 79 FR 17445, 3/28/2014, effective 3/28/2014; Interim rule, 79 FR 45661, 8/5/2014, effective 8/5/2014; Final rule, 79 FR 73488, 12/11/2014, effective 12/11/2014; Final rule, 80 FR 4999, 1/29/2015, effective 1/29/2015; Interim rule, 83 FR 66066, 12/21/2018, effective 12/21/2018; Final rule, 84 FR 12140, 4/1/2019, effective 4/1/2019; Final rule, 84 FR 25188, 5/31/2019, effective 5/31/2019; Final rule, 84 FR 30946, 6/28/2019, effective 6/28/2019; Interim rule, 84 FR 72231, 12/31/2019, effective 12/31/2019; Final rule, 84 FR 72554, 12/31/2019, effective 12/31/2019]

252.204-7008 Compliance with Safeguarding Covered Defense Information Controls.

As prescribed in 204.7304(a), use the following provision:

COMPLIANCE WITH SAFEGUARDING COVERED DEFENSE INFORMATION CONTROLS (OCT 2016)

(a) *Definitions*. As used in this provision—

Controlled technical information, covered contractor information system, covered defense information, cyber incident, information system, and *technical information* are defined in clause 252.204-7012, Safeguarding Covered Defense Information and Cyber Incident Reporting.

(b) The security requirements required by contract clause 252.204-7012 shall be implemented for all covered defense information on all covered contractor information systems that support the performance of this contract.

(c) For covered contractor information systems that are not part of an information technology service or system operated on behalf of the Government (see 252.204-7012(b)(2))—

(1) By submission of this offer, the Offeror represents that it will implement the security requirements specified by National Institute of Standards and Technology (NIST) Special Publication (SP) 800-171, "Protecting Controlled Unclassified Information in Nonfederal Information Systems and Organizations" (see *http://*

dx.doi.org/10.6028/NIST.SP.800-171) that are in effect at the time the solicitation is issued or as authorized by the contracting officer not later than December 31, 2017.

(2) (i) If the Offeror proposes to vary from any of the security requirements specified by NIST SP 800-171 that are in effect at the time the solicitation is issued or as authorized by the Contracting Officer, the Offeror shall submit to the Contracting Officer, for consideration by the DoD Chief Information Officer (CIO), a written explanation of—

(A) Why a particular security requirement is not applicable; or

(B) How an alternative but equally effective, security measure is used to compensate for the inability to satisfy a particular requirement and achieve equivalent protection.

(ii) An authorized representative of the DoD CIO will adjudicate offeror requests to vary from NIST SP 800-171 requirements in writing prior to contract award. Any accepted variance from NIST SP 800-171 shall be incorporated into the resulting contract.

(End of provision)

[Interim rule, 73 FR 42274, 7/21/2008, effective 7/21/2008; Final rule, 75 FR 18029, 4/8/2010, effective 4/8/2010; Final rule, 78 FR 36108, 6/17/2013, effective 6/17/2013; Interim rule, 80 FR 51739, 8/26/2015, effective 8/26/2015; Interim rule, 80 FR 81472, 12/30/2015, effective 12/30/2015; Final rule, 81 FR 72986, 10/21/2016, effective 10/21/2016]

252.204-7009 Limitations on the Use or Disclosure of Third-Party Contractor Reported Cyber Incident Information.

As prescribed in 204.7304(b), use the following clause:

LIMITATIONS ON THE USE OR DISCLOSURE OF THIRD-PARTY CONTRACTOR REPORTED CYBER INCIDENT INFORMATION (OCT 2016)

(a) *Definitions*. As used in this clause—

Compromise means disclosure of information to unauthorized persons, or a violation of the security policy of a system, in which unauthorized intentional or unintentional disclosure, modification, destruction, or loss of an object, or the copying of information to unauthorized media may have occurred.

Controlled technical information means technical information with military or space application that is subject to controls on the access, use, reproduction, modification, performance, display, release, disclosure, or dissemination. Controlled technical information would meet the criteria, if disseminated, for distribution statements B through F using the criteria set forth in DoD Instruction 5230.24, Distribution Statements on Technical Documents. The term does not include information that is lawfully publicly available without restrictions.

Covered defense information means unclassified controlled technical information or other information (as described in the Controlled Unclassified Information (CUI) Registry at *http://www.archives.gov/cui/registry/category-list.html*) that requires safeguarding or dissemination controls pursuant to and consistent with law, regulations, and Governmentwide policies, and is—

(1) Marked or otherwise identified in the contract, task order, or delivery order and provided to the contractor by or on behalf of DoD in support of the performance of the contract; or

(2) Collected, developed, received, transmitted, used, or stored by or on behalf of the contractor in support of the performance of the contract.

Cyber incident means actions taken through the use of computer networks that result in a compromise or an actual or potentially adverse effect on an information system and/or the information residing therein.

Information system means a discrete set of information resources organized for the collection, processing, maintenance, use, sharing, dissemination, or disposition of information.

Media means physical devices or writing surfaces including, but is not limited to, magnetic tapes, optical disks, magnetic disks, large-scale integration memory chips, and printouts onto which covered defense information is recorded, stored, or printed within a covered contractor information system.

Technical information means technical data or computer software, as those terms are defined in the clause at DFARS 252.227-7013, Rights in Technical Data-Noncommercial Items, regardless of whether or not the clause is incorporated in this solicitation or contract. Examples of technical information include research and engineering data, engineering drawings, and associated lists, specifications, standards, process sheets, manuals, technical reports, technical orders, catalog-item identifications, data sets, studies and analyses and related information, and computer software executable code and source code.

(b) *Restrictions.* The Contractor agrees that the following conditions apply to any information it receives or creates in the performance of this contract that is information obtained from a third-party's reporting of a cyber incident pursuant to DFARS clause 252.204-7012, Safeguarding Covered Defense Information and Cyber Incident Reporting (or derived from such information obtained under that clause):

(1) The Contractor shall access and use the information only for the purpose of furnishing advice or technical assistance directly to the Government in support of the Government's activities related to clause 252.204-7012, and shall not be used for any other purpose.

(2) The Contractor shall protect the information against unauthorized release or disclosure.

(3) The Contractor shall ensure that its employees are subject to use and non-disclosure obligations consistent with this clause prior to the employees being provided access to or use of the information.

(4) The third-party contractor that reported the cyber incident is a third-party beneficiary of the non-disclosure agreement between the Government and Contractor, as required by paragraph (b)(3) of this clause.

(5) A breach of these obligations or restrictions may subject the Contractor to—

(i) Criminal, civil, administrative, and contractual actions in law and equity for penalties, damages, and other appropriate remedies by the United States; and

(ii) Civil actions for damages and other appropriate remedies by the third party that reported the cyber incident, as a third party beneficiary of this clause.

(c) *Subcontracts.* The Contractor shall include this clause, including this paragraph (c), in subcontracts, or similar contractual instruments, for services that include support for the Government's activities related to safeguarding covered defense information and cyber incident reporting, including subcontracts for commercial items, without alteration, except to identify the parties.

(End of clause)

[Interim rule, 73 FR 42274, 7/21/2008, effective 7/21/2008; Final rule, 75 FR 18029, 4/8/2010, effective 4/8/2010; Interim rule, 80 FR 51739, 8/26/2015, effective 8/26/2015; Interim rule, 80 FR 81472, 12/30/2015, effective 12/30/2015; Final rule, 81 FR 72986, 10/21/2016, effective 10/21/2016]

252.204-7010 Requirement for Contractor to Notify DoD if the Contractor's Activities are Subject to Reporting Under the U.S.-International Atomic Energy Agency Additional Protocol.

As prescribed in 204.470-3, use the following clause:

REQUIREMENT FOR CONTRACTOR TO NOTIFY DoD IF THE CONTRACTOR'S ACTIVITIES ARE SUBJECT TO REPORTING UNDER THE U.S.-INTERNATIONAL ATOMIC ENERGY AGENCY ADDITIONAL PROTOCOL (JAN 2009)

(a) If the Contractor is required to report any of its activities in accordance with Department of Commerce regulations (15 CFR part 781 et seq.) or Nuclear Regulatory Commission regulations (10 CFR part 75) in order to implement the declarations required by the U.S.-International Atomic Energy Agency Additional Protocol (U.S.-IAEA AP), the Contractor shall—

(1) Immediately provide written notification to the following DoD Program Manager:

[Contracting Officer to insert Program Manager's name, mailing address, e-mail address, telephone number, and facsimile number];

(2) Include in the notification—

(i) Where DoD contract activities or information are located relative to the activities or information to be declared to the Department of Commerce or the Nuclear Regulatory Commission; and

(ii) If or when any current or former DoD contract activities and the activities to be declared to the Department of Commerce or the Nuclear Regulatory Commission have been or will be co-located or located near enough to one another to result in disclosure of the DoD activities during an IAEA inspection or visit; and

(3) Provide a copy of the notification to the Contracting Officer.

(b) After receipt of a notification submitted in accordance with paragraph (a) of this clause, the DoD Program Manager will—

(1) Conduct a security assessment to determine if and by what means access may be granted to the IAEA; or

(2) Provide written justification to the component or agency treaty office for a national security exclusion, in accordance with DoD Instruction 2060.03, Application of the National Security Exclusion to the Agreements Between the United States of America and the International Atomic Energy Agency for the Application of Safeguards in the United States of America. DoD will notify the Contractor if a national security exclusion is applied at the Contractor's location to prohibit access by the IAEA.

(c) If the DoD Program Manager determines that a security assessment is required—

(1) DoD will, at a minimum—

(i) Notify the Contractor that DoD officials intend to conduct an assessment of vulnerabilities to IAEA inspections or visits;

(ii) Notify the Contractor of the time at which the assessment will be conducted, at least 30 days prior to the assessment;

(iii) Provide the Contractor with advance notice of the credentials of the DoD officials who will conduct the assessment; and

(iv) To the maximum extent practicable, conduct the assessment in a manner that does not impede or delay operations at the Contractor's facility; and

(2) The Contractor shall provide access to the site and shall cooperate with DoD officials in the assessment of vulnerabilities to IAEA inspections or visits.

(d) Following a security assessment of the Contractor's facility, DoD officials will notify the Contractor as to—

(1) Whether the Contractor's facility has any vulnerabilities where potentially declarable activities under the U.S.-IAEA AP are taking place;

(2) Whether additional security measures are needed; and

(3) Whether DoD will apply a national security exclusion.

(e) If DoD applies a national security exclusion, the Contractor shall not grant access to IAEA inspectors.

(f) If DoD does not apply a national security exclusion, the Contractor shall apply managed access to prevent disclosure of program activities, locations, or information in the U.S. declaration.

(g) The Contractor shall not delay submission of any reports required by the Department of Commerce or the Nuclear Regulatory Commission while awaiting a DoD response to a notification provided in accordance with this clause.

(h) The Contractor shall incorporate the substance of this clause, including this paragraph (h), in all subcontracts that are subject to the provisions of the U.S.-IAEA AP.

(End of clause)

[Final rule, 74 FR 2411, 1/15/2009, effective 1/15/2009]

252.204-7011 [Removed and Reserved]

[Final rule, 76 FR 58138, 9/20/2011, effective 9/20/2011; Final rule, 83 FR 24886, 5/30/2018, effective 5/30/2018]

252.204-7012 Safeguarding Covered Defense Information and Cyber Incident Reporting.

As prescribed in 204.7304(c), use the following clause:

SAFEGUARDING COVERED DEFENSE INFORMATION AND CYBER INCIDENT REPORTING (DEC 2019)

(a) *Definitions*. As used in this clause—

Adequate security means protective measures that are commensurate with the consequences and probability of loss, misuse, or unauthorized access to, or modification of information.

Compromise means disclosure of information to unauthorized persons, or a violation of the security policy of a system, in which unauthorized intentional or unintentional disclosure, modification, destruction, or loss of an object, or the copying of information to unauthorized media may have occurred.

Contractor attributional/proprietary information means information that identifies the contractor(s), whether directly or indirectly, by the grouping of information that can be traced back to the contractor(s) (e.g., program description, facility locations), personally identifiable information, as well as trade secrets, commercial or financial information, or other commercially sensitive information that is not customarily shared outside of the company.

Controlled technical information means technical information with military or space application that is subject to controls on the access, use, reproduction, modification, performance, display, release, disclosure, or dissemination. Controlled technical information would meet the criteria, if disseminated, for distribution statements B through F using the criteria set forth in DoD Instruction 5230.24, Distribution Statements on Technical Documents. The term does not include information that is lawfully publicly available without restrictions.

Covered contractor information system means an unclassified information system that is owned, or operated by or for, a contractor and that processes, stores, or transmits covered defense information.

Covered defense information means unclassified controlled technical information or other information, as described in the Controlled Unclassified Information (CUI) Registry at *http://www.archives.gov/cui/registry/category-list.html*, that requires safeguarding or dissemination controls pursuant to and consistent with law, regulations, and Governmentwide policies, and is—

(1) Marked or otherwise identified in the contract, task order, or delivery order and provided to the contractor by or on behalf of DoD in support of the performance of the contract; or

(2) Collected, developed, received, transmitted, used, or stored by or on behalf of the contractor in support of the performance of the contract.

Cyber incident means actions taken through the use of computer networks that result in a compromise or an actual or potentially adverse effect on an information system and/or the information residing therein.

Forensic analysis means the practice of gathering, retaining, and analyzing computer-related data for investigative purposes in a manner that maintains the integrity of the data.

Information system means a discrete set of information resources organized for the collection, processing, maintenance, use, sharing, dissemination, or disposition of information.

Malicious software means computer software or firmware intended to perform an unauthorized process that will have adverse impact on the confidentiality, integrity, or availability of an information system. This definition includes a virus, worm, Trojan horse, or other code-based entity that infects a host, as well as spyware and some forms of adware.

Media means physical devices or writing surfaces including, but is not limited to, magnetic tapes, optical disks, magnetic disks, large-scale integration memory chips, and printouts onto which covered defense information is recorded, stored, or printed within a covered contractor information system.

Operationally critical support means supplies or services designated by the Government as critical for airlift, sealift, intermodal transportation services, or logistical support that is essential to the mobilization, deployment, or sustainment of the Armed Forces in a contingency operation.

Rapidly report means within 72 hours of discovery of any cyber incident.

Technical information means technical data or computer software, as those terms are defined in the clause at DFARS 252.227-7013, Rights in Technical Data—Noncommercial Items, regardless of whether or not the clause is incorporated in this solicitation or contract. Examples of technical information include research and engineering data, engineering drawings, and associated lists, specifications, standards, process sheets, manuals, technical reports, technical orders, catalog-item identifications, data sets, studies and analyses and related information, and computer software executable code and source code.

(b) *Adequate security.* The Contractor shall provide adequate security on all covered contractor information systems. To provide adequate security, the Contractor shall implement, at a minimum, the following information security protections:

(1) For covered contractor information systems that are part of an information technology (IT) service or system operated on behalf of the Government, the following security requirements apply:

(i) Cloud computing services shall be subject to the security requirements specified in the clause 252.239-7010, Cloud Computing Services, of this contract.

(ii) Any other such IT service or system (i.e., other than cloud computing) shall be subject to the security requirements specified elsewhere in this contract.

(2) For covered contractor information systems that are not part of an IT service or system operated on behalf of the Government and therefore are not subject to the security requirement specified at paragraph (b)(1) of this clause, the following security requirements apply:

(i) Except as provided in paragraph (b)(2)(ii) of this clause, the covered contractor information system shall be subject to the security requirements in National Institute of Standards and Technology (NIST) Special Publication (SP) 800-171, "Protecting Controlled Unclassified Information in Nonfederal Information Systems and Organizations" (available via the internet at *http://dx.doi.org/10.6028/NIST.SP.800-171*) in effect at the time the solicitation is issued or as authorized by the Contracting Officer.

(ii)(A) The Contractor shall implement NIST SP 800-171, as soon as practical, but not later than December 31, 2017. For all contracts awarded prior to October 1, 2017, the Contractor shall notify the DoD Chief Information Officer (CIO), via email at *osd.dibcsia@mail.mil*, within 30 days of contract award, of any security requirements specified by NIST SP 800-171 not implemented at the time of contract award.

(B) The Contractor shall submit requests to vary from NIST SP 800-171 in writing to the Contracting Officer, for consideration by the DoD CIO. The Contractor need not implement any security requirement adjudicated by an authorized representative of the DoD CIO to be nonapplicable or to have an alternative, but equally effective, security measure that may be implemented in its place.

(C) If the DoD CIO has previously adjudicated the contractor's requests indicating that a requirement is not applicable or that an alternative security measure is equally effective, a copy of that approval shall be provided to the Contracting Officer when requesting its recognition under this contract.

(D) If the Contractor intends to use an external cloud service provider to store, process, or transmit any covered defense information in performance of this contract, the Contractor shall require and ensure that the cloud service provider meets security requirements equivalent to those established by the Government for the Federal Risk and Authorization Management Program (FedRAMP) Moderate baseline (*https://www.fedramp.gov/resources/documents/*) and that the cloud service provider complies with requirements in paragraphs (c) through (g) of this clause for cyber incident reporting, malicious software, media preservation and protection, access to additional information and equipment necessary for forensic analysis, and cyber incident damage assessment.

(3) Apply other information systems security measures when the Contractor reasonably determines that information systems security measures, in addition to those identified in paragraphs (b)(1) and (2) of this clause, may be required to provide adequate security in a dynamic environment or to accommodate special circumstances (e.g., medical devices) and any individual, isolated, or temporary deficiencies based on an assessed risk or vulnerability. These measures may be addressed in a system security plan.

(c) *Cyber incident reporting requirement.*

(1) When the Contractor discovers a cyber incident that affects a covered contractor information system or the covered defense information residing therein, or that affects the contractor's ability to perform the requirements of the contract that are designated as operationally critical support and identified in the contract, the Contractor shall—

(i) Conduct a review for evidence of compromise of covered defense information, including, but not limited to, identifying compromised computers, servers, specific data, and user accounts. This review shall also include analyzing covered contractor information system(s) that were part of the cyber incident, as well as other information systems on the Contractor's network(s), that may have been accessed as a result of the incident in order to identify compromised covered defense information, or that affect the Contractor's ability to provide operationally critical support; and

(ii) Rapidly report cyber incidents to DoD at *https://dibnet.dod.mil.*

(2) *Cyber incident report.* The cyber incident report shall be treated as information created by or for DoD and shall include, at a minimum, the required elements at *https://dibnet.dod.mil.*

(3) *Medium assurance certificate requirement.* In order to report cyber incidents in accordance with this clause, the Contractor or subcontractor shall have or acquire a DoD-approved medium assurance certificate to report cyber incidents. For information on obtaining a DoD-approved medium assurance certificate, see *https://public.cyber.mil/eca/.*

(d) *Malicious software.* When the Contractor or subcontractors discover and isolate malicious software in connection with a reported cyber incident, submit the malicious software to DoD Cyber Crime Center (DC3) in accordance with instructions provided by DC3 or the Contracting Officer. Do not send the malicious software to the Contracting Officer.

(e) *Media preservation and protection.* When a Contractor discovers a cyber incident has occurred, the Contractor shall preserve and protect images of all known affected information systems identified in paragraph (c)(1)(i) of this clause and all relevant monitoring/packet capture data for at least 90 days from the submission of the cyber incident report to allow DoD to request the media or decline interest.

(f) *Access to additional information or equipment necessary for forensic analysis.* Upon request by DoD, the Contractor shall provide DoD with access to additional information or equipment that is necessary to conduct a forensic analysis.

(g) *Cyber incident damage assessment activities.* If DoD elects to conduct a damage assessment, the Contracting Officer will request that the Contractor provide all of the damage assessment information gathered in accordance with paragraph (e) of this clause.

(h) *DoD safeguarding and use of contractor attributional/proprietary information.* The Government shall protect against the unauthorized use or release of information obtained from the contractor (or derived from information obtained from the contractor) under this clause that includes contractor attributional/proprietary information, including such information submitted in accordance with paragraph (c). To the maximum extent practicable, the Contractor shall identify and mark attributional/proprietary information. In making an authorized release of such information, the Government will implement appropriate procedures to minimize the contractor attributional/proprietary information that is included in such authorized release, seeking to include only that information that is necessary for the authorized purpose(s) for which the information is being released.

(i) *Use and release of contractor attributional/proprietary information not created by or for DoD*. Information that is obtained from the contractor (or derived from information obtained from the contractor) under this clause that is not created by or for DoD is authorized to be released outside of DoD—

(1) To entities with missions that may be affected by such information;

(2) To entities that may be called upon to assist in the diagnosis, detection, or mitigation of cyber incidents;

(3) To Government entities that conduct counterintelligence or law enforcement investigations;

(4) For national security purposes, including cyber situational awareness and defense purposes (including with Defense Industrial Base (DIB) participants in the program at 32 CFR part 236); or

(5) To a support services contractor ("recipient") that is directly supporting Government activities under a contract that includes the clause at 252.204-7009, Limitations on the Use or Disclosure of Third-Party Contractor Reported Cyber Incident Information.

(j) *Use and release of contractor attributional/proprietary information created by or for DoD*. Information that is obtained from the contractor (or derived from information obtained from the contractor) under this clause that is created by or for DoD (including the information submitted pursuant to paragraph (c) of this clause) is authorized to be used and released outside of DoD for purposes and activities authorized by paragraph (i) of this clause, and for any other lawful Government purpose or activity, subject to all applicable statutory, regulatory, and policy based restrictions on the Government's use and release of such information.

(k) The Contractor shall conduct activities under this clause in accordance with applicable laws and regulations on the interception, monitoring, access, use, and disclosure of electronic communications and data.

(l) *Other safeguarding or reporting requirements*. The safeguarding and cyber incident reporting required by this clause in no way abrogates the Contractor's responsibility for other safeguarding or cyber incident reporting pertaining to its unclassified information systems as required by other applicable clauses of this contract, or as a result of other applicable U.S. Government statutory or regulatory requirements.

(m) *Subcontracts*. The Contractor shall—

(1) Include this clause, including this paragraph (m), in subcontracts, or similar contractual instruments, for operationally critical support, or for which subcontract performance will involve covered defense information, including subcontracts for commercial items, without alteration, except to identify the parties. The Contractor shall determine if the information required for subcontractor performance retains its identity as covered defense information and will require protection under this clause, and, if necessary, consult with the Contracting Officer; and

(2) Require subcontractors to—

(i) Notify the prime Contractor (or next higher-tier subcontractor) when submitting a request to vary from a NIST SP 800-171 security requirement to the Contracting Officer, in accordance with paragraph (b)(2)(ii)(B) of this clause; and

(ii) Provide the incident report number, automatically assigned by DoD, to the prime Contractor (or next higher-tier subcontractor) as soon as practicable, when reporting a cyber incident to DoD as required in paragraph (c) of this clause.

(End of clause)

[Final rule, 78 FR 69273, 11/18/2013, effective 11/18/2013; Final rule, 79 FR 74652, 12/16/2014, effective 12/16/2014; Interim rule, 80 FR 51739, 8/26/2015, effective 8/26/2015; Final rule, 80 FR 56929, 9/21/2015, effective 9/21/2015; Interim rule, 80 FR 81472, 12/30/2015, effective 12/30/2015; Final rule, 81 FR 72986, 10/21/2016, effective 10/21/2016; Final rule, 84 FR 72563, 12/31/2019, effective 12/31/2019]

252.204-7013 [Removed and Reserved]

[Interim rule, 79 FR 11337, 2/28/2014, effective 2/28/2014; Final rule, 70016.89x, 5/11/2016, effective 5/11/2016; Final rule, 81 FR 28724, 5/10/2016, effective 5/10/2016; Final rule, 84 FR 58331, 10/31/2019, effective 10/31/2019]

252.204-7014 Limitations on the Use or Disclosure of Information by Litigation Support Contractors.

As prescribed in 204.7403(a), use the following clause:

LIMITATIONS ON THE USE OR DISCLOSURE OF INFORMATION BY LITIGATION SUPPORT CONTRACTORS (MAY 2016)

(a) *Definitions*. As used in this clause—

Computer software means computer programs, source code, source code listings, object code listings, design details, algorithms, processes, flow charts, formulae, and related material that would enable the software to be reproduced, recreated, or recompiled. Computer software does not include computer data bases or computer software documentation.

Litigation information means any information, including sensitive information, that is furnished to the contractor by or on behalf of the Government, or that is generated or obtained by the contractor in the performance of litigation support under a contract. The term does not include information that is lawfully, publicly available without restriction, including information contained in a publicly available solicitation.

Litigation support means a contractor (including its experts, technical consultants, subcontractors, and suppliers) providing litigation support under a contract that contains this clause.

Litigation support contractor means a contractor (including an expert or technical consultant) providing litigation support under a contract with the Department of Defense that contains this clause.

Sensitive information means controlled unclassified information of a commercial, financial, proprietary, or privileged nature. The term includes technical data and computer software, but does not include information that is lawfully, publicly available without restriction.

Technical data means recorded information, regardless of the form or method of the recording, of a scientific or technical nature (including computer software documentation). The term does not include computer software or data incidental to contract administration, such as financial and/or management information.

(b) *Limitations on use or disclosure of litigation information*. Notwithstanding any other provision of this contract, the Contractor shall—

(1) Access and use litigation information only for the purpose of providing litigation support under this contract;

(2) Not disclose litigation information to any entity outside the Contractor's organization unless, prior to such disclosure the Contracting Officer has provided written consent to such disclosure;

(3) Take all precautions necessary to prevent unauthorized disclosure of litigation information;

(4) Not use litigation information to compete against a third party for Government or nongovernment contracts; and

(5) Upon completion of the authorized litigation support activities, destroy or return to the Government at the request of the Contracting Officer all litigation information in its possession.

(c) Violation of paragraph (b)(1), (b)(2), (b)(3), (b)(4), or (b)(5) of this clause is a basis for the Government to terminate this contract.

(d) *Indemnification and creation of third party beneficiary rights*. The Contractor agrees—

(1) To indemnify and hold harmless the Government, its agents, and employees from any claim or liability, including attorneys' fees, court costs, and expenses, arising out of, or in any way related to, the misuse or unauthorized modification, reproduction, release, performance, display, or disclosure of any litigation information; and

(2) That any third party holding proprietary rights or any other legally protectable interest in any litigation information, in addition to any other rights it may have, is a third party beneficiary under this contract who shall have a right of direct action against the Contractor, and against any person to whom the Contractor has released or disclosed such litigation information, for any such unauthorized use or disclosure.

(e) *Contractor employees*. The Contractor shall ensure that its employees are subject to use and nondisclosure obligations consistent with this clause prior to the employees being provided access to or use of any litigation information covered by this clause.

(f) *Flowdown*. Include the substance of this clause, including this paragraph (f), in all subcontracts, including subcontracts for commercial items.

(End of clause)

[Interim rule, 79 FR 11337, 2/28/2014, effective 2/28/2014; Final rule, 70016.89x, 5/11/2016, effective 5/11/2016; Final rule, 81 FR 28724, 5/10/2016, effective 5/10/2016; Final rule, 84 FR 58331, 10/31/2019, effective 10/31/2019]

252.204-7015 Notice of Authorized Disclosure of Information for Litigation Support.

As prescribed in 204.7403(b), use the following clause:

NOTICE OF AUTHORIZED DISCLOSURE OF INFORMATION FOR LITIGATION SUPPORT (MAY 2016)

(a) *Definitions*. As used in this clause—

Computer software means computer programs, source code, source code listings, object code listings, design details, algorithms, processes, flow charts, formulae, and related material that would enable the software to be reproduced, recreated, or recompiled. Computer software does not include computer data bases or computer software documentation.

Litigation support means administrative, technical, or professional services provided in support of the Government during or in anticipation of litigation.

Litigation support contractor means a contractor (including its experts, technical consultants, subcontractors, and suppliers) providing litigation support under a contract that contains the clause at 252.204-7014, Limitations on the Use or Disclosure of Information by Litigation Support Contractors.

Sensitive information means controlled unclassified information of a commercial, financial, proprietary, or privileged nature. The term includes technical data and computer software, but does not include information that is lawfully, publicly available without restriction.

Technical data means recorded information, regardless of the form or method of the recording, of a scientific or technical nature (including computer software documentation). The term does not include computer software or data incidental to contract administration, such as financial and/or management information.

(b) *Notice of authorized disclosures*. Notwithstanding any other provision of this solicitation or contract, the Government may disclose to a litigation support contractor, for the sole purpose of litigation support activities, any information, including sensitive information, received—

(1) Within or in connection with a quotation or offer; or

(2) In the performance of or in connection with a contract.

(c) *Flowdown*. Include the substance of this clause, including this paragraph (c), in all subcontracts, including subcontracts for commercial items.

(End of clause)

[Interim rule, 79 FR 11337, 2/28/2014, effective 2/28/2014; Final rule, 81 FR 28724, 5/10/2016, effective 5/10/2016; Final rule, 84 FR 58331, 10/31/2019, effective 10/31/2019]

252.204–7016 Covered Defense Telecommunications Equipment or Services—Representation.

As prescribed in 204.2105(a), use the following provision:

COVERED DEFENSE TELECOMMUNICATIONS EQUIPMENT OR SERVICES—REPRESENTATION (DEC 2019)

(a) *Definitions.* As used in this provision, covered defense telecommunications equipment or services has the meaning provided in the clause 252.204–7018, Prohibition on the Acquisition of Covered Defense Telecommunications Equipment or Services.

(b) *Procedures.* The Offeror shall review the list of excluded parties in the System for Award Management (SAM) (***https://www.sam.gov***) for entities excluded from receiving federal awards for "covered defense telecommunications equipment or services".

(c) *Representation.* The Offeror represents that it [ ] does, [ ] does not provide covered defense telecommunications equipment or services as a part of its offered products or services to the Government in the performance of any contract, subcontract, or other contractual instrument.

(End of provision)

[Interim rule, 84 FR 72231, 12/31/2019, effective 12/31/2019]

252.204–7017 Prohibition on the Acquisition of Covered Defense Telecommunications Equipment or Services—Representation.

As prescribed in 204.2105(b), use the following provision:

PROHIBITION ON THE ACQUISITON OF COVERED DEFENSE TELECOMMUNICATIONS EQUIPMENT OR SERVICES—REPRESENTATION (DEC 2019)

The Offeror is not required to complete the representation in this provision if the Offeror has represented in the provision at 252.204–7016, Covered Defense Telecommunications Equipment or Services—Representation, that it "does not provide covered defense telecommunications equipment or services as a part of its offered products or services to the Government in the performance of any contract, subcontract, or other contractual instrument."

(a) *Definitions. Covered defense telecommunications equipment or services, covered mission, critical technology,* and *substantial or essential component,* as used in this provision, have the meanings given in the 252.204–7018 clause, Prohibition on the Acquisition of Covered Defense Telecommunications Equipment or Services, of this solicitation.

(b) *Prohibition.* Section 1656 of the National Defense Authorization Act for Fiscal Year 2018 (Pub. L. 115–91) prohibits agencies from procuring or obtaining, or extending or renewing a contract to procure or obtain, any equipment, system, or service to carry out covered missions that uses covered defense telecommunications equipment or services as a substantial or essential component of any system, or as critical technology as part of any system.

(c) *Procedures.* The Offeror shall review the list of excluded parties in the System for Award Management (SAM) at ***https://*** ***www.sam.gov*** for entities that are excluded when providing any equipment, system, or service to carry out covered missions that uses covered defense telecommunications equipment or services as a substantial or essential component of any system, or as critical technology as part of any system, unless a waiver is granted.

(d) *Representation.* If in its annual representations and certifications in SAM the Offeror has represented in paragraph (c) of the provision at 252.204–7016, Covered Defense

Telecommunications Equipment or Services—Representation, that it "does" provide covered defense telecommunications equipment or services as a part of its offered products or services to the Government in the performance of any contract, subcontract, or other contractual instrument, then the Offeror shall complete the following additional representation: The Offeror represents that it [ ] will [ ] will not provide covered defense telecommunications equipment or services as a part of its offered products or services to DoD in the performance of any award resulting from this solicitation.

(e) *Disclosures.* If the Offeror has represented in paragraph (d) of this provision that it "will provide covered defense telecommunications equipment or services," the Offeror shall provide the following information as part of the offer:

(1) A description of all covered defense telecommunications equipment and services offered (include brand or manufacturer; product, such as model number, original equipment manufacturer (OEM) number, manufacturer part number, or wholesaler number; and item description, as applicable).

(2) An explanation of the proposed use of covered defense telecommunications equipment and services and any factors relevant to determining if such use would be permissible under the prohibition referenced in paragraph (b) of this provision.

(3) For services, the entity providing the covered defense telecommunications services (include entity name, unique entity identifier, and Commercial and Government Entity (CAGE) code, if known).

(4) For equipment, the entity that produced or provided the covered defense telecommunications equipment (include entity name, unique entity identifier, CAGE code, and whether the entity was the OEM or a distributor, if known).

(End of provision)

[Interim rule, 84 FR 72231, 12/31/2019, effective 12/31/2019]

252.204-7018 Prohibition on the Acquisition of Covered Defense Telecommunications Equipment or Services.

As prescribed in 204.2105(c), use the following clause:

PROHIBITION ON THE ACQUISITION OF COVERED DEFENSE TELECOMMUNICATIONS EQUIPMENT OR SERVICES (DEC 2019)

(a) *Definitions.* As used in this clause—Covered defense telecommunications equipment or services means—

(1) Telecommunications equipment produced by Huawei Technologies Company or ZTE Corporation, or any subsidiary or affiliate of such entities;

(2) Telecommunications services provided by such entities or using such equipment; or

(3) Telecommunications equipment or services produced or provided by an entity that the Secretary of Defense reasonably believes to be an entity owned or controlled by, or otherwise connected to, the government of a covered foreign country.

Covered foreign country means—

(1) The People's Republic of China; or

(2) The Russian Federation.

Covered missions means—

(1) The nuclear deterrence mission of DoD, including with respect to nuclear command, control, and communications, integrated tactical warning and attack assessment, and continuity of Government; or

(2) The homeland defense mission of DoD, including with respect to ballistic missile defense.

Critical technology means—

(1) Defense articles or defense services included on the United States Munitions List set forth in the International Traffic in Arms Regulations under subchapter M of chapter I of title 22, Code of Federal Regulations;

(2) Items included on the Commerce Control List set forth in Supplement No. 1 to part 774 of the Export Administration Regulations under subchapter C of chapter VII of

title 15, Code of Federal Regulations, and controlled—

(i) Pursuant to multilateral regimes, including for reasons relating to national security, chemical and biological weapons proliferation, nuclear nonproliferation, or missile technology; or

(ii) For reasons relating to regional stability or surreptitious listening;

(3) Specially designed and prepared nuclear equipment, parts and components, materials, software, and technology covered by part 810 of title 10, Code of Federal Regulations (relating to assistance to foreign atomic energy activities);

(4) Nuclear facilities, equipment, and material covered by part 110 of title 10, Code of Federal Regulations (relating to export and import of nuclear equipment and material);

(5) Select agents and toxins covered by part 331 of title 7, Code of Federal Regulations, part 121 of title 9 of such Code, or part 73 of title 42 of such Code; or

(6) Emerging and foundational technologies controlled pursuant to section 1758 of the Export Control Reform Act of 2018 (50 U.S.C. 4817).

Substantial or essential component means any component necessary for the proper function or performance of a piece of equipment, system, or service.

(b) *Prohibition.* In accordance with section 1656 of the National Defense Authorization Act for Fiscal Year 2018 (Pub. L. 115–91), the contractor shall not provide to the Government any equipment, system, or service to carry out covered missions that uses covered defense telecommunications equipment or services as a substantial or essential component of any system, or as critical technology as part of any system, unless the covered defense telecommunication equipment or services are covered by a waiver described in Defense Federal Acquisition Regulation Supplement 204.2104.

(c) *Procedures.* The Contractor shall review the list of excluded parties in the System for Award Management (SAM) at *https://www.sam.gov* for entities that are excluded when providing any equipment, system, or service, to carry out covered missions, that uses covered defense telecommunications equipment or services as a substantial or essential component of any system, or as critical technology as part of any system, unless a waiver is granted.

(d) *Reporting.*

(1) In the event the Contractor identifies covered defense telecommunications equipment or services used as a substantial or essential component of any system, or as critical technology as part of any system, during contract performance, the Contractor shall report at *https://dibnet.dod.mil* the information in paragraph (d)(2) of this clause.

(2) The Contractor shall report the following information pursuant to paragraph (d)(1) of this clause:

(i) Within one business day from the date of such identification or notification: The contract number; the order number(s), if applicable; supplier name; brand; model number (original equipment manufacturer number, manufacturer part number, or wholesaler number); item description; and any readily available information about mitigation actions undertaken or recommended.

(ii) Within 10 business days of submitting the information in paragraph (d)(2)(i) of this clause: Any further available information about mitigation actions undertaken or recommended. In addition, the Contractor shall describe the efforts it undertook to prevent use or submission of a covered defense telecommunications equipment or services, and any additional efforts that will be incorporated to prevent future use or submission of covered telecommunications equipment or services.

(e) *Subcontracts.* The Contractor shall insert the substance of this clause, including this paragraph (e), in all subcontracts and other contractual instruments, including subcontracts for the acquisition of commercial items.

(End of clause)

[Interim rule, 84 FR 72231, 12/31/2019, effective 12/31/2019]

252.205 Publicizing Contract Actions, provisions and clauses for DFARS Part 205

252.205-7000 Provision of information to cooperative agreement holders.

As prescribed in 205.470, use the following clause:

PROVISION OF INFORMATION TO COOPERATIVE AGREEMENT HOLDERS (DEC 1991)

(a) *Definition.*

Cooperative agreement holder means a State or local government; a private, nonprofit organization; a tribal organization (as defined in section 4(c) of the Indian Self-Determination and Education Assistance Act (Pub. L. 93-268; 25 U.S.C. 450(c)); or an economic enterprise (as defined in section 3(e) of the Indian Financing Act of 1974 (Pub. L. 93-362; 25 U.S.C. 1452(e)) whether such economic enterprise is organized for profit or nonprofit purposes; which has an agreement with the Defense Logistics Agency to furnish procurement technical assistance to business entities.

(b) The Contractor shall provide cooperative agreement holders, upon their request, with a list of those appropriate employees or offices responsible for entering into subcontracts under defense contracts. The list shall include the business address, telephone number, and area of responsibility of each employee or office.

(c) The Contractor need not provide the listing to a particular cooperative agreement holder more frequently than once a year.

[Final rule, 69 FR 63327, 11/1/2004, effective 1/11/2004]

(End of clause)

252.206 Competition Requirements, provisions and clauses for DFARS Part 206

252.206-7000 Domestic source restriction.

As prescribed at 206.302-3-70, use the following provision:

DOMESTIC SOURCE RESTRICTION (DEC 1991)

This solicitation is restricted to domestic sources under the authority of 10 U.S.C. 2304(c)(3). Foreign sources, except Canadian sources, are not eligible for award.

(End of provision)

252.208 Required Sources of Supplies and Services, provisions and clauses for DFARS Part 208

252.208-7000 Intent to furnish precious metals as Government-furnished material.

As prescribed in 208.7305(a), use the following clause:

INTENT TO FURNISH PRECIOUS METALS AS GOVERNMENT-FURNISHED MATERIAL (DEC 1991)

(a) The Government intends to furnish precious metals required in the manufacture of items to be delivered under the contract if the Contracting Officer determines it to be in the Government's best interest. The use of Government-furnished silver is mandatory when the quantity required is one hundred troy ounces or more. The precious metal(s) will be furnished pursuant to the Government Furnished Property clause of the contract.

(b) The Offeror shall cite the type (silver, gold, platinum, palladium, iridium, rhodium, and ruthenium) and quantity in whole troy ounces of precious metals required in the performance of this contract (including precious metals required for any first article or production sample), and shall specify the national stock number (NSN) and nomenclature, if known, of the deliverable item requiring precious metals.

Precious metal *	Quantity	Deliverable item (NSN and nomenclature)

* If platinum or palladium, specify whether sponge or granules are required.

(c) Offerors shall submit two prices for each deliverable item which contains precious metals—one based on the Government furnishing precious metals, and one based on the Contractor furnishing precious metals. Award will be made on the basis which is in the best interest of the Government.

(d) The Contractor agrees to insert this clause, including this paragraph (d), in solicitations for subcontracts and purchase orders issued in performance of this contract, unless the Contractor knows that the item being purchased contains no precious metals.

(End of clause)

252.209 Contractor Qualifications, provisions and clauses for DFARS Part 209

252.209-7000 [Removed and Reserved]

[DAC 91-9, 60 FR 61586, 11/30/95, effective 11/30/95; Final rule, 69 FR 65088, 11/10/2004, effective 11/10/2004]

252.209-7001 [Removed and Reserved]

[Interim rule, 59 FR 51130, 10/7/94, effective 9/29/94; Interim rule, 63 FR 14836, 3/27/98, effective 3/27/98, finalized without change, 63 FR 64426, 11/20/98; Final rule, 69 FR 55992, 9/17/2004, effective 9/17/2004; Final rule, 71 FR 62566, 10/26/2006, effective 10/26/2006; Final rule, 74 FR 2421, 1/15/2009, effective 1/15/2009; Final rule, 79 FR 73488, 12/11/2014, effective 12/11/2014]

252.209-7002 Disclosure of ownership or control by a foreign government.

As prescribed in 209.104-70, use the following provision:

DISCLOSURE OF OWNERSHIP OR CONTROL BY A FOREIGN GOVERNMENT (JUN 2010)

(a) *Definitions.*

As used in this provision—

(1) *Effectively owned or controlled* means that a foreign government or any entity controlled by a foreign government has the power, either directly or indirectly, whether exercised or exercisable, to control the election, appointment, or tenure of the Offeror's officers or a majority of the Offeror's board of directors by any means, e.g., ownership, contract, or operation of law (or equivalent power for unincorporated organizations).

(2) *Entity controlled by a foreign government*—;

(i) Means—

(A) Any domestic or foreign organization or corporation that is effectively owned or controlled by a foreign government; or

(B) Any individual acting on behalf of a foreign government.

(ii) Does not include an organization or corporation that is owned, but is not controlled, either directly or indirectly, by a foreign government if the ownership of that organization or corporation by that foreign government was effective before October 23, 1992.

(3) *Foreign government* includes the state and the government of any country (other than the United States and its outlying areas) as well as any political subdivision, agency, or instrumentality thereof.

(4) *Proscribed information* means—

(i) Top Secret information;

(ii) Communications security (COMSEC) material, excluding controlled cryptographic items when unkeyed or utilized with unclassified keys;

(iii) Restricted Data as defined in the U.S. Atomic Energy Act of 1954, as amended;

(iv) Special Access Program (SAP) information; or

(v) Sensitive Compartmented Information (SCI).

(b) *Prohibition on award.*

No contract under a national security program may be awarded to an entity controlled by a foreign government if that entity requires access to proscribed information to perform the contract, unless the Secretary of Defense or a designee has waived application of 10 U.S.C. 2536(a).

(c) *Disclosure.*

The Offeror shall disclose any interest a foreign government has in the Offeror when that interest constitutes control by a foreign government as defined in this provision. If the Offeror is a subsidiary, it shall also disclose any reportable interest a foreign government has in any entity that owns or controls the subsidiary, including reportable interest concerning the Offeror's immediate parent, intermediate parents, and the ultimate parent. Use separate paper as needed, and provide the information in the following format:

Offeror's Point of Contact for Questions about Disclosure (Name and Phone Number with Country Code, City Code and Area Code, as applicable)

Name and Address of Offeror

Name and Address of Entity Controlled by a Foreign Government	Description of Interest, Ownership Percentage, and Identification of Foreign Government

(End of provision)

[Interim rule, DAC 91-5, 58 FR 28458, 5/13/93, effective 4/30/93; Final rule, 59 FR 51132, 10/7/94, effective 9/29/94; Final rule, 70 FR 35543, 6/21/2005, effective 6/21/2005; Interim rule, 75 FR 35684, 6/23/2010, effective 6/23/2010; Final rule, 76 FR 21812, 4/19/2011, effective 4/19/2011; Final rule, 79 FR 73488, 12/11/2014, effective 12/11/2014]

252.209-7003 Reserve Officer Training Corps and Military Recruiting on Campus-Representation.

As prescribed in 209.470-4(a), use the following provision:

RESERVE OFFICER TRAINING CORPS AND MILITARY RECRUITING ON CAMPUS—REPRESENTATION (MAR 2012)

(a) *Definition. Institution of higher education*, as used in this provision, is defined in the clause at 252.209-7005, Reserve officer Training Corps and Military Recruiting on Campus.

(b) *Limitation on contract award.* Except as provided in paragraph (c) of this provision, an institution of higher education is ineligible for contract award if the Secretary of Defense determines that the institution has a current policy or practice (regardless of when implemented) that prohibits or in effect prevents—

(1) The Secretary of a military department from maintaining, establishing, or operating a unit of the Senior Reserve Officer Training Corps (ROTC) (in accordance with 10 U.S.C.

654 and other applicable Federal laws) at that institution;

(2) A student at that institution from enrolling in a unit of the Senior ROTC at another institution of higher education;

(3) The Secretary of a military department or the Secretary of Transportation from gaining entry to campuses, or access to students (who are 17 years of age or older) on campuses, for purposes of military recruiting; or

(4) Military recruiters from accessing, for purposes of military recruiting, the following information pertaining to students (who are 17 years of age or older) enrolled at that institution:

(i) Name.

(ii) Address.

(iii) Telephone number.

(iv) Date and place of birth.

(v) Educational level.

(vi) Academic major.

(vii) Degrees received.

(viii) Most recent educational institution enrollment.

(c) *Exception*. The limitation in paragraph (b) of this provision does not apply to an institution of higher education if the Secretary of Defense determines that the institution has a long-standing policy of pacifism based on historical religious affiliation.

(d) *Representation*. By submission of its offer, the offeror represents that the institution does not have any policy or practice described in paragraph (b) of this clause, unless the Secretary of Defense has determined that the institution has a long-standing policy of pacifism based on historical religious affiliation.

(End of provision)

[Removed and reserved by 67 FR 4208, 1/29/2002, effective 1/29/2002; Final rule, 77 FR 19128, 3/30/2012, effective 3/30/2012]

252.209-7004 Subcontracting with Firms that are Owned or Controlled by the Government of a Country that is a State Sponsor of Terrorism.

As prescribed in 209.409, use the following clause:

SUBCONTRACTING WITH FIRMS THAT ARE OWNED OR CONTROLLED BY THE GOVERNMENT OF A COUNTRY THAT IS A STATE SPONSOR OF TERRORISM (MAY 2019)

(a) Unless the Government determines that there is a compelling reason to do so, the Contractor shall not enter into any subcontract in excess of the threshold specified in Federal Acquisition Regulation 9.405-2(b) on the date of subcontract award with a firm, or a subsidiary of a firm, that is identified in the Exclusions section of the System for Award Management System (SAM Exclusions) as being ineligible for the award of Defense contracts or subcontracts because it is owned or controlled by the government of a country that is a state sponsor of terrorism.

(b) A corporate officer or a designee of the Contractor shall notify the Contracting Officer, in writing, before entering into a subcontract with a party that is identified, in SAM Exclusions, as being ineligible for the award of Defense contracts or subcontracts because it is owned or controlled by the government of a country that is a state sponsor of terrorism. The notice must include the name of the proposed subcontractor and the compelling reason(s) for doing business with the subcontractor notwithstanding its inclusion in SAM Exclusions.

(End of clause)

[Interim rule, 63 FR 14836, 3/27/98, effective 3/27/98, finalized without change, 63 FR 64426, 11/20/98; Final rule, 71 FR 75891, 12/19/2006, effective 12/19/2006; Final rule, 79 FR 17445, 3/28/2014, effective 3/28/2014; Final rule, 79 FR 73488, 12/11/2014, effective 12/11/2014; Final rule, 80 FR 36903, 6/26/2015, effective 10/1/2015; Final rule, 84 FR 25186, 5/31/2019, effective 5/31/2019]

252.209-7005 Reserve Officer Training Corps and military recruiting on campus.

As prescribed in 209.470-4(b), use the following clause:

RESERVE OFFICER TRAINING CORPS AND MILITARY RECRUITING ON CAMPUS (MAR 2012)

(a) *Definition. Institution of higher education*, as used in this clause, means an institution that meets the requirements of 20 U.S.C. 1001 and includes all subelements of such an institution.

(b) *Limitation*. Except as provided in paragraph (c) of this clause, the Contractor shall not, during performance of this contract, have any policy or practice that prohibits or in effect prevents—

(1) The Secretary of a military department from maintaining, establishing, or operating a unit of the Senior Reserve Officer Training Corps (ROTC) (in accordance with 10 U.S.C. 654 and other applicable Federal laws) at that institution;

(2) A student at that institution from enrolling in a unit of the Senior ROTC at another institution of higher education;

(3) The Secretary of a military department or the Secretary of Transportation from gaining entry to campuses, or access to students (who are 17 years of age or older) on campuses, for purposes of military recruiting; or

(4) Military recruiters from accessing, for purposes of military recruiting, the following information pertaining to students (who are 17 years of age or older) enrolled at that institution:

(i) Name.

(ii) Address.

(iii) Telephone number.

(iv) Date and place of birth.

(v) Educational level.

(vi) Academic major.

(vii) Degrees received.

(viii) Most recent educational institution enrollment.

(c) *Exception*. The limitation in paragraph (b) of this clause does not apply to an institution of higher education if the Secretary of Defense determines that—

(1) The institution has ceased the policy or practice described in paragraph (b) of this clause; or

(2) The institution has a long-standing policy of pacifism based on historical religious affiliation.

(d) Notwithstanding any other clause of this contract, if the Secretary of Defense determines that the Contractor misrepresented its policies and practices at the time of contract award or has violated the prohibition in paragraph (b) of this clause—

(1) The Contractor will be ineligible for further payments under this and other contracts with the Department of Defense; and

(2) The Government will terminate this contract for default for the Contractor's material failure to comply with the terms and conditions of award.

(End of clause)

[Interim rule, 65 FR 2056, 1/13/2000, effective 1/13/2000; Final rule, 67 FR 49253, 7/30/2002, effective 7/30/2002; Final rule, 77 FR 19128, 3/30/2012, effective 3/30/2012; Final rule, 79 FR 17445, 3/28/2014, effective 3/28/2014]

252.209-7006 Limitations on Contractors Acting as Lead System Integrators.

As prescribed in 209.570-4(a), use the following provision:

LIMITATIONS ON CONTRACTORS ACTING AS LEAD SYSTEM INTEGRATORS (JAN 2008)

(a) *Definitions. Lead system integrator, lead system integrator with system responsibility*, and *lead system integrator without system responsibility*, as used in this provision, have the meanings given in the clause of this solicitation entitled "Prohibited Financial Interests for Lead System Integrators" (DFARS 252.209-7007).

(b) *General*. Unless an exception is granted, no contractor performing lead system integrator functions in the acquisition of a major system by the Department of Defense may have any direct financial interest in the development or construction of any individual system or element of any system of systems.

(c) *Representations.* (1) The offeror represents that it does

[] does not [] propose to perform this contract as a lead system integrator with system responsibility.

(2) The offeror represents that it does [] does not [] propose to perform this contract as a lead system integrator without system responsibility.

(3) If the offeror answered in the affirmative in paragraph (c)(1) or (2) of this provision, the offeror represents that it does [] does not []have any direct financial interest as described in paragraph (b) of this provision with respect to the system(s), subsystem(s), system of systems, or services described in this solicitation.

(d) If the offeror answered in the affirmative in paragraph (c)(3) of this provision, the offeror should contact the Contracting Officer for guidance on the possibility of submitting a mitigation plan and/or requesting an exception.

(e) If the offeror does have a direct financial interest, the offeror may be prohibited from receiving an award under this solicitation, unless the offeror submits to the Contracting Officer appropriate evidence that the offeror was selected by a subcontractor to serve as a lower-tier subcontractor through a process over which the offeror exercised no control.

(f) This provision implements the requirements of 10 U.S.C. 2410p, as added by section 807 of the National Defense Authorization Act for Fiscal Year 2007 (Pub. L. 109-364).

(End of provision)

[Interim rule, 73 FR 1823, 1/10/2008, effective 1/10/2008]

252.209-7007 Prohibited Financial Interests for Lead System Integrators.

As prescribed in 209.570-4(b), use the following clause:

PROHIBITED FINANCIAL INTERESTS FOR LEAD SYSTEM INTEGRATORS (JUL 2009)

(a) *Definitions.* As used in this clause—

(1) *Lead system integrator* includes *lead system integrator with system responsibility* and *lead system integrator without system responsibility.*

(2) *Lead system integrator with system responsibility* means a prime contractor for the development or production of a major system, if the prime contractor is not expected at the time of award to perform a substantial portion of the work on the system and the major subsystems.

(3) *Lead system integrator without system responsibility* means a prime contractor under a contract for the procurement of services, the primary purpose of which is to perform acquisition functions closely associated with inherently governmental functions (see section 7.503(d) of the Federal Acquisition Regulation) with respect to the development or production of a major system.

(b) *Limitations.* The Contracting Officer has determined that the Contractor meets the definition of lead system integrator with [] without [] system responsibility. Unless an exception is granted, the Contractor shall not have any direct financial interest in the development or construction of any individual system or element of any system of systems while performing lead system integrator functions in the acquisition of a major system by the Department of Defense under this contract.

(c) *Agreement.* The Contractor agrees that during performance of this contract it will not acquire any direct financial interest as described in paragraph (b) of this clause, or, if it does acquire or plan to acquire such interest, it will immediately notify the Contracting Officer. The Contractor further agrees to provide to the Contracting Officer all relevant information regarding the change in financial interests so that the Contracting Officer can determine whether an exception applies or whether the Contractor will be allowed to continue performance on this contract. If a direct financial interest cannot be avoided, eliminated, or mitigated to the Contracting Officer's satisfaction, the Contracting Officer may terminate this contract for default for the Contractor's material failure to comply with the terms and conditions of award or may take other remedial measures as appropriate in the Contracting Officer's sole discretion.

(d) Notwithstanding any other clause of this contract, if the Contracting Officer determines that the Contractor misrepresented its financial interests at the time of award or has violated the agreement in paragraph (c) of this clause, the Government may terminate this contract for default for the Contractor's material failure to comply with the terms and conditions of award or may take other remedial measures as appropriate in the Contracting Officer's sole discretion.

(e) This clause implements the requirements of 10 U.S.C. 2410p, as added by Section 807 of the National Defense Authorization Act for Fiscal Year 2007 (Pub. L. 109-364), and Section 802 of the National Defense Authorization Act for Fiscal Year 2008 (Pub. L. 110-181).

(End of clause)

[Interim rule, 73 FR 1823, 1/10/2008, effective 1/10/2008; Interim rule, 74 FR 34266, 7/15/2009, effective 7/15/2009; Final rule, 75 FR 3178, 1/20/2010, effective 1/20/2010]

252.209-7008 Notice of Prohibition Relating to Organizational Conflict of Interest—Major Defense Acquisition Program.

As prescribed in 209.571-8(a), use the following provision:

NOTICE OF PROHIBITION RELATING TO ORGANIZATIONAL CONFLICT OF INTEREST—MAJOR DEFENSE ACQUISITION PROGRAM (DEC 2010)

(a) *Definitions. Major subcontractor* is defined in the clause at 252.209-7009, Organizational Conflict of Interest—Major Defense Acquisition Program.

(b) This solicitation is for the performance of systems engineering and technical assistance for a major defense acquisition program or a pre-major defense acquisition program.

(c) *Prohibition*. As required by paragraph (b)(3) of section 207 of the Weapons System Acquisition Reform Act of 2009 (Pub. L. 111-23), if awarded the contract, the contractor or any affiliate of the contractor is prohibited from participating as a prime contractor or a major subcontractor in the development or production of a weapon system under the major defense acquisition program or pre-major defense acquisition program, unless the offeror submits, and the Government approves, an Organizational Conflict of Interest Mitigation Plan.

(d) *Request for an exception*. If the offeror requests an exception to the prohibition of paragraph (c) of this provision, then the offeror shall submit an Organizational Conflict of Interest Mitigation Plan with its offer for evaluation.

(e) *Incorporation of Organizational Conflict of Interest Mitigation Plan in contract*. If the apparently successful offeror submitted an acceptable Organizational Conflict of Interest Mitigation Plan, and the head of the contracting activity determines that DoD needs the domain experience and expertise of the highly qualified, apparently successful offeror in accordance with FAR 209.571-7(c), then the Contracting Officer will incorporate the Organizational Conflict of Interest Mitigation Plan into the resultant contract, and paragraph (d) of the clause at 252.209-7009 will become applicable.

(End of provision)

[Final rule, 75 FR 81908, 12/29/2010, effective 12/29/2010]

252.209-7009 Organizational Conflict of Interest—Major Defense Acquisition Program.

As prescribed in 209.571-8(b), use the following clause:

ORGANIZATIONAL CONFLICT OF INTEREST—MAJOR DEFENSE ACQUISITION PROGRAM (MAY 2019)

(a) *Definition*. As used in this clause—

Major subcontractor means a subcontractor that is awarded a subcontract that equals or exceeds—

(1) Both the certified cost or pricing data threshold and 10 percent of the value of the contract under which the subcontract is awarded; or

(2) The threshold specified in the definition of *major subcontractor* at Defense Federal Acquisition Regulation Supplement 209.571-1 on the date of subcontract award.

(b) This contract is for the performance of systems engineering and technical assistance for a major defense acquisition program or a pre-major defense acquisition program.

(c) *Prohibition*. Except as provided in paragraph (d) of this clause, as required by paragraph (b)(3) of section 207 of the Weapons System Acquisition Reform Act of 2009 (Pub. L. 111-23), the Contractor or any affiliate of the Contractor is prohibited from participating as a prime contractor or major subcontractor in the development or production of a weapon system under the major defense acquisition program or pre-major defense acquisition program.

(d) *Organizational Conflict of Interest Mitigation Plan*. If the Contractor submitted an acceptable Organizational Conflict of Interest Mitigation Plan that has been incorporated into this contract, then the prohibition in paragraph (c) of this clause does not apply. The Contractor shall comply with the Organizational Conflict of Interest Mitigation Plan. Compliance with the Organizational Conflict of Interest Mitigation Plan is a material requirement of the contract. Failure to comply may result in the Contractor or any affiliate of the Contractor being prohibited from participating as a contractor or major subcontractor in the development or production of a weapon system under the program, in addition to any other remedies available to the Government for noncompliance with a material requirement of a contract.

(End of clause)

[Final rule, 75 FR 81908, 12/29/2010, effective 12/29/2010; Final rule, 77 FR 76939, 12/31/2012, effective 12/31/2012; Final rule, 80 FR 36903, 6/26/2015, effective 10/1/2015; Final rule, 84 FR 25186, 5/31/2019, effective 5/31/2019]

252.209-7010 Critical Safety Items.

As prescribed in 209.270-5, use the following clause:

CRITICAL SAFETY ITEMS (AUG 2011)

(a) *Definitions*.

Aviation critical safety item means a part, an assembly, installation equipment, launch equipment, recovery equipment, or support equipment for an aircraft or aviation weapon system if the part, assembly, or equipment contains a characteristic any failure, malfunction, or absence of which could cause—

(i) A catastrophic or critical failure resulting in the loss of, or serious damage to, the aircraft or weapon system;

(ii) An unacceptable risk of personal injury or loss of life; or

(iii) An uncommanded engine shutdown that jeopardizes safety.

Design control activity. (i) With respect to an aviation critical safety item, means the systems command of a military department that is specifically responsible for ensuring the airworthiness of an aviation system or equipment, in which an aviation critical safety item is to be used; and

(ii) With respect to a ship critical safety item, means the systems command of a military department that is specifically responsible for ensuring the seaworthiness of a ship or ship equipment, in which a ship critical safety item is to be used.

Ship critical safety item means any ship part, assembly, or support equipment containing a characteristic, the failure, malfunction, or absence of which could cause—

(i) A catastrophic or critical failure resulting in loss of, or serious damage to, the ship; or

(ii) An unacceptable risk of personal injury or loss of life.

(b) *Identification of critical safety items*. One or more of the items being procured under this contract is an aviation or ship critical safety item. The following items have been designated aviation critical safety items or ship critical safety items by the designated design control activity:

____

____

____

____

(Insert additional lines as necessary)

(c) *Heightened quality assurance surveillance*. Items designated in paragraph (b) of this clause are subject to heightened, risk-based surveillance by the designated quality assurance representative.

(End of clause)

[Final rule, 76 FR 52138, 8/19/2011, effective 8/19/2011]

252.211 Acquisition and Distribution of Commercial Products, provisions and clauses for DFARS Part 211

252.211-7000 [Removed and Reserved]

[Redesignated from 252.210-7003, DAC 91-9, 60 FR 61586, 11/30/95, effective 11/30/95; Final rule, 75 FR 45072, 8/2/2010, effective 10/1/2010; Final rule, 83 FR 54676, 10/31/2018, effective 10/31/2018]

252.211-7001 [Removed and Reserved]

[Redesignated from 252.210-7001, DAC 91-9, 60 FR 61586, 11/30/95, effective 11/30/95; Final rule, 71 FR 27641, 5/12/2006, effective 5/12/2006; Final rule, 84 FR 25192, 5/31/2019, effective 5/31/2019]

252.211-7002 Availability for examination of specifications, standards, plans, drawings, data item descriptions, and other pertinent documents.

As prescribed in 211.204(c), use the following provision:

AVAILABILITY FOR EXAMINATION OF SPECIFICATIONS, STANDARDS, PLANS, DRAWINGS, DATA ITEM DESCRIPTIONS, AND OTHER PERTINENT DOCUMENTS (DEC 1991)

The specifications, standards, plans, drawings, data item descriptions, and other pertinent documents cited in this solicitation are not available for distribution but may be examined at the following location:

____

(Insert complete address)

(End of provision)

[Redesignated from 252.210-7002, DAC 91-9, 60 FR 61586, 11/30/95, effective 11/30/95; Final rule, 84 FR 25192, 5/31/2019, effective 5/31/2019]

252.211-7003 Item unique identification and valuation.

As prescribed in 211.274-6(a)(1), use the following clause:

ITEM UNIQUE IDENTIFICATION AND VALUATION (MAR 2016)

(a) *Definitions*. As used in this clause:

Automatic identification device means a device, such as a reader or interrogator, used to retrieve data encoded on machine-readable media.

Concatenated unique item identifier means—

(1) For items that are serialized within the enterprise identifier, the linking together of the unique identifier data elements in order of the issuing agency code, enterprise identifier, and unique serial number within the enterprise identifier; or

(2) For items that are serialized within the original part, lot, or batch number, the linking together of the unique identifier data elements in order of the issuing agency code; enterprise identifier; original part, lot, or batch number; and serial number within the original part, lot, or batch number.

Data matrix means a two-dimensional matrix symbology, which is made up of square or, in some cases, round modules arranged within a perimeter finder pattern and uses the Error Checking and Correction 200 (ECC200) specification found within International Standards Organization (ISO)/International Electrotechnical Commission (IEC) 16022.

Data qualifier means a specified character (or string of characters) that immediately precedes a data field that defines the general category or intended use of the data that follows.

DoD recognized unique identification equivalent means a unique identification method that is in commercial use and has been recognized by DoD. All DoD recognized unique identification equivalents are listed at *http://www.acq.osd.mil/dpap/pdi/uid/iuid_equivalents.html.*

DoD item unique identification means a system of marking items delivered to DoD with unique item identifiers that have machine-readable data elements to distinguish an item from all other like and unlike items. For items that are serialized within the enterprise identifier, the unique item identifier shall include the data elements of the enterprise identifier and a unique serial number. For items that are serialized within the part, lot, or batch number within the enterprise identifier, the unique item identifier shall include the data elements of the enterprise identifier; the original part, lot, or batch number; and the serial number.

Enterprise means the entity (*e.g.*, a manufacturer or vendor) responsible for assigning unique item identifiers to items.

Enterprise identifier means a code that is uniquely assigned to an enterprise by an issuing agency.

Government's unit acquisition cost means—

(1) For fixed-price type line, subline, or exhibit line items, the unit price identified in the contract at the time of delivery;

(2) For cost-type or undefinitized line, subline, or exhibit line items, the Contractor's estimated fully burdened unit cost to the Government at the time of delivery; and

(3) For items produced under a time-and-materials contract, the Contractor's estimated fully burdened unit cost to the Government at the time of delivery.

Issuing agency an organization responsible for assigning a globally unique identifier to an enterprise, as indicated in the Register of Issuing Agency Codes for ISO/IEC 15459, located at *http://www.aimglobal.org/ ?Reg_Authority15459.*

Issuing agency code means a code that designates the registration (or controlling) authority for the enterprise identifier.

Item means a single hardware article or a single unit formed by a grouping of subassemblies, components, or constituent parts.

Lot or batch number means an identifying number assigned by the enterprise to a designated group of items, usually referred to as either a lot or a batch, all of which were manufactured under identical conditions.

Machine-readable means an automatic identification technology media, such as bar codes, contact memory buttons, radio frequency identification, or optical memory cards.

Original part number means a combination of numbers or letters assigned by the enterprise at item creation to a class of items with the same form, fit, function, and interface.

Parent item means the item assembly, intermediate component, or subassembly that has an embedded item with a unique item identifier or DoD recognized unique identification equivalent.

Serial number within the enterprise identifier means a combination of numbers, letters, or symbols assigned by the enterprise to an item that provides for the differentiation of that item from any other like and unlike item and is never used again within the enterprise.

Serial number within the part, lot, or batch number means a combination of numbers or letters assigned by the enterprise to an item that provides for the differentiation of that item from any other like item within a part, lot, or batch number assignment.

Serialization within the enterprise identifier means each item produced is assigned a serial number that is unique among all the tangible items produced by the enterprise and is never used again. The enterprise is responsible for ensuring unique serialization within the enterprise identifier.

Serialization within the part, lot, or batch number means each item of a particular part, lot, or batch number is assigned a unique serial number within that part, lot, or batch number assignment. The enterprise is responsible for ensuring unique serialization within the part, lot, or batch number within the enterprise identifier.

Type designation means a combination of letters and numerals assigned by the Government to a major end item, assembly or subassembly, as appropriate, to provide a convenient means of differentiating between items having the same basic name and to indicate modifications and changes thereto.

Unique item identifier means a set of data elements marked on items that is globally unique and unambiguous. The term includes a concatenated unique item identifier or a DoD recognized unique identification equivalent.

Unique item identifier type means a designator to indicate which method of uniquely identifying a part has been used. The current list of accepted unique item identifier types is maintained at *http://www.acq.osd.mil/dpap/pdi/uid/uii_types.html*.

(b) The Contractor shall deliver all items under a contract line, subline, or exhibit line item.

(c) *Unique item identifier.*

(1) The Contractor shall provide a unique item identifier for the following:

(i) Delivered items for which the Government's unit acquisition cost is $5,000 or more, except for the following line items:

Contract line, subline, or exhibit line item No.	Item description

(ii) Items for which the Government's unit acquisition cost is less than $5,000 that are identified in the Schedule or the following table:

Contract line, subline, or exhibit line item No.	Item description

(*If items are identified in the Schedule, insert "See Schedule" in this table.*)

(iii) Subassemblies, components, and parts embedded within delivered items, items with warranty requirements, DoD serially managed reparables and DoD serially managed nonreparables as specified in Attachment Number ll__

(iv) Any item of special tooling or special test equipment as defined in FAR 2.101 that have been designated for preservation and storage for a Major Defense Acquisition Program as specified in Attachment Number ll__

(v) Any item not included in paragraphs (c)(1)(i), (ii), (iii), or (iv) of this clause for which the contractor creates and marks a unique item identifier for traceability.

(2) The unique item identifier assignment and its component data element combination shall not be duplicated on any other item marked or registered in the DoD Item Unique Identification Registry by the contractor.

(3) The unique item identifier component data elements shall be marked on an item using two dimensional data matrix symbology that complies with ISO/IEC International Standard 16022, Information technology—International symbology specification—Data matrix; ECC200 data matrix specification.

(4) *Data syntax and semantics of unique item identifiers.* The Contractor shall ensure that—

(i) The data elements (except issuing agency code) of the unique item identifier are encoded within the data matrix symbol that is marked on the item using one of the following three types of data qualifiers, as determined by the Contractor:

(A) *Application Identifiers* (AIs) (Format Indicator 05 of ISO/IEC International Standard 15434), in accordance with ISO/IEC International Standard 15418, Information Technology—EAN/UCC Application Identifiers and Fact Data Identifiers and Maintenance and ANSI MH 10.8.2 Data Identifier and Application Identifier Standard.

(B) *Data Identifiers (DIs)* (Format Indicator 06 of ISO/IEC International Standard 15434), in accordance with ISO/IEC International Standard 15418, Information Technology—EAN/UCC Application Identifiers and Fact Data Identifiers and Maintenance and ANSI MH 10.8.2 Data Identifier and Application Identifier Standard.

(C) *Text Element Identifiers (TEIs)* (Format Indicator 12 of ISO/IEC International Standard 15434), in accordance with the Air Transport Association Common Support Data Dictionary; and

(ii) The encoded data elements of the unique item identifier conform to the transfer structure, syntax, and coding of messages and data formats specified for Format Indicators 05, 06, and 12 in ISO/ IEC International Standard 15434, Information Technology-Transfer Syntax for High Capacity Automatic Data Capture Media.

(5) *Unique item identifier.*

(i) The Contractor shall—

(A) Determine whether to—

(1) Serialize within the enterprise identifier;

(2) Serialize within the part, lot, or batch number; or

(3) Use a DoD recognized unique identification equivalent (e.g. Vehicle Identification Number); and

(B) Place the data elements of the unique item identifier (enterprise identifier; serial number; DoD recognized unique identification equivalent; and for serialization within the part, lot, or batch number only: Original part, lot, or batch number) on items requiring marking by paragraph (c)(1) of this clause, based on the criteria provided in MIL–STD–130, Identification Marking of U.S. Military Property, latest version;

(C) Label shipments, storage containers and packages that contain uniquely identified items in accordance with the requirements of MIL–STD–129, Military Marking for Shipment and Storage, latest version; and

(D) Verify that the marks on items and labels on shipments, storage containers, and packages are machine readable and conform to the applicable standards. The contractor shall use an automatic identification technology device for this verification that has been programmed to the requirements of Appendix A, MIL–STD–130, latest version.

(ii) The issuing agency code—

(A) Shall not be placed on the item; and

(B) Shall be derived from the data qualifier for the enterprise identifier.

(d) For each item that requires item unique identification under paragraph (c)(1)(i), (ii), or (iv) of this clause or when item unique identification is provided under paragraph (c)(1)(v), in addition to the information provided as part of the Material Inspection and Receiving Report specified elsewhere in this contract, the Contractor shall report at the time of delivery, as part of the Material Inspection and Receiving Report, the following information:

(1) Unique item identifier.

(2) Unique item identifier type.

(3) Issuing agency code (if concatenated unique item identifier is used).

(4) Enterprise identifier (if concatenated unique item identifier is used).

(5) Original part number (if there is serialization within the original part number).

(6) Lot or batch number (if there is serialization within the lot or batch number).

(7) Current part number (optional and only if not the same as the original part number).

(8) Current part number effective date (optional and only if current part number is used).

(9) Serial number (if concatenated unique item identifier is used).

(10) Government's unit acquisition cost.

(11) Unit of measure.

(12) Type designation of the item as specified in the contract schedule, if any.

(13) Whether the item is an item of Special Tooling or Special Test Equipment.

(14) Whether the item is covered by a warranty.

(e) For embedded subassemblies, components, and parts that require DoD item unique identification under paragraph (c)(1)(iii) of this clause or when item unique identification is provided under paragraph (c)(1)(v), the Contractor shall report as part of the Material Inspection and Receiving Report specified elsewhere in this contract, the following information:

(1) Unique item identifier of the parent item under paragraph (c)(1) of this clause that contains the embedded subassembly, component, or part.

(2) Unique item identifier of the embedded subassembly, component, or part.

(3) Unique item identifier type.**

(4) Issuing agency code (if concatenated unique item identifier is used).**

(5) Enterprise identifier (if concatenated unique item identifier is used).**

(6) Original part number (if there is serialization within the original part number).**

(7) Lot or batch number (if there is serialization within the lot or batch number).**

(8) Current part number (optional and only if not the same as the original part number).**

(9) Current part number effective date (optional and only if current part number is used).**

(10) Serial number (if concatenated unique item identifier is used).**

(11) Description.

** Once per item.

(f) The Contractor shall submit the information required by paragraphs (d) and (e) of this clause as follows:

(1) End items shall be reported using the receiving report capability in Wide Area WorkFlow (WAWF) in accordance with the clause at 252.232-7003. If WAWF is not required by this contract, and the contractor is not using WAWF, follow the procedures at *http:// dodprocurementtoolbox.com/site/uidregistry/*.

(2) Embedded items shall be reported by one of the following methods—

(i) Use of the embedded items capability in WAWF;

(ii) Direct data submission to the IUID Registry following the procedures and formats at *http:// dodprocurementtoolbox.com/site/uidregistry/*; or

(iii) Via WAWF as a deliverable attachment for exhibit line item number (fill in) __, Unique Item Identifier Report for Embedded Items, Contract Data Requirements List, DD Form 1423.

(g) Subcontracts. If the Contractor acquires by contract any items for which item unique identification is required in accordance with paragraph (c)(1) of this clause, the Contractor shall include this clause, including this paragraph (g), in the applicable subcontract(s), including subcontracts for commercial items.

(End of clause)

[Removed and reserved, 64 FR 55632, 10/14/99, effective 10/14/99; Interim rule, 68 FR 58631, 10/10/2003, effective 1/1/2004; Interim rule, 68 FR 75196, 12/30/2003, effective 1/1/2004; Final rule, 70 FR 20831, 4/22/2005, effective 4/22/2005; Final rule, 70 FR 35549, 6/21/2005, effective 6/21/2005; Interim rule, 72 FR 52293, 9/13/2007, effective 9/13/2007; Final rule, 73 FR 27464, 5/13/2008, effective 5/13/2008; Final rule, 73 FR 46819, 8/12/2008, effective 8/12/2008; Final rule, 75 FR 59102, 9/27/2010, effective 9/27/2010; Final rule, 76 FR 33166, 6/8/2011, effective 6/8/2011; Final rule, 76 FR 76318, 12/7/2011, effective 12/7/2011; Final rule, 78 FR 37980,

6/25/2013, effective 6/25/2013; Final rule, 78 FR 76067, 12/16/2013, effective 12/16/2013; Final rule, 79 FR 30474, 5/28/2014, effective 5/28/2014; Final rule, 81 FR 17041, 3/25/2016, effective 3/25/2016]

252.211-7004 Alternate preservation, packaging, and packing.

As prescribed in 211.272, use the following provision:

ALTERNATE PRESERVATION, PACKAGING, AND PACKING (DEC 1991)

(a) The Offeror may submit two unit prices for each item—one based on use of the military preservation, packaging, or packing requirements of the solicitation; and an alternate based on use of commercial or industrial preservation, packaging, or packing of equal or better protection than the military.

(b) If the Offeror submits two unit prices, the following information, as a minimum, shall be submitted with the offer to allow evaluation of the alternate—

(1) The per unit/item cost of commercial or industrial preservation, packaging, and packing;

(2) The per unit/item cost of military preservation, packaging, and packing;

(3) The description of commercial or industrial preservation, packaging, and packing procedures, including material specifications, when applicable, to include—

(i) Method of preservation;

(ii) Quantity per unit package;

(iii) Cleaning/drying treatment;

(iv) Preservation treatment;

(v) Wrapping materials;

(vi) Cushioning/dunnage material;

(vii) Thickness of cushioning;

(viii) Unit container;

(ix) Unit package gross weight and dimensions;

(x) Packing; and

(xi) Packing gross weight and dimensions; and

(4) Item characteristics, to include—

(i) Material and finish;

(ii) Net weight;

(iii) Net dimensions; and

(iv) Fragility.

(c) If the Contracting Officer does not evaluate or accept the Offeror's proposed alternate commercial or industrial preservation, packaging, or packing, the Offeror agrees to preserve, package, or pack in accordance with the specified military requirements.

(End of provision)

[Redesignated from 252.210-7004, DAC 91-9, 60 FR 61586, 11/30/95, effective 11/30/95]

252.211-7005 Substitutions for military or Federal specifications and standards.

As prescribed in 211.273-4, use the following clause:

SUBSTITUTIONS FOR MILITARY OR FEDERAL SPECIFICATIONS AND STANDARDS (NOV 2005)

(a) *Definition. SPI process*, as used in this clause, means a management or manufacturing process that has been accepted previously by the Department of Defense under the Single Process Initiative (SPI) for use in lieu of a specific military or Federal specification or standard at specific facilities. Under SPI, these processes are reviewed and accepted by a Management Council, which includes representatives of the Contractor, the Defense Contract Management Agency, the Defense Contract Audit Agency, and the military departments.

(b) Offerors are encouraged to propose SPI processes in lieu of military or Federal specifications and standards cited in the solicitation. A listing of SPI processes accepted at specific facilities is available via the Internet at *http://guidebook.dcma.mil/20/guidebook_process.htm* (paragraph 4.2).

(c) An offeror proposing to use an SPI process in lieu of military or Federal specifications or standards cited in the solicitation shall—

(1) Identify the specific military or Federal specification or standard for which the SPI process has been accepted;

(2) Identify each facility at which the offeror proposes to use the specific SPI process in lieu of military or Federal specifications or standards cited in the solicitation;

(3) Identify the contract line items, subline items, components, or elements affected by the SPI process; and

(4) If the proposed SPI process has been accepted at the facility at which it is proposed for use, but is not yet listed at the Internet site specified in paragraph (b) of this clause, submit documentation of Department of Defense acceptance of the SPI process.

(d) Absent a determination that an SPI process is not acceptable for this procurement, the Contractor shall use the following SPI processes in lieu of military or Federal specifications or standards:

(Offeror insert information for each SPI process)

SPI Process: ________________

Facility: ________________

Military or Federal Specification or Standard: ________________

Affected Contract Line Item Number, Subline Item Number, Component, or Element: _

(e) If a prospective offeror wishes to obtain, prior to the time specified for receipt of offers, verification that an SPI process is an acceptable replacement for military or Federal specifications or standards required by the solicitation, the prospective offeror—

(1) May submit the information required by paragraph (d) of this clause to the Contracting Officer prior to submission of an offer; but

(2) Must submit the information to the Contracting Officer at least 10 working days prior to the date specified for receipt of offers.

(End of clause)

[Final rule, 64 FR 14398, 3/25/99, effective 3/25/99, corrected, 64 FR 28875, 5/27/99; Final rule, 65 FR 52951, 8/31/2000, effective 8/31/2000; Final rule, 66 FR 49860, 10/1/2001, effective 10/1/2001; Final rule, 68 FR 7438, 2/14/2003, effective 2/14/2003; Final rule, 70 FR 67924, 11/9/2005, effective 11/9/2005]

252.211-7006 Passive Radio Frequency Identification.

As prescribed in 211.275-3, use the following clause:

PASSIVE RADIO FREQUENCY IDENTIFICATION (DEC 2019)

(a) *Definitions*. As used in this clause—

Advance shipment notice means an electronic notification used to list the contents of a shipment of goods as well as additional information relating to the shipment, such as passive radio frequency identification (RFID) or item unique identification (IUID) information, order information, product description, physical characteristics, type of packaging, marking, carrier information, and configuration of goods within the transportation equipment.

Bulk commodities means the following commodities, when shipped in rail tank cars, tanker trucks, trailers, other bulk wheeled conveyances, or pipelines:

(1) Sand.

(2) Gravel.

(3) Bulk liquids (water, chemicals, or petroleum products).

(4) Ready-mix concrete or similar construction materials.

(5) Coal or combustibles such as firewood.

(6) Agricultural products such as seeds, grains, or animal feed.

Case means either a MIL-STD-129 defined exterior container within a palletized unit load or a MIL-STD-129 defined individual shipping container.

Electronic Product Code™ (EPC®) means an identification scheme for universally identifying physical objects via RFID tags and other means. The standardized EPC™ data consists of an EPC™ (or EPC™ identifier) that uniquely identifies an individual object, as well as an optional filter value when judged to be necessary to enable effective and efficient reading of the EPC™ tags. In addition to this standardized data, certain classes of EPC™ tags will allow user-defined data. The EPC™ Tag Data Standards will define the length and position of this data, without defining its content.

EPCglobal® means a subscriber-driven organization comprised of industry leaders and organizations focused on creating global standards for the adoption of passive RFID technology.

Exterior container means a MIL-STD-129 defined container, bundle, or assembly that is sufficient by reason of material, design, and construction to protect unit packs and intermediate containers and their contents during shipment and storage. It can be a unit pack or a container with a combination of unit packs or intermediate containers. An exterior container may or may not be used as a shipping container.

Palletized unit load means a MIL-STD-129 defined quantity of items, packed or unpacked, arranged on a pallet in a specified manner and secured, strapped, or fastened on the pallet so that the whole palletized load is handled as a single unit. A palletized or skidded load is not considered to be a shipping container. A loaded 463L System pallet is not considered to be a palletized unit load. Refer to the Defense Transportation Regulation, DoD 4500.9-R, Part II, Chapter 203, for marking of 463L System pallets.

Passive RFID tag means a tag that reflects energy from the reader/interrogator or that receives and temporarily stores a small amount of energy from the reader/interrogator signal in order to generate the tag response. The only acceptable tags are EPC Class 1 passive RFID tags that meet the EPCglobal™ Class 1 Generation 2 standard.

Radio frequency identification (RFID) means an automatic identification and data capture technology comprising one or more reader/interrogators and one or more radio frequency transponders in which data transfer is achieved by means of suitably modulated inductive or radiating electromagnetic carriers.

Shipping container means a MIL-STD-129 defined exterior container that meets carrier regulations and is of sufficient strength, by reason of material, design, and construction, to be shipped safely without further packing (*e.g.*, wooden boxes or crates, fiber and metal drums, and corrugated and solid fiberboard boxes).

(b) (1) Except as provided in paragraph (b) (2) of this clause, the Contractor shall affix passive RFID tags, at the case- and palletized-unit-load packaging levels, for shipments of items that—

(i) Are in any of the following classes of supply, as defined in DoD Manual 4140.01, Volume 6, DoD Supply Chain Materiel Management Procedures: Materiel Returns, Retention, and Disposition:

(A) Subclass of Class I—Packaged operational rations.

(B) Class II—Clothing, individual equipment, tentage, organizational tool kits, hand tools, and administrative and housekeeping supplies and equipment.

(C) Class IIIP—Packaged petroleum, lubricants, oils, preservatives, chemicals, and additives.

(D) Class IV—Construction and barrier materials.

(E) Class VI—Personal demand items (non-military sales items).

(F) Subclass of Class VIII—Medical materials (excluding pharmaceuticals, biologicals, and reagents—suppliers should limit the mixing of excluded and non-excluded materials).

(G) Class IX—Repair parts and components including kits, assemblies and subassemblies, reparable and consumable items required for maintenance support of all equipment, excluding medical-peculiar repair parts; and

(ii) Are being shipped to one of the locations listed at *https://www.acq.osd.mil/log/sci/RFID_ship-to-locations.html* or to—

(A) A location outside the contiguous United States when the shipment has been assigned Transportation Priority 1, or to—

(B) The following location(s) deemed necessary by the requiring activity:

Contract line, subline, or exhibit line item number	Location name	City	State	DoDAAC

(2) The following are excluded from the requirements of paragraph (b)(1) of this clause:

(i) Shipments of bulk commodities.

(ii) Shipments to locations other than Defense Distribution Depots when the contract includes the clause at FAR 52.213-1, Fast Payment Procedures.

(c) The Contractor shall—

(1) Ensure that the data encoded on each passive RFID tag are globally unique (*i.e.*, the tag ID is never repeated across two or more RFID tags) and conforms to the requirements in paragraph (d) of this clause;

(2) Use passive tags that are readable; and

(3) Ensure that the passive tag is affixed at the appropriate location on the specific level of packaging, in accordance with MIL-STD-129 (Section 4.9.2) tag placement specifications.

(d) *Data syntax and standards.* The Contractor shall encode an approved RFID tag using the instructions provided in the EPC™ Tag Data Standards in effect at the time of contract award. The EPC™ Tag Data Standards are available at *http://www.gs1.org/epc-rfid*.

(1) If the Contractor is an EPCglobal™ subscriber and possesses a unique EPC™ company prefix, the Contractor may use any of the identifiers and encoding instructions described in the most recent EPC™ Tag Data Standards document to encode tags.

(2) If the Contractor chooses to employ the DoD identifier, the Contractor shall use its previously assigned Commercial and Government Entity (CAGE) code and shall encode the tags in accordance with the tag identifier details located in the DoD Suppliers' Passive RFID Information Guide at *http://www.acq.osd.mil/log/sci/ait.html* If the Contractor uses a third-party packaging house to encode its tags, the CAGE code of the third-party packaging house is acceptable.

(3) Regardless of the selected encoding scheme, the Contractor with which the Department holds the contract is responsible for ensuring that the tag ID encoded on each passive RFID tag is globally unique, per the requirements in paragraph (c)(1) of this clause.

(e) *Advance shipment notice.* The Contractor shall use Wide Area WorkFlow (WAWF), as required by DFARS 252.232-7003, Electronic Submission of Payment Requests, to electronically submit advance shipment notice(s) with the RFID tag ID(s) (specified in paragraph (d) of this clause) in advance of the shipment in accordance with the procedures at *https://wawf.eb.mil/*.

(End of clause)

[Final rule, 70 FR 53955, 9/13/2005, effective 11/14/2005; Interim rule, 71 FR 29084, 5/19/2006, effective 5/19/2006; Final rule, 72 FR 6480, 2/12/2007, effective 2/12/2007; Final rule, 76 FR 58142, 9/20/2011, effective 9/20/2011; Final rule, 81 FR 36473, 6/7/2016, effective 6/7/2016; Final rule, 82 FR 61479, 12/28/2017, effective 12/28/2017; Final rule, 83 FR 12681, 3/23/2018, effective

3/23/2018; Final rule, 84 FR 72563, 12/31/2019, effective 12/31/2019]

252.211-7007 Reporting of Government-Furnished Property.

As prescribed in 211.274-6(b), use the following clause:

REPORTING OF GOVERNMENT-FURNISHED PROPERTY (AUG 2012)

(a) *Definitions*. As used in this clause—

Commercial and Government entity (CAGE) code means—

(i) A code assigned by the Defense Logistics Agency Logistics Information Service to identify a commercial or Government entity; or

(ii) A code assigned by a member of the North Atlantic Treaty Organization that the Defense Logistics Agency Logistics Information Service records and maintains in the CAGE master file. The type of code is known as an "NCAGE code."

Contractor-acquired property has the meaning given in FAR clause 52.245-1. Upon acceptance by the Government, contractor-acquired property becomes Government-furnished property.

Government-furnished property has the meaning given in FAR clause 52.245-1.

Item unique identification (IUID) means a system of assigning, reporting, and marking DoD property with unique item identifiers that have machine-readable data elements to distinguish an item from all other like and unlike items.

IUID Registry means the DoD data repository that receives input from both industry and Government sources and provides storage of, and access to, data that identifies and describes tangible Government personal property. The IUID Registry is—

(i) The authoritative source of Government unit acquisition cost for items with unique item identification (see DFARS 252.211-7003) that were acquired after January 1, 2004;

(ii) The master data source for Government-furnished property; and

(iii) An authoritative source for establishing the acquisition cost of end-item equipment.

National stock number (NSN) means a 13-digit stock number used to identify items of supply. It consists of a four-digit Federal Supply Code and a nine-digit National Item Identification Number.

Nomenclature means—

(i) The combination of a Government-assigned type designation and an approved item name;

(ii) Names assigned to kinds and groups of products; or

(iii) Formal designations assigned to products by customer or supplier (such as model number or model type, design differentiation, or specific design series or configuration).

Part or identifying number (PIN) means the identifier assigned by the original design activity, or by the controlling nationally recognized standard, that uniquely identifies (relative to that design activity) a specific item.

Reparable means an item, typically in unserviceable condition, furnished to the Contractor for maintenance, repair, modification, or overhaul.

Serially managed item means an item designated by DoD to be uniquely tracked, controlled, or managed in maintenance, repair, and/or supply systems by means of its serial number.

Supply condition code means a classification of materiel in terms of readiness for issue and use or to identify action underway to change the status of materiel (see *http://www2.dla.mil/j-6/dlmso/elibrary/manuals/dlm/dlm_pubs.asp*).

Unique item identifier (UII) means a set of data elements permanently marked on an item that is globally unique and unambiguous and never changes, in order to provide traceability of the item throughout its total life cycle. The term includes a concatenated UII or a DoD recognized unique identification equivalent.

Unit acquisition cost has the meaning given in FAR clause 52.245-1.

(b) *Reporting Government-furnished property to the IUID Registry*. Except as provided in paragraph (c) of this clause, the Contractor shall report, in accordance with paragraph (f), Government-furnished property to the IUID Registry as follows:—

(1) Up to and including December 31, 2013, report serially managed Government-furnished property with a unit-acquisition cost of $5,000 or greater.

(2) Beginning January 1, 2014, report—

(i) All serially managed Government-furnished property, regardless of unit-acquisition cost; and

(ii) Contractor receipt of non-serially managed items. Unless tracked as an individual item, the Contractor shall report non-serially managed items to the Registry in the same unit of packaging, e.g., original manufacturer's package, box, or container, as it was received.

(c) *Exceptions*. Paragraph (b) of this clause does not apply to—

(1) Contractor-acquired property;

(2) Property under any statutory leasing authority;

(3) Property to which the Government has acquired a lien or title solely because of partial, advance, progress, or performance-based payments;

(4) Intellectual property or software;

(5) Real property; or

(6) Property released for work in process.

(d) *Data for reporting to the IUID Registry*. To permit reporting of Government-furnished property to the IUID Registry, the Contractor's property management system shall enable the following data elements in addition to those required by paragraph (f)(1)(iii)(A)(1) through (3), (5), (7), (8), and (10) of the Government Property clause of this contract (FAR 52.245-1):

(1) Received/Sent (shipped) date.

(2) Status code.

(3) Accountable Government contract number.

(4) Commercial and Government Entity (CAGE) code on the accountable Government contract.

(5) Mark record.

(i) Bagged or tagged code (for items too small to individually tag or mark).

(ii) Contents (the type of information recorded on the item, e.g., item internal control number).

(iii) Effective date (date the mark is applied).

(iv) Added or removed code/flag.

(v) Marker code (designates which code is used in the marker identifier, e.g., D=CAGE, UN=DUNS, LD=DODAAC).

(vi) Marker identifier, e.g., Contractor's CAGE code or DUNS number.

(vii) Medium code; how the data is recorded, e.g., barcode, contact memory button.

(viii) Value, e.g., actual text or data string that is recorded in its human-readable form.

(ix) Set (used to group marks when multiple sets exist.

(6) Appropriate supply condition code, required only for reporting of reparables, per Appendix 2 of DoD 4000.25-2-M, Military Standard Transaction Reporting and Accounting Procedures manual (*http://www2.dla.mil/j-6/dlmso/elibrary/manuals/dlm/dlm_pubs.asp*).

(e) When Government-furnished property is in the possession of subcontractors, Contractors shall ensure that reporting is accomplished using the data elements required in paragraph (d) of this clause.

(f) *Procedures for reporting of Government-furnished property*. Except as provided in paragraph (c) of this clause, the Contractor shall establish and report to the IUID Registry the information required by FAR clause 52.245-1, paragraphs (e) and (f)(1)(iii), in accordance with the data submission procedures at *http://www.acq.osd.mil/dpap/pdi/uid/data_submission_information.html*.

(g) *Procedures for updating the IUID Registry.*

(1) Except as provided in paragraph (g)(2), the Contractor shall update the IUID Registry at *https://iuid.logistics information-service.dla.mil/* for changes in status, mark, custody, condition code (for reparables only), or disposition of items that are—

(i) Received by the Contractor;

(ii) Delivered or shipped from the Contractor's plant, under Government instructions, except when shipment is to a subcontractor or other location of the Contractor;

(iii) Consumed or expended, reasonably and properly, or otherwise accounted for, in the performance of the contract as determined by the Government property administrator, including reasonable inventory adjustments;

(iv) Disposed of; or

(v) Transferred to a follow-on or other contract.

(2) The Contractor need not report to the IUID Registry those transactions reported or to be reported to the following DCMA etools:

(i) Plant Clearance Automated Reutilization and Screening System (PCARSS); or

(ii) Lost, Theft, Damaged or Destroyed (LTDD) system.

(3) The contractor shall update the IUID Registry as transactions occur or as otherwise stated in the Contractor's property management procedure.

(End of clause)

[Interim rule, 72 FR 52293, 9/13/2007, effective 9/13/2007; Final rule, 73 FR 70906, 11/24/2008, effective 11/24/2008; Final rule, 73 FR 76971, 12/18/2008, effective 12/18/2008; Final rule, 75 FR 59102, 9/27/2010, effective 9/27/2010; Final rule, 77 FR 52254, 8/29/2012, effective 8/29/2012; Final rule, 78 FR 13543, 2/28/2013, effective 2/28/2013]

252.211-7008 Use of Government-assigned Serial Numbers

As prescribed in 211.274-6(c), use the following clause:

USE OF GOVERNMENT-ASSIGNED SERIAL NUMBERS (SEP 2010)

(a) *Definitions.* As used in this clause—

Government-assigned serial number means a combination of letters or numerals in a fixed human-readable information format (text) conveying information about a major end item, which is provided to a contractor by the requiring activity with accompanying technical data instructions for marking the Government-assigned serial number on major end items to be delivered to the Government.

Major end item means a final combination of component parts and/or materials which is ready for its intended use and of such importance to operational readiness that review and control of inventory management functions (procurement, distribution, maintenance, disposal, and asset reporting) is required at all levels of life cycle management. Major end items include aircraft; ships; boats; motorized wheeled, tracked, and towed vehicles for use on highway or rough terrain; weapon and missile end items; ammunition; and sets, assemblies, or end items having a major end item as a component.

Unique item identifier (UII) means a set of data elements permanently marked on an item that is globally unique and unambiguous and never changes in order to provide traceability of the item throughout its total life cycle. The term includes a concatenated UII or a DoD-recognized unique identification equivalent.

(b) The Contractor shall mark the Government-assigned serial numbers on those major end items as specified by line item in the Schedule, in accordance with the technical instructions for the placement and method of application identified in the terms and conditions of the contract.

(c) The Contractor shall register the Government-assigned serial number along with the major end item's UII at the time of delivery in accordance with the provisions of the clause at DFARS 252.211-7003(d).

(d) The Contractor shall establish the UII for major end items for use throughout the life of the major end item. The Contractor may elect, but is not required, to use the Government-assigned serial number to construct the UII.

(End of clause)

[Final rule, 75 FR 59102, 9/27/2010, effective 9/27/2010]

252.212 Acquisition of commercial items—general, provisions and clauses for DFARS Part 212

252.212-7000 [Removed and Reserved]

[DAC 91-9, 60 FR 61586, 11/30/95, effective 11/30/95; DAC 91-11, 61 FR 50446, 9/26/96, effective 9/26/96; Final rule, 70 FR 35543, 6/21/2005, effective 6/21/2005; Final rule, 78 FR 37980, 6/25/2013, effective 6/25/2013]

252.212-7001 [Removed and Reserved]

[Final rule, 66 FR 55121, 11/1/2001, effective 11/1/2001; Interim rule, 67 FR 20697, 4/26/2002, effective 4/26/2002; Final rule, 67 FR 38020, 5/31/2002, effective 5/31/2002; Final rule, 67 FR 49251, 7/30/2002, effective 7/30/2002; Final rule, 67 FR 70325, 11/22/2002, effective 11/22/2002; Final rule, 67 FR 77937, 12/20/2002, effective 12/20/2002; Interim rule, 68 FR 7441, 2/14/2003, effective 2/14/2003; Interim rule, 68 FR 8450, 2/21/2003, effective 3/1/2003; Final rule, 68 FR 15615, 3/31/2003, effective 4/30/2003; Final rule, 68 FR 33026, 6/3/2003, effective 6/3/2003; Final rule, 68 FR 56560, 10/1/2003, effective 10/1/2003; Interim rule, 68 FR 56561, 10/1/2003, effective 10/1/2003; Final rule, 68 FR 69628, 12/15/2003, effective 12/15/2003; Interim rule, 69 FR 1926, 1/13/2004, effective 1/13/2004; Final rule, 69 FR 26509, 5/13/2004, effective 5/13/2004; Interim rule, 69 FR 26508, 5/13/2004, effective 5/13/2004; Final rule, 69 FR 31910, 6/8/2004, effective 6/8/2004; Final rule, 69 FR 35535, 6/25/2004, effective 6/25/2004; Final rule, 69 FR 55989, 9/17/2004, effective 9/17/2004; Final rule, 69 FR 74991, 12/15/2004, effective 12/15/2004; Interim rule, 70 FR 2361, 1/13/2005, effective 1/13/2005; Final rule, 70 FR 35543, 6/21/2005, effective 6/21/2005; Interim rule, 70 FR 52032, 9/1/2005, effective 9/1/2005; Correction, 70 FR 53716, 9/9/2005, effective 9/9/2005; Final rule, 70 FR 73152, 12/9/2005, effective 12/9/2005; Interim rule, 71 FR 9269, 2/23/2006, effective 2/23/2006; Final rule, 71 FR 14110, 3/21/2006, effective 3/21/2006; Final rule, 71 FR 27643, 5/12/2006, effective 5/12/2006; Interim rule, 71 FR 34834, 6/16/2006, effective 6/16/2006; Final rule, 71 FR 39008, 7/11/2006, effective 7/11/2006; Final rule, 71 FR 53047, 9/8/2006, effective 9/8/2006; Interim rule, 71 FR 58541, 10/4/2006, effective 10/4/2006; Final rule, 71 FR 65752, 11/9/2006, effective 11/9/2006; Interim rule, 72 FR 2637, 1/22/2007, effective 1/22/2007; Final rule, 72 FR 6486, 2/12/2007, effective 2/12/2007; Interim rule, 72 FR 14242, 3/27/2007, effective 3/27/2007; Final rule, 72 FR 14241, 3/27,2007, effective 3/27/2007; Final rule, 72 FR 20761, 72 FR 20765, 4/26/2007, effective 4/26/2007; Final rule 72 FR 42315, 8/2/2007, effective 8/2/2007; Final rule, 73 FR 1830, 1/10/2008, effective 1/10/2008; Final rule, 73 FR 11356, 3/3/2008, effective 3/3/2008; Final rule, 73 FR 53151, 9/15/2008, effective 9/15/2008; Final rule, 73 FR 70913, 11/24/2008, effective 11/24/2008; Final rule, 73 FR 76970, 12/18/2008, effective 12/18/2008; Interim rule, 74 FR 2408, 1/15/2009, effective 1/15/2009; Final rule, 74 FR 37626, 7/29/2009, effective 7/29/2009; Final rule, 74 FR 59913, 11/19/2009, effective 11/19/2009; Interim rule, 74 FR 61045, 11/23/2009, effective 11/23/2009; Final rule, 75 FR 18035, 4/8/2010, effective 4/8/2010; Final rule, 75 FR 33195, 6/11/2010, effective 6/11/2010; Final rule, 75 FR 34943, 6/21/2010, effective 6/21/2010; Final rule, 75 FR 59103, 9/27/2010, effective 9/27/2010; Interim rule, 75 FR 65439, 10/25/2010, effective 10/25/2010; Interim rule, 75 FR 66683, 10/29/2010, effective 10/29/2010; Interim rule, 75 FR 67632,

11/3/2010, effective 11/3/2010; Final rule, 75 FR 76297, 12/8/2010, effective 12/8/2010; Final rule, 75 FR 81915, 12/29/2010, effective 12/29/2010; Final rule, 76 FR 25, 1/3/2011, effective 1/3/2011; Final rule, 76 FR 3536, 1/20/2011, effective 1/20/2011; Interim rule, 76 FR 11363, 3/2/2011, effective 3/2/2011; Final rule, 76 FR 14590, 3/17/2011, effective 3/17/2011; Final rule, 76 FR 32840, 32841, 6/6/2011, effective 6/6/2011; Final rule, 76 FR 38053, 6/29/2011, effective 6/29/2011; Final rule, 76 FR 44282, 7/25/2011, effective 7/25/2011; Interim rule, 76 FR 52133, 8/19/2011, effective 8/19/2011; Final rule, 76 FR 58137, 9/20/2011, effective 9/20/2011; Final rule, 76 FR 58144, 9/20/2011, effective 9/20/201; Final rule, 76 FR 61279, 10/4/2011, effective 10/4/2011; Final rule, 76 FR 61282, 10/4/2011, effective 10/4/2011; Final rule, 76 FR 76318, 12/7/2011, effective 12/7/2011; Interim rule, 76 FR 78858, 12/20/2011, effective 12/20/2011; Final rule, 77 FR 4631, 1/30/2012, effective 1/30/2012; Final rule, 77 FR 10976, 2/24/2012, effective 2/24/2012; Final rule, 77 FR 13013, 3/5/2012, effective 3/5/2012; Final rule, 77 FR 23631, 4/20/2012, effective 4/20/2012; Interim rule, 77 FR 30356, 5/22/2012, effective 5/22/2012; Final rule, 77 FR 30368, 5/22/2012, effective 5/22/2012; Final rule, 77 FR 35879, 6/15/2012, effective 6/15/2012; Final rule, 77 FR 35883, 6/15/2012, effective 6/15/2012; Interim rule, 77 FR 38734, 6/29/2012, effective 6/29/2012; Final rule, 77 FR 38736, 6/29/2012, effective 6/29/2012; Interim rule, 77 FR 68699, 11/16/2012, effective 11/16/2012; Final rule, 77 FR 76941, 12/31/2012, effective 12/31/2012; Final rule, 78 FR 13546, 2/28/2013, effective 2/28/2013; Final rule, 78 FR 13543, 2/28/2013, effective 2/28/2013; Final rule, 78 FR 13544, 2/28/2013, effective 2/28/2013; Final rule, 78 FR 13546, 2/28/2013, effective 2/28/2013; Final rule, 78 FR 18876, 3/28/2013, effective 3/28/2013; Final rule, 78 FR 18877, 3/28/2013, effective 3/28/2013; Final rule, 78 FR 30233, 5/22/2013, effective 5/22/2013; Correction, 78 FR 33994, 6/6/2013, effective 6/6/2013; Final rule, 78 FR 37980, 6/25/2013, effective 6/25/2013]

252.212-7002 Pilot Program for Acquisition of Military-purpose Nondevelopmental Items.

As prescribed in 212.7103, use the following provision:

PILOT PROGRAM FOR ACQUISITION OF MILITARY-PURPOSE NONDEVELOPMENTAL ITEMS (JUN 2016)

(a) *Definitions*. As used in this provision—

Military-purpose nondevelopmental item means a nondevelopmental item that meets a validated military requirement, as determined in writing by the responsible program manager, and has been developed exclusively at private expense. An item shall not be considered to be developed at private expense if development of the item was paid for in whole or in part through—

(1) Independent research and development costs or bid and proposal costs, per the definition in FAR 31.205-18, that have been reimbursed directly or indirectly by a Federal agency or have been submitted to a Federal agency for reimbursement; or

(2) Foreign government funding.

Nondevelopmental item is defined in FAR 2.101 and also includes previously developed items of supply that require modifications other than those customarily available in the commercial marketplace if such modifications are consistent with the requirement at DFARS 212.7102-1(c)(1).

(b) *Notice*. This is a procurement action under section 866 of the National Defense Authorization Act for Fiscal Year 2011, Pilot Program for Acquisition of Military-Purpose Nondevelopmental Items, as modified by section 892 of the National Defense Authorization Act for Fiscal Year 2016 (Pub. L. 114-92), and is subject to the limitations outlined in DFARS 212.7102.

(End of provision)

[Interim rule, 76 FR 38048, 6/29/2011, effective 6/29/201; Final rule, 77 FR 2653, 1/19/2012, effective 1/19/2012; Final rule, 77 FR 35879, 6/15/2012, effective 6/15/2012; Interim rule, 81 FR 42557,

6/30/2016, effective 6/30/2016; Final rule, 81 FR 78012, 11/4/2016, effective 11/4/2016; Publication notice, 20171208]

252.213 Simplified acquisition procedures for DFARS Part 213

252.213-7000 Notice to Prospective Suppliers on Use of Supplier Performance Risk System in Past Performance Evaluations.

As prescribed in 213.106-2-70, use the following provision:

NOTICE TO PROSPECTIVE SUPPLIERS ON USE OF PAST SUPPLIER PERFORMANCE RISK SYSTEM IN PAST PERFORMANCE EVALUATIONS (SEP 2019)

(a) The Supplier Performance Risk System (SPSR) application (*https://www.sprs.csd.disa.mil*) will be used in the evaluation of suppliers' past performance in accordance with DFARS 213.106-2(b) (i).

(b) SPRS collects quality and delivery data on previously awarded contracts and orders from existing Department of Defense reporting systems to classify each supplier's performance history by Federal supply class (FSC) and product or service code (PSC). The SPRS application provides the contracting officer quantifiable past performance information regarding a supplier's quality and delivery performance for the FSC and PSC of the supplies being purchased.

(c) The quality and delivery classifications identified for a supplier in SPRS will be used by the contracting officer to evaluate a supplier's past performance in conjunction with the supplier's references (if requested) and other provisions of this solicitation under the past performance evaluation factor. The Government reserves the right to award to the supplier whose quotation or offer represents the best value to the Government.

(d) SPRS classifications are generated monthly for each contractor and can be reviewed by following the access instructions in the SPRS User's Manual found at *https://www.sprs.csd.disa.mil/reference.htm*. Contractors are granted access to SPRS for their own classifications only. Suppliers are encouraged to review their own classifications, the SPRS reporting procedures and classification methodology detailed in the SPRS User's Manual, and SPRS Evaluation Criteria available from the references at *https://www.sprs.csd.disa.mil/pdf/SPRS_DataEvaluationCriteria.pdf*. The method to challenge a rating generated by SPRS is provided in the User's Manual.

(End of provision)

[Interim rule, 76 FR 38048, 6/29/2011, effective 6/29/201; Final rule, 77 FR 2653, 1/19/2012, effective 1/19/2012; Final rule, 77 FR 35879, 6/15/2012, effective 6/15/2012; Final rule, 80 FR 30117, 5/26/2015, effective 5/26/2015; Final rule, 80 FR 30117, 5/26/2015, effective 5/26/2015; Final rule, 80 FR 36718, 6/26/2015, effective 6/26/2015; Final rule, 83 FR 12681, 3/23/2018, effective 3/23/2018; Final rule, 84 FR 48507, 9/13/2019, effective 9/13/2019]

252.215 Contracting by negotiation, provisions and clauses for DFARS Part 215

252.215-7000 [Removed and Reserved]

[Final rule, 62 FR 40471, 7/29/97, effective 7/29/97; Final rule, 63 FR 55040, 10/14/98, effective 10/14/98; Final rule, 77 FR 76939, 12/31/2012, effective 12/31/2012; Final rule, 78 FR 13543, 2/28/2013, effective 2/28/2013; Final rule, 83 FR 30824, 6/29/2018, effective 6/29/2018]

252.215-7001 [Reserved]

[Reserved, DAC 91-9, 60 FR 61586, 11/30/95, effective 11/30/95]

252.215-7002 Cost estimating system requirements.

As prescribed in 215.408(1), use the following clause:

COST ESTIMATING SYSTEM REQUIREMENTS (DEC 2012)

(a) *Definitions*.

Acceptable estimating system means an estimating system that complies with the system criteria in paragraph (d) of this clause, and provides for a system that—

(1) Is maintained, reliable, and consistently applied;

(2) Produces verifiable, supportable, documented, and timely cost estimates that are an acceptable basis for negotiation of fair and reasonable prices;

(3) Is consistent with and integrated with the Contractor's related management systems; and

(4) Is subject to applicable financial control systems.

Estimating system means the Contractor's policies, procedures, and practices for budgeting and planning controls, and generating estimates of costs and other data included in proposals submitted to customers in the expectation of receiving contract awards. Estimating system includes the Contractor's—

(1) Organizational structure;

(2) Established lines of authority, duties, and responsibilities;

(3) Internal controls and managerial reviews;

(4) Flow of work, coordination, and communication; and

(5) Budgeting, planning, estimating methods, techniques, accumulation of historical costs, and other analyses used to generate cost estimates.

Significant deficiency means a shortcoming in the system that materially affects the ability of officials of the Department of Defense to rely upon data and information produced by the system that is needed for management purposes.

(b) *General*. The Contractor shall establish, maintain, and comply with an acceptable estimating system.

(c) *Applicability*. Paragraphs (d) and (e) of this clause apply if the Contractor is a large business and either—

(1) In its fiscal year preceding award of this contract, received Department of Defense (DoD) prime contracts or subcontracts, totaling $50 million or more for which certified cost or pricing data were required; or

(2) In its fiscal year preceding award of this contract—

(i) Received DoD prime contracts or subcontracts totaling $10 million or more (but less than $50 million) for which certified cost or pricing data were required; and

(ii) Was notified, in writing, by the Contracting Officer that paragraphs (d) and (e) of this clause apply.

(d) *System requirements*. (1) The Contractor shall disclose its estimating system to the Administrative Contracting Officer (ACO), in writing. If the Contractor wishes the Government to protect the data and information as privileged or confidential, the Contractor must mark the documents with the appropriate legends before submission.

(2) An estimating system disclosure is acceptable when the Contractor has provided the ACO with documentation that—

(i) Accurately describes those policies, procedures, and practices that the Contractor currently uses in preparing cost proposals; and

(ii) Provides sufficient detail for the Government to reasonably make an informed judgment regarding the acceptability of the Contractor's estimating practices.

(3) The Contractor shall—

(i) Comply with its disclosed estimating system; and

(ii) Disclose significant changes to the cost estimating system to the ACO on a timely basis.

(4) The Contractor's estimating system shall provide for the use of appropriate source data, utilize sound estimating techniques and good judgment, maintain a consistent approach, and adhere to established policies and procedures. An acceptable estimating system shall accomplish the following functions:

(i) Establish clear responsibility for preparation, review, and approval of cost estimates and budgets.

(ii) Provide a written description of the organization and duties of the personnel responsible for preparing, reviewing, and approving cost estimates and budgets.

(iii) Ensure that relevant personnel have sufficient training, experience, and guidance to perform estimating and budgeting tasks in accordance with the Contractor's established procedures.

(iv) Identify and document the sources of data and the estimating methods and rationale used in developing cost estimates and budgets.

(v) Provide for adequate supervision throughout the estimating and budgeting process.

(vi) Provide for consistent application of estimating and budgeting techniques.

(vii) Provide for detection and timely correction of errors.

(viii) Protect against cost duplication and omissions.

(ix) Provide for the use of historical experience, including historical vendor pricing data, where appropriate.

(x) Require use of appropriate analytical methods.

(xi) Integrate data and information available from other management systems.

(xii) Require management review, including verification of compliance with the company's estimating and budgeting policies.

(xiii) Provide for internal review of, and accountability for, the acceptability of the estimating system, including the budgetary data supporting indirect cost estimates and comparisons of projected results to actual results, and an analysis of any differences.

(xiv) Provide procedures to update cost estimates and notify the Contracting Officer in a timely manner throughout the negotiation process.

(xv) Provide procedures that ensure subcontract prices are reasonable based on a documented review and analysis provided with the prime proposal, when practicable.

(xvi) Provide estimating and budgeting practices that consistently generate sound proposals that are compliant with the provisions of the solicitation and are adequate to serve as a basis to reach a fair and reasonable price.

(xvii) Have an adequate system description, including policies, procedures, and estimating and budgeting practices, that comply with the Federal Acquisition Regulation and Defense Federal Acquisition Regulation Supplement.

(e) *Significant deficiencies*. (1) The Contracting Officer will provide an initial determination to the Contractor, in writing, of any significant deficiencies. The initial determination will describe the deficiency in sufficient detail to allow the Contractor to understand the deficiency.

(2) The Contractor shall respond within 30 days to a written initial determination from the Contracting Officer that identifies significant deficiencies in the Contractor's estimating system. If the Contractor disagrees with the initial determination, the Contractor shall state, in writing, its rationale for disagreeing.

(3) The Contracting Officer will evaluate the Contractor's response and notify the Contractor, in writing, of the Contracting Officer's final determination concerning—

(i) Remaining significant deficiencies;

(ii) The adequacy of any proposed or completed corrective action; and

(iii) System disapproval, if the Contracting Officer determines that one or more significant deficiencies remain.

(f) If the Contractor receives the Contracting Officer's final determination of significant deficiencies, the Contractor shall, within 45 days of receipt of the final determination, either correct the significant deficiencies or submit an acceptable corrective action plan showing milestones and actions to eliminate the significant deficiencies.

(g) *Withholding payments*. If the Contracting Officer makes a final determination to disapprove the Contractor's estimating system, and the contract includes the clause at 252.242-7005, Contractor Business Systems, the Contracting Officer will withhold payments in accordance with that clause.

(End of clause)

[Final rule, 62 FR 40471, 7/29/97, effective 7/29/97; Final rule, 63 FR 55040, 10/14/98, effective 10/14/98; Final rule, 71 FR 69492, 12/1/2006, effective 12/1/2006; Interim rule, 76 FR 28856, 5/18/2011, effective 5/18/2011; Final rule, 77 FR 11355, 2/24/2012, effective 2/24/2012; Final rule, 77 FR 11755, 2/28/2012, effective 2/28/2012; Final rule, 77 FR 76939, 12/31/2012, effective 12/31/2012; Final rule, 83 FR 30824, 6/29/2018, effective 6/29/2018]

252.215-7003 Requirement for Submission of Data Other Than Certified Cost or Pricing Data—Canadian Commercial Corporation.

As prescribed at DFARS 215.408(2)(i), use the following provision:

REQUIREMENT FOR SUBMISSION OF DATA OTHER THAN CERTIFIED COST OR PRICING DATA—CANADIAN COMMERCIAL CORPORATION (JUL 2012)

(a) Submission of certified cost or pricing data is not required.

(b) Canadian Commercial Corporation shall obtain and provide the following:

(i) Profit rate or fee (as applicable).

(ii) Analysis provided by Public Works and Government Services Canada to the Canadian Commercial Corporation to determine a fair and reasonable price (comparable to the analysis required at FAR 15.404-1).

(iii) Data other than certified cost or pricing data necessary to permit a determination by the U.S. Contracting Officer that the proposed price is fair and reasonable [*U.S. Contracting Officer to insert description of the data required in accordance with FAR 15.403-3(a)(1)*].

(c) As specified in FAR 15.403-3(a)(4), an offeror who does not comply with a requirement to submit data that the U.S. Contracting Officer has deemed necessary to determine price reasonableness or cost realism is ineligible for award unless the head of the contracting activity determines that it is in the best interest of the Government to make the award to that offeror.

(End of provision)

[Interim rule, 72 FR 20758, 4/26/2007, effective 4/26/2007; Interim rule, 73 FR 27464, 5/13/2008, effective 5/13/2008; Final rule, 75 FR 49849, 8/16/2010, effective 8/16/2010; Final rule, 77 FR 43470, 7/24/2012, effective 7/24/2012; Final rule, 78 FR 65214, 10/31/2013, effective 10/31/2013; Final rule, 83 FR 30824, 6/29/2018, effective 6/29/2018]

252.215-7004 Requirement for Submission of Data Other Than Certified Cost or Pricing Data—Modifications—Canadian Commercial Corporation.

As prescribed at 215.408(2)(ii), use the following clause:

REQUIREMENT FOR SUBMISSION OF DATA OTHER THAN CERTIFIED COST OR PRICING DATA—MODIFICATIONS—CANADIAN COMMERCIAL CORPORATION (OCT 2013)

This clause, in lieu of FAR 52.215-21, applies only if award is to the Canadian Commercial Corporation.

(a) Submission of certified cost or pricing data is not required.

(b) Canadian Commercial Corporation shall obtain and provide the following for modifications that exceed $150,000 [*or higher dollar value specified by the U.S. Contracting Officer in the solicitation*].

(i) Profit rate or fee (as applicable).

(ii) Analysis provided by Public Works and Government Services Canada to the Canadian Commercial Corporation to determine a fair and reasonable price (comparable to the analysis required at FAR 15.404-1).

(iii) Data other than certified cost or pricing data necessary to permit a determination by the U.S. Contracting Officer that the proposed price is fair and reasonable [*U.S. Contracting Officer to insert description of the data required in accordance with FAR FAR 15.403-3(a)(1)*].

(End of clause)

[Interim rule, 72 FR 20758, 4/26/2007, effective 4/26/2007; Interim rule, 73 FR 27464, 5/13/2008, effective 5/13/2008; Final rule, 75 FR 49849, 8/16/2010, effective 8/16/2010; Final rule, 77 FR 43570, 7/24/2012, effective 7/24/2012; Final rule, 78 FR 65214, 10/31/2013, effective 10/31/2013; Final rule, 83 FR 30824, 6/29/2018, effective 6/29/2018]

252.215-7005 Evaluation Factor for Employing or Subcontracting with Members of the Selected Reserve.

As prescribed in 215.370-3(a), use the following provision:

EVALUATION FACTOR FOR EMPLOYING OR SUBCONTRACTING WITH MEMBERS OF THE SELECTED RESERVE (OCT 2008)

(a) *Definition. Selected Reserve*, as used in this provision, has the meaning given that term in 10 U.S.C. 10143. Selected Reserve members normally attend regular drills throughout the year and are the group of Reserves most readily available to the President.

(b) This solicitation includes an evaluation factor that considers the offeror's intended use of employees, or individual subcontractors, who are members of the Selected Reserve.

(c) If the offeror, in the performance of any contract resulting from this solicitation, intends to use employees or individual subcontractors who are members of the Selected Reserve, the offeror's proposal shall include documentation to support this intent. Such documentation may include, but is not limited to—

(1) Existing company documentation, such as payroll or personnel records, indicating the names of the Selected Reserve members who are currently employed by the company; or

(2) A statement that one or more positions will be set aside to be filled by new hires of Selected Reserve members, along with verifying documentation.

(End of provision)

[Final rule, 73 FR 62211, 10/20/2008, effective 10/20/2008]

252.215-7006 Use of Employees or Individual Subcontractors Who Are Members of the Selected Reserve.

As prescribed in 215.370-3(b), use the following clause:

USE OF EMPLOYEES OR INDIVIDUAL SUBCONTRACTORS WHO ARE MEMBERS OF THE SELECTED RESERVE (OCT 2008)

(a) *Definition. Selected Reserve*, as used in this clause, has the meaning given that term in 10 U.S.C. 10143. Selected Reserve members normally attend regular drills throughout the year and are the group of Reserves most readily available to the President.

(b) If the Contractor stated in its offer that it intends to use members of the Selected Reserve in the performance of this contract—

(1) The Contractor shall use employees, or individual subcontractors, who are members of the Selected Reserve in the performance of the contract to the fullest extent consistent with efficient contract performance; and

(2) The Government has the right to terminate the contract for default if the Contractor willfully or intentionally fails to use members of the Selected Reserve, as employees or individual subcontractors, in the performance of the contract.

(End of clause)

[Final rule, 73 FR 62211, 10/20/2008, effective 10/20/2008]

252.215-7007 Notice of Intent to Resolicit.

As prescribed in 215.371-6, use the following provision:

NOTICE OF INTENT TO RESOLICIT (JUN 2012)

This solicitation provides offerors fewer than 30 days to submit proposals. In the event that only one offer is received in response to this solicitation, the Contracting Officer may cancel the solicitation and resolicit for an additional period of at least 30 days in accordance with 215.371-2.

(End of provision)

[Final rule, 77 FR 39125, 6/29/2012, effective 6/29/2012; Final rule, 78 FR 65214, 10/31/2013, effective 10/31/2013]

252.215-7008 Only One Offer.

As prescribed in 215.408(3), use the following provision:

ONLY ONE OFFER (JUL 2019)

(a) *Cost or pricing data requirements.* After initial submission of offers, if the Contracting Officer notifies the Offeror that only one offer was received, the Offeror agrees to—

(1) Submit any additional cost or pricing data that is required in order to determine whether the price is fair and reasonable or to comply with the statutory requirement for certified cost or pricing data (10 U.S.C. 2306a and FAR 15.403-3); and

(2) Except as provided in paragraph (b) of this provision, if the acquisition exceeds the certified cost or pricing data threshold and an exception to the requirement for certified cost or pricing data at FAR 15.403-1(b)(2) through (5) does not apply, certify all cost or pricing data in accordance with paragraph (c) of DFARS provision 252.215-7010, Requirements for Certified Cost or Pricing Data and Data Other Than Certified Cost or Pricing Data, of this solicitation.

(b) *Canadian Commercial Corporation.* If the Offeror is the Canadian Commercial Corporation, certified cost or pricing data are not required. If the Contracting Officer notifies the Canadian Commercial Corporation that additional data other than certified cost or pricing data are required in accordance with DFARS 225.870-4(c), the Canadian Commercial Corporation shall obtain and provide the following:

(1) Profit rate or fee (as applicable).

(2) Analysis provided by Public Works and Government Services Canada to the Canadian Commercial Corporation to determine a fair and reasonable price (comparable to the analysis required at FAR 15.404-1).

(3) Data other than certified cost or pricing data necessary to permit a determination by the U.S. Contracting Officer that the proposed price is fair and reasonable *[U.S. Contracting Officer to provide description of the data required in accordance with FAR 15.403-3(a)(1) with the notification]*.

(4) As specified in FAR 15.403-3(a)(4), an offeror who does not comply with a requirement to submit data that the U.S. Contracting Officer has deemed necessary to determine price reasonableness or cost realism is ineligible for award unless the head of the contracting activity determines that it is in the best interest of the Government to make the award to that offeror.

(c) *Subcontracts.* Unless the Offeror is the Canadian Commercial Corporation, the Offeror shall insert the substance of this provision, including this paragraph (c), in all subcontracts exceeding the simplified acquisition threshold defined in FAR part 2.

(End of provision)

[Final rule, 77 FR 39125, 6/29/2012, effective 6/29/2012; Final rule, 78 FR 65214, 10/31/2013, effective 10/31/2013; Final rule, 83 FR 30824, 6/29/2018, effective 6/29/2018; Final rule, 84 FR 30947, 6/28/2019, effective 7/31/2019; Final rule, 84 FR 33858, 7/16/2019, effective 7/31/2019]

252.215-7009 Proposal adequacy checklist.

As prescribed in 215.408(4), use the following provision:

PROPOSAL ADEQUACY CHECKLIST (JAN 2014)

The offeror shall complete the following checklist, providing location of requested information, or an explanation of why the requested information is not provided. In preparation of the offeror's checklist, offerors may elect to have their prospective subcontractors use the same or similar checklist as appropriate.

PROPOSAL ADEQUACY CHECKLIST

References	Submission item	Proposal page No.	If not provided EXPLAIN (may use continuation pages)
	GENERAL INSTRUCTIONS		
1. FAR 15.408, Table 15-2, Section I Paragraph A	Is there a properly completed first page of the proposal per FAR 15.408 Table 15-2 I.A or as specified in the solicitation?		
2. FAR 15.408, Table 15-2, Section I Paragraph A(7)	Does the proposal identify the need for Government-furnished material/tooling/test equipment? Include the accountable contract number and contracting officer contact information if known.		
3. FAR 15.408, Table 15-2, Section I Paragraph A(8)	Does the proposal identify and explain notifications of noncompliance with Cost Accounting Standards Board or Cost Accounting Standards (CAS); any proposal inconsistencies with your disclosed practices or applicable CAS; and inconsistencies with your established estimating and accounting principles and procedures?		
4. FAR 15.408, Table 15-2, Section I, Paragraph C(1)	Does the proposal disclose any other known activity that could materially impact the costs?		
FAR 2.101, "Cost or pricing data"	This may include, but is not limited to, such factors as— (1) Vendor quotations; (2) Nonrecurring costs; (3) Information on changes in production methods and in production or purchasing volume; (4) Data supporting projections of business prospects and objectives and related operations costs; (5) Unit-cost trends such as those associated with labor efficiency; (6) Make-or-buy decisions; (7) Estimated resources to attain business goals; and (8) Information on management decisions that could have a significant bearing on costs.		
5. FAR 15.408, Table 15-2, Section I Paragraph B	Is an Index of all certified cost or pricing data and information accompanying or identified in the proposal provided and appropriately referenced?		
6. FAR 15.403-1(b)	Are there any exceptions to submission of certified cost or pricing data pursuant to FAR 15.403-1(b)? If so, is supporting documentation included in the proposal? (Note questions 18-20.)		
7. FAR 15.408, Table 15-2, Section I Paragraph C(2)(i).	Does the proposal disclose the judgmental factors applied and the mathematical or other methods used in the estimate, including those used in projecting from known data?		
8. FAR 15.408, Table 15-2, Section I Paragraph C(2)(ii).	Does the proposal disclose the nature and amount of any contingencies included in the proposed price?		
9. FAR 15.408 Table 15-2, Section II, Paragraph A or B.	Does the proposal explain the basis of all cost estimating relationships (labor hours or material) proposed on other than a discrete basis?		
10. FAR 15.408, Table 15-2, Section I Paragraphs D and E.	Is there a summary of total cost by element of cost and are the elements of cost cross-referenced to the supporting cost or pricing data? (Breakdowns for each cost element must be consistent with your cost accounting system, including breakdown by year.)		

References	Submission item	Proposal page No.	If not provided EXPLAIN (may use continuation pages)
11. FAR 15.408, Table 15-2, Section I Paragraphs D and E.	If more than one Contract Line Item Number (CLIN) or sub Contract Line Item Number (sub-CLIN) is proposed as required by the RFP, are there summary total amounts covering all line items for each element of cost and is it cross-referenced to the supporting cost or pricing data?		
12. FAR 15.408, Table 15-2, Section I Paragraph F	Does the proposal identify any incurred costs for work performed before the submission of the proposal?		
13. FAR 15.408, Table 15-2, Section I Paragraph G	Is there a Government forward pricing rate agreement (FPRA)? If so, the offeror shall identify the official submittal of such rate and factor data. If not, does the proposal include all rates and factors by year that are utilized in the development of the proposal and the basis for those rates and factors?		
	COST ELEMENTS		
	MATERIALS AND SERVICES		
14. FAR 15.408, Table 15-2, Section II Paragraph A	Does the proposal include a consolidated summary of individual material and services, frequently referred to as a Consolidated Bill of Material (CBOM), to include the basis for pricing? The offeror's consolidated summary shall include raw materials, parts, components, assemblies, subcontracts and services to be produced or performed by others, identifying as a minimum the item, source, quantity, and price.		
	SUBCONTRACTS (Purchased materials or services)		
15. DFARS 215.404-3	Has the offeror identified in the proposal those subcontractor proposals, for which the contracting officer has initiated or may need to request field pricing analysis?		
16. FAR 15.404-3(c) FAR 52.244-2	Per the thresholds of FAR 15.404-3(c), Subcontract Pricing Considerations, does the proposal include a copy of the applicable subcontractor's certified cost or pricing data?		
17. FAR 15.408, Table 15-2, Note 1; Section II Paragraph A.	Is there a price/cost analysis establishing the reasonableness of each of the proposed subcontracts included with the proposal? If the offeror's price/cost analyses are not provided with the proposal, does the proposal include a matrix identifying dates for receipt of subcontractor proposal, completion of fact finding for purposes of price/cost analysis, and submission of the price/cost analysis?		
	EXCEPTIONS TO CERTIFIED COST OR PRICING DATA		

References	Submission item	Proposal page No.	If not provided EXPLAIN (may use continuation pages)
18. FAR 52.215-20 FAR 2.101, "commercial item" . . .	Has the offeror submitted an exception to the submission of certified cost or pricing data for commercial items proposed either at the prime or subcontractor level, in accordance with provision 52.215-20? a. Has the offeror specifically identified the type of commercial item claim (FAR 2.101 commercial item definition, paragraphs (1) through (8)), and the basis on which the item meets the definition? b. For modified commercial items (FAR 2.101 commercial item definition paragraph (3)); did the offeror classify the modification(s) as either— i. A modification of a type customarily available in the commercial marketplace (paragraph (3)(i)); or ii. A minor modification (paragraph (3)(ii)) of a type not customarily available in the commercial marketplace made to meet Federal Government requirements not exceeding the thresholds in FAR 15.403-1(c)(3)(iii)(B)? c. For proposed commercial items "of a type", or "evolved" or modified (FAR 2.101 commercial item definition paragraphs (1) through (3)), did the contractor provide a technical description of the differences between the proposed item and the comparison item(s)?		
19.	[Reserved]		
20. FAR 15.408, Table 15-2, Section II Paragraph A(1).	Does the proposal support the degree of competition and the basis for establishing the source and reasonableness of price for each subcontract or purchase order priced on a competitive basis exceeding the threshold for certified cost or pricing data?		
	INTERORGANIZATIONAL TRANSFERS		
21. FAR 15.408, Table 15-2, Section II Paragraph A.(2).	For inter-organizational transfers proposed at cost, does the proposal include a complete cost proposal in compliance with Table 15-2?		
22. FAR 15.408, Table 15-2, Section II Paragraph A(1).	For inter-organizational transfers proposed at price in accordance with FAR 31.205-26(e), does the proposal provide an analysis by the prime that supports the exception from certified cost or pricing data in accordance with FAR 15.403-1?		
	DIRECT LABOR		
23. FAR 15.408, Table 15-2, Section II Paragraph B	Does the proposal include a time phased (i.e.; monthly, quarterly) breakdown of labor hours, rates and costs by category or skill level? If labor is the allocation base for indirect costs, the labor cost must be summarized in order that the applicable overhead rate can be applied.		
24. FAR 15.408, Table 15-2, Section II Paragraph B	For labor Basis of Estimates (BOEs), does the proposal include labor categories, labor hours, and task descriptions—(e.g.; Statement of Work reference, applicable CLIN, Work Breakdown Structure, rationale for estimate, applicable history, and time-phasing)?		
25. FAR subpart 22.10	If covered by the Service Contract Labor Standards statute (41 U.S.C. chapter 67), are the rates in the proposal in compliance with the minimum rates specified in the statute?		
	INDIRECT COSTS		
26. FAR 15.408, Table 15-2, Section II Paragraph C	Does the proposal indicate the basis of estimate for proposed indirect costs and how they are applied? (Support for the indirect rates could consist of cost breakdowns, trends, and budgetary data.)		

References	Submission item	Proposal page No.	If not provided EXPLAIN (may use continuation pages)
	OTHER COSTS		
27. FAR 15.408, Table 15-2, Section II Paragraph D	Does the proposal include other direct costs and the basis for pricing? If travel is included does the proposal include number of trips, number of people, number of days per trip, locations, and rates (e.g. airfare, per diem, hotel, car rental, etc)?		
28. FAR 15.408, Table 15-2, Section II Paragraph E	If royalties exceed $1,500 does the proposal provide the information/data identified by Table 15-2?		
29. FAR 15.408, Table 15-2, Section II Paragraph F	When facilities capital cost of money is proposed, does the proposal include submission of Form CASB-CMF or reference to an FPRA/FPRP and show the calculation of the proposed amount?		
	FORMATS FOR SUBMISSION OF LINE ITEM SUMMARIES		
30. FAR 15.408, Table 15-2, Section III	Are all cost element breakdowns provided using the applicable format prescribed in FAR 15.408, Table 15-2 III? (or alternative format if specified in the request for proposal)		
31. FAR 15.408, Table 15-2, Section III Paragraph B	If the proposal is for a modification or change order, have cost of work deleted (credits) and cost of work added (debits) been provided in the format described in FAR 15.408, Table 15-2.III.B?		
32. FAR 15.408, Table 15-2, Section III Paragraph C	For price revisions/redeterminations, does the proposal follow the format in FAR 15.408, Table 15-2.III.C?		
	OTHER		
33. FAR 16.4	If an incentive contract type, does the proposal include offeror proposed target cost, target profit or fee, share ratio, and, when applicable, minimum/maximum fee, ceiling price?		
34. FAR 16.203-4 and FAR 15.408 Table 15-2, Section II, Paragraphs A, B, C, and D.	If Economic Price Adjustments are being proposed, does the proposal show the rationale and application for the economic price adjustment?		
35. FAR 52.232-28	If the offeror is proposing Performance-Based Payments—did the offeror comply with FAR 52.232-28?		
36. FAR 15.408(n) FAR 52.215-22 FAR 52.215-23	Excessive Pass-through Charges—Identification of Subcontract Effort: If the offeror intends to subcontract more than 70% of the total cost of work to be performed, does the proposal identify: (i) the amount of the offeror's indirect costs and profit applicable to the work to be performed by the proposed subcontractor(s); and (ii) a description of the added value provided by the offeror as related to the work to be performed by the proposed subcontractor(s)?		

(End of provision)

[Final rule, 78 FR 18865, 3/28/2013, effective 3/28/2013; Final rule, 78 FR 65214, 10/31/2013, effective 10/31/2013; Final rule, 79 FR 4633, 1/29/2014, effective 1/29/2014; Final rule, 83 FR 30824, 6/29/2018, effective 6/29/2018]

252.215-7010 Requirements for Certified Cost or Pricing Data and Data Other Than Certified Cost or Pricing Data.

Basic. As prescribed in 215.408(5)(i) and (5)(i)(A), use the following provision:

REQUIREMENTS FOR CERTIFIED COST OR PRICING DATA AND DATA OTHER THAN CERTIFIED COST OR PRICING DATA—BASIC (JUL 2019)

(a) *Definitions*. As used in this provision—

Market prices means current prices that are established in the course of ordinary trade between buyers and sellers free to bargain and that can be substantiated through competition or from sources independent of the offerors.

Non-Government sales means sales of the supplies or services to non-Governmental entities for purposes other than governmental purposes.

Relevant sales data means information provided by an offeror on sales of the same or similar items that can be used to establish price reasonableness taking into consideration the age, volume, and nature of the transactions (including any related discounts, refunds, rebates, offsets, or other adjustments).

Sufficient non-Government sales means relevant sales data that reflects market pricing and contains enough information to make adjustments covered by FAR 15.404-1(b)(2)(ii)(B).

Uncertified cost data means the subset of data other than certified cost or pricing data (see FAR 2.101) that relates to cost.

(b) *Exceptions from certified cost or pricing data.* (1) In lieu of submitting certified cost or pricing data, the Offeror may submit a written request for exception by submitting the information described in paragraphs (b)(1)(i) and (ii) of this provision. The Contracting Officer may require additional supporting information, but only to the extent necessary to determine whether an exception should be granted and whether the price is fair and reasonable.

(i) *Exception for prices set by law or regulation - Identification of the law or regulation establishing the prices offered.* If the prices are controlled under law by periodic rulings, reviews, or similar actions of a governmental body, attach a copy of the controlling document, unless it was previously submitted to the contracting office.

(ii) *Commercial item exception.* For a commercial item exception, the Offeror shall submit, at a minimum, information that is adequate for evaluating the reasonableness of the price for this acquisition, including prices at which the same item or similar items have been sold in the commercial market. Such information shall include—

(A) For items previously determined to be commercial, the contract number and military department, defense agency, or other DoD component that rendered such determination, and if available, a Government point of contact;

(B) For items priced based on a catalog—

(*1*) A copy of or identification of the Offeror's current catalog showing the price for that item; and

(*2*) If the catalog pricing provided with this proposal is not consistent with all relevant sales data, a detailed description of differences or inconsistencies between or among the relevant sales data, the proposed price, and the catalog price (including any related discounts, refunds, rebates, offsets, or other adjustments);

(C) For items priced based on market pricing, a description of the nature of the commercial market, the methodology used to establish a market price, and all relevant sales data. The description shall be adequate to permit the DoD to verify the accuracy of the description;

(D) For items included on an active Federal Supply Service Multiple Award Schedule contract, proof that an exception has been granted for the schedule item; or

(E) For items provided by nontraditional defense contractors, a statement that the entity is not currently performing and has not performed, for at least the 1-year period preceding the solicitation of sources by DoD for the procurement or transaction, any contract or subcontract for DoD that is subject to full coverage under the cost accounting standards prescribed pursuant to 41 U.S.C. 1502 and the regulations implementing such section.

(2) The Offeror grants the Contracting Officer or an authorized representative the right to examine, at any time before award, books, records, documents, or other directly pertinent records to verify any request for an exception under this provision, and to determine the reasonableness of price.

(c) *Requirements for certified cost or pricing data*. If the Offeror is not granted an exception from the requirement to submit certified cost or pricing data, the following applies:

(1) The Offeror shall prepare and submit certified cost or pricing data and supporting attachments in accordance with the instructions contained in Table 15-2 of FAR 15.408, which is incorporated by reference with the same force and effect as though it were inserted here in full text. The instructions in Table 15-2 are incorporated as a mandatory format to be used in any resultant contract, unless the Contracting Officer and the Offeror agree to a different format and change this provision to use Alternate I.

(2) As soon as practicable after agreement on price, but before contract award (except for unpriced actions such as letter contracts), the Offeror shall submit a Certificate of Current Cost or Pricing Data, as prescribed by FAR 15.406-2.

(3) The Offeror is responsible for determining whether a subcontractor qualifies for an exception from the requirement for submission of certified cost or pricing data on the basis of adequate price competition, i.e., two or more responsible offerors, competing independently, submit priced offers that satisfy the Government's expressed requirement in accordance with FAR 15.403-1(c)(1)(i).

(d) *Requirements for data other than certified cost or pricing data*. (1) Data other than certified cost or pricing data submitted in accordance with this provision shall include the minimum information necessary to permit a determination that the proposed price is fair and reasonable, to include the requirements in DFARS 215.402(a)(i) and 215.404-1(b).

(2) In cases in which uncertified cost data is required, the information shall be provided in the form in which it is regularly maintained by the Offeror or prospective subcontractor in its business operations.

(3) Within 10 days of a written request from the Contracting Officer for additional information to permit an adequate evaluation of the proposed price in accordance with FAR 15.403-3, the Offeror shall provide either the requested information, or a written explanation for the inability to fully comply.

(4) *Subcontract price evaluation*. (i) Offerors shall obtain from subcontractors the minimum information necessary to support a determination of price reasonableness, as described in FAR part 15 and DFARS part 215.

(ii) No cost data may be required from a prospective subcontractor in any case in which there are sufficient non-Government sales of the same item to establish reasonableness of price.

(iii) If the Offeror relies on relevant sales data for similar items to determine the price is reasonable, the Offeror shall obtain only that technical information necessary—

(A) To support the conclusion that items are technically similar; and

(B) To explain any technical differences that account for variances between the proposed prices and the sales data presented.

(e) *Subcontracts*. The Offeror shall insert the substance of this provision, including this paragraph (e), in subcontracts exceeding the simplified acquisition threshold defined in FAR part 2. The Offeror shall require prospective subcontractors to adhere to the requirements of—

(1) Paragraphs (c) and (d) of this provision for subcontracts above the threshold for submission of certified cost or pricing data in FAR 15.403-4; and

(2) Paragraph (d) of this provision for subcontracts exceeding the simplified acquisition threshold defined in FAR part 2.

(End of provision)

Alternate I. As prescribed in 215.408(5)(i) and (5)(i)(B), use the following provision, which includes a different paragraph (c)(1).

REQUIREMENTS FOR CERTIFIED COST OR PRICING DATA AND DATA OTHER THAN CERTIFIED COST OR PRICING DATA—ALTERNATE I (JUN 2019)

(a) *Definitions*. As used in this provision—

Market prices means current prices that are established in the course of ordinary trade between buyers and sellers free to bargain and that can be substantiated through competition or from sources independent of the offerors.

Non-Government sales means sales of the supplies or services to non-Governmental entities for purposes other than governmental purposes.

Relevant sales data means information provided by an offeror on sales of the same or similar items that can be used to establish price reasonableness taking into consideration the age, volume, and nature of the transactions (including any related discounts, refunds, rebates, offsets, or other adjustments).

Sufficient non-Government sales means relevant sales data that reflects market pricing and contains enough information to make adjustments covered by FAR 15.404-1(b)(2)(ii)(B).

Uncertified cost data means the subset of data other than certified cost or pricing data (see FAR 2.101) that relates to cost.

(b) *Exceptions from certified cost or pricing data.* (1) In lieu of submitting certified cost or pricing data, the Offeror may submit a written request for exception by submitting the information described in paragraphs (b)(1)(i) and (ii) of this provision. The Contracting Officer may require additional supporting information, but only to the extent necessary to determine whether an exception should be granted and whether the price is fair and reasonable.

(i) *Exception for price set by law or regulation - Identification of the law or regulation establishing the price offered.* If the price is controlled under law by periodic rulings, reviews, or similar actions of a governmental body, attach a copy of the controlling document, unless it was previously submitted to the contracting office.

(ii) *Commercial item exception.* For a commercial item exception, the Offeror shall submit, at a minimum, information that is adequate for evaluating the reasonableness of the price for this acquisition, including prices at which the same item or similar items have been sold in the commercial market. Such information shall include—

(A) For items previously determined to be commercial, the contract number and military department, defense agency, or other DoD component that rendered such determination, and if available, a Government point of contact;

(B) For items priced based on a catalog—

(*1*) A copy of or identification of the Offeror's current catalog showing the price for that item; and

(*2*) If the catalog pricing provided with this proposal is not consistent with all relevant sales data, a detailed description of differences or inconsistencies between or among the relevant sales data, the proposed price, and the catalog price (including any related discounts, refunds, rebates, offsets, or other adjustments);

(C) For items priced based on market pricing, a description of the nature of the commercial market, the methodology used to establish a market price, and all relevant sales data. The description shall be adequate to permit the DoD to verify the accuracy of the description;

(D) For items included on an active Federal Supply Service Multiple Award Schedule contract, proof that an exception has been granted for the schedule item; or

(E) For items provided by nontraditional defense contractors, a statement that the entity is not currently performing and has not performed, for at least the 1-year period preceding the solicitation of sources by the DoD for the procurement or transaction, any contract or subcontract for the DoD that is subject to full coverage under the cost accounting standards prescribed pursuant to 41 U.S.C. 1502 and the regulations implementing such section.

(2) The Offeror grants the Contracting Officer or an authorized representative the right to examine, at any time before award, books, records, documents, or other directly pertinent records to verify any request for an exception under this provision, and to determine the reasonableness of price.

(c) *Requirements for certified cost or pricing data.* If the Offeror is not granted an exception from the requirement to submit certified cost or pricing data, the following applies:

(1) The Offeror shall submit certified cost or pricing data and supporting attachments in the following format: [*Insert description of the data and format that are required, and include access to records necessary to permit an adequate evaluation of the proposed price in accordance with FAR 15.408, Table 15-2, Note 2. The Contracting Officer shall insert the description at the time of issuing the solicitation or specify that the format regularly maintained by the offeror or prospective subcontractor in its business operations will be acceptable. The Contracting Officer may amend the description as the result of negotiations.*]

(2) As soon as practicable after agreement on price, but before contract award (except for unpriced actions such as letter contracts), the Offeror shall submit a Certificate of Current Cost or Pricing Data, as prescribed by FAR 15.406-2.

(3) The Offeror is responsible for determining whether a subcontractor qualifies for an exception from the requirement for submission of certified cost or pricing data on the basis of adequate price competition, i.e., two or more responsible offerors, competing independently, submit priced offers that satisfy the Government's expressed requirement in accordance with FAR 15.403-1(c)(1)(i).

(d) *Requirements for data other than certified cost or pricing data.* (1) Data other than certified cost or pricing data submitted in accordance with this provision shall include all data necessary to permit a determination that the proposed price is fair and reasonable, to include the requirements in DFARS 215.402(a)(i) and 215.404-1(b).

(2) In cases in which uncertified cost data is required, the information shall be provided in the form in which it is regularly maintained by the Offeror or prospective subcontractor in its business operations.

(3) The Offeror shall provide information described as follows: [*Insert description of the data and the format that are required, including access to records necessary to permit an adequate evaluation of the proposed price in accordance with FAR 15.403-3.*]

(4) Within 10 days of a written request from the Contracting Officer for additional information to support proposal analysis, the Offeror shall provide either the requested information, or a written explanation for the inability to fully comply.

(5) *Subcontract price evaluation.* (i) Offerors shall obtain from subcontractors the information necessary to support a determination of price reasonableness, as described in FAR part 15 and DFARS part 215.

(ii) No cost information may be required from a prospective subcontractor in any case in which there are sufficient non-Government sales of the same item to establish reasonableness of price.

(iii) If the Offeror relies on relevant sales data for similar items to determine the price is reasonable, the Offeror shall obtain only that technical information necessary—

(A) To support the conclusion that items are technically similar; and

(B) To explain any technical differences that account for variances between the proposed prices and the sales data presented.

(e) *Subcontracts.* The Offeror shall insert the substance of this provision, including this paragraph (e), in all subcontracts exceeding the simplified acquisition threshold defined in FAR part 2. The Offeror shall require prospective subcontractors to adhere to the requirements of—

(1) Paragraph (c) and (d) of this provision for subcontracts above the threshold for submission of certified cost or pricing data in FAR 15.403-4; and

(2) Paragraph (d) of this provision for subcontracts exceeding the simplified acquisition threshold defined in FAR part 2.

(End of provision)

[Final rule, 83 FR 4431, 1/31/2018, effective 1/31/2018; Final rule, 83 FR 30824, 6/29/2018, effective 6/29/2018; Final rule, 84 FR 30947, 6/28/2019, effective 7/31/2019; Final rule, 84 FR 33858, 7/16/2019, effective 7/31/2019]

252.215-7011 Requirements for Submission of Proposals to the Administrative Contracting Officer and Contract Auditor.

As prescribed in 215.408(5)(ii), use the following provision:

REQUIREMENTS FOR SUBMISSION OF PROPOSALS TO THE ADMINISTRATIVE CONTRACTING OFFICER AND CONTRACT AUDITOR (JAN 2018)

When the proposal is submitted, the Offeror shall also submit one copy each to—

(a) The Administrative Contracting Officer; and

(b) The Contract Auditor.

(End of provision)

[Final rule, 83 FR 4431, 1/31/2018, effective 1/31/2018; Final rule, 83 FR 30824, 6/29/2018, effective 6/29/2018]

252.215-7012 Requirements for Submission of Proposals via Electronic Media.

As prescribed in 215.408(5)(iii), use the following provision:

REQUIREMENTS FOR SUBMISSION OF PROPOSALS VIA ELECTRONIC MEDIA (JAN 2018)

The Offeror shall submit the cost portion of the proposal via the following electronic media: [*Insert media format, e.g., electronic spreadsheet format, electronic mail, etc.*]

(End of provision)

[Final rule, 83 FR 4431, 1/31/2018, effective 1/31/2018; Final rule, 83 FR 30824, 6/29/2018, effective 6/29/2018]

252.215-7013 Supplies and Services Provided by Nontraditional Defense Contractors.

As prescribed in 215.408(6), use the following provision:

SUPPLES AND SERVICES PROVIDED BY NONTRADITIONAL DEFENSE CONTRACTORS (JAN 2018)

Offerors are advised that in accordance with 10 U.S.C. 2380a, supplies and services provided by a nontraditional defense contractor, as defined in DFARS 212.001, may be treated as commercial items. The decision to apply commercial item procedures to the procurement of supplies and services from a nontraditional defense contractor does not require a commercial item determination and does not mean the supplies or services are commercial.

(End of provision)

[Final rule, 83 FR 4431, 1/31/2018, effective 1/31/2018; Final rule, 83 FR 30824, 6/29/2018, effective 6/29/2018]

252.215-7014 Exception from Certified Cost or Pricing Data Requirements for Foreign Military Sales Indirect Offsets.

As prescribed in 215.408(8), use the following clause:

EXCEPTION FROM CERTIFIED COST OR PRICING DATA REQUIREMENTS FOR FOREIGN MILITARY SALES INDIRECT OFFSETS (JUN 2018)

(a) *Definition.* As used in this clause—

Offset means a benefit or obligation agreed to by a contractor and a foreign government or international organization as an inducement or condition to purchase supplies or services pursuant to a foreign military sale (FMS). There are two types of offsets: direct offsets and indirect offsets.

(i) A direct offset involves benefits or obligations, including supplies or services that are directly related to the item being purchased and are integral to the deliverable of the FMS contract. For example, as a condition of a foreign military sale, the contractor may require or agree to permit the customer to produce in its country certain components or subsystems of the item being sold. Generally, direct offsets must be performed within a specified period, because they are integral to the deliverable of the FMS contract.

(ii) An indirect offset involves benefits or obligations, including supplies or services that are not directly related to the specific item(s) being purchased and are not integral to the deliverable of the FMS contract. For example, as a condition of a foreign military sale, the contractor may agree to purchase certain manufactured products, agricultural commodities, raw materials, or services, or make an equity investment or grant of equipment required by the FMS customer, or may agree to build a school, road or other facility. Indirect offsets would also include projects that are related to the FMS contract but not purchased under said contract (e.g., a project to develop or advance a capability, technology transfer, or know-how in a foreign company). Indirect offsets may be accomplished without a clearly defined period of performance.

(b) *Exceptions from certified cost or pricing data requirements.* Notwithstanding the requirements of Federal Acquisition Regulation (FAR) 52.215-20, Requirements for Certified Cost or Pricing Data and Data Other Than Certified Cost or Pricing Data, in the case of this contract or a subcontract, and FAR 52.215-21, Requirements for Certified Cost or Pricing Data and Data Other Than Certified Cost or Pricing Data-Modifications, in the case of modification of this contract or a subcontract, submission of certified cost or pricing data shall not be required to the extent such data relates to an indirect offset (10 U.S.C. 2306a(b)(1)).

(End of provision)

[Final rule, 83 FR 30825, 6/29/2018, effective 6/29/2018]

252.215-7015 Program Should-Cost Review.

As prescribed in 215.408(8), use the following clause:

PROGRAM SHOULD-COST REVIEW (NOV 2019)

(a) The Government has the right to perform a program should-cost review, as described in Federal Acquisition Regulation (FAR) 15.407-4(b). The review may be conducted in support of a particular contract proposal or during contract performance to find opportunities to reduce program costs. The Government will communicate the elements of the proposed should-cost review to the prime contractor (Pub. L. 115-91).

(b) If the Government performs a program should-cost review, upon the Government's request, the Contractor shall provide access to accurate and complete cost data and Contractor facilities and personnel necessary to permit the Government to perform the program should-cost review.

(c) The Government has the right to use third-party experts to supplement the program should-cost review team. The Contractor shall provide access to the Contractor's facilities and information necessary to support the program should-cost review to any third-party experts who have signed non-disclosure agreements in accordance with the FAR 52.203-16.

(End of provision)

[Final rule, 84 FR 65308, 11/27/2019, effective 11/27/2019]

252.216 Types of Contracts, provisions and clauses for DFARS Part 216

252.216-7000 Economic price adjustment—basic steel, aluminum, brass, bronze, or copper mill products.

As prescribed in 216.203-4-70(a)(1), use the following clause:

ECONOMIC PRICE ADJUSTMENT—BASIC STEEL, ALUMINUM, BRASS, BRONZE, OR COPPER MILL PRODUCTS (MAR 2012)

(a) *Definitions.*

As used in this clause—

Established price means a price which is an established catalog or market price for a commercial item sold in substantial quantities to the general public.

Unit price excludes any part of the price which reflects requirements for preservation, packaging, and packing beyond standard commercial practice.

(b) As represented by the Contractor in its offer, the unit price stated for __________ (*Identify the item*) is not in excess of the Contractor's established price in effect on the date set for opening of bids (or the contract date if this is a negotiated contract) for like quantities of the same item. This price is the net price after applying any applicable standard trade discounts offered by the Contractor from its catalog, list, or schedule price.

(c) The Contractor shall promptly notify the Contracting Officer of the amount and effective date of each decrease in any established price.

(1) Each corresponding contract unit price shall be decreased by the same percentage that the established price is decreased.

(2) This decrease shall apply to items delivered on or after the effective date of the decrease in the Contractor's established price.

(3) This contract shall be modified accordingly.

(d) If the Contractor's established price is increased after the date set for opening of bids (or the contract date if this is a negotiated contract), upon the Contractor's written request to the Contracting Officer, the corresponding contract unit price shall be increased by the same percentage that the established price is increased, and this contract shall be modified accordingly, provided—

(1) The aggregate of the increases in any contract unit price under this contract shall not exceed 10 percent of the original contract unit price;

(2) The increased contract unit price shall be effective on the effective date of the increase in the applicable established price if the Contractor's written request is received by the Contracting Officer within ten days of the change. If it is not, the effective date of the increased unit price shall be the date of receipt of the request by the Contracting Officer; and

(3) The increased contract unit price shall not apply to quantities scheduled for delivery before the effective date of the increased contract unit price unless the Contractor's failure to deliver before that date results from causes beyond the control and without the fault or negligence of the Contractor, within the meaning of the Default clause of this contract.

(4) The Contracting Officer shall not execute a modification incorporating an increase in a contract unit price under this clause until the increase is verified.

(e) Within 30 days after receipt of the Contractor's written request, the Contracting Officer may cancel, without liability to either party, any portion of the contract affected by the requested increase and not delivered at the time of such cancellation, except as follows—

(1) The Contractor may, after that time, deliver any items that were completed or in the process of manufacture at the time of receipt of the cancellation notice, provided the Contractor notifies the Contracting Officer of such items within 10 days after the Contractor receives the cancellation notice.

(2) The Government shall pay for those items at the contract unit price increased to the extent provided by paragraph (d) of this clause.

(3) Any standard steel supply item shall be deemed to be in the process of manufacture when the steel for that item is in the state of processing after the beginning of the furnace melt.

(f) Pending any cancellation of this contract under paragraph (e) of this clause, or if there is no cancellation, the Contractor shall continue deliveries according to the delivery schedule of the contract. The Contractor shall be paid for those deliveries at the contract unit price increased to the extent provided by paragraph (d) of this clause.

(End of clause)

[Final rule, 62 FR 2612, 1/17/97, effective 1/17/97; Final rule, 62 FR 40471, 7/29/97, effective 7/29/97; Final rule, 77 FR 19128, 3/30/2012, effective 3/30/2012]

252.216-7001 Economic price adjustment—Nonstandard steel items.

As prescribed in 216.203-4-70(b), use the following clause:

ECONOMIC PRICE ADJUSTMENT—NONSTANDARD STEEL ITEMS (JUL 1997)

(a) *Definitions.*

As used in this clause—

Base labor index means the average of the labor indices for the three months which consist of the month of bid opening (or offer submission) and the months immediately preceding and following that month.

Base steel index means the Contractor's established price (see note 6) including all applicable extras of $____ per ____ (see note 1) for ____ (see note 2) on the date set for bid opening (or the date of submission of the offer).

Current labor index means the average of the labor indices for the month in which delivery of supplies is required to be made and the month preceding.

Current steel index means the Contractor's established price (see note 6) for that item, including all applicable extras in effect ____ days (see note 3) prior to the first day of the month in which delivery is required.

Established price is—

(1) A price which is an established catalog or market price of a commercial item sold in substantial quantities to the general public; and

(2) The net price after applying any applicable standard trade discounts offered by the Contractor from its catalog, list, or schedule price. (But see Note 6.)

Labor index means the average straight time hourly earnings of the Contractor's employees in the ____ shop of the Contractor's ____ plant (see note 4) for any particular month.

Month means calendar month. However, if the Contractor's accounting period does not coincide with the calendar month, then that accounting period shall be used in lieu of *month*.

(b) Each contract unit price shall be subject to revision, under the terms of this clause, to reflect changes in the cost of labor and steel. For purpose of this price revision, the proportion of the contract unit price attributable to costs of labor not otherwise included in the price of the steel item identified under the *base steel index* definition in paragraph (a) shall be ____ percent, and the proportion of the contract unit price attributable to the cost of steel shall be ____ percent. (See note 5.)

(c)(1) Unless otherwise specified in this contract, the labor index shall be computed by dividing the total straight time earnings of the Contractor's employees in the shop identified in paragraph (a) for any given month by the total number of straight time hours worked by those employees in that month.

(2) Any revision in a contract unit price to reflect changes in the cost of labor shall be computed solely by reference to the *base labor index* and the *current labor index*.

(d) Any revision in a contract unit price to reflect changes in the cost of steel shall be computed solely by reference to the *base steel index* and the *current steel index*.

(e)(1) Each contract unit price shall be revised for each month in which delivery of supplies is required to be made.

(2) The revised contract unit price shall apply to the deliveries of those quantities required to be made in that month regardless of when actual delivery is made.

(3) Each revised contract unit price shall be computed by adding—

(i) The adjusted cost of labor (obtained by multiplying ____ percent of the contract unit price by a fraction, of which the numerator shall be the current labor index and the denominator shall be the base labor index);

(ii) The adjusted cost of steel (obtained by multiplying ____ percent of the contract unit price by a fraction, of which the numerator shall be the current steel index and the denominator shall be the base steel index); and

(iii) The amount equal to ____ percent of the original contract unit price (representing that portion of the unit price which relates neither to the cost of labor nor the cost of steel, and which is therefore not subject to revision (see note 5)).

(4) The aggregate of the increases in any contract unit price under this contract shall not exceed ten percent of the original contract unit price.

(5) Computations shall be made to the nearest one-hundredth of one cent.

(f) (1) Pending any revisions of the contract unit prices, the Contractor shall be paid the contract unit price for deliveries made.

(2) Within 30 days after final delivery (or such other period as may be authorized by the Contracting Officer), the Contractor shall furnish a statement identifying the correctness of—

(i) The average straight time hourly earnings of the Contractor's employees in the shop identified in paragraph (a) that are relevant to the computations of the *base labor index* and the *current labor index; and*

(ii) The Contractor's established prices (see note 6), including all applicable extras for like quantities of the item that are relevant to the computation of the *base steel index* and the *current steel index.*

(3) Upon request of the Contracting Officer, the Contractor shall make available all records used in the computation of the labor indices.

(4) Upon receipt of the statement, the Contracting Officer will compute the revised contract unit prices and modify the contract accordingly. No modification to this contract will be made pursuant to this clause until the Contracting Officer has verified the revised established price (see note 6).

(g) (1) In the event any item of this contract is subject to a total or partial termination for convenience, the month in which the Contractor receives notice of the termination, if prior to the month in which delivery is required, shall be considered the month in which delivery of the terminated item is required for the purposes of determining the current labor and steel indices under paragraphs (c) and (d).

(2) For any item which is not terminated for convenience, the month in which delivery is required under the contract shall continue to apply for determining those indices with respect to the quantity of the non-terminated item.

(3) If this contract is terminated for default, any price revision shall be limited to the quantity of the item which has been delivered by the Contractor and accepted by the Government prior to receipt by the Contractor of the notice of termination.

(h) If the Contractor's failure to make delivery of any required quantity arises out of causes beyond the control and without the fault or negligence of the Contractor, within the meaning of the clause of this contract entitled *Default*, the quantity not delivered shall be delivered as promptly as possible after the cessation of the cause of the failure, and the delivery schedule set forth in this contract shall be amended accordingly.

Notes:

1 Offeror insert the unit price and unit measure of the standard steel mill item to be used in the manufacture of the contract item.

2 Offeror identify the standard steel mill item to be used in the manufacture of the contract item.

3 Offeror insert best estimate of the number of days required for processing the standard steel mill item in the shop identified under the *labor index* definition.

4 Offeror identify the shop and plant in which the standard steel mill item identified under the *base steel index* definition will be finally fabricated or processed into the contract item.

5 Offeror insert the same percentage figures for the corresponding blanks in paragraphs (b), (e) (3) (i), and (e) (3) (ii). In paragraph (e) (3) (iii), insert the percentage representing the difference between the sum of the percentages inserted in paragraph (b) and 100 percent.

6 In negotiated acquisitions of nonstandard steel items, when there is no *established price* or when it is not desirable to use this price, this paragraph may refer to another appropriate price basis, *e.g.*, an established interplant price.

(End of clause)

[Final rule, 62 FR 2612, 1/17/97, effective 1/17/97; Final rule, 62 FR 40471, 7/29/97, effective 7/29/97]

252.216-7002 Alternate A, Time-and-Materials/Labor-Hour Proposal Requirements—Non-Commercial

DFARS 252.216-7002

Item Acquisition with Adequate Price Competition.

As prescribed in 216.601(e), substitute the following paragraph (c) for paragraph (c) of the provision at 52.216-29:

ALTERNATE A, TIME-AND-MATERIALS/ LABOR-HOUR PROPOSAL REQUIREMENTS—NON-COMMERCIAL ITEM ACQUISITION WITH ADEQUATE PRICE COMPETITION (FEB 2007)

(c) The offeror must establish fixed hourly rates using separate rates for each category of labor to be performed by each subcontractor and for each category of labor to be performed by the offeror, and for each category of labor to be transferred between divisions, subsidiaries, or affiliates of the offeror under a common control.

[Removed and reserved, DAC 91-12, 62 FR 34114, 6/24/97, effective 6/24/97; Interim rule, 71 FR 74469, 12/12/2006, effective 2/12/2007; Final rule, 72 FR 51189, 9/6/2007, effective 9/6/2007]

252.216-7003 Economic price adjustment—wage rates or material prices controlled by a foreign government.

As prescribed in 216.203-4-70(c)(1), use the following clause:

ECONOMIC PRICE ADJUSTMENT—WAGE RATES OR MATERIAL PRICES CONTROLLED BY A FOREIGN GOVERNMENT (MAR 2012)

(a) As represented by the Contractor in its offer, the prices set forth in this contract—

(1) Are based on the wage rates or material prices established and controlled by the government of the country specified by the Contractor in its offer; and

(2) Do not include contingency allowances to pay for possible increases in wage rates or material prices.

(b) If wage rates or material prices are revised by the government named in paragraph (a) of this clause, the Contracting Officer shall make an equitable adjustment in the contract price and shall modify the contract to the extent that the Contractor's actual costs of performing this contract are increased or decreased, as a direct result of the revision, subject to the following:

(1) For increases in established wage rates or material prices, the increase in contract unit price(s) shall be effective on the same date that the government named in paragraph (a) of this clause increased the applicable wage rate(s) or material price(s), but only if the Contracting Officer receives the Contractor's written request for contract adjustment within 10 days of the change. If the Contractor's request is received later, the effective date shall be the date that the Contracting Officer received the Contractor's request.

(2) For decreases in established wage rates or material prices, the decrease in contract unit price(s) shall be effective on the same date that the government named in paragraph (a) of this clause decreased the applicable wage rate(s) or material price(s). The decrease in contract unit price(s) shall apply to all items delivered on and after the effective date of the governments rate or price decrease.

(c) No modification changing the contract unit price(s) shall be executed until the Contracting Officer has verified the applicable change in the rates or prices set by the government named in paragraph (a) of this clause. The Contractor shall make available its books and records that support a requested change in contract price.

(d) Failure to agree to any adjustment shall be a dispute under the Disputes clause of this contract.

(End of clause)

[DAC 91-12, 62 FR 34114, 6/24/97, effective 6/24/97; Final rule, 77 FR 19128, 3/30/2012, effective 3/30/2012]

252.216-7004 Award Fee Reduction or Denial for Jeopardizing the Health or Safety of Government Personnel.

As prescribed in 216.406(e), use the following clause:

AWARD FEE REDUCTION OR DENIAL FOR JEOPARDIZING THE HEALTH OR SAFETY

OF GOVERNMENT PERSONNEL (SEP 2011)

(a) *Definitions*. As used in this clause—

Covered incident—

(i) Means any incident in which the Contractor, through a criminal, civil, or administrative proceeding that results in a disposition listed in paragraph (a)(ii) of this definition—

(A) Has been determined in the performance of this contract to have caused serious bodily injury or death of any civilian or military personnel of the Government through gross negligence or with reckless disregard for the safety of such personnel; or

(B) Has been determined to be liable for actions of a subcontractor of the Contractor that caused serious bodily injury or death of any civilian or military personnel of the Government through gross negligence or with reckless disregard for the safety of such personnel.

(ii) Includes those incidents that have resulted in any of the following dispositions:

(A) In a criminal proceeding, a conviction.

(B) In a civil proceeding, a finding of fault or liability that results in the payment of a monetary fine, penalty, reimbursement, restitution, or damage of $5,000 or more.

(C) In an administrative proceeding, a finding of fault and liability that results in—

(*1*) The payment of a monetary fine or penalty of $5,000 or more; or

(*2*) The payment of a reimbursement, restitution, or damages in excess of $100,000.

(D) In a criminal, civil, or administrative proceeding, a disposition of the matter by consent or compromise with an acknowledgment of fault by the Contractor if the proceeding could have led to any of the outcomes specified in subparagraphs (a)(ii)(A), (a)(ii)

(B), or (a)(ii)(C).

(E) In a DoD investigation of the Contractor or its subcontractors at any tier not subject to the jurisdiction of the U.S. courts, a final determination by the Secretary of Defense of Contractor or subcontractor fault (see DFARS 216.405-2-70.

Serious bodily injury means a grievous physical harm that results in a permanent disability.

(b) If, in the performance of this contract, the Contractor's or its subcontractor's actions cause serious bodily injury or death of civilian or military Government personnel, the Government may reduce or deny the award fee for the period in which the covered incident occurred, including the recovery of all or part of any award fees paid for any previous period during which the covered incident occurred.

(End of clause)

[Interim rule, 75 FR 69360, 11/12/2010, effective 11/12/2010; Final rule, 76 FR 21812, 4/19/2011, effective 4/19/2011; Interim rule, 76 FR 57674, 9/16/2011, effective 9/16/2011; Final rule, 77 FR 11354, 2/24/2012, effective 2/24/2012; Final rule, 83 FR 49180, 9/28/2018, effective 9/28/2018]

252.216-7005 [Removed and Reserved]

[Final rule, 76 FR 8303, 2/14/2011, effective 2/14/2011; Final rule, 83 FR 49180, 9/28/2018, effective 9/28/2018]

252.216-7006 Ordering.

As prescribed in 216.506(a), use the following clause:

ORDERING (SEP 2019)

(a) Any supplies and services to be furnished under this contract shall be ordered by issuance of delivery orders or task orders by the individuals or activities designated in the contract schedule. Such orders may be issued from ________ through ________ [*insert dates*].

(b) All delivery orders or task orders are subject to the terms and conditions of this contract. In the event of conflict between a delivery order or task order and this contract, the contract shall control.

(c)(1) If issued electronically, the order is considered "issued" when a copy has been posted to the Electronic Data Access system, and notice has been sent to the Contractor.

(2) If mailed or transmitted by facsimile, a delivery order or task order is considered "issued" when the Government deposits the order in the mail or transmits by facsimile. Mailing includes transmittal by U.S. mail or private delivery services.

(3) Orders may be issued orally only if authorized in the schedule.

(End of clause)

[Final rule, 76 FR 25566, 5/5/2011, effective 5/5/2011; Final rule, 84 FR 48510, 9/13/2019, effective 9/13/2019]

252.216-7007 Economic price adjustment—basic steel, aluminum, brass, bronze, or copper mill products-representation.

As prescribed in 216.203-4-70(a)(2), use the following provision:

ECONOMIC PRICE ADJUSTMENT—BASIC STEEL, ALUMINUM, BRASS, BRONZE, OR COPPER MILL PRODUCTS—REPRESENTATION (MAR 2012)

(a) *Definitions.* The terms *established price* and *unit price,* as used in this provision, have the meaning given in the clause 252.216-7000, Economic Price Adjustment—Basic Steel, Aluminum, Brass, Bronze, or Copper Mill Products.

(b) By submission of its offer, the offeror represents that the unit price stated in this offer for __________*(Identify the item)* is not in excess of the offeror's established price in effect on the date set for opening of bids (or the contract date if this is to be a negotiated contract) for like quantities of the same item. This price is the net price after applying any applicable standard trade discounts offered by the offeror from its catalog, list, or schedule price.

(End of provision)

[Final rule, 77 FR 19128, 3/30/2012, effective 3/30/2012]

252.216-7008 Economic price adjustment—wage rates or material prices controlled by a foreign government—representation.

As prescribed in 216.203-4-70(c)(2), use the following provision:

ECONOMIC PRICE ADJUSTMENT—WAGE RATES OR MATERIAL PRICES CONTROLLED BY A FOREIGN GOVERNMENT—REPRESENTATION (MAR 2012)

(a) By submission of its offer, the offeror represents that the prices set forth in this offer—

(1) Are based on the wage rate(s) or material price(s) established and controlled by the government of __________*(Offeror insert name of host country)*; and

(2) Do not include contingency allowances to pay for possible increases in wage rates or material prices.

(End of provision)

[Final rule, 77 FR 19128, 3/30/2012, effective 3/30/2012]

252.216-7009 Allowability of legal costs incurred in connection with a whistleblower proceeding.

As prescribed in 216.307(a), use the following clause:

ALLOWABILITY OF LEGAL COSTS INCURRED IN CONNECTION WITH A WHISTLEBLOWER PROCEEDING (SEP 2013)

Pursuant to section 827 of the National Defense Authorization Act for Fiscal year 2013 (Pub. L. 112-239), notwithstanding FAR clause 52.216-7, Allowable Cost and Payment—

(1) The restrictions of FAR 31.205-47(b) on allowability of costs related to legal and other proceedings also apply to any proceeding brought by a contractor employee submitting a complaint under 10 U.S.C. 2409, entitled "Contractor employees: protection from reprisal for disclosure of certain information;" and

(2) Costs incurred in connection with a proceeding that is brought by a contractor employee submitting a complaint under 10 U.S.C. 2409 are also unallowable if the result

is an order to take corrective action under 10 U.S.C. 2409.

(End of clause)

[Interim rule, 78 FR 59859, 9/30/2013, effective 9/30/2013; Final rule, 80 FR 36719, 6/26/2015, effective 6/26/2015]

252.216-7010 [Removed]

[Final rule, 79 FR 22036, 4/21/2014, effective 4/21/2014; Final rule, 80 FR 36897, 6/26/2015, effective 6/26/2015; Final rule, 83 FR 30587, 6/29/2018, effective 6/29/2018]

252.217 Special Contracting Methods, provisions and clauses for DFARS Part 217

252.217-7000 Exercise of option to fulfill foreign military sales commitments.

Basic. As prescribed in 217.208-70(a) and (a)(1), use the following clause:

EXERCISE OF OPTION TO FULFILL FOREIGN MILITARY SALES COMMITMENTS—BASIC (NOV 2014)

(a) The Government may exercise the option(s) of this contract to fulfill foreign military sales commitments.

(b) The foreign military sales commitments are for:

____

(Insert name of country)

____

(Insert applicable CLIN)

(End of clause)

Alternate I. As prescribed in 217.208-70(a) and (a)(2), substitute the following paragraph (b) for paragraph (b) of the basic clause:

EXERCISE OF OPTION TO FULFILL FOREIGN MILITARY SALES COMMITMENTS—ALTERNATE I (NOV 2014)

(a) The Government may exercise the option(s) of this contract to fulfill foreign military sales commitments.

(b) On the date the option is exercised, the Government shall identify the foreign country for the purpose of negotiating any equitable adjustment attributable to foreign military sales. Failure to agree on an equitable adjustment shall be treated as a dispute under the Disputes clause of this contract.

(End of clause)

[Final rule, 79 FR 65592, 11/5/2014, effective 11/5/2014; Final rule, 80 FR 36897, 6/26/2015, effective 6/26/2015]

252.217-7001 Surge option.

As prescribed in 217.208-70(a)(2), use the following clause, which uses a different paragraph (b) than paragraph (b) of the basic clause:

SURGE OPTION (DEC 2018)

(a) *General*. The Government has the option to—

(1) Increase the quantity of supplies or services called for under this contract by no more than ____ percent or ____ [*insert quantity and description of services or supplies to be increased*]; and/or

(2) Accelerate the rate of delivery called for under this contract, at a price or cost established before contract award or to be established by negotiation as provided in this clause.

(b) *Schedule*. (1) When the Capabilities Analysis Plan (CAP) is included in the contract, the option delivery schedule shall be the production rate provided with the Plan. If the Plan was negotiated before contract award, then the negotiated schedule shall be used.

(2) If there is no CAP in the contract, the Contractor shall, within 30 days from the date of award, furnish the Contracting Officer a delivery schedule showing the maximum sustainable rate of delivery for items in this contract. This delivery schedule shall provide acceleration by month up to the

maximum sustainable rate of delivery achievable within the Contractor's existing facilities, equipment, and subcontracting structure.

(3) The Contractor shall not revise the option delivery schedule without approval from the Contracting Officer.

(c) *Exercise of option.* (1) The Contracting Officer may exercise this option at any time before acceptance by the Government of the final scheduled delivery.

(2) The Contracting Officer will provide a preliminary oral or written notice to the Contractor stating the quantities to be added or accelerated under the terms of this clause, followed by a contract modification incorporating the transmitted information and instructions. The notice and modification will establish a not-to-exceed price equal to the highest contract unit price or cost of the added or accelerated items as of the date of the notice.

(3) The Contractor will not be required to deliver at a rate greater than the maximum sustainable delivery rate under paragraph (b)(2) of this clause, nor will the exercise of this option extend delivery more than 24 months beyond the scheduled final delivery.

(d) *Price negotiation.* (1) Unless the option cost or price was previously agreed upon, the Contractor shall, within 30 days from the date of option exercise, submit to the Contracting Officer a cost or price proposal (including a cost breakdown) for the added or accelerated items.

(2) Failure to agree on a cost or price in negotiations resulting from the exercise of this option shall constitute a dispute concerning a question of fact within the meaning of the Disputes clause of this contract. However, nothing in this clause shall excuse the Contractor from proceeding with the performance of the contract, as modified, while any resulting claim is being settled.

(End of clause)

[DAC 91-3, 57 FR 42633, 9/15/92, effective 8/31/92; Final rule, 83 FR 62502, 12/4/2018, effective 12/4/2018]

252.217-7002 Offering property for exchange.

As prescribed in 217.7005, use the following provision:

OFFERING PROPERTY FOR EXCHANGE (JUN 2012)

(a) The property described in item number ____, is being offered in accordance with the exchange provisions of 40 U.S.C. 503.

(b) The property is located at (insert address). Offerors may inspect the property during the period (insert beginning and ending dates and insert hours during day).

(End of provision)

[DAC 91-3, 57 FR 42633, 9/15/92, effective 8/31/92; Final rule, 77 FR 35879, 6/15/2012, effective 6/15/2012]

252.217-7003 Changes.

As prescribed in 217.7104(a), use the following clause:

CHANGES (DEC 1991)

(a) The Contracting Officer may, at any time and without notice to the sureties, by written change order, make changes within the general scope of any job order issued under the Master Agreement in—

(1) Drawings, designs, plans, and specifications;

(2) Work itemized;

(3) Place of performance of the work;

(4) Time of commencement or completion of the work; and

(5) Any other requirement of the job order.

(b) If a change causes an increase or decrease in the cost of, or time required for, performance of the job order, whether or not changed by the order, the Contracting Officer shall make an equitable adjustment in the price or date of completion, or both, and shall modify the job order in writing.

(1) Within ten days after the Contractor receives notification of the change, the Contractor shall submit to the Contracting Officer a request for price adjustment, together with a written estimate of the increased cost.

(2) The Contracting Officer may grant an extension of this period if the Contractor requests it within the ten day period.

(3) If the circumstances justify it, the Contracting Officer may accept and grant a request for equitable adjustment at any later time prior to final payment under the job order, except that the Contractor may not receive profit on a payment under a late request.

(c) If the Contractor includes in its claim the cost of property made obsolete or excess as a result of a change, the Contracting Officer shall have the right to prescribe the manner of disposition of that property.

(d) Failure to agree to any adjustment shall be a dispute within the meaning of the Disputes clause.

(e) Nothing in this clause shall excuse the Contractor from proceeding with the job order as changed.

(End of clause)

[Final rule, 75 FR 48278, 8/10/2010, effective 8/10/2010; Final rule, 75 FR 49849, 8/16/2010, effective 8/16/2010]

252.217-7004 Job orders and compensation.

As prescribed in 217.7104(a), use the following clause:

JOB ORDERS AND COMPENSATION (MAY 2006)

(a) The Contracting Officer shall solicit bids or proposals and make award of job orders. The issuance of a job order signed by the Contracting Officer constitutes award. The job order shall incorporate the terms and conditions of the Master Agreement.

(b) Whenever the Contracting Officer determines that a vessel, its cargo or stores, would be endangered by delay, or whenever the Contracting Officer determines that military necessity requires that immediate work on a vessel is necessary, the Contracting Officer may issue a written order to perform that work and the Contractor hereby agrees to comply with that order and to perform work on such vessel within its capabilities.

(1) As soon as practicable after the issuance of the order, the Contracting Officer and the Contractor shall negotiate a price for the work and the Contracting Officer shall issue a job order covering the work.

(2) The Contractor shall, upon request, furnish the Contracting Officer with a breakdown of costs incurred by the Contractor and an estimate of costs expected to be incurred in the performance of the work. The Contractor shall maintain, and make available for inspection by the Contracting Officer or the Contracting Officer's representative, records supporting the cost of performing the work.

(3) Failure of the parties to agree upon the price of the work shall constitute a dispute within the meaning of the Disputes clause of the Master Agreement. In the meantime, the Contractor shall diligently proceed to perform the work ordered.

(c) (1) If the nature of any repairs is such that their extent and probable cost cannot be ascertained readily, the Contracting Officer may issue a job order (on a sealed bid or negotiated basis) to determine the nature and extent of required repairs.

(2) Upon determination by the Contracting Officer of what work is necessary, the Contractor, if requested by the Contracting Officer, shall negotiate prices for performance of that work. The prices agreed upon shall be set forth in a modification of the job order.

(3) Failure of the parties to agree upon the price shall constitute a dispute under the Disputes clause. In the meantime, the Contractor shall diligently proceed to perform the work ordered.

(End of clause)

[Final rule, 71 FR 27642, 5/12/2006, effective 5/12/2006; Final rule, 75 FR 48278, 8/10/2010, effective 8/10/2010; Final rule, 75 FR 49849, 8/16/2010, effective 8/16/2010]

252.217-7005 Inspection and manner of doing work.

As prescribed in 217.7104(a), use the following clause:

INSPECTION AND MANNER OF DOING WORK (JUL 2009)

(a) The Contractor shall perform work in accordance with the job order, any drawings and specifications made a part of the job order, and any change or modification issued under the Changes clause of the Master Agreement.

(b)(1) Except as provided in paragraph (b)(2) of this clause, and unless otherwise specifically provided in the job order, all operational practices of the Contractor and all workmanship, material, equipment, and articles used in the performance of work under the Master Agreement shall be in accordance with the best commercial marine practices and the rules and requirements of the American Bureau of Shipping, the U.S. Coast Guard, and the Institute of Electrical and Electronic Engineers, in effect at the time of Contractor's submission of bid (or acceptance of the job order, if negotiated).

(2) When Navy specifications are specified in the job order, the Contractor shall follow Navy standards of material and workmanship. The solicitation shall prescribe the Navy standard whenever applicable.

(c) The Government may inspect and test all material and workmanship at any time during the Contractor's performance of the work.

(1) If, prior to delivery, the Government finds any material or workmanship is defective or not in accordance with the job order, in addition to its rights under the Guarantees clause of the Master Agreement, the Government may reject the defective or nonconforming material or workmanship and require the Contractor to correct or replace it at the Contractor's expense.

(2) If the Contractor fails to proceed promptly with the replacement or correction of the material or workmanship, the Government may replace or correct the defective or nonconforming material or workmanship and charge the Contractor the excess costs incurred.

(3) As specified in the job order, the Contractor shall provide and maintain an inspection system acceptable to the Government.

(4) The Contractor shall maintain complete records of all inspection work and shall make them available to the Government during performance of the job order and for 90 days after the completion of all work required.

(d) The Contractor shall not permit any welder to work on a vessel unless the welder is, at the time of the work, qualified to the standards established by the U.S. Coast Guard, American Bureau of Shipping, or Department of the Navy for the type of welding being performed. Qualifications of a welder shall be as specified in the job order.

(e) The Contractor shall—

(1) Exercise reasonable care to protect the vessel from fire;

(2) Maintain a reasonable system of inspection over activities taking place in the vicinity of the vessel's magazines, fuel oil tanks, or storerooms containing flammable materials;

(3) Maintain a reasonable number of hose lines ready for immediate use on the vessel at all times while the vessel is berthed alongside the Contractor's pier or in dry dock or on a marine railway;

(4) Unless otherwise provided in a job order, provide sufficient security patrols to reasonably maintain a fire watch for protection of the vessel when it is in the Contractor's custody;

(5) To the extent necessary, clean, wash, and steam out or otherwise make safe, all tanks under alteration or repair;

(6) Furnish the Contracting Officer or designated representative with a copy of the "gas-free" or "safe-for-hotwork" certificate, provided by a Marine Chemist or Coast Guard authorized person in accordance with Occupational Safety and Health Administration regulations (29 CFR 1915.14) before any hot work is done on a tank;

(7) Treat the contents of any tank as Government property in accordance with the Government Property clause; and

(8) Dispose of the contents of any tank only at the direction, or with the concurrence, of the Contracting Officer.

(f) Except as otherwise provided in the job order, when the vessel is in the custody of the Contractor or in dry dock or on a marine railway and the temperature is expected to go as low as 35 F, the Contractor shall take all necessary steps to—

(1) Keep all hose pipe lines, fixtures, traps, tanks, and other receptacles on the vessel from freezing; and

(2) Protect the stern tube and propeller hubs from frost damage.

(g) The Contractor shall, whenever practicable—

(1) Perform the required work in a manner that will not interfere with the berthing and messing of Government personnel attached to the vessel; and

(2) Provide Government personnel attached to the vessel access to the vessel at all times.

(h) Government personnel attached to the vessel shall not interfere with the Contractor's work or workers.

(i) (1) The Government does not guarantee the correctness of the dimensions, sizes, and shapes set forth in any job order, sketches, drawings, plans, or specifications prepared or furnished by the Government, unless the job order requires that the Contractor perform the work prior to any opportunity to inspect.

(2) Except as stated in paragraph (i) (1) of this clause, and other than those parts furnished by the Government, the Contractor shall be responsible for the correctness of the dimensions, sizes, and shapes of parts furnished under this agreement.

(j) The Contractor shall at all times keep the site of the work on the vessel free from accumulation of waste material or rubbish caused by its employees or the work. At the completion of the work, unless the job order specifies otherwise, the Contractor shall remove all rubbish from the site of the work and leave the immediate vicinity of the work area "broom clean."

(End of clause)

[Final rule, 62 FR 2612, 1/17/97, effective 1/17/97; Final rule, 74 FR 37645, 7/29/2009, effective 7/29/2009]

252.217-7006 Title.

As prescribed in 217.7104(a), use the following clause:

TITLE (DEC 1991)

(a) Unless otherwise provided, title to all materials and equipment to be incorporated in a vessel in the performance of a job order shall vest in the Government upon delivery at the location specified for the performance of the work.

(b) Upon completion of the job order, or with the approval of the Contracting Officer during performance of the job order, all Contractor-furnished materials and equipment not incorporated in, or placed on, any vessel, shall become the property of the Contractor, unless the Government has reimbursed the Contractor for the cost of the materials and equipment.

(c) The vessel, its equipment, movable stores, cargo, or other ship's materials shall not be considered Government-furnished property.

(End of clause)

252.217-7007 Payments.

As prescribed in 217.7104(a), use the following clause:

PAYMENTS (DEC 1991)

(a) *Progress payments*, as used in this clause, means payments made before completion of work in progress under a job order.

(b) Upon submission by the Contractor of invoices in the form and number of copies directed by the Contracting Officer, and as approved by the Contracting Officer, the Government will make progress payments as work progresses under the job order.

(1) Generally, the Contractor may submit invoices on a semi-monthly basis, unless expenditures justify a more frequent submission.

(2) The Government need not make progress payments for invoices aggregating less than $5,000.

(3) The Contracting Officer shall approve progress payments based on the value, computed on the price of the job order, of labor and materials incorporated in the work, materials suitably stored at the site of the work, and preparatory work completed, less the aggregate of any previous payments.

(4) Upon request, the Contractor will furnish the Contracting Officer any reports concerning expenditures on the work to date that the Contracting Officer may require.

(c) The Government will retain until final completion and acceptance of all work covered by the job order, an amount estimated or approved by the Contracting Officer under paragraph (b) of this clause. The amount retained will be in accordance with the rate authorized by Congress for Naval vessel repair contracts at the time of job order award.

(d) The Contracting Officer may direct that progress payments be based on the price of the job order as adjusted as a result of change orders under the Changes clause of the Master Agreement. If the Contracting Officer does not so direct—

(1) Payments of any increases shall be made from time to time after the amount of the increase is determined under the Changes clause of the Master Agreement; and

(2) Reductions resulting from decreases shall be made for the purposes of subsequent progress payments as soon as the amounts are determined under the Changes clause of the Master Agreement.

(e) Upon completion of the work under a job order and final inspection and acceptance, and upon submission of invoices in such form and with such copies as the Contracting Officer may prescribe, the Contractor shall be paid for the price of the job order, as adjusted pursuant to the Changes clause of the Master Agreement, less any performance reserves deemed necessary by the Contracting Officer, and less the amount of any previous payments.

(f) All materials, equipment, or any other property or work in process covered by the progress payments made by the Government, upon the making of those progress payments, shall become the sole property of the Government, and are subject to the provisions of the Title clause of the Master Agreement.

(End of clause)

252.217-7008 Bonds.

As prescribed in 217.7104(a), use the following clause:

BONDS (DEC 1991)

(a) If the solicitation requires an offeror to submit a bid bond, the Offeror may furnish, instead, an annual bid bond (or evidence thereof) or an annual performance and payment bond (or evidence thereof).

(b) If the solicitation does not require a bid bond, the Offeror shall not include in the price any contingency to cover the premium of such a bond.

(c) Even if the solicitation does not require bonds, the Contracting Officer may nevertheless require a performance and payment bond, in form, amount, and with a surety acceptable to the Contracting Officer. Where performance and payment bond is required, the offer price shall be increased upon the award of the job order in an amount not to exceed the premium of a corporate surety bond.

(d) If any surety upon any bond furnished in connection with a job order under this agreement fails to submit requested reports as to its financial condition or otherwise becomes unacceptable to the Government, the Contracting Officer may require the Contractor to furnish whatever additional security the Contracting Officer determines necessary to protect the interests of the Government and of persons supplying labor or materials in the performance of the work contemplated under the Master Agreement.

(End of clause)

252.217-7009 Default.

As prescribed in 217.7104(a), use the following clause:

DEFAULT (DEC 1991)

(a) The Government may, subject to the provisions of paragraph (b) of this clause, by written notice of default to the Contractor, terminate the whole or any part of a job order if the Contractor fails to—

(1) Make delivery of the supplies or to perform the services within the time specified in a job order or any extension;

(2) Make progress, so as to endanger performance of the job order; or

(3) Perform any of the other provisions of this agreement or a job order.

(b) Except for defaults of subcontractors, the Contractor shall not be liable for any excess costs if failure to perform the job order arises from causes beyond the control and without the fault or negligence of the Contractor. Examples of such causes include acts of God or of the public enemy, acts of the Government in either its sovereign or contractual capacity, fires, floods, epidemics, quarantine restrictions, strikes, freight embargoes, and unusually severe weather.

(c) If the Contractor's failure to perform is caused by the default of a subcontractor, and if such default arises out of causes beyond the control of both the Contractor and subcontractor, and without the fault or negligence of either, the Contractor shall not be liable for any excess costs for failure to perform, unless the supplies or services to be furnished by the subcontractor were obtainable from other sources in sufficient time to permit the Contractor to perform the job order within the time specified.

(d) If the Government terminates the job order in whole or in part as provided in paragraph (a) of this clause—

(1) The Government may, upon such terms and in such manner as the Contracting Officer may deem appropriate, arrange for the completion of the work so terminated, at such plant or plants, including that of the Contractor, as may be designated by the Contracting Officer.

(i) The Contractor shall continue the performance of the job order to the extent not terminated under the provisions of this clause.

(ii) If the work is to be completed at the plant, the Government may use all tools, machinery, facilities, and equipment of the Contractor determined by the Contracting Office to be necessary for that purpose.

(iii) If the cost to the Government of the work procured or completed (after adjusting such cost to exclude the effect of changes in the plans and specifications made subsequent to the date of termination) exceeds the price fixed for work under the job order (after adjusting such price on account of changes in the plans and specifications made before the date of termination), the Contractor, or the Contractor's surety, if any, shall be liable for such excess.

(2) The Government, in addition to any other rights provided in this clause, may require the Contractor to transfer title and delivery to the Government, in the manner and to the extent directed by the Contracting Officer, any completed supplies and such partially completed supplies and materials, parts, tools, dies, jigs, fixtures, plans, drawings, information and contract rights (hereinafter called "manufacturing materials") as the Contractor has specifically produced or specifically acquired for the performance of the terminated part of the job order.

(i) The Contractor shall, upon direction of the Contracting Officer, protect and preserve property in possession of the Contractor in which the Government has an interest.

(ii) The Government shall pay to the Contractor the job order price for completed items of work delivered to and accepted by the Government, and the amount agreed upon by the Contractor and the Contracting Officer for manufacturing materials delivered to and accepted by the Government, and for the protection and preservation of property. Failure to agree shall be a dispute concerning a question of fact within the meaning of the Disputes clause.

(e) If, after notice of termination of the job order, it is determined that the Contractor was not in default, or that the default was excusable, the rights and obligations of the parties shall be the same as if the notice of termination had been issued for the convenience of the Government.

(f) If the Contractor fails to complete the performance of a job order within the time specified, or any extension, the actual damage to the Government for the delay will be difficult or impossible to determine.

(1) In lieu of actual damage, the Contractor shall pay to the Government as fixed, agreed, and liquidated damages for each calendar day of delay the amount, if any, set forth in the job order (prorated to the nearest hour for fractional days).

(2) If the Government terminates the job order, the Contractor shall be liable, in addition to the excess costs provided in paragraph (d) of this clause, for liquidated damages accruing until such time as the Government may reasonably obtain completion of the work.

(3) The Contractor shall not be charged with liquidated damages when the delay arises out of causes beyond the control and without the fault or negligence of the Contractor. Subject to the provisions of the Disputes clause of the Master Agreement, the Contracting Officer shall ascertain the facts and the extent of the delay and shall extend the time for performance when in the judgment of the Contracting Officer, the findings of fact justify an extension.

(g) The rights and remedies of the Government provided in this clause shall not be exclusive and are in addition to any other rights and remedies provided by law under this agreement.

(End of clause)

252.217-7010 Performance.

As prescribed in 217.7104(a), use the following clause:

PERFORMANCE (JUL 2009)

(a) Upon the award of a job order, the Contractor shall promptly start the work specified and shall diligently prosecute the work to completion. The Contractor shall not start work until the job order has been awarded except in the case of emergency work ordered by the Contracting Officer under the Job Orders and Compensation clause of the Master Agreement.

(b) The Government shall deliver the vessel described in the job order at the time and location specified in the job order. Upon completion of the work, the Government shall accept delivery of the vessel at the time and location specified in the job order.

(c) The Contractor shall, without charge and without specific requirement in a job order—

(1) Make available at the plant to personnel of the vessel while in dry dock or on a marine railway, sanitary lavatory and similar facilities acceptable to the Contracting Officer;

(2) Supply and maintain suitable brows and gangways from the pier, dry dock, or marine railway to the vessel;

(3) Treat salvage, scrap or other ship's material of the Government resulting from performance of the work as items of Government-furnished property, in accordance with the Government Property clause;

(4) Perform, or pay the cost of, any repair, reconditioning or replacement made necessary as the result of the use by the Contractor of any of the vessel's machinery, equipment or fittings, including, but not limited to, winches, pumps, rigging, or pipe lines; and

(5) Furnish suitable offices, office equipment and telephones at or near the site of the work for the Government's use.

(d) The job order will state whether dock and sea trials are required to determine whether or not the Contractor has satisfactorily performed the work.

(1) If dock and sea trials are required, the vessel shall be under the control of the vessel's commander and crew.

(2) The Contractor shall not conduct dock and sea trials not specified in the job order without advance approval of the Contracting Officer. Dock and sea trials not specified in the job order shall be at the Contractor's expense and risk.

(3) The Contractor shall provide and install all fittings and appliances necessary for dock and sea trials. The Contractor shall be responsible for care, installation, and re-

moval of instruments and apparatus furnished by the Government for use in the trials.

(End of clause)

[Final rule, 74 FR 37645, 7/29/2009, effective 7/29/2009]

252.217-7011 Access to vessel.

As prescribed at 217.7104(a), use the following clause:

ACCESS TO VESSEL (DEC 1991)

(a) Upon the request of the Contracting Officer, the Contractor shall grant admission to the Contractor's facilities and access to vessel, on a non-interference basis, as necessary to perform their respective responsibilities, to a reasonable number of:

(1) Government and other Government contractor employees (in addition to those Government employees attached to the vessel); and

(2) Representatives of offerors on other contemplated Government work.

(b) All personnel granted access shall comply with Contractor rules governing personnel at its shipyard.

(End of clause)

252.217-7012 Liability and insurance.

As prescribed in 217.7104(a), use the following clause:

LIABILITY AND INSURANCE (AUG 2003)

(a) The Contractor shall exercise its best efforts to prevent accidents, injury, or damage to all employees, persons, and property, in and about the work, and to the vessel or part of the vessel upon which work is done.

(b) *Loss or damage to the vessel, materials, or equipment.* (1) Unless otherwise directed or approved in writing by the Contracting Officer, the Contractor shall not carry insurance against any form of loss or damage to the vessel(s) or to the materials or equipment to which the Government has title or which have been furnished by the Government for installation by the Contractor. The Government assumes the risks of loss of and damage to that property.

(2) The Government does not assume any risk with respect to loss or damage compensated for by insurance or otherwise or resulting from risks with respect to which the Contractor has failed to maintain insurance, if available, as required or approved by the Contracting Officer.

(3) The Government does not assume risk of and will not pay for any costs of the following:

(i) Inspection, repair, replacement, or renewal of any defects in the vessel(s) or material and equipment due to—

(A) Defective workmanship performed by the Contractor or its subcontractors;

(B) Defective materials or equipment furnished by the Contractor or its subcontracts; or

(C) Workmanship, materials, or equipment which do not conform to the requirements of the contract, whether or not the defect is latent or whether or not the nonconformance is the result of negligence.

(ii) Loss, damage, liability, or expense caused by, resulting from, or incurred as a consequence of any delay or disruption, willful misconduct or lack of good faith by the Contractor or any of its representatives that have supervision or direction of—

(A) All or substantially all of the Contractor's business; or

(B) All or substantially all of the Contractor's operation at any one plant.

(4) As to any risk that is assumed by the Government, the Government shall be subrogated to any claim, demand or cause of action against third parties that exists in favor of the Contractor. If required by the Contracting Officer, the Contractor shall execute a formal assignment or transfer of the claim, demand, or cause of action.

(5) No party other than the Contractor shall have any right to proceed directly against the Government or join the Government as a co-defendant in any action.

(6) Notwithstanding the foregoing, the Contractor shall bear the first $50,000 of loss or damage from each occurrence or incident, the risk of which the Government

would have assumed under the provisions of this paragraph (b).

(c) *Indemnification*. The Contractor indemnifies the Government and the vessel and its owners against all claims, demands, or causes of action to which the Government, the vessel or its owner(s) might be subject as a result of damage or injury (including death) to the property or person of anyone other than the Government or its employees, or the vessel or its owner, arising in whole or in part from the negligence or other wrongful act of the Contractor or its agents or employees, or any subcontractor, or its agents or employees.

(1) The Contractor's obligation to indemnify under this paragraph shall not exceed the sum of $300,000 as a consequence of any single occurrence with respect to any one vessel.

(2) The indemnity includes, without limitation, suits, actions, claims, costs, or demands of any kind, resulting from death, personal injury, or property damage occurring during the period of performance of work on the vessel or within 90 days after redelivery of the vessel. For any claim, etc., made after 90 days, the rights of the parties shall be as determined by other provisions of this agreement and by law. The indemnity does apply to death occurring after 90 days where the injury was received during the period covered by the indemnity.

(d) *Insurance*. (1) The Contractor shall, at its own expense, obtain and maintain the following insurance—

(i) Casualty, accident, and liability insurance, as approved by the Contracting Officer, insuring the performance of its obligations under paragraph (c) of this clause.

(ii) Workers Compensation Insurance (or its equivalent) covering the employees engaged on the work.

(2) The Contractor shall ensure that all subcontractors engaged on the work obtain and maintain the insurance required in paragraph (d)(1) of this clause.

(3) Upon request of the Contracting Officer, the Contractor shall provide evidence of the insurance required by paragraph (d) of this clause.

(e) The Contractor shall not make any allowance in the job order price for the inclusion of any premium expense or charge for any reserve made on account of self-insurance for coverage against any risk assumed by the Government under this clause.

(f) The Contractor shall give the Contracting Officer written notice as soon as practicable after the occurrence of a loss or damage for which the Government has assumed the risk.

(1) The notice shall contain full details of the loss or damage.

(2) If a claim or suit is later filed against the Contractor as a result of the event, the Contractor shall immediately deliver to the Government every demand, notice, summons, or other process received by the Contractor or its employees or representatives.

(3) The Contractor shall cooperate with the Government and, upon request, shall assist in effecting settlements, securing and giving evidence, obtaining the attendance of witnesses, and in the conduct of suits. The Government shall reimburse the Contractor for expenses incurred in this effort, other than the cost of maintaining the Contractor's usual organization.

(4) The Contractor shall not, except at its own expense, voluntarily make any payment, assume any obligation, or incur any expense other than what would be imperative for the protection of the vessel(s) at the time of the event.

(g) In the event of loss of or damage to any vessel(s), material, or equipment which may result in a claim against the Government under the insurance provisions of this contract, the Contractor shall promptly notify the Contracting Officer of the loss or damage. The Contracting Officer may, without prejudice to any other right of the Government, either—

(1) Order the Contractor to proceed with replacement or repair, in which event the Contractor shall effect the replacement or repair;

(i) The Contractor shall submit to the Contracting Officer a request for reimbursement of the cost of the replacement or repair together with whatever supporting documentation the Contracting Officer may reasonably require, and shall identify the request as being submitted under the Insurance clause of the agreement.

(ii) If the Government determines that the risk of the loss or damage is within the scope of the risks assumed by the Government under this clause, the Government will reimburse the Contractor for the reasonable, allowable cost of the replacement or repair, plus a reasonable profit (if the work or replacement or repair was performed by the Contractor) less the deductible amount specified in paragraph (b) of this clause.

(iii) Payments by the Government to the Contractor under this clause are outside the scope of and shall not affect the pricing structure of the contract, and are additional to the compensation otherwise payable to the Contractor under this contract; or

(2) In the event the Contracting Officer decides that the loss or damage shall not be replaced or repaired, the Contracting Officer shall—

(i) Modify the contract appropriately, consistent with the reduced requirements reflected by the unreplaced or unrepaired loss or damage; or

(ii) Terminate the repair of any part or all of the vessel(s) under the Termination for Convenience of the Government clause of this agreement.

(End of clause)

[Final rule, 68 FR 50477, 8/21/2003, effective 8/21/2003]

252.217-7013 Guarantees.

As prescribed in 217.7104(a), use the following clause:

GUARANTEES (DEC 1991)

(a) In the event any work performed or materials furnished by the contractor under the Master Agreement prove defective or deficient within 90 days from the date of redelivery of the vessel(s), the Contractor, as directed by the Contracting Officer and at its own expense, shall correct and repair the deficiency to the satisfaction of the Contracting Officer.

(b) If the Contractor or any subcontractor has a guarantee for work performed or materials furnished that exceeds the 90 day period, the Government shall be entitled to rely upon the longer guarantee until its expiration.

(c) With respect to any individual work item identified as incomplete at the time of redelivery of the vessel(s), the guarantee period shall run from the date the item is completed.

(d) If practicable, the Government shall give the Contractor an opportunity to correct the deficiency.

(1) If the Contracting Officer determines it is not practicable or is otherwise not advisable to return the vessel(s) to the Contractor, or the Contractor fails to proceed with the repairs promptly, the Contracting Officer may direct that the repairs be performed elsewhere, at the Contractor's expense.

(2) If correction and repairs are performed by other than the Contractor, the Contracting Officer may discharge the Contractor's liability by making an equitable deduction in the price of the job order.

(e) The Contractor's liability shall extend for an additional 90 day guarantee period on those defects or deficiencies that the Contractor corrected.

(f) At the option of the Contracting Officer, defects and deficiencies may be left uncorrected. In that event, the Contractor and Contracting Officer shall negotiate an equitable reduction in the job price. Failure to agree upon an equitable reduction shall constitute a dispute under the Disputes clause of this agreement.

(End of clause)

252.217-7014 Discharge of liens.

As prescribed in 217.7104(a), use the following clause:

DISCHARGE OF LIENS (DEC 1991)

(a) The Contractor shall immediately discharge, or cause to be discharged, any lien or right *in rem* of any kind, other than in favor of the Government, that exists or arises in connection with work done or material furnished under any job order under this agreement.

(b) If any lien or right *in rem* is not immediately discharged, the Government, at the expense of the Contractor, may discharge, or cause to be discharged, the lien or right.

(End of clause)

252.217-7015 Safety and health.

As prescribed in 217.7104(a), use the following clause:

SAFETY AND HEALTH (DEC 1991)

Nothing contained in the Master Agreement or any job order shall relieve the Contractor of any obligations it may have to comply with—

(a) The Occupational Safety and Health Act of 1970 (29 U.S.C. 651, *et seq.*);

(b) The Safety and Health Regulations for Ship Repairing (29 CFR part 1915); or

(c) Any other applicable Federal, State, and local laws, codes, ordinances, and regulations.

(End of clause)

252.217-7016 Plant protection.

As prescribed in 217.7104(a), use the following clause:

PLANT PROTECTION (DEC 1991)

(a) The Contractor shall provide, for the plant and work in process, reasonable safeguards against all hazards, including unauthorized entry, malicious mischief, theft, vandalism, and fire.

(b) The Contractor shall also provide whatever additional safeguards are necessary to protect the plant and work in process from espionage, sabotage, and enemy action.

(1) The Government shall reimburse the Contractor for that portion of the costs of the additional safeguards that is allocable to the contract in the same manner as if the Contracting Officer had issued a change order for the additional safeguards.

(2) The costs reimbursed shall not include any overhead allowance, unless the overhead is incident to the construction or installation of necessary security devices or equipment.

(c) Upon payment by the Government of the cost of any device or equipment required or approved under paragraph (b) of this clause, title shall vest in the Government.

(1) The Contractor shall comply with the instructions of the Contracting Officer concerning its identification and disposition.

(2) No such device or equipment shall become a fixture as a result of its being affixed to realty not owned by the Government.

(End of clause)

252.217-7017 [Removed and Reserved]

[Final rule, 71 FR 27642, 5/12/2006, effective 5/12/2006]

252.217-7018 [Removed and Reserved]

[Final rule, 71 FR 27642, 5/12/2006, effective 5/12/2006]

252.217-7019 [Removed and Reserved]

[Final rule, 71 FR 27642, 5/12/2006, effective 5/12/2006]

252.217-7020 [Removed and Reserved]

[Final rule, 71 FR 27642, 5/12/2006, effective 5/12/2006]

252.217-7021 [Removed and Reserved]

[Final rule, 71 FR 27642, 5/12/2006, effective 5/12/2006]

252.217-7022 [Removed and Reserved]

[Final rule, 71 FR 27642, 5/12/2006, effective 5/12/2006]

252.217-7023 [Removed and Reserved]

[Final rule, 71 FR 27642, 5/12/2006, effective 5/12/2006]

252.217-7024 [Removed and Reserved]

[Final rule, 71 FR 27642, 5/12/2006, effective 5/12/2006]

252.217-7025 [Removed and Reserved]

[Final rule, 71 FR 27642, 5/12/2006, effective 5/12/2006]

252.217-7026 Identification of sources of supply.

As prescribed in 217.7303, use the following provision:

IDENTIFICATION OF SOURCES OF SUPPLY (NOV 1995)

(a) The Government is required under 10 U.S.C. 2384 to obtain certain information on the actual manufacturer or sources of supplies it acquires.

(b) The apparently successful Offeror agrees to complete and submit the following table before award:

TABLE

Line items (1)	National stock No. (2)	Commercial item (Y or N) (3)	Source of supply			
			Company (4)	Address (4)	Part No. (5)	Actual mfg? (6)
....	....	....				

(1) List each deliverable item of supply and item of technical data.
(2) If there is no national stock number, list "none."
(3) Use "Y" if the item is a commercial item; otherwise use "N." If "Y" is listed, the Offeror need not complete the remaining columns in the table.
(4) For items of supply, list all sources. For technical data, list the source.
(5) For items of supply, list each source's part number for the item.
(6) Use "Y" if the source of supply is the actual manufacturer, "N" if it is not; and "U" if unknown.

(End of provision)

[DAC 91-6, 59 FR 27662, 5/27/94, effective 5/27/94; DAC 91-9, 60 FR 61586, 11/30/95, effective 11/30/95]

252.217-7027 Contract definitization.

As prescribed in 217.7406(b), use the following clause:

CONTRACT DEFINITIZATION (DEC 2012)

(a) A ___ (*insert specific type of contract action*) is contemplated. The Contractor agrees to begin promptly negotiating with the Contracting Officer the terms of a definitive contract that will include (1) all clauses required by the Federal Acquisition Regulation (FAR) on the date of execution of the undefinitized contract action, (2) all clauses required by law on the date of execution of the definitive contract action, and (3) any other mutually agreeable clauses, terms, and conditions. The Contractor agrees to submit a ___ (*insert type of proposal; e.g., fixed-price or cost-and-fee*) proposal and certified cost or pricing data supporting its proposal.

(b) The schedule for definitizing this contract is as follows (*insert target date for definitization of the contract action and dates for submission of proposal, beginning of negotiations, and, if appropriate, submission of the make-or-buy and subcontracting plans and certified cost or pricing data*).

____

____

____

____

(c) If agreement on a definitive contract action to supersede this undefinitized contract action is not reached by the target date in paragraph (b) of this clause, or within any extension of it granted by the Contracting Officer, the Contracting Officer may, with the approval of the head of the contracting activity, determine a reasonable price or fee in accordance with subpart 15.4 and part 31 of the FAR, subject to Contractor appeal as provided in the Disputes clause. In any event, the Contractor shall proceed with completion of the contract, subject only to the Limitation of Government Liability clause.

(1) After the Contracting Officer's determination of price or fee, the contract shall be governed by—

(i) All clauses required by the FAR on the date of execution of this undefinitized contract action for either fixed-price or cost-reimbursement contracts, as determined by the Contracting Officer under this paragraph (c);

(ii) All clauses required by law as of the date of the Contracting Officer's determination; and

(iii) Any other clauses, terms, and conditions mutually agreed upon.

(2) To the extent consistent with paragraph (c)(1) of this clause, all clauses, terms, and conditions included in this undefinitized contract action shall continue in effect, except those that by their nature apply only to an undefinitized contract action.

(d) The definitive contract resulting from this undefinitized contract action will include a negotiated ___ *(insert "cost/price ceiling" or "firm-fixed price")* in no event to exceed ___ *(insert the not-to-exceed amount)*.

(End of clause)

[DAC 91-10, 61 FR 7739, 2/29/96, effective 2/29/96, corrected 61 FR 18195, 4/24/96; Final rule, 63 FR 55040, 10/14/98, effective 10/14/98; Final rule, 71 FR 27642, 5/12/2006, effective 5/12/2006; Final rule, 74 FR 37649, 7/29/2009, effective 7/29/2009; Final rule, 77 FR 76939, 12/31/2012, effective 12/31/2012]

252.217-7028 Over and above work.

As prescribed in 217.7702, use a clause substantially as follows:

OVER AND ABOVE WORK (DEC 1991)

(a) *Definitions.*

As used in this clause—

(1) *Over and above work* means work discovered during the course of performing overhaul, maintenance, and repair efforts that is—

(i) Within the general scope of the contract;

(ii) Not covered by the line item(s) for the basic work under the contract; and

(iii) Necessary in order to satisfactorily complete the contract.

(2) *Work request* means a document prepared by the Contractor which describes over and above work being proposed.

(b) The Contractor and Administrative Contracting Officer shall mutually agree to procedures for Government administration and Contractor performance of over and above work requests. If the parties cannot agree upon the procedures, the Administrative Contracting Officer has the unilateral right to direct the over and above work procedures to be followed. These procedures shall, as a minimum, cover—

(1) The format, content, and submission of work requests by the Contractor. Work requests shall contain data on the type of discrepancy disclosed, the specific location of the discrepancy, and the estimated labor hours and material required to correct the discrepancy. Data shall be sufficient to satisfy contract requirements and obtain the authorization of the Contracting Officer to perform the proposed work;

(2) Government review, verification, and authorization of the work; and

(3) Proposal pricing, submission, negotiation, and definitization.

(c) Upon discovery of the need for over and above work, the Contractor shall prepare and furnish to the Government a work request in accordance with the agreed-to procedures.

(d) The Government shall—

(1) Promptly review the work request;

(2) Verify that the proposed work is required and not covered under the basic contract line item(s);

(3) Verify that the proposed corrective action is appropriate; and

(4) Authorize over and above work as necessary.

(e) The Contractor shall promptly submit to the Contracting Officer, a proposal for the over and above work. The Government and Contractor will then negotiate a settlement for the over and above work. Contract modifications will be executed to definitize all over and above work.

(f) Failure to agree on the price of over and above work shall be a dispute within the meaning of the Disputes clause of this contract.

(End of clause)

252.219 Small Business and Small Disadvantaged Business Concerns, provisions and clauses for DFARS Part 219

252.219-7000 Advancing Small Business Growth.

As prescribed in 219.309(1), use the following provision:

ADVANCING SMALL BUSINESS GROWTH (SEP 2016)

(a) This provision implements 10 U.S.C. 2419.

(b) The Offeror acknowledges by submission of its offer that by acceptance of the contract resulting from this solicitation, the Offeror may exceed the applicable small business size standard of the North American Industry Classification System (NAICS) code assigned to the contract and would no longer qualify as a small business concern for that NAICS code. (Small business size standards matched to industry NAICS codes are published by the Small Business Administration and are available at *http://www.sba.gov/content/table-small-business-size-standards.*) The Offeror is therefore encouraged to develop the capabilities and characteristics typically desired in contractors that are competitive as other-than-small contractors in this industry.

(c) For procurement technical assistance, the Offeror may contact the nearest Procurement Technical Assistance Center (PTAC). PTAC locations are available at *http://www.dla.mil/HQ/SmallBusiness/PTAC.aspx.*

(End of provision)

[Removed and reserved, interim rule, 63 FR 41972, 8/6/98, effective 10/1/98, finalized without change, 64 FR 52670, 9/30/99; Final rule, 80 FR 30115, 5/26/2015, effective 5/26/2015; Final rule, 80 FR 30116, 5/26/2015, effective 5/26/2015; Final rule, 81 FR 65563, 9/23/2016, effective 9/23/2016]

252.219-7001 [Reserved]

[Removed and reserved, interim rule, 63 FR 41972, 8/6/98, effective 10/1/98, finalized without change, 64 FR 52670, 9/30/99]

252.219-7002 [Reserved]

[Removed and reserved, interim rule, 63 FR 41972, 8/6/98, effective 10/1/98, finalized without change, 64 FR 52670, 9/30/99]

252.219-7003 Small Business Subcontracting Plan (DoD Contracts).

Basic. As prescribed in 219.708(b)(1)(A) and (b)(1)(A)(*1*), use the following clause:

SMALL BUSINESS SUBCONTRACTING PLAN (DoD CONTRACTS)—BASIC (DEC 2019)

This clause supplements the Federal Acquisition Regulation 52.219-9, Small Business Subcontracting Plan, clause of this contract.

(a) *Definition.* As used in this clause—

Summary Subcontract Report (SSR) Coordinator means the individual who is registered in the Electronic Subcontracting Reporting System (eSRS) at the Department of Defense level and is responsible for acknowledging receipt or rejecting SSRs submitted under an individual subcontracting plan in eSRS for the Department of Defense.

(b) Subcontracts awarded to qualified nonprofit agencies designated by the Committee for Purchase From People Who Are Blind or Severely Disabled (41 U.S.C. 8502-8504), may be counted toward the Contractor's small business subcontracting goal (section 8025 of Pub. L. 108–87).

(c) A mentor firm, under the Pilot Mentor-Protege Program established under section 831 of Public Law 101-510, as amended, may count toward its small disadvantaged business goal, subcontracts awarded to—

(1) Protege firms which are qualified organizations employing the severely disabled; and

(2) Former protege firms that meet the criteria in section 831(g)(4) of Public Law 101-510.

(d) The master plan is approved by the cognizant contract administration activity for the Contractor.

(e) In those subcontracting plans which specifically identify small businesses, the Contractor shall notify the Administrative Contracting Officer of any substitutions of firms that are not small business firms, for the small business firms specifically identified in the subcontracting plan. Notifications shall be in writing and shall occur within a reasonable period of time after award of the subcontract. Contractor-specified formats shall be acceptable.

(f)(1) For DoD, the Contractor shall submit reports in eSRS as follows:

(i) The Individual Subcontract Report (ISR) shall be submitted to the contracting officer at the procuring contracting office, even when contract administration has been delegated to the Defense Contract Management Agency.

(ii) Submit the consolidated SSR for an individual subcontracting plan to the "Department of Defense."

(2) For DoD, the authority to acknowledge receipt or reject reports in eSRS is as follows:

(i) The authority to acknowledge receipt or reject the ISR resides with the contracting officer who receives it, as described in paragraph (f)(1)(i) of this clause.

(ii) The authority to acknowledge receipt of or reject SSRs submitted under an individual subcontracting plan resides with the SSR Coordinator.

(g) Include the clause at Defense Federal Acquisition Regulation Supplement (DFARS) 252.219-7004, Small Business Subcontracting Plan (Test Program), in subcontracts with subcontractors that participate in the Test Program described in DFARS 219.702-70, if the subcontract is expected to exceed the applicable threshold specified in Federal Acquisition Regulation 19.702(a), and to have further subcontracting opportunities.

(End of clause)

Alternate I. As prescribed in 219.708(b)(1)(A) and (b)(1)(A)(*2*), use the following clause, which uses a different paragraph (f) than the basic clause.

SMALL BUSINESS SUBCONTRACTING PLAN (DoD CONTRACTS)—ALTERNATE I (DEC 2019)

This clause supplements the Federal Acquisition Regulation 52.219-9, Small Business Subcontracting Plan, clause of this contract.

(a) *Definition.* As used in this clause—

Summary Subcontract Report (SSR) Coordinator means the individual who is registered in the Electronic Subcontracting Reporting System (eSRS) at the Department of Defense level and is responsible for acknowledging receipt or rejecting SSRs submitted under an individual subcontracting plan in eSRS for the Department of Defense.

(b) Subcontracts awarded to qualified nonprofit agencies designated by the Committee for Purchase From People Who Are Blind or Severely Disabled (41 U.S.C. 8502-8504), may be counted toward the Contractor's small business subcontracting goal (section 8025 of Pub. L. 108–87).

(c) A mentor firm, under the Pilot Mentor-Protege Program established under section 831 of Public Law 101-510, as amended, may count toward its small disadvantaged business goal, subcontracts awarded to—

(1) Protege firms which are qualified organizations employing the severely disabled; and

(2) Former protege firms that meet the criteria in section 831(g)(4) of Public Law 101-510.

(d) The master plan is approved by the cognizant contract administration activity for the Contractor.

(e) In those subcontracting plans which specifically identify small businesses, the Contractor shall notify the Administrative Contracting Officer of any substitutions of firms that are not small business firms, for the small business firms specifically identified in the subcontracting plan. Notifications shall be in writing and shall occur within a reasonable period of time after award of the subcontract. Contractor-specified formats shall be acceptable.

(f) (1) For DoD, the Contractor shall submit reports in eSRS as follows:

(i) The Standard Form 294, Subcontracting Report for Individual Contracts, shall be submitted in accordance with the instructions on that form.

(ii) Submit the consolidated SSR to the "Department of Defense."

(2) For DoD, the authority to acknowledge receipt of or reject SSRs submitted under an individual subcontracting plan in eSRS resides with the SSR Coordinator.

(g) Include the clause at Defense Federal Acquisition Regulation Supplement (DFARS) 252.219-7004, Small Business Subcontracting Plan (Test Program), in subcontracts with subcontractors that participate in the Test Program described in DFARS 219.702-70, if the subcontract is expected to exceed the applicable threshold specified in Federal Acquisition Regulation 19.702(a), and to have further subcontracting opportunities.

Alternate II. As prescribed in 219.708(b)(1)(A) and (b)(1)(A)(3), use the following clause, which uses different paragraphs (a) and (b) than the basic clause.

SMALL BUSINESS SUBCONTRACTING PLAN (DOD CONTRACTS)—ALTERNATE II (DEC 2019)

(a) *Definitions.* As used in this clause—

Eligible contractor means a business entity operated on a for-profit or nonprofit basis that—

(1) Employs severely disabled individuals at a rate that averages not less than 33 percent of its total workforce over the 12-month period prior to issuance of the solicitation;

(2) Pays not less than the minimum wage prescribed pursuant to 29 U.S.C. 206 to the employees who are severely disabled individuals; and

(3) Provides, for its employees, health insurance and a retirement plan comparable to those provided for employees by business entities of similar size in its industrial sector or geographic region.

Summary Subcontract Report (SSR) Coordinator means the individual who is registered in the Electronic Subcontracting Reporting System (eSRS) at the Department of Defense level and is responsible for acknowledging receipt or rejecting SSRs submitted under an individual subcontracting plan in eSRS for the Department of Defense.

(b) (1) Subcontracts awarded to qualified nonprofit agencies designated by the Committee for Purchase From People Who are Blind or Severely Disabled (41 U.S.C. 8502–8504), may be counted toward the Contractor's small business subcontracting goal (section 8025 of Pub. L. 108–87).

(2) Subcontracts awarded to eligible contractors under the Demonstration Project for Contractors Employing Persons with Disabilities (see Defense Federal Acquisition Regulation Supplement (DFARS) 226.72) may be counted toward the Contractor's small disadvantaged business subcontracting goal (section 853 of Pub. L. 108–136, as amended by division H, section 110 of Pub. L. 108–199).

(c) A mentor firm, under the Pilot Mentor-Protege Program established under section 831 of Public Law 101–510, may count toward its small disadvantaged business goal, subcontracts awarded to—

(1) Protege firms which are qualified organizations employing the severely disabled; and

(2) Former protege firms that meet the criteria in section 831(g)(4) of Public Law 101–510.

(d) The master plan is approved by the cognizant contract administration activity for the Contractor.

(e) In those subcontracting plans which specifically identify small businesses, the Contractor shall notify the Administrative Contracting Officer of any substitutions of firms that are not small business firms, for the small business firms specifically identified in the subcontracting plan. Notifications shall be in writing and shall occur within a reasonable period of time after award of the subcontract. Contractorspecified formats shall be acceptable.

(f) (1) For DoD, the Contractor shall submit reports in eSRS as follows:

(i) The Individual Subcontract Report (ISR) shall be submitted to the contracting officer at the procuring contracting office, even when contract administration has been delegated to the Defense Contract Management Agency.

(ii) Submit the consolidated SSR for an individual subcontracting plan to the "Department of Defense."

(2) For DoD, the authority to acknowledge receipt or reject reports in eSRS is as follows:

(i) The authority to acknowledge receipt or reject the ISR resides with the contracting officer who receives it, as described in paragraph (f) (1) (i) of this clause.

(ii) The authority to acknowledge receipt of or reject SSRs submitted under an individual subcontracting plan resides with the SSR Coordinator.

(g) Include the clause at DFARS 252.219–7004, Small Business Subcontracting Plan (Test Program), in subcontracts with subcontractors that participate in the Test Program described in DFARS 219.702–70, if the subcontract is expected to exceed the applicable threshold specified in Federal Acquisition Regulation 19.702(a) and to have further subcontracting opportunities.

(End of clause)

[DAC 91-5, 58 FR 28458, 5/13/93, effective 4/30/93; Interim rule, 59 FR 22130, 4/29/94, effective 4/21/94; DAC 91-6, 59 FR 27662, 5/27/94, effective 5/27/94; DAC 91-9, 60 FR 61586, 11/30/95, effective 11/30/95; Final rule, 61 FR 18686, 4/29/96, effective 4/29/96; Final rule, 72 FR 20761, 4/26/2007, effective 4/26/2007; Interim rule, 75 FR 65439, 10/25/2010, effective 10/25/2010; Final rule, 76 FR 58137, 9/20/2011, effective 9/20/2011; Final rule, 77 FR 35879, 6/15/2012, effective 6/15/2012; Final rule, 77 FR 52253, 8/29/2012, effective 8/29/2012; Final rule, 78 FR 13546, 2/28/2013, effective 2/28/2013; Interim rule, 79 FR 61579, 10/14/2014, effective 10/14/2014; Final rule, 80 FR 15912, 3/26/2015, effective 3/26/2015; Final rule, 81 FR 17045, 3/25/2016, effective 3/25/2016; Final rule, 83 FR 15996, 4/13/2018, effective 4/13/2018; Final rule, 83 FR 65562, 12/21/2018, effective 12/21/2018; Final rule, 84 FR 25186, 5/31/2019, effective 5/31/2019; Final rule, 84 FR 72554, 12/31/2019, effective 12/31/2019]

252.219-7004 Small Business Subcontracting Plan (Test Program).

As prescribed in 219.708(b) (1)(B), use the following clause:

SMALL BUSINESS SUBCONTRACTING PLAN (TEST PROGRAM) (MAY 2019)

(a) *Definitions.* As used in this clause—

Covered small business concern means a small business concern, veteran-owned small business concern, service-disabled veteran-owned small business concern, HUBZone small business concern, women-owned small business concern, or small disadvantaged business concern, as these terms are defined in FAR 2.101.

Electronic Subcontracting Reporting System (eSRS) means the Governmentwide, electronic, Web-based system for small business subcontracting program reporting. The eSRS is located at *http://www.esrs.gov.*

Failure to make a good faith effort to comply with a comprehensive subcontracting plan means a willful or intentional failure to perform in accordance with the requirements of the Contractor's approved comprehensive subcontracting plan or willful or intentional action to frustrate the plan.

Subcontract means any agreement (other than one involving an employer-employee relationship) entered into by a Federal Government prime Contractor or subcontractor calling for supplies or services required for performance of the contract or subcontract.

(b) *Test Program.* The Contractor's comprehensive small business subcontracting plan and its successors, which are authorized by and approved under the Test Program of 15 U.S.C. 637 note, as amended, shall be included in and made a part of this contract. Upon expulsion from the Test Program or expiration of the Test Program, the Contractor shall negotiate an individual subcontracting plan for all future contracts that meet the requirements of 15 U.S.C. 637(d).

(c) *Eligibility requirements.* To become and remain eligible to participate in the Test Program, a business concern is required to have furnished supplies or services (including construction) under at least three DoD contracts during the preceding fiscal year, having an aggregate value of at least $100 million.

(d) *Reports.* (1) The Contractor shall report semiannually for the 6-month periods ending March 31 and September 30, the information in paragraphs (d)(1)(i) through (v) of this section within 30 days after the end of the reporting period. Submit the report at *https://www.esrs.gov.*

(i) A list of contracts covered under its comprehensive small business subcontracting plan, to include the Commercial and Government Entity (CAGE) code and unique entity identifier.

(ii) The amount of first-tier subcontract dollars awarded during the 6-month period covered by the report to covered small business concerns, with the information set forth separately by—

(A) North American Industrial Classification System (NAICS) code;

(B) Major defense acquisition program, as defined in 10 U.S.C. 2430(a);

(C) Contract number, if the contract is for maintenance, overhaul, repair, servicing, rehabilitation, salvage, modernization, or modification of supplies, systems, or equipment, and the total value of the contract, including options, exceeds $100 million; and

(D) Military department.

(iii) Total number of subcontracts active under the Test Program that would have otherwise required a subcontracting plan.

(iv) Costs incurred in negotiating, complying with, and reporting on its comprehensive subcontracting plan.

(v) Costs avoided through the use of a comprehensive subcontracting plan

(2) The Contractor shall—

(i) Ensure that subcontractors with subcontracting plans agree to submit an Individual Subcontract Report (ISR) and/or Summary Subcontract Report (SSR) using the Electronic Subcontracting Reporting System (eSRS).

(ii) Provide its contract number, its unique entity identifier, and the email address of the Contractor's official responsible for acknowledging or rejecting the ISR to all first-tier subcontractors, who will be required to submit ISRs, so they can enter this information into the eSRS when submitting their reports.

(iii) Require that each subcontractor with a subcontracting plan provide the prime contract number, its own unique entity identifier, and the email address of the subcontractor's official responsible for acknowledging or rejecting the ISRs to its subcontractors with subcontracting plans who will be required to submit ISRs.

(iv) Acknowledge receipt or reject all ISRs submitted by its subcontractors using eSRS.

(3) The Contractor shall submit SSRs using eSRS at *http://www.esrs.gov.* The reports shall provide information on subcontract awards to small business concerns, veteran-owned small business concerns, service-disabled veteran-owned small business concerns, HUBZone small business concerns, small disadvantaged business concerns, and women-owned small business concerns. Purchases from a corporation, company, or subdivision that is an affiliate of the prime Contractor or subcontractor are not included in these reports. Subcontract award data reported by prime contractors and subcontrac-

tors shall be limited to awards made to their immediate next-tier subcontractors. Credit cannot be taken for awards made to lower-tier subcontractors unless the Contractor or subcontractor has been designated to receive a small business or small disadvantaged business credit from a member firm of the Alaska Native—Corporations or an Indian tribe. Only subcontracts involving performance in the U.S. or its outlying areas should be included in these reports.

(i) This report may be submitted on a corporate, company, or subdivision (e.g., plant or division operating as a separate profit center) basis, as negotiated in the comprehensive subcontracting plan with the Defense Contract Management Agency.

(ii) This report encompasses all subcontracting under prime contracts and subcontracts with the Department of Defense, regardless of the dollar value of the subcontracts, and is based on the negotiated comprehensive subcontracting plan.

(iii) The report shall be submitted semiannually for the six months ending March 31 and the twelve months ending September 30. Reports are due 30 days after the close of each reporting period.

(iv) The authority to acknowledge receipt of or reject the SSR resides with the Defense Contract Management Agency.

(e) *Failure to comply.* The failure of the Contractor or subcontractor to comply in good faith with the clause of this contract entitled "Utilization of Small Business Concerns," or an approved plan required by this clause, shall be a material breach of the contract.

(f) *Liquidated damages.* The Contracting Officer designated to manage the comprehensive subcontracting plan will exercise the functions of the Contracting Officer, as identified in paragraphs (f)(1) through (4) of this clause, on behalf of all DoD departments and agencies that awarded contracts covered by the Contractor's comprehensive subcontracting plan.

(1) To determine the need for liquidated damages, the Contracting Officer will conduct a compliance review during the fiscal year after the close of the fiscal year for which the plan is applicable. The Contracting Officer will compare the approved percentage or dollar goals to the total, actual subcontracting dollars covered by the plan.

(2) If the Contractor has failed to meet its approved subcontracting goal(s), the Contracting Officer will provide the Contractor written notice specifying the failure, advising of the potential for assessment of liquidated damages, and permitting the Contractor to demonstrate what good faith efforts have been made. The Contracting Officer may take the Contractor's failure to respond to the notice within 15 working days (or longer period at the Contracting Officer's discretion) as an admission that no valid explanation exists.

(3) If, after consideration of all relevant information, the Contracting Officer determines that the Contractor failed to make a good faith effort to comply with the comprehensive subcontracting plan, the Contracting Officer will issue a final decision to the Contractor to that effect and require the Contractor to pay liquidated damages to the Government in the amount identified in the comprehensive subcontracting plan.

(4) The Contractor shall have the right of appeal under the clause in this contract entitled "Disputes" from any final decision of the Contracting Officer.

(g) *Subcontracts.* The Contractor shall include in subcontracts that offer subcontracting opportunities, are expected to exceed the applicable threshold specified in FAR 19.702(a) on the date of subcontract award, and are required to include the clause at FAR 52.219-8, Utilization of Small Business Concerns, the clauses at—

(1) FAR 52.219-9, Small Business Subcontracting Plan, and Defense Federal Acquisition Regulation Supplement (DFARS) 252.219-7003, Small Business Subcontracting Plan (DoD Contracts)—Basic;

(2) FAR 52.219-9, Small Business Subcontracting Plan, with its Alternate III, and DFARS 252.219-7003, Small Business Subcontracting Plan (DoD Contracts)—Alternate I, to allow for submission of SF 294s in lieu of ISRs; or

(3) DFARS 252.219-7004, Small Business Subcontracting Plan (Test Program), in subcontracts with subcontractors that participate in the Test Program described in DFARS 219.702.

(End of clause)

[Final rule, 60 FR 35668, 7/10/95, effective 7/10/95; Interim rule, 61 FR 39900, 7/31/96, effective 7/31/96; DAC 91-12, 62 FR 34114, 6/24/97, effective 6/24/97; Final rule, 72 FR 20761, 4/26/2007, effective 4/26/2007; Final rule, 73 FR 46813, 8/12/2008, effective 8/12/2008; Interim rule, 75 FR 65439, 10/25/2010, effective 10/25/2010; Final rule, 76 FR 3536, 1/20/2011, effective 1/20/2011; Final rule, 78 FR 13546, 2/28/2013, effective 2/28/2013; Interim rule, 79 FR 61579, 10/14/2014, effective 10/14/2014; Final rule, 80 FR 15912, 3/26/2015, effective 3/26/2015; Final rule, 83 FR 15996, 4/13/2018, effective 4/13/2018; Final rule, 84 FR 25186, 5/31/2019, effective 5/31/2019]

252.219-7005 [Removed and Reserved]

[Removed and reserved, interim rule, 63 FR 64427, 11/20/98, effective 1/1/99, finalized without change, 64 FR 52670, 9/30/99; Added by Final rule, 68 FR 64559, 11/14/2003, effective date 12/15/2003; Final rule, 69 FR 63328, 11/1/2004, effective 11/1/2004]

252.219-7006 [Removed and Reserved]

[Removed and reserved, interim rule, 63 FR 41972, 8/6/98, effective 10/1/98, finalized without change, 64 FR 52670, 9/30/99; Added by Final rule, 68 FR 64559, 11/14/2003, effective 12/15/2003; Final rule, 69 FR 63328, 11/1/2004, effective 11/1/2004]

252.219-7007 [Reserved]

[Removed and reserved, DAC 91-12, 62 FR 34114, 6/24/97, effective 6/24/97]

252.219-7008 [Reserved]

[Removed and reserved, Interim rule, 63 FR 41972, 8/16/98, effective 10/1/98, finalized without change, 64 FR 52670, 9/30/99]

252.219-7009 Section 8(a) Direct Award.

As prescribed in 219.811-3(1), use the following clause:

SECTION 8(a) DIRECT AWARD (OCT 2018)

(a) This contract is issued as a direct award between the contracting office and the 8(a) Contractor pursuant to the Partnership Agreement between the Small Business Administration (SBA) and the Department of Defense. Accordingly, the SBA, even if not identified in Section A of this contract, is the prime contractor and retains responsibility for 8(a) certification, for 8(a) eligibility determinations and related issues, and for providing counseling and assistance to the 8(a) Contractor under the 8(a) Program. The cognizant SBA district office is:

____

____

____

____

[*To be completed by the Contracting Officer at the time of award*]

(b) The contracting office is responsible for administering the contract and for taking any action on behalf of the Government under the terms and conditions of the contract; provided that the contracting office shall give advance notice to the SBA before it issues a final notice terminating performance, either in whole or in part, under the contract. The contracting office also shall coordinate with the SBA prior to processing any novation agreement. The contracting office may assign contract administration functions to a contract administration office.

(c) The 8(a) Contractor agrees that it will notify the Contracting Officer, simultaneous with its notification to the SBA (as required by SBA's 8(a) regulations at 13 CFR 124.515), when the owner or owners upon whom 8(a) eligibility is based plan to relinquish ownership or control of the concern. Consistent with section 407 of Public Law 100-656, transfer of ownership or control shall result in termination of the contract for convenience, unless the SBA waives the requirement for termination prior to the actual relinquishing of ownership and control.

(End of clause)

[Interim rule, 63 FR 33586, 6/19/98, effective 6/19/98, finalized without change, 63 FR 64426, 11/20/98; Interim rule, 67 FR 11435, 3/14/2002, effective 3/14/2002; Final rule, 67 FR 49255, 7/30/2002, effective 7/30/2002; Final rule, 72 FR 51187, 9/6/2007, effective 9/6/2007; Final rule, 83 FR 54681, 10/31/2018, effective 10/31/20181]

252.219-7010 Notification of Competition Limited to Eligible 8(a) Participants—Partnership Agreement.

As prescribed in 219.811-3(2), use the following clause:

NOTIFICATION OF COMPETITION LIMITED TO ELIGIBLE 8(A) PARTICIPANTS—PARTNERSHIP AGREEMENT (OCT 2019)

(a) Offers are solicited only from small business concerns expressly certified by the Small Business Administration (SBA) for participation in SBA's 8(a) Program and which meet the following criteria at the time of submission of offer:

(1) The Offeror is in conformance with the 8(a) support limitation set forth in its approved business plan.

(2) The Offeror is in conformance with the Business Activity Targets set forth in its approved business plan or any remedial action directed by SBA.

(3) If the competition is to be limited to 8(a) concerns within one or more specific SBA regions or districts, then the offeror's approved business plan is on the file and serviced by ____________________. [*Contracting Officer completes by inserting the appropriate SBA District and/or Regional Office(s) as identified by SBA.*]

(b) By submission of its offer, the Offeror represents that it meets all of the criteria set forth in paragraph (a) of this clause.

(c) Any award resulting from this solicitation will be made directly by the Contracting Officer to the successful 8(a) offeror selected through the evaluation criteria set forth in this solicitation.

(d) (1) Unless SBA has waived the requirements of paragraphs (d)(1)(i) through (iii) and (d)(2) of this clause in accordance with 13 CFR 121.1204, a small business concern that provides an end item it did not manufacture, process, or produce, shall—

(i) Provide an end item that a small business has manufactured, processed, or produced in the United States or its outlying areas; for kit assemblers, see paragraph (d)(2) of this clause instead;

(ii) Be primarily engaged in the retail or wholesale trade and normally sell the type of item being supplied; and

(iii) Take ownership or possession of the item(s) with its personnel, equipment, or facilities in a manner consistent with industry practice; for example, providing storage, transportation, or delivery.

(2) When the end item being acquired is a kit of supplies, at least 50 percent of the total cost of the components of the kit shall be manufactured, processed, or produced by small businesses in the United States or its outlying areas.

(3) The requirements of paragraphs (d)(1)(i) through (iii) and (d)(2) of this clause do not apply to construction or service contracts.

(e) The ____________________ [*insert name of SBA's contractor*] will notify the ____________________ [*insert name of contracting agency*] Contracting Officer in writing immediately upon entering an agreement (either oral or written) to transfer all or part of its stock or other ownership interest to any other party.

(End of clause)

[Interim rule, 63 FR 33586, 6/19/98, effective 6/19/98, finalized without change, 63 FR 64426, 11/20/98; Final rule, 81 FR 17045, 3/25/2016, effective 3/25/2016; Final rule, 84 FR 58334, 10/31/2019, effective 10/31/2019]

252.219-7011 Notification to Delay Performance.

As prescribed in 219.811-3(3), use the following clause:

NOTIFICATION TO DELAY PERFORMANCE (JUN 1998)

The Contractor shall not begin performance under this purchase order until 2 working days have passed from the date of its receipt. Unless the Contractor receives notification from the Small Business Administration that it is ineligible for this 8(a) award, or otherwise receives instructions from the Contracting Officer, performance under this purchase order may begin on the third working day following receipt of the purchase order. If a determination of ineligibility is issued within the 2-day period, the purchase order shall be considered canceled.

(End of clause)

[Interim rule, 63 FR 33586, 6/19/98, effective 6/19/98, finalized without change, 63 FR 64426, 11/20/98]

252.219-7012 Competition for Religious-Related Services.

As prescribed in 219.270-3, use the following provision:

COMPETITION FOR RELIGIOUS-RELATED SERVICES (APR 2018)

(a) *Definition.* As used in this provision—

Nonprofit organization means any organization that is—

(1) Described in section 501(c) of the Internal Revenue Code of 1986; and

(2) Exempt from tax under section 501(a) of that Code.

(b) A nonprofit organization is not precluded from competing for a contract for religious-related services to be performed on a U.S. military installation notwithstanding that a nonprofit organization is not a small business concern as identified in FAR 19.000(a)(3).

(c) If the apparently successful offeror has not represented in its offer or quotation that it is a small business concern identified in FAR 19.000(a)(3), as appropriate to the solicitation, the Contracting Officer will verify that the offeror is registered in the System for Award Management (SAM) database as a nonprofit organization.

(End of provision)

[Final rule, 83 FR 16001, 4/13/2018, effective 4/13/2018]

252.222 Application of Labor Laws to Government Acquisitions, provisions and clauses for DFARS Part 222

252.222-7000 Restrictions on employment of personnel.

As prescribed in 222.7004, use the following clause:

RESTRICTIONS ON EMPLOYMENT OF PERSONNEL (MAR 2000)

(a) The Contractor shall employ, for the purpose of performing that portion of the contract work in ______, individuals who are residents thereof and who, in the case of any craft or trade, possess or would be able to acquire promptly the necessary skills to perform the contract.

(b) The Contractor shall insert the substance of this clause, including this paragraph (b), in each subcontract awarded under this contract.

(End of clause)

[Interim rule, 65 FR 14402, 3/16/2000, effective 3/16/2000, finalized without change, 65 FR 50150, 8/17/2000]

252.222-7001 [Removed and Reserved]

[Interim rule, 57 FR 52594, 11/4/92, effective 10/26/92; DAC 91-5, 58 FR 28458, 5/13/93, effective 4/30/93; Final rule, 83 FR 24892, 5/30/2018, effective 5/30/2018]

252.222-7002 Compliance with local labor laws (overseas).

As prescribed in 222.7201(a), use the following clause:

COMPLIANCE WITH LOCAL LABOR LAWS (OVERSEAS) (JUN 1997)

(a) The Contractor shall comply with all—

(1) Local laws, regulations, and labor union agreements governing work hours; and

(2) Labor regulations including collective bargaining agreements, workers' compensation, working conditions, fringe benefits, and labor standards or labor contract matters.

(b) The Contractor indemnifies and holds harmless the United States Government from all claims arising out of the requirements of this clause. This indemnity includes the Contractor's obligation to handle and settle, without cost to the United States Government, any claims or litigation concerning allegations that the Contractor or the United States Government, or both, have not fully complied with local labor laws or regulations relating to the performance of work required by this contract.

(c) Notwithstanding paragraph (b) of this clause, consistent with paragraphs 31.205-15(a) and 31.205-47(d) of the Federal Acquisition Regulation, the Contractor will be reimbursed for the costs of all fines, penalties, and reasonable litigation expenses incurred as a result of compliance with specific contract terms and conditions or written instructions from the Contracting officer.

(End of clause)

[DAC 91-12, 62 FR 34114, 6/24/97, effective 6/24/97]

252.222-7003 Permit from Italian Inspectorate of Labor.

As prescribed in 222.7201(b), use the following clause:

PERMIT FROM ITALIAN INSPECTORATE OF LABOR (JUN 1997)

Prior to the date set for commencement of work and services under this contract, the Contractor shall obtain the prescribed permit from the Inspectorate of Labor having jurisdiction over the work site, in accordance with Article 5g of Italian Law Number 1369, dated October 23, 1960. The Contractor shall ensure that a copy of the permit is available at all reasonable times for inspection by the Contracting Officer or an authorized representative. Failure to obtain such permit may result in termination of the contract for the convenience of the United States Government, at no cost to the United States Government.

(End of clause)

[DAC 91-12, 62 FR 34114, 6/24/97, effective 6/24/97]

252.222-7004 Compliance with Spanish social security laws and regulations.

As prescribed in 222.7201(c), use the following clause:

COMPLIANCE WITH SPANISH SOCIAL SECURITY LAWS AND REGULATIONS (JUN 1997)

(a) The Contractor shall comply with all Spanish Government social security laws and regulations. Within 30 calendar days after the start of contract performance, the Contractor shall ensure that copies of the documents identified in paragraph (a)(1) through (a)(5) of this clause are available at all reasonable times for inspection by the Contracting Officer or an authorized representative. The Contractor shall retain the records in accordance with the Audit and Records clause of this contract.

(1) TC1—Certificate of Social Security Payments;

(2) TC2—List of Employees;

(3) TC2/1—Certificate of Social Security Payments for Trainees;

(4) Nominal (pay statements) signed by both the employee and the Contractor; and

(5) Informa de Situacion de Empressa (Report of the Condition of the Enterprise) from the Ministerio de Trabajo y S.S., Tesoreria General de la Seguridad Social (annotated with the pertinent contract number(s) next to the employee's name).

(b) All TC1's, TC2's, and TC2/1's shall contain a representation that they have been paid by either the Social Security Administration office or the Contractor's bank or savings institution. Failure by the Contractor to comply with the requirements of this clause may result in termination of the contract under the clause of the contract entitled "Default."

(End of clause)

[DAC 91-12, 62 FR 34114, 6/24/97, effective 6/24/97]

252.222-7005 Prohibition on use of nonimmigrant aliens—Guam.

As prescribed in 222.7302, use the following clause:

PROHIBITION ON USE OF NONIMMIGRANT ALIENS—GUAM (SEP 1999)

The work required by this contract shall not be performed by any alien who is issued a visa or otherwise provided nonimmigrant status under Section 101(a)(15)(H)(ii) of the Immigration and Nationality Act (8 U.S.C. 1101(a)(15)(H)(ii)). This prohibition does not apply to the performance of work by lawfully admitted citizens of the freely associated states of the Republic of the Marshall Islands, the Federated States of Micronesia, or the Republic of Palau.

(End of clause)

[Final rule, 64 FR 52672, 9/30/99, effective 9/30/99; Final rule, 72 FR 20764, 4/26/2007, effective 4/26/2007]

252.222-7006 Restrictions on the Use of Mandatory Arbitration Agreements.

As prescribed in 222.7405, use the following clause:

RESTRICTIONS ON THE USE OF MANDATORY ARBITRATION AGREEMENTS (DEC 2010)

(a) *Definitions*. As used in this clause—

Covered subcontractor means any entity that has a subcontract valued in excess of $1 million, except a subcontract for the acquisition of commercial items, including commercially available off-the-shelf items.

Subcontract means any contract, as defined in Federal Acquisition Regulation subpart 2.1, to furnish supplies or services for performance of this contract or a higher-tier subcontract thereunder.

(b) The Contractor—

(1) Agrees not to—

(i) Enter into any agreement with any of its employees or independent contractors that requires, as a condition of employment, that the employee or independent contractor agree to resolve through arbitration—

(A) Any claim under title VII of the Civil Rights Act of 1964; or

(B) Any tort related to or arising out of sexual assault or harassment, including assault and battery, intentional infliction of emotional distress, false imprisonment, or negligent hiring, supervision, or retention; or

(ii) Take any action to enforce any provision of an existing agreement with an employee or independent contractor that mandates that the employee or independent contractor resolve through arbitration—

(A) Any claim under title VII of the Civil Rights Act of 1964; or

(B) Any tort related to or arising out of sexual assault or harassment, including assault and battery, intentional infliction of emotional distress, false imprisonment, or negligent hiring, supervision, or retention; and

(2) Certifies, by signature of the contract, that it requires each covered subcontractor to agree not to enter into, and not to take any action to enforce, any provision of any existing agreements, as described in paragraph (b)(1) of this clause, with respect to any employee or independent contractor performing work related to such subcontract.

(c) The prohibitions of this clause do not apply with respect to a contractor's or subcontractor's agreements with employees or independent contractors that may not be enforced in a court of the United States.

(d) The Secretary of Defense may waive the applicability of the restrictions of paragraph (b) of this clause in accordance with Defense Federal Acquisition Regulation Supplement 222.7404.

(End of clause)

[Interim rule, 71 FR 62560, 10/26/2006, effective 10/26/2006; Final rule, 73 FR 4115, 1/24/2008, effective 1/24/2008; Interim rule, 75 FR 27946, 5/19/2010, effective 5/19/2010; Final rule, 75 FR 40717, 7/13/2010, effective 7/13/2010; Final rule, 75 FR 76295, 12/8/2010, effective 12/8/2010]

252.222-7007 [Removed]

[Final rule, 80 FR 4999, 1/29/2015, effective 1/29/2015; Final rule, 83 FR 24887, 5/30/2018, effective 5/30/2018]

252.223 Environment, Energy and Water Efficiency, Renewable Energy Technology, Occupational Safety, and Drug-Free Workplace, provisions and clauses for DFARS Part 223

252.223-7000 [Reserved]

[Reserved, DAC 91-1, 56 FR 67221, 12/30/91, effective 12/31/91]

252.223-7001 Hazard warning labels.

As prescribed in 223.303, use the following clause:

HAZARD WARNING LABELS (DEC 1991)

(a) *Hazardous material*, as used in this clause, is defined in the Hazardous Material Identification and Material Safety Data clause of this contract.

(b) The Contractor shall label the item package (unit container) of any hazardous material to be delivered under this contract in accordance with the Hazard Communication Standard (29 CFR 1910.1200 *et seq*). The Standard requires that the hazard warning label conform to the requirements of the standard unless the material is otherwise subject to the labelling requirements of one of the following statutes:

(1) Federal Insecticide, Fungicide and Rodenticide Act;

(2) Federal Food, Drug and Cosmetics Act;

(3) Consumer Product Safety Act;

(4) Federal Hazardous Substances Act; or

(5) Federal Alcohol Administration Act.

(c) The Offeror shall list which hazardous material listed in the Hazardous Material Identification and Material Safety Data clause of this contract will be labelled in accordance with one of the Acts in paragraphs (b) (1) through (5) of this clause instead of the Hazard Communication Standard. Any hazardous material not listed will be interpreted to mean that a label is required in accordance with the Hazard Communication Standard.

Material (if none, insert "none.")	Act
________	________
________	________

(d) The apparently successful Offeror agrees to submit, before award, a copy of the hazard warning label for all hazardous materials not listed in paragraph (c) of this clause. The Offeror shall submit the label with the Material Safety Data Sheet being furnished under the Hazardous Material Identification and Material Safety Data clause of this contract.

(e) The Contractor shall also comply with MIL-STD-129, Marking for Shipment and Storage (including revisions adopted during the term of this contract).

(End of clause)

252.223-7002 Safety precautions for ammunition and explosives.

As prescribed in 223.370-5, use the following clause:

SAFETY PRECAUTIONS FOR AMMUNITION AND EXPLOSIVES (MAY 1994)

(a) *Definition. Ammunition and explosives*, as used in this clause—

(1) Means liquid and solid propellants and explosives, pyrotechnics, incendiaries and smokes in the following forms:

(i) Bulk;

(ii) Ammunition;

(iii) Rockets;

(iv) Missiles;

(v) Warheads;

(vi) Devices; and

(vii) Components of (i) through (vi), except for wholly inert items.

(2) This definition does not include the following, unless the Contractor is using or

incorporating these materials for initiation, propulsion, or detonation as an integral or component part of an explosive, an ammunition or explosive end item, or of a weapon system—

(i) Inert components containing no explosives, propellants, or pyrotechnics;

(ii) Flammable liquids;

(iii) Acids;

(iv) Oxidizers

(v) Powdered metals; or

(vi) Other materials having fire or explosive characteristics.

(b) *Safety requirements*. (1) The Contractor shall comply with the requirements of the DoD Contractors' Safety Manual for Ammunition and Explosives, DoD 4145.26-M hereafter referred to as "the manual," in effect on the date of this solicitation for this contract. The Contractor shall also comply with any other additional requirements included in the schedule of this contract.

(2) The Contractor shall allow the Government access to the Contractor's facilities, personnel, and safety program documentation. The Contractor shall allow authorized Government representatives to evaluate safety programs, implementation, and facilities.

(c) *Noncompliance with the manual*. (1) If the Contracting Officer notifies the Contractor of any noncompliance with the manual or schedule provisions, the Contractor shall take immediate steps to correct the noncompliance. The Contractor is not entitled to reimbursement of costs incurred to correct noncompliance unless such reimbursement is specified elsewhere in the contract.

(2) The Contractor has 30 days from the date of notification by the Contracting Officer to correct the noncompliance and inform the Contracting Officer of the actions taken. The Contracting Officer may direct a different time period for the correction of noncompliance.

(3) If the Contractor refuses or fails to correct noncompliance within the time period specified by the Contracting Officer, the Government has the right to direct the Contractor to cease performance on all or part of this contract. The Contractor shall not resume performance until the Contracting Officer is satisfied that the corrective action was effective and the Contracting Officer so informs the Contractor.

(4) The Contracting Officer may remove Government personnel at any time the Contractor is in noncompliance with any safety requirement of this clause.

(5) If the direction to cease work or the removal of Government personnel results in increased costs to the Contractor, the Contractor shall not be entitled to an adjustment in the contract price or a change in the delivery or performance schedule unless the Contracting Officer later determines that the Contractor had in fact complied with the manual or schedule provisions. If the Contractor is entitled to an equitable adjustment, it shall be made in accordance with the Changes clause of this contract.

(d) *Mishaps*. If a mishap involving ammunition or explosives occurs, the Contractor shall—

(1) Notify the Contracting Officer immediately;

(2) Conduct an investigation in accordance with other provisions of this contract or as required by the Contracting Officer; and

(3) Submit a written report to the Contracting Officer.

(e) *Contractor responsibility for safety*. (1) Nothing in this clause, nor any Government action or failure to act in surveillance of this contract, shall relieve the Contractor of its responsibility for the safety of—

(i) The Contractor's personnel and property;

(ii) The Government's personnel and property; or

(iii) The general public.

(2) Nothing in this clause shall relieve the Contractor of its responsibility for complying with applicable Federal, State, and local laws, ordinances, codes, and regulations (including those requiring the obtaining of li-

censes and permits) in connection with the performance of this contract.

(f) *Contractor responsibility for contract performance.* (1) Neither the number or frequency of inspections performed by the Government, nor the degree of surveillance exercised by the Government, relieve the Contractor of its responsibility for contract performance.

(2) If the Government acts or fails to act in surveillance or enforcement of the safety requirements of this contract, this does not impose or add to any liability of the Government.

(g) *Subcontractors.* (1) The Contractor shall insert this clause, including this paragraph (g), in every subcontract that involves ammunition or explosives.

(i) The clause shall include a provision allowing authorized Government safety representatives to evaluate subcontractor safety programs, implementation, and facilities as the Government determines necessary.

(ii) **Note:** The Government Contracting Officer or authorized representative shall notify the prime Contractor of all findings concerning subcontractor safety and compliance with the manual. The Contracting Officer or authorized representative may furnish copies to the subcontractor. The Contractor in turn shall communicate directly with the subcontractor, substituting its name for references to "the Government". The Contractor and higher tier subcontractors shall also include provisions to allow direction to cease performance of the subcontract if a serious uncorrected or recurring safety deficiency potentially causes an imminent hazard to DoD personnel, property, or contract performance.

(2) The Contractor agrees to ensure that the subcontractor complies with all contract safety requirements. The Contractor will determine the best method for verifying the adequacy of the subcontractor's compliance.

(3) The Contractor shall ensure that the subcontractor understands and agrees to the Government's right to access to the subcontractor's facilities, personnel, and safety program documentation to perform safety surveys. The Government performs these safety surveys of subcontractor facilities solely to prevent the occurrence of any mishap which would endanger the safety of DoD personnel or otherwise adversely impact upon the Government's contractual interests.

(4) The Contractor shall notify the Contracting Officer or authorized representative before issuing any subcontract when it involves ammunition or explosives. If the proposed subcontract represents a change in the place of performance, the Contractor shall request approval for such change in accordance with the clause of this contract entitled "Change in Place of Performance—Ammunition and Explosives".

(End of clause)

[DAC 91-6, 59 FR 27662, 5/27/94, effective 5/27/94]

252.223-7003 Change in place of performance—ammunition and explosives.

As prescribed in 223.370-5, use the following clause:

CHANGE IN PLACE OF PERFORMANCE—AMMUNITION AND EXPLOSIVES (DEC 1991)

(a) The Offeror shall identify, in the "Place of Performance" provision of this solicitation, the place of performance of all ammunition and explosives work covered by the Safety Precautions for Ammunition and Explosives clause of this solicitation. Failure to furnish this information with the offer may result in rejection of the offer.

(b) The Offeror agrees not to change the place of performance of any portion of the offer covered by the Safety Precautions for Ammunition and Explosives clause contained in this solicitation after the date set for receipt of offers without the written approval of the Contracting Officer. The Contracting Officer shall grant approval only if there is enough time for the Government to perform the necessary safety reviews on the new proposed place of performance.

(c) If a contract results from this offer, the Contractor agrees not to change any place of performance previously cited without the advance written approval of the Contracting Officer.

(End of clause)

252.223-7004 Drug-free work force.

As prescribed in 223.570-2, use the following clause:

DRUG-FREE WORK FORCE (SEP 1988)

(a) *Definitions.* (1) *Employee in a sensitive position*, as used in this clause, means an employee who has been granted access to classified information; or employees in other positions that the Contractor determines involve national security, health or safety, or functions other than the foregoing requiring a high degree of trust and confidence.

(2) *Illegal drugs*, as used in this clause, means controlled substances included in Schedules I and II, as defined by section 802(6) of title 21 of the United States Code, the possession of which is unlawful under chapter 13 of that Title. The term *illegal drugs* does not mean the use of a controlled substance pursuant to a valid prescription or other uses authorized by law.

(b) The Contractor agrees to institute and maintain a program for achieving the objective of a drug-free work force. While this clause defines criteria for such a program, contractors are encouraged to implement alternative approaches comparable to the criteria in paragraph (c) that are designed to achieve the objectives of this clause.

(c) Contractor programs shall include the following, or appropriate alternatives:

(1) Employee assistance programs emphasizing high level direction, education, counseling, rehabilitation, and coordination with available community resources;

(2) Supervisory training to assist in identifying and addressing illegal drug use by Contractor employees;

(3) Provision for self-referrals as well as supervisory referrals to treatment with maximum respect for individual confidentiality consistent with safety and security issues;

(4) Provision for identifying illegal drug users, including testing on a controlled and carefully monitored basis. Employee drug testing programs shall be established taking account of the following:

(i) The Contractor shall establish a program that provides for testing for the use of illegal drugs by employees in sensitive positions. The extent of and criteria for such testing shall be determined by the Contractor based on considerations that include the nature of the work being performed under the contract, the employee's duties, the efficient use of Contractor resources, and the risks to health, safety, or national security that could result from the failure of an employee adequately to discharge his or her position.

(ii) In addition, the Contractor may establish a program for employee drug testing—

(A) When there is a reasonable suspicion that an employee uses illegal drugs; or

(B) When an employee has been involved in an accident or unsafe practice;

(C) As part of or as a follow-up to counseling or rehabilitation for illegal drug use;

(D) As part of a voluntary employee drug testing program.

(iii) The Contractor may establish a program to test applicants for employment for illegal drug use.

(iv) For the purpose of administering this clause, testing for illegal drugs may be limited to those substances for which testing is prescribed by section 2.1 of subpart B of the "Mandatory Guidelines for Federal Workplace Drug Testing Programs" (53 FR 11980 (April 11, 1988)), issued by the Department of Health and Human Services.

(d) Contractors shall adopt appropriate personnel procedures to deal with employees who are found to be using drugs illegally. Contractors shall not allow any employee to remain on duty or perform in a sensitive position who is found to use illegal drugs until such times as the Contractor, in accordance with procedures established by the Contractor, determines that the employee may perform in such a position.

(e) The provisions of this clause pertaining to drug testing program shall not apply to the extent they are inconsistent with state or local law, or with an existing collective bargaining agreement; provided that with respect to the latter, the Contractor agrees that those issues that are in conflict will be a subject of negotiation at the next collective bargaining session.

(End of clause)

[Interim final rule, 57 FR 32737, 7/23/92, effective 7/16/92, finalized without change, DAC 91-11, 61 FR 50446, 9/26/96; Final rule, 70 FR 73150, 12/9/2005, effective 12/9/2005]

252.223-7005 [Reserved]

[Removed and reserved, final rule, 63 FR 67804, 12/9/98, effective 12/9/98]

252.223-7006 Prohibition on Storage, Treatment, and Disposal of Toxic or Hazardous Materials.

Basic. As prescribed at 223.7106 and 223.7106(a), use the following clause:

PROHIBITION ON STORAGE, TREATMENT, AND DISPOSAL OF TOXIC OR HAZARDOUS MATERIALS—BASIC (SEP 2014)

(a) *Definitions*:

As used in this clause—

Storage means a non-transitory, semipermanent or permanent holding, placement, or leaving of material. It does not include a temporary accumulation of a limited quantity of a material used in or a waste generated or resulting from authorized activities, such as servicing, maintenance, or repair of Department of Defense (DoD) items, equipment, or facilities.

Toxic or hazardous materials means—

(i) Materials referred to in section 101(14) of the Comprehensive Environmental Response, Compensation, and Liability Act (CERCLA) of 1980 (42 U.S.C. 9601(14)) and materials designated under section 102 of CERCLA (42 U.S.C. 9602) (40 CFR Part 302);

(ii) Materials that are of an explosive, flammable, or pyrotechnic nature; or

(iii) Materials otherwise identified by the Secretary of Defense as specified in DoD regulations.

(b) In accordance with 10 U.S.C. 2692, the Contractor is prohibited from storing, treating, or disposing of toxic or hazardous materials not owned by DoD on a DoD installation, except to the extent authorized by a statutory exception to 10 U.S.C. 2692 or as authorized by the Secretary of Defense. A charge may be assessed for any storage or disposal authorized under any of the exceptions to 10 U.S.C. 2692. If a charge is to be assessed, then such assessment shall be identified elsewhere in the contract with payment to the Government on a reimbursable cost basis.

(c) The Contractor shall include the substance of this clause, including this paragraph (c), in all subcontracts that require, may require, or permit a subcontractor access to a DoD installation, at any subcontract tier.

(End of clause)

Alternate I. As prescribed in 223.7106 and 223.7106(b), use the following clause, which add a new paragraph (c) and revises and redesignates paragraph (c) of the basic clause as paragraph (d).

PROHIBITION ON STORAGE, TREATMENT, AND DISPOSAL OF TOXIC OR HAZARDOUS MATERIALS—ALTERNATE I (SEP 2014)

(a) *Definitions.* As used in this clause—

Storage means a non-transitory, semipermanent or permanent holding, placement, or leaving of material. It does not include a temporary accumulation of a limited quantity of a material used in or a waste generated or resulting from authorized activities, such as servicing, maintenance, or repair of Department of Defense (DoD) items, equipment, or facilities.

Toxic or hazardous materials means—

(i) Materials referred to in section 101(14) of the Comprehensive Environmental Response, Compensation, and Liability Act (CERCLA) of 1980 (42 U.S.C. 9601(14)) and materials designated under section 102 of CERCLA (42 U.S.C. 9602) (40 CFR Part 302);

(ii) Materials that are of an explosive, flammable, or pyrotechnic nature; or

(iii) Materials otherwise identified by the Secretary of Defense as specified in DoD regulations.

(b) In accordance with 10 U.S.C. 2692, the Contractor is prohibited from storing, treating, or disposing of toxic or hazardous materials not owned by DoD on a DoD installation, except to the extent authorized by a statutory exception to 10 U.S.C. 2692 or as authorized by the Secretary of Defense. A charge may be assessed for any storage or disposal authorized under any of the exceptions to 10 U.S.C. 2692. If a charge is to be assessed, then such assessment shall be identified elsewhere in the contract with payment to the Government on a reimbursable cost basis.

(c) With respect to treatment or disposal authorized pursuant to DFARS 223.7104(10) (10 U.S.C. 2692(b)(10), and notwithstanding any other provision of the contract, the Contractor assumes all financial and environmental responsibility and liability resulting from any treatment or disposal of toxic or hazardous materials not owned by DoD on a military installation. The Contractor shall indemnify, defend, and hold the Government harmless for all costs, liability, or penalties resulting from the Contractor's treatment or disposal of toxic or hazardous materials not owned by DoD on a military installation.

(d) The Contractor shall include the substance of this clause, including this paragraph (d), in all subcontracts that require, may require, or permit a subcontractor access to a DoD installation, at any tier. Inclusion of the substance of this clause in subcontracts does not relieve the prime Contractor of liability to the Government under paragraph (c) of this clause.

(End of clause)

[Interim rule, DAC 91-5, 58 FR 28458, 5/13/93, effective 4/30/93; DAC 91-6, 59 FR 27662, 5/27/94, effective 5/27/94; interim rule, 60 FR 13075, 3/10/95, effective 3/6/95; DAC 91-9, 60 FR 61586, 11/30/95, effective 11/30/95; Final rule, 77 FR 23631, 4/20/2012, effective 4/20/2012; Final rule, 79 FR 58697, 9/30/2014, effective 9/30/2014; Final rule, 80 FR 36897, 6/26/2015, effective 6/26/2015]

252.223-7007 Safeguarding sensitive conventional arms, ammunition, and explosives.

As prescribed in 223.7203, use the following clause:

SAFEGUARDING SENSITIVE CONVENTIONAL ARMS, AMMUNITION, AND EXPLOSIVES (SEP 1999)

(a) *Definition.*

Arms, ammunition, and explosives (AA&E), as used in this clause, means those items within the scope (chapter 1, paragraph B) of DoD 5100.76-M, Physical Security of Sensitive Conventional Arms, Ammunition, and Explosives.

(b) The requirements of DoD 5100.76-M apply to the following items of AA&E being developed, produced, manufactured, or purchased for the Government, or provided to the Contractor as Government-furnished property under this contract:

Nomenclature	National stock number	Sensitivity category

(c) The Contractor shall comply with the requirements of DoD 5100.76-M, as specified in the statement of work. The edition of DoD 5100.76-M in effect on the date of issuance of the solicitation for this contract shall apply.

(d) The Contractor shall allow representatives of the Defense Security Service (DSS), and representatives of other appropriate offices of the Government, access at all reasonable times into its facilities and those of its subcontractors, for the purpose of performing surveys, inspections, and investigations necessary to review compliance with the physical security standards applicable to this contract.

(e) The Contractor shall notify the cognizant DSS field office of any subcontract involving AA&E within 10 days after award of the subcontract.

(f) The Contractor shall ensure that the requirements of this clause are included in all subcontracts, at every tier—

(1) For the development, production, manufacture, or purchase of AA&E; or

(2) When AA&E will be provided to the subcontractor as Government-furnished property.

(g) Nothing in this clause shall relieve the Contractor of its responsibility for complying with applicable Federal, state, and local laws, ordinances, codes, and regulations (including requirements for obtaining licenses and permits) in connection with the performance of this contract.

(End of clause)

[DAC 91-10, 61 FR 7739, 2/29/96, effective 2/29/96; Final rule, 64 FR 51074, 9/21/99, effective 9/21/99]

252.223-7008 Prohibition of Hexavalent Chromium.

As prescribed in 223.7306, use the following clause:

PROHIBITION OF HEXAVALENT CHROMIUM (JUN 2013)

(a) *Definitions.* As used in this clause— *Homogeneous material* means a material that cannot be mechanically disjointed into different materials and is of uniform composition throughout.

(1) Examples of homogeneous materials include individual types of plastics, ceramics, glass, metals, alloys, paper, board, resins, and surface coatings.

(2) Homogeneous material does not include conversion coatings that chemically modify the substrate.

Mechanically disjointed means that the materials can, in principle, be separated by mechanical actions such as unscrewing, cutting, crushing, grinding, and abrasive processes.

(b) *Prohibition.* (1) Unless otherwise specified by the Contracting Officer, the Contractor shall not provide any deliverable or construction material under this contract that—

(i) Contains hexavalent chromium in a concentration greater than 0.1 percent by weight in any homogenous material; or

(ii) Requires the removal or reapplication of hexavalent chromium materials during subsequent sustainment phases of the deliverable or construction material.

(2) This prohibition does not apply to hexavalent chromium produced as a by-product of manufacturing processes.

(c) If authorization for incorporation of hexavalent chromium in a deliverable or construction material is required, the Contractor shall submit a request to the Contracting Officer.

(d) *Subcontracts.* The Contractor shall include the substance of this clause, including this paragraph (d), in all subcontracts, including subcontracts for commercial items, that are for supplies, maintenance and repair services, or construction materials.

(End of clause)

[Final rule, 76 FR 25569, 5/5/2011, effective 5/5/2011; Final rule, 78 FR 37980, 6/25/2013, effective 6/25/2013]

252.225 Foreign Acquisition, provisions and clauses for DFARS Part 225

252.225-7000 Buy American—Balance of Payments Program Certificate.

Basic. As prescribed in 225.1101(1) and (1)(i), use the following provision:

BUY AMERICAN—BALANCE OF PAYMENTS PROGRAM CERTIFICATE—BASIC (NOV 2014)

(a) *Definitions. Commercially available off-the-shelf (COTS) item, component, domestic end product, foreign end product, qualifying country, qualifying country end product, South Caucasus/Central and South Asian (SC/CASA) state, South Caucasus/Central and South Asian (SC/CASA) state end product,* and *United States*, as used in this provision, have the meanings given in the Buy American and Balance of Payments Program—Basic clause of this solicitation.

(b) *Evaluation.* The Government—

(1) Will evaluate offers in accordance with the policies and procedures of Part 225 of

the Defense Federal Acquisition Regulation Supplement; and

(2) Will evaluate offers of qualifying country end products without regard to the restrictions of the Buy American statute or the Balance of Payments Program.

(c) *Certifications and identification of country of origin.*

(1) For all line items subject to the Buy American and Balance of Payments Program—Basic clause of this solicitation, the offeror certifies that—

(i) Each end product, except those listed in paragraph (c)(2) or (3) of this provision, is a domestic end product; and

(ii) For end products other than COTS items, components of unknown origin are considered to have been mined, produced, or manufactured outside the United States or a qualifying country.

(2) The offeror certifies that the following end products are qualifying country end products:

(Line Item Number)

(Country of Origin)

(3) The following end products are other foreign end products, including end products manufactured in the United States that do not qualify as domestic end products, i.e., an end product that is not a COTS item and does not meet the component test in paragraph (ii) of the definition of "domestic end product":

(Line Item Number)

(Country of Origin)

(End of provision)

Alternate I. As prescribed in 225.1101(1) and (1)(ii), use the following provision, which adds *South Caucasus/Central and South Asian (SC/CASA) state* and *South Caucasus/Central and South Asian (SC/CASA) state end product* in paragraph (a), and replaces *qualifying country end products* in paragraphs (b)(2) and (c)(2) with *qualifying country end products or SC/CASA state end products*:

BUY AMERICAN—BALANCE OF PAYMENTS PROGRAM CERTIFICATE—ALTERNATE I (NOV 2014)

(a) *Definitions. Commercially available off-the-shelf (COTS) item, component, domestic end product, foreign end product, qualifying country, qualifying country end product, South Caucasus/Central and South Asian (SC/CASA) state, South Caucasus/Central and South Asian (SC/CASA) state end product*, and *United States*, as used in this provision, have the meanings given in the Buy American and Balance of Payments Program—Alternate I clause of this solicitation.

(b) *Evaluation.* The Government—

(1) Will evaluate offers in accordance with the policies and procedures of part 225 of the Defense Federal Acquisition Regulation Supplement; and

(2) Will evaluate offers of qualifying country end products or SC/CASA state end products without regard to the restrictions of the Buy American statute or the Balance of Payments Program.

(c) *Certifications and identification of country of origin.*

(1) For all line items subject to the Buy American and Balance of Payments Program—Alternate I clause of this solicitation, the offeror certifies that—

(i) Each end product, except those listed in paragraphs (c)(2) or (3) of this provision, is a domestic end product; and

(ii) For end products other than COTS items, components of unknown origin are considered to have been mined, produced, or manufactured outside the United States or a qualifying country.

(2) The offeror certifies that the following end products are qualifying country end products or SC/CASA state end products:

Line Item Number

Country of Origin

---

(3) The following end products are other foreign end products, including end products manufactured in the United States that do not qualify as domestic end products, i.e., an end product that is not a COTS item and

does not meet the component test in paragraph (ii) of the definition of *domestic end product*:

Line Item Number

Country of Origin (if known)

(End of provision)

[Final rule, 64 FR 51074, 9/21/99, effective 9/21/99; Final rule, 65 FR 19849, 4/13/2000, effective 4/13/2000; Final rule, 68 FR 15615, 3/31/2003, effective 4/30/2003; Final rule, 70 FR 35543, 6/21/2005, effective 6/21/2005; Interim rule, 74 FR 2422, 1/15/2009, effective 1/15/2009; Final rule, 74 FR 68383, 12/24/2009, effective 12/24/2009; Final rule, 74 FR 68384, 12/24/2009, effective 12/24/2009; Final rule, 75 FR 81915, 12/29/2010, effective 12/29/2010; Final rule, 77 FR 35879, 6/15/2012, effective 6/15/2012; Final rule, 79 FR 3519, 1/22/2014, effective 1/22/2014; Final rule, 79 FR 65815, 11/5/2014, effective 11/5/2014; Final rule, 80 FR 36897, 6/26/2015, effective 6/26/2015]

252.225-7001 Buy American and Balance of Payments Program.

Basic. As prescribed in 225.1101(2)(i) and (2)(ii), use the following clause:

BUY AMERICAN AND BALANCE OF PAYMENTS PROGRAM—BASIC (DEC 2017)

(a) *Definitions.* As used in this clause—

Commercially available off-the-shelf (COTS) item—

(i) Means any item of supply (including construction material) that is—

(A) A commercial item (as defined in paragraph (1) of the definition of *commercial item* in section 2.101 of the Federal Acquisition Regulation);

(B) Sold in substantial quantities in the commercial marketplace; and

(C) Offered to the Government, under a contract or subcontract at any tier, without modification, in the same form in which it is sold in the commercial marketplace; and

(ii) Does not include bulk cargo, as defined in 46 U.S.C. 40102(4), such as agricultural products and petroleum products.

Component means an article, material, or supply incorporated directly into an end product.

Domestic end product means—

(i) An unmanufactured end product that has been mined or produced in the United States; or

(ii) An end product manufactured in the United States if—

(A) The cost of its qualifying country components and its components that are mined, produced, or manufactured in the United States exceeds 50 percent of the cost of all its components. The cost of components includes transportation costs to the place of incorporation into the end product and U.S. duty (whether or not a duty-free entry certificate is issued). Scrap generated, collected, and prepared for processing in the United States is considered domestic. A component is considered to have been mined, produced, or manufactured in the United States (regardless of its source in fact) if the end product in which it is incorporated is manufactured in the United States and the component is of a class or kind for which the Government has determined that—

(1) Sufficient and reasonably available commercial quantities of a satisfactory quality are not mined, produced, or manufactured in the United States; or

(2) It is inconsistent with the public interest to apply the restrictions of the Buy American statute; or

(B) The end product is a COTS item.

End product means those articles, materials, and supplies to be acquired under this contract for public use.

Foreign end product means an end product other than a domestic end product.

Qualifying country means a country with a reciprocal defense procurement memorandum of understanding or international agreement with the United States in which both countries agree to remove barriers to purchases of supplies produced in the other country or services performed by sources of the other country, and the memorandum or agreement complies, where applicable, with the requirements of section 36 of the Arms Export Control Act (22 U.S.C. 2776) and with 10 U.S.C. 2457. Accordingly, the following are qualifying countries:

Australia, Austria, Belgium, Canada, Czech Republic, Denmark, Egypt, Estonia, Finland, France, Germany, Greece, Israel, Italy, Japan, Latvia, Luxembourg, Netherlands, Norway, Poland, Portugal, Slovenia, Spain, Sweden, Switzerland, Turkey, United Kingdom of Great Britain and Northern Ireland.

Qualifying country component means a component mined, produced, or manufactured in a qualifying country.

Qualifying country end product means—

(i) An unmanufactured end product mined or produced in a qualifying country; or

(ii) An end product manufactured in a qualifying country if—

(A) The cost of the following types of components exceeds 50 percent of the cost of all its components:

(*1*) Components mined, produced, or manufactured in a qualifying country.

(*2*) Components mined, produced, or manufactured in the United States.

(*3*) Components of foreign origin of a class or kind for which the Government has determined that sufficient and reasonably available commercial quantities of a satisfactory quality are not mined, produced, or manufactured in the United States; or

(B) The end product is a COTS item.

United States means the 50 States, the District of Columbia, and outlying areas.

(b) This clause implements Buy American [41 U.S.C. Chapter 83]. In accordance with 41 U.S.C. 1907, the component test of the Buy American statute is waived for an end product that is a COTS item (see section 12.505(a)(1) of the Federal Acquisition Regulation). Unless otherwise specified, this clause applies to all line items in the contract.

(c) The Contractor shall deliver only domestic end products unless, in its offer, it specified delivery of other end products in the Buy American—Balance of Payments Program Certificate provision of the solicitation. If the Contractor certified in its offer that it will deliver a qualifying country end product, the Contractor shall deliver a qualifying country end product or, at the Contractor's option, a domestic end product.

(d) The contract price does not include duty for end products or components for which the Contractor will claim duty-free entry.

(End of clause)

Alternate I. As prescribed in 225.1101(2)(i) and (2)(iii), use the following clause, which adds *South Caucasus/ Central and South Asian (SC/CASA) state* and *South Caucasus/Central and South Asian (SC/ CASA) state end product* to paragraph (a), and uses different paragraphs (b) and (c) than the basic clause:

BUY AMERICAN AND BALANCE OF PAYMENTS PROGRAM—ALTERNATE I (DEC 2017)

(a) *Definitions.* As used in this clause—*Commercially available off-the-shelf (COTS) item*—

(i) Means any item of supply (including construction material) that is—

(A) A commercial item (as defined in paragraph (1) of the definition of "commercial item" in section 2.101 of the Federal Acquisition Regulation);

(B) Sold in substantial quantities in the commercial marketplace; and

(C) Offered to the Government, under a contract or subcontract at any tier, without modification, in the same form in which it is sold in the commercial marketplace; and

(ii) Does not include bulk cargo, as defined in 46 U.S.C. 40102(4), such as agricultural products and petroleum products.

Component means an article, material, or supply incorporated directly into an end product.

Domestic end product means—

(i) An unmanufactured end product that has been mined or produced in the United States; or

(ii) An end product manufactured in the United States if—

(A) The cost of its qualifying country components and its components that are mined, produced, or manufactured in the United States exceeds 50 percent of the cost of all its components. The cost of components includes transportation costs to the place of incorporation into the end product and U.S. duty (whether or not a duty-free entry certificate is issued). Scrap generated, collected, and prepared for processing in the United States is considered domestic. A component is considered to have been mined, produced, or manufactured in the United States (regardless of its source in fact) if the end product in which it is incorporated is manufactured in the United States and the component is of a class or kind for which the Government has determined that—

(1) Sufficient and reasonably available commercial quantities of a satisfactory quality are not mined, produced, or manufactured in the United States; or

(2) It is inconsistent with the public interest to apply the restrictions of the Buy American statute; or

(B) The end product is a COTS item.

End product means those articles, materials, and supplies to be acquired under this contract for public use.

Foreign end product means an end product other than a domestic end product.

Qualifying country means a country with a reciprocal defense procurement memorandum of understanding or international agreement with the United States in which both countries agree to remove barriers to purchases of supplies produced in the other country or services performed by sources of the other country, and the memorandum or agreement complies, where applicable, with the requirements of section 36 of the Arms Export Control Act (22 U.S.C. 2776) and with 10 U.S.C. 2457. Accordingly, the following are qualifying countries:

Australia

Austria

Belgium

Canada

Czech Republic

Denmark

Egypt

Estonia

Finland

France

Germany

Greece

Israel

Italy

Japan

Latvia

Luxembourg

Netherlands

Norway

Poland

Portugal

Slovenia

Spain

Sweden

Switzerland

Turkey

United Kingdom of Great Britain and Northern Ireland.

Qualifying country component means a component mined, produced, or manufactured in a qualifying country.

Qualifying country end product means—

(i) An unmanufactured end product mined or produced in a qualifying country; or

(ii) An end product manufactured in a qualifying country if—

(A) The cost of the following types of components exceeds 50 percent of the cost of all its components:

(1) Components mined, produced, or manufactured in a qualifying country.

(2) Components mined, produced, or manufactured in the United States.

(3) Components of foreign origin of a class or kind for which the Government has determined that sufficient and reasonably available commercial quantities of a satisfactory quality are not mined, produced, or manufactured in the United States; or

(B) The end product is a COTS item.

South Caucasus/Central and South Asian (SC/CASA) state means Armenia, Azerbaijan, Georgia, Kazakhstan, Kyrgyzstan, Pakistan, Tajikistan, Turkmenistan, or Uzbekistan.

South Caucasus/Central and South Asian (SC/CASA) state end product means an article that—

(i) Is wholly the growth, product, or manufacture of an SC/CASA state; or

(ii) In the case of an article that consists in whole or in part of materials from another country, has been substantially transformed in an SC/CASA state into a new and different article of commerce with a name, character, or use distinct from that of the article or articles from which it was transformed. The term refers to a product offered for purchase under a supply contract, but for purposes of calculating the value of the end product includes services (except transportation services) incidental to its supply, provided that the value of those incidental services does not exceed the value of the product itself.

United States means the 50 States, the District of Columbia, and outlying areas.

(b) This clause implements the Balance of Payments Program. Unless otherwise specified, this clause applies to all line items in the contract.

(c) The Contractor shall deliver only domestic end products unless, in its offer, it specified delivery of other end products in the Buy American Balance of Payments Program Certificate provision of the solicitation. If the Contractor certified in its offer that it will deliver a qualifying country end product or an SC/CASA state end product, the Contractor shall deliver a qualifying country end product, an SC/CASA state end product, or, at the Contractor's option, a domestic end product.

(d) The contract price does not include duty for end products or components for which the Contractor will claim duty-free entry.

(End of clause)

[DAC 91-13, 63 FR 11522, 3/9/98, effective 3/9/98; Final rule, 65 FR 19849, 4/13/2000, effective 4/13/2000; Final rule, 68 FR 15615, 3/31/2003, effective 4/30/2003; Final rule, 70 FR 35543, 6/21/2005, effective 6/21/2005; Interim rule, 74 FR 2422, 1/15/2009, effective 1/15/2009; Final rule, 74 FR 68384, 12/24/2009, effective 12/24/2009; Final rule, 75 FR 81915, 12/29/2010, effective 12/29/2010; Final rule, 76 FR 58137, 9/20/2011, effective 9/20/2011; Final rule, 76 FR 61282, 10/4/2011, effective 10/4/2011; Final rule, 77 FR 35879, 6/15/2012, effective 6/15/2012; Final rule, 77 FR 38736, 6/29/2012, effective 6/29/2012; Final rule, 77 FR 76941, 12/31/2012, effective 12/31/2012; Final rule, 79 FR 3519, 1/22/2014, effective 1/22/2014; Final rule, 79 FR 65815, 11/5/2014, effective 11/5/2014; Final rule, 80 FR 36897, 6/26/2015, effective 6/26/2015; Final rule, 81 FR 50650, 8/2/2016, effective 8/2/2016; Final rule, 81 FR 93840, 12/22/2016, effective 12/22/2016; Final rule, 82 FR 61483, 12/28/2017, effective 12/28/2017]

252.225-7002 Qualifying country sources as subcontractors.

As prescribed in 225.1101(3), use the following clause:

QUALIFYING COUNTRY SOURCES AS SUBCONTRACTORS (DEC 2017)

(a) *Definition. Qualifying country,* as used in this clause, means a country with a reciprocal defense procurement memorandum of understanding or international agreement with the United States in which both countries agree to remove barriers to purchases of supplies produced in the other country or services performed by sources of the other country, and the memorandum or agreement complies, where applicable, with the requirements of section 36 of the Arms Export Control Act (22 U.S.C. 2776) and with 10 U.S.C. 2457. Accordingly, the following are qualifying countries:

Australia

Austria

Belgium

Canada

Czech Republic

Denmark

Egypt

Estonia

France

Germany

Greece

Israel

Italy

Japan

Latvia

Luxembourg

Netherlands

Norway

Poland

Portugal

Slovenia

Spain

Sweden

Switzerland

Turkey

United Kingdom of Great Britain and Northern Ireland

(b) Subject to the restrictions in section 225.872 of the Defense FAR Supplement, the Contractor shall not preclude qualifying country sources or U.S. sources from competing for subcontracts under this contract.

(End of clause)

[Final rule, 68 FR 15615, 3/31/2003, effective 4/30/2003; Final rule, 77 FR 38736, 6/29/2012, effective 6/29/2012; Final rule, 77 FR 76941, 12/31/2012, effective 12/31/2012; Final rule, 81 FR 50650, 8/2/2016, effective 8/2/2016; Final rule, 81 FR 93840, 12/22/2016, effective 12/22/2016; Final rule, 82 FR 61483, 12/28/2017, effective 12/28/2017]

252.225-7003 Report of intended performance outside the United States and Canada—Submission with offer.

As prescribed in 225.7204(a), use the following provision:

REPORT OF INTENDED PERFORMANCE OUTSIDE THE UNITED STATES AND CANADA—SUBMISSION WITH OFFER (OCT 2015)

(a) *Definition. United States*, as used in this provision, means the 50 States, the District of Columbia, and outlying areas.

(b) The offeror shall submit, with its offer, a report of intended performance outside the United States and Canada if—

(1) The offer exceeds $13.5 million in value; and

(2) The offeror is aware that the offeror or a first-tier subcontractor intends to perform any part of the contract outside the United States and Canada that—

(i) Exceeds $700,000 in value; and

(ii) Could be performed inside the United States or Canada.

(c) Information to be reported includes that for—

(1) Subcontracts;

(2) Purchases; and

(3) Intracompany transfers when transfers originate in a foreign location.

(d) The offeror shall submit the report using—

(1) DD Form 2139, Report of Contract Performance Outside the United States; or

(2) A computer-generated report that contains all information required by DD Form 2139.

(e) The offeror may obtain a copy of DD Form 2139 from the Contracting Officer or via the Internet at *http://www.dtic.mil/whs/directives/infomgt/forms/formsprogram.htm.*

(End of provision)

[DAC 91-13, 63 FR 11522, 3/9/98, effective 3/9/98; Final rule, 65 FR 19849, 4/13/2000, effective 4/13/2000; Final rule, 68 FR 15615, 3/31/2003, effective 4/30/2003; Final rule, 70 FR 20838, 4/22/2005, effective 4/22/2005; Final rule, 70 FR 35543, 6/21/2005, effective 6/21/2005; Final rule, 71 FR 75891, 12/19/2006, effective 12/19/2006; Final rule, 75 FR 45072, 8/2/2010, effective 10/1/2010; Final rule, 80 FR 36903, 6/26/2015, effective 10/1/2015]

252.225-7004 Report of Intended Performance Outside the United States and Canada—Submission after Award.

As prescribed in 225.7204(b), use the following clause:

REPORT OF INTENDED PERFORMANCE OUTSIDE THE UNITED STATES AND CANADA—SUBMISSION AFTER AWARD (MAY 2019)

(a) *Definition.* As used in this clause—

United States means the 50 States, the District of Columbia, and outlying areas.

(b) *Reporting requirement.* The Contractor shall submit a report in accordance with this clause, if the Contractor or a first-tier subcontractor will perform any part of this contract outside the United States and Canada that—

(1) Exceeds the threshold specified in Defense Federal Acquisition Regulation Supplement 225.870-4(c)(2)(i)(A)(*1*) on the date of award of this contract; and

(2) Could be performed inside the United States or Canada.

(c) *Submission of reports.* The Contractor—

(1) Shall submit a report as soon as practical after the information is known;

(2) To the maximum extent practicable, shall submit a report regarding a first-tier subcontractor at least 30 days before award of the subcontract;

(3) Need not resubmit information submitted with its offer, unless the information changes;

(4) Shall submit all reports to the Contracting Officer; and

(5) Shall submit a copy of each report to: Deputy Director of Defense Procurement and Acquisition Policy (Contract Policy and International Contracting), OUSD(AT&L) DPAP/CPIC, Washington, DC 20301-3060.

(d) *Report format.* The Contractor—

(1) Shall submit reports using—

(i) DD Form 2139, Report of Contract Performance Outside the United States; or

(ii) A computer-generated report that contains all information required by DD Form 2139; and

(2) May obtain copies of DD Form 2139 from the Contracting Officer or via the Internet at *http://www.dtic.mil/whs/directives/infomgt/forms/formsprogram.htm.*

(End of clause)

[Removed and reserved, DAC 91-12, 62 FR 34114, 6/24/97, effective 6/24/97; Added, Final rule, 68 FR 15615, 3/31/2003, effective 4/30/2003; Final rule, 70 FR 20838, 4/22/2005, effective 4/22/2005; Final rule, 70 FR 35543, 6/21/2005, effective 6/21/2005; Final rule, 71 FR 75891, 12/19/2006, effective 12/19/2006; Final rule, 72 FR 30278, 5/31/2007, effective 5/31/2007; Final rule, 75 FR 45072, 8/2/2010, effective 10/1/2010; Final rule, 78 FR 73450, 12/6/2013, effective 12/6/2013; Final rule, 80 FR 36903, 6/26/2015, effective 10/1/2015; Final rule, 84 FR 25186, 5/31/2019, effective 5/31/2019]

252.225-7005 Identification of expenditures in the United States.

As prescribed in 225.1103(1), use the following clause:

IDENTIFICATION OF EXPENDITURES IN THE UNITED STATES (JUN 2005)

(a) *Definition. United States,* as used in this provision, means the 50 States, the District of Columbia, and outlying areas.

(b) This clause applies only if the Contractor is—

(1) A concern incorporated in the United States (including a subsidiary that is incorporated in the United States, even if the parent corporation is not incorporated in the United States); or

(2) An unincorporated concern having its principal place of business in the United States.

(c) On each invoice, voucher, or other request for payment under this contract, the Contractor shall identify that part of the requested payment that represents estimated expenditures in the United States. The identification—

(1) May be expressed either as dollar amounts or as percentages of the total amount of the request for payment;

(2) Should be based on reasonable estimates; and

(3) Shall state the full amount of the payment requested, subdivided into the following categories:

(i) U.S. products—expenditures for material and equipment manufactured or produced in the United States, including end products, components, or construction material, but excluding transportation;

(ii) U.S. services—expenditures for services performed in the United States, including all charges for overhead, other indirect costs, and profit under construction or service contracts;

(iii) Transportation on U.S. carriers—expenditures for transportation furnished by U.S. flag, ocean, surface, and air carriers; and

(iv) Expenditures not identified under paragraphs (c)(3)(i) through (iii) of this clause.

(d) Nothing in this clause requires the establishment or maintenance of detailed accounting records or gives the U.S. Government any right to audit the Contractor's books or records.

(End of clause)

[Final rule, 65 FR 19849, 4/13/2000, effective 4/13/2000; Final rule 67 FR 20693, 4/26/2002 effective 4/26/2002; Final rule, 70 FR 35543, 6/21/2005, effective 6/21/2005; Correction, 79 FR 75757, 12/19/2014, effective 12/19/2014]

252.225-7006 Acquisition of the American Flag.

As prescribed in 225.7002-3(c), insert the following clause:

ACQUISITION OF THE AMERICAN FLAG (AUG 2015)

(a) *Definition. United States*, as used in this clause, means the 50 States, the District of Columbia, and outlying areas.

(b) If the Contractor is required to deliver under this contract one or more American flags (Product or Service Code 8345), such flag(s), including the materials and components thereof, shall be manufactured in the United States, consistent with the requirements at 10 U.S.C. 2533a (commonly known as the "Berry Amendment").

(c) This clause does not apply to the acquisition of any end items or components related to flying or displaying the flag (e.g., flagpoles and accessories).

[DAC 91-12, 62 FR 34114, 6/27/97, effective 6/24/97; DAC 91-13, 63 FR 11522, 3/9/98, effective 3/9/98; Final rule, 65 FR 19849, 4/13/2000, effective 4/13/2000; Final rule, 67 FR 77937, 12/20/2002, effective 12/20/2002; Final rule, 70 FR 20838, 4/22/2005, effective 4/22/2005; Final rule, 70 FR 35543, 6/21/2005, effective 6/21/2005; Final rule, 71 FR 75891, 12/19/2006, effective 12/19/2006; Final rule, 72 FR 30278, 5/31/2007, effective 5/31/2007; Final rule, 75 FR 45072, 8/2/2010, effective 10/1/2010; Final rule, 78 FR 73450, 12/6/2013, effective 12/6/2013; Final rule, 79 FR 73499, 12/11/2014, effective 12/11/2014; Correction, 79 FR 75757, 12/19/2014, effective 12/19/2014; Final rule, 80 FR 51748, 8/26/2015, effective 8/26/2015]

252.225-7007 Prohibition on Acquisition of Certain Items from Communist Chinese Military Companies.

As prescribed in 225.1103(4), use the following clause:

PROHIBITION ON ACQUISITION OF CERTAIN ITEMS FROM COMMUNIST CHINESE MILITARY COMPANIES (DEC 2018)

(a) *Definitions*. As used in this clause—

600 series of the Commerce Control List means the series of 5-character export control classification numbers (ECCNs) of the Commerce Control List of the Export Administration Regulations in 15 CFR part 774, supplement no. 1, that have a "6" as the third character. The 600 series constitutes the munitions and munitions-related ECCNs within the larger Commerce Control List. (See definition of "600 series" in 15 CFR 772.)

Communist Chinese military company means any entity, regardless of geographic location, that is—

(1) A part of the commercial or defense industrial base of the People's Republic of China (including a subsidiary or affiliate of such entity); or

(2) Owned or controlled by, or affiliated with, an element of the Government or armed forces of the People's Republic of China.

Item means—

(1) A USML defense article, as defined at 22 CFR 120.6;

(2) A USML defense service, as defined at 22 CFR 120.9; or

(3) A 600 series item, as defined at 15 CFR 772.1.

United States Munitions List means the munitions list of the International Traffic in Arms Regulation in 22 CFR part 121.

(b) Any items covered by the United States Munitions List or the 600 series of the Commerce Control List that are delivered under this contract may not be acquired, directly or indirectly, from a Communist Chinese military company.

(c) The Contractor shall insert the substance of this clause, including this paragraph (c), in all subcontracts for items covered by the United States Munitions List or the 600 series of the Commerce Control List.

(End of clause)

[DAC 91-13, 63 FR 11522, 3/9/98, effective 3/9/98; Final rule, 64 FR 8730, 2/23/99, effective 2/23/99; Final rule, 65 FR 19859, 4/13/2000, effective 4/13/2000; Final rule, 65 FR 19849, 4/13/2000, effective 4/13/2000; Final rule, 66 FR 47112, 9/11/2001, effective 9/11/2001; Interim rule, 66 FR 47113, 9/11/2001, effective 9/11/2001, finalized without change, 67 FR 4210, 1/29/2002, effective 1/29/2002; Final rule, 67 FR 65514, 10/25/2002, effective 10/25/2002; Final rule, 67 FR 77937, 12/20/2002, effective 12/20/2002; Interim rule, 71 FR 53045, 9/8/2006, effective 9/8/2006; Final rule, 72 FR 14239, 3/27/2007, effective 3/27/2007; Interim rule, 83 FR 66066, 12/21/2018, effective 12/21/2018; Final rule, 84 FR 25188, 5/31/2019, effective 5/31/2019]

252.225-7008 Restriction on Acquisition of Specialty Metals.

As prescribed in 225.7003-5(a)(1), use the following clause:

RESTRICTION ON ACQUISITION OF SPECIALTY METALS (MAR 2013)

(a) *Definitions*. As used in this clause—

Alloy means a metal consisting of a mixture of a basic metallic element and one or more metallic, or non-metallic, alloying elements.

(i) For alloys named by a single metallic element (*e.g.*, titanium alloy), it means that the alloy contains 50 percent or more of the named metal (by mass).

(ii) If two metals are specified in the name (*e.g.*, nickel-iron alloy), those metals are the two predominant elements in the alloy, and together they constitute 50 percent or more of the alloy (by mass).

Produce means—

(i) Atomization;

(ii) Sputtering; or

(iii) Final consolidation of non-melt derived metal powders.

Specialty metal means—

(i) Steel—

(A) With a maximum alloy content exceeding one or more of the following limits: Manganese, 1.65 percent; silicon, 0.60 percent; or copper, 0.60 percent; or

(B) Containing more than 0.25 percent of any of the following elements: Aluminum, chromium, cobalt, molybdenum, nickel, niobium (columbium), titanium, tungsten, or vanadium;

(ii) Metal alloys consisting of—

(A) Nickel or iron-nickel alloys that contain a total of alloying metals other than nickel and iron in excess of 10 percent; or

(B) Cobalt alloys that contain a total of alloying metals other than cobalt and iron in excess of 10 percent;

(iii) Titanium and titanium alloys; or

(iv) Zirconium and zirconium alloys.

Steel means an iron alloy that includes between .02 and 2 percent carbon and may include other elements.

(b) Any specialty metal delivered under this contract shall be melted or produced in the United States or its outlying areas.

(End of clause)

[DAC 91-13, 63 FR 11522, 3/9/98, effective 3/9/98; Final rule, 65 FR 19849, 4/13/2000, effective 4/13/2000; Final rule, 67 FR 77937, 12/20/2002, effective 12/20/2002; Final rule, 68 FR 15615, 3/31/2003, effective 4/31/2003; Final rule, 74 FR 37626, 7/29/2009, effective 7/29/2009; Final rule, 78 FR 18877, 3/28/2013, effective 3/28/2013; Final rule, 78 FR 37980, 6/25/2013, effective 6/25/2013]

252.225-7009 Restriction on Acquisition of Certain Articles Containing Specialty Metals.

As prescribed in 225.7003-5(a)(2), use the following clause:

RESTRICTION ON ACQUISITION OF CERTAIN ARTICLES CONTAINING SPECIALTY METALS (DEC 2019)

(a) *Definitions*. As used in this clause—

Alloy means a metal consisting of a mixture of a basic metallic element and one or more metallic, or non-metallic, alloying elements.

(i) For alloys named by a single metallic element (e.g., titanium alloy), it means that the alloy contains 50 percent or more of the named metal (by mass).

(ii) If two metals are specified in the name (e.g., nickel-iron alloy), those metals are the two predominant elements in the alloy, and together they constitute 50 percent or more of the alloy (by mass).

Assembly means an item forming a portion of a system or subsystem that—

(i) Can be provisioned and replaced as an entity; and

(ii) Incorporates multiple, replaceable parts.

Commercial derivative military article means an item acquired by the Department of Defense that is or will be produced using the same production facilities, a common supply chain, and the same or similar production processes that are used for the production of articles predominantly used by the general public or by nongovernmental entities for purposes other than governmental purposes.

Commercially available off-the-shelf item—

(i) Means any item of supply that is—

(A) A commercial item (as defined in paragraph (1) of the definition of *commercial item* in section 2.101 of the Federal Acquisition Regulation);

(B) Sold in substantial quantities in the commercial marketplace; and

(C) Offered to the Government, under this contract or a subcontract at any tier, without modification, in the same form in which it is sold in the commercial marketplace; and

(ii) Does not include bulk cargo, as defined in 46 U.S.C. 40102(4), such as agricultural products and petroleum products.

Component means any item supplied to the Government as part of an end item or of another component.

Electronic component means an item that operates by controlling the flow of electrons or other electrically charged particles in circuits, using interconnections of electrical devices such as resistors, inductors, capacitors, diodes, switches, transistors, or integrated circuits. The term does not include structural or mechanical parts of an assembly containing an electronic component, and does not include any high performance magnets that may be used in the electronic component.

End item means the final production product when assembled or completed and ready for delivery under a line item of this contract.

High performance magnet means a permanent magnet that obtains a majority of its magnetic properties from rare earth metals (such as samarium).

Produce means—

(i) Atomization;

(ii) Sputtering; or

(iii) Final consolidation of non-melt derived metal powders.

Qualifying country means any country listed in the definition of *Qualifying country* at 225.003 of the Defense Federal Acquisition Regulation Supplement (DFARS).

Specialty metal means—

(i) Steel—

(A) With a maximum alloy content exceeding one or more of the following limits: Manganese, 1.65 percent; silicon, 0.60 percent; or copper, 0.60 percent; or

(B) Containing more than 0.25 percent of any of the following elements: Aluminum, chromium, cobalt, molybdenum, nickel, niobium (columbium), titanium, tungsten, or vanadium;

(ii) Metal alloys consisting of—

(A) Nickel or iron-nickel alloys that contain a total of alloying metals other than nickel and iron in excess of 10 percent; or

(B) Cobalt alloys that contain a total of alloying metals other than cobalt and iron in excess of 10 percent;

(iii) Titanium and titanium alloys; or

(iv) Zirconium and zirconium alloys.

Steel means an iron alloy that includes between .02 and 2 percent carbon and may include other elements.

Subsystem means a functional grouping of items that combine to perform a major function within an end item, such as electrical power, attitude control, and propulsion.

(b) *Restriction*. Except as provided in paragraph (c) of this clause, any specialty metals incorporated in items delivered under this contract shall be melted or produced in the United States, its outlying areas, or a qualifying country.

(c) *Exceptions*. The restriction in paragraph (b) of this clause does not apply to—

(1) Electronic components.

(2) (i) Commercially available off-the-shelf (COTS) items, other than—

(A) Specialty metal mill products, such as bar, billet, slab, wire, plate, or sheet, that have not been incorporated into COTS end items, subsystems, assemblies, or components;

(B) Forgings or castings of specialty metals, unless the forgings or castings are incorporated into COTS end items, subsystems, or assemblies;

(C) Commercially available high performance magnets that contain specialty metal, unless such high performance magnets are incorporated into COTS end items or subsystems; and

(D) COTS fasteners, unless—

(1) The fasteners are incorporated into COTS end items, subsystems, assemblies, or components; or

(2) The fasteners qualify for the commercial item exception in paragraph (c)(3) of this clause.

(ii) A COTS item is considered to be "without modification" if it is not modified prior to contractual acceptance by the next higher tier in the supply chain.

(A) Specialty metals in a COTS item that was accepted without modification by the next higher tier are excepted from the restriction in paragraph (b) of this clause, and remain excepted, even if a piece of the COTS item subsequently is removed (*e.g.*, the end is removed from a COTS screw or an extra hole is drilled in a COTS bracket).

(B) Specialty metals that were not contained in a COTS item upon acceptance, but are added to the COTS item after acceptance, are subject to the restriction in paragraph (b) of this clause (*e.g.*, a special reinforced handle made of specialty metal is added to a COTS item).

(C) If two or more COTS items are combined in such a way that the resultant item is not a COTS item, only the specialty metals involved in joining the COTS items together are subject to the restriction in paragraph (b) of this clause (*e.g.*, a COTS aircraft is outfitted with a COTS engine that is not the COTS engine normally provided with the aircraft).

(D) For COTS items that are normally sold in the commercial marketplace with various options, items that include such options are also COTS items. However, if a COTS item is offered to the Government with an option that is not normally offered in the commercial marketplace, that option is subject to the restriction in paragraph (b) of this clause (*e.g.*—An aircraft is normally sold to the public with an option for installation kits. The Department of Defense requests a military-unique kit. The aircraft is still a COTS item, but the military-unique kit is not a COTS item and must comply with the restriction in paragraph (b) of this clause unless another exception applies).

(3) Fasteners that are commercial items, if the manufacturer of the fasteners certifies it will purchase, during the relevant calendar year, an amount of domestically melted or produced specialty metal, in the required form, for use in the production of fasteners for sale to the Department of Defense and other customers, that is not less than 50 percent of the total amount of the specialty metal that it will purchase to carry out the production of such fasteners for all customers.

(4) Items manufactured in a qualifying country.

(5) Specialty metals for which the Government has determined in accordance with DFARS 225.7003-3 that specialty metal melted or produced in the United States, its outlying areas, or a qualifying country cannot be acquired as and when needed in—

(i) A satisfactory quality;

(ii) A sufficient quantity; and

(iii) The required form. In accordance with 10 U.S.C. 2533b(m)(4), the term "required form" in this clause refers to the form of the mill product, such as bar, billet, wire, slab, plate, or sheet, in the grade appropriate for the production of a finished end item to be delivered to the Government under this contract; or a finished component assembled into an end item to be delivered to the Government under this contract.

(6) End items containing a minimal amount of otherwise noncompliant specialty metals (*i.e.*, specialty metals not melted or produced in the United States, an outlying area, or a qualifying country, that are not covered by one of the other exceptions in this paragraph (c)), if the total weight of such noncompliant metals does not exceed 2 percent of the total weight of all specialty metals in the end item, as estimated in good faith by the Contractor. This exception does not apply to high performance magnets containing specialty metals.

(d) *Compliance for commercial derivative military articles.*

(1) As an alternative to the compliance required in paragraph (b) of this clause, the Contractor may purchase an amount of domestically melted or produced specialty metals in the required form, for use during the period of contract performance in the production of the commercial derivative military article and the related commercial article, if—

(i) The Contracting Officer has notified the Contractor of the items to be delivered under this contract that have been determined by the Government to meet the definition of "commercial derivative military article"; and

(ii) For each item that has been determined by the Government to meet the definition of *commercial derivative military article*, the Contractor has certified, as specified in the provision of the solicitation entitled *Commercial Derivative Military Article—Specialty Metals Compliance Certificate* (DFARS 252.225-7010), that the Contractor and its subcontractor(s) will enter into a contractual agreement or agreements to purchase an amount of domestically melted or produced specialty metal in the required form, for use during the period of contract performance in the production of each commercial derivative military article and the related commercial article, that is not less than the Contractor's good faith estimate of the greater of—

(A) An amount equivalent to 120 percent of the amount of specialty metal that is required to carry out the production of the commercial derivative military article (including the work performed under each subcontract); or

(B) An amount equivalent to 50 percent of the amount of specialty metal that will be purchased by the Contractor and its subcontractors for use during such period in the production of the commercial derivative military article and the related commercial article.

(2) For the purposes of this alternative, the amount of specialty metal that is required to carry out production of the commercial derivative military article includes specialty metal contained in any item, including COTS items.

(e) *Subcontracts.* (1) The Contractor shall exclude and reserve paragraph (d) and this paragraph (e)(1) when flowing down this clause to subcontracts.

(2) The Contractor shall insert paragraphs (a) through (c) and this paragraph (e)(2) of this clause in subcontracts, including subcontracts for commercial items, that are for items containing specialty metals to ensure compliance of the end products that the Contractor will deliver to the Government. When inserting this clause in subcontracts, the Contractor shall—

(i) Modify paragraph (c)(6) of this clause only as necessary to facilitate management of the minimal content exception at the prime contract level. The minimal content exception does not apply to specialty metals contained in high-performance magnets; and

(ii) Not further alter the clause other than to identify the appropriate parties.

(End of clause)

[DAC 91-1, 56 FR 67221, 12/30/91, effective 12/31/91; DAC 91-7, 60 FR 29491, 6/5/95, effective 5/17/95; Final rule, 62 FR 2612, 1/17/97, effective 1/17/97; DAC 91-13, 63 FR 11522, 3/9/98, effective 3/9/98; Final rule, 65 FR 19849, 4/13/2000, effective 4/13/2000; Final rule, 65 FR 52951, 8/31/2000, effective 8/31/2000, corrected, 65 FR 58607, 9/29/2000; Final rule, 67 FR 77937, 12/20/2002, effective 12/20/2002; Final rule, 68 FR 15615, 3/31/2003, effective 4/30/2003; Final rule, 74 FR 37626, 7/29/2009, effective 7/29/2009; Final rule, 76 FR 3536, 1/20/2011, effective 1/20/2011; Final rule, 77 FR 35879, 6/15/2012, effective 6/15/2012; Final rule, 78 FR 18877, 3/28/2013, effective 3/28/2013; Final rule, 78 FR 37980, 6/25/2013, effective 6/25/2013; Final rule, 79 FR 61584, 10/14/2014, effective 10/14/2014; Final rule, 84 FR 72239, 12/31/2019, effective 12/31/2019]

252.225-7010 Commercial Derivative Military Article—Specialty Metals Compliance Certificate.

As prescribed in 225.7003-5(b), use the following provision:

COMMERCIAL DERIVATIVE MILITARY ARTICLE—SPECIALTY METALS COMPLIANCE CERTIFICATE (JUL 2009)

(a) *Definitions. Commercial derivative military article, commercially available off-the-shelf item, produce, required form,* and *specialty metal*, as used in this provision, have the meanings given in the clause of this solicitation entitled "Restriction on Acquisition of Certain Articles Containing Specialty Metals" (DFARS 252.225-7009).

(b) The offeror shall list in this paragraph any commercial derivative military articles it intends to deliver under any contract resulting from this solicitation using the alternative compliance for commercial derivative military articles, as specified in paragraph (d) of the clause of this solicitation entitled

"Restriction on Acquisition of Certain Articles Containing Specialty Metals" (DFARS 252.225-7009). The offeror's designation of an item as a *commercial derivative military article* will be subject to Government review and approval.

(c) If the offeror has listed any commercial derivative military articles in paragraph (b) of this provision, the offeror certifies that, if awarded a contract as a result of this solicitation, and if the Government approves the designation of the listed item(s) as commercial derivative military articles, the offeror and its subcontractor(s) will demonstrate that individually or collectively they have entered into a contractual agreement or agreements to purchase an amount of domestically melted or produced specialty metal in the required form, for use during the period of contract performance in the production of each commercial derivative military article and the related commercial article, that is not less than the Contractor's good faith estimate of the greater of—

(1) An amount equivalent to 120 percent of the amount of specialty metal that is required to carry out the production of the commercial derivative military article (including the work performed under each subcontract); or

(2) An amount equivalent to 50 percent of the amount of specialty metal that will be purchased by the Contractor and its subcontractors for use during such period in the production of the commercial derivative military article and the related commercial article.

(d) For the purposes of this provision, the amount of specialty metal that is required to carry out the production of the commercial derivative military article includes specialty metal contained in any item, including commercially available off-the-shelf items, incorporated into such commercial derivative military articles.

(End of provision)

[Interim rule, 59 FR 1288, 1/10/94, effective 1/1/94; DAC 91-7, 60 FR 29491, 6/5/95, effective 5/17/95; Final rule, 62 FR 2612, 1/17/97, effective 1/17/97; DAC 91-13, 63 FR 11522, 3/9/98, effective 3/9/98; Final rule, 65 FR 19849, 4/13/2000, effective 4/13/2000; Final rule, 65 FR 52951, 8/31/2000, effective 8/31/2000; Final rule, 67 FR 77937, 12/20/2002, effective 12/20/2002; Final rule, 68 FR 15615, 3/31/2003, effective 4/30/2003; Final rule, 74 FR 37626, 7/29/2009, effective 7/29/2009]

252.225-7011 Restriction on acquisition of supercomputers.

As prescribed in 225.7012-3, use the following clause:

RESTRICTION ON ACQUISITION OF SUPERCOMPUTERS (JUN 2005)

Supercomputers delivered under this contract shall be manufactured in the United States or its outlying areas.

(End of clause)

[Interim rule, 60 FR 34471, 7/3/95, effective 7/3/95; Finalized without change, DAC 91-9, 60 FR 61586, 11/30/95, effective 11/30/95; Final rule, 68 FR 15615, 3/31/2003, effective 4/30/2003; Final rule, 70 FR 35543, 6/21/2005, effective 6/21/2005]

252.225-7012 Preference for certain domestic commodities.

As prescribed in 225.7002-3(a), use the following clause:

PREFERENCE FOR CERTAIN DOMESTIC COMMODITIES (DEC 2017)

(a) *Definitions*. As used in this clause—

Component means any item supplied to the Government as part of an end product or of another component.

End product means supplies delivered under a line item of this contract.

Qualifying country means a country with a reciprocal defense procurement memorandum of understanding or international agreement with the United States in which both countries agree to remove barriers to purchases of supplies produced in the other country or services performed by sources of the other country, and the memorandum or agreement complies, where applicable, with the requirements of section 36 of the Arms Export Control Act (22 U.S.C. 2776) and with 10 U.S.C. 2457. Accordingly, the following are qualifying countries:

Australia

Austria

Belgium

Canada

Czech Republic

Denmark

Egypt

Estonia

Finland

France

Germany

Greece

Israel

Italy

Japan

Latvia

Luxembourg

Netherlands

Norway

Poland

Portugal

Slovenia

Spain

Sweden

Switzerland

Turkey

United Kingdom of Great Britain and Northern Ireland.

Structural component of a tent—

(i) Means a component that contributes to the form and stability of the tent (e.g., poles, frames, flooring, guy ropes, pegs);

(ii) Does not include equipment such as heating, cooling, or lighting.

United States means the 50 States, the District of Columbia, and outlying areas.

U.S.-flag vessel means a vessel of the United States or belonging to the United States, including any vessel registered or having national status under the laws of the United States.

(b) The Contractor shall deliver under this contract only such of the following items, either as end products or components, that have been grown, reprocessed, reused, or produced in the United States:

(1) Food.

(2) Clothing and the materials and components thereof, other than sensors, electronics, or other items added to, and not normally associated with, clothing and the materials and components thereof. Clothing includes items such as outerwear, headwear, underwear, nightwear, footwear, hosiery, handwear, belts, badges, and insignia.

(3)(i) Tents and structural components of tents;

(ii) Tarpaulins; or

(iii) Covers.

(4) Cotton and other natural fiber products.

(5) Woven silk or woven silk blends.

(6) Spun silk yarn for cartridge cloth.

(7) Synthetic fabric, and coated synthetic fabric, including all textile fibers and yarns that are for use in such fabrics.

(8) Canvas products.

(9) Wool (whether in the form of fiber or yarn or contained in fabrics, materials, or manufactured articles).

(10) Any item of individual equipment (Federal Supply Class 8465) manufactured from or containing fibers, yarns, fabrics, or materials listed in this paragraph (b).

(c) This clause does not apply—

(1) To items listed in section 25.104(a) of the Federal Acquisition Regulation (FAR), or other items for which the Government has determined that a satisfactory quality and sufficient quantity cannot be acquired as and when needed at U.S. market prices;

(2) To incidental amounts of cotton, other natural fibers, or wool incorporated in an

end product, for which the estimated value of the cotton, other natural fibers, or wool—

(i) Is not more than 10 percent of the total price of the end product; and

(ii) Does not exceed the simplified acquisition threshold in FAR part 2;

(3) To waste and byproducts of cotton and wool fiber for use in the production of propellants and explosives;

(4) To foods, other than fish, shellfish, or seafood, that have been manufactured or processed in the United States, regardless of where the foods (and any component if applicable) were grown or produced. Fish, shellfish, or seafood manufactured or processed in the United States and fish, shellfish, or seafood contained in foods manufactured or processed in the United States shall be provided in accordance with paragraph (d) of this clause;

(5) To chemical warfare protective clothing produced in a qualifying country; or

(6) To fibers and yarns that are for use in synthetic fabric or coated synthetic fabric (but does apply to the synthetic or coated synthetic fabric itself), if—

(i) The fabric is to be used as a component of an end product that is not a textile product. Examples of textile products, made in whole or in part of fabric, include—

(A) Draperies, floor coverings, furnishings, and bedding (Federal Supply Group 72, Household and Commercial Furnishings and Appliances);

(B) Items made in whole or in part of fabric in Federal Supply Group 83, Textile/leather/furs/apparel/findings/tents/flags, or Federal Supply Group 84, Clothing, Individual Equipment and Insignia;

(C) Upholstered seats (whether for household, office, or other use); and

(D) Parachutes (Federal Supply Class 1670); or

(ii) The fibers and yarns are para-aramid fibers and continuous filament para-aramid yarns manufactured in a qualifying country.

(d)(1) Fish, shellfish, and seafood delivered under this contract, or contained in foods delivered under this contract—

(i) Shall be taken from the sea by U.S.-flag vessels; or

(ii) If not taken from the sea, shall be obtained from fishing within the United States; and

(2) Any processing or manufacturing of the fish, shellfish, or seafood shall be performed on a U.S.-flag vessel or in the United States.

(End of clause)

[DAC 91-6, 59 FR 27662, 5/27/94, effective 5/27/94; DAC 91-9, 60 FR 61586, 11/30/95, effective 11/30/95; DAC 91-11, 61 FR 50446, 9/26/96, effective 9/26/96; Interim rule, 62 FR 5779, 2/7/97, effective 2/7/97; Final rule, 62 FR 47153, 9/8/97, effective 9/8/97; Interim rule, 64 FR 2599, 1/15/99, effective 1/15/99; Final rule, 64 FR 24528, 5/7/99, effective 5/7/99; Final rule, 65 FR 52951, 8/31/2000, effective 8/31/2000; Interim rule, FR 67 20697, 4/26/2002, effective 4/26/2002; Interim rule, 68 FR 7441, 2/14/2003, effective 2/14/2003; Interim rule, 69 FR 26508, 5/13/2004, effective 5/13/2004; Final rule, 69 FR 31910, 6/8/2004, effective 6/8/2004; Final rule, 69 FR 55989, 9/17/2004, effective 9/17/2004; Interim rule, 72 FR 2637, 1/22/2007, effective 1/22/2007; Final rule, 72 FR 42315, 8/2/2007, effective 8/2/2007; Final rule, 73 FR 11354, 3/3/2008, effective 3/3/2008; Final rule, 73 FR 76970, 12/18/2008, effective 12/18/2008; Final rule, 75 FR 34943, 6/21/2010, effective 6/21/2010; Interim rule, 77 FR 38734, 6/29/2012, effective 6/29/2012; Final rule, 77 FR 38736, 6/29/2012, effective 6/29/2012; Final rule, 77 FR 76941, 12/31/2012, effective 12/31/2012; Final rule, 78 FR 13544, 2/28/2013, effective 2/28/2013; Final rule, 81 FR 50650, 8/2/2016, effective 8/2/2016; Final rule, 81 FR 93840, 12/22/2016, effective 12/22/2016; Final rule, 82 FR 61483, 12/28/2017, effective 12/28/2017]

252.225-7013 Duty-free entry.

As prescribed in 225.1101(4), use the following clause:

DUTY-FREE ENTRY (MAY 2016)

(a) *Definitions*. As used in this clause—

Component means any item supplied to the Government as part of an end product or of another component.

Customs territory of the United States means the 50 States, the District of Columbia, and Puerto Rico.

Eligible product means—

(i) *Designated country end product*, as defined in the Trade Agreements (either basic or alternate) clause of this contract;

(ii) *Free Trade Agreement country end product*, other than a *Bahrainian end product*, a *Moroccan end product*, a *Panamanian end product*, or a *Peruvian end product*, as defined in the Buy American—Free Trade Agreements—Balance of Payments Program (either basic or alternate II) clause of this contract;

(iii) *Canadian end product*, as defined in the Buy American—Free Trade Agreements—Balance of Payments Program (either alternate I or alternate III) clause of this contract; or

(iv) *Free Trade Agreement country end product* other than a *Bahrainian end product, Korean end product, Moroccan end product, Panamanian end product*, or *Peruvian end product*, as defined in the Buy American—Free Trade Agreements—Balance of Payments Program (either alternate IV or alternate V) clause of this contract.

Qualifying country and *qualifying country end product* have the meanings given in the Trade Agreements clause, the Buy American and Balance of Payments Program clause, or the Buy American—Free Trade Agreements—Balance of Payments Program clause of this contract, basic or alternate.

(b) Except as provided in paragraph (i) of this clause, or unless supplies were imported into the customs territory of the United States before the date of this contract or the applicable subcontract, the price of this contract shall not include any amount for duty on—

(1) End items that are eligible products or qualifying country end products;

(2) Components (including, without limitation, raw materials and intermediate assemblies) produced or made in qualifying countries, that are to be incorporated in U.S.-made end products to be delivered under this contract; or

(3) Other supplies for which the Contractor estimates that duty will exceed $300 per shipment into the customs territory of the United States.

(c) The Contractor shall—

(1) Claim duty-free entry only for supplies that the Contractor intends to deliver to the Government under this contract, either as end items or components of end items; and

(2) Pay duty on supplies, or any portion thereof, that are diverted to nongovernmental use, other than—

(i) Scrap or salvage; or

(ii) Competitive sale made, directed, or authorized by the Contracting Officer.

(d) Except as the Contractor may otherwise agree, the Government will execute duty-free entry certificates and will afford such assistance as appropriate to obtain the duty-free entry of supplies—

(1) For which no duty is included in the contract price in accordance with paragraph (b) of this clause; and

(2) For which shipping documents bear the notation specified in paragraph (e) of this clause.

(e) For foreign supplies for which the Government will issue duty-free entry certificates in accordance with this clause, shipping documents submitted to Customs shall—

(1) Consign the shipments to the appropriate—

(i) Military department in care of the Contractor, including the Contractor's delivery address; or

(ii) Military installation; and

(2) Include the following information:

(i) Prime contract number and, if applicable, delivery order number.

(ii) Number of the subcontract for foreign supplies, if applicable.

(iii) Identification of the carrier.

(iv) (A) For direct shipments to a U.S. military installation, the notation: "UNITED STATES GOVERNMENT, DEPARTMENT OF DEFENSE Duty-Free Entry to be claimed pursuant to Section XXII, Chapter 98, Subchapter VIII, Item 9808.00.30 of the Harmonized Tariff Schedule of the United States. Upon arrival of shipment at the appropriate port of entry, District Director of Customs, please release shipment under 19 CFR part 142 and notify Commander, Defense Contract Management Agency (DCMA) New York, ATTN: Customs Team, DCMAE-GNTF, 207 New York Avenue, Staten Island, New York, 10305-5013, for execution of Customs Form 7501, 7501A, or 7506 and any required duty-free entry certificates."

(B) If the shipment will be consigned to other than a military installation, e.g., a domestic contractor's plant, the shipping document notation shall be altered to include the name and address of the contractor, agent, or broker who will notify Commander, DCMA New York, for execution of the duty-free entry certificate. (If the shipment will be consigned to a contractor's plant and no duty-free entry certificate is required due to a trade agreement, the Contractor shall claim duty-free entry under the applicable trade agreement and shall comply with the U.S. Customs Service requirements. No notification to Commander, DCMA New York, is required.)

(v) Gross weight in pounds (if freight is based on space tonnage, state cubic feet in addition to gross shipping weight).

(vi) Estimated value in U.S. dollars.

(vii) Activity address number of the contract administration office administering the prime contract, e.g., for DCMA Dayton, S3605A.

(f) Preparation of customs forms.

(1) (i) Except for shipments consigned to a military installation, the Contractor shall—

(A) Prepare any customs forms required for the entry of foreign supplies into the customs territory of the United States in connection with this contract; and

(B) Submit the completed customs forms to the District Director of Customs, with a copy to DCMA NY for execution of any required duty-free entry certificates.

(ii) Shipments consigned directly to a military installation will be released in accordance with sections 10.101 and 10.102 of the U.S. Customs regulations.

(2) For shipments containing both supplies that are to be accorded duty-free entry and supplies that are not, the Contractor shall identify on the customs forms those items that are eligible for duty-free entry.

(g) The Contractor shall—

(1) Prepare (if the Contractor is a foreign supplier), or shall instruct the foreign supplier to prepare, a sufficient number of copies of the bill of lading (or other shipping document) so that at least two of the copies accompanying the shipment will be available for use by the District Director of Customs at the port of entry;

(2) Consign the shipment as specified in paragraph (e) of this clause; and

(3) Mark on the exterior of all packages—

(i) "UNITED STATES GOVERNMENT, DEPARTMENT OF DEFENSE"; and

(ii) The activity address number of the contract administration office administering the prime contract.

(h) The Contractor shall notify the Administrative Contracting Officer (ACO) in writing of any purchase of eligible products or qualifying country supplies to be accorded duty-free entry, that are to be imported into the customs territory of the United States for delivery to the Government or for incorporation in end items to be delivered to the Government. The Contractor shall furnish the notice to the ACO immediately upon award to the supplier and shall include in the notice—

(1) The Contractor's name, address, and Commercial and Government Entity (CAGE) code;

(2) Prime contract number and, if applicable, delivery order number;

(3) Total dollar value of the prime contract or delivery order;

(4) Date of the last scheduled delivery under the prime contract or delivery order;

(5) Foreign supplier's name and address;

(6) Number of the subcontract for foreign supplies;

(7) Total dollar value of the subcontract for foreign supplies;

(8) Date of the last scheduled delivery under the subcontract for foreign supplies;

(9) List of items purchased;

(10) An agreement that the Contractor will pay duty on supplies, or any portion thereof, that are diverted to nongovernmental use other than—

(i) Scrap or salvage; or

(ii) Competitive sale made, directed, or authorized by the Contracting Officer;

(11) Country of origin; and

(12) Scheduled delivery date(s).

(i) This clause does not apply to purchases of eligible products or qualifying country supplies in connection with this contract if—

(1) The supplies are identical in nature to supplies purchased by the Contractor or any subcontractor in connection with its commercial business; and

(2) It is not economical or feasible to account for such supplies so as to ensure that the amount of the supplies for which duty-free entry is claimed does not exceed the amount purchased in connection with this contract.

(j) The Contractor shall—

(1) Insert the substance of this clause, including this paragraph (j), in all subcontracts for

(i) Qualifying country components; or

(ii) Nonqualifying country components for which the Contractor estimates that duty will exceed $200 per unit;

(2) Require subcontractors to include the number of this contract on all shipping documents submitted to Customs for supplies for which duty-free entry is claimed pursuant to this clause; and

(3) Include in applicable subcontracts—

(i) The name and address of the ACO for this contract;

(ii) The name, address, and activity address number of the contract administration office specified in this contract; and

(iii) The information required by paragraphs (h) (1), (2), and (3) of this clause.

(End of clause)

[Removed and reserved, DAC 91-11, 61 FR 50446, 9/26/96, effective 9/26/96; Final rule, 68 FR 15615, 3/31/2003, effective 4/30/2003; Interim rule, 69 FR 1926, 1/13/2004, effective 1/13/2004; Interim rule, 70 FR 2361, 1/13/2005, effective 1/13/2005; Final rule, 70 FR 35543, 6/21/2005, effective 6/21/2005; Final rule, 70 FR 73152, 12/9/2005, effective 12/9/2005; Interim rule, 71 FR 34834, 6/16/2006, effective 6/16/2006; Interim rule, 71 FR 58541, 10/4/2006, effective 10/4/2006; Final rule, 72 FR 6486, 2/12/2007, effective 2/12/2007; Final rule, 72 FR 14241, 3/27/2007, effective 3/27/2007; Final rule, 74 FR 68383, 12/24/2009, effective 12/24/2009; Final rule, 77 FR 35879, 6/15/2012, effective 6/15/2012; Final rule, 78 FR 65221, 10/31/2013, effective 10/31/2013; Final rule, 79 FR 65815, 11/5/2014, effective 11/5/2014; Final rule, 81 FR 28732, 5/10/2016, effective 5/10/2016]

252.225-7014 [Removed and Reserved]

[DAC 91-9, 60 FR 61586, 11/30/95, effective 11/30/95; DAC 91-11, 61 FR 50446, 9/26/96, effective 9/26/96; Interim rule, 62 FR 5779, 2/7/97, effective 2/7/97; DAC 91-13, 63 FR 11522, 3/9/98, effective 3/9/98; Final rule, 68 FR 15615, 3/31/2003, effective 4/30/2003; Final rule, 70 FR 35543, 6/21/2005, effective 6/21/2005; Final rule, 74 FR 37626, 7/29/2009, effective 7/29/2009]

252.225-7015 Restriction on acquisition of hand or measuring tools.

As prescribed in 225.7002-3(b), use the following clause:

RESTRICTION ON ACQUISITION OF HAND OR MEASURING TOOLS (JUN 2005)

Hand or measuring tools delivered under this contract shall be produced in the United States or its outlying areas.

(End of clause)

[DAC 91-6, 59 FR 27662, 5/27/94, effective 5/27/94; DAC 91-11, 61 FR 50446, 9/26/96, effective 9/26/96; Final rule, 68 FR 15615, 3/31/2002, effective 4/30/2003; Final rule, 70 FR 35543, 6/21/2005, effective 6/21/2005; Final rule, 74 FR 37626, 7/29/2009, effective 7/29/2009]

252.225-7016 Restriction on acquisition of ball and roller bearings.

As prescribed in 225.7009-5, use the following clause:

RESTRICTION ON ACQUISITION OF BALL AND ROLLER BEARINGS (JUN 2011)

(a) *Definitions*. As used in this clause—

(1) *Bearing component* means the bearing element, retainer, inner race, or outer race.

(2) *Component*, other than a bearing component, means any item supplied to the Government as part of an end product or of another component.

(3) *End product* means supplies delivered under a line item of this contract.

(b) Except as provided in paragraph (c) of this clause—

(1) Each ball and roller bearing delivered under this contract shall be manufactured in the United States, its outlying areas, or Canada; and

(2) For each ball or roller bearing, the cost of the bearing components manufactured in the United States, its outlying areas, or Canada shall exceed 50 percent of the total cost of the bearing components of that ball or roller bearing.

(c) The restriction in paragraph (b) of this clause does not apply to ball or roller bearings that are acquired as—

(1) Commercial components of a noncommercial end product; or

(2) Commercial or noncommercial components of a commercial component of a noncommercial end product.

(d) The restriction in paragraph (b) of this clause may be waived upon request from the Contractor in accordance with subsection 225.7009-4 of the Defense Federal Acquisition Regulation Supplement.

(e) If this contract includes DFARS clause 252.225-7009, Restriction on Acquisition of Certain Articles Containing Specialty Metals, all bearings that contain specialty metals, as defined in that clause, must meet the requirements of that clause.

(f) The Contractor shall insert the substance of this clause, including this paragraph (f), in all subcontracts, except those for—

(1) Commercial items; or

(2) Items that do not contain ball or roller bearings.

(End of clause)

[DAC 91-11, 61 FR 50446, 9/26/96, effective 9/26/96; DAC 91-12, 62 FR 34114, 6/24/97, effective 6/24/97; Interim rule, 63 FR 5744, 2/4/98, effective 2/4/98; Interim rule, 63 FR 43887, 8/17/98, effective 8/17/98, finalized without change, 63 FR 64426, 11/20/98; Interim rule, 65 FR 77827, 12/13/2000, effective 12/13/2000, finalized without change, 66 FR 49862, 10/1/2001, effective 10/1/2001; Final rule, 68 FR 15615, 3/31/2003, effective 4/30/2003; Final rule, 69 FR 26509, 5/13/2004, effective 5/13/2004; Final rule, 70 FR 35543, 6/21/2005, effective 6/21/2005; Final rule, 71 FR 14110, 3/21/2006, effective 3/21/2006; Final rule, 75 FR 76297, 12/8/2010, effective 12/8/2010; Final rule, 76 FR 32841, 6/6/2011, effective 6/6/2011]

252.225-7017 Photovoltaic Devices.

As prescribed in 225.7017-4(a), use the following clause:

PHOTOVOLTAIC DEVICES (JAN 2020)

(a) *Definitions.* As used in this clause—

Bahrainian photovoltaic device means an a photovoltaic device that—

(1) Is wholly manufactured in Bahrain; or

(2) In the case of a photovoltaic device that consists in whole or in part of materials from another country, has been substantially transformed in Bahrain into a new and different article of commerce with a name, character, or use distinct from that of the article or articles from which it was transformed, provided that the photovoltaic device is not subsequently substantially transformed outside of Bahrain.

Canadian photovoltaic device means a photovoltaic device that has been substantially transformed in Canada into a new and different article of commerce with a name, character, or use distinct from that of the article or articles from which it was transformed, provided that the photovoltaic device is not subsequently substantially transformed outside of Canada.

Caribbean Basin country photovoltaic device means a photovoltaic device that—

(1) Is wholly manufactured in a Caribbean Basin country; or

(2) In the case of a photovoltaic device that consists in whole or in part of materials from another country, has been substantially transformed in a Caribbean Basin country into a new and different article of commerce with a name, character, or use distinct from that of the article or articles from which it was transformed, provided that the photovoltaic device is not subsequently substantially transformed outside of Caribbean Basin country.

Designated country means—

(1) A World Trade Organization Government Procurement Agreement (WTO GPA) country (Armenia, Aruba, Australia, Austria, Belgium, Bulgaria, Canada, Croatia, Cyprus, Czech Republic, Denmark, Estonia, Finland, France, Germany, Greece, Hong Kong, Hungary, Iceland, Ireland, Israel, Italy, Japan, Korea (Republic of), Latvia, Liechtenstein, Lithuania, Luxembourg, Malta, Moldova, Montenegro, Netherlands, New Zealand, Norway, Poland, Portugal, Romania, Singapore, Slovak Republic, Slovenia, Spain, Sweden, Switzerland, Taiwan (known in the World Trade Organization as "the Separate Customs Territory of Taiwan, Penghu, Kinmen, Matsu" (Chinese Taipei)), Ukraine, or the United Kingdom;

(2) A Free Trade Agreement country (Australia, Bahrain, Canada, Chile, Columbia, Costa Rica, Dominican Republic, El Salvador, Guatemala, Honduras, Korea (Republic of), Mexico, Morocco, Nicaragua, Panama, Peru, or Singapore);

(3) A least developed country (Afghanistan, Angola, Bangladesh, Benin, Bhutan, Burkina Faso, Burundi, Cambodia, Central African Republic, Chad, Comoros, Democratic Republic of Congo, Djibouti, Equatorial Guinea, Eritrea, Ethiopia, Gambia, Guinea, Guinea-Bissau, Haiti, Kiribati, Laos, Lesotho, Liberia, Madagascar, Malawi, Mali, Mauritania, Mozambique, Nepal, Niger, Rwanda, Samoa, Sao Tome and Principe, Senegal, Sierra Leone, Solomon Islands, Somalia, South Sudan, Tanzania, Timor-Leste, Togo, Tuvalu, Uganda, Vanuatu, Yemen, or Zambia); or

(4) A Caribbean Basin country (Antigua and Barbuda, Aruba, Bahamas, Barbados, Belize, Bonaire, British Virgin Islands, Curacao, Dominica, Grenada, Guyana, Haiti, Jamaica, Montserrat, Saba, St. Kitts and Nevis, St. Lucia, St. Vincent and the Grenadines, Sint Eustatius, Sint Maarten, or Trinidad and Tobago).

Designated country photovoltaic device means a WTO GPA country photovoltaic device, a Free Trade Agreement country photovoltaic device, a least developed country photovoltaic device, or a Caribbean Basin country photovoltaic device.

Domestic photovoltaic device means a photovoltaic device that is manufactured in the United States.

Foreign photovoltaic device means a photovoltaic device other than a domestic photovoltaic device.

Free Trade Agreement country means Australia, Bahrain, Canada, Chile, Columbia, Costa Rica, Dominican Republic, El Salvador, Guatemala, Honduras, Korea (Republic of), Mexico, Morocco, Nicaragua, Panama, Peru, or Singapore.

Free Trade Agreement country photovoltaic device means a photovoltaic device that—

(1) Is wholly manufactured in a Free Trade Agreement country; or

(2) In the case of a photovoltaic device that consists in whole or in part of materials from another country, has been substantially transformed in a Free Trade Agreement country into a new and different article of commerce with a name, character, or use distinct from that of the article or articles from which it was transformed, provided that the photovoltaic device is not subsequently substantially transformed outside of a Free Trade Agreement country.

Korean photovoltaic device means a photovoltaic device that—

(1) Is wholly manufactured in Korea (Republic of) or

(2) In the case of a photovoltaic device that consists in whole or in part of materials from another country, has been substantially transformed in Korea (Republic of) into a new and different article of commerce with a name, character, or use distinct from that of the article or articles from which it was transformed; provided that the photovoltaic device is not subsequently substantially transformed outside of Korea (Republic of).

Least developed country photovoltaic device means a photovoltaic device that—

(1) Is wholly manufactured in a least developed country; or

(2) In the case of a photovoltaic device that consists in whole or in part of materials from another country, has been substantially transformed in a least developed country into a new and different article of commerce with a name, character, or use distinct from that of the article or articles from which it was transformed, provided that the photovoltaic device is not subsequently substantially transformed outside of a least developed country.

Moroccan photovoltaic device means a photovoltaic device that—

(1) Is wholly manufactured in Morocco; or

(2) In the case of a photovoltaic device that consists in whole or in part of materials from another country, has been substantially transformed in Morocco into a new and different article of commerce with a name, character, or use distinct from that of the article or articles from which it was transformed, provided that the photovoltaic device is not subsequently substantially transformed outside of Morocco.

Panamanian photovoltaic device means a photovoltaic device that—

(1) Is wholly manufactured in Panama; or

(2) In the case of a photovoltaic device that consists in whole or in part of materials from another country, has been substantially transformed in Panama into a new and different article of commerce with a name, character, or use distinct from that of the article or articles from which it was transformed, provided that the photovoltaic device is not subsequently substantially transformed outside of Panama.

Peruvian photovoltaic device means a photovoltaic device that—

(1) Is wholly manufactured in Peru; or

(2) In the case of a photovoltaic device that consists in whole or in part of materials from another country, has been substantially transformed in Peru into a new and different article of commerce with a name, character, or use distinct from that of the article or articles from which it was transformed, provided that the photovoltaic device is not subsequently substantially transformed outside of Peru.

Photovoltaic device means a device that converts light directly into electricity through a solid-state, semiconductor process.

Qualifying country means a country with a reciprocal defense procurement memorandum of understanding or international agreement with the United States in which both countries agree to remove barriers to purchases of supplies produced in the other country or services performed by sources of the other country, and the memorandum or agreement complies, where applicable, with the requirements of section 36 of the Arms Export Control Act (22 U.S.C. 2776) and with 10 U.S.C. 2457. Accordingly, the following are qualifying countries:

Australia

Austria

Belgium

Canada

Czech Republic

Denmark

Egypt

Estonia

Finland

France

Germany

Greece

Israel

Italy

Japan

Latvia

Luxembourg

Netherlands

Norway

Poland

Portugal

Slovenia

Spain

Sweden

Switzerland

Turkey

United Kingdom of Great Britain and Northern Ireland

Qualifying country photovoltaic device means a photovoltaic device manufactured in a qualifying country.

United States means the 50 States, the District of Columbia, and outlying areas.

U.S.-made photovoltaic device means a photovoltaic device that—

(1) Is manufactured in the United States; or

(2) Is substantially transformed in the United States into a new and different article of commerce with a name, character, or use distinct from that of the article or articles from which it was transformed, provided that the photovoltaic device is not subsequently substantially transformed outside of United States.

WTO GPA country photovoltaic device means a photovoltaic device that—

(1) Is wholly manufactured in a WTO GPA country; or

(2) In the case of a photovoltaic device that consists in whole or in part of materials from another country, has been substantially transformed in a WTO GPA country into a new and different article of commerce with a name, character, or use distinct from that of the article or articles from which it was transformed, provided that the photovoltaic device is not subsequently substantially transformed outside of a WTO GPA country.

(b) This clause implements section 846 of the National Defense Authorization Act for Fiscal Year 2011 (Pub. L. 111-383).

(c) *Restriction*. If the Contractor specified in its offer in the Photovoltaic Devices—Certificate provision of the solicitation that the estimated value of the photovoltaic devices to be utilized in performance of this contract would be—

(1) More than the micro-purchase threshold but less than $25,000, then the Contractor shall utilize only domestic photovoltaic devices unless, in its offer, it specified utilization of qualifying country or other foreign photovoltaic devices in paragraph (d)(2) of the Photovoltaic Devices—Certificate provision of the solicitation.

(2) $25,000 or more but less than $83,099, then the Contractor shall utilize in the performance of this contract only domestic photovoltaic devices unless, in its offer, it specified utilization of Canadian, qualifying country, or other foreign photovoltaic devices in paragraph (d)(3) of the Photovoltaic Devices—Certificate provision of the solicitation. If the Contractor certified in its offer that it will utilize a qualifying country photovoltaic device or a Canadian photovoltaic de-

vice, then the Contractor shall utilize a qualifying country photovoltaic device or a Canadian photovoltaic device, or, at the Contractor's option, a domestic photovoltaic device;

(3) $83,099 or more but less than $100,000, then the Contractor shall utilize under this contract only domestic photovoltaic devices, unless, in its offer, it specified utilization of Free Trade Agreement country photovoltaic devices (other than Bahrainian, Korean, Moroccan, Panamanian, or Peruvian photovoltaic devices), qualifying country photovoltaic devices, or other foreign photovoltaic devices in paragraph (d)(4) of the Photovoltaic Devices—Certificate provision of the solicitation. If the Contractor certified in its offer that it will utilize a Free Trade Agreement country photovoltaic device (other than a Bahrainian, Korean, Moroccan, Panamanian, or Peruvian photovoltaic device) or a qualifying country photovoltaic device, then the Contractor shall utilize a Free Trade Agreement country photovoltaic device (other than a Bahrainian, Korean, Moroccan, Panamanian, or Peruvian photovoltaic device) or a qualifying country photovoltaic device; or, at the Contractor's option, a domestic photovoltaic device;

(4) $100,000 or more but less than $182,000, then the Contractor shall utilize under this contract only domestic photovoltaic devices, unless, in its offer it specified utilization of Free Trade Agreement country photovoltaic devices (other than Bahrainian, Moroccan, Panamanian, or Peruvian photovoltaic devices), qualifying country photovoltaic devices, or other foreign photovoltaic devices in paragraph (d)(5) of the Photovoltaic Devices—Certificate provision of the solicitation. If the Contractor certified in its offer that it will utilize a Free Trade Agreement country photovoltaic device (other than a Bahrainian, Moroccan, Panamanian, or Peruvian photovoltaic device) or a qualifying country photovoltaic device, then the Contractor shall utilize a Free Trade Agreement country photovoltaic device (other than a Bahrainian, Moroccan, Panamanian, or Peruvian photovoltaic device) or a qualifying country photovoltaic device; or, at the Contractor's option, a domestic photovoltaic device; or

(5) $182,000 or more, then the Contractor shall utilize under this contract only U.S.-made, designated country, or qualifying country photovoltaic devices.

(End of clause)

[Final rule, 65 FR 6553, 2/10/2000, effective 2/10/2000; Final rule, 68 FR 15615, 3/31/2003, effective 4/30/2003; Interim rule, 76 FR 78858, 12/20/2011, effective 12/20/2011; Final rule, 77 FR 13013, 3/5/2012, effective 3/5/2012; Interim rule, 77 FR 30356, 5/22/2012, effective 5/22/2012; Interim rule, 77 FR 30359, 5/22/2012, effective 5/22/2012; Final rule, 77 FR 30368, 5/22/2012, effective 5/22/2012; Final rule, 77 FR 31536, 5/29/2012, effective 5/29/2012; Final rule, 77 FR 38736, 6/29/2012, effective 6/29/2012; Final rule, 77 FR 52253, 8/29/2012, effective 8/29/2012; Interim rule, 77 FR 68699, 11/16/2012, effective 11/16/2012; Final rule, 77 FR 76941, 12/31/2012, effective 12/31/2012; Final rule, 78 FR 18876, 3/28/2013, effective 3/28/2013; Final rule, 78 FR 18877, 3/28/2013, effective 3/28/2013; Final rule, 78 FR 48333, 8/8/2013, effective 8/8/2013; Final rule, 78 FR 65220, 10/31/2013, effective 10/31/2013; Final rule, 78 FR 65221, 10/31/2013, effective 10/31/2013; Interim rule, 78 FR 76993, 12/20/2013, effective 12/20/2013 Final rule, 78 FR 79620, 12/31/2013, effective 1/1/2014; Final rule, 79 FR 22041, 4/21/2014, effective 4/21/2014; Final rule, 80 FR 36903, 6/26/2015, effective 10/1/2015; Final rule, 80 FR 67253, 10/30/2015, effective 10/30/2015; Final rule, 80 FR 72599, 11/20/2015, effective 11/20/2015; Final rule, 80 FR 81470, 12/30/2015, effective 1/1/2016; Final rule, 81 FR 42563, 6/30/2016, effective 6/30/2016; Final rule, 81 FR 50650, 8/2/2016, effective 8/2/2016; Final rule, 81 FR 65567, 9/23/2016, effective 9/23/2016; Final rule, 81 FR 93840, 12/22/2016, effective 12/22/2016; Final rule, 82 FR 61481, 12/28/2017, effective 1/1/2018; Final rule, 82 FR 61483, 12/28/2017, effective 12/28/2017; Final rule, 83 FR 62498, 12/4/2018, effective

12/5/2018; Final rule, 84 FR 39207, 8/9/2019, effective 8/9/2019; Final rule, 84 FR 72245, 12/31/2019, effective 1/1/2020]

252.225-7018 Photovoltaic Devices—Certificate.

As prescribed in 225.7017-4(b), use the following provision:

PHOTOVOLTAIC DEVICES—CERTIFICATE (JAN 2020)

(a) *Definitions. Bahrainian photovoltaic device, Canadian photovoltaic device, Caribbean Basin photovoltaic device, designated country, designated country photovoltaic device, domestic photovoltaic device, foreign photovoltaic device, Free Trade Agreement country, Free Trade Agreement photovoltaic device, Korean photovoltaic device, least developed country photovoltaic device, Moroccan photovoltaic device, Panamanian photovoltaic device, Peruvian photovoltaic device, photovoltaic device, qualifying country, qualifying country photovoltaic device, United States, U.S.-made photovoltaic device*, and *WTO GPA country photovoltaic device* have the meanings given in the Photovoltaic Devices clause of this solicitation.

(b) *Restrictions.* The following restrictions apply, depending on the estimated aggregate value of photovoltaic devices to be utilized under a resultant contract:

(1) If more than the micro-purchase threshold but less than $182,000, then the Government will not accept an offer specifying the use of other foreign photovoltaic devices in paragraph (d)(2)(ii), (d)(3)(ii), (d)(4)(ii), or (d)(5)(ii) of this provision, unless the offeror documents to the satisfaction of the Contracting Officer that the price of the foreign photovoltaic device plus 50 percent is less than the price of a comparable domestic photovoltaic device.

(2) If $182,000 or more, then the Government will consider only offers that utilize photovoltaic devices that are U.S.-made, qualifying country, or designated country photovoltaic devices.

(c) *Country in which a designated country photovoltaic device was wholly manufactured or was substantially transformed.* If the estimated value of the photovoltaic devices to be utilized under a resultant contract exceeds $25,000, the Offeror's certification that such photovoltaic device (e.g., solar panel) is a designated country photovoltaic device shall be consistent with country of origin determinations by the U.S. Customs and Border Protection with regard to importation of the same or similar photovoltaic devices into the United States. If the Offeror is uncertain as to what the country of origin would be determined to be by the U.S. Customs and Border Protection, the Offeror shall request a determination from U.S. Customs and Border Protection. (See *http://www.cbp.gov/trade/rulings.*)

(d) *Certification and identification of country of origin.* [*The offeror shall check the block and fill in the blank for one of the following paragraphs, based on the estimated value and the country of origin of photovoltaic devices to be utilized in performance of the contract:*]

___ (1) No photovoltaic devices will be utilized in performance of the contract, or such photovoltaic devices have an estimated value that does not exceed the micro-purchase threshold.

(2) If more than the micro-purchase threshold but less than $25,000—

___ (i) The offeror certifies that each photovoltaic device to be utilized in performance of the contract is a domestic photovoltaic device;

___(ii) The offeror certifies that each photovoltaic device to be utilized in performance of the contract is a qualifying country photovoltaic device. [*Offeror to specify country of origin* ________]; or

___ (iii) The foreign (other than qualifying country) photovoltaic devices to be utilized in performance of the contract are the product of________[*Offeror to specify country of origin, if known, and provide documentation that the cost of a domestic photovoltaic device would be unreasonable in comparison to the cost of the proposed foreign photovoltaic device, i.e., that the price of the foreign photovoltaic device plus 50 percent is less than the price of a comparable domestic photovoltaic device.*]

(3) If $25,000 or more but less than $83,099—

___ (i) The offeror certifies that each photovoltaic device to be utilized in performance of the contract is a domestic photovoltaic device;

___ (ii) The offeror certifies that each photovoltaic device to be utilized in performance of the contract is a Canadian photovoltaic device or a qualifying country photovoltaic device [*Offeror to specify country of origin* ___]; or

___(iii) The foreign (other than Canadian or qualifying country) photovoltaic devices to be utilized in performance of the contract are the product of ___. [*Offeror to specify country of origin, if known, and provide documentation that the cost of a domestic photovoltaic device would be unreasonable in comparison to the cost of the proposed foreign photovoltaic device, i.e. that the price of the foreign photovoltaic device plus 50 percent is less than the price of a comparable domestic photovoltaic device.*]

(4) If $83,099 or more but less than $100,000—

___(i) The offeror certifies that each photovoltaic device to be utilized in performance of the contract is a domestic photovoltaic device ;

___(ii) The offeror certifies that each photovoltaic device to be utilized in performance of the contract is a Free Trade Agreement country photovoltaic device (other than a Bahrainian, Korean, Moroccan, Panamanian, or Peruvian photovoltaic device) or a qualifying country photovoltaic device [*Offeror to specify country of origin* ___]; or

___(iii) The offered foreign photovoltaic devices (other than those from countries listed in paragraph (d)(4)(ii) of this provision) are the product of ___. [*Offeror to specify country of origin, if known, and provide documentation that the cost of a domestic photovoltaic device would be unreasonable in comparison to the cost of the proposed foreign photovoltaic device, i.e. that the price of the foreign photovoltaic device plus 50 percent is less than the price of a comparable domestic photovoltaic device.*]

(5) If $100,000 or more but less than $182,000—

___(i) The offeror certifies that each photovoltaic device to be utilized in performance of the contract is a domestic photovoltaic device;

___(ii) The offeror certifies that each photovoltaic device to be utilized in performance of the contract is a Free Trade Agreement country photovoltaic device (other than a Bahrainian, Moroccan, Panamanian, or Peruvian photovoltaic device) or a qualifying country photovoltaic device [*Offeror to specify country of origin* ___]; or

___(iii) The offered foreign photovoltaic devices (other than those from countries listed in paragraph (d)(5)(ii) of this provision) are the product of ___. [*Offeror to specify country of origin, if known, and provide documentation that the cost of a domestic photovoltaic device would be unreasonable in comparison to the cost of the proposed foreign photovoltaic device, i.e. that the price of the foreign photovoltaic device plus 50 percent is less than the price of a comparable domestic photovoltaic device.*]

(6) If $182,000 or more, the Offeror certifies that each photovoltaic device to be used in performance of the contract is—

___(i) A U.S.-made photovoltaic device; or

___(ii) A designated country photovoltaic device or a qualifying country photovoltaic device. [*Offeror to specify country of origin* ___.]

(End of provision)

[DAC 91-6, 59 FR 27662, 5/27/94, effective 5/27/94; Final rule, 62 FR 2612, 1/17/97, effective 1/17/97; Final rule, 68 FR 15615, 3/31/2003, effective 4/30/2003; Final rule, 70 FR 35543, 6/21/2005, effective 6/21/2005; Final rule, 74 FR 53413, 10/19/2009, effective 10/19/2009; Final rule, 76 FR 14589, 3/17/2011, effective 3/17/2011; Interim rule, 76 FR 78858, 12/20/2011, effective 12/20/2011; Final rule, 77 FR 13013, 3/5/2012, effective 3/5/2012; Interim rule, 77 FR 30356, 5/22/2012, effective 5/22/2012; Final rule, 77 FR 30368, 5/22/2012, effective 5/22/2012; Interim rule, 77 FR 68699, 11/16/2012, effective

11/16/2012; Final rule, 78 FR 18876, 3/28/2013, effective 3/28/2013; Final rule, 78 FR 65221, 10/31/2013, effective 10/31/2013; Interim rule, 78 FR 76993, 12/20/2013, effective 12/20/2013; Final rule, 78 FR 79620, 12/31/2013, effective 1/1/2014; Final rule, 79 FR 3519, 1/22/2014, effective 1/22/2014; Final rule, 79 FR 22041, 4/21/2014, effective 4/21/2014; Final rule, 80 FR 36903, 6/26/2015, effective 10/1/2015; Final rule, 80 FR 72599, 11/20/2015, effective 11/20/2015; Final rule, 80 FR 81470, 12/30/2015, effective 1/1/2016; Publication notice, 20171208; Final rule, 82 FR 61481, 12/28/2017, effective 1/1/2018; Final rule, 83 FR 62498, 12/4/2018, effective 12/5/2018; Final rule, 84 FR 72245, 12/31/2019, effective 1/1/2020]

252.225-7019 Restriction on acquisition of anchor and mooring chain.

As prescribed in 225.7007-3, use the following clause:

RESTRICTION ON ACQUISITION OF ANCHOR AND MOORING CHAIN (DEC 2009)

(a) *Definition. Component* as used in this clause, means an article, material, or supply incorporated directly into an end product.

(b) Welded shipboard anchor and mooring chain, four inches or less in diameter, delivered under this contract—

(1) Shall be manufactured in the United States or its outlying areas, including cutting, heat treating, quality control, testing, and welding (both forging and shot blasting process); and

(2) The cost of the components manufactured in the United States or its outlying areas shall exceed 50 percent of the total cost of components.

(c) The Contractor may request a waiver of this restriction if adequate domestic supplies meeting the requirements in paragraph (b) of this clause are not available to meet the contract delivery schedule.

(d) The Contractor shall insert the substance of this clause, including this paragraph (d), in all subcontracts for items containing welded shipboard anchor and mooring chain, four inches or less in diameter.

(End of clause)

[Interim rule, 61 FR 13106, 3/26/96, effective 4/1/96, finalized without change, DAC 91-11, 61 FR 50446, 9/29/96, effective 9/26/96; Final rule, 68 FR 15615, 3/31/2003, effective 4/30/2003; Final rule, 70 FR 35543, 6/21/2005, effective 6/21/2005; Final rule, 74 FR 68383, 12/24/2009, effective 12/24/2009]

252.225-7020 Trade Agreements Certificate.

Basic. As prescribed in 225.1101(5) and (5) (i), use the following provision:

TRADE AGREEMENTS CERTIFICATE—BASIC (NOV 2014)

(a) *Definitions. Designated country end product, nondesignated country end product, qualifying country end product*, and *U.S.-made end product*, as used in this provision have the meanings given in the Trade Agreements—Basic clause of this solicitation.

(b) *Evaluation*. The Government—

(1) Will evaluate offers in accordance with the policies and procedures of part 225 of the Defense Federal Acquisition Regulation Supplement; and

(2) Will consider only offers of end products that are U.S.-made, qualifying country, or designated country end products unless—

(i) There are no offers of such end products;

(ii) The offers of such end products are insufficient to fulfill the Government's requirements; or

(iii) A national interest waiver has been granted.

(c) *Certification and identification of country of origin*.

(1) For all line items subject to the Trade Agreements—Basic of this solicitation, the offeror certifies that each end product to be delivered under this contract, except those listed in paragraph (c) (2) of this provision, is

a U.S.-made, qualifying country, or designated country end product.

(2) The following supplies are other nondesignated country end products:

(Line Item Number)

(Country of Origin)

(End of provision)

Alternate I. As prescribed in 225.1101(5) and (5)(ii), use the following provision, which uses different paragraphs (a), (b)(2), and (c) than the basic provision:

TRADE AGREEMENTS CERTIFICATE—ALTERNATE I (NOV 2014)

(a) *Definitions. Designated country end product, nondesignated country end product, qualifying country end product, South Caucasus/Central and South Asian (SC/ CASA) state, South Caucasus/Central and South Asian (SC/CASA) state end product,* and *U.S.-made end product*, as used in this provision, have the meanings given in the Trade Agreements—Alternate I clause of this solicitation.

(b) *Evaluation*. The Government—

(1) Will evaluate offers in accordance with the policies and procedures of part 225 of the Defense Federal Acquisition Regulation Supplement; and

(2) Will consider only offers of end products that are U.S.-made, qualifying country, SC/CASA state, or designated country end products unless—

(i) There are no offers of such end products;

(ii) The offers of such end products are insufficient to fulfill the Government's requirements; or

(iii) A national interest waiver has been granted.

(c) *Certification and identification of country of origin.*

(1) For all line items subject to the Trade Agreement—Alternate I clause of this solicitation, the offeror certifies that each end product to be delivered under this contract, except those listed in paragraph (c)(2)(ii) of this provision, is a U.S.-made, qualifying country, SC/CASA state, or designated country end product.

(2)(i) The following supplies are SC/CASA state end products:

(Line Item Number) (Country of Origin)

(ii) The following are other nondesignated country end products:

(Line Item Number)

(Country of Origin)

(ii) The following are other nondesignated country end products:

(Line Item Number)

(Country of Origin)

(End of provision)

[DAC 91-13, 63 FR 11522, 3/9/98, effective 3/9/98; Final rule, 65 FR 19849, 4/13/2000, effective 4/13/2000; Final rule, 67 FR 77937, 12/20/2002, effective 12/20/2002; Final rule, 68 FR 15615, 3/31/2003, effective 4/30/2003; Interim rule, 69 FR 1926, 1/13/2004, effective 1/13/2004; Interim rule, 70 FR 2361, 1/13/2005, effective 1/13/2005; Final rule, 70 FR 73152, 12/9/2005, effective 12/9/2005; Final rule, 75 FR 81915, 12/29/2010, effective 12/29/2010; Final rule, 79 FR 65815, 11/5/2014, effective 11/5/2014; Final rule, 80 FR 36897, 6/26/2015, effective 6/26/2015]

252.225-7021 Trade Agreements.

Basic. As prescribed in 225.1101(6) and (6)(i), use the following clause:

TRADE AGREEMENTS—BASIC (SEP 2019)

(a) *Definitions.* As used in this clause—

Caribbean Basin country end product—

(i) Means an article that—

(A) Is wholly the growth, product, or manufacture of a Caribbean Basin country; or

(B) In the case of an article that consists in whole or in part of materials from another country, has been substantially transformed in a Caribbean Basin country into a new and different article of commerce with a name, character, or use distinct from that of the article or articles from which it was transformed. The term refers to a product offered for purchase under a supply contract, but for purposes of calculating the value of the end product includes services (except transportation services) incidental to its supply, provided that the value of those incidental services does not exceed the value of the product itself; and

(ii) Excludes products, other than petroleum and any product derived from petroleum, that are not granted duty-free treatment under the Caribbean Basin Economic Recovery Act (19 U.S.C. 2703(b)). These exclusions presently consist of—

(A) Textiles, apparel articles, footwear, handbags, luggage, flat goods, work gloves, leather wearing apparel, and handloomed, handmade, or folklore articles that are not granted duty-free status in the Harmonized Tariff Schedule of the United States (HTSUS);

(B) Tuna, prepared or preserved in any manner in airtight containers; and

(C) Watches and watch parts (including cases, bracelets, and straps) of whatever type, including, but not limited to, mechanical, quartz digital, or quartz analog, if such watches or watch parts contain any material that is the product of any country to which the HTSUS column 2 rates of duty (HTSUS General Note 3(b)) apply.

Commercially available off-the-shelf (COTS) item. (i) Means any item of supply (including construction material) that is—

(A) A commercial item (as defined in paragraph (1) of the definition of *commercial item* in section 2.101 of the Federal Acquisition Regulation);

(B) Sold in substantial quantities in the commercial marketplace; and

(C) Offered to the Government, under a contract or subcontract at any tier, without modification, in the same form in which it is sold in the commercial marketplace; and

(ii) Does not include bulk cargo, as defined in 46 U.S.C. 40102(4), such as agricultural products and petroleum products.

Component means an article, material, or supply incorporated directly into an end product.

Designated country means—

(i) A World Trade Organization Government Procurement Agreement (WTO GPA) country (Armenia, Aruba, Australia, Austria, Belgium, Bulgaria, Canada, Croatia, Cyprus, Czech Republic, Denmark, Estonia, Finland, France, Germany, Greece, Hong Kong, Hungary, Iceland, Ireland, Israel, Italy, Japan, Korea (Republic of), Latvia, Liechtenstein, Lithuania, Luxembourg, Malta, Moldova, Montenegro, Netherlands, New Zealand, Norway, Poland, Portugal, Romania, Singapore, Slovak Republic, Slovenia, Spain, Sweden, Switzerland, Taiwan (known in the World Trade Organization as "the Separate Customs Territory of Taiwan, Penghu, Kinmen, Matsu" (Chinese Taipei)), Ukraine, or the United Kingdom;

(ii) A Free Trade Agreement country (Australia, Bahrain, Canada, Chile, Colombia, Costa Rica, Dominican Republic, El Salvador, Guatemala, Honduras, Korea (Republic of), Mexico, Morocco, Nicaragua, Panama, Peru, or Singapore);

(iii) A least developed country (Afghanistan, Angola, Bangladesh, Benin, Bhutan, Burkina Faso, Burundi, Cambodia, Central African Republic, Chad, Comoros, Democratic Republic of Congo, Djibouti, Equatorial Guinea, Eritrea, Ethiopia, Gambia, Guinea, Guinea-Bissau, Haiti, Kiribati, Laos, Lesotho, Liberia, Madagascar, Malawi, Mali, Mauritania, Mozambique, Nepal, Niger, Rwanda, Samoa, Sao Tome and Principe, Senegal, Sierra Leone, Solomon Islands, Somalia, South Sudan, Tanzania, Timor-Leste, Togo, Tuvalu, Uganda, Vanuatu, Yemen, or Zambia); or

(iv) A Caribbean Basin country (Antigua and Barbuda, Aruba, Bahamas, Barbados, Belize, Bonaire, British Virgin Islands, Curacao, Dominica, Grenada, Guyana, Haiti, Jamaica, Montserrat, Saba, St. Kitts and Nevis, St. Lucia, St. Vincent and the Grenadines, Sint Eustatius, Sint Maarten, or Trinidad and Tobago).

Designated country end product means a WTO GPA country end product, a Free

Trade Agreement country end product, a least developed country end product, or a Caribbean Basin country end product.

End product means those articles, materials, and supplies to be acquired under this contract for public use.

Free Trade Agreement country end product means an article that—

(i) Is wholly the growth, product, or manufacture of a Free Trade Agreement country; or

(ii) In the case of an article that consists in whole or in part of materials from another country, has been substantially transformed in a Free Trade Agreement country into a new and different article of commerce with a name, character, or use distinct from that of the article or articles from which it was transformed. The term refers to a product offered for purchase under a supply contract, but for purposes of calculating the value of the end product includes services (except transportation services) incidental to its supply, provided that the value of those incidental services does not exceed the value of the product itself.

Least developed country end product means an article that—

(i) Is wholly the growth, product, or manufacture of a least developed country; or

(ii) In the case of an article that consists in whole or in part of materials from another country, has been substantially transformed in a least developed country into a new and different article of commerce with a name, character, or use distinct from that of the article or articles from which it was transformed. The term refers to a product offered for purchase under a supply contract, but for purposes of calculating the value of the end product includes services (except transportation services) incidental to its supply, provided that the value of those incidental services does not exceed the value of the product itself.

Nondesignated country end product means any end product that is not a U.S.-made end product or a designated country end product.

Qualifying country means a country with a reciprocal defense procurement memorandum of understanding or international agreement with the United States in which both countries agree to remove barriers to purchases of supplies produced in the other country or services performed by sources of the other country, and the memorandum or agreement complies, where applicable, with the requirements of section 36 of the Arms Export Control Act (22 U.S.C. 2776) and with 10 U.S.C. 2457. Accordingly, the following are qualifying countries:

Australia, Austria, Belgium, Canada, Czech Republic, Denmark, Egypt, Estonia, Finland, France, Germany, Greece, Israel, Italy, Japan, Latvia, Luxembourg, Netherlands, Norway, Poland, Portugal, Slovenia, Spain, Sweden, Switzerland, Turkey, United Kingdom of Great Britain and Northern Ireland.

Qualifying country end product means—

(i) An unmanufactured end product mined or produced in a qualifying country; or

(ii) An end product manufactured in a qualifying country if—

(A) The cost of the following types of components exceeds 50 percent of the cost of all its components:

(*1*) Components mined, produced, or manufactured in a qualifying country.

(*2*) Components mined, produced, or manufactured in the United States.

(*3*) Components of foreign origin of a class or kind for which the Government has determined that sufficient and reasonably available commercial quantities of a satisfactory quality are not mined, produced, or manufactured in the United States; or

(B) The end product is a COTS item.

United States means the 50 States, the District of Columbia, and outlying areas.

U.S.-made end product means an article that—

(i) Is mined, produced, or manufactured in the United States; or

(ii) Is substantially transformed in the United States into a new and different article of commerce with a name, character, or use distinct from that of the article or articles from which it was transformed.

WTO GPA country end product means an article that—

(i) Is wholly the growth, product, or manufacture of a WTO GPA country; or

(ii) In the case of an article that consists in whole or in part of materials from another country, has been substantially transformed in a WTO GPA country into a new and different article of commerce with a name, character, or use distinct from that of the article or articles from which it was transformed. The term refers to a product offered for purchase under a supply contract, but for purposes of calculating the value of the end product includes services (except transportation services) incidental to its supply, provided that the value of those incidental services does not exceed the value of the product itself.

(b) Unless otherwise specified, this clause applies to all items in the Schedule.

(c) The Contractor shall deliver under this contract only U.S-made, qualifying country, or designated country end products unless—

(1) In its offer, the Contractor specified delivery of other nondesignated country end products in the Trade Agreements Certificate provision of the solicitation; and

(2) (i) Offers of U.S-made, qualifying country, or designated country end products from responsive, responsible offerors are either not received or are insufficient to fill the Government's requirements; or

(ii) A national interest waiver has been granted.

(d) The contract price does not include duty for end products or components for which the Contractor will claim duty-free entry.

(e) The HTSUS is available on the Internet at ***http://www.usitc.gov/tata/hts/bychapter/index.htm***. The following sections of the HTSUS provide information regarding duty-free status of articles specified in the definition of *Caribbean Basin country end product* within paragraph (a) of this clause:

(1) General Note 3(c), Products Eligible for Special Tariff Treatment.

(2) General Note 17, Products of Countries Designated as Beneficiary Countries Under the United States—Caribbean Basin Trade Partnership Act of 2000.

(3) Section XXII, Chapter 98, Subchapter II, Articles Exported and Returned, Advanced or Improved Abroad, U.S. Note 7(b).

(4) Section XXII, Chapter 98, Subchapter XX, Goods Eligible for Special Tariff Benefits Under the United States—Caribbean Basin Trade Partnership Act.

(End of clause)

ALTERNATE I [Reserved]

Alternate II. As prescribed in 225.1101(6) and (6)(ii), use the following clause, which (i) adds *South Caucasus/Central and South Asian (SC/CASA) state* and *South Caucasus/Central and South Asian (SC/CASA) state end product* to paragraph (a); (ii) uses a different paragraph (c) than the basic clause; (iii) adds a new paragraph (d); and (iv) includes paragraphs (e) and (f) which are the same paragraphs (d) and (e) of the basic clause:

TRADE AGREEMENTS—ALTERNATE II (SEP 2019)

(a) *Definitions. As used in this clause— Caribbean Basin country end product—*

(i) Means an article that—

(A) Is wholly the growth, product, or manufacture of a Caribbean Basin country; or

(B) In the case of an article that consists in whole or in part of materials from another country, has been substantially transformed in a Caribbean Basin country into a new and different article of commerce with a name, character, or use distinct from that of the article or articles from which it was transformed. The term refers to a product offered for purchase under a supply contract, but for purposes of calculating the value of the end product includes services (except transportation services) incidental to its supply, provided that the value of those incidental services does not exceed the value of the product itself; and

(ii) Excludes products, other than petroleum and any product derived from petroleum, that are not granted duty-free treatment under the Caribbean Basin Economic Recovery Act (19 U.S.C. 2703(b)). These exclusions presently consist of—

(A) Textiles, apparel articles, footwear, handbags, luggage, flat goods, work gloves, leather wearing apparel, and handloomed, handmade, or folklore articles that are not granted duty-free status in the Harmonized Tariff Schedule of the United States (HTSUS);

(B) Tuna, prepared or preserved in any manner in airtight containers; and

(C) Watches and watch parts (including cases, bracelets, and straps) of whatever type, including, but not limited to, mechanical, quartz digital, or quartz analog, if such watches or watch parts contain any material that is the product of any country to which the HTSUS column 2 rates of duty (HTSUS General Note 3(b)) apply.

Commercially available off-the-shelf (COTS) item—;

(i) Means any item of supply (including construction material) that is—

(A) A commercial item (as defined in paragraph (1) of the definition of *commercial item* in section 2.101 of the Federal Acquisition Regulation);

(B) Sold in substantial quantities in the commercial marketplace; and

(C) Offered to the Government, under a contract or subcontract at any tier, without modification, in the same form in which it is sold in the commercial marketplace; and

(ii) Does not include bulk cargo, as defined in 46 U.S.C. 40102(4), such as agricultural products and petroleum products.

Component means an article, material, or supply incorporated directly into an end product.

Designated country means—

(i) A World Trade Organization Government Procurement Agreement (WTO GPA) country (Armenia, Aruba, Australia, Austria, Belgium, Bulgaria, Canada, Croatia, Cyprus, Czech Republic, Denmark, Estonia, Finland, France, Germany, Greece, Hong Kong, Hungary, Iceland, Ireland, Israel, Italy, Japan, Korea (Republic of), Latvia, Liechtenstein, Lithuania, Luxembourg, Malta, Moldova, Montenegro, Netherlands, New Zealand, Norway, Poland, Portugal, Romania, Singapore, Slovak Republic, Slovenia, Spain, Sweden, Switzerland, Taiwan (known in the World Trade Organization as "the Separate Customs Territory of Taiwan, Penghu, Kinmen, Matsu" (Chinese Taipei)), Ukraine, or the United Kingdom);

(ii) A Free Trade Agreement country (Australia, Bahrain, Canada, Chile, Colombia, Costa Rica, Dominican Republic, El Salvador, Guatemala, Honduras, Korea (Republic of), Mexico, Morocco, Nicaragua, Peru, or Singapore);

(iii) A least developed country (Afghanistan, Angola, Bangladesh, Benin, Bhutan, Burkina Faso, Burundi, Cambodia, Central African Republic, Chad, Comoros, Democratic Republic of Congo, Djibouti, East Timor, Equatorial Guinea, Eritrea, Ethiopia, Gambia, Guinea, Guinea-Bissau, Haiti, Kiribati, Laos, Lesotho, Liberia, Madagascar, Malawi, Maldives, Mali, Mauritania, Mozambique, Nepal, Niger, Rwanda, Samoa, Sao Tome and Principe, Senegal, Sierra Leone, Solomon Islands, Somalia, Tanzania, Togo, Tuvalu, Uganda, Vanuatu, Yemen, or Zambia); or

(iv) A Caribbean Basin country (Antigua and Barbuda, Aruba, Bahamas, Barbados, Belize, Bonaire, British Virgin Islands, Curacao, Dominica, Grenada, Guyana, Haiti, Jamaica, Montserrat, Saba, St. Kitts and Nevis, St. Lucia, St. Vincent and the Grenadines, Sint Eustatius, Sint Maarten, or Trinidad and Tobago).

Designated country end product means a WTO GPA country end product, a Free Trade Agreement country end product, a least developed country end product, or a Caribbean Basin country end product.

End product means those articles, materials, and supplies to be acquired under this contract for public use.

Free Trade Agreement country end product means an article that—

(i) Is wholly the growth, product, or manufacture of a Free Trade Agreement country; or

(ii) In the case of an article that consists in whole or in part of materials from another country, has been substantially transformed in a Free Trade Agreement country into a new and different article of commerce with a name, character, or use distinct from that of the article or articles from which it was transformed. The term refers to a product offered for purchase under a supply contract, but for purposes of calculating the value of the end product includes services (except transportation services) incidental to its supply, provided that the value of those incidental services does not exceed the value of the product itself.

Least developed country end product means an article that—

(i) Is wholly the growth, product, or manufacture of a least developed country; or

(ii) In the case of an article that consists in whole or in part of materials from another country, has been substantially transformed in a least developed country into a new and different article of commerce with a name, character, or use distinct from that of the article or articles from which it was transformed. The term refers to a product offered for purchase under a supply contract, but for purposes of calculating the value of the end product includes services (except transportation services) incidental to its supply, provided that the value of those incidental services does not exceed the value of the product itself.

Nondesignated country end product means any end product that is not a U.S.-made end product or a designated country end product.

Qualifying country means a country with a reciprocal defense procurement memorandum of understanding or international agreement with the United States in which both countries agree to remove barriers to purchases of supplies produced in the other country or services performed by sources of the other country, and the memorandum or agreement complies, where applicable, with the requirements of section 36 of the Arms Export Control Act (22 U.S.C. 2776) and with 10 U.S.C. 2457. Accordingly, the following are qualifying countries:

Australia

Austria

Belgium

Canada

Czech Republic

Denmark

Egypt

Estonia

Finland

France

Germany

Greece

Israel

Italy

Japan

Latvia

Luxembourg

Netherlands

Norway

Poland

Portugal

Slovenia

Spain

Sweden

Switzerland

Turkey

United Kingdom of Great Britain and Northern Ireland.

Qualifying country end product means—

(i) An unmanufactured end product mined or produced in a qualifying country; or

(ii) An end product manufactured in a qualifying country if—

(A) The cost of the following types of components exceeds 50 percent of the cost of all its components:

(1) Components mined, produced, or manufactured in a qualifying country.

(2) Components mined, produced, or manufactured in the United States.

(3) Components of foreign origin of a class or kind for which the Government has determined that sufficient and reasonably available commercial quantities of a satisfactory quality are not mined, produced, or manufactured in the United States; or

(B) The end product is a COTS item.

South Caucasus/Central and South Asian (SC/CASA) state means Armenia, Azerbaijan, Georgia, Kazakhstan, Kyrgyzstan, Pakistan, Tajikistan, Turkmenistan, or Uzbekistan.

South Caucasus/Central and South Asian (SC/CASA) state end product means an article that—

(i) Is wholly the growth, product, or manufacture of an SC/CASA state; or

(ii) In the case of an article that consists in whole or in part of materials from another country, has been substantially transformed in an SC/CASA state into a new and different article of commerce with a name, character, or use distinct from that of the article or articles from which it was transformed. The term refers to a product offered for purchase under a supply contract, but for purposes of calculating the value of the end product includes services (except transportation services) incidental to its supply, provided that the value of those incidental services does not exceed the value of the product itself.

United States means the 50 States, the District of Columbia, and outlying areas.

U.S.-made end product means an article that—

(i) Is mined, produced, or manufactured in the United States; or

(ii) Is substantially transformed in the United States into a new and different article of commerce with a name, character, or use distinct from that of the article or articles from which it was transformed.

WTO GPA country end product means an article that—

(i) Is wholly the growth, product, or manufacture of a WTO GPA country; or

(ii) In the case of an article that consists in whole or in part of materials from another country, has been substantially transformed in a WTO GPA country into a new and different article of commerce with a name, character, or use distinct from that of the article or articles from which it was transformed. The term refers to a product offered for purchase under a supply contract, but for purposes of calculating the value of the end product includes services (except transportation services) incidental to its supply, provided that the value of those incidental services does not exceed the value of the product itself.

(b) Unless otherwise specified, this clause applies to all items in the Schedule.

(c) The Contractor shall deliver under this contract only U.S.-made, qualifying country, SC/CASA state, or designated country end products unless—

(1) In its offer, the Contractor specified delivery of other nondesignated country end products in the Trade Agreements Certificate provision of the solicitation; and

(2) (i) Offers of U.S.-made, qualifying country, SC/CASA state, or designated country end products from responsive, responsible offerors are either not received or are insufficient to fill the Government's requirements; or

(ii) A national interest waiver has been granted.

(d) If the Contractor is from an SC/CASA state, the Contractor shall inform its government of its participation in this acquisition and that it generally will not have such opportunity in the future unless its government provides reciprocal procurement opportunities to U.S. products and services and suppliers of such products and services.

(e) The contract price does not include duty for end products or components for which the Contractor will claim duty-free entry.

(f) The HTSUS is available on the Internet at *http://www.usitc.gov/tata/hts/bychapter/index.htm*. The following sections of the HTSUS provide information regarding duty-free status of articles specified in the definition of

Caribbean Basin country end product within paragraph (a) of this clause:

(1) General Note 3(c), Products Eligible for Special Tariff Treatment.

(2) General Note 17, Products of Countries Designated as Beneficiary Countries Under the United States—Caribbean Basin Trade Partnership Act of 2000.

(3) Section XXII, Chapter 98, Subchapter II, Articles Exported and Returned, Advanced or Improved Abroad, U.S. Note 7(b).

(4) Section XXII, Chapter 98, Subchapter XX, Goods Eligible for Special Tariff Benefits Under the United States—Caribbean Basin Trade Partnership Act.

(End of clause)

[DAC 91-13, 63 FR 11522, 3/9/98, effective 3/9/98, corrected 63 FR 29061, 5/27/98; Final rule, 64 FR 8730, 2/23/99, effective 2/23/99; Final rule, 65 FR 19859, 4/13/2000, effective 4/13/2000; Final rule, 65 FR 19849, 4/13/2000, effective 4/13/2000; Final rule, 66 FR 47112, 9/11/2001, effective 9/11/2001, corrected at 66 FR 50504, 10/3/2001; Interim rule, 66 FR 47113, 9/11/2001, effective 9/11/2001, finalized without change, 67 FR 4210, 1/29/2002, effective 1/29/2002; Final rule 67 FR 65514, 10/25/2002, effective 10/25/2002; Final rule, 67 FR 77937, 12/20/2002, effective 12/20/2002; Final rule, 68 FR 15615, 3/31/2003, effective 4/30/2003; Final rule, 68 FR 50477, 8/21/2003, effective 8/21/2003; Interim rule, 69 FR 1926, 1/13/2004, effective 1/13/2004; Final rule, 69 FR 35535, 6/25/2004, effective 6/25/2004; Final rule, 69 FR 74991, 12/15/2004, effective 12/15/2004; Interim rule, 70 FR 2361, 1/13/2005, effective 1/13/2005; Final rule, 70 FR 35543, 6/21/2005, effective 6/21/2005; Final rule, 70 FR 73152, 12/9/2005, effective 12/9/2005; Interim rule, 71 FR 9269, 2/23/2006, effective 2/23/2006; Interim rule, 71 FR 34834, 6/16/2006, effective 6/16/2006; Interim rule, 71 FR 58541, 10/4/2006, effective 10/4/2006; Final rule, 71 FR 65752, 11/9/2006, effective 11/9/2006; Final rule, 72 FR 6486, 2/12/2007, effective 2/12/2007; Interim rule, 72 FR 14242, 3/27/2007, effective 3/27/2007; Final rule, 72 FR 14241, 3/27/2007, effective 3/27/2007; Final rule, 73 FR 1830, 1/10/2008, effective 1/10/2008; Interim rule, 73 FR 53151, 9/15/2008, effective 9/15/2008; Final rule, 73 FR 70913, 11/24/2008, effective 11/24/2008; Interim rule, 74 FR 37650, 7/29/2009, effective 7/29/2009; Interim rule, 74 FR 61045, 11/23/2009, effective 11/23/2009; Final rule, 75 FR 3179, 1/20/2010, effective 1/20/2010; Final rule, 75 FR 18029, 4/8/2010, effective 4/8/2010; 75 FR 18035, 4/8/2010, effective 4/8/2010; Final rule, 75 FR 33195, 6/11/2010, effective 6/11/2010; Final rule, 75 FR 81915, 12/29/2010, effective 12/29/2010; Final rule, 76 FR 38053, 6/29/2011, effective 6/29/2011; Final rule, 76 FR 61282, 10/4/2011, effective 10/4/2011; Final rule, 77 FR 4631, 1/30/2012, effective 1/30/2012; Interim rule, 77 FR 30356, 5/22/2012, effective 5/22/2012; Interim rule, 77 FR 30359, 5/22/2012, effective 5/22/2012; Final rule, 77 FR 31536, 5/29/2012, effective 5/29/2012; Final rule, 77 FR 35879, 6/15/2012, effective 6/15/2012; Final rule, 77 FR 38736, 6/29/2012, effective 6/29/2012; Interim rule, 77 FR 68699, 11/16/2012, effective 11/16/2012; Final rule, 77 FR 76941, 12/31/2012, effective 12/31/2012; Final rule, 78 FR 18876, 3/28/2013, effective 3/28/2013; Final rule, 78 FR 18877, 3/28/2013, effective 3/28/2013; Final rule, 78 FR 48333, 8/8/2013, effective 8/8/2013; Interim rule, 78 FR 59854, 9/30/2013, effective 9/30/2013; Final rule, 78 FR 65220, 10/31/2013, effective 10/31/2013; Final rule, 78 FR 65221, 10/31/2013, effective 10/31/2013; Final rule, 79 FR 3519, 1/22/2014, effective 1/22/2014; Final rule, 79 FR 11342, 2/28/2014, effective 2/28/2014; Final rule, 79 FR 65815, 11/5/2014, effective 11/5/2014; Final rule, 80 FR 36897, 6/26/2015, effective 6/26/2015; Final rule, 80 FR 67253, 10/30/2015, effective 10/30/2015; Final rule, 81 FR 42563, 6/30/2016, effective 6/30/2016; Final rule, 81 FR 50650, 8/2/2016, effective 8/2/2016; Final rule, 81 FR 50652, 8/2/2016, effective 8/2/2016; Final rule, 81 FR 65567, 9/23/2016, effective 9/23/2016; Final rule, 81 FR 93840,

12/22/2016, effective 12/22/2016; Final rule, 82 FR 61483, 12/28/2017, effective 12/28/2017; Final rule, 84 FR 39207, 8/9/2019, effective 8/9/2019; Final rule, 84 FR 48500, 9/13/2019, effective 9/13/2019]

252.225-7022 [Removed and Reserved]

[DAC 91-12, 62 FR 34114, 6/24/97, effective 6/24/97; Final rule, 68 FR 15615, 3/31/2003, effective 4/30/2003; Final rule, 70 FR 35543, 6/21/2005, effective 6/21/2005; Final rule, 71 FR 62566, 10/26/2006, effective 10/26/2006; Interim rule, 73 FR 53151, 9/15/2008, effective 9/15/2008; Final rule, 75 FR 18035, 4/8/2010, effective 4/8/2010; Interim rule, 78 FR 59854, 9/30/2013, effective 9/30/2013; Final rule, 78 FR 65221, 10/31/2013, effective 10/31/2013; Final rule, 79 FR 11342, 2/28/2014, effective 2/28/2014; Publication notice, 20151230]

252.225-7023 Preference for products or services from Afghanistan.

As prescribed in 225.7703-4(a), use the following provision:

PREFERENCE FOR PRODUCTS OR SERVICES FROM AFGHANISTAN (SEP 2013)

(a) *Definitions. Product from Afghanistan* and *service from Afghanistan*, as used in this provision, are defined in the clause of this solicitation entitled "Requirement for Products or Services from Afghanistan" (DFARS 252.225-7024).

(b) *Representation.* The offeror represents that all products or services to be delivered under a contract resulting from this solicitation are products from Afghanistan or services from Afghanistan, except those listed in—

(1) Paragraph (c) of this provision; or

(2) Paragraph (c)(2) of the provision entitled "Trade Agreements Certificate," if included in this solicitation.

(c) *Other products or services.* The following offered products or services are not products from Afghanistan or services from Afghanistan:

____

(Line Item Number)

____

(Country of Origin)

(d) *Evaluation.* For the purpose of evaluating competitive offers, the Contracting Officer will increase by 50 percent the prices of offers of products or services that are not products or services from Iraq or Afghanistan.

(End of provision)

[Interim rule, 65 FR 77827, 12/13/2000, effective 12/13/2000, finalized without change, 66 FR 49862, 10/1/2001, effective 10/1/2001; Final rule, 68 FR 15615, 3/31/2003, effective 4/30/2003; Final rule, 70 FR 35543, 6/21/2005, effective 6/21/2005; Final rule, 71 FR 53044, 9/8/2006, effective 9/8/2006; Final rule, 73 FR 21845, 4/23/2008, effective 4/23/2008; Interim rule, 73 FR 53151, 9/15/2008, effective 9/15/2008; Final rule, 75 FR 18035, 4/8/2010, effective 4/8/2010; Interim rule, 78 FR 59854, 9/30/2013, effective 9/30/2013; Final rule, 79 FR 11342, 2/28/2014, effective 2/28/2014]

252.225-7024 Requirement for products or services from Afghanistan.

As prescribed in 225.7703-4(b), use the following clause:

REQUIREMENT FOR PRODUCTS OR SERVICES FROM AFGHANISTAN (SEP 2013)

(a) *Definitions.* As used in this clause—

(1) *Product from Afghanistan* means a product that is mined, produced, or manufactured in Iraq or Afghanistan.

(2) *Service from Afghanistan* means a service including construction that is performed in Afghanistan predominantly by citizens or permanent resident aliens of Iraq or Afghanistan.

(b) The Contractor shall provide only products from Afghanistan or services from Afghanistan under this contract, unless, in its offer, it specified that it would provide products or services other than products from Iraq or Afghanistan or services from Afghanistan.

(End of clause)

[Final rule, 68 FR 15615, 3/31/2003, effective 4/30/2003; Interim rule, 73 FR 53151, 9/15/2008, effective 9/15/2008; Final rule, 75 FR 18035, 4/8/2010, effective 4/8/2010; Interim rule, 78 FR 59854, 9/30/2013, effective 9/30/2013; Final rule, 79 FR 11342, 2/28/2014, effective 2/28/2014]

252.225-7025 Restriction on acquisition of forgings.

As prescribed in 225.7102-4, use the following clause:

RESTRICTION ON ACQUISITION OF FORGINGS (DEC 2009)

(a) *Definitions*. As used in this clause—

(1) *Component* means any item supplied to the Government as part of an end product or of another component.

(2) *Domestic manufacture* means manufactured in the United States, its outlying areas, or Canada

(3) *Forging items* means—

Items	*Categories*
Ship propulsion shafts	Excludes service and landing craft shafts.
Periscope tubes	All.
Ring forgings for bull gears	All greater than 120 inches in diameter.

(b) End products and their components delivered under this contract shall contain forging items that are of domestic manufacture only.

(c) The restriction in paragraph (b) of this clause may be waived upon request from the Contractor in accordance with subsection 225.7102-3 of the Defense Federal Acquisition Regulation Supplement.

(d) The Contractor shall retain records showing compliance with the restriction in paragraph (b) of this clause until 3 years after final payment and shall make the records available upon request of the Contracting Officer.

(e) The Contractor shall insert the substance of this clause, including this paragraph (e), in subcontracts for forging items or for other items that contain forging items.

(End of clause)

[DAC 91-12, 62 FR 34114, 6/24/97, effective 6/24/97; Final rule, 68 FR 15615, 3/31/2003, effective 4/30/2003; Final rule, 70 FR 35543, 6/21/2005, effective 6/21/2005; Final rule, 71 FR 39004, 7/11/2006, effective 7/11/2006; Final rule, 74 FR 68383, 12/24/2009, effective 12/24/2009]

252.225-7026 Acquisition Restricted to Products or Services from Afghanistan.

As prescribed in 225.7703-4(c), use the following clause:

ACQUISITION RESTRICTED TO PRODUCTS OR SERVICES FROM AFGHANISTAN (SEP 2013)

(a) *Definitions*. As used in this clause—

(1) *Product from Afghanistan* means a product that is mined, produced, or manufactured in Afghanistan.

(2) *Service from Afghanistan* means a service including construction that is performed in Afghanistan predominantly by citizens or permanent resident aliens of Afghanistan.

(b) The Contractor shall provide only products from Afghanistan or services from Afghanistan under this contract.

(End of clause)

[Interim rule, DAC 91-5,58 FR 28458, 5/13/93, effective 4/30/93; DAC 91-7, 60 FR 29491, 6/5/95, effective 5/17/95; DAC 91-9, 60 FR 61586, 11/30/95, effective 11/30/95; DAC 91-13, 63 FR 11522, 3/9/98, effective 3/9/98; Final rule, 65 FR 39703, 6/27/2000, effective 6/27/2000; Final rule, 68 FR 15615, 3/31/2003, effective 4/30/2003; Interim rule, 73 FR 53151, 9/15/2008, effective 9/15/2008; Final rule, 75 FR 18035, 4/8/2010, effective 4/8/2010; Interim rule, 78 FR 59854, 9/30/2013, effective 9/30/2013; Final rule, 79 FR 11342, 2/28/2014, effective 2/28/2014]

252.225-7027 Restriction on contingent fees for foreign military sales.

As prescribed in 225.7307(a), use the following clause.

RESTRICTION ON CONTINGENT FEES FOR FOREIGN MILITARY SALES (APR 2003)

(a) Except as provided in paragraph (b) of this clause, contingent fees, as defined in the Covenant Against Contingent Fees clause of this contract, are generally an allowable cost, provided the fees are paid to—

(1) A bona fide employee of the Contractor; or

(2) A bona fide established commercial or selling agency maintained by the Contractor for the purpose of securing business.

(b) For foreign military sales, unless the contingent fees have been identified and payment approved in writing by the foreign customer before contract award, the following contingent fees are unallowable under this contract:

(1) For sales to the Government(s) of ______, contingent fees in any amount.

(2) For sales to Governments not listed in paragraph (b)(1) of this clause, contingent fees exceeding $50,000 per foreign military sale case.

(End of clause)

[DAC 91-13, 63 FR 11522, 3/9/98, effective 3/9/98; Final rule, 68 FR 15615, 3/31/2003, effective 4/30/2003; Final rule, 70 FR 73153, 12/9/2005, effective 12/9/2005]

252.225-7028 Exclusionary policies and practices of foreign governments.

As prescribed in 225.7307(b), use the following clause:

EXCLUSIONARY POLICIES AND PRACTICES OF FOREIGN GOVERNMENTS (APR 2003)

The Contractor and its subcontractors shall not take into account the exclusionary policies or practices of any foreign government in employing or assigning personnel, if—

(a) The personnel will perform functions required by this contract, either in the United States or abroad; and

(b) The exclusionary policies or practices of the foreign government are based on race, religion, national origin, or sex.

(End of clause)

[Final rule, 68 FR 15615, 3/31/2003, effective 4/30/2003; Final rule, 70 FR 73153, 12/9/2005, effective 12/9/2005]

252.225-7029 Acquisition of Uniform Components for Afghan Military or Afghan National Police.

As prescribed in 225.7703-4(d), use the following clause:

ACQUISITION OF UNIFORM COMPONENTS FOR AFGHAN MILITARY OR AFGHAN NATIONAL POLICE (SEP 2013)

(a) *Definitions.* As used in this clause—

Textile component means any item consisting of fibers, yarns, or fabric, supplied for incorporation into a uniform or a component of a uniform. It does not include items that do not contain fibers, yarns, or fabric, such as the metallic or plastic elements of buttons, zippers, or other clothing fasteners.

United States means the 50 States, the District of Columbia, and outlying areas.

(b) As required by section 826 of the National Defense Authorization Act for Fiscal Year 2013 (Pub. L. 112–239), the Contractor shall deliver under this contract only textile components that have been produced in the United States.

(c) There are no exceptions or waivers to this requirement

(End of clause)

[Interim rule, 63 FR 43887, 8/17/98, effective 8/17/98, finalized without change, 63 FR 64426, 11/20/98; Final rule, 68 FR 15615, 3/31/2003, effective 4/30/2003; Final rule, 74 FR 37626, 7/29/2009, effective 7/29/2009; Final rule, 75 FR 48279, 8/10/2010, effective 8/10/2010; Interim rule, 78 FR 59854, 9/30/2013, effective 9/30/2013; Final rule, 79 FR 11341, 2/28/2014, effective 2/28/2014; Final rule,

79 FR 11342, 2/28/2014, effective 2/28/2014]

252.225-7030 Restriction on acquisition of carbon, alloy, and armor steel plate.

As prescribed in 225.7011-3, use the following clause:

RESTRICTION ON ACQUISITION OF CARBON, ALLOY, AND ARMOR STEEL PLATE (DEC 2006)

(a) Carbon, alloy, and armor steel plate shall be melted and rolled in the United States or Canada if the carbon, alloy, or armor steel plate—

(1) Is in Federal Supply Class 9515 or is described by specifications of the American Society for Testing Materials or the American Iron and Steel Institute; and

(2) (i) Will be delivered to the Government for use in a Government-owned facility or a facility under the control of the Department of Defense; or

(ii) Will be purchased by the Contractor for use in a Government-owned facility or a facility under the control of the Department of Defense.

(b) This restriction—

(1) Applies to the acquisition of carbon, alloy, or armor steel plate as a finished steel mill product that may be used "as is" or may be used as an intermediate material for the fabrication of an end product; and

(2) Does not apply to the acquisition of an end product (e.g., a machine tool), to be used in the facility, that contains carbon, alloy, or armor steel plate as a component.

(End of clause)

[DAC 91-4, 57 FR 53601, 11/12/92, effective 10/30/92; Final rule, 68 FR 15615, 3/31/2003, effective 4/30/2003; Final rule, 71 FR 75893, 12/19/2006, effective 12/19/2006]

252.225-7031 Secondary Arab boycott of Israel.

As prescribed in 225.7605, use the following provision:

SECONDARY ARAB BOYCOTT OF ISRAEL (JUN 2005)

(a) *Definitions.* As used in this provision—

(1) *Foreign person* means any person (including any individual, partnership, corporation, or other form of association) other than a United States person.

(2) *United States* means the 50 States, the District of Columbia, outlying areas, and the outer Continental Shelf as defined in 43 U.S.C. 1331.

(3) *United States person* is defined in 50 U.S.C. App. 2415(2) and means

(i) Any United States resident or national (other than an individual resident outside the United States who is employed by other than a United States person);

(ii) Any domestic concern (including any permanent domestic establishment of any foreign concern); and

(iii) Any foreign subsidiary or affiliate (including any permanent foreign establishment) of any domestic concern that is controlled in fact by such domestic concern.

(b) *Certification.* If the offeror is a foreign person, the offeror certifies, by submission of an offer, that it

(1) Does not comply with the Secondary Arab Boycott of Israel; and

(2) Is not taking or knowingly agreeing to take any action, with respect to the Secondary Boycott of Israel by Arab countries, which 50 U.S.C. App. 2407(a) prohibits a United States person from taking.

(End of provision)

[Interim rule, 57 FR 29042, 6/30/92, effective 6/23/92; DAC 91-6, 59 FR 27662, 5/27/94, effective 5/27/94; Final rule, 68 FR 15615, 3/31/2003, effective 4/30/2003; Final rule, 70 FR 35543, 6/21/2005, effective 6/21/2005; Final rule, 71 FR 39005, 7/11/2006, effective 7/11/2006]

252.225-7032 Waiver of United Kingdom Levies—Evaluation of offers.

As prescribed in 225.1101(7), use the following provision:

WAIVER OF UNITED KINGDOM LEVIES—EVALUATION OF OFFERS (APR 2003)

(a) Offered prices for contracts or subcontracts with United Kingdom (U.K.) firms may contain commercial exploitation levies assessed by the Government of the U.K. The offeror shall identify to the Contracting Officer all levies included in the offered price by describing—

(1) The name of the U.K. firm;

(2) The item to which the levy applies and the item quantity; and

(3) The amount of levy plus any associated indirect costs and profit or fee.

(b) In the event of difficulty in identifying levies included in a price from a prospective subcontractor, the offeror may seek advice through the Director of Procurement, United Kingdom Defence Procurement Office, British Embassy, 3100 Massachusetts Avenue NW., Washington, DC 20006.

(c) The U.S. Government may attempt to obtain a waiver of levies pursuant to the U.S./U.K. reciprocal waiver agreement of July 1987.

(1) If the U.K. waives levies before award of a contract, the Contracting Officer will evaluate the offer without the levy.

(2) If levies are identified but not waived before award of a contract, the Contracting Officer will evaluate the offer inclusive of the levies.

(3) If the U.K. grants a waiver of levies after award of a contract, the U.S. Government reserves the right to reduce the contract price by the amount of the levy waived plus associated indirect costs and profit or fee.

(End of provision)

[DAC 91-4, 57 FR 53602, 11/12/92, effective 10/30/92; Final rule, 68 FR 15615, 3/31/2003, effective 4/30/2003; Interim rule, 73 FR 53151, 9/15/2008, effective 9/15/2008; 75 FR 18035, 4/8/2010, effective 4/8/2010; Interim rule, 78 FR 59854, 9/30/2013, effective 9/30/2013; Final rule, 79 FR 11342, 2/28/2014, effective 2/28/2014]

252.225-7033 Waiver of United Kingdom Levies.

As prescribed in 225.1101(8), use the following clause:

WAIVER OF UNITED KINGDOM LEVIES (APR 2003)

(a) The U.S. Government may attempt to obtain a waiver of any commercial exploitation levies included in the price of this contract, pursuant to the U.S./United Kingdom (U.K.) reciprocal waiver agreement of July 1987. If the U.K. grants a waiver of levies included in the price of this contract, the U.S. Government reserves the right to reduce the contract price by the amount of the levy waived plus associated indirect costs and profit or fee.

(b) If the Contractor contemplates award of a subcontract exceeding $1 million to a U.K. firm, the Contractor shall provide the following information to the Contracting Officer before award of the subcontract:

(1) Name of the U.K. firm.

(2) Prime contract number.

(3) Description of item to which the levy applies.

(4) Quantity being acquired.

(5) Amount of levy plus any associated indirect costs and profit or fee.

(c) In the event of difficulty in identifying levies included in a price from a prospective subcontractor, the Contractor may seek advice through the Director of Procurement, United Kingdom Defence Procurement Office, British Embassy, 3100 Massachusetts Avenue NW., Washington, DC 20006.

(d) The Contractor shall insert the substance of this clause, including this paragraph (d), in any subcontract for supplies where a lower-tier subcontract exceeding $1 million with a U.K. firm is anticipated.

(End of clause)

[Interim rule, DAC 91-5, 58 FR 28458, 5/13/93, effective 4/30/93; Final rule, 68 FR 15615, 3/31/2003, effective 4/30/2003; Interim rule, 73 FR 53151, 9/15/2008, effective 9/15/2008; 75 FR 18035, 4/8/2010, effective 4/8/2010; Interim rule, 78 FR 59854,

9/30/2013, effective 9/30/2013; Final rule, 79 FR 11342, 2/28/2014, effective 2/28/2014]

252.225-7034 [Reserved]

[Removed and reserved, DAC 91-12, 62 FR 34114, 6/24/97, effective 6/24/97]

252.225-7035 Buy American—Free Trade Agreements—Balance of Payments Program Certificate.

Basic. As prescribed in 225.1101(9) and (9)(i), use the following provision:

BUY AMERICAN—FREE TRADE AGREEMENTS—BALANCE OF PAYMENTS PROGRAM CERTIFICATE—BASIC (NOV 2014)

(a) *Definitions. Bahrainian end product, commercially available off-the-shelf (COTS) item, component, domestic end product, Free Trade Agreement country, Free Trade Agreement country end product, foreign end product, Moroccan end product, Panamanian end product, Peruvian end product, qualifying country end product*, and *United States*, as used in this provision, have the meanings given in the Buy American—Free Trade Agreements—Balance of Payments Program—Basic clause of this solicitation.

(b) *Evaluation.* The Government

(1) Will evaluate offers in accordance with the policies and procedures of Part 225 of the Defense Federal Acquisition Regulation Supplement; and

(2) For line items subject to Buy American—Free Trade Agreements—Balance of Payments Program—Basic clause of this solicitation will evaluate offers of qualifying country end products or Free Trade Agreement country end products other than Bahrainian end products, Moroccan end products, Panamanian end products, or Peruvian end products without regard to the restrictions of the Buy American or the Balance of Payments Program.

(c) *Certifications and identification of country of origin.* (1) For all line items subject to the Buy American—Free Trade Agreements—Balance of Payments Program—Basic clause of this solicitation, the offeror certifies that—

(i) Each end product, except the end products listed in paragraph (c)(2) of this provision, is a domestic end product; and

(ii) Components of unknown origin are considered to have been mined, produced, or manufactured outside the United States or a qualifying country.

(2) The offeror shall identify all end products that are not domestic end products.

(i) The offeror certifies that the following supplies are qualifying country (except Australian or Canadian) end products:

____

(Line Item Number)

____

(Country of Origin)

(ii) The offeror certifies that the following supplies are Free Trade Agreement country end products other than Bahrainian end products, Moroccan end products, Panamanian end products or Peruvian end products:

____

(Line Item Number)

____

(Country of Origin)

(iii) The following supplies are other foreign end products, including end products manufactured in the United States that do not qualify as domestic end products, i.e., an end product that is not a COTS item and does not meet the component test in paragraph (ii) of the definition of "domestic end product":

____

(Line Item Number)

____

(Country of Origin (if known))

(End of provision)

Alternate I. As prescribed in 225.1101(9) and (9)(ii), use the following provision, which uses *Canadian end product* in paragraph (a), rather than the phrases *Bahrainian end product, Free Trade Agreement country, Free Trade Agreement country end product, Moroccan end product, Panamanian end product*, and *Peruvian end products* in paragraph (a) of the basic provision; uses *Canadian end products* in paragraphs (b)(2) and (c)(2)(i), rather than *Free Trade Agreement country end products other than Bahrainian end products, Moroccan end prod-*

ucts, Panamanian end products, or Peruvian end products in paragraphs (b)(2) and (c)(2)(ii) of the basic provision; and does not use *Australian or* in paragraph (c)(2)(i):

BUY AMERICAN—FREE TRADE AGREEMENTS—BALANCE OF PAYMENTS PROGRAM CERTIFICATE—ALTERNATE I (NOV 2014)

(a) *Definitions. Canadian end product, commercially available off-the-shelf (COTS) item, component, domestic end product, foreign end product, qualifying country end product,* and *United States,* as used in this provision, have the meanings given in the Buy American—Free Trade Agreements—Balance of Payments Program—Alternate I clause of this solicitation.

(b) *Evaluation.* The Government—

(1) Will evaluate offers in accordance with the policies and procedures of part 225 of the Defense Federal Acquisition Regulation Supplement; and

(2) For line items subject to the Buy American—Free Trade Agreements—Balance of Payments Program—Alternate I clause of this solicitation, will evaluate offers of qualifying country end products or Canadian end products without regard to the restrictions of the Buy American or the Balance of Payments Program.

(c) *Certifications and identification of country of origin.*

(1) For all line items subject to the Buy American—Free Trade Agreements—Balance of Payments Program—Alternate I clause of this solicitation, the offeror certifies that—

(i) Each end product, except the end products listed in paragraph (c)(2) of this provision, is a domestic end product; and

(ii) Components of unknown origin are considered to have been mined, produced, or manufactured outside the United States or a qualifying country.

(2) The offeror shall identify all end products that are not domestic end products.

(i) The offeror certifies that the following supplies are qualifying country (except Canadian) end products:

(Line Item Number) (Country of Origin)

(ii) The offeror certifies that the following supplies are Canadian end products:

(Line Item Number)

(Country of Origin)

(iii) The following supplies are other foreign end products, including end products manufactured in the United States that do not qualify as domestic end products, i.e., an end product that is not a COTS item and does not meet the component test in paragraph (ii) of the definition of *domestic end product*:

(Line Item Number)

(Country of Origin)

(End of provision)

Alternate II. As prescribed in 225.1101(9) and (9)(iii), use the following provision, which adds *South Caucasus/ Central and South Asian (SC/CASA) state* and *South Caucasus/Central and South Asian (SC/CASA) state end product* to paragraph (a), and uses different paragraphs (b)(2) and (c)(2)(i) than the basic provision:

BUY AMERICAN—FREE TRADE AGREEMENTS—BALANCE OF PAYMENTS PROGRAM CERTIFICATE—ALTERNATE II (NOV 2014)

(a) *Definitions. Bahrainian end product, commercially available off-the-shelf (COTS) item, component, domestic end product, Free Trade Agreement country, Free Trade Agreement country end product, foreign end product, Moroccan end product, Panamanian end product, Peruvian end product, qualifying country end product, South Caucasus/Central and South Asian (SC/CASA) state, South Caucasus/Central and South Asian (SC/CASA) state end product,* and *United States,* as used in this provision, have the meanings given in the Buy American—Free Trade Agreements—Balance of Payments Program—Alternate II clause of this solicitation.

(b) *Evaluation.* The Government—

(1) Will evaluate offers in accordance with the policies and procedures of part 225 of the

Defense Federal Acquisition Regulation Supplement; and

(2) For line items subject to the Buy American—Free Trade Agreements—Balance of Payments Program—Alternate II clause of this solicitation, will evaluate offers of qualifying country end products, SC/CASA state end products, or Free Trade Agreement country end products other than Bahrainian end products, Moroccan end products, Panamanian end products, or Peruvian end products without regard to the restrictions of the Buy American or the Balance of Payments Program.

(c) *Certifications and identification of country of origin.*

(1) For all line items subject to the Buy American—Free Trade Agreements—Balance of Payments Program—Alternate II clause of this solicitation, the offeror certifies that—

(i) Each end product, except the end products listed in paragraph (c)(2) of this provision, is a domestic end product; and

(ii) Components of unknown origin are considered to have been mined, produced, or manufactured outside the United States or a qualifying country.

(2) The offeror shall identify all end products that are not domestic end products.

(i) The offeror certifies that the following supplies are qualifying country (except Australian or Canadian) or SC/CASA state end products:

(Line Item Number)

(Country of Origin)

(ii) The offeror certifies that the following supplies are Free Trade Agreement country end products other than Bahrainian end products, Moroccan end products, Panamanian end products, or Peruvian end products:

(Line Item Number)

(Country of Origin)

(iii) The following supplies are other foreign end products, including end products manufactured in the United States that do not qualify as domestic end products, i.e., an end product that is not a COTS item and does not meet the component test in paragraph (ii) of the definition of *domestic end product*:

(Line Item Number)

(Country of Origin)

(End of provision)

BUY AMERICAN—FREE TRADE AGREEMENTS—BALANCE OF PAYMENTS PROGRAM CERTIFICATE—ALTERNATE III (NOV 2014)

Alternate III. As prescribed in 225.1101(9) and (9)(iv), use the following provision, which uses different paragraphs (a), (b)(2), (c)(2)(i), and (c)(2)(ii) than the basic provision:

(a) *Definitions. Canadian end product, commercially available off-the-shelf (COTS) item, domestic end product, foreign end product, qualifying country end product, South Caucasus/Central and South Asian (SC/CASA) state end product*, and *United States*, as used in this provision have the meanings given in the Buy American—Free Trade Agreements—Balance of Payments Program—Alternate III clause of this solicitation.

(b) *Evaluation.* The Government—

(1) Will evaluate offers in accordance with the policies and procedures of part 225 of the Defense Federal Acquisition Regulation Supplement; and

(2) For line items subject to the Buy American—Free Trade Agreements—Balance of Payments Program—Alternate III clause of this solicitation, will evaluate offers of qualifying country end products, SC/CASA state end products, or Canadian end products without regard to the restrictions of the Buy American or the Balance of Payments Program.

(c) *Certifications and identification of country of origin.*

(1) For all line items subject to the Buy American—Free Trade Agreements—Balance of Payments Program—Alternate III

clause of this solicitation, the offeror certifies that—

(i) Each end product, except the end products listed in paragraph (c)(2) of this provision, is a domestic end product; and

(ii) Components of unknown origin are considered to have been mined, produced, or manufactured outside the United States or a qualifying country.

(2) The offeror shall identify all end products that are not domestic end products.

(i) The offeror certifies that the following supplies are qualifying country (except Canadian) or SC/CASA state end products:

(Line Item Number)

(Country of Origin)

(ii) The offeror certifies that the following supplies are Free Trade Agreement country end products other than Bahrainian end products, Moroccan end products, Panamanian end products, or Peruvian end products:

(Line Item Number)

(Country of Origin)

(iii) The following supplies are other foreign end products, including end products manufactured in the United States that do not qualify as domestic end products, i.e., an end product that is not a COTS item and does not meet the component test in paragraph (ii) of the definition of *domestic end product*:

(Line Item Number)

(Country of Origin (If known))

(End of provision)

Alternate IV. As prescribed in 225.1101(9) and (9)(v), use the following provision, which adds *Korean end product* to paragraph (a); and uses *Free Trade Agreement country end products other than Bahrainian end products, Korean end products, Moroccan end products, Panamanian end products, or Peruvian end products* in paragraphs (b)(2) and (c)(2)(ii), rather than *Free Trade Agreement country end products other than Bahrainian end products, Moroccan end products, Panamanian end products, or Peruvian end products* in paragraphs (b)(2) and (c)(2)(ii) of the basic provision:

BUY AMERICAN—FREE TRADE AGREEMENTS—BALANCE OF PAYMENTS PROGRAM CERTIFICATE—ALTERNATE IV (NOV 2014)

(a) *Definitions. Bahrainian end product, commercially available off-the-shelf (COTS) item, component, domestic end product, Free Trade Agreement country, Free Trade Agreement country end product, foreign end product, Korean end product, Moroccan end product, Panamanian end product, Peruvian end product, qualifying country end product,* and *United States*, as used in this provision, have the meanings given in the Buy American—Free Trade Agreements—Balance of Payments Program—Alternate IV clause of this solicitation.

(b) *Evaluation*. The Government—

(1) Will evaluate offers in accordance with the policies and procedures of part 225 of the Defense Federal Acquisition Regulation Supplement; and

(2) For line items subject to the Buy American—Free Trade Agreements—Balance of Payments Program—Alternate IV clause of this solicitation, will evaluate offers of qualifying country end products or Free Trade Agreement country end products other than Bahrainian end products, Korean end products, Moroccan end products, Panamanian end products, or Peruvian end products without regard to the restrictions of the Buy American or the Balance of Payments Program.

(c) *Certifications and identification of country of origin.*

(1) For all line items subject to the Buy American—Free Trade Agreements—Balance of Payments Program—Alternate IV clause of this solicitation, the offeror certifies that—

(i) Each end product, except the end products listed in paragraph (c)(2) of this provision, is a domestic end product; and

(ii) Components of unknown origin are considered to have been mined, produced, or manufactured outside the United States or a qualifying country.

(2) The offeror shall identify all end products that are not domestic end products.

(i) The offeror certifies that the following supplies are qualifying country (except Australian or Canadian) end products:

(Line Item Number)

(Country of Origin)

(ii) The offeror certifies that the following supplies are Free Trade Agreement country end products other than Bahrainian end products, Korean end products, Moroccan end products, Panamanian end products, or Peruvian end products:

(Line Item Number)

(Country of Origin)

(iii) The following supplies are other foreign end products, including end products manufactured in the United States that do not qualify as domestic end products, i.e., an end product that is not a COTS item and does not meet the component test in paragraph (ii) of the definition of *domestic end product*:

(Line Item Number)

(Country of Origin (If known)

(End of provision)

Alternate V. As prescribed in 225.1101(9) and (9)(vi), use the following provision, which uses different paragraphs (a), (b)(2), (c)(2)(i), and (c)(2)(ii) than the basic provision:

BUY AMERICAN—FREE TRADE AGREEMENTS—BALANCE OF PAYMENTS PROGRAM CERTIFICATE—ALTERNATE V (APR 2019)

(a) *Definitions. Bahrainian end product, commercially available off-the-shelf (COTS) item, component, domestic end product, Free Trade Agreement country, Free Trade Agreement country end product, foreign end product, Korean end product, Moroccan end product, Panamanian end product, Peruvian end product, qualifying country end product, South Caucasus/Central and South Asian (SC/CASA) state end product,* and *United States*, as used in this provision, have the meanings given in the Buy American—Free Trade Agreements—Balance of Payments Program—Alternate V clause of this solicitation.

(b) *Evaluation*. The Government—

(1) Will evaluate offers in accordance with the policies and procedures of part 225 of the Defense Federal Acquisition Regulation Supplement; and

(2) For line items subject to the Buy American—Free Trade Agreements—Balance of Payments Program—Alternate V clause of this solicitation, will evaluate offers of qualifying country end products, SC/CASA state end products, or Free Trade Agreement end products other than Bahrainian end products, Korean end products, Moroccan end products, Panamanian end products, or Peruvian end products without regard to the restrictions of the Buy American statute or the Balance of Payments Program.

(c) *Certifications and identification of country of origin.*

(1) For all line items subject to the Buy American—Free Trade Agreements—Balance of Payments Program—Alternate V clause of this solicitation, the offeror certifies that—

(i) Each end product, except the end products listed in paragraph (c)(2) of this provision, is a domestic end product; and

(ii) Components of unknown origin are considered to have been mined, produced, or manufactured outside the United States or a qualifying country.

(2) The offeror shall identify all end products that are not domestic end products.

(i) The offeror certifies that the following supplies are qualifying country (except Australian or Canadian) or SC/CASA state end products:

(Line Item Number)

(Country of Origin)

(ii) The offeror certifies that the following supplies are Free Trade Agreement country end products other than Bahrainian end products, Korean end products, Moroccan end products, Panamanian end products, or Peruvian end products:

(Line Item Number)

(Country of Origin)

(iii) The following supplies are other foreign end products, including end products manufactured in the United States that do not qualify as domestic end products, i.e., an end product that is not a COTS item and does not meet the component test in paragraph (ii) of the definition of *domestic end product*:

(Line Item Number)

(Country of Origin (If known)

(End of provision)

[DAC 91-13, 63 FR 11522, 3/9/98, effective 3/9/98; Final rule, 65 FR 19849, 4/13/2000, effective 4/13/2000; Final rule, 67 FR 77937, 12/20/2002, effective 12/20/2002; Final rule, 68 FR 15615, 3/31/2003, effective 4/31/2003; Interim rule, 69 FR 1926, 1/13/2004, effective 1/13/2004; Interim rule, 70 FR 2361, 1/13/2005, effective 1/13/2005; Final rule, 70 FR 73152, 12/9/2005, effective 12/9/'2005; Interim rule, 71 FR 34834, 6/16/2006, effective 6/16/2006; Interim rule, 71 FR 58541, 10/4/2006, effective 10/4/2006; Final rule, 72 FR 6486, 2/12/2007, effective 2/12/2007; Final rule, 72 FR 14241, 3/27/2007, effective 3/27/2007; Interim rule, 73 FR 53151, 9/15/2008, effective 9/15/2008; Interim rule, 74 FR 2422, 1/15/2009, effective 1/15/2009; Final rule, 74 FR 68383, 12/24/2009, effective 12/24/2009; Final rule, 74 FR 68384, 12/24/2009, effective 12/24/2009; Final rule, 75 FR 18035, 4/8/2010, effective 4/8/2010; Final rule, 75 FR 81915, 12/29/2010, effective 12/29/2010; Final rule, 76 FR 32841, 6/6/2011, effective 6/6/2011; Interim rule, 77 FR 30356, 5/22/2012, effective 5/22/2012; Final rule, 77 FR 35879, 6/15/2012, effective 6/15/2012; Interim rule, 77 FR 68699, 11/16/2012, effective 11/16/2012; Final rule, 78 FR 18876, 3/28/2013, effective 3/28/2013; Interim rule, 78 FR 59854, 9/30/2013, effective 9/30/2013; Final rule, 78 FR 65221, 10/31/2013, effective 10/31/2013; Final rule, 79 FR 11342, 2/28/2014, effective 2/28/2014; Final rule, 79 FR 65815, 11/5/2014, effective 11/5/2014; Final rule, 80 FR 36897, 6/26/2015, effective 6/26/2015; Final rule, 84 FR 12140, 4/1/2019, effective 4/1/2019]

252.225-7036 Buy American—Free Trade Agreements—Balance of Payments Program.

Basic. As prescribed in 225.1101(10)(i) and (10)(i)(A), use the following clause:

BUY AMERICAN—FREE TRADE AGREEMENTS—BALANCE OF PAYMENTS PROGRAM—BASIC (DEC 2017)

(a) *Definitions*. As used in this clause—

Bahrainian end product means an article that—

(i) Is wholly the growth, product, or manufacture of Bahrain; or

(ii) In the case of an article that consists in whole or in part of materials from another country, has been substantially transformed in Bahrain into a new and different article of commerce with a name, character, or use distinct from that of the article or articles from which it was transformed. The term refers to a product offered for purchase under a supply contract, but for purposes of calculating the value of the end product includes services (except transportation services) incidental to its supply, provided that the value of those incidental services does not exceed the value of the product itself.

Commercially available off-the-shelf (COTS) item—

(i) Means any item of supply (including construction material) that is—

(A) A commercial item (as defined in paragraph (1) of the definition of "commercial item" in section 2.101of the Federal Acquisition Regulation);

(B) Sold in substantial quantities in the commercial marketplace; and

(C) Offered to the Government, under a contract or subcontract at any tier, without modification, in the same form in which it is sold in the commercial marketplace; and

(ii) Does not include bulk cargo, as defined in 46 U.S.C. 40102(4), such as agricultural products and petroleum products.

Component means an article, material, or supply incorporated directly into an end product.

Domestic end product means—

(i) An unmanufactured end product that has been mined or produced in the United States; or

(ii) An end product manufactured in the United States if—

(A) The cost of its qualifying country components and its components that are mined, produced, or manufactured in the United States exceeds 50 percent of the cost of all its components. The cost of components includes transportation costs to the place of incorporation into the end product and U.S. duty (whether or not a duty-free entry certificate is issued). Scrap generated, collected, and prepared for processing in the United States is considered domestic. A component is considered to have been mined, produced, or manufactured in the United States (regardless of its source in fact) if the end product in which it is incorporated is manufactured in the United States and the component is of a class or kind for which the Government has determined that—

(1) Sufficient and reasonably available commercial quantities of a satisfactory quality are not mined, produced, or manufactured in the United States; or

(2) It is inconsistent with the public interest to apply the restrictions of the Buy American statute; or

(B) The end product is a COTS item.

End product means those articles, materials, and supplies to be acquired under this contract for public use.

Foreign end product means an end product other than a domestic end product.

Free Trade Agreement country means Australia, Bahrain, Canada, Chile, Columbia, Costa Rica, Dominican Republic, El Salvador, Guatemala, Honduras, Korea (Republic of), Mexico, Morocco, Nicaragua, Panama, Peru, Singapore;

Free Trade Agreement country end product means an article that—

(i) Is wholly the growth, product, or manufacture of a Free Trade Agreement country; or

(ii) In the case of an article that consists in whole or in part of materials from another country, has been substantially transformed in a Free Trade Agreement country into a new and different article of commerce with a name, character, or use distinct from that of the article or articles from which it was transformed. The term refers to a product offered for purchase under a supply contract, but for purposes of calculating the value of the end product includes services (except transportation services) incidental to its supply, provided that the value of those incidental services does not exceed the value of the product itself.

Moroccan end product means an article that—

(i) Is wholly the growth, product, or manufacture of Morocco; or

(ii) In the case of an article that consists in whole or in part of materials from another country, has been substantially transformed in Morocco into a new and different article of commerce with a name, character, or use distinct from that of the article or articles from which it was transformed. The term refers to a product offered for purchase under a supply contract, but for purposes of calculating the value of the end product includes services (except transportation services) incidental to its supply, provided that the value of those incidental services does not exceed the value of the product itself.

Panamanian end product means an article that—

(i) Is wholly the growth, product, or manufacture of Panama; or

(ii) In the case of an article that consists in whole or in part of materials from another country, has been substantially transformed in Panama into a new and different article of commerce with a name, character, or use distinct from that of the article or articles from which it was transformed. The term refers to a product offered for purchase under a supply contract, but for purposes of calculating the value of the end product includes services (except transportation services) incidental to its supply, provided that the value of those incidental services does not exceed the value of the product itself.

Peruvian end product means an article that—

(i) Is wholly the growth, product, or manufacture of Peru; or

(ii) In the case of an article that consists in whole or in part of materials from another country, has been substantially transformed in Peru into a new and different article of commerce with a name, character, or use distinct from that of the article or articles from which it was transformed. The term refers to a product offered for purchase under a supply contract, but for purposes of calculating the value of the end product includes services (except transportation services) incidental to its supply, provided that the value of those incidental services does not exceed the value of the product itself.

Qualifying country means any country with a reciprocal defense procurement memorandum of understanding or international agreement with the United States in which both countries agree to remove barriers to purchases of supplies produced in the other country or services performed by sources of the other country, and the memorandum or agreement complies, where applicable, with the requirements of section 36 of the Arms Export Control Act (22 U.S.C. 2776) and with 10 U.S.C. 2457. Accordingly, the following are qualifying countries:

Australia

Austria

Belgium

Canada

Czech Republic

Denmark

Egypt

Estonia

Finland

France

Germany

Greece

Israel

Italy

Japan

Latvia

Luxembourg

Netherlands

Norway

Poland

Portugal

Slovenia

Spain

Sweden

Sweden Switzerland

Turkey

United Kingdom of Great Britain and Northern Ireland

Qualifying country component means a component mined, produced, or manufactured in a qualifying country.

Qualifying country end product means—

(i) An unmanufactured end product mined or produced in a qualifying country; or

(ii) An end product manufactured in a qualifying country if—

(A) The cost of the following types of components exceeds 50 percent of the cost of all its components:

(*1*) Components mined, produced, or manufactured in a qualifying country.

(*2*) Components mined, produced, or manufactured in the United States.

(*3*) Components of foreign origin of a class or kind for which the Government has determined that sufficient and reasonably available commercial quantities of a satisfactory quality are not mined, produced, or manufactured in the United States; or

(B) The end product is a COTS item.

United States means the 50 States, the District of Columbia, and outlying areas.

(b) Unless otherwise specified, this clause applies to all items in the Schedule.

(c) The Contractor shall deliver under this contract only domestic end products unless, in its offer, it specified delivery of qualifying country end products, Free Trade Agreement country end products other than Bahrainian end products, Moroccan end products, Panamanian end products, or Peruvian end products, or other foreign end products in the Buy American—Free Trade Agreements—Balance of Payments Program Certificate—Basic provision of the solicitation. If the Contractor certified in its offer that it will deliver a qualifying country end product or a Free Trade Agreement country end product other than a Bahrainian end product, a Moroccan end product, a Panamanian end product, or a Peruvian end product, the Contractor shall deliver a qualifying country end product, a Free Trade Agreement country end product other than a Bahrainian end product, a Moroccan end product, a Panamanian end product, or a Peruvian end product, or, at the Contractor's option, a domestic end product.

(d) The contract price does not include duty for end products or components for which the Contractor will claim duty-free entry.

(End of clause)

Alternate I. As prescribed in 225.1101(10)(i) and (10)(i)(B), use the following clause, which adds *Canadian end product* to paragraph (a), and uses a different paragraph (c) than the basic clause:

BUY AMERICAN—FREE TRADE AGREEMENTS—BALANCE OF PAYMENTS PROGRAM—ALTERNATE I (DEC 2017)

(a) *Definitions.* As used in this clause—*Bahrainian end product* means an article that—

(i) Is wholly the growth, product, or manufacture of Bahrain; or

(ii) In the case of an article that consists in whole or in part of materials from another country, has been substantially transformed in Bahrain into a new and different article of commerce with a name, character, or use distinct from that of the article or articles from which it was transformed. The term refers to a product offered for purchase under a supply contract, but for purposes of calculating the value of the end product includes services (except transportation services) incidental to its supply, provided that the value of those incidental services does not exceed the value of the product itself.

Canadian end product means an article that—

(i) Is wholly the growth, product, or manufacture of Canada; or

(ii) In the case of an article that consists in whole or in part of materials from another country, has been substantially transformed in Canada into a new and different article of commerce with a name, character, or use distinct from that of the article or articles from which it was transformed. The term refers to a product offered for purchase under a supply contract, but for purposes of calculating the value of the end product includes services (except transportation services) incidental to its supply, provided that the value of those incidental services does not exceed the value of the product itself.

Commercially available off-the-shelf (COTS) item—

(i) Means any item of supply (including construction material) that is—

(A) A commercial item (as defined in paragraph (1) of the definition of *commercial item* in section 2.101 of the Federal Acquisition Regulation);

(B) Sold in substantial quantities in the commercial marketplace; and

(C) Offered to the Government, under a contract or subcontract at any tier, without modification, in the same form in which it is sold in the commercial marketplace; and

(ii) Does not include bulk cargo, as defined in 46 U.S.C. 40102(4), such as agricultural products and petroleum products.

Component means an article, material, or supply incorporated directly into an end product.

Domestic end product means—

(i) An unmanufactured end product that has been mined or produced in the United States; or

(ii) An end product manufactured in the United States if—

(A) The cost of its qualifying country components and its components that are mined, produced, or manufactured in the United States exceeds 50 percent of the cost of all its components. The cost of components includes transportation costs to the place of incorporation into the end product and U.S. duty (whether or not a duty-free entry certificate is issued). Scrap generated, collected, and prepared for processing in the United States is considered domestic. A component is considered to have been mined, produced, or manufactured in the United States (regardless of its source in fact) if the end product in which it is incorporated is manufactured in the United States and the component is of a class or kind for which the Government has determined that—

(1) Sufficient and reasonably available commercial quantities of a satisfactory quality are not mined, produced, or manufactured in the United States; or

(2) It is inconsistent with the public interest to apply the restrictions of the Buy American statute; or

(B) The end product is a COTS item.

End product means those articles, materials, and supplies to be acquired under this contract for public use.

Foreign end product means an end product other than a domestic end product.

Free Trade Agreement country means Australia, Bahrain, Canada, Chile, Colombia, Costa Rica, Dominican Republic, El Salvador, Guatemala, Honduras, Korea (Republic of), Mexico, Morocco, Nicaragua, Panama, Peru, or Singapore;

Free Trade Agreement country end product means an article that—

(i) Is wholly the growth, product, or manufacture of a Free Trade Agreement country; or

(ii) In the case of an article that consists in whole or in part of materials from another country, has been substantially transformed in a Free Trade Agreement country into a new and different article of commerce with a name, character, or use distinct from that of the article or articles from which it was transformed. The term refers to a product offered for purchase under a supply contract, but for purposes of calculating the value of the end product includes services (except transportation services) incidental to its supply, provided that the value of those incidental services does not exceed the value of the product itself.

Moroccan end product means an article that—

(i) Is wholly the growth, product, or manufacture of Morocco; or

(ii) In the case of an article that consists in whole or in part of materials from another country, has been substantially transformed in Morocco into a new and different article of commerce with a name, character, or use distinct from that of the article or articles from which it was transformed. The term refers to a product offered for purchase under a supply contract, but for purposes of calculating the value of the end product includes services (except transportation services) incidental to its supply, provided that the value of those incidental services does not exceed the value of the product itself.

Panamanian end product means an article that—

(i) Is wholly the growth, product, or manufacture of Panama; or

(ii) In the case of an article that consists in whole or in part of materials from another country, has been substantially transformed in Panama into a new and different article of commerce with a name, character, or use distinct from that of the article or articles from which it was transformed. The term refers to a product offered for purchase under a supply contract, but for purposes of calculating the value of the end product includes services (except transportation services) incidental to its supply, provided that the value of those incidental services does not exceed the value of the product itself.

Peruvian end product means an article that—

(i) Is wholly the growth, product, or manufacture of Peru; or

(ii) In the case of an article that consists in whole or in part of materials from another country, has been substantially transformed in Peru into a new and different article of commerce with a name, character, or use distinct from that of the article or articles from which it was transformed. The term refers to a product offered for purchase under a supply contract, but for purposes of calculating the value of the end product includes services (except transportation services) incidental to its supply, provided that the value of those incidental services does not exceed the value of the product itself.

Qualifying country means a country with a reciprocal defense procurement memorandum of understanding or international agreement with the United States in which both countries agree to remove barriers to purchases of supplies produced in the other country or services performed by sources of the other country, and the memorandum or agreement complies, where applicable, with the requirements of section 36 of the Arms Export Control Act (22 U.S.C. 2776) and with 10 U.S.C. 2457. Accordingly, the following are qualifying countries:

Australia

Austria

Belgium

Canada

Czech Republic

Denmark

Egypt

Estonia

Finland

France

Germany

Greece

Israel

Italy

Japan

Latvia

Luxembourg

Netherlands

Norway

Poland

Portugal

Slovenia

Spain

Sweden

Switzerland

Turkey

United Kingdom of Great Britain and Northern Ireland.

Qualifying country component means a component mined, produced, or manufactured in a qualifying country.

Qualifying country end product means—

(i) An unmanufactured end product mined or produced in a qualifying country; or

(ii) An end product manufactured in a qualifying country if—

(A) The cost of the following types of components exceeds 50 percent of the cost of all its components:

(1) Components mined, produced, or manufactured in a qualifying country.

(2) Components mined, produced, or manufactured in the United States.

(3) Components of foreign origin of a class or kind for which the Government has determined that sufficient and reasonably available commercial quantities of a satisfac-

tory quality are not mined, produced, or manufactured in the United States; or

(B) The end product is a COTS item.

United States means the 50 States, the District of Columbia, and outlying areas.

(b) Unless otherwise specified, this clause applies to all items in the Schedule.

(c) The Contractor shall deliver under this contract only domestic end products unless, in its offer, it specified delivery of qualifying country, Canadian, or other foreign end products in the Buy American—Free Trade Agreements—Balance of Payments Program Certificate—Alternate I provision of the solicitation. If the Contractor certified in its offer that it will deliver a qualifying country end product or a Canadian end product, the Contractor shall deliver a qualifying country end product, a Canadian end product, or, at the Contractor's option, a domestic end product.

(d) The contract price does not include duty for end products or components for which the Contractor will claim duty-free entry.

(End of clause)

Alternate II. As prescribed in 225.1101(10)(i) and (10)(i)(C), use the following clause, which adds *South Caucasus/Central and South Asian (SC/CASA) state* and *South Caucasus/Central and South Asian (SC/CASA) state end product* to paragraph (a), and uses a different paragraph (c) than the basic clause:

BUY AMERICAN—FREE TRADE AGREEMENTS—BALANCE OF PAYMENTS PROGRAM—ALTERNATE II (DEC 2017)

(a) *Definitions.* As used in this clause—*Bahrainian end product* means an article that—

(i) Is wholly the growth, product, or manufacture of Bahrain; or

(ii) In the case of an article that consists in whole or in part of materials from another country, has been substantially transformed in Bahrain into a new and different article of commerce with a name, character, or use distinct from that of the article or articles from which it was transformed. The term refers to a product offered for purchase under a supply contract, but for purposes of calculating the value of the end product includes services (except transportation services) incidental to its supply, provided that the value of those incidental services does not exceed the value of the product itself.

Commercially available off-the-shelf (COTS) item—

(i) Means any item of supply (including construction material) that is—

(A) A commercial item (as defined in paragraph (1) of the definition of *commercial item* in section 2.101 of the Federal Acquisition Regulation);

(B) Sold in substantial quantities in the commercial marketplace; and

(C) Offered to the Government, under a contract or subcontract at any tier, without modification, in the same form in which it is sold in the commercial marketplace; and

(ii) Does not include bulk cargo, as defined in 46 U.S.C. 40102(4), such as agricultural products and petroleum products.

Component means an article, material, or supply incorporated directly into an end product.

Domestic end product means—

(i) An unmanufactured end product that has been mined or produced in the United States; or

(ii) An end product manufactured in the United States if—

(A) The cost of its qualifying country components and its components that are mined, produced, or manufactured in the United States exceeds 50 percent of the cost of all its components. The cost of components includes transportation costs to the place of incorporation into the end product and U.S. duty (whether or not a duty-free entry certificate is issued). Scrap generated, collected, and prepared for processing in the United States is considered domestic. A component is considered to have been mined, produced, or manufactured in the United States (regardless of its source in fact) if the end product in which it is incorporated is manufactured in the United States and the component is of a class or kind for which the Government has determined that—

(1) Sufficient and reasonably available commercial quantities of a satisfactory quality are not mined, produced, or manufactured in the United States; or

(2) It is inconsistent with the public interest to apply the restrictions of the Buy American statute; or

(B) The end product is a COTS item.

End product means those articles, materials, and supplies to be acquired under this contract for public use.

Foreign end product means an end product other than a domestic end product.

Free Trade Agreement country means Australia, Bahrain, Canada, Chile, Colombia, Costa Rica, Dominican Republic, El Salvador, Guatemala, Honduras, Korea (Republic of), Mexico, Morocco, Nicaragua, Panama, Peru, or Singapore;

Free Trade Agreement country end product means an article that—

(i) Is wholly the growth, product, or manufacture of a Free Trade Agreement country; or

(ii) In the case of an article that consists in whole or in part of materials from another country, has been substantially transformed in a Free Trade Agreement country into a new and different article of commerce with a name, character, or use distinct from that of the article or articles from which it was transformed. The term refers to a product offered for purchase under a supply contract, but for purposes of calculating the value of the end product includes services (except transportation services) incidental to its supply, provided that the value of those incidental services does not exceed the value of the product itself.

Moroccan end product means an article that—

(i) Is wholly the growth, product, or manufacture of Morocco; or

(ii) In the case of an article that consists in whole or in part of materials from another country, has been substantially transformed in Morocco into a new and different article of commerce with a name, character, or use distinct from that of the article or articles from which it was transformed. The term refers to a product offered for purchase under a supply contract, but for purposes of calculating the value of the end product includes services (except transportation services) incidental to its supply, provided that the value of those incidental services does not exceed the value of the product itself.

Panamanian end product means an article that—

(i) Is wholly the growth, product, or manufacture of Panama; or

(ii) In the case of an article that consists in whole or in part of materials from another country, has been substantially transformed in Panama into a new and different article of commerce with a name, character, or use distinct from that of the article or articles from which it was transformed. The term refers to a product offered for purchase under a supply contract, but for purposes of calculating the value of the end product includes services (except transportation services) incidental to its supply, provided that the value of those incidental services does not exceed the value of the product itself.

Peruvian end product means an article that—

(i) Is wholly the growth, product, or manufacture of Peru; or

(ii) In the case of an article that consists in whole or in part of materials from another country, has been substantially transformed in Peru into a new and different article of commerce with a name, character, or use distinct from that of the article or articles from which it was transformed. The term refers to a product offered for purchase under a supply contract, but for purposes of calculating the value of the end product includes services (except transportation services) incidental to its supply, provided that the value of those incidental services does not exceed the value of the product itself.

Qualifying country means a country with a reciprocal defense procurement memorandum of understanding or international agreement with the United States in which both countries agree to remove barriers to purchases of supplies produced in the other country or services performed by sources of the other country, and the memorandum or agreement complies, where applicable, with the requirements of section 36 of the Arms Export Control Act (22 U.S.C. 2776) and with 10 U.S.C. 2457. Accordingly, the following are qualifying countries:

Australia

Austria

Belgium

Canada

Czech Republic

Denmark

Egypt

Estonia

Finland

France

Germany

Greece

Israel

Italy

Japan

Latvia

Luxembourg

Netherlands

Norway

Poland

Portugal

Slovenia

Spain

Sweden

Switzerland

Turkey

United Kingdom of Great Britain and Northern Ireland.

Qualifying country component means a component mined, produced, or manufactured in a qualifying country.

Qualifying country end product means—

(i) An unmanufactured end product mined or produced in a qualifying country; or

(ii) An end product manufactured in a qualifying country if—

(A) The cost of the following types of components exceeds 50 percent of the cost of all its components:

(1) Components mined, produced, or manufactured in a qualifying country.

(2) Components mined, produced, or manufactured in the United States.

(3) Components of foreign origin of a class or kind for which the Government has determined that sufficient and reasonably available commercial quantities of a satisfactory quality are not mined, produced, or manufactured in the United States; or

(B) The end product is a COTS item. *South Caucasus/Central and South Asian (SC/CASA) state* means Armenia, Azerbaijan, Georgia, Kazakhstan, Kyrgyzstan, Pakistan, Tajikistan, Turkmenistan, or Uzbekistan.

South Caucasus/Central and South Asian (SC/CASA) state end product means an article that—

(i) Is wholly the growth, product, or manufacture of an SC/CASA state; or

(ii) In the case of an article that consists in whole or in part of materials from another country, has been substantially transformed in an SC/CASA state into a new and different article of commerce with a name, character, or use distinct from that of the article or articles from which it was transformed. The term refers to a product offered for purchase under a supply contract, but for purposes of calculating the value of the end product includes services (except transportation services) incidental to its supply, provided that the value of those incidental services does not exceed the value of the product itself.

United States means the 50 States, the District of Columbia, and outlying areas.

(b) Unless otherwise specified, this clause applies to all items in the Schedule.

(c) The Contractor shall deliver under this contract only domestic end products unless, in its offer, it specified delivery of qualifying country end products, SC/CASA state end products, Free Trade Agreement country end products other than Bahrainian end products, Moroccan end products, Panamanian end products, or Peruvian end products, or other foreign end products in the Buy American—Free Trade Agreements—Balance of Payments Program Certificate—Alternate II provision of the solicitation. If the Contractor certified in its offer that it will deliver a qualifying country end product, SC/CASA state end products, or a Free Trade Agreement country end product other than a Bahrainian end product, a Moroccan end product, a Panamanian end product, or a Peruvian end product, the Contractor shall deliver a qualifying country end product, an SC/CASA state end product, a Free Trade Agreement country end product other than a Bahrainian end product, a Moroccan end product, a Panamanian end product, or a Peruvian end product or, at the Contractor's option, a domestic end product.

(d) The contract price does not include duty for end products or components for which the Contractor will claim duty-free entry.

(End of clause)

Alternate III. As prescribed in 225.1101(10)(i) and (10)(i)(D), use the following clause, which adds *Canadian end product, South Caucasus/Central and South Asian (SC/CASA) state*, and *South Caucasus/Central and South Asian (SC/CASA) state end product* to paragraph (a) and uses a different paragraph (c) than the basic clause:

BUY AMERICAN—FREE TRADE AGREEMENTS—BALANCE OF PAYMENTS PROGRAM—ALTERNATE III (DEC 2017)

(a) *Definitions*. As used in this clause—*Bahrainian end product* means an article that—

(i) Is wholly the growth, product, or manufacture of Bahrain; or

(ii) In the case of an article that consists in whole or in part of materials from another country, has been substantially transformed in Bahrain into a new and different article of commerce with a name, character, or use distinct from that of the article or articles from which it was transformed. The term refers to a product offered for purchase under a supply contract, but for purposes of calculating the value of the end product includes services (except transportation services) incidental to its supply, provided that the value of those incidental services does not exceed the value of the product itself.

Canadian end product means an article that—

(i) Is wholly the growth, product, or manufacture of Canada; or

(ii) In the case of an article that consists in whole or in part of materials from another country, has been substantially transformed in Canada into a new and different article of commerce with a name, character, or use distinct from that of the article or articles from which it was transformed. The term refers to a product offered for purchase under a supply contract, but for purposes of calculating the value of the end product includes services (except transportation services) incidental to its supply, provided that the value of those incidental services does not exceed the value of the product itself.

Commercially available off-the-shelf (COTS) item—

(i) Means any item of supply (including construction material) that is—

(A) A commercial item (as defined in paragraph (1) of the definition of *commercial item* in section 2.101 of the Federal Acquisition Regulation);

(B) Sold in substantial quantities in the commercial marketplace; and

(C) Offered to the Government, under a contract or subcontract at any tier, without modification, in the same form in which it is sold in the commercial marketplace; and

(ii) Does not include bulk cargo, as defined in 46 U.S.C. 40102(4), such as agricultural products and petroleum products.

Component means an article, material, or supply incorporated directly into an end product.

Domestic end product means—

(i) An unmanufactured end product that has been mined or produced in the United States; or

(ii) An end product manufactured in the United States if—

(A) The cost of its qualifying country components and its components that are mined, produced, or manufactured in the United States exceeds 50 percent of the cost of all its components. The cost of components includes transportation costs to the place of incorporation into the end product and U.S. duty (whether or not a duty-free entry certificate is issued). Scrap generated, collected, and prepared for processing in the United States is considered domestic. A component is considered to have been mined, produced, or manufactured in the United States (regardless of its source in fact) if the end product in which it is incorporated is manufactured in the United States and the component is of a class or kind for which the Government has determined that—

(1) Sufficient and reasonably available commercial quantities of a satisfactory quality are not mined, produced, or manufactured in the United States; or

(2) It is inconsistent with the public interest to apply the restrictions of the Buy American statute; or

(B) The end product is a COTS item.

End product means those articles, materials, and supplies to be acquired under this contract for public use.

Foreign end product means an end product other than a domestic end product.

Free Trade Agreement country means Australia, Bahrain, Canada, Chile, Colombia, Costa Rica, Dominican Republic, El Salvador, Guatemala, Honduras, Korea (Republic of), Mexico, Morocco, Nicaragua, Panama, Peru, or Singapore;

Free Trade Agreement country end product means an article that—

(i) Is wholly the growth, product, or manufacture of a Free Trade Agreement country; or

(ii) In the case of an article that consists in whole or in part of materials from another country, has been substantially transformed in a Free Trade Agreement country into a new and different article of commerce with a name, character, or use distinct from that of the article or articles from which it was transformed. The term refers to a product offered for purchase under a supply contract, but for purposes of calculating the value of the end product includes services (except transportation services) incidental to its supply, provided that the value of those incidental services does not exceed the value of the product itself.

Moroccan end product means an article that—

(i) Is wholly the growth, product, or manufacture of Morocco; or

(ii) In the case of an article that consists in whole or in part of materials from another country, has been substantially transformed in Morocco into a new and different article of commerce with a name, character, or use distinct from that of the article or articles from which it was transformed. The term refers to a product offered for purchase under a supply contract, but for purposes of calculating the value of the end product includes services (except transportation services) incidental to its supply, provided that the value of those incidental services does not exceed the value of the product itself.

Panamanian end product means an article that—

(i) Is wholly the growth, product, or manufacture of Panama; or

(ii) In the case of an article that consists in whole or in part of materials from another country, has been substantially transformed in Panama into a new and different article of commerce with a name, character, or use distinct from that of the article or articles from which it was transformed. The term refers to a product offered for purchase under a supply contract, but for purposes of calculating the value of the end product includes services (except transportation services) incidental to its supply, provided that the value of those incidental services does not exceed the value of the product itself.

Peruvian end product means an article that—

(i) Is wholly the growth, product, or manufacture of Peru; or

(ii) In the case of an article that consists in whole or in part of materials from another country, has been substantially transformed in Peru into a new and different article of commerce with a name, character, or use distinct from that of the article or articles from which it was transformed. The term refers to a product offered for purchase under a supply contract, but for purposes of calculating the value of the end product includes services (except transportation services) incidental to its supply, provided that the value of those incidental services does not exceed the value of the product itself.

Qualifying country means a country with a reciprocal defense procurement memorandum of understanding or international agreement with the United States in which both countries agree to remove barriers to purchases of supplies produced in the other country or services performed by sources of the other country, and the memorandum or agreement complies, where applicable, with the requirements of section 36 of the Arms Export Control Act (22 U.S.C. 2776) and with 10 U.S.C. 2457. Accordingly, the following are qualifying countries:

Australia

Austria

Belgium

Canada

Czech Republic

Denmark

Egypt

Estonia

Finland

France

Germany

Greece

Israel

Italy

Japan

Latvia

Luxembourg

Netherlands

Norway

Poland

Portugal

Slovenia

Spain

Sweden

Switzerland

Turkey

United Kingdom of Great Britain and Northern Ireland.

Qualifying country component means a component mined, produced, or manufactured in a qualifying country.

Qualifying country end product means—

(i) An unmanufactured end product mined or produced in a qualifying country; or

(ii) An end product manufactured in a qualifying country if—

(A) The cost of the following types of components exceeds 50 percent of the cost of all its components:

(*1*) Components mined, produced, or manufactured in a qualifying country.

(*2*) Components mined, produced, or manufactured in the United States.

(*3*) Components of foreign origin of a class or kind for which the Government has determined that sufficient and reasonably available commercial quantities of a satisfactory quality are not mined, produced, or manufactured in the United States; or

(B) The end product is a COTS item.

South Caucasus/Central and South Asian (SC/CASA) state means Armenia, Azerbaijan, Georgia, Kazakhstan, Kyrgyzstan, Pakistan, Tajikistan, Turkmenistan, or Uzbekistan.

South Caucasus/Central and South Asian (SC/CASA) state end product means an article that—

(i) Is wholly the growth, product, or manufacture of an SC/CASA state; or

(ii) In the case of an article that consists in whole or in part of materials from another country, has been substantially transformed in an SC/CASA state into a new and different article of commerce with a name, character, or use distinct from that of the article or articles from which it was transformed. The term refers to a product offered for purchase under a supply contract, but for purposes of calculating the value of the end product includes services (except transportation services) incidental to its supply, provided that the value of those incidental services does not exceed the value of the product itself.

United States means the 50 States, the District of Columbia, and outlying areas.

(b) Unless otherwise specified, this clause applies to all items in the Schedule.

(c) The Contractor shall deliver under this contract only domestic end products unless, in its offer, it specified delivery of qualifying country end products, SC/CASA state end products, Canadian end products, or other foreign end products in the Buy American—Free Trade Agreements—Balance of Payments Program Certificate—Alternate III provision of the solicitation. If the Contractor certified in its offer that it will deliver a qualifying country end product, SC/CASA state end products, or a Canadian end product, the Contractor shall deliver a qualifying country end product, an SC/CASA state end product, a Canadian end product or, at the Contractor's option, a domestic end product.

(d) The contract price does not include duty for end products or components for which the Contractor will claim duty-free entry.

(End of clause)

Alternate IV. As prescribed in 225.1101(10)(i) and (10)(i)(E), use the following clause, which adds *Korean end product* to paragraph (a), and uses a different paragraph (c) than the basic clause:

BUY AMERICAN—FREE TRADE AGREEMENTS—BALANCE OF PAYMENTS PROGRAM—ALTERNATE IV (DEC 2017)

(a) *Definitions.* As used in this clause—

Bahrainian end product means an article that—

(i) Is wholly the growth, product, or manufacture of Bahrain; or

(ii) In the case of an article that consists in whole or in part of materials from another country, has been substantially transformed in Bahrain into a new and different article of commerce with a name, character, or use distinct from that of the article or articles from which it was transformed. The term refers to a product offered for purchase under a supply contract, but for purposes of calculating the value of the end product includes services (except transportation services) incidental to its supply, provided that the value of those incidental services does not exceed the value of the product itself.

Commercially available off-the-shelf (COTS) item—

(i) Means any item of supply (including construction material) that is—

(A) A commercial item (as defined in paragraph (1) of the definition of *commercial item* in section 2.101 of the Federal Acquisition Regulation);

(B) Sold in substantial quantities in the commercial marketplace; and

(C) Offered to the Government, under a contract or subcontract at any tier, without modification, in the same form in which it is sold in the commercial marketplace; and

(ii) Does not include bulk cargo, as defined in 46 U.S.C. 40102(4), such as agricultural products and petroleum products.

Component means an article, material, or supply incorporated directly into an end product.

Domestic end product means—

(i) An unmanufactured end product that has been mined or produced in the United States; or

(ii) An end product manufactured in the United States if—

(A) The cost of its qualifying country components and its components that are mined, produced, or manufactured in the United States exceeds 50 percent of the cost of all its components. The cost of components includes transportation costs to the place of incorporation into the end product and U.S. duty (whether or not a duty-free entry certificate is issued). Scrap generated, collected, and prepared for processing in the United States is considered domestic. A component is considered to have been mined, produced, or manufactured in the United States (regardless of its source in fact) if the end product in which it is incorporated is manufactured in the United States and the component is of a class or kind for which the Government has determined that—

(1) Sufficient and reasonably available commercial quantities of a satisfactory quality are not mined, produced, or manufactured in the United States; or

(2) It is inconsistent with the public interest to apply the restrictions of the Buy American statute; or

(B) The end product is a COTS item.

End product means those articles, materials, and supplies to be acquired under this contract for public use.

Foreign end product means an end product other than a domestic end product.

Free Trade Agreement country means Australia, Bahrain, Canada, Chile, Colombia, Costa Rica, Dominican Republic, El Salvador, Guatemala, Honduras, Korea (Republic of), Mexico, Morocco, Nicaragua, Panama, Peru, or Singapore;

Free Trade Agreement country end product means an article that—

(i) Is wholly the growth, product, or manufacture of a Free Trade Agreement country; or

(ii) In the case of an article that consists in whole or in part of materials from another country, has been substantially transformed in a Free Trade Agreement country into a new and different article of commerce with a name, character, or use distinct from that of the article or articles from which it was transformed. The term refers to a product offered for purchase under a supply contract, but for purposes of calculating the value of the end product includes services (except transportation services) incidental to its supply, provided that the value of those incidental services does not exceed the value of the product itself.

Korean end product means an article that—

(i) Is wholly the growth, product, or manufacture of Korea; or

(ii) In the case of an article that consists in whole or in part of materials from another country, has been substantially transformed in Korea (Republic of) into a new and different article of commerce with a name, character, or use distinct from that of the article or articles from which it was transformed. The term refers to a product offered for purchase under a supply contract, but for purposes of calculating the value of the end product, includes services (except transportation services) incidental to its supply, provided that the value of those incidental services does not exceed the value of the product itself.

Moroccan end product means an article that—

(i) Is wholly the growth, product, or manufacture of Morocco; or

(ii) In the case of an article that consists in whole or in part of materials from another country, has been substantially transformed in Morocco into a new and different article of commerce with a name, character, or use distinct from that of the article or articles from which it was transformed. The term refers to a product offered for purchase under a supply contract, but for purposes of calculating the value of the end product includes services (except transportation services) incidental to its supply, provided that the value of those incidental services does not exceed the value of the product itself.

Panamanian end product means an article that—

(i) Is wholly the growth, product, or manufacture of Panama; or

(ii) In the case of an article that consists in whole or in part of materials from another country, has been substantially transformed in Panama into a new and different article of commerce with a name, character, or use distinct from that of the article or articles from which it was transformed. The term refers to a product offered for purchase under a supply contract, but for purposes of calculating the value of the end product includes services (except transportation services) incidental to its supply, provided that the value of those incidental services does not exceed the value of the product itself.

Peruvian end product means an article that—

(i) Is wholly the growth, product, or manufacture of Peru; or

(ii) In the case of an article that consists in whole or in part of materials from another country, has been substantially transformed in Peru into a new and different article of commerce with a name, character, or use distinct from that of the article or articles from which it was transformed. The term refers to a product offered for purchase under a supply contract, but for purposes of calculating the value of the end product includes services (except transportation services) incidental to its supply, provided that the value of those incidental services does not exceed the value of the product itself.

Qualifying country means a country with a reciprocal defense procurement memorandum of understanding or international agreement with the United States in which both countries agree to remove barriers to purchases of supplies produced in the other country or services performed by sources of the other country, and the memorandum or agreement complies, where applicable, with the requirements of section 36 of the Arms Export Control Act (22 U.S.C. 2776) and with 10 U.S.C. 2457. Accordingly, the following are qualifying countries:

Australia

Austria

Belgium

Canada

Czech Republic

Denmark

Egypt

Estonia

Finland

France

Germany

Greece

Israel

Italy

Japan

Latvia

Luxembourg

Netherlands

Norway

Poland

Portugal

Slovenia

Spain

Sweden

Switzerland

Turkey

United Kingdom of Great Britain and Northern Ireland.

Qualifying country component means a component mined, produced, or manufactured in a qualifying country.

Qualifying country end product means—

(i) An unmanufactured end product mined or produced in a qualifying country; or

(ii) An end product manufactured in a qualifying country if—

(A) The cost of the following types of components exceeds 50 percent of the cost of all its components:

(1) Components mined, produced, or manufactured in a qualifying country.

(2) Components mined, produced, or manufactured in the United States.

(3) Components of foreign origin of a class or kind for which the Government has determined that sufficient and reasonably available commercial quantities of a satisfactory quality are not mined, produced, or manufactured in the United States; or

(B) The end product is a COTS item.

United States means the 50 States, the District of Columbia, and outlying areas.

(b) Unless otherwise specified, this clause applies to all items in the Schedule.

(c) The Contractor shall deliver under this contract only domestic end products unless, in its offer, it specified delivery of qualifying country end products, Free Trade Agreement country end products other than Bahrainian end products, Korean end products, Moroccan end products, Panamanian end products, or Peruvian end products, or other foreign end products in the Buy American—Free Trade Agreements—Balance of Payments Program Certificate—Alternate IV provision of the solicitation. If the Contractor certified in its offer that it will deliver a qualifying country end product or a Free Trade Agreement country end product other than a Bahrainian end product, a Korean end product, a Moroccan end product, a Panamanian end product, or a Peruvian end product, the Contractor shall deliver a qualifying country end product, a Free Trade Agreement country end product other than a Bahrainian end product, a Korean end product, a Moroccan end product, a Panamanian end product, or a Peruvian end product, or, at the Contractor's option, a domestic end product.

(d) The contract price does not include duty for end products or components for which the Contractor will claim duty-free entry.

(End of clause)

Alternate V. As prescribed in 225.1101(10)(i) and (10)(i)(F), use the following clause, which adds *Korean end product, South Caucasus/Central and South Asian (SC/CASA) state,* and *South Caucasus/Central and South Asian (SC/ CASA) state end product* to paragraph (a), and uses a different paragraph (c) than the basic clause:

BUY AMERICAN—FREE TRADE AGREEMENTS—BALANCE OF PAYMENTS PROGRAM—ALTERNATE V (DEC 2017)

(a) *Definitions.* As used in this clause—*Bahrainian end product* means an article that—

(i) Is wholly the growth, product, or manufacture of Bahrain; or

(ii) In the case of an article that consists in whole or in part of materials from another country, has been substantially transformed in Bahrain into a new and different article of commerce with a name, character, or use distinct from that of the article or articles from which it was transformed. The term refers to a product offered for purchase under a supply contract, but for purposes of calculating the value of the end product includes services (except transportation services) incidental to its supply, provided that the value of those incidental services does not exceed the value of the product itself.

Commercially available off-the-shelf (COTS) item—

(i) Means any item of supply (including construction material) that is—

(A) A commercial item (as defined in paragraph (1) of the definition of *commercial item* in section 2.101 of the Federal Acquisition Regulation);

(B) Sold in substantial quantities in the commercial marketplace; and

(C) Offered to the Government, under a contract or subcontract at any tier, without modification, in the same form in which it is sold in the commercial marketplace; and

(ii) Does not include bulk cargo, as defined in 46 U.S.C. 40102(4), such as agricultural products and petroleum products.

Component means an article, material, or supply incorporated directly into an end product.

Domestic end product means—

(i) An unmanufactured end product that has been mined or produced in the United States; or

(ii) An end product manufactured in the United States if—

(A) The cost of its qualifying country components and its components that are mined, produced, or manufactured in the United States exceeds 50 percent of the cost of all its components. The cost of components includes transportation costs to the place of incorporation into the end product and U.S. duty (whether or not a duty-free entry certificate is issued). Scrap generated, collected, and prepared for processing in the United States is considered domestic. A component is considered to have been mined, produced, or manufactured in the United States (regardless of its source in fact) if the end product in which it is incorporated is manufactured in the United States and the component is of a class or kind for which the Government has determined that—

(1) Sufficient and reasonably available commercial quantities of a satisfactory quality are not mined, produced, or manufactured in the United States; or

(2) It is inconsistent with the public interest to apply the restrictions of the Buy American statute; or

(B) The end product is a COTS item.

End product means those articles, materials, and supplies to be acquired under this contract for public use.

Foreign end product means an end product other than a domestic end product.

Free Trade Agreement country means Australia, Bahrain, Canada, Chile, Colombia, Costa Rica, Dominican Republic, El Salvador, Guatemala, Honduras, Korea (Republic of), Mexico, Morocco, Nicaragua, Panama, Peru, or Singapore;

Free Trade Agreement country end product means an article that—

(i) Is wholly the growth, product, or manufacture of a Free Trade Agreement country; or

(ii) In the case of an article that consists in whole or in part of materials from another country, has been substantially transformed in a Free Trade Agreement country into a new and different article of commerce with a name, character, or use distinct from that of the article or articles from which it was transformed. The term refers to a product offered for purchase under a supply contract, but for purposes of calculating the value of the end product includes services (except transportation services) incidental to its supply, provided that the value of those incidental services does not exceed the value of the product itself.

Korean end product means an article that—

(i) Is wholly the growth, product, or manufacture of Korea; or

(ii) In the case of an article that consists in whole or in part of materials from another country, has been substantially transformed in Korea (Republic of) into a new and different article of commerce with a name, character, or use distinct from that of the article or articles from which it was transformed. The term refers to a product offered for purchase under a supply contract, but for purposes of calculating the value of the end product, includes services (except transportation services) incidental to its supply, provided that the value of those incidental services does not exceed the value of the product itself.

Moroccan end product means an article that—

(i) Is wholly the growth, product, or manufacture of Morocco; or

(ii) In the case of an article that consists in whole or in part of materials from another country, has been substantially transformed in Morocco into a new and different article of commerce with a name, character, or use distinct from that of the article or articles from which it was transformed. The term refers to a product offered for purchase under a supply contract, but for purposes of calculating the value of the end product includes services (except transportation services) incidental to its supply, provided that the value of those incidental services does not exceed the value of the product itself.

Panamanian end product means an article that—

(i) Is wholly the growth, product, or manufacture of Panama; or

(ii) In the case of an article that consists in whole or in part of materials from another country, has been substantially transformed in Panama into a new and different article of commerce with a name, character, or use distinct from that of the article or articles from which it was transformed. The term refers to a product offered for purchase under a supply contract, but for purposes of calculating the value of the end product includes services (except transportation services) incidental to its supply, provided that the value of those incidental services does not exceed the value of the product itself.

Peruvian end product means an article that—

(i) Is wholly the growth, product, or manufacture of Peru; or

(ii) In the case of an article that consists in whole or in part of materials from another country, has been substantially transformed in Peru into a new and different article of commerce with a name, character, or use distinct from that of the article or articles from which it was transformed. The term refers to a product offered for purchase under a supply contract, but for purposes of calculating the value of the end product includes services (except transportation services) incidental to its supply, provided that the value of those incidental services does not exceed the value of the product itself.

Qualifying country means a country with a reciprocal defense procurement memorandum of understanding or international agreement with the United States in which both countries agree to remove barriers to purchases of supplies produced in the other country or services performed by sources of the other country, and the memorandum or agreement complies, where applicable, with the requirements of section 36 of the Arms Export Control Act (22 U.S.C. 2776) and with 10 U.S.C. 2457. Accordingly, the following are qualifying countries:

Australia

Austria

Belgium

Canada

Czech Republic

Denmark

Egypt

Estonia

Finland

France

Germany

Greece

Israel

Italy

Japan

Latvia

Luxembourg

Netherlands

Norway

Poland

Portugal

Slovenia

Spain

Sweden

Switzerland

Turkey

United Kingdom of Great Britain and Northern Ireland.

Qualifying country component means a component mined, produced, or manufactured in a qualifying country.

Qualifying country end product means—

(i) An unmanufactured end product mined or produced in a qualifying country; or

(ii) An end product manufactured in a qualifying country if—

(A) The cost of the following types of components exceeds 50 percent of the cost of all its components:

(1) Components mined, produced, or manufactured in a qualifying country.

(2) Components mined, produced, or manufactured in the United States.

(3) Components of foreign origin of a class or kind for which the Government has determined that sufficient and reasonably available commercial quantities of a satisfactory quality are not mined, produced, or manufactured in the United States; or

(B) The end product is a COTS item.

South Caucasus/Central and South Asian (SC/CASA) state means Armenia, Azerbaijan, Georgia, Kazakhstan, Kyrgyzstan, Pakistan, Tajikistan, Turkmenistan, or Uzbekistan.

South Caucasus/Central and South Asian (SC/CASA) state end product means an article that—

(i) Is wholly the growth, product, or manufacture of an SC/CASA state; or

(ii) In the case of an article that consists in whole or in part of materials from another country, has been substantially transformed in an SC/CASA state into a new and different article of commerce with a name, character, or use distinct from that of the article or articles from which it was transformed. The term refers to a product offered for purchase under a supply contract, but for purposes of calculating the value of the end product, includes services (except transportation services) incidental to its supply, provided that the value of those incidental services does not exceed the value of the product itself.

United States means the 50 States, the District of Columbia, and outlying areas.

(b) Unless otherwise specified, this clause applies to all items in the Schedule.

(c) The Contractor shall deliver under this contract only domestic end products unless, in its offer, it specified delivery of qualifying country end products, SC/CASA state end products, Free Trade Agreement country end products other than Bahrainian end products, Korean end products, Moroccan end products, Panamanian end products, or Peruvian end products, or other foreign end products in the Buy American—Free Trade Agreements—Balance of Payments Program Certificate—Alternate V provision of the solicitation. If the Contractor certified in its offer that it will deliver a qualifying country end product, SC/CASA state end products, or a Free Trade Agreement country end product other than a Bahrainian end product, a Korean end product, a Moroccan end product, a Panamanian end product, or a Peruvian end product, the Contractor shall deliver a qualifying country end product, an SC/CASA state end product, a Free Trade Agreement country end product other than a Bahrainian end product, a Korean end product, a Moroccan end product, a Panamanian end product, or a Peruvian end product or, at the Contractor's option, a domestic end product.

(d) The contract price does not include duty for end products or components for which the Contractor will claim duty-free entry.

(End of clause)

[DAC 91-13, 63 FR 11522, 3/9/98, effective 3/9/98; Final rule, 64 FR 51074, 9/21/99, effective 9/21/99; Final rule, 65 FR 19849, 4/13/2000, effective 4/13/2000; Final rule, 67 FR 77937, 12/20/2002, effective 12/20/2002; Final rule, 68 FR 15615, 3/31/2003, effective 4/30/2003; Interim rule, 69 FR 1926, 1/13/2004, effective 1/13/2004; Final rule, 69 FR 74991, 12/15/2004, effective 12/15/2004; Interim rule, 70 FR 2361, 1/13/2005, effective 1/13/2005; Final rule, 70 FR 35543, 6/21/2005, effective 6/21/2005; Final rule, 70 FR 73152, 12/9/2005, effective 12/9/2005; Interim rule, 71 FR 34834, 6/16/2006, effective 6/16/2006; Interim rule, 71 FR 58541, 10/4/2006, effective 10/4/2006; Final rule, 72 FR 6486, 2/12/2007, effective 2/12/2007; Interim rule, 72 FR 14242, 3/27/2007, effective 3/27/2007; Final rule, 72 FR 14241, 3/27/2007, effective 3/27/2007; Final rule, 73 FR 1830, 1/10/2008, effective 1/10/2008; Interim rule, 73 FR 53151, 9/15/2008, effective 9/15/2008; Interim rule, 74 FR 2422, 1/15/2009, effective 1/15/2009; Final rule, 74 FR 37642, 7/29/2009, effective 7/29/2009; Interim rule, 74 FR 37650, 7/29/2009, effective 7/29/2009; Final rule, 74 FR 68384, 12/24/2009, effective 12/24/2009; Final rule, 75 FR 3179, 1/20/2010, effective 1/20/2010; Final rule, 75 FR 18035, 4/8/2010, effective 4/8/2010; Final rule, 75 FR 81915, 12/29/2010, effective 12/29/2010; Final rule, 76 FR 61282, 10/4/2011, effective 10/4/201; Interim rule, 77 FR 30356, 5/22/2012, effective 5/22/2012; Final rule, 77 FR 31536, 5/29/2012, effective 5/29/2012; Final rule, 77 FR 35879, 6/15/2012, effective 6/15/2012; Final rule, 77 FR 38736, 6/29/2012, effective 6/29/2012; Final rule, 77 FR 43470, 7/24/2012, effective 7/24/2012; Interim rule, 77 FR 68699, 11/16/2012, effective 11/16/2012; Final rule,

77 FR 76941, 12/31/2012, effective 12/31/2012; Final rule, 78 FR 18876, 3/28/2013, effective 3/28/2013; Final rule, 78 FR 18877, 3/28/2013, effective 3/28/2013; Interim rule, 78 FR 59854, 9/30/2013, effective 9/30/2013; Final rule, 78 FR 65221, 10/31/2013, effective 10/31/2013; Final rule, 79 FR 11342, 2/28/2014, effective 2/28/2014; Final rule, 79 FR 65815, 11/5/2014, effective 11/5/2014; Final rule, 80 FR 36897, 6/26/2015, effective 6/26/2015; Final rule, 81 FR 50650, 8/2/2016, effective 8/2/2016; Final rule, 81 FR 93840, 12/22/2016, effective 12/22/2016; Final rule, 82 FR 61483, 12/28/2017, effective 12/28/2017; Final rule, 83 FR 65560, 12/21/2018, effective 12/21/2018]

252.225-7037 Evaluation of Offers for Air Circuit Breakers.

As prescribed in 225.7006-4(a), use the following provision:

EVALUATION OF OFFERS FOR AIR CIRCUIT BREAKERS (DEC 2018)

(a) The offeror shall specify, in its offer, any intent to furnish air circuit breakers that are not manufactured in the United States or its outlying areas, Australia, Canada, or the United Kingdom.

(b) The Contracting Officer will evaluate offers by adding a factor of 50 percent to the offered price of air circuit breakers that are not manufactured in the United States or its outlying areas, Australia, Canada, or the United Kingdom.

(End of provision)

[DAC 91-13, 63 FR 11522, 3/9/98, effective 3/9/98; Final rule, 65 FR 19849, 4/13/2000, effective 4/13/2000; Final rule, 65 FR 52951, 8/31/2000, effective 8/31/2000; Final rule, 67 FR 77937, 12/20/2002, effective 12/20/2002; Final rule, 68 FR 15615, 3/31/2003, effective 4/30/2003; Final rule, 70 FR 35543, 6/21/2005, effective 6/21/2005; Final rule, 83 FR 65560, 12/21/2018, effective 12/21/2018]

252.225-7038 Restriction on Acquisition of Air Circuit Breakers.

As prescribed in 225.7006-4(b), use the following clause:

RESTRICTION ON ACQUISITION OF AIR CIRCUIT BREAKERS (DEC 2018)

Unless otherwise specified in its offer, the Contractor shall deliver under this contract air circuit breakers manufactured in the United States or its outlying areas, Australia, Canada, or the United Kingdom.

(End of clause)

[Interim rule, 59 FR 11729, 3/14/94, effective 3/7/94; Corrected, 59 FR 38931, 8/1/94; Final rule, 68 FR 15615, 3/31/2003, effective 4/30/2003; Final rule, 70 FR 35543, 6/21/2005, effective 6/21/2005; Final rule, 83 FR 65560, 12/21/2018, effective 12/21/2018]

252.225-7039 Defense Contractors Performing Private Security Functions Outside the United States.

As prescribed in 225.302-6, insert the following clause:

DEFENSE CONTRACTORS PERFORMING PRIVATE SECURITY FUNCTIONS OUTSIDE THE UNITED STATES (JUN 2016)

(a) *Definitions.* As used in this clause—

Full cooperation—(1) Means disclosure to the Government of the information sufficient to identify the nature and extent of the incident and the individuals responsible for the conduct. It includes providing timely and complete response to Government auditors' and investigators' requests for documents and access to employees with information;

(2) Does not foreclose any contractor rights arising in law, the FAR or the terms of the contract. It does not require—

(i) The contractor to waive its attorney-client privilege or the protections afforded by the attorney work product doctrine; or

(ii) Any officer, director, owner, or employee of the contractor, including a sole proprietor, to waive his or her attorney-client privilege or Fifth Amendment rights; and

(3) Does not restrict the contractor from—

(i) Conducting an internal investigation; or

(ii) Defending a proceeding or dispute arising under the contract or related to a potential or disclosed violation.

Private security functions means the following activities engaged in by a contractor:

(1) Guarding of personnel, facilities, designated sites or property of a Federal agency, the contractor or subcontractor, or a third party.

(2) Any other activity for which personnel are required to carry weapons in the performance of their duties in accordance with the terms of this contract.

(b) *Applicability.* If this contract is performed both in a designated area and in an area that is not designated, the clause only applies to performance in the designated area. Designated areas are areas outside the United States of—

(1) Contingency operations;

(2) Combat operations, as designated by the Secretary of Defense;

(3) Other significant military operations (as defined in 32 CFR part 159), designated by the Secretary of Defense upon agreement of the Secretary of State;

(4) Peace operations, consistent with Joint Publication 3- 07.3; or

(5) Other military operations or military exercises, when designated by the Combatant Commander.

(c) *Requirements.* The Contractor shall—

(1) Ensure that all Contractor personnel who are responsible for performing private security functions under this contract comply with 32 CFR part 159 and any orders, directives, or instructions to contractors performing private security functions that are identified in the contract for—

(i) Registering, processing, accounting for, managing, overseeing and keeping appropriate records of personnel performing private security functions;

(ii) Authorizing, accounting for and registering in Synchronized Predeployment and Operational Tracker (SPOT), weapons to be carried by or available to be used by personnel performing private security functions;

(iii) Identifying and registering in SPOT armored vehicles, helicopters and other military vehicles operated by Contractors performing private security functions; and

(iv) In accordance with orders and instructions established by the applicable Combatant Commander, reporting incidents in which—

(A) A weapon is discharged by personnel performing private security functions;

(B) Personnel performing private security functions are attacked, killed, or injured;

(C) Persons are killed or injured or property is destroyed as a result of conduct by Contractor personnel;

(D) A weapon is discharged against personnel performing private security functions or personnel performing such functions believe a weapon was so discharged; or

(E) Active, non-lethal countermeasures (other than the discharge of a weapon) are employed by personnel performing private security functions in response to a perceived immediate threat;

(2) Ensure that Contractor personnel who are responsible for performing private security functions under this contract are briefed on and understand their obligation to comply with—

(i) Qualification, training, screening (including, if applicable, thorough background checks) and security requirements established by 32 CFR part 159;

(ii) Applicable laws and regulations of the United States and the host country and applicable treaties and international agreements regarding performance of private security functions;

(iii) Orders, directives, and instructions issued by the applicable Combatant Commander or relevant Chief of Mission relating to weapons, equipment, force protection, security, health, safety, or relations and interaction with locals; and

(iv) Rules on the use of force issued by the applicable Combatant Commander or relevant Chief of Mission for personnel performing private security functions;

(3) Provide full cooperation with any Government-authorized investigation of incidents reported pursuant to paragraph (c)(1)(iv) of this clause and incidents of alleged misconduct by personnel performing private security functions under this contract by providing—

(i) Access to employees performing private security functions; and

(ii) Relevant information in the possession of the Contractor regarding the incident concerned; and

(4) Comply with ANSI/ASIS PSC.1-2012, American National Standard, Management System for Quality of Private Security Company Operations—Requirements with Guidance or the International Standard ISO 18788, Management System for Private Security Operations—Requirements with Guidance (located at *http://www.acq.osd.mil/log/PS/psc.html*).

(d) *Remedies.* In addition to other remedies available to the Government—

(1) The Contracting Officer may direct the Contractor, at its own expense, to remove and replace any Contractor or subcontractor personnel performing private security functions who fail to comply with or violate applicable requirements of this clause or 32 CFR part 159. Such action may be taken at the Government's discretion without prejudice to its rights under any other provision of this contract;

(2) The Contractor's failure to comply with the requirements of this clause will be included in appropriate databases of past performance and considered in any responsibility determination or evaluation of past performance; and

(3) If this is an award-fee contract, the Contractor's failure to comply with the requirements of this clause shall be considered in the evaluation of the Contractor's performance during the relevant evaluation period, and the Contracting Officer may treat such failure to comply as a basis for reducing or denying award fees for such period or for recovering all or part of award fees previously paid for such period.

(e) *Rule of construction.* The duty of the Contractor to comply with the requirements of this clause shall not be reduced or diminished by the failure of a higher- or lower-tier Contractor or subcontractor to comply with the clause requirements or by a failure of the contracting activity to provide required oversight.

(f) *Subcontracts.* The Contractor shall include the substance of this clause, including this paragraph (b), in subcontracts, including subcontracts for commercial items, when private security functions will be performed outside the United States in areas of—

(1) Contingency operations;

(2) Combat operations, as designated by the Secretary of Defense;

(3) Other significant military operations (as defined in 32 CFR part 159), designated by the Secretary of Defense upon agreement of the Secretary of State;

(4) Peace operations, consistent with Joint Publication 3- 07.3; or

(5) Other military operations or military exercises, when designated by the Combatant Commander.

(End of clause)

[Interim rule, 59 FR 19145, 4/22/94, effective 4/13/94; Interim rule, 61 FR 13106, 3/26/96, effective 4/1/96, finalized without change, DAC 91-11, 61 FR 50446, 9/26/96; Final rule, 70 FR 52030, 9/1/2005, effective 9/1/2005; Interim rule, 76 FR 52133, 8/19/2011, effective 8/19/2011; Final rule, 77 FR 35883, 6/15/2012, effective 6/15/2012; Final rule, 78 FR 37980, 6/25/2013, effective 6/25/2013; Final rule, 78 FR 69282, 11/18/2013, effective 11/18/2013; Final rule, 80 FR 4997, 1/29/2015, effective 1/29/2015; Final rule, 81 FR 42559, 6/30/2016, effective 6/30/2016]

252.225-7040 Contractor Personnel Supporting U.S. Armed Forces Deployed Outside the United States.

As prescribed in 225.371-5(a), use the following clause:

CONTRACTOR PERSONNEL SUPPORTING U.S. ARMED FORCES DEPLOYED OUTSIDE THE UNITED STATES (OCT 2015)

(a) *Definitions.* As used in this clause—

Combatant Commander means the commander of a unified or specified combatant command established in accordance with 10 U.S.C. 161.

Contractors authorized to accompany the Force, or *CAAF,* means contractor personnel, including all tiers of subcontractor personnel, who are authorized to accompany U.S. Armed Forces in applicable operations and have been afforded CAAF status through a letter of authorization. CAAF generally include all U.S. citizen and third-country national employees not normally residing within the operational area whose area of performance is in the direct vicinity of U.S. Armed Forces and who routinely are collocated with the U.S. Armed Forces (especially in non-permissive environments). Personnel collocated with U.S. Armed Forces shall be afforded CAAF status through a letter of authorization. In some cases, Combatant Commander subordinate commanders may designate mission-essential host nation or local national contractor employees (e.g., interpreters) as CAAF. CAAF includes contractors previously identified as contractors deploying with the U.S. Armed Forces. CAAF status does not apply to contractor personnel in support of applicable operations within the boundaries and territories of the United States.

Designated operational area means a geographic area designated by the combatant commander or subordinate joint force commander for the conduct or support of specified military operations.

Designated reception site means the designated place for the reception, staging, integration, and onward movement of contractors deploying during a contingency. The designated reception site includes assigned joint reception centers and other Service or private reception sites.

Law of war means that part of international law that regulates the conduct of armed hostilities. The law of war encompasses all international law for the conduct of hostilities binding on the United States or its individual citizens, including treaties and international agreements to which the United States is a party, and applicable customary international law.

Non-CAAF means personnel who are not designated as CAAF, such as local national (LN) employees and non-LN employees who are permanent residents in the operational area or third-country nationals not routinely residing with U.S. Armed Forces (and third-country national expatriates who are permanent residents in the operational area) who perform support functions away from the close proximity of, and do not reside with, U.S. Armed Forces. Government-furnished support to non-CAAF is typically limited to force protection, emergency medical care, and basic human needs (e.g., bottled water, latrine facilities, security, and food when necessary) when performing their jobs in the direct vicinity of U.S. Armed Forces. Non-CAAF status does not apply to contractor personnel in support of applicable operations within the boundaries and territories of the United States.

Subordinate joint force commander means a sub-unified commander or joint task force commander.

(b) *General.*

(1) This clause applies to both CAAF and non-CAAF when performing in a designated operational area outside the United States to support U.S. Armed Forces deployed outside the United States in—

(i) Contingency operations;

(ii) Peace operations, consistent with Joint Publication 3-07.3; or

(iii) Other military operations or military exercises, when designated by the Combatant Commander or as directed by the Secretary of Defense.

(2) Contract performance in support of U.S. Armed Forces deployed outside the

United States may require work in dangerous or austere conditions. Except as otherwise provided in the contract, the Contractor accepts the risks associated with required contract performance in such operations.

(3) When authorized in accordance with paragraph (j) of this clause to carry arms for personal protection, Contractor personnel are only authorized to use force for individual self-defense.

(4) Unless immune from host nation jurisdiction by virtue of an international agreement or international law, inappropriate use of force by contractor personnel supporting the U.S. Armed Forces can subject such personnel to United States or host nation prosecution and civil liability (see paragraphs (d) and (j)(3) of this clause).

(5) Service performed by Contractor personnel subject to this clause is not active duty or service under 38 U.S.C. 106 note.

(c) *Support*. (1)(i) The Combatant Commander will develop a security plan for protection of Contractor personnel in locations where there is not sufficient or legitimate civil authority, when the Combatant Commander decides it is in the interests of the Government to provide security because—

(A) The Contractor cannot obtain effective security services;

(B) Effective security services are unavailable at a reasonable cost; or

(C) Threat conditions necessitate security through military means.

(ii) In appropriate cases, the Combatant Commander may provide security through military means, commensurate with the level of security provided DoD civilians.

(2)(i) Generally, CAAF will be afforded emergency medical and dental care if injured while supporting applicable operations. Additionally, non-CAAF employees who are injured while in the vicinity of U. S. Armed Forces will normally receive emergency medical and dental care. Emergency medical and dental care includes medical care situations in which life, limb, or eyesight is jeopardized. Examples of emergency medical and dental care include examination and initial treatment of victims of sexual assault; refills of prescriptions for life-dependent drugs; repair of broken bones, lacerations, infections; and traumatic injuries to the dentition. Hospitalization will be limited to stabilization and short-term medical treatment with an emphasis on return to duty or placement in the patient movement system.

(ii) When the Government provides medical treatment or transportation of Contractor personnel to a selected civilian facility, the Contractor shall ensure that the Government is reimbursed for any costs associated with such treatment or transportation.

(iii) Medical or dental care beyond this standard is not authorized.

(3) Contractor personnel must have a Synchronized Predeployment and Operational Tracker (SPOT)-generated letter of authorization signed by the Contracting Officer in order to process through a deployment center or to travel to, from, or within the designated operational area. The letter of authorization also will identify any additional authorizations, privileges, or Government support that Contractor personnel are entitled to under this contract. Contractor personnel who are issued a letter of authorization shall carry it with them at all times while deployed.

(4) Unless specified elsewhere in this contract, the Contractor is responsible for all other support required for its personnel engaged in the designated operational area under this contract.

(d) *Compliance with laws and regulations*. (1) The Contractor shall comply with, and shall ensure that its personnel supporting U.S. Armed Forces deployed outside the United States as specified in paragraph (b)(1) of this clause are familiar with and comply with, all applicable—

(i) United States, host country, and third country national laws;

(ii) Provisions of the law of war, as well as any other applicable treaties and international agreements;

(iii) United States regulations, directives, instructions, policies, and procedures; and

(iv) Orders, directives, and instructions issued by the Combatant Commander, including those relating to force protection, security, health, safety, or relations and interaction with local nationals.

(2) The Contractor shall institute and implement an effective program to prevent violations of the law of war by its employees and subcontractors, including law of war training in accordance with paragraph (e) (1) (vii) of this clause.

(3) The Contractor shall ensure that CAAF and non-CAAF are aware—

(i) Of the DoD definition of "sexual assault" in DoD Directive 6495.01, Sexual Assault Prevention and Response Program;

(ii) That many of the offenses addressed by the definition are covered under the Uniform Code of Military Justice (see paragraph (e) (2) (iv) of this clause). Other sexual misconduct may constitute offenses under the Uniform Code of Military Justice, Federal law, such as the Military Extraterritorial Jurisdiction Act, or host nation laws;

(iii) That the offenses not covered by the Uniform Code of Military Justice may nevertheless have consequences to the contractor employees (see paragraph (h) (1) of this clause).

(4) The Contractor shall report to the appropriate investigative authorities, identified in paragraph (d) (6) of this clause, any alleged offenses under—

(i) The Uniform Code of Military Justice (chapter 47 of title 10, United States Code) (applicable to contractors serving with or accompanying an armed force in the field during a declared war or contingency operations); or

(ii) The Military Extraterritorial Jurisdiction Act (chapter 212 of title 18, United States Code).

(5) The Contractor shall provide to all contractor personnel who will perform work on a contract in the deployed area, before beginning such work, information on the following:

(i) How and where to report an alleged crime described in paragraph (d) (4) of this clause.

(ii) Where to seek victim and witness protection and assistance available to contractor personnel in connection with an alleged offense described in paragraph (4) of this clause.

(iii) That this section does not create any rights or privileges that are not authorized by law or DoD policy.

(6) The appropriate investigative authorities to which suspected crimes shall be reported include the following—

(i) US Army Criminal Investigation Command at *http://www.cid.army.mil/reportacrime.html*;

(ii) Air Force Office of Special Investigations at *http://www.osi.andrews.af.mil/library/factsheets/factsheet.asp?id=14522*;

(iii) Navy Criminal Investigative Service at *http://www.ncis.navy.mil/Pages/publicdefault.aspx*;

(iv) Defense Criminal Investigative Service at *http://www.dodig.mil/HOTLINE/index.html*;

(v) To any command of any supported military element or the command of any base.

(7) Personnel seeking whistleblower protection from reprisals for reporting criminal acts shall seek guidance through the DoD Inspector General hotline at 800-424-9098 or *www.dodig.mil/HOTLINE/index.html*. Personnel seeking other forms of victim or witness protections should contact the nearest military law enforcement office.

(8) (i) The Contractor shall ensure that Contractor employees supporting the U.S. Armed Forces are aware of their rights to—

(A) Hold their own identity or immigration documents, such as passport or driver's license, regardless of the documents' issuing authority;

(B) Receive agreed upon wages on time;

(C) Take lunch and work-breaks;

(D) Elect to terminate employment at any time;

(E) Identify grievances without fear of reprisal;

(F) Have a copy of their employment contract in a language they understand;

(G) Receive wages that are not below the legal host-country minimum wage;

(H) Be notified of their rights, wages, and prohibited activities prior to signing their employment contract; and

(I) If housing is provided, live in housing that meets host-country housing and safety standards.

(ii) The Contractor shall post these rights in employee work spaces in English and in any foreign language(s) spoken by a significant portion of the workforce.

(iii) The Contractor shall enforce the rights of Contractor personnel supporting the U.S. Armed Forces.

(e) *Preliminary personnel requirements.* (1) The Contractor shall ensure that the following requirements are met prior to deploying CAAF (specific requirements for each category will be specified in the statement of work or elsewhere in the contract):

(i) All required security and background checks are complete and acceptable.

(ii) All CAAF deploying in support of an applicable operation—

(A) Are medically, dentally, and psychologically fit for deployment and performance of their contracted duties;

(B) Meet the minimum medical screening requirements, including theater-specific medical qualifications as established by the geographic Combatant Commander (as posted to the Geographic Combatant Commander's website or other venue); and

(C) Have received all required immunizations as specified in the contract.

(1) During predeployment processing, the Government will provide, at no cost to the Contractor, any military-specific immunizations and/or medications not available to the general public

(2) All other immunizations shall be obtained prior to arrival at the deployment center.

(3) All CAAF and selected non-CAAF, as specified in the statement of work, shall bring to the designated operational area a copy of the U.S. Centers for Disease Control and Prevention (CDC) Form 731, International Certificate of Vaccination or Prophylaxis as Approved by the World Health Organization, (also known as "shot record" or "Yellow Card") that shows vaccinations are current.

(iii) Deploying personnel have all necessary passports, visas, and other documents required to enter and exit a designated operational area and have a Geneva Conventions identification card, or other appropriate DoD identity credential, from the deployment center.

(iv) Special area, country, and theater clearance is obtained for all personnel deploying. Clearance requirements are in DoD Directive 4500.54E, DoD Foreign Clearance Program. For this purpose, CAAF are considered non-DoD contractor personnel traveling under DoD sponsorship.

(v) All deploying personnel have received personal security training. At a minimum, the training shall—

(A) Cover safety and security issues facing employees overseas;

(B) Identify safety and security contingency planning activities; and

(C) Identify ways to utilize safety and security personnel and other resources appropriately.

(vi) All personnel have received isolated personnel training, if specified in the contract, in accordance with DoD Instruction 1300.23, Isolated Personnel Training for DoD Civilian and Contractors.

(vii) Personnel have received law of war training as follows:

(A) Basic training is required for all CAAF. The basic training will be provided through—

(1) A military-run training center; or

(2) A web-based source, if specified in the contract or approved by the Contracting Officer.

(B) Advanced training, commensurate with their duties and responsibilities, may be required for some Contractor personnel as specified in the contract.

(2) The Contractor shall notify all personnel who are not a host country national, or who are not ordinarily resident in the host country, that—

(i) Such employees, and dependents residing with such employees, who engage in conduct outside the United States that would constitute an offense punishable by imprisonment for more than one year if the conduct had been engaged in within the special maritime and territorial jurisdiction of the United States, may potentially be subject to the criminal jurisdiction of the United States in accordance with the Military Extraterritorial Jurisdiction Act of 2000 (18 U.S.C. 3621, *et seq.*);

(ii) Pursuant to the War Crimes Act (18 U.S.C. 2441), Federal criminal jurisdiction also extends to conduct that is determined to constitute a war crime when committed by a civilian national of the United States;

(iii) Other laws may provide for prosecution of U.S. nationals who commit offenses on the premises of U.S. diplomatic, consular, military or other U.S. Government missions outside the United States (18 U.S.C. 7(9)); and

(iv) In time of declared war or a contingency operation, CAAF are subject to the jurisdiction of the Uniform Code of Military Justice under 10 U.S.C. 802(a)(10).

(v) Such employees are required to report offenses alleged to have been committed by or against Contractor personnel to appropriate investigative authorities.

(vi) Such employees will be provided victim and witness protection and assistance.

(f) *Processing and departure points.* CAAF shall—

(1) Process through the deployment center designated in the contract, or as otherwise directed by the Contracting Officer, prior to deploying. The deployment center will conduct deployment processing to ensure visibility and accountability of Contractor personnel and to ensure that all deployment requirements are met, including the requirements specified in paragraph (e)(1) of this clause;

(2) Use the point of departure and transportation mode directed by the Contracting Officer; and

(3) Process through a designated reception site (DRS) upon arrival at the deployed location. The DRS will validate personnel accountability, ensure that specific designated operational area entrance requirements are met, and brief Contractor personnel on theater-specific policies and procedures.

(g) *Personnel data.* (1) The Contractor shall use the Synchronized Predeployment and Operational Tracker (SPOT) web-based system, to enter and maintain the data for all CAAF and, as designated by USD(AT&L) or the Combatant Commander, non-CAAF supporting U.S. Armed Forces deployed outside the United States as specified in paragraph (b)(1) of this clause.

(2) The Contractor shall enter the required information about their contractor personnel prior to deployment and shall continue to use the SPOT web-based system at *https://spot.dmdc.mil* to maintain accurate, up-to-date information throughout the deployment for all Contractor personnel. Changes to status of individual Contractor personnel relating to their in-theater arrival date and their duty location, to include closing out the deployment with their proper status (e.g., mission complete, killed, wounded) shall be annotated within the SPOT database in accordance with the timelines established in the SPOT Business Rules at ***http://www.acq.osd.mil/log/PS/ctr mgt_accountability.html.***.

(h) *Contractor personnel.* (1) The Contracting Officer may direct the Contractor, at its own expense, to remove and replace any Contractor personnel who jeopardize or interfere with mission accomplishment or who fail to comply with or violate applicable requirements of this contract. Such action may be taken at the Government's discretion without prejudice to its rights under any other provision of this contract, including the Termination for Default clause.

(2) The Contractor shall identify all personnel who occupy a position designated as mission essential and ensure the continuity of essential Contractor services during designated operations, unless, after consultation with the Contracting Officer, Contracting Officer's representative, or local commander, the Contracting Officer directs withdrawal due to security conditions.

(3) The Contractor shall ensure that Contractor personnel follow the guidance at paragraph (e)(2)(v) of this clause and any specific Combatant Commander guidance on reporting offenses alleged to have been committed by or against Contractor personnel to appropriate investigative authorities.

(4) Contractor personnel shall return all U.S. Government-issued identification, to include the Common Access Card, to appropriate U.S. Government authorities at the end of their deployment (or, for non-CAAF, at the end of their employment under this contract).

(i) *Military clothing and protective equipment*. (1) Contractor personnel are prohibited from wearing military clothing unless specifically authorized in writing by the Combatant Commander. If authorized to wear military clothing, Contractor personnel must—

(i) Wear distinctive patches, arm bands, nametags, or headgear, in order to be distinguishable from military personnel, consistent with force protection measures; and

(ii) Carry the written authorization with them at all times.

(2) Contractor personnel may wear military-unique organizational clothing and individual equipment (OCIE) required for safety and security, such as ballistic, nuclear, biological, or chemical protective equipment.

(3) The deployment center, or the Combatant Commander, shall issue OCIE and shall provide training, if necessary, to ensure the safety and security of Contractor personnel.

(4) The Contractor shall ensure that all issued OCIE is returned to the point of issue, unless otherwise directed by the Contracting Officer.

(j) *Weapons*. (1) If the Contractor requests that its personnel performing in the designated operational area be authorized to carry weapons for individual self-defense, the request shall be made through the Contracting Officer to the Combatant Commander, in accordance with DoD Instruction 3020.41, Operational Contractor Support. The Combatant Commander will determine whether to authorize in-theater Contractor personnel to carry weapons and what weapons and ammunition will be allowed.

(2) If Contractor personnel are authorized to carry weapons in accordance with paragraph (j)(1) of this clause, the Contracting Officer will notify the Contractor what weapons and ammunition are authorized.

(3) The Contractor shall ensure that its personnel who are authorized to carry weapons—

(i) Are adequately trained to carry and use them—

(A) Safely;

(B) With full understanding of, and adherence to, the rules of the use of force issued by the Combatant Commander; and

(C) In compliance with applicable agency policies, agreements, rules, regulations, and other applicable law;

(ii) Are not barred from possession of a firearm by 18 U.S.C. 922;

(iii) Adhere to all guidance and orders issued by the Combatant Commander regarding possession, use, safety, and accountability of weapons and ammunition;

(iv) Comply with applicable Combatant Commander and local commander force-protection policies; and

(v) Understand that the inappropriate use of force could subject them to U.S. or host-nation prosecution and civil liability.

(4) Whether or not weapons are Government-furnished, all liability for the use of any weapon by Contractor personnel rests solely with the Contractor and the Contractor employee using such weapon.

(5) Upon redeployment or revocation by the Combatant Commander of the Contrac-

tor's authorization to issue firearms, the Contractor shall ensure that all Government-issued weapons and unexpended ammunition are returned as directed by the Contracting Officer.

(k) *Vehicle or equipment licenses.* Contractor personnel shall possess the required licenses to operate all vehicles or equipment necessary to perform the contract in the designated operational area.

(l) *Purchase of scarce goods and services.* If the Combatant Commander has established an organization for the designated operational area whose function is to determine that certain items are scarce goods or services, the Contractor shall coordinate with that organization local purchases of goods and services designated as scarce, in accordance with instructions provided by the Contracting Officer.

(m) *Evacuation.* (1) If the Combatant Commander orders a mandatory evacuation of some or all personnel, the Government will provide assistance, to the extent available, to United States and third country national Contractor personnel.

(2) In the event of a non-mandatory evacuation order, unless authorized in writing by the Contracting Officer, the Contractor shall maintain personnel on location sufficient to meet obligations under this contract.

(n) *Next of kin notification and personnel recovery.* (1) The Contractor shall be responsible for notification of the employee-designated next of kin in the event an employee dies, requires evacuation due to an injury, or is isolated, missing, detained, captured, or abducted.

(2) In the case of isolated, missing, detained, captured, or abducted Contractor personnel, the Government will assist in personnel recovery actions in accordance with DoD Directive 3002.01E, Personnel Recovery in the Department of Defense

(o) *Mortuary affairs.* Contractor personnel who die while in support of the U.S. Armed Forces shall be covered by the DoD mortuary affairs program as described in DoD Directive 1300.22, Mortuary Affairs Policy, and DoD Instruction 3020.41, Operational Contractor Support.

(p) *Changes.* In addition to the changes otherwise authorized by the Changes clause of this contract, the Contracting Officer may, at any time, by written order identified as a change order, make changes in the place of performance or Government-furnished facilities, equipment, material, services, or site. Any change order issued in accordance with this paragraph (p) shall be subject to the provisions of the Changes clause of this contract.

(q) *Subcontracts.* The Contractor shall incorporate the substance of this clause, including this paragraph (q), in all subcontracts when subcontractor personnel are supporting U.S. Armed Forces deployed outside the United States in—

(1) Contingency operations;

(2) Peace operations consistent with Joint Publication 3-07.3; or

(3) Other military operations or military exercises, when designated by the Combatant Commander or as directed by the Secretary of Defense.

(End of clause)

[DAC 91-12, 62 FR 34114, 6/24/97, effective 6/24/97; Final rule, 68 FR 15615, 3/31/2003, effective 4/30/2003; Final rule, 70 FR 23790, 5/5/2005, effective 6/6/2005; Interim rule, 71 FR 34826, 6/16/2006, effective 6/16/2006; Final rule, 73 FR 16764, 3/31/2008, effective 3/31/2008; Final rule, 74 FR 2418, 1/15/2009, effective 1/15/2009; Final rule, 74 FR 34264, 7/15/2009, effective 7/15/2009; Final rule, 76 FR 36883, 6/23/2011, effective 6/23/2011; Final rule, 76 FR 38051, 6/29/2011, effective 6/29/2011; Final rule, 78 FR 13547, 2/28/2013, effective 2/28/2013; Final rule, 79 FR 30469, 5/28/2014, effective 5/28/2014; Final rule, 80 FR 4999, 1/29/2015, effective 1/29/2015; Final rule, 80 FR 36900, 6/26/2015, effective 6/26/2015; Final rule, 80 FR 51752, 8/26/2015, effective 8/26/2015; Final rule, 80 FR 67254, 10/30/2015, effective 10/30/2015; Final rule, 80 FR 67254, 10/30/2015, effective 10/30/2015]

252.225-7041 Correspondence in English.

As prescribed in 225.1103(2), use the following clause:

CORRESPONDENCE IN ENGLISH (JUN 1997)

The Contractor shall ensure that all contract correspondence that is addressed to the United States Government is submitted in English or with an English translation.

(End of clause)

[DAC 91-12, 62 FR 34114, 6/24/97, effective 6/24/97; Final rule, 65 FR 19849, 4/13/2000, effective 4/13/2000; Final rule, 68 FR 15615, 3/31/2003, effective 4/30/2003; Final rule, 71 FR 39005, 7/11/2006, effective 7/11/2006]

252.225-7042 Authorization to perform.

As prescribed in 225.1103(3), use the following provision:

AUTHORIZATION TO PERFORM (APR 2003)

The offeror represents that it has been duly authorized to operate and to do business in the country or countries in which the contract is to be performed.

(End of provision)

[DAC 91-12, 62 FR 34114, 6/24/97, effective 6/24/97; Final rule, 65 FR 19849, 4/13/2000, effective 4/13/2000; Final rule, 68 FR 15615, 3/31/2003, effective 4/30/2003; Final rule, 71 FR 39005, 7/11/2006, effective 7/11/2006]

252.225-7043 Antiterrorism/force protection policy for defense contractors outside the United States.

As prescribed in 225.372-2, use the following clause:

ANTITERRORISM/FORCE PROTECTION POLICY FOR DEFENSE CONTRACTORS OUTSIDE THE UNITED STATES (JUN 2015)

(a) *Definition. United States*, as used in this clause, means, the 50 States, the District of Columbia, and outlying areas.

(b) Except as provided in paragraph (c) of this clause, the Contractor and its subcontractors, if performing or traveling outside the United States under this contract, shall—

(1) Affiliate with the Overseas Security Advisory Council, if the Contractor or subcontractor is a U.S. entity;

(2) Ensure that Contractor and subcontractor personnel who are U.S. nationals and are in-country on a non-transitory basis, register with the U.S. Embassy, and that Contractor and subcontractor personnel who are third country nationals comply with any security related requirements of the Embassy of their nationality;

(3) Provide, to Contractor and subcontractor personnel, antiterrorism/force protection awareness information commensurate with that which the Department of Defense (DoD) provides to its military and civilian personnel and their families, to the extent such information can be made available prior to travel outside the United States; and

(4) Obtain and comply with the most current antiterrorism/force protection guidance for Contractor and subcontractor personnel.

(c) The requirements of this clause do not apply to any subcontractor that is—

(1) A foreign government;

(2) A representative of a foreign government; or

(3) A foreign corporation wholly owned by a foreign government.

(d) Information and guidance pertaining to DoD antiterrorism/force protection can be obtained from [*Contracting Officer to insert applicable information cited in PGI 225.372-1–1*].

(End of clause)

[Interim rule, 63 FR 31936, 6/11/98, effective 6/11/98, finalized without change, 64 FR 24529, 5/7/99; Final rule, 70 FR 23790, 5/5/2005, effective 6/6/2005; Final rule, 70 FR 35543, 6/21/2005, effective 6/21/2005; Final rule, 71 FR 14099, 3/21/2006, effective 3/21/2006; Final rule, 80 FR 36900, 6/26/2015, effective 6/26/2015]

252.225-7044 Balance of Payments Program—Construction Material.

Basic. As prescribed in 225.7503(a) and (a)(1), use the following clause:

BALANCE OF PAYMENTS PROGRAM—CONSTRUCTION MATERIAL—BASIC (NOV 2014)

(a) *Definitions.* As used in this clause–

Commercially available off-the-shelf (COTS) item—

(i) Means any item of supply (including construction material) that is—

(A) A commercial item (as defined in paragraph (1) of the definition of *commercial item* in section 2.101of the Federal Acquisition Regulation);

(B) Sold in substantial quantities in the commercial marketplace; and

(C) Offered to the Government, under a contract or subcontract at any tier, without modification, in the same form in which it is sold in the commercial marketplace; and

(ii) Does not include bulk cargo, as defined in 46 U.S.C. 40102(4), such as agricultural products and petroleum products.

Component means any article, material, or supply incorporated directly into construction material.

Construction material means an article, material, or supply brought to the construction site by the Contractor or a subcontractor for incorporation into the building or work. The term also includes an item brought to the site preassembled from articles, materials, or supplies. However, emergency life safety systems, such as emergency lighting, fire alarm, and audio evacuation systems, that are discrete systems incorporated into a public building or work and that are produced as complete systems, are evaluated as a single and distinct construction material regardless of when or how the individual parts or components of those systems are delivered to the construction site. Materials purchased directly by the Government are supplies, not construction material.

Cost of components means—

(i) For components purchased by the Contractor, the acquisition cost, including transportation costs to the place of incorporation into the end product (whether or not such costs are paid to a domestic firm), and any applicable duty (whether or not a duty-free entry certificate is issued); or

(ii) For components manufactured by the Contractor, all costs associated with the manufacture of the component, including transportation costs as described in paragraph (1) of this definition, plus allocable overhead costs, but excluding profit. Cost of components does not include any costs associated with the manufacture of the construction material.

Domestic construction material means—

(i) An unmanufactured construction material mined or produced in the United States; or

(ii) A construction material manufactured in the United States, if—

(A) The cost of its components mined, produced, or manufactured in the United States exceeds 50 percent of the cost of all its components. Components of foreign origin of the same class or kind for which nonavailability determinations have been made are treated as domestic; or

(B) The construction material is a COTS item.

United States means the 50 States, the District of Columbia, and outlying areas.

(b) Domestic preference. This clause implements the Balance of Payments Program by providing a preference for domestic construction material. The Contractor shall use only domestic construction material in performing this contract, except for—

(1) Construction material valued at or below the simplified acquisition threshold in part 2 of the Federal Acquisition Regulation;

(2) Information technology that is a commercial item; or

(3) The construction material or components listed by the Government as follows:

[*Contracting Officer to list applicable excepted materials or indicate none*]

Alternate I. As prescribed in 225.7503(a) and (a)(2), use the following clause, which adds definitions for *South Caucasus/Central and South Asian (SC/ CASA) state* and *SC/ CASA state construction material* to paragraph (a), and uses *domestic construction material or SC/CASA state construction material* instead of *domestic construction material* in the second sentence of paragraph (b):

BALANCE OF PAYMENTS PROGRAM—CONSTRUCTION MATERIAL—ALTERNATE I (NOV 2014)

(a) *Definitions*. As used in this clause—*Commercially available off-the-shelf (COTS) item*—

(i) Means any item of supply (including construction material) that is—

(A) A commercial item (as defined in paragraph (1) of the definition of *commercial item* in section 2.101 of the Federal Acquisition Regulation);

(B) Sold in substantial quantities in the commercial marketplace; and

(C) Offered to the Government, under a contract or subcontract at any tier, without modification, in the same form in which it is sold in the commercial marketplace; and

(ii) Does not include bulk cargo, as defined in 46 U.S.C. 40102(4), such as agricultural products and petroleum products.

Component means any article, material, or supply incorporated directly into construction material.

Construction material means an article, material, or supply brought to the construction site by the Contractor or a subcontractor for incorporation into the building or work. The term also includes an item brought to the site preassembled from articles, materials, or supplies. However, emergency life safety systems, such as emergency lighting, fire alarm, and audio evacuation systems, that are discrete systems incorporated into a public building or work and that are produced as complete systems, are evaluated as a single and distinct construction material regardless of when or how the individual parts or components of those systems are delivered to the construction site. Materials purchased directly by the Government are supplies, not construction material.

Cost of components means—

(i) For components purchased by the Contractor, the acquisition cost, including transportation costs to the place of incorporation into the end product (whether or not such costs are paid to a domestic firm), and any applicable duty (whether or not a duty-free entry certificate is issued); or

(ii) For components manufactured by the Contractor, all costs associated with the manufacture of the component, including transportation costs as described in paragraph (1) of this definition, plus allocable overhead costs, but excluding profit. Cost of components does not include any costs associated with the manufacture of the construction material.

Domestic construction material means—

(i) An unmanufactured construction material mined or produced in the United States; or

(ii) A construction material manufactured in the United States, if—

(A) The cost of its components mined, produced, or manufactured in the United States exceeds 50 percent of the cost of all its components. Components of foreign origin of the same class or kind for which nonavailability determinations have been made are treated as domestic; or

(B) The construction material is a COTS item.

South Caucasus/Central and South Asian (SC/CASA) state means Armenia, Azerbaijan, Georgia, Kazakhstan, Kyrgyzstan, Pakistan, Tajikistan, Turkmenistan, or Uzbekistan.

SC/CASA state construction material means construction material that—

(i) Is wholly the growth, product, or manufacture of an SC/CASA state; or

(ii) In the case of a construction material that consists in whole or in part of materials from another country, has been substantially transformed in an SC/CASA state into a new and different construction material distinct from the material from which it was transformed.

United States means the 50 States, the District of Columbia, and outlying areas.

(b) *Domestic preference*. This clause implements the Balance of Payments Program by providing a preference for domestic construction material. The Contractor shall use only domestic construction material or SC/CASA state construction material in performing this contract, except for—

(1) Construction material valued at or below the simplified acquisition threshold in part 2 of the Federal Acquisition Regulation;

(2) Information technology that is a commercial item; or

(3) The construction material or components listed by the Government as follows:

[*Contracting Officer to list applicable excepted materials or indicate "none"*].

(End of clause)

[Interim rule, 70 FR 2361, 1/13/2005, effective 1/13/2005; Final rule, 70 FR 35543, 6/21/2005, effective 6/21/2005; Final rule, 70 FR 73152, 12/9/2005, effective 12/9/2005; Interim rule, 74 FR 2422, 1/15/2009, effective 1/15/2009; Final rule, 74 FR 68384, 12/24/2009, effective 12/24/2009; Final rule, 75 FR 66686, 10/29/2010, effective 10/29/2010; Final rule, 75 FR 81915, 12/29/2010, effective 12/29/2010; Final rule,, 77 FR 35879, 6/15/2012, effective 6/15/2012; Final rule, 79 FR 65815, 11/5/2014, effective 11/5/2014; Final rule, 80 FR 36897, 6/26/2015, effective 6/26/2015]

252.225-7045 Balance of Payments Program—Construction Material Under Trade Agreements.

Basic. As prescribed in 225.7503(b) and (b)(1), use the following clause:

BALANCE OF PAYMENTS PROGRAM—CONSTRUCTION MATERIAL UNDER TRADE AGREEMENTS—BASIC (AUG 2019)

(a) *Definitions.* As used in this clause—

Caribbean Basin country construction material means a construction material that—

(i) Is wholly the growth, product, or manufacture of a Caribbean Basin country; or

(ii) In the case of a construction material that consists in whole or in part of materials from another country, has been substantially transformed in a Caribbean Basin country into a new and different construction material distinct from the materials from which it was transformed.

Commercially available off-the-shelf (COTS) item—

(i) Means any item of supply (including construction material) that is—

(A) A commercial item (as defined in paragraph (1) of the definition of "commercial item" in section 2.101of the Federal Acquisition Regulation);

(B) Sold in substantial quantities in the commercial marketplace; and

(C) Offered to the Government, under a contract or subcontract at any tier, without modification, in the same form in which it is sold in the commercial marketplace; and

(ii) Does not include bulk cargo, as defined in section 3 of the Shipping Act of 1984 (46 U.S.C. 40102), such as agricultural products and petroleum products.

Component means any article, material, or supply incorporated directly into construction material.

Construction material means an article, material, or supply brought to the construction site by the Contractor or a subcontractor for incorporation into the building or work. The term also includes an item brought to the site preassembled from articles, materials, or supplies. However, emergency life safety systems, such as emergency lighting, fire alarm, and audio evacuation systems, that are discrete systems incorporated into a public building or work and that are produced as complete systems, are evaluated as a single and distinct construction material regardless of when or how the individual parts or components of those systems are delivered to the construction site. Materials purchased directly by the Government are supplies, not construction material.

Cost of components means—

(1) For components purchased by the Contractor, the acquisition cost, including transportation costs to the place of incorporation into the end product (whether or not such costs are paid to a domestic firm), and any applicable duty (whether or not a duty-free entry certificate is issued); or

(2) For components manufactured by the Contractor, all costs associated with the manufacture of the component, including transportation costs as described in paragraph (1) of this definition, plus allocable overhead costs, but excluding profit. Cost of components does not include any costs associated with the manufacture of the construction material.

Designated country means—

(i) A World Trade Organization Government Procurement Agreement (WTO GPA) country (Armenia, Aruba, Australia, Austria, Belgium, Bulgaria, Canada, Croatia, Cyprus, Czech Republic, Denmark, Estonia, Finland, France, Germany, Greece, Hong Kong, Hungary, Iceland, Ireland, Israel, Italy, Japan, Korea (Republic of), Latvia, Liechtenstein, Lithuania, Luxembourg, Malta, Moldova, Montenegro, Netherlands, New Zealand, Norway, Poland, Portugal, Romania, Singapore, Slovak Republic, Slovenia, Spain, Sweden, Switzerland, Taiwan (known in the World Trade Organization as "the Separate Customs Territory of Taiwan, Penghu, Kinmen, Matsu" (Chinese Taipei)), Ukraine, or the United Kingdom);

(ii) A Free Trade Agreement country (Australia, Bahrain, Canada, Chile, Colombia, Costa Rica, Dominican Republic, El Salvador, Guatemala, Honduras, Korea (Republic of), Mexico, Morocco, Nicaragua, Panama, Peru, or Singapore);

(iii) A least developed country (Afghanistan, Angola, Bangladesh, Benin, Bhutan, Burkina Faso, Burundi, Cambodia, Central African Republic, Chad, Comoros, Democratic Republic of Congo, Djibouti, Equatorial Guinea, Eritrea, Ethiopia, Gambia, Guinea, Guinea-Bissau, Haiti, Kiribati, Laos, Lesotho, Liberia, Madagascar, Malawi, Mali, Mauritania, Mozambique, Nepal, Niger, Rwanda, Samoa, Sao Tome and Principe, Senegal, Sierra Leone, Solomon Islands, Somalia, South Sudan, Tanzania, Timor-Leste, Togo, Tuvalu, Uganda, Vanuatu, Yemen, or Zambia); or

(iv) A Caribbean Basin country (Antigua and Barbuda, Aruba, Bahamas, Barbados, Belize, Bonaire, British Virgin Islands, Curacao, Dominica, Grenada, Guyana, Haiti, Jamaica, Montserrat, Saba, St. Kitts and Nevis, St. Lucia, St. Vincent and the Grenadines, Sint Eustatius, Sint Maarten, or Trinidad and Tobago).

Designated country construction material means a construction material that is a WTO GPA country construction material, a Free Trade Agreement country construction material, a least developed country construction material, or a Caribbean Basin country construction material.

Domestic construction material means—

(i) An unmanufactured construction material mined or produced in the United States; or

(ii) A construction material manufactured in the United States, if—

(A) The cost of its components mined, produced, or manufactured in the United States exceeds 50 percent of the cost of all its components. Components of foreign origin of the same class or kind for which nonavailability determinations have been made are treated as domestic; or

(B) The construction material is a COTS item.

Free Trade Agreement country construction material means a construction material that—

(i) Is wholly the growth, product, or manufacture of a Free Trade Agreement country; or

(ii) In the case of a construction material that consists in whole or in part of materials from another country, has been substantially transformed in a Free Trade Agreement country into a new and different construction material distinct from the material from which it was transformed.

Least developed country construction material means a construction material that—

(i) Is wholly the growth, product, or manufacture of a least developed country; or

(ii) In the case of a construction material that consists in whole or in part of materials from another country has been substantially transformed in a least developed country into a new and different construction material distinct from the materials from which it was transformed.

United States means the 50 States, the District of Columbia, and outlying areas.

WTO GPA country construction material means a construction material that—

(1) Is wholly the growth, product, or manufacture of a WTO GPA country; or

(2) In the case of a construction material that consists in whole or in part of materials from another country, has been substantially transformed in a WTO GPA country into a new and different construction material distinct from the materials from which it was transformed.

(b) This clause implements the Balance of Payments Program by providing a preference for domestic construction material. In addition, the Contracting Officer has determined that the WTO GPA and Free Trade Agreements apply to this acquisition. Therefore, the Balance of Payments Program restrictions are waived for designated country construction materials.

(c) The Contractor shall use only domestic or designated country construction material in performing this contract, except for—

(1) Construction material valued at or below the simplified acquisition threshold in part 2 of the Federal Acquisition Regulation;

(2) Information technology that is a commercial item; or

(3) The construction material or components listed by the Government as follows:

[*Contracting Officer to list applicable excepted materials or indicate none*]

(End of clause)

Alternate I. As prescribed in 225.7503(b) and (b)(2), use the following clause, which adds *Bahrainian or Mexican construction material* to paragraph (a), and uses a different paragraph (b) and (c) than the basic clause:

BALANCE OF PAYMENTS PROGRAM—CONSTRUCTION MATERIAL UNDER TRADE AGREEMENTS—ALTERNATE I (AUG 2019)

(a) *Definitions.* As used in this clause—*Bahrainian or Mexican construction material* means a construction material that—

(i) Is wholly the growth, product, or manufacture of Bahrain or Mexico; or

(ii) In the case of a construction material that consists in whole or in part of materials from another country, has been substantially transformed in Bahrain or Mexico into a new and different construction material distinct from the materials from which it was transformed.

Caribbean Basin country construction material means a construction material that—

(i) Is wholly the growth, product, or manufacture of a Caribbean Basin country; or

(ii) In the case of a construction material that consists in whole or in part of materials from another country, has been substantially transformed in a Caribbean Basin country into a new and different construction material distinct from the materials from which it was transformed.

Commercially available off-the-shelf (COTS) item—

(i) Means any item of supply (including construction material) that is—

(A) A commercial item (as defined in paragraph (1) of the definition of *commercial item* in section 2.101 of the Federal Acquisition Regulation);

(B) Sold in substantial quantities in the commercial marketplace; and

(C) Offered to the Government, under a contract or subcontract at any tier, without modification, in the same form in which it is sold in the commercial marketplace; and

(ii) Does not include bulk cargo, as defined in section 3 of the Shipping Act of 1984 (46 U.S.C. 40102), such as agricultural products and petroleum products.

Component means any article, material, or supply incorporated directly into construction material.

Construction material means an article, material, or supply brought to the construction site by the Contractor or a subcontractor for incorporation into the building or work. The term also includes an item brought to the site preassembled from articles, materials, or supplies. However, emergency life safety systems, such as emergency lighting, fire alarm, and audio evacuation systems, that are discrete systems incorporated into a public building or work and that are produced as complete systems, are evaluated as a single and distinct construction material regardless of when or how the individual parts or components of those systems are delivered to the construction site. Materials purchased directly by the Government are supplies, not construction material.

Cost of components means—

(i) For components purchased by the Contractor, the acquisition cost, including transportation costs to the place of incorporation into the end product (whether or not such costs are paid to a domestic firm), and any applicable duty (whether or not a duty-free entry certificate is issued); or

(ii) For components manufactured by the Contractor, all costs associated with the manufacture of the component, including transportation costs as described in paragraph (1) of this definition, plus allocable overhead costs, but excluding profit. Cost of components does not include any costs associated with the manufacture of the construction material.

Designated country means—

(i) A World Trade Organization Government Procurement Agreement (WTO GPA) country (Armenia, Aruba, Australia, Austria, Belgium, Bulgaria, Canada, Croatia, Cyprus, Czech Republic, Denmark, Estonia, Finland, France, Germany, Greece, Hong Kong, Hungary, Iceland, Ireland, Israel, Italy, Japan, Korea (Republic of), Latvia, Liechtenstein, Lithuania, Luxembourg, Malta, Moldova, Montenegro, Netherlands, New Zealand, Norway, Poland, Portugal, Romania, Singapore, Slovak Republic, Slovenia, Spain, Sweden, Switzerland, Taiwan (known in the World Trade Organization as "the Separate Customs Territory of Taiwan, Penghu, Kinmen, Matsu" (Chinese Taipei)), Ukraine, or the United Kingdom);

(ii) A Free Trade Agreement country (Australia, Bahrain, Canada, Chile, Colombia, Costa Rica, Dominican Republic, El Salvador, Guatemala, Honduras, Korea (Republic of), Mexico, Morocco, Nicaragua, Panama, Peru, or Singapore);

(iii) A least developed country (Afghanistan, Angola, Bangladesh, Benin, Bhutan, Burkina Faso, Burundi, Cambodia, Central African Republic, Chad, Comoros, Democratic Republic of Congo, Djibouti, Equatorial Guinea, Eritrea, Ethiopia, Gambia, Guinea, Guinea-Bissau, Haiti, Kiribati, Laos, Lesotho, Liberia, Madagascar, Malawi, Mali, Mauritania, Mozambique, Nepal, Niger, Rwanda, Samoa, Sao Tome and Principe, Senegal, Sierra Leone, Solomon Islands, Somalia, South Sudan, Tanzania, Timor-Leste, Togo, Tuvalu, Uganda, Vanuatu, Yemen, or Zambia); or

(iv) A Caribbean Basin country (Antigua and Barbuda, Aruba, Bahamas, Barbados, Belize, Bonaire, British Virgin Islands, Curacao, Dominica, Grenada, Guyana, Haiti, Jamaica, Montserrat, Saba, St. Kitts and Nevis, St. Lucia, St. Vincent and the Grenadines, Sint Eustatius, Sint Maarten, or Trinidad and Tobago).

Designated country construction material means a construction material that is a WTO GPA country construction material, a Free Trade Agreement country construction material, a least developed country construction material, or a Caribbean Basin country construction material.

Domestic construction material means—

(i) An unmanufactured construction material mined or produced in the United States; or

(ii) A construction material manufactured in the United States, if—

(A) The cost of its components mined, produced, or manufactured in the United States exceeds 50 percent of the cost of all its components. Components of foreign origin of the same class or kind for which nonavailability determinations have been made are treated as domestic; or

(B) The construction material is a COTS item.

Free Trade Agreement country construction material means a construction material that—

(i) Is wholly the growth, product, or manufacture of a Free Trade Agreement country; or

(ii) In the case of a construction material that consists in whole or in part of materials from another country, has been substantially transformed in a Free Trade Agreement country into a new and different construction material distinct from the material from which it was transformed.

Least developed country construction material means a construction material that—

(i) Is wholly the growth, product, or manufacture of a least developed country; or

(ii) In the case of a construction material that consists in whole or in part of materials from another country, has been substantially transformed in a least developed country into a new and different construction material distinct from the materials from which it was transformed.

United States means the 50 States, the District of Columbia, and outlying areas.

WTO GPA country construction material means a construction material that—

(i) Is wholly the growth, product, or manufacture of a WTO GPA country; or

(ii) In the case of a construction material that consists in whole or in part of materials from another country, has been substantially transformed in a WTO GPA country into a new and different construction material distinct from the materials from which it was transformed.

(b) This clause implements the Balance of Payments Program by providing a preference for domestic construction material. In addition, the Contracting Officer has determined that the WTO GPA and all Free Trade Agreements except NAFTA and the Bahrain Free Trade Agreement apply to this acquisition. Therefore, the Balance of Payments Program restrictions are waived for designated country construction material other than Bahrainian or Mexican construction material.

(c) The Contractor shall use only domestic or designated country construction material other than Bahrainian or Mexican construction material in performing this contract, except for—

(1) Construction material valued at or below the simplified acquisition threshold in part 2 of the Federal Acquisition Regulation; or

(2) Information technology that is a commercial item; or

(3) The construction material or components listed by the Government as follows:

____

[*Contracting Officer to list applicable excepted materials or indicate "none"*].

(End of clause)

Alternate II. As prescribed in 225.7503(b) and (b)(3), use the following clause, which adds *South Caucasus/Central and South Asian (SC/CASA) state* and *SC/CASA state construction material* to paragraph (a), uses a different paragraph (b) and introductory text for paragraph (c) than the basic clause, and adds paragraph (d):

BALANCE OF PAYMENTS PROGRAM—CONSTRUCTION MATERIAL UNDER TRADE AGREEMENTS—ALTERNATE II (AUG 2019)

(a) *Definitions.* As used in this clause—

Caribbean Basin country construction material means a construction material that—

(i) Is wholly the growth, product, or manufacture of a Caribbean Basin country; or

(ii) In the case of a construction material that consists in whole or in part of materials from another country, has been substantially transformed in a Caribbean Basin country into a new and different construction material distinct from the materials from which it was transformed.

Commercially available off-the-shelf (COTS) item—

(i) Means any item of supply (including construction material) that is—

(A) A commercial item (as defined in paragraph (1) of the definition of *commercial item* in section 2.101 of the Federal Acquisition Regulation);

(B) Sold in substantial quantities in the commercial marketplace; and

(C) Offered to the Government, under a contract or subcontract at any tier, without modification, in the same form in which it is sold in the commercial marketplace; and

(ii) Does not include bulk cargo, as defined in section 3 of the Shipping Act of 1984 (46 U.S.C. 40102), such as agricultural products and petroleum products.

Component means any article, material, or supply incorporated directly into construction material.

Construction material means an article, material, or supply brought to the construction site by the Contractor or a subcontractor for incorporation into the building or work. The term also includes an item brought to the site preassembled from articles, materials, or supplies. However, emergency life safety systems, such as emergency lighting, fire alarm, and audio evacuation systems, that are discrete systems incorporated into a public building or work and that are produced as complete systems, are evaluated as a single and distinct construction material regardless of when or how the individual parts or components of those systems are delivered to the construction site. Materials purchased directly by the Government are supplies, not construction material.

Cost of components means—

(i) For components purchased by the Contractor, the acquisition cost, including transportation costs to the place of incorporation into the end product (whether or not such costs are paid to a domestic firm), and any applicable duty (whether or not a duty-free entry certificate is issued); or

(ii) For components manufactured by the Contractor, all costs associated with the manufacture of the component, including transportation costs as described in paragraph (1) of this definition, plus allocable overhead costs, but excluding profit. Cost of components does not include any costs associated with the manufacture of the construction material.

Designated country means—

(i) A World Trade Organization Government Procurement Agreement (WTO GPA) country (Armenia, Aruba, Australia, Austria, Belgium, Bulgaria, Canada, Croatia, Cyprus, Czech Republic, Denmark, Estonia, Finland, France, Germany, Greece, Hong Kong, Hungary, Iceland, Ireland, Israel, Italy, Japan, Korea (Republic of), Latvia, Liechtenstein, Lithuania, Luxembourg, Malta, Moldova, Montenegro, Netherlands, New Zealand, Norway, Poland, Portugal, Romania, Singapore, Slovak Republic, Slovenia, Spain, Sweden, Switzerland, Taiwan (known in the World Trade Organization as "the Separate Customs Territory of Taiwan, Penghu, Kinmen, Matsu" (Chinese Taipei)), Ukraine, or the United Kingdom);

(ii) A Free Trade Agreement country (Australia, Bahrain, Canada, Chile, Colombia, Costa Rica, Dominican Republic, El Salvador, Guatemala, Honduras, Korea (Republic of), Mexico, Morocco, Nicaragua, Panama, Peru, or Singapore);

(iii) A least developed country (Afghanistan, Angola, Bangladesh, Benin, Bhutan, Burkina Faso, Burundi, Cambodia, Central African Republic, Chad, Comoros, Democratic Republic of Congo, Djibouti, Equatorial Guinea, Eritrea, Ethiopia, Gambia, Guinea, Guinea-Bissau, Haiti, Kiribati, Laos, Lesotho, Liberia, Madagascar, Malawi, Mali, Mauritania, Mozambique, Nepal, Niger, Rwanda, Samoa, Sao Tome and Principe, Senegal, Sierra Leone, Solomon Islands, Somalia, South Sudan, Tanzania, Timor-Leste, Togo, Tuvalu, Uganda, Vanuatu, Yemen, or Zambia); or

(iv) A Caribbean Basin country (Antigua and Barbuda, Aruba, Bahamas, Barbados, Belize, Bonaire, British Virgin Islands, Curacao, Dominica, Grenada, Guyana, Haiti, Jamaica, Montserrat, Saba, St. Kitts and Nevis, St. Lucia, St. Vincent and the Grenadines, Sint Eustatius, Sint Maarten, or Trinidad and Tobago).

Designated country construction material means a construction material that is a WTO GPA country construction material, a Free Trade Agreement country construction material, a least developed country construction material, or a Caribbean Basin country construction material.

Domestic construction material means—

(i) An unmanufactured construction material mined or produced in the United States; or

(ii) A construction material manufactured in the United States, if—

(A) The cost of its components mined, produced, or manufactured in the United States exceeds 50 percent of the cost of all its components. Components of foreign origin of the same class or kind for which nonavailability determinations have been made are treated as domestic; or

(B) The construction material is a COTS item.

Free Trade Agreement country construction material means a construction material that—

(i) Is wholly the growth, product, or manufacture of a Free Trade Agreement country; or

(ii) In the case of a construction material that consists in whole or in part of materials from another country, has been substantially transformed in a Free Trade Agreement country into a new and different construction material distinct from the material from which it was transformed.

Least developed country construction material means a construction material that—

(i) Is wholly the growth, product, or manufacture of a least developed country; or

(ii) In the case of a construction material that consists in whole or in part of materials from another country, has been substantially transformed in a least developed country into a new and different construction material distinct from the materials from which it was transformed.

South Caucasus/Central and South Asian (SC/CASA) state means Armenia, Azerbaijan, Georgia, Kazakhstan, Kyrgyzstan, Pakistan, Tajikistan, Turkmenistan, or Uzbekistan.

SC/CASA state construction material means construction material that—

(i) Is wholly the growth, product, or manufacture of an SC/CASA state; or

(ii) In the case of a construction material that consists in whole or in part of materials from another country, has been substantially transformed in an SC/CASA state into a new and different construction material distinct from the material from which it was transformed.

United States means the 50 States, the District of Columbia, and outlying areas.

WTO GPA country construction material means a construction material that—

(i) Is wholly the growth, product, or manufacture of a WTO GPA country; or

(ii) In the case of a construction material that consists in whole or in part of materials from another country, has been substantially transformed in a WTO GPA country into a new and different construction material distinct from the materials from which it was transformed.

(b) This clause implements the Balance of Payments Program by providing a preference for domestic construction material. In addition, the Contracting Officer has determined that the WTO GPA, Free Trade Agreements, and other waivers relating to acquisitions in support of operations in Afghanistan apply to this acquisition. Therefore, the Balance of Payments Program restrictions are waived for SC/CASA state and designated country construction materials.

(c) The Contractor shall use only domestic, SC/CASA state, or designated country construction material in performing this contract, except for—

(1) Construction material valued at or below the simplified acquisition threshold in part 2 of the Federal Acquisition Regulation;

(2) Information technology that is a commercial item; or

(3) The construction material or components listed by the Government as follows:

____

[*Contracting Officer to list applicable excepted materials or indicate "none"*].

(d) If the Contractor is from an SC/CASA state, the Contractor shall inform its government of its participation in this acquisition and that it generally will not have such opportunity in the future unless its government provides reciprocal procurement opportunities to U.S. products and services and suppliers of such products and services.

(End of clause)

Alternate III. As prescribed in 225.7503(b) and (b)(4), use the following clause, which adds *South Caucasus/Central and South Asian (SC/CASA state* and *SC/CASA state construction material* to paragraph (a), uses a different paragraph (b) and introductory text for paragraph (c) than the basic clause, and adds paragraph (d):

BALANCE OF PAYMENTS PROGRAM—CONSTRUCTION MATERIAL UNDER TRADE AGREEMENTS—ALTERNATE III (AUG 2019)

(a) *Definitions*. As used in this clause—

Caribbean Basin country construction material means a construction material that—

(i) Is wholly the growth, product, or manufacture of a Caribbean Basin country; or

(ii) In the case of a construction material that consists in whole or in part of materials from another country, has been substantially transformed in a Caribbean Basin country into a new and different construction material distinct from the materials from which it was transformed.

Commercially available off-the-shelf (COTS) item—

(i) Means any item of supply (including construction material) that is—

(A) A commercial item (as defined in paragraph (1) of the definition of *commercial item* in section 2.101 of the Federal Acquisition Regulation);

(B) Sold in substantial quantities in the commercial marketplace; and

(C) Offered to the Government, under a contract or subcontract at any tier, without modification, in the same form in which it is sold in the commercial marketplace; and

(ii) Does not include bulk cargo, as defined in section 3 of the Shipping Act of 1984 (46 U.S.C. 40102), such as agricultural products and petroleum products.

Component means any article, material, or supply incorporated directly into construction material.

Construction material means an article, material, or supply brought to the construction site by the Contractor or a subcontractor for incorporation into the building or work. The term also includes an item brought to the site preassembled from articles, materials, or supplies. However, emergency life safety systems, such as emergency lighting, fire alarm, and audio evacuation systems, that are discrete systems incorporated into a public building or work and that are produced as complete systems, are evaluated as a single and distinct construction material regardless of when or how the individual parts or components of those systems are delivered to the construction site. Materials purchased directly by the Government are supplies, not construction material.

Cost of components means—

(i) For components purchased by the Contractor, the acquisition cost, including transportation costs to the place of incorporation into the end product (whether or not such costs are paid to a domestic firm), and any applicable duty (whether or not a duty-free entry certificate is issued); or

(ii) For components manufactured by the Contractor, all costs associated with the manufacture of the component, including transportation costs as described in

paragraph (1) of this definition, plus

allocable overhead costs, but excluding profit. Cost of components does not include any costs associated with the manufacture of the construction material.

Designated country means—

(i) A World Trade Organization Government Procurement Agreement (WTO GPA) country (Armenia, Aruba, Australia, Austria, Belgium, Bulgaria, Canada, Croatia, Cyprus, Czech Republic, Denmark, Estonia, Finland, France, Germany, Greece, Hong Kong, Hungary, Iceland, Ireland, Israel, Italy, Japan, Korea (Republic of), Latvia, Liechtenstein, Lithuania, Luxembourg, Malta, Moldova, Montenegro, Netherlands, New Zealand, Norway, Poland, Portugal, Romania, Singapore, Slovak Republic, Slovenia, Spain, Sweden, Switzerland, Taiwan (known in the World Trade Organization as "the Separate Customs Territory of Taiwan, Penghu, Kinmen, Matsu" (Chinese Taipei)), Ukraine, or the United Kingdom);

(ii) A Free Trade Agreement country (Australia, Bahrain, Canada, Chile, Colombia, Costa Rica, Dominican Republic, El Salvador, Guatemala, Honduras, Korea (Republic of), Mexico, Morocco, Nicaragua, Panama, Peru, or Singapore);

(iii) A least developed country (Afghanistan, Angola, Bangladesh, Benin, Bhutan, Burkina Faso, Burundi, Cambodia, Central African Republic, Chad, Comoros, Democratic Republic of Congo, Djibouti, Equatorial Guinea, Eritrea, Ethiopia, Gambia, Guinea, Guinea-Bissau, Haiti, Kiribati, Laos, Lesotho, Liberia, Madagascar, Malawi, Mali, Mauritania, Mozambique, Nepal, Niger, Rwanda, Samoa, Sao Tome and Principe, Senegal, Sierra Leone, Solomon Islands, Somalia, South Sudan, Tanzania, Timor-Leste, Togo, Tuvalu, Uganda, Vanuatu, Yemen, or Zambia); or

(iv) A Caribbean Basin country (Antigua and Barbuda, Aruba, Bahamas, Barbados, Belize, Bonaire, British Virgin Islands, Curacao, Dominica, Grenada, Guyana, Haiti, Jamaica, Montserrat, Saba, St. Kitts and Nevis, St. Lucia, St. Vincent and the Grenadines, Sint Eustatius, Sint Maarten, or Trinidad and Tobago).

Designated country construction material means a construction material that is a WTO GPA country construction material, a Free Trade Agreement country construction material, a least developed country construction material, or a Caribbean Basin country construction material.

Domestic construction material means—

(i) An unmanufactured construction material mined or produced in the United States; or

(ii) A construction material manufactured in the United States, if—

(A) The cost of its components mined, produced, or manufactured in the United States exceeds 50 percent of the cost of all its components. Components of foreign origin of the same class or kind for which nonavailability determinations have been made are treated as domestic; or

(B) The construction material is a COTS item.

Free Trade Agreement country construction material means a construction material that—

(i) Is wholly the growth, product, or manufacture of a Free Trade Agreement country; or

(ii) In the case of a construction material that consists in whole or in part of materials from another country, has been substantially transformed in a Free Trade Agreement country into a new and different construction material distinct from the material from which it was transformed.

Least developed country construction material means a construction material that—

(i) Is wholly the growth, product, or manufacture of a least developed country; or

(ii) In the case of a construction material that consists in whole or in part of materials from another country, has been substantially transformed in a least developed country into a new and different construction material distinct from the materials from which it was transformed.

South Caucasus/Central and South Asian (SC/CASA) state means Armenia, Azerbaijan, Georgia, Kazakhstan, Kyrgyzstan, Pakistan, Tajikistan, Turkmenistan, or Uzbekistan.

SC/CASA state construction material means construction material that—

(i) Is wholly the growth, product, or manufacture of An SC/CASA state; or

(ii) In the case of a construction material that consists in whole or in part of materials from another country, has been substantially transformed in an SC/CASA state into a new and different construction material distinct from the material from which it was transformed.

United States means the 50 States, the District of Columbia, and outlying areas.

WTO GPA country construction material means a construction material that—

(i) Is wholly the growth, product, or manufacture of a WTO GPA country; or

(ii) In the case of a construction material that consists in whole or in part of materials from another country, has been substantially transformed in a WTO GPA country into a new and different construction material distinct from the materials from which it was transformed.

(b) This clause implements the Balance of Payments Program by providing a preference for domestic construction material. In addition, the Contracting Officer has determined that the WTO GPA, all Free Trade Agreements except NAFTA and the Bahrain Free Trade Agreement, and other waivers relating to acquisitions in support of operations in Afghanistan apply to this acquisition. Therefore, the Balance of Payments Program restrictions are waived for SC/CASA state and designated country construction material other than Bahrainian or Mexican construction material.

(c) The Contractor shall use only domestic, SC/CASA state, or designated country construction material other than Bahrainian or Mexican construction material in performing this contract, except for—

(1) Construction material valued at or below the simplified acquisition threshold in part 2 of the Federal Acquisition Regulation;

(2) Information technology that is a commercial item; or

(3) The construction material or components listed by the Government as follows:

[*Contracting Officer to list applicable excepted materials or indicate "none"*].

(d) If the Contractor is from an SC/CASA state, the Contractor shall inform its government of its participation in this acquisition and that it generally will not have such opportunity in the future unless its government provides reciprocal procurement opportunities to U.S. products and services and suppliers of such products and services.

(End of clause)

[Final rule, 67 FR 20693, 4/26/2002, effective 4/26/2002; Interim rule, 69 FR 1926, 1/13/2004, effective 1/13/2004; Final rule, 69 FR 35535, 6/25/2004, effective 6/25/2004; Final rule, 69 FR 74991, 12/15/2004, effective 12/15/2004; Interim rule, 70 FR 2361, 1/13/2005, effective 1/13/2005; Final rule, 70 FR 35543, 6/21/2005, effective 6/21/2005; Final rule, 70 FR 73152, 12/9/2005, effective 12/9/2005; Interim rule, 71 FR 9269, 2/23/2006, effective 2/23/2006; Interim rule, 71 FR 34834, 6/16/2006, effective 6/16/2006; Interim rule, 71 FR 58541, 10/4/2006, effective 10/4/2006; Final rule, 71 FR 65752, 11/9/2006, effective 11/9/2006; Final rule, 72 FR 6486, 2/12/2007, effective 2/12/2007; Interim rule, 72 FR 14242, 3/27/2007, effective 3/27/2007; Final rule, 72 FR 14241, 3/27/2007, effective 3/27/2007; Final rule, 73 FR 1830, 1/10/2008, effective 1/10/2008; Final rule, 73 FR 70913, 11/24/2008, effective 11/24/2008; Interim rule, 74 FR 2422, 1/15/2009, effective 1/15/2009; Interim rule, 74 FR 37650, 7/29/2009, effective 7/29/2009; Interim rule, 74 FR 61045, 11/23/2009, effective 11/23/2009; Final rule, 74 FR 68384, 12/24/2009, effective 12/24/2009; Final rule, 75 FR 3179, 1/20/2010, effective 1/20/2010; Final rule, 75 FR 33195, 6/11/2010, effective 6/11/2010; Final rule, 75 FR 66686, 10/29/2010, effective 10/29/2010; Final rule, 75 FR 81915, 12/29/2010, effective

12/29/2010; Final rule, 76 FR 32841, 6/6/2011, effective 6/6/2011; Final rule, 76 FR 38053, 6/29/2011, effective 6/29/2011; Final rule, 77 FR 4631, 1/30/2012, effective 1/30/2012; Interim rule, 77 FR 30356, 5/22/2012, effective 5/22/2012; Interim rule, 77 FR 30359, 5/22/2012, effective 5/22/2012; Final rule, 77 FR 31536, 5/29/2012, effective 5/29/2012; Interim rule, 77 FR 68699, 11/16/2012, effective 11/16/2012; Final rule, 78 FR 18876, 3/28/2013, effective 3/28/2013; Final rule, 78 FR 18877, 3/28/2013, effective 3/28/2013; Final rule, 78 FR 48333, 8/8/2013, effective 8/8/2013; Final rule, 78 FR 65220, 10/31/2013, effective 10/31/2013; Final rule, 78 FR 65221, 10/31/2013, effective 10/31/2013; Final rule, 79 FR 65815, 11/5/2014, effective 11/5/2014; Final rule, 80 FR 36897, 6/26/2015, effective 6/26/2015; Final rule, 80 FR 67253, 10/30/2015, effective 10/30/2015; Final rule, 81 FR 42563, 6/30/2016, effective 6/30/2016; Final rule, 81 FR 65567, 9/23/2016, effective 9/23/2016; Final rule, 84 FR 39207, 8/9/2019, effective 8/9/2019]

252.225-7046 Exports by Approved Community Members in Response to the Solicitation.

As prescribed in 225.7902-5(a), use the following provision:

EXPORTS BY APPROVED COMMUNITY MEMBERS IN RESPONSE TO THE SOLICITATION (JUN 2013)

(a) *Definitions*. The definitions of *Approved Community, defense articles, Defense Trade Cooperation (DTC) Treaty, export, Implementing Arrangement, qualifying defense articles, transfer*, and *U.S. DoD Treaty-eligible requirements* in DFARS clause 252.225-7047 apply to this provision.

(b) All contract line items in the contemplated contract, except any identified in this paragraph, are intended to satisfy U.S. DoD Treaty-eligible requirements. Specific defense articles that are not U.S. DoD Treaty-eligible will be identified as such in those contract line items that are otherwise U.S. DoD Treaty-eligible.

CONTRACT LINE ITEMS NOT INTENDED TO SATISFY U.S. DoD TREATY-ELIGIBLE REQUIREMENTS:

____

[*Enter Contract Line Item Number(s) or enter "None"*]

(c) Approved Community members responding to the solicitation may only export or transfer defense articles that specifically respond to the stated requirements of the solicitation.

(d) Subject to the other terms and conditions of the solicitation and the contemplated contract that affect the acceptability of foreign sources or foreign end products, components, parts, or materials, Approved Community members are permitted, but not required, to use the DTC Treaties for exports or transfers of qualifying defense articles in preparing a response to this solicitation.

(e) Any conduct by an offeror responding to this solicitation that falls outside the scope of the DTC Treaties, the Implementing Arrangements, and the implementing regulations of the Department of State in 22 CFR 126.16 (Australia), 22 CFR 126.17 (United Kingdom), and 22 CFR 126 Supplement No. 1 (exempted technologies list) is subject to all applicable International Traffic in Arms Regulations (ITAR) requirements, including any criminal, civil, and administrative penalties or sanctions, as well as all other United States statutory and regulatory requirements outside of ITAR.

(f) If the offeror uses the procedures established pursuant to the DTC Treaties, the offeror agrees that, with regard to the export or transfer of a qualifying defense article associated with responding to the solicitation, the offeror shall—

(1) Comply with the requirements and provisions of the applicable DTC Treaties, the Implementing Arrangements, and corresponding regulations (including the ITAR) of the U.S. Government and the government of Australia or of the United Kingdom, as applicable; and

(2) Prior to the export or transfer of a qualifying defense article—

(i) Mark, identify, transmit, store, and handle any defense articles provided for the purpose of responding to such solicitations, as well as any defense articles provided with or developed pursuant to their responses to such solicitations, in accordance with the DTC Treaties, the Implementing Arrangements, and corresponding regulations of the United States Government and the government of Australia or the government of the United Kingdom, as applicable, including, but not limited to, the marking and classification requirements described in the applicable regulations;

(ii) Comply with the re-transfer or re-export provisions of the DTC Treaties, the Implementing Arrangements, and corresponding regulations of the United States Government and the government of Australia or the government of the United Kingdom, as applicable, including, but not limited to, the re-transfer and re-export requirements described in the applicable regulations; and

(iii) Acknowledge that any conduct that falls outside or in violation of the DTC Treaties, Implementing Arrangements, and implementing regulations of the applicable government including, but not limited to, unauthorized re-transfer or re-export in violation of the procedures established in the applicable Implementing Arrangement and implementing regulations, remains subject to applicable licensing requirements of the government of Australia, the government of the United Kingdom, and the United States Government, as applicable, including any criminal, civil, and administrative penalties or sanctions contained therein.

(g) *Representation*. The offeror shall check one of the following boxes and sign the representation:

☐ The offeror represents that export(s) or transfer(s) of qualifying defense articles were made in preparing its response to this solicitation and that such export(s) or transfer(s) complied with the requirements of this provision.

____

Name/Title of Duly Authorized Representative   Date

☐ The offeror represents that no export(s) or transfer(s) of qualifying defense articles were made in preparing its response to this solicitation.

____

Name/Title of Duly Authorized Representative   Date

(h) *Subcontracts*. The offeror shall flow down the substance of this provision, including this paragraph (h), but excluding the representation at paragraph (g), to any subcontractor at any tier intending to use the DTC Treaties in responding to this solicitation.

(End of provision)

[Interim rule, 77 FR 30361, 5/22/2012, effective 5/22/2012; Final rule, 78 FR 36108, 6/17/2013, effective 6/17/2013]

252.225-7047 Exports by Approved Community Members in Performance of the Contract.

As prescribed in 225.7902-5(b), use the following clause:

EXPORTS BY APPROVED COMMUNITY MEMBERS IN PERFORMANCE OF THE CONTRACT (JUN 2013)

(a) *Definitions*. As used in this clause—

Approved Community means the U.S. Government, U.S. entities that are registered and eligible exporters, and certain government and industry facilities in Australia or the United Kingdom that are approved and listed by the U.S. Government.

Australia Community member means an Australian government authority or nongovernmental entity or facility on the Australia Community list accessible at *http://pmddtc.state.gov/treaties/index.html*.

Defense articles means articles, services, and related technical data, including software, in tangible or intangible form, listed on the United States Munitions List of the International Traffic in Arms Regulations (ITAR), as modified or amended.

Defense Trade Cooperation (DTC) Treaty means—

(1) The Treaty Between the Government of the United States of America and the government of the United Kingdom of Great Britain and Northern Ireland concerning Defense Trade Cooperation, signed at Washington and London on June 21 and 26, 2007; or

(2) The Treaty Between the Government of the United States of America and the Government of Australia Concerning Defense Trade Cooperation, signed at Sydney on September 5, 2007].

Export means the initial movement of defense articles from the United States Community to the United Kingdom Community and the Australia Community.

Implementing Arrangement means—

(1) The Implementing Arrangement Pursuant to the Treaty between the Government of the United States of America and the Government of the United Kingdom of Great Britain and Northern Ireland Concerning Defense Trade Cooperation, signed on February 14, 2008; or

(2) The Implementing Arrangement Pursuant to the Treaty between the Government of the United States of America and the Government of Australia Concerning Defense Trade Cooperation, signed on March 14, 2008.

Qualifying defense articles means defense articles that are not exempt from the scope of the DTC Treaties as defined in 22 CFR 126.16(g) and 22 CFR 126.17(g).

Transfer means the movement of previously exported defense articles within the Approved Community.

United Kingdom Community member means a United Kingdom government authority or nongovernmental entity or facility on the United Kingdom Community list accessible at *http://pmddtc.state.gov*.

United States Community means—

(1) Departments and agencies of the U.S. Government, including their personnel, with, as appropriate, security accreditation and a need-to-know; and

(2) Nongovernmental U.S. entities registered with the Department of State and eligible to export defense articles under U.S. law and regulation, including their employees, with, as appropriate, security accreditation and a need-to-know.

U.S. DoD Treaty-eligible requirements means any defense article acquired by the DoD for use in a combined military or counterterrorism operation, cooperative research, development, production or support program, or DoD end use, as described in Article 3 of the U.S.-U.K. DTC Treaty and sections 2 and 3 of the associated Implementing Arrangement; and Article 3 of the U.S.-Australia DTC Treaty and sections 2 and 3 of the associated Implementing Arrangement.

(b) All contract line items in this contract, except any identified in this paragraph, are intended to satisfy U.S. DoD Treaty-eligible requirements. Specific defense articles that are not U.S. DoD Treaty-eligible will be identified as such in those contract line items that are otherwise U.S. DoD Treaty-eligible.

CONTRACT LINE ITEMS NOT INTENDED TO SATISFY U.S. DoD TREATY-ELIGIBLE REQUIREMENTS:

[*Enter Contract Line Item Number(s) or enter "None"*]

(c) Subject to the other terms and conditions of this contract that affect the acceptability of foreign sources or foreign end products, components, parts, or materials, Approved Community members are permitted, but not required, to use the DTC Treaties for exports or transfers of qualifying defense articles in performance of the contract.

(d) Any conduct by the Contractor that falls outside the scope of the DTC Treaties, the Implementing Arrangements, and 22 CFR 126.16(g) and 22 CFR 126.17(g) is subject to all applicable ITAR requirements, including any criminal, civil, and administrative penalties or sanctions, as well as all other United States statutory and regulatory requirements outside of ITAR, including, but not limited to, regulations issued by the Bureau of Alcohol, Tobacco, Firearms and Explosives found at 27 CFR parts 447, 478, and 479, which are unaffected by the DTC Treaties.

(e) If the Contractor is an Approved Community member, the Contractor agrees that—

(1) The Contractor shall comply with the requirements of the DTC Treaties, the Implementing Arrangements, the ITAR, and corresponding regulations of the U.S. Government and the government of Australia or the government of the United Kingdom, as applicable; and

(2) Prior to the export or transfer of a qualifying defense article the Contractor—

(i) Shall mark, identify, transmit, store, and handle any defense articles provided for the purpose of responding to such solicitations, as well as any defense articles provided with or developed pursuant to their responses to such solicitations, in accordance with the DTC Treaties, the Implementing Arrangements, and corresponding regulations of the United States Government and the government of Australia or the government of the United Kingdom, as applicable, including, but not limited to, the marking and classification requirements described in the applicable regulations;

(ii) Shall comply with the re-transfer or re-export provisions of the DTC Treaties, the Implementing Arrangements, and corresponding regulations of the United States Government and the government of Australia or the government of the United Kingdom, as applicable, including, but not limited to, the re-transfer and re-export requirements described in the applicable regulations; and

(iii) Shall acknowledge that any conduct that falls outside or in violation of the DTC Treaties, Implementing Arrangements, and implementing regulations of the applicable government including, but not limited to, unauthorized re-transfer or re-export in violation of the procedures established in the applicable Implementing Arrangement and implementing regulations, remains subject to applicable licensing requirements of the government of Australia, the government of the United Kingdom, and the United States Government, including any criminal, civil, and administrative penalties or sanctions contained therein.

(f) The contractor shall include the substance of this clause, including this paragraph (f), in all subcontracts that may require exports or transfers of qualifying defense articles in connection with deliveries under the contract.

(End of clause)

[Interim rule, 77 FR 30361, 5/22/2012, effective 5/22/2012; Final rule, 78 FR 36108, 6/17/2013, effective 6/17/2013; Final rule, 78 FR 38235, 6/26/2013, effective 6/26/2013]

252.225-7048 Export-Controlled Items.

As prescribed in 225.7901-4, use the following clause:

EXPORT-CONTROLLED ITEMS (JUN 2013)

(a) *Definition. Export-controlled items*, as used in this clause, means items subject to the Export Administration Regulations (EAR) (15 CFR Parts 730-774) or the International Traffic in Arms Regulations (ITAR) (22 CFR Parts 120-130). The term includes—

(1) *Defense items*, defined in the Arms Export Control Act, 22 U.S.C. 2778(j)(4)(A), as defense articles, defense services, and related technical data, and further defined in the ITAR, 22 CFR Part 120; and

(2) *Items*, defined in the EAR as *commodities*, *software*, and *technology*, terms that are also defined in the EAR, 15 CFR 772.1.

(b) The Contractor shall comply with all applicable laws and regulations regarding export-controlled items, including, but not limited to, the requirement for contractors to register with the Department of State in accordance with the ITAR. The Contractor shall consult with the Department of State regarding any questions relating to compliance with the ITAR and shall consult with the Department of Commerce regarding any questions relating to compliance with the EAR.

(c) The Contractor's responsibility to comply with all applicable laws and regulations regarding export-controlled items exists independent of, and is not established or limited by, the information provided by this clause.

(d) Nothing in the terms of this contract adds, changes, supersedes, or waives any of the requirements of applicable Federal laws, Executive orders, and regulations, including but not limited to—

(1) The Export Administration Act of 1979, as amended (50 U.S.C. App. 2401, *et seq.*);

(2) The Arms Export Control Act (22 U.S.C. 2751, *et seq.*);

(3) The International Emergency Economic Powers Act (50 U.S.C. 1701, *et seq.*);

(4) The Export Administration Regulations (15 CFR Parts 730-774);

(5) The International Traffic in Arms Regulations (22 CFR Parts 120-130); and

(6) Executive Order 13222, as extended.

(e) The Contractor shall include the substance of this clause, including this paragraph (e), in all subcontracts.

(End of clause)

[Final rule, 78 FR 36108, 6/17/2013, effective 6/17/2013]

252.225-7049 Prohibition on Acquisition of Certain Foreign Commercial Satellite Services—Representations.

As prescribed in 225.772-5(a), use the following provision:

PROHIBITION ON ACQUISITION OF CERTAIN FOREIGN COMMERCIAL SATELLITE SERVICES—REPRESENTATIONS (DEC 2018)

(a) *Definitions*. As used in this provision—

Covered foreign country, foreign entity, government of a covered foreign country, launch vehicle, satellite services, and *state sponsor of terrorism* are defined in the clause at Defense Federal Acquisition Regulation Supplement (DFARS) 252.225-7051, Prohibition on Acquisition of Certain Commercial Satellite Services.

Cybersecurity risk means threats to and vulnerabilities of information or information systems and any related consequences caused by or resulting from unauthorized access, use, disclosure, degradation, disruption, modification, or destruction of such information or information systems, including such related consequences caused by an act of terrorism. (10 U.S.C. 2279)]

(b) *Prohibition on award*. In accordance with 10 U.S.C. 2279, unless an exception is determined to apply in accordance with DFARS 225.772-4, no contract for commercial satellite services may be awarded to—

(1) (i) A foreign entity if the Under Secretary of Defense for Acquisition and Sustainment or the Under Secretary of Defense for Policy reasonably believes that—

(A) The foreign entity is an entity in which the government of a covered foreign country has an ownership interest that enables the government to affect satellite operations;

(B) The foreign entity plans to, or is expected to, provide satellite services under the contract from a covered foreign country; or

(C) Entering into such contract would create an unacceptable cybersecurity risk for DoD; or

(ii) An offeror that is offering to provide the commercial satellite services of a foreign entity as described in paragraph (b)(1) of this provision; or

(2) (i) Any entity, except as provided in paragraph (b)(2)(ii) of this provision, for a launch that occurs on or after December 31, 2022, if the Under Secretary of Defense for Acquisition and Sustainment or the Under Secretary of Defense for Policy reasonably believes that such satellite service will be provided using satellites that will be—

(A) Designed or manufactured—

(*1*) In a covered foreign country; or

(*2*) By an entity controlled in whole or in part by, or acting on behalf of, the government of a covered foreign country; or

(B) Launched outside the United States using a launch vehicle that is—

(*1*) Designed or manufactured in a covered foreign country; or

(*2*) Provided by—

(*i*) The government of a covered foreign country; or

(*ii*) An entity controlled in whole or in part by, or acting on behalf of, the government of a covered foreign country.

(ii) The prohibition in paragraph (b)(2)(i)(B) of this provision does not apply with respect to launch vehicles for which the satellite service provider has a contract or other agreement relating to launch services that, prior to June 10, 2018, was either fully paid for by the satellite service provider or covered by a legally binding commitment of the satellite service provider to pay for such services.

(c) *Representations*. The Offeror represents that—

(1) It [ ] is, [ ] is not a foreign entity in which the government of a covered foreign country has an ownership interest that enables the government to affect satellite operations. If affirmative, identify the covered foreign country: __________;

(2) It [ ] is, [ ] is not a foreign entity that plans to provide satellite services under the contract from a covered foreign country. If affirmative, identify the covered foreign country: __________;

(3) It [ ] is, [ ] is not offering commercial satellite services provided by a foreign entity in which the government of a covered foreign country has an ownership interest that enables the government to affect satellite operations. If affirmative, identify the foreign entity and the covered foreign country: __________;

(4) It [ ] is, [ ] is not offering commercial satellite services provided by a foreign entity that plans to or is expected to provide satellite services under the contract from a covered foreign country. If affirmative, identify the foreign entity and the covered foreign country: __________;

(5) It [ ] is, [ ] is not offering commercial satellite services that will use satellites, launched on or after December 31, 2022, that will be designed or manufactured in a covered foreign country. If affirmative, identify the covered foreign country: __________;

(6) It [ ] is, [ ] is not offering commercial satellite services that will use satellites, launched on or after December 31, 2022, that will be designed or manufactured by an entity controlled in whole or in part by, or acting on behalf of, the government of a covered foreign country. If affirmative, identify the entity, the covered foreign country, and the relationship of the entity to the government of the covered foreign country: __________;

(7) It [ ] is, [ ] is not offering commercial satellite services that will use satellites, launched outside the United States on or after December 31, 2022, using a launch vehicle that is designed or manufactured in a covered foreign country. If affirmative, identify the covered foreign country: __________;

(8) It [ ] is, [ ] is not offering commercial satellite services that will use satellites, launched outside the United States on or after December 31, 2022, using a launch vehicle that is provided by the government of a covered foreign country. If affirmative, identify the covered foreign country: __________; and

(9) It [ ] is, [ ] is not offering commercial satellite services that will use satellites, launched outside the United States on or after December 31, 2022, using a launch vehicle that is provided by an entity controlled in whole or in part by, or acting on behalf of, the government of a covered foreign country. If affirmative, identify the entity, the covered foreign country, and the relationship of the entity to the government of the covered foreign country: __________;

(d) If the Offeror has responded affirmatively to any representation in paragraphs (c)(7) through (9) of this provision, and if such launches are covered in whole or in part by a contract or other agreement relating to launch services that, prior to June 10, 2018, was either fully paid for by the satellite service provider or covered by a legally binding commitment of the satellite service provider to pay for such services, provide the following information:

(1) The entity awarded the contract or other agreement: ________.

(2) The date the contract or other agreement was awarded: ________.

(3) The period of performance for the contract or other agreement: ________.

(e) The representations in paragraph (c) of this provision are a material representation of fact upon which reliance will be placed when making award. If it is later determined that the Offeror knowingly rendered an erroneous representation, in addition to other remedies available to the Government, the Contracting Officer may terminate the contract resulting from this solicitation for default.

(End of provision)

[Interim rule, 79 FR 45661, 8/5/2014, effective 8/5/2014; Final rule, 79 FR 73490, 12/11/2014, effective 12/11/2014; Final rule, 80 FR 67252, 10/30/2015, effective 10/30/2015; Final rule, 83 FR 4447, 1/31/2018, effective 1/31/2018; Interim rule, 83 FR 66066, 12/21/2018, effective 12/21/2018; Interim rule, 83 FR 66066, 12/21/2018, effective 12/21/2018; Final rule, 84 FR 25188, 5/31/2019, effective 5/31/2019]

252.225-7050 Disclosure of Ownership or Control by the Government of a Country that is a State Sponsor of Terrorism.

As prescribed in 225.771–5, use the following provision:

DISCLOSURE OF OWNERSHIP OR CONTROL BY THE GOVERNMENT OF A COUNTRY THAT IS A STATE SPONSOR OF TERRORISM (DEC 2018)

(a) *Definitions*. As used in this provision—

Government of a country that is a state sponsor of terrorism includes the state and the government of a country that is a state sponsor of terrorism, as well as any political subdivision, agency, or instrumentality thereof.

Significant interest means—

(i) Ownership of or beneficial interest in 5 percent or more of the firm's or subsidiary's securities. Beneficial interest includes holding 5 percent or more of any class of the firm's securities in "nominee shares," "street names," or some other method of holding securities that does not disclose the beneficial owner;

(ii) Holding a management position in the firm, such as a director or officer;

(iii) Ability to control or influence the election, appointment, or tenure of directors or officers in the firm;

(iv) Ownership of 10 percent or more of the assets of a firm such as equipment, buildings, real estate, or other tangible assets of the firm; or

(v) Holding 50 percent or more of the indebtedness of a firm.

State sponsor of terrorism means a country determined by the Secretary of State, under section 1754(c)(1)(A)(i) of the Export Control Reform Act of 2018 (Title XVII, Subtitle B, of the National Defense Authorization Act for Fiscal Year 2019, Pub. L. 115-232), to be a country the government of which has repeatedly provided support for acts of international terrorism. As of the date of this provision, state sponsors of terrorism include: Iran, North Korea, Sudan, and Syria.

(b) *Prohibition on award*. In accordance with 10 U.S.C. 2327, unless a waiver is granted by the Secretary of Defense, no contract may be awarded to a firm if the government of a country that is a state sponsor of terrorism owns or controls a significant interest in—

(1) The firm;

(2) A subsidiary of the firm; or

(3) Any other firm that owns or controls the firm.

(c) *Representations*. Unless the Offeror submits with its offer the disclosure required in paragraph (d) of this provision, the Offeror represents, by submission of its offer, that the government of a country that is a state sponsor of terrorism does not own or control a significant interest in—

(1) The Offeror;

(2) A subsidiary of the Offeror; or

(3) Any other firm that owns or controls the Offeror.

(d) *Disclosure.* (1) The Offeror shall disclose in an attachment to its offer if the government of a country that is a state sponsor of terrorism owns or controls a significant interest in the Offeror; a subsidiary of the Offeror; or any other firm that owns or controls the Offeror.

(2) The disclosure shall include—

(i) Identification of each government holding a significant interest; and

(ii) A description of the significant interest held by each government.

(End of provision)

[Final rule, 79 FR 73488, 12/11/2014, effective 12/11/2014; Final rule, 80 FR 67252, 10/30/2015, effective 10/30/2015; Final rule, 83 FR 4447, 1/31/2018, effective 1/31/2018; Interim rule, 83 FR 66066, 12/21/2018, effective 12/21/2018; Final rule, 84 FR 25188, 5/31/2019, effective 5/31/2019]

252.225-7051 Prohibition on Acquisition of Certain Foreign Commercial Satellite Services.

As prescribed in 225.772-5, use the following clause:

PROHIBITION ON ACQUISITION OF CERTAIN FOREIGN COMMERCIAL SATELLITE SERVICES (DEC 2018)

(a) *Definitions.* As used in this clause—

Covered foreign country means—

(i) The People's Republic of China;

(ii) North Korea;

(iii) The Russian Federation; or

(iv) Any country that is a state sponsor of terrorism. (10 U.S.C. 2279)

Foreign entity means—

(i) Any branch, partnership, group or sub-group, association, estate, trust, corporation or division of a corporation, or organization organized under the laws of a foreign state if either its principal place of business is outside the United States or its equity securities are primarily traded on one or more foreign exchanges.

(ii) Notwithstanding paragraph (i) of this definition, any branch, partnership, group or sub-group, association, estate, trust, corporation or division of a corporation, or organization that demonstrates that a majority of the equity interest in such entity is ultimately owned by U.S. nationals is not a foreign entity. (31 CFR 800.212)

Government of a covered foreign country includes the state and the government of a covered foreign country, as well as any political subdivision, agency, or instrumentality thereof.

Launch vehicle means a fully integrated space launch vehicle. (10 U.S.C. 2279)

Satellite services means communications capabilities that utilize an on-orbit satellite for transmitting the signal from one location to another.

State sponsor of terrorism means a country determined by the Secretary of State, under section 1754(c)(1)(A)(i) of the Export Control Reform Act of 2018 (Title XVII, Subtitle B, of the National Defense Authorization Act for Fiscal Year 2019, Pub. L. 115-232), to be a country the government of which has repeatedly provided support for acts of international terrorism. As of the date of this provision, state sponsors of terrorism include: Iran, North Korea, Sudan, and Syria. (10 U.S.C. 2327)

(b) *Limitation.* Unless specified in its offer, the Contractor shall not provide satellite services under this contract that—

(1) Are from a covered foreign country; or

(2) Except as provided in paragraph (c) of this provision, use satellites that will be—

(i) Designed or manufactured—

(A) In a covered foreign country; or

(B) By an entity controlled in whole or in part by, or acting on behalf of, the government of a covered foreign country; or

(ii) Launched outside the United States using a launch vehicle that is designed or manufactured—

(A) In a covered foreign country; or

(B) Provided by—

(*1*) The government of a covered foreign country;

(*2*) An entity controlled in whole or in part by, or acting on behalf of, the government of a covered foreign country.

(c) *Exception*. The limitation in paragraph (b)(2) of this provision shall not apply with respect to—

(1) A launch that occurs prior to December 31, 2022; or

(2) A satellite service provider that has a contract or other agreement relating to launch services that, prior to June 10, 2018, was either fully paid for by the satellite service provider or covered by a legally binding commitment of the satellite service provider to pay for such services.

(End of provision)

[Interim rule, 83 FR 66066, 12/21/2018, effective 12/21/2018; Final rule, 84 FR 25188, 5/31/2019, effective 5/31/2019]

252.225-7052 Restriction on the Acquisition of Certain Magnets and Tungsten.

As prescribed in 225.7018-5, use the following clause:

RESTRICTION ON THE ACQUISITION OF CERTAIN MAGNETS AND TUNGSTEN (DEC 2019)

(a) *Definitions*. As used in this clause—

Assembly means an item forming a portion of a system or subsystem that—

(1) Can be provisioned and replaced as an entity; and

(2) Incorporates multiple, replaceable parts.

Commercially available off-the-shelf item—

(1) Means any item of supply that is—

(i) A commercial item (as defined in paragraph (1) of the definition of *commercial item* in section 2.101 of the Federal Acquisition Regulation);

(ii) Sold in substantial quantities in the commercial marketplace; and

(iii) Offered to the Government, under this contract or a subcontract at any tier, without modification, in the same form in which it is sold in the commercial marketplace; and

(2) Does not include bulk cargo, as defined in 46 U.S.C. 40102(4), such as agricultural products and petroleum products.

Component means any item supplied to the Government as part of an end item or of another component.

Covered country means—

(1) The Democratic People's Republic of North Korea;

(2) The People's Republic of China;

(3) The Russian Federation; and

(4) The Islamic Republic of Iran.

Covered material means—

(1) Samarium-cobalt magnets;

(2) Neodymium-iron-boron magnets;

(3) Tungsten metal powder; and

(4) Tungsten heavy alloy or any finished or semi-finished component containing tungsten heavy alloy.

Electronic device means an item that operates by controlling the flow of electrons or other electrically charged particles in circuits, using interconnections such as resistors, inductors, capacitors, diodes, switches, transistors, or integrated circuits.

End item means the final production product when assembled or completed and ready for delivery under a line item of this contract.

Subsystem means a functional grouping of items that combine to perform a major function within an end item, such as electrical power, attitude control, and propulsion.

Tungsten heavy alloy means a tungsten base pseudo alloy that—

(1) Meets the specifications of ASTM B777 or SAE–AMS–T–21014 for a particular class of tungsten heavy alloy; or

(2) Contains at least 90 percent tungsten in a matrix of other metals (such as nickel-iron or nickel-copper) and has density of at least 16.5 g/cm3).

(b) *Restriction*. (1) Except as provided in paragraph (c) of this clause, the Contractor shall not deliver under this contract any covered material melted or produced in any covered country, or any end item, manufactured in any covered country, that contains a covered material (10 U.S.C. 2533c).

(2) (i) For samarium-cobalt magnets and neodymium iron-boron magnets, this restriction includes—

(A) Melting samarium with cobalt to produce the samarium-cobalt alloy or melting neodymium with iron and boron to produce the neodymium-iron-boron alloy; and

(B) All subsequent phases of production of the magnets, such as powder formation, pressing, sintering or bonding, and magnetization.

(ii) The restriction on melting and producing of samarium-cobalt magnets is in addition to any applicable restrictions on melting of specialty metals if the clause at 252.225-7009, Restriction on Acquisition of Certain Articles Containing Specialty Metals, is included in the contract.

(3) For production of tungsten metal powder and tungsten heavy alloy, this restriction includes—

(i) Atomization;

(ii) Calcination and reduction into powder;

(iii) Final consolidation of non-melt derived metal powders; and

(iv) All subsequent phases of production of tungsten metal powder, tungsten heavy alloy, or any finished or semi-finished component containing tungsten heavy alloy.

(c) *Exceptions*. This clause does not apply—

(1) To an end item that is—

(i) A commercially available off-the-shelf item, other than—

(A) A commercially available off-the-shelf item that is 50 percent or more tungsten by weight; or

(B) A tungsten heavy alloy mill product, such as bar, billet, slab, wire, cube, sphere, block, blank, plate, or sheet, that has not been incorporated into an end item, subsystem, assembly, or component;

(ii) An electronic device, unless otherwise specified in the contract; or

(iii) A neodymium-iron-boron magnet manufactured from recycled material if the milling of the recycled material and sintering of the final magnet takes place in the United States.

(2) If the authorized agency official concerned has made a nonavailability determination, in accordance with section 225.7018–4 of the Defense Federal Acquisition Regulation Supplement, that compliant covered materials of satisfactory quality and quantity, in the required form, cannot be procured as and when needed at a reasonable price.

(i) For tungsten heavy alloy, the term "required form" refers to the form of the mill product, such as bar, billet, wire, slab, plate, or sheet, in the grade appropriate for the production of a finished end item to be delivered to the Government under this contract; or a finished component assembled into an end item to be delivered to the Government under the contract.

(ii) For samarium-cobalt magnets or neodymium-iron-boron magnets, the term "required form" refers to the form and properties of the magnets.

(d) The Contractor shall insert the substance of this clause, including this paragraph (d), in subcontracts and other contractual instruments that are for items containing a covered material, including subcontracts and other contractual instruments for commercial items, unless an exception in paragraph (c) of this clause applies. The Contractor shall not alter this clause other than to identify the appropriate parties.

(End of clause)

[Interim rule, 84 FR 18156, 4/30/2019, effective 4/30/2019; Final rule, 84 FR 72239, 12/31/2019, effective 12/31/2019]

252.226 Other Socioeconomic Programs, provisions and clauses for DFARS Part 226

252.226-7000 [Removed]

[Interim rule, 59 FR 22130, 4/29/94, effective 4/21/94; Final rule, 70 FR 73148, 12/9/2005, effective 12/9/2005; Final rule, 75 FR 81915, 12/29/2010, effective 12/29/2010; Interim rule, 79 FR 61579, 10/14/2014, effective 10/14/2014; Final rule, 80 FR 15912, 3/26/2015, effective 3/26/2015]

252.226-7001 Utilization of Indian organizations, Indian-owned economic enterprises, and native Hawaiian small business concerns.

As prescribed in 226.104, use the following clause:

UTILIZATION OF INDIAN ORGANIZATIONS, INDIAN-OWNED ECONOMIC ENTERPRISES AND NATIVE HAWAIIAN SMALL BUSINESS CONCERNS (APR 2019)

(a) *Definitions.* As used in this clause—

Indian means—

(1) Any person who is a member of any Indian tribe, band, group, pueblo, or community that is recognized by the Federal Government as eligible for services from the Bureau of Indian Affairs (BIA) in accordance with 25 U.S.C. 1452(c); and

(2) Any *Native* as defined in the Alaska Native Claims Settlement Act (43 U.S.C. 1601).

Indian organization means the governing body of any Indian tribe or entity established or recognized by the governing body of an Indian tribe for the purposes of 25 U.S.C. chapter 17.

Indian-owned economic enterprise means any Indian-owned (as determined by the Secretary of the Interior) commercial, industrial, or business activity established or organized for the purpose of profit, provided that Indian ownership constitutes not less than 51 percent of the enterprise.

Indian tribe means any Indian tribe, band, group, pueblo, or community, including native villages and native groups (including corporations organized by Kenai, Juneau, Sitka, and Kodiak) as defined in the Alaska Native Claims Settlement Act, that is recognized by the Federal Government as eligible for services from BIA in accordance with 25 U.S.C. 1452(c).

Interested party means a contractor or an actual or prospective offeror whose direct economic interest would be affected by the award of a subcontract or by the failure to award a subcontract.

Native Hawaiian small business concern means an entity that is—

(1) A small business concern as defined in section 3 of the Small Business Act (15 U.S.C. 632) and relevant implementing regulations; and

(2) Owned and controlled by a Native Hawaiian as defined in 25 U.S.C. 4221(9).

(b) The Contractor shall use its best efforts to give Indian organizations, Indian-owned economic enterprises, and Native Hawaiian small business concerns the maximum practicable opportunity to participate in the subcontracts it awards, to the fullest extent consistent with efficient performance of the contract.

(c) The Contracting Officer and the Contractor, acting in good faith, may rely on the representation of an Indian organization, Indian-owned economic enterprise, or Native Hawaiian small business concern as to its eligibility, unless an interested party challenges its status or the Contracting Officer has independent reason to question that status.

(d) In the event of a challenge to the representation of a subcontractor, the Contracting Officer will refer the matter to—

(1) (i) For matters relating to Indian organizations or Indian-owned economic enterprises:

U.S. Department of the Interior, Bureau of Indian Affairs, Attn: Bureau Procurement Chief, 12220 Sunrise Valley Drive, Reston, VA 20191, Phone: 703–390–6433, Website: *https://www.bia.gov/*.

(ii) The BIA will determine the eligibility and will notify the Contracting Officer.

(2) (i) For matters relating to Native Hawaiian small business concerns:

Department of Hawaiian Home Lands, P.O. Box 1879, Honolulu, HI 96805, Phone: 808–620–9500, Website: *http://dhhl.hawaii.gov/*.

(ii) The Department of Hawaiian Home Lands will determine the eligibility and will notify the Contracting Officer.

(e) No incentive payment will be made—

(1) While a challenge is pending; or

(2) If a subcontractor is determined to be an ineligible participant.

(f) (1) The Contractor, on its own behalf or on behalf of a subcontractor at any tier, may request an incentive payment in accordance with this clause.

(2) The incentive amount that may be requested is 5 percent of the estimated cost, target cost, or fixed price included in the subcontract at the time of award to the Indian organization, Indian- owned economic enterprise, or Native Hawaiian small business concern.

(3) In the case of a subcontract for commercial items, the Contractor may receive an incentive payment only if the subcontracted items are produced or manufactured in whole or in part by an Indian organization, Indian-owned economic enterprise, or Native Hawaiian small business concern.

(4) The Contractor has the burden of proving the amount claimed and shall assert its request for an incentive payment prior to completion of contract performance.

(5) The Contracting Officer, subject to the terms and conditions of the contract and the availability of funds, will authorize an incentive payment of 5 percent of the estimated cost, target cost, or fixed price included in the subcontract awarded to the Indian organization, Indian-owned economic enterprise, or Native Hawaiian small business concern.

(6) If the Contractor requests and receives an incentive payment on behalf of a subcontractor, the Contractor is obligated to pay the subcontractor the incentive amount.

(g) The Contractor shall insert the substance of this clause, including this paragraph (g), in all subcontracts exceeding $500,000.

(End of Clause)

[Interim rule, 66 FR 47110, 9/11/2001, effective 9/11/2001, corrected 66 FR 50504, 10/3/2001; Final rule, 67 FR 38022, 5/31/2002, effective 5/31/2002; Interim rule, 68 FR 56561, 10/1/2003, effective 10/1/2003; Final rule, 69 FR 55989, 9/17/2004, effective 9/17/2004; Final rule, 84 FR 12141, 4/1/2019, effective 4/1/2019]

252.226-7002 Representation for Demonstration Project for Contractors Employing Persons with Disabilities.

As prescribed in 226.7203, use the following provision:

REPRESENTATION FOR DEMONSTRATION PROJECT FOR CONTRACTORS EMPLOYING PERSONS WITH DISABILITIES (DEC 2019)

(a) *Definitions.* As used in this provision—

Eligible contractor means a business entity operated on a for-profit or nonprofit basis that—

(1) Employs severely disabled individuals at a rate that averages not less than 33 percent of its total workforce over the 12-month period prior to issuance of the solicitation;

(2) Pays not less than the minimum wage prescribed pursuant to 29 U.S.C. 206 to the employees who are severely disabled individuals; and

(3) Provides, for its employees, health insurance and a retirement plan comparable to those provided for employees by business entities of similar size in its industrial sector or geographic region.

Severely disabled individual means an individual with a disability (as defined in 42 U.S.C. 12102) who has a severe physical or mental impairment that seriously limits one or more functional capacities.

(b) *Demonstration Project.* This solicitation is issued pursuant to the Demonstration Project for Contractors Employing Persons with Disabilities. The purpose of the Demonstration Project is to provide defense contracting opportunities for entities that employ severely disabled individuals. To be eligible for award, an offeror must be an eligible contractor as defined in paragraph (a) of this provision.

(c) *Representation.* The offeror represents that it []is [] is not an eligible contractor as defined in paragraph (a) of this provision.

(End of provision)

[Interim rule, 66 FR 47110, 9/11/2001, effective 9/11/2001, corrected 66 FR 50504, 10/3/2001; Final rule, 67 FR 38022, 5/31/2002, effective 5/31/2002; Interim rule, 68 FR 56561, 10/1/2003, effective 10/1/2003; Final rule, 69 FR 55989, 9/17/2004, effective 9/17/2004; Final rule, 84 FR 12141, 4/1/2019, effective 4/1/2019; Final rule, 84 FR 72554, 12/31/2019, effective 12/31/2019]

252.227 Patents, Data, and Copyrights, provisions and clauses for DFARS Part 227

252.227-7000 Non-estoppel.

As prescribed at 227.7009-1, insert the following clause in patent releases, license agreements, and assignments:

NON-ESTOPPEL (OCT 1966)

The Government reserves the right at any time to contest the enforceability, validity, scope of, or the title to any patent or patent application herein licensed without waiving or forfeiting any right under this contract.

(End of clause)

252.227-7001 Release of past infringement.

As prescribed at 227.7009-2(a), insert the following clause in patent releases, license agreements, and assignments:

RELEASE OF PAST INFRINGEMENT (SEP 2019)

The Contractor hereby releases each and every claim and demand which the Contractor now has or may hereafter have against the Government for the manufacture or use by or for the Government prior to the effective date of this contract, of any inventions covered by (i) any of the patents and applications for patent identified in this contract, and (ii) any other patent or application for patent owned or hereafter acquired by the Contractor, insofar as and only to the extent that such other patent or patent application covers the manufacture, use, or disposition of [description of subject matter].*

*Bracketed portions of the clause may be omitted when not appropriate or not encompassed by the release as negotiated.

(End of clause)

[Final rule, 84 FR 48499, 9/13/2019, effective 9/13/2019]

252.227-7002 Readjustment of payments.

As prescribed at 227.7009-2(b), insert the following clause in patent releases, license agreements, and assignments:

READJUSTMENT OF PAYMENTS (SEP 2019)

(a) If any license, under substantially the same patents and authorizing substantially the same acts which are authorized under this contract, has been or shall hereafter be granted within the United States, on royalty terms which are more favorable to the licensee than those contained herein, the Government shall be entitled to the benefit of such more favorable terms with respect to all royalties accruing under this contract after the date such more favorable terms become effective, and the Contractor shall promptly notify the Contracting Officer in writing of the granting of such more favorable terms.

(b) In the event any claim of any patent hereby licensed is construed or held invalid by decision of a court of competent jurisdiction, the requirement to pay royalties under this contract insofar as it arises solely by reason of such claim, and any other claim not materially different therefrom, shall be interpreted in conformity with the court's decision as to the scope of validity of such claims; *Provided*, however, that in the event such decision is modified or reversed on appeal, the requirement to pay royalties under this contract shall be interpreted in conformity with the final decision rendered on such appeal.

(End of clause)

[Final rule, 84 FR 48501, 9/13/2019, effective 9/13/2019]

252.227-7003 Termination.

As prescribed at 227.7009-2(c), insert the following clause in patent releases, license agreements, and assignments:

TERMINATION (AUG 1984)

Notwithstanding any other provision of this contract, the Government shall have the right to terminate the within license, in whole or in part, by giving the Contractor not less than thirty (30) days notice in writing of the date such termination is to be effective; provided, however, that such termination shall not affect the obligation of the Government to pay royalties which have accrued prior to the effective date of such termination.

(End of clause)

252.227-7004 License grant.

As prescribed at 227.7009-3(a), insert the following clause in patent releases, license agreements, and assignments:

LICENSE GRANT (AUG 1984)

(a) The Contractor hereby grants to the Government an irrevocable, nonexclusive, nontransferable, and paid up license under the following patents, applications for patent, and any patents granted on such applications, and under any patents which may issue as the result of any reissue, division or continuation thereof, to practice by or cause to be practiced for the Government throughout the world, any and all of the inventions thereunder, in the manufacture and use of any article or material, in the use of any method or process, and in the disposition of any article or material in accordance with law:

U.S. Patent No. ____________________
Date ____________________
Application Serial No. ____________________
Filing Date ____________________

together with corresponding foreign patents and foreign applications for patents, insofar as the Contractor has the right to grant licenses thereunder without incurring an obligation to pay royalties or other compensation to others solely on account of such grant.

(b) No rights are granted or implied by the agreement under any other patents other than as provided above or by operation of law.

(c) Nothing contained herein shall limit any rights which the Government may have obtained by virtue of prior contracts or by operation of law or otherwise.

(End of clause)

252.227-7005 License term.

As prescribed at 227.7009-3(b), insert one of the following clauses in patent releases, license agreements, and assignments:

LICENSE TERM (OCT 2001)

ALTERNATE I (AUG 1984)

The license hereby granted shall remain in full force and effect for the full term of each of the patents referred to in the "License Grant" clause of this contract and any and all patents hereafter issued on applications for patent referred to in such "License Grant" clause.

ALTERNATE II (OCT 2001)

The license hereby granted shall terminate on the ____ day of ____,____; *Provided*, however, that said termination shall be without prejudice to the completion of any contract entered into by the Government prior to said date of termination or to the use or disposition thereafter of any articles or materials manufactured by or for the Government under this license.

[Final rule, 66 FR 49860, 10/1/2001, effective 10/1/2001]

252.227-7006 License grant—running royalty.

As prescribed at 227.7009-4(a), insert the following clause in patent releases, license agreements, and assignments:

LICENSE GRANT—RUNNING ROYALTY (AUG 1984)

(a) The Contractor hereby grants to the Government, as represented by the Secretary of ____, an irrevocable, nonexclusive, nontransferable license under the following patents, applications for patent, and any patents granted on such applications, and under any patents which may issue as the result of any reissue, division, or continuation thereunder to practice by or cause to be practiced for the Department of ____, throughout the world, any and all of the inventions thereunder in the manufacture and use of any article or material, in the use of any method or process, and in the disposition of any article or material in accordance with law:

U.S. Patent No. ____
Date ____
Application Serial No. ____
Filing Date ____

together with corresponding foreign patents and foreign applications for patent, insofar as the Contractor has the right to grant licenses thereunder without incurring an obligation to pay royalties or other compensation to others solely on account of such grant.

(b) No rights are granted or implied by the agreement under any other patents other than as provided above or by operation of law.

(c) Nothing contained herein shall limit any rights which the Government may have obtained by virtue of prior contracts or by operation of law or otherwise.

(End of clause)

252.227-7007 License term—running royalty.

As prescribed at 227.7009-4(b), insert the following clause in patent releases, license agreements, and assignments:

LICENSE TERM—RUNNING ROYALTY (AUG 1984)

The license hereby granted shall remain in full force and effect for the full term of each of the patents referred to in the "License Grant" clause of this contract and any and all patents hereafter issued on applications for patent referred to above unless sooner terminated as elsewhere herein provided.

(End of clause)

252.227-7008 Computation of royalties.

As prescribed at 227.7009-4(c), insert the following clause in patent releases, license agreements, and assignments:

COMPUTATION OF ROYALTIES (AUG 1984)

Subject to the conditions hereinafter stated, royalties shall accrue to the Contractor under this agreement on all articles or materials embodying, or manufactured by the use of, any or all inventions claimed under any unexpired United States patent licensed herein, upon acceptance thereof by the Department of ____ at the rate of ____ percent of the net selling price of such articles or materials (amount) per (name of item)* whether manufactured by the Government or procured under a fixed price contract, and at the rate of (amount) per (name of item) acquired or manufactured by a Contractor performing under a cost-reimbursement contract. With respect to such articles or materials made by the Department of ____, "net selling price," as used in this paragraph, means the actual cost of direct labor and materials without allowance for overhead and supervision.

(End of clause)

* Use bracketed matter as appropriate.

252.227-7009 Reporting and payment of royalties.

As prescribed at 227.7009-4(d), insert the following clause in patent releases, license agreements, and assignments:

REPORTING AND PAYMENT OF ROYALTIES (SEP 2019)

(a) The [*insert the Contracting Officer or the name of the designated office, in accordance with agency procedures*] shall, on or before the sixtieth (60th) day next following the end of each yearly* period ending ____ during which royalties have accrued under this license, deliver to the Contractor, subject to military security regulations, a report in writing furnishing necessary information relative to royalties which have accrued under this contract.

(b) Royalties which have accrued under this contract during the yearly* period ending ____ shall be paid to the Contractor (if appropriations therefor are available or become available) within sixty (60) days next following the receipt of a voucher from the Contractor submitted in accordance with the report referred to in (a) of this clause; *Provided*, that the Government shall not be obligated to pay, in respect of any such yearly period, on account of the combined royalties accruing under this contract directly and under any separate licenses granted pursuant to the "License to Other Government Agencies" clause (if any) of this contract, an amount greater than ____ dollars ($____), and if such combined royalties exceed the said maximum yearly obligation, each department or agency shall pay a pro rata share of the said maximum yearly obligation as determined by the proportion its accrued royalties bear to the combined total of accrued royalties.

* The frequency, date, and length of reporting periods should be elected as appropriate to the particular circumstances of the contract.

(End of clause)

[Final rule, 84 FR 48503, 9/13/2019, effective 9/13/2019]

252.227-7010 License to other government agencies.

As prescribed at 227.7009-4(e), insert the following clause in patent releases, license agreements, and assignments:

LICENSE TO OTHER GOVERNMENT AGENCIES (AUG 1984)

The Contractor hereby agrees to grant a separate license under the patents, applications for patents, and improvements referred to in the "License Grant" clause of this contract, on the same terms and conditions as appear in this license contract, to any other department or agency of the Government at any time on receipt of a written request for such a license from such department or agency; *Provided*, however, that as to royalties which accrue under such separate licenses, reports and payments shall be made directly to the Contractor by each such other department or agency pursuant to the terms of such separate licenses. The Contractor shall notify the Licensee hereunder promptly upon receipt of any request for license hereunder.

(End of clause)

252.227-7011 Assignments.

As prescribed at 227.7010, insert the following clause in assignments.

ASSIGNMENT (AUG 1984)

The Contractor hereby conveys to the Government, as represented by the Secretary of ____, the entire right, title, and interest in and to the following patents (and applications for patent), in and to the inventions thereof, and in and to all claims and demands whatsoever for infringement thereof heretofore accrued, the same to be held and enjoyed by the Government through its duly appointed representatives to the full end of the term of said patents (and to the full end of the terms of all patents which may be granted upon said applications for patent, or upon any division, continuation-in-part or continuation thereof):

U.S. Patent No. ____

Date ____

Name of Inventor ____

U.S. Application Serial No. ____

Filing Date ____

Name of Inventor ____

together with corresponding foreign patents and applications for patent insofar as the Contractor has the right to assign the same.

(End of clause)

252.227-7012 Patent license and release contract.

As prescribed at 227.7012, insert the following clause in patent releases, license agreements, and assignments:

(Contract No.) ____

PATENT LICENSE AND RELEASE CONTRACT (SEP 1999)

This CONTRACT is effective as of the ____ day of [month, year], between the UNITED STATES OF AMERICA (hereinafter called the Government), and ____ (hereinafter called the Contractor), (a corporation organized and existing under the laws of the State of ____ (a partnership consisting of ____), (an individual trading as ____), of the City of ____, in the State of ____.

Whereas, the Contractor warrants that it has the right to grant the within license and release, and the Government desires to procure the same, and

Whereas, this contract is authorized by law, including 10 U.S.C. 2386.

Now Therefore, in consideration of the grant, release and agreements hereinafter recited, the parties have agreed as follows:

Article 1. License Grant.*

(Insert the clause at 252.227-7004 for a paid up license, or the clause at 252.227-7006 for a license on a running royalty basis.)

Article 2. License Term.*

(Insert the appropriate alternative clause at 252.227-7005 for a paid up license, or the clause at 252.227-7007 for a license on a running royalty basis.)

Article 3. Release of Past Infringement.

(Insert the clause at 252.227-7001.)

Article 4. Non-Estoppel.

(Insert the clause at 252.227-7000.)

Article 5. Payment.

The Contractor shall be paid the sum of ____ Dollars ($____) in full compensation for the rights herein granted and agreed to be granted. (For a license on a running royalty basis, insert the clause at 252.227-7006 in accordance with the instructions therein, and also the clause as specified at 252.227-7002 and 252.227-7009 and 252.227-7010.)

Article 6. Covenant Against Contingent Fees.

(Insert the clause at FAR 52.203-5.)

Article 7. Assignment of Claims.

(Insert the clause at FAR 52.232-23.)

Article 8. Gratuities.

(Insert the clause at FAR 52.203-3.)

Article 9. Disputes.

(Insert the clause at FAR 52.233-1.)

Article 10. Successors and Assignees.

This Agreement shall be binding upon the Contractor, its successors** and assignees, but nothing contained in this Article shall authorize an assignment of any claim against the Government otherwise than as permitted by law.

In Witness Whereof, the parties hereto have executed this contract.

THE UNITED STATES OF AMERICA

By ____

Date ____

(Signature and Title of Contractor Representative) ____

By ____

Date ____

* If only a release is procured, delete this article; if an assignment is procured, use the clause at 252.227-7011.

** When the Contractor is an individual, change "successors" to "heirs"; if a partnership, modify appropriately.

(End of clause)

[Final rule, 64 FR 49684, 9/14/99, effective 9/14/99]

252.227-7013 Rights in technical data—Noncommercial items.

As prescribed in 227.7103-6(a), use the following clause:

RIGHTS IN TECHNICAL DATA—NONCOMMERCIAL ITEMS (FEB 2014)

(a) *Definitions*. As used in this clause—

(1) *Computer data base* means a collection of data recorded in a form capable of being processed by a computer. The term does not include computer software.

(2) *Computer program* means a set of instructions, rules, or routines recorded in a form that is capable of causing a computer to perform a specific operation or series of operations.

(3) *Computer software* means computer programs, source code, source code listings, object code listings, design details, algorithms, processes, flow charts, formulae and related material that would enable the software to be reproduced, recreated, or recompiled. Computer software does not include computer data bases or computer software documentation.

(4) *Computer software documentation* means owner's manuals, user's manuals, installation instructions, operating instructions, and other similar items, regardless of storage medium, that explain the capabilities of the computer software or provide instructions for using the software.

(5) *Covered Government support contractor* means a contractor (other than a litigation support contractor covered by 252.204-7014) under a contract, the primary purpose of which is to furnish independent and impartial advice or technical assistance directly to the Government in support of the Government's management and oversight of a program or effort (rather than to directly furnish an end item or service to accomplish a program or effort), provided that the contractor—

(i) Is not affiliated with the prime contractor or a first-tier subcontractor on the program or effort, or with any direct competitor of such prime contractor or any such first-tier subcontractor in furnishing end items or services of the type developed or produced on the program or effort; and

(ii) Receives access to technical data or computer software for performance of a Government contract that contains the clause at 252.227-7025, Limitations on the Use or Disclosure of Government-Furnished Information Marked with Restrictive Legends.

(6) *Detailed manufacturing or process data* means technical data that describe the steps, sequences, and conditions of manufacturing, processing or assembly used by the manufacturer to produce an item or component or to perform a process.

(7) *Developed* means that an item, component, or process exists and is workable. Thus, the item or component must have been constructed or the process practiced. Workability is generally established when the item, component, or process has been analyzed or tested sufficiently to demonstrate to reasonable people skilled in the applicable art that there is a high probability that it will operate as intended. Whether, how much, and what type of analysis or testing is required to establish workability depends on the nature of the item, component, or process, and the state of the art. To be considered "developed," the item, component, or process need not be at the stage where it could be offered for sale or sold on the commercial market, nor must the item, component, or process be actually reduced to practice within the meaning of Title 35 of the United States Code.

(8) *Developed exclusively at private expense* means development was accomplished entirely with costs charged to indirect cost pools, costs not allocated to a government contract, or any combination thereof.

(i) Private expense determinations should be made at the lowest practicable level.

(ii) Under fixed-price contracts, when total costs are greater than the firm-fixed-price or ceiling price of the contract, the additional development costs necessary to complete development shall not be considered when determining whether development was at government, private, or mixed expense.

(9) *Developed exclusively with government funds* means development was not accomplished exclusively or partially at private expense.

(10) *Developed with mixed funding* means development was accomplished partially with costs charged to indirect cost pools and/or costs not allocated to a government contract, and partially with costs charged directly to a government contract.

(11) *Form, fit, and function data* means technical data that describes the required overall physical, functional, and performance

characteristics (along with the qualification requirements, if applicable) of an item, component, or process to the extent necessary to permit identification of physically and functionally interchangeable items.

(12) *Government purpose* means any activity in which the United States Government is a party, including cooperative agreements with international or multi-national defense organizations, or sales or transfers by the United States Government to foreign governments or international organizations. Government purposes include competitive procurement, but do not include the rights to use, modify, reproduce, release, perform, display, or disclose technical data for commercial purposes or authorize others to do so.

(13) *Government purpose rights* means the rights to—

(i) Use, modify, reproduce, release, perform, display, or disclose technical data within the Government without restriction; and

(ii) Release or disclose technical data outside the Government and authorize persons to whom release or disclosure has been made to use, modify, reproduce, release, perform, display, or disclose that data for United States government purposes.

(14) *Limited rights* means the rights to use, modify, reproduce, release, perform, display, or disclose technical data, in whole or in part, within the Government. The Government may not, without the written permission of the party asserting limited rights, release or disclose the technical data outside the Government, use the technical data for manufacture, or authorize the technical data to be used by another party, except that the Government may reproduce, release, or disclose such data or authorize the use or reproduction of the data by persons outside the Government if—

(i) The reproduction, release, disclosure, or use is—

(A) Necessary for emergency repair and overhaul; or

(B) A release or disclosure to—

(*1*) A covered Government support contractor in performance of its covered Government support contract for use, modification, reproduction, performance, display, or release or disclosure to a person authorized to receive limited rights technical data; or

(*2*) A foreign government, of technical data other than detailed manufacturing or process data, when use of such data by the foreign government is in the interest of the Government and is required for evaluational or informational purposes;

(ii) The recipient of the technical data is subject to a prohibition on the further reproduction, release, disclosure, or use of the technical data; and

(iii) The contractor or subcontractor asserting the restriction is notified of such reproduction, release, disclosure, or use.

(15) *Technical data* means recorded information, regardless of the form or method of the recording, of a scientific or technical nature (including computer software documentation). The term does not include computer software or data incidental to contract administration, such as financial and/or management information.

(16) *Unlimited rights* means rights to use, modify, reproduce, perform, display, release, or disclose technical data in whole or in part, in any manner, and for any purpose whatsoever, and to have or authorize others to do so.

(b) *Rights in technical data*. The Contractor grants or shall obtain for the Government the following royalty free, world-wide, nonexclusive, irrevocable license rights in technical data other than computer software documentation (see the Rights in Noncommercial Computer Software and Noncommercial Computer Software Documentation clause of this contract for rights in computer software documentation):

(1) *Unlimited rights.*

The Government shall have unlimited rights in technical data that are—

(i) Data pertaining to an item, component, or process which has been or will be developed exclusively with Government funds;

(ii) Studies, analyses, test data, or similar data produced for this contract, when the study, analysis, test, or similar work was specified as an element of performance;

(iii) Created exclusively with Government funds in the performance of a contract that does not require the development, manufacture, construction, or production of items, components, or processes;

(iv) Form, fit, and function data;

(v) Necessary for installation, operation, maintenance, or training purposes (other than detailed manufacturing or process data);

(vi) Corrections or changes to technical data furnished to the Contractor by the Government;

(vii) Otherwise publicly available or have been released or disclosed by the Contractor or subcontractor without restrictions on further use, release or disclosure, other than a release or disclosure resulting from the sale, transfer, or other assignment of interest in the technical data to another party or the sale or transfer of some or all of a business entity or its assets to another party;

(viii) Data in which the Government has obtained unlimited rights under another Government contract or as a result of negotiations; or

(ix) Data furnished to the Government, under this or any other Government contract or subcontract thereunder, with—

(A) Government purpose license rights or limited rights and the restrictive condition(s) has/have expired; or

(B) Government purpose rights and the Contractor's exclusive right to use such data for commercial purposes has expired.

(2) *Government purpose rights.*

(i) The Government shall have government purpose rights for a five-year period, or such other period as may be negotiated, in technical data—

(A) That pertain to items, components, or processes developed with mixed funding except when the Government is entitled to unlimited rights in such data as provided in paragraphs (b)(1)(ii) and (b)(1)(iv) through (b)(ix) of this clause; or

(B) Created with mixed funding in the performance of a contract that does not require the development, manufacture, construction, or production of items, components, or processes.

(ii) The five-year period, or such other period as may have been negotiated, shall commence upon execution of the contract, subcontract, letter contract (or similar contractual instrument), contract modification, or option exercise that required development of the items, components, or processes or creation of the data described in paragraph (b)(2)(i)(B) of this clause. Upon expiration of the five-year or other negotiated period, the Government shall have unlimited rights in the technical data.

(iii) The Government shall not release or disclose technical data in which it has government purpose rights unless—

(A) Prior to release or disclosure, the intended recipient is subject to the non-disclosure agreement at 227.7103-7 of the Defense Federal Acquisition Regulation Supplement (DFARS); or

(B) The recipient is a Government contractor receiving access to the data for performance of a Government contract that contains the clause at DFARS 252.227-7025, Limitations on the Use or Disclosure of Government-Furnished Information Marked with Restrictive Legends.

(iv) The Contractor has the exclusive right, including the right to license others, to use technical data in which the Government has obtained government purpose rights under this contract for any commercial purpose during the time period specified in the government purpose rights legend prescribed in paragraph (f)(2) of this clause.

(3) *Limited rights.*

(i) Except as provided in paragraphs (b)(1)(ii) and (b)(1)(iv) through (b)(1)(ix) of this clause, the Government shall have limited rights in technical data—

(A) Pertaining to items, components, or processes developed exclusively at private expense and marked with the limited rights legend prescribed in paragraph (f) of this clause; or

(B) Created exclusively at private expense in the performance of a contract that does not require the development, manufacture, construction, or production of items, components, or processes.

(ii) The Government shall require a recipient of limited rights data for emergency repair or overhaul to destroy the data and all copies in its possession promptly following completion of the emergency repair/overhaul and to notify the Contractor that the data have been destroyed.

(iii) The Contractor, its subcontractors, and suppliers are not required to provide the Government additional rights to use, modify, reproduce, release, perform, display, or disclose technical data furnished to the Government with limited rights. However, if the Government desires to obtain additional rights in technical data in which it has limited rights, the Contractor agrees to promptly enter into negotiations with the Contracting Officer to determine whether there are acceptable terms for transferring such rights. All technical data in which the Contractor has granted the Government additional rights shall be listed or described in a license agreement made part of the contract. The license shall enumerate the additional rights granted the Government in such data.

(iv) The Contractor acknowledges that—

(A) Limited rights data are authorized to be released or disclosed to covered Government support contractors;

(B) The Contractor will be notified of such release or disclosure;

(C) The Contractor (or the party asserting restrictions as identified in the limited rights legend) may require each such covered Government support contractor to enter into a non-disclosure agreement directly with the Contractor (or the party asserting restrictions) regarding the covered Government support contractor's use of such data, or alternatively, that the Contractor (or party asserting restrictions) may waive in writing the requirement for a non-disclosure agreement; and

(D) Any such non-disclosure agreement shall address the restrictions on the covered Government support contractor's use of the limited rights data as set forth in the clause at 252.227-7025, Limitations on the Use or Disclosure of Government-Furnished Information Marked with Restrictive Legends. The non-disclosure agreement shall not include any additional terms and conditions unless mutually agreed to by the parties to the non-disclosure agreement.

(4) *Specifically negotiated license rights.*

The standard license rights granted to the Government under paragraphs (b)(1) through (b)(3) of this clause, including the period during which the Government shall have government purpose rights in technical data, may be modified by mutual agreement to provide such rights as the parties consider appropriate but shall not provide the Government lesser rights than are enumerated in paragraph (a)(14) of this clause. Any rights so negotiated shall be identified in a license agreement made part of this contract.

(5) *Prior government rights.*

Technical data that will be delivered, furnished, or otherwise provided to the Government under this contract, in which the Government has previously obtained rights shall be delivered, furnished, or provided with the pre-existing rights, unless—

(i) The parties have agreed otherwise; or

(ii) Any restrictions on the Government's rights to use, modify, reproduce, release, perform, display, or disclose the data have expired or no longer apply.

(6) *Release from liability.*

The Contractor agrees to release the Government from liability for any release or disclosure of technical data made in accordance with paragraph (a)(14) or (b)(2)(iii) of this clause, in accordance with the terms of a license negotiated under paragraph (b)(4) of this clause, or by others to whom the recipient has released or disclosed the data and to seek relief solely from the party who has improperly used, modified, reproduced, released, performed, displayed, or disclosed Contractor data marked with restrictive legends.

(c) *Contractor rights in technical data*. All rights not granted to the Government are retained by the Contractor.

(d) *Third party copyrighted data*. The Contractor shall not, without the written approval of the Contracting Officer, incorporate any copyrighted data in the technical data to be delivered under this contract unless the Contractor is the copyright owner or has obtained for the Government the license rights necessary to perfect a license or licenses in the deliverable data of the appropriate scope set forth in paragraph (b) of this clause, and has affixed a statement of the license or licenses obtained on behalf of the Government and other persons to the data transmittal document.

(e) *Identification and delivery of data to be furnished with restrictions on use, release, or disclosure.*

(1) This paragraph does not apply to restrictions based solely on copyright.

(2) Except as provided in paragraph (e)(3) of this clause, technical data that the Contractor asserts should be furnished to the Government with restrictions on use, release, or disclosure are identified in an attachment to this contract (the Attachment). The Contractor shall not deliver any data with restrictive markings unless the data are listed on the Attachment.

(3) In addition to the assertions made in the Attachment, other assertions may be identified after award when based on new information or inadvertent omissions unless the inadvertent omissions would have materially affected the source selection decision. Such identification and assertion shall be submitted to the Contracting Officer as soon as practicable prior to the scheduled date for delivery of the data, in the following format, and signed by an official authorized to contractually obligate the Contractor: Identification and Assertion of Restrictions on the Government's Use, Release, or Disclosure of Technical Data.

The Contractor asserts for itself, or the persons identified below, that the Government's rights to use, release, or disclose the following technical data should be restricted—

Technical data to be furnished with restrictions [1]	Basis for assertion [2]	Asserted rights category [3]	Name of person asserting restrictions [4]
(LIST) . .	(LIST) .	(LIST) . .	(LIST) .

[1]If the assertion is applicable to items, components or processes developed at private expense, identify both the data and each such items, component, or process.

[2]Generally, the development of an item, component, or process at private expense, either exclusively or partially, is the only basis for asserting restrictions on the Government's rights to use, release, or disclose technical data pertaining to such items, components, or processes. Indicate whether development was exclusively or partially at private expense. If development was not at private expense, enter the specific reason for asserting that the Government's rights should be restricted.

[3]Enter asserted rights category (e.g., government purpose license rights from a prior contract, rights in SBIR data generated under another contract, limited or government purpose rights under this or a prior contract, or specifically negotiated licenses).

[4]Corporation, individual, or other person, as appropriate.

Date ______________

Printed Name and Title ______________

____

Signature ______________

(End of identification and assertion)

(4) When requested by the Contracting Officer, the Contractor shall provide sufficient information to enable the Contracting Officer to evaluate the Contractor's assertions. The Contracting Officer reserves the

right to add the Contractor's assertions to the Attachment and validate any listed assertion, at a later date, in accordance with the procedures of the Validation of Restrictive Markings on Technical Data clause of this contract.

(f) *Marking requirements*. The Contractor, and its subcontractors or suppliers, may only assert restrictions on the Government's rights to use, modify, reproduce, release, perform, display, or disclose technical data to be delivered under this contract by marking the deliverable data subject to restriction. Except as provided in paragraph (f)(5) of this clause, only the following legends are authorized under this contract: the government purpose rights legend at paragraph (f)(2) of this clause; the limited rights legend at paragraph (f)(3) of this clause; or the special license rights legend at paragraph (f)(4) of this clause; and/or a notice of copyright as prescribed under 17 U.S.C. 401 or 402.

(1) *General marking instructions*. The Contractor, or its subcontractors or suppliers, shall conspicuously and legibly mark the appropriate legend on all technical data that qualify for such markings. The authorized legends shall be placed on the transmittal document or storage container and, for printed material, each page of the printed material containing technical data for which restrictions are asserted. When only portions of a page of printed material are subject to the asserted restrictions, such portions shall be identified by circling, underscoring, with a note, or other appropriate identifier. Technical data transmitted directly from one computer or computer terminal to another shall contain a notice of asserted restrictions. Reproductions of technical data or any portions thereof subject to asserted restrictions shall also reproduce the asserted restrictions.

(2) *Government purpose rights markings*. Data delivered or otherwise furnished to the Government with government purpose rights shall be marked as follows:

Government Purpose Rights

Contract No. ______

Contractor Name ______

Contractor Address ______

______

Expiration Date ______

The Government's rights to use, modify, reproduce, release, perform, display, or disclose these technical data are restricted by paragraph (b)(2) of the Rights in Technical Data—Noncommercial Items clause contained in the above identified contract. No restrictions apply after the expiration date shown above. Any reproduction of technical data or portions thereof marked with this legend must also reproduce the markings.

(End of legend)

(3) *Limited rights markings*. Data delivered or otherwise furnished to the Government with limited rights shall be marked with the following legend:

Limited Rights

Contract No. ______

Contractor Name ______

Contractor Address ______

______

The Government's rights to use, modify, reproduce, release, perform, display, or disclose these technical data are restricted by paragraph (b)(3) of the Rights in Technical Data—Noncommercial Items clause contained in the above identified contract. Any reproduction of technical data or portions thereof marked with this legend must also reproduce the markings. Any person, other than the Government, who has been provided access to such data must promptly notify the above named Contractor.

(End of legend)

(4) *Special license rights markings*. (i) Data in which the Government's rights stem from a specifically negotiated license shall be marked with the following legend:

Special License Rights

The Government's rights to use, modify, reproduce, release, perform, display, or disclose these data are restricted by Contract No. ___ (Insert contract number) ___, License No. ___ (Insert license identifier) ___. Any reproduction of technical data or portions thereof marked with this legend must also reproduce the markings.

(End of legend)

(ii) For purposes of this clause, special licenses do not include government purpose license rights acquired under a prior contract (see paragraph (b)(5) of this clause).

(5) *Pre-existing data markings.* If the terms of a prior contract or license permitted the Contractor to restrict the Government's rights to use, modify, reproduce, release, perform, display, or disclose technical data deliverable under this contract, and those restrictions are still applicable, the Contractor may mark such data with the appropriate restrictive legend for which the data qualified under the prior contract or license. The marking procedures in paragraph (f)(1) of this clause shall be followed.

(g) *Contractor procedures and records.* Throughout performance of this contract, the Contractor and its subcontractors or suppliers that will deliver technical data with other than unlimited rights, shall—

(1) Have, maintain, and follow written procedures sufficient to assure that restrictive markings are used only when authorized by the terms of this clause; and

(2) Maintain records sufficient to justify the validity of any restrictive markings on technical data delivered under this contract.

(h) *Removal of unjustified and nonconforming markings.*—(1) *Unjustified technical data markings.* The rights and obligations of the parties regarding the validation of restrictive markings on technical data furnished or to be furnished under this contract are contained in the Validation of Restrictive Markings on Technical Data clause of this contract. Notwithstanding any provision of this contract concerning inspection and acceptance, the Government may ignore or, at the Contractor's expense, correct or strike a marking if, in accordance with the procedures in the Validation of Restrictive Markings on Technical Data clause of this contract, a restrictive marking is determined to be unjustified.

(2) *Nonconforming technical data markings.* A nonconforming marking is a marking placed on technical data delivered or otherwise furnished to the Government under this contract that is not in the format authorized by this contract. Correction of nonconforming markings is not subject to the Validation of Restrictive Markings on Technical Data clause of this contract. If the Contracting Officer notifies the Contractor of a nonconforming marking and the Contractor fails to remove or correct such marking within sixty (60) days, the Government may ignore or, at the Contractor's expense, remove or correct any nonconforming marking.

(i) *Relation to patents.* Nothing contained in this clause shall imply a license to the Government under any patent or be construed as affecting the scope of any license or other right otherwise granted to the Government under any patent.

(j) *Limitation on charges for rights in technical data.*

(1) The Contractor shall not charge to this contract any cost, including, but not limited to, license fees, royalties, or similar charges, for rights in technical data to be delivered under this contract when

(i) The Government has acquired, by any means, the same or greater rights in the data; or

(ii) The data are available to the public without restrictions.

(2) The limitation in paragraph (j)(1) of this clause—

(i) Includes costs charged by a subcontractor or supplier, at any tier, or costs incurred by the Contractor to acquire rights in subcontractor or supplier technical data, if the subcontractor or supplier has been paid for such rights under any other Government contract or under a license conveying the rights to the Government; and

(ii) Does not include the reasonable costs of reproducing, handling, or mailing the documents or other media in which the technical data will be delivered.

(k) *Applicability to subcontractors or suppliers.*

(1) The Contractor shall ensure that the rights afforded its subcontractors and suppli-

ers under 10 U.S.C. 2320, 10 U.S.C. 2321, and the identification, assertion, and delivery processes of paragraph (e) of this clause are recognized and protected.

(2) Whenever any technical data for noncommercial items, or for commercial items developed in any part at Government expense, is to be obtained from a subcontractor or supplier for delivery to the Government under this contract, the Contractor shall use this same clause in the subcontract or other contractual instrument, including subcontracts or other contractual instruments for commercial items, and require its subcontractors or suppliers to do so, without alteration, except to identify the parties. This clause will govern the technical data pertaining to noncommercial items or to any portion of a commercial item that was developed in any part at Government expense, and the clause at 252.227-7015 will govern the technical data pertaining to any portion of a commercial item that was developed exclusively at private expense. No other clause shall be used to enlarge or diminish the Government's, the Contractor's, or a higher-tier subcontractor's or supplier's rights in a subcontractor's or supplier's technical data.

(3) Technical data required to be delivered by a subcontractor or supplier shall normally be delivered to the next higher-tier contractor, subcontractor, or supplier. However, when there is a requirement in the prime contract for data which may be submitted with other than unlimited rights by a subcontractor or supplier, then said subcontractor or supplier may fulfill its requirement by submitting such data directly to the Government, rather than through a higher-tier contractor, subcontractor, or supplier.

(4) The Contractor and higher-tier subcontractors or suppliers shall not use their power to award contracts as economic leverage to obtain rights in technical data from their subcontractors or suppliers.

(5) In no event shall the Contractor use its obligation to recognize and protect subcontractor or supplier rights in technical data as an excuse for failing to satisfy its contractual obligations to the Government.

(End of clause)

ALTERNATE I (JUN 2006)

As prescribed in 227.7103-6(b)(1), add the following paragraph (l) to the basic clause:

(l) *Publication for sale.*

(1) This paragraph only applies to technical data in which the Government has obtained unlimited rights or a license to make an unrestricted release of technical data.

(2) The Government shall not publish a deliverable technical data item or items identified in this contract as being subject to paragraph (l) of this clause or authorize others to publish such data on its behalf if, prior to publication for sale by the Government and within twenty-four (24) months following the date specified in this contract for delivery of such data or the removal of any national security or export control restrictions, whichever is later, the Contractor publishes that item or items for sale and promptly notifies the Contracting Officer of such publication(s). Any such publication shall include a notice identifying the number of this contract and the Government's rights in the published data.

(3) This limitation on the Government's right to publish for sale shall continue as long as the data are reasonably available to the public for purchase.

ALTERNATE II (MAR 2011)

As prescribed in 227.7103-6(b)(2), add the following paragraphs (a)(17) and (b)(7) to the basic clause:

(a)(17) *Vessel design* means the design of a vessel, boat, or craft, and its components, including the hull, decks, superstructure, and the exterior surface shape of all external shipboard equipment and systems. The term includes designs covered by 10 U.S.C. 7317, and designs protectable under 17 U.S.C. 1301, *et seq.*

(b)(7) *Vessel designs.* For a vessel design (including a vessel design embodied in a useful article) that is developed or delivered under this contract, the Government shall have the right to make and have made any useful article that embodies the vessel design, to import the article, to sell the article, and to distribute the article for sale or to use the article in trade, to the same extent that the Government is granted rights in the technical data pertaining to the vessel design.

[DAC 91-8, 60 FR 33464, 6/28/95, effective 6/30/95; DAC 91-9, 60 FR 61586, 11/30/95, effective 11/30/95; Interim rule, 74 FR 61043, 11/23/2009, effective 11/23/2009; Final rule, 75 FR 54527, 9/8/2010, effective 9/8/2010; Interim rule, 76 FR 11363, 3/2/2011, effective 3/2/2011; Final rule 76 FR 58144, 9/20/2011, effective 9/20/2011; Final rule, 77 FR 10976, 2/24/2012, effective 2/24/2012; Final rule, 78 FR 30233, 5/22/2013, effective 5/22/2013; Final rule, 78 FR 37980, 6/25/2013, effective 6/25/2013; Interim rule, 79 FR 11337, 2/28/2014, effective 2/28/2014; Final rule, 81 FR 28724, 5/10/2016, effective 5/10/2016]

252.227-7014 Rights in noncommercial computer software and noncommercial computer software documentation.

As prescribed in 227.7203-6(a)(1), use the following clause.

RIGHTS IN NONCOMMERCIAL COMPUTER SOFTWARE AND NONCOMMERCIAL COMPUTER SOFTWARE DOCUMENTATION (FEB 2014)

(a) *Definitions*. As used in this clause—

(1) *Commercial computer software* means software developed or regularly used for nongovernmental purposes which—

(i) Has been sold, leased, or licensed to the public;

(ii) Has been offered for sale, lease, or license to the public;

(iii) Has not been offered, sold, leased, or licensed to the public but will be available for commercial sale, lease, or license in time to satisfy the delivery requirements of this contract; or

(iv) Satisfies a criterion expressed in paragraph (a)(1) (i), (ii), or (iii) of this clause and would require only minor modification to meet the requirements of this contract.

(2) *Computer database* means a collection of recorded data in a form capable of being processed by a computer. The term does not include computer software.

(3) *Computer program* means a set of instructions, rules, or routines, recorded in a form that is capable of causing a computer to perform a specific operation or series of operations.

(4) *Computer software* means computer programs, source code, source code listings, object code listings, design details, algorithms, processes, flow charts, formulae, and related material that would enable the software to be reproduced, recreated, or recompiled. Computer software does not include computer databases or computer software documentation.

(5) *Computer software documentation* means owner's manuals, user's manuals, installation instructions, operating instructions, and other similar items, regardless of storage medium, that explain the capabilities of the computer software or provide instructions for using the software.

(6) *Covered Government support contractor* means a contractor (other than a litigation support contractor covered by 252.204-7014) under a contract, the primary purpose of which is to furnish independent and impartial advice or technical assistance directly to the Government in support of the Government's management and oversight of a program or effort (rather than to directly furnish an end item or service to accomplish a program or effort), provided that the contractor—

(i) Is not affiliated with the prime contractor or a first-tier subcontractor on the program or effort, or with any direct competitor of such prime contractor or any such first-tier subcontractor in furnishing end items or services of the type developed or produced on the program or effort; and

(ii) Receives access to technical data or computer software for performance of a Government contract that contains the clause at 252.227-7025, Limitations on the Use or Disclosure of Government-Furnished Information Marked with Restrictive Legends.

(7) *Developed* means that—

(i) A computer program has been successfully operated in a computer and tested to the extent sufficient to demonstrate to reasonable persons skilled in the art that the program can reasonably be expected to perform its intended purpose;

(ii) Computer software, other than computer programs, has been tested or analyzed to the extent sufficient to demonstrate to reasonable persons skilled in the art that the software can reasonably be expected to perform its intended purpose; or

(iii) Computer software documentation required to be delivered under a contract has been written, in any medium, in sufficient detail to comply with requirements under that contract.

(8) *Developed exclusively at private expense* means development was accomplished entirely with costs charged to indirect cost pools, costs not allocated to a government contract, or any combination thereof.

(i) Private expense determinations should be made at the lowest practicable level.

(ii) Under fixed-price contracts, when total costs are greater than the firm-fixed-price or ceiling price of the contract, the additional development costs necessary to complete development shall not be considered when determining whether development was at government, private, or mixed expense.

(9) *Developed exclusively with government funds* means development was not accomplished exclusively or partially at private expense.

(10) *Developed with mixed funding* means development was accomplished partially with costs charged to indirect cost pools and/or costs not allocated to a government contract, and partially with costs charged directly to a government contract.

(11) *Government purpose* means any activity in which the United States Government is a party, including cooperative agreements with international or multi-national defense organizations or sales or transfers by the United States Government to foreign governments or international organizations. Government purposes include competitive procurement, but do not include the rights to use, modify, reproduce, release, perform, display, or disclose computer software or computer software documentation for commercial purposes or authorize others to do so.

(12) *Government purpose rights* means the rights to—

(i) Use, modify, reproduce, release, perform, display, or disclose computer software or computer software documentation within the Government without restriction; and

(ii) Release or disclose computer software or computer software documentation outside the Government and authorize persons to whom release or disclosure has been made to use, modify, reproduce, release, perform, display, or disclose the software or documentation for United States government purposes.

(13) *Minor modification* means a modification that does not significantly alter the nongovernmental function or purpose of the software or is of the type customarily provided in the commercial marketplace.

(14) *Noncommercial computer software* means software that does not qualify as commercial computer software under paragraph (a)(1) of this clause.

(15) *Restricted rights* apply only to noncommercial computer software and mean the Government's rights to—

(i) Use a computer program with one computer at one time. The program may not be accessed by more than one terminal or central processing unit or time shared unless otherwise permitted by this contract;

(ii) Transfer a computer program to another Government agency without the further permission of the Contractor if the transferor destroys all copies of the program and related computer software documentation in its possession and notifies the licensor of the transfer. Transferred programs remain subject to the provisions of this clause;

(iii) Make the minimum number of copies of the computer software required for safekeeping (archive), backup, or modification purposes;

(iv) Modify computer software provided that the Government may—

(A) Use the modified software only as provided in paragraphs (a)(15)(i) and (iii) of this clause; and

(B) Not release or disclose the modified software except as provided in paragraphs (a)(15)(ii), (v), (vi) and (vii) of this clause;

(v) Permit contractors or subcontractors performing service contracts (see 37.101 of the Federal Acquisition Regulation) in support of this or a related contract to use computer software to diagnose and correct deficiencies in a computer program, to modify computer software to enable a computer program to be combined with, adapted to, or merged with other computer programs or when necessary to respond to urgent tactical situations, provided that—

(A) The Government notifies the party which has granted restricted rights that a release or disclosure to particular contractors or subcontractors was made;

(B) Such contractors or subcontractors are subject to the use and non-disclosure agreement at 227.7103-7 of the Defense Federal Acquisition Regulation Supplement (DFARS) or are Government contractors receiving access to the software for performance of a Government contract that contains the clause at DFARS 252.227-7025, Limitations on the Use or Disclosure of Government-Furnished Information Marked with Restrictive Legends;

(C) The Government shall not permit the recipient to decompile, disassemble, or reverse engineer the software, or use software decompiled, disassembled, or reverse engineered by the Government pursuant to paragraph (a)(15)(iv) of this clause, for any other purpose; and

(D) Such use is subject to the limitations in paragraphs (a)(15)(i) through (iii) of this clause;

(vi) Permit contractors or subcontractors performing emergency repairs or overhaul of items or components of items procured under this or a related contract to use the computer software when necessary to perform the repairs or overhaul, or to modify the computer software to reflect the repairs or overhaul made, provided that—

(A) The intended recipient is subject to the use and non-disclosure agreement at DFARS 227.7103-7 or is a Government contractor receiving access to the software for performance of a Government contract that contains the clause at DFARS 252.227-7025, Limitations on the Use or Disclosure of Government-Furnished Information Marked with Restrictive Legends;

(B) The Government shall not permit the recipient to decompile, disassemble, or reverse engineer the software, or use software decompiled, disassembled, or reverse engineered by the Government pursuant to paragraph (a)(15)(iv) of this clause, for any other purpose; and

(C) Such use is subject to the limitations in paragraphs (a)(15)(i) through (iii) of this clause; and

(vii) Permit covered Government support contractors in the performance of covered Government support contracts that contain the clause at 252.227-7025, Limitations on the Use or Disclosure of Government-Furnished Information Marked with Restrictive Legends, to use, modify, reproduce, perform, display, or release or disclose the computer software to a person authorized to receive restricted rights computer software, provided that—

(A) The Government shall not permit the covered Government support contractor to decompile, disassemble, or reverse engineer the software, or use software decompiled, disassembled, or reverse engineered by the Government pursuant to paragraph (a)(15)(iv) of this clause, for any other purpose; and

(B) Such use is subject to the limitations in paragraphs (a)(15)(i) through (iv) of this clause.

(16) *Unlimited rights* means rights to use, modify, reproduce, release, perform, display, or disclose computer software or computer software documentation in whole or in part, in any manner and for any purpose whatsoever, and to have or authorize others to do so.

(b) *Rights in computer software or computer software documentation*. The Contractor grants or shall obtain for the Government the following royalty free, world-wide, nonexclusive, irrevocable license rights in noncommercial computer software or computer software documentation. All rights not granted to the Government are retained by the Contractor.

(1) *Unlimited rights*. The Government shall have unlimited rights in—

(i) Computer software developed exclusively with Government funds;

(ii) Computer software documentation required to be delivered under this contract;

(iii) Corrections or changes to computer software or computer software documentation furnished to the Contractor by the Government;

(iv) Computer software or computer software documentation that is otherwise publicly available or has been released or disclosed by the Contractor or subcontractor without restriction on further use, release or disclosure, other than a release or disclosure resulting from the sale, transfer, or other assignment of interest in the software to another party or the sale or transfer of some or all of a business entity or its assets to another party;

(v) Computer software or computer software documentation obtained with unlimited rights under another Government contract or as a result of negotiations; or

(vi) Computer software or computer software documentation furnished to the Government, under this or any other Government contract or subcontract thereunder with—

(A) Restricted rights in computer software, limited rights in technical data, or government purpose license rights and the restrictive conditions have expired; or

(B) Government purpose rights and the Contractor's exclusive right to use such software or documentation for commercial purposes has expired.

(2) *Government purpose rights*.

(i) Except as provided in paragraph (b)(1) of this clause, the Government shall have government purpose rights in computer software development with mixed funding.

(ii) Government purpose rights shall remain in effect for a period of five years unless a different period has been negotiated. Upon expiration of the five-year or other negotiated period, the Government shall have unlimited rights in the computer software or computer software documentation. The government purpose rights period shall commence upon execution of the contract, subcontract, letter contract (or similar contractual instrument), contract modification, or option exercise that required development of the computer software.

(iii) The Government shall not release or disclose computer software in which it has government purpose rights to any other person unless—

(A) Prior to release or disclosure, the intended recipient is subject to the use and non-disclosure agreement at DFARS 227.7103-7; or

(B) The recipient is a Government contractor receiving access to the software or documentation for performance of a Government contract that contains the clause at DFARS 252.227-7025, Limitations on the Use or Disclosure of Government Furnished Information Marked with Restrictive Legends.

(3) *Restricted rights*.

(i) The Government shall have restricted rights in noncommercial computer software required to be delivered or otherwise provided to the Government under this contract that were developed exclusively at private expense.

(ii) The Contractor, its subcontractors, or suppliers are not required to provide the Government additional rights in noncommercial computer software delivered or otherwise provided to the Government with restricted rights. However, if the Government desires to obtain additional rights in such software, the Contractor agrees to promptly enter into negotiations with the Contracting Officer to determine whether there are acceptable terms for transferring such rights. All noncommercial computer software in which the Contractor has granted the Government additional rights shall be listed or described in a license agreement made part of the contract (see paragraph (b)(4) of this clause). The license shall enumerate the additional rights granted the Government.

(iii) The Contractor acknowledges that—

(A) Restricted rights computer software is authorized to be released or disclosed to covered Government support contractors;

(B) The Contractor will be notified of such release or disclosure;

(C) The Contractor (or the party asserting restrictions, as identified in the restricted rights legend) may require each such covered Government support contractor to enter into a non-disclosure agreement directly with the Contractor (or the party asserting restrictions) regarding the covered Government support contractor's use of such software, or alternatively, that the Contractor (or party asserting restrictions) may waive in writing the requirement for a non-disclosure agreement; and

(D) Any such non-disclosure agreement shall address the restrictions on the covered Government support contractor's use of the restricted rights software as set forth in the clause at 252.227-7025, Limitations on the Use or Disclosure of Government-Furnished Information Marked with Restrictive Legends. The non-disclosure agreement shall not include any additional terms and conditions unless mutually agreed to by the parties to the non-disclosure agreement.

(4) *Specifically negotiated license rights.* (i) The standard license rights granted to the Government under paragraphs (b)(1) through (b)(3) of this clause, including the period during which the Government shall have government purpose rights in computer software, may be modified by mutual agreement to provide such rights as the parties consider appropriate but shall not provide the Government lesser rights in computer software than are enumerated in paragraph (a)(15) of this clause or lesser rights in computer software documentation than are enumerated in paragraph (a)(14) of the Rights in Technical Data—Noncommercial Items clause of this contract.

(ii) Any rights so negotiated shall be identified in a license agreement made part of this contract.

(5) *Prior government rights.* Computer software or computer software documentation that will be delivered, furnished, or otherwise provided to the Government under this contract, in which the Government has previously obtained rights shall be delivered, furnished, or provided with the pre-existing rights, unless—

(i) The parties have agreed otherwise; or

(ii) Any restrictions on the Government's rights to use, modify, reproduce, release, perform, display, or disclose the data have expired or no longer apply.

(6) *Release from liability.* The Contractor agrees to release the Government from liability for any release or disclosure of computer software made in accordance with paragraph (a)(15) or (b)(2)(iii) of this clause, in accordance with the terms of a license negotiated under paragraph (b)(4) of this clause, or by others to whom the recipient has released or disclosed the software, and to seek relief solely from the party who has improperly used, modified, reproduced, released, performed, displayed, or disclosed Contractor software marked with restrictive legends.

(c) *Rights in derivative computer software or computer software documentation.* The Government shall retain its rights in the unchanged portions of any computer software or computer software documentation delivered under this contract that the Contractor uses to prepare, or includes in, derivative computer software or computer software documentation.

(d) *Third party copyrighted computer software or computer software documentation.* The Contractor shall not, without the written approval of the Contracting Officer, incorporate any copyrighted computer software or computer software documentation in the software or documentation to be delivered under this contract unless the Contractor is the copyright owner or has obtained for the

Government the license rights necessary to perfect a license or licenses in the deliverable software or documentation of the appropriate scope set forth in paragraph (b) of this clause, and prior to delivery of such—

(1) Computer software, has provided a statement of the license rights obtained in a form acceptable to the Contracting Officer; or

(2) Computer software documentation, has affixed to the transmittal document a statement of the license rights obtained.

(e) *Identification and delivery of computer software and computer software documentation to be furnished with restrictions on use, release, or disclosure.*

(1) This paragraph does not apply to restrictions based solely on copyright.

(2) Except as provided in paragraph (e)(3) of this clause, computer software that the Contractor asserts should be furnished to the Government with restrictions on use, release, or disclosure is identified in an attachment to this contract (the Attachment). The Contractor shall not deliver any software with restrictive markings unless the software is listed on the Attachment.

(3) In addition to the assertions made in the Attachment, other assertions may be identified after award when based on new information or inadvertent omissions unless the inadvertent omissions would have materially affected the source selection decision. Such identification and assertion shall be submitted to the Contracting Officer as soon as practicable prior to the scheduled data for delivery of the software, in the following format, and signed by an official authorized to contractually obligate the Contractor: Identification and Assertion of Restrictions on the Government's Use, Release, or Disclosure of Computer Software.

The Contractor asserts for itself, or the persons identified below, that the Government's rights to use, release, or disclose the following computer software should be restricted:

Computer Software to be Furnished With Restrictions*	Basis for Assertion**	Asserted Rights Category***	Name of Person Asserting Restrictions****
(LIST)	(LIST)	(LIST)	(LIST)

* Generally, development at private expense, either exclusively or partially, is the only basis for asserting restrictions on the Government's rights to use, release, or disclose computer software.

** Indicate whether development was exclusively or partially at private expense. If development was not a private expense, enter the specific reason for asserting that the Government's rights should be restricted.

*** Enter asserted rights category (e.g., restricted or government purpose rights in computer software, government purpose license rights from a prior contract, rights in SBIR software generated under another contract, or specifically negotiated licenses).

**** Corporation, individual, or other person, as appropriate.

Date ______________________

Printed Name and Title ______________________

____

Signature ______________________

(End of identification and assertion)

(4) When requested by the Contracting Officer, the Contractor shall provide sufficient information to enable the Contracting Officer to evaluate the Contractor's assertions. The Contracting Officer reserves the right to add the Contractor's assertions to the Attachment and validate any listed assertion, at a later date, in accordance with the procedures of the Validation of Asserted Restrictions—Computer Software clause of this contract.

(f) *Marking requirements.* The Contractor, and its subcontractors or suppliers, may only assert restrictions on the Government's rights to use, modify, reproduce, release, perform, display, or disclose computer software by marking the deliverable software or documentation subject to restriction. Except as provided in paragraph (f)(5) of this clause, only the following legends are authorized under this contract; the government purpose rights legend at paragraph (f)(2) of this clause; the restricted rights legend at paragraph (f)(3) of this clause; or the special license rights legend at paragraph (f)(4) of this clause; and/or a notice of copyright as prescribed under 17 U.S.C. 401 or 402.

(1) *General marking instructions*. The Contractor, or its subcontractors or suppliers, shall conspicuously and legibly mark the appropriate legend on all computer software that qualify for such markings. The authorized legends shall be placed on the transmitted document or software storage container and each page, or portions thereof, of printed material containing computer software for which restrictions are asserted. Computer software transmitted directly from one computer or computer terminal to another shall contain a notice of asserted restrictions. However, instructions that interfere with or delay the operation of computer software in order to display a restrictive rights legend or other license statement at any time prior to or during use of the computer software, or otherwise cause such interference or delay, shall not be inserted in software that will or might be used in combat or situations that simulate combat conditions, unless the Contracting Officer's written permission to deliver such software has been obtained prior to delivery. Reproductions of computer software or any portions thereof subject to asserted restrictions, shall also reproduce the asserted restrictions.

(2) *Government purpose rights markings*. Computer software delivered or otherwise furnished to the Government with government purpose rights shall be marked as follows:

GOVERNMENT PURPOSE RIGHTS

Contract No. __________

Contractor Name __________

Contractor Address __________

____

Expiration Date __________

The Government's rights to use, modify, reproduce, release, perform, display, or disclose this software are restricted by paragraph (b)(2) of the Rights in Noncommercial Computer Software and Noncommercial Computer Software Documentation clause contained in the above identified contract. No restrictions apply after the expiration date shown above. Any reproduction of the software or portions thereof marked with this legend must also reproduce the markings.

(End of legend)

(3) *Restricted rights markings*. Software delivered or otherwise furnished to the Government with restricted rights shall be marked with the following legend:

RESTRICTED RIGHTS

Contract No. __________

Contractor Name __________

Contractor Address __________

____

The Government's rights to use, modify, reproduce, release, perform, display, or disclose this software are restricted by paragraph (b)(3) of the Rights in Noncommercial Computer Software and Noncommercial Computer Software Documentation clause contained in the above identified contract. Any reproduction of computer software or portions thereof marked with this legend must also reproduce the markings. Any person, other than the Government, who has been provided access to such software must promptly notify the above named Contractor.

(End of legend)

(4) *Special license rights markings*. (i) Computer software or computer documentation in which the Government's rights stem from a specifically negotiated license shall be marked with the following legend:

SPECIAL LICENSE RIGHTS

The Government's rights to use, modify, reproduce, release, perform, display, or disclose this software are restricted by Contract No. ___ (Insert contract number) ___, License No. ___ (Insert license identifier) ___. Any reproduction of computer software, computer software documentation, or portions thereof marked with this legend must also reproduce the markings.

(End of legend)

(ii) For purposes of this clause, special licenses do not include government purpose license rights acquired under a prior contract (see paragraph (b)(5) of this clause).

(5) *Pre-existing markings.* If the terms of a prior contract or license permitted the Contractor to restrict the Government's rights to use, modify, release, perform, display, or disclose computer software or computer software documentation and those restrictions are still applicable, the Contractor may mark such software or documentation with the appropriate restrictive legend for which the software qualified under the prior contract or license. The marking procedures in paragraph (f)(1) of this clause shall be followed.

(g) *Contractor procedures and records.* Throughout performance of this contract, the Contractor and its subcontractors or suppliers that will deliver computer software or computer software documentation with other than unlimited rights, shall—

(1) Have, maintain, and follow written procedures sufficient to assure that restrictive markings are used only when authorized by the terms of this clause; and

(2) Maintain records sufficient to justify the validity of any restrictive markings on computer software or computer software documentation delivered under this contract.

(h) *Removal of unjustified and nonconforming markings.*—(1) *Unjustified computer software or computer software documentation markings.* The rights and obligations of the parties regarding the validation of restrictive markings on computer software or computer software documentation furnished or to be furnished under this contract are contained in the Validation of Asserted Restrictions—Computer Software and the Validation of Restrictive Markings on Technical Data clauses of this contract, respectively. Notwithstanding any provision of this contract concerning inspection and acceptance, the Government may ignore or, at the Contractor's expense, correct or strike a marking if, in accordance with the procedures of those clauses, a restrictive marking is determined to be unjustified.

(2) *Nonconforming computer software or computer software documentation markings.* A nonconforming marking is a marking placed on computer software or computer software documentation delivered or otherwise furnished to the Government under this contract that is not in the format authorized by this contract. Correction of nonconforming markings is not subject to the Validation of Asserted Restrictions—Computer Software or the Validation of Restrictive Markings on Technical Data clause of this contract. If the Contracting Officer notifies the Contractor of a nonconforming marking or markings and the Contractor fails to remove or correct such markings within sixty (60) days, the Government may ignore or, at the Contractor's expense, remove or correct any nonconforming markings.

(i) *Relation to patents.* Nothing contained in this clause shall imply a license to the Government under any patent or be construed as affecting the scope of any license or other right otherwise granted to the Government under any patent.

(j) *Limitation on charges for rights in computer software or computer software documentation.*

(1) The Contractor shall not charge to this contract any cost, including but not limited to license fees, royalties, or similar charges, for rights in computer software or computer software documentation to be delivered under this contract when—

(i) The Government has acquired, by any means, the same or greater rights in the software or documentation; or

(ii) The software or documentation are available to the public without restrictions.

(2) The limitation in paragraph (j)(1) of this clause—

(i) Includes costs charged by a subcontractor or supplier, at any tier, or costs incurred by the Contractor to acquire rights in subcontractor or supplier computer software or computer software documentation, if the subcontractor or supplier has been paid for such rights under any other Government contract or under a license conveying the rights to the Government; and

(ii) Does not include the reasonable costs of reproducing, handling, or mailing the documents or other media in which the software or documentation will be delivered.

(k) *Applicability to subcontractors or suppliers.*

(1) Whenever any noncommercial computer software or computer software documentation is to be obtained from a subcontractor or supplier for delivery to the Government under this contract, the Contractor shall use this same clause in its subcontracts or other contractual instruments, and require its subcontractors or suppliers to do so, without alteration, except to identify the parties. No other clause shall be used to enlarge or diminish the Government's, the Contractor's, or a higher tier subcontractor's or supplier's rights in a subcontractor's or supplier's computer software or computer software documentation.

(2) The Contractor and higher tier subcontractors or suppliers shall not use their power to award contracts as economic leverage to obtain rights in computer software or computer software documentation from their subcontractors or suppliers.

(3) The Contractor shall ensure that subcontractor or supplier rights are recognized and protected in the identification, assertion, and delivery processes required by paragraph (e) of this clause.

(4) In no event shall the Contractor use its obligation to recognize and protect subcontractor or supplier rights in computer software or computer software documentation as an excuse for failing to satisfy its contractual obligation to the Government.

(End of clause)

ALTERNATE I (JUN 1995)

As prescribed in 227.7203-6(a)(2), add the following paragraph (l) to the basic clause:

(l) *Publication for sale.*

(1) This paragraph only applies to computer software or computer software documentation in which the Government has obtained unlimited rights or a license to make an unrestricted release of the software or documentation.

(2) The Government shall not publish a deliverable item or items of computer software or computer software documentation identified in this contract as being subject to paragraph (l) of this clause or authorize others to publish such software or documentation on its behalf if, prior to publication for sale by the Government and within twenty-four (24) months following the date specified in this contract for delivery of such software or documentation, or the removal of any national security or export control restrictions, whichever is later, the Contractor publishes that item or items for sale and promptly notifies the Contracting Officer of such publication(s). Any such publication shall include a notice identifying the number of this contract and the Government's rights in the published software or documentation.

(3) This limitation on the Government's rights to publish for sale shall continue as long as the software or documentation are reasonably available to the public for purchase.

[DAC 91-8, 60 FR 33464, 6/28/95, effective 6/30/95; Interim rule, 76 FR 11363, 3/2/2011, effective 3/2/2011; Final rule, 77 FR 10976, 2/24/2012, effective 2/24/2012; Final rule, 78 FR 30233, 5/22/2013, effective 5/22/2013; Correction, 78 FR 33994, 6/6/2013, effective 6/6/2013; Interim rule, 79 FR 11337, 2/28/2014, effective 2/28/2014; Final rule, 81 FR 28724, 5/10/2016, effective 5/10/2016]

252.227-7015 Technical data—Commercial items.

As prescribed in 227.7102-4 (a)(1), use the following clause:

TECHNICAL DATA—COMMERCIAL ITEMS (FEB 2014)

(a) *Definitions.* As used in this clause—

(1) *Commercial item* does not include commercial computer software.

(2) *Covered Government support contractor* means a contractor (other than a litigation support contractor covered by 252.204-7014) under a contract, the primary purpose of which is to furnish independent and impar-

tial advice or technical assistance directly to the Government in support of the Government's management and oversight of a program or effort (rather than to directly furnish an end item or service to accomplish a program or effort), provided that the contractor—

(i) Is not affiliated with the prime contractor or a first-tier subcontractor on the program or effort, or with any direct competitor of such prime contractor or any such first-tier subcontractor in furnishing end items or services of the type developed or produced on the program or effort; and

(ii) Receives access to technical data or computer software for performance of a Government contract that contains the clause at 252.227-7025, Limitations on the Use or Disclosure of Government-Furnished Information Marked with Restrictive Legends.

(3) *Form, fit, and function data* means technical data that describes the required overall physical, functional, and performance characteristics (along with the qualification requirements, if applicable) of an item, component, or process to the extent necessary to permit identification of physically and functionally interchangeable items.

(4) The term *item* includes components or processes.

(5) *Technical data* means recorded information, regardless of the form or method of recording, of a scientific or technical nature (including computer software documentation). The term does not include computer software or data incidental to contract administration, such as financial and/or management information.

(b) *License.* (1) The Government shall have the unrestricted right to use, modify, reproduce, release, perform, display, or disclose technical data, and to permit others to do so, that—

(i) Have been provided to the Government or others without restrictions on use, modification, reproduction, release, or further disclosure other than a release or disclosure resulting from the sale, transfer, or other assignment of interest in the technical data to another party or the sale or transfer of some or all of a business entity or its assets to another party;

(ii) Are form, fit, and function data;

(iii) Are a correction or change to technical data furnished to the Contractor by the Government;

(iv) Are necessary for operation, maintenance, installation, or training (other than detailed manufacturing or process data); or

(v) Have been provided to the Government under a prior contract or licensing agreement through which the Government has acquired the rights to use, modify, reproduce, release, perform, display, or disclose the data without restrictions.

(2) Except as provided in paragraph (b)(1) of this clause, the Government may use, modify, reproduce, release, perform, display, or disclose technical data within the Government only. The Government shall not—

(i) Use the technical data to manufacture additional quantities of the commercial items; or

(ii) Release, perform, display, disclose, or authorize use of the technical data outside the Government without the Contractor's written permission unless a release, disclosure, or permitted use is necessary for emergency repair or overhaul of the commercial items furnished under this contract, or for performance of work by covered Government support contractors.

(3) The Contractor acknowledges that—

(i) Technical data covered by paragraph (b)(2) of this clause are authorized to be released or disclosed to covered Government support contractors;

(ii) The Contractor will be notified of such release or disclosure;

(iii) The Contractor (or the party asserting restrictions as identified in a restrictive legend) may require each such covered Government support contractor to enter into a non-disclosure agreement directly with the Contractor (or the party asserting restrictions) regarding the covered Government support contractor's use of such data, or alternatively, that the Contractor (or party asserting restrictions) may waive in writing the requirement for an non-disclosure agreement; and

(iv) Any such non-disclosure agreement shall address the restrictions on the covered Government support contractor's use of the data as set forth in the clause at 252.227-7025, Limitations on the Use or Disclosure of Government-Furnished Information Marked with Restrictive Legends. The non-disclosure agreement shall not include any additional terms and conditions unless mutually agreed to by the parties to the non-disclosure agreement.

(c) *Additional license rights.* The Contractor, its subcontractors, and suppliers are not required to provide the Government additional rights to use, modify, reproduce, release, perform, display, or disclose technical data. However, if the Government desires to obtain additional rights in technical data, the Contractor agrees to promptly enter into negotiations with the Contracting Officer to determine whether there are acceptable terms for transferring such rights. All technical data in which the Contractor has granted the Government additional rights shall be listed or described in a special license agreement made part of this contract. The license shall enumerate the additional rights granted the Government in such data.

(d) *Release from liability.* The Contractor agrees that the Government, and other persons to whom the Government may have released or disclosed technical data delivered or otherwise furnished under this contract, shall have no liability for any release or disclosure of technical data that are not marked to indicate that such data are licensed data subject to use, modification, reproduction, release, performance, display, or disclosure restrictions.

(e) *Applicability to subcontractors or suppliers.*

(1) The Contractor shall recognize and protect the rights afforded its subcontractors and suppliers under 10 U.S.C. 2320 and 10 U.S.C. 2321.

(2) Whenever any technical data related to commercial items developed in any part at private expense will be obtained from a subcontractor or supplier for delivery to the Government under this contract, the Contractor shall use this same clause in the subcontract or other contractual instrument, including subcontracts and other contractual instruments for commercial items, and require its subcontractors or suppliers to do so, without alteration, except to identify the parties. This clause will govern the technical data pertaining to any portion of a commercial item that was developed exclusively at private expense, and the clause at 252.227-7013 will govern the technical data pertaining to any portion of a commercial item that was developed in any part at Government expense.

(End of clause)

ALTERNATE I (DEC 2011)

As prescribed in 227.7102-4(a)(2), add the following paragraphs (a)(6) and (b)(4) to the basic clause:

(a)(6) *Vessel design* means the design of a vessel, boat, or craft, and its components, including the hull, decks, superstructure, and the exterior surface shape of all external shipboard equipment and systems. The term includes designs covered by 10 U.S.C. 7317, and designs protectable under 17 U.S.C. 1301, *et seq.*

(b)(4) *Vessel designs.* For a vessel design (including a vessel design embodied in a useful article) that is developed or delivered under this contract, the Government shall have the right to make and have made any useful article that embodies the vessel design, to import the article, to sell the article, and to distribute the article for sale or to use the article in trade, to the same extent that the Government is granted rights in the technical data pertaining to the vessel design.

[DAC 91-8, 60 FR 33464, 6/28/95, effective 6/30/95; DAC 91-9, 60 FR 61586, 11/30/95, effective 11/30/95; Interim rule, 74 FR 61043, 11/23/2009, effective 11/23/2009; Final rule, 75 FR 54527, 9/8/2010, effective 9/8/2010; Interim rule, 76 FR 11363, 3/2/2011, effective 3/2/2011; Final rule 76 FR 58144, 9/20/2011, effective 9/20/2011; Final rule, 76 FR 76318, 12/7/2011, effective 12/7/2011; Final rule,

78 FR 30233, 5/22/2013, effective 5/22/2013; Final rule, 78 FR 37980, 6/25/2013, effective 6/25/2013; Interim rule, 79 FR 11337, 2/28/2014, effective 2/28/2014; Final rule, 81 FR 28724, 5/10/2016, effective 5/10/2016]

252.227-7016 Rights in bid or proposal information.

As prescribed in 227.7103-6(e)(1), 227.7104(e)(1), or 227.7203-6(b), use the following clause:

RIGHTS IN BID OR PROPOSAL INFORMATION (JAN 2011)

(a) *Definitions.*

(1) For contracts that require the delivery of technical data, the terms *technical data* and *computer software* are defined in the Rights in Technical Data—Noncommercial Item clause of this contract or, if this is a contract awarded under the Small Business Innovative Research Program, the Rights in Noncommercial Technical Data and Computer Software—Small Business Innovation Research (SBIR) Program clause of this contract.

(2) For contracts that do not require the delivery of technical data, the term *computer software* is defined in the Rights in Noncommercial Computer and Noncommercial Computer Software Documentation clause of this contract or, if this is a contract awarded under the Small Business Innovative Research Program, the Rights in Noncommercial Technical Data and Computer Software—Small Business Innovation Research (SBIR) Program clause of this contract.

(b) *Government rights to contract award.* By submission of its offer, the Offeror agrees that the Government—

(1) May reproduce the bid or proposal, or any portions thereof, to the extent necessary to evaluate the offer.

(2) Except as provided in paragraph (d) of this clause, shall use information contained in the bid or proposal only for evaluational purposes and shall not disclose, directly or indirectly, such information to any person including potential evaluators, unless that person has been authorized by the head of the agency, his or her designee, or the Contracting Officer to receive such information.

(c) *Government rights subsequent to contract award.* The Contractor agrees—

(1) Except as provided in paragraphs (c)((2), (d), and (e) of this clause, the Government shall have the rights to use, modify, reproduce, release, perform, display, or disclose information contained in the Contractor's bid or proposal within the Government. The Government shall not release, perform, display, or disclose such information outside the Government without the Contractor's written permission.

(2) The Government's right to use, modify, reproduce, release, perform, display, or disclose information that is technical data or computer software required to be delivered under this contract are determined by the Rights in Technical Data—Noncommercial Items, Rights in Noncommercial Computer Software and Noncommercial Computer Software Documentation, or Rights in Noncommercial Technical Data and Computer Software—Small Business Innovation Research (SBIR) Program clause(s) of this contract.

(d) *Government-furnished information.* The Government's rights with respect to technical data or computer software contained in the Contractor's bid or proposal that were provided to the Contractor by the Government are subject only to restrictions on use, modification, reproduction, release, performance, display, or disclosure, if any, imposed by the developer or licensor of such data or software.

(e) *Information available without restrictions.* The Government's rights to use, modify, reproduce, release, perform, display, or, disclose information contained in a bid or proposal, including technical data or computer software, and to permit others to do so, shall not be restricted in any manner if such information has been released or disclosed to the Government or to other persons without restrictions other than a release or disclosure resulting from the sale, transfer, or other assignment of interest in the information to another party or the sale or transfer of some or all of a business entity or its assets to another party.

(f) *Flowdown*. Contractor shall include this clause in all subcontracts or similar contractual instruments and require its subcontractors or suppliers to do so without alteration, except to identify the parties.

(End of clause)

[DAC 91-8, 60 FR 33464, 6/28/95, effective 6/30/95; Final rule, 76 FR 3536, 1/20/2011, effective 1/20/2011]

252.227-7017 Identification and assertion of use, release, or disclosure restrictions.

As prescribed in 227.7103-3(b), 227.7104(e)(2), or 227.7203-3(a), use the following provision:

IDENTIFICATION AND ASSERTION OF USE, RELEASE, OR DISCLOSURE RESTRICTIONS (JAN 2011)

(a) The terms used in this provision are defined in following clause or clauses contained in this solicitation—

(1) If a successful offeror will be required to deliver technical data, the Rights in Technical Data—Noncommercial Items clause, or, if this solicitation contemplates a contract under the Small Business Innovative Research Program, the Rights in Noncommercial Technical Data and Computer Software—Small Business Innovation Research (SBIR) Program clause.

(2) If a successful offeror will not be required to deliver technical data, the Rights in Noncommercial Computer Software and Noncommercial Computer Software Documentation clause, or, if this solicitation contemplates a contract under the Small Business Innovative Research Program, the Rights in Noncommercial Technical Data and Computer Software—Small Business Innovation Research (SBIR) Program clause.

(b) The identification and assertion requirements in this provision apply only to technical data, including computer software documents, or computer software to be delivered with other than unlimited rights. For contracts to be awarded under the Small Business Innovation Research Program, the notification requirements do not apply to technical data or computer software that will be generated under the resulting contract. Notification and identification is not required for restrictions based solely on copyright.

(c) Offers submitted in response to this solicitation shall identify, to the extent known at the time an offer is submitted to the Government, the technical data or computer software that the Offeror, its subcontractors or suppliers, or potential subcontractors or suppliers, assert should be furnished to the Government with restrictions on use, release, or disclosure.

(d) The Offeror's assertions, including the assertions of its subcontractors or suppliers or potential subcontractors or suppliers shall be submitted as an attachment to its offer in the following format, dated and signed by an official authorized to contractually obligate the Offeror:

Identification and Assertion of Restrictions on the Government's Use, Release, or Disclosure of Technical Data or Computer Software.

The Offeror asserts for itself, or the persons identified below, that the Government's rights to use, release, or disclose the following technical data or computer software should be restricted:

Technical Data or Computer Software to be Furnished With Restrictions*	Basis for Assertion**	Asserted Rights Category***	Name of Person Asserting Restrictions****
(LIST)*****	(LIST)	(LIST)	(LIST)

* For technical data (other than computer software documentation) pertaining to items, components, or processes developed at private expense, identify both the deliverable technical data and each such items, component, or process. For computer software or computer software documentation identify the software or documentation.

** Generally, development at private expense, either exclusively or partially, is the only basis for asserting restrictions. For technical data, other than computer software documentation, development refers to development of the item, component, or process to which the data pertain. The Government's rights in computer software documentation generally may not be restricted. For computer software, development refers to the software. Indicate whether development was accomplished exclusively or partially at private expense. If development was not accomplished at private expense, or for computer software documentation, enter the specific basis for asserting restrictions.
*** Enter asserted rights category (e.g., government purpose license rights from a prior contract, rights in SBIR data generated under another contract, limited, restricted, or government purpose rights under this or a prior contract, or specially negotiated licenses).
**** Corporation, individual, or other person, as appropriate.
***** Enter "none" when all data or software will be submitted without restrictions.

Date ____________________

Printed Name and Title ____________________

____

Signature ____________________

(End of identification and assertion)

(e) An offeror's failure to submit, complete, or sign the notification and identification required by paragraph (d) of this provision with its offer may render the offer ineligible for award.

(f) If the Offeror is awarded a contract, the assertions identified in paragraph (d) of this provision shall be listed in an attachment to that contract. Upon request by the Contracting Officer, the Offeror shall provide sufficient information to enable the Contracting Officer to evaluate any listed assertion.

(End of provision)

[DAC 91-8, 60 FR 33464, 6/28/95, effective 6/30/95; Final rule, 76 FR 3536, 1/20/2011, effective 1/20/2011]

252.227-7018 Rights in noncommercial technical data and computer software—Small Business Innovation Research (SBIR) Program.

As prescribed in 227.7104(a), use the following clause:

RIGHTS IN NONCOMMERCIAL TECHNICAL DATA AND COMPUTER SOFTWARE—SMALL BUSINESS INNOVATION RESEARCH (SBIR) PROGRAM (FEB 2014)

(a) *Definitions.* As used in this clause—

(1) *Commercial computer software* means software developed or regularly used for nongovernmental purposes which—

(i) Has been sold, leased, or licensed to the public;

(ii) Has been offered for sale, lease, or license to the public;

(iii) Has not been offered, sold, leased, or licensed to the public but will be available for commercial sale, lease, or license in time to satisfy the delivery requirements of this contract; or

(iv) Satisfies a criterion expressed in paragraph (a) (1) (i), (ii), or (iii) of this clause and would require only minor modification to meet the requirements of this contract.

(2) *Computer database* means a collection of recorded data in a form capable of being processed by a computer. The term does not include computer software.

(3) *Computer program* means a set of instructions, rules, or routines, recorded in a form that is capable of causing a computer to perform a specific operation or series of operations.

(4) *Computer software* means computer programs, source code, source code listings, object code listings, design details, algorithms, processes, flow charts, formulae, and related material that would enable the software to be reproduced, recreated, or recompiled. Computer software does not include computer databases or computer software documentation.

(5) *Computer software documentation* means owner's manuals, user's manuals, installation instructions, operating instructions, and other similar items, regardless of storage medium, that explain the capabilities of the computer software or provide instructions for using the software.

(6) *Covered Government support contractor* means a contractor (other than a litigation support contractor covered by 252.204-7014) under a contract, the primary purpose of which is to furnish independent and impar-

tial advice or technical assistance directly to the Government in support of the Government's management and oversight of a program or effort (rather than to directly furnish an end item or service to accomplish a program or effort), provided that the contractor—

(i) Is not affiliated with the prime contractor or a first-tier subcontractor on the program or effort, or with any direct competitor of such prime contractor or any such first-tier subcontractor in furnishing end items or services of the type developed or produced on the program or effort; and

(ii) Receives access to the technical data or computer software for performance of a Government contract that contains the clause at 252.227-7025, Limitations on the Use or Disclosure of Government-Furnished Information Marked with Restrictive Legends.

(7) *Detailed manufacturing or process data* means technical data that describe the steps, sequences, and conditions of manufacturing, processing or assembly used by the manufacturer to produce an item or component or to perform a process.

(8) *Developed* means—

(i) (Applicable to technical data other than computer software documentation.) An item, component, or process, exists and is workable. Thus, the item or component must have been constructed or the process practiced. Workability is generally established when the item, component, or process has been analyzed or tested sufficiently to demonstrate to reasonable people skilled in the applicable art that there is a high probability that it will operate as intended. Whether, how much, and what type of analysis or testing is required to establish workability depends on the nature of the item, component, or process, and the state of the art. To be considered "developed," the item, component, or process need not be at the stage where it could be offered for sale or sold on the commercial market, nor must the item, component or process be actually reduced to practice within the meaning of Title 35 of the United States Code;

(ii) A computer program has been successfully operated in a computer and tested to the extent sufficient to demonstrate to reasonable persons skilled in the art that the program can reasonably be expected to perform its intended purpose;

(iii) Computer software, other than computer programs, has been tested or analyzed to the extent sufficient to demonstrate to reasonable persons skilled in the art that the software can reasonably be expected to perform its intended purpose; or

(iv) Computer software documentation required to be delivered under a contract has been written, in any medium, in sufficient detail to comply with requirements under that contract.

(9) *Developed exclusively at private expense* means development was accomplished entirely with costs charged to indirect cost pools, costs not allocated to a government contract, or any combination thereof.

(i) Private expense determinations should be made at the lowest practicable level.

(ii) Under fixed-price contracts, when total costs are greater than the firm-fixed-price or ceiling price of the contract, the additional development costs necessary to complete development shall not be considered when determining whether development was at government, private, or mixed expense.

(10) *Developed exclusively with government funds* means development was not accomplished exclusively or partially at private expense.

(11) *Developed with mixed funding* means development was accomplished partially with costs charged to indirect cost pools and/or costs not allocated to a government contract, and partially with costs charged directly to a government contract.

(12) *Form, fit, and function data* means technical data that describe the required overall physical, functional, and performance characteristics (along with the qualification requirements, if applicable) of an item, component, or process to the extent necessary to permit identification of physically and functionally interchangeable items.

(13) *Generated* means technical data or computer software first created in the performance of this contract.

(14) *Government purpose* means any activity in which the United States Government is a party, including cooperative agreements with international or multi-national defense organizations or sales or transfers by the United States Government to foreign governments or international organizations. Government purposes include competitive procurement, but do not include the rights to use, modify, reproduce, release, perform, display, or disclose technical data or computer software for commercial purposes or authorize others to do so.

(15) *Limited rights* means the rights to use, modify, reproduce, release, perform, display, or disclose technical data, in whole or in part, within the Government. The Government may not, without the written permission of the party asserting limited rights, release or disclose the technical data outside the Government, use the technical data for manufacture, or authorize the technical data to be used by another party, except that the Government may reproduce, release, or disclose such data or authorize the use or reproduction of the data by persons outside the Government if—

(i) The reproduction, release, disclosure, or use is—

(A) Necessary for emergency repair and overhaul; or

(B) A release or disclosure to—

(*1*) A covered Government support contractor in performance of its covered Government support contracts for use, modification, reproduction, performance, display, or release or disclosure to a person authorized to receive limited rights technical data; or

(*2*) A foreign government, of technical data other than detailed manufacturing or process data, when use of such data by the foreign government is in the interest of the Government and is required for evaluational or informational purposes;

(ii) The recipient of the technical data is subject to a prohibition on the further reproduction, release, disclosure, or use of the technical data; and

(iii) The contractor or subcontractor asserting the restriction is notified of such reproduction, release, disclosure, or use.

(16) *Minor modification* means a modification that does not significantly alter the nongovernmental function or purpose of computer software or is of the type customarily provided in the commercial marketplace.

(17) *Noncommercial computer software* means software that does not qualify as commercial computer software under paragraph (a) (1) of this clause.

(18) *Restricted rights* apply only to noncommercial computer software and mean the Government's rights to—

(i) Use a computer program with one computer at one time. The program may not be accessed by more than one terminal or central processing unit or time shared unless otherwise permitted by this contract;

(ii) Transfer a computer program to another Government agency without the further permission of the Contractor if the transferor destroys all copies of the program and related computer software documentation in its possession and notifies the licensor of the transfer. Transferred programs remain subject to the provisions of this clause;

(iii) Make the minimum number of copies of the computer software required for safekeeping (archive), backup, or modification purposes;

(iv) Modify computer software provided that the Government may—

(A) Use the modified software only as provided in paragraphs (a) (18) (i) and (iii) of this clause; and

(B) Not release or disclose the modified software except as provided in paragraphs (a) (18) (ii), (v), (vi), and (vii) of this clause;

(v) Permit contractors or subcontractors performing service contracts (see 37.101 of the Federal Acquisition Regulation) in support of this or a related contract to use computer software to diagnose and correct deficiencies in a computer program, to modify computer software to enable a computer program to be combined with, adapted to, or merged with other computer programs or when necessary to respond to urgent tactical situations, provided that—

(A) The Government notifies the party which has granted restricted rights that a release or disclosure to particular contractors or subcontractors was made;

(B) Such contractors or subcontractors are subject to the non-disclosure agreement at 227.7103-7 of the Defense Federal Acquisition Regulation Supplement or are Government contractors receiving access to the software for performance of a Government contract that contains the clause at 252.227-7025, Limitations on the Use or Disclosure of Government-Furnished Information Marked with Restrictive Legends;

(C) The Government shall not permit the recipient to decompile, disassemble, or reverse engineer the software, or use software decompiled, disassembled, or reverse engineered by the Government pursuant to paragraph (a)(18)(iv) of this clause, for any other purpose; and

(D) Such use is subject to the limitations in paragraphs (a)(18)(i) through (iii) of this clause;

(vi) Permit contractors or subcontractors performing emergency repairs or overhaul of items or components of items procured under this or a related contract to use the computer software when necessary to perform the repairs or overhaul, or to modify the computer software to reflect the repairs or overhaul made, provided that—

(A) The intended recipient is subject to the non-disclosure agreement at 227.7103-7 or is a Government contractor receiving access to the software for performance of a Government contract that contains the clause at 252.227-7025, Limitations on the Use or Disclosure of Government Furnished Information Marked with Restrictive Legends;

(B) The Government shall not permit the recipient to decompile, disassemble, or reverse engineer the software, or use software decompiled, disassembled, or reverse engineered by the Government pursuant to paragraph (a)(18)(iv) of this clause, for any other purpose; and

(C) Such use is subject to the limitations in paragraphs (a)(18)(i) through (iii) of this clause; and

(vii) Permit covered Government support contractors in the performance of Government contracts that contain the clause at 252.227-7025, Limitations on the Use or Disclosure of Government-Furnished Information Marked with Restrictive Legends, to use, modify, reproduce, perform, display, or release or disclose the computer software to a person authorized to receive restricted rights computer software, provided that—

(A) The Government shall not permit the covered Government support contractor to decompile, disassemble, or reverse engineer the software, or use software decompiled, disassembled, or reverse engineered by the Government pursuant to paragraph (a)(18)(iv) of this clause, for any other purpose; and

(B) Such use is subject to the limitations in paragraphs (a)(18)(i) through (iv) of this clause.

(19) *SBIR data rights* means the Government's rights during the SBIR data protection period (specified in paragraph (b)(4) of this clause) to use, modify, reproduce, release, perform, display, or disclose technical data or computer software generated a SBIR award as follows:

(i) Limited rights in such SBIR technical data; and

(ii) Restricted rights in such SBIR computer software.

(20) *Technical data* means recorded information, regardless of the form or method of the recording, of a scientific or technical nature (including computer software documentation). The term does not include computer software or data incidental to contract administration, such as financial and/or management information.

(21) *Unlimited rights* means rights to use, modify, reproduce, release, perform, display, or disclose, technical data or computer software in whole or in part, in any manner

and for any purpose whatsoever, and to have or authorize others to do so.

(b) *Rights in technical data and computer software.* The Contractor grants or shall obtain for the Government the following royalty-free, world-wide, nonexclusive, irrevocable license rights in technical data or noncommercial computer software. All rights not granted to the Government are retained by the Contractor.

(1) *Unlimited rights.* The Government shall have unlimited rights in technical data, including computer software documentation, or computer software generated under this contract that are—

(i) Form, fit, and function data;

(ii) Necessary for installation, operation, maintenance, or training purposes (other than detailed manufacturing or process data);

(iii) Corrections or changes to Government-furnished technical data or computer software;

(iv) Otherwise publicly available or have been released or disclosed by the Contractor or a subcontractor without restrictions on further use, release or disclosure other than a release or disclosure resulting from the sale, transfer, or other assignment of interest in the technical data or computer software to another party or the sale or transfer of some or all of a business entity or its assets to another party;

(v) Data or software in which the Government has acquired previously unlimited rights under another Government contract or through a specific license; and

(vi) SBIR data upon expiration of the SBIR data rights period.

(2) *Limited rights.* The Government shall have limited rights in technical data, that were not generated under this contract, pertain to items, components or processes developed exclusively at private expense, and are marked, in accordance with the marking instructions in paragraph (f)(1) of this clause, with the legend prescribed in paragraph (f)(2) of this clause.

(3) *Restricted rights in computer software.* The Government shall have restricted rights in noncommercial computer software required to be delivered or otherwise furnished to the Government under this contract that were developed exclusively at private expense and were not generated under this contract.

(4) *SBIR data rights.* Except for technical data, including computer software documentation, or computer software in which the Government has unlimited rights under paragraph (b)(1) of this clause, the Government shall have SBIR data rights in all technical data or computer software generated under this contract during the period commencing with contract award and ending upon the date five years after completion of the project from which such data were generated.

(5) *Specifically negotiated license rights.* The standard license rights granted to the Government under paragraphs (b)(1) through (b)(4) of this clause may be modified by mutual agreement to provide such rights as the parties consider appropriate but shall not provide the Government lesser rights in technical data, including computer software documentation, than are enumerated in paragraph (a)(15) of this clause or lesser rights in computer software than are enumerated in paragraph (a)(18) of this clause. Any rights so negotiated shall be identified in a license agreement made part of this contract.

(6) *Prior government rights.* Technical data, including computer software documentation, or computer software that will be delivered, furnished, or otherwise provided to the Government under this contract, in which the Government has previously obtained rights shall be delivered, furnished, or provided with the pre-existing rights, unless—

(i) The parties have agreed otherwise; or

(ii) Any restrictions on the Government's rights to use, modify, release, perform, display, or disclose the technical data or computer software have expired or no longer apply.

(7) *Release from liability.* The Contractor agrees to release the Government from lia-

bility for any release or disclosure of technical data, computer software, or computer software documentation made in accordance with paragraph (a)(14), (a)(17), or (b)(4) of this clause, or in accordance with the terms of a license negotiated under paragraph (b)(5) of this clause, or by others to whom the recipient has released or disclosed the data, software, or documentation and to seek relief solely from the party who has improperly used, modified, reproduced, released, performed, displayed, or disclosed Contractor data or software marked with restrictive legends.

(8) *Covered Government support contractors.* The Contractor acknowledges that—

(i) Limited rights technical data and restricted rights computer software are authorized to be released or disclosed to covered Government support contractors;

(ii) The Contractor will be notified of such release or disclosure;

(iii) The Contractor may require each such covered Government support contractor to enter into a non-disclosure agreement directly with the Contractor (or the party asserting restrictions as identified in a restrictive legend) regarding the covered Government support contractor's use of such data or software, or alternatively that the Contractor (or party asserting restrictions) may waive in writing the requirement for a non-disclosure agreement; and

(iv) Any such non-disclosure agreement shall address the restrictions on the covered Government support contractor's use of the data or software as set forth in the clause at 252.227-7025, Limitations on the Use or Disclosure of Government-Furnished Information Marked with Restrictive Legends. The non-disclosure agreement shall not include any additional terms and conditions unless mutually agreed to by the parties to the non-disclosure agreement.

(c) *Rights in derivative computer software or computer software documentation.* The Government shall retain its rights in the unchanged portions of any computer software or computer software documentation delivered under this contract that the Contractor uses to prepare, or includes in, derivative software or documentation.

(d) *Third party copyrighted technical data and computer software.* The Contractor shall not, without the written approval of the Contracting Officer, incorporate any copyrighted technical data, including computer software documentation, or computer software in the data or software to be delivered under this contract unless the Contractor is the copyright owner or has obtained for the Government the license rights necessary to perfect a license or licenses in the deliverable data or software of the appropriate scope set forth in paragraph (b) of this clause and, prior to delivery of such—

(1) Technical data, has affixed to the transmittal document a statement of the license rights obtained; or

(2) Computer software, has provided a statement of the license rights obtained in a form acceptable to the Contracting Officer.

(e) *Identification and delivery of technical data or computer software to be furnished with restrictions on use, release, or disclosure.* (1) This paragraph does not apply to technical data or computer software that were or will be generated under this contract or to restrictions based solely on copyright.

(2) Except as provided in paragraph (e)(3) of this clause, technical data or computer software that the Contractor asserts should be furnished to the Government with restrictions on use, release, or disclosure is identified in an attachment to this contract (the Attachment). The Contractor shall not deliver any technical data or computer software with restrictive markings unless the technical data or computer software are listed on the Attachment.

(3) In addition to the assertions made in the Attachment, other assertions may be identified after award when based on new information or inadvertent omissions unless the inadvertent omissions would have materially affected the source selection decision. Such identification and assertion shall be submitted to the Contracting Officer as soon as practicable prior to the scheduled date for delivery of the technical data or computer software, in the following format, and signed

by an official authorized to contractually obligate the Contractor:

Identification and Assertion of Restrictions on the Government's Use, Release, or Disclosure of Technical Data or Computer Software.

The Contractor asserts for itself, or the persons identified below, that the Government's rights to use, release, or disclose the following technical data or computer software should be restricted:

Technical data or computer software to be furnished with restrictions*	Basis for assertion**	Asserted rights category***	Name of person asserting restrictions****
(LIST)	(LIST)	(LIST)	(LIST)

* If the assertion is applicable to items, components, or processes developed at private expense, identify both the technical data and each such item, component, or process.

** Generally, the development at private expense, either exclusively or partially, is the only basis for asserting restrictions on the Government's rights to use, release, or disclose technical data or computer software. Indicate whether development was exclusively or partially at private expense. If development was not at private expense, enter the specific reason for asserting that the Government's rights should be restricted.

*** Enter asserted rights category (e.g., limited rights, restricted rights, government purpose rights, or government purpose license rights from a prior contract, SBIR data rights under another contract, or specifically negotiated licenses).

**** Corporation, individual, or other person, as appropriate.

Date ______________________

Printed Name and Title ______________________

____

Signature ______________________

(End of identification and assertion)

(4) When requested by the Contracting Officer, the Contractor shall provide sufficient information to enable the Contracting Officer to evaluate the Contractor's assertions. The Contracting Officer reserves the right to add the Contractor's assertions to the Attachment and validate any listed assertions, at a later date, in accordance with the procedures of the Validation of Asserted Restrictions—Computer Software and/or Validation of Restrictive Markings on Technical Data clauses of this contract.

(f) *Marking requirements*. The Contractor, and its subcontractors or suppliers, may only assert restrictions on the Government's rights to use, modify, reproduce, release, perform, display, or disclose technical data or computer software to be delivered under this contract by marking the deliverable data or software subject to restriction. Except as provided in paragraph (f)(6) of this clause, only the following markings are authorized under this contract: the limited rights legend at paragraph (f)(2) of this clause; the restricted rights legend at paragraph (f)(3) of this clause, the SBIR data rights legend at paragraph (f)(4) of this clause, or the special license rights legend at paragraphs (f)(5) of this clause; and/or a notice of copyright as prescribed under 17 U.S.C. 401 or 402.

(1) *General marking instructions*. The Contractor, or its subcontractors or suppliers, shall conspicuously and legibly mark the appropriate legend to all technical data and computer software that qualify for such markings. The authorized legends shall be placed on the transmittal document or storage container and, for printed material, each page of the printed material containing technical data or computer software for which restrictions are asserted. When only portions of a page of printed material are subject to the asserted restrictions, such portions shall be identified by circling, underscoring, with a note, or other appropriate identifier. Technical data or computer software transmitted directly from one computer or computer terminal to another shall contain a notice of asserted restrictions. However, instructions that interfere with or delay the operation of computer software in order to display a restrictive rights legend or other

license statement at any time prior to or during use of the computer software, or otherwise cause such interference or delay, shall not be inserted in software that will or might be used in combat or situations that simulate combat conditions, unless the Contracting Officer's written permission to deliver such software has been obtained prior to delivery. Reproductions of technical data, computer software, or any portions thereof subject to asserted restrictions shall also reproduce the asserted restrictions.

(2) *Limited rights markings*. Technical data not generated under this contract that pertain to items, components, or processes developed exclusively at private expense and delivered or otherwise furnished with limited rights shall be marked with the following legend:

Limited Rights

Contract No. __________

Contractor Name __________

Contractor Address __________

____

The Government's rights to use, modify, reproduce, release, perform, display, or disclose these technical data are restricted by paragraph (b)(2) of the Rights in Noncommercial Technical Data and Computer Software—Small Business Innovation Research (SBIR) Program clause contained in the above identified contract. Any reproduction of technical data or portions thereof marked with this legend must also reproduce the markings. Any person, other than the Government, who has been provided access to such data must promptly notify the above named Contractor.

(End of legend)

(3) *Restricted rights markings*. Computer software delivered or otherwise furnished to the Government with restricted rights shall be marked with the following legend:

Restricted Rights

Contract No. __________

Contractor Name __________

Contractor Address __________

____

The Government's rights to use, modify, reproduce, release, perform, display, or disclose this software are restricted by paragraph (b)(3) of the Rights in Noncommercial Technical Data and Computer Software—Small Business Innovation Research (SBIR) Program clause contained in the above identified contract. Any reproduction of computer software or portions thereof marked with this legend must also reproduce the markings. Any person, other than the Government, who has been provided access to such data must promptly notify the above named Contractor.

(End of legend)

(4) *SBIR data rights markings*: Except for technical data or computer software in which the Government has acquired unlimited rights under paragraph (b)(1) of this clause, or negotiated special license rights as provided in paragraph (b)(5) of this clause, technical data or computer software generated under this contract shall be marked with the following legend. The Contractor shall enter the expiration date for the SBIR data rights period on the legend:

SBIR Data Rights

Contract No. __________

Contractor Name __________

Address __________

____

Expiration of SBIR Data Rights Period __________

The Government's rights to use, modify, reproduce, release, perform, display, or disclose technical data or computer software marked with this legend are restricted during the period shown as provided in paragraph (b)(4) of the Rights in Noncommercial Technical Data and Computer Software—Small Business Innovation Research (SBIR) Program clause contained in the above identified contract. No restrictions apply after the expiration date shown above. Any reproduction of technical data, computer software, or portions thereof marked with this legend must also reproduce the markings.

(End of legend)

(5) *Special license rights markings.* (i) Technical data or computer software in which the Government's rights stem from a specifically negotiated license shall be marked with the following legend:

Special License Rights

The Government's rights to use, modify, reproduce, release, perform, display, or disclose this technical data or computer software are restricted by Contract No. ___ (Insert contract number), License No. ___ (Insert license identifier). Any reproduction of technical data, computer software, or portions thereof marked with this legend must also reproduce the markings.

(End of legend)

(ii) For purposes of this clause, special licenses do not include government purpose license rights acquired under a prior contract (see paragraph (b)(6) of this clause).

(6) *Pre-existing data markings.* If the terms of a prior contract or license permitted the Contractor to restrict the Government's rights to use, modify, reproduce, release, perform, display, or disclose technical data or computer software, and those restrictions are still applicable, the Contractor may mark such data or software with the appropriate restrictive legend for which the data or software qualified under the prior contract or license. The marking procedures in paragraph (f)(1) of this clause shall be followed.

(g) *Contractor procedures and records.* Throughout performance of this contract, the Contractor, and its subcontractors or suppliers that will deliver technical data or computer software with other than unlimited rights, shall—

(1) Have, maintain, and follow written procedures sufficient to assure that restrictive markings are used only when authorized by the terms of this clause; and

(2) Maintain records sufficient to justify the validity of any restrictive markings on technical data or computer software delivered under this contract.

(h) *Removal of unjustified and nonconforming markings.*

(1) *Unjustified markings.* The rights and obligations of the parties regarding the validation of restrictive markings on technical data or computer software furnished or to be furnished under this contract are contained in the Validation of Restrictive Markings on Technical Data and the Validation of Asserted Restrictions—Computer Software clauses of this contract, respectively. Notwithstanding any provision of this contract concerning inspection and acceptance, the Government may ignore or, at the Contractor's expense, correct or strike a marking if, in accordance with the applicable procedures of those clauses, a restrictive marking is determined to be unjustified.

(2) *Nonconforming markings.* A nonconforming marking is a marking placed on technical data or computer software delivered or otherwise furnished to the Government under this contract that is not in the format authorized by this contract. Correction of nonconforming markings is not subject to the Validation of Restrictive Markings on Technical Data or the Validation of Asserted Restrictions—Computer Software clause of this contract. If the Contracting Officer notifies the Contractor of a nonconforming marking or markings and the Contractor fails to remove or correct such markings within sixty (6)) days, the Government may ignore or, at the Contractor's expense, remove or correct any nonconforming markings.

(i) *Relation to patents.* Nothing contained in this clause shall imply a license to the Government under any patent or be construed as affecting the scope of any license or other right otherwise granted to the Government under any patent.

(j) *Limitation on charges for rights in technical data or computer software.* (1) The Contractor shall not charge to this contract any cost, including but not limited to, license fees, royalties, or similar charges, for rights in technical data or computer software to be delivered under this contract when—

(i) the Government has acquired, by any means, the same or greater rights in the data or software; or

(ii) The data are available to the public without restrictions.

(2) The limitation in paragraph (j)(1) of this clause—

(i) Includes costs charged by a subcontractor or supplier, at any tier, or costs incurred by the Contractor to acquire rights in subcontractor of supplier technical data or computer software, if the subcontractor or supplier has been paid for such rights under any other Government contract or under a license conveying the rights to the Government; and

(ii) Does not include the reasonable costs of reproducing, handling, or mailing the documents or other media in which the technical data or computer software will be delivered.

(k) *Applicability to subcontractors or suppliers*. (1) the Contractor shall assure that the rights afforded its subcontractors and suppliers under 10 U.S.C. 2320, 10 U.S.C. 2321, and the identification, assertion, and delivery processes required by paragraph (e) of this clause are recognized and protected.

(2) Whenever any noncommercial technical data or computer software is to be obtained from a subcontractor or supplier for delivery to the Government under this contract, the Contractor shall use this same clause in the subcontract or other contractual instrument, and require its subcontractors or suppliers to do so, without alteration, except to identify the parties. The Contractor shall use the Technical Data—Commercial Items clause of this contract to obtain technical data pertaining to commercial items, components, or processes. No other clause shall be used to enlarge or diminish the Government's, the Contractor's, or a higher tier subcontractor's or supplier's rights in a subcontractor's or supplier's technical data or computer software.

(3) Technical data required to be delivered by a subcontractor or supplier shall normally be delivered to the next higher tier contractor, subcontractor, or supplier. However, when there is a requirement in the prime contract for technical data which may be submitted with other than unlimited rights by a subcontractor or supplier, then said subcontractor or supplier may fulfill its requirement by submitting such technical data directly to the Government, rather than through a higher tier contractor, subcontractor, or supplier.

(4) The Contractor and higher tier subcontractors or suppliers shall not use their power to award contracts as economic leverage to obtain rights in technical data or computer software from their subcontractors or suppliers.

(5) In no event shall the Contractor use its obligation to recognize and protect subcontractor or supplier rights in technical data or computer software as an excuse for failing to satisfy its contractual obligation to the Government.

(End of clause)

ALTERNATE I (JUN 1995)

As prescribed in 227.7104(d), add the following paragraph (l) to the basic clause:

(l) *Publication for sale*. (1) This paragraph applies only to technical data or computer software delivered to the Government with SBIR data rights.

(2) Upon expiration of the SBIR data rights period, the Government will not exercise its right to publish or authorize others to publish an item of technical data or computer software identified in this contract as being subject to paragraph (l) of this clause if the Contractor, prior to the expiration of the SBIR data rights period, or within two years following delivery of the data or software item, or within twenty-four months following the removal of any national security or export control restrictions, whichever is later, publishes such data or software item(s) and promptly notifies the Contracting Officer of such publication(s). Any such publication(s) shall include a notice identifying the number of this contract and the Government's rights in the published data.

(3) This limitation on the Government's right to publish for sale shall continue as long as the technical data or computer software are reasonably available to the public for purchase.

[DAC 91-8, 60 FR 33464, 6/28/95, effective 6/30/95; DAC 91-9, 60 FR 61586, 11/30/95, effective 11/30/95; Final rule, 76 FR 3536, 1/20/2011, effective 1/20/2011; Interim rule, 76 FR 11363, 3/2/2011, effective 3/2/2011; Final rule, 78 FR 30233, 5/22/2013, effective 5/22/2013; Interim rule, 79 FR 11337, 2/28/2014, effective 2/28/2014; Final rule, 81 FR 28724, 5/10/2016, effective 5/10/2016]

252.227-7019 Validation of asserted restrictions—Computer software.

As prescribed in 227.7104(e)(3) or 227.7203-6(c), use the following clause:

VALIDATION OF ASSERTED RESTRICTIONS—COMPUTER SOFTWARE (SEP 2016)

(a) *Definitions.* (1) As used in this clause, unless otherwise specifically indicated, the term *Contractor* means the Contractor and its subcontractors or suppliers.

(2) Other terms used in this clause are defined in the Rights in Noncommercial Computer Software and Noncommercial Computer Software Documentation clause of this contract.

(b) *Justification.* The Contractor shall maintain records sufficient to justify the validity of any markings that assert restrictions on the Government's rights to use, modify, reproduce, perform, display, release, or disclose computer software delivered or required to be delivered under this contract and shall be prepared to furnish to the Contracting Officer a written justification for such restrictive markings in response to a request for information under paragraph (d) or a challenge under paragraph (f) of this clause.

(c) *Direct contact with subcontractors or suppliers.* The Contractor agrees that the Contracting Officer may transact matters under this clause directly with subcontractors or suppliers at any tier who assert restrictions on the Government's right to use, modify, reproduce, release, perform, display, or disclose computer software. Neither this clause, nor any action taken by the Government under this clause, creates or implies privity of contract between the Government and the Contractor's subcontractors or suppliers.

(d) *Requests for information.* (1) The Contracting Officer may request the Contractor to provide sufficient information to enable the Contracting Officer to evaluate the Contractor's asserted restrictions. Such information shall be based upon the records required by this clause or other information reasonably available to the Contractor.

(2) Based upon the information provided, if the—

(i) Contractor agrees that an asserted restriction is not valid, the Contracting Officer may—

(A) Strike or correct the unjustified marking at the Contractor's expense; or

(B) Return the computer software to the Contractor for correction at the Contractor's expense. If the Contractor fails to correct or strike the unjustified restrictions and return the corrected software to the Contracting Officer within sixty (60) days following receipt of the software, the Contracting Officer may correct the strike the markings at the Contractor's expense.

(ii) Contracting Officer concludes that the asserted restriction is appropriate for this contract, the Contracting Officer shall so notify the Contractor in writing.

(3) The Contractor's failure to provide a timely response to a Contracting Officer's request for information or failure to provide sufficient information to enable the Contracting Officer to evaluate an asserted restriction shall constitute reasonable grounds for questioning the validity of an asserted restriction.

(e) *Government right to challenge and validate asserted restrictions.* (1) The Government, when there are reasonable grounds to do so, has the right to review and challenge the validity of any restrictions asserted by the Contractor on the Government's rights to use, modify, reproduce, release, perform, display, or disclose computer software delivered, to be delivered under this contract, or otherwise provided to the Government in the performance of this contract. Except for software that is publicly available, has been furnished to the Government without restrictions, or has been otherwise made available without restrictions, the Government may exercise this right only within three years after the date(s) the software is delivered or otherwise furnished to the Government, or three years following final payment under this contract, whichever is later.

(2) The absence of a challenge to an asserted restriction shall not constitute validation under this clause. Only a Contracting Officer's final decision or actions of an agency Board of Contract Appeals or a court of competent jurisdiction that sustain the validity of an asserted restriction constitute validation of the restriction.

(f) *Challenge procedures*. (1) A challenge must be in writing and shall—

(i) State the specific grounds for challenging the asserted restriction;

(ii) Require the Contractor to respond within sixty (60) days;

(iii) Require the Contractor to provide justification for the assertion based upon records kept in accordance with paragraph (b) of this clause and such other documentation that are reasonably available to the Contractor, in sufficient detail to enable the Contracting Officer to determine the validity of the asserted restrictions; and

(iv) State that a Contracting Officer's final decision, during the three-year period preceding this challenge, or action of a court of competent jurisdiction or Board of Contract Appeals that sustained the validity of an identical assertion made by the Contractor (or a licensee) shall serve as justification for the asserted restriction.

(2) The Contracting Officer shall extend the time for response if the Contractor submits a written request showing the need for additional time to prepare a response.

(3) The Contracting Officer may request additional supporting documentation if, in the Contracting Officer's opinion, the Contractor's explanation does not provide sufficient evidence to justify the validity of the asserted restrictions. The Contractor agrees to promptly respond to the Contracting Officer's request for additional supporting documentation.

(4) Notwithstanding challenge by the Contracting Officer, the parties may agree on the disposition of an asserted restriction at any time prior to a Contracting Officer's final decision or, if the Contractor has appealed that decision, filed suit, or provided notice of an intent to file suit, at any time prior to a decision by a court of competent jurisdiction or Board of Contract Appeals.

(5) If the Contractor fails to respond to the Contracting Officer's request for information or additional information under paragraph (f)(1) of this clause, the Contracting Officer shall issue a final decision, in accordance with the Disputes clause of this contract, pertaining to the validity of the asserted restriction.

(6) If the Contracting Officer, after reviewing any available information pertaining to the validity of an asserted restriction, determines that the asserted restriction has—

(i) Not been justified, the Contracting Officer shall issue promptly a final decision, in accordance with the Disputes clause of this contract, denying the validity of the asserted restriction; or

(ii) Been justified, the Contracting Officer shall issue promptly a final decision, in accordance with the Disputes clause of this contract, validating the asserted restriction.

(7) A Contractor receiving challenges to the same asserted restriction(s) from more than one Contracting Officer shall notify each Contracting Officer of the other challenges. The notice shall also state which Contracting Officer initiated the first in time unanswered challenge. The Contracting Officer who initiated the first in time unanswered challenge, after consultation with the other Contracting Officers who have challenged the restrictions and the Contractor, shall formulate and distribute a schedule that provides the contractor a reasonable opportunity for responding to each challenge.

(g) *Contractor appeal—Government obligation*. (1) The Government agrees that, notwithstanding a Contracting Officer's final decision denying the validity of an asserted restriction and except as provided in paragraph (g)(3) of this clause, it will honor the asserted restriction—

(i) For a period of ninety (90) days from the date of the Contracting Officer's final decision to allow the Contractor to appeal to the appropriate Board of Contract Appeals or to file suit in an appropriate court;

(ii) For a period of one year from the date of the Contracting Officer's final decision if, within the first ninety (90) days following the Contracting Officer's final decision, the Contractor has provided notice of an intent to file suit in an appropriate court; or

(iii) Until final disposition by the appropriate Board of Contract Appeals or court of competent jurisdiction, if the Contractor has: (A) appealed to the Board of Contract Appeals or filed suit an appropriate court within ninety (90) days; or (B) submitted, within ninety (90) days, a notice of intent to file suit in an appropriate court and filed suit within one year.

(2) The Contractor agrees that the Government may strike, correct, or ignore the restrictive markings if the Contractor fails to—

(i) Appeal to a Board of Contract Appeals within ninety (90) days from the date of the Contracting Officer's final decision;

(ii) File suit in an appropriate court within ninety (90) days from such date; or

(iii) File suit within one year after the date of the Contracting Officer's final decision if the Contractor had provided notice of intent to file suit within ninety (90) days following the date of the Contracting Officer's final decision.

(3) The agency head, on a nondelegable basis, may determine that urgent or compelling circumstances do not permit awaiting the filing of suit in an appropriate court, or the rendering of a decision by a court of competent jurisdiction or Board of Contract Appeals. In that event, the agency head shall notify the Contractor of the urgent or compelling circumstances. Notwithstanding paragraph (g)(1) of this clause, the Contractor agrees that the agency may use, modify, reproduce, release, perform, display, or disclose computer software marked with (i) government purpose legends for any purpose, and authorize others to do so; or (ii) restricted or special license rights for government purposes only. The Government agrees not to release or disclose such software unless, prior to release or disclosure, the intended recipient is subject to the use and nondisclosure agreement at 227.7103-7 of the Defense Federal Acquisition Regulation Supplement (DFARS), or is a Government contractor receiving access to the software for performance of a Government contract that contains the clause at DFARS 252.227-7025, Limitations on the Use or Disclosure of Government-Furnished Information Marked with Restrictive Legends. The agency head's determination may be made at any time after the date of the Contracting Officer's final decision and shall not affect the Contractor's right to damages against the United States, or other relief provided by law, if its asserted restrictions are ultimately upheld.

(h) *Final disposition of appeal or suit.* If the Contractor appeals or files suit and if, upon final disposition of the appeal or suit, the Contracting Officer's decision is:

(1) Sustained—

(i) Any restrictive marking on such computer software shall be struck or corrected at the contractor's expense or ignored; and

(ii) If the asserted restriction is found not to be substantially justified, the Contractor shall be liable to the Government for payment of the cost to the Government of reviewing the asserted restriction and the fees and other expenses (as defined in 28 U.S.C. 2412(d)(2)(A)) incurred by the Government in challenging the restriction, unless special circumstances would make such payment unjust.

(2) Not sustained—

(i) The Government shall be bound by the asserted restriction; and

(ii) If the challenge by the Government is found not to have been made in good faith, the Government shall be liable to the Contractor for payment of fees and other expenses (as defined in 28 U.S.C. 2412(d)(2)(A)) incurred by the Contractor in defending the restriction.

(i) *Flowdown*. The Contractor shall insert this clause in all contracts, purchase orders, and other similar instruments with its subcontractors or suppliers, at any tier, who will be furnishing computer software to the Government in the performance of this contract. The clause may not be altered other than to identify the appropriate parties.

(End of clause)

[DAC 91-8, 60 FR 33464, 6/28/95, effective 6/30/95; Final rule, 76 FR 58144, 9/20/2011, effective 9/20/2011; Final rule, 81 FR 65565, 9/23/2016, effective 9/23/2016]

252.227-7020 Rights in special works.

As prescribed in 227.7105-3, 227.7106(a) or 227.7205(a), use the following clause:

RIGHTS IN SPECIAL WORKS (JUN 1995)

(a) *Applicability*. This clause applies to works first created, generated, or produced and required to be delivered under this contract.

(b) *Definitions*. As used in this clause:

(1) *Computer data base* means a collection of data recorded in a form capable of being processed by a computer. The term does not include computer software.

(2) *Computer program* means a set of instructions, rules, or routines recorded in a form that is capable of causing a computer to perform a specific operation or series of operations.

(3) *Computer software* means computer programs, source code, source code listings, object code listings, design details, algorithms, processes, flow charts, formulae and related material that would enable the software to be reproduced, recreated, or recompiled. Computer software does not include computer data bases or computer software documentation.

(4) *Computer software documentation* means owner's manuals, user's manuals, installation instructions, operating instructions, and other similar items, regardless of storage medium, that explain the capabilities of the computer software or provide instructions for using the software.

(5) *Unlimited rights* means the rights to use, modify, reproduce, perform, display, release, or disclose a work in whole or in part, in any manner, and for any purpose whatsoever, and to have or authorize others to do so.

(6) The term *works* includes computer data bases, computer software, or computer software documentation; literary, musical, choreographic, or dramatic compositions; pantomimes; pictorial, graphic, or sculptural compositions; motion pictures and other audiovisual compositions; sound recordings in any medium; or, items of similar nature.

(c) *License rights*. (1) The Government shall have unlimited rights in works first produced, created, or generated and required to be delivered under this contract.

(2) When a work is first produced, created, or generated under this contract, and such work is required to be delivered under this contract, the Contractor shall assign copyright in those works to the Government. The Contractor, unless directed to the contrary by the Contracting Officer, shall place the following notice on such works: "© (*Year date of delivery*) United States Government, as represented by the Secretary of (*department*). All rights reserved."

For phonorecords, the "©" markings shall be replaced by a "P".

(3) The Contractor grants to the Government a royalty-free, world-wide, nonexclusive, irrevocable license to reproduce, prepare derivative works from, distribute, perform, or display, and to have or authorize others to do so, the Contractor's copyrighted works not first produced, created, or generated under this contract that have been incorporated into the works deliverable under this contract.

(d) *Third party copyrighted data*. The Contractor shall not incorporate, without the written approval of the Contracting Officer, any copyrighted works in the works to be delivered under this contract unless the Contractor is the copyright owner or has obtained for the Government the license rights necessary to perfect a license of the scope identified in paragraph (c)(3) of this clause and, prior to delivery of such works—

(1) Has affixed to the transmittal document a statement of the license rights obtained; or

(2) For computer software, has provided a statement of the license rights obtained in a form acceptable to the Contracting Officer.

(e) *Indemnification*. The Contractor shall indemnify and save and hold harmless the Government, and its officers, agents and employees acting for the Government, against any liability, including costs and expenses, (1) for violation of proprietary rights, copyrights, or rights of privacy or publicity, arising out of the creation, delivery, use, modification, reproduction, release, performance, display, or disclosure of any works furnished under this contract, or (2) based upon any libelous or other unlawful matter contained in such works.

(f) *Government-furnished information*. Paragraphs (d) and (e) of this clause are not applicable to information furnished to the Contractor by the Government and incorporated in the works delivered under this contract.

(End of clause)

[DAC 91-8, 60 FR 33464, 6/28/95, effective 6/30/95]

252.227-7021 Rights in data—existing works.

As prescribed at 227.7105-2(a), use the following clause:

RIGHTS IN DATA—EXISTING WORKS (MAR 1979)

(a) The term *works* as used herein includes literary, musical, and dramatic works; pantomimes and choreographic works; pictorial, graphic and sculptural works; motion pictures and other audiovisual works; sound recordings; and works of a similar nature. The term does not include financial reports, cost analyses, and other information incidental to contract administration.

(b) Except as otherwise provided in this contract, the Contractor hereby grants to the Government a nonexclusive, paid-up license throughout the world (1) to distribute, perform publicly, and display publicly the works called for under this contract and (2) to authorize others to do so for Government purposes.

(c) The Contractor shall indemnify and save and hold harmless the Government, and its officers, agents, and employees acting for the Government, against any liability, including costs and expenses, (1) for violation of proprietary rights, copyrights, or rights of privacy or publicity arising out of the creation, delivery, or use, of any works furnished under this contract, or (2) based upon any libelous or other unlawful matter contained in same works.

(End of clause)

[DAC 91-8, 60 FR 33464, 6/28/95, effective 6/30/95]

252.227-7022 Government rights (unlimited).

As prescribed at 227.7107-1(a), use the following clause:

GOVERNMENT RIGHTS (UNLIMITED) (MAR 1979)

The Government shall have unlimited rights, in all drawings, designs, specifications, notes and other works developed in the performance of this contract, including the right to use same on any other Government design or construction without additional compensation to the Contractor. The Contractor hereby grants to the Government a paid-up license throughout the world to all such works to which he may assert or establish any claim under design patent or copyright laws. The Contractor for a period of three (3) years after completion of the project agrees to furnish the original or copies of all such works on the request of the Contracting Officer.

(End of clause)

[DAC 91-8, 60 FR 33464, 6/28/95, effective 6/30/95]

252.227-7023 Drawings and other data to become property of government.

As prescribed at 227.7107-1(b), use the following clause:

DRAWINGS AND OTHER DATA TO BECOME PROPERTY OF GOVERNMENT (MAR 1979)

All designs, drawings, specifications, notes and other works developed in the performance of this contract shall become the sole property of the Government and may be used on any other design or construction without additional compensation to the Contractor. The Government shall be considered the "person for whom the work was prepared" for the purpose of authorship in any copyrightable work under 17 U.S.C. 201(b). With respect thereto, the Contractor agrees not to assert or authorize others to assert any rights nor establish any claim under the design patent or copyright laws. The Contractor for a period of three (3) years after completion of the project agrees to furnish all retained works on the request of the Contracting Officer. Unless otherwise provided in this contract, the Contractor shall have the right to retain copies of all works beyond such period.

(End of clause)

[DAC 91-8, 60 FR 33464, 6/28/95, effective 6/30/95]

252.227-7024 Notice and approval of restricted designs.

As prescribed at 227.7107-3, use the following clause:

NOTICE AND APPROVAL OF RESTRICTED DESIGNS (APR 1984)

In the performance of this contract, the Contractor shall, to the extent practicable, make maximum use of structures, machines, products, materials, construction methods, and equipment that are readily available through Government or competitive commercial channels, or through standard or proven production techniques, methods, and processes. Unless approved by the Contracting Officer, the Contractor shall not produce a design or specification that requires in this construction work the use of structures, products, materials, construction equipment, or processes that are known by the Contractor to be available only from a sole source. The Contractor shall promptly report any such design or specification to the Contracting Officer and give the reason why it is considered necessary to so restrict the design or specification.

(End of clause)

[DAC 91-8, 60 FR 33464, 6/28/95, effective 6/30/95]

252.227-7025 Limitations on the Use or Disclosure of Government-Furnished Information Marked with Restrictive Legends.

As prescribed in 227.7103-6(c), 227.7104(f)(1), or 227.7203-6(d), use the following clause:

LIMITATIONS ON THE USE OR DISCLOSURE OF GOVERNMENT-FURNISHED INFORMATION MARKED WITH RESTRICTIVE LEGENDS (MAY 2013)

(a)(1) For contracts in which the Government will furnish the Contractor with technical data, the terms *covered Government support contractor, limited rights*, and *Government purpose rights* are defined in the clause at 252.227-7013, Rights in Technical Data-Noncommercial Items.

(2) For contracts in which the Government will furnish the Contractor with computer software or computer software documentation, the terms *covered Government support contractor government purpose rights* and *restricted rights* are defined in the clause at 252.227-7014, Rights in Noncommercial Computer Software and Noncommercial Computer Software Documentation.

(3) For Small Business Innovation Research program contracts, the terms *covered Government support contractor, limited rights, restricted rights* and *SBIR data rights* are defined in the clause at 252.227-7018, Rights in Noncommercial Technical Data and Computer Software—Small Business Innovation Research (SBIR) Program.

(b) Technical data or computer software provided to the Contractor as Government-furnished information (GFI) under this contract may be subject to restrictions on use, modification, reproduction, release, performance, display, or further disclosure.

(1) *GFI marked with limited rights, restricted rights, or SBIR data rights legends.*

(i) The Contractor shall use, modify, reproduce, perform, or display technical data received from the Government with limited rights legends, computer software received with restricted rights legends, or SBIR technical data or computer software received with SBIR data rights legends (during the SBIR data protection period) only in the performance of this contract. The Contractor shall not, without the express written permission of the party whose name appears in the legend, release or disclose such data or software to any unauthorized person.

(ii) If the Contractor is a covered Government support contractor, the Contractor is also subject to the additional terms and conditions at paragraph (b)(5) of this clause

(2) *GFI marked with government purpose rights legends.* The Contractor shall use technical data or computer software received from the Government with government purpose rights legends for government purposes only. The Contractor shall not, without the express written permission of the party whose name appears in the restrictive legend, use, modify, reproduce, release, perform, or display such data or software for any commercial purpose or disclose such data or software to a person other than its subcontractors, suppliers, or prospective subcontractors or suppliers, who require the data or software to submit offers for, or perform, contracts under this contract. Prior to disclosing the data or software, the Contractor shall require the persons to whom disclosure will be made to complete and sign the non-disclosure agreement at 227.7103-7.

(3) *GFI marked with specially negotiated license rights legends.*

(i) The Contractor shall use, modify, reproduce, release, perform, or display technical data or computer software received from the Government with specially negotiated license legends only as permitted in the license. Such data or software may not be released or disclosed to other persons unless permitted by the license and, prior to release or disclosure, the intended recipient has completed the non-disclosure agreement at 227.7103-7. The Contractor shall modify paragraph (1)(c) of the non-disclosure agreement to reflect the recipient's obligations regarding use, modification, reproduction, release, performance, display, and disclosure of the data or software.

(ii) If the Contractor is a covered Government support contractor, the Contractor may also be subject to some or all of the additional terms and conditions at paragraph (b)(5) of this clause, to the extent such terms and conditions are required by the specially negotiated license.

(4) *GFI technical data marked with commercial restrictive legends.*

(i) The Contractor shall use, modify, reproduce, perform, or display technical data that is or pertains to a commercial item and is received from the Government with a commercial restrictive legend (i.e., marked to indicate that such data are subject to use, modification, reproduction, release, performance, display, or disclosure restrictions) only in the performance of this contract. The Contractor shall not, without the express written permission of the party whose name appears in the legend, use the technical data to manufacture additional quantities of the commercial items, or release or disclose such data to any unauthorized person.

(ii) If the Contractor is a covered Government support contractor, the Contractor is also subject to the additional terms and conditions at paragraph (b)(5) of this clause

(5) *Covered Government support contractors.* If the Contractor is a covered Government support contractor receiving technical data or computer software marked with restrictive legends pursuant to paragraphs (b)(1)(ii), (b)(3)(ii), or (b)(4)(ii) of this clause, the Contractor further agrees and acknowledges that—

(i) The technical data or computer software will be accessed and used for the sole purpose of furnishing independent and impartial advice or technical assistance directly to the Government in support of the Government's management and oversight of the program or effort to which such technical data or computer software relates, as stated in this contract, and shall not be used to compete for any Government or non-Government contract;

(ii) The Contractor will take all reasonable steps to protect the technical data or computer software against any unauthorized release or disclosure;

(iii) The Contractor will ensure that the party whose name appears in the legend is notified of the access or use within thirty (30) days of the Contractor's access or use of such data or software;

(iv) The Contractor will enter into a non-disclosure agreement with the party whose name appears in the legend, if required to do so by that party, and that any such non-disclosure agreement will implement the restrictions on the Contractor's use of such data or software as set forth in this clause. The non-disclosure agreement shall not include any additional terms and conditions unless mutually agreed to by the parties to the non-disclosure agreement; and

(v) That a breach of these obligations or restrictions may subject the Contractor to—

(A) Criminal, civil, administrative, and contractual actions in law and equity for penalties, damages, and other appropriate remedies by the United States; and

(B) Civil actions for damages and other appropriate remedies by the party whose name appears in the legend.

(c) *Indemnification and creation of third party beneficiary rights*. The Contractor agrees—

(1) To indemnify and hold harmless the Government, its agents, and employees from every claim or liability, including attorneys fees, court costs, and expenses, arising out of, or in any way related to, the misuse or unauthorized modification, reproduction, release, performance, display, or disclosure of technical data or computer software received from the Government with restrictive legends by the Contractor or any person to whom the Contractor has released or disclosed such data or software; and

(2) That the party whose name appears on the restrictive legend, in addition to any other rights it may have, is a third party beneficiary who has the right of direct action against the Contractor, or any person to whom the Contractor has released or disclosed such data or software, for the unauthorized duplication, release, or disclosure of technical data or computer software subject to restrictive legends.

(d) The Contractor shall ensure that its employees are subject to use and non-disclosure obligations consistent with this clause prior to the employees being provided access to or use of any GFI covered by this clause.

(End of clause)

[DAC 91-8, 60 FR 33464, 6/28/95, effective 6/30/95; Final rule, 76 FR 3536, 1/20/2011, effective 1/20/2011; Interim rule, 76 FR 11363, 3/2/2011, effective 3/2/2011; Final rule, 78 FR 30233, 5/22/2013, effective 5/22/2013]

252.227-7026 Deferred delivery of technical data or computer software.

As prescribed at 227.7103-8(a), use the following clause:

DEFERRED DELIVERY OF TECHNICAL DATA OR COMPUTER SOFTWARE (APR 1988)

The Government shall have the right to require, at any time during the performance of this contract, within two (2) years after either acceptance of all items (other than data or computer software) to be delivered under this contract or termination of this contract, whichever is later, delivery of any technical data or computer software item identified in this contract as "deferred delivery" data or computer software. The obligation to furnish such technical data required to be prepared by a subcontractor and pertaining to an item obtained from him shall expire two (2) years after the date Contractor accepts the last delivery of that item from that subcontractor for use in performing this contract.

(End of clause)

[DAC 91-8, 60 FR 33464, 6/28/95, effective 6/30/95]

252.227-7027 Deferred ordering of technical data or computer software.

As prescribed at 227.7103-8(b), use the following clause:

DEFERRED ORDERING OF TECHNICAL DATA OR COMPUTER SOFTWARE (APR 1988)

In addition to technical data or computer software specified elsewhere in this contract to be delivered hereunder, the Government may, at any time during the performance of this contract or within a period of three (3) years after acceptance of all items (other than technical data or computer software) to be delivered under this contract or the termination of this contract, order any technical data or computer software generated in the performance of this contract or any subcontract hereunder. When the technical data or computer software is ordered, the Contractor shall be compensated for converting the data or computer software into the prescribed form, for reproduction and delivery. The obligation to deliver the technical data of a subcontractor and pertaining to an item obtained from him shall expire three (3) years after the date the Contractor accepts the last delivery of that item from that subcontractor under this contract. The Government's rights to use said data or computer software shall be pursuant to the "Rights in Technical Data and Computer Software" clause of this contract.

(End of clause)

[DAC 91-8, 60 FR 33464, 6/28/95, effective 6/30/95]

252.227-7028 Technical data or computer software previously delivered to the government.

As prescribed in 227.7103-6(d), 227.7104(f)(2), or 227.7203-6(e), use the following provision:

TECHNICAL DATA OR COMPUTER SOFTWARE PREVIOUSLY DELIVERED TO THE GOVERNMENT (JUN 1995)

The Offeror shall attach to its offer an identification of all documents or other media incorporating technical data or computer software it intends to deliver under this contract with other than unlimited rights that are identical or substantially similar to documents or other media that the Offeror has produced for, delivered to, or is obligated to deliver to the Government under any contract or subcontract. The attachment shall identify—

(a) The contract number under which the data or software were produced;

(b) The contract number under which, and the name and address of the organization to whom, the data or software were most recently delivered or will be delivered; and

(c) Any limitations on the Government's rights to use or disclose the data or software, including, when applicable, identification of the earliest date the limitations expire.

(End of provision)

[DAC 91-8, 60 FR 33464, 6/28/95, effective 6/30/95]

252.227-7029 [Reserved]

[DAC 91-8, 60 FR 33464, 6/28/95, effective 6/30/95]

252.227-7030 Technical data—withholding of payment.

As prescribed at 227.7103-6(e)(2) or 227.7104(e)(4), use the following clause:

TECHNICAL DATA—WITHHOLDING OF PAYMENT (MAR 2000)

(a) If technical data specified to be delivered under this contract, is not delivered within the time specified by this contract or is deficient upon delivery (including having restrictive markings not identified in the list described in the clause at 252.227-7013(e)(2) or 252.227-7018(e)(2) of this contract), the Contracting Officer may until such data is accepted by the Government, withhold payment to the Contractor of ten percent (10%) of the total contract price or amount unless a lesser withholding is specified in the contract. Payments shall not be withheld nor any other action taken pursuant to this paragraph when the Contractor's failure to make timely delivery or to deliver such data without deficiencies arises out of causes beyond the control and without the fault or negligence of the Contractor.

(b) The withholding of any amount or subsequent payment to the Contractor shall not be construed as a waiver of any rights accruing to the Government under this contract.

(End of clause)

[DAC 91-8, 60 FR 33464, 6/28/95, effective 6/30/95; DAC 91-12, 62 FR 34114, 6/24/97, effective 6/24/97; Final rule, 65 FR 14397, 3/16/2000, effective 3/16/2000]

252.227-7031 [Reserved]

[DAC 91-8, 60 FR 33464, 6/28/95, effective 6/30/95]

252.227-7032 Rights in technical data and computer software (foreign).

As prescribed in 227.7103-17, use the following clause:

RIGHTS IN TECHNICAL DATA AND COMPUTER SOFTWARE (FOREIGN) (JUN 1975)

The United States Government may duplicate, use, and disclose in any manner for any purposes whatsoever, including delivery to other governments for the furtherance of mutual defense of the United States Government and other governments, all technical data including reports, drawings and blueprints, and all computer software, specified to be delivered by the Contractor to the United States Government under this contract.

(End of clause)

[DAC 91-8, 60 FR 33464, 6/28/95, effective 6/30/95]

252.227-7033 Rights in shop drawings.

As prescribed at 227.7107-1(c), use the following clause:

RIGHTS IN SHOP DRAWINGS (APR 1966)

(a) *Shop drawings for construction* means drawings, submitted to the Government by the Construction Contractor, subcontractor or any lower-tier subcontractor pursuant to a construction contract, showing in detail (i) the proposed fabrication and assembly of structural elements and (ii) the installation (i.e., form, fit, and attachment details) of materials or equipment. The Government may duplicate, use, and disclose in any manner and for any purpose shop drawings delivered under this contract.

(b) This clause, including this paragraph (b), shall be included in all subcontracts hereunder at any tier.

(End of clause)

[DAC 91-8, 60 FR 33464, 6/28/95, effective 6/30/95]

252.227-7034 [Reserved]

[Final rule, 72 FR 69159, 12/7/2007, effective 12/7/2007]

252.227-7035 [Reserved]

252.227-7036 [Reserved]

[Final rule, 62 FR 2612, 1/17/97, effective 1/17/97; Interim rule, 69 FR 31911, 6/8/2004, effective 6/8/2004; Final rule, 69 FR 67856, 11/22/2004, effective 11/22/2004]

252.227-7037 Validation of restrictive markings on technical data.

As prescribed in 227.7102-4(c), 227.7103-6(e)(3), 227.7104(e)(5), or 227.7203-6(f), use the following clause:

VALIDATION OF RESTRICTIVE MARKINGS ON TECHNICAL DATA (SEP 2016)

(a) *Definitions*. The terms used in this clause are defined in the Rights in Technical Data—Noncommercial Items clause of this contract.

(b) *Presumption regarding development exclusively at private expense.*

(1) *Commercial items*. (i) Except as provided in paragraph (b)(2) of this clause, the Contracting Officer will presume that the Contractor's or a subcontractor's asserted use or release restrictions with respect to a commercial item is justified on the basis that the item was developed exclusively at private expense.

(ii) The Contracting Officer will not challenge such assertions unless the Contracting Officer has information that demonstrates that the commercial item was not developed exclusively at private expense.

(2) *Major weapon systems.* In the case of a challenge to a use or release restriction that is asserted with respect to data of the Contractor or a subcontractor for a major weapon system or a subsystem or component thereof on the basis that the major weapon system, subsystem, or component was developed exclusively at private expense—

(i) The presumption in paragraph (b)(1) of this clause applies to—

(A) A commercial subsystem or component of a major weapon system, if the major weapon system was acquired as a commercial item in accordance with DFARS subpart 234.70 (10 U.S.C. 2379(a));

(B) A component of a subsystem, if the subsystem was acquired as a commercial item in accordance with DFARS subpart 234.70 (10 U.S.C. 2379(b)); and

(C) Any other component, if the component is a commercially available off-the-shelf item or a commercially available off-the-shelf item with modifications of a type customarily available in the commercial marketplace or minor modifications made to meet Federal Government requirements; and

(ii) In all other cases, the challenge to the use or release restriction will be sustained unless information provided by the Contractor or a subcontractor demonstrates that the item or process was developed exclusively at private expense.

(c) *Justification.* The Contractor or subcontractor at any tier is responsible for maintaining records sufficient to justify the validity of its markings that impose restrictions on the Government and others to use, duplicate, or disclose technical data delivered or required to be delivered under the contract or subcontract. Except as provided in paragraph (b)(1) of this clause, the Contractor or subcontractor shall be prepared to furnish to the Contracting Officer a written justification for such restrictive markings in response to a challenge under paragraph (e) of this clause.

(d) *Prechallenge request for information.* (1) The Contracting Officer may request the Contractor or subcontractor to furnish a written explanation for any restriction asserted by the Contractor or subcontractor on the right of the United States or others to use technical data. If, upon review of the explanation submitted, the Contracting Officer remains unable to ascertain the basis of the restrictive marking, the Contracting Officer may further request the Contractor or subcontractor to furnish additional information in the records of, or otherwise in the possession of or reasonably available to, the Contractor or subcontractor to justify the validity of any restrictive marking on technical data delivered or to be delivered under the contract or subcontract (e.g., a statement of facts accompanied with supporting documentation). The Contractor or subcontractor shall submit such written data as requested by the Contracting Officer within the time required or such longer period as may be mutually agreed.

(2) If the Contracting Officer, after reviewing the written data furnished pursuant to paragraph (d)(1) of this clause, or any other available information pertaining to the validity of a restrictive marking, determines that reasonable grounds exist to question the current validity of the marking and that continued adherence to the marking would make impracticable the subsequent competitive acquisition of the item, component, or process to which the technical data relates, the Contracting Officer shall follow the procedures in paragraph (e) of this clause.

(3) If the Contractor or subcontractor fails to respond to the Contracting Officer's request for information under paragraph (d)(1) of this clause, and the Contracting Officer determines that continued adherence to the marking would make impracticable the subsequent competitive acquisition of the item, component, or process to which the technical data relates, the Contracting Officer may challenge the validity of the marking as described in paragraph (e) of this clause.

(e) *Challenge.* (1) Notwithstanding any provision of this contract concerning inspection and acceptance, if the Contracting Officer determines that a challenge to the restrictive marking is warranted, the Contracting Officer shall send a written challenge notice to the Contractor or subcontractor asserting the restrictive markings. Such challenge shall—

(i) State the specific grounds for challenging the asserted restriction;

(ii) Require a response within sixty (60) days justifying and providing sufficient evidence as to the current validity of the asserted restriction;

(iii) State that a DoD Contracting Officer's final decision, issued pursuant to paragraph (g) of this clause, sustaining the validity of a restrictive marking identical to the asserted restriction, within the three-year period preceding the challenge, shall serve as justification for the asserted restriction if the validated restriction was asserted by the same Contractor or subcontractor (or any licensee of such Contractor or subcontractor) to which such notice is being provided; and

(iv) State that failure to respond to the challenge notice may result in issuance of a final decision pursuant to paragraph (f) of this clause.

(2) The Contracting Officer shall extend the time for response as appropriate if the Contractor or subcontractor submits a written request showing the need for additional time to prepare a response.

(3) The Contractor's or subcontractor's written response shall be considered a claim within the meaning of the 41 U.S.C. 7101, Contract Disputes, and shall be certified in the form prescribed at 33.207 of the Federal Acquisition Regulation, regardless of dollar amount.

(4) A Contractor or subcontractor receiving challenges to the same restrictive markings from more than one Contracting Officer shall notify each Contracting Officer of the existence of more than one challenge. The notice shall also state which Contracting Officer initiated the first in time unanswered challenge. The Contracting Officer initiating the first in time unanswered challenge after consultation with the Contractor or subcontractor and the other Contracting Officers, shall formulate and distribute a schedule for responding to each of the challenge notices to all interested parties. The schedule shall afford the Contractor or subcontractor an opportunity to respond to each challenge notice. All parties will be bound by this schedule.

(f) *Final decision when Contractor or subcontractor fails to respond.* Upon a failure of a Contractor or subcontractor to submit any response to the challenge notice the Contracting Officer will issue a final decision to the Contractor or subcontractor in accordance with paragraph (b) of this clause and the Disputes clause of this contract pertaining to the validity of the asserted restriction. This final decision shall be issued as soon as possible after the expiration of the time period of paragraph (e) (1) (ii) or (e) (2) of this clause. Following issuance of the final decision, the Contracting Officer will comply with the procedures in paragraphs (g) (2) (ii) through (iv) of this clause.

(g) *Final decision when Contractor or subcontractor responds.* (1) if the Contracting Officer determines that the Contractor or subcontractor has justified the validity of the restrictive marking, the Contracting Officer shall issue a final decision to the Contractor or subcontractor sustaining the validity of the restrictive marking, and stating that the Government will continue to be bound by the restrictive marking. This final decision shall be issued within sixty (60) days after receipt of the Contractor's or subcontractor's response to the challenge notice, or within such longer period that the Contracting Officer has notified the Contractor or subcontractor that the Government will require. The notification of a longer period for issuance of a final decision will be made within sixty (60) days after receipt of the response to the challenge notice.

(2) (i) If the Contracting Officer determines that the validity of the restrictive marking is not justified, the Contracting Officer shall issue a final decision to the Contractor or subcontractor in accordance with the Disputes clause of this contract. Notwithstanding paragraph (e) of the Disputes clause, the final decision shall be issued within sixty (60) days after receipt of the Contractor's or subcontractor's response to the challenge notice, or within such longer

period that the Contracting Officer has notified the Contractor or subcontractor of the longer period that the Government will require. The notification of a longer period for issuance of a final decision will be made within sixty (60) days after receipt of the response to the challenge notice.

(ii) The Government agrees that it will continue to be bound by the restrictive marking of a period of ninety (90) days from the issuance of the Contracting Officer's final decision under paragraph (g)(2)(i) of this clause. The Contractor or subcontractor agrees that, if it intends to file suit in the United States Claims Court it will provide a notice of intent to file suit to the Contracting Officer within ninety (90) days from the issuance of the Contracting Officer's final decision under paragraph (g)(2)(i) of this clause. If the Contractor or subcontractor fails to appeal, file suit, or provide a notice of intent to file suit to the Contracting Officer within the ninety (90)-day period, the Government may cancel or ignore the restrictive markings, and the failure of the Contractor or subcontractor to take the required action constitutes agreement with such Government action.

(iii) The Government agrees that it will continue to be bound by the restrictive marking where a notice of intent to file suit in the United States Claims Court is provided to the Contracting Officer within ninety (90) days from the issuance of the final decision under paragraph (g)(2)(i) of this clause. The Government will no longer be bound, and the Contractor or subcontractor agrees that the Government may strike or ignore the restrictive markings, if the Contractor or subcontractor fails to file its suit within one (1) year after issuance of the final decision. Notwithstanding the foregoing, where the head of an agency determines, on a nondelegable basis, that urgent or compelling circumstances will not permit waiting for the filing of a suit in the United States Claims Court, the Contractor or subcontractor agrees that the agency may, following notice to the Contractor or subcontractor, authorize release or disclosure of the technical data. Such agency determination may be made at any time after issuance of the final decision and will not affect the Contractor's or subcontractor's right to damages against the United States where its restrictive markings are ultimately upheld or to pursue other relief, if any, as may be provided by law.

(iv) The Government agrees that it will be bound by the restrictive marking where an appeal or suit is filed pursuant to the Contract Disputes statute until final disposition by an agency Board of Contract Appeals or the United States Claims Court. Notwithstanding the foregoing, where the head of an agency determines, on a nondelegable basis, following notice to the Contractor that urgent or compelling circumstances will not permit awaiting the decision by such Board of Contract Appeals or the United States Claims Court, the Contractor or subcontractor agrees that the agency may authorize release or disclosure of the technical data. Such agency determination may be made at any time after issuance of the final decision and will not affect the Contractor's or subcontractor's right to damages against the United States where its restrictive markings are ultimately upheld or to pursue other relief, if any, as may be provided by law.

(h) *Final disposition of appeal or suit.* (1) If the Contractor or subcontractor appeals or files suit and if, upon final disposition of the appeal or suit, the Contracting Officer's decision is sustained—

(i) The restrictive marking on the technical data shall be cancelled, corrected or ignored; and

(ii) If the restrictive marking is found not to be substantially justified, the Contractor or subcontractor, as appropriate, shall be liable to the Government for payment of the cost to the Government of reviewing the restrictive marking and the fees and other expenses (as defined in 28 U.S.C. 2412(d)(2)(A)) incurred by the Government in challenging the marking, unless special circumstances would make such payment unjust.

(2) If the Contractor or subcontractor appeals or files suit and if, upon final disposition of the appeal or suit, the Contracting Officer's decision is not sustained—

(i) The Government shall continue to be bound by the restrictive marking; and

(ii) The Government shall be liable to the Contractor or subcontractor for payment of fees and other expenses (as defined in 28 U.S.C. 2412(d)(2)(A)) incurred by the Contractor or subcontractor in defending the marking, if the challenge by the Government is found not to have been made in good faith.

(i) *Duration of right to challenge.* The Government may review the validity of any restriction on technical data, delivered or to be delivered under a contract, asserted by the Contractor or subcontractor. During the period within three (3) years of final payment on a contract or within three (3) years of delivery of the technical data to the Government, whichever is later, the Contracting Officer may review and make a written determination to challenge the restriction. The Government may, however, challenge a restriction on the release, disclosure or use of technical data at any time if such technical data—

(1) Is publicly available;

(2) Has been furnished to the United States without restriction; or

(3) Has been otherwise made available without restriction. Only the Contracting Officer's final decision resolving a formal challenge by sustaining the validity of a restrictive marking constitutes "validation" as addressed in 10 U.S.C. 2321.

(j) *Decision not to challenge.* A decision by the Government, or a determination by the Contracting Officer, to not challenge the restrictive marking or asserted restriction shall not constitute "validation."

(k) *Privity of contract.* The Contractor or subcontractor agrees that the Contracting Officer may transact matters under this clause directly with subcontractors at any tier that assert restrictive markings. However, this clause neither creates nor implies privity of contract between the Government and subcontractors.

(l) *Flowdown.* The Contractor or subcontractor agrees to insert this clause in contractual instruments, including subcontracts and other contractual instruments for commercial items, with its subcontractors or suppliers at any tier requiring the delivery of technical data.

(End of clause)

[DAC 91-8, 60 FR 33464, 6/28/95, effective 6/30/95; DAC 91-9, 60 FR 61586, 11/30/95, effective 11/30/95; Final rule, 64 FR 51074 9/21/99, effective 9/21/99; Interim rule, 69 FR 31911, 6/8/2004, effective 6/8/2004; Final rule, 69 FR 67856, 11/22/2004, effective 11/22/2004; Final rule, 76 FR 58137, 9/20/2011, effective 9/20/2011; Final rule, 76 FR 58144, 9/20/2011, effective 9/20/2011; Final rule, 77 FR 23631, 4/20/2012, effective 4/20/2012; Final rule, 77 FR 35879, 6/15/2012, effective 6/15/2012; Final rule, 77 FR 76936, 12/31/2012, effective 12/31/2012; Final rule, 78 FR 37980, 6/25/2013, effective 6/25/2013; Final rule, 81 FR 65565, 9/23/2016, effective 9/23/2016]

252.227-7038 Patent Rights—Ownership by the Contractor (Large Business).

As prescribed in 227.303(2), use the following clause:

PATENT RIGHTS—OWNERSHIP BY THE CONTRACTOR (LARGE BUSINESS) (JUN 2012)

(a) *Definitions.* As used in this clause—
Invention means—

(1) Any invention or discovery that is or may be patentable or otherwise protectable under Title 35 of the United States Code; or

(2) Any variety of plant that is or may be protectable under the Plant Variety Protection statute (7 U.S.C. 2321, *et seq.*).

Made—

(1) When used in relation to any invention other than a plant variety, means the conception or first actual reduction to practice of the invention; or

(2) When used in relation to a plant variety, means that the Contractor has at least tentatively determined that the variety has been reproduced with recognized characteristics.

Nonprofit organization means—

(1) A university or other institution of higher education;

(2) An organization of the type described in the Internal Revenue Code at 26 U.S.C. 501(c)(3) and exempt from taxation under 26 U.S.C. 501(a); or

(3) Any nonprofit scientific or educational organization qualified under a State nonprofit organization statute.

Practical application means—

(1)(i) To manufacture, in the case of a composition or product;

(ii) To practice, in the case of a process or method; or

(iii) To operate, in the case of a machine or system; and

(2) In each case, under such conditions as to establish that—

(i) The invention is being utilized; and

(ii) The benefits of the invention are, to the extent permitted by law or Government regulations, available to the public on reasonable terms.

Subject invention means any invention of the Contractor made in the performance of work under this contract.

(b) *Contractor's rights*—(1) *Ownership*. The Contractor may elect to retain ownership of each subject invention throughout the world in accordance with the provisions of this clause.

(2) *License*. (i) The Contractor shall retain a nonexclusive royalty-free license throughout the world in each subject invention to which the Government obtains title, unless the Contractor fails to disclose the invention within the times specified in paragraph (c) of this clause. The Contractor's license—

(A) Extends to any domestic subsidiaries and affiliates within the corporate structure of which the Contractor is a part;

(B) Includes the right to grant sublicenses to the extent the Contractor was legally obligated to do so at the time of contract award; and

(C) Is transferable only with the approval of the agency, except when transferred to the successor of that part of the Contractor's business to which the invention pertains.

(ii) The agency—

(A) May revoke or modify the Contractor's domestic license to the extent necessary to achieve expeditious practical application of the subject invention pursuant to an application for an exclusive license submitted in accordance with 37 CFR Part 404 and agency licensing regulations;

(B) Will not revoke the license in that field of use or the geographical areas in which the Contractor has achieved practical application and continues to make the benefits of the invention reasonably accessible to the public; and

(C) May revoke or modify the license in any foreign country to the extent the Contractor, its licensees, or the domestic subsidiaries or affiliates have failed to achieve practical application in that foreign country.

(iii) Before revoking or modifying the license, the agency—

(A) Will furnish the Contractor a written notice of its intention to revoke or modify the license; and

(B) Will allow the Contractor 30 days (or such other time as the funding agency may authorize for good cause shown by the Contractor) after the notice to show cause why the license should not be revoked or modified.

(iv) The Contractor has the right to appeal, in accordance with 37 CFR Part 404 and agency regulations, concerning the licensing of Government-owned inventions, any decision concerning the revocation or modification of the license.

(c) *Contractor's obligations*. (1) The Contractor shall—

(i) Disclose, in writing, each subject invention to the Contracting Officer within 2 months after the inventor discloses it in writing to Contractor personnel responsible for patent matters, or within 6 months after the Contractor first becomes aware that a subject invention has been made, whichever is earlier;

(ii) Include in the disclosure—

(A) The inventor(s) and the contract under which the invention was made;

(B) Sufficient technical detail to convey a clear understanding of the invention; and

(C) Any publication, on sale (i.e., sale or offer for sale), or public use of the invention and whether a manuscript describing the invention has been submitted for publication and, if so, whether it has been accepted for publication; and

(iii) After submission of the disclosure, promptly notify the Contracting Officer of the acceptance of any manuscript describing the invention for publication and of any on sale or public use.

(2) The Contractor shall elect in writing whether or not to retain ownership of any subject invention by notifying the Contracting Officer at the time of disclosure or within 8 months of disclosure, as to those countries (including the United States) in which the Contractor will retain ownership. However, in any case where publication, on sale, or public use has initiated the 1-year statutory period during which valid patent protection can be obtained in the United States, the agency may shorten the period of election of title to a date that is no more than 60 days prior to the end of the statutory period.

(3) The Contractor shall—

(i) File either a provisional or a nonprovisional patent application on an elected subject invention within 1 year after election, provided that in all cases the application is filed prior to the end of any statutory period wherein valid patent protection can be obtained in the United States after a publication, on sale, or public use;

(ii) File a nonprovisional application within 10 months of the filing of any provisional application; and

(iii) File patent applications in additional countries or international patent offices within either 10 months of the first filed patent application (whether provisional or nonprovisional) or 6 months from the date the Commissioner of Patents grants permission to file foreign patent applications where such filing has been prohibited by a Secrecy Order.

(4) The Contractor may request extensions of time for disclosure, election, or filing under paragraphs (c)(1), (2), and (3) of this clause. The Contracting Officer will normally grant the extension unless there is reason to believe the extension would prejudice the Government's interests.

(d) *Government's rights*—(1) *Ownership*. The Contractor shall assign to the agency, upon written request, title to any subject invention—

(i) If the Contractor elects not to retain title to a subject invention;

(ii) If the Contractor fails to disclose or elect the subject invention within the times specified in paragraph (c) of this clause and the agency requests title within 60 days after learning of the Contractor's failure to report or elect within the specified times;

(iii) In those countries in which the Contractor fails to file patent applications within the times specified in paragraph (c) of this clause, provided that, if the Contractor has filed a patent application in a country after the times specified in paragraph (c) of this clause, but prior to its receipt of the written request of the agency, the Contractor shall continue to retain ownership in that country; and

(iv) In any country in which the Contractor decides not to continue the prosecution of any application for, to pay the maintenance fees on, or defend in reexamination or opposition proceeding on, a patent on a subject invention.

(2) *License*. If the Contractor retains ownership of any subject invention, the Government shall have a nonexclusive, nontransferable, irrevocable, paid-up license to practice, or have practiced for or on behalf of the United States, the subject invention throughout the world.

(e) *Contractor action to protect the Government's interest.* (1) The Contractor shall execute or have executed and promptly deliver to the agency all instruments necessary to—

(i) Establish or confirm the rights the Government has throughout the world in those subject inventions in which the Contractor elects to retain ownership; and

(ii) Assign title to the agency when requested under paragraph (d)(1) of this clause and enable the Government to obtain patent protection for that subject invention in any country.

(2) The Contractor shall—

(i) Require, by written agreement, its employees, other than clerical and nontechnical employees, to—

(A) Disclose each subject invention promptly in writing to personnel identified as responsible for the administration of patent matters, so that the Contractor can comply with the disclosure provisions in paragraph (c) of this clause; and

(B) Provide the disclosure in the Contractor's format, which should require, as a minimum, the information required by paragraph (c)(1) of this clause;

(ii) Instruct its employees, through employee agreements or other suitable educational programs, as to the importance of reporting inventions in sufficient time to permit the filing of patent applications prior to U.S. or statutory foreign bars; and

(iii) Execute all papers necessary to file patent applications on subject inventions and to establish the Government's rights in the subject inventions.

(3) The Contractor shall notify the Contracting Officer of any decisions not to file a nonprovisional patent application, continue the prosecution of a patent application, pay maintenance fees, or defend in a reexamination or opposition proceeding on a patent, in any country, not less than 30 days before the expiration of the response or filing period required by the relevant patent office.

(4) The Contractor shall include, within the specification of any United States nonprovisional patent application and any patent issuing thereon covering a subject invention, the following statement: "This invention was made with Government support under (identify the contract) awarded by (identify the agency). The Government has certain rights in this invention."

(5) The Contractor shall—

(i) Establish and maintain active and effective procedures to ensure that subject inventions are promptly identified and disclosed to Contractor personnel responsible for patent matters;

(ii) Include in these procedures the maintenance of—

(A) Laboratory notebooks or equivalent records and other records as are reasonably necessary to document the conception and/ or the first actual reduction to practice of subject inventions; and

(B) Records that show that the procedures for identifying and disclosing the inventions are followed; and

(iii) Upon request, furnish the Contracting Officer a description of these procedures for evaluation and for determination as to their effectiveness.

(6) The Contractor shall, when licensing a subject invention, arrange to—

(i) Avoid royalty charges on acquisitions involving Government funds, including funds derived through the Government's Military Assistance Program or otherwise derived through the Government;

(ii) Refund any amounts received as royalty charges on the subject inventions in acquisitions for, or on behalf of, the Government; and

(iii) Provide for the refund in any instrument transferring rights in the invention to any party.

(7) The Contractor shall furnish to the Contracting Officer the following:

(i) Interim reports every 12 months (or any longer period as may be specified by the Contracting Officer) from the date of the contract, listing subject inventions during that period and stating that all subject inventions have been disclosed or that there are no subject inventions.

(ii) A final report, within 3 months after completion of the contracted work, listing all subject inventions or stating that there were no subject inventions, and listing all subcontracts at any tier containing a patent rights clause or stating that there were no subcontracts.

(8) (i) The Contractor shall promptly notify the Contracting Officer in writing upon the award of any subcontract at any tier containing a patent rights clause by identifying—

(A) The subcontractor;

(B) The applicable patent rights clause;

(C) The work to be performed under the subcontract; and

(D) The dates of award and estimated completion.

(ii) The Contractor shall furnish, upon request, a copy of the subcontract, and no more frequently than annually, a listing of the subcontracts that have been awarded.

(9) In the event of a refusal by a prospective subcontractor to accept one of the clauses specified in paragraph (l) (1) of this clause, the Contractor—

(i) Shall promptly submit a written notice to the Contracting Officer setting forth the subcontractor's reasons for the refusal and other pertinent information that may expedite disposition of the matter; and

(ii) Shall not proceed with that subcontract without the written authorization of the Contracting Officer.

(10) The Contractor shall provide to the Contracting Officer, upon request, the following information for any subject invention for which the Contractor has retained ownership:

(i) Filing date.

(ii) Serial number and title.

(iii) A copy of any patent application (including an English-language version if filed in a language other than English).

(iv) Patent number and issue date.

(11) The Contractor shall furnish to the Government, upon request, an irrevocable power to inspect and make copies of any patent application file.

(f) *Reporting on utilization of subject inventions.* (1) The Contractor shall—

(i) Submit upon request periodic reports no more frequently than annually on the utilization of a subject invention or on efforts in obtaining utilization of the subject invention that are being made by the Contractor or its licensees or assignees;

(ii) Include in the reports information regarding the status of development, date of first commercial sale or use, gross royalties received by the Contractor, and other information as the agency may reasonably specify; and

(iii) Provide additional reports that the agency may request in connection with any march-in proceedings undertaken by the agency in accordance with paragraph (h) of this clause.

(2) To the extent permitted by law, the agency shall not disclose the information provided under paragraph (f) (1) of this clause to persons outside the Government without the Contractor's permission, if the data or information is considered by the Contractor or its licensee or assignee to be "privileged and confidential" (see 5 U.S.C. 552(b) (4)) and is so marked.

(g) *Preference for United States industry.* Notwithstanding any other provision of this clause, the Contractor agrees that neither the Contractor nor any assignee shall grant to any person the exclusive right to use or sell any subject invention in the United States unless the person agrees that any products embodying the subject invention or produced through the use of the subject invention will be manufactured substantially in the United States. However, in individual cases, the agency may waive the requirement for an exclusive license agreement upon a showing by the Contractor or its assignee that—

(1) Reasonable but unsuccessful efforts have been made to grant licenses on similar terms to potential licensees that would be likely to manufacture substantially in the United States; or

(2) Under the circumstances, domestic manufacture is not commercially feasible.

(h) *March-in rights*. The Contractor acknowledges that, with respect to any subject invention in which it has retained ownership, the agency has the right to require licensing pursuant to 35 U.S.C. 203 and 210(c), 37 CFR 401.6, and any supplemental regulations of the agency in effect on the date of contract award.

(i) *Other inventions*. Nothing contained in this clause shall be deemed to grant to the Government any rights with respect to any invention other than a subject invention.

(j) *Examination of records relating to inventions*. (1) The Contracting Officer or any authorized representative shall, until 3 years after final payment under this contract, have the right to examine any books (including laboratory notebooks), records, and documents of the Contractor relating to the conception or first reduction to practice of inventions in the same field of technology as the work under this contract to determine whether—

(i) Any inventions are subject inventions;

(ii) The Contractor has established procedures required by paragraph (e)(5) of this clause; and

(iii) The Contractor and its inventors have complied with the procedures.

(2) If the Contracting Officer learns of an unreported Contractor invention that the Contracting Officer believes may be a subject invention, the Contractor shall be required to disclose the invention to the agency for a determination of ownership rights.

(3) Any examination of records under this paragraph (j) shall be subject to appropriate conditions to protect the confidentiality of the information involved.

(k) *Withholding of payment (this paragraph does not apply to subcontracts)*. (1) Any time before final payment under this contract, the Contracting Officer may, in the Government's interest, withhold payment until a reserve not exceeding $50,000 or 5 percent of the amount of the contract, whichever is less, is set aside if, in the Contracting Officer's opinion, the Contractor fails to—

(i) Establish, maintain, and follow effective procedures for identifying and disclosing subject inventions pursuant to paragraph (e)(5) of this clause;

(ii) Disclose any subject invention pursuant to paragraph (c)(1) of this clause;

(iii) Deliver acceptable interim reports pursuant to paragraph (e)(7)(i) of this clause; or

(iv) Provide the information regarding subcontracts pursuant to paragraph (e)(8) of this clause.

(2) The reserve or balance shall be withheld until the Contracting Officer has determined that the Contractor has rectified whatever deficiencies exist and has delivered all reports, disclosures, and other information required by this clause.

(3) The Government will not make final payment under this contract before the Contractor delivers to the Contracting Officer—

(i) All disclosures of subject inventions required by paragraph (c)(1) of this clause;

(ii) An acceptable final report pursuant to paragraph (e)(7)(ii) of this clause; and

(iii) All past due confirmatory instruments.

(4) The Contracting Officer may decrease or increase the sums withheld up to the maximum authorized in paragraph (k)(1) of this clause. No amount shall be withheld under this paragraph while the amount specified by this paragraph is being withheld under other provisions of the contract. The withholding of any amount or the subsequent payment thereof shall not be construed as a waiver of any Government right.

(l) *Subcontracts*. (1) The Contractor—

(i) Shall include the substance of the Patent Rights-Ownership by the Contractor clause set forth at 52.227-11 of the Federal Acquisition Regulation (FAR), in all subcontracts for experimental, developmental, or research work to be performed by a small business concern or nonprofit organization; and

(ii) Shall include the substance of this clause, including this paragraph (l), in all other subcontracts for experimental, developmental, or research work, unless a different patent rights clause is required by FAR 27.303.

(2) For subcontracts at any tier—

(i) The patents rights clause included in the subcontract shall retain all references to the Government and shall provide to the subcontractor all the rights and obligations provided to the Contractor in the clause. The Contractor shall not, as consideration for awarding the subcontract, obtain rights in the subcontractor's subject inventions; and

(ii) The Government, the Contractor, and the subcontractor agree that the mutual obligations of the parties created by this clause constitute a contract between the subcontractor and the Government with respect to those matters covered by this clause. However, nothing in this paragraph is intended to confer any jurisdiction under the Contract Disputes statute in connection with proceedings under paragraph (h) of this clause.

(End of clause)

ALTERNATE I (DEC 2007)

As prescribed in 227.303(2)(ii), add the following paragraph (b)(2)(v) to the basic clause:

(v) The license shall include the right of the Government to sublicense foreign governments, their nationals, and international organizations pursuant to the following treaties or international agreements: ____*____.

[Contracting Officer to complete with the names of applicable existing treaties or international agreements. This paragraph is not intended to apply to treaties or agreements that are in effect on the date of the award but are not listed.]*

ALTERNATE II (DEC 2007)

As prescribed in 227.303(2)(iii), add the following paragraph (b)(2)(v) to the basic clause:

(v) The agency reserves the right to—

(A) Unilaterally amend this contract to identify specific treaties or international agreements entered into or to be entered into by the Government after the effective date of this contract; and

(B) Exercise those license or other rights that are necessary for the Government to meet its obligations to foreign governments, their nationals, and international organizations under any treaties or international agreement with respect to subject inventions made after the date of the amendment.

[Final rule, 72 FR 69159, 12/7/2007, effective 12/7/2007; Final rule, 77 FR 35879, 6/15/2012, effective 6/15/2012; Final rule, 77 FR 76936, 12/31/2012, effective 12/31/2012]

252.227-7039 Patents—reporting of subject inventions.

As prescribed in 227.303(1), use the following clause:

PATENTS—REPORTING OF SUBJECT INVENTIONS (APR 1990)

The Contractor shall furnish the Contracting Officer the following:

(a) Interim reports every twelve (12) months (or such longer period as may be specified by the Contracting Officer) from the date of the contract, listing subject inventions during that period and stating that all subject inventions have been disclosed or that there are no such inventions.

(b) A final report, within three (3) months after completion of the contracted work, listing all subject inventions or stating that there were no such inventions.

(c) Upon request, the filing date, serial number and title, a copy of the patent application and patent number, and issue data for any subject invention for which the Contractor has retained title.

(d) Upon request, the Contractor shall furnish the Government an irrevocable power to inspect and make copies of the patent application file.

(End of clause)

[Final rule, 72 FR 69159, 12/7/2007, effective 12/7/2007]

252.228 Bonds and Insurance, provisions and clauses for DFARS Part 228

252.228-7000 Reimbursement for war-hazard losses.

As prescribed in 228.370(a), use the following clause:

REIMBURSEMENT FOR WAR-HAZARD LOSSES (DEC 1991)

(a) Costs for providing employee war-hazard benefits in accordance with paragraph (b) of the Workers' Compensation and War-Hazard Insurance clause of this contract are allowable if the Contractor—

(1) Submits proof of loss files to support payment or denial of each claim;

(2) Subject to Contracting Officer approval, makes lump sum final settlement of any open claims and obtains necessary release documents within one year of the expiration or termination of this contract, unless otherwise extended by the Contracting Officer; and

(3) Provides the Contracting Officer at the time of final settlement of this contract—

(i) An investigation report and evaluation of any potential claim; and

(ii) An estimate of the dollar amount involved should the potential claim mature.

(b) The cost of insurance for liabilities reimbursable under this clause is not allowable.

(c) The Contracting Officer may require the Contractor to assign to the Government all right, title, and interest to any refund, rebate, or recapture arising out of any claim settlements.

(d) The Contractor agrees to—

(1) Investigate and promptly notify the Contracting Officer in writing of any occurrence which may give rise to a claim or potential claim, including the estimated amount of the claim;

(2) Give the Contracting Officer immediate written notice of any suit or action filed which may result in a payment under this clause; and

(3) Provide assistance to the Government in connection with any third party suit or claim relating to this clause which the Government elects to prosecute or defend in its own behalf.

(End of clause)

252.228-7001 Ground and flight risk.

As prescribed in 228.370(b), use the following clause:

GROUND AND FLIGHT RISK (JUN 2010)

(a) *Definitions*. As used in this clause—

(1) *Aircraft*, unless otherwise provided in the contract Schedule, means—

(i) Aircraft to be delivered to the Government under this contract (either before or after Government acceptance), including complete aircraft and aircraft in the process of being manufactured, disassembled, or reassembled; provided that an engine, portion of a wing, or a wing is attached to a fuselage of the aircraft;

(ii) Aircraft, whether in a state of disassembly or reassembly, furnished by the Government to the Contractor under this contract, including all Government property installed, in the process of installation, or temporarily removed; provided that the aircraft and property are not covered by a separate bailment agreement;

(iii) Aircraft furnished by the Contractor under this contract (either before or after Government acceptance); or

(iv) Conventional winged aircraft, as well as helicopters, vertical take-off or landing aircraft, lighter-than-air airships, unmanned aerial vehicles, or other nonconventional aircraft specified in this contract.

(2) *Contractor's managerial personnel* means the Contractor's directors, officers, and any of the Contractor's managers, superintendents, or other equivalent representatives who have supervision or direction of—

(i) All or substantially all of the Contractor's business;

(ii) All or substantially all of the Contractor's operation at any one plant or separate location; or

(iii) A separate and complete major industrial operation.

(3) *Contractor's premises* means those premises, including subcontractors' premises, designated in the Schedule or in writing by the Contracting Officer, and any other place the aircraft is moved for safeguarding.

(4) *Flight* means any flight demonstration, flight test, taxi test, or other flight made in the performance of this contract, or for the purpose of safeguarding the aircraft, or previously approved in writing by the Contracting Officer.

(i) For land-based aircraft, *flight* begins with the taxi roll from a flight line on the Contractor's premises and continues until the aircraft has completed the taxi roll in returning to a flight line on the Contractor's premises.

(ii) For seaplanes, *flight* begins with the launching from a ramp on the Contractor's premises and continues until the aircraft has completed its landing run and is beached at a ramp on the Contractor's premises.

(iii) For helicopters, *flight* begins upon engagement of the rotors for the purpose of take-off from the Contractor's premises and continues until the aircraft has returned to the ground on the Contractor's premises and the rotors are disengaged.

(iv) For vertical take-off or landing aircraft, *flight* begins upon disengagement from any launching platform or device on the Contractor's premises and continues until the aircraft has been engaged to any launching platform or device on the Contractor's premises.

(v) All aircraft off the Contractor's premises shall be considered to be in flight when on the ground or water for reasonable periods of time following emergency landings, landings made in performance of this contract, or landings approved in writing by the Contracting Officer.

(5) *Flight crew member* means the pilot, the co-pilot, and, unless otherwise provided in the Schedule, the flight engineer, navigator, and bombardier-navigator when assigned to their respective crew positions for the purpose of conducting any flight on behalf of the Contractor. It also includes any pilot or operator of an unmanned aerial vehicle. If required, a defense systems operator may also be assigned as a flight crew member.

(6) *In the open* means located wholly outside of buildings on the Contractor's premises or other places described in the Schedule as being *in the open*. Government-furnished aircraft shall be considered to be located *in the open* at all times while in the Contractor's possession, care, custody, or control.

(7) *Operation* means operations and tests of the aircraft and its installed equipment, accessories, and power plants, while the aircraft is in the open or in motion. The term does not apply to aircraft on any production line or in flight.

(b) *Combined regulation/instruction*. The Contractor shall be bound by the operating procedures contained in the combined regulation/instruction entitled *Contractor's Flight and Ground Operations* (Air Force Instruction 10-220, Army Regulation 95-20, NAVAIR Instruction 3710.1 (Series), Coast Guard Instruction M13020.3, and Defense Contract Management Agency Instruction 8210.1) in effect on the date of contract award.

(c) *Government as self-insurer*. Subject to the conditions in paragraph (d) of this clause, the Government self-insures and assumes the risk of damage to, or loss or destruction of aircraft *in the open*, during *operation*, and in *flight*, except as may be specifically provided in the Schedule as an exception to this clause. The Contractor shall not be liable to the Government for such damage, loss, or destruction beyond the Contractor's share of loss amount under the Government's self-insurance.

(d) *Conditions for Government's self-insurance*. The Government's assumption of risk for aircraft in the open shall continue unless the Contracting Officer finds that the Contractor has failed to comply with paragraph (b) of this clause, or that the aircraft is in the open under unreasonable conditions, and the Contractor fails to take prompt corrective action.

(1) The Contracting Officer, when finding that the Contractor has failed to comply with paragraph (b) of this clause or that the aircraft is in the open under unreasonable conditions, shall notify the Contractor in writing and shall require the Contractor to make corrections within a reasonable time.

(2) Upon receipt of the notice, the Contractor shall promptly correct the cited conditions, regardless of whether there is agreement that the conditions are unreasonable.

(i) If the Contracting Officer later determines that the cited conditions were not unreasonable, an equitable adjustment shall be made in the contract price for any additional costs incurred in correcting the conditions.

(ii) Any dispute as to the unreasonableness of the conditions or the equitable adjustment shall be considered a dispute under the Disputes clause of this contract.

(3) If the Contracting Officer finds that the Contractor failed to act promptly to correct the cited conditions or failed to correct the conditions within a reasonable time, the Contracting Officer may terminate the Government's assumption of risk for any aircraft in the open under the cited conditions. The termination will be effective at 12:01 a.m. on the fifteenth day following the day the written notice is received by the Contractor.

(i) If the Contracting Officer later determines that the Contractor acted promptly to correct the cited conditions or that the time taken by the Contractor was not unreasonable, an equitable adjustment shall be made in the contract price for any additional costs incurred as a result of termination of the Government's assumption of risk.

(ii) Any dispute as to the timeliness of the Contractor's action or the equitable adjustment shall be considered a dispute under the Disputes clause of this contract.

(4) If the Government terminates its assumption of risk pursuant to the terms of this clause—

(i) The Contractor shall thereafter assume the entire risk for damage, loss, or destruction of the affected aircraft;

(ii) Any costs incurred by the Contractor (including the costs of the Contractor's self-insurance, insurance premiums paid to insure the Contractor's assumption of risk, deductibles associated with such purchased insurance, etc.) to mitigate its assumption of risk are unallowable costs; and

(iii) The liability provisions of the Government Property clause of this contract are not applicable to the affected aircraft.

(5) The Contractor shall promptly notify the Contracting Officer when unreasonable conditions have been corrected.

(i) If, upon receipt of the Contractor's notice of the correction of the unreasonable conditions, the Government elects to again assume the risk of loss and relieve the Contractor of its liability for damage, loss, or destruction of the aircraft, the Contracting Officer will notify the Contractor of the Contracting Officer's decision to resume the Government's risk of loss. The Contractor shall be entitled to an equitable adjustment in the contract price for any insurance costs extending from the end of the third working day after the Government's receipt of the Contractor's notice of correction until the Contractor is notified that the Government will resume the risk of loss.

(ii) If the Government does not again assume the risk of loss and the unreasonable conditions have been corrected, the Contractor shall be entitled to an equitable adjustment for insurance costs, if any, extending after the third working day after the Government's receipt of the Contractor's notice of correction.

(6) The Government's termination of its assumption of risk of loss does not relieve the Contractor of its obligation to comply with all other provisions of this clause, including the combined regulation/instruction entitled *Contractor's Flight and Ground Operations*.

(e) *Exclusions from the Government's assumption of risk*. The Government's assumption of risk shall not extend to damage, loss, or destruction of aircraft which—

(1) Results from failure of the Contractor, due to willful misconduct or lack of good

faith of any of the Contractor's managerial personnel, to maintain and administer a program for the protection and preservation of aircraft in the open and during operation in accordance with sound industrial practice, including oversight of a subcontractor's program;

(2) Is sustained during flight if either the flight or the flight crew members have not been approved in advance of any flight in writing by the Government Flight Representative, who has been authorized in accordance with the combined regulation/instruction entitled *Contractor's Flight and Ground Operations*;

(3) Occurs in the course of transportation by rail, or by conveyance on public streets, highways, or waterways, except for Government-furnished property;

(4) Is covered by insurance;

(5) Consists of wear and tear; deterioration (including rust and corrosion); freezing; or mechanical, structural, or electrical breakdown or failure, unless these are the result of other loss, damage or destruction covered by this clause. (This exclusion does not apply to Government-furnished property if damage consists of reasonable wear and tear or deterioration, or results from inherent vice, *e.g.*, a known condition or design defect in the property); or

(6) Is sustained while the aircraft is being worked on and is a direct result of the work unless such damage, loss, or destruction would be covered by insurance which would have been maintained by the Contractor, but for the Government's assumption of risk.

(f) *Contractor's share of loss and Contractor's deductible under the Government's self-insurance.*

(1) The Contractor assumes the risk of loss and shall be responsible for the Contractor's share of loss under the Government's self-insurance. That share is the lesser of—

(i) The first $100,000 of loss or damage to aircraft in the open, during operation, or in flight resulting from each separate event, except for reasonable wear and tear and to the extent the loss or damage is caused by negligence of Government personnel; or

(ii) Twenty percent of the price or estimated cost of this contract.

(2) If the Government elects to require that the aircraft be replaced or restored by the Contractor to its condition immediately prior to the damage, the equitable adjustment in the price authorized by paragraph (j) of this clause shall not include the dollar amount of the risk assumed by the Contractor.

(3) In the event the Government does not elect repair or replacement, the Contractor agrees to credit the contract price or pay the Government, as directed by the Contracting Officer, the lesser of—

(i) $100,000;

(ii) Twenty percent of the price or estimated cost of this contract; or

(iii) The amount of the loss.

(4) For task order and delivery order contracts, the Contractor's share of the loss shall be the lesser of $100,000 or twenty percent of the combined total price or total estimated cost of those orders issued to date to which the clause applies.

(5) The costs incurred by the Contractor for its share of the loss and for insuring against that loss are unallowable costs, including but not limited to—

(i) The Contractor's share of loss under the Government's self-insurance;

(ii) The costs of the Contractor's self-insurance;

(iii) The deductible for any Contractor-purchased insurance;

(iv) Insurance premiums paid for Contractor-purchased insurance; and

(v) Costs associated with determining, litigating, and defending against the Contractor's liability.

(g) *Subcontractor possession or control.* The Contractor shall not be relieved from liability for damage, loss, or destruction of aircraft while such aircraft is in the possession or control of its subcontractors, except to the extent that the subcontract, with the written approval of the Contracting Officer, provides for relief from each liability. In the absence of approval, the subcontract shall contain provisions requiring the return of aircraft in as good condition as when received, except for reasonable wear and tear or for the utilization of the property in accordance with the provisions of this contract.

(h) *Contractor's exclusion of insurance costs.* The Contractor warrants that the contract price does not and will not include, except as may be authorized in this clause, any charge or contingency reserve for insurance covering damage, loss, or destruction of aircraft while in the open, during operation, or in flight when the risk has been assumed by the Government, including the Contractor share of loss in this clause, even if the assumption may be terminated for aircraft in the open.

(i) *Procedures in the event of loss.*

(1) In the event of damage, loss, or destruction of aircraft in the open, during operation, or in flight, the Contractor shall take all reasonable steps to protect the aircraft from further damage, to separate damaged and undamaged aircraft, and to put all aircraft in the best possible order. Except in cases covered by paragraph (f)(2) of this clause, the Contractor shall furnish to the Contracting Officer a statement of—

(i) The damaged, lost, or destroyed aircraft;

(ii) The time and origin of the damage, loss, or destruction;

(iii) All known interests in commingled property of which aircraft are a part; and

(iv) The insurance, if any, covering the interest in commingled property.

(2) The Contracting Officer will make an equitable adjustment for expenditures made by the Contractor in performing the obligations under this paragraph.

(j) *Loss prior to delivery.*

(1) If prior to delivery and acceptance by the Government, aircraft is damaged, lost, or destroyed and the Government assumed the risk, the Government shall either—

(i) Require that the aircraft be replaced or restored by the Contractor to the condition immediately prior to the damage, in which event the Contracting Officer will make an equitable adjustment in the contract price and the time for contract performance; or

(ii) Terminate this contract with respect to the aircraft. Notwithstanding the provisions in any other termination clause under this contract, in the event of termination, the Contractor shall be paid the contract price for the aircraft (or, if applicable, any work to be performed on the aircraft) less any amount the Contracting Officer determines—

(A) It would have cost the Contractor to complete the aircraft (or any work to be performed on the aircraft) together with anticipated profit on uncompleted work; and

(B) Would be the value of the damaged aircraft or any salvage retained by the Contractor.

(2) The Contracting Officer shall prescribe the manner of disposition of the damaged, lost, or destroyed aircraft, or any parts of the aircraft. If any additional costs of such disposition are incurred by the Contractor, a further equitable adjustment will be made in the amount due the Contractor. Failure of the parties to agree upon termination costs or an equitable adjustment with respect to any aircraft shall be considered a dispute under the Disputes clause of this contract.

(k) *Reimbursement from a third party.* In the event the Contractor is reimbursed or compensated by a third party for damage, loss, or destruction of aircraft and has also been compensated by the Government, the Contractor shall equitably reimburse the Government. The Contractor shall do nothing to prejudice the Government's right to recover against third parties for damage, loss, or destruction. Upon the request of the Contracting Officer or authorized representative, the Contractor shall at Government expense furnish to the Government all reasonable assistance and cooperation (including the prosecution of suit and the execution of instruments of assignment or subrogation) in obtaining recovery.

(l) *Government acceptance of liability.* To the extent the Government has accepted such liability under other provisions of this contract, the Contractor shall not be reimbursed for liability to third persons for loss or damage to property or for death or bodily injury caused by aircraft during flight unless the flight crew members previously have been approved for this flight in writing by the Government Flight Representative, who has been authorized in accordance with the combined regulation entitled *Contractor's Flight and Ground Operations*.

(m) *Subcontracts*. The Contractor shall incorporate the requirements of this clause, including this paragraph (m), in all subcontracts.

(End of clause)

[DAC 91-1, 56 FR 67222, 12/30/91, effective 12/31/91; DAC 91-11, 61 FR 50446, 9/26/96, effective 9/26/96; Final rule, 75 FR 32642, 6/8/2010, effective 6/8/2010]

252.228-7002 [Removed and Reserved]

[DAC 91-11, 61 FR 50446, 9/26/96, effective 9/26/96; Final rule, 75 FR 32642, 6/8/2010, effective 6/8/2010]

252.228-7003 Capture and detention.

As prescribed in 228.370(c), use the following clause:

CAPTURE AND DETENTION (DEC 1991)

(a) As used in this clause—

(1) *Captured person* means any employee of the Contractor who is—

(i) Assigned to duty outside the United States for the performance of this contract; and

(ii) Found to be missing from his or her place of employment under circumstances that make it appear probable that the absence is due to the action of the force of any power not allied with the United States in a common military effort; or

(iii) Known to have been taken prisoner, hostage, or otherwise detained by the force of such power, whether or not actually engaged in employment at the time of capture; provided, that at the time of capture or detention, the person was either—

(A) Engaged in activity directly arising out of and in the course of employment under this contract; or

(B) Captured in an area where required to be only in order to perform this contract.

(2) A *period of detention* begins with the day of capture and continues until the captured person is returned to the place of employment, the United States, or is able to be returned to the jurisdiction of the United States, or until the person's death is established or legally presumed to have occurred by evidence satisfactory to the Contracting Officer, whichever occurs first.

(3) *United States* comprises geographically the 50 states and the District of Columbia.

(4) *War Hazards Compensation Act* refers to the statute compiled in chapter 12 of title 42, U.S. Code (sections 1701-1717), as amended.

(b) If pursuant to an agreement entered into prior to capture, the Contractor is obligated to pay and has paid detention benefits to a captured person, or the person's dependents, the Government will reimburse the Contractor up to an amount equal to the lesser of—

(1) Total wage or salary being paid at the time of capture due from the Contractor to the captured person for the period of detention; or

(2) That amount which would have been payable if the detention had occurred under circumstances covered by the War Hazards Compensation Act.

(c) The period of detention shall not be considered as time spent in contract performance, and the Government shall not be obligated to make payment for that time except as provided in this clause.

(d) The obligation of the Government shall apply to the entire period of detention, except that it is subject to the availability of funds from which payment can be made. The rights and obligations of the parties under this clause shall survive prior expiration, completion, or termination of this contract.

(e) The Contractor shall not be reimbursed under this clause for payments made if the employees were entitled to compensation for capture and detention under the War Hazards Compensation Act, as amended.

(End of clause)

[DAC 91-3, 57 FR 42633, 9/15/92, effective 8/31/92; Final rule, 75 FR 32642, 6/8/2010, effective 6/8/2010]

252.228-7004 [Removed and Reserved]

[Final rule, 83 FR 54679, 10/31/2018, effective 10/31/2018]

252.228-7005 Mishap reporting and investigation involving aircraft, missiles, and space launch vehicles.

As prescribed in 228.370(d), use the following clause:

MISHAP REPORTING AND INVESTIGATION INVOLVING AIRCRAFT, MISSILES, AND SPACE LAUNCH VEHICLES (NOV 2019)

(a) The Contractor shall report promptly to the Administrative Contracting Officer all pertinent facts relating to each mishap involving an aircraft, missile, or space launch vehicle being manufactured, modified, repaired, or overhauled in connection with this contract.

(b) If the Government conducts an investigation of the mishap, the Contractor shall cooperate and assist the Government's personnel until the investigation is complete.

(c) The Contractor shall include a clause in subcontracts under this contract to require subcontractor cooperation and assistance in mishap investigations.

(End of clause)

[Final rule, 75 FR 32642, 6/8/2010, effective 6/8/2010; Final rule, 84 FR 65311, 11/27/2019, effective 11/27/2019]

252.228-7006 Compliance with Spanish laws and insurance.

As prescribed at 228.370(e), use the following clause:

COMPLIANCE WITH SPANISH LAWS AND INSURANCE (DEC 1998)

(a) The requirements of this clause apply only if the Contractor is not a Spanish concern.

(b) The Contractor shall, without additional expense to the United States Government, comply with all applicable Spanish Government laws pertaining to sanitation, traffic, security, employment of labor, and all other laws relevant to the performance of this contract. The Contractor shall hold the United States Government harmless and free from any liability resulting from the Contractor's failure to comply with such laws.

(c) The contractor shall, at its own expense, provide and maintain during the entire performance of this contract, all workmen's compensation, employees' liability, bodily injury insurance, and other required insurance adequate to cover the risk assumed by the Contractor. The Contractor shall indemnify and hold harmless the United States Government from liability resulting from all claims for damages as a result of death or injury to personnel or damage to real or personal property related to the performance of this contract.

(d) The Contractor agrees to represent in writing to the Contracting Officer, prior to commencement of work and not later than 15 days after the date of the Notice to Proceed, that the Contractor has obtained the required types of insurance in the following minimum amounts. The representation also shall state that the Contractor will promptly notify the Contracting Officer of any notice of cancellation of insurance or material change in insurance coverage that could affect the United States Government's interests.

Type of insurance	Coverage per person	Coverage per accident	Property damage
Comprehensive General Liability	$300,000	$1,000,000	$100,000

(e) The Contractor shall provide the Contracting Officer with a similar representation for all subcontracts with non-Spanish concerns that will perform work in Spain under this contract.

(f) Insurance policies required herein shall be purchased from Spanish insurance companies or other insurance companies legally authorized to conduct business in Spain. Such policies shall conform to Spanish laws and regulations and shall—

(1) Contain provisions requiring submission to Spanish law and jurisdiction of any problem that may arise with regard to the interpretation or application of the clauses and conditions of the insurance policy;

(2) Contain a provision authorizing the insurance company, as subrogee of the insured entity, to assume and attend to directly, with respect to any person damaged, the legal consequences arising from the occurrence of such damages;

(3) Contain a provision worded as follows: "The insurance company waives any right of subrogation against the United States of America that may arise by reason of any payment under this policy.";

(4) Not contain any deductible amount or similar limitation; and

(5) Not contain any provisions requiring submission to any type of arbitration.

(End of clause)

[DAC 91-12, 62 FR 34114, 6/24/97, effective 6/24/97; Final rule, 63 FR 69006, 12/15/98, effective 12/15/98; Final rule, 75 FR 32642, 6/8/2010, effective 6/8/2010]

252.229 Taxes, provisions and clauses for DFARS Part 229

252.229-7000 Invoices exclusive of taxes or duties.

As prescribed in 229.402-1, use the following clause:

INVOICES EXCLUSIVE OF TAXES OR DUTIES (JUN 1997)

Invoices submitted in accordance with the terms and conditions of this contract shall be exclusive of all taxes or duties for which relief is available.

(End of clause)

[DAC 91-12, 62 FR 34114, 6/24/97, effective 6/24/97]

252.229-7001 Tax Relief.

Basic. As prescribed at 229.402–70(a) and (a)(1), use the following clause:

TAX RELIEF—BASIC (SEP 2014)

(a) Prices set forth in this contract are exclusive of all taxes and duties from which the United States Government is exempt by virtue of tax agreements between the United States Government and the Contractor's government. The following taxes or duties have been excluded from the contract price:

NAME OF TAX: (*Offeror Insert*)

RATE (PERCENTAGE): (*Offeror Insert*)

(b) The Contractor's invoice shall list separately the gross price, amount of tax deducted, and net price charged.

(c) When items manufactured to United States Government specifications are being acquired, the Contractor shall identify the materials or components intended to be imported in order to ensure that relief from import duties is obtained. If the Contractor intends to use imported products from inventories on hand, the price of which includes a factor for import duties, the Contractor shall ensure the United States Government's exemption from these taxes. The Contractor may obtain a refund of the import duties from its government or request the duty-free import of an amount of supplies or components corresponding to that used from inventory for this contract.

(End of clause)

Alternate I. As prescribed at 229.402–70(a) and (a)(2), use the following clause, which adds a paragraph (d) not included in the basic clause.

TAX RELIEF—ALTERNATE I (SEP 2014)

(a) Prices set forth in this contract are exclusive of all taxes and duties from which the United States Government is exempt by virtue of tax agreements between the United States Government and the Contractor's government. The following taxes or duties have been excluded from the contract price:

NAME OF TAX: [*Offeror insert*]

RATE (PERCENTAGE): [*Offeror insert*]

(b) The Contractor's invoice shall list separately the gross price, amount of tax deducted, and net price charged.

(c) When items manufactured to United States Government specifications are being acquired, the Contractor shall identify the materials or components intended to be imported in order to ensure that relief from import duties is obtained. If the Contractor intends to use imported products from inventories on hand, the price of which includes a factor for import duties, the Contractor shall ensure the United States Government's exemption from these taxes. The Contractor may obtain a refund of the import duties from its government or request the duty-free import of an amount of supplies or components corresponding to that used from inventory for this contract.

(d) Tax relief will be claimed in Germany pursuant to the provisions of the Agreement Between the United States of America and Germany Concerning Tax Relief to be Accorded by Germany to United States Expenditures in the Interest of Common Defense. The Contractor shall use Abwicklungsschein fuer abgabenbeguenstigte Lieferungen/Leistungen nach dem Offshore Steuerabkommen (Performance Certificate for Tax-Free Deliveries/Performance according to the Offshore Tax Relief Agreement) or other documentary evidence acceptable to the German tax authorities. All purchases made and paid for on a tax-free basis during a 30-day period may be accumulated, totaled, and reported as tax-free.

(End of clause)

[DAC 91-12, 62 FR 34114, 6/24/97, effective 6/24/97; Final rule, 79 FR 58699, 9/30/2014, effective 9/30/2014; Final rule, 80 FR 36897, 6/26/2015, effective 6/26/2015]

252.229-7002 Customs exemptions (Germany).

As prescribed in 229.402-70(b), use the following clause:

CUSTOMS EXEMPTIONS (GERMANY) (JUN 1997)

Imported products required for the direct benefit of the United States Forces are authorized to be acquired duty-free by the Contractor in accordance with the provisions of the Agreement Between the United States of America and Germany Concerning Tax Relief to be Accorded by Germany to United States Expenditures in the Interest of Common Defense.

(End of clause)

[DAC 91-12, 62 FR 34114, 6/24/97, effective 6/24/97]

252.229-7003 Tax exemptions (Italy).

As prescribed in 229.402-70(c)(1), use the following clause:

TAX EXEMPTIONS (ITALY) (MAR 2012)

(a) As the Contractor represented in its offer, the contract price, including the prices in subcontracts awarded under this contract, does not include taxes from which the United States Government is exempt.

(b) The United States Government is exempt from payment of Imposta Valore Aggiunto (IVA) tax in accordance with Article 72 of the IVA implementing decree on all supplies and services sold to United States Military Commands in Italy.

(1) The Contractor shall include the following information on invoices submitted to the United States Government:

(i) The contract number.

(ii) The IVA tax exemption claimed pursuant to Article 72 of Decree Law 633, dated October 26, 1972.

(iii) The following fiscal code(s): [*Contracting Officer must insert the applicable fiscal code(s) for military activities within Italy: 80028250241 for Army, 80156020630 for Navy, or 91000190933 for Air Force*].

(2)(i) Upon receipt of the invoice, the paying office will include the following certification on one copy of the invoice:

"I certify that this invoice is true and correct and reflects expenditures made in Italy for the Common Defense by the United

States Government pursuant to international agreements. The amount to be paid does not include the IVA tax, because this transaction is not subject to the tax in accordance with Article 72 of Decree Law 633, dated October 26, 1972." An authorized United States Government official will sign the copy of the invoice containing this certification.

(ii) The paying office will return the certified copy together with payment to the Contractor. The payment will not include the amount of the IVA tax.

(iii) The Contractor shall retain the certified copy to substantiate non-payment of the IVA tax.

(3) The Contractor may address questions regarding the IVA tax to the Ministry of Finance, IVA Office, Rome (06) 520741.

(c) In addition to the IVA tax, purchases by the United States Forces in Italy are exempt from the following taxes:

(1) Imposta di Fabbricazione (Production Tax for Petroleum Products).

(2) Imposta di Consumo (Consumption Tax for Electrical Power).

(3) Dazi Doganali (Customs Duties).

(4) Tassa di Sbarco e d'Imbarco sulle Merci Transportate per Via Aerea e per Via Maritima (Port Fees).

(5) Tassa de Circolazione sui Veicoli (Vehicle Circulation Tax).

(6) Imposta di Registro (Registration Tax).

(7) Imposta di Bollo (Stamp Tax).

(End of clause)

[Final rule, 67 FR 4209, 1/29/2002, effective 1/29/2002; Final rule, 77 FR 19128, 3/30/2012, effective 3/30/2012]

252.229-7004 Status of contractor as a direct contractor (Spain).

As prescribed in 229.402-70(d), use the following clause:

STATUS OF CONTRACTOR AS A DIRECT CONTRACTOR (SPAIN) (JUN 1997)

(a) *Direct Contractor*, as used in this clause, means an individual, company, or entity with whom an agency of the United States Department of Defense has executed a written agreement that allows duty-free import of equipment, materials, and supplies into Spain for the construction, development, maintenance, and operation of Spanish-American installations and facilities.

(b) The Contractor is hereby designated as a Direct Contractor under the provisions of Complementary Agreement 5, articles 11, 14, 15, 17, and 18 of the Agreement on Friendship, Defense and Cooperation between the United States Government and the Kingdom of Spain, dated July 2, 1982. The Agreement relates to contacts to be performed in whole or part in Spain, the provisions of which are hereby incorporated into and made a part of this contract by reference.

(c) The Contractor shall apply to the appropriate Spanish authorities for approval of status as a Direct Contractor in order to complete duty-free import of non-Spanish equipment, materials, and supplies represented as necessary for contract performance by the Contracting Officer. Orders for equipment, materials, and supplies placed prior to official notification of such approval shall be at the Contractor's own risk. The Contractor must submit its documentation in sufficient time to permit processing by the appropriate United States and Spanish Government agencies prior to the arrival of the equipment, material, or supplies in Spain. Seasonal variations in processing times are common, and the Contractor should program its projects accordingly. Any delay or expense arising directly or indirectly from this process shall not excuse untimely performance (except as expressly allowed in other provisions of this contract), constitute a direct or constructive change, or otherwise provide a basis for additional compensation or adjustment of any kind.

(d) To ensure that all duty-free imports are properly accounted for, exported, or disposed of, in accordance with Spanish law, the Contractor shall obtain a written bank letter of guaranty payable to the Treasurer of the United States, or such other authority as may be designated by the Contracting Officer, in the amount set forth in paragraph

(g) of this clause, prior to effecting any duty-free imports for the performance of this contract.

(e) If the Contractor fails to obtain the required guaranty, the Contractor agrees that the Contracting Officer may withhold a portion of the contract payments in order to establish a fund in the amount set forth in paragraph (g) of this clause. The fund shall be used for the payment of import taxes in the event that the Contractor fails to properly account for, export, or dispose of equipment, materials, or supplies imported on a duty-free basis.

(f) The amount of the bank letter of guaranty or size of the fund required under paragraph (d) or (e) of this clause normally shall be 5 percent of the contract value. However, if the Contractor demonstrates to the Contracting Officer's satisfaction that the amount retained by the United States Government or guaranteed by the bank is excessive, the amount shall be reduced to an amount commensurate with contingent import tax and duty-free liability. This bank guaranty or fund shall not be released to the Contractor until the Spanish General Directorate of Customs verifies the accounting, export, or disposition of the equipment, material, or supplies imported on a duty-free basis.

(g) The amount required under paragraph (d), (e), or (f) of this clause is (*Contracting Officer insert amount at time of contract award*).

(h) The Contractor agrees to insert the provisions of this clause, including this paragraph (h), in all subcontracts.

(End of clause)

[DAC 91-12, 62 FR 34114, 6/24/97, effective 6/24/97; DAC 91-13, 63 FR 11522, 3/9/98, effective 3/9/98]

252.229-7005 Tax exemptions (Spain).

As prescribed in 229.402-70(e)(1), use the following clause:

TAX EXEMPTIONS (SPAIN) (MAR 2012)

(a) As the Contractor represented in its offer, the contract price, including the prices in subcontracts awarded under this contract, does not include taxes from which the United States Government is exempt.

(b) In accordance with tax relief agreements between the United States Government and the Spanish Government, and because the incumbent contract arises from the activities of the United States Forces in Spain, the contract will be exempt from the following excise, luxury, and transaction taxes:

(1) Derechos de Aduana (Customs Duties).

(2) Impuesto de Compensacion a la Importacion (Compensation Tax on Imports).

(3) Transmisiones Patrionomiales (Property Transfer Tax).

(4) Impuesto Sobre el Lujo (Luxury Tax).

(5) Actos Juridocos Documentados (Legal Official Transactions).

(6) Impuesto Sobre el Trafico de Empresas (Business Trade Tax).

(7) Impuestos Especiales de Fabricacion (Special Products Tax).

(8) Impuesto Sobre el Petroleo y Derivados (Tax on Petroleum and its By-Products).

(9) Impuesto Sobre el Uso de Telefona (Telephone Tax).

(10) Impuesto General Sobre la Renta de Sociedades y demas Entidades Juridicas (General Corporation Income Tax).

(11) Impuesto Industrial (Industrial Tax).

(12) Impuesto de Rentas Sobre el Capital (Capital Gains Tax).

(13) Plus Vailia (Increase on Real Property).

(14) Contribucion Territorial Urbana (Metropolitan Real Estate Tax).

(15) Contribucion Territorial Rustica y Pecuaria (Farmland Real Estate Tax).

(16) Impuestos de la Diputacion (County Service Charges).

(17) Impuestos Municipal y Tasas Parafiscales (Municipal Tax and Charges).

(End of clause)

[DAC 91-12, 62 FR 34114, 6/24/97, effective 6/24/97; Final rule, 77 FR 19128, 3/30/2012, effective 3/30/2012]

252.229-7006 Value Added Tax Exclusion (United Kingdom).

As prescribed in 229.402-70(f), use the following clause:

VALUE ADDED TAX EXCLUSION (UNITED KINGDOM) (DEC 2011)

The supplies or services identified in this contract are to be delivered at a price exclusive of value added tax under arrangements between the appropriate United States authorities and Her Majesty's Revenue and Customs (HMRC) (Reference HMRC Notice 431, entitled "Relief from Customs Duty and/or Value Added Tax on United States Government Expenditures in the United Kingdom"). By executing this contract, the Contracting Officer certifies that these supplies or services are being purchased for United States Government official purposes only. (End of clause)

(End of clause)

[DAC 91-12, 62 FR 34114, 6/24/97, effective 6/24/97; Final rule, 76 FR 76318, 12/7/2011, effective 12/7/2011]

252.229-7007 Verification of United States receipt of goods.

As prescribed in 229.402-70(g), use the following clause:

VERIFICATION OF UNITED STATES RECEIPT OF GOODS (JUN 1997)

The Contractor shall insert the following statement on all Material Inspection and Receiving Reports (DD Form 250 series) for Contracting Officer approval: "I certify that the items listed on this invoice have been received by the United States."

(End of clause)

[DAC 91-12, 62 FR 34114, 6/24/97, effective 6/24/97]

252.229-7008 Relief from Import Duty (United Kingdom).

As prescribed in 229.402-70(h), use the following clause:

RELIEF FROM IMPORT DUTY (UNITED KINGDOM) (DEC 2011)

Any import dutiable articles, components, or raw materials supplied to the United States Government under this contract shall be exclusive of any United Kingdom import duties. Any imported items supplied for which import duty already has been paid will be supplied at a price exclusive of the amount of import duty paid. The Contractor is advised to contact Her Majesty's Revenue and Customs (HMRC) to obtain a refund upon completion of the contract (Reference HMRC Notice No. 431, entitled "Relief from Customs Duty and/or Value Added Tax on United States Government Expenditures in the United Kingdom"). (End of clause)

(End of clause)

[DAC 91-12, 62 FR 34114, 6/24/97, effective 6/24/97; Final rule, 76 FR 76318, 12/7/2011, effective 12/7/2011]

252.229-7009 Relief from customs duty and value added tax on fuel (passenger vehicles) (United Kingdom).

As prescribed in 229.402-70(i), use the following clause:

RELIEF FROM CUSTOMS DUTY AND VALUE ADDED TAX ON FUEL (PASSENGER VEHICLES) (UNITED KINGDOM) (JUN 1997)

(a) Pursuant to an agreement between the United States Government and Her Majesty's (HM) Customs and Excise, fuels and lubricants used by passenger vehicles (except taxis) in the performance of this contract will be exempt from customs duty and value added tax. Therefore, the procedures outlined in HM Customs and Excise Notice No. 431B, August 1982, and any amendment thereto, shall be used to obtain relief from both customs duty and value added tax for fuel used under the contract. These procedures shall apply to both loaded and unloaded miles. The unit prices shall be based on the recoupment by the Contractor of customs duty in accordance with the following allowances:

(1) Vehicles (except taxis) with a seating capacity of less than 29, one gallon for every 27 miles.

(2) Vehicles with a seating capacity of 29-53, one gallon for every 13 miles.

(3) Vehicles with a seating capacity of 54 or more, one gallon for every 10 miles.

(b) In the event the mileage of any route is increased or decreased within 10 percent, resulting in no change in route price, the customs duty shall be reclaimed from HM Customs and Excise on actual mileage performed.

(End of clause)

[DAC 91-12, 62 FR 34114, 6/24/97, effective 6/24/97; Final rule, 79 FR 61584, 10/14/2014, effective 10/14/2014]

252.229-7010 Relief from customs duty on fuel (United Kingdom).

As prescribed in 229.402-70(j), use the following clause:

RELIEF FROM CUSTOMS DUTY ON FUEL (UNITED KINGDOM) (JUN 1997)

(a) Pursuant to an agreement between the United States Government and Her Majesty's (HM) Customs and Excise, it is possible to obtain relief from customs duty on fuels and lubricants used in support of certain contracts. If vehicle fuels and lubricants are used in support of this contract, the Contractor shall seek relief from customs duty in accordance with HM Customs Notice No. 431, February 1973, entitled "Relief from Customs Duty and/or Value Added Tax on United States Government Expenditures in the United Kingdom." Application should be sent to the Contractor's local Customs and Excise Office.

(b) Specific information should be included in the request for tax relief, such as the number of vehicles involved, types of vehicles, rating of vehicles, fuel consumption, estimated mileage per contract period, and any other information that will assist HM Customs and Excise in determining the amount of relief to be granted.

(c) Within 30 days after the award of this contract, the Contractor shall provide the Contracting Officer with evidence that an attempt to obtain such relief has been initiated. In the event the Contractor does not attempt to obtain relief within the time specified, the Contracting Officer may deduct from the contract price the amount of relief that would have been allowed if HM Customs and Excise had favorably considered the request for relief.

(d) The amount of any rebate granted by HM Customs and Excise shall be paid in full to the United States Government. Checks shall be made payable to the Treasurer of the United States and forwarded to the Administrative Contracting Officer.

(End of clause)

[DAC 91-12, 62 FR 34114, 6/24/97, effective 6/24/97]

252.229-7011 Reporting of Foreign Taxes—U.S. Assistance Programs.

As prescribed in 229.170-4, use the following clause:

REPORTING OF FOREIGN TAXES—U.S. ASSISTANCE PROGRAMS (SEP 2005)

(a) *Definition. Commodities,* as used in this clause, means any materials, articles, supplies, goods, or equipment.

(b) Commodities acquired under this contract shall be exempt from all value added taxes and customs duties imposed by the recipient country. This exemption is in addition to any other tax exemption provided through separate agreements or other means.

(c) The Contractor shall inform the foreign government of the tax exemption, as documented in the Letter of Offer and Acceptance, country-to-country agreement, or interagency agreement.

(d) If the foreign government or entity nevertheless imposes taxes, the Contractor shall promptly notify the Contracting Officer and shall provide documentation showing that the foreign government was apprised of the tax exemption in accordance with paragraph (c) of this clause.

(e) The Contractor shall insert the substance of this clause, including this paragraph (e), in all subcontracts for commodities that exceed $500.

(End of clause)

[Interim rule, 70 FR 57191, 9/30/2005, effective 9/30/2005; Final rule, 71 FR 18671, 4/12/2006, effective 4/12/2006]

252.229-7012 Tax exemptions (Italy)—representation.

As prescribed in 229.402-70(c)(2), use the following provision:

TAX EXEMPTIONS (ITALY)—
REPRESENTATION (MAR 2012)

(a) *Exemptions*. The United States Government is exempt from payment of—

(1) Imposta Valore Aggiunto (IVA) tax in accordance with Article 72 of the IVA implementing decree on all supplies and services sold to United States Military Commands in Italy; and

(2) The other taxes specified in paragraph (c) of the clause DFARS 252.229-7003, Tax Exemptions (Italy).

(b) *Representation*. By submission of its offer, the offeror represents that the offered price, including the prices of subcontracts to be awarded under the contract, does not include the taxes identified herein, or any other taxes from which the United States Government is exempt.

(End of provision)

[Final rule, 77 FR 19128, 3/30/2012, effective 3/30/2012]

252.229-7013 Tax exemptions (Spain)—representation.

As prescribed in 229.402-70(e)(2), use the following provision:

TAX EXEMPTIONS (SPAIN)—
REPRESENTATION (APR 2012)

(a) *Exemptions*. In accordance with tax relief agreements between the United States Government and the Spanish Government, and because the resultant contract arises from the activities of the United States Forces in Spain, the contract will be exempt from the excise, luxury, and transaction taxes listed in paragraph (b) of the clause DFARS 252.229-7005, Tax Exemptions (Spain).

(b) *Representation*. By submission of its offer, the offeror represents that the offered price, including the prices of subcontracts to be awarded under the contract, does not include the taxes identified herein, or any other taxes from which the United States Government is exempt.

(End of provision)

[Final rule, 77 FR 19128, 3/30/2012, effective 3/30/2012; Final rule, 77 FR 23631, 4/20/2012, effective 4/20/2012]

252.229-7014 Taxes—Foreign Contracts in Afghanistan.

As prescribed in 229.402-70(k), use the following provision:

TAXES—FOREIGN CONTRACTS IN
AFGHANISTAN (DEC 2015)

(a) This acquisition is covered by the Security and Defense Cooperation Agreement (the Agreement) between the Islamic Republic of Afghanistan and the United States of America signed on September 30, 2014, and entered into force on January 1, 2015.

(b) The Agreement exempts the Department of Defense (DoD), and its contractors and subcontractors (other than those that are Afghan legal entities or residents), from paying any tax or similar charge assessed on activities associated with this contract within Afghanistan. The Agreement also exempts the acquisition, importation, exportation, reexportation, transportation, and use of supplies and services in Afghanistan, by or on behalf of DoD, from any taxes, customs, duties, fees, or similar charges in Afghanistan.

(c) The Contractor shall exclude any Afghan taxes, customs, duties, fees, or similar charges from the contract price, other than those charged to Afghan legal entities or residents.

(d) The Agreement does not exempt Afghan employees of DoD contractors and subcontractors from Afghan tax laws. To the extent required by Afghan law, the Contractor shall withhold tax from the wages of these employees and remit those payments to the appropriate Afghanistan taxing authority. These withholdings are an individual's liability, not a tax against the Contractor.

(e) The Contractor shall include the substance of this clause, including this paragraph (e), in all subcontracts, including subcontracts for commercial items.

(End of clause)

[Final rule, 80 FR 81467, 12/30/2015, effective 12/30/2015]

252.229-7015 Taxes—Foreign Contracts in Afghanistan (North Atlantic Treaty Organization Status of Forces Agreement).

As prescribed in 229.402-70(l), use the following provision:

TAXES—FOREIGN CONTRACTS IN AFGHANISTAN (NORTH ATLANTIC TREATY ORGANIZATION STATUS OF FORCES AGREEMENT) (DEC 2015)

(a) This acquisition is covered by the Status of Forces Agreement (SOFA) entered into between the North Atlantic Treaty Organization (NATO) and the Islamic Republic of Afghanistan issued on September 30, 2014, and entered into force on January 1, 2015.

(b) The SOFA exempts NATO Forces and its contractors and subcontractors (other than those that are Afghan legal entities or residents) from paying any tax or similar charge assessed within Afghanistan. The SOFA also exempts the acquisition, importation, exportation, reexportation, transportation and use of supplies and services in Afghanistan from all Afghan taxes, customs, duties, fees, or similar charges.

(c) The Contractor shall exclude any Afghan taxes, customs, duties, fees or similar charges from the contract price, other than those that are Afghan legal entities or residents.

(d) Afghan citizens employed by NATO contractors and subcontractors are subject to Afghan tax laws. To the extent required by Afghan law, the Contractor shall withhold tax from the wages of these employees and remit those withholdings to the Afghanistan Revenue Department. These withholdings are an individual's liability, not a tax against the Contractor.

(e) The Contractor shall include the substance of this clause, including this paragraph (e), in all subcontracts including subcontracts for commercial items.

(End of clause)

[Final rule, 80 FR 81467, 12/30/2015, effective 12/30/2015]

252.231 Contract Cost Principles and Procedures, provisions and clauses for DFARS Part 231

252.231-7000 Supplemental cost principles.

As prescribed in 231.100-70, use the following clause:

SUPPLEMENTAL COST PRINCIPLES (DEC 1991)

When the allowability of costs under this contract is determined in accordance with part 31 of the Federal Acquisition Regulation (FAR), allowability shall also be determined in accordance with part 231 of the Defense FAR Supplement, in effect on the date of this contract.

(End of clause)

252.232 Contract Financing, provisions and clauses for DFARS Part 232

252.232-7000 Advance payment pool.

As prescribed in 232.412-70(a), use the following clause:

ADVANCE PAYMENT POOL (DEC 1991)

(a) Notwithstanding any other provision of this contract, advance payments will be made for contract performance in accordance with the Determinations, Findings, and Authorization for Advance payment dated ____.

(b) Payments made in accordance with this clause shall be governed by the terms and conditions of the Advance Payment Pool Agreement between the United States of America and (*insert the name of the contractor*). The Agreement is incorporated in the contract by reference.

(End of clause)

252.232-7001 Disposition of payments.

As prescribed in 232.412-70(b), use the following clause:

DISPOSITION OF PAYMENT (DEC 1991)

Payment will be by a dual payee Treasury check made payable to the contractor or the (*insert the name of the disbursing office in the advance payment pool agreement*), and will be forwarded to that disbursing office for appropriate disposition.

(End of clause)

[DAC 91-3 57 FR 42633, 9/15/92, effective 8/31/92]

252.232-7002 Progress payments for foreign military sales acquisitions.

As prescribed in 232.502-4-70(a), use the following clause:

PROGRESS PAYMENTS FOR FOREIGN MILITARY SALES ACQUISITIONS (DEC 1991)

If this contract includes foreign military sales (FMS) requirements, the Contractor shall—

(a) Submit a separate progress payment request for each progress payment rate; and

(b) Submit a supporting schedule showing—

(1) The amount of each request distributed to each country's requirements; and

(2) Total price per contract line item applicable to each separate progress payment rate.

(c) Identify in each progress payment request the contract requirements to which it applies (i.e., FMS or U.S.);

(d) Calculate each request on the basis of the prices, costs (including costs to complete), subcontractor progress payments, and progress payment liquidations of the contract requirements to which it applies; and

(e) Distribute costs among contract line items and countries in a manner acceptable to the Administrative Contracting Officer.

(End of clause)

252.232-7003 Electronic submission of payment requests and receiving reports.

As prescribed in 232.7004(a), use the following clause:

ELECTRONIC SUBMISSION OF PAYMENT REQUESTS AND RECEIVING REPORTS (DEC 2018)

(a) *Definitions.* As used in this clause—

Contract financing payment means an authorized Government disbursement of monies to a contractor prior to acceptance of supplies or services by the Government.

(1) Contract financing payments include—

(i) Advance payments;

(ii) Performance-based payments;

(iii) Commercial advance and interim payments;

(iv) Progress payments based on cost under the clause at Federal Acquisition Regulation (FAR) 52.232-16, Progress Payments;

(v) Progress payments based on a percentage or stage of completion (see FAR 32.102(e)), except those made under the clause at FAR 52.232-5, Payments Under Fixed-Price Construction Contracts, or the clause at FAR 52.232-10, Payments Under Fixed-Price Architect-Engineer Contracts; and

(vi) Interim payments under a cost reimbursement contract, except for a cost reimbursement contract for services when Alternate I of the clause at FAR 52.232-25, Prompt Payment, is used.

(2) Contract financing payments do not include—

(i) Invoice payments;

(ii) Payments for partial deliveries; or

(iii) Lease and rental payments.

Electronic form means any automated system that transmits information electronically from the initiating system to affected systems.

Invoice payment means a Government disbursement of monies to a contractor under a contract or other authorization for supplies or services accepted by the Government.

(1) Invoice payments include—

(i) Payments for partial deliveries that have been accepted by the Government;

(ii) Final cost or fee payments where amounts owed have been settled between the Government and the contractor;

(iii) For purposes of subpart 32.9 only, all payments made under the clause at 52.232-5, Payments Under Fixed-Price Construction Contracts, and the clause at 52.232-10, Payments Under Fixed-Price Architect-Engineer Contracts; and

(iv) Interim payments under a cost-reimbursement contract for services when Alternate I of the clause at 52.232-25, Prompt Payment, is used.

(2) Invoice payments do not include contract financing payments.

Payment request means any request for contract financing payment or invoice payment submitted by the Contractor under this contract or task or delivery order.

Receiving report means the data prepared in the manner and to the extent required by Appendix F, Material Inspection and Receiving Report, of the Defense Federal Acquisition Regulation Supplement.

(b) Except as provided in paragraph (d) of this clause, the Contractor shall submit payment requests and receiving reports in electronic form using Wide Area WorkFlow (WAWF). The Contractor shall prepare and furnish to the Government a receiving report at the time of each delivery of supplies or services under this contract or task or delivery order.

(c) Submit payment requests and receiving reports to WAWF in one of the following electronic formats:

(1) Electronic Data Interchange.

(2) Secure File Transfer Protocol.

(3) Direct input through the WAWF website.

(d) The Contractor may submit a payment request and receiving report using methods other than WAWF only when—

(1) The Contractor has requested permission in writing to do so, and the Contracting Officer has provided instructions for a temporary alternative method of submission of payment requests and receiving reports in the contract administration data section of this contract or task or delivery order;

(2) DoD makes payment for commercial transportation services provided under a Government rate tender or a contract for transportation services using a DoD-approved electronic third party payment system or other exempted vendor payment/invoicing system (*e.g.*, PowerTrack, Transportation Financial Management System, and Cargo and Billing System);

(3) DoD makes payment on a contract or task or delivery order for rendered health care services using the TRICARE Encounter Data System; or

(4) The Governmentwide commercial purchase card is used as the method of payment, in which case submission of only the receiving report in WAWF is required.

(e) Information regarding WAWF is available at *https://wawf.eb.mil/*.

(f) In addition to the requirements of this clause, the Contractor shall meet the requirements of the appropriate payment clauses in this contract when submitting payment requests.

(End of clause)

[Removed and reserved, Final rule, 64 FR 8731, 2/23/99, effective 2/23/99; Interim rule, 68 FR 8450, 2/21/2003, effective 3/1/2003; Final rule, 68 FR 15380, 3/31/2003, effective 3/31/2003; Final rule, 68 FR 69628, 12/15/2003, effective 12/15/2003; Final rule, 69 FR 1926, 1/13/2004, effective 1/13/2004; Final rule, 71 FR 27643, 5/12/2006, effective 5/12/2006; Final rule, 72 FR 14240, 3/27/2007, effective 3/27/2007; Final rule, 73 FR 11356, 3/3/2008, effective 3/3/2008; Final rule, 77 FR 38731, 6/29/2012, effectively 6/29/2012; Final rule, 83 FR 66062, 12/21/2018, effective 12/21/2018]

252.232-7004 DoD progress payment rates.

As prescribed in 232.502-4-70(b), use the following clause:

DoD PROGRESS PAYMENT RATES (OCT 2014)

If the Contractor is a small business concern, the Progress Payments clause of this contract is modified to change each mention of the progress payment rate and liquidations rate (excepting paragraph (k), Limitations on Undefinitized Contract Actions) to 90 percent.

(End of clause)

[Final rule, 66 FR 49864, 10/1/2001, effective 10/1/2001; Interim rule, 79 FR 61579, 10/14/2014, effective 10/14/2014; Final rule, 80 FR 15912, 3/26/2015, effective 3/26/2015]

252.232-7005 Reimbursement of subcontractor advance payments—DoD pilot mentor-protege program.

As prescribed in 232.412-70(c), use the following clause:

REIMBURSEMENT OF SUBCONTRACTOR ADVANCE PAYMENTS—DoD PILOT MENTOR-PROTEGE PROGRAM (SEP 2001)

(a) The Government will reimburse the Contractor for any advance payments made by the Contractor, as a mentor firm, to a protege firm, pursuant to an approved mentor-protege agreement, provided—

(1) The Contractor's subcontract with the protege firm includes a provision substantially the same as FAR 52.232-12, Advance Payments;

(2) The Contractor has administered the advance payments in accordance with the policies of FAR subpart 32.4; and

(3) The Contractor agrees that any financial loss resulting from the failure or inability of the protege firm to repay any unliquidated advance payments is the sole financial responsibility of the Contractor.

(b) For a fixed price type contract, advance payments made to a protege firm shall be paid and administered as if they were 100 percent progress payments. The Contractor shall include as a separate attachment with each Standard Form (SF) 1443, Contractor's Request for Progress Payment, a request for reimbursement of advance payments made to a protege firm. The attachment shall provide a separate calculation of lines 14a through 14e of SF 1443 for each protege, reflecting the status of advance payments made to that protege.

(c) For cost reimbursable contracts, reimbursement of advance payments shall be made via public voucher. The Contractor shall show the amounts of advance payments made to each protege on the public voucher, in the form and detail directed by the cognizant contracting officer or contract auditor.

(End of clause)

[DAC 91-1, 56 FR 67221, 12/30/91, effective 12/31/91; DAC 91-4, 57 FR 53602, 11/12/92, effective 10/30/92; Interim rule, 66 FR 47108, 9/11/2001, effective 9/11/2001, finalized without change, 67 FR 11435, 3/14/2002, effective 3/14/2002]

252.232-7006 Wide Area WorkFlow Payment Instructions.

As prescribed in 232.7004(b), use the following clause:

WIDE AREA WORKFLOW PAYMENT INSTRUCTIONS (DEC 2018)

(a) *Definitions*. As used in this clause—

Department of Defense Activity Address Code (DoDAAC) is a six position code that uniquely identifies a unit, activity, or organization.

Document type means the type of payment request or receiving report available for creation in Wide Area WorkFlow (WAWF).

Local processing office (LPO) is the office responsible for payment certification when payment certification is done external to the entitlement system.

Payment request and *receiving report* are defined in the clause at 252.232-7003, Electronic Submission of Payment Requests and Receiving Reports.

(b) *Electronic invoicing*. The WAWF system provides the method to electronically process vendor payment requests and receiving reports, as authorized by Defense Federal Acquisition Regulation System (DFARS) 252.232-7003, Electronic Submission of Payment Requests and Receiving Reports.

(c) *WAWF access*. To access WAWF, the Contractor shall—

(1) Have a designated electronic business point of contact in the System for Award Management at *https://www.sam.gov*; and

(2) Be registered to use WAWF at *https://wawf.eb.mil/* following the step-by-step procedures for self-registration available at this Web site.

(d) *WAWF training*. The Contractor should follow the training instructions of the WAWF Web-Based Training Course and use the Practice Training Site before submitting payment requests through WAWF. Both can be accessed by selecting the "Web Based Training" link on the WAWF home page at *https://wawf.eb.mil/*.

(e) *WAWF methods of document submission*. Document submissions may be via Web entry, Electronic Data Interchange, or File Transfer Protocol.

(f) *WAWF payment instructions*. The Contractor shall use the following information when submitting payment requests and receiving reports in WAWF for this contract or task or delivery order:

(1) *Document type*. The Contractor shall submit payment requests using the following document type(s):

(i) For cost-type line items, including labor-hour or time-and-materials, submit a cost voucher.

(ii) For fixed price line items—

(A) That require shipment of a deliverable, submit the invoice and receiving report specified by the Contracting Officer.

(Contracting Officer: Insert applicable invoice and receiving report document type(s) for fixed price line items that require shipment of a deliverable.)

(B) For services that do not require shipment of a deliverable, submit either the Invoice 2in1, which meets the requirements for the invoice and receiving report, or the applicable invoice and receiving report, as specified by the Contracting Officer.

(Contracting Officer: Insert either "Invoice 2in1" or the applicable invoice and receiving report document type(s) for fixed price line items for services.)

(iii) For customary progress payments based on costs incurred, submit a progress payment request.

(iv) For performance based payments, submit a performance based payment request.

(v) For commercial item financing, submit a commercial item financing request.

(2) Fast Pay requests are only permitted when Federal Acquisition Regulation (FAR) 52.213-1 is included in the contract.

[Note: The Contractor may use a WAWF "combo" document type to create some combinations of invoice and receiving report in one step.]

(3) *Document routing*. The Contractor shall use the information in the Routing Data Table below only to fill in applicable fields in WAWF when creating payment requests and receiving reports in the system.

ROUTING DATA TABLE*

Field name in WAWF	Data to be entered in WAWF
Pay Official DoDAAC.	
Issue By DoDAAC.	
Admin DoDAAC**.	
Inspect By DoDAAC.	

DFARS 252.232-7006

Field name in WAWF	Data to be entered in WAWF
Ship To Code.	
Ship From Code.	
Mark For Code.	
Service Approver (DoDAAC).	
Service Acceptor (DoDAAC).	
Accept at Other DoDAAC.	
LPO DoDAAC.	
DCAA Auditor DoDAAC.	
Other DoDAAC(s).	

(*Contracting Officer: Insert applicable DoDAAC information. If multiple ship to/acceptance locations apply, insert "See Schedule" or "Not applicable.")

(**Contracting Officer: If the contract provides for progress payments or performance-based payments, insert the DoDAAC for the contract administration office assigned the functions under FAR 42.302(a)(13).)

(4) *Payment request.* The Contractor shall ensure a payment request includes documentation appropriate to the type of payment request in accordance with the payment clause, contract financing clause, or Federal Acquisition Regulation 52.216-7, Allowable Cost and Payment, as applicable.

(5) *Receiving report.* The Contractor shall ensure a receiving report meets the requirements of DFARS Appendix F.

(g) *WAWF point of contact.* (1) The Contractor may obtain clarification regarding invoicing in WAWF from the following contracting activity's WAWF point of contact.

____

(*Contracting Officer: Insert applicable information or "Not applicable."*)

(2) Contact the WAWF helpdesk at 866-618-5988, if assistance is needed.

(End of clause)

[Final rule, 68 FR 69631, 12/15/2003, effective 12/15/2003; Final rule, 73 FR 4116, 1/24/2008, effective 1/24/2008; Final rule, 77 FR 38731, 6/29/2012, effectively 6/29/2012; Final rule, 78 FR 28756, 5/16/2013, effective 5/16/2013; Final rule, 78 FR 30232, 5/22/2013, effective 5/22/2013; Final rule, 83 FR 66062, 12/21/2018, effective 12/21/2018]

252.232-7007 Limitation of Government's obligation.

As prescribed in 232.705-70, use the following clause:

LIMITATION OF GOVERNMENT'S OBLIGATION (APR 2014)

(a) Contract line item(s) [*Contracting Officer insert after negotiations*] is/are incrementally funded. For this/these item(s), the sum of $__________[*Contracting Officer insert after negotiations*] of the total price is presently available for payment and allotted to this contract. An allotment schedule is set forth in paragraph (j) of this clause.

(b) For item(s) identified in paragraph (a) of this clause, the Contractor agrees to perform up to the point at which the total amount payable by the Government, including reimbursement in the event of termination of those item(s) for the Government's convenience, approximates the total amount currently allotted to the contract. The Contractor is not authorized to continue work on those item(s) beyond that point. The Government will not be obligated in any event to reimburse the Contractor in excess of the amount allotted to the contract for those item(s) regardless of anything to the contrary in the clause entitled "Termination for Convenience of the Government." As used in this clause, the total amount payable by the

Government in the event of termination of applicable contract line item(s) for convenience includes costs, profit, and estimated termination settlement costs for those item(s).

(c) Notwithstanding the dates specified in the allotment schedule in paragraph (j) of this clause, the Contractor will notify the Contracting Officer in writing at least ninety days prior to the date when, in the Contractor's best judgment, the work will reach the point at which the total amount payable by the Government, including any cost for termination for convenience, will approximate 85 percent of the total amount then allotted to the contract for performance of the applicable item(s). The notification will state (1) the estimated date when that point will be reached and (2) an estimate of additional funding, if any, needed to continue performance of applicable line items up to the next scheduled date for allotment of funds identified in paragraph (j) of this clause, or to a mutually agreed upon substitute date. The notification will also advise the Contracting Officer of the estimated amount of additional funds that will be required for the timely performance of the item(s) funded pursuant to this clause, for a subsequent period as may be specified in the allotment schedule in paragraph (j) of this clause or otherwise agreed to by the parties. If after such notification additional funds are not allotted by the date identified in the Contractor's notification, or by an agreed substitute date, the Contracting Officer will terminate any item(s) for which additional funds have not been allotted, pursuant to the clause of this contract entitled "Termination for Convenience of the Government."

(d) When additional funds are allotted for continued performance of the contract line item(s) identified in paragraph (a) of this clause, the parties will agree as to the period of contract performance which will be covered by the funds. The provisions of paragraphs (b) through (d) of this clause will apply in like manner to the additional allotted funds and agreed substitute date, and the contract will be modified accordingly.

(e) If, solely by reason of failure of the Government to allot additional funds, by the dates indicated below, in amounts sufficient for timely performance of the contract line item(s) identified in paragraph (a) of this clause, the Contractor incurs additional costs or is delayed in the performance of the work under this contract and if additional funds are allotted, an equitable adjustment will be made in the price or prices (including appropriate target, billing, and ceiling prices where applicable) of the item(s), or in the time of delivery, or both. Failure to agree to any such equitable adjustment hereunder will be a dispute concerning a question of fact within the meaning of the clause entitled "Disputes."

(f) The Government may at any time prior to termination allot additional funds for the performance of the contract line item(s) identified in paragraph (a) of this clause.

(g) The termination provisions of this clause do not limit the rights of the Government under the clause entitled "Default." The provisions of this clause are limited to the work and allotment of funds for the contract line item(s) set forth in paragraph (a) of this clause. This clause no longer applies once the contract is fully funded except with regard to the rights or obligations of the parties concerning equitable adjustments negotiated under paragraphs (d) or (e) of this clause.

(h) Nothing in this clause affects the right of the Government to terminate this contract pursuant to the clause of this contract entitled "Termination for Convenience of the Government."

(i) Nothing in this clause shall be construed as authorization of voluntary services whose acceptance is otherwise prohibited under 31 U.S.C. 1342.

(j) The parties contemplate that the Government will allot funds to this contract in accordance with the following schedule:

On execution of contract $____

(month) (day), (year) $____

(month) (day), (year) $____

(month) (day), (year) $____

(End of clause)

[Interim rule, 58 FR 46091, 9/1/93, effective 8/23/93; Final rule, 71 FR 18671, 4/12/2006, effective 4/12/2006; Final rule, 71 FR 27643, 5/12/2006, effective 5/12/2006; Final rule, 79 FR 22042, 4/21/2014, effective 4/21/2014]

252.232-7008 Assignment of claims (overseas).

As prescribed in 232.806(a)(1), use the following clause:

ASSIGNMENT OF CLAIMS (OVERSEAS) (JUN 1997)

(a) No claims for monies due, or to become due, shall be assigned by the Contractor unless—

(1) Approved in writing by the Contracting Officer;

(2) Made in accordance with the laws and regulations of the United States of America; and

(3) Permitted by the laws and regulations of the Contractor's country.

(b) In no event shall copies of this contract of any plans, specifications, or other similar documents relating to work under this contract, if marked "Top Secret," "Secret," or "Confidential" be furnished to any assignee of any claim arising under this contract or to any other person not entitled to receive such documents. However, a copy of any part or all of this contract so marked may be furnished, or any information contained herein may be disclosed, to such assignee upon the Contracting Officer's prior written authorization.

(c) Any assignment under this contract shall cover all amounts payable under this contract and not already paid, and shall not be made to more than one party, except that any such assignment may be made to one party as agent or trustee for two or more parties participating in such financing. On each invoice or voucher submitted for payment under this contract to which any assignment applies, and for which direct payment thereof is to be made to an assignee, the Contractor shall—

(1) Identify the assignee by name and complete address; and

(2) Acknowledge the validity of the assignment and the right of the named assignee to receive payment in the amount invoiced or vouchered.

(End of clause)

[DAC 91-12, 62 FR 34114, 6/24/97, effective 6/24/97]

252.232-7009 Mandatory payment by Governmentwide commercial purchase card.

As prescribed in 232.1110, use the following clause:

MANDATORY PAYMENT BY GOVERNMENTWIDE COMMERCIAL PURCHASE CARD (MAY 2018)

The Contractor agrees to accept the Government wide commercial purchase card as the method of payment for orders or calls valued at or below the micro-purchase threshold in part 202 of the Defense Federal Acquisition Regulation Supplement, under this contract or agreement.

(End of clause)

[Final rule, 65 FR 46625, 7/31/2000, effective 7/31/2000; Final rule, 71 FR 75891, 12/19/2006, effective 12/19/2006; Final rule, 83 FR 24895, 5/30/2018, effective 5/30/2018]

252.232-7010 Levies on Contract Payments.

As prescribed in 232.7102, use the following clause:

LEVIES ON CONTRACT PAYMENTS (DEC 2006)

(a) 26 U.S.C. 6331(h) authorizes the Internal Revenue Service (IRS) to continuously levy up to 100 percent of contract payments, up to the amount of tax debt.

(b) When a levy is imposed on a payment under this contract and the Contractor believes that the levy may result in an inability to perform the contract, the Contractor shall promptly notify the Procuring Contracting Officer in writing, with a copy to the Administrative Contracting Officer, and shall provide—

(1) The total dollar amount of the levy;

(2) A statement that the Contractor believes that the levy may result in an inability to perform the contract, including rationale and adequate supporting documentation; and

(3) Advice as to whether the inability to perform may adversely affect national security, including rationale and adequate supporting documentation.

(c) DoD shall promptly review the Contractor's assessment, and the Procuring Contracting Officer shall provide a written notification to the Contractor including—

(1) A statement as to whether DoD agrees that the levy may result in an inability to perform the contract; and

(2) (i) If the levy may result in an inability to perform the contract and the lack of performance will adversely affect national security, the total amount of the monies collected that should be returned to the Contractor; or

(ii) If the levy may result in an inability to perform the contract but will not impact national security, a recommendation that the Contractor promptly notify the IRS to attempt to resolve the tax situation.

(d) Any DoD determination under this clause is not subject to appeal under the Contract Disputes Act.

(End of clause)

[Interim rule, 70 FR 52031, 9/1/2005, effective 9/1/2005; Final rule, 71 FR 69489, 12/1/2006, effective 12/1/2006]

252.232-7011 Payments in Support of Emergencies and Contingency Operations.

As prescribed in section 232.908, use the following clause:

PAYMENTS IN SUPPORT OF EMERGENCIES AND CONTINGENCY OPERATIONS (MAY 2013)

(a) Definitions of pertinent terms are set forth in sections 2.101, 32.001, and 32.902 of the Federal Acquisition Regulation.

(b) Notwithstanding any other payment clause in this contract, the Government will make invoice payments under the terms and conditions specified in this clause. The Government considers payment as being made on the day a check is dated or the date of an electronic funds transfer

(c) *Invoice payments.*

(1) *Due date.*

(i) Payment will be made as soon as possible once a proper invoice is received and matched with the contract and the receiving/acceptance report.

(ii) If the contract does not require submission of an invoice for payment (*e.g.*, periodic lease payments), the due date will be as specified in the contract.

(2) *Contractor's invoice.* The Contractor shall prepare and submit invoices to the designated billing office specified in the contract. A proper invoice should include the items listed in paragraphs (c) (2) (i) through (c) (2) (x) of this clause.

(i) Name and address of the Contractor.

(ii) Invoice date and invoice number. (The Contractor should date invoices as close as possible to the date of the mailing or transmission.)

(iii) Contract number or other authorization for supplies delivered or services performed (including order number and contract line item number).

(iv) Description, quantity, unit of measure, unit price, and extended price of supplies delivered or services performed.

(v) Shipping and payment terms (*e.g.*, shipment number and date of shipment, discount for prompt payment terms). Bill of lading number and weight of shipment will be shown for shipments on Government bills of lading.

(vi) Name and address of Contractor official to whom payment is to be sent (must be the same as that in the contract or in a proper notice of assignment).

(vii) Name (where practicable), title, phone number, and mailing address of person to notify in the event of a defective invoice.

(viii) Taxpayer Identification Number (when required). The taxpayer identification number is required for all payees subject to the U.S. Internal Revenue Code.

(ix) Electronic funds transfer banking information.

(A) The Contractor shall include electronic funds transfer banking information on the invoice only if required elsewhere in this contract.

(B) If electronic funds transfer banking information is not required to be on the invoice, in order for the invoice to be a proper invoice, the Contractor shall have submitted correct electronic funds transfer banking information in accordance with the applicable solicitation provision (e.g., FAR 52.232-38, Submission of Electronic Funds Transfer Information with Offer), contract clause (e.g., FAR 52.232-33, Payment by Electronic Funds Transfer—System for Award Management, or FAR 52.232-34, Payment by Electronic Funds Transfer—Other Than System for Award Management), or applicable agency procedures.

(C) Electronic funds transfer banking information is not required if the Government waived the requirement to pay by electronic funds transfer.

(x) Any other information or documentation required by the contract (*e.g.*, evidence of shipment).

(3) *Discounts for prompt payment*. The designated payment office will take cost-effective discounts if the payment is made within the discount terms of the contract.

(4) *Contract financing payment*. If this contract provides for contract financing, the Government will make contract financing payments in accordance with the applicable contract financing clause.

(5) *Overpayments*. If the Contractor becomes aware of a duplicate contract financing or invoice payment or that the Government has otherwise overpaid on a contract financing or invoice payment, the Contractor shall—

(i) Remit the overpayment amount to the payment office cited in the contract along with a description of the overpayment, including the—

(A) Circumstances of the overpayment (*e.g.*, duplicate payment, erroneous payment, liquidation errors, date(s) of overpayment);

(B) Affected contract number and delivery order number, if applicable;

(C) Affected contract line item or subline item, if applicable; and

(D) Contractor point of contact; and

(ii) Provide a copy of the remittance and supporting documentation to the Contracting Officer.

(d) This clause is applicable until otherwise notified by the Contracting Officer. Upon notification by issuance of a contract modification, the appropriate FAR Prompt Payment clause in the contract becomes applicable.

(End of clause)

[Interim rule, 75 FR 40711, 7/13/2010, effective 7/13/2010; Final rule, 76 FR 11371, 3/2/2011, effective 3/2/2011; Final rule, 78 FR 28756, 5/16/2013, effective 5/16/2013; Final rule, 78 FR 30232, 5/22/2013, effective 5/22/2013]

252.232-7012 Performance-Based Payments—Whole-Contract Basis.

As prescribed in 232.1005-70(a), use the following clause:

PERFORMANCE-BASED PAYMENTS—WHOLE-CONTRACT BASIS (MAR 2014)

(a) Performance-based payments shall form the basis for the contract financing payments provided under this contract, and shall apply to the whole contract. The performance-based payments schedule (Contract Attachment ______) describes the basis for payment, to include identification of the individual payment events, evidence of completion, and amount of payment due upon completion of each event.

(b) (i) At no time shall cumulative performance-based payments exceed cumulative contract cost incurred under this contract. To ensure compliance with this requirement, the Contractor shall, in addition to providing the information required by FAR 52.232-32, submit supporting information for all payment requests using the following format:

Current performance-based payment(s) event(s) addressed by this request:		
Contractor shall identify—	Amount	Totals
(1a) Negotiated value of all previously completed performance-based payment(s) event(s);		
(1b) Negotiated value of the current performance-based payment(s) event(s);		
(1c) Cumulative negotiated value of performance-based payment(s) events completed to date (1a) + (1b);		
(2) Total costs incurred to date;		
(3) Enter the amount from (1c) or (2), whichever is less;		
(4) Cumulative amount of payments previously requested; and		
(5) Payment amount requested for the current performance-based payment(s) event(s) (3) - (4).		

(ii) The Contractor shall not submit payment requests more frequently than monthly.

(iii) Incurred cost is determined by the Contractor's accounting books and records, which the contractor shall provide access to upon request of the Contracting Officer for the administration of this clause.

(End of clause)

[Final rule, 79 FR 17931, 3/31/2014, effective 3/31/2014]

252.232-7013 Performance-Based Payments—Deliverable-Item Basis.

As prescribed in 232.1005-70(b), use the following clause:

PERFORMANCE-BASED PAYMENTS—DELIVERABLE-ITEM BASIS (APR 2014)

(a) Performance-based payments shall form the basis for the contract financing payments provided under this contract and shall apply to Contract Line Item Number(s) (CLIN(s)) [Contracting Officer insert applicable CLIN(s)]. The performance-based payments schedule (Contract Attachment ___) describes the basis for payment, to include identification of the individual payment events, CLINs to which each event applies, evidence of completion, and amount of payment due upon completion of each event.

(b) (i) At no time shall cumulative performance-based payments exceed cumulative contract cost incurred under CLIN(s) [Contracting Officer insert applicable CLIN(s)]. To ensure compliance with this requirement, the Contractor shall, in addition to providing the information required by FAR 52.232-32, submit supporting information for all payment requests using the following format:

Current performance-based payment(s) event(s) addressed by this request:		
Contractor shall identify—	Amount	Totals

(1a) Negotiated value of all previously completed performance-based payment(s) event(s);
(1b) Negotiated value of the current performance-based payment(s) event(s);
(1c) Cumulative negotiated value of performance-based payment(s) event(s) completed to date (1a) + (1b);
(2) Total costs incurred to date;
(3) Enter the amount from (1c) or (2), whichever is less;
(4) Cumulative amount of payments previously requested; and
(5) Payment amount requested for the current performance-based payment(s) event(s) (3) - (4).

(ii) The Contractor shall not submit payment requests more frequently than monthly.

(iii) Incurred cost is determined by the Contractor's accounting books and records, which the contractor shall provide access to upon request of the Contracting Officer for the administration of this clause.

(End of clause)

[Final rule, 79 FR 17931, 3/31/2014, effective 3/31/2014; Final rule, 79 FR 23278, 4/28/2014, effective 4/28/2014]

252.232-7014 Notification of Payment in Local Currency (Afghanistan).

As prescribed in 232.7202, use the following provision:

NOTIFICATION OF PAYMENT IN LOCAL CURRENCY (AFGHANISTAN) (SEP 2014)

(a) The contract resulting from this solicitation will be paid in Afghani (local currency) if the contract is awarded to a host nation vendor (Afghan), pursuant to the authority of USCENTCOM Fragmentary Order (FRAGO) 09–1567 and FRAGO 10–143. Contract payment will be made in Afghani (local currency) via electronic funds transfer (EFT) to a local (Afghan) banking institution, unless an exception in paragraph (c) applies. Contracts shall not be awarded to host nation vendors who do not bank locally. If award is made to other than a host nation vendor, the contract will be awarded in U.S. dollars.

(b) Vendors shall submit quotations and offers in U.S. dollars. If the contract is awarded to an Afghan vendor, the quotation or offer will be converted to Afghani using a Government budget rate of [*Insert current budget rate here.*] Afghani per U.S. dollar.

(c) By exception, the following forms of payment are acceptable, in the following order of priority, when the local finance office determines that EFT using *ITS.gov* is not available:

(1) EFT using Limited Depository Account (LDA).

(2) Check from the local finance office LDA.

(3) Local currency cash payments in Afghani (must be approved in writing by the local finance office and contracting office prior to contract award). Payments in cash are restricted to contracts when—

(i) The vendor provides proof via a letter from the host nation banking institution that it is not EFT capable; and

(ii) The local finance office validates that the vendor's banking institution is not EFT capable. Cash payments will be made in Afghani.

(End of provision)

[Interim rule, 75 FR 40711, 7/13/2010, effective 7/13/2010; Final rule, 76 FR 11371, 3/2/2011, effective 3/2/2011; Final rule, 78 FR 28756, 5/16/2013, effective 5/16/2013; Final rule, 78 FR 30232, 5/22/2013, effective 5/22/2013; Final rule, 79 FR 58694, 9/30/2014, effective 9/30/2014]

252.233 Protests, Disputes, and Appeals, provisions and clauses for DFARS Part 233

252.233-7000 [Reserved]

[Reserved, DAC 91-12, 62 FR 34114, 6/24/97, effective 6/24/97]

252.233-7001 Choice of law (overseas).

As prescribed in 233.215-70, use the following clause:

CHOICE OF LAW (OVERSEAS) (JUN 1997)

This contract shall be construed and interpreted in accordance with the substantive laws of the United States of America. By the execution of this contract, the Contractor expressly agrees to waive any rights to invoke the jurisdiction of local national courts where this contract is performed and agrees to accept the exclusive jurisdiction of the United States Armed Services Board of Contract Appeals and the United States Court of Federal Claims for hearing and determination of any and all disputes that may arise under the Disputes clause of this contract.

(End of clause)

[DAC 91-12, 62 FR 34114, 6/24/97, effective 6/24/97]

252.234 Major System Acquisition, provisions and clauses for DFARS Part 234

252.234-7000 [Removed]

[Interim rule, 62 FR 9990, 3/5/97, effective 3/5/97, corrected 62 FR 49305, 9/19/97; DAC 91-12, 62 FR 34114, 6/24/97, effective 6/24/97; DAC 91-13, 63 FR 11522, 3/9/98, effective 3/9/98; Final rule, 70 FR 14574, 3/23/2005, effective 3/23/2005]

252.234-7001 Notice of Earned Value Management System.

As prescribed in 234.203(1), use the following provision:

NOTICE OF EARNED VALUE MANAGEMENT SYSTEM (APR 2008)

(a) If the offeror submits a proposal in the amount of $50,000,000 or more—

(1) The offeror shall provide documentation that the Cognizant Federal Agency (CFA) has determined that the proposed Earned Value Management System (EVMS) complies with the EVMS guidelines in the American National Standards Institute/Electronic Industries Alliance Standard 748, Earned Value Management Systems (ANSI/EIA-748) (current version at time of solicitation). The Government reserves the right to perform reviews of the EVMS when deemed necessary to verify compliance.

(2) If the offeror proposes to use a system that has not been determined to be in compliance with the requirements of paragraph (a)(1) of this provision, the offeror shall submit a comprehensive plan for compliance with the guidelines in ANSI/EIA-748.

(i) The plan shall—

(A) Describe the EVMS the offeror intends to use in performance of the contract, and how the proposed EVMS complies with the EVMS guidelines in ANSI/EIA-748;

(B) Distinguish between the offeror's existing management system and modifications proposed to meet the EVMS guidelines;

(C) Describe the management system and its application in terms of the EVMS guidelines;

(D) Describe the proposed procedure for administration of the EVMS guidelines as applied to subcontractors; and

(E) Describe the process the offeror will use to determine subcontractor compliance with ANSI/EIA-748.

(ii) The offeror shall provide information and assistance as required by the Contracting Officer to support review of the plan.

(iii) The offeror's EVMS plan must provide milestones that indicate when the offeror anticipates that the EVMS will be compliant with the guidelines in ANSI/EIA-748.

(b) If the offeror submits a proposal in an amount less than $50,000,000—

(1) The offeror shall submit a written description of the management procedures it will use and maintain in the performance of any resultant contract to comply with the requirements of the Earned Value Management System clause of the contract. The description shall include—

(i) A matrix that correlates each guideline in ANSI/EIA-748 (current version at time of solicitation) to the corresponding process in the offeror's written management procedures; and

(ii) The process the offeror will use to determine subcontractor compliance with ANSI/EIA-748.

(2) If the offeror proposes to use an EVMS that has been determined by the CFA to be in compliance with the EVMS guidelines in ANSI/EIA-748, the offeror may submit a copy of the documentation of such determination instead of the written description required by paragraph (b)(1) of this provision.

(c) The offeror shall identify the subcontractors (or the subcontracted effort if subcontractors have not been selected) to whom the EVMS requirements will apply. The offeror and the Government shall agree to the subcontractors or the subcontracted effort selected for application of the EVMS requirements. The offeror shall be responsible for ensuring that the selected subcontractors comply with the requirements of the Earned Value Management System clause of the contract.

(End of provision)

[DAC 91-13, 63 FR 11522, 3/9/98, effective 3/9/98; Final rule, 70 FR 14574, 3/23/2005, effective 3/23/2005; Final rule, 73 FR 21846, 4/23/2008, effective 4/23/2008]

252.234-7002 Earned Value Management System.

As prescribed in 234.203(2), use the following clause:

EARNED VALUE MANAGEMENT SYSTEM (MAY 2011)

(a) *Definitions*. As used in this clause—

Acceptable earned value management system means an earned value management system that generally complies with system criteria in paragraph (b) of this clause.

Earned value management system means an earned value management system that complies with the earned value management system guidelines in the ANSI/EIA-748.

Significant deficiency means a shortcoming in the system that materially affects the ability of officials of the Department of Defense to rely upon information produced by the system that is needed for management purposes.

(b) *System criteria*. In the performance of this contract, the Contractor shall use—

(1) An Earned Value Management System (EVMS) that complies with the EVMS guidelines in the American National Standards Institute/Electronic Industries Alliance Standard 748, Earned Value Management Systems (ANSI/EIA-748); and

(2) Management procedures that provide for generation of timely, reliable, and verifiable information for the Contract Performance Report (CPR) and the Integrated Master Schedule (IMS) required by the CPR and IMS data items of this contract.

(c) If this contract has a value of $50 million or more, the Contractor shall use an EVMS that has been determined to be acceptable by the Cognizant Federal Agency (CFA). If, at the time of award, the Contractor's EVMS has not been determined by the CFA to be in compliance with the EVMS guidelines as stated in paragraph (b)(1) of this clause, the Contractor shall apply its current system to the contract and shall take necessary actions to meet the milestones in the Contractor's EVMS plan.

(d) If this contract has a value of less than $50 million, the Government will not make a formal determination that the Contractor's EVMS complies with the EVMS guidelines in ANSI/EIA-748 with respect to the contract. The use of the Contractor's EVMS for this contract does not imply a Government determination of the Contractor's compliance with the EVMS guidelines in ANSI/EIA-748 for application to future contracts. The Government will allow the use of a Contractor's EVMS that has been formally reviewed and determined by the CFA to be in compliance with the EVMS guidelines in ANSI/EIA-748.

(e) The Contractor shall submit notification of any proposed substantive changes to the EVMS procedures and the impact of those changes to the CFA. If this contract has a value of $50 million or more, unless a waiver is granted by the CFA, any EVMS changes proposed by the Contractor require approval of the CFA prior to implementation. The CFA will advise the Contractor of the acceptability of such changes as soon as practicable (generally within 30 calendar days) after receipt of the Contractor's notice of proposed changes. If the CFA waives the advance approval requirements, the Contractor shall disclose EVMS changes to the CFA at least 14 calendar days prior to the effective date of implementation.

(f) The Government will schedule integrated baseline reviews as early as practicable, and the review process will be conducted not later than 180 calendar days after—

(1) Contract award;

(2) The exercise of significant contract options; and

(3) The incorporation of major modifications.

During such reviews, the Government and the Contractor will jointly assess the Contractor's baseline to be used for performance measurement to ensure complete coverage of the statement of work, logical scheduling of the work activities, adequate resource, and identification of inherent risks.

(g) The Contractor shall provide access to all pertinent records and data requested by the Contracting Officer or duly authorized representative as necessary to permit Government surveillance to ensure that the EVMS complies, and continues to comply, with the performance criteria referenced in paragraph (b) of this clause.

(h) When indicated by contract performance, the Contractor shall submit a request for approval to initiate an over-target baseline or over-target schedule to the Contracting Officer. The request shall include a top-level projection of cost and/or schedule growth, a determination of whether or not performance variances will be retained, and a schedule of implementation for the rebaselining. The Government will acknowledge receipt of the request in a timely manner (generally within 30 calendar days).

(i) *Significant deficiencies*. (1) The Contracting Officer will provide an initial determination to the Contractor, in writing, on any significant deficiencies. The initial determination will describe the deficiency in sufficient detail to allow the Contractor to understand the deficiency.

(2) The Contractor shall respond within 30 days to a written initial determination from the Contracting Officer that identifies significant deficiencies in the Contractor's EVMS. If the Contractor disagrees with the initial determination, the Contractor shall state, in writing, its rationale for disagreeing.

(3) The Contracting Officer will evaluate the Contractor's response and notify the Contractor, in writing, of the Contracting Officer's final determination concerning—

(i) Remaining significant deficiencies;

(ii) The adequacy of any proposed or completed corrective action;

(iii) System noncompliance, when the Contractor's existing EVMS fails to comply with the earned value management system guidelines in the ANSI/EIA-748; and

(iv) System disapproval, if initial EVMS validation is not successfully completed within the timeframe approved by the Contracting Officer, or if the Contracting Officer determines that the Contractor's earned value management system contains one or more significant deficiencies in high-risk guidelines in ANSI/EIA-748 standards (guidelines 1, 3, 6, 7, 8, 9, 10, 12, 16, 21, 23, 26, 27, 28, 30, or 32). When the Contracting Officer determines that the existing earned value management system contains one or more significant deficiencies in one or more of the remaining 16 guidelines in ANSI/EIA-748 standards, the contracting officer will use discretion to disapprove the system based on input received from functional specialists and the auditor.

(4) If the Contractor receives the Contracting Officer's final determination of significant deficiencies, the Contractor shall, within 45 days of receipt of the final determination, either correct the significant deficiencies or submit an acceptable corrective action plan showing milestones and actions to eliminate the significant deficiencies.

(j) *Withholding payments*. If the Contracting Officer makes a final determination to disapprove the Contractor's EVMS, and the contract includes the clause at 252.242-7005, Contractor Business Systems, the Contracting Officer will withhold payments in accordance with that clause.

(k) With the exception of paragraphs (i) and (j) of this clause, the Contractor shall require its subcontractors to comply with EVMS requirements as follows:

(1) For subcontracts valued at $50 million or more, the following subcontractors shall comply with the requirements of this clause:

[*Contracting Officer to insert names of subcontractors (or subcontracted effort if subcontractors have not been selected) designated for application of the EVMS requirements of this clause.*]

____

____

____

____

(2) For subcontracts valued at less than $50 million, the following subcontractors shall comply with the requirements of this clause, excluding the requirements of paragraph (c) of this clause:

[*Contracting Officer to insert names of subcontractors (or subcontracted effort if subcontractors have not been selected) designated for application of the EVMS requirements of this clause.*]

____

____

____

____

(End of clause)

[Final rule, 73 FR 21846, 4/23/2008, effective 4/23/2008; Interim rule, 76 FR 28856, 5/18/2011, effective 5/18/2011; Final rule, 77 FR 11355, 2/24/2012, effective 2/24/2012]

252.234-7003 Notice of Cost and Software Data Reporting System.

Basic. As prescribed in 234.7101(a) and (a)(1), use the following provision:

NOTICE OF COST AND SOFTWARE DATA REPORTING SYSTEM—BASIC (NOV 2014)

(a) This solicitation includes—

(1) The Government-approved cost and software data reporting (CSDR) plan for the contract, DD Form 2794; and

(2) The related Resource Distribution Table.

(b) As part of its proposal, the Offeror shall—

(1) Describe the process to be used to satisfy the requirements of the DoD 5000.04-M-1, CSDR Manual, and the Government-approved CSDR plan for the proposed contract;

(2) Demonstrate how contractor cost and data reporting (CCDR) will be based, to the maximum extent possible, upon actual cost transactions and not cost allocations;

(3) Demonstrate how the data from its accounting system will be mapped into the standard reporting categories required in the CCDR data item descriptions;

(4) Describe how recurring and nonrecurring costs will be segregated;

(5) Provide comments on the adequacy of the CSDR contract plan and related Resource Distribution Table; and

(6) Submit the DD Form 1921, Cost Data Summary Report, and DD Form 1921-1,

Functional Cost-Hour Report, with its pricing proposal.

(c) CSDR reporting will be required for selected subcontractors identified in the CSR contract plan as requiring such reporting. The offeror shall identify, by providing comments on the Resource Distribution Table, the subcontractors, or, if the subcontractors have not been selected, the subcontracted effort.

(End of provision)

Alternate I. As prescribed in 234.7101(a) and (a)(2), use the following provision, which uses a different paragraph (c) than the basic provision:

NOTICE OF COST AND SOFTWARE DATA REPORTING SYSTEM—ALTERNATE I (NOV 2014)

(a) This solicitation includes—

(1) The Government-approved cost and software data reporting (CSDR) plan for the contract, DD Form 2794; and

(2) The related Resource Distribution Table.

(b) As part of its proposal, the Offeror shall—

(1) Describe the process to be used to satisfy the requirements of the DoD 5000.04–M–1, CSDR Manual, and the Government approved CSDR plan for the proposed contract;

(2) Demonstrate how contractor cost and data reporting (CCDR) will be based, to the maximum extent possible, upon actual cost transactions and not cost allocations;

(3) Demonstrate how the data from its accounting system will be mapped into the standard reporting categories required in the CCDR data item descriptions;

(4) Describe how recurring and nonrecurring costs will be segregated;

(5) Provide comments on the adequacy of the CSDR contract plan and related Resource Distribution Table; and

(6) Submit the DD Form 1921, Cost Data Summary Report, and DD Form 1921–1, Functional Cost-Hour Report, with its pricing proposal.

(c) CSDR reporting will be required for subcontractors for selected subcontracts identified in the CSDR contract plan as requiring such reporting. The offeror shall identify, by providing comments on the Resource Distribution Table, the subcontractors, or, if the subcontractors have not been selected, the subcontracted effort.

(End of provision)

[Final rule, 75 FR 71560, 11/24/2010, effective 11/24/2010; Final rule, 79 FR 65592, 11/5/2014, effective 11/5/2014; Final rule, 80 FR 36897, 6/26/2015, effective 6/26/2015]

252.234-7004 Cost and Software Data Reporting System.

Basic. As prescribed at 234.7101(b) and (b)(1), use the following clause:

COST AND SOFTWARE DATA REPORTING SYSTEM—BASIC (NOV 2014)

(a) In the performance of this contract, the Contractor shall use—

(1) A documented standard cost and software data reporting (CSDR) process that satisfies the guidelines contained in the DoD 5000.04–M–1, CSDR Manual;

(2) Management procedures that provide for generation of timely and reliable information for the contractor cost data reports (CCDRs) and software resources data reports (SRDRs) required by the CCDR and SRDR data items of this contract; and

(3) The Government-approved CSDR plan for this contract, DD Form 2794, and the related Resource Distribution Table as the basis for reporting in accordance with the required CSDR data item descriptions (DIDs).

(b) The Contractor shall require CSDR reporting from subcontractors at any tier with a subcontract that exceeds $50 million. If, for subcontracts that exceed $50 million, the Contractor changes subcontractors or makes new subcontract awards, the Contractor shall notify the Government.

(End of clause)

Alternate I. As prescribed in 234.7101 (b) and (b)(2), use the following clause, which uses a different paragraph (b) than the basic clause:

COST AND SOFTWARE DATA REPORTING SYSTEM—ALTERNATE I (NOV 2014)

(a) In the performance of this contract, the Contractor shall use—

(1) A documented standard cost and software data reporting (CSDR) process that satisfies the guidelines contained in the DoD 5000.04–M–1, CSDR Manual;

(2) Management procedures that provide for generation of timely and reliable information for the contractor cost data reports (CCDRs) and software resources data reports (SRDRs) required by the CCDR and SRDR data items of this contract; and

(3) The Government-approved CSDR plan for this contract, DD Form 2794, and the related Resource Distribution Table as the basis for reporting in accordance with the required CSDR data item descriptions (DIDs).

(b) The Contractor shall require CSDR reporting from selected subcontractors identified in the CSDR contract plan as requiring such reporting. If the Contractor changes subcontractors or makes new awards for selected subcontract effort, the Contractor shall notify the Government.

(End of clause)

[Final rule, 75 FR 71560, 11/24/2010, effective 11/24/2010; Final rule, 79 FR 65592, 11/5/2014, effective 11/5/2014; Final rule, 80 FR 36897, 6/26/2015, effective 6/26/2015]

252.235 Research and Development Contracting, provisions and clauses for DFARS Part 235

252.235-7000 Indemnification under 10 U.S.C. 2354—fixed price.

As prescribed in 235.070-3, use the following clause:

INDEMNIFICATION UNDER 10 U.S.C. 2354—FIXED PRICE (DEC 1991)

(a) This clause provides for indemnification under 10 U.S.C. 2354 if the Contractor meets all the terms and conditions of this clause.

(b) Claims, losses, and damages covered—

(1) Claims by third persons for death, bodily injury, sickness, or disease, or the loss, damage, or lost use of property. Claims include those for reasonable expenses of litigation or settlement. The term *third persons* includes employees of the contractor;

(2) The loss, damage, and lost use of the Contractor's property, but excluding lost profit; and

(3) Loss, damage, or lost use of the Government's property.

(c) The claim, loss, or damage—

(1) Must arise from the direct performance of this contract;

(2) Must not be compensated by insurance or other means, or be within deductible amounts of the Contractor's insurance;

(3) Must result from an unusually hazardous risk as specifically defined in the contract;

(4) Must not result from willful misconduct or lack of good faith on the part of any of the Contractor's directors or officers, managers, superintendents, or other equivalent representatives who have supervision or direction of—

(i) All or substantially all of the Contractor's business;

(ii) All or substantially all of the Contractor's operations at any one plant or separate location where this contract is being performed; or

(iii) A separate and complete major industrial operation connected with the performance of this contract;

(5) Must not be a liability assumed under any contract or agreement (except for subcontracts covered by paragraph (h) of this clause), unless the Contracting Officer (or in contracts with the Department of the Navy, the Department) specifically approved the assumption of liability; and

(6) Must be certified as just and reasonable by the Secretary of the department or designated representative.

(d) The Contractor shall buy and maintain, to the extent available, insurance against unusually hazardous risks in the form, amount, period(s) of time, at the rate(s), and with such insurers, as the Contracting Officer (or, for Navy contracts, the Department) may from time to time require and approve. If the cost of this insurance is higher than the cost of the insurance the Contractor had as of the date of the contract, the Government shall reimburse the Contractor for the difference in cost, as long as it is properly allocable to this contract and is not included in the contract price. The Government shall not be liable for claims, loss, or damage if insurance was available and is either required or approved under this paragraph.

(e) A reduction of the insurance coverage maintained by the Contractor on the date of the execution of this contract shall not increase the Government's liability under this clause unless the Contracting Officer consents, and the contract price is equitably adjusted, if appropriate, to reflect the Contractor's consideration for the Government's assumption of increased liability.

(f) *Notice*. The Contractor shall—

(1) Promptly notify the Contracting Officer of any occurrence, action, or claim that might trigger the Government's liability under this clause;

(2) Furnish the proof or evidence of any claim, loss, or damage in the form and manner that the Government requires; and

(3) Immediately provide copies of all pertinent papers that the Contractor receives or has received.

(g) The Government may direct, participate in, and supervise the settlement or defense of the claim or action. The Contractor shall comply with the Government's directions and execute any authorizations required.

(h) *Flowdown*. The Government shall indemnify the Contractor if the Contractor has an obligation to indemnify a subcontractor under any subcontract at any tier under this contract for the unusually hazardous risk identified in this contract only if—

(1) The Contracting Officer gave prior written approval for the Contractor to provide in a subcontract for the Contractor to indemnify the subcontractor for unusually hazardous risks defined in this contract;

(2) The Contracting Officer approved those indemnification provisions;

(3) The subcontract indemnification provisions entitle the Contractor, or the Government, or both, to direct, participate in, and supervise the settlement or defense of relevant actions and claims; and

(4) The subcontract provides the same rights and duties, the same provisions for notice, furnishing of papers and the like, between the Contractor and the subcontractor, as exist between the Government and the Contractor under this clause.

(i) The Government may discharge its obligations under paragraph (h) of this clause by making payments directly to subcontractors or to persons to whom the subcontractors may be liable.

(j) The rights and obligations of the parties under this clause shall survive the termination, expiration, or completion of this contract.

(End of clause)

252.235-7001 Indemnification under 10 U.S.C. 2354—cost reimbursement.

As prescribed in 235.070-3, use the following clause:

INDEMNIFICATION UNDER 10 U.S.C. 2354—COST REIMBURSEMENT (DEC 1991)

(a) This clause provides for indemnification under 10 U.S.C. 2354 if the Contractor meets all the terms and conditions of this clause.

(b) Claims, losses, and damages covered—

(1) Claims by third persons for death, bodily injury, sickness, or disease, or the loss, damage, or lost use of property. Claims include those for reasonable expenses of litigation or settlement. The term "third persons" includes employees of the Contractor;

(2) The loss, damage, and lost use of the Contractor's property, but excluding lost profit; and

(3) Loss, damage, or lost use of the Government's property.

(c) The claim, loss, or damage—

(1) Must arise from the direct performance of this contract;

(2) Must not be compensated by insurance or other means, or be within deductible amounts of the Contractor's insurance;

(3) Must result from an unusually hazardous risk as specifically defined in the contract;

(4) Must not result from willful misconduct or lack of good faith on the part of any of the Contractor's directors or officers, managers, superintendents, or other equivalent representatives who have supervision or direction of—

(i) All or substantially all of the Contractor's business;

(ii) All or substantially all of the Contractor's operations at any one plant or separate location where this contract is being performed; or

(iii) A separate and complete major industrial operation connected with the performance of this contract;

(5) Must not be a liability assumed under any contract or agreement (except for subcontracts covered by paragraph (i) of this clause), unless the Contracting Officer (or in contracts with the Department of the Navy, the Department) specifically approved the assumption of liability; and

(6) Must be certified as just and reasonable by the Secretary of the department or designated representative.

(d) A reduction of the insurance coverage maintained by the Contractor on the date of the execution of this contract shall not increase the Government's liability under this clause unless the Contracting Officer consents, and the contract price is equitably adjusted, if appropriate, to reflect the Contractor's consideration for the Government's assumption of increased liability.

(e) *Notice*. The Insurance—Liability to Third Persons clause of this contract applies also to claims under this clause. In addition, the Contractor shall—

(1) Promptly notify the Contracting Officer of any occurrence, action, or claim that might trigger the Government's liability under this clause;

(2) Furnish the proof or evidence of any claim, loss, or damage in the form and manner that the Government requires; and

(3) Immediately provide copies of all pertinent papers that the contractor receives or has received.

(f) The Government may direct, participate in, and supervise the settlement or defense of the claim or action. The Contractor shall comply with the Government's directions, and execute any authorizations required.

(g) The Limitation of Cost clause of this contract does not apply to the Government's obligations under this clause. The obligations under this clause are excepted from the release required by the Allowable Cost, Fee, and Payment clause of this contract.

(h) Under this clause, a claim, loss, or damage arises from the direct performance of this contract if the cause of the claim, loss, or damage occurred during the period of performance of this contract or as a result of the performance of this contract.

(i) *Flowdown*. The Government shall indemnify the Contractor if the Contractor has an obligation to indemnify a subcontractor under any subcontract at any tier under this contract for the unusually hazardous risk identified in this contract only if—

(1) The Contracting Officer gave prior written approval for the Contractor to provide in a subcontract for the Contractor to indemnify the subcontractor for unusually hazardous risks defined in this contract;

(2) The Contracting Officer approved those indemnification provisions;

(3) The subcontract indemnification provisions entitle the Contractor, or the Government, or both, to direct, participate in, and

supervise the settlement or defense of relevant actions and claims; and

(4) The subcontract provides the same rights and duties, the same provisions for notice, furnishing of paper and the like, between the Contractor and the subcontractor, as exist between the Government and the Contractor under this clause.

(j) The Government may discharge its obligations under paragraph (i) of this clause by making payments directly to subcontractors or to persons to whom the subcontractors may be liable.

(k) The rights and obligations of the parties under this clause shall survive the termination, expiration, or completion of this contract.

(End of clause)

252.235-7002 Animal welfare.

As prescribed in 235.072(a), use the following clause:

ANIMAL WELFARE (DEC 2014)

(a) (1) The Contractor shall register its research, development, test, and evaluation or training facility with the Secretary of Agriculture in accordance with 7 U.S.C. 2136 and 9 CFR subpart C, and section 2.30, unless otherwise exempt from this requirement by meeting the conditions in 7 U.S.C. 2136 and 9 CFR parts 1 through 4 for the duration of the activity. The Contractor shall have its proposed animal use approved in accordance with Department of Defense Instruction (DoDI) 3216.01, Use of Animals in DoD Programs, by a DoD Component Headquarters Oversight Office. The Contractor shall furnish evidence of such registration and approval to the Contracting Officer before beginning work under this contract.

(2) The Contractor shall make its animals, and all premises, facilities, vehicles, equipment, and records that support animal care available during business hours and at other times mutually agreeable to the Contractor and the United States Department of Agriculture Office of Animal and Plant Health Inspection Service (USDA/APHIS) representative, personnel representing the DoD component oversight offices, as well as the Contracting Officer, to ascertain that the Contractor is compliant with 7 U.S.C. 2131-2159 and 9 CFR parts 1 through 4.

(b) The Contractor shall acquire animals in accordance with DoDI 3216.01, current at time of award (*http://www.dtic.mil/whs/directives/corres/pdf/321601p.pdf*).

(c) The Contractor agrees that the care and use of animals will conform with the pertinent laws of the United States, regulations of the Department of Agriculture, and policies and procedures of the Department of Defense (see 7 U.S.C. 2131 et seq., and 9 CFR subchapter A, parts 1 through 4, DoDI 3216.01, Army Regulation 40-33/SECNAVINST 3900.38C/AFMAN 40-401(I)/DARPAINST 18/USUHSINST 3203). The Contractor shall also comply with DoDI 1322.24, Medical Readiness Training, if this contract includes acquisition of training.

(d) The Contracting Officer may immediately suspend, in whole or in part, work and further payments under this contract for failure to comply with the requirements of paragraphs (a) through (c) of this clause.

(1) The suspension will stay in effect until the Contractor complies with the requirements.

(2) Failure to complete corrective action within the time specified by the Contracting Officer may result in termination of this contract and, if applicable, removal of the Contractor's name from the approved vendor list for live animals used in medical training.

(e) The Contractor may request registration of its facility by contacting USDA/APHIS/AC, 4700 River Road, Unit 84, Riverdale, MD 20737-1234, or via the APHIS Animal Care website at: *http://www.aphis.usda.gov/wps/portal/aphis/ourfocus/animalwelfare*.

(f) The Contractor shall include the substance of this clause, including this paragraph (f), in all subcontracts involving research, development, test, and evaluation or training that use live vertebrate animals.

(End of clause)

[Interim rule, 73 FR 42274, 7/21/2008, effective 7/21/2008; Final rule, 75 FR 18029,

4/8/2010, effective 4/8/2010; Final rule, 76 FR 76318, 12/7/2011, effective 12/7/2011; Final rule, 70016.834 79 FR 73500, 12/11/2014, effective 12/11/2014]

252.235-7003 Frequency authorization.

Basic. As prescribed in 235.072(b) and (b)(1), use one of the following clauses:

FREQUENCY AUTHORIZATION—BASIC (MAR 2014)

(a) The Contractor shall obtain authorization for radio frequencies required in support of this contract.

(b) For any experimental, developmental, or operational equipment for which the appropriate frequency allocation has not been made, the Contractor shall provide the technical operating characteristics of the proposed electromagnetic radiating device to the Contracting Officer during the initial planning, experimental, or developmental phase of contract performance.

(c) The Contracting Officer shall furnish the procedures for obtaining radio frequency authorization.

(d) The Contractor shall include this clause, including this paragraph (d), in all subcontracts requiring the development, production, construction, testing, or operation of a device for which a radio frequency authorization is required.

(End of clause)

Alternate I. As prescribed at 235.072((b) and (b)(2), use the following clause, which uses a different paragraph (c) than the basic clause:

FREQUENCY AUTHORIZATION—ALTERNATE I (MAR 2014)

(a) The Contractor shall obtain authorization for radio frequencies required in support of this contract.

(b) For any experimental, developmental, or operational equipment for which the appropriate frequency allocation has not been made, the Contractor shall provide the technical operating characteristics of the proposed electromagnetic radiating device to the Contracting Officer during the initial planning, experimental, or developmental phase of contract performance.

(c) The Contractor shall use DD Form 1494, Application for Equipment Frequency Allocation, to obtain radio frequency authorization.

(d) The Contractor shall include this clause, including this paragraph (d), in all subcontracts requiring the development, production, construction, testing, or operation of a device for which a radio frequency authorization is required.

(End of clause)

[Interim rule, 73 FR 42274, 7/21/2008, effective 7/21/2008; Final rule, 73 FR 46817, 8/12/2008, effective 8/12/2008; Final rule, 75 FR 18029, 4/8/2010, effective 4/8/2010; Final rule, 79 FR 17447, 3/28/2014, effective 3/28/2014; Final rule, 80 FR 36897, 6/26/2015, effective 6/26/2015]

252.235-7004 Protection of Human Subjects.

As prescribed in 235.072(e), use the following clause:

PROTECTION OF HUMAN SUBJECTS (JUL 2009)

(a) *Definitions*. As used in this clause—

(1) *Assurance of compliance* means a written assurance that an institution will comply with requirements of 32 CFR Part 219, as well as the terms of the assurance, which the Human Research Protection Official determines to be appropriate for the research supported by the Department of Defense (DoD) component (32 CFR 219.103).

(2) *Human Research Protection Official (HRPO)* means the individual designated by the head of the applicable DoD component and identified in the component's Human Research Protection Management Plan as the official who is responsible for the oversight and execution of the requirements of this clause, although some DoD components may use a different title for this position.

(3) *Human subject* means a living individual about whom an investigator (whether professional or student) conducting research obtains data through intervention or interaction with the individual, or identifiable pri-

vate information (32 CFR 219.102(f)). For example, this could include the use of human organs, tissue, and body fluids from individually identifiable living human subjects as well as graphic, written, or recorded information derived from individually identifiable living human subjects.

(4) *Institution* means any public or private entity or agency (32 CFR 219.102(b)).

(5) *Institutional Review Board (IRB)* means a board established for the purposes expressed in 32 CFR Part 219 (32 CFR 219.102(g)).

(6) *IRB approval* means the determination of the IRB that the research has been reviewed and may be conducted at an institution within the constraints set forth by the IRB and by other institutional and Federal requirements (32 CFR 219.102(h)).

(7) *Research* means a systematic investigation, including research, development, testing, and evaluation, designed to develop or contribute to generalizable knowledge. Activities that meet this definition constitute research for purposes of 32 CFR Part 219, whether or not they are conducted or supported under a program that is considered research for other purposes. For example, some demonstration and service programs may include research activities (32 CFR 219.102(d)).

(b) The Contractor shall oversee the execution of the research to ensure compliance with this clause. The Contractor shall comply fully with 32 CFR Part 219 and DoD Directive 3216.02, applicable DoD component policies, 10 U.S.C. 980, and, when applicable, Food and Drug Administration policies and regulations.

(c) The Contractor shall not commence performance of research involving human subjects that is covered under 32 CFR Part 219 or that meets exemption criteria under 32 CFR 219.101(b), or expend funding on such effort, until and unless the conditions of either the following paragraph (c)(1) or (c)(2) have been met:

(1) The Contractor furnishes to the HRPO, with a copy to the Contracting Officer, an assurance of compliance and IRB approval and receives notification from the Contracting Officer that the HRPO has approved the assurance as appropriate for the research under the Statement of Work and also that the HRPO has reviewed the protocol and accepted the IRB approval for compliance with the DoD component policies. The Contractor may furnish evidence of an existing assurance of compliance for acceptance by the HRPO, if an appropriate assurance has been approved in connection with previous research. The Contractor shall notify the Contracting Officer immediately of any suspensions or terminations of the assurance.

(2) The Contractor furnishes to the HRPO, with a copy to the Contracting Officer, a determination that the human research proposed meets exemption criteria in 32 CFR 219.101(b) and receives written notification from the Contracting Officer that the exemption is determined acceptable. The determination shall include citation of the exemption category under 32 CFR 219.101(b) and a rationale statement. In the event of a disagreement regarding the Contractor's furnished exemption determination, the HRPO retains final judgment on what research activities or classes of research are covered or are exempt under the contract.

(d) DoD staff, consultants, and advisory groups may independently review and inspect the Contractor's research and research procedures involving human subjects and, based on such findings, DoD may prohibit research that presents unacceptable hazards or otherwise fails to comply with DoD procedures.

(e) Failure of the Contractor to comply with the requirements of this clause will result in the issuance of a stop-work order under Federal Acquisition Regulation clause 52.242-15to immediately suspend, in whole or in part, work and further payment under this contract, or will result in other issuance of suspension of work and further payment for as long as determined necessary at the discretion of the Contracting Officer.

(f) The Contractor shall include the substance of this clause, including this paragraph (f), in all subcontracts that may include research involving human subjects in accordance with 32 CFR Part 219, DoD Directive 3216.02, and 10 U.S.C. 980, including research that meets exemption criteria under 32 CFR 219.101(b). This clause does not apply to subcontracts that involve only the use of cadaver materials.

(End of clause)

[Removed and reserved, Final rule, 64 FR 39431, 7/22/99, effective 7/22/99; Final rule, 74 FR 37648, 7/29/2009, effective 7/29/2009]

252.235-7005 [Reserved]

[Removed and reserved, Final rule, 64 FR 39431, 7/22/99, effective 7/22/99]

252.235-7006 [Reserved]

[Removed and reserved, Final rule, 64 FR 39431, 7/22/99, effective 7/22/99]

252.235-7007 [Reserved]

[Removed and reserved, Final rule, 64 FR 39431, 7/22/99, effective 7/22/99]

252.235-7008 [Reserved]

[Removed and reserved, Final rule, 64 FR 39431, 7/22/99, effective 7/22/99]

252.235-7009 [Reserved]

[Removed and reserved, Final rule, 64 FR 39431, 7/22/99, effective 7/22/99]

252.235-7010 Acknowledgment of support and disclaimer.

As prescribed in 235.072(c), use the following clause:

ACKNOWLEDGMENT OF SUPPORT AND DISCLAIMER (MAY 1995)

(a) The Contractor shall include an acknowledgment of the Government's support in the publication of any material based on or developed under this contract, stated in the following terms: This material is based upon work supported by the (name of contracting agency(ies)) under Contract No. (Contracting agency(ies) contract number(s)).

(b) All material, except scientific articles or papers published in scientific journals, must, in addition to any notices or disclaimers by the Contractor, also contain the following disclaimer: Any opinions, findings and conclusions or recommendations expressed in this material are those of the author(s) and do not necessarily reflect the views of the (name of contracting agency(ies)).

(End of clause)

[DAC 91-7, 60 FR 29491, 6/5/95, effective 5/17/95; Interim rule, 73 FR 42274, 7/21/2008, effective 7/21/2008; Final rule, 75 FR 18029, 4/8/2010, effective 4/8/2010]

252.235-7011 Final scientific or technical report.

As prescribed in 235.072(d), use the following clause:

FINAL SCIENTIFIC OR TECHNICAL REPORT (DEC 2019)

The Contractor shall—

(a) Submit an electronic copy of the approved final scientific or technical report, not a summary, delivered under this contract to the Defense Technical Information Center (DTIC) through the web-based input system at *https://discover. dtic.mil/submit-documents/* as required by DoD Instruction 3200.12, DoD Scientific and Technical Information Program (STIP). Include a completed Standard Form (SF) 298, Report Documentation Page, in the document, or complete the web-based SF 298.

(b) For instructions on submitting multimedia reports, follow the instructions at *https://discover. dtic.mil/submit-documents/*.

(c) Email classified reports (up to Secret) to *dtic.belvoir.da.mbx.tr@mail.smil.mil*. If a SIPRNET email capability is not available, follow the classified submission instructions at *https://discover. dtic.mil/submit-documents/*.

(End of clause)

[DAC 91-7, 60 FR 29491, 6/5/95, effective 5/1/795; Final rule, 64 FR 51074 9/21/99, effective 9/21/99; Final rule, 69 FR 65091, 11/10/2004, effective 11/10/2004; Interim rule, 73 FR 42274, 7/21/2008, effective 7/21/2008; Final rule, 75 FR 18029, 4/8/2010, effective 4/8/2010; Final rule, 80 FR 4806, 1/29/2015, effective 1/29/2015; Final rule, 84 FR 72563, 12/31/2019, effective 12/31/2019]

252.236 Construction and Architect-Engineer Contracts, provisions and clauses for DFARS Part 236

252.236-7000 Modification proposals—price breakdown.

As prescribed in 236.570(a), use the following clause:

MODIFICATION PROPOSALS—PRICE BREAKDOWN (DEC 1991)

(a) The Contractor shall furnish a price breakdown, itemized as required and within the time specified by the Contracting Officer, with any proposal for a contract modification.

(b) The price breakdown—

(1) Must include sufficient detail to permit an analysis of profit, and of all costs for—

(i) Material;

(ii) Labor;

(iii) Equipment;

(iv) Subcontracts; and

(v) Overhead; and

(2) Must cover all work involved in the modification, whether the work was deleted, added, or changed.

(c) The Contractor shall provide similar price breakdowns to support any amounts claimed for subcontracts.

(d) The Contractor's proposal shall include a justification for any time extension proposed.

(End of clause)

252.236-7001 Contract drawings and specifications.

As prescribed in 236.570(a), use the following clause:

CONTRACT DRAWINGS AND SPECIFICATIONS (AUG 2000)

(a) The Government will provide to the Contractor, without charge, one set of contract drawings and specifications, except publications incorporated into the technical provisions by reference, in electronic or paper media as chosen by the Contracting Officer.

(b) The Contractor shall—

(1) Check all drawings furnished immediately upon receipt;

(2) Compare all drawings and verify the figures before laying out the work;

(3) Promptly notify the Contracting Officer of any discrepancies;

(4) Be responsible for any errors that might have been avoided by complying with this paragraph (b); and

(5) Reproduce and print contract drawings and specifications as needed.

(c) In general—

(1) Large-scale drawings shall govern small-scale drawings; and

(2) The Contractor shall follow figures marked on drawings in preference to scale measurements.

(d) Omissions from the drawings or specifications or the misdescription of details of work that are manifestly necessary to carry out the intent of the drawings and specifications, or that are customarily performed, shall not relieve the Contractor from performing such omitted or misdescribed details of the work. The Contractor shall perform such details as if fully and correctly set forth and described in the drawings and specifications.

(e) The work shall conform to the specifications and the contract drawings identified on the following index of drawings:

Title	File	Drawing No.

(End of clause)

[Final rule, 65 FR 50152, 8/17/2000, effective 8/17/2000]

252.236-7002 Obstruction of navigable waterways.

As prescribed in 236.570(b)(1), use the following clause:

OBSTRUCTION OF NAVIGABLE WATERWAYS (DEC 1991)

(a) The Contractor shall—

(1) Promptly recover and remove any material, plant, machinery, or appliance which the contractor loses, dumps, throws over-

board, sinks, or misplaces, and which, in the opinion of the Contracting Officer, may be dangerous to or obstruct navigation;

(2) Give immediate notice, with description and locations of any such obstructions, to the Contracting Officer; and

(3) When required by the Contracting Officer, mark or buoy such obstructions until the same are removed.

(b) The Contracting Officer may—

(1) Remove the obstructions by contract or otherwise should the Contractor refuse, neglect, or delay compliance with paragraph (a) of this clause; and

(2) Deduct the cost of removal from any monies due or to become due to the Contractor; or

(3) Recover the cost of removal under the Contractor's bond.

(c) The Contractor's liability for the removal of a vessel wrecked or sunk without fault or negligence is limited to that provided in sections 15, 19, and 20 of the River and Harbor Act of March 3, 1899 (33 U.S.C. 410 *et. seq.*).

(End of clause)

252.236-7003 Payment for mobilization and preparatory work.

As prescribed in 236.570(b)(2), use the following clause:

PAYMENT FOR MOBILIZATION AND PREPARATORY WORK (JAN 1997)

(a) The Government will make payment to the Contractor under the procedures in this clause for mobilization and preparatory work under item no. ____.

(b) Payments will be made for actual payments by the Contractor on work preparatory to commencing actual work on the construction items for which payment is provided under the terms of this contract, as follows—

(1) For construction plant and equipment exceeding $25,000 in value per unit (as appraised by the Contracting Officer at the work site) acquired for the execution of the work;

(2) Transportation of all plant and equipment to the site;

(3) Material purchased for the prosecution of the contract, but not to be incorporated in the work;

(4) Construction of access roads or railroads, camps, trailer courts, mess halls, dormitories or living quarters, field headquarters facilities, and construction yards;

(5) Personal services; and

(6) Hire of plant.

(c) Requests for payment must include—

(1) An account of the Contractor's actual expenditures;

(2) Supporting documentation, including receipted bills or copies of payrolls and freight bills; and

(3) The Contractor's documentation—

(i) Showing that it has acquired the construction plant, equipment, and material free from all encumbrances;

(ii) Agreeing that the construction plant, equipment, and material will not be removed from the site without the written permission of the Contracting Officer; and

(iii) Agreeing that structures and facilities prepared or erected for the prosecution of the contract work will be maintained and not dismantled prior to the completion and acceptance of the entire work, without the written permission of the Contracting Officer.

(d) Upon receiving a request for payment, the Government will make payment, less any prescribed retained percentage, if—

(1) The Contracting Officer finds the—

(i) Construction plant, material, equipment, and the mobilization and preparatory work performed are suitable and necessary to the efficient prosecution of the contract; and

(ii) Preparatory work has been done with proper economy and efficiency.

(2) Payments for construction plant, equipment, material, and structures and facilities prepared or erected for prosecution of the contract work do not exceed—

(i) The Contractor's cost for the work performed less the estimated value upon completion of the contract; and

(ii) 100 percent of the cost to the contractor of any items having no appreciable salvage value; and

(iii) 75 percent of the cost to the contractor of items which do have an appreciable salvage value.

(e) (1) Payments will continue to be made for item no. ____, and all payments will be deducted from the contract price for this item, until the total deductions reduce this item to zero, after which no further payments will be made under this item.

(2) If the total of payments so made does not reduce this item to zero, the balance will be paid to the Contractor in the final payment under the contract.

(3) The retained percentage will be paid in accordance with the Payments to Contractor clause of this contract.

(f) The Contracting Officer shall determine the value and suitability of the construction plant, equipment, materials, structures and facilities. The Contracting Officer's determinations are not subject to appeal.

(End of clause)

[Final rule, 62 FR 2612, 1/17/97, effective 1/17/97]

252.236-7004 Payment for mobilization and demobilization.

As prescribed in 236.570(b)(2), use the following clause:

PAYMENT FOR MOBILIZATION AND DEMOBILIZATION (DEC 1991)

(a) The Government will pay all costs for the mobilization and demobilization of all of the Contractor's plant and equipment at the contract lump sum price for this item.

(1) ____ percent of the lump sum price upon completion of the contractor's mobilization at the work site.

(2) The remaining ____ percent upon completion of demobilization.

(b) The Contracting Officer may require the Contractor to furnish cost data to justify this portion of the bid if the Contracting Officer believes that the percentages in paragraphs (a)(1) and (2) of this clause do not bear a reasonable relation to the cost of the work in this contract.

(1) Failure to justify such price to the satisfaction of the Contracting Officer will result in payment, as determined by the Contracting Officer, of—

(i) Actual mobilization costs at completion of mobilization;

(ii) Actual demobilization costs at completion of demobilization; and

(iii) The remainder of this item in the final payment under this contract.

(2) The Contracting Officer's determination of the actual costs in paragraph (b)(1) of this clause is not subject to appeal.

(End of clause)

252.236-7005 Airfield safety precautions.

As prescribed in 236.570(b)(3), use the following clause. At some airfields, the width of the primary surface is 1,500 feet (750 feet on each side of the runway centerline). In such instances, substitute the proper width in the clause.

AIRFIELD SAFETY PRECAUTIONS (DEC 1991)

(a) *Definitions*. As used in this clause—

(1) *Landing areas* means—

(i) The primary surfaces, comprising the surface of the runway, runway shoulders, and lateral safety zones. The length of each primary surface is the same as the runway length. The width of each primary surface is 2,000 feet (1,000 feet on each side of the runway centerline);

(ii) The *clear zone* beyond the ends of each runway, i.e., the extension of the primary surface for a distance of 1,000 feet beyond each end of each runway;

(iii) All taxiways, plus the lateral clearance zones along each side for the length of the taxiways (the outer edge of each lateral clearance zone is laterally 250 feet from the far or opposite edge of the taxiway, e.g., a 75-foot-wide taxiway would have a combined width of taxiway and lateral clearance zones of 425 feet); and

(iv) All aircraft parking aprons, plus the area 125 feet in width extending beyond each edge all around the aprons.

(2) *Safety precaution areas* means those portions of approach-departure clearance zones and transitional zones where placement of objects incident to contract performance might result in vertical projections at or above the approach-departure clearance, or the transitional surface.

(i) The *approach-departure clearance surface* is an extension of the primary surface and the clear zone at each end of each runway, for a distance of 50,000 feet, first along an inclined plane (glide angle) and then along a horizontal plane, both flaring symmetrically about the runway centerline extended.

(A) The inclined plane (glide angle) begins in the clear zone 200 feet past the end of the runway (and primary surface) at the same elevation as the end of the runway. It continues upward at a slope of 50:1 (1 foot vertically for each 50 feet horizontally) to an elevation of 500 feet above the established airfield elevation. At that point the plane becomes horizontal, continuing at that same uniform elevation to a point 50,000 feet longitudinally from the beginning of the inclined plane (glide angle) and ending there.

(B) The width of the surface at the beginning of the inclined plane (glide angle) is the same as the width of the clear zone. It then flares uniformly, reaching the maximum width of 16,000 feet at the end.

(ii) The *approach-departure clearance zone* is the ground area under the approach-departure clearance surface.

(iii) The *transitional surface* is a sideways extension of all primary surfaces, clear zones, and approach-departure clearance surfaces along inclined planes.

(A) The inclined plane in each case begins at the edge of the surface.

(B) The slope of the incline plane is 7:1 (1 foot vertically for each 7 feet horizontally). It continues to the point of intersection with the—

(*1*) Inner horizontal surface (which is the horizontal plane 150 feet above the established airfield elevation); or

(*2*) Outer horizontal surface (which is the horizontal plane 500 feet above the established airfield elevation), whichever is applicable.

(iv) The *transitional zone* is the ground area under the transitional surface. (It adjoins the primary surface, clear zone, and approach-departure clearance zone.)

(b) *General.* (1) The Contractor shall comply with the requirements of this clause while—

(i) Operating all ground equipment (mobile or stationary);

(ii) Placing all materials; and

(iii) Performing all work, upon and around all airfields.

(2) The requirements of this clause are in addition to any other safety requirements of this contract.

(c) The Contractor shall—

(1) Report to the Contracting Officer before initiating any work;

(2) Notify the Contracting Officer of proposed changes to locations and operations;

(3) Not permit either its equipment or personnel to use any runway for purposes other than aircraft operation without permission of the Contracting Officer, unless the runway is—

(i) Closed by order of the Contracting Officer; and

(ii) Marked as provided in paragraph (d)(2) of this clause;

(4) Keep all paved surfaces, such as runways, taxiways, and hardstands, clean at all times and, specifically, free from small stones which might damage aircraft propellers or jet aircraft;

(5) Operate mobile equipment according to the safety provisions of this clause, while actually performing work on the airfield. At

all other times, the Contractor shall remove all mobile equipment to locations—

(i) Approved by the Contracting Officer;

(ii) At a distance of at least 750 feet from the runway centerline, plus any additional distance; and

(iii) Necessary to ensure compliance with the other provisions of this clause; and

(6) Not open a trench unless material is on hand and ready for placing in the trench. As soon as practicable after material has been placed and work approved, the Contractor shall backfill and compact trenches as required by the contract. Meanwhile, all hazardous conditions shall be marked and lighted in accordance with the other provisions of this clause.

(d) *Landing areas*. The Contractor shall—

(1) Place nothing upon the landing areas without the authorization of the Contracting Officer;

(2) Outline those landing areas hazardous to aircraft, using (unless otherwise authorized by the Contracting Officer) red flags by day, and electric, battery-operated low-intensity red flasher lights by night;

(3) Obtain, at an airfield where flying is controlled, additional permission from the control tower operator every time before entering any landing area, unless the landing area is marked as hazardous in accordance with paragraph (d)(2) of this clause;

(4) Identify all vehicles it operates in landing areas by means of a flag on a staff attached to, and flying above, the vehicle. The flag shall be three feet square, and consist of a checkered pattern of international orange and white squares of 1 foot on each side (except that the flag may vary up to ten percent from each of these dimensions);

(5) Mark all other equipment and materials in the landing areas, using the same marking devices as in paragraph (d)(2) of this clause; and

(6) Perform work so as to leave that portion of the landing area which is available to aircraft free from hazards, holes, piles of material, and projecting shoulders that might damage an airplane tire.

(e) *Safety precaution areas*. The Contractor shall—

(1) Place nothing upon the safety precaution areas without authorization of the Contracting Officer;

(2) Mark all equipment and materials in safety precaution areas, using (unless otherwise authorized by the Contracting Officer) red flags by day, and electric, battery-operated, low-intensity red flasher lights by night; and

(3) Provide all objects placed in safety precaution areas with a red light or red lantern at night, if the objects project above the approach-departure clearance surface or above the transitional surface.

(End of clause)

252.236-7006 Cost limitation.

As prescribed in 236.570(b)(4), use the following provision:

COST LIMITATION (JAN 1997)

(a) Certain items in this solicitation are subject to statutory cost limitations. The limitations are stated in the Schedule.

(b) An offer which does not state separate prices for the items identified in the Schedule as subject to a cost limitation may be considered nonresponsive.

(c) Prices stated in offers for items subject to cost limitations shall include an appropriate apportionment of all costs, direct and indirect, overhead, and profit.

(d) Offers may be rejected which—

(1) Are materially unbalanced for the purpose of bringing items within cost limitations; or

(2) Exceed the cost limitations, unless the limitations have been waived by the Government prior to award.

(End of provision)

[Final rule, 62 FR 2612, 1/17/97, effective 1/17/97]

252.236-7007 Additive or deductive items.

As prescribed in 236.570(b)(5), use the following provision:

ADDITIVE OR DEDUCTIVE ITEMS (DEC 1991)

(a) The low offeror and the items to be awarded shall be determined as follows—

(1) Prior to the opening of bids, the Government will determine the amount of funds available for the project.

(2) The low offeror shall be the Offeror that—

(i) Is otherwise eligible for award; and

(ii) Offers the lowest aggregate amount for the first or base bid item, plus or minus (in the order stated in the list of priorities in the bid schedule) those additive or deductive items that provide the most features within the funds determined available.

(3) The Contracting Officer shall evaluate all bids on the basis of the same additive or deductive items.

(i) If adding another item from the bid schedule list of priorities would make the award exceed the available funds for all offerors, the Contracting Officer will skip that item and go to the next item from the bid schedule of priorities; and

(ii) Add that next item if an award may be made that includes that item and is within the available funds.

(b) The Contracting Officer will use the list of priorities in the bid schedule only to determine the low offeror. After determining the low offeror, an award may be made on any combination of items if—

(1) It is in the best interest of the Government;

(2) Funds are available at the time of award; and

(3) The low offeror's price for the combination to be awarded is less than the price offered by any other responsive, responsible offeror.

(c) *Example*. The amount available is $100,000. Offeror A's base bid and four additives (in the order stated in the list of priorities in the bid Schedule) are $85,000, $10,000, $8,000, $6,000, and $4,000. Offeror B's base bid and four additives are $80,000, $16,000, $9,000, $7,000, and $4,000. Offeror A is the low offeror. The aggregate amount of offeror A's bid for purposes of award would be $99,000, which includes a base bid plus the first and fourth additives. The second and third additives were skipped because each of them would cause the aggregate bid to exceed $100,000.

(End of provision)

252.236-7008 Contract prices—bidding schedules.

As prescribed in 236.570(b)(6), use the following provision:

CONTRACT PRICES—BIDDING SCHEDULES (DEC 1991)

(a) The Government's payment for the items listed in the Bidding Schedule shall constitute full compensation to the Contractor for—

(1) Furnishing all plant, labor, equipment, appliances, and materials; and

(2) Performing all operations required to complete the work in conformity with the drawings and specifications.

(b) The Contractor shall include in the prices for the items listed in the Bidding Schedule all costs for work in the specifications, whether or not specifically listed in the Bidding Schedule.

(End of provision)

252.236-7009 [Removed and Reserved]

[Final rule, 83 FR 54680, 10/31/2018, effective 10/31/2018]

252.236-7010 Overseas military construction—Preference for United States firms.

As prescribed in 236.570(c)(1), use the following provision:

OVERSEAS MILITARY CONSTRUCTION—PREFERENCE FOR UNITED STATES FIRMS (JAN 1997)

(a) *Definition*. *United States firm*, as used in this provision, means a firm incorporated in the United States that complies with the following:

(1) The corporate headquarters are in the United States;

(2) The firm has filed corporate and employment tax returns in the United States for a minimum of 2 years (if required), has filed State and Federal income tax returns (if required) for 2 years, and has paid any taxes due as a result of these filings; and

(3) The firm employs United States citizens in key management positions.

(b) *Evaluation*. Offers from firms that do not qualify as United States firms will be evaluated by adding 20 percent to the offer.

(c) *Status*. The offeror ___ is, ___ is not a United States firm.

(End of provision)

[Interim rule, 62 FR 2856, 1/17/97, effective 1/17/97, finalized without change, DAC 91-12, 62 FR 34114, 6/24/97, effective 6/24/97; DAC 91-13, 63 FR 11522, 3/9/98, effective 3/9/98, finalized without change, 63 FR 64426, 11/20/98]

252.236-7011 Overseas architect-engineer services—Restriction to United States firms.

As prescribed in 236.609-70, use the following provision:

OVERSEAS ARCHITECT-ENGINEER SERVICES—RESTRICTION TO UNITED STATES FIRMS (JAN 1997)

(a) *Definition*. *United States firm*, as used in this provision, means a firm incorporated in the United States that complies with the following:

(1) The corporate headquarters are in the United States;

(2) The firm has filed corporate and employment tax returns in the United States for a minimum of 12 years (if required), has filed State and Federal income tax returns (if required) for 2 years, and has paid any taxes due as a result of these filings; and

(3) The firm employs United States citizens in key management positions.

(b) *Restriction*. Military construction appropriations acts restrict award of a contract, resulting from this solicitation, to a United States firm or a joint venture of United States and host nation firms.

(c) *Status*. The offeror confirms, by submission of its offer, that it is a United States firm or a joint venture of United States and host nation firms.

(End of provision)

[Interim rule, 62 FR 2857, 1/17/97, effective 1/17/97, finalized without change, DAC 91-12, 62 FR 34114, 6/24/97, effective 6/24/97; Final rule, 83 FR 54680, 10/31/2018, effective 10/31/2018]

252.236-7012 Military construction on Kwajalein Atoll—evaluation preference.

As prescribed in 236.570(c)(2), use the following provision:

MILITARY CONSTRUCTION ON KWAJALEIN ATOLL—EVALUATION PREFERENCE (MAR 1998)

(a) *Definitions*. As used in this provision—

(1) *Marshallese firm* means a local firm incorporated in the Marshall Islands, or otherwise legally organized under the laws of the Marshall Islands, that—

(i) Is more than 50 percent owned by citizens of the Marshall Islands; or

(ii) Complies with the following:

(A) The firm has done business in the Marshall Islands on a continuing basis for not less than 3 years prior to the date of issuance of this solicitation;

(B) Substantially all of the firm's directors of local operations, senior staff, and operating personnel are resident in the Marshall Islands or are U.S. citizens; and

(C) Most of the operating equipment and physical plant are in the Marshall Islands.

(2) *United States firm* means a firm incorporated in the United States that complies with the following:

(i) The corporate headquarters are in the United States;

(ii) The firm has filed corporate and employment tax returns in the United States for a minimum of 2 years (if required), has filed State and Federal income tax returns (if required) for 2 years, and has paid any taxes due as a result of these filings; and

(iii) The firm employs United States citizens in key management positions.

(b) *Evaluation*. Offers from firms that do not qualify as United States firms or Marshallese firms will be evaluated by adding 20 percent to the offer, unless application of the factor would not result in award to a United States firm.

(c) *Status*. The offeror is ___ a United States firm; ___ a Marshallese firm; ___ Other.

(End of provision)

[DAC 91-13, 63 FR 11522, 3/9/98, effective 3/9/98, finalized without change, 63 FR 64426, 11/20/98]

252.236-7013 Requirement for competition opportunity for American steel producers, fabricators, and manufacturers.

As prescribed in 236.570(d), use the following clause:

REQUIREMENT FOR COMPETITION OPPORTUNITY FOR AMERICAN STEEL PRODUCERS, FABRICATORS, AND MANUFACTURERS (JUN 2013)

(a) *Definition. Construction material*, as used in this clause, means an article, material, or supply brought to the construction site by the Contractor or a subcontractor for incorporation into the building or work.

(b) The Contractor shall provide American steel producers, fabricators, and manufacturers the opportunity to compete when acquiring steel as a construction material (e.g., steel beams, rods, cables, plates).

(c) The Contractor shall insert the substance of this clause, including this paragraph (c), in any subcontract that involves the acquisition of steel as a construction material, including subcontracts for the acquisition of commercial items.

(End of provision)

[Interim rule, 74 FR 2417, 1/15/2009, effective 1/15/2009; Final rule, 74 FR 59916, 11/19/2009, effective 11/19/2009; Final rule, 78 FR 37980, 6/25/2013, effective 6/25/2013]

252.237 Service Contracting, provisions and clauses for DFARS Part 237

252.237-7000 Notice of special standards of responsibility.

As prescribed in 237.270(d)(1), use the following provision:

NOTICE OF SPECIAL STANDARDS OF RESPONSIBILITY (DEC 1991)

(a) To be determined responsible, the Offeror must meet the general standards of responsibility set forth at FAR 9.104-1 and the following criteria, as described in Chapter 3, General Standards, of "Government Auditing Standards."

(1) Qualifications;

(2) Independence; and

(3) Quality Control.

(b) "Government Auditing Standards" is issued by the Comptroller General of the United States and is available for sale from the: Superintendent of Documents, U.S. Government Printing Office. Washington, DC 20401, Stock number 020-000-00243-3.

(c) The apparently successful Offeror, before award, shall give the Contracting Officer evidence that it is licensed by the cognizant licensing authority in the state or other political jurisdiction where the Offeror operates its professional practice.

(End of provision)

[Final rule, 66 FR 49860, 10/1/2001, effective 10/1/2001]

252.237-7001 Compliance with audit standards.

As prescribed in 237.270(d)(2), use the following clause:

COMPLIANCE WITH AUDIT STANDARDS (MAY 2000)

The Contractor, in performance of all audit services under this contract, shall comply with "Government Auditing Standards" issued by the Comptroller General of the United States.

(End of clause)

[Final rule, 65 FR 32041, 5/22/2000, effective 5/22/2000]

252.237-7002 [Removed and Reserved]

[Final rule, 71 FR 3415, 1/23/2006, effective 1/23/2006; Final rule, 79 FR 65592, 11/5/2014, effective 11/5/2014; Final rule, 80 FR 36897, 6/26/2015, effective 6/26/2015; Final rule, 84 FR 48504, 9/13/2019, effective 9/13/2019]

252.237-7003 Requirements.

As prescribed in 237.7003(a) and (a)(1), use the following clause:

REQUIREMENTS (DEC 1991)

(a) Except as provided in paragraphs (c) and (d) of this clause, the Government will order from the Contractor all of its requirements in the area of performance for the supplies and services listed in the schedule of this contract.

(b) Each order will be issued as a delivery order and will list—

(1) The supplies or services being ordered;

(2) The quantities to be furnished;

(3) Delivery or performance dates;

(4) Place of delivery or performance;

(5) Packing and shipping instructions;

(6) The address to send invoices; and

(7) The funds from which payment will be made.

(c) The Government may elect not to order supplies and services under this contract in instances where the body is removed from the area for medical, scientific, or other reason.

(d) In an epidemic or other emergency, the contracting activity may obtain services beyond the capacity of the Contractor's facilities from other sources.

(e) Contracting Officers of the following activities may order services and supplies under this contract—

(End of clause)

[Final rule, 71 FR 3415, 1/23/2006, effective 1/23/2006; Final rule, 84 FR 48504, 9/13/2019, effective 9/13/2019]

252.237-7004 Area of performance.

As prescribed in 237.7003(a) and (a)(2), use the following clause:

AREA OF PERFORMANCE (DEC 1991)

(a) The area of performance is as specified in the contract.

(b) The Contractor shall take possession of the remains at the place where they are located, transport them to the Contractor's place of preparation, and later transport them to a place designated by the Contracting Officer.

(c) The Contractor will not be reimbursed for transportation when both the place where the remains were located and the delivery point are within the area of performance.

(d) If remains are located outside the area of performance, the Contracting Officer may place an order with the Contractor under this contract or may obtain the services elsewhere. If the Contracting Officer requires the Contractor to transport the remains into the area of performance, the Contractor shall be paid the amount per mile in the schedule for the number of miles required to transport the remains by a reasonable route from the point where located to the boundary of the area of performance.

(e) The Contracting Officer may require the Contractor to deliver remains to any point within 100 miles of the area of performance. In this case, the Contractor shall be paid the amount per mile in the schedule for the number of miles required to transport the remains by a reasonable route from the boundary of the area of performance to the delivery point.

(End of clause)

[Final rule, 71 FR 3415, 1/23/2006, effective 1/23/2006; Final rule, 84 FR 48504, 9/13/2019, effective 9/13/2019]

252.237-7005 Performance and delivery.

As prescribed in 237.7003(a) and (a)(3), use the following clause:

PERFORMANCE AND DELIVERY (DEC 1991)

(a) The Contractor shall furnish the material ordered and perform the services specified as promptly as possible but not later than 36 hours after receiving notification to remove the remains, excluding the time necessary for the Government to inspect and check results of preparation.

(b) The Government may, at no additional charge, require the Contractor to hold the remains for an additional period not to exceed 72 hours from the time the remains are casketed and final inspection completed.

(End of clause)

[Final rule, 71 FR 3415, 1/23/2006, effective 1/23/2006; Final rule, 84 FR 48504, 9/13/2019, effective 9/13/2019]

252.237-7006 Subcontracting.

As prescribed in 237.7003(a) and (a)(4), use the following clause:

SUBCONTRACTING (DEC 1991)

The Contractor shall not subcontract any work under this contract without the Contracting Officer's written approval. This clause does not apply to contracts of employment between the Contractor and its personnel.

(End of clause)

[Final rule, 71 FR 3415, 1/23/2006, effective 1/23/2006; Final rule, 84 FR 48504, 9/13/2019, effective 9/13/2019]

252.237-7007 Termination for default.

As prescribed in 237.7003(a) and (a)(5), use the following clause:

TERMINATION FOR DEFAULT (DEC 1991)

(a) This clause supplements and is in addition to the Default clause of this contract.

(b) The Contracting Officer may terminate this contract for default by written notice without the ten day notice required by paragraph (a)(2) of the Default clause if—

(1) The Contractor, through circumstances reasonably within its control or that of its employees, performs any act under or in connection with this contract, or fails in the performance of any service under this contract and the act or failures may reasonably be considered to reflect discredit upon the Department of Defense in fulfilling its responsibility for proper care of remains;

(2) The Contractor, or its employees, solicits relatives or friends of the deceased to purchase supplies or services not under this contract. (The Contractor may furnish supplies or arrange for services not under this contract, only if representatives of the deceased voluntarily request, select, and pay for them.);

(3) The services or any part of the services are performed by anyone other than the Contractor or the Contractor's employees without the written authorization of the Contracting Officer;

(4) The Contractor refuses to perform the services required for any particular remains; or

(5) The Contractor mentions or otherwise uses this contract in its advertising in any way.

(End of clause)

[Final rule, 71 FR 3415, 1/23/2006, effective 1/23/2006; Final rule, 84 FR 48504, 9/13/2019, effective 9/13/2019]

252.237-7008 Group interment.

As prescribed in 237.7003(a) and (a)(6), use the following clause:

GROUP INTERMENT (DEC 1991)

The Government will pay the Contractor for supplies and services provided for remains interred as a group on the basis of the number of caskets furnished, rather than on the basis of the number of persons in the group.

(End of clause)

[Final rule, 71 FR 3415, 1/23/2006, effective 1/23/2006; Final rule, 84 FR 48504, 9/13/2019, effective 9/13/2019]

252.237-7009 Permits.

As prescribed in 237.7003(a) and (a)(7), use the following clause:

PERMITS (DEC 1991)

The Contractor shall meet all State and local licensing requirements and obtain and furnish all necessary health department and shipping permits at no additional cost to the Government. The Contractor shall ensure that all necessary health department permits are in order for disposition of the remains.

(End of clause)

[Final rule, 71 FR 3415, 1/23/2006, effective 1/23/2006; Final rule, 84 FR 48504, 9/13/2019, effective 9/13/2019]

252.237-7010 Prohibition on interrogation of detainees by contractor personnel.

As prescribed in 237.173-5, use the following clause:

PROHIBITION ON INTERROGATION OF DETAINEES BY CONTRACTOR PERSONNEL (JUN 2013)

(a) *Definitions.* As used in this clause—

Detainee means any person captured, detained, held, or otherwise under the effective control of DoD personnel (military or civilian) in connection with hostilities. This includes, but is not limited to, enemy prisoners of war, civilian internees, and retained personnel. This does not include DoD personnel or DoD contractor personnel being held for law enforcement purposes.

Interrogation of detainees means a systematic process of formally and officially questioning a detainee for the purpose of obtaining reliable information to satisfy foreign intelligence collection requirements.

(b) Contractor personnel shall not interrogate detainees.

(c) Subcontracts. The Contractor shall include the substance of this clause, including this paragraph (c), in all subcontracts, including subcontracts for commercial items, that may require subcontractor personnel to interact with detainees in the course of their duties.

(End of clause)

[Final rule, 71 FR 3415, 1/23/2006, effective 1/23/2006; Interim rule, 75 FR 67632, 11/3/2010, effective 11/3/2010; Final rule, 76 FR 44282, 7/25/2011, effective 7/25/2011; Final rule, 78 FR 37980, 6/25/2013, effective 6/25/2013]

252.237-7011 Preparation history.

As prescribed in 237.7003(a) and (a)(8), use the following clause:

PREPARATION HISTORY (DEC 1991)

For each body prepared, or for each casket handled in a group interment, the Contractor shall state briefly the results of the embalming process on a certificate furnished by the Contracting Officer.

(End of clause)

[Final rule, 71 FR 3415, 1/23/2006, effective 1/23/2006; Final rule, 84 FR 48504, 9/13/2019, effective 9/13/2019]

252.237-7012 Instruction to offerors (count-of-articles).

As prescribed in 237.7101(a), use the following provision:

INSTRUCTION TO OFFERORS (COUNT-OF-ARTICLES) (DEC 1991)

(a) The Offeror shall include unit prices for each item in a lot. Unit prices shall include all costs to the Government of providing the services, including pickup and delivery charges.

(b) Failure to offer on any item in a lot shall be cause for rejection of the offer on that lot. The Contracting Officer will evaluate offers based on the estimated quantities in the solicitation.

(c) Award generally will be made to a single offeror for all lots. However, the Contracting Officer may award by individual lot when it is more advantageous to the Government.

(d) Prospective offerors may inspect the types of articles to be serviced. Contact the Contracting Officer to make inspection arrangements.

(End of provision)

[Final rule, 71 FR 3415, 1/23/2006, effective 1/23/2006]

252.237-7013 Instruction to offerors (bulk weight).

As prescribed in 237.7101(b), use the following provision:

INSTRUCTION TO OFFERORS (BULK WEIGHT) (DEC 1991)

(a) Offers shall be submitted on a unit price per pound of serviced laundry. Unit prices shall include all costs to the Government of providing the service, including pickup and delivery charges.

(b) The Contracting Officer will evaluate bids based on the estimated pounds of serviced laundry stated in the solicitation.

(c) Award generally will be made to a single offeror for all lots. However, the Contracting Officer may award by individual lot when it is more advantageous to the Government.

(d) Prospective offerors may inspect the types of articles to be serviced. Contact the Contracting Officer to make inspection arrangements.

(End of provision)

[Final rule, 71 FR 3415, 1/23/2006, effective 1/23/2006]

252.237-7014 Loss or damage (count-of-articles).

As prescribed in 237.7101(c), use the following clause:

LOSS OR DAMAGE (COUNT-OF-ARTICLES) (DEC 1991)

(a) The count-of-articles will be—

(1) The count of the Contracting Officer; or

(2) The count agreed upon as a result of a joint count by the Contractor and the Contracting Officer at the time of delivery to the Contractor.

(b) The Contractor shall—

(1) Be liable for return of the number and kind of articles furnished for service under this contract; and

(2) Shall indemnify the Government for any loss or damage to such articles.

(c) The Contractor shall pay to the Government the value of any lost or damaged property using Federal supply schedule price lists. If the property is not on these price lists, the Contracting Officer shall determine a fair and reasonable price.

(d) The Contracting Officer will allow credit for any depreciation in the value of the property at the time of loss or damage. The Contracting Officer and the Contractor shall mutually determine the amount of the allowable credit.

(e) Failure to agree upon the value of the property or on the amount of credit due will be treated as a dispute under the Disputes clause of this contract.

(f) In case of damage to any property that the Contracting Officer and the Contractor agree can be satisfactorily repaired, the Contractor may repair the property at its expense in a manner satisfactory to the Contracting Officer, rather than make payment under paragraph (c) of this clause.

(End of clause)

[Final rule, 71 FR 3415, 1/23/2006, effective 1/23/2006]

252.237-7015 Loss or damage (weight of articles).

As prescribed in 237.7101(d), use the following clause:

LOSS OR DAMAGE (WEIGHT OF ARTICLES) (DEC 1991)

(a) The Contractor shall—

(1) Be liable for return of the articles furnished for service under this contract; and

(2) Indemnify the Government for any articles delivered to the Contractor for servicing under this contract that are lost or damaged, and in the opinion of the Contracting Officer, cannot be repaired satisfactorily.

(b) The Contractor shall pay to the Government ____ per pound for lost or damaged articles. The Contractor shall pay the Government only for losses which exceed the maximum weight loss in paragraph (e) of this clause.

(c) Failure to agree on the amount of credit due will be treated as a dispute under the Disputes clause of this contract.

(d) In the case of damage to any articles that the Contracting Officer and the Contractor agree can be satisfactorily repaired, the Contractor shall repair the articles at its expense in a manner satisfactory to the Contracting Officer.

(e) The maximum weight loss allowable in servicing the laundry is ____ percent of the weight recorded on delivery tickets when the laundry is picked up. Any weight loss in excess of this amount shall be subject to the loss provisions of this clause.

(End of clause)

[Final rule, 71 FR 3415, 1/23/2006, effective 1/23/2006]

252.237-7016 Delivery tickets.

Basic. As prescribed in 237.7101(e) and (e)(1), use the following clause:

DELIVERY TICKETS—BASIC (NOV 2014)

(a) The Contractor shall complete delivery tickets in the number of copies required and in the form approved by the Contracting Officer, when it receives the articles to be serviced.

(b) The Contractor shall include one copy of each delivery ticket with its invoice for payment.

(End of clause)

Alternate I. As prescribed in 237.7101(e) and (e)(2), use the following clause, which includes paragraphs (c), (d), and (e) not included in the basic clause:

DELIVERY TICKETS—ALTERNATE I (NOV 2014)

(a) The Contractor shall complete delivery tickets in the number of copies required and in the form approved by the Contracting Officer, when it receives the articles to be serviced.

(b) The Contractor shall include one copy of each delivery ticket with its invoice for payment.

(c) Before the Contractor picks up articles for service under this contract, the Contracting Officer will ensure that—

(1) Each bag contains only articles within a single bag type as specified in the schedule; and

(2) Each bag is weighed and the weight and bag type are identified on the bag.

(d) The Contractor shall, at time of pickup—

(1) Verify the weight and bag type and record them on the delivery ticket; and

(2) Provide the Contracting Officer, or representative, a copy of the delivery ticket.

(e) At the time of delivery, the Contractor shall record the weight and bag type of serviced laundry on the delivery ticket. The Contracting Officer will ensure that this weight and bag type are verified at time of delivery.

(End of clause)

Alternate II. As prescribed in 237.7101(e) and (e)(3), use the following clause, which includes paragraphs (c), (d), and (e) not included in the basic clause:

DELIVERY TICKETS—ALTERNATE II (NOV 2014)

(a) The Contractor shall complete delivery tickets in the number of copies required and in the form approved by the Contracting Officer, when it receives the articles to be serviced.

(b) The Contractor shall include one copy of each delivery ticket with its invoice for payment.

(c) Before the Contractor picks up articles for service under this contract, the Contracting Officer will ensure that each bag is weighed and that the weight is identified on the bag.

(d) The Contractor, at time of pickup, shall verify and record the weight on the delivery ticket and shall provide the Contracting Officer, or representative, a copy of the delivery ticket.

(e) At the time of delivery, the Contractor shall record the weight of serviced laundry on the delivery ticket. The Contracting Officer will ensure that this weight is verified at time of delivery.

(End of clause)

[Final rule, 71 FR 3415, 1/23/2006, effective 1/23/2006; Final rule, 79 FR 65592, 11/5/2014, effective 11/5/2014; Final rule, 80 FR 36897, 6/26/2015, effective 6/26/2015]

252.237-7017 Individual laundry.

As prescribed in 237.7101(f), use the following clause:

INDIVIDUAL LAUNDRY (DEC 1991)

(a) The Contractor shall provide laundry service under this contract on both a unit bundle and on a piece-rate bundle basis for individual personnel.

(b) The total number of pieces listed in the "Estimated Quantity" column in the schedule is the estimated amount of individual laundry for this contract. The estimate is for information only and is not a representation of the amount of individual laundry to be ordered. Individuals may elect whether or not to use the laundry services.

(c) Charges for individual laundry will be on a per unit bundle or a piece-rate basis. The Contractor shall provide individual laundry bundle delivery tickets for use by the individuals in designating whether the laundry is a unit bundle or a piece-rate bundle. An individual laundry bundle will be accompanied by a delivery ticket listing the contents of the bundle.

(d) The maximum number of pieces to be allowed per bundle is as specified in the schedule and as follows—

(1) *Bundle consisting of 26 pieces, including laundry bag.* This bundle will contain approximately ____ pieces of outer garments which shall be starched and pressed. Outer garments include, but are not limited to, shirts, trousers, jackets, dresses, and coats.

(2) *Bundle consisting of 13 pieces, including laundry bag.* This bundle will contain approximately ____ pieces of outer garments which shall be starched and pressed. Outer garments include, but are not limited to, shirts, trousers, jackets, dresses, and coats.

(End of clause)

[Final rule, 71 FR 3415, 1/23/2006, effective 1/23/2006]

252.237-7018 Special definitions of Government property.

As prescribed in 237.7101(g), use the following clause:

SPECIAL DEFINITIONS OF GOVERNMENT PROPERTY (DEC 1991)

Articles delivered to the Contractor to be laundered or dry-cleaned, including any articles which are actually owned by individual Government personnel, are Government-owned property, not Government-furnished property. Government-owned property does not fall under the requirements of any Government-furnished property clause of this contract.

(End of clause)

[Final rule, 71 FR 3415, 1/23/2006, effective 1/23/2006]

252.237-7019 Training for Contractor Personnel Interacting with Detainees.

As prescribed in 237.171-4, use the following clause:

TRAINING FOR CONTRACTOR PERSONNEL INTERACTING WITH DETAINEES (JUN 2013)

(a) *Definitions.* As used in this clause—

Combatant Commander means the commander of a unified or specified combatant command established in accordance with 10 U.S.C. 161.

Detainee means a person in the custody or under the physical control of the Department of Defense on behalf of the United States Government as a result of armed conflict or other military operation by the United States armed forces.

Personnel interacting with detainees means personnel who, in the course of duties, are expected to interact with detainees.

(b) *Training requirement.* This clause implements Section 1092 of the National Defense Authorization Act for Fiscal Year 2005 (Pub. L. 108-375).

(1) The Combatant Commander responsible for the area where a detention or interrogation facility is located will arrange for training to be provided to contractor personnel interacting with detainees. The training will address the international obligations and laws of the United States applicable to the detention of personnel, including the Geneva Conventions. The Combatant Commander will arrange for a training receipt document to be provided to personnel who have completed the training.

(2) (i) The Contractor shall arrange for its personnel interacting with detainees to—

(A) Receive the training specified in paragraph (b) (1) of this clause—

(1) Prior to interacting with detainees, or as soon as possible if, for compelling reasons, the Contracting Officer authorizes interaction with detainees prior to receipt of such training; and

(2) Annually thereafter; and

(B) Provide a copy of the training receipt document specified in paragraph (b) (1) of this clause to the Contractor for retention.

(ii) To make these arrangements, the following points of contact apply:

[*Contracting Officer to insert applicable point of contact information cited in PGI 237.171-3(b).*]

(3) The Contractor shall retain a copy of the training receipt document(s) provided in accordance with paragraphs (b) (1) and (2) of this clause until the contract is closed, or 3 years after all work required by the contract has been completed and accepted by the Government, whichever is sooner.

(c) *Subcontracts*. The Contractor shall include the substance of this clause, including this paragraph (c), in all subcontracts, including subcontracts for commercial items, that may require subcontractor personnel to interact with detainees in the course of their duties.

(End of clause)

[Removed and reserved, DAC 91-13, 63 FR 11522, 3/9/98, effective 3/9/98; Interim rule, 70 FR 52032, 9/1/2005, effective 9/1/2005; Final rule, 71 FR 53047, 9/8/2006, effective 9/8/2006; Final rule, 78 FR 37980, 6/25/2013, effective 6/25/2013]

252.237-7020 [Reserved]

252.237-7021 [Reserved]

252.237-7022 Services at installations being closed.

As prescribed in 237.7402, use the following clause:

SERVICES AT INSTALLATIONS BEING CLOSED (MAY 1995)

Professional employees shall be used by the local government to provide services under this contract to the extent that professionals are available in the area under the jurisdiction of such government.

(End of clause)

[Interim rule, 59 FR 36088, 7/15/94, effective 7/8/94; DAC 91-7, 60 FR 29491, 6/5/95, effective 5/17/95]

252.237-7023 Continuation of Essential Contractor Services.

As prescribed in 237.7603(a), use the following clause:

CONTINUATION OF ESSENTIAL CONTRACTOR SERVICES (OCT 2010)

(a) *Definitions*. As used in this clause—

(1) *Essential contractor service* means a service provided by a firm or individual under contract to DoD to support mission-essential functions, such as support of vital systems, including ships owned, leased, or operated in support of military missions or roles at sea; associated support activities, including installation, garrison, and base support services; and similar services provided to foreign military sales customers under the Security Assistance Program. Services are essential if the effectiveness of defense systems or operations has the potential to be seriously impaired by the interruption of these services, as determined by the appropriate functional commander or civilian equivalent.

(2) *Mission-essential functions* means those organizational activities that must be performed under all circumstances to achieve DoD component missions or responsibili-

ties, as determined by the appropriate functional commander or civilian equivalent. Failure to perform or sustain these functions would significantly affect DoD's ability to provide vital services or exercise authority, direction, and control.

(b) The Government has identified all or a portion of the contractor services performed under this contract as essential contractor services in support of mission-essential functions. These services are listed in attachment ____, Mission-Essential Contractor Services, dated ____.

(c)(1) The Mission-Essential Contractor Services Plan submitted by the Contractor, is incorporated in this contract.

(2) The Contractor shall maintain and update its plan as necessary. The Contractor shall provide all plan updates to the Contracting Officer for approval.

(3) As directed by the Contracting Officer, the Contractor shall participate in training events, exercises, and drills associated with Government efforts to test the effectiveness of continuity of operations procedures and practices.

(d)(1) Notwithstanding any other clause of this contract, the Contractor shall be responsible to perform those services identified as essential contractor services during crisis situations (as directed by the Contracting Officer), in accordance with its Mission-Essential Contractor Services Plan.

(2) In the event the Contractor anticipates not being able to perform any of the essential contractor services identified in accordance with paragraph (b) of this clause during a crisis situation, the Contractor shall notify the Contracting Officer or other designated representative as expeditiously as possible and use its best efforts to cooperate with the Government in the Government's efforts to maintain the continuity of operations.

(e) The Government reserves the right in such crisis situations to use Federal employees, military personnel, or contract support from other contractors, or to enter into new contracts for essential contractor services.

(f) *Changes.* The Contractor shall segregate and separately identify all costs incurred in continuing performance of essential services in a crisis situation. The Contractor shall notify the Contracting Officer of an increase or decrease in costs within ninety days after continued performance has been directed by the Contracting Officer, or within any additional period that the Contracting Officer approves in writing, but not later than the date of final payment under the contract. The Contractor's notice shall include the Contractor's proposal for an equitable adjustment and any data supporting the increase or decrease in the form prescribed by the Contracting Officer. The parties shall negotiate an equitable price adjustment to the contract price, delivery schedule, or both as soon as is practicable after receipt of the Contractor's proposal.

(g) The Contractor shall include the substance of this clause, including this paragraph (g), in subcontracts for the essential services.

(End of clause)

[Interim rule, 75 FR 10191, 3/5/2010, effective 3/5/2010; Final rule, 75 FR 66680, 10/29/2010, effective 10/29/2010]

252.237-7024 Notice of Continuation of Essential Contractor Services.

As prescribed in 237.7603(b), use the following provision:

NOTICE OF CONTINUATION OF ESSENTIAL CONTRACTOR SERVICES (OCT 2010)

(a) *Definitions. Essential contractor service* and *mission-essential functions* have the meanings given in the clause at 252.237-7023, Continuation of Essential Contractor Services, in this solicitation.

(b) The offeror shall provide with its offer a written plan describing how it will continue to perform the essential contractor services listed in attachment ____, Mission Essential Contractor Services, dated ____, during periods of crisis. The offeror shall—

(1) Identify provisions made for the acquisition of essential personnel and resources, if

necessary, for continuity of operations for up to 30 days or until normal operations can be resumed;

(2) Address in the plan, at a minimum—

(i) Challenges associated with maintaining essential contractor services during an extended event, such as a pandemic that occurs in repeated waves;

(ii) The time lapse associated with the initiation of the acquisition of essential personnel and resources and their actual availability on site;

(iii) The components, processes, and requirements for the identification, training, and preparedness of personnel who are capable of relocating to alternate facilities or performing work from home;

(iv) Any established alert and notification procedures for mobilizing identified "essential contractor service" personnel; and

(v) The approach for communicating expectations to contractor employees regarding their roles and responsibilities during a crisis.

(End of provision)

[Final rule, 75 FR 66680, 10/29/2010, effective 10/29/2010]

252.239 Acquisition of Information Resources, provisions and clauses for DFARS Part 239

252.239-7000 Protection against compromising emanations.

As prescribed in 239.7103 (a), use the following clause:

PROTECTION AGAINST COMPROMISING EMANATIONS (OCT 2019)

(a) The Contractor shall provide or use only information technology, as specified by the Government, that has been accredited to meet the appropriate information assurance requirements of—

(1) The National Security Agency National TEMPEST Standards (NSTISSAM TEMPEST 1-92, Compromising Emanations Laboratory Test Requirements, Electromagnetics (U)); or

(2) Other standards specified by this contract, including the date through which the required accreditation is current or valid for the contract.

(b) Upon request of the Contracting Officer, the Contractor shall provide documentation supporting the accreditation.

(c) The Government may, as part of its inspection and acceptance, conduct additional tests to ensure that information technology delivered under this contract satisfies the information assurance standards specified. The Government may conduct additional tests—

(1) At the installation site or contractor's facility; and

(2) Notwithstanding the existence of valid accreditations of information technology prior to the award of this contract.

(d) Unless otherwise provided in this contract under the Warranty of Supplies or Warranty of Systems and Equipment clause, the Contractor shall correct or replace accepted information technology found to be deficient within 1 year after proper installations.

(1) The correction or replacement shall be at no cost to the Government.

(2) Should a modification to the delivered information technology be made by the Contractor, the 1-year period applies to the modification upon its proper installation.

(3) This paragraph (d) applies regardless of f.o.b. point or the point of acceptance of the deficient information technology.

(End of clause)

[DAC 91-1, 56 FR 67222, 12/30/91, effective 12/31/91; Final rule, 66 FR 49860, 10/1/2001, effective 10/1/2001; Final rule, 69 FR 35533, 6/25/2004, effective 6/25/2004; Final rule, 73 FR 1828, 1/10/2008, effective 1/10/2008; Final rule, 84 FR 58336, 10/31/2019, effective 10/31/2019]

252.239-7001 Information Assurance Contractor Training and Certification.

As prescribed in 239.7103(b), use the following clause:

INFORMATION ASSURANCE CONTRACTOR TRAINING AND CERTIFICATION (JAN 2008)

(a) The Contractor shall ensure that personnel accessing information systems have the proper and current information assurance certification to perform information assurance functions in accordance with DoD 8570.01-M, Information Assurance Workforce Improvement Program. The Contractor shall meet the applicable information assurance certification requirements, including—

(1) DoD-approved information assurance workforce certifications appropriate for each category and level as listed in the current version of DoD 8570.01-M; and

(2) Appropriate operating system certification for information assurance technical positions as required by DoD 8570.01-M.

(b) Upon request by the Government, the Contractor shall provide documentation supporting the information assurance certification status of personnel performing information assurance functions.

(c) Contractor personnel who do not have proper and current certifications shall be denied access to DoD information systems for the purpose of performing information assurance functions.

(End of clause)

[Final rule, 73 FR 1828, 1/10/2008, effective 1/10/2008]

252.239-7002 Access.

As prescribed in 239.7411(a), use the following clause:

ACCESS (DEC 1991)

(a) Subject to military security regulations, the Government shall permit the Contractor access at all reasonable times to Contractor furnished facilities. However, if the Government is unable to permit access, the Government at its own risk and expense shall maintain these facilities and the Contractor shall not be responsible for the service involving any of these facilities during the period of nonaccess, unless the service failure results from the Contractor's fault or negligence.

(b) During periods when the Government does not permit Contractor access, the Government will reimburse the Contractor at mutually acceptable rates for the loss of or damage to the equipment due to the fault or negligence of the Government. Failure to agree shall be a dispute concerning a question of fact within the meaning of the Disputes clause of this contract.

(End of clause)

252.239-7003 [Removed and Reserved]

[Final rule, 70 FR 67919, 11/9/2005, effective 11/9/2005]

252.239-7004 Orders for facilities and services.

As prescribed in 239.7411(a), use the following clause:

ORDERS FOR FACILITIES AND SERVICES (SEP 2019)

(a) *Definitions.* As used in this clause—

Governmental regulatory body means the Federal Communications Commission, any statewide regulatory body, or any body with less than statewide jurisdiction when operating under the state authority. Regulatory bodies whose decisions are not subject to judicial appeal and regulatory bodies which regulate a company owned by the same entity that creates the regulatory body are not governmental regulatory bodies.

(b) The Contractor shall acknowledge a communication service authorization or other type order for supplies and facilities by—

(1) Commencing performance after receipt of an order; or

(2) Written acceptance by a duly authorized representative.

(c) The Contractor shall furnish the services and facilities under this agreement/contract in accordance with all applicable tariffs, rates, charges, regulations, requirements, terms, and conditions of—

(1) Service and facilities furnished or offered by the Contractor to the general public or the Contractor's subscribers; or

(2) Service as lawfully established by a governmental regulatory body.

(d) The Government will not prepay for services.

(e) For nontariffed services, the Contractor shall charge the Government at the lowest rate and under the most favorable terms and conditions for similar service and facilities offered to any other customer.

(f) Recurring charges for services and facilities shall, in each case, start with the satisfactory beginning of service or provision of facilities or equipment and are payable monthly in arrears.

(g) Expediting charges are costs necessary to get services earlier than normal. Examples are overtime pay or special shipment. When authorized, expediting charges shall be the additional costs incurred by the Contractor and the subcontractor. The Government shall pay expediting charges only when—

(1) They are provided for in the tariff established by a governmental regulatory body; or

(2) They are authorized in a communication service authorization or other contractual document.

(h) When services normally provided are technically unacceptable and the development, fabrication, or manufacture of special equipment is required, the Government may—

(1) Provide the equipment; or

(2) Direct the Contractor to acquire the equipment or facilities. If the Contractor acquires the equipment or facilities, the acquisition shall be competitive, if practicable.

(i) If at any time the Government defers or changes its orders for any of the services but does not cancel or terminate them, the amount paid or payable to the Contractor for the services deferred or modified shall be equitably adjusted under applicable tariffs filed by the Contractor with the regulatory commission in effect at the time of deferral or change. If no tariffs are in effect, the Government and the Contractor shall equitably adjust the rates by mutual agreement. Failure to agree on any adjustment shall be a dispute concerning a question of fact within the meaning of the Disputes clause of this contract.

(End of clause)

[Final rule, 70 FR 67919, 11/9/2005, effective 11/9/2005; Final rule, 84 FR 48498, 9/13/2019, effective 9/13/2019]

252.239-7005 [Removed and Reserved]

[Final rule, 70 FR 67919, 11/9/2005, effective 11/9/2005; Final rule, 84 FR 48498, 9/13/2019, effective 9/13/2019]

252.239-7006 Tariff information.

As prescribed in 239.7411(a), use the following clause:

TARIFF INFORMATION (JUL 1997)

(a) The Contractor shall provide to the Contracting Officer—

(1) Upon request, a copy of the Contractor's current existing tariffs (including changes);

(2) Before filing, any application to a Federal, State, or any other regulatory agency for new or changes to, rates, charges, services, or regulations relating to any tariff or any of the facilities or services to be furnished solely or primarily to the Government; and

(3) Upon request, a copy of all information, material, and data developed or prepared in support of or in connection with an application under paragraph (a)(2) of this clause.

(b) The Contractor shall notify the Contracting Officer of any application that anyone other than the Contractor files with a governmental regulatory body which affects or will affect the rate or conditions of services under this agreement/contract. These requirements also apply to applications pending on the effective date of this agreement/contract.

(End of clause)

[Final rule, 62 FR 40471, 7/29/97, effective 7/29/97]

252.239-7007 Cancellation or termination of orders.

As prescribed in 239.7411(a), use the following clause:

CANCELLATION OR TERMINATION OF ORDERS (SEP 2019)

(a) *Definitions.* As used in this clause—

Actual nonrecoverable costs means the installed costs of the facilities and equipment, less cost of reusable materials, and less net salvage value.

Basic cancellation liability means the actual nonrecoverable cost, which the Government shall reimburse the Contractor at the time services are cancelled.

Basic termination liability means the nonrecoverable cost amortized in equal monthly increments throughout the liability period.

Installed costs means the actual cost of equipment and materials specifically provided or used, plus the actual cost of installing (including engineering, labor, supervision, transportation, rights-of-way, and any other items which are chargeable to the capital accounts of the Contractor), less any costs the government may have directly reimbursed the Contractor under the Special Construction and Equipment Charges clause of this agreement/contract.

Net salvage value means the salvage value less the cost of removal.

(b) If the Government cancels any of the services ordered under this agreement/contract, before the services are made available to the Government, or terminates any of these services after they are made available to the Government, the Government will reimburse the Contractor for the actual nonrecoverable costs the Contractor has reasonably incurred in providing facilities and equipment for which the Contractor has no foreseeable reuse. The Government will not reimburse the Contractor for any actual nonrecoverable costs incurred after notice of award, but prior to execution of the order.

(c) When feasible, the Contractor shall reuse cancelled or terminated facilities or equipment to minimize the charges to the Government.

(d) If at any time the Government requires that telecommunications facilities or equipment be relocated within the Contractor's service area, the Government will have the option of paying the costs of relocating the facilities or equipment in lieu of paying any termination or cancellation charge under this clause. The basic cancellation liability or basic termination liability applicable to the facilities or equipment in their former location shall continue to apply to the facilities and equipment in their new location. Monthly recurring charges shall continue to be paid during the period.

(e) When there is another requirement or foreseeable reuse in place of cancelled or terminated facilities or equipment, no charge shall apply and the basic cancellation liability or basic termination liability shall be appropriately reduced. When feasible, the Contractor shall promptly reuse discontinued channels or facilities, including equipment for which the Government is obligated to pay a minimum service charge.

(f) The amount of the Government's liability upon cancellation or termination of any of the services ordered under this agreement/contract will be determined under applicable tariffs governing cancellation and termination charges which—

(1) Are filed by the Contractor with a governmental regulatory body, as defined in the Orders For Facilities and Services clause of this agreement/contract;

(2) Are in effect on the date of termination; and

(3) Provide specific cancellation or termination charges for the facilities and equipment involved or show how to determine the charges.

(g) The amount of the Government's liability upon cancellation or termination of any of the services ordered under this agreement/contract, which are not subject to a governmental regulatory body, will be determined under a mutually agreed schedule in the communication services authorization (CSA) or other contractual document.

(h) If no applicable tariffs are in effect on the date of cancellation or termination or set forth in the applicable CSA or other contractual document, the Government's liability will be determined under the following settlement procedures—

(1) The Contractor agrees to provide the Contracting Officer, in such reasonable detail as the Contracting Officer may require, inventory schedules covering all items of property or facilities in the Contractor's possession, the cost of which is included in the Basic Cancellation or Termination Liability for which the Contractor has no foreseeable reuse.

(2) The Contractor shall use its best efforts to sell property or facilities when the Contractor has no foreseeable reuse or when the Government has not exercised its option to take title under the Title to Telecommunications Facilities and Equipment clause of this agreement/contract. The Contractor shall apply any proceeds of the sale to reduce any payments by the Government to the Contractor under a cancellation or termination settlement.

(3) The Contractor shall record actual nonrecoverable costs under established accounting procedures prescribed by the cognizant governmental regulatory authority or, if no such procedures have been prescribed, under generally accepted accounting procedures applicable to the provision of telecommunication services for public use.

(4) The net salvage value shall be deducted from the Contractor's installed cost. In determining net salvage value, the Contractor shall consider the foreseeable reuse of the facilities and equipment by the Contractor. The Contractor shall make allowance for the cost of dismantling, removal, reconditioning, and disposal of the facilities and equipment when necessary either for the sale of facilities or their reuse by the Contractor in another location.

(5) Upon termination of services, the Government will reimburse the Contractor for the nonrecoverable cost less such costs amortized to the date services are terminated and establish the liability period as mutually agreed to but not to exceed ten years. In the case of either a cancellation or a termination, the Government's presumed maximum liability will be capped by the unpaid nonrecurring charges and the monthly recurring charges set out in the contract/agreement. The presumed maximum liability for monthly recurring charges shall be capped at monthly recurring charges for the minimum service period and any required notice period.

(6) When the basic cancellation liability or basic termination liability established by the CSA or other contractual document is based on estimated costs, the Contractor agrees to settle on the basis of actual cost at the time of cancellation or termination.

(7) The Contractor agrees that, if after settlement but within the termination liability period of the services, should the Contractor make reuse of equipment or facilities which were treated as nonreusable or nonsalvable in the settlement, the Contractor shall reimburse the Government for the value of the equipment or facilities.

(8) The Contractor agrees to exclude—

(i) Any costs which are not included in determining cancellation and termination charges under the Contractor's standard practices or procedures; and

(ii) Charges not ordinarily made by the Contractor for similar facilities or equipment, furnished under similar circumstances.

(i) The Government may, under such terms and conditions as it may prescribe, make partial payments and payments on account against costs incurred by the Contractor in connection with the cancelled or terminated portion of this agreement/contract. The Government may make these payments if the Contracting Officer determines that the total of the payments is within the amount the Contractor is entitled. If the total of the payments is in excess of the amount finally agreed or determined to be due under this clause, the Contractor shall pay the excess to the Government upon demand.

(j) Failure to agree shall be a dispute concerning a question of fact within the meaning of the Disputes clause.

(End of clause)

[Final rule, 62 FR 2612, 1/17/97, effective 1/17/97; Final rule, 70 FR 67919, 11/9/2005, effective 11/9/2005; Final rule, 84 FR 48496, 9/13/2019, effective 9/13/2019]

252.239-7008 [Removed and Reserved]

[Final rule, 84 FR 48496, 9/13/2019, effective 9/13/2019]

252.239-7009 Representation of Use of Cloud Computing.

As prescribed in 239.7604(a), use the following provision:

REPRESENTATION OF USE OF CLOUD COMPUTING (SEP 2015)

(a) *Definition. Cloud computing*, as used in this provision, means a model for enabling ubiquitous, convenient, on-demand network access to a shared pool of configurable computing resources (e.g., networks, servers, storage, applications, and services) that can be rapidly provisioned and released with minimal management effort or service provider interaction. This includes other commercial terms, such as on-demand self-service, broad network access, resource pooling, rapid elasticity, and measured service. It also includes commercial offerings for software-as-a-service, infrastructure-as-a-service, and platform-as-a-service.

(b) The Offeror shall indicate by checking the appropriate blank in paragraph (c) of this provision whether the use of cloud computing is anticipated under the resultant contract.

(c) *Representation*. The Offeror represents that it—

_ Does anticipate that cloud computing services will be used in the performance of any contract or subcontract resulting from this solicitation.

_ Does not anticipate that cloud computing services will be used in the performance of any contract or subcontract resulting from this solicitation.

(End of provision)

[Removed and reserved, final rule, 62 FR 40471, 7/29/97, effective 7/29/97; Interim rule, 80 FR 51739, 8/26/2015, effective 8/26/2015; Final rule, 80 FR 56929, 9/21/2015, effective 9/21/2015; Final rule, 80 FR 74694, 11/30/2015, effective 11/30/2015]

252.239-7010 Cloud Computing Services.

As prescribed in 239.7604(b), use the following clause:

CLOUD COMPUTING SERVICES (OCT 2016)

(a) *Definitions*. As used in this clause—

Authorizing official, as described in DoD Instruction 8510.01, Risk Management Framework (RMF) for DoD Information Technology (IT), means the senior Federal official or executive with the authority to formally assume responsibility for operating an information system at an acceptable level of risk to organizational operations (including mission, functions, image, or reputation), organizational assets, individuals, other organizations, and the Nation.

Cloud computing means a model for enabling ubiquitous, convenient, on-demand network access to a shared pool of configurable computing resources (e.g., networks, servers, storage, applications, and services) that can be rapidly provisioned and released with minimal management effort or service provider interaction. This includes other commercial terms, such as on-demand self-service, broad network access, resource pooling, rapid elasticity, and measured service. It also includes commercial offerings for software-as-a-service, infrastructure-as-a-service, and platform-as-a-service.

Compromise means disclosure of information to unauthorized persons, or a violation of the security policy of a system, in which unauthorized intentional or unintentional disclosure, modification, destruction, or loss of an object, or the copying of information to unauthorized media may have occurred.

Cyber incident means actions taken through the use of computer networks that result in a compromise or an actual or potentially adverse effect on an information system and/or the information residing therein.

Government data means any information, document, media, or machine readable material regardless of physical form or characteristics, that is created or obtained by the Government in the course of official Government business.

Government-related data means any information, document, media, or machine readable material regardless of physical form or characteristics that is created or obtained by a contractor through the storage, processing, or communication of Government data. This does not include contractor's business records e.g. financial records, legal records etc. or data such as operating procedures, software coding or algorithms that are not uniquely applied to the Government data.

Information system means a discrete set of information resources organized for the collection, processing, maintenance, use, sharing, dissemination, or disposition of information.

Media means physical devices or writing surfaces including, but not limited to, magnetic tapes, optical disks, magnetic disks, large-scale integration memory chips, and printouts onto which information is recorded, stored, or printed within an information system.

Spillage security incident that results in the transfer of classified or controlled unclassified information onto an information system not accredited (i.e., authorized) for the appropriate security level.

(b) *Cloud computing security requirements.* The requirements of this clause are applicable when using cloud computing to provide information technology services in the performance of the contract.

(1) If the Contractor indicated in its offer that it "does not anticipate the use of cloud computing services in the performance of a resultant contract," in response to provision 252.239-7009, Representation of Use of Cloud Computing, and after the award of this contract, the Contractor proposes to use cloud computing services in the performance of the contract, the Contractor shall obtain approval from the Contracting Officer prior to utilizing cloud computing services in performance of the contract.

(2) The Contractor shall implement and maintain administrative, technical, and physical safeguards and controls with the security level and services required in accordance with the Cloud Computing Security Requirements Guide (SRG) (version in effect at the time the solicitation is issued or as authorized by the Contracting Officer) found at *http://iase.disa.mil/cloudsecurity/Pages/index.aspx.*, unless notified by the Contracting Officer that this requirement has been waived by the DoD Chief Information Officer

(3) The Contractor shall maintain within the United States or outlying areas all Government data that is not physically located on DoD premises, unless the Contractor receives written notification from the Contracting Officer to use another location, in accordance with DFARS 239.7602-2(a).

(c) *Limitations on access to, and use and disclosure of* Government data and Government-related data.

(1) The Contractor shall not access, use, or disclose Government data unless specifically authorized by the terms of this contract or a task order or delivery order issued hereunder.

(i) If authorized by the terms of this contract or a task order or delivery order issued hereunder, any access to, or use or disclosure of, Government data shall only be for purposes specified in this contract or task order or delivery order.

(ii) The Contractor shall ensure that its employees are subject to all such access, use, and disclosure prohibitions and obligations.

(iii) These access, use, and disclosure prohibitions and obligations shall survive the expiration or termination of this contract.

(2) The Contractor shall use Government-related data only to manage the operational environment that supports the Government data and for no other purpose unless otherwise permitted with the prior written approval of the Contracting Officer.

(d) *Cloud computing services cyber incident reporting.* The Contractor shall report all cyber incidents that are related to the cloud computing service provided under this contract.

Reports shall be submitted to DoD via *http://dibnet.dod.mil/*.

(e) *Malicious software*. The Contractor or subcontractors that discover and isolate malicious software in connection with a reported cyber incident shall submit the malicious software in accordance with instructions provided by the Contracting Officer.

(f) *Media preservation and protection*. When a Contractor discovers a cyber incident has occurred, the Contractor shall preserve and protect images of all known affected information systems identified in the cyber incident report (see paragraph (d) of this clause) and all relevant monitoring/packet capture data for at least 90 days from the submission of the cyber incident report to allow DoD to request the media or decline interest.

(g) *Access to additional information or equipment necessary for forensic analysis*. Upon request by DoD, the Contractor shall provide DoD with access to additional information or equipment that is necessary to conduct a forensic analysis.

(h) *Cyber incident damage assessment activities*. If DoD elects to conduct a damage assessment, the Contracting Officer will request that the Contractor provide all of the damage assessment information gathered in accordance with paragraph (f) of this clause.

(i) *Records management and facility access*.

(1) The Contractor shall provide the Contracting Officer all Government data and Government-related data in the format specified in the contract.

(2) The Contractor shall dispose of Government data and Government-related data in accordance with the terms of the contract and provide the confirmation of disposition to the Contracting Officer in accordance with contract closeout procedures.

(3) The Contractor shall provide the Government, or its authorized representatives, access to all Government data and Government-related data, access to contractor personnel involved in performance of the contract, and physical access to any Contractor facility with Government data, for the purpose of audits, investigations, inspections, or other similar activities, as authorized by law or regulation.

(j) *Notification of third party access requests*. The Contractor shall notify the Contracting Officer promptly of any requests from a third party for access to Government data or Government-related data, including any warrants, seizures, or subpoenas it receives, including those from another Federal, State, or local agency. The Contractor shall cooperate with the Contracting Officer to take all measures to protect Government data and Government-related data from any unauthorized disclosure.

(k) *Spillage*. Upon notification by the Government of a spillage, or upon the Contractor's discovery of a spillage, the Contractor shall cooperate with the Contracting Officer to address the spillage in compliance with agency procedures.

(l) *Subcontracts*. The Contractor shall include this clause, including this paragraph (l), in all subcontracts that involve or may involve cloud services, including subcontracts for commercial items.

(End of clause)

[Removed and reserved, final rule, 62 FR 40471, 7/29/97, effective 7/29/97; Interim rule, 80 FR 51739, 8/26/2015, effective 8/26/2015; Final rule, 80 FR 74694, 11/30/2015, effective 11/30/2015; Final rule, 81 FR 72986, 10/21/2016, effective 10/21/2016]

252.239-7011 Special construction and equipment charges.

As prescribed in 239.7411(b), use the following clause:

SPECIAL CONSTRUCTION AND EQUIPMENT CHARGES (DEC 1991)

(a) The Government will not directly reimburse the Contractor for the cost of constructing any facilities or providing any equipment, unless the Contracting Officer authorizes direct reimbursement.

(b) If the Contractor stops using facilities or equipment which the Government has, in whole or part, directly reimbursed, the Contractor shall allow the Government credit for the value of the facilities or equipment attributable to the Government's contribution. Determine the value of the facilities and equipment on the basis of their foreseeable reuse by the Contractor at the time their use is discontinued or on the basis of the net salvage value, whichever is greater. The Contractor shall promptly pay the Government the amount of any credit.

(c) The amount of the direct special construction charge shall not exceed—

(1) The actual costs to the Contractor; and

(2) An amount properly allocable to the services to be provided to the Government.

(d) The amount of the direct special construction charge shall not include costs incurred by the Contractor which are covered by—

(1) A cancellation or termination liability; or

(2) The Contractor's recurring or other nonrecurring charges.

(e) The Contractor represents that—

(1) Recurring charges for the services, facilities, and equipment do not include in the rate base any costs that have been reimbursed by the Government to the Contractor; and

(2) Depreciation charges are based only on the cost of facilities and equipment paid by the Contractor and not reimbursed by the Government.

(f) If it becomes necessary for the Contractor to incur costs to replace any facilities or equipment, the Government shall assume those costs or reimburse the Contractor for replacement costs at mutually acceptable rates under the following circumstances—

(1) The Government paid direct special construction charges; or

(2) The Government reimbursed the Contractor for those facilities or equipment as a part of the recurring charges; and

(3) The need for replacement was due to circumstances beyond the control and without the fault of the Contractor.

(g) Before incurring any costs under paragraph (f) of this clause, the Government shall have the right to terminate the service under the Cancellation or Termination of Orders clause of this contract.

(End of clause)

252.239-7012 Title to telecommunication facilities and equipment.

As prescribed in 239.7411(b), use the following clause:

TITLE TO TELECOMMUNICATION FACILITIES AND EQUIPMENT (DEC 1991)

(a) Title to all Contractor furnished facilities and equipment used under this agreement/contract shall remain with the Contractor even if the Government paid the costs of constructing the facilities or equipment. A mutually accepted communications service authorization may provide for exceptions.

(b) The Contractor shall operate and maintain all telecommunication facilities and equipment used under this agreement/contract whether the Government or the Contractor has title.

(End of clause)

252.239-7013 Term of Agreement and Continuation of Services.

Basic. As prescribed in 239.7411(c)(1), use the following clause:

TERM OF AGREEMENT AND CONTINUATION OF SERVICES–BASIC (OCT 2019)

(a) This basic agreement is not a contract. The Government incurs liability only upon issuance of a communication service authorization, which is a contract that incorporates the terms and conditions of this basic agreement.

(b) This agreement shall continue in force from year to year, unless terminated by either party by 30 days' written notice. Termination of this basic agreement does not terminate or cancel any communication service authorizations issued under this basic agreement prior to the termination.

(c) Communication service authorizations issued under this basic agreement may be modified to incorporate the terms and conditions of a new basic agreement negotiated with the Contractor.

(End of clause)

Alternate I. As prescribed in 239.7411(c)(2), use the following clause, which uses a different paragraph (c) than the basic clause and adds a new paragraph (d).

TERM OF AGREEMENT AND CONTINUATION OF SERVICES–ALTERNATE I (OCT 2019)

(a) This basic agreement is not a contract. The Government incurs liability only upon issuance of a communication service authorization, which is a contract that incorporates the terms and conditions of this basic agreement.

(b) This agreement shall continue in force from year to year, unless terminated by either party by 30 days' written notice. Termination of this basic agreement does not terminate or cancel any communication service authorizations issued under this basic agreement prior to the termination.

(c) The Contractor's current communication services authorizations have been modified to incorporate the terms and conditions of this basic agreement.

(1) All current communication service authorizations issued by ________ that incorporate Basic Agreement Number ________, dated ________, are modified to incorporate this basic agreement.

(2) Current communication service authorizations, issued by the activity in paragraph (c)(1) of this clause, that incorporate other agreements with the Contractor may also be modified to incorporate this basic agreement.

(d) Communication service authorizations issued under this basic agreement may be modified to incorporate a new basic agreement with the Contractor.

(End of clause)

[Final rule, 71 FR 39010, 7/11/2006, effective 7/11/2006; Final rule, 84 FR 58337, 10/31/2019, effective 10/31/2019]

252.239-7014 [Removed and Reserved]

[Final rule, 84 FR 58337, 10/31/2019, effective 10/31/2019]

252.239-7015 [Removed and Reserved]

[Final rule, 71 FR 39010, 7/11/2006, effective 7/11/2006; Final rule, 84 FR 58337, 10/31/2019, effective 10/31/2019]

252.239-7016 Telecommunications security equipment, devices, techniques, and services.

As prescribed in 239.7411(d), use the following clause:

TELECOMMUNICATIONS SECURITY EQUIPMENT, DEVICES, TECHNIQUES, AND SERVICES (DEC 1991)

(a) *Definitions.* As used in this clause—

(1) *Securing* means the application of Government-approved telecommunications security equipment, devices, techniques, or services to contractor telecommunications systems.

(2) *Sensitive information* means any information the loss, misuse, or modification of which, or unauthorized access to, could adversely affect the national interest or the conduct of Federal programs, or the privacy to which individuals are entitled under 5 U.S.C. 552a (the Privacy Act), but which has not been specifically authorized under criteria established by an Executive Order or Act of Congress to be kept secret in the interest of national defense or foreign policy.

(3) *Telecommunications systems* means voice, record, and data communications, including management information systems and local data networks that connect to external transmission media, when employed by Government agencies, contractors, and subcontractors to transmit—

(i) Classified or sensitive information;

(ii) Matters involving intelligence activities, cryptologic activities related to national security, the command and control of military forces, or equipment that is an integral part of a weapon or weapons system; or

(iii) Matters critical to the direct fulfillment of military or intelligence missions.

(b) This solicitation/contract identifies classified or sensitive information that requires securing during telecommunications and requires the Contractor to secure telecommunications systems. The Contractor agrees to secure information and systems at the following location: (Identify the location.)

(c) To provide the security, the Contractor shall use Government-approved telecommunications equipment, devices, techniques, or services. A list of the approved equipment, etc. may be obtained from (identify where list can be obtained). Equipment, devices, techniques, or services used by the Contractor must be compatible or interoperable with (list and identify the location of any telecommunications security equipment, device, technique, or service currently being used by the technical or requirements organization or other offices with which the Contractor must communicate).

(d) Except as may be provided elsewhere in this contract, the Contractor shall furnish all telecommunications security equipment, devices, techniques, or services necessary to perform this contract. The Contractor must meet ownership eligibility conditions for communications security equipment designated as controlled cryptographic items.

(e) The Contractor agrees to include this clause, including this paragraph (e), in all subcontracts which require securing telecommunications.

(End of clause)

252.239-7017 Notice of supply chain risk.

As prescribed in 239.7306(a), use the following provision:

NOTICE OF SUPPLY CHAIN RISK (FEB 2019)

(a) *Definition*. *Supply chain risk*, as used in this provision, means the risk that an adversary may sabotage, maliciously introduce unwanted function, or otherwise subvert the design, integrity, manufacturing, production, distribution, installation, operation, or maintenance of a covered system so as to surveil, deny, disrupt, or otherwise degrade the function, use, or operation of such system (see 10 U.S.C. 2339a).

(b) In order to manage supply chain risk, the Government may use the authorities provided by 10 U.S.C. 2339a. In exercising these authorities, the Government may consider information, public and non-public, including all-source intelligence, relating to an offeror and its supply chain.

(c) If the Government exercises the authority provided in 10 U.S.C. 2339a to limit disclosure of information, no action undertaken by the Government under such authority shall be subject to review in a bid protest before the Government Accountability Office or in any Federal court.

(End of provision)

[Interim rule, 78 FR 69276, 11/18/2013, effective 11/18/2013; Final rule, 80 FR 67243, 10/30/2015, effective 10/30/2015; Final rule, 84 FR 4368, 2/15/2019, effective 2/15/2019]

252.239-7018 Supply chain risk.

As prescribed in 239.7306(b), use the following clause:

SUPPLY CHAIN RISK (FEB 2019)

(a) *Definition*. As used in this clause—

Information technology (see 40 U.S.C 11101(6)) means, in lieu of the definition at FAR 2.1, any equipment, or interconnected system(s) or subsystem(s) of equipment, that is used in the automatic acquisition, storage, analysis, evaluation, manipulation, management, movement, control, display, switching, interchange, transmission, or reception of data or information by the agency.

(1) For purposes of this definition, equipment is used by an agency if the equipment is used by the agency directly or is used by a contractor under a contract with the agency that requires—

(i) Its use; or

(ii) To a significant extent, its use in the performance of a service or the furnishing of a product.

(2) The term *information technology* includes computers, ancillary equipment (including imaging peripherals, input, output, and storage devices necessary for security and surveillance), peripheral equipment designed to be controlled by the central processing unit of a computer, software, firmware and similar procedures, services (including support services), and related resources.

(3) The term *information technology* does not include any equipment acquired by a contractor incidental to a contract.

Supply chain risk means the risk that an adversary may sabotage, maliciously introduce unwanted function, or otherwise subvert the design, integrity, manufacturing, production, distribution, installation, operation, or maintenance of a covered system so as to surveil, deny, disrupt, or otherwise degrade the function, use, or operation of such system (see 10 U.S.C. 2339a).

(b) The Contractor shall mitigate supply chain risk in the provision of supplies and services to the Government.

(c) In order to manage supply chain risk, the Government may use the authorities provided by 10 U.S.C. 2339a. In exercising these authorities, the Government may consider information, public and non-public, including all-source intelligence, relating to a Contractor's supply chain.

(d) If the Government exercises the authority provided in 10 U.S.C. 2339a to limit disclosure of information, no action undertaken by the Government under such authority shall be subject to review in a bid protest before the Government Accountability Office or in any Federal court.

(End of clause)

[Interim rule, 78 FR 69276, 11/18/2013, effective 11/18/2013; Final rule, 80 FR 67243, 10/30/2015, effective 10/30/2015; Final rule, 84 FR 4368, 2/15/2019, effective 2/15/2019]

252.241 Acquisition of Utility Services, provisions and clauses for DFARS Part 241

252.241-7000 Superseding contract.

As prescribed in 241.501-70(a), use the following clause:

SUPERSEDING CONTRACT (DEC 1991)

This contract supersedes contract No. __, dated ____ which provided similar services. Any capital credits accrued to the Government, any remaining credits due to the Government under the connection charge, or any termination liability are transferred to this contract, as follows:

Capital Credits

(List years and accrued credits by year and separate delivery points.)

Outstanding Connection Charge Credits

(List by month and year the amount credited and show the remaining amount of outstanding credits due the Government.)

Termination Liability Charges

(List by month and year the amount of monthly facility cost recovered and show the remaining amount of facility cost to be recovered.)

(End of clause)

[DAC 91-13, 63 FR 11522, 3/9/98, effective 3/9/98]

252.241-7001 Government access.

As prescribed in 241.501-70(b), use the following clause:

GOVERNMENT ACCESS (DEC 1991)

Authorized representatives of the Government may have access to the Contractor's on-base facilities upon reasonable notice or in case of emergency.

(End of clause)

[DAC 91-13, 63 FR 11522, 3/9/98, effective 3/9/98]

252.242 Contract Administration, provisions and clauses for DFARS Part 242

252.242-7000 [Removed and Reserved]

[Final rule, 70 FR 67919, 11/9/2005, effective 11/9/2005]

252.242-7001 [Removed and Reserved]

[DAC 91-9, 60 FR 61586, 11/30/95, effective 11/30/95; Final rule, 70 FR 14574, 3/23/2005, effective 3/23/2005; Final rule, 73 FR 21846, 4/23/2008, effective 4/23/2008]

252.242-7002 [Removed and Reserved]

[DAC 91-12, 62 FR 34114, 6/24/97, effective 6/24/97; Final rule, 70 FR 14574, 3/23/2005, effective 3/23/2005; Final rule, 73 FR 21846, 4/23/2008, effective 4/23/2008]

252.242-7003 [Removed and Reserved]

[DAC 91-12, 62 FR 34114, 6/24/97, effective 6/24/97; Final rule, 77 FR 39140, 6/29/2012, effective 6/29/2012]

252.242-7004 Material Management and Accounting System.

As prescribed in 242.7204, use the following clause:

MATERIAL MANAGEMENT AND ACCOUNTING SYSTEM (MAY 2011)

(a) *Definitions*. As used in this clause—

(1) *Material management and accounting system (MMAS)* means the Contractor's system or systems for planning, controlling, and accounting for the acquisition, use, issuing, and disposition of material. Material management and accounting systems may be manual or automated. They may be stand-alone systems or they may be integrated with planning, engineering, estimating, purchasing, inventory, accounting, or other systems.

(2) *Valid time-phased requirements* means material that is—

(i) Needed to fulfill the production plan, including reasonable quantities for scrap, shrinkage, yield, *etc.*; and

(ii) Charged/billed to contracts or other cost objectives in a manner consistent with the need to fulfill the production plan.

(3) *Contractor* means a business unit as defined in section 31.001 of the Federal Acquisition Regulation (FAR).

(4) *Acceptable material management and accounting system* means a MMAS that generally complies with the system criteria in paragraph (d) of this clause.

(5) *Significant deficiency* means a shortcoming in the system that materially affects the ability of officials of the Department of Defense to rely upon information produced by the system that is needed for management purposes.

(b) *General*. The Contractor shall—

(1) Maintain an MMAS that—

(i) Reasonably forecasts material requirements;

(ii) Ensures that costs of purchased and fabricated material charged or allocated to a contract are based on valid time-phased requirements; and

(iii) Maintains a consistent, equitable, and unbiased logic for costing of material transactions; and

(2) Assess its MMAS and take reasonable action to comply with the MMAS standards in paragraph (e) of this clause.

(c) *Disclosure and maintenance requirements*. The Contractor shall—

(1) Have policies, procedures, and operating instructions that adequately describe its MMAS;

(2) Provide to the Administrative Contracting Officer (ACO), upon request, the results of internal reviews that it has conducted to ensure compliance with established MMAS policies, procedures, and operating instructions; and

(3) Disclose significant changes in its MMAS to the ACO at least 30 days prior to implementation.

(d) *System criteria*. The MMAS shall have adequate internal controls to ensure system and data integrity, and shall—

(1) Have an adequate system description including policies, procedures, and operating instructions that comply with the Federal Acquisition Regulation and Defense Federal Acquisition Regulation Supplement;

(2) Ensure that costs of purchased and fabricated material charged or allocated to a contract are based on valid time-phased requirements as impacted by minimum/economic order quantity restrictions.

(i) A 98 percent bill of material accuracy and a 95 percent master production schedule accuracy are desirable as a goal in order to ensure that requirements are both valid and appropriately time-phased.

(ii) If systems have accuracy levels below these, the Contractor shall provide adequate evidence that—

(A) There is no material harm to the Government due to lower accuracy levels; and

(B) The cost to meet the accuracy goals is excessive in relation to the impact on the Government;

(3) Provide a mechanism to identify, report, and resolve system control weaknesses and manual override. Systems should identify operational exceptions, such as excess/residual inventory, as soon as known;

(4) Provide audit trails and maintain records (manual and those in machine-readable form) necessary to evaluate system logic and to verify through transaction testing that the system is operating as desired;

(5) Establish and maintain adequate levels of record accuracy, and include reconciliation of recorded inventory quantities to physical inventory by part number on a periodic basis. A 95 percent accuracy level is desirable. If systems have an accuracy level below 95 percent, the Contractor shall provide adequate evidence that—

(i) There is no material harm to the Government due to lower accuracy levels; and

(ii) The cost to meet the accuracy goal is excessive in relation to the impact on the Government;

(6) Provide detailed descriptions of circumstances that will result in manual or system generated transfers of parts;

(7) Maintain a consistent, equitable, and unbiased logic for costing of material transactions as follows:

(i) The Contractor shall maintain and disclose written policies describing the transfer methodology and the loan/pay-back technique.

(ii) The costing methodology may be standard or actual cost, or any of the inventory costing methods in 48 CFR 9904.411-50(b). The Contractor shall maintain consistency across all contract and customer types, and from accounting period to accounting period for initial charging and transfer charging.

(iii) The system should transfer parts and associated costs within the same billing period. In the few instances where this may not be appropriate, the Contractor may accomplish the material transaction using a loan/pay-back technique. The "loan/pay-back technique" means that the physical part is moved temporarily from the contract, but the cost of the part remains on the contract. The procedures for the loan/pay-back technique must be approved by the ACO. When the technique is used, the Contractor shall have controls to ensure—

(A) Parts are paid back expeditiously;

(B) Procedures and controls are in place to correct any overbilling that might occur;

(C) Monthly, at a minimum, identification of the borrowing contract and the date the part was borrowed; and

(D) The cost of the replacement part is charged to the borrowing contract;

(8) Where allocations from common inventory accounts are used, have controls (in addition to those in paragraphs (d)(2) and (7) of this clause) to ensure that—

(i) Reallocations and any credit due are processed no less frequently than the routine billing cycle;

(ii) Inventories retained for requirements that are not under contract are not allocated to contracts; and

(iii) Algorithms are maintained based on valid and current data;

(9) Have adequate controls to ensure that physically commingled inventories that may include material for which costs are charged or allocated to fixed-price, cost-reimbursement, and commercial contracts do not compromise requirements of any of the standards in paragraphs (d)(1) through (8) of this clause. Government-furnished material shall not be—

(i) Physically commingled with other material; or

(ii) Used on commercial work; and

(10) Be subjected to periodic internal reviews to ensure compliance with established policies and procedures.

(e) *Significant deficiencies.* (1) The Contracting Officer will provide an initial determination to the Contractor, in writing, of any significant deficiencies. The initial determination will describe the deficiency in sufficient detail to allow the Contractor to understand the deficiency.

(2) The Contractor shall respond within 30 days to a written initial determination from the Contracting Officer that identifies significant deficiencies in the Contractor's MMAS. If the Contractor disagrees with the initial determination, the Contractor shall state, in writing, its rationale for disagreeing.

(3) The Contracting Officer will evaluate the Contractor's response and notify the Contractor, in writing, of the Contracting Officer's final determination concerning—

(i) Remaining significant deficiencies;

(ii) The adequacy of any proposed or completed corrective action; and

(iii) System disapproval if the Contracting Officer determines that one or more significant deficiencies remain.

(f) If the Contractor receives the Contracting Officer's final determination of significant deficiencies, the Contractor shall, within 45 days of receipt of the final determination, either correct the significant deficiencies or submit an acceptable corrective action plan showing milestones and actions to eliminate the significant deficiencies.

(g) *Withholding payments.* If the Contracting Officer makes a final determination to disapprove the Contractor's MMAS, and the contract includes the clause at 252.242-7005, Contractor Business Systems, the Contracting Officer will withhold payments in accordance with that clause.

(End of clause)

[Final rule, 65 FR 77832, 12/13/2000, effective 12/13/2000; Final rule, 70 FR 67919, 11/9/2005, effective 11/9/2005; Final rule, 74 FR 37645, 7/29/2009, effective 7/29/2009; Interim rule, 76 FR 28856, 5/18/2011, effective 5/18/2011; Final rule, 77 FR 11355, 2/24/2012, effective 2/24/2012; Publication notice, 20171208]

252.242-7005 Contractor business systems.

As prescribed in 242.7001, use the following clause:

CONTRACTOR BUSINESS SYSTEMS (FEB 2012)

(a) This clause only applies to covered contracts that are subject to the Cost Accounting Standards under 41 U.S.C. chapter 15, as implemented in regulations found at 48 CFR 9903.201-1 (see the FAR Appendix).

(b) *Definitions.* As used in this clause—

Acceptable contractor business systems means contractor business systems that comply with the terms and conditions of the applicable business system clauses listed in the definition of *contractor business systems* in this clause.

Contractor business systems means—

(1) Accounting system, if this contract includes the clause at 252.242-7006, Accounting System Administration;

(2) Earned value management system, if this contract includes the clause at 252.234-7002, Earned Value Management System;

(3) Estimating system, if this contract includes the clause at 252.215-7002, Cost Estimating System Requirements;

(4) Material management and accounting system, if this contract includes the clause at

252.242-7004, Material Management and Accounting System;

(5) Property management system, if this contract includes the clause at 252.245-7003, Contractor Property Management System Administration; and

(6) Purchasing system, if this contract includes the clause at 252.244-7001, Contractor Purchasing System Administration.

Significant deficiency, in the case of a contractor business system, means a shortcoming in the system that materially affects the ability of officials of the Department of Defense to rely upon information produced by the system that is needed for management purposes.

(c) *General.* The Contractor shall establish and maintain acceptable business systems in accordance with the terms and conditions of this contract.

(d) *Significant deficiencies.* (1) The Contractor shall respond, in writing, within 30 days to an initial determination that there are one or more significant deficiencies in one or more of the Contractor's business systems.

(2) The Contracting Officer will evaluate the Contractor's response and notify the Contractor, in writing, of the final determination as to whether the Contractor's business system contains significant deficiencies. If the Contracting Officer determines that the Contractor's business system contains significant deficiencies, the final determination will include a notice to withhold payments.

(e) *Withholding payments.* (1) If the Contracting Officer issues the final determination with a notice to withhold payments for significant deficiencies in a contractor business system required under this contract, the Contracting Officer will withhold five percent of amounts due from progress payments and performance-based payments, and direct the Contractor, in writing, to withhold five percent from its billings on interim cost vouchers on cost-reimbursement, labor-hour, and time-and-materials contracts until the Contracting Officer has determined that the Contractor has corrected all significant deficiencies as directed by the Contracting Officer's final determination. The Contractor shall, within 45 days of receipt of the notice, either correct the deficiencies or submit an acceptable corrective action plan showing milestones and actions to eliminate the deficiencies.

(2) If the Contractor submits an acceptable corrective action plan within 45 days of receipt of a notice of the Contracting Officer's intent to withhold payments, and the Contracting Officer, in consultation with the auditor or functional specialist, determines that the Contractor is effectively implementing such plan, the Contracting Officer will reduce withholding directly related to the significant deficiencies covered under the corrective action plan, to two percent from progress payments and performance-based payments, and direct the Contractor, in writing, to reduce the percentage withheld on interim cost vouchers to two percent until the Contracting Officer determines the Contractor has corrected all significant deficiencies as directed by the Contracting Officer's final determination. However, if at any time, the Contracting Officer determines that the Contractor has failed to follow the accepted corrective action plan, the Contracting Officer will increase withholding from progress payments and performance-based payments, and direct the Contractor, in writing, to increase the percentage withheld on interim cost vouchers to the percentage initially withheld, until the Contracting Officer determines that the Contractor has corrected all significant deficiencies as directed by the Contracting Officer's final determination.

(3) *Payment withhold percentage limits.*

(i) The total percentage of payments withheld on amounts due under each progress payment, performance-based payment, or interim cost voucher, on this contract shall not exceed—

(A) Five percent for one or more significant deficiencies in any single contractor business system; and

(B) Ten percent for significant deficiencies in multiple contractor business systems.

(ii) If this contract contains pre-existing withholds, and the application of any subsequent payment withholds will cause withholding under this clause to exceed the payment withhold percentage limits in paragraph (e)(3)(i) of this clause, the Contracting Officer will reduce the payment withhold percentage in the final determination to an amount that will not exceed the payment withhold percentage limits.

(4) For the purpose of this clause, payment means any of the following payments authorized under this contract:

(i) Interim payments under—

(A) Cost-reimbursement contracts;

(B) Incentive type contracts;

(C) Time-and-materials contracts;

(D) Labor-hour contracts.

(ii) Progress payments.

(iii) Performance-based payments.

(5) Payment withholding shall not apply to payments on fixed-price line items where performance is complete and the items were accepted by the Government.

(6) The withholding of any amount or subsequent payment to the Contractor shall not be construed as a waiver of any rights or remedies the Government has under this contract.

(7) Notwithstanding the provisions of any clause in this contract providing for interim, partial, or other payment withholding on any basis, the Contracting Officer may withhold payment in accordance with the provisions of this clause.

(8) The payment withholding authorized in this clause is not subject to the interest-penalty provisions of the Prompt Payment Act.

(f) *Correction of deficiencies.* (1) The Contractor shall notify the Contracting Officer, in writing, when the Contractor has corrected the business system's deficiencies.

(2) Once the Contractor has notified the Contracting Officer that all deficiencies have been corrected, the Contracting Officer will take one of the following actions:

(i) If the Contracting Officer determines that the Contractor has corrected all significant deficiencies as directed by the Contracting Officer's final determination, the Contracting Officer will, as appropriate, discontinue the withholding of progress payments and performance-based payments, and direct the Contractor, in writing, to discontinue the payment withholding from billings on interim cost vouchers under this contract associated with the Contracting Officer's final determination, and authorize the Contractor to bill for any monies previously withheld that are not also being withheld due to other significant deficiencies. Any payment withholding under this contract due to other significant deficiencies, will remain in effect until the Contracting Officer determines that those significant deficiencies are corrected.

(ii) If the Contracting Officer determines that the Contractor still has significant deficiencies, the Contracting Officer will continue the withholding of progress payments and performance-based payments, and the Contractor shall continue withholding amounts from its billings on interim cost vouchers in accordance with paragraph (e) of this clause, and not bill for any monies previously withheld.

(iii) If the Contracting Officer determines, based on evidence submitted by the Contractor, that there is a reasonable expectation that the corrective actions have been implemented and are expected to correct the significant deficiencies, the Contracting Officer will discontinue withholding payments, and release any payments previously withheld directly related to the significant deficiencies identified in the Contractor notification, and direct the Contractor, in writing, to discontinue the payment withholding from billings on interim cost vouchers associated with the Contracting Officer's final determination, and authorize the Contractor to bill for any monies previously withheld.

(iv) If, within 90 days of receipt of the Contractor notification that the Contractor corrected the significant deficiencies, the Contracting Officer has not made a determination in accordance with paragraphs (f)(2)(i), (ii), or (iii) of this clause, the Contracting Officer will reduce withholding directly related to the significant deficiencies identified in the Contractor notification by at least 50 percent of the amount being withheld from progress payments and performance-based payments, and direct the Contractor, in writing, to reduce the payment withholding from billings on interim cost vouchers directly related to the significant deficiencies identified in the Contractor notification by a specified percentage that is at least 50 percent, but not authorize the Contractor to bill for any monies previously withheld until the Contracting Officer makes a determination in accordance with paragraphs (f)(2)(i), (ii), or (iii) of this clause.

(iv) If, within 90 days of receipt of the Contractor notification that the Contractor has corrected the significant deficiencies, the Contracting Officer has not made a determination whether the Contractor has corrected all significant deficiencies as directed by the Contracting Officer's final determination, or has not made a determination whether there is a reasonable expectation that the corrective actions have been implemented, the Contracting Officer will reduce withholding directly related to the significant deficiencies covered under the corrective action plan by at least 50 percent of the amount being withheld from progress payments and performance-based payments, and direct the Contractor, in writing, to reduce the percentage withheld on interim cost vouchers by at least 50 percent, until the Contracting Officer makes a determination whether the Contractor has corrected all significant deficiencies as directed by the Contracting Officer's final determination, or has made a determination whether there is a reasonable expectation that the corrective actions have been implemented.

(v) At any time after the Contracting Officer reduces or discontinues the withholding of progress payments and performance-based payments, or directs the Contractor to reduce or discontinue the payment withholding from billings on interim cost vouchers under this contract, if the Contracting Officer determines that the Contractor has failed to correct the significant deficiencies identified in the Contractor's notification, the Contracting Officer will reinstate or increase withholding from progress payments and performance-based payments, and direct the Contractor, in writing, to reinstate or increase the percentage withheld on interim cost vouchers to the percentage initially withheld, until the Contracting Officer determines that the Contractor has corrected all significant deficiencies as directed by the Contracting Officer's final determination.

(End of clause)

[Interim rule, 62 FR 9990, 3/5/97, effective 3/5/97; DAC 91-12, 62 FR 34114, 6/24/97, effective 6/24/97; DAC 91-13, 63 FR 11522, 3/9/98, effective 3/9/98; Final rule, 70 FR 14574, 3/23/2005, effective 3/23/2005; Final rule, 73 FR 21846, 4/23/2008, effective 4/23/2008; Interim rule, 76 FR 28856, 5/18/2011, effective 5/18/2011; Final rule, 77 FR 11355, 2/24/2012, effective 2/24/2012]

252.242-7006 Accounting system administration.

As prescribed in 242.7503, use the following clause:

ACCOUNTING SYSTEM ADMINISTRATION (FEB 2012)

(a) *Definitions*. As used in this clause—

(1) *Acceptable accounting system* means a system that complies with the system criteria in paragraph (c) of this clause to provide reasonable assurance that—

(i) Applicable laws and regulations are complied with;

(ii) The accounting system and cost data are reliable;

(iii) Risk of misallocations and mischarges are minimized; and

(iv) Contract allocations and charges are consistent with billing procedures.

(2) *Accounting system* means the Contractor's system or systems for accounting methods, procedures, and controls established to gather, record, classify, analyze, summarize, interpret, and present accurate and timely financial data for reporting in compliance with applicable laws, regulations, and management decisions, and may include subsystems for specific areas such as indirect and

other direct costs, compensation, billing, labor, and general information technology.

(3) *Significant deficiency* means a shortcoming in the system that materially affects the ability of officials of the Department of Defense to rely upon information produced by the system that is needed for management purposes.

(b) *General*. The Contractor shall establish and maintain an acceptable accounting system. Failure to maintain an acceptable accounting system, as defined in this clause, shall result in the withholding of payments if the contract includes the clause at 252.242-7005, Contractor Business Systems, and also may result in disapproval of the system.

(c) *System criteria*. The Contractor's accounting system shall provide for—

(1) A sound internal control environment, accounting framework, and organizational structure;

(2) Proper segregation of direct costs from indirect costs;

(3) Identification and accumulation of direct costs by contract;

(4) A logical and consistent method for the accumulation and allocation of indirect costs to intermediate and final cost objectives;

(5) Accumulation of costs under general ledger control;

(6) Reconciliation of subsidiary cost ledgers and cost objectives to general ledger;

(7) Approval and documentation of adjusting entries;

(8) Management reviews or internal audits of the system to ensure compliance with the Contractor's established policies, procedures, and accounting practices;

(9) A timekeeping system that identifies employees' labor by intermediate or final cost objectives;

(10) A labor distribution system that charges direct and indirect labor to the appropriate cost objectives;

(11) Interim (at least monthly) determination of costs charged to a contract through routine posting of books of account;

(12) Exclusion from costs charged to Government contracts of amounts which are not allowable in terms of Federal Acquisition Regulation (FAR) part 31, Contract Cost Principles and Procedures, and other contract provisions;

(13) Identification of costs by contract line item and by units (as if each unit or line item were a separate contract), if required by the contract;

(14) Segregation of preproduction costs from production costs, as applicable;

(15) Cost accounting information, as required—

(i) By contract clauses concerning limitation of cost (FAR 52.232-20), limitation of funds (FAR 52.232-22), or allowable cost and payment (FAR 52.216-7); and

(ii) To readily calculate indirect cost rates from the books of accounts;

(16) Billings that can be reconciled to the cost accounts for both current and cumulative amounts claimed and comply with contract terms;

(17) Adequate, reliable data for use in pricing follow-on acquisitions; and

(18) Accounting practices in accordance with standards promulgated by the Cost Accounting Standards Board, if applicable, otherwise, Generally Accepted Accounting Principles.

(d) *Significant deficiencies*. (1) The Contracting Officer will provide an initial determination to the Contractor, in writing, on any significant deficiencies. The initial determination will describe the deficiency in sufficient detail to allow the Contractor to understand the deficiency.

(2) The Contractor shall respond within 30 days to a written initial determination from the Contracting Officer that identifies significant deficiencies in the Contractor's accounting system. If the Contractor disagrees with the initial determination, the Contractor shall state, in writing, its rationale for disagreeing.

(3) The Contracting Officer will evaluate the Contractor's response and notify the Contractor, in writing, of the Contracting Officer's final determination concerning—

(i) Remaining significant deficiencies;

(ii) The adequacy of any proposed or completed corrective action; and

(iii) System disapproval, if the Contracting Officer determines that one or more significant deficiencies remain.

(e) If the Contractor receives the Contracting Officer's final determination of significant deficiencies, the Contractor shall, within 45 days of receipt of the final determination, either correct the significant deficiencies or submit an acceptable corrective action plan showing milestones and actions to eliminate the significant deficiencies.

(f) *Withholding payments.* If the Contracting Officer makes a final determination to disapprove the Contractor's accounting system, and the contract includes the clause at 252.242-7005, Contractor Business Systems, the Contracting Officer will withhold payments in accordance with that clause.

(End of clause)

[Interim rule, 62 FR 9990, 3/5/97, effective 3/5/97, adopted as final, DAC 91-13, 63 FR 11522, 3/9/98; DAC 91-12, 62 FR 34114, 6/24/97, effective 6/24/97; Final rule, 70 FR 14574, 3/23/2005, effective 3/23/2005; Final rule, 73 FR 21846, 4/23/2008, effective 4/23/2008; Interim rule, 76 FR 28856, 5/18/2011, effective 5/18/2011; Final rule, 77 FR 11355, 2/24/2012, effective 2/24/2012]

252.243 Contract Modifications, provisions and clauses for DFARS Part 243

252.243-7000 [Reserved]

[Removed and reserved, 66 FR 49865, 10/1/2001, effective 10/1/2001]

252.243-7001 Pricing of contract modifications.

As prescribed in 243.205-70, use the following clause:

PRICING OF CONTRACT MODIFICATIONS (DEC 1991)

When costs are a factor in any price adjustment under this contract, the contract cost principles and procedures in FAR Part 31 and DFARS Part 231, in effect on the date of this contract, apply.

(End of clause)

[Final rule, 66 FR 49865, 10/1/2001, effective 10/1/2001]

252.243-7002 Requests for equitable adjustment.

As prescribed in 243.205-71, use the following clause:

REQUESTS FOR EQUITABLE ADJUSTMENT (DEC 2012)

(a) The amount of any request for equitable adjustment to contract terms shall accurately reflect the contract adjustment for which the Contractor believes the Government is liable. The request shall include only costs for performing the change, and shall not include any costs that already have been reimbursed or that have been separately claimed. All indirect costs included in the request shall be properly allocable to the change in accordance with applicable acquisition regulations.

(b) In accordance with 10 U.S.C. 2410(a), any request for equitable adjustment to contract terms that exceeds the simplified acquisition threshold shall bear, at the time of submission, the following certificate executed by an individual authorized to certify the request on behalf of the Contractor:

I certify that the request is made in good faith, and that the supporting data are accurate and complete to the best of my knowledge and belief.

____

(Official's Name)

____

(Title)

(c) The certification in paragraph (b) of this clause requires full disclosure of all relevant facts, including—

(1) Certified cost or pricing data if required in accordance with subsection 15.403-4 of the Federal Acquisition Regulation (FAR); and

(2) Data other than certified cost or pricing data, in accordance with subsection 15.403-3 of the FAR, including actual cost data and data to support any estimated costs, even if certified cost or pricing data are not required.

(d) The certification requirement in paragraph (b) of this clause does not apply to—

(1) Requests for routine contract payments; for example, requests for payment for accepted supplies and services, routine vouchers under a cost-reimbursement type contract, or progress payment invoices; or

(2) Final adjustment under an incentive provision of the contract.

(End of clause)

[DAC 91-13, 63 FR 11522, 3/9/98, effective 3/9/98; Final rule, 66 FR 49865, 10/1/2001, effective 10/1/2001; Final rule, 77 FR 76939, 12/31/2012, effective 12/31/2012]

252.244 Subcontracting Policies and Procedures, provisions and clauses for DFARS Part 244

252.244-7000 Subcontracts for Commercial Items.

As prescribed in 244.403, use the following clause:

SUBCONTRACTS FOR COMMERCIAL ITEMS (JUN 2013)

(a) The Contractor is not required to flow down the terms of any Defense Federal Acquisition Regulation Supplement (DFARS) clause in subcontracts for commercial items at any tier under this contract, unless so specified in the particular clause.

(b) While not required, the Contractor may flow down to subcontracts for commercial items a minimal number of additional clauses necessary to satisfy its contractual obligation.

(c) The Contractor shall include the terms of this clause, including this paragraph (c), in subcontracts awarded under this contract, including subcontracts for the acquisition of commercial items.

(End of clause)

[Final rule, 65 FR 14400, 3/16/2000, effective 3/16/2000; Final rule, 70 FR 67922, 11/9/2005, effective 11/9/2005; Final rule, 72 FR 2633, 1/22/2007, effective 1/22/2007; Interim rule, 74 FR 2417, 1/15/2009, effective 1/15/2009; Final rule, 74 FR 42779, 8/25/2009, effective 8/25/2009; Final rule, 74 FR 59916, 11/19/2009, effective 11/19/2009; Interim rule, 75 FR 67632, 11/3/2010, effective 11/3/2010; Final rule, 76 FR 44282, 7/25/2011, effective 7/25/2011; Interim rule, 76 FR 52133, 8/19/2011, effective 8/19/2011; Final rule, 76 FR 58144, 9/20/2011, effective 9/20/2011; Final rule, 77 FR 35883, 6/15/2012, effective 6/15/2012; Final rule, 77 FR 39141, 6/29/2012, effective 6/29/2012; Final rule, 78 FR 18877, 3/28/2013, effective 3/28/2013; Final rule, 78 FR 37980, 6/25/2013, effective 6/25/2013]

252.244-7001 Contractor purchasing system administration.

Basic. As prescribed in 244.305-71 and 244.305-71(a), use the following clause.

CONTRACTOR PURCHASING SYSTEM ADMINISTRATION (MAY 2014)

(a) *Definitions.* As used in this clause—

Acceptable purchasing system means a purchasing system that complies with the system criteria in paragraph (c) of this clause.

Purchasing system means the Contractor's system or systems for purchasing and subcontracting, including make-or-buy decisions, the selection of vendors, analysis of quoted prices, negotiation of prices with vendors, placing and administering of orders, and expediting delivery of materials.

Significant deficiency means a shortcoming in the system that materially affects the ability of officials of the Department of Defense to rely upon information produced by the system that is needed for management purposes.

(b) *General*. The Contractor shall establish and maintain an acceptable purchasing system. Failure to maintain an acceptable purchasing system, as defined in this clause, may result in disapproval of the system by the Contracting Officer and/or withholding of payments.

(c) *System criteria*. The Contractor's purchasing system shall—

(1) Have an adequate system description including policies, procedures, and purchasing practices that comply with the Federal Acquisition Regulation (FAR) and the Defense Federal Acquisition Regulation Supplement (DFARS);

(2) Ensure that all applicable purchase orders and subcontracts contain all flowdown clauses, including terms and conditions and any other clauses needed to carry out the requirements of the prime contract;

(3) Maintain an organization plan that establishes clear lines of authority and responsibility;

(4) Ensure all purchase orders are based on authorized requisitions and include a complete and accurate history of purchase transactions to support vendor selected, price paid, and document the subcontract/purchase order files which are subject to Government review;

(5) Establish and maintain adequate documentation to provide a complete and accurate history of purchase transactions to support vendors selected and prices paid;

(6) Apply a consistent make-or-buy policy that is in the best interest of the Government;

(7) Use competitive sourcing to the maximum extent practicable, and ensure debarred or suspended contractors are properly excluded from contract award;

(8) Evaluate price, quality, delivery, technical capabilities, and financial capabilities of competing vendors to ensure fair and reasonable prices;

(9) Require management level justification and adequate cost or price analysis, as applicable, for any sole or single source award;

(10) Perform timely and adequate cost or price analysis and technical evaluation for each subcontractor and supplier proposal or quote to ensure fair and reasonable subcontract prices;

(11) Document negotiations in accordance with FAR 15.406-3;

(12) Seek, take, and document economically feasible purchase discounts, including cash discounts, trade discounts, quantity discounts, rebates, freight allowances, and company-wide volume discounts;

(13) Ensure proper type of contract selection and prohibit issuance of cost-plus-a-percentage-of-cost subcontracts;

(14) Maintain subcontract surveillance to ensure timely delivery of an acceptable product and procedures to notify the Government of potential subcontract problems that may impact delivery, quantity, or price;

(15) Document and justify reasons for subcontract changes that affect cost or price;

(16) Notify the Government of the award of all subcontracts that contain the FAR and DFARS flowdown clauses that allow for Government audit of those subcontracts, and ensure the performance of audits of those subcontracts;

(17) Enforce adequate policies on conflict of interest, gifts, and gratuities, including the requirements of the 41 U.S.C. chapter 87, Kickbacks Act;

(18) Perform internal audits or management reviews, training, and maintain policies and procedures for the purchasing department to ensure the integrity of the purchasing system;

(19) Establish and maintain policies and procedures to ensure purchase orders and subcontracts contain mandatory and applicable flowdown clauses, as required by the FAR and DFARS, including terms and conditions required by the prime contract and any clauses required to carry out the requirements of the prime contract, including the requirements of 252.246-7007, Contractor Counterfeit Electronic Part Detection and Avoidance System, if applicable;

(20) Provide for an organizational and administrative structure that ensures effective and efficient procurement of required quality materials and parts at the best value from responsible and reliable sources, including the requirements of 252.246-7007, Contractor Counterfeit Electronic Part Detection and Avoidance System, if applicable;

(21) Establish and maintain selection processes to ensure the most responsive and responsible sources for furnishing required quality parts and materials and to promote competitive sourcing among dependable suppliers so that purchases are reasonably priced and from sources that meet contractor quality requirements, including the requirements of 252.246-7007, Contractor Counterfeit Electronic Part Detection and Avoidance System, and the item marking requirements of 252.211-7003, Item Unique Identification and Valuation, if applicable;

(22) Establish and maintain procedures to ensure performance of adequate price or cost analysis on purchasing actions;

(23) Establish and maintain procedures to ensure that proper types of subcontracts are selected, and that there are controls over subcontracting, including oversight and surveillance of subcontracted effort; and

(24) Establish and maintain procedures to timely notify the Contracting Officer, in writing, if—

(i) The Contractor changes the amount of subcontract effort after award such that it exceeds 70 percent of the total cost of the work to be performed under the contract, task order, or delivery order. The notification shall identify the revised cost of the subcontract effort and shall include verification that the Contractor will provide added value; or

(ii) Any subcontractor changes the amount of lower-tier subcontractor effort after award such that it exceeds 70 percent of the total cost of the work to be performed under its subcontract. The notification shall identify the revised cost of the subcontract effort and shall include verification that the subcontractor will provide added value as related to the work to be performed by the lower-tier subcontractor(s).

(d) *Significant deficiencies.* (1) The Contracting Officer will provide notification of initial determination to the Contractor, in writing, of any significant deficiencies. The initial determination will describe the deficiency in sufficient detail to allow the Contractor to understand the deficiency.

(2) The Contractor shall respond within 30 days to a written initial determination from the Contracting Officer that identifies significant deficiencies in the Contractor's purchasing system. If the Contractor disagrees with the initial determination, the Contractor shall state, in writing, its rationale for disagreeing.

(3) The Contracting Officer will evaluate the Contractor's response and notify the Contractor, in writing, of the Contracting Officer's final determination concerning—

(i) Remaining significant deficiencies;

(ii) The adequacy of any proposed or completed corrective action; and

(iii) System disapproval, if the Contracting Officer determines that one or more significant deficiencies remain.

(e) If the Contractor receives the Contracting Officer's final determination of significant deficiencies, the Contractor shall, within 45 days of receipt of the final determination, either correct the significant deficiencies or submit an acceptable corrective action plan showing milestones and actions to eliminate the deficiencies.

(f) *Withholding payments.* If the Contracting Officer makes a final determination to disapprove the Contractor's purchasing system, and the contract includes the clause at 252.242-7005, Contractor Business Systems, the Contracting Officer will withhold payments in accordance with that clause.

(End of clause)

Alternate I. As prescribed in 244.305-71 and 244.305-71(b), use the following clause, which amends paragraph (c) of the basic clause by deleting paragraphs (c)(1) through (c)(18) and (c)(22) through (c)(24), and revising and renumbering paragraphs (c)(19) through (c)(21) of the basic clause:

CONTRACTOR PURCHASING SYSTEM ADMINISTRATION—ALTERNATE I (MAY 2014)

The following paragraphs (a) through (f) of this clause do not apply unless the Contractor is subject to the Cost Accounting Standards under 41 U.S.C. chapter 15, as implemented in regulations found at 48 CFR 9903.201-1.

(a) *Definitions.* As used in this clause—

Acceptable purchasing system means a purchasing system that complies with the system criteria in paragraph (c) of this clause.

Purchasing system means the Contractor's system or systems for purchasing and subcontracting, including make-or-buy decisions, the selection of vendors, analysis of quoted prices, negotiation of prices with vendors, placing and administering of orders, and expediting delivery of materials.

Significant deficiency means a shortcoming in the system that materially affects the ability of officials of the Department of Defense to rely upon information produced by the system that is needed for management purposes.

(b) *Acceptable purchasing system.* The Contractor shall establish and maintain an acceptable purchasing system. Failure to maintain an acceptable purchasing system, as defined in this clause, may result in disapproval of the system by the Contracting Officer and/or withholding of payments.

(c) *System criteria.* The Contractor's purchasing system shall—

(1) Establish and maintain policies and procedures to ensure purchase orders and subcontracts contain mandatory and applicable flowdown clauses, as required by the FAR and DFARS, including terms and conditions required by the prime contract and any clauses required to carry out the requirements of the prime contract, including the requirements of 252.246-7007, Contractor Counterfeit Electronic Part Detection and Avoidance System;

(2) Provide for an organizational and administrative structure that ensures effective and efficient procurement of required quality materials and parts at the best value from responsible and reliable sources, including the requirements of 252.246-7007, Contractor Counterfeit Electronic Part Detection and Avoidance System, and, if applicable, the item marking requirements of 252.211-7003, Item Unique Identification and Valuation; and

(3) Establish and maintain selection processes to ensure the most responsive and responsible sources for furnishing required quality parts and materials and to promote competitive sourcing among dependable suppliers so that purchases are from sources that meet contractor quality requirements, including the requirements of 252.246-7007, Contractor Counterfeit Electronic Part Detection and Avoidance System.

(d) *Significant deficiencies.* (1) The Contracting Officer will provide notification of initial determination to the Contractor, in writing, of any significant deficiencies. The initial determination will describe the deficiency in sufficient detail to allow the Contractor to understand the deficiency.

(2) The Contractor shall respond within 30 days to a written initial determination from the Contracting Officer that identifies significant deficiencies in the Contractor's purchasing system. If the Contractor disagrees with the initial determination, the Contractor shall state, in writing, its rationale for disagreeing.

(3) The Contracting Officer will evaluate the Contractor's response and notify the Contractor, in writing, of the Contracting Officer's final determination concerning—

(i) Remaining significant deficiencies;

(ii) The adequacy of any proposed or completed corrective action; and

(iii) System disapproval, if the Contracting Officer determines that one or more significant deficiencies remain.

(e) If the Contractor receives the Contracting Officer's final determination of significant deficiencies, the Contractor shall, within 45 days of receipt of the final determination, either correct the significant deficiencies or submit an acceptable corrective action plan showing milestones and actions to eliminate the deficiencies.

(f) *Withholding payments*. If the Contracting Officer makes a final determination to disapprove the Contractor's purchasing system, and the contract includes the clause at 252.242-7005, Contractor Business Systems, the Contracting Officer will withhold payments in accordance with that clause.

(End of clause)

[Interim rule, 76 FR 28856, 5/18/2011, effective 5/18/2011; Final rule, 77 FR 11355, 2/24/2012, effective 2/24/2012; Final rule, 77 FR 35879, 6/15/2012, effective 6/15/2012; Final rule 79 FR 26091, 5/6/2014, effective 5/6/2014; Final rule, 80 FR 36897, 6/26/2015, effective 6/26/2015]

252.245 Government Property, provisions and clauses for DFARS Part 245

252.245-7000 Government-furnished mapping, charting, and geodesy property.

As prescribed in 245.107(1), use the following clause:

GOVERNMENT-FURNISHED MAPPING, CHARTING, AND GEODESY PROPERTY (APR 2012)

(a) *Definition—Mapping, charting, and geodesy (MC&G) property* means geodetic, geomagnetic, gravimetric, aeronautical, topographic, hydrographic, cultural, and toponymic data presented in the form of topographic, planimetric, relief, or thematic maps and graphics; nautical and aeronautical charts and publications; and in simulated, photographic, digital, or computerized formats.

(b) The Contractor shall not duplicate, copy, or otherwise reproduce MC&G property for purposes other than those necessary for performance of the contract.

(c) At the completion of performance of the contract, the Contractor, as directed by the Contracting Officer, shall either destroy or return to the Government all Government-furnished MC&G property not consumed in the performance of this contract.

(End of clause)

[Final rule, 74 FR 37645, 7/29/2009, effective 7/29/2009; Final rule, 76 FR 6004, 2/2/2011, effective 2/2/2011; Final rule, 77 FR 23631, 4/20/2012, effective 4/20/2012]

252.245-7001 Tagging, labeling, and marking of government-furnished property.

As prescribed in 245.107(2), use the following clause:

TAGGING, LABELING, AND MARKING OF GOVERNMENT-FURNISHED PROPERTY (APR 2012)

(a) *Definitions*. As used in this clause—

Government-furnished property is defined in the clause at FAR 52.245-1, Government Property.

Serially-managed item means an item designated by DoD to be uniquely tracked, controlled, or managed in maintenance, repair, and/or supply systems by means of its serial number.

(b) The Contractor shall tag, label, or mark Government-furnished property items identified in the contract as subject to serialized item management (serially-managed items).

(c) The Contractor is not required to tag, label, or mark Government-furnished property previously tagged, labeled, or marked.

(End of clause)

[DAC 91-6, 59 FR 27662, 5/27/94, effective 5/27/94; Interim rule, 72 FR 52293, 9/13/2007, effective 9/13/2007; Final rule, 73 FR 70906, 11/24/2008, effective 11/24/2008; Final rule, 76 FR 6004, 2/2/2011, effective 2/2/2011; Final rule, 77 FR 23631, 4/20/2012, effective 4/20/2012]

252.245-7002 Reporting Loss of Government Property.

As prescribed in 245.107(3), use the following clause:

REPORTING LOSS OF GOVERNMENT PROPERTY (DEC 2017)

(a) *Definitions*. As used in this clause—

Government property is defined in the clause at FAR 52.245-1, Government Property.

Loss of Government property means unintended, unforeseen, or accidental loss, damage, or destruction of Government property that reduces the Government's expected economic benefits of the property. Loss of Government property does not include purposeful destructive testing, obsolescence, normal wear and tear, or manufacturing defects. Loss of Government property includes, but is not limited to—

(1) Items that cannot be found after a reasonable search;

(2) Theft;

(3) Damage resulting in unexpected harm to property requiring repair to restore the item to usable condition; or

(4) Destruction resulting from incidents that render the item useless for its intended purpose or beyond economical repair.

Unit acquisition cost means—

(1) For Government-furnished property, the dollar value assigned by the Government and identified in the contract; and

(2) For Contractor-acquired property, the cost derived from the Contractor's records that reflect consistently applied, generally acceptable accounting principles.

(b) *Reporting loss of Government property.* (1) The Contractor shall use the Defense Contract Management Agency (DCMA) eTools software application for reporting loss of Government property. Reporting value shall be at unit acquisition cost. The eTools "LTDD of Government Property" toolset can be accessed from the DCMA home page External Web Access Management application at *http://www.dcma.mil/WBT/propertyloss/*.

(2) Unless otherwise provided for in this contract, the requirements of paragraph (b)(1) of this clause do not apply to normal and reasonable inventory adjustments, i.e., losses of low-risk consumable material such as common hardware, as agreed to by the Contractor and the Government Property Administrator. Such losses are typically a product of normal process variation. The Contractor shall ensure that its property management system provides adequate management control measures, e.g., statistical process controls, as a means of managing such variation.

(3) The Contractor shall report losses of Government property outside normal process variation, e.g., losses due to—

(i) Theft;

(ii) Inadequate storage;

(iii) Lack of physical security; or

(iv) "Acts of God."

(4) This reporting requirement does not change any liability provisions or other reporting requirements that may exist under this contract.

(End of clause)

[Final rule, 76 FR 6004, 2/2/2011, effective 2/2/2011; Final rule, 77 FR 23631, 4/20/2012, effective 4/20/2012; Final rule, 82 FR 61479, 12/28/2017, effective 12/28/2017]

252.245-7003 Contractor Property Management System Administration.

As prescribed in 245.107(4), use the following clause:

CONTRACTOR PROPERTY MANAGEMENT SYSTEM ADMINISTRATION (APR 2012)

(a) *Definitions.* As used in this clause—

Acceptable property management system means a property system that complies with the system criteria in paragraph (c) of this clause.

Property management system means the Contractor's system or systems for managing and controlling Government property.

Significant deficiency means a shortcoming in the system that materially affects the ability of officials of the Department of Defense to rely upon information produced by the system that is needed for management purposes.

(b) *General.* The Contractor shall establish and maintain an acceptable property management system. Failure to maintain an acceptable property management system, as defined in this clause, may result in disapproval of the system by the Contracting Officer and/or withholding of payments.

(c) *System criteria*. The Contractor's property management system shall be in accordance with paragraph (f) of the contract clause at Federal Acquisition Regulation 52.245-1.

(d) *Significant deficiencies*. (1) The Contracting Officer will provide an initial determination to the Contractor, in writing, of any significant deficiencies. The initial determination will describe the deficiency in sufficient detail to allow the Contractor to understand the deficiency.

(2) The Contractor shall respond within 30 days to a written initial determination from the Contracting Officer that identifies significant deficiencies in the Contractor's property management system. If the Contractor disagrees with the initial determination, the Contractor shall state, in writing, its rationale for disagreeing.

(3) The Contracting Officer will evaluate the Contractor's response and notify the Contractor, in writing, of the Contracting Officer's final determination concerning—

(i) Remaining significant deficiencies;

(ii) The adequacy of any proposed or completed corrective action; and

(iii) System disapproval, if the Contracting Officer determines that one or more significant deficiencies remain.

(e) If the Contractor receives the Contracting Officer's final determination of significant deficiencies, the Contractor shall, within 45 days of receipt of the final determination, either correct the significant deficiencies or submit an acceptable corrective action plan showing milestones and actions to eliminate the significant deficiencies.

(f) *Withholding payments*. If the Contracting Officer makes a final determination to disapprove the Contractor's property management system, and the contract includes the clause at 252.242-7005, Contractor Business Systems, the Contracting Officer will withhold payments in accordance with that clause.

(End of clause)

[Interim rule, 76 FR 28856, 5/18/2011, effective 5/18/2011; Final rule, 77 FR 11355, 2/24/2012, effective 2/24/2012; Final rule, 77 FR 23631, 4/20/2012, effective 4/20/2012]

252.245-7004 Reporting, Reutilization, and Disposal.

As prescribed in 245.107(5), use the following clause:

REPORTING, REUTILIZATION, AND DISPOSAL (DEC 2017)

(a) *Definitions*. As used in this clause—

(1) *Demilitarization* means the act of eliminating the functional capabilities and inherent military design features from DoD personal property. Methods and degree range from removal and destruction of critical features to total destruction by cutting, tearing, crushing, mangling, shredding, melting, burning, etc.

(2) *Export-controlled items* means items subject to the Export Administration Regulations (EAR) (15 CFR parts 730-774) or the International Traffic in Arms Regulations (ITAR) (22 CFR parts 120-130). The term includes—

(i) *Defense items*, defined in the Arms Export Control Act, 22 U.S.C. 2778(j)(4)(A), as defense articles, defense services, and related technical data, etc.; and

(ii) *Items*, defined in the EAR as *commodities*, *software*, and *technology*, terms that are also defined in the EAR, 15 CFR 772.1.

(3) *Ineligible transferees* means individuals, entities, or countries—

(i) Excluded from Federal programs by the General Services Administration as identified in the System for Award Management Exclusions located at *https://www.acquisition.gov/*;

(ii) Delinquent on obligations to the U.S. Government under surplus sales contracts;

(iii) Designated by the Department of Defense as ineligible, debarred, or suspended from defense contracts; or

(iv) Subject to denial, debarment, or other sanctions under export control laws and related laws and regulations, and orders administered by the Department of State, the Department of Commerce, the Department of Homeland Security, or the Department of the Treasury.

(4) *Scrap* means property that has no value except for its basic material content. For purposes of demilitarization, scrap is defined as recyclable waste and discarded materials derived from items that have been rendered useless beyond repair, rehabilitation, or restoration such that the item's original identity, utility, form, fit, and function have been destroyed. Items can be classified as scrap if processed by cutting, tearing, crushing, mangling, shredding, or melting. Intact or recognizable components and parts are not *scrap*.

(5) *Serviceable or usable property* means property with potential for reutilization or sale "as is" or with minor repairs or alterations.

(b) *Inventory disposal schedules.* Unless disposition instructions are otherwise included in this contract, the Contractor shall complete SF 1428, Inventory Schedule B, within the Plant Clearance Automated Reutilization Screening System (PCARSS). Information on PCARSS can be obtained from the plant clearance officer and at *http://www.dcma.mil/WBT/PCARSS/*.

(1) The SF 1428 shall contain the following:

(i) If known, the applicable Federal Supply Code (FSC) for all items, except items in scrap condition.

(ii) If known, the manufacturer name for all aircraft components under Federal Supply Group (FSG) 16 or 17 and FSCs 2620, 2810, 2915, 2925, 2935, 2945, 2995, 4920, 5821, 5826, 5841, 6340, and 6615.

(iii) The manufacturer name, make, model number, model year, and serial number for all aircraft under FSCs 1510 and 1520.

(iv) *Appropriate Federal Condition Codes.* See Appendix 2 of DLM 4000.25-2, Military Standard Transaction Reporting and Accounting Procedures (MILSTRAP) manual, edition in effect as of the date of this contract. Information on Federal Condition Codes can be obtained at *http://www.dla.mil/HQ/InformationOperations/DLMS/elibrary/manuals/MILSTRAP/*.

(2) If the schedules are acceptable, the plant clearance officer shall complete and send the Contractor a DD Form 1637, Notice of Acceptance of Inventory.

(c) *Proceeds from sales of surplus property.* Unless otherwise provided in the contract, the proceeds of any sale, purchase, or retention shall be—

(1) Forwarded to the Contracting Officer;

(2) Credited to the Government as part of the settlement agreement;

(3) Credited to the price or cost of the contract; or

(4) Applied as otherwise directed by the Contracting Officer.

(d) *Demilitarization, mutilation, and destruction.* If demilitarization, mutilation, or destruction of contractor inventory is required, the Contractor shall demilitarize, mutilate, or destroy contractor inventory, in accordance with the terms and conditions of the contract and consistent with Defense Demilitarization Manual, DoDM 4160.28-M, edition in effect as of the date of this contract. The plant clearance officer may authorize the purchaser to demilitarize, mutilate, or destroy as a condition of sale provided the property is not inherently dangerous to public health and safety.

(e) *Classified Contractor inventory.* The Contractor shall dispose of classified contractor inventory in accordance with applicable security guides and regulations or as directed by the Contracting Officer.

(f) *Inherently dangerous Contractor inventory.* Contractor inventory dangerous to public health or safety shall not be disposed of unless rendered innocuous or until adequate safeguards are provided.

(g) *Contractor inventory located in foreign countries.* Consistent with contract terms and conditions, property disposition shall be in accordance with foreign and U.S. laws and regulations, including laws and regulations involving export controls, host nation requirements, Final Governing Standards, and

Government-to-Government agreements. The Contractor's responsibility to comply with all applicable laws and regulations regarding export-controlled items exists independent of, and is not established or limited by, the information provided by this clause.

(h) *Disposal of scrap*. (1) *Contractor with scrap procedures*. (i) The Contractor shall include within its property management procedure, a process for the accountability and management of Government-owned scrap. The process shall, at a minimum, provide for the effective and efficient disposition of scrap, including sales to scrap dealers, so as to minimize costs, maximize sales proceeds, and, contain the necessary internal controls for mitigating the improper release of non-scrap property.

(ii) The Contractor may commingle Government and contractor-owned scrap and provide routine disposal of scrap, with plant clearance officer concurrence, when determined to be effective and efficient.

(2) *Scrap warranty*. The plant clearance officer may require the Contractor to secure from scrap buyers a DD Form 1639, Scrap Warranty.

(i) *Sale of surplus Contractor inventory*. (1) The Contractor shall conduct sales of contractor inventory (both usable property and scrap) in accordance with the requirements of this contract and plant clearance officer direction.

(2) Any sales contracts or other documents transferring title shall include the following statement:

"The Purchaser certifies that the property covered by this contract will be used in (name of country). In the event of resale or export by the Purchaser of any of the property, the Purchaser agrees to obtain the appropriate U.S. and foreign export or re-export license approval."

(j) *Restrictions on purchase or retention of Contractor inventory*. (1) The Contractor may not knowingly sell the inventory to any person or that person's agent, employee, or household member if that person—

(i) Is a civilian employee of the DoD or the U.S. Coast Guard;

(ii) Is a member of the armed forces of the United States, including the U.S. Coast Guard; or

(iii) Has any functional or supervisory responsibilities for or within the DoD's property disposal/disposition or plant clearance programs or for the disposal of contractor inventory.

(2) The Contractor may conduct Internet-based sales, to include use of a third party.

(3) If the Contractor wishes to bid on the sale, the Contractor or its employees shall submit bids to the plant clearance officer prior to soliciting bids from other prospective bidders.

(4) The Contractor shall solicit a sufficient number of bidders to obtain adequate competition. Informal bid procedures shall be used, unless the plant clearance officer directs otherwise. The Contractor shall include in its invitation for bids, the sales terms and conditions provided by the plant clearance officer.

(5) The Contractor shall solicit bids at least 15 calendar days before bid opening to allow adequate opportunity to inspect the property and prepare bids.

(6) For large sales, the Contractor may use summary lists of items offered as bid sheets with detailed descriptions attached.

(7) In addition to mailing or delivering notice of the proposed sale to prospective bidders, the Contractor may (when the results are expected to justify the additional expense) display a notice of the proposed sale in appropriate public places, e.g., publish a sales notice on the Internet in appropriate trade journals or magazines and local newspapers.

(8) The plant clearance officer or representative will witness the bid opening. The Contractor shall submit, either electronically or manually, two copies of the bid abstract.

(9) The following terms and conditions shall be included in sales contracts involving the demilitarization, mutilation, or destruction of property:

(i) *Demilitarization, mutilation, or destruction on Contractor or subcontractor premises*.

Item(s) _____ require demilitarization, mutilation, or destruction by the Purchaser. Insert item number(s) and specific demilitarization, mutilation, or destruction requirements for item(s) shown in Defense Demilitarization Manual, DoDM 4160.28-M, edition in effect as of the date of this contract. Demilitarization shall be witnessed and verified by a Government representative using DRMS Form 145 or equivalent.

(ii) *Demilitarization, mutilation, or destruction off Contractor or subcontractor premises.*

(A) Item(s) _____ require demilitarization, mutilation, or destruction by the Purchaser. Insert item number(s) and specific demilitarization, mutilation, or destruction requirements for item(s) shown in Defense Demilitarization Manual, DoDM 4160.28-M, edition in effect as of the date of this contract. Demilitarization shall be witnessed and verified by a Government representative using DRMS Form 145 or equivalent.

(B) Property requiring demilitarization shall not be removed, and title shall not pass to the Purchaser, until demilitarization has been accomplished and verified by a Government representative. Demilitarization will be accomplished as specified in the sales contract. Demilitarization shall be witnessed and verified by a Government representative using DRMS Form 145 or equivalent.

(C) The Purchaser agrees to assume all costs incident to the demilitarization and to restore the working area to its present condition after removing the demilitarized property.

(iii) *Failure to demilitarize.* If the Purchaser fails to demilitarize, mutilate, or destroy the property as specified in the contract, the Contractor may, upon giving 10 days written notice from date of mailing to the Purchaser—

(A) Repossess, demilitarize, and return the property to the Purchaser, in which case the Purchaser hereby agrees to pay to the Contractor, prior to the return of the property, all costs incurred by the Contractor in repossessing, demilitarizing, and returning the property;

(B) Repossess, demilitarize, and resell the property, and charge the defaulting Purchaser with all costs incurred by the Contractor. The Contractor shall deduct these costs from the purchase price and refund the balance of the purchase price, if any, to the Purchaser. In the event the costs exceed the purchase price, the defaulting Purchaser hereby agrees to pay these costs to the Contractor; or

(C) Repossess and resell the property under similar terms and conditions. In the event this option is exercised, the Contractor shall charge the defaulting Purchaser with all costs incurred by the Contractor. The Contractor shall deduct these costs from the original purchase price and refund the balance of the purchase price, if any, to the defaulting Purchaser. Should the excess costs to the Contractor exceed the purchase price, the defaulting Purchaser hereby agrees to pay these costs to the Contractor.

(End of clause)

[Final rule, 76 FR 52139, 8/19/2011, effective 8/19/2011; Final rule, 77 FR 23631, 4/20/2012, effective 4/20/2012; Final rule, 78 FR 28756, 5/16/2013, effective 5/16/2013; Final rule, 78 FR 30232, 5/22/2013, effective 5/22/2013; Final rule, 80 FR 15912, 3/26/2015, effective 3/26/2015; Final rule, 80 FR 15912, 3/26/2015, effective 3/26/2015; Final rule, 81 FR 65563, 9/23/2016, effective 9/23/2016; Final rule, 82 FR 61479, 12/28/2017, effective 12/28/2017]

252.246 Quality Assurance, provisions and clauses for DFARS Part 246

252.246-7000 [Removed and Reserved]

[Interim rule, 68 FR 8450, 2/21/2003, effective 3/1/2003; Final rule, 73 FR 1830, 1/10/2008, effective 1/10/2008; Final rule, 73 FR 11356, 3/3/2008, effective 3/3/2008; Final rule, 83 FR 66062, 12/21/2018, effective 12/21/2018]

252.246-7001 Warranty of data.

Basic. As prescribed at 246.710(1) and 246.710(1)(i), use the following clause.

WARRANTY OF DATA—BASIC (MAR 2014)

(a) *Definition—Technical data* has the same meaning as given in the clause in this contract entitled, Rights in Technical Data and Computer Software.

(b) *Warranty.* Notwithstanding inspection and acceptance by the Government of technical data furnished under this contract, and notwithstanding any provision of this contract concerning the conclusiveness of acceptance, the Contractor warrants that all technical data delivered under this contract will at the time of delivery conform with the specifications and all other requirements of this contract. The warranty period shall extend for three years after completion of the delivery of the line item of data (as identified in DD Form 1423, Contract Data Requirements List) of which the data forms a part; or any longer period specified in the contract.

(c) *Contractor notification.* The Contractor agrees to notify the Contracting Officer in writing immediately of any breach of the above warranty which the Contractor discovers within the warranty period.

(d) *Remedies.* The following remedies shall apply to all breaches of the warranty, whether the Contractor notifies the Contracting Officer in accordance with paragraph (c) of this clause or if the Government notifies the Contractor of the breach in writing within the warranty period:

(1) Within a reasonable time after such notification, the Contracting Officer may—

(i) By written notice, direct the Contractor to correct or replace at the Contractor's expense the nonconforming technical data promptly; or

(ii) If the Contracting Officer determines that the Government no longer has a requirement for correction or replacement of the data, or that the data can be more reasonably corrected by the Government, inform the Contractor by written notice that the Government elects a price or fee adjustment instead of correction or replacement.

(2) If the Contractor refuses or fails to comply with a direction under paragraph (d)(1)(i) of this clause, the Contracting Officer may, within a reasonable time of the refusal or failure—

(i) By contract or otherwise, correct or replace the nonconforming technical data and charge the cost to the Contractor; or

(ii) Elect a price or fee adjustment instead of correction or replacement.

(3) The remedies in this clause represent the only way to enforce the Government's rights under this clause.

(e) The provisions of this clause apply anew to that portion of any corrected or replaced technical data furnished to the Government under paragraph (d)(1)(i) of this clause.

(End of clause)

Alternate I. As prescribed in 246.710(1) and (1)(ii), use the following clause, which uses a different paragraph (d)(3) than the basic clause:

WARRANTY OF DATA—ALTERNATE I (MAR 2014)

(a) *Definition.* Technical data has the same meaning as given in the clause in this contract entitled "Rights in Technical Data and Computer Software".

(b) *Warranty.* Notwithstanding inspection and acceptance by the Government of technical data furnished under this contract, and notwithstanding any provision of this contract concerning the conclusiveness of acceptance, the Contractor warrants that all technical data delivered under this contract will at the time of delivery conform with the specifications and all other requirements of this contract. The warranty period shall extend for three years after completion of the delivery of the line item of data (as identified in DD Form 1423, Contract Data Requirements List) of which the data forms a part; or any longer period specified in the contract.

(c) *Contractor Notification.* The Contractor agrees to notify the Contracting Officer in writing immediately of any breach of the above warranty which the Contractor discovers within the warranty period.

(d) *Remedies.* The following remedies shall apply to all breaches of the warranty, whether the Contractor notifies the Contracting Officer in accordance with paragraph (c) of this clause or if the Government notifies the Contractor of the breach in writing within the warranty period:

(1) Within a reasonable time after such notification, the Contracting Officer may—

(i) By written notice, direct the Contractor to correct or replace at the Contractor's expense the nonconforming technical data promptly; or

(ii) If the Contracting Officer determines that the Government no longer has a requirement for correction or replacement of the data, or that the data can be more reasonably corrected by the Government, inform the Contractor by written notice that the Government elects a price or fee adjustment instead of correction or replacement.

(2) If the Contractor refuses or fails to comply with a direction under paragraph (d)(1)(i) of this clause, the Contracting Officer may, within a reasonable time of the refusal or failure—

(i) By contract or otherwise, correct or replace the nonconforming technical data and charge the cost to the Contractor; or

(ii) Elect a price or fee adjustment instead of correction or replacement.]

(3) In addition to the remedies under paragraphs (d)(1) and (2) of this clause, the Contractor shall be liable to the Government for all damages to the Government as a result of the breach of warranty.

(i) The additional liability under paragraph (d)(3) of this clause shall not exceed 75 percent of the target profit.

(ii) If the breach of the warranty is with respect to the data supplied by an equipment subcontractor, the limit of the Contractor's liability shall be—

(A) Ten percent of the total subcontract price in a firm-fixed-price subcontract;

(B) Seventy-five percent of the total subcontract fee in a cost-plus-fixed-fee or cost-plus-award-fee subcontract; or

(C) Seventy-five percent of the total subcontract target profit or fee in a fixed-price-incentive or cost-plus-incentive subcontract.

(iii) Damages due the Government under the provisions of this warranty are not an allowable cost.

(iv) The additional liability in paragraph (d)(3) of this clause shall not apply—

(A) With respect to the requirements for product drawings and associated lists, special inspection equipment (SIE) drawings and associated lists, special tooling drawings and associated lists, SIE operating instructions, SIE descriptive documentation, and SIE calibration procedures under MIL–T–31000, General Specification for Technical Data Packages, Amendment 1, or MIL–T–47500, General Specification for Technical Data Packages, Supp 1, or drawings and associated lists under level 2 or level 3 of MIL–D–1000A, Engineering and Associated Data Drawings, or DoD–D–1000B, Engineering and Associated Lists Drawings (Inactive for New Design) Amendment 4, Notice 1; or drawings and associated lists under category E or I of MIL–D–1000, Engineering and Associated Lists Drawings, provided that the data furnished by the Contractor was current, accurate at time of submission, and did not involve a significant omission of data necessary to comply with the requirements; or

(B) To defects the Contractor discovers and gives written notice to the Government before the Government discovers the error.

(e) The provisions of this clause apply anew to that portion of any corrected or replaced technical data furnished to the Government under paragraph (d)(1)(i) of this clause.

(End of clause)

Alternate II. As prescribed at 246.710(1) and (1)(iii), use the following clause, which uses a different paragraph (d)(3) than the basic clause:

WARRANTY OF DATA—ALTERNATE II (MAR 2014)

(a) *Definition*. Technical data has the same meaning as given in the clause in this contract entitled "Rights in Technical Data and Computer Software."

(b) *Warranty.* Notwithstanding inspection and acceptance by the Government of technical data furnished under this contract, and notwithstanding any provision of this contract concerning the conclusiveness of acceptance, the Contractor warrants that all technical data delivered under this contract will at the time of delivery conform with the specifications and all other requirements of this contract. The warranty period shall extend for three years after completion of the delivery of the line item of data (as identified in DD Form 1423, Contract Data Requirements List) of which the data forms a part; or any longer period specified in the contract.

(c) *Contractor Notification.* The Contractor agrees to notify the Contracting Officer in writing immediately of any breach of the above warranty which the Contractor discovers within the warranty period.

(d) *Remedies.* The following remedies shall apply to all breaches of the warranty, whether the Contractor notifies the Contracting Officer in accordance with paragraph (c) of this clause or if the Government notifies the Contractor of the breach in writing within the warranty period:

(1) Within a reasonable time after such notification, the Contracting Officer may—

(i) By written notice, direct the Contractor to correct or replace at the Contractor's expense the nonconforming technical data promptly; or

(ii) If the Contracting Officer determines that the Government no longer has a requirement for correction or replacement of the data, or that the data can be more reasonably corrected by the Government, inform the Contractor by written notice that the Government elects a price or fee adjustment instead of correction or replacement.

(2) If the Contractor refuses or fails to comply with a direction under paragraph (d)(1)(i) of this clause, the Contracting Officer may, within a reasonable time of the refusal or failure—

(i) By contract or otherwise, correct or replace the nonconforming technical data and charge the cost to the Contractor; or

(ii) Elect a price or fee adjustment instead of correction or replacement.

(3) In addition to the remedies under paragraphs (d)(1) and (2) of this clause, the Contractor shall be liable to the Government for all damages to the Government as a result of the breach of the warranty.

(i) The additional liability under paragraph (d)(3) of this clause shall not exceed ten percent of the total contract price.

(ii) If the breach of the warranty is with respect to the data supplied by an equipment subcontractor, the limit of the Contractor's liability shall be—

(A) Ten percent of the total subcontract price in a firm-fixed-price subcontract;

(B) Seventy-five percent of the total subcontract fee in a cost-plus-fixed-fee or cost-plus-award-fee subcontract; or

(C) Seventy-five percent of the total subcontract target profit or fee in a fixed-price-incentive or cost-plus-incentive subcontract.

(iii) The additional liability specified in paragraph (d)(3) of this clause shall not apply—

(A) With respect to the requirements for product drawings and associated lists, special inspection equipment (SIE) drawings and associated lists, special tooling drawings and associated lists, SIE operating instructions, SIE descriptive documentation, and SIE calibration procedures under MIL–T–31000, General Specification for Technical Data Packages, Amendment 1, or MIL–T–47500, General Specification for Technical Data Packages, Supp 1, or drawings and associated lists under level 2 or level 3 of MIL–D–1000A, Engineering and Associated Data Drawings, or DoD–D–1000B, Engineering and Associated Lists Drawings (Inactive for New Design) Amendment 4, Notice 1; or drawings and associated lists under category E or I of MIL–D–1000, Engineering and Associated Lists Drawings, provided that the data furnished by the Contractor was current, accurate at time of submission, and did not involve a significant omission of data necessary to comply with the requirements; or

(B) To defects the Contractor discovers and gives written notice to the Government before the Government discovers the error.

(e) The provisions of this clause apply anew to that portion of any corrected or replaced technical data furnished to the Government under paragraph (d)(1)(i) of this clause.

(End of clause)

[Final rule, 79 FR 17448, 3/28/2014, effective 3/28/2014; Final rule, 80 FR 36897, 6/26/2015, effective 6/26/2015]

252.246-7002 Warranty of construction (Germany).

As prescribed in 246.710(2), use the following clause:

WARRANTY OF CONSTRUCTION (GERMANY) (JUN 1997)

(a) In addition to any other representations in this contract, the Contractor warrants, except as provided in paragraph (j) of this clause, that the work performed under this contract conforms to the contract requirements and is free of any defect of equipment, material, or design furnished or workmanship performed by the Contractor or any subcontractor or supplier at any tier.

(b) This warranty shall continue for the period(s) specified in Section 13, VOB, Part B, commencing from the date of final acceptance of the work under this contract. If the Government takes possession of any part of the work before final acceptance, this warranty shall continue for the period(s) specified in Section 13, VOB, Part B, from the date the Government takes possession.

(c) The Contractor shall remedy, at the Contractor's expense, any failure to conform or any defect. In addition, the Contractor shall remedy, at the Contractor's expense, any damage to Government-owned or controlled real or personal property when that damage is the result of—

(1) The Contractor's failure to conform to contract requirements; or

(2) Any defect of equipment, material, or design furnished or workmanship performed.

(d) The Contractor shall restore any work damaged in fulfilling the terms and conditions of this clause.

(e) The Contracting Officer shall notify the Contractor, in writing, within a reasonable period of time after the discovery of any failure, defect, or damage.

(f) If the Contractor fails to remedy any failure, defect, or damage within a reasonable period of time after receipt of notice, the Government shall have the right to replace, repair, or otherwise remedy the failure, defect, or damage at the Contractor's expense.

(g) With respect to all warranties, express or implied, from subcontractors, manufacturers, or suppliers for work performed and materials furnished under this contract, the Contractor shall—

(1) Obtain all warranties that would be given in normal commercial practice;

(2) Require all warranties to be executed in writing, for the benefit of the Government, if directed by the Contracting Officer; and

(3) Enforce all warranties for the benefit of the Government as directed by the Contracting Officer.

(h) In the event the Contractor's warranty under paragraph (b) of this clause has expired, the Government may bring suit at its expense to enforce a subcontractor's, manufacturer's, or supplier's warranty.

(i) Unless a defect is caused by the Contractor's negligence, or the negligence of a subcontractor or supplier at any tier, the Contractor shall not be liable for the repair of any defects of material or design furnished by the Government or for the repair of any damage resulting from any defect in Government-furnished material or design.

(j) This warranty shall not limit the Government's right under the Inspection clause of this contract, with respect to latent defects, gross mistakes, or fraud.

(End of clause)

[DAC 91-12, 62 FR 34114, 6/24/97, effective 6/24/97, corrected 62 FR 49306, 9/19/97; Final rule, 79 FR 17448, 3/28/2014, effective 3/28/2014]

252.246-7003 Notification of Potential Safety Issues.

As prescribed in 246.370(a), use the following clause:

NOTIFICATION OF POTENTIAL SAFETY ISSUES (JUN 2013)

(a) *Definitions.* As used in this clause—

Credible information means information that, considering its source and the surrounding circumstances, supports a reasonable belief that an event has occurred or will occur.

Critical safety item means a part, subassembly, assembly, subsystem, installation equipment, or support equipment for a system that contains a characteristic, any failure, malfunction, or absence of which could have a safety impact.

Safety impact means the occurrence of death, permanent total disability, permanent partial disability, or injury or occupational illness requiring hospitalization; loss of a weapon system; or property damage exceeding $1,000,000.

Subcontractor means any supplier, distributor, vendor, or firm that furnishes supplies or services to or for the Contractor or another subcontractor under this contract.

(b) The Contractor shall provide notification, in accordance with paragraph (c) of this clause, of—

(1) All nonconformances for parts identified as critical safety items acquired by the Government under this contract; and

(2) All nonconformances or deficiencies that may result in a safety impact for systems, or subsystems, assemblies, subassemblies, or parts integral to a system, acquired by or serviced for the Government under this contract.

(c) The Contractor—

(1) Shall notify the Administrative Contracting Officer (ACO) and the Procuring Contracting Officer (PCO) as soon as practicable, but not later than 72 hours, after discovering or acquiring credible information concerning nonconformances and deficiencies described in paragraph (b) of this clause; and

(2) Shall provide a written notification to the ACO and the PCO within 5 working days that includes—

(i) A summary of the defect or nonconformance;

(ii) A chronology of pertinent events;

(iii) The identification of potentially affected items to the extent known at the time of notification;

(iv) A point of contact to coordinate problem analysis and resolution; and

(v) Any other relevant information.

(d) The Contractor—

(1) Is responsible for the notification of potential safety issues occurring with regard to an item furnished by any subcontractor; and

(2) Shall facilitate direct communication between the Government and the subcontractor as necessary.

(e) Notification of safety issues under this clause shall be considered neither an admission of responsibility nor a release of liability for the defect or its consequences. This clause does not affect any right of the Government or the Contractor established elsewhere in this contract.

(f)(1) The Contractor shall include the substance of this clause, including this paragraph (f), in subcontracts for—

(i) Parts identified as critical safety items;

(ii) Systems and subsystems, assemblies, and subassemblies integral to a system; or

(iii) Repair, maintenance, logistics support, or overhaul services for systems and subsystems, assemblies, subassemblies, and parts integral to a system.

(2) For those subcontracts, including subcontracts for commercial items, described in paragraph (f)(1) of this clause, the Contractor shall require the subcontractor to pro-

vide the notification required by paragraph (c) of this clause to—

(i) The Contractor or higher-tier subcontractor; and

(ii) The ACO and the PCO, if the subcontractor is aware of the ACO and the PCO for the contract.

(End of clause)

[Final rule, 72 FR 2633, 1/22/2007, effective 1/22/2007; Final rule, 78 FR 37980, 6/25/2013, effective 6/25/2013; Final rule, 83 FR 66062, 12/21/2018, effective 12/21/2018]

252.246-7004 Safety of Facilities, Infrastructure, and Equipment for Military Operations.

As prescribed in 246.270-4, use the following clause:

SAFETY OF FACILITIES, INFRASTRUCTURE, AND EQUIPMENT FOR MILITARY OPERATIONS (OCT 2010)

(a) *Definition. Discipline Working Group*, as used in this clause, means representatives from the DoD Components, as defined in MIL-STD-3007F, who are responsible for the unification and maintenance of the Unified Facilities Criteria (UFC) documents for a particular discipline area.

(b) The Contractor shall ensure, consistent with the requirements of the applicable inspection clause in this contract, that the facilities, infrastructure, and equipment acquired, constructed, installed, repaired, maintained, or operated under this contract comply with Unified Facilities Criteria (UFC) 1-200-01 for—

(1) Fire protection;

(2) Structural integrity;

(3) Electrical systems;

(4) Plumbing;

(5) Water treatment;

(6) Waste disposal; and

(7) Telecommunications networks.

(c) The Contractor may apply a standard equivalent to or more stringent than UFC 1-200-01 upon a written determination of the acceptability of the standard by the Contracting Officer with the concurrence of the relevant Discipline Working Group.

(End of clause)

[Interim rule, 75 FR 66683, 10/29/2010, effective 10/29/2010; Final rule, 76 FR 14590, 3/17/2011, effective 3/17/2011]

252.246-7005 Notice of Warranty Tracking of Serialized Items.

As prescribed in 246.710(3)(i), use the following provision:

NOTICE OF WARRANTY TRACKING OF SERIALIZED ITEMS (MAR 2016)

(a) *Definitions. Duration, enterprise, enterprise identifier, fixed expiration, item type, serialized item, starting event, unique item identifier, usage, warranty administrator, warranty guarantor*, and *warranty tracking* are defined in the clause at252.246-7006, Warranty Tracking of Serialized Items.

(b) *Reporting of data for warranty tracking and administration.* (1) The Offeror shall provide the information required by the attachment entitled "Warranty Tracking Information" on each contract line item number, subline item number, or exhibit line item number for warranted items with its offer. Information required in the warranty attachment for each warranted item shall include such information as duration, fixed expiration, item type, starting event, usage, warranty administrator enterprise identifier, and warranty guarantor enterprise identifier.

(2) The successful offeror will be required to provide the following information no later than when the warranted items are presented for receipt and/or acceptance, in accordance with the clause at 252.246-7006—

(i) The unique item identifier for each warranted item required by the attachment entitled "Warranty Tracking Information;" and

(ii) All information required by the attachment entitled "Source of Repair Instructions" for each warranted item.

(3) For additional information on warranty attachments, see the "Warranty and Source of Repair" training and "Warranty and

Source of Repair Tracking User Guide" accessible on the Product Data Reporting and Evaluation Program (PDREP) website at *https://www.pdrep.csd.disa.mil/pdrep_files/other/wsr.htm*.

(End of provision)

[Final rule, 76 FR 33166, 6/8/2011, effective 6/8/2011; Final rule, 79 FR 17448, 3/28/2014, effective 3/28/2014; Final rule, 81 FR 17041, 3/25/2016, effective 3/25/2016]

252.246-7006 Warranty Tracking of Serialized Items.

As prescribed in 246.710(3)(ii), use the following provision:

WARRANTY TRACKING OF SERIALIZED ITEMS (MAR 2016)

(a) *Definitions*. As used in this clause—

Duration means the warranty period. This period may be a stated period of time, amount of usage, or the occurrence of a specified event, after formal acceptance of delivery, for the Government to assert a contractual right for the correction of defects.

Enterprise means the entity (*e.g.*, a manufacturer or vendor) responsible for granting the warranty and/or assigning unique item identifiers to serialized warranty items.

Enterprise identifier means a code that is uniquely assigned to an enterprise by an issuing agency.

First use means the initial or first-time use of a product by the Government.

Fixed expiration means the date the warranty expires and the Contractor's obligation to provide for a remedy or corrective action ends.

Installation means the date a unit is inserted into a higher level assembly in order to make that assembly operational.

Issuing agency means an organization responsible for assigning a globally unique identifier to an enterprise, as indicated in the Register of Issuing Agency Codes for International Standards Organization/International Electrotechnical Commission 15459, located at *http://www.aimglobal.org/?Reg_Authority15459*.

Item type means a coded representation of the description of the item being warranted, consisting of the codes C—component procured separate from end item, S—subassembly procured separate from end item or subassembly, E—embedded in component, subassembly or end item parent, and P—parent end item.

Serialized item means each item produced is assigned a serial number that is unique among all the collective tangible items produced by the enterprise, or each item of a particular part, lot, or batch number is assigned a unique serial number within that part, lot, or batch number assignment within the enterprise identifier. The enterprise is responsible for ensuring unique serialization within the enterprise identifier or within the part, lot, or batch numbers, and that serial numbers, once assigned, are never used again.

Starting event means the event or action that initiates the warranty, such as first use or upon installation.

Unique item identifier means a set of data elements marked on an item that is globally unique and unambiguous.

Usage means the quantity and an associated unit of measure that specifies the amount of a characteristic subject to the contractor's obligation to provide for remedy or corrective action, such as a number of miles, hours, or cycles.

Warranty administrator means the organization specified by the guarantor for managing the warranty.

Warranty guarantor means the enterprise that provides the warranty under the terms and conditions of a contract.

Warranty repair source means the organization specified by a warranty guarantor for receiving and managing warranty items that are returned by a customer.

Warranty tracking means the ability to trace a warranted item from delivery through completion of the effectivity of the warranty.

(b) *Reporting of data for warranty tracking and administration*. (1) The Contractor shall provide the information required by the attachment entitled "Warranty Tracking Information" on each contract line item number, subline item number, or exhibit line item number for warranted items no later than the time of award. Information required in the warranty attachment shall include such information as duration, fixed expiration, item type, starting event, usage, warranty administrator enterprise identifier, and warranty guarantor enterprise identifier.

(2) The Contractor shall provide the following information no later than when the warranted items are presented for receipt and/or acceptance—

(i) The unique item identifier for each warranted item required by the attachment entitled "Warranty Tracking Information;" and

(ii) The warranty repair source information and instructions for each warranted item required by the attachment entitled "Source of Repair Instructions".

(3) The Contractor shall submit the data for warranty tracking to the Contracting Officer with a copy to the requiring activity and the Contracting Officer Representative.

(4) For additional information on warranty attachments, see the "Warranty and Source of Repair" training and "Warranty and Source of Repair Tracking User Guide" accessible on the Product Data Reporting and Evaluation Program (PDREP) website at *https://www.pdrep.csd.disa.mil/pdrep_files/other/wsr.htm*.

(c) *Reservation of rights*. The terms of this clause shall not be construed to limit the Government's rights or remedies under any other contract clause.

(End of clause)

[Final rule, 76 FR 33166, 6/8/2011, effective 6/8/2011; Final rule, 79 FR 17448, 3/28/2014, effective 3/28/2014; Final rule, 81 FR 17041, 3/25/2016, effective 3/25/2016]

252.246-7007 Contractor Counterfeit Electronic Part Detection and Avoidance System.

As prescribed in 246.870-3(a), use the following clause:

CONTRACTOR COUNTERFEIT ELECTRONIC PART DETECTION AND AVOIDANCE SYSTEM (AUG 2016)

The following paragraphs (a) through (e) of this clause do not apply unless the Contractor is subject to the Cost Accounting Standards under 41 U.S.C. chapter 15, as implemented in regulations found at 48 CFR 9903.201-1.

(a) *Definitions*. As used in this clause—

Authorized aftermarket manufacturer means an organization that fabricates a part under a contract with, or with the express written authority of, the original component manufacturer based on the original component manufacturer's designs, formulas, and/or specifications.

Authorized supplier means a supplier, distributor, or an aftermarket manufacturer with a contractual arrangement with, or the express written authority of, the original manufacturer or current design activity to buy, stock, repackage, sell, or distribute the part.

Contract manufacturer means a company that produces goods under contract for another company under the label or brand name of that company.

Contractor-approved supplier means a supplier that does not have a contractual agreement with the original component manufacturer for a transaction, but has been identified as trustworthy by a contractor or subcontractor.

Counterfeit electronic part means an unlawful or unauthorized reproduction, substitution, or alteration that has been knowingly mismarked, misidentified, or otherwise misrepresented to be an authentic, unmodified electronic part from the original manufacturer, or a source with the express written authority of the original manufacturer or current design activity, including an authorized aftermarket manufacturer. Unlawful or unauthorized substitution includes used electronic parts represented as new, or the false identification of grade, serial number, lot number, date code, or performance characteristics.

Electronic part means an integrated circuit, a discrete electronic component (including, but not limited to, a transistor, capacitor, resistor, or diode), or a circuit assembly (section 818(f)(2) of Pub. L. 112-81).

Obsolete electronic part means an electronic part that is no longer available from the original manufacturer or an authorized aftermarket manufacturer.

Original component manufacturer means an organization that designs and/or engineers a part and is entitled to any intellectual property rights to that part.

Original equipment manufacturer means a company that manufactures products that it has designed from purchased components and sells those products under the company's brand name.

Original manufacturer means the original component manufacturer, the original equipment manufacturer, or the contract manufacturer.

Suspect counterfeit electronic part means an electronic part for which credible evidence (including, but not limited to, visual inspection or testing) provides reasonable doubt that the electronic part is authentic.

(b) *Acceptable counterfeit electronic part detection and avoidance system.* The Contractor shall establish and maintain an acceptable counterfeit electronic part detection and avoidance system. Failure to maintain an acceptable counterfeit electronic part detection and avoidance system, as defined in this clause, may result in disapproval of the purchasing system by the Contracting Officer and/or withholding of payments and affect the allowability of costs of counterfeit electronic parts or suspect counterfeit electronic parts and the cost of rework or corrective action that may be required to remedy the use or inclusion of such parts (see DFARS 231.205-71).

(c) *System criteria.* A counterfeit electronic part detection and avoidance system shall include risk-based policies and procedures that address, at a minimum, the following areas:

(1) The training of personnel.

(2) The inspection and testing of electronic parts, including criteria for acceptance and rejection. Tests and inspections shall be performed in accordance with accepted Government- and industry-recognized techniques. Selection of tests and inspections shall be based on minimizing risk to the Government. Determination of risk shall be based on the assessed probability of receiving a counterfeit electronic part; the probability that the inspection or test selected will detect a counterfeit electronic part; and the potential negative consequences of a counterfeit electronic part being installed (e.g., human safety, mission success) where such consequences are made known to the Contractor.

(3) Processes to abolish counterfeit parts proliferation.

(4) Risk-based processes that enable tracking of electronic parts from the original manufacturer to product acceptance by the Government, whether the electronic parts are supplied as discrete electronic parts or are contained in assemblies, in accordance with paragraph (c) of the clause at 252.246-7008, Sources of Electronic Parts (also see paragraph (c)(2) of this clause).

(5) Use of suppliers in accordance with the clause at 252.246-7008.

(6) Reporting and quarantining of counterfeit electronic parts and suspect counterfeit electronic parts. Reporting is required to the Contracting Officer and to the Government-Industry Data Exchange Program (GIDEP) when the Contractor becomes aware of, or has reason to suspect that, any electronic part or end item, component, part, or assembly containing electronic parts purchased by the DoD, or purchased by a Contractor for delivery to, or on behalf of, the DoD, contains counterfeit electronic parts or suspect counterfeit electronic parts. Counterfeit electronic parts and suspect counterfeit electronic parts shall not be returned to the seller or otherwise returned to the supply chain until such time that the parts are determined to be authentic.

(7) Methodologies to identify suspect counterfeit parts and to rapidly determine if

a suspect counterfeit part is, in fact, counterfeit.

(8) Design, operation, and maintenance of systems to detect and avoid counterfeit electronic parts and suspect counterfeit electronic parts. The Contractor may elect to use current Government- or industry-recognized standards to meet this requirement.

(9) Flowdown of counterfeit detection and avoidance requirements, including applicable system criteria provided herein, to subcontractors at all levels in the supply chain that are responsible for buying or selling electronic parts or assemblies containing electronic parts, or for performing authentication testing.

(10) Process for keeping continually informed of current counterfeiting information and trends, including detection and avoidance techniques contained in appropriate industry standards, and using such information and techniques for continuously upgrading internal processes.

(11) Process for screening GIDEP reports and other credible sources of counterfeiting information to avoid the purchase or use of counterfeit electronic parts.

(12) Control of obsolete electronic parts in order to maximize the availability and use of authentic, originally designed, and qualified electronic parts throughout the product's life cycle.

(d) Government review and evaluation of the Contractor's policies and procedures will be accomplished as part of the evaluation of the Contractor's purchasing system in accordance with 252.244-7001, Contractor Purchasing System Administration—Basic, or Contractor Purchasing System Administration—Alternate I.

(e) The Contractor shall include the substance of this clause, excluding the introductory text and including only paragraphs (a) through (e), in subcontracts, including subcontracts for commercial items, for electronic parts or assemblies containing electronic parts.

(End of clause)

[Final rule 79 FR 26091, 5/6/2014, effective 5/6/2014; Final rule, 81 FR 50635, 8/2/2016, effective 8/2/2016]

252.246-7008 Sources of Electronic Parts.

As prescribed in 246.870-3(b), use the following clause:

SOURCES OF ELECTRONIC PARTS (MAY 2018)

(a) *Definitions*. As used in this clause—

Authorized aftermarket manufacturer means an organization that fabricates a part under a contract with, or with the express written authority of, the original component manufacturer based on the original component manufacturer's designs, formulas, and/or specifications.

Authorized supplier means a supplier, distributor, or an aftermarket manufacturer with a contractual arrangement with, or the express written authority of, the original manufacturer or current design activity to buy, stock, repackage, sell, or distribute the part.

Contract manufacturer means a company that produces goods under contract for another company under the label or brand name of that company.

Contractor-approved supplier means a supplier that does not have a contractual agreement with the original component manufacturer for a transaction, but has been identified as trustworthy by a contractor or subcontractor.

Electronic part means an integrated circuit, a discrete electronic component (including, but not limited to, a transistor, capacitor, resistor, or diode), or a circuit assembly (section 818(f)(2) of Pub. L. 112-81).

Original component manufacturer means an organization that designs and/or engineers a part and is entitled to any intellectual property rights to that part.

Original equipment manufacturer means a company that manufactures products that it has designed from purchased components and sells those products under the company's brand name.

Original manufacturer means the original component manufacturer, the original equipment manufacturer, or the contract manufacturer.

(b) *Selecting suppliers*. In accordance with section 818(c)(3) of the National Defense Authorization Act for Fiscal Year 2012 (Pub. L. 112-81), as amended by section 817 of the National Defense Authorization Act for Fiscal Year 2015 (Pub. L. 113-291) and section 885 of the National Defense Authorization Act for Fiscal Year 2016 (Pub. L. 114-92), the Contractor shall—

(1) First obtain electronic parts that are in production by the original manufacturer or an authorized aftermarket manufacturer or currently available in stock from—

(i) The original manufacturers of the parts;

(ii) Their authorized suppliers; or

(iii) Suppliers that obtain such parts exclusively from the original manufacturers of the parts or their authorized suppliers;

(2) If electronic parts are not available as provided in paragraph (b)(1) of this clause, obtain electronic parts that are not in production by the original manufacturer or an authorized aftermarket manufacturer, and that are not currently available in stock from a source listed in paragraph (b)(1) of this clause, from suppliers identified by the Contractor as contractor-approved suppliers, provided that—

(i) For identifying and approving such contractor-approved suppliers, the Contractor uses established counterfeit prevention industry standards and processes (including inspection, testing, and authentication), such as the DoD-adopted standards at *https://assist.dla.mil*;

(ii) The Contractor assumes responsibility for the authenticity of parts provided by such contractor-approved suppliers; and

(iii) The Contractor's selection of such contractor-approved suppliers is subject to review, audit, and approval by the Government, generally in conjunction with a contractor purchasing system review or other surveillance of purchasing practices by the contract administration office, or if the Government obtains credible evidence that a contractor-approved supplier has provided counterfeit parts. The Contractor may proceed with the acquisition of electronic parts from a contractor-approved supplier unless otherwise notified by DoD; or

(3)(i) Take the actions in paragraph (b)(3)(ii) of this clause if the Contractor—

(A) Obtains an electronic part from—

(*1*) A source other than any of the sources identified in paragraph (b)(1) or (b)(2) of this clause, due to nonavailability from such sources; or

(*2*) A subcontractor (other than the original manufacturer) that refuses to accept flowdown of this clause; or

(B) Cannot confirm that an electronic part is new or previously unused and that it has not been commingled in supplier new production or stock with used, refurbished, reclaimed, or returned parts.

(ii) If the contractor obtains an electronic part or cannot confirm an electronic part pursuant to paragraph (b)(3)(i) of this clause—

(A) Promptly notify the Contracting Officer in writing. If such notification is required for an electronic part to be used in a designated lot of assemblies to be acquired under a single contract, the Contractor may submit one notification for the lot, providing identification of the assemblies containing the parts (e.g., serial numbers);

(B) Be responsible for inspection, testing, and authentication, in accordance with existing applicable industry standards; and

(C) Make documentation of inspection, testing, and authentication of such electronic parts available to the Government upon request.

(c) *Traceability*. If the Contractor is not the original manufacturer of, or authorized supplier for, an electronic part, the Contractor shall—

(1) Have risk-based processes (taking into consideration the consequences of failure of

an electronic part) that enable tracking of electronic parts from the original manufacturer to product acceptance by the Government, whether the electronic part is supplied as a discrete electronic part or is contained in an assembly;

(2) If the Contractor cannot establish this traceability from the original manufacturer for a specific electronic part, be responsible for inspection, testing, and authentication, in accordance with existing applicable industry standards; and

(3) (i) Maintain documentation of traceability (paragraph (c) (1) of this clause) or the inspection, testing, and authentication required when traceability cannot be established (paragraph (c) (2) of this clause) in accordance with FAR subpart 4.7; and

(ii) Make such documentation available to the Government upon request.

(d) *Government sources*. Contractors and subcontractors are still required to comply with the requirements of paragraphs (b) and (c) of this clause, as applicable, if—

(1) Authorized to purchase electronic parts from the Federal Supply Schedule;

(2) Purchasing electronic parts from suppliers accredited by the Defense Microelectronics Activity; or

(3) Requisitioning electronic parts from Government inventory/stock under the authority of 252.251-7000, Ordering from Government Supply Sources.

(i) The cost of any required inspection, testing, and authentication of such parts may be charged as a direct cost.

(ii) The Government is responsible for the authenticity of the requisitioned parts. If any such part is subsequently found to be counterfeit or suspect counterfeit, the Government will—

(A) Promptly replace such part at no charge; and

(B) Consider an adjustment in the contract schedule to the extent that replacement of the counterfeit or suspect counterfeit electronic parts caused a delay in performance.

(e) *Subcontracts*. The Contractor shall include the substance of this clause, including this paragraph (e), in subcontracts, including subcontracts for commercial items, that are for electronic parts or assemblies containing electronic parts, unless the subcontractor is the original manufacturer.

(End of clause)

[Final rule, 81 FR 50635, 8/2/2016, effective 8/2/2016; Final rule, 81 FR 72738, 10/21/2016, effective 10/21/2016; Final rule, 82 FR 61479, 12/28/2017, effective 12/28/2017; Final rule, 83 FR 19641, 5/4/2018, effective 5/4/2018]

252.247 Transportation, provisions and clauses for DFARS Part 247

252.247-7000 Hardship conditions.

As prescribed in 247.270-4(a), use the following clause:

HARDSHIP CONDITIONS (AUG 2000)

(a) If the Contractor finds unusual ship, dock, or cargo conditions associated with loading or unloading a particular cargo, that will work a hardship on the Contractor if loaded or unloaded at the basic commodity rates, the Contractor shall—

(1) Notify the Contracting Officer before performing the work, if feasible, but no later than the vessel sailing time; and

(2) Submit any associated request for price adjustment to the Contracting Officer within 10 working days of the vessel sailing time.

(b) Unusual conditions include, but are not limited to, inaccessibility of place of stowage to the ship's cargo gear, side port operations, and small quantities of cargo in any one hatch.

(c) The Contracting Officer will investigate the conditions promptly after receiving the notice. If the Contracting Officer finds that the conditions are unusual and do materially affect the cost of loading or unloading, the Contracting Officer will authorize payment at the applicable man-hour rates set forth in the schedule of rates of this contract.

(End of clause)

[Final rule, 65 FR 50143, 8/17/2000, effective 8/17/2000; Final rule, 75 FR 51416, 8/20/2010, effective 8/20/2010]

252.247-7001 [Removed and Reserved]

[Final rule, 62 FR 2612, 1/17/97, effective 1/17/97; Final rule, 65 FR 50143, 8/17/2000, effective 8/17/2000; Final rule, 75 FR 51416, 8/20/2010, effective 8/20/2010; Final rule, 84 FR 30952, 6/28/2019, effective 6/28/2019]

252.247-7002 Revision of prices.

As prescribed in 247.270-4(b), use the following clause:

REVISION OF PRICES (DEC 1991)

(a) *Definition. Wage adjustment*, as used in this clause, means a change in the wages, salaries, or other terms or conditions of employment which—

(1) Substantially affects the cost of performing this contract;

(2) Is generally applicable to the port where work under this contract is performed; and

(3) Applies to operations by the Contractor on non-Government work as well as to work under this contract.

(b) *General*. The prices fixed in this contract are based on wages and working conditions established by collective bargaining agreements, and on other conditions in effect on the date of this contract. The Contracting Officer and the Contractor may agree to increase or decrease such prices in accordance with this clause.

(c) *Demand for negotiation*. (1) At any time, subject to the limitations specified in this clause, either the Contracting Officer or the Contractor may deliver to the other a written demand that the parties negotiate to revise the prices under this contract.

(2) No such demand shall be made before 90 days after the date of this contract, and thereafter neither party shall make a demand having an effective date within 90 days of the effective date of any prior demand. However, this limitation does not apply to a wage adjustment during the 90 day period.

(3) Each demand shall specify a date (the same as or subsequent to the date of the delivery of the demand) as to when the revised prices shall be effective. This date is the effective date of the price revision.

(i) If the Contractor makes a demand under this clause, the demand shall briefly state the basis of the demand and include the statements and data referred to in paragraph (d) of this clause.

(ii) If the demand is made by the Contracting Officer, the Contractor shall furnish the statements and data within 30 days of the delivery of the demand.

(d) *Submission of data*. At the times specified in paragraphs (c)(3)(i) and (ii) of this clause, the Contractor shall submit—

(1) A new estimate and breakdown of the unit cost and the proposed prices for the services the Contractor will perform under this contract after the effective date of the price revision, itemized to be consistent with the original negotiations of the contract;

(2) An explanation of the difference between the original (or last preceding) estimate and the new estimate;

(3) Such relevant operating data, cost records, overhead absorption reports, and accounting statements as may be of assistance in determining the accuracy and reliability of the new estimate;

(4) A statement of the actual costs of performance under this contract to the extent that they are available at the time of the negotiation of the revision of prices under this clause; and

(5) Any other relevant data usually furnished in the case of negotiations of prices under a new contract. The Government may examine and audit the Contractor's accounts, records, and books as the Contracting Officer considers necessary.

(e) *Negotiations*. (1) Upon the filing of the statements and data required by paragraph (d) of this clause, the Contractor and the Contracting Officer shall negotiate promptly in good faith to agree upon prices for services the Contractor will perform on and after the effective date of the price revision.

(2) If the prices in this contract were established by competitive negotiation, they shall not be revised upward unless justified by changes in conditions occurring after the contract was awarded.

(3) The agreement reached after each negotiation will be incorporated into the contract by supplemental agreement.

(f) *Disagreements*. If, within 30 days after the date on which statements and data are required pursuant to paragraph (c) of this clause, the Contracting Officer and the Contractor fail to agree to revised prices, the failure to agree shall be resolved in accordance with the Disputes clause of this contract. The prices fixed by the Contracting Officer will remain in effect for the balance of the contract, and the Contractor shall continue performance.

(g) *Retroactive changes in wages or working conditions*. (1) In the event of a retroactive wage adjustment, the Contractor or the Contracting Officer may request an equitable adjustment in the prices in this contract.

(2) The Contractor shall request a price adjustment within 30 days of any retroactive wage adjustment. The Contractor shall support its request with—

(i) An estimate of the changes in cost resulting from the retroactive wage adjustment;

(ii) Complete information upon which the estimate is based; and

(iii) A certified copy of the collective bargaining agreement, arbitration award, or other document evidencing the retroactive wage adjustment.

(3) Subject to the limitation in paragraph (g) (2) of this clause as to the time of making a request, completion or termination of this contract shall not affect the Contractor's right under paragraph (g) of this clause.

(4) In case of disagreement concerning any question of fact, including whether any adjustment should be made, or the amount of such adjustment, the disagreement will be resolved in accordance with the Disputes clause of this contract.

(5) The Contractor shall notify the Contracting Officer in writing of any request by or on behalf of the employees of the Contractor which may result in a retroactive wage adjustment. The notice shall be given within 20 days after the request, or if the request occurs before contract execution, at the time of execution.

(End of clause)

[Final rule, 65 FR 50143, 8/17/2000, effective 8/17/2000; Final rule, 75 FR 51416, 8/20/2010, effective 8/20/2010; Final rule, 84 FR 30952, 6/28/2019, effective 6/28/2019]

252.247-7003 Pass-Through of Motor Carrier Fuel Surcharge Adjustment To The Cost Bearer.

As prescribed in 247.207, use the following clause:

PASS-THROUGH OF MOTOR CARRIER FUEL SURCHARGE ADJUSTMENT TO THE COST BEARER (JUN 2013)

(a) This clause implements section 884 of the National Defense Authorization Act for Fiscal Year 2009 (Pub. L. 110-417).

(b) Unless an exception is authorized by the Contracting Officer, the Contractor shall pass through any motor carrier fuel-related surcharge adjustments to the person, corporation, or entity that directly bears the cost of fuel for shipment(s) transported under this contract.

(c) The Contractor shall insert the substance of this clause, including this paragraph (c), in all subcontracts, including subcontracts for commercial items, with motor carriers, brokers, or freight forwarders.

(End of clause)

[Removed and reserved, Final rule, 65 FR 50143, 8/17/2000, effective 8/17/2000; Interim rule, 74 FR 37652, 7/29/2009, effective 7/29/2009; Final rule, 75 FR 59103, 9/27/2010, effective 9/27/2010; Final rule, 78 FR 37980, 6/25/2013, effective 6/25/2013]

252.247-7004 [Removed and Reserved]

[Final rule, 65 FR 50143, 8/17/2000, effective 8/17/2000; Final rule, 75 FR 51416, 8/20/2010, effective 8/20/2010; Final rule, 83 FR 49181, 9/28/2018, effective 9/28/2018]

252.247-7005 [Removed and Reserved]

[Final rule, 65 FR 50143, 8/17/2000, effective 8/17/2000; Final rule, 75 FR 51416, 8/20/2010, effective 8/20/2010; Final rule, 83 FR 49179, 9/28/2018, effective 9/28/2018]

252.247-7006 [Removed and Reserved]

[Final rule, 65 FR 50143, 8/17/2000, effective 8/17/2000; Final rule, 75 FR 51416, 8/20/2010, effective 8/20/2010; Final rule, 83 FR 42788, 8/24/2018, effective 8/24/2018]

252.247-7007 Liability and insurance.

As prescribed in 247.270-4(c), use the following clause;

LIABILITY AND INSURANCE (DEC 1991)

(a) The Contractor shall be—

(1) Liable to the Government for loss or damage to property, real and personal, owned by the Government or for which the Government is liable;

(2) Responsible for, and hold the Government harmless from, loss of or damage to property not included in paragraph (a)(1); and

(3) Responsible for, and hold the Government harmless from, bodily injury and death of persons, resulting either in whole or in part from the negligence or fault of the Contractor, its officers, agents, or employees in the performance of work under this contract.

(b) For the purpose of this clause, all cargo loaded or unloaded under this contract is agreed to be property owned by the Government or property for which the Government is liable.

(1) The amount of the loss or damage as determined by the Contracting Officer will be withheld from payments otherwise due the Contractor.

(2) Determination of liability and responsibility by the Contracting Officer will constitute questions of fact within the meaning of the Disputes clause of this contract.

(c) The general liability and responsibility of the Contractor under this clause are subject only to the following specific limitations. The Contractor is not responsible to the Government for, and does not agree to hold the Government harmless from, loss or damage to property or bodily injury to or death of persons if—

(1) The unseaworthiness of the vessel, or failure or defect of the gear or equipment furnished by the Government, contributed jointly with the fault or negligence of the Contractor in causing such damage, injury, or death; and

(i) The Contractor, his officers, agents, and employees, by the exercise of due diligence, could not have discovered such unseaworthiness or defect of gear or equipment; or

(ii) Through the exercise of due diligence could not otherwise have avoided such damage, injury, or death.

(2) The damage, injury, or death resulted solely from an act or omission of the Government or its employees, or resulted solely from proper compliance by officers, agents, or employees of the Contractor with specific directions of the Contracting Officer.

(d) The Contractor shall at its own expense acquire and maintain insurance during the term of this contract, as follows—

(1) Standard workmen's compensation and employer's liability insurance and longshoremen's and harbor workers' compensation insurance, or such of these as may be proper under applicable state or Federal statutes.

(i) The Contractor may, with the prior approval of the Contracting Officer, be a self-insurer against the risk of this paragraph (d)(1).

(ii) This approval will be given upon receipt of satisfactory evidence that the Contractor has qualified as a self-insurer under applicable provision of law.

(2) Bodily injury liability insurance in an amount of not less than $300,000 on account of any one occurrence.

(3) Property damage liability insurance (which shall include any and all property, whether or not in the care, custody, or control of the Contractor) in an amount of not less than $300,000 for any one occurrence.

(e) Each policy shall provide, by appropriate endorsement or otherwise, that cancellation or material change in the policy shall not be effective until after a 30 day written notice is furnished the Contracting Officer.

(f) The Contractor shall furnish the Contracting Officer with satisfactory evidence of the insurance required in paragraph (d) before performance of any work under this contract.

(g) The Contractor shall, at its own cost and expense, defend any suits, demands, claims, or actions, in which the United States might be named as a co-defendant of the Contractor, resulting from the Contractor's performance of work under this contract. This requirement is without regard to whether such suit, demand, claim, or action was the result of the Contractor's negligence. The Government shall have the right to appear in such suit, participate in defense, and take such actions as may be necessary to protect the interest of the United States.

(h) It is expressly agreed that the provisions in paragraphs (d) through (g) of this clause shall not in any manner limit the liability or extend the liability of the Contractor as provided in paragraphs (a) through (c) of this clause.

(i) The Contractor shall—

(1) Equitably reimburse the Government if the Contractor is indemnified, reimbursed, or relieved of any loss or damage to Government property;

(2) Do nothing to prevent the Government's right to recover against third parties for any such loss or damage; and

(3) Furnish the Government, upon the request of the Contracting Officer, at the Government's expense, all reasonable assistance and cooperation in obtaining recovery, including the prosecution of suit and the execution of instruments of assignment in favor of the Government.

(End of clause)

[Final rule, 65 FR 50143, 8/17/2000, effective 8/17/2000; Final rule, 75 FR 51416, 8/20/2010, effective 8/20/2010; Final rule, 83 FR 42788, 8/24/2018, effective 8/24/2018; Final rule, 83 FR 49179, 9/28/2018, effective 9/28/2018; Final rule, 83 FR 49181, 9/28/2018, effective 9/28/2018; Final rule, 84 FR 30952, 6/28/2019, effective 6/28/2019]

252.247-7008 [Removed and Reserved]

[Final rule, 75 FR 51416, 8/20/2010, effective 8/20/2010; Final rule, 79 FR 22036, 4/21/2014, effective 4/21/2014; Final rule, 80 FR 36897, 6/26/2015, effective 6/26/2015; Final rule, 84 FR 30950, 6/28/2019, effective 6/28/2019]

252.247-7009 [Removed and Reserved]

[Final rule, 75 FR 51416, 8/20/2010, effective 8/20/2010; Final rule, 84 FR 30950, 6/28/2019, effective 6/28/2019]

252.247-7010 [Removed and Reserved]

[Final rule, 75 FR 51416, 8/20/2010, effective 8/20/2010; Final rule, 84 FR 30950, 6/28/2019, effective 6/28/2019]

252.247-7011 [Removed and Reserved]

[Final rule, 56 FR 36479, 7/31/91; Final rule, 66 FR 49860, 10/1/2001, effective 10/1/2001; Final rule, 75 FR 51416, 8/20/2010, effective 8/20/2010; Final rule, 84 FR 30950, 6/28/2019, effective 6/28/2019]

252.247-7012 [Removed and Reserved]

[Final rule, 75 FR 51416, 8/20/2010, effective 8/20/2010; Final rule, 84 FR 25194, 5/31/2019, effective 5/31/2019]

252.247-7013 [Removed and Reserved]

[Final rule, 75 FR 51416, 8/20/2010, effective 8/20/2010; Final rule, 84 FR 25194, 5/31/2019, effective 5/31/2019; Final rule, 84 FR 30950, 6/28/2019, effective 6/28/2019]

252.247-7014 Demurrage.

As prescribed in 247.271-3(c), use the following clause:

DEMURRAGE (DEC 1991)

The Contractor shall be liable for all demurrage, detention, or other charges as a result of its failure to load or unload trucks, freight cars, freight terminals, vessel piers, or warehouses within the free time allowed under applicable rules and tariffs.

(End of clause)

[Final rule, 75 FR 51416, 8/20/2010, effective 8/20/2010; Final rule, 84 FR 25194, 5/31/2019, effective 5/31/2019; Final rule, 84 FR 30950, 6/28/2019, effective 6/28/2019]

252.247-7015 [Removed and Reserved]

[Final rule, 65 FR 63804, 10/25/2000, effective 10/25/2000, Removed and reserved, Final rule, 79 FR 22036, 4/21/2014, effective 4/21/2014]

252.247-7016 Contractor liability for loss or damage.

As prescribed in 247.271-3(d), use the following clause:

CONTRACTOR LIABILITY FOR LOSS OR DAMAGE (DEC 1991)

(a) *Definitions.*

As used in this clause—

Article means any shipping piece or package and its contents.

Schedule means the level of service for which specific types of traffic apply as described in DoD 4500.34-R, Personal Property Traffic Management Regulation.

(b) For shipments picked up under Schedule I, Outbound Services, or delivered under Schedule II, Inbound Services—

(1) If notified within one year after delivery that the owner has discovered loss or damage to the owner's property, the Contractor agrees to indemnify the Government for loss or damage to the property which arises from any cause while it is in the Contractor's possession. The Contractor's liability is—

(i) *Non-negligent damage.* For any cause, other than the Contractor's negligence, indemnification shall be at a rate not to exceed sixty cents per pound per article.

(ii) *Negligent damage.* When loss or damage is caused by the negligence of the Contractor, the liability is for the full cost of satisfactory repair or for the current replacement value of the article.

(2) The Contractor shall make prompt payment to the owner of the property for any loss or damage for which the Contractor is liable.

(3) In the absence of evidence or supporting documentation which places liability on a carrier or another contractor, the destination contractor shall be presumed to be liable for the loss or damage, if timely notified.

(c) For shipments picked up or delivered under Schedule III, Intra-City and Intra-Area—

(1) If notified of loss or damage within 75 days following delivery, the Contractor agrees to indemnify the Government for loss or damage to the owner's property.

(2) The Contractor's liability shall be for the full cost of satisfactory repair, or for the current replacement value of the article less depreciation, up to a maximum liability of $1.25 per pound times the net weight of the shipment.

(3) The Contractor has full salvage rights to damaged items which are not repairable and for which the Government has received compensation at replacement value.

(End of clause)

[Final rule, 75 FR 51416, 8/20/2010, effective 8/20/2010; Final rule, 84 FR 25194, 5/31/2019, effective 5/31/2019; Final rule, 84 FR 30950, 6/28/2019, effective 6/28/2019]

252.247-7017 [Removed and Reserved]

[Final rule, 75 FR 51416, 8/20/2010, effective 8/20/2010; Final rule, 84 FR 25194, 5/31/2019, effective 5/31/2019; Final rule, 84 FR 30950, 6/28/2019, effective 6/28/2019]

252.247-7018 [Removed and Reserved]

[Final rule, 75 FR 51416, 8/20/2010, effective 8/20/2010; Final rule, 84 FR 25194, 5/31/2019, effective 5/31/2019; Final rule, 84 FR 30950, 6/28/2019, effective 6/28/2019]

252.247-7019 [Removed and Reserved]

[Final rule, 75 FR 51416, 8/20/2010, effective 8/20/2010; Final rule, 84 FR 25194, 5/31/2019, effective 5/31/2019; Final rule, 84 FR 30950, 6/28/2019, effective 6/28/2019]

252.247-7020 [Removed and Reserved]

[Final rule, 65 FR 50143, 8/17/2000, effective 8/17/2000; Final rule, 75 FR 51416, 8/20/2010, effective 8/20/2010; Final rule, 82 FR 61479, 12/28/2017, effective 12/28/2017; Final rule, 83 FR 49178, 9/28/2018, effective 9/28/2018]

252.247-7021 [Removed and Reserved]

[DAC 91-7, 60 FR 29491, 6/5/95, effective 5/17/95; Final rule, 84 FR 48506, 9/13/2019, effective 9/13/2019]

252.247-7022 Representation of extent of transportation by sea.

As prescribed in 247.574(a), use the following provision:

REPRESENTATION OF EXTENT OF TRANSPORTATION BY SEA (JUN 2019)

(a) The Offeror shall indicate by checking the appropriate blank in paragraph (b) of this provision whether transportation of supplies by sea is anticipated under the resultant contract. The term *supplies* is defined in the Transportation of Supplies by Sea clause of this solicitation.

(b) *Representation*. The Offeror represents that it

__Does anticipate that supplies will be transported by sea in the performance of any contract or subcontract resulting from this solicitation.

__Does not anticipate that supplies will be transported by sea in the performance of any contract or subcontract resulting from this solicitation.

(c) Any contract resulting from this solicitation will include the Transportation of Supplies by Sea clause.

(End of provision)

[DAC 91-3, 57 FR 42633, 9/15/92, effective 8/31/92; Interim rule, 72 49204, 8/28/2007, effective 8/28/2007; Final rule, 73 FR 70909, 11/24/2008, effective 11/24/2008; Final rule, 84 FR 30950, 6/28/2019, effective 6/28/2019]

252.247-7023 Transportation of Supplies by Sea.

Basic. As prescribed in 247.574(b) and (b)(1), use the following clause.

TRANSPORTATION OF SUPPLIES BY SEA—BASIC (FEB 2019)

(a) *Definitions*. As used in this clause—

Components means articles, materials, and supplies incorporated directly into end products at any level of manufacture, fabrication, or assembly by the Contractor or any subcontractor.

Department of Defense (DoD) means the Army, Navy, Air Force, Marine Corps, and defense agencies.

Foreign-flag vessel means any vessel that is not a U.S.-flag vessel.

Ocean transportation means any transportation aboard a ship, vessel, boat, barge, or ferry through international waters.

Subcontractor means a supplier, materialman, distributor, or vendor at any level below the prime contractor whose contractual obligation to perform results from, or is conditioned upon, award of the prime contract and who is performing any part of the work or other requirement of the prime contract.

Supplies means all property, except land and interests in land, that is clearly identifiable for eventual use by or owned by the DoD at the time of transportation by sea.

(i) An item is clearly identifiable for eventual use by the DoD if, for example, the contract documentation contains a reference to a DoD contract number or a military destination.

(ii) *Supplies* includes (but is not limited to) public works; buildings and facilities; ships; floating equipment and vessels of every character, type, and description, with parts, subassemblies, accessories, and equipment; machine tools; material; equipment; stores of all kinds; end items; construction materials; and components of the foregoing.

U.S.-flag vessel means a vessel of the United States or belonging to the United States, including any vessel registered or having national status under the laws of the United States.

(b)(1) The Contractor shall use U.S.-flag vessels when transporting any supplies by sea under this contract.

(2) A subcontractor transporting supplies by sea under this contract shall use U.S.-flag vessels if—

(i) This contract is a construction contract; or

(ii) The supplies being transported are—

(A) Noncommercial items; or

(B) Commercial items that—

(*1*) The Contractor is reselling or distributing to the Government without adding value (generally, the Contractor does not add value to items that it contracts for f.o.b. destination shipment);

(*2*) Are shipped in direct support of U.S. military contingency operations, exercises, or forces deployed in humanitarian or peacekeeping operations; or

(*3*) Are commissary or exchange cargoes transported outside of the Defense Transportation System in accordance with 10 U.S.C. 2643.

(c) The Contractor and its subcontractors may request that the Contracting Officer authorize shipment in foreign-flag vessels, or designate available U.S.-flag vessels, if the Contractor or a subcontractor believes that—

(1) U.S.-flag vessels are not available for timely shipment;

(2) The freight charges are inordinately excessive or unreasonable; or

(3) Freight charges are higher than charges to private persons for transportation of like goods.

(d) The Contractor must submit any request for use of foreign-flag vessels in writing to the Contracting Officer at least 45 days prior to the sailing date necessary to meet its delivery schedules. The Contracting Officer will process requests submitted after such date(s) as expeditiously as possible, but the Contracting Officer's failure to grant approvals to meet the shipper's sailing date will not of itself constitute a compensable delay under this or any other clause of this contract. Requests shall contain at a minimum—

(1) Type, weight, and cube of cargo;

(2) Required shipping date;

(3) Special handling and discharge requirements;

(4) Loading and discharge points;

(5) Name of shipper and consignee;

(6) Prime contract number; and

(7) A documented description of efforts made to secure U.S.-flag vessels, including points of contact (with names and telephone numbers) with at least two U.S.-flag carriers contacted. Copies of telephone notes, telegraphic and facsimile messages or letters will be sufficient for this purpose.

(e) The Contractor shall, within 30 days after each shipment covered by this clause, provide the Contracting Officer and the Maritime Administration, Office of Cargo Preference, U.S. Department of Transportation, 400 Seventh Street SW., Washington, DC 20590, one copy of the rated on board vessel operating carrier's ocean bill of lading, which shall contain the following information:

(1) Prime contract number;

(2) Name of vessel;

(3) Vessel flag of registry;

(4) Date of loading;

(5) Port of loading;

(6) Port of final discharge;

(7) Description of commodity;

(8) Gross weight in pounds and cubic feet if available;

(9) Total ocean freight in U.S. dollars; and

(10) Name of the steamship company.

(f) If this contract exceeds the simplified acquisition threshold, the Contractor shall provide with its final invoice under this contract a representation that to the best of its knowledge and belief—

(1) No ocean transportation was used in the performance of this contract;

(2) Ocean transportation was used and only U.S.-flag vessels were used for all ocean shipments under the contract;

(3) Ocean transportation was used, and the Contractor had the written consent of the Contracting Officer for all foreign-flag ocean transportation; or

(4) Ocean transportation was used and some or all of the shipments were made on foreign-flag vessels without the written consent of the Contracting Officer. The Contractor shall describe these shipments in the following format:

Item Description	Contract Line items	Quantity
Total		

(g) If this contract exceeds the simplified acquisition threshold and the final invoice does not include the required representation, the Government will reject and return it to the Contractor as an improper invoice for the purposes of the Prompt Payment clause of this contract. In the event there has been unauthorized use of foreign-flag vessels in the performance of this contract, the Contracting Officer is entitled to equitably adjust the contract, based on the unauthorized use.

(h) If the Contractor has indicated by the response to the solicitation provision, Representation of Extent of Transportation by Sea, that it did not anticipate transporting by sea any supplies; however, after the award of this contract, the Contractor learns that supplies will be transported by sea, the Contractor—

(1) Shall notify the Contracting Officer of that fact; and

(2) Hereby agrees to comply with all the terms and conditions of this clause.

(i) In the award of subcontracts for the types of supplies described in paragraph (b)(2) of this clause, including subcontracts for commercial items, the Contractor shall flow down the requirements of this clause as follows:

(1) The Contractor shall insert the substance of this clause, including this paragraph (i), in subcontracts that exceed the simplified acquisition threshold in part 2 of the Federal Acquisition Regulation.

(2) The Contractor shall insert the substance of paragraphs (a) through (e) of this clause, and this paragraph (i), in subcontracts that are at or below the simplified acquisition threshold in part 2 of the Federal Acquisition Regulation.

(End of clause)

Alternate I. As prescribed in 247.574(b) and (b)(2), use the following clause, which uses a different paragraph (b) than the basic clause:

TRANSPORTATION OF SUPPLIES BY SEA—ALTERNATE I (FEB 2019)

(a) *Definitions.* As used in this clause—

Components means articles, materials, and supplies incorporated directly into end products at any level of manufacture, fabrication, or assembly by the Contractor or any subcontractor.

Department of Defense (DoD) means the Army, Navy, Air Force, Marine Corps, and defense agencies.

Foreign-flag vessel means any vessel that is not a U.S.-flag vessel.

Ocean transportation means any transportation aboard a ship, vessel, boat, barge, or ferry through international waters.

Subcontractor means a supplier, materialman, distributor, or vendor at any level below the prime contractor whose contractual obligation to perform results from, or is conditioned upon, award of the prime contract and who is performing any part of the work or other requirement of the prime contract.

Supplies means all property, except land and interests in land, that is clearly identifiable for eventual use by or owned by the DoD at the time of transportation by sea.

(i) An item is clearly identifiable for eventual use by the DoD if, for example, the contract documentation contains a reference to a DoD contract number or a military destination.

(ii) *Supplies* includes (but is not limited to) public works; buildings and facilities; ships; floating equipment and vessels of every character, type, and description, with parts, subassemblies, accessories, and equipment; machine tools; material; equipment; stores of all kinds; end items; construction materials; and components of the foregoing.

U.S.-flag vessel means a vessel of the United States or belonging to the United States, including any vessel registered or having national status under the laws of the United States.

(b)(1) The Contractor shall use U.S.-flag vessels when transporting any supplies by sea under this contract.

(2) A subcontractor transporting supplies by sea under this contract shall use U.S.-flag vessels if the supplies being transported are—

(i) Noncommercial items; or

(ii) Commercial items that—

(A) The Contractor is reselling or distributing to the Government without adding value (generally, the Contractor does not add value to items that it subcontracts for f.o.b. destination shipment);

(B) Are shipped in direct support of U.S. military contingency operations, exercises, or forces deployed in humanitarian or peacekeeping operations (Note: This contract requires shipment of commercial items in direct support of U.S. military contingency operations, exercises, or forces deployed in humanitarian or peacekeeping operations); or

(C) Are commissary or exchange cargoes transported outside of the Defense Transportation System in accordance with 10 U.S.C. 2643.

(c) The Contractor and its subcontractors may request that the Contracting Officer authorize shipment in foreign-flag vessels, or designate available U.S.-flag vessels, if the Contractor or a subcontractor believes that—

(1) U.S.-flag vessels are not available for timely shipment;

(2) The freight charges are inordinately excessive or unreasonable; or

(3) Freight charges are higher than charges to private persons for transportation of like goods.

(d) The Contractor must submit any request for use of foreign flag vessels in writing to the Contracting Officer at least 45 days prior to the sailing date necessary to meet its delivery schedules. The Contracting Officer will process requests submitted after such date(s) as expeditiously as possible, but the Contracting Officer's failure to grant approvals to meet the shipper's sailing date will not of itself constitute a compensable delay under this or any other clause of this contract. Requests shall contain at a minimum—

(1) Type, weight, and cube of cargo;

(2) Required shipping date;

(3) Special handling and discharge requirements;

(4) Loading and discharge points;

(5) Name of shipper and consignee;

(6) Prime contract number; and

(7) A documented description of efforts made to secure U.S.- flag vessels, including points of contact (with names and telephone numbers) with at least two U.S.-flag carriers contacted. Copies of telephone notes, tele-

graphic and facsimile message or letters will be sufficient for this purpose.

(e) The Contractor shall, within 30 days after each shipment covered by this clause, provide the Contracting Officer and the Maritime Administration, Office of Cargo Preference, U.S. Department of Transportation, 400 Seventh Street SW, Washington, DC 20590, one copy of the rated on board vessel operating carrier's ocean bill of lading, which shall contain the following information:

(1) Prime contract number;

(2) Name of vessel;

(3) Vessel flag of registry;

(4) Date of loading;

(5) Port of loading;

(6) Port of final discharge;

(7) Description of commodity;

(8) Gross weight in pounds and cubic feet if available;

(9) Total ocean freight in U.S. dollars; and

(10) Name of steamship company.

(f) If this contract exceeds the simplified acquisition threshold, the Contractor shall provide with its final invoice under this contract a representation that to the best of its knowledge and belief—

(1) No ocean transportation was used in the performance of this contract;

(2) Ocean transportation was used and only U.S.-flag vessels were used for all ocean shipments under the contract;

(3) Ocean transportation was used, and the Contractor had the written consent of the Contracting Officer for all foreign-flag ocean transportation; or

(4) Ocean transportation was used and some or all of the shipments were made on foreign-flag vessels without the written consent of the Contracting Officer. The Contractor shall describe these shipments in the following format:

Item Description	Contract Line items	Quantity
Total		

(g) If this contract exceeds the simplified acquisition threshold and the final invoice does not include the required representation, the Government will reject and return it to the Contractor as an improper invoice for the purposes of the Prompt Payment clause of this contract. In the event there has been unauthorized use of foreign-flag vessels in the performance of this contract, the Contracting Officer is entitled to equitably adjust the contract, based on the unauthorized use.

(h) If the Contractor has indicated by the response to the solicitation provision, Representation of Extent of Transportation by Sea, that it did not anticipate transporting by sea any supplies; however, after the award of this contract, the Contractor learns that supplies will be transported by sea, the Contractor—

(1) Shall notify the Contracting Officer of that fact; and

(2) Hereby agrees to comply with all the terms and conditions of this clause.

(i) In the award of subcontracts for the types of supplies described in paragraph (b)(2) of this clause, including subcontracts for commercial items, the Contractor shall flow down the requirements of this clause as follows:

(1) The Contractor shall insert the substance of this clause, including this paragraph (i), in subcontracts that exceed the simplified acquisition threshold in part 2 of the Federal Acquisition Regulation.

(2) The Contractor shall insert the substance of paragraphs (a) through (e) of this clause, and this paragraph (i), in subcontracts that are at or below the simplified acquisition threshold in part 2 of the Federal Acquisition Regulation.

(End of clause)

Alternate II. As prescribed in 247.574(b) and (b)(3), use the following clause, which uses a different paragraph (b) than the basic clause:

TRANSPORTATION OF SUPPLIES BY SEA—ALTERNATE II (FEB 2019)

(a) *Definitions*. As used in this clause—

Components means articles, materials, and supplies incorporated directly into end products at any level of manufacture, fabrication, or assembly by the Contractor or any subcontractor.

Department of Defense (DoD) means the Army, Navy, Air Force, Marine Corps, and defense agencies.

Foreign-flag vessel means any vessel that is not a U.S.-flag vessel.

Ocean transportation means any transportation aboard a ship, vessel, boat, barge, or ferry through international waters.

Subcontractor means a supplier, materialman, distributor, or vendor at any level below the prime contractor whose contractual obligation to perform results from, or is conditioned upon, award of the prime contract and who is performing any part of the work or other requirement of the prime contract.

Supplies means all property, except land and interests in land, that is clearly identifiable for eventual use by or owned by the DoD at the time of transportation by sea.

(i) An item is clearly identifiable for eventual use by the DoD if, for example, the contract documentation contains a reference to a DoD contract number or a military destination.

(ii) *Supplies* includes (but is not limited to) public works; buildings and facilities; ships; floating equipment and vessels of every character, type, and description, with parts, subassemblies, accessories, and equipment; machine tools; material; equipment; stores of all kinds; end items; construction materials; and components of the foregoing.

U.S.-flag vessel means a vessel of the United States or belonging to the United States, including any vessel registered or having national status under the laws of the United States.

(b)(1) The Contractor shall use U.S.-flag vessels when transporting any supplies by sea under this contract.

(2) A subcontractor transporting supplies by sea under this contract shall use U.S.-flag vessels if the supplies being transported are—

(i) Noncommercial items; or

(ii) Commercial items that—

(A) The Contractor is reselling or distributing to the Government without adding value (generally, the Contractor does not add value to items that it subcontracts for f.o.b. destination shipment);

(B) Are shipped in direct support of U.S. military contingency operations, exercises, or forces deployed in humanitarian or peacekeeping operations; or

(C) Are commissary or exchange cargoes transported outside of the Defense Transportation System in accordance with 10 U.S.C. 2643 (Note: This contract requires transportation of commissary or exchange cargoes outside of the Defense Transportation System in accordance with 10 U.S.C. 2643).

(c) The Contractor and its subcontractors may request that the Contracting Officer authorize shipment in foreign-flag vessels, or designate available U.S.-flag vessels, if the Contractor or a subcontractor believes that—

(1) U.S.-flag vessels are not available for timely shipment;

(2) The freight charges are inordinately excessive or unreasonable; or

(3) Freight charges are higher than charges to private persons for transportation of like goods.

(d) The Contractor must submit any request for use of foreign flag vessels in writing to the Contracting Officer at least 45 days prior to the sailing date necessary to meet its delivery schedules. The Contracting Officer will process requests submitted after such date(s) as expeditiously as possible, but the Contracting Officer's failure to grant approvals to meet the shipper's sailing date will not of itself constitute a compensable delay under this or any other clause of this contract. Requests shall contain at a minimum—

(1) Type, weight, and cube of cargo;

(2) Required shipping date;

3) Special handling and discharge requirements;

(4) Loading and discharge points;

(5) Name of shipper and consignee;

(6) Prime contract number; and

(7) A documented description of efforts made to secure U.S.- flag vessels, including points of contact (with names and telephone numbers) with at least two U.S.-flag carriers contacted. Copies of telephone notes, telegraphic and facsimile message or letters will be sufficient for this purpose.

(e) The Contractor shall, within 30 days after each shipment covered by this clause, provide the Contracting Officer and the Maritime Administration, Office of Cargo Preference, U.S. Department of Transportation, 400 Seventh Street SW, Washington, DC 20590, one copy of the rated on board vessel operating carrier's ocean bill of lading, which shall contain the following information:

(1) Prime contract number;

(2) Name of vessel;

(3) Vessel flag of registry;

(4) Date of loading;

(5) Port of loading;

(6) Port of final discharge;

(7) Description of commodity;

(8) Gross weight in pounds and cubic feet if available;

(9) Total ocean freight in U.S. dollars; and

(10) Name of steamship company.

(f) If this contract exceeds the simplified acquisition threshold, the Contractor shall provide with its final invoice under this contract a representation that to the best of its knowledge and belief—

(1) No ocean transportation was used in the performance of this contract;

(2) Ocean transportation was used and only U.S.-flag vessels were used for all ocean shipments under the contract;

(3) Ocean transportation was used, and the Contractor had the written consent of the Contracting Officer for all foreign-flag ocean transportation; or

(4) Ocean transportation was used and some or all of the shipments were made on foreign-flag vessels without the written consent of the Contracting Officer. The Contractor shall describe these shipments in the following format:

Item Description	Contract Line items	Quantity
Total		

(g) If this contract exceeds the simplified acquisition threshold and the final invoice does not include the required representation, the Government will reject and return it to the Contractor as an improper invoice for the purposes of the Prompt Payment clause of this contract. In the event there has been unauthorized use of foreign-flag vessels in the performance of this contract, the Contracting Officer is entitled to equitably adjust the contract, based on the unauthorized use.

(h) If the Contractor has indicated by the response to the solicitation provision, Representation of Extent of Transportation by Sea, that it did not anticipate transporting by sea any supplies, but the contractor learns after the award of the contract that supplies will be transported by sea, the Contractor shall notify the Contracting Officer of that fact.

(i) In the award of subcontracts for the types of supplies described in paragraph (b)(2) of this clause, including subcontracts for commercial items, the Contractor shall flow down the requirements of this clause as follows:

(1) The Contractor shall insert the substance of this clause, including this paragraph (i), in subcontracts that exceed the simplified acquisition threshold in part 2 of the Federal Acquisition Regulation.

(2) The Contractor shall insert the substance of paragraphs (a) through (e) of this clause, and this paragraph (i), in subcontracts that are at or below the simplified acquisition threshold in part 2 of the Federal Acquisition Regulation.

(End of clause)

[DAC 91-9, 60 FR 61586, 11/30/95, effective 11/30/95; Final rule, 65 FR 14400, 3/16/2000, effective 3/16/2000; Final rule, 67 FR 38020, 5/31/2002, effective 5/31/2002; Final rule, 67 FR 49251, 7/30/2002, effective 7/30/2002; Interim rule, 72 FR 49204, 8/28/2007, effective 8/28/2007; Final rule, 73 FR 70909, 11/24/2008, effective 11/24/2008; Final rule, 77 FR 76936, 12/31/2012, effective 12/31/2012; Final rule, 78 FR 37980, 6/25/2013, effective 6/25/2013; Final rule, 79 FR 22036, 4/21/2014, effective 4/21/2014; Final rule, 80 FR 36897, 6/26/2015, effective 6/26/2015; Final rule, 84 FR 4370, 2/15/2019, effective 2/15/2019]

252.247-7024 [Removed and Reserved]

[DAC 91-9, 60 FR 61586, 11/30/95, effective 11/30/95; Final rule, 65 FR 14400, 3/16/2000, effective 3/16/2000; Interim rule, 72 FR 49204, 8/28/2007, effective 8/28/2007; Final rule, 73 FR 70909, 11/24/2008, effective 11/24/2008; Final rule, 84 FR 4370, 2/15/2019, effective 2/15/2019]

252.247-7025 Reflagging or Repair Work.

As prescribed in 247.574(c), use the following clause:

REFLAGGING OR REPAIR WORK (JUN 2005)

(a) *Definition. Reflagging or repair work*, as used in this clause, means work performed on a vessel—

(1) To enable the vessel to meet applicable standards to become a vessel of the United States; or

(2) To convert the vessel to a more useful military configuration.

(b) *Requirement*. Unless the Secretary of Defense waives this requirement, reflagging or repair work shall be performed in the United States or its outlying areas, if the reflagging or repair work is performed—

(1) On a vessel for which the Contractor submitted an offer in response to the solicitation for this contract; and

(2) Prior to acceptance of the vessel by the Government.

(End of clause)

[DAC 91-7, 60 FR 29491, 6/5/95, effective 5/17/95; Final rule, 70 FR 35543, 6/21/2005, effective 6/21/2005; Interim rule, 72 FR 49204, 8/28/2007, effective 8/28/2007; Final rule, 73 FR 70909, 11/24/2008, effective 11/24/2008; Final rule, 84 FR 4370, 2/15/2019, effective 2/15/2019]

252.247-7026 Evaluation Preference for Use of Domestic Shipyards—Applicable to Acquisition of Carriage by Vessel for DoD Cargo in the Coastwise or Noncontiguous Trade.

As prescribed in 247.574(d), use the following provision:

EVALUATION PREFERENCE FOR USE OF DOMESTIC SHIPYARDS—APPLICABLE TO ACQUISITION OF CARRIAGE BY VESSEL FOR DoD CARGO IN THE COASTWISE OR NONCONTIGUOUS TRADE (NOV 2008)

(a) *Definitions*. As used in this provision—

Covered vessel means a vessel—

(1) Owned, operated, or controlled by the offeror; and

(2) Qualified to engage in the carriage of cargo in the coastwise or noncontiguous trade under Section 27 of the Merchant Marine Act, 1920 (46 U.S.C. 12101, 12132, and 55102), commonly referred to as "Jones Act"; 46 U.S.C. 12102, 12112, and 12119; and Section 2 of the Shipping Act, 1916 (46 U.S.C. 50501).

Foreign shipyard means a shipyard that is not a U.S. shipyard.

Overhaul, repair, and maintenance work means work requiring a shipyard period greater than or equal to 5 calendar days.

Shipyard means a facility capable of performing overhaul, repair, and maintenance work on covered vessels.

U.S. shipyard means a shipyard that is located in any State of the United States or in Guam.

(b) This solicitation includes an evaluation criterion that considers the extent to which the offeror has had overhaul, repair, and maintenance work for covered vessels performed in U.S. shipyards.

(c) The offeror shall provide the following information with its offer, addressing all covered vessels for which overhaul, repair, and maintenance work has been performed during the period covering the current calendar year, up to the date of proposal submission, and the preceding four calendar years:

(1) Name of vessel.

(2) Description and cost of qualifying shipyard work performed in U.S. shipyards.

(3) Description and cost of qualifying shipyard work performed in foreign shipyards and whether—

(i) Such work was performed as emergency repairs in foreign shipyards due to accident, emergency, Act of God, or an infirmity to the vessel, and safety considerations warranted taking the vessel to a foreign shipyard; or

(ii) Such work was paid for or reimbursed by the U.S. Government.

(4) Names of shipyards that performed the work.

(5) Inclusive dates of work performed.

(d) Offerors are responsible for submitting accurate information. The Contracting Officer—

(1) Will use the information to evaluate offers in accordance with the criteria specified in the solicitation; and

(2) Reserves the right to request supporting documentation if determined necessary in the proposal evaluation process.

(e) The Department of Defense will provide the information submitted in response to this provision to the congressional defense committees, as required by Section 1017 of Public Law 109-364.

(End of provision)

[Interim rule, 72 FR 49204, 8/28/2007, effective 8/28/2007; Final rule, 73 FR 70909, 11/24/2008, effective 11/24/2008; Final rule, 84 FR 4370, 2/15/2019, effective 2/15/2019]

252.247-7027 Riding gang member requirements.

As prescribed in 247.574(e), use the following clause:

RIDING GANG MEMBER REQUIREMENTS (MAY 2018)

(a) *Definition. Riding gang member,* as used in this clause, has the same definition as *riding gang member* in title 46 U.S.C. 2101.

(b) *Requirements relating to riding gang members.* Notwithstanding 46 U.S.C. 8106, the Contractor shall ensure each riding gang member holds a valid U.S. Merchant Mariner's Document issued under 46 U.S.C. chapter 73, or a transportation security card issued under section 70105 of such title.

(c) *Exemption.*

(1) An individual is exempt from the requirements of paragraph (b) of this clause and shall not be treated as a riding gang member for the purposes of section 8106 of title 46, if that individual is on a vessel for purposes other than engaging in the operation or maintenance of the vessel and is—

(i) One of the personnel who accompanies, supervises, guards, or maintains unit equipment aboard a ship, commonly referred to as supercargo personnel;

(ii) One of the force protection personnel of the vessel;

(iii) A specialized repair technician; or

(iv) An individual who is otherwise required by the Secretary of Defense or designee to be aboard the vessel.

(2) Any individual who is exempt under paragraph (c)(1) of this clause must pass a DoD background check before going aboard the vessel.

(i) The Contractor shall—

(A) Render all necessary assistance to U.S. Armed Forces personnel with respect to the identification and screening of exempted individuals. This will require, at a minimum, the Contractor to submit the name and other biographical information necessary to the Government official specified in the contract for the purposes of conducting a background check; and

(B) Deny access or immediately remove any individual(s) from the vessel deemed unsuitable for any reason by the Government agency conducting the background checks. The Contractor agrees to replace any such individual promptly and require such replacements to fully comply with all screening requirements.

(ii) The head of the contracting activity may waive this requirement if the individual possesses a valid U.S. Merchant Mariner's Document issued under 46 U.S.C. chapter 73, or a transportation security card issued under section 70105 of such title.

(3) An individual exempted under paragraph (c)(1) of this clause is not treated as a riding gang member and shall not be counted as an individual in addition to the crew for the purposes of 46 U.S.C. 3304.

(End of clause)

[Interim rule, 75 FR 65437, 10/25/2010, effective 10/25/2010; Final rule, 76 FR 61279, 10/4/2011, effective 10/4/2011; Final rule, 83 FR 24891, 5/30/2018, effective 5/30/2018; Final rule, 84 FR 4370, 2/15/2019, effective 2/15/2019]

252.247-7028 Application for U.S. Government Shipping Documentation/Instructions.

As prescribed in 247.207, use the following clause:

APPLICATION FOR U.S. GOVERNMENT SHIPPING DOCUMENTATION/ INSTRUCTIONS (JUN 2012)

(a) Except as provided in paragraph (b) of this clause, the Contractor shall request bills of lading by submitting a DD Form 1659, Application for U.S. Government Shipping Documentation/Instructions, to the—

(1) Transportation Officer, if named in the contract schedule; or

(2) Contract administration office.

(b) If an automated system is available for shipment requests, use service/agency systems (e.g., Navy's Global Freight Management-Electronic Transportation Acquisition (GFM-ETA) and Financial Air Clearance Transportation System (FACTS) Shipment Processing Module, Air Force's Cargo Movement Operations System, DCMA's Shipment Instruction Request (SIR) E-tool, and DLA's Distribution Standard System Vendor Shipment Module in lieu of DD Form 1659.

(End of clause)

[Final rule, 77 FR 39140, 6/29/2012, effective 6/29/2012]

252.248 Value Engineering, provisions and clauses for DFARS Part 248

252.248-7000 [Removed]

[Removed by 66 FR 49865, 10/1/2001, effective 10/1/2001, corrected at 66 FR 51515, 10/9/2001]

252.249 Termination of Contracts, provisions and clauses for DFARS Part 249

252.249-7000 Special termination costs.

As prescribed in 249.501-70, use the following clause:

SPECIAL TERMINATION COSTS (DEC 1991)

(a) *Definition. Special termination costs,* as used in this clause, means only costs in the following categories as defined in part 31 of the Federal Acquisition Regulation (FAR)

(1) Severance pay, as provided in FAR 31.205-6(g);

(2) Reasonable costs continuing after termination, as provided in FAR 31.205-42(b);

(3) Settlement of expenses, as provided in FAR 31.205-42(g);

(4) Costs of return of field service personnel from sites, as provided in FAR 31.205-35 and FAR 31.205-46(c); and

(5) Costs in paragraphs (a) (1), (2), (3), and (4) of this clause to which subcontractors may be entitled in the event of termination.

(b) Notwithstanding the Limitation of Cost/Limitation of Funds clause of this contract, the Contractor shall not include in its estimate of costs incurred or to be incurred, any amount for special termination costs to which the Contractor may be entitled in the event this contract is terminated for the convenience of the Government.

(c) The Contractor agrees to perform this contract in such a manner that the Contractor's claim for special termination costs will not exceed $______. The Government shall have no obligation to pay the Contractor any amount for the special termination costs in excess of this amount.

(d) In the event of termination for the convenience of the Government, this clause shall not be construed as affecting the allowability of special termination costs in any manner other than limiting the maximum amount of the costs payable by the Government.

(e) This clause shall remain in full force and effect until this contract is fully funded.

(End of clause)

252.249-7001 [Reserved]

[Reserved, Final rule, 61 FR 67952, 12/26/96, effective 12/26/96]

252.249-7002 Notification of Anticipated Contract Termination or Reduction.

As prescribed in 249.7003(c), use the following clause:

NOTIFICATION OF ANTICIPATED CONTRACT TERMINATION OR REDUCTION (MAY 2019)

(a) *Definition*. As used in this clause—

Major defense program means a program that is carried out to produce or acquire a major system (as defined in 10 U.S.C. 2302(5)).

(b) Section 1372 of the National Defense Authorization Act for Fiscal Year 1994 (Pub. L. 103-160) and Section 824 of the National Defense Authorization Act for Fiscal Year 1997 (Pub. L. 104-201) are intended to help establish benefit eligibility under the Job Training Partnership Act (29 U.S.C. 1661 and 1662) for employees of DoD contractors and subcontractors adversely affected by contract terminations or substantial reductions under major defense programs.

(c) Notice to employees and state and local officials. Within 2 weeks after the Contracting Officer notifies the Contractor that contract funding will be terminated or substantially reduced, the Contractor shall provide notice of such anticipated termination or reduction to—

(1) Each employee representative of the Contractor's employees whose work is directly related to the defense contract; or

(2) If there is no such representative, each such employee;

(3) The State dislocated worker unit or office described in section 311(b)(2) of the Job Training Partnership Act (29 U.S.C. 1661(b)(2)); and

(4) The chief elected official of the unit of general local government within which the adverse effect may occur.

(d) *Notice to subcontractors*. Not later than 60 days after the Contractor receives the Contracting Officer's notice of the anticipated termination or reduction, the Contractor shall—

(1) Provide notice of the anticipated termination or reduction to each first-tier subcontractor with a subcontract that equals or exceeds the threshold specified in Defense Federal Acquisition Regulation Supplement (DFARS) 225.870-4(c)(2)(i)(A)(*1*) at the time of the notice; and

(2) Require that each such subcontractor—

(i) Provide notice to each of its subcontractors with a subcontract that equals or exceeds the threshold specified in DFARS 225.870-4(c)(2)(i)(C) at the time of the notice; and

(ii) Impose a similar notice and flowdown requirement to subcontractors with subcontracts that equal or exceed the threshold specified in DFARS 225.870-4(c)(2)(i)(C) at the time of the notice.

(e) The notice provided an employee under paragraph (c) of this clause shall have the same effect as a notice of termination to the employee for the purposes of determining whether such employee is eligible for training, adjustment assistance, and employment services under section 325 or 325A of the Job Training Partnership Act (29 U.S.C. 1662d, 1662d-1). If the Contractor has specified that the anticipated contract termination or reduction is not likely to result in plant closure or mass layoff, as defined in 29 U.S.C. 2101, the employee shall be eligible only for services under section 314(b) and paragraphs (1) through (14), (16), and (18) of section 314(c) of the Job Training Partnership Act (29 U.S.C. 1661c(b) and paragraphs (1) through (14), (16), and (18) of section 1661c(c)).

(End of clause)

[Interim rule, 61 FR 64636, 12/6/96, effective 12/6/96, finalized without change, DAC 91-12, 62 FR 34114, 6/24/97, effective 6/24/97; Final rule, 71 FR 75891, 12/19/2006, effective 12/19/2006; Final rule, 75 FR 45072, 8/2/2010, effective 10/1/2010; Final rule, 80 FR 36903, 6/26/2015, effective 10/1/2015; Final rule, 84 FR 25186, 5/31/2019, effective 5/31/2019]

252.251 Use of Government Sources by Contractors, provisions and clauses for DFARS Part 251

252.251-7000 Ordering from Government supply sources.

As prescribed in 251.107, use the following clause:

ORDERING FROM GOVERNMENT SUPPLY SOURCES (AUG 2012)

(a) When placing orders under Federal Supply Schedules, Personal Property Rehabilitation Price Schedules, or Enterprise Software Agreements, the Contractor shall follow the terms of the applicable schedule or agreement and authorization. Include in each order:

(1) A copy of the authorization (unless a copy was previously furnished to the Federal Supply Schedule, Personal Property Rehabilitation Price Schedule, or Enterprise Software Agreement contractor).

(2) The following statement: Any price reductions negotiated as part of an Enterprise Software Agreement issued under a Federal Supply Schedule contract shall control. In the event of any other inconsistencies between an Enterprise Software Agreement, established as a Federal Supply Schedule blanket purchase agreement, and the Federal Supply Schedule contract, the latter shall govern.

(3) The completed address(es) to which the Contractor's mail, freight, and billing documents are to be directed.

(b) When placing orders under nonmandatory schedule contracts and requirements contracts, issued by the General Services Administration (GSA) Office of Information Resources Management, for automated data processing equipment, software and maintenance, communications equipment and supplies, and teleprocessing services, the Contractor shall follow the terms of the applicable contract and the procedures in paragraph (a) of this clause.

(c) When placing orders for Government stock on a reimbursable basis, the Contractor shall—

(1) Comply with the requirements of the Contracting Officer's authorization, using FEDSTRIP or MILSTRIP procedures, as appropriate;

(2) Use only the GSA Form 1948-A, Retail Services Shopping Plate, when ordering from GSA Self-Service Stores;

(3) Order only those items required in the performance of Government contracts; and

(4) Pay invoices from Government supply sources promptly. For purchases made from DoD supply sources, this means within 30 days of the date of a proper invoice. The contractor shall annotate each invoice with the date of receipt. For purposes of computing interest for late Contractor payments, the Government's invoice is deemed to be a demand for payment in accordance with the Interest clause of this contract. The Contractor's failure to pay may also result in the DoD supply source refusing to honor the requisition (see DFARS 251.102(f)) or in the Contracting Officer terminating the Contractor's authorization to use DoD supply sources. In the event the Contracting Officer decides to terminate the authorization due to the Contractor's failure to pay in a timely manner, the Contracting Officer shall provide the Contractor with prompt written no-

tice of the intent to terminate the authorization and the basis for such action. The Contractor shall have 10 days after receipt of the Government's notice in which to provide additional information as to why the authorization should not be terminated. The termination shall not provide the Contractor with an excusable delay for failure to perform or complete the contract in accordance with the terms of the contract, and the Contractor shall be solely responsible for any increased costs.

(d) When placing orders for Government stock on a non-reimbursable basis, the Contractor shall—

(1) Comply with the requirements of the Contracting Officer's authorization; and

(2) When using electronic transactions to submit requisitions on a non-reimbursable basis only, place orders by authorizing contract number using the Defense Logistics Management System (DLMS) Supplement to Federal Implementation Convention 511R, Requisition; and acknowledge receipts by authorizing contract number using the DLMS Supplement 527R, Receipt, Inquiry, Response and Material Receipt Acknowledgment.

(e) Only the Contractor may request authorization for subcontractor use of Government supply sources. The Contracting Officer will not grant authorizations for subcontractor use without approval of the Contractor.

(f) Government invoices shall be submitted to the Contractor's billing address, and Contractor payments shall be sent to the Government remittance address specified below:

Contractor's Billing Address (include point of contact and telephone number):

Government Remittance Address (include point of contact and telephone number):

(End of clause)

[DAC 91-7, 60 FR 29491, 6/5/95, effective 5/17/95; Final rule, 67 FR 65509, 10/25/2002, effective 10/25/2002; Final rule, 69 FR 67858, 11/22/2004, effective 11/22/2004; Final rule, 77 FR 52254, 8/29/2012, effective 8/29/2012]

252.251-7001 Use of Interagency Fleet Management System (IFMS) Vehicles and related services.

As prescribed in 251.205, use the following clause:

USE OF INTERAGENCY FLEET MANAGEMENT SYSTEM (IFMS) VEHICLES AND RELATED SERVICES (DEC 1991)

(a) The Contractor, if authorized use of IFMS vehicles, shall submit requests for five or fewer vehicles and related services in writing to the appropriate General Services Administration (GSA) Regional Customer Service Bureau, Attention: Motor Equipment Activity. Submit requests for more than five vehicles to GSA headquarters: General Services Administration, FTM, Washington, DC 20406. Include the following in each request:

(1) Two copies of the agency authorization to obtain vehicles and related services from GSA.

(2) The number of vehicles and related services required and the period of use.

(3) A list of the Contractor's employees authorized to request vehicles and related services.

(4) A list of the makes, models, and serial numbers of Contractor-owned or leased equipment authorized to be serviced.

(5) Billing instructions and address.

(b) The Contractor should make requests for any unusual quantities of vehicles as far in advance as possible.

(c) The Contractor shall establish and enforce suitable penalties for employees who use or authorize the use of Government vehicles for other than performance of Government contracts.

(d) The Contractor shall assume, without the right of reimbursement from the Government, the cost or expense of any use of IFMS vehicles and services not related to the performance of the contract.

(e) Only the Contractor may request authorization for subcontractor use of IFMS vehicles. The Contracting Officer will not grant authorization for subcontractor use without approval of the Contractor.

(End of clause)

Defense Federal Acquisition Regulation Supplement Part 253

FORMS

Table of Contents

Page

SUBCHAPTER H—CLAUSES AND FORMS

Part 253—Forms 1029

See page 39 for an explanation of the numbering of the DFARS.

PART 253—FORMS

Table of Contents

Subpart 253.2—Prescription of Forms

[Removed] 253.204
[Removed] 253.204-70
[Removed] 253.204-71
Required sources of supplies and services 253.208
DD Form 448, Military Interdepartmental Purchase Request 253.208-1
DD Form 448-2, Acceptance of MIPR 253.208-2
Contractor qualifications 253.209
Responsible prospective contractors 253.209-1
Simplified Acquisition Procedures (SF's 18, 30, 44, 1165, 1449, and OF's 336, 347, 348) 253.213
Completion of DD Form 1155, order for supplies or services 253.213-70
Contracting by negotiation 253.215
DD Form 1547, Record of Weighted Guidelines Application 253.215-70

Subpart 253.3—Illustration of Forms

Agency forms 253.303
Material Inspection and Receiving Report 253.303-250
Material Inspection and Receiving Report—Continuation Sheet 253.303-250c
Tanker/Barge Material Inspection and Receiving Report 253.303-250-1
Individual Contracting Action Report (over $25,000) 253.303-350
Purchase Request for Coal, Coke or Briquettes 253.303-416
Communication Service Authorization 253.303-428
Military Interdepartmental Purchase Request 253.303-448
Acceptance of MIPR 253.303-448-2
Statement of Compliance 253.303-879
Report of Inventions and Subcontracts 253.303-882
Monthly Summary of Contracting Actions 253.303-1057
Cash Collection Voucher 253.303-1131
Requisition and Invoice/Shipping Document 253.303-1149
Order for Supplies or Services 253.303-1155
Order for Supplies or Services (Commissary Continuation Sheet) 253.303-1155c-1
DoD Property Record 253.303-1342
DoD Single Line Item Requisition System Document (Manual) 253.303-1348
DoD Single Line Item Requisition System Document (Mechanical) 253.303-1348m
Issue Release/Receipt Document 253.303-1348- 1A
Issue Release/Receipt Document with Address Label 253.303-1348-2
Transportation Control and Movement Document 253.303-1384
FY—Military Construction Project Data 253.303-1391
FY—Military Construction Project Data (Continuation) 253.303-1391c
DoD Industrial Plant Equipment Requisition 253.303-1419
Contract Data Requirements List 253.303-1423
Contract Data Requirements List (1 Data Item) 253.303-1423-1

Contract Data Requirements List (2 Data Items) 253.303-1423-2
Post-Award Conference Record 253.303-1484
Record of Weighted Guidelines Application 253.303-1547
Contract Administration Completion Record 253.303-1593
Contract Completion Statement 253.303-1594
Contract Closeout Check-List 253.303-1597
Contract Termination Status Report 253.303-1598
Plant Clearance Case Register 253.303-1635
Notice of Acceptance of Inventory Schedules 253.303-1637
Report of Disposition of Contractor Inventory 253.303-1638
Scrap Warranty 253.303-1639
Request for Plant Clearance 253.303-1640
Disposal Determination Approval 253.303-1641
Transportation Data for Solicitations 253.303-1653
Evaluation of Transportation Cost Factors 253.303-1654
Application for U.S. Government Shipping Documentation/
Instructions 253.303-1659
DoD Property in the Custody of Contractors 253.303-1662
Data Item Description 253.303-1664
Information to Offerors or Quoters 253.303-1707
Contract Facilities Capital Cost of Money 253.303-1861
Cost Data Summary Report 253.303-1921
Functional Cost-Hour Report 253.303-1921-1
Request for Assignment of a Commercial and Government Entity
(CAGE) Code 253.303-2051
Request for Information/Verification of Commercial and
Government Entity (CAGE) Code 253.303-2051-1
Report of Contract Performance Outside the United States 253.303-2139
Small Business Coordination Record 253.303-2579
Performance Evaluation (Construction) 253.303-2626
Performance Evaluation (Architect-Engineer) 253.303-2631

PART 253—FORMS

SUBPART 253.2—PRESCRIPTION OF FORMS

253.204 [Removed]

[Final rule, 74 FR 37644, 7/29/2009, effective 7/29/2009]

253.204-70 [Removed]

[Final rule, 66 FR 47096, 9/11/2001, effective 10/1/2001, corrected at 66 FR 48621, 9/21/2001, corrected at 66 FR 50504, 10/3/2001; Final rule, 66 FR 55121, 11/1/2001, effective 11/1/2001; Final rule, 67 FR 46112, 7/12/2002, effective 10/1/2002; Final rule, 68 FR 7438, 2/14/2003, effective 2/14/2003; Final rule, 68 FR 26945, 6/20/2003, effective 10/1/2003; Final rule, 71 FR 44926, 8/8/2006, effective 8/8/2006; Final rule, 74 FR 37644, 7/29/2009, effective 7/29/2009]

253.204-71 [Removed]

[Final rule, 65 FR 39707, 6/27/2000, effective 10/1/2000; Final rule, 66 FR 47096, 9/11/2001, effective 10/1/2001; Final rule, 68 FR 7438, 2/14/2003, effective 2/14/2003; Final rule, 71 FR 44926, 8/8/2006, effective 8/8/2006]

253.208 Required sources of supplies and services. (No Text)

253.208-1 DD Form 448, Military Interdepartmental Purchase Request.

Follow the procedures at PGI 253.208-1 for use of DD Form 448.

[Final rule, 65 FR 52951, 8/31/2000, effective 8/31/2000; Final rule, 71 FR 39004, 7/11/2006, effective 7/11/2006]

253.208-2 DD Form 448-2, Acceptance of MIPR.

Follow the procedures at PGI 253.208-2 for use of DD Form 448-2.

[Final rule, 71 FR 39004, 7/11/2006, effective 7/11/2006]

253.209 Contractor qualifications. (No Text)

253.209-1 Responsible prospective contractors.

(a) *SF 1403, Preaward Survey of Prospective Contractor (General)*. (i) The factors in Section III, Block 19, generally mean—

(A) *Technical Capability.* An assessment of the prospective contractor's key management personnel to determine if they have the basic technical knowledge, experience, and understanding of the requirements necessary to produce the required product or provide the required service.

(B) *Production Capability.* An evaluation of the prospective contractor's ability to plan, control, and integrate manpower, facilities, and other resources necessary for successful contract completion. This includes—

(1) An assessment of the prospective contractor's possession of, or the ability to acquire, the necessary facilities, material, equipment, and labor; and

(2) A determination that the prospective contractor's system provides for timely placement of orders and for vendor follow-up and control.

(C) *Quality Assurance Capability.* An assessment of the prospective contractor's capability to meet the quality assurance requirements of the proposed contract. It may involve an evaluation of the prospective contractor's quality assurance system, personnel, facilities, and equipment.

(D) *Financial Capability.* A determination that the prospective contractor has or can get adequate financial resources to obtain needed facilities, equipment, materials, etc.

(E) *Accounting system and related internal controls.* An assessment by the auditor of the adequacy of the prospective contractor's accounting system and related internal controls as defined in 242.7501, Definition. Normally, a contracting officer will request an accounting system review when soliciting and awarding cost-reimbursement or incentive type contracts, or contracts which provide for progress payments based on costs or on a percentage or stage of completion.

(ii) The factors in section III, Block 20, generally mean—

(A) *Government Property Control.* An assessment of the prospective contractor's capability to manage and control Government property.

(B) *Transportation.* An assessment of the prospective contractor's capability to follow the laws and regulations applicable to the movement of Government material, or overweight, oversized, hazardous cargo, etc.

(C) *Packaging.* An assessment of the prospective contractor's ability to meet all contractual packaging requirements including preservation, unit pack, packing, marking, and unitizing for shipment.

(D) *Security Clearance.* A determination that the prospective contractor's facility security clearance is adequate and current. (When checked, the surveying activity will refer this factor to the Defense Security Service (DSS)).

(E) *Plant Safety.* An assessment of the prospective contractor's ability to meet the safety requirements in the solicitation.

(F) *Environmental/Energy Consideration.* An evaluation of the prospective contractor's ability to meet specific environmental and energy requirements in the solicitation.

(G) *Flight Operations and Flight Safety.* An evaluation of the prospective contractor's ability to meet flight operation and flight safety requirements on solicitations involving the overhaul and repair of aircraft.

(H) *Other.* If the contracting officer wants an assessment of other than major factors A-E and other factors A-G, check this factor. Explain the desired information in the Remarks sections.

[DAC 91-7, 60 FR 29491, 6/5/95, effective 5/17/95; Final rule, 64 FR 51074, 9/21/99, effective 9/21/99]

253.213 Simplified acquisition procedures (SF's 18, 30, 44, 1165, 1449, and OF's 336, 347, and 348).

(f) DoD uses the DD Form 1155, Order for Supplies or Services, instead of OF 347; and OF 336, Continuation Sheet, instead of OF 348. Follow the procedures at PGI 253.213(f) for use of forms.

[Final rule, 64 FR 2595, 1/15/99, effective 1/15/99; Final rule, 71 FR 3412, 1/23/2006, effective 1/23/2006]

253.213-70 Completion of DD Form 1155, order for supplies or services.

Follow the procedures at PGI 253.213-70 for completion of DD Form 1155.

[DAC 91-10, 61 FR 7739, 2/29/96, effective 2/29/96; Final rule, 64 FR 2600, 1/15/99, effective 1/15/99; Final rule, 65 FR 39703, 6/27/2000, effective 6/27/2000; Final rule, 65 FR 52951, 8/31/2000, effective 8/31/2000; Final rule, 70 FR 35543, 6/21/2005, effective 6/21/2005; Final rule, 71 FR 3412, 1/23/2006, effective 1/23/2006]

253.215 Contracting by negotiation. (No Text)

253.215-70 DD Form 1547, Record of Weighted Guidelines Application.

Follow the procedures at PGI 253.215-70 for completing DD Form 1547.

[Final rule, 66 FR 49862, 10/1/2001, effective 10/1/2001; Final rule, 67 FR 49254, 7/30/2002, effective 7/30/2002; Final rule, 71 FR 69492, 12/1/2006, effective 12/1/2006]

SUBPART 253.3—ILLUSTRATION OF FORMS

Note: Department of Defense Acquisition Forms are not published in the Federal Register or the Code of Federal Regulations. For the convenience of the user, the list set forth below includes section numbers, form numbers, and titles.

253.303-250 Material Inspection and Receiving Report.

253.303-250c Material Inspection and Receiving Report-Continuation Sheet.

253.303-250-1 Tanker/Barge Material Inspection and Receiving Report.

253.303-350 Individual Contracting Action Report.

253.303-416 Purchase Request for Coal, Coke or Briquettes.

253.303-428 Communication Service Authorization.

253.303-448 Military Interdepartmental Purchase Request.

253.303-448-2 Acceptance of MIPR.

253.303-879 Statement of Compliance.

253.303-882 Report of Inventions and Subcontracts.

253.303-1057 Monthly Summary of Contracting Actions.

253.303-1131 Cash Collection Voucher.

253.303-1149 Requisition and Invoice/Shipping Document.

253.303-1155 Order for Supplies or Services.

253.303-1155c-1 Order for Supplies or Services (Commissary Continuation Sheet).

253.303-1342 Property Record.

253.303-1348 Single Line Item Requisition System Document (Manual).

253.303-1348m Single Line Item Requisition System Document (Mechanical).

253.303-1348-1A—Issue Release/Receipt Document.

253.303-1348-2—Issue Release/Receipt Document with Address Label.

253.303-1384 Transportation Control and Movement Document.

253.303-1391 FY—Military Construction Project Data.

253.303-1391c FY—Military Construction Project Data (Continuation).

253.303-1419 Industrial Plant Equipment Requisition.

253.303-1423 Contract Data Requirements List

253.303-1423-1 Contract Data Requirements List (1 Data Item).

253.303-1423-2 Contract Data Requirements List (2 Data Items).

253.303-1484 Post-Award Conference Record.

253.303-1547 Record of Weighted Guidelines Application.

253.303-1593 Contract Administration Completion Record.

253.303-1594 Contract Completion Statement.

253.303-1597 Contract Closeout Check-List.

253.303-1598 Contract Termination Status Report.

253.303-1635 Plant Clearance Case Register.

253.303-1637 Notice of Acceptance of Inventory Schedules.

253.303-1638 Report of Disposition of Contractor Inventory.

253.303-1639 Scrap Warranty.

253.303-1640 Request for Plant Clearance.

253.303-1641 Disposal Determination Approval.

253.303-1653 Transportation Data for Solicitations.

253.303-1654 Evaluation of Transportation Cost Factors.

253.303-1659 Application for U.S. Government Shipping Documentation/Instructions.

253.303-1662 Property in the Custody of Contractors.

253.303-1664 Data Item Description.

253.303-1707 Information to Offerors or Quoters.

253.303-1861 Contract Facilities Capital Cost of Money.

253.303-1921 Cost Data Summary Report.

253.303-1921-1 Functional Cost-Hour Report.

253.303-2051 Request for Assignment of a Commercial and Government Entity (CAGE) Code.

253.303-2051-1 Request for Information/Verification of Commercial and Government Entity (CAGE) Code.

253.303-2139 Report of Contract Performance Outside the United States.

253.303-2579 Small Business Coordination Record.

253.303-2626 Performance Evaluation (Construction)

253.303-2631 Performance Evaluation (Architect-Engineer)

[DAC 91-7, 60 FR 29491, 6/5/95, effective 5/17/95; Final rule, 61 FR 51030, 9/30/96, effective 10/1/96; DAC 91-12, 62 FR 34114,

6/24/97, effective 6/24/97; Final rule, 63 FR 43889, 8/17/98, effective 8/17/98; Final rule, 63 FR 55040, 10/14/98, effective 10/14/98; Final rule, 63 FR 63799, 11/17/98, effective 11/17/98; Final rule, 63 FR 69007, 12/15/98, effective 12/15/98; Final rule, 64 FR 8727, 2/23/99, effective 2/23/99; Final rule, 64 FR 28109, 5/25/99, effective 5/25/99; Final rule, 65 FR 2055, 1/13/2000, effective 1/13/2000; Final rule, 65 FR 39722, 6/27/2000, effective 6/27/2000; Final rule, 65 FR 39707, 6/27/2000, effective 10/1/2000; Final rule, 65 FR 39703, 6/27/2000, effective 6/27/2000; Final rule, 65 FR 52951, 8/31/2000, effective 8/31/2000]

253.303 Agency forms.

DoD forms are available at *http://www.dtic.mil/whs/directives/infomgt/forms/formsprogram.htm.*

[Final rule, 72 FR 14239, 3/27/2007, effective 3/27/2007]

253.303-250 DD Form 250: Material Inspection and Receiving Report

[DAC 91-6, 5/27/94]

MATERIAL INSPECTION AND RECEIVING REPORT

Form Approved OMB No. 0704-0248

The public reporting burden for this collection of information is estimated to average 30 minutes per response, including the time for reviewing instructions, searching existing data sources, gathering and maintaining the data needed, and completing and reviewing the collection of information. Send comments regarding this burden estimate or any other aspect of this collection of information, including suggestions for reducing the burden, to Department of Defense, Washington Headquarters Services, Directorate for Information Operations and Reports (0704-0248), 1215 Jefferson Davis Highway, Suite 1204, Arlington, VA 22202-4302. Respondents should be aware that notwithstanding any other provision of law, no person shall be subject to any penalty for failing to comply with a collection of information if it does not display a currently valid OMB control number.

PLEASE DO NOT RETURN YOUR COMPLETED FORM TO THE ABOVE ADDRESS.
SEND THIS FORM IN ACCORDANCE WITH THE INSTRUCTIONS CONTAINED IN THE DFARS, APPENDIX F-401.

1. PROCUREMENT INSTRUMENT IDENTIFICATION (CONTRACT) NO. | ORDER NO. | 6. INVOICE NO./DATE | 7. PAGE | OF | 8. ACCEPTANCE POINT

2. SHIPMENT NO. | 3. DATE SHIPPED | 4. B/L TCN | 5. DISCOUNT TERMS

9. PRIME CONTRACTOR CODE | 10. ADMINISTERED BY CODE

11. SHIPPED FROM *(If other than 9)* CODE | FOB: | 12. PAYMENT WILL BE MADE BY CODE

13. SHIPPED TO CODE | 14. MARKED FOR CODE

15. ITEM NO.	16. STOCK/PART NO. DESCRIPTION *(Indicate number of shipping containers - type of container - container number.)*	17. QUANTITY SHIP/REC'D*	18. UNIT	19. UNIT PRICE	20. AMOUNT

21. CONTRACT QUALITY ASSURANCE

a. ORIGIN

☐ CQA ☐ ACCEPTANCE of listed items has been made by me or under my supervision and they conform to contract, except as noted herein or on supporting documents.

DATE — SIGNATURE OF AUTHORIZED GOVERNMENT REPRESENTATIVE

TYPED NAME:

TITLE:

MAILING ADDRESS:

COMMERCIAL TELEPHONE NUMBER:

b. DESTINATION

☐ CQA ☐ ACCEPTANCE of listed items has been made by me or under my supervision and they conform to contract, except as noted herein or on supporting documents.

DATE — SIGNATURE OF AUTHORIZED GOVERNMENT REPRESENTATIVE

TYPED NAME:

TITLE:

MAILING ADDRESS:

COMMERCIAL TELEPHONE NUMBER:

22. RECEIVER'S USE

Quantities shown in column 17 were received in apparent good condition except as noted.

DATE RECEIVED — SIGNATURE OF AUTHORIZED GOVERNMENT REPRESENTATIVE

TYPED NAME:

TITLE:

MAILING ADDRESS:

COMMERCIAL TELEPHONE NUMBER:

** If quantity received by the Government is the same as quantity shipped, indicate by (X) mark; if different, enter actual quantity received below quantity shipped and encircle.*

23. CONTRACTOR USE ONLY

DD FORM 250, AUG 2000 PREVIOUS EDITION IS OBSOLETE.

253.303-250c DD Form 250c: Material Inspection and Receiving Report—Continuation Sheet

[DAC 91-6, 5/27/94]

MATERIAL INSPECTION AND RECEIVING REPORT - *CONTINUATION SHEET*	PAGE	OF	*Form Approved OMB No. 0704-0248*

The public reporting burden for this collection of information is estimated to average 30 minutes per response, including the time for reviewing instructions, searching existing data sources, gathering and maintaining the data needed, and completing and reviewing the collection of information. Send comments regarding this burden estimate or any other aspect of this collection of information, including suggestions for reducing the burden, to the Department of Defense, Executive Services and Communications Directorate (0704-0248). Respondents should be aware that notwithstanding any other provision of law, no person shall be subject to any penalty for failing to comply with a collection of information if it does not display a currently valid OMB control number.

PLEASE DO NOT RETURN YOUR COMPLETED FORM TOTHE ABOVE ORGANIZATION.
SEND THIS FORM IN ACCORDANCE WITH THE INSTRUCTIONS CONTAINED IN THE DFARS, APPENDIX F-401.

SHIPMENT NO.	DATE SHIPPED	PROC INSTRUMENT IDEN. (CONTRACT)	(ORDER) NO.	INVOICE NO.

ITEM NO.	STOCK/PART NO. DESCRIPTION (*Indicate number of shipping containers - type of container - container number.)*	QUANTITY SHIP/REC'D	UNIT	UNIT PRICE	AMOUNT

253.303-250-1 DD Form 250-1: Tanker/Barge Material Inspection and Receiving Report

[DAC 91-6, 5/27/94]

TANKER/BARGE MATERIAL INSPECTION AND RECEIVING REPORT

Form Approved
OMB No. 0704-0248

The public reporting burden for this collection of information is estimated to average 30 minutes per response, including the time for reviewing instructions, searching existing data sources, gathering and maintaining the data needed, and completing and reviewing the collection of information. Send comments regarding this burden estimate or any other aspect of this collection of information, including suggestions for reducing the burden, to the Department of Defense, Executive Services Directorate (0704-0248). Respondents should be aware that notwithstanding any other provision of law, no person shall be subject to any penalty for failing to comply with a collection of information if it does not display a currently valid OMB control number.

PLEASE DO NOT RETURN YOUR COMPLETED FORM TO THE ABOVE ORGANIZATION.
SEND THIS FORM IN ACCORDANCE WITH THE INSTRUCTIONS CONTAINED IN THE DFARS, APPENDIX F-401.

1. TANKER/BARGE ☐ LOADING REPORT ☐ DISCHARGE REPORT
2. INSPECTION OFFICE
3. REPORT NUMBER
4. AGENCY PLACING ORDER ON SHIPPER, CITY, STATE AND/OR LOCAL ADDRESS *(Loading)*
5. DEPARTMENT
6. PRIME CONTRACT OR P.O. NUMBER
7. NAME OF PRIME CONTRACTOR, CITY, STATE AND/OR LOCAL ADDRESS *(Loading)*
8. STORAGE CONTRACT
9. TERMINAL OR REFINERY SHIPPED FROM, CITY, STATE AND/OR LOCAL ADDRESS *(Loading)*
10. ORDER NUMBER ON SUPPLIER
11. SHIPPED TO *(Receiving Activity, City, State and/or Local Address)*
12. B/L NUMBER
13. REQN. OR REQUEST NO.
14. CARGO NUMBER
15. VESSEL
16. DRAFT ARRIVAL — FORE — AFT
17. DRAFT SAILING — FORE — AFT
18. PREVIOUS TWO CARGOES — FIRST — LAST
19. PRIOR INSPECTION
20. CONDITION OF SHORE PIPELINE
21. APPROPRIATION *(Loading)*
22. CONTRACT ITEM NO.
23. PRODUCT
24. SPECIFICATIONS

25. STATEMENT OF QUANTITY	LOADED	DISCHARGED	LOSS/GAIN	PER CENT
BARRELS *(42 Gals) (Net)*				
GALLONS *(Net)*				
TONS *(Long)*				

26. STATEMENT OF QUALITY

TESTS	SPECIFICATION LIMITS	TEST RESULTS

27. TIME STATEMENT	DATE	TIME
NOTICE OF READINESS TO LOAD DISCHARGE		
VESSEL ARRIVED IN ROADS		
MOORED ALONGSIDE		
STARTED BALLAST DISCHARGE		
FINISHED BALLAST DISCHARGE		
INSPECTED AND READY TO LOAD DISCHARGE		
CARGO HOSES CONNECTED		
COMMENCED LOADING DISCHARGE		
STOPPED LOADING DISCHARGING		
RESUMED LOADING DISCHARGING		
FINISHED LOADING DISCHARGING		
CARGO HOSES REMOVED		
VESSEL RELEASED BY INSPECTOR		
COMMENCED BUNKERING		
FINISHED BUNKERING		
VESSEL LEFT BERTH *(Actual/Estimated)*		

28. REMARKS *(Note in detail cause of delays such as repairs, breakdown, slow operation, stoppages, etc.)*

29. COMPANY OR RECEIVING TERMINAL

(Signature)

30. I CERTIFY THAT THE CARGO WAS INSPECTED, ACCEPTED AND LOADED/DISCHARGED AS INDICATED HEREON.

(Date) *(Signature of Authorized Government Representative)*

31. I HEREBY CERTIFY THAT THIS TIME STATEMENT IS CORRECT.

(Master or Agent)

253.303-350 DD Form 350: Individual Contracting Action Report

INDIVIDUAL CONTRACTING ACTION REPORT

Report Control Symbol DD-AT&L(M)1014

A1 Type of Report ____ (0) Original; (1) Canceling; or (2) Correcting
A2 Report Number ____________
A3 Contracting Office
A3A Reporting Agency FIPS 95 Code
A3B Contracting Office Code ____________
A4 Name of Contracting Office ____________________________

B1 Contract Identification Information
B1A Contract Number ____________________
B1B Origin of Contract ____ (A) DoD; (B) NASA; or (C) Other Non-DoD Agency
B1C Bundled Contract ____ (Y) Yes; or (N) No
B1D Bundled Contract Exception ____ (A) Mission Critical; (B) OMB Circular A-76; or (C) Other
B1E Performance-Based Service Contract ____ (Y) Yes; or (N) No
B2 Modification, Order, or Other ID Number
B2A Order, or Other ID Number ____________________
B2B Modification Number ____________
B3 Action Date (*yyyymmdd*) ____________________
B4 Completion Date (*yyyymmdd*) ____________________
B5 Contractor Identification Information
B5A Contractor Identification Number (DUNS) ____________
B5B Government Agency ____ (Y) Yes; or (N) No
B5D Contractor Name and Division Name
Contractor ____________________________
Division ____________________________
B5E Contractor Address
Street or PO Box ____________________
City or Town ____________________
State or Country ____________ Zip Code ____________
B5F Taxpayer Identification Number ____________
B5G Parent Taxpayer Identification Number ____________
B5H Parent Name ____________________________
B6 Principal Place of Performance
B6A City or Place Code ____________
B6B State or Country Code ____________
B6C City or Place and State or Country Name ____________________
B7 Type Obligation ____ (1) Obligation; (2) Deobligation; or (3) No Dollars Obligated or Deobligated
B8 Obligated or Deobligated Dollars *(Enter Whole Dollars Only)* ____________
B9 Foreign Military Sale ____ (Y) Yes; or (N) No
B10 Multiyear Contract ____ (Y) Yes; or (N) No
B11 Total Estimated Contract Value *(Enter Whole Dollars Only)* ____________
B12 Principal Product or Service
B12A Federal Supply Class or Service Code ________
B12B DoD Claimant Program Code ________
B12C MDAP, MAIS, or Other Program Code ________

INDIVIDUAL CONTRACTING ACTION REPORT

Report Control Symbol DD-AT&L(M)1014

B12D NAICS Code ________
B12E Name or Description ________
B12F EPA-Designated Product(s) ____ (A) EPA-Designated Product(s) with Minimum Recovered Material Content; (B) FAR 23.405(c)(1) Justification; (C) FAR 23.405(c)(2) Justification; (D) FAR 23.405(c)(3) Justification; or (E) No EPA-Designated Product(s) Acquired
B12G Recovered Material Clauses ____ (A) FAR 52.223-4; or (B) FAR 52.223-4 and FAR 52.223-9
B13 Kind of Action
B13A Contract or Order ____ (1) Letter Contract; (3) Definitive Contract; (4) Order under an Agreement; (5) Order under Indefinite-Delivery Contract; (6) Order under Federal Schedule; (7) BPA Order under Federal Schedule; (8) Order from UNICOR or JWOD; or (9) Award under FAR Part 13
B13B Type of Indefinite-Delivery Contract ____ (A) Requirements Contract (FAR 52.216-21); (B) Indefinite-Quantity Contract (FAR 52.216-22); or (C) Definite-Quantity Contract (FAR 52.216-20)
B13C Multiple or Single Award Indefinite-Delivery Contract ____ (M) Multiple Award; or (S) Single Award
B13D Modification ____ (A) Additional Work (new agreement); (B) Additional Work (other); (C) Funding Action; (D) Change Order; (E) Termination for Default; (F) Termination for Convenience; (G) Cancellation; (H) Exercise of an Option; or (J) Definitization
B13E Multiple Award Contract Fair Opportunity ____ (A) Fair Opportunity Process; (B) Urgency;(C) One/Unique Source; (D) Follow-On Contract; or (E) Minimum Guarantee
B13F Indefinite-Delivery Contract Use ____ (A) Government-Wide; (B) DoD-Wide; (C) DoD Department or Agency Only; or (D) Contracting Office Only
B13G Indefinite-Delivery Contract Ordering Period Ending Date (*yyyymmdd*)
B14 CICA Applicability ____ (A) Pre-CICA; (B) CICA Applicable; (C) Simplified Acquisition Procedures Other than FAR Subpart 13.5; or (D) Simplified Acquisition Procedures Pursuant to FAR Subpart 13.5
B15 Information Technology Products or Services ____(A) Commercially Available Off-the-Shelf Item; (B) Other Commercial Item of Supply; (C) Nondevelopmental Item Other than Commercial Item; (D) Other Noncommercial Item of Supply; (E) Commercial Service; or (F) Noncommercial Service.
B16 Clinger-Cohen Act Planning Compliance ____ (Y) Yes; or (N) No

Do not complete Part C if Line B5B is coded Y.

C1 Synopsis ____ (A) Synopsis Only; (B) Combined Synopsis/Solicitation; or (N) Not Synopsized
C2 Reason Not Synopsized ____ (A) Urgency; (B) FAR 5.202(a)(13); (C) SBA/OFPP Pilot Program; or (Z) Other Reason
C3 Extent Competed ____ (A) Competed Action; (B) Not Available for Competition; (C) Follow-On to Competed Action; or (D) Not Competed
C4 Sea Transportation ____ (Y) Yes - Positive Response to DFARS 252.247-7022 or 252.212-7000(c)(2); (N) No - Negative Response to DFARS 252.247-7022 or 252.212-7000(c)(2); or (U) Unknown - No Response or Provision Not Included in Solicitation

INDIVIDUAL CONTRACTING ACTION REPORT

Report Control Symbol DD-AT&L(M)1014

C5 Type of Contract ____ (A) Fixed-Price Redetermination; (J) Firm-Fixed-Price; (K) Fixed-Price Economic Price Adjustment; (L) Fixed-Price Incentive; (M) Fixed-Price-Award-Fee; (R) Cost-Plus-Award-Fee; (S) Cost Contract; (T) Cost-Sharing; (U) Cost-Plus-Fixed-Fee; (V) Cost-Plus-Incentive-Fee; (Y) Time-and-Materials; or (Z) Labor-Hour

C6 Number of Offerors Solicited ____(1) One; or (2) More than One

C7 Number of Offers Received ________

C8 Solicitation Procedures ____ (A) Full and Open Competition – Sealed Bid; (B) Full and Open Competition – Competitive Proposal; (C) Full and Open Competition – Combination; (D) Architect-Engineer; (E) Basic Research; (F) Multiple Award Schedule; (G) Alternative Sources; (K) Set-Aside; or (N) Other than Full and Open Competition

C9 Authority for Other Than Full and Open Competition ____ (1A) Unique Source; (1B) Follow-On Contract; (1C) Unsolicited Research Proposal; (1D) Patent or Data Rights; (1E) Utilities; (1F) Standardization; (1G) Only One Source – Other; (2A) Urgency; (3A) Particular Sources; (4A) International Agreement; (5A) Authorized by Statute; (5B) Authorized Resale; (6A) National Security; or (7A) Public Interest

C10 Subject to Labor Standards Statutes ____ (A) Walsh-Healey Act; (C) Service Contract Act; (D) Davis-Bacon Act; or (Z) Not Applicable

C11 Cost or Pricing Data ____ (Y) Yes – Obtained; (N) No – Not Obtained; or (W) Not Obtained - Waived

C12 Contract Financing ____ (A) FAR 52.232-16; (C) Percentage of Completion Progress Payments; (D) Unusual Progress Payments or Advance Payments; (E) Commercial Financing; (F) Performance-Based Financing; or (Z) Not Applicable

C13 Foreign Trade Data

C13A Place of Manufacture ____ (A) U.S.; or (B) Foreign

C13B Country of Origin Code ______

C14 Commercial Item ____(Y) Yes – FAR 52.212-4 Included; or (N) No – FAR 52.212-4 Not Included

Do not complete Part D if Line B5B is coded Y or if Line B13A is coded 6.

D1 Type of Contractor

D1A Type of Entity ____(A) Small Disadvantaged Business (SDB) Performing in U.S.; (B) Other Small Business (SB) Performing in U.S.; (C) Large Business Performing in U.S.; (D) JWOD Participating Nonprofit Agency; (F) Hospital; (L) Foreign Concern or Entity; (M) Domestic Firm Performing Outside U.S.; (T) Historically Black College or University (HBCU); (U) Minority Institution (MI); (V) Other Educational or (Z) Other Nonprofit

D1B Women-Owned Business ____ (Y) Yes; (N) No; or (U) Uncertified

D1C HUBZone Representation ____(Y) Yes; or (N) No

D1D Ethnic Group ____ (A) Asian-Indian American; (B) Asian-Pacific American; (C) Black American; (D) Hispanic American; (E) Native American; (F) Other SDB Certified or Determined by SBA; or (Z) No Representation

D1E Veteran-Owned Small Business ____ (A) Service-Disabled Veteran; or (B) Other Veteran

INDIVIDUAL CONTRACTING ACTION REPORT
Report Control Symbol DD-AT&L(M)1014

D2 Reason Not Awarded to SDB ____ (A) No Known SDB Source; (B) SDB Not Solicited; (C) SDB Solicited and No Offer Received; (D) SDB Solicited and Offer Was Not Low; or (Z) Other Reason

D3 Reason Not Awarded to SB ____ (A) No Known SB Source; (B) SB Not Solicited; (C) SB Solicited and No Offer Received; (D) SB Solicited and Offer Was Not Low; or (Z) Other Reason

D4 Set-Aside or Preference Program

D4A Type of Set-Aside ____ (A) None; (B) Total SB Set-Aside; (C) Partial SB Set-Aside; (D) Section 8(a) Set-Aside or Sole Source; (E) Total SDB Set-Aside; (F) HBCU or MI – Total Set-Aside; (G) HBCU or MI – Partial Set-Aside; (H) Very Small Business Set-Aside; (J) Emerging Small Business Set-Aside; (K) HUBZone Set-Aside or Sole Source; (L) Combination HUBZone and 8(a)

D4B Type of Preference ____ (A) None; (B) SDB Price Evaluation Adjustment – Unrestricted; (C) SDB Preferential Consideration - Partial SB Set-Aside; (D) HUBZone Price Evaluation Preference; or (E) Combination HUBZone Price Evaluation Preference and SDB Price Evaluation Adjustment

D4C Premium Percent __________

D7 Small Business Innovation Research (SBIR) Program ___(A) Not a SBIR Program Phase I, II, or III; (B) SBIR Program Phase I Action; (C) SBIR Program Phase II Action; or (D) SBIR Program Phase III Action

D8 Subcontracting Plan - SB, SDB, HBCU, or MI ____ (A) Plan Not Included – No Subcontracting Possibilities; (B) Plan Not Required; (C) Plan Required – Incentive Not Included; or (D) Plan Required – Incentive Included

D9 Small Business Competitiveness Demonstration Program ____ (Y) Yes; or (N) No

D10 Size of Small Business ____

Employees		Annual Gross Revenues
	(A) 50 or fewer	
	(B) 51 - 100	(M) $1 million or less
	(C) 101 - 250	(N) Over $1 million - $2 million
	(D) 251 - 500	(P) Over $2 million - $3.5 million
	(E) 501 - 750	(R) Over $3.5 million - $5 million
	(F) 751 - 1000	(S) Over $5 million - $10 million
	(G) Over 1000	(T) Over $10 million - $17 million
		(U) Over $17 million.

D11 Emerging Small Business ____ (Y) Yes; or (N) No

E1 Contingency, Humanitarian, or Peacekeeping Operation ____ (Y) Yes; or Leave Blank

E2 Cost Accounting Standards Clause ____ (Y) Yes; or Leave Blank

E3 Requesting Agency Code (FIPS 95) ________

E4 Requesting Activity Code ________

E5 Number of Actions ________

E6 Payment by Governmentwide Purchase Card ____ (Y) Yes; or Leave Blank

F1 Name of Contracting Officer or Representative ______________________________

F2 Signature ____

F3 Telephone Number __________________

F4 Date (*yyyymmdd*) __________________

253.303-416 DD Form 416: Purchase Request for Coal, Coke or Briquettes

Purchase Request for Coal, Coke or Briquettes	**Instructions** Prepare separate request for each kind of Coal (See reverse)	1. For 12 Month Period *(From - Thru)* 2. Program Number

3. Thru	4. From *(Department, Agency or Installation)*
5. To *(Chief of Service)*	6. Consign To
	7. Purchase Request Number / 8. Date

9. Kind *(Anthracite, bituminous, sub-bituminous, lignite, or coke.)*	10. Tons in Storage	11. Storage Capacity	14. Size *(In Inches)*			
			a. Top		b. Bottom	
	12. Tons Due on Existing Contracts	13. Actual Consumption *(Last 12 Months)*	(1) Maximum	(2) Minimum	(1) Maximum	(2) Minimum

15. Analytical Specifications Required	a. Min	b. Max	c. Dust Suppressant (Check if applicable) ☐ / d. Freeze Conditioning (Check if applicable) ☐	Do Not Write In These Columns — 16. Approved Analytical Specifications	a. Min	b. Max	c. Dust Suppressant (Check if applicable) ☐ / d. Freeze Conditioning (Check if applicable) ☐ / e. Approved Tonnage
(1) Moisture				(1) Moisture			
DRY COAL (2) Vol				DRY COAL (2) Vol			
(3) Ash				(3) Ash			
(4) Sul				(4) Sul			
(5) Btu				(5) Btu			
(6) AST °F				(6) AST °F			
(7) Hardgrove Grindability				(7) H. Grind			
(8) FSI				(8) FSI			

17. Tentative Ship Schedule	
a. Month & Year	b. Estimated Tons
Jan 20	
Feb 20	
Mar 20	
Apr 20	
May 20	
Jun 20	
Jul 20	
Aug 20	
Sep 20	
Oct 20	
Nov 20	
Dec 20	

18. Screen Size (Round Hole)	a. Maximum % Retained On	b. Maximum % Passing THRU
(1) Top		
(2) Bottom		

19. Preferred Method of Delivery *(Check One)*: ☐ a. Rail ☐ b. Truck ☐ c. Rail or Truck ☐ d.Barge

20. Delivering Railroad

21. Total Purchase Request *(Tons)* 0

22. Railhead for Carload Shipments

23a. Alternate Method of Delivery

23b. Estimated Additional Cost

24. Type of Railroad Cars Required

25. Estimated Charges for Labor and Equipment if Commercial Service is Required for Unloading, Hauling and Storage of Coal

26. State or Local Regulatory Sulfur Dioxide Emission Limits *(Show Units)*

27. Spur Track To Installation *(Check One)* ☐ a. Yes ☐ b. No

28. Remarks

29. Technical Point of Contact at Requesting Activity

a. Typed Name *(Last, First, Middle Initial)*	b. E-mail Address	c. Telephone No.

30. Prepared By

a. Typed Name *(Last, First, Middle Initial)*	b. Signature	c. E-mail Address	d. Telephone No.

31. Approved at Requesting Activity By

a. Typed Name *(Last, First, Middle Initial)*	b. Signature	c. E-mail Address	d. Telephone No.

32. Approved By

a. Typed Name *(Last, First, Middle Initial)*	b. Signature	c. E-mail Address	d. Telephone No.

Instructions for completion of DD Form 416, Purchase Request for Coal, Coke or Briquettes	
Block	
1.	FOR 12 MONTH PERIOD. Enter the 12 month period of request (i.e., 1 May 08 - 30 Apr 09).
2.	PROGRAM NUMBER. As stated.
3.	THRU. Enter name and mailing address of organization request is submitted thru.
4.	FROM. Enter name and address of Department, Agency or Installation. (i.e., CDR, Red River Army Depot, Houston, TX 77507-5000).
5.	TO. Enter To (Chief of Service) organization.
6.	CONSIGN TO. Enter Consign to location (i.e., Red River Army Depot).
7.	PURCHASE REQUEST NUMBER. As stated.
8.	DATE. As Stated.
9.	KIND. As stated.
10.	TONS IN STORAGE. As stated
11.	STORAGE CAPACITY. As stated.
12.	TONS DUE ON EXISTING CONTRACTS. As stated.
13.	ACTUAL CONSUMPTION. Enter last 12 months actual consumption.
14.	SIZE. Enter in inches and maximum and minimum size for Top and Bottom
15.	ANALYTICAL SPECIFICATIONS REQUIRED. Enter minimum and maximum specifications. Check if DUST SUPPRESSANT and/or FREEZE CONDITIONING is required. (State time frame in Blk 28 "Remarks")
16.	APPROVED ANALYTICAL SPECIFICATIONS. APC or DESC use only.
17.	TENTATIVE SHIP SCHEDULE. As stated
18.	SCREEN SIZE (Round Hole). Enter Screen Size.
19.	PREFERRED METHOD OF DELIVERY. Check Rail, Truck, Rail or Truck, or Barge.
20.	DELIVERING RAILROAD. As Stated.
21.	TOTAL PURCHASE REQUEST. Enter Tons.
22.	RAILHEAD FOR CARLOAD SHIPMENTS. Enter Name/location of Railhead.
23a.	ALTERNATE METHOD OF DELIVERY. Enter Rail, Truck, Rail or Truck, or Barge.
23b.	ESTIMATED ADDITIONAL COST. As stated.
24.	TYPE OF RAILROAD CARS REQUIRED. As stated.
25.	ESTIMATED CHARGES FOR LABOR AND EQUIPMENT IF COMMERCIAL SERVICE IS REQUIRED FOR UNLOADING, HAULING AND STORAGE OF COAL. As stated.
26.	STATE OR LOCAL REGULATORY SULFUR DIOXIDE EMISSION LIMITS. Enter in units.
27.	SPUR TRACK TO INSTALLATION. Check yes or no.
28.	REMARKS. (Include special conditions and distribution e-mail addresses) Or use separate attachment.
29.	TECHNICAL POINT OF CONTACT REQUESTING ACTIVITY. Enter typed name, e-mail, and telephone.
30.	PREPARED BY. Enter typed name, signature, e-mail, and telephone.
31.	APPROVED AT REQUESTING ACTIVITY BY. Enter typed name, signature, e-mail, and telephone of approving official.
32.	APPROVED BY. Enter typed name, signature, e-mail, and telephone of approving official.

253.303-428 DD Form 428: Communication Service Authorization

[DAC 91-10, 2/29/96]

COMMUNICATION SERVICE AUTHORIZATION

1. AUTHORIZATION a. NUMBER	1. b. DATE (YYYYMMDD)	2. AUTHORIZATION a. NUMBER	2. b. DATE (YYYYMMDD)	3. CIRCUIT OR BILL NUMBER

4. FROM (Include ZIP Code)	5. SUBMIT BILLS FOR CERTIFICATION TO (Include ZIP Code)

6. TO (Communications Company)
- a. COMPANY NAME
- b. ADDRESS
  - (1) STREET
  - (2) CITY
  - (3) STATE
  - (4) ZIP CODE

7. TELEPHONE NUMBER TO CONTACT FOR DETAILS (Include Area Code)

8. AUTHORIZATION. In accordance with provisions of the contract indicated above of which this authorization forms a part, authority is hereby given to Communications Company indicated in Item 6 to establish or perform services for official use as prescribed below at:

9. SERVICE(S)

DESCRIPTION a.	NUMBER b.	NON-RECURRING CHARGE c.	d. RATE PER MONTH PER UNIT (1)	d. RATE PER MONTH TOTAL (2)

10. DISBURSING OFFICER MAKING PAYMENT
- a. NAME (Last, First, Middle Initial)
- b. GRADE

11. DISTRIBUTION

12. AUTHORIZING OFFICIAL
- a. SIGNATURE
- b. TITLE
- c. GRADE

13. ACCEPTANCE
- a. NAME OF CONTRACTING FIRM
- b. SIGNATURE OF CONTRACTOR'S REPRESENTATIVE
- c. DATE SIGNED (YYYYMMDD)

DD FORM 428, MAY 1999 PREVIOUS EDITION IS OBSOLETE.

253.303-448 DD Form 448: Military Interdepartmental Purchase Request

MILITARY INTERDEPARTMENTAL PURCHASE REQUEST

1. PAGE 1 OF PAGES

2. FSC	3. CONTROL SYMBOL NO.	4. DATE PREPARED	5. MIPR NUMBER	6. AMEND NO.

7. TO:	8. FROM: (Agency, name, telephone number of originator)

9. ITEMS ☐ ARE ☐ ARE NOT INCLUDED IN THE INTERSERVICE SUPPLY SUPPORT PROGRAM AND REQUIRED INTERSERVICE SCREENING ☐ HAS ☐ HAS NOT BEEN ACCOMPLISHED

ITEM NO. a	DESCRIPTION (Federal stock number, nomenclature, specification and/or drawing No., etc.) b	QTY c	UNIT d	ESTIMATED UNIT PRICE e	ESTIMATED TOTAL PRICE f

10. SEE ATTACHED PAGES FOR DELIVERY SCHEDULES, PRESERVATION AND PACKAGING INSTRUCTIONS, SHIPPING INSTRUCTIONS AND INSTRUCTIONS FOR DISTRIBUTION OF CONTRACTS AND RELATED DOCUMENTS.

11. GRAND TOTAL

12. TRANSPORTATION ALLOTMENT (Used if FOB Contractor's plant)	13. MAIL INVOICES TO (Payment will be made by)
	PAY OFFICE DODAAD

14. FUNDS FOR PROCUREMENT ARE PROPERLY CHARGEABLE TO THE ALLOTMENTS SET FORTH BELOW, THE AVAILABLE BALANCES OF WHICH ARE SUFFICIENT TO COVER THE ESTIMATED TOTAL PRICE.

ACRN	APPROPRIATION	LIMIT/ SUBHEAD	SUPPLEMENTAL ACCOUNTING CLASSIFICATION	ACCTG STA DODAAD	AMOUNT

15. AUTHORIZING OFFICER (Type name and title)	16. SIGNATURE	17. DATE

DD Form 448, JUN 72 PREVIOUS EDITION IS OBSOLETE. 164/073

253.303-448-2 DD Form 448-2: Acceptance of MIPR

ACCEPTANCE OF MIPR

1. TO (Requiring Activity Address) *(Include ZIP Code)*	2. MIPR NUMBER	3. AMENDMENT NO.
	4. DATE *(MIPR Signature date)*	5. AMOUNT *(As Listed on the MIPR)*

6. The MIPR identified above is accepted and the items requested will be provided as follows: *(Check as Applicable)*

a. ☐ ALL ITEMS WILL BE PROVIDED THROUGH REIMBURSEMENT *(Category I)*

b. ☐ ALL ITEMS WILL BE PROCURED BY THE DIRECT CITATION OF FUNDS *(Category II)*

c. ☐ ITEMS WILL BE PROVIDED BY BOTH CATEGORY I AND CATEGORY II AS INDICATED BELOW

d. ☐ THIS ACCEPTANCE, FOR CATEGORY I ITEMS, IS QUALIFIED BECAUSE OF ANTICIPATED CONTINGENCIES AS TO FINAL PRICE. CHANGES IN THIS ACCEPTANCE FIGURE WILL BE FURNISHED PERIODICALLY UPON DETERMINATION OF DEFINITIZED PRICES, BUT PRIOR TO SUBMISSION OF BILLINGS.

7. ☐ MIPR ITEM NUMBER(S) IDENTIFIED IN BLOCK 13, "REMARKS" IS NOT ACCEPTED (IS REJECTED) FOR THE REASONS INDICATED.

8. TO BE PROVIDED THROUGH REIMBURSEMENT CATEGORY I			9. TO BE PROCURED BY DIRECT CITATION OF FUNDS CATEGORY II		
ITEM NO. a.	QUANTITY b.	ESTIMATED PRICE c.	ITEM NO. a.	QUANTITY b.	ESTIMATED PRICE c.
d. TOTAL ESTIMATED PRICE			d. TOTAL ESTIMATED PRICE		
10. ANTICIPATED DATE OF OBLIGATION FOR CATEGORY II ITEMS			11. GRAND TOTAL ESTIMATED PRICE OF ALL ITEMS		

12. FUNDS DATA *(Check if Applicable)*

a. ☐ ADDITIONAL FUNDS IN THE AMOUNT OF $ ________ ARE REQUIRED *(See Justification in Block 13)*

b. ☐ FUNDS IN THE AMOUNT OF $ ________ ARE NOT REQUIRED AND MAY BE WITHDRAWN

13. REMARKS

14. ACCEPTING ACTIVITY *(Complete Address)*	15. TYPED NAME AND TITLE OF AUTHORIZED OFFICIAL	
	16. SIGNATURE	17. DATE

DD Form 448-2, JUL 71 PREVIOUS EDITION WILL BE USED UNTIL EXHAUSTED.

253.303-879 DD Form 879: Statement of Compliance

[DAC 91-7, 5/17/95]

STATEMENT OF COMPLIANCE	*Form Approved OMB No. 1215-0149 Expires June 30, 2000*

The public reporting burden for this collection of information is estimated to average 16 minutes per response, including the time for reviewing instructions, searching existing data sources, gathering and maintaining the data needed, and completing and reviewing the collection of information. Send comments regarding this burden estimate or any other aspect of this collection of information, including suggestions for reducing the burden, to the Department of Defense, Executive Services and Communications Directorate (1215-0149). Respondents should be aware that notwithstanding any other provision of law, no person shall be subject to any penalty for failing to comply with a collection of information if it does not display a currently valid OMB control number.

PLEASE DO NOT RETURN YOUR COMPLETED FORM TO THE ABOVE ORGANIZATION. RETURN THE COMPLETED FORM TO THE CONTRACTING OFFICER.

1. PAYROLL NUMBER	2. PAYROLL PAYMENT DATE *(YYYYMMDD)*	3. CONTRACT NUMBER	4. DATE *(YYYYMMDD)*

I, ______________ *(Name of signatory party)*, ______________ *(Title)* do hereby state

(1) That I pay or supervise the payment of the persons employed by ______________ *(Contractor or subcontractor)*

on the ______________ *(Building or work)*; that during the payroll period commencing on the ______ day of ______, ______, and ending the ______ day of ______, ______, all persons employed

on said project have been paid the full weekly wages earned, that no rebates have been or will be made either directly or indirectly to or on

behalf of said ______________ *(Contractor or subcontractor)* from the full weekly wages earned by any person

and that no deductions have been made either directly or indirectly from the full wages earned by any person, other than permissible deductions as defined in Regulations, Part 3 (29 CFR Subtitle A), issued by the Secretary of Labor under the Copeland Act, as amended *(48 Stat. 948, 63 Stat. 108, 72 Stat. 967; 76 Stat. 357; 40 U.S.C. 276c)*, and described below:

(2) That any payrolls otherwise under this contract required to be submitted for the above period are correct and complete; that the wage rates for laborers or mechanics contained therein are not less than the applicable wage rates contained in any wage determination incorporated into the contract; that the classifications set forth therein for each laborer or mechanic conform with the work performed.

(3) That any apprentices employed in the above period are duly registered in a bona fide apprenticeship program registered with a State apprenticeship agency recognized by the Bureau of Apprenticeship and Training, United States Department of Labor, or if no such recognized agency exists in a State, are registered with the Bureau of Apprenticeship and Training, United States Department of Labor.

(4) That:

(a) **WHERE FRINGE BENEFITS ARE PAID TO APPROVED PLANS, FUNDS, OR PROGRAMS**

☐ - In addition to the basic hourly wage rates paid to each laborer or mechanic listed in the above referenced payroll, payments of fringe benefits as listed in the contract have been or will be made to appropriate programs for the benefit of such employees, except as noted in Section 4(c) below.

(b) **WHERE FRINGE BENEFITS ARE PAID IN CASH**

☐ - Each laborer or mechanic listed in the above referenced payroll has been paid as indicated on the payroll, an amount not less than the sum of the applicable basic hourly wage rate plus the amount of the required fringe benefits as listed in the contract, except as noted in Section 4(c) below.

(c) **EXCEPTIONS**

EXCEPTION *(Craft)*	EXPLANATION

5. REMARKS

6. NAME *(Last, First, Middle Initial)*	7. TITLE	8. SIGNATURE

The willful falsification of any of the above statements may subject the contractor or subcontractor to civil or criminal prosecution. See Section 1001 of Title 18 and Section 3729 of Title 31 of the United States Code.

INSTRUCTIONS FOR PREPARATION OF DD FORM 879, STATEMENT OF COMPLIANCE

This statement of compliance meets requirements resulting from the Davis-Bacon Act (40 U.S.C. 276a - 276a-7). Under this law, the contractor is required to pay minimum wage rates and fringe benefits as predetermined by the Department of Labor. The contractor's obligation to pay fringe benefits may be met by payment of the fringes to approved plans, funds, or programs or by making these payments to the employees as cash in lieu of fringes.

The contractor should show on the face of its payroll all monies paid to the employees whether as basic rates or as cash in lieu of fringes. The contractor shall represent in the statement of compliance that either it is paying fringes required by the contract to approved plans, funds, or programs, or it is paying employees cash in lieu of fringes. Detailed instructions follow:

CONTRACTORS THAT PAY ALL REQUIRED FRINGE BENEFITS

A contractor that pays fringe benefits to approved plans, funds, or programs in amounts not less than were determined in the applicable wage decision of the Secretary of Labor shall show on the face of the payroll the basic cash hourly rate and overtime rate paid to employees. Such a contractor shall check Section 4(a) of the statement to indicate that payment is also being made to approved plans, funds, or programs not less than the amount predetermined as fringe benefits for each craft. Any exception shall be noted in Section 4(c).

CONTRACTORS THAT PAY NO FRINGE BENEFITS

A contractor that pays no fringe benefits shall pay to the employee and insert in the straight time hourly rate column of the payroll an amount not less than the predetermined rate for each classification plus the amount of fringe benefits determined for each classification in the applicable wage decision. Inasmuch as it is not necessary to pay time and a half on cash paid in lieu of fringes, the overtime rate shall be not less than the sum of the basic predetermined rate, plus the half time premium on the basic or regular rate, plus the required cash in lieu of fringes at the straight time rate. To simplify computation of overtime, it is suggested that the straight time basic rate and cash in lieu of fringes be separately stated in the hourly rate column, thus $X.XX/$X.XX. In addition, the contractor shall mark Section 4(b) of the statement to indicate that payment of fringe benefits is being made in cash directly to employees. Any exceptions shall be noted in Section 4(c).

USE OF SECTION 4(c), EXCEPTIONS

Any contractor that is making payment to approved plans, funds, or programs in amounts less than the wage determination required is obliged to pay the deficiency directly to the employees as cash in lieu of fringes. Any exceptions to Section 4(a) or 4(b), whichever the contractor may mark, shall be entered in Section 4(c). Enter in the Exception column the craft, and enter in the Explanation column the hourly amount paid the employees as cash in lieu of fringes, and the hourly amount paid to plans, funds, or programs as fringes.

253.303-882 DD Form 882: Report of Inventions and Subcontracts (Pursuant to "Patent Rights" Contract Clause)

[DAC 91-11, 9/26/96]

REPORT OF INVENTIONS AND SUBCONTRACTS
(Pursuant to "Patent Rights" Contract Clause) (See Instructions on back)

Form Approved
OMB No. 9000-0095
Expires Jan 31, 2008

The public reporting burden for this collection of information is estimated to average 1 hour per response, including the time for reviewing instructions, searching existing data sources, gathering and maintaining the data needed, and completing and reviewing the collection of information. Send comments regarding this burden estimate or any other aspect of this collection of information, including suggestions for reducing the burden, to the Department of Defense, Executive Services Directorate (9000-0095). Respondents should be aware that notwithstanding any other provision of law, no person shall be subject to any penalty for failing to comply with a collection of information if it does not display a currently valid OMB control number.

PLEASE DO NOT RETURN YOUR COMPLETED FORM TO THE ABOVE ORGANIZATION. RETURN COMPLETED FORM TO THE CONTRACTING OFFICER.

1.a. NAME OF CONTRACTOR/SUBCONTRACTOR	c. CONTRACT NUMBER	2.a. NAME OF GOVERNMENT PRIME CONTRACTOR	c. CONTRACT NUMBER	3. TYPE OF REPORT *(X one)*: a. INTERIM / b. FINAL
b. ADDRESS *(Include ZIP Code)*	d. AWARD DATE *(YYYYMMDD)*	b. ADDRESS *(Include ZIP Code)*	d. AWARD DATE *(YYYYMMDD)*	4. REPORTING PERIOD *(YYYYMMDD)*: a. FROM / b. TO

SECTION I - SUBJECT INVENTIONS

5. "SUBJECT INVENTIONS" REQUIRED TO BE REPORTED BY CONTRACTOR/SUBCONTRACTOR *(If "None," so state)*

NAME(S) OF INVENTOR(S) *(Last, First, Middle Initial)* a.	TITLE OF INVENTION(S) b.	DISCLOSURE NUMBER, PATENT APPLICATION SERIAL NUMBER OR PATENT NUMBER c.	ELECTION TO FILE PATENT APPLICATIONS *(X)* d. (1) UNITED STATES (a) YES	(1) UNITED STATES (b) NO	(2) FOREIGN (a) YES	(2) FOREIGN (b) NO	CONFIRMATORY INSTRUMENT OR ASSIGNMENT FORWARDED TO CONTRACTING OFFICER *(X)* e. (a) YES	(b) NO

f. EMPLOYER OF INVENTOR(S) NOT EMPLOYED BY CONTRACTOR/SUBCONTRACTOR		g. ELECTED FOREIGN COUNTRIES IN WHICH A PATENT APPLICATION WILL BE FILED	
(1) (a) NAME OF INVENTOR *(Last, First, Middle Initial)*	(2) (a) NAME OF INVENTOR *(Last, First, Middle Initial)*	(1) TITLE OF INVENTION	(2) FOREIGN COUNTRIES OF PATENT APPLICATION
(b) NAME OF EMPLOYER	(b) NAME OF EMPLOYER		
(c) ADDRESS OF EMPLOYER *(Include ZIP Code)*	(c) ADDRESS OF EMPLOYER *(Include ZIP Code)*		

SECTION II - SUBCONTRACTS *(Containing a "Patent Rights" clause)*

6. SUBCONTRACTS AWARDED BY CONTRACTOR/SUBCONTRACTOR *(If "None," so state)*

NAME OF SUBCONTRACTOR(S) a.	ADDRESS *(Include ZIP Code)* b.	SUBCONTRACT NUMBER(S) c.	FAR "PATENT RIGHTS" d. (1) CLAUSE NUMBER	(2) DATE *(YYYYMM)*	DESCRIPTION OF WORK TO BE PERFORMED UNDER SUBCONTRACT(S) e.	SUBCONTRACT DATES *(YYYYMMDD)* f. (1) AWARD	(2) ESTIMATED COMPLETION

SECTION III - CERTIFICATION

7. CERTIFICATION OF REPORT BY CONTRACTOR/SUBCONTRACTOR *(Not required if: (X as appropriate))* ☐ SMALL BUSINESS or ☐ NONPROFIT ORGANIZATION

I certify that the reporting party has procedures for prompt identification and timely disclosure of "Subject Inventions," that such procedures have been followed and that all "Subject Inventions" have been reported.

a. NAME OF AUTHORIZED CONTRACTOR/SUBCONTRACTOR OFFICIAL *(Last, First, Middle Initial)*	b. TITLE	c. SIGNATURE	d. DATE SIGNED

DD FORM 882 INSTRUCTIONS

GENERAL

This form is for use in submitting INTERIM and FINAL invention reports to the Contracting Officer and for use in reporting the award of subcontracts containing a "Patent Rights" clause. If the form does not afford sufficient space, multiple forms may be used or plain sheets of paper with proper identification of information by item number may be attached.

An INTERIM report is due at least every 12 months from the date of contract award and shall include (a) a listing of "Subject Inventions" during the reporting period, (b) a certification of compliance with required invention identification and disclosure procedures together with a certification of reporting of all "Subject Inventions," and (c) any required information not previously reported on subcontracts containing a "Patent Rights" clause.

A FINAL report is due within 6 months if contractor is a small business firm or domestic nonprofit organization and within 3 months for all others after completion of the contract work and shall include (a) a listing of all "Subject Inventions" required by the contract to be reported, and (b) any required information not previously reported on subcontracts awarded during the course of or under the contract and containing a "Patent Rights" clause.

While the form may be used for simultaneously reporting inventions and subcontracts, it may also be used for reporting, promptly after award, subcontracts containing a "Patent Rights" clause.

Dates shall be entered where indicated in certain items on this form and shall be entered in six or eight digit numbers in the order of year and month (YYYYMM) or year, month and day (YYYYMMDD). Example: April 2005 should be entered as 200504 and April 15, 2005 should be entered as 20050415.

1.a. Self-explanatory.

1.b. Self-explanatory.

1.c. If "same" as Item 2.c., so state.

1.d. Self-explanatory.

2.a. If "same" as Item 1.a., so state.

2.b. Self-explanatory.

2.c. Procurement Instrument Identification (PII) number of contract (DFARS 204.7003).

2.d. through 5.e. Self-explanatory.

5.f. The name and address of the employer of each inventor not employed by the contractor or subcontractor is needed because the Government's rights in a reported invention may not be determined solely by the terms of the "Patent Rights" clause in the contract.

Example 1: If an invention is made by a Government employee assigned to work with a contractor, the Government rights in such an invention will be determined under Executive Order 10096.

Example 2: If an invention is made under a contract by joint inventors and one of the inventors is a Government employee, the Government's rights in such an inventor's interest in the invention will also be determined under Executive Order 10096, except where the contractor is a small business or nonprofit organization, in which case the provisions of 35 U.S.C. 202(e) will apply.

5.g.(1) Self-explanatory.

5.g.(2) Self-explanatory with the exception that the contractor or subcontractor shall indicate, if known at the time of this report, whether applications will be filed under either the Patent Cooperation Treaty (PCT) or the European Patent Convention (EPC). If such is known, the letters PCT or EPC shall be entered after each listed country.

6.a. Self-explanatory.

6.b. Self-explanatory.

6.c. Self-explanatory.

6.d. Patent Rights Clauses are located in FAR 52.227.

6.e. Self-explanatory.

6.f. Self-explanatory.

7. Certification not required by small business firms and domestic nonprofit organizations.

7.a. through 7.d. Self-explanatory.

253.303-1057 DD Form 1057: Monthly Summary of Contracting Actions

[DAC 91-1, 12/31/91.]

MONTHLY SUMMARY OF CONTRACTING ACTIONS

Report Control Symbol DD-AT&L(M)1015

	Section A – General Information		
A1	Report Month		
A2	Name of Contracting Office		
A2a	Name		
A2b	Address		
A3	Contracting Office Codes		
A3a	Reporting Agency FIPS 95 Code		
A3b	Contracting Office Code		

	Section B – Contracting Actions (1) Category	(2) Actions	(3) Dollars
B1	Tariff or Regulated Acquisitions		
B2	Foreign or Interagency		
B2a	FMS or International Agreements		
B2b	Actions with UNICOR		
B2c	Actions with Other Government Agencies		
B3	Small Business		
B3a	Simplified Acquisition Procedures		
B3b	GSA Schedule Orders		
B3c	Other Federal Schedule Orders		
B3d	All Other Orders		
B3e	Other Contracting Actions		
B4	Large Business		
B4a	Simplified Acquisition Procedures		
B4b	GSA Schedule Orders		
B4c	Other Federal Schedule Orders		
B4d	All Other Orders		
B4e	Other Contracting Actions		
B5	Domestic or Foreign Entities Performing Outside the U.S.		
B5a	Simplified Acquisition Procedures		
B5b	GSA Schedule Orders		
B5c	Other Federal Schedule Orders		
B5d	All Other Orders		
B5e	Other Contracting Actions		
B6	Educational		
B6a	Simplified Acquisition Procedures		
B6b	GSA Schedule Orders		
B6c	Other Federal Schedule Orders		
B6d	All Other Orders		
B6e	Other Contracting Actions		
B7	Nonprofit and Other		
B7a	Simplified Acquisition Procedures		
B7b	GSA Schedule Orders		
B7c	Other Federal Schedule Orders		
B7d	All Other Orders		
B7e	Other Contracting Actions		

PREVIOUS EDITION IS OBSOLETE.

DD FORM 1057, OCT 2001 1

MONTHLY SUMMARY OF CONTRACTING ACTIONS

Report Control Symbol DD-AT&L(M)1015

	(1) Category	(2) Actions	(3) Dollars
B8	Total Contracting Actions		
B8a	Simplified Acquisition Procedures		
B8b	GSA Schedule Orders		
B8c	Other Federal Schedule Orders		
B8d	All Other Orders		
B8e	Other Contracting Actions		
B9	Total Modifications Excluding Simplified Acquisition Procedures		
	Section C – Extent Competed		
C1	Competed		
C1a	Small Business Concerns		
C1b	Large Business Concerns		
C1c	Domestic or Foreign Entities Performing Outside the U.S.		
C1d	Educational		
C1e	Nonprofit and Other		
C2	Not Available for Competition		
C2a	Small Business Concerns		
C2b	Large Business Concerns		
C2c	Domestic or Foreign Entities Performing Outside the U.S.		
C2d	Educational		
C2e	Nonprofit and Other		
C3	Not Competed		
C3a	Small Business Concerns		
C3b	Large Business Concerns		
C3c	Domestic or Foreign Entities Performing Outside the U.S.		
C3d	Educational		
C3e	Nonprofit and Other		
	Section D – RDT&E Actions		
D1	Small Business		
D2	Large Business		
D3	Domestic or Foreign Entities Performing Outside the U.S.		
D4	Historically Black Colleges and Universities (HBCU)		
D5	Minority Institutions (MI)		
D6	Other Educational		
D7	Other Entities		

DD FORM 1057, OCT 2001 2

MONTHLY SUMMARY OF CONTRACTING ACTIONS

Report Control Symbol DD-AT&L(M)1015

	(1) Category	(2) Actions	(3) Dollars
	Section E – Selected Socioeconomic Statistics		
E1	Small Business (SB) Set-Aside	________	________
E1a	SB Set-Aside Using Simplified Acquisition Procedures	________	________
E1b	SB Set-Aside	________	________
E1c	Reserved	________	________
E2	Small Disadvantaged Business (SDB) Actions	________	________
E2a	Through SBA—Section 8(a)	________	________
E2b	SDB Set-Aside, SDB Preference, or SDB Evaluation Adjustment	________	________
E2c	SB Set-Aside Using Simplified Acquisition Procedures	________	________
E2d	SB Set-Aside	________	________
E2e	Other	________	________
E3	SDB Federal Schedule Orders	________	________
E4	Women-Owned Small Business	________	________
E5	Women-Owned Small Business Federal Schedule Orders	________	________
E6	HBCU	________	________
E7	MI	________	________
E8	JWOD Participating Nonprofit Agencies	________	________
E9	Exempt from Small Business Act Requirements	________	________
E10	HUBZone	________	________
E10a	HUBZone Set-Aside	________	________
E10b	HUBZone Price Evaluation Preference	________	________
E10c	HUBZone Sole Source	________	________
E10d	HUBZone Concern – Other	________	________
E11	Service-Related Disabled Veteran-Owned Small Business	________	________
E12	Other Veteran-Owned Small Business	________	________
	Section F – Simplified Acquisition Procedures – Ranges		
F1	$0.01 to $2,500.00	________	________
F2	$2,500.01 to $10,000.00	________	________
F3	$10,000.01 to $25,000.00	________	________
	Section G – Contingency Actions		
G1	Total Actions	________	________
G1a	Competed	________	________
G1b	Not Available for Competition	________	________
G1c	Not Competed	________	________

Section H – Remarks and Authentication

H1 Remarks: ________________________________

H2 Contracting Officer

H2a Name ________________________________

H2b Signature ________________________

H2c Telephone Number ________________

H2d Date Report Submitted *(yyyymmdd)* ________________

DD FORM 1057, OCT 2001 3

253.303-1131 DD Form 1131: Cash Collection Voucher

CASH COLLECTION VOUCHER

1. DISBURSING OFFICE COLLECTION VOUCHER NUMBER

2. RECEIVING OFFICE COLLECTION VOUCHER NUMBER

3. RECEIVING OFFICE

a. ACTIVITY *(Name and Location) (Include ZIP Code)*

b. RECEIVED AND FORWARDED BY *(Printed Name, Title and Signature)*

d. DATE *(YYYYMMDD)*

c. TELEPHONE NUMBER *(Include Area Code)*:
COMMERCIAL: DSN:

4. DISBURSING OFFICE

a. ACTIVITY *(Name and Location) (Include ZIP Code)*

b. DISBURSING OFFICER *(Printed Name, Title and Signature)*

d. DISBURSING STATION SYMBOL NUMBER

c. TELEPHONE NUMBER *(Include Area Code)*:
COMMERCIAL: DSN:

e. DATE *(YYYYMMDD)*

5. PERIOD: a. FROM: b. TO:

6. DATE RECEIVED	7. NAME OF REMITTER DESCRIPTION OF REMITTANCE	8. DETAILED DESCRIPTION OF PURPOSE FOR WHICH COLLECTIONS WERE RECEIVED	9. AMOUNT	10. ACCOUNTING CLASSIFICATION
		11. TOTAL	0.00	

253.303-1149 DD Form 1149: Requisition and Invoice/Shipping Document

[DAC 91-6, 5/27/94]

REQUISITION AND INVOICE/SHIPPING DOCUMENT	OMB No. 0704-0246 *OMB approval expires Apr 30, 2009*

The public reporting burden for this collection of information is estimated to average 1 hour per response, including the time for reviewing instructions, searching existing data sources, gathering and maintaining the data needed, and completing and reviewing the collection of information. Send comments regarding this burden estimate or any other aspect of this collection of information, including suggestions for reducing the burden, to the Department of Defense, Executive Services Directorate (0704-0246). Respondents should be aware that notwithstanding any other provision of law, no person shall be subject to any penalty for failing to comply with a collection of information if it does not display a currently valid OMB control number.

PLEASE DO NOT RETURN YOUR FORM TO THE ABOVE ORGANIZATION. RETURN COMPLETED FORM TO THE ADDRESS IN ITEM 2.

1. FROM: *(Include ZIP Code)*	SHEET NO.	NO. OF SHEETS	5. REQUISITION DATE	6. REQUISITION NUMBER
	7. DATE MATERIAL REQUIRED *(YYYYMMDD)*			8. PRIORITY
2. TO: *(Include ZIP Code)*	9. AUTHORITY OR PURPOSE			
	10. SIGNATURE			11a. VOUCHER NUMBER & DATE *(YYYYMMDD)*
3. SHIP TO - MARK FOR	12. DATE SHIPPED *(YYYYMMDD)*			b.
	13. MODE OF SHIPMENT			14. BILL OF LADING NUMBER
	15. AIR MOVEMENT DESIGNATOR OR PORT REFERENCE NO.			
4. APPROPRIATIONS DATA				AMOUNT

ITEM NO. (a)	FEDERAL STOCK NUMBER, DESCRIPTION, AND CODING OF MATERIEL AND/OR SERVICES (b)	UNIT OF ISSUE (c)	QUANTITY REQUESTED (d)	SUPPLY ACTION (e)	TYPE CON-TAINER (f)	CON-TAINER NOS. (g)	UNIT PRICE (h)	TOTAL COST (i)
								0.00
								0.00
								0.00
								0.00
								0.00

16. TRANSPORTATION VIA AMC OR MSC CHARGEABLE TO	17. SPECIAL HANDLING

18. RECAPITULATION OF SHIPMENT	TOTAL CON-TAINERS	TYPE CON-TAINER	DESCRIPTION	TOTAL WEIGHT	TOTAL CUBE	19. RECEIPT	DATE	BY	
ISSUED BY						CONTAINERS RECEIVED EXCEPT AS NOTED	DATE *(YYYYMMDD)*	BY	SHEET TOTAL 0.00
CHECKED BY						QUANTITIES RECEIVED EXCEPT AS NOTED	DATE *(YYYYMMDD)*	BY	GRAND TOTAL
PACKED BY			← TOTAL →			POSTED	DATE *(YYYYMMDD)*	BY	20. RECEIVER'S VOUCHER NO.

REQUISITION AND INVOICE/SHIPPING DOCUMENT *(Continuation Sheet)*

OMB No. 0704-0246
OMB approval expires Apr 30, 2009

The public reporting burden for this collection of information is estimated to average 1 hour per response, including the time for reviewing instructions, searching existing data sources, gathering and maintaining the data needed, and completing and reviewing the collection of information. Send comments regarding this burden estimate or any other aspect of this collection of information, including suggestions for reducing the burden, to the Department of Defense, Executive Services Directorate (0704-0246). Respondents should be aware that notwithstanding any other provision of law, no person shall be subject to any penalty for failing to comply with a collection of information if it does not display a currently valid OMB control number.

PLEASE DO NOT RETURN YOUR FORM TO THIS ADDRESS. RETURN COMPLETED FORM TO THE ADDRESS IN ITEM 2 OF DD FORM 1149.

SHEET NO.	NO. OF SHEETS	6. REQUISITION NUMBER	11a. VOUCHER NUMBER AND DATE	b. VOUCHER NUMBER AND DATE

ITEM NO. (a)	FEDERAL STOCK NUMBER, DESCRIPTION, AND CODING OF MATERIEL AND/OR SERVICES (b)	UNIT OF ISSUE (c)	QUANTITY REQUESTED (d)	SUPPLY ACTION (e)	TYPE CON-TAINER (f)	CON-TAINER NOS. (g)	UNIT PRICE (h)	TOTAL COST (i)
								0.00
								0.00
								0.00
								0.00
								0.00
								0.00
								0.00
								0.00
								0.00
							SHEET TOTAL	0.00

253.303-1155 DD Form 1155: Order for Supplies or Services

[DAC 91-7, 5/17/95]

ORDER FOR SUPPLIES OR SERVICES — PAGE 1 OF

1. CONTRACT/PURCH ORDER/AGREEMENT NO.
2. DELIVERY ORDER/CALL NO.
3. DATE OF ORDER/CALL (YYYYMMMDD)
4. REQUISITION/PURCH REQUEST NO.
5. PRIORITY

6. ISSUED BY — CODE
7. ADMINISTERED BY (If other than 6) — CODE
8. DELIVERY FOB — DESTINATION — OTHER (See Schedule if other)

9. CONTRACTOR — CODE — FACILITY
NAME AND ADDRESS
10. DELIVER TO FOB POINT BY (Date) (YYYYMMMDD)
11. X IF BUSINESS IS — SMALL — SMALL DISAD-VANTAGED — WOMEN-OWNED
12. DISCOUNT TERMS
13. MAIL INVOICES TO THE ADDRESS IN BLOCK

14. SHIP TO — CODE
15. PAYMENT WILL BE MADE BY — CODE
MARK ALL PACKAGES AND PAPERS WITH IDENTIFICATION NUMBERS IN BLOCKS 1 AND 2.

16. TYPE OF ORDER
- DELIVERY/CALL — This delivery order/call is issued on another Government agency or in accordance with and subject to terms and conditions of above numbered contract.
- PURCHASE — Reference your ______ furnish the following on terms specified herein.

ACCEPTANCE THE CONTRACTOR HEREBY ACCEPTS THE OFFER REPRESENTED BY THE NUMBERED PURCHASE ORDER AS IT MAY PREVIOUSLY HAVE BEEN OR IS NOW MODIFIED, SUBJECT TO ALL OF THE TERMS AND CONDITIONS SET FORTH, AND AGREES TO PERFORM THE SAME.

NAME OF CONTRACTOR — SIGNATURE — TYPED NAME AND TITLE — DATE SIGNED (YYYYMMMDD)

If this box is marked, supplier must sign Acceptance and return the following number of copies:

17. ACCOUNTING AND APPROPRIATION DATA/LOCAL USE

18. ITEM NO.	19. SCHEDULE OF SUPPLIES/SERVICES	20. QUANTITY ORDERED/ ACCEPTED*	21. UNIT	22. UNIT PRICE	23. AMOUNT

* If quantity accepted by the Government is same as quantity ordered, indicate by X. If different, enter actual quantity accepted below quantity ordered and encircle.

24. UNITED STATES OF AMERICA
BY: — CONTRACTING/ORDERING OFFICER
25. TOTAL
26. DIFFERENCES

27a. QUANTITY IN COLUMN 20 HAS BEEN
INSPECTED — RECEIVED — ACCEPTED, AND CONFORMS TO THE CONTRACT EXCEPT AS NOTED: ______

b. SIGNATURE OF AUTHORIZED GOVERNMENT REPRESENTATIVE
c. DATE (YYYYMMMDD)
d. PRINTED NAME AND TITLE OF AUTHORIZED GOVERNMENT REPRESENTATIVE

e. MAILING ADDRESS OF AUTHORIZED GOVERNMENT REPRESENTATIVE
28. SHIP. NO. — PARTIAL — FINAL
29. D.O. VOUCHER NO.
30. INITIALS

f. TELEPHONE NUMBER
g. E-MAIL ADDRESS
31. PAYMENT — COMPLETE — PARTIAL — FINAL
32. PAID BY
33. AMOUNT VERIFIED CORRECT FOR
34. CHECK NUMBER
35. BILL OF LADING NO.

36. I CERTIFY THIS ACCOUNT IS CORRECT AND PROPER FOR PAYMENT.
a. DATE (YYYYMMMDD)
b. SIGNATURE AND TITLE OF CERTIFYING OFFICER

37. RECEIVED AT
38. RECEIVED BY (Print)
39. DATE RECEIVED (YYYYMMMDD)
40. TOTAL CONTAINERS
41. S/R ACCOUNT NUMBER
42. S/R VOUCHER NO.

DD FORM 1155, DEC 2001 — PREVIOUS EDITION IS OBSOLETE.

253.303-1155c-1 DD Form 1155c-1: Order for Supplies or Services (Commissary Continuation Sheet)

[DAC 91-7, 5/17/95]

ORDER FOR SUPPLIES OR SERVICES
(Commissary Continuation Sheet)

1. CONTRACTOR				2. PURCHASE OR DELIVERY ORDER NUMBER	3. DATE OF ORDER	4. PAGE NO.	5. NO. OF PAGES
6. ISSUED BY				7. CONTRACT NUMBER	8. VENDOR INVOICE NUMBER	9. RECEIVING REPORT NUMBER	

10. ITEM NO.	11. SCHEDULE OF SUPPLIES/SERVICES	12. QUANTITY ORDERED*	13. QUANTITY ACCEPTED*	14. UNIT	15. UNIT PRICE	16. AMOUNT	17. RETAIL a. UNIT PRICE	17. RETAIL b. EXTENSION
						$0.00		
						$0.00		
						$0.00		
						$0.00		
						$0.00		
						$0.00		
						$0.00		
						$0.00		
						$0.00		
						$0.00		

*The supplies or services listed in the "Quantity Ordered" column were inspected and accepted, and quantities shown therein were received, unless otherwise noted in the "Quantity Accepted" column.	18. DATE	19. AUTHORIZED GOVERNMENT REPRESENTATIVE

DD FORM 1155C-1, JAN 1998 (EG) PREVIOUS EDITION MAY BE USED. Designed using Perform Pro, WHS/DIOR, Jan 98

253.303-1342 DD Form 1342: DoD Property Record

[DAC 91-6, 5/27/94]

DOD PROPERTY RECORD

Form Approved OMB No. 0704-0246 Expires Feb 28, 2006

The public reporting burden for this collection of information is estimated to average 2.5 hours per response, including the time for reviewing instructions, searching existing data sources, gathering and maintaining the data needed, and completing and reviewing the collection of information. Send comments regarding this burden estimate or any other aspect of this collection of information, including suggestions for reducing the burden, to the Department of Defense, Executive Services and Communications Directorate (0704-0246). Respondents should be aware that notwithstanding any other provision of law, no person shall be subject to any penalty for failing to comply with a collection of information if it does not display a currently valid OMB control number.

PLEASE DO NOT RETURN YOUR COMPLETED FORM TO THE ABOVE ORGANIZATION. RETURN COMPLETED FORM TO THE CONTRACT ADMINISTRATION OFFICE

1.	a. ACTIVE	b. INITIAL	c. IDLE	d. CHANGE	2. JULIAN DATE	3. I.D./GOVERNMENT TAG NO.

SECTION I - INVENTORY RECORD

4. COMMODITY CODE	5. STOCK NUMBER	6. ACQUISITION COST	7. TYPE CODE	8. YR OF MFG.	9. POWER CODE	10. STATUS CODE	11. SVC CODE	12. COMMAND CODE	13. ADM OFFICE CODE

14. NAME OF MANUFACTURER	15. MFR'S CODE	16. MANUFACTURER'S MODEL NO.	17. MANUFACTURER'S SERIAL NO.

18. LENGTH	19. WIDTH	20. HEIGHT	21. WEIGHT	22. CERTIFICATE OF NON-AVAILABILITY NUMBER	23. PEP NO.	24. ARD	25. CONTRACT NUMBER

26. DESCRIPTION AND CAPACITY

CONTINUED ON BACK OF FORM ☐ YES ☐ NO

27. ELECTRICAL CHARACTERISTICS

a. QTY	b. HORSEPOWER	c. VOLTS	d. PHASE	e. CYCLE	f. AC	g. DC	h. SPEED	i. TYPE AND FRAME NUMBER

28a. PRESENT LOCATION	28b. DIPEC CONTROL NO.
	29. POSSESSOR CODE

SECTION II - INSPECTION RECORD *(If explanation is required, respond in Remarks)*

	YES	NO		YES	NO
30. Can items be stored and maintained on site for at least 12 months?			42. Must item be repaired/rebuilt/overhauled to perform all functions? $		
31. Has item been rebuilt/overhauled? If so, when? Date					
32. Has item been modified from original configuration? If so, explain.			43. Do QC records indicate satisfactory performance? If no, explain.		
33. Was item inspected under power? If no, explain.			44. Are manually operated mechanisms in working order? If no, describe.		
34. Are maintenance costs normal? If no, explain.			45. Are scales, dials, and gauges working and readable? If no, describe.		
35. Are safety devices adequate and satisfactory? If no, explain.			46. Are hydraulic pumps, valves/fittings operating properly? If no, describe.		
36. Are installation instructions available for transfer?			47. Are electronic systems and controls operating properly? If no, explain.		
37. Are operating instructions available for transfer?			48. How many hours was item used by current possessor?		
38. Was item last used on a finishing operation?			49. Explain last use of equipment described in item 26 above.		
39. Will adjustments or calibration correct deficiencies?			50. Estimated cost for packing, crating, handling. $		
40. Is item severable without damage to components? If not, give their replacement cost. $			51. Indicate date item will be available for redistribution.		
			52. Condition code.		
41. Is item in operable condition?			53. Operating test code.		

SECTION III - REMARKS

54. REMARKS

CONTINUED ON BACK OF FORM ☐ YES ☐ NO

SECTION IV - VALIDATION RECORD

55. VALIDATION *(Typed name(s) and signature(s))*

1. a. ACTIVE | b. INITIAL | c. IDLE | d. CHANGE

2. JULIAN DATE

3. I.D./GOVERNMENT TAG NO.

SECTION V - NUMERICALLY CONTROLLED MACHINE DATA

56. CONTROL MFR

57. MODEL

58. SERIAL NO.

59. MFG. DATE

60. CONTROL DESIGN
a. I.C. | b. CNC | c. STORED PROG. | d. EDIT | e. SOLID STATE | f. VACUUM TUBE | g. OTHER *(List)*

61. TYPE NUMERICAL CONTROL SYSTEM
a. POSITIONING | b. CONTOURING | c. CONTOURING/ POSITIONING

62. DIRECT NC
a. NO | b. YES *(If yes, X (1), (2) and/or (3))*
(1) READER BY-PASS | (2) MGT. DATA | (3) DEDICATED COMPUTER

63. AXES NAMED PER RS-267 FIGURE

64. EIA FORMAT DETAIL

65. EIA FORMAT CLASSIFICATION SHORTHAND

66. ROTARY MOTIONS UNDER NC *(Name and identify)*

67. SPECIFY AXES UNDER POSITIONING CONTROL

68. SPECIFY AXES UNDER CONTOURING CONTROL

69. AXES MAXIMUM TRAVEL *(Enter axes: X, Y, Z, etc., and specify inches or mm)*

70. POSITIONING RATE, MAX

71. FEED RANGE
a. ROTARY, RPM | b. LINEAR, XY | c. LINEAR, Z

72. SPINDLE DATA →
a. NO. OF SPINDLES | b. NO. OF SPDL MOTORS | c. HP/SPDL MOTOR | d. TAPER | e. SPEED RANGE | f. NO. OF INCREMENTS | g. TAPE CONTROL (1) YES (2) NO

73. EIA ASSIGNED "G" FUNCTION CODES *(Identify functions in Remarks that are not EIA assigned)*

74. EIA ASSIGNED "M" FUNCTION CODES *(Identify functions in Remarks that are not EIA assigned)*

75. INPUT DATA →
a. STANDARD: (1) RS-273 | (2) RS-274 | (3) RS-326
b. FORMAT: (1) WORD ADD | (2) TAB SEQ | (3) FIXED SEQ | (4) CL DATA
c. CODE: (1) RS-244aa | (2) RS-358 | (3) BINARY
d. DIMENSIONAL INPUT: (1) INCH | (2) METRIC | (3) BOTH

76. TOOL CHANGE DATA →
a. NO. OF TURRETS | b. NO. STA-TIONS | c. AUTO. CHANGER: YES / NO | d. NO. OF TOOLS | e. SELECTION: (1) SEQUENTIAL 2 / (2) RANDOM | f. MAX. TOOL DIA. | g. TOOL LENGTH | h. MAX. TOOL WT. | i. TOOL CODING METHOD

77. ROTABLE TABLE DATA →
a. INDEXING: (1) MANUAL / (2) NC | b. NO. OF STOPS | c. POSITIONING, NC: (1) YES / (2) NO | d. NO. OF POSITIONS | e. CONTOURING, NC: (1) YES / (2) NO | f. FEED RANGE: RPM

78. NO. OF READERS

79. READER TYPE
a. MECH | b. PHOTO | c. OTHER *(List)*

80. READER SPEED

81. INTERPOLATION
a. PARABOLIC | b. LINEAR | c. CIRCULAR | d. NONE

82. BUFFER STORAGE
a. YES | b. NO

83. THREAD-CUTTING MAX. LEAD.

84. CUTTER DIA. COMPENSATIONS
a. NUMBER OF | b. MAX. AMOUNT

85. TOOL OFFSETS
a. NO. TOOL OFFSETS | b. MAX. AMOUNT

86. READOUTS
a. SEQ. NO. | b. POSITION | c. COMMAND DATA | d. OTHER *(List)*

87. FEEDBACK DEVICE
a. ANALOG | b. NONE | c. DIGITAL

88. MIN. PROGRAMMABLE INCREMENT

89. MOTOR DRIVE
a. STEPPING | b. DC | c. HYDRAULIC

90. POST PROCESSOR *(Name)*

91. DEVELOPED BY *(Name)*

92. COMPUTER LANGUAGE USED

93. PART PROGRAM LANGUAGE

94. APPLICABLE COMPUTER *(Name, Model and Min. Core Storage)*

95. REQUIRED MANUALS *(Title and Manual Edition)*

96. REMARKS *(Features not covered above, functions not EIA assigned, etc.)*

253.303-1348 DD Form 1348: DoD Single Line Item Requisition System Document (Manual)

USE TYPEWRITER OR BALL POINT PEN
PRESS HERE
TO ASSURE LEGIBILITY ON ALL COPIES

D O D SINGLE LINE ITEM
DD FORM 1348 JUL 91 (EG) REQUISITION SYSTEM DOCUMENT (MANUAL)

SEND TO:

REQUISITION IS FROM:

REMARKS

PREVIOUS EDITIONS MAY BE USED

253.303-1348m DD Form 1348m: DoD Single Line Item Requisition System Document (Mechanical)

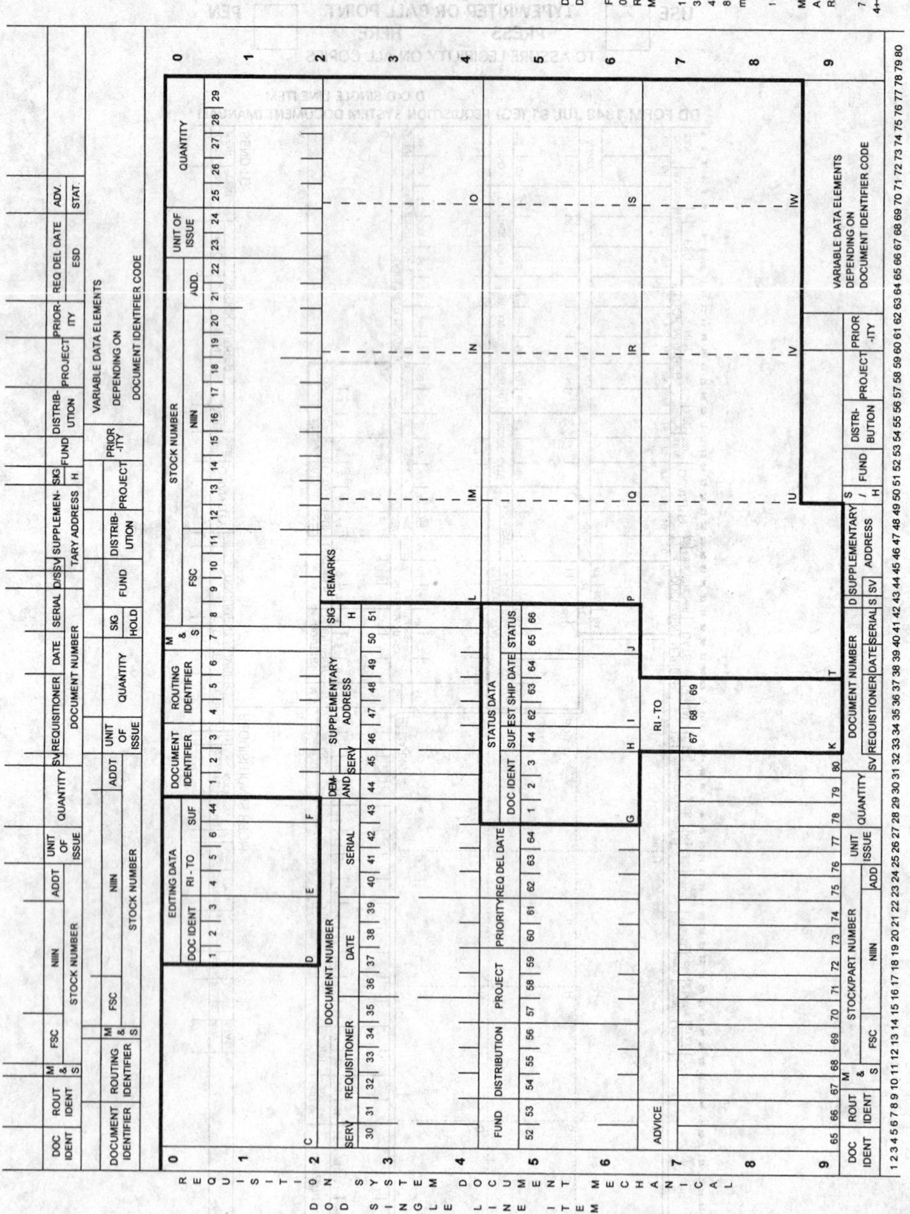
DD FORM 1348m 1 MAR 74

REQUISITION DOCUMENT SYSTEM SINGLE LINE ITEM DOCUMENT MECHANICAL

DOC IDENT	ROUT IDENT	M & S	FSC	NIIN (STOCK NUMBER)	ADDT	UNIT OF ISSUE	QUANTITY	SV	REQUISITIONER	DATE	SERIAL	D/SSV	SUPPLEMENTARY ADDRESS	SIG	FUND	DISTRIBUTION	PROJECT	PRIORITY	REQ DEL DATE (ESD)	ADV. STAT.
								DOCUMENT NUMBER												

DOCUMENT IDENTIFIER	ROUTING IDENTIFIER	M & S	FSC	NIIN (STOCK NUMBER)	ADDT	UNIT OF ISSUE	QUANTITY	SIG HOLD	FUND	DISTRIBUTION	PROJECT	PRIORITY	VARIABLE DATA ELEMENTS DEPENDING ON DOCUMENT IDENTIFIER CODE

EDITING DATA: DOC IDENT 1 2 3 | RI-TO 4 5 6 | SUF 44

DOCUMENT IDENTIFIER 1 2 3 | ROUTING IDENTIFIER 4 5 6 | M & S 7 | STOCK NUMBER: FSC 8 9 10 11, NIIN 12 13 14 15 16 17 18 19 20, ADD. 21 22 | UNIT OF ISSUE 23 24 | QUANTITY 25 26 27 28 29

DOCUMENT NUMBER: SERV 30 | REQUISITIONER 31 32 33 34 | DATE 35 36 37 38 | SERIAL 39 40 41 42 43 | DEMAND 44 | SUPPLEMENTARY ADDRESS: SERV 45, 46 47 48 49 50 | SIG 51 | REMARKS

FUND 52 53 | DISTRIBUTION 54 55 56 | PROJECT 57 58 59 | PRIORITY 60 61 | REQ DEL DATE 62 63 64

STATUS DATA: DOC IDENT 1 2 3 | SUF 44 | EST SHIP DATE 62 63 64 | STATUS 65 66

RI-TO 67 68 69

ADVICE 65 66 67 68 69 70 71 72 73 74 75 76 77 78 79 80

C D E F G H I J K L M N O P T

IM IN IO IQ IR IS IU IV IW

DOC IDENT	ROUT IDENT	M & S	FSC	NIIN	ADD	UNIT ISSUE	QUANTITY	SV	REQUISITIONER	DATE	SERIAL	S	D	SV	SUPPLEMENTARY ADDRESS	S/H	FUND	DISTRIBUTION	PROJECT	PRIORITY	VARIABLE DATA ELEMENTS DEPENDING ON DOCUMENT IDENTIFIER CODE
			STOCK/PART NUMBER						DOCUMENT NUMBER												

1 2 3 4 5 6 7 8 9 10 11 12 13 14 15 16 17 18 19 20 21 22 23 24 25 26 27 28 29 30 31 32 33 34 35 36 37 38 39 40 41 42 43 44 45 46 47 48 49 50 51 52 53 54 55 56 57 58 59 60 61 62 63 64 65 66 67 68 69 70 71 72 73 74 75 76 77 78 79 80

253.303-1348-1A DD Form 1348-1A: Issue Release/Receipt Document

DD FORM 1348-1A, JUL 91 (EG) ISSUE RELEASE/RECEIPT DOCUMENT

27. ADDITIONAL DATA

26. RIC (4-6) UI (23-24) QTY (25-29) CON CODE (71) DIST (55-56) UP (74-80)

25. NATIONAL STOCK NO. & ADD (8-22)

24. DOCUMENT NUMBER & SUFFIX (30-44)

DOC IDENT | RI FROM | M&S | UI | NSN | QUANTITY | SUPPLEMENTARY ADDRESS | SIG | FUND | DISTRIBUTION | PROJECT | PRI | REQD DEL DATE | ADV | RI | O/P | COND | MGT | UNIT PRICE DOLLARS CTS

1. TOTAL PRICE DOLLARS CTS

2. SHIP FROM

3. SHIP TO

4. MARK FOR

5. DOC DATE

6. NMFC

7. FRT RATE

8. TYPE CARGO

9. PS

10. QTY. REC'D

11. UP

12. UNIT WEIGHT

13. UNIT CUBE

14. UFC

15. SL

16. FREIGHT CLASSIFICATION NOMENCLATURE

17. ITEM NOMENCLATURE

18. TY CONT

19. NO CONT

20. TOTAL WEIGHT

21. TOTAL CUBE

22. RECEIVED BY

23. DATE RECEIVED

PerFORM (DLA)

PREVIOUS EDITION MAY BE USED

253.303-1348-2 DD Form 1348-2: Issue Release/Receipt Document with Address Label

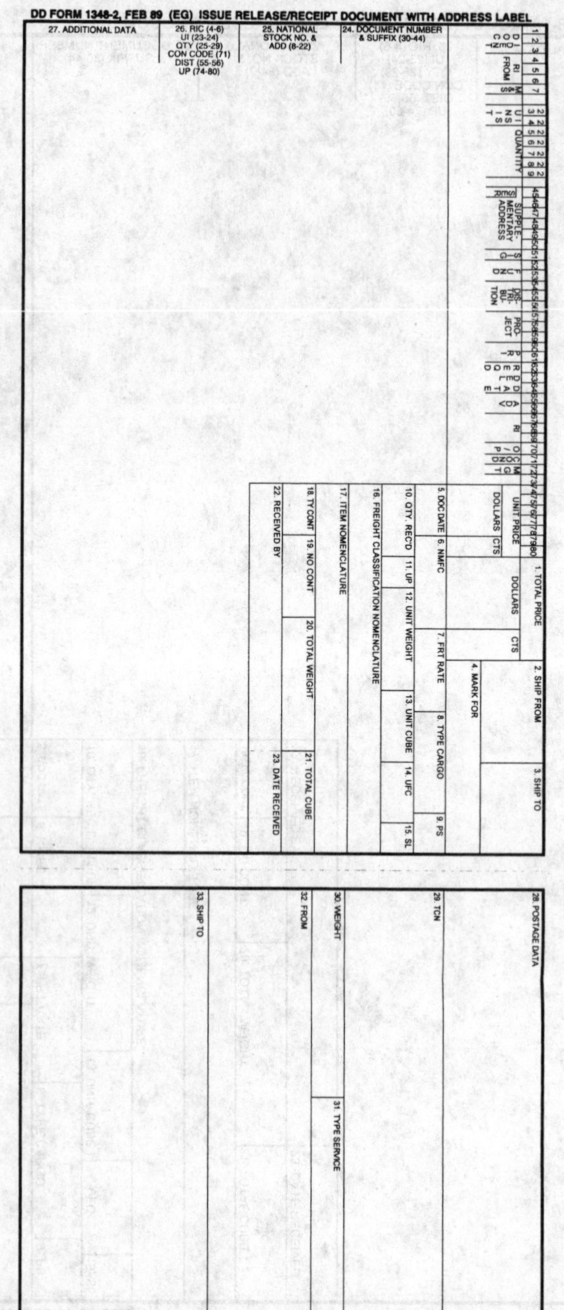

DD FORM 1348-2, FEB 89 (EG) ISSUE RELEASE/RECEIPT DOCUMENT WITH ADDRESS LABEL

DOC IDENT | RI FROM | M & S | UI | QUANTITY | SUPPLEMENTARY ADDRESS | SIG | FUND | DISTRIBUTION | PROJECT | PRI | REQ'D DEL DATE | ADV | RI | O/P | COND | MGT | UNIT PRICE DOLLARS CTS

1. TOTAL PRICE DOLLARS CTS
2. SHIP FROM
3. SHIP TO
4. MARK FOR
5. DOC DATE
6. NMFC
7. FRT RATE
8. TYPE CARGO
9. PS
10. QTY. REC'D
11. UP
12. UNIT WEIGHT
13. UNIT CUBE
14. UFC
15. SL
16. FREIGHT CLASSIFICATION NOMENCLATURE
17. ITEM NOMENCLATURE
18. TY CONT
19. NO CONT
20. TOTAL WEIGHT
21. TOTAL CUBE
22. RECEIVED BY
23. DATE RECEIVED
24. DOCUMENT NUMBER & SUFFIX (30-44)
25. NATIONAL STOCK NO. & ADD (8-22)
26. RIC (4-6) UI (23-24) QTY (25-29) CON CODE (71) DIST (55-56) UP (74-80)
27. ADDITIONAL DATA

28. POSTAGE DATA
29. TCN
30. WEIGHT
31. TYPE SERVICE
32. FROM
33. SHIP TO

253.303-1384 DoD Form 1384: Transportation Control and Movement Document

TRANSPORTATION CONTROL AND MOVEMENT DOCUMENT

PAGE NO.

1. DOC ID	2. TRLR CTR	3. CONSIGNOR	4. COMMODITY SPECIAL HANDLING	5. AIR DIM	6. POE	7. POD

8. MODE	9. PACK	10. TRANSPORTATION CONTROL NO.	11. CONSIGNEE	12. PRI	13. RDD	14. PROJ	15. DATE SHPD	16. ETA	17. TR ACCT

18. CARRIER	19. FLIGHT-TRUCK-VOY-DOC NO.	20. REF	21. REMARKS	22. PIECES	23. WEIGHT	24. CUBE

a. Transship Point	b. Date Rec	c. Bay Whse	d. Date Shpd	e. Mode Carrier	f. Flight-Truck-Voy Doc No.	g. Ref	h. Stow Loc	i. Split	j. Cond	k. Signature-Remarks
25.										
26.										
27.										

28. CONSIGNEE	29. DATE RECEIVED/OFFERED *(Sign)*	30. CONDITION	31. REMARKS

32. DOC ID	33. TRAILER - CON- TAINER	34. CONSIGNOR COMM ABBR OTHER	35. COMMODITY SPECIAL HANDLING	36. VOY NO Air Dim a.	36. VOY NO POE b.	37. POD	38. MODE	39. TYPE PACK	40. TRANSPORTATION CONTROL NUMBER	41. CONSIGNEE	42. PRI	43. REMARKS AND/OR RDD a.	Proj b.	Stow Loc Shpd c.	Stow Loc ETA d.	Tac e.	44. ADDITIONAL REMARKS OR Pieces a.	Weight b.	Cube C.

DD FORM 1384, OCT 2000 PREVIOUS EDITIONS MAY BE USED.

253.303-1391 DD Form 1391: FY— Military Construction Project Data

1. COMPONENT	FY ______ MILITARY CONSTRUCTION PROJECT DATA			2. DATE (YYYYMMDD)	REPORT CONTROL SYMBOL DD-AT&L(A)1610
3. INSTALLATION AND LOCATION		4. PROJECT TITLE			
5. PROGRAM ELEMENT	6. CATEGORY CODE	7. PROJECT NUMBER		8. PROJECT COST ($000) $0	
9. COST ESTIMATES					
ITEM		U/M	QUANTITY	UNIT COST	COST ($000)
					0.00
					0.00
					0.00
					0.00
					0.00
					0.00
					0.00
					0.00
10. DESCRIPTION OF PROPOSED CONSTRUCTION					

DD FORM 1391, JUL 1999 PREVIOUS EDITION IS OBSOLETE. PAGE NO.

253.303-1391c DD Form 1391c: FY— Military Construction Project Data (Continuation)

1. COMPONENT	FY _______ MILITARY CONSTRUCTION PROJECT DATA *(Continuation)*		2. DATE *(YYYYMMDD)*	REPORT CONTROL SYMBOL DD-AT&L(A)1610
3. INSTALLATION AND LOCATION		4. PROJECT TITLE		
5. PROGRAM ELEMENT	6. CATEGORY CODE	7. PROJECT NUMBER	8. PROJECT COST ($000)	

DD FORM 1391C, JUL 1999 PREVIOUS EDITION IS OBSOLETE. PAGE NO.

253.303-1419 DD Form 1419: DoD Industrial Plant Equipment Requisition

[DAC 91-6, 5/27/94]

DOD INDUSTRIAL PLANT EQUIPMENT REQUISITION | REQUISITION NUMBER | *Form Approved OMB No. 0704-0246 Expires Feb 28, 2006*

The public reporting burden for this collection of information is estimated to average 1.5 hours per response, including the time for reviewing instructions, searching existing data sources, gathering and maintaining the data needed, and completing and reviewing the collection of information. Send comments regarding this burden estimate or any other aspect of this collection of information, including suggestions for reducing the burden, to Department of Defense, Washington Headquarters Services, Directorate for Information Operations and Reports (0704-0246), 1215 Jefferson Davis Highway, Suite 1204, Arlington, VA 22202-4302. Respondents should be aware that notwithstanding any other provision of law, no person shall be subject to any penalty for failing to comply with a collection of information if it does not display a currently valid OMB control number.

PLEASE DO NOT RETURN YOUR FORM TO THIS ADDRESS. RETURN COMPLETED FORM TO DEFENSE SUPPLY CENTER RICHMOND, ATTN: JH, 8000 JEFFERSON DAVIS HIGHWAY, RICHMOND, VA 28297-5100

SECTION I - ITEM DESCRIPTION

1. COMMODITY CODE | 2. MANUFACTURER | 3. MODEL NUMBER

4. STOCK NUMBER | 5. POWER CODE | 6. ESTIMATED COST | 7. PHYSICAL INSPECTION REQUIRED *(X one)* YES NO | 8. PROCUREMENT SPECIFICATION ATTACHED *(X one)* YES NO

9. DESCRIPTION

CONTINUED UNDER REMARKS SECTION YES NO

SECTION II - ROUTING AGENCY/FACILITY/CONTRACTOR

10. NAME AND ADDRESS *(Include ZIP Code)* | 11. CONTRACT NUMBER | 12. DATE *(YYYYMMDD)* | 13. COMMAND CODE

14. PROGRAM *(X one)* MILITARY CONTRACTOR

15. INTENDED USE | 16. DATE ITEM REQUIRED AT DESTINATION *(YYYYMMDD)* | 17. DATE CERT. N/A REQUIRED *(YYYYMMDD)* | 18. PRIORITY

19. BASIS FOR AUTHORIZATION *(X one)* PRODUCTION MOBILIZATION REPLACEMENT | 20. PROCUREMENT PLANNED *(X one)* YES NO *(If "YES," cite Appropriation)* | 21. REBUILD/OVERHAUL CANDIDATE YES

22. TYPED NAME AND TITLE OF REQUESTING OFFICIAL | 23. SIGNATURE OF REQUESTING OFFICIAL | 24. DATE *(YYYYMMDD)*

25. CERTIFICATION OF NEED BY ADMINISTERING ACTIVITY | a. ADMINISTERING OFFICE CODE

b. NAME AND ADDRESS *(Include ZIP Code)* | c. TYPED NAME AND SIGNATURE OF PRODUCTION REPRESENTATIVE | d. DATE *(YYYYMMDD)*

e. SIGNATURE OF ADMIN. CONTRACTING OFFICER | f. DATE *(YYYYMMDD)*

SECTION III - APPROVAL AUTHORITY

26. NAME AND ADDRESS *(Include ZIP Code)* | 27. TITLE, SYMBOL AND TELEPHONE NO. OF APPROVING OFFICIAL

28. TYPED NAME & SIGNATURE OF APPROVING OFFICIAL | 29. DATE *(YYYYMMDD)*

SECTION IV - ALLOCATION AND AUTHORITY TO INSPECT *(To be completed by DSCR)*

30. COMMODITY CODE | 31. I.D./GOVERNMENT TAG NUMBER | 32. DESCRIPTION *(See attached copy of DD Form 1342, dated)*

33. PRESENT LOCATION *(Name, address and ZIP Code)* | 34. SHIPPED TO *(Name, address and ZIP Code)*

35. ESTIMATED TIME REQUIRED FOR SHIPMENT FROM DATE OF ACCEPTANCE *(Enter number of days)*

a. AS IS CONDITION | b. TEST REQUIRED | c. REPAIR REQUIRED | d. REPAIR/OVERHAUL REQUIRED | e. STANDARD ATTACHMENTS REQUIRED

36. TYPED NAME AND SIGNATURE OF ALLOCATING OFFICIAL | 37. DATE *(YYYYMMDD)* | 38. DATE OFFER EXPIRES *(YYYYMMDD)*

SECTION V - NON-AVAILABILITY CERTIFICATE *(To be completed by DSCR)*

39. The item described in Section I of this form has been screened by DSCR against the idle inventory of the Department of Defense and it is hereby certified as not available or cannot be delivered on or before the date specified in Section II *(Item 16)*. Procurement action resulting from this Certification of Non-Availability must be initiated within 45 calendar days of the date included in this Section *(Item 42)* or complete rescreening is required. Equipment offered by DSCR in Section IV must be considered if the supplier cannot deliver new equipment before expiration of the period specified in Section IV *(Item 35)*.

40. TYPED NAME AND SIGNATURE OF CERTIFYING OFFICIAL | 41. DATE CERTIFICATE ISSUED *(YYYYMMDD)* | 42. DATE CERTIFICATE EXPIRES *(YYYYMMDD)* | 43. CERTIFICATE NUMBER

SECTION VI - CERTIFICATE OF ACCEPTANCE				
44. THE ITEM ALLOCATED IN SECTION IV OF THIS FORM *(X as applicable)*				
a. HAS BEEN PHYSICALLY INSPECTED AND IS ACCEPTABLE		b. IS ACCEPTABLE WITHOUT PHYSICAL INSPECTION		
c. IS ACCEPTED UNDER ONE OF THESE CONDITIONS:				
(1) AS IS CONDITION	(2) REPAIR REQUIRED	(3) TEST REQUIRED	(4) REBUILD/OVERHAUL REQUIRED	
(5) OTHER				
d. IS NOT ACCEPTABLE *(A complete description of conditions making item unacceptable must be stated under REMARKS below)*				
45. TYPED NAME AND TITLE OF CERTIFYING OFFICIAL		46. SIGNATURE OF CERTIFYING OFFICIAL		47. DATE *(YYYYMMDD)*

SECTION VII - SPECIAL SHIPPING INSTRUCTIONS		
48. SHIP TO *(Include ZIP Code)*		49. FOR TRANSSHIPMENT TO *(Include ZIP Code)*
50. MARK FOR		
51. APPROPRIATION CHARGEABLE FOR		d. PAYING OFFICE/ACTIVITY NAME AND ADDRESS *(Include ZIP Code)*
a. PACKING/CRATING/HANDLING		
b. TRANSPORTATION		
c. OTHER		
52. SPECIAL DISTRIBUTION OF SHIPPING DOCUMENTS AND OTHER INSTRUCTIONS		

SECTION VIII - REMARKS
53. REMARKS

253.303-1423 DD Form 1423: Contract Data Requirements List

CONTRACT DATA REQUIREMENTS LIST	*Form Approved OMB No. 0704-0188*

The public reporting burden for this collection of information is estimated to average 440 hours per response, including the time for reviewing instructions, searching existing data sources, gathering and maintaining the data needed, and completing and reviewing the collection of information. Send comments regarding this burden estimate or any other aspect of this collection of information, including suggestions for reducing the burden, to the Department of Defense, Executive Services Directorate (0704-0188). Respondents should be aware that notwithstanding any other provision of law, no person shall be subject to any penalty for failing to comply with a collection of information if it does not display a currently valid OMB control number. **Please do not return your form to the above organization. Send completed form to the Government Issuing Contracting Officer for the Contract/PR No. listed in Block E.**

A. CONTRACT LINE ITEM NO.	B. EXHIBIT	C. CATEGORY: TDP ___ TM ___ OTHER ___
D. SYSTEM/ITEM	E. CONTRACT/PR NO.	F. CONTRACTOR

1. DATA ITEM NO.	2. TITLE OF DATA ITEM		3. SUBTITLE					17. PRICE GROUP
4. AUTHORITY *(Data Acquisition Document No.)*		5. CONTRACT REFERENCE	6. REQUIRING OFFICE					18. ESTIMATED TOTAL PRICE
7. DD 250 REQ	9. DIST STATEMENT REQUIRED	10. FREQUENCY	12. DATE OF FIRST SUBMISSION	14. DISTRIBUTION				
8. APP CODE		11. AS OF DATE	13. DATE OF SUBSEQUENT SUBMISSION	a. ADDRESSEE	b. COPIES: Draft	Final: Reg	Final: Repro	
16. REMARKS								
				15. TOTAL →	0	0	0	

1. DATA ITEM NO.	2. TITLE OF DATA ITEM		3. SUBTITLE					17. PRICE GROUP
4. AUTHORITY *(Data Acquisition Document No.)*		5. CONTRACT REFERENCE	6. REQUIRING OFFICE					18. ESTIMATED TOTAL PRICE
7. DD 250 REQ	9. DIST STATEMENT REQUIRED	10. FREQUENCY	12. DATE OF FIRST SUBMISSION	14. DISTRIBUTION				
8. APP CODE		11. AS OF DATE	13. DATE OF SUBSEQUENT SUBMISSION	a. ADDRESSEE	b. COPIES: Draft	Final: Reg	Final: Repro	
16. REMARKS								
				15. TOTAL →	0	0	0	

1. DATA ITEM NO.	2. TITLE OF DATA ITEM		3. SUBTITLE					17. PRICE GROUP
4. AUTHORITY *(Data Acquisition Document No.)*		5. CONTRACT REFERENCE	6. REQUIRING OFFICE					18. ESTIMATED TOTAL PRICE
7. DD 250 REQ	9. DIST STATEMENT REQUIRED	10. FREQUENCY	12. DATE OF FIRST SUBMISSION	14. DISTRIBUTION				
8. APP CODE		11. AS OF DATE	13. DATE OF SUBSEQUENT SUBMISSION	a. ADDRESSEE	b. COPIES: Draft	Final: Reg	Final: Repro	
16. REMARKS								
				15. TOTAL →	0	0	0	

1. DATA ITEM NO.	2. TITLE OF DATA ITEM		3. SUBTITLE					17. PRICE GROUP
4. AUTHORITY *(Data Acquisition Document No.)*		5. CONTRACT REFERENCE	6. REQUIRING OFFICE					18. ESTIMATED TOTAL PRICE
7. DD 250 REQ	9. DIST STATEMENT REQUIRED	10. FREQUENCY	12. DATE OF FIRST SUBMISSION	14. DISTRIBUTION				
8. APP CODE		11. AS OF DATE	13. DATE OF SUBSEQUENT SUBMISSION	a. ADDRESSEE	b. COPIES: Draft	Final: Reg	Final: Repro	
16. REMARKS								
				15. TOTAL →	0	0	0	

G. PREPARED BY	H. DATE	I. APPROVED BY	J. DATE

INSTRUCTIONS FOR COMPLETING DD FORM 1423

(See DoD 5010.12-M for detailed instructions.)

FOR GOVERNMENT PERSONNEL

Item A. Self-explanatory.

Item B. Self-explanatory.

Item C. Mark (X) appropriate category: TDP - Technical Data Package; TM - Technical Manual; Other - other category of data, such as "Provisioning,""Configuration Management," etc.

Item D. Enter name of system/item being acquired that data will support.

Item E. Self-explanatory (to be filled in after contract award).

Item F. Self-explanatory (to be filled in after contract award).

Item G. Signature of preparer of CDRL.

Item H. Date CDRL was prepared.

Item I. Signature of CDRL approval authority.

Item J. Date CDRL was approved.

Item 1. See DoD FAR Supplement Subpart 4.71 for proper numbering.

Item 2. Enter title as it appears on data acquisition document cited in Item 4.

Item 3. Enter subtitle of data item for further definition of data item (optional entry).

Item 4. Enter Data Item Description (DID) number, military specification number, or military standard number listed in DoD 5010.12-L (AMSDL), or one-time DID number, that defines data content and format requirements.

Item 5. Enter reference to tasking in contract that generates requirement for the data item (e.g., Statement of Work paragraph number).

Item 6. Enter technical office responsible for ensuring adequacy of the data item.

Item 7. Specify requirement for inspection/acceptance of the data item by the Government.

Item 8. Specify requirement for approval of a draft before preparation of the final data item.

Item 9. For technical data, specify requirement for contractor to mark the appropriate distribution statement on the data (ref. DoDD 5230.24).

Item 10. Specify number of times data items are to be delivered.

Item 11. Specify as-of date of data item, when applicable.

Item 12. Specify when first submittal is required.

Item 13. Specify when subsequent submittals are required, when applicable.

Item 14. Enter addressees and number of draft/final copies to be delivered to each addressee. Explain reproducible copies in Item 16.

Item 15. Enter total number of draft/final copies to be delivered.

Item 16. Use for additional/clarifying information for Items 1 through 15. Examples are: Tailoring of documents cited in Item 4; Clarification of submittal dates in Items 12 and 13; Explanation of reproducible copies in Item 14.; Desired medium for delivery of the data item.

FOR THE CONTRACTOR

Item 17. Specify appropriate price group from one of the following groups of effort in developing estimated prices for each data item listed on the DD Form 1423.

a. Group I. Definition - Data which is not otherwise essential to the contractor's performance of the primary contracted effort (production, development, testing, and administration) but which is required by DD Form 1423.

Estimated Price - Costs to be included under Group I are those applicable to preparing and assembling the data item in conformance with Government requirements, and the administration and other expenses related to reproducing and delivering such data items to the Government.

b. Group II. Definition - Data which is essential to the performance of the primary contracted effort but the contractor is required to perform additional work to conform to Government requirements with regard to depth of content, format, frequency of submittal, preparation, control, or quality of the data item.

Estimated Price - Costs to be included under Group II are those incurred over and above the cost of the essential data item without conforming to Government requirements, and the administrative and other expenses related to reproducing and delivering such data item to the Government.

c. Group III. Definition - Data which the contractor must develop for his internal use in performance of the primary contracted effort and does not require any substantial change to conform to Government requirements with regard to depth of content, format, frequency of submittal, preparation, control, and quality of the data item.

Estimated Price - Costs to be included under Group III are the administrative and other expenses related to reproducing and delivering such data item to the Government.

d. Group IV. Definition - Data which is developed by the contractor as part of his normal operating procedures and his effort in supplying these data to the Government is minimal.

Estimated Price - Group IV items should normally be shown on the DD Form 1423 at no cost.

Item 18. For each data item, enter an amount equal to that portion of the total price which is estimated to be attributable to the production or development for the Government of that item of data. These estimated data prices shall be developed only from those costs which will be incurred as a direct result of the requirement to supply the data, over and above those costs which would otherwise be incurred in performance of the contract if no data were required. The estimated data prices shall not include any amount for rights in data. The Government's right to use the data shall be governed by the pertinent provisions of the contract.

253.303-1423-1 DD Form 1423-1: Contract Data Requirements List (1 Data Item)

CONTRACT DATA REQUIREMENTS LIST (1 Data Item)							Form Approved OMB No. 0704-0188				
The public reporting burden for this collection of information is estimated to average 110 hours per response, including the time for reviewing instructions, searching existing data sources, gathering and maintaining the data needed, and completing and reviewing the collection of information. Send comments regarding this burden estimate or any other aspect of this collection of information, including suggestions for reducing the burden, to the Department of Defense, Executive Services Directorate (0704-0188). Respondents should be aware that notwithstanding any other provision of law, no person shall be subject to any penalty for failing to comply with a collection of information if it does not display a currently valid OMB control number. **Please do not return your form to the above organization. Send completed form to the Government Issuing Contracting Officer for the Contract/PR No. listed in Block E.**											
A. CONTRACT LINE ITEM NO.	B. EXHIBIT	C. CATEGORY: TDP ___ TM ___ OTHER									
D. SYSTEM/ITEM		E. CONTRACT/PR NO.		F. CONTRACTOR							
1. DATA ITEM NO.	2. TITLE OF DATA ITEM			3. SUBTITLE							17. PRICE GROUP
4. AUTHORITY *(Data Acquisition Document No.)*		5. CONTRACT REFERENCE			6. REQUIRING OFFICE						18. ESTIMATED TOTAL PRICE
7. DD 250 REQ	9. DIST STATEMENT REQUIRED	10. FREQUENCY	12. DATE OF FIRST SUBMISSION		14. DISTRIBUTION						
8. APP CODE		11. AS OF DATE	13. DATE OF SUBSEQUENT SUBMISSION		a. ADDRESSEE	b. COPIES					
						Draft	Final				
							Reg	Repro			
16. REMARKS											
					15. TOTAL →	0	0	0			
G. PREPARED BY		H. DATE	I. APPROVED BY			J. DATE					

CONTRACT DATA REQUIREMENTS LIST
(1 Data Item)

A. CONTRACT LINE ITEM NO.	B. EXHIBIT	C. CATEGORY: TDP ____ TM ____ OTHER
D. SYSTEM/ITEM	**E. CONTRACT/PR NO.**	**F. CONTRACTOR**

16. REMARKS *(Continued)*

INSTRUCTIONS FOR COMPLETING DD FORM 1423

(See DoD 5010.12-M for detailed instructions.)

FOR GOVERNMENT PERSONNEL

Item A. Self-explanatory.

Item B. Self-explanatory.

Item C. Mark (X) appropriate category: TDP - Technical Data Package; TM - Technical Manual; Other - other category of data, such as "Provisioning,""Configuration Management," etc.

Item D. Enter name of system/item being acquired that data will support.

Item E. Self-explanatory (to be filled in after contract award).

Item F. Self-explanatory (to be filled in after contract award).

Item G. Signature of preparer of CDRL.

Item H. Date CDRL was prepared.

Item I. Signature of CDRL approval authority.

Item J. Date CDRL was approved.

Item 1. See DoD FAR Supplement Subpart 4.71 for proper numbering.

Item 2. Enter title as it appears on data acquisition document cited in Item 4.

Item 3. Enter subtitle of data item for further definition of data item (optional entry).

Item 4. Enter Data Item Description (DID) number, military specification number, or military standard number listed in DoD 5010.12-L (AMSDL), or one-time DID number, that defines data content and format requirements.

Item 5. Enter reference to tasking in contract that generates requirement for the data item (e.g., Statement of Work paragraph number).

Item 6. Enter technical office responsible for ensuring adequacy of the data item.

Item 7. Specify requirement for inspection/acceptance of the data item by the Government.

Item 8. Specify requirement for approval of a draft before preparation of the final data item.

Item 9. For technical data, specify requirement for contractor to mark the appropriate distribution statement on the data (ref. DoDD 5230.24).

Item 10. Specify number of times data items are to be delivered.

Item 11. Specify as-of date of data item, when applicable.

Item 12. Specify when first submittal is required.

Item 13. Specify when subsequent submittals are required, when applicable.

Item 14. Enter addressees and number of draft/final copies to be delivered to each addressee. Explain reproducible copies in Item 16.

Item 15. Enter total number of draft/final copies to be delivered.

Item 16. Use for additional/clarifying information for Items 1 through 15. Examples are: Tailoring of documents cited in Item 4; Clarification of submittal dates in Items 12 and 13; Explanation of reproducible copies in Item 14.; Desired medium for delivery of the data item.

FOR THE CONTRACTOR

Item 17. Specify appropriate price group from one of the following groups of effort in developing estimated prices for each data item listed on the DD Form 1423.

a. Group I. Definition - Data which is not otherwise essential to the contractor's performance of the primary contracted effort (production, development, testing, and administration) but which is required by DD Form 1423.

Estimated Price - Costs to be included under Group I are those applicable to preparing and assembling the data item in conformance with Government requirements, and the administration and other expenses related to reproducing and delivering such data items to the Government.

b. Group II. Definition - Data which is essential to the performance of the primary contracted effort but the contractor is required to perform additional work to conform to Government requirements with regard to depth of content, format, frequency of submittal, preparation, control, or quality of the data item.

Estimated Price - Costs to be included under Group II are those incurred over and above the cost of the essential data item without conforming to Government requirements, and the administrative and other expenses related to reproducing and delivering such data item to the Government.

c. Group III. Definition - Data which the contractor must develop for his internal use in performance of the primary contracted effort and does not require any substantial change to conform to Government requirements with regard to depth of content, format, frequency of submittal, preparation, control, and quality of the data item.

Estimated Price - Costs to be included under Group III are the administrative and other expenses related to reproducing and delivering such data item to the Government.

d. Group IV. Definition - Data which is developed by the contractor as part of his normal operating procedures and his effort in supplying these data to the Government is minimal.

Estimated Price - Group IV items should normally be shown on the DD Form 1423 at no cost.

Item 18. For each data item, enter an amount equal to that portion of the total price which is estimated to be attributable to the production or development for the Government of that item of data. These estimated data prices shall be developed only from those costs which will be incurred as a direct result of the requirement to supply the data, over and above those costs which would otherwise be incurred in performance of the contract if no data were required. The estimated data prices shall not include any amount for rights in data. The Government's right to use the data shall be governed by the pertinent provisions of the contract.

253.303-1423-2 DD Form 1423-2: Contract Data Requirements List (2 Data Items)

CONTRACT DATA REQUIREMENTS LIST
(2 Data Items)

Form Approved
OMB No. 0704-0188

The public reporting burden for this collection of information is estimated to average 220 hours per response, including the time for reviewing instructions, searching existing data sources, gathering and maintaining the data needed, and completing and reviewing the collection of information. Send comments regarding this burden estimate or any other aspect of this collection of information, including suggestions for reducing the burden, to the Department of Defense, Executive Services Directorate (0704-0188). Respondents should be aware that notwithstanding any other provision of law, no person shall be subject to any penalty for failing to comply with a collection of information if it does not display a currently valid OMB control number. **Please do not return your form to the above organization. Send completed form to the Government Issuing Contracting Officer for the Contract/PR No. listed in Block E.**

A. CONTRACT LINE ITEM NO.	B. EXHIBIT	C. CATEGORY: TDP ____ TM ____ OTHER ____
D. SYSTEM/ITEM	E. CONTRACT/PR NO.	F. CONTRACTOR

1. DATA ITEM NO.	2. TITLE OF DATA ITEM		3. SUBTITLE				17. PRICE GROUP
4. AUTHORITY *(Data Acquisition Document No.)*		5. CONTRACT REFERENCE		6. REQUIRING OFFICE			18. ESTIMATED TOTAL PRICE
7. DD 250 REQ	9. DIST STATEMENT REQUIRED	10. FREQUENCY	12. DATE OF FIRST SUBMISSION	14. DISTRIBUTION			
8. APP CODE		11. AS OF DATE	13. DATE OF SUBSEQUENT SUBMISSION	a. ADDRESSEE	b. COPIES: Draft	Final: Reg	Final: Repro
16. REMARKS							
				15. TOTAL →	0	0	0

1. DATA ITEM NO.	2. TITLE OF DATA ITEM		3. SUBTITLE				17. PRICE GROUP
4. AUTHORITY *(Data Acquisition Document No.)*		5. CONTRACT REFERENCE		6. REQUIRING OFFICE			18. ESTIMATED TOTAL PRICE
7. DD 250 REQ	9. DIST STATEMENT REQUIRED	10. FREQUENCY	12. DATE OF FIRST SUBMISSION	14. DISTRIBUTION			
8. APP CODE		11. AS OF DATE	13. DATE OF SUBSEQUENT SUBMISSION	a. ADDRESSEE	b. COPIES: Draft	Final: Reg	Final: Repro
16. REMARKS							
				15. TOTAL →	0	0	0

G. PREPARED BY	H. DATE	I. APPROVED BY	J. DATE

INSTRUCTIONS FOR COMPLETING DD FORM 1423

(See DoD 5010.12-M for detailed instructions.)

FOR GOVERNMENT PERSONNEL

Item A. Self-explanatory.

Item B. Self-explanatory.

Item C. Mark (X) appropriate category: TDP - Technical Data Package; TM - Technical Manual; Other - other category of data, such as "Provisioning,""Configuration Management," etc.

Item D. Enter name of system/item being acquired that data will support.

Item E. Self-explanatory (to be filled in after contract award).

Item F. Self-explanatory (to be filled in after contract award).

Item G. Signature of preparer of CDRL.

Item H. Date CDRL was prepared.

Item I. Signature of CDRL approval authority.

Item J. Date CDRL was approved.

Item 1. See DoD FAR Supplement Subpart 4.71 for proper numbering.

Item 2. Enter title as it appears on data acquisition document cited in Item 4.

Item 3. Enter subtitle of data item for further definition of data item (optional entry).

Item 4. Enter Data Item Description (DID) number, military specification number, or military standard number listed in DoD 5010.12-L (AMSDL), or one-time DID number, that defines data content and format requirements.

Item 5. Enter reference to tasking in contract that generates requirement for the data item (e.g., Statement of Work paragraph number).

Item 6. Enter technical office responsible for ensuring adequacy of the data item.

Item 7. Specify requirement for inspection/acceptance of the data item by the Government.

Item 8. Specify requirement for approval of a draft before preparation of the final data item.

Item 9. For technical data, specify requirement for contractor to mark the appropriate distribution statement on the data (ref. DoDD 5230.24).

Item 10. Specify number of times data items are to be delivered.

Item 11. Specify as-of date of data item, when applicable.

Item 12. Specify when first submittal is required.

Item 13. Specify when subsequent submittals are required, when applicable.

Item 14. Enter addressees and number of draft/final copies to be delivered to each addressee. Explain reproducible copies in Item 16.

Item 15. Enter total number of draft/final copies to be delivered.

Item 16. Use for additional/clarifying information for Items 1 through 15. Examples are: Tailoring of documents cited in Item 4; Clarification of submittal dates in Items 12 and 13; Explanation of reproducible copies in Item 14.; Desired medium for delivery of the data item.

FOR THE CONTRACTOR

Item 17. Specify appropriate price group from one of the following groups of effort in developing estimated prices for each data item listed on the DD Form 1423.

a. Group I. Definition - Data which is not otherwise essential to the contractor's performance of the primary contracted effort (production, development, testing, and administration) but which is required by DD Form 1423.

Estimated Price - Costs to be included under Group I are those applicable to preparing and assembling the data item in conformance with Government requirements, and the administration and other expenses related to reproducing and delivering such data items to the Government.

b. Group II. Definition - Data which is essential to the performance of the primary contracted effort but the contractor is required to perform additional work to conform to Government requirements with regard to depth of content, format, frequency of submittal, preparation, control, or quality of the data item.

Estimated Price - Costs to be included under Group II are those incurred over and above the cost of the essential data item without conforming to Government requirements, and the administrative and other expenses related to reproducing and delivering such data item to the Government.

c. Group III. Definition - Data which the contractor must develop for his internal use in performance of the primary contracted effort and does not require any substantial change to conform to Government requirements with regard to depth of content, format, frequency of submittal, preparation, control, and quality of the data item.

Estimated Price - Costs to be included under Group III are the administrative and other expenses related to reproducing and delivering such data item to the Government.

d. Group IV. Definition - Data which is developed by the contractor as part of his normal operating procedures and his effort in supplying these data to the Government is minimal.

Estimated Price - Group IV items should normally be shown on the DD Form 1423 at no cost.

Item 18. For each data item, enter an amount equal to that portion of the total price which is estimated to be attributable to the production or development for the Government of that item of data. These estimated data prices shall be developed only from those costs which will be incurred as a direct result of the requirement to supply the data, over and above those costs which would otherwise be incurred in performance of the contract if no data were required. The estimated data prices shall not include any amount for rights in data. The Government's right to use the data shall be governed by the pertinent provisions of the contract.

253.303-1484 DD Form 1484: Post-Award Conference Record

POST-AWARD CONFERENCE RECORD

PART I - GENERAL

1. CONTRACT NO.		2. TOTAL AMOUNT	3. TYPE OF CONTRACT	4. DATE OF CONFERENCE
5. PRIORITY OF PROCUREMENT (1-28) IDENTIFY	6. PREAWARD SURVEY MADE *(x one)* a. YES b. NO	7. CONTRACTOR NAME	8. CONTRACTOR ADDRESS *(include ZIP Code)*	

PART II - CONFEREES

1. CONTRACTOR	2. GOVERNMENT

PART III - CONFERENCE PROGRAM

SECTION 1. CONTRACT ADMINISTRATION - GENERAL

SUBJECT (a)	ITEMS DISCUSSED *(x if applicable)* *(b)*	CLAUSE NO. *(if applicable* *(c)*	INDICATE SIGNIFICANT CONCLUSIONS AND ANY FURTHER ACTION TO BE TAKEN *(d)*
A. GENERAL			
1. FUNCTION AND AUTHORITY OF U.S. GOVERNMENT PERSONNEL			
2. ROUTING OF CORRESPONDENCE			
3. OMISSIONS OR CONFLICTING PROVISIONS			
4. OTHER			
B. REPORTS: PREPARATION AND SUBMITTAL			
1. WORK PROGRESS			
2. FINANCIAL REPORTS			
3. ROYALTY REPORT			
4. PATENT REPORT			
5. OTHER (Specify)			
C. SUBCONTRACTS			
1. CONSENT TO PLACEMENT			
2. PRIME'S RESPONSIBILITY FOR ADMINISTRATION			
3. CERTIFICATE OF CURRENT COST OR PRICING DATA			
4. SOURCE INSPECTION			
5. CORPORATION INTERDIVISIONAL ORDERS			
6. CLASSIFIED SUBCONTRACTS			
a. SECURITY REQUIREMENTS CHECK LIST (DD Form 254) - APPROVAL REQUIRED			
b. SPECIAL PROCEDURE FOR FOREIGN SUPPLIERS			
7. DUTY-FREE ENTRY CERTIFICATE			
8. OTHER *(Specify)*			

DD Form 1484, APR 86 *Previous editions are obsolete.* 464/226

253.303-1484 DD Form 1484: Post-Award Conference Record—Continued (Page 2)

SUBJECT (a)	ITEMS DISCUSSED *(x if applicable)* (b)	CLAUSE NO *(if applicable)* (C)	INDICATE SIGNIFICANT CONCLUSIONS AND ANY FURTHER ACTION TO BE TAKEN (d)
D. SMALL BUSINESS SUBCONTRACTING			
1. CONTRACTUAL REQUIREMENTS			
2. PROGRAM DESIGNED TO FACILITATE SUBCONTRACTING TO SMALL BUSINESS			
3. DEFENSE SMALL BUSINESS SUBCONTRACTING REPORT (SF 295-quarterly; SF 294 semiannually)			
4. PROPOSED NUMBER OF SUBCONTRACTS AWARDED SMALL BUSINESS % OF DOLLAR VALUE			
E. CONTRACT MODIFICATIONS			
F. GOVERNMENT PROPERTY			
1. USE OF FACILITIES AND TOOLING			
2. MAINTENANCE AND PRESERVATION			
3. PROPERTY PROCEDURE APPROVAL			
4. OTHER *(Specify)*			
G. SPECIAL PROVISIONS			
1. REPRICING			
2. LIQUIDATED DAMAGES			
3. GOVERNMENT FINANCING (Progress Payments, etc)			
4. SPECIAL TOOLING			
5. OVERTIME			
6. BILL OF MATERIALS			
7. DATA RIGHTS			
8. WARRANTIES			
9. OTHER *(Specify)*			
H. GENERAL PROVISIONS			
1. LIMITATION OF COST			
2. ALLOWABILITY OF COST			
3. OTHER *(Specify)*			
I. DELIVERY SCHEDULES			
J. TRANSPORTATION			
K. INVOICING AND BILLING INSTRUCTIONS			
L. PROCESSING COST AND PRICE PROPOSALS			
M. LABOR			
1. ACTUAL AND POTENTIAL LABOR DISPUTES			
2. DAVIS-BACON ACT			
3. WORK HOURS ACT			
4. WALSH-HEALEY PUBLIC CONTRACTS ACT			
5. COPELAND ANTI-KICKBACK ACT			
6. EQUAL OPPORTUNITY PROGRAM			

DD Form 1484, APR 86 PAGE 2

253.303-1484 DD Form 1484: Post-Award Conference Record—Continued (Page 3)

SUBJECT (a)	ITEMS DISCUSSED *(x if applicable)* (b)	CLAUSE NO. *(if applicable)* (c)	INDICATE SIGNIFICANT CONCLUSIONS AND ANY FURTHER ACTION TO BE TAKEN *(d)*
SECTION 2. QUALITY ASSURANCE AND ENGINEERING			
A. QUALITY ASSURANCE SYSTEM			
1. MIL-Q-9658			
2. MIL-I-45206-A			
3. *OTHER(Specify)*			
B. WAIVERS AND DEVIATIONS			
C. DRAWING/DESIGN APPROVAL			
D. MANUALS			
E. PRE-PRODUCTION SAMPLE			
F. QUALIFICATION AND ENVIRONMENTAL TESTS			
G. INSPECTION AND ACCEPTANCE			
H. SPECIFICATION INTERPRETATION			
I. LABORATORY FACILITIES			
J. VALUE ENGINEERING CLAUSE			
K. OTHER			
SECTION 3. PRODUCTION			
A. PRODUCTION PLANNING			
B. MILESTONES AND OTHER MONITORING DEVICES			
C. PRODUCTION SURVEILLANCE			
D. PRIORITIES ASSISTANCE			
E. SAFETY			
SECTION 4. SECURITY			
A. SPECIAL SECURITY HANDLING			
B. DISPOSITION OF CLASSIFIED MATERIAL			
SECTION 5. CONTRACT TERMINATION AND PROPERTY DISPOSAL			
A. PRIME CONTRACTOR GENERATED CANCELLATION OF SUBCONTRACTS			
B. PROPERTY DISPOSAL			
C. OTHER *(Identify)*			

DD Form 1484, APR 86 PAGE 3

253.303-1484 DD Form 1484: Post-Award Conference Record—Continued (Page 4)

SECTION 6. OTHER ITEMS *(Identify)*			
SUBJECT (a)	ITEMS DISCUSSED *(x if applicable)* (b)	CLAUSE NO. *(if applicable)* (C)	INDICATE SIGNIFICANT CONCLUSIONS AND ANY FURTHER ACTION TO BE TAKEN (d)

SIGNATURE OF CHAIRMAN	DATE

DD Form 1484, APR 86

PAGE 4

253.303-1547 DD Form 1547: Record of Weighted Guidelines Application

RECORD OF WEIGHTED GUIDELINES APPLICATION						REPORT CONTROL SYMBOL DD-AT&L(Q)1751	
1. REPORT NO.	2. BASIC PROCUREMENT INSTRUMENT IDENTIFICATION NO. a. PURCHASING OFFICE	b. FY	c. TYPE PROC INST CODE	d. PRISN	3. SPIIN	4. DATE OF ACTION a. YEAR	b. MONTH

		ITEM	COST CATEGORY	OBJECTIVE
5. CONTRACTING OFFICE CODE				
6. NAME OF CONTRACTOR		13.	MATERIAL	
		14.	SUBCONTRACTS	
7. DUNS NUMBER	8. FEDERAL SUPPLY CODE	15.	DIRECT LABOR	
		16.	INDIRECT EXPENSES	
9. DOD CLAIMANT PROGRAM	10. CONTRACT TYPE CODE	17.	OTHER DIRECT CHARGES	
		18.	SUBTOTAL COSTS *(13 thru 17)*	
11. TYPE EFFORT	12. USE CODE	19.	GENERAL AND ADMINISTRATIVE	
		20.	TOTAL COSTS *(18 + 19)*	

WEIGHTED GUIDELINES PROFIT FACTORS

ITEM	CONTRACTOR RISK FACTORS	ASSIGNED WEIGHTING	ASSIGNED VALUE	BASE *(Item 20)*	PROFIT OBJECTIVE
21.	TECHNICAL	%			
22.	MANAGEMENT/COST CONTROL	%			
23.	PERFORMANCE RISK (COMPOSITE)				
24.	CONTRACT TYPE RISK				
		COSTS FINANCED	LENGTH FACTOR	INTEREST RATE	
25.	WORKING CAPITAL			%	
	CONTRACTOR FACILITIES CAPITAL EMPLOYED		ASSIGNED VALUE	AMOUNT EMPLOYED	
26.	LAND				
27.	BUILDINGS				
28.	EQUIPMENT				
			ASSIGNED VALUE	BASE *(Item 20)*	
29.	COST EFFICIENCY FACTOR		%		
30.				TOTAL PROFIT OBJECTIVE	

NEGOTIATED SUMMARY

		PROPOSED	OBJECTIVE	NEGOTIATED
31.	TOTAL COSTS			
32.	FACILITIES CAPITAL COST OF MONEY *(DD Form 1861)*			
33.	PROFIT			
34.	TOTAL PRICE *(Line 31 + 32 + 33)*			
35.	MARKUP RATE *(Line 32 + 33 divided by 31)*	%	%	%

CONTRACTING OFFICER APPROVAL

36. TYPED/PRINTED NAME OF CONTRACTING OFFICER *(Last, First, Middle Initial)*	37. SIGNATURE OF CONTRACTING OFFICER	38. TELEPHONE NO.	39. DATE SUBMITTED *(YYYYMMDD)*

OPTIONAL USE

96.	97.	98.	99.

DD FORM 1547, JUL 2002

PREVIOUS EDITION IS OBSOLETE.

253.303-1593 DD Form 1593: Contract Administration Completion Record

CONTRACT ADMINISTRATION COMPLETION RECORD	1. SUSPENSE DATE
2. FROM:	3. CONTRACT NUMBER AS AMENDED BY MODIFICATIONS NUMBERED THROUGH ______
4. TO: *(Organizational element performing function checked below)*	5. NAME OF CONTRACTOR

The contract identified above has been physically completed *(i.e., all required deliveries or shipments have been made and/or services performed or terminated).*

Request column 6c and 6d and 6e and 6f be completed with regard to the function checked in column 6a and this form returned by the suspense date indicated in Item 1. If only an anticipated date of completion of required actions can be given the suspense date, a subsequest advice of final action is requested.

If contract being closed is classified, send signed copy of this form marked "INFORMATION COPY" to cognizant Industrial Security Office.

6. STATUS OF ACTION(S)

"X" *a*	FUNCTION *b*	"X" IF REQUIRED ACTION(S) COMPLETED *c*	ANTICIPATED DATE FOR COMPLETION OF ACTION(S) *d*	SIGNATURE *e*	DATE *f*
	PROPERTY ADMINISTRATION				
	PLANT CLEARANCE				
	CONTRACT TERMINATION				
	OTHER *(Specify)*				

7. REMARKS

8. TYPED NAME OF RESPONSIBLE OFFICIAL	9. SIGNATURE	10. DATE

DD Form 1593, APR 69 REPLACES EDITION OF 1 FEB 67 WHICH IS OBSOLETE. 172/261

253.303-1594 DD Form 1594: Contract Completion Statement

CONTRACT COMPLETION STATEMENT

1. **FROM:** *(Contract Administration Office)*

2a. PII NUMBER

2b. LAST MODIFICATION NUMBER

2c. CALL / ORDER NUMBER

3. **TO:** *(Name and Address of Purchasing Office and Office Symbol of the PCO, if known)*

4. CONTRACT IDENTITY CODE AND ADDRESS

5. EXCESS FUNDS ☐ YES ☐ NO
$

6a. IF FINAL PAYMENT HAS BEEN MADE, COMPLETE ITEMS 6b., AND 6c.	6b. VOUCHER NUMBER	6c. DATE
7a. IF FINAL APPROVED INVOICE FORWARDED TO D.O. OF ANOTHER ACTIVITY AND STATUS OF PAYMENT IS UNKNOWN, COMPLETE ITEMS 7b. AND 7c.	7b. INVOICE NUMBER	7c. DATE FORWARDED

8. REMARKS

9a. ALL ADMINISTRATION OFFICE ACTIONS REQUIRED HAVE BEEN FULLY AND SATISFACTORILY ACCOMPLISHED. THIS INCLUDES FINAL SETTLEMENT IN THE CASE OF A PRICE REVISION CONTRACT.

9b. TYPED NAME OF RESPONSIBLE OFFICIAL	9c. SIGNATURE	9d. DATE

FOR PURCHASING OFFICE USE ONLY

10a. ALL PURCHASING OFFICE ACTIONS REQUIRED HAVE BEEN FULLY AND SATISFACTORILY ACCOMPLISHED. CONTRACT FILE OF THIS OFFICE IS HEREBY CLOSED AS OF:

☐ DATE SHOWN IN ITEM 9d. ABOVE.

☐ DATE SHOWN IN ITEM 10e. BELOW. *(Check this box only if final completion of any significant purchasing office action extends more than three months beyond close-out date shown in item 9d. above. In such cases, submit a copy of the completed form upon final accomplishment of all purchasing office actions to the contract administration office, (Upon receipt, the contract administration office shall extend its contract file close-out date accordingly.))*

10b. REMARKS

10c. TYPED NAME OF RESPONSIBLE OFFICIAL	10d. SIGNATURE	10e. DATE

DD Form 1594, FEB 70 REPLACES EDITION OF 1 JUN 68 WHICH IS OBSOLETE 222/261

253.303-1597 DD Form 1597: Contract Closeout Check-List

CONTRACT CLOSEOUT CHECK-LIST *(Use a separate page to attach any comments.)*	1. CONTRACT NUMBER
	2. CONTRACT MODIFICATION NUMBERS *(If applicable)*
3. NAME OF CONTRACTOR	

4. DATE OF PHYSICAL COMPLETION *(YYYYMMDD)*		6. MILESTONES/CALENDAR MONTHS AFTER PHYSICAL COMPLETION *(FAR 4.804-1)*			7. FORECAST COMPLETION DATE *(YYYYMMDD)*	8. DATE ACTION COMPLETED *(YYYYMMDD)* *(NA if not applicable)*
5. ACTION ITEMS		Category 2	Category 3	Category 4		
a. DISPOSITION OF CLASSIFIED MATERIAL COMPLETED						
b. FINAL PATENT REPORT SUBMITTED *(Inventions Disclosures)*	DD 882					
c. FINAL ROYALTY REPORT SUBMITTED						
d. FINAL PATENT REPORT CLEARED *(Inventions Disclosures)*						
e. FINAL ROYALTY REPORT CLEARED						
f. ISSUANCE OF REPORT OF CONTRACT COMPLETION						
g. NO OUTSTANDING VALUE ENGINEERING CHANGE PROPOSAL *(VECP)*						
h. PLANT CLEARANCE REPORT RECEIVED	DD 1593					
i. PROPERTY CLEARANCE RECEIVED	DD 1593					
j. SETTLEMENT OF ALL INTERIM OR DISALLOWED COSTS *(DCAA Form 1)*						
k. PRICE REVISION COMPLETED						
l. SETTLEMENT OF SUBCONTRACTS BY THE PRIME CONTRACTOR						
m. PRIOR YEAR OVERHEAD RATES COMPLETED						
n. CONTRACTOR'S CLOSING STATEMENT RECEIVED						
o. FINAL SUBCONTRACTING PLAN REPORT SUBMITTED						
p. TERMINATION DOCKET COMPLETED	DD 1593					
q. CONTRACT AUDIT COMPLETED						
r. CONTRACTOR'S CLOSING STATEMENT COMPLETED						
s. FINAL VOUCHER SUBMITTED	SF 1034					
t. FINAL PAID VOUCHER RECEIVED	SF 1034					
u. FINAL REMOVAL OF EXCESS FUNDS RECOMMENDED						
v. ISSUANCE OF CONTRACT COMPLETION STATEMENT *(Or MILSCAP Format Identifier PK9)*		6	36	20		
w. OTHER REQUIREMENTS COMPLETED *(Specify)*						

9. RESPONSIBLE OFFICIAL	
a. TYPED NAME *(Last, First, Middle Initial)*	b. TITLE
c. SIGNATURE *(Sign only upon completion of all actions)*	d. DATE SIGNED *(YYYYMMDD)*

DD FORM 1597, APR 2000 PREVIOUS EDITION MAY BE USED.

253.303-1598 DD Form 1598: Contract Termination Status Report

CONTRACT TERMINATION STATUS REPORT	STATUS REPORT NUMBER	REPORT CONTROL SYMBOL DD-AT&L(AR)1411 DATE *(YYYYMMDD)*
SECTION I		
1. NAME OF CONTRACTOR *(25 positions)*	2. ADDRESS OF CONTRACTOR *(15 positions)*	
3. BRIEF DESCRIPTION OF ITEM TERMINATED *(15 positions)*		
	DATA	
4. REGION/DISTRICT/PLANT		
5. CONTRACT NUMBER		
SECTION II		
6. EFFECTIVE DATE OF TERMINATION		
7. DATE OF ASSIGNMENT		
8. TERMINATION *(P - Partial, C - Complete)*		
9. TYPE OF CONTRACT, FP-FPI-CPF-CPIF-LETTER		
10. AMOUNT OF CONTRACT INCLUDING ALL SUPPLEMENTS		
11. CONTRACT PRICE OF ITEMS TERMINATED		
12. AMOUNT OF EXCESS FUNDS RELEASED		
SECTION III		
13. STATUS OF SETTLEMENT *(See Instructions)*		
14. DATE CONTRACTOR'S CLAIM RECEIVED *(Interim - Final)*		
15. AMOUNT OF PRIME CONTRACTOR'S OWN CHARGES		
16. AMOUNT OF COST VOUCHERS PAID TO DATE - CPF - CPIF		
17. AMOUNT OF ADVANCE PROGRESS OR PARTIAL PAYMENTS		
18. VALUE OF TERMINATION INVENTORY		
19. AMOUNT OF DISPOSAL CREDITS		
20. GROSS SETTLEMENT AMOUNT *(VO-RE-NC-NS-UD) (See Instructions)*		
21. NET SETTLEMENT AMOUNT *(VO-RE-NC-NS-UD) (See Instructions)*		
22. CLOSING DATE		
SECTION IV		
23. NUMBER OF SUBCONTRACTORS' CLAIMS SUBMITTED		
24. NUMBER OF SUBCONTRACTORS' CLAIMS APPROVED		
a. APPROVED BY TCO		
b. APPROVED BY CONTRACTOR UNDER DELEGATION		
25. AMOUNT OF SUBCONTRACTORS' CLAIMS SUBMITTED		
26. AMOUNT OF SUBCONTRACTORS' CLAIMS APPROVED		
SECTION V		
27. TYPE OF REPORT *(See Instructions)*		
28. DOCKET NUMBER		
29. ADVANCE SUPPLEMENTAL AGREEMENT OR AMENDMENT NUMBER		
30. a. CONTRACTING ACTIVITY NAME		
b. PROCURING CONTRACTING OFFICER NAME/CODE		
c. MAILING ADDRESS		
31. TYPED NAME OF TERMINATION CONTRACTING OFFICER	32. SIGNATURE	

DD FORM 1598, JAN 2001 PREVIOUS EDITION MAY BE USED. LOCAL REPRODUCTION AUTHORIZED.

253.303-1598 DD Form 1598: Contract Termination Status Report—Continued

INSTRUCTIONS

GENERAL. Required information shall be inserted in the clear. Dollar entries shall be rounded to the nearest dollar.

STATUS REPORT NUMBER. Number reports consecutively; the closing report will be marked "Final."

DATE. Enter as YYYYMMDD (Example: June 1, 2001 = 20010601).

ITEM 4. Identify activity responsible for settlement.

ITEM 8. Insert, in addition, immediately following parenthetical instruction, the supplementary Procurement Instrument Identification (PII) number assigned to the termination notice. If multiple termination notices apply to the same docket number, insert under "Remarks" the supplementary PII number assigned to each termination notice.

ITEM 11. For cost-reimbursement type contract, enter estimate of cost of work terminated.

ITEM 13. Use the following status codes:

a. Docket established and assigned to TCO
b. Initial conference held
c. Claim expected
d. Interim claim received
e. Final claim received
f. Audit requested
g. Contractor vouchering costs
h. Audit report received
i. Negotiations in process
j. Negotiations completed
k. Supplemental agreement forwarded for signature
l. Determination issued

ITEM 14. Insert after date "I" for interim and "F" for final claims.

ITEM 15. For final settlement proposals on hand for fixed-priced contracts, insert, in addition under "Remarks" the gross amount of the claim.

ITEM 20 and 21.
VO - Vouchering Out
RE - Rescinded
NC - No Cost
NS - Negotiated Settlement
UD - Unilateral Determination

ITEMS 23 THROUGH 26. Insert cumulative data.

ITEM 27.
O - Opening
C - Closing
R - Revision
T - Transfer
I - Inactive
S - Semiannual

Report cases before the ASBCA or in litigation that preclude settlement as inactive.

ITEM 28. Docket number will be assigned in accordance with departmental instructions.

REMARKS *(The TCO will set forth below explanatory or clarifying remarks with respect to any line of data and the status of settlement. Where a settlement has been pending in an administration office for more than 6 months, the TCO is required to furnish: (a) Current Status; (b) Reasons for Delay in Settlement; (c) Estimated Date of Settlement.)*

DD FORM 1598 (BACK), JAN 2001

253.303-1635 DD Form 1635: Plant Clearance Case Register

PLANT CLEARANCE CASE REGISTER

CASE NUMBER	DATE	CONTRACT NUMBER or PURCHASE ORDER NUMBER	CONTRACTOR'S NAME	CONTRACTOR'S REFERENCE NUMBER	LOCATION OF PROPERTY	TERMINATION OR OTHER INVENTORY	DEPT AGENCY SERVICED	INVENTORY DOLLAR VALUE	TOTAL NO OF LINE ITEMS	PLANT CLEARANCE OFFICER ASSIGNED	DATE CLOSED	PART NUMBER

DD Form 1635, (modified), Jan 69

253.303-1637 DD Form 1637: Notice of Acceptance of Inventory Schedules

[DAC 91-6, 5/27/94]

NOTICE OF ACCEPTANCE OF INVENTORY SCHEDULES

1. PLANT CLEARANCE CASE NUMBER

Form Approved OMB No. 0704-0246 Expires Feb 28, 2006

The public reporting burden for this collection of information is estimated to average 30 minutes per response, including the time for reviewing instructions, searching existing data sources, gathering and maintaining the data needed, and completing and reviewing the collection of information. Send comments regarding this burden estimate or any other aspect of this collection of information, including suggestions for reducing the burden, to the Department of Defense, Executive Services and Communications Directorate (0704-0246). Respondents should be aware that notwithstanding any other provision of law, no person shall be subject to any penalty for failing to comply with a collection of information if it does not display a currently valid OMB control number.

PLEASE DO NOT RETURN YOUR COMPLETED FORM TO THE ABOVE ORGANIZATION. RETURN COMPLETED FORM TO ADDRESS IN BLOCK 2

ALL FUTURE DOCUMENTS CONCERNING THIS CASE MUST BEAR THE PLANT CLEARANCE CASE NUMBER SHOWN ABOVE.

2. TO *(Include ZIP Code)*

3. FROM *(Include ZIP Code)*

NOTE TO CONTRACTOR

This office accepts the inventory schedules listed below as being satisfactory in form for storage or removal purposes. Acceptance of the inventory schedules as satisfactory in form will not affect the Government's right to require additional information on any listed item, nor prejudice the Government's right to contest the cost, quantities, and allocability of any item or items. Within a few days, a Government representative will visit your plant to verify the inventory submitted, review your bill of material, and confirm allocability of the inventory submitted.

4. PROCUREMENT INSTRUMENT IDENTIFICATION NUMBER

5. SUBCONTRACT OR PURCHASE ORDER NUMBER

6. CHANGE ORDER NUMBER

7. TERMINATION DOCKET NUMBER

8. CONTRACTOR'S REFERENCE NUMBER

9. TYPE OF CONTRACT *(X one)*

- a. FIXED PRICE
- b. COST TYPE
- c. FACILITY
- d. LEASE
- e. BAILMENT
- f. STORAGE

10. TYPE OF INVENTORY *(X one)*

- a. TERMINATION
- b. RESIDUAL TO CONTRACT
- c. CHANGE ORDER
- d. EXCESS GFP
- e. PRODUCTION EQUIPMENT

11. COST OF INVENTORY SCHEDULES

a. STANDARD FORM 1426 *(Schedule A)*	$
b. STANDARD FORM 1428 *(Schedule B)*	$
c. STANDARD FORM 1430 *(Schedule C)*	$
d. STANDARD FORM 1432 *(Schedule D)*	$
e. DD FORM 1342	$
f. STANDARD FORM 1434	$
g. TOTAL	$ 0.00

12. LOCATION OF PROPERTY

13. CONTRACTOR OR SUBCONTRACTOR

a. NAME *(Identify as Prime Contractor or Subcontractor)*

b. ADDRESS OF CONTRACTOR OR SUBCONTRACTOR *(Include ZIP Code)*

14. COMMENTS *(Continue on additional sheets if necessary.)*

15. PLANT CLEARANCE OFFICER

a. TYPED NAME *(Last, First, Middle Initial)*

b. SIGNATURE

c. DATE

253.303-1638 DD Form 1638: Report of Disposition of Contractor Inventory

REPORT OF DISPOSITION OF CONTRACTOR INVENTORY	TO (Include ZIP Code)			FROM (Include ZIP Code)			REPORT CONTROL SYMBOL DD-P&L(Q)1430 REPORT PERIOD		
SECTION I - SUMMARY	INDUSTRIAL PLANT EQUIPMENT			OTHER CONTRACTOR INVENTORY			TOTAL		
	CASES	LINE ITEMS	ACQUISITION COST	CASES	LINE ITEMS	ACQUISITION COST	CASES	LINE ITEMS	ACQUISITION COST
1. ON HAND - BEGINNING OF REPORT PERIOD									
2. ADJUSTMENTS									
3. RECEIPTS									
4. AVAILABLE FOR DISPOSITION (Total lines 1 - 3)									
5. COMPLETIONS (Line 18 - Section 8)									
6.									
7. ON HAND - END OF REPORT PERIOD									

SECTION 11 - DETAILS OF DISPOSITION ACTIONS	INDUSTRIAL PLANT EQUIPMENT		OTHER CONTRACTOR INVENTORY		TOTAL	
	ACQUISITION COST	PROCEEDS	ACQUISITION COST	PROCEEDS	ACQUISITION COST	PROCEEDS
8. PURCHASES OR RETENTIONS AT COST						
9. RETURN TO SUPPLIERS						
10. TOTAL REDISTRIBUTIONS						
a. Within Owning Agency						
b. Other Agencies						
c.						
d.						
11. DONATIONS						
12. SALES						
13. SALES - PROCEEDS TO OVERHEAD						
14. OTHER						
15.						
16. DESTROYED OR ABANDONED						
17.						
18. TOTAL DISPOSITIONS						

SECTION III - REMARKS

19. APPROVING OFFICIAL			
a. NAME (Last, First, Middle Initial)	b. TITLE	c. SIGNATURE	d. DATE SIGNED

DD Form 1638, OCT 86 Previous editions are obsolete. 148/267

253.303-1639 DD Form 1639: Scrap Warranty

[DAC 91-6, 5/27/94]

SCRAP WARRANTY

Form Approved
OMB No. 0704-0246
Expires Feb 28, 2006

The public reporting burden for this collection of information is estimated to average 30 minutes per response, including the time for reviewing instructions, searching existing data sources, gathering and maintaining the data needed, and completing and reviewing the collection of information. Send comments regarding this burden estimate or any other aspect of this collection of information, including suggestions for reducing the burden, to the Department of Defense, Executive Services and Communications Directorate (0704-0246). Respondents should be aware that notwithstanding any other provision of law, no person shall be subject to any penalty for failing to comply with a collection of information if it does not display a currently valid OMB control number.

PLEASE DO NOT RETURN YOUR COMPLETED FORM TO THE ABOVE ORGANIZATION.
RETURN COMPLETED FORM TO THE CONTRACT ADMINISTRATION OFFICE.

1. PLANT CLEARANCE CASE NUMBER	2. CONTRACT NUMBER

3. CONTRACTOR	4. INVENTORY REFERENCE

5. WARRANTY

a. This scrap warranty covers materials listed below at indicated procurement cost and selling prices as approved by the Plant Clearance Officer and as sold by ______________________________

PAGE (1)	ITEM (2)	DESCRIPTION (3)	WEIGHT (4)	ACQUISITION COST (5)	SELLING COST (6)

b. In consideration of the transfer to the undersigned of the property covered by this agreement at a value based upon its being used as scrap, the undersigned represents and warrants to the United States as follows:

(1) The property covered by this agreement will be used only as scrap, either in its existing condition or after further preparation, unless and until the undersigned is released from this warranty.

(2) In the event the undersigned is released from this warranty, any payment agreed on as consideration for such release shall be made to the United States regardless of whether this warranty shall have been executed at the request of the United States.

(3) In the event the undersigned sells the property covered by this agreement prior to release of this warranty, the undersigned will obtain from the purchaser and tender to the United States a warranty identical to this executed by the purchaser, and upon receipt of such other warranty this warranty will be released by the United States.

(4) All obligations of the undersigned under this warranty shall expire five years from the date hereof.

6. PURCHASER

a. TYPED NAME *(Last, First, Middle Initial)*		b. ADDRESS *(Street, City, State, and ZIP Code)*
c. SIGNATURE	d. DATE SIGNED *(YYYYMMDD)*	

253.303-1640 DD Form 1640: Request for Plant Clearance

[DAC 91-6, 5/27/94]

REQUEST FOR PLANT CLEARANCE

1. DATE PREPARED *(YYYYMMDD)*

Form Approved OMB No. 0704-0246 Expires Feb 28, 2006

The public reporting burden for this collection of information is estimated to average 1 hour per response, including the time for reviewing instructions, searching existing data sources, gathering and maintaining the data needed, and completing and reviewing the collection of information. Send comments regarding this burden estimate or any other aspect of this collection of information, including suggestions for reducing the burden, to the Department of Defense, Executive Services and Communications Directorate (0704-0246). Respondents should be aware that notwithstanding any other provision of law, no person shall be subject to any penalty for failing to comply with a collection of information if it does not display a currently valid OMB control number.

PLEASE DO NOT RETURN YOUR COMPLETED FORM TO THE ABOVE ORGANIZATION. RETURN COMPLETED FORM TO ADDRESS IN ITEM 2.

2. TO *(Include ZIP Code)*

3. FROM *(Include ZIP Code)*

It is requested that plant clearance, including prescribed screening and disposal actions, be accomplished with respect to the contractor inventory described in the enclosed schedules. Plant clearance authority is hereby delegated for the purpose of this referral.

4. GROSS VALUE OF INVENTORY SCHEDULES *($)*

5. SCHEDULE PARTIAL NUMBER

6. PROCUREMENT INSTRUMENT IDENTIFICATION NUMBER

7. PRIME CONTRACT END ITEM

8. SUBCONTRACT NUMBER

9. NAME AND ADDRESS OF PRIME CONTRACTOR *(Include ZIP Code)*

10. NAME AND ADDRESS OF SUBCONTRACTOR *(Include ZIP Code)*

11. LOCATION OF PROPERTY

12. TYPE OF CONTRACT *(X one)*

a. FIXED PRICE	b. COST TYPE	c. FACILITY
d. LEASE AGREEMENT	e. FORMAL STORAGE AGREEMENT	f. BAILMENT

13. TYPE OF INVENTORY *(X one)*

a. TERMINATION	b. RESIDUAL TO COMPLETED CONTRACT	c. CHANGE ORDER
d. EXCESS TO ACTIVE CONTRACT	e. PRODUCTION EQUIPMENT	

14. REMARKS

15. ENCLOSURE(S) *(Include Prime Contractor's Certificate of Allocability and Statement of No Further Requirements for the Property)*

16. REQUESTING OFFICIAL

a. TYPED NAME *(Last, First, Middle Initial)*

b. TITLE

c. SIGNATURE

d. DATE SIGNED *(YYYYMMDD)*

FIRST ENDORSEMENT

17. TO *(Include ZIP Code)*

18. FROM *(Include ZIP Code)*

19. DATE *(YYYYMMDD)*

(1) Disposition will be accomplished under case number ______________________ .

(2) It is requested that all correspondence with this office pertaining to enclosure(s) make reference to the assigned case number.

20. PLANT CLEARANCE OFFICER

a. TYPED NAME *(Last, First, Middle Initial)*

b. TITLE

c. SIGNATURE

d. DATE SIGNED *(YYYYMMDD)*

253.303-1641 DD Form 1641: Disposal Determination Approval

DISPOSAL DETERMINATION APPROVAL		1. PLANT CLEARANCE CASE NO.	2. DATE *(YYYYMMDD)*
3. TYPE OF CONTRACT *(X one)* a. FIXED PRICE b. COST TYPE c. FACILITY d. LEASE e. BAILMENT	4. INVENTORY SCHEDULE NO. *(Attach copy)*	5. TYPE OF INVENTORY *(X one)* a. TERMINATION b. RESIDUAL TO CONTRACT c. CHANGE ORDER d. EXCESS GFP e. PRODUCTION EQUIPMENT	
6.a. NAME OF PRIME CONTRACTOR		7.a. NAME OF SUBCONTRACTOR	
b. ADDRESS OF PRIME CONTRACTOR *(Include ZIP code)*		b. ADDRESS OF SUBCONTRACTOR *(Include ZIP code)*	
c. PROCUREMENT INSTRUMENT ID NUMBER		c. SUBCONTRACT NUMBER	

8. DISPOSAL RATIONALE CODES *(Select alpha and numeric codes that apply and insert in the "Code(s)" column below.)*

CATEGORY A Rationale For Scrap or Salvage	CATEGORY B Rationale For Abandonment	CATEGORY C Rationale For Sale Without Competitive Bids *(Enter sale price)*
1. Beyond economical repair/estimated cost of repair in excess of 65% of acquisition. 2. Without value except for basic content. 3. Obsolete. 4. Specialized design. 5. Incomplete condition. 6. No reasonable prospect of sale or use as serviceable property without major repairs or alterations. 7. Other *(Specify)*.	1. No commercial value. 2. Donation is not feasible. 3. Estimated cost of continued care and handling exceeds estimated proceeds of sale. 4. Offered for sale and no bids received. 5. Value so little and cost of continued care and handling so great advertising for sale not justified. 6. Abandonment required by considerations of health, safety, or security. 7. Other *(Specify)*.	1. Sale price equals (or exceeds) current market value. 2. Sale price is fair and reasonable based on (a) test of market or (b) recent sale price of similar property. 3. Sale price equals (or exceeds) that which could be realized through competitive sale, cost of sale, and/or additional storage costs; would more than offset any potential increased return. 4. Other *(Specify)*. CATEGORY D Other Disposal Action(s) Requiring Documentation *(Attach rationale)*

CODE(S) a.	ITEM NUMBER(S) b.	ACQUISITION COST c.	CODE(S) a.	ITEM NUMBER(S) b.	ACQUISITION COST c.
d. SUBTOTAL *(This column)* ➔			d. SUBTOTAL *(This column)* ➔		
		e. TOTAL COST			

9. PLANT CLEARANCE OFFICER	10. REVIEW BOARD CHAIRMAN APPROVAL *(If required)*	
a. TYPED NAME *(Last, First, Middle Initial)*	a. TYPED NAME *(Last, First, Middle Initial)*	
b. SIGNATURE	b. SIGNATURE	c. DATE SIGNED *(YYYYMMDD)*

DD FORM 1641, APR 2000 PREVIOUS EDITION MAY BE USED.

253.303-1653 DD Form 1653: Transportation Data for Solicitations

TRANSPORTATION DATA FOR SOLICITATIONS (*Use back for additional remarks.*)	1. PR, PD OR MIPR NUMBER	2. DATE (*YYYYMMDD*)
3. COMMODITY		4. STOCK NUMBER

5. F.O.B. TERMS RECOMMENDED AS BEST SUITED FOR THIS PROCUREMENT (*X as applicable*)

	a. ORIGIN		c. OTHER (*Specify*)
	b. DESTINATION		

	6. TRANSPORTATION PROVISIONS AND CLAUSES (*X as applicable*)	7. FAR CITATION
	a. F.O.B. ORIGIN - GOVERNMENT BILLS OF LADING OR PREPAID POSTAGE	
	b. REPORT OF SHIPMENT (*Reship*)	
	c. COMMERCIAL BILL OF LADING NOTATIONS	
	d. F.O.B. ORIGIN	
	e. F.O.B. ORIGIN, WITH DIFFERENTIALS	
	f. F.O.B. DESTINATION	
	g. F.O.B. ORIGIN AND/OR DESTINATION	
	h. SHIPPING POINT(S) USED IN EVALUATION OF F.O.B. ORIGIN OFFERS	
	i. EVALUATION - F.O.B. ORIGIN	
	j. F.O.B. DESTINATION - EVIDENCE OF SHIPMENT	
	k. DESTINATION - UNKNOWN	
	l. NO EVALUATION OF TRANSPORTATION COSTS	
	m. EVALUATION OF EXPORT OFFERS	
	n. CLEARANCE AND DOCUMENTATION REQUIREMENTS	
	o. FREIGHT CLASSIFICATION DESCRIPTION	
	p. DIVERSION OF SHIPMENT UNDER F.O.B. DESTINATION CONTRACTS	
	q. F.O.B. POINT FOR DELIVERY OF GOVERNMENT-FURNISHED PROPERTY	
	r. TRANSIT ARRANGEMENTS	
	s. TRANSPORTATION TRANSIT PRIVILEGE CREDITS	
	t. LOADING, BLOCKING, AND BRACING OF FREIGHT CARS	
	u. F.O.B. ORIGIN - CARLOAD AND TRUCKLOAD SHIPMENTS	
	v. GUARANTEED MAXIMUM SHIPPING WEIGHTS AND DIMENSIONS	
	w. F.O.B. ORIGIN - MINIMUM SIZE OF SHIPMENTS	
	x. MARKING OF SHIPMENTS	

8. EVALUATION OF PORT BIDS OR PROPOSAL (*Ports and combined handling and transportation charges per measurement ton used by the Government for evaluation purposes*)

a. DESTINATION COUNTRIES	b. ORIGIN PORTS (*Air or water*)				

9. TRANSPORTATION SPECIALIST

a. TYPED OR PRINTED NAME (*Last, First, Middle Initial*)	b. SIGNATURE	c. DATE SIGNED (*YYYYMMDD*)

DD FORM 1653, APR 1999 (EG) PREVIOUS EDITION IS OBSOLETE. WHS/DIOR, Apr 99

253.303-1654 DD Form 1654: Evaluation of Transportation Cost Factors

EVALUATION OF TRANSPORTATION COST FACTORS
(See Instructions on back before completion.)

1. PR, PD OR MIPR NUMBER	2. SOLICITATION NUMBER	3. BID OPENING OR PROPOSAL CLOSING DATE	4. DATE REQUIRED
5. FMS *(X one)* ☐ YES ☐ NO	6. UFC	7. NMFC	

TRANSPORTATION DATA

NAME OF COMPETITOR	ITEM NO.	FMS	ORIGIN	DESTINATION	NO. OF SHIPMENTS	QUANTITY	NUMBER OF UNITS PER CONTAINER	WEIGHT OF EACH CONTAINER *(Lbs.)*	SIZE OF CONTAINER IN INCHES *(LWH)*	GROSS SHIPPING WEIGHT	MODE	RATE PER CWT OR	TOTAL COST OF TRANSPORTATION
A	B	C	D	E	F	G	H	I	J	K	L	M	N

8. BUYER/NEGOTIATOR		10. TENDER/TARIFF	
a. NAME *(Last, First, Middle Initial)*	b. SYMBOL/EXT.		
9. CONTRACTING OFFICER		**11. TRANSPORTATION OFFICER**	
a. TYPED OR PRINTED NAME *(Last, First, Middle Initial)*	b. SYMBOL/EXT.	a. TYPED OR PRINTED NAME *(Last, First, Middle Initial)*	b. SYMBOL/EXT.
c. SIGNATURE	d. DATE SIGNED *(YYYYMMDD)*	c. SIGNATURE	d. DATE SIGNED *(YYYYMMDD)*

DD FORM 1654, APR 1999 (EG) PREVIOUS EDITION IS OBSOLETE. Page of Pages WHS/DIOR, Apr 99

INSTRUCTIONS FOR PREPARATION OF DD FORM 1654

In order to facilitate processing the "Evaluation of Transportation Cost Factors," DD Form 1654 should be prepared in duplicate by the Contracting Officer, Buyer, or Negotiator and submitted to the Transportation Officer with the following information in Items 1 through 5, 8 and 9, and columns A through K.

ITEM NUMBER	REQUIREMENT
1.	PR, PD, or MIPR Number.
2.	Solicitation Number.
3.	Bid Opening or Proposal Closing Date *(only required on first page if multiple pages used).*
4.	Date the DD Form 1654 is required by the C.O., Buyer or Negotiator - allow a minimum of 5 working days.
5.	FMS - Mark (X) Yes or No. If Yes, identify each FMS portion in Column C with an X.
6.	UFC - Uniform Freight Class. *(To be provided by Transportation Officer.)*
7.	NMFC - National Motor Freight Class. *(To be provided by Transportation Officer.)*
A.	Name of Competitor - to be provided in ascending order by price.
B.	Item Number.
C.	Insert an "X" for each FMS increment.
D.	Origin - City, State and Zip Code.
E.	Destination - City, State and Zip Code, or Military Installation and Zip Code.
F.	Number of Shipments.
G.	Quantity - to be shipped each shipment.
H, I, J, K.	Units, weight, size, and gross weight when known.
L.	Insert Mode of Shipment Code(s) from DoD 4500.32-R (MILSTAMP) appendix B. *(To be provided by Transportation Officer.)*
M.	Freight rate to be specified as per CWT, gallon, vehicle used, mile, ton or whatever unit of measure rate is based. *(To be provided by Transportation Officer.)*
N.	To be provided by Transportation Officer.
8 and 9.	Self explanatory. *(Items 8 and 9 shall be completed only on first page if multiple pages are used.)*
10.	Tariff Authority from which rates are obtained *(To be provided by Transportation Officer).*
11.	Self explanatory.

DD FORM 1654 (BACK), APR 1999

253.303-1659 DD Form 1659: Application for U.S. Government Shipping Documentation/Instructions

[DAC 91-10, 2/29/96]

APPLICATION FOR U.S. GOVERNMENT SHIPPING DOCUMENTATION/INSTRUCTIONS
(See Instructions and Legend on back before completion)

TYPE OF APPLICATION *(X all that apply)*
- GOVERNMENT BILL(S) OF LADING
- DOMESTIC ROUTE ORDER
- EXPORT OR FMS SHIPMENT

Form Approved
OMB No. 0704-0250
Expires Jul 31, 2009

The public reporting burden for this collection of information is estimated to average 15 minutes per response, including the time for reviewing instructions, searching existing data sources, gathering and maintaining the data needed, and completing and reviewing the collection of information. Send comments regarding this burden estimate or any other aspect of this collection of information, including suggestions for reducing the burden, to the Department of Defense, Executive Services Directorate, Information Management Division, 1155 Defense Pentagon, Washington, DC 20301-1155 (0704-0250). Respondents should be aware that notwithstanding any other provision of law, no person shall be subject to any penalty for failing to comply with a collection of information if it does not display a currently valid OMB control number.
PLEASE DO NOT RETURN YOUR COMPLETED FORM TO THE ABOVE ORGANIZATION. SEND YOUR COMPLETED FORM TO THE APPROPRIATE TRANSPORTATION OFFICE.

1. TO *(Name and Address of Transportation Officer providing shipping instructions) (Include ZIP Code)*	**2. AGENCY ID NO.** **3. CONTRACTOR'S APPLICATION NO.**	**4. FROM** *(Name and Address of Contractor) (Include ZIP Code)*
5. DESTINATION *(Name and Address) (Include ZIP Code)*	**6. SPLC** *(Destination)* **7. SPLC** *(Origin)*	**8. ORIGIN** *(Name and Address) (Include ZIP Code)*
9. CONSIGNEE *(Name and Address) (Include ZIP Code)*	**10. DODAAC** **11. CAGE CODE**	**12. SHIPPER** *(Name and Address) (Include ZIP Code)*

13. MARKS AND ANNOTATIONS	**14. DATE SHIPMENT AVAILABLE** *(YYYYMMDD)*	**15. REQ. DATE AT DESTINATION** *(YYYYMMDD)*	**16. TP**

17. IF CARLOAD OR TRUCKLOAD, INDICATE TYPE AND SIZE REQUIRED FOR EACH	**18. SPECIAL ROUTING CONDITIONS**

19. RAIL CARRIER SERVING

a. CONSIGNOR	SCAC	c. PRIVATE SIDING *(X if applicable or indicate nearest point of delivery)*	SPLC
b. CONSIGNEE	SCAC		SPLC

20. HAZARDOUS MATERIALS *(X and complete as applicable)*

a. THIS SHIPMENT DOES NOT CONTAIN HAZARDOUS MATERIAL.	INITIALS	b. THIS SHIPMENT CONTAINS HAZARDOUS MATERIAL. (1) PSN	(2) UN/NA No.

21. CONTAINER AND COMMODITY DATA

CONTRACT ITEM NO. a.	UNITS PER PKG/COS b.	PKG/COS c. (1) NO.	PKG/COS c. (2) TYPE	DESCRIPTION OF COMMODITY *(NSN No., Freight classification including UFC/NMFC Item No.) (For all package sizes show dimensions in INCHES.)* d.	WT. PER PKG/COS *(Pounds)* e.	CUBE PER PKG/COS *(Feet)* f.
g. TOTALS		0			0	0

22. CONTRACT (PII) NUMBER	**23. FOB CONTRACT TERMS**	**24. FOB POINT** *(City and State)*

25. REQUESTER

a. TYPED OR PRINTED NAME *(Last, First, Middle Initial)*	b. TELEPHONE NO./EXTENSION *(Include Area Code)*	c. SIGNATURE	d. DATE SIGNED *(YYYYMMDD)*

26. REMARKS		
To be completed by Transportation Officer		
27. CARRIER(S) OR ROUTING(S)	28. TARIFF OR TENDER NO. AND DATE	29. ROUTE ORDER/RELEASE NO. 30. TRANSPORTATION FUNDS
31. FREIGHT RATE SPECIALIST		
a. SIGNATURE	b. TELEPHONE NO. *(Include Area Code)*	c. DATE SIGNED *(YYYYMMDD)*

LEGEND

CAGE	Contractor and Government Entity	IPG	Issue Priority Group	TP	Transportation Priority
CONUS	Continental United States	NSN	National Stock Number	UN/NA	United Nations/North America
COS	Containers	PII	Procurement Instrument Identification	UFC/NMFC	Uniform Freight Classification/ National Motor Freight Classification
DODAAC	DoD Activity Address Code	POE	Point of Embarkation		
FAS	Free Alongside	PSN	Proper Shipping Name		
FMS	Foreign Military Sales	SCAC	Standard Carrier Alpha Code		
FOB	Free On Board	SPLC	Standard Point Location Code		

INSTRUCTIONS FOR COMPLETION OF DD FORM 1659

GENERAL.

This form will be used to obtain: (a) Government Bills of Lading under FOB origin contracts, (b) a Domestic Route Order under FOB origin contracts, (c) an Export Traffic Release regardless of FOB terms, or (d) FMS shipment instructions, in compliance with DoD regulations and procedures. Prepare separate forms for each contract/purchase order or destination.

To ensure that shipments are accomplished in accordance with contract delivery schedule, application(s) should be submitted in duplicate, at least 10 days in advance of actual shipping date, to the Transportation Office of the contract administration office. Applications must be submitted 15 days in advance for FMS shipments.

To avoid excess cost, do not order or load carrier's equipment until routing instructions are received.

Export shipments require marking in accordance with MIL-STD-129, "Marking for Shipment and Storage." Markings should not be applied until complete and accurate shipment information has been provided by the Transportation Office.

Items 1, 3, 4, 24, 25, and 27 through 31 are self-explanatory.

2. Leave blank. The transportation office will complete if necessary.

5. Enter the city, town or point, state and ZIP Code, according to the shipping mode when the destination is located in CONUS. Show the address found in the contract if the destination is overseas. Identify a water terminal only when the contract terms are FOB/FAS Port.

6. Specify the SPLC, if known, for the CONUS destination shown in Item 5. Leave blank for overseas destinations.

7. Enter the SPLC for the origin point in Item 8.

8. Designate the actual location where shipment will be tendered to a carrier.

9. Enter the name and address of the ultimate consignee shown in the contract. Do not show a POE.

10. Record the 6-digit DoDAAC assigned to the ultimate consignee as found in the contract. The DoDAAC should be identical to the one which will be recorded in Item 13, DD Form 250.

11. Annotate the CAGE Code assigned to the actual shipper. Show the CAGE Code for a packaging facility if the shipment will be tendered at that location.

12. Enter the name of the actual shipper, prime or subcontractor as appropriate, and address if different from Item 8.

13. Identify data shown in the contract which affects marking, transportation, delivery, and export of packages or shipping containers.

14. Specify the earliest date your shipment can be tendered to a carrier.

15. Enter a date only when specific instructions indicate the shipment must be delivered on or before that date.

16. Indicate the TP or the IPG for the shipment as stated in the contract or shipping instructions. If not available, leave blank.

17. Enter type and size of equipment needed to accommodate a full load.

18. Enter any special handling or protective instructions required for hazardous, sensitive, or classified material, temperature limitatons, fragility, etc. FOR TRANSPORTATION OFFICES: Add transit information for a route order request, if appropriate.

19. Show the rail carrier including the SCAC serving the origin point. FOR TRANSPORTATION OFFICES: Complete consignee information when applicable.

20. The appropriate statement MUST be marked. If shipment contains hazardous material, enter PSN in accordance with 49 CFR, Section 172.101 and UN/NA number(s).

21. Enter data as described. Totals in line g. must describe entire shipment. Include unit of packaging in column b.; e.g., "30/COS." Be sure to state dimensions in INCHES.

22. Enter the PII number. Specify also the delivery order number when added to the basic contract or the shipping authority when different than the contract.

23. Indicate the FOB term *(origin, destination, etc.)* as stated in the contract.

26. Record necessary data not otherwise shown. If the application covers multiple shipments, specify the number of the shipments, total weight and cube for each shipment, transportation priority, and dates shipments will be available.

253.303-1662 DD Form 1662: DoD Property in the Custody of Contractors

[DAC 91-6, 5/27/94]

DOD PROPERTY IN THE CUSTODY OF CONTRACTORS (DFARS 245.505-14) *(See Instructions on back before completing this form.)*	REPORT AS OF 30 SEP ______ OR __________	*Form Approved* *OMB No. 0704-0246* *Expires Feb 28, 2006*

The public reporting burden for this collection of information is estimated to average 1 hour per response, including the time for reviewing instructions, searching existing data sources, gathering and maintaining the data needed, and completing and reviewing the collection of information. Send comments regarding this burden estimate or any other aspect of this collection of information, including suggestions for reducing the burden, to the Department of Defense, Executive Services and Communications Directorate (0704-0246). Respondents should be aware that notwithstanding any other provision of law, no person shall be subject to any penalty for failing to comply with a collection of information if it does not display a currently valid OMB control number.

PLEASE DO NOT RETURN YOUR COMPLETED FORM TO THE ABOVE ORGANIZATION.
RETURN COMPLETED FORM TO THE ADDRESS IN ITEM 1.

1. TO *(Enter name and address of property administrator)*	2. FROM *(Enter full name, address and CAGE code of contractor)*

3. IF GOVERNMENT-OWNED, CONTRACTOR-OPERATED PLANT, ENTER GOVERNMENT NAME OF PLANT

4. CONTRACT NO. *(PIIN)*	5. CONTRACT PURPOSE	6. BUSINESS TYPE *(Enter L, S, or N)*	7. OFFICIAL NAME OF PARENT COMPANY

8. PROPERTY LOCATION(S)	9. PLANT EQUIPMENT PACKAGE *(PEP No. and use)*

a. PROPERTY *(Type or Account)*	b. BALANCE START OF PERIOD (1) ACQUISITION COST *(in dollars)*	b. BALANCE START OF PERIOD (2) QUANTITY *(in units or acres)*	c. ADDITIONS *(in dollars)*	d. DELETIONS *(in dollars)*	e. BALANCE END OF PERIOD (1) ACQUISITION COST *(in dollars)*	e. BALANCE END OF PERIOD (2) QUANTITY *(in units or acres)*
10. LAND						
11. OTHER REAL PROPERTY						
12. OTHER PLANT EQUIPMENT						
13. INDUSTRIAL PLANT EQUIPMENT						
14. SPECIAL TEST EQUIPMENT						
15. SPECIAL TOOLING *(Government Title Only)*						
16. MILITARY PROPERTY *(Agency-Peculiar)*						
17. GOVERNMENT MATERIAL *(Government-Furnished)*						
18. GOVERNMENT MATERIAL *(Contractor-Acquired)*						

19. CONTRACTOR REPRESENTATIVE

a. TYPED NAME *(Last, First, Middle Initial)*	b. SIGNATURE	c. DATE SIGNED *(YYYYMMDD)*

20. DOD PROPERTY REPRESENTATIVE

a. TYPED NAME *(Last, First, Middle Initial)*	c. SIGNATURE	d. DATE SIGNED *(YYYYMMDD)*
b. TELEPHONE NUMBERS *(Commercial and DSN)*		

REPORTING INSTRUCTIONS

GENERAL. The prime contractor shall report all DoD property (as indicated) in its custody or in that of its subcontractors as of September 30 to the Government Property Representative by October 31 of each year. Also report zero end of period balances when no DoD property remains accountable to the contract. Report data from records maintained in accordance with FAR Subpart 45.5 and DFARS Subpart 245.5.

REPORT AS OF 30 SEP ______. Fill in the appropriate year *(or other date).*

ITEM 1 - TO. Enter the name of the Government Property Representative, the Contract Administration Office or other office the Government Property Representative works for, and the full mailing address *(including City, State, and ZIP+4).*

ITEM 2 - FROM. Enter the full name and address of the reporting contractor with the Division name stated after the Corporate name. Use the name as it appears on the contract but omit articles and insert spaces between company names that are made up of letters like XYZ Inc., for example. Also enter the Commercial and Government Entity (CAGE) Code.

ITEM 3 - IF GOVERNMENT-OWNED CONTRACTOR-OPERATED PLANT, ENTER GOVERNMENT NAME OF PLANT. Enter the Government name of the plant if the plant is Government-owned and Contractor-operated. Leave blank if it is a contractor-owned plant.

ITEM 4 - CONTRACT NO. (PIIN). Enter the 13-digit contract number or Procurement Instrument Identification Number (PIIN) under which the Government property is accountable. Use format XXXXXX-XX-X-XXXX.

ITEM 5 - CONTRACT PURPOSE. Enter one of the following 1-character alphabetic codes to identify the general purposes of the contract:

A. RDT&E

B. Supplies and Equipment *(deliverable end items)*

C. Facilities Contract

D. Lease of facilities by the contractor

E. Maintenance, Repair, Modification, or Rebuilding of Equipment

F. Operation of Government-Owned Plant or Facilities including test sites, ranges, installations

G. Service contract performed primarily on Military Installations, test facilities, ranges or sites

H. Contract for storage of Government Property

I. Others

ITEM 6 - BUSINESS TYPE. Enter a 1-character alphabetic code indicating the type of business concern:

L = Large S = Small N = Non-profit

(See FAR Part 19 for definition of Small Business and FAR 31.701 for definition of Non-profit Organizations.)

ITEM 7 - OFFICIAL NAME OF PARENT COMPANY. Enter the name of the Parent Corporation of the Reporting Contractor. The Parent Corporation is one in which common stock has been issued whether or not the stock is publicly traded and which is not a subsidiary of another corporation.

ITEM 8 - PROPERTY LOCATION(S). Enter the primary location(s) of the property if it is located at site(s) other than that of the Reporting Contractor, e.g., location of subcontract property or property at alternate sites of the prime contractor. Location is the City, State and Zip or the Military Installation or the Foreign site. Limit input to 69 characters. NOTE: Can be used as a "REMARKS" field.

ITEM 9 - PLANT EQUIPMENT PACKAGE. Enter the Number and Use of a Plant Equipment Package (PEP) if one exists on this contract. Leave blank otherwise. Example: ARMY PEP #570 - 81 mm Shells.

ITEMS 10 - 18.b.(1) - ACQUISITION COST (BALANCE AT THE BEGINNING OF THE FISCAL YEAR). Enter the acquisition cost for each type of property as defined in FAR 45.5 or DFARS 245.5. The amounts reported must agree with the amounts reported in the previous year for BALANCE AT END OF PERIOD.

ITEMS 10, 12 - 16.b.(2) - QUANTITY (BALANCE AT BEGINNING OF THE FISCAL YEAR). Enter the quantity for all categories of Government property except for Other Real Property and Material on hand at the beginning of the fiscal year. The amounts reported must agree with the amounts reported in the previous year for BALANCE AT END OF PERIOD.

ITEMS 10 - 15.c. - ADDITIONS *(in dollars).* For the property categories indicated, enter the acquisition cost for the total additions to the contract from any source during the fiscal year. Do not enter for Government Material or Military Property.

ITEMS 10 - 15.d. - DELETIONS *(in dollars).* For the property categories indicated, enter the acquisition cost for the total deletions from the contract during the fiscal year. Do not enter for Government Material or Military Property.

ITEMS 10 - 18.e.(1) - ACQUISITION COST (BALANCE AT THE END OF THE FISCAL YEAR). Enter the acquisition cost for each type of property as defined in FAR 45.5 or DFARS 245.5.

ITEMS 10, 12-16.e.(2) - QUANTITY (BALANCE AT END OF FISCAL YEAR). Enter the quantity for all categories of Government Property except for Other Real Property and Material on hand at the end of the fiscal year. These will be carried forward to reflect the balance at the beginning of the following year.

ITEMS 17 and 18 - GOVERNMENT MATERIAL. Report material as reflected on inventory records in accordance with FAR 45.505-3.

ITEM 19 - CONTRACTOR REPRESENTATIVE. Type the name of the contractor representative authorized by the property control system to sign this report.

ITEM 20 - DOD PROPERTY REPRESENTATIVE. Type the name of the DoD Property Administrator or other Authorized Property Representative, plus that individual's commercial area code and telephone number and DSN number *(if one exists).* Signature and date.

NOTE TO CONTRACTOR: When reporting more than one contract from the same location and the same contractor, you may elect to fill out Data Elements 1, 3, 6, 7, and 19 only once as long as each form can be readily identified if any form becomes separated from the others.

253.303-1664 DD Form 1664: Data Item Description

DATA ITEM DESCRIPTION			Form Approved OMB No. 0704-0188
The public reporting burden for this collection of information is estimated to average 110 hours per response, including the time for reviewing instructions, searching existing data sources, gathering and maintaining the data needed, and completing and reviewing the collection of information. Send comments regarding this burden estimate or any other aspect of this collection of information, including suggestions for reducing the burden, to Department of Defense, Washington Headquarters Services, Directorate for Information Operations and Reports (0704-0188), 1215 Jefferson Davis Highway, Suite 1204, Arlington, VA 22202-4302. Respondents should be aware that notwithstanding any other provision of law, no person shall be subject to any penalty for failing to comply with a collection of information if it does not display a currently valid OMB control number. **PLEASE DO NOT RETURN YOUR FORM TO THE ABOVE ADDRESS.**			
1. TITLE		2. IDENTIFICATION NUMBER	
3. DESCRIPTION/PURPOSE			
4. APPROVAL DATE *(YYYYMMDD)*	5. OFFICE OF PRIMARY RESPONSIBILITY (OPR)	6a. DTIC APPLICABLE	6b. GIDEP APPLICABLE
7. APPLICATION/INTERRELATIONSHIP			
8. APPROVAL LIMITATION	9a. APPLICABLE FORMS		9b. AMSC NUMBER
10. PREPARATION INSTRUCTIONS			
11. DISTRIBUTION STATEMENT			

DD FORM 1664, AUG 96 (EG) PREVIOUS EDITION MAY BE USED. Page ___ of _____ Pages

253.303-1707 DD Form 1707: Information to Offerors or Quoters

INFORMATION TO OFFERORS OR QUOTERS
SECTION A - COVER SHEET

Form Approved
OMB No. 9000-0002
Expires Oct 31, 2004

The public reporting burden for this collection of information is estimated to average 35 minutes per response, including the time for reviewing instructions, searching existing data sources, gathering and maintaining the data needed, and completing and reviewing the collection of information. Send comments regarding this burden estimate or any other aspect of this collection of information, including suggestions for reducing the burden, to Department of Defense, Washington Headquarters Services, Directorate for Information Operations and Reports (9000-0002), 1215 Jefferson Davis Highway, Suite 1204, Arlington, VA 22202-4302. Respondents should be aware that notwithstanding any other provision of law, no person will be subject to any penalty for failing to comply with a collection of information if it does not display a currently valid OMB control number.

PLEASE DO NOT RETURN YOUR FORM TO THE ABOVE ADDRESS. RETURN COMPLETED FORM TO THE ADDRESS IN BLOCK 4 BELOW.

1. SOLICITATION NUMBER	2. *(X one)*	3. DATE/TIME RESPONSE DUE
	☐ a. INVITATION FOR BID (IFB) ☐ b. REQUEST FOR PROPOSAL (RFP) ☐ c. REQUEST FOR QUOTATION (RFQ)	

INSTRUCTIONS

NOTE: The provision entitled "Required Central Contractor Registration" applies to most solicitations.

1. If you are not submitting a response, complete the information in Blocks 9 through 11 and return to the issuing office in Block 4 unless a different return address is indicated in Block 7.

2. Offerors or quoters must include full, accurate, and complete information in their responses as required by this solicitation (including attachments). "Fill-ins" are provided on Standard Form 18, Standard Form 33, and other solicitation documents. Examine the entire solicitation carefully. The penalty for making false statements is prescribed in 18 U.S.C. 1001.

3. Offerors or quoters must plainly mark their responses with the Solicitation Number and the date and local time for bid opening or receipt of proposals that is in the solicitation document.

4. Information regarding the timeliness of response is addressed in the provision of this solicitation entitled either "Late Submissions, Modifications, and Withdrawals of Bids" or "Instructions to Offerors - Competitive Acquisitions".

4. ISSUING OFFICE *(Complete mailing address, including ZIP Code)*	5. ITEMS TO BE PURCHASED *(Brief description)*

6. PROCUREMENT INFORMATION *(X and complete as applicable)*

☐	a. THIS PROCUREMENT IS UNRESTRICTED
☐	b. THIS PROCUREMENT IS ______ % SET-ASIDE FOR SMALL BUSINESS. THE APPLICABLE NAICS CODE IS: ______
☐	c. THIS PROCUREMENT IS ______ % SET-ASIDE FOR HUB ZONE CONCERNS. THE APPLICABLE NAICS CODE IS: ______
☐	d. THIS PROCUREMENT IS RESTRICTED TO FIRMS ELIGIBLE UNDER SECTION 8(a) OF THE SMALL BUSINESS ACT.

7. ADDITIONAL INFORMATION

8. POINT OF CONTACT FOR INFORMATION

a. NAME *(Last, First, Middle Initial)*		b. ADDRESS *(Include Zip Code)*
c. TELEPHONE NUMBER *(Include Area Code and Extension)*	d. E-MAIL ADDRESS	

9. REASONS FOR NO RESPONSE *(X all that apply)*

☐	a. CANNOT COMPLY WITH SPECIFICATIONS	☐	d. DO NOT REGULARLY MANUFACTURE OR SELL THE TYPE OF ITEMS INVOLVED
☐	b. UNABLE TO IDENTIFY THE ITEM(S)	☐	e. OTHER *(Specify)*
☐	c. CANNOT MEET DELIVERY REQUIREMENT		

10. MAILING LIST INFORMATION *(X one)*

WE ☐ DO ☐ DO NOT DESIRE TO BE RETAINED ON THE MAILING LIST FOR FUTURE PROCUREMENT OF THE TYPE INVOLVED.

11a. COMPANY NAME	b. ADDRESS *(Include Zip Code)*

c. ACTION OFFICER

(1) TYPED OR PRINTED NAME *(Last, First, Middle Initial)*	(2) TITLE
(3) SIGNATURE	(4) DATE SIGNED *(YYYYMMDD)*

DD FORM 1707, FEB 2002 PREVIOUS EDITION IS OBSOLETE.

DD FORM 1707 (BACK), FEB 2002

FOLD

FOLD

FROM

AFFIX
STAMP
HERE

SOLICITATION NUMBER	
DATE *(YYYYMMDD)*	LOCAL TIME

253.303-1861 DD Form 1861: Contract Facilities Capital Cost of Money

[DAC 91-6, 5/27/94]

CONTRACT FACILITIES CAPITAL COST OF MONEY			OMB No. 0704-0267 OMB approval expires Jul 31, 2007
The public reporting burden for this collection of information is estimated to average 10 hours per response, including the time for reviewing instructions, searching existing data sources, gathering and maintaining the data needed, and completing and reviewing the collection of information. Send comments regarding this burden estimate or any other aspect of this collection of information, including suggestions for reducing the burden, to the Department of Defense, Executive Services Directorate (0704-0267). Respondents should be aware that notwithstanding any other provision of law, no person shall be subject to any penalty for failing to comply with a collection of information if it does not display a currently valid OMB control number. **PLEASE DO NOT RETURN YOUR COMPLETED FORM TO THE ABOVE ORGANIZATION. RETURN COMPLETED FORM TO YOUR CONTRACTING OFFICIAL.**			
1. CONTRACTOR NAME		2. CONTRACTOR ADDRESS	
3. BUSINESS UNIT			
4. RFP/CONTRACT PIIN NUMBER		5. PERFORMANCE PERIOD	
6. DISTRIBUTION OF FACILITIES CAPITAL COST OF MONEY			
POOL a.	ALLOCATION BASE b.	FACILITIES CAPITAL COST OF MONEY c. FACTOR (1)	AMOUNT (2)
d. TOTAL			$0.00
e. TREASURY RATE			%
f. FACILITIES CAPITAL EMPLOYED (TOTAL DIVIDED BY TREASURY RATE)			
7. DISTRIBUTION OF FACILITIES CAPITAL EMPLOYED			
		PERCENTAGE a.	AMOUNT b.
(1) LAND		%	
(2) BUILDINGS		%	
(3) EQUIPMENT		%	
(4) FACILITIES CAPITAL EMPLOYED		100%	$0.00

253.303-1921 DD Form 1921: Cost Data Summary Report

The public reporting burden for this collection of information is estimated to average 10 hours per response, including the time for reviewing instructions, searching existing data sources, gathering and maintaining the data needed, and completing and reviewing the collection of information. Send comments regarding this burden estimate or any other aspect of this collection of information, including suggestions for reducing the burden, to Department of Defense, Washington Headquarters Services, Directorate for Information Operations and Reports (0704-0188), 1215 Jefferson Davis Highway, Suite 1204, Arlington, VA 22202-4302. Respondents should be aware that notwithstanding any other provision of law, no person shall be subject to any penalty for failing to comply with a collection of information if it does not display a currently valid OMB control number. PLEASE DO NOT RETURN YOUR FORM TO THIS ADDRESS.

SECURITY CLASSIFICATION

Form Approved OMB No. 0704-0188

COST DATA SUMMARY REPORT (*Dollars in* ________)	1. PROGRAM	2. ☐ CONTRACT NO.: LATEST AMENDMENT: ☐ RFP NO: ☐ PROGRAM ESTIMATE	3. ☐ RDT&E ☐ PROCUREMENT / 4. MULTIPLE YEAR CONTRACT ☐ YES ☐ NO	5. REPORT AS OF / 6. FY FUNDED
7. CONTRACT TYPE / 8. CONTRACT PRICE	9. CONTRACT CEILING	10. ☐ PRIME/ASSOCIATE ☐ SUBCONTRACTOR (*Name and Address, Include ZIP Code*)	11. NAME OF CUSTOMER (*Subcontractor Use Only*)	

CONTRACT LINE ITEM A	REPORTING ELEMENTS B	ELEMENT CODE C	TO DATE COSTS INCURRED: NONRECURRING D	RECURRING E	TOTAL F	AT COMPLETION: NUMBER OF UNITS G	COSTS INCURRED: NONRECURRING H	RECURRING I	TOTAL J

12. REMARKS			
13. NAME OF PERSON TO BE CONTACTED	14. TELEPHONE NO.	15. SIGNATURE	16. DATE

DD FORM 1921, AUG 96 (EG) PREVIOUS EDITION MAY BE USED.

SECURITY CLASSIFICATION

253.303-1921-1 DD Form 1921-1: Functional Cost-Hour Report

SECURITY CLASSIFICATION

FUNCTIONAL COST-HOUR REPORT

Form Approved
OMB No. 0704-0188

The public reporting burden for this collection of information is estimated to average 10 hours per response, including the time for reviewing instructions, searching existing data sources, gathering and maintaining the data needed, and completing and reviewing the collection of information. Send comments regarding this burden estimate or any other aspect of this collection of information, including suggestions for reducing the burden, to Department of Defense, Washington Headquarters Services, Directorate for Information Operations and Reports (0704-0188), 1215 Jefferson Davis Highway, Suite 1204, Arlington, VA 22202-4302. Respondents should be aware that notwithstanding any other provision of law, no person shall be subject to any penalty for failing to comply with a collection of information if it does not display a currently valid OMB control number.
PLEASE DO NOT RETURN YOUR FORM TO THIS ADDRESS.

SECTION A

1. PROGRAM	2. REPORT AS OF	3. DOLLARS IN	4. HOURS IN

5. [ ] CONTRACT NO. ______ LATEST AMENDMENT ______ [ ] RFP NO. ______ [ ] PROGRAM ESTIMATE ______

6. [ ] NON-RECURRING [ ] RECURRING [ ] TOTAL 7. [ ] RDT&E [ ] PROCUREMENT [ ] OTHER

8. MULTIPLE YEAR CONTRACT [ ] YES [ ] NO

9. FY FUNDED

10. [ ] PRIME/ASSOCIATE [ ] SUBCONTRACTOR
(Name and address; include ZIP Code)

11. NAME OF CUSTOMER *(Subcontractor use only)*

12. REPORTING ELEMENT

13. QUANTITY

SECTION B

14. FUNCTIONAL CATEGORIES	ADJUSTMENTS TO PREVIOUS REPORTS a.	CONTRACTOR TO DATE b.	CONTRACTOR AT COMPL. c.	SUBCONTRACT OR OUTSIDE PRODUCTION AND SERVICES TO DATE d.	SUBCONTRACT OR OUTSIDE PRODUCTION AND SERVICES AT COMPL. e.	TOTAL TO DATE f.	TOTAL AT COMPL. g.
ENGINEERING							
(1) DIRECT LABOR HOURS						0	0
(2) DIRECT LABOR DOLLARS						0.00	0.00
(3) OVERHEAD						0.00	0.00
(4) MATERIAL						0.00	0.00
(5) OTHER DIRECT CHARGES *(Specify)*						0.00	0.00
(6) TOTAL ENGINEERING DOLLARS	0.00	0.00	0.00	0.00	0.00	0.00	0.00
TOOLING							
(7) DIRECT LABOR HOURS						0	0
(8) DIRECT LABOR DOLLARS						0.00	0.00
(9) OVERHEAD						0.00	0.00
(10) MATERIALS AND PURCHASED TOOLS						0.00	0.00
(11) OTHER DIRECT CHARGES *(Specify)*						0.00	0.00
(12) TOTAL TOOLING DOLLARS	0.00	0.00	0.00	0.00	0.00	0.00	0.00
QUALITY CONTROL							
(13) DIRECT LABOR HOURS						0	0
(14) DIRECT LABOR DOLLARS						0.00	0.00
(15) OVERHEAD						0.00	0.00
(16) OTHER DIRECT CHARGES *(Specify)*						0.00	0.00
(17) TOTAL QUALITY CONTROL DOLLARS	0.00	0.00	0.00	0.00	0.00	0.00	0.00
MANUFACTURING							
(18) DIRECT LABOR HOURS							
(19) DIRECT LABOR DOLLARS						0.00	0.00
(20) OVERHEAD						0.00	0.00
(21) MATERIALS AND PURCHASED PARTS						0.00	0.00
(22) OTHER DIRECT CHARGES *(Specify)*						0.00	0.00
(23) TOTAL MANUFACTURING DOLLARS	0.00	0.00	0.00	0.00	0.00	0.00	0.00
(24) PURCHASED EQUIPMENT						0.00	0.00
(25) MATERIAL OVERHEAD						0.00	0.00
(26) OTHER COSTS NOT SHOWN ELSEWHERE							
(27) TOTAL COST LESS G&A	0.00	0	0	0	0	0	0
(28) G&A						0.00	0.00
(29) TOTAL COST PLUS G&A	0.00	0.00	0.00	0.00	0.00	0.00	0.00
(30) FEE OR PROFIT						0.00	0.00
(31) TOTAL OF LINES (29) AND (30)	0.00	0.00	0.00	0.00	0.00	0.00	0.00

DD FORM 1921-1, AUG 2000 PREVIOUS EDITION IS OBSOLETE.

SECURITY CLASSIFICATION

SECURITY CLASSIFICATION

15. REMARKS			
16. NAME OF PERSON TO BE CONTACTED	17. TELEPHONE NO.	18. SIGNATURE	19. DATE

DD FORM 1921-1, (BACK), AUG 2000

SECURITY CLASSIFICATION

253.303-2051 DD Form 2051: Request for Assignment of a Commercial and Government Entity (CAGE) Code

REQUEST FOR ASSIGNMENT OF A COMMERCIAL AND GOVERNMENT ENTITY (CAGE) CODE

(See Instructions on back)

OMB No. 0704-0225
OMB approval expires Oct 31, 2007

The public reporting burden for this collection of information is estimated to average 7 minutes per response, including the time for reviewing instructions, searching existing data sources, gathering and maintaining the data needed, and completing and reviewing the collection of information. Send comments regarding this burden estimate or any other aspect of this collection of information, including suggestions for reducing the burden, to the Department of Defense, Executive Services Directorate (0704-0225). Respondents should be aware that notwithstanding any other provision of law, no person shall be subject to any penalty for failing to comply with a collection of information if it does not display a currently valid OMB control number.

PLEASE DO NOT RETURN YOUR FORM TO THE ABOVE ORGANIZATION. SEND COMPLETED FORM TO ADDRESS ON BACK.

SECTION A - TO BE COMPLETED BY INITIATOR

1. REQUESTING GOVERNMENT AGENCY/ACTIVITY

a. NAME	b. ADDRESS STREET		
2. TYPE CODE REQUESTED *(X one)* a. TYPE A b. TYPE F	**3. EXCEPTION CODES** a. CAO b. ADP		
	CITY	STATE	ZIP CODE

4. INITIATOR

a. TYPED NAME *(Last, First, Middle Initial)*	b. OFFICE SYMBOL	c. SIGNATURE	d. TELEPHONE NO. *(Include area code)*

SECTION B - TO BE COMPLETED BY FIRM TO BE CODED

5. FIRM

a. NAME *(Include Branch of, Division of, etc.)*	b. ADDRESS STREET		
c. CAGE CODE *(If previously assigned)*	CITY	STATE	ZIP CODE

6. IF FIRM PREVIOUSLY OPERATED UNDER OTHER NAME(S) OR OTHER ADDRESS(ES) SPECIFY THE PREVIOUS NAME(S) AND/OR ADDRESS(ES) *(Use separate sheet of paper, if necessary)*

7. PARENT COMPANY AND AFFILIATED FIRMS *(X one, and complete as applicable)*

- a. NONE
- b. CURRENTLY AFFILIATED WITH OTHER FIRMS *(List name(s) and address(es) of such firms on a separate sheet of paper)*
- c. PREVIOUSLY AFFILIATED WITH OTHER FIRMS *(List name(s) and address(es) of such firms on a separate sheet of paper)*

8. PRIMARY BUSINESS CATEGORY *(X one)*

- a. MANUFACTURER
- b. DEALER/DISTRIBUTOR
- c. CONSTRUCTION FIRM
- d. SERVICE COMPANY
- e. SALES OFFICE
- f. OTHER *(Specify)*

9. SMALL DISADVANTAGED BUSINESS STATUS *(X one)*

- a. APPROVED BY SMALL BUSINESS ADMINISTRATION (SBA) FOR SECTION 8(a) PROGRAM
- b. OTHER SMALL DISADVANTAGED BUSINESS CONCERN
- c. NOT SMALL DISADVANTAGED BUSINESS CONCERN

10. NUMBER OF EMPLOYEES

11. WOMEN-OWNED BUSINESS CONCERN *(X one)* a. YES b. NO

12. NORTH AMERICAN INDUSTRY CLASSIFICATION SYSTEM (NAICS) CODES

- a. PRIMARY
- b. OTHER *(Specify)*

13. REMARKS

14. FIRM OFFICIAL

a. TYPED NAME *(Last, First, Middle Initial)*	b. DATE SIGNED *(YYYYMMDD)*	c. SIGNATURE	d. TELEPHONE NO. *(Include area code)*

INSTRUCTIONS FOR COMPLETING DD FORM 2051

GENERAL NOTE FOR PERSONNEL PREPARING OR PROCESSING THIS REPORT

Coding must be as indicated in the instructions. Noncompliance with the coding instructions contained herein will make the organization that fails to comply responsible for required concessions in data base communication.

SPECIFIC INSTRUCTIONS

SECTION A - TO BE COMPLETED BY THE INITIATING GOVERNMENT ACTIVITY

Item 1. Self-explanatory.

Item 2. Mark the type of code being requested.

a. Type A - Manufacturers Code, which is used in the Federal Catalog System to identify a certain facility at a specific location that is a possible source for the manufacture and/or design control of items cataloged by the Federal Government; or,

b. Type F - Non-manufacturers Code, which is required for identifying an organization/function in MILSCAP. These are assigned to contractors that are non-manufacturers or that are manufacturers not qualifying for a Type A Code.

Item 3. If applicable, enter the exception DoD Activity Address Code for the Servicing Contract Administration Office (CAO) or ADP point.

Item 4. Self-explanatory.

SECTION B - TO BE COMPLETED BY THE FIRM TO WHICH THE CODE WILL BE ASSIGNED

Item 5.a. and b. Self-explanatory.

c. If a CAGE Code (Type A or Type F) was previously assigned, enter it in this block.

Item 6. Self-explanatory.

Item 7. If a block other than "None" is marked, identify the Parent company by a (P) beside the firm name.

Item 8. Self-explanatory.

SECTION B - *(Continued)*

Item 9. A small disadvantaged business concern is defined in Section 19.001 of the Federal Acquisition Regulation.

Item 10. Enter the number of employees. This number should include the employees of all affiliates.

Item 11. A women-owned business concern is defined in Section 52.204-5 of the Federal Acquisition Regulation.

Item 12. The NAICS Code is a Government Index that is used to identify business activity and that indicates the function (manufacturer, wholesaler, retailer, or service) and the line of business in which the company is engaged. If multiple NAICS Codes apply, indicate the primary first, then next important, etc.

Item 13. Self-explanatory.

Item 14. Self-explanatory.

NOTE: When any future changes are made to the coded facility (e.g. name change, location change, business sold, or operations discontinued), written notification stating the appropriate change should be sent to:

Commander
Defense Logistics Services Center
ATTN: DLSC-SBB
Federal Center
74 North Washington
Battle Creek, MI 49017-3084

253.303-2051-1 DD Form 2051-1: Request for Information/Verification of Commercial and Government Entity (CAGE) Code

REQUEST FOR INFORMATION/VERIFICATION OF COMMERCIAL AND GOVERNMENT ENTITY (CAGE) CODE

OMB No. 0704-0225
OMB approval expires Oct 31, 2007

The public reporting burden for this collection of information is estimated to average 7 minutes per response, including the time for reviewing instructions, searching existing data sources, gathering and maintaining the data needed, and completing and reviewing the collection of information. Send comments regarding this burden estimate or any other aspect of this collection of information, including suggestions for reducing the burden, to the Department of Defense, Executive Services Directorate (0704-0225). Respondents should be aware that notwithstanding any other provision of law, no person shall be subject to any penalty for failing to comply with a collection of information if it does not display a currently valid OMB control number.

PLEASE DO NOT RETURN YOUR COMPLETED FORM TO THE ABOVE ORGANIZATION. RETURN COMPLETED FORM TO: DEFENSE LOGISTICS SERVICE CENTER, ATTN: DLSC-SBB, FEDERAL CENTER, 74 NORTH WASHINGTON, BATTLE CREEK, MICHIGAN 49017-3084.

INSTRUCTIONS

The CAGE Code listed below is assigned to your company to ensure that your production items are properly cataloged and contracting services are administered correctly. This verification of contractor status is forwarded periodically for any necessary changes to your name, address, etc. Please complete the following to assist us:

1. Please review the above address and annotate any changes. If unchanged, X this box →

2. If any affiliated companies have been sold, indicate in Item 8, Remarks, to whom and to what extent *(include design control, patents, drawings, product line, etc.)* as this could affect the code assigned.

3. If any of the facilities have been merged to form another division, indicate here which CAGE Codes are involved.

4. If any operation has been discontinued and its items now manufactured elsewhere, include this information in Item 8, Remarks, as well as the name of the current manufacturer.

5. **SOURCE DEVELOPMENT PROFILE DATA.** In the following four categories, if there is a letter printed in the space next to the category title, verify the data against the tables immediately following each category. If a change is required, circle the appropriate letter in each category. If the space is blank, circle one letter in each category that best describes your firm.

a. SIZE OF BUSINESS	b. PRIMARY BUSINESS CATEGORY	c. SMALL DISADVANTAGED BUSINESS STATUS*	d. WOMEN-OWNED** BUSINESS
A - Under 500 employees	F - Construction Firm	H - Approved by Small Business Administration (SBA) for Section 8(a) Program	Y - Women-Owned Business Concern
B - 501 to 750 employees	G - Service Company	I - Other Small Disadvantaged Business Concern	N - Not Women-Owned Business Concern
C - 701 to 1000 employees	J - Manufacturer	X - Not Small Disadvantaged Business Concern	
D - 1001 to 1500 employees	K - Regular Dealer/Distributor		
E - Over 1500 employees	L - Sales Office		

*Small Disadvantaged Business Concern is defined in Section 19.001 of the Federal Acquisition Regulation.

**Women-Owned Business Concern is defined in Section 52.204-5 of the Federal Acquisition Regulation.

6. **NORTH AMERICAN INDUSTRY CLASSIFICATION SYSTEM (NAICS) CODE.** The NAICS Code is a government index used to identify business activity and indicates the function (manufacturer, wholesaler, retailer, or service) and the line of business in which the company is engaged. If your business has multiple NAICS Codes, indicate primary NAICS Code first, next important, etc.

NAICS CODES

7. **TELEPHONE NUMBER.** Enter the telephone number of the office designated to answer queries from the Federal Government with regard to contracting and/or procurement actions.

8. **REMARKS**

9. **CAGE CODE** *(Federal Supply Code Manufacturer/Non-Manufacturer)* | *(For DLSC Use Only)*

10. **PERSON AUTHORIZED TO SIGN**

a. TYPED OR PRINTED NAME *(Last, First, Middle Initial)*	b. SIGNATURE	c. DATE SIGNED *(YYYYMMDD)*

d. TITLE	e. TELEPHONE NUMBER *(Include Area Code)*

253.303-2139 DD Form 2139: Report of Contract Performance Outside the United States

[DAC 91-11, 9/26/96]

REPORT OF CONTRACT PERFORMANCE OUTSIDE THE UNITED STATES	*OMB No. 0704-0229* *OMB approval expires* *Jul 31, 2010*
The public reporting burden for this collection of information is estimated to average 20 minutes per response, including the time for reviewing instructions, searching existing data sources, gathering and maintaining the data needed, and completing and reviewing the collection of information. Send comments regarding this burden estimate or any other aspect of this collection of information, including suggestions for reducing the burden, to the Department of Defense, Executive Services Directorate, Information Management Division, 1155 Defense Pentagon, Washington, DC 20301-1155 (0704-0229). Respondents should be aware that notwithstanding any other provision of law, no person shall be subject to any penalty for failing to comply with a collection of information if it does not display a currently valid OMB control number. **PLEASE DO NOT RETURN YOUR COMPLETED FORM TO THE ABOVE ORGANIZATION.** **RETURN COMPLETED FORM TO: DEPUTY DIRECTOR OF DEFENSE PROCUREMENT (FOREIGN CONTRACTING), OUSD(A&T)DP(FC), WASHINGTON, DC 20301-3060**	
1.a. PRIME CONTRACT NUMBER *(Use solicitation number when report is submitted with offer)*	**1.b. PURCHASE ORDER NUMBER** *(If applicable)*
2. PROGRAM IDENTIFICATION *(e.g., F-16 aircraft, F-100 engine, AN/APN-59 radar, or type of services) (Please avoid use of acronyms.)*	
3. NAME AND DIVISION OF PRIME CONTRACTOR	
4. ADDRESS OF PRIME CONTRACTOR *(Street, City, State, and 9-digit ZIP Code)*	
5. NAME OF SUBCONTRACTOR OR FOREIGN DIVISION OF PRIME CONTRACTOR *(If subcontractor, identify whether first- or second-tier)* ☐ **FIRST-TIER SUBCONTRACTOR** ☐ **SECOND-TIER SUBCONTRACTOR**	
6. ADDRESS OF SUBCONTRACTOR OR FOREIGN DIVISION OF PRIME CONTRACTOR *(Street, City, State, 9-digit ZIP Code, and Country)*	
7. VALUE *(in dollars)* **OF EFFORT PERFORMED OUTSIDE THE UNITED STATES FOR THIS ACTION ONLY. DO NOT INCLUDE AMOUNTS PREVIOUSLY REPORTED.**	**8. COUNTRY OF ORIGIN** *(Enter city and country of actual producer of supplies or firm providing services)*
9. DESCRIPTION OF SUPPLIES OR SERVICES OBTAINED OUTSIDE THE UNITED STATES *(e.g., vertical stabilizer, F-15; Bomb Nav System, FB-111; or repair of F-16 wings) (Please avoid use of acronyms.)*	
10. NAME OF COMPANY SUBMITTING REPORT *(Prime contractor for reports on first-tier subcontracts or first-tier subcontractor for reports on second-tier subcontracts)*	
11. NAME OF SUBMITTER *(LAST, First, Middle Initial)*	**12. TELEPHONE NUMBER** *(Include Area Code)*
13. SIGNATURE	**14. DATE** *(YYYYMMDD)*

253.303-2579 DD Form 2579: Small Business Coordination Record

SMALL BUSINESS COORDINATION RECORD

REPORT CONTROL SYMBOL DD-AT&L(AR)1862

1. CONTROL NO. *(Optional)*
2. PURCHASE REQUEST NO./ REQUISITION NO.
3. TOTAL ESTIMATED VALUE *(Including options)*
4. SOLICITATION NO./CONTRACT MODIFICATION NO.

5. BUYER
a. NAME *(Last, First, Middle Initial)*
b. OFFICE SYMBOL
c. TELEPHONE *(Include Area Code)*

6. ITEM DESCRIPTION *(Including quantity)*
6a. FEDERAL SUPPLY CLASS/SERVICE (FSC/SVC) CODE

7. TYPE OF COORDINATION *(X one)*
INITIAL CONTACT
MODIFICATION
WITHDRAWAL

8. SMALL BUSINESS SIZE STANDARD
a. NORTH AMERICAN INDUSTRY CLASSIFICATION SYSTEM (NAICS) CODE
b. NO. OF EMPLOYEES
c. DOLLARS

9. RECOMMENDATION *(X as applicable)*

YES	NO	*(If all recommendations are "No," explain in Remarks.)*
		a. SECTION 8(a) *(X one)*
		(1) COMPETITIVE (2) SOLE SOURCE
		b. SMALL DISADVANTAGED BUSINESS (SDB) SET-ASIDE
		c. HISTORICALLY BLACK COLLEGES AND UNIVERSITIES/ MINORITY INSTITUTIONS (HBCU/MI) SET-ASIDE *(List percentage)* %
		d. SMALL BUSINESS (SB) SET-ASIDE *(List percentage)* %
		e. EMERGING SMALL BUSINESS SET-ASIDE
		f. EVALUATION PREFERENCE FOR SDBs
		g. HUBZONE SET-ASIDE
		h. HUBZONE SOLE SOURCE
		i. HUBZONE PRICE EVALUATION PREFERENCE

10. ACQUISITION HISTORY *(X one)*
a. FIRST TIME BUY
b. PREVIOUS ACQUISITION *(X all that apply)*
(1) SECTION 8(a)
(2) SDB SET-ASIDE
(3) HBCU/MI SET-ASIDE
(4) SB SET-ASIDE
(5) OTHER *(Specify)*
(6) TWO OR MORE RESPONSIVE SB OFFERS ON PRIOR ACQUISITION
(7) ONE OR MORE RESPONSIVE SDB OFFER(S) WITHIN 10% OF AWARD PRICE OF PRIOR ACQUISITION
(8) WOMAN OWNED SB
(9) SERVICE-DISABLED VETERAN SB

11. SB PROGRESS PAYMENTS *(X one)*
YES NO

12. SUBCONTRACTING PLAN REQUIRED *(X one)*
YES NO

13. SYNOPSIS REQUIRED *(X one) (If "No," cite FAR 5.202 exception)*
YES NO

14. REMARKS

15. REVIEWED BY SMALL BUSINESS ADMINISTRATION (SBA) REPRESENTATIVE
a. NAME *(Last, First, Middle Initial)*
b. SIGNATURE
c. DATE SIGNED *(YYYYMMDD)*

16. LOCAL USE

17. CONTRACTING OFFICER *(X one)*
CONCURS
REJECTS
a. RECOMMENDATIONS *(Document rejections on reverse side)*
b. NAME *(Last, First, Middle Initial)*
c. SIGNATURE
d. DATE SIGNED *(YYYYMMDD)*

18. SMALL BUSINESS SPECIALIST *(X one)*
CONCURS
APPEALS

NOTE: Any change in the acquisition plan this coordination record describes will require return for re-evaluation by the SB specialist.

a. NAME *(Last, First, Middle Initial)*
b. SIGNATURE
c. DATE SIGNED *(YYYYMMDD)*

DD FORM 2579, DEC 2000 PREVIOUS EDITION IS OBSOLETE.

253.303-2626 DD Form 2626: Performance Evaluation (Construction)

FOR OFFICIAL USE ONLY (WHEN COMPLETED)

PERFORMANCE EVALUATION (CONSTRUCTION)

1. CONTRACT NUMBER
2. CEC NUMBER

IMPORTANT: Be sure to complete Part III - Evaluation of Performance Elements on Page 2.

PART I - GENERAL CONTRACT DATA

3. TYPE OF EVALUATION (X one)
 INTERIM (List percentage ______%) FINAL AMENDED
4. TERMINATED FOR DEFAULT
5. CONTRACTOR (Name, Address, and ZIP Code)
6.a. PROCUREMENT METHOD (X one)
 SEALED BID NEGOTIATED
b. TYPE OF CONTRACT (X one)
 FIRM FIXED PRICE COST REIMBURSEMENT
 OTHER (Specify)
7. DESCRIPTION AND LOCATION OF WORK
8. TYPE AND PERCENT OF SUBCONTRACTING

9. FISCAL DATA	a. AMOUNT OF BASIC CONTRACT $	b. TOTAL AMOUNT OF MODIFICATIONS $	c. LIQUIDATED DAMAGES ASSESSED $	d. NET AMOUNT PAID CONTRACTOR $
10. SIGNIFICANT DATES	a. DATE OF AWARD	b. ORIGINAL CONTRACT COMPLETION DATE	c. REVISED CONTRACT COMPLETION DATE	d. DATE WORK ACCEPTED

PART II - PERFORMANCE EVALUATION OF CONTRACTOR

11. OVERALL RATING (X appropriate block)
 OUTSTANDING ABOVE AVERAGE SATISFACTORY MARGINAL UNSATISFACTORY (Explain in Item 20 on Page 2)

12. EVALUATED BY
a. ORGANIZATION (Name and Address (Include ZIP Code))
b. TELEPHONE NUMBER (Include Area Code)
c. NAME AND TITLE
d. SIGNATURE
e. DATE

13. EVALUATION REVIEWED BY
a. ORGANIZATION (Name and Address (Include ZIP Code))
b. TELEPHONE NUMBER (Include Area Code)
c. NAME AND TITLE
d. SIGNATURE
e. DATE

14. AGENCY USE (Distribution, etc.)

DD FORM 2626, JUN 94

EXCEPTION APPROVED BY

DAC 91 -10

253.303-2626 DD Form 2626: Performance Evaluation (Construction) (Back)

[DAC 91-10, 2/29/96]

FOR OFFICIAL USE ONLY (WHEN COMPLETED)

PART III - EVALUATION OF PERFORMANCE ELEMENTS

N/A = NOT APPLICABLE 0 = OUTSTANDING A = ABOVE AVERAGE S = SATISFACTORY M = MARGINAL U = UNSATISFACTORY

15. QUALITY CONTROL	N/A	O	A	S	M	U
a. QUALITY OF WORKMANSHIP						
b. ADEQUACY OF THE CQC PLAN						
c. IMPLEMENTATION OF THE CQC PLAN						
d. QUALITY OF QC DOCUMENTATION						
e. STORAGE OF MATERIALS						
f. ADEQUACY OF MATERIALS						
g. ADEQUACY OF SUBMITTALS						
h. ADEQUACY OF QC TESTING						
i. ADEQUACY OF AS-BUILTS						
l. USE OF SPECIFIED MATERIALS						
k. IDENTIFICATION/ CORRECTION OF DEFICIENT WORK IN A TIMELY MANNER						

16. EFFECTIVENESS OF MANAGEMENT	N/A	O	A	S	M	U
a. COOPERATION AND RESPONSIVENESS						
b. MANAGEMENT OF RESOURCES/ PERSONNEL						
c. COORDINATION AND CONTROL OF SUBCONTRACTOR(S)						
d. ADEQUACY OF SITE CLEAN-UP						
e. EFFECTIVENESS OF JOB-SITE SUPERVISION						
f. COMPLIANCE WITH LAWS AND REGULATIONS						
g. PROFESSIONAL CONDUCT						
h. REVIEW / RESOLUTION OF SUBCONTRACTOR'S ISSUES						
j. IMPLEMENTATION OF SUBCONTRACTING PLAN						

17. TIMELY PERFORMANCE	N/A	O	A	S	M	U
a. ADEQUACY OF INITIAL PROGRESS SCHEDULE						
b. ADHERENCE TO APPROVED SCHEDULE						
c. RESOLUTION OF DELAYS						
d. SUBMISSION OF REQUIRED DOCUMENTATION						
e. COMPLETION OF PUNCHLIST ITEMS						
f. SUBMISSION OF UPDATED AND REVISED PROGRESS SCHEDULES						
g. WARRANTY RESPONSE						

18. COMPLIANCE WITH LABOR STANDARDS	N/A	O	A	S	M	U
a. CORRECTION OF NOTED DEFICIENCIES						
b. PAYROLLS PROPERLY COMPLETED AND SUBMITTED						
c. COMPLIANCE WITH LABOR LAWS AND REGULATIONS WITH SPECIFIC ATTENTION TO THE DAVIS-BACON ACT AND EEO REQUIREMENTS						

19. COMPLIANCE WITH SAFETY STANDARDS	N/A	O	A	S	M	U
a. ADEQUACY OF SAFETY PLAN						
b. IMPLEMENTATION OF SAFETY PLAN						
c. CORRECTION OF NOTED DEFICIENCIES						

20. REMARKS (Explanation of unsatisfactory evaluation is required. Other comments are optional. Provide facts concerning specific events or actions to justify the evaluation. These data must be in sufficient detail to assist contracting officers in determining the contractor's responsibility. Continue on separate sheet(s), if needed.)

DD FORM 2626, JUN 94 (PAGE 2)

253.303-2631 DD Form 2631: Performance Evaluation (Architect-Engineer)

[DAC 91-10, 2/29/96]

PERFORMANCE EVALUATION (ARCHITECT-ENGINEER)

A-E CONTRACTOR I.D. NUMBER *(For ACASS use only)*

1. A-E CONTRACT NUMBER

2. CONSTRUCTION CONTRACT NUMBER

IMPORTANT: Be sure to complete back of form. If additional space is necessary for any item, use Remarks section on back.

3. TYPE OF EVALUATION
 - a. PHASE OF COMPLETION: INTERIM (_____%) / FINAL
 - b. COMPLETION *(X one)*: DESIGN / ENGINEERING SERVICES / CONSTRUCTION
 - c. X IF APPLICABLE: TERMINATION *(Explain in Remarks)*

4. PROJECT NUMBER

5. DELIVERY ORDER NO.(S) *(if applicable)*

6. NAME AND ADDRESS OF A-E CONTRACTOR

7a. PROJECT TITLE AND LOCATION

7b. DESCRIPTION OF PROJECT IF NOT EXPLAINED BY TITLE

8. NAME, ADDRESS AND PHONE NUMBER OF OFFICE RESPONSIBLE FOR:
 - a. SELECTION OF A-E CONTRACTOR
 - b. NEGOTIATION/AWARD OF A-E CONTRACT
 - c. ADMINISTRATION OF A-E CONTRACT
 - d. ADMINISTRATION OF CONSTRUCTION CONTRACT

9. A-E CONTRACT DATA *(Items 9d thru 9g are not applicable during construction unless there are modifications to the A-E contract.)*
 - a. TYPE OF WORK *(Design, study, etc.)*
 - b. TYPE OF CONTRACT: FIRM FIXED-PRICE / COST-REIMBURSEMENT / INDEFINITE DELIVERY/INDEFINITE QUANTITY (ID/IQ) / TASK ORDER UNDER ID/IQ / OTHER *(Specify)*
 - c. PROJECT COMPLEXITY: DIFFICULT / ROUTINE
 - d. CONTRACT OR TASK ORDER AMOUNT
   - (1) INITIAL FEE $
   - (2) CONTRACT OR TASK ORDER MODIFICATIONS: NO. / AMOUNT $
   - (3) TOTAL FEE $
 - e. CONTRACT OR TASK ORDER AWARD DATE
 - f. NEGOTIATED CONTRACT OR TASK ORDER COMPLETION DATE *(or number of days)* *(Including extensions)*
 - g. ACTUAL CONTRACT OR TASK ORDER COMPLETION DATE *(or number of days)*

10. CONSTRUCTION CONTRACT DATA *(Not applicable at completion of design or engineering services not involving construction.)*

a. CONSTRUCTION COSTS	(1) AUTHORIZED CONSTRUCTION COST $	(2) A-E ESTIMATE FOR BID ITEMS AWARDED $	(3) AWARD AMOUNT $
b. DATA AT TIME OF CONSTRUCTION COMPLETION *(Completion date __________)*		NUMBER	TOTAL COST
(1) CONSTRUCTION MODIFICATIONS			$
(2) CONSTRUCTION MODIFICATIONS ARISING FROM DESIGN DEFICIENCIES			$

11. A-E LIABILITY: NONE / UNDETERMINED / PENDING $ / SETTLEMENT $

12. OVERALL RATING: EXCEPTIONAL / VERY GOOD / SATISFACTORY / MARGINAL / UNSATISFACTORY

13. RECOMMENDED FOR FUTURE CONTRACTS? YES / CONDITIONALLY / NO *(Explain "No" or "Conditionally" in Remarks.)*

14a. NAME, TITLE AND OFFICE OF RATING OFFICIAL

TELEPHONE NUMBER:

b. SIGNATURE

c. DATE

15a. NAME, TITLE AND OFFICE OF REVIEWING OFFICIAL

TELEPHONE NUMBER:

b. SIGNATURE

c. DATE *(Official Report date)*

AGENCY USE: *(Distribution, etc.)*

DD FORM 2631, APR 1999 (EG) PREVIOUS EDITION IS OBSOLETE. Exception to SF 1421 Approved by GSA/IRMS 11-92. WHS/DIOR, Apr 99

16. QUALITY OF A-E SERVICES BY DISCIPLINE *(Completion mandatory for both DESIGN and CONSTRUCTION phases and Engineering Services)*

a. DISCIPLINES *(If applicable)*	DESIGN/SERVICES					CONSTRUCTION				
	EXCEP-TIONAL	VERY GOOD	SATIS-FACTORY	MARGINAL	UNSATIS-FACTORY	EXCEP-TIONAL	VERY GOOD	SATIS-FACTORY	MARGINAL	UNSATIS-FACTORY
Architectural										
Structural										
Civil										
Mechanical										
Electrical										
Fire Protection										
Surveying, Mapping, & Geospatial Information Svcs.										
Cost Estimating										
Value Engineering										
Environmental Engineering										
Geotechnical Engineering										
Master Planning										
Hydrology										
Chemical Engineering										
Geology										
Chemistry										
Risk Assessment										
Safety/Occupational Health										
Hydrographic Surveying										

17. DESIGN PHASE OR ENGINEERING SERVICES *(Quality of A-E Services Evaluation)*

ATTRIBUTES *(If applicable)*	EXCEP-TIONAL	VERY GOOD	SATIS-FACTORY	MARGINAL	UNSATIS-FACTORY
Thoroughness of Site Investigation/Field Analysis					
Quality Control Procedures and Execution					
Plans/Specs Accurate and Coordinated					
Plans Clear and Detailed Sufficiently					
Management and Adherence to Schedules					
Meeting Cost Limitations					
Suitability of Design or Study Results					
Solution Environmentally Suitable					
Cooperativeness and Responsiveness					
Quality of Briefing and Presentations					
Innovative Approaches/Technologies					
Implementation of Sm. Business Subcontracting Plan					

16b. DISCIPLINE, NAME AND ADDRESS OF KEY CONSULTANT(S) *(If applicable)*

18. HOW MANY 100% FINAL RESUBMITTALS WERE REQUIRED BECAUSE OF POOR A-E PERFORMANCE?

19. CONSTRUCTION PHASE *(Quality of A-E Services Evaluation)*

ATTRIBUTES *(If applicable)*	EXCEP-TIONAL	VERY GOOD	SATIS-FACTORY	MARGINAL	UNSATIS-FACTORY
Plans Clear and Detailed Sufficiently					
Drawings Reflect True Conditions					
Plans/Specs Accurate and Coordinated					
Design Constructibility					
Cooperativeness and Responsiveness					
Timeliness and Quality of Processing Submittals					
Product & Equipment Selections Readily Available					
Timeliness of Answers to Design Questions					
Field Consultation and Investigations					
Quality of Construction Support Services					

20. REMARKS *(Attach additional sheet(s) or documentation if necessary)*

DD FORM 2631 (BACK), APR 1999

Defense Federal Acquisition Regulation

APPENDICES

Table of Contents

Appendix **Page**

A—Armed Services Board of Contract Appeals 1119
B—[Removed] 1139
D—[Removed and Reserved] 1143
E—[Removed] 1147
F—Material Inspection and Receiving Report 1151
G—[Removed] 1177
H—Debarment and Suspension Procedures.......... 1181
I—Policy and Procedures for the DoD Pilot
Mentor-Protege Program 1185

See page 39 for an explanation of the numbering of the DFARS.

APPENDIX A—ARMED SERVICES BOARD OF CONTRACT APPEALS

Table of Contents

Charter . . . . Part 1
Rules . . . . Part 2

APPENDIX A—ARMED SERVICES BOARD OF CONTRACT APPEALS

APPENDIX A to Chapter 2—Armed Services Board of Contract Appeals

Armed Services Board of Contract Appeals

Approved 1 May 1962

Revised 1 May 1969

Revised 1 September 1973

Revised 1 July 1979

Revised 14 May 2007

Revised 9 April 2018

Revised 23 May 2019

Part 1—Charter

1. There is created the Armed Services Board of Contract Appeals which is hereby designated as the authorized representative of the Secretary of Defense, the Secretary of the Army, the Secretary of the Navy, and the Secretary of the Air Force, in hearing, considering and determining appeals by contractors from decisions of contracting officers or their authorized representatives or other authorities on disputed questions. These appeals may be taken (a) pursuant to the Contract Disputes Act of 1978 (41 U.S.C. Sections 7101–7109), (b) pursuant to the provisions of contracts requiring the decision by the Secretary of Defense or by a Secretary of a Military Department or their duly authorized representative, or (c) pursuant to the provisions of any directive whereby the Secretary of Defense or the Secretary of a Military Department or their authorized representative has granted a right of appeal not contained in the contract on any matter consistent with the contract appeals procedure. The Board may determine contract disputes for other departments and agencies by agreement as permitted by law. The Board shall operate under general policies established or approved by the Under Secretary of Defense responsible for acquisition and may perform other duties as directed not inconsistent with the Contract Disputes Act of 1978. The Board shall decide the matters before it independently.

2. Membership of the Board shall consist of attorneys at law who have been qualified in the manner prescribed by the Contract Disputes Act of 1978. Appointment of Board members shall be made by the Secretary of Defense. Members of the Board are hereby designated Administrative Judges. There shall be designated from among the appointed Judges of the Board a Chairman and two or more Vice Chairmen. Designation of the Chairman and Vice Chairmen shall be made by the Secretary of Defense, of nominees from Judges of the Board recommended by the Under Secretary of Defense responsible for acquisition, in coordination with the General Counsel of the Department of Defense, and the Assistant Secretaries of the Military Departments responsible for acquisition. When there is a vacancy, the incumbent is unavailable, or for appropriate Board administrative reasons, the Under Secretary of Defense responsible for acquisition or the Chairman may designate a Judge of the Board to serve as an Acting Chairman or Acting Vice Chairman.

3. The Chairman of the Board shall be responsible for establishing appropriate divisions of the Board to provide for the most effective and expeditious handling of appeals. The Chairman shall have authority to establish procedures for the issuance of Board decisions. The Chairman may refer an appeal of unusual difficulty, significant precedential importance, or serious dispute within the normal decision process for decision by a Senior Deciding Group established by the Chairman which shall have the authority to overturn prior Board precedent.

4. It shall be the duty and obligation of the Judges of the Armed Services Board of Contract Appeals to decide appeals on the record of the appeal to the best of their knowledge and ability in accordance with applicable contract provisions and in accordance with law and regulation pertinent thereto.

5. Any Judge of the Board or any examiner, designated by the Chairman, shall be authorized to hold hearings, examine witnesses, and receive evidence and argument. A Judge of the Board shall have authority to administer oaths and issue subpoenas as specified in the Contract Disputes Act of 1978. In cases of contumacy or refusal to

obey a subpoena, the Chairman may request orders of the court in the manner prescribed in the Contract Disputes Act of 1978.

6. The Board shall have all powers necessary and incident to the proper performance of its duties. The Board has the authority to issue methods of procedure and rules and regulations for its conduct and for the preparation and presentation of appeals and issuance of opinions.

7. The Chairman shall be responsible for the internal organization of the Board and for its administration. The Chairman shall provide within approved ceilings for the staffing of the Board with non-Judge personnel, including hearing examiners, as may be required for the performance of the functions of the Board. The Chairman shall appoint a Recorder of the Board. All personnel shall be responsible to and shall function under the direction, supervision and control of the Chairman.

8. The Board will be serviced by the Department of the Army for administrative support as required for its operations. Administrative support will include budgeting, funding, fiscal control, manpower control and utilization, personnel administration, security administration, supplies, and other administrative services. The Departments of the Army, Navy, Air Force and the Office of the Secretary of Defense will participate in financing the Board's operations on an equal basis and to the extent determined by the Under Secretary of Defense (Comptroller). The cost of processing appeals for departments and agencies other than those in the Department of Defense will be reimbursed.

9. Within 30 days following the close of a fiscal year, the Chairman shall forward a report of the Board's transactions and proceedings for the preceding fiscal year to the Under Secretary of Defense responsible for acquisition, the General Counsel of the Department of Defense, and the Assistant Secretaries of the Military Departments responsible for acquisition.

10. The Board shall have a seal bearing the following inscription: "Armed Services Board of Contract Appeals." This seal shall be affixed to all authentications of copies of records and to such other instruments as the Board may determine.

11. This revised charter is effective upon the date of the signature of the Secretary of Defense.

Approved: Patrick M. Shanahan (23 May 2019),

Acting Secretary of Defense.

[Final rule, 75 FR 14095, 3/24/2010, effective 3/24/2010; Final rule, 76 FR 76318, 12/7/2011, effective 12/7/2011; Final rule, 84 FR 4360, 2/15/2019, effective 2/15/2019; Final rule, 84 FR 48508, 9/13/2019, effective 9/13/2019]

PART 2—RULES

Approved 15 July 1963

Revised 1 May 1969

Revised 1 September 1973

Revised 30 June 1980

Revised 11 May 2011

Revised 21 July 2014

PREFACE

I. Jurisdiction for Considering Appeals

The Armed Services Board of Contract Appeals (referred to herein as the Board) has jurisdiction to decide any appeal from a final decision of a contracting officer, pursuant to the Contract Disputes Act, 41 U.S.C. 7101-7109, or its Charter, 48 CFR Chap. 2, App. A, Pt. 1, relative to a contract made by the Department of Defense, the Department of the Army, the Department of the Navy, the Department of the Air Force, the National Aeronautics and Space Administration or any other department or agency, as permitted by law.

II. Location and Organization of the Board

(a) The Board's address is Skyline Six, Room 703, 5109 Leesburg Pike, Falls Church, VA 22041-3208; telephone 703-681-8500 (general), 703-681-8502 (Recorder). The Board's facsimile number is 703-681-8535. The Board's Recorder's email address is *asbca.recorder@mail.mil*. The Board's Web site address is ***http://*** *www.asbca.mil*.

(b) The Board consists of a Chairman, two or more Vice Chairmen, and other Members, all of whom are attorneys at law duly licensed by a state, commonwealth, territory, or the District of Columbia. Board Members are designated Administrative Judges.

(c) There are a number of divisions of the Board, established by the Chairman in such manner as to provide for the most effective and expeditious handling of appeals. The Chairman and a Vice Chairman act as members of each division. Hearings may be held by an Administrative Judge or by a duly authorized examiner. Except for appeals processed under the expedited or accelerated procedure (see Rules 12.2(c) and 12.3(c)), the decision of a majority of a division constitutes the decision of the Board, unless the Chairman refers the appeal to the Board's Senior Deciding Group (consisting of the Chairman, Vice Chairmen, all division heads, and the Judge who drafted the decision), in which event a decision of a majority of that group constitutes the decision of the Board. Appeals referred to the Senior Deciding Group are those of unusual difficulty or significant precedential importance, or that have occasioned serious dispute within the normal division decision process.

(d) The Board will to the fullest extent practicable provide informal, expeditious, and inexpensive resolution of disputes.

Table of Contents

Rules of the Armed Services Board of Contract Appeals

Preliminary Procedures

Rule 1 Appeals

Rule 2 Filing Documents

Rule 3 Service Upon Other Parties

Rule 4 Preparation, Content, Organization, Forwarding, and Status of Appeal File

Rule 5 Time, Computation, and Extensions

Rule 6 Pleadings

Rule 7 Motions

Rule 8 Discovery

Rule 9 Pre-hearing or Pre-submission Conference

Rule 10 Hearings

Rule 11 Submission Without a Hearing

Rule 12 Optional Small Claims (Expedited) and Accelerated Procedures

Rule 13 Settling the Record in Appeals with a Hearing

Rule 14 Briefs

Rule 15 Representation

Rule 16 Sanctions

Rule 17 Dismissal or Default for Failure to Prosecute or Defend

Rule 18 Suspensions; Dismissal without Prejudice

Rule 19 Decisions

Rule 20 Motion for Reconsideration

Rule 21 Remand from Court

Rule 22 Subpoenas

Rule 23 Ex Parte Communications

Rule 24 Effective Date

Addendums

Addendum I: Equal Access to Justice Act Procedures

Addendum II: Alternative Methods of Dispute Resolution

[Final rule, 65 FR 39703, 6/27/2000, effective 6/27/2000; CFR correction, 76 FR 11969, 3/4/2011, effective 3/4/2011; Final rule, 76 FR 27274, 5/11/2011, effective 5/11/2011; Final rule, 79 FR 42214 , 7/21/2014, effective 7/21/2014]

RULES

Rule 1. Appeals

(a) *Taking an Appeal*—For appeals subject to the Contract Disputes Act, notice of an appeal shall be in writing and mailed or otherwise furnished to the Board within 90 days from the date of receipt of a contracting officer's decision. The appellant (contractor) should also furnish a copy of the notice of appeal to the contracting officer. For appeals not subject to the Contract Disputes Act, the contractor should refer to the Disputes clause in its contract for the time period in which it must file a notice of appeal.

(1) Where the contractor has submitted a claim of $100,000 or less to the contracting officer and has requested a written decision within 60 days from receipt of the request, and the contracting officer has not provided a decision within that period, or where such a contractor request has not been made and the contracting officer has not issued a decision within a reasonable time, the contractor may file a notice of appeal as provided in paragraph (a) of this Rule, citing the failure of the contracting officer to issue a decision.

(2) Where the contractor has submitted a properly certified claim over $100,000 to the contracting officer or has submitted a claim that involves no monetary amount, and the contracting officer, within 60 days of receipt of the claim, fails to issue a decision or fails to provide the contractor with a reasonable date by which a decision will be issued, and the contracting officer has failed to issue a decision within a reasonable time, the contractor may file a notice of appeal as provided in paragraph (a) of this Rule, citing the failure of the contracting officer to issue a decision.

(3) A reasonable time shall be determined by taking into account such factors as the size and complexity of the claim and the adequacy of the information provided by the contractor to support the claim.

(4) Where an appeal is before the Board pursuant to paragraph (a)(1) or (a)(2) of this Rule, the Board may, at its option, stay further proceedings pending issuance of a final decision by the contracting officer within such period of time as is determined by the Board.

(5) In lieu of filing a notice of appeal under paragraph (a)(1) or (a)(2) of this Rule, the contractor may petition the Board to direct the contracting officer to issue a decision in a specified period of time as determined by the Board.

(b) *Contents of Notice of Appeal*—A notice of appeal shall indicate that an appeal is being taken and should identify the contract by number, the department and/or agency involved in the dispute, the decision from which the appeal is taken, and the amount in dispute, if any. A copy of the contracting officer's final decision, if any, should be attached to the notice of appeal. The notice of appeal should be signed by the appellant or by the appellant's duly authorized representative or attorney. The complaint referred to in Rule 6 may be filed with the notice of appeal, or the appellant may designate the notice of appeal as a complaint, if it otherwise fulfills the requirements of a complaint.

(c) *Docketing of Appeal*—When a notice of appeal has been received by the Board, it will be docketed. The Board will provide a written notice of docketing to the appellant and to the Government.

Rule 2. Filing Documents

(a) Documents may be filed with the Board by the following methods:

(1) *Governmental Postal Service*—Documents may be filed via a governmental postal service. Filing occurs when the document, properly addressed and with sufficient postage, is transferred into the custody of the postal service. Contact the Recorder before submitting classified documents.

(2) *Courier*—Documents may be filed via courier. Filing occurs when the document is delivered to the Board. Contact the Recorder before submitting classified documents.

(3) *Electronic Mail*—Documents, except appeal files submitted pursuant to Rule 4, hearing exhibits, classified documents, and documents submitted in camera or under a protective order, may be filed via electronic mail (email). Email attachments should be in PDF format and the attachments may not exceed 10 megabytes total. The transmittal email should include the ASBCA docket number(s), if applicable, and the name of the appellant in the "Subject:" line. Filing occurs upon receipt by the Board's email server. When a document is successfully filed via email, the document should not also be submitted by any other means, unless so directed by the Board. Submit emails to: *asbca.recorder@mail.mil*.

(4) *Facsimile Transmission*—Documents, except appeal files submitted pursuant to Rule 4, hearing exhibits, classified documents, and documents submitted in camera or under a protective order, may be filed via facsimile (fax) machine. Due to equipment constraints, transmissions over 10 pages

should not be made absent Board permission. Filing occurs upon receipt by the Board. When a document is successfully filed via fax, the document should not also be submitted by any other means, unless so directed by the Board.

(b) *Copies to Opposing Party*—The party filing any document with the Board will send a copy to the opposing party unless the Board directs otherwise, noting on the document filed with the Board that a copy has been so furnished.

Rule 3. Service Upon Other Parties

Documents may be served personally or by mail, addressed to the party upon whom service is to be made, unless the parties have agreed to an alternate means of service. Subpoenas shall be served as provided in Rule 22.

Rule 4. Preparation, Content, Organization, Forwarding, and Status of Appeal File

(a) *Duties of the Government*—Within 30 days of notice that an appeal has been filed, the Government shall transmit to the Board and the appellant an appeal file consisting of the documents the Government considers relevant to the appeal, including:

(1) The decision from which the appeal is taken;

(2) The contract, including pertinent specifications, amendments, plans, and drawings;

(3) All correspondence between the parties relevant to the appeal, including any claim in response to which the decision was issued.

The Government's appeal file may be supplemented at such times as are fair and reasonable and as ordered by the Board.

(b) *Duties of the Appellant*—Within 30 days after receipt of a copy of the Government's appeal file, the appellant shall transmit to the Board and the Government any documents not contained therein that the appellant considers relevant to the appeal. Appellant's appeal file may be supplemented at such times as are fair and reasonable and as ordered by the Board.

(c) *Organization of Appeal File*—Documents in the appeal file may be originals or legible copies, and shall be arranged in chronological order where practicable, tabbed with sequential numbers, and indexed to identify the contents of the file. Any document without internal page numbers shall have page numbers added. All documents must be in English or include an English translation. Documents shall be submitted in 3-ring binders, with spines not wider than 3 inches wide, with labels identifying the name of the appeal, ASBCA number and tab numbers contained in each volume, on the front and spine of each volume. Each volume shall contain an index of the documents contained in the entire Rule 4 submission.

(d) *Status of Documents in Appeal File*—Documents contained in the appeal file are considered, without further action by the parties, as part of the record upon which the Board will render its decision. However, a party may object, for reasons stated, to the admissibility of a particular document reasonably in advance of hearing or, if there is no hearing, of settling the record, or in any case as ordered by the Board. If such objection is made, the Board will constructively remove the document from the appeal file and permit the party offering the document to move its admission as evidence in accordance with Rules 10, 11, and 13.

Rule 5. Time, Computation, and Extensions

(a) Where practicable, actions should be taken in less time than the time allowed. Where appropriate and justified, however, extensions of time will be granted. All requests for extensions of time should be in writing and indicate that the other party was contacted to seek its concurrence.

(b) In computing any period of time, the day of the event from which the designated period of time begins to run will not be included, but the last day of the period will be included unless it is a Saturday, Sunday, or a Federal holiday, in which event the period will run to the next business day.

Rule 6. Pleadings

(a) *Appellant*—Within 30 days after receipt of notice of docketing of the appeal, the appellant shall file with the Board a complaint setting forth simple, concise, and direct statements of each of its claims. The complaint shall also set forth the basis, with appropriate reference to contract provisions, of each claim and the dollar amount claimed, if any. This pleading shall fulfill the generally recognized requirements of a complaint, although no particular form is required. Should the complaint not be timely received, the appellant's claim and notice of appeal may be deemed to set forth its complaint if, in the opinion of the Board, the issues before the Board are sufficiently defined, and the parties will be notified.

(b) *Government*—Within 30 days from receipt of the complaint, or the aforesaid notice from the Board, the Government shall file with the Board an answer thereto. The answer shall admit or deny the allegations of the complaint and shall set forth simple, concise, and direct statements of the Government's defenses to each claim asserted by the appellant, including any affirmative defenses. Should the answer not be timely received, the Board may enter a general denial on behalf of the Government, and the parties will be notified.

(c) *Foreign Law*—A party who intends to raise an issue concerning the law of a foreign country shall give notice in its pleadings or other reasonable written notice. The Board, in determining foreign law, may consider any relevant material or source, including testimony, whether or not submitted by a party or admissible under Rules 10, 11, or 13. The determination of foreign law shall be treated as a ruling on a question of law.

(d) *Further Pleadings*—The Board upon its own initiative or upon motion may order a party to make a more definite statement of the complaint or answer, or to reply to an answer. The Board may permit either party to amend its pleading upon conditions fair to both parties. When issues within the proper scope of the appeal, but not raised by the pleadings, are tried by express or implied consent of the parties, or by permission of the Board, they shall be treated in all respects as if they had been raised therein. In such instances, motions to amend the pleadings to conform to the proof may be entered, but are not required. If evidence is objected to at a hearing on the ground that it is not within the issues raised by the pleadings, it may be admitted within the proper scope of the appeal, provided however, that the objecting party may be granted an opportunity to meet such evidence.

Rule 7. Motions

(a) *Motions Generally*—The Board may entertain and rule upon motions and may defer ruling as appropriate. The Board will rule on motions so as to secure, to the fullest extent practicable, the informal, expeditious, and inexpensive resolution of appeals. All motions should be filed as separate documents with an appropriate heading describing the motion. Oral argument on motions is subject to the discretion of the Board.

(b) *Jurisdictional Motions*—Any motion addressed to the jurisdiction of the Board should be promptly filed. An evidentiary hearing to address disputed jurisdictional facts will be afforded on application of either party or by order of the Board. The Board may defer its decision on the motion pending hearing on the merits. The Board may at any time and on its own initiative raise the issue of its jurisdiction, and shall do so by an appropriate order, affording the parties an opportunity to be heard thereon.

(c) *Summary Judgment Motions*—

(1) To facilitate disposition of such a motion, the parties should adhere to the following procedures. Where the parties agree that disposition by summary judgment or partial summary judgment is appropriate, they may file a stipulation of all material facts necessary for the Board to rule on the motion. Otherwise, the moving party should file with its motion a "Statement of Undisputed Material Facts," setting forth the claimed undisputed material facts in separate, numbered paragraphs. The non-moving party should file a "Statement of Genuine Issues of Material Fact," responding to each numbered paragraph proposed, demonstrating, where appropriate, the existence of material facts in dispute and if appropriate propose additional facts. The moving party and the non-moving party should submit a memorandum of law supporting or opposing summary judgment.

(2) In deciding motions for summary judgment, the Board looks to Rule 56 of the Federal Rules of Civil Procedure for gui-

dance. The parties should explicitly state and support by specific evidence all facts and legal arguments necessary to sustain a party's position. Each party should cite to the record and attach any additional evidence upon which it relies (e.g., affidavits, declarations, excerpts from depositions, answers to interrogatories, admissions). The Board may accept a fact properly proposed and supported by one party as undisputed, unless the opposing party properly responds and establishes that it is in dispute.

(d) *Response to Motions*—A non-moving party has 30 days from receipt of a motion to file its response, unless a different period is ordered by the Board. A moving party has 30 days from receipt of a non-moving party's response to file a reply, unless a different period is ordered by the Board.

Rule 8. Discovery

(a) *General Policy and Protective Orders*—The parties are encouraged to engage in voluntary discovery procedures. Within 45 days after the pleadings have been filed, the parties must confer concerning each party's discovery needs, including the scheduling of discovery and the production of electronically stored information. Absent stipulation or a Board order, no discovery may be served prior to this conference. Any motion pertaining to a discovery dispute shall include a statement that the movant has in good faith attempted to resolve the discovery dispute without involvement of the Board. In connection with any discovery procedure, the Board may issue orders to protect a party or person from annoyance, embarrassment, or undue burden or expense. Those orders may include limitations on the scope, method, time, and place for discovery, and provisions for governing the disclosure of information or documents. Any discovery under this Rule shall be subject to the provisions of Rule 16 with respect to sanctions.

(b) *Depositions—When Permitted*—Subject to paragraph (a) of this Rule, a party may take, or the Board may upon motion order the taking of, testimony of any person by deposition upon oral examination or written interrogatories before any officer authorized to administer oaths at the place of examination, for use as evidence or for purpose of discovery. The Board expects the parties to make persons under their control available for deposition. The motion for an order shall specify whether the purpose of the deposition is discovery or for use as evidence.

(1) *Depositions—Orders*—The time, place, and manner of taking depositions shall be as mutually agreed by the parties, or failing such agreement, governed by order of the Board.

(2) *Depositions—Use as Evidence*—No testimony taken by deposition shall be considered as part of the evidence in the hearing of an appeal until such testimony is offered and received in evidence at such hearing. It will not ordinarily be received in evidence if the deponent can testify at the hearing. The deposition may be used to contradict or impeach the testimony of the deponent given at a hearing. In cases submitted on the record, the Board may receive depositions to supplement the record.

(3) *Depositions—Expenses*—Each party shall bear its own expenses associated with the taking of any deposition, absent an agreement by the parties or a Board order to the contrary.

(4) *Depositions—Subpoenas*—Where appropriate, a party may request the issuance of a subpoena under the provisions of Rule 22.

(c) *Interrogatories, Requests for Admissions, Requests for Production*—Subject to paragraph (a) of this Rule, a party may serve, or the Board may upon motion order:

(1) Written interrogatories to be answered separately in writing, signed under oath and answered or objected to within 45 days after service;

(2) A request for the admission of specified facts and/or of the authenticity of any documents, to be answered or objected to within 45 days after service, the factual statements and/or the authenticity of the documents to be deemed admitted upon failure of a party to respond to the request; and

(3) A request for the production, inspection, and copying of any documents, electronic or otherwise, or objects, not privileged, which reasonably may lead to the

discovery of admissible evidence, to be answered or objected to within 45 days after service. The Board may allow a shorter or longer time.

Rule 9. Pre-hearing or Pre-submission Conference

The Board may, upon its own initiative, or upon the request of either party, arrange a conference or order the parties to appear before an Administrative Judge or examiner for a conference to address any issue related to the prosecution of the appeal.

Rule 10. Hearings

(a) *Where and When Held*—Hearings will be held at such times and places determined by the Board to best serve the interests of the parties and the Board.

(b) *Unexcused Absence*—The unexcused absence of a party at the time and place set for hearing will not be occasion for delay. In the event of such absence, the hearing will proceed and the evidentiary record will consist solely of the evidence of record at the conclusion of the hearing, except as ordered otherwise by the Board.

(c) *Nature of Hearings*—Hearings shall be as informal as may be reasonable and appropriate under the circumstances. The parties may offer such evidence as they deem appropriate and as would be admissible under the Federal Rules of Evidence or in the sound discretion of the presiding Administrative Judge or examiner. The Federal Rules of Evidence are not binding on the Board but may guide the Board's rulings. The parties may stipulate the testimony that would be given by a witness if the witness were present. The Board may require evidence in addition to that offered by the parties.

(d) *Examination of Witnesses*—Witnesses will be examined orally under oath or affirmation, unless the presiding Administrative Judge or examiner shall otherwise order. If the testimony of a witness is not given under oath or affirmation, the Board may advise the witness that his or her testimony may be subject to any provision of law imposing penalties for knowingly making false representations in connection with claims.

(e) *Interpreters*—In appropriate cases, the Board may order that an interpreter be used. An interpreter must be qualified and must be placed under oath or affirmation to give a complete and true translation.

(f) *Transcripts*—Testimony and argument at hearings will be reported verbatim, unless the Board otherwise orders. The Board will contract for a reporter. No other recordings of the proceedings will be made.

Rule 11. Submission Without a Hearing

(a) Either party may elect to waive a hearing and to submit its case upon the record. Submission of a case without hearing does not relieve the parties from the necessity of proving the facts supporting their allegations or defenses. Affidavits, declarations, depositions, admissions, answers to interrogatories, and stipulations may be employed in addition to the Rule 4 file if moved and accepted into evidence. Such submissions may be supplemented by briefs. The Board may designate, with notice to the parties, any document to be made part of the record.

(b) As appropriate, the Board may also rely on pleadings, prehearing conference memoranda, orders, briefs, stipulations and other documents contained in the Board's file.

(c) Except as the Board may otherwise order, no evidence will be received after notification by the Board that the record is closed.

(d) The weight to be given to any evidence will rest within the discretion of the Board. The Board may require either party, with appropriate notice to the other party, to submit additional evidence on any matter relevant to the appeal.

(e) The record will at all reasonable times be available for inspection by the parties at the offices of the Board.

Rule 12. Optional Small Claims (Expedited) and Accelerated Procedures

12.1 Elections To Utilize Small Claims (Expedited) and Accelerated Procedures

(a) In appeals where the amount in dispute is $50,000 or less, or in the case of a small business concern (as defined in the Small Business Act and regulations under that Act), $150,000 or less, the appellant may elect to have the appeal processed under a

Small Claims (Expedited) procedure requiring decision of the appeal, whenever possible, within 120 days after the Board receives written notice of the appellant's election to utilize this procedure. The details of this procedure appear in section 12.2 of this Rule. An appellant may elect the Accelerated procedure rather than the Small Claims (Expedited) procedure for any appeal where the amount in dispute is $50,000 or less.

(b) In appeals where the amount in dispute is $100,000 or less, the appellant may elect to have the appeal processed under an Accelerated procedure requiring decision of the appeal, whenever possible, within 180 days after the Board receives written notice of the appellant's election to utilize this procedure. The details of this procedure appear in section 12.3 of this Rule.

(c) The appellant's election of either the Small Claims (Expedited) procedure or the Accelerated procedure shall be made by written notice within 60 days after receipt of notice of docketing, unless such period is extended by the Board for good cause. The election, once made, may not be changed or withdrawn except with permission of the Board and for good cause.

(d) The 45-day conference required by Rule 8(a) does not apply to Rule 12 appeals.

12.2 Small Claims (Expedited) Procedure

(a) In appeals proceeding under the Small Claims (Expedited) procedure, the following time periods shall apply:

(1) Within 10 days from the Government's receipt of the appellant's notice of election of the Small Claims (Expedited) procedure, the Government shall send the Board a copy of the contract, the contracting officer's final decision, and the appellant's claim letter or letters, if any. Any other documents required under Rule 4 shall be submitted in accordance with times specified in that Rule unless the Board otherwise directs.

(2) Within 15 days after the Board has acknowledged receipt of the appellant's notice of election, the assigned Administrative Judge should take the following actions, if feasible, in a pre-hearing conference:

(i) Identify and simplify the issues;

(ii) Establish a simplified procedure, including discovery, appropriate to the particular appeal involved;

(iii) Determine whether either party elects a hearing, and if so, fix a time and place therefor; and

(iv) Establish an expedited schedule for the timely resolution of the appeal.

(b) Pleadings, discovery, and other prehearing activity will be allowed only as consistent with the requirement to conduct a hearing, or if no hearing is elected, to close the record on a date that will allow the timely issuance of the decision. The Board may shorten time periods prescribed or allowed under these Rules as necessary to enable the Board to decide the appeal within the 120-day period.

(c) Written decisions by the Board in appeals processed under the Small Claims (Expedited) procedure will be short and will contain only summary findings of fact and conclusions. Decisions will be rendered for the Board by a single Administrative Judge. If there has been a hearing, the Administrative Judge presiding at the hearing may at the conclusion of the hearing and after entertaining such oral argument as deemed appropriate, render on the record oral summary findings of fact, conclusions, and a decision of the appeal. Whenever such an oral decision is rendered, the Board will subsequently furnish the parties an authenticated copy of such oral decision for record and payment purposes and to establish the starting date for the period for filing a motion for reconsideration under Rule 20.

(d) A decision under Rule 12.2 shall have no value as precedent, and in the absence of fraud, shall be final and conclusive and may not be appealed or set aside.

12.3 The Accelerated Procedure

(a) In appeals proceeding under the Accelerated procedure, the parties are encouraged, to the extent possible consistent with adequate presentation of their factual and legal positions, to waive pleadings, discovery, and briefs. The Board may shorten time periods prescribed or allowed under these Rules as necessary to enable the

Board to decide the appeal within the 180-day period.

(b) Within 30 days after the Board has acknowledged receipt of the appellant's notice of election, the assigned Administrative Judge should take the following actions, if feasible, in a pre-hearing conference:

(1) Identify and simplify the issues;

(2) Establish a simplified procedure, including discovery, appropriate to the particular appeal involved;

(3) Determine whether either party elects a hearing, and if so, fix a time and place therefor; and

(4) Establish an accelerated schedule for the timely resolution of the appeal.

(c) Written decisions by the Board in appeals processed under the Accelerated procedure will normally be short and contain only summary findings of fact and conclusions. Decisions will be rendered for the Board by a single Administrative Judge with the concurrence of a Vice Chairman, or by a majority among these two and the Chairman in case of disagreement.

12.4 Motions for Reconsideration in Rule 12 Appeals

Motions for reconsideration of appeals decided under either the Small Claims (Expedited) procedure or the Accelerated procedure need not be decided within the original 120-day or 180-day limit, but all such motions will be processed and decided promptly so as to be consistent with the intent of this Rule.

Rule 13. Settling the Record in Appeals With a Hearing

(a) The record upon which the Board's decision will be rendered consists of the documents admitted under Rule 4, the documents admitted into evidence as hearing exhibits, together with the hearing transcript. The Board may designate with notice to the parties, any document to be made part of the record.

(b) As appropriate, the Board may also rely on pleadings, pre-hearing conference memoranda, orders, briefs, stipulations, and other documents contained in the Board's file.

(c) Except as the Board may otherwise order, no evidence will be received after completion of an oral hearing.

(d) The weight to be given to any evidence will rest within the discretion of the Board. The Board may require either party, with appropriate notice to the other party, to submit additional evidence on any matter relevant to the appeal.

(e) The record will at all reasonable times be available for inspection by the parties at the offices of the Board.

Rule 14. Briefs

(a) *Pre-Hearing Briefs*—The Board may require the parties to submit pre-hearing briefs. If the Board does not require pre-hearing briefs, either party may, upon appropriate and sufficient notice to the other party, furnish a pre-hearing brief to the Board.

(b) *Post-Hearing Briefs*—Post-hearing briefs may be submitted upon such terms as may be directed by the presiding Administrative Judge or examiner at the conclusion of the hearing.

Rule 15. Representation

(a) An individual appellant may represent his or her interests before the Board; a corporation may be represented by one of its officers; and a partnership or joint venture by one of its members; or any of these by an attorney at law duly licensed in any state, commonwealth, territory, the District of Columbia, or in a foreign country. Anyone representing an appellant shall file a written notice of appearance with the Board.

(b) The Government shall be represented by counsel. Counsel for the Government shall file a written notice of appearance with the Board.

Rule 16. Sanctions

If any party fails to obey an order issued by the Board, the Board may impose such sanctions as it considers necessary to the just and expeditious conduct of the appeal.

Rule 17. Dismissal or Default for Failure to Prosecute or Defend

Whenever the record discloses the failure of either party to file documents required by these Rules, respond to notices or correspondence from the Board, comply with orders of the Board, or otherwise indicates an intention not to continue the prosecution or defense of an appeal, the Board may, in the case of a default by the appellant, issue an order to show cause why the appeal should not be dismissed with prejudice for failure to prosecute. In the case of a default by the Government, the Board may issue an order to show cause why the Board should not act thereon pursuant to Rule 16. If good cause is not shown, the Board may take appropriate action.

Rule 18. Suspensions; Dismissal Without Prejudice

(a) The Board may suspend the proceedings by agreement of the parties for settlement discussions, or for good cause shown.

(b) In certain cases, appeals docketed before the Board are required to be placed in a suspense status and the Board is unable to proceed with disposition thereof for reasons not within the control of the Board. Where the suspension has continued, or may continue, for an inordinate length of time, the Board may dismiss such appeals from its docket for a period of time without prejudice to their restoration. Unless either party or the Board moves to reinstate the appeal within the time period set forth in the dismissal order, or if no time period is set forth, within one year from the date of the dismissal order, the dismissal shall be deemed to be with prejudice.

Rule 19. Decisions

(a) Decisions of the Board will be made in writing and authenticated copies of the decision will be sent simultaneously to both parties. All orders and decisions, except those as may be required by law to be held confidential, will be available to the public. Decisions of the Board will be made solely upon the record.

(b) Any monetary award shall be promptly paid.

(c) In awards that may be paid from the Judgment Fund, 31 U.S.C. 1304, the Recorder will forward the required forms to each party with the decision. If the parties do not contemplate an appeal or motion for reconsideration, they will execute the forms indicating that no judicial review will be sought. The Government agency will forward the required forms with a copy of the decision to the Department of the Treasury for certification of payment.

(d) When the parties settle an appeal in favor of the appellant, they may file with the Board a stipulation setting forth the amount of the settlement due to the appellant. By joint motion, the parties may request that the Board issue a decision in the nature of a consent judgment, awarding the stipulated amount to the appellant. These decisions will be processed in accordance with paragraph (c) of this Rule.

(e) After a decision has become final the Board may, upon request of a party and after notice to the other party, grant the withdrawal of original exhibits, or any part thereof. The Board may require the substitution of true copies of exhibits or any part thereof as a condition of granting permission for such withdrawal.

Rule 20. Motion for Reconsideration

A motion for reconsideration may be filed by either party. It shall set forth specifically the grounds relied upon to grant the motion. The motion must be filed within 30 days from the date of the receipt of a copy of the decision of the Board by the party filing the motion. An opposing party must file any cross-motion for reconsideration within 30 days from its receipt of the motion for reconsideration. Extensions in the period to file a motion will not be granted. Extensions to file a memorandum in support of a timely-filed motion may be granted.

Rule 21. Remand from Court

Whenever any Court remands an appeal to the Board for further proceedings, each of the parties shall, within 30 days of receipt of such remand, submit a report to the Board recommending procedures to be followed so as to comply with the Court's remand. The Board will consider the reports and enter an order governing the remanded appeal.

Rule 22. Subpoenas

(a) *Voluntary Cooperation*—Each party is expected:

(1) To cooperate and make available witnesses and evidence under its control as requested by the other party without issuance of a subpoena, and

(2) To secure voluntary attendance of desired third-party witnesses and production of desired third-party books, records, documents, or tangible things whenever possible.

(b) *General*—Upon written request of either party, or on his or her own initiative, an Administrative Judge may issue a subpoena requiring:

(1) *Testimony at a deposition*—The deposing of a witness in the city or county where the witness resides or is employed or transacts business in person, or at another location convenient for the witness that is specifically determined by the Board;

(2) *Testimony at a hearing*—The attendance of a witness for the purpose of taking testimony at a hearing; and

(3) *Production of books and records*—The production by the witness at the deposition or hearing of books and records (including electronically stored information and other tangible things) designated in the subpoena.

(c) *Request for Subpoena*—

(1) A request for subpoena shall normally be filed at least:

(i) 15 days before a scheduled deposition where the attendance of a witness at a deposition is sought; or

(ii) 30 days before a scheduled hearing where the attendance of a witness at a hearing is sought.

(2) The Board may honor a request for subpoena not made within the time limitations set forth in paragraph (c)(1) of this Rule.

(3) A request for a subpoena shall state the reasonable scope and general relevance to the case of the testimony and of any books and records sought. The Board may require resubmission of a request that does not provide this information.

(d) *Requests to Quash or Modify*—Upon written request by the person subpoenaed or by a party, made within 10 days after service but in any event not later than the time specified in the subpoena for compliance, the Board may quash or modify the subpoena if it is unreasonable or oppressive or for other good cause shown, or require the person in whose behalf the subpoena was issued to advance the reasonable cost of producing subpoenaed books and papers. Where circumstances require, the Board may act upon such a request at any time after a copy of the request has been served upon the opposing party.

(e) *Form of Subpoena*—

(1) Every subpoena shall state the name of the Board and the caption of the appeal, and shall command each person to whom it is directed to attend and give testimony, and if appropriate, to produce specified books and records at a time and place therein specified. In issuing a subpoena to a requesting party, the Administrative Judge will sign the subpoena, enter the name of the witness and may otherwise leave it blank. The party to whom the subpoena is issued shall complete the subpoena before service.

(2) Where the witness is located in a foreign country, a letter rogatory may be issued and served under the circumstances and in the manner provided in 28 U.S.C. 1781.

(f) *Service*—

(1) The party requesting issuance of a subpoena shall arrange for service.

(2) A subpoena requiring the attendance of a witness at a deposition or hearing may be served in any state, commonwealth, territory, or the District of Columbia. A subpoena may be served by a United States marshal or deputy marshal, or by any other person who is not a party and not less than 18 years of age. Service of a subpoena upon a person named therein shall be made by personally delivering a copy to that person and tendering the fees for one day's attendance and the mileage provided by 28 U.S.C. 1821 or other applicable law. However, where the subpoena is issued on behalf of the Government, payment need not be tendered in advance of attendance.

(3) The party at whose instance a subpoena is issued shall be responsible for the payment of fees and mileage of the witness and of the officer who serves the subpoena. The failure to make payment of such

charges on demand may be deemed by the Board as a sufficient ground for striking such evidence as the Board deems appropriate.

(g) *Contumacy or Refusal to Obey a Subpoena*—In case of contumacy or refusal to obey a subpoena by a person who resides, is found, or transacts business within the jurisdiction of a United States District Court, the Board may apply to the Court through the Attorney General of the United States for an order requiring the person to appear before the Board to give testimony or produce evidence or both. Any failure of any such person to obey the order of the Court may be punished by the Court as a contempt thereof.

Rule 23. Post-Hearing Briefs

No member of the Board or of the Board's staff shall entertain, nor shall any person directly or indirectly involved in an appeal, submit to the Board or the Board's staff, ex parte, any evidence, explanation, analysis, or advice, whether written or oral, regarding any matter at issue in an appeal. This Rule does not apply to consultation among Board members or its staff or to ex parte communications concerning the Board's administrative functions or procedures.

Rule 24. Effective Date

These rules and addendums are applicable to appeals processed under the Contract Disputes Act (CDA), 41 U.S.C. 7101-7109, and other appeals to the extent consistent with law. They apply to all appeals filed on or after the date of final publication in the **Federal Register**, and to those appeals filed before that date, unless that application is inequitable or unfair.

ADDENDUM I

EQUAL ACCESS TO JUSTICE ACT PROCEDURES

(a) *Definitions*—

For the purpose of these procedures:

(1) "Equal Access to Justice Act," or "EAJA," means 5 U.S.C. 504, as amended;

(2) "Board" means the Armed Services Board of Contract Appeals; and

(3) "Contract Disputes Act" means the Contract Disputes Act, 41 U.S.C. 7101-7109 (CDA).

(b) *Scope of procedures*—These procedures are intended to assist the parties in the processing of EAJA applications for award of fees and other expenses incurred in connection with appeals pursuant to the CDA.

(c) *Eligibility of applicants*—

(1) To be eligible for an EAJA award, an applicant must be a party appellant that has prevailed in a CDA appeal before the Board and must be one of the following:

(i) An individual with a net worth which did not exceed $2,000,000 at the time the appeal was filed; or

(ii) Any owner of an unincorporated business, or any partnership, corporation, association, unit of local Government, or organization, the net worth of which does not exceed $7,000,000 and which does not have more than 500 employees; except:

(A) Certain charitable organizations or cooperative associations; and

(B) For the purposes of 5 U.S.C. 504(a)(4), a small entity as defined in 5 U.S.C. 601, need not comply with any net worth requirement (see 5 U.S.C. 504(b)(1)(B)).

(2) For the purpose of eligibility, the net worth and number of employees of an applicant shall be determined as of the date the underlying CDA appeal was filed with the Board.

(d) *Standards of awards*—A prevailing eligible applicant shall receive an award of fees and expenses incurred in connection with a CDA appeal, unless the position of the Government over which the applicant prevailed was substantially justified, or if special circumstances make the award unjust.

(e) *Allowable fees and other expenses*—

(1) Fees and other expenses must be reasonable. Awards will be based upon the prevailing market rates, subject to paragraph (e)(2) of this section, for the kind and quality of services furnished by attorneys, agents, and expert witnesses.

(2) No award for the fee of an attorney or agent may exceed $125 per hour. No expert witness shall be compensated at a rate in excess of the highest rate of compensation for expert witnesses paid by the agency involved.

(3) The reasonable cost of any study, analysis, engineering report, test, or project, prepared on behalf of a party may be awarded, to the extent that the study or other matter was necessary in connection with the appeal and the charge for the service does not exceed the prevailing rate for similar services.

(f) *Time for filing of applications*—An application may be filed after an appellant has prevailed in the CDA appeal within 30 days after the Board's disposition of the appeal has become final.

(g) *Application contents*—

(1) An EAJA application shall comply with each of the following:

(i) Show that the applicant is a prevailing party;

(ii) Show that the applicant is eligible to receive an award;

(iii) Allege that the position of the government was not substantially justified; and

(iv) Show the amount of fees and other expenses sought, including an itemized statement thereof.

(2) An original and one copy of the application and exhibits should be filed with the Board. The applicant will forward one copy to the Government.

(3) When a compliant application has been timely filed, the Board, in order to obtain more detailed information, may require supplementation of the application.

(h) *Net worth exhibit*—Each applicant for which a determination of net worth is required under the EAJA should provide with its application a detailed net worth exhibit showing the net worth of the applicant when the CDA appeal was filed. The exhibit may be in any form convenient to the applicant that provides full disclosure of assets, liabilities, and net worth.

(i) *Fees and other expenses exhibit*—The application should be accompanied by a detailed fees and other expenses exhibit fully documenting the fees and other expenses, including the cost of any study, analysis, engineering report, test, or project, for which an award is sought. The date and a description of all services rendered or costs incurred should be indicated. A separate itemized statement should be submitted for each professional firm or individual whose services are covered by the application showing the hours spent in connection with the CDA appeal by each individual, a description of the particular services performed by specific date, the rate at which each fee has been computed, any expenses for which reimbursement is sought, the total amount claimed, and the total amount paid or payable by the applicant or by any other person or entity for the services provided. The Board may require the applicant to provide vouchers, receipts, or other substantiation for any expenses sought.

(j) *Answer to application*—

(1) Within 30 days after receipt by the Government of an application, the Government may file an answer. Unless the Government requests an extension of time for filing or files a statement of intent to negotiate under paragraph (2) below, failure to file an answer within the 30-day period may be treated by the Board at its discretion as a general denial to the application on behalf of the Government.

(2) If the Government and the applicant believe that the matters raised in the application can be resolved by mutual agreement, they may jointly file a statement of intent to negotiate a settlement. Filing of this statement will extend the time for filing an answer for an additional 30 days. Further extensions may be requested by the parties.

(3) The answer will explain in detail any objections to the award requested and identify the facts relied upon in support of the Government's position.

(4) An original and one copy of the answer should be filed with the Board. The Government will forward one copy to the applicant.

(k) *Reply*—Within 15 days after receipt of an answer, the applicant may file a reply. An original and one copy of the reply will be filed with the Board. The applicant will forward one copy to the Government.

(l) *Award proceedings*—

(1) The Board may enter an order prescribing the procedure to be followed or take such other action as may be deemed appropriate under the EAJA. Further proceedings will be held only when necessary for full and fair resolution of the issues arising from the application.

(2) A request that the Board order further proceedings under this paragraph will describe the disputed issues, explain why the additional proceedings are deemed necessary to resolve the issues and specifically identify any information sought and its relationship to the disputed issues.

(m) *Evidence*—

(1) *Decisions on the merits*—When a CDA appeal is decided on the merits, other than by a consent judgment, the record relating to whether the Government's position under the EAJA was substantially justified will be limited to the record in the CDA appeal. Evidence relevant to other issues in the award proceeding may be submitted.

(2) *Other dispositions*—When a CDA appeal is settled, or decided by a consent judgment, either party in proceedings under the EAJA may, for good cause shown, supplement the record established in the CDA appeal with affidavits and other supporting evidence relating to whether the position of the agency was substantially justified or other issues in the award proceeding.

(n) *Decision*—Decisions under the EAJA will be rendered by the Administrative Judge or a majority of the judges who would have participated in a motion for reconsideration of the underlying CDA appeal. The decision of the Board will include written findings and conclusions and the basis therefor. The Board's decision on an application for fees and other expenses under the EAJA will be the final administrative decision regarding the EAJA application.

(o) *Motions for reconsideration*—Either party may file a motion for reconsideration. Motions for reconsideration must be filed within 30 days of receipt of the Board's EAJA decision. Extensions in the period to file a motion will not be granted. Extensions to file a memorandum in support of a timely filed motion may be granted.

(p) *Payment of Awards*—The Board's EAJA awards will be paid directly by the contracting agency over which the applicant prevailed in the underlying CDA appeal.

ADDENDUM II

Alternative Methods of Dispute Resolution

1. The Contract Disputes Act (CDA), 41 U.S.C. 7105(g)(1), states that boards of contract appeals "shall . . . to the fullest extent practicable provide informal, expeditious, and inexpensive resolution of disputes." Resolution of a dispute at the earliest stage feasible, by the fastest and least expensive method possible, benefits both parties. To that end, the parties are encouraged to consider Alternative Dispute Resolution (ADR) procedures for pre-claim and pre-final decision matters, as well as appeals pending before the Board. The Board may also conduct ADRs for any Federal agency. However, if the matter is not pending before the Board under its CDA jurisdiction, any settlement may not be paid out of the Judgment Fund.

2. The ADR methods described in this Addendum are intended to suggest techniques that have worked in the past. Any appropriate method that brings the parties together in settlement, or partial settlement, of their disputes is a good method. The ADR methods listed are not intended to preclude the parties' use of other ADR techniques that do not require the Board's participation, such as settlement negotiations, fact-finding conferences or procedures, mediation, or minitrials not involving use of the Board's personnel. Any method, or combination of methods, including one that will result in a binding decision, may be selected by the parties without regard to the dollar amount in dispute.

3. The parties must jointly request ADR procedures at the Board. The request must be approved by the Board. The Board may also schedule a conference to explore the desirability and selection of an ADR method and related procedures. If an ADR involving the Board's participation is requested and

approved by the Board, a Neutral will be appointed. If an Administrative Judge has already been assigned to an appeal, the same judge will normally be assigned to be the Neutral in an ADR. If an Administrative Judge has not yet been assigned to the appeal, or if the subject of the ADR is a matter pending before the contracting officer prior to any appeal, the Board will appoint an Administrative Judge to be the Neutral. In such instances, as well as situations in which the parties prefer that an assigned Administrative Judge not be appointed to serve as the Neutral, the parties may submit a list of at least three preferred Administrative Judges and the Board will endeavor to accommodate their preferences.

4. To facilitate full, frank and open discussion and presentations, any Neutral who has participated in a non-binding ADR procedure that has failed to resolve the underlying dispute will be recused from further participation in the matter unless the parties expressly agree otherwise in writing and the Board concurs. Further, the recused Neutral will not discuss the merits of the dispute or substantive matters involved in the ADR proceedings with other Board personnel.

5. Written material prepared specifically for use in an ADR proceeding, oral presentations made at an ADR proceeding, and all discussions in connection with such proceedings between the parties and the Neutral are confidential and, unless otherwise specifically agreed by the parties, inadmissible as evidence in any pending or future Board proceeding involving the parties or matter in dispute. However, evidence otherwise admissible before the Board is not rendered inadmissible because of its use in the ADR proceeding.

6. The ADR method and the procedures and requirements implementing the ADR method will be prescribed by the written agreement of the parties and approved by the Board. ADR methods can be used successfully at any stage of the litigation.

7. The following are examples of ADR methods commonly used at the Board:

(a) *Nonbinding*—

Mediations: A Neutral is an Administrative Judge who will not normally hear or have any formal or informal decision-making authority in the matter and who is appointed for the purpose of facilitating settlement. In many circumstances, settlement can be fostered by a frank, in-depth discussion of the strengths and weaknesses of each party's position with the Neutral. The agenda for meetings with the Neutral will be flexible to accommodate the requirements of the case. To further the settlement effort, the Neutral may meet with the parties either jointly or individually. A Neutral's recommendations are not binding on the parties. When this method is selected, the ADR agreement must contain a provision in which the parties and counsel agree not to subpoena the Neutral in any legal action or administrative proceeding of any kind to produce any notes or documents related to the ADR proceeding or to testify concerning any such notes or documents or concerning his/her thoughts or impressions.

(b) *Binding*—

Summary Proceeding With Binding Decision: A summary proceeding with binding decision is a procedure whereby the resolution of the appeal is expedited and the parties try their appeal informally before an Administrative Judge. A binding "bench" decision may be issued upon conclusion of the proceeding, or a binding summary written decision will be issued by the judge no later than ten days following the later of conclusion of the proceeding or receipt of a transcript. The parties must agree in the ADR agreement that all decisions, rulings, and orders by the Board under this method shall be final, conclusive, not appealable, and may not be set aside, except for fraud. All such decisions, rulings, and orders will have no precedential value. Pre-hearing, hearing, and post-hearing procedures and rules applicable to appeals generally will be modified or eliminated to expedite resolution of the appeal.

(c) *Other Agreed Methods*—

The parties and the Board may agree upon other informal methods, binding or nonbinding that are structured and tailored to suit the requirements of the individual case.

8. The above-listed ADR procedures are intended to shorten and simplify the Board's more formalized procedures. Generally, if the parties resolve their dispute by agreement, they benefit in terms of cost and time savings and maintenance or restoration of amicable relations. The Board will not view the parties' participation in ADR proceedings as a sign of weakness. Any method adopted for dispute resolution depends upon both parties having a firm, good faith commitment to resolve their differences. Absent such intention, the best structured dispute resolution procedure is unlikely to be successful.

[Final rule, 76 FR 27274, 5/11/2011, effective 5/11/2011; Final rule, 79 FR 42214, 7/21/2014, effective 7/21/2014]

APPENDIX B—COORDINATED ACQUISITION ASSIGNMENTS

Part 1—6—[Removed]

APPENDIX B—COORDINATED ACQUISITION ASSIGNMENTS

PARTS 1-6 [REMOVED]

[Removed, final rule, 64 FR 8726, 2/23/99, effective 2/23/99; Final rule, 71 FR 39004, 7/11/2006, effective 7/11/2006]

APPENDIX D—COMPONENT BREAKOUT

[Removed and Reserved]

APPENDIX D—COMPONENT BREAKOUT

D-100 [Removed and reserved]

[Final rule, 71 FR 14101, 3/21/2006, effective 3/21/2006]

D-101 [Removed and reserved]

[Final rule, 71 FR 14101, 3/21/2006, effective 3/21/2006]

D-102 [Removed and reserved]

[Final rule, 71 FR 14101, 3/21/2006, effective 3/21/2006]

D-103 [Removed and reserved]

[Final rule, 71 FR 14101, 3/21/2006, effective 3/21/2006]

D-104 [Removed and reserved]

[Final rule, 71 FR 14101, 3/21/2006, effective 3/21/2006]

D-105 [Removed and reserved]

[DAC 91-3, 57 FR 42634, 9/15/92, effective 8/31/92; 58 FR 37868, 7/14/93; Final rule, 71 FR 14101, 3/21/2006, effective 3/21/2006]

APPENDIX E—DOD SPARE PARTS BREAKOUT PROGRAM

Parts 1-5—[Removed]

APPENDIX E—DOD SPARE PARTS BREAKOUT PROGRAM

PARTS 1-5 [REMOVED]

[Removed, final rule, 71 FR 27642, 5/12/2006, effective 5/12/2006]

APPENDIX F—MATERIAL INSPECTION AND RECEIVING REPORT

Table of Contents

Part 1—Introduction

General F-101
Applicability F-102
Use F-103
Application F-104

Part 2—Contract Quality Assurance on Shipments Between Contractors

Procedures F-201

Part 3—Preparation of the Wide Area Workflow (WAWF) Receiving Report (RR) and WAWF Energy RR

Preparation instructions F-301
Mode/method of shipment codes F-302
Consolidated shipments F-303
Correction instructions F-304
Invoice instructions F-305
Packing list instructions F-306
Receiving instructions F-307

Part 4—Preparation of the DD Form 250 and DD Form 250C

Preparation instructions F-401
Mode/method of shipment codes F-402
Consolidated shipments F-403
Multiple consignee instructions F-404
Correction instructions F-405
Invoice instructions F-406
Packing list instructions F-407
Receiving instructions F-408

Part 5—Distribution of Wide Area Workflow Receiving Report (WAWF RR), DD Form 250 and DD Form 250C

Distribution of WAWF RR F-501
Distribution of DD Form 250 and DD Form 250C F-502

Part 6—Preparation of the DD Form 250-1 (Loading Report)

Instructions F-601

Part 7—Preparation of the DD Form 250-1 (Discharge Report)

Instructions F-701

Part 8—Distribution of the DD Form 250-1

Distribution. F-801
Corrected DD Form 250-1 . . . . F-802

APPENDIX F—MATERIAL INSPECTION AND RECEIVING REPORT

PART 1—INTRODUCTION

F-101 General.

(a) This appendix contains procedures and instructions for the use, preparation, and distribution of the Wide Area WorkFlow (WAWF) Receiving Report (RR), WAWF Reparable Receiving Report (WAWF RRR), the WAWF Energy RR, and commercial shipping/packing lists used to document Government contract quality assurance. The WAWF RR is the electronic equivalent of the DD Form 250, Material Inspection and Receiving Report (MIRR). The WAWF Energy RR is the electronic equivalent of the DD Form 250 for overland shipments and DD Form 250-1, Tanker/Barge Material Inspection and Receiving Report, for waterborne shipments. The WAWF RRR is the electronic equivalent of the DD Form 250 for repair, maintenance, or overhaul of Government-furnished property.

(b) The use of the DD Form 250 series documents is on an exception basis (see DFARS 232.7002(a)) because use of the WAWF RR is now required by most DoD contracts. WAWF provides for electronic preparation and documentation of acceptance of supplies and services, and electronic invoicing. In addition WAWF allows the printing of a RR that can be used as a packing list or when a signed copy is required.

[Final rule, 76 FR 58122, 9/20/2011, effective 9/20/2011; Final rule, 80 FR 29983, 5/26/2015, effective 5/26/2015; Final rule, 81 FR 59515, 8/30/2016, effective 9/29/2016]

F-102 Applicability.

(a) DFARS 252.232-7003, Electronic Submission of Payment Requests and Receiving Reports, requires payment requests and receiving reports using WAWF in nearly all cases.

(b) When DoD provides quality assurance or acceptance services for non-DoD activities, prepare a MIRR using the instructions in this appendix, unless otherwise specified in the contract.

[Final rule, 76 FR 58122, 9/20/2011, effective 9/20/2011; Final rule, 83 FR 66062, 12/21/2018, effective 12/21/2018]

F-103 Use.

(a) The WAWF RR, WAWF RRR, and the DD Form 250 are multipurpose reports used—

(1) To provide evidence of Government contract quality assurance at origin or destination;

(2) To provide evidence of acceptance at origin, destination, or other;

(3) For packing lists;

(4) For receiving;

(5) For shipping;

(6) As a contractor invoice (the WAWF RR, WAWF RRR, or DD Form 250 alone cannot be used as an invoice, however the option exists to create an invoice from the Receiving Report or a Combo (Invoice and Receiving Report) both of which minimize data entry); and

(7) As commercial invoice support.

(b) Do not use the WAWF RR, WAWF RRR, or the DD Form 250 for shipments—

(1) By subcontractors, unless the subcontractor is shipping directly to the Government; or

(2) Of contract inventory. The WAWF Property Transfer document should be used for this type of shipment. Training for the preparation of this document type is available at *https://wawftraining.eb.mil*, under the Property Transfer and Receipt section.

(c) The contractor prepares the WAWF RR, WAWF RRR, or the DD Form 250, except for entries that an authorized Government representative is required to complete. When using a paper DD Form 250, the contractor shall furnish sufficient copies of the completed form, as directed by the Government representative.

(d) Use the WAWF Energy RR or the DD Form 250-1:

(1) For bulk movements of petroleum products by tanker or barge to cover—

(i) Origin or destination acceptance of cargo; or

(ii) Shipment or receipt of Government owned products.

(2) To send quality data to the point of acceptance in the case of origin inspection on FOB destination deliveries or preinspection at product source. Annotate the forms with the words "INSPECTED FOR QUALITY ONLY."

(e) In addition to the above uses, the WAWF RR and WAWF RRR provide additional functionality, not provided by the paper DD Form 250 that complies with the following requirements:

(1) Item Unique Identification (IUID), when the clause at DFARS 252.211-7003, Item Unique Identification and Valuation is used in the contract, reporting of IUID data is required. WAWF captures the IUID data and forwards the data to the IUID registry after acceptance. WAWF shall be used to report Unique Item Identifiers (UIIs) at the line item level, unless an exception to WAWF applies, and can also be used to report UIIs embedded at the line item level.

(2) Radio Frequency Identification (RFID), when the clause at DFARS 252.211-7006, Radio Frequency Identification, is used in the contract, WAWF will capture the RFID information and forward the data to the receiving location. Using WAWF is the only way a contractor can comply with the clause to furnish RFID data via an Advance Shipping Notice (ASN). The RFID information may be added at time of submission, or via the WAWF Pack Later functionality after acceptance.

(3) Reporting of Government-furnished property, when the clause at DFARS 252.211-7007, Reporting of Government-Furnished Property, is used in the contract, use of the WAWF RRR will capture the shipment of Government-furnished property items after acceptance of repair services and forward the data to the IUID registry. WAWF is the only way a contractor can report the transfer of Government-furnished property items in the IUID registry.

[Final rule, 71 FR 75890, 12/19/2006, effective 12/19/2006; Final rule, 76 FR 58122, 9/20/2011, effective 9/20/2011; Final rule, 78 FR 76067, 12/16/2013, effective 12/16/2013; Final rule, 80 FR 29983, 5/26/2015, effective 5/26/2015; Final rule, 81 FR 59515, 8/30/2016, effective 9/29/2016]

F-104 Application.

(a) *WAWF RR and DD Form 250.*

(1) Use the WAWF RR or DD Form 250 for delivery of contract line, subline, exhibit line, or exhibit subline items. Do not use the WAWF RR or DD Form 250 for those exhibit line or exhibit subline items on a DD Form 1423, Contract Data Requirements List, which indicate no DD Form 250 is required.

(2) If the shipped to, marked for, shipped from, mode of shipment, contract quality assurance and acceptance data are the same for more than one shipment made on the same day under the same contract, contractors may prepare one WAWF RR or DD Form 250 to cover all such shipments.

(3) If the volume of the shipment precludes the use of a single car, truck, or other vehicle, prepare a separate WAWF RR or DD Form 250 for the contents of each vehicle.

(4) When a shipment is consigned to an Air Force activity and the shipment includes items of more than one Federal supply class (FSC) or material management code (MMC), prepare a separate WAWF RR or DD Form 250 for items of each of the FSCs or MMCs in the shipment. However, the cognizant Government representative may authorize a single WAWF RR or DD Form 250, listing each of the FSCs or MMCs included in the shipment on a separate continuation sheet. The MMC appears as a suffix to the national stock number applicable to the item.

(5) *Consolidation of Petroleum Shipments on a Single WAWF RR or DD Form 250.*

(i) *Contiguous United States.* Contractors may consolidate multiple car or truck load shipments of petroleum made on the same day, to the same destination, against the same contract line item, on one WAWF RR or DD Form 250. To permit verification of motor deliveries, assign each load a load number which can be identified to the shipment number in Block 2 of the DD Form 250. Include a shipping document (commercial or Government) with each individual load showing as a minimum—

(A) The shipper;

(B) Shipping point;

(C) Consignee;

(D) Contract and line item number;

(E) Product identification;

(F) Gross gallons (bulk only);

(G) Loading temperature (bulk only);

(H) American Petroleum Institute gravity (bulk only);

(I) Identification of carrier's equipment;

(J) Serial number of all seals applied; and

(K) Signature of supplier's representative.

When acceptance is at destination, the receiving activity retains the shipping document(s) to verify the entries on the consignee copy of the DD Form 250 forwarded by the contractor (reference F-401, Table 1) before signing Block 21b.

(ii) *Overseas.* The same criteria as for contiguous United States applies, except the consolidation period may be extended, if acceptable to the receiving activity, shipping activity, Government finance office, and the authorized Government representative having cognizance at the contractor's facility. In addition, the contractor may include more than one contract line item in each WAWF RR or DD Form 250 if the shipped to, marked for, shipped from, mode of shipment, contract quality assurance, and acceptance data are the same for all line items.

(6) *Consolidation of Coal Shipments on a Single WAWF RR or DD Form 250.* Contractors may consolidate multiple railcar or truck shipments of coal made on the same day, to the same destination, against the same contract line items, on one WAWF RR or DD Form 250. To permit verification of truck deliveries, assign each load a load number which can be identified to the shipment number in Block 2 of the DD Form 250 and the analytical test report. Include a commercial shipping document with each individual truck load showing as a minimum—

(i) The shipper;

(ii) The name or names;

(iii) Location and shipping point of the mine or mines from which the coal originates;

(iv) The contract number;

(v) The exact size of the coal shipped; and

(vi) A certified weighmaster's certification of weight for the truckload.

Include a waybill with each rail shipment showing the identical information. To permit verification of rail deliveries, identify each railcar number comprising the shipment to the shipment number in Block 2 of the DD Form 250 and the analytical test report. When acceptance is at destination, the receiving activity must retain the shipping document(s) to verify the entries on the consignee copy of the DD Form 250.

(b) *WAWF RRR or DD Form 250.* Use as in paragraph (a) of this section for delivery of services for repair, overhaul, or maintenance.

(c) *WAWF Energy RR or the DD Form 250-1.*

(1) Use a separate form for each tanker or barge cargo loaded.

(2) The contractor may report more than one barge in the same tow on a single form if on the same contract and consigned to the same destination.

(3) When liftings involve more than one contract, prepare separate forms to cover the portion of cargo loaded on each contract.

(4) Prepare a separate form for each product or grade of product loaded.

(5) Use a separate document for each tanker or barge cargo and each grade of product discharged.

(6) For discharge, the contractor may report more than one barge in the same tow on a single form if from the same loading source.

[Final rule, 65 FR 63802, 10/25/2000, effective 10/25/2000; Final rule, 70 FR 35543, 6/21/2005, effective 6/21/2005; Final rule, 76 FR 58122, 9/20/2011, effective 9/20/2011; Final rule, 80 FR 29983, 5/26/2015, effective 5/26/2015; Final rule,

81 FR 59515, 8/30/2016, effective 9/29/2016]

PART 2—CONTRACT QUALITY ASSURANCE ON SHIPMENTS BETWEEN CONTRACTORS

F-201 Procedures.

Follow the procedures at PGI F-201 for evidence of required Government contract quality assurance at a subcontractor's facility.

[Final rule, 71 FR 75890, 12/19/2006, effective 12/19/2006; Final rule, 76 FR 58122, 9/20/2011, effective 9/20/2011]

PART 3—PREPARATION OF THE WIDE AREA WORKFLOW (WAWF) RECEIVING REPORT (RR), WAWF REPARABLE RECEIVING REPORT (WAWF RRR), AND WAWF ENERGY RR

F-301 Preparation instructions.

(a) *General.*

(1) Preparation instructions and training for the WAWF RR are available at *https://wawftraining.eb.mil.* The instructions on preparing a WAWF RR are part of the Vendor Training section.

(2) Prime contractors can direct subcontractors to prepare and submit documents in WAWF by giving their subcontractors access to WAWF via the creation of a Commercial and Government Entity (CAGE) extension to the prime CAGE.

(3) If the contract is in Electronic Data Access (EDA) (DoD's contract repository), then the WAWF system will automatically populate all available and applicable contract data.

(i) When source acceptance is required, WAWF will populate the "Inspect By" with the "Admin by" Department of Defense Activity Address Code (DoDAAC). The vendor shall change the DoDAAC if Government Source Inspection (GSI) is performed at other than the "Admin By."

(ii) Any fields that have been pre-filled may be changed.

(iii) WAWF will also verify that CAGE codes are valid and active in the System for Award Management (SAM), and that DoDAACs and Military Assistance Program Address Codes (MAPACs) are valid in Defense Automatic Addressing System (DAAS).

(4) WAWF will populate the address information for CAGE codes, DODAACs, and MAPACs from SAM and DAAS. These sites are the DoD definitive sources for address information. Any fields that have been prefilled may be changed or additional information added.

(5) Do not include classified information in WAWF.

(b) *Completion instructions.*

(1) Contract no/delivery order no.

(i) For stand-alone contracts, enter the 13-position alpha-numeric basic Procurement Instrument Identifier (PIID) of the contract. For task and delivery orders numbered in accordance with FAR 4.1603 and DFARS 204.1603, enter the 13-character order number. The contract or agreement number under which the order was placed may be omitted from the WAWF RR. Alternatively, the contractor may choose to enter the contract number on the WAWF RR in addition to the 13-character order number. If the order has only a four-position alphanumeric call or order serial number, enter both the 13-position basic contract PIID and the four-position order number.

(ii) Except as indicated in paragraph (b)(1)(iii) of this appendix, do not enter supplementary numbers used in conjunction with basic PIIDs to identify—

(A) Modifications of contracts and agreements;

(B) Modifications to calls or orders; or

(C) Document numbers representing contracts written between contractors.

(iii) When shipping instructions are furnished and shipment is made before receipt of the confirming contract modification (SF 30, Amendment of Solicitation/Modification of Contract), enter a comment in the Misc. Info Tab to this effect. This will appear in the Comments section of the printed WAWF RR.

(iv) For DoD delivery orders on non-DoD contracts, enter the non-DoD contract number in the contract number field and enter the DoD contract number and, when applicable, delivery order number in the delivery order field.

(2) Shipment No.

(i) The shipment number format requires first three data positions to be alpha, fourth position alpha-numeric and last three positions numeric, *e.g.,* DFAR001 or DAR0001. Any document used as a packing list must include the shipment number information.

(A) The prime contractor shall control and assign the shipment number prefix. The shipment number shall consist of three alphabetic characters for each "Shipped From" address. The shipment number prefix shall be different for each "Shipped From" address and shall remain constant throughout the life of the contract. The prime contractor may assign separate prefixes when shipments are made from different locations within a facility identified by one "Shipped From" address.

(B) Number the first shipment 0001 for shipments made under the contract or contract and order number from each "Shipped From" address, or shipping location within the "Shipped From" address. Consecutively number all subsequent shipments with the identical shipment number prefix. While shipments should be created sequentially they can be released and accepted out of sequence.

(1) Use alpha-numeric serial numbers when more than 9,999 numbers are required. Serially assign alpha-numeric numbers with the alpha in the first position (the letters I and O shall not be used) followed by the three-position numeric serial number. Use the following alpha-numeric sequence: A000 through A999 (10,000 through 10,999) B000 through B999 (11,000 through 11,999) Z000 through Z999 (34,000 through 34,999)

(2) When this series is completely used, the shipment number prefix will have to be changed when the series is completely used. WAWF will not allow duplicate shipment numbers to be created against a contract or contract and delivery order.

(ii) Reassign the shipment number of the initial shipment where a "Replacement Shipment" is involved (see paragraph (b)(16)(iv)(F) of this appendix).

(iii) The prime contractor shall control deliveries and on the final shipment of the contract shall end the shipment number with a "Z." Where the final shipment is from other than the prime contractor's plant, the prime contractor may elect either to—

(A) Direct the subcontractor making the final shipment to end that shipment number with a "Z"; or

(B) Upon determination that all subcontractors have completed their shipments, to correct the DD Form 250 (see F-304) covering the final shipment made from the prime contractor's plant by addition of a "Z" to that shipment number.

(iv) Contractors follow the procedures in F-305 to use commercial invoices.

(3) Date shipped. Enter the date the shipment is released to the carrier or the date the services are completed. If the shipment will be released after the date of contract quality assurance and/or acceptance, enter the estimated date of release. When the date is estimated, enter an "E" or select an "E" from the drop down menu in the "Estimated" block after the date. Do not delay submission of the WAWF RR for lack of entry of the actual shipping date. Correction of the WAWF RR is not required to show the actual shipping date (see F-303). Once the document is submitted the shipment date cannot be changed.

(4) B/L TCN. When applicable, enter—

(i) The commercial or Government bill of lading number after "B/L;" WAWF provides the capability to separately and correctly identify the Government Bill of Lading (GBL) from a Commercial Bill of Lading (CBL). An authorized user will select whether the entered bill of lading number is either a GBL number or a CBL number.

(ii) The transportation control number must be a 17 alpha/numeric digit min/max field, and WAWF provides the capability to enter two secondary transportation tracking numbers.

(5) Line haul mode. Select the Line Haul Mode of Shipment code from a drop down menu in WAWF.

(6) Inspection and acceptance point. Enter an "S" for Origin or "D" for Destination. In addition to "S" and "D," WAWF allows acceptance at Other (O). For purposes of conforming to contract, "O" is equivalent to "D". In WAWF, destination acceptance is performed by the "Ship to" DODAAC organization and "Other" permits the acceptance of destination documents at a location other than the "Ship to." The goods or services will be shipped to one location and the paperwork will be routed to another location for the actual acceptance.

(7) Prime contractor/code. Enter the prime CAGE code to which the contract was awarded.

(8) Administered by/code. Enter the DoDAAC code of the contract administration office cited in the contract.

(9) Shipped from/code.

(i) Enter the CAGE or DoDAAC code of the "Shipped From" location. If it is the same as the CAGE code leave blank.

(ii) For performance of services line items which do not require delivery of items upon completion of services, enter the code of the location at which the services were performed. As mentioned in (i) above, if identical to the prime CAGE code leave blank.

(10) FOB. Enter an "S" for Origin or "D" for Destination as specified in the contract. Enter an alphabetic "O" if the "FOB" point cited in the contract is other than origin or destination.

(11) Payment will be made by/code. Enter the DoDAAC code of the payment office cited in the contract.

(12) Shipped to/code. Enter the DoDAAC, MAPAC, or CAGE code from the contract or shipping instructions.

(13) Marked for/code. Enter the code from the contract or shipping instructions. Only valid DoDAACs, MAPACs, or CAGE codes can be entered. Vendors should use the WAWF "Mark for Rep" and "Mark for Secondary" fields for textual marking information specified in the contract. Enter the three-character project code when provided in the contract or shipping instructions.

(14) Item No. Enter the item number used in the contract. Use a valid 4 or 6 character line item number under the Uniform Contract Line Item Numbering System (see 204.71). Line item numbers with 6 characters with numbers in the final two positions are not deliverable or billable.

(15) Stock/part number/description.

(i) Enter the following for each line item:

(A) The national stock number (NSN) or noncatalog number. If the contract contains NSNs as well as other identification (*e.g.*, part numbers) the contractor should place the NSN information in the Stock Part Number field and the remaining numbers in the line item description field. The data entered in the NSN field must reflect the NSN of the material item being shipped and should be a valid NSN, 13 positions in length. In the "Type" drop-down field, select the corresponding type for the data entered. If no National Stock Number (NSN) or other valid "Type" is available, the word "NONE" may be entered for the Stock/Part Number, with a corresponding "Type" of any value other than NSN selected from the drop-down box.

(B) In the description field, if required by the contract for control purposes, enter: The make, model, serial number, lot, batch, hazard indicator, or similar description.

(C) The Military Standard Requisitioning and Issue Procedures (MILSTRIP) must be placed on the MILSTRIP Tab, not in the line item description field. Enter the MILSTRIP data for each CLIN when MILSTRIP data is identified in the contract.

(ii) For service line items, select SV for "SERVICE" in the type field followed by as short a description as is possible in the description field. Some examples of service line items are maintenance, repair, alteration, rehabilitation, engineering, research, development, training, and testing.

(A) For WAWF RRRs, the "Ship To" code is the DoDAAC, MAPAC, or CAGE code from the contract or shipping instructions.

(B) For service line items not using a WAWF RRR, the "Ship To" code and the

"Unit" shall be filled out. The "Ship To" code is the destination Service Acceptor Code for WAWF. If source inspected and accepted, enter the service performance location as the "Ship To" code.

(iii) For all contracts administered by the Defense Contract Management Agency, with the exception of fast pay procedures, enter the gross weight of the shipment.

(iv) In the description field enter the following as appropriate (entries may be extended through Block 20).

(A) Enter in capital letters any special handling instructions/limits for material environmental control, such as temperature, humidity, aging, freezing, shock, etc.

(B) When a shipment is chargeable to Navy appropriation 17X4911, enter the appropriation, bureau control number (BCN), and authorization accounting activity (AAA) number (*e.g.*, 17X4911-14003-104).

(C) When the Navy transaction type code (TC), "2T" or "7T" is included in the appropriation data, enter "TC 2T" or "TC 7T."

(D) When an NSN is required by but not cited in a contract and has not been furnished by the Government, the contractor may make shipment without the NSN at the direction of the contracting officer. Enter the authority for such shipment.

(E) When Government furnished property (GFP) is included with or incorporated into the line item, enter the letters "GFP."

(F) On shipments of Government furnished aeronautical equipment (GFAE) under Air Force contracts, enter the assignment AERNO control number, *e.g.*, "AERNO 60-6354."

(G) For items shipped with missing components, enter and complete the following:

"Item(s) shipped short of the following component(s): NSN or comparable identification ______, Quantity ______, Estimated Value ______, Authority ______"

(H) When shipment is made of components which were short on a prior shipment, enter and complete the following:

"These components were listed as shortages on shipment number ______, date shipped ______"

(I) When shipments involve drums, cylinders, reels, containers, skids, etc., designated as returnable under contract provisions, enter and complete the following:

"Return to ______, Quantity ______, Item ______, Ownership (Government/contractor)."

(J) Enter the total number of shipping containers, the type of containers, and the container number(s) assigned for the shipment.

(K) On foreign military sales (FMS) shipments, enter the special markings, and FMS case identifier from the contract. Also enter the gross weight.

(L) When test/evaluation results are a condition of acceptance and are not available prior to shipment, the following note shall be entered if the shipment is approved by the contracting officer:

"Note: Acceptance and payment are contingent upon receipt of approved test/evaluation results."

The contracting officer will advise—

(1) The consignee of the results (approval/disapproval); and

(2) The contractor to withhold invoicing pending attachment of the approved test/evaluation results.

(M) For clothing and textile contracts containing a bailment clause, enter the words "GFP UNIT VALUE."

(N) When the initial unit incorporating an approved value engineering change proposal (VECP) is shipped, enter the following statement:

This is the initial unit delivered which incorporates VECP No. ______, Contract Modification No. ______, dated ______

(16) Quantity shipped/received.

(i) Enter the quantity shipped, using the unit of measure in the contract for payment. When a second unit of measure is used for purposes other than payment, enter the appropriate quantity in the description field.

(ii) On the final shipment of a line item of a contract containing a clause permitting a variation of quantity and an underrun condition exists, the prime contractor shall choose the Ship Advice Code "Z". Where the final shipment is from other than the prime contractor's plant and an underrun condition exists, the prime contractor may elect to direct the subcontractor making the final shipment to choose the Ship Advice Code "Z";

(iii) When the Government is performing destination acceptance the acceptor should enter actual quantity received in apparent good condition in the "Qty. Accepted" field of the Acceptor Line Item Tab.

(17) Unit of measure. Enter the abbreviation of the unit measure as indicated in the contract for payment. Where a second unit of measure is indicated in the contract for purposes other than payment or used for shipping purposes, enter the second unit of measure in the description field. Authorized abbreviations are listed in MIL-STD-129, Marking for Shipping and Storage and in the WAWF Unit of Measure Table Link. For example, LB for pound, SH for sheet.

(18) Unit price. When using the WAWF RRR, the unit price is the price of the repair, overhaul, or maintenance service from the contract.

(i) The contractor may, at its option, enter unit prices on the WAWF RR, except when the contract has IUID requirements and the receiving report is being processed in WAWF, the unit price must represent the acquisition cost that will be recorded in the IUID registry. Therefore, in such cases, the unit price is required. See DFARS 252.211-7003, Item Unique Identification and Valuation).

(ii) The contractor shall enter unit prices for each item of property fabricated or acquired for the Government and delivered to a contractor as Government furnished property (GFP). Get the unit price from Section B of the contract. If the unit price is not available, use an estimate. The estimated price should be the contractor's estimate of what the items cost the Government. When the price is estimated, enter "Estimated Unit Price" in the description field. When delivering GFP via WAWF to another contractor, WAWF will initiate a property transfer if the vendor who is initiating the WAWF RR is also registered as a vendor property shipper in WAWF and the vendor receiving the property is also a vendor property receiver in WAWF.

(iii) For clothing and textile contracts containing a bailment clause, enter the cited Government furnished property unit value as "GFP UNIT VALUE" in the description field.

(iv) For all copies of DD Forms 250 for FMS shipments, enter actual prices, if available. If actual prices are not available, use estimated prices. When the price is estimated, enter an "E" after the price.

(19) Amount. WAWF will calculate and populate the amount by multiplying the unit price times the quantity.

(20) Contract Quality Assurance (CQA).

(i) The words "conform to contract" contained in the text above the signature block in the WAWF RR Header Tab relate to quality and to the quantity of the items on the report. Enter notes taking exception in Misc. Info Tab comment field or on attached supporting documents with an appropriate block cross-reference.

(ii) When a shipment is authorized under an alternative release procedure, contractors will execute the alternative release procedure in WAWF by including the appropriate indicator in the electronic transaction rather than through inclusion or attachment of the text of the certificate. The alternative release procedure only provides for release of shipment; Government acceptance must still be indicated by a Government official's signature on the WAWF RR.

(iii) When contract terms provide for use of Certificate of Conformance and shipment is made under these terms, contractors will execute Certificates in WAWF by including the appropriate indicator in the electronic transaction rather than through inclusion or attachment of the text of the certificate. Government acceptance must still be indicated by a Government official's signature on the WAWF RR.

(iv) Origin.

(A) The authorized Government representative must:—

(1) Place an "X" in the appropriate CQA and/or acceptance box(es) to show origin CQA and/or acceptance; and

(2) Sign and date.

WAWF will enter the typed, stamped, or printed name, title, email address, and commercial telephone number.

(B) When fast pay procedures apply, the contractor or subcontractor shall select "FAST PAY" when creating the WAWF RR. When CQA is required, the authorized Government representative shall execute the block as required by paragraph (A).

(v) Destination. When CQA and acceptance or acceptance is at destination, the authorized Government representative must—

(A) Place an "X" in the appropriate box(es); and

(B) Sign and date.

WAWF will enter the typed, stamped, or printed name, title, email address, and commercial telephone number.

(21) Contractor use only. MISC. INFO. Self explanatory.

[Final rule, 65 FR 52951, 8/31/2000, effective 8/31/2000; Final rule, 65 FR 63802, 10/25/2000, effective 10/25/2000; Final rule, 71 FR 75890, 12/19/2006, effective 12/19/2006; Final rule, 76 FR 58122, 9/20/2011, effective 9/20/2011; Final rule, 78 FR 28756, 5/16/2013, effective 5/16/2013; Final rule, 78 FR 76067, 12/16/2013, effective 12/16/2013; Final rule, 80 FR 29983, 5/26/2015, effective 5/26/2015; Final rule 81 FR 9783, 2/26/2016, effective 2/26/2016; Final rule, 81 FR 59515, 8/30/2016, effective 9/29/2016; Final rule, 83 FR 66062, 12/21/2018, effective 12/21/2018; Final rule, 84 FR 48510, 9/13/2019, effective 9/13/2019]

F-302 Mode/method of shipment codes.

Code	Description
A	Motor, truckload.
B	Motor, less than truckload.
C	Van (unpacked, uncrated personal or Government property).
D	Driveaway, truckaway, towaway.
E	Bus.
F	Air Mobility Command (Channel and Special Assignment Airlift Mission)
G	Surface parcel post.
H	Air parcel post.
I	Government trucks, for shipment outside local delivery area.
J	Air, small package carrier.
K	Rail, carload.[1]
L	Rail, less than carload.[1]
M	Surface, freight forwarder.
N	LOGAIR.
O	Organic military air (including aircraft of foreign governments).
P	Through Government Bill of Lading (TGBL).
Q	Commercial air freight (includes regular and expedited service provided by major airlines; charters and air taxis).
R	European Distribution System or Pacific Distribution System.
S	Scheduled Truck Service (STS) (applies to contract carriage, guaranteed traffic routings and/or scheduled service).
T	Air freight forwarder.
U	QUICKTRANS.
V	SEAVAN.
W	Water, river, lake, coastal (commercial).
X	Bearer, walk-thru (customer pickup of material).
Y	Military Intratheater Airlift Service.
Z	Military Sealift Command (MSC) (controlled contract or arranged space).
2	Government watercraft, barge, lighter.
3	Roll-on Roll-off (RORO) service.
4	Armed Forces Courier Service (AFRCOS).
5	Surface, small package carrier.
6	Military official mail (MOM).
7	Express mail.
8	Pipeline.
9	Local delivery by Government or commercial truck (includes on base transfers; deliveries between air, water, or motor terminals; and adjacent activities). Local delivery areas are identified in commercial carriers' tariffs which are filed and approved by regulatory authorities.

[1] Includes trailer/container-on-flat-car (excluding SEAVAN).

[DAC 91-6, 59 FR 27662, 5/27/94, effective 5/27/94; Final rule, 76 FR 58122, 9/20/2011, effective 9/20/2011]

F-303 Consolidated shipments.

When individual shipments are held at the contractor's plant for authorized transportation consolidation to a single bill of lading, the contractor may prepare the WAWF RR or WAWF RRR at the time of CQA or acceptance prior to the time of actual shipment.

[Final rule, 76 FR 58122, 9/20/2011, effective 9/20/2011; Final rule, 81 FR 59515, 8/30/2016, effective 9/29/2016]

F-304 Correction instructions.

Functionality for correcting a WAWF RR or WAWF RRR is available for Defense Contract Management Agency administered contracts paid using the Mechanization of Contract Administration Services system with source acceptance. Preparation instructions and training for corrections is available at *https://wawftraining.eb.mil*. The instructions are part of the Vendor Training section.

[Final rule, 76 FR 58122, 9/20/2011, effective 9/20/2011; Final rule, 81 FR 59515, 8/30/2016, effective 9/29/2016]

F-305 Invoice instructions.

Contractors shall submit payment requests and receiving reports in accordance with paragraph (b) of the clause at DFARS 252.232-7003 unless one of the exceptions in paragraph (d) of that clause applies.

[Final rule, 76 FR 58122, 9/20/2011, effective 9/20/2011; Final rule, 83 FR 66062, 12/21/2018, effective 12/21/2018]

F-306 Packing list instructions.

(a) Contractors may use a WAWF processed RR or the WAWF RRR, as a packing list. WAWF provides an option to print the RR or RRR. Contractors can print a RR or RRR from a system other than WAWF if a signed copy is required. In such cases, the contractor shall print the WAWF RR or RRR only after a signature is applied by the Government inspector or authorized acceptor in WAWF. Copies printed from the contractor's system shall be annotated with "\\original signed in WAWF\\" in lieu of the inspector or acceptor's signature. Ensure a copy is visible on the outside and one is placed inside the package.

(b) If the contract requires Government source inspection and acceptance at origin, the contractor shall ensure that its packaging documentation includes a RR or RRR that documents inspection, acceptance, or both by the Government inspector or authorized acceptor. A paper DD Form 250 may be used in lieu of WAWF generated RRs or RRRs when one of the exceptions in paragraph (d) of the clause at DFARS 252.232-7003 applies.

[Final rule, 70 FR 58980, 10/11/2005, effective 10/11/2005; Final rule, 73 FR 11356, 3/3/2008, effective 3/3/2008; Final rule, 76 FR 58122, 9/20/2011, effective 9/20/2011; Final rule, 81 FR 59515, 8/30/2016, effective 9/29/2016; Final rule, 83 FR 66062, 12/21/2018, effective 12/21/2018]

F-307 Receiving instructions.

If CQA and acceptance or acceptance of supplies is required upon arrival at destination, see F-301(b)(20)(v) for instructions.

[Final rule, 76 FR 58122, 9/20/2011, effective 9/20/2011; Final rule, 80 FR 29983, 5/26/2015, effective 5/26/2015]

PART 4—PREPARATION OF THE DD FORM 250 AND DD FORM 250C

F-401 Preparation instructions.

(a) *General.*

(1) Dates must use nine spaces consisting of the four digits of the year, three-position alphabetic month abbreviation, and two digits for the day. For example, 2000AUG07, 2000SEP24.

(2) Addresses must consist of the name, street address/P.O. box, city, state, and ZIP code.

(3) Enter to the right of and on the same line as the word "Code" in Blocks 9 through 12 and in Block 14—

(i) The Commercial and Government Entity Handbook (H4/H8) code;

(ii) The DoD activity address code (DoDAAC) as it appears in the DoD Activity Address Directory (DoDAAD), DoD 4000.25-6-M; or

(iii) The Military Assistance Program Address Directory (MAPAD) code.

(4) Enter the DoDAAC, CAGE (H4/H8), or MAPAD code in Block 13.

(5) The data entered in the blocks at the top of the DD Form 250c must be identical to the comparable entries in Blocks 1, 2, 3, and 6 of the DD Form 250.

(6) Enter overflow data from the DD Form 250 in Block 16 or in the body of the DD Form 250c with an appropriate cross-reference. Do not number or distribute additional

DD Form 250c sheets, solely for continuation of Block 23 data as part of the MIRR.

(7) Do not include classified information in the MIRR. MIRRs must not be classified.

(b) *Completion instructions.*

(1) Block 1—Procurement instrument identification (Contract) NO. See paragraph F-301(b)(1).

(2) Block 2—Shipment no. See F-301(b)(2), Shipment no. When the series is completely used, change the shipment number prefix and start with 0001.

(3) Block 3—Date shipped. Enter the date the shipment is released to the carrier or the date the services are completed. If the shipment will be released after the date of CQA and/or acceptance, enter the estimated date of release. When the date is estimated, enter an "E" after the date. Do not delay distribution of the MIRR for entry of the actual shipping date. Reissuance of the MIRR is not required to show the actual shipping date (see F-403).

(4) Block 4—B/L TCN. When applicable, enter—

(i) The commercial or Government bill of lading number after "B/L;"

(ii) The transportation control number after "TCN" (when a TCN is assigned for each line item on the DD Form 250 under Block 16 instructions, insert "See Block 16"); and

(iii) The initial (line haul) mode of shipment code in the lower right corner of the block (see F-402).

(5) Block 5—Discount terms.

(i) The contractor may enter the discount in terms of percentages on all copies of the MIRR.

(ii) Use the procedures in F-406 when the MIRR is used as an invoice.

(6) Block 6—Invoice no./date.

(i) The contractor may enter the invoice number and actual or estimated date of invoice submission on all copies of the MIRR. When the date is estimated, enter an "E" after the date. Do not correct MIRRs other than invoice copies to reflect the actual date of invoice submission.

(ii) Use the procedures in F-406 when the MIRR is used as an invoice.

(7) Block 7—Page/of. Consecutively number the pages of the MIRR. On each page enter the total number of pages of the MIRR.

(8) Block 8—Acceptance point. Enter an "S" for Origin or "D" for destination.

(9) Block 9—Prime contractor/code. Enter the code and address.

(10) Block 10—Administered by/code. Enter the code and address of the contract administration office cited in the contract.

(11) Block 11—Shipped from/code/fob.

(i) Enter the code and address of the "Shipped From" location. If identical to Block 9, enter "See Block 9."

(ii) For performance of services line items which do not require delivery of items upon completion of services, enter the code and address of the location at which the services were performed. If the DD Form 250 covers performance at multiple locations, or if identical to Block 9, enter "See Block 9."

(iii) Enter on the same line and to the right of "FOB" an "S" for Origin or "D" for Destination as specified in the contract. Enter an alphabetic "O" if the "FOB" point cited in the contract is other than origin or destination.

(iv) For destination or origin acceptance shipments involving discount terms, enter "DISCOUNT EXPEDITE" in at least one-half inch outline-type style letters across Blocks 11 and 12. Do not obliterate other information in these blocks.

(12) Block 12—Payment will be made by/code. Enter the code and address of the payment office cited in the contract.

(13) Block 13—Shipped to/code. Enter the code and address from the contract or shipping instructions.

(14) Block 14—Marked for/code. Enter the code and address from the contract or shipping instructions. When three-character project codes are provided in the contract or shipping instructions, enter the code in the body of the block, prefixed by "Proj"; do not enter in the Code block.

(15) Block 15—Item No. See paragraph F-301(b)(14) with the exception to F301(b)(2)(B)2 that line item numbers not in accordance with the Uniform Contract Line Item Numbering System may be entered without regard to positioning.

(16) Block 16—Stock/part No./description.

(i) Use single or double spacing between line items when there are less than four line items. Use double spacing when there are four or more line items. Enter the following for each line item:

(A) The national stock number (NSN) or noncatalog number. Where applicable, include a prefix or suffix. If a number is not provided, or it is necessary to supplement the number, include other identification such as the manufacturer's name or Federal supply code (as published in Cataloging Handbook H4-1), and the part number. Show additional part numbers in parentheses or slashes. Show the descriptive noun of the item nomenclature and if provided, the Government assigned management/material control code. The contractor may use the following technique in the case of equal kind supply items. The first entry shall be the description without regard to kind. For example, "Shoe-Low Quarter-Black," "Resistor," "Vacuum Tube," etc. Below this description, enter the contract line item number in Block 15 and Stock/Part number followed by the size or type in Block 16.

(B) On the next printing line, if required by the contract for control purposes, enter: The make, model, serial number, lot, batch, hazard indicator, or similar description.

(C) On the next printing lines enter—

(1) The MIPR number prefixed by "MIPR" or the MILSTRIP requisition number(s) when provided in the contract; or

(2) Shipping instructions followed on the same line (when more than one requisition is entered) by the unit for payment and the quantity shipped against each requisition.

Example: V04696-185-750XY19059A—EA 5 N0018801776038XY3211BA—EA 200 AT650803050051AAT6391J—EA 1000

(D) When a TCN is assigned for each line item, enter on the next line the transportation control number prefixed by "TCN."

(ii) For service line items, enter the word "SERVICE" followed by as short a description as is possible in no more than 20 additional characters. Some examples of service line items are maintenance, repair, alteration, rehabilitation, engineering, research, development, training, and testing. Do not complete Blocks 4, 13, and 14 when there is no shipment of material.

(iii) For all contracts administered by the Defense Contract Management Agency, with the exception of fast pay procedures, enter and complete the following:

Gross Shipping Wt.

____

State weight in pounds only.

(iv) Starting with the next line, enter the following as appropriate (entries may be extended through Block 20). When entries apply to more than one line item in the MIRR, enter them only once after the last line item entry. Reference applicable line item numbers.

(A) Enter in capital letters any special handling instructions/limits for material environmental control, such as temperature, humidity, aging, freezing, shock, etc.

(B) When a shipment is chargeable to Navy appropriation 17X4911, enter the appropriation, bureau control number (BCN), and authorization accounting activity (AAA) number (*e.g.,* 17X4911-14003-104).

(C) When the Navy transaction type code (TC), "2T" or "7T" is included in the appropriation data, enter "TC 2T" or "TC 7T."

(D) When an NSN is required by but not cited in a contract and has not been furnished by the Government, the contractor may make shipment without the NSN at the direction of the contracting officer. Enter the authority for such shipment.

(E) When Government furnished property (GFP) is included with or incorporated into the line item, enter the letters "GFP."

(F) When shipment consists of replacements for supplies previously furnished, enter in capital letters "REPLACEMENT

SHIPMENT." (See F-401, Block 17, for replacement indicators.)

(G) On shipments of Government furnished aeronautical equipment (GFAE) under Air Force contracts, enter the assignment AERNO control number, *e.g.,* "AERNO 60-6354."

(H) For items shipped with missing components, enter and complete the following:

"Item(s) shipped short of the following component(s):

NSN or comparable identification ________, Quantity ________, Estimated Value ________, Authority ________"

(I) When shipment is made of components which were short on a prior shipment, enter and complete the following:

"These components were listed as shortages on shipment number ________, date shipped ________"

(J) When shipments involve drums, cylinders, reels, containers, skids, etc., designated as returnable under contract provisions, enter and complete the following:

"Return to ________, Quantity ________, Item ________, Ownership (Government/contractor)."

(K) Enter the total number of shipping containers, the type of containers, and the container number(s) assigned for the shipment.

(L) On foreign military sales (FMS) shipments, enter the special markings, and FMS case identifier from the contract. Also enter the gross weight.

(M) When test/evaluation results are a condition of acceptance and are not available prior to shipment, the following note shall be entered if the shipment is approved by the contracting officer:

"Note: Acceptance and payment are contingent upon receipt of approved test/evaluation results."

The contracting officer will advise—

(1) The consignee of the results (approval/disapproval); and

(2) The contractor to withhold invoicing pending attachment of the approved test/evaluation results.

(N) The copy of the DD Form 250 required to support payment for destination acceptance (top copy of those with shipment) or ARP origin acceptance shall be identified as follows: enter "PAYMENT COPY" in approximately one-half inch outline type style letters with "FORWARD TO BLOCK 12 ADDRESS" in approximately one-quarter inch letters immediately below. Do not obliterate any other entries.

(O) For clothing and textile contracts containing a bailment clause, enter the words "GFP UNIT VALUE."

(P) When the initial unit incorporating an approved value engineering change proposal (VECP) is shipped, enter the following statement:

This is the initial unit delivered which incorporates VECP No. ________, Contract Modification No. ________, dated ________

(17) Block 17—Quantity shipped/received.

(i) Enter the quantity shipped, using the unit of measure in the contract for payment. When a second unit of measure is used for purposes other than payment, enter the appropriate quantity directly below in parentheses.

(ii) On the final shipment of a line item of a contract containing a clause permitting a variation of quantity and an underrun condition exists, the prime contractor shall enter a "Z" below the last digit of the quantity. Where the final shipment is from other than the prime contractor's plant and an underrun condition exists, the prime contractor may elect either to—

(A) Direct the subcontractor making the final shipment to enter a "Z" below the quantity; or

(B) Upon determination that all subcontractors have completed their shipments, correct the DD Form 250 (see F-405) covering the final shipment of the line item from the prime contractor's plant by addition of a "Z" below the quantity. Do not use the "Z" on deliveries which equal or exceed the contract line item quantity.

(iii) For replacement shipments, enter "A" below the last digit of the quantity, to designate first replacement, "B" for second replacement, etc. Do not use the final shipment indicator "Z" on underrun deliveries when a final line item shipment is replaced.

17. QUANTITY SHIP/REC'D

1000

(10)

Z

(iv) If the quantity received is the same quantity shipped and all items are in apparent good condition, enter by a check mark. If different, enter actual quantity received in apparent good condition below quantity shipped and circle. The receiving activity will annotate the DD Form 250 stating the reason for the difference.

(18) Block 18—Unit. Enter the abbreviation of the unit measure as indicated in the contract for payment. Where a second unit of measure is indicated in the contract for purposes other than payment or used for shipping purposes, enter the second unit of measure directly below in parentheses. Authorized abbreviations are listed in MIL-STD-129, Marking for Shipping and Storage. For example, LB for pound, SH for sheet.

18. UNIT

LB

(SH)

(19) Block 19—Unit price. The contractor may, at its option, enter unit prices on all MIRR copies, except as a minimum:

(i) The contractor shall enter unit prices on all MIRR copies for each item of property fabricated or acquired for the Government and delivered to a contractor as Government furnished property (GFP). Get the unit price from Section B of the contract. If the unit price is not available, use an estimate. The estimated price should be the contractor's estimate of what the items will cost the Government. When the price is estimated, enter an "E" after the unit price.

(ii) Use the procedures in F-406 when the MIRR is used as an invoice.

(iii) For clothing and textile contracts containing a bailment clause, enter the cited Government furnished property unit value opposite "GFP UNIT VALUE" entry in Block 16.

(iv) Price all copies of DD Forms 250 for FMS shipments with actual prices, if available. If actual price are not available, use estimated prices. When the price is estimated, enter an "E" after the price.

(20) Block 20—AMOUNT. Enter the extended amount when the unit price is entered in Block 19.

(21) Block 21—Contract quality assurance (CQA).

(i) The words "conform to contract" contained in the printed statements in Blocks 21a and 21b relate to quality and to the quantity of the items on the report. Do not modify the statements. Enter notes taking exception in Block 16 or on attached supporting documents with an appropriate block cross-reference.

(ii) When a shipment is authorized under alternative release procedure, attach or include the appropriate contractor signed certificate on the top copy of the DD Form 250 copies distributed to the payment office or attach or include the appropriate contractor certificate on the contract administration office copy when contract administration (Block 10 of the DD Form 250) is performed by the Defense Contract Management Agency.

(iii) When contract terms provide for use of Certificate of Conformance and shipment is made under these terms, the contractor shall enter in capital letters "CERTIFICATE OF CONFORMANCE" in Block 21a on the next line following the CQA and acceptance statements. Attach or include the appropriate contractor signed certificate on the top copy of the DD Form 250 copies distributed to the payment office or attach or include the appropriate certificate on the contract administration office copy when contract administration (Block 10 of the DD Form 250) is performed by the Defense Contract Management Agency. In addition, attach a copy of the signed certificate to, or enter on, copies of the MIRR sent with shipment.

(iv) Origin.

(A) The authorized Government representative must—

(1) Place an "X" in the appropriate CQA and/or acceptance box(es) to show origin CQA and/or acceptance. When the contract requires CQA at destination in addition to origin CQA, enter an asterisk at the end of the statement and an explanatory note in Block 16;

(2) Sign and date;

(3) Enter the typed, stamped, or printed name, title, mailing address, and commercial telephone number.

(B) When alternative release procedures apply—

(1) The contractor or subcontractor shall complete the entries required under paragraph (A) and enter in capital letters "ALTERNATIVE RELEASE PROCEDURE" on the next line following the printed CQA/acceptance statement.

(2) When acceptance is at origin and contract administration is performed by an office other than the Defense Contract Management Agency, the contractor shall furnish the four payment office copies of the MIRR to the authorized Government representative for dating and signing of one copy and forwarding of all copies to the payment office.

(3) When acceptance is at origin and contract administration is performed by the Defense Contract Management Agency, furnish the contract administration office copy of the MIRR to the authorized Government representative for dating and signing and forwarding to the contract administration office (see F-501, Table 1).

(C) When fast pay procedures apply, the contractor or subcontractor shall enter in capital letters "FAST PAY" on the next line following the printed CQA/acceptance statement. When CQA is required, the authorized Government representative shall execute the block as required by paragraph (A).

(D) When Certificate of Conformance procedures apply, inspection or inspection and acceptance are at source, and the contractor's Certificate of Conformance is required, the contractor shall enter in capital letters "CERTIFICATE OF CONFORMANCE" as required by paragraph (b)(21)(iii) of this appendix.

(1) For contracts administered by an office other than the Defense Contract Management Agency, furnish the four payment office copies of the MIRR to the authorized Government representative for dating and signing of one copy, and forwarding of all copies to the payment office.

(2) For contracts administered by the Defense Contract Management Agency, furnish the contract administration office copy of the MIRR to the authorized Government representative for dating and signing and forwarding to the contract administration office (see F-401, Table 1).

(3) When acceptance is at destination, no entry shall be made other than "CERTIFICATE OF CONFORMANCE."

(v) Destination.

(A) When acceptance at origin is indicated in Block 21a, make no entries in Block 21b.

(B) When CQA and acceptance or acceptance is at destination, the authorized Government representative must—

(1) Place an "X" in the appropriate box(es);

(2) Sign and date; and

(3) Enter typed, stamped, or printed name, title, mailing address, and commercial telephone number.

(C) When "ALTERNATIVE RELEASE PROCEDURE" is entered in Block 21a and acceptance is at destination, the authorized Government representative must complete the entries required by paragraph (b)(21)(v)(B) of this appendix.

(D) Forward the executed payment copy or MILSCAP format identifier PKN or PKP to the payment office cited in Block 12 within four work days (five days when MILSCAP Format is used) after delivery and acceptance of the shipment by the receiving activity. Forward one executed copy of the final DD Form 250 to the contract administration office cited in Block 10 for implementing contract closeout procedures.

(E) When "FAST PAY" is entered in Block 21a, make no entries in this block.

(22) Block 22—Receiver's use. The authorized representative of the receiving activity (Government or contractor) must use this block to show receipt, quantity, and condition. The authorized representative must—

(i) Enter the date the supplies arrived. For example, when off-loading or in-checking occurs subsequent to the day of arrival of the carrier at the installation, the date of the carrier's arrival is the date received for purposes of this block;

(ii) Sign; and

(iii) Enter typed, stamped, or printed name, title, mailing address, and commercial telephone number.

(23) Block 23—Contractor use only. Self explanatory.

[DAC 91-4, 57 FR 53602, 11/12/92, effective 10/30/92; DAC 91-6, 59 FR 27662, 5/27/94, effective 5/27/94; DAC 91-9, 60 FR 61586, 11/30/95, effective 11/30/95; Final rule, 65 FR 52951, 8/31/2000, effective 8/31/2000; Final rule, 65 FR 63804, 10/25/2000, effective 10/25/2000; Final rule, 65 FR 63802, 10/25/2000, effective 10/25/2000; Final rule, 73 FR 1830, 1/10/2008, effective 1/10/2008; Final rule, 73 11356, 3/3/2008, effective 3/3/2008; Final rule, 76 FR 58122, 9/20/2011, effective 9/20/2011]

F-402 Mode/method of shipment codes.

See paragraph F-302.

[Final rule, 76 FR 58122, 9/20/2011, effective 9/20/2011]

F-403 Consolidated shipments.

When individual shipments are held at the contractor's plant for authorized transportation consolidation to a single bill of lading, the contractor may prepare the DD Forms 250 at the time of CQA or acceptance prior to the time of actual shipment (see Block 3).

[Final rule, 76 FR 58122, 9/20/2011, effective 9/20/2011]

F-404 Multiple consignee instructions.

The contractor may prepare one MIRR when the identical line item(s) of a contract are to be shipped to more than one consignee, with the same or varying quantities, and the shipment requires origin acceptance. Prepare the MIRR using the procedures in this appendix with the following changes:

(a) Blocks 2, 4, 13, and, if applicable, 14—Enter "See Attached Distribution List."

(b) Block 15—The contractor may group item numbers for identical stock/part number and description.

(c) Block 17—Enter the "total" quantity shipped by line item or, if applicable, grouped identical line items.

(d) Use the DD Form 250c to list each individual "Shipped To" and "Marked For" with—

(1) Code(s) and complete shipping address and a sequential shipment number for each;

(2) Line item number(s);

(3) Quantity;

(4) MIPR number(s), preceded by "MIPR," or the MILSTRIP requisition number, and quantity for each when provided in the contract or shipping instructions; and

(5) If applicable, bill of lading number, TCN, and mode of shipment code.

(e) The contractor may omit those distribution list pages of the DD Form 250c that are not applicable to the consignee. Provide a complete MIRR for all other distribution.

[Final rule, 76 FR 58122, 9/20/2011, effective 9/20/2011]

F-405 Correction instructions.

Make a new revised MIRR or correct the original when, because of errors or omissions, it is necessary to correct the MIRR after distribution has been made. Use data identical to that of the original MIRR. Do not correct MIRRs for Blocks 19 and 20 entries. Make the corrections as follows—

(a) Circle the error and place the corrected information in the same block; if space is limited, enter the corrected information in Block 16 referencing the error page and block. Enter omissions in Block 16 referencing omission page and block. For example—

2. SHIPMENT NO.

(AAA0001)

See Block 16

---

17. QUANTITY

SHIP/REC'D

19

(17)

---

16. STOCK/PART NO. DESCRIPTION CORRECTIONS:

Refer Block 2: Change shipment No. AAA001 to AAA0010 on all pages of the MIRR.

Refer Blocks 15, 16, 17, and 18, page 2: Delete in entirety Line Item No. 0006. This item was not shipped.

(b) When corrections have been made to entries for line items (Block 15) or quantity (Block 17), enter the words "CORRECTIONS HAVE BEEN VERIFIED" on page 1. The authorized Government representative will date and sign immediately below the statement. This verification statement and signature are not required for other corrections.

(c) Clearly mark the pages of the MIRR requiring correction with the words "CORRECTED COPY." Avoid obliterating any other entries. Where corrections are made only on continuation sheets, also mark page number 1 with the words "CORRECTED COPY."

(d) Page 1 and only those continuation pages marked "CORRECTED COPY" shall be distributed to the initial distribution. A complete MIRR with corrections shall be distributed to new addressee(s) created by error corrections.

[Final rule, 76 FR 58122, 9/20/2011, effective 9/20/2011]

F-406 Invoice instructions.

(a) Contractors shall submit payment requests and receiving reports in electronic form, unless an exception in DFARS 232.7002applies. Contractor submission of the material inspection and receiving information required by this appendix by using the WAWF electronic form (see paragraph (b) of the clause at DFARS 252.232-7003) fulfills the requirement for an MIRR.

(b) If the contracting officer authorizes the contractor to submit an invoice in paper form, the Government encourages, but does not require, the contractor to use the MIRR as an invoice, in lieu of a commercial form. If commercial forms are used, identify the related MIRR shipment number(s) on the form. If using the MIRR as an invoice, prepare the MIRR and forward the required number of copies to the payment office as follows:

(1) Complete Blocks 5, 6, 19, and 20. Block 6 shall contain the invoice number and date. Column 20 shall be totaled.

(2) Mark in letters approximately one inch high, first copy: "ORIGINAL INVOICE," for all invoice submissions; and three copies: "INVOICE COPY," when the payment office requires four copies. Questions regarding the appropriate number of copies (*i.e.,* one or four) should be directed to the applicable payment office.

(3) Forward the appropriate number of copies to the payment office (Block 12 address), except when acceptance is at destination and a Navy finance office will make payment, forward to destination.

(4) Separate the copies of the MIRR used as an invoice from the copies of the MIRR used as a receiving report.

[Final rule, 76 FR 58122, 9/20/2011, effective 9/20/2011]

F-407 Packing list instructions.

Contractors may use copies of the MIRR as a packing list. The packing list copies are in addition to the copies of the MIRR required for standard distribution (see F-501). Mark them "PACKING LIST."

[Final rule, 76 FR 58122, 9/20/2011, effective 9/20/2011]

F-408 Receiving instructions.

When the MIRR is used for receiving purposes, local directives shall prescribe procedures. If CQA and acceptance or acceptance of supplies is required upon arrival at destination, see F-401(b)(21)(v) for instructions.

[Final rule, 76 FR 58122, 9/20/2011, effective 9/20/2011]

PART 5—DISTRIBUTION OF WIDE AREA WORKFLOW RECEIVING REPORT (WAWF RR), DD FORM 250 AND DD FORM 250C

F-501 Distribution of WAWF RR.

Use of the WAWF electronic form satisfies the distribution requirements of this section, except for the copies required to accompany shipment.

[Final rule, 76 FR 58122, 9/20/2011, effective 9/20/2011]

F-502 Distribution of DD Form 250 and DD Form 250C.

(a) The contractor is responsible for distributing the DD Form 250, Material Inspection and Receiving Report (MIRR) including mailing and payment of postage.

(b) Contractors shall distribute MIRRs using the instructions in Tables 1 and 2.

(c) Contractors shall distribute MIRRs on non-DoD contracts using this appendix as amended by the contract.

(d) Contractors shall make distribution promptly, but no later than the close of business of the work day following—

(1) Signing of the DD Form 250 (Block 21a) by the authorized Government representative; or

(2) Shipment when authorized under terms of alternative release, certificate of conformance, or fast pay procedures; or

(3) Shipment when CQA and acceptance are to be performed at destination.

(e) Do not send the consignee copies (via mail) on overseas shipments to port of embarkation (POE). Send them to consignee at APO/FPO address.

(f) Copies of the MIRR forwarded to a location for more than one recipient shall clearly identify each recipient.

Material Inspection And Receiving Report

MATERIAL INSPECTION AND RECEIVING REPORT TABLE 1—STANDARD DISTRIBUTION

Standard distribution	Number of copies
With Shipment*	2
Consignee (via mail)	1
(For Navy procurement, include unit price.)	
(For foreign military sales, consignee copies are not required.)	
Contract Administration Office (CAO)	1
(Forward direct to address in Block 10 except when addressee is a Defense Contract Management Agency (DCMA) office and a certificate of conformance or the alternative release procedures (see F-301, Block 21) is involved, and acceptance is at origin; then, forward through the authorized Government representative.)	
Purchasing Office	1
Payment Office**	2
(Forward direct to address in Block 12 except—	
(i) When address in Block 10 is a DCMA office and payment office in Block 12 is the Defense Finance and Accounting Service, Columbus Center, do not make distribution to the Block 12 addressee;	

Standard distribution	Number of copies
(ii) When address in Block 12 is the Defense Finance and Accounting Service, Columbus Center/Albuquerque Office (DFAS-CO/ALQ), Kirtland AFB, NM, attach only one copy to the required number of copies of the contractor's invoice;	
(iii) When acceptance is at destination and a Navy finance office will make payment, forward to destination; and	
(iv) When a certificate of conformance or the alternative release procedures (see F-301, Block 21) are involved and acceptance is at origin, forward the copies through the authorized Government representative.)	
ADP Point for CAO (applicable to Air Force only)	1
(When DFAS-CO/ALQ is the payment office in Block 12, send one copy to DFAS-CO/ALQ immediately after signature. If submission of delivery data is made electronically, distribution of this hard copy need not be made to DFAS-CO/ALQ.)	
CAO of Contractor Receiving GFP	1
(For items fabricated or acquired for the Government and shipped to a contractor as Government furnished property, send one copy directly to the CAO cognizant of the receiving contractor, ATTN: Property Administrator (see DoD 4105.59-H).)	

* Attach as follows:

Type of shipment	Location
Carload or truckload	Affix to the shipment where it will be readily visible and available upon receipt.
Less than carload or truckload	Affix to container number one or container truckload bearing lowest number.
Mail, including parcel post	Attach to outside or include in the package. Include a copy in each additional package of multi-package shipments.
Pipeline, tank car, or railroad cars for coal movements	Forward with consignee copies.

**Payment by Defense Finance and Accounting Service, Columbus Center will be based on the source acceptance copies of DD Forms 250 forwarded to the contract administration office.

[Final rule, 76 FR 58122, 9/20/2011, effective 9/20/2011; Final rule, 83 FR 66062, 12/21/2018, effective 12/21/2018]

PART 6—PREPARATION OF THE DD FORM 250-1 (LOADING REPORT)

F-601 Instructions.

Prepare the DD Form 250-1 using the following instructions when applied to a tanker or barge cargo lifting. If space is limited, use abbreviations. The block numbers correspond to those on the form.

(a) Block 1—Tanker/barge. Line out "TANKER" or "BARGE" as appropriate and place an "X" to indicate loading report.

(b) Block 2—Inspection office. Enter the name and location of the Government office conducting the inspection.

(c) Block 3—Report No. Number each form consecutively, starting with number 1, to correspond to the number of shipments made against the contract. If shipment is made from more than one location against the same contract, use this numbering system at each location.

(d) Block 4—Agency placing order on shipper, city, state and/or local address (loading). Enter the applicable Government activity.

(e) Block 5—Department. Enter military department owning product being shipped.

(f) Block 6—Prime contract or P.O. No. Enter the contract or purchase order number.

(g) Block 7—Name of prime contractor, city, state and/or local address (loading). Enter the name and address of the contractor as shown in the contract.

(h) Block 8—Storage contract. Enter storage contract number if applicable.

(i) Block 9—Terminal or refinery shipped from, city, state and/or local address. Enter the name and location of the contractor facility from which shipment is made. Also enter delivery point in this space as either "FOB Origin" or "FOB Destination."

(j) Block 10—Order No. on supplier. Enter number of the delivery order, purchase order, subcontract or suborder placed on the supplier.

(k) Block 11—Shipped to: (receiving activity, city, state and/or local address). Enter the name and geographical address of the consignee as shown on the shipping order.

(l) Block 12—B/L number. If applicable, enter the initials and number of the bill of lading. If a commercial bill of lading is later authorized to be converted to a Government bill of lading, show "Com. B/L to GB/L."

(m) Block 13—Reqn. or request No. Enter number and date from the shipping instructions.

(n) Block 14—Cargo No. Enter the cargo number furnished by the ordering office.

(o) Block 15—Vessel. Enter the name of tanker or barge.

(p) Block 16—Draft arrival. Enter the vessel's draft on arrival.

(q) Block 17—Draft sailing. Enter the vessel's draft on completion of loading.

(r) Block 18—Previous two cargoes. Enter the type of product constituting previous two cargoes.

(s) Block 19—Prior inspection. Leave blank.

(t) Block 20—Condition of shore pipeline. Enter condition of line (full or empty) before and after loading.

(u) Block 21—Appropriation (loading). Enter the appropriation number shown on the contract, purchase order or distribution plan. If the shipment is made from departmentally owned stock, show "Army, Navy, or Air Force (as appropriate) owned stock."

(v) Block 22—Contract item no. Enter the contract item number applicable to the shipment.

(w) Block 23—Product. Enter the product nomenclature and grade as shown in the contract or specification, the stock or class number, and the NATO symbol.

(x) Block 24—Specifications. Enter the specification and amendment number shown in the contract.

(y) Block 25—Statement of quantity. Enter in the "LOADED" column, the net barrels, net gallons, and long tons for the cargo loaded. NOTE: If more than 1.2 of 1 percent difference exists between the ship and shore quantity figures, the contractor shall immediately investigate to determine the cause of the difference. If necessary, prepare corrected documents; otherwise, put a statement in Block 28 as to the probable or actual cause of the difference.

(z) Block 26—Statement of quality.

(1) Under the heading "TESTS" list all inspection acceptance tests of the specification and any other quality requirements of the contract.

(2) Under the heading "SPECIFICATION LIMITS" list the limits or requirements as stated in the specification or contract directly opposite each entry in the "TESTS" column. List waivers to technical requirements.

(3) Under the heading "TEST RESULTS" list the test results applicable to the storage tank or tanks from which the cargo was lifted. If more than one storage tank is involved, list the tests applicable to each tank in separate columns headed by the tank number, the date the product in the tank was approved, and the quantity loaded from the tank. Each column shall also list such product characteristics as amount and type of corrosion inhibitor, etc.

(aa) Block 27—Time statement. Line out "DISCHARGE" and "DISCHARGING." Complete all applicable entries of the time statement using local time. Take these dates and times from either the vessel or shore facility log. The Government representative shall ensure that the logs are in agreement on those entries used. If the vessel and shore facility logs are not in agreement, the Government representative will explain the reasons in Block 28—REMARKS. Do not enter the date and time the vessel left berth on documents placed aboard the vessel. The date and time shall appear on all other copies. Express all dates in sequence of day, month, and year with the month spelled out or abbreviated (*e.g.,* 10 Sept. 67). The term FINISHED BALLAST DISCHARGE is meant to include all times needed to complete deballasting and mopping/drying of ship's tanks. The inspection of ship's tanks for loading is normally performed immediately upon completion of drying tanks.

(bb) Block 28—Remarks. Use this space for reporting:

(1) All delays, their cause and responsible party (vessel, shore facility, Government representative, or other).

(2) Details of loading abnormalities such as product losses due to overflow, leaks, delivery of product from low level in shore tanks, etc.

(3) In the case of multiple consignees, enter each consignee, the amount consigned to each, and if applicable, the storage contract numbers appearing on the delivery order.

(4) When product title is vested in the U.S. Government, insert in capital letters "U.S. GOVERNMENT OWNED CARGO." If title to the product remains with the contractor and inspection is performed at source with acceptance at destination, insert in capital letters "CONTRACTOR OWNED CARGO."

(5) Seal numbers and location of seals. If space is not adequate, place this information on the ullage report or an attached supplemental sheet.

(cc) Block 29—Company or receiving terminal. Line out "OR RECEIVING TERMINAL" and get the signature of the supplier's representative.

(dd) Block 30—Certification by government representative. Line out "discharged." The Government representative shall date and sign the form to certify inspection and acceptance, as applicable, by the Government. The name of the individual signing this certification, as well as the names applied in Blocks 29 and 31, shall be typed or hand lettered. The signature in Block 30 must agree with the typed or lettered name to be acceptable to the paying office.

(ee) Block 31—Certification by master or agent. Obtain the signature of the master of the vessel or its agent.

[Final rule, 76 FR 58122, 9/20/2011, effective 9/20/2011]

PART 7—PREPARATION OF THE DD FORM 250-1 (DISCHARGE REPORT)

F-701 Instructions.

Prepare the DD Form 250-1 using the following instructions when applied to a tanker or barge discharge. If space is limited, use abbreviations. The block numbers correspond to those on the form.

(a) Block 1—Tanker/barge. Line out "TANKER" or "BARGE" as applicable and place an "X" to enter discharge report.

(b) Block 2—Inspection office. Enter Government activity performing inspection on the cargo received.

(c) Block 3—Report No. Leave blank.

(d) Block 4—Agency placing order on shipper, city, state and/or local address (loading). Enter Government agency shown on loading report.

(e) Block 5—Department. Enter Department owning product being received.

(f) Block 6—Prime contract or P.O. No. Enter the contract or purchase order number shown on the loading report.

(g) Block 7—Name of prime contractor, city, state and/or local address (loading). Enter the name and location of contractor who loaded the cargo.

(h) Block 8—Storage contract. Enter the number of the contract under which material is placed in commercial storage where applicable.

(i) Block 9—Terminal or refinery shipped from, city, state and/or local address. Enter source of cargo.

(j) Block 10—Order No. on supplier. Make same entry appearing on loading report.

(k) Block 11—Shipped to: (RECEIVING ACTIVITY, CITY, STATE AND/OR LOCAL ADDRESS). Enter receiving activity's name and location.

(l) Block 12—B/L number. Enter as appears on loading report.

(m) Block 13—Reqn. or request No. Leave blank.

(n) Block 14—Cargo No. Enter cargo number shown on loading report.

(o) Block 15—Vessel. Enter name of tanker or barge discharging cargo.

(p) Block 16—Draft arrival. Enter draft of vessel upon arrival at dock.

(q) Block 17—Draft sailing. Enter draft of vessel after discharging.

(r) Block 18—Previous two cargoes. Leave blank.

(s) Block 19—Prior inspection. Enter the name and location of the Government office which inspected the cargo loading.

(t) Block 20—Condition of shore pipeline. Enter condition of line (full or empty) before and after discharging.

(u) Block 21—Appropriation (loading). Leave blank.

(v) Block 22—Contract item No. Enter the item number shown on the loading report.

(w) Block 23—Product. Enter information appearing in Block 23 of the loading report.

(x) Block 24—Specifications. Enter information appearing in Block 24 of the loading report.

(y) Block 25—Statement of quantity. Enter applicable data in proper columns.

(1) Take "LOADED" figures from the loading report.

(2) Determine quantities discharged from shore tank gauges at destination.

(3) If a grade of product is discharged at more than one point, calculate the loss or gain for that product by the final discharge point.

Report amounts previously discharged on discharge reports prepared by the previous discharge points. Transmit volume figures by routine message to the final discharge point in advance of mailed documents to expedite the loss or gain calculation and provide proration data when more than one department is involved.

(4) The loss or gain percentage shall be entered in the "PERCENT" column followed by "LOSS" or "GAIN," as applicable.

(5) On destination acceptance shipments, accomplish the "DISCHARGED" column only, unless instructed to the contrary.

(z) Block 26—Statement of quality.

(1) Under the heading "TESTS" enter the verification tests performed on the cargo preparatory to discharge.

(2) Under "SPECIFICATION LIMITS" enter the limits, including authorized departures (if any) appearing on the loading report, for the tests performed.

(3) Enter the results of tests performed under the heading "TEST RESULTS."

(aa) Block 27—Time statement. Line out "LOAD" and "LOADING." Complete all applicable entries of the time statement using local time. Take the dates and times from either the vessel or shore facility log. The Government representative shall ensure that these logs are in agreement with entries used. If the vessel and shore facility logs are not in agreement, the Government representative will explain the reason(s) in Block

28—REMARKS. Do not enter the date and time the vessel left berth on documents placed aboard the vessel. The date and time shall appear on all other copies. Express all dates in sequence of day, month, and year with the month spelled out or abbreviated (*e.g.,* 10 Sept. 67).

(bb) Block 28—Remarks. Use this space for reporting important facts such as:

(1) Delays, their cause, and responsible party (vessel, shore facility, Government representative, or others).

(2) Abnormal individual losses contributing to the total loss. Enter the cause of such losses as well as actual or estimated volumes involved. Such losses shall include, but not be restricted to, product remaining aboard (enter tanks in which contained), spillages, line breaks, etc. Note where gravity group change of receiving tank contents results in a fictitious loss or gain. Note irregularities observed on comparing vessel ullages obtained at loading point with those at the discharge point if they indicate an abnormal transportation loss or contamination.

(cc) Block 29—Company or receiving terminal. Line out "COMPANY OR." Secure the signature of a representative of the receiving terminal.

(dd) Block 30—Certification by government representative. Line out "loaded." The Government representative shall date and sign the form to certify inspection and acceptance, as applicable, by the Government. The name of the individual signing the certification as well as the names applied in Blocks 29 and 31 shall be typed or hand lettered on the master or all copies of the form. The signature in Block 30 must agree with the typed or lettered name to be acceptable to the paying office.

(ee) Block 31—Certification by master or agent. Obtain the signature of the master of the vessel or the vessel's agent.

[Final rule, 71 FR 75890, 12/19/2006, effective 12/19/2006; Final rule, 76 FR 58122, 9/20/2011, effective 9/20/2011]

PART 8—DISTRIBUTION OF THE DD FORM 250-1

F-801 Distribution.

Follow the procedures at PGI F-801 for distribution of DD Form 250-1.

[Final rule, 76 FR 58122, 9/20/2011, effective 9/20/2011]

F-802 Corrected DD Form 250-1.

Follow the procedures at PGI F-802 when corrections to DD Form 250-1 are needed.

[Final rule, 76 FR 58122, 9/20/2011, effective 9/20/2011]

APPENDIX G—ACTIVITY ADDRESS NUMBERS

Parts 1-14—[Removed]

APPENDIX G—ACTIVITY ADDRESS NUMBERS

PARTS 1-14 [REMOVED]

[Removed, final rule, 68 FR 64555, 11/14/2003, effective 11/14/2003]

APPENDIX H—DEBARMENT AND SUSPENSION PROCEDURES

Table of Contents

Scope H-100
Notification H-101
Nature of proceeding H-102
Presentation of matters in opposition H-103
Fact-finding H-104
Timing requirements H-105
Subsequent to fact-finding H-106

APPENDIX H—DEBARMENT AND SUSPENSION PROCEDURES

H-100 Scope.

This appendix provides uniform debarment and suspension procedures to be followed by all debarring and suspending officials.

[DAC 91-6, 59 FR 27662, 5/27/94, effective 5/27/94]

H-101 Notification.

Contractors will be notified of the proposed debarment or suspension in accordance with FAR 9.406-3 or 9.407-3. A copy of the record which formed the basis for the decision by the debarring and suspending official will be made available to the contractor. If there is a reason to withhold from the contractor any portion of the record, the contractor will be informed of what is withheld and the reasons for such withholding.

[DAC 91-6, 59 FR 27662, 5/27/94, effective 5/27/94]

H-102 Nature of proceeding.

There are two distinct proceedings which may be involved in the suspension or debarment process. The first is the presentation of matters in opposition to the suspension or proposed debarment by the contractor.

The second is fact-finding which occurs only in cases in which the contractor's presentation of matters in opposition raises a genuine dispute over one or more material facts. In a suspension action based upon an indictment or in a proposed debarment action based upon a conviction or civil judgment, there will be no fact-finding proceeding concerning the matters alleged in the indictment, or the facts underlying the convictions or civil judgment. However, to the extent that the proposed action stems from the contractor's affiliation with an individual or firm indicted or convicted, or the subject of a civil judgment, fact-finding is permitted if a genuine dispute of fact is raised as to the question of affiliation as defined in FAR 9.403.

[DAC 91-6, 59 FR 27662, 5/27/94, effective 5/27/94]

H-103 Presentation of matters in opposition.

(a) In accordance with FAR 9.406-3(c) and 9.407-3(c), matters in opposition may be presented in person, in writing, or through a representative. Matters in opposition may be presented through any combination of the foregoing methods, but if a contractor desires to present matters in person or through a representative, any written material should be delivered at least 5 working days in advance of the presentation. Usually, all matters in opposition are presented in a single proceeding. A contractor who becomes aware of a pending indictment or allegations of wrongdoing that the contractor believes may lead to suspension or debarment action may contact the debarring and suspending official or designee to provide information as to the contractor's present responsibility.

(b) An in-person presentation is an informal meeting, nonadversarial in nature. The debarring and suspending official and/or other agency representatives may ask questions of the contractor or its representative making the presentation. The contractor may select the individuals who will attend the meeting on the contractor's behalf; individual respondents or principals of a business firm respondent may attend and speak for themselves.

(c) In accordance with FAR 9.406-3(c) and 9.407-3(c), the contractor may submit matters in opposition within 30 days from receipt of the notice of suspension or proposed debarment.

(d) The opportunity to present matters in opposition to debarment includes the opportunity to present matters concerning the duration of the debarment.

[DAC 91-6, 59 FR 27662, 5/27/94, effective 5/27/94]

H-104 Fact-finding.

(a) The debarring and suspending official will determine whether the contractor's presentation has raised a genuine dispute of material fact(s). If the debarring and suspending official has decided against debarment or continued suspension, or the provisions of FAR 9.4 preclude fact-finding, no fact-finding will be conducted. If the debarring and suspending official has determined a genuine dispute of material fact(s) exists, a designated fact-finder will conduct the fact-finding proceeding. The proceeding before the fact-finder will be limited to a finding of the facts in dispute as determined by the debarring and suspending official.

(b) The designated fact-finder will establish the date for a fact-finding proceeding, normally to be held within 45 working days of the contractor's presentation of matters in opposition. An official record will be made of the fact-finding proceeding.

(c) The Government's representative and the contractor will have an opportunity to present evidence relevant to the facts at issue. The contractor may appear in person or through a representative in the fact-finding proceeding.

(d) Neither the Federal Rules of Evidence nor the Federal Rules of Civil Procedure govern fact-finding. Hearsay evidence may be presented and will be given appropriate weight by the fact-finder.

(e) Witnesses may testify in person. Witnesses will be reminded of the official nature of the proceeding and that any false testimony given is subject to criminal prosecution. Witnesses are subject to cross-examination.

[DAC 91-6, 59 FR 27662, 5/27/94, effective 5/27/94]

H-105 Timing requirements.

All timing requirements set forth in these procedures may be extended by the debarring and suspending official for good cause.

[DAC 91-6, 59 FR 27662, 5/27/94, effective 5/27/94]

H-106 Subsequent to fact-finding.

(a) Written findings of fact will be prepared by the fact-finder as mandated by FAR 9.406-3(d)(2)(i) and 9.407-3(d)(2)(i).

(b) The fact-finder will determine the disputed fact(s) by a preponderance of the evidence. A copy of the findings of fact will be provided to the debarring and suspending official, the Government's representative, and the contractor.

(c) The debarring and suspending official will determine whether to continue the suspension or to debar the contractor based upon the entire administrative record, including the findings of fact.

(d) Prompt written notice of the debarring and suspending official's decision will be sent to the contractor and any affiliates involved, in compliance with FAR 9.406-3(e) and 9.407-3(d)(4).

[DAC 91-6, 59 FR 27662, 5/27/94, effective 5/27/94]

APPENDIX I—POLICY AND PROCEDURES FOR THE DOD PILOT MENTOR-PROTEGE PROGRAM

Table of Contents

Purpose I-100
Definitions I-101
Affiliation I-101.1
Minority institution of higher education I-101.2
Nontraditional Defense Contractor I-101.3
Eligible entity employing the severely disabled I-101.4
Severely disabled individual I-101.5
Women-owned small business I-101.6
Service-disabled veteran-owned small business I-101.7
Participant eligibility I-102
Program duration I-103
Selection of protege firms I-104
Mentor approval process I-105
Development of mentor-protege agreements mentor firms I-106
Elements of a mentor-protege agreements I-107
Submission and approval of mentor-protege agreements I-108
Reimburseable Agreements I-109
Credit agreements I-110
Program provisions applicable to credit agreements I-110.1
Credit adjustments I-110.2
Agreement terminations I-111
Reporting requirements I-112
Reporting requirements applicable to Individual Subcontract Reports (ISR), Summary Subcontract Reports (SSR) and Standard Forms 294 . . . . I-112.1
Program specific reporting requirements I-112.2
Performance reviews I-113

APPENDIX I—POLICY AND PROCEDURES FOR THE DOD PILOT MENTOR-PROTEGE PROGRAM

I-100 Purpose.

(a) This Appendix I to 48 CFR chapter 2 implements the Pilot Mentor-Protégé Program (hereafter referred to as the "Program") established under section 831 of Public Law 101-510, the National Defense Authorization Act for Fiscal Year 1991 (10 U.S.C. 2302 note), as amended through November 25, 2015. The purpose of the Program is to provide incentives to major DoD contractors to furnish eligible small business concerns with assistance designed to—

(1) Enhance the capabilities of eligible small business concerns to perform as subcontractors and suppliers under DoD contracts and other contracts and subcontracts; and

(2) Increase the participation of such business concerns as subcontractors and suppliers under DoD contracts, other Federal Government contracts, and commercial contracts.

(b) Under the Program, eligible companies approved as mentor firms will enter into mentor-protege agreements with eligible protege firms to provide appropriate developmental assistance to enhance the capabilities of the protege firms to perform as subcontractors and suppliers. DoD may provide the mentor firm with either cost reimbursement or credit against applicable subcontracting goals established under contracts with DoD or other Federal agencies.

(c) DoD will measure the overall success of the Program by the extent to which the Program results in—

(1) An increase in the dollar value of contract and subcontract awards to protege firms (under DoD contracts, contracts awarded by other Federal agencies, and commercial contracts) from the date of their entry into the Program until 2 years after the conclusion of the agreement;

(2) An increase in the number and dollar value of subcontracts awarded to a protege firm (or former protege firm) by its mentor firm (or former mentor firm);

(3) An increase in the employment level of protege firms from the date of entry into the Program until 2 years after the completion of the agreement.

(d) This policy sets forth the procedures for participation in the Program applicable to companies that are interested in receiving—

(1) Reimbursement through a separate contract line item in a DoD contract or a separate contract with DoD; or

(2) Credit toward applicable subcontracting goals for costs incurred under the Program.

[Interim rule, 66 FR 47108, 9/11/2001, effective 9/11/2001, finalized without change, 67 FR 11435, 3/14/2002, effective 3/14/2002; Final rule, 69 FR 74995, 12/15/2004, effective 12/15/2004; Final rule, 83 FR 12682, 3/23/2018, effective 3/23/2018]

I-101 Definitions. (No Text)

I-101.1 Affiliation.

With respect to a relationship between a mentor firm and a protege firm, a relationship described under 13 CFR 121.103.

[Final rule, 83 FR 54677, 10/31/2018, effective 10/31/2018]

I-101.2 Minority institution of higher education.

An institution of higher education with a student body that reflects the composition specified in section 312(b)(3), (4), and (5) of the Higher Education Act of 1965 (20 U.S.C. 1058(b)(3), (4), and (5)).

[Interim rule, 65 FR 6554, 2/10/2000, effective 2/10/2000, finalized without change, 65 FR 50149, 8/17/2000; Final rule, 69 FR 74995, 12/15/2004, effective 12/15/2004; Final rule, 83 FR 12682, 3/23/2018, effective 3/23/2018; Final rule, 83 FR 54677, 10/31/2018, effective 10/31/2018]

I-101.3 Nontraditional Defense Contractor

An entity that is not currently performing and has not performed any contract or subcontract for DoD that is subject to full coverage under the cost accounting standards prescribed pursuant to 41 U.S.C. 1502 and the regulations implementing such section, for at least the 1-year period preceding the solicitation of sources by DoD for the procurement (10 U.S.C. 2302(9)).

[Final rule, 83 FR 12682, 3/23/2018, effective 3/23/2018; Final rule, 83 FR 54677, 10/31/2018, effective 10/31/2018]

I-101.4 Eligible entity employing the severely disabled.

A business entity operated on a for-profit or nonprofit basis that—

(a) Uses rehabilitative engineering to provide employment opportunities for severely disabled individuals and integrates severely disabled individuals into its workforce;

(b) Employs severely disabled individuals at a rate that averages not less than 20 percent of its total workforce;

(c) Employs each severely disabled individual in its workforce generally on the basis of 40 hours per week; and

(d) Pays not less than the minimum wage prescribed pursuant to section 6 of the Fair Labor Standards Act (29 U.S.C. 206) to those employees who are severely disabled individuals.

[Final rule, 69 FR 74995, 12/15/2004, effective 12/15/2004; Final rule, 83 FR 54677, 10/31/2018, effective 10/31/2018]

I-101.5 Severely disabled individual.

An individual who is blind or severely disabled as defined in 41 U.S.C. 8501.

[Final rule, 69 FR 74995, 12/15/2004, effective 12/15/2004; Final rule, 76 FR 58137, 9/20/2011, effective 9/20/2011; Final rule, 77 FR 35879, 6/15/2012, effective 6/15/2012; Final rule, 83 FR 12682, 3/23/2018, effective 3/23/2018; Final rule, 83 FR 54677, 10/31/2018, effective 10/31/2018]

I-101.6 Women-owned small business.

A small business concern owned and controlled by women as defined in section 8(d)(3)(D) of the Small Business Act (15 U.S.C. 637(d)(3)(D)).

[Final rule, 69 FR 74995, 12/15/2004, effective 12/15/2004; Interim rule, 70 FR 29644, 5/24/2005, effective 5/24/2005; Final rule, 71 FR 3414, 1/23/2006, effective 1/23/2006; Final rule, 83 FR 12682, 3/23/2018, effective 3/23/2018; Final rule, 83 FR 54677, 10/31/2018, effective 10/31/2018]

I-101.7 Service-disabled veteran-owned small business.

A small business concern owned and controlled by service-disabled veterans as defined in section 8(d)(3) of the Small Business Act (15 U.S.C. 637(d)(3)).

[Interim rule, 70 FR 29644, 5/24/2005, effective 5/245/2005; Final rule, 71 FR 3414, 1/23/2006, effective 1/23/2006; Final rule, 83 FR 12682, 3/23/2018, effective 3/23/2018; Final rule, 83 FR 54677, 10/31/2018, effective 10/31/2018]

I-102 Participant eligibility.

(a) To be eligible to participate as a mentor, an entity must—

(1) Be eligible for the award of Federal contracts;

(2) Demonstrate that it—

(i) Is qualified to provide assistance that will contribute to the purpose of the Program;

(ii) Is of good financial health and character; and

(iii) Is not on a Federal list of debarred or suspended contractors; and

(3) Be capable of imparting value to a protégé firm because of experience gained as a DoD contractor or through knowledge of general business operations and Government contracting, as demonstrated by evidence that such entity—

(i) Received DoD contracts and subcontracts equal to or greater than $100 million during the previous fiscal year;

(ii) Is an other-than-small business, unless a waiver to the small business exception has been obtained from the Director, Small Business Programs (SBP), OUSD(A&S);

(iii) Is a prime contractor to DoD with an active subcontracting plan; or

(iv) Has graduated from the 8(a) Business Development Program and provides documentation of its ability to serve as a mentor.

(b) To be eligible to participate as a protégé, an entity must be—

(1) A small business concern;

(2) Eligible for the award of Federal contracts;

(3) Less than half the Small Business Administration (SBA) size standard for its primary North American Industry Classification System (NAICS) code;

(4) Not owned or managed by individuals or entities that directly or indirectly have stock options or convertible securities in the mentor firm; and

(5) At least one of the following:

(i) A qualified HUBZone small business concern.

(ii) A women-owned small business concern.

(iii) A service-disabled veteran-owned small business concern.

(iv) An entity owned and controlled by an Indian tribe.

(v) An entity owned and controlled by a Native Hawaiian organization.

(vi) An entity owned and controlled by socially and economically disadvantaged individuals.

(vii) A qualified organization employing severely disabled individuals.

(viii) A nontraditional defense contractor.

(ix) An entity that currently provides goods or services in the private sector that are critical to enhancing the capabilities of the defense supplier base and fulfilling key DoD needs.

(c) Mentor firms may rely in good faith on a written representation that the entity meets the requirements of paragraph (b) of this section, except that a mentor firm is required to confirm a protégé's status as a HUBZone small business concern (see FAR 19.703(d)).

(d) If at any time the SBA (or DoD in the case of entities employing severely disabled individuals) determines that a protégé is ineligible, assistance that the mentor firm furnishes to the protégé after the date of the determination may not be considered assistance furnished under the Program.

(e) A mentor firm may not enter into an agreement with a protegé firm if SBA has made a determination of affiliation. If SBA has not made such a determination and if the DoD Office of Small Business Programs (OSBP) has reason to believe, based on SBA's regulations regarding affiliation, that the mentor firm is affiliated with the protégé firm, then DoD OSBP will request a determination regarding affiliation from SBA.

(f) A company may not be approved for participation in the Program as a mentor firm if, at the time of requesting participation in the Program, it is currently debarred or suspended from contracting with the Federal Government pursuant to FAR subpart 9.4.

(g) If the mentor firm is suspended or debarred while performing under an approved mentor-protege agreement, the mentor firm—

(1) May continue to provide assistance to its protege firms pursuant to approved mentor-protege agreements entered into prior to the imposition of such suspension or debarment;

(2) May not be reimbursed or take credit for any costs of providing developmental assistance to its protege firm, incurred more than 30 days after the imposition of such suspension or debarment; and

(3) Must promptly give notice of its suspension or debarment to its protege firm and the cognizant Component Director, SBP.

[Interim rule, 65 FR 6554, 2/10/2000, effective 2/10/2000, finalized without change, 65 FR 50149, 8/17/2000; Interim rule, 66 FR 47108, 9/11/2001, effective 9/11/2001, finalized without change, 67 FR 11435, 3/14/2002, effective 3/14/2002; Final rule, 67 FR 77936, 12/20/2002, effective 12/20/2002; Final rule, 69 FR 74995, 12/15/2004, effective 12/15/2004; Interim rule, 70 FR 29644, 5/24/2005, effective

5/24/2005; Final rule, 71 FR 3414, 1/23/2006, effective 1/23/2006; Final rule, 73 FR 46813, 8/12/2008, effective 8/12/2008; Final rule, 83 FR 12682, 3/23/2018, effective 3/23/2018; Final rule, 83 FR 54677, 10/31/2018, effective 10/31/2018]

I-103 Program duration.

(a) New mentor-protege agreements may be submitted and approved through September 30, 2018.

(b) Mentors incurring costs prior to September 30, 2021, pursuant to an approved mentor-protege agreement may be eligible for—

(1) Credit toward the attainment of its applicable subcontracting goals for unreimbursed costs incurred in providing developmental assistance to its protege firm(s);

(2) Reimbursement pursuant to the execution of a separately priced contract line item added to a DoD contract; or

(3) Reimbursement pursuant to entering into a separate DoD contract upon determination by the cognizant Component Director, SBP, that unusual circumstances justify using a separate contract.

[Interim rule, 65 FR 6554, 2/10/2000, effective 2/10/2000, corrected 65 FR 30191, 5/10/2000, finalized without change, 65 FR 50149, 8/17/2000; Interim rule, 66 FR 47108, 9/11/2001, effective 9/11/2001, finalized without change, 67 FR 11435, 3/14/2002, effective 3/14/2002; Final rule, 67 FR 77936, 12/20/2002, effective 12/20/2002; Final rule, 69 FR 74995, 12/15/2004, effective 12/15/2004; Interim rule, 70 FR 29644, 5/24/2005, effective 5/24/2005; Final rule, 71 FR 3414, 1/23/2006, effective 1/23/2006; Final rule, 73 FR 46813, 8/12/2008, effective 8/12/2008; Final rule, 76 FR 71467, 11/18/2011, effective 11/18/2011; Final rule, 77 FR 11367, 2/24/2012, effective 2/24/2012; Final rule, 83 FR 12682, 3/23/2018, effective 3/23/2018]

I-104 Selection of protege firms.

(a) Mentor firms will be solely responsible for selecting protégé firms that qualify under I-102(b). Mentor firms are encouraged to identify and select concerns that have not previously received significant prime contract awards from DoD or any other Federal agency.

(b) The selection of protege firms by mentor firms may not be protested, except as in paragraph (c) of this section.

(c) In the event of a protest regarding the size or disadvantaged status of an entity selected to be a protege firm, the mentor firm must refer the protest to the SBA to resolve in accordance with 13 CFR part 121 (with respect to size) or 13 CFR part 124 (with respect to disadvantaged status).

(d) For purposes of the Small Business Act, no determination of affiliation or control (either direct or indirect) may be found between a protege firm and its mentor firm on the basis that the mentor firm has agreed to furnish (or has furnished) to its protege firm, pursuant to a mentor-protege agreement, any form of developmental assistance described in I-106(d)(d).

(e) A protégé firm may not be a party to more than one DoD mentor-protégé agreement at a time, and may only participate in the Program during the 5-year period beginning on the date the protégé firm enters into its first mentor-protégé agreement.

[Interim rule, 66 FR 47108, 9/11/2001, effective 9/11/2001, finalized without change, 67 FR 11435, 3/14/2002, effective 3/14/2002; Final rule, 69 FR 74995, 12/15/2004, effective 12/15/2004; Interim rule, 70 FR 29644, 5/24/2005, effective 5/24/2005; Final rule, 71 FR 3414, 1/23/2006, effective 1/23/2006; Final rule, 83 FR 12682, 3/23/2018, effective 3/23/2018]

I-105 Mentor approval process.

(a) An entity seeking to participate as a mentor must apply to the cognizant Component Director, SBP, to establish its initial eligibility as a mentor. This application may accompany its initial mentor-protege agreement.

(b) The application must provide the following information:

(1) A statement that the entity meets the requirements in I-102(a), specifying the cri-

teria in I-102(a)(3) under which the entity is applying.

(2) A summary of the entity's historical and recent activities and accomplishments under its small and disadvantaged business utilization program.

(3) The total dollar amount of DoD contracts and subcontracts that the entity received during the 2 preceding fiscal years. (Show prime contracts and subcontracts separately per year.)

(4) The total dollar amount of all other Federal agency contracts and subcontracts that the entity received during the 2 preceding fiscal years. (Show prime contracts and subcontracts separately per year.)

(5) The total dollar amount of subcontracts that the entity awarded under DoD contracts during the 2 preceding fiscal years.

(6) The total dollar amount of subcontracts that the entity awarded under all other Federal agency contracts during the 2 preceding fiscal years.

(7) The total dollar amount and percentage of subcontracts that the entity awarded to firms qualifying under I-102(b)(5)(ii) through (viii) during the 2 preceding fiscal years. (Show DoD subcontract awards separately.) If the entity was required to submit a Summary Subcontract Report (SSR) in the Electronic Subcontracting Reporting System, the request must include copies of the final reports for the 2 preceding fiscal years.

(8) Information on the company's ability to provide developmental assistance to eligible proteges.

(c) A template of the mentor application is available at: *http://www.acq.osd.mil/osbp/sb/programs/mpp/resources.shtml*.

(d) Companies that apply for participation and are not approved will be provided the reasons and an opportunity to submit additional information for reconsideration.

[Final rule, 69 FR 74995, 12/15/2004, effective 12/15/2004; Interim rule, 70 FR 29644, 5/24/2005, effective 5/24/2005; Final rule, 71 FR 3414, 1/23/2006, effective 1/23/2006; Final rule, 73 FR 46813, 8/12/2008, effective 8/12/2008; Interim rule, 75 FR 65439, 10/25/2010, effective 10/25/2010; Final rule, 83 FR 12682, 3/23/2018, effective 3/23/2018]

I-106 Development of mentor-protege agreements.

(a) Prospective mentors and their proteges may choose to execute letters of intent prior to negotiation of mentor-protege agreements.

(b) The agreements should be structured after completion of a preliminary assessment of the developmental needs of the protege firm and mutual agreement regarding the developmental assistance to be provided to address those needs and enhance the protege's ability to perform successfully under contracts or subcontracts.

(c) A mentor firm may not require a protege firm to enter into a mentor-protege agreement as a condition for award of a contract by the mentor firm, including a subcontract under a DoD contract awarded to the mentor firm.

(d) The mentor-protege agreement may provide for the mentor firm to furnish any or all of the following types of developmental assistance:

(1) Assistance by mentor firm personnel in—

(i) General business management, including organizational management, financial management, and personnel management, marketing, and overall business planning;

(ii) Engineering and technical matters such as production inventory control and quality assurance; and

(iii) Any other assistance designed to develop the capabilities of the protege firm under the developmental program described in I-107(g).

(2) Award of subcontracts to the protégé firm under DoD contracts or other contracts on a noncompetitive basis.

(3) Payment of progress payments for the performance of subcontracts by a protege firm in amounts as provided for in the subcontract; but in no event may any such progress payment exceed 100 percent of the costs incurred by the protege firm for the performance of the subcontract. Provision of progress payments by a mentor firm to a

protege firm at a rate other than the customary rate for the firm must be implemented in accordance with FAR 32.504(c).

(4) Advance payments under such subcontracts. The mentor firm must administer advance payments in accordance with FAR Subpart 32.4.

(5) Loans.

(6) Assistance that the mentor firm obtains for the protege firm from one or more of the following:

(i) Small Business Development Centers established pursuant to section 21 of the Small Business Act (15 U.S.C. 648).

(ii) Entities providing procurement technical assistance pursuant to 10 U.S.C. Chapter 142 (Procurement Technical Assistance Centers).

(iii) Historically Black colleges and universities.

(iv) Minority institutions of higher education.

(v) Women's business centers described in section 29 of the Small Business Act (15 U.S.C. 656).

(e) Pursuant to FAR 31.109, approved mentor firms seeking either reimbursement or credit are strongly encouraged to enter into an advance agreement with the contracting officer responsible for determining final indirect cost rates under FAR 42.705. The purpose of the advance agreement is to establish the accounting treatment of the costs of the developmental assistance pursuant to the mentor-protege agreement prior to the incurring of any costs by the mentor firm. An advance agreement is an attempt by both the Government and the mentor firm to avoid possible subsequent dispute based on questions related to reasonableness, allocability, or allowability of the costs of developmental assistance under the Program. Absent an advance agreement, mentor firms are advised to establish the accounting treatment of such costs and to address the need for any changes to their cost accounting practices that may result from the implementation of a mentor-protege agreement, prior to incurring any costs, and irrespective of whether costs will be reimbursed or credited.

(f) Developmental assistance provided under an approved mentor-protege agreement is distinct from, and must not duplicate, any effort that is the normal and expected product of the award and administration of the mentor firm's subcontracts. Costs associated with the latter must be accumulated and charged in accordance with the contractor's approved accounting practices; they are not considered developmental assistance costs eligible for either credit or reimbursement under the Program.

[Final rule, 69 FR 74995, 12/15/2004, effective 12/15/2004; Final rule, 83 FR 12682, 3/23/2018, effective 3/23/2018; Final rule, 83 FR 54677, 10/31/2018, effective 10/31/2018]

I-107 Elements of a mentor-protege agreement.

Each mentor-protege agreement shall contain—

(a) The name, address, e-mail address, and telephone number of the mentor and protege points of contact;

(b) The NAICS code(s) that represent the contemplated supplies or services to be provided by the protégé firm to the mentor firm and a statement that, at the time the agreement is submitted for approval, the protégé firm does not exceed the size standard in I-102(b)(3);

(c) A statement that the protege firm is eligible to participate in accordance with I-102(a);

(d) A statement that the mentor is eligible to participate in accordance with I-102(a);

(e) Assurances that—

(1) The mentor firm does not share, directly or indirectly, with the protégé firm ownership or management of the protégé firm;

(2) The mentor firm does not have an agreement, at the time the mentor firm enters into a mentor-protégé agreement, to merge with the protégé firm;

(3) The owners and managers of the mentor firm are not the parent, child, spouse,

sibling, aunt, uncle, niece, nephew, grandparent, grandchild, or first cousin of an owner or manager of the protégé firm;

(4) The mentor firm has not, during the 2-year period before entering into a mentor-protégé agreement, employed any officer, director, principal stock holder, managing member, or key employee of the protégé firm;

(5) The mentor firm has not engaged in a joint venture with the protégé firm during the 2-year period before entering into a mentor-protégé agreement, unless such joint venture was approved by SBA prior to making any offer on a contract;

(6) The mentor firm is not, directly or indirectly, the primary party providing contracts to the protégé firm, as measured by the dollar value of the contracts; and

(7) The SBA has not made a determination of affiliation or control;

(f) A preliminary assessment of the developmental needs of the protégé firm;

(g) A developmental program for the protégé firm including—

(1) The type of assistance the mentor will provide to the protégé and how that assistance will—

(i) Increase the protégé's ability to participate in DoD, Federal, and/or commercial contracts and subcontracts; and

(ii) Increase small business subcontracting opportunities in industry categories where eligible protégés or other small business firms are not dominant in the company's vendor base;

(2) Factors to assess the protégé firm's developmental progress under the Program, including specific milestones for providing each element of the identified assistance;

(3) A description of the quantitative and qualitative benefits to DoD from the agreement, if applicable; and

(4) Goals for additional awards for which the protégé firm can compete outside the Program;

(h) The assistance the mentor will provide to the protégé firm in understanding Federal contract regulations, including the FAR and DFARS, after award of a subcontract under the Program, if applicable;

(i) An estimate of the dollar value and type of subcontracts that the mentor firm will award to the protege firm, and the period of time over which the subcontracts will be awarded;

(j) A statement from the protege firm indicating its commitment to comply with the requirements for reporting and for review of the agreement during the duration of the agreement and for 2 years thereafter;

(k) A program participation term for the agreement that does not exceed 3 years. Requests for an extension of the agreement for a period not to exceed an additional 2 years are subject to the approval of the cognizant Component Director, SBP. The justification must detail the unusual circumstances that warrant a term in excess of 3 years;

(l) Procedures for the mentor firm to notify the protege firm in writing at least 30 days in advance of the mentor firm's intent to voluntarily withdraw its participation in the Program. A mentor firm may voluntarily terminate its mentor-protege agreement(s) only if it no longer wants to be a participant in the Program as a mentor firm. Otherwise, a mentor firm must terminate a mentor-protege agreement for cause;

(m) Procedures for the mentor firm to terminate the mentor-protege agreement for cause which provide that—

(1) The mentor firm must furnish the protege firm a written notice of the proposed termination, stating the specific reasons for such action, at least 30 days in advance of the effective date of such proposed termination;

(2) The protege firm must have 30 days to respond to such notice of proposed termination, and may rebut any findings believed to be erroneous and offer a remedial program;

(3) Upon prompt consideration of the protege firm's response, the mentor firm must either withdraw the notice of proposed termination and continue the protege firm's participation, or issue the notice of termination; and

(4) The decision of the mentor firm regarding termination for cause, conforming with the requirements of this section, will be final and is not reviewable by DoD;

(n) Procedures for a protege firm to notify the mentor firm in writing at least 30 days in advance of the protege firm's intent to voluntarily terminate the mentor-protege agreement;

(o) Additional terms and conditions as may be agreed upon by both parties; and

(p) Signatures and dates for both parties to the mentor-protege agreement.

[Final rule, 69 FR 74995, 12/15/2004, effective 12/15/2004; Interim rule, 70 FR 29644, 5/24/2005, effective 5/24/2005; Final rule, 71 FR 3414, 1/23/2006, effective 1/23/2006; Final rule, 73 FR 46813, 8/12/2008, effective 8/12/2008; Final rule, 83 FR 12682, 3/23/2018, effective 3/23/2018; Final rule, 83 FR 54677, 10/31/2018, effective 10/31/2018]

I-108 Submission and approval of mentor-protege agreements.

(a) Upon solicitation or as determined by the cognizant DoD component, mentors will submit—

(1) A mentor application pursuant to I-105, if the mentor has not been previously approved to participate;

(2) A signed mentor-protege agreement pursuant to I-107;

(3) A statement as to whether the mentor is seeking credit or reimbursement of costs incurred;

(4) The estimated cost of the technical assistance to be provided, broken out per year;

(5) A justification if program participation term is greater than 3 years (Term of agreements may not exceed 5 years); and

(6) For reimbursable agreements, a specific justification for developmental costs in excess of $1,000,000 per year.

(b) When seeking reimbursement of costs, cognizant DoD components may require additional information.

(c) The mentor-protege agreement must be approved by the cognizant Component Director, SBP, prior to incurring costs eligible for credit.

(d) The cognizant DoD component will execute a contract modification or a separate contract, if justified pursuant to I-103(b)(3), prior to the mentor's incurring costs eligible for reimbursement.

(e) Credit agreements that are not associated with an existing DoD program and/or component will be submitted for approval to Director, SBP, Defense Contract Management Agency (DCMA), via the mentor's cognizant administrative contracting officer.

(f) A prospective mentor that has identified Program funds to be made available from a DoD program manager must provide the information in paragraph (a) of this section through the program manager to the cognizant Component Director, SBP, with a letter signed by the program manager indicating the amount of funding that has been identified for the developmental assistance program.

[Final rule, 69 FR 74995, 12/15/2004, effective 12/15/2004; Final rule, 73 FR 46813, 8/12/2008, effective 8/12/2008]

I-109 Reimburseable Agreements.

The following program provisions apply to all reimbursable mentor-protege agreements:

(a) Assistance provided in the form of progress payments to a protege firm in excess of the customary progress payment rate for the firm will be reimbursed only if implemented in accordance with FAR 32.504(c).

(b) Assistance provided in the form of advance payments will be reimbursed only if the payments have been provided to a protege firm under subcontract terms and conditions similar to those in the clause at FAR 52.232-12, Advance Payments. Reimbursement of any advance payments will be made pursuant to the inclusion of the clause at DFARS 252.232-7005, Reimbursement of Subcontractor Advance Payments—DoD Pilot Mentor-protege Program, in appropriate contracts. In requesting reimbursement, the mentor firm agrees that the risk of any financial loss due to the failure or inability of a protege firm to repay any unliquidated advance payments will be the sole responsibility of the mentor firm.

(c) The primary forms of developmental assistance authorized for reimbursement under the Program are identified in I-106(d). On a case-by-case basis, Component Directors, SBP, at their discretion, may approve additional incidental expenses for reimbursement, provided these expenses do not exceed 10 percent of the total estimated cost of the agreement.

(d) The total amount reimbursed to a mentor firm for costs of assistance furnished to a protege firm in a fiscal year may not exceed $1,000,000 unless the cognizant Component Director, SBP, determines in writing that unusual circumstances justify reimbursement at a higher amount. Request for authority to reimburse in excess of $1,000,000 must detail the unusual circumstances and must be endorsed and submitted by the program manager to the cognizant Component Director, SBP.

(e) DoD may not reimburse any fee to the mentor firm for services provided to the protégé firm pursuant to I-106(d)(6) or for business development expenses incurred by the mentor firm under a contract awarded to the mentor firm while participating in a joint venture with the protégé firm.

(f) Developmental assistance costs that are incurred pursuant to an approved reimbursable mentor-protege agreement, and have been charged to, but not reimbursed through, a separate contract, or through a separately priced contract line item added to a DoD contract, will not be otherwise reimbursed, as either a direct or indirect cost, under any other DoD contract, irrespective of whether the costs have been recognized for credit against applicable subcontracting goals.

[Final rule, 69 FR 74995, 12/15/2004, effective 12/15/2004; Final rule, 73 FR 46813, 8/12/2008, effective 8/12/2008; Final rule, 83 FR 12682, 3/23/2018, effective 3/23/2018]

I-110 Credit agreements. (No Text)

I-110.1 Program provisions applicable to credit agreements.

(a) Developmental assistance costs incurred by a mentor firm for providing assistance to a protege firm pursuant to an approved credit mentor-protege agreement may be credited as if the costs were incurred under a subcontract award to that protege, for the purpose of determining the performance of the mentor firm in attaining an applicable subcontracting goal established under any contract containing a subcontracting plan pursuant to the clause at FAR 52.219-9, Small Business Subcontracting Plan, or the provisions of the DoD Test Program for Negotiation of Comprehensive Small Business Subcontracting Plans. Unreimbursed developmental assistance costs incurred for a protege firm that is an eligible entity employing severely disabled individuals may be credited toward the mentor firm's small disadvantaged business subcontracting goal, even if the protege firm is not a small disadvantaged business concern.

(b) Costs that have been reimbursed through inclusion in indirect expense pools may also be credited as subcontract awards for determining the performance of the mentor firm in attaining an applicable subcontracting goal established under any contract containing a subcontracting plan. However, costs that have not been reimbursed because they are not reasonable, allocable, or allowable will not be recognized for crediting purposes.

(c) Other costs that are not eligible for reimbursement pursuant to I-106(d) may be recognized for credit only if requested, identified, and incorporated in an approved mentor-protege agreement.

(d) The amount of credit a mentor firm may receive for any such unreimbursed developmental assistance costs must be equal to—

(1) Four times the total amount of such costs attributable to assistance provided by small business development centers, historically Black colleges and universities, minority institutions, and procurement technical assistance centers.

(2) Three times the total amount of such costs attributable to assistance furnished by the mentor's employees.

(3) Two times the total amount of other such costs incurred by the mentor in carrying out the developmental assistance program.

[Final rule, 69 FR 74995, 12/15/2004, effective 12/15/2004; Final rule, 83 FR 12682, 3/23/2018, effective 3/23/2018]

I-110.2 Credit adjustments.

(a) Adjustments may be made to the amount of credit claimed if the Director, SBP, OUSD(A&S), determines that—

(1) A mentor firm's performance in the attainment of its subcontracting goals through actual subcontract awards declined from the prior fiscal year without justifiable cause; and

(2) Imposition of such a limitation on credit appears to be warranted to prevent abuse of this incentive for the mentor firm's participation in the Program.

(b) The mentor firm must be afforded the opportunity to explain the decline in small business subcontract awards before imposition of any such limitation on credit. In making the final decision to impose a limitation on credit, the Director, SBP, OUSD(A&S), must consider—

(1) The mentor firm's overall small business participation rates (in terms of percentages of subcontract awards and dollars awarded) as compared to the participation rates existing during the 2 fiscal years prior to the firm's admission to the Program;

(2) The mentor firm's aggregate prime contract awards during the prior 2 fiscal years and the total amount of subcontract awards under such contracts; and

(3) Such other information the mentor firm may wish to submit.

(c) The decision of the Director, SBP, OUSD(A&S), regarding the imposition of a limitation on credit will be final.

[Final rule, 69 FR 74995, 12/15/2004, effective 12/15/2004; Final rule, 73 FR 46813, 8/12/2008, effective 8/12/2008; Final rule, 83 FR 12682, 3/23/2018, effective 3/23/2018]

I-111 Agreement terminations.

(a) Mentors and/or proteges must send a copy of any termination notices to the cognizant Component Director, SBP, that approved the agreement, and the DCMA administrative contracting officer responsible for conducting the annual review pursuant to I-113.

(b) For reimbursable agreements, mentors must also send copies of any termination to the program manager and to the contracting officer.

(c) Termination of a mentor-protege agreement will not impair the obligations of the mentor firm to perform pursuant to its contractual obligations under Government contracts and subcontracts.

(d) Termination of all or part of the mentor-protege agreement will not impair the obligations of the protege firm to perform pursuant to its contractual obligations under any contract awarded to the protege firm by the mentor firm.

(e) Mentors and proteges will follow provisions of the mentor-protege agreement developed in compliance with I-107(l) through (n).

[Final rule, 69 FR 74995, 12/15/2004, effective 12/15/2004; Final rule, 73 FR 46813, 8/12/2008, effective 8/12/2008; Final rule, 83 FR 54677, 10/31/2018, effective 10/31/2018]

I-112 Reporting requirements. (No Text)

I-112.1 Reporting requirements applicable to Individual Subcontract Reports (ISR), Summary Subcontract Reports (SSR) and Standard Forms 294.

(a) Amounts credited toward applicable subcontracting goal(s) for unreimbursed costs under the Program must be separately identified on the appropriate ISR, SSR or SF294 reports from the amounts credited toward the goal(s) resulting from the award of actual subcontracts to protege firms. The combination of the two must equal the mentor firm's overall accomplishment toward the applicable goal(s).

(b) A mentor firm may receive credit toward the attainment of an applicable subcontracting goal for each subcontract awarded by the mentor firm to an entity that qualifies as a protege firm pursuant to I-102(b).

[Final rule, 69 FR 74995, 12/15/2004, effective 12/15/2004; Interim rule, 75 FR 65439, 10/25/2010, effective 10/25/2010; Interim rule, 79 FR 61579, 10/14/2014, effective 10/14/2014; Final rule, 83 FR 12682, 3/23/2018, effective 3/23/2018]

I-112.2 Program specific reporting requirements.

(a) Mentors must report on the progress made under active mentor-protégé agreements semiannually for the periods ending March 31st and September 30th throughout the Program participation term of the agreement. The September 30th report must address the entire fiscal year.

(1) Reports are due 30 days after the close of each reporting period.

(2) Each report must include the following data on performance under the mentor-protégé agreement:

(i) Dollars obligated (for reimbursable agreements).

(ii) Expenditures.

(iii) Dollars credited, if any, toward applicable subcontracting goals as a result of developmental assistance provided to the protégé and a copy of the ISR or SF 294 and/or SSR for each contract where developmental assistance was credited.

(iv) Any new awards of subcontracts on a competitive or noncompetitive basis to the protégé firm under DoD contracts or other contracts, including the value of such subcontracts.

(v) All technical or management assistance provided by mentor firm personnel for the purposes described in I-106(d).

(vi) Any extensions, increases in the scope of work, or additional payments not previously reported for prior awards of subcontracts on a competitive or noncompetitive basis to the protégé firm under DoD contracts or other contracts, including the value of such subcontracts.

(vii) The amount of any payment of progress payments or advance payments made to the protégé firm for performance under any subcontract made under the Program.

(viii) Any loans made by the mentor firm to the protégé firm.

(ix) All Federal contracts awarded to the mentor firm and the protégé firm as a joint venture, designating whether the award was a restricted competition or a full and open competition.

(x) Any assistance obtained by the mentor firm for the protégé firm from the entities listed at I-106(d)(6).

(xi) Whether there have been any changes to the terms of the mentor-protégé agreement.

(xii) A narrative describing the following:

(A) The success assistance provided under I-106(d) has had in addressing the developmental needs of the protégé firm.

(B) The impact on DoD contracts.

(C) Any problems encountered.

(D) Any milestones achieved in the protégé firm's developmental program.

(E) Impact of the agreement in terms of capabilities enhanced, certifications received, and technology transferred.

(3) In accordance with section 861, paragraph (b)(2), of the National Defense Authorization Act for Fiscal Year 2016 (Pub. L. 114-92), the reporting requirements specified in paragraphs (a)(2)(iv) through (a)(2)(xii)(C) of this section apply retroactively to mentor-protégé agreements that were in effect on November 25, 2015. Mentors must submit reports as described in paragraph (a) of this section.

(4) A recommended reporting format and guidance for its submission are available at: *http://www.acq.osd.mil/osbp/sb/programs/mpp/resources.shtml.*

(b) The protégé must provide data, annually by October 31st, on the progress made during the prior fiscal year by the protégé in employment, revenues, and participation in DoD contracts during—

(1) Each fiscal year of the Program participation term; and

(2) Each of the 2 fiscal years following the expiration of the Program participation term.

(c) The protégé report required by paragraph (b) of this section may be provided as part of the mentor report for the period ending September 30th required by paragraph (a) of this section.

(d) Progress reports must be submitted—

(1) For credit agreements, to the cognizant Component Director, SBP, that approved the agreement, and the mentor's cognizant DCMA administrative contracting officer; and

(2) For reimbursable agreements, to the cognizant Component Director, SBP, the contracting officer, the DCMA administrative contracting officer, and the program manager.

[Final rule, 69 FR 74995, 12/15/2004, effective 12/15/2004; Final rule, 73 FR 46813, 8/12/2008, effective 8/12/2008; Interim rule, 75 FR 65439, 10/25/2010, effective 10/25/2010; Final rule, 78 FR 13546, 2/28/2013, effective 2/28/2013; Final rule, 83 FR 12682, 3/23/2018, effective 3/23/2018]

I-113 Performance reviews.

(a) DCMA will conduct annual performance reviews of the progress and accomplishments realized under approved mentor-protege agreements. These reviews must verify data provided on the semiannual reports and must provide information as to—

(1) Whether all costs reimbursed to the mentor firm under the agreement were reasonably incurred to furnish assistance to the protege in accordance with the mentor-protege agreement and applicable regulations and procedures; and

(2) Whether the mentor and protege accurately reported progress made by the protege in employment, revenues, and participation in DoD contracts during the Program participation term and for 2 fiscal years following the expiration of the Program participation term.

(b) A checklist for annual performance reviews is available at *http://www.acq.osd.mil/osbp/mentor_protege/*.

[Final rule, 69 FR 74995, 12/15/2004, effective 12/15/2004; Final rule, 73 FR 46813, 8/12/2008, effective 8/12/2008]

Procedures, Guidance, and Information

DoD Procedures, Guidance, and Information Parts 201—253

Table of Contents

Page

SUBCHAPTER A—GENERAL

Part 201—Federal Acquisition Regulations System 1205
Part 202—Definitions of Words and Terms 1219
Part 203—Improper Business Practices and Personal Conflicts of Interest 1223
Part 204—Administrative Matters 1227

SUBCHAPTER B—COMPETITION AND ACQUISITION PLANNING

Part 205—Publicizing Contract Actions 1281
Part 206—Competition Requirements 1285
Part 207—Acquisition Planning 1291
Part 208—Required Sources of Supplies and Services 1301
Part 209—Contractor Qualifcations 1333
Part 210—Market Research 1341
Part 211—Describing Agency Needs 1345
Part 212—Acquisition of Commercial Items 1351

SUBCHAPTER C—CONTRACTING METHODS AND CONTRACT TYPES

Part 213—Simplified Acquisition Procedures 1355
Part 215—Contracting by Negotiation 1361
Part 216—Types of Contracts 1379
Part 217—Special Contracting Methods 1393
Part 218—Emergency Acquisitions 1427

SUBCHAPTER D—SOCIOECONOMIC PROGRAMS

Part 219—Small Business Programs 1431
Part 222—Application of Labor Laws to Government Acquisitions 1437

Page

Part 223—Environment, Energy and Water Efficiency, Renewable Energy Technologies, Occupational Safety and Drug-Free Workplace 1447
Part 225—Foreign Acquisition 1451
Part 226—Other Socioeconomic Programs 1489

SUBCHAPTER E—GENERAL CONTRACTING REQUIREMENTS

Part 228—Bonds and Insurance 1493
Part 229—Taxes 1499
Part 230—Cost Accounting Standards Administration 1505
Part 231—Contract Cost Principles and Procedures 1509
Part 232—Contract Financing 1513
Part 233—Protests, Disputes, and Appeals 1521

SUBCHAPTER F—SPECIAL CATEGORIES OF CONTRACTING

Part 234—Major System Acquisition 1525
Part 235—Research and Development Contracting 1529
Part 236—Construction and Architect-Engineer Contracts 1533
Part 237—Service Contracting 1539
Part 239—Acquisition of Information Technology . . . 1547
Part 241—Acquisition of Utility Services 1553

SUBCHAPTER G—CONTRACT MANAGEMENT

Part 242—Contract Administration and Audit Services 1557
Part 243—Contract Modifications 1571
Part 244—Subcontracting Policies and Procedures 1575
Part 245—Government Property 1579
Part 246—Quality Assurance 1591
Part 247—Transportation 1597
Part 249—Termination of Contracts 1605

Page

Part 250—Extraordinary Contractual Actions and the Safety Act 1615
Part 251—Use of Government Sources by Contractors 1621

SUBCHAPTER H—CLAUSES AND FORMS

Part 252—Solicitation Provisions and Contract Clauses 1625
Part 253—Forms 1629

APPENDICES

F—Material Inspection and Receiving Report 1641

PART 201—FEDERAL ACQUISITION REGULATIONS SYSTEM

Table of Contents

Subpart 201.1—Purpose, Authority, Issuance

OMB approval under the Paperwork Reduction Act 201.106
Statutory acquisition-related dollar thresholds—adjustment for inflation . 201.109
Peer Reviews 201.170
Objective of Peer Reviews 201.170-1
Pre-award Peer Reviews 201.170-2
Post-award Peer Reviews of service contracts 201.170-3
Administration of Peer Reviews 201.170-4

Subpart 201.3—Agency Acquisition Regulations

Policy 201.301
Agency control and compliance procedures 201.304

Subpart 201.6—Career Development, Contracting Authority and Responsibilities

Contracting officers 201.602
Responsibilities 201.602-2

PART 201—FEDERAL ACQUISITION REGULATIONS SYSTEM

SUBPART 201.1—PURPOSE, AUTHORITY, ISSUANCE

201.106 OMB approval under the Paperwork Reduction Act.

The information collection and recordkeeping requirements contained in the Defense Federal Acquisition Regulations Supplement (DFARS) and Procedures, Guidance, and Information (PGI) have been approved by the Office of Management and Budget. The following OMB control numbers apply:

DFARS Segment	OMB Control No.
215.403-5	0704-0497
217.7004(a)	0704-0214
217.7404-3(b)	0704-0214
217.7505(d)	0704-0214
231.205-18	0704-0483
232.10	0704-0359
239.7408	0704-0341
242.1106	0704-0250
245.302(1)(i)	0704-0246
245.604-3(b) and3(d)	0704-0246
252.204-7000	0704-0225
252.204-7008	0704-0478
252.204-7010	0704-0454
252.204-7012	0704-0478
252.205-7000	0704-0286
252.208-7000	0704-0187
252.209-7001	0704-0187
252.209-7002	0704-0187
252.209-7004	0704-0187
252.209-7008	0704-0477
252.211-7004	0704-0398
252.211-7005	0704-0398
252.211-7006	0704-0434
252.211-7007	0704-0398

DFARS Segment	OMB Control No.
252.215-7002	0704-0232
252.215-7005	0704-0446
252.216-7000	0704-0259
252.216-7001	0704-0259
252.216-7003	0704-0259
252.217-7012	0704-0214
252.217-7026	0704-0214
252.217-7028	0704-0214
252.219-7003	0704-0386
252.223-7001	0704-0272
252.223-7002	0704-0272
252.223-7003	0704-0272
252.223-7004	0704-0272
252.223-7007	0704-0272
252.225-7000	0704-0229
252.225-7003	0704-0229
252.225-7004	0704-0229
252.225-7005	0704-0229
252.225-7010	0704-0229
252.225-7013	0704-0229
252.225-7018	0704-0229
252.225-7020	0704-0229
252.225-7021	0704-0229
252.225-7023	0704-0229
252.225-7025	0704-0229
252.225-7032	0704-0229
252.225-7033	0704-0229
252.225-7035	0704-0229
252.225-7039	0704-0549

DFARS Segment	OMB Control No.
252.225-7040	0704-0460
252.225-7046	0704-0229
252.225-7049	0704-0525
252.225-7050	0704-0187
252.227-7013	0704-0369
252.227-7014	0704-0369
252.227-7017	0704-0369
252.227-7018	0704-0369
252.227-7019	0704-0369
252.227-7025	0704-0369
252.227-7028	0704-0369
252.227-7037	0704-0369
252.228-7000	0704-0216
252.228-7005	0704-0216
252.228-7006	0704-0216
252.229-7010	0704-0390
252.232-7002	0704-0321
252.232-7007	0704-0359
252.234-7002	0704-0479
252.235-7000	0704-0187
252.235-7001	0704-0187
252.235-7003	0704-0187
252.236-7000	0704-0255
252.236-7002	0704-0255
252.236-7003	0704-0255
252.236-7004	0704-0255
252.236-7010	0704-0255
252.236-7012	0704-0255
252.237-7000	0704-0231

DFARS Segment	OMB Control No.
252.237-7011	0704-0231
252.237-7023	0704-0231
252.237-7024	0704-0231
252.239-7000	0704-0341
252.239-7006	0704-0341
252.239-7009	0704-0478
252.239-7010	0704-0478
252.242-7004	0704-0250
252.243-7002	0704-0397
252.244-7001	0704-0253
252.245-7003	0704-0246
252.246-7003	0704-0441
252.246-7005	0704-0481
252.246-7006	0704-0481
252.246-7008	0704-0541
252.247-7000	0704-0245
252.247-7001	0704-0245
252.247-7002	0704-0245
252.247-7007	0704-0245
252.247-7022	0704-0245
252.247-7023	0704-0245
252.247-7026	0704-0245
252.247-7028	0704-0245
252.249-7002	0704-0533
252.251-7000	0704-0252
Appendix F	0704-0248
Appendix I	0704-0332
DD Form 1348-1A	0704-0246
DD Form 1639	0704-0246

PGI 201.106

DFARS Segment	OMB Control No.
DD Form 1659	0704-0245
DD Form 2063	0704-0231
DD Form 2139	0704-0229
DD Form 250	0704-0248
DD Form 250-1	0704-0248

[Publication notice, 20151030, Publication notice, 20161104; Publication notice, 20171208; Publication notice, 20180323; Final rule, 84 FR 4370, 2/15/2019, effective 2/15/2019]

201.109 Statutory acquisition-related dollar thresholds—adjustment for inflation.

Statutory acquisition-related dollar thresholds are reviewed every 5 years to calculate adjustment for inflation, as required by Section 807 of the National Defense Authorization Act for Fiscal Year 2005 (Public Law 108-375). The matrix showing the most recent escalation adjustments of statutory acquisition-related dollar thresholds in the DFARS is available at *http://www.acq.osd.mil/dpap/dars/pgi/attachments/Matrix%20PGI.xls*.

[Final rule, 71 FR 75891, 12/19/2006, effective 12/19/2006; Final rule, 80 FR 58630, 9/30/2015, effective 9/30/2015]

201.170 Peer reviews. (No Text)

[Final rule, 74 FR 37625, 7/29/2009, effective 7/29/2009]

201.170-1 Objective of peer reviews.

The objectives of Peer Reviews are to—

(a) Ensure that DoD contracting officers are implementing policy and regulations in a consistent and appropriate manner;

(b) Continue to improve the quality of contracting processes throughout DoD; and

(c) Facilitate cross-sharing of best practices and lessons learned throughout DoD Defense Procurement and Acquisition Policy maintains a database of Peer Review recommendations, lessons learned, and best practices that is available at: *http://www.acq.osd.mil/dpap/cpic/cp/peerreviews.html*.

[Final rule, 74 FR 37625, 7/29/2009, effective 7/29/2009; Publication notice, 20101025; Final rule, 80 FR 58630, 9/30/2015, effective 9/30/2015]

201.170-2 Pre-award Peer Reviews.

(a) Pre-award Peer Reviews for competitive acquisitions shall be conducted prior to each of the following three phases of the acquisition:

(1) Issuance of the solicitation.

(2) Request for final proposal revisions (if applicable).

(3) Contract award.

(b) Pre-award Peer Reviews for non-competitive acquisitions shall be conducted prior to each of the following two phases of the acquisition:

(1) Negotiation.

(2) Contract award.

[Final rule, 74 FR 37625, 7/29/2009, effective 7/29/2009; Final rule, 80 FR 58630, 9/30/2015, effective 9/30/2015]

201.170-3 Post-award Peer Reviews of service contracts.

(a) If the base period of performance is greater than one year, the first post-award Peer Review should take place at the mid-point of the base period of performance. If the base period of performance is one year or less, the post-award Peer Review should occur prior to exercise of the first option year. Post-award Peer Reviews should occur prior to every option period thereafter.

(b) Post-award Peer Reviews shall be focused on—

(1) The adequacy of competition;

(2) An assessment of actual contract performance; and

(3) The adequacy of Government surveillance of contract performance.

[Final rule, 74 FR 37625, 7/29/2009, effective 7/29/2009; Final rule, 80 FR 58630, 9/30/2015, effective 9/30/2015]

201.170-4 Administration of Peer Reviews.

(a) The results and recommendations that are products of Peer Reviews are intended to be advisory in nature; however, in the event the Peer Review report includes a recommendation that is identified as "significant" and the contracting officer does not intend to follow that recommendation, the senior procurement official of the contracting activity for the reviewed organization must be made aware of this fact before action is taken (or inaction, as applicable) that is contrary to the recommendation. Reviews will be conducted in a manner that preserves the authority, judgment, and discretion of the contracting officer and the senior officials of the acquiring activity.

(b) Peer Review teams will be comprised of senior contracting officials and attorneys from throughout DoD. A senior official designated by the OSD Office of Small Business Programs will participate as a team member on Peer Reviews of services acquisitions. Teams will include civilian employees or military personnel external to the department, agency, or component that is the subject of the Peer Review.

(c) Generally, each review will be conducted at the location of the executing contracting organization.

(d) A list of the documents that must be made available to the review team, along with the specific elements the team will examine, is provided at the end of this PGI section.

(e) The review team observations and recommendations will be communicated to the contracting officer and the senior procurement official immediately upon completion of a review.

(f) The contracting officer shall document the disposition of all Peer Review recommendations (i.e., state whether the recommendation will be followed and, if not, why not) as a signed memorandum for the record in the applicable contract file. This memorandum must be executed prior to the next phase Peer Review or prior to contract award for Phase 3 reviews. For post-award Peer Reviews of services acquisitions, the memorandum must be executed prior to the next option exercise. The contracting officer shall provide a copy of the memorandum to: Deputy Director, Defense Procurement and Acquisition Policy (Contract Policy and International Contracting), 3060 Defense Pentagon, Washington, DC 20301-3060.

Pre-award Peer Reviews Required Documents and Elements

Required Documents: At a minimum, Peer Review teams shall have access to the following documents (as applicable):

1. The requirements document, to include the Acquisition Decision Memorandum;

2. The acquisition strategy, or acquisition plan;

3. The source selection plan;

4. The initial Request for Proposals (RFP) and all amendments to include what, if any, RFP requirements (technical and contractual) were changed and why;

5. The Source Selection Evaluation Board (SSEB) analysis and findings to ensure the evaluation of offers was consistent with the Source Selection Plan and RFP criteria;

6. Any meeting minutes memorializing discussions between the Government and offerors;

7. All evaluation notices generated as a result of deficiencies in the offerors' proposals as well as the offerors' responses to those evaluation notices;

8. All minutes memorializing the conduct of Source Selection Advisory Council (SSAC) deliberations held to date;

9. The offerors' responses to the request for Final Proposal Revision;

10. The final SSAC deliberations;

11. The final SSA determination and source selection decision;

12. Award/incentive fee arrangements, documentation of any required HCA D&Fs regarding non-availability of objective criteria;

13. Justification and Approval for use of non-competitive procedures; and

14. Documentation of pre-negotiation objectives, cost/price negotiation and the assessment of contractor risk in determining profit or fee.

Elements to be addressed:

1. The process was well understood by both Government and Industry;

2. Source Selection was carried out in accordance with the Source Selection Plan and RFP;

3. The SSEB evaluation was clearly documented;

4. The SSAC advisory panel recommendation was clearly documented;

5. The SSA decision was clearly derived from the conduct of the source selection process;

6. All source selection documentation is consistent with the Section M evaluation criteria; and

7. The business arrangement.

Post-award Peer Reviews Required Documents and Elements

Required Documents: At a minimum, Peer Review teams shall have access to the following documents (as applicable):

1. The requirements document;

2. The business arrangement, including business case analysis;

3. Market research documentation;

4. The business clearance, including documentation of cost/price negotiation and the assessment of contractor risk in determining profit or fee.

5. Contractor surveillance documentation to include metrics, quality assurance surveillance plans; and

6. The contract and modifications thereof.

Elements to be addressed, at a minimum, in every post-award review:

1. Contract performance in terms of cost, schedule, and requirements;

2. Use of contracting mechanisms, including the use of competition, the contract structure and type, the definition of contract requirements, cost or pricing methods, the award and negotiation of task orders, and management and oversight mechanisms;

3. Contractor's use, management, and oversight of subcontractors;

4. Staffing of contract management and oversight functions; and

5. Extent of any pass-throughs, and excessive pass-through charges by the contractor (as defined in section 852 of the National Defense Authorization Act for Fiscal Year 2007, Public Law 109-364).

6. Steps taken to mitigate the risk that, as implemented and administered, non-personal services contracts may become de facto personal services contracts.

Elements to be addressed in post-award reviews of contracts under which one contractor provides oversight for services performed by other contractors:

1. Extent of the DoD component's reliance on the contractor to perform acquisition functions closely associated with inherently governmental functions as defined in 10 U.S.C. 2383(b)(3); and

2. The financial interest of any prime contractor performing acquisition functions described in paragraph (1) in any contract or subcontract with regard to which the contractor provided advice or recommendations to the agency.

[Final rule, 74 FR 37625, 7/29/2009, effective 7/29/2009; Interim rule, 75 FR 54524, 9/8/2010, effective 9/8/2010; Publication notice, 20101025; Final rule, 80 FR 58630, 9/30/2015, effective 9/30/2015]

SUBPART 201.3—AGENCY ACQUISITION REGULATIONS

201.301 Policy.

(b)(i) Contract clauses and solicitation provisions developed by departments and agencies (local clauses) that constitute a significant revision, as defined at FAR 1.501-1, shall be—

(A) Published for public comment in the Federal Register in accordance with FAR 1.501; and

(B) Approved in accordance with DFARS 201.304.

(ii) A local clause is considered a significant revision, as defined at FAR 1.501-1, if the clause—

(A) Contains a new certification requirement for contractors or offerors that is not imposed by statute (see FAR 1.107 and DFARS 201.107 and 201.304(2));

(B) Constitutes a deviation (as defined at FAR 1.401) from the parts and subparts identified at DFARS 201.402(1); or

(C) Will be used on a repetitive basis; and

(*1*) Imposes a new requirement for the collection of information from 10 or more members of the public (see FAR 1.106); or

(*2*) Has any cost or administrative impact on contractors or offerors beyond that contained in the FAR or DFARS.

(iii) A local clause is not considered a significant revision as defined at FAR 1.501-1, if the clause—

(A) Is for a single-use intended to meet the needs of an individual acquisition (e.g. a clause developed as a result of negotiations and documented in the business clearance or similar document), except for clauses that constitute a deviation (as defined at FAR 1.401) from the parts and subparts identified at DFARS 201.402(1); or

(B) May be used on a repetitive basis and has no new or additional cost or administrative impact on contractors or offerors beyond any cost or administrative impact contained in existing FAR or DFARS coverage.

[Publication notice, 20150626; Publication notice, 20150826]

201.304 Agency control and compliance procedures.

(4) Plans for controlling the use of clauses or provisions other than those prescribed by the FAR or DFARS (local clauses), as required by DFARS 201.304(4), shall include procedures to ensure that a local clause—

(A) Is evaluated to determine whether the local clause constitutes a significant revision (see 201.301(b));

(B) Is numbered in accordance with FAR 52.1 and DFARS 252.1 (see 252.103);

(C) Is accompanied by a prescription in the appropriate part and subpart of the department or agency FAR supplement where the subject matter of the clause receives its primary treatment;

(D) If it constitutes a significant revision—

(*1*) Is published for public comment in the Federal Register in accordance with FAR 1.501 and DFARS 201.501;

(*2*) Complies with the Paperwork Reduction Act 1980 (44 USC chapter 35), in accordance with FAR 1.106 and 1.301;

(*3*) Complies with the Regulatory Flexibility Act (5 U.S.C. 601, *et seq.*), in accordance with FAR 1.301; and

(*4*) Is approved in accordance with DFARS 201.304; and

(E) Is published with a prescription as a final rule in the Federal Register in order to amend the department or agency's chapter of Title 48 of the Code of Federal Regulations (CFR), if it is to be used on a repetitive basis.

(5) (A) Prior to publication for public comment in the Federal Register of a local clause that constitutes a significant revision (see 201.301(b)), departments and agencies shall submit, in accordance with agency procedures, the following information electronically via email to the Director, Defense Acquisition Regulation (DAR) Council, at *osd.clause.control@mail.mil*:

(*1*) The name of the requesting department or agency.

(*2*) The name, email address and phone number of the point of contract for the local clause and the department or agency clause control point of contact.

(*3*) A detailed rationale for the request, to include—

(*i*) Why existing FAR or DFARS clauses or provisions do not satisfy, or could not be tailored to meet, the department or agency's needs;

(*ii*) What contracting problem or situation will be avoided, corrected, or improved if the local clause is approved; and

(*iii*) Identification of other DoD Components that have expressed interest in use of the clause for consideration for incorporation into the DFARS.

(*4*) The draft rule to be published in the Federal Register to solicit public comments on the proposal to amend the department and agency's chapter of Title 48 of the CFR to incorporate the local clause.

(*5*) The initial regulatory flexibility analysis. For additional information on the Regulatory Flexibility Act (5 U.S.C. 601, *et seq.*) see Appendix 8 of the FAR Operating Guide accessible via the Defense Acquisition Regulation System (DARS) website at *http://www.acq.osd.mil/dpap/dars/about.html.*

(*6*) If applicable, the request package to be submitted to the Office of Management and Budget for any new information collection requirement imposed by the local clause. For additional information on the Paperwork Reduction Act (44 USC Chapter 35) see Appendix 9 of the FAR Operating Guide accessible via the DARS website at *http://www.acq.osd.mil/dpap/dars/about.html.*

(*7*) Evidence of coordination with the department or agency's legal counsel.

(*8*) Evidence of coordination with the appropriate stakeholders (e.g., Chief Information Officer, Office of Small Business Programs, etc.).

(B) The Director, DAR Council, shall—

(*1*) Determine whether the local clause unnecessarily duplicates coverage currently contained within the FAR or DFARS;

(*2*) Determine whether the local clause constitutes a deviation from the FAR or DFARS (see FAR 1.401) and requires approval in accordance with DFARS 201.4;

(*3*) Coordinate the local clause with the appropriate stakeholders;

(*4*) Coordinate local clauses, as appropriate, with the DAR Council for consideration of the local clause for incorporation in the DFARS; and

(*5*) Provide recommendations regarding the local clause package.

(C) Requests for Director, Defense Procurement and Acquisition Policy (DPAP), approval of local clauses that have been published for public comment in the Federal Register, shall be submitted electronically via email through the Director, DAR Council, at *osd.clause.control@mail.mil* and shall include the following:

(*1*) A memorandum requesting Director, DPAP, approval of the local clause.

(*2*) A copy of the notice of the rule published in the Federal Register.

(*3*) A copy of all public comments received in response to the Federal Register notice.

(*4*) An analysis of, and responses to, any public comments received.

(*5*) The draft final rule to be published in the Federal Register to amend the department or agency's chapter of Title 48 of the CFR to incorporate the local clause.

(*6*) The final regulatory flexibility analysis. For additional information on the Regulatory Flexibility Act (5 U.S.C. 601, *et seq.*) see Appendix 8 of the FAR Operating Guide accessible via the DARS website at *http://www.acq.osd.mil/dpap/dars/about.html.*

(*7*) If applicable, a copy of the Office of Management and Budget's approval of any new information collection requirement imposed by the local clause. For additional information on the Paperwork Reduction Act (44 USC chapter 35) see Appendix 9 of the FAR Operating Guide accessible via the DARS website at *http://www.acq.osd.mil/dpap/dars/about.html.*

(*8*) Evidence of coordination with the department or agency's legal counsel.

(*9*) Evidence of coordination with the appropriate stakeholders (e.g., Chief Information Officer, Office of Small Business Programs, etc.).

(*10*) A copy of any initial recommendations received from the Director, DAR Council on the proposed rule.

[Publication notice, 20150626; Publication notice, 20150826]

SUBPART 201.6—CAREER DEVELOPMENT, CONTRACTING AUTHORITY AND RESPONSIBILITIES

201.602 Contracting officers. (No Text)

[Final rule, 70 FR 75411, 12/20/2005, effective 12/20/2005; Final rule, 71 FR 69488, 12/1/2006, effective 12/1/2006]

201.602-2 Responsibilities.

Contracting officers shall inform all individuals performing on their behalf of their delegated roles and responsibilities, and the relationships among the parties.

(d) (i) When designating Department of State personnel as a contracting officer's representative (COR for contracts executed by DoD in support of Department of State in Iraq), follow the procedures in the Director, Defense Procurement and Acquisition Policy memorandum dated *July 11, 2011, Contracting Officer's Representative Designation—Iraq*.

(ii) DoD COR certification standards define minimum COR competencies, experience, and training requirements according to the nature and complexity of the requirement and contract performance risk. These COR certification standards should be considered when developing service requirements, soliciting proposals, and performing surveillance during contract performance. The DoD standards and policy are provided in *DoD Instruction 5000.72, DoD Standard for Contracting Officer's Representative (COR) Certification*.

(iii) Guidance on the appointment and duties of CORs is provided in the *https://www.acq.osd.mil/dpap/cpic/cp/docs/USA001390-12_DoD_COR_Handbook_Signed.pdf*.

(iv) DoD agencies and components shall use the DoD Contracting Officer Representative Tracking (CORT) Tool to electronically track COR nominations, appointments, terminations, and training certifications for service contracts. Further guidance on using this tool is provided in *OUSD(AT&L) memorandum, dated February 10, 2014, Update to the Department of Defense Contracting Officer Representative Tracking Tool*. The link to the CORT Tool is *https://wawf.eb.mil*.

(v) A COR assists in the technical monitoring or administration of a contract.

(A) Contracting officers shall designate a COR for all service contracts, including both firm-fixed-price and other than firm-fixed-price contracts, awarded by a DoD component or by any other Federal agency on behalf of DoD. The surveillance activities performed by CORs should be tailored to the dollar value/complexity of the specific contract for which they are designated. For geographically dispersed large contracts with multiple task orders, contracting officers should consider appointing multiple or alternate CORs to assist with surveillance duties. These CORs should have specific duties based on criteria, such as geographic region or distinct task areas, to avoid conflicting or duplicative direction. Contracting officers may exempt service contracts from this requirement when the following three conditions are met:

(1) The contract will be awarded using simplified acquisition procedures;

(2) The requirement is not complex; and

(3) The contracting officer documents the file, in writing, with the specific reasons why the appointment of a COR is unnecessary.

(B) For cost reimbursement contracts that are not service contracts, contracting officers shall either retain or delegate surveillance activities to a COR or DCMA.

(C) The contracting officer shall include a copy of the written designation required by FAR 1.602-2(d) (7) in the CORT Tool.

(vi) A COR shall maintain an electronic file in the CORT Tool for each contract assigned. This file must include, as a minimum—

(A) A copy of the contracting officer's letter of designation and other documentation describing the COR's duties and responsibilities; and

(B) Documentation of actions taken in accordance with the delegation of authority.

(vii) Contracting officers, as well as the requiring activities (or the COR's supervisor), shall, as a minimum, annually review the COR's files for accuracy and completeness. The results of the contracting officer's review shall be documented in the CORT Tool.

(viii) Prior to contract closeout, the COR will deliver the COR files for the assigned contract to the contracting officer for incorporation into the contract file.

[Final rule, 70 FR 75411, 12/20/2005, effective 12/20/2005; Final rule, 71 FR 69488, 12/1/2006, effective 12/1/2006; Change notice, 20091002; Final rule, 76 FR 58136, 9/20/2011, effective 9/20/2011; Publication notice 20120615; 6/15/2012; Publication notice 20130311, 3/11/2014; Final rule, 79 FR 22036, 4/21/2014, effective 4/21/2014; Publication notice, 20151030; Publication notice, 20191231]

PART 202—DEFINITIONS OF WORDS AND TERMS

Table of Contents

Subpart 202.1—Definitions

Definitions 202.101

PART 202—DEFINITIONS OF WORDS AND TERMS

SUBPART 202.1—DEFINITIONS

202.101 Definitions.

DoD contracting activities are—

(1) *Department of Defense.*

Department of Defense Education Activity

Joint Improvised Explosive Device Defeat Organization

Washington Headquarters Services, Acquisition Directorate

Inspector General of the Department of Defense (limited contracting authority for use of the Governmentwide commercial purchase card)

(2) *Department of the Air Force.*

Office of the Assistant Secretary of the Air Force (Acquisition)

Office of the Deputy Assistant Secretary (Contracting)

Air Force Materiel Command

Air Force Space Command

Air Combat Command

Air Mobility Command

Air Education and Training Command

Pacific Air Forces

United States Air Forces in Europe

Air Force Special Operations Command

Air Force Reserve Command

Air Force Global Strike Command

Air Force Life Cycle Management Center

Air Force District of Washington

United States Air Force Academy

Air Force Operational Test and Evaluation Center

Space and Missile Systems Center

(3) *Department of the Army.*

Deputy Assistant Secretary of the Army (Procurement)

Headquarters, U.S. Army Materiel Command

Headquarters, U.S. Army Medical Command

National Guard Bureau

U.S. Army Corps of Engineers

(4) *Department of the Navy.*

Deputy Assistant Secretary of the Navy (Acquisition and Procurement)

Marine Corps Systems Command

Military Sealift Command

Installations and Logistics, Headquarters, U.S. Marine Corps

Naval Air Systems Command

Naval Facilities Engineering Command

Naval Sea Systems Command

Naval Supply Systems Command

Office of Naval Research

Space and Naval Warfare Systems Command

Strategic Systems Programs

(5) *Defense Advanced Research Projects Agency.*

Office of the Deputy Director, Management

(6) *Defense Commissary Agency.*

Directorate of Contracting

(7) *Defense Contract Management Agency.*

Office of the Executive Director, Contracts, Defense Contract Management Agency

(8) *Defense Finance and Accounting Service.*

External Services, Defense Finance and Accounting Service

(9) *Defense Health Agency.*

Directorate of Procurement

(10) *Defense Information Systems Agency.*

Defense Information Technology Contracting Organization

(11) *Defense Intelligence Agency.*

Office of Procurement

(12) *Defense Logistics Agency.*

DLA Acquisition (J-7)

DLA Aviation

DLA Energy

DLA Land and Maritime

DLA Troop Support

(13) *Defense Security Cooperation Agency.*

Contracting Division

(14) *Defense Security Service.*

Office of Acquisitions

(15) *Defense Threat Reduction Agency.*

Acquisition Management Office

(16) *Missile Defense Agency.*

Headquarters, Missile Defense Agency

(17) *National Geospatial-Intelligence Agency.*

Procurement and Contracting Office

(18) *National Security Agency.*

Headquarters, National Security Agency

(19) *United States Special Operations Command.*

Headquarters, United States Special Operations Command

(20) *United States Transportation Command.*

Directorate of Acquisition

[Final rule, 77 FR 76938, 12/31/2012, effective 1/30/2013; Publication notice, 20130228; Publication notice, 20140328; Publication notice, 20140919; Publication notice, 20171208; Publication notice, 20180323]

PART 203—IMPROPER BUSINESS PRACTICES AND PERSONAL CONFLICTS OF INTEREST

Table of Contents

Subpart 203.1—[Removed]

Subpart 203.5—Other Improper Business Practices

Prohibition on persons convicted of fraud or other defense-contract related felonies 203.570
Scope 203.570-1
Prohibition period 203.570-2

Subpart 203.8—Limitations on the Payment of Funds to Influence Federal Transactions

Limitations on the payment of funds to influence federal transactions . . . 203.8

PART 203—IMPROPER BUSINESS PRACTICES AND PERSONAL CONFLICTS OF INTEREST

SUBPART 203.1—[REMOVED]

203.170 [Removed]

[Final rule, 74 FR 2407, 1/15/2009, effective 1/15/2009; Final rule, 78 FR 54968, 9/9/2013, effective 9/9/2013; Final rule, 79 FR 73487, 12/11/2014, effective 12/11/2014]

SUBPART 203.5—OTHER IMPROPER BUSINESS PRACTICES

203.570 Prohibition on persons convicted of fraud or other defense-contract-related felonies. (No Text)

203.570-1 Scope.

The complete text of 10 U.S.C. 2408, Prohibition on Persons Convicted of Defense-Contract Related Felonies and Related Criminal Penalty on Defense Contractors, is available at *http://uscode.house.gov/* (Select "Search the U.S. Code"; then type "10 USC Sec. 2408" (including the quotation marks) in the search engine window and click on the search button).

[Final rule, 71 FR 14099, 3/21/2006, effective 3/21/2006; Change notice, 20060321]

203.570-2 Prohibition period.

(a) (1) The contracting officer shall—

(i) Review any request for waiver; and

(ii) Deny the request if the contracting officer decides the waiver is not required in the interests of national security; or

(iii) Forward the request to the head of the agency or designee for approval if the contracting officer decides the waiver may be in the interest of national security.

(2) The head of the agency or designee shall report all waivers granted, and the reasons for granting the waiver, to the Under Secretary of Defense (Acquisition, Technology, and Logistics), who will forward the report to Congress as required by 10 U.S.C. 2408(a)(3).

(3) Guidance on using the Exclusions section of the System for Award Management is available at PGI 209.105-1.

(b) Submit a copy of the determination to Bureau of Justice Assistance, U.S. Department of Justice, 810 Seventh Street, NW, Washington, DC 20531.

[Final rule, 69 FR 74989, 12/15/2004, effective 12/15/2004; Publication notice, 20140328]

SUBPART 203.8—LIMITATIONS ON THE PAYMENT OF FUNDS TO INFLUENCE FEDERAL TRANSACTIONS

203.8 Limitations on the Payment of Funds to Influence Federal Transactions.

(a) Report violations or potential violations of the Lobbying Disclosure Act (31 U.S.C. 1352) through agency channels to the Deputy Director, Defense Procurement and Acquisition Policy (Contracting Policy and International Contracting), *osd.pentagon.ousd-atl.mbx.cpic@mail.mil.*

(b) Click *here* [*http://www.acq.osd.mil/dpap/policy/policyvault/USA000430-12-DPAP.pdf*] to view OUSD(AT&L) memorandum dated March 5, 2012, Department of Defense Inspector General (DODIG) Report 2012-030, Contractor Compliance Varies with Classification of Lobbying Costs and Reporting of Lobbying Activities (Project No. D2010-DOOOCF-0145.000).

[Final rule, 77 FR 19128, 3/30/2012, effective 3/30/2012; Final rule, 78 FR 54968, 9/9/2013, effective 9/9/2013]

PART 204—ADMINISTRATIVE MATTERS

Table of Contents

Subpart 204.1—Contract Execution

Contracting officer's signature 204.101

Subpart 204.2—Contract Distribution

Procedures 204.201
Electronic Document Access 204.270
Procedures 204.270.2

Subpart 204.4—Safeguarding Classified Information Within Industry

General 204.402
Responsibilities of contracting officers 204.403

Subpart 204.6—Contract Reporting

General 204.602
Responsibilities 204.604
Reporting data 204.606

Subpart 204.8—Contract Files

Closeout of contract files 204.804
Closeout by the office administering the contract 204.804-1
Closeout of the contracting office files if another office administers the contract 204.804-2
Closeout of paying office contract files 204.804-3

Subpart 204.11—System for Award Management

Procedures 204.1103

Subpart 204.16—Uniform Procurement Instrument Identifiers

Policy 204.1601
Procedures 204.1603
Cross reference to Federal Procurement Data System 204.1670

Subpart 204.18—Commercial and Government Entity Code

Procedures 204.1870
Instructions to contracting officers 204.1870-1
Maintenance of the CAGE file 204.1870-2

Subpart 204.70—PROCUREMENT ACQUISITION LEAD TIME

Procedures 204.7001

Subpart 204.71—Uniform Contract Line Item Numbering System

Contract line items 204.7103
Numbering procedures 204.7103-2
Contract subline items 204.7104
Numbering procedures 204.7104-2
Contract exhibits and attachments 204.7105
Contract accounting classification reference number (ACRN) 204.7107
Payment instructions 204.7108

Subpart 204.72—[Removed]

[Removed] 204.7202

Subpart 204.73—Safeguarding Covered Defense Information and Cyber Incident Reporting

[Removed] 204.7302
Procedures 204.7303
General 204.7303-1
Safeguarding controls and requirements 204.7303-2
Cyber incident and compromise reporting 204.7303-3
DoD damage assessment activities 204.7303-4
[Removed] 204.7304

PART 204—ADMINISTRATIVE MATTERS

SUBPART 204.1—CONTRACT EXECUTION

204.101 Contracting officer's signature.

(1) Include the contracting officer's telephone number and, when available, e-mail/Internet address on contracts and modifications.

(2) The contracting officer may sign bilateral modifications of a letter contract before signature by the contractor.

[Final rule, 71 FR 9267, 2/23/2006, effective 2/23/2006]

SUBPART 204.2—CONTRACT DISTRIBUTION

204.201 Procedures.

(1) The procuring contracting officer (PCO) retains the original signed contract for the contract file. Administrative contracting officers and termination contracting officers provide the original of each modification to the PCO for retention in the contract file. Unless otherwise directed by department/agency procedures, the office issuing the orders maintains the original of orders under basic ordering agreements and the original of provisioning orders; and

(2) Ensure that distribution of contracts and modifications is consistent with security directives.

(3) Use the following distribution procedures instead of those at FAR 4.201(b) through (f):

(i) Contracts and modifications shall be distributed electronically (except as provided at DFARS 204.270-1(a)) using the following methods:

(A) Indexed Portable Document Format files shall be sent via the Global Exchange system (GEX) to the Electronic Data Access (EDA) (*http://eda.ogden.disa.mil*) system to provide a human-readable copy of contract documents.

(B) Electronic data files depicting the contract shall be sent in at least one of the following formats via the GEX to EDA and to systems supporting specific offices as set forth in paragraph (ii) below. (Note that the GEX can be used to translate from the formats below to other formats. Organizations should send both formats in parallel unless validation failures have been eliminated.)

(1) American National Standards Institute X.12 Electronic Data Interchange standard transaction sets 850 and 860.

(2) Department of Defense Procurement Data Standard (PDS) Extensible Markup Language (XML) format: *http://www.acq.osd.mil/dpap/pdi/eb/procurement_data_standard.html*

(ii) After contract execution, provide an electronic data file copy of the contract and modifications in either X.12 or PDS XML to the following:

(A) The contract administration office, if the contracting officer delegates contract administration to another office (see FAR subpart 42.2). The contracting officer also should provide the contract administration office with a copy of the contract distribution list, indicating those offices that should receive copies of modifications, and any changes to the list as they occur.

(B) The payment office. Provide any modification that changes the payment office to both the new and the old payment offices.

(C) Each accounting office whose funds are cited in the contract.

(D) Each consignee specified in the contract. A transshipping terminal is not a consignee. The Defense Logistics Agency (DLA) is authorized to prescribe alternate procedures for distribution of contract documents in DLA Europe and Africa.

(E) The military interdepartmental purchase request requiring activity in the case of coordinated acquisition.

(F) The receiving activity, if the contract or modification provides initial or amended shipping instructions under DFARS 204.1603(b)(2)(ii)(*1*)(*ii*) and (*iii*).

(iii) Provide electronic notice of award via EDA to the following:

(A) *(1)* The appropriate Defense Contract Audit Agency (DCAA) office, as listed in

DCAAP 5100.1, Directory of DCAA Offices, or as obtained through the DCAA cognizant field audit office locator, both available via the Internet at *http://www.dcaa.mil*, if the contract or modification is one of the following types:

(i) Cost-reimbursement.

(ii) Time-and-materials.

(iii) Labor-hour.

(iv) Fixed-price with provisions for redetermination, cost incentives, economic price adjustment based on cost, or cost allowability.

(v) Any other contract that requires audit service.

(2) If there is a question as to the appropriate DCAA field audit office, request the assistance of the DCAA financial liaison advisor or the nearest DCAA field audit office.

(B) Those organizations required to perform contract administration support functions (e.g., when manufacturing is performed at multiple sites, provide a copy to the contract administration office cognizant of each location).

(C) The cognizant administrative contracting officer when the contract is not assigned for administration but contains a Cost Accounting Standards clause. Indicate that the copy is provided "For Cost Accounting Standards Administration Only" (see FAR 30.601(b)); and

(D) The cognizant Defense Security Service office listed in DoD 5100.76-M, Physical Security of Sensitive Conventional Arms, Ammunition, and Explosives, when the clause at DFARS 252.223-7007, Safeguarding Sensitive Conventional Arms, Ammunition, and Explosives, is included in the contract. An extract of the pertinent information can be provided instead of the contract.

(iv) If electronic distribution is not available, provide one paper copy to each location identified in paragraphs (3)(i) through (iii) of this section.

[Final rule, 70 FR 58980, 10/11/2005, effective 10/11/2005; Change notice, 20080423; Change notice, 20090904; Change notice, 20091002; Publication notice, 20110419; Publication notice, 20121212, 12/12/2012; Final rule, 80 FR 58630, 9/30/2015, effective 9/30/2015; Final rule, 81 FR 9783, 2/26/2016, effective 2/26/2016; Publication notice, 20190913]

204.270 Electronic Document Access. (No Text)

[Final rule, 80 FR 58630, 9/30/2015, effective 9/30/2015]

204.270-2 Procedures.

(a) Contracting officers shall maintain an account in Wide Area WorkFlow (WAWF), which provides access to Electronic Data Access (EDA) to ensure their ability to validate and verify data and documents distributed to EDA, as necessary.

(b) Agencies shall perform, upon deployment of any contract writing system or other source of contractual documents to be posted to EDA, an analysis to verify adequate controls are in place to ensure that contract documents including attachments, and contract data posted to EDA are accurate representations of the contract. Analyses performed shall include the following—

(1) For documents posted in document formats (e.g., Portable Document Format (PDF)), verification that the electronic versions of contract documents posted to EDA are accurate representations of the contract; however, the electronic version is not required to display visual signatures; and

(2) For data sent to EDA in the data standards at PGI 204.201, review of the data posted to EDA against the contract documents verified under PGI 204.270(b)(1) to ensure the contract data rendered in EDA is an accurate representation of the underlying contract. To facilitate this review process, all feeds of data to EDA in the Procurement Data Standard are initially placed in a view only evaluation mode, where the data is not available to other systems or outside users pending verification. Upon completion of the review of data, contracting organizations shall notify the EDA program office of the results of the review, with a list of the issuing offices of the contractual actions, the identifier of the system sending the actions, the version or versions of the data standards to which the review applies, and the loca-

tions of the systems sending the actions, directing one of the following decisions—

(i) Delete all data sent to date (in this case the system remains in evaluation status pending further review);

(ii) Delete all data sent to date, and change all subsequent data from 'evaluation' to 'compliant' status; or

(iii) Retain all data sent to date, and change all subsequent data from 'evaluation' to 'compliant' status.

(c) *Contract deficiency reports.*

(1) Contracting officers and all individuals tasked with creating, managing, or viewing contract deficiency reports (CDRs) shall establish and maintain an account in WAWF.

(2) Agencies that award or administer contracts, or perform pay office functions, should assign individuals within their organization to create, manage, and view CDRs within WAWF based on the following CDR user roles: initiator, reviewer, assignee, and view only.

(3) The contracting officer shall correct contract deficiencies identified in a CDR and document the steps taken to resolve the deficiency in the CDR.

(4) *The CDR process.*

(i) *Creation.* A CDR is created when a deficiency is identified in the procurement instrument. A list of types of CDR deficiencies is available at ***http://www.acq.osd.mil/dpap/pdi/eb/procurement_data_standard.html***. The specifics of the deficiency shall be documented in the description in enough detail to provide the assignee an understanding of the problem.

(ii) *Approval.* Once a CDR is created, the initiator shall route the CDR to their local approval official for review.

(iii) *Assignment.* Once a CDR is approved, it is routed to the appropriate contracting activity for action.

(iv) *Acceptance.* A CDR must be accepted or returned by the contracting activity. If a CDR is determined to have been incorrectly assigned, the contracting activity can reassign the CDR to the proper organization (if known) or reject the CDR.

(v) *Resolution.* The assignee shall document the actions taken to resolve a CDR. If a modification has been issued to resolve the deficiency, it shall be identified in the CDR. Once all deficiencies identified on a CDR have been resolved, mark the CDR as resolved. All CDRs should be resolved within 30 days of approval.

(vi) *Close.* After resolution of a CDR, the initiator of the CDR can accept the resolution and manually close the CDR or return it to the assignee for further action. CDRs not manually closed or returned by the initiator to the assignee within 60 days after resolution will automatically be closed. Once the CDR is closed, a notification is generated advising that the CDR is closed.

(5) Additional information on the CDR module of WAWF is available at ***https://wawf.eb.mil.***

[Final rule, 80 FR 58630, 9/30/2015, effective 9/30/2015; Publication notice, 20161021; Publication notice, 20190913]

SUBPART 204.4—SAFEGUARDING CLASSIFIED INFORMATION WITHIN INDUSTRY

204.402 General.

(1) The use of "Not Releasable to Foreign Nationals" (NOFORN) caveat on Department of Defense (DoD) Information, to include contract documents, shall not be applied to non-intelligence information except for Naval Nuclear Propulsion Information and the National Disclosure Policy document (NDP-1).

(2) Agencies shall not restrict procurements on the basis of foreign origin but rather on the level of security clearance required by industry to submit an offer and perform on the contract.

PGI 204.403 Responsibilities of Contracting Officers.

Consistent with the requirements at FAR subpart 4.403, contracting officers shall ensure that solicitations, to include any Broad Agency Announcement (BAA) or notice to industry, that requires industry access to classified information and/or controlled unclassified information (***see policy memos***), shall contain one or more of the following:

(1) Draft DoD Form DD 254, DoD Contract Security Classification Specification. See Defense Security Service (DSS) guide for the preparation of the DD Form 254: *http://www.dss.mil/seta/seta.html* (select security-related brochures and guides, followed by selecting "A Guide for the Preparation of a DD Form 254").

(2) The clause at FAR 52.204-2, Security Requirements.

(3) Detailed agency instructions for industry requirements to request access to classified information and/or controlled unclassified information. Agency instructions shall clearly reference and be in accordance with the National Industrial Security Program Operating Manual (NISPOM) (DoD 5220-22-M) and Industrial Security Regulation (DoD 5220.22-R).

(4) The following is a template of agency instructions to industry:

"Offerors must have a valid U.S. security clearance of [to be filled in by the contracting officer] or higher in order to respond to this RFP (Announcement), because the RFP (Announcement) includes an annex (information) classified at the [to be filled in by the contracting officer] level which will be released only to offerors possessing the appropriate clearance. All classified material must be handled in accordance with the National Industrial Security Program Operating Manual (NISPOM) (DoD 5220-22-M) and Industrial Security Regulation (DoD 5220.22-R)."

[Publication notice, 20110920]

204.403 Responsibilities of contracting officers.

(i) Consistent with the requirements at FAR subpart 4.403, contracting officers shall ensure that solicitations, to include any Broad Agency Announcement (BAA) or notice to industry, that requires industry access to classified information and/or controlled unclassified information (see policy memos [*http://www.acq.osd.mil/dpap/dars/pgi/docs/CUI_policy_memos_2011-P018.pdf*]), shall contain one or more of the following:

(ii) Draft DoD Form DD 254, DoD Contract Security Classification Specification. See Defense Security Service (DSS) guide for the preparation of the DD Form 254 at *http://www.dss.mil/isp/tools.html* and select the "A Guide for the Preparation of a DD Form 254).

(2) The clause at FAR 52.204-2, Security Requirements.

(iii) Detailed agency instructions for industry requirements to request access to classified information and/or controlled unclassified information. Agency instructions shall clearly reference and be in accordance with the National Industrial Security Program Operating Manual (NISPOM) (DoD 5220-22-M) and Industrial Security Regulation (DoD 5220.22-R).

(iv) The following is a template of agency instructions to industry:

"Offerors must have a valid U.S. security clearance of [*to be filled in by the contracting officer*] or higher in order to respond to this RFP (Announcement), because the RFP (Announcement) includes an annex (information) classified at the [*to be filled in by the contracting officer*] level which will be released only to offerors possessing the appropriate clearance. All classified material must be handled in accordance with the National Industrial Security Program Operating Manual (NISPOM) (DoD 5220-22-M) and Industrial Security Regulation (DoD 5220.22-R)."

(2) Fundamental research project determination.

(i) Projects being scoped as fundamental research may include the entire contract effort or a specified portion of the statement of work, and must be documented in the written determination and in the contract.

(ii) The determination of fundamental research shall occur when the project is added to the statement of work, either prior to award or during a contract modification that modified the statement of work.

(iii) Fundamental research is defined in the USD(AT&L) memorandum on Fundamental Research, dated May 24, 2010.

(iv) See clause 252.204-7000(a)(3), concerning disclosure of information for fundamental research projects.

[Publication notice 20110920; Publication notice 20130228; Final rule, 79 FR 56278, 9/19/2014, effective 9/19/2014]

204.6 SUBPART 204.6—CONTRACT REPORTING

As used in this subpart, the unique entity identifier is currently the Data Universal Numbering System (DUNS) number.

[Publication notice, 20171208; Publication notice, 20191231]

204.602 General.

(1) *Helpful documents.* The Federal Procurement Data System (FPDS) website at *https://www.fpds.gov* provides useful documents and on-line training to assist with FPDS data entry. Key manuals can be found at the top of the website homepage under the "Training" and "Worksite" drop-down links to include:

(i) *FPDS Data Element Dictionary.* The data dictionary outlines relevant information for each data field. The Data Dictionary identifies whether a data field is "Required," "Optional," "Propagates from the base action," "Not Applicable," or "System Generated," for each type of data entry screen (Awards, Indefinite-Delivery Vehicles, and Transactions/Modifications). It also identifies the source of data entry (e.g., Contracting Officer, System for Award Management (SAM), FPDS); the format of the field; and whether the field input is derived from entries in other fields. At the back of the Data Dictionary is a useful summary.

(ii) *FPDS Data Validations.* This document identifies all the validation rules that are applied to data entry. The majority of the rules apply Governmentwide. DoD specific validation rules appear at "5.5.1 DoD Specific Validations."

(iii) *FPDS Users Manual.* This manual provides guidance on the various types of data entry screens and addresses whether a particular field is: "[R]" –requires contracting officer/buyer entry; "[A]" –pre-populated by FPDS or a contract writing system, if using machine-to-machine process; or "[C]" –calculated by FPDS for each type of data entry screen. However, the nature of the field is determined based on Governmentwide requirements. To determine DoD-specific requirements, refer to J3 "DoD Use Case Summary" in the FPDS Data Element Dictionary. The FPDS User Manual is not a policy document; it is intended only for general guidance. Refer to this PGI section for specific FPDS reporting entries.

(2) *Reporting technical or policy issues.*

(i) *Technical issues.* To report an FPDS technical issue—

(A) (*1*) Users of the Standard Procurement System (SPS) should contact their local SPS Help Desk (authorized SPS caller);

(*2*) Users of other contract writing systems should contact the local contract writing system administrator to determine the appropriate procedures; and

(*3*) Web users should contact their local system administrator, who will then contact the FPDS Help Desk; or

(B) If the issue is an obvious FPDS technical issue that needs to be documented and corrected by the system, the user should contact the Federal Service Desk (FSD), by telephone at 866-606-8220 (U.S. or DSN), or 334-206-7828 (International), or submit a comment or request at *www.fsd.gov.* When e-mailing FSD, also send a copy to the applicable agency representative identified in paragraph (2)(iii) of this section.

(ii) *Policy issues.* Report policy issues to the applicable agency representative identified in paragraph (2)(iii) of this section.

(iii) *Agency representatives.* Department and component FPDS representatives and their contact information can be found on the DPC website at *http://www.acq.osd.mil/dpap/pdi/eb/federal_procurement_data_system_-_next_generation_fpds-ng.html* under "Additional Resources."

[Final rule, 74 FR 37644, 7/29/2009, effective 7/29/2009; Publication notice, 20100324; Publication notice, 20100802; Publication notice, 20100810; Publication notice, 20110920; Final rule, 78 FR 28756, 5/16/2013, effective 5/16/2013; Publication notice, 20160923;

Publication notice, 20171208; Publication notice, 20191231]

204.604 Responsibilities.

(1) The OSD Procurement Data Improvement Plan, posted at ***http://www.acq.osd.mil/dpap/pdi/eb/dataimp.html#***, applies to each of the military services and agencies with procurement authority, and identifies the data validation requirements and responsibilities that support the annual Department of Defense certification identified at FAR 4.604(c). These review requirements encompass contract action reports submitted to FPDS, terminations for default and other documents submitted to the Federal Awardee Performance and Integrity Information System (FAPIIS), and other reporting and posting requirements.

(2) Contract action reports (CARs) must be completed in compliance with the timelines established in FAR 4.604(b)(2) and (3). CARs or their data are not available for public view or for non-DoD use until 90 days after the "Date Signed" data element in order to minimize risk to military operations.

[Publication notice, 20140731; Publication notice, 20160923; Publication notice, 20171208; Publication notice, 20191231]

204.606 Reporting data.

Do not enter a generic DUNS number used for reporting to the Federal Procurement Data System (FPDS) (see FAR subpart 4.6), nor a generic CAGE code that corresponds to a generic DUNS number, on any contractual document. These generic codes shall only be used for reporting to FPDS. Using the generic codes on actual contract actions masks the true identity of the vendor and immediately makes any accurate electronic processing of invoices, receiving reports, and payments impossible; and can, in fact, result in misdirected payments. As a reminder FAR subpart 4.18 requires each contractor be identified by its actual CAGE code on contract actions; there is no exemption to the requirement for an actual CAGE code.

(1) *Methods of reporting to FPDS.*

(i) *Individual contract action report (CAR) (one CAR per contract action)*. The normal method of reporting to FPDS is through the use of individual CARs.

(A) An individual CAR is required to be reported for each of the following types of awards regardless of the estimated value of the award:

(*1*) Indefinite-delivery contract.

(*2*) Blanket purchase agreement (prescribed by FAR parts 8 or 13).

(*3*) Basic ordering agreement.

(*4*) Basic agreement (only if the agreement has a value and potential obligations greater than $0).

(*5*) Task and delivery orders and calls issued under any agreement or indefinite-delivery contract (including Federal Supply Schedules, Governmentwide acquisition contracts, or multi-agency contracts).

(*6*) Modification to any contract, agreement, order, or call where a CAR is required for the base award regardless of the amount being obligated or deobligated on the modification.

(B)(*1*) An individual CAR is required to be reported for each of the following types of awards when the award process was conducted using other than micro-purchase procedures and the value is greater than the micro-purchase threshold (MPT):

(*i*) Purchase order.

(*ii*) Definitive contract.

(*2*) Although a contract action report is not required for these awards when micro-purchase procedures were followed and the value is less than the MPT, it is encouraged as a best practice if the award was not accomplished using the Governmentwide commercial purchase card (GPC) or a Standard Form 44. Additionally, when the purchase order or definitive contract being awarded is in response to a contingency, an individual report is required when the value of the award is greater than $25,000, not the MPT of $30,000 referenced in FAR part 2.

(C) See paragraphs (1)(ii) and (iii) of this section for exceptions to individual reporting.

(ii) *Multiple CARs (more than one CAR per contract action)*.

(A) Prepare multiple CARs if the contract or order award is anticipated to include both foreign funding and U.S. funding.

(B) The determination of whether multiple CARs are needed for the situations described in paragraph (1)(ii)(A) of this section is made when the contract or order is awarded. Contracting officers are not required to delete and re-enter CARs in FPDS as multiple CARs if, during the life of the contract or order, subsequent unanticipated modifications make the award eligible for multiple CARs.

(C) The following multiple CAR transaction identification numbers have been established for reporting multiple CARs and shall be used by all DoD contracting offices. Do not use transaction numbers other than "0" if the requirements for multiple CARs in paragraphs (1)(ii)(A) and (B) of this section do not apply at the time of contract or order award. When reporting modifications, include the transaction number that was reported on the initial base award in order to properly identify the referenced contract action report. If the situation described in paragraph (1)(ii)(A) of this section exists, transaction numbers should be assigned based on foreign military sales (FMS) and non-FMS rather than by type of contract pricing arrangement. Do not use multiple CARs with transaction numbers other than "0" if the entire award is expected to be funded by foreign funding.

Transaction Type	Transaction Number
No multiple CARs	0
FMS	14
Non-FMS	16

(iii) *Express reporting (consolidated reporting of multiple contract actions, to be submitted at least monthly)*.

(A) Express reporting may be used for—

(*1*) Multiple contract actions against a single contract or agreement, when monthly volume of actions is such that individual contract action reporting is overly burdensome (e.g., orders placed by the Defense Commissary Agency; installation housing maintenance; and recurring blanket purchase agreement actions);

(*2*) Multiple contract actions accomplished away from the contracting office, such as ships away from home port; contingency, humanitarian, or peacekeeping operations; or other remote deployments;

(*3*) Multiple delivery orders that use the GPC as both the method of purchase and payment under Federal Supply Schedules, Governmentwide acquisition contracts (GWACs), blanket purchase agreements (BPAs), basic ordering agreements (BOAs), and other indefinite-delivery type contracts;

(*4*) Multiple contract actions for energy-related supplies and associated services accomplished by Defense Logistics Agency (DLA) Energy; and

(*5*) Orders under communications service agreements for local dial tone services, in accordance with agency procedures.

(B) When express reports reflect more than one contractor for overseas actions or consolidated delivery orders made using the GPC where identification of the contract or agreement is not possible, use the appropriate generic DUNS number.

(C) When express reports are used, sum all of the actions and enter in the "Number of Actions" data field. Also sum all of the obligations and enter in the "Action Obligation," "Base and Exercised Options Value," and "Base and All Options Value" data fields. Express reports shall be submitted no less frequently than monthly.

(D) When express reports are used, the contracting officer must maintain a log of individual actions being summarized on the express reports and ensure it is available for audit purposes. Logs must include the following, at a minimum, for each action: procurement instrument identifier (PIID) used for the express report under which action is summarized, referenced Indefinite-Delivery Vehicles (IDV) PIID (if the express report is summarizing task/delivery/call orders), date of award, obligation amount, vendor name, and DUNS number (if known).

(2) *Actions not reported.* In addition, to the types of actions listed in FAR 4.606(c), do not report the following types of actions to FPDS:

(i) Orders placed by ordering officers against IDVs awarded by—

(A) The United States Transportation Command (USTRANSCOM) or its components for decentralized transportation-related services. USTRANSCOM will report these orders. Contracting officers shall submit consolidated reports of orders (bookings/bills of lading) at least annually to USTRANSCOM; or

(B) DLA Energy for energy-related supplies and associated services using defensewide working capital funds. DLA Energy will report these orders. It is the responsibility of the contracting office to ensure that orders placed against these vehicles using other than defensewide working capital funds are reported to FPDS.

(ii) Contracts, agreements, or orders that are themselves classified.

(3) *Specific instructions for entering data in FPDS.*

(i) Contracting officers shall choose the correct FPDS format (e.g., purchase order, basic ordering agreement (BOA), blanket purchase agreement (BPA)) to report the award of a new contract, agreement, or order. Note that prior to fiscal year (FY)10, DoD offices reported BOAs and BPAs as IDCs in FPDS; BPA calls issued under those pre-FY10 reported BPAs are reported using the task/delivery order format in FPDS. BPA calls issued under DoD issued BPAs reported FY10 or later or any civilian agency issued BPA should be reported using the BPA call format.

(ii) The remaining instructions in this section cover the different sections of an FPDS contract action report, as presented to the user in the system. Not every data element is addressed here, as many are self-explanatory. Users should also consult the FPDS User Manual referenced in PGI 204.602(1)(iii) for more complete descriptions and examples. Also, the instructions in this section use data field names based on what is shown to the user while entering data in FPDS; for more specific information, review the FPDS Data Element Dictionary referenced in PGI 204.602(1)(i).

(iii) *FPDS Entry – Document Information Section.*

(A) Enter the new contract, agreement, or order number in the "Procurement Instrument Identifier" data field. Note that new awards will be reflected as Modification 0 in FPDS.

(B) If the action is a BPA awarded against a Federal Supply Schedule, enter the Federal Supply Schedule contract number in the "Referenced IDV ID" data field.

(C) If the action is a delivery order awarded against a Federal Supply Schedule, Governmentwide acquisition contract (GWAC), BOA, or other IDC; enter that contract or BOA number in the "Referenced IDV ID" data field.

(D) If the action is a BPA call awarded against a BPA, enter the BPA number in the "Referenced IDV ID" data field.

(E) If the action is a modification, enter the contract, agreement, or order number in the "Procurement Instrument Identifier" data field and the modification number in the "Modification Number" data field.

(F) If multiple reports are required by paragraph (1)(ii) of this section, then enter the appropriate transaction number in the "Transaction Number" data field.

(G) If the award is associated with a solicitation, enter the solicitation number in the "Solicitation ID" data field.

(H) If the award is associated with an initiative identified in FPDS (e.g., American Recovery and Reinvestment Act), choose the appropriate value in the "Treasury Account Symbol Initiative" data field.

(iv) *FPDS Entry–Treasury Account Symbol (TAS) data fields.*

(A) TAS data fields are no longer required to be entered in FPDS (as of July 2016) and should be left blank; however, if correcting TAS data fields on a previously reported contract action report follow the instructions in this section.

(B) The TAS should be provided by the requiring organization with the purchase request, and is often part of the line of accounting. The list of valid TAS is maintained by the Department of Treasury in the

FASTBook; an on-line version of the FASTBook is available at *http://www.fms.treas.gov/fastbook/index.html*. Each TAS reported to FPDS includes a character agency identifier and a four character main account code (example: 97 0100). Some TAS also require a three character subaccount code. Note that the Department of Treasury FASTBook indicates a transition from a two character agency identifier to a three character agency identifier. However at this time, DoD contracting officers are advised to drop the leading zero (0) from a three character agency identifier, and enter the next two characters in FPDS (e.g., 097 becomes 97).

(C) Report the TAS on CARs for each contract action with an obligation amount other than $0. The TAS that is reported on a CAR should represent the predominant type of funding in terms of absolute dollars obligated and deobligated on the specific contract action being reported.

(D) For contract actions awarded by working capital funds offices, and the original type of funds received from the customer are not tied to specific procurements or otherwise identifiable, use the TAS that represents the working capital funds provided.

(E) For contract actions funded by foreign governments, and those funds are not considered under the Foreign Military Financing Program identified by the Department of Treasury in its FASTBook, in order to report the action to FPDS using the code that most closely approximates the use of the funds, then enter—

(*1*) 97 0100 (Operation and Maintenance, Defense-Wide, Defense) as the TAS for requirements that can be categorized as operations and maintenance in nature;

(*2*) 97 0300 (Procurement, Defense-Wide) as the TAS for requirements that can be categorized as procurement in nature; or

(*3*) 97 0400 (Research, Development, Test, and Evaluation, Defense-Wide) as the TAS for requirements that can be categorized as research and development in nature.

(F) USTRANSCOM should use 97 0100 (Operation and Maintenance, Defense-Wide, Defense) as the TAS when reporting the consolidated orders of from their decentralized transportation-related services contracts.

(v) *FPDS Entry – Dates Section.*

(A) The "Date Signed" data field represents the date the contracting officer signed or otherwise awarded the contract action.

(B) The "Effective Date" data field represents the date the period of performance begins. For actions where an authorization to proceed was given prior to the signed contract action, use the date of the authorization in this data element.

(C) The date entered in the "Completion Date" data field shall be the latest period of performance / delivery date of all of the exercised line items on the contract or order. This data field shall be updated on the contract action report used to report the modification whenever line items are added or exercised by modification that extend the period of performance / delivery date beyond what was previously entered, including the exercise of any option years.

(D) The date entered in the "Estimated Ultimate Completion Date" data field shall be the latest period of performance / delivery date of all line items on the contract or order, including unexercised line items and option years. This data field shall be updated on the contract action report used to report the modification whenever line items are added or changed by modification that extend the period of performance/delivery date beyond what was previously entered.

(E) The date entered in the "Last Date to Order" data field on IDCs, BOAs, and BPAs shall be the last date allowed by the contract for the contractor to accept orders. This data field shall be updated whenever this date is changed by modification from what was previously entered.

(F) The "Solicitation Date" data field generally represents the date an Invitation for Bids, Request for Quotation, or Request for Proposal was issued to potential bidders or offerors. However, follow the instructions below for other situations where an IFB, RFQ, or RFP is not issued:

(*1*) When the action is the award of an order using existing pre-priced line items under an ordering instrument where no proposal is required (i.e., there are no elements of the delivery or performance to negotiate)—

(*i*) *Orders under single-award indefinite delivery vehicles, BPA calls under single-award BPAs issued under FAR part 8, and BPA calls under BPAs issued under FAR part 13.* Use the date the procurement-ready requirements package (including funded purchase request or MIPR) was provided to the contracting office as the "Solicitation Date". If unknown, use the date of the award of the order as the "Solicitation Date".

(*ii*) *Orders under multiple-award indefinite delivery contracts and BPA calls issued under multiple-award BPAs issued under FAR part 8.* Use the date of the survey of the multiple-award contracts or BPAs prices in accordance with FAR part 8 or 16 procedures.

(*2*) When the action is the award of a contract under a broad agency announcement (BAA), use the date when a final (not draft) combined synopsis/solicitation is issued as the "Solicitation Date" except—

(*i*) For two-step BAAs, including white paper submissions for review, selection, and subsequent request for full proposals, the "Solicitation Date" is the date when the contracting officer signs the proposal request;

(*ii*) Under BAAs with calls, the "Solicitation Date" is the date when the individual call is issued; or

(iii) For open BAAs, when white papers and/or proposals are accepted for review over an extended period (typically open for a year or longer), the "Solicitation Date" is either the date when the contracting officer signs a proposal request (white papers) or the date on which the proposal is submitted, whichever is earlier.

(*3*) For awards made in response to unsolicited proposals, the "Solicitation Date" is the date when the offeror is notified of proposal acceptance for negotiations and/or award.

(vi) *FPDS Entry – Amounts Section.*

(A) When entering a net deobligation on a contract action, include the minus (-) sign.

(B) The amount entered in the "Base and Exercised Options Value" for new awards shall be the total value (represented in U.S. dollars and cents) of all the exercised line items on the contract or order regardless of whether they are partially or fully funded. This data field shall be updated on the contract action report used to report the modification whenever the current value of the contract or order is changed by modification, including when options are exercised. When reporting such a modification, report the net value of the change itself in "Current" field; FPDS will calculate the new total Base and Exercised Options Value. When an Administrative Contracting Officer (ACO) executes a modification and the previous value reported in FPDS is incorrect, the ACO shall notify the procuring contract office of the discrepancy and enter the appropriate value in the "Current" field of the "Base and Exercised Options Value" to ensure a correct total is represented. The ACO shall document the correction of the discrepancy in the contract file.

(C) The amount entered in the "Base and All Options Value" for new awards shall be the total potential value of the award (represented in U.S. dollars and cents) (e.g., total price, total not-to-exceed amount, maximum award amount, etc.), including the value of all unexercised line items and options. For blanket purchase agreements and basic ordering agreements, enter the total expected amount for orders that will be issued. Note: on IDV formats in FPDS, this data element is named "Base and All Options Value (Total Contract Value)."

(*1*) For each IDC resulting from a solicitation where multiple awards were contemplated, this is the maximum for that resulting specific contract. Note: this amount is not always the same as the ceiling for the program under which multiple contracts were awarded. Each contract shall have a specific ceiling identified for that specific period (see FAR 16.504(a)(4)(ii)).

(*2*) This data field shall be updated on the contract action report used to report the modification whenever the total potential value is changed by modification, including changes made as a result of overruns or claims. When reporting such a modification, report the net value of the change itself in

"Current" field; FPDS will calculate the new total Base and All Options Value. When an ACO executes a modification and the previous value reported in FPDS is incorrect, the ACO shall notify the procuring contract office of the discrepancy and enter the appropriate value in the "Current" field of the "Base and All Options Value" to ensure a correct total is represented. The ACO shall document the discrepancy correction in the contract file.

(D) The amount entered in the "Action Obligation" for new awards shall be the total value of all the obligated funds on the contract or order, represented in U.S. dollars and cents. When reporting a modification, report the net value of the change in funding accomplished by the modification in the "Current" field; FPDS will calculate the new total action obligation value. When an ACO executes a modification and the previous value reported in FPDS is incorrect, the ACO shall notify the procuring contract office of the discrepancy and enter the appropriate value in the "Current" field of the "Action Obligation Value" field to ensure a correct total is represented. The ACO shall document the discrepancy correction in the contract file.

(E) The amount entered in the "Total Estimated Order Value" for new IDC awards shall be the total estimated value of all anticipated orders to be placed under the contract. For DoD, this value should match the "Base and All Options" value, as DoD does not obligate funds on indefinite-delivery contracts themselves.

(vii) *FPDS Entry – Purchaser Information Section.*

(A) Enter the contracting office's DoD Activity Address Code (DoDAAC) in as the "Contracting Office ID" data field.

(B) If the requiring organization is a DoD organization, enter the DoDAAC for the requiring office in the "Funding Office ID" data field. This is normally the DoDAAC that is included on the purchase request in the purchase request number. If the contract action is supporting working capital funded efforts and the specific requiring office is unknown, enter the DoDAAC for the working capital funded office. Do not enter the DoDAAC from the contracting office in the "Funding Office ID" field unless the contracting office is also the requiring organization.

(C) If the requiring organization is not a DoD organization, enter the Funding Office ID provided on the interagency agreement in the "Funding Office ID" data field.

(D) Choose the appropriate value in the "Foreign Funding" data field as to whether or not the action includes foreign funding that is identified as FMS. If the action does not include foreign funds, choose "Not Applicable."

(viii) *FPDS Entry – Contractor Information Section.*

(A) Enter the DUNS number for the vendor in the "DUNS Number" data field. This DUNS number will be used to pull the associated current record from the System for Award Management (SAM) database.

(B) If a SAM exception applies to the procurement, ensure the correct exception is chosen from the "SAM Exception" data field. In this case the DUNS number entered in the "DUNS Number" data field will be used to pull the contractor's name and location information from Dun & Bradstreet's database.

(ix) *FPDS Entry – Contract Data Section.*

(A) On the contract action report used to report the base award, choose the type of contract pricing in the "Type of Contract" data field that is applicable to the predominant amount of the action, based on the value of the line items. This value will automatically populate any subsequent contract action reports for modifications.

(B) If the procurement is for services, enter the appropriate Inherently Governmental Functions indicator:

(*1*) "Closely Associated" means functions that are closely associated with inherently governmental functions; those contractor duties that could expand to become inherently governmental functions without sufficient management controls or oversight on the part of the Government. Office of Federal Procurement Policy (OFPP) Policy Letter 11–01, Performance of Inherently Governmental and Critical Functions, provides examples of work that is inherently governmental and therefore must be performed by Federal employees and work that is closely associated with inherently governmental functions that may be performed by either Federal employees or contractors.

(*2*) "Critical Functions" means functions that are necessary to the agency being able to effectively perform and maintain control of its mission and operations. Typically, critical functions are recurring and long-term in duration.

(*3*) "Other Functions" means neither "Closely Associated Functions" nor "Critical Functions."

(*4*) For services that include performing both "Closely Associated" and "Critical Functions," select "Closely Associated, Critical Functions."

(*5*) If services include performing "Other Functions" and either "Closely Associated" or "Critical Functions," select only the "Closely Associated" or "Critical Functions" value.

(C) Enter "Yes" in the "Multiyear Contract" field if the procurement is a multiyear contract in accordance with FAR 17.1; otherwise enter "No."

(D) Enter the full name of the program, not an acronym or abbreviation, in the "Major Program" field if there is an associated program name. Contracts and agreements with ordering provisions established as multi-agency contracts or for wide use within an agency shall always include a program name in order to ensure they are correctly represented in the Interagency Contract Directory (ICD) (see FAR 7.105(b)(1) for website).

(E) If the procurement is as a result of a requirement responding specifically to a National Interest Action that is listed in this field (for example, "Hurricane Sandy" or "Operation Enduring Freedom (OEF),") then select the appropriate value. Otherwise, enter "None."

(F) For indefinite-delivery contracts, enter the appropriate type of IDC in the "Type of IDC" field: Indefinite Quantity, Requirements, or Definite Quantity.

(G) For IDVs in the "Multiple or Single Award IDV" field:

(*1*) Select "Multiple Award" when the contract action is—

(*i*) One of several indefinite-delivery indefinite-quantity (IDIQ) contracts awarded under a single solicitation in accordance with FAR 16.504(c);

(*ii*) One of several blanket purchase agreements (BPAs) awarded against a Federal Supply Schedule in accordance with FAR 8.405-3;

(*iii*) Any other IDIQ contract that an agency enters into with two or more sources under the same solicitation that requires contracting officers to compare or compete their requirements among several vendors; or

(*iv*) A part 13 BPA or Basic Ordering Agreement (BOA) with multiple awards.

(*2*) Select "Single Award" when the contract does not satisfy any of the above criteria for a multiple award.

(H) When reporting the initial award of IDCs and agreements that allow orders to be placed by other contracting offices, enter the acronym or short abbreviation of the program name for the program supported by the contract or agreement with ordering provisions in the "Program Acronym" field. Contracts and agreements with ordering provisions established as multi-agency contracts or for wide use within an agency shall always include an acronym or abbreviated program name, and the first five characters of this field shall be:

(*1*) "FSSI-" for a federal strategic sourcing initiative (FSSI) vehicle.

(*2*) "MMAC-" for a multiple-award multi-agency contract.

(*3*) "SMAC-" for a single-award multi-agency contract.

(*4*) "MBPA-" for a blanket purchase agreement available for use outside of the Department of Defense.

(*5*) "AGYV-" for an agency-wide acquisition vehicle. For the purpose of this section, an agency-wide acquisition vehicle is an IDC, BPA, or basic ordering agreement intended for the sole use of the Department of

Defense. These may be for DoD-wide use or limited to one or more specific Military Services or Defense Agencies.

(I) In the "Cost or Pricing Data" field, enter "Yes" if certified cost and pricing data were obtained. Enter "Not Obtained – Waived" if the requirement for certified cost and pricing data was waived. Enter "No" if certified cost or pricing data were not obtained and no waiver was required. See FAR 15.403 for the requirements for certified cost and pricing data.

(J) Enter "Yes" in the "Purchase Card as Payment Method" field if the GPC was used as the method of payment or as both the method of purchase and payment for the contract action. Enter "No" if neither was the case.

(K) In the "Undefinitized Action" field, enter "Letter Contract" if the procurement is a letter contract that meets the description in FAR 16.603-1. Enter "Other Undefinitized Action" if the procurement is for any other unpriced action that shall be subsequently definitized. Enter "No" if neither of these situations is applicable.

(L) Enter "Yes" in the "Performance Based Service Acquisition" field if the procurement is for services and performance based acquisition procedures were used. Enter "No" if the procurement is for services and performance based acquisition procedures were not used. Enter "Not Applicable" if the procurement is not for services.

(M) In the "Contingency Humanitarian Peacekeeping Operation" field, enter "Contingency" if the procurement is in response to a contingency operation as defined in 10 U.S.C. 101(a)(13) or "Humanitarian" if the procurement is in response to a humanitarian or peacekeeping operation as defined in 10 U.S.C. 2302(8). Otherwise, enter "Not Applicable."

(N) In the "Cost Accounting Standards Clause" field, enter "Yes" if the procurement was subject to cost accounting standards (CAS) and the associated clauses were included in the contract. Enter "No – CAS Waiver Approved" if the procurement is subject to CAS but a waiver was approved. Enter "Not Applicable" if neither situation applies.

(O) *Consolidated Contract.*

(*1*) Enter "Consolidated Requirements" when the requirements meet the definition of "Consolidation or consolidated requirement" at FAR 2.101 but a written determination was not made because the estimated value of the requirements were at or below $2 million, or the requirements are bundled and a written determination for bundling is required.

(*2*) Enter "Consolidated Requirements with Written Determination" when the requirements meet the definition of "Consolidation or consolidated requirement" at FAR 2.101 and a written determination is made in accordance with FAR 7.107-2.

(*3*) Enter "Consolidated Requirements Under FAR 7.107-1(b) Exceptions" when the requirements meet the definition of "Consolidation or consolidated requirement" at FAR 2.101 but do not require a written determination in accordance with FAR 7.107-1(b).

(*4*) Enter "Not Consolidated" when the requirements do not meet the definition of "Consolidation or consolidated requirement" at FAR 2.101.

(P) Enter "1" in the "Number of Actions" data field unless using Express Reporting procedures described in paragraph (1)(iii) of this section.

(x) *FPDS Entry – Legislative Mandates Section.*

(A) For the "Clinger-Cohen Act," "Labor Standards," "Materials, Supplies, Articles, and Equipment," and "Construction Wage Rate Requirements" data elements, answer "Yes" if the acts apply to any of the line items on the award. Choose "Not Applicable" if the act itself is not applicable based on implementation requirements in the FAR for each act (see FAR subparts 22.10, 22.6, and 22.4, respectively), or choose "No" if the act is applicable, but the associated clauses were not included in the award. For the "Clinger-Cohen Act", choose "No" if either the Act is not applicable or the planning requirements from the act were not accomplished.

(B) Indicate in the "Interagency Contracting Authority" data field if the action is subject to the Economy Act, a different statutory authority, or if interagency authorities are not applicable. If the contracting officer selects "Other Statutory Authority" in the "Interagency Contracting Authority", they shall enter the name of the other authority in the associated text box.

(C) In the "Additional Reporting" data field, select each value that represents reporting to be accomplished by the contractor that is required by the contract. Multiple values may be selected.

(1) If none of the reporting requirements apply, select "None of the Above."

(2) Select "Service Contract Inventory FAR 4.17" if FAR clause 52.204-14, Service Contract Reporting Requirements, is present in the contract.

(3) Select "Employment Eligibility Verification (52.222-54)" if FAR clause 52.222-54, Employment Eligibility Verification, is included in the contract or if 52.212-5, Contract Terms and Conditions Required to Implement Statutes or Executive Orders—Commercial, is included in the contract and subparagraph (34) is checked for 52.222-54, Employment Eligibility Verification.

(xi) *FPDS Entry – Principal Place of Performance Section.*

(A) For supplies, the data entered in this section shall reflect the predominant place where manufacturing occurred or where procured finished products were taken out of inventory. Do not enter the Government delivery location. When the manufacturing or inventory location is unknown, and the contractor has not provided a separate address for the place of performance in FAR provision 52.214-14 or 52.215-6 with its offer, enter the contractor's physical address that corresponds with its registration in the System for Award Management (SAM) that is identified by its DUNS number and CAGE code.

(B) For services, identify the location that represents the predominant place the services are performed. For services that start performance in one location and complete performance in a different location, such as transportation and cargo shipment services, the completion or destination location shall be entered. If the contract or order has multiple destination locations, enter the location where the predominant amount is being delivered.

(C) For place of performance based in the United States, ensure the zip code + 4 data element is entered. This will populate the city and state fields accordingly. Zip codes and their +4 extensions can be identified at the United States Postal Service website (*www.usps.com*). When a "+4" extension cannot be determined for a zip code (for example, in a highly rural area or at a location with a vanity address), choose the "+4" extension that represents the area nearest to the place of performance.

(xii) *FPDS Entry – Contract Marketing Data Section.* This section applies to IDVs (i.e., BOAs, BPAs, and IDCs) only.

(A) Enter the website in the "Website URL" data field where a new user would find the best information about ordering under the vehicle. This is an optional field, but each multi-agency contract being reported should include one.

(B) In the "Who Can Use" data field, choose the value that best represents which agencies are allowed to have their contracting officers place orders under the vehicle. If only the office that awarded the IDV is allowed to place orders under the vehicle, choose "Only My Agency". Do not list codes or text under the "Codes" or "Other" options unless the vehicle only allows very specific parts of agencies to place orders.

(C) Include in the "Email Contact" data element the specific email of the contracting officer responsible for the IDV who is able to answer questions concerning ordering. A group email address may only be used in this field if it is continuously monitored.

(D) Enter the maximum dollar value of each order that may be issued under the vehicle in the "Individual Order / Call Limit" field.

(E) Enter the fee charged to the ordering agency for allowing the ordering agency to place an order under the specific vehicle. The fee may be identified as a fixed percentage, an upper and lower amount if based on a varying factor, or as "no fee." This is not the fee paid to a contracting office for placing an order on behalf of a requiring office.

(F) Enter a brief description of ordering instructions in the "Ordering Procedure" data field. If the "Website URL" field is entered, this field is not required to be completed; however, ensure that the website provided gives the user enough information to be able to place an order.

(xiii) *FPDS Entry – Product or Service Information Section*.

(A) For the "Product or service code (PSC)" data field choose the code that best represents the predominant amount of supplies or services being procured on the award. The list of active PSCs for use in FPDS reporting is available on the FPDS website under the "Worksite" section under "Reference."

(B) For the "Principal NAICS code" data field, enter the NAICS code that best represents the type of industry related to the predominant amount of supplies or services being procured on the award. If the award was a result of a solicitation that included any of the following provisions, use the NAICS code that was included in the provision: 52.204-8, Annual Representations and Certifications; 52.212-3, Offeror Representations and Certifications – Commercial Items; or 52.219-1, Small Business Program Representations. The list of active NAICS codes for use in FPDS reporting is available on the FPDS website under the "Worksite" section under "Reference".

(C) *Contract bundling*.

(*1*) Enter "Bundled Requirements" when the requirements meet the definition of "Bundling" at FAR 2.101.

(*2*) Enter "Substantially Bundled Requirements" when the requirements meet the definition of "Bundling" at FAR 2.101 but has an estimated value outlined at FAR 7.107-4, Substantial bundling.

(*3*) Enter "Bundled Requirements Under a FAR 7.107-1(b) Exception" when the requirements meet the definition of "Bundling" at FAR 2.101 but do not require a written determination in accordance with FAR 7.107-1(b).

(*4*) Enter "Not Bundled" when the requirements do not meet the definition of "Bundling" at FAR 2.101.

(D) Enter in the "DoD Acquisition Program" data field—

(1) The Major Defense Acquisition Program (MDAP) or Major Automated Information System (MAIS) program number (PNO) if a new award is in support of an Acquisition Category (ACAT) I MDAP or MAIS. If needed, use the code look-up table provided for the data element in the CAR to identify the code for an ACAT I MDAP/MAIS.

(2) The appropriate following code if a new award is associated with one of the following programs or activities:

(*i*) ZBL – for Performance-Based Logistics (PBL) support.

(*ii*) ZRS – for Randolph-Sheppard Act dining facilities.

(*iii*) ZBC – for Base Realignment and Closure (BRAC) environmental activities.

(*iv*) ZDE – for Defense environmental and restoration programs.

(*v*) ZOP – for other environmental programs.

(*vi*) ZSE – for Environmental Protection Agency (EPA) Superfund activities.

(*vii*) ZSF – prescribed under a Status of Forces Agreement (SOFA).

(3) "000" if neither (1) or (2) in this section apply.

(E) Enter the country code where products were manufactured or performance of services occurred in the "Country of Product or Service Origin" data field. If needed, use the code look-up table provided for the data element in the CAR to identify the code for a country.

(F) *Place of Manufacture*.

(*1*) Choose "Not a Manufactured End Product" when the procurement is for services or for unmanufactured end products (e.g., ores, food, animals).

(*2*) Choose "Manufactured Outside the U.S. – Use Outside the U.S." when the procurement is for supplies acquired for use outside the United States.

(*3*) If the procurement is for supplies to be used inside the United States, choose one of the following:

(*i*) "Manufactured in the U.S." when the supplies that are considered domestic end products (see FAR 25.101).

(*ii*) "Manufactured Outside the U.S. – Trade Agreements" when the supplies are acquired subject to a Trade Agreement (see FAR 25.4) where the Buy American Act requirements have been waived.

(*iii*) The exception to the Buy American Act that was used in the procurement when the supplies are considered foreign end products (see FAR 25.103):

(*A*) "Manufactured Outside the U.S. – Public Interest."

(*B*) "Manufactured Outside the U.S. – Domestic Nonavailability."

(*C*) "Manufactured Outside the U.S. – Unreasonable Cost."

(*D*) "Manufactured Outside the U.S. – Resale."

(*E*) "Manufactured Outside the U.S. – Commercial Information Technology."

(*F*) "Manufactured Outside the U.S. – Qualifying Country." Only choose "Manufactured Outside the United States – Qualifying Country" if the country of product or service origin is one of the current qualifying countries at DFARS 225.003.

(G) In the "Domestic or Foreign Entity" data field, choose the most applicable answer regarding the ownership of the contractor.

(H) Indicate whether Government Furnished Property (GFP), (see FAR 45.101), is included on the award in the "GFE/GFP Provided Under This Action" data field.

(*1*) When reporting modifications to previously reported award, the CAR should carry the same value for this data element as was on the CAR for the initial award unless the modification itself is specifically adding GFP where the originally was none. There is no need to create a CAR solely to report the return of GFP at the end of performance.

(*2*) When reporting task, delivery, or call orders under indefinite-delivery contracts or agreements, this data element reflects whether GFP is or is not included specifically as a part of the order itself. The value for the underlying contract or agreement is collected separately.

(I) For the "Description of requirement" data field, enter a short description of what is being procured by the action. This should be entered in plain English with no acronyms or military jargon such that the public can understand what is being acquired by the Department. Do not use national stock numbers, part numbers, or other identifiers without also including associated plain English descriptions. When reporting modifications, do not use this field to explain what type of procurement process is accomplished (e.g., exercise option year, incremental funding); continue to address what is being procured.

(J) For the "Recovered materials/sustainability" data field, choose the value from the list below that reflects the requirements of sustainability incorporated into the contract or order. If there is a combination of the attributes on the contract that does not exist in the list below, choose the one from the list that most closely reflects the situation on the contract.

(1) FAR 52.223-4 included. Use when the contract includes the requirement for recovered materials in accordance with FAR subpart 23.4 and provision 52.223-4, Recovered Material Certification, was included in the solicitation.

(2) FAR 52.223-4 and 52.223-9 included. Use when the contract includes the requirement for recovered materials in accordance with FAR subpart 23.4, provision 52.223-4 was included in the solicitation, and clause 52.223-9 is included in the contract.

(3) No clauses included and no sustainability included. Use when the contract includes neither requirements nor provisions/clauses for recovered materials or energy efficient, biobased, or environmentally preferable products or services.

(4) Energy efficient. Use when the contract includes the requirement for energy efficient products or services in accordance with FAR subpart 23.2.

(5) Biobased. Use when the contract includes the requirement for biobased products or services in accordance with FAR subpart 23.4.

(6) Environmentally preferable. Use when the contract includes the requirement for environmentally preferable products or services in accordance with FAR subpart 23.7.

(7) FAR 52.223-4 and energy efficient. Use when the contract includes the requirement for–

(*i*) Recovered materials in accordance with FAR subpart 23.4 and provision 52.223-4 was included in the solicitation; and

(*ii*) Energy efficient products or services in accordance with FAR subpart 23.2.

(8) FAR 52.223-4 and biobased. Use when the contract includes the requirement for–

(*i*) Recovered materials in accordance with FAR subpart 23.4 and provision 52.223-4 was included in the solicitation; and

(*ii*) Biobased products or services in accordance with FAR subpart 23.4.

(9) FAR 52.223-4 and environmentally preferable. Use when the contract includes the requirement for–

(*i*) Recovered materials in accordance with FAR subpart 23.4 and provision 52.223-4 was included in the solicitation; and

(*ii*) Environmentally preferable products or services in accordance with FAR subpart 23.7.

(10) FAR 52.223-4, biobased and energy efficient. Use when the contract includes the requirement for–

(*i*) Recovered materials in accordance with FAR subpart 23.4 and provision 52.223-4 was included in the solicitation;

(*ii*) Energy efficient products or services in accordance with FAR subpart 23.2; and

(*iii*) Biobased products or services in accordance with FAR subpart 23.4.

(11) FAR 52.223-4, biobased and environmentally preferable. Use when the contract includes the requirement for–

(*i*) Recovered materials in accordance with FAR subpart 23.4 and provision 52.223-4 was included in the solicitation;

(*ii*) Biobased products or services in accordance with FAR subpart 23.4; and

(*iii*) Environmentally preferable products or services in accordance with FAR subpart 23.7.

(12) FAR 52.223-4, biobased, energy efficient and environmentally preferable. Use when the contract includes the requirement for–

(*i*) Recovered materials in accordance with FAR subpart 23.4 and provision 52.223-4 was included in the solicitation;

(*ii*) Energy efficient products or services in accordance with FAR subpart 23.2;

(*iii*) Biobased products or services in accordance with FAR subpart 23.4; and

(*iv*) Environmentally preferable products or services in accordance with FAR subpart 23.7.

(*xiv*) *FPDS Entry – Competition Information Section.*

(A) *Solicitation procedures.* Select the appropriate entry from the following list:

(1) Simplified Acquisition. Report this code for competitive and noncompetitive contract actions that used simplified acquisition procedures in accordance with FAR part 13, to include acquisitions using the Commercial Items Test Program. However, if the action is noncompetitive and the reason for other than full and open competition is other than "Authorized by Statute," "Authorized Resale," or "SAP Noncompetition," then enter "Only One Source Solicited" as the solicitation procedure. (Note that most times when in conflict, the reason for other than full and open competition takes precedence over the type of solicitation procedure used.)

(2) Only One Source Solicited. Use this code if no solicitation procedure was used or only one source is solicited for the action.

(3) Negotiated Proposal/Quote. Use this code for competitive contract actions that use negotiated procedures (FAR parts 12, 13, or 15).

(4) Sealed Bid. Use this code for contract actions using sealed bid procedures (FAR part 14).

(5) Two Step. Use this code for contract actions that use a combination of sealed bids and negotiated procedures (FAR 6.102).

(6) Architect-Engineer FAR 6.102. Use this code if the action resulted from selection of sources for architect-engineer contracts pursuant to FAR 6.102(d)(1).

(7) Basic Research. Use this code if the action resulted from a competitive selection of basic research proposals pursuant to FAR 6.102(d)(2).

(8) Alternative Sources. Use this code if the action resulted from use of procedures that provided for full and open competition after exclusion of sources to establish or maintain alternative sources pursuant to FAR 6.202.

(9) Subject to Multiple Award Fair Opportunity. FPDS will automatically populate this entry for orders placed against multiple award contracts (to include Federal Supply Schedules) and FAR part 8 BPAs (and orders issued under such BPAs that are subject to fair opportunity pursuant to FAR 16.505(b)(1).

(B) *Extent Competed.* Select the appropriate entry from the following list. The extent competed for any modification or order against a task or delivery order contract pulls from the basic contract and is shown in the "Extent competed for referenced IDV" data field.

(1) Competed under SAP. Report this for competitive contract actions that were awarded using FAR part 13 Simplified Acquisition Procedures (i.e., solicitation procedures were "Simplified Acquisition"), to include for the Commercial Item Test Program.

(2) Full and Open Competition (F&OC). Report this if the contract action resulted from an award pursuant to FAR 6.102(a), Sealed bids; FAR 6.102(b), Competitive proposals; FAR 6.102(c), Combination; or any other competitive method that did not exclude sources of any type.

(3) F&OC after Exclusion of Sources. Report this when sources are excluded before competition. (Note: This terminology is broader than FAR subpart 6.2, which includes set-aside actions and actions to establish or maintain alternate sources, in that it also includes actions justified by a justification and approval that provided for competition).

(4) Not Available for Competition. Report this if the contract action is not available for competition (i.e., contract actions where the solicitation procedure was "Only One Source" and the reason not competed is "Authorized by Statute," "International Agreement," "Utilities," or "Authorized Resale.") Note that sole source awards for 8a firms, HUBZone firms, and service-related disabled veteran-owned concerns should always be identified as "Authorized by Statute" as the reason for other than full and open competition.

(5) Not Competed under SAP. Report this for non-competitive contract actions that were awarded using FAR part 13, Simplified Acquisition Procedures (i.e., solicitation procedures were "Simplified Acquisition").

(6) Not Competed. Report this when the contract action is not competed and the solicitation procedures are "Only One Source."

(C) *Type of Set-Aside.*

(1) If the contract action is a result of a set-aside or sole source authorized under part 19 of the FAR, choose the applicable value. In order to indicate a FAR part 19 set-aside or sole source on an order under a multiple-award contract, see paragraph (F) of this section.

(2) Note that the type of set-aside is collected on the original award. In the case of a task or delivery order being reported, the user will see the type of set-aside from the original contract in the "Type Set Aside" data element. The "Type of Set-Aside Source" data element is system generated to indicate whether the data in the "Type Set Aside" data element was entered on the specific CAR being viewed or if it was pre-populated from the original contract award.

(D) *SBIR/STTR.* Ensure the "SBIR/STTR" data field is completed if the contract action is a result of a Small Business Innovative Research (SBIR) or Small Technology Transfer Research (STTR) Program. SBIR and STTR Phase III awards require that a previous SBIR or STTR award exists.

(E) *Other than Full and Open Competition.*

(1) Simplified Acquisition Procedures (SAP). Select only "SAP Non-Competition," "Authorized by Statute" if a sole source set-aside shall also be noted, or "Authorized for Resale" when the award is noncompetitive and simplified acquisition procedures were used, including those awards under the commercial items test program. Do not choose other values from the list.

(2) *Other than Simplified Acquisition Procedures.* Select from available values the one that matches the FAR part 6 authority referenced in the Justification & Authorization document for using other than competitive procedures. Do not choose "SAP Non-competition."

(3) *Acquiring Products or Services from Afghanistan.* When DFARS 225.7703-1(a)(2) or (3) procedures are used to limit competition to products or services from Afghanistan, or to award a contract to a particular source or sources from Afghanistan, select "Authorized by Statute" in the "Other than Full and Open Competition" data field.

(F) *Fair Opportunity/Limited Sources.* This field is the basis for determining whether competition is provided for on orders placed against multiple-award contracts (to include DoD contracts, Governmentwide Acquisition Contracts, Federal Supply Schedules, and BPAs issued under the Federal Supply Schedules). If a Federal Supply Schedule contract or a Governmentwide multiple-award contract is not coded as a multiple-award vehicle, thereby preventing completion of this field, the FPDS user should advise the agency FPDS so that the contracting office for the multiple-award contract can be notified and pursue correction.

(1) Urgency. Report this if the action was justified pursuant to FAR 8.405-6(a)(1)(i)(A) or 16.505(b)(2)(i)(A).

(2) Only One Source. Other – Report if the action was justified pursuant to FAR 8.405-6(a)(1)(i)(B) or 16.505(b)(2)(i)(B).

(3) Follow-On Delivery Order Following Competitive Initial Order. Report this if the action was justified pursuant to FAR 8.405-6(a)(1)(i)(C) or 16.505(b)(2)(i)(C).

(4) Minimum Guarantee. Report this if it was necessary to place an order to satisfy a minimum amount guaranteed to the contractor. See FAR 16.505(b)(2)(i)(D).

(5) Other Statutory Authority. Report this if a statute expressly authorizes or requires that the purchase by made from a specified source. See FAR16.505(b)(2)(i)(E).

(6) Fair Opportunity Given. Report this if fair opportunity was given pursuant to FAR 16.505(b)(1).

(7) Competitive Set-Aside. Report this if the order was set aside pursuant to FAR 19.502-4(c) and a sub-set of multiple-award contract holders meeting the set-aside criteria were provided fair opportunity to submit an offer. If this value is selected, also choose the appropriate set-aside in the "Type of Set-Aside" field. Do not select this value if the original multiple award contract itself was set-aside or partially set-aside.

(8) Sole Source. Report this if the order was issued pursuant to FAR 19.502-4(c) and awarded to a single contract holder meeting the socio-economic criteria without providing fair opportunity to other multiple-award contract holders. If this value is selected, also choose the appropriate value in the "Type of Set-Aside" field.

(G) If an award did not provide for full and open competition; or in the case of simplified acquisition, did not provide the maximum extent of competition practicable; select the value in the "Other Than Full and Open Competition" field that represents the justification used.

(H) In the "Commercial Item Acquisition Procedures" data field, indicate whether commercial procedures were (1) used for commercial items, (2) used for supplies or services pursuant to FAR 12.102(f), (3) used for services pursuant to FAR 12.102(g), or (4) not used.

(I) In the "Simplified Procedures for Certain Commercial Items" data field, indicate if the contract action utilized procedures under FAR 13.5.

(J) In the "A-76 Action" data field, indicate if the contract action resulted from an A-76 / FAIR Act competitive sourcing process. Note, however, that DoD is currently under a moratorium from procuring services using these procedures. See *PGI 207.302* for more information.

(K) In the "Local Area Set Aside" data field, indicate if the contract action resulted from a local area set-aside in accordance with FAR 26.202.

(L) In the "FedBizOpps" data field, enter "Yes" if the award was greater than $25,000 in value and subject to FAR 5.2 synopsis requirements. Enter "No" if the award was greater than $25,000 in value, but an exception to synopsis requirements applied. Enter "Not Applicable" if the award was less than or equal to $25,000 in value.

(M) *Number of Offers.*

(*1*) Enter the specific number of offers received in response to the solicitation. In the case of contracts awarded as a result of a Broad Agency Announcement, enter the number of proposals received under the specific announcement. In the case of orders under a multiple-award contract (including Federal Supply Schedules and GWACs), BOAs, and BPAs, enter the number of offers received for the specific order.

(*2*) Note that the "Number of Offers Received" is collected on the original award. In the case of a task or delivery order being reported, the user will see the number of offers from the original contract in the "IDV Number of Offers" data element. The "Number of Offers Source" data element is system generated to indicate whether the data in the "Number of Offers Received" data element was entered on the specific CAR being viewed or if it was pre-populated from the original contract award.

(xv) *FPDS Entry – Preference Programs / Other Data Section.*

(A) *Contracting Officer's Business Size Selection—*

(*1*) When entering a new contract, purchase order, or agreement award in FPDS, contracting officers shall ensure they appropriately choose "Small Business" or "Other than Small Business" in the "Contracting Officer's Determination of Business Size" data field according to the NAICS code applied to the award, its associated size standard, and the contractor's response to provision 52.212-3 or 52.219-1. The contracting officer shall enter "Other than Small Business" for awards where the contractor has not certified to its status in one of these provisions.

(*2*) If the "Contracting Officer's Determination of Business Size" data field is completed with "Small Business", the contractor's other socio-economic information that it has entered or the Small Business Administration (SBA) has provided to the System for Award Management (SAM) database will be included in the contract action report. This includes designations such as SBA-Certified 8(a), Women-owned Small Business, Service Disabled Veteran Owned.

(*3*) Contracting officers will not be allowed to identify types of set-asides in FPDS unless the "Contracting Officer's Determination of Business Size" field is completed with "Small Business," and other required socio-economic designations are present in the Contractor's SAM record (e.g., contractor shall have the SBA-Certified 8(a) designation in order to identify an 8(a) type set-aside in FPDS).

(*4*) All subsequent modifications and delivery orders under the initial award will be automatically populated with the same designations.

(B) *Subcontracting Plan.* Select whether a subcontracting plan is required for the contract action, and, if so, which type applies from the following values:

(*1*) Plan Not Required;

(*2*) Plan Not Included, No Subcontracting Possibilities;

(*3*) Individual Subcontracting Plan;

(*4*) Commercial Subcontracting Plan; or

(*5*) DoD Comprehensive Subcontracting Plan.

(4) *Reporting modifications to FPDS.*

(i) Modifications against previously reported contracts, agreements, and orders are required to be reported to FPDS if they include any obligation or deobligation amount. They are also required to be reported to FPDS if there is no obligation or deobligation amount and involve a change to the data reported in any data field in the contract action report (e.g., vendor name, completion date, place of performance).

(ii) Contracting officers should choose the "Reason for Modification" value that best represents the purpose of the modification action. If more than one reason for modification applies, choose the more specific value. When a name, address, DUNS number, or CAGE code change occurs as the result of the modification, choose "Novation," "Vendor DUNS Change," or "Vendor Address Change," per the instructions at paragraphs (4)(v), (vi) and (vii), rather than other values that may also apply to the action (e.g., Exercise Option).

(iii) Do not use "Close Out" as the reason for modification in FPDS unless the modification being reported actually accomplishes the close out of the award.

(iv) DoD offices shall not use the "Transfer Action" value in the "Reason for Modification" field unless transferring the contract to a non-DoD contracting office (e.g., Department of Interior).

(v) Modifications for novations (see FAR subpart 42.12 and DFARS subpart 242.12) shall use "Novation Agreement" in the "Reason for Modification" field.

(A) When this value is used, the contracting officer shall enter the appropriate DUNS number for the contractor in the modification contract action report. FPDS will then bring over the current vendor name and address from the contractor's SAM record for that DUNS number into the modification contract action report. Subsequent contract action reports will show the updated DUNS number and vendor name.

(B) When this value is used, FPDS also allows the contracting officer to update the "Contracting Officer's Determination of Business Size" data field. The contracting officer shall ensure that the contractor's current size status is appropriately recorded on the modification contract action report. Subsequent contract action reports will reflect the size entered on this modification contract action report (see FAR subparts 19.301-2 and 19.301-3).

(vi) Modifications for contractor name changes that do not require a novation (see FAR subpart 42.12 and DFARS subpart 242.12) shall use "Vendor DUNS Change" in the "Reason for Modification" field. When this value is used, the contracting officer shall enter the appropriate DUNS number for the contractor in the modification contract action report. FPDS will then bring over the current vendor name and address from the contractor's SAM record for that DUNS number into the modification contract action report. Subsequent contract action reports will show the updated DUNS number and vendor name.

(vii) Modifications for contractor address changes that do not require a novation shall use "Vendor Address Change" in the "Reason for Modification" field. When this value is used, FPDS will bring over the current address from the contractor's SAM record into the modification contract action report. Subsequent contract action reports will show the updated address.

(viii) Modifications for re-representation actions (see FAR 19.301-2 and 19.301-3) shall use either "Re-representation" or "Re-representation of Non-Novated Merger/Acquisition", as appropriate, in the "Reason for Modification" field. When this value is used, FPDS allows the contracting officer to update the "Contracting Officer's Determination of Business Size" data field. The contracting officer shall ensure that the contractor's current size status is appropriately recorded on the modification contract action report. Subsequent contract action reports will reflect the size entered on this modification contract action report.

(ix) When a modification is reported with "Termination for Default" or "Termination for Cause" in the "Reason for Modification" data field, the user must also report the termination to the Federal Awardee Performance and Integrity Information System (FAPIIS) in accordance with FAR 42.1503(h) requirements.

(5) *Reporting awards where the GPC is both the method of purchase and payment.*

(i) Do not report open-market purchases (i.e., not under a Federal Supply schedule, agreement, or contract) made with the GPC valued less than the micro-purchase threshold to FPDS.

(ii) Purchases made using the GPC as the method of both purchase and payment under federal schedules, agreements, or contracts are required to be reported to FPDS regardless of value. Contracting offices shall ensure all such purchases made by their authorized cardholders are reported to FPDS no less frequently than monthly. Any individual purchase valued greater than $25,000 shall be reported individually to FPDS. For individual purchases valued less than $25,000, there are three acceptable methods for reporting to FPDS. They are, in preferred order of use—

(A) Report each order individually to FPDS;

(B) Report a consolidated express report to FPDS using the delivery order or BPA call format that references the individual contract or BPA, respectively; or

(C) Report a consolidated express report to FPDS using the purchase order format that uses the generic DUNS 136721250 for "GPC Consolidated Reporting" or 136721292 for "GPC Foreign Contractor Consolidated Reporting", as appropriate, as the identifier. Note that when a generic DUNS number is used to report these actions, only "Other than Small Business" is allowed as the "Contracting Officer's Determination of Business Size" selection.

(iii) For orders placed on FedMall, contracting officers are not required to separately report such awards to FPDS.

(6) *Using generic DUNS numbers*.

(i) Generic DUNS numbers may only be used for reporting to FPDS in accordance with FAR 4.605(c) or paragraph 204.606(5)(ii)(C) of this section. Note that if a generic DUNS number is used on the report to FPDS, systems that prepopulate data based on the DUNS number reported to FPDS may not be able to use the DUNS number for further reporting on that contract action because the contractor identification information is not accurately reflected. For example, assessing officials cannot report past performance reports to the Contractor Performance Assessment Reporting System (CPARS) (see FAR subpart 42.15) if a generic DUNS number was used to report the action to FPDS. Additionally, some reporting requirements placed on the contractor, such as subcontract reporting required by FAR subparts 4.14 and 19.7, are not able to be completed. Therefore, it is important that the use of generic DUNS numbers in reporting to FPDS be rare and only when necessary.

(ii) The following generic DUNS numbers are available for use in contract reporting only if the conditions in FAR 4.605(c) or paragraph 204.606(5)(ii)(C) of this section apply:

(A) DUNS 167445928 – Student Workers in Laboratories. Used to report actions awarded to student workers providing goods/services in government laboratories (or other government facilities) when obtaining a DUNS number would place a financial hardship on the student. Corresponding CAGE code in the System for Award Management (SAM): 35HL9.

(B) DUNS 123456787 – Miscellaneous Foreign Awardees. Used to report actions awarded to vendors located outside the United States providing goods/services when a specific DUNS number is not available. Corresponding CAGE code in SAM: 35KC0.

(C) DUNS 136666505 – Spouses of Service Personnel. Used to report actions awarded to service personnel dependents located and providing goods/services outside the United States when obtaining a DUNS number would place a financial hardship on the dependent. Corresponding CAGE code in SAM: 3JDV7.

(D) DUNS 167446249 – Navy Vessel Purchases In Foreign Ports. Used to report actions awarded to vendors located outside the United States providing goods/services in support of vessels located in foreign ports when a specific DUNS number is not available. Corresponding CAGE code in SAM: 35KD3.

(E) DUNS 153906193 – Foreign Utility Consolidated Reporting. Used to report procurement actions awarded to vendors located outside the United States providing utilities goods/services when a specific

DUNS number is not available. Corresponding CAGE code in SAM: 3JDX5.

(F) DUNS 790238638 – Domestic Awardees (Undisclosed). Used to report actions awarded to vendors located in the United States where identifying the vendor could cause harm to the mission or the vendor (for example, domestic shelters). Corresponding CAGE code in SAM: 3JEH0.

(G) DUNS 790238851 – Foreign Awardees (Undisclosed). Used to report actions awarded to vendors located outside the United States when identifying the vendor could cause harm to the mission or the vendor. Corresponding CAGE code in SAM: 3JEV3.

(H) DUNS 136721250 – GPC Consolidated Reporting. Used to report orders and calls issued via the GPC under indefinite-delivery type contracts and agreements to businesses located in the United States, and the identity of the DUNS number for the vendor is not available to the office reporting the action. Corresponding CAGE code in SAM: 3JDW4.

(I) DUNS 136721292 – GPC Foreign Contractor Consolidated Reporting. Used to report orders and calls issued via the GPC under indefinite delivery type contracts and agreements to businesses located outside the United States, and the identity of the DUNS number for the vendor is not available to the office reporting the action. Corresponding CAGE code in SAM: 3JDV9.

(7) *Contract Action Report Status.*

(i) The "Status" data element on contract action reports indicates whether an award is still open or officially "closed" and applies to the family of actions comprising the contract or order (i.e., includes all modifications to that contract or order). Values in this field will either be null (blank), indicating that the contract is still open; or "Closed," indicating the contract or order has completed closeout activities in accordance with FAR 4.804, as supplemented. Awards without the "Closed" status are assumed to still be open and either still within the established delivery dates or period of performance, or in a post-performance period preparing for closeout.

(ii) The "Status" is changed to "Closed" in one of three ways:

(A) User reports a modification using "Closeout" in the "Reason for Modification" field. This should be rare and only occur when a modification being issued actually closes the award in that modification (not just prepares for it). If a contract action report is finalized with "Closeout" as the value, it will no longer be able to be corrected by the user. Users will need to contact the FPDS help desk to perform any corrections.

(B) User with "Closeout" privileges in FPDS marks the award as closed. This will be rare in DoD; only the DoD and Service lead system administrators will be given these privileges.

(C) An agency system sends a "Close" notice via web services to FPDS.

(iii) When the "Status" is changed to "Closed" that status is applied to the contract or order and all of its subsequent modifications. Closed notices received for task, delivery, and call orders placed under IDCs or agreements do not cause the IDC or agreement to be closed. Closed notices received for IDCs or agreements do not cause task, delivery, and call orders placed under them to be closed.

(iv) Once a contract or order, and its modifications, has been marked as "Closed" the user or agency cannot change the status and will need to contact the FPDS help desk to remove the status if it was marked in error.

[Final rule, 74 FR 37644, 7/29/2009, effective 7/29/2009; Publication notice, 20100802; Publication notice, 20110920; Procurement notice, 20111220; Publication notice 20120420, 4/20/2012; Final rule, 77 FR 38736, 6/29/2012, effective 6/29/2012; Final rule, 77 FR 76941, 12/31/2012, effective 12/31/2012; Final rule, 78 FR 28756, 5/16/2013, effective 5/16/2013; Final rule, 78 FR 37980, 6/25/2013, effective 6/25/2013; Publication notice 20140512, effective 5/12/2014; Publication notice, 20140731; Final rule, 79 FR 73487, 12/11/2014, effective 12/11/2014; Final rule, 81 FR 93840, 12/22/2016, effective 12/22/2016; Publication notice, 20171208; Publication notice, 20191231]

SUBPART 204.8—CONTRACT FILES

204.804 Closeout of contract files.

Data supporting contract closeout (e.g., DD Form 1594, Contract Completion Statement) are electronically transmitted throughout DoD. The Defense Logistics Manual, 4000.25 Volume 7, Contract Administration, Chapter 4, Contract Completion Status Reporting, available at *http://www.dla.mil/j-6/dlmso/elibrary/manuals/dlm/dlm_pubs.asp*, contains detailed instructions regarding closeout and electronic data transmission.

(1) The administration office closeout date for file purposes will be the date in Block 9d of the DD Form 1594 or agency equivalent.

(2) If the contracting office must do a major closeout action that will take longer than 3 months after the date shown in Block 9d of the DD Form 1594—

(i) The purchasing office closeout date for file purposes will be the date in Block 10e of the DD Form 1594 or agency equivalent; and

(ii) The contracting office shall notify the contract administration office of the revised closeout date by either sending a copy of the completed DD Form 1594 or by electronically transmitting the data.

[Final rule, 73 FR 4113, 1/24/2008, effective 1/24/2008; Publication notice, 20131216; Final rule, 80 FR 58630, 9/30/2015, effective 9/30/2015]

204.804-1 Closeout by the office administering the contract.

(1) Locally developed forms or a statement of completion may be used instead of the DD Form 1594, Contract Completion Statement, and use the administration office closeout date. Whichever method is used, the form shall be retained in the contract file and copies sent to Electronic Data Access (EDA) and financial systems using the American National Standards Institute (ANSI) X12 Electronic Data Interchange (EDI) 567 transaction set.

(2) For contracts valued above the simplified acquisition threshold and not subject to the automated closeout procedures at PGI 204.804-3, prepare a DD Form 1597, Contract Closeout Check List (or agency equivalent), to ensure that all required contract actions have been satisfactorily accomplished.

[Final rule, 73 FR 4113, 1/24/2008, effective 1/24/2008; Publication notice, 20131216; Final rule, 80 FR 58630, 9/30/2015, effective 9/30/2015; Publication notice, 20190913]

204.804-2 Closeout of the contracting office files if another office administers the contract.

(1) When an office other than the contracting office administers the contract, the administering office shall—

(i) Provide the contracting office an interim contract completion statement when the contract is physically completed using the ANSI X12 567;

(ii) Prepare a DD Form 1597, Contract Closeout Check List or agency equivalent, if necessary, to determine that all the required actions have been completed;

(iii) Initiate DD Form 1593, Contract Administration Completion Record, if necessary to obtain statements from other organizational elements that they have completed the actions for which they are responsible; and

(iv) Upon final payment—

(A) Process a DD Form 1594 or the electronic equivalent verifying that all contract administration office actions have been completed; and

(B) Send the original DD Form 1594 or the electronic equivalent to the contracting office for filing in the contract file and send a copy to EDA and financial systems using the ANSI X12 567.

(2) If the administrative contracting officer (ACO) cannot close out a contract within the specified time period (see FAR 4.804-1), the ACO shall notify the procuring contracting officer (PCO) within 45 days after the expiration of the time period of—

(i) The reasons for the delay; and

(ii) The new target date for closeout.

(3) If the contract still is not closed out by the new target date, the ACO shall again notify the PCO with the reasons for delay and a new target date.

[Final rule, 73 FR 4113, 1/24/2008, effective 1/24/2008; Publication notice, 20131216; Final rule, 80 FR 58630, 9/30/2015, effective 9/30/2015]

204.804-3 Closeout of paying office contract files.

(1) *Automated contract closeout.* As permitted by FAR 4.804-5(a), automated contract closeout allows a system to initiate and execute the closeout action. The contract qualifies for the automated closeout process if the contract—

(i) Is firm-fixed priced;

(ii) Does not exceed a total contract value of $500,000 (inclusive of exercised options); and

(iii) Does not contain any of the following provisions requiring administrative action at closeout:

(A) FAR 52.211-11 Liquidated Damages—Supplies, Services, or Research and Development.

(B) FAR 52.216-7 Allowable Cost and Payment.

(C) FAR 52.227-9 Refund of Royalties.

(D) FAR 52.227-11 Patent Rights—Ownership by the Contractor.

(E) FAR 52.227-13 Patent Rights—Ownership by the Government.

(F) FAR 52.232-16 Progress Payments.

(G) FAR 52.232-29 Terms for Financing of Purchases of Commercial Items.

(H) FAR 52.232-30 Installment Payments for Commercial Items.

(I) FAR 52.232-32 Performance-Based Payments.

(J) FAR 52.245-1 Government Property.

(K) FAR 52.248-1 Value Engineering.

(2) Components may apply additional conditions not listed above, as necessary to ensure all contract requirements have been completed prior to closeout.

[Publication notice, 20131216; Final rule, 80 FR 58630, 9/30/2015, effective 9/30/2015]

SUBPART 204.11—SYSTEM FOR AWARD MANAGEMENT

204.1103 Procedures.

(i) Use the CCR database as the primary source of contractor information for contract award and administration, to include supporting contract writing, management, and administration systems. Do not request or use contractor information from other sources, unless another source, such as the On-Line Representations and Certifications Application (ORCA), is specifically authorized. At a minimum, supporting systems shall use the CCR database as the authoritative source for the following data elements, as applicable by system, when CCR is required in accordance with FAR Subpart 4.11:

(i) Use the SAM database as the primary source of contractor information for contract award and administration, to include supporting contract writing, management, and administration systems. Do not request or use contractor information from other sources, unless another source is specifically authorized. At a minimum, supporting systems shall use the SAM database as the authoritative source for the following data elements, as applicable by system, when SAM is required in accordance with FAR Subpart 4.11:

(A) Data Universal Number System (DUNS) Number.

(B) DUNS+4 Number.

(C) Commercial and Government Entity (CAGE) Code.

(D) Taxpayer Identification Number (TIN).

(E) Legal Business Name.

(F) Doing Business As (DBA) Name.

(G) Physical Address.

(H) Mailing Address.

(I) Electronic Funds Transfer (EFT) information (includes American Banking Association (ABA) Routing Number, Account Number, and Account Type).

(ii) Ensure that SAM non-disclosure requirements regarding TIN and EFT information are followed.

[Final rule, 74 FR 37642, 7/29/2009, effective 7/29/2009; Final rule, 78 FR 28756, 5/16/2013, effective 5/16/2013]

SUBPART 204.16—UNIFORM PROCUREMENT INSTRUMENT IDENTIFIERS

204.1601 Policy.

(b) Transition of PIID numbering. Components are encouraged to transition to the Procurement Instrument Identifier (PIID) numbering schema as soon as possible, but no later than the date specified at DFARS 204.1601(b).

(c) (i) A continued contract is issued solely for administrative reasons. When issuing a continued contract, the contracting officer shall perform the following tasks:

(A) Obtain approval at a level above the contracting officer before issuance of the continued contract.

(B) Assign a PIID to the continued contract that is different from the PIID assigned to the predecessor contract, using the uniform PIID numbering system prescribed in FAR 4.1603 and DFARS 204.1603. The predecessor contract will retain the PIID originally assigned to it.

(C) Find a clear breaking point (e.g., between issuance of orders, exercise of options, or establishment of a new line of accounting) to issue the continued contract.

(D) Clearly segregate contractual requirements for purposes of Government inspection, acceptance, payment, and closeout. Supplies already delivered and services already performed under the predecessor contract will remain under the predecessor contract. This will allow the predecessor contract to be closed out when all inspection, acceptance, payment, and other closeout issues associated with supplies delivered and services performed under the predecessor contract are complete.

(E) Include in the continued contract all terms and conditions of the predecessor contract that pertain to the supplies and services yet to be delivered or performed. At the time it is issued, the continued contract may not in any way alter the prices or terms and conditions established in the predecessor contract.

(F) Provide advance notice to the contractor before issuance of the continued contract, to include the PIID and the effective date of the continued contract.

(G) Modify the predecessor contract to—

(1) Reflect any necessary administrative changes such as transfer of Government property, and make the Government property accountable under the continued contract;

(2) Clearly state that future performance (e.g., issuance of orders or exercise of options) will be accomplished under the continued contract; and

(3) Specify the administrative reason for issuing the continued contract.

(H) Reference the predecessor contract PIID on the face page of the continued contract to ensure traceability.

(ii) Sample language for the administrative modification to the predecessor contract follows:

> This modification is issued for administrative purposes to facilitate continued contract performance due to [state the reason for assigning an additional PIID]. This modification is authorized in accordance with FAR 4.1601 and DFARS 204.1601.
>
> Supplies and services already acquired under this contract number shall remain solely under this contract number for purposes of Government inspection, acceptance, payment, and closeout. All future [delivery orders] [task orders] [options exercised] will be accomplished under continued contract [insert contract number].

[Final rule, 81 FR 9783, 2/26/2016, effective 2/26/2016; Publication notice, 20160923]

204.1603 Procedures.

(a) (3) (A) (*3*) Legacy contract writing systems authorized to use the letter T in position 9 of the PIID for automated requests for quotation include the following:

(*i*) Department of Navy's Item Management and Procurement (ITIMP) system.

(*ii*) Defense Logistics Agency's Enterprise Business System (EBS).

(b) Elements of a supplementary PIID.

(1) Examples of proper numbering for positions 2-6 (the first position will be either A or P) are as follows:

Normal modification	Provisioned items order (reserved for exclusive use by the Air Force only)	Shipping Instructions
00001 — 99999	K0001 — K9999	S0001 — S9999
then	KA001 — KZ999	SA001 — SZ999
A0001 — A9999	L0001 — L9999	T0001 — T9999
B0001 — B9999	LA001 — LZ999	TA001 — TZ999
and so on to	M0001 — M9999	U0001 — U9999
H0001 — H9999	MA001 — MZ999	UA001 — UZ999
then	N0001 — N9999	V0001 — V9999
J0001 — J9999	NA001 — NZ999	VA001 — VZ999
then	P0001 — P9999	W0001 — W9999
R0001 — R9999	PA001 — PZ999	WA001 — WZ999
then	Q0001 — Q9999	X0001 — X9999
AA001 — HZ999	QA001 — QZ999	XA001 — XZ999
then		
JA001 — JZ999		Y0001 — Y9999
RA001 — RZ999		YA001 — YZ999

(2) If the contract administration office is changing the contract administration or disbursement office for the first time and is using computer generated modifications to notify many offices, it uses the six position supplementary number ARZ999. If either office has to be changed again during the life of the contract, the supplementary number will be ARZ998, and on down as needed.

[Final rule, 81 FR 9783, 2/26/2016, effective 2/26/2016]

204.1670 Cross reference to Federal Procurement Data System.

The following matrices should be used as a cross reference between the terms used in the FAR, DFARS, and the Federal Procurement Data System (FPDS).

STRUCTURE OF REQUIRED IDENTIFIERS

Key and Description	Format			
A - DoD Procurement Instrument Identifier (PIID)	Consists of the concatenation of the following four fields:			
	Enterprise Identifier - DODAAC of contracting office	Fiscal Year in which award is made	Procurement Instrument Type Code	Serialized Identifier

Key and Description	Format			
	Six alpha-numeric characters excluding I and O	Two numeric characters	One alpha character excluding I and O	Four alpha-numeric characters excluding I and O. 0000 is not an acceptable value.
B - DoD Order Number (Supplementary PIID)	Four alpha-numeric characters excluding I and O. A and P are prohibited in the first position. 0000 is not an acceptable value. *(NOTE: Four character supplementary PIID order numbers are only allowed to be issued through FY16. Subsequently, all orders must be in the format shown above in section A of this table. DoD activities are encouraged to transition as soon as possible in FY16 to this new method for numbering orders under DoD contracts and agreements. Transition must be completed no later than October 1, 2016.)*			
C - DoD Procurement Instrument Modification Identifier (Supplementary PIID)	Six alpha-numeric characters beginning with A or P, excluding I and O. P00000 and A00000 are not acceptable values.			
D - DoD Order Modification Identifier (Supplementary PIID)	Two alpha-numeric characters excluding I and O. 00 is not an acceptable value. *(NOTE: Two character supplementary PIID modification numbers are only allowed to be issued to DoD orders issued through FY16. Modification to DoD orders issued after the transition to the new method of numbering orders under DoD contracts and agreements must be in the form shown in section C of this table.)*			
E - Non DoD Procurement Instrument Number	4 to 50 Alpha-numeric characters			

ELEMENTS NEEDED TO IDENTIFY A DEPARTMENT OF DEFENSE PROCUREMENT ACTION

		Required as shown below to uniquely identify the action.		
Procurement Instrument Action Type	**Reference Procurement Instrument (Reference Use Only)**	**Procurement Instrument Identifier (PIID) (Contract Number)**	**Order Number**	**Modification Number**

Key and Description	Format			
BPA or Order under a Schedule or other non-DoD Instrument		E	A	
Order against a BPA under a Schedule (FY16 and later)	E	A	A	
Order against a BPA under a Schedule (Pre-FY16)	E	A	B	
DoD Contract, Purchase Order, BOA, BPA not under a Schedule, or other instrument		A		
Order against a DoD Contract, BOA, BPA not under a Schedule, or other instrument (FY16 and later)		A	A	
Order against a DoD Contract, BOA, BPA not under a Schedule or other instrument (Pre-FY16)		A	B	
Modification to a BPA or Order under a Schedule or other non-DoD instrument	E	A		C
Modification to an Order against a BPA under a Schedule (FY16 and later)	E	A	A	C
Modification to an Order against a BPA under a Schedule (Pre-FY16)	E	A	B	D
Modification to a DoD Contract, Purchase Order, BOA, BPA not under a Schedule, or other instrument		A		C

Key and Description	Format			
Modification to an Order against a DoD Contract, BOA, or BPA not under a schedule (FY16 and later)		A	A	C
Modification to an Order against a DoD Contract, BOA, or BPA not under a schedule (Pre-FY16)		A	B	D

FPDS Crosswalk	FPDS FIELD NAME			
	REF_IDV PIID	REF_IDV_ MODIFICATION NUMBER	PIID	MODIFICATION_ NUMBER
BPA or Order under a Schedule or other non-DoD Instrument	E	Use 0	A	Use 0
Order against a BPA under a Schedule (FY16 and later)	A	Use 0	A	Use 0
Order against a BPA under a Schedule (Pre-FY16)	A	Use 0	B*	Use 0
DoD Contract, Purchase Order, BOA, BPA not under a Schedule, or other instrument			A	Use 0
Order against a DoD Contract, BOA, BPA not under a Schedule, or other instrument (FY16 and later)	A	Use 0	A	C
Order against a DoD Contract, BOA, BPA not under a Schedule, or other instrument (Pre-FY16)	A	Use 0	B*	D*

	FPDS FIELD NAME			
FPDS Crosswalk	REF_IDV PIID	REF_IDV_ MODIFICATION NUMBER	PIID	MODIFICATION_ NUMBER
Modification to a BPA or Order under a Schedule or other non-DoD Instrument			A	C
Modification to an Order against a BPA under a Schedule (FY16 and later)	A	Use 0	A	C
Modification to an Order against a BPA under a Schedule (Pre-FY16)	A	Use 0	B*	D*
Modification to a DoD Contract, Purchase Order, BOA, BPA not under a Schedule, or other instrument			A	C
Modification to an Order against a DoD Contract, BOA, or BPA not under a Schedule (FY16 and later)	A	Use 0	A	C
Modification to an Order against a DoD Contract, BOA, or BPA not under a Schedule (Pre-FY16)	A	Use 0	B*	D*

** Note that FPDS strips leading zeroes, so that modification 02 to order 0024 is shown as modification 2 to order 24.*

[Final rule, 81 FR 9783, 2/26/2016, effective 2/26/2016; Publication notice, 20171208]

SUBPART 204.18—COMMERCIAL AND GOVERNMENT ENTITY CODE

204.1870 Procedures. (No Text)

[Final rule, 79 FR 73492, 12/11/2014, effective 12/11/2014]

204.1870-1 Instructions to contracting officers.

Contracting officers shall—

(a) Assist offerors in obtaining the required Commercial and Government Entity (CAGE) codes. Note that if an offeror's facility requires security clearance in accordance with a potential contract, the offeror is required to have a CAGE code assigned to that facility. If the facility is a location other than the offeror's office submitting the proposal, that facility is not required to be separately registered in the System for Award Management (SAM) in order to have a CAGE code assigned. Offerors may be directed to the DLA CAGE Branch (see PGI 204.1870-2(c) for contact information);

(b) Not deny a potential offeror a solicitation package because the offeror does not have a CAGE code, DUNS number, or TIN;

(c) Not require a contractor to register sections or locations of their organization in SAM for reasons not already required by clauses present in their contracts in order to obtain a CAGE code; and

(d) Not require a contractor to obtain new CAGE codes or change CAGE code records assigned to their locations solely for Government administration purposes (such as a result of a Government reorganization, change in Government contracting officer or office) or for distinction in Government systems beyond physical address and Electronic Funds Transfer (EFT) data.

[Final rule, 79 FR 73492, 12/11/2014, effective 12/11/2014]

204.1870-2 Maintenance of the CAGE file.

The following information and procedures are provided to assist contracting officers.

(a) *Assignment of CAGE codes for entities located in the United States or its outlying areas.*

(1) CAGE codes are assigned per legal entity at individual physical addresses (i.e., the same entity at the same physical address will not be assigned two or more CAGE codes). The only exception to this rule is when an entity has a registration in the SAM with multiple EFT addresses identified by multiple DUNS+4 numbers. In this case, each DUNS+4 number record is assigned a separate CAGE code to assist in correct processing of payments.

(2) CAGE codes are not assigned to mailing addresses; a physical address shall be provided. Neither U.S. Post Office boxes nor addresses that can be identified as belonging to commercial mail and/or shipping provider locations will be accepted as physical addresses.

(3) CAGE codes are not assigned to entities where the provided physical address is identified as a short-term virtual location, such as mobile offices, commercial packaging/mailing facilities (e.g., UPS stores, FedEx stores), mailbox rentals and certain business incubator locations if the majority of the operations are not performed from that incubator location. A sole proprietor, partnership, corporate entity, or other business organization shall have a principal place of business, even if it is a home office, from where the business operates and record books are maintained. In that case, a home address of an officer of the company or board member would be required.

(4) Individuals who register in SAM as sole proprietors are assigned CAGE codes. However, there may not be multiple CAGE codes assigned to the same location even if the entity names are differentiated by establishing a Limited Liability Corporation (LLC) (e.g., "John Smith" and "John Smith, LLC"). Additionally, the standard for the legal business name for sole proprietors, driven by Internal Revenue Service (IRS) standards, is the use of the individual's personal name. Any additional name used for the sole proprietorship should be identified as a doing business as (DBA) name (e.g., "John Smith" is the legal business name, "Smith Construction" is the DBA).

(5) Authorized agents or brokers may be assigned CAGE codes for identification and processing purposes. A single CAGE code will be assigned to the agent or broker entity in addition to any codes assigned to the entities represented by the agent or broker (i.e., only one code will be assigned to a specific agent or broker entity regardless of the number of firms represented by that agent or broker). Codes will not be assigned to an agent or broker in care of the entity being represented or in any way infer that the agent or broker is a separate establishment bearing the name of the entity represented by the agent or broker.

(6) There are some cases where both the owner of real property and a separate legal

entity located at the same address as the real property each are required to have CAGE codes assigned. Examples are an office building owner and a tenant in the office building, or a land owner and a company using all or a portion of the land to farm. Additional cases exist where two separate entities may lease office space in the same building and both require CAGE codes. In both of these situations, the most specific physical address will be requested (i.e., specific additions of suites, floors, or room numbers) to distinguish between the two entities. If no more specific physical address is able to be identified, then documentation such as that listed in PGI 204.1870-2(c)(3)(i)(A) will be requested to ensure that the entities are separate legal entities.

(b) *NCAGE code assignment for entities located outside the United States and its outlying areas managed via established NATO processes.*

SAM records received by the CAGE code system for validation shall—

(1) Include an NCAGE that has been received from the NATO Support Agency's (NSPA's) common database. The frequency with which local country code bureaus update the common database differs by the country. While most updates occur within a week, it can take up to a month to process. The CAGE code system will hold a validation request from SAM for three (3) days before rejecting it because the NCAGE does not appear to exist; and

(2) Include a legal business name and physical address that matches the address on the NSPA database in order to be validated.

(c) *Changes of information on the CAGE code record.*

(1) The DLA CAGE Branch accepts written requests for changes to CAGE files from the following sources:

(i) The company, organization, or sole proprietor entity identified by the code, if located in the United States or its outlying areas.

(A) For CAGE records for which there is a corresponding registration in SAM, the entity shall update their Dun & Bradstreet (D&B) record to begin the process and then proceed to update and submit their SAM registration for validation. If the update includes a change to the entity's legal business name, the additional steps at PGI 204.1870-2(c)(3)(i)(C) will be necessary.

(B) For CAGE records for which there is not a corresponding registration in SAM, the entity shall use company letterhead to request a change to their CAGE code record. Submit requests for changes to CAGE files, when there is not a corresponding SAM record, at *https://cage.dla.mil* or using a DD Form 2051 (available at *http://dtic.mil/whs/directives/forms/eforms/dd2051.pdf*). The form may be emailed to *cagemail@dla.mil*, or a hard copy mailed to—

DLA CAGE Branch

74 Washington Avenue

Battle Creek, MI 49037

Telephone Number: toll-free 877-352-2255

(ii) The Government contracting office on agency letterhead.

(iii) The Government contract administration office on agency letterhead.

(2) The DLA CAGE branch refers requests for changes to CAGE files from entities located outside the United States and its outlying areas as follows:

(i) Entities located in a NATO or NATO-sponsored nation shall contact their codification bureau. A listing of codification bureaus is found at *http://www.nato.int/structur/AC/135/main/links/contacts.htm*.

(ii) Entities located in a country that is neither in NATO nor sponsored by NATO shall contact the NATO Support Agency (NSPA) at ncage@nspa.nato.int or request update after searching for their CAGE code at *https://eportal.nspa.nato.int/AC135Public/scage/CageList.aspx*.

(3) When a request is received by DLA (either directly or via an entity-updated SAM registration submitted for validation) that includes a change to the entity's legal business name as recorded within the CAGE file, the DLA team will contact the entity and process the request in accordance with the following procedure:

(i) If the entity indicates that it does not hold any active federal Government contracts or any outstanding invoices on a physically complete contract, the entity will be asked to provide the following to DLA—

(A) Signed legal documentation that confirms the formal name change and accurately reflects the change requested. Examples of acceptable documentation include: Articles of Incorporation, Articles of Organization, Bill of Sale, Asset Purchase Agreement, Secretary of State documentation, and Legal Merger or Acquisition documentation. DLA will not accept Internal Review Service (IRS) documentation or validation, as the IRS does not require the use of the legal business name. Sole proprietors will need to provide their filings for one of the following: Fictitious Business Name, Assumed Name, Trade Style Name, or Business License. DLA may use information found at state government websites in lieu of requesting documentation from the entity to confirm the name if it is available;

(B) Written statement that they do not have active federal contracts or any outstanding invoices on a physically complete contract; and

(C) After receipt of the documentation in (A) and (B), DLA will process the change. If the initial request was received from SAM as a part of the CAGE validation process, the processed change will be communicated back to SAM.

(ii) If the entity indicates it does hold active Federal Government contracts, the entity will be asked to provide an indication in writing (may be provided by email) if the change in legal business name is a result of an acquisition, merger, or other situation related to recognition of a successor in interest to Federal Government contracts when contractor assets are transferred, which would necessitate a novation agreement be executed.

(A) If the entity indicates that the change in legal business name is not a result of an acquisition merger or other situation as indicated above; the entity will be asked to confirm, in writing (may be provided by email) that it has advised each of the respective Government contracting officers necessary to process name-change agreements in accordance with FAR subpart 42.12 requirements. Additionally, DLA will ask the entity to provide a copy of the change-of-name agreement (see FAR 42.1205) signed by the entity. DLA will not process a change to the CAGE file without a copy of the signed change-of-name agreement, or confirmation from the cognizant Government contracting officer that processing a change to the CAGE file prior to the signed change-of-name agreement being completed is permissible. Note that the modification action that incorporates the change-of-name agreement into the contract is an acceptable method of providing the change-of-name agreement. However, if the modification is not able to be issued until the CAGE code information is updated, the change-of-name agreement itself will suffice.

(B) If the entity indicates that the change in legal business name is a result of an acquisition, merger, or other situation as indicated above, DLA will request the entity to provide the Novation Agreement that has been executed by the cognizant Government contracting officer (see FAR 42.1204) as well as the contact information for that contracting officer. DLA may, based on the content of the Novation Agreement, request that the contracting officer provide additional information regarding any Government interest in whether CAGE codes are transferred to the successor in interest. DLA will not process a change to the CAGE file without a copy of the executed Novation Agreement, or confirmation from the cognizant Government contracting officer that processing a change to the CAGE file prior to the novation agreement being completed is permissible. Note that the modification action that incorporates the Novation Agreement into the contract is an acceptable method of providing the Novation Agreement. However, if the modification is not able to be issued until the CAGE code information is updated, the Novation Agreement itself will suffice.

(1) When contacted by DLA in relation to a name change resulting from a novation, contracting officers shall provide DLA the following information:

(i) Name(s), address(es), and code(s) of the contractor(s) transferring the original contractual rights and obligations (transferor).

(ii) Name(s), address(es), and code(s) (if any) of the entity who is the successor in interest (transferee).

iii) Name(s), address(es), and code(s) (if any) of the entity who is retaining or receiving the rights to the technical data.

iv) Description of the circumstances surrounding the novation agreement and especially the relationship of each entity to the other.

(2) Note that if the name change request was received as a part of a registration from SAM update, and this situation applies, the update will be sent back to SAM as rejected by CAGE validation if a copy of the executed Novation Agreement or confirmation from the cognizant Government contracting officer is not available within 10 business days. The entity may resubmit the update in SAM with the changed legal name at such point this information becomes available.

(4) If the initial request was received from SAM as a part of the CAGE validation process, a processed change will be communicated back to SAM.

(5) Note that DLA does not follow the process outlined in (c)(3) above for minor changes in the legal business name received from SAM during validation, such as changing an "and" to "&"; inserting or removing abbreviations, such as changing "Co." to "Company"; inserting or removing a space between words in an entity's name; or inserting or removing acronyms or wording identifying a type of incorporated status, such as "Inc." or "LLC". These changes are processed and communicated back to SAM.

[Final rule, 79 FR 73492, 12/11/2014, effective 12/11/2014; Publication notice, 20160226]

SUBPART 204.70—PROCUREMENT ACQUISITION LEAD TIME

204.7001 Procedures.

(a) When conducting an acquisition with an estimated value greater than $250 million, agencies shall ensure planned and actual procurement administrative lead time (PALT) milestone dates are entered into the Procurement Integrated Enterprise Environment (PIEE) module. The PIEE module can be accessed at *https://wawf.eb.mil/*.

(b) The "planned" date indicates when the milestone is initially expected to be completed and the "actual" date is when the milestone is complete.

(c) The following PALT milestones shall be entered into the PIEE module, if applicable:

(1) The acquisition strategy/acquisition plan approval date.

(2) The date the justification and approval is approved.

(3) The date a funded purchase request is received by the contracting officer.

(4) The date a procurement-ready requirements package is received by the contracting officer.

(5) The solicitation issuance date.

(6) The proposal receipt date.

(7) The date the technical evaluation is complete.

(8) The audit completion date.

(9) The date the business clearance is approved.

(10) The date negotiations/discussions are complete.

(11) The date the contract clearance is complete.

(12) The contract award date.

(d) Planned milestone dates shall be entered into the PIEE module within one week of establishment of the milestones, but no later than the approval date of the acquisition strategy or plan. Actual milestone dates shall be entered into the PIEE module no later than one week after occurrence. Milestone dates shall be updated, as necessary, to reflect any changes.

(e) A PowerPoint presentation with screenshots introducing the module is available on the DPC Procurement Toolbox at *https://dodprocurementtoolbox.com/site-pages/palt*.

[Final rule, 71 FR 27640, 5/12/2006, effective 5/12/2006; Final rule, 81 FR 9783, 2/26/2016, effective 2/26/2016; Publication notice, 20191231]

204.7005 [Removed]

[Final rule, 76 FR 38046, 6/29/2011, Removed 6/29/2011; Publication notice, 20120829; Publication notice, 20120906; Final rule, 78 FR 54968, 9/9/2013, effective 9/9/2013; Final rule, 81 FR 9783, 2/26/2016, effective 2/26/2016]

204.7006 [Removed]

[Publication notice, 20100917; Publication notice, 20101124; Final rule, 81 FR 9783, 2/26/2016, effective 2/26/2016]

SUBPART 204.71—UNIFORM CONTRACT LINE ITEM NUMBERING SYSTEM

204.7103 Contract line items.

(a) Separately identifiable contract line and subline items (i.e., all except those with characteristics described in DFARS 204.7103-1(a)(2)(iii) or 204.7104-1(a)) shall include a description of the item or service being procured, the associated Product or Service Code (PSC), the quantity, a unit of measure, defined acceptance and inspection locations and requirements, and the delivery schedule or performance period. Contracts for contingency operations shall include the project code at the line item level on each contract action. The list of applicable codes is maintained at *http://www.dla.mil/j-6/dlmso/elibrary/ServicePoints/CD_ProjCd_nopoc.docx*. The contracting officer is responsible for coordinating any changes from the purchase request to the contract with the requiring activity.

(1) The list of active PSCs is available on the Federal Procurement Data System website under the 'Worksite' section under 'Reference'.

(2) The list of available units of measure is on the Defense Procurement and Acquisition Policy website at *http://www.acq.osd.mil/dpap/pdi/eb/docs/Line_Item_UoM_List.xlsx*.

(3) Delivery and acceptance locations shall be defined using Activity Address Codes published in (1) DoD Activity Address Directory (DODAAD), DoD 4000.25-6-M, or (2) Military Assistance Program Address Directory System (MAPAD), DoD 4000.25-8-M and available for verification at *https://www.daas.dla.mil/daasinq/default.asp*.

(4) No activity shall be assigned acceptance responsibility unless that activity has acceptors registered in Wide Area WorkFlow (WAWF). Available roles for an Activity Address Code can be verified at the Active DoDAACs & Roles link on the WAWF homepage at *https://wawf.eb.mil/*.

(b) Fixed price line items shall include unit prices and total prices. Cost type line items shall not include unit prices, but shall contain the appropriate elements in accordance with FAR part 16. Not separately priced line items shall be so labeled. The notation "No Charge" shall not be used.

(c) The requirements at paragraph (a) and (b) shall be included in the appropriate parts of the contract Schedule.

(d) In structuring line items, especially on fixed-price contracts, due consideration shall be given to the effect of the chosen units of measure on administration and payment. No contract line item shall contain a quantity less than the number of deliveries anticipated on the line item. Contracting officers shall consider the need for periodic deliveries and payments in selecting a unit of measure. Included in this analysis shall be the impact of any financing arrangements under FAR part 32.

(i) Supplies: Line item quantities shall match the actual count of the supplies to be provided. For instance, if more than one delivery is expected, the quantity cannot be "1."

(ii) Services: Line item quantities shall match the frequency with which performance will be reviewed, and on fixed-price line items, payment made. For example, a contract with a twelve-month period of performance should have a quantity and unit of measure suited to how the contract will be managed. If the intent is to review, accept, and pay for the services monthly, then the quantity should be 12, with a unit of measure such as "Months" or "Lots." If the intent is to review, accept, and pay for the services quarterly, then the quantity should be 4, with a unit of measure such as "Lot". If the quantity used is 1, then no payment for delivery can occur until the end of the period of performance. Services with tangible deliveries, such as repairs, shall be structured like supply line items.

(e) The following examples illustrate when the requirements at paragraph (a) apply—

(1) Separately identifiable subline items. The rule applies to subline items 0001AA and 0001AB. It does not apply to the line item 0001, because it does not have a deliverable.

ITEM NO.	SUPPLIES/SERVICE	QUANTITY	UNIT	UNIT PRICE	AMOUNT
0001	Widgets				
0001AA	Red painted widgets	6	EA	$10.00	$60.00
0001AB	Unpainted widgets	6	EA	$9.50	$57.00

(2) Informational subline items. The rule applies to line item 0001. It does not apply to subline items 000101, 000102, and 000103 because they do not have deliverables.

ITEM NO.	SUPPLIES/SERVICE	QUANTITY	UNIT	UNIT PRICE	AMOUNT
0001	Widget implementation Joint Service Study	1	LOT	$60,000	$60,000
000101	Army funding (AA: $20,000)				
000102	Navy funding (AB: $20,000)				
000103	Air Force funding (AC: $20,000)				

(3) Line item with no subline items. The rule applies.

ITEM NO.	SUPPLIES/SERVICE	QUANTITY	UNIT	UNIT PRICE	AMOUNT
0001	Red painted widgets	6	EA	$10.00	$60.00

(4) Line item is parent to an exhibit. The rule applies to the exhibit lines.

ITEM NO.	SUPPLIES/SERVICE	QUANTITY	UNIT	UNIT PRICE	AMOUNT
0001	See exhibit A ($117.00)				
A001	Red painted widgets	6	EA	$10.00	$60.00
A002	Unpainted widgets	6	EA	$9.50	$57.00

(5) Line is parent to a subline item which refers to an exhibit. The rule applies to the exhibit lines.

ITEM NO.	SUPPLIES/SERVICE	QUANTITY	UNIT	UNIT PRICE	AMOUNT
0001	Widget program				
0001AA	Design and develop widgets	1	LOT	$500.00	$500.00
0001AB	See exhibit A ($117.00)				
A001	Red painted widgets	6	EA	$10.00	$60.00
A002	Unpainted widgets	6	EA	$9.50	$57.00

[Final rule, 70 FR 58980, 10/11/2005, effective 10/11/2005; Publication notice, 20121212, 12/12/2012; Publication notice, 20140624; Final rule, 79 FR 51264, 8/28/2014, effective 8/28/2014]

204.7103-2 Numbering procedures.

(a) Contract line items shall consist of four numeric digits 0001 through 9999. Do not use numbers beyond 9999. Within a given contract, the item numbers shall be sequential but need not be consecutive.

(b) The contract line item number shall be the same as the solicitation line item number unless there is a valid reason for using different numbers.

(c) Once a contract line item number has been assigned, it shall not be assigned to another, different, contract line item in the same contract.

[Final rule, 70 FR 58980, 10/11/2005, effective 10/11/2005]

204.7104 Contract subline items. (No Text)

[Final rule, 70 FR 58980, 10/11/2005, effective 10/11/2005]

204.7104-2 Numbering procedures.

(a) Number subline items by adding either two numeric characters or two alpha characters to the basic contract line item number.

(1) *Information subline item numbers.* Use numeric characters only for information subline items, running 01 through 99. Do not use spaces or special characters to separate the subline item number from the contract line item number that is its root. For example, if the contract line item number is 0001, the first three subline items would be 000101, 000102, and 000103. Do not use a designation more than once within a contract line item.

(2) *Separately identified subline items.* Use alpha characters only for separately identified subline items, running AA through ZZ. Do not use spaces or special characters to separate the subline item number from the contract line item number that is its root. For example, if the contract line item number is 0001, the first three subline items would be 0001AA, 0001AB, and 0001AC.

(i) Do not use the letters I or O as alpha characters.

(ii) Use all 24 available alpha characters in the second position before selecting a different alpha character for the first position. For example, AA, AB, AC, through AZ before beginning BA, BB, and BC.

(b) Within a given contract line item, the subline item numbers shall be sequential but need not be consecutive.

(c) Exhibits may be used as an alternative to setting forth in the schedule a long list of contract subline items. If exhibits are used, create a contract subline item citing the exhibit's identifier. See DFARS 204.7105.

(d) If a contract line item involves ancillary functions, like packaging and handling, transportation, payment of state or local taxes, or use of reusable containers, and these functions are normally performed by the contractor and the contractor is normally entitled to reimbursement for performing these functions, do not establish a separate subline item solely to account for these functions. However, do identify the functions in the contract schedule. If an offeror separately prices these functions, the contracting officer may establish separate subline items for the functions; however, the separate subline items must conform to the requirements of DFARS 204.7104-1.

(e) The following examples illustrate subline items numbering—

(1) Subline items structured to identify destinations for identical items, identically priced (delivery schedule shall be established for each subline item, not the contract line item).

ITEM NO.	SUPPLIES/SERVICE	QUANTITY	UNIT	UNIT PRICE	AMOUNT
0001	NSN 1615-00-591-6620 Shim, Aluminum Alloy, . . . Apbl, Rotor, Helicopter PRON A1-9-63821-M1-M1 ACRN:AA				
0001AA	A3168R-9030-4025 A2537M IPD: 2 RDD: 334 PROJ: 501	10	EA	$100.00	$1,000.00
0001AB	A3168R-9030-4026 A51AXBM IPD: 2 RDD: 325 PROJ: 502	10	EA	$100.00	$1,000.00
0001AC	A3168R-9030-4027 A67KBCM IPD: 2 RDD: 349 PROJ: 503	15	EA	$100.00	$1,500.00

(2) Subline items structured to identify destinations for identical items, not identically priced (delivery schedule shall be established for each subline item, not the contract line item).

ITEM NO.	SUPPLIES/SERVICE	QUANTITY	UNIT	UNIT PRICE	AMOUNT
0001	NSN 1615-00-591-6620 Shim, Aluminum Alloy, . . . Apbl, Rotor, Helicopter PRON A1-9-63821-M1-M1 ACRN:AA				
0001AA	A3168R-9030-4025 A2537M IPD: 2 RDD: 334 PROJ: 501	10	EA	$100.00	$1,000.00
0001AB	A3168R-9030-4026 A51AXBM IPD: 2 RDD: 325 PROJ: 502	20	EA	$99.00	$1,980.00
0001AC	A3168R-9030-4027 A67KBCM IPD: 2 RDD: 349 PROJ: 503	30	EA	$98.00	$2,940.00

NOTE: Difference in prices for identical items is due to separate destinations for FOB destination delivery.

(3) Subline items structured to identify different sizes of an item that are identically priced (delivery schedule shall be established for each subline item, not the contract line item).

ITEM NO.	SUPPLIES/SERVICE	QUANTITY	UNIT	UNIT PRICE	AMOUNT
0013	Boots Insulated, Cold Weather White, Type II, Class 1		PR	$38.35	$13,422.50
0013AA	8430-00-655-5541 Size 5N	50			
0013AB	8430-00-655-5544 Size 8N	70			
0013AC	8430-00-655-5551 Size 9N	30			
0013AD	8430-00-655-5535 Size 9R	200			

NOTE: Unit price and total amount shown at line item level rather than at subline item level.

(4) Subline items structured to identify different sizes of an item that are not identically priced (delivery schedule shall be established for each subline item, not the contract line item).

ITEM NO.	SUPPLIES/SERVICE	QUANTITY	UNIT	UNIT PRICE	AMOUNT
0002	Body Armor Ground Troops Variable Type Small Arms, Fragmentation Protective Nylon Felt Vest, Front and Back Plates, Ceramic Plate, Type I				
0002AA	First Article	1	LO	NSP	
0002AB	8470-00-141-0935 Medium Regular	1936	SE	$331.77	$642,306.72
0002AC	8470-00-141-0936 Large Regular	625	SE	$355.77	$222,356.25
0002AD	8470-00-141-0937, Medium Long	1237	SE	$346.77	$428,954.49
0002AE	8470-00-141-0938, Large Long	804	SE	$365.77	$294,079.08

(5) Subline items structured to provide the capability for relating subordinate separately priced packaging costs to the overall contract line item. (Separate delivery schedules shall be established for the subline item identifying the contractor's product and for the subline item identifying packaging. No schedule will be established for the contract line item.)

ITEM NO.	SUPPLIES/SERVICE	QUANTITY	UNIT	UNIT PRICE	AMOUNT
0001	6105-00-635-6568 50380 Ref No 63504-WZ Armature Motor ACRN: AA				
0001AA	6105-00-635-6568 50380 Ref No 63504-WZ Armature Motor ACRN: AA	2	EA	$2,895.87	$5,791.74
0001AB	Packaging ACRN:AA	2	EA	$289.58	$579.16

(6) Subline items structured to identify different accounting classifications for identical items (delivery schedule shall be established for each subline item, not the contract line item).

AJ: 17X1505183503150691000001 92B000000000000000000

AK: 17X15051837031756910000 0192B000000000000000000

AL: 17X150519350314369100000192B000000000000000000

ITEM NO.	SUPPLIES/SERVICE	QUANTITY	UNIT	UNIT PRICE	AMOUNT
0002	Pulse Decoder KY-312/A5Q-19		EA	$3,037.40	
0002AA	Pulse Decoder KY-312/A5Q-19 ACRN: AJ	2			$6,074.80
0002AB	Pulse Decoder KY-312/A5Q-19 ACRN: AK	6			$18,224.40
0002AC	Pulse Decoder KY-312/A5Q-19 ACRN: AL	2			$6,074.80

NOTE: Unit price may be shown at line item level and total amounts shown at subline item level.

(7) Informational subline items established to identify multiple accounting classification citations assigned to a single contract line item.

ITEM NO.	SUPPLIES/SERVICE	QUANTITY	UNIT	UNIT PRICE	AMOUNT
0001	Air Vehicle 000101 ACRN:AA $3,300,000 000102 ACRN:AB $2,000,000 000103 ACRN:AC $1,400,000	1	EA	$6,700,000	$6,700,000

(8) Subline items structured to identify parts of an assembly (delivery schedule and price shall be established for each identified part at the subline item level, not for the assembly at the contract line item level).

ITEM NO.	SUPPLIES/SERVICE	QUANTITY	UNIT	UNIT PRICE	AMOUNT
0003	Automatic Degausing System Consisting of: (2 ea @ $52,061; $104,122 total)				
0003AA	Switchboard	2	EA	$52,061.00	$104,122.00

ITEM NO.	SUPPLIES/SERVICE	QUANTITY	UNIT	UNIT PRICE	AMOUNT
0003AB	Remote Control Panel	2	EA	NSP	
0003AC	Power Supply (M Coil) SSM Type 145 Amps, 220 V DC)	2	EA	NSP	
*	*	*		*	*
0003AF	Power Supply (A Coil) SSM Type (118 Amps, 220 V DC)	2	EA	NSP	

(9) Subline items structured to identify parts of a kit (delivery schedule and price shall be established for each identified part at the subline item level, not for the kit at the contract line item level).

ITEM NO.	SUPPLIES/SERVICE	QUANTITY	UNIT	UNIT PRICE	AMOUNT
0031	Conversion Kit to Convert Torpedo MK 45 Mod 0 to Torpedo MK 45 Mod 1 (50 Kt @ $10,868.52; $543,426 total)				
0031AA	Integrator Assy LD 620106	50	EA	$10,868.52	$543,426.00
0031AB	Pulse Generator Assy LD 587569	50	EA	NSP	
0031AC	Drive Shaft Assy LD 587559	50	EA	NSP	
*	*	*		*	
0031BF	Actual Panel Assy LD 542924	50	EA	NSP	

NOTE: In this example, the prices of subline items 0031AB through 0031BF are included in the Integrator Assembly.

[Final rule, 70 FR 58980, 10/11/2005, effective 10/11/2005]

204.7105 Contract exhibits and attachments.

(a) *Use of exhibits.*

(1) Exhibits may be used instead of putting a long list of contract line items or subline items in the contract schedule. Exhibits are particularly useful in buying spare parts.

(2) When using exhibits, establish a contract line or subline item and refer to the exhibit.

(3) Identify exhibits individually.

(4) Each exhibit shall apply to only one contract line item or subline item.

(5) More than one exhibit may apply to a single contract line item.

(6) Data items on a DD Form 1423, Contract Data Requirements List, may be either separately priced or not separately priced.

(i) *Separately priced.* When data are separately priced, enter the price in Section B of the contract.

(ii) *Not separately priced.* Include prices in a priced contract line item or subline item.

(7) The contracting officer may append attachments to exhibits, as long as the attachment does not identify a deliverable requirement that has not been established by a contract line item or subline item or exhibit line item.

(8) Include exhibit line items and associated information in the electronically distributed contract documents identified in PGI 204.201(3) (i) (A) and (B).

(b) *Numbering exhibits and attachments.*

(1) Use alpha characters to identify exhibits. The alpha characters shall be either single or double capital letters. Do not use the letters I or O.

(2) Once an identifier has been assigned to an exhibit, do not use it on another exhibit in the same contract.

(3) The identifier shall always appear in the first or first and second positions of all applicable exhibit line item numbers.

(4) If the exhibit has more than one page, cite the procurement instrument identification number, exhibit identifier, and applicable contract line or subline item number on each page.

(5) Use numbers to identify attachments.

(c) *Numbering exhibit line items.*

(1) *Criteria for establishing.* The criteria for establishing exhibit line items are the

same as those for establishing contract line items (see DFARS 204.7103.

(2) *Procedures for numbering.*

(i) Number items in an exhibit in a manner similar to contract line items.

(ii) Number line items using a four-position number.

(A) The first position or the first and second position contain the exhibit identifier.

(B) The third and fourth positions contain the alpha or numeric character serial numbers assigned to the line item when using a double letter exhibit identifier. The second, third and fourth positions contain the alpha or numeric character serial numbers assigned to the line item when using a single letter exhibit identifier.

(iii) Exhibit line item numbers shall be sequential within the exhibit.

(3) *Examples.*

(i) Two-position serial number for double letter exhibit identifier.

Cumulative No. of Line Items	*Serial Number Sequence*
1-33	01 thru 09, then 0A thru 0Z, then
34-67	10 thru 19, then 1A thru 1Z, then
68-101	20 thru 29, then 2A thru 2Z, then
102-135	30 thru 39, then 3A thru 3Z, then
136-169	40 thru 49, then 4A thru 4Z, then
170-203	50 thru 59, then 5A thru 5Z, then
204-237	60 thru 69, then 6A thru 6Z, then
238-271	70 thru 79, then 7A thru 7Z, then
272-305	80 thru 89, then 8A thru 8Z, then
306-339	90 thru 99, then 9A thru 9Z, then
340-373	A0 thru A9, then AA thru AZ, then
374-407	B0 thru B9, then BA thru BZ, then
408-441	C0 thru C9, then CA thru CZ, then
442-475	D0 thru D9, then DA thru DZ, then
476-509	E0 thru E9, then EA thru EZ, then
510-543	F0 thru F9, then FA thru FZ, then
544-577	G0 thru G9, then GA thru GZ, then
578-611	H0 thru H9, then HA thru HZ, then
612-645	J0 thru J9, then JA thru JZ, then
646-679	K0 thru K9, then KA thru KZ, then
680-713	L0 thru L9, then LA thru LZ, then
714-747	M0 thru M9, then MA thru MZ, then
748-781	N0 thru N9, then NA thru NZ, then
782-815	P0 thru P9, then PA thru PZ, then
816-849	Q0 thru Q9, then QA thru QZ, then
850-883	R0 thru R9, then RA thru RZ, then
884-917	S0 thru S9, then SA thru SZ, then
918-951	T0 thru T9, then TA thru TZ, then
952-985	U0 thru U9, then UA thru UZ, then
986-1019	V0 thru V9, then VA thru VZ, then
1020-1053	W0 thru W9, then WA thru WZ, then

Cumulative No. of Line Items	Serial Number Sequence
1054-1087	X0 thru X9, then XA thru XZ, then
1088-1121	Y0 thru Y9, then YA thru YZ, then
1122-1155	Z0 thru Z9, then ZA thru ZZ

(ii) Three-position numbers.

Cumulative No. of Line Items	Serial Number Sequence
1-33	01 thru 009, then 00A thru 00Z, then
34-67	010 thru 019, then 01A thru 01Z, then
68-101	020 thru 029, then 02A thru 02Z, then
102-135	030 thru 039, then 03A thru 03Z and
136-305	so on to
306-339	090 thru 099, then 09A thru 09Z, then
340-373	0A0 thru 0A9, then 0AA thru 0AZ, then
374-407	0B0 thru 0B9, then 0BB thru 0BZ, then
408-441	0C0 thru 0C9, then 0CA thru 0CZ, and
442-1121	so on to
1122-1155	0Z0 thru 0Z9, then 0ZA thru 0ZZ, then
1156-1189	100 thru 109, then 10A thru 10Z, then
1190-1223	110 thru 119, then 11A thru 11Z, then
1224-1257	120 thru 129, then 12A thru 12Z, and
1258-1461	so on to
1462-1495	190 thru 199, then 19A thru 19Z, then
1496-1529	1A0 thru 1A9, then 1AA thru 1AZ, then
1530-1563	1B0 thru 1B9, then 1BA thru 1BZ, and
1564-2277	so on to
2278-2311	1Z0 thru 1Z9, then 1ZA thru 1ZB, then
2312-2345	200 thru 109, then 10A thru 10Z, then
2346-2379	210 thru 219, then 21A thru 21Z, then
2380-2413	220 thru 229, then 22A thru 22Z, and
2414-2617	so on to
2618-2651	290 thru 299, then 29A thru 29Z, then
2652-2685	2A0 thru 2A9, then 2AA thru 2AZ, then
2686-2719	2B0 thru 2B9, then 2BA thru 2BZ, and
2720-3433	so on to
3434-3467	2Z0 thru 2Z9, then 2ZA thru 2ZZ, then
3468-3501	300 thru 309, then 30Z thru 30Z, and
3502-10403	so on to
10404-10437	900 thru 909, then 90A thru 90Z, then
10438-10471	910 thru 919, then 91A thru 91Z, and
10472-10709	so on to
10710-10743	990 thru 999, then 99A thru 99Z, then

Cumulative No. of Line Items	Serial Number Sequence
10744-10777	9A0 thru 9A9, then 9AA thru 9AZ, then
10778-10811	9B0 thru 9B9, then 9BA thru 9BZ, and
10812-11525	so on to
11526-11559	9Z0 thru 9Z9, then 9ZA thru 9ZZ

[Final rule, 71 FR 9268, 2/23/2006, effective 2/23/2006; Change notice, 20070531; Publication notice, 20120829; Publication notice, 20120906]

204.7107 Contract accounting classification reference number (ACRN) and agency accounting identifier (AAI).

(a) Establishing the contract ACRN.

(1) The contracting office issuing the contract is responsible for assigning ACRNs. This authority shall not be delegated. If more than one office will use the contract (e.g., ordering officers, other contracting officers), the contract must contain instructions for assigning ACRNs.

(2) ACRNs shall be established in accordance with the following guidelines:

(i) Do not use the letters I and O.

(ii) In no case shall an ACRN apply to more than one accounting classification citation, nor shall more than one ACRN be assigned to one accounting classification citation.

(b) *Establishing an AAI*. An AAI, as detailed *http://www.acq.osd.mil/dpap/policy/policyvault/USA002246-09-DPAP.pdf*, is a six-digit data element that identifies a system in which accounting for specific funds is performed. The funding office will provide to the contracting office the AAI associated with the funding for each line item.

(c) Capturing accounting and appropriations data in procurement. Procurement instruments shall identify the funding used for the effort in one of two ways.

(1) In legacy system environments where the contracting and accounting processes are not sufficiently integrated to ensure use of the Procurement Instrument Identifiers (PIIDs) (see DFARS subpart 204.16) and line item numbers as common keys, the contract shall include the accounting and appropriations data and ACRN as follows:

(i) Show the ACRN as a detached prefix to the accounting classification citation in the accounting and appropriations data block or, if there are too many accounting classification citations to fit reasonably in that block, in section G (Contract Administration Data).

(ii) ACRNs need not prefix accounting classification citations if the accounting classification citations are present in the contract only for the transportation officer to cite to Government bills of lading.

(iii) If the contracting officer is making a modification to a contract and using the same accounting classification citations, which have had ACRNs assigned to them, the modification need cite only the ACRNs in the accounting and appropriations data block or on the continuation sheets.

(iv) Showing the ACRN in the contract. If there is more than one ACRN in a contract, all the ACRNs will appear in several places in the schedule (e.g., ACRN: AA).

(A) Ship-to/mark-for block. Show the ACRN beside the identity code of each activity in the ship-to/mark-for block unless only one accounting classification citation applies to a line item or subline item. Only one ACRN may be assigned to the same ship-to/mark-for within the same contract line or subline item number unless multiple accounting classification citations apply to a single nonseverable deliverable unit such that the item cannot be related to an individual accounting classification citation.

(B) Supplies/services column.

(1) If only one accounting classification citation applies to a line item or a subline item, the ACRN shall be shown in the supplies/services column near the item description.

(2) If more than one accounting classification citation applies to a single contract line item, identify each assigned ACRN and the amount of associated funds using informational subline items (see DFARS 204.7104-1(a)).

(2) The contract shall include AAIs and ACRNs in system environments where the accounting systems are able to use PIIDs and line item numbers as common keys to enable traceability of funding to contract actions. Include AAIs and ACRNs as follows:

(i) Showing the ACRN in the contract. If there is more than one ACRN in a contract, all the ACRNs will appear in several places in the schedule (e.g., ACRN: AA).

(A) Ship-to/mark-for block. Show the ACRN beside the identity code of each activity in the ship-to/mark-for block unless only one accounting classification citation applies to a line item or subline item. Only one ACRN may be assigned to the same ship-to/mark-for within the same contract line or subline item number unless multiple accounting classification citations apply to a single nonseverable deliverable unit such that the item cannot be related to an individual accounting classification citation.

(B) Supplies/services column.

(1) If only one accounting classification citation applies to a line item or a subline item, the ACRN shall be shown in the supplies/services column near the item description.

(2) If more than one accounting classification citation applies to a single contract line item, identify each assigned ACRN and the amount of associated funds using informational subline items (see DFARS 204.7104-1(a)).

(ii) Showing the AAI in the contract. If there is more than one AAI in a contract, show the AAI in the supplies/services column of the Schedule next to the ACRN. A sample showing the AAI is as follows:

ITEM NO	SUPPLIES/SERVICES	QUANTITY	UNIT	UNIT PRICE	AMOUNT
0002	BRU-32 B/A Ejector Bomb Rack	23	Each	$22,206.00	$510,738.00

[Final rule, 70 FR 58980, 10/11/2005, effective 10/11/2005; Final rule, 74 FR 52895, 10/15/2009, effective 10/15/2009; Final rule, 81 FR 9783, 2/26/2016, effective 2/26/2016]

204.7108 Payment instructions.

(a) *Scope*. This section applies to contracts and orders that are funded by multiple accounting classification citations and—

(1) Include deliverable line items or deliverable subline items (see FAR 4.1005-1) that are funded by multiple accounting classification citations;

(2) Contain cost-reimbursement or time-and-materials/labor-hour line items; or

(3) Authorize financing payments.

(b) For contracts and orders covered by this subpart—

(1) The contracting officer shall insert the table at (b)(2)), or a link to the table at (b)(2) (*https://www.acq.osd.mil/dpap/dars/pgi/pgi_htm/current/PGI204_71.htm#payment_instructions*) in Section G of the contract, or equivalent, including contracts with incrementally funded line items. When some, but not all, of the fixed price line items in a contract are subject to contract financing payments, the contracting officer shall clearly identify to which line items the payment clause(s) included in Section I apply.

(2) The payment office shall allocate and record the amounts paid to the accounting classification citations in the contract using the table below based on the type of payment request submitted (see DFARS 252.232-7006) and the type of effort.

For Government Use Only

Contract/Order Payment Clause	Type of Payment Request	Supply	Service	Construction	Payment Office Allocation Method
52.212-4 (Alt I), Contract Terms and Conditions—Commercial Items 52.216-7, Allowable Cost and Payment 52.232-7, Payments under Time-and-Materials and Labor-Hour Contracts	Cost Voucher	X	X	N/A	Line item specific proration. If there is more than one ACRN within a deliverable line or deliverable subline item, the funds will be allocated in the same proportion as the amount of funding currently unliquidated for each ACRN on the deliverable line or deliverable subline item for which payment is requested.
52.232-1, Payments	Navy Shipbuilding Invoice (Fixed Price)	X	N/A	N/A	Line Item specific by fiscal year. If there is more than one ACRN within a deliverable line or deliverable subline item, the funds will be allocated using the oldest funds. In the event of a deliverable line or deliverable subline item with two ACRNs with the same fiscal year, those amounts will be prorated to the available unliquidated funds for that year.

52.232-1, Payments; 52.232-2, Payments under Fixed-Price Research and Development Contracts; 52.232-3, Payments under Personal Services Contracts; 52.232-4, Payments under Transportation Contracts and Transportation-Related Services Contracts; and 52.232-6, Payments under Communication Service Contracts with Common Carriers	Invoice	X	X	N/A	Line Item Specific proration. If there is more than one ACRN within a deliverable line or deliverable subline item, the funds will be allocated in the same proportion as the amount of funding currently unliquidated for each ACRN on the deliverable line or deliverable subline item for which payment is requested.
52.232-5, Payments Under Fixed-Price Construction Contracts	Construction Payment Invoice	N/A	Na/A	X	Line Item specific by fiscal year. If there is more than one ACRN within a deliverable line or deliverable subline item, the funds will be allocated using the oldest funds. In the event of a deliverable line or deliverable subline item with two ACRNs with the same fiscal year, those amounts will be prorated to the available unliquidated funds for that year.
52.232-16, Progress Payments	Progress Payment*	X	X	N/A	Contract-wide proration. Funds shall be allocated in the same proportion as the amount of funding currently unliquidated for each ACRN. Progress Payments are considered contract level financing, and the "contract price" shall reflect the fixed price portion of the contract per FAR 32.501-3.

52.232-29, Terms for Financing of Purchases of Commercial Items; 52.232-30, Installment Payments for Commercial Items	Commercial Item Financing*	X	X	N/A	Specified in approved payment. The contracting officer shall specify the amount to be paid and the account(s) to be charged for each payment approval in accordance with FAR 32.207(b)(2) and 32.1007(b)(2).
52.232-32, Performance-Based Payments	Performance-Based Payments*	X	X	N/A	Specified in approved payment. The contracting officer shall specify the amount to be paid and the account(s) to be charged for each payment approval in accordance with FAR 32.207(b)(2) and 32.1007(b)(2).
252.232-7002, Progress Payments for Foreign Military Sales Acquisitions	Progress Payment*	X	X	N/A	Allocate costs among line items and countries in a manner acceptable to the Administrative Contracting Officer.

*Liquidation of Financing Payments. Liquidation will be applied by the payment office against those ACRNs which are identified by the payment instructions for the delivery payment and in keeping with the liquidation provision of the applicable contract financing clause (i.e., progress payment, performance-based payment, or commercial item financing).

(c) Reserved.

(d) The numbered payment instructions ((d)(1) through (11)) are replaced by the table at paragraph (b)(2) of this section.

(1) *Line item specific: single funding.* If there is only one source of funding for the contract line item (i.e., one ACRN), insert the following:

252.204-0001 Line Item Specific: Single Funding. (SEP 2009)

The payment office shall make payment using the ACRN funding of the line item being billed.

(2) *Line item specific: sequential ACRN order.* If there is more than one ACRN within a contract line item (i.e., informational subline items contain separate ACRNs), and the contracting officer intends funds to be liquidated in ACRN order, insert the following:

252.204-0002 Line Item Specific: Sequential ACRN Order. (SEP 2009)

The payment office shall make payment in sequential ACRN order within the line item, exhausting all funds in the previous ACRN before paying from the next ACRN using the following sequential order: Alpha/Alpha; Alpha/numeric; numeric/alpha; and numeric/numeric.

(3) *Line item specific: contracting officer specified ACRN order.* If there is more than one ACRN within a contract line item, (i.e. informational sub-line items contain separate ACRNs), and the contracting officer intends the funds to be liquidated in a specified ACRN order, insert the following, including the specified order in the instruction:

252.204-0003 Line Item Specific: Contracting Officer Specified ACRN Order. (SEP 2009)

The payment office shall make payment within the line item in the sequence ACRN order specified below, exhausting all funds in the previous ACRN before paying from the next ACRN.

Line Item ACRN Order

__________ ____________________

__________ ____________________

(4) *Line item specific: by fiscal year.* If there is more than one ACRN within a contract line item, [(i.e. informational sub-line items contain separate ACRNs), and the contracting officer intends the funds to be liquidated using the oldest funds first, insert the following:

252.204-0004 Line Item Specific: by Fiscal Year. (SEP 2009)

The payment office shall make payment using the oldest fiscal year appropriations first, exhausting all funds in the previous fiscal year before disbursing from the next fiscal year. In the event there is more than one ACRN associated with the same fiscal year, the payment amount shall be disbursed from each ACRN within a fiscal year in the same proportion as the amount of funding obligated for each ACRN within the fiscal year.

(5) *Line item specific: by cancellation date.* If there is more than one ACRN within a contract line item, (i.e. informational sub-line items contain separate ACRNs), and the contracting officer intends the funds to be liquidated using the ACRN with the earliest cancellation date first, insert the following:

252.204-0005 Line Item Specific: by Cancellation Date. (SEP 2009)

The payment office shall make payment using the ACRN with the earliest cancellation date first, exhausting all funds in that ACRN before disbursing funds from the next. In the event there is more than one ACRN associated with the same cancellation date, the payment amount shall be disbursed from each ACRN with the same cancellation date in the same proportion as the amount of funding obligated for each ACRN with the same cancellation date.

(6) *Line item specific: proration.* If there is more than one ACRN within a contract line item, (i.e. informational sub-line items contain separate ACRNs), and the contracting officer intends the funds to be liquidated in the same proportion as the amount of funding currently unliquidated for each ACRN, insert the following:

252.204-0006 Line Item Specific: Proration. (SEP 2009)

The payment office shall make payment from each ACRN in the same proportion as the amount of funding currently unliquidated for each ACRN.

(7) *Contract-wide: sequential ACRN order.* If the contracting officer intends the funds to be liquidated in sequential ACRN order, insert the following:

252.204-0007 Contract-wide: Sequential ACRN Order. (SEP 2009)

The payment office shall make payment in sequential ACRN order within the contract or order, exhausting all funds in the previous ACRN before paying from the next ACRN using the following sequential order: alpha/alpha; alpha/numeric; numeric/alpha; and numeric/numeric.

(8) *Contract-wide: contracting officer specified ACRN order.* If the contracting officer intends the funds to be liquidated in a specified ACRN order, insert the following, including the specified order in the instruction:

252.204-0008 Contract-wide: Contracting Officer Specified ACRN Order. (SEP 2009)

The payment office shall make payment in sequential ACRN order within the contract or order, exhausting all funds in the previous ACRN before paying from the next ACRN in the sequence order specified below:

ACRN Order

____

____

(9) *Contract-wide: by fiscal year.* If the contracting officer intends the funds to be liquidated in fiscal year order, insert the following:

252.204-0009 Contract-wide: by Fiscal Year. (SEP 2009)

The payment office shall make payment using the oldest fiscal year appropriations first, exhausting all funds in the previous fiscal year before disbursing from the next fiscal year. In the event there is more than one ACRN associated with the same fiscal year, the payment amount shall be disbursed from each ACRN within a fiscal year in the same proportion as the amount of funding obligated for each ACRN within the fiscal year.

(10) *Contract-wide: by cancellation date.* If the contracting officer intends the funds to be liquidated in fiscal year order, insert the following:

252.204-0010 Contract-wide: by Cancellation Date. (SEP 2009)

The payment office shall make payment using the ACRN with the earliest cancellation date first, exhausting all funds in that ACRN before disbursing funds from the next. In the event there is more than one ACRN associated with the same cancellation date, the payment amount shall be disbursed from each ACRN with the same cancellation date in the same proportion as the amount of funding obligated for each ACRN with the same cancellation date.

(11) *Contract-wide: proration.* If the contract or order that provides for progress payments based on costs, (unless the administrative contracting officer authorizes use of one of the other options), or if the contracting officer intends the funds to be liquidated in the same proportion as the amount of funding currently unliquidated for each ACRN, insert the following:

252.204-0011 Contract-wide: Proration. (SEP 2009)

The payment office shall make payment from each ACRN within the contract or order in the same proportion as the amount of funding currently unliquidated for each ACRN.

(12) *Other.* If none of the payment instructions identified in paragraph (b)(2) of this section are appropriate (i.e., multiple lot progress payments), the contracting officer may insert other payment instructions, provided the other payment instructions—

(i) Provide a significantly better reflection of how funds will be expended in support of contract performance; and

(ii) Are agreed to by the payment office and the contract administration office. A copy of the agreement will be kept in the contract file.

[Final rule, 70 FR 58980, 10/11/2005, effective 10/11/2005; Change notice, 20070531; Publication notice, 20171201; Publication notice, 20180323]

SUBPART 204.72—[REMOVED]

204.7202 [Removed]

[Publication notice, 20140512; Final rule, 79 FR 73492, 12/11/2014, effective 12/11/2014]

SUBPART 204.73—SAFEGUARDING COVERED DEFENSE INFORMATION AND CYBER INCIDENT REPORTING

204.7302 [Removed]

[Interim rule, 73 FR 42274, 7/21/2008, effective 7/21/2008; Final rule, 75 FR 18029, 4/8/2010, effective 4/8/2010; Final rule, 78 FR 36108, 6/17/2013, effective 6/17/2013]

204.7303 Procedures. (No Text)

204.7303-1 General.

(a) The contracting officer will be notified by the requiring activity when a solicitation is expected to result in a contract, task order, or delivery order that will involve—

(1) Covered defense information; or

(2) Operationally critical support.

(b) The contracting officer shall—

(1) Ensure that the requiring activity provides a work statement or specification that includes the identification of covered defense information or operationally critical support consistent with paragraph (a).

(2) Ensure that the solicitation and resultant contract, task order, or delivery order includes the requirement (such as a contract data requirements list), as provided by the requiring activity, for the contractor to apply markings, when appropriate, on covered defense information.

[Publication notice, 20151118; Publication notice, 20171201]

204.7303-2 Safeguarding controls and requirements.

(a) When an offeror proposes to vary from any of the security requirements specified by National Institute of Standards and Technology (NIST) Special Publication (SP) 800-171, "Protecting Controlled Unclassified Information in Nonfederal Information Systems and Organizations," in accordance with paragraph (c)(2) of the solicitation provision at DFARS 252.204-7008, or in accordance with paragraphs (b)(2)(ii)(B) of DFARS clause 252.204-7012, the contracting officer shall submit the offeror's explanation of the proposed variance to the DoD Chief Information Officer via email at *osd.dibcsia@mail.mil* for adjudication.

(b) For additional information on safeguarding controls and requirements, see the Frequently Asked Questions document at *http://www.acq.osd.mil/dpap/pdi/network_penetration_reporting_and_contracting.html*.

[Publication notice, 20151118; Interim rule, 80 FR 81472, 12/30/2015, effective 12/30/2015; Publication notice, 20171201]

204.7303-3 Cyber incident and compromise reporting.

(a) When a cyber incident is reported by a contractor, the DoD Cyber Crime Center (DC3) will send an unclassified encrypted email containing the cyber incident report to the contracting officer(s) identified on the Incident Collection Format (ICF). The DC3 may request the contracting officer send a digitally signed e-mail to DC3.

(1) The procuring contracting officer (PCO) shall notify the requiring activities that have contracts identified in the ICF. In cases where an administrative contracting officer (ACO) receives the cyber incident report, in lieu of the PCO, the ACO shall notify the PCO for each affected contract, who will then notify the requiring activity.

(2) In cases of cyber incidents involving multiple contracts, the DoD components will collaboratively designate a single contracting officer to coordinate additional actions required of the contractor, on behalf of the affected DoD components. The requiring activity will notify the contracting officer once a lead is designated.

(3) If the requiring activity requests an assessment of compliance with the requirements of the clause at DFARS 252.204-7012 related to the cyber incident, the contracting officer shall—

(i) Consult with the DoD component Chief Information Officer (CIO)/cyber security office;

(ii) Request a description of the contractor's implementation of the security requirements in NIST SP 800-171, "Protecting Controlled Unclassified Information in Nonfederal Information Systems and Organizations" (see *http://dx.doi.org/10.6028/NIST.SP.800-171*) in order to support evaluation of whether any of the controls were inadequate, or if any of the controls were not implemented at the time of the incident; and

(iii) Provide a copy of the assessment of contractor compliance to the requiring activity, the DoD CIO at *osd.dibcsia@mail.mil*, and the other contracting officers listed in the cyber incident report.

(b) When requested by the contractor, the contracting officer shall provide the contractor with the "Instructions for Malware Submission" document available at *http://www.acq.osd.mil/dpap/pdi/docs/Instructions_for_Malware_Submission.docx*. The contracting officer should never receive malicious software directly from the contractor.

(c) If the requiring activity requests access to contractor information or equipment, in accordance with DFARS 252.204-7012(f), the contracting officer shall provide a written request to the contractor.

(d) For additional information on cyber incident reporting, see the Frequently Asked Questions document at *http://www.acq.osd.mil/dpap/pdi/network_penetration_reporting_and_contracting.html*.

[Publication notice, 20151118; Publication notice, 20171201]

204.7303-4 DoD damage assessment activities.

(a) Prior to initiating damage assessment activities, the contracting officer shall verify that any contract identified in the cyber incident report includes the clause at DFARS 252.204-7012. If the contracting officer determines that a contract identified in the report does not contain the clause, the contracting officer shall notify the requiring activity that damage assessment activities, if required, may be determined to constitute a change to the contract.

(b) In cases of cyber incidents involving multiple contracts, a single contracting officer will be designated to coordinate with the contractor regarding media submission (see 204.7303-3(a)(2)).

(c) If the requiring activity requests the contracting officer to obtain media, as defined in DFARS 252.204-7012, from the contractor, the contracting officer shall—

(1) Provide a written request for the media;

(2) Provide the contractor with the "Instructions for Media Submission" document available at *http://www.acq.osd.mil/dpap/dars/pgi/docs/Instructions_for_Submitting_Media.docx*; and

(3) Provide a copy of the request to DC3, electronically via email at *dcise@dc3.mil*, and the requiring activity.

(d) If the contracting officer is notified by the requiring activity that media are not required, the contracting officer shall notify the contractor and simultaneously provide a copy of the notice to DC3 and the requiring activity.

(e) The contracting officer shall document the action taken as required by paragraph (c) or (d) of this section, in the contract file.

(f) Upon receipt of the contractor media, DC3 will confirm receipt in writing to the contractor and the requesting contracting officer.

(g) Once the requiring activity determines that the damage assessment activities are complete, the requiring activity will provide the contracting officer with a report documenting the actions taken to close out the cyber incident.

[Publication notice, 20151118; Publication notice, 20171201]

204.7304 [Removed]

[Interim rule, 73 FR 42274, 7/21/2008, effective 7/21/2008; Final rule, 75 FR 18029, 4/8/2010, effective 4/8/2010]

PART 205—PUBLICIZING CONTRACT ACTIONS

Table of Contents

Subpart 205.2—Synopses of Proposed Contract Actions

Preparation and transmittal of synopses 205.207

PART 205—PUBLICIZING CONTRACT ACTIONS

SUBPART 205.2—SYNOPSES OF PROPOSED CONTRACT ACTIONS

205.207 Preparation and transmittal of synopses.

(a) (i) *Notice numbering.*

(1) For a particular procurement, when submitting notices at different stages of the acquisition (i.e., sources sought notice, presolicitation notice, award notice), ensure the solicitation number is entered exactly the same way in order to allow all to be retrieved when a search is performed.

(2) Use only alpha-numeric characters in the solicitation and award number data elements in the GPE. Do not include hyphens, slashes, or other special characters.

(d) Special notices for small business events. When advertising an event for small businesses, post a 'special notice' notice type and ensure the "title" data field begins with "Small Business Event". This will enable the public to easily search the GPE using the small business event calendar on the website.

[Final rule, 69 FR 63327, 11/1/2004, effective 11/1/2004; Publication notice, 20110920; Interim rule, 79 FR 61579, 10/14/2014, effective 10/14/2014]

PART 206—COMPETITION REQUIREMENTS

Table of Contents

Scope of part 206.000

Subpart 206.2—Full and Open Competition After Exclusion of Sources

Establishing or maintaining alternative sources 206.202

Subpart 206.3—Other Than Full and Open Competition

Circumstances permitting other than full and open competition 206.302
Only one responsible source and no other supplies or services will satisfy agency requirements 206.302-1
Unusual and compelling urgency 206.302-2
Justifications 206.303
Content 206.303-2
Approval of the justification 206.304
Availability of the justification 206.305

PART 206—COMPETITION REQUIREMENTS

206.000 Scope of part.

For information on various approaches that may be used to competitively fulfill DoD requirements, see the Office of the Under Secretary of Defense for Acquisition, Technology, and Logistics Guidelines for Creating and Maintaining a Competitive Environment for Supplies and Services in the Department of Defense [*bbp.dau.mil/docs/BBP%202-0%20Competition%20Guidelines%20(Published%2022%20Aug%202014).pdf*].

[Final rule, 80 FR 21656, 4/20/2015, effective 4/20/2015]

SUBPART 206.2—FULL AND OPEN COMPETITION AFTER EXCLUSION OF SOURCES

206.202 Establishing or maintaining alternative sources.

(b)(i) Include the following information, as applicable, and any other information that may be pertinent, in the supporting documentation:

(A) The acquisition history of the supplies or services, including sources, prices, quantities, and dates of award.

(B) The circumstances that make it necessary to exclude the particular source from the contract action, including—

(1) The reasons for the lack of or potential loss of alternative sources; e.g., the technical complexity and criticality of the supplies or services; and

(2) The current annual requirement and projected needs for the supplies or services.

(C) Whether the existing source must be totally excluded from the contract action or whether a partial exclusion is sufficient.

(D) The potential effect of exclusion on the excluded source in terms of loss of capability to furnish the supplies or services in the future.

(E) When FAR 6.202(a)(1) is the authority, the basis for—

(1) The determination of future competition; and

(2) The determination of reduced overall costs. Include, as a minimum, a discussion of start-up costs, facility costs, duplicative administration costs, economic order quantities, and life cycle cost considerations.

(F) When FAR 6.202(a)(2) is the authority-

(1) The current annual and mobilization requirements for the supplies or services, citing the source of, or the basis for, the data;

(2) A comparison of current production capacity with that necessary to meet mobilization requirements;

(3) An analysis of the risks of relying on the present source; and

(4) A projection of the time required for a new source to acquire the necessary facilities and achieve the production capacity necessary to meet mobilization requirements.

(ii) The following is a sample format for Determination and Findings citing the authority of FAR 6.202(a):

Determination and Findings

Authority to Exclude a Source

In accordance with 10 U.S.C. 2304(b)(1), it is my determination that the following contract action may be awarded using full and open competition after exclusion of ____________________*:

(Describe requirement.)

Findings

The exclusion of ____________________*

Alternate 1: will increase or maintain competition for this requirement and is expected to result in a reduction of $________ in overall costs for the present and future acquisition of these supplies or services. (Describe how estimate was derived.)

Alternate 2: is in the interest of national defense because it will result in having a supplier available for furnishing these supplies or services in case of a national emergency or industrial mobilization. (Explain circumstances requiring exclusion of source.)

Alternate 3: is in the interest of national defense because it will result in establishment or maintenance of an essential engineering, research or development capability to be provided by an educational or other nonprofit institution or a federally funded research and development center. (Explain circumstances requiring exclusion of source.)

* Identify source being excluded.

[Final rule, 69 FR 74990, 12/15/2004, effective 12/1/2004]

SUBPART 206.3—OTHER THAN FULL AND OPEN COMPETITION

206.302 Circumstances permitting other than full and open competition. (No Text)

206.302-1 Only one responsible source and no other supplies or services will satisfy agency requirements.

(d) *Limitations.* When utilizing the authority at FAR 6.302-1, the contracting officer shall post a request for information or a sources sought notice, and shall include the results of this inquiry in the justification required by FAR 6.303. This requirement to post may be waived by the Head of the Contracting Activity, or designee. The waiver authority may not be delegated lower than a general or flag officer or a member of the Senior Executive Service.

[Final rule, 80 FR 21656, 4/20/2015, effective 4/20/2015]

206.302-2 Unusual and compelling urgency.

(b) *Application.* The circumstances under which use of this authority may be appropriate include, but are not limited to, the following:

(i) Supplies, services, or construction needed at once because of fire, flood, explosion, or other disaster.

(ii) Essential equipment or repair needed at once to—

(A) Comply with orders for a ship;

(B) Perform the operational mission of an aircraft; or

(C) Preclude impairment of launch capabilities or mission performance of missiles or missile support equipment.

(iii) Construction needed at once to preserve a structure or its contents from damage.

(iv) Purchase requests citing an issue priority designator under DoD Manual 4140.01, Volume 5, DoD Supply Chain Materiel Management Procedures: Delivery of Material, of 4 or higher, or citing "Electronic Warfare QRC Priority."

[Final rule, 69 74990, 12/15/2004, effective 12/15/2004; Publication notice, 20171228]

206.303 Justifications. (No Text)

206.303-2 Content.

(b) (i) Justifications citing the authority at FAR 6.302-1 to permit the use of other than full and open competition, shall–

(A) Include the results of the request for information or sources sought notice posted in accordance with PGI 206.302-1 (unless the requirement to post has been waived); and

(B) For non-competitive follow-on acquisitions of supplies or services previously awarded on a non-competitive basis, include a copy of the previous justification to assist the approval authority in determining whether the planned actions to remove any barriers to competition cited on the previous justification were completed.

[Final rule, 80 FR 21656, 4/20/2015, effective 4/20/2015]

206.304 Approval of the justification.

(a) (S-70) For a non-competitive follow-on to a previous award for the same supply or service supported by a justification for other than full and open competition citing the authority at FAR 6.302-1—

(i) The justification shall include a copy of the previous justification to assist the approval authority in determining whether the planned actions to remove any barriers to competition cited on the previous justification were completed; and

(ii) The approval authority shall determine whether the planned actions were completed. If the actions were not completed, the justification for the follow-on acquisition shall be approved by the approval authority one-level above the approval authority for the previous justification (see FAR 6.304). If the previous justification was approved by the Senior Procurement Executive (SPE), the approval remains at the SPE level.

[Final rule, 80 FR 21656, 4/20/2015, effective 4/20/2015]

206.305 Availability of the justification.

See OUSD(AT&L) DPAP memorandum, "*Noncompetitive Contracts Awarded Based on Urgency*," dated April 13, 2015, for further guidance on the justification and approval documents required for contracts awarded using the unusual and compelling urgency exception.

[Publication notice, 20151030]

PART 207—ACQUISITION PLANNING

Table of Contents

Subpart 207.1—Acquisition Plans

Agency-head responsibilities 207.103
Contents of written acquisition plans 207.105
Component breakout 207.171
Procedures 207.171-4

Subpart 207.3—Contractor Versus Government Performance

Policy 207.302

Subpart 207.4—Equipment Lease or Purchase

Statutory requirements 207.470

Subpart 207.5—Inherently Governmental Functions

Policy 207.503

PART 207—ACQUISITION PLANNING

SUBPART 207.1—ACQUISITION PLANS

207.103 Agency-head responsibilities.

(h) Submit acquisition plans for procurement of conventional ammunition to—

Program Executive Officer, Ammunition
ATTN: SFAE-AMO
Building 171
Picatinny Arsenal, NJ 07806-5000
Telephone: Commercial (973) 724-7101; DSN 880-7101.

[Final rule, 71 FR 53044, 9/8/2006, effective 9/8/2006]

207.105 Contents of written acquisition plans.

For acquisitions covered by DFARS 207.103(d)(i)(A) and (B), correlate the plan to the DoD Future Years Defense Program, applicable budget submissions, and the decision coordinating paper/program memorandum, as appropriate. It is incumbent upon the planner to coordinate the plan with all those who have a responsibility for the development, management, or administration of the acquisition. The acquisition plan should be provided to the contract administration organization to facilitate resource allocation and planning for the evaluation, identification, and management of contractor performance risk.

(a) *Acquisition background and objectives.*

(1) *Statement of need. Include—*

(A) Applicability of an acquisition decision document, a milestone decision review, or a service review, as appropriate.

(B) The date approval for operational use has been or will be obtained. If waivers are requested, describe the need for the waivers.

(C) A milestone chart depicting the acquisition objectives.

(D) Milestones for updating the acquisition plan. Indicate when the plan will be updated. Program managers should schedule updates to coincide with DAB reviews and the transition from one phase to another (e.g., system development and demonstration to production and deployment).

(E) *Supplies and services.* To determine if acquisitions for supplies or services are covered by DFARS 208.7, acquisition officials shall use the AbilityOne Program Procurement List published by the Committee for Purchase From People Who Are Blind or Severely Disabled at *http://www.abilityone.gov/procurement_list/index.html* (see FAR Part 8.7).

(3)(i) Life-cycle cost. When acquiring tents or other temporary structures, consider total life-cycle costs in accordance with DFARS 215.101.

(8) *Acquisition streamlining.* See DoDD 5000.1, The Defense Acquisition System, and the Defense Acquisition Guidebook at *https://dag.dau.mil/Pages/Default.aspx.*

(b) *Plan of action.*

(2) *Competition.* For information on various approaches that may be used to competitively fulfill DoD requirements, see the Office of the Under Secretary of Defense for Acquisition, Technology, and Logistics *Guidelines for Creating and Maintaining a Competitive Environment for Supplies and Services in the Department of Defense.*

(4) *Acquisition considerations.* When supplies or services will be acquired by placing an order under a non-DoD contract (e.g., a Federal Supply Schedule contract), regardless of whether the order is placed by DoD or by another agency on behalf of DoD, address the method of ensuring that the order will be consistent with DoD statutory and regulatory requirements applicable to the acquisition and the requirements for use of DoD appropriated funds.

(5) *Budgeting and funding.* Include specific references to budget line items and program elements, where applicable, estimated production unit cost, and the total cost for remaining production.

(6) *Product or service descriptions.* For development acquisitions, describe the market research undertaken to identify commercial items, commercial items with modifications,

or nondevelopmental items (see FAR Part 10) that could satisfy the acquisition objectives.

(14) *Logistics considerations.*

(i) Describe the extent of integrated logistics support planning, including total life cycle system management and performance-based logistics. Reference approved plans. See PGI 245.103-73 for information on reporting requirements for Government inventory held by contractors under sustainment contracts in accordance with DoD Manual 4140.01, Volume 6, DoD Supply Chain Materiel Management Procedures: Materiel Returns, Retention, and Disposition.

(ii) *(1)* Discuss the mission profile, reliability, and maintainability (R&M) program plan, R&M predictions, redundancy, qualified parts lists, parts and material qualification, R&M requirements imposed on vendors, failure analysis, corrective action and feedback, and R&M design reviews and trade-off studies. Also discuss corrosion prevention and mitigation plans.

(2) See the Under Secretary of Defense Acquisition and Sustainment Policy Memo, dated January 31, 2019, entitled "*Implementation of 10 U.S.C. 2443—Sustainment Factors in Weapon System Design*" and DoD Instruction 5000.02, Operation of the Defense Acquisition System, policies and procedures.

(iii) For all acquisitions, see Subpart 227.71 regarding technical data and associated license rights, and Subpart 227.72 regarding computer software and associated license rights. For acquisitions involving major weapon systems and subsystems of major weapon systems, see the additional requirements at DFARS 207.106(S-70).

(iv) See DoD 4120.24-M, Defense Standardization Program (DSP) Policies and Procedures.

(S-70) Describe the extent of Computer-Aided Acquisition and Logistics Support (CALS) implementation (see MIL-STD-1840C, Automated Interchange of Technical Information).

(17) *Environmental and energy conservation objectives.*

(i) Discuss actions taken to ensure either elimination of or authorization to use class I ozone-depleting chemicals and substances (see DFARS Subpart 223.8).

(ii) Ensure compliance with DoDI 4715.23, Integrated Recycling and Solid Waste Management.

(20) *Other considerations.*

(A) *National Technology and Industrial Base.* For major defense acquisition programs, address the following (10 U.S.C. 2506)—

(1) An analysis of the capabilities of the national technology and industrial base to develop, produce, maintain, and support such program, including consideration of the following factors related to foreign dependency (10 U.S.C. 2505)—

(i) The availability of essential raw materials, special alloys, composite materials, components, tooling, and production test equipment for the sustained production of systems fully capable of meeting the performance objectives established for those systems; the uninterrupted maintenance and repair of such systems; and the sustained operation of such systems.

(ii) The identification of items specified in paragraph (b)(19)(A)(1)(i) of this section that are available only from sources outside the national technology and industrial base.

(iii) The availability of alternatives for obtaining such items from within the national technology and industrial base if such items become unavailable from sources outside the national technology and industrial base; and an analysis of any military vulnerability that could result from the lack of reasonable alternatives.

(iv) The effects on the national technology and industrial base that result from foreign acquisition of firms in the United States.

(2) Consideration of requirements for efficient manufacture during the design and production of the systems to be procured under the program.

(3) The use of advanced manufacturing technology, processes, and systems during the research and development phase and the production phase of the program.

(4) To the maximum extent practicable, the use of contract solicitations that encourage competing offerors to acquire, for use in the performance of the contract, modern technology, production equipment, and production systems (including hardware and software) that increase the productivity of the offerors and reduce the life-cycle costs.

(5) Methods to encourage investment by U.S. domestic sources in advanced manufacturing technology production equipment and processes through—

(i) Recognition of the contractor's investment in advanced manufacturing technology production equipment, processes, and organization of work systems that build on workers' skill and experience, and work force skill development in the development of the contract objective; and

(ii) Increased emphasis in source selection on the efficiency of production.

(6) Expanded use of commercial manufacturing processes rather than processes specified by DoD.

(7) Elimination of barriers to, and facilitation of, the integrated manufacture of commercial items and items being produced under DoD contracts.

(8) Expanded use of commercial items, commercial items with modifications, or to the extent commercial items are not available, nondevelopmental items (see FAR Part 10).

(9) Acquisition of major weapon systems as commercial items (see DFARS Subpart 234.70).

(B) *Industrial Capability (IC).*

(1) Provide the program's IC strategy that assesses the capability of the U.S. industrial base to achieve identified surge and mobilization goals. If no IC strategy has been developed, provide supporting rationale for this position.

(2) If, in the IC strategy, the development of a detailed IC plan was determined to be applicable, include the plan by text or by reference. If the development of the IC plan was determined not to be applicable, summarize the details of the analysis forming the basis of this decision.

(3) If the program involves peacetime and wartime hardware configurations that are supported by logistics support plans, identify their impact on the IC plan.

(C) *Special considerations for acquisition planning for crisis situations.* Ensure that the requirements of DoD Instruction 1100.22, Policy and Procedures for Determining Workforce Mix, are addressed. Also—

(1) Acquisition planning must consider whether a contract is likely to be performed in crisis situations outside the United States and must develop appropriately detailed measures for inclusion in the contract. Combatant commanders establish operational plans identifying essential services that must continue during crisis. DoDI 1100.22 requires Combatant Commanders to develop contingency plans if they have a reasonable doubt that a contractor will continue to provide essential services during a mobilization or crisis. When planning the acquisition, consider these operational plans and the resources available to carry out these plans.

(2) During acquisition planning, identify which services have been declared so essential that they must continue during a crisis situation. A best practice is to create a separate section, paragraph, line, or other designation in the contract for these essential services so they can be tracked to an option or separate contract line item.

(3) The requirements for the contractor written plan for continuity of essential services and the criteria for assessing the sufficiency of the plan will be determined/tailored for each acquisition of essential services by the contracting officer in coordination with the functional manager. The contractor's written plan, including prices/cost, shall be considered and evaluated in conjunction with the technical evaluation of offers.

(4) Operational-specific contractor policies and requirements resulting from combatant commander "integrated planning" will be described in operation plans (OPLAN), operation orders (OPORD) or separate annexes, and must be incorporated into applicable contracts. The plans may include rules for theater entry, country clearance, use of weapons, living on-base, etc. Therefore, the

requiring activity is responsible for obtaining pertinent OPLANs, OPORDs, and annexes (or unclassified extracts) from the affected combatant command or military service element or component and for ensuring that the contract is consistent with the theater OPLAN and OPORD.

(5) Ask the requiring activity to confirm that the appropriate personnel department has determined that inherently Governmental functions are not included in the contract requirements. If contract services will become inherently Governmental during a time of crisis, ensure that the contract states that work will be removed from the contract (temporarily or permanently) upon the occurrence of a triggering event (specified in the contract) or upon notice from the contracting officer that informs the contractor when its responsibility to perform affected duties will stop or restart. The contract should require the contractor to have a plan for restarting performance after the crisis ends.

(6) If the combatant commander's contingency plan requires military members to replace contractor employees during a crisis or contingency, acquisition planning must consider whether the contract should require the contractor to train military members to do that.

(7) For acquisitions that have or may have some portion of delivery of items or performance in a foreign country, address considerations and requirements set forth in DFARS 225.370, Contracts requiring performance or delivery in a foreign country; 225.371, Contractor personnel supporting U.S. Armed Forces deployed outside the United States; 225.372, Antiterrorism/force protection, and 225.373, Contract administration in support of contingency operations.

(8) Contract administration planning considerations for contracts in support of contingency operations.

(i) When delegation of contract administration services to a contracting officer located in a different geographic area to support a contract for the delivery of items or performance in a joint operations area will or may occur, address the resourcing of contract administration and oversight personnel, including administrative contracting officers, quality assurance specialists, contract administrators, property administrators, and contracting officers' representatives.

(ii) If contract delivery of items or performance in support of contingency operations will or may occur in an austere, uncertain, or hostile environment, address the need for logistics support of contract administration and oversight personnel.

(iii) When some portion of contract delivery of items or performance may take place in a contingency area, address pertinent combatant commander or joint force commander requirements and considerations for contract administration. Such requirements will be maintained on the particular combatant commander operational contract support website, *http://www.acq.osd.mil/dpap/pacc/cc/areas_of_responsibility.html.*

(iv) When contracts are awarded for performance in a contingency area, the head of the contracting activity is responsible for planning to ensure that contingency contracts will be closed in a timely manner considering personnel turnover and preaward, contract administration, and other contracting workload. A plan for reachback support of contract closeouts should be included, if required.

(9) For contracts that will incorporate the clause at DFARS 252.225-7040, Contractor Personnel Supporting U.S. Armed Forces Deployed Outside the United States, in accordance with DFARS 225.371-5(a), or otherwise require accountability for contractor personnel, consider the requirements and resources necessary for both the Government and contractor to keep the Synchronized Predeployment and Operational Tracker (SPOT) current in accordance with the SPOT business rules available at the website provided at *http://www.acq.osd.mil/log/PS/ctr_mgt_accountability.html.*

(10) For contracts that will incorporate the clause at FAR 52.222-50, Combating Trafficking in Persons, consider the requirements and resources necessary for both the Government and contractor to implement and maintain compliance with Federal and DoD trafficking in persons requirements, including PGI 222.1703.

(D) *Software and software maintenance.* When acquiring software or software maintenance, see DFARS 212.212.

(E) *Procurement Support for Theater Security Cooperation Efforts.* When planning procurement support for theater security cooperation efforts (e.g., military exercises/training, base operations, weapons procurement, aviation fuels, construction, or the President's Emergency Plan for Aids Relief projects), planners should be aware that Department of State (DoS) missions (embassies and consulates) do not provide such contracting support; however, these missions can provide support for routine, noncomplex services and supplies used by U.S. Government personnel, even if funded with foreignmilitary-sales case money (see DFARS PGI 225.78). Planners shall take the following steps:

(1) Become familiar with DoS Cable 11 STATE 030953, "Procurement Roles and Responsibilities – General Services Officer and DoD Personnel" (see also DFARS PGI 225.78).

(2) Request general guidance from the combatant-command coordinator on past practices in the particular location for which procurement support is to be requested;

(3) Contact the Defense Attaché Office and/or General Services Officer (normally the embassy/consulate contracting officer) at the DoS mission at least 60 days prior to the requirement, or as soon as practicable, to obtain information on–

(i) Availability of, and procedures associated with, requesting DoS mission procurement support;

(ii) Local sources of supplies and services; and

(iii) Business payment practices to support DoD procurement of specific theater security cooperation procurement requirements.

(4) Ascertain whether payment support is available from the DoS mission.

(5) When DoS contracting support is determined to be unavailable or not allowed, ensure the party of DoD military and/or civilians deploying to support the particular Theater Security Cooperation effort either pre-arranges DoD contracting support through reach-back, if possible, or if necessary, includes a warranted contracting officer, fieldordering officer, or credit-card holder, and, if necessary, a paying agent.

[Final rule, 70 FR 23790, 5/5/2005, effective 6/6/2005; Final rule, 71 FR 14099, 3/21/2006, effective 3/21/2006; Change notice, 20060321; Final rule, 71 FR 53044, 9/8/2006, effective 9/8/2006; Interim rule, 71 FR 58537, 10/4/2006, effective 10/4/2006; Final rule, 72 FR 14239, 3/27/2007, effective 3/27/2007; Interim rule, 72 FR 51188, 9/6/2007, effective 9/6/2007; Final rule, 74 FR 34269, 7/15/2009, effective 7/15/2009; Interim rule, 75 FR 10191, 3/5/2010, effective 3/5/2010; Publication notice, 20100519; Final rule, 75 FR 66680, 10/29/2010, effective 10/29/2010; Final rule, 76 FR 27274, 5/11/2011, effective 5/11/2011; Final rule, 76 FR 36883, 6/23/2011, effective 6/23/2011; Final rule, 76 FR 71830, 11/18/2011, effective 11/18/2011; Final rule, 77 FR 30366, 5/22/2012, effective 5/22/2012; Final rule, 77 FR 38734, 6/29/2012, effective 6/29/2012; Final rule, 78 FR 13544, 2/28/2013, effective 2/28/2013; Final rule, 79 FR 51264, 8/28/2014, effective 8/28/2014; Final rule, 80 FR 21656, 4/20/2015, effective 4/20/2015; Final rule, 80 FR 36900, 6/26/2015, effective 6/26/2015; Publication notice, 20160923; Final rule, 81 FR 78011, 11/4/2016, effective 11/4/2016; Publication notice, 20171228; Final rule, 84 FR 4362, 2/15/2019, effective 2/15/2019; Final rule, 84 FR 58332, 10/31/2019, effective 10/31/2019]

207.171 Component breakout. (No text)

207.171-4 Procedures.

(1) *Responsibility.*

(i) Agencies are responsible for ensuring that—

(A) Breakout reviews are performed on components meeting the criteria in DFARS 207.171-3(a) and (b);

(B) Components susceptible to breakout are earmarked for consideration in future acquisitions;

(C) Components earmarked for breakout are considered during requirements determination and appropriate decisions are made; and

(D) Components are broken out when required.

(ii) The program manager or other official responsible for the material program concerned is responsible for breakout selection, review, and decision.

(iii) The contracting officer or buyer and other specialists (e.g., small business specialist, engineering, production, logistics, and maintenance) support the program manager in implementing the breakout program.

(2) *Breakout review and decision.*

(i) A breakout review and decision includes—

(A) An assessment of the potential risks to the end item from possibilities such as delayed delivery and reduced reliability of the component;

(B) A calculation of estimated net cost savings (i.e., estimated acquisition savings less any offsetting costs); and

(C) An analysis of the technical, operational, logistics, and administrative factors involved.

(ii) The decision must be supported by adequate explanatory information, including an assessment by the end item contractor when feasible.

(iii) The following questions should be used in the decision process:

(A) Is the end item contractor likely to do further design or engineering effort on the component?

(B) Is a suitable data package available with rights to use it for Government acquisition? (Note that breakout may be warranted even though competitive acquisition is not possible.)

(C) Can any quality control and reliability problems of the component be resolved without requiring effort by the end item contractor?

(D) Will the component require further technical support (e.g., development of specifications, testing requirements, or quality assurance requirements)? If so, does the Government have the resources (manpower, technical competence, facilities, etc.) to provide such support? Or, can the support be obtained from the end item contractor (even though the component is broken out) or other source?

(E) Will breakout impair logistics support (e.g., by jeopardizing standardization of components)?

(F) Will breakout unduly fragment administration, management, or performance of the end item contract (e.g., by complicating production scheduling or preventing identification of responsibility for end item failure caused by a defective component)?

(G) Can breakout be accomplished without jeopardizing delivery requirements of the end item?

(H) If a decision is made to break out a component, can advance acquisition funds be made available to provide the new source any necessary additional lead time?

(I) Is there a source other than the present manufacturer capable of supplying the component?

(J) Has the component been (or is it going to be) acquired directly by the Government as a support item in the supply system or as Government-furnished equipment in other end items?

(K) Will the financial risks and other responsibilities assumed by the Government after breakout be acceptable?

(L) Will breakout result in substantial net cost savings? Develop estimates of probable savings in cost considering all offsetting costs such as increases in the cost of requirements determination and control, contracting, contract administration, data package purchase, material inspection, qualification or preproduction testing, ground support and test equipment, transportation, security, storage, distribution, and technical support.

(iv) If answers to the questions reveal conditions unfavorable to breakout, the program manager should explore whether the unfavorable conditions can be eliminated. For example, where adequate technical support is not available from Government resources, consider contracting for the necessary services from the end item contractor or other qualified source.

(3) *Records.*

(i) The contracting activity shall maintain records on components reviewed for breakout. Records should evidence whether the components—

(A) Have no potential for breakout;

(B) Have been earmarked as potential breakout candidates; or

(C) Have been, or will be, broken out.

(ii) The program manager or other designated official must sign the records.

(iii) Records must reflect the facts and conditions of the case, including any assessment by the contractor, and the basis for the decision. The records must contain the assessments, calculations, and analyses discussed in paragraph 2 of this section, including the trade-off analysis between savings and increased risk to the Government because of responsibility for Government-furnished equipment.

[Final rule, 71 FR 14101, 3/21/2006, effective 3/21/2006]

SUBPART 207.3—CONTRACTOR VERSUS GOVERNMENT PERFORMANCE

207.302 Policy.

See the memorandum from Assistant Secretary of Defense (Manpower and Reserve Affairs) dated April 21, 2016, entitled "Update on OMB Circular A-76 Public-Private Competition Prohibitions-FY 2016," regarding the ongoing Governmentwide moratorium and restrictions on public-private competitions. The restrictions prohibit the conversion of any work currently performed (or designated for performance) by civilian personnel to contract performance.

[Final rule, 81 FR 36473, 6/7/2016, effective 6/7/2016]

SUBPART 207.4—EQUIPMENT LEASE OR PURCHASE

207.470 Statutory requirements.

The contracting officer should obtain additional information on the definition of *substantial termination liability* by contacting the servicing legal adviser.

[Final rule, 74 FR 34265, 7/15/2009, effective 7/15/2009]

SUBPART 207.5—INHERENTLY GOVERNMENTAL FUNCTIONS

207.503 Policy.

(S-70) Section 804 of the National Defense Authorization Act for Fiscal Year 2005 (Public Law 108-375) limits contractor performance of acquisition functions closely associated with inherently Governmental functions (see related conference language).

[Interim rule, 70 FR 14572, 3/23/2005, effective 3/23/2005]

PART 208—REQUIRED SOURCES OF SUPPLIES AND SERVICES

Table of Contents

Subpart 208.4—Federal Supply Schedules

[Removed] 208.404
Limiting sources 208.405-6
[Removed] 208.405-70
Ordering activity responsibilities 208.406
Order placement 208.406-1

Subpart 208.7—Acquisition from Nonprofit Agencies Employing People Who are Blind or Severely Disabled

Procedures 208.705

Subpart 208.70—Coordinated Acquisition

Assignment authority 208.7002
Acquiring department responsibilities 208.7002-1
Requiring department responsibilities 208.7002-2
Applicability 208.7003
Assignments under integrated material management (IMM) 208.7003-1
Procedures 208.7004
Purchase authorization from requiring department 208.7004-1
Acceptance by acquiring department 208.7004-2
Use of advance MIPRs 208.7004-3
Cutoff dates for submission of Category II MIPRs 208.7004-4
Notification of inability to obligate on Category II MIPRs 208.7004-5
Cancellation of requirements 208.7004-6
Termination for default 208.7004-7
Transportation funding 208.7004-8
Status reporting 208.7004-9
Administrative costs 208.7004-10
Coordinated acquisition assignments 208.7006

Subpart 208.71—Acquisition for National Aeronautics and Space Administration (NASA)

Procedures 208.7102
General 208.7102-1
Purchase request and acceptance 208.7102-2
Changes in estimated total prices 208.7102-3
Payments 208.7102-4

Subpart 208.73—Use of Government-Owned Precious Metals

Definitions 208.7301
Procedures 208.7303
Refined precious metals 208.7304

Subpart 208.74—Enterprise Software Agreements

Definitions 208.7401
Acquisition procedures 208.7403

PART 208—REQUIRED SOURCES OF SUPPLIES AND SERVICES

SUBPART 208.4—FEDERAL SUPPLY SCHEDULES

208.404 [Removed]

[Final rule, 69 FR 63327, 11/1/2004, effective 11/1/2004; Removed Final rule 71 FR 14106, 3/21/2006, effective 3/21/2006]

208.405-6 Limiting sources.

For an order or blanket purchase agreement (BPA) exceeding the simplified acquisition threshold that is a follow-on to an order or BPA for the same supply or services previously issued based on a limiting sources justification citing the authority at FAR 8.405-6(a)(1)(i)(B) or (C)—

(1) The limited sources justification shall include a copy of the previous justification to assist the approval authority in determining whether the planned actions to remove any barriers that led to the restricted consideration cited on the previous justification were completed; and

(2) The approval authority shall determine whether the planned actions were completed. If the actions were not completed, the justification for the follow-on action must be approved by the approval authority one-level above the approval authority for the previous justification (see FAR 8.405-6(d)). If the previous justification was approved by the Senior Procurement Executive (SPE), the approval remains at the SPE level.

[Final rule, 80 FR 21656, 4/20/2015, effective 4/20/2015]

208.405-70 [Removed]

[Final rule, 71 FR 14106, 3/21/2006, effective 3/21/2006; Final rule, 78 FR 38234, 6/26/2013, effective 6/26/2013]

208.406 Ordering activity responsibilities. (No Text)

[Final rule, 71 FR 14106, 3/21/2006, effective 3/21/2006]

208.406-1 Order placement.

(1) When ordering from schedules, ordering offices—

(i) May use DD Form 1155, Order for Supplies or Services, to place orders for—

(A) Commercial items at or below the simplified acquisition threshold; and

(B) Other than commercial items at any dollar value (see PGI 213.307);

(ii) Shall use SF 1449, Solicitation/Contract/Order for Commercial Items, to place orders for commercial items exceeding the simplified acquisition threshold (see FAR 12.204); and

(iii) May use SF 1449 to place orders for other than commercial items at any dollar value.

(2) Schedule orders may be placed orally if—

(i) The contractor agrees to furnish a delivery ticket for each shipment under the order (in the number of copies required by the ordering office). The ticket must include the?

(A) Contract number;

(B) Order number under the contract;

(C) Date of order;

(D) Name and title of person placing the order;

(E) Itemized listing of supplies or services furnished; and

(F) Date of delivery or shipment; and

(ii) Invoicing procedures are agreed upon. Optional methods of submitting invoices for payment are permitted, such as—

(A) An individual invoice with a receipted copy of the delivery ticket;

(B) A summarized monthly invoice covering all oral orders made during the month, with receipted copies of the delivery tickets (this option is preferred if there are many oral orders); or

(C) A contracting officer statement that the Government has received the supplies.

(3) For purchases where cash payment is an advantage, the use of imprest funds in accordance with DFARS 213.305 is authorized when—

(i) The order does not exceed the threshold at FAR 13.305-3(a); and

(ii) The contractor agrees to the procedure.

(4) If permitted under the schedule contract, use of the Governmentwide commercial purchase card—

(i) Is mandatory for placement of orders valued at or below the micro-purchase threshold; and

(ii) Is optional for placement of orders valued above the micro-purchase threshold.

[Final rule, 71 FR 14106, 3/21/2006, effective 3/21/2006]

SUBPART 208.7—ACQUISITION FROM NONPROFIT AGENCIES EMPLOYING PEOPLE WHO ARE BLIND OR SEVERELY DISABLED

208.705 Procedures.

Ordering offices may use DD Form 1155, Order for Supplies or Services, to place orders with central nonprofit agencies.

[Final rule, 71 FR 39004, 7/11/2006, effective 7/11/2006; Change notice, 20080812]

SUBPART 208.70—COORDINATED ACQUISITION

208.7002 Assignment authority. (No Text)

208.7002-1 Acquiring department responsibilities.

The acquiring department generally is responsible under coordinated acquisition for—

(1) Operational aspects of acquisition planning (phasing the submission of requirements to contracting, consolidating or dividing requirements, analyzing the market, and determining patterns for the phased placement of orders to avoid unnecessary production fluctuations and meet the needs of requiring departments at the lowest price);

(2) Purchasing;

(3) Performing or assigning contract administration, including follow-up and expediting of inspection and transportation; and

(4) Obtaining licenses under patents and settling patent infringement claims arising out of the acquisition. (Acquiring departments must obtain approval from the department whose funds are to be charged for obtaining licenses or settling claims.)

[Final rule, 71 FR 39004, 7/11/2006, effective 7/11/2006]

208.7002-2 Requiring department responsibilities.

The requiring department is responsible for—

(1) Ensuring compliance with the order of priority in FAR 8.001 for use of Government supply sources before submitting a requirement to the acquiring department for contracting action.

(2) Providing the acquiring department—

(i) The complete and certified documentation required by FAR 6.303-2(b). A requiring department official, equivalent to the appropriate level in FAR 6.304, must approve the documentation before submission of the military interdepartmental purchase request (MIPR) to the acquiring department;

(ii) Any additional supporting data that the acquiring department contracting officer requests (e.g., the results of any market survey or why none was conducted, and actions the requiring department will take to overcome barriers to competition in the future);

(iii) The executed determination and findings required by FAR 6.302-7(c)(1);

(iv) When a requiring department requests an acquiring department to contract for supplies or services using full and open competition after exclusion of sources, all data required by FAR 6.202(b)(2);

(v) When the requiring department specifies a foreign end product, any determinations required by DFARS Part 225 or FAR Part 25;

(vi) A complete definition of the requirements, including a list (or copies) of specifications, drawings, and other data required for the acquisition. The requiring department need not furnish Federal, military, departmental, or other specifications or drawings or data that are available to the acquiring department;

(vii) Justification required by FAR 17.205(a) for any option quantities requested;

(viii) A statement as to whether used or reconditioned material, former Government surplus property, or residual inventory will be acceptable, and if so—

(A) A list of any supplies that need not be new; and

(B) The basis for determining the acceptability of such supplies (see FAR 11.302(b));

(ix) A statement as to whether the acquiring department may exceed the total MIPR estimate and, if so, by what amount; and

(x) Unless otherwise agreed between the departments, an original and six copies of each MIPR and its attachments (except specifications, drawings, and other data).

[Final rule, 71 FR 39004, 7/11/2006, effective 7/11/2006]

208.7003 Applicability. (No Text)

208.7003-1 Assignments under integrated materiel management (IMM).

(b) When an item assigned for IMM is to be acquired by the requiring activity under DFARS 208.7003-1(a)(3), the contracting officer must—

(i) Document the contract file with a statement of the specific advantage of local purchase for an acquisition exceeding the micro-purchase threshold in FAR Part 2; and

(ii) Ensure that a waiver is obtained from the IMM manager before initiating an acquisition exceeding the simplified acquisition threshold in FAR Part 2, if the IMM assignment is to the General Services Administration (GSA), the Defense Logistics Agency (DLA), or the Army Materiel Command (AMC). Submit requests for waiver—

(A) For GSA, to: Commissioner (F)

Federal Supply Service

Washington, DC 20406

(B) For DLA, to: DLA Land and Maritime

ATTN: DSCC-BDL

P.O. Box 3990

Columbus, OH 43216-5000

DLA Energy

ATTN: DESC-CPA

8725 John J. Kingman Road

Fort Belvoir, VA 22060-6222

DLA Aviation

ATTN: DSCR-BA

8000 Jefferson Davis Highway

Richmond, VA 23297-5000

DLA Troop Support

ATTN: DSCP-ILSI (for General and Industrial)

DSCP-OCS (for Medical, Clothing, and Textiles)

700 Robbins Avenue, Bldg. 4

Philadelphia, PA 19111-5096

(iii) In addition, forward a copy of each request to:

Defense Logistics Agency

Logistics Operations

ATTN: J-335

8725 John J. Kingman Road

Fort Belvoir, VA 22060-6221

For AMC: HQ, Army Materiel Command

ATTN: AMCLG-SL

4400 Martin Road

Redstone Arsenal, AL 35898

[Final rule, 71 FR 39004, 7/11/2006, effective 7/11/2006; Change notice, 20080721; Publication notice, 20110419; Publication notice, 20140421; Publication notice, 20171208]

208.7004 Procedures. (No Text)

208.7004-1 Purchase authorization from requiring department.

(1) Requiring departments send their requirements to acquiring departments on either a DD Form 448, Military Interdepartmental Purchase Request (MIPR), or a DD Form 416, Requisition for Coal, Coke or Briquettes. A MIPR or a DD Form 416 is the acquiring department's authority to acquire the supplies or services on behalf of the requiring department.

(2) The acquiring department is authorized to create obligations against the funds

cited in a MIPR without further referral to the requiring department. The acquiring department has no responsibility to determine the validity of a stated requirement in an approved MIPR, but it should bring apparent errors in the requirement to the attention of the requiring department.

(3) Changes that affect the contents of the MIPR must be processed as a MIPR amendment regardless of the status of the MIPR. The requiring department may initially transmit changes electronically or by some other expedited means, but must confirm changes by a MIPR amendment.

(4) The requiring department must submit requirements for additional line items of supplies or services not provided for in the original MIPR as a new MIPR. The requiring department may use a MIPR amendment for increased quantities only if—

(i) The original MIPR requirements have not been released for solicitation; and

(ii) The acquiring department agrees.

[Final rule, 71 FR 39004, 7/11/2006, effective 7/11/2006]

208.7004-2 Acceptance by acquiring department.

(1) Acquiring departments formally accept a MIPR by DD Form 448-2, Acceptance of MIPR, as soon as practicable, but no later than 30 days after receipt of the MIPR. If the 30 day time limit cannot be met, the acquiring department must inform the requiring department of the reason for the delay, and the anticipated date the MIPR will be accepted. The acquiring department must accept MIPRs in writing before expiration of the funds.

(2) The acquiring department in accepting a MIPR will determine whether to use Category I (reimbursable funds citation) or Category II (direct funds citation) methods of funding.

(i) Category I method of funding is used under the following circumstances and results in citing the funds of the acquiring department in the contract:

(A) Delivery is from existing inventories of the acquiring department;

(B) Delivery is by diversion from existing contracts of the acquiring department;

(C) Production or assembly is through Government work orders in Government-owned plants;

(D) Production quantities are allocated among users from one or more contracts, and the identification of specific quantities of the end item to individual contracts is not feasible at the time of MIPR acceptance;

(E) Acquisition of the end items involves separate acquisition of components to be assembled by the acquiring department;

(F) Payments will be made without reference to deliveries of end items (e.g., cost-reimbursement type contracts and fixed-price contracts with progress payment clauses); or

(G) Category II method of funding is not feasible and economical.

(ii) Category II method of funding is used in circumstances other than those in paragraph (2)(i) of this subsection. Category II funding results in citation of the requiring department's funds and MIPR number in the resultant contract.

(3) When the acquiring departments accepts a MIPR for Category I funding—

(i) The DD Form 448-2, Acceptance of MIPR, is the authority for the requiring department to record the obligation of funds;

(ii) The acquiring department will annotate the DD Form 448-2 if contingencies, price revisions, or variations in quantities are anticipated. The acquiring department will periodically advise the requiring department, prior to submission of billings, of any changes in the acceptance figure so that the requiring department may issue an amendment to the MIPR, and the recorded obligation may be adjusted to reflect the current price;

(iii) If the acquiring department does not qualify the acceptance of a MIPR for anticipated contingencies, the price on the acceptance will be final and will be billed at time of delivery; and

(iv) Upon receipt of the final billing (SF 1080, Voucher for Transferring Funds), the requiring department may adjust the fiscal records accordingly without authorization from or notice to the acquiring department.

(4) When the MIPR is accepted for Category II funding, a conformed copy of the contract (see DFARS 204.802(1)(ii)) is the authority to record the obligation. When all awards have been placed to satisfy the total MIPR requirement, any unused funds remaining on the MIPR become excess to the acquiring department. The acquiring department will immediately notify the requiring department of the excess funds by submitting an Acceptance of MIPR (DD Form 448-2). This amendment is authorization for the requiring department to withdraw the funds. The acquiring department is prohibited from further use of such excess funds.

(5) When the acquiring department requires additional funds to complete the contracting action for the requiring department, the request for additional funds must identify the exact items involved, and the reason why additional funds are required. The requiring department shall act quickly to—

(i) Provide the funds by an amendment of the MIPR; or

(ii) Reduce the requirements.

(6) The accepting activity of the acquiring department shall remain responsible for the MIPR even though that activity may split the MIPR into segments for action by other contracting activities.

[Final rule, 71 FR 39004, 7/11/2006, effective 7/11/2006]

208.7004-3 Use of advance MIPRs.

(1) An advance MIPR is an unfunded MIPR provided to the acquiring department in advance of the funded MIPR so that initial steps in planning the contract action can begin at an earlier date.

(2) In order to use an advance MIPR, the acquiring department and the requiring department must agree that its use will be beneficial. The departments may execute a blanket agreement to use advance MIPRs.

(3) The requiring department shall not release an advance MIPR to the acquiring department without obtaining proper internal approval of the requirement.

(4) When advance MIPRs are used, mark "ADVANCE MIPR" prominently on the DD Form 448.

(5) For urgent requirements, the advance MIPR may be transmitted electronically.

(6) On the basis of an advance MIPR, the acquiring department may take the initial steps toward awarding a contract, such as obtaining internal coordination and preparing an acquisition plan. Acquiring departments may determine the extent of these initial actions but shall not award contracts on the basis of advance MIPRs.

[Final rule, 71 FR 39004, 7/11/2006, effective 7/11/2006]

208.7004-4 Cutoff dates for submission of Category II MIPRs.

(1) Unless otherwise agreed between the departments, May 31 is the cutoff date for the receipt of MIPRs citing expiring appropriations which must be obligated by September 30 of that fiscal year. If circumstances arise that require the submission of MIPRs citing expiring appropriations after the cutoff date, the requiring department will communicate with the acquiring department before submission to find out whether the acquiring department can execute a contract or otherwise obligate the funds by the end of the fiscal year. Acquiring departments will make every effort to obligate funds for all such MIPRs accepted after the cutoff date. However, acceptance of a late MIPR does not constitute assurance by the acquiring department that all such funds will be obligated.

(2) Nothing in these instructions is intended to restrict the processing of MIPRs when the acquiring department is capable of executing contracts or otherwise obligating funds before the end of the fiscal year.

(3) The May 31 cutoff date does not apply to MIPRs citing continuing appropriations.

[Final rule, 71 FR 39004, 7/11/2006, effective 7/11/2006]

208.7004-5 Notification of inability to obligate on Category II MIPRs.

On August 1, the acquiring department will advise the requiring department of any Category II MIPRs on hand citing expiring appropriations it will be unable to obligate prior to the fund expiration date. If an unforeseen situation develops after August 1 that will prevent execution of a contract, the acquiring department will notify the requiring department as quickly as possible and will return the MIPR. The letter of transmittal returning the MIPR will authorize purchase by the requiring department and state the reason that the acquisition could not be accomplished.

[Final rule, 71 FR 39004, 7/11/2006, effective 7/11/2006]

208.7004-6 Cancellation of requirements.

(1) *Category I MIPRs.* The requiring department will notify the acquiring department by electronic or other immediate means when cancelling all or part of the supplies or services requested in the MIPR. Within 30 days, the acquiring department will notify the requiring department of the quantity of items available for termination and the amount of funds in excess of the estimated settlement costs. Upon receipt of this information, the requiring department will issue a MIPR amendment to reduce the quantities and funds accordingly.

(2) *Category II MIPRs.* The requiring department will notify the acquiring department electronically or by other immediate means when cancelling all or any part of the supplies or services requested in the MIPR.

(i) If the acquiring department has not entered into a contract for the supplies or services to be cancelled, the acquiring department will immediately notify the requiring department. Upon receipt of such notification, the requiring department shall initiate a MIPR amendment to revoke the estimated amount shown on the original MIPR for the cancelled items.

(ii) If the items to be cancelled have already been placed under contract—

(A) As soon as practicable, but in no event more than 45 days after receipt of the cancellation notice from the requiring department, the contracting officer shall issue a termination data letter to the requiring department (original and four copies) containing, as a minimum, the information in Table 8-1, Termination Data Letter.

(B) The termination contracting officer (TCO) will review the proceedings at least every 60 days to reassess the Government's probable obligation. If any additional funds are excess to the probable settlement requirements, or if it appears that previous release of excess funds will result in a shortage of the amount that will be required for settlement, the TCO will promptly notify the contracting office which will amend the termination data letter. The requiring department will process a MIPR amendment to reflect the reinstatement of funds within 30 days after receiving the amended termination data letter.

(C) Upon receipt of a copy of the termination settlement agreement, the requiring department will prepare a MIPR amendment, if required, to remove any remaining excess funds.

TABLE 8-1, TERMINATION DATA LETTER

SUBJECT: Termination Data Re:

Contract No.

____

Termination No.

____

Contract

____

(a) As termination action is now in progress on the above contract, the following information is submitted:

(1) Brief Description of items terminated.

(2) You are notified that the sum of $______ is available for release under the subject contract. This sum represents the difference between $______, the value of items terminated under the contract, and $______, estimated to be required for settlement of the terminated contract. The estimated amount available for release is allocated by the appropriations cited on the contract as follows:

MIPR NO.______ ACCOUNTING CLASSIFICATION______ AMOUNT______

Total available for release at this time $________

(b) Request you forward an amendment to MIPR ________ on DD Form 448-2 to reflect the reduced quantity and amount of funds available for release.

(c) Periodic reviews (not less than 60 days) will be made as termination proceedings progress to redetermine the Government's probable obligation.

____

Contracting Officer

[Final rule, 71 FR 39004, 7/11/2006, effective 7/11/2006]

208.7004-7 Termination for default.

(1) When the acquiring department terminates a contract for default, it will ask the requiring department if the supplies or services to be terminated are still required so that repurchase action can be started.

(2) The requiring department will not deobligate funds on a contract terminated for default until receipt of a settlement modification or other written evidence from the acquiring department authorizing release of funds.

(3) On the repurchase action, the acquiring department will not exceed the unliquidated funds on the defaulted contract without receiving additional funds from the requiring department.

[Final rule, 71 FR 39004, 7/11/2006, effective 7/11/2006]

208.7004-8 Transportation funding.

The requiring department will advise the acquiring department or the transportation officer in the contract administration office of the fund account to be charged for transportation costs. The requiring department may cite the fund account on each MIPR or provide the funding cite to the transportation officer at the beginning of each fiscal year for use on Government bills of lading. When issuing a Government bill of lading, show the requiring department as the department to be billed and cite the appropriate fund account.

[Final rule, 71 FR 39004, 7/11/2006, effective 7/11/2006]

208.7004-9 Status reporting.

(1) The acquiring department will maintain a system of MIPR follow-up to inform the requiring department of the current status of its requests. In addition, the contract administration office will maintain a system of follow-up in order to advise the acquiring department on contract performance.

(2) If requested by the requiring department, the acquiring department will furnish the requiring department a copy of the solicitation when the MIPR is satisfied through Category II funding.

(3) Any reimbursement billings, shipping document, contractual documents, project orders, or related documentation furnished to the requiring department will identify the requiring department's MIPR number, quantities of items, and funding information.

[Final rule, 71 FR 39004, 7/11/2006, effective 7/11/2006]

208.7004-10 Administrative costs.

The acquiring department bears the administrative costs of acquiring supplies for the requiring department. However, when an acquisition responsibility is transferred to another department, funds appropriated or to be appropriated for administrative costs will transfer to the successor acquiring department. The new acquiring department must assume budget cognizance as soon as possible.

[Final rule, 71 FR 39004, 7/11/2006, effective 7/11/2006]

208.7006 Coordinated acquisition assignments.

PART 1—ARMY ASSIGNMENTS

Federal Supply Class Code	*Commodity*
	Electronic Equipment
	Each department is assigned acquisition responsibility for those items which the department either designed or for which it sponsored development. See FSC 5821 under Navy listings for assignment of certain commercially developed radio sets (i.e., developed without the use of Government funds).
1005 P*	Guns, through 30mm This partial assignment applies to guns, through 30mm, and parts and equipment therefor, as listed in Department of Army Supply Manuals/Catalogs. It does not apply to Navy ordnance type guns; MK 11 and MK 12, 20mm gun; and aircraft gun mounts.
1010 P*	Guns, over 30mm up to 75mm
	This partial assignment applies to guns, over 30mm and up to 75mm, and parts and equipment therefor, as listed in Department of the Army Supply Manuals/Catalogs. It does not apply to Naval ordnance type guns and aircraft gun mounts.
1015 P*	Guns, 75mm through 125mm
	This partial assignment applies to guns, 75mm through 125mm, and parts and equipment therefor, as listed in Department of Army Supply Manuals/Catalogs. It does not apply to Naval ordnance type guns.
1020 P*	Guns over 125mm through 150mm
1025 P*	Guns over 150mm through 200mm
1030 P*	Guns over 200mm through 300mm
1035 P*	Guns over 300mm
	These partial assignments apply to guns, over 125mm, and parts and equipment therefor, as listed in Department of Army Supply Manuals/Catalogs. They do not apply to Naval ordnance type guns.
1040	Chemical Weapons and Equipment
1055 P*	Launchers, Rocket and Pyrotechnic
	This partial assignment applies to launchers, rocket and pyrotechnic, as listed in Department of Army Supply Manuals/Catalogs does not apply to Naval ordnance type and airborne type, with the exception of 2.75 inch rocket launchers which are included in this partial FSC assignment to the Department of the Army.
1090 P	Assemblies Interchangeable Between Weapons in Two or More Classes
	This partial assignment applies to the following items:
	National stock number nomenclature
	1090-563-7232 Staff Section, Class
	1090-699-0633 Staff Section
	1090-796-8760 Power Supply
	1090-885-8451 Wrench Corrector
	1090-986-9707 Reticle Assembly

("P" after the FSC number indicates a partial FSC assignment)

Federal Supply Class Code	*Commodity*
1095 P*	Miscellaneous Weapons
	This partial assignment applies to miscellaneous weapons, and parts and equipment therefor, as listed in Department of Army Supply Manuals/Catalogs. It does not apply to Naval ordnance type; line throwing guns (which are under DoD Coordinated Acquisition assignment to the Department of the Navy); and aircraft type miscellaneous weapons.

Federal Supply Class Code	Commodity
1210 P*	Fire Control Directors
1220 P*	Fire Control Computing Sights and Devices
1230 P*	Fire Control Systems, Complete
1240 P*	Optical Sighting and Ranging Equipment
1250 P*	Fire Control Stabilizing Mechanisms
1260 P*	Fire Control Designating and Indicating Equipment
1265 P*	Fire Control Transmitting and Receiving Equipment, Except Airborne
1285 P*	Fire Control Radar Equipment, Except Airborne
1290 P*	Miscellaneous Fire Control Equipment
	The above nine partial FSC assignments apply to fire control equipment, as listed in Department of the Army Supply Manuals/Catalogs. They do not apply to Naval ordnance type and aircraft type.
1305 P*	Ammunition, through 30mm
	This partial assignment applies to ammunition through 30mm as listed in Department of Army Supply Manuals/Catalogs. It does not apply to Naval ordnance type and ammunition for the MK 11 and MK 12, 20mm gun
1310 P*	Ammunition, over 30mm up to 75mm
	This partial assignment applies to ammunition, over 30mm up to 75mm, as listed in Department of Army Supply Manuals/Catalogs. It does not apply to Naval ordnance type and to 40mm ammunition (which is under DoD Coordinated Acquisition assignment to the Navy). The Army is responsible for the acquisition of fillers and the loading, assembling, and packing of toxicological, incapacitating riot control, smoke and incendiary munitions.
1315 P*	Ammunition, 75mm through 125mm
	This partial assignment applies to ammunition, 75mm through 125mm, as listed in Department of Army Supply Manuals/Catalogs. It does not apply to Naval ordnance type. The Army is responsible for the acquisition of fillers and the loading, assembling, and packing of toxicological, incapacitating riot control, smoke and incendiary munitions.
1320 P*	Ammunition, over 125mm
	This partial assignment applies to ammunition over 125mm, as listed in Department of Army Supply Manuals/Catalogs. It does not apply to Naval ordnance type. The Army is responsible for the acquisition of fillers and the loading, assembling, and packing of toxicological, incapacitating riot control, smoke and incendiary munitions.
1325 P	Bombs

Federal Supply Class Code	Commodity
	This partial assignment applies to bombs as listed in Department of Army Supply Manuals/Catalogs. It does not apply to Navy assigned bombs as shown in list of assignments to the Navy; however, the Department of the Army is responsible for the acquisition of fillers and the loading, assembling, and packing of toxicological, incapacitating riot control, smoke and incendiary munitions, and for other loading, assembling, and packing in excess of Navy owned capacity.
1330	Grenades
1340 P	Rockets and Rocket Ammunition
	This partial assignment applies to:
	66mm Rocket, HEAT, M72
	2.75" Rocket FFAR, Service and Practice
	Heads MK5 and Mods (HEAT)
	HE, M151
	HE, XM229 (17 lb Warhead)
	HE, XM157 (Spotting Red)
	HE, XM158 (Spotting Yellow)
	MK61 Practice (5 lb Slug)
	XM230 Practice (10 lb)
	Motors MK4 and Mods (High Performance Aircraft)
	MK40 and Mods (Low Performance Aircraft)
	3.5 inch Rocket Heat, M35
	Practice, M36
	Smoke, WP, M30
	4.5 inch Motor, Drill, M24
	HE, M32
	Practice, M33
	Incendiary and toxicological rockets, as listed in Army Supply Bulletins. It does not apply to Navy assigned rockets as shown in the list of assignments to the Navy. However, the Department of the Army is responsible for acquisition of filler and for filling of all smoke and toxicological rockets.
1345	Land Mines
1365	Military Chemical Agents
1370 P	Pyrotechnics
	This partial assignment does not apply to shipboard and aircraft pyrotechnics.
1375 P	Demolition Materials
	This partial assignment applies to Blasting Agents and supplies such as:
	Bangalore torpedo
	Blocks, demolition
	Caps, blasting, electric and nonelectric
	Charge, cratering
	Charge, shaped and demolition
	Chests, demolition platoon and squad
	Cord detonating
	Demolition equipment sets, with ancillary items
	Detonators, all types
	Dynamite
	Firing devices
	Fuze, safety
	Kit, demolition
	Lighter, fuse
	Machine, blasting
	Primer, percussion cap
	It does not apply to Navy underwater demolition requirements.
1376 P	Bulk Explosives

Federal Supply Class Code	*Commodity*
	This partial assignment applies to solid propellants and explosives such as: Ammonium Picrate (Explosive D) JAN-A-166A Trinitrotoluene (TNT) MIL-T-248A Tetryl JAN-T-339 Pantaerythrite Tetranitrate (PETN) JAN-P-387 RDX Composition B Composition B-3 Pentolite, 50 Composition C-3 Composition A-3 Composition A-4 Nitroguanidine (Picrate) It does not apply to production capacity for any of the above listed explosives at the U.S. Naval Propellant Plant, Indian Head, Maryland.
1377 P	Cartridge and Propellant Actuated Devices and Components This partial assignment is reserved pending Services agreement as to items to be included in the assignment.
1380	Military Biological Agents
1390 P*	Fuzes and Primers This partial assignment applies to Fuzes and Primers for Army assigned ammunition. It does not apply to Naval ordnance type, which is under DoD Coordinated Acquisition assignment to the Department of the Navy; and guided missile fuzes.
2210	Locomotives
2220	Rail Cars
2240	Locomotive and Rail Car Accessories and Components
2250	Track Materials, Railroad
2310 P	Passenger Motor Vehicles
2320 P	Trucks and Truck Tractors These two partial assignments apply to tactical vehicles and the following types of vehicles: Bus, convertible to ambulance Truck, 4 × 4, convertible to ambulance Truck 4 × 4 dump, 9,000 GVW, with cut-down cab These assignments do not apply to tracked landing vehicles which are not under DoD Coordinated Acquisition assignment, and airport crash rescue vehicles, which are under DoD Coordinated Acquisition assignment to the Department of the Air Force. With the exception of the types enumerated above, these assignments do not apply to commercial, non-tactical, passenger carrying vehicles and trucks which are assigned for DoD Coordinated Acquisition to the General Services Administration.
2330 P	Trailers This partial assignment does not apply to two wheel lubrication trailers, two wheel steam cleaning trailers, and troop transporter semitrailers which are not under DoD Coordinated Acquisition assignment, and airport crash rescue trailer units which are under DoD Coordinated Acquisition assignment to the Department of the Air Force.
2340 P	Motorcycles, Motor Scooters, and Bicycles This partial assignment does not apply to bicycles and tricycles.
2350	Tanks and Self-propelled Weapons
2430	Tractors, Track Laying, High-Speed

Federal Supply Class Code	*Commodity*
2510 P**	Vehicular Cab, Body, and Frame Structural Components
2520 P**	Vehicular Power Transmission Components
2530 P**	Vehicular Brake, Steering, Axle, Wheel, and Track Components
2540 P**	Vehicular Furniture and Accessories
2590 P**	Miscellaneous Vehicular Components
2610	Tires and Tubes, Pneumatic, except Aircraft
2630	Tires, solid and cushion
2640	Tire Rebuilding and Tire and Tube Repair Materials
2805 P**	Gasoline Reciprocating Engines, except Aircraft and Components
2910 P**	Engine Fuel System Components, Nonaircraft
2920 P**	Engine Electrical System Components, Nonaircraft
2930 P**	Engine Cooling System Components, Nonaircraft
2940 P**	Engine Air and Oil Filters, Strainers and Cleaners, Nonaircraft
2990 P**	Miscellaneous Engine Accessories, Nonaircraft
4210 P	Fire Fighting Equipment This partial assignment applies only to equipment developed by or under the sponsorship of the Department of the Army.
4230 P	Decontaminating and Impregnating Equipment This partial assignment applies only to items peculiar to chemical warfare.
4240 P	Safety and Rescue Equipment This partial assignment applies only to military respiratory protective equipment for chemical warfare.
5805 P	Telephone and Telegraph Equipment This partial assignment applies only to military (wire) equipment, field type.
5815 P	Teletype and Facsimile Equipment This partial assignment applies only to military (wire) equipment, field type.
5830 P	Intercommunication and Public Address Systems; except Airborne This partial assignment applies only to military (wire) equipment, field type.
6135 P	Batteries, Primary This partial assignment applies to MIL type, dry cell batteries, only.
6625 P	Electrical and Electronic Properties Measuring and Testing Instruments This partial assignment applies only to instruments for testing military (wire) equipment, field type.
6645 P	Time Measuring Instruments This partial assignment applies to the following watches; aircraft instrument panel clocks; cases and spare parts therefor: Master navigation watches; pocket watches; stop watches; second setting wrist watches; wrist watches; athletic timers; aircraft clocks; aircraft panel clocks; mechanical aircraft clocks; navigation watch cases; pocket watch cases; watch holders; watch case assemblies and watch movements.
6660 P	Meteorological Instruments and Apparatus

Federal Supply Class Code	Commodity
	Each department is assigned acquisition responsibility for those systems, instruments and end items in FSC 6660 which the department either designed or sponsored development. For purposes of this assignment, the developing department is the department which awarded the developmental contract, notwithstanding that other departments may have provided funds for the development.
6665 P	Hazard-Detecting Instruments and Apparatus
	This partial assignment applies only to items peculiar to chemical warfare.
6695 P	Combination and Miscellaneous Instruments
	This partial assignment applies to jewel bearings only.
6820 P	Dyes
	This partial assignment applies only to items peculiar to chemical warfare.
6910 P	Training Aids
	This partial assignment applies only to items peculiar to Army assignments under weapons, fire control equipment, ammunition and explosives, and chemical and biological warfare.
6920 P	Armament Training Devices
	This partial assignment applies to armament training devices as listed in Department of Army Catalogs SC 6910, ML/IL and SC 6920 ML/IL. It does not apply to clay pigeons in Department of Army Catalogs SC 6910, ML/IL and SC 6920 ML/IL. It does not apply to clay pigeons.
6940 P	Communication Training Devices
	This partial assignment applies only to code training sets, code practice equipment, and other telephone and telegraph training devices.
8130 P	Reels and Spools
	This partial assignment applies only to reels and spools for military (wire) equipment, field type.
8140 P	Ammunition Boxes, Packages, and Special Containers
	This partial assignment applies only to boxes, packages, and containers peculiar to Army assignments under ammunitions, explosives, and chemical and biological warfare as listed in Department of Army Catalog SC 8140 IL and SC 8140 ML.

* For contracting purposes, Naval ordnance comprises all arms, armor, and armament for the Department of the Navy and includes all offensive and defensive weapons, together with their components, controlling devices and ammunition used in executing the Navy's mission in National Defense (except small arms and those items of aviation ordnance acquired from the Army).

** These partial FSC assignments apply only to repair parts peculiar to combat and tactical vehicles. In addition, the assignment in FSC 2805 applies to military standard engines 1.5 HP through 20 HP and parts peculiar therefor. Balance of these FSCs are assigned to the Defense Logistics Agency (DLA Land and Maritime).

PART 2—NAVY ASSIGNMENTS

Federal Supply Class Code	Commodity
	Electronic Equipment Each department is assigned acquisition responsibility for those items which the department either designed or sponsored development. See FSC 5821 for assignment of certain commercially developed radio sets to the Department of the Navy (i.e., developed without the use of Government funds).
1095 P	Miscellaneous Weapons This partial assignment applies to line throwing guns only.
1310 P	Ammunition, over 30mm up to 75mm This partial assignment applies only to reels and spools for military.
1325 P	Bombs This partial assignment applies to armor-piercing; depth bombs; externally suspended low drag bombs; and components and practice bombs therefor, as listed in Ord Pamphlets, and the MK 43, Target Detecting Device. The Department of the Army is responsible for the acquisition of fillers and the loading, assembling, and packing of toxicological, incapacitating riot control, smoke and incendiary munitions, and for other loading, assembling, and packing in excess of Navy-owned capacity.
1340 P	Rockets and Rocket Ammunition This partial assignment applies to: Fuze, Rocket, V.T., MK93-0 2.25 inch Rocket SCAR, Practice Heads MK3 and Mods Motors MK15 and Mods MK16 and Mods 5 inch Rocket HVAR, service and practice Heads MK2 and Mods (common) MK6 and Mods (GP) MK4 and Mods (smoke) MK25 and Mods (ATAR) Motors MK10 and Mods 5 inch Rocket FFAR service and practice Heads MK24 and Mods (General Purposes) MK32 and Mods (Shaped Charged) MK26 and Mods (Illum) Motor MK16 and Mods The Department of the Army is responsible for acquisition of filler and for filling of all smoke and toxicological rockets.
1390 P	Fuzes and Primers This partial assignment applies to fuzes and primers for Navy assigned ammunition.
1550 P	Drones This partial assignment applies only to Drone, Model BQM34E.

("P" after the FSC number indicates a partial FSC assignment).

Federal Supply Class Code	Commodity
1905 P	Combat Ships and Landing Vessels This partial assignment applies to landing vessels only.
1910 P	Transport Vessels, Passenger and Troop This partial assignment applies to ferryboats only.
1920	Fishing Vessels
1925	Special Service Vessels
1930	Barges and Lighters, Cargo
1935 P	Barges and Lighters, Special Purpose

Federal Supply Class Code	Commodity
	This partial assignment does not apply to derricks, pile drivers, rock cutters, concrete mixing plants, mechanical bank grader barges, other bank revetment barges, and barge power plants.
1940	Small Craft
1945 P	Pontoons and Floating Docks
	This partial assignment applies only to Naval Facilities Engineering Command type pontoons.
1950	Floating Drydocks
1990 P	Miscellaneous Vessels
	This partial assignment applies to commercial sailing vessels only.
2010	Ship and Boat Propulsion Components
2020	Rigging and Rigging Gear
2030	Deck Machinery
2040	Marine Hardware and Hull Items
2060	Commercial Fishing Equipment
2090	Miscellaneous Ship and Marine Equipment
2820 P	Steam Engines, Reciprocating and Components
	This partial assignment applies to marine main propulsion steam engines only.
2825 P	Steam Turbines and Components
	This partial assignment applies to marine steam turbines only.
4210 P	Fire Fighting Equipment
	This partial assignment applies only to fire fighting equipment developed by or under the sponsorship of the Department of Navy.
4410 P	Industrial Boilers
	This partial assignment applies only to boilers for use aboard those ships assigned to the Navy for coordinated acquisition.
4420 P	Heat Exchangers and Steam Condensers
	This partial assignment applies only to heat exchangers for use aboard those ships assigned to the Navy for coordinated acquisition.
4925 P	Ammunition Maintenance and Repair Shop Specialized Equipment
	This partial assignment applies to sets, kits, and outfits of tools and equipment for explosive ordnance as defined in military service regulations and documents.
5821 P	Radio and Television Communication Equipment, Airborne
	This partial assignment applies only to the following commercially developed radio sets. (The term "commercially developed" means that no Government funds were provided for development purposes.) HF-101, 102, 103, 104, 105, 106, 107, 108, 109, 111, 113, ARC-94, 102, 105, 110, 112, 119, 120; MRC-95, 108; VC-102, 104, 105, 106, 109, 110; and components of the foregoing including the 490T antenna coupler.
6125 P	Converters, Electrical, Rotating
	This partial assignment applies only to motor-generated sets for use aboard ships assigned to the Navy for coordinated acquisition.
6320 P	Shipboard Alarm and Signal System
	This partial assignment applies only to alarm systems, fire alarm systems, indicating systems, telegraph systems (signal and signaling) (less electronic type) for use aboard ships assigned to the Navy for coordinated acquisition.
6605 P	Navigational Instruments

Federal Supply Class Code	Commodity
	This partial assignment applies only to lifeboat and raft compasses, aircraft sextants, hand leads (soundings), lead reels, sounding machines and pelorus stands for use aboard ships assigned to the Navy for coordinated acquisition.
6645 P	Time Measuring Instruments
	This partial assignment applies to the following instruments, cases, and spare parts therefor:
	Chronometers including gimbal, padded, and make break circuit
	Clocks, alarm, boat, deck, direct reading, electrical, floor, interval timer, marine, mechanical, master control, master program, master regulating, mechanical message center, nurses, program, shelf, stop, wall, watchman's
	Counters, time period
	Meters, engine running time, hour recording, and electrical time totalizing
	Timers; bombing, engine hours, sequential, stop, and program
	Program control instrument
	Cases; chronometer, including gimbal and padded, chronometer carrying; makebreak circuit chronometer
	Cans, chronometer shipping and storage
	Clock keys; clock movements, clock motors
6650 P	Optical Instruments
	This partial assignment applies only to stands, telescope, for use aboard ships assigned to the Navy for coordinated acquisition.
6660 P	Meteorological Instruments and Apparatus
	Each department is assigned acquisition responsibility for those systems, instruments, and end items in FSC 6660 for which the department either designed or sponsored development. For purposes of this assignment, the developing department is the department which awarded the developmental contract, notwithstanding that other departments may have provided funds for the development.
6665 P	Hazard-Detecting Instruments and Apparatus
	This partial assignment applies only to hazard determining safety devices, for use aboard ships assigned to the Navy for coordinated acquisition.
8140 P	Ammunition Boxes, Packages, and Special Containers
	This partial assignment applies only to boxes, packages, and containers for 40mm ammunition.

PART 3—AIR FORCE ASSIGNMENTS

Federal Supply Class Code	Commodity
	Electronic Equipment
	Each department is assigned acquisition responsibility for those items which the department either designed or sponsored development. See FSC 5821 under Navy listing for assignment of certain commercially developed radio sets (i.e., developed without the use of Government funds).
1550 P	Drones
	This partial assignment applies only to the following model drones:
	Model 147
	Model 154

Federal Supply Class Code	Commodity
	BQM 34A MQM 34D
2320 P	Trucks and Truck Tractors This partial assignment applies only to airport crash rescue vehicles.
2330 P	Trailers This partial assignment applies only to airport crash rescue trailer units.
4210 P	Fire Fighting Equipment This partial assignment applies only to fire fighting equipment developed by or under the sponsorship of the Department of the Air Force.
6660 P	Meteorological Instruments and Apparatus Each department is assigned acquisition responsibility for those systems, instruments, and end items in FSC 6660 for which the department either designed or sponsored development. The developing department is the department which awarded the developmental contract, notwithstanding that other departments may have provided funds for the development.
6710 P*	Cameras, Motion Picture This partial assignment does not apply to submarine periscope and underwater cameras.
6720 P*	Cameras, Still Picture This partial assignment does not apply to submarine periscope and underwater cameras.
6730 P*	Photographic Projection Equipment This partial assignment does not apply to 35mm theater projectors.
6740*	Photographic Developing and Finishing Equipment
6760*	Photographic Equipment and Accessories
6780*	Photographic Sets, Kits, and Outfits

("P" after the FSC number indicates a partial FSC assignment).

Federal Supply Class Code	Commodity
8820 P	Live Animals Not Raised for Food This partial assignment applies only to the following types of working dogs: Scout Sentry Patrol Mine/tunnel Tracker Detector-narcotic/contraband Sledge Bloodhound Water dog Patrol/detector

* This partial FSC assignment does not apply to photographic equipment controlled by the Congressional Joint Committee on Printing and Micro-Film Equipment and Supplies.

PART 4—DEFENSE LOGISTICS AGENCY ASSIGNMENTS

Federal Supply Class Code	Commodity	DLA Center[6]
2230	Right of Way Construction and Maintenance Equipment, Railroad	DSCP
2410	Tractor, Full Track, Low-Speed	DSCP
2420	Tractor, Wheeled	DSCP
2510 P[2]	Vehicular Cab, Body, and Frame, Structural Components	DSCC

Federal Supply Class Code	Commodity	DLA Center[6]
2520 P[2]	Vehicular Power Transmission Components	DSCC
2530 P[2]	Vehicular Brake, Steering, Axle, Wheel, and Track Components	DSCC
2540 P[2]	Vehicular Furniture and Accessories	DSCC
2590 P[2]	Miscellaneous Vehicular Components	DSCC
2805 P[2]	Gasoline Reciprocating Engines, Except Aircraft; and Components	DSCC
2815	Diesel Engines and Components	DSCC
2895	Miscellaneous Engines and Components	DSCC
2910 P[2]	Engine Fuel System Components, Nonaircraft	DSCC
2920 P[2]	Engine Electrical System Components, Nonaircraft	DSCC
2930 P[2]	Engine Cooling System Components, Nonaircraft	DSCC
2940 P[2]	Engine Air and Oil Filters, Strainers and Cleaners, Nonaircraft	DSCC
2990 P[2]	Miscellaneous Engine Accessories, Nonaircraft	DSCC
3020	Gears, Pulleys, Sprockets and Transmission Chain	DSCC
3030	Belting, Drive Belts, Fan Belts, and Accessories	DSCP
3040	Miscellaneous Power Transmission Equipment	DSCC
3110	Bearings, Antifriction, Unmounted	DSCR
3120	Bearings, Plain Unmounted	DSCR
3130	Bearings, Mounted	DSCR
3210	Sawmill and Planing Mill Machinery	DSCP
3220	Woodworking Machines	DSCP
3230	Tools and Attachments for Woodworking Machinery	DSCP
3405	Saws and Filing Machines	DSCR
3408	Machining Centers and Way-Type Machines	DSCR
3410	Electrical and Ultrasonic Erosion Machines	DSCR
3411	Boring Machines	DSCR
3412	Broaching Machines	DSCR
3413	Drilling and Tapping Machines	DSCR
3414	Gear Cutting and Finishing Machines	DSCR
3415	Grinding Machines	DSCR
3416	Lathes	DSCR
3417	Milling Machines	DSCR
3418	Planers and Shapers	DSCR
3419	Miscellaneous Machine Tools	DSCR
3422	Rolling Mills and Drawing Machines	DSCR

("P" after the FSC number indicates a partial FSC assignment)

Federal Supply Class Code	Commodity	DLA Center[6]
3424	Metal Heat Treating Equipment	DSCR
3426	Metal Finishing Equipment	DSCR
3431	Electric Arc Welding Equipment	DSCR
3432	Electric Resistance Welding Equipment	DSCR
3433	Gas Welding, Heat Cutting & Metalizing Equipment	DSCR
3436	Welding Positioners and Manipulators	DSCR
3438	Miscellaneous Welding Equipment	DSCR
3439	Miscellaneous Welding, Soldering and Brazing Supplies and Accessories	DSCR
3441	Bending and Forming Machines	DSCR
3442	Hydraulic and Pneumatic Presses, Power Driven	DSCR
3443	Mechanical Presses, Power Driven	DSCR

Federal Supply Class Code	*Commodity*	*DLA Center*[6]
3444	Manual Presses	DSCR
3445	Punching and Shearing Machines	DSCR
3446	Forging Machinery and Hammers	DSCR
3447	Wire and Metal Ribbon Forming Machinery	DSCR
3448	Riveting Machines	DSCR
3449	Misc. Secondary Metal Forming and Cutting Machines	DSCR
3450	Machine Tools, Portable	DSCR
3455	Cutting Tools for Machine Tools	DSCR
3456	Cutting and Forming Tools for Secondary Metal Working Machines	DSCR
3460	Machine Tool Accessories	DSCR
3461	Accessories for Secondary Metal Working Machinery	DSCR
3465	Production Jigs, Fixtures and Templates	DSCR
3470	Machine Shop Sets, Kits, and Outfits	DSCR
3510	Laundry and Dry Cleaning Equipment	DSCP
3520	Shoe Repairing Equipment	DSCP
3530	Industrial Sewing Machines & Mobile Textile Repair Shops	DSCP
3610	Printing, Duplicating, and Bookbinding Equipment	DSCR
3611 P[9]	Industrial Marking Machines	DSCR
3620 P[9]	Rubber and Plastics Working Machinery	DSCR
3635 P[9]	Crystal and Glass Industries Machinery	DSCR
3650 P[9]	Chemical & Pharmaceutical Products Manufacturing Machinery	DSCR
3655	Gas Generating and Dispensing Systems, Fixed or Mobile	DSCR
3660 P[9]	Industrial Size Reduction Machinery	DSCR
3680 P[9]	Foundry Machinery, Related Equipment and Supplies	DSCR
3685 P[9]	Specialized Metal Container Manufacturing Machinery and Related Equipment	DSCR
3693 P[9]	Industrial Assembly Machines	DSCR
3694 P[9]	Clean Work Stations, Controlled Environment & Related Equipment	DSCR
3695	Miscellaneous Special Industry Machinery	DSCR
3710	Soil Preparation Equipment	DSCP
3720	Harvesting Equipment	DSCP
3740	Pest, Disease, and Frost Control Equipment	DSCR
3770	Saddlery, Harness, Whips and Related Animal Furnishings	DSCP
3805	Earth Moving and Excavating Equipment	DSCP
3810	Cranes and Crane-Shovels	DSCP
3815	Crane and Crane-Shovel Attachments	DSCP
3820	Mining, Rock Drilling, Earth Boring, and Related Equipment	DSCP
3825	Road Clearing and Cleaning Equipment	DSCP
3830	Truck and Tractor Attachments	DSCP
3835	Petroleum Production and Distribution Equipment	DSCP
3895	Miscellaneous Construction Equipment	DSCP
3910	Conveyors	DSCP
3920	Materials Handling Equipment, Nonself-Propelled	DSCP
3930	Warehouse Trucks and Tractors, Self-Propelled	DSCP
3940	Blocks, Tackle, Rigging, and Slings	DSCP
3950	Winches, Hoists, Cranes, and Derricks	DSCC

Federal Supply Class Code	Commodity	DLA Center[6]
3990	Miscellaneous Materials Handling Equipment	DSCP
4010	Chain and Wire Rope	DSCR
4020	Fiber Rope, Cordage and Twine	DSCP
4030	Fittings for Rope, Cable, and Chain	DSCC
4110	Refrigeration Equipment	DSCP
4120	Air Conditioning Equipment	DSCP
4130	Refrigeration and Air Conditioning Components	DSCP
4140	Fans, Air Circulators, and Blower Equipment	DSCP
4210 P[3]	Fire Fighting Equipment	DSCP
4220	Marine Lifesaving and Diving Equipment	DSCP
4310	Compressors and Vacuum Pumps	DSCC
4320	Power and Hand Pumps	DSCC
4330	Centrifugals, Separators, and Pressure and Vacuum Filters	DSCC
4440	Driers, Dehydrators, and Anhydrators	DSCC
4450	Industrial Fan and Blower Equipment	DSCC
4460	Air Purification Equipment	DSCC
4510	Plumbing Fixtures and Accessories	DSCP
4520	Space Heating Equipment and Domestic Water Heaters	DSCP
4530	Fuel Burning Equipment Units	DSCP
4540	Miscellaneous Plumbing, Heating, and Sanitation Equipment	DSCP
4610	Water Purification Equipment	DSCC
4620	Water Distillation Equipment, Marine and Industrial	DSCC
4630	Sewage Treatment Equipment	DSCP
4710	Pipe and Tube	DSCC
4720	Hose and Tubing, Flexible	DSCC
4730	Fittings and Specialities; Hose, Pipe, and Tube	DSCC
4810	Valves, Powered	DSCC
4820	Valves, Nonpowered	DSCC
4930	Lubrication and Fuel Dispensing Equipment	DSCP
5280	Sets, Kits, and Outfits of Measuring Tools	DSCP
5305	Screws	DSCP
5306	Bolts	DSCP
5307	Studs	DSCP
5310	Nuts and Washers	DSCP
5315	Nails, Keys, and Pins	DSCP
5320	Rivets	DSCP
5325	Fastening Devices	DSCP
5330	Packing and Gasket Materials	DSCP
5335	Metal Screening	DSCP
5340	Miscellaneous Hardware	DSCP
5355	Knobs and Pointers	DSCP
5360	Coil, Flat and Wire Springs	DSCP
5365	Rings, Shims, and Spacers	DSCR
5410	Prefabricated and Portable Buildings	DSCP
5420	Bridges, Fixed and Floating	DSCC
5430	Storage Tanks	DSCP
5440	Scaffolding Equipment and Concrete Forms	DSCP
5445	Prefabricated Tower Structures	DSCP
5450	Miscellaneous Prefabricated Structures	DSCP
5510	Lumber and Related Basic Wood Materials	DSCP
5520	Millwork	DSCP
5530	Plywood and Veneer	DSCP
5660	Fencing, Fences and Gates	DSCP
5680 P	Miscellaneous Construction Materials	

Federal Supply Class Code	*Commodity*	*DLA Center*[6]
	This partial assignment applies only to airplane landing mat. (Also, see footnote 1 at end of list relative to purchase of DLA managed items in GSA assigned classes.)	DSCC
5820 P[10]	Radio and Television Communication Equipment, except Airborne	T-ASA (DMC)
5905	Resistors	DSCC
5910	Capacitors	DSCC
5915	Filters and Networks	DSCC
5920	Fuses and Lightning Arrestors	DSCC
5925	Circuit Breakers	DSCC
5930	Switches	DSCC
5935	Connectors, Electrical	DSCC
5940	Lugs, Terminals, and Terminals Strips	DSCR
5945	Relays, Contractors, and Solenoids	DSCC
5950	Coils and Transformers	DSCC
5955	Piezoelectric Crystals	DSCC
5960	Electron Tubes and Associated Hardware	DSCC
5961	Semiconductor Devices and Associated Hardware	DSCC
5962	Microelectronic Circuit Devices	DSCC
5965	Headsets, Handsets, Microphones, and Speakers	DSCC
5970	Electrical Insulators and Insulating Materials	DSCR
5975	Electrical Hardware and Supplies	DSCR
5977	Electrical Contact Brushes and Electrodes	DSCR
5985	Antennas, Waveguides, and Related Equipment	DSCC
5990	Synchros and Resolvers	DSCC
5995	Cable, Cord, and Wire Assemblies; Communication Equipment	DSCR
5999	Miscellaneous Electrical and Electronic Components	DSCC
6105	Motors, Electrical	DSCR
6110	Electrical Control Equipment	DSCR
6115 P[8]	Generators and Generator Sets, Electrical	DSCR
6120	Transformers; Distribution and Power Station	DSCR
6145	Wire and Cable, Electrical	DSCC
6150	Miscellaneous Electric Power and Distribution Equipment	DSCR
6210	Indoor and Outdoor Electric Lighting Fixtures	DSCP
6220	Electric Vehicular Lights and Fixtures	DSCP
6230	Electric Portable and Hand Lighting Equipment	DSCP
6240	Electric Lamps	DSCP
6250	Ballasts, Lampholders and Starters	DSCP
6260	Nonelectrical Lighting Fixtures	DSCP
6350	Miscellaneous Alarm and Signal Systems	DSCP
6505[4]	Drugs, Biologicals, and Official Reagents	DSCP
6508[4]	Medicated Cosmetics and Toiletries	DSCP
6510[4]	Surgical Dressing Materials	DSCP
6515[4]	Medical and Surgical Instruments, Equipment and Supplies	DSCP
6520[4]	Dental Instruments, Equipment and Supplies	DSCP
6525[4]	X-Ray Equipment and Supplies; Medical, Dental and Veterinary	DSCP
6530[4]	Hospital Furniture, Equipment, Utensils, and Supplies	DSCP
6532	Hospital and Surgical Clothing and Textile Special Purpose Items	DSCP

Federal Supply Class Code	*Commodity*	*DLA Center*[6]
6540[4]	Opticians' Instruments, Equipment and Supplies	DSCP
6545[4]	Medical Sets, Kits, and Outfits	DSCP
6630	Chemical Analysis Instruments	DSCP
6635	Physical Properties Testing Equipment	DSCR
6640	Laboratory Equipment and Supplies	DSCP
6655	Geophysical and Astronomical Instruments	DSCR
6670	Scales and Balances	DSCR
6675	Drafting, Surveying, and Mapping Instruments	DSCP
6680	Liquid and Gas Flow, Liquid Level and Mechanical Motion Measuring Instruments	DSCR
6750	Photographic Supplies	DSCP
6810[7]	Chemicals	DSCR
6820	Dyes	DSCR
6830	Gases; Compressed and Liquified	DSCR
6840	Pest Control Agents and Disinfectants	DSCR
6850[7]	Miscellaneous Chemical Specialties	DSCR
7210	Household Furnishings	DSCP
7310	Food Cooking, Baking, and Serving Equipment	DSCP
7320	Kitchen Equipment and Appliances	DSCP
7360	Sets, Kits, and Outfits; Food Preparation and Serving	DSCP
7610	Books and Pamphlets	DSCP
7660	Sheet and Book Music	DSCP
7690	Miscellaneous Printed Matter	DSCP
8110	Drums and Cans	DSCP
8120	Commercial and Industrial Gas Cylinders	DSCR
8125	Bottles and Jars	DSCP
8305	Textile Fabrics	DSCP
	FSC 8305 does not include laminated cloth used exclusively in the repair of lighter than air envelopes.	
8310	Yarn and Thread	DSCP
8315	Notions and Apparel Findings	DSCP
	FSC 8315 does not include coated cloth tape used exclusively in the repair of lighter than air envelopes.	
8320	Padding and Stuffing Materials	DSCP
8325	Fur Materials	DSCP
8330	Leather	DSCP
8335	Shoe Findings and Soling Materials	DSCP
8340	Tents and Tarpaulins	DSCP
8345	Flags and Pennants	DSCP
8405	Outerwear, Men's	DSCP
8410	Outerwear, Women's	DSCP
8415	Clothing, Special Purpose	DSCP
	FSC 8415 includes all submarine clothing.	
8420	Underwear and Nightwear, Men's	DSCP
8425	Underwear and Nightwear, Women's	DSCP
8430	Footwear, Men's	DSCP
8435	Footwear, Women's	DSCP
8440	Hosiery, Handwear, and Clothing Accessories, Men's	DSCP
8445	Hosiery, Handwear, and Clothing Accessories, Women's	DSCP
8450	Children's and Infant's Apparel and Accessories	DSCP
8455	Badges and Insignia	DSCP
8460	Luggage	DSCP
8465	Individual Equipment	DSCP
8470	Armor, Personal	DSCP
8475	Specialized Flight Clothing and Accessories	DSCP
8905[5]	Meat, Poultry, and Fish	DSCP

Federal Supply Class Code	Commodity	DLA Center[6]
8910[5]	Dairy Foods and Eggs	DSCP
8915[5]	Fruits and Vegetables	DSCP
8920[5]	Bakery and Cereal Products	DSCP
8925[5]	Sugar, Confectionery, and Nuts	DSCP
8930[5]	Jams, Jellies, and Preserves	DSCP
8935[5]	Soups and Bouillons	DSCP
8940[5]	Special Dietary Foods and Food Specialty Preparations	DSCP
8945[5]	Food Oils and Fats	DSCP
8950[5]	Condiments and Related Products	DSCP
8955[5]	Coffee, Tea, and Cocoa	DSCP
8960[5]	Beverages, Nonalcoholic	DSCP
8970[5]	Composite Food Packages	DSCP
8975[5]	Tobacco Products	DSCP
9110	Fuels, Solid	DSCP
9130	Liquid Propellants and Fuels, Petroleum Base	DESC
9140	Fuel Oils	DESC
9150	Oils and Greases; Cutting, Lubricating, and Hydraulic	DSCR
9160	Miscellaneous Waxes, Oils, and Fats	DSCP
9320	Rubber Fabricated Materials	DSCP
9330	Plastic Fabricated Materials	DSCP
9340	Glass Fabricated Materials	DSCP
9350	Refractories and Fire Surfacing Materials	DSCP
9390	Miscellaneous Fabricated Nonmetallic Materials	DSCP
9420 P	Fibers; Vegetable, Animal, and Synthetic	
	This partial FSC assignment applies only to raw cotton and raw wool.	DSCP
9430 P	Miscellaneous Crude Animal Products, Inedible	
	This partial assignment applies only to crude hides.	DSCP
9505	Wire, Nonelectrical, Iron and Steel	DSCP
9510	Bars and Rods, Iron and Steel	DSCP
9515	Plate, Sheet, and Strip, Iron and Steel	DSCP
9520	Structural Shapes, Iron and Steel	DSCP
9525	Wire, Nonelectrical, Nonferrous Base Metal	DSCP
9530	Bars and Rods, Nonferrous Base Metal	DSCP
9535	Plate, Sheet, Strip, and Foil, Nonferrous Base Metal	DSCP
9540	Structural Shapes, Nonferrous Base Metal	DSCP
9545	Plate, Sheet, Strip, Foil and Wire, Precious Metal	DSCP
9620 P	Minerals, Natural and Synthetic	
	This partial assignment applies only to crude petroleum and crude shale oil.	DSCP
9925	Ecclesiastical Equipment, Furnishings and Supplies	DSCP
9930	Memorials, Cemeterial and Mortuary Equipment and Supplies	DSCP
9999	Miscellaneous Items	DSCP

[1] These assignments do not apply to items decentralized by the DLA Center Commander, i.e., designated for purchase by each military department, and to those items in DLA assigned federal supply classes, which may be assigned to GSA for supply management. In addition, see DFARS Subpart 208.70, which describes conditions under which a military service may purchase (contract for) military service supply managed items in DLA assigned federal supply classes. See notes 2 and 3 for further exceptions pertaining to certain DLA assignments.

[2] DLA assignments in FSC 2510, 2520, 2530, 2540, 2590, 2805, 2910, 2920, 2930, 2940, and 2990 do not apply to repair parts peculiar to combat and tactical vehicles, which are assigned for coordinated acquisition to the Department of the Army. In addition, the assignment in FSC 2805 does not apply to military standard engines 1.5 HP through 20 HP and parts peculiar therefor, which are assigned for coordinated acquisition to the Department of the Army.

[3] This partial FSC assignment in FSC 4210 does not apply to Fire Fighting Equipment developed by or under the sponsorship of a military department. The contracting responsibility for such equipment is assigned to the department which developed or sponsored its development.

[4] DLA has contracting responsibility for all the items in the classes of FS Group 65. In addition, DLA has contracting responsibility for all equipment and supplies related to the medical, dental, veterinary professions in Non-group 65 classes where the military medical services have the sole or prime interest in such items. The specific item coverage of these Non-group 65 items is published in the DoD section of the Federal Supply Catalog for medical material C3-1 through C3-12, inclusive.

[5] This assignment includes health and comfort items listed in AR 700-23. It also includes resale items for commissary stores (including brand name items).

[6] DLA centers are identified as follows—
DSCC — DLA Land and Maritime
DESC — DLA Energy
DSCR — DLA Aviation
DSCP — DLA Troop Support
DLA also serves as the head of the contracting activity for the Defense Media Center (DMC).

[7] DLA Energy is responsible for contracting for only petroleum base items in FSC 6810 and 6850.

[8] This partial FSC assignment in FSC 6115 does not apply to Mobile Electric Power Generating Sources (MEPGS). The contracting direction responsibility for MEPGS is assigned to the DoD Project Manager, Mobile Electric Power, by DoDD 4120.11. DoD components desiring to use other than the DoD Standard Family of Generator Sets, contained in MIL-STD 633, shall process a Request for Deviation in accordance with Joint Operating Procedures, AR 700-101, AFR 400-50, NAVMATINST 4120.100A, MCO 11310.8c and DLAR 4120.7, Subject: Management and Standardization of Mobile Electric Power Generating Sources, prior to initiating an acquisition.

[9] This partial assignment applies only to secondary items not otherwise assigned, as listed in the applicable Federal Supply Catalog Management Data lists of each respective service.

[10] This partial assignment applies to broadcasting, visual information, and graphics presentation communications equipment used by the American Forces Radio and Television Services, centralized visual information support activities, media centers, closed circuit educational and training programs, language training activities, combat camera units, and individual base visual information centers. This assignment does not apply to equipment with airborne applications. Examples of the types of equipment covered by this assignment include radio and television transmitters, video recording and playback equipment, video cameras, editing and switching equipment, electronic imaging equipment, language training equipment, monitors, audio equipment, and other nontactical, off-the-shelf, commercially available, nondevelopmental electronic equipment used to support broadcast and visual information missions.

PART 5—DEFENSE THREAT REDUCTION AGENCY ASSIGNMENTS

Federal Supply Class Code	*Commodity*
1105	Nuclear Bombs
1110	Nuclear Projectiles
1115	Nuclear Warheads and Warhead Sections
1120	Nuclear Depth Charges
1125	Nuclear Demolition Charges
1127	Nuclear Rockets
1130	Conversion Kits, Nuclear Ordnance
1135	Fuzing and Firing Devices, Nuclear Ordnance
1140	Nuclear Components
1145	Explosive and Pyrotechnic Components, Nuclear Ordnance
1190	Specialized Test and Handling Equipment, Nuclear Ordnance
1195	Miscellaneous Nuclear Ordnance

In addition to the above, assignments to the Defense Threat Reduction Agency (DTRA) include all items for which DTRA provides logistics management or has integrated management responsibilities in accordance with the DTRA Charter.

PART 6—GENERAL SERVICES ADMINISTRATION ASSIGNMENTS

Federal Supply Class Code	*Commodity*
2310 P	Passenger Motor Vehicles
2320 P	Trucks and Truck Tractors
	These two partial assignments apply to all commercial, non-tactical, passenger carrying vehicles and trucks except the following types which are assigned for DoD Coordinated Acquisition to the Department of the Army—
	Bus, convertible to ambulance
	Truck, 4×4, convertible to ambulance
	Truck, 4×4, dump, 9,000 pounds GVW, with cut-down cab
	(See Army Coordinated Acquisition assignments in FSC 2310 and 2320.)
3540	Wrapping and Packaging Machinery
3550	Vending and Coin Operated Machines
3590	Miscellaneous Service and Trade Equipment
3750	Gardening Implements and Tools
5110	Hand Tools, Edged, Nonpowered
5120	Hand Tools, Nonedged, Nonpowered
5130	Hand Tools, Power Driven
5133	Drill Bits, Counterbores, and Countersinks; Hand and Machine
5136	Taps, Dies, and Collects; Hand and Machine
5140	Tool and Hardware Boxes
5180	Sets, Kits, and Outfits of Hand Tools
5210	Measuring Tools, Craftmen's
5345	Disks and Stones, Abrasive
5350	Abrasive Materials
5610	Mineral Construction Materials, Bulk
5620	Building Glass, Tile, Brick, and Block
5630	Pipe and Conduit, Nonmetallic
5640	Wallboard, Building Paper, and Thermal Insulation Materials
5650	Roofing and Siding Materials
5670	Architectural and Related Metal Products
5680 P*	Miscellaneous Construction Materials
7105	Household Furniture
7110	Office Furniture

Federal Supply Class Code	*Commodity*
7125	Cabinets, Lockers, Bins, and Shelving
7195	Miscellaneous Furniture and Fixtures
7220	Floor Coverings
7230	Draperies, Awnings, and Shades
7240	Household and Commercial Utility Containers
7290	Miscellaneous Household and Commercial Furnishings and Appliances
7330	Kitchen Hand Tools and Utensils
7340	Cutlery and Flatware
7350	Tableware
7410	Punched Card System Machines
7420	Accounting and Calculating Machines

("P" after FSC number indicates partial FSC assignment.)

Federal Supply Class Code	*Commodity*
7430	Typewriters and Office-type Composing Machines
	This assignment does not apply to machines controlled by the Congressional Joint Committee on Printing.
7450	Office-type Sound Recording and Reproducing Machines
7460	Visible Record Equipment
7490	Miscellaneous Office Machines
	This assignment does not apply to equipment controlled by the Congressional Joint Committee on Printing.
7510	Office Supplies
	This assignment does not apply to office supplies, including special inks, when DoD requirements of such items are acquired through Government Printing Office channels.
7520	Office Devices and Accessories
	This assignment does not apply to office devices and accessories when DoD requirements of such items are acquired through Government Printing Office channels.
7530	Stationery and Record Forms
	This assignment does not apply to stationery and record forms when DoD requirements of such items are acquired through Government Printing Office channels including those items covered by term contracts issued by GPO for tabulating cards and marginally punched continuous forms.
7710	Musical Instruments
7720	Musical Instrument Parts and Accessories
7730	Phonographs, Radios, and Television Sets; Home Type
7740	Phonograph Records
7810	Athletic and Sporting Equipment
7820	Games, Toys, and Wheeled Goods
7830	Recreational and Gymnastic Equipment
7910	Floor Polishers and Vacuum Cleaning Equipment
7920	Brooms, Brushes, Mops, and Sponges
7930	Cleaning and Polishing Compounds and Preparations
8010	Paints, Dopes, Varnishes, and Related Products
8020	Paint and Artists Brushes
8030	Preservative and Sealing Compounds
8040	Adhesives
8105	Bags and Sacks
8115	Boxes, Cartons and Crates
8135	Packaging and Packing Bulk Materials
8510	Perfumes, Toilet Preparations and Powders

Federal Supply Class Code	Commodity
8520	Toilet Soap, Shaving Preparations and Dentifrices
8530	Personal Toiletry Articles
8540	Toiletry Paper Products
8710	Forage and Feed
8720	Fertilizers
8730	Seeds and Nursery Stock
9310	Paper and Paperboard
9905	Signs, Advertising Displays, and Identification Plates
9910	Jewelry
9915	Collector's Items
9920	Smokers' Articles and Matches

These GSA assignments do not apply to items as described under FSC 7430, 7490, 7510, 7520, and 7530, and those items in the GSA assigned federal supply classes which have been retained for DLA supply management as listed in the applicable Federal Supply Catalog Management Data lists. In addition, see DFARS Subpart 208.70, which describes conditions under which a military service may contract for military service managed items in GSA assigned federal supply classes.

---

* This partial FSC assignment does not include landing mats which are assigned to the Defense Logistics Agency.

[Final rule, 71 FR 39004, 7/11/2006, effective 7/11/2006; Publication notice, 20110419; Publication notice, 20140421]

SUBPART 208.71—ACQUISITION FOR NATIONAL AERONAUTICS AND SPACE ADMINISTRATION (NASA)

208.7102 Procedures. (No Text)

[Final rule, 71 FR 39004, 7/11/2006, effective 7/11/2006]

208.7102-1 General.

(1) Departments and agencies shall not claim reimbursement for administrative costs incident to acquisitions for NASA, unless agreed otherwise prior to the time the services are performed.

(2) When contracting or performing field service functions for NASA, departments and agencies—

(i) Will use their own methods, except when otherwise required by the terms of the agreement; and

(ii) Normally will use their own funds and will not cite NASA funds on any defense obligation or payment document.

[Final rule, 71 FR 39004, 7/11/2006, effective 7/11/2006]

208.7102-2 Purchase request and acceptance.

(1) NASA will use NASA Form 523, NASA-Defense Purchase Request, to request acquisition of supplies or services.

(2) Except as provided in paragraph (4) of this subsection, departments and agencies will respond within 30 days to a NASA purchase request by forwarding DD Form 448-2, Acceptance of MIPR. Forward each DD Form 448-2 in quadruplicate and indicate action status as well as the name and address of the DoD acquisition activity for future use by the NASA initiator.

(3) To the extent feasible, all documents related to the NASA action will reference the NASA-Defense Purchase Request number and the item number when appropriate.

(4) Departments and agencies are not required to accept NASA-Defense Purchase Requests for common-use standard stock items that the supplying department has on hand or on order for prompt delivery at published prices.

[Final rule, 71 FR 39004, 7/11/2006, effective 7/11/2006]

208.7102-3 Changes in estimated total prices.

When a department or agency determines that the estimated total price (Block 6F, NASA Form 523) for NASA items is not sufficient to cover the required reimbursement, or is in excess of the amount required, the department/agency will forward a request for amendment to the NASA originating office. Indicate in the request a specific dollar amount, rather than a percentage, and include justification for any upward adjustment requested. Upon approval of a request, NASA will forward an amendment of its purchase request to the contracting activity.

[Final rule, 71 FR 39004, 7/11/2006, effective 7/11/2006]

208.7102-4 Payments.

Departments and agencies will submit SF 1080, Voucher for Transferring Funds, billings to the NASA office designated in Block 9 of the NASA-Defense Purchase Request, except where agreements provide that reimbursement is not required. Departments and agencies will support billings in the same manner as billings between departments and agencies.

[Final rule, 71 FR 39004, 7/11/2006, effective 7/11/2006]

SUBPART 208.73—USE OF GOVERNMENT-OWNED PRECIOUS METALS

208.7301 Definitions.

As used in this subpart—

Dual pricing evaluation procedure means a procedure where offerors submit two prices for precious metals bearing items—one based on Government-furnished precious metals and one based on contractor-furnished precious metals. The contracting officer evaluates the prices to determine which is in the Government's best interest.

Precious Metals Indicator Code (PMIC) means a single-digit, alpha-numeric code assigned to national stock numbered items in the Defense Integrated Data System Total Item Record used to indicate the presence or absence of precious metals in the item. PMICs and the content value of corresponding items are listed in DoD 4100.39-M, Federal Logistics Information System (FLIS) Procedures Manual, Volume 10, Chapter 4, Table 160.

208.7303 Procedures.

(1) Item managers and contracting officers will use the PMIC and/or other relevant data furnished with a purchase request to determine the applicability of this subpart.

(2) When an offeror advises of a precious metals requirement, the contracting officer shall use the procedures in Chapter 11 of DoD 4160.21-M, Defense Materiel Disposition Manual, to determine availability of required precious metal assets and current Government-furnished materiel (GFM) unit prices. If the precious metals are available, the contracting officer shall evaluate offers and award the contract on the basis of the offer that is in the best interest of the Government.

(3) When the clause prescribed by DFARS 208.7305 is included in a solicitation, the contracting officer shall ensure that Section B, Schedule of Supplies or Services and Prices, is structured to—

(i) Permit insertion of alternate prices for each deliverable contract line item number that uses precious metals; and

(ii) Use dual pricing evaluation procedures.

[Final rule, 71 FR 39004, 7/11/2006, effective 7/11/2006]

208.7304 Refined precious metals.

The following refined precious metals are currently managed by-DSCP:

Precious Metal	*National Stock Number (NSN)*
Gold	9660-00-042-7733
Silver	9660-00-106-9432
Platinum Granules	9660-00-042-7768
Platinum Sponge	9660-00-151-4050
Palladium Granules	9660-00-042-7765
Palladium Sponge	9660-01-039-0320
Rhodium	9660-01-010-2625
Iridium	9660-00-011-1937
Ruthenium	9660-01-039-0313

[Final rule, 71 FR 39004, 7/11/2006, effective 7/11/2006; Publication notice, 20110419]

SUBPART 208.74—ENTERPRISE SOFTWARE AGREEMENTS

208.7401 Definitions.

As used in this subpart—

Golden Disk means a purchased license or entitlement to distribute an unlimited or bulk number of copies of software throughout DoD.

Software product manager means the Government official who manages an enterprise software agreement.

[Final rule, 71 FR 39004, 7/11/2006, effective 7/11/2006]

208.7403 Acquisition procedures.

(1) After requirements are determined, the requiring official shall review the information at the ESI website to determine if the required commercial software or related services are available from DoD inventory (e.g., Golden Disks and DoD-wide software maintenance agreements). If the software or services are available, the requiring official shall fulfill the requirement from the DoD inventory.

(2) If the required commercial software or related services are not in the DoD inventory, and not on an ESA, the contracting officer or requiring official may fulfill the requirement by other means. Existing ESAs are listed on the ESI website.

(3) If the commercial software or related services are on an ESA, the contracting officer or requiring official shall review the terms and conditions and prices in accordance with otherwise applicable source selection requirements.

(4) If an ESA's terms and conditions and prices represent the best value to the Government, the contracting officer or requiring official shall fulfill the requirement for software or services through the ESA.

(5) If existing ESAs do not represent the best value to the Government, the software product manager (SPM) shall be given an opportunity to provide the same or a better value to the Government under the ESAs before the contracting officer or requiring official may continue with alternate acquisition methods.

(i) The contracting officer or requiring official shall notify the SPM of specific concerns about existing ESA terms and conditions or prices through the ESI webpage.

(ii) The SPM shall consider adjusting, within the scope of the ESA, terms and conditions or prices to provide the best value to the customer.

(A) Within 3 working days, the SPM shall—

(1) Update the ESA;

(2) Provide an estimated date by which the update will be accomplished; or

(3) Inform the contracting officer or requiring official that no change will be made to the ESA.

(B) If the SPM informs the contracting officer or requiring official that no change will be made to the ESA terms and conditions or prices, the contracting officer or requiring official may fulfill the requirement by other means.

(C) If the SPM does not respond within 3 working days or does not plan to adjust the ESA within 90 days, the contracting officer or requiring official may fulfill the requirement by other means.

(iii) A management official designated by the department or agency may waive the requirement to obtain commercial software or related services through an ESA after the steps in paragraphs (5)(i) and (5)(ii)(A) of this section are complete. The rationale for use of an alternate source shall be included in the waiver request and shall be provided to the SPM.

[Final rule, 71 FR 39004, 7/11/2006, effective 7/11/2006]

PART 209—CONTRACTOR QUALIFICATIONS

Table of Contents

Subpart 209.1—Responsible Prospective Contractors

Obtaining information 209.105-1
[Removed] 209.105-2
Preaward surveys 209.106
Conditions for preaward surveys 209.106-1
Requests for preaward surveys 209.106-2

Subpart 209.2—Qualifications Requirements

Policy 209.202
Aviation and ship critical safety items 209.270
Procedures 209.270-4

Subpart 209.4—Debarment, Suspension, and Ineligibility

Effect of listing 209.405
Debarment 209.406
Procedures 209.406-3
Suspension 209.407
Procedures 209.407-3

Subpart 209.5—Organizational and Consultant Conflicts of Interest

Limitations on contractors acting as lead system integrators 209.570
Definitions 209.570-1
Procedures 209.570-3
Organizational conflicts of interest in major defense acquisition programs . 209.571
Systems engineering and technical assistance contracts 209.571-7

PART 209—CONTRACTOR QUALIFICATIONS

SUBPART 209.1—RESPONSIBLE PROSPECTIVE CONTRACTORS

209.105-1 Obtaining Information.

GSA's System for Award Management (SAM), which is available at *http://www.acquisition.gov/*, identifies entities excluded throughout the U.S. Government (unless otherwise noted) from receiving Federal contracts or certain subcontracts and from certain types of Federal financial and non-financial assistance and benefits. The SAM website provides useful documents and on-line training to assist with SAM navigation and data entry. User Guides and Demonstration Videos can be found in the User Help section after clicking the HELP link at the top of the website homepage. The former Excluded Parties List System (EPLS) information is within the Performance Information functional area of SAM, and is maintained as "Exclusions" data. Exclusions are located in the Data Access area of SAM which can be accessed by navigating the following path after logging into the SAM website. Select Tab – MYSAM, Tab - Data Access, and Tab – Exclusions.

(1) Multiple agencies have the authority to suspend or debar entities from "doing business" with the Government. There are approximately 71 separate cause and treatment codes under which entities have been suspended or debarred or excluded. New exclusion records created in SAM will no longer be identified with cause and treatment codes. Exclusions will be associated with one of four exclusion types: Preliminarily Ineligible (Proceedings Pending), Ineligible (Proceedings Completed), Prohibition/Restriction, Voluntary Exclusion. Each cause and treatment code is linked to one exclusion type.

(2) The exclusion type advises readers of the nature of the exclusion, debarment, or suspension and how those listed in the SAM Exclusions should be treated. However, the fact that an entity is listed in the SAM Exclusions does not necessarily mean the entity is ineligible for contract award. Review of the exclusion type is crucial in ensuring that listed entities are not deprived of their "liberty interest" in conducting business with the Government.

(3) When the Department of Justice Bureau of Justice Assistance debars individuals under 10 U.S.C. 2408, they are placed in the SAM Exclusions under cause and treatment code FF (Reciprocal), which is now linked to exclusion type, Ineligible (Proceedings Completed). The records for individuals currently entered into EPLS and listed under this cause and treatment code can be found in the SAM Exclusions. Records created in EPLS have both a cause and treatment code and an exclusion type listed.

(4) A "Public User's Manual" is available on the EPLS website to assist users in navigating the system. Definitions of Procurement, Nonprocurement, and Reciprocal exclusions can be found in Chapter 4 of the manual.

[Final rule, 71 FR 14099, 3/21/2006, effective 3/21/2006; Change notice, 20060321; Final rule, 78 FR 28756, 5/16/2013, effective 5/16/2013]

209.105-2 [Removed]

[Final rule, 69 FR 74989, 12/15/2004, effective 12/15/2004; Change notice, 20060321; Change notice 20061026]

209.106 Preaward surveys. (No Text)

209.106-1 Conditions for preaward surveys.

(a) If a preaward survey is requested, include the rationale in Block 23 of the SF 1403, Preaward Survey of Prospective Contractor (General).

[Final rule, 69 FR 65088, 11/10/2004, effective 11/10/2004; Change notice, 20060321; Final rule, 76 FR 71464, 11/18/2011, effective 11/18/2011]

209.106-2 Requests for preaward surveys.

(1) The surveying activity is the cognizant contract administration office as listed in the Federal Directory of Contract Administration Services Components, available at *https://pubapp.dcma.mil/CASD/main.jsp*.

When information is required as part of the survey on the adequacy of the contractor's accounting system or its suitability for administration of the proposed type of contract, the surveying activity will obtain the information from the auditor.

(2) Limited information may be requested by telephone.

(3) The contracting officer may request a formal survey by telephone but must confirm immediately with SF 1403, Preaward Survey of Prospective Contractor (General). For a formal survey, send original and three copies of SF 1403, including necessary drawings and specifications.

List additional factors in Item H, Section III of the SF 1403 and explain them in Block 23. For example—

(A) Information needed to determine a prospective contractor's eligibility under the Walsh-Healey Public Contracts Act. (Note that the Walsh-Healey Public Contracts Act, Block 12 of Section I, only indicates what the contractor has represented its classification to be under Walsh-Healey.)

(B) Evaluation of a contractor as a planned producer when the offered item is or may appear on the Industrial Preparedness Planning List (IPPL). When the preaward survey results in a recommendation for award, ask the office responsible for industrial preparedness planning to consider designating the prospective contractor as a planned producer. If the item is already on the IPPL or the prospective contractor is already a planned producer, note the information in Block 23.

(C) Evaluation of the prospective contractor's performance against small business subcontracting plans.

(4) On base level preaward surveys, technical personnel from the requiring installation should participate when there is concern about the ability of a prospective contractor to perform a base level service or construction contract.

(5) Allow more time for—

(i) Complex items;

(ii) New or inexperienced DoD contractors; and

(iii) Surveys with time-consuming requirements, e.g., secondary survey, accounting system review, financial capability analysis, or purchasing office participation.

(6) Only request those factors essential to the determination of responsibility. See DFARS 253.209-1(a) for an explanation of the factors in Section III, Blocks 19 and 20 of the SF 1403.

[Final rule, 69 FR 65088, 11/10/2004, effective 11/10/2004; Change notice, 20060321; Publication notice, 20120130]

SUBPART 209.2—QUALIFICATIONS REQUIREMENTS

209.202 Policy.

(a)(1) The inclusion of qualification requirements in specifications for products that are to be included on a Qualified Products List, or manufactured by business firms included on a Qualified Manufacturers List, requires approval by the departmental standardization office in accordance with DoD 4120.24-M, Defense Standardization Program (DSP) Policies and Procedures. The inclusion of other qualification requirements in an acquisition or group of acquisitions requires approval by the chief of the contracting office.

[Final rule, 69 FR 65088, 11/10/2004, effective 11/10/2004; Change notice, 20080110]

209.270 Aviation and ship critical safety items. (No Text)

[Final rule, 70 FR 57188, 9/30/2005, effective 9/30/2005; Change notice, 20080110]

209.270-4 Procedures.

(1) Policies and procedures applicable to aviation critical safety item design control activities are in DoD Manual 4140.01, Volume 11, DoD Supply Chain Materiel Management Procedures: Inventory Accountability and Special Management and Handling, DoD Aviation Critical Safety Item (CSI)/Flight Safety Critical Aircraft Part (FSCAP) Program. This regulation provides direction on establishing criticality determinations, identification of aviation critical safety items in the Federal Logistics Information System, and related requirements.

(2) Procedures for management of aviation critical safety items and ship critical safety items are available at *http://www.dscr.dla.mil/ExternalWeb/UserWeb/AviationEngineering/TechnicalOversight/CSI.htm*. This web site provides detailed lifecycle procedures for aviation and ship critical safety items, from initial identification through disposal, as well as a detailed list of definitions applicable to aviation and ship critical safety items.

[Final rule, 70 FR 57188, 9/30/2005, effective 9/30/2005; Change notice, 20080110; Change notice, 20080812; Publication notice, 20140212; Publication notice, 20171228]

SUBPART 209.4—DEBARMENT, SUSPENSION, AND INELIGIBILITY

209.405 Effect of listing.

(1) Environmental Protection Agency (EPA) responsibilities under Executive Order 11738, Providing for Administration of the Clean Air Act and the Federal Water Pollution Control Act With Respect to Federal Contracts, Grants, or Loans, have been delegated to the EPA Suspending and Debarring Official (EPA SDO).

(i) Submit notifications and reports required by DFARS 209.405(b) to the EPA SDO at the following address:

Office of Grants and Debarments
U.S. Environmental Protection Agency
Ariel Rios Building
1200 Pennsylvania Avenue NW
Washington, DC 20640

Telephone: 202-564-5399

(ii) Unless agency procedures specify otherwise, coordinate submissions to the EPA SDO through the applicable agency suspending and debarring official.

(2) Executive Order 11738 is available at *http://www.epa.gov/isdc/eo11738.htm*.

(3) Contracting officers are required to review the System for Award Management (SAM) Exclusions twice, once after opening of bids/receipt of proposals (FAR 9.405(d)(1)) and again immediately prior to award (FAR 9.405(d)(4)). The contracting officer shall document the contract file for both searches; the documentation may include a copy of the SAM Exclusions search results.

[Final rule, 74 FR 2414, 1/15/2009, effective 1/15/2009; Publication notice, 20111102; Final rule, 78 FR 28756, 5/16/2013, effective 5/16/2013]

209.406 Debarment. (No Text)

209.406-3 Procedures.

(i) *Investigation and referral*. When referring any matter to the agency debarring and suspending official for consideration, provide the following specific information and documentation, to the extent practicable. Send two copies (one paper and one electronic) of each report, including enclosures.

(ii) For all referrals, provide the following:

(A) Name, address, and telephone number of the point of contact for the activity making the report.

(B) Name and address of the referred individual/contractor, CAGE code, and DUNS number, if applicable.

(C) Name and addresses of the members of the board, principal officers, partners, owners, and managers of the referred contractor.

(D) Name and addresses of all known affiliates, subsidiaries, or parent firms, and the nature of the business relationship to the referred individual/contractor.

(E) If a contracting office initiates the report, the comments and recommendations of the contracting officer and of each higher-level contracting review authority regarding—

(*1*) Whether to suspend or debar the contractor;

(*2*) Whether to apply limitations to the suspension or debarment;

(*3*) The period of any recommended debarment; and

(*4*) Whether to continue any current contracts with the contractor (or explain why a recommendation regarding current contracts is not included).

(F) To the extent that this information is available through FPDS-NG, a list of other agencies that hold current contracts with the referred individual/contractor.

(iii) For referrals based on judicial actions (indictments, convictions, civil judgments, etc.), provide the following:

(A) Copies of indictments, judgments, and sentencing actions.

(B) Copies of investigative reports when authorized by the investigative agency.

(C) Witness statements or affidavits when authorized by the investigative agency.

(D) If judicial action is contract-related, the contract number, description of supplies or services, and contract amount.

(iv) For "fact-based" referrals (no judicial action), for each contract affected by the misconduct or poor performance being reported, provide the following:

(A) The contract number, description of supplies or services, contract amount, percentage of completion, and amounts paid to and withheld from the contractor.

(B) Whether the contract is assigned under the Assignment of Claims Act and, if so, to whom.

(C) The contract fund citations involved, to expedite accurate return of funds to open accounts and commands, as appropriate.

(D) For any other contracts outstanding with the contractor or any of its affiliates, the contract number, description of supplies or services, and contract amount.

(E) A complete summary of all pertinent evidence and the status of any legal proceedings involving the contractor.

(F) An estimate of any damages sustained by the Government as a result of the contractor's action (explain how the estimate was calculated).

(G) A copy of pertinent extracts of each pertinent contract.

(H) Copies of investigative reports when authorized by the investigative agency.

(I) Witness statements or affidavits when authorized by the investigative agency.

(J) A copy of any available determinations of nonresponsibility in accordance with FAR 9.105-2(a)(1).

(K) Any other appropriate exhibits or documentation.

(b) Decisionmaking process.

(i) The agency debarring and suspending official shall follow the procedures and decisionmaking process stated in FAR 9.406-3(c) for proposed debarments and debarments) and FAR 9.407-3 (for suspensions), DFARS Appendix H, and any agency-specific procedures that are to be provided to the individual/contractor with the notice of proposed debarment or suspension, either by enclosure or electronic reference.

(ii) The absence of a referral in accordance with this section, or the absence of any information specified in this section, will not preclude the debarring and suspending official from making decisions to suspend, propose for debarment, or debar an individual/contractor.

(iii) The signature of the debarring and suspending official on the notice of suspension, proposed debarment, or debarment is sufficient evidence that the debarring and suspending official has made the specified decision.

(iv) If a debarring and suspending official determines that a referral lacks sufficient evidence of a cause for suspension or debarment, the debarring and suspending official may refer the matter for further review or investigation, as appropriate, by an appropriate agency or other Government entity, including a contracting activity, inspector general, auditing agency, or a criminal investigative agency.

[Final rule, 69 FR 74989, 12/15/2004, effective 12/15/2004; Change notice, 20060321; Publication notice 20120615, 6/15/2012; Publication notice, 20121212, 12/12/2012]

209.407 Suspension. (No Text)

209.407-3 Procedures.

Use similar procedures as in DFARS PGI 209.406-3 for suspensions.

[Final rule, 69 FR 74989, 12/15/2004, effective 12/15/2004; Change notice, 20060321; Publication notice 20120615, 6/15/2012]

SUBPART 209.5—ORGANIZATIONAL AND CONSULTANT CONFLICTS OF INTEREST

209.570 Limitations on contractors acting as lead system integrators. (No Text)

[Interim rule, 73 FR 1823, 1/10/2008, effective 1/10/2008]

209.570-1 Definitions.

The phrase *substantial portion of the work,* as used in the definition of *lead system integrator with system responsibility* in the clause at DFARS 252.209-7007, may relate to the dollar value of the effort or to the criticality of the effort to be performed.

[Interim rule, 73 FR 1823, 1/10/2008, effective 1/10/2008]

209.570-3 Procedures.

(1) After assessing the offeror's direct financial interests in the development or construction of any individual system or element of any system of systems, if the offeror—

(i) Has no direct financial interest in such systems, the contracting officer shall document the contract file to that effect and may then further consider the offeror for award of the contract;

(ii) Has a direct financial interest in such systems, but the exception in DFARS 209.570-2(b)(2) applies, the contracting officer shall document the contract file to that effect and may then further consider the offeror for award of the contract;

(iii) Has a direct financial interest in such systems and the exception in DFARS 209.570-2(b)(2) does not apply, but the conditions in DFARS 209.570-2(b)(1)(i) and (ii) do apply, the contracting officer—

(A) Shall document the contract file to that effect;

(B) May, in coordination with program officials, request an exception for the offeror from the Secretary of Defense, in accordance with paragraph (2) of this subsection; and

(C) Shall not award to the offeror unless the Secretary of Defense grants the exception and provides the required certification to Congress; or

(iv) Has a direct financial interest in such systems and the exceptions in DFARS 209.570-2(b)(1) and (2) do not apply, the contracting officer shall not award to the offeror.

(2)(i) To process an exception under DFARS 209.570-2(b)(1), the contracting officer shall submit the request and appropriate documentation to—

Director, Defense Procurement and Acquisition Policy
ATTN: OUSD(AT&L)DPAP/PACC
3060 Defense Pentagon
Washington, DC 20301-3060.
Phone: 703-695-4235
FAX: 703-693-9616

(ii) The action officer in the Office of the Director, Defense Procurement and Acquisition Policy, Program Acquisition and Contingency Contracting (DPAP/PACC), will process the request through the Office of the Secretary of Defense and, if approved, to the appropriate committees of Congress. The contracting officer shall not award a contract to the affected offeror until notified by the DPAP/PACC action officer that the exception has been approved and transmitted to Congress.

[Interim rule, 73 FR 1823, 1/10/2008, effective 1/10/2008; Final rule, 78 FR 54968, 9/9/2013, effective 9/9/2013]

209.571 Organizational conflicts of interest in major defense acquisition programs. (No Text)

[Final rule, 75 FR 81908, 12/29/2010, effective 12/29/2010]

209.571-7 Systems engineering and technical assistance contracts.

Because of the special organizational conflict of interest restrictions that relate to systems engineering and technical assistance contracts, it is more practical to separate systems engineering and technical assistance-type work from design- and development-type work, and not include both types of work in the same task order or other contract vehicle.

[Final rule, 75 FR 81908, 12/29/2010, effective 12/29/2010]

PART 210—MARKET RESEARCH

Table of Contents

Subpart 210.0—Market Research

Procedures 210.002
Market research report guide for improving the tradecraft in services acquisition 210.070

PART 210—MARKET RESEARCH

SUBPART 210.0—MARKET RESEARCH

210.002 Procedures.

(e) (ii) Contracting officers are encouraged to retain information on potential offerors that express an interest in an acquisition, in order to solicit feedback in instances when only one offer is received on a competitive solicitation (see PGI 215.371-2).

(iii) Contracting officers should ensure that the contract file includes—

(A) The methods used to conduct market research;

(B) The timeframe in which market research was conducted;

(C) The analysis of the capabilities of the potential sources that were identified during market research; and

(D) Any conclusion(s) reached as a result of market research analysis.

[Publication notice, 20120829; Final rule, 80 FR 21656, 4/20/2015, effective 4/20/2015; Publication notice, 20160923]

210.070 Market research report guide for improving the tradecraft in services acquisition.

The "Market Research Report Guide for Improving the Tradecraft in Services Acquisition" is designed to effect the collection and sharing of standardized market research information across the Department. The guide is available for download at *http://www.acq.osd.mil/dpap/cpic/cp/marketresearch.html.*

[Publication notice, 20120829]

PART 211—DESCRIBING AGENCY NEEDS

Table of Contents

Subpart 211.1—Selecting and Developing Requirements Documents

Items peculiar to one manufacturer 211.105

Subpart 211.2—Using and Maintaining Requirements Documents

Identification and availability of specifications 211.201
Substitutions for military or Federal specifications and standards 211.273
Procedures 211.273–3
Item identification and valuation requirements 211.274
Policy for unique item identification 211.274-2

Subpart 211.70—Purchase Requests

Procedures 211.105

PART 211—DESCRIBING AGENCY NEEDS

SUBPART 211.1—SELECTING AND DEVELOPING REQUIREMENTS DOCUMENTS

211.105 Items peculiar to one manufacturer.

Office of Federal Procurement memorandum of April 11, 2005, Subject: Use of Brand Name Specifications, reinforces the need to maintain vendor and technology neutral contract specifications, and asks agencies to publish the supporting justification when using brand name specifications in a solicitation.

Office of Federal Procurement Policy memorandum of April 17, 2006, Subject: Publication of Brand Name Justifications, provides additional guidance regarding publication of justifications for use of brand name specifications.

[Final rule, 70 FR 23804, 5/5/2005, effective 5/5/2005; Change notice 20060814]

SUBPART 211.2—USING AND MAINTAINING REQUIREMENTS DOCUMENTS

211.201 Identification and availability of specifications.

(1) Specifications, standards, and data item descriptions are indexed in the Acquisition Streamlining and Standardization Information System (ASSIST).

(2) Most unclassified specifications, standards, and data item descriptions, and DoD adoption notices on voluntary consensus standards may be downloaded from the ASSIST database (*https://assist.dla.mil/* or *http://quicksearch.dla.mil/*). Documents contained in ASSIST that are not available for download may be identified and obtained by following the instructions at *http://assist.dla.mil/online/faqs/overview.cfm.*

[Final rule, 71 FR 27641, 5/12/2006, effective 5/12/2006; Publication notice, 20160325; Final rule, 84 FR 4366, 2/15/2019, effective 2/15/2019]

211.273 Substitutions for military or Federal specifications and standards. (No Text)

[Final rule, 71 FR 27641, 5/12/2006, effective 5/12/2006]

211.273-3 Procedures.

(1) Solicitations for previously developed items shall encourage offerors to identify Single Process Initiative (SPI) processes for use instead of military or Federal specifications and standards cited in the solicitation. Use of the clause at DFARS 252.211-7005, Substitutions for Military or Federal Specifications and Standards, satisfies this requirement.

(2) Contracting officers shall ensure that—

(i) Concurrence of the requiring activity is obtained for any proposed substitutions prior to contract award;

(ii) Any necessary additional information regarding the SPI process identified in the proposal is obtained from the cognizant administrative contracting officer; and

(iii) In competitive procurements, prospective offerors are provided the opportunity to obtain verification that an SPI process is an acceptable replacement for a military or Federal specification or standard for the particular procurement prior to the date specified for receipt of offers.

(3) Any determination that an SPI process is not acceptable for a specific procurement shall be made prior to contract award at the head of the contracting activity or program executive officer level. This authority may not be delegated.

[Final rule, 71 FR 27641, 5/12/2006, effective 5/12/2006]

211.274 Item identification and valuation requirements. (No Text)

[Final rule, 77 FR 52254, 8/29/2012, effective 8/29/2012; Publication notice, 20120829]

211.274-2 Policy for unique item identification.

(b) (2) (ii) Send the copy of the determination and findings required by DFARS 211.274-2(b) (2) (i) to DPAP/Program Development and Implementation, Deputy Director, 3060 Defense Pentagon, 3B855, Washington, DC 20301-3060; or via email to: *osd.pentagon.ousd-atl.mbx.pdi@mail.mil*.

[Final rule, 77 FR 52254, 8/29/2012, effective 8/29/2012; Publication notice, 20120829; Publication notice, 20160923]

SUBPART 211.70—PURCHASE REQUESTS

211.7001 Procedures.

Requiring activities are responsible for developing and distributing purchase requests, except for the requirements for Military Interdepartmental Purchase Requests (MIPRs) (DD Form 448) addressed in *253.208-1*.

(a) Agencies may use a combined numbering series for MIPRs and internal purchase requests, following the rules at 253.208-1(c) (1) for both. If using a separate numbering sequence for internal purchase requests, procedures shall be in place to ensure that the same number cannot be assigned to both a MIPR and an internal purchase request. Use of a purely internal tracking number in addition to the purchase request number is authorized and supported by the data standards. Number the purchase request by using—

(1) The requiring activity's Department of Defense Activity Address Code (DODAAC), as described in DLM 4000.25 Volume 6, Chapter 2. DODAACs may be verified at ***https://www.transactionservices.dla.mil/daasinq***.

(2) A serial number of eight alphanumeric characters, excluding "I" and "O"; and

(3) A revision number, with the original request being assigned zero and subsequent revisions or amendments being numbered consecutively.

(b) Prior to taking action on a purchase request, contracting officers shall ensure that the requiring activity has prepared the purchase requests in uniform contract format (see FAR 14.201-1 and 15.204), except for procurement of construction (see part 36), which should follow the current edition of the Construction Specifications Institute format. Purchase requests shall include all supporting documentation required by local contract procedures.

(c) Prior to taking action on a purchase request, contracting officers shall ensure that the purchase requests follow the line item rules and data requirements in DFARS 204.71. Purchase requests for individual supplies (i.e., not bulk commodities such as oil) shall identify whether the item to be acquired is subject to the item unique identification requirements of DFARS 211.274-2.

(d) (1) Purchase requests may be unfunded for planning purposes, partially funded, or fully funded.

(2) Funding data in purchase requests will, at a minimum, identify the following elements of the funding source: Department Code (e.g. 21 Army), Main Account (e.g. 1804, Operation and Maintenance, Navy), Subaccount (where applicable), and Fiscal Year. Lists of these codes are published in Supplement 1 to Volume I of the Treasury Financial Manual, Federal Account Symbols and Titles, generally referred to as The FAST Book.

(3) Agencies shall have sufficient procedures in place to enable traceability of line items identified in the purchase request to those in the resulting contract. In developing such procedures, agencies shall ensure that provisions are made for circumstances in which the deliverables may be more completely defined during the process of soliciting offers and making an award.

(e) Contracting officers shall not obligate funds that have not been certified as currently available and suitable. All purchase requests shall be reviewed and certified after agreement on price and prior to award to ensure that the funds are—

(1) Suitable and available for the purpose and amount of the contract; and

(2) Traceable from the purchase request to the resultant contract.

(f) Purchase requests transmitted between requiring systems and contract writing systems shall be transmitted via the Global EXchange system (GEX) using the Purchase Request Data Standard Extensible Markup Language (XML) format (*http://www.acq.osd.mil/dpap/pdi/eb/procurement_data_standard.html*). Copies shall be sent via the GEX to the Electronic Data Access (EDA) (*http://eda.ogden.disa.mil*) system. Requiring systems and contract writing systems may use a format that can be translated to or from the purchase request Data Standard Extensible Markup Language (XML) format.

[Final rule, 71 FR 27641, 5/12/2006, effective 5/12/2006; Publication notice, 20140828; Publication notice, 20161021; Publication notice, 20190913; Publication notice, 20191231]

PART 212—ACQUISITION OF COMMERCIAL ITEMS

Table of Contents

Subpart 212.1—Acquisition of Commercial Items—General

Applicability 212.102

Subpart 212.4—[Removed]

Subpart 212.70—[Removed]

Subpart 212.71—Pilot Program for Acquisition of Military-Purpose Nondevelopmental Items

Pilot Program 212.7102
Reporting requirements 212.7102-3

PART 212—ACQUISITION OF COMMERCIAL ITEMS

SUBPART 212.1—ACQUISITION OF COMMERCIAL ITEMS—GENERAL

212.102 Applicability.

Applicability.

(a) (i) *Commercial item determination.*

(1) *Making the commercial item determination.*

(A) The contracting officer may make the commercial item determination or request a Defense Contract Management Agency (DCMA) Commercial Item Group (CIG) contracting officer make the determination. To request a determination from a DCMA CIG contracting officer, the contracting officer shall send a request to the e-mail address at paragraph (a) (i) (3). The contracting officer may withdraw the request for a CIG commercial item determination at any point prior to the determination being made. Contracting officers shall include the completed commercial item determination in the contract file.

(B) Before making a commercial item determination, the contracting officer shall search for a prior DoD commercial item determination for the same item within the DoD Commercial Item Database located on the website identified in paragraph (a) (iii) (2).

(C) Particular care must be taken to document determinations involving "modifications of a type customarily available in the marketplace," and items only "offered for sale, lease, or license to the general public," but not yet actually sold, leased, or licensed. In these situations, the documentation must clearly detail the particulars of the modifications and sales offers. When such items lack sufficient market pricing histories, additional diligence must be given to determinations that prices are fair and reasonable as required by FAR subpart 15.4.

(2) *Documenting the commercial item determination.* The contracting officer making the determination shall document the market research and rationale supporting a conclusion that the item is commercial.

(3) *DoD commercial item database.* Within 30 days of making a commercial item determination, the contracting officer shall e-mail the commercial item determination to DCMA CIG at *dcma.boston-ma.eastern-rc.mbx.Commercial@mail.mil* so that it can be uploaded by the CIG to the DoD Commercial Item Database.

(ii) *Prior commercial item determination.* If a prior DoD commercial item determination for the same item is made by a military department, defense agency, or another component of DoD, contracting officers may presume that the prior commercial item determination shall serve as a determination for subsequent procurements of such item, unless the process is followed to overturn the prior determination (see DFARS 212.102(a) (ii) (B)).

(iii) *Commercial item support.*

(1) *Commercial item guidebook.* See the Department of Defense Guidebook for Acquiring Commercial Items, Part A: Commercial Item Determination, for detailed guidance and practical examples on improving the consistency and timeliness of commercial item determinations to include a template for new commercial item determinations and for general information related to commercial items.

(2) *DCMA CIG.* Contracting officers are able to request support and assistance on market research, price reasonableness, and commercial item determinations from the DCMA CIG. The DCMA CIG contact information is available at *http://www.dcma.mil/commercial-item-group/*.

[Final rule, 73 FR 4114, 1/24/2008, effective 1/24/2008; Final rule, 83 FR 4431, 1/31/2018, effective 1/31/2018; Publication notice, 20190809]

SUBPART 212.4—[REMOVED]

[Change notice, 20080722; Publication notice, 20101029]

SUBPART 212.70—[REMOVED]

[Final rule, 74 FR 34264, 7/15/2009, effective 7/15/2009]

SUBPART 212.71—PILOT PROGRAM FOR ACQUISITION OF MILITARY-PURPOSE NONDEVELOPMENTAL ITEMS

212.7102 Pilot Program.

Contracting officers shall ensure that contract files fully and adequately document the market research and rationale supporting a conclusion that the military-purpose nondevelopmental item definition in DFARS 212.7101 has been satisfied.

[Interim rule, 76 FR 38048, 6/29/2011, effective 6/29/2011; Final rule, 77 FR 2653, 1/19/2012, effective 1/19/2012; Interim rule, 81 FR 42557, 6/30/2016, effective 6/30/2016]

212.7102-3 Reporting requirements.

(a) By October 31 each year, departments and agencies shall submit a consolidated report identifying all contracts awarded under the Pilot Program on Acquisition of Military Purpose Nondevelopmental Items during the preceding fiscal year. Submit the required information via email at *osd.pentagon.ousd-atl.mbx.cpic@mail.mil*.

(b) The report shall include the following:

(1) Name of the contractor receiving a contract award under the pilot described in this subpart.

(2) Description of the item or items to be acquired.

(3) The military purpose to be served by such item or items.

(4) The amount of the contract.

(5) Actions taken by the contracting officer to ensure that the price paid for such item(s) is fair and reasonable.

(c) The required format for the report is available at *http://www.acq.osd.mil/dpap/dars/pgi/docs/Template_for_Annual_Report_(PGI_212-7102-3_Pilot_for_Military_Purpose_Nondevelopmental%20Items).xlsx*.

[Interim rule, 76 FR 38048, 6/29/2011, effective 6/29/2011; Final rule, 77 FR 2653, 1/19/2012, effective 1/19/2012; Interim rule, 81 FR 42557, 6/30/2016, effective 6/30/2016]

PART 213—SIMPLIFIED ACQUISITION PROCEDURES

Table of Contents

Subpart 213.1—Procedures

Promoting competition. 213.104

Subpart 213.2—Actions at or below the Micro-Purchase Threshold

General 213.201

Subpart 213.3—Simplified Acquisition Methods

Governmentwide commercial purchase card 213.301
Purchase orders 213.302
Obtaining contractor acceptance and modifying purchase orders 213.302-3
SF 44, Purchase Order-Invoice-Voucher 213.306
Forms 213.307

PART 213—SIMPLIFIED ACQUISITION PROCEDURES

SUBPART 213.1—PROCEDURES

213.104 Promoting competition.

For information on the various approaches that may be used to competitively fulfill DoD requirements, see the Office of the Under Secretary of Defense for Acquisition, Technology, and Logistics Guidelines for Creating and Maintaining a Competitive Environment for Supplies and Services in the Department of Defense [*bbp.dau.mil/docs/BBP%202-0%20Competition%20Guidelines%20(Published%2022%20Aug%202014).pdf*].

[Final rule, 80 FR 21656, 4/20/2015, effective 4/20/2015]

SUBPART 213.2—ACTIONS AT OR BELOW THE MICRO-PURCHASE THRESHOLD

213.201 General.

(g) (i) The higher micro-purchase thresholds in FAR 13.201(g) are authorized for purchases that have a clear and direct relationship to the support of a declared contingency operation; to facilitate defense against or recovery from cyber, nuclear, biological, chemical, or radiological attack; to support a request from the Secretary of State or the Administrator of the United States Agency for International Development to facilitate provision of international disaster assistance pursuant to 22 U.S.C. 2292 et seq.; or to support response to an emergency or major disaster (42 U.S.C. 5122). To determine if a declaration has been made that authorizes the use of the higher micropurchase thresholds review the following websites:

(A) Declared domestic contingency operations are listed at *http://www.acq.osd.mil/dpap/pacc/cc/domestic_emergencies.html*.

(B) Declared overseas contingency operations are listed at *http://www.acq.osd.mil/dpap/pacc/cc/international_operations.html*.

(ii) *United States*, as used in this section, is defined in FAR 2.101(b).

(iii) Except as provided in paragraph (iv) of this section, the following tables illustrate the micro-purchase threshold based on the physical location of the Government purchaser and, for services, the place of performance:

(A) For supplies—

Government Purchaser Physical Location	Authorized Micro-Purchase Threshold
Inside United States	$20,000
Outside United States	$30,000

(B) For services, including acquisitions of services subject to 41 U.S.C. chapter 67, Service Contract Labor Standards—

Government Purchaser Physical Location	Place of Performance	Authorized Micro-Purchase Threshold
Inside United States	Inside or Outside United States	$20,000
Outside United States	Inside United States	$20,000
Outside United States	Outside United States	$30,000

(iv) (A) Government purchasers located inside the United States are prohibited from using the $30,000 contingency micro-purchase threshold, unless specifically authorized by statute.

(B) The $2,000 micro-purchase threshold for acquisitions of construction subject to 40 U.S.C. chapter 31, subchapter IV, Wage Rate Requirements (Construction), remains unchanged in the event of a declared contingency operation; a cyber, nuclear, biological, chemical, or radiological attack; a request from the Secretary of State or the Administrator of the United States Agency for International Development to facilitate provision of international disaster assistance pursuant to 22 U.S.C. 2292 et seq.; or an emergency or major disaster (42 U.S.C. 5122), regardless of the criteria described above.

[Final rule, 81 FR 53045, 8/11/2016, effective 8/11/2016; Final rule, 83 FR 24888, 5/30/2018, effective 5/30/2018]

SUBPART 213.3—SIMPLIFIED ACQUISITION METHODS

213.301 Governmentwide commercial purchase card.

(1) A Governmentwide commercial purchase card program is a program that is authorized pursuant to a delegation of contracting authority and designation as a DoD contracting activity for the purpose of streamlining the purchase and payment processes for supplies and services by use of a Government-issued purchase card.

(2) Governmentwide commercial purchase card programs cannot be established or operated unless contracting authority is granted in accordance with governing laws and regulations, and delegated through a contracting activity identified at PGI 202.101. Further guidance regarding establishment, operation, and oversight of Governmentwide commercial purchase card programs can be found in the "Department of Defense Government Charge Card Guidebook for Establishing and Managing Purchase, Travel, and Fuel Card Programs" at *http://www.acq.osd.mil/dpap/pdi/pc/policy_documents.html*.

[Final rule, 79 FR 56278, 9/19/2014, effective 9/19/2014]

213.302 Purchase orders. (No Text)

[Final rule, 71 FR 3412, 1/23/2006, effective 1/23/2006]

213.302-3 Obtaining contractor acceptance and modifying purchase orders.

Generally, use unilateral modifications (see FAR 43.103) for—

(1) No-cost amended shipping instructions if—

(i) The amended shipping instructions modify a unilateral purchase order; and

(ii) The contractor agrees orally or in writing; and

(2) Any change made before work begins if—

(i) The change is within the scope of the original order;

(ii) The contractor agrees;

(iii) The modification references the contractor's oral or written agreement; and

(iv) Block 13D of Standard Form 30, Amendment of Solicitation/Modification of Contract, is annotated to reflect the authority for issuance of the modification.

[Final rule, 71 FR 3412, 1/23/2006, effective 1/23/2006]

213.306 SF 44, Purchase Order-Invoice-Voucher.

1) For DoD customers, contact the Service or Agency Component Program Manager (CPM) for fuel cards (see *http://www.desc.dla.mil/DCM/Files/CPMPOCs06022010.pdf*; and

(2) For non-DoD customers, contact the designated Account Manager identified at *http://www.desc.dla.mil/DCM/DCMPage.asp?pageid=41*.

(B) Purchases using the AIR Card® and SEA Card® shall follow the guidance found at *http://www.desc.dla.mil/DCM/DCMPage.asp?pageid=28*.

[Final rule, 76 FR 58149, 9/20/2011, effective 9/20/2011]

213.307 Forms.

(a) If SF 1449 is not used, use DD Form 1155 in accordance with paragraph (b)(i) of this section.

(b)(i) Use DD Form 1155, Order for Supplies or Services, for purchases made using simplified acquisition procedures.

(A) The DD Form 1155 serves as a—

(1) Purchase order or blanket purchase agreement;

(2) Delivery order or task order;

(3) Receiving and inspection report;

(4) Property voucher;

(5) Document for acceptance by the supplier; and

(6) Public voucher, when used as—

(i) A delivery order;

(ii) The basis for payment of an invoice against blanket purchase agreements or basic ordering agreements when a firm-fixed-price has been established; or

(iii) A purchase order for acquisitions using simplified acquisition procedures.

(B) The DD Form 1155 is also authorized for use for—

(1) Orders placed in accordance with FAR Subparts 8.4, 8.6, 8.7, and 16.5; and

(2) Classified acquisitions when the purchase is made within the United States or its outlying areas. Attach the DD Form 254, Contract Security Classification Specification, to the purchase order.

(ii) Do not use Optional Form 347, Order for Supplies or Services, or Optional Form 348, Order for Supplies or Services Schedule—Continuation.

(iii) Use Standard Form 30, Amendment of Solicitation/Modification of Contract, to—

(A) Modify a purchase order; or

(B) Cancel a unilateral purchase order.

[Final rule, 71 FR 3412, 1/23/2006, effective 1/23/2006]

PART 215—CONTRACTING BY NEGOTIATION

Table of Contents

Subpart 215.1—Source Selection Processes and Techniques

Limitations and Prohibitions 215.101-2-70

Subpart 215.3—Source Selection

Scope of subpart 215.300
Responsibilities 215.303
Evaluation factors and significant subfactors 215.304
Evaluation factor for employing or subcontracting with members of the Selected Reserve 215.370
Evaluation factor 215.370-2
Only one offer 215.371
Promote competition 215.371

Subpart 215.4—Contract Pricing

Pricing policy 215.402
Obtaining certified cost or pricing data 215.403
Prohibition on obtaining certified cost or pricing data (10 U.S.C. 2306a and 41 U.S.C. chapter 35) 215.403-1
Requiring data other than certified cost or pricing data 215.403-3
[Removed] 215.403-5
Proposal analysis 215.404
Proposal analysis techniques 215.404-1
Data to support proposal analysis 215.404-2
Subcontract pricing considerations 215.404-3
DD Form 1547, Record of Weighted Guidelines Method Application 215.404-70
Weighted guidelines method 215.404-71
Facilities capital employed 215.404-71-4
Reporting profit and fee statistics 215.404-76
Prenegotiation objectives 215.406-1
Certificate of Current Cost or Pricing Data 215.406-2
Documenting the negotiation 215.406-3
Make-or-buy programs 215.407-2
Should-cost review 215.407-4
Estimating systems 215.407-5
Disclosure, maintenance, and review requirements 215.407-5-70
Estimated data prices 215.470

PART 215—CONTRACTING BY NEGOTIATION

SUBPART 215.1—SOURCE SELECTION PROCESSES AND TECHNIQUES

215.101-2-70 Limitations and Prohibitions.

(a) *Limitations.*

(1) (vi) Contracting officers shall obtain guidance from the requiring activity when it is unclear whether a supply is "predominately expendable in nature" or "nontechnical," or has a "short life expectancy" or "short shelf life."

(vii) The contracting officer shall document the contract file with a determination from the requiring activity that the lowest priced offer reflects full life-cycle costs for the supply or service (see DoD Instruction 4140.01, DoD Supply Chain Material Management Policy for additional information on life-cycle costs for supplies).

[Final rule, 84 FR 50785, 9/26/2019, effective 10/1/2019]

SUBPART 215.3—SOURCE SELECTION

215.300 Scope of subpart.

See the policy tab for Director, Defense Procurement and Acquisition Policy memorandum dated April 1, 2016, entitled, *Department of Defense Source Selection Procedures*, which provides the procedures to be used within DoD when conducting negotiated, competitive acquisitions utilizing FAR part 15 procedures.

[Publication notice, 20110307; Final rule, 81 FR 28729, 5/10/2016, effective 5/10/2016]

215.303 Responsibilities.

(b) (2) The source selection plan—

(A) Shall be prepared and maintained by a person designated by the source selection authority or as prescribed by agency procedures;

(B) Shall be coordinated with the contracting officer and senior advisory group, if any, within the source selection organization; and

(C) Shall include, as a minimum—

(1) The organization, membership, and responsibilities of the source selection team;

(2) A statement of the proposed evaluation factors and any significant subfactors and their relative importance;

(3) A description of the evaluation process, including specific procedures and techniques to be used in evaluating proposals; and

(4) A schedule of significant events in the source selection process, including documentation of the source selection decision and announcement of the source selection decision.

[Final rule, 71 FR 3413, 1/23/2006, effective 1/23/2006]

215.304 Evaluation factors and significant subfactors.

(c) (i) (A) Evaluation factors may include—

(1) The extent to which such firms are specifically identified in proposals;

(2) The extent of commitment to use such firms (for example, enforceable commitments are to be weighted more heavily than non-enforceable ones);

(3) The complexity and variety of the work small firms are to perform;

(4) The realism of the proposal;

(5) Past performance of the offerors in complying with requirements of the clauses at FAR 52.219-8, Utilization of Small Business Concerns, and 52.219-9, Small Business Subcontracting Plan; and

(6) The extent of participation of such firms in terms of the value of the total acquisition.

(v) Using authority granted in section 806 of Pub. L. 111-383 to exclude a source based on supply chain risk requires an evaluation factor for supply chain risk, as specified at DFARS 239.73. Evaluating supply chain risk requires review of the supply chain, including all information technology subcontractors and suppliers that are proposed for use at any time in the performance of the contract and may involve the use of all-source intelligence information. The requiring activity is responsible for obtaining any necessary all-source intelligence information and must inform the contracting officer and source selection authority of the results of the review for use in evaluating offers

[Final rule, 71 FR 3413, 1/23/2006, effective 1/23/2006; Final rule, 80 FR 67243, 10/30/2015, effective 10/30/2015]

215.370 Evaluation factor for employing or subcontracting with members of the Selected Reserve. (No Text)

[Final rule, 73 FR 62211, 10/20/2008, effective 10/20/2008]

215.370-2 Evaluation factor.

(1) This evaluation factor may be used as an incentive to encourage contractors to use employees or individual subcontractors who are members of the Selected Reserve.

(2) As with all evaluation factors and subfactors, the contracting officer should consider the impact the inclusion of this factor will have on the resulting contract and weight it accordingly.

(3) The solicitation provision at 252.215-7005 requires an offeror to provide supporting documentation when stating an intent to use members of the Selected Reserve in the performance of the contract.

[Final rule, 73 FR 62211, 10/20/2008, effective 10/20/2008]

215.371 Only one offer. (No Text)

[Final rule, 80 FR 21656, 4/20/2015, effective 4/20/2015]

215.371-2 Promote competition.

(a) For competitive solicitations in which more than one potential offeror expressed an interest in an acquisition, but only one offer was ultimately received, the Contracting Officer shall—

(1) Seek feedback (e.g., issue an RFI) after award from potential offerors expected to submit an offer; and

(2) Document any feedback received in the contract file.

(b) Agencies shall use any feedback received when considering how to overcome barriers to competition for future requirements.

[Final rule, 80 FR 21656, 4/20/2015, effective 4/20/2015]

SUBPART 215.4—CONTRACT PRICING

215.402 Pricing policy.

(1) Contracting officers must purchase supplies and services from responsible sources at fair and reasonable prices. The Truth in Negotiations Act (TINA) (10 U.S.C. 2306a and 41 U.S.C. chapter 35) requires offerors to submit certified cost or pricing data if a procurement exceeds the TINA threshold and none of the exceptions to certified cost or pricing data requirements applies. Under TINA, the contracting officer obtains accurate, complete, and current data from offerors to establish a fair and reasonable price (see FAR 15.403). TINA also allows for a price adjustment remedy if it is later found that a contractor did not provide accurate, complete, and current data.

(2) When certified cost or pricing data are not required, and the contracting officer does not have sufficient data to determine price reasonableness, FAR 15.402(a)(2) requires the offeror to provide whatever data the contracting officer needs in order to determine fair and reasonable prices.

(3) Obtaining sufficient data from the offeror is particularly critical in situations where an item is determined to be a commercial item in accordance with FAR 2.101 and the contract is being awarded on a sole source basis. This includes commercial sales data of items sold in similar quantities and, if such data is insufficient, cost data to support the proposed price.

(4) See PGI 215.404-1 and the Department of Defense Guidebook for Acquiring Commercial Items, Part B: Pricing Commercial Items, for more detailed procedures and guidance on obtaining data needed to determine fair and reasonable prices.

[Change notice, 2007053; Final rule, 76 FR 58137, 9/20/2011, effective 9/20/2011; Final rule, 77 FR 76939, 12/31/2012, effective 12/31/2012; Final rule, 83 FR 4431,

1/31/2018, effective 1/31/2018; Publication notice, 20191231]

215.403 Obtaining certified cost or pricing data.

[Final rule, 71 FR 69492, 12/1/2006, effective 12/1/2006; Final rule, 77 FR 76939, 12/31/2012, effective 12/31/2012; Publication notice, 20191231]

215.403-1 Prohibition on obtaining certified cost or pricing data (10 U.S.C. 2306a and 41 U.S.C. chapter 35).

(b) *Exceptions to certified cost or pricing data requirements.* Even if an exception to certified cost or pricing data applies, the contracting officer is still required to determine price reasonableness. In order to make this determination, the contracting officer may require data other than certified cost or pricing data, including data related to prices and cost data that would otherwise be defined as certified cost or pricing data if certified.

(c)(3) *Commercial items.*

(A) See the Department of Defense Guidebook for Acquiring Commercial Items, *Part B: Pricing Commercial Items,* for detailed guidance about techniques and approaches to pricing commercial products and services.

(B) *(1) Report Content.* The annual report of commercial item exceptions to Truth in Negotiations Act (TINA) requirements shall include the following:

Title: Commercial Item Exceptions to TINA Requirements

(1) Contract number, including modification number, if applicable, and program name.

(2) Contractor name.

(3) Contracting activity.

(4) Total dollar amount of exception.

(5) Brief explanation of the basis for determining that the item(s) are commercial.

(6) Brief description of the specific steps taken to ensure price reasonableness.

(2) Pricing Actions Reported. The intent of this requirement is to report when a commercial item exception was determined. Therefore, the reporting of the commercial item exceptions are for pricing actions at the point the contracting officer makes a determination that the commercial item exception applies. For example—

Example 1: The contracting officer determined that a commercial item exception applies for an entire indefinite-delivery indefinite-quantity (IDIQ) contract and expected the subsequent orders to exceed $19.5 million (based on the estimated maximum amount for the IDIQ or other supportable estimate of future orders). The organization would report this in accordance with DFARS 215.403-1(c)(3) for the period in which the IDIQ contract was awarded, and would include the total dollar amount of subsequent orders under the exception expected at the time of award.

Example 2: The contracting officer awards an IDIQ contract with no commercial item exceptions anticipated. The contracting officer later modifies the contract for an order that will meet commercial item exceptions, and the subsequent order(s) are expected to exceed $19.5 million. Reporting (in the year the modification was issued) will include this IDIQ contract, the amount of this order, and any other expected future orders that will use the exception.

(i) For the above examples, after the contract is reported as receiving the exception with expected awards over $19.5 million, there would be no further report, e.g., when a subsequent order under that contract exceeds $19.5 million, because reporting for that contract was already accomplished.

(ii) When explaining price reasonableness in accordance with paragraph (c)(3)(B)(*1*)(6) of this subsection, if pricing was accomplished when the IDIQ contract was awarded, also explain how price reasonableness was determined. In circumstances where pricing will take place on the order at a future date, explain how pricing techniques at FAR 15.404-1 will be used, including obtaining cost data, if that is the only way to determine price reasonableness.

(4) *Waivers.*

(A) *Exceptional case TINA waiver.*

(1) In determining that an exceptional case TINA waiver is appropriate, the head of

the contracting activity must exercise care to ensure that the supplies or services could not be obtained without the waiver and that the determination is clearly documented. *See DPAP March 23, 2007, policy memorandum.* The intent is not to relieve entities that normally perform Government contracts subject to TINA from an obligation to certify that cost or pricing data are accurate, complete, and current. Instead, waivers must be used judiciously, in situations where the Government could not otherwise obtain a needed item without a waiver. A prime example would be when a particular company offers an item that is essential to DoD's mission but is not available from other sources, and the company refuses to submit certified cost or pricing data. In such cases, a waiver may be appropriate. However, the procuring agency should, in conjunction with the waiver, develop a strategy for procuring the item in the future that will not require such a waiver (e.g., develop a second source, develop an alternative product that satisfies the department's needs, or have DoD produce the item).

(2) Senior procurement executive coordination. An exceptional case TINA waiver that exceeds $100 million shall be coordinated with the senior procurement executive prior to granting the waiver.

(3) Waiver for part of a proposal. The requirement for submission of certified cost or pricing data may be waived for part of an offeror's proposed price when it is possible to clearly identify that part of the offeror's cost proposal to which the waiver applies as separate and distinct from the balance of the proposal. In granting a partial waiver, in addition to complying with the requirements in DFARS 215.403-1(c)(4), the head of the contracting activity must address why it is in the Government's best interests to grant a partial waiver, given that the offeror has no objection to certifying to the balance of its cost proposal.

(4) Waivers for unpriced supplies or services. Because there is no price, unpriced supplies or services cannot be subject to cost or pricing data certification requirements. The Government cannot agree in advance to waive certification requirements for unpriced supplies or services, and may only consider a waiver at such time as an offeror proposes a price that would otherwise be subject to certification requirements.

(B) The annual report of waiver of TINA requirements shall include the following: Title: Waiver of TINA Requirements

(1) Contract number, including modification number, if applicable, and program name.

(2) Contractor name.

(3) Contracting activity.

(4) Total dollar amount waived.

(5) Brief description of why the item(s) could not be obtained without a waiver. *See DPAP March 23, 2007, policy memorandum.*

(6) Brief description of the specific steps taken to ensure price reasonableness.

(7) Brief description of the demonstrated benefits of granting the waiver.

[Final rule, 71 FR 69492, 12/1/2006, effective 12/1/2006; Change notice, 20070531; Final rule, 76 FR 58137, 9/20/2011, effective 9/20/2011; Final rule, 77 FR 76939, 12/31/2012, effective 12/31/2012; Final rule, 83 FR 4431, 1/31/2018, effective 1/31/2018; Publication notice, 20180131; Publication notice, 20191231]

215.403-3 Requiring data other than certified cost or pricing data.

To the extent that certified cost or pricing data are not required by FAR 15.403-4 and there is no other means for the contracting officer to determine that prices are fair and reasonable, the offeror is required to submit "data other than certified cost or pricing data" (see definition at FAR 2.101). In accordance with FAR 15.403-3(a), the offeror must provide appropriate data on the prices at which the same or similar items have previously been sold, adequate for determining the reasonableness of the price. The following clarifies these requirements:

(1) *Data other than certified cost or pricing data.* When certified cost or pricing data are not required, the contracting officer must obtain whatever data is necessary in order to determine the reasonableness of the price. The FAR defines this as "data other than

certified cost or pricing data." When TINA does not apply and there is no other means of determining that prices are fair and reasonable, the contracting officer must obtain appropriate data on the prices at which the same or similar items have been sold previously, adequate for evaluating the reasonableness of the price. Sales data must be comparable to the quantities, capabilities, specifications, etc., of the product or service proposed. Sufficient steps must be taken to verify the integrity of the sales data, to include assistance from the Defense Contract Management Agency, the Defense Contract Audit Agency, and/or other agencies if required. See PGI 215.404-1 for more detailed procedures for obtaining data from offerors to determine price reasonableness.

(2) *Previously been sold.* Contracting officers shall request offerors to provide data related to prior sales (or "offered for sale") in support of price reasonableness determinations.

(3) *Adequacy of sales data for pricing.* The contracting officer must determine if the prior sales data is sufficient for determining that prices are fair and reasonable. If the sales data is not sufficient, additional data shall be obtained, including cost data if necessary. See PGI 215.404-1 for more detailed procedures for obtaining whatever data is needed to determine fair and reasonable prices.

(4) *Reliance on prior prices paid by the Government.* Before relying on a prior price paid by the Government, the contracting officer must verify and document that sufficient analysis was performed to determine that the prior price was fair and reasonable. Sometimes, due to exigent situations, supplies or services are purchased even though an adequate price or cost analysis could not be performed. The problem is exacerbated when other contracting officers assume these prices were adequately analyzed and determined to be fair and reasonable. The contracting officer also must verify that the prices previously paid were for quantities consistent with the current solicitation. Not verifying that a previous analysis was performed, or the consistencies in quantities, has been a recurring issue on sole source commercial items reported by oversight organizations. Sole source commercial items require extra attention to verify that previous prices paid on Government contracts were sufficiently analyzed and determined to be fair and reasonable. At a minimum, a contracting officer reviewing price history shall discuss the basis of previous prices paid with the contracting organization that previously bought the item. These discussions shall be documented in the contract file.

(5) *Canadian Commercial Corporation.* All contracts with the Canadian Commercial Corporation (CCC) are placed in accordance with the practices, policies and procedures of the Government of Canada covering procurement for defense purposes (see PGI 225.870). Contracting Officers may rely on the confirmation and endorsement of the offer from the Canadian Commercial Corporation at 225.870-3(a) as an endorsement of the cost/price as no more than would be charged to the Canadian government.

(i) When 252.215-7003 or 252.215-7004 are included in a solicitation with the Canadian Commercial Corporation, the data required by paragraph (b)(i) and (ii), in concert with the confirmation and endorsement of the offer, is intended to meet the requirements of FAR 15.404-1 for documentation of fair and reasonable pricing.

(ii) Use of 252.215-7003 or 252.215-7004 in sole source acquisitions not meeting the threshold at 215.408(2)(i)(A) or (ii)(A)*(1)* or competitive acquisitions at any dollar value shall be supported by a determination and finding justifying the anticipated need for data other than certified cost or pricing data to determine a fair and reasonable price.

(iii) When the contracting officer anticipates the need for additional data to establish a fair and reasonable price, specific data should be requested at time of solicitation as detailed in DFARS 252.215-7003.

(iv) Examples of clause use:

Scenario	Requirement
Sole source to CCC, fixed price, with estimated value of $600 million.	Include provision and clause in accordance with 215.408(2)(i)(A)*(2)* and (ii)(A(*1*)*(ii)*, respectively, because estimated value exceeds $500 million.
Sole source to CCC, cost reimbursement, with estimated value of $800,000.	Include provision and clause in accordance with 215.408(2)(i)(A)*(1)* and (ii)(A(*1*)*(i)*, respectively, because estimated value exceeds $750,000.
Sole source to CCC, cost-reimbursement, with estimated value of $500,000.	Do not include provision and clause, unless D&F is approved in accordance with 215.408(2)(i)(B) and (ii)(A)(*2*)), respectively, because estimated value does not exceed $750.000.
Sole source to CCC, fixed price, with estimated value of $800,000	Do not include provision and clause, unless D&F is approved in accordance with 215.408(2)(i)(B) and (ii)(A)(*2*)), respectively, because estimated value does not exceed $500 million.
Modifications to contracts that include the clause 252.215-7004.	If 252.215-7004 is included in the contract, then data are required for modifications valued above the simplified acquisition threshold, or a higher threshold specified in the solicitation by the contracting officer, in accordance with 252.215-7004(b).

[Change notice, 20070531; Publication notice 20121212, 12/12/2012; Publication notice, 20160510; Final rule, 83 FR 30824, 6/29/2018, effective 6/29/2018; Publication notice, 20191231]

215.403-5 [Removed]

[Final rule, 71 FR 69492, 12/1/2006, effective 12/1/2006; Final rule, 75 FR 71560, 11/24/2010, effective 11/24/2010]

215.404 Proposal analysis.

[Final rule, 71 FR 69492, 12/1/2006, effective 12/1/2006]

215.404-1 Proposal analysis techniques.

(a) *General.*

(i) The objective of proposal analysis is to ensure that the final agreed-to price is fair and reasonable.

(A) When the contracting officer needs data to determine price reasonableness and the offeror will not furnish that data, use the following sequence of steps to resolve the issue:

(*i*) The contracting officer should make it clear what data is required and why it is needed to determine fair and reasonable prices, and should be flexible in requesting data in existing formats with appropriate explanations from the offeror.

(*ii*) If the offeror refuses to provide the data, the contracting officer should elevate the issue within the contracting activity.

(*iii*) Contracting activity management shall, with support from the contracting officer, discuss the issue with appropriate levels of the offeror's management.

(*iv*) If the offeror continues to refuse to provide the data, contracting activity management shall elevate the issue to the head of the contracting activity for a decision in accordance with FAR 15.403-3(a)(4).

(*v*) The contracting officer shall document the contract file to describe—

(a) The data requested and the contracting officer's need for that data;

(b) Why there is currently no other alternative but to procure the item from this particular source; and

(c) A written plan for avoiding this situation in the future (e.g., develop a second source by . . .; bring the procurement in house to the Government by . . .).

(*vi*) Consistent with the requirements at FAR 15.304 and 42.1502 and the DoD Guide to Collection and Use of Past Performance Information, Version 3, dated May 2003, the contracting officer shall provide input into the past performance system, noting the offeror's refusal to provide the requested information.

(B) In some cases, supplies or services that are not subject to TINA may require a cost analysis (see paragraph (b)(iv) of this section). This will occur when a price analysis is not sufficient for determining prices to be fair and reasonable. In such cases, the contracting officer should consider the need for a Defense Contract Audit Agency audit of the cost data.

(C) Particular attention should be paid to sole source commercial supplies or services. While the order of preference at FAR 15.402 must be followed, if the contracting officer cannot determine price reasonableness without obtaining data other than cost or pricing data from the offeror, at a minimum, the contracting officer must obtain appropriate data on the prices at which the same or similar items have been sold previously (often previous sales data was the basis of the commercial item determination and must be requested during price analysis of the data provided by the offeror). If previous sales data is not sufficient to determine price reasonableness, the contracting officer must obtain "data other than certified cost or pricing data" and, if necessary, perform a cost analysis.

(D) Analysis of termination proposals, including termination of any contract scope, should not rely solely on earned value management budgets or estimates for estimating the costs of all work deleted, or the cost of deleted work already performed (reference FAR subpart 15.4, Table 15-2—Instructions for Submitting Cost/Price Proposals When Certified Cost or Pricing Data are Required, columns (2) and (3) of section III.B., Change Orders, Modifications, and Claims).

(b) *Price analysis for commercial and noncommercial items.*

(i) See the Department of Defense Guidebook for Acquiring Commercial Items, *Part B: Pricing Commercial Items*, for detailed guidance about techniques and approaches to pricing commercial products and services.

(v) Contracting officers must obtain and document sufficient data to confirm that previous prices paid by the Government were based on a thorough price and/or cost analysis. For example, it would not be sufficient to use price(s) from a database paid by another contracting officer without understanding the type of analysis that was performed to determine the price(s), and without verifying that the quantities were similar for pricing purposes. This does not necessarily need to be another analysis, but there should be coordination with the other office that acknowledges an analysis was performed previously.

(vii) See the Department of Defense Guidebook for Acquiring Commercial Items, *Part B: Pricing Commercial Items*, for information about how to obtain advisory assistance from the DoD cadre of experts in the Defense Contract Management Agency (DCMA) Commercial Item Group (CIG) via email at *commercial@dcma.mil* or at *http://www.dcma.mil/commercial-item-group/*.

(c) *Cost analysis.*

(i) When the contracting officer cannot obtain sufficient data to perform a price analysis in accordance with the pricing steps in FAR 15.404-1(b), a cost analysis is required.

(ii) When a solicitation is not subject to TINA and a cost analysis is required, the contracting officer must clearly communicate to the offeror the cost data that will be needed to determine if the proposed price is fair and reasonable.

(iii) To the extent possible, when cost or pricing data are not required to be submitted in accordance with Table 15-2 of FAR 15.408, the contracting officer should accept the cost data in a format consistent with the offeror's records.

(iv) The contracting officer must always consider the need for field pricing support from the Defense Contract Management Agency, the Defense Contract Audit Agency, and/or other agencies.

(e) *Technical analysis.*

Requesting technical assistance is particularly important when evaluating pricing related to items that are "similar to" items being purchased or commercial items that are "of a type" or require "minor modifications." Technical analysis can assist in pricing these types of items by identifying any differences between the item being acquired and the "similar to" item. In particular, the technical review can assist in evaluating the changes that are required to get from the "similar to" item, to the item being solicited, so the contracting officer can determine sufficient price/cost analysis techniques when evaluating that the price for the item being solicited is fair and reasonable. See the Department of Defense Guidebook for Acquiring Commercial Items, *Part B: Pricing Commercial Items*, for information about how to obtain advisory assistance from the DoD cadre of experts in the Defense Contract Management Agency (DCMA) Commercial Item Group (CIG) via email at *commercial@dcma.mil* or at *http://www.dcma.mil/commercial-item-group/*.

(h) *Review and justification of pass-through contracts.*

(2) (A) This requirement applies to acquisitions that include the clause at FAR 52.215-23, Limitations on Pass-Through Charges, as prescribed at FAR 15.408(n) (2) (i) (B). When considering alternative approaches or making the determination that the contracting approach selected is in the best interest of the Government as required by FAR 15.404-1(h) (2), consider the following elements:

(*1*) The requirement, proposed prime contractor, and overall proposed contract value.

(*2*) The information provided in response to the provision at FAR 52.215-22, Limitations on Pass-Through Charges—Identification of Subcontract Effort, regarding the subcontracts, and the estimated value of the proposed subcontracts.

(*3*) The availability of alternative existing contracts that would allow direct access to the subcontractor, such as existing indefinite delivery/indefinite quantity contracts, Federal Supply Schedule contracts, or Governmentwide agency contracts. Perform market research as appropriate.

(*4*) Potential cost savings of directly contracting with the subcontractor.

(*5*) Feasibility of competition for the subcontracted effort or justification for single source procurement.

(*6*) Potential impacts to the contracting and program schedule for implementing a direct contract with the subcontractors or conducting a competition for the subcontracted effort.

(*7*) Changes in performance risk as result of eliminating prime contractor oversight and substituting direct government oversight. Risks may include loss of prime contractor knowledge of integration and program requirements, availability of government contracting and contract administration personnel, reduced system or program accountability of the prime contractor who is no longer responsible for the entire effort, impact on warranties.

(*8*) Subcontractor past performance and experience directly managing programs of this size.

(B) DoD components shall include reviews of compliance in routine procurement management reviews or other inspections.

[Change notice, 20070531; Final rule, 77 FR 76939, 12/31/2012, effective 12/31/2012; Publication notice, 20150930; Final rule, 83 FR 4431, 1/31/2018, effective 1/31/2018; Publication notice, 20191231]

215.404-2 Data to support proposal analysis.

(a) *Field pricing assistance.*

(i) The contracting officer should consider requesting field pricing assistance (See PGI 215.404-2(c) for when audit assistance should be requested) for—

(A) Fixed-price proposals exceeding the certified cost or pricing data threshold;

(B) Cost-type proposals exceeding the certified cost or pricing data threshold from offerors with significant estimating system deficiencies (see DFARS 215.407-5-70(a)(4) and (c)(2)(i)); or

(C) Cost-type proposals exceeding $10 million from offerors without significant estimating system deficiencies.

(ii) The contracting officer should not request field pricing support for proposed contracts or modifications in an amount less than that specified in paragraph (a)(i) of this subsection. An exception may be made when a reasonable pricing result cannot be established because of—

(A) A lack of knowledge of the particular offeror; or

(B) Sensitive conditions (e.g., a change in, or unusual problems with, an offeror's internal systems).

(c) *Audit assistance for prime contracts or subcontracts.*

(i) The contracting officer should consider requesting audit assistance from DCAA for—

(A) Fixed-price proposals exceeding $10 million;

(B) Cost-type proposals exceeding $100 million.

(ii) The contracting officer should not request DCAA audit assistance for proposed contracts or modifications in an amount less than that specified in paragraph (c)(i) of this subsection unless there are exceptional circumstances explained in the request for audit. (See PGI 215.404-2(a)(i) for requesting field pricing assistance without a DCAA audit.)

(iii) If, in the opinion of the contracting officer or auditor, the review of a prime contractor's proposal requires further review of subcontractors' cost estimates at the subcontractors' plants (after due consideration of reviews performed by the prime contractor), the contracting officer should inform the administrative contracting officer (ACO) having cognizance of the prime contractor before the review is initiated.

(iv) Notify the appropriate contract administration activities when extensive, special, or expedited field pricing assistance will be needed to review and evaluate subcontractors' proposals under a major weapon system acquisition. If audit reports are received on contracting actions that are subsequently cancelled, notify the cognizant auditor in writing.

(v) Requests for audit assistance for subcontracts should use the same criteria as established in paragraphs (c)(i) and (c)(ii) of this subsection.

[Final rule, 71 FR 69492, 12/1/2006, effective 12/1/2006; Publication notice, 20100917; Final rule, 77 FR 76939, 12/31/2012, effective 12/31/2012; Publication notice, 20191231]

215.404-3 Subcontract pricing considerations.

(a) The contracting officer should consider the need for field pricing analysis and evaluation of lower-tier subcontractor proposals, and assistance to prime contractors when they are being denied access to lower-tier subcontractor records.

(i) When obtaining field pricing assistance on a prime contractor's proposal, the contracting officer should request audit or field pricing assistance to analyze and evaluate the proposal of a subcontractor at any tier (notwithstanding availability of data or analyses performed by the prime contractor) if the contracting officer believes that such assistance is necessary to ensure the reasonableness of the total proposed price. Such assistance may be appropriate when, for example—

(A) There is a business relationship between the contractor and the subcontractor not conducive to independence and objectivity;

(B) The contractor is a sole source supplier and the subcontract costs represent a substantial part of the contract cost;

(C) The contractor has been denied access to the subcontractor's records;

(D) The contracting officer determines that, because of factors such as the size of the proposed subcontract price, audit or field pricing assistance for a subcontract at any tier is critical to a fully detailed analysis of the prime contractor's proposal;

(E) The contractor or higher-tier subcontractor has been cited for having significant estimating system deficiencies in the area of subcontract pricing, especially the failure to perform adequate cost analyses of proposed subcontract costs or to perform subcontract analyses prior to negotiation of the prime contract with the Government; or

(F) A lower-tier subcontractor has been cited as having significant estimating system deficiencies.

(ii) It may be appropriate for the contracting officer or the ACO to provide assistance to a contractor or subcontractor at any tier, when the contractor or higher-tier subcontractor has been denied access to a subcontractor's records in carrying out the responsibilities at FAR 15.404-3 to conduct price or cost analysis to determine the reasonableness of proposed subcontract prices. Under these circumstances, the contracting officer or the ACO should consider whether providing audit or field pricing assistance will serve a valid Government interest.

(iii) When DoD performs the subcontract analysis, DoD shall furnish to the prime contractor or higher-tier subcontractor, with the consent of the subcontractor reviewed, a summary of the analysis performed in determining any unacceptable costs included in the subcontract proposal. If the subcontractor withholds consent, DoD shall furnish a range of unacceptable costs for each element in such a way as to prevent disclosure of subcontractor proprietary data.

(iv) Price redeterminable or fixed-price incentive contracts may include subcontracts placed on the same basis. When the contracting officer wants to reprice the prime contract even though the contractor has not yet established final prices for the subcontracts, the contracting officer may negotiate a firm contract price—

(A) If certified cost or pricing data on the subcontracts show the amounts to be reasonable and realistic; or

(B) If certified cost or pricing data on the subcontracts are too indefinite to determine whether the amounts are reasonable and realistic, but—

(1) Circumstances require prompt negotiation; and

(2) A statement substantially as follows is included in the repricing modification of the prime contract:

> As soon as the Contractor establishes firm prices for each subcontract listed below, the Contractor shall submit (in the format and with the level of detail specified by the Contracting Officer) to the Contracting Officer the subcontractor's cost incurred in performing the subcontract and the final subcontract price. The Contractor and the Contracting Officer shall negotiate an equitable adjustment in the total amount paid or to be paid under this contract to reflect the final subcontract price.

(v) If the selection of the subcontractor is based on a trade-off among cost or price and other non-cost factors rather than lowest price, the analysis supporting subcontractor selection should include a discussion of the factors considered in the selection (also see FAR 15.101 and 15.304 and DFARS *215.304*). If the contractor's analysis is not adequate, return it for correction of deficiencies.

(vi) The contracting officer shall make every effort to ensure that fees negotiated by contractors for cost-plus-fixed-fee subcontracts do not exceed the fee limitations in FAR 15.404-4(c)(4).

[Final rule, 71 FR 69492, 12/1/2006, effective 12/1/2006; Final rule, 77 FR 76939, 12/31/2012, effective 12/31/2012; Publication notice, 20191231]

215.404-70 DD Form 1547, Record of Weighted Guidelines Method Application.

(1) The DD Form 1547—

(i) Provides a vehicle for performing the analysis necessary to develop a profit objective; and

(ii) Provides a format for summarizing profit amounts subsequently negotiated as part of the contract price.

(2) The contracting officer shall—

(i) Use and prepare a DD Form 1547 whenever a structured approach to profit analysis is required by DFARS 215.404-4(b) (see DFARS 215.404-71, 215.404-72, and 215.404-73 for guidance on using the structured approaches). Administrative instructions for completing the form are in *PGI 253.215-70*.

(ii) Ensure that the DD Form 1547 is accurately completed. The contracting officer is responsible for the correction of any errors detected by the management system auditing process.

[Final rule, 71 FR 69492, 12/1/2006, effective 12/1/2006; Publication notice, 20151030; Publication notice, 20191231]

215.404-71 Weighted guidelines method.

[Final rule, 71 FR 69492, 12/1/2006, effective 12/1/2006; Publication notice, 20151030; Publication notice, 20191231]

215.404-71-4 Facilities capital employed.

(c) *Use of DD Form 1861 - Field pricing support.*

(i) The contracting officer may ask the ACO to complete the forms as part of field pricing support.

(ii) When the Weighted Guidelines Method is used, completion of the DD Form 1861 requires data not included on the Form CASB-CMF, i.e., distribution percentages of land, building, and equipment for the business unit performing the contract. Choose the most practical method for obtaining this data, for example—

(A) Contract administration offices could obtain the data through the process used to establish factors for facilities capital cost of money or could establish advance agreements on distribution percentages for inclusion in field pricing reports;

(B) The corporate ACO could obtain distribution percentages; or

(C) The contracting officer could request the data through a solicitation provision.

[Final rule, 71 FR 69492, 12/1/2006, effective 12/1/2006; Final rule, 77 FR 76939, 12/31/2012, effective 12/31/2012; Publication notice, 20191231]

215.406-1 Prenegotiation objectives.

(a) Also consider—

(i) Data resulting from application of work measurement systems in developing prenegotiation objectives; and

(ii) Field pricing assistance personnel participation in planned prenegotiation and negotiation activities.

(b) Prenegotiation objectives, including objectives related to disposition of findings and recommendations contained in preaward and postaward contract audit and other advisory reports, shall be documented and reviewed in accordance with departmental procedures.

(i) *Significant Disagreements.* (A) Contracting officers and contract auditors have complementary roles in the contracting process and are expected to collaborate to determine fair and reasonable contract values, in accordance with *Director, Defense Procurement and Acquisition Policy memorandum dated December 4, 2009, Subject: Resolving Contract Audit Recommendations.* When a significant disagreement arises on questioned costs, the contracting officer and the auditor shall discuss the basis of the disagreement. The contracting officer shall document that discussion and their disagreement in a written communication to the auditor. The contracting officer shall also document the disagreement in the prenegotiation objective (or pre-business clearance). The contracting officer may then proceed with negotiations when the prenegotiation objectives are approved.

(B) A significant disagreement is defined as the contracting officer planning to sustain less than 75-percent of the total recommended questioned costs in a Defense Contract Audit Agency (DCAA) audit report of a contractor proposal for an initial contract or a contract modification with a value equal to or greater than $10 million. It does not apply to costs that DCAA has categorized as unsupported or unresolved in its audit report.

(ii) *Adjudication Procedures.* DCAA has three days to elevate the issues within the contracting officer's activity after receipt of the contracting officers' written communication confirming the disagreement. Furthermore, DCAA may appeal the significant issues up the chain of command as established in each Component's "Resolving Contract Audit Recommendations" policy. If issues remain, the Director, DCAA may escalate from the Defense Component's Head of Contracting Activity or Senior Procurement Executive, to the Director, Defense Procurement and Acquisition Policy (DPAP). If the DCAA Director believes that the Director, DPAP has not adequately addressed the matter, the disagreement may finally be elevated to the Under Secretary of Defense for Acquisition, Technology, and Logistics, and the Comptroller.

(iii) Notwithstanding the above, the Director, DCAA, may always raise audit issues to the Director, DPAP.

(c) *Cost estimates for program baselines and contract negotiations for Major Defense Acquisition and Major Automated Information System Programs.*

(i) For the purpose of contract negotiations and obligation of funds under this paragraph, the Government shall prepare cost analyses and targets based on the Government's reasonable expectation of successful contractor performance in accordance with the contractor's proposal and previous experience.

(ii) Cost estimates developed for baseline descriptions and other program purposes by the Director of Cost Assessment and Program Evaluation pursuant to its functions, do not meet the criteria described in paragraph (c) (i) of this subsection and, thus, shall not be used for purposes of developing the Government's contract negotiation position or for the obligation of funds. However, the Government may consider the data used to develop such estimates when developing the cost analyses and targets described in paragraph (c) (i) of this subsection.

(d) See Frequently asked 'Questions and Answers" at *http://www.acq.osd.mil/dpap/cpic/cp/sec_808_NDAA.html* relating to the limitations placed on the Department of Defense for aggregate annual amounts available for contracted services in accordance with section 808 of the National Defense Authorization Act for Fiscal year 2012, P.L. 112-81 and DFARS Class Deviation 2012-O0012, Limitation on Amounts Available for Contracted Services, dated July 31, 2012.

[Final rule, 71 FR 69492, 12/1/2006, effective 12/1/2006; Publication notice, 20011102; Final rule, 77 FR 76939, 12/31/2012, effective 12/31/2012; Publication notice, 20130228; Publication notice, 20191231]

215.406-2 Certificate of Current Cost or Pricing Data.

(c) (i) Prior to the start of negotiations, contracting officers should notify offerors and contractors that—

(A) A Certificate of Current Cost or Pricing Data, as prescribed in FAR 15.406-2, shall be submitted as soon as practicable after agreement on price (preferably within 5 days after price agreement), but before contract award or execution of a modification, except for unpriced actions such as letter contracts.

(B) A Certificate of Current Cost or Pricing Data that deviates from the language specified in FAR 15.406-2, or has been amended to include certification of data submitted after the date of price agreement, will not be accepted.

(ii) If any data is submitted after the date of price agreement, contracting officers shall—

(A) Notify offerors in writing that such data will not be reviewed until after contract award and will be dispositioned in accordance with FAR 15.407-1 and FAR clause 52.215-10 or 52.215-11, as applicable; or

(B) Consider the previous price agreement null and void, and prior to award—

(*1*) Reopen negotiations to assess the impact of the data submitted after the date of price agreement ("sweep data");

(*2*) Reestablish price agreement based on cost or pricing data that is accurate, complete, and current as of the date of the revised agreement on price; and

(*3*) Request a new Certificate of Current Cost or Pricing Data, as prescribed by FAR 15.406-2, to include the sweep data and any new or revised data submitted after the previous certification.

(iii) If a contractor persistently submits untimely "sweep" data or fails to timely submit cost or pricing data or the certification that the data are accurate, complete, and current as of the data of price agreement, the contracting officer should refer the matter to the Defense Contract Audit Agency (DCAA) via the Administrative Contracting Officer, Divisional Administrative Contracting Officer, or Corporate Administrative Contracting Officer, as appropriate, for consideration in DCAA's review of the adequacy of the contractor's estimating system.

[Final rule, 84 FR 25194, 5/31/2019, effective 5/31/2019]

215.406-3 Documenting the negotiation.

(a) (7) Include the principal factors related to the disposition of findings and recommendations contained in preaward and postaward contract audit and other advisory reports.

(10) The documentation—

(A) Shall address significant deviations from the prenegotiation profit objective;

(B) Should include the DD Form 1547, Record of Weighted Guidelines Application (see DFARS 215.404-70), if used, with supporting rationale;

(C) Shall address the rationale for not using the weighted guidelines method when its use would otherwise be required by DFARS *215.404-70;* and

(D) Shall be marked "FOR OFFICIAL USE ONLY", as appropriate and in accordance with *DoD Manual 5200.01,* Volume 4.

(11) The contracting officer is responsible to ensure the approved pre- and postnegotiation noncompetitive business clearance documents (e.g., price negotiation memoranda) are uploaded into the Contract Business Analysis Repository (CBAR) at *https://eadf.dcma.mil/ewam2/registration/setup.do* for the purpose of sharing negotiation experience with other contracting officers preparing to negotiate. This includes both noncompetitive actions using the procedures at FAR part 12, Acquisition of Commercial Items, as well as noncompetitive actions using the procedures at FAR part 15, Contracting by Negotiation, that are valued in excess of $25 million and awarded on or after June 24, 2013 (and for all definitized or awarded actions over $100 million, which occurred on or after October 1, 2012).

(A) Business clearance documents uploaded to CBAR shall be marked "FOR OFFICIAL USE ONLY (FOUO)" at the top and bottom of the face or cover page, and on the bottom of each page containing FOUO, including the back page or cover.

(B) The business clearance documents uploaded to CBAR shall be signed by the contracting officer and shall include all other signatures required by local policy/ procedure.

(C) The documentation shall be uploaded to CBAR no later than 30 days after award of the contract action associated with the negotiation and shall include both the prenegotiation objectives required by FAR 15.406-1 and PGI 215.406-1, and the record of negotiations (i.e. the Price Negotiation Memoranda required by FAR 15.406-3 and PGI 215.406-3). The contracting officer shall complete the "description of acquisition" field with keywords and searchable terms to identify the products and services acquired. Additionally, the contracting officer shall complete the "comments" field of the CBAR record to summarize unique features and aspects of the negotiation in order to prompt other contracting teams to inquire further to learn from their peers' prior experience.

(D) If an initial indefinite-delivery indefinite-quantity (IDIQ) task or delivery order contract contemplates issuance of task or delivery orders that will invoke negotiated rates or values from the basic contract, then the business clearance record for the basic IDIQ contract shall be uploaded if the estimated value of the contract (e.g. ceiling price) exceeds the prescribed dollar threshold. To the extent individual task or delivery orders entail a negotiation (i.e. did not simply incorporate prices established at the basic contract level), a business clearance record for the individual task or delivery orders that exceed the prescribed dollar thresholds shall be uploaded to CBAR.

(E) For additional information about obtaining access to and training for the CBAR database, see the Director, Defense Contract Management Agency memorandum, dated April 2, 2013. *Click here*.

[Final rule, 71 FR 69492, 12/1/2006, effective 12/1/200; Final rule, 78 FR 21850, 4/12/2013, effective 4/12/2013; Publication notice, 20131118; Publication notice 20140528; Publication notice, 20150921; Publication notice, 20151230; Publication notice, 20180131; Publication notice, 20191231]

215.407-2 Make-or-buy programs.

(d) *Solicitation Requirements*. Consider the following factors when deciding whether to request a make-or-buy plan—

(1) The prime contractor's assumption of risk;

(2) The prime contractor's plant capacity;

(3) The prime contractor's degree of vertical integration;

(4) The prime contractor's internal resources;

(5) The anticipated contract type;

(6) The complexity, uniqueness, or configuration maturity associated with the end item or its subsystems;

(7) Critical path items;

(8) The impact on contract overhead rates with respect to maintaining work in-house;

(9) The industrial base that could potentially satisfy some system requirements, based on market survey;

(10) Proprietary data and/or trade secrets;

(11) Potential product quality concerns associated with items that would be subject to subcontracting;

(12) Integrated master schedule timelines and their tolerances for variation;

(13) The availability and experience of program office personnel to credibly analyze and evaluate a submission; and

(14) Socioeconomic considerations, e.g. small business or labor surplus area concerns.

(f) *Evaluation, negotiation, and Agreement*. When a make-or-buy plan is required, listed below are factors that may be considered when evaluating a submission—

(1) Prime contractor past performance, especially with respect to subcontract management;

(2) Prime contractor make-or-buy history;

(3) Adequacy of contractor's existing make-or-buy processes, including cost and technical risk considerations;

(4) Component availability through existing sources, e.g. available inventory, or other Government contracts;

(5) Prime contractor plant capacity;

(6) The adequacy of the prime contractor's technical, financial and personnel capabilities; and

(7) Prime contractor justification that is provided with respect to items it does not normally make.

[Final rule, 76 FR 73618, 12/7/2011, effective 12/7/2011; Publication notice, 20191231]

215.407-4 Should-cost review.

(b) *Program should-cost review*.

(2) DoD contracting activities should consider performing a program should-cost review before award of a definitive contract for a major system as defined by DoDI 5000.2. See DoDI 5000.2 regarding industry participation.

(c) *Overhead should-cost review*.

(1) Contact the Defense Contract Management Agency (DCMA) (*http://www.dcma.mil/*) for questions on overhead should-cost analysis.

(2) (A) DCMA or the military department responsible for performing contract administration functions (e.g., Navy SUPSHIP) should consider, based on risk assessment, performing an overhead should-cost review of a contractor business unit (as defined in FAR 2.101) when all of the following conditions exist:

(1) Projected annual sales to DoD exceed $1 billion;

(2) Projected DoD versus total business exceeds 30 percent;

(3) Level of sole-source DoD contracts is high;

(4) Significant volume of proposal activity is anticipated;

(5) Production or development of a major weapon system or program is anticipated; and

(6) Contractor cost control/reduction initiatives appear inadequate.

(B) The head of the contracting activity may request an overhead should-cost review for a business unit that does not meet the criteria in paragraph (c) (2) (A) of this subsection.

(C) Overhead should-cost reviews are labor intensive. These reviews generally involve participation by the contracting, contract administration, and contract audit elements. The extent of availability of military department, contract administration, and contract audit resources to support DCMA-led teams should be considered when determining whether a review will be conducted. Overhead should-cost reviews generally should not be conducted at a contractor business segment more frequently than every 3 years.

[Final rule, 71 FR 69492, 12/1/2006, effective 12/1/2006; Publication notice, 20191231]

215.407-5 Estimating systems.

[Final rule, 71 FR 69492, 12/1/2006, effective 12/1/2006; Publication notice, 20191231]

215.407-5-70 Disclosure, maintenance, and review requirements.

(e) *Disposition of findings.*

(2) *Initial determination.*

(ii) (A) Within 10 days of receiving the report, if the contracting officer makes a determination that there is a significant deficiency, the contracting officer should provide an initial determination of deficiencies and a copy of the report to the contractor and require the contractor to submit a written response.

(C) *Evaluation of contractor's response.* Within 30 days of receiving the contractor's response, the contracting officer, in consultation with the auditor or cognizant functional specialist, should evaluate the contractor's response and make a final determination.

(3) *Final Determination.*

(ii) (A) *Monitoring contractor's corrective action.* The auditor and the contracting officer shall monitor the contractor's progress in correcting deficiencies. If the contractor fails to make adequate progress, the contracting officer shall take whatever action is necessary to ensure that the contractor corrects the deficiencies. Examples of actions the contracting officer can take are: bringing the issue to the attention of higher level management, reducing or suspending progress payments (see FAR 32.503-6), implementing or increasing the withholding in accordance with 252.242-7005, Contractor Business Systems, if applicable, and recommending non-award of potential contracts.

(B) *Correction of significant deficiencies.*

(*1*) When the contractor notifies the contracting officer, in writing, that the contractor has corrected the significant deficiencies, the contracting officer shall request that the auditor review the correction to determine if the deficiencies have been resolved.

(*2*) The contracting officer shall determine if the contractor has corrected the deficiencies.

(*3*) If the contracting officer determines the contractor has corrected the deficiencies, the contracting officer's notification shall be sent to the auditor; payment office; appropriate action officers responsible for reporting past performance at the requiring activities; and each contracting and contract administration office having substantial business with the contractor, as applicable.

[Final rule, 71 FR 69492, 12/1/2006, effective 12/1/2006; Interim rule, 76 FR 28856, 5/18/2011, effective 5/18/2011; Final rule, 77 FR 11355, 2/24/2012, effective 2/24/2012; Publication notice, 20191231]

215.470 Estimated data prices.

(b) (i) The form and the provision included in the solicitation request the offeror to state what portion of the total price is estimated to be attributable to the production or development of the listed data for the Government (not to the sale of rights in the data). However, offerors' estimated prices may not reflect all such costs; and different offerors may reflect these costs in a different manner, for the following reasons—

(A) Differences in business practices in competitive situations;

(B) Differences in accounting systems among offerors;

(C) Use of factors or rates on some portions of the data;

(D) Application of common effort to two or more data items; and

(E) Differences in data preparation methods among offerors.

(ii) Data price estimates should not be used for contract pricing purposes without further analysis.

[Final rule, 71 FR 69492, 12/1/2006, effective 12/1/2006; Publication notice, 20191231]

PART 216—TYPES OF CONTRACTS

Table of Contents

Subpart 216.1—Selecting Contract Types

Factors in selecting contract type 216.104
Research and development 216.104-70

Subpart 216.2—Fixed-Price Contracts

Fixed-price contracts with economic price adjustment 216.203
Contract clauses 216.203-4

Subpart 216.4—Incentive Contracts

General 216.401
[Removed] 216.401-70
Application of predetermined, formula-type incentives 216.402
Technical performance incentives 216.402-2
Fixed-price incentive contracts 216.403
Fixed-price incentive (firm target) contracts 216.403-1
Fixed-price incentive (successive targets) contracts 216.403-2
Cost-reimbursement incentive contracts 216.405
Cost-plus-incentive fee contracts 216.405-1
Cost-plus-award-fee contracts 216.405-2
Other applications of award fees 216.470

Subpart 216.5—Indefinite-Delivery Contracts

Ordering 216.505

Subpart 216.7—Agreements

Basic ordering agreements 216.703

PART 216—TYPES OF CONTRACTS

SUBPART 216.1—SELECTING CONTRACT TYPES

216.104 Factors in selecting contract type.

See the policy tab for Director, Defense Procurement and Acquisition Policy memorandum dated April 1, 2016, entitled *"Guidance on Using Incentive and Other Contract Types*, when selecting and negotiating the most appropriate contract type for a given procurement.

[Final rule, 81 FR 28729, 5/10/2016, effective 5/10/2016]

216.104-70 Research and development.

(1) *General*. There are several categories of research and development (R&D) contracts: research, exploratory development, advanced development, engineering development, and operational systems development (see DFARS 235.001for definitions). Each category has a primary technical or functional objective. Different parts of a project may fit several categories. The contract type must fit the work required, not just the classification of the overall program.

(2) *Research and exploratory development*.

(i) Price is not necessarily the primary factor in determining the contract type.

(ii) The nature of the work to be performed will usually result in a cost-plus award fee, cost-plus fixed fee term, cost-no-fee, or cost-sharing contract.

(iii) If the Government and the contractor can identify and agree upon the level of contractor effort required, the contracting officer may select a firm fixed-price level-of-effort contract, except see DFARS 235.006.

(iv) If the Government and the contractor agree that an incentive arrangement is desirable and capable of being evaluated after completion of the work, the contracting officer may use an incentive type contract.

(3) *Advanced development*.

(i) The nature of the work to be performed often results in a cost-plus fixed fee completion type contract.

(ii) Contracting officers may select incentive contracts if—

(A) Realistic and measurable targets are identified; and

(B) Achievement of those targets is predictable with a reasonable degree of accuracy.

(iii) Contracting officers should not use contracts with only cost incentives where—

(A) There will be a large number of major technical changes; or

(B) Actions beyond the control of the contractor may influence the contractor's achievement of cost targets.

(4) *Engineering development and operational systems development.*

(i) When selecting contract types, also consider—

(A) The degree to which the project is clearly defined, which in turn affects the contractor's ability to provide accurate cost estimates;

(B) The need for effort that will overlap that of earlier stages;

(C) The need for firm technical direction by the Government; and

(D) The degree of configuration control the Government will exercise.

(ii) For development efforts, particularly for major defense systems, the preferred contract type is cost reimbursement.

(iii) Contracting officers should use fixed-price type contracts when risk has been reduced to the extent that realistic pricing can occur; e.g., when a program has reached the final stages of development and technical risks are minimal, except see DFARS 235.006.

[Final rule, 71 FR 39006, 7/11/2006, effective 7/11/2006]

SUBPART 216.2—FIXED-PRICE CONTRACTS

216.203 Fixed-price contracts with economic price adjustment. (No Text)

216.203-4 Contract clauses.

Contracting officers should use caution when incorporating Economic Price Adjustment (EPA) provisions in contracts. EPA provisions can result in significant and unanticipated price increases which can have major adverse impacts to a program. EPA provisions should be used only when general economic factors make the estimating of future costs too unpredictable within a fixed-price contract. The primary factors that should be considered before using an EPA provision include volatility of labor and/or material costs and contract length. In cases where cost volatility and/or contract length warrant using an EPA provision, the provision must be carefully crafted to ensure an equitable adjustment to the contract. Accordingly, contracting officers should always request assistance from their local pricing office, the Defense Contract Management Agency, or the Defense Contract Audit Agency when contemplating the use of an EPA provision.

For adjustments based on cost indexes of labor or material, use the following guidelines:

(1) Do not make the clause unnecessarily complex.

(2) Normally, the clause should not provide either a ceiling or a floor for adjustment unless adjustment is based on indices below the six-digit level of the Bureau of Labor Statistics (BLS)—

(i) Producer Price Index;

(ii) Employment Cost Index for wages and salaries, benefits, and compensation costs for aerospace industries (but see paragraphs (3) and (6) of this subsection); or

(iii) North American Industry Classification System (NAICS) Product Code.

(3) DoD contracting officers may no longer use the BLS employment cost index for total compensation, aircraft manufacturing (NAICS Product Code 336411, formerly Standard Industrial Classification Code 3721, Aircraft) in any EPA clause in DoD contracts. This index is ineffective for use as the basis for labor cost adjustments in EPA clauses in DoD contracts.

The BLS employment cost index for wages and salaries, aircraft manufacturing may still be used in EPA clauses for labor costs. If a BLS index for benefits is desired, contracting officers should use a broader based index that will smooth the effects of any large pension contributions, such as the employment cost index for benefits, total private industry. If a total compensation index is desired, contracting officers should consider the creation of a hybrid index by combining the above referenced indices at a predetermined percentage. For example, a hybrid total compensation index could consist of 68 percent employment cost index for wages and salaries, aircraft manufacturing, and 32 percent of the employment cost index for benefits, private industry.

(4) Normally, the clause should cover potential economic fluctuations within the original contract period of performance using a trigger band. Unless the economic fluctuation exceeds the trigger value, no EPA clause adjustments are made.

(5) The clause must accurately identify the index(es) upon which adjustments will be based.

(i) It must provide for a means to adjust for appropriate economic fluctuation in the event publication of the movement of the designated index is discontinued. This might include the substitution of another index if the time remaining would justify doing so and an appropriate index is reasonably available, or some other method for repricing the remaining portion of work to be performed.

(ii) Normally, there should be no need to make an adjustment if computation of the identified index is altered. However, it may be appropriate to provide for adjustment of the economic fluctuation computations in the event there is such a substantial alteration in the method of computing the index that the original intent of the parties is negated.

(iii) When an index to be used is subject to revision (e.g., the BLS Producer Price

Indexes), the EPA clause must specify that any economic price adjustment will be based on a revised index and must identify which revision to the index will be used.

(6) The basis of the index should not be so large and diverse that it is significantly affected by fluctuations not relevant to contract performance, but it must be broad enough to minimize the effect of any single company, including the anticipated contractor(s).

(7) Construction of an index is largely dependent upon three general series published by the U.S. Department of Labor, BLS. These are the—

(i) Industrial Commodities portion of the Producer Price Index;

(ii) Employment Cost Index for wages and salaries, benefits, and compensation costs for aerospace industries (but see paragraphs (3) and (6) of this subsection); and

(iii) NAICS Product Code.

(8) Normally, do not use more than two indices, i.e., one for labor and one for material.

(9) The clause must establish and properly identify a base period comparable to the contract periods for which adjustments are to be made as a reference point for application of an index.

(10) The clause should not provide for an adjustment beyond the original contract performance period, including options. The start date for the adjustment may be the beginning of the contract or a later time, as appropriate, based on the projected rate of expenditures.

(11) The expenditure profile for both labor and material should be based on a predetermined rate of expenditure (expressed as the percentage of material or labor usage as it relates to the total contract price) in lieu of actual cost incurred.

(i) If the clause is to be used in a competitive acquisition, determine the labor and material allocations, with regard to both mix of labor and material and rate of expenditure by percentage, in a manner which will, as nearly as possible, approximate the average expenditure profile of all companies to be solicited so that all companies may compete on an equal basis.

(ii) If the clause is to be used in a noncompetitive acquisition, the labor and material allocations may be subject to negotiation and agreement.

(iii) For multiyear contracts, establish predetermined expenditure profile tables for each of the annual increments in the multiyear buy. Each of the second and subsequent year tables must be cumulative to reflect the total expenditures for all increments funded through the latest multiyear funding.

(12) The clause should state the percentage of the contract price subject to price adjustment.

(i) Normally, do not apply adjustments to the profit portion of the contract.

(ii) Examine the labor and material portions of the contract to exclude any areas that do not require adjustment. For example, it may be possible to exclude—

(A) Subcontracting for short periods of time during the early life of the contract which could be covered by firm-fixed-priced subcontracting;

(B) Certain areas of overhead, e.g., depreciation charges, prepaid insurance costs, rental costs, leases, certain taxes, and utility charges;

(C) Labor costs for which a definitive union agreement exists; and

(D) Those costs not likely to be affected by fluctuation in the economy.

(iii) Allocate that part of the contract price subject to adjustment to specific periods of time (e.g., quarterly, semiannually, etc.) based on the most probable expenditure or commitment basis (expenditure profile).

(13) The clause should provide for definite times or events that trigger price adjustments. Adjustments should be frequent enough to afford the contractor appropriate economic protection without creating a burdensome administrative effort. The adjustment period should normally range from quarterly to annually.

(14) When the contract contains cost incentives, any sums paid to the contractor on

account of EPA provisions must be subtracted from the total of the contractor's allowable costs for the purpose of establishing the total costs to which the cost incentive provisions apply. If the incentive arrangement is cited in percentage ranges, rather than dollar ranges, above and below target costs, structure the EPA clause to maintain the original contract incentive range in dollars.

(15) The EPA clause should provide that once the labor and material allocations and the portion of the contract price subject to price adjustment have been established, they remain fixed through the life of the contract and shall not be modified except in the event of significant changes in the scope of the contract. The clause should state that pricing actions pursuant to the Changes clause or other provisions of the contract will be priced as though there were no provisions for economic price adjustment. However, subsequent modifications may include a change to the delivery schedule or significantly change the amount of, or mix of, labor or material for the contract. In such cases, it may be appropriate to prospectively apply EPA coverage. This may be accomplished by—

(i) Using an EPA clause that applies only to the effort covered by the modification;

(ii) Revising the baseline data or period in the EPA clause for the basic contract to include the new work; or

(iii) Using an entirely new EPA clause for the entire contract, including the new work.

(16) Consistent with the factors in paragraphs (1) through (15) of this subsection, it may also be appropriate to provide in the prime contract for similar EPA arrangements between the prime contractor and affected subcontractors to allocate risks properly and ensure that those subcontractors are provided similar economic protection.

(17) When EPA clauses are included in contracts that do not require submission of certified cost or pricing data as provided for in FAR 15.403-1, the contracting officer must obtain adequate data to establish the baseline from which adjustments will be made. The contracting officer may require verification of the data submitted to the extent necessary to permit reliance upon the data as a reasonable baseline.

[Final rule, 71 FR 39004, 7/11/2006, effective 7/11/2006; Change notice, 20080110; Final rule, 77 FR 76939, 12/31/2012, effective 12/31/2012]

SUBPART 216.4—INCENTIVE CONTRACTS

216.401 General.

(c) Incentive contracts. DoD has established the Award and Incentive Fees Community of Practice (CoP) under the leadership of the Defense Acquisition University (DAU). The CoP serves as the repository for all related materials including policy information, related training courses, examples of good award fee arrangements, and other supporting resources. The CoP is available on the DAU Acquisition Community Connection at https://acc.dau.mil/awardandincentivefees. Additional information can be found on the MAX website maintained by the Office of Management and Budget at: https://max.omb.gov.

(e) Award-fee contracts.

(i) It is DoD policy to utilize objective criteria, whenever possible, to measure contract performance. In cases where an award-fee contract must be used due to lack of objective criteria, the contracting officer shall consult with the program manager and the fee determining official when developing the award-fee plan. Award-fee criteria shall be linked directly to contract cost, schedule, and performance outcomes objectives.

(ii) Award fees must be tied to identifiable interim outcomes, discrete events or milestones, as much as possible. Examples of such interim milestones include timely completion of preliminary design review, critical design review, and successful system demonstration. In situations where there may be no identifiable milestone for a year or more, consideration should be given to apportioning some of the award fee pool for a predetermined interim period of time based on assessing progress toward milestones. In any case, award fee provisions must clearly explain how a contractor's performance will be evaluated.

(iii) The head of the contracting activity for each defense agency shall retain the D&F for (a) all acquisition category (ACAT) I or II) programs, and (b) all non-ACAT I or II contracts with an estimated value of $50 million or more. The head of the contracting activity shall forward the D&Fs for ACAT I programs to Defense Pricing and Contracting/Contract Policy directorate DPC/CP) within 1 month of the end of the quarter. Copies of D&Fs on all contracts shall also be included in the contract file.

[Change notice, 12102010; Publication notice, 20120906; Publication notice 20140919; Final rule, 84 FR 65304, 11/27/2019, effective 11/27/2019]

216.401-70 [Removed]

[Change notice, 12102010; Publication notice, 20120829; Publication notice 20140919; Final rule, 80 FR 18323 , 4/6/2015, effective 4/6/2015; Publication notice, 20150406]

216.402 Application of predetermined, formula-type incentives. (No Text)

216.402-2 Technical performance incentives.

(2) Contractor performance incentives should relate to specific performance areas of milestones, such as delivery or test schedules, quality controls, maintenance requirements, and achievement of design specification requirements for reliability and maintainability.

[Final rule, 71 FR 39004, 7/11/2006, effective 7/11/2006; Final rule, 84 FR 58332, 10/31/2019, effective 10/31/2019]

216.403 Fixed-price incentive contracts. (No Text)

216.403-1 Fixed-price incentive (firm target) contracts.

(1) *Use of FPIF contract. (i) Not mandatory.* DFARS 216.403-1(b)(1) directs the contracting officer to give particular consideration to the use of fixed-price incentive (firm target) (FPIF) contracts, especially for acquisitions moving from development to production. DFARS does not mandate the use of FPIF for initial production and each acquisition situation must be evaluated in terms of the degree and nature of the risk presented in order to select the proper contract type.

(ii) *Considerations.* Volume 4, chapter 1, of the Contract Pricing Reference Guide provides a detailed discussion of the considerations involved in selecting the proper contract type. For example:

(A) It is not in the Government's best interest to use FPIF when the cost risk is so great that establishing a ceiling price is unrealistic.

(B) It is also not in the Government's best interest to use firm-fixed-price (FFP) contracts on production programs until costs have become stable. Therefore, FPIF contracts should be considered in production programs where actual costs on prior FFP contracts have varied by more than four percent from the costs considered negotiated. Contracting officers are reminded that actual costs on prior contracts for the same item, regardless of contract type or data reporting requirements of the prior contract, are cost and pricing data on the pending contract, and should be obtained from the contractor on production programs when cost or pricing data are required.

(2) *Incentive arrangement.* DFARS 216.403-1(b)(2) directs the contracting officer to pay particular attention to share lines and ceiling prices for fixed-price incentive (firm target) contracts, with 120 percent ceiling and a 50/50 share ratio as the point of departure for establishing the incentive arrangement. While DFARS does not mandate the use of these share ratios or ceiling percentage, it is not unreasonable to expect that upon entering into production, risks have been mitigated to the point that the DFARS recommended point of departure for an FPIF incentive arrangement would be normal.

(3) *Analyzing risk.*

(i) *Quantification of risk.*

(A) The first step is establishing a target cost for which the probability of an underrun and overrun are considered equal and therefore, the risks and rewards are shared equally, hence the 50/50 share is the point of departure. Equally important is determining that the contractor has a high probability of being able to accomplish the effort within a ceiling percentage of 120 percent. In accomplishing both these steps, the analysis of risk is essential.

(B) Too often, risk is evaluated only in general terms without attempting to quantify the risk posed by the various elements of cost. Also, a contracting officer may incorrectly fall back on the share ratios and ceiling percentages negotiated on prior contracts or other programs, without examining the specific risks.

(C) Whether being used to select the proper contract type or establishing share lines and ceiling price on an FPIF contract, the analysis of risk as it pertains to the prime contractor is key. From a contractor's perspective, all risks, including technical and schedule risk, have financial ramifications. Technical and schedule risks, if realized, generally translate into increased effort, which means increased cost. Therefore, all risk can be translated into cost risk and quantified. Risk always has two components that must be considered in the quantification: the magnitude of the impact and the probability that it will occur.

(D) When cost risk is quantified, it is much easier to establish a reasonable ceiling percentage. The ceiling percentage is applicable to the target cost on the prime contract. It is important to understand the degree of risk that various cost elements pose in relation to that target cost. A discussion of the major cost elements and the risk implications follows in paragraphs (3)(ii) through (iv) of this section.

(ii) *Subcontracts and material cost and risk.*

(A) In many prime contractors' contracts, a substantial amount of risk is borne by subcontractors, not the prime contractor, via negotiated firm-fixed-price (FFP) subcontracts. In the case of FFP subcontracts, the subcontractor is obligated to deliver at the negotiated price. The risk to the prime contractor is the supplier's failure to perform or perform on time. Generally, that risk is considered to be low by both the prime and the subcontractor as evidenced by the FFP contract type. In addition, the prime contractor will normally have priced effort for material management or subcontract administration to ensure timely performance on the part of the suppliers. This effort may be bid directly or indirectly (e.g., as part of an overhead expense) depending on the contractor's accounting practices.

(B) The impact of negotiated FFP subcontracts on the prime contractor's risk can be significant. A prime contract with a 120 percent ceiling price provides overrun protection to the prime contractor equal to 20 percent of the target cost on the contract. However, if FFP subcontracts represent half of the total contract cost, then half of the target cost is subject to little or no cost risk on the part of the prime contractor. Therefore, the overrun protection provided by 20 percent of the target cost is really closer to 40 percent protection of the prime's cost that is truly at risk to the prime contractor, which likely is significantly overstated. Thus, a ceiling price less than 120 percent in this risk situation would be more appropriate.

(C) For subcontracts that have not yet been negotiated between the prime and subcontractor at the time of negotiation of the prime contract, the degree of risk is essentially limited to the difference between the price proposed by the subcontractor and the subcontract value included in the prime contractor's proposal.

(D) For subcontracts that are not FFP, the risk to the prime is based on the risk represented by the subcontractors' contractual relationship with the prime. If the subcontract is FPIF and has a 50/50 share ratio and 120 percent ceiling, the prime's risk is 50 percent of each dollar of overrun up to the ceiling amount. An analysis of the subcontractor's risk would be necessary to determine the probability of reaching the ceiling price.

(iii) *Direct labor cost and risk.*

(A) The risk in direct labor is in the hours needed to perform the effort and the risk in the labor rates paid to employees. There is generally little risk in the direct labor rates. However, there are various levels of risk in the direct labor hours needed by the prime contractor to accomplish the contract requirements. This risk can be driven by a number of factors including technical complexity, schedule constraints, or availability of personnel, parts, or tooling. Risks vary by task and the key is to identify the major tasks and assess the "what if" impact at the total contract cost level.

(B) Schedule is often correctly cited as a risk factor, but it is important to understand and quantify the probability and impact of a potential schedule slip. Generally, any schedule slip can only affect the prime contractor's in-house cost. Therefore, any schedule impact should be assessed on the impact it would have on the prime contractor's performance of its tasks.

(C) However, it is wrong to assume the worst-case scenario that a schedule delay results in an extension of the entire prime contractor workforce for the period of the delay. A responsible contractor will take steps to minimize both the delay and the impact of that delay. For instance, a production schedule assumes an optimal sequencing of tasks which presumes the timely arrival and availability of parts from suppliers or other in-house sources. A delay in receiving parts as planned could require a resequencing of tasks and could adversely affect the efficiency of performing a number of tasks, but it will not cause the entire workforce to be idle during the delay.

(iv) *Indirect (e.g., overhead) cost and risk.* Overhead and other indirect costs (e.g., general and administrative expense) can represent a significant portion of the prime contractor's in-house cost. Indirect expense (hereafter referred to as overhead) poses potential cost growth risk or the opportunity for cost reduction from the following two perspectives:

(A) *Actual overhead rate. (1)* First, the actual overhead rate could be different than that proposed. Proposed overhead rates, even those covered by a forward pricing rate agreement, are based on forecasts of overhead expenses and the bases to which they are applied. The final overhead rate that is actually applied (charged) to a contract will be based on the actual overhead expenses and the actual base, each of which could be considerably different than estimated. The net effect could be a higher or lower overhead rate than estimated.

(2) In general, the risk in an overhead rate tends to be driven more by fluctuations in the base than in the expenses. This is because overhead expenses are made up of expenses that consist of "fixed" (e.g., depreciation) and variable (e.g., fringe benefits) in nature. When the actual base turns out to be lower than the estimated base, the fixed costs are spread over a smaller base resulting in a higher overhead rate. In general, if the actual base is greater than estimated, a lower overhead rate will result.

(3) In assessing this risk, the contracting officer should consider the contractor's ability to predict overhead rates based on comparing proposed versus actual rates for prior years. In making this comparison, it is important to do so in a manner consistent with the proposal being reviewed. For instance, if the majority of overhead costs on the proposal being reviewed occur two years in the future, the comparison should look at the contractor's accuracy in predicting overhead rates two years in advance. For example, in looking at the 2009 actual overhead rate, what did the contractor propose for 2009 in its 2007 forward pricing rate proposal?

(B) *Actual base cost.* If the actual base cost on the contract (e.g., direct labor dollars) is different than that proposed, the contract will be charged overhead costs according to the actual base costs on that contract. If the contractor overruns direct labor, even if the actual labor overhead rate was the same as proposed, that rate would be applied to a higher base resulting in increased overhead dollars on that contract. The opposite would be true if the contractor underruns direct labor on the contract. Since this aspect of risk is tied to the base cost on the contract, the risk is the same as it is for those base costs (e.g., direct labor, material).

[Final rule, 76 FR 57677, 9/16/2011, effective 9/16/2011; Publication notice, 20120906; Publication notice, 20140129]

216.403-2 Fixed-price incentive (successive targets) contracts.

The formula specified in FAR 16.403-2(a)(1)(iii) does not apply for the life of the contract. It is used to fix the firm target profit for the contract. To provide an incentive consistent with the circumstances, the formula should reflect the relative risk involved in establishing an incentive arrangement where cost and pricing information were not sufficient to permit the negotiation of firm targets at the outset.

[Final rule, 71 FR 39004, 7/11/2006, effective 7/11/2006]

216.405 Cost-reimbursement incentive contracts. (No Text)

216.405-1 Cost-plus-incentive-fee contracts.

Give appropriate weight to basic acquisition objectives in negotiating the range of fee and the fee adjustment formula. For example—

(1) In an initial product development contract, it may be appropriate to provide for relatively small adjustments in fee tied to the cost incentive feature, but provide for significant adjustments if the contractor meets or surpasses performance targets; and

(2) In subsequent development and test contracts, it may be appropriate to negotiate an incentive formula tied primarily to the contractor's success in controlling costs.

[Final rule, 71 FR 39004, 7/11/2006, effective 7/11/2006]

216.405-2 Cost-plus-award-fee contracts.

(1) Although weighted guidelines do not apply per DFARS 216.405-2(3)(ii) when definitizing a contract action, the contracting officer shall, nevertheless, separately assess and document the reduced cost risk on the contract for—

(i) The period up to the date of definitization; as well as

(ii) The remaining period of performance (see DFARS 217.7404-6)

(2) The basis for all award fee determinations shall be documented in the contract file.

(3) The cost-plus-award-fee contract is also suitable for level of effort contracts where mission feasibility is established but measurement of achievement must be by subjective evaluation rather than objective measurement. See Table 16-1, Performance Evaluation Criteria, for sample performance evaluation criteria and Table 16-2, Contractor Performance Evaluation Report, for a sample evaluation report.

(4) The contracting activity may—

(i) Establish a board to—

(A) Evaluate the contractor's performance; and

(B) Determine the amount of the award or recommend an amount to the contracting officer; and

(ii) Afford the contractor an opportunity to present information on its own behalf.

[Final rule, 71 FR 39004, 7/11/2006, effective 7/11/2006; Publication notice, 20110617]

216.470 Other applications of award fees.

The *award amount* portion of the fee may be used in other types of contracts under the following conditions:

(1) The Government wishes to motivate and reward a contractor for—

(i) Purchase of capital assets (including machine tools) manufactured in the United States, on major defense acquisition programs; or

(ii) Management performance in areas which cannot be measured objectively and where normal incentive provisions cannot be used. For example, logistics support, quality, timeliness, ingenuity, and cost effectiveness are areas under the control of management which may be susceptible only to subjective measurement and evaluation.

(2) The *base fee* (fixed amount portion) is not used.

(3) The chief of the contracting office approves the use of the "award amount."

(4) An award review board and procedures are established for conduct of the evaluation.

(5) The administrative costs of evaluation do not exceed the expected benefits.

TABLE 16-1, PERFORMANCE EVALUATION CRITERIA

		Submarginal	Marginal	Good	Very Good	Excellent
A Time of Delivery.	(A-1) Adherence to plan schedule.	Consistently late on 20% plans	Late on 10% plans w/o prior agreement	Occasional plan late w/o justification.	Meets plan schedule.	Delivers all plans on schedule & meets prod. Change requirements on schedule
—	(A-2) Action on Anticipated delays.	Does not expose changes or resolve them as soon as recognized.	Exposes changes but is dilatory in resolution on plans.	Anticipates changes, advise Shipyard but misses completion of design plans 10%.	Keeps Yard posted on delays, resolves independently on plans.	Anticipates in good time, advises Shipyard, resolves independently and meets production requirements.
—	(A-3) Plan Maintenance.	Does not complete interrelated systems studies concurrently.	System studies completed but constr. Plan changes delayed.	Major work plans coordinated in time to meet production schedules.	Design changes from studies and interrelated plant issued in time to meet product schedules.	Design changes, studies resolved and test data issued ahead of production requirements.
B Quality of Work.	(B-1) Work Appearance.	25% dwgs. Not compatible with Shipyard repro. processes and use.	20% not compatible with Shipyard repro. processes and use.	10% not compatible with Shipyard repro. processes and use.	0% dwgs prepared by Des. Agent not compatible with Shipyard repro. processes and use.	0% dwgs. Presented incl. Des. Agent, vendors, subcontr. Not compatible with Shipyard repro processes and use.
—	(B-2) Thoroughness and Accuracy of Work.	Is brief on plans tending to leave questionable situations for Shipyard to resolve.	Has followed guidance, type and standard dwgs.	Has followed guidance, type and standard dwgs. Questioning and resolving doubtful areas.	Work complete with notes and thorough explanations for anticipated questionable areas.	Work of highest caliber incorporating all pertinent data required including related activities.
—	(B-3) Engineering Competence.	Tendency to follow past practice with no variation to meet reqmts. job in hand.	Adequate engrg. To use & adapt existing designs to suit job on hand for routine work.	Engineered to satisfy specs., guidance plans and material provided.	Displays excellent knowledge of constr. Reqmts. considering systems aspect, cost, shop capabilities and procurement problems.	Exceptional knowledge of Naval shipwork & adaptability to work process incorporating knowledge of future planning in Design.
—	(B-4) Liaison Effectiveness	Indifferent to requirements of associated activities, related systems, and Shipyard advice.	Satisfactory but dependent on Shipyard of force resolution of problems without constructive recommendations to subcontr. or vendors.	Maintains normal contract with associated activities depending on Shipyard for problems requiring military resolution.	Maintains independent contact with all associated activities, keeping them informed to produce compatible design with little assistance for Yard.	Maintains expert contact, keeping Yard informed, obtaining info from equip, supplies w/o prompting of Shipyard.

		Submarginal	Marginal	Good	Very Good	Excellent
—	(B-5)	Constant surveillance required to keep job from slipping—assign to low priority to satisfy needs.	Requires occasional prodding to stay on schedule & expects Shipyard resolution of most problems.	Normal interest and desire to provide workable plans with average assistance & direction by Shipyard.	Complete & accurate job. Free of incompatibilities with little or no direction by Shipyard.	Develops complete and accurate plans, seeks out problem areas and resolves with assoc. act. ahead of schedule.
C Effectiveness in Controlling and/or Reducing Costs	(C-1) Utilization of Personnel	Planning of work left to designers on drafting boards.	Supervision sets & reviews goals for designers.	System planning by supervisory, personnel, studies checked by engineers.	Design parameters established by system engineers & held in design plans.	Mods. to design plans limited to less than 5% as result lack engrg. System correlation.
—	(C-2) Control Direct Charges (Except Labor)	Expenditures not controlled for services.	Expenditures reviewed occasionally by supervision.	Direct charges set & accounted for on each work package.	Provides services as part of normal design function w/o extra charges.	No cost overruns on original estimates absorbs service demands by Shipyard.
—	(C-3) Performance to Cost Estimate	Does not meet cost estimate for original work or changes 30% time.	Does not meet cost estimate for original work or changes 20% time.	Exceeds original est. on change orders 10% time and meets original design costs.	Exceeds original est. on changing orders 5% time.	Never exceeds estimates of original package or change orders.

TABLE 16-2, CONTRACTOR PERFORMANCE EVALUATION REPORT

Ratings	
Excellent	Period of
	Contract Number
Very Good	Contractor
Marginal	Date of Report
Submarginal	PNS Technical Monitor/s

CATEGORY	CRITERIA	RATING		ITEM FACTOR		EVALUATION RATING	CATEGORY FACTOR		EFFICIENCY RATING
A	TIME OF DELIVERY A-1 Adherence to Plan Schedule	______	×	.40	=	______			
	A-2 Action on Anticipated Delays	______	×	.30	=	______			
	A-3 Plan Maintenance	______	×	.30	=	______			
	Total Item Weighed Rating					______	× .30	=	______
B	QUALITY OF WORK B-1 Work Appearance	______	×	.15	=	______			

CATEGORY	CRITERIA	RATING	ITEM FACTOR	EVALUATION RATING	CATEGORY FACTOR	EFFICIENCY RATING
	B-2 Thoroughness and Accuracy of Work	______	× .30	= ______		
	B-3 Engineering Competence.	______	× .20	= ______		
	B-4 Liaison Effectiveness	______	× .15	= ______		
	B-5 Independence and Initiative	______	× .15	= ______		
	Total Item Weighed Rating			______	× .40	= ______
C	EFFECTIVENESS IN CONTROLLING AND/OR REDUCING COSTS					
	C-1 Utilization of Personnel	______	× .30	= ______		
	C-2 Control of all Direct Charges Other than Labor	______	× .30	= ______		
	C-3 Performance to Cost Estimate	______	× .40	= ______		
	Total Item Weighed Rating			______	× .30	= ______
	TOTAL WEIGHT RATING ______					
	Rated by: ______					
	Signature(s) ______					

NOTE: Provide supporting data and/or justification for below average or outstanding item ratings.

[Final rule, 71 FR 39004, 7/11/2006, effective 7/11/2006]

SUBPART 216.5—INDEFINITE-DELIVERY CONTRACTS

216.505 Ordering.

(b) (2) Exceptions to the fair opportunity process. For an order exceeding the simplified acquisition threshold, that is a follow-on to an order previously issued for the same supply or service based on a justification for an exception to fair opportunity citing the authority at FAR 16.505(b) (2) (i) (B) or (C)—

(A) The justification shall include a copy of the previous justification to assist the approval authority in determining whether the actions to remove or overcome any barriers that led to the exception to fair opportunity cited on the previous justification were completed; and

(B) The approval authority shall determine whether the planned actions were completed. If the actions were not completed, the justification for the follow-on action must be approved by the approval authority one-level above the approval authority for the previous justification (see FAR 16.505(b) (2) (ii) (C)). If the previous justification was approved by the Senior Procurement Executive (SPE), the approval remains at the SPE level.

[Final rule, 80 FR 21656, 4/20/2015, effective 4/20/2015]

SUBPART 216.7—AGREEMENTS

216.703 Basic ordering agreements.

(d) (i) Individual orders under a basic ordering agreement shall be individually closed following completion of the orders (see FAR 4.804).

(ii) The office issuing the agreement shall furnish all authorized ordering offices sufficient information for the ordering office to complete its contract reporting responsibilities under DFARS 204.670-2or, in the case of civilian agencies, the Federal Procurement Data System reporting requirement. Data furnished to civilian agencies must contain uncoded information about the data elements and the meanings of the codes to permit these users to translate the data into the federal format. This data must be furnished to the ordering activity in sufficient time for the activity to prepare its report for the action within 3 working days of the order.

(iii) Any activity listed in the agreement may issue orders on DD Form 1155, Order for Supplies or Services, or Standard Form 26, Award/Contract.

[Final rule, 71 FR 39004, 7/11/2006, effective 7/11/2006]

PART 217—SPECIAL CONTRACTING METHODS

Table of Contents

Subpart 217.1—Multiyear Contracting

[Removed] 217.100
Multiyear contracts for electricity from renewable energy sources. 217.174

Subpart 217.2—Options

Use of options 217.202
[Removed] 217.204
Exercise of options 217.207

Subpart 217.5—Interagency Acquisitions

Procedures 217.502
General 217.502-1

Subpart 217.7—Interagency Acquisitions: Acquisitions by Nondefense Agencies on Behalf of the Department of Defense

Procedures 217.770

Subpart 217.71—Master Agreement for Repair and Alteration of Vessels

Master agreements and job orders 217.7103
Content and format of master agreements 217.7103–1
Solicitations for job orders 217.7103–3
Emergency work 217.7103–4
Repair costs not readily ascertainable 217.7103–5

Subpart 217.74—Undefinitized Contract Actions

Authorization 217.7404-1
Price ceiling 217.7404-2
Definitization schedule 217.7404-3
Allowable profit 217.7404-6
Plans and reports 217.7405

Subpart 217.75—Acquisition of Replenishment Parts

Spares acquisition integrated with production. 217.7503
Acquisition of parts when data is not available. 217.7504
Spare parts breakout program 217.7506

Subpart 217.76—Contracts with Provisioning Requirements

Provisioning 217.7601

Subpart 217.77—Over and Above Work

Procedures 217.7701

Subpart 217.78—[Removed]

PART 217—SPECIAL CONTRACTING METHODS

SUBPART 217.1—MULTIYEAR CONTRACTING

217.100 [Removed]

[Interim rule, 70 FR 24323, 5/9/2005, effective 5/9/2005; Final rule, 76 FR 58152, 9/20/2011, effective 9/20/2011]

217.174 Multiyear contracts for electricity from renewable energy sources.

The business case analysis template and guidance for the head of the contracting activity determination to enter into a contract for a period in excess of 5 years is available here: Renewable *Electricity Acquisition Business Case Analysis Template and Guidance.*

[Interim rule, 70 FR 24323, 5/9/2005, effective 5/9/2005; Final rule, 76 FR 58152, 9/20/2011, effective 9/20/2011]

SUBPART 217.2—OPTIONS

217.202 Use of options.

(1) Options may be used for foreign military sales requirements.

(2) Consider use of surge options to support industrial capability. A surge option allows the Government, prior to final delivery, to—

(i) Accelerate the contractor's production rate in accordance with a surge production plan or a delivery schedule provided by the contractor under the terms of the contract; and

(ii) Purchase additional quantities of supplies or services.

(3) See DFARS Subpart 217.74 for limitations on the use of undefinitized options.

[Final rule, 71 FR 27642, 5/12/2006, effective 5/12/2006]

217.204 [Removed]

[Interim rule, 69 FR 74992, 12/15/2004, effective 12/15/2004; Final rule, 70 FR 73151, 12/9/2005, effective 12/9/2005; Final rule, 71 FR 27642, 5/12/2006, effective 5/12/2006; Publication notice, 20110202]

217.207 Exercise of options.

Before exercising an option for firm-fixed-price contracts containing spare parts, the contracting officer shall perform a cost or price analysis of the proposed spare parts. The contracting officer shall use an appropriate sampling technique or request field pricing assistance, and document the contract file with the results of the cost or price analysis.

[Publication notice, 20120111]

SUBPART 217.5—INTERAGENCY ACQUISITIONS

217.502 Procedures. (No Text).

[Final rule, 80 FR 74694, 11/30/2015, effective 11/30/2015]

217.502-1 General.

(a) *Written agreement on responsibility for management and administration—*

(1) *Assisted acquisitions.* When the contracting activity of one DoD Component provides acquisition assistance to deployed units or personnel from another DoD Component—

(A) The written interagency agreement between the servicing DoD Component and the requesting DoD Component, required by FAR 17.502-1(a)(1), shall be documented on the DD Form 1144, Support Agreement (see template at *http://www.acq.osd.mil/dpap/pacc/cc/resources.html*);

(B) Procurement support should be on a nonreimbursable basis, unless the parties mutually agree, in writing, for reimbursable support; and

(C) The DD Form 448, Military Interdepartmental Purchase Request (MIPR), shall be used to provide a description of the supplies/services and certification of funds available to support the requirement.

[Final rule, 80 FR 74694, 11/30/2015, effective 11/30/2015; Final rule, 83 FR 62501, 12/4/2018, effective 12/4/2018]

SUBPART 217.7—INTERAGENCY ACQUISITIONS: ACQUISITIONS BY NONDEFENSE AGENCIES ON

BEHALF OF THE DEPARTMENT OF DEFENSE

217.770 Procedures.

(a)(3)

(i) Departments and agencies shall ensure full awareness of the total costs of all fees associated with use of a non-DoD contracting vehicle. In order to ensure full awareness, the DoD acquisition official shall require the servicing agency to—

(A) Provide notification if its acquisition approach will use another agency's contract vehicle; and

(B) Identify all fees (direct and indirect) associated with the assisted acquisition.

(ii) The DoD acquisition official shall document in the business decision the rationale to continue with the assisted acquisition given the total fees (direct and indirect) involved.

[Final rule, 80 FR 51750, 8/26/2015, effective 8/26/2015]

SUBPART 217.71—MASTER AGREEMENT FOR REPAIR AND ALTERATION OF VESSELS

217.7103 Master agreements and job orders. (No Text)

[Final rule, 71 FR 27642, 5/12/2006, effective 5/12/2006]

217.7103-1 Content and format of master agreements.

(1) A master agreement shall contain all clauses required by DFARS 217.7104(a), statute, and Executive order.

(2) The following format may be adapted to fit specific circumstances:

MASTER AGREEMENT FOR REPAIR AND ALTERATION OF VESSELS

1. This agreement is entered into this ____ day of ______________ , ____, by the United States of America (the "Government":) represented by ____________, the Contracting Officer, and ______________ ______________, a corporation organized and existing under the laws of the State of ______ ______________________ (the "Contractor").

2. The clauses in this agreement, shall be incorporated, by reference or attachment, in job orders issued under this agreement to effect repairs, alterations, and/or additions to vessels.

3. By giving 30 days written notice, either party to this agreement has the right to cancel it without affecting the rights and liabilities under any job order existing at the time of cancellation. The Contractor shall perform, under the terms of this agreement, all work covered by any job order awarded before the effective date of the cancellation.

4. This agreement may be modified only by mutual agreement of the parties. A modification of this agreement shall not affect any job order in existence at the time of modification, unless the parties agree otherwise.

5. The rights and obligations of the parties to this agreement are set forth in this agreement and the clauses of any job orders issued under this agreement. In the event there is an inconsistency between this agreement and any job order, the provisions of this agreement shall govern.

6. This agreement shall remain in effect until cancelled by either party.

THE UNITED STATES OF AMERICA

by (Contracting Officer)

____
(Contractor)

by (Authorized Individual)

____
(Title)

[Final rule, 71 FR 27642, 5/12/2006, effective 5/12/2006]

217.7103-3 Solicitations for job orders.

(1) Include in the solicitation—

(i) The nature of the work to be performed;

(ii) The date the vessel will be available to the contractor;

(iii) The date the work is to be completed; and

(iv) Whether bulk ammunition is aboard the vessel.

(2) Unless the solicitation states otherwise, offers are to be based on performance at the contractor's site.

(3) Solicitations processed under negotiated acquisition procedures shall require offerors to include a breakdown of the price with reasonable supporting detail in whatever format and detail the contracting officer may request.

(4) Where practicable, afford potential offerors an opportunity to inspect the item needing repair or alteration.

[Final rule, 71 FR 27642, 5/12/2006, effective 5/12/2006]

217.7103-4 Emergency work.

Process this type of undefinitized contract action in accordance with DFARS Subpart 217.74. Negotiate a price as soon as practicable after the issuance of an undefinitized order and definitize the job order upon completing negotiations.

[Final rule, 71 FR 27642, 5/12/2006, effective 5/12/2006]

217.7103-5 Repair costs not readily ascertainable.

If the nature of any repairs is such that their extent and probable cost cannot be ascertained readily, the solicitation should—

(1) Solicit offers for determining the nature and extent of the repairs;

(2) Provide that upon determination by the contracting officer of what work is necessary, the contractor, if requested by the contracting officer, shall negotiate prices for performance of the repairs; and

(3) Provide that prices for the repairs, if ordered, will be set forth in a modification of the job order.

[Final rule, 71 FR 27642, 5/12/2006, effective 5/12/2006]

SUBPART 217.74—UNDEFINITIZED CONTRACT ACTIONS

217.7404-1 Authorization.

(1) The requiring activity, in coordination with the contracting office, will prepare the request for approval package for an undefinitized contract action (UCA) requirement. The approval package shall—

(i) Document why a UCA is required (for letter contracts see DFARS 216.603);

(ii) Provide a detailed explanation for the need to begin performance before definitization;

(iii) Address the adverse impact on agency requirements that would result from delays in beginning performance;

(iv) Identify the risk of using a UCA and the means by which the Government will mitigate such risk;

(v) Identify and justify the specific contractual instrument to be used;

(vi) Establish limitations on the obligation of funds; and

(vii) Provide the definitization schedule of agreed-upon events that support timely definitization.

(2) A sample format with certain variations for letter contracts is provided here at this website: [*http://www.acq.osd.mil/dpap/dars/pgi/docs*].

[Publication notice 20120615, 6/15/2012; Publication notice, 20160325]

217.7404-2 Price ceiling.

(1) The rationale for the not-to-exceed price will be documented and retained in the contract file. Examples of such supporting rationale include—

(i) The Independent Government Cost Estimate;

(ii) Price analysis based on prior buys; and

(iii) The contractor's proposal.

(2) The maximum not-to-exceed price is the firm-fixed price for firm-fixed price contracts, the ceiling price for fixed-price incentive contracts, and the estimated cost and fee for cost-reimbursement contracts.

[Publication notice 20120615, 6/15/2012]

217.7404-3 Definitization schedule.

In order to meet the definitization dates, the contracting officer shall closely coordinate and monitor each UCA. Contracting officers should frequently communicate with the program office and requiring officials as appropriate to actively manage the definitization of UCAs. The contracting officer should alert the approval authority if, for any reason, the definitization schedule appears to be in jeopardy.

[Publication notice 20120615, 6/15/2012]

217.7404-6 Allowable profit.

To improve the documentation and provide guidance on determining the profit for UCAs with substantial incurred cost, contracting officers shall follow the mandatory instructions at DFARS 215.404-71-3(d)(2) regarding lowering contract type risk assessments for the incurred costs when performing weighted guidelines analysis. Additional guidance on analyzing profit or fee (DAU continuous learning course 104) is provided here at this website: [*http://learn.dau.mil/atlas2/faces/page/atlas SE/login*].

[Publication notice 20120615, 6/15/2012; Publication notice, 20160325]

217.7405 Plans and reports.

(1) By October 31 and April 30 of each year, departments and agencies shall submit an updated Consolidated UCA Management Plan, and a Consolidated UCA Management Report, identifying each UCA with a value exceeding $5 million. In addition, departments and agencies shall submit a copy of the record of weighted guidelines for each definitized UCA with a value of $100 million or more. If there is no record of weighted guidelines (e.g., not required for a cost plus award fee contract per DFARS 215.404-74), then departments and agencies shall submit alternative documentation that addresses appropriate recognition of the contractor's reduced cost risk during the undefinitized performance period. Submit the required information to—

Deputy Director, Defense Procurement and Acquisition Policy
(Contract Policy and International Contracting)
3060 Defense Pentagon
Washington, DC 20301-3060.

(2) The Consolidated UCA Management Plan and the Consolidated UCA Management Report shall be prepared using the following formats:

(i) Consolidated UCA Management Plan:

Title: Consolidated Undefinitized Contract Action (UCA) Management Plan Period Covered:

1. Applicable military department, defense agency, or DoD component.

a. Headquarters point of contact.

b. Contact information.

2. Description of actions planned and taken to ensure:

a. Appropriate use of UCAs.

b. Timely definitization of UCAs.

c. Minimized obligation amounts at the time of UCA award, consistent with the contractor's requirements for the undefinitized period.

d. In determining profit/fee, appropriate recognition of the contractor's reduced cost risk during the undefinitized performance period.

e. Documentation of the risk assessment in the contract file.

3. Milestones for completion of planned events.

4. Other.

(ii) Consolidated UCA Management Report:

The required format for the Consolidated UCA Management Report is available at this website: [*http://www.acq.osd.mil/dpap/dars/pgi/docs/uca_management_report_2015(updated22Mar16).xlsx*].

(3) A list of Frequently Asked Questions about UCA reporting requirements is available at this website: [*http://www.acq.osd.mil/dpap/dars/pgi/docs/faq_201603.docx*].

[Publication notice 20120615, 6/15/2012; Publication notice, 20160325]

SUBPART 217.75—ACQUISITION OF REPLENISHMENT PARTS

217.7503 Spares acquisition integrated with production.

(1) Spares acquisition integrated with production (SAIP) is a technique used to acquire replenishment parts concurrently with parts being produced for the end item.

(2) Include appropriately tailored provisions in the contract when SAIP is used.

[Final rule, 71 FR 27642, 5/12/2006, effective 5/12/2006]

217.7504 Acquisition of parts when data is not available.

When acquiring a part for which the Government does not have necessary data with rights to use in a specification or drawing for competitive acquisition, use one of the following procedures in order of preference:

(1) When items of identical design are not required, the acquisition may still be conducted through full and open competition by using a performance specification or other similar technical requirement or purchase description that does not contain data with restricted rights. Two methods are—

(i) Two-step sealed bidding; and

(ii) Brand name or equal purchase descriptions.

(2) When other than full and open competition is authorized under FAR Part 6, acquire the part from the firm that developed or designed the item or process, or its licensees, provided productive capacity and quality are adequate and the price is fair and reasonable.

(3) When additional sources are needed and the procedures in paragraph (1) of this section are not practicable, consider the following alternatives:

(i) Encourage the developer to license others to manufacture the parts;

(ii) Acquire the necessary rights in data;

(iii) Use a leader company acquisition technique (FAR Subpart 17.4) when complex technical equipment is involved and establishing satisfactory additional sources will require technical assistance as well as data; or

(iv) Incorporate a priced option in the contract that allows the Government to require the contractor to establish a second source.

(4) As a last alternative, the contracting activity may develop a design specification for competitive acquisition through reverse engineering. Contracting activities shall not do reverse engineering unless—

(i) Significant cost savings can be demonstrated; and

(ii) The action is authorized by the head of the contracting activity.

[Final rule, 71 FR 27642, 5/12/2006, effective 5/12/2006]

217.7506 Spare Parts Breakout Program.

PART 1 GENERAL

1-101 Applicability.

(a) The Spare Parts Breakout Program applies to—

(1) Any centrally managed replenishment or provisioned part (hereinafter referred to as "part") for military systems and equipment; and

(2) All DoD personnel involved with design control, acquisition, and management of such parts including, but not limited to, project/program/system managers, technical personnel, contracting officers, legal counsel, inventory managers, inspectors, and small business specialists and technical advisors.

(b) The Spare Parts Breakout Program does not apply to—

(1) Component breakout (see DFARS 207.171);

(2) Foreign military sale peculiar items;

(3) Insurance items (e.g., one-time buy);

(4) Obsolete items;

(5) Phase-out items (e.g., life-of-type buy);

(6) Items with annual buy values below the thresholds developed by DoD components or field activities;

(7) Parts being acquired under other specifically defined initial support programs; or

(8) Parts acquired through local purchase.

1-102 General.

(a) Significant resources are dedicated to the acquisition and management of parts for military systems and equipment. The ability to competitively buy spares must be considered early in a weapon system acquisition. Initially, repairable or consumable parts are identified and acquired through a provisioning process; repairable or consumable parts acquired thereafter are for replenishment.

(b) The objective of the DoD Spare Parts Breakout Program is to reduce costs through the use of competitive procurement methods, or the purchase of parts directly from the actual manufacturer rather than the prime contractor, while maintaining the integrity of the systems and equipment in which the parts are to be used. The program is based on the application of sound management and engineering judgment in—

(1) Determining the feasibility of acquiring parts by competitive procedures or direct purchase from actual manufacturers; and

(2) Overcoming or removing constraints to breakout identified through the screening process (technical review) described in 3-302.

(c) The breakout program includes procedures for screening and coding parts in order to provide contracting officers summary information regarding technical data and sources of supply to meet the Government's minimum requirements. This information assists the contracting officer in selecting the method of contracting, identifying sources of supply, and making other decisions in the preaward and award phases, with consideration for established parameters of system and equipment integrity, readiness, and the opportunities to competitively acquire parts (see FAR/DFARS Part 6). The identification of sources for parts, for example, requires knowledge of manufacturing sources, additional operations performed after manufacture of parts possessing safety or other critical characteristics, and the availability of technical data.

(d) The result of the screening process (technical review is indicated by an acquisition method code (AMC) and an acquisition method suffix code (AMSC). The breakout program provides procedures for both the initial assignment of an AMC and an AMSC to a part, and for the recurring review of these codes (see 2-202 and 2-203(b)).

1-103 Definitions. (No Text)

1-103.1 Acquisition method code (AMC).

A single digit numeric code, assigned by a DoD activity, to describe to the contracting officer and other Government personnel the results of a technical review of a part and its suitability for breakout.

1-103.2 Acquisition method code conference.

A conference that is generally held at the contractor's facility for the purpose of reviewing contractor technical information codes (CTICs) and corresponding substantiating data for breakout.

1-103.3 Acquisition method suffix code (AMSC).

A single digit alpha code, assigned by a DoD activity, that provides the contracting officer and other Government personnel with engineering, manufacturing, and technical information.

1-103.4 Actual manufacturer.

An individual, activity, or organization that performs the physical fabrication processes that produce the deliverable part or other items of supply for the Government. The actual manufacturer must produce the part in-house. The actual manufacturer may or may not be the design control activity.

1-103.5 Altered item drawing.

See current version of DoD STD-100, paragraphs 201.4.4 and 703.

1-103.6 Annual buy quantity.

The forecast quantity of a part required for the next 12 months.

1-103.7 Annual buy value (ABV).

The annual buy quantity of a part multiplied by its unit price.

1-103.8 Bailment.

The process whereby a part is loaned to a recipient with the agreement that the part will be returned at an appointed time. The government retains legal title to such material even though the borrowing organization has possession during the stated period.

1-103.9 Breakout.

The improvement of the acquisition status of a part resulting from a technical review and a deliberate management decision. Examples are—

(a) The competitive acquisition of a part previously purchased noncompetitively; and

(b) The direct purchase of a part previously purchased from a prime contractor who is not the actual manufacturer of the part.

1-103.10 Competition.

A contract action where two or more responsible sources, acting independently, can be solicited to satisfy the Government's requirement.

1-103.11 Contractor technical information code (CTIC).

A two-digit alpha code assigned to a part by a prime contractor to furnish specific information regarding the engineering, manufacturing, and technical aspects of that part.

1-103.12 Design control activity.

A contractor or Government activity having responsibility for the design of a given part, and for the preparation and currency of engineering drawings and other technical data for that part. The design control activity may or may not be the actual manufacturer. The design control activity is synonymous with design activity as used by DoD STD-100.

1-103.13 Direct purchase.

The acquisition of a part from the actual manufacturer, including a prime contractor who is an actual manufacturer of the part.

1-103.14 Engineering drawings.

See current versions of DoD STD-100 and DoDD 1000.

1-103.15 Extended dollar value.

The contract unit price of a part multiplied by the quantity purchased.

1-103.16 Full and open competition.

A contract action where all responsible sources are permitted to compete.

1-103.17 Full screening.

A detailed parts breakout process, including data collection, data evaluation, data completion, technical evaluation, economic evaluation, and supply feedback, used to determine if parts can be purchased directly from the actual manufacturer(s) or can be competed.

1-103.18 Immediate (live) buy.

A buy that must be executed as soon as possible to prevent unacceptable equipment readiness reduction, unacceptable disruption in operational capability, and increased safety risks, or to avoid other costs.

1-103.19 Life cycle buy value.

The total dollar value of all acquisitions that are estimated to occur over a part's remaining life cycle.

1-103.20 Limited competition.

A competitive contract action where the provisions of full and open competition do not exist.

1-103.21 Limited screening.

A parts breakout process covering only selected points of data and technical evaluations, and should only be used to support immediate buy requirements (see 3-301.3).

1-103.22 Manufacture.

The physical fabrication process that produces a part, or other item of supply. The physical fabrication processes include, but are not limited to, machining, welding, soldering, brazing, heat treating, braking, riveting, pressing, and chemical treatment.

1-103.23 Prime contractor.

A contractor having responsibility for design control and/or delivery of a system/equipment such as aircraft, engines, ships, tanks, vehicles, guns and missiles, ground communications and electronics systems, and test equipment.

1-103.24 Provisioning.

The process of determining and acquiring the range and quantity (depth) of spare and repair parts, and support and test equipment required to operate and maintain an end item of materiel for an initial period of service.

1-103.25 Qualification.

Any action (contractual or precontractual) that results in approval for a firm to supply items to the Government without further testing beyond quality assurance demonstrations incident to acceptance of an item. When prequalification is required, the Government must have a justification on file—

(a) Stating the need for qualification and why it must be done prior to award;

(b) Estimating likely cost of qualification; and

(c) Specifying all qualification requirements.

1-103.26 Replenishment part.

A part, repairable or consumable, purchased after provisioning of that part, for: replacement; replenishment of stock; or use in the maintenance, overhaul, and repair of equipment such as aircraft, engines, ships, tanks, vehicles, guns and missiles, ground communications and electronic systems, ground support, and test equipment. As used in the breakout program, except when distinction is necessary, the term "part" includes subassemblies, components, and subsystems as defined by the current version of MIL-STD-280.

1-103.27 Reverse engineering.

A process by which parts are examined and analyzed to determine how they were manufactured, for the purpose of developing a complete technical data package. The normal, expected result of reverse engineering is the creation of a technical data package suitable for manufacture of an item by new sources.

1-103.28 Selected item drawing.

See current version of DoD-STD-100, paragraph 201.4.5.

1-103.29 Source.

Any commercial or noncommercial organization that can supply a specified part. For coding purposes, sources include actual manufacturers, prime contractors, vendors, dealers, surplus dealers, distributors, and other firms.

1-103.30 Source approval.

The Government review that must be completed before contract award.

1-103.31 Source control drawing.

See the current version of DoD-STD-100, paragraph 201.4.3.

1-103.32 Technical data.

Specifications, plans, drawings, standards, purchase descriptions, and such other data to describe the Government's requirements for acquisition.

1-104 General policies.

(a) The identification, selection, and screening of parts for breakout shall be made as early as possible to determine the technical and economic considerations of the opportunities for breakout to competition or direct purchase. Full and open competition is the preferred result of breakout screening.

(b) A part shall be made a candidate for breakout screening based on its cost effectiveness for breakout. Resources should be assigned and priority given to those parts with the greatest expected return given their annual buy value, life cycle buy value, and likelihood of successful breakout, given technical characteristics such as design and performance stability. Consideration of all such factors is necessary to ensure the maximum return on investment in a given breakout program. Occasionally, an item will not meet strict economic considerations for breakout, but action may be required due to other considerations to avoid overpricing situations. Accordingly, there is no minimum DoD threshold for breakout screening actions. DoD components and field activities will develop annual buy thresholds for breakout screening that are consistent with economic considerations and resources. Every effort should be made to complete the full screening of parts that are expected to be subsequently replenished as they enter the inventory.

(c) Breakout improvement efforts shall continue through the life cycle of a part to improve its breakout status (see 2-203) or until such time as the part is coded 1G, 2G, 1K, 2K, 1M, 2M, 1N, 2N, 1T, 2T, 1Z, or 2Z.

(d) No firm shall be denied the opportunity to demonstrate its ability to furnish a part that meets the Government's needs, without regard to a part's annual buy value, where a restrictive AMC/AMSC is assigned (see FAR 9.202). A firm must clearly demonstrate, normally at its own expense, that it can satisfy the Government's requirements. The Government shall make a vigorous effort to expedite its evaluation of such demonstration and to furnish a decision to the demonstrating firm within a reasonable period of time. If a resolution cannot be made within 60 days, the offeror must be advised of the status of the request and be provided with a good faith estimate of the date the evaluation will be completed. Every reasonable effort shall be made to complete the review before a subsequent acquisition is made. Also, restrictive codes and low annual buy value do not preclude consideration of a surplus dealer or other nonmanufacturing source when the part offered was manufactured by an approved source (see FAR 11.302). A potential surplus dealer or other nonmanufacturing source must provide the Government with all the necessary evidence that proves the proposed part meets the Government's requirements.

(e) The experience and knowledge accrued by contractors in the development, design, manufacture and test of equipment may enhance the breakout decision making process. DoD activities may obtain technical information from contractors when it is considered requisite to an informed coding decision. The procedure for contracting for this information is provided in Part 4 of this document. Contractor's technical information will be designated by CTICs. Only DoD activities shall assign AMCs and AMSCs.

(f) DoD activities with breakout screening responsibilities shall develop, document, and advertise programs that promote the development of qualified sources for parts that are currently being purchased sole source. These programs should provide fair and reasonable technical assistance (engineering or other technical data, parts on bailment, etc.) to contractors who prove they have potential for becoming a qualified second source for an item. These programs should also provide specially tailored incentives to successful firms so as to stimulate their investment in becoming qualified, e.g., Government furnished equipment (GFE) or Government furnished material (GFM) for reverse engineering and technical data package review and assistance.

(g) Departments and agencies shall identify the engineering support activity, design control activity, actual manufacturer, and prime contractor for each part such that the information is readily available to breakout and acquisition personnel.

1-105 Responsibilities.

(a) The Under Secretary of Defense (Acquisition, Technology, and Logistics) has authority for direction and management of the DoD Spare Parts Breakout Program, including the establishment and maintenance of implementing regulations.

(b) Departments and agencies shall perform audits to ensure that their respective activities comply with the provisions of this program.

(c) Commanders of DoD activities with breakout screening responsibility shall—

(1) Implement a breakout program consistent with the requirements of this document.

(2) Assist in the identification and acquisition of necessary data rights and technical data, and the review of restrictive legends on technical data, during system/equipment development and production to allow, when feasible, breakout of parts.

(3) Designate a program manager to serve as the central focal point, communicate breakout policy, ensure cost-effectiveness of screening actions and breakout program, provide assistance in implementing breakout screening, monitor ongoing breakout efforts and achievements, and provide surveillance over implementation of the breakout program. The program manager shall report only to the Commander, or deputy, of the activity with breakout screening responsibility.

(4) Ensure that actions to remove impediments to breakout are continued as long as it is cost-effective, or until no further breakout improvements can be made.

(5) Invite the activity's small business specialist and the resident small business administration's procurement center representative, if any, to participate in all acquisition method coding conferences at Government and contractor locations.

(6) Ensure timely engineering and technical support to other breakout activities regardless of location.

(i) In the case of parts where contracting or inventory management responsibility has been transferred, support shall include—

(A) Assignment of an AMC/AMSC prior to the transfer;

(B) Assignment of an AMC/AMSC when requested by the receiving activity to parts transferred without such codes. The requesting activity may recommend an AMC/AMSC; and

(C) Full support of the receiving activities' breakout effort by providing timely engineering support in revising existing AMC/AMSCs.

(ii) In all cases, support shall include, but not be limited to, furnishing all necessary technical data and other information (such as code suspense date and procurement history) to permit acquisition in accordance with the assigned AMC/AMSC (see 1-105(d)(6)).

(7) Ensure that appropriate surveillance is given to first time breakout parts.

(d) Breakout program managers shall be responsible for—

(1) Initiating the breakout process during the early phases of development and continuing the process during the life of the part;

(2) Considering the need for contractor technical information codes (CTICs) and, when needed, initiating a contract data requirement;

(3) Identifying, selecting, and screening in accordance with Part 3 of this document;

(4) Assigning an AMC/AMSC, using all available data, including CTICs;

(5) Responding promptly to a request for evaluation of additional sources or a review of assigned codes. An evaluation not completed prior to an immediate buy shall be promptly completed for future buys; and

(6) Documenting all assignments and changes, to include rationale for assigning the chosen code, in a permanent file for each part. As a minimum, the file should identify the engineering support activity, cognizant design control activity, actual manufacturer, prime contractor, known sources of supply, and any other information needed to support AMC/AMSC assignments.

(e) Contracting officers responsible for the acquisition of replenishment parts shall—

(1) Consider the AMC/AMSC when developing the method of contracting, the list of sources to be solicited, the type of contract, etc.; and

(2) Provide information that is inconsistent with the assigned AMC/AMSC (e.g., availability of technical data or possible sources) to the activity responsible for code assignment with a request for timely evaluation of the additional information. An urgent immediate buy need not be delayed if an evaluation of the additional information cannot be completed in time to meet the required delivery date.

PART 2 BREAKOUT CODING

2-200 Scope.

This part provides parts breakout codes and prescribes responsibilities for their assignment and management.

2-201 Coding.

Three types of codes are used in the breakout program.

2-201.1 Acquisition method codes.

The following codes shall be assigned by DoD activities to describe the results of the spare parts breakout screening:

(a) *AMC 0.* The part was not assigned AMC 1 through 5 when it entered the inventory, nor has it ever completed screening. Use of this code is sometimes necessary but discouraged. Maximum effort to determine the applicability of an alternate AMC is the objective. This code will never be used to recode a part that already has AMC 1 through 5 assigned, and shall never be assigned as a result of breakout screening. Maximum effort to determine the applicability of AMC 1 through 5 is the objective.

(b) *AMC 1.* Suitable for competitive acquisition for the second or subsequent time.

(c) *AMC 2.* Suitable for competitive acquisition for the first time.

(d) *AMC 3.* Acquire, for the second or subsequent time, directly from the actual manufacturer.

(e) *AMC 4.* Acquire, for the first time, directly from the actual manufacturer.

(f) *AMC 5.* Acquire directly from a sole source contractor which is not the actual manufacturer.

2-201.2 Acquisition method suffix codes.

The following codes shall be assigned by DoD activities to further describe the acquisition method code. Valid combinations of AMCs/AMSCs are indicated in paragraphs (a) through (z) of this subsection and summarized in Exhibit I.

(a) *AMSC A.* The Government's right to use data in its possession is questionable. This code is only applicable to parts under immediate buy requirements and for as long thereafter as rights to data are still under review for resolution and appropriate coding. This code is assigned only at the conclusion of limited screening, and it remains assigned until the full screening process resolves the Government's rights to use data and results in assignment of a different AMSC. If one source is available, AMCs 3, 4, or 5 are valid. If at least two sources exist, or if the data is adequate for an alternate source to qualify in accordance with the design control activity's procedures, AMCs 1 or 2 are valid.

(b) *AMSC B.* This part must be acquired from a manufacturing source(s) specified on a source control or selected item drawing as defined by the current version of DoD-STD-100. Suitable technical data, Government data rights, or manufacturing knowledge are not available to permit acquisition from other sources, nor qualification testing of another part, nor use of a second source part in the intended application. Although, by DoD-STD-100 definition, altered and selected items shall have an adequate technical data package, data review discloses that required data or data rights are not in Government possession and cannot be economically obtained. If one source is available, AMCs 3, 4, or 5 are valid. If at least two sources exist, AMCs 1 or 2 are valid.

(c) *AMSC C.* This part requires engineering source approval by the design control activity in order to maintain the quality of the part. Existing unique design capability, engineering skills, and manufacturing knowledge by the qualified source(s) require acquisition of the part from the approved source(s). The approved source(s) retain data rights, manufacturing knowledge, or technical data that are not economically available to the Government, and the data or knowledge is essential to maintaining the quality of the part. An alternate source must qualify in accordance with the design control activity's procedures, as approved by the cognizant Government engineering activity. The qualification procedures must be approved by the Government engineering activity having jurisdiction over the part in the intended application. If one source is approved, AMCs 3, 4, or 5 are valid. If at least two sources are approved or if data is adequate for an alternate source to qualify in accordance with the design control activity's procedures, AMCs 1 or 2 are valid.

(d) *AMSC D.* The data needed to acquire this part competitively is not physically available, it cannot be obtained economically, nor is it possible to draft adequate specifications or any other adequate, economical description of the material for a competitive solicitation. AMCS 3, 4, or 5 are valid.

(e) *AMSC E.* (Reserved)

(f) *AMSC F.* (Reserved)

(g) *AMSC G.* The Government has rights to the technical data, the data package is complete, and there are no technical data, engineering, tooling or manufacturing restrictions. (This is the only AMSC that implies that parts are candidates for full and open competition. Other AMSCs such as K,

M, N, Q, and S may imply limited competition when two or more independent sources exist yet the technical data package is inadequate for full and open competition.) AMCs 1 or 2 are valid.

(h) *AMSC H.* The Government physically does not have in its possession sufficient, accurate, or legible data to purchase this part from other than the current source(s). This code is applicable only to parts under immediate buy requirements and only for as long thereafter as the deficiency is under review for resolution and appropriate recoding. This code is only assigned at the conclusion of limited screening, and it remains assigned until the full screening process resolves physical data questions and results in assignment of a different AMSC. If one source is available, AMCs 3, 4, or 5 are valid. If at least two sources exist, AMCs 1 or 2 are valid.

(i) *AMSC I.* (Not authorized)

(j) *AMSC J.* (Reserved)

(k) *AMSC K.* This part must be produced from class 1 castings and similar type forgings as approved (controlled) by procedures contained in the current version of MIL-STD-2175. If one source has such castings and cannot provide them to other sources, AMCs 3, 4, or 5 are valid. If at least two sources have such castings or they can be provided to other sources AMCs 1 or 2 or valid.

(l) *AMSC L.* The annual buy value of this part falls below the screening threshold established by DoD components and field activities. However, this part has been screened for additional known sources, resulting in either confirmation that the initial source exists or that other sources may supply the part. No additional screening was performed to identify the competitive or noncompetitive conditions that would result in assignment of a different AMSC. This code shall not be used when screening parts entering the inventory. This code shall be used only to replace AMSC O for parts under the established screening threshold. If one source is available, AMCs 3, 4, or 5 are valid. If at least two sources exist, AMCs 1 or 2 are valid.

(m) *AMSC M.* Manufacture of this part requires use of master or coordinated tooling. If only one set of tooling exists and cannot be made available to another source for manufacture of this part, AMCs 3, 4, or 5 are valid. When the availability of existent or refurbishable tooling is available to two or more sources, then AMCs 1 or 2 are valid.

(n) *AMSC N.* Manufacture of this part requires special test and/or inspection facilities to determine and maintain ultra-precision quality for its function or system integrity. Substantiation and inspection of the precision or quality cannot be accomplished without such specialized test or inspection facilities. If the test cannot be made available for the competitive manufacture of the part, the required test or inspection knowledge cannot be documented for reliable replication, or the required physical test or inspection facilities and processes cannot be economically documented in a TDP, valid AMCs are 3, 4, or 5. If the facilities or tests can be made available to two or more competitive sources, AMCs 1 or 2 are valid.

(o) *AMSC O.* The part was not assigned an AMSC when it entered the inventory, nor has it ever completed screening. Use of this code in conjunction with AMC 0 is sometimes necessary but discouraged. Maximum effort to determine the applicability of an alternate AMSC is the objective. Only AMC O is valid.

(p) *AMSC P.* The rights to use the data needed to purchase this part from additional source(s) are not owned by the Government and cannot be purchased, developed, or otherwise obtained. It is uneconomical to reverse engineer this part. This code is used in situations where the Government has the data but does not own the rights to the data. If only one source has the rights or data to manufacture this item, AMCs 3, 4, or 5 are valid. If two or more sources have the rights or data to manufacture this item, AMCs 1 or 2 are valid.

(q) *AMSC Q.* The Government does not have adequate data, lacks rights to data, or both needed to purchase this part from additional sources. The Government has been unable to economically buy the data or rights to the data, although the part has been undergoing full screening for 12 or more months. Breakout to competition has not been achieved, but current, continuing actions to obtain necessary rights to data or adequate, reprocurement technical data indicate breakout to competition is expected to be achieved. This part may be a candidate for reverse engineering or other techniques to obtain technical data. All AMSC Q items are required to be reviewed within the timeframes cited in 2-203(b). If one source is available, AMCs 3, 4, or 5 are valid. If at least two sources exist, AMCs 1 or 2 are valid.

(r) *AMSC R.* The Government does not own the data or the rights to the data needed to purchase this part from additional sources. It has been determined to be uneconomical to buy the data or rights to the data. It is uneconomical to reverse engineer the part. This code is used when the Government did not initially purchase the data and/or rights. If only one source has the rights or data to manufacture this item, AMCs 3, 4, or 5 are valid. If two or more sources have the rights or data to manufacture this item, AMCs 1 or 2 are valid.

(s) *AMSC S.* Acquisition of this item is restricted to Government approved source(s) because the production of this item involves unclassified but militarily sensitive technology (see FAR Subpart 6.3). If one source is approved, AMCs 3, 4, or 5 are valid. If at least two sources are approved, AMCs 1 or 2 are valid.

(t) *AMSC T.* Acquisition of this part is controlled by qualified products list (QPL) procedures. Competition for this part is limited to sources which are listed on or are qualified for listing on the QPL at the time of award (see FAR Part 9 and DFARS Part 209). AMCs 1 or 2 are valid.

(u) *AMSC U.* The cost to the Government to breakout this part and acquire it competitively has been determined to exceed the projected savings over the life span of the part. If one source is available, AMCs 3, 4, or 5 are valid. If at least two sources exist, AMCs 1 or 2 are valid.

(v) *AMSC V.* This part has been designated a high reliability part under a formal reliability program. Probability of failure would be unacceptable from the standpoint of safety of personnel and/or equipment. The cognizant engineering activity has determined that data to define and control reliability limits cannot be obtained nor is it possible to draft adequate specifications for this purpose. If one source is available, AMCs 3, 4, or 5 are valid. If at least two sources are available, AMCs 1 or 2 are valid.

(w) *AMSC W.* (Reserved)

(x) *AMSC X.* (Not authorized)

(y) *AMSC Y.* The design of this part is unstable. Engineering, manufacturing, or performance characteristics indicate that the required design objectives have not been achieved. Major changes are contemplated because the part has a low process yield or has demonstrated marginal performance during tests or service use. These changes will render the present part obsolete and unusable in its present configuration. Limited acquisition from the present source is anticipated pending configuration changes. If one source is available, AMCs 3, 4, or 5 are valid. If at least two sources exist, AMCs 1 or 2 are valid.

(z) *AMSC Z.* This part is a commercial/nondevelopmental/off-the-shelf item. Commercial item descriptions, commercial vendor catalog or price lists or commercial manuals assigned a technical manual number apply. If one source is available, AMCs 3, 4, or 5 are valid. If at least two sources are available, AMCs 1 or 2 are valid.

2-201.3 Contractor technical information codes.

The following two-digit alpha codes shall be used by contractors, when contractor's assistance is requested. These codes are assigned in accordance with the current version of MIL-STD-789 and shall be considered during the initial assignment of an AMC/AMSC. For spare parts breakout, requirements for contractor assistance through CTIC submission shall be accomplished as stated in Part 4 of this document. Each CTIC submitted by a contractor must be accompanied by supporting documentation that justifies the proposed code. These codes and supporting documentation, transmitted by DD Form 1418, Contractor Technical Information Record, and DD Form 1418-1, Technical Data Identification Checklist, are useful not only for code assignment during acquisition coding conferences, but also for personnel conducting both full and limited screening of breakout candidates. Personnel conducting full and limited screening of breakout candidates should use the supporting documentation provided with CTICs as a source of information. However, they should not allow this information to substitute for careful analysis and further investigation of the possibilities of acquiring a part through competition or by direct purchase. The definitions for CTICs are—

(a) *CTIC CB.* Source(s) are specified on source control, altered item, or selected item drawings/documents. (The contractor shall furnish a list of the sources with this code.)

(b) *CTIC CC.* Requires engineering source approval by the design control activity in order to maintain the quality of the part. An alternate source must qualify in accordance with the design control activity's procedures, as approved by the cognizant Government engineering activity.

(c) *CTIC CG.* There are no technical restrictions to competition.

(d) *CTIC CK.* Produced from class 1 castings (see the current version of MIL-STD-2175) and similar type forgings. The process of developing and proving the acceptability of high-integrity castings and forgings requires repetitive performance by a controlled source. Each casting or forging must be produced along identical lines to those that resulted in initial acceptability of the part. (The contractor shall furnish a list of known sources for obtaining castings/forgings with this code.)

(e) *CTIC CM.* Master or coordinated tooling is required to produce this part. This tooling is not owned by the Government or, where owned, cannot be made available to other sources. (The contractor shall furnish a list of the firms possessing the master or coordinated tooling with this code.)

(f) *CTIC CN.* Requires special test and/or inspection facilities to determine and maintain ultra-precision quality for function or system integrity. Substantiation and inspection of the precision or quality cannot be accomplished without such specialized test or inspection facilities. Other sources in industry do not possess, nor would it be economically feasible for them to acquire facilities. (The contractor shall furnish a list of the required facilities and their locations with this code.)

(g) *CTIC CP.* The rights to use the data needed to purchase this part from additional sources are not owned by the Government and cannot be purchased.

(h) *CTIC CV.* A high reliability part under a formal reliability program. Probability of failure would be unacceptable from the standpoint of safety of personnel and/or equipment. The cognizant engineering activity has determined that data to define and control reliability limits cannot be obtained nor is it possible to draft adequate specifications for this purpose. Continued control by the existing source is necessary to ensure acceptable reliability. (The contractor shall identify the existing source with this code.)

(i) *CTIC CY.* The design of this part is unstable. Engineering, manufacturing, or performance characteristics indicate that the required design objectives have not been achieved. Major changes are contemplated because the part has a low process yield or has demonstrated marginal performance during tests or service use. These changes will render the present part obsolete and unusable in its present configuration. Limited acquisition from the present source is anticipated pending configuration changes. (The contractor shall identify the existing source with this code.)

2-202 Assignment of codes.

The purpose of AMC/AMSC assignments is to provide the best possible technical assessment of how a part can be acquired. The technical assessment should not be based on issues such as: are the known sources actual manufacturers, or are there two actual manufacturers in existence; but rather on factors such as the availability of adequate technical data, the Government's rights to use the data, technical restrictions placed on the hardware (criticality, reliability, special testing, master tooling, source approval, etc.) and the cost to breakout vice projected savings. In cases where there is additional technical information that affects the way a part can be acquired, it should be made available to the contracting officer, with the AMC/AMSC. Concerning the assignment of AMCs and AMSCs, it is DoD policy that—

(a) The assignment of AMC/AMSCs to parts is the responsibility of the DoD component introducing the equipment or system for which the parts are needed in the inventory. Subsequent screening is the responsibility of the DoD component assigned technical responsibility.

(b) When two or more AMSCs apply, the most technically restrictive code will be assigned.

(c) Restricted combinations of AMC/AMSCs are reflected in the AMSC definitions. The Defense Logistics Information Service will reject invalid code combinations, as shown in Exhibit I, submitted for entry into the Federal catalog program (see 2-204.2).

(d) One-time acquisition of a part by a method other than indicated by the code does not require a change to the AMC (e.g., when only one of a number of sources can meet a short delivery date, or when only one manufacturing source is known but acceptable surplus parts are available from other sources).

(e) After the first acquisition under AMC 2 or 4, the AMC shall be recoded 1 or 3 respectively.

(f) Both full and limited screening will result in the assignment or reassignment of an AMC/AMSC. This assignment shall be based on the best technical judgment of breakout personnel and on information gathered during the screening process.

(g) A part need not be coded as noncompetitive based on an initial market survey that only uncovers one interested source. If the Government has sufficient technical data in its possession to enable other sources to manufacture an acceptable part, and there are no technical restrictions on the part that would preclude other sources from manufacturing it, the part should be coded competitive.

2-203 Improving part status.

(a) *General.* An effective breakout program requires that all reasonable actions be taken to improve the acquisition status of parts. The potential for improvement of the acquisition status will vary with individual circumstances. On one end of the spectrum are those parts with acquisition method suffix codes of a temporary nature requiring vigorous follow-through improvement action (e.g., AMSCs A and H); on the other end are those parts with codes suggesting a relative degree of permanence (e.g., AMSC P). A code assigned to a part should never be considered fixed with respect to either technical circumstance or time; today's technical constraint may be overcome by tomorrow's technology and a contractor's rights to data, so zealously protected today, often become less important with time. The application of breakout improvement effort must always consider individual circumstances and overall benefits expected to be obtained.

(b) *Code suspense dates.* Every part whose breakout status can be improved shall be suspended for rescreening as appropriate. In general, the following codes cannot be improved: 1G, 2G, 1K, 2K, 1M, 2M, 1N, 2N, 1T, 2T, 1Z, or 2Z. The period between suspensions is a period for which an assigned AMC/AMSC is considered active, and routine rescreening of parts with "valid" codes is not required. Suspense dates may vary with the circumstance surrounding each part. A code reached as a result of limited screening (3-304) shall not be assigned a suspense date exceeding 12 months; a code reached as a result of full screening (3-303) shall not be assigned a suspense date exceeding 3 years. In exceptional cases, where circumstances indicate that no change can be expected in a code over an extended period, a suspense date not exceeding 5 years may be assigned in accordance with controls established by the breakout activity. Items with a 1G or 2G code do not require a suspense date.

2-204 Communication of codes. (No Text)

2-204.1 Communication media.

Use the Federal catalog program formats, set forth in DoD Manual 4100.39-M, Defense Integrated Data System (DIDS) Procedural Manual, communication media and operating instructions as augmented by this document to disseminate AMCs and AMSCs.

2-204.2 Responsibilities.

(a) The Defense Logistics Information Service (DLIS) will—

(1) Receive and disseminate AMCs and AMSCs for each national stock number (NSN) to all appropriate Government activities in consonance with scheduled Federal catalog program computer cycles;

(2) Make the AMCs and AMSCs a part of the data bank of NSN item intelligence;

(3) Perpetuate the codes in all subsequent Federal catalog program transactions; e.g., entry of new NSNs and Federal supply code (FSC) changes; and

(4) Reject invalid code combinations submitted for entry into the Federal catalog program.

(b) DoD activities responsible for the assignment of AMCs and AMSCs will—

(1) Transmit assigned codes for each NSN through normal cataloging channels to DLIS under existing Federal catalog program procedures; and

(2) Notify DLIS by normal Federal catalog program maintenance procedures when a change in coding is made.

PART 3 IDENTIFICATION, SELECTION, AND SCREENING OF PARTS

3-300 General.

This part sets forth procedures for the identification, selection, and screening of parts.

3-301 Identification and selection procedures. (No Text)

3-301.1 Parts entering the inventory.

The breakout process should begin at the earliest possible stage of weapon systems acquisition. Generally, a provisioned part will require subsequent replenishment. Provisioning or similar lists of new parts are, therefore, the appropriate bases for selecting parts for screening. This is not to imply that breakout must be done on all items as part of the provisioning process. Priorities shall be applied to those parts offering the greatest opportunity for breakout and potential savings. The major factors in making this determination are—

(a) The unit price;

(b) The projected quantity to be purchased over the part's life cycle; and

(c) The potential for screening to result in a part being successfully broken out, e.g., item stability, cost, and completeness of technical data, etc.

3-301.2 Annual buy forecasts.

Annually, lists shall be prepared that identify all parts projected for purchase during the subsequent 12-month period. Priority should be given to those parts with the greatest expected return given their annual buy value, life cycle buy value, and likelihood of successful breakout, given technical characteristics such as design and performance stability and the availability of technical data. Parts with an expired suspense date or a suspense date that will expire during the forecast period (see 2-203(b)), need only be subjected to the necessary steps of the full screening procedure (see 3-303). Parts with a valid code that will not expire during the forecast period need not be screened. Parts coded 0O shall be selected for full screening.

3-301.3 Immediate buy requirements.

An immediate buy requirement will be identified by the user or the item manager in consonance with department/agency regulations. When an immediate buy requirement meeting the screening criteria (see 1-104(b)) is generated for a part not assigned a current

AMC/AMSC, the part shall be promptly screened in accordance with either the full or limited screening procedures (see 3-303 and 3-304).

3-301.4 Suspect AMC/AMSC.

Whenever an AMC/AMSC is suspected of being inaccurate by anyone, including the contracting officer, a rescreening shall be conducted for that part. Suspect codes include codes composed of invalid combinations of AMCs and AMSCs, those which do not truly reflect how a part is actually being acquired, and those suspected of being more restrictive than necessary for the next buy.

3-302 Screening.

(a) Screening procedures include consideration and recording of the relevant facts pertaining to breakout decisions. The objective of screening is to improve the acquisition status by determining the potential for competition, or purchase from an actual manufacturer. Consideration of any reasonable approach to establishing competition should be an integral part of the breakout process.

(b) Screening procedures may vary depending on circumstances related to the parts. No set rules will provide complete guidance for making acquisition method decisions under all conditions encountered in actual practice. An informed coding decision can be made without following the procedures step-by-step in every case.

(c) Activities involved in screening are encouraged to develop supplemental procedures that prove effective in meeting this program's objectives. These procedures should be tailored to the particular activity's operating environment and the characteristics of the parts for which it is responsible. Nevertheless, care should be taken in all cases to assure that—

(1) Responsible judgment is applied to all elements involved in the review of a part;

(2) The necessary supporting facts are produced, considered, and recorded in the breakout screening file. The breakout screening file contains technical data and other documents concerning screening of the part;

(3) All cost-effective alternatives are considered for establishing competition, or purchase from an actual manufacturer (see 1-105(d)(6)); and

(4) When possible, the sequence of the review allows for accomplishing several screening steps concurrently.

(d) Contractor participation in the decision making process extends only to providing technical information. This technical information is provided by supporting documentation (DD Forms 1418, Contractor Technical Information Record, and DD Form 1418-1, Technical Data Identification Checklist) which includes the CTIC assignment. Government personnel shall substantiate the breakout decision by reference to the CTIC and by careful review of the supporting documentation. However, the CTIC provides guidance only, and it should be used as one of the inputs to arrive at an acceptable AMC and AMSC coding.

(e) Contractor's technical information furnished in accordance with MIL-STD-789 may indicate areas requiring additional research by the Government before screening can be completed. Seldom will industry's contribution to the screening process enable the Government to assign an AMC or AMSC without additional review.

(f) During the screening process, it may be appropriate to communicate with industry, particularly potential manufacturers of a part, to determine the feasibility of establishing a competitive source and to estimate the costs and technical risks involved.

(g) Coding conferences with industry shall be documented.

(h) Screening may disclose that a part is not suitable for competitive acquisition, but it may be possible to break out the part for direct purchase from the actual manufacturer or to establish a second source. Parts particularly suited to direct purchase are those where neither the design control activity nor the prime contractor contribute additional value or whose data belong to the actual manufacturer and will not be acquired by the Government, and where that manufacturer exercises total responsibility for the part (design and quality control, testing, etc.), and where additional operations performed by the prime contractor can be performed by the actual manufacturer or by the Government.

(i) For each part that is screened, a file shall be established to document and justify the decisions and results of all screening effort (see 1-105(d)(6)).

(j) Full and limited screening procedures are two elements of breakout programs. Other spare parts initiatives to enhance breakout are reverse engineering, bailment, data rights challenges, and publication of intended buy lists. Integration of other initiatives within the screening processes developed at each activity is encouraged.

3-303 Full screening procedures.

(a) Full screening procedures should be developed so that the potential is fully evaluated for establishing competition or purchase from an actual manufacturer. Also, full screening procedures should facilitate accurate and consistent acquisition method code assignment. It is expected that each activity will develop its own operational screening procedures. A general model, full screening decision process is provided below to support the development of activity level procedures and to provide guidance regarding the general scope of these procedures. The full screening procedures involve 65 steps in the decision process, and are divided into the following phases:

(1) Data collection.

(2) Data evaluation.

(3) Data completion.

(4) Technical evaluation.

(5) Economic evaluation.

(6) Supply feedback.

(b) The six phases describe different functions that must be achieved during screening. The nature of the screening process does not permit clear distinction of one phase from another. Further, the order of performance of these phases may not correspond to the order listed here. In fact, the phases will often overlap and may be performed simultaneously. Their purpose is to identify the different functions comprising the screening process.

(c) A summary flow chart of the decision steps is provided as Exhibit II to assist in understanding the logical order of the full screening steps for various conditions. Use of the flow chart in connection with the text that follows is essential to fully understand the order of the steps in the process.

3-303.1 Data collection phase (step 1).

(a) Assemble all available data and establish a file for each part. Collect identification data, relevant data obtained from industry, contracting and technical history data and current status of the part, including—

(1) Normal identification required for cataloging and standardization review;

(2) All known sources;

(3) Historical contracting information, including the more recent awards, date of awards, and unit price(s) for the quantities prescribed;

(4) Identification of the actual manufacturer(s), the latest unit price, and the quantity on which the price is based. (When the actual manufacturer is not the design control activity, the design control activity may be consulted to ensure the latest version of the item is being procured from the actual manufacturer);

(5) Identification of the activity, Government or industry, having design control over the part and, if industry, the cognizant Government engineering activity;

(6) The expected life in the military supply system;

(7) Record of any prior review for breakout, with results or findings; and

(8) Annual demand.

(b) In the case of complex items requiring large numbers of drawings, collection of a reasonable technical data sample is sufficient for the initial technical data evaluation phase (steps 2-14).

3-303.2 Data evaluation phase (steps 2-14).

(a) Data evaluation is crucial to the whole review procedure. It involves determination of the adequacy of the technical data package and the Government's rights to use the data for acquisition purposes.

(b) The data evaluation process may be divided into two stages:

(1) A brief but intensive analysis of available data and documents regarding both technical matters and data rights, leading to a decision whether to proceed with screening; and

(2) If the decision is to proceed with screening, further work is necessary to produce an adequate technical data package, such as research of contract provisions, engineering work on data and drawings, and requests to contractors for additional data.

(c) The steps in this phase are—

(1) *Step 2.* Are full Government rights established by the available data package? Evidence for an affirmative answer would include the identification of Government drawings, incorporation by reference of Government specifications or process descriptions in the public domain, or reference to contract provisions giving the Government rights to data. If the answer is negative, proceed to step 3; if positive, proceed to step 6.

(2) *Step 3.* Are the contractor's limitations of the Government's rights to data established by the available data package?

(i) The questions in step 2 and 3 are not exclusive. The incorporation in a drawing of contract provisions reserving rights to the manufacturer, either in the whole design or in certain manufacturing processes, would establish a clear affirmative answer to step 3 where there is substantiating Government documentation. Parts not in this group shall be retained for further processing (see step 20). Data rights that cannot be substantiated shall be challenged (see DFARS Part 227, validation procedures).

(ii) In the case of clear contractor ownership of rights, proceed with steps 4 and 5.

(3) *Step 4.* Are there bases for competitive acquisition without using data subject to limitations on use? This question requires consideration, for example, of the possibility of using performance specifications or substitution of military or commercial specifications or bulletins for limited elements of the manufacturing process. The use of sample copies is another possibility.

(4) *Step 5.* Can the Government buy the necessary rights to data? This is a preliminary question to the full analysis (in steps 20 and 21 below) and is designed primarily to eliminate from further consideration those items which incorporate established data restrictions and for which there are no other bases for competitive acquisition nor is purchase of rights possible or feasible.

(5) *Steps 6 and 7.* Is the present technical data package adequate for competitive acquisition of a reliable part?

(6) *Steps 8 and 9.* Specify omissions. The question in steps 6 and 7 requires a critical engineering evaluation and should deal first with the physical completeness of the date—are any essential dimensions, tolerances, processes, finishes, material specifications, or other vital elements of data lacking from the package? If so, these omissions should be specified. A second element deals with adequacy of the existing package to produce a part of the required performance, compatibility, quality, and reliability. This will, of course, be related to the completeness of data. In some cases, qualified engineering judgment may decide that, in spite of apparently complete data, the high performance or other critical characteristics of the item require retention of the present source. If such decision is made, the file shall include documentation in the form of specific information, such as difficulties experienced by the present manufacturer in producing a satisfactory item or the existence of unique production skills in the present source.

(7) *Steps 10 and 11.* Can the data be developed to make up a reliable technical data package? This implies a survey of the specified omissions with careful consideration to determine the resources available to supply each missing element. Such resources will vary from simple referencing of standard engineering publications to more complex development of drawings with the alternatives of either obtaining such drawings or developing performance specifications. In some cases, certain elements of data are missing because they have been properly restricted. If, however, there has been no advance sub-

stantiation of the right to restrict, the part should be further researched. If the answer to this question is negative, proceed to step 12; if positive, proceed to step 13 or 14.

(8) *Step 12.* If the answer to the question in steps 10 and 11 is no, which condition is the prime element in this decision, the lack of data or the unreliability of the data? Specific documentation is needed to support this decision.

(9) *Step 13 and 14.* Estimate the time required to complete the data package. In those cases where the data package is found inadequate and specific additions need to be developed, an estimate of the time required for completion must be made in order to determine if breakout of the part is feasible during this review cycle and to estimate at what point in the remaining life of the part the data package could be available.

3-303.3 Data completion phase (steps 15-21).

(a) The data completion phase involves acquiring or developing the missing elements of information to reach a determination on both adequacy of the technical data package and the restriction of rights to data. It may involve various functional responsibilities, such as examination of past contracts, queries directed to industry or to other Government agencies, inspection of the part, reverse or other engineering work to develop drawings and write specifications, arrangements with the present source for licensing or technical assistance to new manufacturers, and negotiations for purchase of rights to data. Additional research and information requests should be expeditiously initiated on those parts where there is a reasonable expectation of breakout. Because this phase is time-consuming, it should take place concurrently with other phases of the review.

(b) At the beginning of the data completion phase, the part falls into one of the following four steps:

(1) *Step 15.* The data package is complete and adequate and the Government has sufficient rights for acquisition purposes. Such parts require no further data analysis. Proceed to step 22.

(2) *Step 16.* The Government has rights to existing data. The data package is incomplete but there is a reasonable expectation that the missing elements can be supplied. Proceed to step 19.

(3) *Step 17.* The data package is complete, but suitable Government rights to the data have not been established. Proceed to step 20.

(4) *Step 18.* Neither rights nor completeness of data is adequately established; therefore, the part requires further research. Proceed to step 20.

(c) *Step 19.* Obtain or develop the necessary data for a suitable data package. Reverse engineering to develop acquisition data may be used if there is a clear indication that the costs of reverse engineering will be less than the savings anticipated from competitive acquisition. If there is a choice between reverse engineering and the purchase of data (step 21), the decision shall be made on the basis of relative costs, quality, time, and other pertinent factors.

(d) *Step 20.* Establish the Government's and contractor's rights to the data. Where drawings and data cannot be identified to a contract, the following guidelines should be applied:

(1) Where drawings and data bear legends that warn of copyright or patent rights, the effect of such legends shall be resolved according to law and policy; however, the existence of patent or copyright restrictions does not per se preclude securing competition with respect to the parts described (see FAR Subpart 27.3/DFARS Subpart 227.3).

(2) If the technical data bears legends that limit the Government's right to use the data for breakout and it is determined that reasonable grounds exist to question the current validity of the restrictive markings, the contracting officer will be notified to initiate the validation procedures at DFARS Subpart 227.4.

(3) Where drawings and data are unmarked and, therefore, free of limitation on their use, they shall be considered available for use in acquisition, unless the acquiring office has clear evidence to the contrary (see DFARS Subpart 227.4).

(4) The decision process in situations described in paragraphs (d)(1), (2), and (3) of this subsection requires the exercise of sound discretion and judgment and embraces legal considerations. In no case shall a decision be made without review and approval of that decision by legal counsel.

(5) If the validation procedures in paragraph (d)(2) of this subsection establish the Government's right to use the data for breakout, the Government shall attempt to obtain competition pursuant to the decisions resulting from concurrent technical and economic evaluation.

(e) *Step 21.* If restrictions on the use of data are established, determine whether the Government can buy rights to the required data. Use the procedure in DFARS Subpart 227.4.

3-303.4 Technical evaluation phase (steps 22-37).

(a) *Introduction.*

(1) The purposes of technical evaluation are to determine the development status, design stability, high performance, and/or critical characteristics such as safety of personnel and equipment; the reliability and effective operation of the system and equipment in which the parts are to be used; and to exercise technical judgment as to the feasibility of breaking out the parts. No simple and universal rules apply to each determination. The application of experience and responsible judgment is required. Technical considerations arise in several elements of the decision process, e.g., in determining adequacy of the data package (steps 6-14).

(2) Certain manufacturing conditions may reduce the field of potential sources. However, these conditions do not justify the restriction of competition by the assignment of restrictive AMCs for the following reasons:

(i) *Parts produced from class 1 castings and similar type forgings.* The process of developing and providing the acceptability of high-integrity castings and forgings requires repetitive performance by a controlled source for each casting or forging along identical lines to those which result in initial acceptability of the item. The particular manufacturer's process becomes the controlling factor with regard to the acceptability of any such item. However, other firms can produce class 1 castings and similar type forgings and provide the necessary inspection, or the part may be acquired from other sources that use castings or forgings from approved (controlled) source(s).

(ii) *Parts produced from master or coordinated tooling, e.g., numerically controlled tapes.* Such parts have features (contoured surfaces, hole locations, etc.) delineated according to unique master tooling or tapes and are manufactured to minimum/maximum limits and must be replaceable without additional tailoring or fitting. These parts cannot be manufactured or configured by a secondary pattern or jigs independent of the master tooling and cannot be manufactured to requisite tolerances of fit by use of commercial precision machinery. In this context, jigs and fixtures used only for ease of production are not considered master tooling. However, master tooling may be reproduced.

(iii) *Parts requiring special test and/or inspection facilities to determine and maintain ultra-precision quality for the function or system integrity.* Substantiation and inspection of the precision or quality cannot be accomplished without specialized test or inspection facilities. Testing is often done by the actual manufacturer under actual operating use. However, such special test inspection facilities may be available at other firms.

(b) *Design procedures (steps 22-31).*

(1) *Step 22.* Will a design change occur during anticipated lead time? If affirmative, proceed to step 23; if negative, proceed to step 24.

(2) *Step 23.* Specify the design change and assign an appropriate code.

(3) *Step 24.* Is a satisfactory part now being produced? Concurrently with the research and completion of data, a technical determination is required as to the developmental status of the part. With the frequent telescoping of the development/production cycle as well as constant product improvement throughout the active life of equipment, parts are frequently subject to design changes. The present source, if a prime con-

tractor, is usually committed to incorporate the latest changes in any deliveries under a production order. In considering the part for breakout, an assessment must be made of the stability of design, so that in buying from a new source the Government will not be purchasing an obsolete or incompatible part. The question of obsolescence or noncompatibility is to some extent under Government control. Screening for breakout on parts that are anticipated to undergo design change should be deferred until design stability is attained.

(4) *Step 25.* Can a satisfactory part be produced by a new source? Determine whether technical reasons prohibit seeking a new source. The fact that the present source has not yet been able to produce a satisfactory part (step 24) does not preclude another source from being successful. If the answer to steps 24 or 25 is affirmative, proceed simultaneously to steps 27 and 38. If the answer to step 25 is negative, proceed to step 26.

(5) *Step 26.* If the present source is producing an unsatisfactory part, but technical reasons prohibit seeking a new source, specify the reasons.

(6) *Step 27.* Does the part require prior qualification or other approval testing? If the answer is positive, proceed to step 28; if negative, proceed to step 32.

(8) *Step 28.* Specify the requirement.

(9) *Step 29.* Estimate the time required to qualify a new source.

(10) *Step 30.* Is there currently a qualified source?

(11) *Step 31.* Who is responsible for qualifications of the subcontractor, present prime contractor, the Government, or an independent testing agency?

(i) If a qualified source is currently in existence, the review should consider who will be responsible for qualification in the event of competitive acquisition. If qualification testing is such that it can be performed by the selected source under a preproduction or first article clause in the contract, the costs of initial approval should be reflected in the offers received. If the part requires initial qualification tests by some other agency such as the present prime contractor, the Government, an independent testing agent outside the Government, or by technical facilities within the departments, out-of-pocket costs may be incurred if the part is competed. An estimate of qualification costs should then be made and recorded in such cases.

(ii) Where facilities within the Government are not adequate for testing or qualification, or outside agencies such as the equipment contractor cannot or will not do the job, the economics of qualification may be unreasonable, and a narrative statement of these facts should replace the cost estimate. Whenever possible, such as in the case of engine qualification tests, economy of combined qualification tests should be considered.

(c) *Quality assurance procedures (steps 32-33).* Quality control and inspection is a primary consideration when making a decision to breakout. Where the prime contractor performs quality assurance functions beyond those of the part manufacturer or other sources, the Government may—

(1) Develop the same quality control and inspection capability in the manufacturer's plant;

(2) Assume the responsibility for quality; or

(3) Undertake to obtain the quality assurance services from another source, possibly the prime contractor.

(4) *Step 32.* Who is now responsible for quality control and inspection of the part?

(5) *Step 33.* Can a new source be assigned responsibility for quality control? Is the level of the quality assurance requirements specified in the system contract necessary for the screened part? The minimum quality assurance procedures for each part shall be confirmed.

(i) A new source shall be considered if—

(A) Any essential responsibility (e.g., burn-in, reliability, maintainability) retained by the prime contractor for the part and its relationship to the end item can be eliminated, shifted to the new source, or assumed by the Government;

(B) The prime contractor will provide the needed quality assurance services;

(C) The Government can obtain competent, impartial services to perform quality assurance responsibility; or

(D) The new source can maintain an adequate quality assurance program, inspection system, or inspection appropriate for the part.

(ii) If the prime contractor has responsibility for quality that a new source cannot assume or obtain, or that the Government cannot undertake or eliminate, consideration of the new source is precluded.

(d) *Tooling procedures (steps 34-37).*

(1) *Step 34.* Is tooling or other special equipment required?

(2) *Step 35.* Specify the type of tooling.

(3) *Step 36.* Estimate additional acquisition leadtime for setup and for tooling.

(4) *Step 37.* Does the Government possess this tooling? If tooling or special equipment is required for production of the part, the types and quantities should be specified. Investigation can then be made as to whether the Government possesses such tooling and can make it available to a new source. A requirement for special tooling is not necessarily a deterrent to competitive solicitation for parts. The Government may find it desirable to purchase the needed tooling and furnish it to the new source. In this case, the costs can be determined with reasonable accuracy. However, if new sources can provide the tooling or special equipment, this will be reflected in competitive prices and should not normally require further analysis.

3-303.5 Economic evaluation phase (steps 38-56).

(a) Economic evaluation concerns identification and estimation of breakout savings and direct cost offsets to breakout. The economic evaluation phase is composed of the three segments detailed in paragraphs (b) through (d) of this subsection.

(b) *Development of savings data (steps 38-40).*

(1) *Step 38.* Estimate remaining program life cycle buy value.

(2) *Step 39.* Apply either a savings factor of 25 percent or one determined under local conditions and experience.

(3) *Step 40.* Multiply the remaining program life cycle buy value by the savings factor to obtain the expected future savings, if the part is coded for breakout.

(c) *Computation of breakout costs (steps 41-47).* Several groups of costs must be collected, summarized and compared to estimated savings to properly determine the economics of breakout. These costs include—

(1) *Direct costs (steps 41-45).* Direct costs of breakout normally include all expenditures that are direct and wholly identifiable to a specific, successful breakout action, and that are not reflected in the part unit price. Examples of direct costs include Government tooling or special test equipment, qualification testing, quality control expenses, and industry participation costs (such as completion of the Contractor Technical Information Data Record) if borne by the Government.

(i) *Step 41.* Estimate the cost to the Government for tooling or special equipment.

(ii) *Step 42.* Estimate the cost, if any, to the Government for qualifying the new source.

(iii) *Step 43.* Estimate the cost, if any, to the Government for assuring quality control, or the cost of contracting for quality control.

(iv) *Step 44.* Estimate the cost to the Government for purchasing rights to data.

(v) *Step 45.* Add estimated total direct costs to the Government to breakout the item.

(2) *Performance specification costs (steps 46-47).*

(i) *Step 46.* Is the breakout candidate constructed to a performance specification?

(ii) *Step 47.* If the answer is yes in step 46, add performance specification breakout cost estimate elements to the result of step 45. The addition of an unknown number of nonstocked parts that must be stocked by the supply system for repairs is a significant element of cost associated with the decision to compete a performance specification assembly. (The same situation does not arise with respect to a design specification assembly, since virtually all spare parts used to repair such an assembly are essentially identical to parts already in the assembly.) The cost of introducing these nonstocked parts into the system includes—

(A) Additional catalog costs. The number of nonstocked parts forecasted to be in the competed assembly, multiplied by the variable cost of cataloging per line item.

(B) Additional bin opening costs. The number of nonstocked parts forecasted to be in the competed assembly, multiplied by the variable cost of a bin opening at each of the locations where the part is to be stocked.

(C) Additional management costs. The number of nonstocked parts forecasted to be in the competed assembly, multiplied by the variable cost of management per line item.

(D) Additional technical data costs. The cost of a new set of technical data for the competed assembly, including the variable expenses of its production, reproduction, and distribution.

(E) Additional repair tools and test equipment costs. The costs of additional special tools and test equipment not otherwise required by the existing assembly.

(F) Additional logistics support costs. The costs associated with the new item such as spare and repair parts, technical manuals, and training.

(d) *Comparison of savings and costs (steps 48-56)*. Compare estimated breakout costs to forecasted breakout savings. If costs exceed estimated savings, it will be uneconomical to compete the part. Performance specification parts should be analyzed to ensure that pertinent breakout costs have been considered and, if it is not economical to breakout the part, whether an appropriate detailed design data package reduces costs sufficiently to make breakout economical.

(1) *Step 48*. Compare total costs of breakout (step 47) to estimated savings (step 40).

(2) *Step 49*. Are costs of breakout greater or less than estimated savings? If greater, proceed to step 50; if yes, proceed to step 51.

(3) *Step 50*. Is the breakout candidate constructed to a performance specification? If no, proceed to step 54; if yes, proceed to step 57.

(4) *Step 51*. Is it appropriate to obtain a detailed design data package? If yes, proceed to step 52; if no, proceed to step 54. The decision to change a performance specification part to a detailed design part obviously requires a critical engineering examination of the part itself, as well as a review of the impact such a change might have on the operational effectiveness of the system in which the equipment is to be employed. Acquisition of a performance specification part by a subsequently acquired design specification subjects the Government to the additional hazard of losing the money paid for the development of the design specification, should the design be altered during the contracting leadtime period. Accordingly, the engineering evaluation should closely review design stability over the anticipated contracting leadtime in order to avoid acquiring an obsolete or nonstandard part if the decision is made to compete it.

(5) *Step 52*. Add the estimated cost of obtaining a detailed design data package to the results of step 45.

(6) *Step 53*. If the results of step 52 are less than the estimated savings, initiate action to obtain a detailed design data package. Proceed to step 54 to code the part for a period until it can be rescreened using the design specification package. The code determined in this screening shall be assigned a suspense date commensurate with the leadtime required to obtain the detailed design data package (see 2-203(b)).

(7) *Step 54*. Is the part manufactured by the prime contractor? If yes, code the part AMC 3; if no, proceed to step 55.

(8) *Step 55*. Can the part be acquired directly from the actual manufacturer? If no, proceed to step 56; if yes, code the part AMC 3 or 4, as applicable.

(9) *Step 56*. Specify the reasons for inability to obtain the part from the actual manufacturer. Code the part AMC 5.

3-303.6 Supply feedback phase (steps 57-65).

(a) The supply feedback phase of the analysis is the final screening phase for breakout parts. This phase in completed for all AMC 2 parts to determine if sufficient time is available to break out on the immediate buy and to communicate this information to the inventory manager responsible for the requirement. First, all additional time factors required to break out the part are added. Total time is subtracted from the immediate and future buy date and the result compared to the current date. (Note: Not all time factors listed apply to each part screened.) If the result is the same or earlier than the required contract date, the part is coded competitive and action is begun to qualify additional sources as necessary. If the result is later than the required contract date, action to compete the immediate buy quantity should be initiated if the inventory manager can find some means of accepting later delivery. If this is impossible, the appropriate records should be annotated for competitive acquisition of the next replenishment buy quantity. If late delivery is acceptable, the inventory manager should compute requirements for the part and initiate an appropriate purchase requisition.

(b) *Procedures.*

(1) *Step 57.* Add all additional time factors required to break out the part (steps 13, 14, 29, and 36).

(2) *Step 58.* Add the results of step 57 to the date of this review.

(3) *Step 59.* Compare the result of step 58 to the date that the contract or order must be placed.

(4) *Step 60.* Is the result of step 59 earlier than, later than, or the same as the contract or order date? (If earlier or the same, proceed to step 61; if later, proceed to step 63.)

(5) *Step 61.* Can supply accept late delivery? If yes, proceed to step 62; if no, proceed to step 63.

(6) *Step 62.* Notify the inventory manager to compute requirements and initiate a purchase requisition. Proceed to step 64.

(7) *Step 63.* Code the part AMC 2. Insufficient time to compete on this buy.

(8) *Step 64.* Code the part AMC 2.

(9) *Step 65.* Begin actions to qualify new sources, if required and possible.

3-304 Limited screening procedures.

(a) Limited screening procedures are only appropriate when the full screening process cannot be completed for a part in sufficient time to support an immediate buy requirement. If limited screening does not result in a competitive AMC and the part is characterized by a high buy value and high buy quantity in the annual buy forecast, full screening procedures shall be immediately initiated.

(b) Limited screening procedures cover only the essential points of data and technical evaluations more completely described in full screening procedures (see 3-303). Extensive legal review of rights or technical review of data is not required; nor is backup information on type and extent of qualification testing, quality control procedures and master tooling required. A summary flow chart of the limited screening decision steps is provided at Exhibit III.

(c) The limited screening decision steps are followed sequentially if the answer to the question in each step is affirmative. If any step is answered in the negative, proceed directly to step 10.

(1) *Step 1.* Assemble all available data and establish a file for each part. Collect identification data, relevant data obtained from industry, contracting and technical history data and current status of the part (see 3-303.1).

(2) *Step 2.* Do the available documents establish Government rights to use the data for acquisition purposes? If the Government's rights to use data in its possession is questionable, resolution of the rights must continue beyond award of the immediate buy.

(3) *Step 3.* Is the data package sufficient, accurate, and legible? If the Government does not have in its possession sufficient, accurate, or legible data, action shall be promptly initiated to resolve the deficiency for the next buy.

(4) *Step 4.* Is the design of the part stable over the anticipated acquisition lead time?

(5) *Step 5.* Is a satisfactory part now being produced?

(6) *Step 6.* Can the part be acquired from a new source without prior qualification testing or other approval testing?

(7) *Step 7.* Can the Government or a new source be responsible for quality assurance?

(8) *Step 8.* Can the part be manufactured without master or coordinated tooling or other special equipment; if no, is there more than one source that has the tooling or special equipment?

(9) *Step 9.* Assign AMC 2. Proceed to step 11.

(10) *Step 10.* Assign AMC 3, 4, or 5, as appropriate.

(11) *Step 11.* Establish the date of the next review (see 1-104(c) and 2-203(b)).

PART 4 CONTRACTOR'S ASSISTANCE

4-400 General.

(a) Contractor's assistance in screening shall be requested on provisioned and replenishment parts after consideration of the benefit expected from the contractor's technical information and the cost to the Government of obtaining such assistance.

(b) Contractor's assistance shall not be requested for parts covered by Government/industry specifications, commercially available parts or parts for which data is already available.

(c) Arrangements entered into with contractors to obtain technical information shall provide that—

(1) Contractors will exert their best effort to make impartial technical evaluations using applicable technical data and the experience of competent personnel; and

(2) No costs to the Government will be incurred for duplicate screening of parts.

4-401 Contractor's technical evaluation procedures.

(a) Contractor's technical evaluation for the screening process shall be required contractually by incorporating MIL-STD-789, which delineates the contractor's responsibilities and procedures and prescribes use of the contractor DD Form 1418, Technical Information Record, and the DD Form 1418-1, Technical Data Identification Checklist, a copy of each document listed on DD Form 1418-1, and other substantive data that was used in developing the contractor's recommendations.

(b) When MIL-STD-789 is incorporated in a contract, the DD Form 1423, Contract Data Requirements List, shall specify the requirement for the submission of DD Form 1418, Technical Information Record, and DD Form 1418-1, Technical Data Identification Checklist, in accordance with MIL-STD-789.

PART 5 REPORTING SYSTEM

5-500 General.

This part prescribes reports regarding the breakout program that cannot be obtained from other sources. These reports are used to evaluate the effectiveness of breakout programs, establish a baseline for all spare part acquisitions, and identify trends in spare parts acquisition.

5-501 Reports.

(a) *Spare Parts Breakout Screening Report (RCS DD P&L(Q&SA)714A).* This is a cumulative semi-annual report reflecting the accomplishments of the breakout program. The report describes the results of full and limited screening for provisioning and replenishment parts by number of different NSNs for each AMC. Departments and agencies shall also maintain actual cost data attributable to the Spare Parts Breakout Program which shall be forwarded on this report semi-annually.

(b) *Spare Parts Acquisition Report (RCS DD P&L(Q&SA) 714B).* This is a cumulative semi-annual report for all purchases made of spare parts during the current fiscal year. This report describes the number and extended dollar value of different NSNs purchased for each AMC. Departments and agencies shall also maintain actual savings (or cost avoidance) data attributable to the Spare Parts Breakout Program which shall be forwarded on this report semi-annually. Because of extraneous factors such as contracting lead times and changes in spare parts requirements, this report will not always reflect the acquisition of the parts screened during a reporting period (contained on the Spare Parts Breakout Screening Report). Also, it will not show in all instances how the part was actually acquired. This report is intended to be an indication of the success of the breakout program, and designed to show trends in the coding and data available to buyers in the acquisition package.

5-502 Reporting procedures.

(a) Departments and agencies shall maintain and forward semi-annual reports. The second semi-annual report in a fiscal year shall reflect cumulative totals for the current fiscal year using the formats in Exhibits IV and V.

(b) The reports will be due no later than 45 days after the end of each period designated.

(c) Submissions will be made to the Under Secretary of Defense (Acquisition, Technology, and Logistics).

5-503 Reporting instructions.

(a) *Spare parts breakout screening report.* Using the format in Exhibit IV, provide the following—

(1) Enter reporting activity name, fiscal year, and period ending.

(2) For each AMC/AMSC listed, enter the number of different NSNs for which screening was completed during the period. Show zeros where applicable. This should be done for both full and limited screening.

(3) Report the total costs of the breakout program incurred for the period. Although this will be primarily labor costs, it should also include appropriate prorated costs of ADP services, office overhead, data retrieval service costs, etc. (see 3-303.5).

(b) *Spare parts acquisition report.* Using the format in Exhibit V, provide the following:

(1) Enter reporting activity name, fiscal year, and period ending.

(2) For each AMC/AMSC listed, enter the number of different NSNs purchased during the current fiscal year and their extended dollar value.

(3) Report the actual breakout program savings or cost avoidances as measured by completed acquisition (not anticipated acquisitions). Price differentials should be measured on each acquisition where a breakout action has taken place. They should equal the difference between the previous contract unit price and the current contract unit price, times the number of units purchased.

EXHIBIT I VALID AMC/AMSC COMBINATIONS

	Acquisition Method Code (AMC)					
AMSC	0	1	2	3	4	5
A	X	○	○	○	○	○
B	X	○	○	○	○	○
C	X	○	○	○	○	○
D	X	X	X	○	○	○
G	X	○	○	X	X	X
H	X	○	○	○	○	○
K	X	○	○	○	○	○
L	X	○	○	○	○	○
M	X	○	○	○	○	○
N	X	○	○	○	○	○
O	○	X	X	X	X	X
P	X	○	○	○	○	○

	Acquisition Method Code (AMC)					
AMSC	0	1	2	3	4	5
Q	X	○	○	○	○	○
R	X	○	○	○	○	○
S	X	○	○	○	○	○
T	X	○	○	X	X	X
U	X	○	○	○	○	○
V	X	○	○	○	○	○
Y	X	○	○	○	○	○
Z	X	○	○	○	○	○

○ = VALID COMBINATION

X = INVALID COMBINATIONS

EXHIBIT II— FULL SCREENING DECISION PROCESS SUMMARY FLOW CHART

NOTE: Copies of Exhibit II can be obtained from: Defense Acquisition Regulations System, OUSD(AT&L)DPAP/DARS, 3062 Defense Pentagon, Washington, DC 20301-3060; facsimile (703) 602-0350; e-mail: *osd.pentagon.ousd-atl.mbx.dfars@mail.mil*.

EXHIBIT III— LIMITED SCREENING DECISION PROCESS SUMMARY FLOW CHART

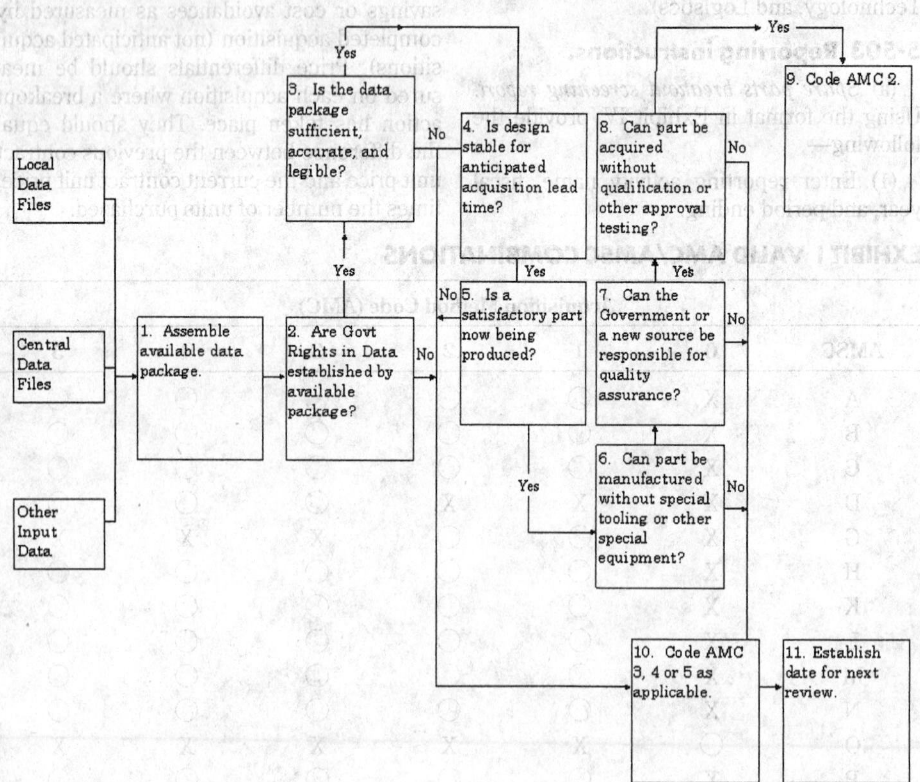

EXHIBIT IV— SPARE PARTS BREAKOUT SCREENING REPORT

SPARE PARTS BREAKOUT SCREENING REPORT

Report Activity ______ Fiscal Year ______ Period Ending

NUMBER OF NSNs

AMC/AMSC	LIMITED SCREENING	FULL SCREENING	TOTAL SCREENING
*1G Only			
1			
**2G Only			
2			
3			
4			
5			
TOTAL			

SPARE PARTS BREAKOUT PROGRAM COSTS $ ______

* Excluded from AMC 1 data
** Excluded from AMC 2 data

EXHIBIT V— SPARE PARTS ACQUISITION REPORT

SPARE PARTS ACQUISITION REPORT

Report Activity Fiscal Year ______ Period Ending

PURCHASE MADE

AMC/AMSC	NUMBER OF NSNs	EXTENDED DOLLAR VALUE
*1G Only		
1		
**2G Only		
2		
3		
4		
5		
TOTAL		

SPARE PARTS BREAKOUT PROGRAM SAVINGS OR COST AVOIDANCES $ ______

* Excluded from AMC 1 data
** Excluded from AMC 2 data

[Final rule, 71 FR 27642, 5/12/2006, effective 5/12/2006; Publication notice, 20101103; Publication notice, 20101112; Final rule, 78 FR 54968, 9/9/2013, effective 9/9/2013]

SUBPART 217.76—CONTRACTS WITH PROVISIONING REQUIREMENTS

217.7601 Provisioning.

(1) *Definitions.* As used in this section—

(i) *Provisioning* means the process of determining and acquiring the range and quantity of spare and repair parts, and support and test equipment required to operate and maintain an end item for an initial period of service.

(ii) *Provisioned item* means any item selected under provisioning procedures.

(iii) *Provisioned items order* means an undefinitized order issued under a contract that includes the Government's requirements for provisioned items. (Provisioned items with firm prices are acquired by supplemental agreement or by separate contract.)

(iv) *Provisioning activity* means the organization responsible for selecting and determining requirements for provisioned items.

(v) *Provisioning requirements statement* means the contractual document listing the specific provisioning requirements for that contract. The statement normally includes—

(A) Instructions, such as the provisioning method to be used;

(B) The extent of provisioning technical documentation and data needed (including administrative requirements for submission and distribution);

(C) The type and location of provisioning conferences;

(D) Sample article requirements;

(E) The delivery schedule;

(F) Packaging and marking requirements for provisioned items; and

(G) Requirements for provisioning screening.

(vi) *Provisioning technical documentation* means the data needed for the identification, selection, determination of initial requirements, and cataloging of support items to be acquired through the provisioning process. It includes such things as provisioning lists and logistics support analysis summaries. Descriptive data such as drawings and photographs are referred to as *supplementary provisioning technical documentation.*

(2) *Contractual provisions.* Contracts containing provisioning requirements shall—

(i) List the provisioning functions to be performed and who will perform them;

(ii) Include a provisioning requirements statement or specify a time limit for its incorporation into the contract by modification (revisions to the provisioning requirements statement shall also be incorporated by contract modification);

(iii) Include on the DD Form 1423, Contract Data Requirements List, a schedule for delivery of provisioning technical documentation, or provide for the schedule to be incorporated later by contract modification;

(iv) Require flow down of the appropriate provisioning technical documentation requirement when the subcontractor prepares the documentation;

(v) Specify any applicable procedures for interim release by the contractor of long lead time items, and include ordering and funding instructions for such items. As a minimum, the instructions shall require the contractor to advise the contracting officer or provisioning activity at least 30 days before release of the items, their estimated costs, and the effective date of release;

(vi) Specify the activity designated to issue provisioned items orders, i.e., contracting officer, provisioning activity, or administrative contracting officer. When it is expected that more than one activity will place provisioned items orders against the contract, state the requirements for provisioned items of each activity as separate contract line items;

(vii) Provide a definitization schedule (normally 120 days after receipt of the contractor's proposal) and a time frame for the contractor to furnish price proposals for provisioned items orders (normally 60 days after order issuance);

(viii) Specify exhibit identifiers applicable to the contract line/subline items; and

(ix) Include procedures for processing changes (including cancellations) in quantities of items ordered.

(3) *Issuance of provisioned items orders.*

(i) Use the Standard Form 30, Amendment of Solicitation/Modification of Contract, to—

(A) Issue provisioned items orders;

(B) Decrease or cancel quantities of items ordered; and

(C) Cover the contractor's interim release of long lead items when the contracting officer approves the release (if the release is not approved, the contracting officer shall notify the contractor to cancel the items).

(ii) Include in Block 14 of the Standard Form 30—

(A) The term PROVISIONED ITEMS ORDER in capital letters and underlined; and

(B) The appropriate exhibit identifier(s) for all attached exhibits.

(iii) Obligate funds to cover the estimated price of the items being ordered. Show individual estimated prices for each exhibit line item on the accounting and payment office copies.

(iv) Distribution is the same as for the basic contract (see FAR Subpart 4.2). However, if the exhibits are voluminous, the contracting officer may restrict distribution of the exhibits to the contract administration office.

(v) See DFARS Subpart 217.74 for additional guidance and limitations on the use of undefinitized contract actions.

(4) *Provisioning conferences.* When requested by the contracting officer or provisioning activity, the contract administration office shall assist the contracting officer or provisioning activity in scheduling and determining the types of provisioning conferences required, e.g., guidance meetings, long lead time items conferences, source coding meetings.

(5) *Contract administration office monitoring.*

The contract administration office (CAO) shall monitor contracts containing provisioning requirements. As a minimum the CAO shall—

(i) Ensure that the contractor understands the provisioning requirements;

(ii) Review contractor progress in the preparation of provisioning technical documentation and, if requested by the contracting officer or provisioning activity, inspect it for format and content;

(iii) Ensure the prime contractor flows down provisioning requirements to any subcontractor charged with preparation of documentation;

(iv) Advise the contracting office or provisioning activity of delays in delivery of provisioning technical documentation or other related problems (see FAR Subpart 42.11);

(v) Ensure contractor compliance with contract requirements concerning the assignment of national stock numbers; and

(vi) Ensure that the contractor complies with contractual criteria for release of long lead time items.

(6) *Negotiating and executing supplemental agreements.*

(i) The administrative contracting officer (ACO) shall definitize provisioned items orders within the prescribed schedule.

(ii) If the provisioned items order does not contain a delivery date, or the contractor cannot meet the date, the ACO shall coordinate the negotiated schedule with the contracting officer or provisioning activity before execution of the supplemental agreement.

(iii) The ACO shall maintain records of provisioned items orders showing—

(A) The adequacy of obligated funds;

(B) Due dates for price proposals; and

(C) Actions taken to obtain additional funds or to deobligate excess funds.

[Final rule, 71 FR 27642, 5/12/2006, effective 5/12/2006]

SUBPART 217.77—OVER AND ABOVE WORK

217.7701 Procedures.

(1) Contracts for the performance of maintenance, overhaul, modification, and repair of various items (e.g., aircraft, engines, ground support equipment, ships) generally contain over and above work requirements. When they do, the contracting officer shall establish a separate contract line item for the over and above work.

(2) Over and above requirements task the contractor to identify needed repairs and recommend corrective action during contract performance. The contractor submits a work request to identify the over and above work and, as appropriate, the Government authorizes the contractor to proceed.

(3) The clause at DFARS *252.217-7028*, Over and Above Work, requires the contractor and the contracting officer responsible for administering the contract to negotiate specific procedures for Government administration and contractor performance of over and above work requests.

(4) The contracting officer may issue a blanket work request authorization describing the manner in which individual over and above work requests will be administered and setting forth a dollar limitation for all over and above work under the contract. The blanket work request authorization may be in the form of a letter or contract modification (Standard Form 30).

(5) Over and above work requests are within the scope of the contract. Therefore, procedures in DFARS subpart *217.74*, Undefinitized Contract Actions, do not apply.

(6) To the maximum extent practical, over and above work shall be negotiated prior to performance of the work.

[Final rule, 71 FR 14102, 3/21/2006, effective 3/21/2006; Final rule, 71 FR 27642, 5/12/2006, effective 5/12/2006; Publication notice, 20171208]

SUBPART 217.78—REMOVED

217.7802 [Removed]

[Final rule, 71 FR 14102, 3/21/2006, effective 3/21/2006; Change notice 20071108; Interim rule, 74 FR 34270, 7/15/2009, effective 7/15/2009; Final rule, 75 FR 6819, 2/11/2010, effective 3/15/2010; Final rule, 79 FR 56278, 9/19/2014, effective 9/19/2014; Final rule, 80 FR 51750, 8/26/2015, effective 8/26/2015]

PART 218—EMERGENCY ACQUISITIONS

Table of Contents

Subpart 218.2—Emergency Acquisition Flexibilities

Use of electronic business tools 218.271

PART 218—EMERGENCY ACQUISITIONS

SUBPART 218.2—EMERGENCY ACQUISITION FLEXIBILITIES

218.271 Use of electronic business tools.

(a) Use of electronic business (e-business) acquisition tools greatly enhances the efficacy of the contracting process in a contingency business environment (CBE). The CBE involves specific tools, policies, roles and responsibilities, and processes necessary to streamline delivery of goods and services to the end user and to implement an e-business program with the capabilities necessary to support an end-to-end electronic acquisition process in order to quickly obtain goods and services for the warfighter in an operational area. For information and procedures to effectively utilize CBE e-business tools, and additional policy references supporting use of the e-business tools, see the DoD CBE Guidebook at *http://www.acq.osd.mil/dpap/pacc/cc/docs/CBE_Guidebook.docx*.

(b) Use of the following CBE e-business tools is mandatory when supporting a contingency or humanitarian or peacekeeping operation as defined in FAR 2.101:

(1) The 3in1 Tool. The 3in1 Tool automates the field order, receipt, and purchase processes previously executed manually using the paper Standard Form (SF) 44. The 3in1 handheld device records and transmits cash and carry type purchases and payment data to the prime database for remote reconciliation and review, when conducting on-the-spot, over-the-counter field purchases where use of the Government Purchase Card is appropriate, but not feasible. The 3in1 database may be accessed on the Joint Contingency Contracting Systems (JCCS) website at *https://www.jccs.gov/olvr/*.

(2) The Acquisition Cross-Servicing Agreements (ACSA) Global Automated Tracking and Reporting System (AGATRS). AGATRS is an automated tool that tracks and provides visibility into worldwide ACSAs that may satisfy a requirement through support from the host nation or other nations supporting the contingency. ACSA transactions that are used in support of contingency or humanitarian or peacekeeping operations are required to be documented and tracked in AGATRS as required by the Chairman of the Joint Chiefs of Staff Instruction 2120.01C, Acquisition Cross Servicing Agreements (*http://dtic.mil/cjcs_directives/cdata/unlimit/2120_01.pdf*). AGATRS is accessible on the JCCS website at *https://www.jccs.gov/olvr*.

(c) No other electronic tools may be used to fulfill the same capabilities as 3in1 and AGATRS.

(d) See PGI 225.370(a)(ii) regarding use of the Theater Business Clearance CBE e-business tool.

[Final rule, 80 FR 10390, 2/26/2015, effective 2/26/2015; Final rule, 80 FR 36900, 6/26/2015, effective 6/26/2015; Final rule, 83 FR 24888, 5/30/2018, effective 5/30/2018]

PART 219—SMALL BUSINESS PROGRAMS

Table of Contents

Subpart 219.2—Policies

General policy 219.201

Subpart 219.6—Certificates of Competency

Procedures 219.602
Referral 219.602-1
Resolving differences between the agency and the Small Business Administration 219.603

Subpart 219.7—The Small Business Subcontracting Program

[Removed] 219.702
Responsibilities of the contracting officer under the subcontracting assistance program 219.705
Reviewing the subcontracting plan 219.705-4
Postaward responsibilities of the contracting officer 219.705-6

Subpart 219.8—Contracting with the Small Business Administration (The 8(a) Program)

General 219.800
Selecting acquisitions for the 8(a) Program 219.803
Evaluation, offering, and acceptance 219.804
Agency offering 219.804-2
SBA acceptance 219.804-3
Competitive 8(a) 219.805
Procedures 219.805-2
Contract negotiations 219.808
Sole source 219.808-1
Preparing the contracts 219.811
Sole source 219.811-1
Competitive 219.811-2

PART 219—SMALL BUSINESS PROGRAMS

SUBPART 219.2—POLICIES

219.201 General policy.

(c) (10) *(1)* Agencies are not precluded from requiring that actions over $10,000, but under $150,000, that are totally set aside for small business be reviewed by the small business specialist. One example of when an agency may choose to require this review is when the agency determines that such a review is necessary to assist contracting officers in identifying opportunities for other small business set-aside programs (e.g., HUBZone, service-disabled veteran-owned, small disadvantaged business, women-owned small business) in order to meet small business goals.

(2) Modifications that increase the scope of the contract, or the order under a Federal Supply Schedule contract, should be reviewed by the small business specialist. At a minimum, these actions might impact the small business subcontracting plan. However, funding modifications or modifications that do not increase the scope of the contract generally should not be reviewed, because the value that a small business specialist review would add in these instances would be minimal compared to the resources that would be expended.

(d) Small business specialists are appointed and perform functions in accordance with DoD Instruction (DoDI) 4205.01, DoD Small Business Programs. In the DoDI, small business specialists are called "small business professionals."

[Final rule, 71 FR 44926, 8/8/2006, effective 8/8/2006; Interim rule, 79 FR 61579, 10/14/2014, effective 10/14/2014; Final rule, 79 FR 67356, 11/13/2014, effective 11/13/2014; Publication notice, 20161222]

SUBPART 219.6—CERTIFICATES OF COMPETENCY

219.602 Procedures. (No Text)

[Final rule, 72 FR 20761, 4/26/2007, effective 4/26/2007]

219.602-1 Referral.

When making a nonresponsibility determination on a small business concern, the contracting officer shall notify the contracting activity's small business specialist.

[Final rule, 72 FR 20761, 4/26/2007, effective 4/26/2007]

219.602-3 Resolving differences between the agency and the Small Business Administration.

(a) (3) (A) If the contracting officer believes the agency should appeal, the contracting officer shall immediately inform the departmental director of the Office of Small Business Programs and shall send the director, through departmental channels—

(1) A request for appeal, summarizing the issues. The request must be sent to arrive within 5 working days after receipt of the SBA Headquarters' written position; and

(2) An appeal file, documenting the contracting activity's position. The file must be sent to arrive within 5 working days after transmission of the request.

(B) The departmental director will determine whether the agency will appeal and will notify the SBA of the agency's intent.

[Final rule, 72 FR 20761, 4/26/2007, effective 4/26/2007; Final rule, 73 FR 46813, 8/12/2008, effective 8/12/2008]

SUBPART 219.7—SMALL BUSINESS SUBCONTRACTING PROGRAM

219.702 [Removed]

[Final rule, 72 FR 20761, 4/26/2007, effective 4/26/2007; Final rule, 77 FR 11367, 2/24/2012, effective 2/24/2012; Final rule, 83 FR 15996, 4/13/2018, effective 4/13/2018]

219.705 Responsibilities of the contracting officer under the subcontracting assistance program. (No Text)

[Publication notice, 20171201]

219.705-4 Reviewing the subcontracting plan.

When reviewing the subcontracting plan, contracting officers may use the document entitled "DoD Checklist for Reviewing Subcontracting Plans." The document is available at *http://business.defense.gov/Acquisition/Subcontracting/*.

[Publication notice, 20171201]

219.705-6 Postaward responsibilities of the contracting officer.

(f) When reviewing subcontracting reports, contracting officers may use the document entitled "DoD Subcontracting Program—Business Rules and Processes for (1) Electronic Subcontracting Reporting System (eSRS) and (2) Preparing and Reviewing Related Subcontract Reports." The document is available at *http://business.defense.gov/Acquisition/Subcontracting/*.

[Publication notice, 20171201]

SUBPART 219.8—CONTRACTING WITH THE SMALL BUSINESS ADMINISTRATION (THE 8(a) PROGRAM)

219.800 General.

A copy of the Partnership Agreement (PA) between DoD and the Small Business Administration (SBA) is available *here: http://www.acq.osd.mil/dpap/dars/pgi/docs/PA.pdf*.

[Final rule, 72 FR 20761, 4/26/2007, effective 4/26/2007]

219.803 Selecting acquisitions for 8(a) Program.

(1) Contracting activities should respond to SBA requests for contract support within 30 calendar days after receipt.

(2) Before considering a small business set-aside, review the acquisition for offering under the 8(a) Program.

[Final rule, 72 FR 20761, 4/26/2007, effective 4/26/2007]

219.804 Evaluation, offering, and acceptance. (No Text)

[Final rule, 72 FR 20761, 4/26/2007, effective 4/26/2007]

219.804-2 Agency offering.

(1) For requirements processed under the PA cited in DFARS 219.800 (but see paragraph (2) of this subsection for procedures related to purchase orders that do not exceed the simplified acquisition threshold), the notification to the SBA shall clearly indicate that the requirement is being processed under the PA. All notifications should be submitted in writing, using facsimile or electronic mail, when possible, and shall specify that—

(i) Under the PA, an SBA acceptance or rejection of the offering is required within 5 working days of receipt of the offering; and

(ii) (A) For sole source requirements, an SBA acceptance shall include a size verification and a determination of the 8(a) firm's program eligibility, and, upon acceptance, the contracting officer will solicit a proposal, conduct negotiations, and make award directly to the 8(a) firm; or

(B) For competitive requirements, upon acceptance, the contracting officer will solicit offers, conduct source selection, and, upon receipt of an eligibility verification, award a contract directly to the selected 8(a) firm.

(2) Under the PA cited in DFARS 219.800, no separate agency offering or SBA acceptance is needed for requirements that are issued under purchase orders that do not exceed the simplified acquisition threshold. After an 8(a) contractor has been identified, the contracting officer shall establish the prices, terms, and conditions with the 8(a) contractor and shall prepare a purchase order consistent with the procedures in FAR Part 13 and DFARS Part 213, including the applicable clauses required by DFARS Subpart 219.8. No later than the day that the purchase order is provided to the 8(a) contractor, the contracting officer shall provide to the cognizant SBA Business Opportunity Specialist, using facsimile, electronic mail, or any other means acceptable to the SBA district office—

(i) A copy of the signed purchase order; and

(ii) A notice stating that the purchase order is being processed under the PA. The notice also shall indicate that the 8(a) contractor will be deemed eligible for award and will automatically begin work under the purchase order unless, within 2 working days after SBA's receipt of the purchase order, the 8(a) contractor and the contracting officer are notified that the 8(a) contractor is ineligible for award.

(3) The notification to SBA shall identify any joint venture proposed for performance of the contract. SBA shall approve a joint venture before award of an 8(a) contract involving the joint venture.

(4) For competitive requirements for construction to be performed overseas, submit the notification to SBA Headquarters.

[Final rule, 72 FR 20761, 4/26/2007, effective 4/26/2007]

219.804-3 SBA acceptance.

For requirements processed under the PA cited in DFARS 219.800, SBA's acceptance is required within 5 working days (but see PGI 219.804-2 (2) for purchase orders that do not exceed the simplified acquisition threshold).

[Final rule, 72 FR 20761, 4/26/2007, effective 4/26/2007]

219.805 Competitive 8(a). (No Text)

[Final rule, 72 FR 20761, 4/26/2007, effective 4/26/2007]

219.805-2 Procedures.

For requirements processed under the PA cited in DFARS 219.800—

(1) For sealed bid and negotiated acquisitions, the SBA will determine the eligibility of the firms and will advise the contracting officer within 2 working days after its receipt of a request for an eligibility determination; and

(2) For negotiated acquisitions, the contracting officer may submit a request for an eligibility determination on all firms in the competitive range if discussions are to be conducted, or on all firms with a realistic chance of award if no discussions are to be conducted.

[Final rule, 72 FR 20761, 4/26/2007, effective 4/26/2007]

219.808 Contract negotiations. (No Text)

[Final rule, 72 FR 20761, 4/26/2007, effective 4/26/2007]

219.808-1 Sole source.

For requirements processed under the PA cited in DFARS 219.800—

(1) The agency may negotiate directly with the 8(a) contractor. The contracting officer is responsible for initiating negotiations;

(2) The 8(a) contractor is responsible for negotiating within the time established by the contracting officer;

(3) If the 8(a) contractor does not negotiate within the established time and the agency cannot allow additional time, the contracting officer may, after notifying the SBA, proceed with the acquisition from other sources;

(4) If requested by the 8(a) contractor, the SBA may participate in negotiations; and

(5) SBA approval of the contract is not required.

[Final rule, 72 FR 20761, 4/26/2007, effective 4/26/2007]

219.811 Preparing the contracts. (No Text)

[Final rule, 72 FR 20761, 4/26/2007, effective 4/26/2007]

219.811-1 Sole source.

(1) Awards under the PA cited in DFARS 219.800 may be made directly to the 8(a) contractor and, except as provided in paragraph (2) of this subsection and in DFARS 219.811-3, award documents shall be prepared in accordance with procedures established for non-8(a) contracts, using any otherwise authorized award forms. The "Issued by" block shall identify the awarding DoD contracting office. The contractor's name and address shall be that of the 8(a) participant.

(2) Use the following alternative procedures for direct awards made under the PA cited in DFARS 219.800:

(i) Cite 10 U.S.C. 2304(c)(5) as the authority for use of other than full and open competition.

(ii) Include the clause at DFARS 252.219-7009, Section 8(a) Direct Award, in accordance with the prescription at DFARS 219.811-3(1). Identify the cognizant SBA district office for the 8(a) contractor.

(iii) No SBA contract number is required.

(iv) Do not require an SBA signature on the award document.

[Final rule, 72 FR 20761, 4/26/2007, effective 4/26/2007]

219.811-2 Competitive.

Awards made under the PA cited in DFARS 219.800shall be prepared in accordance with the procedures in PGI 219.811-1.

[Final rule, 72 FR 20761, 4/26/2007, effective 4/26/2007]

PART 222—APPLICATION OF LABOR LAWS TO GOVERNMENT ACQUISITIONS

Table of Contents

Subpart 222.1—Basic Labor Policies

Labor relations 222.101
General 222.101-1
Reporting labor disputes 222.101-3
Impact of labor disputes on defense programs 222.101-3-70
Removal of items from contractors' facilities affected by work stoppages . . 222.101-4

Subpart 222.4—Labor Standards for Contracts Involving Construction

Construction Wage Rate Requirements statute wage determinations 222.404
General requirements 222.404-2
Administration and enforcement 222.406
Investigations 222.406-8

Subpart 222.8—Equal Employment Opportunity

Exemptions 222.807

Subpart 222.10—Service Contract Labor Standards

Obtaining wage determinations 222.1008-1

Subpart 222.13—Special Disabled and Vietnam Era Veterans

Waivers 222.1305

Subpart 222.17—Combating Trafficking in Persons

Policy 222.1703
Violations and remedies 222.1704
[Removed] 222.1704-70

Subpart 222.17—Restrictions on the Use of Mandatory Arbitration Agreements

Waiver 222.7404

PART 222—APPLICATION OF LABOR LAWS TO GOVERNMENT ACQUISITIONS

SUBPART 222.1—BASIC LABOR POLICIES

222.101 Labor relations. (No Text)

[Final rule, 71 FR 18669, 4/12/2006, effective 4/12/2006]

222.101-1 General.

The contracting offices shall obtain approval from the labor advisor before—

(1) Contacting a national office of a labor organization, a Government agency headquarters, or any other organization on a labor relations matters or disputes; or

(2) Making recommendations for plant seizure or injunctive action relating to potential or actual work stoppages.

[Final rule, 71 FR 18669, 4/12/2006, effective 4/12/2006; Change notice, 20070426]

222.101-3 Reporting labor disputes.

The contract administration office shall—

(1) Notify the labor advisor, the contracting officer, and the head of the contracting activity when interference is likely; and

(2) Disseminate information on labor disputes in accordance with departmental procedures.

[Final rule, 71 FR 18669, 4/12/2006, effective 4/12/2006]

222.101-3-70 Impact of labor disputes on defense programs.

If the dispute involves a product, project (including construction), or service that must be obtained in order to meet schedules for urgently needed military programs or requirements, each department and agency shall consider the degree of impact of potential or actual labor disputes, and each contracting activity involved shall obtain and develop data reflecting the impact of a labor dispute. Upon determining the impact, the head of the contracting activity shall submit a report of findings and recommendations to the labor advisor.

(b)(i) The report to the labor advisor must be in narrative form and must include—

(A) Location of dispute and name of contractor or subcontractor involved;

(B) A description of the impact, including how the specific items or services affect the specific programs or requirements;

(C) Identity of alternate sources available to furnish the supply or service within the time required; and

(D) A description of any action taken to reduce the impact.

(ii) The head of the contracting activity shall submit impact reports to the agency head when—

(A) Specifically requested; or

(B) The department or agency considers the impact to be of sufficient urgency to warrant the attention of the agency head.

(iii) The labor advisor will expand the report submitted under paragraph (b)(ii) of this subsection by addressing the following, as appropriate:

(A) *Description of military program, project, or service.* Identify item, project, or service that will be or is being affected by the work stoppage. Describe its normal use and current functions in combat, combat support, or deterrent operations. For components or raw materials, identify the end item(s) for which they are used.

(B) *Requirements and assets.* Identify requirements and assets in appropriate detail in terms commonly used by the DoD component.

(1) For production programs, include requirements for each using military service. Where applicable, state in detail production schedule, inventory objectives, assets against these objectives, and critical shortages. For spares and highly expendable items, such as ground and air ammunition, show usage (consumption) rates and assets in absolute terms and in terms of daily, weekly, or monthly supplies. For components, include requirements for spares.

(2) For projects, describe the potential adverse effects of a delay in meeting schedules, and its impact on the national security.

(3) For services, describe how a loss or interruption affects the ability to support Defense operations in terms of traffic requirements, assets, testing programs, etc.

(C) *Possible measures to minimize strike impact.* Describe—

(1) Capabilities, if any, to substitute items or to use alternate sources and indicate the number of other facilities available and the relative capabilities of such facilities in meeting total requirements;

(2) How much time would be required to replace the loss of the facilities or service affected by a work stoppage; and

(3) The feasibility of transferring assets from theater to theater to relieve deficits in some areas of urgency.

(D) *Conclusion.*

(1) Describe the impact on operations of a 15-30, 30-60, and a 60-90 day work stoppage.

(2) Project the degree of criticality of a program, project, or service resulting from a work stoppage on a calendar basis, indicating the increased impact, if any, as the stoppage lengthens. Criticality is measured by the number of days required for the work stoppage to have an effect on operational capability. This time must be stated in terms of days.

[Final rule, 71 FR 18669, 4/12/2006, effective 4/12/2006; Change notice, 20070426; Publication notice, 20150921]

222.101-4 Removal of items from contractors' facilities affected by work stoppages.

(a) (ii) Include the following information in the request:

(1) Contract number.

(2) A statement as to the urgency and criticality of the item needed.

(3) A description of the items to be moved (nature of the item, amount, approximate weight and cubic feet, item number, etc.).

(4) Mode of transportation by which the items are to be moved, if different than in the contract, and whether by Government or commercial bill of lading.

(5) Destination of the material, if different from that specified in the contract.

[Final rule, 71 FR 18669, 4/12/2006, effective 4/12/2006]

SUBPART 222.4—LABOR STANDARDS FOR CONTRACTS INVOLVING CONSTRUCTION

222.404 Construction Wage Rate Requirements statute wage determinations. (No Text)

[Final rule, 77 FR 35879, 6/15/2012, effective 6/15/2012]

222.404-2 General requirements.

(c) (5) Clarification concerning the proper application of wage rate schedules to the type or types of construction involved shall be obtained from—

(A) For the Army-The appropriate district commander, Corps of Engineers.

(B) For the Navy-The cognizant Naval Facilities Engineering Command division.

(C) For the Air Force-The appropriate Regional Industrial Relations Office.

[Final rule, 71 FR 18669, 4/12/2006, effective 4/12/2006; Change notice, 20070426]

222.406 Administration and enforcement. (No Text)

[Change notice, 20070426]

222.406-8 Investigations.

(a) Under Reorganization Plan No. 14 of 1950, contracting agencies are tasked with the primary responsibility for the conduct of labor standards compliance activities for construction contracts subject to the Construction Wage Rate Requirements statute. When such compliance assurance activities disclose potential violations that are substantial in amount (wage underpayments in excess of $1,000) or when requested by the Department of Labor, the contracting officer or a designee should take the following steps to ensure compliance with the investigative requirements of the Department of Labor:

(i) *Beginning of the investigation.* The investigator shall—

(A) Inform the contractor of the investigation in advance;

(B) Verify the exact legal name of the contractor, its address, and the names and titles of its principal officers;

(C) Outline the general scope of the investigation, including the examination of pertinent records and the interview of employees;

(D) Inform the contractor that the names of the employees to be interviewed will not be divulged to the contractor; and

(E) When requested, provide a letter from the contracting officer verifying the investigator's authority.

(ii) *Conduct of the investigation*. Labor standards investigations are comprised of the following essential components:

(A) *Review of the contract.*

(1) Verify that all required labor standards and clauses and wage determinations are included in the contract.

(2) Review the following items in the contract file, if applicable:

(i) List of subcontractors.

(ii) Payroll statements for the contractor and subcontractors.

(iii) Approvals of additional classifications.

(iv) Data regarding apprentices and trainees as required by FAR 22.406-4.

(v) Daily inspector's report or other inspection reports.

(vi) Employee interview statements.

(vii) Standard Form (SF) 1413, Statement and Acknowledgment.

(B) *Interview of the complainant.* If the investigation is based upon the receipt of a complaint, the investigator should interview the complainant unless this is impractical. The interview shall cover all aspects of the complaint to ensure that all pertinent information is obtained. Whenever an investigation does not include an interview of the complainant, explain such omission in the investigator's report.

(C) *Interview of employees and former employees.*

(1) Interview a sufficient number of employees or former employees, who represent all classifications, to develop information regarding the method and amount of payments, deductions, hours worked, and the type of work performed.

(2) Interview employees at the job site if the interviews can be conducted privately and in such a manner so as to cause the least inconvenience to the employer and employees.

(3) Former employees may be interviewed elsewhere.

(4) Do not disclose to any employee any information, finding, recommendation, or conclusion relating to the investigation except to the extent necessary to obtain required information.

(5) Do not disclose any employee's statement to anyone, except a Government representative working on the case, without the employee's written permission.

(6) Obtain information by mail when personal interviews are impractical.

(7) Use SF 1445, Labor Standards Interview, for employee interviews.

(8) Ask employees to sign their statements and to initial any changes.

(9) Provide an evaluation of each employee's credibility.

(D) *Interview of foremen.* Interview foremen to obtain information concerning the contractor's compliance with the labor standards provisions with respect to employees under the foreman's supervision and the correctness of the foreman's classification as a supervisory employee. All procedures established for the conduct of employee interviews, and the recording and use of information obtained, apply to foremen interviews.

(E) *Interview of the contractor.*

(1) Interview the contractor whenever the investigation indicates the possibility of a violation.

(2) Inform the contractor that—

(i) The interview does not mean that a violation has been found or that a requirement for corrective action exists; and

(ii) The purpose of the interview is to obtain only such data as the contractor may desire to present in connection with the investigation.

(3) Do not disclose the identity of any individual who filed a complaint or was interviewed.

(F) *Review of contractor and subcontractor records.*

(1) Review contractor and subcontractor records such as basic time cards, books, cancelled payroll checks, fringe benefits, and payment records. Compare them with submitted payrolls. When discrepancies are found, include pertinent excerpts or copies of the records in the investigation report with a statement of the discrepancy and any explanation the investigator obtains. When wages include contributions or anticipated costs for fringe payments requiring approval of the Secretary of Labor, examine the contractor records to ensure such approval has been obtained and that any requirements specified in the approval have been met. (See FAR 22.406-2(a)(3).)

(2) Review contractor's and subcontractor's weekly payrolls and payroll statements for completeness and accuracy regarding the following:

(i) Identification of employees, payroll amount, the contract, contractor, subcontractor, and payroll period.

(ii) Inclusion of only job classifications and wage rates specified in the contract specifications, or otherwise established for the contract or subcontract.

(iii) Computation of daily and weekly hours.

(iv) Computation of time-and-one half for work in excess of 40 hours per week in accordance with FAR 22.406-2(c).

(v) Gross weekly wages.

(vi) Deductions.

(vii) Computation of net weekly wages paid to each employee.

(viii) Ratio of helpers, apprentices, and trainees to laborers and mechanics.

(ix) Apprenticeship and trainee registration and ratios.

(x) Computation of fringe benefits payments.

(3) Transcribe the contractor's records whenever they contain information at variance with payrolls or other submitted documents.

(i) Make the transcriptions in sufficient detail to permit them to be used to check computations of restitution and to determine amounts to be withheld from the contractor.

(ii) Follow the form used by the contractor.

(iii) Place comments or explanations concerning the transcriptions on separate memoranda or in the narrative report.

(iv) Determine whether the wage determination, any modifications of the determination, and any additional classifications are posted as required.

(iii) *Submission of the report of investigation.* The investigator shall submit a report of the investigation in accordance with agency procedures. Each report shall include at least—

(A) The basis for the investigation, including the name of the complainant;

(B) Names and addresses of prime contractors and subcontractors involved, and names and titles of their principal officers;

(C) Contract number, date, dollar value of prime contract, and date and number of wage determination included in the contract;

(D) Description of the contract and subcontract work involved;

(E) Summary of the findings with respect to each of the items listed in *PGI 222.406-8*(a)(ii);

(F) Concluding statement concerning—

(1) The types of violations, including the amount of kickbacks under the Copeland Act, underpayments of basic hourly rates and fringe benefits under Wage Rate Requirements statute, or underpayments and liquidated damages under the Contract Work Hours and Safety Standards statute;

(2) Whether violations are considered to be willful or due to the negligence of the contractor or its agent;

(3) The amount of funds withheld from the contractor; and

(4) Other violations found; and

(G) Exhibits indexed and appropriately tabbed, including copies of the following, when applicable—

(1) Complaint letter;

(2) Contract wage determination;

(3) Preconstruction letter and memorandum of preconstruction conference;

(4) Payrolls and statements indicating violations;

(5) Transcripts of pertinent records of the contractor, and approvals of fringe benefit payments;

(6) Employee interview statements;

(7) Foreman interview statements;

(8) Statements of others interviewed, including Government personnel;

(9) Detailed computations showing kickbacks, underpayments, and liquidated damages;

(10) Summary of all payments due to each employee or to a fund plan or program, and liquidated damages; and

(11) Receipts and cancelled checks.

(d) *Contracting officer's report.* This report shall include at least—

(i) SF 1446, Labor Standards Investigation Summary Sheet;

(ii) Contracting officer's findings;

(iii) Statement as to the disposition of any contractor rebuttal to the findings;

(iv) Statement as to whether the contractor has accepted the findings and has paid any restitution or liquidated damages;

(v) Statement as to the disposition of funds available;

(vi) Recommendations as to disposition or further handling of the case (when appropriate, include recommendations as to the reduction, waiver, or assessment of liquidated damages, whether the contractor should be debarred, and whether the file should be referred for possible criminal prosecution); and

(vii) When applicable, the following exhibits:

(A) Investigator's report.

(B) Copy of the contractor's written rebuttal or a summary of the contractor's oral rebuttal of the contracting officer's findings.

(C) Copies of correspondence between the contractor and contracting officer, including a statement of specific violations found, corrective action requested, and the contractor's letter of acceptance or rejection.

(D) Evidence of the contractor's payment of restitution or liquidated damages (copies of receipts, cancelled checks, or supplemental payrolls).

(E) Letter from the contractor requesting relief from the liquidated damage provisions of the Contract Work Hours and Safety Standard statute.

[Final rule, 71 FR 18669, 4/12/2006, effective 4/12/2006; Change notice, 20070426; Final rule, 77 FR 35879, 6/15/2012, effective 6/15/2012]

SUBPART 222.8—EQUAL EMPLOYMENT OPPORTUNITY

222.807 Exemptions.

(c) When seeking an exemption from the requirements of Executive Order 11246, submit the request with a justification through contracting channels to the labor advisor, who will forward the request to the agency head. If the request is submitted under FAR 22.807(a)(1), the agency head shall act on the request. If the exemption is granted, the agency head shall notify the Director, Office of Federal Contract Compliance Programs (OFCCP), of such action within 30 days. If the request is submitted under FAR 22.807(a)(2) or (b)(5), the agency head will forward it to the Director, OFCCP, for action.

[Final rule, 71 FR 18669, 4/12/2006, effective 4/12/2006; Change notice, 20070426]

SUBPART 222.10—SERVICE CONTRACT LABOR STANDARDS

222.1008-1 Obtaining wage determinations.

(1) The contracting officer shall secure the assistance of cognizant customer/technical personnel to ensure maximum use of the Service Contract Act Directory of Occupations (Directory) and incorporation of all service employee classes (Directory and nondirectory) expected to be utilized.

(2) When the statement of work job title, for which there is a Directory equivalent, differs from the Directory job title, provide a cross-reference on the e98.

(3) Include and note as such any classifications and minimum hourly wage rates conformed under any predecessor contract. When a previously conformed classification is not included in the Directory, include the job description on the e98.

[Final rule, 71 FR 18669, 4/12/2006, effective 4/12/2006; Change notice, 20070426]

SUBPART 222.13—SPECIAL DISABLED AND VIETNAM ERA VETERANS

222.1305 Waivers.

(c) When seeking a waiver of any of the terms of the clause at FAR 52.222-35, Equal Opportunity for Special Disabled Veterans, Veterans of the Vietnam Era, and Other Eligible Veterans, submit a waiver request through contracting channels to the labor advisor. If the request is justified, the labor advisor will endorse the request and forward it for action to—

(i) The agency head for waivers under FAR 22.1305(a); or

(ii) The Secretary of Defense, without the power of redelegation, for waivers under FAR 22.1305(b).

[Final rule, 71 FR 18669, 4/12/2006, effective 4/12/2006; Change notice, 20070426]

SUBPART 222.17—COMBATING TRAFFICKING IN PERSONS

[For sample checklist for auditing compliance with Combating Trafficking in Persons policy, click *www.acq.osd.mil*]

222.1703 Policy.

(1) The Office of the Under Secretary of Defense for Personnel and Readiness (OUSD(P&R)) is responsible for developing overall guidance on personnel policy issues relating to Combating Trafficking in Persons (CTIP). The DoD CTIP website is *http://ctip.defense.gov/*. The website includes DoD policy on CTIP, CTIP training information, and links to the National TIP hotline, the DoD IG website, the Department of State Office to Monitor and Combat Trafficking in Persons, and other Government and non-Government organization websites.

(2) Department of Defense Instruction 2200.01, reissued September 15, 2010, entitled Combating Trafficking in Persons, (located at *http://www.dtic.mil/whs/directives/corres/pdf/220001p.pdf*), requires the incorporation of terms and conditions in contracts performed either inside or outside the United States that—

(i) Prohibit any activities on the part of contractor employees that support or promote trafficking in persons; and

(ii) Impose suitable penalties on contractors who fail to monitor the conduct of their employees.

(3) DoD Instruction 5525.11, Criminal Jurisdiction Over Civilians Employed By or Accompanying the Armed Forces Outside the United States, Certain Service Members, and Former Service Members, dated March 3, 2005, located at *http://www.dtic.mil/whs/directives/corres/pdf/552511p.pdf*, and as supplemented by Directive-Type Memorandum 09-015 at *http://www.dtic.mil/whs/directives/corres/pdf/DTM-09-015.pdf*, implements policies and procedures, and assigns responsibilities, under the Military Extraterritorial Jurisdiction Act of 2000, as amended by section 1088 of the National Defense Authorization Act for Fiscal Year 2005, for exercising extraterritorial criminal jurisdiction over certain current and former members of the U.S. Armed Forces, and over civilians employed by or accompanying the U.S. Armed Forces outside the United States.

(4) Quality assurance surveillance plans (QASPs) that are developed in accordance with DFARS 237.172 should appropriately describe how the contracting officer's representative will monitor the contractor's performance regarding trafficking in persons such that non-compliance with FAR clause 52.222-50, Combating Trafficking in Persons, is brought to the immediate attention of the contracting officer.

(5) PD2 users shall not use system overrides or other administrative methods of developing clauses for use in PD2-generated contracts to avoid the inclusion of the clause at FAR 52.222-50, with its Alternate I, if appropriate, in solicitations and contracts.

(6) The contracting officer shall rely on the requiring activity to ascertain the existence of any additional Geographic Combatant Commander's (GCC's)/Subordinate Joint Force Commander, Trafficking In Persons, Directives or Notices, as required under PGI 225.370, checklist item #12, that would require the use of Alternate I with the clause at FAR 52.222-50, Combating Trafficking in Persons, as required by FAR 22.1705 for contracts performed outside the United States. The webpage is provided at *http://www.acq.osd.mil/dpap/pacc/cc/areas_of_responsibility.html* and by clicking on the pertinent GCC Area of Responsibility.

[Interim rule, 71 FR 62560, 10/26/2006, effective 10/26/2006; Publication notice, 20100810; Publication notice, 20110105; Final rule, 76 FR 71830, 11/18/2011, effective 11/18/2011; Publication notice, 20130516; Final rule, 80 FR 36900, 6/26/2015, effective 6/26/2015]

222.1704 Violations and remedies.

(1) If the contracting officer receives information indicating that the contractor, a contractor employee, a subcontractor, or a subcontractor employee has failed to comply with the requirements of the clause at FAR 52.222-50, the contracting officer shall—

(i) Through the contracting officer's local commander or other designated representative, immediately notify the Combatant Commander responsible for the geographical area in which the incident has occurred; and

(ii) Provide information for any investigation and enforcement to—

Program Manager

DoD CTIP Policy and Programs Support

OUSD (P&R)

4800 Mark Center Dr. Suite 06J25-01

Alexandria, VA 22350-4000

(2) Reports may be made to the DoD Inspector General Hotline at *http://www.dodig.mil/hotline/* or 800-424-9098, first and foremost.

(3) Reports also may be made to the Program Manager on-line at *http://ctip.defense.gov/* or by e-mail to *ctipreports@osd.pentagon.mil.*

(4) Reports also may be made to the National CTIP Hotline at 1-888-373-7888 or to the CTIP Hotline website at *http://www.polarisproject.org/*.

[Interim rule, 71 FR 62560, 10/26/2006, effective 10/26/2006; Final rule, 73 FR 4115, 1/24/2008, effective 1/24/2008; Publication notice, 20100810; Publication notice, 20130516]

222.1704-70 [Removed]

[Interim rule, 71 FR 62560, 10/26/2006, effective 10/26/2006; Final rule, 73 FR 4115, 1/24/2008, effective 1/24/2008]

SUBPART 222.74—RESTRICTIONS ON THE USE OF MANDATORY ARBITRATION AGREEMENTS

222.7404 Waiver.

(c) Requests for waivers to the policy at DFARS 222.7402 must be submitted to the Secretary of Defense through Contract Policy and International Contracting of Defense Procurement and Acquisition Policy, OUSD (AT&L) DPAP/CPIC at 3060 Defense Pentagon, Room 5E621, Washington, D.C. 20301-3060. Requests for waivers may be submitted electronically to the following CPIC email address: *osd.pentagon.ousd-atl.mbx.cpic@mail.mil.* Include "Waiver-Mandatory Arbitration" in the subject line of the message.

[Final rule, 78 FR 36113, 6/17/2013, effective 6/17/2013; Final rule, 78 FR 54968, 9/9/2013, effective 9/9/2013]

PART 223—ENVIRONMENT, ENERGY AND WATER EFFICIENCY, RENEWABLE ENERGY TECHNOLOGIES, OCCUPATIONAL SAFETY, AND DRUG-FREE WORKPLACE

Table of Contents

Subpart 223.3—Hazardous Material Identification and Material Safety Data

Safety precautions for ammunition and explosives 223.370
Procedures 223.370-4

Subpart 223.4—Use of Recovered Materials

Procedures 223.405
Solicitation provisions and contract clauses 223.406

Subpart 223.73—Minimizing the Use of Materials Containing Hexavalent Chromium

Authorization and approval 223.7305

PART 223—ENVIRONMENT, ENERGY AND WATER EFFICIENCY, RENEWABLE ENERGY TECHNOLOGIES, OCCUPATIONAL SAFETY, AND DRUG-FREE WORKPLACE

SUBPART 223.3—HAZARDOUS MATERIAL IDENTIFICATION AND MATERIAL SAFETY DATA

223.370 Safety precautions for ammunition and explosives. (No Text)

[Final rule, 70 FR 73150, 12/9/2005, effective 12/9/2005]

223.370-4 Procedures.

(1) *Preaward phase.*

(i) *Waiver of the mandatory requirements.*

(A) Before either omitting the clause at DFARS 252.223-7002, Safety Precautions for Ammunition and Explosives, from solicitations and contracts or waiving the mandatory requirements of the manual, obtain approval of—

(1) The safety personnel responsible for ammunition and explosives safety; and

(2) The head of the contracting activity.

(B) If the contracting officer decides to waive the mandatory requirements before award, the contracting officer shall set forth in the solicitation, or in an amendment of the solicitation, the specific requirements to be waived.

(C) If the head of the contracting activity declines to approve a request for waiver, but the prospective contractor agrees to take corrective action to bring the operation into compliance, make the corrective action a part of the resulting contract.

(ii) *Transportation considerations.* If shipment of ammunition and explosives is involved in the contract, address in the Schedule of the contract the applicable Department of Transportation or Military Surface Deployment and Distribution Command requirements and any other requirements for transportation, packaging, marking, and labeling.

(iii) *Disposition of excess.* Include instructions within the contract concerning final disposition of excess Government furnished material containing ammunition and explosives, including defective or rejected supplies.

(iv) *Preaward survey.* Before awarding any contract, including purchase orders, involving ammunition and explosives, obtain a preaward ammunition and explosives safety survey. If the prospective contractor proposes subcontracting any ammunitions or explosive work, include a review of the subcontractor's facility in the preaward survey.

(2) *Postaward phase.*

(i) *Contract administration office responsibility.*

(A) The contract administration office is responsible for verifying that the safety requirements of the clause at DFARS 252.223-7002, Safety Precautions for Ammunition and Explosives, are being implemented in a manner that will reduce, to the maximum extent practicable, or eliminate the probability of a mishap occurring.

(B) The clause at DFARS 252.223-7002, Safety Precautions for Ammunition and Explosives, requires compliance with DoD 4145.26-M, Contractors' Safety Manual for Ammunition and Explosives. This manual requires the contractor to submit to the administrative contracting officer (ACO) any postaward requests for a waiver of the contract safety standards, a site plan modification, or a construction review. The ACO shall review any request and make recommendations to the contracting officer. The contracting officer shall make a decision after considering recommendations of the ACO and safety personnel responsible for ammunition and explosive safety.

(1) If the request arrives at the contracting office without evidence that the ACO has seen it, immediately send it to the ACO for review and recommendations.

(2) When the contracting officer has made a determination approving or disapproving the contractor's request, send the determination to the ACO for transmission to the contractor.

(ii) *Subcontracts.*

(A) The clause at DFARS 252.223-7002, Safety Precautions for Ammunition and Explosives, requires the contractor to notify the contracting officer when placing a subcontract for ammunition and explosives. The contracting officer should coordinate with the safety personnel and request supporting contract administration in accordance with FAR 42.202(e). If the contracting officer believes the nature of the subcontract work poses a potential danger to Government property, Government personnel, production capability, or contract completion, request supporting contract administration.

(B) If the preaward safety survey identified areas in which a subcontractor was not complying with the manual, and the subcontractor was supposed to correct the deficiencies before start-up, the contracting officer shall require a preoperations survey to verify that the corrections were made.

(C) When postaward safety reviews by the Government uncover any safety deficiencies in the subcontractor's operation, the review team shall inform the ACO cognizant of the subcontractor, who shall immediately notify the ACO cognizant of the prime contractor. The ACO cognizant of the prime shall inform the prime contractor of deficiencies requiring correction. The notifications shall be made by the most expeditious means appropriate to the circumstance. If a critical safety deficiency poses an imminent danger, the ACO cognizant of the prime shall make the notifications by the most expeditious means available.

[Final rule, 70 FR 73150, 12/9/2005, effective 12/9/2005]

SUBPART 223.4—USE OF RECOVERED MATERIALS

223.405 Procedures.

Departments and agencies must centrally collect information submitted in accordance with the clause at FAR 52.223-9 for reporting to the Office of the Deputy Under Secretary of Defense (Installations and Environment). The information is collected in the Federal Procurement Data System (FPDS).

[Final rule, 70 FR 73150, 12/9/2005, effective 12/9/2005; Change notice, 20060412; Final rule, 74 FR 37644, 7/29/2009, effective 7/29/2009]

223.406 Solicitation provisions and contract clauses.

(b) FAR 23.406(b) prescribes the use of the clause at FAR 52.223-2, Affirmative Procurement of Biobased Products Under Service and Construction Contracts. Paragraph (d) of this clause requires the insertion of an environmental point of contact. Use the list below to identify the appropriate environmental point of contact for use in the clause:

Organization	POC	Phone	E-mail
Air Force	Maj David Pugh	571-256-4397	*david.pugh@pentagon.af.mil*
Army	Robert Luther	703-697-4032	*roberte.luther.civ@mail.mil*
DLA	Karen Moran	703-767-6237	*karen.moran@dla.mil*
Navy	John Bendick	717-605-9144	*john.bendick@navy.mil]*

[Publication notice, 20120312]

SUBPART 223.73—MINIMIZING THE USE OF MATERIALS CONTAINING HEXAVALENT CHROMIUM

223.7305 Authorization and approval.

The contracting officer shall ensure that the appropriate authorizations from the program executive office are included in the solicitation and contract. The contracting officer shall forward proposals submitted by an offeror or requests from a Contractor seeking authorization to use hexavalent chromium in a deliverable item, to the cognizant program executive office for evaluation and, if necessary, authorization by the appropriate official.

[Final rule, 76 FR 25569, 5/5/2011, effective 5/5/2011]

PART 225—FOREIGN ACQUISITION

Table of Contents

General 225.001
Reporting of acquisition of end products manufactured outside the United States 225.070

Subpart 225.3—Contracts Performed Outside the United States

Contracts requiring performance or delivery in a foreign country 225.370
Contractor personnel supporting U.S. Armed Forces deployed outside the United States 225.371
Definitions 225.371-2
Government support 225.371-3
Contract clauses 225.371-5
Antiterrorism/force protection 225.372
General 225.372-1
Contract administration in support of contingency operations 225.373

Subpart 225.7—Prohibited Sources

Prohibition on acquisition of United States Munitions List items from Communist Chinese military companies 225.770
Definitions 225.770-1
Identifying USML items 225.770-4
Waiver of prohibition 225.770-5
Prohibition on contracting or subcontracting with a firm that is owned or controlled by the government or a country that is a state sponsor of terrorism 225.771
Notification 225.771-3
Procedures 225.772-3

Subpart 225.8—Other International Agreements and Coordination

Procedures 225.802
Contracts for performance outside the United States and Canada 225.802-70
Contracting with Canadian contractors 225.870
General 225.870-1
Contract administration 225.870-5
Acceptance of Canadian supplies 225.870-7
North Atlantic Treaty Organization (NATO) cooperative projects 225.871
Statutory waivers 225.871-4
Directed subcontracting 225.871-5
Contracting with qualifying country sources 225.872
Individual determinations 225.872-4
Contract administration 225.872-5
Request for audit services 225.872-6
Waiver of United Kingdom commercial exploitation levies 225.873
Procedures 225.873-2

Subpart 225.9—Customs and Duties

Procedures 225.902
Exempted supplies 225.903

Subpart 225.70—Authorization Acts, Appropriations Acts, and Other Statutory Restrictions on Foreign Acquisition

Restrictions on food, clothing, fabrics, and hand or measuring tools 225.7002
Restrictions 225.7002-1
Exceptions 225.7002-2
Restrictions on acquisition of specialty metals 225.7003
Restrictions 225.7003-2
Exceptions 225.7003-2-3
[Removed] 225.7016
[Removed] 225.7016-3
Utilization of domestic photovoltaic devices 225.7017
[Removed] 225.7017-4
Restriction on acquisition of certain magnets and tungsten 225.7018
Exceptions 225.7018-3
Nonavailability determination 225.7018-4

Subpart 225.72—Reporting Contract Performance Outside the United States

Contracting officer distribution of reports 225.7203

Subpart 225.73—Acquisitions for Foreign Military Sales

Scope of subpart 225.7300
General 225.7301
Preparation of letter of offer and acceptance 225.7302
Pricing acquisitions for FMS 225.7303
Cost of doing business with a foreign government or an international organization 225.7303-2
[Removed] 225.7303-3

Subpart 225.74—[Removed]

Subpart 225.75—Balance of Payments Program

Procedures 225.7502

Subpart 225.76—Secondary Arab Boycott of Israel

Waivers 225.7604

Subpart 225.77—Acquisitions in Support of Operations in Afghanistan

Enhanced authority to acquire products or services from Afghanistan 225.7703
Acquisition procedures 225.7703-1
Determination requirements 225.7703-2
[Removed] 225.7703-3
Reporting requirement 225.7703-4

Subpart 225.78—Acquisitions in Support of Geographic Combatant Command's Theater Security Cooperation Efforts

Policy 225.7801

Subpart 225.79—Export Control

Export-controlled items 225.7901
General 225.7901-2
Defense Trade Cooperation Treaty with the United Kingdom 225.7902
Purpose 225.7902-2
Procedures 225.7902-4

PART 225—FOREIGN ACQUISITION

225.001 General.

Consider the following when evaluating offers of foreign end products:

(1) *Statutory or policy restrictions.*

(i) Determine whether the product is restricted by—

(A) Statute (see DFARS subpart 225.70); or

(B) DoD policy (see DFARS subpart 225.71, FAR 6.302-3, and DoD Directive 5230.11, Disclosure of Classified Military Information to Foreign Governments and International Organizations).

(ii) If an exception to or waiver of a restriction in DFARS subpart 225.70 or 225.71 would result in award of a foreign end product, apply the policies and procedures of the Buy American statute or the Balance of Payments Program, and, if applicable, the trade agreements.

(2) *Memoranda of understanding or other international agreements.* Determine whether the offered product is the product of one of the qualifying countries listed in DFARS 225.872-1.

(3) *Trade agreements.* If the product is not an eligible product, a qualifying country end product, or a U.S.-made end product, purchase of the foreign end product may be prohibited (see FAR 25.403(c) and DFARS 225.403(c)).

(4) *Other trade sanctions and prohibited sources.*

(i) Determine whether the offeror complies with the secondary Arab boycott of Israel. Award to such offerors may be prohibited (see DFARS subpart 225.76).

(ii) Determine whether the offeror is a prohibited source (see FAR subpart 25.7 and DFARS Subpart 225.7).

(5) *Buy American and Balance of Payments Program.* See the evaluation procedures in DFARS subpart 225.5.

[Final rule, 70 FR 73153, 12/9/2005, effective 12/9/2005; Final rule, 77 FR 35879, 6/15/2012, effective 6/15/2012]

225.070 Reporting of acquisition of end products manufactured outside the United States.

(1) *Definitions. Manufactured end product* and *place of manufacture* are defined in the provision at FAR 52.225-18, Place of Manufacture.

(2) Use the Federal Procurement Data System data field "Place of Manufacture," under the section on Product or Service Information, to enter data on the acquisition of end products manufactured outside the United States for contracts awarded and orders issued in fiscal year 2007 and subsequent fiscal years. Select the appropriate description in accordance with the following table:

Place of Manufacture

Short Description as viewed in drop down box	Long Description
Manufactured or performed outside United States (Actions prior to FY 2007 only)	The action is for (i) Any foreign end product manufactured outside the United States; or (ii) Services performed outside the United States by a foreign concern.
Mfg in U.S.	The action is predominantly for acquisition of manufactured end products that are manufactured in the United States.
Mfg outside U.S. - Commercial information technology	The foreign manufactured end products are predominantly commercial information technology items (FAR 25.103(e)).

Short Description as viewed in drop down box	Long Description
Mfg outside U.S. - Domestic nonavailability	The foreign manufactured end products were predominantly not domestically available as shown by one of the following: • The item is listed at FAR 25.104 (FAR 25.103(b)(1)). • The agency did an individual determination (FAR 25.103(b)(2)). • No offer of a domestic end product was received, even though the acquisition was synopsized and conducted through full and open competition (FAR 25.103(b)(3)).
Mfg outside U.S - Public interest determination	The head of the agency has made a determination that domestic preferences would be inconsistent with the public interest (FAR 25.103(a)).
Mfg outside U.S. - Qualifying country	For DoD only, the foreign manufactured end products are predominantly qualifying country end products (DFARS 225.003 and 225.872-1).
Mfg outside U.S. - Resale	The foreign manufactured end products acquired are predominantly for resale (FAR 25.103(d)).
Mfg outside U.S. - Trade Agreements	The foreign manufactured end products are predominantly eligible products acquired under Trade Agreements (FAR 25.402(a)(1)).
Mfg outside U.S. - Unreasonable cost	The cost of the offered domestic end products was unreasonable (FAR 25.103(c), 25.105, and Subpart 25.5).
Mfg outside U.S. - Use outside the United States	The foreign manufactured end products acquired are predominantly for use outside the United States (FAR 25.100).
More than 50% of foreign content, but manufactured in United States (Actions prior to FY 2007 only)	The action is for (i) A foreign end product that is manufactured in the United States but still determined to be foreign because 50 percent or more of the cost of the components is not mined, produced, or manufactured inside the United States or qualifying countries; or (ii) Services performed in the United States by a foreign concern.
Not applicable	The action is NOT predominantly for acquisition of manufactured end products.

(3) Note that the first and second from the last options in the drop down box are to be used only for reporting of contracts awarded or orders issued prior to October 1, 2006.

(4) The other options in the drop down box apply only to contracts awarded and orders issued on or after October 1, 2006. If the solicitation for the contract contains the provision at FAR 52.225-18, Place of Manufacture (or the commercial item equivalent at FAR 52.212-3(j)), the contracting officer must review the successful offeror's response to this provision to select the correct option.

(i) Enter "Mfg in U.S." if the offeror has checked the box "In the United States."

(ii) If the offeror has checked the box "Outside the United States," enter one of the other options, depending on the predominant reason for acquiring end products manufactured outside the United States. These reasons correspond to the exceptions to the

Buy American statute (FAR subpart 25.1 and DFARS subpart 225.1). Further explanation of these exceptions to the Buy American statute are available at the FAR and DFARS references provided in the long description for each option.

(5) For any contract awarded on or after October 1, 2006, when the solicitation did not include the provision at FAR 52.225-18, Place of Manufacture (or FAR 52.212-3(j)), and for any order placed on or after October 1, 2006, under a contract that did not include one of these provisions, the contracting officer shall use best judgment in estimating whether the acquisition is predominantly for manufactured end products and whether the end products were predominantly end products manufactured in the United States or outside the United States, using the place of performance or other information that may be available to the contracting officer to assist in forming this judgment.

[Final rule, 71 FR 62559, 10/26/2006, effective 10/26/2006; Change notice 20070802; Final rule, 77 FR 35879, 6/15/2012, effective 6/15/2012; Redesignated, Final rule, 79 FR 11341, 2/28/2014, effective 2/28/2014]

SUBPART 225.3—CONTRACTS PERFORMED OUTSIDE THE UNITED STATES

225.370 Contracts requiring performance or delivery in a foreign country.

(a) If the acquisition requires the performance of services or delivery of supplies in an area outside the United States, the contracting officer shall—

(i) Ensure that the solicitation and contract include any applicable host country and designated operational area performance considerations. Failure to provide such information—

(A) May result in a contract that does not reflect the respective support relationships between the contractor and the Government, ultimately affecting the ability of the contractor to fulfill the contract terms and conditions;

(B) May result in unplanned support burdens being placed on the Government in a theater of operations;

(C) May result in contractor personnel conflicting with theater operations or performing in violation of a theater commander's directives or host country laws; or

(D) May cause contractor personnel to be wrongly subjected to host country laws;

(ii) Comply with any theater business clearance and contract administration delegation requirements set forth in memorandum (click here) entitled Theater Business Clearance/Contract Administration Delegation Update—Integration of TBC with the Joint Contingency Contracting System Platform (which must be consistent with the combat support agency's established functions and responsibilities) and set forth by the geographic combatant commander during declared contingency operations for all solicitations and contracts that relate to the delivery of supplies and services to the designated area(s) of operation.

(A) Theater business clearance ensures—

(*1*) Contracted effort to be accomplished in designated area(s) of operations, along with any associated contractor personnel, is visible to the combatant commander;

(*2*) Contracted effort is in consonance with in-country commanders' plans;

(*3*) Solicitations and contracts contain appropriate terms and conditions;

(*4*) Contracted effort will be properly overseen in designated area(s) of operation;.

(*5*) Any Government-furnished support requirements associated with contractor personnel are properly addressed in the contract terms and conditions.

(B) Contract administration delegation—

(*1*) Allows the combatant commander to exercise control over the assignment of contract administration (which must be consistent with the combat support agency's established functions and responsibilities) for that portion of contracted effort that relates to performance in, or delivery to, designated area(s) of operation.

(*2*) Allows the combatant commander to exercise oversight to ensure the contractor's compliance with combatant commander and subordinate task force commander policies, directives, and terms and conditions;

(iii) Refer to the website at *http://www.acq.osd.mil/dpap/pacc/cc/index.html*, which contains required procedures and applicable guidance and information;

(iv) Follow specific guidance for the combatant command in whose area the contractor will be performing services or delivering supplies. This guidance is contained on the respective combatant commander's operational contract support webpage, which is linked to the procedures at *http://www.acq.osd.mil/dpap/pacc/cc/areas_of_responsibility.html*, at the weblink for the combatant command for the area in which the contractor will be performing services or delivering items. These pages list prevailing regulations, policies, requirements, host nation laws, orders/fragmentary orders, combatant commander's directives, unique clauses, and other considerations necessary for soliciting and awarding a contract for performance in, or delivery of items to, that combatant commander's area of responsibility;

(v) To determine the appropriate point(s) of contact for contracting matters within the combatant commander's area of responsibility, contact the overseas contracting office by accessing the link for the combatant command in whose area of responsibility the contractor will be performing services or delivering items. From the combatant command website, link to the contracting office supporting the combatant command to identify the appropriate point of contact; and

(vi) Use the following checklist as a guide to document consideration of each listed issue, as applicable, and retain a copy of the completed checklist in the contract file.

CHECKLIST

The contracting officer shall verify that the requiring activity has considered the following when building its requirements package, as applicable:

____ (1) Whether the contemplated acquisition will duplicate or otherwise conflict with existing work being performed or items already provided in the area, and whether economies of scope/schedule can be leveraged if there are already existing contracts in place for similar work or items.

____(2) The availability of technically qualified and properly trained Government civilian and/or military personnel to oversee the performance of the contract in the combatant commander's area of responsibility (e.g., contracting officer's representatives, quality assurance representatives, and property administrators).

____(3) The applicability of any international agreements to the acquisition. (Some agreements may be classified and must be handled appropriately.)

____(4) Compliance with area-specific, anti-terrorism security guidance set forth by the command anti-terrorism officer, to include soliciting anti-terrorism officer guidance on the particular requirement and the location of delivery and/or execution of services, and incorporating recommended security measures into the requirements package.

____(5) Whether there are any requirements for use of foreign currencies, including applicability of U.S. holdings of excess foreign currencies.

____(6) Information on taxes and duties from which the Government may be exempt.

____ (7) If the acquisition requires performance of work in the foreign country, whether there are standards of conduct for the prospective contractor and, if so, the consequences for violation of such standards of conduct.

____ (8) The availability of logistical and other Government-furnished support and equipment for contractor personnel. This includes, but is not limited to: berthing and messing; intra-theater transportation; medical support; morale, welfare, and recreation support; postal support; force protection support; organizational clothing and personal protective gear (e.g., body armor and gas masks.)

____(9) If the contractor will employ foreign workers, whether a waiver of the Defense Base Act will be required (see FAR 28.305).

____(10) Whether contractor personnel will need authorization to carry weapons for the performance of the contract.

____(11) If the contract will include the clause at DFARS 252.225-7040, Contractor Personnel Supporting U.S. Armed Forces Deployed Outside the United States, the Government official authorized to receive DD Form 93, Record of Emergency Data Card, to enable the contracting officer to provide that information to the contractor, as required by paragraph (g) of the clause.

____ (12) Ascertain the existence of and detail any Geographic Combatant Commander's (GCC's)/Subordinate Joint Force Commander Combating Trafficking in Persons Directives or Notices applying to Combating Trafficking in Persons (as required by FAR 22.1705 for contracts performed outside the United States) that would require the contracting officer to use Alternate I of the clause at FAR 52.222-50 detailing these requirements. This information can be ascertained from review of content on the cognizant Geographic Combatant Command Operational Contract Support webpage referred to in (a)(iv) of this PGI section.

____(13) Other requirements associated with contractor personnel to include deployment-related training, accountability (registration in Synchronized Pre-deployment and Operational Tracker), medical and dental qualifications, theater entrance and country clearance requirements

____ (14) Any other requirements of the website for the country in which the contract will be performed or the designated operational area to which deliveries will be made.

The contracting officer shall provide the following information to the applicable overseas contracting office (see PGI 225.370(a)(v)):

____(1) The solicitation number, the estimated dollar value of the acquisition, and a brief description of the work to be performed or the items to be delivered.

____ (2) Notice of contract award, including contract number, dollar value, and a brief description of the work to be performed or the items to be delivered.

____ (3) Any additional information requested by the applicable contracting office to ensure full compliance with policies, procedures, and objectives of the applicable country or designated operational area.

(c) For work performed in Japan or Korea, U.S.-Japan or U.S.-Korea bilateral agreements govern the status of contractors and employees, criminal jurisdiction, and taxation. U.S. Forces Japan (USFJ) and U.S. Forces Korea (USFK) are sub-unified commands of Pacific Command (PACOM). The PACOM Staff Judge Advocate contact information is available at *http://www.pacom.mil/web/Site_Pages/Staff%20Directory/J0/J0.shtml* or by clicking on Staff Directory/Special Staff on the PACOM website. Links to USFJ and USFK websites can be found at the PACOM website at *http://www.pacom.mil* by clicking on "Regional Resources - Links".

(i) For work performed in Japan—

(A) U.S.-Japan bilateral agreements govern the status of contractors and employees, criminal jurisdiction, and taxation;

(B) USFJ and component policy, as well as U.S.-Japan bilateral agreements, govern logistic support and base privileges of contractor employees;

(C) The Commander, USFJ, is primarily responsible for interpreting the Status of Forces Agreement (SOFA) and local laws applicable to U.S. Forces in Japan and for requirements in support of USFJ; and

(D)(*1*) To ensure that the solicitation and resultant contract reflect an accurate description of available logistics support and application of the U.S.-Japan SOFA, review the information on Contract Performance in Japan at the USFJ website, *http://www.usfj.mil*; or

(*2*) Contact the Staff Judge Advocate at (commercial) 011-81-3117-55-7717, or DSN 315-225-7717.

(ii) For work performed in Korea—

(A) U.S.-Korea bilateral agreements govern the status of contractors and employees, criminal jurisdiction, and taxation;

(B) USFK and component policy, as well as U.S.-Korea bilateral agreements, govern logistics support and base privileges of contractor employees;

(C) The Commander, USFK, is primarily responsible for interpreting the SOFA and local laws applicable to U.S. Forces in Korea and for requirements in support of USFK; and

(D) To ensure that the solicitation and resultant contract reflect an accurate description of available logistics support and application of the U.S.-Korea SOFA, review the SOFA information found at the USFK website at *http://www.usfk.mil/usfk/* under "Publications", or at *http://www.usfk.mil/usfk/sofadocuments.aspx*. Contact information for the Commander is also available at *http://www.usfk.mil/usfk/leadership.aspx*; and

(E) Additional applicable directives and regulations are available at http://www.usfk.mil/usfk/ , click on the drop down menu for "Publications".

(d) For work performed in specified countries in the USCENTCOM area of responsibility, follow theater business clearance/contract administration delegation policy as set forth in OSD policy letters linked to this PGI, and specific theater business clearance/contract administration delegation instructions as implemented by USCENTCOM's Joint Theater Support Contracting Command and found under contracting guidance at *http://www.acq.osd.mil/dpap/pacc/cc/areas_of_responsibility.html* (click on CENTCOM area of responsibility).

[Final rule, 80 FR 36900, 6/26/2015, effective 6/26/2015]

225.371 Contractor personnel supporting U.S. Armed Forces deployed outside the United States.

(1) DoDI 3020.41, Operational Contract Support (OCS), establishes policy, assigns responsibilities and provides procedures for OCS, including OCS Program Management, contract support integration, and integration of defense contractor personnel into contingency operations outside the United States. This instruction serves as a comprehensive source of DoD policy and procedures concerning DoD contractor and subcontractor personnel supporting the U.S. Armed Forces deployed outside the United States.

(2) Also see PGI 207.105(b)(20)(C)(9) for special considerations for acquisition planning for crisis situations outside the United States.

[Final rule, 80 FR 36900, 6/26/2015, effective 6/26/2015]

225.371-2 Definitions.

Designated operational areas include, but are not limited to, such descriptors as theater of war, theater of operations, joint operations area, amphibious objective area, joint special operations area, and area of operations. See DoD Joint Publication 3-0, Joint Operations, Chapter IV, Paragraph 2, "Understanding the Operational Environment," at *http://www.dtic.mil/doctrine/new_pubs/jp3_0.pdf*.

[Final rule, 80 FR 36900, 6/26/2015, effective 6/26/2015]

225.371-3 Government support.

(a) Support that may be authorized or required when contractor personnel are deployed with or otherwise provide support in the theater of operations to U.S. military forces deployed outside the United States may include, but are not limited to—

(i) Deployment in-processing centers;

(ii) Training;

(iii) Transportation to operation area;

(iv) Transportation within operation area;

(v) Physical security;

(vi) Force protection;

(vii) Organizational clothing and individual equipment;

(viii) Emergency medical care;

(ix) Mess operations;

(x) Quarters;

(xi) Postal service;

(xii) Phone service;

(xiii) Emergency notification;

(xiv) Laundry; and

(xv) Religious services.

(d) *Medical support of contractor personnel.*

(1) Contractors are required to ensure that the Government is reimbursed for any costs associated with medical or dental care provided to contractor employees accompanying the forces (see 252.225-7040(c)(2)).

(2) If questions arise concerning Defense Finance and Accounting Services (DFAS) billing to contractors for medical or dental care provided, contracting officers may refer the individual to any of the following resources:

(i) For in-patient and out-patient billing rates, go to *http://comptroller.defense.gov/FinancialManagement/Reports/rates2013.asp* x, click on the appropriate fiscal year, and select Deployed/Non-Fixed Medical Facility Billing Rates.

(ii) For Military Service-appointed points of contact (POCs) responsible for resolving medical billing disputes, see the POCs listed in the *memoranda of agreements between DFAS and the military services*).

(iii) For general information on medical support of deployed contractor personnel in applicable contingency operations, see DoDI 3020.41.

(3) Contracting officers are not responsible for adjudicating DFAS bills to contractors for such medical or dental reimbursement. However, contracting officers are required to assist the Military Service POCs in resolving billing disputes.

(e) *Letter of Authorization.*

(i) If authorized by the contracting officer, a contracting officer's representative may approve a SPOT-generated LOA. Contractor travel orders will be prepared by the supporting installation.

(ii) The LOA will state the intended length of assignment in the theater of operations and will identify planned use of Government facilities and privileges in the theater of operations, as authorized by the contract. Authorizations may include such privileges as access to the exchange facilities and the commissary, and use of Government messing and billeting. The LOA must include the name of the approving Government official.

(iii) Approved, standard DoD format for LOA: (See sample LOA, Business Rules for the Synchronized Predeployment and Operational Tracker, at *http://www.acq.osd.mil/log/PS/spot.html*.

[Final rule, 80 FR 36900, 6/26/2015, effective 6/26/2015]

225.371-5 Contract clauses.

Performance, as used in *Class Deviation 2015-O0009*, Contractor Personnel Performing in the United States Central Command Area of Responsibility, means performance of a service or construction, as required by the contract. For supply contracts, production of the supplies or associated overhead functions are not covered by the Class Deviation, but services associated with the acquisition of the supplies are covered (e.g., installation or maintenance)

(b) When using the clause at DFARS 252.225-7040, Contractor Personnel Supporting U.S. Armed Forces Deployed Outside the United States, consider the applicability of the following clauses:

(i) The clause at DFARS 252.225-7043, Antiterrorism/Force Protection Policy for Defense Contractors Outside the United States, as prescribed at DFARS 225.372-2.

(ii) Either the clause at FAR 52.228-3, Workers' Compensation Insurance (Defense Base Act), or the clause at FAR 52.228-4, Workers' Compensation and War-Hazard Insurance Overseas, as prescribed at FAR 28.309(a) and (b).

(iii) The clause at FAR 52.228-7, Insurance—Liability to Third Persons, in cost-reimbursement contracts as prescribed at DFARS 228.311-1.

(iv) The clause at DFARS 252.228-7003, Capture and Detention, as prescribed at DFARS 228.370(d).

(v) The clause at DFARS 252.237-7019, Training for Contractor Personnel Interacting with Detainees, as prescribed at DFARS 237.171-4.

(vi) The clause at FAR 52.249-14, Excusable Delays, as prescribed at FAR 49.505(b).

(vii) The clauses at FAR 52.251-1, Government Supply Sources, as prescribed at FAR 51.107, and DFARS 252.251-7000, Ordering from Government Supply Sources, as prescribed at DFARS 251.107. See also Class

Deviation 2013-O0012, Authorization for Contractors to Use Government Supply Sources in Support of Operation Enduring Freedom.

[Final rule, 80 FR 36900, 6/26/2015, effective 6/26/2015]

225.372 Antiterrorism/force protection. (No Text)

[Final rule, 80 FR 36900, 6/26/2015, effective 6/26/2015]

225.372-1 General.

Information and guidance pertaining to DoD antiterrorism/force protection policy for contracts that require performance or travel outside the United States can be obtained from the following offices:

(1) For Army contracts: HQDA-AT; telephone, DSN 222-9832 or commercial (703) 692-9832.

(2) For Navy contracts: Naval Criminal Investigative Service (NCIS), Code 21; telephone, DSN 288-9077 or commercial (202) 433-9077.

(3) For Marine Corps contracts: CMC Code POS-10; telephone, DSN 224-4177 or commercial (703) 614-4177.

(4) For Air Force and Combatant Command contracts: The appropriate Antiterrorism/Force Protection Office at the Command Headquarters. Also see *https://atep.dtic.mil*.

(5) For defense agency contracts: The appropriate agency security office.

(6) For additional information: Assistant Secretary of Defense for Homeland Defense and Global Security, ASD (HS/GS); telephone, DSN 227-6566 or 260-8350 or commercial (703) 697-6566 or (571) 256-8350.

[Final rule, 80 FR 36900, 6/26/2015, effective 6/26/2015; Final rule, 84 FR 4362, 2/15/2019, effective 2/15/2019]

225.373 Contract administration in support of contingency operations.

(1) In accordance with Joint Publication 1, Doctrine for the Armed Forces of the United States, at *http://www.apexnet.org/docs/Joint_Publication_1.pdf*, the geographic combatant commander or subordinate joint force commander, through his command authority to exercise operational control, has the authority to exercise control over the combat support agency's established mission functions, responsibilities, and core competencies, for contracts requiring delivery of items or performance within the area of operations.

(2) In certain contingency operations, the combatant commander or joint force commander may promulgate theater or joint operations area guidance for contracting that may include establishing—

(i) A contracting command and control structure;

(ii) Head of contracting activity responsibilities, specific orders, and policies, including local clauses;

(iii) Roles and responsibilities of DoD components and supporting agencies in contract formation and execution; and

(iv) Procedures and requirements for contract clearance and contract administration of contracts requiring delivery of items and performance within the area of operations.

(3) When a combat support agency is tasked by the combatant commander to provide contingency contract administration services in support of contingency operations and such support will be required for a long duration, the combat support agency shall initiate a memorandum of agreement with the combatant commander or joint force commander. This agreement shall clearly delineate the purpose of the support, respective responsibilities of the combat support agency and the joint, lead service, or service contracting activity requesting the support, combat support agency support parameters, and a resolution process for resolving support issues.

(i) The memorandum of agreement should focus on maximizing the combat support agency's core competencies to address the more critical, complex, high-risk, and specialized oversight requirements

(ii) The memorandum of agreement should take into consideration the combat support agency's core competencies, workload priorities, and contract administration services support parameters for accepting requests for contract administration services support.

(iii) A combat support agency shall not be assigned to perform tasks outside its mission functions, responsibilities, or core competencies.

(iv) Contracting officers contemplating requesting contract administration support in a contingency area from a combat support agency should first ascertain whether such a memorandum of agreement exists by contacting their combat support agency point of contact and/or checking the combatant commander operational contract support website (referenced in DFARS PGI 225.370).

(v) The following is a notional format for a memorandum of agreement for contract administration services support;

(A) Purpose: Outline formal procedures for requesting contract administration services support, describe objectives associated with combat support agency providing such support.

(B) Reference: Key documents or reference(s) associated with the execution of the contract administration services support.

(C) Clearinghouse functions performed by the designated joint or lead component contracting activity in the operational area–

(1) Contract clearance parameters – when required;

(2) Contract delegation parameters – when required.

(D) Contract administration services support parameters—

(1) Acceptable for delegation - contract types that will be accepted by the combat support agency based on risk, dollar threshold, geographic dispersion of performance, service type, criticality of acceptance, or other criteria;

(2) Generally not be delegated – below-threshold contract types;

(3) Will not be delegated – no agency expertise to oversee.

(E) Delegation process – process for accepting and assigning contract administration services tasks within the combat support agency. (F) Joint resolution process – procedures in the event of disagreement on actions to be supported by the combat support agency.

(F) Joint resolution process – procedures in the event of disagreement on actions to be supported by the combat support agency.

(G) Term of the Agreement and Modification - length of time the agreement will be in effect and procedures for the parties to modify or terminate it.

(4) Disputes regarding requested support should be resolved at the lowest management level possible, through a predetermined resolution process. When support issues arise that affect the ability of a combat support agency to provide contract administration support that cannot be resolved at lower management levels, follow procedures set forth in DoDI 3000.06, Combat Support Agencies, paragraphs 5.6.8 and 5.6.9, (*http://www.dtic.mil/whs/directives/corres/pdf/300006p.pdf*).

(5) Responsibilities of the head of the contracting activity for contingency contract closeout are addressed at DFARS 204.804(2). See also planning considerations at PGI 207.105(b)(20)(C)(8).

[Final rule, 80 FR 36900, 6/26/2015, effective 6/26/2015]

SUBPART 225.7—PROHIBITED SOURCES

225.770 Prohibition on acquisition of United States Munitions List items from Communist Chinese military companies.

(1) The Department of State is the lead agency responsible for the regulations governing the export of defense articles, which are identified on the United States Munitions List. The Department of State has issued the International Traffic in Arms Regulations, which implement the Arms Export Control Act (22 U.S.C. 2751) and include the United States Munitions List.

(2) The official version of the International Traffic in Arms Regulations can be found in Title 22, Parts 120 through 130, of the Code of Federal Regulations (22 CFR 120-130), published by the U.S. Government Printing Office and available at *http://*

www.gpoaccess.gov/cfr/index.html. The Department of State also publishes an on-line version at *http://pmddtc.state.gov/consolidated_itar.htm*.

[Interim rule, 71 FR 53045, 9/8/2006, effective 9/8/2006; Final rule, 72 FR 14239, 3/27/2007, effective 3/27/2007]

225.770-1 Definitions.

In accordance with 22 CFR 121.8—

(1) A *major component* includes any assembled element that forms a portion of an end item without which the end item is inoperable. Examples of major components are airframes, tail sections, transmissions, tank treads, and hulls;

(2) A *minor component* includes any assembled element of a major component; and

(3) Examples of *parts* are rivets, wires, and bolts.

[Interim rule, 71 FR 53045, 9/8/2006, effective 9/8/2006]

225.770-4 Identifying USML items.

(1) The 21 categories of items on the United States Munitions List (USML) can be found at *https://pmddtc.state.gov/docs/ITAR/2006/ITAR_Part_221.pdf*. Where applicable, the categories also contain a statement with regard to the coverage of components and parts of items included in a category. For example, a category may include all components and parts of covered items, only those components and parts specifically designed or modified for military use.

(2) In addition to the list of covered items, the USML provides explanation of terms needed to determine whether a particular item is or is not covered by the USML.

(3) Within DoD, the experts on export control and the USML are in the Defense Technology Security Administration (DTSA).

(i) Official authorities and responsibilities of DTSA are in DoD Directive 5105.72, available at *http://www.dtic.mil/whs/directives/corres/html/510572.htm*.

(ii) Additional information on DTSA and a correspondence link are available at *http://www.dod.mil/policy/sections/policy_offices/dtsa/index.html*.

[Interim rule, 71 FR 53045, 9/8/2006, effective 9/8/2006; Final rule, 72 FR 14239, 3/27/2007, effective 3/27/2007]

225.770-5 Waiver of prohibition.

(c) Send the DPAP copy of the report to:

Director, Defense Procurement and Acquisition Policy

ATTN: OUSD (AT&L) DPAP (CPIC)

3060 Defense Pentagon.

Washington, DC 20301-3060..

[Final rule, 77 FR 30365, 5/22/2012, effective 5/22/2012]

225.771 Prohibition on contracting or subcontracting with a firm that is owned or controlled by the government of a country that is a state sponsor of terrorism. (No Text)

[Final rule, 79 FR 73488, 12/11/2014, effective 12/11/2014]

225.771-3 Notification.

Forward any information indicating that a firm, a subsidiary of a firm, or any other firm that owns or controls the firm, may be owned or controlled by the government of a country that is a state sponsor of terrorism, through agency channels, to: Deputy Director, Defense Procurement (Contract Policy and International Contracting, OUSD (AT&L) DPAP/CPIC), 3060 Defense Pentagon, Washington, DC 20301-3060.

[Final rule, 79 FR 73488, 12/11/2014, effective 12/11/2014]

225.772-3 Prohibition on acquisition of commercial satellite services from certain foreign entities.

(1) Forward any information required in accordance with 225.772-3 or requests for an exception to:

Director, Defense Pricing and Contracting

ATTN: OUSD (A&S) DPC/CP

3060 Defense Pentagon

Washington, DC 20301-3060.

(2) Consult with OUSD (A&S) DPC/CP, as required in accordance with

225.772-3(c)(2), by telephone at 703-697-0895 or 703-695-8569.

[Interim rule, 83 FR 66066, 12/21/2018, effective 12/21/2018; Final rule, 84 FR 25188, 5/31/2019, effective 5/31/2019]

SUBPART 225.8—OTHER INTERNATIONAL AGREEMENTS AND COORDINATION

225.802 Procedures.

(b) Information on specific memoranda of understanding and other international agreements is available as follows:

(i) Memoranda of understanding and other international agreements between the United States and the countries listed in DFARS 225.872-1 are maintained in the Office of the Director of Defense Procurement and Acquisition Policy (Contract Policy and International Contracting) ((703) 697-9351, DSN 227-9351) and are available at *http://www.acq.osd.mil/dpap/cpic/ic/reciprocal_procurement_memoranda_of_understanding.html.*

(ii) Military Assistance Advisory Groups, Naval Missions, and Joint U.S. Military Aid Groups normally have copies of the agreements applicable to the countries concerned.

(iii) Copies of international agreements covering the United Kingdom of Great Britain and Northern Ireland, Western European countries, North Africa, and the Middle East are filed with the U.S. European Command.

(iv) Agreements with countries in the Pacific and Far East are filed with the U.S. Pacific Command.

[Final rule, 70 FR 23790, 5/5/2005, effective 6/6/2005; Final rule, 70 FR 73153, 12/9/2005, effective 12/9/2005; Change notice, 20061109; Change notice, 20070531; Change notice, 20071108]

225.802-70 Contracts for performance outside the United States and Canada.

When a contracting office anticipates placement of a contract for performance outside the United States and Canada, and the contracting office is not under the jurisdiction of a command for the country involved, the contracting office shall maintain liaison with the cognizant contract administration office (CAO) during preaward negotiations and postaward administration. The cognizant CAO can be found at *http://home.dcma.mil/cassites/district.htm*. The CAO will provide pertinent information for contract negotiations, effect appropriate coordination, and obtain required approvals for the performance of the contract.

[Final rule, 70 FR 23790, 5/5/2005, effective 6/6/2005]

225.870 Contracting with Canadian contractors. (No Text)

[Final rule, 70 FR 73153, 12/9/2005, effective 12/9/2005]

225.870-1 General.

(d)(i) The Canadian Commercial Corporation uses provisions in contracts with Canadian or U.S. concerns that give DoD the same production rights, data, and information that DoD would obtain in contracts with U.S. concerns.

(ii) The Government of Canada will provide the following services under contracts with the Canadian Commercial Corporation without charge to DoD:

(A) Contract administration services, including—

(1) Cost and price analysis;

(2) Industrial security;

(3) Accountability and disposal of Government property;

(4) Production expediting;

(5) Compliance with Canadian labor laws;

(6) Processing of termination claims and disposal of termination inventory;

(7) Customs documentation;

(8) Processing of disputes and appeals; and

(9) Such other related contract administration functions as may be required with respect to the Canadian Commercial Corporation contract with the Canadian supplier.

(B) *Audits.* The Public Works and Government Services Canada (PWGSC) performs audits, when needed, for contracts overseen by the Canadian Commercial Corporation, in accordance with international agreement.

(C) *Inspection.* The Department of National Defence (Canada) provides inspection personnel, services, and facilities, at no charge to DoD departments and agencies (see DFARS 225.870-7).

(iii) In accordance with DPAP Policy Memorandum dated June 5, 2013, PWGSC will perform audits without charge to DoD, including accounting system and interim voucher reviews, when needed for—

(A) DoD contracts awarded directly to Canadian firms;

(B) Subcontracts with Canadian firms under such direct contracts with Canadian firms; and

(C) Subcontracts with Canadian firms under DoD contracts with U.S.

[Publication notice, 20130703; Publication notice, 20131031]

225.870-5 Contract administration.

(1) Assign contract administration in accordance with DFARS Part 242. When the Defense Contract Management Agency will perform contract administration in Canada, name in the contract the following payment office for disbursement of DoD funds (DoD Department Code: 17-Navy; 21-Army; 57-Air Force; 97-all other DoD components), whether payment is in Canadian or U.S. dollars:

DFAS Columbus Center
DFAS-CO/North Entitlement Operations
PO Box 182266
Columbus, OH 43218-2266.

(2) The following procedures apply to cost-reimbursement type contracts:

(i) The PWGSC automatically arranges audits on contracts with the Canadian Commercial Corporation. Upon advice from PWGSC, the Canadian Commercial Corporation certifies the invoice and forwards it with Standard Form (SF) 1034, Public Voucher, to the administrative contracting officer for further processing and transmittal to the disbursing office.

(ii) For contracts placed directly with Canadian firms, the administrative contracting officer requests audits from the PWGSC, Ottawa, Ontario, Canada. Route requests for audit of non-Canadian Commercial Corporation contracts and subcontracts with Canadian contractors through the cognizant contract management office of the Defense Contract Management Agency.

(A) Within 25 days of the date of the audit request, PWGSC will provide—

(1) An acknowledgment of receipt form:

(2) An estimate of completion form; and

(3) A single point of contact to report the status of audit requests and the progress of audits.

(B) Audits will be completed within 24 months of the requested date for post-award audits.

(C) PWGSC will provide information to support the determination that the price is fair and reasonable.

(D) The CAC/PWGSC—

(1) Approves invoices on a provisional basis pending completion of the contract and final audit.

(2) Forwards these invoices, accompanied by SF 1034, Public Voucher, to the administrative contracting officer for further processing and transmittal to the disbursing officer; and

(3) Furnishes periodic advisory audit reports directly to the administrative contracting officer.

[Final rule, 70 FR 73153, 12/9/2005, effective 12/9/2005; Publication notice, 20130703; Publication notice, 20131031]

225.870-7 Acceptance of Canadian supplies.

(1) For contracts placed in Canada, either with the Canadian Commercial Corporation or directly with Canadian suppliers, the Department of National Defence (Canada) will perform any necessary contract quality assurance and/or acceptance, as applicable.

(2) Signature by the Department of National Defence (Canada) quality assurance representative on the DoD inspection and acceptance form is satisfactory evidence of acceptance for payment purposes.

[Final rule, 70 FR 73153, 12/9/2005, effective 12/9/2005]

225.871 North Atlantic Treaty Organization (NATO) cooperative projects. (No Text)

[Final rule, 70 FR 73153, 12/9/2005, effective 12/9/2005]

225.871-4 Statutory waivers.

Forward any request for waiver under a cooperative project to the Deputy Secretary of Defense, through the Director of Defense Procurement and Acquisition Policy, Office of the Under Secretary of Defense (Acquisition, Technology, and Logistics). The waiver request shall include a draft Determination and Findings for signature by the Deputy Secretary of Defense establishing that the waiver is necessary to significantly further NATO standardization, rationalization, and interoperability.

[Final rule, 71 FR 62565, 10/26/2006, effective 10/26/2006]

225.871-5 Directed subcontracting.

The cooperative project agreement is the authority for a contractual provision requiring the contractor to place certain subcontracts with particular subcontractors. No separate justification and approval during the acquisition process is required.

[Final rule, 70 FR 73153, 12/9/2005, effective 12/9/2005]

225.872 Contracting with qualifying country sources. (No Text)

[Final rule, 70 FR 73153, 12/9/2005, effective 12/9/2005]

225.872-4 Individual determinations.

(1) Obtain signature of the determination and findings—

(i) At a level above the contracting officer, for acquisitions valued at or below the simplified acquisition threshold; or

(ii) By the chief of the contracting office, for acquisitions with a value greater than the simplified acquisition threshold.

(2) Prepare the determination and findings substantially as follows:

SERVICE OR AGENCY

Exemption of the Buy American and Balance of Payments Program

Determination and Findings

Upon the basis of the following findings and determination which I hereby make in accordance with the provisions of FAR 25.103(a), the acquisition of a qualifying country end product may be made as follows:

Findings

1. The (*contracting office*) proposes to purchase under contract number ________________, (*describe item*) mined, produced, or manufactured in (*qualifying country of origin*). The total estimated cost of this acquisition is ________________.

2. The United States Government and the Government of ____________ have agreed to remove barriers to procurement at the prime and subcontract level for defense equipment produced in each other's countries insofar as laws and regulations permit.

3. The agreement provides that the Department of Defense will evaluate competitive offers of qualifying country end products mined, produced, or manufactured in (*qualifying country*) without imposing any price differential under the Buy American statute or the Balance of Payments Program and without taking applicable U.S. customs and duties into consideration so that such items may better compete for sales of defense equipment to the Department of Defense. In addition, the Agreement stipulates that acquisitions of such items shall fully satisfy Department of Defense requirements for performance, quality, and delivery and shall cost the Department of Defense no more than would comparable U.S. source or other foreign source defense equipment eligible for award.

4. To achieve the foregoing objectives, the solicitation contained the clause (*title and number of the Buy American clause contained in the contract*). Offers were solicited from other sources and

the offer receive from (*offeror*) is found to be otherwise eligible for award.

Determination

I hereby determine that it is inconsistent with the public interest to apply the restrictions of the Buy American statute or the Balance of Payments Program to the offer described in this determination and findings.

____________ ____________

(Date)

[Final rule, 70 FR 73153, 12/9/2005, effective 12/9/2005; Final rule, 77 FR 35879, 6/15/2012, effective 6/15/2012]

225.872-5 Contract administration.

(b) (i) When contract administration services are required on contracts to be performed in qualifying countries, direct the request to the cognizant activity listed in the Federal Directory of Contract Administration Services. The cognizant activity also will arrange contract administration services for DoD subcontracts that qualifying country sources place in the United States.

(ii) The contract administration activity receiving a delegation shall determine whether any portions of the delegation are covered by memoranda of understanding annexes and, if so, shall delegate those functions to the appropriate organization in the qualifying country's government.

[Final rule, 70 FR 73153, 12/9/2005, effective 12/9/2005]

225.872-6 Request for audit services.

(1) Send requests for audit services in France, Germany, the Netherlands, or the United Kingdom to the administrative contracting officer at the cognizant activity listed in Section 2B of the Federal Directory of Contract Administration Services. See DFARS *225.870, PGI 225.870-1*, and *PGI 225.870-5* for procedures to request audit services for contracts overseen by the Canadian Commercial Corporation.

(2) Complete requests for audit services in France, Germany, the Netherlands, or the United Kingdom using the forms and information sheet with form completion instructions available at ***http://www.dcma.mil/Contact-Us/Division_I/*** (click on "DCMA Foreign Contractors Pricing Support and Assist Audit Information Sheet").

[Final rule, 70 FR 73153, 12/9/2005, effective 12/9/2005; Change notice, 20070531; Final rule, 81 FR 59510, 8/30/2016, effective 8/30/2016; Publication notice, 20171208]

225.873 Waiver of United Kingdom commercial exploitation levies. (No Text)

[Final rule, 70 FR 73153, 12/9/2005, effective 12/9/2005]

225.873-2 Procedures.

(1) The Government of the U.K. shall approve waiver of U.K. levies. When an offeror or contractor identifies a levy included in an offered or contract price, the contracting officer shall provide written notification to the Defense Security Cooperation Agency, ATTN: PSD-PMD, 1111 Jefferson Davis Highway, Arlington, VA 22202-4306, telephone (703) 601-3864. The Defense Security Cooperation Agency will request a waiver of the levy from the Government of the U.K. The notification shall include—

(i) Name of the U.K. firm;

(ii) Prime contract number;

(iii) Description of item for which waiver is being sought;

(iv) Quantity being acquired; and

(v) Amount of levy.

(2) Waiver may occur after contract award. If levies are waived before contract award, evaluate the offer without the levy. If levies are identified but not waived before contract award, evaluate the offer inclusive of the levies.

[Final rule, 70 FR 73153, 12/9/2005, effective 12/9/2005]

SUBPART 225.9—CUSTOMS AND DUTIES

225.902 Procedures.

(1) Formal entry and release.

(i) The administrative contracting officer shall—

(A) Ensure that contractors are aware of and understand any Duty-Free Entry clause requirements. Contractors should understand that failure by them or their subcontractors to provide the data required by the clause will result in treatment of the shipment as without benefit of free entry under Section XXII, Chapter 98, Subchapter VIII, Item 9808.00.30 of the Harmonized Tariff Schedule of the United States.

(B) Upon receipt of the required notice of purchase of foreign supplies from the contractor or any tier subcontractor—

(1) Verify the duty-free entitlement of supplies entering under the contract; and

(2) Review the prime contract to ensure that performance of the contract requires the foreign supplies (quantity and price) identified in the notice.

(C) Within 20 days after receiving the notification of purchase of foreign supplies, forward the following information in the format indicated to the Commander, DCMA New York, ATTN: Customs Team, DCMAE-GNTF, 207 New York Avenue, Building 120, Staten Island, NY 10305-5013:

We have received a contractor notification of the purchase of foreign supplies. I have verified that foreign supplies are required for the performance of the contract.

Prime Contractor Name and Address:

Prime Contractor CAGE Code:

Prime Contract Number plus Delivery Order Number, if applicable:

Total Dollar Value of the Prime Contract or Delivery Order:

Expiration Date of the Prime Contract or Delivery Order:

Foreign Supplier Name and Address:

Number of Subcontract/Purchase Order for Foreign Supplies:

Total Dollar Value of the Subcontract for Foreign Supplies:

Expiration Date of the Subcontract for Foreign Supplies:

CAO Activity Address Number:

ACO Name and Telephone Number:

ACO Code:

Signature:

Title:

(D) If a contract modification results in a change to any data verifying duty-free entitlement previously furnished, forward a revised notification including the changed data to DCMA New York.

(ii) The Customs Team, DCMAE-GNTF, DCMA New York—

(A) Is responsible for issuing duty-free entry certificates for foreign supplies purchased under a DoD contract or subcontract; and

(B) Upon receipt of import documentation for incoming shipments from the contractor, its agent, or the U.S. Customs Service, will verify the duty-free entitlement and execute the duty-free entry certificate.

(iii) Upon arrival of foreign supplies at ports of entry, the consignee, generally the contractor or its agent (import broker) for shipments to other than a military installation, will file U.S. Customs Form 7501, 7501A, or 7506, with the District Director of Customs.

(2) Immediate entry and release. Importations made in the name of a DoD military facility or shipped directly to a military facility are entitled to release under the immediate delivery procedure.

(i) A DoD immediate delivery application has been approved and is on file at Customs Headquarters.

(ii) The application is for an indefinite period and is good for all Customs districts, areas, and ports.

[Final rule, 70 FR 73153, 12/9/2005, effective 12/9/2005]

225.903 Exempted supplies.

(b) (i) The term *supplies*

(A) Includes

(1) Articles known as *stores*, such as food, medicines, and toiletries; and

(2) All consumable articles necessary and appropriate for the propulsion, operation, and maintenance of the vessel or aircraft, such as fuel, oil, gasoline, grease, paint, cleansing compounds, solvents, wiping rags, and polishes; and

(B) Does not include portable articles necessary and appropriate for the navigation, operation, or maintenance of the vessel or aircraft and for the comfort and safety of the persons on board, such as rope, bolts and nuts, bedding, china and cutlery, which are included in the term *equipment*.

(ii) Format for duty-free certificate.

(Date) ____________________

I certify that the acquisition of this material constituted a purchase of supplies by the United States for vessels or aircraft operated by the United States, and is admissible free of duty pursuant to 19 U.S.C. 1309.

(Name) ____________________

(Title) ____________________

(Organization)

____

[Final rule, 70 FR 73153, 1292005, effective 1292005]

SUBPART 225.70—AUTHORIZATION ACTS, APPROPRIATIONS ACTS, AND OTHER STATUTORY RESTRICTIONS ON FOREIGN ACQUISITION

225.7002 Restrictions on food, clothing, fabrics, and hand or measuring tools.

[Final rule, 70 FR 43073, 7/26/2005, effective 7/26/2005; Interim rule, 72 FR 2637, 1/22/2007, effective 1/22/2007; Change notice, 20080110; Final rule, 74 FR 37626, 7/29/2009, effective 7/29/2009; Publication notice, 20191231]

225.7002-1 Restrictions.

(a) (1) (ii) (*1*) The following are examples, not all-inclusive, of Product and Service Codes (PSCs) that contain items of clothing:

(i) Clothing apparel (such as outerwear, headwear, underwear, nightwear, footwear, hosiery, or handwear) listed in PSC 8405, 8410, 8415, 8420, 8425, 8450, or 8475.

(ii) Footwear listed in PSC 8430 or 8435.

(iii) Hosiery, handwear, or other items of clothing apparel, such as belts and suspenders, listed in PSC 8440 or 8445.

(iv) Badges or insignia listed in PSC 8455.

(2) The PSCs listed in paragraph (a) (1) (ii) (*1*) of this section also contain items that are not clothing, such as—

(i) Visors;

(ii) Kevlar helmets;

(iii) Handbags; and

(iv) Plastic identification tags.

(3) Each item should be individually analyzed to determine if it is clothing, rather than relying on the PSC alone to make that determination.

(4) The fact that an item is excluded from the foreign source restriction of the Berry Amendment applicable to clothing does not preclude application of another Berry Amendment restriction in DFARS *225.7002-1* to the components of the item.

(5) Small arms protective inserts (SAPI plates) are an example of items added to, and not normally associated with, clothing. Therefore, SAPI plates are not covered under the Berry Amendment as clothing. However, fabrics used in the SAPI plate are still subject to the foreign source restrictions of the Berry Amendment. If the fabric used in the SAPI plate is a synthetic fabric or a coated synthetic fabric, the fibers and yarns used in the fabric are not covered by the Berry Amendment, because the fabric is a component of an end product that is not a textile product (see DFARS *225.7002-2*(m)).

Example: A SAPI plate is compliant with the Berry Amendment if the synthetic fiber or yarn is obtained from foreign country X and woven into synthetic fabric in the United States, which is then incorporated into a SAPI plate manufactured in foreign country Y.

(2) *Hand or measuring tools.*

(A) As applied to hand or measuring tools, "produced in the United States" means that the hand or measuring tool was assembled in the United States out of components, or otherwise made from raw materials into the finished product that is to be provided to the Government.

(B) If a hand or measuring tool was assembled in a country other than the United States, then disassembled and reassembled in the United States, the hand or measuring tool was not produced in the United States.

(C) The requirement to buy hand or measuring tools produced in the United States does not impose any restriction on the source of the components of the hand or measuring tools. This is unlike the Berry Amendment restriction on clothing (see 225.7002-1(a)(1)(ii)), which explicitly requires domestic source for the materials and components of clothing (other than unusual components such as sensors or electronics), as well as the additional separate restrictions on various types of fibers and fabrics that might be components of the clothing.

(D) If the acquisition of the hand or measuring tools is also subject to the Buy American statute (see FAR subpart 25.1), then in order to qualify as a domestic end product, the cost of the components mined, produced, or manufactured in the United States or a qualifying country, must exceed 50 percent of the cost of all the components of the hand or measuring tool.

[Final rule, 71 FR 39008, 7/11/2006, effective 7/11/2006; Interim rule, 72 FR 2637, 1/22/2007, effective 1/22/2007; 72 FR 42315, 8/2/2007, effective 8/2/2007; Change notice, 20080110; Final rule, 74 FR 37626, 7/29/2009, effective 7/29/2009; Publication notice, 20110725; Final rule, 77 FR 35879, 6/15/2012, effective 6/15/2012; Final rule, 80 FR 51750, 8/26/2015, effective 8/26/2015; Publication notice, 20191231]

225.7002-2 Exceptions.

(b) *Domestic nonavailability determinations.*

(3) *Defense agencies other than the Defense Logistics Agency.*

(A) A defense agency requesting a domestic nonavailability determination must submit the request, including the proposed determination, to—

Principal Director, Defense Pricing and Contracting

ATTN: OUSD(A&S) DPC/CP

3060 Defense Pentagon

Washington, DC 20301-3060.

(B) The Principal Director, Defense Pricing and Contracting, will forward the request to the Under Secretary of Defense (Acquisition and Sustainment) (USD(A&S)) as appropriate.

[Final rule, 70 FR 43073, 7/26/2005, effective 7/26/2005; Interim rule, 72 FR 2637, 1/22/2007, effective 1/22/2007; Change notice, 20070327; Change notice, 20070426; Change notice, 20070531; Change notice, 20070802; Change notice, 20071108; Change notice, 20080110; Final rule, 74 FR 37626, 7/29/2009, effective 7/29/2009; Final rule, 74 FR 53413, 10/19/2009, effective 10/19/2009; Publication Notice, 20100713; Final rule, 77 FR 35879, 6/15/2012, effective 6/15/2012; Final rule, 78 FR 54968, 9/9/2013, effective 9/9/2013; Publication notice, 20150626; Final rule, 84 FR 72239, 12/31/2019, effective 12/31/2019]

225.7002-3 [Removed]

[Final rule, 74 FR 37626, 7/29/2009, effective 7/29/2009]

225.7003 Restrictions on acquisition of specialty metals.

[Final rule, 74 FR 37626, 7/29/2009, effective 7/29/2009; Publication notice, 20191231]

225.7003-2 Restrictions.

(a)(i) This restriction applies to the item containing the specialty metal, not just the specialty metal, as was true when the restriction was part of 10 U.S.C. 2533a. The previous practice of withholding payment while conditionally accepting noncompliant items is not permissible for—

(A) Contracts entered into on or after November 16, 2006; or

(B) New procurements or out-of-scope changes accomplished on or after November 16, 2006, through the use of bilateral modifications to contracts originally awarded prior to November 16, 2006.

(ii) Consistent with the definition of "component" in the clause at DFARS

252.225-7009, a component is any item supplied to the Government as part of an end item or of another component. Items that are not incorporated into any of the items listed in DFARS *225.7003-2*(a) are not components of those items. For example, test equipment, ground support equipment, or shipping containers are not components of the missile system.

[Final rule, 74 FR 37626, 7/29/2009, effective 7/29/2009; Publication notice, 20191231]

225.7003-3 Exceptions.

(b) (2) *Report of COTS items.*

If a department or agency uses the exception at DFARS 225.7003-3(b)(2) for an acquisition of COTS end items valued at $5 million or more per item, the department or agency shall address use of the exception in a year-end report, to be prepared and submitted as follows:

(A) Entitle the report "COTS Specialty Metal Exceptions Granted During Fiscal Year ________."

(B) For each excepted COTS item purchased during the fiscal year, include in the report, at a minimum, the applicable—

(1) Contract number and any applicable delivery order number;

(2) Dollar value; and

(3) Item description.

(C) Submit the report by October 31 of each year to:

Principal Director, Defense Pricing and Contracting

ATTN: OUSD(A&S) DPC/CP

3060 Defense Pentagon

Washington, DC 20301-3060.

(4) For samarium-cobalt magnets contained in an item listed in 225.7003-2(a) manufactured in a qualifying country, see paragraph (b)(6)(C) of this section.

(5) Domestic specialty metals nonavailable as and when needed. (A) *Determining availability.*

(*1*) FAR 15.402 requires that contracting officers purchase supplies and services at fair and reasonable prices. Thus, contracting officers must determine whether any increase in contract price that results from providing compliant specialty metal is fair and reasonable, given the circumstances of the particular situation. In those cases where the contracting officer determines that the price would not be fair and reasonable, the Secretary of the military department concerned may use that information in determining whether the unreasonable price causes the compliant metal to be effectively "nonavailable." Where these "reasonableness" limits should be drawn is a case-by-case decision.

(*2*) A similar approach may be used to determine whether delays associated with incorporating compliant specialty metals into items being acquired results in the metals being effectively nonavailable.

(B) (*1*) A department or agency requesting a determination or approval from USD(A&S) in accordance with DFARS 225.7003-3(b)(5) shall submit the request, including the proposed determination, to—

Principal Director, Defense Pricing and Contracting

ATTN: OUSD(A&S) DPC/CP

3060 Defense Pentagon

Washington, DC 20301-3060.

(2) The Principal Director, Defense Pricing and Contracting, will forward the request to USD(A&S) as appropriate.

(C) For domestic nonavailability determinations with regard to samarium-cobalt high performance magnets, see paragraph (b)(6)(D) of this section.

(6) *Application of specialty metals restrictions to magnets.*

(A) The two most common types of high performance magnets are samarium-cobalt magnets and neodymium-iron-boron magnets. Only samarium-cobalt magnets contain specialty metals and are subject to the restrictions of 10 U.S.C. 2533b in this section, as well as the restrictions of 10 U.S.C. 2533c at *225.7018*. Neodymium-iron-boron magnets are only subject to the restrictions of 10 U.S.C. 2533c at 225.7018, because they do not contain specialty metals. There are no other commonly used magnets that contain specialty metals.

(B) Table.

HPM = High performance magnet

COTS = Commercially available off-the-shelf

SmCo = Samarium Cobalt

Magnet made of specialty metal is:	Commercially available, SmCo HPM	NOT Commercially available, SmCo HPM
Incorporated into COTS subsystem or COTS end item	NOT restricted	*
NOT incorporated into COTS subsystem or COTS end item	Restricted	Restricted
Included in 2 percent minimum content?	Cannot be included in 2 percent minimum content	Cannot be included in 2 percent minimum content

* By definition, COTS assemblies and COTS end items will not include a HPM that is not commercially available.

(C) Samarium-cobalt magnets contained in an item manufactured in a qualifying country are still subject to the requirements of 10 U.S.C. 2533c, because there is no exception in 10 U.S.C. 2533c for items manufactured in a qualifying country comparable to the exception at *225.7003-3*(b)(4) to the specialty metal restrictions of 10 U.S.C. 2533b.

(D) Even if samarium-cobalt magnets are determined to be domestically nonavailable under this section, the restrictions of 10 U.S.C. 2533c still apply unless samarium-cobalt magnets melted or produced outside a covered country are also determined to be nonavailable in accordance with *225.7018-4*.

(c) *Compliance for commercial derivative military articles.*

(i) A department or agency requesting a determination or approval from USD(A&S) in accordance with DFARS 225.7003-3(c) shall submit the request, including the proposed determination, to—

Principal Director, Defense Pricing and Contracting

ATTN: OUSD(A&S) DPC/CP

3060 Defense Pentagon

Washington, DC 20301-3060.

(ii) The Principal Director, Defense Pricing and Contracting, will forward the request to USD(A&S) as appropriate.

(d) *National security waiver.*

(i) A department or agency shall request a national security waiver of the restrictions of 10 U.S.C. 2533b from USD(A&S) in accordance with DFARS 225.7003-3(d) in a timely manner after discovering or being informed of a specialty metals noncompliance in an item, or component thereof, listed at 225.7003-2(a) and covered by 10 U.S.C. 2533b. The department or agency shall submit the request, via the chain of command, including the draft determination and draft letters of notification to the congressional defense committees, as follows:

Principal Director, Defense Pricing and Contracting

ATTN: OUSD(A&S) DPC/CP

3060 Defense Pentagon

Washington, DC 20301-3060

(ii) The request shall include—

(A) The quantity of end items to which the waiver would apply;

(B) The time period that the waiver will cover;

(C) How and when the noncompliance was discovered—

(1) By the subcontractor(s);

(2) By the contractor; and

(3) By the department or agency;

(D) A complete description of all of the items or systems containing noncompliant specialty metals;

(E) The contract number(s), date(s), duration, and subcontractor(s) associated with the noncompliance;

(F) The manufacturer and country of origin of the noncompliant material, if known;

(G) Whether the contractor flowed down the DFARS clause to the subcontractors and in what format (e.g., exact quote or substantially the same?);

(H) A technical description of the affected parts, their role in the larger assembly, and their function in the end item;

(I) Estimated cost and schedule to replace noncompliant parts if a national security waiver is not granted;

(J) Operational and safety implications;

(K) Other national security considerations (such as how the requested waiver will contribute to national security policy or operational security);

(L) A description of the contractor's efforts to develop and implement a corrective plan to ensure future compliance; and

(M) Information helpful to a determination as to whether any noncompliance was knowing and willful.

(iii) The Director, Defense Procurement and Acquisition Policy, will forward the request to USD(AT&L) as appropriate.

[Final rule, 74 FR 37626, 7/29/2009, effective 7/29/2009; Final rule, 78 FR 54968, 9/9/2013, effective 9/9/2013; Publication notice, 20140328; Publication notice, 20140624; Publication notice, 20150626; Final rule, 84 FR 72239, 12/31/2019, effective 12/31/2019]

225.7016 [Removed]

[Final rule, 70 FR 43073, 7/26/2005, effective 7/26/2005; Interim rule, 72 FR 2637, 1/22/2007, effective 1/22/2007; Change notice, 20080110; Change notice, 20091019; Redesignated, Final rule, 74 FR 53413, 10/19/2009, effective 10/19/2009; Final rule, 75 FR 14589, 3/17/2011, effective 2/17/2011]

225.7016-3 [Removed]

[Final rule, 71 FR 62565, 10/26/2006, effective 10/26/2006; Interim rule, 72 FR 2637, 1/22/2007, effective 1/22/2007; Change notice, 20080110; Change notice, 20091019; Redesignated, Final rule, 74 FR 53413, 10/19/2009, effective 10/19/2009; Final rule, 75 FR 14589, 3/17/2011, effective 3/17/2011]

225.7017 Utilization of domestic photovoltaic devices. (No Text)

[Final rule, 80 FR 72599, 11/20/2015, effective 11/20/2015; Final rule, 83 FR 62498, 12/4/2018, effective 12/5/2018]

225.7017-4 [Removed]

[Final rule, 80 FR 72599, 11/20/2015, effective 11/20/2015; Final rule, 83 FR 62498, 12/4/2018, effective 12/5/2018]

225.7018 Restriction on acquisition of certain magnets and tungsten.

[Publication notice, 20191231]

225.7018-3 Exceptions.

(c) (1) (i) Commercially available off-the-shelf samarium-cobalt magnets are still subject to the restrictions of 10 U.S.C. 2533b unless incorporated into commercially available off-the-shelf end items or subsystems (see 225.7003-3(b)(2)(i)(C)).

(ii) A samarium-cobalt magnet that is exempt from 10 U.S.C. 2533c because it is incorporated in an electronic device is still subject to the restrictions of 10 U.S.C. 2533b, because the exemption under that statute applies to "electronic component," which excludes any high performance magnet used in the electronic component (see definition of "electronic component" at 225.7003-1).

[Final rule, 84 FR 72239, 12/31/2019, effective 12/31/2019]

225.7018-4 Nonavailability determination.

(a) (3) Provide a copy of signed individual nonavailability determination and supporting documentation or notification when an individual waiver is requested, but denied to:

OUSD(A&S)

DASD, Industrial Policy

U.S. Department of Defense
3330 Defense Pentagon, Room 3B854
Washington, DC 20301-3330

(b) (i) When requesting a class nonavailability determination, submit the request, including the proposed determination, to—

Principal Director, Defense Pricing and Contracting
ATTN: OUSD(A&S) DPC/CP
3060 Defense Pentagon
Washington, DC 20301-3060.

(ii) The Principal Director, Defense Pricing and Contracting, will forward the request to the Under Secretary of Defense (Acquisition and Sustainment) (USD(A&S)) as appropriate.

[Publication notice, 20191231]

SUBPART 225.72—REPORTING CONTRACT PERFORMANCE OUTSIDE THE UNITED STATES

225.7203 Contracting officer distribution of reports.

Before contract award, forward a copy of any reports that are submitted with offers in accordance with the provision at 252.225-7003, Report of Intended Performance Outside the United States and Canada-Submission with Offer, to the Deputy Director of Defense Procurement and Acquisition Policy (Contract Policy and International Contracting), OUSD(AT&L)DPAP/CPIC, Washington, DC 20301-3060. This is necessary to satisfy the requirement of 10 U.S.C. 2410g that notifications (or copies) of contract performance outside the United States and Canada be maintained in compiled form for 5 years after the date of submission.

[Final rule, 70 FR 20838, 4/22/2005, effective 4/22/2005; Change notice, 20070531; Final rule, 78 FR 54968, 9/9/2013, effective 9/9/2013]

SUBPART 225.73—ACQUISITIONS FOR FOREIGN MILITARY SALES

225.7300 Scope of subpart.

(a) The Foreign Military Sales (FMS) acquisition infrastructure is also used to execute cases funded with U.S. appropriated funds under special authority to build international partner capacity. These Building Partner Capacity (BPC) cases are implemented using Pseudo Letter of Offer and Acceptance (LOA) documents.

[Publication notice, 20120312]

225.7301 General.

(c) (i) Separately identify known FMS requirements and the FMS customer in solicitations.

(ii) Clearly identify contracts for known FMS requirements by the case identifier code in section B of the Schedule.

(iii) Ensure that the FMS LOA terms and conditions are incorporated into the signed contract.

(iv) Ensure that the shipping terms for any contract of FMS materiel are stated as free on board (f.o.b.) origin.

(v) For Pseudo LOAs, ensure that the period of performance in the contract is consistent with the period of availability of appropriated funds, as provided by the financial resource manager.

(vi) Consistent with the Defense Transportation Regulations (DTR) 4500.9-R-Part II, Cargo Movement, *http://www.transcom.mil/dtr/part-ii/*, Appendix E, contracting officers shall ensure that contracts involving the acquisition and delivery of FMS materiel comply with the policies, procedures, packaging, labeling, and documentation requirements specified by the DTR.

(vii) The Government representative responsible for acceptance shall ensure that the contractor prepares material inspection and receiving reports in compliance with—

(A) Appendix F, F-301(b)(15)(iv)(K) for Wide Area WorkFlow (WAWF) Receiving Report; or

(B) F-401(b)(16)(iv)(L) for a paper DD Form 250, Material Inspection and Receiving Report, if an exception to the use of WAWF at 232.7003 applies.

(viii) Prior to contract award, contracting officers shall ensure that—

(A) If a contracting officer's representative is assigned, detailed point of contact information (email, phone number with international dialing protocols, and physical and mailing address) clearly visible;

(B) Unique country requirements are specified in the contract (i.e., additional documentation requirements for use in country customs clearance (Levy Exemption waiver));

(C) Commodity-unique requirements are specified in the contract (i.e., responsibility for obtaining/paying for/affixing active Radio Frequency Identification tags and Transportation Control Number construction/usage); and

(D) The FMS Transportation Accounting Code is stated in the contract.

[Final rule, 70 FR 73153, 12/9/2005, effective 12/9/2005; Publication notice, 20120312; Publication notice, 20120829; Interim rule, 80 FR 31309, 6/2/2015, effective 6/2/2015]

225.7302 Preparation of letter or offer and acceptance.

(2) The contracting officer shall—

(i) Assist the DoD implementing agency, as necessary, in preparation of the Letter of Offer and Acceptance;

(ii) Identify and explain all unusual contractual requirements or requests for deviations; and

(iii) Assist in preparing the price and availability data.

[Final rule, 70 FR 73153, 12/9/2005, effective 12/9/2005; Publication notice, 20120312; Final rule, 77 FR 76939, 12/31/2012, effective 12/31/2012; Final rule, 78 FR 73450, 12/6/2013, effective 12/6/2013]

225.7303 Pricing acquisition for FMS. (No Text)

[Interim rule, 80 FR 31309, 6/2/2015, effective 6/2/2015]

225.7303-2 Cost of doing business with a foreign government or an international organization.

(a) (3) *Offsets.*

(A) Offsets are the entire range of industrial and commercial benefits provided to foreign governments as an inducement or condition to purchase military supplies or services, including benefits such as coproduction, licensed production, subcontracting, technology transfer, in-county procurement, marketing and financial assistance, and joint ventures (Defense Offsets Disclosure Act of 1999, Pub. L. 106-113, section 1243(3)). There are two types of offsets: direct offsets and indirect offsets.

(i) A direct offset involves benefits, including supplies or services that are directly related to the item being purchased. For example, as a condition of a U.S. sale, the contractor may require or agree to permit the purchaser to produce in its country certain components or subsystems of the item being sold. Generally, direct offsets must be performed within a specified period because they are integral to the deliverable of the FMS contract

(ii) An indirect offset involves benefits, including supplies or services that are unrelated to the item being purchased. For example, as a condition of a sale the contractor may agree to purchase certain of the customer's manufactured products, agricultural commodities, raw materials, or services. Indirect offsets may be accomplished without a clearly defined period of performance.

(B) Offset costs are the costs to the contractor of providing any direct or indirect offsets required (explicitly or implicitly) as a condition of purchase in a government-to-government sale of defense articles and/or defense services as defined by the Arms Export Control Act and the International Traffic in Arms Regulations.

(C) An offset agreement is the contractual arrangement between the FMS customer and the U.S. defense contractor that identifies the offset obligation imposed by the FMS customer that has been accepted by the U.S. defense contractor as a condition of the FMS customer's purchase. These agreements are distinct and independent of the LOA and the FMS contract. Further information about offsets and LOAs may be found in the Defense Security Cooperation Agency (DSCA) Security Assistance Management Manual (DSCA 5105.38-M), chapter 6, paragraph 6.3.9. (*http://samm.dsca.mil/chapter/chapter-6*).

[Interim rule, 80 FR 31309, 6/2/2015, effective 6/2/2015; Final rule, 81 FR 28729, 5/10/2016, effective 5/10/2016]

225.7303-3 [Removed]

[Final rule, 80 FR 72599, 11/20/2015, effective 11/20/2015]

SUBPART 225.74—[REMOVED]

SUBPART 225.75—BALANCE OF PAYMENTS PROGRAM

225.7502 Procedures.

If the Balance of Payments Program applies, use the following procedures:

(1) Solicitation of offers. Identify, in the solicitation, supplies and construction material known in advance to be exempt from the Balance of Payments Program.

(2) Evaluation of offers.

(i) Supplies. Unless the entire acquisition is exempt from the Balance of Payments Program, evaluate offers for supplies that are subject to the Balance of Payments Program using the evaluation procedures in DFARS Subpart 225.5. However, treatment of duty may differ when delivery is overseas.

(A) Duty may not be applicable to nonqualifying country offers.

(B) The U.S. Government cannot guarantee the exemption of duty for components or end products imported into foreign countries.

(C) Foreign governments may impose duties. Evaluate offers including such duties as offered.

(ii) Construction. Because the contracting officer evaluates the estimated cost of foreign and domestic construction material in accordance with DFARS 225.7501(a)(6)(iv) before issuing the solicitation, no special procedures are required for evaluation of construction offers.

(3) *Postaward.* For construction contracts, the procedures at FAR 25.206, for noncompliance under the Buy American statute, also apply to noncompliance under the Balance of Payments Program.

[Final rule, 70 FR 23790, 5/5/2005, effective 6/6/2005; Change notice, 20060412; Interim rule, 71 FR 34826, 6/16/2006, effective 6/16/2006; Change notice, 20060616; Final rule, 71 FR 62565, 10/26/2006, effective 10/26/2006; Final rule, 77 FR 35879, 6/15/2012, effective 6/15/2012]

SUBPART 225.76—SECONDARY ARAB BOYCOTT OF ISRAEL

225.7604 Waivers.

Forward waiver requests to the Director, Defense Procurement and Acquisition Policy, ATTN: OUSD(AT&L)DPAP/CPIC, 3060 Defense Pentagon, Washington, DC 20301-3060.

[Final rule, 70 FR 23790, 5/5/2005, effective 6/6/2005; Change notice, 20060412; Interim rule, 71 FR 34826, 6/16/2006, effective 6/16/2006; Change notice, 20060616; Final rule, 71 FR 62565, 10/26/2006, effective 10/26/2006; Change notice, 20070531; Final rule, 78 FR 54968, 9/9/2013, effective 9/9/2013]

SUBPART 225.77—ACQUISITIONS IN SUPPORT OF OPERATIONS IN AFGHANISTAN

225.7703 Enhanced authority to acquire products or services from Afghanistan.

[Interim rule, 73 FR 53151, 9/15/2008, effective 9/15/2008; Final rule, 75 FR 18035, 4/8/2010, effective 4/8/2010; Final rule, 79 FR 58694, 9/30/2014, effective 9/30/2014; Publication notice, 20191231]

225.7703-1 Acquisition procedures.

(c) When issuing solicitations and contracts for performance in Afghanistan, follow the guidance for CENTCOM Operational Contract Support Policies and Procedures, Theater Business Clearance, at *https://www2.centcom.mil/sites/contracts/Pages/GCO.aspx*, and use the applicable solicitation provisions and contract clauses:

(1) The provision at DFARS *252.232-7014*, Notification of Payment in Local Currency (Afghanistan), as prescribed at DFARS *232.7202*.

[Interim rule, 73 FR 53151, 9/15/2008, effective 9/15/2008; Final rule, 75 FR 18035, 4/8/2010, effective 4/8/2010; Final rule, 79

FR 58694, 9/30/2014, effective 9/30/2014; Publication notice, 20141014; Publication notice, 20160510; Publication notice, 20191231]

225.7703-2 Determination requirements.

(b) Subject matter experts for defense industrial base matters are as follows:

For Army: SAAL-PA, Army Industrial Base Policy, telephone 703-695-2488.

For DLA: DLA J-74, Acquisition Programs and Industrial Capabilities Division, telephone 703-767-1427.

For Navy: Ship Programs, DASN Ships, telephone 703-697-1710.

For Air Force: Air Force Research Laboratory, Materials Manufacturing Directorate, telephone 703-588-7777.

For Other Defense Agencies: Personnel at defense agencies without industrial base expertise on staff should contact the Office of the Deputy Assistant Secretary of Defense for Industrial Policy (Acquisition and Sustainment), telephone 703-697-0051.

(c) Determination formats.

(i) Prepare an individual determination and findings substantially as follows:

DEPARTMENT OR AGENCY

Authority to Acquire Products or Services from Afghanistan

Determination and Findings

Upon the basis of the following findings and determination which I hereby make in accordance with the provisions of DFARS 225.7703-2, the acquisition of a product or service, other than small arms, in support of operations in Afghanistan may be made as follows:

Findings

1. The *[contracting office]* proposes to purchase under contract number__________, *[describe item]*. The total estimated cost of this acquisition is__________.

2. The product or service is to be used by *[describe the entity(ies) that are the intended user(s) of the product or service]*.

3. The contracting officer recommends conducting the acquisition using the following procedure, which, given this determination, is authorized by section 886 of Public Law 110-181, as amended by section 842 of Public Law 112-239 and section 886 of Public Law 114-92:

[Select one of the following:]

Provide a preference for products or services from Afghanistan.

Limit competition to products or services from Afghanistan.

Use procedures other than competitive procedures to award a contract to a particular source or sources from Afghanistan.

4. To implement the recommended procedure, the solicitation will contain [title and number of the applicable provision and/or clause prescribed at DFARS 225.7703-4].

5. The proposed acquisition will provide a stable source of jobs in Afghanistan because__________.

6. The proposed use of other than full and open competition is necessary to provide this stable source of jobs in Afghanistan.

7. The proposed use of other than full and open competition will not adversely affect military operations or stability operations in Afghanistan, because__________. This is the opinion of the *[title of the official responsible for operations in the area involved]*.

8. The proposed use of other than full and open competition will not adversely affect the United States industrial base.

9. *[If a preference will be provided for products or services from Afghanistan, or if competition will be limited to products or services from Afghanistan, include—*

(1) A description of efforts made to ensure that offers are solicited from as many potential sources as is practicable; and

(2) Whether a notice was or will be publicized as required by FAR subpart 5.2 and, if not, which exception in FAR 5.202 applies.]

[If procedures other than competitive procedures will be used to award a contract to a particular source or sources from Afghanistan, include—

(1) A description of the market research conducted in accordance with FAR part 10 and the results; or a statement of the reason market research was not conducted;

(2) A listing of the sources, if any, that expressed, in writing, an interest in the acquisition;

(3) A demonstration that the proposed contractor's unique qualifications require the use of a noncompetitive acquisition, or an explanation of the other reasons for use of a noncompetitive acquisition; and

(4) A certification by the contracting officer that the information in paragraphs (1) through (3) above is accurate and complete to the best of the contracting officer's knowledge and belief.]

Determination

I hereby determine that it is in the national security interest of the United States to use the acquisition procedure described above, because the procedure is necessary to provide a stable source of jobs in Afghanistan and it will not adversely affect (1) Operations in Afghanistan or (2) the United States industrial base.

____

(Date)

(ii) Prepare a determination and findings for a class of acquisitions substantially as follows:

DEPARTMENT OR AGENCY

Authority to Acquire Products or Services from Afghanistan

Determination and Findings

Upon the basis of the following findings and determination which I hereby make in accordance with the provisions of DFARS *225.7703-2*, the acquisition of products or services, other than small arms, in support of operations in Afghanistan may be made as follows:

Findings

1. It is anticipated that *[applicable departments/agencies/components] will* need to award contracts during the period from ________ to ________ in order to acquire *[describe the type(s) of products or services]* for *[describe the purpose, if the purpose for which the items will be acquired is a defining characteristic of the class of acquisitions to be covered by the class determination]*.

2. The products or services to be acquired under the contemplated contracts are to be used by *[describe the entity(ies) intended to use the products or services]*.

3. This class of acquisitions should be conducted using the following procedure, which, given this determination, is authorized by section 886 of Public Law 110-181, as amended by section 842 of Public Law 112-239 and section 886 of Public Law 114-92:

[Select one of the following:]

Provide a preference for products or services from Afghanistan.

Limit competition to products or services from Afghanistan.

Use procedures other than competitive procedures to award a contract to a particular source or sources from Afghanistan.

4. To implement the recommended procedure, solicitations will contain *[title and number of the applicable provision and/or clause prescribed at DFARS 225.7703-4]*.

5. Each of the contemplated contracts will provide a stable source of jobs in Afghanistan, because__________.

6. The proposed use of other than full and open competition for this class of acquisitions is necessary to provide this stable source of jobs in Afghanistan.

7. The proposed use of other than full and open competition for this class of acquisitions will not adversely affect operations in Afghanistan, because__________. This is the opinion of the *[title of the official responsible for operations in the area involved]*.

8. The proposed use of other than full and open competition for this class of acquisitions will not adversely affect the United States industrial base.

9. *[If a preference will be provided for products or services from Afghanistan, or if competition will be limited to products or services from Afghanistan, include—*

(1) A description of the efforts that will be made to ensure that offers are solicited from as many potential sources as is practicable; and

(2) Whether a notice will be publicized as required by FAR subpart 5.2 and, if not, which exception in FAR 5.202 applies.]

- or -

[If procedures other than competitive procedures will be used to award contracts to a particular source or sources from Afghanistan, include—

(1) A description of the market research conducted in accordance with FAR part 10 and the results; or a statement of the reason market research was not conducted;

(2) A listing of the sources, if any, that expressed, in writing, an interest in this class of acquisitions;

(3) A demonstration that the proposed contractor's unique qualifications require the use of a noncompetitive acquisition, or an explanation of the other reasons for use of a noncompetitive acquisition; and

(4) A certification by the contracting officer that the information in paragraphs (1) through (3) above is accurate and complete to the best of the contracting officer's knowledge and belief.

Determination

I hereby determine that it is in the national security interest of the United States to use the acquisition procedure described above for *[description of the class of acquisitions to which this determination is intended to apply]*, because the procedure is necessary to provide a stable source of jobs Afghanistan and it will not adversely affect (1) Operations in Afghanistan or (2) the United States industrial base.

____

(Date)

____

(iii) Prepare a determination and findings for acquisitions issued pursuant to *Class Deviation 2020-O0002,* to Acquire Products and Services Produced in Afghanistan or in Countries along a Major Route of Supply to Afghanistan, substantially as follows:

DEPARTMENT OR AGENCY

AUTHORITY TO ACQUIRE PRODUCTS OR SERVICES FROM

1

Determination and Findings

Upon the basis of the following findings and determination, which I hereby make in accordance with the provisions of DFARS 225.7799-2 (DEVIATION *2020-O0002*), the acquisition of a product or service, other than small arms, in support of operations in Afghanistan may be made as follows:

FINDINGS

1. The *1A* proposes to purchase under solicitation number *1B, 1C.* The total estimated cost of this acquisition is *1D.*

2. The product or service is to be used by *2.*

3. The contracting officer recommends conducting the acquisition using the following procedure, which, given this determination, is authorized by section 801 of Public Law 111-84, as amended by section 886 of Public Law 114-92 and section 1212 of Public Law 116-92, and section 886 of Public Law 110-181, as amended by section 842 of Public Law 112-239 and section 886 of Public Law 114-92:

3.

4. To implement the recommended procedure, the solicitation will contain:

a. DFARS 252.225-7998, Preference for Products or Services from Afghanistan, a Central Asian state, Pakistan, or the South Caucasus (DEC 2019) (DEVIATION *2020-O0002*), and DFARS 252.225-7999, Requirement for Products or Services from Afghanistan, a Central Asian state, Pakistan, or the South Caucasus (DEC 2019) (DEVIATION *2020-O0002*); or

b. DFARS 252.225-7996, Acquisition Restricted to Products or Services from Afghanistan, a Central Asian state, Pakistan, or the South Caucasus (DEC 2019) (DEVIATION *2020-O0002*).

5. The proposed acquisition will provide a product or service that is to be used *5.*

6.a. For products or services from Afghanistan, a Central Asian state, Pakistan, or the South Caucasus, it is in the national security interest of the United States to use a procedure specified in 225.7799-1(a) (DEVIATION *2020-O0002*) because the procedure is necessary to *6A.*

Use of the procedure for acquisition of products or services from Afghanistan, a Central Asian state, Pakistan, or the South Caucasus will not adversely affect military or stability operations in Afghanistan or the United States industrial base (*see* 6B).

b. For products or services from Afghanistan, it is in the national security interest of the United States to use a procedure specified in 225.7799-1(a) (DEVIATION *2020-O0002*) because the procedure is necessary to provide a stable source of jobs in Afghanistan.

Use of the procedure for acquisition of products or services from Afghanistan will not adversely affect military or stability operations in Afghanistan or the United States industrial base (*see* 6B). (see 6C)

7. Acquisitions conducted using the procedures specified in DFARS 225.7799-1(a) (DEVIATION *2020-O0002*), (see para. 3. above), are authorized to use other than full and open competition procedures and do not require the justification and approval addressed in FAR subpart 6.3.

8. Requirement will be/was synopsized: YES [__________] NO [__________]. If not synopsized, exception at FAR 5.202(a) applies.

__________ Date: __________

CONTRACTING OFFICER

Name: __________

Office Symbol: __________

DETERMINATION

In accordance with the authorization outlined in DFARS 225.7799-2(b)(1)(i) (DEVIATION *2020-O0002*) and under the authority of section 801 of Public Law 111-84, as amended by section 886 of Public Law 114-92 and section 1212 of Public Law 116-92, and section 886 of Public Law 110-181, as amended by section 842 of Public Law 112-239 and section 886 of Public Law 114-02, I hereby determinethat it is in the national security interest of the United States to use the acquisition procedure described above because the procedure is necessary to encourage countries along a major route of supply in support of military and stability operations in Afghanistan. This procedure will not adversely affect military or stability operations in Afghanistan or the United States industrial base.

__________ Date: __________

INSTRUCTIONS FOR COMPLETING DETERMINATION

1 Afghanistan, a Central Asian state, Pakistan, or the South Caucasus

1A Office symbol of your contracting office

1B RFP/RFQ/IFB number

1C Description of the items to be purchased

1D Estimated amount of the requirement (in USD)

2 Describe the entity(ies) that are the intended user(s) of the product or service

3 *Select and include one of the following:*

a. Provide a preference for products or services from Afghanistan, a Central Asian state, Pakistan, or the South Caucasus in accordance with the evaluation procedures at 225.7799-3 (DEVIATION *2020-O0002*).

b. Limit competition to products or services from Afghanistan, a Central Asian state, Pakistan, or the South Caucasus DEVIATION *2020-O0002*).

5 *Select and include one of the following:*

In the country that is the source of the product or service.

In the course of efforts by the United States and the Forces to ship goods to or from Afghanistan in support of operations in Afghanistan.

By the military forces, police, or other security personnel of Afghanistan.

By the United States or coalition forces in Afghanistan.

6Ai Paragraph (6.a. may be deleted if the product or service is for use by the military forces, police, or other security personnel of Afghanistan.

6Aii *Select and include one of the following:*

Reduce the overall United States transportation costs and risks in shipping goods in support of operations in Afghanistan.

Encourage states of Central Asia, Pakistan, and the South Caucasus to cooperate in expanding supply routes through their territory in support of operations in Afghanistan.

Help develop more robust and enduring routes of supply to or from Afghanistan.

6B The contracting officer generally may presume that there will not be an adverse effect on the U.S. industrial base. However, when in doubt the contracting officer should coordinate with the applicable subject matter experts.

6C Delete paragraph 6.b. if the product or service concerned is to be used only by the military forces, police, or other security personnel of Afghanistan.

7 Include a description of efforts made to ensure offers are solicited from as many potential sources as is practicable.

[Interim rule, 73 FR 53151, 9/15/2008, effective 9/15/2008; Change notice, 20091208; Final rule, 75 FR 18035, 4/8/2010, effective 4/8/2010; Publication notice, 20100917; Publication notice, 20120130; Publication notice, 20120909; Publication notice, 20131216; Publication notice, 20140407; Publication notice 20160510; Publication notice, 20191231]

225.7703-3 Evaluating offers.

[Publication notice, 20130703; Publication notice, 20140407; Final rule, 79 FR 56278, 9/19/2014, effective 9/19/2014; Publication notice, 20141014]

225.7703-4 Reporting requirement.

(1) Reports for Class Deviation 2009-O0012, Class Deviation to Implement Temporary Authority to Acquire Products and Services Produced in Countries along a Major Route of Supply to Afghanistan and Class Deviation 2012-O0009, Revise Implementation of Temporary Authority to Acquire Products and Services (Including Construction) from Countries along a Major Supply Route to Afghanistan, shall include—

(i) The number of occasions on which a determination under Class Deviation 2009-O0012 or 2012-O0009 was made with respect to the exercise of the authority, regardless of whether or not the determination resulted in the exercise of such authority;

(ii) The total dollar amount of contracts issued pursuant to the exercise of such authority displayed—

(A) Separately for each country (Georgia, the Kyrgyz Republic, Pakistan, the Republic of Armenia, the Republic of Azerbaijan, the Republic of Kazakhstan, the Republic of Tajikistan, the Republic of Uzbekistan, or Turkmenistan for Class Deviation 2009-O0012) (the Kyrgyz Republic, the Republic of Kazakhstan, the Republic of Tajikistan, the Republic of Uzbekistan, or Turkmenistan for Class Deviation 2012-O0009); and

(B) Combined total for all countries pursuant to each deviation; and

(iii) A description and assessment of the extent to which procurements pursuant to the exercise of such authority furthered the national security interest of the United States to—

(A) Improve local market and transportation infrastructure in order to reduce overall United States transportation costs and risks in shipping goods in support of operations in Afghanistan; or

(B) Encourage states along the major supply route to Afghanistan to cooperate in expanding supply routes through their territory in support of operations in Afghanistan.

(2) Reports for the period of January 1, 2012, through October 27, 2012, shall be submitted no later than November 30, 2012, separately reporting determinations and resultant contract actions under the authority of Class Deviation 2001-O0012, and Class Deviation 2012-O0009.

[Interim rule, 73 FR 53151, 9/15/2008, effective 9/15/2008; Change notice, 20091208; Final rule, 75 FR 18035, 4/8/2010, effective 4/8/2010; Publication notice, 20120130; Publication notice, 20120906]

SUBPART 225.78—ACQUISITIONS IN SUPPORT OF GEOGRAPHIC

COMBATANT COMMAND'S THEATER SECURITY COOPERATION EFFORTS

225.7801 Policy.

DoD components are responsible for providing procurement and contracting support of theater security cooperation efforts conducted in support of combatant commander/ Chief of Mission, to include military exercises/training, base operations, weapons procurement, aviation fuels and construction and the President's Emergency Plan for Aids relief. By *Director, Defense Procurement and Acquisition Policy (DPAP) memorandum dated May 6, 2011* and its attachment, Department of State (DoS) Cable 11 STATE 030953, "Procurement Roles and Responsibilities – General Services Officer and DoD Personnel," DoS procurement support is normally restricted to those routine non-complex supplies and services used by U. S. Government personnel permanently assigned at post and acquired for U. S. Government employee direct use. Follow all guidance set forth in this Director, DPAP-approved cable and associated planning considerations at *PGI 207.105* (b) (20) (E).

[Final rule, 76 FR 27274, 5/11/2011, effective 5/11/2011; Final rule, 84 FR 4362, 2/15/2019, effective 2/15/2019]

SUBPART 225.79—EXPORT CONTROL

225.7901 Export-controlled items. (No Text)

[Final rule, 78 36108, 6/17/2013, effective 6/17/2013]

225.7901-2 General.

(1) DoD Focal Point on Export Controls.

(i) Within DoD, the focal point on export controls is the Defense Technology Security Administration (DTSA). Official authorities and responsibilities of DTSA are established in DoD Directive 5105.72.

(ii) Initial DoD acquisition workforce questions regarding the applicability of the Export Administration Regulations (EAR) or the International Traffic in Arms Regulations (ITAR) to specific procurements or items, or interpretation of DoD issuances regarding export controls, may be directed to the DTSA Policy Directorate, by phone at 571-372- 2438/2377 or by visiting the DTSA web site at: *http://www.dtsa.mil/SitePages/contactus/default.aspx*.

(2) Regulations. The Department of State and the Department of Commerce are the lead agencies responsible for regulations governing the export of defense articles, commercial items, and dual use items.

(i) The International Traffic in Arms Regulations (ITAR), issued by the Department of State, control the export of defense-related articles and services, including technical data, ensuring compliance with the Arms Export Control Act (22 U.S.C. 2751 et seq.). The United States Munitions List (USML) identifies defense articles, services, and related technical data that are inherently military in character and could, if exported, jeopardize national security or foreign policy interests of the United States.

(A) The ITAR is published in Title 22 of the Code of Federal Regulations (CFR), Parts 120 through 130 (22 CFR 120-130). The official version of the ITAR is maintained at *http://www.gpoaccess.gov/cfr/index.html*. The Department of State also maintains an on-line version at *http://www.pmddtc.state.gov/regulations_laws/itar_official.html*.

(B) The USML is part of the ITAR, in 22 CFR Part 121, and is available at the web sites in paragraph (2) (i) (A) of this section.

(C) The Department of State is responsible for compliance with the ITAR. Depending on the nature of questions you may have, you may contact the following Department of State office to obtain additional information:

U.S. Department of State

Bureau of Political Military Affairs

Directorate of Defense Trade Controls

Office of Defense Trade Controls Compliance

http://www.pmddtc.state.gov/about/contact_information.html.

(D) Contracting officers should not answer any questions a contractor may ask regarding how to comply with the ITAR. If asked, the contracting officer should direct the contractor's attention to paragraph (c) of the clause at DFARS 252.225-7048 and may inform the contractor that the Department of State publishes guidance regarding ITAR compliance at *http://www.pmddtc.state.gov/compliance/index.html.*

(E) Contracting officers should not answer any questions a contractor may ask regarding the State Department requirement, mentioned in the clause at 252.225-7048, for contractors to register with the Department of State in accordance with the ITAR. If asked, the contracting officer should direct the contractor's attention to paragraph (b) of the clause, which directs the contractor to consult with the Department of State regarding any questions relating to compliance with the ITAR. (The registration requirements are in Subpart 122.1 of the ITAR. Subpart 122.1 requires any person who engages in the United States in the business of either manufacturing or exporting defense articles or furnishing defense services to register with the Directorate of Defense Trade Controls.)

(ii) The Export Administration Regulations (EAR), issued by the Department of Commerce, control the export of dual-use items, (items that have both commercial and military or proliferation applications) and purely commercial items. These items include commodities, software, and technology. Many items subject to the EAR are set forth by Export Control Classification Number on the Commerce Control List.

(A) The EAR is published in Title 15 of the Code of Federal Regulations, Parts 730 through 774 (15 CFR Parts 730-774), *available at http://www.gpoaccess.gov/cfr/index.html* and *http://www.access.gpo.gov/bis/ear/ear_data.html.*

(B) The Commerce Control List is part of the EAR, in Supplement No. 1 to 15 CFR Part 774, and is available at *http://www.gpoaccess.gov/cfr/index.html* and *http://www.access.gpo.gov/bis/ear/ear_data.html.*

(C) The Department of Commerce is responsible for compliance with the EAR. Depending on the nature of questions you may have, you may contact the following Department of Commerce office to obtain additional information:

U.S. Department of Commerce

Bureau of Industry and Security

Office of Exporter Services (OExS)

OExS Hotline: 202-482-4811.

(D) Contracting officers should not answer any questions a contractor may ask regarding how to comply with the EAR. If asked, the contracting officer should direct the contractor's attention to paragraph (b) of the clause at DFARS 252.225-7048 and may inform the contractor that the Department of Commerce publishes guidance regarding EAR compliance at *http://www.bis.doc.gov/.*

(3) National Security Decision Directive (NSDD) 189, National Policy on the Transfer of Scientific, Technical, and Engineering Information.

(i) NSDD 189 establishes a national policy that, to the maximum extent possible, the products of fundamental research shall remain unrestricted. NSDD 189 provides that no restrictions may be placed upon the conduct or reporting of federally funded fundamental research that has not received national security classification, except as provided in applicable U.S. statutes. As a result, contracts confined to the performance of unclassified fundamental research generally do not involve any export-controlled items, as defined in paragraph (a) of the clause at DFARS 252.225-7048.

(ii) NSDD 189 does not take precedence over statutes. NSDD 189 does not exempt any research, whether basic, fundamental, or applied, from statutes that apply to export controls such as the Arms Export Control Act, the Export Administration Act of 1979, as amended, or the U.S. International Emergency Economic Powers Act, or the regulations that implement those statutes (the ITAR and the EAR). Thus, if export-controlled items are used to conduct research or are generated as part of the research efforts, the export control laws and regulations apply to the controlled items.

(iii) NSDD 189 is available at *http://www.fas.org/irp/offdocs/nsdd/nsdd-189.htm.*

(4) DoD Instruction 2040.02, International Transfers of Technology, Articles, and Services. This DoD instruction provides gui-

dance to manage and control transfers of technology, articles, and services consistent with U.S. foreign policy and national security objectives. DoD Instruction 2040.02 is available at *http://www.dtic.mil/whs/directives/*.

(5) Other DoD Issuances. Other DoD issuances that address export control matters include those listed below. Except as otherwise noted, these issuances are available at *http://www.dtic.mil/whs/directives/*.

- DoD Instruction 2015.4, Defense Research, Development, Test and Evaluation (RDT&E) Information Exchange Program (IEP).
- DoD Directive 5000.1, The Defense Acquisition System.
- DoD Instruction 5000.2, Operation of the Defense Acquisition System.
- DoD Directive 5105.72, Defense Technology Security Administration (DTSA).
- DoD Publication 5200.1-M, Acquisition Systems Protection Program.
- DoD Instruction 5200.39, Critical Program Information (CPI) Protection Within the Department of Defense.
- DoD Publication 5220.22-M, National Industrial Security Program Operating Manual (NISPOM).
- DoD Directive 5230.25, Withholding of Unclassified Technical Data From Public Disclosure.
- DoD Instruction 5230.27, Presentation of DoD-Related Scientific and Technical Papers at Meetings.
- Defense Acquisition Guidebook, available at *http://akss.dau.mil/dag/DoD5000.asp?view=document&doc=1*.
- Under Secretary of Defense (Intelligence) Memorandum, Subject: Policy and Procedures for Sanitization of Department of Defense (DoD) Classified or Controlled Unclassified Information Prior to Public Release, is available here *http://www.dod.mil/pubs/foi/dfoipo/docs/NewRedactionPolicy.pdf*

Link to online training on export controls:

CLM 036 Technology Transfer and Export Control Fundamentals, *http://icatalog.dau.mil/onlinecatalog/courses.aspx?crs_id=306*

[Final rule, 78 36108, 6/17/2013, effective 6/17/2013; Publication notice, 20160510]

225.7902 Defense Trade Cooperation Treaties.

The following documents are accessible at: *http://pmddtc.state.gov*:

- DTC Treaties.
- Implementing Arrangements.
- The provisions of the International Traffic in Arms Regulations (ITAR) (22 CFR 126.16 (United Kingdom)) pertaining to the DCT Treaty.
- List of Defense Articles Exempted from DCT Treaty Coverage (also in 22 CFR 126 Supplement No. 1).
- List of Approved Community Members.
- Definitions.

[Interim rule, 77 FR 30361, 5/22/2012, effective 5/22/2012; Final rule, 78 36108, 6/17/2013, effective 6/17/2013]

225.7902-2 Purpose.

(1) Background.

(i) The U.S. Government controls exports of defense articles, technical data, and defense services. The controls are imposed by the Arms Export Control Act (AECA) and the Department of State regulation that implements the AECA export controls. That regulation is the ITAR. See PGI 204.7302(2)(i) for more information about the ITAR.

(ii) Under the ITAR, the Department of State manages an export licensing system in which government approvals are often necessary for companies to hold discussions about potential projects, pursue joint activities, ship hardware, or transfer know-how to one another, and even sometimes to move engineers and other personnel within branches of the same company located in different countries. This process can be challenging for U.S. exporters and for foreign firms in their supply chains.

(iii) Given the close allied relationship of the United States with Australia and the United Kingdom, the President and the respective Prime Ministers decided to reform the defense trade system between their countries with the goal of facilitating the exchange of certain defense articles, technical data, and defense services between their militaries and security authorities, and their industries. They negotiated bilateral Defense Trade Cooperation DTC Treaties to achieve this goal. These bilateral DTC Treaties establish permissions for export without export licenses for each country, if an export meets the DTC Treaty requirements. Other exports remain under the AECA and the ITAR. The DTC Treaties are intended solely to waive certain requirements of the ITAR for specific transactions within the scope of the DTC Treaties not remove any requirements for contractors to comply with domestic U.S. law.

(iv) The Department of State regulations implementing the DTC Treaties are in the ITAR.

(2) How the DTC Treaties work.

(i) The DTC Treaties establish Approved Communities. The "Approved Community" for each DTC Treaty is defined in DFARS clause 252.225-7047. Exports of most U.S. defense articles, technical data, and defense services are permitted to go into and to move within the Approved Community, without the need for government approvals and export licenses (provided that all persons comply with statutory and regulatory requirements outside of DFARS and ITAR concerning the import of defense articles and defense services or the possession or transfer of defense articles, including, but not limited to, regulations issued by the Bureau of Alcohol, Tobacco, Firearms and Explosives found at 27 C.F.R. Parts 447, 478, and 479, which are unaffected by the DTC Treaties) when in support of the following:

- Combined U.S.-Australia or U.S.-U.K. military or counterterrorism operations.

- U.S.-Australia or U.S.-U.K. cooperative security and defense research, development, production, and support programs.

- Specific security and defense projects that are for the government of Australia or the government of the United Kingdom use only.

- U.S. Government end use.

(ii) Under the DTC Treaties, instead of a U.S. exporter preparing and requesting Department of State approval of an export license or other written authorization for a project, the exporter may elect to use the applicable DTC Treaty if Treaty conditions are met. If using a DTC Treaty, the exporter will check the Department of State website (*http://pmddtc.state.gov/*) or other appropriate reference and verify that—

- The Australian or U.K. partner is on the list of approved companies/facilities (i.e., a member of the Approved Community);

- The effort is in support of at least one of the scope areas identified in paragraph (2)(i) of this section; and

- The defense article is not on the exempted technology list. (Also in 22 CFR 126 Supplement No. 1).

If all three conditions are met, then the U.S. exporter and the Australian or U.K. partner may use the DTC Treaty exemptions in the ITAR to move qualifying defense articles without the need to obtain export licenses or other written authorizations, provided compliance with paragraph (2)(i) of this section.

(iii) A company using a DTC Treaty, in addition to checking the three lists (as explained in paragraph (2)(ii) of this section), must also comply with requirements in the applicable DTC Treaty and the associated Implementing Arrangements, and the provisions of the ITAR pertaining to the DTC Treaty. These include marking and recordkeeping requirements to ensure that export-controlled items are recognized as such and treated accordingly. For example, instead of normal ITAR requirements, the provisions of the ITAR pertaining to the DTC Treaties establish the requirements that apply. Similarly, DFARS 225.7902 implements requirements that relate to exports that a prospective contractor may make under a DoD solicitation or that a contractor may make in performance of a DoD contract. The company must continue to comply with domestic laws and regulations, including those pertaining to the movement of defense articles within the United States.

[Interim rule, 77 FR 30361, 5/22/2012, effective 5/22/2012; Final rule, 78 36108, 6/17/2013, effective 6/17/2013]

225.7902-4 Procedures.

(1) Since the DTC Treaties apply only to eligible items, a solicitation or contract falls within the scope of the DTC Treaties, and is thus eligible for DTC Treaty coverage (i.e., falls within the scope of the DTC Treaties) if it will acquire at least one defense article that is not otherwise exempt from the DTC Treaties and is required for—

(i) (i) Combined military or counterterrorism operations as described in the Implementing Arrangements;

(ii) Cooperative security and defense research, development, production, and support programs that are identified pursuant to the Implementing Arrangements;

(iii) Cases where the government or Australia or the government of the United Kingdom is the end user in mutually agreed specific security and defense projects, that are identified pursuant to the Implementing Arrangements; or

(iv) U.S. Government end use under a solicitation or contract.

(2) Since the DTC Treaties apply only to eligible items, a solicitation or contract falls within the scope of the DTC Treaties and is thus eligible for DTC Treaty coverage when it will acquire at least one defense article that is DTC Treaty-eligible and the contract falls within the scope of the DTC Treaties. Article 3, section (2) of each DTC Treaty and Section 4 of each Implementing Arrangement require the DTC Treaty Participants to maintain lists of defense articles to be exempted from the scope of the DTC Treaties. These exempted technology lists are incorporated in Supplement No. 1 to part of the ITAR and are accessible at: *http://www.pmddtc.state.gov/treaties/index.html.*

(3) The DTC Treaties do not apply to defense articles initially being acquired pursuant to the U.S. Foreign Military Sales (FMS) program, although, once the defense articles are acquired by the Australia or United Kingdom under an FMS case, the DTC Treaty applies as though the defense articles were exported under the DTC Treaty, subject to PGI 225.7902-2.

(4) If a company obtains an export license, or other authorization, for the export of defense articles that might otherwise have been eligible for export without a license under a DTC Treaty, the terms of the export license, or other authorization, shall apply unless and until the company obtains approval to transition to DTC Treaty coverage. The process and requirements for transition are described in 22 CFR 126.16(i) and 22 CFR 126.17(i), respectively.

[Interim rule, 77 FR 30361, 5/22/2012, effective 5/22/2012; Final rule, 78 36108, 6/17/2013, effective 6/17/2013]

PART 226—OTHER SOCIOECONOMIC PROGRAMS

Table of Contents

Subpart 226.1—Indian Incentive Program

Procedures 226.103

PART 226—OTHER SOCIOECONOMIC PROGRAMS

SUBPART 226.1—INDIAN INCENTIVE PROGRAM

226.103 Procedures.

(1) Submit a request for funding of the Indian incentive to the Office of Small Business Programs, Office of the Under Secretary of Defense (Acquisition, Technology, and Logistics) (OUSD(AT&L)SBP), 201 12th Street South, Suite 406, Arlington, VA 22202.

(2) Upon receipt of funding from OUSD(AT&L) SBP, issue a contract modification to add the Indian incentive funding for payment of the contractor's request for adjustment as described in the clause at DFARS 252.226-7001, Utilization of Indian Organizations, Indian-Owned Economic Enterprises, and Native Hawaiian Small Business Concerns.

[Final rule, 70 FR 73148, 12/9/2005, effective 12/9/2005; Final rule, 73 FR 46813, 8/12/2008, effective 8/12/2008; Final rule, 78 FR 54968, 9/9/2013, effective 9/9/2013]

PART 228—BONDS AND INSURANCE

Table of Contents

Subpart 228.3—Insurance

Risk pooling arrangements 228.304
Overseas workers' compensation and war-hazard insurance 228.305
Additional clauses 228.370

PART 228—BONDS AND INSURANCE

SUBPART 228.3—INSURANCE

228.304 Risk-pooling arrangements.

(1) The plan—

(i) Is implemented by attaching an endorsement to standard insurance policy forms for workers' compensation, employer's liability, comprehensive general, and automobile liability. The endorsement states that the instant policy is subject to the National Defense Projects Rating Plan.

(ii) Applies to eligible defense projects of one or more departments/agencies. For purposes of this section, a defense project is any eligible contract or group of contracts with the same contractor.

(A) A defense project is eligible when—

(1) Eligible contracts represent, at the inception of the plan, at least 90 percent of the payroll for the total operations at project locations; and

(2) The annual insurance premium is estimated to be at least $10,000.

(B) A contract is eligible when it is—

(1) Either domestic or foreign;

(2) Cost-reimbursement type; or

(3) Fixed price with redetermination provisions.

(2) Under construction contracts, include construction subcontractors in the prime contractor's plan only when subcontractor operations are at the project site, and the subcontract provides that the prime contractor will furnish insurance.

(3) Use the agreement in Table 28-1, Insurance Rating Plan Agreement, when the Government assumes contractor premium payments upon contract termination or completion.

(4) The Federal Tort Claims Act provides protection for Government employees while driving Government-owned vehicles in the performance of their assigned duties. Include the endorsement in Table 28-2, Automobile Insurance Policy Endorsement, in automobile liability insurance policies provided under the National Defense Projects Rating Plan.

TABLE 28-1, INSURANCE RATING PLAN RATING AGREEMENT

Special Casualty Insurance Rating Plan

Assignment-Assumption of Premium Obligations

It is agreed that 100 percent* of the return premiums and premium refunds (and dividends) due or to become due the prime contractor under the policies to which the National Defense Projects Rating Plan Endorsement made a part of policy ______ applies are hereby assigned to and shall be paid to the United States of America, and the prime contractor directs the Company to make such payments to the office designated for contract administration acting for and on account of the United States of America.

The United States of America hereby assumes and agrees to fulfill all present and future obligations of the prime contractor with respect to the payment of 100 percent* of the premiums under said policies.

This agreement, upon acceptance by the prime contractor, the United States of America, and the Company shall be effective from

Accepted___	(Date)
______	(Name of Insurance Company)
By ___	(Title of Official Signing)
Accepted___	(Date)
United States of America	
By ___	(Authorized Representative)
Accepted___	(Date)
______	(Prime Contractor)
By ___	(Authorized Representative)

*In the event the Government has less than a 100 percent interest in premium funds or dividends, modify the assignment to reflect the percentage of interest and extent of the Government's assumption of additional premium obligation.

TABLE 28-2, AUTOMOBILE INSURANCE POLICY ENDORSEMENT

It is agreed that insurance provided by the policy with respect to the ownership, maintenance, or use of automobiles, including loading and unloading thereof, does not apply to the following as insureds: The United States of America, any of its agencies, or any of its officers or employees.

[Final rule, 69 FR 65090, 11/10/2004, effective 11/10/2004]

228.305 Overseas workers' compensation and war-hazard insurance.

(d) Submit requests for waiver through department/agency channels. Include the following in the request:

(ii) Contract number.

(iii) Date of award.

(iv) Place of performance.

(v) Name of insurance company providing Defense Base Act coverage.

(vi) Nationality of employees to whom waiver is to apply.

(vii) Reason for waiver.

[Final rule, 69 FR 65090, 11/10/2004, effective 11/10/2004]

228.370 Additional clauses.

(b) (3) DFARS 252.228-7001, Ground and Flight Risk Clause, requires the assignment of a Government Flight Representative (GFR) to administer the requirements of the combined instruction *Contractor's Flight and*

Ground Operations, (DCMA INST 8210.1, AFI 10-220, AR 95-20, NAVAIRINST 3710.1 (Series), and COMDTINST M13020.3). At the time the solicitation is issued, contracting officers shall contact DCMA Aircraft Operations (AO) and the appropriate Military Service to obtain technical advice and allow adequate lead time for assigning a GFR. Make requests for assignment of a GFR to—

HQ DCMA: DCMA-AO

8000 Jefferson Davis Highway

Building 4A

Richmond, VA 23297

804-279-6322

Email: *AOInbox@dcma.mil* (include "Ground and Flight Risk Clause" on the subject line)

Army: HQ, Army Materiel Command

ATTN: AMCOL-CA

4400 Martin Road

Redstone Arsenal, AL 35898

256–450-7021

Navy: Commander, Naval Air Systems Command (AIR-09F)

22541 Millstone Road, Unit 10

Patuxent River, MD 20670-1601

301–342–7233

Air Force: HQ AFMC/A3V

508 W. Choctawhatchee

Eglin AFB, FL 32542-5713

850–882–7890

Workflow: *afmc.a3v@us.af.mil*

Coast Guard: Commanding Officer

Aviation Logistics Center

U.S. Coast Guard

1664 Weeksville Road, Building 63

Elizabeth City, NC 27909-6725

[Final rule, 75 FR 32642, 6/8/2010, effective 6/8/2010; Publication notice, 20140421; Publication notice, 20160325]

PART 229—TAXES

Table of Contents

Subpart 229.1—General

Resolving tax problems 229.101
Reporting of foreign taxation on U.S. assistance programs 229.170
Reports 229.170-3

Subpart 229.70—Special Procedures for Overseas Contracts

Scope of subpart 229.7000
Tax exemption in Spain 229.7001
Tax exemption in the United Kingdom 229.7002
Value added tax 229.7002-1
Import duty 229.7002-2
Value added tax of import duty problem resolution 229.7002-3
Information required by HM Customs and Excise 229.7002-4

PART 229—TAXES

SUBPART 229.1—GENERAL

229.101 Resolving tax problems.

(a) For the military departments, the Defense Logistics Agency, and the Defense Contract Management Agency, the members of the DFARS Tax Committee are the designated legal counsel for tax matters within their respective departments/agencies. A list of the members of the DFARS Tax Committee is available at *http://www.acq.osd.mil/dpap/dars/dfars_committees.html#taxes.*

(b) Information on fuel excise taxes, including applicability, exemptions, and refunds, is available as follows:

(i) The DLA Energy website at *www.desc.dla.mil* provides information on Federal, State, and local excise taxes.

(ii) Internal Revenue Service Publications 510 and 378, available on the Internal Revenue Service website at *www.irs.gov*, provide information on Federal excise taxes.

(c) The contracting officer may direct the contractor to litigate the applicability of a particular tax if—

(i) The contract is either a cost-reimbursement type or a fixed-price type with a tax escalation clause such as FAR 52.229-4; and

(ii) The direction is coordinated with the DoD Tax Policy and Advisory Group through the agency-designated legal counsel.

(d) (i) Tax relief agreements between the United States and foreign governments in Europe that exempt the United States from payment of specific taxes on purchases made for common defense purposes are maintained by the United States European Command (USEUCOM). For further information, contact HQ USEUCOM, ATTN: ECLA, Unit 30400, Box 1000, APO AE09128; Telephone: DSN 430-8001/7263, Commercial 49-0711-680-8001/7263; facsimile: 49-0711-680-5732.

(ii) Other international treaties may exempt the United States from the payment of specific taxes. The Department of State publishes a list of treaties on its website at *www.state.gov.*

(iii) Tax relief also may be available in countries that have not signed tax relief agreements. The potential for such relief should be explored in accordance with paragraph (d) (iv) of this section.

(iv) DoD Directive 5100.64, DoD Foreign Tax Relief Program, defines DoD tax relief policy and requires designation of a military commander as the single point of contact for investigation and resolution of specific matters related to the foreign tax relief program within the country for which the commander is designated. Those military commanders are the same as the ones designated under DoD Directive 5525.1, Status of Forces Policy and Information, and specified in Appendix C of Army Regulation 27-50/SECNAVINST 5820.4G, Status of Forces Policies, Procedures, and Information. Appendix C of Army Regulation 27-50/SECNAVINST 5820.4G is available at *http://www.army.mil/usapa/epubs/xml_pubs/r27_50/main.xml#appc.*

(A) DoD Directive 5100.64 is available at *http://www.dtic.mil/whs/directives/corres/html/510064.htm.*

(B) DoD Directive 5525.1 is available at *http://www.dtic.mil/whs/directives/corres/html/552501.htm.*

(C) Appendix C of Army Regulation 27-50/SECNAVINST 5820.4G is available at *http://www.army.mil/usapa/epubs/xml_pubs/r27_50/main.xml#appc.*

(v) Also see PGI 229.70 for special procedures for obtaining tax relief and duty-free import privileges when conducting U.S. Government acquisitions in certain foreign countries.

[Final rule, 70 FR 8538, 2/22/2005, effective 2/22/2005; Final rule, 71 FR 14099, 3/21/2006, effective 3/21/2006; Change notice, 20060321; Change notice 20060412; Change notice, 20070531; Change notice, 20070626; Change notice, 20071108; Publication notice, 20110419]

229.170 Reporting of foreign taxation on U.S. assistance programs. (No Text)

[Interim rule, 70 FR 57191, 9/30/2005, effective 9/30/2005]

229.170-3 Reports.

(1) Upon receipt of a notification under the clause at DFARS 252.229-7011, that a foreign tax has been imposed, submit the following information to the applicable office identified in paragraph (2) of this subsection.

(i) Contractor name.

(ii) Contract number.

(iii) Contractor point of contact (Name, phone number, FAX number, and e-mail address).

(iv) Amount of foreign taxes assessed by each foreign government.

(v) Amount of any foreign taxes reimbursed by each foreign government.

(2) Submit the information required by paragraph (1) of this subsection to—

(i) For Army contracts:

Commander, U.S. Army Security Assistance Command

ATTN: AMSAC-SR

5701 21st Street

Fort Belvoir, VA 22060-5940.

(ii) For Navy contracts:

Navy International Programs Office

ATTN: IPO 02C2F

Nebraska Avenue Complex

4255 Mt. Vernon Dr., Suite 17100

Washington, DC 20393-5445.

(iii) For Air Force contracts:

Secretary of the Air Force/International Affairs

ATTN: SAF/IAPC

1080 Air Force, Pentagon

Washington, DC 20330-1080.

(iv) For Marine Corps contracts:

Navy International Programs Office

ATTN: IPO 02C2F

Nebraska Avenue Complex

4255 Mt. Vernon Dr., Suite 17100

Washington, DC 20393-5445.

(v) For all other DoD contracts:

Defense Security Cooperation Agency

ATTN: DBO-CFD

201 12th Street South, Suite 203

Arlington, VA 22202-5408.

[Interim rule, 70 FR 57191, 9/30/2005, effective 9/30/2005; Change notice, 20060321]

SUBPART 229.70—SPECIAL PROCEDURES FOR OVERSEAS CONTRACTS

229.7000 Scope of subpart.

This subpart prescribes procedures to be used by contracting officers to obtain tax relief and duty-free import privileges when conducting U.S. Government acquisitions in certain foreign countries.

[Final rule, 70 FR 6375, 2/7/2005, effective 2/7/2005]

229.7001 Tax exemption in Spain.

(a) The Joint United States Military Group (JUSMG), Spain Policy Directive 400.4, or subsequent directive, applies to U.S. contracting offices acquiring supplies or services in Spain when the introduction of material or equipment into Spain is required for contract performance.

(b) Upon award of a contract with a Direct Contractor, as defined in the clause at DFARS 252.229-7004, the contracting officer will notify JUSMG-MAAG Madrid, Spain, and HQ 16AF/LGTT and will forward three copies of the contract to JUSMG-MAAG, Spain.

(c) If copies of the contract are not available and duty-free import of equipment or materials is urgent, the contracting officer will send JUSMG-MAAG three copies of the Letter of Intent or a similar document indicating the pending award. In these cases, authorization for duty-free import will be issued by the Government of Spain. Upon formal award, the contracting officer will forward three copies of the completed contract to JUSMG-MAAG, Spain.

(d) The contracting officer will notify JUSMG-MAAG, Spain, and HQ 16AF/LGTT of ports-of-entry and identify the customs agents who will clear property on their behalf. Additional documents required for port-of-entry and customs clearance can be obtained by contacting HQ 16AF/LGTT. This information will be passed to the Secretaria General Tecnica del Ministerio de Hacienda (Technical General Secretariat of the Ministry of Finance). A list of customs agents may be obtained from the 600 ABG, APO AE 09646.

[Final rule, 70 FR 6375, 2/7/2005, effective 2/7/2005]

229.7002 Tax exemption in the United Kingdom.

This section contains procedures to be followed in securing relief from the British value added tax and import duties.

[Final rule, 70 FR 6375, 2/7/2005, effective 2/7/2005]

229.7002-1 Value added tax.

(a) U.S. Government purchases qualifying for tax relief are equipment, materials, facilities, and services for the common defense effort and for foreign aid programs.

(b) To facilitate the resolution of issues concerning specific waivers of import duty or tax exemption for U.S. Government purchases (see PGI 229.7002-3), contracting offices shall provide the name and activity address of personnel who have been granted warranted contracting authority to Her Majesty's (HM) Customs and Excise at the following address: HM Customs and Excise, International Customs Division G, Branch 4, Adelaide House, London Bridge, London EC4R 9DB.

[Final rule, 70 FR 6375, 2/7/2005, effective 2/7/2005]

229.7002-2 Import duty.

No import duty shall be paid by the United States and contract prices shall be exclusive of duty, except when the administrative cost compared to the low dollar value of a contract makes it impracticable to obtain relief from contract import duty. In this instance, the contracting officer shall document the contract file with a statement that—

(a) The administrative burden of securing tax relief under the contract was out of proportion to the tax relief involved;

(b) It is impracticable to secure tax relief;

(c) Tax relief is therefore not being secured; and

(d) The acquisition does not involve the expenditure of any funds to establish a permanent military installation.

[Final rule, 70 FR 6375, 2/7/2005, effective 2/7/2005]

229.7002-3 Value added tax or import duty problem resolution.

In the event a value added tax or import duty problem cannot be resolved at the contracting officer's level, refer the issue to HQ Third Air Force, Staff Judge Advocate, Unit 4840, Box 45, APO AE 09459. Direct contact with HM Customs and Excise in London is prohibited.

[Final rule, 70 FR 6375, 2/7/2005, effective 2/7/2005]

229.7002-4 Information required by HM Customs and Excise.

(a) *School bus contracts.* Provide one copy of the contract and all modifications to HM Customs and Excise.

(b) *Road fuel contracts.* For contracts that involve an application for relief from duty on the road fuel used in performance of the contract, provide—

(1) To HM Customs and Excise—

(i) Contract number;

(ii) Name and address of contractor;

(iii) Type of work (e.g., laundry, transportation);

(iv) Area of work; and

(v) Period of performance.

(2) To the regional office of HM Customs and Excise to which the contractor applied for relief from the duty on road fuel—one copy of the contract.

(c) *Other contracts awarded to United Kingdom firms.* Provide information when requested by HM Customs and Excise.

[Final rule, 70 FR 6375, 2/7/2005, effective 2/7/2005]

PART 230—COST ACCOUNTING STANDARDS ADMINISTRATION

Table of Contents

Subpart 230.2—CAS Program Requirements

Waiver 230.201-5

PART 230—COST ACCOUNTING STANDARDS ADMINISTRATION

SUBPART 230.2—CAS PROGRAM REQUIREMENTS

230.201-5 Waiver.

(a)(1)(i) Unless otherwise authorized by the Director of Defense Procurement and Acquisition Policy, Office of the Under Secretary of Defense (Acquisition, Technology, and Logistics), the military departments must submit each CAS waiver request to the Director of Defense Procurement and Acquisition Policy for review at least 14 days before granting the waiver.

(ii) DoD contracting activities that are not within a military department must submit CAS waiver requests that meet the conditions in FAR 30.201-5(b) to the Director of Defense Procurement and Acquisition Policy for approval at least 30 days before the anticipated contract award date.

(e) The annual report of exceptional case CAS waivers shall include the following:

Title: Waiver of CAS Requirements

(1) Contract number, including modification number, if applicable, and program name.

(2) Contractor name.

(3) Contracting activity.

(4) Total dollar amount waived.

(5) Brief description of why the item(s) could not be obtained without a waiver.

(6) Brief description of the specific steps taken to ensure price reasonableness.

(7) Brief description of the demonstrated benefits of granting the waiver.

[Final rule, 71 FR 69492, 12/1/2006, effective 12/1/2006; Change notice, 20071108]

PART 231—CONTRACT COST PRINCIPLES AND PROCEDURES

Table of Contents

Subpart 231.2—Contracts with Commercial Organizations

External restructuring costs 231.205-70

PART 231—CONTRACT COST PRINCIPLES AND PROCEDURES

SUBPART 231.2—CONTRACTS WITH COMMERCIAL ORGANIZATIONS

231.205-70 External restructuring costs.

(d) *Procedures and ACO responsibilities.* The cognizant ACO shall—

(i) Promptly execute a novation agreement, if one is required, in accordance with FAR Subpart 42.12and DFARS Subpart 242.12 and include the provision at DFARS 242.1204(i).

(ii) Direct the contractor to segregate restructuring costs and to suspend these amounts from any billings, final contract price settlements, and overhead settlements until the determination in DFARS 231.205-70(c)(4)(i) is obtained.

(iii) Require the contractor to submit an overall plan of restructuring activities and an adequately supported proposal for planned restructuring projects. The proposal must include a breakout by year by cost element, showing the present value of projected restructuring costs and projected restructuring savings.

(iv) Notify major buying activities of contractor restructuring actions and inform them about any potential monetary impacts on major weapons programs, when known.

(v) Upon receipt of the contractor's proposal, as soon as practicable, adjust forward pricing rates to reflect the impact of projected restructuring savings. If restructuring costs are included in forward pricing rates prior to execution of an advance agreement in accordance with paragraph (d)(8) of this subsection, the contracting officer shall include a repricing clause in each fixed-price action that is priced based on the rates. The repricing clause must provide for a downward price adjustment to remove restructuring costs if the determination required by DFARS 231.205-70(c)(4)(i) is not obtained.

(vi) Upon receipt of the contractor's proposal, immediately request an audit review of the contractor's proposal.

(vii) Upon receipt of the audit report, determine on a present value basis if—

(A) The audited projected restructuring savings for DoD will exceed the restructuring costs allowed by a factor of at least two to on, as required by DFARS 231.205-70(c)(4)(i)(A); or

(B) If the audited projected restructuring savings will exceed the restructuring costs allowed in a case where the business combination will result in the preservation of a critical capability that otherwise might be lost to DoD, as required by DFARS 231.205-70(c)(4)(i)(B).

(viii) Negotiate an advance agreement with the contractor setting forth, at a minimum, a cumulative cost ceiling for restructuring projects and, when necessary, a cost amortization schedule. The costs may not exceed the amount of projected restructuring savings on a present value basis. The advance agreement shall not be executed until determination required by DFARS 231.205-70(c)(4)(i) is obtained.

(ix) (A) Submit a recommendation for determination to-

(1) The Director of Defense Procurement and Acquisition Policy, Office of the Under Secretary of Defense (Acquisition, Technology, and Logistics), ATTN: OUSD(AT&L)DPAP(P), if DFARS 231.205-70(c)(4)(ii)(A) applies; or

(2) To the Director of the Defense Contract Management Agency, ATTN: HQ DCMA-OCB, if DFARS 231.205-70(c)(4)(ii)(B) applies.

(B) Include the information described in DFARS 231.205-70(e).

(x) Consult with the Director of Defense Procurement and Acquisition Policy, Office of the Under Secretary of Defense (Acquisition, Technology, and Logistics), or with the Director of the Defense Contract Management Agency, as appropriate, when DFARS 231.205-70(c)(4)(i)(B) applies.

[Final rule, 69 FR 63331, 11/1/2004, effective 11/1/2004; Final rule 70 FR 43074, 7/26/2005, effective 7/26/2005]

PART 232—CONTRACT FINANCING

Table of Contents

Responsibilities 232.070

Subpart 232.4—Advance Payments for Non-Commercial Items

Recommendation for approval 232.409-1
Findings, determination, and authorization 232.410

Subpart 232.5—Progress Payments Based on Costs

Unusual progress payments 232.501-2

Subpart 232.6—Contracts Debts

Debt determination and collection 232.603
Demand for payment 232.604
Transfer of responsibility for debt collection 232.670
Bankruptcy reporting 232.671

Subpart 232.10—Performance-Based Payments

Policy 232.1001

Subpart 232.70—Electronic Submission and Processing of Payment Requests and Receiving Reports

Contract clause instructions 232.7004

Subpart 232.71—Levies on Contract Payments

Policy and procedures 232.7101

PART 232—CONTRACT FINANCING

232.070 Responsibilities.

(c) The Under or Assistant Secretary, or other designated official, responsible for the comptroller function within the department or agency is the focal point for financing matters at the department/agency headquarters. Departments and agencies may establish contract financing offices at operational levels.

(i) Department/agency contract financing offices are:

(A) Army: Office of the Assistant Secretary of the Army (Financial Management).

(B) Navy: Office of the Assistant Secretary of the Navy (Financial Management and Comptroller), Office of Financial Operations.

(C) Air Force: Air Force Contract Financing Office (SAF/FMPB).

(D) Defense agencies: Office of the agency comptroller.

(ii) Contract financing offices should participate in?

(A) Developing regulations for contract financing;

(B) Developing contract provisions for contract financing; and

(C) Resolving specific cases that involve unusual contract financing requirements.

[Final rule, 70 FR 75412, 12/20/2005, effective 12/20/2005]

SUBPART 232.4—ADVANCE PAYMENTS FOR NON-COMMERCIAL ITEMS

232.409-1 Recommendation for approval.

To ensure uniform application of this subpart (see FAR 32.402(e)(1)), the departmental/agency contract financing office shall prepare the documents required by FAR 32.409-1(e) and (f).

[Final rule, 70 FR 75412, 12/20/2005, effective 12/20/2005]

232.410 Findings, determination, and authorization.

If an advance payment procedure is used without a special bank account, replace paragraph (a)(4) of the Findings, Determination, and Authorization for Advance Payments at FAR 32.410 with:

"(4) The proposed advance payment clause contains appropriate provisions as security for advance payments. These provisions include a requirement that the outstanding advance payments will be liquidated from cost reimbursements as they become due the contractor. This security is considered adequate to protect the interest of the Government."

[Final rule, 70 FR 75412, 12/20/2005, effective 12/20/2005]

SUBPART 232.5—PROGRESS PAYMENTS BASED ON COSTS

232.501-2 Unusual progress payments.

Unusual progress payment arrangements require the advance approval of the Director of Defense Procurement and Acquisition Policy, Office of the Under Secretary of Defense (Acquisition, Technology, and Logistics) (OUSD) AT&L DPAP). Contracting officers must submit all unusual progress payment requests to the department or agency contract financing office for approval and submission to OUSD(AT&L)DPAP.

[Final rule, 70 FR 75412, 12/20/2005, effective 12/20/2005; Final rule, 78 FR 54968, 9/9/2013, effective 9/9/2013]

SUBPART 232.6—CONTRACT DEBTS

232.603 Debt determination and collection.

Upon transfer of a case to the contract financing office, the contracting officer shall close the debt record by reference to the date of transfer.

[Final rule, 70 FR 75412, 12/20/2005, effective 12/20/2005; Final rule, 80 FR 58632, 9/30/2015, effective 9/30/2015]

232.604 Demand for payment.

(1) For contract debts resulting from other than a termination for default, the office that first determines an amount due, whether it be the contract administration of-

fice, the contracting office, the disbursing office, or the selling office/agency, shall—

(i) Make a demand for payment; and

(ii) Provide a copy of the demand to the payment office cited in the contract.

(2) For contract debts resulting from a termination for default, the contracting officer shall make the demand and direct the debtor to make such payment to the designated office.

[Publication notice, 20161222]

232.670 Transfer of responsibility for debt collection.

Disbursing officers will transfer responsibility for debt collection to department/agency contract financing offices in accordance with comptroller regulations. Notwithstanding the transfer of the debt collection responsibility, contracting officers shall continue to provide assistance as requested by the debt collection office.

[Final rule, 70 FR 75412, 12/20/2005, effective 12/20/2005; Final rule, 80 FR 58632, 9/30/2015, effective 9/30/2015]

232.671 Bankruptcy reporting.

(1) For those debts covered by this subpart, the department or agency that awarded the contract shall furnish the Department of Justice any claims in bankruptcy, insolvency, or in proceedings for reorganization or arrangement. Furnish claims that—

(i) Have been transferred to a contract financing office;

(ii) Are on the way to a contract financing office at the inception of bankruptcy or insolvency proceedings;

(iii) Are pending and not forwarded to a contract financing office at the inception of bankruptcy or insolvency proceedings; and

(iv) Are the result of bankruptcy or insolvency proceedings.

(2) The contract financing office or other office designated within a department or agency will furnish proof of claims to the Department of Justice.

(3) The office of origin of a debt will provide, as soon as possible, information on a bankruptcy, insolvency, reorganization, or rearrangement to the office designated within a department/agency to receive this information.

(4) The information and proof of claim requirements in paragraphs (2) and (3) of this section do not apply to debts of less than $600.

[Final rule, 70 FR 75412, 12/20/2005, effective 12/20/2005; Final rule, 80 FR 58632, 9/30/2015, effective 9/30/2015]

SUBPART 232.10—PERFORMANCE-BASED PAYMENTS

232.1001 Policy.

(a) Contracting officer action. Performance-based payments are not practical for use on all fixed price contracts and require considerable effort between the contractor and Government to identify the appropriate performance-based payment events and establish the proper completion criteria for those events. Additionally, FAR 32.1003 prohibits contracts from having both progress payments and performance-based payment financing on a contract at the same time. Additional information and instruction on performance-based payments are provided in the DoD Performance-based Payments Guide on the DPAP website in the Cost, Pricing & Finance section under the Performance Based Payments – Guide Book & Analysis Tool tab: *http://www.acq.osd.mil/dpap/cpic/cp/Performance_based payments.html*.

[Final rule, 79 FR 17931, 3/31/2014, effective 3/31/2014]

SUBPART 232.70—ELECTRONIC SUBMISSION AND PROCESSING OF PAYMENT REQUESTS AND RECEIVING REPORTS

232.7004 Contract clause instructions.

(b) (1) The clause 252.232-7006, Wide Area WorkFlow Payment Instructions, shall be located in the contract administration section of the contract (e.g., Section G).

(2) Complete paragraph (f) (1) of the clause by selecting a document type from the list in (i) through (xix) below. Document

type selection is contingent on contract type (e.g., fixed price, cost reimbursement), nature of the work being performed or product being acquired, and the entitlement system of the DoD Component. Use the guidance for Wide Area WorkFlow (WAWF) payment instructions found at *https://wawf.eb.mil/* to determine which document types are available for each entitlement system. WAWF document types include—

(i) Invoice (stand-alone) and Receiving Report (stand-alone);

(ii) Fast Pay (FAR 52.213-1) Invoice (stand-alone) and Receiving Report (stand-alone);

(iii) Invoice 2-in-1 (Services only);

(iv) Commercial Item Financing;

(v) Performance-Based Payment;

(vi) Progress Payment;

(vii) Invoice and Receiving Report (Combo) (see paragraph (3) of this section);

(viii) Fast Pay (FAR 52.213-1) Invoice and Receiving Report (Combo) (see paragraph (3) of this section);

(ix) Cost Voucher (FAR 52.216-7, 52.232-7);

(x) Cost Voucher-Shipbuilding;

(xi) Grant Voucher;

(xii) Navy Construction/Facilities Management Invoice;

(xiii) Navy Shipbuilding Invoice—Fixed Price;

(xiv) Telecom Invoice (Contractual);

(xv) Reparables Receiving Report;

(xvi) Energy Invoice and Energy Receiving Report (Combo) (see paragraph (3) of this section);

(xvii) Energy Invoice (stand-alone) and Energy Receiving Report (stand-alone);

(xviii) Construction Payment Invoice; and

(xix) Other document type, exactly as it appears in the WAWF system, as mutually agreed to by the contracting parties.

(3) A Combo document may be used with the stand-alone alternative, separated by "or" e.g. "(vii) Invoice and Receiving Report (Combo) or (i) Invoice (stand-alone) and Receiving Report (stand-alone)"; or "(viii) Fast Pay (FAR 52.213-1) Invoice and Receiving Report Combo or (ii) Fast Pay (FAR 52.213-1) Invoice (stand-alone) and Receiving Report (standalone)."

(4) Complete paragraph (f)(2) of the clause only when document types, "Invoice (standalone) and Receiving Report (standalone)" and "Invoice and Receiving Report (Combo)" are used. Identify the applicable inspection and acceptance locations from the clause as follows:

(i) Inspection location: (select either "Source," "Destination," or "Other").

(ii) Acceptance location: (select either "Source," "Destination," or "Other").

(5) Complete paragraph (f)(3) of the clause before contract award. Selection of applicable DoDAACs is dependent on the document type and the entitlement system used by the DoD Component.

(i) To determine applicable DoDAACs, use the guidance for WAWF payment instructions at *https://wawf.eb.mil/*.

(ii) If a DoDAAC field is not listed in paragraph (f)(3) Routing Data Table, select "Other DoDAAC(s)" and list the DoDAAC field name(s) as they appear in the WAWF system and applicable DoDAAC(s).

(iii) When multiple "Ship to" and inspection/acceptance locations" (i.e. DoDAACs) exist, enter "See schedule." The corresponding schedule in the contract/order must cite all applicable DoDAACs.

(iv) Validate DoDAACs using the following resources:

(A) For inspector, acceptor and local processing office roles, use *https://wawf.eb.mil/* and click on the "Active DoDAACs & Roles link" in the "Help" section on the home page to validate active DoDAACs and user roles in WAWF.

(B) For all other DoDAACs, use *https://www.daas.dla.mil/daasinq/*.

(6) Complete paragraph (f)(5) by entering e-mail addresses of other Government personnel requiring status of the payment request, if applicable.

(7) Complete paragraph (g) by entering the WAWF point of contact information, if applicable.

[Final rule, 77 FR 38731, 6/29/2012, effective 6/29/2012; Publication notice, 20120829; Publication notice, 20130705]

SUBPART 232.71—LEVIES ON CONTRACT PAYMENTS

232.7101 Policy and procedures.

Background. The Internal Revenue Service (IRS) is authorized to collect overdue taxes through a continuous levy up to 100 percent of the debt on certain vendor contract payments disbursed by the Defense Finance and Accounting Service. The levy is continuous until the overdue taxes are paid in full, or other arrangements are made to satisfy the debt. Contractors are required to promptly notify the procuring contracting officer when a tax levy that may result in an inability to perform the contract is imposed, so that the contracting officer and the Director, Defense Procurement and Acquisition Policy (DPAP), can take appropriate action to mitigate any possible adverse effect on national security.

(b) *Procuring contracting officer procedures for reviewing the contractor's rationale and submitting the required documentation.*

(i) When the procuring contracting officer receives notification from the contractor that the tax levy may result in an inability to perform the contract, the procuring contracting officer shall promptly review the contractor's assessment and either agree or disagree that the levy may result in an inability to perform. The procuring contracting officer shall alert the administrative contracting officer and the cognizant contract auditor when a notice of levy has been received, and shall obtain any necessary assistance from the administrative contracting officer or contract auditor when performing this review.

(ii) If the procuring contracting officer does not agree with the contractor's assessment, the procuring contracting officer shall notify the contractor of this determination and no further action will be taken.

(iii) If the procuring contracting officer agrees with the contractor's assessment that the levy may result in an inability to perform the contract, the procuring contracting officer shall document, in writing, whether the inability to perform—

(A) Adversely affects national security; and/or

(B) Will result in significant additional costs to the Government (e.g., cost of re-procurement, loss of contract financing payments when the product produced to date is not salvageable).

(iv) If the procuring contracting officer believes that the levy will impact national security and/or result in significant additional costs to DoD, the procuring contracting officer shall, in accordance with agency procedures, promptly notify the Director, DPAP, by e-mail or facsimile. The notification to the Director, DPAP, shall include—

(A) The rationale supporting the recommendation that the levy may result in an inability to perform the contract;

(B) A description of the adverse effect on national security, if applicable; and

(C) A description and estimate of the additional costs to the Government, if applicable. Since prompt notification to the Director, DPAP, is essential, the procuring contracting officer should not delay the notification while trying to achieve more precise data.

(c) *Director, DPAP, procedures.* The Director, DPAP, will promptly evaluate the procuring contracting officer's notification package.

(i) If the Director, DPAP, disagrees with the recommendation of the procuring contracting officer, the Director, DPAP, will notify the procuring contracting officer through the same agency channels that were used for submission of the notification.

(ii) If the Director, DPAP, agrees with the recommendation of the procuring contracting officer—

(A) When there is an adverse effect on national security, the Director, DPAP, will notify the payment office, the IRS, and the procuring contracting officer that the total amount of the levy should be promptly returned to the contractor; or

(B) When there is not an adverse effect on national security but the levy will result in significant additional costs to DoD, the Director, DPAP, will promptly notify the procuring contracting officer and the IRS. The Director, DPAP, notification to the IRS will-

(1) State that the procuring contracting officer has notified the contractor and has recommended that the contractor contact the IRS to resolve the situation;

(2) Request that the IRS expedite resolution of the situation with the contractor; and

(3) Include an estimate of additional costs to DoD that will result if the contractor is unable to perform on the contract.

(d) *Procuring contracting officer procedures for notifying the contractor of the decision of the Director, DPAP.* The procuring contracting officer shall promptly notify the contractor, in writing, of the decision made by the Director, DPAP, including the actions to be taken (if any).

[Interim rule, 70 FR 52032, 9/1/2005, effective 9/1/2005; Final rule, 71 FR 69489, 12/1/2006, effective 12/1/2006]

PART 233—PROTESTS, DISPUTES, AND APPEALS

Table of Contents

Subpart 233.1—Protests

Briefing requirement for protested acquisitions valued at $1 billion or more 233.170
Reporting requirement for protests of solicitations or awards 233.171

Subpart 233.2—Disputes and Appeals

Contracting officer's authority 233.210

PART 233—PROTESTS, DISPUTES, AND APPEALS

SUBPART 233.1—PROTESTS

233.170 Briefing requirement for protested acquisitions valued at $1 billion or more.

In the event of a protest of a competitively awarded Major Defense Acquisition Program or of an acquisition of services valued at $1 billion or more, the agency concerned shall provide a briefing to the Principal Director, Defense Pricing and Contracting, within 10 days of the filing of the protest. The briefing must outline—

(a) The basis of the protest;

(b) The agency's position; and

(c) Any other information the agency deems relevant to the protest.

[Change notice, 20081112; Final rule, 84 FR 25194, 5/31/2019, effective 5/31/2019]

233.171 Reporting requirement for protests of solicitations or awards.

The Protest Tracker on the Procurement Integrated Enterprise Environment (PIEE) (accessible at https://wawf.eb.mil/) is the bid protest data repository required by section 822(c) of the National Defense Authorization Act for Fiscal Year 2019 (Pub. L. 115-232). When protests involving the same contract or proposed award, valued at any amount, have been filed at both the Government Accountability Office and the United States Court of Federal Claims (COFC), the contracting officer shall report the protest information required in the Protest Tracker no later than 10 days after the outcome of the protest at the COFC. Instructions on reporting protest information in the Protest Tracker are available on the PIEE webpage.

[Final rule, 84 FR 25194, 5/31/2019, effective 5/31/2019]

SUBPART 233.2—DISPUTES AND APPEALS

233.210 Contracting officer's authority.

When it would be helpful in reviewing the current claim, the contracting officer should get information on claims previously filed by the contractor. Such information may provide a historical perspective of the nature and accuracy of the claims submitted by the contractor and how they were settled. Potential sources for the information include the contracting activity's office of legal counsel, other contracting activities, and the Defense Contract Audit Agency.

[Final rule, 72 FR 6485, 2/12/2007, effective 2/12/2007]

PART 234—MAJOR SYSTEM ACQUISITION

Table of Contents

Subpart 234.2—Earned Value Management System

Policy 234.201

Subpart 234.70—Acquisition of Major Weapon Systems as Commercial Items

Policy 234.7002

Subpart 234.71—Cost and Software Data Reporting

Policy 234.7100

PART 234—MAJOR SYSTEM ACQUISITION

SUBPART 234.2—EARNED VALUE MANAGEMENT SYSTEM

234.201 Policy.

(iii) When the program manager decides to implement earned value management on contracts and subcontracts valued at less than $20,000,000, a cost-benefit analysis shall be conducted and the results documented in the contract file. Considerations for determining the effectiveness of applying earned value management in these situations and guidance for tailoring reporting can be found in—

(1) The Defense Acquisition Guidebook, Chapter 11, Section 11.3, at *https://akss.dau.mil/dag/DoD5000.asp?view=document;* and

(2) The DoD Earned Value Management Implementation Guide at *https://acc.dau.mil/CommunityBrowser.aspx?id=19557.*

(iv) In extraordinary cases where cost/schedule visibility is required and cannot be obtained using other means, the program manager shall request a waiver for individual contracts from the Milestone Decision Authority. In these cases, the program manager will conduct a business case analysis that includes rationale as to why a cost or fixed-price incentive contract was not an appropriate contracting vehicle. Considerations for determining the effectiveness of applying earned value management in these situations and guidance for tailoring reporting can be found in—

(1) The Defense Acquisition Guidebook, Chapter 11, Section 11.3, at *https://akss.dau.mil/dag/DoD5000.asp?view=document;* and

(2) The DoD Earned Value Management Implementation Guide at *https://acc.dau.mil/CommunityBrowser.aspx?id=19557.*

(2) The procuring contracting officer shall obtain the assistance of the administrative contracting officer in determining the adequacy of an earned value management system (EVMS) plan that an offeror proposes for compliance with ANSI/EIA-748, under the provision at DFARS 252.234-7001, Notice of Earned Value Management System. The Government will review and approve the offeror's EVMS plan before contract award. Instructions for performing EVMS plan reviews can be found at *http://guidebook.dcma.mil/39/instructions.htm.*

(4) Additional guidance on earned value management can be found in—

(A) The Guidebook for Earned Value Management System (EVMS) System-Level Surveillance at *http://guidebook.dcma.mil/79/instructions.htm;*

(B) The Guidebook for Earned Value Management System - Program Analysis at *http://guidebook.dcma.mil/248/guidebook_process.htm;* and

(C) The Program Managers' Guide to the Integrated Baseline Review Process (the IBR Guide) at *http://www.acq.osd.mil/pm/currentpolicy/currentpolicy.html.*

(7) *Disposition of findings.*

(ii) *Initial determination.*

(B) (1) Within 10 days of receiving the report, if the contracting officer makes a determination that there is a significant deficiency, the contracting officer should provide an initial determination of deficiencies and a copy of the report to the contractor and require the contractor to submit a written response.

(3) *Evaluation of contractor's response.* Within 30 days of receiving the contractor's response, the contracting officer, in consultation with the auditor or cognizant functional specialist, should evaluate the contractor's response and make a final determination.

(iii) *Final determination.*

(B) (1) *Monitoring contractor's corrective action.* The contracting officer and cognizant functional specialist or auditor shall monitor the contractor's progress in correcting deficiencies. If the contractor fails to make adequate progress, the contracting officer shall take whatever action is necessary to ensure that the contractor corrects the deficiencies. Examples of actions the contracting officer can take are: bringing the issue to the attention of higher level management, implementing or increasing the withholding in accordance with 252.242-7005, Contractor Business Systems.

(2) *Correction of significant deficiencies.*

(i) When the contractor notifies the contracting officer that the contractor has corrected the significant deficiencies, the contracting officer shall request the cognizant functional specialist or auditor to review the correction to determine if the deficiencies have been resolved.

(ii) The contracting officer shall determine if the contractor has corrected the deficiencies.

(iii) If the contracting officer determines the contractor has corrected the deficiencies, the contracting officer's notification shall be sent to the cognizant functional specialist; auditor; payment office; appropriate action officers at the requiring activities; and each contracting and contract administration office having substantial business with the contractor as applicable.

[Final rule, 73 FR 21845, 4/23/2008, effective 4/23/2008; Interim rule, 76 FR 28856, 5/18/2011, effective 5/18/2011; Final rule, 77 FR 11355, 2/24/2012, effective 2/24/2012]

SUBPART 234.70—ACQUISITION OF MAJOR WEAPON SYSTEMS AS COMMERCIAL ITEMS

234.7002 Policy.

Departments and agencies shall obtain a determination by the Secretary of Defense and shall notify the congressional defense committees before acquiring a major weapon system as a commercial item.

[Interim rule, 71 FR 58537, 10/4/2006, effective 10/4/2006]

SUBPART 234.71—COST AND SOFTWARE DATA REPORTING

234.7100 Policy.

The OSD Deputy Director, Cost Assessment, may be contacted at—

Defense Cost and Resource Center

201 12th Street, Suite 220

Arlington, VA 22202-5408

703-601-4850

703-604-1012 (fax)

DSN: 329-4850

DCARC@osd.mil

osd.pentagon.cape.mbx.dcarc@mail.mil.pae.osd.mil
http://dcarc.pae.osd.mil

[Final rule, 75 FR 71560, 11/24/2010, effective 11/24/2010; Final rule, 78 FR 54968, 9/9/2013, effective 9/9/2013]

PART 235—RESEARCH AND DEVELOPMENT CONTRACTING

Table of Contents

Subpart 235.0—Research and Development Contracting

Scientific and technical reports 235.010

PART 235—RESEARCH AND DEVELOPMENT CONTRACTING

SUBPART 235.0—RESEARCH AND DEVELOPMENT CONTRACTING

235.010 Scientific and technical reports.

(b) The Defense Technical Information Center (DTIC) is responsible for collecting all scientific or technological observations, findings, recommendations, and results derived from DoD endeavors, including both in-house and contracted efforts. The DTIC has eligibility and registration requirements for use of its services. Requests for eligibility and registration information should be addressed to DTIC-BC Registration, 8725 John J. Kingman Road, Fort Belvoir, VA 22060-6218, or may be obtained at *http://www.dtic.mil.*

[Final rule, 69 FR 65091, 11/10/2004, effective 11/10/2004]

PART 236—CONSTRUCTION AND ARCHITECT-ENGINEER CONTRACTS

Table of Contents

Subpart 236.2—Special Aspects of Contracting for Construction

[Removed] 236.201
Government estimate of construction costs 236.203
Pricing Fixed-Price Construction Contracts. 236.207
Special procedures for sealed bidding in construction contracting 236.213
Construction in foreign countries 236.273

Subpart 236.6—Architect-Engineer Services

Selection of firms for architect-engineer contracts 236.602
Selection criteria 236.602-1

PART 236—CONSTRUCTION AND ARCHITECT-ENGINEER CONTRACTS

SUBPART 236.2—SPECIAL ASPECTS OF CONTRACTING FOR CONSTRUCTION

236.201 [Removed]

[Final rule, 71 FR 9272, 2/23/2006, effective 2/23/2006; Final rule, 75 FR 45072, 8/2/2010, effective 10/1/2010; Final rule, 76 58155, 9/20/2011, effective 9/20/2011]

236.203 Government estimate of construction costs.

(1) Designate the Government estimate as "For Official Use Only," unless the information is classified. If it is, handle the estimate in accordance with security regulations.

(2) For sealed bid acquisitions—

(i) File a sealed copy of the Government estimate with the bids. (In the case of two-step acquisitions, this is done in the second step.)

(ii) After the bids are read and recorded, remove the "For Official Use Only" designation and read and record the estimate as if it were a bid, in the same detail as the bids.

[Final rule, 71 FR 9272, 2/23/2006, effective 2/23/2006]

236.207 Pricing Fixed-Price Construction Contracts.

(a) (70) *Definition: lump sum* means a single payment of money, as opposed to a series of payments made over time.

(i) An example of a line item with lump sum pricing in accordance with DFARS 204.71 is as follows:

ITEM NO.	SUPPLIES/SERVICE	QUANTITY	UNIT	UNIT PRICE	AMOUNT
0001	Repave runway 4 at Joint Base Andrews Firm Fixed Price PSC: Z1BD ACRN: AA	1	Job	$1,501,866.08	$1,501,866.08

Note that payment would occur upon completion and acceptance of the entire effort. Progress payments based on estimates of the percentage of completion (see FAR 52.232-5—Payments Under Fixed-Price Construction Contracts) could occur prior to that point.

(ii) An example of a line item with unit pricing in accordance with DFARS 204.71 is as follows:

ITEM NO.	SUPPLIES/SERVICE	QUANTITY	UNIT	UNIT PRICE	AMOUNT
0001	Repave runway 4 at Joint Base Andrews Firm Fixed Price PSC: Z1BD ACRN: AA	525,128	Square Foot	$2.86	$1,501,866.08

Note that this allows the contractor to invoice for completed quantities of work, in accordance with FAR 32.102(d), as those are accepted. Progress payments based on estimates of the percentage of completion (see FAR 52.232-5—Payments Under Fixed-Price Construction Contracts) could also occur prior to that point.

[Publication notice, 20140624]

236.213 Special procedures for sealed bidding in construction contracting.

For additive or deductive items—

(1) Use a bid schedule with—

(i) A first or base bid item covering the work generally as specified; and

(ii) A list of priorities that contains one or more additive or deductive bid items that progressively add or omit specified features of the work in a stated order of priority. (Normally, do not mix additive and deductive bid items in the same solicitation.)

(2) Before opening the bids, record in the contract file the amount of funds available for the project.

(3) Determine the low bidder and the items to be awarded in accordance with the procedures in the clause at 252.236-7007, Additive or Deductive Items.

[Final rule, 71 FR 9272, 2/23/2006, effective 2/23/2006]

236.273 Construction in foreign countries.

(b) When a technical working agreement with a foreign government is required for a construction contract—

(i) Consider inviting the Army Office of the Chief of Engineers, or the Naval Facilities Engineering Command, to participate in the negotiations.

(ii) The agreement should, as feasible and where not otherwise provided for in other agreements, cover all elements necessary for the construction that are required by laws, regulations, and customs of the United States and the foreign government, including—

(A) Acquisition of all necessary rights;

(B) Expeditious, duty-free importation of labor, material, and equipment;

(C) Payment of taxes applicable to contractors, personnel, materials, and equipment;

(D) Applicability of workers' compensation and other labor laws to citizens of the United States, the host country, and other countries;

(E) Provision of utility services;

(F) Disposition of surplus materials and equipment;

(G) Handling of claims and litigation; and

(H) Resolution of any other foreseeable problems that can be appropriately included in the agreement.

[Final rule, 71 FR 9272, 2/23/2006, effective 2/23/2006]

SUBPART 236.6—ARCHITECT-ENGINEER SERVICES

236.602 Selection of firms for architect-engineer contracts. (No Text)

236.602-1 Selection criteria.

(a) The evaluation criteria should be project specific. Use the information in the DD Form 1391, FY__ Military Construction Project Data, when available, and other pertinent project data in preparing the evaluation criteria.

(4) Use performance evaluation data from the Contractor Performance Assessment Report System (CPARS).

(6) The primary factor in architect-engineer contractor selection is the determination of the most highly qualified firm. Also consider secondary factors such as geographic proximity and equitable distribution of work, but do not attribute greater significance to the secondary factors than to qualifications and past performance. Do not reject the overall most highly qualified firm solely in the interest of equitable distribution of contracts.

(A) Consider the volume of work awarded by DoD during the previous 12 months. In considering equitable distribution of work among architect-engineer contractor firms, include small business concerns; historically black colleges and universities and minority institutions; firms that have not had prior DoD contracts; and small disadvantaged business concerns and joint ventures with small disadvantaged business participants if the North American Industry Classification System (NAICS) Industry Subsector of the acquisition is one in which use of a price evaluation adjustment is currently authorized (see FAR 19.201(b)).

(1) Use data extracted from the Federal Procurement Data System (FPDS).

(2) Do not consider awards to overseas offices for projects outside the United States, its territories and possessions. Do not consider awards to a subsidiary if the subsidiary is not normally subject to management decisions, bookkeeping, and policies of a holding or parent company or an incorporated sub-

sidiary that operates under a firm name different from the parent company. This allows greater competition.

(B) Consider as appropriate superior performance evaluations on recently completed DoD contracts.

(C) Consider the extent to which potential contractors identify and commit to small business, to small disadvantaged business (SDB) if the NAICS Industry Subsector of the subcontracted effort is one in which use of an evaluation factor or subfactor for participation of SDB concerns is currently authorized (see FAR 19.201(b)), and to historically black college or university and minority institution performance as subcontractors.

[Final rule, 69 FR 75000, 12/15/2004, effective 12/15/2004; Final rule, 74 FR 37644, 7/29/2009, effective 7/29/2009; Final rule, 76 FR 58155, 9/20/2011, effective 9/20/2011; Publication notice, 20121212, 12/12/2012]

PART 237—SERVICE CONTRACTING

Table of Contents

Subpart 237.1—Service Contracting—General

Prohibition on contracting for firefighting or security-guard functions 237.102-70
Limitation on service contracts for military flight simulators 237.102-71
Prohibition on contracts for services of senior mentors 237.102-73
Taxonomy for the acquisition of services and supplies & equipment 237.102-74
Review criteria for the acquisition of services 237.102-76
Automated requirements roadmap tool 237.102-77
Market research report guide for improving the tradecraft in services acquisition 237.102-78
Private sector notification requirements in support of in-sourcing actions. . 237.102-79
Training for contractor personnel interacting with detainees 237.171
Policy 237.171-3
Service contracts surveillance 237.172

Subpart 237.2—Advisory and Assistance Services

Acquisition of audit services 237.270

Subpart 237.5—Management Oversight of Service Contracts

Agency-head responsibilities 237.503

Subpart 237.70—Mortuary Services

Area of performance and distribution of contracts 237.7002

PART 237—SERVICE CONTRACTING

SUBPART 237.1—SERVICE CONTRACTS—GENERAL

237.102-70 Prohibition on contracting for firefighting or security-guard functions.

(c) (i) To ensure that the personnel limitations in DFARS 237.102-70(c) (1) (iv) are not exceeded, there is an office of primary responsibility (OPR) within each department or agency that is responsible for managing the total number of security-guard personnel on contract for the department or agency.

(ii) Before finalizing a contract action that affects the number of security-guard personnel on contract, the contracting officer shall request, from the requiring activity, evidence of the OPR's approval for the contract action. This requirement also applies to renewal or exercise of options for the same number of security-guard personnel, to ensure compliance with the statutory limitations/reductions specified for each fiscal year.

(iii) If the evidence of approval is not provided by the requiring activity, the contracting officer shall directly contact the applicable OPR for approval before finalizing the contract action. OPRs are as follows:

(A) U.S. Army:

HQ Department of the Army

Office of the Provost Marshal General

2800 Army Pentagon

Washington, DC 20310

Phone: 703-695-4210 or 703-614-2597.

(B) U.S. Navy:

Commander, Navy Installations

Command (CNIC) N3

2715 Mitscher Road, Suite 300

Anacostia Annex

Washington, DC 20373

Phone: 202-409-4053.

(C) U.S. Marine Corps:

HQ U.S. Marine Corps

Assistant Deputy Commandant, Plans, Policy, & Operations (Security)

3000 Marine Corps Pentagon

Washington, DC 20350

Phone: 571-201-3633.

(D) U.S. Air Force:

HQ Air Force

Directorate of Security Forces

Programs & Resources Division (A7SX)

1340 AF Pentagon

Washington, DC 20330

Phone: 703-588-0027 or 703-588-0012.

(E) Pentagon Force Protection Agency:

Pentagon Force Protection Agency

9000 Defense Pentagon

Washington, DC 20301

Phone: 703-693-3685.

[Final rule, 70 FR 14576, 3/23/2005, effective 3/23/2005; Change notice, 20051209; Interim rule, 71 FR 34833, 6/16/2006, effective 6/16/2006; Interim rule, 72 FR 51192, 9/6/2007, effective 9/6/2007; Change notice, 20080812; Final rule, 84 FR 65310, 11/27/2019, effective 11/27/2019; Publication notice, 20191231]

237.102-71 Limitation on service contracts for military flight simulators.

(1) To process a request for waiver, the contracting officer shall submit the request and appropriate documentation relating to the requirements of DFARS 237.102-71(b) to:

Director, Defense Procurement and Acquisition Policy

ATTN: OUSD(AT&L) DPAP/CPIC

3060 Defense Pentagon

Washington, DC 20301-3060

Phone: 703-697-8334 FAX: 703-614-1254

(2) The action officer in the Office of the Director, Defense Procurement and Acquisition Policy, Contract Policy and International Contracting (DPAP/CPIC), will process the request through the Office of the Secretary of Defense and will forward the appropriate

documentation to the congressional defense committees. The contracting officer shall not award a contract until notified by the DPAP/CPIC action officer that the waiver has been approved, the appropriate documentation has been transmitted to the congressional defense committees, and the required 30 days have passed.

[Final rule, 72 FR 51193, 9/6/2007, effective 9/6/2007; Final rule, 78 FR 54968, 9/9/2013, effective 9/9/2013; Publication notice, 20191231]

237.102-73 Prohibition on contracts for services of senior mentors.

DoD policies on senior mentors are set forth in (1) Secretary of Defense memorandum, subject: Policy on Senior Mentors (April 1, 2010) (*https://www.acq.osd.mil/dpap/dars/docs/SeniorMentorPolicy.pdf*) and (2) Deputy Secretary of Defense memorandum, subject: Implementation Guidance on Senior Mentors Policy (July 8, 2010) (*https://www.acq.osd.mil/dpap/dars/docs/Updated%20Conversion%20Guidance%208%20Jul%202010.pdf*).

[Interim rule, 75 FR 54524, 9/8/2010, effective 9/8/2010; Publication notice, 20100908; Final rule, 75 FR 71563, 11/24/2010, effective 11/24/2010; Publication notice, 20191231]

237.102-74 Taxonomy for the acquisition of services and supplies & equipment.

Click *https://www.acq.osd.mil/dpap/policy/policyvault/USA004219-12-DPAP.pdf* for OUSD(AT&L) DPAP memorandum, "Taxonomy for the Acquisition of Services and Supplies & Equipment," dated August 27, 2012. An Excel version of "Acquisition of Services and Supplies & Equipment Taxonomy" is available *Acquisition_services_taxonomy*.

[Publication notice, 20101210; Final rule, 75 FR 78619, 12/16/2010, effective 12/16/2010; Publication notice, 20121212, 12/12/2012; Publication notice, 20191231]

237.102-75 Defense Acquisition Guidebook.

The Defense Acquisition Guidebook, Chapter 10, Acquisition of Services, is available via the internet at *https://www.dau.mil/tools/dag*. Chapter 10 provides acquisition teams with a step-by-step guide explaining the process of acquiring services.

[Final rule, 81 FR 36473, 6/7/2016, effective 6/7/2016; Publication notice, 20171228; Publication notice, 20191231]

237.102-76 Review criteria for the acquisition of services.

The tenets of the DoD-wide architecture for the acquisition of services along with the associated review criteria are available *Criteria_for_Acquisition_of_Services_(Pre_and_Postaward)*. These matrices are to be used when conducting reviews in the preaward phase (Review/Approval of Acquisition Strategies or Preaward Peer Reviews) and in the postaward phase (Postaward Peer Reviews). See DFARS 201.170, Peer reviews, and PGI 201.170, Peer reviews.

[Publication notice, 20191231]

237.102-77 Acquisition requirements roadmap tool.

The Acquisition Requirements Roadmap Tool (ARRT) is a tool that enables requiring activities to develop and organize performance requirements into draft versions of the performance work statement, the quality assurance surveillance plan, and the performance requirements summary. ARRT provides a standard template for these documents and some default text that can be modified to reflect a particular requirement. This tool should be used to prepare these documents for all performance-based acquisitions for services. ARRT is available for download at *https://www.dau.edu/tools/Documents/SAM/resources/ARRT_Home.html*.

[Publication notice, 20120829; Final rule, 81 FR 36473, 6/7/2016, effective 6/7/2016; Publication notice, 20191231]

237.102-78 Market research report guide for improving the tradecraft in services acquisition.

See PGI 210.070 for guidance on use of the market research report guide to conduct and document market research for service acquisitions.

[Publication notice, 20120829; Publication notice, 20191231]

237.102-79 Private sector notification requirements in support of in-sourcing actions.

Click *https://www.acq.osd.mil/dpap/dars/pgi/docs/Private_Sector_Notificaton_Requirements_in_Support_of_In-sourcing_Actions.pdf* for OUSD (RFM) memorandum, "Private Sector Notification Requirements in Support of In-sourcing Actions," dated January 29, 2013.

[Final rule, 78 FR 21850, 4/12/2013, effective 4/12/2013; Interim rule, 78 FR 65218, 10/31/2013, effective 10/31/2013; Final rule 79 FR 35700, 6/24/2014, effective 6/24/2014; Publication notice, 20191231]

237.171 Training for contractor personnel interacting with detainees.

[Final rule, 71 FR 53047, 9/8/2006, effective 9/8/2006; Publication notice, 20191231]

237.171-3 Policy.

(b) (i) *Geographic areas of responsibility.* With regard to training for contractor personnel interacting with detainees—

(A) The Commander, U.S. Southern Command, is responsible for the U.S. military detention center at Guantanamo Bay, Cuba.

(B) The Commander, U.S. Joint Forces Command, is responsible for the Navy Consolidated Brig, Charleston, SC.

(C) The other combatant commander geographic areas of responsibility are identified in the Unified Command Plan, 1 March 2005, which can be found at: *www.defenselink.mil/specials/unifiedcommand/.*

(ii) *Point of contact information for each command:*

US Central Command (USCENTCOM)
Commander, Combined Forces Land Component Commander (CFLCC)
a.k.a. Third Army, Ft. McPherson, Atlanta, GA
Staff Judge Advocate (SJA) Forward, Kuwait
POC: Lieutenant Colonel Gary Kluka
E-mail: Gary.Kluka@arifjan.arcent.army.mil
Comm: 011-965-389-6303; DSN: 318-430-6303; Alt. US numbers: 404-464-3721 or 404-464-4219

US European Command (USEUCOM)
Logistics and Security Assistance Directorate
Chief, Contingency Contracting and Contract Policy Division (USEUCOM J4-LS)
POC: Major Michael Debreczini
debreczm@eucom.smil.mil
Comm: 011-49-711-680-7202; DSN: 314-0430-7202

US Joint Forces Command (USJFCOM)
**Applicable to potential detainees in the United States at Navy Consolidated Brig, Charleston, SC
Headquarters, USJFCOM (J355)
Personnel Recovery & Special Operations Division (J355)
POC: Lieutenant Colonel John Maraia
Comm: 757-836-5799; DSN: 836-5799

US Northern Command (USNORTHCOM)
Not applicable to USNORTHCOM; see US Joint Forces Command

US Pacific Command (USPACOM)
Headquarters, Office of the Staff Judge Advocate (SJA)
Deputy Staff Judge Advocate
POC: Lieutenant Colonel James Buckels, USAF
james.buckels@pacom.mil
Comm: 808-477-1193

US Southern Command (USSOUTHCOM)
Headquarters, Office of the Staff Judge Advocate (SJA)
Joint Task Force Guanatanamo Bay
POC: Lieutenant Commander Tony Dealicante
DealicanteTF@JTFGTMO.southcom.mil
Comm: 011-5399-9916; DSN: 660-9916

US Special Operations Command (USSOCOM)
Headquarters, Office of the Staff Judge Advocate (SJA)
Attn: Staff Judge Advocate
POC: Colonel Dana Chipman

chipmad@socom.mil
Comm: 813-828-3288; DSN: 299-3288

[Interim rule, 70 FR 52032, 9/1/2005, effective 9/1/2005; Final rule, 71 FR 53047, 9/8/2006, effective 9/8/2006; Publication notice, 20191231]

237.172 Service contracts surveillance.

The contracting officer shall remind requirements personnel, when they are preparing the quality assurance surveillance plan for contracts, to include a requirement for surveillance of the contractor's implementation of the clause at FAR 52. 222-50, Combating Trafficking in Persons (see PGI 222.1703).

[Publication notice, 20130516; Publication notice, 20191231]

SUBPART 237.2—ADVISORY AND ASSISTANCE SERVICES

237.270 Acquisition of audit services.

The following DoD publications govern the conduct of audits:

(1) DoDD 7600.2, Audit Policies-Provides DoD audit policies.

(2) DoDI 7600.6, Audit of Nonappropriated Fund Instrumentalities and Related Activities-Provides guidance to audit organizations for audits of nonappropriated fund organizations.

(3) DoD 7600.7-M, DoD Audit Manual-Provides policy and guidance to DoD audit organizations for the monitoring of audit services provided by non-Federal auditors.

[Final rule, 70 FR 57193, 9/30/2005, effective 9/30/2005; Publication notice, 20140828]

SUBPART 237.5—MANAGEMENT OVERSIGHT OF SERVICE CONTRACTS

237.503 Agency-head responsibilities.

(c) To comply with the certification requirement at DFARS 237.503, complete a certification substantially the same as the following and include a copy in the contract file:

Certification of Nonpersonal Services

This certification and enclosed worksheet is designed to ensure that the agency does not award a personal-services contract unless specifically authorized by statute (e.g., 10 U.S.C. 129b, 5 U.S.C. 3109, or 10 U.S.C. 1091). Therefore, this documentation should be completed in conjunction with the submission of a service-contract requirement to the contracting officer.

A personal services contract is characterized by the employer-employee relationship it creates between the Government and the contractor's personnel. The Government is normally required to obtain its employees by direct hire under competitive appointment procedures required by civil service laws. Obtaining personal services by contract, rather than by direct hire, circumvents those laws unless Congress has specifically authorized acquisition of the services by contract.

An employer-employee relationship under a service contract occurs when the Government exercises relatively continuous supervision and control over contractor personnel performing the contract.

Upon considering the information above and the worksheet below, I certify that this requirement does not include an unauthorized personal services arrangement, either in the way the work statement is written or in the manner in which the resulting contract will be managed and overseen.

____

Printed Name, Grade, Title, and Date

Signature:____________________

	Personal Services (The following descriptive elements from FAR 37.104 should be used as a guide to assess whether or not a proposed contract is personal in nature. If the answer to any of the items below is "YES," then additional measures should be taken to ensure the contract is not administered so as to create an employer-employee relationship between the Government and the contractor's personnel and result in an unauthorized personal services contract.)	YES	NO
1.	Contractor personnel are performing on a Government site.		
2.	Principal tools and equipment are furnished by the Government.		
3	Services are applied directly to the integral effort of the agency or an organizational subpart in furtherance of assigned function or mission.		
4	Comparable services meeting comparable needs are performed in this agency or similar agencies using civil-service personnel.		
5.	The need for the service provided can reasonably be expected to last beyond one year.		
6.	The inherent nature of the service, or the manner in which it is to be provided, reasonably requires (directly or indirectly) Government direction or supervision of contractor employees in order to: (a) adequately protect the Government's interest; (b) retain control of the function involved; or (c) retain full personal responsibility for the function supported in a duly authorized Federal officer or employee.		

[Interim rule, 75 FR 54524, 9/8/2010, effective 9/80/2010; Final rule, 76 FR 25565, 5/5/2011, effective 5/5/2011]

SUBPART 237.70—MORTUARY SERVICES

237.7002 Area of performance and distribution of contracts.

(1) Determine and define the geographical area to be covered by the contract using the following general guidelines:

(i) Use political boundaries, streets, or other features as demarcation lines.

(ii) The size should be roughly equivalent to the contiguous metropolitan or municipal area enlarged to include the activities served.

(iii) If the area of performance best suited to the needs of a particular contract is not large enough to include a carrier terminal commonly used by people within the area, the contract area of performance shall specifically state that it includes the terminal as a pickup or delivery point.

(2) In addition to normal contract distribution, send three copies of each contract to each activity authorized to use the contract, and two copies to each of the following:

(i) HQDA (TAPC-PEC-D), Alexandria, VA 22331.

(ii) Commander, Naval Medical Command, Department of the Navy (MED 3141), 23rd and E Streets NW, Washington, DC 20372.

(iii) Headquarters, AFMPC-MPCCM.

[Final rule, 71 FR 3415, 1/23/2006, effective 1/23/2006]

PART 239—ACQUISITION OF INFORMATION TECHNOLOGY

Table of Contents

Subpart 239.71—Security and Privacy for Computer Systems

Policy and responsibilities 239.7102
Information assurance contractor training and certification 239.7102-3

Subpart 239.74—Telecommunications Services

Policy 239.7402
Delegated authority for telecommunications resources 239.7405
Certified cost or pricing data and data other than certified cost or pricing data 239.7406
Type of contract 239.7407

Subpart 239.76—Cloud Computing

Policy and responsibilities 239.7602
General 239.7602-1
Required storage of data within the United States or outlying areas 239.7602-2
Procedures 239.7603
General 239.7603-1
Notification of third party access requests 239.7603-2
Cyber incident and compromise reporting 239.7603-3
DoD damage assessment activities 239.7603-4

PART 239—ACQUISITION OF INFORMATION TECHNOLOGY

SUBPART 239.71—SECURITY AND PRIVACY FOR COMPUTER SYSTEMS

239.7102 Policy and responsibilities. (No Text)

[Final rule, 73 FR 1828, 1/10/2008, effective 1/10/2008]

239.7102-3 Information assurance contractor training and certification.

(1) The designated contracting officer's representative will document the current information assurance certification status of contractor personnel by category and level, in the Defense Eligibility Enrollment Reporting System, as required by DoD Manual 8570.01-M, Information Assurance Workforce Improvement Program.

(2) DoD 8570.01-M, paragraphs C3.2.4.8.1 and C4.2.3.7.1, requires modification of existing contracts to specify contractor training and certification requirements, in accordance with the phased implementation plan in Chapter 9 of DoD 8570.01-M. As with all modifications, any change to contract requirements shall be with appropriate consideration.

[Final rule, 73 FR 1828, 1/10/2008, effective 1/10/2008]

SUBPART 239.74—TELECOMMUNICATIONS SERVICES

239.7402 Policy.

(c) *Foreign carriers.*

(i) Frequently, foreign carriers are owned by the government of the country in which they operate. The foreign governments often prescribe the methods of doing business.

(ii) In contracts for telecommunications services in foreign countries, describe the rates and practices in as much detail as possible. It is DoD policy not to pay discriminatory rates. DoD will pay a reasonable rate for telecommunications services or the rate charged the military of that country, whichever is less.

(iii) Refer special problems with telecommunications acquisition in foreign countries to higher headquarters for resolution with appropriate State Department representatives.

(d) *Long-haul telecommunications services.* DISA will acquire all long-haul telecommunications services for *DoD. See DoD Directive 5105.19*, Defense Information Systems Agency (DISA).

[Final rule, 71 FR 39010, 7/11/2006, effective 7/11/2006; Final rule, 81 FR 28732, 5/10/2016, effective 5/10/2016]

239.7405 Delegated authority for telecommunications resources.

Related Documents:

Documents related to DoD's delegated authority to enter into telecommunications service contracts are available *here*.

[Final rule, 70 FR 67918, 11/9/2005, effective 11/9/2005]

239.7406 Certified cost or pricing data and data other than certified cost or pricing data.

Examples of instances where certified cost or pricing data, if required in accordance with FAR 15.403-4, or data other than certified cost or pricing data, if required in accordance with FAR 15.403-3, may be necessary to support price reasonableness include—

(1) Nontariffed services;

(2) Special rates and charges not included in a tariff, whether filed or to be filed;

(3) Special assembly rates and charges;

(4) Special construction and equipment charges;

(5) Contingent liabilities that are fixed at the outset of the service;

(6) Proposed cancellation and termination charges under the clause at 252.239-7007, Cancellation or Termination of Orders, and reuse arrangements under the clause at 252.239-7008, Reuse Arrangements;

(7) Rates contained in voluntary tariffs filed by nondominant common carriers; or

(8) A tariff, whether filed or to be filed, for new services installed or developed primarily for Government use.

[Final rule, 71 FR 39010, 7/11/2006, effective 7/11/2006; Final rule, 77 FR 76939, 12/31/2012, effective 12/31/2012; Final rule, 84 FR 48496, 9/13/2019, effective 9/13/2019]

239.7407 Type of contract.

When using a basic agreement in conjunction with a communication service authorization—

(1) Use DD Form 428, Communication Service Authorization (CSA), or an electronic data processing substitute to award, modify, cancel, or terminate telecommunications services. The CSA shall—

(i) Refer to the basic agreement;

(ii) Specify the types and quantities and equipment to be provided as well as the tariff (or other price if a tariff is not available) of those services and equipment;

(iii) Specify the premises involved;

(iv) Cite the address for billing;

(v) Identify the disbursing office;

(vi) Provide funding information; and

(vii) Include an expiration date.

(2) Before awarding a CSA, comply with the requirements in FAR and DFARS, e.g., for competition, reviews, approvals, and determinations and findings.

[Final rule, 71 FR 27644, 5/12/2006, effective 5/12/2006]

SUBPART 239.76—CLOUD COMPUTING

239.7602 Policy and responsibilities. (No Text)

239.7602-1 General.

(c) (6) When the clause at DFARS 252.239-7010 applies, the contracting officer shall provide the contractor with the name of the responsible Government official to contact in response to any spillage occurring in connection with the cloud computing services being provided. The requiring activity will provide the contracting officer with the name of the responsible official in accordance with agency procedures, as required by Enclosure 7 of DoDM 5200.01-V3, DoD Information Security Program: Protection of Classified Information.

[Publication notice, 20151118]

239.7602-2 Required storage of data within the United States or outlying areas.

(b) Prior to authorizing storage of data outside the United States and outlying areas, the contracting officer must receive written authorization from the authorizing official.

[Publication notice, 20151118]

239.7603 Procedures.

239.7603-1 General.

(a) When the apparently successful offeror indicates in the provision at DFARS 252.239-7009 that cloud computing services will be used in the performance of the contract, the contracting officer shall review the DoD Cloud Service Catalog at *http://www.disa.mil/Computing/Cloud-Services/Cloud-Support* (look under the "Additional Information" tab for "Service Catalog") to verify that the cloud service provider's offering to be used in the performance of the contract has a provisional authorization prior to award (see DFARS 239.7602-1(b)).

(b) When the contractor indicated in the provision at DFARS 252.239-7009 that it did not anticipate the use of cloud computing services in the performance of the contract and requests, after award, in accordance with the clause at DFARS 252.239-7010(b)(1), that the contracting officer approve the use of cloud computing services in the performance of the contract, the contracting officer shall—

(1) Request approval from the requiring activity for the contractor to use cloud computing services; and

(2) If the requiring activity provides approval, review the DoD Cloud Service Catalog at *http://www.disa.mil/Computing/Cloud-Services/Cloud-Support* (look under the "Additional Information" tab for "Service Catalog") to verify that the cloud service provider's offering to be used in the performance of the contract has a provisional authorization (see DFARS 239.7602-1(b)).

[Publication notice, 20151118]

239.7603-2 Notification of third party access requests.

When a contractor provides notification of a request from a third party for access to Government data or Government-related data, in accordance with DFARS 252.239-7010(j), the contracting officer shall convey the request to the requiring activity. The requiring activity will coordinate a response with the mission or data owner.

[Publication notice, 20151118]

239.7603-3 Cyber incident and compromise reporting.

(a) When a cyber incident is reported by a contractor, the DoD Cyber Crime Center (DC3) will send an unclassified encrypted email containing the cyber incident report to the contracting officer(s) identified on the Incident Collection Format (ICF). The DC3 may request the contracting officer to send a digitally signed email to DC3.

(1) The procuring contracting officer (PCO) shall notify the requiring activities that have contracts identified in the ICF. In cases where an administrative contracting officer (ACO) receives the cyber incident report, in lieu of the PCO, the ACO shall notify the PCO for each affected contract, who will then notify the requiring activity.

(2) In cases of cyber incidents involving multiple contracts, the DoD components will work together to designate a single contracting officer to coordinate the effort. The requiring activity will notify the contracting officer once a lead is designated.

(b) When requested by the contractor, the contracting officer shall provide the contractor with the "Instructions for Malware Submission" document available at *http://www.acq.osd.mil/dpap/dars/pgi/docs/Instructions for Submitting Malware.docx*. The contracting officer should never receive malicious software directly from the contractor.

(c) If the requiring activity requests access to contractor information or equipment, in accordance with DFARS 252.239-7010(g), the contracting officer shall provide a written request to the contractor.

(d) For additional information on cyber incident reporting, see the frequently asked question document at *http://www.acq.osd.mil/dpap/pdi/network penetration reporting and contracting.html*.

[Publication notice, 20151118]

239.7603-4 DoD damage assessment activities.

(a) Prior to initiating damage assessment activities, the contracting officer shall verify that a contract(s) identified in the cyber incident report include(s) the clause at DFARS 252.239-7010. If the contracting officer determines that a contract identified in the report does not contain the clause, the contracting officer shall notify the requiring activity that damage assessment activities, if required, may be determined to constitute a change to the contract.

(b) In cases of cyber incidents involving multiple contracts, a single contracting officer will be designated to coordinate with the contractor regarding media submission.

(c) If the requiring activity requests the contracting officer obtain media, as defined at DFARS 252.239-7010, from the contractor, the contracting officer shall—

(1) Provide a written request for the media;

(2) Provide the contractor with the "Instructions for Media Submission" document available at *http://www.acq.osd.mil/dpap/dars/pgi/docs/Instructions for Submitting Media.docx*; and

(3) Provide a copy of the request to DC3, electronically via email at *dcise@dc3.mil*, and the requiring activity.

(d) If the contracting officer is notified by the requiring activity that media are not required, the contracting officer shall notify the contractor and simultaneously provide a copy of the notice to DC3 and the requiring activity.

(e) The contracting officer shall document the action taken as required by paragraph (c) or (d) of this section, in the contract file.

(f) Upon receipt of the contractor media, DC3 will confirm receipt in writing to the contractor and the requesting contracting officer.

(g) When the requiring activity determines that the damage assessment activities are complete, the requiring activity will provide the contracting officer with a report documenting the findings from the damage assessment activities affecting covered defense information.

(h) The contracting officer shall include the report documenting the findings in the contract file(s) and provide a copy to the contractor.

[Publication notice, 20151118]

PART 241—ACQUISITION OF UTILITY SERVICES

Table of Contents

Subpart 241.1—General

Statutory and delegated authority 241.103

Subpart 241.2—Acquiring Utility Services

Procedures 241.202
Separate contracts 241.205

PART 241—ACQUISITION OF UTILITY SERVICES

SUBPART 241.1—GENERAL

241.103 Statutory and delegated authority.

Summary of Statutory Authority for Utility/Energy Purchases

Acquisition Type	Authority	Maximum Term (years)
Energy Commodities (purchased as supplies) (Natural Gas & Electricity) *	10 U.S.C. 2306b/10 U.S.C. 2829	5 (4)**
Utility Service Contracts (in support of Privatization)	10 U.S.C. 2688(d)(2)	50
Utility Service Contracts*** (when not in support of Privatization)	10 U.S.C. 2304 40 U.S.C. 113(e)(3)	10

* Section 8093 of Public Law 100-202 specifically precludes the Federal Government from expending appropriated funds to purchase electricity in a manner inconsistent with State law and regulation.

** 5 years in support of facilities and installations (10 U.S.C. 2306b) and 4 years for military family housing (10 U.S.C. 2829).

*** GSA has delegated to DoD its authority, under 40 U.S.C. 501(b), to enter into utility service contracts for periods not exceeding 10 years. Absent this authority, the length of DoD utility service contracts in support of facilities and installations would be limited to 5 years (10 U.S.C. 2306c) and, for military family housing, would be limited to 4 years (10 U.S.C. 2829).

[Final rule, 71 FR 3416, 1/23/2006, effective 1/23/2006; Final rule, 74 FR 52895, 10/15/2009, effective 10/15/2009]

SUBPART 241.2—ACQUIRING UTILITY SERVICES

241.202 Procedures.

(2)(A) Do not use the connection charge provisions for the installation of Government-owned distribution lines and facilities. The acquisition of such facilities must be authorized by legislation and accomplished in accordance with FAR Part 36. Also, do not use the connection charge provisions for the installation of new facilities related to the supplier's production and general "backbone" system unless authorized by legislation.

(B) Construction labor standards ordinarily do not apply to construction accomplished under the connection charge provisions of this part. However, if installation includes construction of a public building or public work as defined in FAR 36.102, construction labor standards may apply.

[Final rule, 71 FR 3416, 1/23/2006, effective 1/23/2006]

241.205 Separate contracts.

(1) *Definitions*. As used in this section-

Definite term contract means a contract for utility services for a definite period of not less than one nor more than ten years.

Indefinite term contract means a month-to-month contract for utility services that may be terminated by the Government upon proper notice.

(2) Requests for proposals shall state the anticipated service period in terms of months or years. If the period extends beyond the current fiscal year, evaluate offers of incentives for a definite term contract.

(3) The solicitation may permit offerors the choice of proposing on the basis of-

(i) A definite term not to exceed the anticipated service period; or

(ii) An indefinite term contract.

(4) If the expected service period is less than the current fiscal year, the solicitation shall be on the basis of an indefinite term contract.

(5) Contracts for utility services for leased premises shall identify the lease document on the face of the contract.

(6) Use an indefinite term utility service contract when it is considered to be in the Government's best interest to-

(i) Have the right to terminate on a 30-day (or longer) notice. A notice of up to one year may be granted by an installation if needed to obtain a more favorable rate, more advantageous conditions, or for other valid reasons; or

(ii) Grant the supplier the right to terminate the contract when of benefit to the Government in the form of lower rates, larger discounts, or more favorable terms and conditions.

[Final rule, 71 FR 3416, 1/23/2006, effective 1/23/2006]

PART 242—CONTRACT ADMINISTRATION AND AUDIT SERVICES

Table of Contents

Subpart 242.0—Interagency Agreements

Interagency agreements 242.002

Subpart 242.3—Contract Administration Office Functions

Contract administration functions 242.302
Surveillance of the contractor's implementation of the Synchronized Predeployment and Operational Tracker (SPOT) . . . . 242.302(a)(S-72)
Monitoring contractor costs . . . . 242.302(a)(S-75)

Subpart 242.7—Indirect Cost Rates

Final indirect cost rates 242.705
Contracting officer determination procedure 242.705-1

Subpart 242.12—Novation and Change-of-Name Agreements

Processing agreements 242.1203

Subpart 242.70—Contractor Business Systems

Contractor business system deficiencies 242.7000

Subpart 242.71—Voluntary Refunds

General 242.7100

Subpart 242.72—Contractor Material Management and Accounting System

Review procedures 242.7203

Subpart 242.73—Contractor Insurance/Pension Review

[Removed] 242.7302
Responsibilities 242.7303

Subpart 242.74—Technical Representation at Contractor Facilities

Procedures 242.7401

Subpart 242.75—Contractor Accounting Systems and Related Controls

Policy 242.7502

PART 242—CONTRACT ADMINISTRATION AND AUDIT SERVICES

SUBPART 242.0—INTERAGENCY AGREEMENTS

242.002 Interagency agreements.

(S-70) (iii) Upon receipt of a request for contract administration services, the CCP shall—

(A) Determine whether the request is from a friendly foreign government or an international agency in which the United States is a participant;

(B) Determine whether the services are consistent with the DoD mutual security program policies (the Assistant Secretary of Defense (International Security Affairs) is the source of information for questions as to the eligibility of foreign governments to receive services);

(C) Ensure that the reimbursement arrangements are consistent with DFARS 242.002 (b);

(D) Coordinate with appropriate contract administration offices to determine whether DoD can provide the services;

(E) Notify the requestor that the request is accepted, or provide reasons why it cannot be accepted;

(F) Distribute the acquisition documents and related materials to contract administration offices; and

(G) Receive statements of costs incurred by contract administration offices for reimbursable services and forward them for billing to the Security Assistance Accounting Center.

[Final rule, 70 FR 67919, 11/9/2005, effective 11/9/2005]

SUBPART 242.3—CONTRACT ADMINISTRATION FUNCTIONS

242.302 Contract administration functions.

(a) (13) (B) *(1)* For contracts assigned to DCMA for contract administration, designate as the payment office—

(i) The cognizant Defense Finance and Accounting Service (DFAS) payment office as specified in the Federal Directory of Contract Administration Services Components (available via the Internet at *https://pubapps.dcma.mil/CASD/main.jsp*), for contracts funded with DoD funds;

(ii) The department or agency payment office, if authorized by defense financial management regulations or if the contract is funded with non-DoD funds; or

(iii) Multiple payment offices under paragraphs (a) (13) (B) *(1) (i)* and *(ii)* of this section, if the contract is funded with both DoD and non-DoD funds.

(2) For contracts not assigned to DCMA, select a payment office or offices under department/agency procedures. DoD personnel may use the DFAS Reference Tool, available via the Internet at *http://referencetool.dfas.mil*, to identify cognizant DFAS payment offices.

[Final rule, 71 FR 44928, 8/8/2006, effective 8/8/2006; Publication notice, 20120130]

242.302(a)(S72) Surveillance of the contractor's implementation of the Synchronized Predeployment and Operational Tracker (SPOT).

For suggested criteria to assess a contractor's implementation of SPOT, see SPOT Compliance Checklist at *http://www.acq.osd.mil/log/PS/ctr_mgt_accountability.html*.

(2) (i) For visibility into certain discrepant records in SPOT, use the following audit compliance reports (ACRs) available via the Total Operational Picture Support System (TOPSS):

(A) *Deployment Status Report (ACR–01)*. Lists all deployment requests that were submitted less than 10 days prior to the estimated deployment start date.

(B) *In-Theater Arrival Date (ITAD) Report (ACR–02)*. Lists all records where the ITAD was entered more than one day after the actual ITAD.

(C) *Primary Duty Station Report (ACR–03)*. Lists all deployments where the primary duty station arrival date was entered more than three days after the actual duty station arrival date.

(D) *Closeout Deployment Report (ACR–05)*. Lists all deployments where the primary duty station arrival date was entered more than three days after the actual duty station arrival date.

(E) *Open/Blank In-Theater Arrival Date (ITAD) Report (ACR–06)*. Lists where the ITAD was not entered into SPOT within 15 days after the estimated deployment start date.

(ii) Contracting Officers shall obtain a TOPSS account by following the TOPPS PKI Certificate Registration instructions at *http://www.acq.osd.mil/log/PS/ctr_mgt_accountability.html.*

(3) Contracting Officers shall–

(i) Take immediate action to notify contractors of non-compliance with SPOT (e.g., issue one of the delinquency notices identified at FAR 49.607).

(ii) Document performance deficiencies related to SPOT non-compliance that will be relevant to past performance evaluations for future contract opportunities in accordance with FAR subpart 42.15.

[Publication notice, 20130228; Publication notice, 20151230]

242.302(a)(S-75) Monitoring contractor costs.

(a) *Scope.*

This section provides guidelines for—

(1) Monitoring the policies, procedures, and practices used by contractors to control direct and indirect costs related to Government business; and

(2) Eliminating duplication in Government monitoring of contractors' costs.

(b) *Policy.*

Effective management of contract costs is essential to the efficient and economical performance of Government contracts. Contractors are responsible for managing and controlling their direct and indirect costs; however, DoD must systematically monitor the management of contractors' costs to ensure these responsibilities are met.

(c) *Responsibilities.*

(1) Departments and agencies.

(i) Departments and agencies should conduct a formal program of Government monitoring of contractor policies, procedures, and practices for controlling costs (cost monitoring) at contractor locations where—

(A) Sales to the Government, as determined by the contract administration offices, during the contractor's next fiscal year are expected to exceed $200 million in contracts—

(1) Based on costs incurred; or

(2) Negotiated based on projected costs.

(B) The contract administration office determines the cost benefits derived from monitoring the individual contractors with less than $200 million in other than firm fixed-price and fixed-price with economic price adjustment contracts to be warranted; or

(C) Significant Government business exists and is specifically directed by the head of the contracting activity.

(ii) Departments and agencies are responsible for designating the cost monitoring sites and discontinuing them when the criteria are no longer met.

(2) Contract administration offices.

(i) Contract administration offices (CAOs), which are designated as cost monitoring sites, are responsible for—

(A) Assigning a cost monitoring specialist (CMS) to conduct the program. The CMS may be the administrative contracting officer (ACO) or any other CAO employee whose normal function relates to evaluation of contractor performance.

(B) Reviewing and approving the cost monitoring plan for the next fiscal year and the cost monitoring report from the concluding fiscal year.

(ii) The ACO is responsible for—

(A) In the absence of a CMS, ensuring completion of the CMS duties referenced in paragraph (iii) of this section;

(B) Considering review results in direct and indirect rate negotiations and contract negotiations;

(C) Ensuring the contractor implements corrective action recommended in the cost monitoring review reports; and

(D) Resolving disputes with the contractor regarding cost monitoring review findings, conclusions, or recommendations.

(iii) The CMS is responsible for managing the cost monitoring effort within the CAO and coordinating planned effort with the contract auditor. This includes—

(A) Preparing and maintaining an annual written cost monitoring plan for reviewing contractor operations (see paragraph (d));

(B) Maintaining an inventory of planned and completed CAO, Defense Contract Audit Agency (DCAA), and other Government reviews and audits in order to mitigate duplication of efforts;

(C) Monitoring contractor direct and indirect rates and factors during the year, making comparisons to historical actual costs and to contractor proposed or negotiated forward pricing rates and factors, and providing rate recommendations based on their analysis;

(D) Performing approved functional reviews of contractor activities, to include assisting Government personnel in obtaining access to pertinent contractor policies, procedures, and related data;

(E) Advising the ACO and CAO management of corrective action recommended to improve inefficient or uneconomical contractor conditions, policies, or practices, to include preparing, for the ACO's consideration when appropriate, a Notice of Intent to Disallow or Not Recognize Costs;

(F) Continuously tracking the status of recommendations made to the contractor concerning cost performance stemming from all Government reports;

(G) Keeping the contracting officer, program manager, contract auditor, and other responsible officials informed of issues affecting economical contract performance;

(H) Maintaining current organizational charts of the operations identifiable to the contractor's functional centers of its cost control functions; and

(I) Preparing a final cost monitoring report summarizing all of the cost monitoring functions performed during the Government fiscal year.

(3) *Audit and other organizations.*

(i) The contract auditor is responsible for assisting the CMS by performing the portion of cost monitoring plan and related analyses that requires access to the contractor's financial and accounting records supporting the cost or pricing data. (This does not preclude the program manager, contracting officer, ACO, CMS, or other representatives from reviewing contractor records and data necessary to the performance of their duties.)

(ii) Audit organizations, program offices, contracting activities, and any other DoD organizations with responsibility for reviewing contractor operations for the purpose of monitoring contractor policies, procedures, and practices to control costs, shall submit to the CMS—

(A) An annual schedule of planned and tentative visits, oversight reviews, and audits to be performed at cost monitoring locations; and

(B) Revisions to scheduled visits or audit plans, within 30 days of issuance.

(d) *Annual cost monitoring plan.*

(1) Description.

The annual cost monitoring plan is a strategy for monitoring, reviewing, negotiating, and approving contractor's direct and indirect rates, business systems, corrective actions to deficient processes, and cost controls by coordinating the capabilities of the CAO, DCAA, and other Government representatives in an effort to reduce unreasonable, erroneous, or improper costs to Government contracts.

(2) *Contents of the plan.*

(i) The plan should—

(A) Provide coverage for each significant activity of the contractor over a period of five to ten years;

(B) Provide coverage for contractor future years dependent on the period of forward pricing years the contractor proposes and the expected length of executed Government programs;

(C) Be updated to reflect changed conditions as the year progresses; and

(D) Be consistent with the approved schedule, and any deviations should be explained in the final cost monitoring report.

(ii) The plan must identify the organizations having the primary responsibility for performing the reviews.

(iii) The plan should include reviews required by the ACO and DFARS. Reviews will be performed by the assigned organization during the coordination phase of the cost monitoring plan, except when DFARS makes a specific organizational assignment. For example, Subpart 244.301 makes the ACO responsible for leading contractor purchasing system reviews and 215.407-5-70(c)(3) makes the DCAA auditor responsible for leading estimating system reviews on behalf of the ACO.

(3) *Selecting the activities.*

(i) The CAO selects the activities for the cost monitoring plan. DCAA will complete its annual audit plan independently and communicate the approved audit plan to ensure the most effective monitoring approach. To ensure all Government interests are considered in the selection, the CMS should invite CAO, DCAA, and other interested Government representatives to a meeting before the beginning of each Government fiscal year to identify and prioritize the areas to be reviewed during the coming year, to ensure a fully communicated Government cost monitoring plan.

(ii) The selection team should consider the following data and assign primary responsibility in the selection process—

(A) Contractor forecasts for the coming years supporting direct and indirect costs by functional centers of its cost control system and the results of the latest survey performed of such systems;

(B) Organizational charts for the contractor's entire operation;

(C) Outline of the contractor's accounting system showing the flow of costs by function;

(D) Determination of Government participation in the dollars attributable to the operations and cost accounts under consideration;

(E) List of recent reviews and audits performed by CAO, DCAA, and other Government representatives; list should show outstanding weakness and deficiencies in the contractor's operations that will be considered for follow-up reviews or audits;

(F) Evidence of contractor under or over staffing;

(G) Significant departures from established contractor productivity standards;

(H) Major financial variances from forecasts in prior years;

(I) Evidences of idle or under-used capacity;

(J) Any visits or audit plans scheduled by other Government organizations and identified to the CMS; and

(K) Any other significant information or business changes which could have an adverse effect or cause a significant change to on the contractor's management of contract costs.

(4) *Prioritizing the plan.*

(i) The CMS should prioritize the plan to review contractor activity by considering—

(A) The extent of competition in awarded contracts;

(B) The contractor's operating methods;

(C) The nature of the work;

(D) Acquisition cycle stage;

(E) Business and industry practices;

(F) Types of contracts involved;

(G) Degree of technical and financial risk;

(H) Previously reported findings and deficiencies;

(I) Ratio of Government/commercial work;

(J) Significant changes in the level (dollars) of the contractor's work and backlog; and

(K) The extent performance efficiencies have been previously demonstrated.

(5) *Plan approval and submission.*

(i) The local DCAA office will provide an approved annual audit plan to the ACO within 30 days after the first day of each fiscal year.

(ii) The CMS will submit an adequate cost monitoring plan to the head of the local CAO within 45 days after the first day of each fiscal year.

(iii) The head of the local CAO, or designee, will approve the annual cost monitoring plan within 15 days of an adequate submission. The head of the local CAO will ensure that adequate coordination of the cost monitoring plan was performed with the DCAA and other responsible Government representatives.

(6) *Reviews and analysis.*

(i) Perform functional reviews and audits as scheduled in accordance with the cost monitoring plan.

(ii) Hold interim meetings with the contractor as necessary to clarify information. Hold an exit conference at the conclusion of reviews.

(iii) Prepare reports at the conclusion of reviews. The ACO will determine whether a Government review or audit report will be provided to a contractor based on specific regulatory requirements or the impact to pending negotiations or litigation.

(iv) Prepare periodic reports on the results of the CMS analysis and monitoring of the contractors rates and factors, which should address the causes for significant deviations from historical and negotiated forward pricing rates and factors.

(e) *Annual cost monitoring report.*

(1) *Description.*

The annual cost monitoring report is a culmination of the Government activities performed during the fiscal year in an effort to conduct and maintain a formal monitoring program of contractor policies, procedures, and practices for controlling costs charged to Government contracts.

(2) *Contents of the report.*

(i) The report should—

(A) Provide a brief introduction of the contractor and the products it provides to the Government;

(B) Summarize each review and audit completed during the reporting period along with any deviations from the cost monitoring plan;

(C) Highlight open deficiencies, corrected deficiencies, and any newly reported deficiencies; and

(D) Include the current status of all final, billing, and forward pricing rates.

(ii) The annual cost monitoring report is the primary responsibility of the CAO. Incorporate the final DCAA audit reports by summary and reference.

(3) *Report approval and submission.*

(i) The head of the local CAO, or designee, will approve the annual cost monitoring report within 60 days of the end of the Government fiscal year.

(ii) A copy of the approved report will be provided to the head of the local DCAA office within 15 days of approval.

[Procurement notice, 20111220; Final rule, 77 FR 23631, 4/20/2012, effective 4/20/2012; Publication notice, 20130228]

SUBPART 242.7—INDIRECT COST RATES

242.705 Final indirect cost rates. (No Text)

[Final rule, 70 FR 67919, 11/9/2005, effective 11/9/2005]

242.705-1 Contracting officer determination procedure.

(a) *Applicability and responsibility.*

(1) When negotiations are conducted on a coordinated basis, individual administrative contracting officers are responsible for coordinating with the corporate administrative contracting officer to ensure consistency of cost determinations.

[Final rule, 70 FR 67919, 11/9/2005, effective 11/9/2005]

SUBPART 242.11—CONTRACT ADMINISTRATION AND AUDIT SERVICES

242.1106 [Removed]

[Final rule, 73 FR 21845, 4/23/2008, effective 4/23/2008]

SUBPART 242.12—NOVATION AND CHANGE-OF-NAME AGREEMENTS

242.1203 Processing agreements.

(1) For contracts awarded by the military departments, provide notices to the following addressees instead of individual contracting or contract administration offices:

Army	HQ, Army Materiel Command ATTN: AMCCC 4400 Martin Road Redstone Arsenal, AL 35898
Navy	Office of the Assistant Secretary of the Navy Research, Development & Acquisition Deputy Assistant Secretary for Acquisition and Logistics Management 1000 Navy Pentagon, Room BF992 Washington, DC 20350-1000
Air Force	HQ Air Force Materiel Command ATTN: HQ AFMC/PKQ 4375 Chidlaw Road Wright Patterson AFB, OH 45433-5006
National Aeronautics and Space Administration	National Aeronautics and Space Administration ATTN: Office of Procurement Director, Program Operations Division 300 E Street, SW Washington, DC 20546-0001

(2) Lists of affected contracts accompanying a notice of successor in interest should include the information at FAR 42.1204 (e) (2).

(3) Lists of affected contracts accompanying a notice of a name change should include the information at FAR 42.1205 (a) (3).

(4) On notices sent to the addressees in paragraph (1) of this section, include a consolidated list for all subordinate contracting offices of the addressee.

(5) Before making any substantial alterations or additions to the novation agreement format at FAR 42.1204 (i), coordinate with the addressees in paragraph (1) of this section that have contracts with the contractor. Resolve any objections before executing the agreement.

(6) If the National Aeronautics and Space Administration (NASA) wants a separate agreement with the contractor, continue to process the agreement only for DoD.

(7) In addition to the requirements of FAR 42.1203 (g), make distribution to—

(i) The addressees in paragraph (1) of this section - two copies; and

(ii) The appropriate Military Surface Deployment and Distribution Command area command for agreements affecting contracts and basic agreements for storage and related services for personal property of military and civilian personnel — two copies:

Commander	Commander
Eastern Area	Western Area
Military Surface Deployment and Distribution Command	Military Surface Deployment and Distribution Command
ATTN: MTE-LO	Oakland Army Base
Bayonne, NJ 07002	ATTN: MTW-LO Oakland, CA 94626

(8) In addition to the distribution requirements of FAR 42.1203 (h) (4)—

(i) Send two copies to the address in paragraph (1) of this section. The list of contracts may be confined to those issued by that department.

(ii) Do not send copies to NASA or the commands in paragraph (7) (ii) of this section. They will issue their own modifications.

(9) Report the novation agreement or name change modification for each of the effected contracts to FPDS (see PGI 204.606(4) (iv) and (v)).

(10) The contracting officer responsible for execution of a change-of-name agreement (see FAR subpart 42.12) must submit the agreement to DLIS-SBB. If there are no current contracts, each contracting and contract administration office receiving notification of changes from the commercial entity must forward a copy of the change notice annotated with the CAGE code to DLIS-SBB unless the change notice indicates that DLIS-SBB already has been notified.

[Final rule, 70 FR 67919, 11/9/2005, effective 11/9/2005; Change notice, 20060412; Change notice, 20080331; Publication notice 20110920; Publication notice, 20111004; Publication notice, 20140421; Final rule, 79 FR 73492, 12/11/2014, effective 12/11/2014; Publication notice, 20190430]

SUBPART 242.70—CONTRACTOR BUSINESS SYSTEMS

242.7000 Contractor business system deficiencies.

(b) *Determination to withhold payments.* The following are sample formats for written notifications of contracting officer determinations to initiate payment withholding, reduce payment withholding, and discontinue payment withholding in accordance with the clause at DFARS 252.242-7005, Contractor Business Systems:

(1) Use this sample format for written final determinations to implement payment withholding:

Payment Withholding

(i) The purpose of this final determination is to disapprove your [*identify the contractor business system(s)*] and implement payment withholding per the terms of the DFARS clause at 252.242-7005, Contractor Business Systems.

(ii) It is my final determination that XXX System(s) contains the following significant deficiencies:

— [*list all significant deficiencies*]

(iii) Effective immediately, five percent (or a lesser percentage if five percent will exceed the withhold limitations in the DFARS clause at 252.242-7005) of each request for payment under the contracts in Attachment A will be withheld as described below for significant deficiencies in XXX system. Upon receipt of an acceptable corrective action plan and my determination that this corrective action plan is being effectively implemented, I will issue a notification with respect to reducing the percentage being withheld to two percent until I determine that all significant deficiencies, as identified in this final determination, have been corrected. Failure to follow the accepted corrective action plan will result in an increase in the percentage withheld against each payment under this contract to five percent (or a lesser percentage if five percent will exceed the withhold limitations in DFARS 252.242-7005). [*Repeat this paragraph, as necessary, if multiple withholds are being applied to multiple systems in accordance with 252.242-7005(d)*]

(iv) For payments under cost, labor-hour, or time-and-material contracts: The Contractor shall apply a five percent (or a lesser percentage if five percent will exceed the withhold limitations in DFARS 252.242-7005) withhold to the amount being billed and prepare a cost voucher in Wide Area WorkFlow (WAWF) for the net amount due. The Contractor shall show the amount withheld on the current billing, as well as the cumulative amount withheld to date on this contract in accordance with DFARS clause 252.242-7005, in the Comments block of the Miscellaneous Info Tab in WAWF.

(v) For progress payments: The Contractor shall prepare the request in WAWF without applying any withhold percentage. The Contracting Officer will reduce the approved amount by five percent (or a lesser percentage if five percent will exceed the withhold limitations in DFARS 252.242-7005) and record the amount being withheld on the progress payment request, as well the cumulative amount withheld on this contract in accordance with DFARS clause 252.242-7005, in the Comments block of the Miscellaneous Info Tab in WAWF.

(vi) For performance-based payments: The Contractor shall prepare the request in WAWF without applying any withhold percentage to the performance based payment event schedule amounts. The Contracting Officer will reduce the amount approved by five percent (or a lesser percentage if five percent will exceed the withhold limitations in DFARS 252.242-7005) and record the amount being withheld on the performance based payment as well as the cumulative amount withheld on this contract in accordance with the DFARS clause 252.242-7005 in the Comments block of the of the Miscellaneous Info Tab in WAWF.

(2) Use this sample format for determinations to reduce payment withholding:

Reduction of Temporary Payment Withholding

(i) The purpose of this determination is to reduce the payment withholding percentage per the terms of the DFARS clause at 252.242-7005, Contractor Business Systems, as a result of receiving an acceptable corrective action plan from the contractor, dated YYYY/MM/DD, for resolving deficiencies in its XXX system(s) as identified in the Contracting Officer's determination, dated YYYY/MM/DD. This reduction is prospective and previous amounts withheld will not be reduced or released at this time.

(ii) Effective immediately, two percent of each request for payment under this contract will be withheld as described below. The two percent being withheld will remain in effect until the Contracting Officer determines that the Contractor has corrected all significant deficiencies as directed by the Contracting Officer's determination. Failure to follow the accepted corrective action plan will result in an increase in the percentage withheld against each payment under this contract to five percent (or a lesser percentage if five percent will exceed the withhold limitations in DFARS 252.242-7005).

(iii) For payments under cost, labor-hour, or time-and-material contracts: The Contractor shall apply a two percent withhold to the amount being billed and prepare a cost voucher in Wide Area WorkFlow (WAWF) for the net amount due. The Contractor shall show the amount withheld on the current billing, as well as the cumulative amount withheld to date on this contract in accordance with DFARS clause 252.242-7005, in the Comments block of the Miscellaneous Info Tab in WAWF.

(iv) For progress payments: The Contractor shall prepare the request in WAWF without applying any withhold percentage. The Contracting Officer will reduce the approved amount by two percent and record the amount being withheld on the progress payment request, as well the cumulative amount withheld on this contract in accordance with DFARS clause 252.242-7005, in the Comments block of the Miscellaneous Info Tab in WAWF.

(v) For performance-based payments: The Contractor shall prepare the request in WAWF without applying any withhold percentage to the performance-based payment event schedule amounts. The Contracting Officer will reduce the amount approved by two percent and record the amount being withheld on the performance-based payment as well as the cumulative amount withheld on this contract in accordance with the DFARS clause 252.242-7005 in the Comments block of the of the Miscellaneous Info Tab in WAWF.

(3) Use the sample format below if payment withholding is discontinued pending receipt of auditor or functional specialist verification and based on evidence that the Contractor has corrected all significant deficiencies, in accordance with DFARS clause 252.242-7005, Contractor Business Systems:

Discontinuation of Payment Withholding Pending Verification

(i) The purpose of this determination is to approve your [*identify system(s)*] pending verification, discontinue the payment withhold as identified in the Contracting Officer's determination dated YYYY/MM/DD, and release previous amounts withheld on the contracts in Attachment A, in accordance with DFARS clause 252.242-7005, Contractor Business Systems.

(ii) The discontinuation of the payment withhold is made pending receipt of verification and based on my review of the evidence submitted by the Contractor that all the Contractor's system(s) deficiencies identified in the Contracting Officer's determination dated YYYY/MM/DD have been corrected.

(iii) The Contractor is authorized to submit a bill in the amount of $XXXXXXXX. The billed amount should be submitted on the same type of invoice as the withhold was originally taken, as appropriate.

(4) Use the sample format below if payment withholding is discontinued after auditor or functional specialist verification that the Contractor has corrected all significant deficiencies, in accordance with DFARS clause 252.242-7005, Contractor Business Systems:

Discontinuation of Payment Withholding

(i) The purpose of this determination is to approve your [identify system(s)], discontinue the payment withhold as identified in the Contracting Officer's determination dated YYYY/MM/DD, and release previous amounts withheld on the contracts in Attachment A, in accordance with DFARS clause 252.242-7005, Contractor Business Systems.

(ii) The discontinuation of the payment withhold is made based on verification that all the Contractor's system(s) deficiencies identified in the Contracting Officer's final determination dated YYYY/MM/DD have been corrected.

(iii) The Contractor is authorized to submit a bill in the amount of $XXXXXXXX. The billed amount should be submitted on the same type of invoice as the withhold was originally taken, as appropriate.

[Interim rule, 76 FR 28856, 51/18/2011, effective 5/18/2011; Final rule, 79 FR 3519, 1/22/2014, effective 1/22/2014]

SUBPART 242.71—VOLUNTARY REFUNDS

242.7100 General.

(1) A voluntary refund may be solicited (requested by the Government) or unsolicited.

(i) Generally, request voluntary refunds only after determining that no contractual remedy is readily available to recover the amount sought.

(ii) Acceptance of unsolicited refunds does not prejudice remedies otherwise available to the Government.

(2) Before soliciting a voluntary refund or accepting an unsolicited one, the contracting officer should have legal counsel review the contract and related data to—

(i) Confirm that there are no readily available contractual remedies; and

(ii) Advise whether the proposed action would jeopardize or impair the Government's rights.

(3) Request voluntary refunds only when—

(i) The contracting officer concludes that the contractor overcharged under a contract, or inadequately compensated the Government for the use of Government-owned property, or inadequately compensated the Government in the disposition of contractor inventory; and

(ii) Retention of the amount in question by the contractor or subcontractor would be contrary to good conscience and equity.

(4) Do not solicit voluntary refunds without approval of the head of the contracting activity, or as provided in department/agency regulations.

(5) Voluntary refunds may be requested during or after contract performance.

(6) A contract modification, rather than a check, is the preferred means of effecting a solicited or unsolicited refund transacted before final payment.

(i) For modifications, adjust the price for the refund and credit the refund to the applicable appropriation cited in the contract.

(ii) For checks—

(A) Advise the contractor to—

(1) Make the check payable to the agency that awarded the contract;

(2) Forward the check to the contracting officer or, when the contract is assigned to another office for administration, to that office; and

(3) Include a letter with the check—

(i) Identifying it as a voluntary refund;

(ii) Giving the contract number involved; and

(iii) Where possible, giving the appropriation and account number to be credited; and

(B) Forward the check to the office responsible for control of funds.

[Final rule, 70 FR 67919, 11/9/2005, effective 11/9/2005]

SUBPART 242.72—CONTRACTOR MATERIAL MANAGEMENT AND ACCOUNTING SYSTEM

242.7203 Review procedures.

(c) *Disposition of findings.*

(2) *Initial determination.*

(ii) (A) Within 10 days of receiving the report, if the contracting officer makes a determination that there is a significant deficiency, the contracting officer should provide an initial determination of deficiencies and a copy of the report to the contractor and require the contractor to submit a written response.

(C) Evaluation of contractor's response. Within 30 days of receiving the contractor's response, the contracting officer, in consultation with the auditor or cognizant functional specialist, should evaluate the contractor's response and make a final determination.

(3) *Final Determination.*

(ii) (A) Monitoring contractor's corrective action. The contracting officer, with the assistance of the auditor, shall monitor the contractor's progress in correcting deficiencies. If the contractor fails to make adequate progress, the contracting officer shall take whatever action is necessary to ensure that the contractor corrects the deficiencies. Examples of actions the contracting officer can take are: disapprove the contractor's MMAS; bringing the issue to the attention of higher level management; implementing or increasing the withholding in accordance with 252.242-7005, Contractor Business Systems, if applicable; and recommending non-award of potential contracts.

(B) *Correction of significant deficiencies.*

(1) When the contractor notifies the contracting officer that the contractor has corrected the significant deficiencies, the contracting officer shall request that the auditor review the correction to determine if the deficiencies have been resolved.

(2) The contracting officer shall determine if the contractor has corrected the deficiencies.

(3) If the contracting officer determines the contractor has corrected the deficiencies, the contracting officer's notification shall be sent to the auditor; payment office; appropriate action officers responsible for reporting past performance at the requiring activities; and each contracting and contract administration office having substantial business with the contractor as applicable.

[Interim rule, 76 FR 28856, 51/18/2011, effective 5/18/2011; Final rule, 77 FR 11355, 2/24/2012, effective 2/24/2012]

SUBPART 242.73—CONTRACTOR INSURANCE/PENSION REVIEW

242.7302 [Removed]

[Final rule, 71 FR 9273, 2/23/2006, effective 2/23/2006; Final rule, 75 FR 71564, 11/24/2010, effective 11/24/2010]

242.7303 Responsibilities.

(1) The ACO is responsible for—

(i) Determining the need for a CIPR in accordance with the procedures at PGI 242.7302;

(ii) Requesting and scheduling the reviews with the appropriate DCMA activity;

(iii) Notifying the contractor of the proposed date and purpose of the review, and obtaining any preliminary data needed by the DCMA insurance/pension specialist or the DCAA auditor;

(iv) Reviewing the CIPR report, advising the contractor of the recommendations contained within the report, considering contractor comments, and rendering a decision based on those recommendations;

(v) Providing other interested contracting officers copies of documents related to the CIPR;

(vi) Ensuring adequate follow-up on all CIPR recommendations; and

(vii) Performing contract administration responsibilities related to Cost Accounting Standards administration as described in FAR Subparts 30.2 and 30.6.

(2) The DCMA insurance/pension specialist is responsible for—

(i) Issuing a technical report on the contractor's insurance/pension plans for incorporation into the final CIPR report based on an analysis of the contractor's pension plans, insurance programs, and other related data;

(ii) Leading the team that conducts the review. Another individual may serve as the team leader when both the insurance/pension specialist and that individual agree. The team leader is responsible for—

(A) Maintaining complete documentation for CIPR reports;

(B) To the extent possible, resolving discrepancies between audit reports and CIPR draft reports prior to releasing the final CIPR report;

(C) Preparing and distributing the final CIPR report;

(D) Providing the final audit report and/or the insurance/pension specialist's report as an attachment to the CIPR report; and

(E) Preparing a draft letter for the administrative contracting officer's use in notifying the contractor of CIPR results; and

(iii) When requested, advising administrative contracting officers and other Government representatives concerning contractor insurance/pension matters.

(3) The DCAA auditor is responsible for—

(i) Participating as a member of the CIPR team or serving as the team leader (see paragraph (2)(ii) of this section);

(ii) Issuing an audit report for incorporation into the final CIPR report based on an analysis of the contractor's books, accounting records, and other related data; and

(iii) Performing contract audit responsibilities related to Cost Accounting Standards administration as described in FAR Subparts 30.2 and 30.6.

[Final rule, 71 FR 9273, 2/23/2006, effective 2/23/2006]

SUBPART 242.74—TECHNICAL REPRESENTATION AT CONTRACTOR FACILITIES

242.7401 Procedures.

(1) When the program, project, or system manager determines that a technical representative is required, the manager shall issue a letter of intent to the contract administration office commander listing the assignment location, starting and ending assignment dates, technical duties assigned, delegated authority, and support required from the contract administration office. Any issues regarding the assignment of a technical representative should be resolved promptly. However, final decision on the assignment remains with the program manager. Issues regarding the assignment of technical duties that cannot be resolved between the program office and the on-site DoD Contract administration office will be elevated.

(2) The program, project, or system manager will furnish the designated technical representative a letter of assignment of delegated technical duties, with copies to the contract administration office, the contracting officer, and the contractor, at least 30 days before the assignment date (or termination date). Any changes to the requirements of the assignment letter will be made by a new letter of intent and processed in accordance with paragraph (1) of this section.

(3) The contract administration office normally provides the technical representative with office space, equipment, supplies, and part-time clerical support. The program, project, or system manager provides supervision, technical direction, administrative services (e.g., pay, travel, maintenance of

personnel records), and, when required, full-time clerical support.

(4) The program manager or designee and the contract administration office, at the local level, shall negotiate a memorandum of agreement (MOA) delineating their functional administrative interrelationships, with annual updates as necessary. The agreements may be included in an existing MOA, if one exists, or as a separate MOA.

(5) The technical representative shall keep the contract administration office commander fully informed of matters discussed with the contractor. The contract administration office shall also keep the technical representative fully informed of contractor discussions that relate to technical matters within the purview of the technical representative's assigned duties.

[Final rule, 70 FR 67919, 11/9/2005, effective 11/9/2005; Change notice, 20061109]

SUBPART 242.75—CONTRACTOR ACCOUNTING SYSTEMS AND RELATED CONTROLS

242.7502 Policy.

(d) *Disposition of findings.*

(2) *Initial determination.*

(ii) (A) Within 10 days of receiving the report, if the contracting officer makes a determination that there is a significant deficiency, the contracting officer should provide an initial determination of deficiencies and a copy of the report to the contractor and require the contractor to submit a written response.

(C) *Evaluation of contractor's response.* Within 30 days of receiving the contractor's response, the contracting officer, in consultation with the auditor or cognizant functional specialist, should evaluate the contractor's response and make a final determination.

(3) *Final Determination.*

(ii) (A) *Monitoring contractor's corrective action.* The auditor and the contracting officer shall monitor the contractor's progress in correcting deficiencies. If the contractor fails to make adequate progress, the contracting officer shall take whatever action is necessary to ensure that the contractor corrects the deficiencies. Examples of actions the contracting officer can take are: disapproving the system; bringing the issue to the attention of higher level management; implementing or increasing the withholding in accordance with 252.242-7005, Contractor Business Systems, if applicable; and recommending non-award of potential contracts.

(B) *Correction of significant deficiencies.*

(1) When the contractor notifies the contracting officer that the contractor has corrected the significant deficiencies, the contracting officer shall request that the auditor review the correction to determine if the deficiencies have been resolved.

(2) The contracting officer shall determine if the contractor has corrected the deficiencies.

(3) If the contracting officer determines the contractor has corrected the deficiencies, the contracting officer's notification shall be sent to the auditor; payment office; appropriate action officers responsible for reporting past performance at the requiring activities; and each contracting and contract administration office having substantial business with the contractor as applicable.

(g) Mitigating the risk of accounting system deficiencies on specific proposals.

(2) In the event that a contractor's accounting system contains deficiencies, even if it has been disapproved, a cost reimbursement contract is not prohibited if the contracting officer determines that the contractor's accounting system is adequate for determining costs applicable to the contract or order.

[Interim rule, 76 FR 28856, 51/18/2011, effective 5/18/2011; Final rule, 77 FR 11355, 2/24/2012, effective 2/24/2012; Final rule, 80 FR 10390, 2/26/2015, effective 2/26/2015]

PART 243—CONTRACT MODIFICATIONS

Table of Contents

Subpart 243.1—General

Identification of foreign military sale (FMS) requirements 243.170
Obligation or deobligation of funds 243.171

Subpart 243.2—Change Orders

Administration 243.204
Certification of requests for equitable adjustment 243.204-71

PART 243—CONTRACT MODIFICATIONS

SUBPART 243.1—GENERAL

243.170 Identification of foreign military sale (FMS) requirements.

When adding FMS requirements using a contract modification, the contracting officer shall—

(1) Clearly indicate "FMS Requirement" on the front of the modification; and

(2) Refer to each FMS case identifier code by line/subline item number within the modification, e.g., FMS Case Identifier GY-D-DCA.

[Final rule, 70 FR 67921, 11/9/2005, effective 11/9/2005; Change notice, 20060711]

243.171 Obligation or deobligation of funds.

The contracting officer shall include sufficient information in each contract modification to permit the paying office to readily identify the changes for each contract line and subline item.

(1) Include the information under the heading "Summary for the Payment Office" in—

(i) Section G, Contract Administration Data (Uniform Contract Format); or

(ii) The contract schedule (Simplified Contract Format).

(2) The information normally should contain—

(i) The amount of funds obligated by prior contract actions, to include—

(A) The total cost and fee if a cost-type contract;

(B) The target fee at time of contract award if a cost-plus-incentive-fee contract;

(C) The base fee if a cost-plus-award-fee contract; or

(D) The target price and target profit if a fixed-price incentive contract;

(ii) The amount of funds obligated or deobligated by the instant modification, categorized by the types of contracts specified in paragraph (2) (i) of this section; and

(iii) The total cumulative amount of obligated or deobligated funds, categorized by the types of contracts specified in paragraph (2) (i) of this section.

[Final rule, 70 FR 67921, 11/9/2005, effective 11/9/2005; Change notice, 20060711]

SUBPART 243.2—CHANGE ORDERS

243.204 Administration.

(1) Whenever practicable, the contracting officer should provide advance notice of a proposed change order to the administrative contracting officer (ACO).

(i) The ACO shall review the proposed change order to ensure compatibility with the status of performance.

(ii) If the contractor has progressed beyond the effective point specified in the proposed change order, the ACO shall determine the earliest practical point at which the change order could be made effective and shall advise the contracting officer.

(2) If a change order has been issued and the effective date has been determined to be impracticable, the contracting officer shall—

(i) Issue another change order to correct, revise, or supersede the first change order; then

(ii) Definitize by supplemental agreement citing both change orders.

[Final rule, 70 FR 67921, 11/9/2005, effective 11/9/2005; Change notice, 20060711; Final rule, 75 FR 48276, 8/10/2010, effective 8/10/2010]

243.204-71 Certification of requests for equitable adjustment.

(b) For example, a request for equitable adjustment that involves both an increase of $100,000 and a decrease of $105,000 has an absolute value of $205,000 ($100,000 + $105,000, regardless of whether the amounts are plus or minus), which exceeds the simplified acquisition threshold.

[Final rule, 70 FR 67921, 11/9/2005, effective 11/9/2005; Final rule, 75 FR 48276, 8/10/2010, effective 8/10/2010; Publication notice, 20121212, 12/12/2012]

PART 244—SUBCONTRACTING POLICIES AND PROCEDURES

Table of Contents

Subpart 244.3—Contractors' Purchasing Systems Reviews

Consent and advance notification requirements 244.201
Consent requirements 244.201-1
Surveillance 244.304
Policy 244.305-70

PART 244—SUBCONTRACTING POLICIES AND PROCEDURES

SUBPART 244.2—CONSENT TO SUBCONTRACT

244.201 Consent and advance notification requirements.

[Final rule, 80 FR 67243, 10/30/2015, effective 10/30/2015]

244.201-1 Consent requirements.

When contracting for a covered system or covered item of supply, work with the requiring activity to determine if, based on the criticality of the component or system to be supplied and potential concerns about supply chain risk, written consent to subcontract by the contracting officer is necessary when subcontractors are selected or modified during the course of contract performance. Should the requiring activity conclude that a potential subcontractor is beyond the risk tolerance of the system and mission, the requiring activity must inform the contracting officer and the authority granted in section 806 of Pub. L. 111-383 may be used to withhold consent for the contractor to subcontract with a particular source or exclude a source from consideration as specified in DFARS 239.73.

[Final rule, 80 FR 67243, 10/30/2015, effective 10/30/2015]

SUBPART 244.3—CONTRACTORS' PURCHASING SYSTEMS REVIEWS

244.304 Surveillance.

(b) Weaknesses

(i) May arise because of—

(A) Major changes in the contractor's purchasing policies, procedures, or key personnel; or

(B) Changes in plant workload or type of work; and

(ii) May be discovered—

(A) During reviews of subcontracts submitted under advance notification and consent (FAR Subpart 44.2); or

(B) From information provided by Government personnel.

[Final rule, 70 FR 67922, 11/9/2005, effective 11/9/2005; Change notice, 20061109]

244.305-70 Policy.

(c) *Disposition of findings.*

(2) *Initial determination.*

(ii) (A) Within 10 days of receiving the report, if the contracting officer makes a determination that there is a significant deficiency, the contracting officer should provide an initial determination of deficiencies and a copy of the report to the contractor and require the contractor to submit a written response.

(C) *Evaluation of contractor's response.* Within 30 days of receiving the contractor's response, the contracting officer, in consultation with the auditor or cognizant functional specialist, should evaluate the contractor's response and make a final determination.

(3) *Final Determination.*

(ii) (A) *Monitoring contractors' corrective action.* The contracting officer and Purchasing System Analyst (PSA) or auditor shall monitor the contractor's progress in correcting deficiencies. If the contractor fails to make adequate progress, the contracting officer shall take whatever action is necessary to ensure that the contractor corrects the deficiencies. Examples of actions the contracting officer can take are: withdraw or withhold approval of the system; bringing the issue to the attention of higher level management, implementing or increasing the withholding in accordance with 252.242-7005, Contractor Business Systems, and recommending non-award of potential contracts.

(B) *Correction of significant deficiencies.*

(1) When the contractor notifies the contracting officer that the contractor has corrected the significant deficiencies, the contracting officer shall request the PSA or auditor to review the correction to determine if the deficiencies have been resolved.

(2) The contracting officer shall determine if the contractor has corrected the deficiencies.

(3) If the contracting officer determines the contractor has corrected the deficiencies, the contracting officer's notification shall be sent to the PSA; auditor; payment

office; appropriate action officers responsible for reporting past performance at the requiring activities; and each contracting and contract administration office having substantial business with the contractor as applicable.

[Interim rule, 76 FR 28856, 5/18/2011, effective 5/18/2011; Final rule, 77 FR 11355, 2/24/2012, effective 2/24/2012]

PART 245—GOVERNMENT PROPERTY

Table of Contents

Subpart 245.1—General

Policy 245.102-70
General 245.103
Furnishing Government property to contractors 245.103-70
Transferring Government property accountability 245.103-71
Government-furnished property attachments to solicitations and awards . . 245.103-72
Government property under sustainment contracts 245.103-73
Contracting office responsibilities 245.103-74
Contractor's property management system compliance 245.105

Subpart 245.2—Solicitation and Evaluation Procedures

Solicitation 245.201
Definitions 245.201-70
Security classification 245.201-71

Subpart 245.4—Title to Government Property

Title to contractor-acquired property 245.402
Policy 245.402-70
Delivery of contractor-acquired property 245.402-71

Subpart 245.6—Reporting, Reutilization, and Disposal

Plant clearance procedures 245.602-70

PART 245—GOVERNMENT PROPERTY

SUBPART 245.1—GENERAL

245.102-70 Policy.

(1) A basic principle of the Federal Acquisition Regulations System is that, upon contract award, contractors bring all the necessary organization, experience, accounting and operational controls, property, and technical skills, or the ability to obtain them (reference FAR 9.104-1 (e), (f), and (g) of General Standards). Therefore, upon contract award, responsible contractors should have the means to provide effective and efficient stewardship of Government property.

(2) Government property, as defined at FAR 45.101, must be contractually accountable to a single contract and only one contract at a time. This requirement applies to both Government-furnished property and contractor-acquired property. Although accountable to only one contract at a time, contract terms and conditions may allow Government property to be used on other contracts (see FAR 52.245-9, Use and Charges).

[Publication notice, 20100723; Publication notice, 20141106]

245.103 General. (No Text)

[Publication notice, 20100723]

245.103-70 Furnishing Government property to contractors.

(1) The requiring activity (project or program manager, or purchase request generator), as part of its responsibility for acquisition planning (FAR part 7, Acquisition Planning), is the decision point as to whether or not to furnish property to contractors. The basis for any decision to provide Government property shall be documented by the requiring activity and provided to the contracting officer. Such documentation is not required when contractors are furnished property for repair, modification, or overhaul under a contract.

(2) Prior to furnishing Government property to the contractor, the contracting officer shall ensure that each of the requirements of FAR 45.102 are addressed as follows, and documented in the contracting file—

(i) *Element 1: In the Government's best interest.* Discussion should be specific, factual, and where necessary, address actual or projected dollars and percentages. Merely selecting one or two objectives supported by a general, perfunctory discussion does not address this element satisfactorily. Discussion should address the following factors:

(A) Economy - Furnishing Government property is the lowest cost or price alternative.

(B) Standardization - There is a critical need for precise replication.

(C) Security - Government property is needed due to national security issues/concerns.

(D) Expedite production - Government property is crucial to achieving timely or accelerated delivery of a supply item or service.

(E) Scarcity - The Government can obtain scarce items, or is the only source of property necessary for successful execution of a contract.

(F) Maintain the industrial base - Government property is needed to ensure future capability to obtain a particular supply item or service.

(G) Contract type - Government property will enable the Government to obtain a more favorable contract type.

(ii) *Element 2: Overall benefit.* Demonstrate that the overall benefit to the acquisition significantly outweighs the increased cost of administration, including property disposal.

(A) Property in the hands of contractors drives program costs. Therefore, in order to make the case that providing Government property to the contractor is worthwhile, the associated costs must be considered and the business decision justified. The costs of Government property removal and disposal, including demilitarization and disposal of environmentally-regulated property, must be included.

(B) Costs must be either less than what the contractor might otherwise incur, or the demonstrated benefit to the Government must outweigh these additional contract costs.

(iii) *Element 3: Government assumption of risk.* Demonstrate that providing the property does not substantially increase the Government's risk.

(A) Risk must be discussed and documented. A risk analysis is warranted to demonstrate that the Government is not substantially increasing its risk. For example, when furnishing Government property, the Government is ordinarily responsible for suitability of use, timely delivery, and replacement of defective Government property.

(B) Other risks may need to be considered, discussed, and documented.

(iv) *Element 4: Government requirements cannot otherwise be met.* Document why the furnishing of Government property is critical and significant to meeting acquisition plan objectives.

[Publication notice, 20100723]

245.103-71 Transferring Government property accountability.

(1) Use only the Standard Form 30 to execute transfers of Government property accountability between existing contracts. No other forms or documents, such as the DD Form 1149, Requisition and Invoice/Shipping Document, are authorized for the transfer of Government property accountability from one contract to another.

(2) Modifications for the transfer of Government property accountability shall:

(i) Use the fillable PDF formats prescribed at PGI 245.103-72.

(ii) Incorporate FAR clauses 52.245-1, Government Property, and 52.245-9, Use and Charges, and the associated DFARS clauses (see 245.107, Contract clauses) to the extent that the gaining contract lacks the required clauses.

[Publication notice, 20100723; Publication notice, 20141106]

245.103-72 Government-furnished property attachments to solicitations and awards.

(a) When Government-furnished property (GFP) is anticipated, include the fillable electronic "Requisitioned Government Furnished Property" and/or "Scheduled Government Furnished Property" formats provided at the URLs listed in paragraphs (b) and (c) in solicitations and awards to—

(1) Specify the required GFP data elements; and

(2) Accomplish the electronic transmission of requisitioned GFP lists and/or scheduled GFP lists.

(b) *Requisitioned Government-furnished property.* This format is a listing of Government Property to be authorized for contractor requisition from DoD supply sources in accordance with the clause at FAR 52.251-1. The fillable PDF format for this attachment is available at *http://dodprocurementtoolbox.org/site/detail/id/26*. In accordance with PGI 204.7105(b)(5), enter a numerical sequence number for the attachment.

(c) *Scheduled Government-furnished property.* This format is a listing of the Government property to be provided, including when major end items are being provided under a modification or upgrade contract; or when reparables are being provided under a repair, modification, or overhaul contract. The fillable PDF format for this attachment is available at *http://dodprocurementtoolbox.org/site/detail/id/26*. In accordance with PGI 204.7105(b)(5), enter a numerical sequence number for the attachment.

[Publication notice, 20121212, 12/12/2012; Publication notice, 20140421]

245.103-73 Government property under sustainment contracts.

(1) Sustainment contracts, including those for performance-based logistics, sustainment support, contractor logistics support, life-cycle product support, and weapon systems product support (see 10 U.S.C. 2337(c)), may require the contractor to hold or manage Government inventory. In such cases, regularly scheduled (typically, semi-annually) inventory reporting from the contractor

is required to ensure that inventory levels meet program requirements and Government inventory in excess of authorized amounts is identified. The requiring activity is responsible for providing the contracting officer with reporting requirements for Government inventory. See the Data Item Description DI-ILSS-80727, Government Furnished Material (GFM) by National Stock Number, and the instructions for completing the DD Form 1423 Contract Data Requirements List (CDRL) for inventory reporting requirements on sustainment contracts available at *http://dodprocurementtoolbox.com/site-pages/gfp-resources*.

(2) During acquisition planning, pricing contracts, exercising options, and assessing past performance, contracting officers should review the requiring activity's assessment of the information generated by the inventory reporting requirements.

[Publication notice, 20121212; Publication notice, 20141106; Publication notice, 20171228; Publication notice, 20180323]

245.103-74 Contracting office responsibilities.

(1) Prepare modifications to execute transfers of Government property accountability between existing contracts in accordance with *PGI 245.103-71*.

(2) Prepare the GFP attachments in accordance with the procedures in *PGI 245.103-72*.

(3) Maintain the GFP attachments in the contract.

(4) Include in applicable solicitations and contracts the CDRL provided by the requiring activity for reporting Government inventory held under sustainment contracts (see *PGI 245.103-73*).

[Publication notice, 20171228]

245.105 Contractor's property management system compliance.

(d) *Disposition of findings.*

(2) *Initial determination.*

(ii) (A) Within 10 days of receiving the report, if the contracting officer makes a determination that there is a significant deficiency, the contracting officer should provide an initial determination of deficiencies and a copy of the report to the contractor and require the contractor to submit a written response.

(C) *Evaluation of contractor's response.* Within 30 days of receiving the contractor's response, the contracting officer, in consultation with the auditor or cognizant functional specialist, should evaluate the contractor's response and make a final determination.

(3) *Final Determination.*

(ii) (A) *Monitoring contractor's corrective action.* The contracting officer and property administrator shall monitor the contractor's progress in correcting deficiencies. If the contractor fails to make adequate progress, the contracting officer shall take whatever action is necessary to ensure that the contractor corrects the deficiencies. Examples of actions the contracting officer can take are: withdraw or withhold approval of the system; bringing the issue to the attention of higher level management, implementing or increasing the withholding in accordance with the clause at 252.242-7005, Contractor Business Systems, and recommending non-award of potential contracts.

(B) *Correction of significant deficiencies.*

(1) When the contractor notifies the contracting officer that the contractor has corrected the significant deficiencies, the contracting officer shall request the property administrator to review the correction to determine if the deficiencies have been resolved.

(2) The contracting officer shall determine if the contractor has corrected the deficiencies.

(3) If the contracting officer determines the contractor has corrected the deficiencies, the contracting officer's notification shall be sent to the property administrator; auditor; payment office; appropriate action officers responsible for reporting past performance at the requiring activities; and each contracting and contract administration office having substantial business with the contractor as applicable.

[Interim rule 76 FR 28856, 5/18/2011, effective 5/18/2011; Final rule, 77 FR 11355, 2/24/2012, effective 2/24/2012]

SUBPART 245.2—SOLICITATION AND EVALUATION PROCEDURES

245.201 Solicitation. (No Text)

[Publication notice, 20100723; Publication notice 20100816]

245.201-70 Definitions.

As used in this section—

(1) "As is" means that the Government may, at its option, furnish Government property in an "as-is" condition. In such cases, the Government makes no warranty with respect to the serviceability and/or suitability of the Government property for contract performance. Any repairs, replacement, and/or refurbishment shall be at the contractor's expense.

(2) "Commercial and Government entity (CAGE) code" means: (i) A code assigned by the Defense Logistics Information Service (DLIS) to identify a commercial or Government entity; or (ii) A code assigned by a member of the North Atlantic Treaty Organization that DLIS records and maintains in the CAGE master file. This type of code is known as an "NCAGE code". As defined in the DoD 4100.39-M, Federal Logistics Information System Glossary, the CAGE Code is a five-character data element assigned to establishments that are manufacturers or have design control of items of supply procured by the Federal Government. In the United States, the first and last positions of a CAGE code will be numeric.

(3) "Contractor-acquired property." See FAR 45.101.

(4) "Description" means a collection and compilation of data to describe an item. The descriptive noun of the item nomenclature, as defined in DoD 4100.39-M, Glossary.

(5) "Government property." See FAR 45.101.

(6) "Government-furnished property." See FAR 45.101.

(7) "Major end item" means a final combination of end products that is ready for its intended use; e.g., launchers, tanks, mobile machine shops, aircraft, and vehicles.

(8) "National stock number (NSN)" means a 13-digit stock number used to identify items of supply. It consists of a four-digit Federal Supply Classification code and a nine-digit national item identification number (NIIN), as defined in DoD Manual 4140.01, Volume 9, DoD Supply Chain Materiel Management Procedures: Material Programs.

(9) "NIIN" means the last nine digits of the NSN that differentiates each individual supply item from all other supply items. The first two digits signify the National Codification Bureau that assigned the NIIN, wherein the last seven digits are non-significant and are sequentially assigned by the Federal Logistics Information System. All United States-manufactured items have a National Codification Bureau code of "00" (cataloged before 1975) or "01" (cataloged in 1975, or later).

(10) "Nomenclature" means: (i) The combination of a Government-assigned type designation and an approved item name; (ii) Names assigned to kinds and groups of products; or (iii) Formal designations assigned to products by customer or supplier (such as model number, or model type, design differentiation, specific design series, or configuration).

(11) "Part or identifying number (PIN)" means the identifier assigned by the original design activity, or by the controlling nationally recognized standard, that uniquely identifies (relative to that design activity) a specific item, as defined by Military Standard 130, Standard Practice for Identification Marking of U. S. Military Property, latest version.

(12) "Quantity" means a numeric value for such characteristics as dimensions, measure, magnitude, electrical rating, etc. Also, the numerical designator for a unit of issue described in table 53, unit of issue codes, DoD 4100.39-M, Federal Logistics Information System (FLIS) Procedures, volume 10. See *http://www.dla.mil/HQ/InformationOperations/Offers/Services/TrainingandReference/FLISProcedures.aspx*.

(13) "Reparable." See DFARS clause *252.211-7007*.

(14) "Requiring activity" means the DoD organization, or part of an organization, that

identifies and defines a requirement for supplies or services, and requests the initiation of, and provides funding for, an acquisition to fulfill the requirement.

(15) "Serial number" means an assigned designation that provides a means of identifying a specific individual item, as defined by Military Standard 130, Standard Practice for Identification Marking of U. S. Military Property, latest version.

(16) "Type Designation" means a combination of letters and numbers arranged in a specific sequence to provide a short, significant method of identification for an item. The various type designators are as follows:

(i) Electronics: MIL-STD-196, Joint Electronics Type Designation System, February 17, 1998.

(ii) Aerospace Vehicles: DoD 4120.15-L, Model Designation of Military Aerospace Vehicles, May 12, 2004.

(iii) Aerospace Engines and Equipment: MIL-HDBK-1812, Type Designation, Assignment and Method of Obtaining, February 14, 1997.

(iv) Ships: SECNAVINST 5030.8, Classification of Naval Ships and Craft, November 21, 2006.

(v) Army Watercraft: AR 56-9, Watercraft, February 7, 2002

(vi) Army Nomenclature: MIL-STD-1464A (AR), Army Nomenclature System, May 15, 1987.

(vii) Navy Nomenclature: MIL-STD-1661(OS), Mark and Mod Nomenclature System, August 1, 1978.

(17) "Unique item identifier (UII)." See DFARS clause 252.211-7003.

(18) "Unit of measure" means a measurement term, as listed in Table 81, Unit of Measure Designations, Volume 10, DoD 4100.39-M, Federal Logistics Information System, used in conjunction with a unit of issue of related national stock numbers.

[Publication notice, 20100723; Publication notice 20100816; Publication notice, 20171208; Publication notice, 20171228]

245.201-71 Security classification.

Classified contracts are not exempt from including GFP attachments solely because the contracts are classified.

[Publication notice, 20100723; Publication notice 20100816; Publication notice, 20121212]

SUBPART 245.4—TITLE TO GOVERNMENT PROPERTY

245.402 Title to contractor-acquired property. (No Text)

[Publication notice, 20100723; Publication notice 20100816; Publication notice 20110112]

245.402-70 Policy.

Title vests in the Government for all property acquired or fabricated by the contractor in accordance with paragraph (e)(3) of the clause at FAR 52.245-1, Government Property. Oversight and visibility of contractor-acquired property (CAP) is accomplished through reviews and audits of contractor business systems, including—

(1) Accounting systems (see DFARS *242.75*);

(2) Property management systems (see DFARS *245.105*); and

(3) Material management and accounting systems (see DFARS *242.72*).

[Publication notice, 20100723; Publication notice 20100816; Publication notice 20110112; Final rule, 81 FR 50652, 8/2/2016, effective 8/2/2016]

245.402-71 Delivery of contractor-acquired property.

(1) The contractual transfer of accountability of CAP from one contract to another is prohibited. Only upon delivery under a line item can property be transferred to other contracts as Government-furnished property (GFP) (see PGI 245.103-71).

(2) Upon delivery and acceptance by the Government, and when retained by the contractor for use under a contract, the delivered CAP items become GFP and shall be added to the contract GFP attachment (see PGI 245.103-72).

(3) *Contractor-acquired property not anticipated at time of contract award.*

(i) For CAP not anticipated at the time of contract award, or not otherwise specified for delivery on an existing line item, the contracting officer shall direct delivery of the CAP items to the Government on a not separately priced (NSP) line item (e.g. contract line item, exhibit line item, etc.). Such items are typically identified through—

(A) Plant clearance in accordance with the clause at DFARS *252.245-7004*, Reporting, reutilization, and Disposal;

(B) Inventory reports provided by the contractor in accordance with FAR clause 52.245-1; or

(C) Other reporting requirements specified in the contract.

(ii) The contracting officer shall direct delivery of CAP on a line item as soon as the CAP item is identified, if—

(A) The value of the item meets or exceeds the capitalization threshold as identified in the memorandum issued jointly by the Under Secretary of Defense (USD) Comptroller and the USD (Acquisition, Technology, and Logistics) on 20 September 2013, entitled, "Elimination of Military Equipment Definition and Increase to Capitalization Thresholds for General Property, Plant and Equipment" (available at *http://www.acq.osd.mil/pepolicy/pdfs/FinancialReportingGPPEMemo.pdf*) or;

(B) The item is special tooling, special test equipment, or equipment designated for preservation and storage under a major defense acquisition program (reference: Section 815 of the National Defense Authorization Act for Fiscal Year 2009 (Pub. L. 110-417)).

(iii) Each NSP line item of CAP to be delivered to the Government shall include the following information:

Contractor-Acquired Property Delivery NSP Line Item

LI	Item Description/ Nomenclature	Type Designation	NSN	PIN	Quantity	Unit of Measure	Serial Number (UII)*	Unit Acquisition Cost	Date Placed in Service by the Contractor
x	x	As required	x	x	x	x	If known	x	x

* Contractor-acquired property items shall be marked as required by DFARS clause 252.211-7003.

(A) The value of any delivered CAP item shall be at the contractor provided fully burdened cost, i.e., normal or provisional burdens to the direct costs in accordance with the applicable disclosed accounting practices, including an appropriate amount for fee or profit (as reflected in the contract under which the estimate is prepared) in addition to the direct and indirect costs. This is consistent with DFARS *211.274-3*, Policy for valuation, regarding unit acquisition cost.

(B) Unless otherwise noted by the contractor at the time of delivery to the Government, the placed-in-service date shall be the date of acquisition or, if fabricated, the date of completed manufacture.

(4) *Special circumstances.* In some circumstances, such as contractor-performed logistics support, interim contractor support, or performance-based logistics support under fixed-price contracts, contract deliverables consist of non-hardware items, such as operational readiness rate goals or mean-time-between failures of a system. In order to meet these deliverables, contractors are required to provide certain property items to the Government. In such cases, the contract does not include specific delivery line items requiring formal delivery of the property. By extension, the Government will not have title to the property at the time contractor provides the property. In such cases, title to the property passes to the Government upon Government acceptance (as defined in FAR 46.101) of the items at the destination stated in the contract. Contracting officers shall ensure that the contract—

(i) Clearly defines how and when acceptance will be performed; and

(ii) Includes applicable requirements for quality assurance, part marking, anticounterfeiting, or other requirement for the delivery of the property.

[Publication notice, 20100723; Publication notice, 20100816; Publication notice, 20110112; Publication notice, 20130228; Final rule, 81 FR 50652, 8/2/2016, effective 8/2/2016]

SUBPART 245.6—REPORTING, REUTILIZATION, AND DISPOSAL

245.602-70 Plant clearance procedures.

(1) Upon receipt of acceptable inventory schedules, the plant clearance officer (PLCO) shall assign a plant clearance case number using DD Form 1635 (or an automated equivalent) and establish a case file.

(2) The plant clearance case number shall be established using a three-part, 11-character number as follows:

(i) Part 1: DoD Activity Address Code (six-character alphanumeric code) assigned to the contract administration activity.

(ii) Part 2: Locally assigned four-character consecutive alphanumeric code, beginning each calendar year with "001" continuing as necessary through "zzz". The fourth character is the last digit of the calendar year, e.g., "0013" for the first case of calendar year 2003.

(iii) Part 3: The 11th character is a single letter identifying the department or agency:

C-Army

Q-Navy

E-Air Force

L-Marine Corps

U-Defense Logistics Agency

N-Defense Threat Reduction Agency

M-National Geospatial-Intelligence Agency

S-NASA

D-Other DoD activities

O-Non-DoD activities

(3) The case file shall contain copies of all documents relevant to the case, e.g., correspondence, review board findings, antitrust clearances, and reports.

(4) PLCOs will use DD Form 1638, Report of Disposition of Contractor Inventory, or an automated equivalent to report the disposition of contractor inventory. Do not include disposition actions transferred to other offices. Complete only the column total for each line of this report. The report is self-explanatory except—

(i) Line 1–insert totals from line 7 of the preceding report;

(ii) Line 2–insert net changes due to shortages, overages, errors, or withdrawals (other than purchases or retention at cost);

(iii) Line 3–insert total excess inventory reported by contractors during the report period;

(iv) Line 5–insert total plant clearance cases completed during the report period. Do not report cases as completed until all property has been disposed. Acquisition cost must equal line 19;

(v) Line 8–insert amount retained or withdrawn at full cost;

(vi) Line 9–insert acquisition cost in the "Acquisition Cost" column and insert acquisition cost less handling, transportation, or restocking charges, in the "Proceeds" column;

(vii) Line 10–insert acquisition cost of all transfers completed during the report period. On lines 10A through 10H, insert subtotals representing transfers to the agency indicated. Exclude amounts on lines 10A through 10H when computing line 19 totals;

(viii) Line 12–insert the acquisition cost and gross proceeds;

(ix) Lines 14 and 15–used to identify and report other transactions, and

(x) Line 18–insert section II totals. Line 18 acquisition cost must equal acquisition cost on line 5.

(5) The PLCO will prepare quarterly reports for periods ending March 31, June 30, September 30, and December 31. Activities preparing manual reports will submit duplicate reports to the headquarters of the administering activity within 10 working days

after the close of the report period (Report Control Symbol DD(I&L) (Q) 1430 applies).

(6) Upon completion of the plant clearance action, the PLCO shall prepare a Standard Form 1424, Inventory Disposal Report. The form is self-explanatory except–

(i) Item 12–insert net change due to shortages, overages, errors, pricing, or withdrawals, etc. Explain in item 18, Remarks;

(ii) Item 14–insert amount contractor is retaining or purchasing at acquisition cost;

(iii) Item 15–insert acquisition cost and net credit (full credit less approved handling, transportation, and restocking charges for items returned to supplier);

(iv) Item 16–insert the acquisition cost for all transfers accomplished. For lines 16A and 16B, insert subtotals as indicated;

(v) Item 18–insert acquisition cost and gross proceeds;

(vi) Items 20 and 21–use to identify and report transactions not otherwise identified, such as items shipped to a Government precious metals reclamation activity, etc. Further explanation may be provided in item 26, Remarks, if necessary;

(vii) Item 26–show the specific disposition of proceeds reported in items 14, 15, and 18. Also, indicate amounts deleted for specific contractor claims, or applied as a credit to the claim; and

(viii) Item 27–total dispositions must equal the amounts on line 13, and must reflect all disposal actions within the case.

(7) When contractor inventory with an estimated fair market value of $3 million or more, or any patents, processes, techniques, or inventions, regardless of cost, are sold or otherwise disposed of to private interests, notify the Attorney General and the General Services Administration (GSA) of the proposed terms and conditions of disposal. Submit the following information to the Department of Justice and GSA through contract administration agency channels (Report Control Symbol DD-ACQ (AR) 1492 applies):

(i) Location and description of property (specify tonnage if scrap).

(ii) Proposed sale price (explain if the proposed purchaser was not highest bidder).

(iii) Acquisition cost of property.

(iv) Manner of sale, indicating whether by—

(A) Sealed bid (specify number of bidders solicited and bids received);

(B) Auction or spot bid (state how sale was advertised);

(C) Negotiation (explain why property was not sold competitively);

(D) Proposed purchaser's name, address, and trade name (if any) under which proposed purchaser is doing business;

(E) If a corporation, provide state and date of incorporation, and name and address of—

(1) Each holder of 25 percent or more of the corporate stock;

(2) Each subsidiary; and

(3) Each company under common control with proposed purchaser.

(4) If a partnership, provide—

(a) Name and address of each partner; and

(b) Other business connections of each partner;

(c) Nature of proposed purchaser's business (indicate whether its scope is local, statewide, regional, or national);

(d) Estimated dollar volume of sales of proposed purchaser (as of latest calendar or fiscal year);

(e) Estimated net worth of proposed purchaser; and

(f) Intended use of property.

(8) Do not dispose of property until the Attorney General determines whether the proposed disposal action would tend to create or maintain a situation inconsistent with the antitrust laws.

(9) If the Attorney General advises that the proposed disposition is inconsistent with the antitrust laws, do not continue with the proposed disposition.

(10) Under noncompetitive sales, the prospective purchaser shall be informed that

final consummation of the sale is subject to determination by the Attorney General.

(11) The disposal of contractor inventory is the responsibility of the contractor. However, the disposal/sales services of the Defense Logistics Agency (DLA) Disposition Services or a Federal agency, e.g., GSA, may be used in unusual or compelling circumstances, as determined by the contracting officer to be in the best interest of the Government, and provided DLA Disposition Services/the agency agrees. In such cases, disposal/sales services may be provided on a reimbursable basis, with any sale proceeds credited in compliance with FAR 45.604-4, Proceeds from sales of surplus property. If sale services are needed, the plant clearance officer will document the reasons in the case file and make arrangements directly with DLA Disposition Services, GSA, other Federal agency, or third-party. The arrangements will include a requirement to return all proceeds to the plant clearance officer for crediting in compliance with FAR 45.604-4.

(12) The PLCO shall, prior to sales contract award—

(i) Ensure the prospective buyer is not an ineligible transferee, including those on found in the System for Award Management (SAM) Exclusions. For additional information see *http://www.acquisition.gov*;

(ii) Cross-reference contractor inventory to a National Stock Number and Demilitarization code. For additional information, see FED LOG or WEBFLIS at *http://www.dlis.dla.mil/webflis/* and the current edition of the DoD Demilitarization Manual at *http://www.dtic.mil/whs/directives*;

(iii) Consult with the DoD Demilitarization (Demil)/Trade Security Control (TSC) Program office to determine if the contractor inventory can be sold to the public; and if a TSC assessment of the prospective buyer is required. Reference DoD Instruction 2030.08, Implementation of Trade Security Controls (TSC) for Transfers of DoD U.S. Munitions List (USML) and Commerce Control List (CCL) Personal Property to Parties Outside DoD Control; and Defense Demilitarization Manual, DoD 4160.28-M;

(iv) If TSC is required, provide the DoD Demil/TSC Program office with a completed DLA Form 1822 End-Use Certificate (EUC) for the prospective buyer. Note: TSC assessments/EUCs are typically not required for scrap sales; and

(v) Upon TSC clearance (if required) of the prospective buyer, authorize the contractor to complete the sale, as applicable.

(13) To the extent that demilitarization, mutilation, or destruction is required, the PLCO may authorize the contractor to perform such action as follows:

(i) Demilitarization, mutilation, or destruction by the contractor or buyer as a condition of sale;

(ii) Shipment to a DoD disposal activity (contingent upon packing, crating, handling, and transportation funding), or

(iii) Such other actions as are included in the terms and conditions of the contract.

(14) Security assistance transfers or foreign military sales shall be conducted in accordance with the terms and conditions of the contract and consistent with DoD 5105.38-M Security Assistance Management Manual.

(15) The plant clearance officer may send a notice of proposed surplus sale to FedBizOpps (*http://www.fbo.gov*) if the items have potentially high public interest.

[Final rule, 76 FR 52139, 8/19/2011, effective 8/19/2011; Final rule, 78 FR 28756, 5/16/2013, effective 5/16/2013]

PART 246—QUALITY ASSURANCE

Table of Contents

Subpart 246.1—General

Contracting office responsibilities 246.103

Subpart 246.3—Contract Clauses

Notification of potential safety issues 246.371

Subpart 246.4—Government Contract Quality Assurance

Noncomforming supplies or services 246.407
Single-agency assignments of Government contract quality assurance 246.408
Aircraft 246.408-71
Government contract quality assurance actions 246.470
Quality evaluation data 246.470–2
Inspection stamping 246.472

Subpart 246.7—Warranties

Definitions 246.701
Warranty attachments 246.710-70

PART 246—QUALITY ASSURANCE

SUBPART 246.1—GENERAL

246.103 Contracting office responsibilities.

(2) (i) In preparing instructions for Government inspections, the technical activity shall consider, as applicable—

(A) The past quality history of the contractor;

(B) The criticality of the material procured in relation to its intended use, considering factors such as—

(1) Reliability;

(2) Safety;

(3) Interchangeability; and

(4) Maintainability;

(C) Problems encountered in the development of the material;

(D) Problems encountered in other procurements of the same or similar material;

(E) Available feedback data from contract administration, receiving, testing, or using activities; and

(F) The experience of other contractors in overcoming manufacturing problems.

(ii) The instructions shall—

(A) Be kept to a minimum;

(B) Ensure that the activities requested are in direct relation to contract quality requirements to serve as objective evidence of quality conformance; and

(C) Be prepared on a contract-by-contract basis.

(iii) The instructions shall not—

(A) Serve as a substitute for incomplete contract quality requirements;

(B) Impose greater inspection requirements than are in the contract;

(C) Use broad or general designations such as—

(1) All requirements;

(2) All characteristics; or

(3) All characteristics in the classification of defects;

(D) Be used for routine administrative procedures; or

(E) Specify continued inspection requirements when statistically sound sampling will provide an adequate degree of protection.

(iv) After issuing the instructions, the technical activity must—

(A) Provide the contract administration office with available information regarding those factors that resulted in the requirement for Government inspection;

(B) Periodically analyze the need to continue, change, or discontinue the instructions; and

(C) Advise the contract administration office of the results of the periodic analyses.

[Final rule, 71 FR 27646, 5/12/2006, effective 5/12/2006]

SUBPART 246.3—CONTRACT CLAUSES

246.371 Notification of potential safety issues.

(1) The objective of this requirement is to ensure that the Government receives timely notification of potential safety defects so that—

(i) Systems and equipment likely affected by the situation can be identified; and

(ii) An appropriate engineering investigation and follow-on actions can be taken to establish and mitigate risk.

(2) The notification is intended to be neither an admission of nor a release from liability.

(3) Upon notification of a potential safety nonconformance or deficiency—

(i) The procuring contracting officer must—

(A) Advise the affected program office(s) or integrated materiel manager(s); and

(B) Request a point of contact from the affected program office(s) or materiel management organization to assess the impact of the situation, address technical concerns, and provide recommendations;

(ii) The administrative contracting officer must—

(A) Confirm that potentially affected program offices, integrated materiel managers, and other contract management offices that may be recipients of the suspect items are aware of the situation; and

(B) Identify a point of contact to provide support and technical assistance to the investigative team; and

(iii) For replenishment parts, the integrated materiel manager must—

(A) Identify any potentially affected programs or equipment; and

(B) Request engineering assistance from affected engineering support activities, as prescribed by—

(1) DLAI 3200.1/PAM 715.13/NAVSUPINST 4120.30A/AFI 21-408/MCO 4000.18, Engineering Support Instruction for Items Supplied by Defense Logistics Agency;

(2) SECNAVINST 4140.2/AFI 20-106/DA PAM 95-9/DLAI 3200.4/DCMA INST CSI (AV), Management of Aviation Critical Safety Items;

(3) DA PAM 738-751, Functional Users Manual for the Army Maintenance Management System—Aviation (TAMMS-A);

(4) AMCOM REG 702-7, Flight Safety Parts/New Source Testing Program Management; or

(5) Internal agency procedures.

[Final rule, 72 FR 2633, 1/22/2007, effective 1/22/2007]

SUBPART 246.4—GOVERNMENT CONTRACT QUALITY ASSURANCE

246.407 Nonconforming supplies or services.

Additional information on delegation of authority for acceptance of minor nonconformances in aviation and ship critical safety items is available at *http://www.aviation.dla.mil/UserWeb/AviationEngineering/EngineeringSupport/Documents/AviationCSIHandbook.pdf.*

[Publication notice, 20140919]

246.408 Single-agency assignments of Government contract quality assurance. (No Text)

[Publication notice 20130419, 4/19/2013]

246.408-71 Aircraft.

(c) The CAO shall ensure that—.

(i) A detailed consultation with the FAA Military Certification Office (MCO) (contact the MCO here: (*http://www.faq.gov/about/office_org/headquaters_offices/air/directorates_field/small_airplanes/mco*) is documented regarding the scope of the acquisition or modification project;

(ii) Supporting contractual documents (meeting minutes, an email record of consultations, memoranda, etc.) demonstrate that the scope of work is feasible and compatible with FAA regulations and policy;

(iii) The period of performance and contract deliverable dates are consistent with FAA capabilities; and

(iv) Contract provisions requiring FAA approval or processes are coordinated with the MCO prior to a solicitation.

[Publication notice 20130419, 4/19/2013]

246.470 Government contract quality assurance actions. (No Text)

[Final rule, 71 FR 27646, 5/12/2006, effective 5/12/2006; Change notice 2008110]

246.470-2 Quality evaluation data.

Types of quality evaluation data are—

(1) Quality data developed by the contractor during performance;

(2) Data developed by the Government through contract quality assurance actions; and

(3) Reports by users and customers.

[Final rule, 71 FR 27646, 5/12/2006, effective 5/12/2006; Change notice, 2008110]

246.472 Inspection stamping.

(a) (i) There are two DoD quality inspection approval marking designs (stamps).

(A) Both stamps are used—

(1) Only by, or under the direct supervision of, the Government representative; and

(2) For both prime and subcontracts.

(B) The designs of the two stamps and the differences in their uses are—

(1) Partial (Circle) Inspection Approval Stamp.

(i) This circular stamp is used to identify material inspected for conformance to only a portion of the contract quality requirements.

(ii) Further inspection is to be performed at another time and/or place.

(iii) Material not inspected is so listed on the associated DD Form 250 (Material Inspection and Receiving Report), packing list, or comparable document.

(2) Complete (Square) Inspection Approval Stamp.

(i) This square stamp is used to identify material completely inspected for all contract quality requirements at source.

(ii) The material satisfies all contract quality requirements and is in complete conformance with all contract quality requirements applicable at the time and place of inspection.

(iii) Complete inspection approval establishes that material that once was partially approved has subsequently been completely approved.

(iv) One imprint of the square stamp voids multiple imprints of the circle stamp.

(ii) The marking of each item is neither required nor prohibited. Ordinarily, the stamping of shipping containers, packing lists, or routing tickets serves to adequately indicate the status of the material and to control or facilitate its movement.

(iii) Stamping material does not mean that it has been accepted by the Government. Evidence of acceptance is ordinarily a signed acceptance certificate on the DD Form 250, Material Inspection and Receiving Report.

[Final rule, 71 FR 27646, 5/12/2006, effective 5/12/2006; Change notice, 2008110]

SUBPART 246.7—WARRANTIES

246.701 Definitions.

Duration, *fixed expiration*, *starting event*, *usage*, and *warranty repair source* are defined in the clause at 252.246-7006, Warranty Tracking of Serialized Items.

[Final rule, 81 FR 17041, 3/25/2016, effective 3/25/2016]

246.710-70 Warranty attachments.

(1) The following attachments shall be included in solicitations and awards to specify the required data elements for warranties of serialized items:

(i) *Warranty Tracking Information*. This format is used to specify the required warranty tracking data elements and accomplish the electronic transmission of the list of warranty items. All fields of this attachment must be completed at the time of award, except the unique item identifier field, which may be completed after the time of award, but no later than when the warranted items are presented for receipt and/or acceptance.

(ii) *Source of Repair Instructions*. This format is used to specify the required warranty source of repair data elements and accomplish the electronic transmission of the source of repair data for each warranty item. This attachment shall be completed no later than when the warranted items are presented for receipt and/or acceptance.

(2) Warranty attachments shall be—

(i) Completed electronically using the fillable PDF format or downloadable Excel format available on the Product Data Reporting and Evaluation Program (PDREP) website at *https://www.pdrep.csd.disa.mil/pdrep_files/other/wsr.htm*; and

(ii) Numbered in accordance with PGI 204.7105(b)(5).

(3) If the Government specifies a warranty, the contracting officer shall request the requiring activity to provide information to ensure that the "Warranty Tracking Information" attachment is populated with data specifying the Government's required warranty terms by contract line item number, subline item number, or exhibit line item number prior to solicitation. One of the following is required to populate the attachment for each warranted item: starting event, usage, duration, or fixed expiration date.

(4) If the Government does not specify a warranty, the contracting officer may require offerors to provide warranty data by populat-

ing the "Warranty Tracking Information" attachment, as appropriate, and include the attachment as part of its offer, in accordance with the provision at 252.246-7005, Notice of Warranty Tracking of Serialized Items.

(5) As required in the clause at 252.246-7006, Warranty Tracking of Serialized Items, the contractor is required to provide the following information no later than the time of receipt and/or acceptance of warranted items:

(i) The unique item identifier for each warranted item on the "Warranty Tracking Information" attachment.

(ii) The warranty repair source information and instructions required by the "Source of Repair Instructions" attachment.

(6) The contracting officer shall ensure the completed warranty attachments are uploaded to the Electronic Data Access (EDA) system (see DFARS 204.270 for information on obtaining an EDA account).

(7) For additional information on the warranty attachments, see the "Warranty and Source of Repair" training and "Warranty and Source of Repair Tracking User Guide" accessible on the PDREP site at *https://www.pdrep.csd.disa.mil/pdrep_files/other/wsr.htm*.

[Final rule, 81 FR 17041, 3/25/2016, effective 3/25/2016; Publication notice, 20190913]

PART 247—TRANSPORTATION

Table of Contents

Definitions 247.001

Subpart 247.2—Contracts for Transportation or for Transportation-Related Services

Scope of subpart 247.200
Procedures 247.271-2
Solicitation provisions, schedule formats, and contract clauses 247.271-3

Subpart 247.3—Transportation in Supply Contracts

General 247.301
Solicitation provisions, contract clauses, and transportation factors 247.305
Packing, marking, and consignment instructions 247.305-10
DD Form 1384, Transportation Control and Movement 247.370

Subpart 247.5—Ocean Transportation by U.S.-Flag Vessels

General 247.573

PART 247—TRANSPORTATION

247.001 Definitions.

For more information about the Voluntary Intermodal Sealift Agreement (VISA) program, see *http://www.marad.dot.gov/ships_shipping_landing_page/national_security/vol_intermodal_sealift_agreement/vol_intermodal_sealift_agreement.htm.*

[Final rule, 75 FR 51416, 8/20/2010, effective 8/20/2010]

SUBPART 247.2—CONTRACTS FOR TRANSPORTATION OR FOR TRANSPORTATION-RELATED SERVICES

247.200 Scope of subpart.

For general cargo provisions, see DTR 4500.9-R, Defense Transportation Regulation (DTR), Part II, Chapter 201, paragraphs L, M, N, and S (available at *http://www.transcom.mil//dtr/part-ii/part_ii 201.pdf*).

[Final rule, 75 FR 51416, 8/20/2010, effective 8/20/2010; Publication notice, 20140930]

247.271-2 Procedures.

(a) *Contiguous United States military activities assigned multi-service personal property areas of responsibility.*

(1) When two or more military installations or activities have personal property responsibilities in a given area, one activity must contract for the estimated requirements of all activities in the area. The installation commanders concerned must designate the activity by mutual agreement.

(2) The Commander, Military Surface Deployment and Distribution Command (SDDC), must designate the contracting activity when local commanders are unable to reach agreement.

(b) *Additional services and excess requirements.*

(1) When requiring activities need additional services that exceed contractor capabilities available under contracts, contracting officers should use simplified acquisition procedures to satisfy those excess requirements.

(2) Additional services are those not specified in the bid items.

(i) Additional services may include—

(A) Hoisting or lowering of articles;

(B) Waiting time;

(C) Special packaging; and

(D) Stuffing or unstuffing of sea van containers.

(ii) Contracting officers should consider contracting for local moves that do not require drayage by using hourly rate or constructive weight methods. The rate will include those services necessary for completion of the movement, including—

(A) Packing and unpacking;

(B) Movement;

(C) Inventorying; and

(D) Removal of debris.

(iii) Each personal property shipping activity must determine if local requirements exist for any additional services.

(iv) The contracting officer may obtain additional services by—

(A) Including them as items within the contract, provided they are not used in the evaluation of bids (see DFARS 252.247-7008, Evaluation of Bids); or

(B) Using simplified acquisition procedures.

(v) Either predetermine prices for additional services with the contractor, or negotiate them on a case-by-case basis.

(vi) The contracting officer must authorize the contractor to perform any additional services, other than attempted pick up or delivery, regardless of the contracting method.

(vii) To the maximum extent possible, identify additional services required that are incidental to an order before placing the order, or, when applicable, during the premove survey.

(c) Contract distribution.

(1) Contiguous United States personal property shipping activities must send the copy to the Commander, Military Surface Deployment and Distribution Command

(SDDC), ATTN: AMSSD-PP, 709 Ward Drive, Scott AFB IL 62225.

(2) In the European and Pacific areas, personal property shipping activities must send the copy to either the Property Directorate, SDDC Europe, or the Field Office-Pacific.

(3) Other overseas personal property shipping activities must send the copy to the Commander, Military Surface Deployment and Distribution Command, ATTN: AMSSD-PP, 709 Ward Drive, Scott AFB IL 62225.

(d) When preparing solicitations for personal property for shipment or storage, and intra-area or intra-city movement, contracting officers should follow the procedures in DTR 4500.9-R, Part IV, Chapter 404 at *http://www.transcom.mil/dtr/part-iv/dtr-part-4-404.pdf*, and Appendix G at *http://www.transcom.mil/dtr/part-iv/dtr-part-4-app-g.pdf*.

[Final rule, 75 FR 51416, 8/20/2010, effective 8/20/2010; Publication notice, 2014 0930; Final rule, 81 FR 78011, 11/4/2016, effective 11/4/2016]

247.271-3 Solicitation provisions, schedule formats, and contract clauses.

(c) DTR 4500.9-R, Defense Transportation Regulation, Part IV, Appendix G-3 (available at *http://www.transcom.mil/dtr/part-iv/dtr-part-4-app-g3.pdf*), contains guidance on schedules as follows:

Schedule I Outbound Services, Pages 6-12.

Schedule II Inbound Services, Pages 13-17.

Schedule III Intra-City and Intra-Area Moves, Page 18.

(1) *Demurrage and detention charges.*

(i) Carrier demurrage/detention is a charge made against a consignor (shipper) or consignee (receiver) for the extended use of carrier- furnished equipment when delays attributable to the consignor or consignee occur. Carrier demurrage/detention rules usually allow a period of free time for loading, unloading, or holding equipment.

(ii) Carrier-published demurrage/detention rules and charges are not uniform from one carrier to another. Contracting officers should specifically address them in the contract. While demurrage/detention rules are published in individual carrier tariffs or agency tenders, Contracting Officers may negotiate contract-specific demurrage/detention rules and charges independent of any existing tariffs or tenders.

(6) Process any modification of schedule format, other than those authorized in paragraph (c) of this subsection, as a request for deviation to the Commander, SDDC.

[Final rule, 75 FR 51416, 8/20/2010, effective 8/20/2010; Publication notice, 20140930]

SUBPART 247.3—TRANSPORTATION IN SUPPLY CONTRACTS

247.301 General.

Transportation guidance relating to Governmentwide commercial purchase card purchases is available in the Department of Defense Government Charge Card Guidebook for Establishing and Managing Purchase, Travel, and Fuel Card Programs, Appendix C, at *http://www.acq.osd.mil/dpap/pdi/pc/policy_documents.html*.

[Final rule, 75 FR 51416, 8/20/2010, effective 8/20/2010; Publication notice, 20140930; Final rule, 81 FR 78011, 11/4/2016, effective 11/4/2016]

247.305 Solicitation provisions, contract clauses, and transportation factors. (No Text)

[Final rule, 75 FR 51416, 8/20/2010, effective 8/20/2010]

247.305-10 Packing, marking, and consignment instructions.

Follow the procedures in DTR 4500.9-R, Defense Transportation Regulation, Part II, Chapter 208 *http://www.transcom.mil/j5/pt/dtrpart2/dtr_part_ii_208.pdf*.

Additional guidance for marking can be found at MIL-STD-129P (Document ID 129P) at *http://quicksearch.dla.mil* and AR 700-15 at *http://www.apd.army.mil/jw2/xmldemo/r700_15/cover.asp*.

Consignment locations can be found in the Transportation Facilities Guide (TFG) on the SDDC website at *https://eta.sddc.army.mil/default.asp?fa=general.* Access to this site requires an Electronic Transportation Account.

[Final rule, 75 FR 51416, 8/20/2010, effective 8/20/2010; Publication notice, 20140930]

247.370 DD Form 1384, Transportation Control and Movement.

DTR 4500.9-R, Defense Transportation Regulation, Part II, Chapter 203 is available at *http://www.transcom.mil/dtr/part-ii/dtr_part_ii_203.pdf.*]

[Final rule, 75 FR 51416, 8/20/2010, effective 8/20/2010; Publication notice, 20140930]

SUBPART 247.5—OCEAN TRANSPORTATION BY U.S.-FLAG VESSELS

247.573 General.

(a) *Delegated Authority.* The authority to make determinations of excessive ocean liner rates and excessive charter rates is delegated in *Secretary of Defense Memorandum dated February 7, 2012.*

(b) *Procedures.*

(1) Contracting officers shall follow these procedures when ocean transportation is not the principal purpose of the contract, and the cargo to be transported is owned by DoD or is clearly identifiable for eventual use by DoD.

(i) DD Form 1653, Transportation Data for Solicitations, shall be used—

(A) By the requesting activity in developing the Government estimate for transportation costs; and

(B) By the contracting officer in ensuring that valid shipping instructions and delivery terms are included in solicitations and contracts that may involve transportation of supplies by sea.

(ii) (A) If the contractor notifies the contracting officer that the contractor or a subcontractor considers that no U.S.-flag vessels are available, the contracting officer shall request confirmation of the nonavailability from—

(*1*) The Commander, Military Sealift Command (MSC), through the Contracts and Business Management Directorate, MSC (*msc.n101.ffw@navy.mil*), for voyage and time charters; or

(*2*) The Commander, Military Surface Deployment and Distribution (SDDC), through the SDDC global e-mailbox (*usarmy.scott.sddc.mbx.ffw-team@mail.mil*) for ocean liner and intermodal transportation.

(B) If the contractor notifies the contracting officer that the contractor or a subcontractor considers that the proposed freight charges to the Government, the contractor, or any subcontractor are higher than charges for transportation of like goods to private persons, the contracting officer may approve a request for an exception to the requirement to ship on U.S.-flag vessels for a particular shipment.

(*1*) Prior to granting an exception, the contracting officer shall request advice, oral or written, from the Commander, MSC, through the Contracts and Business Management Directorate, MSC (*msc.n101.ffw@navy.mil*), for voyage and time charters; or the USTRANSCOM Director of Acquisition, through the Sealift Services Division (*transcom.scott.tcaq.mbx.i-foreign-flag-waiver@mail.mil*), for ocean liner and intermodal transportation.

(*2*) In advising the contracting officer whether to grant the exception, evidence from the following sources shall be considered, as appropriate—

(i) Published tariffs;

(ii) Industry publications;

(iii) The U.S. Maritime Administration; and

(iv) Other available sources.

(C) If the contractor notifies the contracting officer that the contractor or a subcontractor considers that the freight charges proposed by U.S.-flag carriers are excessive or otherwise unreasonable—

(*1*) The contracting officer shall prepare a report in determination and findings format, and shall—

(i) Take into consideration that the 1904 Act is, in part, a subsidy of the U.S.-flag commercial shipping industry that recognizes that lower prices may be available from foreign-flag carriers. Therefore, a lower price for use of a foreign-flag vessel is not a sufficient basis, on its own, to determine that the freight rate proposed by the U.S.-flag carrier is excessive or otherwise unreasonable. However, such a price differential may indicate a need for further review;

(ii) Consider, accordingly, not only excessive profits to the carrier (to include vessel owner or operator), if ascertainable, but also excessive costs to the Government (i.e., costs beyond the economic penalty normally incurred by excluding foreign competition) resulting from the use of U.S.-flag vessels in extraordinarily inefficient circumstances; and

(iii) Include an analysis of whether the cost is excessive, taking into account factors such as—

(*a*) The differential between the freight charges proposed by the U.S.-flag carrier and an estimate of what foreign-flag carriers would charge based upon a price analysis;

(*b*) A comparison of U.S.-flag rates charged on comparable routes;

(*c*) Efficiency of operation regardless of rate differential (e.g., suitability of the vessel for the required transportation in terms of cargo requirements or vessel capacity, and the commercial reasonableness of vessel positioning required); and

(*d*) Any other relevant economic and financial considerations; and

(*2*) The contracting officer shall forward the report to—

(i) The Commander, MSC, through the Contracts and Business Management Directorate, MSC (*msc.n101.ffw@navy.mil*), for voyage and time charters; or

(ii) The USTRANSCOM Director of Acquisition, through the Sealift Services Division (*transcom.scott.tcaq.mbx.i-foreign-flag-waiver@mail.mil*), for ocean liner and intermodal transportation.

(*3*) The Commander, MSC, or the USTRANSCOM Director of Acquisition, will forward the report to the Secretary of the Navy or the Commander, USTRANSCOM, respectively, for a determination as to whether the proposed freight charges are excessive or otherwise unreasonable. Upon receipt of a determination by the Secretary of the Navy or the Commander, USTRANSCOM, respectively, that U.S. flag rates are excessive or unreasonable, the contracting officer shall provide the contractor with written approval to use a non-U.S. flag carrier, in accordance with that determination.

(2) Contracting officers shall follow these procedures when the direct purchase of ocean transportation services is the principal purpose of the contract.

(i) Direct purchase of ocean transportation may include—

(A) Time charters;

(B) Voyage charters;

(C) Contracts for charter vessel services;

(D) Dedicated contractor contracts for charter vessel services;

(E) Ocean bills of lading;

(F) Subcontracts under Government contracts or agreements for ocean transportation services; and

(G) Ocean liner contracts (including contracts where ocean liner transportation is part of an intermodal movement).

(ii) Coordinate these acquisitions, as appropriate, with USTRANSCOM, the DoD single manager for commercial transportation and related services, other than Service-unique or theater-assigned transportation assets, in accordance with DoDD 5158.4, United States Transportation Command.

(iii) All solicitations within the scope of this section shall provide—

(A) A preference for U.S.-flag vessels in accordance with the 1904 Act;

(B) An evaluation criterion for offeror participation in the Voluntary Intermodal Sealift Agreement; and

(C) An evaluation criterion considering the extent to which offerors have had overhaul, repair, and maintenance work for all covered vessels in an offeror's fleet performed in shipyards located in the United States or Guam. Work performed in foreign shipyards shall not be considered if—

(*1*) Such work was performed as emergency repairs in foreign shipyards due to accident, emergency, Act of God, or an infirmity to the vessel, and safety considerations warranted taking the vessel to a foreign shipyard; or

(*2*) Such work was paid for or reimbursed by the U.S. Government.

(iv) Do not award a contract of the type described in paragraph (b)(2) of this section for a foreign-flag vessel unless—

(A) The Commander, MSC, or the Commander, SDDC, determines that no U.S.-flag vessels are available;

(*1*) The Commander, MSC, and the Commander, SDDC, are authorized to make any determinations as to the availability of U.S.-flag vessels to ensure the proper use of Government and private U.S. vessels.

(*2*) The contracting officer shall request such determinations—

(i) For voyage and time charters, through the Contracts and Business Management Directorate, MSC (*msc.n101.ffw@navy.mil*); and

(ii) For ocean liner and intermodal transportation, including contracts for shipment of military household goods and privately-owned vehicles, through the SDDC global e-mailbox (*usarmy.scott.sddc.mbx.ffw-team@mail.mil*).

(*3*) In the absence of regularly scheduled U.S.-flag service to fulfill stated DoD requirements, the Commander, SDDC, may grant, on a case-by-case basis, an on-going non-availability determination for foreign-flag service approval with predetermined review date(s);

(B) The contracting officer determines that the U.S.-flag carrier has proposed to the Government freight charges that are higher than charges to private persons for transportation of like goods, and obtains the approval of the Commander, MSC, through the Contracts and Business Management Directorate, MSC (*msc.n101.ffw@navy.mil*), or the USTRANSCOM Director of Acquisition, through the Sealift Services Division, (*transcom.scott.tcaq.mbx.i-foreign-flag-waiver@mail.mil*); or

(C) The Secretary of the Navy, for voyage and time charters, or the Commander, USTRANSCOM, for ocean liner and intermodal transportation, determines that the proposed freight charges for U.S.-flag vessels are excessive or otherwise unreasonable.

(*1*) After considering the factors in paragraphs (b)(1)(ii)(C)(*1*)(*i*) and (*ii*) of this section, if the contracting officer concludes that the freight charges proposed by U.S.-flag carriers may be excessive or otherwise unreasonable, the contracting officer shall prepare a report in determination and findings format that includes, as appropriate—

(*i*) An analysis of the carrier's costs in accordance with FAR subpart 15.4, or profit in accordance with DFARS *215.404-4*. The costs or profit should not be so high as to make it unreasonable to apply the preference for U.S.-flag vessels;

(ii) A description of efforts taken pursuant to FAR 15.405 to negotiate a reasonable price. For the purpose of FAR 15.405(d), this report is the referral to a level above the contracting officer; and

(iii) An analysis of whether the costs are excessive (i.e., costs beyond the economic penalty normally incurred by excluding foreign competition), taking into consideration factors such as those listed at paragraph (b)(1)(ii)(C)(*1*)(*iii*) of this section.

(*2*) The contracting officer shall forward the report to—

(i) The Commander, MSC, through the Contracts and Business Management Directorate, MSC (*msc.n101.ffw@navy.mil*), for voyage and time charters; or

(ii) The USTRANSCOM Director of Acquisition, through the Sealift Services Division (*transcom.scott.tcaq.mbx.i-foreign-flag-waiver@mail.mil*).

(*3*) The Commander, MSC, or the USTRANSCOM Director of Acquisition, will forward the report to the Secretary of the Navy or the Commander, USTRANSCOM, respectively, for a determination as to whether the proposed freight charges are excessive or otherwise unreasonable. Upon receipt of a determination by the Secretary of the Navy or the Commander, USTRANSCOM, respectively, that U.S. flag rates are excessive or unreasonable, the contracting officer shall provide the contractor with written approval to use a non-U.S. flag carrier, in accordance with that determination.

(3) The following annual reporting requirement procedures relate to the DFARS solicitation provision at *252.247-7026*, Evaluation Preference for Use of Domestic Shipyards—Applicable to Acquisition of Carriage by Vessel for DoD Cargo in the Coastwise of Noncontiguous Trade.

(i) No later than February 15th of each year, departments and agencies shall—

(A) Prepare a report containing all information received from all offerors in response to the DFARS provision at *252.247-7026*, Evaluation Preference for Use of Domestic Shipyards—Applicable to Acquisition of Carriage by Vessel for DoD Cargo in the Coastwise of Noncontiguous Trade during the previous calendar year; and

(B) Submit the report to: Directorate of Acquisition, U.S. Transportation Command, ATTN: TCAQ, 508 Scott Drive, Scott AFB, IL 62225-5357.

(ii) The Director of Acquisition, U.S. Transportation Command, will submit a consolidated annual report to the congressional defense committees, by June 1st of each year, in accordance with section 1017 of Pub. L. 109-364.

(4) (i) Contracting officers shall ensure the following procedures have been followed when security background checks are required pursuant to the DFARS clause at *252.247-7027*, Riding Gang Member Requirements, when exercising the exemption provided by 10 U.S.C. 2401 note. The contracting officer shall coordinate as necessary with the Government official specified in the contract pursuant to paragraph *252.247-7027*(c) (2) (i) (A).

(ii) Contracting officers shall ensure that security background checks are processed by the Military Sealift Command (MSC) using the procedures contained in COMSC Instruction 5521.1 series, Security Screening of Persons with Access to MSC Ships (FOUO). Force Protection for Military Sealift Command (COMSC N3) will act as the executive agent for DoD utilizing the U.S. Government's El Paso Intelligence Center (EPIC) to perform required background checks as required by 10 U.S.C. 2401 note, and COMSC N34 Director of Force Protection or COMSC Antiterrorism Officer at *mschq_n34_epic@navy.mil* will facilitate the processes necessary to conduct background checks.

[Final rule, 79 FR 61583, 10/14/2014, effective 10/14/2014; Publication notice, 20171208]

PART 249—TERMINATION OF CONTRACTS

Table of Contents

Subpart 249.1—General Principles

Duties of termination contracting officer after issuance of notice of termination 249.105
Termination status reports 249.105–1
Release of excess funds 249.105–2
Settlement agreements 249.109
Settlement by determination 249.109–7
Limitation on pricing of the terminated effort 249.109–70
Settlement negotiation memorandum 249.110

Subpart 249.4—[Removed]

Subpart 249.70—Special Termination Requirements

Congressional notification on significant contract terminations 249.7001

PART 249—TERMINATION OF CONTRACTS

SUBPART 249.1—GENERAL PRINCIPLES

249.105 Duties of termination contracting officer after issuance of notice of termination. (No Text)

[Final rule, 71 FR 27644, 5/12/2006, effective 5/12/2006]

249.105-1 Termination status reports.

When the contract administration office receives a termination notice, it will, under Report Control Symbol DD-AT&L(AR)1411—

(1) Prepare a DD Form 1598, Contract Termination Status Report;

(2) Within 30 days, send one copy to the purchasing office and one copy to the headquarters office to which the contract administration office is directly responsible;

(3) Continue reporting semiannually to cover the six-month periods ending March and September. The semiannual reports must be submitted within 30 days after the end of the reporting period; and

(4) Submit a final report within 30 days after closing the termination case.

[Final rule, 71 FR 27644, 5/12/2006, effective 5/12/2006]

249.105-2 Release of excess funds.

The DD Form 1598, Contract Termination Status Report, may be used to recommend the release of excess funds. Include the accounting classification reference numbers, funds citations, and allocated amounts in any recommendation for release of excess funds.

[Final rule, 71 FR 27644, 5/12/2006, effective 5/12/2006]

249.109 Settlement agreements. (No Text)

[Final rule, 71 FR 27644, 5/12/2006, effective 5/12/2006]

249.109-7 Settlement by determination.

(1) Use a Standard Form 30(SF 30), Amendment of Solicitation/Modification of Contract, to settle a convenience termination by determination—

(i) When the contractor has lost its right of appeal because it failed to submit a timely settlement proposal; and

(ii) To confirm the determination when the contractor does not appeal the termination contracting officer's decision.

(2) The effective date of the SF 30 shall be the same as the date of the letter of determination. Do not assign a supplementary procurement instrument identification number to the letter of determination. Send a copy of the SF 30 to the contractor by certified mail return receipt requested.

[Final rule, 71 FR 27644, 5/12/2006, effective 5/12/2006]

249.109-70 Limitation on pricing of the terminated effort.

When there is a termination for convenience (partial or whole) or a change that reduces scope, the price of the terminated or reduced effort that the contractor is required to credit back to the Government shall not be more than the original amount placed on contract for that effort.

[Final rule, 84 FR 30953, 6/28/2019, effective 6/28/2019]

249.110 Settlement negotiation memorandum.

(1) *Fixed-price contracts.* Use the format in Table 49-1, Settlement Memorandum Fixed-Price Contracts, for the termination contracting officer's settlement memorandum for fixed-price contracts terminated for the convenience of the Government. Encourage contractors and subcontractors to use this format, appropriately modified, for subcontract settlements submitted for review and approval.

(2) *Cost-reimbursement contracts.* Use Part I of the format in Table 49-1 and Part II of the format in Table 49-2, Settlement Memorandum for Cost-Reimbursement Contracts, for the termination contracting officer's settlement memorandum for cost-reimbursement contracts:

TABLE 49-1, SETTLEMENT MEMORANDUM FIXED-PRICE CONTRACTS

PART I—GENERAL INFORMATION

1. *Identification.* (Identify memorandum as to its purpose and content.)

a. Name and address of the contractor. Comment on any pertinent affiliation between prime and subcontractors relative to the overall settlement.

b. Names and titles of both contractor and Government personnel who participated in the negotiation.

2. *Description of terminated contract.*

a. Date of contract and contract number.

b. Type of contract (e.g., fixed-price, fixed-price incentive).

c. General description of contract items.

d. Total contract price.

e. Furnish reference to the contract termination clauses (cite FAR/DFARS designation or other special provisions).

3. *Termination notice.*

a. Reference termination notice and state effective date of termination.

b. Scope and nature of termination (complete or partial), items terminated, and unit price and total price of items terminated.

c. State whether termination notice was amended, and explain any amendment.

d. State whether contractor stopped work on effective termination date. If not, furnish details.

e. State whether the contractor promptly terminated subcontracts.

f. Statement as to the diversion of common items and return of goods to suppliers, if any.

g. Furnish information as to contract performance and timeliness of deliveries by the contractor.

4. *Contractor's settlement proposal.*

a. *Date and amount.* Indicate date and location where claim was filed. State gross amount of claim. (If interim settlement proposals were filed, furnished information for each claim.)

b. *Basis of claim.* State whether claim was filed on inventory, total cost, or other basis. Explain rationale for approval when claim is filed on other than inventory basis.

c. *Examination of proposal.* State type of reviews made and by whom (audit, engineering, legal, or other).

PART II—SUMMARY OF CONTRACTOR'S CLAIM AND NEGOTIATED SETTLEMENT

Prepare a summary substantially as follows:

Item Claimed	Contractor's Proposal	Dollars Accepted	Costs Questioned	Unresolved Items	TCO Negotiated Amount
1. Contractor's costs as set forth on settlement proposal. Metals, raw materials, etc.					
Total					
2. Profit					
3. Settlement expenses					
4. Total					
5. Settlement with subs					

Item Claimed	Contractor's Proposal	Dollars Accepted	Costs Questioned	Unresolved Items	TCO Negotiated Amount
6. Acceptable finished product					
7. Gross Total					
8. Disposal and other credits					
9. Net settlement					
10. Partial progress & advance payments					
11. Net payments requested					

PART III—DISCUSSION OF SETTLEMENT

1. *Contractor's cost.*

a. If the settlement was negotiated on the basis of individual items, specify the factors and consideration for each item.

b. In the case of a lump-sum settlement, comment on the general basis for and major factors concerning each element of cost and profit included.

c. Comment on any important adjustments made to costs claimed or any significant amounts in relation to the total claim.

d. If a partial termination is involved, state whether the contractor has requested an equitable adjustment in the price of the continued portion of the contract.

e. Comment on any unadjusted contractual changes that are included in the settlement.

f. Comment on whether or not a loss would have been incurred and explain adjustment for loss, if any.

g. Furnish other information believed helpful to any reviewing authority in understanding the recommended settlement.

2. *Profit.* Explain the basis and factors considered in arriving at a fair profit.

3. *Settlement expenses.* Comment on and summarize those expenses not included in the audit review.

4. *Subcontractor's settlements.* Include the number of no-cost settlements, settlements concluded by the contractor under delegation of authority and those approved by the termination contracting officer, as well as the net amount of each.

5. *Partial payments.* Furnish the total amount of partial payments, if any.

6. *Progress or advance payments.* Furnish the total of unliquidated amounts, if any.

7. *Claims of the Government against the contractor included in settlement agreement reservations.* List all outstanding claims, if any, that the Government has against the contractor in connection with the terminated contract or terminated portion of the contract.

8. *Assignments.* List any assignments, giving name and address of assignee.

9. *Disposal credits.* Furnish information as to applicable disposal credits and give dollar amounts of all disposal credits.

10. *Plant clearance.* State whether plant clearance action has been completed and all inventory sold, retained, or otherwise properly disposed of in accordance with applicable plant clearance regulations. Comment on any unusual matters pertaining to plant clearances. Attach consolidated closing plant clearance report.

11. *Government property.* State whether all Government property has been accounted for.

12. *Special tooling.* If involved, furnish comment on disposition.

13. *Summary of settlement.* Summarize the settlement in tabular form substantially as follows:

TABULAR SUMMARY FOR COMPLETE OR PARTIAL TERMINATION

	Amount *Claimed*	Amount *Allowed*
Prime contractors charges (before disposal credits)		
Plus: Subcontractor charges (after disposal credits)		
Gross settlement:		
Less: disposal credits—Prime		
Net settlement—Less:		
Prior payment credits (this settlement)		
Previous partial settlements		
Other credits or deductions		
Net payment:		
Total contract price (complete termination)		
Contract Price of Items Terminated (for partial termination)—Less:		
Total payments to date		
Net payment from this settlement		
Fund reserved for reservations		
Reduction in contract price		

14. *Exclusions.* Describe any proposed reservation of rights to the Government or to the contractor.

15. *Include a statement that the settlement is fair and reasonable for the Government and the contractor.* The contracting officer shall sign and date the memorandum.

(End of memorandum)

TABLE 49-2, SETTLEMENT MEMORANDUM FOR COST-REIMBURSEMENT CONTRACTS

PART II—SUMMARY OF SETTLEMENT

1. *Summary.* Summarize the proposed settlement in tabular form substantially as shown in Tables 49-3 and 49-4. Partial settlements may be summarized on Table 49-4.

2. *Comments.* Explain tabular summaries.

a. Summary of final settlement (see Table 49-3).

(1) Explain why the auditor's final report was not available for consideration, if applicable.

(2) Explain how the fixed-fee was adjusted. Identify basis used, such as percentage of completion. Include a description of factors considered and how they were considered. Include any tabular summaries and breakdowns deemed helpful to an understanding of the process. Factors that may be given consideration are outlined in FAR 49.305.

(3) Briefly identify matters included in liability for property and other charges against the contractor arising from the contract.

(4) Identify reservations included in the settlement that are other than standard reservations required by regulations and that are concerned with pending claims and refunds.

(5) Explain substantial or otherwise important adjustments made in cost figures submitted by the contractor in arriving at the proposed settlement.

(6) If unreimbursed costs were settled on a lump sum basis, explain the general basis

for and the major factors considered in arriving at this settlement.

(7) Comment on any unusual items of cost included in the claim and on any phase of cost allocation requiring particular attention and not covered above.

(8) If the auditor's recommendations for nonacceptance were not followed, explain briefly the main reasons why such recommendations were not followed.

(9) On items recommended for further consideration by the auditor, explain, in general, the basis for the action taken.

(10) If any cost previously disallowed by a contracting officer is included in the proposed settlement, identify and explain the reason for inclusion of such costs.

(11) Show number and amounts of settlements with subcontractors.

(12) Use the following summary where settlement includes costs and fixed-fee in a complete termination:

Gross settlement		$_____
Less: Disposal credits		_____
Net settlement		_____
Less: Prior payments	_____	
Other credits or deductions	_____	
Total		_____
Net payment		$_____
Total contract estimated cost plus fixed fee		_____
Less: Net settlement	_____	
Estimated reserve for exclusions	_____	
Final contract price (Consisting of $_____ for reimbursement of costs and $_____ for adjusted fixed fee)	_____	_____
Reduction in contract price (credit)		_____

(13) *Plant clearance.* Indicate dollar value of termination inventory and state whether plant clearance has been completed. Attach consolidated plant clearance report (SF 1424, Inventory Disposal Report).

(14) *Government property.* State whether all Government property has been accounted for.

(15) *Include a statement that the settlement is fair and reasonable to the Government and the contractor.* The contracting officer shall sign and date the memorandum.

(End of memorandum)

TABLE 49-3, SUMMARY OF SETTLEMENT

		AMOUNT CLAIMED	AMOUNT ALLOWED
1.	Previous reimbursed costs—Prime and Subs	$_____	$_____
2.	Previous unreimbursed costs	$_____	$_____
3.	Total cost settlement	$_____	$_____
4.	Previous fees paid—Prime	$_____	$_____
5.	Previous fees unpaid—Prime	$_____	$_____

		AMOUNT CLAIMED	AMOUNT ALLOWED
6.	Total fee settlement	$______	$______
7.	Gross settlement	$______	$______
		$______	$______
	Less: Deductions not reflected in Items 1-7		
	a. Disposal credits $______		
	b. Other charges against contractor arising from contract $______		
8.	Net settlement		$______
	Less: Prior payment credits		$______
9.	Net payment		$______
10.	Recapitulation of previous settlements (insert number of previous partial settlements effected on account of this particular termination):		
	Aggregate gross amount of previous settlements		$______
	Aggregate net amount of previous partial settlements		$______
	Aggregate net payment provided in previous partial settlements		$______
	Aggregate amount allowed for prime contractor acquired property taken over by the Government in connection with previous partial settlements		$______

TABLE 49-4, UNREIMBURSED COSTS SUBMITTED ON SF 1437*

Costs	Amounts Claimed by Contractor's Proposal	Auditor's Recommendation: Cost Questioned	Auditor's Recommendation: Unresolved Items	TCO's Computation
1. Direct material				
2. Direct labor				
3. Indirect factory expense				
4. Dies, jigs, fixtures and special tools				
5. Other costs				
6. General and administrative expenses				
7. Fee				
8. Settlement expense				
9. Settlement with subs				

Costs	Amounts Claimed by Contractor's Proposal	Auditor's Recommendation		TCO's Computation
		Cost Questioned	Unresolved Items	
10. Total costs (Items 1-9)				

*Expand the format to include recommendations of technical personnel as required.

[Final rule, 71 FR 27644, 5/12/2006, effective 5/12/2006]

SUBPART 249.4—[REMOVED]

[Change notice, 20080722; Publication notice, 20101029]

SUBPART 249.70—SPECIAL TERMINATION REQUIREMENTS

249.7001 Congressional notification on significant contract terminations.

(1) Department and agency liaison offices will coordinate timing of the congressional notification and public release of the information with release of the termination notice to the contractor. Department and agency liaison offices are—

(i) Army - Chief, Legislative Liaison (SALL-SPA).

(ii) Navy - Chief of Legislative Affairs (OLA-N).

(iii) Air Force - SAF/AQC.

(iv) Defense Advanced Research Projects Agency – CMO.

(v) Defense Information Systems Agency - Contract Management Division (Code 260).

(vi) Defense Intelligence Agency – RSQ.

(vii) Defense Logistics Agency - DLSC-P.

(viii) National Geospatial-Intelligence Agency - NGA(A).

(ix) Defense Threat Reduction Agency - Acquisition Management Office (AM).

(x) National Security Agency/Central Security Service - Chief, Office of Contracting.

(xi) Missile Defense Agency - Director of Contracts (MDA-DCT).

(2) Request clearance to release information in accordance with departmental procedures as soon as possible after the decision to terminate is made. Until clearance has been obtained, treat this information as "For Official Use Only" unless the information is classified.

(3) Include in the request for clearance—

(i) Contract number, date, and type of contract;

(ii) Name of the company;

(iii) Nature of contract or end item;

(iv) The reason for the termination;

(v) Contract price of the items terminated;

(vi) Total number of contractor employees involved, including the Government's estimate of the number who may be discharged;

(vii) Statement of anticipated impact on the company and the community;

(viii) The area labor category, whether the contractor is a large or small business, and any known impact on hard core disadvantaged employment programs;

(ix) Total number of subcontractors involved and the impact in this area; and

(x) An unclassified draft of a suggested press release.

(4) To minimize termination costs, liaison offices will act promptly on all requests for clearance and will provide a response not later than two working days after receipt of the request.

(5) This reporting requirement is assigned Report Control Symbol DD-AT & L (AR)1412.

[Final rule, 71 FR 27644, 5/12/2006, effective 5/12/2006; Final rule, 74 FR 42779, 8/25/2009, effective 8/25/2009]

PART 250—EXTRAORDINARY CONTRACTUAL ACTIONS AND THE SAFETY ACT

Table of Contents

Subpart 250.1—Extraordinary Contractual Actions

General 250.101
Records 250.101-3
Contract adjustments 250.103
Processing cases 250.103-5
Disposition 250.103-6

PART 250—EXTRAORDINARY CONTRACTUAL ACTIONS AND THE SAFETY ACT

SUBPART 250.1—EXTRAORDINARY CONTRACTUAL ACTIONS

250.101 General. (No Text)

[Final rule, 73 FR 46814, 8/12/2008, effective 8/12/2008]

250.101-3 Records.

(1) Departments and agencies shall—

(i) Prepare a preliminary record when a request for a contract adjustment under FAR 50.103 is filed (see DFARS 250.103-5 (1).

(ii) Prepare a final record stating the disposition of the request (see PGI 250.103-6).

(iii) Designate the offices or officials responsible for preparing, submitting, and receiving all records required by DFARS Subpart 250.1. Records shall be maintained by the contract adjustment boards of the Army, Navy, and Air Force, respectively, and by the headquarters of the defense agencies.

(2) A suggested format for the record is the Record of Request for Adjustment shown at the end of this section. This format permits the information required for the preliminary and final records to be combined on one form. The following instructions are provided for those items in the format that are not self-explanatory:

(i) *Extent of performance as of date of request.* State the degree of completion of the contract; e.g., 50 percent completed or performance not yet begun. If work is completed, state the date of completion and whether final payment has been made.

(ii) *Award procedure.* State whether the contract was awarded under sealed bidding or negotiated procedures. Cite the specific authority for using other than full and open competition, if applicable, e.g., 10 U.S.C. 2304(c)(1).

(iii) *Type of contract.* State the type of contract (see FAR Part 16); e.g., FFP (firm-fixed-price).

(iv) *Category of case.* State whether the request involves a modification without consideration, a mistake, or an informal commitment. If the case involves more than one category, identify both; list the most significant category first.

(v) *Amount or description of request.* If the request is expressed in dollars, state the amount and whether it is an increase or decrease. If the request cannot be expressed in monetary terms, provide a brief description; e.g., "Cancellation" or "Modification." Even if the adjustment is not easily expressed in terms of dollars, if the contractor has made an estimate in the request, that estimate should be stated.

(vi) *Action below Secretarial level.* State the disposition of the case, the office that took the action and the date the action was taken. The disposition should be stated as "Withdrawn," "Denied," "Approved," or "Forwarded." If the request was approved, in whole or in part, state the dollar amount or nature of the action (as explained in paragraph (2)(v) of this section). The date should correspond with the date of the memorandum of decision or of the letter forwarding the request to the contract adjustment board or other deciding body.

(vii) *Action by contract adjustment board and date.* State the disposition and date of disposition of the case by the contract adjustment board. Provide the same information as for paragraph (2)(vi) of this section.

(viii) *Implementation and date.* State the appropriate action; e.g., "Modification," "New Contract," or "Letter of Denial."

<table>
<tr><td>☐ PRELIMINARY</td><td colspan="2">RECORD OF
REQUEST FOR ADJUSTMENT
PUBLIC LAW 85-804</td><td>FINAL ☐</td></tr>
<tr><td>DATE OF REQUEST</td><td colspan="2"></td><td>DATE RECEIVED BY GOVERNMENT</td></tr>
<tr><td colspan="4">CONTRACTOR'S NAME AND ADDRESS
☐ SMALL BUSINESS</td></tr>
<tr><td colspan="4">NAME AND ADDRESS OF CONTRACTOR'S REPRESENTATIVE, IF ANY</td></tr>
<tr><td colspan="2">COGNIZANT CONTRACTING OFFICER OR OFFICE</td><td colspan="2">PROCURING ACTIVITY</td></tr>
<tr><td colspan="2">PROPERTY OR SERVICE INVOLVED</td><td colspan="2">EXTENT OF PERFORMANCE AS OF DATE OF REQUEST</td></tr>
<tr><td>CONTRACT NUMBER</td><td>DATE</td><td>ADVERTISED OR NEGOTIATED</td><td>TYPE OF CONTRACT</td></tr>
<tr><td colspan="2">CATEGORY OF CASE</td><td colspan="2">AMOUNT OF DESCRIPTION OF REQUEST</td></tr>
<tr><td colspan="3">ACTION BELOW SECRETARIAL LEVEL</td><td>DATE</td></tr>
<tr><td colspan="3">ACTION BY CAB</td><td>DATE</td></tr>
<tr><td colspan="3">IMPLEMENTATION</td><td>DATE</td></tr>
<tr><td colspan="4">ADDITIONAL DATA OR REMARKS</td></tr>
<tr><td colspan="2">DATE THIS RECORD SIGNED</td><td colspan="2">SIGNATURE</td></tr>
</table>

[Final rule, 70 FR 67923, 11/9/2005, effective 11/9/2005; Final rule, 73 FR 46814, 8/12/2008, effective 8/12/2008]

250.103 Contract adjustments. (No Text)

[Final rule, 73 FR 46814, 8/12/2008, effective 8/12/2008]

250.103-5 Processing cases.

(1) The officer or official responsible for the case shall forward to the contract adjustment board, through departmental channels, two copies of the following:

(i) A letter stating—

(A) The nature of the case;

(B) The basis for the board's authority to act;

(C) The findings of fact essential to the case (see FAR 50.103-4). Arrange the findings chronologically with cross-references to supporting enclosures;

(D) The conclusions drawn;

(E) The recommended disposition; and

(F) If contractual action is recommended, a statement by the signer that the action will facilitate the national defense.

(ii) The contractor's request.

(iii) All evidentiary materials.

(iv) All endorsements, reports and comments of cognizant Government officials.

(2) A letter to the Board recommending an amendment without consideration where essentiality is a factor (see FAR 50.103-2 (a)(1)) should also provide—

(i) The information required by FAR 50.103-4(a) and (b), and

(ii) Findings as to—

(A) The contractor's performance record, including the quality of product, rate of production, and promptness of deliveries;

(B) The importance to the Government, particularly to the active duty military, of the performance of the contract and the importance of the contractor to the national defense;

(C) The forecast of future contracts with the contractor; and

(D) Other available sources of supply for the supplies or services covered by the contract, and the time and cost of having contract performance completed by such other sources.

[Final rule, 70 FR 67923, 11/9/2005, effective 11/9/2005; Final rule, 73 FR 46814, 8/12/2008, effective 8/12/2008]

250.103-6 Disposition.

(1) When the request for relief is denied or approved below the Secretarial level, submit the following documents to the appropriate office within 30 days after the close of the month in which the decision is executed:

(i) Two copies of the memorandum of decision.

(ii) Except for the Army, one copy of the contractual document implementing any decision approving contractual action.

(iii) One copy of a final record, as described at PGI 250.101-3.

(2) When a contract adjustment board decision is implemented, the activity that forwarded the case to the board shall prepare and submit to the board the documents identified in paragraphs (1)(ii) and (iii) of this section.

[Final rule, 70 FR 67923, 11/9/2005, effective 11/9/2005; Final rule, 73 FR 46814, 8/12/2008, effective 8/12/2008]

PART 251—USE OF GOVERNMENT SOURCES BY CONTRACTORS

Table of Contents

Subpart 251.1—Contractor Use of Government Supply Sources

Authorization to use Government supply sources 251.102
Contracting office responsibilities 251.102-70

PART 251—CONTRACTOR USE OF GOVERNMENT SUPPLY SOURCES

SUBPART 251.1—CONTRACTOR USE OF GOVERNMENT SUPPLY SOURCES

251.102 Authorization to use Government supply sources.

Use a format substantially the same as the following when authorizing contractor use of Government Supply Sources. Specify the terms of the purchase, including contractor acceptance of any Government materiel, payment terms, and the addresses required by paragraph (e) of the clause at 252.251-7000, Ordering from Government Supply Sources.

AUTHORIZATION TO PURCHASE FROM GOVERNMENT SUPPLY SOURCES (SAMPLE FORMAT)

SUBJECT: Authorization to Purchase from Government Supply Sources

____

(Contractor's Name)

____

(Contractor's Address)

____

(CAGE Code)

1. You are hereby authorized to use Government sources in performing Contract No. _______________ for *[insert the requiring activity's DoD Activity Address Code (doDAAC)]*,, as follows: *[Insert applicable purchasing authority given to the contractor.]*

2.a. Purchase Orders Under Federal Supply Schedules or Personal Property Rehabilitation Price Schedules. Place orders in accordance with the terms and conditions of the attached Schedule(s) and this authorization. Attach a copy of this authorization to the order (unless a copy was previously furnished to the Federal Supply Schedule or Personal Property Rehabilitation Price Schedule contractor). Insert the following statement in the order:

This order is placed under written authorization from ____________________ dated __________ (* __________). In the event of any inconsistency between the terms and conditions of this order and those of the Federal Supply Schedule or Personal Property Rehabilitation Price Schedule contract, the latter will govern.

b. Requisitioning from the General Services Administration (GSA) or the Department of Defense (DoD). Place orders in accordance with this authorization and, as appropriate, the following:

(1) Federal Standard Requisitioning and Issue Procedures (FEDSTRIP) (GSA FEDSTRIP Operating Guide: FPMR 101-26.2 (41 CFR 101-26.2)). Copies are available from the Superintendent of Documents, Government Printing Office, Washington, DC 20402; telephone (202) 512-1800; facsimile (202) 512-2250.

(2) Military Standard Requisitioning and Issue Procedures (MILSTRIP) (DoD 4000.25-1-M). Copies are available from the Defense Logistics Agency, Administrative Support Center East, ATTN: ASCE-WS, 14 Dedication Drive, Suite 3, POD 43, New Cumberland, PA 17070-5011; telephone 1-888-DLA-PUBS(352-7827), or (717) 770-6034; facsimile (717) 770-4817.

c. Enterprise Software Initiative. Place orders in accordance with the terms and conditions of the attached Enterprise Software Agreement(s), or instructions for obtaining commercial software or software maintenance from Enterprise Software Initiative inventories, and this authorization. Attach a copy of this authorization to the order (unless a copy was previously furnished to the Enterprise Software Agreement contractor). Insert the following statement in the order:

This order is placed under written authorization from ____________________ dated__________ (*__________). In the event of any inconsistency between the terms and conditions of this order, and those of the Enterprise Software Agreement, the latter will govern.

3. [*Insert other provisions as necessary.*]

---

* Insert "a copy of which is attached," "a copy of which you have on file," or other suitable language, as appropriate.

4. This authority is not transferable or assignable.

5. The DoD Activity Address Directory (DoDAAD) (DLM 4000.25, Volume 6, Chapter 2) Activity Address Code** to which this Authorization applies is ________.

6. This Authorization expires ________________________.

__________ (Contracting Officer)

[Final rule, 69 FR 67858, 11/22/2004, effective 11/22/2004; Publication notice, 20121212, 12/12/2012; Publication notice, 20130516; Publication notice, 20140228]

251.102-70 Contracting office responsibilities.

(a) The DoD Activity Address Code (DoDAAC) assigned in accordance with paragraph 5 of the authorization format in PGI 251.102 shall be assigned to the contractor for authorization to use Government supply sources only for the contract number cited in paragraph 1 of the authorization format.

(b) The authorization to use Government sources of supply is unique to each contract and shall not be transferred or assigned to any other contractor or contract. Therefore, the same DoDAAC shall not be assigned to any other contract number during the period of performance for the contract. After 24 months has lapsed beyond contract closeout, the DoDAAC may be reused for another contract.

[Publication notice, 20140228]

** The sponsoring service assumes responsibility for monitoring and controlling all activity address codes used in the letters of authority.

PART 252—SOLICITATION PROVISIONS AND CONTRACT CLAUSES

Table of Contents

Subpart 252.1—Instructions for Using Provisions and Clauses

Identification of provisions and clauses. 252.103

PART 252—SOLICITATION PROVISIONS AND CONTRACT CLAUSES

SUBPART 252.1—INSTRUCTIONS FOR USING PROVISIONS AND CLAUSES

252.103 Identification of provisions and clauses.

(c) Local provisions and clauses developed by departments and agencies for a single-use intended to meet the needs of an individual acquisition shall be identified by the title, date, and name of the department or agency that developed the local clause. For example, if "X" Agency negotiated a single-use clause for use of special government facilities during discussions, such clause would be identified in the contract as follows:

"Special Use of Government Facilities (DATE) X Agency"

(d) (1) (A) Local provisions and clauses that will be used on a repetitive basis shall be identified by—

(*1*) The chapter assigned to the department or agency under Title 48 of the Code of Federal Regulations (CFR);

(*2*) FAR subpart "52.2";

(*3*) The applicable FAR part;

(*4*) A four-digit sequential number in the 9000 series for the suffix (see DFARS 252.101(b) (2) (ii) (B));

(*5*) Title; and

(*6*) Date.

(B) For example, if "Y" Agency is assigned a CFR chapter number 99, and has developed a provision regarding an evaluation factor for past performance to be used on a repetitive basis in negotiated acquisitions, such provision would be identified as follows:

"9952.215-9XXX Past Performance Evaluation Factor (AUG 2015)"

[Final rule, 80 FR 36718, 6/26/2015, effective 6/26/2015; Publication notice, 20150826]

PART 253—FORMS

Table of Contents

Subpart 253.2—Prescription of Forms

[Removed] 253.204

Required sources of supplies and services 253.208

DD Form 448, Military Interdepartmental Purchase Request 253.208-1

DD Form 448-2, Acceptance of MIPR 253.208-2

Simplified acquisition procedures (SF's 18, 30, 44, 1165, 1449, and OF's 336, 347, and 348) 253.213

Completion of DD Form 1155, Order for Supplies or Services 253.213-70

Contracting by Negotiation 253.215

DD Form 1547, Record of Weighted Guidelines Application 253.215-70

Small Business Programs. 253.219

DD Form 2579, Small Business Coordination Record. 253.219-70

PART 253—FORMS

SUBPART 253.2—PRESCRIPTION OF FORMS

253.204 [Removed]

[Final rule, 71 FR 44926, 8/8/2006, effective 8/8/2006; Final rule, 74 FR 37644, 7/29/2009, effective 7/29/2009]

253.208 Required sources of supplies and services. (No Text)

[Final rule, 71 FR 39004, 7/11/2006, effective 7/11/2006]

253.208-1 DD Form 448, Military Interdepartmental Purchase Request.

(a) Use the DD Form 448 as prescribed in PGI 208.70.

(b) Prepare MIPR information in uniform contract format when possible. Overprint of fixed repetitive information is authorized.

(c) Instructions for completion of DD Form 448.

(1) BLOCK 5–MIPR NUMBER. Number the MIPR by using—

(i) The requiring department identification code as prescribed in DoD 4000.25-6-M, Department of Defense Activity Address Directory (DoDAAD);

(ii) The last digit of the fiscal year; and

(iii) The number of the particular MIPR (numbered consecutively by the requiring activity).

(2) BLOCK 6–AMEND NO. Assign a suffix number. Assign amendments of the same MIPR consecutive suffix numbers.

(3) BLOCK 9.

(i) Conduct interdepartmental screening of items in accordance with FAR 8.001. Requisition items which are available from stocks of other departments as follows:

(A) Obtain items within the scope of MILSTRIP (see DoD 4000.25-1-M, Military Standard Requisitioning and Issue Procedures (MILSTRIP)) by use of DD Form 1348 (Single Line Item Requisition System Document (Manual), DoD))/1348M (Single Line Item Requisition System Document, DoD (Mechanical)).

(B) Obtain items not covered by MILSTRIP using DD Form 1149, Requisition and Invoice/Shipping Document.

(C) If, after receipt of a MIPR, it is determined the requested items are available from stock, the acquiring department shall use the MIPR to obtain the item.

(ii) Normally restrict a MIPR to one major end item, including its required spare parts, ground support equipment, and similar related items. For other than major end items, limit MIPRs to items within a single Federal supply class when possible.

(4) BLOCK 10.

(i) Delivery Schedules.

(A) The requiring department must clearly state the required time of delivery or performance in each MIPR, taking into consideration the normal administrative lead time of the particular commodity. Delivery and performance schedules on MIPRs must be realistic (see FAR Subpart 11.4). If the acquiring department cannot accept the delivery schedule in the MIPR, the acquiring department will note that on DD Form 448-2, Acceptance of MIPR. Changes in the requested delivery schedule must be made by MIPR amendment.

(B) When a short delivery schedule is mandatory, the requiring department shall mark the MIPR "URGENT" in bold letters and provide justification for the marking.

(ii) Requiring activities must provide MILSTRIP requisition data prescribed in Appendix B of the MILSTRIP Manual for each line item which is to be delivered to each "ship to" address. Repetitive data applicable to all lines on the MIPR may be overprinted.

(iii) The requiring activity will furnish estimated weight, cube, and dimensions for each line item or a statement explaining why these data are not available.

(iv) The requiring activity shall include the name and telephone number of an individual who is thoroughly familiar with the MIPR, its attachments, and technical requirements.

(v) Prepare attachments to MIPRs in sufficient numbers so that each copy of a MIPR submitted to the acquiring department is complete with a copy of all attachments. “Ship To and Mark For” addresses in shipping instructions must include the clear text identification and DoDAAD code if assigned.

(5) BLOCK 12–TRANSPORTATION ALLOTMENT. Enter allotment data for transportation of supplies at Government expense if appropriate.

(6) BLOCK 13–MAIL INVOICES TO. Use this block to identify the name and address of the office to receive invoices and make payment.

(i) Complete the block only if—

(A) The resulting contract is not to be paid by the Defense Finance and Accounting Service; and

(B) The office to receive invoices and make payment is known at the time of preparation of the MIPR.

(ii) If payment is to be made by an office designated to receive invoices, also enter the DoDAAD code of that office.

(iii) If payment is to be made by an office other than the office to which the invoice is to be mailed, include the name, address, and DoDAAD code of the payment office as an attachment to the MIPR.

(iv) If multiple offices are to receive invoices and make payment, include the names and addresses of those offices as an attachment to the MIPR. Also include the DoDAAD code of each payment office.

(v) Whenever the payment office is included in an attachment, include a reference to the attachment in this block.

(vi) If the names and addresses of invoicing and payment offices are provided the acquiring department after submission of the MIPR, the requiring department also must provide the DoDAAD code for each payment office.

(7) BLOCK 14. Enter allotment data for the acquisition of supplies. Enter each citation in Item 14 in the appropriate space as follows:

(i) Accounting Classification Reference Number (ACRN). If the ACRN procedures of PGI 204.7107 are used in the MIPR to relate allotment data to the MIPR item or delivery, enter the ACRN for each fund citation. (The acquiring department, when preparing the contract, is not required to use the ACRN assigned to a fund citation in the MIPR.)

(ii) Appropriation. Enter the ten positions as follows:

(A) First and second - Treasury Department number identifying the department or agency to which the appropriation applies or has been transferred.

(B) Third and fourth - Treasury Department number identifying the department or agency from which an appropriation has been transferred; leave blank if no transfer is involved.

(C) Fifth and sixth - Identify the appropriation fiscal year. For multiple-year appropriations, the fifth position shall be the last digit of the first year of availability, and the sixth position shall be the last digit of the final year of availability. For annual appropriations, the fifth position shall be blank, and the sixth position shall be the last digit of the fiscal year. For no-year (continuing) appropriations, the fifth position shall be blank, and the sixth position shall be “X.”

(D) Seventh through tenth - Treasury Department appropriation serial number.

(iii) Limit/Subhead. Up to four characters; if less than four characters, leave empty spaces blank.

(iv) Supplemental Accounting Classification Data. Not to exceed 36 characters. Enter in accordance with departmental or agency regulations.

(v) Accounting Station. Enter the six character DoDAAD code of the accounting station (not used with Navy and Marine Corps funds).

(vi) Amount. Enter the amount for each fund citation if more than one allotment is cited.

(vii) Additional Citations. If space is required for additional fund citations, include as an attachment and reference the attachment on the form.

(d) When preparing a MIPR amendment, always fill out the basic information in Blocks 1 through 8. Fill out only those other blocks which vary from the data shown on the basic MIPR or a prior amendment. Insert "n/c" in items where there is no change.

(e) Change of a disbursing office cited on a DoD funded MIPR does not require a MIPR amendment when the resultant contract is assigned for administration to the Defense Contract Management Agency. The administrative contracting office may issue an administrative contract modification, copies of which will be provided to the contracting officer for transmittal to the requiring activity.

(f) Signed or official record copies of MIPRs, and any amendments, shall be distributed electronically using both of the following methods:

(1) Indexed Portable Document Format files shall be manually uploaded or sent via the Global Exchange system (GEX) to the Electronic Data Access (EDA) (*http://eda.ogden.disa.mil*) system to provide a human-readable copy.

(2) Electronic data files shall be sent via the GEX in Department of Defense Purchase Request Data Standard Extensible Markup Language (XML) format.

[Final rule, 71 FR 39004, 7/11/2006, effective 7/11/2006; Publication notice, 20130516; Publication notice, 20190913]

253.208-2 DD Form 448-2, Acceptance of MIPR.

(a) Use the DD Form 448-2 as prescribed in PGI 208.70.

(b) Instructions for completion of DD Form 448-2. (Complete only the applicable blocks.)

(1) *BLOCK 6.* Check the specific terms under which the MIPR is being accepted.

(2) *BLOCK 7.* If any one of the MIPR line items is not accepted, check Block 7 and record the affected MIPR line item number and reason in Block 13.

(3) *BLOCKS 8 AND 9.* Use Blocks 8 and 9 only—

(i) When Block 6c acceptance is indicated (indicate the MIPR line item numbers that will be provided under each method of financing in Blocks 8a and 9a, respectively); or

(ii) If quantities or estimated costs cited in a MIPR require adjustment (list the affected MIPR line item numbers together with the adjusted quantities or estimated costs in the columns provided under Blocks 8 and 9, as appropriate).

(4) *BLOCK 10.* Whenever a MIPR is accepted in part or in total under Category II funding, forecast the estimated date of contract award.

(5) *BLOCK 11.* Enter the total amount of funds required to fund the MIPR items, as accepted.

(6) *BLOCK 12.*

(i) Complete this block only in those cases where the amount recorded in Block 11 is not in agreement with the amount recorded in Block 5. This will serve either—

(A) As a request to the requiring department to issue a MIPR amendment to provide the additional funds; or

(B) Authority for the requiring department to withdraw the available excess funds.

(ii) When funds of two or more appropriations are involved, provide proper breakdown information in Block 13.

(7) *BLOCK 13.* Use this block to record—

(i) Justification, by MIPR line item, for any additional funds required;

(ii) Explanation for rejection of MIPR whether in part or in total;

(iii) Appropriation and subhead data cited on the MIPR; and

(iv) Other pertinent data.

(c) Complete a DD Form 448-2 for all MIPR amendments involving an adjustment of funds or delivery schedule, or if requested by the requiring department.

(d) Unless otherwise agreed, provide the requiring department an original and three copies of each DD Form 448-2.

[Final rule, 71 FR 39004, 7/11/2006, effective 7/11/2006]

253.213 Simplified acquisition procedures (SF's 18, 30, 44, 1165, 1449, and OF's 336, 347, and 348).

(f) (i) Use the OF 336, or a sheet of paper, as a continuation sheet for the DD Form

1155. Continuation sheets may be printed on the reverse of the DD Form 1155.

(ii) DD Form 1155c-1, Order for Supplies or Services (Commissary Continuation Sheet) may be used for commissary acquisitions.

[Final rule, 71 FR 3412, 1/23/2006, effective 1/23/2006]

253.213-70 Completion of DD Form 1155, Order for Supplies or Services.

(a) The following instructions are mandatory if—

(1) Contract administration has been assigned outside the purchasing office; or

(2) The contractor is located in the contiguous United States or Canada.

(b) The entity codes (address codes) referenced in this subsection are codes published in—

(1) DoD Activity Address Directory (DODAAD), DoD 4000.25-6-M.

(2) Military Assistance Program Address Directory System (MAPAD), DoD 4000.25-8-M.

(3) Commercial and Government Entity (CAGE) Codes Handbook H4/H8.

(c) For orders requiring payment in Canadian currency—

(1) State the contract price in terms of Canadian dollars, followed by the initials CN; e.g., $1,647.23CN.

(2) Indicate on the face of the order—

(i) The U.S./Canadian conversion rate in effect at the time of the award; and

(ii) The U.S. dollar equivalent of the Canadian dollar amount.

(d) When the DD Form 1155 includes FMS requirements, clearly mark "FMS Requirement" on its face. Specify within the order each FMS case identifier code by line or subline item number.

(e) Instructions for DD Form 1155 entries. (Instructions apply to purchase orders, delivery orders, and calls, except Block 2, which applies only to delivery orders and calls, and Block 12, which applies only to purchase orders.)

BLOCK

1 CONTRACT/PURCH ORDER/AGREEMENT NO.—Enter the Procurement Instrument Identification (PII) number and, when applicable, the supplementary identification number for contracts, purchase orders, and agreements as prescribed in DFARS subpart 204.16.

2 DELIVERY ORDER/CALL NO.—Enter the PII number for delivery orders/calls, when applicable, as prescribed in DFARS subpart 204.16.

3 DATE OF ORDER/CALL—Enter the four-position numeric year, three-position alpha month, and two-position numeric day.

4 REQUISITION/PURCH REQUEST NO.—Enter the number authorizing the purchase. When the number differs by line item, list it in the Schedule and annotate this block, "See Schedule."

5 PRIORITY—Enter the appropriate Program Identification Code as identified in Schedule I to the Defense Priorities and Allocations System Regulation.

6 ISSUED BY—Enter the name and address of the issuing office. In the code block, enter the DoDAAD code for the issuing office. Directly below the address, enter: Buyer/Symbol: followed by the buyer's name and routing symbol. Directly below the buyer/symbol, enter: Phone: followed by the buyer's phone number and extension.

7 ADMINISTERED BY—Enter the name and address of the contract administration activity. On purchase orders retained by purchasing offices for administration, mark this block, "See Block 6." Enter in the code block the DODAAD code of the contract administration activity. In the lower right or left-hand corner, enter the criticality designator code from FAR 42.1105.

8 DELIVERY FOB—Check the applicable box.

9 CONTRACTOR—

(1) Enter the full business name and address of the contractor. Enter in the first code block, the CAGE code of the contractor.

(2) If it is known that all the work covered by the order is to be performed at an address different from the address represented

by the contractor's code, and any contract administration function will be required at that facility, enter in the facility code block the organizational entity code for that facility, i.e., H8-1/H8-2 code for a non-Government entity or DODAAD code for a Government entity. (Use DODAAD codes only to indicate "performed at" locations for orders specifying services at a Government location.) If it is known that multiple facilities are involved, enter the codes for all facilities at which work is to be performed, including the contractor's code if work is performed at that address, in the Optional Form 336 Continuation Sheet and mark the facility code block with "See Schedule."

10 DELIVER TO FOB POINT BY (Date)—If a single date of delivery applies to the entire order, enter date in this block. List multiple delivery dates in the schedule and mark this block "See Schedule."

11 MARK IF BUSINESS—Check all applicable blocks.

12 DISCOUNT TERMS—Enter the discount for prompt payment in terms of percentages and corresponding days. Express the percentages in whole numbers and decimals, e.g., 3.25% - 10 days; 0.50% - 20 days.

13 MAIL INVOICES TO THE ADDRESS IN BLOCK—Enter a reference to the block number containing the address to which invoices are to be mailed. When not in Block 6, 7, 14, or 15, insert in Block 13, "See Schedule."

14 SHIP TO—If a single ship-to point applies to the entire order, enter the name and address of that point in this block and a DODAAD code in the code block. For FMS shipments, enter the MAPAD code in the code block and an instruction for the contractor to contact the transportation office of the administering activity to obtain a name and a shipping address. Enter multiple ship-to points in the Schedule and mark this block, "See Schedule."

15 PAYMENT WILL BE MADE BY—Enter the name and address of the activity making payment. Enter in the code block, the DODAAD code of the paying activity. When a purchase card is used for payment, enter "CRCARD" in the code block.

16 TYPE OF ORDER—Check the appropriate box. If a purchase order:

(1) Identify the type of quotation, e.g., oral, letter, e-mail, on which the order is based.

(2) Check the box when acceptance of the purchase order is required and enter the number of copies of the order to be returned to the issuing office.

17 ACCOUNTING AND APPROPRIATION DATA/LOCAL USE—Enter the accounting classification and the accounting classification reference number(s) in accordance with DFARS 204.7107.

18 ITEM NO.—Enter an item number for each item of supply or service in accordance with DFARS Subpart 204.71.

19 SCHEDULE OF SUPPLIES/SERVICES—The Schedule contains several elements of data. The order and arrangement of data in the Schedule is mandatory for purchase and delivery orders assigned to the Defense Contract Management Agency or the military departments for administration and is encouraged for all orders.

(1) *National Stock Number (NSN)*—Total item quantity for the line or subline item number followed by the appropriate national stock number or the word "none" if an NSN has not been assigned. On the same line and adjacent to NSN, enter the words "Total Item Quantity." This phrase is used in conjunction with the total quantity, unit of issue, unit price, and dollar amount of the stock number or item cited (see entries for Blocks 20, 21, 22, and 23).

(2) *Item Identification*—Enter first the most descriptive noun or verb of the supplies or services to be furnished, supplemented by additional description as prescribed in FAR Part 10. If multiple accounting classifications apply to the contract, enter the accounting classification reference number.

(3) *Quantity Variance*—Enter the quantity variance permitted for the line item in terms of percentages, indicating whether the per-

centage is plus or minus and if applicable to each destination.

(4) *Inspection/Acceptance*—Enter the point at which inspection/acceptance will take place.

(5) *Preservation and Packaging*—Enter the preservation requirements for the item described. These requirements may be expressed in terms of MIL-STD-2073-1, DoD Material Procedures for Development and Application of Packaging Requirements, and MIL-STD-2073-2, Packaging Requirements, codes. They may also be expressed by reference to applicable specifications.

(6) *Packing*—When required, enter the packing level designator and specification, standard, or document in which the requirements are stated or state the specific requirements.

(7) *Unitization*—When desired by the requiring activity, a requirement for cargo unitization for a particular destination should be specified for shipments involving two or more shipping containers having an aggregate total of not less than 20 cubic feet or 200 pounds.

(8) *Ship To*—Enter the DODAAD or MILSCAP H8-1/H8-2 (cage) as appropriate for the entity code of the ship-to point on the first line and the corresponding name and address on succeeding lines. If multiple accounting classifications apply to the same line or subline item, enter the accounting classification reference number. When several items are to be shipped to the same point, the code will be listed; but it will not be necessary to repeat the address.

(9) *Delivery Date*—When multiple delivery dates apply, enter the required date of delivery on the same line with ship-to code.

(10) *Mark For*—Enter the DODAAD or MILSCAP H8-1/H8-2 (cage) as appropriate for the entity code on the first line and name and address of the ultimate recipient of the supplies and services on succeeding lines.

20 QUANTITY ORDERED/ACCEPTED—Enter the total quantity ordered for the line item. If applicable, enter the breakdown on quantities for each ship-to point within the line item.

21 UNIT—Enter the unit of measure applicable to the line item.

22 UNIT PRICE—Enter the unit price applicable to the line item.

23 AMOUNT—Enter the extended dollar amount (quantity x unit price) for each line item.

24 CONTRACTING/ORDERING OFFICER—Enter the contracting/ordering officer's signature.

25 TOTAL AMOUNT—Enter the total dollar amount for all line items on the order.

26 thru 42 These blocks are used in the receiving and payment functions. Procedures for making entries are prescribed by the respective departments.

[Final rule, 71 FR 3412, 1/23/2006, effective 1/23/2006; Change notice, 20090715; Final rule, 81 FR 9783, 2/26/2016, effective 2/26/2016]

253.215 Contracting by negotiation. (No Text)

[Final rule, 71 FR 69492, 12/1/2006, effective 12/1/2006]

253.215-70 DD Form 1547, Record of Weighted Guidelines Application.

(a) Use the DD Form 1547 as prescribed in DFARS DFARS 215.404-70 and 215.404-71.

(b) *General instructions*.

(1) Report amounts as they relate to the price of the contract action without regard to funding status (e.g., amounts obligated).

(2) Express all dollar values to the nearest whole value (e.g., $200,008.55 = $200,009).

(3) Do not express percentages beyond the nearest thousandth (e.g., interest rate—8.257%).

(4) If the contracting office is exempt from reporting to the DoD management information system on profit and fee statistics (see PGI 215.404-76), do not complete Block 1, 4, 5, 6, 7, 8, 9, 10, 11, or 12.

(5) Report an option amount for additional quantities as a separate contract action when exercised.

(6) Even though fixed-price type contract actions are negotiated on the basis of total price, prepare the negotiation summary por-

tion of the DD Form 1547 showing the contracting officer's best estimates of cost and profit.

(7) For indefinite-delivery type contracts, prepare a consolidated DD Form 1547 for annual requirements expected to exceed the certified cost or pricing data threshold.

(8) Prepare a consolidated DD Form 1547, if possible, when multiple profit rates apply to a single negotiation.

(c) *Specific instructions for completion of DD Form 1547.*

(1) BLOCK 1—REPORT NO. Enter the four-digit local control number followed by a dash and the last two digits of the fiscal year (e.g., 0004-06 for 4th action in fiscal year 2006). Each field contracting office participating in profit reporting shall establish a control system for consecutively numbering completed DD Forms 1547. Always start with 0001 at the beginning of each fiscal year and always use four digits. This number will identify the specific DD Form 1547 in DoD's management information system and will be used for follow-up actions.

(2) BLOCK 2—BASIC PROCUREMENT INSTRUMENT IDENTIFICATION NO. Enter the identifying contract number assigned per DFARS Subpart 204.16DFARS subpart.

(3) BLOCK 3—SPIIN. Enter the supplemental procurement instrument identification number for supplemental agreements or other modifications, assigned per DFARS Subpart 204.16.

(4) BLOCK 4—DATE OF ACTION.

(i) Year. Enter the last two digits of the year the action was negotiated (e.g., 06 for 2006).

(ii) Month. Enter the two-digit number for the month the action was negotiated (e.g., 09 for September).

(5) BLOCK 5—CONTRACTING OFFICE CODE. Enter the code assigned the contracting office per DoD Procurement Coding Manual, Volume III.

(6) BLOCK 6—NAME OF CONTRACTOR. Enter the contractor's name (including division name).

(7) BLOCK 7—DUNS NUMBER. Enter the contractor establishment code number.

(8) BLOCK 8—FEDERAL SUPPLY CODE.

(9) BLOCK 9—DOD CLAIMANT PROGRAM.

(10) BLOCK 10—CONTRACT TYPE CODE. Enter the appropriate code—

Description	Code
FPR (all types)	A
FPI (all types)	L
FFP	J
FP(E)	K
CPFF	U
CPIF (all types)	V

(11) BLOCK 11—TYPE EFFORT. Enter the appropriate code—

Description	Code
Manufacturing	1
Research and Development	2
Services	3

(12) BLOCK 12—USE CODE. Enter the appropriate code for use of the weighted guidelines method—

Description	Code
Standard weighted guidelines method (DFARS 215.404-71-2(c)(1))	2
Alternate structured approach (DFARS 215.404-73)	4
Modified weighted guidelines approach (DFARS 215.404-72)	5
Technology incentive (DFARS 215.404-71-2(c)(2))	6

(13) BLOCKS 13 through 20—COST CATEGORY OBJECTIVE. Enter the prenegotiation objectives. Include contractor independent research and development/bid and proposal in the general and administrative expenses in Block 19.

(14) BLOCKS 21 through 29—WEIGHTED GUIDELINES PROFIT FAC-

TORS. Enter the amounts determined in accordance with DFARS 215.404-71 or 215.404-72. This section is not required to be completed when using an alternate structured approach (DFARS 215.404-73).

(15) BLOCK 30—TOTAL PROFIT OBJECTIVE. Enter the total of Blocks 23, 24, 25, 27, 28, and 29. This section is not required to be completed when using an alternate structured approach ((DFARS 215.404-73)).

(16) BLOCKS 31 through 35—NEGOTIATION SUMMARY. Complete as indicated on the form. For fixed-price type contracts negotiated on a total price basis, enter the contracting officer's best estimates of cost and profit. When using an alternate structured approach, see DFARS 215.404-73(b)(2) for offsets.

(17) BLOCKS 36 through 39—CONTRACTING OFFICER APPROVAL. The contracting officer shall sign the form. Include a complete (with area code) commercial telephone number to facilitate any follow-up actions.

(18) BLOCKS 96 through 99—OPTIONAL USE. Complete in accordance with department/agency procedures, if any.

[Final rule, 71 FR 69492, 12/1/2006, effective 12/1/2006; Final rule, 77 FR 76939, 12/31/2012, effective 12/31/2012; Final rule, 81 FR 9783, 2/26/2016, effective 2/26/2016]

253.219 Small Business Programs.

[Publication notice, 20150826]

253.219-70 DD Form 2579, Small Business Coordination Record.

(a) Use the DD Form 2579 as prescribed in DFARS 219.201(10)(B).

(b) General instructions.

(1) The Contracting Officer is responsible for the coordination and completion of the form.

(2) Coordination on this form is not required when the agency will satisfy a requirement through the use of a mandatory source listed at FAR 8.002 or FAR 8.003.

(c) Specific instructions for completion of DD Form 2579.

(1) BLOCK 1—CONTROL NO. Reserved for use by the Small Business Professional to create a unique identification number for each coordination record.

(2) BLOCK 2—PURCHASE REQUEST/REQUISITION NO. Locally assigned purchase request/requisition number.

(3) BLOCK 3—TOTAL ESTIMATED VALUE. Enter the total estimated value for the acquisition, including all options. For multiple award task or delivery order contracts, enter the total estimated value of the entire acquisition including all orders expected to be awarded.

(4) BLOCKS 4a and 4b:

(i) Block 4a—PROCUREMENT INSTRUMENT IDENTIFIER (PIID). Enter the PIID assigned to the solicitation, contract, or order in Block 4a. (FAR 4.1601, DFARS 204.1601).

(ii) Block 4b—INDEFINITE DELIVERY VEHICLE (IDV) PIID. If applicable, enter the PIID assigned to the IDV against which the solicitation or order identified in Block 4a is issued.

(5) BLOCK 5—MODIFICATION/AMENDMENT NUMBER (MOD/AMDMT No.). Enter the contract or order modification number or solicitation amendment number. (FAR 4.1601, DFARS 204.1601).

(6) BLOCKS 6a through 6e—CONTRACTING OFFICER NAME, DOD ACTIVITY ADDRESS CODE (DODAAC), OFFICE SYMBOL, EMAIL ADDRESS, PHONE NO. Enter the appropriate information in Blocks 6a through 6e.

(7) BLOCKS 7a through 7d:

(i) BLOCK 7a—ITEM and/or SERVICE DESCRIPTION. Enter description of planned acquisition, including quantity, unique delivery requirements, and other descriptors. For services, include the type of service and place of performance, and attach a copy of the Performance Work Statement (PWS), Statement of Work (SOW), Statement of Objectives (SOO), or other specifications and statements as appropriate.

(ii) BLOCK 7b—PRODUCT OR SERVICE CODE (PSC). For the Product and Service Codes Manual, go to http://acquisition.gov.

(iii) BLOCK 7c—NORTH AMERICAN INDUSTRY CLASSIFICATION (NAICS) CODE. For the NAICS codes and definitions, go to http://www.census.gov/eos/www/naics.

(iv) BLOCK 7d—SMALL BUSINESS SIZE STANDARD. For the applicable small business size standard, go to http://www.sba.gov/content/table-small-business-size-standards.

(8) BLOCK 8—PERIOD OF PERFORMANCE/DELIVERY DATES. Enter the estimated beginning and end dates.

(9) BLOCK 9—PURPOSE OF COORDINATION. Check one box indicating the purpose of the action being reviewed: Initial Coordination, Withdrawal (see FAR 19.506), or a Change to the form. Note: Any significant change in the acquisition strategy or plan described on this form will require re-evaluation by the Small Business Professional and the Small Business Administration (SBA) Procurement Center Representative (PCR), if applicable.

(10) BLOCKS 10a through 10j—RECOMMENDATION. Check all that apply, e.g., a small business set-aside could also be a multiple-award. For Blocks 10c through 10d, attach justification if applicable in accordance with FAR 19.1306(a), and 19.1406(a), respectively.

(11) BLOCKS 11a through 11c:

(i) BLOCK 11a—ACQUISITION PLAN/MARKET RESEARCH. Attach the written acquisition plan (FAR 7.104(d)), if required, and the results of market research, including any resulting justification and approval (FAR 6.3) or sole source/brand name justification (FAR 13.106 or 13.501). Include findings that demonstrate efforts to locate qualified small business sources e.g., sources sought (FAR 5.205), requests for information synopses, or waivers to the nonmanufacturer rule (FAR 19.5) and attach additional pages as necessary).

(ii) BLOCK 11b—SYNOPSIS REQUIRED. Check "Yes" or "No." If "No," provide explanation and the exception under FAR 5.202, if applicable.

(iii) BLOCK 11c—SMALL BUSINESS PROGRESS PAYMENTS. Check "Yes" or "No" (DFARS 232.501-1(a)).

(12) BLOCK 12—CONSOLIDATED OR BUNDLED. Select either "Consolidated" or "Bundled," and check "Yes" or "No" for each. If "Yes," attach required documentation for consolidation or bundling (FAR 7.107).

(13) BLOCK 13—SUBCONTRACTING PLAN REQUIRED. Check "Yes" or "No." For recommendations 10g, 10h, or IA or if Block 12 recommendation is "Yes," specify actions that will be taken to maximize small business participation. Consider requirements of FAR 19.7, acquisition history, anticipated subcontracting goals, market research to identify small business capability at the subcontract level, source selection evaluation factor for small business utilization (DFARS 215.304, 215.305), incentives, contract performance metrics, etc. State detailed objectives for subcontract (attach additional pages as necessary).

(14) BLOCKS a through 14c—ACQUISITION HISTORY:

(i) BLOCK 14a—NEW REQUIREMENT. Check "Yes" or "No" and follow the applicable guidance for each selection.

(ii) BLOCK 14b—PREVIOUSLY CONSOLIDATED OR BUNDLED. Check "Yes" or "No" for each. If "Yes," attach required documentation for previous acquisition. (See FAR 7.107).

(iii) BLOCK 14c—DETAILS OF PREVIOUS AWARD(S). For each contractor that received an award for any portion of the immediately preceding acquisition, include the following information—

—Name and CAGE code.

—Small business socioeconomic categories of the awardee.

—PIID.

—NAICS code and size standard.

—Contract type.

—Period of performance.

—Total contract value.

—Subcontracting History. (Small business subcontracting goal achievement (CPARS and eSRS data) and any additional small business utilization requirements included in the contract resulting from a source selection factor used when making the previous contract award.)

(15) BLOCK 15a through 15d—CONTRACTING OFFICER SIGNATURE. Complete 15a through 15d. Digital signature is desired.

(16) BLOCKS 16 through 16f—SMALL BUSINESS PROFESSIONAL/SMALL BUSINESS DIRECTOR REVIEW. Complete 16 through 16f. Digital signature is desired. If "non-concur" is checked, attach rationale or include in Block 16f, along with any other remarks. Block 16e must be completed when any of the conditions in FAR 19.202-1(e) applies to indicate when the acquisition package was provided to the Small Business Administration (SBA).

(17) BLOCKS 17 through 17e—SBA PROCUREMENT CENTER REPRESENTATIVE (PCR) REVIEW. Complete 17 through 17e (see FAR 19.402(a) when a PCR is not assigned to the contracting activity or administration office). Digital signature is desired. If "non-concur" is checked, the PCR shall attach rationale and recommendations or include in Block 17e, along with any other remarks (see FAR 19.402).

(18) BLOCKS 18 through18c—CONTRACTING OFFICER REVIEW. The Contracting Officer shall complete this block if the Small Business Professional and/or the SBA PCR have "non-concurred" in Blocks 16 and 17. Block 18c shall include the Contracting Officer's rationale for decision. Send copies of the completed form to the Small Business Professional and the SBA PCR within 5 working days if rejecting the PCR's recommendation, in accordance with FAR 19.505.

[Publication notice, 20150826; Final rule, 81 FR 9783, 2/26/2016, effective 2/26/2016; Publication notice, 20171201; Final rule, 83 FR 15995, 4/13/2018, effective 4/13/2018]

APPENDIX F—MATERIAL INSPECTION AND RECEIVING REPORT

Table of Contents

Part 2—Contract Quality Assurance on shipments Between Contractors

Procedures F-201

Part 8—Distribution of the DD Form 250-1

Distribution F-801
Corrected DD Form 250-1 . . . . F-802

APPENDIX F—MATERIAL INSPECTION AND RECEIVING REPORT

PART 2—CONTRACT QUALITY ASSURANCE ON SHIPMENTS BETWEEN CONTRACTORS

F-201 Procedures.

(1) Use the supplier's commercial shipping document/packing list to enter performance of required contract quality assurance (CQA) actions at the subcontract level. Make the following entries on the supplier's commercial shipping document/packing list:

Required CQA of listed items has been performed.

_______________ (Signature of Authorized Government Representative or DoD Stamp)

_______________ (Date)

_______________ (Typed Name and Office)

(2) Distribution for Government purposes shall be—

(i) One copy with shipment;

(ii) One copy for the Government representative at consignee (via mail); and

(iii) One copy for the Government representative at consignor.

[Final rule, 71 FR 75890, 12/19/2006, effective 12/19/2006; Publication notice, 20110419]

PART 8—DISTRIBUTION OF THE DD FORM 250-1

F-801 Distribution.

(1) The Government representative shall distribute the completed DD Form 250-1 using Table 3 on the following pages, as amended by the provisions of the contract or shipping order.

(2) The contractor shall furnish the Government representative sufficient copies of the completed form to permit the required distribution.

(3) Distribution of the form shall be made as soon as possible, but not later than 24 hours following completion of the form.

[Final rule, 71 FR 75890, 12/19/2006, effective 12/19/2006; Publication notice, 20110419; Final rule, 76 FR 58122, 9/20/2011, effective 9/20/2011]

F-802 Corrected DD Form 250-1.

When errors are made in entries on the form that would affect payment or accountability—

(1) Make corrected copies;

(2) Circle the corrected entries on all copies and mark the form "CORRECTED COPY";

(3) Enter the statement "Corrections Have Been Verified" in Block 26, with the authorized Government representative's dated signature directly below; and

(4) Make distribution of the certified corrected copy to all recipients of the original distribution.

TABLE 3

TYPE OF SHIPMENT	RECIPIENT OF DD FORM 250-1	NUMBER OF COPIES: LOADING (Prepared by shipper or Government representative)		NUMBER OF COPIES: DISCHARGE (Prepared by receiving activity)	
		TANKER	BARGE	TANKER	BARGE
All (On overseas shipments, provide for a minimum of 4 consignees. Place 1 copy, attached to ullege report, in each of 4 envelopes. Mark the envelopes, "Consignee - First Destination", "Consignee - Second Destination", etc. Deliver via the vessel).	Each Consignee (By mail contiguous United States only).	2	1	As Required	As Required
	With Shipment.	1	1	As Required	As Required
	Master of Vessel.	1	1	1	1
	Tanker or Barge Agent.	2	2	2	2
	Contractor.	As Required	As Required	As Required	As Required
	Cognizant Inspection Office.	1	1	1	1
	Government Representative responsible for quality at each destination.	1	1	1	1
	Government Representative at Cargo Loading Point.	1	1	1*	1*
On all USNS tankers and all MSC chartered tankers and MSC chartered barges.	Military Sealift Command, Code N322, Washington, DC 20396-5100.	2	2	2	2

TABLE 3

TYPE OF SHIPMENT	RECIPIENT OF DD FORM 250-1	NUMBER OF COPIES			
		LOADING (Prepared by shipper or Government representative)		DISCHARGE (Prepared by receiving activity)	
		TANKER	BARGE	TANKER	BARGE
See the contract or shipping order for finance documentation and any supplemental requirements for Government-owned product shipments and receipts.	Payment Office: If this is DFAS-CO, send copies to: DLA Energy, ATTN: DESC-FII, 8725 John J. Kingman Road, Fort Belvoir, VA 22060-6221 (do not send copies to DFAS-CO).	2	2	2	2
For shipments and receipts of DLA Energy-financed cargoes for which DFAS-CO is not the paying office.	DLA Energy, ATTN: DESC-FII, 8725 John J. Kingman Road, Fort Belvoir, VA 22060-6221.	1	1	1	1
For shipments on all USNS tankers, MSC chartered tankers and barges, and FOB destination tankers with copy of ullage report.	DLA Energy, ATTN: DESC-BID, 8725 John J. Kingman Road, Fort Belvoir, VA 22060-6221.	1	1	1**	1
On Army ILP shipments.	U.S. Army International Logistics Center, New Cumberland Army Depot, New Cumberland, PA 17070-5001.	2	2	2	2
On all shipments to Navy Operated Terminals.	DLA Energy, ATTN: DESC-FII, 8725 John J. Kingman Road, Fort Belvoir, VA 22060-6221.	2	1	2	1

TABLE 3

TYPE OF SHIPMENT	RECIPIENT OF DD FORM 250-1	NUMBER OF COPIES: LOADING (Prepared by shipper or Government representative)		NUMBER OF COPIES: DISCHARGE (Prepared by receiving activity)	
		TANKER	BARGE	TANKER	BARGE
On all shipments to Air Force Bases.	Directorate of Energy Management, SA ALC(SFT), Kelly AFB, TX 78241-5000.	1	1	1	1
On all contiguous United States loadings.	DLA Energy Region(s) cognizant of shipping point.	1	1	1	1
On all shipments to contiguous United States destinations.	DLA Energy Region(s) cognizant of shipping and receiving point.****	1	1	0	0
For all discharges of cargoes originating at DLA Energy Support Points and discharging at activities not Defense Energy Support Points.	DLA Energy, ATTN: DESC-BID, 8725 John J. Kingman Road, Fort Belvoir, VA 22060-6221.			1***	1***

*With copy of ullage report.

**Dry tank certificate to accompany DD Form 250-1 and ullage report.

***Copies of the DD Form 250-1, forwarded by bases, will include the following in Block 11: Shipped to: Supplementary Address, if applicable; Signed Code; and Fund Code.

****See Table 4.

TABLE 4

FUEL REGION LOCATIONS AND AREAS OF RESPONSIBILITY

a.	DLA Energy Americas	DLA Energy Americas Federal Office Building 2320 La Branch Street, Suite 2118 Houston, TX 74004-1091
	Area of Responsibility:	Colorado, Connecticut, Delaware, District of Columbia, Illinois, Indiana, Iowa, Kansas, Kentucky, Maine, Maryland, Massachusetts, Michigan, Minnesota, Missouri, Nebraska, New Hampshire, New Jersey, New York, North Dakota, Ohio, Pennsylvania, Rhode Island, South Dakota, Vermont, Virginia, West Virginia, Wisconsin, and Wyoming
b.	DLA Energy Americas East	DLA Energy Americas East Federal Office Building 2320 La Branch, Room 1005 Houston, TX 77004-1091
	Area of Responsibility:	Alabama, Arizona, Arkansas, Caribbean Area, Florida, Georgia, Louisiana, Mexico, Mississippi, New Mexico, North Carolina, Oklahoma, Puerto Rico, South Carolina, Tennessee, Texas, West Indies, Central America, and South America
c.	DLA Energy Americas West	DLA Energy Americas West 3171 N. Gaffney Street San Pedro, CA 90731-1099
	Area of Responsibility:	California, Idaho, Montana, Nevada, Oregon, Utah, and Washington
d.	DLA Energy Alaska	DLA Energy Alaska 10480 22nd Street Elmendorf AFB, Alaska 99506-2500
	Area of Responsibility:	Alaska and Aleutians
e.	DLA Europe and Africa	DLA Europe & Africa Building 2304 APO New York 09128-4105

	Area of Responsibility:	Continental Europe, United Kingdom, Mediterranean Area, Turkey, and Africa (less Djibouti, Egypt, Ethiopia, Kenya, Somalia)
f.	DLA Energy Middle East	DLA Energy Middle East PSC 451 Box DESC-ME FPO AE 09834-2800
	Area of Responsibility:	Afghanistan, Bahrain, Djibouti, Egypt, Ethiopia, Iran, Iraq, Jordan, Kenya, Kuwait, Oman, Pakistan, Qatar, Saudi Arabia, Somalia, Sudan, United Arab Emirates, and Yemen
g.	DLA Energy Pacific	DLA Energy Pacific Camp H. M. Smith Honolulu, HI 96861-5000
	Area of Responsibility:	Australia, Burma, East Indies, Hawaii, Indian Ocean, Japan, Korea, Malaya, Marianas, New Zealand, Philippines, Ryukyu Islands, South Pacific Islands, Sri Lanka, Taiwan, and Thailand

[Final rule, 71 FR 75890, 12/19/2006, effective 12/19/2006; Publication notice, 20110419; Final rule, 76 FR 58122, 9/20/2011, effective 9/20/2011; Final rule, 81 FR 78011, 11/4/2016, effective 11/4/2016]

Defense Federal Acquisition Regulation

TOPICAL INDEX

Table of Contents

Topical Index **Page**

Topical Index 1651

See page 39 for an explanation of the numbering of the DFARS.

Defense Federal Acquisition Regulation Supplement

Topical Index
References are to section (§) numbers

A

Accounting classification reference number (ACRN) . . . 204.7107

Accounting systems
. material management and accounting system (MMAS)
. . contract clause . . . 242.7204; 252.242-7004
. . definitions . . . 252.242-7004
. . policy . . . 242.7202
. . review procedures . . . 242.7203
. . scope . . . 242.7200
. policy . . . 242.7502
. procedures . . . 242.7503

Acquisition planning
. agency-head responsibilities . . . 207.103
. buy-to-budget—additional quantities of end items
. . authority . . . 207.7002
. . definition of end item . . . 207.7001
. . limitation . . . 207.7003
. commercial items
. . applicability of FAR Part 12 . . . 212.102
. . policy for written determination . . . 207.102
. component breakout
. . definition of component . . . 207.171-2
. . policy . . . 207.171-3
. . procedures . . . 207.171-4
. . scope . . . 207.171-1
. contractor versus government performance
. . policy . . . 207.302
. equipment lease or purchase
. . considerations . . . 207.401
. . funding requirements . . . 207.471
. . statutory requirements . . . 207.470
. human research . . . 207.172
. inherently governmental functions
. . policy . . . 207.503
. . scope . . . 207.500
. major systems requirements . . . 207.106
. procedures for peer reviews . . . 207.104
. use of brand name or equal purchase descriptions . . . 211.104
. use of proprietary specifications or standards . . . 211.170
. written plan, contents . . . 207.105

Administration of contracts
. accounting systems and related controls
. . policy . . . 242.7502
. . procedures . . . 242.7503
. assignment of contract administration . . . 242.202
. system for award management
. . contract clause and solicitation provision . . . 204.1105; 252.204-7004

Administration of contracts—continued
. system for award management—continued
. . procedures . . . 204.1103
. commercial and government entity (CAGE) codes
. . procedures . . . 204.1870
. contract clauses and solicitation provisions
. . annual representations and certifications, Alternate A . . . 252.204-7007
. . contracts involving export-controlled items . . . 252.225-7048
. . control of government personnel work product . . . 252.204-7003
. . disclosure of information . . . 252.204-7000
. . material management and accounting system . . . 252.242-7004
. . payment for subline items not separately priced . . . 252.204-7002
. . postaward conference . . . 252.242-7000
. contract distribution
. . procedures . . . 204.201
. . taxpayer identification information . . . 204.203
. contract execution
. . contracting officer's signature . . . 204.101
. contract reporting
. . federal procurement data system, general . . . 204.602
. . federal procurement data system, reporting data . . . 204.606
. . federal procurement data system, responsibilities . . . 204.604
. . individual contracting action report, DD Form 350 . . . 253.303-350
. . monthly summary of contracting actions, DD Form 1057 . . . 253.303-1057
. contractor accounting systems and related controls
. . contract clause . . . 242.7503
. . definitions . . . 242.7501
. . policy . . . 242.7502
. contractor business systems
. . contract clause . . . 242.7001
. . deficiencies . . . 242.7000
. contractor identification
. . CAGE codes . . . 204.1870
. . taxpayer identification numbers . . . 204.203
. contractor insurance/pension review
. . general . . . 242.7301
. . requirements . . . 242.7302
. . responsibilities . . . 242.7303
. corporate administrative contracting officer
. . assignment and location . . . 242.602
. DD Form 1593, contract administration completion record . . . 253.303-1593
. disallowance of costs . . . 242.803

Administration of contracts—continued
. disclosure of information to litigation support contractors
. . contract clause . . . 252.204-7014; 252.204-7015
. . definitions . . . 204.7401
. . policy . . . 204.7402
. . scope of subpart . . . 204.7400
. . solicitation provision . . . 252.204-7013
. . solicitation provision and contract clauses . . . 204.7403
. electronic document access
. . policy . . . 204.270-1
. . procedures . . . 204.270-2; 204.270
. Federal Procurement Data System, cross-reference . . . 204.1670
. files
. . closeout . . . 204.804
. . closeout by administrating office . . . 204.804-1
. . closeout if another office administers contract . . . 204.804-2
. . contents . . . 204.802
. . disposal . . . 204.805
. final indirect cost rates
. . auditor determination procedure . . . 242.705-2
. . contracting officer determination procedure . . . 242.705-1
. forms
. . contract administration completion record, DD Form 1593 . . . 204.804-2
. . contract closeout check list, DD Form 1597 . . . 204.804-2
. . contract completion statement, DD Form 1594 . . . 204.804
. independent research and development and bid and proposal costs
. . policy . . . 242.771-2
. . responsibilities . . . 242.771-3
. . scope . . . 242.771-1
. interagency agreements . . . 242.002
. labor standards
. . disputes . . . 222.406-10
. . investigations . . . 222.406-8
. . payrolls and statements . . . 222.406-6
. . policy . . . 222.406-1
. . preconstruction letters and conferences . . . 222.406-1
. . semiannual enforcement reports . . . 222.406-13
. . withholding/suspension of payments . . . 222.406-9
. line items . . . 204.7103
. material management and accounting system (MMAS)
. . contract clause . . . 242.7204; 252.242-7004
. . definitions . . . 252.242-7004
. . policy . . . 242.7202
. . review procedures . . . 242.7203
. . scope . . . 242.7200
. novation and change-of-name agreements
. . agreement to recognize a successor in interest . . . 242.1204
. . processing agreements . . . 242.1203

Administration of contracts—continued
. office functions . . . 242.301; 242.302
. postaward conference procedure . . . 242.503-2
. production surveillance and reporting
. . assignment of criticality designator . . . 242.1105
. . reporting requirements . . . 242.1106
. . surveillance requirements . . . 242.1104
. safeguarding classified information
. . atomic energy agency additional protocol . . . 204.470-1
. . contract clause . . . 204.470-3
. . contract clause prescriptions . . . 204.404
. . contracting officer responsibilities . . . 204.403
. . general . . . 204.402
. . national security exclusion . . . 204.470-2
. support of contingency operations . . . 225.373
. . use of electronic business tools . . . 225.374
. taxpayer identification number information
. . contractor identification . . . 204.203; 204.7202-3
. . individual contracting action report, DD Form 350 . . . 204.902
. technical representation at contractor facilities
. . general . . . 242.7400
. . procedures . . . 242.7401
. traffic and transportation management
. . policies . . . 247.101
. . application for U.S. government shipping documentation/instructions . . . 252.247-7028
. uniform contract line item numbering system
. . accounting classification reference number (ACRN) . . . 204.7107
. . contract clause . . . 204.7109; 252.204-7006
. . contract modifications . . . 204.7106
. . definitions . . . 204.7101
. . exhibits and attachments . . . 204.7105
. . line items, criteria for establishing . . . 204.7103-1
. . numbering procedures . . . 204.7103-2; 204.7104-2
. . payment instructions . . . 204.7108
. . policy . . . 204.7102
. . scope . . . 204.7100
. . subline items, criteria for establishing . . . 204.7104-1
. uniform procurement instrument identifiers
. . Federal Procurement Data System . . . 204.1670
. . order of application for modifications . . . 204.1671
. . policy . . . 204.1601
. . procedures . . . 204.1603
. voluntary refunds . . . 242.7100

Advance payments—see also Contract financing
. contract clause
. . contract clause . . . 232.412-70; 252.232-7005
. noncommercial items
. . advance payment pool . . . 232.470
. . approval recommendation . . . 232.409-1
. . contract clause prescription . . . 232.412-70
. . exclusions . . . 232.404
. . findings, determination, and authorization . . . 232.410

Advisory and assistance services—see also Consultants
. audit services . . . 237.270

Agency acquisition regulations
. agency control and compliance procedures . . . 201.304
. interagency acquisitions under the Economy Act
. . ordering procedures . . . 217.503
. . general . . . 217.502-1
. . procedures . . . 217.502
. . scope of subpart . . . 217.500
. non-DoD agency contracts
. . definitions . . . 217.701
. . procedures . . . 217.770
. . scope . . . 217.700
. policy . . . 201.301
. publication and codification . . . 201.303

Agency needs, describing
. contract clauses and solicitation provisions
. . acquisition streamlining . . . 211.002-70
. . alternate preservation, packaging, and packing . . . 252.211-7004; 211.272
. . government-assigned serial numbers, policy . . . 211.274-5
. . item identification and valuation . . . 211.274-6; 252.211-7003
. . contract clauses . . . 211.503
. . radio frequency identification . . . 211.275-3; 252.211-7006
. . substitutions for military or federal specifications and standards . . . 211.273-4
. definitions . . . 211.273-1
. item identification and valuation
. . contract clause . . . 211.274-6; 252.211-7003
. . general . . . 211.274-1
. . government-assigned serial numbers, policy . . . 211.274-5
. . identification policy . . . 211.274-4
. . valuation policy . . . 211.274-3
. liquidated damages, construction contracts . . . 211.503
. liquidated damages, scope of subpart . . . 211.500
. policy . . . 211.002
. priorities and allocations . . . 211.503; 211.602
. purchase requests
. . procedures . . . 211.7001
. radio frequency identification
. . contract clause . . . 211.275-3; 252.211-7006
. . definitions . . . 211.275-1; 252.211-7006
. . policy . . . 211.275-2
. requirements documents
. . alternate preservation, packaging, and packing . . . 211.272
. . contract clauses and solicitation provisions prescriptions . . . 211.107; 211.204
. . elimination of use of class I ozone-depleting substances . . . 211.271
. . identification and availability of specifications . . . 211.201

Agency needs, describing—continued
. requirements documents—continued
. . items peculiar to one manufacturer . . . 211.105
. . service contracts . . . 211.106
. substitutions for military or federal specifications and standards
. . contract clause . . . 211.273-4; 252.211-7005
. . definition of SPI process . . . 211.273-1
. . policy . . . 211.273-2
. . procedures . . . 211.273-3

Air circuit breakers for naval vessels
. contract clause and solicitation provision prescriptions . . . 225.7006-4
. exceptions . . . 225.7006-2
. restriction . . . 225.7006-1
. waiver . . . 225.7006-3

Aircraft quality assurance . . . 246.408-71; 246.504

Ammunition and explosives
. safeguarding sensitive arms, ammunition and explosives
. . contract clause . . . 252.223-7007; 223.7203
. . definition . . . 223.7200
. . policy . . . 223.7201
. . preaward responsibilities . . . 223.7202
. safety precautions
. . contract clause prescriptions . . . 223.370-5
. . definition of ammunition and explosives . . . 223.370-2; 252.223-7002
. . policy . . . 223.370-3
. . procedures . . . 223.370-4
. . scope . . . 223.370-1

Anchor and mooring chain
. contract clause . . . 225.7007-3; 252.225-7019
. restriction . . . 225.7007-1
. waiver . . . 225.7007-2

Annual representations and certifications
. contract clause and solicitation provision . . . 204.1202; 252.204-7007

Antiterrorism awareness training
. contract clause . . . 252.204-7004
. contract clause prescription . . . 204.7203
. definition . . . 204.7201
. policy . . . 204.7202
. scope of subpart . . . 204.7200

Antiterrorism/force protection
. contract clause . . . 225.7403-2; 252.225-7043
. general . . . 225.372-1

Arab boycott of Israel
. exceptions . . . 225.7603
. procedures . . . 225.7602
. restriction . . . 225.7601
. solicitation provision . . . 225.7604; 252.225-7031
. waivers . . . 225.7604

Architect-engineer services—see also Construction contracts
. contract clause and solicitation provision . . . 236.609-70

Architect-engineer services—see also Construction contracts—continued
. forms
. . DD Form 2631, performance evaluation (architect-engineer) . . . 253.303-2631
. . prescription . . . 236.701
. performance evaluation . . . 236.604
. policy . . . 236.601
. restriction on steel acquisition for military construction . . . 236.274
. rights in software or software documentation . . . 227.7206
. rights in technical data
. . approval of restricted designs . . . 227.7107-3
. . construction supplies and research and development work . . . 227.7107-2
. . contract clause prescriptions . . . 227.7107-1
. . contracts . . . 227.7107
. selection of firms . . . 236.602-1
. statutory fee limitation . . . 236.606-70

Arms—see also Ammunition and explosives
. international traffic in arms regulations . . . 227.675-1

Assignment of claims—see also Contract financing
. contract clause . . . 232.806; 252.232-7008

Audit services . . . 237.270

Authority, delegation of
. contract adjustment boards . . . 250.102-2
. general . . . 250.101

Automatic data processing equipment (ADPE)
. provision to contractors . . . 245.302

Aviation critical safety items
. definitions . . . 209.270-2
. policy . . . 209.270-3
. procedures . . . 209.270-4
. scope . . . 209.270-1

Aviation into-plane reimbursement (AIR) card . . . 213.306

Awards—see also Selection of contractor
. exchange of personal property . . . 217.7004
. synopses of
. . announcement . . . 205.303
. . general . . . 205.301

B

Balance of Payments Program—see also Foreign acquisitions
. contract clause prescriptions . . . 225.7503
. policy . . . 225.7501
. procedures . . . 225.7502
. scope . . . 225.7500

Ball and roller bearings . . . 225.7009
. contract clause . . . 225.7009-5; 252.225-7016
. exception . . . 225.7009-3
. restriction . . . 225.7009-2
. scope . . . 225.7009-1
. waiver . . . 225.7009-4

Ballistic missile defense research
. definitions . . . 225.7017-1
. exceptions . . . 225.7017-3
. restriction . . . 225.7017-2
. solicitation provision . . . 225.7017-4

Basic ordering agreements . . . 216.703

Bid and proposal costs
. commercial organization contracts . . . 231.205-18
. legislative lobbying costs . . . 231.205-22
. policy . . . 242.771-2
. responsibilities . . . 242.771-3
. scope . . . 242.771-1

Bid evaluations
. evaluation factors and subfactors . . . 215.304
. only one offer . . . 214.209; 214.404-1
. past performance evaluation . . . 215.305
. stevedoring contracts . . . 247.270-3
. tiered evaluation of offers . . . 213.106-1-70; 215.203-70

Bid solicitation
. alternate bids
. . sale of surplus contractor inventory . . . 245.7302-3
. DD Form 1707, information to offerors or quoters . . . 253.303-1707
. exchange of personal property . . . 217.7004
. negotiated procurement contracts . . . 215.203-70
. options use . . . 217.202
. sale of surplus contractor inventory . . . 245.7302-1
. sealed bidding
. . descriptive literature . . . 214.202
. . invitation for bids requirements . . . 214.202

Bidders mailing lists
. sale of surplus contractor inventory . . . 245.7302-5

Blanket purchase agreements (BPAs) . . . 213.303-5

Bonds
. contract clauses and solicitation provisions
. . accident reporting and investigation involving aircraft, missiles, and space launch vehicles . . . 252.228-7005
. . capture and detention . . . 252.228-7003
. . ground and flight risk . . . 252.228-7001
. . reimbursement for war-hazard losses . . . 252.228-7000
. Defense Environmental Restoration Program, construction contracts . . . 228.102-70
. fidelity and forgery bonds . . . 228.105
. general . . . 228.102-1
. performance and payment bonds
. . contract clause . . . 245.7310-2
. withholding contract payments . . . 228.106-7

Buy American—see also Foreign acquisitions
. construction materials
. . exceptions . . . 225.202
. . nonavailability determination . . . 225.202
. . noncompliance . . . 225.206

Buy American—see also Foreign acquisitions—continued
. supplies
. . acquisition from or through other government agencies . . . 225.170
. . determining reasonableness of cost . . . 225.105
. . exceptions . . . 225.103
. . general . . . 225.101
. . nonavailable articles . . . 225.104

Buy-to-budget additional quantities of end items
. authority . . . 207.7002
. definition of end item . . . 207.7001
. limitation . . . 207.7003

C

Canadian contracting
. acceptance of supplies . . . 225.870-7
. contract administration . . . 225.870-5
. contract clause . . . 215.408; 252.215-7004
. contracting procedures . . . 225.870-4
. general . . . 225.870-1
. industrial security . . . 225.870-8
. solicitation of contractors . . . 225.870-2
. solicitation provision . . . 252.215-7003; 215.408
. submission of offers . . . 225.870-3
. termination procedures . . . 225.870-6; 249.7000

Cancellation
. of invitations for bids after opening . . . 214.404-1
. of invitations for bids before opening . . . 214.209
. telecommunications services . . . 239.7410

Carbon, alloy, and armor steel plate
. contract clause . . . 225.7011-3; 252.225-7030
. restriction . . . 225.7011-1
. waiver . . . 225.7011-2

System for award management
. contract clause and solicitation provision . . . 204.1105; 252.204-7004
. procedures . . . 204.1103

Certificates of competency and determinations of responsibility—see also Small business programs
. agency and Small Business Administration differences resolution . . . 219.602-3
. procedures
. referral . . . 219.602-1

Change orders—see also Modification of contracts
. administration . . . 243.204
. certification of requests for equitable adjustment . . . 243.204-71
. contract clauses
. . pricing of contract modifications . . . 252.243-7001; 243.205-70
. . requests for equitable adjustments . . . 243.205-71; 252.243-7002
. definitization . . . 243.204-70
. . allowable profit . . . 243.204-70-6
. . exceptions . . . 243.204-70-5

Change orders—see also Modification of contracts—continued
. definitization—continued
. . limitations on obligations . . . 243.204-70-4
. . plans and reports . . . 243.204-70-7
. . price ceiling . . . 243.204-70-2
. . schedule . . . 243.204-70-3
. . scope . . . 243.204-70-1
. unpriced change orders . . . 243.205-72

Chemical weapons antidote
. exception . . . 225.7005-2
. restriction . . . 225.7005-1
. waiver . . . 225.7005-3

China
. Communist Chinese military company, defined . . . 252.225-7007
. exceptions to prohibition . . . 225.770-3
. prohibition on acquisition of items from . . . 225.770-2

Classified information
. safeguarding
. . contract clause prescriptions . . . 204.404
. . contracting officer responsibilities . . . 204.403
. . general . . . 204.402

Commercial and government entity (CAGE) codes
. forms
. . DD Form 2051-1, request for information/verification of commercial and government entity (CAGE) code . . . 253.303-2051
. . DD Form 2051, request for assignment of commercial and government entity (CAGE) code . . . 253.303-2051
. . request for assignment of commercial and government entity (CAGE) code, DD Form 2051 . . . 253.303-2051
. . request for information/verification of commercial and government entity (CAGE) code, DD Form 2051-1 . . . 253.303-2051
. procedures . . . 204.1870

Commercial item acquisition
. applicability of certain laws
. . laws not applicable to executive agency contracts . . . 212.503
. . laws not applicable to strategic materials
. . laws not applicable to subcontracts . . . 212.504
. applicability of FAR Part 12
. . documentation requirements . . . 212.102
. contract clauses and solicitation provisions
. . alternate preservation, packaging, and packing . . . 252.211-7004
. . availability for examination of specifications, standards, plans, drawings, data item descriptions, and other pertinent documents . . . 252.211-7002
. . availability of specifications and standards not listed in acquisition streamlining and standardization information system (ASSIST) . . . 211.204
. . financing . . . 232.206
. . prescriptions . . . 212.301; 232.206

Commercial item acquisition—continued
. contract clauses and solicitation provisions—continued
. . substitutions for military or federal specifications and standards . . . 252.211-7005
. . tailoring of . . . 212.302
. contract financing
. . contract clauses and solicitation provisions . . . 232.206
. . security for government financing . . . 232.202-4
. contract type . . . 212.207
. limitation on acquisition of right-hand drive passenger sedans . . . 212.271
. only one offer . . . 212.205
. requirement for written determination, policy . . . 207.102
. rights in technical data . . . 227.7102
. security for government financing . . . 232.202-4
. software
. . contract clause prescription . . . 227.7202-4
. . policy . . . 227.7202-1
. . rights in . . . 227.7202-3
. special requirements
. . computer software . . . 212.212
. . major weapon systems . . . 212.270
. . technical data . . . 212.211
. streamlined procedures
. . evaluation of offers . . . 212.602
. subcontracting
. . contract clause prescriptions . . . 244.403
. . policy requirements . . . 244.402

Commercial organizations, contracts with
. bid and proposal costs . . . 231.205-18
. compensation for personal services . . . 231.205-6
. external restructuring costs . . . 231.205-70
. independent research and development costs . . . 231.205-18
. legislative lobbying costs . . . 231.205-22
. public relations and advertising costs . . . 231.205-1

Competition requirements
. applicability . . . 206.001
. contractor versus government performance
. . policy . . . 207.302
. full and open competition after exclusion of sources
. . establishing, maintaining alternate sources . . . 206.202
. offers . . . 212.205
. other than full and open competition
. . authorized or required by statute . . . 206.302-5
. . availability of justification . . . 206.305
. . domestic source restriction . . . 206.302-3; 252.206-7000
. . international agreement . . . 206.302-4
. . justification approval . . . 206.304
. . only one responsible source . . . 206.302-1
. . public interest . . . 206.302-7
. . unusual and compelling urgency . . . 206.302-2

Competition requirements—continued
. Section 8(a) program
. . contract preparation . . . 219.811-2
. . exceptions . . . 219.805-1
. . procedures . . . 219.805-2
. solicitation provision
. . domestic source restriction . . . 206.302-3; 252.206-7000
. tiered evaluation of offers . . . 213.106-1-70; 215.203-70

Component breakout
. definition of component . . . 207.171-2
. policy . . . 207.171-3
. procedures . . . 207.171-4
. scope . . . 207.171-1

Congressional Medal of Honor, unlawful manufacture of . . . 209.471

Congressional notification
. contract termination . . . 249.7001

Construction contracts
. architect-engineer services
. . contract clause and solicitation provision . . . 236.609-70
. . forms . . . 236.701
. . performance evaluation . . . 236.604
. . policy . . . 236.601
. . restriction on steel acquisition for military construction . . . 236.274
. . selection of firms . . . 236.602-1
. . statutory fee limitation . . . 236.606-70
. contract clauses and solicitation provisions
. . additive or deductive items . . . 252.236-7007
. . airfield safety precautions . . . 252.236-7005
. . contract drawings and specifications . . . 252.236-7001
. . contract clauses and solicitation provisions . . . 252.236-7008
. . cost limitation . . . 252.236-7006
. . contract clauses and solicitation provisions . . . 252.236-7012; 252.236-7000
. . obstruction of navigable waterways . . . 252.236-7002
. . contract clauses and solicitation provisions . . . 252.236-7011; 252.236-7008; 252.236-7010
. . payment for mobilization and demobilization . . . 252.236-7004
. . payment for mobilization and preparatory work . . . 252.236-7003
. . prescriptions . . . 236.570
. contractor performance evaluation . . . 236.201
. cost estimates . . . 236.203
. cost-plus-fixed-fee contracts . . . 236.271
. definitions . . . 236.102
. demolition contracts . . . 236.701
. disclosure of the magnitude of construction projects . . . 236.204
. expediting contracts . . . 236.270
. foreign countries, construction in . . . 236.273

Construction contracts—continued
. forms
. . DD Form 2626, performance evaluation (construction) . . . 253.303-2626
. . prescription . . . 236.701
. industrial resources, facilities projects . . . 236.275
. labor standards
. . administration and enforcement policy . . . 222.406-1
. . construction wage rate requirements determinations . . . 222.404
. . Department of Labor regulations . . . 222.403-4
. . disposition of disputes . . . 222.406-10
. . installation support contracts . . . 222.402-70
. . investigations . . . 222.406-8
. . payrolls and statements . . . 222.406-6
. . preconstruction letters and conferences . . . 222.406-1
. . semiannual enforcement reports . . . 222.406-13
. . wage rate schedules
. . withholding/suspension of contract payments . . . 222.406-9
. liquidated damages . . . 236.206
. network analysis systems . . . 236.273
. option for supervision and inspection services
. . contract clause prescription . . . 236.609-70
. prequalification of sources . . . 236.272
. restriction on award of overseas architect-engineer contracts to foreign firms . . . 236.602-70
. sealed bidding . . . 236.213
. special construction, telecommunications services
. . applicability of construction labor standards . . . 239.7408-2
. . general . . . 239.7408-1
. special procedures for cost-reimbursement contracts for construction . . . 236.215

Construction or repair of vessels in foreign shipyards, restrictions . . . 225.7013

Construction wage rate requirements statute—see also Labor laws
. wage determination . . . 222.404

Consultants
. cost principles . . . 231.205-6
. funding and term of service . . . 237.106
. lead system integrators, limitations . . . 209.570
. personal services contracts . . . 237.104

Contingent fees
. foreign military sales acquisition . . . 225.7303-4

Contract adjustments—see also Modification of contracts
. disposition . . . 250.103-6

Contract clauses and solicitation provisions
. access (communications) . . . 252.239-7002
. . prescription . . . 239.7411
. access to vessel . . . 252.217-7011
. . contract clauses prescriptions . . . 217.7104

Contract clauses and solicitation provisions—continued
. accident reporting and investigation involving aircraft, missiles, and space launch vehicles 252.228-7005
. . prescription . . . 228.370
. accounting system administration . . . 252.242-7006
. . prescription . . . 242.7503
. acknowledgment of support and disclaimer . . . 252.235-7010
. . prescriptions . . . 235.072
. acquisition of the American flag . . . 252.225-7006
. . prescription . . . 225.7002-3
. acquisition of uniform components for Afghan military or national police . . . 252.225-7029
. acquisition streamlining
. . prescription . . . 211.002-70
. additional services (transportation) . . . 252.247-7020
. . prescription . . . 247.271-3
. additive or deductive items . . . 252.236-7007
. . prescription . . . 236.570
. advance payment pool . . . 252.232-7000
. . prescription . . . 232.412-70
. advancing small business growth
. . prescription . . . 219.309; 252.219-7000
. agency office of inspector general . . . 252.203-7003
. . prescription . . . 203.1004
. aircraft flight risk
. . prescription . . . 228.370
. airfield safety precautions . . . 252.236-7005
. . prescription . . . 236.570
. alternate preservation, packaging, and packing . . . 252.211-7004
. . prescription . . . 211.272
. alternative line item . . . 252.204-7011
. . prescription . . . 204.7109
. animal welfare . . . 252.235-7002
. . prescription . . . 235.072; 237.175
. annual representations and certifications, Alternate A . . . 252.204-7007
. . prescription . . . 204.1202
. antiterrorism awareness training for contractors . . . 252.204-7004
. . prescription . . . 252.7203
. antiterrorism/force protection policy for defense contractors outside the U.S . . . 252.225-7043
. . prescription . . . 225.371
. allowability of legal costs incurred in connection with a whistleblower proceeding . . . 252.216-7009
. . prescription . . . 216.307
. antitrust clearance
. . prescription . . . 245.7310-8
. application for U.S. government shipping documentation/instructions . . . 252.247-7028
. . prescription . . . 247.207
. area of performance (mortuary services) . . . 252.237-7004
. . prescription . . . 237.7003
. assignment of claims
. . prescription . . . 227.7009-1

Contract clauses and solicitation provisions— continued
. assignment of claims (overseas) . . . 252.232-7008
. . prescription . . . 232.806
. assignments . . . 252.227-7011
. . prescription . . . 227.7010
. atomic energy agency additional protocol reporting requirements . . . 252.204-7010
. . prescription . . . 204.470-3
. authorization to perform . . . 252.225-7042
. . prescription . . . 225.1103
. availability for examination of specifications, standards, plans, drawings, data item descriptions, and other pertinent documents . . . 252.211-7002
. . prescription . . . 211.204
. availability of specifications and standards not listed in acquisition streamlining and standardization information system (ASSIST)
. . prescription . . . 211.204
. award fee . . . 252.216-7005
. . prescription . . . 216.406
. award fee reduction or denial, jeopardizing health or safety . . . 252.216-7004
. . prescription . . . 216.406
. award to single offeror . . . 252.237-7002
. . prescription . . . 237.7003
. award (transportation)
. . prescription . . . 247.271-3
. billing instructions . . . 252.204-7006
. . prescription . . . 204.7109
. bonds or other security
. . prescription . . . 228.170
. bonds (vessel repair) . . . 252.217-7008
. . prescription . . . 217.7104
. Buy American—Balance of Payments Program certificate . . . 252.225-7000
. . prescription . . . 212.301; 225.1101
. Buy American—Free Trade Agreements—Balance of Payments Program . . . 252.225-7036
. Buy American—Free Trade Agreements—Balance of Payments Program certificate . . . 252.225-7035
. Buy American—Free Trade Agreements—Balance of Payments Program
. . prescription . . . 213.302-5; 225.1101
. Buy American—Free Trade Agreements—Balance of Payments Program certificate
. . prescription . . . 212.301; 225.1101
. Buy American and Balance of Payments Program . . . 252.225-7001
. . prescription . . . 213.302-5; 225.1103
. cancellation or termination of orders (communications) . . . 252.239-7007
. . prescription . . . 239.7411
. capture and detention . . . 252.228-7003
. . prescription . . . 228.370
. system for award management
. . alternate A . . . 252.204-7004
. . prescription . . . 204.1105

Contract clauses and solicitation provisions— continued
. certification of technical data conformity
. . prescription . . . 227.7104
. change in place of performance—ammunition and explosives . . . 252.223-7003
. . prescription . . . 223.370-5
. changes (vessel repair) . . . 252.217-7003
. . prescription . . . 217.7104
. charges (transportation)
. . prescription . . . 247.271-3
. choice of law (overseas) . . . 252.233-7001
. . prescription . . . 233.215-70
. cloud computing services . . . 252.239-7010
. . prescription . . . 239.7604
. commercial derivative military article, specialty metals compliance certificate . . . 252.225-7010
. . prescription . . . 225.7003-5
. compensation of former DoD officials . . . 252.203-7000
. . prescription . . . 203.171-4
. competition for religious-related services . . . 252.219-7012
. . prescription . . . 219.270-3
. competition opportunity for American steel producers . . . 252.236-7013
. . prescription . . . 236.570
. compliance with audit standards . . . 252.237-7001
. . prescription . . . 237.270
. compliance with local labor laws (overseas) . . . 252.222-7002
. . prescription . . . 222.7201
. compliance with safeguarding covered defense information controls . . . 252.204-7008
. prescription . . . 204.7304
. compliance with Spanish laws and insurance . . . 252.228-7006
. . prescription . . . 228.370
. compliance with Spanish social security laws and regulations . . . 252.222-7004
. . prescription . . . 222.7201
. computation of royalties . . . 252.227-7008
. . prescription . . . 227.7009-4
. continuation of communication service authorizations (communications) . . . 252.239-7015
. . prescription . . . 239.7411
. continuation of essential contractor services . . . 252.237-7023
. . prescription . . . 237.7603
. contract areas of performance (transportation)
. . prescription . . . 247.271-3
. contract definitization . . . 252.217-7027
. . prescriptions . . . 216.603-4; 217.7406
. contract drawings and specifications . . . 252.236-7001
. . prescription . . . 236.570
. contract prices—bidding schedule . . . 252.236-7008
. . prescription . . . 236.570

Contract clauses and solicitation provisions—continued
. contract terms and conditions required to implement statutes applicable to defense acquisitions of commercial items
. . prescription . . . 212.301
. contracting officer's representative . . . 252.201-7000
. . prescription . . . 201.602-70
. contractor business systems . . . 252.242-7005
. . prescription . . . 242.7001
. contractor counterfeit electronic part detection and avoidance system . . . 252.246-7007
. . prescription . . . 246.870-3
. contractor liability for loss or damage (transportation) . . . 252.247-7016
. . prescription . . . 247.271-3
. contractor management system administration . . . 252.245-7003
. . prescription . . . 245.107
. contractor personnel authorized to accompany U.S. armed forces deployed outside the United States
. . prescription . . . 212.301
. contractor purchasing system administration . . . 252.244-7001
. . prescription . . . 244.305-71
. contractors performing private security functions . . . 252.225-7039
. . prescription . . . 225.370-6
. control of government personnel work product . . . 252.204-7003
. . prescription . . . 204.404-70
. correspondence in English . . . 252.225-7041
. . prescription . . . 225.1103
. cost and software data reporting system . . . 252.234-7004
. . prescription . . . 234.7101
. cost estimating system requirements . . . 252.215-7002
. . prescription . . . 215.408
. cost limitation . . . 252.236-7006
. . prescription . . . 236.570
. covenant against contingent fees
. . prescription . . . 227.7009-1
. critical safety items . . . 252.209-7010
. . prescription . . . 209.270-5
. customs exemptions (Germany) . . . 252.229-7002
. . prescription . . . 229.402-70
. dangerous property
. . prescription . . . 245.7310-4
. declaration of technical data conformity
. . prescription . . . 227.7103-6; 227.7104
. default (vessel repair) . . . 252.217-7009
. . prescription . . . 217.7104
. defense contractors performing private security functions outside the United States . . . 52.225-7039
. . prescription . . . 225.302-6
. deferred delivery of technical data or computer software . . . 227.7103-8; 252.227-7026
. . prescription . . . 227.7203-8

Contract clauses and solicitation provisions—continued
. deferred ordering of technical data or computer software . . . 252.227-7027
. . prescriptions . . . 227.7103-8; 227.7203-8
. delivery tickets (laundry and dry cleaning) . . . 252.237-7016
. . prescription . . . 237.7101
. demilitarization
. . prescription . . . 245.7310-1
. demurrage (transportation) . . . 252.247-7014
. . prescription . . . 247.271-3
. discharge of liens (vessel repair) . . . 252.217-7014
. . prescription . . . 217.7104
. disclosure of information . . . 252.204-7000
. . prescription . . . 204.404-70
. disclosure of information to litigation support contractors . . . 252.204-7015
. . prescription . . . 204.7403
. disclosure of ownership or control by a foreign government . . . 252.209-7002
. . prescription . . . 209.104-70
. disclosure of ownership or control by the government of a country that is a state sponsor of terrorism . . . 252.225-7050
. . prescription . . . 225.771-5
. display of DoD hotline poster
. . prescription . . . 203.1004
. display of fraud hotline poster(s) . . . 252.203-7004
. . prescription . . . 203.1004
. disposition of payments . . . 252.232-7001
. . prescription . . . 232.412-70
. DoD progress payment rates . . . 252.232-7004
. . prescription . . . 232.502-4
. domestic source restriction . . . 252.206-7000
. . prescription . . . 206.302-3
. drawings and other data to become property of government . . . 252.227-7023
. . prescription . . . 227.7107-1
. drayage (transportation)
. . prescription . . . 247.271-3
. drug-free work force . . . 252.223-7004
. . prescription . . . 223.370-4
. duty-free entry . . . 252.225-7013
. . prescription . . . 225.1101
. earned value management system . . . 252.234-7002
. . prescription . . . 234.203
. economic price adjustment—basic steel, aluminum, brass, bronze or copper mill products . . . 252.216-7000
. . prescription . . . 216.203-4
. economic price adjustment—nonstandard steel items . . . 252.216-7001
. . prescription . . . 216.203-4
. economic price adjustment—wage rates or material prices controlled by a foreign government . . . 252.216-7003
. . prescription . . . 216.203-4

Contract clauses and solicitation provisions— continued
. economic price adjustment—basic steel, aluminum, brass, bronze, or copper mill products—representation . . . 252.216-7007
. . prescription . . . 216.203-4-70
. economic price adjustment—wage rates or material prices controlled by a foreign government—representation . . . 252.216-7008
. . prescription . . . 216.203-4-70
. wide area workflow payment instructions . . . 252.232-7006
. . prescription . . . 232.7004
. erroneous shipments
. . prescription . . . 247.271-3
. evaluation factor for employing or subcontracting with members of selective service . . . 252.215-7006
. . prescription . . . 215.370-3
. evaluation of bids (transportation)
. . prescription . . . 247.271-3
. evaluation of offers for air circuit breakers . . . 252.225-7037
. . prescription . . . 225.7006-4
. evaluation preference for domestic shipyards
. . prescription
. exception from certified cost or pricing data requirements for foreign military sales indirect offsets . . . 252.215-7014
. . prescription . . . 215.408
. excessive pass-through charges
. . prescription
. exclusionary policies and practices of foreign governments . . . 252.225-7028
. exercise of option to fulfill foreign military sales commitments . . . 252.217-7000
. . prescription . . . 217.208-70
. export-controlled items
. . prescription . . . 225.7901-4
. exports by approved community members in performance of the contract . . . 252.225-7047
. . prescription . . . 225.7902-5
. exports by approved community members in response to the solicitation . . . 252.225-7046
. . prescription . . . 225.7902-5
. facility requirements (mortuary services)
. . prescription . . . 237.7003
. fast payment procedures
. . prescription . . . 242.1404-2
. final scientific or technical report . . . 252.235-7011
. . prescription . . . 235.072
. flexible progress payments
. . prescription . . . 232.502-4
. frequency authorization . . . 252.235-7003
. . prescription . . . 235.072
. government access . . . 252.241-7001
. . prescription . . . 241.501-70
. government-furnished mapping, charting and geodesy property . . . 252.245-7000
. government-furnished property (short form)
. . prescription . . . 237.7003

Contract clauses and solicitation provisions— continued
. government rights (unlimited) . . . 252.227-7022
. . prescription . . . 227.7107-1
. gratuities
. . prescription . . . 227.7009-1
. ground and flight risk . . . 252.228-7001
. . prescription . . . 228.370
. group interment (mortuary services) . . . 252.237-7008
. . prescription . . . 237.7003
. guarantees (vessel repair) . . . 252.217-7013
. . prescription . . . 217.7104
. hardship conditions (transportation) . . . 252.247-7000
. . prescription . . . 247.270-4
. hazard warning labels . . . 252.223-7001
. . prescription . . . 223.303
. human research subjects . . . 252.235-7004
. . prescription . . . 235.072
. identification and assertion of use, release, or disclosure restrictions . . . 252.227-7017
. . prescription . . . 227.7103-10; 227.7104; 227.7203-3
. identification of expenditures in the U.S. . . . 252.225-7005
. . prescription . . . 225.1103
. identification of provisions and clauses . . . 252.103
. identification of sources of supply
. . prescription . . . 217.7303
. indefinite quantities—fixed charges (transportation) . . . 252.247-7004
. . prescription . . . 247.270-4
. indefinite quantities—no fixed charges (transportation) . . . 252.247-7005
. . prescription . . . 247.270-4
. indemnification under 10 U.S.C. 2354—cost-reimbursement . . . 252.235-7001
. indemnification under 10 U.S.C. 2354—fixed-price . . . 252.235-7000
. . prescription . . . 235.070-3
. indemnification under 10 U.S.C. 2354—cost-reimbursement
. . prescription . . . 235.070-3
. individual laundry . . . 252.237-7017
. information assurance contractor training and certification . . . 252.239-7001
. . prescription . . . 239.7103
. information for duty-free entry evaluation
. . prescription . . . 225.1103
. inspection and manner of doing work (vessel repair) . . . 252.217-7005
. . prescription . . . 217.7104
. instructions for use
. . numbering . . . 252.101
. . using Part 252 . . . 252.101
. instructions to offerors (bulk weight) (laundry and dry cleaning) . . . 252.237-7013

Contract clauses and solicitation provisions—
continued
. instructions to offerors (count-of-articles) (laundry and dry cleaning) . . . 252.237-7012
. . prescription . . . 237.7101
. insurance—liability to third persons
. . prescription . . . 228.311-1
. intent to furnish precious metals as government-furnished material . . . 252.208-7000
. . prescription . . . 208.7305
. invoices exclusive of taxes or duties . . . 252.229-7000
. . prescription . . . 229.402-1
. item identification and valuation . . . 252.211-7003
. . prescription . . . 211.274-6
. item unique identification of government property
. . prescription
. job orders and compensation (vessel repair) . . . 252.217-7004
. . prescription . . . 217.7104
. levies on contract payments . . . 252.232-7010
. . prescription . . . 212.301; 232.7102
. liability and insurance (stevedoring) . . . 252.247-7007
. . prescriptions . . . 245.7310-3; 247.270-4
. liability and insurance (vessel repair) . . . 252.217-7012
. . prescription . . . 217.7104
. license grant . . . 252.227-7004
. . prescription . . . 227.7009-3
. license grant—running royalty . . . 252.227-7006
. . prescription . . . 227.7009-4
. license term . . . 252.227-7005
. . prescription . . . 227.7009-3
. license term—running royalty . . . 252.227-7007
. . prescription . . . 227.7009-4
. license to other government agencies . . . 252.227-7010
. . prescription . . . 227.7009-4
. limitation of government liability
. . prescription . . . 216.603-4; 217.7406
. limitation of government's obligation . . . 252.232-7007
. . prescription . . . 232.705-70
. limitations on contractors acting as lead systerm integrators . . . 252.209-7006
. . prescription . . . 209.570-4
. limitations on the use or disclosure of government-furnished information marked with restrictive legends . . . 252.227-7025
. . prescriptions . . . 227.7103-6; 227.7104; 227.7203-6
. limitations on the use or disclosure of information by litigation support solicitation offerors . . . 252.204-7013
. limitations on the use or disclosure of information by litigation support contractors . . . 252.204-7014
. . prescription . . . 204.7403

Contract clauses and solicitation provisions—
continued
. limitations on the use or disclosure of information by litigation support solicitation offerors
. . prescription . . . 204.7403
. limitations on the use or disclosure of third-party contractor reported cyber incident information . . . 252.204-7009
. . prescription . . . 204.7304
. loss or damage (count-of-articles) (laundry and dry cleaning) . . . 252.237-7014
. . prescription . . . 237.7101
. loss or damage (weight of articles) (laundry and dry cleaning) . . . 252.237-7015
. . prescription . . . 237.7101
. mandatory payment by governmentwide commercial purchase card . . . 252.232-7009
. . prescription . . . 212.301
. material inspection and receiving report . . . 252.246-7000
. . prescription . . . 246.370
. material management and accounting system . . . 252.242-7004
. . prescription . . . 242.7204
. military construction on Kwajalein Atoll—evaluation preference . . . 252.236-7012
. . prescription . . . 236.570
. modification proposals—price breakdown . . . 252.236-7000
. . prescription . . . 236.570
. non-estoppel . . . 252.227-7000
. . prescription . . . 227.7009-1
. notice and approval of restricted designs . . . 252.227-7024
. . prescription . . . 227.7107-3
. notice of continuation of essential contractor services . . . 252.237-7024
. . prescription . . . 237.7603
. notice of cost and software data reporting system . . . 252.234-7003
. . prescription . . . 234.7101
. notice of earned value management system . . . 252.234-7001
. . prescription . . . 234.203
. notice of intent to resolicit . . . 252.215-7007
. . prescription . . . 215.371-6
. notice of prohibition of certain contracts with foreign entities for conduct of ballistic missile defense research, development, test, and evaluation
. . prescription . . . 225.7017-4
. notice of prohibition relating to organizational conflict of interest . . . 252.209-7008
. . prescription . . . 209.571-8
. notice of special standards of responsibility (audits) . . . 252.237-7000
. . prescription . . . 237.270
. notice of supply chain risk . . . 252.239-7017
. . prescrption . . . 239.7306

Contract clauses and solicitation provisions— continued
. notice of warranty tracking of serialized items . . . 252.246-7005
. . prescription . . . 246.710
. notice to prospective suppliers on use of Past Performance Information Retrieval System-statistical reporting in past performance evaluations . . . 252.213-7000
. . prescription . . . 213.106-2-70
. report of intended performance outside United States and Canada . . . 252.249-7002
. notification of anticipated contract terminations or reductions
. . prescription . . . 249.7003
. notification of competition limited to eligible concern
. . prescription . . . 219.811-3
. notification of payment in local currency (Afghanistan) . . . 252.232-7014
. . prescription . . . 232.7202
. notification of potential safety issues . . . 252.246-7003
. . prescription . . . 246.371
. notification of transportation of supplies by sea
. . prescription . . . 244.403; 247.574
. notification to delay performance . . . 252.219-7011
. . prescription . . . 219.811-3
. obligation of the government (communications) . . . 252.239-7013
. . prescription . . . 239.7411
. obstruction of navigable waterways . . . 252.236-7002
. . prescription . . . 236.570
. offering property for exchange . . . 252.217-7002
. . prescription . . . 217.7005
. offeror representations and certifications—commercial items
. . prescription . . . 212.301
. only one offer . . . 252.215-7008
. . prescription . . . 215.408
. option for supervision and inspection services
. . prescription . . . 236.609-70
. oral attestation of security responsibilities
. . prescription . . . 204.404-70
. ordering . . . 252.216-7006
. . prescription . . . 216.506
. ordering from government supply sources . . . 252.251-7000
. . prescription . . . 251.107
. ordering limitation (transportation) . . . 252.247-7012
. . prescription . . . 247.271-3
. ordering (transportation)
. . prescription . . . 247.271-3
. organizational conflict of interest, major defense acquisition program . . . 252.209-7009
. . prescription . . . 209.571-8
. over and above work . . . 252.217-7028
. . prescription . . . 217.7702
. overseas architect-engineer services—restriction to U.S. firms . . . 252.236-7011
. . prescription . . . 236.609-70

Contract clauses and solicitation provisions— continued
. overseas military construction—preference for U.S. firms . . . 252.236-7010
. . prescription . . . 236.570
. pass-through of motor carrier fuel surcharge adjustment . . . 252.247-7003
. . prescription . . . 247.207
. passive radio frequency identification . . . 52.211-7006
. . prescription . . . 211.275-3
. patent license and release contract . . . 252.227-7012
. . prescription . . . 227.7012
. patents—ownership by large business contractor
. . prescription
. patents—reporting of subject inventions . . . 252.227-7039
. . prescription . . . 227.303
. payment for mobilization and demobilization . . . 252.236-7004
. . prescription . . . 236.570
. payment for mobilization and preparatory work . . . 252.236-7003
. . prescription . . . 236.570
. payment for subline items not separately priced . . . 252.204-7002
. . prescription . . . 204.7104-1
. payments in support of emergencies and contingency operations . . . 252.232-7011
. . prescription . . . 232.908
. payments under personal services contracts
. . prescription . . . 237.7303
. payments under time-and-materials and labor-hour contracts
. . alternate A, prescription . . . 252.232-7011
. payments (vessel repair) . . . 252.217-7007
. . prescription . . . 217.7104
. performance and delivery (mortuary services) . . . 252.237-7005
. . prescription . . . 237.7003
. performance-based payments—deliverable-item basis . . . 252.232-7013
. . prescription . . . 232.1005-70
. performance-based payments—whole-contract basis . . . 252.232-7012
. . prescription . . . 232.1005-70
. performance (vessel repair) . . . 252.217-7010
. . prescription . . . 217.7104
. period of contract (transportation)
. . prescription . . . 247.271-3
. permit from Italian inspectorate of labor . . . 252.222-7003
. . prescription . . . 222.7201
. permits, authorities, or franchises (transportation)
. . prescription . . . 247.271-3
. permits (mortuary services) . . . 252.237-7009
. . prescription . . . 237.7003
. photovoltaic devices . . . 252.225-7017
. . solicitation provision and contract clause . . . 225.7017-5

Contract clauses and solicitation provisions—
continued
. photovoltaic devices, certificate . . . 252.225-7018
. . prescription . . . 252.225-7018
. plant protection (vessel repair) . . . 252.217-7016
. . prescription . . . 217.7104
. preference for certain domestic commodities . . . 252.225-7012
. . prescription . . . 225.7002-3
. preference for domestic hand or measuring tools
. . prescription . . . 225.7002-3
. preference for domestic specialty metals
. . prescription . . . 225.7002-3; 244.403
. preparation history (mortuary services) . . . 252.237-7011
. . prescription . . . 237.7003
. price adjustment (transportation) . . . 252.247-7001
. . prescription . . . 247.270-4
. pricing adjustments
. . prescription . . . 215.408
. pricing of contract modifications . . . 252.243-7001
. . prescriptions . . . 213.302-5; 243.205-70
. progress payments for foreign military sales acquisitions . . . 252.232-7002
. . prescription . . . 232.502-4
. prohibited financial interests for lead system integrators . . . 252.209-7007
. . prescription . . . 209.570-4
. prohibition of hexavalent chromium . . . 252.223-7008
. . prescription . . . 223.7306
. prohibition on acquisition of commercial satellite services from certain foreign entities . . . 52.225-7049
. . definitions . . . 225.772-1
. . prescription . . . 225.872-5
. prohibition on acquisition of munitions list items from communist Chinese military . . . 252.225-7007
. . prescription . . . 225.1103
. prohibition on interrogation of detainees by contractor personnel . . . 252.237-7010
. . prescription . . . 237.173-5
. prohibition on persons convicted of fraud or other defense-contract-related felonies . . . 252.203-7001
. . prescription . . . 203.570-3
. prohibition on storage, treatment, and disposal of toxic or hazardous materials . . . 252.223-7006
. . prescription . . . 223.7103
. prohibition on use of nonimmigrant aliens—Guam . . . 252.222-7005
. . prescription . . . 222.7302
. proposal adequacy checklist . . . 52.215-7009
. . prescription . . . 215.408
. protection against compromising emanations . . . 239.7103; 252.239-7000
. . prescription . . . 239.7102-3
. provision of information to cooperative agreement holders . . . 252.205-7000
. . prescription . . . 205.470

Contract clauses and solicitation provisions—
continued
. qualifying country sources as subcontractors . . . 252.225-7002
. . prescription . . . 225.1103
. radio frequency identification . . . 252.211-7006
. . prescription . . . 211.275-3; 212.301
. radioactive material
. . prescription . . . 245.7310-6
. rates, charges, and services (communications) . . . 252.239-7005
. . prescription . . . 239.7411
. readjustment of payments . . . 252.227-7002
. . prescription . . . 227.7009-2
. reflagging or repair work . . . 252.247-7025
. . prescription . . . 247.574
. reimbursement for war-hazard losses . . . 252.228-7000
. . prescription . . . 228.370
. reimbursement of subcontractor advance payments—DoD pilot mentor-protege program . . . 252.232-7005
. . prescription . . . 232.412-70
. release of past infringement . . . 252.227-7001
. . prescription . . . 227.7009-2
. relief from customs duty and value added tax on fuel (passenger vehicles) (United Kingdom) . . . 252.229-7009
. . prescription . . . 229.402-70
. relief from customs duty on fuel (United Kingdom) . . . 252.229-7010
. . prescription . . . 229.402-70
. relief from import duty (United Kingdom) . . . 252.229-7008
. . prescription . . . 229.402-70
. removal of contractor's employees (transportation)
. . prescription . . . 247.270-4
. report of intended performance outside the U.S. and Canada—submission after award . . . 252.225-7004
. report of intended performance outside the U.S. and Canada—submission with offer . . . 252.225-7003
. report of intended performance outside the U.S. and Canada—submission after award
. . prescription . . . 225.7203
. report of intended performance outside the U.S. and Canada—submission with offer
. . prescription . . . 225.7204
. reporting and payment of royalties . . . 252.227-7009
. . prescription . . . 227.7009-4
. reporting loss of government property . . . 252.245-7002
. . prescription . . . 245.107
. reporting of foreign taxes—U.S. assistance programs . . . 252.229-7011
. . prescription . . . 229.170-4
. reporting of government-furnished property . . . 252.211-7007
. . prescription . . . 211.274-6

Contract clauses and solicitation provisions— continued
. reporting, reutilization, and disposal . . . 252.245-7004
. . prescription . . . 245.107
. representation of extent of transportation by sea . . . 252.247-7022
. . prescription . . . 247.574
. representation of use of cloud computing . . . 252.239-7009
. . prescription . . . 239.7604
. representation regarding combatting trafficking in persons . . . 252.222-7007
. . prescription . . . 222.1771
. representation relating to compensation of former DoD officials . . . 252.203-7005
. . prescription . . . 203.171-4
. requests for equitable adjustment . . . 252.243-7002
. . prescription . . . 243.205-71
. requirement for submission of data other than certified cost or pricing data—modifications—Canadian Commercial Corporation . . . 252.215-7004
. requirement for submission of data other than certified cost or pricing data—Canadian Commercial Corporation . . . 252.215-7004
. . prescription . . . 215.408
. requirement for submission of data other than certified cost or pricing data—modifications—Canadian Commercial Corporation
. . prescription . . . 215.408
. requirement to inform employees of whistleblower rights . . . 252.203-7002
. . prescription . . . 203.970
. requirements (mortuary services) . . . 252.237-7003
. . prescription . . . 237.7003
. requirements (transportation)
. . prescription . . . 247.271-3
. reserve officer training corps and military recruiting on campus . . . 252.209-7005
. . prescription . . . 209.470-4
. restriction on acquisition of air circuit breakers . . . 252.225-7038
. . prescription . . . 225.7006-4
. restriction on acquisition of anchor and mooring chain . . . 252.225-7019
. . prescription . . . 225.7007-3
. restriction on acquisition of ball and roller bearings . . . 252.225-7016
. . prescription . . . 225.7009-5
. restriction on acquisition of carbon, alloy, and armor steel plate . . . 252.225-7030
. . prescriptions . . . 225.7011-3
. restriction on acquisition of forgings . . . 252.225-7025
. . prescription . . . 225.7102-4
. restriction on acquisition of hand or measuring tools . . . 252.225-7015
. . prescription . . . 225.7002-3

Contract clauses and solicitation provisions— continued
. restriction on acquisition of supercomputers . . . 252.225-7011
. . prescription . . . 225.7012-3
. restriction on acquisition of vessel propellers
. . prescription . . . 225.7010-4
. restriction on acquistion of specialty metals . . . 252.225-7008
. . prescription . . . 225.7003-5
. restriction on contingent fees for foreign military sales . . . 252.225-7027
. . prescription . . . 225.7307
. restrictions on employment of personnel . . . 252.222-7000
. . prescription . . . 222.7004
. restrictions on use of mandatory arbitration agreements . . . 252.222-7006
. . prescription . . . 222.7405
. returnable containers other than cylinders . . . 252.247-7021
. . prescription . . . 247.305-70
. reuse arrangements (communications) . . . 252.239-7008
. . prescription . . . 239.7411
. revision of prices (transportation) . . . 252.247-7002
. . prescription . . . 247.270-4
. riding gang member requirements . . . 252.247-7027
. . prescription . . . 247.574
. right of first refusal of employment—closure of military installations . . . 252.222-7001
. . prescription . . . 222.7102
. rights in bid or proposal information . . . 252.227-7016
. . prescription . . . 227.7104; 227.7203-6; 227.7103-6
. rights in data—existing works . . . 252.227-7021
. . prescription . . . 227.7105-2
. rights in noncommercial computer software and noncommercial software documentation . . . 252.227-7014
. . prescriptions . . . 227.7203-6; 227.7203-11
. rights in noncommercial technical data and computer software—small business innovation research (SBIR) program . . . 252.227-7018
. . prescription . . . 227.7104
. rights in shop drawings . . . 252.227-7033
. . prescription . . . 227.7107-1
. rights in special works . . . 252.227-7020
. . prescription . . . 227.7105-3; 227.7205
. rights in technical data—noncommercial items . . . 252.227-7013
. . prescription . . . 227.7103-6; 227.7103-9; 227.7103-10
. rights in technical data and computer software . . . 252.227-7013
. . prescription . . . 227.7103-6; 246.710
. rights in technical data and computer software (foreign) . . . 252.227-7032
. . prescription . . . 227.7103-17

Contract clauses and solicitation provisions— continued
. safeguarding sensitive conventional arms, ammunition, and explosives . . . 252.223-7007
. . prescription . . . 223.7203
. safety and health (vessel repair) . . . 252.217-7015
. . prescription . . . 217.7104
. safety of facilities, infrastructure, and equipment for military operations . . . 252.246-7004
. . prescription . . . 246.270-4
. safety precautions for ammunition and explosives . . . 252.223-7002
. . prescription . . . 223.370-5
. scope of contract (transportation)
. . prescription (personal property shipment or storage) . . . 247.271-3
. scrap warranty
. . prescription . . . 245.7310-7
. secondary Arab boycott of Israel . . . 252.225-7031
. . prescription . . . 225.7605
. Section 8(a) direct award . . . 252.219-7009
. . alternate A . . . 252.219-7010
. . prescription . . . 219.811-3
. services at installations being closed . . . 237.7402; 252.237-7020; 252.237-7022
. . prescription . . . 237.7402
. small business subcontracting plan (DoD contracts) . . . 252.219-7003
. . prescription
. small business subcontracting plan (test program) . . . 252.219-7004
. . prescription . . . 219.708
. sources of electronic parts . . . 252.242-7008
. . prescription . . . 246.870-3
. special construction and equipment charges (communications) . . . 252.239-7011
. . prescription . . . 239.7411
. special definitions of government property (laundry and dry cleaning) . . . 252.237-7018
. special termination costs . . . 252.249-7000
. . prescription . . . 249.501-70
. status of contractor as a direct contractor (Spain) . . . 252.229-7004
. . prescription . . . 229.402-70
. subcontracting
. . prescription . . . 247.271-3
. subcontracting (mortuary services) . . . 252.237-7006
. . prescription . . . 237.7003
. subcontracting with firms that are owned or controlled by the government of a country that is a state sponsor of terrorism . . . 252.209-7004
. subcontracting with firms that are owned or controlled by the government of a terrorist country
. . prescription . . . 209.409
. subcontractor advance payments—DoD pilot mentor-protege program
. . prescription . . . 232.412-70
. subcontracts for commercial items . . . 252.244-7000

Contract clauses and solicitation provisions— continued
. subcontracts for commercial items and commercial components (DoD contracts)
. . prescription . . . 244.403
. substitutions for military or federal specifications and standards . . . 252.211-7005
. . prescription . . . 211.273-4
. superseding contract (utility services) . . . 252.241-7000
. . prescription . . . 252.241-7000
. supplemental cost principles . . . 252.231-7000
. . prescription . . . 231.100-70
. supplies to be accorded duty-free entry
. . prescription . . . 225.1103
. supply chain risk . . . 252.239-7017
. . prescription . . . 239.7306
. surge option . . . 252.217-7001
. . prescription . . . 217.208-70
. tagging, labeling, and marking government-furnished property . . . 252.245-7001
. . prescription . . . 245.107
. tariff information (communications) . . . 252.239-7006
. . prescription . . . 239.7411
. tax exemptions (Italy) . . . 252.229-7003
. . prescription . . . 229.402-70
. tax exemptions (Italy)—representation . . . 252.229-7012
. . prescription . . . 229.402-70
. tax exemptions (Spain) . . . 252.229-7005
. . prescription . . . 229.402-70
. tax exemptions (Spain)—representation . . . 252.229-7013
. . prescription . . . 229.402-70
. tax relief . . . 252.229-7001
. . prescription . . . 229.402-70
. taxes, foreign contracts in Afghanistan . . . 252.229-7014
. . prescription . . . 229.402-70
. taxes, foreign contracts in Afghanistan (North Atlantic Treaty Organization Status of Forces Agreement)
. Taxes, Foreign Contracts in Afghanistan (North Atlantic Treaty Organization Status of Forces Agreement)
. . prescription . . . 229.402-70
. technical data—commercial items . . . 252.227-7015
. . prescription . . . 227.7102-4
. technical data—withholding of payment . . . 252.227-7030
. . prescriptions . . . 227.7103-6; 227.7104
. technical data or computer software previously delivered to the government . . . 252.227-7028
. . prescription . . . 227.7103-6; 227.7104; 227.7203-6
. telecommunications security equipment, devices, techniques, and services . . . 252.239-7016
. . prescription . . . 239.7411
. term of agreement (communications) . . . 252.239-7014
. . prescription . . . 239.7411

Contract clauses and solicitation provisions—
continued
. termination . . . 252.227-7003
. . prescription . . . 227.7009-2
. termination for default (mortuary services) . . . 252.237-7007
. . prescription . . . 237.7003
. termination (personal services)
. . prescription . . . 237.7303
. time-and-materials/labor-hour proposal requirements—noncommercial item acquisition with adequate price competition . . . 252.216-7002
. . prescription . . . 216.601
. title to communication facilities and equipment (communications)
. . prescription . . . 239.7411
. title to telecommunication facilities and equipment (communications) . . . 252.239-7012
. . prescription . . . 239.7411
. title (vessel repair) . . . 252.217-7006
. . prescription . . . 217.7104
. trade agreements . . . 252.225-7021
. . prescription . . . 225.1103
. trade agreements certificate . . . 252.225-7020
. . prescription . . . 225.1103
. training for contractor personnel interacting with detainees . . . 252.237-7019
. . prescription . . . 237.171-4
. transportation of supplies by sea . . . 252.247-7023
. . prescriptions . . . 244.403; 247.574
. use of employees or subcontractors who are members of selective reserve . . . 252.215-7006
. . prescription . . . 215.370-3
. use of interagency fleet management system (IFMS) vehicles and related services . . . 252.251-7001
. . prescription . . . 251.205
. utilization of Indian organizations and Indian-owned economic enterprises and Native Hawaiian small business concerns . . . 252.226-7001
. utilization of Indian organizations and Indian-owned economic enterprises
. . prescription . . . 226.104
. validation of asserted restrictions—computer software . . . 252.227-7019
. . prescription . . . 227.7104; 227.7203-6; 227.7203-11
. validation of restrictive markings on technical data . . . 252.227-7037
. . prescription . . . 227.7102-4; 227.7103-6; 227.7103-11; 227.7104; 227.7203-6
. value added tax exclusion (United Kingdom) . . . 252.229-7006
. . prescription . . . 229.402-70
. verification of U.S. receipt of goods . . . 252.229-7007
. . prescription . . . 229.402-70
. waiver of United Kingdom levies . . . 252.225-7033
. . prescription . . . 225.1101
. waiver of United Kingdom levies—evaluation of offers . . . 252.225-7032
. . prescription . . . 225.1101

Contract clauses and solicitation provisions—
continued
. warranty of construction (Germany) . . . 252.246-7002
. . prescription . . . 246.710
. warranty of data . . . 252.246-7001
. . prescription . . . 246.710
. warranty of systems and equipment under performance specifications or design criteria
. . prescription . . . 246.710
. warranty tracking of serialized items . . . 252.246-7006
. workers' compensation and war-hazard insurance overseas
. . prescription . . . 228.370
. acquisition of uniform components for Afghan military or national police
. . prescription . . . 52.225-7029

Contract disputes
. contract clauses and solicitation provisions
. . choice of law (overseas) . . . 233.215-70; 252.233-7001
. . prescriptions . . . 233.215
. contracting officer's authority . . . 233.210
. labor disputes
. . construction contracts . . . 222.406-10
. . impact on defense programs . . . 222.101-3
. . removal of items from affected facility . . . 222.101-4
. . reporting requirement . . . 222.101-3
. . stevedoring services acquisition during . . . 222.101-70
. . work stoppages . . . 222.101-4
. limitations on payment . . . 233.204-70

Contract financing
. administration and payment . . . 232.207
. advance payments for noncommercial items
. . advance payment pool . . . 232.470
. . approval recommendation . . . 232.409-1
. . contract clause prescriptions . . . 232.412-70
. . exclusions . . . 232.404
. . findings, determination, and authorization . . . 232.410
. assignment of claims
. . contract clause . . . 232.806; 252.232-7008
. . policies . . . 232.803
. . procedure . . . 232.805
. commercial item purchase financing
. . contract clauses and solicitation provisions . . . 232.206
. . security for government financing . . . 232.202-4
. contract clauses and solicitation provisions
. . advance payment pool . . . 252.232-7000
. . assignment of claims (overseas) . . . 252.232-7008
. . disposition of payments . . . 252.232-7001
. . DoD progress payment rates . . . 252.232-7004
. . limitation of government's obligation . . . 252.232-7007
. . notification of payment in local currency (Afghanistan) . . . 252.232-7014

Contract financing—continued
. contract clauses and solicitation provisions—continued
. . payments in support of emergencies and contingency operations . . . 252.232-7011
. . progress payments for foreign military sales acquisitions . . . 252.232-7002
. . reimbursement of subcontractor advance payments, DoD pilot mentor-protege program . . . 252.232-7005
. . wide area workflow payment instructions . . . 252.232-7006
. debts
. . bankruptcy reporting . . . 232.671
. . compromising debts . . . 232.610
. . contract clause . . . 232.611
. . demand for payment . . . 232.604
. . debt determination . . . 232.603
. . responsibilities . . . 232.602
. . transfer of responsibility for debt collection . . . 232.670
. electronic funds transfer
. . contract clause and solicitation provision . . . 232.1110; 252.232-7009
. funding
. . contract clause . . . 232.705-70; 252.232-7007
. . contracts crossing fiscal years . . . 232.703-3
. . general requirements . . . 232.703-1
. . incrementally funded fixed-price contracts . . . 232.704-70
. . limitation of costs or funds . . . 232.704-70
. . military construction appropriations act restriction . . . 232.703-70
. . policy . . . 232.702
. general
. . appropriate information, obtaining . . . 232.072-2
. . cash flow forecasts . . . 232.072-3
. . financial responsibility of contractors . . . 232.072
. . payments, policy . . . 232.007
. . reduction or suspension of payments upon finding of fraud . . . 232.006-5
. . required financial reviews . . . 232.072-1
. . responsibilities . . . 232.070
. levies on payments
. . contract clause . . . 232.7102; 252.232-7010
. . policy and procedures . . . 232.7101
. . scope . . . 232.7100
. loan guarantees for defense production
. . authority . . . 232.302
. noncommercial item purchase financing
. . description of financing methods . . . 232.102
. . financial consultation . . . 232.108
. . providing contract financing . . . 232.104
. . provisional delivery payments . . . 232.102-70
. payment in local currency (Afghanistan)
. . policy and procedures . . . 232.7201
. . scope of subpart . . . 232.7200
. . solicitation provision . . . 252.232-7014; 232.7202

Contract financing—continued
. performance-based payments
. . contract clauses . . . 232.1005-70; 252.232-7012; 252.232-7013
. . criteria for use . . . 232.1003-70
. . policy . . . 232.1001
. . procedure . . . 232.1004
. postaward matters
. . application of government title terms . . . 232.503-15
. . suspension or reduction of payments . . . 232.503-6
. progress payments based on costs
. . application of government title terms . . . 232.503-15
. . contract clause prescriptions . . . 232.502-4
. . contract price and . . . 232.501-3
. . customary progress payment rates . . . 232.501-1
. . suspension or reduction of payments . . . 232.503-6
. . unusual . . . 232.501-2
. prompt payment
. . applicability . . . 232.901
. . contract clauses . . . 232.908
. . determining payment due dates . . . 232.904
. . making payments . . . 232.906
. . payment documentation and process . . . 232.905
. . responsibilities . . . 232.903
. requests, submission and processing of
. . contract clause . . . 252.232-7006
. . prescription . . . 232.7004
. . contract clause . . . 252.232-7003
. . definitions . . . 232.7001; 252.232-7003
. . policy . . . 232.7002
. . procedures . . . 232.7003
. . scope . . . 232.7000
. wide area workflow payment instructions
. . contract clause . . . 252.232-7006
. . prescription . . . 232.7004

Contract types
. award fees and . . . 216.470
. basic ordering agreements . . . 216.703
. commercial items . . . 212.207
. contract clauses and solicitation provisions
. . contract definitization . . . 216.603-4; 252.217-7027
. . contract clauses and solicitation provisions . . . 216.203-4; 252.216-7000; 216.203-4; 252.216-7001; 216.203-4; 252.216-7003
. . requirements . . . 216.506
. cost-plus-fixed-fee contracts . . . 216.306
. . limittaions . . . 216.301-1
. factors for selection . . . 216.104
. fixed-price contracts
. . incentive contracts . . . 216.403
. . incentive contracts; firm targets . . . 216.403-1
. . incentive (successive targets) contracts . . . 216.403-2
. . with economic price adjustments . . . 216.203-4
. incentive contracts
. . cost-plus-award-fee contracts . . . 216.405-2
. . cost-plus-incentive-fee contracts . . . 216.405-1

Contract types—continued
. incentive contracts—continued
. . cost-reimbursement incentive contracts . . . 216.405
. . fixed-price incentive contracts . . . 216.403
. . fixed-price incentive (firm targets) contracts . . . 216.403-1
. . fixed-price incentive (successive targets) contracts . . . 216.403-2
. . objective criteria . . . 216.401-71
. . procedures and information . . . 216.401
. . technical performance incentives . . . 216.402-2
. indefinite delivery contracts
. . contract clause and solicitation provision prescription . . . 216.506
. . ordering . . . 216.505
. . orders under multiple award contracts . . . 216.505-70
. indefinite-quantity contracts . . . 216.504
. letter contracts
. . contract clause prescriptions . . . 216.603-4
. . limitations . . . 216.603-3
. management and operating contracts . . . 217.600
. policies . . . 216.102
. research and development contracts . . . 216.104-70; 235.006
. time-and-materials contracts . . . 216.601

Contract work hours and safety standards
. liquidated damages and overtime pay . . . 222.302

Contracting authority—see also Contracting officers
. agency-head responsibilities . . . 207.103
. appointment . . . 201.603-3
. contract clause . . . 201.602-70; 252.201-7000
. contracting officer's signature . . . 204.101
. paid advertisements in newspapers . . . 205.502
. selection . . . 201.603-2

Contracting officers
. agency-head responsibilities . . . 207.103
. appointment . . . 201.603-3
. contracting officer's representative . . . 201.602-2; 252.201-7000
. corporate administrative contracting officer
. . assignment and location . . . 242.602
. . determination of final indirect cost rates . . . 242.705-1
. responsibilities . . . 201.602-2
. selection . . . 201.603
. signature . . . 204.101
. termination duties . . . 249.105-1; 249.105-2

Contractor insurance/pension review (CIPR)
. general . . . 242.7301
. requirements . . . 242.7302
. responsibilities . . . 242.7303

Contractor purchasing system reviews
. extent of review . . . 244.303
. granting, withholding, or withdrawing approval . . . 244.305-70
. objective . . . 244.301

Contractor qualifications
. architect-engineer services
. . selection criteria . . . 236.602-1
. aviation critical safety items
. . definitions . . . 209.270-2
. . policy . . . 209.270-3
. . procedures . . . 209.270-4
. . scope . . . 209.270-1
. contract clauses and solicitation provisions
. . disclosure of ownership or control by a foreign government . . . 209.104-70; 252.209-7002
. . organizational and consultant conflicts of interest . . . 209.570-4; 252.209-7006; 252.209-7007
. . reserve officer training corps and military recruiting on campus—representation . . . 252.209-7003
. . reserve officer training corps and military recruiting on campus . . . 209.470-4
. . subcontracting with firms that are owned or controlled by the government of a country that is a state sponsor of terrorism . . . 209.409; 252.209-7004
. critical safety items
. . contract clause . . . 252.209-7010
. . contract clause prescription . . . 209.270-5
. debarment, suspension, and ineligibility
. . causes for debarment . . . 209.406-2
. . debarment policy . . . 209.406-1
. . debarment procedures . . . 209.406-3
. . definitions . . . 209.403
. . effect of listing . . . 209.405
. . general policy . . . 209.402
. . policy . . . 209.402
. . reserve officer training corps and military recruiting on campus . . . 209.470
. . restrictions on subcontracting . . . 209.405-2
. . suspension procedures . . . 209.407-3
. . unlawful manufacture of Congressional Medal of Honor . . . 209.471
. excluded parties list system . . . 209.105-1
. Federal Awardee Performance and Integrity Information System . . . 209.105-2
. general requirements, policy . . . 209.202
. organizational and consultant conflicts of interest
. . limitations on contractors acting as lead system integrators . . . 209.570
. organizational conflicts of interest
. . applicability . . . 209.571-2
. . definitions . . . 209.571-1
. . identification . . . 209.571-6
. . lead system integrators . . . 209.571-5
. . major defense acquisition program, contract clause . . . 252.209-7009
. . mitigation . . . 209.571-4
. . notice of prohibition, solicitation provision . . . 252.209-7008
. . policy . . . 209.571-3
. . prescription, contract clause . . . 209.571-8
. . prescription, solicitation provision . . . 209.571-8
. . scope of subpart . . . 209.571-0

Contractor qualifications—continued
. organizational conflicts of interest—continued
. . systems engineering contracts . . . 209.571-7
. . technical assistance contracts . . . 209.571-7
. responsible prospective contractors, identifying
. . definitions . . . 209.101
. . determinations and documentation . . . 209.105-2
. . general standards . . . 209.104-1
. . preaward surveys . . . 209.106
. . prescription of forms . . . 253.209-1
. . subcontractor responsibility . . . 209.104-4

Contractors
. financial responsibility . . . 232.072
. . appropriate information, obtaining . . . 232.072-2
. . cash flow forecasts . . . 232.072-3
. . required reviews . . . 232.072-1
. identification of
. . CAGE codes . . . 204.1870
. performance evaluations . . . 236.201; 236.604
. qualifications
. . obtaining access to proprietary information . . . 209.505-4

Copyrights—see also Rights in software and software documentation; Rights in technical data
. infringement claims . . . 227.7003
. rights in technical data . . . 227.7103-9
. scope . . . 227.400
. software or software documentation . . . 227.7203-9

Cost accounting standards
. waiver of program requirements . . . 230.201-5

Cost efficiency factor . . . 215.404-71

Cost-plus-award-fee contracts . . . 216.405-2
. fee requirements . . . 215.404-74

Cost-plus-fixed-fee contracts . . . 216.306; 236.271
. limitations . . . 216.301-1

Cost-plus-incentive-fee contracts . . . 216.405-1

Cost principles and procedures
. commercial organizations, contracts with
. . bid and proposal costs . . . 231.205-18
. . compensation for personal services . . . 231.205-6
. . external restructuring costs . . . 231.205-70
. . independent research and development costs . . . 231.205-18
. . insurance and indemnification . . . 231.205-19
. . legislative lobbying costs . . . 231.205-22
. . public relations and advertising costs . . . 231.205-1
. contract clause . . . 231.100-70; 252.231-7000
. cost of remedy for use or inclusion of cocounterfeit electronic parts and suspect counterfeit electronic parts . . . 231.205-71
. educational institutions, contracts with . . . 231.303
. Indian tribal governments, contracts with . . . 231.603
. nonprofit organizations, contracts with . . . 231.703

Cost-reimbursement contracts
. cost-plus contracts
. . limitations . . . 216.301-3
. cost-plus-fixed-fee contracts . . . 216.306

Cost-reimbursement contracts—continued
. incentive contracts . . . 216.405
. settlement memorandum . . . 249.110

Costs, disallowance of . . . 242.803

Counterfeit electronic parts
. contract clauses
. . contractor counterfeit electronic part detection and avoidance system . . . 252.246-7007
. . contractor purchasing system administration . . . 252.244-7001
. . sources of electronic parts . . . 252.246-7008
. contractor counterfeit electronic part detection and avoidance . . . 246.870
. . contract clause . . . 252.246-7007; 252.246-7008
. . contract clauses . . . 246.870-3
. . definition . . . 246.870-1
. . policy . . . 246.870-2
. . scope . . . 246.870-0
. cost principle
. . use or inclusion of counterfeit electronic parts and suspect counterfeit electronic parts . . . 231.205-71

Customs and duties—see also Foreign acquisitions
. component, definition of . . . 225.900-70
. exempted supplies . . . 225.903
. policy . . . 225.901
. procedures . . . 225.902

D

Debarment, suspension, and ineligibility
. contract clauses and solicitation provisions
. . reserve officer training corps and military recruiting on campus . . . 209.470-4; 252.209-7005
. . reserve officer training corps and military recruiting on campus—representation . . . 252.209-7003
. . subcontracting with firms that are owned or controlled by the government of a country that is a state sponsor of terrorism . . . 209.409; 252.209-7004
. debarment
. . causes for . . . 209.406-2
. . general . . . 209.406-1
. . procedures . . . 209.406-3
. . unlawful manufacture of Congressional Medal of Honor . . . 209.470-3
. definitions . . . 209.403
. general policy . . . 209.402
. list of parties excluded
. . effect of listing . . . 209.405
. . restrictions on subcontracting . . . 209.405-2
. reserve officer training corps and military recruiting on campus
. . contract clause . . . 209.470-3; 252.209-7005
. . definition of institution of higher education . . . 209.470-1
. . policy . . . 209.470-2
. . procedures . . . 209.470-3
. suspension procedures . . . 209.407-3

Debarment, suspension, and ineligibility—continued
. unlawful manufacture of Congressional Medal of Honor . . . 209.471

Debts—see also Contract financing
. bankruptcy reporting . . . 232.671
. compromising debts . . . 232.610
. contract clause . . . 232.611
. demand for payment . . . 232.604
. debt determination . . . 232.603
. responsibilities . . . 232.602
. transfer of responsibility for debt collection . . . 232.670

Defense Environmental Restoration Program . . . 228.102-70

Definitions
. A-E . . . 236.102
. acceptable estimating system . . . 215.404-71
. acceptance . . . 246.701
. accounting classification reference number (ACRN) . . . 204.7101
. acquiring department . . . 208.7001
. advance procurement . . . 217.103
. ammunition and explosives . . . 223.370-2; 252.223-7002
. arms, ammunition, and explosives (AA&E) . . . 223.7200
. assisted acquisition . . . 217.701
. attachment . . . 204.7101
. aviation critical safety item . . . 209.270-2
. bearing components . . . 225.7001
. Caribbean Basin country end product . . . 225.003
. catalog . . . 237.7204
. commodity rate . . . 247.270-1
. common carrier . . . 239.7401
. Communist Chinese military company . . . 252.225-7007
. component . . . 225.770-1; 225.7001; 225.900-70
. congressional defense committees . . . 202.101
. construction activity . . . 236.102
. contract action . . . 217.7401
. contract administration office . . . 202.101
. contracting activities . . . 202.101
. contracting officer's representative . . . 202.101
. contractor . . . 215.404-71; 227.7101; 227.7201
. cooperative project . . . 225.871-2
. course . . . 237.7204
. covered contractor . . . 222.7401
. curriculum . . . 237.7204
. debarring official . . . 209.403
. defect (warranties) . . . 246.701
. defense equipment . . . 225.003
. Defense Supply Center, Philadelphia (DSCP) . . . 208.7301
. definitization . . . 217.7401
. definitized item . . . 204.7101
. Department of Defense (DoD) . . . 202.101
. departments and agencies . . . 202.101
. design control activity . . . 209.270-2
. detainee . . . 237.173-2

Definitions—continued
. direct acquisition . . . 217.701
. discipline working group . . . 246.101
. domestic concern . . . 225.003
. domestic end product . . . 225.003
. domestic manufacture . . . 252.225-7025
. eligible product . . . 225.003
. end item . . . 207.7001
. enterprise software agreement . . . 208.7401
. enterprise software initiative . . . 208.7401
. entity controlled by a foreign government . . . 209.101
. estimating system . . . 215.404-71
. exchange (trade-in) property . . . 217.7001
. executive agency . . . 202.101
. exhibit . . . 204.7101
. facilities project . . . 237.7501—245-301
. fees . . . 237.7204
. foreign carrier . . . 239.7401
. foreign concern . . . 225.003
. gang cost . . . 247.270-1
. governmental regulatory body . . . 239.7401
. hand or measuring tools . . . 225.7001
. head of the agency . . . 202.101
. increased performance of security-guard functions . . . 237.101
. incremental funding . . . 232.001
. independent regulatory body . . . 241.101
. institution of higher learning . . . 237.7301
. integrated logistics managers . . . 247.301-70
. integrated materiel management . . . 208.7001
. internal controls . . . 242.7501
. interrogation of detainees . . . 237.173-2
. job order . . . 217.7101
. labor advisor . . . 222.001
. major weapon system . . . 234.7001
. mapping, charting, and geodesy (MC&G) property . . . 245.101
. Marshallese firm . . . 236.102
. master agreement for repair and alteration of vessels . . . 217.7101
. military installation . . . 217.103
. noncommon carrier . . . 239.7401
. noncontiguous state . . . 222.7001
. nonindependent regulatory body . . . 241.101
. nonprofit organization . . . 215.404-72; 237.7301
. nonqualifying country . . . 225.003
. nonqualifying country offer . . . 225.003
. nonseverable deliverable . . . 204.7101
. offeror . . . 227.7101; 227.7201
. offset . . . 202.101
. organizational conflicts of interest, major defense acquisition program . . . 209.571-1
. other participant . . . 225.871-2
. part . . . 225.770-1
. procedures, guidance, and information (PGI) . . . 202.101
. property . . . 217.7001
. provisioned item . . . 217.7601
. provisioned items order (PIO) . . . 217.7601
. provisioning . . . 217.7601

Definitions—continued
. provisioning activity . . . 217.7601
. provisioning requirements statement . . . 217.7601
. provisioning technical documentation . . . 217.7601
. qualifying country . . . 225.003
. qualifying country component . . . 225.003
. qualifying country offer . . . 225.003
. qualifying proposal . . . 217.7401
. refined precious metal . . . 208.7301
. regulated utility supplier . . . 241.101
. replenishment parts . . . 217.7501
. research and development . . . 235.001
. research facility . . . 235.015-70
. secretarial level . . . 250.1
. securing . . . 252.239-7016
. senior mentor . . . 237.101
. senior procurement executive . . . 202.101
. sensitive information . . . 252.239-7016
. service power procurement officer . . . 241.101
. shipyards
. significant estimating system deficiency . . . 215.404-71
. simplified acquisition threshold . . . 202.101
. software maintenance . . . 208.7401
. source . . . 225.003
. special use allowance . . . 235.015-70
. specialty metals . . . 225.7003-1
. SPI process . . . 211.273-1
. state sponsor of terrorism . . . 225.771-1
. stevedoring . . . 247.270-1
. student . . . 237.7301
. technical support . . . 237.7301
. telecommunications . . . 239.7401
. telecommunications services . . . 239.7401
. telecommunications systems . . . 252.239-7016
. term . . . 237.7204
. third party logistics providers . . . 247.301-70
. tiered evaluation of offers . . . 202.101
. tuition . . . 237.7204
. undefinitized contract action . . . 217.7401
. undefinitized item . . . 204.7101
. United States firm . . . 236.102
. United States Munitions List . . . 252.225-7007

Definitization
. contract clause . . . 217.7406; 252.217-7027
. definition . . . 217.7401
. definitization schedules . . . 217.7404-3
. plans and reports . . . 217.7405

Demurrage . . . 242.1470
. contract clause . . . 247.271-3; 252.247-7014

Department of Defense (DoD)
. contracting activities, list of . . . 202.101
. hotline poster . . . 203.1004

Department of Labor
. construction contracts . . . 222.403-4

Drug-free workplace
. contract clause . . . 223.570-2; 252.223-7004
. policy . . . 223.570-1

DUNS numbers . . . 204.7202-2

E

Economic quantity procurement
. multiyear contracting . . . 217.174

Educational institutions—see also Historically black colleges and universities and minority institutions
. cost principles . . . 231.303
. educational service agreements
. . agreement . . . 237.7201
. . contract clause prescriptions . . . 237.7204
. . contract format . . . 237.7204
. . definitions . . . 237.7204
. . duration . . . 237.7203
. . limitations . . . 237.7202
. . scope . . . 237.7200
. services of students at R&D laboratories
. . contract clause prescription . . . 237.7303
. . definitions . . . 237.7301
. . general . . . 237.7302
. . scope . . . 237.7300
. special use allowances for research facilities . . . 235.015-70

Electronic funds transfer
. contract clause and solicitation provision
. . mandatory payment by governmentwide commercial purchase card . . . 232.1110; 252.232-7009
. payment by governmentwide commercial purchase card . . . 232.1108

Electronic submission and processing of payment requests
. contract clause . . . 252.232-7006; 252.232-7003
. prescription . . . 232.7004
. definitions . . . 252.232-7006; 232.7001; 252.232-7003
. policy . . . 232.7002
. procedures . . . 232.7003
. scope . . . 232.7000

Emergency acquisitions
. acquisition flexibilities . . . 218.170
. contingency operation . . . 218.201
. defense or recovery from certain attacks . . . 218.202
. head of contracting activity determinations . . . 218.271
. humanitarian or peacekeeping operation . . . 218.270
. incidents of national significance, emergency declaration, or major disaster declaration . . . 218.203
. use of electronic business tools . . . 218.272

End items, acquisition of additional quantities
. authority . . . 207.7002
. definition of end item . . . 207.7001
. limitation . . . 207.7003

Enterprise software agreements
. acquisition procedures . . . 208.7403
. definitions . . . 208.7401

Enterprise software agreements—continued
. general . . . 208.7402
. scope . . . 208.7400

Environment and conservation—see also Occupational safety
. contract clauses and solicitation provisions
. . contract clauses and solicitation provisions . . . 223.370-5; 252.223-7003
. . drug-free work force . . . 223.570-2; 252.223-7004
. . hazard warning labels . . . 223.303; 252.223-7001
. . notification of potential safety issues . . . 246.371; 252.246-7003
. . prohibition on storage and disposal of hazardous and toxic waste . . . 223.7103
. . prohibition on storage, treatment, and disposal of toxic or hazardous materials . . . 252.223-7006
. . safeguarding sensitive conventional arms, ammunition, and explosives . . . 223.7203; 252.223-7007
. . safety of facilities, infrastructure, and equipment for military operations . . . 252.246-7004
. . safety precautions for ammunitions and explosives . . . 223.370-5; 252.223-7002
. Defense Environmental Restoration Program, construction contracts . . . 228.102-70
. drug-free workplace
. . contract clause . . . 223.570-2; 252.223-7004
. . policy . . . 223.570-1
. hazardous material identification/material safety data
. . contract clause . . . 223.303; 252.223-7001
. . policy . . . 223.302
. minimizing use of materials containing hexavalent chromium
. . authorities . . . 223.7302
. . authorization and approval . . . 223.7305
. . contract clause . . . 223.7306
. . definition . . . 223.7300
. . exceptions . . . 223.7304
. . policy . . . 223.7301
. . prohibition . . . 223.7303
. ozone-depleting substances . . . 223.803
. recovered materials, use of . . . 223.405
. safety precautions for ammunition and explosives
. . contract clause prescriptions . . . 223.370-5
. . definition of ammunition and explosives . . . 223.370-2; 252.223-7002
. . policy . . . 223.370-3
. . procedures . . . 223.370-4
. . scope . . . 223.370-1
. sensitive conventional arms, ammunition and explosives, safeguarding
. . contract clause . . . 223.7203; 252.223-7007
. . definition . . . 223.7200
. . policy . . . 223.7201
. . preaward responsibilities . . . 223.7202
. storage and disposal of toxic and hazardous materials
. . contract clause . . . 223.7106; 252.223-7006
. . exceptions . . . 223.7104

Environment and conservation—see also Occupational safety—continued
. storage and disposal of toxic and hazardous materials—continued
. . policy . . . 223.7102
. . definitions . . . 223.7101
. . procedures . . . 223.7103
. . reimbursement . . . 223.7105

Equal employment opportunity—see also Labor laws
. exemptions . . . 222.807
. inquiries . . . 222.806

Equipment lease or purchase
. considerations . . . 207.401
. funding requirements . . . 207.471
. statutory requirements . . . 207.470

Equitable adjustment requests . . . 243.204-71
. contract clause . . . 243.205-71; 252.243-7002

Estimating systems
. definitions . . . 215.407-5
. disclosure, maintenance, and review requirements . . . 215.407-5
. general . . . 215.407-5

Exchange of personal property
. definitions . . . 217.7001
. policy . . . 217.7002
. purchase request . . . 217.7003
. scope . . . 217.7000
. solicitation and award . . . 217.7004
. solicitation provision . . . 217.7005; 252.217-7002

Excluded parties list system
. effect of listing . . . 209.405
. restrictions on subcontracting . . . 209.405-2
. use of . . . 209.105-1

Export control
. contract clause . . . 225.7901-4
. Defense Trade Cooperation Treaty with the United Kingdom . . . 225.7902
. definitions . . . 225.7901-1
. export-controlled items . . . 225.7901
. general . . . 225.7901-2
. policy . . . 225.7901-3
. procedures . . . 225.7902-4
. purpose . . . 225.7902-2
. scope of subpart . . . 225.7900
. solicitation provision and contract clause . . . 225.7902-5
. . exports by approved community members in performance of the contract . . . 252.225-7047
. . exports by approved community members in response to the solicitation . . . 252.225-7046

External restructuring costs . . . 231.205-70

Extraordinary contractual actions
. authority
. . contract adjustment boards . . . 250.102-2
. . delegations, military . . . 250.102-1-70
. . delegation of authority . . . 250.102-1

Extraordinary contractual actions—continued
. contract adjustments
. . contractor requests . . . 250.103-3
. . disposition . . . 250.103-6
. . processing cases . . . 250.103-5
. definition of secretarial level . . . 250.100
. limitations on payments . . . 250.101-2-70
. recordkeeping requirements . . . 250.101-3
. residual powers
. . indemnification . . . 250.104-3-70

F

Facilities capital . . . 215.404-71
. contract facilities capital cost of money, DD Form 1861 . . . 253.303-1861
Facilities contracts
. facilities projects
. . definition . . . 237.7501
. . policy . . . 237.7502
. provision of government facilities to contractors
. . optional property-related clauses for facilities contracts . . . 245.103-72
. . policy . . . 245.102
Fast payment procedure . . . 213.402
Federal Acquisition Regulations System
. acquisition-related dollar thresholds, adjustment for inflation . . . 201.109
. administration
. . maintenance of FAR . . . 201.201
. . maintenance of procedures, guidance, and information . . . 201.201-70
. . two councils . . . 201.201-1
. agency acquisition regulations
. . agency control and compliance procedures . . . 201.304
. . policy . . . 201.301
. . publication and codification . . . 201.303
. applicability . . . 201.104
. certifications . . . 201.107
. contracting authority and responsibilities
. . appointment of contracting officer . . . 201.603-3
. . contract clause . . . 201.602-70; 252.201-7000
. . contracting officers . . . 201.602
. . responsibilities . . . 201.602-2
. . selection of contracting officer . . . 201.603-2
. contracting officer's representative . . . 201.602-2; 252.201-7000
. copies of procedures, guidance and information . . . 201.105-3
. deviations from FAR
. . class . . . 201.404
. . individual . . . 201.403
. . policy . . . 201.402
. issuance . . . 201.105
. OMB approval under Paperwork Reduction Act . . . 201.106
. peer reviews . . . 201.170
. policy . . . 201.402

Federal Prison Industries, Inc.
. market share . . . 208.602-70
Federal Supply Schedules
. general . . . 208.404
. order placement . . . 208.406-1
Federally funded research and development centers (FFRDCs)
. fee requirements . . . 215.404-75
. policy . . . 235.017
. sponsoring agreements . . . 235.017-1
Fee limitations, architect-engineer services . . . 236.606-70
Fidelity and forgery bonds . . . 228.105
Final indirect cost rates
. auditor determination procedure . . . 242.705-2
. contracting officer determination procedure . . . 242.705-1
Firefighting service contracting . . . 237.102-70
Fixed-price contracts
. contract funding . . . 232.703-1; 232.704-70
. economic price adjustments
. . contract clause prescriptions . . . 216.203-4-70
. foreign concerns . . . 229.402-1
. incentive contracts . . . 216.403-2
. . firm target . . . 216.403-1
. incentives . . . 216.402-2
. settlement memorandum . . . 249.110
Fixed-price incentive contracts . . . 216.403
. successive targets . . . 216.403-2
Fleet management system
. authorization . . . 251.202
. contract clause . . . 251.205; 252.251-7001
Food, clothing, fabrics, and hand or measuring tools . . . 225.7002
. contract clause prescriptions . . . 225.7002-3
. exceptions . . . 225.7002-2
. restrictions . . . 225.7002-1
. waiver of restrictions of 10 U.S.C. 2534 . . . 225.7008
Foods, quality assurance . . . 246.408-70
Foreign acquisitions
. acquisitions in support of operations in Afghanistan
. . applicability of Balance of Payments Program . . . 225.7704-2
. . applicability of trade agreements . . . 225.7704-1
. . contract clause prescription . . . 225.7704-3
. . solicitation provision prescription . . . 225.7704-3
. antiterrorism/force protection
. . contract clause . . . 225.7403-2; 252.225-7043
. . general . . . 225.372-1
. authorization acts
. . prohibition on requiring use of fire-resistant rayon fiber . . . 225.7016
. . use of fire-resistant rayon fiber . . . 211.170
. . utilization of domestic photovoltaic devices . . . 225.7017

Foreign acquisitions—continued
. Balance of Payments Program
. . acquisitions in support of operations in Afghanistan . . . 225.7704-2
. . contract clause prescriptions . . . 225.7503
. . policy . . . 225.7501
. . procedures . . . 225.7502
. . scope . . . 225.7500
. Canadian contracting
. . acceptance of supplies . . . 225.870-7
. . contract clause . . . 252.215-7004; 215.408
. . contracting procedures . . . 225.870-4
. . solicitation of contractors . . . 225.870-2
. . solicitation provision . . . 215.408
. competition requirements . . . 206.302-4
. contract administration
. . support of contingency operations . . . 225.373
. . use of electronic business tools . . . 225.374
. contract clauses and solicitation provisions
. . authorization to perform . . . 252.225-7042
. . contract clauses and solicitation provisions . . . 225.7503; 252.225-7044; 225.7503; 252.225-7045; 225.1101; 252.225-7000; 225.1101; 252.225-7035; 252.225-7036; 225.1101
. . Buy American and Balance of Payments Program . . . 225.1101; 252.225-7001
. . clause deviations in overseas contracts . . . 225.1070
. . contingent fees for foreign military sales . . . 225.7307; 252.225-7027
. . contractors performing private security functions . . . 252.225-7039
. . correspondence in English . . . 225.1103; 252.225-7041
. . disclosure of ownership or control by the government of a country that is a state sponsor of terrorism . . . 252.225-7050; 225.771-5
. . duty-free entry . . . 225.1101; 252.225-7013
. . contract clauses and solicitation provisions . . . 252.225-7037
. . exception from certified cost or pricing data requirements for foreign military sales indirect offsets . . . 252.715-7014
. . exclusionary policies and practices of foreign governments . . . 225.7307; 252.225-7028
. . export control . . . 225.7902-5
. . exports by approved community members in performance of the contract . . . 252.225-7047
. . exports by approved community members in response to the solicitation . . . 252.225-7046
. . identification of expenditures in the U.S . . . 225.1103; 252.225-7005
. . identification of expenditures in U.S . . . 252.225-7005
. . information for duty-free entry evaluation . . . 252.225-7003
. . personnel supporting U.S. armed forces deployed outside the U.S . . . 225.7402-5; 252.225-7040
. . photovoltaic devices . . . 252.225-7017

Foreign acquisitions—continued
. contract clauses and solicitation provisions—continued
. . photovoltaic devices, certificate . . . 252.225-7018
. . preference for certain domestic commodities . . . 252.225-7012
. . preference for domestic hand or measuring tools . . . 252.225-7015
. . prohibition on acquisition of munitions list items from communist Chinese military . . . 225.1103; 252.225-7007
. . qualifying country sources as subcontractors . . . 225.1101; 252.225-7002
. . quarterly reporting of actual contract performance outside the U.S . . . 225.7204
. . report of intended performance outside the U.S. and Canada . . . 225.7204; 252.225-7003
. . contract clauses and solicitation provisions . . . 225.7204; 252.225-7004
. . restriction on acquisition of aircraft fuel cells . . . 252.225-7038
. . restriction on acquisition of ball and roller bearings . . . 252.225-7016
. . restriction on acquisition of carbon, alloy, and armor steel plates . . . 252.225-7030
. . restriction on acquisition of forgings . . . 225.7102-4; 252.225-7025
. . restriction on acquisition of four ton dolly jacks . . . 252.225-7033
. . restriction on acquisition of supercomputers . . . 252.225-7011
. . secondary Arab boycott of Israel . . . 252.225-7031
. . supplemental cost principles . . . 252.231-7000
. . trade agreements . . . 225.1101; 252.225-7021
. . trade agreements certificate . . . 225.1101; 252.225-7020
. . waiver of United Kingdom levies . . . 225.1101; 252.225-7032; 252.225-7033
. . contract clauses and solicitation provisions . . . 225.1101; 252.225-7032
. contracts performed outside the United States
. . contractors performing private security functions . . . 225.370
. customs and duties
. . exempted supplies . . . 225.903
. . policy . . . 225.901
. . procedures . . . 225.902
. . definition . . . 225.900-70
. defense contractors outside the U.S.
. . antiterrorism/force protection . . . 225.372
. . performance or delivery in foreign country . . . 225.370
. . personnel authorized to accompany U.S. armed forces deployed outside the U.S . . . 225.7042
. definitions . . . 225.003; 225.7001; 225.7017-1; 225.7017-1; 225.900-70; 225.7101
. evaluating foreign offers—supply contracts
. . application . . . 225.502
. . examples . . . 225.504
. . group offers . . . 225.503

Foreign acquisitions—continued
. export control
. . Defense Trade Cooperation Treaty with the United Kingdom . . . 225.7902
. . definitions . . . 225.7902-1
. . exports by approved community members in performance of the contract . . . 252.225-7047
. . exports by approved community members in response to the solicitation . . . 252.225-7046
. . policy . . . 225.7902-3
. . procedures . . . 225.7902-4
. . purpose . . . 225.7902-2
. . scope . . . 225.7900
. . solicitation provision and contract clause . . . 225.7902-5
. foreign military sales acquisition
. . acquisitions paid for from nonrepayable funds . . . 225.7303-5
. . contingent fees . . . 225.7303-4
. . contract clause prescriptions . . . 225.7307
. . contractor sales to other foreign customers . . . 225.7303-1
. . cost of doing business with a foreign government or international organization . . . 225.7303-2
. . customer involvement . . . 225.7304
. . general . . . 225.7301
. . government-to-government agreements . . . 225.7303-3
. . limitation of liability . . . 225.7305
. . offset arrangements . . . 225.7306
. . pricing . . . 225.7303
. . preparation of letter of offer and acceptance . . . 225.7302
. . scope . . . 225.7300
. forgings
. . contract clause . . . 225.7102-4; 252.225-7025
. . exceptions . . . 225.7102-2
. . policy . . . 225.7102-1
. . waiver . . . 225.7102-3
. general guidelines . . . 225.001
. NATO cooperative projects
. . congressional notification . . . 225.871-7
. . definitions . . . 225.871-2
. . directed subcontracting . . . 225.871-5
. . disposal of property . . . 225.871-6
. . general . . . 225.871-3
. . scope . . . 225.871-1
. . statutory waivers . . . 225.871-4
. offset arrangements negotiated pursuant to FMS agreements . . . 225.7307
. personnel supporting U.S. armed forces deployed outside the U.S.
. . contract clause . . . 225.7402-5; 252.225-7040
. . definitions . . . 225.7402-2
. . government support . . . 225.7402-3
. . law of war training . . . 225.7402-4
. . scope . . . 225.370-1
. prohibited sources
. . Communist Chinese military companies . . . 225.770-2

Foreign acquisitions—continued
. prohibited sources—continued
. . definitions . . . 225.770-1
. . exceptions . . . 225.701-70; 225.770-3
. . identifying United States Munitions List items . . . 225.770-4
. . restrictions on . . . 225.701
. . waiver of prohibition . . . 225.770-5
. prohibition on acquisition of commercial satellite services from certain foreign entities
. . definitions . . . 225.772-1
. . exception . . . 225.772-4
. . procedures . . . 225.772-3
. . prohibition . . . 225.772-2
. . scope . . . 225.772-0
. . solicitation prescription . . . 225.772-5
. . solicitation provision . . . 52.225-7049
. prohibition on contracting with firms owned or controlled by governments that are state sponsors of terrorism
. . definition . . . 225.771-1
. . notification . . . 225.771-3
. . prohibition . . . 225.771-2
. . scope . . . 225.771-0
. . solicitation provision . . . 252.225-7050; 225.771-5
. . waiver of prohibition . . . 225.771-4
. prohibition on use of funds for contracts of certain programs and projects in Afghanistan that cannot be safely accessed
. . procedures . . . 225.7705-3
. . prohibition . . . 225.7705-1
. . waiver of prohibition . . . 225.7705-2; 225.7705-2
. qualifying country sources
. . applicability . . . 225.872-2
. . audit . . . 225.872-6
. . contract administration . . . 225.872-5
. . general . . . 225.872-1
. . individual determinations . . . 225.872-4
. . industrial security . . . 225.872-7
. . solicitation procedures . . . 225.872-3
. . subcontracting with . . . 225.872-8
. quality assurance . . . 246.406
. reporting . . . 225.070
. reporting of contract performance outside the United States
. . contract clause and solicitation provision prescriptions . . . 225.7204
. . distribution of reports . . . 225.7203
. . exception . . . 225.7202
. . policy . . . 225.7201
. . scope of subpart . . . 225.7300
. secondary Arab boycott of Israel
. . exceptions . . . 225.7603
. . procedures . . . 225.7602
. . restriction . . . 225.7601
. . solicitation provision . . . 225.7604; 252.225-7031
. . waivers . . . 225.7604
. statutory restrictions
. . acquisition of foreign buses . . . 225.7004
. . air circuit breakers for naval vessels . . . 225.7006

Foreign acquisitions—continued
. statutory restrictions—continued
. . anchor and mooring chain . . . 225.7007
. . ball and roller bearings . . . 225.7009
. . carbon, alloy, and armor steel plate . . . 225.7011
. . chemical weapons antidote . . . 225.7005
. . construction or repair of vessels in foreign shipyards . . . 225.7013
. . definitions . . . 225.7001
. . overseas architect-engineer services . . . 225.7015
. . overseas military construction . . . 225.7014
. . restrictions on acquisitions of specialty metals . . . 225.7003
. . restrictions on food, clothing, fabrics, and hand or measuring tools . . . 225.7002-2
. . scope . . . 225.7000
. . supercomputers . . . 225.7012
. trade agreements
. . acquisitions in support of operations in Afghanistan . . . 225.7704-1
. . exceptions . . . 225.401
. . general . . . 225.402
. . procedures . . . 225.408
. . products subject to . . . 225.401-70
. . World Trade Organization government procurement agreement . . . 225.403
. utilization of domestic photovoltaic devices
. . definitions . . . 225.7017-1
. . exceptions . . . 225.7017-3
. . solicitation provision and contract clause . . . 225.7017-5
. . restriction . . . 225.7017-2
. . waivers . . . 225.7017-4
. waiver of United Kingdom commercial exploitation levies
. . policy . . . 225.873-1
. . procedures . . . 225.873-2

Foreign buses
. applicability . . . 225.7004-2
. exceptions . . . 225.7004-3
. restriction . . . 225.7004-1
. waiver . . . 225.7004-4

Foreign governments—see also International agreements
. labor laws
. . compliance with local labor laws (overseas) . . . 252.222-7002; 222.7201
. . compliance with Spanish social security laws and regulations . . . 222.7201; 252.222-7004
. . permit from Italian inspectorate of labor . . . 222.7201; 252.222-7003

Foreign license and technical assistance agreements
. agreements between the government and domestic concerns . . . 227.673
. foreign patent interchange agreements . . . 227.676
. general . . . 227.671
. international traffic in arms regulations . . . 227.675-1

Foreign license and technical assistance agreements—continued
. policy . . . 227.672
. review of agreements . . . 227.675-2
. scope . . . 227.670
. supply contracts between the government and foreign concerns . . . 227.674

Foreign military sales—see also Foreign acquisitions
. acquisitions paid for from nonrepayable funds . . . 225.7303-5
. contingent fees . . . 225.7303-4
. contract clauses and solicitation provisions
. . exclusionary policies and practices of foreign governments . . . 252.225-7028
. . prescriptions . . . 225.7307
. . restriction on contingent fees for foreign military sales . . . 252.225-7027
. contractor sales to other foreign customers . . . 225.7303-1
. cost of doing business with a foreign government or international organization . . . 225.7303-2
. customer involvement . . . 225.7304
. general . . . 225.7301
. government-to-government agreements . . . 225.7303-3
. limitation of liability . . . 225.7305
. modifications to contracts . . . 243.170
. offset arrangements . . . 225.7306
. options use . . . 217.202
. pricing . . . 225.7303
. preparation of letter of offer and acceptance . . . 225.7302
. scope . . . 225.7300

Forgery bonds . . . 228.105

Forgings
. contract clause . . . 225.7102-4; 252.225-7025
. exceptions . . . 225.7102-2
. policy . . . 225.7102-1
. waiver . . . 225.7102-3

Forms
. acceptance of MIPR, DD Form 448-2 . . . 253.303-448
. . prescription . . . 253.208-2
. agency forms, internet availability
. application for U.S. government shipping documentation/instructions, DD Form 1659 . . . 253.303-1659
. architect-engineering contracts
. . prescription . . . 236.701
. cash collection voucher, DD Form 1131 . . . 253.303-1131
. certificate of release of motor vehicle, SF 97
. . prescription . . . 245.7001-1
. communication service authorization, DD Form 428 . . . 253.303-428
. construction contracts
. . prescription . . . 236.701

Forms—continued
. contract administration completion record, DD Form 1593 . . . 253.303-1593
. contract closeout check-list, DD Form 1597 . . . 253.303-1597
. contract completion statement, DD Form 1594 . . . 253.303-1594
. contract data requirements list, DD Form 1423 . . . 253.303-1423
. . one data item, DD Form 1423-1 . . . 253.303-1423
. . two data items, DD Form 1423-2 . . . 253.303-1423
. contract facilities capital cost of money, DD Form 1861 . . . 253.303-1861
. contract termination status report, DD Form 1598 . . . 253.303-1598
. cost data summary report, DD Form 1921 . . . 253.303-1921
. cost-hour report, DD Form 1921-1 . . . 253.303-1921
. data item description, DD Form 1664 . . . 253.303-1664
. DD Form 250-1, tanker/barge material inspection and receiving report . . . 253.303-250; 253.303-250
. DD Form 250, material inspection and receiving report, DD Form 250 . . . 253.303-250
. DD Form 250c, material inspection and receiving report, continuation sheet . . . 253.303-250c
. DD Form 416, purchase request for coal, coke or briquettes . . . 253.303-416
. DD Form 428, communication service authorization . . . 253.303-428
. DD Form 448-2, acceptance of MIPR . . . 253.303-448
. . prescription . . . 253.208-2
. DD Form 448, military interdepartmental purchase request . . . 253.303-448
. . prescription . . . 253.208-1
. DD Form 879 . . . 222.406-6
. DD Form 879, statement of compliance . . . 253.303-879
. DD Form 882, report of inventions and subcontracts (pursuant to "patent rights" contract clause) . . . 253.303-882
. DD Form 1057, monthly summary of contracting actions . . . 253.303-1057
. DD Form 1131, cash collection voucher . . . 253.303-1131
. DD Form 1149, requisition and invoice/shipping document . . . 253.303-1149
. . prescription . . . 245.7001-2
. DD Form 1155, order for supplies or services . . . 253.303-1155
. . instructions for completion . . . 253.213-70
. DD Form 1155c-1, order for supplies or services, commissary continuation sheet . . . 253.303-1155c
. DD Form 1342, DoD property record . . . 253.303-1342
. DD Form 1348-1A, DoD single line item release/ receipt document
. . prescription . . . 245.7001-3

Forms—continued
. DD Form 1348-2, issue release/receipt document with address label . . . 253.303-1348
. DD Form 1348, DoD single line item requisition system document (manual) . . . 253.303-1348
. DD Form 1348m, DoD single line item requisition system document (mechanical), DD . . . 253.303-1348m
. DD Form 1349-2, issue release/receipt document with address label . . . 253.303-1348
. DD Form 1384, transportation control and movement document . . . 253.303-1384
. . prescription . . . 247.370
. DD Form 1391, FY—military construction project data . . . 253.303-1391
. DD Form 1391c, FY—military construction project data (continuation) . . . 253.303-1391c
. DD Form 1419, DoD industrial plant equipment requisition . . . 253.303-1419
. DD Form 1423-1, contract data requirements list, one data item . . . 253.303-1423
. DD Form 1423-2, contract data requirements list, two data items . . . 253.303-1423
. DD Form 1423, contract data requirements list . . . 253.303-1423
. DD Form 1484, postaward conference record . . . 253.303-1484
. DD Form 1541, disposal determination approval . . . 253.303-1641
. DD Form 1547, record of weighted guidelines application . . . 253.303-1547
. . prescriptions . . . 215.404-70; 253.215-70
. DD Form 1593, contract administration completion record . . . 253.303-1593
. DD Form 1594, contract completion statement . . . 253.303-1594
. DD Form 1597, contract closeout check-list . . . 253.303-1597
. DD Form 1598, contract termination status report . . . 253.303-1598
. DD Form 1635, plant clearance case register . . . 253.303-1635
. DD Form 1637, notice of acceptance of inventory schedules . . . 253.303-1637
. DD Form 1638, report of disposition of contractor inventory . . . 253.303-1638
. DD Form 1639, scrap warranty . . . 253.303-1639
. DD Form 1640, request for plant clearance . . . 245.7001-4; 253.303-1640
. . prescription . . . 245.7001-4
. DD Form 1653, transportation data for solicitations . . . 253.303-1653
. . prescription . . . 247.371
. DD Form 1654, evaluation of transportation cost factors . . . 253.303-1654
. . prescription . . . 247.372
. DD Form 1659, application for U.S. government shipping documentation/instructions . . . 253.303-1659

Forms—continued
. DD Form 1662, DoD property in custody of contractors . . . 253.303-1662
. DD Form 1664, data item description . . . 253.303-1664
. DD Form 1707, information to offerors or quoters . . . 253.303-1707
. DD Form 1861, contract facilities capital cost of money . . . 253.303-1861
. DD Form 1921-1, functional cost-hour report . . . 253.303-1921
. DD Form 1921, cost data summary report . . . 253.303-1921
. DD Form 2051-1, request for information/verification of commercial and government entity (CAGE) code . . . 253.303-2051
. DD Form 2051, request for assignment of commercial and government entity (CAGE) code . . . 253.303-2051
. DD Form 2139, report of contract performance outside the United States . . . 253.303-2139
. DD Form 2579, small business coordination record . . . 253.303-2579
. DD Form 2626, performance evaluation (construction) . . . 253.303-2626
. DD Form 2631, performance evaluation (architect-engineer) . . . 253.303-2631
. demolition contracts
. . prescription . . . 236.701
. disposal determination approval, DD Form 1641 . . . 253.303-1641
. DoD forms, list of . . . 253.3
. DoD industrial plant equipment requisition, DD Form 1419 . . . 253.303-1419
. DoD property in custody of contractors, DD Form 1662 . . . 253.303-1662
. DoD property record, DD Form 1342 . . . 253.303-1342
. DoD single line item issue release/receipt document, DD Form 1348-1A . . . 253.303-1348
. DoD single line item release/receipt document, DD Form 1348-1
. . prescription . . . 245.7001-3
. DoD single line item requisition system document (manual), DD Form 1348 . . . 253.303-1348
. DoD single line item requisition system document (mechanical), DD Form 1348m . . . 253.303-1348m
. evaluation of transportation cost factors, DD Form 1654 . . . 253.303-1654
. . prescription . . . 247.372
. functional cost-hour report, DD Form 1921-1 . . . 253.303-1921
. FY—military construction project data, DD Form 1391 . . . 253.303-1391
. FY—military construction project data, DD Form 1391c (continuation) . . . 253.303-1391c
. individual contracting action report, DD Form 350 . . . 253.303-350

Forms—continued
. information to offerors or quoters, DD Form 1707 . . . 253.303-1707
. issue release/receipt document with address label . . . 253.303-1348
. material inspection and receiving report, DD Form 250 . . . 253.303-250
. . continuation sheet, DD Form 250c . . . 253.303-250
. military interdepartmental purchase request, DD Form 448 . . . 253.303-448
. . prescription . . . 253.208-1
. monthly summary of contracting actions, DD Form 1057 . . . 253.303-1057
. notice of acceptance of inventory schedules, DD Form 1637 . . . 253.303-1637
. OF 336
. . prescription . . . 253.213
. OF 347
. . prescription . . . 253.213
. OF 348
. . prescription . . . 253.213
. order for supplies or services, DD Form 1155 . . . 253.303-1155
. . commissary continuation sheet, DD Form 1155c-1 . . . 253.303-1155c
. . instructions for completion . . . 253.213-70
. performance evaluation (architect-engineer), DD Form 2631 . . . 253.303-2631
. performance evaluation (construction), DD Form 2626 . . . 253.303-2626
. plant clearance case register, DD Form 1635 . . . 253.303-1635
. postaward conference record, DD Form 1484 . . . 253.303-1484
. preaward survey of prospective contractors (general), SF 1403
. . prescription . . . 253.209-1
. purchase order-invoice-voucher, SF 44 . . . 213.306
. purchase request for coal, coke or briquettes, DD Form 416 . . . 253.303-416
. record of weighted guidelines application, DD Form 1547 . . . 253.303-1547
. . prescription . . . 253.215-70
. report of contract performance outside the United States, DD Form 2139 . . . 253.303-2139
. report of disposition of contractor inventory, DD Form 1638 . . . 253.303-1638
. report of inventions and subcontracts (pursuant to "patent rights" contract clause), DD Form 882 . . . 253.303-882
. request for assignment of commercial and government entity (CAGE) code, DD Form 2051 . . . 253.303-2051
. request for information/verification of commercial and government entity (CAGE) code, DD Form 2051-1 . . . 253.303-2051
. request for plant clearance, DD Form 1640 . . . 253.303-1640
. . prescription . . . 245.7001-4

Forms—continued
. requisition and invoice/shipping document, DD Form 1149 . . . 253.303-1149
. . prescription . . . 245.7001-2
. responsible prospective contractors (general)
. . prescription . . . 253.209-1
. scrap warranty, DD Form 1639 . . . 253.303-1639
. SF 18
. . prescription . . . 253.213
. SF 30, amendment of solicitation/modification of contract
. . prescriptions . . . 253.213
. SF 44, purchase order-invoice-voucher . . . 213.306
. . prescription . . . 253.213
. SF 97 certificate of release of motor vehicle
. . prescription . . . 245.7001-1
. SF 1165
. . prescription . . . 253.213
. SF 1403, preaward survey of prospective contractors (general)
. . prescription . . . 253.209-1
. SF 1449
. . prescription . . . 253.213
. simplified acquisition method . . . 213.307
. simplified acquisition procedures, OFs 336, 347, 348
. . prescription . . . 253.213
. simplified acquisition procedures, SFs 18, 30, 44, 1165, 1449
. . prescription . . . 253.213
. small business coordination record, DD Form 2579 . . . 253.303-2579
. statement of compliance, DD Form 879 . . . 253.303-879
. tanker/barge material inspection and receiving report, DD Form 250-1 . . . 253.303-250
. transportation control and movement document, DD Form 1384 . . . 253.303-1384
. . prescription . . . 247.370
. transportation data for solicitations, DD Form 1653 . . . 253.303-1653
. . prescription . . . 247.371

Forward pricing rate agreements . . . 215.407-3

Freedom of Information Act . . . 224.203

Full and open competition
. broad agency announcement . . . 235.016
. use of competitive procedures . . . 206.102

G

Government property
. appointment of property administrators and plant clearance officers . . . 201.670
. contract clauses and solicitation provisions
. . government-furnished mapping, charting and geodesy property . . . 252.245-7000
. . reporting of government-furnished property . . . 252.211-7007
. . reporting, reutilization, and disposal . . . 252.225-7004

Government property—continued
. contract clauses and solicitation provisions—continued
. . restriction on acquisition of carbon, alloy, and armor steel plate . . . 252.225-7030
. disposal of surplus property
. . sale of surplus property . . . 245.604-3
. facilities, provision of to contractors
. . contract clause . . . 245.302; 252.225-7030
. . contracts, termination of . . . 245.302
. . policy . . . 245.402-70
. forms
. . certificate of release of a motor vehicle, SF 97 . . . 245.7001-1
. . DD form 1149, requisition and invoice shipping document . . . 245.7001-2
. . DD Form 1348-1, DoD single line item release/receipt document . . . 245.7001-3
. . DD Form 1640, request for plant clearance . . . 245.7001-4
. . DD Form 1641, disposal determination/approval . . . 245.7001-6
. . DD Form 1822, end user certificate . . . 245.7001-6
. furnishing property to contractors
. . attachments to solicitations and awards . . . 245.103-72
. . contracting office responsibilities . . . 245.103-74
. . government property under sustainment contracts . . . 245.103-73
. . procedures . . . 245.103
. inventory schedules
. . acceptance . . . 245.602-1
. item unique identification
. mapping, charting and geodesy property . . . 252.245-7000
. plant clearance
. . forms . . . 245.7001
. policy for reporting of government-furnished property . . . 211.274-4
. . contract clause . . . 252.211-7007
. precious metals
. . contract clause . . . 208.7305; 252.208-7000
. . definitions . . . 208.7301
. . policy . . . 208.7302
. . procedures . . . 208.7303
. . refined precious metals . . . 208.7304
. property control systems . . . 245.104
. reporting, reutilization, and disposal . . . 245.602-1
. . contract clause . . . 252.225-7004
. reutilization
. . inventory disposal schedules . . . 245.602-1
. . plant clearance procedures . . . 245.602-70
. . screening . . . 245.602-3
. Self-insurance
. . Responsibility and liability . . . 245.107
. solicitation and evaluation procedures
. . definitions . . . 245.201-70
. . security classification . . . 245.201-71
. special instructions . . . 245.7201

Government property—continued
. support government property administration
. . storage at government's expense . . . 245.570
. title
. . delivery of contractor acquired property . . . 245.402-71
. . policy . . . 245.402-70

Government supply sources—see also Sources of supplies and services
. contract clause . . . 252.251-7000; 251.107
. contractor authorization . . . 251.102
. priorities for use . . . 208.002

Governmentwide commercial purchase card
. actions at or below micro-purchase threshold . . . 213.270
. general . . . 213.201
. simplified acquisition methods . . . 213.301

Group insurance . . . 228.307-1

Guam, contracts performed on
. contract clause . . . 222.7302; 252.222-7005
. exception . . . 222.7302
. prohibition on use of nonimmigrant aliens . . . 222.7301
. scope . . . 222.7300

H

Handicapped individuals, employment of
. labor laws
. . complaint procedure . . . 222.1406
. . waivers . . . 222.1403
. nonprofit agencies employing blind and other severely handicapped . . . 208.705

Hawaiian small businesses
. utilization of Indian organizations and Indian-owned economic enterprises and Native Hawaiian small business concerns . . . 252.226-7001

Hazardous materials
. contract clauses and solicitation provisions
. . contract clauses and solicitation provisions . . . 223.370-5; 252.223-7003
. . hazard warning labels . . . 223.303; 252.223-7001
. . safety precautions for ammunition and explosives . . . 223.370-5; 252.223-7002
. policy . . . 223.302
. safety precautions for ammunition and explosives
. . contract clause prescriptions . . . 223.370-5
. . definition of ammunition and explosives . . . 252.223-7002; 223.370-2
. . policy . . . 223.370-3
. . procedures . . . 223.370-4
. . scope . . . 223.370-1
. sensitive conventional arms, ammunition and explosives, safeguarding
. . contract clause . . . 223.7203; 252.223-7007
. . definition . . . 223.7200
. . policy . . . 223.7201
. . preaward responsibilities . . . 223.7202

Hazardous materials—continued
. storage and disposal
. . contract clause . . . 223.7106; 252.223-7006
. . exceptions . . . 223.7104
. . policy . . . 223.7102
. . definitions . . . 223.7101
. . procedures . . . 223.7103
. . reimbursement . . . 223.7105
. warning labels . . . 223.302

Hazardous risks
. contract clause prescriptions . . . 235.070-3; 235.072
. indemnification under contract involving both research and development and other work . . . 235.070-2
. indemnification under research and development contracts . . . 235.070-1

Historically black colleges and universities and minority institutions
. scope . . . 226.7100

Historically underutilized business zone (HUBZone) program
. price evaluation preference . . . 219.1307

I

Identification of unique items
. contract clause . . . 211.274-6; 252.211-7003
. general . . . 211.274-1
. government-assigned serial numbers . . . 211.274-5
. policy . . . 211.274-2

Imprest funds
. conditions for use . . . 213.305-3
. general . . . 213.305-1
. simplified acquisition . . . 213.305

Incentive contracts
. award fee reduction or denial, contract clause prescription . . . 216.406
. award fee reduction or denial, jeopardizing health or safety
. . contract clause . . . 252.216-7004
. contractor performance evaluation report . . . 216.470
. cost-reimbursement contracts . . . 216.405
. . cost-plus-award-fee . . . 216.405-2
. . cost-plus-incentive-fee . . . 216.405-1
. . other applications of award fees . . . 216.470
. fixed-price contracts . . . 216.403
. . firm targets . . . 216.403-1
. . successive targets . . . 216.403-2
. performance evaluation criteria . . . 216.470
. procedures and information . . . 216.401
. technical performance incentives . . . 216.402-2

Indefinite delivery contracts
. contract clause and solicitation provision . . . 216.506
. contract clause and solicitation provision prescription . . . 216.506
. indefinite-quantity contracts . . . 216.504
. ordering . . . 216.505
. orders under multiple award contracts . . . 216.505-70

Independent research and development work—see also Research and development contracts
. contract clause prescriptions . . . 227.7107-2
. costs
. . cost principles . . . 231.205-18
. . policy . . . 242.771-2
. . responsibilities . . . 242.771-3
. . scope . . . 242.771-1

Indian incentive program
. contract clause . . . 226.104; 252.226-7001
. procedures . . . 226.103

Indian tribal governments, contracts with . . . 231.603

Indirect cost rates
. auditor determination procedure . . . 242.705-2
. contracting officer determination procedure . . . 242.705-1
. independent research and development/ bid and proposal costs
. . policy . . . 242.771-2
. . responsibilities . . . 242.771-3
. . scope of subpart . . . 242.771-1

Industrial plant equipment
. DD Form 1419, DoD industrial plant equipment requisition . . . 253.303-1419
. provision to contractors
. . policy . . . 245.102

Industrial security
. Canadian contracting . . . 225.870-8
. qualifying country sources . . . 225.872-7

Information technology acquisitions
. applicability . . . 239.001
. cloud computing
. . contract clause . . . 252.239-7010
. . definitions . . . 239.7602
. . policy and responsibilities . . . 239.7602-1
. . prescription of solicitation provision and contract clause . . . 239.7604
. . procedures . . . 239.7603
. . required storage of data within the United States or outlying areas . . . 239.7602-2
. . scope of subpart . . . 239.7601
. . solicitation provision . . . 252.239-7009
. contract clauses and solicitation provisions
. . access . . . 252.239-7002
. . cancellation or termination of orders . . . 252.239-7007
. . cloud computing services . . . 252.239-7010
. . compliance with safeguarding covered defense information controls . . . 252.204-7008
. . information assurance contractor training and certification . . . 252.239-7001
. . limitations on the use or disclosure of third-party contractor reported cyber incident information . . . 252.204-7009
. . notice of supply chain risk . . . 252.239-7017
. . obligation of the government . . . 252.239-7013

Information technology acquisitions—continued
. contract clauses and solicitation provisions—continued
. . orders for facilities and services . . . 252.239-7004
. . prescriptions . . . 239.7103; 239.7411
. . protection against compromising emanations . . . 239.7103; 252.239-7000
. . rates, charges, and services . . . 252.239-7005
. . representation of use of cloud computing . . . 252.239-7009
. . reuse arrangements . . . 252.239-7008
. . special construction and equipment charges . . . 252.239-7011
. . supply chain risk . . . 252.239-7018
. . tariff information . . . 252.239-7006
. . telecommunications security equipment, devices, techniques, and services . . . 252.239-7016
. . term of agreement . . . 252.239-7014
. . title to telecommunication facilities and equipment . . . 252.236-7012
. contractor training and certification, information assurance . . . 239.7102
. definition . . . 202.101
. exchange or sale of information technology (IT) . . . 239.7001
. policy . . . 239.101
. security and privacy for computer systems
. . compromising emanations, TEMPEST or other standard . . . 239.7102-2
. . contract clause . . . 239.7103; 252.239-7000
. . definition of information assurance . . . 239.7101
. . general policy . . . 239.7102-1
. . privacy protection procedures . . . 224.103
. . scope . . . 239.7100
. . security against compromising emanations . . . 239.7102-1
. solicitation requirements . . . 239.7201
. supply chain risk
. . applicability . . . 239.7302
. . authorized individuals . . . 239.7303
. . definitions . . . 239.7301
. . determination and notification . . . 239.7304
. . exclusion and limitation on disclosure . . . 239.7305
. . scope . . . 239.7300
. . solicitation provision and contract clause prescription . . . 239.7306
. telecommunications services
. . applicability of construction labor standards . . . 239.7408-2
. . authority to contract . . . 239.7405
. . cancellation and termination . . . 239.7410
. . contract clause prescriptions . . . 239.7411
. . certified cost or pricing data . . . 239.7406
. . definitions . . . 239.7401
. . policy . . . 239.7402
. . scope . . . 239.7400
. . special assembly . . . 239.7409
. . special construction . . . 239.7408-1
. . type of contract . . . 239.7407

Inherently governmental functions, acquisition of
. policy . . . 207.503
. scope . . . 207.500

Inspection stamping . . . 246.472

Installation support contracts . . . 222.402-70

Insurance
. contract clauses and solicitation provisions
. . accident reporting and investigation involving aircraft, missiles, and space launch vehicles . . . 252.228-7005
. . capture and detention . . . 252.228-7003
. . compliance with Spanish laws and insurance . . . 252.228-7006
. . ground and flight risk . . . 252.228-7001
. . prescriptions . . . 228.311-1; 228.370
. . reimbursement for war-hazard losses . . . 252.228-7000
. contractor insurance/pension review (CIPR)
. . general . . . 242.7301
. . requirements . . . 242.7302
. . responsibilities . . . 242.7303
. cost principle . . . 231.205-19
. cost-reimbursement contracts
. . contract clause prescription . . . 228.311-1
. . group insurance plans . . . 228.307-1
. overseas workers' compensation and war-hazard insurance . . . 228.305
. risk-pooling arrangements . . . 228.304
. war hazard insurance overseas . . . 228.305

Integrated materiel management program . . . 208.7000

Interagency acquisitions
. contract administration . . . 242.002
. ordering procedures . . . 217.503
. procedures . . . 217.502
. . general . . . 217.502-1
. scope of subpart . . . 217.500

Interagency fleet management system (IFMS) vehicles
. authorization . . . 251.202
. contract clause . . . 251.205; 252.251-7001

Interdepartmental purchase requests
. DD Form 448-2, acceptance of MIPR . . . 253.208-2; 253.303-448
. DD Form 448, military interdepartmental purchase request . . . 253.208-1; 253.303-448
. procedures . . . 208.7005

International agreements
. Canadian contracting
. . acceptance of supplies . . . 225.870-7
. . contract administration . . . 225.870-5
. . contract clause . . . 252.215-7004; 215.408
. . contracting procedures . . . 225.870-4
. . general . . . 225.870-1
. . industrial security . . . 225.870-8
. . solicitation of contractors . . . 225.870-2
. . solicitation provision . . . 252.215-7003; 215.408

International agreements—continued
. Canadian contracting—continued
. . submission of offers . . . 225.870-3
. . termination procedures . . . 225.870-6
. competition requirements . . . 206.302-4
. contracts for performance outside the U.S. and Canada . . . 225.802-70
. end use certificates . . . 225.802-70
. memoranda of understanding . . . 225.802
. NATO cooperative projects
. . congressional notification . . . 225.871-7
. . definitions . . . 225.871-2
. . directed subcontracting . . . 225.871-5
. . disposal of property . . . 225.871-6
. . general . . . 225.871-3
. . scope . . . 225.871-1
. . statutory waivers . . . 225.871-4
. performance outside U.S. or Canada . . . 225.802-70
. procedures . . . 225.802
. qualifying country sources
. . applicability . . . 225.872-2
. . audit . . . 225.872-6
. . contract administration . . . 225.872-5
. . general . . . 225.872-1
. . individual determinations . . . 225.872-4
. . industrial security . . . 225.872-7
. . solicitation procedures . . . 225.872-3
. . subcontracting with . . . 225.872-8
. waiver of United Kingdom commercial exploitation levies
. . policy . . . 225.873-1
. . procedures . . . 225.873-2

International traffic in arms regulations . . . 227.675-1

Inventory—see also Government property
. forms
. . DD Form 1342 . . . 253.303-1342
. . DD Form 1637, notice of acceptance of inventory schedules . . . 253.303-1637
. . DD Form 1638, report of disposition of contractor inventory . . . 253.303-1638
. . DD Form 1639, scrap warranty . . . 253.303-1639

Investigations
. construction contracts, labor standards . . . 222.406-8

Israel, Arab boycott of
. exceptions . . . 225.7603
. procedures . . . 225.7602
. restriction . . . 225.7601
. solicitation provision . . . 225.7604; 252.225-7031
. waivers . . . 225.7604

K

Kickbacks . . . 203.502-2

L

Labor laws
. closure of military installations
. . contract clause . . . 222.7102; 252.222-7001

Labor laws—continued
. closure of military installations—continued
. . policy . . . 222.7101
. combating trafficking in persons
. . auditing compliance procedures . . . 222.1770
. . policy . . . 222.1703
. . violations and remedies . . . 222.1704
. construction contracts
. . administration and enforcement policy . . . 222.406-1
. . construction wage rate requirements statute wage determinations . . . 222.404
. . Department of Labor regulations . . . 222.403-4
. . disposition of disputes . . . 222.406-10
. . installation support contracts . . . 222.402-70
. . investigations . . . 222.406-8
. . payrolls and statements . . . 222.406-6
. . preconstruction letters and conferences . . . 222.406-1
. . semiannual enforcement reports . . . 222.406-13
. . wage rate schedules
. . withholding/suspension of contract payments . . . 222.406-9
. contract clauses and solicitation provisions
. . compliance with local labor laws (overseas) . . . 252.222-7002
. . compliance with Spanish social security laws and regulations . . . 252.222-7004
. . permit from Italian inspectorate of labor . . . 252.222-7003
. . prohibition on use of nonimmigrant aliens-Guam . . . 222.7302; 252.222-7005
. . restrictions on employment of personnel . . . 252.222-7000
. . contract clauses and solicitation provisions . . . 222.7102; 252.222-7001
. contract work hours and safety standards
. . liquidated damages and overtime pay . . . 222.302
. construction wage rate requirements statute
. . wage determinations . . . 222.404
. definitions . . . 222.001; 222.7001
. disputes
. . construction contracts . . . 222.406-10
. . impact on defense programs . . . 222.101-3
. . removal of items from affected facility . . . 222.101-4
. . reporting requirement . . . 222.101-3
. . stevedoring services acquisition during . . . 222.101-70
. . work stoppages . . . 222.101-4
. equal employment opportunity
. . exemptions . . . 222.807
. . inquiries . . . 222.806
. federal and state requirements
. . overtime approvals . . . 222.103-4
. . policy . . . 222.102-1
. foreign governments
. . compliance with local labor laws (overseas) . . . 222.7201; 252.222-7002
. . compliance with Spanish social security laws and regulations . . . 222.7201; 252.222-7004

Labor laws—continued
. foreign governments—continued
. . permit from Italian inspectorate of labor . . . 222.7201; 252.222-7003
. Guam, contracts performed on
. . contract clause . . . 222.7302; 252.222-7005
. . exception . . . 222.7302
. . prohibition on use of nonimmigrant aliens . . . 222.7301
. . scope . . . 222.7300
. handicapped employment
. . complaint procedures . . . 222.1406
. . waivers . . . 222.1403
. noncontiguous states employment restrictions
. . contract clause prescription . . . 222.7004
. . definition of noncontiguous state . . . 222.7001
. . general . . . 222.7002
. . scope . . . 222.7000
. . waivers . . . 222.7003
. overtime
. . approvals . . . 222.103-4
. . under contract work hours and safety standards statute . . . 222.302
. restrictions on use of mandatory arbitration agreements
. . applicability . . . 222.7403
. . contract clause . . . 252.222-7006
. . clause prescription . . . 222.7405
. . definition, covered contractor . . . 222.7401
. . policy . . . 222.7402
. . scope of subpart . . . 222.7400
. . waiver . . . 222.7404
. right of first refusal of employment
. . contract clause . . . 222.7102; 252.222-7001
. . policy . . . 222.7101
. service contract labor standards statute
. . applicability . . . 222.1003-1
. veterans
. . complaint procedures . . . 222.1308
. . contract clause and solicitation provision prescription . . . 222.1310
. . waivers . . . 222.1305
. Walsh-Healey Public Contracts Act
. . regulatory exemptions . . . 222.604-2
. whistleblower protections for contractor employees
. . contract clause . . . 252.203-7002
. . classified information . . . 203.903
. . policy . . . 203.903
. . procedures for filing complaints . . . 203.904
. . procedures for investigating complaints . . . 203.905
. . remedies . . . 203.906
. . scope . . . 203.900
. . definition . . . 203.901

Laundry and dry cleaning services
. contract clauses and solicitation provisions
. . delivery tickets (laundry and dry cleaning) . . . 237.7101; 252.237-7016
. . individual laundry . . . 237.7101; 252.237-7017

Laundry and dry cleaning services—continued
. contract clauses and solicitation provisions—continued
. . instruction to offerors (bulk weight) (laundry and dry cleaning) . . . 237.7101; 252.237-7013
. . instruction to offerors (count-of-articles) (laundry and dry cleaning) . . . 237.7101; 252.237-7012
. . loss or damage (count-of-articles) (laundry and dry cleaning) . . . 237.7101; 252.237-7014
. . loss or damage (weight of articles) (laundry and dry cleaning) . . . 237.7101; 252.237-7015
. . special definitions of government property (laundry and dry cleaning) . . . 237.7101; 252.237-7018
. scope . . . 237.7100

Legislative lobbying costs . . . 231.205-22

Letter contracts
. application . . . 216.603-2
. contract clause prescriptions . . . 216.603-4
. limitations . . . 216.603-3

Levies on payments
. contract clause . . . 232.7102; 252.232-7010
. policy and procedures . . . 232.7101
. scope . . . 232.7100

Licensing—see also Patents
. foreign license and technical assistance agreements
. . agreements between the government and domestic concerns . . . 227.673
. . foreign patent interchange agreements . . . 227.676
. . general . . . 227.671
. . international traffic in arms regulations . . . 227.675-1
. . policy . . . 227.672
. . review of agreements . . . 227.675-2
. . scope . . . 227.670
. . supply contracts between the government and foreign concerns . . . 227.674
. rights in technical data . . . 227.7103-4
. software or software documentation . . . 227.7203-4

Line items—see also Uniform contract line item numbering system
. forms
. . DD Form 1348-1A, DoD single line item release/receipt document . . . 253.303-1348
. . DD Form 1348-2, issue release/receipt document with address label . . . 253.303-1348
. . DD Form 1348, DoD single line item requisition system document (manual) . . . 253.303-1348
. . DD Form 1348m, DoD single line item requisition system document (mechanical), DD . . . 253.303-1348m
. . DD Form 1349-2, issue release/receipt document with address label . . . 253.303-1348

Liquidated damages
. construction contracts
. . adjustment for incorrect assessment . . . 222.406-9
. . contract clause prescription . . . 211.503
. . scope of subpart . . . 211.500
. . special aspects . . . 236.206

Liquidated damages—continued
. under contract work hours and safety standards statute . . . 222.302

Loan guarantees for defense production—see also Contract financing
. authority . . . 232.302

Lobbying costs . . . 231.205-22

M

Major system acquisition
. acquisition strategy, lead system integrators . . . 234.004
. competition . . . 234.005-1
. contract clauses and solicitation provisions
. . earned value management system . . . 252.234-7002
. . notice of earned value management systems . . . 252.234-7001
. contracts for management services . . . 237.102-72
. cost and software data reporting
. . policy . . . 234.7100
. . solicitation provision and contract clause . . . 234.7101
. definition . . . 234.001
. earned value management system
. . notice . . . 252.234-7001
. . policy . . . 234.201
. . solicitation provisions and contract clause . . . 234.203
. planning requirements . . . 207.106
. responsibilities . . . 234.003
. weapons systems . . . 212.270
. . definition . . . 234.7001
. . policy . . . 234.7002
. . scope . . . 234.7000

Make-or-buy programs . . . 215.407-2

Management and operating contracts . . . 217.600

Manufacturing technology program . . . 235.006-70

Market research
. policy . . . 210.001
. procedures . . . 210.002

Material inspection and receiving reports (Appendix F)
. contract clause . . . 246.370; 252.246-7000
. DD Form 250-1 . . . 253.303-250
. DD Forms 250 and 250c . . . 253.303-250; 253.303-250c
. introduction
. . general F-101 . . . 246.601

Material management and accounting system (MMAS)
. contract clause . . . 242.7204; 252.242-7004
. definitions . . . 252.242-7004
. policy . . . 242.7202
. review procedures . . . 242.7203
. scope . . . 242.7200

Medal of Honor, unlawful manufacture of . . . 209.471

Military construction
. contract clauses and solicitation provisions
. . contract clauses and solicitation provisions . . . 252.236-7012; 252.236-7008; 252.236-7010
. forms
. . forms . . . 253.303-1391; 253.303-1391c
. restrictions . . . 225.7014; 232.703-70

Military installations, closure of
. contract clause . . . 222.7102; 252.222-7001
. policy . . . 222.7101
. service contracts . . . 252.237-7022
. . contract clause . . . 237.7402; 252.237-7022
. . policy . . . 237.7401
. . scope . . . 237.7400

Military interdepartmental purchase request (MIPR)
. DD Form 448 . . . 253.208-1; 253.303-448
. DD Form 448-2, acceptance of MIPR . . . 253.208-2; 253.303-448
. procedures . . . 208.7005

Military recruiting on campus
. contract clause . . . 209.470-3; 252.209-7005
. definition of institution of higher education . . . 209.470-1
. policy . . . 209.470-2
. procedures . . . 209.470-3

Photovoltaic devices
. definitions . . . 225.7017-1
. exceptions . . . 225.7017-3
. restriction . . . 225.7017-2
. waivers . . . 225.7017-4

Mistakes
. preaward disclosure of . . . 214.407-3

Modification of contracts
. amendment of solicitation/modification of contract, SF 30 (transportation) . . . 247.370
. application of modifications . . . 243.172
. change orders
. . administration . . . 243.204
. . certification of requests for equitable adjustment . . . 243.204-71
. . definitization . . . 243.204-70
. contract adjustments
. . disposition . . . 250.103-6
. . processing cases . . . 250.103-5
. contract clauses
. . pricing of contract modifications . . . 243.205-70; 252.243-7001
. . requests for equitable adjustments . . . 243.205-71; 252.243-7002
. identification of foreign military sale requirements . . . 243.170
. notification of substantial impact on employment . . . 243.107-70
. obligation or deobligation of funds . . . 243.171
. order of application for modifications . . . 204.1671

Mortuary services
. acquisition method . . . 237.7001
. area of performance . . . 237.7002
. contract clauses and solicitation provisions
. . area of performance (mortuary services) . . . 237.7003; 252.237-7004
. . award to single offeror (mortuary services) . . . 237.7003; 252.237-7002
. . default termination (mortuary services) . . . 237.7003; 252.237-7007
. . facility requirements (mortuary services) . . . 237.7003; 252.237-7010
. . group interment (mortuary services) . . . 237.7003; 252.237-7008
. . performance and delivery (mortuary services) . . . 237.7003; 252.237-7005
. . permits (mortuary services) . . . 237.7003; 252.237-7009
. . preparation history (mortuary services) . . . 237.7003; 252.237-7011
. . requirements (mortuary services) . . . 237.7003; 252.237-7003
. . subcontracting (mortuary services) . . . 237.7003; 252.237-7006
. distribution of contracts . . . 237.7003
. scope . . . 237.7000

Multiyear contracting
. contracts for electricity from renewable energy sources . . . 217.174
. definitions . . . 217.103
. economic order quantity procurement . . . 217.174
. general . . . 217.170
. services . . . 217.171
. supplies . . . 217.172
. weapon systems . . . 217.173

N

NASA procurement
. authorization . . . 208.7100
. policy . . . 208.7101
. procedures . . . 208.7102

Native Hawaiian small businesses
. utilization of Indian organizations and Indian-owned economic enterprises and Native Hawaiian small business concerns . . . 252.226-7001

NATO cooperative projects—see also Foreign acquisitions
. congressional notification . . . 225.871-7
. definitions . . . 225.871-2
. directed subcontracting . . . 225.871-5
. disposal of property . . . 225.871-6
. general . . . 225.871-3
. quality assurance . . . 246.406
. scope . . . 225.871-1
. statutory waivers . . . 225.871-4

Negotiated procurement
. certificate of current cost or pricing data . . . 215.406-2

Negotiated procurement—continued
. contract clauses and solicitation provisions
. . cost estimating system . . . 215.408; 252.215-7002
. . cost estimating system requirements . . . 252.215-7002
. . notice of intent to resolicit . . . 252.215-7007; 215.408
. . only one offer . . . 252.215-7008; 215.408
. . prescriptions . . . 215.408
. . pricing adjustments . . . 215.408
. contract pricing
. . alternate structured approaches . . . 215.404-73
. . checklist, certified cost or pricing data . . . 215.403-5
. . contract type risk . . . 215.404-71
. . cost efficiency factor . . . 215.404-71
. . definitions . . . 215.407-5
. . disclosure, maintenance, and review requirements . . . 215.407-5
. . documenting the negotiation . . . 215.406-3
. . estimated data prices . . . 215.470
. . estimating systems . . . 215.407-5
. . facilities capital . . . 215.404-71
. . fee requirements for cost-plus-award-fee contracts . . . 215.404-74
. . fee requirements for FFRDCs . . . 215.404-75
. . forward pricing rate agreements . . . 215.407-3
. . information to support proposal analysis . . . 215.404-2
. . instructions for submission of certified cost or pricing data and data other than certified cost or pricing data . . . 215.403-5; 215.403-5
. . make-or-buy programs . . . 215.407-2
. . modified weighted guidelines method for nonprofit organizations . . . 215.404-72
. . obtaining certified cost or pricing data . . . 215.403
. . performance risk . . . 215.404-71
. . prenegotiation objectives . . . 215.406-1
. . pricing policy
. . profit . . . 215.404-4
. . prohibition on obtaining cost or pricing data . . . 215.403-1
. . proposal analysis techniques . . . 215.404-1
. . requiring information other than cost or pricing data . . . 215.403-3
. . should-cost review . . . 215.407-4
. . sole source commercial items . . . 215.402
. . subcontract pricing considerations . . . 215.404-3
. . weighted guidelines method . . . 215.404-71
. . working capital adjustment . . . 215.404-71
. evaluation factors
. . consideration of selected reserve for employment or subcontracting . . . 215.370-2
. . definition of selected reserve . . . 215.370-1
. . solicitation provision and contract clause . . . 215.370-3
. exchanges with offerors after receipt of proposals . . . 215.209

Negotiated procurement—continued
. forms
. . record of weighted guidelines application, DD Form 1547 . . . 215.404-70; 253.215-70; 253.303-1547
. solicitation and receipt of proposals and information
. . peer reviews . . . 215.270
. . tiered evaluation of offers . . . 215.203-70
. source selection
. . evaluation factors and subfactors . . . 215.304
. . exceptions . . . 215.371-4
. . fair and reasonable price . . . 215.371-3
. . policy . . . 215.371-1
. . promote competition . . . 215.371-2
. . proposal evaluation . . . 215.305
. . responsibilities . . . 215.303
. . waiver . . . 215.371-5

Non-DoD agency contracts
. procedures . . . 217.7802
. scope . . . 217.700

Noncommercial item acquisitions
. advance payments
. . advance payment pool . . . 232.470
. . approval recommendation . . . 232.409-1
. . contract clause prescriptions . . . 232.412-70
. . exclusions . . . 232.404
. . findings, determination, and authorization . . . 232.410
. contract financing
. . description of financing methods . . . 232.102
. . provisional delivery payments . . . 232.102-70
. rights in software and software documentation
. . acquisition . . . 227.7203-2
. . conformity, acceptance, and warranty . . . 227.7203-14
. . contract clause prescriptions . . . 227.7203-6
. . contractor procedures and records . . . 227.7203-11
. . copyright . . . 227.7203-9
. . deferred delivery and ordering . . . 227.7203-8
. . early identification to be furnished to the government . . . 227.7203-3
. . government right to establish conformity of markings . . . 227.7203-12
. . government right to review, verify, challenge and validate asserted restrictions . . . 227.7203-13
. . government rights . . . 227.7203-5
. . identification and marking . . . 227.7203-10
. . license rights . . . 227.7203-4
. . overseas contracts with foreign sources . . . 227.7203-17
. . policy . . . 227.7203-1
. . providing documentation to foreign concerns . . . 227.7203-16
. . subcontractor rights . . . 227.7203-15
. rights in technical data
. . acquisition of technical data . . . 227.7103-2
. . conformity, acceptance, and warranty . . . 227.7103-14
. . contract clause prescriptions . . . 227.7103-6

Noncommercial item acquisitions—continued
. rights in technical data—continued
. . contractor identification and marking . . . 227.7103-10
. . contractor procedures and records . . . 227.7103-11
. . copyright license . . . 227.7103-9
. . deferred delivery and ordering . . . 227.7103-8
. . early identification of technical data to be furnished to the government . . . 227.7103-3
. . government right to establish conformity of markings . . . 227.7103-12
. . government right to review, verify, challenge and validate asserted restrictions . . . 227.7103-13
. . government rights . . . 227.7103-5
. . license rights . . . 227.7103-4
. . overseas contracts with foreign sources . . . 227.7103-17
. . policy . . . 227.7103-1
. . providing to foreign concerns . . . 227.7103-16
. . subcontractor rights . . . 227.7103-15
. . use and non-disclosure agreement . . . 227.7103-7

Noncontiguous states employment restrictions
. contract clause prescription . . . 222.7004
. definition of noncontiguous state . . . 222.7001
. general . . . 222.7002
. scope . . . 222.7000
. waivers . . . 222.7003

Nonprofit agencies employing the blind or severely disabled
. assignment authority . . . 208.7002
. assignments under coordinated acquisition . . . 208.7003-2; 208.7006
. assignments under integrated materiel management (IMM) . . . 208.7003-1
. definitions . . . 208.7001
. military interdepartmental purchase requests . . . 208.7005
. policy and procedures . . . 208.7000
. procedures . . . 208.7004
. responsibilities of acquiring department . . . 208.7002-1
. responsibilities of requiring department . . . 208.7002-2
. scope . . . 208.7000

Nonprofit organizations
. cost principles . . . 231.703
. definitions . . . 215.404-72; 237.7301
. modified weighted guidelines method . . . 215.404-72
. ordering from . . . 208.705

Novation and change-of-name agreements
. agreement to recognize a successor in interest . . . 242.1204
. processing . . . 242.1203

Numbering systems
. DUNS numbers . . . 204.7202-2
. uniform contract line item numbering system
. . accounting classification reference number (ACRN) . . . 204.7107

Numbering systems—continued
. uniform contract line item numbering system—continued
. . contract clause . . . 204.7109; 252.204-7006
. . contract modifications . . . 204.7106
. . definitions . . . 204.7101
. . exhibits and attachments . . . 204.7105
. . line items, criteria for establishing . . . 204.7103-1
. . numbering procedures . . . 204.7103-2; 204.7104-2
. . payment instructions . . . 204.7108
. . policy . . . 204.7102
. . scope . . . 204.7100
. . subline items, criteria for establishing . . . 204.7104-1
. uniform procurement instrument identifiers
. . policy . . . 204.1601
. . procedures . . . 204.1603
. . Federal Procurement Data System . . . 204.1670
. . order of application for modifications . . . 204.1671

O

Occupational safety—see also Environment and conservation
. drug-free workplace
. . contract clause . . . 223.570-2; 252.223-7004
. . policy . . . 223.570-1

Ocean transportation by U.S.-flag vessels
. annual reporting requirement
. contract clauses and solicitation provision prescriptions . . . 247.574
. definitions
. policy . . . 247.572
. general . . . 247.573
. scope . . . 247.570

Offset arrangements
. foreign military sales . . . 225.7306

Options
. competition . . . 234.005-1
. contract clauses and solicitation provisions
. . exercise of option to fulfill foreign military sales commitments . . . 217.208-70; 252.217-7000
. . prescriptions . . . 217.208-70
. . surge option . . . 217.208-70; 252.217-7001
. exercise of . . . 217.207
. extension of ordering periods . . . 217.204
. use of . . . 217.202

Organizational and consultant conflicts of interest
. limitations on contractors acting as lead system integrators
. . definitions . . . 209.570-1
. . policy . . . 209.570-2
. . procedures . . . 209.570-3
. . solicitation provisions and contract clause . . . 209.570-4
. representation relating to compensation of former DoD officials
. . contract clause . . . 252.203-7005

Organizational conflicts of interest, major defense acquisition program
. applicability . . . 209.571-2
. definitions . . . 209.571-1
. identification . . . 209.571-6
. lead system integrators . . . 209.571-5
. mitigation . . . 209.571-4
. notice of prohibition relating to organizational conflict of interest . . . 252.209-7008
. . prescription . . . 209.571-8
. organizational conflict of interest, contract clause . . . 252.209-7009
. . prescription . . . 209.571-8
. policy . . . 209.571-3
. systems engineering contracts . . . 209.571-7
. technical assistance contracts . . . 209.571-7

Over and above contract work
. contract clause . . . 217.7702; 252.217-7028
. procedures . . . 217.7701

Overseas contracts—see also Foreign acquisitions
. architect-engineer services, restrictions on . . . 225.7015; 236.602-70
. assignment of claims (overseas) . . . 252.232-7008
. choice of law (overseas) . . . 252.233-7001
. compliance with local labor laws (overseas) . . . 252.222-7002
. contract clauses
. . assignment of claims (overseas) . . . 232.806
. . choice of law (overseas) . . . 233.215-70
. . compliance with local labor laws (overseas) . . . 222.7201
. . contract clauses . . . 236.609-70; 252.236-7011; 236.570; 252.236-7010
. . workers' compensation and war-hazard insurance overseas . . . 228.370; 252.228-7000
. DD Form 2139, report of contract performance outside the United States . . . 253.303-2139
. military construction, restrictions on . . . 225.7014
. reporting of acquisition of end products manufacturing outside of U.S . . . 225.070
. rights in software and software documentation . . . 227.7203-17
. rights in technical data . . . 227.7103-17
. special tax procedures . . . 229.101
. workers' compensation and war-hazard insurance . . . 228.305

Overtime
. approvals . . . 222.103-4
. under contract work hours and safety standards statute . . . 222.302

Ozone-depleting substances
. policy . . . 223.803
. requirements documents restrictions . . . 211.271

P

Patents—see also Rights in software and software documentation; Rights in technical data
. assignments . . . 227.7010

Patents—see also Rights in software and software documentation; Rights in technical data— continued
. contract clauses
. . assignments . . . 227.7010; 252.227-7011
. . computation of royalties . . . 227.7009-4; 252.227-7008
. . license grant . . . 227.7009-3; 252.227-7004
. . license grant—running royalty . . . 227.7009-4; 252.227-7006
. . license term . . . 227.7009-3; 252.227-7005
. . license term—running royalty . . . 227.7009-4; 252.227-7007
. . license to other government agencies . . . 227.7009-4; 227.7011; 252.227-7010
. . non-estoppel . . . 252.227-7000
. . patent releases, license agreements, and assignments . . . 227.7009; 227.7009
. . patents—ownership rights of large business contractor
. . patents—reporting of subject inventions . . . 227.303; 252.227-7039
. . readjustment of payments . . . 227.7009-2; 252.227-7002
. . release of past infringement . . . 227.7009-2; 252.227-7001
. . reporting and payment of royalties . . . 227.7009-4; 252.227-7009
. . required clauses . . . 227.7009-1
. . termination . . . 227.7009-2; 252.227-7003
. contract format . . . 227.7012; 252.227-7012
. DD Form 882, report of inventions and subcontracts (pursuant to "patent rights" contract clause) . . . 253.303-882
. foreign license and technical assistance agreements
. . agreements between the government and domestic concerns . . . 227.673
. . foreign patent interchange agreements . . . 227.676
. . general . . . 227.671
. . international traffic in arms regulations . . . 227.675-1
. . policy . . . 227.672
. . review of agreements . . . 227.675-2
. . scope . . . 227.670
. . supply contracts between the government and foreign concerns . . . 227.674
. general procedures . . . 227.304-1
. infringement claims, licenses, and assignments
. . assignments . . . 227.7010
. . contract clause prescriptions . . . 227.7009
. . contract format . . . 227.7012
. . copyright infringement . . . 227.7003
. . filing . . . 227.7004
. . indirect notice of . . . 227.7005
. . investigation and disposition of claims . . . 227.7006
. . notification and disclosure to claimants . . . 227.7007
. . policy . . . 227.7001
. . procurement of rights in inventions, patents, and copyrights . . . 227.7011

Patents—see also Rights in software and software documentation; Rights in technical data— continued
. infringement claims, licenses, and assignments—continued
. . recordation . . . 227.7013
. . scope . . . 227.7000
. . settlement of indemnified claims . . . 227.7008
. . statutes . . . 227.7002
. subcontracts . . . 227.304-4

Payment bonds . . . 245.7310-2

Payments
. advance
. . advance payment pool . . . 232.470
. . approval recommendation . . . 232.409-1
. . contract clause prescriptions . . . 232.412-70
. . exclusions . . . 232.404
. . findings, determination, and authorization . . . 232.410
. . advance . . . 252.232-7005
. contract financing . . . 232.007
. electronic funds transfer
. . contract clauses and solicitation provisions . . . 232.1110
. . payment by governmentwide commercial purchase card . . . 232.1108
. electronic submission and processing of payment requests
. . prescription . . : 232.7004
. . contract clause . . . 252.232-7003; 252.232-7006
. . definitions . . . 252.232-7006; 232.7001; 252.232-7003
. . policy . . . 232.7002
. . procedures . . . 232.7003
. . scope . . . 232.7000
. fast payment procedure . . . 213.402
. levies on
. . contract clause . . . 232.7102; 252.232-7010
. . policy and procedures . . . 232.7101
. . scope . . . 232.7100
. payment in local currency (Afghanistan)
. . policy and procedures . . . 232.7201
. . scope of subpart . . . 232.7200
. . solicitation provision . . . 232.7202; 252.232-7014
. performance-based
. . administration and payment . . . 232.1007
. . contract clauses . . . 232.1005-70; 252.232-7012; 252.232-7013
. . criteria for use . . . 232.1003-70
. . policy . . . 232.1001
. . procedure . . . 232.1004
. progress payments based on costs
. . application of government title terms . . . 232.503-15
. . contract clause prescriptions . . . 232.502-4
. . contract price and . . . 232.501-3
. . customary progress payment rates . . . 232.501-1
. . suspension or reduction of payments . . . 232.503-6
. . unusual . . . 232.501-2

Payments—continued
. prompt payment
. . contract clauses . . . 232.908
. . determining payment due dates . . . 232.904
. . payment documentation and process . . . 232.905
. . making payments . . . 232.906
. . applicability . . . 232.901
. . responsibilities . . . 232.903
. requests, submission and processing of
. . prescription . . . 232.7004
. . contract clause . . . 252.232-7003; 252.232-7006
. . definitions . . . 232.7001; 252.232-7003
. . policy . . . 232.7002
. . procedures . . . 232.7003
. . scope . . . 232.7000
. voluntary refunds . . . 242.7100
. wide area workflow payment instructions
. . contract clause . . . 252.232-7006
. . prescription . . . 232.7004
. withholding/suspension
. . bonds and . . . 228.106-7
. . construction contracts . . . 222.406-9
. . withholding/suspension . . . 227.7103-6; 227.7103-14; 227.7104; 252.227-7030

Payrolls
. forms, construction contracts . . . 222.406-6

Peer reviews
. acquisition procedures . . . 207.104
. negotiated procurements . . . 215.270
. requirements . . . 201.170

Pensions
. contractor insurance/pension review (CIPR)
. . general . . . 242.7301
. . requirements . . . 242.7302
. . responsibilities . . . 242.7303

Performance-based payments
. contract clauses . . . 232.1005-70; 252.232-7012; 252.232-7013
. policy . . . 232.1001
. criteria for use . . . 232.1003-70
. procedure . . . 232.1004

Performance bonds . . . 245.7310-2

Performance evaluation
. architect-engineer services . . . 236.604
. contractors . . . 236.201
. forms
. . DD Form 2626, performance evaluation (construction) . . . 253.303-2626
. . DD Form 2631, performance evaluation (architect-engineer) . . . 253.303-2631
. past performance . . . 215.305

Personal property
. exchange of
. . definitions . . . 217.7001
. . policy . . . 217.7002
. . purchase request . . . 217.7003
. . scope . . . 217.7000

Personal property—continued
. exchange of—continued
. . solicitation and award . . . 217.7004
. . solicitation provision . . . 217.7005; 252.217-7002
. shipment or storage
. . policy . . . 247.271-1
. . procedures . . . 247.271-2
. . solicitation provision, schedule formats, and contract clauses . . . 247.271-3

Personal services—see also Service contracting
. contracts . . . 237.104
. cost principles . . . 231.205-6
. funding and term of service . . . 237.106

Photovoltaic devices
. solicitation provision and contract clause . . . 225.7017-5

Pilot mentor-protege program—see also Small disadvantaged business concerns
. contracting officer responsibilities . . . 219.7103-2
. developmental assistance costs eligible for reimbursement or credit . . . 219.7104
. general . . . 219.7102
. performance reviews I-113 . . . 219.7106
. policy . . . 219.7101
. procedures . . . 219.7103-1
. reporting . . . 219.7105
. scope . . . 219.7100

Plant clearance
. forms
. . DD Form 1635, plant clearance case register . . . 253.303-1635

Postaward matters
. application of government title terms . . . 232.503-15
. DD Form 1484, postaward conference record . . . 253.303-1484
. postaward conference . . . 242.503-2; 252.242-7000
. suspension or reduction of payments . . . 232.503-6

Preaward surveys . . . 209.106
. SF 1403, preaward survey of prospective contractors (general) . . . 253.209-1

Precious metals, government furnished
. contract clause . . . 208.7305; 252.208-7000
. definitions . . . 208.7301
. policy . . . 208.7302
. procedures . . . 208.7303
. refined precious metals . . . 208.7304

Prenegotiation objectives . . . 215.406-1

Prescriptions . . . 237.171-4

Price and pricing—see also Indirect cost rates
. contract clauses and solicitation provisions
. . contract clauses and solicitation provisions . . . 236.570; 252.236-7008; 216.203-4; 252.216-7000; 216.203-4; 252.216-7001; 216.203-4; 252.216-7003; 235.070-3; 252.235-7000; 252.236-7000; 236.570

Price and pricing—see also Indirect cost rates—continued
. contract clauses and solicitation provisions—continued
. . payment for subline items not separately priced . . . 204.7104-1; 252.204-7002
. . price adjustment (transportation) . . . 247.270-4; 252.247-7001
. . pricing adjustments . . . 215.408
. . pricing of contract modifications . . . 213.302-5; 243.205-70; 252.243-7001
. . revision of prices (transportation) . . . 247.270-4; 252.247-7002
. . contract clauses and solicitation provisions . . . 216.601; 252.216-7002
. fee limitations, architect-engineer services . . . 236.606-70
. foreign military sales acquisition . . . 225.7303
. HUBZone program, price evaluation preference . . . 219.1307
. negotiated procurement contracts
. . alternate structured approaches . . . 215.404-73
. . checklist, certified cost or pricing data . . . 215.403-5
. . contract type risk . . . 215.404-71
. . cost efficiency factor . . . 215.404-71
. . DD Form 1547 . . . 215.404-70
. . definitions . . . 215.407-5
. . disclosure, maintenance, and review requirements . . . 215.407-5
. . documenting the negotiation . . . 215.406-3
. . estimated data prices . . . 215.470
. . estimating systems . . . 215.407-5
. . facilities capital . . . 215.404-71
. . fee requirements for cost-plus-award-fee contracts . . . 215.404-74
. . fee requirements for FFRDCs . . . 215.404-75
. . forward pricing rate agreements . . . 215.407-3
. . data to support proposal analysis . . . 215.404-2
. . instructions for submission of certified cost or pricing data and data other than certified cost or pricing data . . . 215.403-5
. . make-or-buy programs . . . 215.407-2
. . modified weighted guidelines method for nonprofit organizations . . . 215.404-72
. . obtaining certified cost or pricing data . . . 215.403
. . performance risk . . . 215.404-71
. . prenegotiation objectives . . . 215.406-1
. . pricing policy
. . profit . . . 215.404-4
. . prohibition on obtaining cost or pricing data . . . 215.403-1
. . proposal analysis techniques . . . 215.404-1
. . requiring information other than certified cost or pricing data . . . 215.403-3
. . should-cost review . . . 215.407-4
. . sole source commercial items . . . 215.402
. . subcontract pricing considerations . . . 215.404-3
. . weighted guidelines method . . . 215.404-71
. . working capital adjustment . . . 215.404-71

Price and pricing—see also Indirect cost rates— continued
. Section 8(a) contracts . . . 219.806
. telecommunications services . . . 239.7406

Priorities and allocations . . . 211.602

Privacy protection
. Freedom of Information Act . . . 224.203
. procedures . . . 224.103

Procedures, Guidance, and Information (PGI)
. copies of, obtaining . . . 201.105
. definition . . . 202.101
. maintenance . . . 201.201-70

Production surveillance and reporting
. assignment of criticality designator . . . 242.1105
. reporting requirements . . . 242.1106
. surveillance requirements . . . 242.1104

Profit
. negotiated procurement contracts . . . 215.404-4
. undefinitized contract actions . . . 217.7404-6

Progress payments based on costs—see also Contract financing
. application of government title terms . . . 232.503-15
. contract clause prescriptions . . . 232.502-4
. contract price and . . . 232.501-3
. customary progress payment rates . . . 232.501-1
. suspension or reduction of payments . . . 232.503-6
. unusual . . . 232.501-2

Prohibited practices
. business practices, best practice policies . . . 203.170
. contract clauses and solicitation provisions
. . agency office of inspector general . . . 252.203-7003
. . prohibition on persons convicted of fraud or other defense-contract-related felonies . . . 203.570-3; 252.203-7001
. . special prohibition on employment . . . 252.203-7001
. . statutory prohibition on compensation to former DoD employees . . . 252.203-7000
. employment prohibitions on persons convicted of fraud or other defense contract-related felonies
. . contract clause . . . 203.570-3; 252.203-7001
. . prohibition period . . . 203.570-2
. . scope . . . 203.570-1
. limitations on payment of funds to influence federal transactions
. . processing suspected violations . . . 203.806
. procurement integrity . . . 203.104
. . contractor bid or proposal information protection . . . 203.104-4
. . disclosure of proprietary and source selection information . . . 203.104-5
. reporting violations and suspected violations . . . 203.070

Prohibited practices—continued
. senior DoD officials seeking employment with defense contractors . . . 203.171
. . compensation of former DoD officials . . . 252.203-7000
. . contract clause . . . 203.171-4
. . definition . . . 203.171-2
. . policy . . . 203.171-3
. . scope . . . 203.171-1
. standards of conduct
. . DoD hotline poster address . . . 203.1004
. . requirements . . . 203.1003
. subcontractor kickbacks . . . 203.502-2
. voiding and rescinding contracts . . . 203.703
. whistleblower protections for contractor employees
. . contract clause . . . 252.203-7002
. . classified information . . . 203.903
. . policy . . . 203.903
. . procedures for filing complaints . . . 203.904
. . procedures for investigating complaints . . . 203.904
. . remedies . . . 203.906
. . scope . . . 203.900
. . definition . . . 203.901

Prohibited sources
. Communist Chinese military companies . . . 225.770-2
. definitions . . . 225.770-1
. exceptions . . . 225.701-70; 225.770-3
. identifying United States Munitions List items . . . 225.770-4
. restrictions on . . . 225.701
. secondary Arab boycott of Israel
. . exceptions . . . 225.7603
. . procedures . . . 225.7602
. . restriction . . . 225.7601
. . solicitation provision . . . 225.7604; 252.225-7031
. . waivers . . . 225.7604
. waiver of prohibition . . . 225.770-5

Prohibition on interrogation of detainees by contractor personnel
. contract clause . . . 252.237-7010
. contract clause prescription . . . 237.173-5
. definitions . . . 237.173-3
. scope . . . 237.173-1
. waiver . . . 237.173-4

Prompt payment
. applicability . . . 232.901
. conctract clauses . . . 232.908
. making payments . . . 232.906
. payment documentation and process . . . 232.905
. responsibilities . . . 232.903
. determining payment due dates . . . 232.904

Property control systems . . . 245.104

Proposed contract actions—see also Publicizing contract actions
. synopses of
. . notification of bundling . . . 205.205

Proposed contract actions—see also Publicizing contract actions—continued
. synopses of—continued
. . preparation and transmittal of synopses . . . 205.207
. . publicizing and response time . . . 205.203

Protection for defense contractors outside the U.S.
. antiterrorism/force protection
. . contract clause . . . 225.372-2; 252.225-7043
. . general . . . 225.372-1
. personnel supporting U.S. armed forces deployed outside the U.S.
. . contract clause . . . 225.371-5; 252.225-7040
. . definitions . . . 225.371-2; 252.225-7040
. . government support . . . 225.371-3
. . law of war training . . . 225.371-4
. . scope . . . 225.371-1

Provisioning requirements, contracts with . . . 217.7601

Public interest
. competition requirements and . . . 206.302-7

Publicizing contract actions
. contract clause and solicitation provision
. . provision of information to cooperative agreement holders . . . 205.470; 252.205-7000
. paid advertisements . . . 205.502
. purchase order-invoice-voucher, SF 44 . . . 213.306
. synopses of contract awards
. . announcement . . . 205.303
. . general . . . 205.301
. synopses of proposed contract actions
. . notification of bundling . . . 205.205-70
. . preparation and transmittal of synopses . . . 205.207
. . publicizing and response time . . . 205.203

Purchase orders
. simplified acquisition procedures
. . contract clause prescriptions . . . 213.302-5
. . obtaining contractor acceptance and modifying purchase orders . . . 213.302-3
. under Section 8(a) . . . 213.7002

Q

Qualifying country sources—see also Foreign acquisitions
. applicability . . . 225.872-2
. audit . . . 225.872-6
. contract administration . . . 225.872-5
. general . . . 225.872-1
. individual determinations . . . 225.872-4
. industrial security . . . 225.872-7
. solicitation procedures . . . 225.872-3
. subcontracting with . . . 225.872-8

Quality assurance—see also Warranties
. acquisitions at or below simplified acquisition threshold . . . 246.404
. aircraft . . . 246.408-71

Quality assurance—see also Warranties—continued
. assessment of additional costs . . . 246.470-1
. at source . . . 246.402
. authorizing shipment of supplies . . . 246.471
. certificate of conformance . . . 246.504
. contract clauses
. . contractor counterfeit electronic part detection and avoidance system . . . 252.246-7007
. . material inspection and receiving report . . . 246.370; 252.246-7000
. . sources of electronic parts . . . 252.246-7008
. . warranty of construction (Germany) . . . 246.710; 252.246-7002
. . warranty of data . . . 246.710; 252.246-7001
. contract quality requirements
. . higher-level requirements . . . 246.202-4
. contracting office responsibilities . . . 246.103
. contractor counterfeit electronic part detection and avoidance . . . 246.870
. . contract clause . . . 252.246-7007; 252.246-7008
. . contract clauses . . . 246.870-3
. . definition . . . 246.870-1
. . policy . . . 246.870-2
. . scope . . . 246.870-0
. definition, discipline working group . . . 246.101
. foreign governments . . . 246.406
. inspection stamping . . . 246.472
. material inspection and receiving reports . . . 246.601
. nonconforming supplies or services . . . 246.407
. notification of potential safety issues . . . 246.371; 252.246-7003
. policy . . . 246.102
. quality evaluation data . . . 246.470-2
. safety of facilities, infrastructure, and equipment for military operations . . . 246.270
. . contract clause . . . 252.246-7004
. . contract clause prescription . . . 246.270-4
. . exceptions . . . 246.270-3
. . policy . . . 246.270-2
. . scope . . . 246.270-1
. contract surveillance . . . 246.401
. single-agency assignments
. . aircraft . . . 246.408-71
. . subsistence . . . 246.408-70
. warranties
. . authority for use . . . 246.704
. . contract clause prescriptions . . . 246.710
. . definitions . . . 246.701
. . limitations . . . 246.705
. . software and software documentation . . . 227.7203-14
. . technical data . . . 227.7103-14; 246.708
. . terms and conditions . . . 246.706
. warranty attachment . . . 246.710-70

Quasi-military armed forces . . . 237.109

R

Radio frequency identification
. contract clause . . . 211.275-3; 252.211-7006

Radio frequency identification—continued
. definitions . . . 211.275-1; 252.211-7006
. policy . . . 211.275-2

Recovered materials, use of . . . 223.405

Remedies
. trafficking in persons . . . 222.1704

Replenishment parts acquisition
. definition . . . 217.7501
. general . . . 217.7502
. limitations on price increases . . . 217.7505
. scope . . . 217.7500
. spare parts breakout program . . . 217.7506
. spares acquisition integrated with production (SAIP) . . . 217.7503
. when data not available . . . 217.7504

Reporting requirements
. contract performance outside the United States
. . contract clause and solicitation provision prescriptions . . . 225.7204
. . distribution of reports . . . 225.7203
. . exception . . . 225.7202
. . policy . . . 225.7201
. . scope of subpart . . . 225.7000
. contract reporting
. . contract action reporting requirements . . . 204.670
. . individual contracting action report, DD Form 350 . . . 253.303-350
. . monthly summary of contracting actions, DD Form 1057 . . . 252.303-1057
. cost and software data
. . policy . . . 234.7100
. . solicitation provision and contract clause, prescription . . . 234.7101
. federal procurement data system
. . general . . . 204.602
. . reporting data . . . 204.606
. . responsibilities . . . 204.604
. foreign acquisitions . . . 225.070
. labor disputes . . . 222.101-3
. production surveillance . . . 242.1106
. protests of solicitations or awards . . . 233.171
. reduction or suspension of contract payments upon finding of fraud . . . 232.006-5
. scientific and technical reports . . . 235.010
. semiannual enforcement reports, labor standards . . . 222.406-13

Research and development contracts—see also Independent research and development work
. competition . . . 235.006-71
. contract clauses and solicitation provisions
. . acknowledgment of support and disclaimer . . . 235.072; 252.235-7010
. . animal welfare . . . 235.072; 252.235-7002
. . final scientific or technical report . . . 235.072; 252.235-7011
. . frequency authorization . . . 235.072; 252.235-7003

Research and development contracts—see also Independent research and development work—continued
. contract clauses and solicitation provisions—continued
. . human research subjects . . . 235.072; 252.235-7004
. . contract clauses and solicitation provisions . . . 235.070-3; 252.235-7001; 235.070-3; 252.235-7000
. . prescriptions . . . 235.070-3; 235.072
. contracting methods and contract types . . . 216.104-70; 235.006
. definitions . . . 234.001; 235.001; 235.015-70
. educational institutions
. . special use allowances for research facilities . . . 235.015-70
. evaluation for award, lead system integrators . . . 235.008
. export-controlled items . . . 235.071
. federally funded research and development centers . . . 235.017
. general . . . 216.104-70; 235.006
. human research . . . 207.172
. manufacturing technology program . . . 235.006-70
. methods . . . 235.006
. scientific and technical reports . . . 235.010
. services of students at R&D laboratories
. . contract clause prescription . . . 237.7303
. . definitions . . . 237.7301
. . general . . . 237.7302
. . scope . . . 237.7300
. sponsoring agreements . . . 235.017-1
. unusually hazardous risks
. . contract clause prescriptions . . . 235.070-3; 235.072
. . indemnification under contract involving both research and development and other work . . . 235.070-2
. . indemnification under research and development contracts . . . 235.070-1

Reserve officer training corps and military recruiting on campus
. contract clause . . . 209.470-3; 252.209-7005
. definition of institution of higher education . . . 209.470-1
. policy . . . 209.470-2
. procedures . . . 209.470-3

Residual powers
. extraordinary contractual actions . . . 250.104

Responsible prospective contractors, identifying
. definitions . . . 209.101
. determinations and documentation . . . 209.105-2
. general standards . . . 209.104-1
. preaward surveys . . . 209.106
. SF 1403, preaward survey of prospective contractors (general) . . . 253.209-1
. subcontractor responsibility . . . 209.104-4

Restrictions on foreign acquisitions—see also Foreign acquisitions
. air circuit breakers for naval vessels
. . contract clause and solicitation provision prescriptions . . . 225.7006-4
. . exceptions . . . 225.7006-2
. . restriction . . . 225.7006-1
. . waiver . . . 225.7006-3
. anchor and mooring chain
. . contract clause . . . 225.7007-3; 252.225-7019
. . restriction . . . 225.7007-1
. . waiver . . . 225.7007-2
. ball and roller bearings . . . 225.7009
. . contract clause . . . 225.7009-5
. . exception . . . 225.7009-3
. . restriction . . . 225.7009-2
. . scope . . . 225.7009-1
. . waiver . . . 225.7009-4
. photovoltaic devices
. . definitions . . . 225.7017-1
. . exceptions . . . 225.7017-3
. . restriction . . . 225.7017-2
. . waivers . . . 225.7017-4
. carbon, alloy, and armor steel plate
. . contract clause . . . 225.7011-3; 252.225-7030
. . restriction . . . 225.7011-1
. . waiver . . . 225.7011-2
. chemical weapons antidote
. . exception . . . 225.7005-2
. . restriction . . . 225.7005-1
. . waiver . . . 225.7005-3
. construction or repair of vessels in foreign shipyards . . . 225.7013
. definitions . . . 225.7001
. food, clothing, fabrics, and hand or measuring tools
. . waiver of restrictions of 10 U.S.C. 2534 . . . 225.7008
. . contract clause prescriptions . . . 225.7002-3
. . exceptions . . . 225.7002-2
. . restrictions . . . 225.7002-1
. foreign buses
. . applicability . . . 225.7004-2
. . exceptions . . . 225.7004-3
. . restriction . . . 225.7004-1
. . waiver . . . 225.7004-4
. military construction . . . 232.703-70
. overseas architect-engineer services . . . 225.7015; 236.602-70
. overseas military construction . . . 225.7014
. photovoltaic devices
. . solicitation provision and contract clause . . . 225.7017-5
. scope . . . 225.7000
. specialty metals . . . 225.7003
. . contract clause prescriptions . . . 225.7003-5
. . contract clauses . . . 252.225-7008; 252.225-7009; 252.225-7010
. . definitions . . . 225.7003-1
. . exceptions . . . 225.7003-3
. . one-time waiver . . . 225.7003-4

Restrictions on foreign acquisitions—see also Foreign acquisitions—continued
. specialty metals—continued
. . restrictions . . . 225.7003-2
. . waiver of restrictions of 10 U.S.C. 2534 . . . 225.7008
. supercomputers
. . contract clause . . . 225.7012-3; 252.225-7011
. . restriction . . . 225.7012-1
. . waiver . . . 225.7012-2

Right of first refusal of employment
. contract clause . . . 222.7102; 252.222-7001
. policy . . . 222.7101

Rights in software and software documentation—see also Patents
. commercial software
. . contract clause prescription . . . 227.7202-4
. . policy . . . 227.7202-1
. . rights in . . . 227.7202-3
. contract clauses and solicitation provisions
. . deferred delivery of technical data or computer software . . . 227.7203-8; 252.227-7026
. . deferred ordering of technical data or computer software . . . 227.7203-8; 252.227-7027
. . identification and assertion of use, release, or disclosure restrictions . . . 227.7203-3; 227.7203-10; 252.227-7017
. . limitations on the use or disclosure of government furnished information marked with restrictive legends . . . 227.7203-5; 227.7203-6; 227.7203-15; 252.227-7025
. . rights in bid or proposal information . . . 227.7203-6; 252.227-7016
. . rights in noncommercial computer software and noncommercial computer software documentation . . . 227.7201; 227.7203; 252.227-7014
. . rights in special works . . . 227.7205; 252.227-7020
. . technical data or computer software previously delivered to the government . . . 227.7203-6; 227.7203-15; 252.227-7028
. . validation of asserted restrictions computer software . . . 227.7203-11; 227.7203-13; 227.7203-15; 252.227-7019
. . validation of restrictive markings on technical data . . . 227.7203-15; 252.227-7037; 227.7203-6; 227.7203-12; 227.7203-13
. contractor data repositories . . . 227.7207
. contracts for architect-engineer services . . . 227.7206
. contracts for special works . . . 227.7205
. definitions . . . 227.7201; 252.227-7014
. noncommercial software
. . acquisition . . . 227.7203-2
. . conformity, acceptance, and warranty . . . 227.7203-14
. . contract clause prescriptions . . . 227.7203-6
. . contractor procedures and records . . . 227.7203-11
. . copyright . . . 227.7203-9

Rights in software and software documentation—see also Patents—continued
. noncommercial software—continued
. . deferred delivery and ordering . . . 227.7203-8
. . early identification to be furnished to the government . . . 227.7203-3
. . government right to establish conformity of markings . . . 227.7203-12
. . government right to review, verify, challenge and validate asserted restrictions . . . 227.7203-13
. . government rights . . . 227.7203-5
. . identification and marking . . . 227.7203-10
. . license rights . . . 227.7203-4
. . overseas contracts with foreign sources . . . 227.7203-17
. . policy . . . 227.7203-1
. . providing documentation to foreign concerns . . . 227.7203-16
. . subcontractor rights . . . 227.7203-15
. scope . . . 227.7200
. Small Business Innovative Research (SBIR) Program . . . 227.7204
. contract clauses and solicitation provisions
. . contract clauses and solicitation provisions . . . 227.7203-9; 227.7203-17; 252.227-7013; 227.7203-6

Rights in technical data—see also Foreign license and technical assistance agreements; Patents
. acquisition of existing works without modification . . . 227.7105-2
. acquisition of modified existing works . . . 227.7105-3
. approval of restricted designs . . . 227.7107-3
. architectural designs and clauses for architect-engineer or construction contracts . . . 227.7107-1
. commercial items, components, or processes . . . 212.211; 227.7102
. contract clauses and solicitation provisions
. . deferred delivery of technical data or computer software . . . 227.7103-8; 252.227-7026
. . deferred ordering of technical data or computer software . . . 252.227-7027; 227.7103-8
. . drawings and other data to become property of government . . . 227.7107-1; 252.227-7023
. . government rights to review, verify, challenge, and validate asserted restrictions . . . 227.7102-3
. . government rights (unlimited) . . . 227.7107-1; 252.227-7022
. . identification and assertion of use, release, or disclosure restrictions . . . 227.7103-3; 227.7103-10; 227.7104; 252.227-7017
. . limitations on the use or disclosure of government furnished information marked with restrictive legends . . . 227.7103; 227.7104; 252.227-7025
. . notice and approval of restricted designs . . . 227.7107-2; 252.227-7024
. . rights in bid or proposal information . . . 227.7103-6; 227.7104; 227.7203-6; 252.227-7016
. . rights in data existing works . . . 227.7105-2; 252.227-7021

Rights in technical data—see also Foreign license and technical assistance agreements; Patents—continued
. contract clauses and solicitation provisions—continued
. . rights in noncommercial technical data and compute . . . 227.7104; 252.227-7018
. . rights in shop drawings . . . 227.7107-1; 252.227-7033
. . rights in special works . . . 227.7105-3; 227.7106; 252.227-7020
. . rights in technical data and computer software (foreign) . . . 227.7103-17; 252.227-7032
. . rights in technical data noncommercial items . . . 227.7106; 252.227-7013; 227.7101; 227.7102; 227.7103
. . technical data commercial items . . . 227.7102-2; 227.7102-4; 252.227-7015
. . technical data or computer software previously delivered to the government . . . 227.7103-6; 227.7103-15; 227.7104; 252.227-7028
. . technical data withholding of payment . . . 227.7103-6; 227.7103-14; 227.7104; 252.227-7030
. . validation of asserted restrictions computer softw . . . 252.227-7019; 227.7104
. . validation of restrictive markings on technical data . . . 227.7103; 227.7102-4; 227.7104; 252.227-7037
. . warranty of data . . . 227.7103-14; 252.246-7001
. contractor data repositories . . . 227.7108
. contracts for acquisition of existing works . . . 227.7105-1
. contracts for architect-engineer services . . . 227.7107
. contracts for construction supplies and research and development work . . . 227.7107-2
. contracts for special works . . . 227.7106
. definitions . . . 227.7101
. noncommercial items or processes
. . acquisition of technical data . . . 227.7103-2
. . conformity, acceptance, and warranty . . . 227.7103-14
. . contract clause prescriptions . . . 227.7103-6
. . contractor identification and marking . . . 227.7103-10
. . contractor procedures and records . . . 227.7103-11
. . copyright license . . . 227.7103-9
. . deferred delivery and ordering . . . 227.7103-8
. . early identification of technical data to be furnished to the government . . . 227.7103-3
. . government right to establish conformity of markings . . . 227.7103-12
. . government right to review, verify, challenge and validate asserted restrictions . . . 227.7103-13
. . government rights . . . 227.7103-5
. . license rights . . . 227.7103-4
. . overseas contracts with foreign sources . . . 227.7103-17
. . policy . . . 227.7103-1

Rights in technical data—see also Foreign license and technical assistance agreements; Patents— continued
. noncommercial items or processes—continued
. . providing to foreign concerns . . . 227.7103-16
. . subcontractor rights . . . 227.7103-15
. . use and non-disclosure agreement . . . 227.7103-7
. policy . . . 227.7102-1
. scope . . . 227.7100
. Small Business Innovation Research (SBIR) Program . . . 227.7104
Risk-pooling arrangements . . . 228.304

S

Scrap material
. DD Form 1639, scrap warranty . . . 253.303-1639
. sale of surplus contractor inventory . . . 245.7310-7
Sealed bidding
. award
. . general . . . 214.408-1
. bid solicitation
. . cancellation of invitations before opening . . . 214.209
. . descriptive literature . . . 214.202
. . invitation for bids requirements . . . 214.202
. . solicitation provisions . . . 214.201-6
. cancellation of invitations after opening . . . 214.404-1
. construction contracts, special procedures . . . 236.213
. mistakes in bids
. . disclosure before award . . . 214.407-3
. notice of intent to resolicit
. . presciption . . . 214.201-6
. . solicitation provisions . . . 252.215-7007
. only one offer
. . presciption . . . 214.201-6
. . solicitation provision . . . 252.215-7008
. representations and instructions . . . 214.201-5
. two-step sealed bidding
. . step one procedures . . . 214.503-1
Secondary Arab boycott of Israel
. exceptions . . . 225.7603
. procedures . . . 225.7602
. restriction . . . 225.7601
. solicitation provision . . . 225.7604; 252.225-7031
. waivers . . . 225.7604
Section 8(a) program
. acceptance by Small Business Administration . . . 219.804-3
. acquisition selection . . . 219.803
. agency evaluation . . . 219.804-1
. agency offering . . . 219.804-2
. competition exceptions . . . 219.805-1
. competition procedures . . . 219.805-2
. competitive contract preparation . . . 219.811-2
. contract clause prescriptions . . . 219.811-3
. general . . . 219.800
. pricing the 8(a) contract . . . 219.806
Section 8(a) program—continued
. simplified acquisition procedures
. . procedures . . . 213.7001
. . purchase orders . . . 213.7002
. sole source, contract preparation . . . 219.811
. sole source negotiations . . . 219.808-1; 219.811-1
Security considerations—see also Bonds
. antiterrorism/force protection
. . contract clause . . . 225.372-2; 252.225-7043
. . general . . . 225.372-1
. computer systems
. . compromising emanations, TEMPEST or other standard . . . 239.7102-2
. . contract clause . . . 239.7103; 252.239-7000
. . definition of information assurance . . . 239.7101
. . general policy . . . 239.7102-1
. . privacy protection procedures . . . 224.103
. . scope . . . 239.7100
. . security against compromising emanations . . . 239.7102-1
. contract financing . . . 232.202-4
. industrial security
. . Canadian contracting . . . 225.870-8
. . qualifying country sources . . . 225.872-7
. personnel authorized to accompany U.S. armed forces deployed outside the U.S.
. . contract clause . . . 252.225-7040; 225.371-5
. . definitions . . . 252.225-7040; 225.371-2
. . government support . . . 225.7402-3
. . law of war training . . . 225.371-4
. . scope . . . 225.371-1
. telecommunications security equipment, devices, techniques, and services . . . 252.239-7016
Security-guard service contracting . . . 237.101; 237.102-70
Selection of contractor—see also Contractor qualifications; Responsible prospective contractors, identifying
. architect-engineer contracts
. . contract clause prescription . . . 236.609-70
. . criteria . . . 236.602-1
. . performance evaluation . . . 236.604
. only one offer
. . exceptions . . . 215.371-4
. . fair and reasonable price . . . 215.371-3
. . policy . . . 215.371-1
. . prescription . . . 215.408
. . promote competition . . . 215.371-2
. . solicitation provision . . . 252.215-7007; 252.215-7008
. . waiver . . . 215.371-5
Service contract labor standards statute
. applicability . . . 222.1003-1
Service contracting—see also Telecommunications services; Utility services
. approval
. . requirements . . . 237.170-2
. . scope . . . 237.170-1

Service contracting—see also Telecommunications services; Utility services—continued
. audit services . . . 237.270
. automated requirements roadmap tool . . . 237.102-77
. competition for religious-related services
. . definition . . . 237.7701
. . policy . . . 237.7702
. . scope of subpart . . . 237.7700
. continuation of essential contractor services
. . contract clause and solicitation provision prescription . . . 237.7603
. . definitions . . . 237.7601
. . policy . . . 237.7602
. . scope . . . 237.7600
. contract clauses and solicitation provisions
. . animal welfare . . . 237.175; 252.235-7002
. . area of performance (mortuary services) . . . 252.237-7004; 237.7003
. . award to single offeror (mortuary services) . . . 237.7003; 252.237-7002
. . continuation of essential contractor services . . . 252.237-7023
. . contractor personnel supporting a force deployed outside the U.S . . . 252.225-7040
. . default termination (mortuary services) . . . 237.7003; 252.237-7007
. . delivery tickets (laundry and dry cleaning) . . . 252.237-7016; 237.7101
. . facility requirements (mortuary services) . . . 252.237-7010; 237.7003
. . group interment (mortuary services) . . . 252.237-7008; 237.7003
. . individual laundry . . . 252.237-7017; 237.7101
. . instruction to offerors (bulk weight) (laundry and dry cleaning) . . . 237.7101; 252.237-7013
. . instruction to offerors (count-of-articles) (laundry and dry cleaning) . . . 237.7101; 252.237-7012
. . loss or damage (count-of-articles) (laundry and dry cleaning) . . . 237.7101; 252.237-7014
. . loss or damage (weight of articles) (laundry and dry cleaning) . . . 237.7101; 252.237-7015
. . notice of continuation of essential contractor services . . . 252.237-7024
. . notice of special standards of responsibility (audits) . . . 252.237-7000
. . performance and delivery (mortuary services) . . . 252.237-7005; 237.7003
. . permits (mortuary services) . . . 237.7003; 252.237-7009
. . preparation history (mortuary services) . . . 237.7003; 252.237-7011
. . requirements (mortuary services) . . . 237.7003; 252.237-7003
. . services at installations being closed . . . 237.7402; 252.237-7022
. . special definitions of government property (laundry and dry cleaning) . . . 252.237-7018; 237.7101
. . subcontracting (mortuary services) . . . 252.237-7006; 237.7003

Service contracting—see also Telecommunications services; Utility services—continued
. contract clauses and solicitation provisions—continued
. . training for contractor personnel interacting with detainees . . . 252.237-7019
. . training for interacting with detainees . . . 237.171-4; 252.237-7019
. definitions . . . 237.101; 237.7301
. disclosure of information to litigation support contractors . . . 237.174
. educational service agreements
. . contract clause prescriptions . . . 237.7204
. . contract format . . . 237.7204
. . definitions . . . 237.7204
. . duration . . . 237.7203
. . general . . . 237.7201
. . limitations . . . 237.7202
. . scope . . . 237.7200
. firefighting functions . . . 237.102-70
. forms
. . DD Form 1155, order for supplies and services . . . 253.213-70
. . DD Form 1155c-1, order for supplies or services, commissary continuation sheet . . . 253.303-1155c
. functions exempt from private sector performance
. . policy . . . 237.102
. funding and term . . . 237.106
. guidebook for acquisition of services . . . 237.102-75
. industrial resources . . . 237.75
. . definition, facilities project . . . 237.7501
. . policy . . . 237.7502
. laundry and dry cleaning services
. . contract clause and solicitation provision prescriptions . . . 237.7101
. . scope . . . 237.7100
. management oversight
. . agency-head responsibilities . . . 237.503
. management services . . . 237.102-72
. market research report guide . . . 237.102-78
. military flight simulators, limitation on service contracts
. mortuary services
. . acquisition method . . . 237.7001
. . area of performance . . . 237.7002
. . distribution of contracts . . . 237.7003
. . scope . . . 237.7000
. multiyear contracts . . . 217.171
. personal services contracts . . . 237.104; 237.106
. private sector notification requirements, in-sourcing actions . . . 237.102-79
. prohibition on interrogation of detainees by contractor personnel . . . 237.173
. quasi-military armed forces . . . 237.109
. review criteria for the acquisition of services . . . 237.102-76
. security-guard functions . . . 237.102-70
. service contracts survelliance . . . 237.172

Service contracting—see also Telecommunications services; Utility services—continued
. services at installations being closed . . . 252.237-7022
. . contract clause . . . 237.7402; 252.237-7022
. . policy . . . 237.7401
. . scope . . . 237.7400
. services of students at R&D laboratories
. . contract clause prescription . . . 237.7303
. . definitions . . . 237.7301
. . general . . . 237.7302
. . scope . . . 237.7300
. taxonomy . . . 237.102-74
. training that uses live vertebrate animals . . . 237.175

Set-asides—see also Small business programs
. rejection of Small Business Administration recommendation . . . 219.505
. requirements . . . 219.502-1
. total . . . 219.502-2

Settlement agreements—see also Termination of contracts
. negotiation memorandum . . . 249.110
. settlement by determination . . . 249.109-7

Ship critical safety items
. definitions . . . 209.270-2
. policy . . . 209.270-3
. procedures . . . 209.270-4
. scope . . . 209.270-1

Should-cost review . . . 215.407-4

Simplified acquisition procedures
. aviation into-plane reimbursement (AIR) card . . . 213.306
. blanket purchase agreements (BPAs) . . . 213.303-5
. contract clauses and solicitation provisions
. . contract clauses and solicitation provisions . . . 252.225-7036
. . Buy American and Balance of Payments Program . . . 252.225-7001
. . pricing of contract modifications . . . 213.302-5; 252.243-7001
. evaluation of quotations or offers . . . 213.106-2
. fast payment procedure . . . 213.402
. forms
. . prescriptions . . . 213.307; 253.213
. . purchase order-invoice-voucher, SF 44 . . . 213.306
. promoting competition . . . 213.102
. general . . . 213.101
. governmentwide commercial purchase card
. . actions at or below micro-purchase threshold . . . 213.270
. . general . . . 213.201
. . simplified acquisition methods . . . 213.301
. imprest funds . . . 213.305
. purchase orders
. . contract clause prescriptions . . . 213.302-5
. . obtaining contractor acceptance and modifying purchase orders . . . 213.302-3
. . under Section 8(a) . . . 213.7002

Simplified acquisition procedures—continued
. Section 8(a) program
. . procedures . . . 213.7001
. . purchase orders . . . 213.7002
. soliciting competition . . . 213.106-1-70; 213.106-1
. tiered evaluation of offers . . . 213.106-1-70

Single process initiative (SPI)
. contract clause . . . 211.273-4; 252.211-7005
. definition of SPI process . . . 211.273-1
. policy . . . 211.273-2
. procedures . . . 211.273-3

Small Business Innovative Research (SBIR) Program
. rights in software and software documentation . . . 227.7204
. rights in technical data . . . 227.7104

Small business programs
. certificates of competency and determinations of eligibility
. . procedures
. . referral . . . 219.602-1
. contract clauses and solicitation provisions
. . advancing small business growth . . . 252.219-7000
. . utilization of Indian organizations and Indian-owned economic enterprises and Native Hawaiian small business concerns . . . 252.226-7001
. cooperation with the Small Business Administration . . . 219.401
. determining North American Industry Classification System (NAICS) codes and size standards . . . 219.303
. HUBZone small business concerns
. . price evaluation preference . . . 219.1307
. pilot mentor-protege program—see Pilot mentor-protege program
. policies
. . encouraging small business participation in acquisitions . . . 219.202-1
. . general policy . . . 219.201
. . rerepresentation by non-small business concern contractor . . . 219.301-3
. . rerepresentation by small business concern contractor . . . 219.301-3
. preference for local and small businesses
. . definition of vicinity . . . 226.7101
. . other considerations . . . 226.7104
. . policy . . . 226.7102
. . procedure . . . 226.7103
. . scope of subpart . . . 226.7100
. religious-related services inclusion of nonprofit organizations
. . definition . . . 219.270-1
. . procedures . . . 219.270-2
. . solicitation provision prescription . . . 219.270-3
. . solicitation provision . . . 252.219-7012
. resolving differences between agency and Small Business Administration . . . 219.602-3

Small business programs—continued
. Section 8(a) program
. . acceptance by Small Business Administration . . . 219.804-3
. . acquisition selection . . . 219.803
. . agency evaluation . . . 219.804-1
. . agency offering . . . 219.804-2
. . competition exceptions . . . 219.805-1
. . competition procedures . . . 219.805-2
. . competitive contract preparation . . . 219.811-2
. . general . . . 219.800
. . pricing the 8(a) contract . . . 219.806
. . sole source, contract preparation . . . 219.811
. . sole source negotiations . . . 219.808-1; 219.811-1
. set-asides
. . rejection of Small Business Administration recommendations . . . 219.505
. . requirements . . . 219.502-1
. . total . . . 219.502-2
. Small Business Innovation Research (SBIR) Program . . . 227.7104
. subcontracting
. . cognizant administrative contracting officer responsibility . . . 219.706
. . contract clauses . . . 219.708
. . eligibility determinations . . . 219.703
. . plan review . . . 219.705-4
. . postaward responsibilities of contracting officer . . . 219.705-6
. . statutory requirements . . . 219.702
. . subcontracting plan requirements . . . 219.704
. tiered evaluation of offers . . . 213.106-1-70

Small purchases—see also Simplified acquisition procedures
. actions at or below the micro-purchase threshold . . . 213.270
. forms
. . DD Form 1155, order for supplies and services . . . 253.213-70
. . DD Form 1155c-1, order for supplies or services, commissary continuation sheet . . . 253.303-1155c
. . OF 346, 347, 348 . . . 253.213
. . SF 18, 30, 44, 1165, 1449 . . . 253.213
. general . . . 213.101; 213.201
. governmentwide commercial purchase card . . . 213.301
. soliciting competition . . . 213.106-1-70
. tiered evaluation of offers . . . 213.106-1-70

Socioeconomic programs—see also Labor laws; Small business programs
. Freedom of Information Act . . . 224.203
. historically black colleges and universities and minority institutions
. . scope . . . 226.7100
. Indian incentive program
. . contract clause . . . 226.104; 252.226-7001
. . procedures . . . 226.103

Socioeconomic programs—see also Labor laws; Small business programs—continued
. preference for local and small businesses
. . definition of vicinity . . . 226.7101
. . other considerations . . . 226.7104
. . policy . . . 226.7102
. . procedure . . . 226.7103
. . scope of subpart . . . 226.7100
. privacy protection . . . 224.102

Software—see also Rights in software and software documentation
. acquisition . . . 212.211
. enterprise software agreements
. . acquisition procedures . . . 208.7403
. . definitions . . . 208.7401
. . general . . . 208.7402
. . scope . . . 208.7400

Sole source acquisitions
. authority . . . 206.302-1
. contract pricing . . . 215.402
. Section 8(a) program
. . contract preparation . . . 219.811
. . negotiations . . . 219.811-1; 219.808-1

Sources of supplies and services—see also International agreements
. acceptance of MIPR, DD Form 448-2 . . . 253.208-2; 253.303-448
. contract clauses and solicitation provisions
. . identification of sources of supply . . . 252.217-7026
. . intent to furnish precious metals as government-furnished material . . . 208.7305; 252.208-7000
. . ordering from government supply sources . . . 252.251-7000
. . use of interagency fleet management system (IFMS) vehicles and related services . . . 252.251-7001
. coordinated acquisition
. . assignment authority . . . 208.7002
. . assignments under coordinated acquisition . . . 208.7003-2; 208.7006
. . assignments under integrated materiel management (IMM) . . . 208.7003-1
. . definitions . . . 208.7001
. . military interdepartmental purchase requests . . . 208.7005
. . policy and procedures . . . 208.7000
. . procedures . . . 208.7004
. . responsibilities of acquiring department . . . 208.7002-1
. . responsibilities of requiring department . . . 208.7002-2
. . scope . . . 208.7000
. enterprise software agreements
. . acquisition procedures . . . 208.7403
. . definitions . . . 208.7401
. . general . . . 208.7402
. . scope . . . 208.7400
. federal prison industries
. . market share . . . 208.602-70

Sources of supplies and services—see also International agreements—continued
. Federal Supply Schedules
. . general . . . 208.404
. . order placement . . . 208.406-1
. government-owned precious metals
. . contract clause . . . 252.208-7000; 208.7305
. . definitions . . . 208.7301
. . policy . . . 208.7302
. . procedures . . . 208.7303
. . refined precious metals . . . 208.7304
. government sources
. . contract clause . . . 251.107; 252.251-7000
. . contractor authorization . . . 251.102
. identification of
. . policy . . . 217.7301
. . procedures . . . 217.7302
. . scope . . . 217.7300
. . solicitation provision . . . 217.7303; 252.217-7026
. industrial preparedness production planning . . . 208.7202
. . authority . . . 208.7203
. . definitions . . . 208.7201
. . procedures . . . 208.7204
. integrated materiel management program . . . 208.7000
. interagency fleet management system vehicles
. . authorization . . . 251.202
. . contract clause . . . 252.251-7001; 251.205
. military interdepartmental purchase request, DD Form 448
. . prescription . . . 253.208-1
. military interdepartmental purchase requests . . . 208.7005
. NASA procurement
. . authorization . . . 208.7100
. . policy . . . 208.7101
. . procedures . . . 208.7102
. nonprofit agencies employing blind and other severely handicapped
. . procedures . . . 208.705
. prequalification . . . 236.272
. priorities for use . . . 208.002
. prohibited sources
. . Communist Chinese military companies . . . 225.770-2
. . definitions . . . 225.770-1
. . exceptions . . . 225.701-70; 225.770-3
. . identifying United States Munitions List items . . . 225.770-4
. . restrictions on . . . 225.701
. . secondary Arab boycott of Israel . . . 225.7601
. . waiver of prohibition . . . 225.770-5
. qualifying country sources
. . applicability . . . 225.872-2
. . audit . . . 225.872-6
. . contract administration . . . 225.872-5
. . general . . . 225.872-1
. . individual determinations . . . 225.872-4
. . industrial security . . . 225.872-7

Sources of supplies and services—see also International agreements—continued
. qualifying country sources—continued
. . solicitation procedures . . . 225.872-3
. . subcontracting with . . . 225.872-8

Spare parts
. acquiring with end items . . . 217.7503
. breakout program . . . 217.7506

Specialty metals
. contract clauses
. . commercial derivative military article—specialty metals compliance certificate . . . 252.225-7010
. . restriction on acquisition of certain articles containing specialty metals . . . 252.225-7009
. . restriction on acquisition of specialty metals . . . 252.225-7008
. definitions . . . 225.7003-1
. exceptions . . . 225.7003-3
. one-time waiver . . . 225.7003-4
. restrictions . . . 225.7003-2
. prescriptions . . . 225.7003-5
. waiver of restrictions of 10 U.S.C. 2534 . . . 225.7008

State laws
. labor requirements
. . overtime approvals . . . 222.103-4
. . policy . . . 222.102-1

Stevedoring contracts
. acquisition of services during labor disputes . . . 222.101-70
. contract clause prescriptions . . . 247.270-4
. definitions . . . 247.270-1
. evaluation of bids and proposals . . . 247.270-3
. technical provisions . . . 247.270-2

Streamlined procedures—see also Simplified acquisition procedures
. commercial item acquisition . . . 212.602
. contract clause . . . 211.002-70

Subcontracting
. commercial items and components
. . contract clause prescriptions . . . 244.403
. . policy requirements . . . 244.402
. competitiveness demonstration program . . . 219.1007
. contract clauses and solicitation provisions
. . notification of transportation of supplies by sea . . . 244.403
. . preference for domestic specialty metals, alternate I . . . 244.403
. . subcontracts for commercial items and commercial components . . . 244.403
. . subcontracts for commercial items . . . 252.244-7000
. . transportation of supplies by sea . . . 244.403; 252.247-7023
. contracting officer's evaluation and consent . . . 244.202-2
. contractor purchasing system reviews
. . extent of review . . . 244.303

Subcontracting—continued
. contractor purchasing system reviews—continued
. . granting, withholding, or withdrawing approval . . . 244.305-70
. . objective . . . 244.301
. foreign
. . qualifying country sources . . . 225.872-8
. . reporting of overseas subcontracts . . . 225.7201
. kickbacks . . . 203.502-2
. NATO cooperative projects . . . 225.871-5
. negotiated procurement contracts . . . 215.404-3
. policy
. . definitions . . . 244.101
. rights in software or software documentation . . . 227.7203-15
. rights in technical data . . . 227.7103-15
. small business programs
. . cognizant administrative contracting officer responsibility . . . 219.706
. . contract clauses and solicitation provision prescriptions . . . 219.708
. . eligibility determinations . . . 219.703
. . subcontracting plan review . . . 219.705-4

Subsistence, quality assurance . . . 246.408-70

Supercomputers
. contract clause . . . 225.7012-3; 252.225-7011
. restriction . . . 225.7012-1
. waiver . . . 225.7012-2

Supply contracts
. evaluating foreign offers
. . application . . . 225.502
. . examples . . . 225.504
. . group offers . . . 225.503
. forms
. . DD Form 1155, order for supplies and services . . . 253.213-70
. . DD Form 1155c-1, order for supplies or services, commissary continuation sheet . . . 253.303-1155c
. multiyear contracting . . . 217.172
. transportation
. . DD Form 1384, transportation control and movement document . . . 247.370
. . DD Form 1653, transportation data for solicitations . . . 247.371
. . DD Form 1654, evaluation of transportation cost factors . . . 247.372
. . definition . . . 247.301-70
. . evaluation factor or subfactor . . . 247.301-71
. . packing, marking, and consignment instructions . . . 247.305-10
. . returnable containers other than cylinders . . . 247.305-70
. with foreign governments or concerns . . . 227.674

T

Taxes
. contract clauses and solicitation provisions
. . customs exemptions (Germany) . . . 229.402-70; 252.229-7002
. . invoices exclusive of taxes or duties . . . 229.402-1; 252.229-7000
. . pass-through of motor carrier fuel surcharge adjustment . . . 252.247-7003; 247.207
. . relief from customs duty and value added tax on fuel (passenger vehicles) (United Kingdom) . . . 229.402-70; 252.229-7009
. . relief from customs duty on fuel (United Kingdom) . . . 229.402-70; 252.229-7010
. . relief from import duty (United Kingdom) . . . 229.402-70; 252.229-7008
. . status of contractor as a direct contractor (Spain) . . . 229.402-70; 252.229-7004
. . tax exemption (Spain) . . . 229.402-70; 252.229-7005
. . tax exemption (Spain)—representation . . . 252.229-7013
. . tax exemptions (Italy) . . . 229.402-70; 252.229-7003
. . tax exemptions (Italy)—representation . . . 252.229-7012
. . tax relief . . . 229.402-70; 252.229-7001
. . taxes, foreign contracts in Afghanistan . . . 252.229-7014
. . taxes, foreign contracts in Afghanistan (North Atlantic Treaty Organization Status of Forces Agreement) . . . 52.229-7015
. . value added tax exclusion (United Kingdom) . . . 229.402-70; 252.229-7006
. . verification of U.S. receipt of goods . . . 229.402-70; 252.229-7007
. foreign contracts . . . 229.402
. problem resolution . . . 229.101
. reporting of foreign taxation on U.S. assistance programs
. . contract clause . . . 229.170-4; 252.229-7011
. . definition of commodities . . . 229.170-1
. . policy . . . 229.170-2
. . reports . . . 229.170-3
. special procedures for overseas contracts . . . 229.70

Taxonomy for acquisition of services, supplies and equipment . . . 237.102-74

Taxpayer identification number information
. contractor identification . . . 204.203; 204.7202-3
. individual contracting action report, DD Form 350 . . . 204.902; 253.303-350

Technical performance incentives . . . 216.402-2

Technical representation at contractor facilities
. general . . . 242.7400
. procedures . . . 242.7401

Telecommunications services
. authority to contract . . . 239.7405

Telecommunications services—continued
. cancellation and termination . . . 239.7410
. contract clause prescriptions . . . 239.7411
. contract clauses and solicitation provisions
. . access . . . 252.239-7002
. . cancellation or termination of orders . . . 252.239-7007
. . continuation of communication service authorizations . . . 252.239-7015
. . obligation of the government . . . 252.239-7013
. . orders for facilities and services . . . 252.239-7004
. . prescriptions . . . 239.7411
. . rates, charges, and services . . . 252.239-7005
. . reuse arrangements . . . 252.239-7008
. . special construction and equipment charges . . . 252.239-7011
. . tariff information . . . 252.239-7006
. . telecommunications security equipment, devices, techniques, and services . . . 252.239-7016
. . term of agreement . . . 252.239-7014
. . title to telecommunication facilities and equipment . . . 252.236-7012
. certified cost or pricing data . . . 239.7406
. definitions . . . 239.7401
. policy . . . 239.7402
. scope . . . 239.7400
. special assembly . . . 239.7409
. special construction
. . applicability of construction labor standards . . . 239.7408-2
. . general . . . 239.7408-1
. type of contract . . . 239.7407

TEMPEST standard . . . 239.7102-2

Termination of contracts
. Canadian Commercial Corporation . . . 249.7000
. congressional notification . . . 249.7001
. contract clauses
. . notification of anticipated contract terminations or reductions . . . 249.7003
. . report of intended performance outside United States and Canada . . . 252.249-7002
. . special termination costs . . . 249.501-70; 252.249-7000
. duties of termination contracting officer
. . release of excess funds . . . 249.105-2
. . termination status report . . . 249.105-1
. forms
. . contract closeout check list, DD Form 1597 . . . 204.804-2
. . contract termination status report, DD Form 1598 . . . 253.303-1598
. limitation on pricing of terminated effort . . . 249.109-70
. notification of anticipated contract terminations or reductions . . . 249.7003
. settlement by determination . . . 249.109-7
. settlement negotiation memorandum . . . 249.110
. telecommunications services . . . 239.7410
. termination status reports . . . 249.105-1

Time-and-materials contracts . . . 216.601

Trade agreements—see also Foreign acquisitions; International agreements
. contract clauses and solicitation provisions
. . trade agreements . . . 252.225-7021
. . trade agreements certificate . . . 252.225-7020
. exceptions . . . 225.401
. general . . . 225.402
. procedures . . . 225.408
. products subject to . . . 225.401-70
. World Trade Organization government procurement agreement . . . 225.403

Traffic and transportation management—see also Transportation
. contract clauses
. . prescription . . . 247.207
. . application for U.S. government shipping documentation/instructions . . . 252.247-7028
. policies . . . 247.101

Trafficking in persons, combating
. policy . . . 222.1703
. violations and remedies . . . 222.1704

Training for contractor personnel interacting with detainees
. contract clause . . . 252.237-7019
. . prescription . . . 237.171-4
. definitions . . . 237.171-2; 252.237-7019
. policy . . . 237.171-3
. scope . . . 237.171-1

Transportation—See also Traffic and transportation management
. contract clauses and solicitation provisions
. . additional services . . . 247.271-3; 252.247-7020
. . award . . . 247.271-3
. . contract areas of performance . . . 247.271-3
. . contractor liability for loss or damage . . . 247.271-3; 252.247-7016
. . demurrage . . . 247.271-3; 252.247-7014
. . drayage . . . 247.271-3
. . erroneous shipments . . . 247.271-3
. . evaluation of bids . . . 247.271-3
. . hardship conditions . . . 247.270-4; 252.247-7000
. . contract clauses and solicitation provisions . . . 252.247-7004; 252.247-7005
. . liability and insurance . . . 247.270-4; 252.247-7007
. . notification of transportation of supplies by sea . . . 247.574
. . ordering limitation . . . 247.271-3; 252.247-7012
. . pass-through of motor carrier fuel surcharge adjustment . . . 247.207; 252.247-7003
. . period of contract . . . 247.271-3
. . price adjustment . . . 247.270-4; 252.247-7001
. . reflagging or repair work . . . 247.574; 252.247-7025
. . removal of contractor's employees . . . 247.270-4
. . representation of extent of transportation by sea . . . 247.574; 252.247-7022

Transportation—See also Traffic and transportation management—continued
. contract clauses and solicitation provisions—continued
. . returnable containers other than cylinders . . . 247.305-70; 252.247-7021
. . revision of prices . . . 247.270-4; 252.247-7002
. . riding gang member requirements . . . 252.247-7027
. . scope of contract . . . 247.271-3
. . subcontracting . . . 247.271-3
. . transportation of supplies by sea . . . 247.574; 252.247-7023
. contracts
. . preparation of solicitations and contracts . . . 247.206
. . scope . . . 247.200
. definitions . . . 247.001; 247.270-1; 247.301-70
. forms
. . evaluation of transportation cost factors, DD Form 1654 . . . 247.372
. . transportation control and movement document, DD Form 1384 . . . 247.370
. . transportation data for IFBs and RFPs, DD Form 1653 . . . 247.371
. general
. . policies . . . 247.101
. ocean transportation by U.S.-flag vessels
. . contract clauses and solicitation provision prescriptions . . . 247.574
. . policy . . . 247.572
. . scope . . . 247.570
. preparation of personal property for shipment or storage
. . policy . . . 247.271-1
. . procedures . . . 247.271-2
. . solicitation provision, schedule formats, and contract clauses . . . 247.271-3
. stevedoring contracts
. . acquisition of services during labor disputes . . . 222.101-70
. . contract clause prescriptions . . . 247.270-4
. . definitions . . . 247.270-1
. . evaluation of bids and proposals . . . 247.270-3
. . technical provisions . . . 247.270-2
. supply contracts
. . DD Form 1384, transportation control and movement document . . . 247.370
. . DD Form 1653, transportation data for solicitations . . . 247.371
. . DD Form 1654, evaluation of transportation cost factors . . . 247.372
. . definition . . . 247.301-70
. . evaluation factor or subfactor . . . 247.301-71
. . packing, marking, and consignment instructions . . . 247.305-10
. . returnable containers other than cylinders . . . 247.305-70

Two-phase design-build selection procedures
. phase one . . . 236.303-1

U

Undefinitized contract actions
. allowable profit . . . 217.7404-6
. authorization . . . 217.7404-1
. contract clause . . . 217.7406
. definitions . . . 217.7401
. definitization schedule . . . 217.7404-3
. exception for initial spares . . . 217.7404-5
. exceptions . . . 217.7402
. limitations on obligations . . . 217.7404-4
. plans and reports . . . 217.7405
. policy . . . 217.7403
. price ceiling . . . 217.7404-2
. scope . . . 217.7400

Uniform contract line item numbering system
. accounting classification reference number (ACRN) . . . 204.7107
. contract clause . . . 204.7109; 252.204-7006
. definitions . . . 204.7101
. exhibits and attachments . . . 204.7105
. line items, criteria for establishing . . . 204.7103-1
. numbering procedures . . . 204.7103-2; 204.7104-2
. payment instructions . . . 204.7108
. subline items, criteria for establishing . . . 204.7104-1

Uniform procurement instrument identifiers
. procedures . . . 204.1603
. Federal Procurement Data System . . . 204.1670
. order of application for modifications . . . 204.1671
. policy . . . 204.1601

Unique item identification and valuation
. contract clause . . . 211.274-6; 252.211-7003
. general . . . 211.274-1
. government-assigned serial numbers, policy . . . 211.274-5
. identification policy . . . 211.274-2
. valuation policy . . . 211.274-3

United Kingdom commercial exploitation levies
. policy . . . 225.873-1
. procedures . . . 225.873-2

U.S. armed forces deployed outside the U.S., personnel supporting
. contract clause . . . 225.371-5; 252.225-7040
. definitions . . . 225.371-2; 252.225-7040
. government support . . . 225.371-3
. law of war training . . . 225.371-4
. scope . . . 225.371-1

United States Munitions List
. definition . . . 252.225-7007
. identifying covered items . . . 225.770-4
. prohibited items . . . 225.770-2

Unusually hazardous risks
. contract clause prescriptions . . . 235.070-3; 235.072

Unusually hazardous risks—continued
. indemnification under contract involving both research and development and other work . . . 235.070-2
. indemnification under research and development contracts . . . 235.070-1

Utility services
. applicability . . . 241.102
. authority . . . 241.103
. contract clauses and solicitation provisions
. . government access . . . 252.241-7001
. . prescriptions . . . 241.501-70
. . superseding contract . . . 252.241-7000
. definitions . . . 241.101
. policy . . . 241.201
. procedures . . . 241.202
. separate contracts . . . 241.205

V

Valuation of unique items
. contract clause . . . 211.274-4; 252.211-7003
. general . . . 211.274-1
. policy . . . 211.274-3

Value engineering
. contract clauses and solicitation provisions
. . preparation of value engineering change proposals . . . 252.248-7000

Vehicles
. interagency fleet management system
. . authorization . . . 251.202
. . contract clause . . . 251.205; 252.251-7001
. SF 97, certificate of release of a motor vehicle . . . 245.7001-1

Vessel repair and alteration
. construction or repair of in foreign shipyards, restrictions . . . 225.7013
. content and format . . . 217.7103-1
. contract clauses and solicitation provisions
. . access to vessel . . . 252.217-7011
. . bonds . . . 252.217-7008
. . changes . . . 252.217-7003
. . default . . . 252.217-7009
. . discharge of liens . . . 252.217-7014
. . guarantees . . . 252.217-7013
. . inspection and manner of doing work . . . 252.217-7005
. . job orders and compensation . . . 252.217-7004
. . liability and insurance . . . 252.217-7012
. . payments . . . 252.217-7007
. . performance . . . 252.217-7010
. . plant protection . . . 252.217-7016
. . prescriptions . . . 217.7104
. . safety and health . . . 252.217-7015
. . title . . . 252.217-7006
. definitions . . . 217.7101
. emergency work . . . 217.7103-4
. general . . . 217.7102

Vessel repair and alteration—continued
. modification of . . . 217.7103-6
. period of agreement . . . 217.7103-2
. repair costs not readily ascertainable . . . 217.7103-5
. scope . . . 217.7100
. solicitations for job orders . . . 217.7103-3

Veterans
. labor laws
. . complaint procedures . . . 222.1308
. . contract clause and solicitation provision prescription . . . 222.1310
. . waivers . . . 222.1305

Voluntary refunds . . . 242.7100

W

Wage determinations
. preparation
. procedures

Walsh-Healey Public Contracts Act
. regulatory exemptions . . . 222.604-2

War-hazard insurance . . . 228.305

Warning labels . . . 223.302
. contract clause . . . 223.303; 252.223-7001

Warranties—see also Quality assurance
. authority for use . . . 246.704
. contract clause prescriptions . . . 246.710
. definitions . . . 246.701
. limitations . . . 246.705
. technical data . . . 246.708
. terms and conditions . . . 246.706

Weapons systems
. major system acquisition
. . definition . . . 234.7001
. . policy . . . 234.7002
. . scope . . . 234.7000
. multiyear contracting . . . 217.173

Weighted guidelines method
. alternate structured approaches . . . 215.404-73
. contract type risk and working capital adjustment . . . 215.404-71
. cost efficiency factor . . . 215.404-71
. facilities capital . . . 215.404-71
. general . . . 215.404-71
. nonprofit organizations . . . 215.404-72
. performance risk . . . 215.404-71

Work over and above contract
. contract clause . . . 217.7702; 252.217-7028
. procedures . . . 217.7701

Work stoppages
. removal of items from contractor's facilities . . . 222.101-4

Working capital adjustment
. negotiated procurement . . . 215.404-71

World Trade Organization
. government procurement agreement . . . 225.403